International GAAP® 2018

Generally Accepted Accounting Practice under International Financial Reporting Standards

Jeremy Barnes
Martin Beyersdorff
Mike Bonham
Linzi Carr
Rob Carrington
Victor Chan
Wei Li Chan
Larissa Connor
Angela Covic
Pieter Dekker
Julie Dempers
Tim Denton
Dennis Deysel
Dennis Esterhuizen
Diego Fernandez
Alan Garry
Prahalad Halgeri
Jane Hurworth
Ted Jones
Parbin Khatun
Bernd Kremp
Sanjeev Kumar
Max Lienhard
Dean Lockhart
Sharon MacIntyre
Takahiro Makino
Amanda Marrion
Richard Moore
Margaret Pankhurst
Tina Patel
Michael Pratt
Tim Rogerson
Serene Seah-Tan
Vadim Shelaginov
Anna Sirocka
Claire Taylor
Michael Varila
Tracey Waring
Jane Watson

WILEY

This edition first published in 2018 by John Wiley & Sons Ltd.

http://www.internationalgaap.com

Registered office
John Wiley & Sons Ltd, The Atrium, Southern Gate, Chichester, West Sussex, PO19 8SQ, United Kingdom

For details of our global editorial offices, for customer services and for information about how to apply for permission to reuse the copyright material in this book please see our website at www.wiley.com

ISBN 978-1-119-46372-6 (paperback)
[EY personnel only ISBN 978-1-119-46364-1]

ISBN 978-1-119-46375-7 (ebk)
ISBN 978-1-119-46373-3 (ebk)

A catalogue record for this book is available from the British Library.

Printed and bound by CPI Group (UK) Ltd, Croydon, CR0 4YY

This book is printed on acid-free paper responsibly manufactured from sustainable forestry.

About this book

The 2018 edition of International GAAP® has been fully revised and updated in order to:

- Include a new chapter on the new insurance contracts standard IFRS 17 (*Insurance Contracts*). IFRS 17 solves the comparison problems created by IFRS 4 by requiring all insurance contracts to be accounted for in a consistent manner, benefiting both investors and insurance companies. Insurance obligations will be accounted for using current values, instead of a mixture of diverse accounting models based largely on previous local GAAP. The information will be updated regularly, providing more useful information to users of financial statements. Due to the range of accounting methods in use today, some countries will see more significant changes than others with the introduction of the new Standard.
- Explore the implementation issues arising as entities adopt, in 2018, IFRS 9 (*Financial Instruments*) and IFRS 15 (*Revenue from Contracts with Customers*), and plan for the adoption of IFRS 16 (*Leases*) in 2019.
- Address amended standards and new interpretations issued since the preparation of the 2017 edition.
- Explain the many other initiatives that are currently being discussed by the IASB and by the IFRS Interpretations Committee and the potential consequential changes to accounting requirements. In particular the conceptual framework project for financial reporting may result in significant changes to current accounting practice.
- Provide insight on the many issues relating to the practical application of IFRS, based on the extensive experience of the book's authors in dealing with current issues.

The book is published in three volumes. The 56 chapters – listed on pages ix to xi – are split between the three volumes as follows:

- Volume 1 - Chapters 1 to 23,
- Volume 2 - Chapters 24 to 41,
- Volume 3 - Chapters 42 to 56.

Each chapter includes a detailed list of contents and list of illustrative examples.

Each of the three volumes contains the following indexes covering all three volumes:

- an index of extracts from financial statements,
- an index of references to standards and interpretations,
- a general index.

Preface

In June 2017, the IASB brought to a close an era in which its agenda was dominated by four major standard-setting projects: financial instruments, revenue recognition, leases and insurance contracts. The completion of these projects with the publication of IFRS 17 – *Insurance Contracts* – is a major achievement that cements the position of IFRS as one of essentially only two global-scale frameworks of financial reporting.

The four projects are also largely responsible for how the IASB is perceived today. On the one hand, the IFRS Reputation Research Report 2017 notes that the IFRS Foundation is seen as successfully harmonising global accounting standards and is highly rated for its transparency, independence and people. On the other hand, these decades-long projects have fed into the perception that accounting standard-setting is not timely and that it does not respond quickly enough to a changing world.

It is therefore crucial for the IASB to strike the right balance between taking on ambitious long-term projects and maintaining the flexibility to respond to emerging issues.

In November 2016, the IASB published its work plan for the period from 2017 until 2021, which can be divided into three elements. Firstly, the Board is working on the Better Communication in Financial Reporting initiative, which aims to address the concern that it can be difficult to identify the most useful information in financial statements, as it is often presented poorly and not communicated effectively. This initiative comprises a number of projects:

- *Primary Financial Statements* is examining targeted improvements to the structure and content of the primary financial statements;
- *Principles of Disclosure* is about developing principles governing what, how and where information should be disclosed in the financial statements;
- Materiality Practice Statement helps companies make materiality judgements in the preparation of IFRS financial statements;
- *Definition of Material* is proposing to clarify and align the definition of 'material' across standards; and
- *IFRS Taxonomy* is targeting the delivery of electronically readable content.

The Better Communications initiative raises important questions about the role of the IASB, because financial reporting is only one part of the broader notion of corporate reporting, which also covers among other things: integrated, environmental, social and governance reporting. Currently, many organisations, including EY, are working on the various individual aspects of corporate reporting that have links to financial reporting. Although the IASB has limited resources and does not have in-depth expertise in each of these areas, we believe it should take an active role when it comes to the efforts to improve the 'broader financial report'. In our view, better communication in financial reporting requires integration with and/or links to the explanatory information that is provided in other parts of the corporate report.

Secondly, as part of its active research agenda, the IASB is planning to publish discussion papers in 2018 on business combinations under common control, financial instruments with characteristics of equity, dynamic risk management, and rate-regulated activities. Although technically complex, these are important projects as they deal with issues that have been the source of many accounting questions. The IASB also plans to issue a discussion paper on goodwill and impairment that reconsiders the existing impairment test for goodwill, whether goodwill should be amortised and which intangible assets should be separated from goodwill. Any improvements and simplifications that may follow from this project would be welcomed by preparers, users and auditors alike.

Thirdly, the Board is working on implementation and adoption support activities, carrying out post-implementation reviews, and completing its remaining standard-setting projects. The Conceptual Framework project, which is now expected to be completed in early 2018, will introduce some improvements but will not address questions around measurement and financial performance in detail.

The publication of IFRS 17, which is effective from 1 January 2021 onwards, marks the completion of a project that started 20 years earlier under the Board's predecessor body, the International Accounting Standards Committee. The standard requires all insurance contracts to be accounted for consistently using current estimates, rather than historical cost, which is expected to provide more useful information to users of financial statements. This is a major change compared to IFRS 4 – *Insurance Contracts*, which permits a wide range of accounting policies and exempts entities from applying the accounting hierarchy in IAS 8 – *Accounting Policies, Changes in Accounting Estimates and Errors*. As insurance companies have different starting points under IFRS 4 they are likely to be affected differently by IFRS 17. The Transition Resource Group for Insurance Contracts, that has been set up to help the Board determine what action is needed to address implementation questions, will play a vital role in the transition process.

Over the past few years, constituents have spent much time and effort in the implementation of IFRS 9 – *Financial Instruments* – and IFRS 15 – *Revenue from Contracts with Customers*, which are effective from 1 January 2018 onwards, and IFRS 16 – *Leases*, which is effective from 1 January 2019 onwards. Each of these standards introduces changes that have given rise to implementation challenges and questions about the recognition, measurement, presentation and disclosure requirements.

This edition of *International GAAP* covers the many interpretations, practices and solutions that have now been developed based on our work with clients, and discussions with regulators, standard-setters and other professionals. We believe that *International GAAP*, now in its thirteenth edition, plays an important role in helping companies as they apply these standards for the first time. Our team of authors and reviewers hails from all parts of the world and includes not only our global technical experts but also senior client-facing staff. This gives us an in-depth knowledge of practice in many different countries and industry sectors, enabling us to go beyond mere recitation of the requirements of standards to explaining their application in many varied situations.

We are deeply indebted to many of our colleagues within the global organisation of EY for their selfless assistance and support in the publication of this book. It has been a truly international effort, with valuable contributions from EY people around the globe.

Our thanks go particularly to those who reviewed, edited and assisted in the preparation of drafts, most notably: Elisa Alfieri, John Alton, Mark Barton, Paul Beswick, Silke Blaschke, Brian Byrne, Larissa Clark, Tony Clifford, Muriel Courel, Tai Danmola, Chantelle Duffy, Josh Forgione, Peter Gittens, Lindsay Gotsman, Laure Guégan, Paul Hebditch, Jennifer Hillenmeyer, Junyoung Jeong, Deborah Jones, Guy Jones, Yoshiki Kashioka, Akashi Kohno, Steinar Kvifte, Vincent de La Bachelerie, Twan van Limpt, Meredith Lloyd, Michiel van der Lof, James Luke, Mark Mahar, Steve Martin, Joseph McGrath, John O'Grady, Eric Ohlund, Sander de Ruiter, Gerard van Santen, Alison Spivey, Leo van der Tas, Paula Tashima, Evangelia Tsakiroglou, Hans van der Veen, Jana Wahrisch, Arne Weber and Luci Wright.

Our thanks also go to everyone who directly or indirectly contributed to the book's creation, including the following members of the Financial Reporting Group in the UK: Denise Brand, Anna Malcolm, Archibald Groenewald, Maria Kingston, Andrea Maylor, Anna Pickup and Anke Wick.

We also thank Jeremy Gugenheim for his assistance with the production technology throughout the period of writing.

London,	*Jeremy Barnes*	*Dennis Esterhuizen*	*Amanda Marrion*
October 2017	*Martin Beyersdorff*	*Diego Fernandez*	*Richard Moore*
	Mike Bonham	*Alan Garry*	*Margaret Pankhurst*
	Linzi Carr	*Prahalad Halgeri*	*Tina Patel*
	Rob Carrington	*Jane Hurworth*	*Michael Pratt*
	Victor Chan	*Ted Jones*	*Tim Rogerson*
	Wei Li Chan	*Parbin Khatun*	*Serene Seah-Tan*
	Larissa Connor	*Bernd Kremp*	*Vadim Shelaginov*
	Angela Covic	*Sanjeev Kumar*	*Anna Sirocka*
	Pieter Dekker	*Max Lienhard*	*Claire Taylor*
	Julie Dempers	*Dean Lockhart*	*Michael Varila*
	Tim Denton	*Sharon MacIntyre*	*Tracey Waring*
	Dennis Deysel	*Takahiro Makino*	*Jane Watson*

Lists of chapters

Volume 1

The lists of chapters in volumes 2 and 3 follow overleaf.

Volume 2

The list of chapters in volume 3 follows overleaf.

Volume 3

Abbreviations

The following abbreviations are used in this book:

Professional and regulatory bodies:

AASB	Australian Accounting Standards Board
AcSB	Accounting Standards Board of Canada
AICPA	American Institute of Certified Public Accountants
AOSSG	Asian-Oceanian Standard-Setters Group
APB	Accounting Principles Board (of the AICPA, predecessor of the FASB)
ARC	Accounting Regulatory Committee of representatives of EU Member States
ASAF	Accounting Standards Advisory Forum
ASB	Accounting Standards Board in the UK
ASBJ	Accounting Standards Board of Japan
ASU	Accounting Standards Update
CASC	China Accounting Standards Committee
CESR	Committee of European Securities Regulators, an independent committee whose members comprised senior representatives from EU securities regulators (replaced by ESMA)
CICA	Canadian Institute of Chartered Accountants
EC	European Commission
ECB	European Central Bank
ECOFIN	The Economic and Financial Affairs Council
EDTF	Enhanced Disclosure Task Force of the (FSB)
EFRAG	European Financial Reporting Advisory Group
EITF	Emerging Issues Task Force in the US
EPRA	European Public Real Estate Association
ESMA	European Securities and Markets Authority (see CESR)
EU	European Union
FAF	Financial Accounting Foundation
FASB	Financial Accounting Standards Board in the US
FCAG	Financial Crisis Advisory Group
FEE	Federation of European Accountants

FSB	Financial Stability Board (successor to the FSF)
FSF	Financial Stability Forum
G4+1	The (now disbanded) group of four plus 1, actually with six members, that comprised an informal 'think tank' of staff from the standard setters from Australia, Canada, New Zealand, UK, and USA, plus the IASC
G7	The Group of Seven Finance Ministers (successor to G8)
G8	The Group of Eight Finance Ministers
G20	The Group of Twenty Finance Ministers and Central Bank Governors
GPPC	Global Public Policy Committee of the six largest accounting networks
HKICPA	Hong Kong Institute of Certified Public Accountants
ICAI	Institute of Chartered Accountants of India
IASB	International Accounting Standards Board
IASC	International Accounting Standards Committee. The former Board of the IASC was the predecessor of the IASB
IASCF	International Accounting Standards Committee Foundation (predecessor of the IFRS Foundation)
ICAEW	Institute of Chartered Accountants in England and Wales
ICAS	Institute of Chartered Accountants of Scotland
IFAC	International Federation of Accountants
IFASS	International Forum of Accounting Standard Setters
IFRIC	The IFRS Interpretations Committee (formerly the International Financial Reporting Interpretations Committee) of the IASB
IGC	Implementation Guidance Committee on IAS 39 (now disbanded)
IOSCO	International Organisation of Securities Commissions
IPSASB	International Public Sector Accounting Standards Board
IPTF	International Practices Task Force (a task force of the SEC Regulations Committee)
ISDA	International Swaps and Derivatives Association
IVSC	International Valuation Standards Council
KASB	Korea Accounting Standards Board
RICS	Royal Institution of Chartered Surveyors
SAC	Standards Advisory Council, predecessor of the IFRS Advisory Council which provides advice to the IASB on a wide range of issues
SEC	Securities and Exchange Commission (the US securities regulator)
SIC	Standing Interpretations Committee of the IASC (replaced by IFRIC)
TEG	Technical Expert Group, an advisor to the European Commission
TRG	Joint Transition Resource Group for Revenue Recognition

Accounting related terms:

ADS	American Depositary Shares
AFS	Available-for-sale investment
ARB	Accounting Research Bulletins (issued by the AICPA)
ARS	Accounting Research Studies (issued by the APB)
ASC	Accounting Standards Codification®. The single source of authoritative US GAAP recognised by the FASB, to be applied to non-governmental entities for interim and accounting periods ending after 15 September 2009
ASU	Accounting Standards Update
CCIRS	Cross Currency Interest Rate Swap
CDO	Collateralised Debt Obligation
CGU	Cash-generating Unit
CU	Currency Unit
DD&A	Depreciation, Depletion and Amortisation
DPF	Discretionary Participation Feature
E&E	Exploration and Evaluation
EBIT	Earnings Before Interest and Taxes
EBITDA	Earnings Before Interest, Taxes, Depreciation and Amortisation
EIR	Effective Interest Rate
EPS	Earnings per Share
FAS	Financial Accounting Standards (issued by the FASB). Superseded by Accounting Standards Codification® (ASC)
FC	Foreign currency
FICE	Financial Instruments with the Characteristics of Equity
FIFO	First-In, First-Out basis of valuation
FRS	Financial Reporting Standard (issued by the ASB)
FTA	First-time Adoption
FVLCD	Fair value less costs of disposal
FVLCS	Fair value less costs to sell (following the issue of IFRS 13, generally replaced by FVLCD)
FVPL	Fair value through profit and loss
FVOCI	Fair value through other comprehensive income
GAAP	Generally accepted accounting practice (as it applies under IFRS), or generally accepted accounting principles (as it applies to the US)
HTM	Held-to-maturity investment
IAS	International Accounting Standard (issued by the former board of the IASC)
IBNR	Incurred but not reported claims
IFRS	International Financial Reporting Standard (issued by the IASB)

IGC Q&A	Implementation guidance to the original version of IAS 39 (issued by the IGC)
IPO	Initial Public Offering
IPR&D	In-process Research and Development
IPSAS	International Public Sector Accounting Standard
IRR	Internal Rate of Return
IRS	Interest Rate Swap
JA	Joint Arrangement
JCA	Jointly Controlled Asset
JCE	Jointly Controlled Entity
JCO	Jointly Controlled Operation
JO	Joint Operation
JV	Joint Venture
LAT	Liability Adequacy Test
LC	Local Currency
LIBOR	London Inter Bank Offered Rate
LIFO	Last-In, First-Out basis of valuation
NCI	Non-controlling Interest
NBV	Net Book Value
NPV	Net Present Value
NRV	Net Realisable Value
OCI	Other Comprehensive Income
PP&E	Property, Plant and Equipment
R&D	Research and Development
SCA	Service Concession Arrangement
SE	Structured Entity
SFAC	Statement of Financial Accounting Concepts (issued by the FASB as part of its conceptual framework project)
SFAS	Statement of Financial Accounting Standards (issued by the FASB). Superseded by Accounting Standards Codification® (ASC)
SME	Small or medium-sized entity
SPE	Special Purpose Entity
SV	Separate Vehicle
TSR	Total Shareholder Return
VIU	Value In Use
WACC	Weighted Average Cost of Capital

References to IFRSs, IASs, Interpretations and supporting documentation:

AG	Application Guidance
AV	Alternative View
BCZ	Basis for Conclusions on IASs
BC	Basis for Conclusions on IFRSs and IASs
DI	Draft Interpretation
DO	Dissenting Opinion
DP	Discussion Paper
ED	Exposure Draft
IE	Illustrative Examples on IFRSs and IASs
IG	Implementation Guidance
IN	Introduction to IFRSs and IASs
PIR	Post-implementation Review

Authoritative literature

The content of this book takes into account all accounting standards and other relevant rules issued up to September 2017. Consequently, it covers the IASB's *Conceptual Framework for Financial Reporting* and authoritative literature listed below.

References in the main text of each chapter to the pronouncements below are generally to the versions of those pronouncements as approved and expected to be included in the Blue Book edition of the Bound Volume 2018 International Financial Reporting Standards – IFRS – Consolidated without early application – Official pronouncements applicable on 1 January 2018, to be published by the IASB.

References to those pronouncements below which have an effective date after 1 January 2018 (such as IFRS 16 – *Leases*) are to the versions of those pronouncements as denoted by the ISBN references noted below. These are expected to be included in the Red Book edition of the Bound Volume 2018 International Financial Reporting Standards – IFRS – Official pronouncements issued at 1 January 2018, to be published by the IASB.

US GAAP accounting standards are organised within a comprehensive FASB Accounting Standards Codification®, which is now the single source of authoritative US GAAP recognised by the FASB to be applied to non-governmental entities and has been applied in this publication.

† The standards and interpretations marked with a dagger have been withdrawn or superseded.

		IASB Framework
		The Conceptual Framework for Financial Reporting
		International Financial Reporting Standards (2018 Bound Volume)
	IFRS 1	First-time Adoption of International Financial Reporting Standards
	IFRS 2	Share-based Payment
	IFRS 3	Business Combinations
†	IFRS 4	Insurance Contracts
	IFRS 5	Non-current Assets Held for Sale and Discontinued Operations
	IFRS 6	Exploration for and Evaluation of Mineral Resources
	IFRS 7	Financial Instruments: Disclosures
	IFRS 8	Operating Segments
	IFRS 9	Financial Instruments
	IFRS 10	Consolidated Financial Statements
	IFRS 11	Joint Arrangements

IFRS 12	Disclosure of Interests in Other Entities
IFRS 13	Fair Value Measurement
IFRS 14	Regulatory Deferral Accounts
IFRS 15	Revenue from Contracts with Customers

International Financial Reporting Standards (mandatory after 1 January 2018)

IFRS 16	Leases
IFRS 17	Insurance Contracts

International Accounting Standards (2018 Bound Volume)

IAS 1	Presentation of Financial Statements
IAS 2	Inventories
IAS 7	Statement of Cash Flows
IAS 8	Accounting Policies, Changes in Accounting Estimates and Errors
IAS 10	Events after the Reporting Period
IAS 12	Income Taxes
IAS 16	Property, Plant and Equipment
† IAS 17	Leases
IAS 19	Employee Benefits
IAS 20	Accounting for Government Grants and Disclosure of Government Assistance
IAS 21	The Effects of Changes in Foreign Exchange Rates
IAS 23	Borrowing Costs
IAS 24	Related Party Disclosures
IAS 26	Accounting and Reporting by Retirement Benefit Plans
IAS 27	Separate Financial Statements
IAS 28	Investments in Associates and Joint Ventures
IAS 29	Financial Reporting in Hyperinflationary Economies
IAS 32	Financial Instruments: Presentation
IAS 33	Earnings per Share
IAS 34	Interim Financial Reporting
IAS 36	Impairment of Assets
IAS 37	Provisions, Contingent Liabilities and Contingent Assets
IAS 38	Intangible Assets
IAS 39	Financial Instruments: Recognition and Measurement
IAS 40	Investment Property
IAS 41	Agriculture

	IFRS Interpretations Committee Interpretations	
	IFRIC 1	Changes in Existing Decommissioning, Restoration and Similar Liabilities
	IFRIC 2	Members' Shares in Co-operative Entities and Similar Instruments
†	IFRIC 4	Determining whether an Arrangement contains a Lease
	IFRIC 5	Rights to Interests arising from Decommissioning, Restoration and Environmental Rehabilitation Funds
	IFRIC 6	Liabilities arising from Participating in a Specific Market – Waste Electrical and Electronic Equipment
	IFRIC 7	Applying the Restatement Approach under IAS 29 Financial Reporting in Hyperinflationary Economies
	IFRIC 10	Interim Financial Reporting and Impairment
	IFRIC 12	Service Concession Arrangements
	IFRIC 14	IAS 19 – The Limit on a Defined Benefit Asset, Minimum Funding Requirements and their Interaction
	IFRIC 16	Hedges of a Net Investment in a Foreign Operation
	IFRIC 17	Distributions of Non-cash Assets to Owners
	IFRIC 19	Extinguishing Financial Liabilities with Equity Instruments
	IFRIC 20	Stripping Costs in the Production Phase of a Surface Mine
	IFRIC 21	Levies
	IFRIC 22	Foreign Currency Transactions and Advance Consideration

	IFRS Interpretations Committee Interpretations (mandatory after 1 January 2018)	
	IFRIC 23	Uncertainty over Income Tax Treatments

	Standing Interpretations Committee Interpretations	
	SIC-7	Introduction of the Euro
	SIC-10	Government Assistance – No Specific Relation to Operating Activities
†	SIC-15	Operating Leases – Incentives
	SIC-25	Income Taxes – Changes in the Tax Status of an Entity or its Shareholders
†	SIC-27	Evaluating the Substance of Transactions Involving the Legal Form of a Lease
	SIC-29	Service Concession Arrangements: Disclosures
	SIC-32	Intangible Assets – Web Site Costs

IASB Exposure Drafts	
ED/2015/1	Classification of Liabilities (Proposed amendments to IAS 1)
ED/2015/3	Conceptual Framework for Financial Reporting
ED/2015/4	Updating References to the Conceptual Framework (Proposed amendments to IFRS 2, IFRS 3, IFRS 4, IFRS 6, IAS 1, IAS 8, IAS 34, SIC-27 and SIC-32)
ED/2015/5	Remeasurement on a Plan Amendment, Curtailment or Settlement/Availability of a Refund from a Defined Benefit Plan (Proposed amendments to IAS 19 and IFRIC 14)

ED/2015/7	Effective Date of Amendments to IFRS 10 and IAS 28
ED/2016/1	Definition of a Business and Accounting for Previously Held Interests (Proposed amendments to IFRS 3 and IFRS 11)
ED/2017/1	Annual Improvements to IFRS Standards 2015—2017 Cycle
ED/2017/2	Improvements to IFRS 8 Operating Segments (Proposed amendments to IFRS 8 and IAS 34)
ED/2017/3	Prepayment Features with Negative Compensation (Proposed amendments to IFRS 9)
ED/2017/4	Property, Plant and Equipment—Proceeds before Intended Use (Proposed amendments to IAS 16)
ED/2017/5	Accounting Policies and Accounting Estimates (Proposed amendments to IAS 8)
ED/2017/6	Definition of Material (Proposed amendments to IAS 1 and IAS 8)

IASB Discussion Papers

DP/2014/1	Accounting for Dynamic Risk Management: a Portfolio Revaluation Approach to Macro Hedging
DP/2014/2	Reporting the Financial Effects of Rate Regulation
DP/2017/1	Disclosure Initiative—Principles of Disclosure

Other IASB publications

IFRS for SMEs	International Financial Reporting Standard (IFRS) for Small and Medium-sized Entities (SMEs)

Chapter 1 International GAAP

Chapter 1 International GAAP

1 WHY INTERNATIONAL FINANCIAL REPORTING STANDARDS MATTER

With globalisation has come the increasing integration of world markets for goods, services and capital – with the result that companies that traditionally were reliant on their domestic capital markets for financing now have substantially increased access to debt and equity capital, both inside and outside their national borders.

Yet – perhaps not entirely surprisingly – the world of financial reporting was slow to respond reflecting, no doubt, a widespread nationalism in respect of countries' own standards.

Undoubtedly, one of the main advantages of a single set of global accounting standards is that it would enable the international capital markets to assess and compare inter-company performance in a much more meaningful, effective and efficient way. This should increase companies' access to global capital and ultimately reduce the cost thereof. Thus the request for global standards came both from regulatory bodies and from preparers of financial statements. As early as 1989 the International Organisation of Securities Commissions (IOSCO), the world's primary forum for co-operation among securities regulators, prepared a paper noting that cross border security offerings would be facilitated by the development of internationally accepted standards. For preparers, greater comparability in financial reporting with their global peers had obvious attractions.

Notwithstanding these anticipated benefits, it has only been since 2000 that there has been a serious effort made toward such global standards. This came about largely as a result of the European Commission's announcement in June 2000 that it would present proposals to introduce the requirement that all listed European Union (EU) companies report in accordance with International Accounting Standards by 2005. This requirement not only changed the face of European financial reporting, but global reporting as well after many other countries followed Europe's lead. Indeed, the IFRS Foundation reports that 126 jurisdictions require International Financial Reporting Standards (IFRS) for 'all or most public companies'.[1]

Thus global financial reporting has ceased to be characterised by numerous disparate national systems to the point at which there are today essentially only two – IFRS and US GAAP.

2 THE IFRS FOUNDATION AND THE IASB

2.1 The standard-setting structure

The diagram below illustrates the structure within which standards are set by the International Accounting Standards Board (IASB).

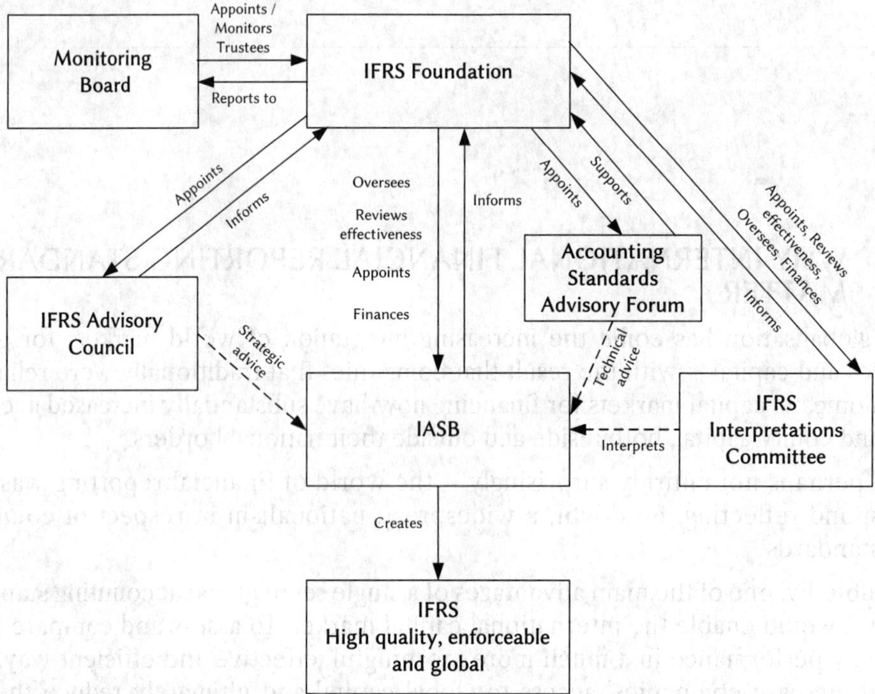

The various elements of the structure are discussed further below.

Unless indicated otherwise, references to IFRS include the following:

- International Financial Reporting Standards – standards developed by the IASB;
- International Accounting Standards (IAS) – standards developed by the International Accounting Standards Committee (IASC), the predecessor to the IASB;
- Interpretations developed by the IFRS Interpretations Committee (Interpretations Committee) or its predecessor, the Standing Interpretations Committee (SIC); and
- International Financial Reporting Standards for Small and Medium-sized Entities (IFRS for SMEs) – a stand-alone standard for general purpose financial statements of small and medium-sized entities (as defined).

2.2 The IFRS Foundation

The governance of the IFRS Foundation primarily rests with the Trustees of the IFRS Foundation (Trustees) who, in turn, act under the terms of the IFRS Foundation Constitution (the Constitution).[2] Section 17 of the Constitution requires a review, every five years, of the structure and effectiveness of the IFRS Foundation. The last review was completed in 2016 and, as a result, the Constitution was revised effective from 1 December 2016.

It is a requirement of the Constitution that, in order to ensure a broad international basis, there must be:[3]

- six Trustees appointed from the Asia/Oceania region;
- six Trustees appointed from Europe;
- six Trustees appointed from the Americas;
- one Trustee appointed from Africa; and
- three Trustees appointed from any area, subject to maintaining overall geographical balance.

The appointment of Trustees to fill vacancies caused by routine retirement or other reasons is the responsibility of the remaining Trustees but subject to the approval of the Monitoring Board as discussed in 2.3 below. The appointment of the Trustees is normally for a term of three years, renewable once.[4]

The Constitution requires that the Trustees comprise individuals that, as a group, provide a balance of professional backgrounds, and have an interest in promoting and maintaining transparency in corporate reporting globally. This includes individuals with global experience at a senior level in securities market regulators, firms representing investors, international audit networks, preparers, users, academics and officials serving the public interest. To achieve such a balance, Trustees are selected after consultation with the accounting and audit profession, the securities market and other public interest bodies, regulators, investors, preparers, users and academics. The Trustees are required to establish procedures for inviting suggestions for appointments from these relevant organisations and for allowing individuals to put forward their own names, including advertising vacant positions.[5]

The Constitution provides that 'all Trustees shall be required to show a firm commitment to the IFRS Foundation and the IASB as a high quality global standard-setter, to be financially knowledgeable, and to have an ability to meet the time commitment. Each Trustee shall have an understanding of, and be sensitive to, the challenges associated with the adoption and application of high quality global accounting standards developed for use in the world's capital markets and by other users.'[6]

The Trustees are responsible also for appointing the members of the IASB, Interpretations Committee, IFRS Advisory Council (the Advisory Council)[7] and the Accounting Standards Advisory Forum (ASAF).[8] In addition, their duties include the following:[9]

- appointing the Executive Director, in consultation with the IASB Chair, and establishing his or her contract of service and performance criteria;
- reviewing annually the strategy of the IFRS Foundation and the IASB and its effectiveness, including consideration, but not determination, of the IASB's agenda;
- assuming responsibility for establishing and maintaining appropriate financing arrangements;
- approving annually the budget of the IFRS Foundation and determining the basis for funding;
- reviewing broad strategic issues affecting financial reporting standards, promoting the IFRS Foundation and its work and promoting the objective of rigorous

application of IFRS, provided that the Trustees are excluded from involvement in technical matters relating to financial reporting standards;

- establishing or amending operating procedures for the Trustees;
- establishing and amending operating procedures, consultative arrangements and due process for the IASB, the Interpretations Committee and the Advisory Council and reviewing their compliance;
- approving amendments to the Constitution after following a due process, including consultation with the Advisory Council and publication of an exposure draft for public comment and subject to the voting requirements given in the Constitution;
- exercising all powers of the IFRS Foundation except for those expressly reserved to the IASB, the Interpretations Committee and the Advisory Council;
- fostering and reviewing the development of educational programmes and materials that are consistent with the IFRS Foundation's objectives; and
- publishing an annual report on the IFRS Foundation's activities, including audited financial statements and priorities for the coming year.

The IFRS Foundation's funding is derived primarily from voluntary contributions from jurisdictions that have put in place national financing regimes. While funding mechanisms differ, most jurisdictions have established either a levy on companies or a system of publicly supported financing. The IFRS Foundation's goal is the contribution from each jurisdiction to be a proportion of its Gross Domestic Product (GDP), calculated as a percentage of the total GDP of all contributing jurisdictions using the International Monetary Fund's (IMF) latest GDP data.[10] In 2016, the major funders of the IFRS Foundation were the international accounting firms, the European Commission, China and Japan.[11]

2.3 The Monitoring Board

The Monitoring Board was created to address a perceived lack of accountability and responsiveness by the IASB and the IFRS Foundation to the concerns of its constituents. The Monitoring Board provides a formal link between the Trustees and public authorities. This relationship seeks to replicate, on an international basis, the link between accounting standard-setters and those public authorities that have generally overseen accounting standard-setters.[12]

The Charter of the Monitoring Board notes that the Monitoring Board's mission is:[13]

- to cooperate to promote the continued development of IFRS as a high quality set of global accounting standards;
- to monitor and reinforce the public interest oversight function of the IFRS Foundation, while preserving the independence of the IASB. In that regard;
  - to participate in the selection and approval of the Trustee appointments;
  - to advise the Trustees with respect to the fulfilment of their responsibilities, in particular with respect to regulatory, legal and policy developments that are pertinent to the IFRS Foundation's oversight of the IASB and appropriate sources of IFRS Foundation funding; and
  - to discuss issues and share views relating to IFRS, as well as regulatory and market developments affecting the development and functioning of these standards.

The responsibilities of the Monitoring Board are to:[14]

- participate in the process for appointing Trustees and approve the appointment of Trustees;
- review and provide advice to the Trustees on the fulfilment of their responsibilities – there is an obligation on the Trustees to report annually to the Monitoring Board; and
- meet with the Trustees or a sub-group thereof at least annually; the Monitoring Board has the authority to request meetings with the Trustees or separately with the chair of the Trustees and with the chair of the IASB to discuss any area of the work of the Trustees or the IASB.

At the time of writing, the Monitoring Board comprises representatives of:[15]

- the IOSCO Board;
- the Securities and Exchange Commission (SEC), United States of America;
- the European Commission;
- the Financial Services Agency, Japan;
- the IOSCO Growth and Emerging Markets Committee;
- the Comissão de Valores Mobiliários, Brazil;
- the Financial Services Commission, Republic of Korea;
- the Ministry of Finance, People's Republic of China; and
- the Basel Committee on Banking Supervision (observer).

The current chairman is the representative of the IOSCO Board.

Membership of the Monitoring Board is assessed based on the following criteria:[16]

- the member must be a capital market authority responsible for setting the form and content of financial reporting in its jurisdiction;
- the jurisdiction has made a clear commitment to moving towards application of IFRS and promoting global acceptance of a single set of high-quality international accounting standards as the final goal;
- the IFRSs to be applied should be essentially aligned with IFRSs developed by the IASB;
- the jurisdiction can be regarded as a major market for capital-raising based on the size of market capitalization, the number of listed companies and capital market activity;
- the jurisdiction makes financial contributions to setting IFRS;
- the jurisdiction has a robust enforcement mechanism to ensure proper implementation of relevant accounting standards; and
- the relevant national or regional standard-setting body is committed to contributing actively to the development of IFRS.

Historically the motivation for the use of IFRS was to facilitate cross-border capital raising and, therefore, the membership of the Monitoring Board was focused on capital markets authorities that were committed to the development of high-quality global accounting standards. While this continues to be a criterion for membership, beginning with the 2016 review of its members, the Monitoring Board will evaluate the integration of IFRS for domestic issuers in that member's jurisdiction.[17]

2.4 The International Accounting Standards Board (IASB)

The members of the IASB are appointed by the Trustees.[18] As of 30 June 2017, the IASB comprises 12 members, although the Constitution requires there be normally 14 members. The main qualifications for membership of the IASB are professional competence and recent relevant professional experience.[19]

The Trustees are required to select IASB members so that the IASB, as a group, will comprise the best available combination of technical expertise and diversity of international business and market experience, including auditors, preparers, users, academics and market and/or financial regulators. No individual should be both a Trustee and a member of the IASB at the same time.[20] Furthermore, the IASB, in consultation with the Trustees, is expected to establish and maintain liaison with national standard-setters and other official bodies concerned with standard-setting to assist in the development of IFRS and to promote the convergence of national accounting standards and IFRS.[21]

The IASB will normally be required to comprise:[22]

- four members from Asia/Oceania;
- four members from Europe;
- four members from the Americas;
- one member from Africa; and
- one member appointed from any area, subject to maintaining overall geographical balance.

The responsibilities of the IASB are listed in Section 36 of the Constitution. Its primary role is to have complete responsibility for all IASB technical matters including preparing and issuing IFRSs (other than interpretations) and exposure drafts, each of which is required to include any dissenting opinions; and final approval of and issuing interpretations developed by the Interpretations Committee.[23]

Approval by at least eight members of the IASB is required for the publication of an exposure draft and IFRS (which includes final interpretations of the Interpretations Committee), if there are fewer than 14 members of the IASB. If there are 14 members, approval is required by at least nine members.[24] Other decisions of the IASB, including the publication of a discussion paper, require a simple majority of the members present at a meeting that is attended by at least 60% of the members.[25] The IASB has full discretion over its technical agenda and over project assignments on technical matters. It must, however, consult the Trustees on its agenda, and the Advisory Council on major projects, agenda decisions and work priorities. In addition, the IASB is required to carry out public consultation every five years in developing its technical agenda.[26] The most recent agenda consultation took place in August 2015. In November 2016, the IASB published the *IASB® Work Plan 2017-2021 (Feedback Statement on the 2015 Agenda Consultation)* on its agenda consultation and its five-year plan. The IASB adopted a central theme for its activities: 'Better Communication in Financial Reporting'.[27]

The IASB meets monthly, but not in August. These meetings are open to the public and meeting materials are available on the IASB's website.

2.5 The IFRS Interpretations Committee (the Interpretations Committee)

For IFRS to be truly global standards, consistent application and interpretation is required. The objectives of the Interpretations Committee are to interpret the application of IFRS, provide timely guidance on financial reporting issues that are not specifically addressed in IFRS and undertake other tasks at the request of the IASB.[28]

The national accounting standard-setting bodies and regional bodies involved with accounting standard-setting are normally consulted on issues referred to the Interpretations Committee.[29] The Interpretations Committee is expected to address issues:[30]

'(a) that have widespread effect and have, or are expected to have, a material effect on those affected;

(b) where financial reporting would be improved through the elimination, or reduction, of diverse reporting methods; and

(c) that can be resolved efficiently within the confines of existing IFRSs and the *Conceptual Framework for Financial Reporting*.'

In addition to developing interpretations, the Interpretations Committee develops minor or narrow scope amendments, including 'Annual Improvements'. The 'Annual Improvements Process' is designed to deal with 'non-urgent, minor amendments to IFRSs'. Issues dealt with in this process arise from matters raised by the Interpretations Committee and suggestions from IASB staff or practitioners, and focus on areas of inconsistency in IFRS or where clarification of wording is required.

The premise behind the Annual Improvements Process is to streamline the IASB's standard-setting process. If a number of minor amendments are processed together, there will be benefits both to constituents and the IASB. The Interpretations Committee assists the IASB by reviewing and recommending potential amendments to IFRS. 'Annual Improvements' is on the IASB's work plan like its other projects and is subject to the same due process.

If the Interpretations Committee does not plan to add an item to its work programme, it publishes a tentative rejection notice in the *IFRIC Update* and on the IFRS Foundation website and requests comments on the matter. The comment period for rejection notices is normally at least 60 days. After considering comments received, the Interpretations Committee will either confirm its decision and issue a rejection notice, add the issue to its work programme or refer the matter to the IASB. Rejection notices do not have the authority of IFRSs and, therefore, do not provide mandatory requirements. However, they should be seen as helpful, informative and persuasive. The IASB does not ratify rejection notices.[31]

The Interpretations Committee has 14 voting members. The chair, who is appointed by the Trustees, is a member of the IASB, the Director of Technical Activities or an appropriately qualified individual. The chair does not have the right to vote. The Trustees may appoint representatives of regulatory organisations, who have the right to attend and speak at meetings but not the right to vote.[32] Currently, the European Commission and IOSCO have observer status. The quorum for a meeting is 10 members,[33] and approval of draft or final interpretations requires that not more than four voting members vote against the draft or final interpretation.[34]

The Interpretations Committee meets six times a year. All technical decisions are taken at sessions that are open to public observation. The Interpretations Committee supports the IASB in improving financial reporting through timely identification, discussion and resolution of financial reporting issues within the IFRS framework.[35] Although the Interpretations Committee develops interpretations, because they are part of the respective IFRSs, they must be ratified by the IASB.[36]

2.6 The IASB's and IFRS Interpretations Committee's Due Process Handbook

The Trustees' Due Process Oversight Committee (DPOC) is responsible for overseeing the due process procedures of the IASB and Interpretations Committee throughout all the development stages of a standard or an interpretation, including agenda-setting and post-implementation reviews (PIRs).[37]

The *Due Process Handbook for the IASB and IFRS Interpretations Committee* (the Handbook) describes the due process requirements of the IASB and Interpretations Committee.[38] The requirements are built on the following principles:[39]

- transparency – the IASB conducts its standard-setting process in a transparent manner;
- full and fair consultation – considering the perspectives of those affected by IFRS globally; and
- accountability – the IASB analyses the potential effects of its proposals on affected parties and explains the rationale for why it made the decisions it reached in developing or changing a standard.

In order to gain a wide range of views from interested parties throughout all stages of the development of IFRS, the Trustees and the IASB have established consultative procedures with the objective of ensuring that, in exercising its independent decision-making, the IASB conducts its standard-setting process in a transparent manner.[40] The Trustees of the IFRS Foundation published an updated version of the Handbook in June 2016 which includes an enhanced due process for the development and maintenance of the IFRS Taxonomy.[41] The Handbook specifies some minimum steps that the IASB and the Interpretations Committee are required to follow before a standard or interpretation can be issued.[42] The following due process steps are mandatory:[43]

- debating any proposals in one or more public meetings;
- exposing for public comment a draft of any proposed new standard, proposed amendment to a standard or proposed interpretation with minimum comment periods;
- considering in a timely manner those comment letters received on the proposals;
- considering whether the proposals should be exposed again;
- reporting to the IFRS Advisory Council (see 2.7 below) on the technical programme, major projects, project proposals and work priorities; and
- ratification of an interpretation by the IASB.

The steps specified in the Constitution that are 'non-mandatory' include:[44]

- publishing a discussion document (for example, a discussion paper) before an exposure draft is developed;
- establishing consultative groups or other types of specialist advisory groups;
- holding public hearings; and
- undertaking fieldwork.

If the IASB decides not to undertake any of the non-mandatory steps, it is required to inform the DPOC of its decision and reason (known as the 'comply or explain' approach). Those explanations must be published in the decision summaries and in the basis for conclusions with the exposure draft or IFRS in question.[45]

Although not mandatory, the IASB conducts public meetings and roundtables to ensure that it has appropriate input from its constituents.

The IASB normally allows a minimum period of 120 days for comment on an exposure draft. If the matter is narrow in scope and urgent, the IASB may consider a comment period of no less than 30 days, but it will only set a period of less than 120 days after consulting, and obtaining approval from, the DPOC.[46]

Under a 'fast track' comment process, if the matter is exceptionally urgent, and only after formally requesting and obtaining prior approval from 75% of the Trustees, 'the IASB may reduce the period for public comment on an exposure draft to below 30 days but may not dispense with a comment period.'[47]

2.7 The IFRS Advisory Council (the Advisory Council)

The Advisory Council (whose members are appointed by the Trustees) provides a forum for geographically and functionally diverse organisations and individuals with an interest in international financial reporting to:

- provide input on the IASB's agenda, project timetable and project priorities; and
- give advice on projects, with emphasis on application and implementation issues, including matters that may warrant the attention of the Interpretations Committee.[48]

A secondary objective of the Advisory Council is 'to encourage broad participation in the development of IFRS as high-quality, globally-accepted standards.'[49]

The Advisory Council comprises thirty or more members, having a diversity of geographical and professional backgrounds. The chair of the Council is appointed by the Trustees, and may not be a member of the IASB or a member of its staff.[50] The Advisory Council normally meets at least two times a year, and its meetings are open to the public. It is required to be consulted by the IASB in advance of the IASB's decisions on major projects and by the Trustees in advance of any proposed changes to the Constitution.[51]

Members are appointed for an initial term of three years and may be asked to remain for up to three additional years.[52]

2.8 Accounting Standards Advisory Forum (ASAF)

The ASAF, established in 2013, is an advisory group consisting of national accounting standard-setters and regional bodies, the purpose of which is to provide technical advice and feedback to the IASB.

The membership of the ASAF consists of 12 non-voting members (appointed by the Trustees), plus the chair, who is the IASB chair or vice-chair. To ensure a broad geographical representation, the members are from the following geographic regions:[53]

- one member from Africa;
- three members from the Americas (North and South);
- three members from the Asia/Oceania region;
- three members from Europe (including non-EU); and
- two members appointed from any area of the world at large, subject to maintaining overall geographic balance.

The ASAF meets four times a year, and its meetings are open to the public.

The objective of the ASAF is 'to provide an advisory forum where members can constructively contribute towards the achievement of the IASB's goal of developing globally accepted high-quality accounting standards.' The ASAF was established to:[54]

- support the IFRS Foundation in its objectives, and contribute towards the development of a single set of high quality understandable, enforceable and globally accepted financial reporting standards;
- formalise and streamline the IASB's collective engagement with the global community of national standard setters and regional bodies in its standard setting process to ensure that a broad range of national and regional input on major technical issues related to the IASB's standard setting activities are discussed and considered; and
- facilitate effective technical discussions on standard setting issues, with representatives at a high level of professional capability and with a good knowledge of their jurisdictions.

As required by the ASAF's Terms of Reference, the Trustees commenced a review of the ASAF in November 2014; the results were published in May 2015. The feedback, which was received from ASAF members, national standard setters and regional groups, IASB members, audit firms, academics and others, was positive, with support to continue the ASAF. Among other decisions resulting from the review, the Trustees decided to amend the Terms of Reference to, among other things, extend the term of the ASAF members to three years.[55]

2.9 Other advisory bodies

In addition to the Advisory Council and the ASAF, discussed in 2.7 and 2.8, respectively, above, the IASB has a number of other formal advisory bodies that provide input on its work and resources to consult. Meetings with the advisory bodies are held in public and meeting materials are available on the IASB's website.

The IASB's other advisory bodies are as follows:[56]

- Capital Markets Advisory Committee – provides the IASB with regular input from the international community of users of financial statements;
- Emerging Economies Group – enhances the participation of emerging economies in the development of IFRSs;
- Global Preparers Forum – provides the IASB with input from the international preparer community;
- Islamic Finance Consultative Group – focuses on potential challenges linked to applying IFRS to Shariah-compliant instruments and transactions;
- IFRS Taxonomy Consultative Group – helps develop the IFRS Taxonomy;
- SME Implementation Group – supports the international adoption of the *IFRS for SMEs* and monitors its implementation;
- World Standard-setters Conferences –helps achieve the G20-endorsed objective of global accounting standards;
- Transition Resource Group for Impairment of Financial Instruments – discusses questions from stakeholders about the new impairment requirements for financial instruments;
- Transition Resource Group for Revenue Recognition – informs the IASB and the US Financial Accounting Standards Board (FASB) about potential implementation issues that could arise when entities implement the new revenue recognition standard;
- Transition Resource Group for Insurance Contracts – aids the implementation of IFRS 17 – *Insurance Contracts*;
- Consultative Group for Rate Regulation – informs the project on rate regulation; and
- Temporary *ad hoc* expert advisory groups – the IASB may create temporary *ad hoc* expert advisory groups to assist the IASB in specific project related areas.

3 THE IASB'S TECHNICAL AGENDA AND CONVERGENCE WITH US GAAP

3.1 The IASB's current priorities and future agenda

The IASB's 2017 activities focused on:[57]

- completing its work on the insurance project, with a new standard published;
- finalising an update to the *Conceptual Framework for Financial Reporting* to provide a more complete, clear and updated set of concepts;
- finalising a Practice Statement – *Making Materiality Judgements* – to provide guidance on how to apply judgement in deciding what financial information is material in preparing IFRS financial statements;
- clarifying the definition of what information is material in preparing financial statements in an exposure draft – *Definition of Material (Proposed amendments to IAS 1 and IAS 8)*;
- exploring whether the existing standards should be amended to reflect the effects of rate regulation; and
- working on a number of research projects.

At the time of writing, the IASB's work plan reflects that work on a number of these projects will continue into 2018 and beyond.

The IASB conducted its most recent agenda consultation in August 2015, the outcome of which set the technical priorities until 2021. The work plan has been revised in response to feedback received during the agenda consultation. The IASB has adopted the theme 'Better Communication in Financial Reporting' and much of the work will focus on making the financial information more relevant and improving the communication of that information.

3.2 IFRS/US GAAP convergence

'Convergence' is a term used to describe the coming together of national systems of financial reporting and IFRS. As discussed below, between 2002 and 2013, the IASB and FASB had various projects to both improve IFRS and US GAAP, respectively, and to achieve their convergence. In addition, the US Securities and Exchange Commission (SEC) have taken some steps towards the acceptance of IFRS in the US. In 2007, the SEC began permitting foreign private issuers to file IFRS financial statements without reconciliation to US GAAP. In 2008, the SEC set out a proposed roadmap outlining the milestones and conditions that, if met, could lead to the use of IFRS in the US by domestic registrants. In 2011, the SEC staff issued a work plan to explore the incorporation of IFRS into the US financial reporting system. The SEC staff has since published its final report on the IFRS work plan that raised significant concerns about the further incorporation of IFRS in the US capital markets.

In 2013, the convergence process between the IASB and the FASB largely came to an end. One of the messages the IASB staff received from respondents outside of the US to the 2011 agenda consultation was for the IASB to consider whether convergence should continue to be a priority. Ultimately, developing 'a single set of high-quality, understandable, enforceable and globally accepted financial reporting standards'[58] has largely superseded convergence as a significant driver of the IASB's agenda setting process. In fact, the Handbook, which was revised in 2013, removed convergence from the list of factors that are influential in setting the agenda.

Progress was made during the decade or so of focused convergence activities, however, during which differences in accounting were minimised in many areas, notably share-based payments, segment reporting, business combinations, consolidated financial statements, fair value measurement, joint arrangements, investment entities and revenue (with the issuance of largely converged standards). Although projects on leases, insurance and financial instruments started out as joint projects, the IASB and the FASB ultimately reached different decisions on each of them and none will be considered converged standards. No new convergence projects are planned.

In a speech in March 2014 dealing with the IASB's response to the global financial crisis, Hans Hoogervorst, IASB Chair, said the following: 'This inability to deliver compatible outcomes with the FASB clearly demonstrates the inherent instability of convergence as a means to achieve a single set of global accounting standards.

For this reason, our Trustees wisely concluded that convergence can never be a substitute for adoption of IFRS.'[59]

In December 2016, Wesley Bricker, the SEC Chief Accountant, on the question of possible further use of IFRS for domestic issuers, expressed the view that, for at least the foreseeable future, the FASB's independent standard setting process and US GAAP would continue to best serve the needs of investors and other users who rely on financial reporting by US issuers. That said, he strongly encouraged the FASB and IASB to continue to work together to eliminate differences between their standards where such efforts would strengthen the standards and be in the best interests of investors in the US public capital markets, as well as in other markets. He further commented that both the FASB and the IASB would benefit from continued collaboration as both boards continue to eliminate differences as a means of achieving progress towards the objective of high-quality accounting standards in the US and globally.[60]

We continue to support the objective of a single set of high-quality global accounting standards that are consistently applied. We acknowledge the significant challenges in achieving this aspirational goal. The past 10 years or so have presented many challenges. However, our reservations about the practicality do not negate the need to continue to work toward the goal of a single set of high-quality accounting standards globally. We believe the capital markets, investors and other users of financial information would benefit from continued progress toward the ultimate goal.

4 THE ADOPTION OF IFRS AROUND THE WORLD

4.1 Worldwide adoption

Since 2001, there has been a tremendous increase in the adoption of IFRS around the world. The precise way in which this has happened has varied among jurisdictions. This section sets out a brief description of how a number of key jurisdictions in each continent have approached the adoption. Some have adopted full IFRS, i.e. IFRS as issued by the IASB. Other jurisdictions have converged, or have a plan to converge, their standards with IFRS.

An entity is required to apply IFRS 1 – *First-time Adoption of International Financial Reporting Standards* – when it first asserts compliance with IFRS. The IASB has, therefore, established unambiguously the principle that full application of its standards and related interpretations is necessary for an entity to be able to assert that its financial statements comply with IFRS (as issued by the IASB). Consequently, it is necessary for countries that align their national standards with IFRS to require the application of IFRS 1 so that entities reporting under those standards can assert compliance with IFRS. In addition, an entity that applies IFRS as amended by a local authority cannot assert compliance with IFRS.

The following table summarises IFRS adoption (generally for consolidated financial statements) in countries with domestic market capitalisation exceeding US$500 billion as at 30 June 2017. For further details on selected countries/regions, see 4.2 to 4.6 below. In addition, the IFRS Foundation is developing profiles of application of IFRS. At the time of writing, profiles for 150 jurisdictions have been completed and are available on the IASB's website.

Country	IFRS Status	IFRS Permitted
Australia	Required for all publicly accountable entities and any entity preparing general purpose financial statements that elects not to apply the framework under the Reduced Disclosure Regime (RDR). Non-publicly accountable entities are required to apply IFRS recognition and measurement requirements with simplified disclosures of the RDR.	
Brazil	Required for regulated public companies, with exemptions for banks and real estate companies; other companies must follow converged national standards.	
Canada	Required for publicly accountable entities.	Permitted for all other entities.
Mainland China	Substantially converged national standards.	
European Union	IFRS as adopted by the EU (EU IFRS – see 4.2.1 below) required for consolidated financial statements of all listed companies and some unlisted companies. Exemption for non-EU companies applying for listing on an EU regulated market that apply certain GAAP's determined by the European Commission to be equivalent to EU IFRS.	EU member states may permit or require the application of EU IFRS by unlisted companies and in separate financial statements.
France	See European Union.	EU IFRS permitted for the consolidated financial statements of non-listed entities.
Germany	See European Union.	EU IFRS permitted for the consolidated financial statements of non-listed entities.
Hong Kong	HKFRS (converged with IFRS) is required for all Hong Kong incorporated companies (listed and non-listed).	Permitted for listed companies incorporated overseas.
India	IFRS converged Indian Accounting Standards (Ind AS), with some mandatory and numerous optional departures from IFRS, to apply in phases from financial years beginning on or after 1 April 2016.	Until Ind AS was introduced, listed companies with subsidiaries were permitted to apply IFRS in consolidated financial statements. This option is no longer available.
Italy	See European Union. EU IFRS is required in the separate financial statements of companies on the Italian regulated stock exchange except insurance companies. Scope of EU IFRS extended to certain financial institutions.	EU IFRS permitted in the statutory separate and consolidated financial statements of all other non-listed entities and non-regulated enterprises (except SMEs).
Japan	Considering mandatory adoption.	Permitted for most companies that are listed or planning to be listed on a domestic stock exchange.
Korea	IFRS as adopted by Korea (K-IFRS) is required for all listed entities, unlisted financial institutions and state-owned entities.	K-IFRS permitted for non-listed entities.

Country	IFRS Status	IFRS Permitted
Russia	Required for banks, insurance entities, non-state pension funds, clearing institutions, certain investment management entities, listed companies and for some state unitary enterprises and state-owned public joint-stock companies. Substantially converged national standards applicable to statutory stand-alone financial statements.	
Singapore	Converged national standards with modifications (Singapore Financial Reporting Standards – SFRS). Foreign entities that are listed on the Singapore Exchange are required to file financial statements prepared in accordance with SFRS, IFRS or US GAAP. Singapore listed companies will be required to file financial statements prepared under an IFRS-identical financial reporting framework for annual periods beginning on or after 1 January 2018. For all non-listed Singapore-incorporated companies, the option to file financial statements under an IFRS-identical financial reporting framework will also be made available for voluntary application at the same time.	Singapore incorporated entities are permitted to file IFRS financial statements with approval.
South Africa	Required for all listed companies. From December 2012, non-listed companies generally use either IFRS or IFRS for SMEs.	
Spain	See European Union.	EU IFRS permitted for non-listed groups for consolidated financial statements; no reversion to local GAAP once an entity has applied EU IFRS.
Switzerland	Issuers of equity securities that are incorporated in Switzerland and listed under the International Standard on the SIX Swiss Exchange (SIX) must apply either IFRS or US GAAP. Other listed entities incorporated in Switzerland must apply IFRS, US GAAP or Swiss GAAP-FER. Entities not incorporated in Switzerland must apply IFRS, US GAAP or a national GAAP deemed by the SIX to be equivalent.	IFRS permitted in consolidated statutory financial statements of non-listed entities.
Taiwan	Standards and interpretations endorsed by the local regulators apply for financial statements beginning on or after 1 January 2017. The effective dates for standards and interpretations for Taiwan IFRS are mostly aligned with global effective dates; however, early adoption is generally not permitted.	IFRS permitted for foreign issuers, with reconciliation to 'Taiwan-IFRS'.
United Kingdom	See European Union. In addition, EU IFRS is mandatory when a company admitted to the UK Alternative Investment Market (AIM) is incorporated in the European Economic Area (EEA) unless such company is not a parent.	EU IFRS permitted for all companies, except in the charities sector; restrictions on reversion to local GAAP once an entity has adopted EU IFRS.

Country	IFRS Status	IFRS Permitted
United States	Substantial convergence of selected standards.	Permitted for foreign private issuers preparing financial statements in accordance with IFRS as issued by the IASB.

4.2 Europe

4.2.1 EU

In July 2002, the European Parliament adopted Regulation No. 1606/2002 (the Regulation), which required publicly traded EU incorporated companies[61] to prepare, by 2005 at the latest, their consolidated financial statements under IFRS 'adopted' (as discussed further below) for application within the EU.

Although an EU regulation has direct effect on companies, without the need for national legislation, the Regulation provides an option for EU member states to permit or require the application of adopted IFRS in the preparation of annual unconsolidated financial statements and to permit or require the application of adopted IFRS by unlisted companies. This means that EU member states can require the uniform application of adopted IFRS by important sectors, such as banking or insurance, regardless of whether or not companies are listed. An analysis of the implementation of the Regulation published in 2012 shows that nearly all EU member states use the option to permit the application of adopted IFRS in the consolidated accounts of some or all types of unlisted companies. More than half of the EU member states also permit the application of adopted IFRS in the annual financial statements of some or all types of unlisted companies.[62]

The Regulation established the basic rules for the creation of an endorsement mechanism for the adoption of IFRS, the timetable for implementation and a review clause to permit an assessment of the overall approach proposed. The European Commission took the view that an endorsement mechanism was needed to provide the necessary public oversight. The European Commission considered also that it was not appropriate, politically or legally, to delegate accounting standard-setting unconditionally and irrevocably to a private organisation over which the European Commission had no influence. In addition, the endorsement mechanism is responsible for examining whether the standards adopted by the IASB satisfy relevant EU public policy criteria.

The role of the endorsement mechanism is not to reformulate or replace IFRS, but to oversee the adoption of new standards and interpretations, intervening only when they contain material deficiencies or have failed to cater for features specific to the EU economic or legal environments. The central task of this mechanism is to confirm that IFRS provides a suitable basis for financial reporting by listed EU companies. The mechanism is based on a two-tier structure, combining a regulatory level with an expert level, to assist the European Commission in its endorsement role.

The recitals to the Regulation state that the endorsement mechanism should act expeditiously and also be a means to deliberate, reflect and exchange information on international accounting standards among the main parties concerned, in particular national accounting standard setters, supervisors in the fields of securities, banking and insurance, central banks including the European Central Bank (ECB), the accounting profession and users and preparers of accounts. The mechanism should be a means of fostering common understanding of adopted international accounting standards in the EU community.[63]

The European Commission is advised on IFRS by the European Financial Reporting Advisory Group (EFRAG). EFRAG is a private sector body established by the European organisations prominent in European capital markets, e.g. the Federation of European Accountants (FEE) and the European Banking Federation. In addition to advising the European Commission on endorsement of IFRS, EFRAG is the mechanism by which Europe as a whole can participate in the global debate on accounting standards and it coordinates European responses to IASB proposals. EFRAG plays a proactive role issuing discussion papers, field-test reports and feedback statements on outreach events. The objective of the proactive work is to involve European stakeholders at an early stage in identifying necessary improvements to financial reporting so as to influence the IASB.

In addition to EFRAG, the European Commission seeks approval from its member states through the Accounting Regulatory Committee. In 2013, a special adviser for the EU was named to develop recommendations for enhancing the EU's role in international accounting standard-setting. As a result, the so-called Maystadt Report was published in November 2013, which included, among other things, recommended changes in the governance of EFRAG, e.g. establishing a new high-level board to approve of all EFRAG's positions and endorsement advice letters.

The recommendations from the Maystadt Report were implemented in 2014 and resulted in a new governance structure effective from 31 October 2014. The EFRAG Board now includes, in equal numbers, representatives of European stakeholder organisations and national standard setters and is led by the President of the EFRAG Board, who is nominated by the European Commission. The EFRAG Board is responsible for all EFRAG positions and operates on the basis of a consensus-based decision-making process with the objective of Europe speaking with one voice. The European Commission, the European supervisory authorities and the ECB participate in the EFRAG Board in an observer capacity. The EFRAG Board takes all its decisions after considering the advice of the EFRAG Technical Expert Group (EFRAG TEG) and the results of EFRAG's due process, and after hearing from the Accounting Regulatory Committee and making all assessments deemed relevant from a political perspective. Following the implementation of the Maystadt reform in 2014, EFRAG's activities include assessments of whether the IASB's proposals and IFRS requirements are conducive to the European public good. This includes the interaction with economic concerns, such as financial stability and growth.

Concerns have been expressed about the EU endorsement process but to date, apart from the carve out from IAS 39 – *Financial Instruments: Recognition and Measurement* (refer to Chapter 48) and the decision not to endorse IFRS 14 – *Regulatory Deferral Accounts*,[64] all IASB standards have ultimately been endorsed. However, there are standards and a number of Interpretations Committee interpretations that have had delayed application dates. The most notable is the effective date for IFRS 10 – *Consolidated Financial Statements*, IFRS 11 – *Joint Arrangements*, IFRS 12 – *Disclosure of Interests in Other Entities*, IAS 27 – *Separate Financial Statements* – and IAS 28 – *Investments in Associates and Joint Ventures* – for which the European Commission permitted a one-year deferral to the mandatory effective date set by the IASB.

However, there is another potential departure from the requirements of IASB standards arising from the endorsement of *Applying IFRS 9 Financial Instruments with IFRS 4 Insurance Contracts (Amendments to IFRS 4).* In July 2017, the European Commission included in its proposed regulation submitted to the European Parliament and the Council of the European Union an additional deferral option not included in the original standard.[65] According to Article 2 of the proposed regulation, a financial conglomerate would be allowed to elect that none of its entities operating in the insurance sector apply IFRS 9 in the consolidated financial statements for financial years beginning before 1 January 2021 when certain conditions are met. The European Commission added this deferral option as it considers that the amendments to IFRS 4 – *Insurance Contracts* – are not sufficiently broad in scope to meet the needs of all significant insurance entities in the EU especially when those are operating within a financial conglomerate.

In 2014, the European Commission started an evaluation of the Regulation on the application of IFRS to assess whether:

- the Regulation achieved its objective in an efficient and effective manner;
- the criteria that all new IFRS should meet to become EU law are appropriate and whether the process for adoption of standards works properly; and
- the governance structure of the bodies developing the standards and advising the Commission is appropriate.

The evaluation mainly included a public consultation, an informal expert group, and a review of literature on the impact of the mandatory adoption of IFRS in the EU and on the performance of IFRS during the financial crisis. The results were included in a report issued on 18 June 2015. The key findings showed that IFRS was successful in creating a common accounting language for capital markets and that there is still no well-defined alternative to IFRS. The evidence from the evaluation also showed that the objectives of the Regulation remain relevant. Companies that responded to the public consultation were mostly positive about their experience of using IFRS and in most cases, benefits outweighed costs. Investors also largely supported IFRS for improving the transparency and comparability of financial statements. Most stakeholders considered that the process through which IFRS become part of EU law works well.

However, the report identifies room for improvement in some areas. Amongst others, it was noted that the coherence of standards with EU laws should continue to be assessed during standard development and endorsement. In addition, the Commission announced that it will look at whether the powers of the European supervisory authorities are sufficient and will consider measures to simplify the endorsement process. Further, the Commission suggested that the IASB strengthen its impact analysis and consider the needs of long-term investors when developing standards.

The European Commission followed up on this issue in March 2017 when it launched a public consultation on the operation of the European Supervisory Authorities (ESAs) one of which is the European Securities and Markets Authority (ESMA).[66] The consultation document suggested that the review of the ESAs' operation might also be used to streamline the endorsement process in the EU and that this could be achieved by giving ESMA an advisory role in the endorsement process. The feedback from numerous stakeholders, however, was not favourable for the proposals and a vast majority of the respondents were of the view that there is no reason to change the current endorsement process or the role of EFRAG.[67] In addition, stakeholders emphasised that a clear separation of powers between standard setting and enforcement should be maintained to avoid conflicts of interest. ESMA itself proposed in its comment letter to increase its role in the endorsement process for IFRS by imposing a formal requirement for it to give the Commission advice on the European public good and financial stability.[68]

4.2.2 Russia

Since 1998, Russian Accounting Principles (RAP) have been gradually converging towards IFRS. Most of RAP are substantially based on IFRS, although some IFRSs have no comparable RAP standard and some RAP standards that are based on IFRS have not been updated for recent changes to the comparable IFRS. Statutory financial statements are required to be prepared by all legal entities in accordance with RAP.

Since 2004, the Central Bank of the Russian Federation (CBR) has required credit institutions to file financial statements prepared in accordance with IFRS as issued by the IASB. For public reporting purposes, 'A-listed' Russian companies were also required to present financial statements in accordance with IFRS or US GAAP.

In 2010 the Russian Federal Law *On consolidated financial statements* (the Law) introduced a legislative requirement on mandatory application of IFRS for the preparation and presentation of consolidated financial statements by certain Russian entities. Initially only credit institutions, insurance companies and listed companies were in the scope of the Law.

Amendments to the Law adopted in 2014 (2014 Law) broadened its scope by requiring non-state pension funds; management companies of investment funds, mutual funds and non-state pension funds; and clearing institutions to present IFRS financial statements. The 2014 Law established a right for the government to require certain state unitary enterprises and state-owned companies to present financial statements in accordance with IFRS. In 2015, the Russian government issued a regulation that required those state unitary enterprises and state-owned public joint stock companies to present their consolidated financial statements in accordance with IFRS, starting with their annual financial statements for 2016. The 2014 Law also clarified that IFRS financial statements are required to be presented by Russian entities that otherwise are in the scope of the Law but have no subsidiaries. The Law was further amended in 2016 to require credit institutions and listed companies to present their half-year interim consolidated financial statements under IFRS starting from 2017.

The Law also established an IFRS endorsement process in Russia. Under the Law, individual IFRSs (standards and interpretations) become mandatory starting from the effective date specified in the IFRS or from the date of its endorsement if it is later. IFRSs can be voluntarily applied after they are endorsed but before their effective date. In practice, the time period between the IASB issuing a new or amended standard and its endorsement in Russia is not significant, which allows Russian companies to early adopt IFRSs and amendments.

The IFRS endorsement process involves an analysis of the Russian language text of an IFRS, provided by the IFRS Foundation, by the National Organization for Financial

Accounting and Reporting Standards Foundation (NOFA), an independent, non-commercial organisation identified by the Ministry of Finance of the Russian Federation (Ministry of Finance). NOFA performs an analysis of an individual IFRS's suitability for the Russian financial reporting system. NOFA advises the Ministry of Finance whether an IFRS should be endorsed as issued by the IASB or whether certain requirements should be 'carved out' to meet the needs of the financial reporting system in Russia. The Ministry of Finance, after consultation with the CBR, makes the final decision on endorsement and publication of an IFRS.

At the time of writing, the Ministry of Finance endorsed, without any 'carve outs', all IFRSs effective from 1 January 2017. IFRS 9 – *Financial Instruments*, IFRS 15 – *Revenue from Contracts with Customers* – and IFRS 16 – *Leases*, were also endorsed and, therefore, are available for early adoption by Russian companies. IFRS 17, two newly issued interpretations IFRIC 22 – *Foreign Currency Transactions and Advance Consideration* – and IFRIC 23 – *Uncertainty over Income Tax Treatments* – and certain amendments to existing standards are in the process of endorsement.

4.3 Americas

4.3.1 US

See 3.2 above for a discussion of the status of US adoption of IFRS.

4.3.2 Canada

For publicly accountable enterprises, the Accounting Standards Board (AcSB) adopted IFRS as Canadian GAAP for fiscal years beginning on or after 1 January 2011, with some deferrals for certain types of entities, which have now expired, and with the exception of pension plans and benefit plans that have characteristics similar to pension plans. Such plans follow the accounting standards for pension plans issued by the AcSB as of 1 January 2011, rather than IAS 26 – *Accounting and Reporting by Retirement Benefit Plans.*

The definition of 'publicly accountable enterprises' is essentially the same as 'publicly accountable entity' in IFRS for SMEs. Canadian publicly accountable enterprises that are registered with the US SEC are permitted to apply US accounting standards rather than IFRS. SEC registered Canadian entities operating in industries dominated by US entities tend to favour US accounting standards over IFRS. In addition, securities regulators have indicated that they will consider permitting the use of US standards by Canadian rate-regulated entities that file with Canadian securities commissions even if they are not SEC registered. A number of these entities have been granted permission to use US standards.

For non-publicly accountable enterprises and not-for-profit organisations, the AcSB has developed new bases of accounting that are derived from Canadian standards rather than IFRS, although IFRS is also available for use by those entities on a voluntary basis.

The adoption of IFRS in Canada for publicly accountable enterprises means that the AcSB has effectively ceased to make final decisions on most matters affecting the technical content and timing of implementation of standards applied to publicly accountable enterprises in Canada. The AcSB's plans for incorporating new or amended IFRS into Canadian standards include reviewing all IASB documents issued for comment. As part of this process, the AcSB seeks the input of Canadian stakeholders by issuing its own 'wraparound exposure draft' of the IASB proposals, together with a document highlighting the key elements of the IASB proposals that are particularly relevant to Canadian stakeholders. In addition, the AcSB may perform outreach activities such as public roundtables. Any changes to IFRS must be approved by the AcSB before becoming part of Canadian GAAP.

While the AcSB retains the power to modify or add to the requirements of IFRS, it intends to avoid changing IFRS when adopting them as Canadian GAAP. Accordingly, the AcSB does not expect to eliminate any options within existing IFRS. As issues relevant to Canadian users of financial information arise in the future, the AcSB will work to resolve them through the Interpretations Committee or the IASB. In the event that a resolution by the Interpretations Committee or IASB is not possible, the AcSB will stand ready to develop additional temporary guidance.

The AcSB has an IFRS Discussion Group to provide a public forum to discuss the application of IFRS in Canada and to identify matters that should be forwarded to the Interpretations Committee for further consideration. The Group does not interpret IFRS or seek consensus on its application in Canada. It meets in public up to four times per year and has generated several submissions for the Interpretations Committee's agenda.

4.3.3 Brazil

Local accounting standards in Brazil (CPCs) have been converged with IFRS since 2010 and public companies regulated by the 'Comissão de Valores Mobiliários' (CVM) are also required to make a formal statement of compliance with IFRS as issued by the IASB for their consolidated financial statements. The only exception is for homebuilding companies, which are temporarily permitted to continue to apply IAS 11 – *Construction Contracts* – rather than IAS 18 – *Revenue* – under IFRIC 15 – *Agreements for the Construction of Real Estate*. Due to the upcoming adoption of IFRS 15, this matter is currently being reconsidered.

Banks are regulated by the Brazilian Central Bank, which continues to require preparation of financial statements under its pre-existing rules. However, larger companies, as defined by law, including banks, are also required to prepare annual financial statements in accordance with IFRS since 2010, which must be made publicly available. Insurance companies were required to adopt the local CPCs, and hence IFRS, in 2011.

Non-public companies outside financial services are required to apply the CPCs. Smaller non-public companies are permitted to apply CPCs for SMEs which is an equivalent of IFRS for SMEs.

4.4 Asia

4.4.1 China

4.4.1.A Mainland China

The Ministry of Finance in China (the MOF) – through its Accounting Regulatory Department – is responsible for the promulgation of accounting standards, which are applicable to various business enterprises.

Representatives of the China Accounting Standards Committee (CASC), which falls under the Accounting Regulatory Department of the MOF, and the IASB met in Beijing in November 2005 to discuss a range of issues relating to the convergence of Chinese accounting standards with IFRS. At the conclusion of the meeting, the two delegations released a joint statement setting out key points of agreement, including the following:

- the CASC stated that convergence is one of the fundamental goals of its standard-setting programme, with the intention that an enterprise applying Chinese accounting standards should produce financial statements that are the same as those of an enterprise that applies IFRS; and
- the delegation acknowledged that convergence with IFRS will take time and how to converge with IFRS is a matter for China to determine.

Since February 2006, the MOF issued a series of new and revised Accounting Standards for Business Enterprises (ASBE), which included the Basic Standard and 41 specific accounting standards. In April 2010, the MOF issued the Road Map for Continual Convergence of the ASBE with IFRS (the MOF Road Map), which requires the application of ASBE by all listed companies, some non-listed financial enterprises and central state-owned enterprises, and most large and medium-sized enterprises. The MOF Road Map also states that ASBE will continue to maintain convergence with IFRS.

To maintain continuous convergence with IFRS, during the period from August 2016 to July 2017, the MOF released seven new and revised accounting standards, covering revenue, non-current assets held for sale, disposal groups and discontinued operations, government grants, and financial instruments, which are generally converged with the relevant IFRSs.

ASBE, to a large extent, represents convergence with IFRS, with due consideration being given to specific situations in China. ASBE covers the recognition, measurement, presentation and disclosure of most transactions and events, financial reporting, and nearly all the topics covered by current IFRS. Most of ASBE is substantially in line with the corresponding IFRS, with a more simplified form of disclosures. However, there are ASBE that do not have an IFRS equivalent, such as that on non-monetary transactions and common control business combinations, and there are certain standards that restrict or eliminate measurement alternatives that exist in IFRS. For example, the ASBE on investment property permits the use of the fair value model only when certain strict criteria are met. Whilst ASBE is not identical to IFRS, the substantive difference from IFRS is that the ASBE on impairment of assets prohibits the reversal of an impairment loss for long-lived assets in all situations.

4.4.1.B Hong Kong

The Hong Kong Institute of Certified Public Accountants (HKICPA) is the principal source of accounting principles in Hong Kong. These include a series of Hong Kong Financial Reporting Standards, accounting standards referred to as Hong Kong Accounting Standards (HKAS) and Interpretations issued by the HKICPA. The term 'Hong Kong Financial Reporting Standards' (HKFRS) is deemed to include all of the foregoing.

HKFRS was fully converged with IFRS (subject to the exceptions discussed below) with effect from 1 January 2005. The HKICPA Council supports the integration of its standard-setting process with that of the IASB.

Although the HKICPA Council has a policy of maintaining convergence of HKFRS with IFRS, the HKICPA Council may consider it appropriate to include additional disclosure requirements in an HKFRS or, in some exceptional cases, to deviate from an IFRS. Each HKFRS contains information about the extent of compliance with the equivalent IFRS. When the requirements of an HKFRS and an IFRS differ, the HKFRS is required to be followed by entities reporting within the area of application of HKFRS. However in practice, exceptions to IFRS are few and relate to certain transitional provisions.

Certain smaller companies or groups meeting the necessary requirements and size criteria are permitted (but not required) to adopt the HKICPA's locally developed small and medium-sized financial reporting framework and financial reporting standards.

4.4.2 Japan

Gradual convergence of Japanese GAAP and IFRS has been ongoing for a number of years; however, full mandatory adoption of IFRS in Japan has been put on hold for the time being.

In June 2009, the Business Advisory Council (BAC), a key advisory body to the Financial Services Agency, approved a roadmap for the adoption of IFRS in Japan. This roadmap gives the option of voluntary adoption to companies that meet certain conditions.

In June 2013, the BAC published an 'Interim Policy Relating to IFRS' (the Policy), which further encourages the voluntary adoption of IFRS. The Policy states that although it is not yet the right time to determine whether or not to require mandatory implementation of IFRS in Japan, the BAC recognises that it is important to expand greater voluntary adoption of IFRS in Japan. Accordingly, conditions for voluntary adoption of IFRS have been relaxed, and some other measures have been taken to make the dual reporting of IFRS in consolidated financial statements and Japanese GAAP in standalone financial statements less of a burden on preparers.

The ruling Liberal Democratic Party (LDP) issued a 'Statement on Approach to IFRS' (the Statement) in June 2013. In contrast to the Policy issued by the BAC, the Statement puts more emphasis on preparation for the future adoption of IFRS. The Statement highlights key points to expand greater voluntary adoption of IFRS in Japan.

All IFRSs issued by the IASB are the basis of voluntary adoption of IFRS in Japan, but a further endorsement mechanism was put in place in 2015. It is contemplated that under this endorsement mechanism, each IFRS would be reviewed and amended only after careful consideration of situations specific to Japan. However, the endorsement mechanism has been used to introduce a 'carved-out version' of IFRS to make transition to IFRS as issued by the IASB easier for Japanese companies. In June 2015, *Japan's Modified International Standards (JMIS): Accounting Standards Comprising IFRSs and the ASBJ Modifications* was issued by the Accounting Standards Board of Japan (ASBJ). JMIS may be adopted in annual periods ending on or after 31 March 2016. JMIS differs from IFRS in that it requires goodwill to be amortised and requires all items recorded in other comprehensive income be recycled to profit or loss eventually. At the time of writing, no Japanese companies have announced plans to apply JMIS. It should be noted that despite the introduction of JMIS, there is no change in the option of Japanese companies to use IFRS as issued by the IASB if they so elect.

Following all of the above actions, the number of the companies voluntarily adopting IFRS in Japan has increased to approximately 60, mostly larger, companies. Although that number seems low, these companies represent a significant and growing part of the market capitalisation of the Tokyo Stock Exchange.

4.4.3 India

Accounting standards in India are issued by the Institute of Chartered Accountants of India (ICAI) and are 'notified' by the Ministry of Corporate Affairs (MCA) under the Companies Act. Until the financial year ended 31 March 2016, all companies registered under the Companies Act were required to follow Indian GAAP standards, which are based on old versions of IFRS and contain many key differences from IFRS.

In February 2015, the MCA notified the Companies (Indian Accounting Standards) Rules, 2015[69] laying down the roadmap for application of IFRS converged standards, known as Indian Accounting Standards (Ind AS), to Indian companies other than banking companies, insurance companies and non-banking finance companies (NBFCs). The Ind AS standards have also been notified.

In January 2016, the MCA issued the phasing-in dates of Ind AS applicability for NBFCs. The Reserve Bank of India also issued the Ind AS applicability dates in phases for banks starting from 1 April 2018. The Insurance Regulatory and Development Authority of India initially expected to apply Ind AS to insurers from the same date as banks. However, due to the issuance of IFRS 17 by the IASB, the applicability of Ind AS to insurers is deferred by two years.

All companies applying Ind AS are required to present comparative information according to Ind AS for at least one year. Ind AS will apply to both standalone financial statements and consolidated financial statements of companies covered under the roadmap.

Companies not covered under the roadmap can either apply Ind AS voluntarily or continue applying existing standards, i.e. current Indian GAAP. If Ind AS is applied voluntarily, this option will be irrevocable.

In 2009, the Securities and Exchange Board of India (SEBI), the securities regulator in India, permitted listed companies with subsidiaries to submit their consolidated financial statements in accordance with IFRS as issued by the IASB. Few companies in India had availed themselves of this option. The option is no longer available for companies. Ind AS contains certain departures from IFRS, including:

- mandatory deviations from IFRS, such as, accounting for foreign currency convertible bonds, accounting for a bargain purchase gain (i.e. 'negative goodwill') in a business combination and current/non-current classification of liabilities on breach of loan covenants;
- optional carve-outs, such as, measurement of property, plant and equipment on first-time adoption and accounting for foreign exchange differences on long-term monetary items that exist at the date of transition;

- removal of accounting options under IFRS, such as, removal of the fair value measurement option for investment properties and the removal of the two-statement approach for the statement of comprehensive income;
- additional guidance under Ind AS, such as for common control business combinations, foreign exchange differences regarded as an adjustment of borrowing costs and treatment of security deposits; and
- companies are required to apply Ind AS 109 *Financial Instruments*, corresponding to IFRS 9, from the date of initial application of Ind AS. There is no Ind AS corresponding to IAS 39. Also, Ind AS 115 – *Revenue from Contracts with Customers*, corresponding to IFRS 15 is deferred.

Consequently, financial statements prepared in accordance with Ind AS may not comply with IFRS.

4.5 Australia

Australia has a regime in which IFRSs are issued under its legal framework as Australian Accounting Standards. These are essentially word-for-word copies of IFRSs. Australian Accounting Standards also include some additional Australian specific standards for entities such as superannuation entities, general insurance and life insurance entities (the insurance standards will be replaced by AASB 17 – *Insurance Contracts*, which is equivalent to IFRS 17, once effective) and some additional disclosures within certain standards.

Compliance by Australian private sector for-profit entities with Australian Accounting Standards will result in compliance with IFRS as issued by the IASB. Explicit statements to this effect are made by the preparers (in the notes to the financial statements and in the Directors' Declaration required by the Corporations Act), as well by the auditors in their reports. Not-for-profit and public sector entities broadly follow for-profit Australian Accounting Standards and hence IFRS, but there are some differences.

Australia has not adopted IFRS for SMEs, and does not appear likely to in the near future because of measurement differences and the removal of options as compared to IFRS.

Australia has a Reduced Disclosure Regime for entities that are not publicly accountable (per the IFRS for SMEs definition). This framework requires such entities to apply all of the recognition and measurement requirements of Australian Accounting Standards, but have reduced disclosure requirements. The Reduced Disclosure Regime disclosures are mandated and are based on the principles adopted by the IASB in its development of the IFRS for SMEs. Financial statements prepared under the Reduced Disclosure Regime are general purpose financial statements but will not comply with IFRS as issued by the IASB.

Australia also permits non-reporting entities (as defined by Australian Accounting Standards) to prepare special purpose financial statements. Preparers are encouraged to follow the recognition and measurement requirements of Australian Accounting Standards and have a great deal of flexibility as to the level of disclosure to provide. Research undertaken by the Australian Accounting Standards Board in 2014 has raised some fundamental questions about the adequacy of special purpose financial statements and is undertaking work to address the issues raised.

4.6 Africa – South Africa

For periods beginning on or after 1 January 2005, the South African securities exchange, JSE Limited (JSE), has required that all listed companies prepare financial statements under IFRS.

Effective 1 May 2011, the South African Companies Act permits different accounting frameworks to apply to different categories of companies based on their 'public interest score'. Listed companies are required to use IFRS, however other companies (depending on their public interest score) may apply IFRS, IFRS for SMEs, or in certain situations (introduced, in particular, for micro-entities) entity specific accounting policies as determined by themselves.

In addition to the disclosure requirements of IFRS and IFRS for SMEs, the South African Companies Act and the JSE impose certain additional disclosure requirements on reporting entities. Further, the previous South African standard setter – the Accounting Practices Board – issued four interpretations. While these interpretations are specific to issues in the South African environment, IFRS reporters in South Africa make use of them as they are based on a framework equivalent to that used for IFRS. These are updated for developments in IFRS.

5 CONSISTENCY IN APPLICATION OF IFRS

The use of a consistent set of accounting standards by companies throughout the world has the potential to improve the comparability and transparency of financial information. The provision of higher quality information has been shown to reduce financial statement preparation costs and, it is believed, to enable capital markets participants to make better decisions. The global adoption of IFRS is a necessary condition for global comparability, but, on its own, it is insufficient. Global comparability cannot be achieved without a rigorous and consistent application of the standards. However, consistent application of the standards cannot be achieved unless countries adopt IFRS without modifying the standards issued by the IASB.

Studies into the impact of the use of IFRS indicate reduced cost of capital and improvements in share prices and trading, resulting in part from increased disclosure and enhanced information comparability. However, the research concludes that these improvements occur in countries with strong legal enforcement.[70] The adoption of IFRS alone is, therefore, unlikely to produce uniform financial reporting. The standards need to be applied, audited and enforced on a consistent basis in order to get the most out of comparability.[71]

Practitioners and regulators agree that enforcement of accounting standards is an integral part of achieving accounting quality under IFRS. With this in mind, ESMA has agreed on common enforcement priorities and has made the consistent application of IFRS one of its primary objectives. In December 2014, ESMA's guidelines on enforcement of financial information (the Guidelines) became effective. They replace earlier versions of the guidelines from ESMA and its predecessor, the Council of European Securities Regulators (CESR). The Guidelines apply to all EU national competent authorities and other bodies in the EU that undertake enforcement responsibilities. The Guidelines build on a common approach to the enforcement of financial information and reinforce coordination among European enforcers. In addition, the Guidelines codify European common enforcement priorities and include a requirement to discuss views on accounting matters prior to taking enforcement decisions.[72]

In addition to enforcement, ESMA contributes to the standard-setting process by engaging with the IASB and the Interpretations Committee by submitting comment letters and identifying areas of diversity in practice (including areas in which a lack of clarity in standards could lead to diversity in practice). In addition, the IFRS Foundation and ESMA have entered into a joint Statement of Protocols, which reaffirms the cooperation between the two entities as well as describes additional areas of cooperation including electronic reporting, the implementation of new standards and emerging financial reporting issues.[73]

The IFRS Foundation and IOSCO have entered into a joint Statement of Protocols to facilitate consistency in the application of IFRS. This is in addition to the memorandum of understanding between the capital markets authorities that formed the Monitoring Board (see 2.3 above) and the IFRS Foundation.[74]

The SEC stresses the importance of enforcing IFRS, not only through its filing review process of foreign private issuers, but also through its collaboration with foreign counterparts bilaterally and through IOSCO.[75]

Although consistent application of IFRS is not the primary responsibility of the IASB, it understandably takes a keen interest. The ASAF was established (see 2.8 above) to coordinate interaction with national and regional standard-setting bodies to, among other things, identify where divergence occurs across borders.[76] The post-implementation reviews of all major standards and interpretations are intended to identify and rectify difficulties in consistency that are identified only after the standard is used. The Interpretations Committee plays a key role as well.

Much has been written about consistency in IFRS, but a recurring message is that it requires a coordinated effort by standard-setters, preparers, regulators and auditors.

6 SUMMARY

IFRS is now, together with US GAAP, one of the two globally recognised financial reporting frameworks. Although the goal of a single set of high-quality global accounting standards has not been fulfilled, given the number of countries that have adopted or converged with IFRS or have plans to in the future, it is safe to say that IFRS has become 'International GAAP'.

References

1 IFRS Foundation website http://www.ifrs.org/use-around-the-world/use-of-ifrs-standards-by-jurisdiction/#analysis (accessed 23 August 2017).
2 IFRS Foundation Constitution, December 2016, Section 3.
3 IFRS Foundation Constitution, December 2016, Section 6.
4 IFRS Foundation Constitution, December 2016, Section 8.
5 IFRS Foundation Constitution, December 2016, Section 7.
6 IFRS Foundation Constitution, December 2016, Section 6.
7 IFRS Foundation Constitution, December 2016, Sections 15(a) and (c).
8 Accounting Standards Advisory Forum: Terms of Reference/Charter.
9 IFRS Foundation Constitution, December 2016, Sections 13 and 15.
10 IFRS Foundation website, http://www.ifrs.org/about-us/who-we-are/#funding (accessed 23 August 2017).
11 IFRS Foundation Annual Report 2016, '2016 Financial Supporters'.
12 IFRS Foundation Constitution, December 2016, Section 18.
13 Charter of the IFRSF Monitoring Board, February 2016.
14 IFRS Foundation Constitution, December 2016, Section 19.
15 IOSCO website, https://www.iosco.org/about/?subSection=monitoring_board&subSection1=members (accessed 1 September 2017).
16 Charter of the IFRSF Monitoring Board, February 2016, Appendix A.
17 IFRS Foundation Monitoring Board Press Release, *Monitoring Board finalizes assessment approach for membership criteria and announces Chair selection*, 1 March 2013.
18 IFRS Foundation Constitution, December 2016, Section 24.
19 IFRS Foundation Constitution, December 2016, Section 25.
20 IFRS Foundation Constitution, December 2016, Section 25.
21 IFRS Foundation Constitution, December 2016, Section 27.
22 IFRS Foundation Constitution, December 2016, Section 26.
23 IFRS Foundation Constitution, December 2016, Section 36(a).
24 IFRS Foundation Constitution, December 2016, Section 35.
25 IFRS Foundation Constitution, December 2016, Section 35.
26 IFRS Foundation Constitution, December 2016, Section 36(d), (e) and (h).
27 IFRS Foundation website, http://www.ifrs.org/projects/2016/2015-agenda-consultation/#current-stage (accessed on 24 August 2017).
28 Due Process Handbook for the IASB and IFRS Interpretations Committee, February 2013, para. 5.15.
29 Due Process Handbook for the IASB and IFRS Interpretations Committee, February 2013, para. 5.16.
30 Due Process Handbook for the IASB and IFRS Interpretations Committee, February 2013, para. 5.16.
31 Due Process Handbook for the IASB and IFRS Interpretations Committee, February 2013, para. 5.22.
32 IFRS Foundation Constitution, December 2016, Section 39.
33 Due Process Handbook for the IASB and IFRS Interpretations Committee, February 2013, para. 3.18.
34 IFRS Foundation Constitution, December 2016, Section 41.
35 Due Process Handbook for the IASB and IFRS Interpretations Committee, February 2013, para. 1.3.
36 Due Process Handbook for the IASB and IFRS Interpretations Committee, February 2013, para. 7.1.
37 Due Process Handbook for the IASB and IFRS Interpretations Committee, February 2013, para. 2.2 and 2.4.
38 Due Process Handbook for the IASB and IFRS Interpretations Committee, February 2013, para. 1.5.
39 Due Process Handbook for the IASB and IFRS Interpretations Committee, February 2013, para. 3.1.
40 Due Process Handbook for the IASB and IFRS Interpretations Committee, February 2013, para. 1.2.
41 IFRS Foundation Press Release, *IFRS Foundation revises Due Process Handbook to incorporate IFRS Taxonomy*, 23 June 2016.
42 Due Process Handbook for IASB and IFRS Interpretations Committee, February 2013, para. 3.42.

43 Due Process Handbook for the IASB and IFRS Interpretations Committee, February 2013, para. 3.43.
44 Due Process Handbook for the IASB and IFRS Interpretations Committee, February 2013, para. 3.44.
45 Due Process Handbook for the IASB and IFRS Interpretations Committee, February 2013, para. 3.45.
46 Due Process Handbook for the IASB and IFRS Interpretations Committee, February 2013, para. 6.7.
47 Due Process Handbook for the IASB and IFRS Interpretations Committee, February 2013, para. 6.8.
48 IFRS Advisory Council, Terms of reference and operating procedures, July 2014.
49 IFRS Advisory Council, Terms of reference and operating procedures, July 2014.
50 IFRS Foundation Constitution, December 2016, Section 44.
51 IFRS Foundation Constitution, December 2016, Section 45.
52 IFRS Advisory Council, Terms of reference and operating procedures, July 2014.
53 Accounting Standards Advisory Forum: Terms of Reference/Charter.
54 Accounting Standards Advisory Forum: Terms of Reference/Charter.
55 Feedback Statement, *Review of the Accounting Standards Advisory Forum*, May 2015.
56 IFRS Foundation website, http://www.ifrs.org/about-us/consultative-bodies/ (accessed 30 August 2017).
57 IFRS Foundation website, http://www.ifrs.org/projects/current-areas-of-focus/ (accessed on 30 August 2017).
58 IFRS Foundation Constitution, January 2013, Section 2(a).
59 Speech by Hans Hoogervorst, 'Closing the accounting chapter of the financial crisis', Asia-Oceania Regional Policy Forum, 8 March 2014.
60 Speech by Wesley R. Bricker, 'Working together to advance high quality information in the capital markets', 2016 AICPA Conference on Current SEC and PCAOB Developments, 5 December 2016.
61 This means those with their securities admitted to trading on a regulated market within the meaning of Article 1(13) of Council Directive 93/22/EEC (on investment services in the securities field) or those offered to the public in view of their admission to such trading under Council Directive 80/390/EEC (coordinating the requirements for the drawing up, scrutiny and distribution of the listing particulars to be published for the admission of securities to official stock exchange listing).
62 European Commission, *Implementation of the IAS Regulation (1606/2002) in the EU and EEA*, 7 February 2012.
63 European Commission, Regulation (EC) No 1606/2002 of the European Parliament and of the Council of 19 July 2002, Recital 11.
64 European Financial Reporting Advisory Group website, http://www.efrag.org/Assets/Download?assetUrl=%2Fsites%2Fwebpublishing%2FLists%2FPublic%20News%2FAttachments%2F117%2FEFRAG%20Endorsement%20Status%20Report%206%20July%202017.pdf (accessed on 30 August 2017).
65 European Commission website, http://ec.europa.eu/transparency/regcomitology/index.cfm?do=search.documentdetail&Dos_ID=14524&DS_ID=51300&Version=2 (accessed on 30 August 2017).
66 European Commission, *Public consultation on the operations of the European Supervisory Authorities*, 21 March 2017.
67 European Commission, *Feedback statement on the public consultation on the operations of the European Supervisory Authorities*, 20 June 2017.
68 European Commission, *Feedback statement on the public consultation on the operations of the European Supervisory Authorities*, 20 June 2017.
69 The Gazette of India, Extraordinary, Part-II, Section 3, Sub-section (i), February 19, 2015.
70 Li, S. (2010) *Does mandatory adoption of International Financial Reporting Standards in the European Union reduce the cost of equity capital?* The Accounting Review, 85(2), 607-636.
71 Speech by Hans Hoogervorst, 'The Search for Consistency in Financial Reporting', Ernst & Young/Cass Business School, 17 January 2013.
72 European Securities and Markets Authority, *ESMA Report on Enforcement and Regulatory Activities of Accounting Enforcers in 2014*, 31 March 2015.
73 IFRS Foundation and ESMA Press Release, *IFRS Foundation and ESMA sign joint Statement of Protocols*, 15 July 2014.
74 IOSCO and IFRS Foundation, Statement of Protocols for Cooperation on International Financial Reporting Standards, 16 September 2013.
75 Speech by Mary Jo White, 'Regulation in a Global Financial System', Investment Company Institute General Membership Meeting, 1 May 2013.
76 IFRS Foundation, *Report of the Trustees' Strategy Review 2011, IFRSs as the Global Standards: Setting a Strategy for the Foundation's Second Decade*, February 2012.

Chapter 2 The IASB's Conceptual Framework

Chapter 2 The IASB's Conceptual Framework

1 INTRODUCTION

There have been numerous attempts over many decades to define the purpose and nature of accounting. Perhaps not surprisingly, most of the earlier studies were carried out by individual academics and academic committees in the US; for example, the writings in 1940 of Paton and Littleton[1] were intended to present a framework of accounting theory that would be regarded as a coherent and consistent foundation for the development of accounting standards, whilst the studies carried out over the years by various committees of the American Accounting Association have made a significant contribution to accounting theory.[2] In addition to the research carried out by individuals and academic committees, professional accounting bodies around the world have also, from time to time, issued statements that deal with various aspects of accounting theory. These can be seen as the first attempts at developing some form of conceptual framework.

With the globalisation of business and the increased access to the world's capital markets that goes with it, there are essentially only two truly global systems of financial reporting – IFRS and US GAAP.

In 2004 the IASB and FASB began a joint project to develop a single conceptual framework, the first phase of which was completed in September 2010. The IASB's current conceptual framework, discussed more fully at 2 below, comprises two sections finalised in this first phase of the joint project with the FASB, together with other material carried forward from the conceptual framework issued by the former IASC in 1989 ('the 1989 Framework'), which was originally intended to be replaced in a second phase of the joint framework project. The 1989 Framework, although not jointly developed with the FASB, nevertheless drew heavily on the FASB's then current conceptual framework. This close direct and indirect relationship between the IASB's and FASB's frameworks goes some way to explain the progress that the two Boards have made towards convergence at the individual standard level.

Following the completion of the first phase in 2010, the joint project with the FASB stalled somewhat until, in 2012, the IASB indicated that it no longer saw convergence between IFRS and US GAAP in the area of the conceptual framework as a primary objective and, moreover, that active work on the conceptual framework would resume shortly. This resulted in the publication by the IASB in July 2013 of a discussion paper DP/2013/1 – *A Review of the Conceptual Framework for Financial Reporting*. The discussion paper noted this was no longer a joint project with the FASB, but the IASB's own project.[3] The IASB followed the discussion paper with an exposure draft of an updated framework in May 2015 (*Exposure Draft ED/2015/3: Conceptual Framework for Financial Reporting*). The key proposals of the ED are discussed at 3 below.

1.1 What is a conceptual framework?

In general terms, a conceptual framework is a statement of generally accepted theoretical principles which form the frame of reference for a particular field of enquiry. In terms of financial reporting, these theoretical principles provide the basis for both the development of new reporting practices and the evaluation of existing ones. Since the financial reporting process is concerned with the provision of information that is useful in making business and economic decisions, a conceptual framework will form the theoretical basis for determining which events should be accounted for, how they should be measured and how they should be communicated. Therefore, although it is theoretical in nature, a conceptual framework for financial reporting has a highly practical end in view.

1.2 Why is a conceptual framework necessary?

A conceptual framework for financial reporting should be a theory of accounting against which practical problems can be tested objectively, and the utility of which is decided by the adequacy of the practical solutions it provides. However, the various standard-setting bodies around the world initially often attempted to resolve practical accounting and reporting problems through the development of accounting standards, without such an accepted theoretical frame of reference. The end result was that standard-setters determined the form and content of external financial reports, without resolving such fundamental issues as:

- What are the objectives of these reports?
- Who are the users of these reports?
- What are the informational needs of these users?
- What types of report will best satisfy their needs?

Consequently, standards were often produced on a haphazard and 'fire-fighting' basis with the danger of mutual inconsistencies. By contrast, an agreed framework would, in principle, provide standard-setters with a basis for designing standards that facilitate more consistent external financial reports that meet the needs of the user.

Whilst the main role of a conceptual framework may be to assist the standard-setter (the focus of the discussion in the remainder of this section), the IASB sees its own framework as a point of reference not only for itself, but also for other (national) standard-setters, preparers, auditors and users (see 2.2.2.A below).

It is key that any framework is 'agreed'. The IASB's original 1989 Framework was clearly derived from the FASB framework, which had been developed much earlier. However, the way in which the two Boards then translated the common principles of their frameworks into detailed rules within the accounting standards issued by each Board can result in very different accounting treatments.

Experience of the last thirty years also shows that, in the absence of an agreed comprehensive conceptual framework, the same theoretical issues were revisited on numerous occasions by different standard-setting bodies. This inevitably sometimes resulted in the development of standards that were internally inconsistent and inconsistent with each other, or which were founded on incompatible concepts. For example, inconsistencies and conflicts have existed between and within individual standards concerning the emphasis placed on substance versus form; neutrality versus prudence; and whether earnings should be determined through balance sheet measurements or by matching costs and revenue. Some standard-setters have permitted two or more methods of accounting for the same set of circumstances, whilst others permitted certain accounting practices to be followed on an arbitrary or unspecified basis. These inconsistencies and irrationalities perhaps reflect the fundamental difficulty of determining what is required in order to give a faithful representation of economic phenomena.

Standard setters have adopted different approaches to the realisation of their conceptual frameworks in specific accounting standards. This can be seen by comparing the standards issued by the FASB with those issued by the IASB. In the US the FASB, in spite of its pioneering work on a conceptual framework, has produced a large number of highly detailed accounting rules. The IASB, on the other hand has tended to produce less detailed standards, relying on preparers and auditors to consider the general principles on which they are based in applying them to specific situations. Clearly, the proliferation of accounting standards in the US stems from many factors, not least the legal and regulatory environment. However, a more satisfactory conceptual framework might reduce the need for such a large number of highly detailed standards, since the emphasis would be on general principles rather than specific rules. Indeed this change of emphasis has been specifically considered by the US authorities following the financial reporting problems that led, in the US, to the Sarbanes-Oxley Act and the establishment of the Public Company Accounting Oversight Board. This is not to say that the IASB's more general 'principles-based' approach to standard setting is necessarily more satisfactory than the FASB's; rather, the legal and regulatory environment within which non-US businesses habitually work is quite different from that of the USA.

The political and economic environment influences not only the approach taken to standard setting, but also the nature of the conceptual framework on which standards are based. Following the widespread incorporation of IFRS into the national GAAPs of many other countries, the IASB is faced with many stakeholders with a variety of needs and expectations. These different stakeholders often express differing views on proposals issued by the IASB and expect their views to be taken into account. Under these circumstances, an agreed conceptual framework is of great value, although the best defence against undue interference in the standard-setting process is the need of the capital markets for financial reporting that provides a sound basis for decision making, which in turn implies a system of financial reporting characterised by relevance, faithful representation, practicality and understandability. While it is probable that these characteristics are more likely to be achieved using a sound theoretical foundation, the converse also applies: namely that the framework must result in standards that account appropriately for actual business practice and economic reality. Otherwise how, for example, is an industry to be persuaded that a particular accounting treatment perceived as adversely affecting its economic interests is better than one which does not?

An agreed framework is therefore not the panacea for all accounting problems. Nor does it obviate the need for judgement to be exercised in the process of resolving accounting issues. What it can provide is a framework within which those judgements can be made. Indeed this is happening, as the principles expressed in the IASB's framework are frequently referred to in IFRSs and during the process of their development. Unfortunately, there is also evidence of the IASB issuing standards that contravene its own conceptual framework. For example, IAS 38 – *Intangible Assets* – requires the capitalisation of goodwill as an asset, despite the fact that goodwill does not meet the definition of an asset in the IASB's framework. Similarly IAS 12 – *Income Taxes* – requires recognition of deferred tax assets and liabilities that arguably do not meet the definitions of asset and liability under the framework.

2 THE IASB'S CONCEPTUAL FRAMEWORK

2.1 Development of the IASB's Conceptual Framework

The IASB issued *Conceptual Framework for Financial Reporting 2010* ('the *Conceptual Framework*') in September 2010. This was effectively work-in-progress, comprising two chapters developed in the first phase of the then joint project of the IASB and FASB to develop an agreed framework (see 1 above), together with material carried forward from the former IASC's 1989 Framework (which was adopted in 2001 by the then newly-constituted IASB).

Following the completion of the first phase in 2010, the joint project with the FASB stalled somewhat until, in 2012, the IASB indicated that it no longer saw convergence between IFRS and US GAAP in the area of the conceptual framework as a primary objective and, moreover, that active work on the conceptual framework would resume shortly. This resulted in the publication by the IASB in July 2013 of a discussion paper DP/2013/1 – *A Review of the Conceptual Framework for Financial Reporting*. The discussion paper noted this was no longer a joint project with the FASB, but the IASB's own project.[4] The IASB followed the discussion paper with an exposure draft of an updated framework in May 2015 (*Exposure Draft ED/2015/3: Conceptual Framework for Financial Reporting*).

The exposure draft proposes comprehensive changes to the Framework. In particular, it proposes revisions to the definitions of elements in the financial statements, includes guidance on derecognition, discussions on measurement bases, principles for including items in other comprehensive income (OCI) in relation to performance reporting, and includes high-level concepts for presentation and disclosure. The exposure draft is discussed at 3 below.

2.2 Contents, purpose and scope of the IASB's Conceptual Framework

2.2.1 Contents of the Conceptual Framework

The *Conceptual Framework* comprises an introduction (discussed here and at 2.2.2 and 2.3.1 below), and four chapters:

- Chapter 1 – *The objective of general purpose financial reporting* (discussed at 2.3 below);
- Chapter 2 – *The reporting entity.* This is a 'place-holder' chapter pending completion of this phase of the IASB's framework (discussed at 2.4 below);
- Chapter 3 – *Qualitative characteristics of useful financial information* (discussed at 2.5 below);
- Chapter 4 – *The Framework (1989): the remaining text* (discussed at 2.6 below), comprising
  - Underlying assumption (discussed at 2.6.1 below);
  - The elements of financial statements (discussed at 2.6.2 below);
  - Recognition of the elements of financial statements (discussed at 2.6.3 below);
  - Measurement of the elements of financial statements (discussed at 2.6.4 below); and
  - Concepts of capital and capital maintenance (discussed at 2.6.5 below).

2.2.2 Purpose and scope of the Conceptual Framework

2.2.2.A Purpose

The purpose of the *Conceptual Framework* is to:

- assist the Board in the development of future IFRSs and in its review of existing IFRSs;
- assist the Board in promoting harmonisation of regulations, accounting standards and procedures relating to the presentation of financial statements by providing a basis for reducing the number of alternative accounting treatments permitted by IFRSs;
- assist national standard-setting bodies in developing national standards;
- assist preparers of financial statements in applying IFRSs and in dealing with topics that have yet to form the subject of an IFRS;
- assist auditors in forming an opinion on whether financial statements comply with IFRSs;
- assist users of financial statements in interpreting the information contained in financial statements prepared in compliance with IFRSs; and
- provide those who are interested in the work of the IASB with information about its approach to the formulation of IFRSs. *[Framework Purpose and status].*

The *Conceptual Framework* is not an IFRS, and nothing in it overrides any specific IFRS, including an IFRS that is in some respect in conflict with the framework. As the Board will be guided by the framework both in developing future standards, and in reviewing existing ones, the number of such conflicts is expected to reduce over time. *[Framework Purpose and status].* However, any revision of the framework (such as those proposed in the IASB's recent exposure draft – see 3 below) might actually increase such conflicts, at least in the shorter term. Nevertheless, the *Conceptual Framework* is a source of guidance for determining an accounting treatment where a standard does not provide specific guidance (see Chapter 3 at 4.3).

The framework will be revised from time to time in the light of the IASB's experience of working with it. *[Framework Purpose and status].*

2.2.2.B Scope

The *Conceptual Framework* deals with:

- the objective of financial reporting;
- the qualitative characteristics of useful financial information;
- the definition, recognition and measurement of the elements from which financial statements are constructed; and
- concepts of capital and capital maintenance. *[Framework Scope].*

2.3 Chapter 1: The objective of general purpose financial reporting

Chapter 1 of the *Conceptual Framework* discusses the objective of general purpose financial reporting, which – in the IASB's view – forms the foundation of the framework. Other aspects of the framework (a reporting entity concept, the qualitative characteristics of, and the constraint on, useful financial information, elements of financial statements, recognition, measurement, presentation and disclosure) flow logically from the objective. *[Framework OB1].*

The Chapter is divided into two main sections dealing with:

- the objective, usefulness and limitations of general purpose financial reporting (see 2.3.1 below); and
- information about a reporting entity's economic resources, claims, and changes in resources and claims (see 2.3.2 below).

2.3.1 Objective, usefulness and limitations of general purpose financial reporting

2.3.1.A Objective and usefulness

The *Conceptual Framework* defines the objective of general purpose financial reporting as being:

> 'to provide financial information about the reporting entity that is useful to existing and potential investors, lenders and other creditors in making decisions about providing resources to the entity. Those decisions involve buying, selling or holding equity and debt instruments, and providing or settling loans and other forms of credit.' *[Framework OB2].*

Existing and potential investors, lenders and other creditors (collectively, 'providers of capital') cannot generally require reporting entities to provide information directly to them and must rely on general purpose financial reports for much of the financial information they need. Consequently, they are the primary users to whom general purpose financial reports are directed. *[Framework OB5].*

The IASB sees the main need of such providers of capital as being information to enable them to assess:

- the prospects for future net cash inflows to an entity. This is because all decisions made by such providers of capital (whether equity investors, lenders or other creditors) depend on their assessment of the amount, timing and uncertainty of (i.e. the prospects for) the entity's future net cash inflows; *[Framework OB3]*

- the resources of, and claims against, the entity. These are discussed further at 2.3.2 below; *[Framework OB4]* and
- how efficiently and effectively the entity's management and governing board have discharged their responsibilities to use the entity's resources. Examples of such responsibilities include protecting the entity's resources from unfavourable effects of economic factors such as price and technological changes and ensuring that the entity complies with applicable laws, regulations and contractual provisions. Information about management's discharge of its responsibilities is also useful for decisions by existing providers of capital who have the right to vote on or otherwise influence management's actions. *[Framework OB4]*.

  The discharge of management's responsibilities referred to in this last bullet point is commonly referred to as 'stewardship', and indeed was described as such in the 1989 Framework (as it still is in the Introduction to the revised framework – see below). The IASB clarifies that it replaced the specific word 'stewardship' with this description of its underlying concepts, because of the potential difficulty of translating the word 'stewardship' into other languages. *[Framework BC1.27-1.28]*.

Chapter 2

The *Conceptual Framework* identifies only providers of capital as the main users of financial statements, in contrast to the 1989 Framework which referred to 'a wide range of users'. The IASB felt it was necessary for the revised framework to focus on a more narrowly-defined group of primary users in order to avoid becoming unduly abstract or vague. *[Framework BC1.14]*. Moreover, the IASB attributes some of the inconsistency between national standards to the fact that different countries take account of the needs of different groups of users when setting national requirements. *[Framework Introduction.1]*.

However, the IASB argues that general purpose financial statements will meet the needs of most users, because they are nearly all making economic decisions, for example:

- to decide when to buy, hold or sell an equity investment;
- to assess the stewardship or accountability of management;
- to assess the ability of the entity to pay and provide other benefits to its employees;
- to assess the security for amounts lent to the entity;
- to determine taxation policies;
- to determine distributable profits and dividends;
- to prepare and use national income statistics; or
- to regulate the activities of entities. *[Framework Introduction.4]*.

However, the IASB stresses that general purpose financial reports are not primarily directed at users other than providers of capital. *[Framework OB10]*.

2.3.1.B Limitations

The *Conceptual Framework* acknowledges that general purpose financial reports do not, and cannot, provide all of the information needed by providers of capital. Users of financial reports need to consider other pertinent information, such as general economic and political conditions, and industry and company outlooks. Moreover, general purpose financial reports are not designed to show the value of a reporting entity, but to provide information to allow users to estimate it for themselves. *[Framework OB6, OB7]*.

General purpose financial reports are focused on meeting the needs of the maximum number of primary users, who may have different, and possibly conflicting, needs for information. However, this does not preclude a reporting entity from including additional information that is most useful to a particular subset of primary users. *[Framework OB8]*. Management of an entity need not rely on general purpose financial reports, since the relevant information can be obtained internally. *[Framework OB9]*.

The IASB notes that, to a large extent, financial reports are based on estimates, judgements and models rather than exact depictions. The *Conceptual Framework* establishes the concepts that underlie those estimates, judgements and models. The concepts should be seen as a goal which the IASB and preparers should strive towards, but are unlikely to achieve in full, at least in the short term, because it takes time to understand, accept and implement new ways of analysing transactions and other events. Nevertheless, the IASB believes that setting such a goal is essential if financial reporting is to evolve so as to improve its usefulness. *[Framework OB11]*.

2.3.2 Information about economic resources, claims and changes in resources and claims

General purpose financial reports provide information about:

- the financial position of a reporting entity (the economic resources of, and claims against, the entity) – see 2.3.2.A below; and
- the effects of transactions and other events that change the economic resources of, and claims against, the entity – see 2.3.2.B below.

Both types of information provide useful input for decisions about providing resources to an entity. *[Framework OB12]*.

2.3.2.A Economic resources and claims

Information about the nature and amounts of a reporting entity's economic resources and claims can help users to:

- identify the entity's financial strengths and weaknesses; and
- assess the entity's liquidity and solvency, its needs for additional financing and how successful it is likely to be in obtaining that financing.

Information about the priorities and payment requirements of existing claims helps users to predict how future cash flows will be distributed among lenders and creditors. *[Framework OB13]*.

Different types of economic resources affect a user's assessment of the entity's prospects for future cash flows in different ways. Some future cash flows result directly from existing economic resources, such as accounts receivable. Other cash flows result from the entity using several resources in combination to produce and market goods or services to customers. Although those cash flows cannot be identified with individual economic resources (or claims), users need to know the nature and amount of the resources available for use in an entity's operations. *[Framework OB14]*.

2.3.2.B Changes in economic resources and claims

Changes in a reporting entity's economic resources and claims result from that entity's financial performance and from other events or transactions such as issuing debt or equity instruments. In order to assess properly the prospects for future cash flows of the entity, users need to know the extent to which the reporting entity has increased its available economic resources, and thus its capacity for generating net cash inflows through its operations rather than by obtaining additional resources directly from providers of capital. *[Framework OB15, 18, 21].*

Information about a reporting entity's financial performance helps users to understand the return that the entity has produced on its economic resources. Information about the return provides an indication of how well management has discharged its responsibilities to make efficient and effective use of the reporting entity's resources. Information about the variability and components of that return is also important, especially in assessing the uncertainty of future cash flows. Information about a reporting entity's past financial performance and how its management discharged its responsibilities is usually helpful in predicting the entity's future returns on its economic resources. *[Framework OB16].*

Financial performance is reflected by changes in the entity's economic resources and claims other than by obtaining additional resources directly from providers of capital. *[Framework OB15, 18].* This is sometimes described as a 'balance sheet approach' to recording financial performance, whereby financial performance for a period is essentially derived as part of the overall movement in the entity's financial position during that period. This is discussed more explicitly in the section of the *Conceptual Framework* dealing with the elements of financial statements (see 2.6.2 below).

Consistent with this 'balance sheet approach', financial performance is based on accrual accounting, which depicts the effects of transactions and other events and circumstances on a reporting entity's economic resources and claims in the periods in which those effects occur, even if the resulting cash receipts and payments occur in a different period. This provides a better basis for assessing the entity's past and future performance than information based solely on cash flows. *[Framework OB17].*

Information about an entity's financial performance may also indicate the extent to which events such as changes in market prices or interest rates have changed the entity's economic resources and claims, thereby affecting the entity's ability to generate net cash inflows. *[Framework OB19].* Nevertheless, information about an entity's cash flows during a period also helps users to assess the entity's ability to generate future net cash inflows, understand the entity's operations, evaluate its financing and investing activities, assess its liquidity or solvency and interpret other information about financial performance. *[Framework OB20].*

2.4 Chapter 2: The reporting entity

Historically there has been no clear definition of the 'reporting entity' and this has led to some uncertainty as to when general purpose financial statements could be prepared in accordance with IFRS. For example:

- Does a reporting entity have to be a legal entity or a legal group?
- Can parts only of a legal entity be a reporting entity?

This is one of the areas the IASB proposes to deal with in more detail. The proposals in the exposure draft published in 2015 are summarised at 3 below.

2.5 Chapter 3: Qualitative characteristics of useful financial information

The *Conceptual Framework* states that the types of information likely to be most useful to providers of capital are identified by various qualitative characteristics, *[Framework QC1]*, comprising:

- two 'fundamental qualitative characteristics' (see 2.5.1 below):
  - relevance; and
  - faithful representation; *[Framework QC5]* supplemented by
- four 'enhancing qualitative characteristics' (see 2.5.2 below):
  - comparability;
  - verifiability;
  - timeliness; and
  - understandability. *[Framework QC19]*.

Chapter 3 of the *Conceptual Framework* also notes the role of cost as a 'pervasive constraint' on a reporting entity's ability to provide useful financial information. This is discussed further at 2.5.3 below.

The relationship between the objective, fundamental characteristics, enhancing characteristics and the pervasive cost constraint can be represented diagrammatically:

Figure 2.1 Components of the Conceptual Framework

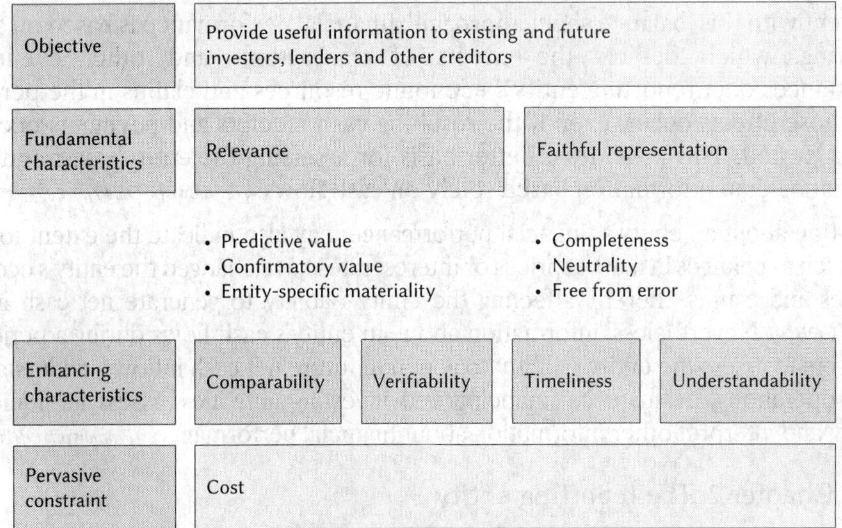

Financial reports provide information about the reporting entity's economic resources, claims against the reporting entity and the effects of transactions and other events and conditions that change those resources and claims (collectively referred to in the *Conceptual Framework* as 'the economic phenomena'). Some financial reports also include explanatory material about management's expectations and strategies for the reporting entity, and other types of forward-looking information. *[Framework QC2]*.

The qualitative characteristics of useful financial information apply to all financial information, whether provided in financial statements or in other ways. All financial information is also subject to a pervasive cost constraint on the reporting entity's ability to provide useful financial information. However, the considerations in applying the qualitative characteristics and the cost constraint may be different for different types of information. For example, applying them to forward-looking information may be different from applying them to information about existing economic resources and claims and to changes in those resources and claims. *[Framework QC3].*

2.5.1 Fundamental qualitative characteristics

In order to be useful, financial information must be relevant (see 2.5.1.A below) and faithfully represent what it purports to represent (see 2.5.1.B below). *[Framework QC4].*

2.5.1.A Relevance (including materiality)

Relevant financial information is that which is capable of making a difference to the decisions made by users, irrespective of whether some users choose not to take advantage of it or are already aware of it from other sources. Financial information is capable of making a difference in decisions if it has predictive value, confirmatory value or both. *[Framework QC6, QC7].*

Financial information has predictive value if it can be used as an input to processes employed by users to predict future outcomes. Financial information with predictive value need not itself be a prediction or forecast, but is employed by users in making their own predictions. Financial information has confirmatory value if it confirms or changes previous evaluations. *[Framework QC8, QC9].*

The predictive value and confirmatory value of financial information are interrelated. For example, information on revenue for the current year can be used both as the basis for predicting revenues in future years, and as a point of comparison with predictions made in prior years of revenue for the current year. The results of those comparisons can help a user to correct and improve the processes that were used to make those previous predictions. *[Framework QC10].*

The *Conceptual Framework* refers to materiality as 'an entity-specific aspect of relevance based on the nature or magnitude, or both, of the items to which the information relates in the context of an individual entity's financial report'. In other words, information is material (and therefore relevant) if omitting or misstating it could influence the decisions of users of financial information about a specific reporting entity. Because of the specificity of materiality to a particular reporting entity, the IASB cannot specify a uniform quantitative threshold for materiality or predetermine what could be material in a particular situation. *[Framework QC11].*

2.5.1.B Faithful representation

The *Conceptual Framework* observes that financial reports represent economic phenomena in words and numbers. To be useful, financial information must not only represent relevant phenomena, but it must also faithfully represent the phenomena that it purports to represent. A perfectly faithful representation would be:

- complete,
- neutral, and
- free from error.

The IASB's objective is to maximise those qualities to the extent possible, while acknowledging that perfection is seldom, if ever, achievable. *[Framework QC12].*

A complete depiction includes all information, including all necessary descriptions and explanations, necessary for a user to understand the phenomenon being depicted. For example, a complete depiction of a group of assets would include, at a minimum:

- a description of the nature of the assets;
- a numerical depiction of the assets; and
- a description of what the numerical depiction represents (for example, original cost, adjusted cost or fair value).

For some items, a complete depiction may also entail explanations of significant facts about the quality and nature of those items, factors and circumstances that might affect their quality and nature, and the process used to determine the numerical depiction. *[Framework QC13].*

A neutral depiction is one without bias in the selection or presentation of financial information. A neutral depiction is not slanted, weighted, emphasised, de-emphasised or otherwise manipulated to increase the probability that financial information will be received favourably or unfavourably by users. That is not to imply that neutral information has no purpose or no influence on behaviour. On the contrary, relevant financial information is, by definition, capable of making a difference in users' decisions. *[Framework QC14].*

The *Conceptual Framework* stresses that the term 'free from error' does not necessarily imply that information is accurate in all respects. Rather, information is 'free from error' if there are no errors or omissions either in the description of the economic phenomenon being depicted or in the selection or application of the process used to produce the reported information. For example, an estimate of an unobservable price or value cannot be determined to be accurate or inaccurate. However, a representation of that estimate can be faithful if the amount is described clearly and accurately as being an estimate, the nature and limitations of the estimating process are explained, and no errors have been made in selecting and applying an appropriate process for developing the estimate. *[Framework QC15].*

The *Conceptual Framework* also notes the apparent paradox that a faithful representation does not, by itself, necessarily result in useful information. It gives the example of a reporting entity receiving property, plant and equipment at no cost through a government grant. To report that the entity had acquired an asset at no cost would be a faithful representation of the cost of the asset, but the resulting information would probably not be very useful.

Another example is an estimate of the adjustment required to the carrying amount of an impaired asset. That estimate can be a faithful representation if the entity has properly applied an appropriate process, properly described the estimate and explained any uncertainties that significantly affect the estimate. However, an estimate subject to a high level of uncertainty will not be particularly useful. In other words, 'the relevance of the asset being faithfully represented is questionable'. If there is no alternative representation that is more faithful, that estimate may provide the best available information. *[Framework QC16]*. Some may be surprised by the implication that information of questionable relevance about an economic phenomenon may nevertheless give a faithful representation of that phenomenon.

The IASB notes that a faithful representation requires a transaction to be reported in accordance with its economic substance rather than its legal form. *[Framework BC3.26]*.

The characteristic of 'faithful representation' in the 2010 *Conceptual Framework* replaces that of 'reliability' in the 1989 Framework, which defined it in the following terms:

> 'Information has the quality of reliability when it is free from material error and bias and can be depended upon by users to represent faithfully that which it either purports to represent or could reasonably be expected to represent'.

The IASB explains that it decided to replace the term 'reliability' because there was a lack of clarity as to its meaning both in the 1989 Framework and the original FASB Concepts Statement 2, from which the 1989 Framework was derived. Moreover, the IASB notes that comments received on numerous proposed standards have indicated a lack of a common understanding of the term 'reliability'. Some respondents 'focused on verifiability or free from material error to the virtual exclusion of faithful representation. Others focused more on faithful representation, perhaps combined with neutrality'. The IASB appears surprised that some respondents 'apparently think that reliability refers primarily to precision', even though precision is intrinsic to the normal English meaning of 'reliability'. For these reasons, the IASB decided to replace 'reliability' with what it regards as the more precisely defined 'faithful representation'. *[Framework BC3.20-BC3.26]*.

2.5.1.C Applying the fundamental qualitative characteristics

In order to be useful, information must be both relevant and provide a faithful representation. In the IASB's words 'neither a faithful representation of an irrelevant phenomenon nor an unfaithful representation of a relevant phenomenon helps users make good decisions'.

The most efficient and effective process for applying the fundamental qualitative characteristics would, subject to the effects of the enhancing qualitative characteristics (see 2.5.2 below) and the cost constraint (see 2.5.3 below), usually be as follows:

- identify an economic phenomenon that has the potential to be useful to users of the reporting entity's financial information;
- identify the type of information about that phenomenon that would be most relevant if it were available and able to be faithfully represented; and
- determine whether that information is in fact available and able to be faithfully represented.

If so, the process of satisfying the fundamental qualitative characteristics ends at that point. If not, the process is repeated with the next most relevant type of information. *[Framework QC17, QC18]*.

2.5.2 Enhancing qualitative characteristics

The usefulness of relevant and faithfully represented financial information is enhanced by the characteristics of comparability (see 2.5.2.A below), verifiability (see 2.5.2.B below), timeliness (see 2.5.2.C below) and understandability (see 2.5.2.D below).

These enhancing characteristics may also help determine which of two ways should be used to depict a phenomenon if both are considered equally relevant and faithfully represented. *[Framework QC4, QC19]*.

2.5.2.A Comparability

The IASB notes that decisions made by users of financial information involve choices between alternatives, such as selling or holding an investment, or investing in one entity or another. Consequently, information about a reporting entity is more useful if it can be compared with similar information about other entities, and about the same entity for another period or as at another date. *[Framework QC20]*.

Comparability is the qualitative characteristic that enables users to identify and understand similarities in, and differences among, items. Unlike the other qualitative characteristics, comparability does not relate to a single item, since – by definition – a comparison requires at least two items. The IASB clarifies that, for information to be comparable, like things must look alike and different things must look different, adding that 'comparability of financial information is not enhanced by making unlike things look alike any more than it is enhanced by making like things look different.' *[Framework QC21-QC23]*. Although a single economic phenomenon can be faithfully represented in more than one way, permitting alternative accounting methods for the same economic phenomenon diminishes comparability. *[Framework QC25]*.

The *Conceptual Framework* stresses that consistency (i.e. the use of the same methods for the same items, either from period to period within a reporting entity or in a single period across entities) helps to achieve comparability, but is not the same as comparability. The IASB adds that comparability is not the same as uniformity, but without any definition of 'uniformity' or clarification of how it differs from comparability. Some degree of comparability is likely to be attained simply by satisfying the fundamental qualitative characteristics. In other words, a faithful representation of a relevant economic phenomenon by one entity should naturally be comparable with a faithful representation of a similar relevant economic phenomenon by another entity. *[Framework QC23, QC24]*.

2.5.2.B Verifiability

Verifiability helps assure users that information faithfully represents the economic phenomena that it purports to depict. Verifiability means that different knowledgeable and independent observers could reach a consensus, although not necessarily complete agreement, that a particular depiction is a faithful representation. Quantified information need not be a single point estimate to be verifiable. A range of possible amounts and their related probabilities can also be verified. *[Framework QC26]*.

The IASB notes that verification can be direct or indirect. Direct verification means verifying an amount or other representation through direct observation. Indirect verification means checking the inputs to a model, formula or other technique and recalculating the outputs using the same methodology. Some explanations and forward-looking financial information may not be verifiable until a future period, if at all. To help users decide whether to use such information, it would normally be necessary to disclose the assumptions, other factors and circumstances underlying the information, together with the methods of compiling the information. *[Framework QC27-QC28]*.

2.5.2.C Timeliness

Timeliness means that information is available to decision-makers in time to be capable of influencing their decisions. Generally, the older the information is the less useful it is. However, some information may continue to be timely long after the end of a reporting period, for example because some users may need to identify and assess trends. *[Framework QC29]*.

2.5.2.D Understandability

Information is made understandable by classifying, characterising and presenting it clearly and concisely. *[Framework QC30]*. The IASB concedes that some phenomena are so inherently complex and difficult to understand that financial reports might be easier to understand if information about those phenomena were excluded. However, reports prepared without that information would be incomplete and therefore potentially misleading. Moreover, financial reports are prepared for users with a reasonable knowledge of business and economic activities who can review and analyse the information diligently. Even such users, however, may need to seek specialist advice in order to understand information about complex economic phenomena. *[Framework QC31, QC32]*.

2.5.2.E Applying the enhancing qualitative characteristics

The *Conceptual Framework* stresses that, while the enhancing qualitative characteristics should be maximised to the extent possible, they cannot, either individually or as a group, make information useful if that information is irrelevant or not faithfully represented. *[Framework QC33]*.

Applying the enhancing qualitative characteristics is an iterative process that does not follow a prescribed order. Sometimes, one enhancing qualitative characteristic may have to be diminished in order to maximise another. For example, applying a new financial reporting standard prospectively (i.e. with no restatement of prior periods) will reduce comparability in the short term. However, that may be a price worth paying for improved relevance or faithful representation in the longer term. Appropriate disclosures may partially compensate for the lack of comparability. *[Framework QC34]*.

2.5.3 The cost constraint

The IASB acknowledges that cost is a pervasive constraint on the information provided by financial reporting, and that the cost of producing information must be justified by the benefits that it provides. Interestingly, the IASB argues that, while there is clearly an explicit cost to the preparers of financial information, the cost is ultimately borne by users, since any cost incurred by the reporting entity reduces the returns earned by users. In addition, users incur costs not only in analysing and interpreting any information that is provided, but also in obtaining or estimating any information that is not provided. *[Framework QC35, QC36, QC38]*.

Relevant and faithfully representative financial information helps users to make decisions with more confidence, resulting in a more efficient functioning of capital markets and a lower cost of capital for the economy as a whole. An individual provider of capital also receives benefits by making more informed decisions. However, it is not possible for general purpose financial reports to provide all information relevant to every user. *[Framework QC37]*.

In assessing whether the benefits of reporting particular information are likely to justify the cost, the IASB seeks information from providers of financial information, users, auditors, academics and others about the expected nature and quantity of the benefits and costs of that standard. In most situations, assessments are based on a combination of quantitative and qualitative information, and will normally be considered in relation to financial reporting generally, and not in relation to individual reporting entities. However, an assessment of costs and benefits will not always justify the same reporting requirements for all entities. Differences may be appropriate because of different sizes of entities, different ways of raising capital (publicly or privately), different needs of users or other factors. *[Framework QC38, QC39].*

2.6 Chapter 4: The Framework (1989): the remaining text

Chapter 4 of the *Conceptual Framework* essentially represents those parts of the 1989 Framework not superseded as the result of the completion of Phase A of the then joint IASB-FASB framework project (see 1 above). It comprises:

- Underlying assumption (see 2.6.1 below);
- The elements of financial statements (see 2.6.2 below);
- Recognition of the elements of financial statements (see 2.6.3 below);
- Measurement of the elements of financial statements (see 2.6.4 below); and
- Concepts of capital and capital maintenance (see 2.6.5 below).

2.6.1 Underlying assumption (going concern)

Financial statements are normally prepared on the assumption that the reporting entity is a going concern and will continue in operation for the foreseeable future. Hence, it is assumed that the entity has neither the intention nor the need to liquidate or curtail materially the scale of its operations. If such an intention or need exists, the financial statements may have to be prepared on a different basis and, if so, the basis used is disclosed. *[Framework 4.1].*

2.6.2 The elements of financial statements

Financial statements portray the financial effects of transactions and other events by grouping them according to their economic characteristics into broad classes termed the elements of financial statements. The elements directly related to the measurement of financial position in the statement of financial position are assets, liabilities and equity. The elements directly related to the measurement of performance in the income statement are income and expenses. The framework identifies no elements that are unique to the statement of changes in equity, since this is comprised of items that appear in the statement of financial position or the income statement, or both. *[Framework 4.2].*

These elements are typically subject to further sub-classification before presentation in the statement of financial position and the income statement. For example, assets and liabilities may be classified by their nature or function in order to display information in the most useful manner to users. *[Framework 4.3].*

2.6.2.A Statement of financial position

The elements related to the measurement of financial position are assets, liabilities and equity.

An asset is 'a resource controlled by the entity as a result of past events and from which future economic benefits are expected to flow to the entity.' Assets are discussed further at 2.6.2.B below.

A liability is 'a present obligation of the entity arising from past events, the settlement of which is expected to result in an outflow from the entity of resources embodying economic benefits.' Liabilities are discussed further at 2.6.2.C below.

Equity is 'the residual interest in the assets of the entity after deducting all its liabilities.' Equity is discussed further at 2.6.2.D below. *[Framework 4.4]*

The *Conceptual Framework* stresses that an item that meets the definition of an asset or a liability is not necessarily recognised in the financial statements. An asset or liability is recognised only where there is a sufficient certainty that there will be a future inflow or outflow of economic benefit. *[Framework 4.5]*. Recognition is discussed more generally at 2.6.3 below.

Any assessment of whether an item meets the definition of an asset, liability or equity must have regard to its underlying substance and economic reality, and not merely its legal form. For example, a finance lease economically gives the lessee a right (which meets the definition of an asset) to use the leased asset for most of its useful life and liability to pay for that right an amount approximating to the fair value of the right plus a finance charge. Hence, a finance lease gives rise to the recognition of both an asset and a liability. *[Framework 4.6]*.

The *Conceptual Framework* comments that specific IFRSs may require items that do not meet the definitions of 'asset' or 'liability' to be recognised in the statement of financial position. Nevertheless, these definitions will underpin reviews of existing IFRSs, and the development of new standards. *[Framework 4.7]*. The *Conceptual Framework* does not give examples of such items, but some would argue that they include:

- goodwill (since this is not controlled by the entity); and
- deferred taxes (since these represent the amount by which future assets or liabilities will be greater or less than they would have been but for the occurrence of one or more past transactions or events, rather than present assets or liabilities).

2.6.2.B Assets

As noted in 2.6.2.A above, a characteristic of an asset is that future economic benefits are expected to flow from it. Those 'future economic benefits' are the potential for the asset to contribute, directly or indirectly, to the flow of cash and cash equivalents to the entity. This may be a productive potential, forming part of the operating activities of the entity. It may also take the form of convertibility into cash or cash equivalents or a capability to reduce cash outflows, such as when an alternative manufacturing process lowers the costs of production. *[Framework 4.8]*.

Assets are typically deployed in order to produce goods or services for customers, who are prepared to pay for them and hence contribute to the cash flow of the entity. Cash – it is asserted – itself renders a service to the entity because of its command over other resources. *[Framework 4.9]*.

An asset may give rise to an inflow of future economic benefits to the entity in a number of ways, for example by being:

- used (singly or in combination with other assets) in the production of goods or services to be sold by the entity;
- exchanged for other assets;
- used to settle a liability; or
- distributed to the owners of the entity. *[Framework 4.10]*.

Many assets, such as property, plant and equipment, have a physical form. However, physical form is not essential to the existence of an asset. For example, patents and copyrights are assets if future economic benefits are expected to flow from them to the entity and if they are controlled by the entity. *[Framework 4.11]*.

Many assets, such as receivables and property, are associated with legal rights, including the right of ownership. However, ownership is not essential in determining the existence of an asset. For example, leased property is an asset if the entity controls the benefits which are expected to flow from the property. Some items may satisfy the definition of an asset even when there is no legal control, such as internally generated know-how where, by keeping the know-how secret, the entity controls the benefits that are expected to flow from it. *[Framework 4.12]*.

Assets of an entity result from past transactions or other past events. Assets are normally purchased or produced, but they may arise from other transactions or events. For example, government may transfer property to an entity to encourage economic growth in an area, or the entity may discover mineral deposits. An expected future transaction or event (such as an intention to purchase inventory) does not give rise to an asset. *[Framework 4.13]*.

The *Conceptual Framework* notes that there is a close – but not a necessary – link between incurring expenditure and generating assets. Expenditure may provide evidence that future economic benefits were sought, but is not conclusive proof that an asset has been obtained. Similarly, the absence of expenditure does not indicate that no asset has been obtained. For example, an item donated to the entity may satisfy the definition of an asset. *[Framework 4.14]*.

The definition of an asset in the *Conceptual Framework* is adopted from the FASB's framework, with one important difference. The US framework refers to benefits 'obtained or controlled', by the entity, while the IASB's definition refers solely to resources 'controlled' by the entity. This has the effect, as noted above, that goodwill (which the IASB itself acknowledges to be an asset) may fall outside the definition of 'asset' in the IASB's own framework.

This shortcoming in the current definition may be tacitly acknowledged by the fact that the discussion of the objective of general purpose financial reporting now refers to information about the economic resources 'of' an entity (see 2.3.2 above), whereas the equivalent discussion in the 1989 Framework referred to the economic resources 'controlled by' an entity.

2.6.2.C Liabilities

An essential characteristic of a liability is that the entity has a present obligation (that is, a duty or responsibility to act or perform in a certain way). An obligation may be legally enforceable under a binding contract or statutory requirement. This is normally the case for amounts payable for goods and services received. However, obligations also arise, from normal business custom and practice, or a desire to maintain good business relations or act in an equitable manner. For example, if an entity has a policy to rectify product faults, even when these become apparent after the warranty period has expired, the amounts that are expected to be expended in respect of goods already sold are liabilities. *[Framework 4.15]*. Such non-legally binding obligations are reflected in the concept of the 'constructive obligation' in IAS 37 – *Provisions, Contingent Liabilities and Contingent Assets* (see Chapter 28 at 3.1.1).

The *Conceptual Framework* stresses that a decision by management – for example to acquire an asset – does not, of itself, give rise to a present obligation. An obligation normally arises only when the asset is delivered, or the entity enters into an irrevocable agreement to acquire it. Such an agreement typically provides for substantial financial penalty for failing to honour the obligation, leaving the entity with little or no discretion to avoid the outflow of resources. *[Framework 4.16]*. This distinction between decisions of management and actual obligations or commitments is a significant feature of IAS 37 (see Chapter 28, particularly at 5).

The settlement of a present obligation usually involves the entity giving up resources embodying economic benefits in order to satisfy the claim of the other party, for example, by:

- payment of cash;
- transfer of other assets;
- provision of services;
- replacement of the obligation being settled with another obligation; or
- conversion of the obligation to equity.

An obligation may also be extinguished by other means, such as a creditor waiving or forfeiting its rights. *[Framework 4.17]*.

Liabilities result from past transactions or other past events. Thus, for example, the acquisition of goods or the use of services gives rise to trade payables (unless paid for in advance or on delivery), and the receipt of a bank loan results in an obligation to repay it. A liability may arise for a rebate offered to customers for minimum levels of purchases. In this case, the sale of the goods in the past is the transaction that gives rise to the liability. *[Framework 4.18]*.

Liabilities that can be measured only by using a substantial degree of estimation (often described as provisions) are liabilities as defined in the *Conceptual Framework*. A provision that involves a present obligation, and satisfies the rest of the definition, is a liability even if its amount has to be estimated. Examples include a provision for payments to be made under existing warranties and a provision to cover pension obligations. *[Framework 4.19]*. Provisions are discussed more broadly in Chapter 28.

2.6.2.D Equity

Although equity is defined as a residual amount (assets less liabilities – see 2.6.2.A above), it may be sub-classified in the statement of financial position. A corporate entity might classify its total equity into:

- funds contributed by shareholders;
- retained earnings;
- reserves representing appropriations of retained earnings; and
- reserves representing capital maintenance adjustments.

Such classifications can be relevant to the decision-making needs of the users of financial statements when they indicate legal or other restrictions on the ability of the entity to distribute or otherwise apply its equity. They may also reflect the differing rights of parties with ownership interests as regards dividends or the repayment of contributed equity. *[Framework 4.20]*.

Statute or other law may require the entity to create reserves in order to protect the entity and its creditors from the effect of losses. National tax law may grant exemptions from, or reductions in, taxation liabilities when transfers are made to such reserves. The existence and size of these legal, statutory and tax reserves is information that can be relevant to the decision-making needs of users. However, transfers to such reserves are appropriations of retained earnings rather than expenses. *[Framework 4.21]*.

The amount of equity in the statement of financial position depends on the measurement of assets and liabilities. Other than by coincidence, the carrying amount of equity will not normally correspond to the aggregate market value of the shares of the entity, or to the sum that could be raised by disposing of either the net assets on a piecemeal basis or the entity as a whole on a going concern basis. *[Framework 4.22]*.

Commercial, industrial and business activities are often undertaken by means of entities such as sole proprietorships, partnerships and trusts and various types of government business undertakings. The legal and regulatory framework for such entities is often different from that applying to corporate entities. For example, there may be few or no restrictions on distributions to owners. Nevertheless, the definition of equity and the other aspects of the *Conceptual Framework* that deal with equity are appropriate for such entities. *[Framework 4.23]*.

2.6.2.E Performance

Profit is frequently used as a measure of performance or as the basis for other measures, such as return on investment or earnings per share. The elements directly related to the measurement of profit are income and expenses. The recognition and measurement of income and expenses, and hence profit, depend in part on the concepts of capital and capital maintenance used by the entity in preparing its financial statements (see 2.6.5 below). *[Framework 4.24]*.

Income is 'increases in economic benefits during the accounting period in the form of inflows or enhancements of assets or decreases of liabilities that result in increases in equity, other than those relating to contributions from equity participants'. Income is discussed at 2.6.2.F below.

Expenses are 'decreases in economic benefits during the accounting period in the form of outflows or depletions of assets or incurrences of liabilities that result in decreases in equity, other than those relating to distributions to equity participants'. Expenses are discussed at 2.6.2.G below. *[Framework 4.25].*

As is the case with assets and liabilities (see 2.6.2.A above), items may meet the definitions of income and expenses but not satisfy the requirements of the *Conceptual Framework* for recognition in the income statement. *[Framework 4.26].* The recognition criteria are discussed at 2.6.3 below.

Income and expenses may be presented in the income statement in different ways. In particular, items of income and expenses that arise in the course of the ordinary activities of the entity are commonly differentiated from those that do not. This helps users to evaluate the entity's ability to generate cash in the future (since incidental activities such as the disposal of a long-term investment are unlikely to recur on a regular basis). Any such distinction between items must have regard to the nature of the entity and its operations. Items that arise from the ordinary activities of one entity may be unusual in respect of another. *[Framework 4.27].*

Distinguishing between items of income and expense and combining them in different ways also permits an entity to display several measures of performance with differing degrees of inclusiveness. For example, the income statement could display gross margin, profit or loss from ordinary activities before taxation, profit or loss from ordinary activities after taxation, and profit or loss. *[Framework 4.28].*

2.6.2.F Income

Income encompasses both revenue and gains. Revenue arises in the course of the ordinary activities of an entity. Gains are other items that meet the definition of income whether or not they arise in the course of the ordinary activities of an entity. Because gains represent increases in economic benefits, they are no different in nature from revenue, and are not regarded a separate element in the *Conceptual Framework*. *[Framework 4.29-30].*

The IASB gives this analysis, in part, in order to explain why it did not follow the approach of the US conceptual framework, which distinguishes revenue from gains, and further differentiates gains arising from central operations from those that do not.

Gains include, for example, those arising on the disposal of non-current assets. The definition of income also includes unrealised gains, such as those arising from the revaluation of marketable securities, exchange differences or increases in the carrying amount of long-term assets. Gains recognised in the income statement are usually displayed separately and are often reported net of related expenses. *[Framework 4.31].*

Income gives rise to the receipt, or enhancement, of various kinds of assets. For example, cash, receivables and goods and services may be received in exchange for goods and services supplied. Income may also result from the settlement of liabilities. For example, an entity may provide goods and services to a lender in lieu of cash settlement of an outstanding loan. *[Framework 4.32].*

2.6.2.G Expenses

The definition of expenses encompasses losses as well as expenses arising in the course of ordinary activities, such as cost of sales, wages and depreciation. Expenses usually take the form of an outflow or depletion of assets such as cash and cash equivalents, inventory, or property, plant and equipment. *[Framework 4.33].*

Losses represent other items that meet the definition of expenses, whether or not they arise in the course of the ordinary activities of the entity. Losses represent decreases in economic benefits. As such, they are no different in nature from other expenses and are not regarded as a separate element in the *Conceptual Framework*. *[Framework 4.34].*

Examples of losses include those resulting from disasters such as fire and flood, and arising on the disposal of non-current assets. The definition of expenses also includes unrealised losses, such as those arising from the revaluation of marketable securities or exchange rate differences. Losses recognised in the income statement are usually displayed separately because knowledge of them is useful for the purpose of making economic decisions, and are often reported net of related income. *[Framework 4.35].*

2.6.2.H Realisation

The realisation principle – that income and expenditure, particularly income, should be recognised only when its conversion into cash has occurred or is reasonably certain – is a fundamental concept in a number of national GAAPs, for example those of members of the European Union.

The realisation principle is not discussed in the *Conceptual Framework*, except to the extent that it is made clear that income and expenses include both realised and unrealised gains and losses (see 2.6.2.E and 2.6.2.F above). However, the realisation principle appears to have significantly influenced the distinction between items required to be included in profit or loss and those required to be included in other comprehensive income (see 2.6.2.E above). Many (but not all) items included in other comprehensive income under IFRS would generally be regarded as unrealised.

2.6.2.I Transactions with owners acting in another capacity

The *Conceptual Framework* does not address the treatment of transactions with an owner of the reporting entity who also transacts with the entity in another capacity. Such transactions may take many forms, for example:

- an owner may be paid for the provision of goods or services to the entity; or
- a shareholder may lend cash to the entity.

In our view the nature of such transactions needs to be considered on a case-by-case basis. Where an owner supplies goods or services on arm's length terms, the presumption must be that the consideration paid by the entity is paid to the owner in his capacity as a supplier (an expense) rather than in his capacity as an owner (a distribution). Where, however, the amount paid is significantly lower or higher than the arm's length price, the entity needs to consider whether the transaction in fact comprises two elements:

- an expense for the arm's length price; and
- either a distribution to, or contribution from, the owner for any amount paid, respectively, in excess of or below the arm's length price.

This is discussed in the context of intragroup transactions in Chapter 8.

Similarly, where an owner makes a loan to the entity on arm's length terms, the presumption would be that the loan is made in the owner's capacity as lender (a financial liability) rather than as owner (an increase in equity). If, however, the loan is subsequently forgiven, it will generally be a more appropriate analysis that the shareholder acts in the capacity of an owner (an increase in equity) rather than in the capacity as lender (a gain). This is because a third-party lender would be extremely unlikely to forgive a loan for no consideration, whereas it is entirely consistent for an owner of a distressed business to choose to inject more capital.

2.6.2.J Capital maintenance adjustments

The *Conceptual Framework* notes that the revaluation or restatement of assets and liabilities gives rise to increases or decreases in equity that meet the definition of income and expenses, but – under certain concepts of capital maintenance – are included in equity as capital maintenance adjustments or revaluation reserves. *[Framework 4.36].* Concepts of capital maintenance are discussed at 2.6.5 below.

2.6.3 Recognition of the elements of financial statements

An item is recognised in the financial statements when:

- it meets the definition of an element (see 2.6.2 above);
- it is probable that any future economic benefit associated with the item will flow to or from the entity (see 2.6.3.A below); and
- the item has a cost or value that can be measured reliably (see 2.6.3.B below).

Recognition involves the depiction of the item in words and by a monetary amount, and the inclusion of that amount in the financial statements. A failure to recognise an item meeting these criteria is not rectified by disclosure of the accounting policies used nor by notes or explanatory material. The entity must consider the materiality of an item in assessing whether it qualifies for recognition in the financial statements. *[Framework 4.37-39].*

An item that fails to meet the recognition criteria above at a particular point in time may qualify for recognition at a later date as a result of subsequent circumstances or events. *[Framework 4.42].*

2.6.3.A Probability of future economic benefit or outflow

The recognition criteria above use the concept of probability to refer to the degree of uncertainty that future economic benefits will flow to or from the entity. Assessments of the degree of uncertainty attaching to the flow of future economic benefits are made on the basis of the evidence available when the financial statements are prepared. For example, it is appropriate to recognise a receivable as an asset when it is probable that it will be paid. For a large population of receivables, however, because some non-payment is normally considered probable, an expense representing the expected reduction in economic benefits is recognised. *[Framework 4.40].*

2.6.3.B Reliability of measurement

A further criterion for the recognition of an item is that it can be measured reliably, which, the *Conceptual Framework* notes (perhaps surprisingly) will include the use of 'reasonable estimates' where necessary. However, when a reasonable estimate cannot be made, the item is not recognised. An item that fails to meet the criteria for recognition may nonetheless warrant disclosure in the notes or other explanatory material, when knowledge of the item is relevant to the evaluation of the entity by the users of financial statements.

For example, the expected proceeds from a lawsuit may meet the definitions of 'asset' and 'income' and satisfy the probability criterion for recognition. However, if it is not possible for the claim to be measured reliably, it should not be recognised, although its existence would be disclosed in the notes or other explanatory material. *[Framework 4.41, 43]*.

2.6.3.C Recognition of assets

As discussed above, an asset is recognised when it is probable that future economic benefits will flow to the entity and the asset can be measured reliably. Conversely, an asset is not recognised when expenditure has been incurred for which it is considered improbable that economic benefits will flow to the entity beyond the current accounting period – such a transaction results in an expense. This does not imply either that management incurred expenditure with no intention to generate future economic benefits or that management was misguided. The only implication is that it is not sufficiently certain that economic benefits will flow to the entity beyond the current accounting period to warrant the recognition of an asset. *[Framework 4.44-45]*.

2.6.3.D Recognition of liabilities

A liability is recognised in the statement of financial position when it is probable that the settlement of a present obligation will result in an outflow of economic benefits that can be measured reliably. In practice, liabilities are not generally recognised for obligations under executory contracts that are unperformed to the same extent by both parties (for example, liabilities for inventory ordered but not yet received). However, such obligations may meet the definition of liabilities and, provided the recognition criteria are met in the particular circumstances, may qualify for recognition. In such circumstances, recognition of liabilities entails recognition of related assets or expenses. *[Framework 4.46]*.

2.6.3.E Recognition of income

Income is recognised when there has been an increase in an asset or decrease of a liability that can be measured reliably. Procedures adopted in practice for recognising income (for example, the requirement that revenue should be earned) are applications of the recognition criteria in the *Conceptual Framework*, aimed at ensuring that items are recognised as income only when they can be measured reliably and have a sufficient degree of certainty. *[Framework 4.47-48]*.

2.6.3.F Recognition of expenses

An expense is recognised when there has been a decrease of an asset or increase in a liability that can be measured reliably. Expenses are recognised in the income statement on the basis of a direct association between the costs incurred and the earning of specific items of income (commonly referred to as 'matching'). For example, the various components of expense making up the cost of goods sold are recognised at the same time as the income from the sale. However, the *Conceptual Framework* does not allow 'matching' when it would result in the recognition of items in the statement of financial position that do not meet the definition of assets or liabilities. *[Framework 4.49-50]*.

When economic benefits associated with expenditure arise over several accounting periods, and there is only a broad or indirect association between income and expenses, expenses are recognised using systematic and rational allocation procedures. This is often necessary in recognising the expenses associated with the consumption of assets such as property, plant, equipment, goodwill, patents and trademarks, referred to as depreciation or amortisation. These allocation procedures are intended to recognise expenses in the accounting periods in which the economic benefits associated with those items are consumed or expire. *[Framework 4.51]*.

An expense is recognised immediately when an expenditure produces no future economic benefits or when, and to the extent that, future economic benefits do not qualify, or cease to qualify, for recognition as an asset. An expense is also recognised in the income statement when a liability is incurred without the recognition of an asset, as when a liability arises under a product warranty. *[Framework 4.52-53]*.

2.6.4 Measurement of the elements of financial statements

Measurement is 'the process of determining the monetary amounts at which the elements of the financial statements are to be recognised and carried in the balance sheet and income statement'. *[Framework 4.54]*.

A number of different measurement bases are employed to different degrees and in varying combinations in financial statements, including:

- *Historical cost*

  Assets are recorded at the amount of cash or cash equivalents paid, or the fair value of the consideration given to acquire them, at the time of their acquisition. Liabilities are recorded at the amount of proceeds received in exchange for the obligation, or at the amounts of cash or cash equivalents expected to be paid to satisfy the liability in the normal course of business.

- *Current cost*

  Assets are carried at the amount of cash or cash equivalents that would have to be paid if the same or an equivalent asset was acquired currently. Liabilities are carried at the undiscounted amount of cash or cash equivalents that would be required to settle the obligation currently.

- *Realisable (settlement) value*

  Assets are carried at the amount of cash or cash equivalents that could currently be obtained by selling the asset in an orderly disposal. Liabilities are carried at the undiscounted amounts of cash or cash equivalents expected to be paid to satisfy the liabilities in the normal course of business.

- *Present value*

  Assets are carried at the present discounted value of the future net cash inflows that the item is expected to generate in the normal course of business. Liabilities are carried at the present discounted value of the future net cash outflows that are expected to be required to settle the liabilities in the normal course of business. *[Framework 4.55]*.

The most commonly adopted measurement basis is historical cost, usually combined with other measurement bases. For example, under IFRS inventories are usually carried at the lower of cost and net realisable value (see Chapter 22), marketable securities at market value (see Chapter 48), and pension liabilities are carried at their present value (see Chapter 33). Furthermore, some entities use the current cost basis as a response to the inability of the historical cost accounting model to deal with the effects of changing prices of non-monetary assets. *[Framework 4.56]*.

The treatment of measurement in the *Conceptual Framework* is not altogether satisfactory. As can be seen from the summary above, the discussion essentially describes various practices, without any conceptual analysis of the relative strengths and weaknesses of each method.

The description of the historical cost model might surprise some by its reference to the cost of an item acquired for non-cash consideration being the 'fair value of the consideration at the time of acquisition'. That implies that, when a non-cash asset is exchanged for another, a gain should be recognised for any excess at the time of exchange of the fair value of the asset exchanged over its historical cost. Many proponents of the historical cost model would argue that no such gain should be recognised, and that the newly acquired second asset should be measured at the historical cost of the asset given up in exchange for it.

It is also curious that fair value is not one of the four bases for measurement in the *Conceptual Framework*, in spite of its frequent use in the IASB's standards. IFRS 13 – *Fair Value Measurement* – defines fair value as 'the price that would be received to sell an asset or to transfer a liability in an orderly transaction between market participants at the measurement date' – see Chapter 14. This essentially means that the term fair value has been adopted to mean essentially what the *Conceptual Framework* refers to as realisable value.

2.6.5 Concepts of capital and capital maintenance

The concept of capital maintenance is concerned with how an entity defines the capital that it seeks to maintain. It is a prerequisite for distinguishing between an entity's return *on* capital (i.e. profit) and its return *of* capital. In general terms, an entity has maintained its capital if it has as much capital at the end of the period as it had at the beginning of the period. Any amount over and above that required to maintain the capital at the beginning of the period is profit. *[Framework 4.60, 62]*.

The *Conceptual Framework* identifies two broad concepts of capital maintenance:

- financial capital maintenance (see 2.6.5.A below); and
- physical capital maintenance (see 2.6.5.B below).

The principal difference between the two concepts of capital maintenance is the treatment of the effects of changes in the prices of assets and liabilities of the entity. *[Framework 4.62]*. The selection of the appropriate concept of capital by an entity should be based on the needs of the users of its financial statements. *[Framework 4.58]*.

The concept of capital maintenance chosen by an entity will determine the accounting model used in the preparation of its financial statements. Most entities adopt a financial concept of capital. Different accounting models exhibit different degrees of relevance and reliability, and it is for management to seek a balance between relevance and reliability (see 2.5.1 above). The *Conceptual Framework* notes that the IASB does not prescribe a particular model other than in exceptional circumstances, such as in a hyperinflationary economy (see Chapter 16). This intention will, however, be reviewed in the light of world developments. *[Framework 4.57, 65]*.

2.6.5.A *Financial capital maintenance*

Under a financial concept of capital, such as invested money or invested purchasing power, capital is synonymous with the net assets or equity of the entity. Under this concept a profit is earned only if the financial (or money) amount of the net assets at the end of the period exceeds the financial (or money) amount of net assets at the beginning of the period, after excluding any distributions to, and contributions from, owners during the period. *[Framework 4.57, 59(a)]*.

Financial capital maintenance can be measured in either nominal monetary units or units of constant purchasing power. *[Framework 4.59(a)]*. The financial capital maintenance concept does not require a particular measurement basis to be used. Rather, the basis selected depends upon the type of financial capital that the entity is seeking to maintain. *[Framework 4.61]*.

Where capital is defined in terms of nominal monetary units, profit represents the increase in nominal money capital over the period. This has the implication that increases in the prices of assets held over the period, conventionally referred to as holding gains, are conceptually profits. They may not be recognised as such, however, until the assets are disposed of in an exchange transaction. *[Framework 4.63]*.

When the concept of financial capital maintenance is defined in terms of constant purchasing power units, profit represents the increase in invested purchasing power over the period. Thus, only that part of the increase in the prices of assets that exceeds the increase in the general level of prices is regarded as profit. The rest of the increase is treated as a capital maintenance adjustment and, hence, as part of equity. *[Framework 4.63]*.

2.6.5.B *Physical capital maintenance*

Under this concept a profit is earned only if the physical productive capacity (or operating capability) of the entity (or the resources or funds needed to achieve that capacity) at the end of the period exceeds the physical productive capacity at the beginning of the period, after excluding any distributions to, and contributions from, owners during the period. *[Framework 4.59(b)]*. The physical capital maintenance concept requires the current cost basis of measurement to be adopted. *[Framework 4.61]*.

Because capital is defined in terms of the physical productive capacity, profit represents the increase in that capital over the period. Price changes affecting the assets and liabilities of the entity are changes in the physical productive capacity of the entity, which are therefore treated as capital maintenance adjustments within equity and not as profit. *[Framework 4.64]*.

2.7 Management commentary

Over a number of years, a number of individual countries have issued regulations or guidance requiring or encouraging the preparation of narrative 'management commentary' to accompany the financial statements.

In December 2010 the IASB published its first guidance on management commentary – *Management Commentary – A Framework for Presentation* – as a non-binding 'IFRS Practice Statement'. The introduction to the Practice Statement clarifies that it is neither an IFRS nor part of the *Conceptual Framework*. However, it has been prepared on the basis that management commentary meets the definition of other financial reporting in the *Preface to International Financial Reporting Standards*, and is therefore within the scope of the *Conceptual Framework*. Consequently, the Statement should be read 'in the context of' the *Conceptual Framework*. *[MC.IN2, IN4]*.

Management commentary is described as a narrative report that relates to financial statements that have been prepared in accordance with IFRSs. Management commentary provides users with historical explanations of the amounts presented in the financial statements, specifically the entity's financial position, financial performance and cash flows. It also provides commentary on an entity's prospects and other information not presented in the financial statements. Management commentary also serves as a basis for understanding management's objectives and its strategies for achieving those objectives. *[MC Appendix]*. For many entities, management commentary is already an important element of their communication with the capital markets, supplementing as well as complementing the financial statements. *[MC.IN3]*.

The Practice Statement is intended to set out a broad framework for the preparation of management commentaries, to be applied by management of individual reporting entities to their own specific circumstances. *[MC.IN5]*. However, the IASB believes that that all management commentary should:

- provide management's view of the entity's performance, position and progress; and
- supplement and complement information presented in the financial statements. *[MC.12]*.

Management commentary should include information that is forward-looking and has the qualitative characteristics referred to in the *Conceptual Framework*. *[MC.13]*.

The IASB also envisages that any management commentary will include the following elements:

- the nature of the business;
- management's objectives and strategies for meeting those objectives;
- the entity's most significant resources, risks and relationships;
- the results of operations and prospects; and
- the critical performance measures and indicators that management uses to evaluate the entity's performance against stated objectives. *[MC.24]*.

3 FUTURE DEVELOPMENTS

As noted at 1 above, in May 2015 the IASB issued an exposure draft of proposed changes to the *Conceptual Framework*. The ED gave a comment deadline of November 2015 and the Board is now considering the comments received. An overview of the tentative decisions made by the Board since the publication of the ED is given at 3.8 below. The IASB intends to finalise a revised framework around the end of 2017.[5]

The topics covered in the ED are:

- Objective of general purpose financial reporting (GPFR);
- Qualitative characteristics of useful financial information;
- General purpose financial statements (GPFS) and reporting entities;
- Elements of financial statements;
- Recognition and derecognition;
- Measurement;
- Presentation and disclosure; and
- Concepts of capital and capital maintenance.

These proposals are discussed in the rest of this section.

3.1 Objective of GPFR and qualitative characteristics of useful financial information

The IASB has proposed limited amendments to these sections of the existing *Conceptual Framework*.

One of the amendments relates to the discussion of management's stewardship of an entity's resources. The existing *Conceptual Framework* does not use the term 'stewardship', but, instead, describes what stewardship encapsulates. The IASB has proposed to include the term stewardship in order to emphasise the need for information required to assess the stewardship function, as a necessary part of the overall objective of financial reporting.

In the existing *Conceptual Framework*'s section on qualitative characteristics of useful financial information, the IASB had not included a discussion on prudence, stating that prudence is inconsistent with neutrality. After considering feedback from constituents, the IASB decided to reinstate the concept of prudence in the ED. The Board believes that prudence is best described as caution when making judgements under conditions of uncertainty, that it has a role to play in financial reporting, and can help achieve neutrality. The IASB has further clarified that prudence works both ways: assets and liabilities should be neither overstated nor understated.

3.2 Reporting entities

The ED describes a reporting entity as an entity that chooses, or is required, to prepare GPFS, and it proposes guidance on how to set the boundary of a reporting entity. The Board proposes that the boundary can be determined by either direct control (which results in unconsolidated or individual financial statements) or by direct and indirect control (which results in consolidated financial statements).

The Board also acknowledges the need for combined financial statements in certain circumstances, but does not discuss in the ED when or how entities could or should prepare them, stating a preference to undertake a standard or standards-level project on this subject rather than deal with it in any great detail in the *Conceptual Framework*.

3.3 Elements of financial statements

The ED proposes to revise the current definitions of assets and liabilities. The ED defines an asset as 'a present economic resource controlled by the entity as a result of past events'. The term 'economic resource' focuses on rights (or a bundle of rights) which have the potential to produce economic benefits. This represents a greater focus on accounting for different rights that compose economic resources, which encapsulates the notion of accounting for both tangible and intangible assets. The IASB has retained the concept of control in the definition, in order to assert that an entity must have both the ability to direct the use of, and rights to obtain, the benefits from the economic resource. The proposed definition of a liability, 'a present obligation of the entity to transfer an economic resource as a result of past events', places emphasis on an entity's obligation at the reporting date, as a consequence of a past transaction or other event that imposed the obligation on the entity. The ED also contains further guidance on what a present obligation is, which would essentially include any obligation arising from past events that an entity has no practical ability to avoid.

For the definitions of both assets and liabilities, the IASB decided not to retain the notion of an 'expected inflow or outflow of resources' in acknowledgement of concerns about varied interpretations of the term 'expected' and the notion of a threshold level of probability. The Board believes that this is best addressed within the recognition guidance.

3.4 Recognition and derecognition

3.4.1 Recognition

The recognition criteria in the current *Conceptual Framework* require that an item be recognised if it is: a) probable that any future economic benefit associated with it will flow to or from the entity; and b) it has a cost or value that can be measured with reliability. The Board observed that, across current standards, the application of the probability criterion is inconsistent.

For example, in IFRS 9 – *Financial Instruments*, there is no probability recognition criterion, otherwise instruments such as derivatives would not be recognised.

Therefore, the IASB proposed that the Conceptual Framework should set out criteria for recognition based on the qualitative characteristics of useful financial information. An asset or liability (and any related income, expense or change in equity) is recognised if:

- it provides users of financial statements with relevant information about the asset or liability and any resulting income, expense or change in equity;
- it provides a faithful representation of the asset or liability and of any resulting income, expense or change in equity; and
- the benefit of the information provided by recognising the asset or liability outweighs the cost of doing so.

3.4.2 Existence uncertainty

One of the challenges of recognition is existence uncertainty. In trying to address this issue, the IASB decided to propose listing existence uncertainty of an asset or liability as one of the indicators that may lead to a conclusion that recognition of that asset or liability may not produce relevant information. The IASB believes that it would not be useful to provide more detailed guidance on how to address existence uncertainty because the facts are likely to depend very much on particular circumstances.

3.4.3 Derecognition

The existing Conceptual Framework does not provide guidance on derecognition and, currently, there are inconsistent approaches to derecognition being applied across the standards. In the ED, the IASB has included the following guidance:

- consider to whom the asset or liability has been transferred, i.e. whether the transferee is acting as an agent, in which case, derecognition may not be appropriate;
- consider the exposure retained by the entity after the transaction; and
- the assets and liabilities retained and any changes in the entity's assets and liabilities should be faithfully represented.

3.5 Measurement

During development of the ED, the Board considered whether the *Conceptual Framework* should advocate the use of a single measurement basis.

Considering the different assets and liabilities being measured, relevance and the cost constraint, the Board eventually concluded that a multiple measurement approach is more appropriate. The proposed measurement guidance in the ED would cover a significant gap in the existing *Conceptual Framework* literature.

The ED covers:

- a description of various measurement bases (historical cost and current value measures) and the information that these measurement bases provide;
- factors to consider when selecting a measurement basis;
- situations when more than one measurement basis provides relevant information; and
- measurement of equity.

3.6 Presentation and disclosure

The ED proposes high-level concepts that describe the information that should be included in financial statements and how that information should be presented and disclosed. These concepts will guide the IASB in setting presentation and disclosure requirements in individual standards and will guide entities in providing information in financial statements. In addition, the IASB is undertaking a Disclosure Initiative, a collection of implementation and research projects aimed at improving disclosure in IFRS financial reporting. In the Disclosure Initiative, the IASB will seek to provide additional specific guidance to support the application of the concepts.

The presentation and disclosure objectives and principles discussed in the ED are:

- the balance between entities' flexibility to provide relevant information that faithfully represents the entity's assets and liabilities and the transactions and other events of the period, and comparability among entities and across reporting periods;
- entity-specific information is more useful than boilerplate language for efficient and effective communication; and
- duplication of information in various sections of the financial statements is unnecessary and makes financial statements less understandable.

3.6.1 *Reporting financial performance and other comprehensive income*

In the discussion of information about financial performance, the ED states that income and expenses in the statement(s) of financial performance are classified into either the statement of profit or loss (P/L) or OCI. The purpose of the P/L is to depict the return an entity has made on its economic resources during the period and to provide information that is helpful in assessing future cash flows and management's stewardship of the entity's resources. Therefore, income and expenses included in the P/L are the primary source of information about an entity's financial performance for the period. As such, there is a presumption that all income and all expenses will be included in the P/L.

The ED continues to explain that there are circumstances in which the exclusion of some income or expenses from the P/L resulting from a change in a current measure of an asset or liability would enhance the relevance of the information in the P/L. When this is the case, that income or expense is recognised in OCI. However, for an item recognised in OCI in one period, there is a presumption that it will be included in the P/L in a future period, unless there is no clear basis for identifying the period in which reclassification would enhance the relevance of the information in the P/L.

3.7 Transition and effective date

The IASB has considered how entities should account for changes in accounting policies resulting from the revision of the *Conceptual Framework*, and proposes that such changes in accounting policy should be accounted for retrospectively in accordance with IAS 8 – *Accounting Policies, Changes in Accounting Estimates and Errors* (see Chapter 3).

The IASB proposes to set an effective date that will allow a transition period of approximately 18 months between the issue of the revised *Conceptual Framework* and its effective date for entities, with early application permitted.

This would allow entities time to review the effects of the revised concepts on their policies and prepare for retrospective application of the changes.

3.8 Tentative decisions of the Board regarding the progression of the ED to a revised framework

As noted above, the Board has made a number of tentative decisions in light of comments on, and its redeliberation of, the ED. These are summarised below.

On 20 April 2016 the Board tentatively decided that it would redeliberate the topics that have proved controversial or those where new information has become available. On other topics, the Board intends to confirm the proposals in the ED but not to undertake significant additional analysis.

The Board tentatively decided that, in analysing the effects of the Conceptual Framework, the staff:[6]

- would not be asked to perform a comprehensive analysis of:
  - the effects of the revised Conceptual Framework on future standard-setting; or
  - inconsistencies between the revised Conceptual Framework and Standards.

- would be asked to:
  - perform a more extensive analysis of the effects that the proposed definitions of assets and liabilities and the concepts supporting those definitions could have for current projects;
  - analyse additional inconsistencies between the revised Conceptual Framework and Standards suggested by respondents; and
  - perform a more detailed analysis of the effects of the revised Conceptual Framework on preparers.

The staff has continued with this work and the Board has discussed the project at its subsequent meetings. In July 2016 the staff published *IASB Staff Paper* – Effect of Board redeliberations on the Exposure Draft *Conceptual Framework for Financial Reporting* (available from the IASB website). The paper indicated where and how the proposals in the ED would change as a result of the Board's tentative decisions and reflected such decisions made up to and including its meeting on the 18 July 2016. Many of these tentative decisions confirmed and clarified, rather than changed, the proposals in the ED. The expectation at the time of that paper was that a final version of the Framework would be published 'early in 2017'.

This expectation was not met, and the Board continued to discuss the project at each of its meetings in 2016 and into 2017. In June 2017 a paper entitled 'Conceptual Framework for Financial Reporting Summary of tentative decisions' was produce (available on the IASB website). It lists the Board's tentative decisions made in meetings up to and including 21 March 2017. The document runs to 27 pages and lists 37 agenda papers which have been discussed by the Board in its meetings from April 2016 to March 2017.

Areas that may be of particular interest include: measurement uncertainty; identifying liabilities; and, selection of measurement basis.

The Board now expects to finalise the project with the publication of the revised Framework 'around the end of' 2017.

References

---

1 W. A. Paton and A. C. Littleton, *An Introduction to Corporate Accounting Standards*, Monograph No. 3, American Accounting Association, 1940.

2 See, for example: American Accounting Association, Executive Committee, 'A Tentative Statement of Accounting Principles Affecting Corporate Reports', *Accounting Review*, June 1936, pp.187-191; American Accounting Association, Executive Committee, 'Accounting Principles Underlying Corporate Financial Statements', *Accounting Review*, June 1941, pp.133-139; American Accounting Association, Committee to Prepare a Statement of Basic Accounting Theory, *A Statement of Basic Accounting Theory*, 1966; American Accounting Association, Committee on Concepts and Standards for External Financial Reports, *Statement on Accounting Theory and Theory Acceptance*, 1977. The 1977 report concluded that closure on the debate was not feasible, which is perhaps indicative of the complexity of the problem.

3 Discussion Paper – *A Review of the Conceptual Framework for Financial Reporting*, IASB, July 2013, ('DP'), para. 1.5.

4 Discussion Paper – *A Review of the Conceptual Framework for Financial Reporting*, IASB, July 2013, ('DP'), para. 1.5.

5 IASB website August 2017.

6 IASB website August 2016.

Chapter 2

References

Chapter 3 Presentation of financial statements and accounting policies

List of examples

Chapter 3

Chapter 3 Presentation of financial statements and accounting policies

1 INTRODUCTION

There is no single International Accounting Standard dealing with the form, content and structure of financial statements and the accounting policies to be applied in their preparation. Of course, all international accounting standards specify some required disclosures and many mention the level of prominence required (such as on the face of a primary statement rather than in the notes). The subject of just what financial statements are, their purpose, contents and presentation is addressed principally by three standards.

IAS 1 – *Presentation of Financial Statements* – is the main standard dealing with the overall requirements for the presentation of financial statements, including their purpose, form, content and structure. IAS 8 – *Accounting Policies, Changes in Accounting Estimates and Errors* – deals with the requirements for the selection and application of accounting policies. It also deals with the requirements as to when changes in accounting policies should be made, and how such changes should be accounted for and disclosed. This chapter deals with the requirements of IAS 1 and IAS 8. Chapter 4 discusses the requirements of IFRS 5 – *Non-current Assets Held for Sale and Discontinued Operations.* That standard principally deals with the classification and presentation of non-current assets held for sale in the statement of financial position, and the presentation of the results of discontinued operations, although it also sets out the measurement requirements for such items. The statement of cash flows is discussed in Chapter 38.

1.1 Objective and scope of IAS 1

IAS 1 deals with the components of financial statements, fair presentation, fundamental accounting concepts, disclosure of accounting policies, and the structure and content of financial statements.

IAS 1 applies to what it calls 'general purpose financial statements' (financial statements), that is those intended to meet the needs of users who are not in a position to require an entity to prepare reports tailored to meet their particular information needs, and it should be applied to all such financial statements prepared in accordance with

International Financial Reporting Standards (IFRSs). *[IAS 1.2, 7]*. Although International Financial Reporting Standards is probably a self-explanatory phrase, both IAS 1 and IAS 8 define it as 'Standards and Interpretations issued by the International Accounting Standards Board (IASB). They comprise:

(a) International Financial Reporting Standards;

(b) International Accounting Standards;

(c) IFRIC Interpretations; and

(d) SIC Interpretations'. *[IAS 1.7, IAS 8.5]*.

An important point here is that implementation guidance for standards issued by the IASB does not form part of those standards, and therefore does not contain requirements for financial statements. *[IAS 8.9]*. Accordingly, the often voluminous implementation guidance accompanying standards is not, strictly speaking, part of 'IFRS'. We would generally be surprised, though, at entities not following such guidance.

The standard applies equally to all entities including those that present consolidated financial statements and those that present separate financial statements (discussed in Chapter 8 at 1.1). IAS 1 does not apply to the structure and content of condensed interim financial statements prepared in accordance with IAS 34 – *Interim Financial Reporting* (discussed in Chapter 39 at 3.2), although its provisions relating to fair presentation, compliance with IFRS and fundamental accounting principles do apply to interims. *[IAS 1.4]*. These provisions of IAS 1 are discussed at 4.1 below.

The objective of the standard is to prescribe the basis for presentation of general purpose financial statements, and by doing so to ensure comparability both with the entity's financial statements of previous periods and with the financial statements of other entities. The standard sets out overall requirements for the presentation of financial statements, guidelines for their structure and minimum requirements for their content. The recognition, measurement and disclosure of specific transactions and other events are dealt with in other standards and in interpretations. *[IAS 1.1, 3]*.

IAS 1 is primarily directed at profit oriented entities (including public sector business entities), and this is reflected in the terminology it uses and its requirements. It acknowledges that entities with not-for-profit activities in the private sector, public sector or government may want to apply the standard and that such entities may need to amend the descriptions used for particular line items in the financial statements and for the financial statements themselves. *[IAS 1.5]*. Furthermore, IAS 1 is a general standard that does not address issues specific to particular industries. It does observe, though, that entities without equity (such as some mutual funds) or whose share capital is not equity (such as some co-operative entities) may need to adapt the presentation of members' or unit holders' interests. *[IAS 1.6]*.

1.2 Objective and scope of IAS 8

IAS 8 applies to selecting and applying accounting policies, and accounting for changes in accounting policies, changes in accounting estimates and corrections of prior period errors. *[IAS 8.3]*. Its objective is to prescribe the criteria for selecting and changing accounting policies, together with the accounting treatment and disclosure of changes in accounting policies, changes in accounting estimates and corrections of errors. The standard's intention is to enhance the relevance and reliability of an entity's financial statements and the comparability of those financial statements over time and with the financial statements of other entities. *[IAS 8.1]*.

Two particular issues which one might expect to be dealt with regarding the above are discussed in other standards and cross-referred to by IAS 8:

- disclosure requirements for accounting policies, except those for changes in accounting policies, are dealt with in IAS 1; *[IAS 8.2]* and
- accounting and disclosure requirements regarding the tax effects of corrections of prior period errors and of retrospective adjustments made to apply changes in accounting policies are dealt with in IAS 12 – *Income Taxes* (discussed in Chapter 31 at 10.2). *[IAS 8.4]*.

2 THE PURPOSE AND COMPOSITION OF FINANCIAL STATEMENTS

What financial statements are and what they are for are important basic questions for any body of accounting literature, and answering them is one of the main purposes of IAS 1.

2.1 The purpose of financial statements

IAS 1 describes financial statements as a structured representation of the financial position and financial performance of an entity. It states that the objective of financial statements is to provide information about the financial position, financial performance and cash flows of an entity that is useful to a wide range of users in making economic decisions. A focus on assisting decision making by the users of financial statements is seeking (at least in part) a forward looking or predictive quality. This is reflected by some requirements of accounting standards. For example: the disclosure of discontinued operations (discussed in Chapter 4 at 3); the use of profit from continuing operations as the control number in calculating diluted earnings per share (discussed in Chapter 35 at 6.3.1); and also, the desire of some entities to present performance measures excluding what they see as unusual or infrequent items (discussed at 3.2.6 below).

IAS 1 also acknowledges a second important role of financial statements. That is, that they also show the results of management's stewardship of the resources entrusted to it.

To meet this objective for financial statements, IAS 1 requires that they provide information about an entity's:

(a) assets;

(b) liabilities;

(c) equity;

(d) income and expenses, including gains and losses;

(e) contributions by owners and distributions to owners in their capacity as owners (owners being defined as holders of instruments classified as equity); *[IAS 1.7]* and

(f) cash flows.

The standard observes that this information, along with other information in the notes, assists users of financial statements in predicting the entity's future cash flows and, in particular, their timing and certainty. *[IAS 1.9]*.

2.2 Frequency of reporting and period covered

IAS 1 requires that a complete set of financial statements (including comparative information, see 2.4 below) be presented 'at least annually'. Whilst this drafting is not exactly precise, it does not seem to mean that financial statements must never be more than a year apart (which is perhaps the most natural meaning of the phrase). This is because the standard goes on to mention that the end of an entity's reporting period may change, and that the annual financial statements are therefore presented for a period *longer* or shorter than one year. When this is the case, IAS 1 requires disclosure of, in addition to the period covered by the financial statements:

(a) the reason for using a longer or shorter period; and

(b) the fact that amounts presented in the financial statements are not entirely comparable. *[IAS 1.36].*

Normally financial statements are consistently prepared covering a one year period. Some entities, particularly in the retail sector, traditionally present financial statements for a 52-week period. IAS 1 does not preclude this practice. *[IAS 1.37].*

2.3 The components of a complete set of financial statements

A complete set of financial statements under IAS 1 comprises the following, each of which should be presented with equal prominence: *[IAS 1.10-11]*

(a) a statement of financial position as at the end of the period;

(b) a statement of profit or loss and other comprehensive income for the period to be presented either as:

  (i) one single statement of comprehensive income with a section for profit and loss followed immediately by a section for other comprehensive income; or

  (ii) a separate statement of profit or loss and statement of comprehensive income. In this case, the former must be presented immediately before the latter;

(c) a statement of changes in equity for the period;

(d) a statement of cash flows for the period;

(e) notes, comprising significant accounting policies and other explanatory information;

(f) comparative information in respect of the preceding period; and

(g) a statement of financial position as at the beginning of the preceding period when:

  (i) an accounting policy has been applied retrospectively; or

  (ii) a retrospective restatement has been made; or

  (iii) items have been reclassified.

The titles of the statements need not be those used in the standard (shown above).

The standard explains that notes contain information in addition to that presented in the statements above, and provide narrative descriptions or disaggregations of items presented in those statements and information about items that do not qualify for recognition in those statements. *[IAS 1.7].*

In addition to information about the reporting period, IAS 1 also requires information about the preceding period. Comparative information is discussed at 2.4 below.

Financial statements are usually published as part of a larger annual report, with the accompanying discussions and analyses often being more voluminous than the financial statements themselves. IAS 1 acknowledges this, but makes clear that such reports and statements (including financial reviews, environmental reports and value added statements) presented outside financial statements are outside the scope of IFRS. *[IAS 1.14]*.

Notwithstanding that this type of information is not within the scope of IFRS, IAS 1 devotes two paragraphs to discussing what this information may comprise, observing that:

- a financial review by management may describe and explain the main features of the entity's financial performance and financial position and the principal uncertainties it faces and that it may include a review of:
  - the main factors and influences determining financial performance, including changes in the environment in which the entity operates, the entity's response to those changes and their effect, and the entity's policy for investment to maintain and enhance financial performance, including its dividend policy;
  - the entity's sources of funding and its targeted ratio of liabilities to equity (IAS 1 itself requires certain disclosures about capital. These are discussed at 5.4 below); and
  - the entity's resources not recognised in the statement of financial position in accordance with IFRS. *[IAS 1.13]*.
- reports and statements such as environmental reports and value added statements may be presented, particularly in industries in which environmental factors are significant and when employees are regarded as an important user group. *[IAS 1.14]*.

At first glance it may seem strange that an accounting standard would concern itself with a discussion of matters outside its scope in this way. However, discursive reports accompanying financial statements are not just common (indeed, required by most markets) but also clearly useful, so perhaps the IASB's discussion is attempting to encourage and support their preparation. Furthermore, the interaction between information in financial statements and information elsewhere in an annual report is one of the issues in the ongoing debate about disclosure effectiveness (see 6 below).

In December 2010 the IASB published a practice statement on management commentary. The practice statement is a broad, non-binding framework for the presentation of narrative reporting to accompany financial statements prepared in accordance with IFRS.

Although management commentaries add helpful and relevant information beyond what is included in the financial statements, IFRS requires the financial statements to provide a fair presentation of the financial position, financial performance and cash flows of an entity on a stand-alone basis.

The Board continues to consider wider aspects of corporate reporting. At its March 2017 meeting, it discussed options for a more active role in wider corporate reporting and tentatively decided to consider a project to revise and update the practice statement. The Board commissioned the staff to do further analysis, including consulting with the IFRS Advisory Council, before preparing a formal proposal to add a project to the active research agenda.[1]

2.4 Comparative information

IAS 1 requires, except when IFRSs permit or require otherwise, comparative information to be disclosed in respect of the previous period for all amounts reported in the current period's financial statements. *[IAS 1.38].* If any information is voluntarily presented, there will by definition be no standard or interpretation providing a dispensation from comparatives. Accordingly, comparative information is necessary for any voluntarily presented current period disclosure.

The above requirement for two sets of statements and notes represents the minimum which is required in all circumstances. *[IAS 1.38A].*

An entity may present comparative information in addition to the minimum comparative financial statements required by IFRS, as long as that information is prepared in accordance with IFRSs. This comparative information may consist of one or more primary statements, but need not comprise a complete set of financial statements. When this is the case, IAS 1 requires an entity to present related note information for those additional statements. *[IAS 1.38C].*

For example, an entity may present a third statement of profit or loss and other comprehensive income (thereby presenting the current period, the preceding period and one additional comparative period). In such circumstances, IAS 1 does not require a third statement of financial position, a third statement of cash flows or a third statement of changes in equity (i.e. an additional comparative financial statement). The entity is required to present, in the notes to the financial statements, the comparative information related to that additional statement of profit or loss and other comprehensive income. *[IAS 1.38D].*

However, further comparative information is required by IAS 1 in certain circumstances. Whenever an entity:

(a) applies an accounting policy retrospectively; or

(b) makes a retrospective restatement; or

(c) reclassifies items in its financial statements;

an additional statement of financial position is required as at the beginning of the preceding period if the change has a material effect on that additional statement. *[IAS 1.40A].* As such restatements are considered, by the IASB, narrow, specific and limited, no notes are required for this additional statement of financial position. *[IAS 1.40C, BC32C].*

It is important to note that 'reclassifies', as that word is used by IAS 1 in this context (at (c) above), is not referring to a 'reclassification adjustment'. 'Reclassification adjustments' is a term defined by IAS 1 which describes the recognition of items in profit or loss which were previously recognised in other comprehensive income (often referred to as 'recycling'). IAS 1 applies this definition when setting out the required presentation and disclosure of such items (see 3.2.4.B below).

Comparative information is also required for narrative and descriptive information when it is relevant to an understanding of the current period's financial statements. *[IAS 1.38].* The standard illustrates the current year relevance of the previous year's narratives with a legal dispute, the outcome of which was uncertain at the previous period and is yet to be resolved (the disclosure of contingent liabilities is discussed in

Chapter 28 at 7.2). It observes that users benefit from information that the uncertainty existed at the end of the previous period, and about the steps that have been taken during the period to resolve the uncertainty. *[IAS 1.38B]*.

Another example would be the required disclosure of material items (see 3.2.6 below). IAS 1 requires that the nature and amount of such items be disclosed separately. *[IAS 1.97]*. Often a simple caption or line item heading will be sufficient to convey the 'nature' of material items. Sometimes, though, a more extensive description in the notes may be needed to do this. In that case, the same information is likely to be relevant the following year.

As noted at 1.1 above, one of the objectives of IAS 1 is to ensure the comparability of financial statements with previous periods. The standard notes that enhancing the inter-period comparability of information assists users in making economic decisions, especially by allowing the assessment of trends in financial information for predictive purposes. *[IAS 1.43]*. Requiring the presentation of comparatives allows such a comparison to be made within one set of financial statements. For a comparison to be meaningful, the amounts for prior periods need to be reclassified whenever the presentation or classification of items in the financial statements is amended. When this is the case, disclosure is required of the nature, amount and reasons for the reclassification (including as at the beginning of the preceding period). *[IAS 1.41]*.

The standard acknowledges, though, that in some circumstances it is impracticable to reclassify comparative information for a particular prior period to achieve comparability with the current period. For these purposes, reclassification is impracticable when it cannot be done after making every reasonable effort to do so. *[IAS 1.7]*. An example given by the standard is that data may not have been collected in the prior period(s) in a way that allows reclassification, and it may not be practicable to recreate the information. *[IAS 1.43]*. When it proves impracticable to reclassify comparative data, IAS 1 requires disclosure of the reason for this and also the nature of the adjustments that would have been made if the amounts had been reclassified. *[IAS 1.42]*.

As well as reclassification to reflect current period classifications as required by IAS 1, a change to comparatives as they were originally reported could be necessary:

(a) following a change in accounting policy (discussed at 4.4 below);

(b) to correct an error discovered in previous financial statements (discussed at 4.6 below); or

(c) in relation to discontinued operations (discussed in Chapter 4 at 3.2).

2.5 Identification of the financial statements and accompanying information

2.5.1 Identification of financial statements

It is commonly the case that financial statements will form only part of a larger annual report, regulatory filing or other document. As IFRS only applies to financial statements, it is important that the financial statements are clearly identified so that users of the report can distinguish information that is prepared using IFRS from other information that may be useful but is not the subject of those requirements. *[IAS 1.49-50]*.

This requirement will be particularly important when an entity chooses to locate information required by IFRS outside of the financial statements and incorporate it into them by cross-reference.

As well as requiring that the financial statements be clearly distinguished, IAS 1 also requires that each financial statement and the notes be identified clearly. Furthermore, the following is required to be displayed prominently, and repeated when that is necessary for the information presented to be understandable:

(a) the name of the reporting entity or other means of identification, and any change in that information from the end of the preceding period;

(b) whether the financial statements are of an individual entity or a group of entities;

(c) the date of the end of the reporting period or the period covered by the set of financial statements or the notes (presumably whichever is appropriate to that component of the financial statements);

(d) the presentation currency, as defined in IAS 21 – *The Effects of Changes in Foreign Exchange Rates* (discussed in Chapter 15 at 3); and

(e) the level of rounding used in presenting amounts in the financial statements. *[IAS 1.51]*.

These requirements are met by the use of appropriate headings for pages, statements, notes, and columns etc. The standard notes that judgement is required in determining the best way of presenting such information. For example, when the financial statements are presented electronically, separate pages are not always used; the above items then need to be presented to ensure that the information included in the financial statements can be understood. *[IAS 1.52]*. IAS 1 considers that financial statements are often made more understandable by presenting information in thousands or millions of units of the presentation currency. It considers this acceptable as long as the level of rounding in presentation is disclosed and material information is not omitted. *[IAS 1.53]*.

2.5.2 Statement of compliance with IFRS

As well as identifying which particular part of any larger document constitutes the financial statements, IAS 1 also requires that financial statements complying with IFRS make an explicit and unreserved statement of such compliance in the notes. *[IAS 1.16]*. As this statement itself is required for full compliance, its absence would render the whole financial statements non-compliant, even if there was otherwise full compliance. The standard goes on to say that 'an entity shall not describe financial statements as complying with IFRSs unless they comply with all the requirements of IFRSs.' *[IAS 1.16]*.

The note containing this statement of compliance is also usually where entities provide any other compliance statement required by local regulation. For example, entities required to comply with IFRS as adopted for use in the EU would typically state compliance with that requirement alongside the statement of compliance with IFRS itself (assuming, of course, that the financial statements were in full compliance with both).

3 THE STRUCTURE OF FINANCIAL STATEMENTS

As noted at 2.3 above, a complete set of financial statements under IAS 1 comprises the following, each of which should be presented with equal prominence: *[IAS 1.10-11]*

(a) a statement of financial position as at the end of the period;

(b) a statement of profit or loss and other comprehensive income for the period to be presented either as:

  (i) one single statement of comprehensive income with a section for profit and loss followed immediately by a section for other comprehensive income; or

  (ii) a separate statement of profit or loss and statement of comprehensive income. In this case, the former must be presented immediately before the latter;

(c) a statement of changes in equity for the period;

(d) a statement of cash flows for the period;

(e) notes, comprising significant accounting policies and other explanatory information; and

(f) a statement of financial position as at the beginning of the preceding period in certain circumstances (see 2.4 above). *[IAS 1.10-10A].*

Chapter 3

The standard adopts a generally permissive stance, by setting out minimum levels of required items to be shown in each statement (sometimes specifically on the face of the statement, and sometimes either on the face or in the notes) whilst allowing great flexibility of order and layout. The standard notes that sometimes it uses the term 'disclosure' in a broad sense, encompassing items 'presented in the financial statements'. It observes that other IFRSs also require disclosures and that, unless specified to the contrary, they may be made 'in the financial statements'. *[IAS 1.48].* This begs the question: if not in 'the financial statements' then where else could they be made? We suspect this stems from, or is reflective of, an ambiguous use of similar words and phrases. In particular, 'financial statements' appears to be restricted to the 'primary' statements (statement of financial position, statement of profit or loss and other comprehensive income, statement of changes in equity and statement of cash flows) when describing what a 'complete set of financial statements' comprises (see 2.3 above). This is because a complete set also includes notes. For the purposes of specifying where a particular required disclosure should be made, we consider the term 'in the financial statements' is intended to mean *anywhere* within the 'complete set of financial statements' – in other words the primary statements or notes.

IAS 1 observes that cash flow information provides users of financial statements with a basis to assess the ability of the entity to generate cash and cash equivalents and the needs of the entity to utilise those cash flows. Requirements for the presentation of the statement of cash flows and related disclosures are set out IAS 7 – *Statement of Cash Flows. [IAS 1.111].* Statements of cash flows are discussed in Chapter 38; each of the other primary statements listed above is discussed in the following sections.

3.1 The statement of financial position

3.1.1 The distinction between current/non-current assets and liabilities

In most situations (but see the exception discussed below, and the treatment of non-current assets held for sale discussed in Chapter 4 at 2.2.4) IAS 1 requires statements of financial position to distinguish current assets and liabilities from non-current ones. *[IAS 1.60].* The standard uses the term 'non-current' to include tangible, intangible and financial assets of a long-term nature. It does not prohibit the use of alternative descriptions as long as the meaning is clear. *[IAS 1.67].*

The standard explains the requirement to present current and non-current items separately by observing that when an entity supplies goods or services within a clearly identifiable operating cycle, separate classification of current and non-current assets and liabilities on the face of the statement of financial position will provide useful information by distinguishing the net assets that are continuously circulating as working capital from those used in long-term operations. Furthermore, the analysis will also highlight assets that are expected to be realised within the current operating cycle, and liabilities that are due for settlement within the same period. *[IAS 1.62].* The distinction between current and non-current items therefore depends on the length of the entity's operating cycle. The standard states that the operating cycle of an entity is the time between the acquisition of assets for processing and their realisation in cash or cash equivalents. However, when the entity's normal operating cycle is not clearly identifiable, it is assumed to be twelve months. *[IAS 1.68, 70].* The standard does not provide any guidance on how to determine if an entity's operating cycle is 'clearly identifiable'. In some businesses the time involved in producing goods or providing services varies significantly from one customer project to another. In such cases, it may be difficult to determine what the normal operating cycle is. In the end, management must consider all facts and circumstances and judgment to determine whether it is appropriate to consider that the operating cycle is clearly identifiable, or whether the twelve months default is to be used.

Once assets have been classified as non-current they should not normally be reclassified as current assets until they meet the criteria to be classified as held for sale in accordance with IFRS 5 (see Chapter 4 at 2.1). However, an entity which routinely sells items of property plant and equipment previously held for rental should transfer such items to inventory when they cease to be rented and become held for sale. *[IAS 16.68A].* Assets of a class that an entity would normally regard as non-current that are acquired exclusively with a view to resale also should not be classified as current unless they meet these criteria in IFRS 5. *[IFRS 5.3].*

The basic requirement of the standard is that current and non-current assets, and current and non-current liabilities, should be presented as separate classifications on the face of the statement of financial position. *[IAS 1.60].* The standard defines current assets and current liabilities (discussed at 3.1.3 and 3.1.4 below), with the non-current category being the residual. *[IAS 1.66, 69].* Example 3.2 at 3.1.7 below provides an illustration of a statement of financial position presenting this classification.

An exception to this requirement is when a presentation based on liquidity provides information that is reliable and is more relevant. When that exception applies, all assets and liabilities are required to be presented broadly in order of liquidity. *[IAS 1.60]*. The reason for this exception given by the standard is that some entities (such as financial institutions) do not supply goods or services within a clearly identifiable operating cycle, and for these entities a presentation of assets and liabilities in increasing or decreasing order of liquidity provides information that is reliable and more relevant than a current/non-current presentation. *[IAS 1.63]*.

The standard also makes clear that an entity is permitted to present some of its assets and liabilities using a current/non-current classification and others in order of liquidity when this provides information that is reliable and more relevant. It goes on to observe that the need for a mixed basis of presentation might arise when an entity has diverse operations. *[IAS 1.64]*.

Whichever method of presentation is adopted, IAS 1 requires for each asset and liability line item that combines amounts expected to be recovered or settled:

(a) no more than twelve months after the reporting period; and

(b) more than twelve months after the reporting period;

disclosure of the amount expected to be recovered or settled after more than twelve months. *[IAS 1.61]*.

The standard explains this requirement by noting that information about expected dates of realisation of assets and liabilities is useful in assessing the liquidity and solvency of an entity. In this vein, IAS 1 contains a reminder that IFRS 7 – *Financial Instruments: Disclosures* – requires disclosure of the maturity dates of financial assets (including trade and other receivables) and financial liabilities (including trade and other payables). This assertion in IAS 1 is not strictly correct, as IFRS 7 in fact only requires a maturity *analysis* (rather than maturity dates) and only requires this for financial liabilities (see Chapter 54 at 5.2.4). Similarly, IAS 1 views information on the expected date of recovery and settlement of non-monetary assets and liabilities such as inventories and provisions as also useful, whether assets and liabilities are classified as current or as non-current. An example of this given by the standard is that an entity should disclose the amount of inventories that are expected to be recovered more than twelve months after the reporting period. *[IAS 1.65]*.

3.1.2 Non-current assets and disposal groups held for sale or distribution

The general requirement to classify items as current or non-current (or present them broadly in order of liquidity) is overlaid with further requirements by IFRS 5 regarding non-current assets and disposal groups held for sale or distribution (discussed in Chapter 4 at 3). The aim of IFRS 5 is that entities should present and disclose information that enables users of the financial statements to evaluate the financial effects of disposals of non-current assets (or disposal groups). *[IFRS 5.30]*. In pursuit of this aim, IFRS 5 requires:

- non-current assets and the assets of a disposal group classified as held for sale or distribution to be presented separately from other assets in the statement of financial position; and
- the liabilities of a disposal group classified as held for sale or distribution to be presented separately from other liabilities in the statement of financial position.

These assets and liabilities should not be offset and presented as a single amount. In addition:

(a) major classes of assets and liabilities classified as held for sale or distribution should generally be separately disclosed either on the face of the statement of financial position or in the notes (see 3.1.6 below). However, this is not necessary for a disposal group if it is a subsidiary that met the criteria to be classified as held for sale or distribution on acquisition; and

(b) any cumulative income or expense recognised in other comprehensive income relating to a non-current asset (or disposal group) classified as held for sale or distribution should be presented separately. *[IFRS 5.38-39].*

3.1.3 Current assets

IAS 1 requires an asset to be classified as current when it satisfies any of the following criteria, with all other assets classified as non-current. The criteria are:

(a) it is expected to be realised in, or is intended for sale or consumption in, the entity's normal operating cycle (discussed at 3.1.1 above);

(b) it is held primarily for the purpose of trading;

(c) it is expected to be realised within twelve months after the end of the reporting period; or

(d) it is cash or a cash equivalent (as defined in IAS 7, see Chapter 38 at 1.1) unless it is restricted from being exchanged or used to settle a liability for at least twelve months after the end of the reporting period. *[IAS 1.66].*

As an exception to this, deferred tax assets are never allowed to be classified as current. *[IAS 1.56].*

Current assets include assets (such as inventories and trade receivables) that are sold, consumed or realised as part of the normal operating cycle even when they are not expected to be realised within twelve months after the reporting period. Current assets also include assets held primarily for the purpose of being traded, for example, some financial assets that meet the definition of held for trading in IFRS 9 – *Financial Instruments* – and the current portion of non-current financial assets. *[IAS 1.68].*

3.1.4 Current liabilities

IAS 1 requires a liability to be classified as current when it satisfies any of the following criteria, with all other liabilities classified as non-current. The criteria for classifying a liability as current are:

(a) it is expected to be settled in the entity's normal operating cycle (discussed at 3.1.1 above);

(b) it is held primarily for the purpose of trading;

(c) it is due to be settled within twelve months after the end of the reporting period; or

(d) the entity does not have an unconditional right to defer settlement of the liability for at least twelve months after the end of the reporting period. Terms of a liability that could, at the option of the counterparty, result in its settlement by the issue of equity instruments do not affect its classification. *[IAS 1.69].*

As an exception to this, deferred tax liabilities are never allowed to be classified as current. *[IAS 1.56].*

In its November 2010 newsletter the Interpretations Committee reconfirmed (d) above by stating that a debt scheduled for repayment after more than a year which is, however, payable on demand of the lender is a current liability.

The standard notes that some current liabilities, such as trade payables and some accruals for employee and other operating costs, are part of the working capital used in the entity's normal operating cycle. Such operating items are classified as current liabilities even if they are due to be settled more than twelve months after the end of the reporting period. *[IAS 1.70]*.

However, neither IAS 19 – *Employee Benefits* – nor IAS 1 specifies where in the statement of financial position an asset or liability in respect of a defined benefit plan should be presented, nor whether such balances should be shown separately on the face of the statement or only in the notes – this is left to the judgement of the reporting entity (see 3.1.5 below). When the format of the statement of financial position distinguishes current assets and liabilities from non-current ones, the question arises as to whether this split needs also to be made for defined benefit plan balances. IAS 19 does not specify whether such a split should be made, on the grounds that it may sometimes be arbitrary. *[IAS 19.133, BC200]*. In practice few, if any, entities make this split.

Some current liabilities are not settled as part of the normal operating cycle, but are due for settlement within twelve months after the end of the reporting period or held primarily for the purpose of being traded. Examples given by the standard are some (but not necessarily all) financial liabilities that meet the definition of held for trading in accordance with IFRS 9, bank overdrafts, and the current portion of non-current financial liabilities, dividends payable, income taxes and other non-trade payables. Financial liabilities that provide financing on a long-term basis (i.e. are not part of the working capital used in the entity's normal operating cycle) and are not due for settlement within twelve months after the end of the reporting period are non-current liabilities. *[IAS 1.71]*.

The assessment of a liability as current or non-current is applied very strictly in IAS 1. In particular, a liability should be classified as current:

(a) when it is due to be settled within twelve months after the end of the reporting period, even if:
   (i) the original term was for a period longer than twelve months; and
   (ii) an agreement to refinance, or to reschedule payments, on a long-term basis is completed after the period end and before the financial statements are authorised for issue (although disclosure of the post period end refinancing would be required); *[IAS 1.72, 76]* or

(b) when an entity breaches a provision of a long-term loan arrangement on or before the period end with the effect that the liability becomes payable on demand. This is the case even if the lender agreed, after the period end and before the authorisation of the financial statements for issue, not to demand payment as a consequence of the breach (although the post period end agreement would be disclosed). The meaning of the term 'authorised for issue' is discussed in Chapter 36 at 2.1.1. The standard explains that the liability should be classified as current because, at the period end, the entity does not have an unconditional right to defer its settlement for at least twelve months after that date. *[IAS 1.74, 76].* However, the liability would be classified as non-current if the lender agreed by the period end to provide a period of grace ending at least twelve months after the reporting period, within which the entity can rectify the breach and during which the lender cannot demand immediate repayment. *[IAS 1.75].*

The key point here is that for a liability to be classified as non-current requires that the entity has *at the end of the reporting period* an unconditional right to defer its settlement for at least twelve months thereafter. Accordingly, the standard explains that liabilities would be non-current if an entity expects, and has the discretion, to refinance or roll over an obligation for at least twelve months after the period end under an existing loan facility, even if it would otherwise be due within a shorter period. However, when refinancing or rolling over the obligation is not at the discretion of the entity the obligation is classified as current. *[IAS 1.73].*

Some common scenarios are illustrated in the following example.

Example 3.1: Determining whether liabilities should be presented as current or non-current

Scenario 1

An entity has a long-term loan arrangement containing a debt covenant. The specific requirements in the debt covenant have to be met as at 31 December every year. The loan is due in more than 12 months. The entity breaches the debt covenant at or before the period end. As a result, the loan becomes payable on demand.

Scenario 2

Same as scenario 1, but the loan arrangement stipulates that the entity has a grace period of 3 months to rectify the breach and during which the lender cannot demand immediate repayment.

Scenario 3

Same as scenario 1, but the lender agreed not to demand repayment as a consequence of the breach. The entity obtains this waiver:

(a) at or before the period end and the waiver is for a period of more than 12 months after the period end;

(b) at or before the period end and the waiver is for a period of less than 12 months after the period end;

(c) after the period end but before the financial statements are authorised for issue.

Scenario 4

An entity has a long-term loan arrangement containing a debt covenant. The loan is due in more than 12 months. At the period end, the debt covenants are met. However, circumstances change unexpectedly and the entity breaches the debt covenant after the period end but before the financial statements are authorised for issue.

As discussed in Chapter 54 at 4.4.9, IFRS 7 requires the following disclosures for any loans payable recognised at the reporting date:

- details of any defaults during the period of principal, interest, sinking fund, or redemption terms;
- the carrying amount of the loans payable in default at the reporting date; and
- whether the default was remedied, or the terms of the loans payable were renegotiated, before the financial statements were authorised for issue.

If, during the period, there were breaches of loan agreement terms other than those described above, the same information should be disclosed if those breaches permitted the lender to demand accelerated repayment (unless the breaches were remedied, or the terms of the loan were renegotiated, on or before the reporting date).

As noted at 5.5 below, IAS 1 requires certain disclosures of refinancing and rectification of loan agreement breaches which happen after the end of the reporting period and before the accounts are authorised for issue.

The table below sets out whether debt is to be presented as current or non-current and whether the above disclosures are required.

	Scenario 1	Scenario 2	Scenario 3(a)	Scenario 3(b)	Scenario 3(c)	Scenario 4
At the period end, does the entity have an unconditional right to defer the settlement of the liability for at least 12 months?	no	no	yes	no	no	yes
Classification of the liability	current	current	non-current	current	current	non-current
Are the above IFRS 7 disclosures required?	yes	yes	no	yes	yes	no
Are the disclosures in IAS 1 required?	no	no	no	no	yes	no

3.1.5 Information required on the face of the statement of financial position

IAS 1 does not contain a prescriptive format or order for the statement of financial position. *[IAS 1.57].* Rather, it contains two mechanisms which require certain information to be shown on the face of the statement. First, it contains a list of specific items for which this is required, on the basis that they are sufficiently different in nature or function to warrant separate presentation. *[IAS 1.54, 57].* Second, it stipulates that: additional line items (including the disaggregation of those items specifically required), headings and subtotals should be presented on the face of the statement of financial position when such presentation is relevant to an understanding of the entity's financial position. *[IAS 1.55].* Clearly this is a highly judgemental decision for entities to make when preparing a statement of financial position, and allows a wide variety of possible presentations. The judgement as to whether additional items should be presented separately is based on an assessment of:

(a) the nature and liquidity of assets;

(b) the function of assets within the entity; and

(c) the amounts, nature and timing of liabilities. *[IAS 1.58].*

IAS 1 indicates that the use of different measurement bases for different classes of assets suggests that their nature or function differs and, therefore, that they should be presented as separate line items. For example, different classes of property, plant and equipment can be carried at cost or revalued amounts in accordance with IAS 16 – *Property, Plant and Equipment. [IAS 1.59].*

The face of the statement of financial position should include line items that present the following amounts: *[IAS 1.54]*

(a) property, plant and equipment;
(b) investment property;
(c) intangible assets;
(d) financial assets (excluding amounts shown under (e), (h) and (i));
(e) investments accounted for using the equity method;
(f) biological assets;
(g) inventories;
(h) trade and other receivables;
(i) cash and cash equivalents;
(j) the total of assets classified as held for sale and assets included in disposal groups classified as held for sale in accordance with IFRS 5;
(k) trade and other payables;
(l) provisions;
(m) financial liabilities (excluding amounts shown under (k) and (l));
(n) liabilities and assets for current tax, as defined in IAS 12;
(o) deferred tax liabilities and deferred tax assets, as defined in IAS 12;
(p) liabilities included in disposal groups classified as held for sale in accordance with IFRS 5;
(q) non-controlling interests, presented within equity; and
(r) issued capital and reserves attributable to owners of the parent.

The standard notes that items above represent a list of items that are sufficiently different in nature or function to warrant separate presentation on the face of the statement of financial position. In addition:

(a) line items should be included when the size, nature or function of an item or aggregation of similar items is such that separate presentation is relevant to an understanding of the entity's financial position; and
(b) the descriptions used and the ordering of items or aggregation of similar items may be amended according to the nature of the entity and its transactions, to provide information that is relevant to an understanding of the entity's financial position. For example, a financial institution may amend the above descriptions to provide information that is relevant to the operations of a financial institution. *[IAS 1.57]*.

As noted above, when relevant to an understanding of financial position, additional line items and subtotals should be presented. Regarding subtotals, IAS 1 requires that they should:

(a) be comprised of line items made up of amounts recognised and measured in accordance with IFRS;
(b) be presented and labelled in a manner that makes the line items that constitute the subtotal clear and understandable;
(c) be consistent from period to period (see 4.1.4 below); and
(d) not be displayed with more prominence than the subtotals and totals required in IFRS for the statement of financial position. *[IAS 1.55A, BC38.G].*

The distinction between trade and financial liabilities in certain supplier finance arrangements is discussed in Chapter 51 at 6.5.

3.1.6 Information required either on the face of the statement of financial position or in the notes

IAS 1 requires further sub-classifications of the line items shown on the face of the statement of financial position to be presented either on the face of the statement or in the notes. The requirements for these further sub-classifications are approached by the standard in a similar manner to those for line items on the face of the statement of financial position. There is a prescriptive list of items required (see below) and also a more general requirement that the sub-classifications should be made in a manner appropriate to the entity's operations. *[IAS 1.77].* The standard notes that the detail provided in sub-classifications depends on the requirements of IFRSs (as numerous disclosures are required by other standards) and on the size, nature and function of the amounts involved. *[IAS 1.78].*

Aside of the specific requirements, deciding what level of detailed disclosure is necessary is clearly a judgemental exercise. As is the case for items on the face of the statement of financial position, IAS 1 requires that the judgement as to whether additional items should be presented separately should be based on an assessment of:

(a) the nature and liquidity of assets;
(b) the function of assets within the entity; and
(c) the amounts, nature and timing of liabilities. *[IAS 1.58, 78].*

The disclosures will also vary for each item, examples given by the standard are:

(a) items of property, plant and equipment are disaggregated into classes in accordance with IAS 16;
(b) receivables are disaggregated into amounts receivable from trade customers, receivables from related parties, prepayments and other amounts;
(c) inventories are disaggregated, in accordance with IAS 2 – *Inventories*, into classifications such as merchandise, production supplies, materials, work in progress and finished goods;
(d) provisions are disaggregated into provisions for employee benefits and other items; and
(e) equity capital and reserves are disaggregated into various classes, such as paid-in capital, share premium and reserves. *[IAS 1.78].*

IAS 1 specifically requires the following information regarding equity and share capital to be shown either on the face of the statement of financial position or in the notes:

(a) for each class of share capital:
   - (i) the number of shares authorised;
   - (ii) the number of shares issued and fully paid, and issued but not fully paid;
   - (iii) par value per share, or that the shares have no par value;
   - (iv) a reconciliation of the number of shares outstanding at the beginning and at the end of the period;
   - (v) the rights, preferences and restrictions attaching to that class including restrictions on the distribution of dividends and the repayment of capital;
   - (vi) shares in the entity held by the entity or by its subsidiaries or associates; and
   - (vii) shares reserved for issue under options and contracts for the sale of shares, including the terms and amounts; and

(b) a description of the nature and purpose of each reserve within equity. *[IAS 1.79].*

An entity without share capital (such as a partnership or trust) should disclose information equivalent to that required by (a) above, showing changes during the period in each category of equity interest, and the rights, preferences and restrictions attaching to each category of equity interest. *[IAS 1.80].*

IAS 32 – *Financial Instruments: Presentation* – allows two specific classes of liabilities to be reported as equity. These are:

- puttable financial instruments; and
- instruments that impose on the entity an obligation to deliver to another party a *pro rata* share of the net assets of the entity only on liquidation.

Both terms are defined and discussed at length in IAS 32 (see Chapter 45 at 4.6).

If an entity reclassifies one of these items between financial liabilities and equity, IAS 1 requires disclosure of:

- the amount reclassified into and out of each category (financial liabilities or equity); and
- the timing and reason for that reclassification. *[IAS 1.80A].*

3.1.7 Illustrative statements of financial position

The implementation guidance accompanying IAS 1 provides an illustration of a statement of financial position presented to distinguish current and non-current items. It makes clear that other formats may be equally appropriate, as long as the distinction is clear. *[IAS 1.IG3].* As discussed in Chapter 4 at 2.2.4, IFRS 5 provides further guidance relating to the presentation of non-current assets and disposal groups held for sale. *[IAS 1.IG Part I].*

Example 3.2: Illustrative statement of financial position

XYZ GROUP – STATEMENT OF FINANCIAL POSITION AS AT 31 DECEMBER 2018

(in thousands of Euros)

	2018	2017
ASSETS		
Non-current assets		
Property, plant and equipment	350,700	360,020
Goodwill	80,800	91,200
Other intangible assets	227,470	227,470
Investments in associates	100,150	110,770
Investments in equity instruments	142,500	156,000
	901,620	945,460
Current assets		
Inventories	135,230	132,500
Trade receivables	91,600	110,800
Other current assets	25,650	12,540
Cash and cash equivalents	312,400	322,900
	564,880	578,740
Total assets	1,466,500	1,524,200

	2018	2017
EQUITY AND LIABILITIES		
Equity attributable to owners of the parent		
Share capital	650,000	600,000
Retained earnings	243,500	161,700
Other components of equity	10,200	21,200
	903,700	782,900
Non-controlling interests	70,050	48,600
Total equity	973,750	831,500
Non-current liabilities		
Long-term borrowings	120,000	160,000
Deferred tax	28,800	26,040
Long-term provisions	28,850	52,240
Total non-current liabilities	177,650	238,280
Current liabilities		
Trade and other payables	115,100	187,620
Short-term borrowings	150,000	200,000
Current portion of long-term borrowings	10,000	20,000
Current tax payable	35,000	42,000
Short-term provisions	5,000	4,800
Total current liabilities	315,100	454,420
Total liabilities	492,750	692,700
Total equity and liabilities	1,466,500	1,524,200

3.2 The statement of comprehensive income and the statement of profit or loss

3.2.1 Profit and loss and comprehensive income

The IASB regards all changes in net assets (other than the introduction and return of capital) and not just more traditional realised profits, as 'performance' in its widest sense. Accordingly, IAS 1 requires a performance statement showing such changes and calls it a statement of comprehensive income.

Total comprehensive income is defined by IAS 1 as the change in equity during a period resulting from transactions and other events, other than those changes resulting from transactions with owners in their capacity as owners. It comprises all components of 'profit or loss' and of 'other comprehensive income'. These two terms are defined as follows:

- profit or loss is the total of income less expenses, excluding the components of other comprehensive income; and
- other comprehensive income comprises items of income and expense (including reclassification adjustments) that are not recognised in profit or loss as required or permitted by other IFRSs. *[IAS 1.7]*.

The use of a variety of terminology is recognised by IAS 1 which notes the following. 'Although this Standard uses the terms "other comprehensive income", "profit or loss" and "total comprehensive income", an entity may use other terms to describe the totals as long as the meaning is clear. For example, an entity may use the term "net income" to describe profit or loss.' *[IAS 1.8]*.

What this means is that profit and loss is the default category – all comprehensive income is part of profit and loss unless a provision of IFRS say it is or may be 'other' comprehensive income. *[IAS 1.88]*.

IAS 1 sets out the following items which are included in other comprehensive income:

(a) changes in revaluation surplus relating to property, plant and equipment and intangible assets;

(b) remeasurements on defined benefit plans in accordance with IAS 19;

(c) gains and losses arising from translating the financial statements of a foreign operation;

(d) gains and losses from investments in equity instruments designated at fair value through other comprehensive income;

(e) gains and losses on financial assets measured at fair value through other comprehensive income;

(f) the effective portion of gains and losses on hedging instruments in a cash flow hedge and the gains and losses on hedging instruments that hedge investments in equity instruments measured at fair value through other comprehensive income;

(g) for particular liabilities designated as at fair value through profit and loss, the amount of the fair value changes attributable to changes in the liability's credit risk;

(h) changes in the value of the time value of options when separating the intrinsic value and time value of an option contract and designating as the hedging instrument only the changes in the intrinsic value; and

(i) changes in the value of the forward elements of forward contracts when separating the forward element and spot element of a forward contract and designating as the hedging instrument only the changes in the spot element, and changes in the value of the foreign currency basis spread of a financial instrument when excluding it from the designation of that financial instrument as the hedging instrument. *[IAS 1.7]*.

IAS requires that all items of income and expense be presented either:

(a) in a single statement of profit or loss and other comprehensive income (with a separate section for each in the order stated); or

(b) in two separate statements:

   (i) a statement of profit or loss; and

   (ii) a statement of comprehensive income beginning with profit and loss and containing components of other comprehensive income. *[IAS 1.10A]*.

If the approach in (b) is followed, the statement of profit or loss must be displayed immediately before the statement of comprehensive income. *[IAS 1.10A]*.

In addition to this choice, IAS 1 provides that different titles may be used for these statements. *[IAS 1.10]*.

Many entities continue to present a separate statement of profit or loss (often titled 'income statement'), and this section is structured in these terms. However, the requirements are the same whether total comprehensive income is presented in one or two statements.

IAS 1 adopts an essentially permissive approach to the format of the statement of profit or loss and statement of comprehensive income. It observes that, because the effects of an entity's various activities, transactions and other events differ in frequency, potential for gain or loss and predictability, disclosing the components of financial performance assists users in understanding the financial performance achieved and in making projections of future performance. *[IAS 1.86]*. In other words, some analysis of the make-up of net profit and other comprehensive income is needed, but a wide variety of presentations would all be acceptable.

Whether one or two statements are presented, IAS 1 requires certain specific items to appear on the face of the statement(s) and then supplements this with a more general requirement that:

- additional line items be presented (including the disaggregation of those specifically required) on the face of the statement(s); and
- the descriptions used and the ordering of items be amended;

when this is relevant to an understanding of the entity's financial performance. *[IAS 1.85-86]*. The standard explains that additional line items should be included, and the descriptions used and the ordering of items amended when this is necessary to explain the elements of financial performance. Factors to be considered would include materiality and the nature and function of the items of income and expense. An example of this is that a financial institution may amend the descriptions to provide information that is relevant to the operations of a financial institution. *[IAS 1.86]*.

When additional subtotals are presented, line items should be given that reconcile those subtotals with the subtotals or totals required in IFRS. *[IAS 1.85B]*.

When such additional subtotals are presented, they should:

(a) be comprised of line items made up of amounts recognised and measured in accordance with IFRS;

(b) be presented and labelled in a manner that makes the line items that constitute the subtotal clear and understandable;

(c) be consistent from period to period (see 4.1.4 below); and

(d) not be displayed with more prominence than the subtotals and totals required in IFRS for the statement(s) presenting profit or loss and other comprehensive income. *[IAS 1.85A]*.

3.2.2 Information required on the face of the statement of profit or loss

As is the case for the statement of financial position, IAS 1 sets out certain items which must appear on the face of the statement of profit or loss and other required disclosures which may be made either on the face or in the notes.

The face of the statement of profit or loss should include, in addition to items required by other IFRSs, line items that present the following amounts (although as noted above, the order and description of the items should be amended as necessary):

(a) revenue, presenting separately interest revenue calculated using the effective interest method;

(b) gains and losses from the derecognition of financial assets measured at amortised cost;

(c) finance costs;

(d) impairment losses (including reversals of impairment losses or impairment gains) determined under IFRS 9;

(e) share of the profit or loss of associates and joint ventures accounted for using the equity method;

(f) any difference between fair value and the previous carrying amount at the date of reclassification when a financial asset is reclassified out of the amortised cost category to be measured at fair value through profit or loss;

(g) any accumulated gain or loss previously recognised in other comprehensive income that is reclassified to profit or loss when a financial asset is reclassified out of the fair value through other comprehensive income category so that it is measured at fair value through profit or loss;

(h) tax expense;

(i) a single amount comprising the total of:

  (i) the post-tax profit or loss of discontinued operations; and

  (ii) the post-tax gain or loss recognised on the measurement to fair value less costs to sell or on the disposal of the assets or disposal group(s) constituting the discontinued operation; *[IFRS 5.33(a)(ii)]*

(j) profit or loss; *[IAS 1.81A]* and

(k) the following as allocations of profit or loss for the period:

  (i) profit or loss attributable to non-controlling interests; and

  (ii) profit or loss attributable to owners of the parent. *[IAS 1.81B]*.

As discussed at 3.2.3 below, an analysis of expenses is required based either on their nature or their function. IAS 1 encourages, but does not require this to be shown on the face of the statement of profit or loss. *[IAS 1.99-100]*.

The implementation guidance accompanying the standard provides an illustrative example of a statement of profit or loss (see Example 3.4 at 3.2.3.A below).

3.2.2.A Operating profit

The current IAS 1 has omitted the requirement in the 1997 version to disclose the results of operating activities as a line item on the face of the statement of profit or loss. The reason given for this in the Basis for Conclusions to the standard is that 'Operating activities' are not defined in the standard, and the Board decided not to require disclosure of an undefined item. *[IAS 1.BC55]*.

The Basis for Conclusions to IAS 1 goes on to state that

'The Board recognises that an entity may elect to disclose the results of operating activities, or a similar line item, even though this term is not defined. In such cases, the Board notes that the entity should ensure the amount disclosed is representative of activities that would normally be considered to be "operating".

'In the Board's view, it would be misleading and would impair the comparability of financial statements if items of an operating nature were excluded from the results of operating activities, even if that had been industry practice. For example, it would be inappropriate to exclude items clearly related to operations (such as inventory write-downs and restructuring and relocation expenses) because they occur irregularly or infrequently or are unusual in amount. Similarly, it would be inappropriate to exclude items on the grounds that they do not involve cash flows, such as depreciation and amortisation expenses.' *[IAS 1.BC56]*.

As noted at 3.2.2 above, IAS 1 requires the face of the statement of profit or loss to show the share of the profit or loss of associates and joint ventures accounted for using the equity method.

For entities presenting a measure of operating profit, in our view it is acceptable for an entity to determine which such investments form part of its operating activities and include their results in that measure, with the results of non-operating investments excluded from it.

Another acceptable alternative would be to exclude the results of all associates and joint ventures from operating profit.

3.2.3 Classification of expenses recognised in profit or loss by nature or function

IAS 1 states that components of financial performance may differ in terms of frequency, potential for gain or loss and predictability, and requires that expenses should be sub-classified to highlight this. *[IAS 1.101]*. To achieve this, the standard requires the presentation of an analysis of expenses (but only those recognised in profit or loss) using a classification based on either their nature or their function within the entity, whichever provides information that is reliable and more relevant. *[IAS 1.99]*. It is because each method of presentation has merit for different types of entities, that the standard requires management to make this selection. *[IAS 1.105]*. As noted at 3.2.2 above IAS 1 encourages, but does not require the chosen analysis to be shown on the face of the statement of profit or loss. *[IAS 1.100]*. This means that entities are permitted to disclose the classification on the face on a mixed basis, as long as the required classification is provided in the notes. Indeed, the IASB itself produces an example of such a statement of profit or loss in an illustrative example to IAS 7. *[IAS 7.IE A]*.

The standard also notes that the choice between the function of expense method and the nature of expense method will depend on historical and industry factors and the nature of the entity. Both methods provide an indication of those costs that might vary, directly or indirectly, with the level of sales or production of the entity. However, because information on the nature of expenses is useful in predicting future cash flows, additional disclosure is required when the function of expense classification is used (see 3.2.3.B below). *[IAS 1.105]*.

3.2.3.A Analysis of expenses by nature

For some entities, 'reliable and more relevant information' may be achieved by aggregating expenses for display in profit or loss according to their nature (for example, depreciation, purchases of materials, transport costs, employee benefits and advertising costs), and not reallocating them among various functions within the entity. IAS 1 observes that this method may be simple to apply because no allocations of expenses to functional classifications are necessary. The standard illustrates a classification using the nature of expense method as follows: *[IAS 1.102]*

Example 3.3: Example of classification of expenses by nature

Revenue		×
Other income		×
Changes in inventories of finished goods and work in progress	×	
Raw materials and consumables used	×	
Employee benefits expense	×	
Depreciation and amortisation expense	×	
Other expenses	×	
Total expenses		(×)
Profit before tax		×

The implementation guidance accompanying the standard provides a further example of a statement of profit or loss analysing expenses by nature. Whilst very similar to the above, it is expanded to show further captions as follows: *[IAS 1.IG Part I]*

Example 3.4: Illustrative statement of profit or loss with expenses classified by nature

XYZ GROUP – STATEMENT OF PROFIT OR LOSS FOR THE YEAR ENDED 31 DECEMBER 2018

(in thousands of Euros)

	2018	2017
Revenue	390,000	355,000
Other income	20,667	11,300
Changes in inventories of finished goods and work in progress	(115,100)	(107,900)
Work performed by the entity and capitalised	16,000	15,000
Raw material and consumables used	(96,000)	(92,000)
Employee benefits expense	(45,000)	(43,000)
Depreciation and amortisation expense	(19,000)	(17,000)
Impairment of property, plant and equipment	(4,000)	–
Other expenses	(6,000)	(5,500)
Finance costs	(15,000)	(18,000)
Share of profit of associates	35,100	30,100
Profit before tax	161,667	128,000
Income tax expense	(40,417)	(32,000)
Profit for the year from continuing operations	121,250	96,000
Loss for the year from discontinued operations	–	(30,500)
Profit for the year	121,250	65,500
Profit attributable to:		
Owners of the parent	97,000	52,400
Non-controlling interests	24,250	13,100
	121,250	65,500
Earnings per share (€)		
Basic and diluted	0.46	0.30

A footnote to the illustrative examples explains that 'share of profits of associates' means share of the profit attributable to the owners of the associates and hence is after tax and non-controlling interests.

Example 3.4 above is an example of presenting comprehensive income in two statements. Example 3.6 below illustrates the presentation of comprehensive income in a single statement. An entity using the approach above would need to give a second statement presenting items of other comprehensive income – this would simply be the bottom portion of Example 3.6, starting with 'Profit for the year' and omitting earnings per share and the analysis of profit between owners and non-controlling interests. This is illustrated in Example 3.8 below.

Chapter 3

3.2.3.B Analysis of expenses by function

For some entities, 'reliable and more relevant information' may be achieved by aggregating expenses for display purposes according to their function for example, as part of cost of sales, the costs of distribution or administrative activities. Under this method, IAS 1 requires as a minimum, disclosure of cost of sales separately from other expenses. The standard observes that this method can provide more relevant information to users than the classification of expenses by nature, but that allocating costs to functions may require arbitrary allocations and involve considerable judgement. An example of classification using the function of expense method given by the standard set out below. *[IAS 1.103]*.

Example 3.5: Example of classification of expenses by function

Revenue	×
Cost of sales	(×)
Gross profit	×
Other income	×
Distribution costs	(×)
Administrative expenses	(×)
Other expenses	(×)
Profit before tax	×

Entities classifying expenses by function are required by IAS 1 to disclose additional information on the nature of expenses. The standard highlights that this requirement also applies to depreciation and amortisation expense and employee benefits expense. *[IAS 1.104]*, which seems a redundant considering that the disclosure of these items (broken down into their components) is specifically required by IAS 16, IAS 19 and IAS 38 – *Intangible Assets*.

The standard gives another illustration of expenses classified by function in the profit and loss section of the single statement of comprehensive income – see Example 3.6 below.

3.2.4 The statement of comprehensive income

3.2.4.A The face of the statement of comprehensive income

Whether presented as a separate statement or as a section of a combined statement (see 3.2.1 above), the face of the statement of comprehensive income should set out the items below. The items in (b) and, separately, the items in (c) should be presented in two groups, one including items which may subsequently be reclassified into profit or loss and another including items which will not: *[IAS 1.81A-82A]*

(a) profit or loss (if two statements are presented this will be a single line item);

(b) each item of comprehensive income, classified by nature, which include:

  (i) changes in revaluation surplus relating to property, plant and equipment and intangible assets;

  (ii) remeasurements on defined benefit plans in accordance with IAS 19;

  (iii) gains and losses arising from translating the financial statements of a foreign operation;

(iv) gains and losses from investments in equity instruments designated at fair value through other comprehensive income;

(v) gains and losses on financial assets measured at fair value through other comprehensive income;

(vi) the effective portion of gains and losses on hedging instruments in a cash flow hedge and the gains and losses on hedging instruments that hedge investments in equity instruments measured at fair value through other comprehensive income;

(vii) for particular liabilities designated as at fair value through profit and loss, fair value changes attributable to changes in the liability's credit risk; *[IAS 1.7]*

(viii) changes in the value of the time value of options when separating the intrinsic value and time value of an option contract and designating as the hedging instrument only the changes in the intrinsic value;

(ix) changes in the value of the forward elements of forward contracts when separating the forward element and spot element of a forward contract and designating as the hedging instrument only the changes in the spot element, and changes in the value of the foreign currency basis spread of a financial instrument when excluding it from the designation of that financial instrument as the hedging instrument;

(x) the aggregate amount of tax relating to components of comprehensive income, unless the components are shown individually net of tax (see 3.2.4.C below). Tax should be allocated between the two groups mentioned above. *[IAS 1.91]*.

(c) share of the items of other comprehensive income of associates and joint ventures accounted for using the equity method;

(d) reclassification adjustments, unless the components of comprehensive income are shown after any related reclassification adjustments (see B below); *[IAS 1.94]* and

(e) total comprehensive income.

In a separate statement of other comprehensive income IAS 1 also requires an analysis of total comprehensive income for the period between that attributable to:

(a) non-controlling interests, and

(b) owners of the parent. *[IAS 1.81B]*.

In a combined statement of total comprehensive income, the equivalent analysis of profit and loss would also be required as would earnings per share disclosures (discussed in Chapter 35 at 7). When two separate statements are presented, these would appear on the statement of profit or loss. *[IAS 33.67A]*.

IAS 1 provides an illustration of both the 'one statement' and 'two statement' approach in its implementation guidance. An illustration of a single statement of comprehensive income is given in Example 3.6 below. *[IAS 1 IG Part I]*. An illustration of a separate statement of profit or loss is given in Example 3.4 above and an illustrative separate statement of other comprehensive income is given in Example 3.8 below.

Example 3.6: Presentation of comprehensive income in one statement and the classification of expenses by function

XYZ Group – Statement of profit or loss and other comprehensive income for the year ended 31 December 2018

(in thousands of currency units)	2018	2017
Revenue	390,000	355,000
Cost of sales	(245,000)	(230,000)
Gross profit	145,000	125,000
Other income	20,667	11,300
Distribution costs	(9,000)	(8,700)
Administrative expenses	(20,000)	(21,000)
Other expenses	(2,100)	(1,200)
Finance costs	(8,000)	(7,500)
Share of profit of associates[(1)]	35,100	30,100
Profit before tax	161,667	128,000
Income tax expense	(40,417)	(32,000)
Profit for the year from continuing operations	121,250	96,000
Loss for the year from discontinued operations	–	(30,500)
PROFIT FOR THE YEAR	121,250	65,500
Other comprehensive income:		
Items that will not be reclassified to profit or loss:		
Gains on property revaluation	933	3,367
Investments in equity instruments	(24,000)	26,667
Remeasurements of defined benefit pension plans	(667)	1,333
Share of other comprehensive income of associates[(2)]	400	(700)
Income tax relating to items that will not be reclassified[(3)]	5,834	(7,667)
	(17,500)	23,000
Items that may be reclassified subsequently to profit or loss:		
Exchange differences on translating foreign operations[(4)]	5,334	10,667
Cash flow hedges[(4)]	(667)	(4,000)
Income tax relating to items that may be reclassified[(3)]	(1,167)	(1,667)
	3,500	5,000
Other comprehensive income for the year, net of tax	(14,000)	28,000
TOTAL COMPREHENSIVE INCOME FOR THE YEAR	107,250	93,500
Profit attributable to:		
Owners of the parent	97,000	52,400
Non-controlling interests	24,250	13,100
	121,250	65,500
Total comprehensive income attributable to:		
Owners of the parent	85,800	74,800
Non-controlling interests	21,450	18,700
	107,250	93,500
Earnings per share (in currency units):		
Basic and diluted	0.46	0.30

Alternatively, items of other comprehensive income could be presented in the statement of profit or loss and other comprehensive income net of tax.

Other comprehensive income for the year, after tax:	2018	2017
Items that will not be reclassified to profit or loss:		
Gains on property revaluation	600	2,700
Investments in equity instruments	(18,000)	20,000
Remeasurements of defined benefit pension plans	(500)	1,000
Share of other comprehensive income of associates	400	(700)
	(17,500)	23,000
Items that may be reclassified subsequently to profit or loss:		
Exchange differences on translating foreign operations	4,000	8,000
Cash flow hedges	(500)	(3,000)
	3,500	5,000
Other comprehensive income for the year, net of tax[(3)]	(14,000)	28,000

(1) This means the share of associates' profit attributable to owners of the associates, i.e. it is after tax and non-controlling interests in the associates.

(2) This means the share of associates' other comprehensive income attributable to owners of the associates, i.e. it is after tax and non-controlling interests in the associates. In this example, the other comprehensive income of associates consists only of items that will not be subsequently reclassified to profit or loss. Entities whose associates' other comprehensive income includes items that may be subsequently reclassified to profit or loss are required to present that amount in a separate line.

(3) The income tax relating to each item of other comprehensive income is disclosed in the notes.

(4) This illustrates the aggregated presentation, with disclosure of the current year gain or loss and reclassification adjustment presented in the notes. Alternatively, a gross presentation can be used.

The illustrative examples in the standard all use the option, which is discussed at 3.2.4.B below, to present components of other comprehensive income net of related reclassification adjustments. The disclosure of those reclassification adjustments in a note is reproduced in Example 3.7 below. This note also demonstrates a reclassification adjustment not to profit and loss but to the statement of financial position. Whilst not addressed explicitly by the standard, evidently these items (like reclassifications to profit or loss) need not be shown on the face of the statement.

3.2.4.B Reclassification adjustments

'Reclassification adjustments' are items recognised in profit or loss which were previously recognised in other comprehensive income (commonly referred to as 'recycling') and IAS 1 requires their disclosure. *[IAS 1.7, 92-93, 95].* Examples include adjustments arising in relation to the disposal of a foreign operation and hedged forecast transactions affecting profit or loss.

The standard allows a choice of how reclassification adjustments are presented. They may either be presented 'gross' on the face of the statement, or alternatively shown in the notes. In the latter case, components of comprehensive income on the face of the statement are shown net of any related reclassification adjustments. *[IAS 1.94].*

IAS 1 illustrates this requirement as follows: *[IAS 1 IG Part I]*

Example 3.7: Note disclosure of components of other comprehensive income

XYZ Group

Disclosure of components of other comprehensive income [(1)]
Notes – Year ended 31 December 2018
(in thousands of currency units)

		2018		2017
Other comprehensive income				
Exchange differences on translating foreign operations[(2)]		5,334		10,667
Investments in equity instruments		(24,000)		26,667
Cash flow hedges:				
Gains (losses) arising during the year	(4,667)		(4,000)	
Less: reclassification adjustments for gains (losses) included in profit or loss	4,000		–	
		(667)		(4,000)
Gains on property revaluation		933		3,367
Remeasurements of defined benefit pension plans		(667)		1,333
Share of other comprehensive income of associates		400		(700)
Other comprehensive income		(18,667)		37,334
Income tax relating to components of other comprehensive income[(3)]		4,667		(9,334)
Other comprehensive income for the year		**(14,000)**		**28,000**

(1) When an entity chooses an aggregated presentation in the statement of comprehensive income, the amounts for reclassification adjustments and current year gain or loss are presented in the notes.

(2) There was no disposal of a foreign operation. Therefore, there is no reclassification adjustment for the years presented.

(3) The income tax relating to each component of other comprehensive income is disclosed in the notes.

Some IFRSs require that gains and losses recognised in other comprehensive income should not be 'recycled' to profit and loss, and hence will not give rise to reclassification adjustments. IAS 1 gives the following examples:

(a) revaluation surpluses for revalued property, plant and equipment, and intangible assets; and

(b) remeasurements on defined benefit plans.

The standard observes that whilst items in (a) are not reclassified to profit or loss they may be transferred to retained earnings as the assets concerned are used or derecognised. *[IAS 1.96]*. This is illustrated in Example 3.9 below.

3.2.4.C Tax on items of other comprehensive income

IAS 1 requires disclosure of the amount of income tax relating to each item of other comprehensive income, including reclassification adjustments, either on the face of the statement or in the notes. *[IAS 1.90]*. This may be done by presenting the items of other comprehensive income either:

(a) net of related tax effects; or

(b) before related tax effects with one amount shown for the aggregate amount of income tax relating to those items.

If the alternative at (b) is selected, the tax should be allocated between the items that might be reclassified subsequently to profit and loss and those that will not. *[IAS 1.91]*.

The reference to reclassification adjustments here and in the definition of other comprehensive income (see 3.2.1 above) seems to suggest that such adjustments are themselves 'components' of other comprehensive income. That would mean that the standard requires disclosure of tax related to reclassification adjustments. The implementation guidance, however, suggests this is not required because the note illustrating the presentation in (b) above allocates tax only to items of comprehensive income themselves net of related reclassification adjustments.

IAS 1 provides an illustration of both approaches in its implementation guidance.

The statement of comprehensive income and related note analysing tax are illustrated in Example 3.8 below (the related separate statement of profit or loss is shown in Example 3.4 above). *[IAS 1 IG Part I]*.

Example 3.8: Statement of comprehensive income illustrating the presentation of comprehensive income in two statements with note disclosure of the tax effects relating to components of other comprehensive income

XYZ Group – Statement of profit or loss and other comprehensive income for the year ended 31 December 2018

(in thousands of currency units)

	2018	2017
Profit for the year	121,250	65,500
Other comprehensive income:		
Items that will not be reclassified to profit or loss:		
Gains on property revaluation	933	3,367
Remeasurements of defined benefit pension plans	(667)	1,333
Share of other comprehensive income of associates[1]	400	(700)
Income tax relating to items that will not be reclassified[2]	(166)	(1,000)
	500	3,000
Items that may be reclassified subsequently to profit or loss:		
Exchange differences on translating foreign operations	5,334	10,667
Investments in equity instruments	(24,000)	26,667
Cash flow hedges	(667)	(4,000)
Income tax relating to items that may be reclassified[2]	4,833	(8,334)
	(14,500)	25,000
Other comprehensive income for the year, net of tax	(14,000)	28,000
TOTAL COMPREHENSIVE INCOME FOR THE YEAR	107,250	93,500
Total comprehensive income attributable to:		
Owners of the parent	85,800	74,800
Non-controlling interests	21,450	18,700
	107,250	93,500

Disclosure of tax effects relating to each component of other comprehensive income

Notes	2018 Before-tax amount	2018 Tax (expense) benefit	2018 Net-of-tax amount	2017 Before-tax amount	2017 Tax (expense) benefit	2017 Net-of-tax amount
Exchange differences on translating foreign operations	5,334	(1,334)	4,000	10,667	(2,667)	8,000
Investments in equity instruments	(24,000)	6,000	(18,000)	26,667	(6,667)	20,000
Cash flow hedges	(667)	167	(500)	(4,000)	1,000	(3,000)
Gains on property revaluation	933	(333)	600	3,367	(667)	2,700
Remeasurements of defined benefit pension plans	(667)	167	(500)	1,333	(333)	1,000
Share of other comprehensive income of associates	400	–	400	(700)	–	(700)
Other comprehensive income	(18,667)	4,667	(14,000)	37,334	(9,334)	28,000

(1) This means the share of associates' other comprehensive income attributable to owners of the associates, i.e. it is after tax and non-controlling interests in the associates. In this example, the other comprehensive income of associates consists only of items that will not be subsequently reclassified to profit or loss. Entities whose associates' other comprehensive income includes items that may be subsequently reclassified to profit or loss are required to present that amount in a separate line.

(2) The income tax relating to each item of other comprehensive income is disclosed in the notes.

3.2.5 Discontinued operations

As discussed in Chapter 4 at 3.2, IFRS 5 requires the presentation of a single amount on the face of the statement of profit or loss relating to discontinued operations, with further analysis either on the face of the statement or in the notes.

3.2.6 Material and extraordinary items

3.2.6.A Material items

IAS 1 requires that when items of income or expense (a term covering both profit and loss, and other comprehensive income) are material, their nature and amount should be disclosed separately. *[IAS 1.97]*. Materiality is discussed at 4.1.5.A below. The standard goes on to suggest that circumstances that would give rise to the separate disclosure of items of income and expense include:

(a) write-downs of inventories to net realisable value or of property, plant and equipment to recoverable amount, as well as reversals of such write-downs;

(b) restructurings of the activities of an entity and reversals of any provisions for the costs of restructuring;

(c) disposals of items of property, plant and equipment;

(d) disposals of investments;

(e) discontinued operations;

(f) litigation settlements; and

(g) other reversals of provisions. *[IAS 1.98]*.

This information may be given on the face of the statement of profit or loss, on the face of the statement of comprehensive income or in the notes. In line with the permissive approach taken to the format of the performance statements discussed above, the level of prominence given to such items is left to the judgement of the entity concerned. However, regarding (e) above, IFRS 5 requires certain information to be presented on the face of the statement of profit or loss (see Chapter 4 at 3.2).

3.2.6.B Ordinary activities and extraordinary items

IAS 1 states that an entity 'shall not present any items of income or expense as extraordinary items, in the statement(s) presenting profit or loss and other comprehensive income, or in the notes.' *[IAS 1.87].*

This derives from the fact that earlier versions of the standard required a distinction to be made between ordinary activities (and the results of them) and extraordinary items.

The basis for conclusions to IAS 1 explains that the removal of this distinction, and the prohibition on the presentation of extraordinary items, was made to avoid arbitrary segregation of an entity's performance. *[IAS 1.64].*

3.3 The statement of changes in equity

IAS 1 requires the presentation of a statement of changes in equity showing: *[IAS 1.106]*

(a) total comprehensive income for the period (comprising profit and loss and other comprehensive income – see 3.2.1 above) showing separately the total amounts attributable to owner of the parent and to non-controlling interests;

(b) for each component of equity, the effects of retrospective application or retrospective restatement recognised in accordance with IAS 8 (discussed at 4.4 and 4.6 below); and

(c) for each component of equity, a reconciliation between the carrying amount at the beginning and the end of the period, separately disclosing changes resulting from:
   - (i) profit or loss;
   - (ii) other comprehensive income; and
   - (iii) transactions with owners in their capacity as owners, showing separately contributions by and distributions to owners and changes in ownership interests in subsidiaries that do not result in a loss of control.

The reconciliation in (c)(ii) above must show each item of other comprehensive income, although that detail may be shown in the notes. *[IAS 1.106A].*

The amounts of dividends shown as distributions to owners and the amounts of dividends per share should be shown either on the face of the statement or in the notes. *[IAS 1.107].*

It can be seen that (a) above is effectively a sub-total of all the items required by (c)(i) and (c)(ii).

For these purposes, 'components' of equity include each class of contributed equity, the accumulated balance of each class of other comprehensive income and retained earnings. *[IAS 1.108].*

This analysis reflects the focus of the IASB on the statement of financial position – whereby any changes in net assets (aside of those arising from transactions with owners) are gains and losses, regarded as performance. In this vein, IAS 1 observes that changes in an entity's equity between two reporting dates reflect the increase or decrease in its net assets during the period. Except for changes resulting from transactions with owners acting in their capacity as owners (such as equity contributions, reacquisitions of the entity's own equity instruments and dividends) and transaction costs directly related to such transactions, the overall change in equity during a period represents the total amount of income and expenses, including gains and losses, generated by the entity's activities during that period. *[IAS 1.109]*.

After taking account of total gains and losses and owner transactions in this way, any other changes in equity will result from the restatement of prior periods. Point (b) above reflects this. IAS 8 requires retrospective adjustments to effect changes in accounting policies, to the extent practicable, except when the transitional provisions in another IFRS require otherwise. IAS 8 also requires that restatements to correct errors are made retrospectively, to the extent practicable. These are discussed at 4 below. IAS 1 observes that retrospective adjustments and retrospective restatements 'are not changes in equity but they are adjustments to the opening balance of retained earnings, except when an IFRS requires retrospective adjustment of another component of equity.' Point (b) above therefore requires disclosure in the statement of changes in equity of the total adjustment to each component of equity resulting, separately, from changes in accounting policies and from corrections of errors. These adjustments should be disclosed for each prior period and the beginning of the period. *[IAS 1.110]*.

The illustrative statement from the implementation guidance accompanying IAS 1 is set out below. *[IAS 1 IG Part I]*.

Example 3.9: Combined statement of all changes in equity

XYZ Group – Statement of changes in equity for the year ended 31 December 2018

(in thousands of currency units)

	Share capital	Retained earnings	Translation of foreign operations	Investments in equity instruments	Cash flow hedge	Revaluation surplus	Total	Non-controlling interest	Total equity
Balance at 1 January 2017	600,000	118,100	(4,000)	1,600	2,000	–	717,700	29,800	747,500
Changes in accounting policy	–	400	–	–	–	–	400	100	500
Restated balance	600,000	118,500	(4,000)	1,600	2,000	–	718,100	29,900	748,000
Changes in equity for 2017									
Dividends	–	(10,000)	–	–	–	–	(10,000)	–	(10,000)
Total comprehensive income for the year[(1)]	–	53,200	6,400	16,000	(2,400)	1,600	74,800	18,700	93,500
Balance at 31 December 2017	600,000	161,700	2,400	17,600	(400)	1,600	782,900	48,600	831,500

Changes in equity for 2018									
Issue of share capital	50,000	–	–	–	–	–	50,000	–	50,000
Dividends	–	(15,000)	–	–	–	–	(15,000)	–	(15,000)
Total comprehensive income for the year[(2)]	–	96,600	3,200	(14,400)	(400)	800	85,800	21,450	107,250
Transfer to retained earnings	–	200	–	–	–	(200)	–	–	–
Balance at 31 December 2018	650,000	243,500	5,600	3,200	(800)	2,200	903,700	70,050	973,750

(1) The amount included in retained earnings for 2017 of 53,200 represents profit attributable to owners of the parent of 52,400 plus remeasurements of defined benefit pension plans of 800 (1,333, less tax 333, less non-controlling interest 200).

The amount included in the translation, investments in equity instruments and cash flow hedge reserves represent other comprehensive income for each component, net of tax and non-controlling interest, e.g. other comprehensive income related to investments in equity instruments for 2018 of 16,000 is 26,667, less tax 6,667, less non-controlling interest 4,000.

The amount included in the revaluation surplus of 1,600 represents the share of other comprehensive income of associates of (700) plus gains on property revaluation of 2,300 (3,367, less tax 667, less non-controlling interest 400). Other comprehensive income of associates relates solely to gains or losses on property revaluation.

(2) The amount included in retained earnings of 2018 of 96,600 represents profit attributable to owners of the parent of 97,000 less remeasurements of defined benefit pension plans of 400 (667, less tax 167, less non-controlling interest 100).

The amount included in the translation, investments in equity instruments and cash flow hedge reserves represent other comprehensive income for each component, net of tax and non-controlling interest, e.g. other comprehensive income related to the translation of foreign operations for 2018 of 3,200 is 5,334, less tax 1,334, less non-controlling interest 800.

The amount included in the revaluation surplus of 800 represents the share of other comprehensive income of associates of 400 plus gains on property revaluation of 400 (933, less tax 333, less non-controlling interest 200). Other comprehensive income of associates relates solely to gains or losses on property revaluation.

3.4 The notes to the financial statements

IAS 1 requires the presentation of notes to the financial statements that:

(a) present information about the basis of preparation of the financial statements and the specific accounting policies used (see 5.1 below);

(b) disclose the information required by IFRS that is not presented elsewhere in the financial statements; and

(c) provide additional information that is not presented elsewhere in the financial statements, but is relevant to an understanding of any of them. *[IAS 1.112]*.

The notes should, as far as practicable, be presented in a systematic manner, determined in consideration of its effect on the understandability and comparability of the financial statements. Each item on the face of the primary statements should be cross-referenced to any related information in the notes. *[IAS 1.113]*.

There is, perhaps, a trade-off to be made between understandability and comparability, in that allowing entities to structure their notes to, for instance, reflect their business model or perceived importance may reduce the comparability between one entity and another. The standard does not prescribe a specific order, but in the Basis for Conclusions the consistency dimension of comparability is highlighted, and it is clarified that the ordering of the notes generally should not be changed from period to period. *[IAS 1.BC76E]*. Examples given in the standard of the systematic ordering or grouping of the notes are as follows:

(a) giving prominence to the areas of its activities that the entity considers to be most relevant to an understanding of its financial performance and financial position, such as grouping together information about particular operating activities;

(b) grouping together information about items measured similarly such as assets measured at fair value; or

(c) following the order of the line items in the statement(s) of profit or loss and other comprehensive income and the statement of financial position, such as:

   (i) a statement of compliance with IFRS (see 2.5.2 above);

   (ii) significant accounting policies applied (see 5.1.1 below);

   (iii) supporting information for items presented on the face of the primary statements, in the order in which each statement and each line item is presented; and

   (iv) other disclosures, including: contingent liabilities, unrecognised contractual commitments and non-financial disclosures such as financial risk management objectives and policies. *[IAS 1.114]*.

The standard also allows that notes providing information about the basis of preparation of the financial statements and specific accounting policies may be presented as a separate component of the financial statements. *[IAS 1.116]*.

4 ACCOUNTING POLICIES

The selection and application of accounting policies is obviously crucial in the preparation of financial statements. As a general premise, the whole purpose of accounting standards is to specify required accounting policies, presentation and disclosure. However, judgement will always remain; many standards may allow choices to accommodate different views, and no body of accounting literature could hope to prescribe precise treatments for all possible situations.

In the broadest sense, accounting policies are discussed by both IAS 1 and IAS 8. Whilst, as its title suggests, IAS 8 deals explicitly with accounting policies, IAS 1 deals with what one might describe as overarching or general principles.

4.1 General principles

IAS 1 deals with some general principles relating to accounting policies, with IAS 8 discussing the detail of selection and application of individual accounting policies and their disclosure.

The general principles discussed by IAS 1 can be described as follows:

- fair presentation and compliance with accounting standards;
- going concern;
- the accrual basis of accounting;
- consistency;
- materiality and aggregation;

- offsetting; and
- profit or loss for the period.

These are discussed in the sections that follow.

4.1.1 Fair presentation

4.1.1.A Fair presentation and compliance with IFRS

Consistent with its objective and statement of the purpose of financial statements, IAS 1 requires that financial statements present fairly the financial position, financial performance and cash flows of an entity. Fair presentation for these purposes requires the faithful representation of the effects of transactions, other events and conditions in accordance with the definitions and recognition criteria for assets, liabilities, income and expenses set out in the *Conceptual Framework* (discussed in Chapter 2).

The main premise of the standard is that application of IFRS, with additional disclosure when necessary, is presumed to result in financial statements that achieve a fair presentation. *[IAS 1.15]*. As noted at 1.1 above, an important point here is that implementation guidance for standards issued by the IASB does not form part of those standards (unless they are explicitly 'scoped-in'), and therefore does not contain requirements for financial statements. *[IAS 8.8]*. In contrast, any application guidance appended to a standard forms an integral part of that standard.

Accordingly, the often voluminous implementation guidance accompanying standards is not, strictly speaking, part of IFRS. We would generally be surprised, though, at entities not following such guidance. The presumption that application of IFRS (with any necessary additional disclosure) results in a fair presentation is potentially rebuttable, as discussed at 4.1.1.B below.

A fair presentation also requires an entity to:

(a) select and apply accounting policies in accordance with IAS 8, which also sets out a hierarchy of authoritative guidance that should be considered in the absence of an IFRS that specifically applies to an item (see 4.3 below);

(b) present information, including accounting policies, in a manner that provides relevant, reliable, comparable and understandable information; and

(c) provide additional disclosures when compliance with the specific requirements in IFRS is insufficient to enable users to understand the impact of particular transactions, other events and conditions on the entity's financial position and financial performance. *[IAS 1.17]*.

However, the standard makes clear that inappropriate accounting policies are not rectified either by disclosure of the accounting policies used or by notes or explanatory material. *[IAS 1.18]*. We support this position, however the IASB has (admittedly only in rare situations) essentially delegated standard setting to the authors of 'relevant regulatory frameworks' in this regard. As discussed at 4.1.1.B below, it is possible that a rare circumstance arises where departure from a provision of IFRS is needed to achieve fair presentation. This is only allowed by IAS 1, however, if permitted by such a regulatory framework. *[IAS 1.19]*.

4.1.1.B The fair presentation override

The presumption that the application of IFRS, with additional disclosure when necessary, results in financial statements that achieve a fair presentation is a rebuttable one, although the standard makes clear that in virtually all situations a fair presentation is achieved through compliance. *[IAS 1.19]*.

The standard observes that an item of information would conflict with the objective of financial statements when it does not represent faithfully the transactions, other events and conditions that it either purports to represent or could reasonably be expected to represent and, consequently, it would be likely to influence economic decisions made by users of financial statements. When assessing whether complying with a specific requirement in an IFRS would be so misleading that it would conflict with the objective of financial statements, IAS 1 requires consideration of:

(a) why the objective of financial statements is not achieved in the particular circumstances; and

(b) how the entity's circumstances differ from those of other entities that comply with the requirement. If other entities in similar circumstances comply with the requirement, there is a rebuttable presumption that the entity's compliance with the requirement would not be so misleading that it would conflict with the objective of financial statements. *[IAS 1.24]*.

In the extremely rare circumstances in which management concludes that compliance with a requirement in an IFRS would be so misleading that it would conflict with the objective of financial statements, IAS 1 requires departure from that requirement. However, this is only permitted if the 'relevant regulatory framework requires, or otherwise does not prohibit, such a departure', which is discussed further below. *[IAS 1.19]*.

When the relevant regulatory framework allows a departure, an entity should make it and also disclose:

(a) that management has concluded that the financial statements present fairly the entity's financial position, financial performance and cash flows;

(b) that it has complied with applicable IFRSs, except that it has departed from a particular requirement to achieve a fair presentation;

(c) the title of the IFRS from which the entity has departed, the nature of the departure, including:
   (i) the treatment that the IFRS would require;
   (ii) the reason why that treatment would be so misleading in the circumstances that it would conflict with the objective of financial statements set out in the *Framework*; and
   (iii) the treatment adopted;

(d) for each period presented, the financial impact of the departure on each item in the financial statements that would have been reported in complying with the requirement; and

(e) when there has been a departure from a requirement of an IFRS in a prior period, and that departure affects the amounts recognised in the financial statements for the current period, the disclosures set out in (c) and (d) above. *[IAS 1.20-21]*.

Regarding (e) above, the standard explains that the requirement could apply, for example, when an entity departed in a prior period from a requirement in an IFRS for the measurement of assets or liabilities and that departure affects the measurement of changes in assets and liabilities recognised in the current period's financial statements. *[IAS 1.22]*.

When the relevant regulatory framework does not allow a departure from IFRS, IAS 1 accepts that, notwithstanding the failure to achieve fair presentation, that it should not be made. Although intended to occur only in extremely rare circumstances, this is a very important provision of the standard as it allows a 'relevant regulatory framework' to override the requirement of IFRS to achieve a fair presentation. In that light, it is perhaps surprising that there is no definition or discussion in the standard of what a relevant regulatory framework is.

When a departure otherwise required by IAS 1 is not allowed by the relevant regulatory framework, the standard requires that the perceived misleading aspects of compliance are reduced, to the maximum extent possible, by the disclosure of:

(a) the title of the IFRS in question, the nature of the requirement, and the reason why management has concluded that complying with that requirement is so misleading in the circumstances that it conflicts with the objective of financial statements set out in the *Framework*; and

(b) for each period presented, the adjustments to each item in the financial statements that management has concluded would be necessary to achieve a fair presentation. *[IAS 1.23]*.

Overall, this strikes us as a fairly uncomfortable compromise. However, the rule is reasonably clear and in our view such a circumstance will indeed be a rare one.

4.1.2 Going concern

When preparing financial statements, IAS 1 requires management to make an assessment of an entity's ability to continue as a going concern. This term is not defined, but its meaning is implicit in the requirement of the standard that financial statements should be prepared on a going concern basis unless management either intends to liquidate the entity or to cease trading, or has no realistic alternative but to do so. The standard goes on to require that when management is aware, in making its assessment, of material uncertainties related to events or conditions that may cast significant doubt upon the entity's ability to continue as a going concern, those uncertainties should be disclosed. Beyond requiring disclosure of the uncertainties, the standard does not specify more precisely what information should be disclosed. The Interpretations Committee recommended, in January 2013, that the IASB make a narrow-scope amendment to IAS 1 that would address when these disclosures should be made and what information should be disclosed. Although the IASB acknowledged that more prescriptive requirements would lead to useful information to investors and creditors, it also had the expectation that such requirements may result in 'boilerplate' disclosures that would obscure relevant disclosures about going concern and thus would contribute to disclosure overload. It also observed that this is a topic that is better handled through local regulator or audit guidance.[2]

When financial statements are not prepared on a going concern basis, that fact should be disclosed, together with the basis on which the financial statements are prepared and the reason why the entity is not regarded as a going concern. *[IAS 1.25]*.

In assessing whether the going concern assumption is appropriate, the standard requires that all available information about the future, which is at least, but is not limited to, twelve months from the end of the reporting period should be taken into account. The degree of consideration required will depend on the facts in each case. When an entity has a history of profitable operations and ready access to financial resources, a conclusion that the going concern basis of accounting is appropriate may be reached without detailed analysis. In other cases, management may need to consider a wide range of factors relating to current and expected profitability, debt repayment schedules and potential sources of replacement financing before it can satisfy itself that the going concern basis is appropriate. *[IAS 1.26]*.

There is no guidance in the standard concerning what impact there should be on the financial statements if it is determined that the going concern basis is not appropriate. Accordingly, entities will need to consider carefully their individual circumstances to arrive at an appropriate basis.

4.1.3 *The accrual basis of accounting*

IAS 1 requires that financial statements be prepared, except for cash flow information, using the accrual basis of accounting. *[IAS 1.27]*. No definition of this is given by the standard, but an explanation is presented that 'When the accrual basis of accounting is used, items are recognised as assets, liabilities, equity, income and expenses (the elements of financial statements) when they satisfy the definitions and recognition criteria for those elements in the *Framework*.' *[IAS 1.28]*.

The *Conceptual Framework* explains the accruals basis as follows. 'Accrual accounting depicts the effects of transactions and other events and circumstances on a reporting entity's economic resources and claims in the periods in which those effects occur, even if the resulting cash receipts and payments occur in a different period. This is important because information about a reporting entity's economic resources and claims and changes in its economic resources and claims during a period provides a better basis for assessing the entity's past and future performance than information solely about cash receipts and payments during that period.' *[Framework OB17]*.

The requirements of the *Conceptual Framework* are discussed in more detail in Chapter 2.

4.1.4 *Consistency*

As noted at 1.1 and 1.2 above, one of the objectives of both IAS 1 and IAS 8 is to ensure the comparability of financial statements with those of previous periods. To this end, each standard addresses the principle of consistency.

IAS 1 requires that the 'presentation and classification' of items in the financial statements be retained from one period to the next unless:

(a) it is apparent, following a significant change in the nature of the entity's operations or a review of its financial statements, that another presentation or classification would be more appropriate having regard to the criteria for the selection and application of accounting policies in IAS 8 (see 4.3 below); or

(b) an IFRS requires a change in presentation. *[IAS 1.45]*.

The standard goes on to amplify this by explaining that a significant acquisition or disposal, or a review of the presentation of the financial statements, might suggest that the financial statements need to be presented differently. An entity should change the presentation of its financial statements only if the changed presentation provides information that is reliable and is more relevant to users of the financial statements and the revised structure is likely to continue, so that comparability is not impaired. When making such changes in presentation, an entity will need to reclassify its comparative information as discussed at 2.4 above. *[IAS 1.46].*

IAS 8 addresses consistency of accounting policies and observes that users of financial statements need to be able to compare the financial statements of an entity over time to identify trends in its financial position, financial performance and cash flows. For this reason, the same accounting policies need to be applied within each period and from one period to the next unless a change in accounting policy meets certain criteria (changes in accounting policy are discussed at 4.4 below). *[IAS 8.15].* Accordingly, the standard requires that accounting policies be selected and applied consistently for similar transactions, other events and conditions, unless an IFRS specifically requires or permits categorisation of items for which different policies may be appropriate. If an IFRS requires or permits such categorisation, an appropriate accounting policy should be selected and applied consistently to each category. *[IAS 8.13].*

4.1.5 Materiality, aggregation and offset

4.1.5.A Materiality and aggregation

Financial statements result from processing large numbers of transactions or other events that are aggregated into classes according to their nature or function. The final stage in the process of aggregation and classification is the presentation of condensed and classified data, which form line items in the financial statements, or in the notes. *[IAS 1.30].* The extent of aggregation versus detailed analysis is clearly a judgemental one, with either extreme eroding the usefulness of the information.

IAS 1 resolves this issue with the concept of materiality, by requiring:

- each material class of similar items to be presented separately in the financial statements; and
- items of a dissimilar nature or function to be presented separately unless they are immaterial. *[IAS 1.29].*

The standard also states when applying IAS 1 and other IFRSs an entity should decide, taking into consideration all relevant facts and circumstances, how it aggregates information in the financial statements, which include the notes. In particular, the understandability of financial statements should not be reduced by obscuring material information with immaterial information or by aggregating material items that have different natures or functions. *[IAS 1.30A].*

Materiality is defined by both IAS 1 and IAS 8 as follows. 'Omissions or misstatements of items are material if they could, individually or collectively, influence the economic decisions that users make on the basis of the financial statements. Materiality depends on the size and nature of the omission or misstatement judged in the surrounding circumstances. The size or nature of the item, or a combination of both, could be the determining factor.' *[IAS 1.7, IAS 8.5]*. At a general level, applying the concept of materiality means that a specific disclosure required by an IFRS to be given in the financial statements (including the notes) need not be provided if the information resulting from that disclosure is not material. This is the case even if the IFRS contains a list of specific requirements or describes them as minimum requirements. On the other hand, the provision of additional disclosures should be considered when compliance with the specific requirements in IFRS is insufficient to enable users of financial statements to understand the impact of particular transactions, other events and conditions on the entity's financial position and financial performance. *[IAS 1.31]*.

IAS 1 and IAS 8 go on to observe that assessing whether an omission or misstatement could influence economic decisions of users, and so be material, requires consideration of the characteristics of those users. For these purposes users are assumed to have a reasonable knowledge of business and economic activities and accounting and a willingness to study the information with reasonable diligence. Therefore, the assessment of materiality needs to take into account how users with such attributes could reasonably be expected to be influenced in making economic decisions. *[IAS 1.7, IAS 8.6]*.

Regarding the presentation of financial statements, IAS 1 requires that if a line item is not individually material, it should be aggregated with other items either on the face of those statements or in the notes. The standard also states that an item that is not sufficiently material to warrant separate presentation on the face of those statements may nevertheless be sufficiently material for it to be presented separately in the notes. *[IAS 1.30]*.

4.1.5.B Offset

IAS 1 considers it important that assets and liabilities, and income and expenses, are reported separately. This is because offsetting in the statement of profit or loss or statement of comprehensive income or the statement of financial position, except when offsetting reflects the substance of the transaction or other event, detracts from the ability of users both to understand the transactions, other events and conditions that have occurred and to assess the entity's future cash flows. It clarifies, though, that measuring assets net of valuation allowances – for example, obsolescence allowances on inventories and doubtful debts allowances on receivables – is not offsetting. *[IAS 1.33]*.

Accordingly, IAS 1 requires that assets and liabilities, and income and expenses, should not be offset unless required or permitted by an IFRS. *[IAS 1.32]*.

Just what constitutes offsetting, particularly given the rider noted above of 'reflecting the substance of the transaction', is not always obvious. IAS 1 expands on its meaning as follows. It notes that:

(a) IFRS 15 – *Revenue from Contracts with Customers* – defines revenue from contracts with customers and requires it to be measured at the amount of consideration to which the entity expects to be entitled in exchange for transferring promised goods or services, taking into account the amount of any trade discounts and volume rebates allowed by the entity – in other words a notional 'gross' revenue and a discount should not be shown separately, but should be 'offset'. Revenue from contracts with customers is discussed in Chapter 30;

(b) entities can undertake, in the course of their ordinary activities, other transactions that do not generate revenue but are incidental to the main revenue-generating activities. The results of such transactions should be presented, when this presentation reflects the substance of the transaction or other event, by netting any income with related expenses arising on the same transaction. For example:
   (i) gains and losses on the disposal of non-current assets, including investments and operating assets, should be reported by deducting from the proceeds on disposal the carrying amount of the asset and related selling expenses; and
   (ii) expenditure related to a provision that is recognised in accordance with IAS 37 – *Provisions, Contingent Liabilities and Contingent Assets* – and reimbursed under a contractual arrangement with a third party (for example, a supplier's warranty agreement) may be netted against the related reimbursement; *[IAS 1.34]* and

(c) gains and losses arising from a group of similar transactions should be reported on a net basis, for example, foreign exchange gains and losses or gains and losses arising on financial instruments held for trading. However, such gains and losses should be reported separately if they are material. *[IAS 1.35]*.

4.1.6 Profit or loss for the period

The final provision of IAS 1 which we term a general principle is a very important one. It is that, unless an IFRS requires or permits otherwise, all items of income and expense recognised in a period should be included in profit or loss. *[IAS 1.88]*. This is the case whether one combined statement of comprehensive income is presented or whether a separate statement of profit or loss is presented (discussed at 3.2.1 above).

Income and expense are not defined by the standard, but they are defined by the *Conceptual Framework* as follows:

(a) income is increases in economic benefits during the accounting period in the form of inflows or enhancements of assets or decreases of liabilities that result in increases in equity, other than those relating to contributions from equity participants; and

(b) expenses are decreases in economic benefits during the accounting period in the form of outflows or depletions of assets or incurrences of liabilities that result in decreases in equity, other than those relating to distributions to equity participants. *[Framework 4.25]*.

This clearly indicates to us that the terms do not have what many would consider their natural meaning, as they encompass all gains and losses (for example, capital appreciation in a non-current asset like property). There is a somewhat awkward compromise with various gains and losses either required or permitted to bypass profit or loss and be reported instead in 'other comprehensive income'. Importantly, as discussed at 3.2.1 above, profit and loss, and other comprehensive income may each be reported as a separate statement.

IAS 1 notes that normally, all items of income and expense recognised in a period are included in profit or loss, and that this includes the effects of changes in accounting estimates. However, circumstances may exist when particular items may be excluded from profit or loss for the current period. IAS 8 deals with two such circumstances: the correction of errors and the effect of changes in accounting policies (discussed at 4.6 and 4.5 below). *[IAS 1.89]*. Other IFRSs deal with items that may meet the *Framework's* definitions of income or expense but are usually excluded from profit or loss. Examples include:

(a) changes in revaluation surplus relating to property, plant and equipment and intangible assets;

(b) remeasurements on defined benefit plans in accordance with IAS 19;

(c) gains and losses arising from translating the financial statements of a foreign operation;

(d) gains and losses from investments in equity instruments designated at fair value through other comprehensive income;

(e) gains and losses on financial assets measured at fair value through other comprehensive income;

(f) the effective portion of gains and losses on hedging instruments in a cash flow hedge and the gains and losses on hedging instruments that hedge investments in equity instruments measured at fair value through other comprehensive income;

(g) for particular liabilities designated as at fair value through profit and loss, fair value changes attributable to changes in the liability's credit risk;

(h) changes in the value of the time value of options when separating the intrinsic value and time value of an option contract and designating as the hedging instrument only the changes in the intrinsic value; and

(i) changes in the value of the forward elements of forward contracts when separating the forward element and spot element of a forward contract and designating as the hedging instrument only the changes in the spot element, and changes in the value of the foreign currency basis spread of a financial instrument when excluding it from the designation of that financial instrument as the hedging instrument. *[IAS 1.7, 89]*.

4.2 The distinction between accounting policies and accounting estimates

IAS 8 defines accounting policies as 'the specific principles, bases, conventions, rules and practices applied by an entity in preparing and presenting financial statements.' *[IAS 8.5]*. In particular, IAS 8 considers a change in 'measurement basis' to be a change in accounting policy (rather than a change in estimate). *[IAS 8.35]*. Although not a defined term, IAS 1 (when requiring disclosure of them) gives examples of measurement bases as follows:

- historical cost;
- current cost;
- net realisable value;
- fair value; and
- recoverable amount. *[IAS 1.118]*.

'Accounting estimates' is not a term defined directly by the standards. However, it is indirectly defined by the definition in IAS 8 of a change in an accounting estimate as follows. A change in accounting estimate is an adjustment of the carrying amount of an asset or a liability, or the amount of the periodic consumption of an asset, that results from the assessment of the present status of, and expected future benefits and obligations associated with, assets and liabilities. Changes in accounting estimates result from new information or new developments and, accordingly, are not corrections of errors. *[IAS 8.5].* Examples given by the IASB are estimates of bad debts and the estimated useful life of, or the expected pattern of consumption of the future economic benefits embodied in, a depreciable asset. *[IAS 8.38].*

The standard also notes that corrections of errors should be distinguished from changes in accounting estimates. Accounting estimates by their nature are approximations that may need revision as additional information becomes known. For example, the gain or loss recognised on the outcome of a contingency is not the correction of an error. *[IAS 8.48].*

The distinction between an accounting policy and an accounting estimate is particularly important because a very different treatment is required when there are changes in accounting policies or accounting estimates (discussed at 4.4 and 4.5 below). When it is difficult to distinguish a change in an accounting policy from a change in an accounting estimate, IAS 8 requires the change to be treated as a change in an accounting estimate. *[IAS 8.35].*

4.3 The selection and application of accounting policies

Entities complying with IFRS (which is a defined term, discussed at 1.1 above) do not have a free hand in selecting accounting policies; indeed the very purpose of a body of accounting literature is to confine such choices.

IFRSs set out accounting policies that the IASB has concluded result in financial statements containing relevant and reliable information about the transactions, other events and conditions to which they apply. *[IAS 8.8].*

To this end, IAS 8's starting point is that when an IFRS specifically applies to a transaction, other event or condition, the accounting policy or policies applied to that item should be determined by applying the IFRS and considering any relevant implementation guidance issued by the IASB for the IFRS. *[IAS 8.7].* This draws out the distinction that IFRS must be *applied* whereas implementation guidance (which, as discussed at 1.1 above, is not part of IFRS) must be *considered*. As noted earlier, though, we would generally be surprised at entities not following such guidance.

Those policies need not be applied when the effect of applying them is immaterial. However, it is inappropriate to make, or leave uncorrected, immaterial departures from IFRS to achieve a particular presentation of an entity's financial position, financial performance or cash flows (see 4.6 below). *[IAS 8.8].* The concept of materiality is discussed at 4.1.5 above.

There will be circumstances where a particular event, transaction or other condition is not specifically addressed by IFRS. When this is the case, IAS 8 sets out a hierarchy of guidance to be considered in the selection of an accounting policy.

The primary requirement of the standard is that management should use its judgement in developing and applying an accounting policy that results in information that is:

(a) relevant to the economic decision-making needs of users; and

(b) reliable, in that the financial statements:

 (i) represent faithfully the financial position, financial performance and cash flows of the entity;

 (ii) reflect the economic substance of transactions, other events and conditions, and not merely the legal form;

 (iii) are neutral, i.e. free from bias;

 (iv) are prudent; and

 (v) are complete in all material respects. *[IAS 8.10]*.

There is, in our view, clearly a tension between (b) (iii) and (b) (iv) above. Prudence and neutrality are not defined or otherwise discussed by IAS 8. Before its revision in September 2010, the *Framework* discussed them and went some way to addressing this tension as follows. 'To be reliable, the information contained in financial statements must be neutral, that is, free from bias. Financial statements are not neutral if, by the selection or presentation of information, they influence the making of a decision or judgement in order to achieve a predetermined result or outcome.'

'The preparers of financial statements do, however, have to contend with the uncertainties that inevitably surround many events and circumstances, such as the collectability of doubtful receivables, the probable useful life of plant and equipment and the number of warranty claims that may occur. Such uncertainties are recognised by the disclosure of their nature and extent and by the exercise of prudence in the preparation of the financial statements. Prudence is the inclusion of a degree of caution in the exercise of the judgements needed in making the estimates required under conditions of uncertainty, such that assets or income are not overstated and liabilities or expenses are not understated. However, the exercise of prudence does not allow, for example, the creation of hidden reserves or excessive provisions, the deliberate understatement of assets or income, or the deliberate overstatement of liabilities or expenses, because the financial statements would not be neutral and, therefore, not have the quality of reliability.' *[Framework (1989) 36-37]*.

In revising the *Framework* in September 2010 the IASB removed the concept of prudence, stating the following. 'Chapter 3 does not include prudence or conservatism as an aspect of faithful representation because including either would be inconsistent with neutrality.' *[Framework BC.3.27]*. However, the Board is now proposing, in its latest exposure draft, to re-introduce the concept (discussed in Chapter 2 at 3.1).

In support of this primary requirement, the standard gives guidance on how management should apply this judgement. This guidance comes in two 'strengths' – certain things which management is required to consider, and others which it 'may' consider, as follows.

In making this judgement, management *shall* refer to, and consider the applicability of, the following sources in descending order:

(a) the requirements and guidance in IFRSs dealing with similar and related issues; and

(b) the definitions, recognition criteria and measurement concepts for assets, liabilities, income and expenses in the *Framework*; *[IAS 8.11]* and

in making this judgement, management *may* also consider the most recent pronouncements of other standard-setting bodies that use a similar conceptual framework to develop accounting standards, other accounting literature and accepted industry practices, to the extent that these do not conflict with the sources in (a) and (b) above. *[IAS 8.12]*. If an entity considers pronouncements of other standard-setting bodies in making its judgment in developing and applying an accounting policy, it should, in our view, consider all the contents of the pronouncements that are relevant to the issue. In other words, it should not adopt a selective or 'cherry-picking' approach.

In its March 2011 newsletter, the Interpretations Committee noted the following. 'The Committee observed that when management develops an accounting policy through analogy to an IFRS dealing with similar and related matters, it needs to use its judgement in applying all aspects of the IFRS that are applicable to the particular issue.' The committee concluded that the issue of developing accounting policies by analogy requires no further clarification, so did not add the matter to its agenda.

4.4 Changes in accounting policies

As discussed at 4.1.4 above, consistency of accounting policies and presentation is a basic principle in both IAS 1 and IAS 8. Accordingly, IAS 8 only permits a change in accounting policies if the change:

(a) is required by an IFRS; or

(b) results in the financial statements providing reliable and more relevant information about the effects of transactions, other events or conditions on the entity's financial position, financial performance or cash flows. *[IAS 8.14]*.

IAS 8 addresses changes of accounting policy arising from three sources:

(a) the initial application (including early application) of an IFRS containing specific transitional provisions;

(b) the initial application of an IFRS which does not contain specific transitional provisions; and

(c) voluntary changes in accounting policy.

Policy changes under (a) should be accounted for in accordance with the specific transitional provisions of that IFRS.

A change of accounting policy under (b) or (c) should be applied retrospectively, that is applied to transactions, other events and conditions as if it had always been applied. *[IAS 8.5, 19-20]*. The standard goes on to explain that retrospective application requires adjustment of the opening balance of each affected component of equity for the earliest prior period presented and the other comparative amounts disclosed for each prior period presented as if the new accounting policy had always been applied. *[IAS 8.22]*. The standard observes that the amount of the resulting adjustment relating to periods before those presented in the financial statements (which is made to the opening balance of each affected component of equity of the earliest prior period presented) will usually be made to retained earnings. However, it goes on to note that the adjustment may be made to another component of equity (for example, to comply with an IFRS). IAS 8 also makes clear that any other information about prior periods, such as historical summaries of financial data, should be also adjusted. *[IAS 8.26]*.

Frequently it will be straightforward to apply a change in accounting policy retrospectively. However, the standard accepts that sometimes it may be impractical to do so. Accordingly, retrospective application of a change in accounting policy is not required to the extent that it is impracticable to determine either the period-specific effects or the cumulative effect of the change. *[IAS 8.23]*. This is discussed further at 4.7 below. As noted at 4.3 above, in the absence of a specifically applicable IFRS an entity may apply an accounting policy from the most recent pronouncements of another standard-setting body that use a similar conceptual framework. The standard makes clear that a change in accounting policy reflecting a change in such a pronouncement is a voluntary change in accounting policy which should be accounted for and disclosed as such. *[IAS 8.21]*.

The standard clarifies that the following are not changes in accounting policy:

- the application of an accounting policy for transactions, other events or conditions that differ in substance from those previously occurring; and
- the application of a new accounting policy for transactions, other events or conditions that did not occur previously or were immaterial. *[IAS 8.16]*.

More importantly, the standard requires that a change to a policy of revaluing intangible assets or property plant and equipment in accordance with IAS 38 and IAS 16 respectively is not to be accounted for under IAS 8 as a change in accounting policy. Rather, such a change should be dealt with as a revaluation in accordance with the relevant standards (discussed in Chapters 17 at 8.2 and 18 at 6). *[IAS 8.17-18]*. What this means is that it is not permissible to restate prior periods for the carrying value and depreciation charge of the assets concerned. Aside of this particular exception, the standard makes clear that a change in measurement basis is a change in an accounting policy, and not a change in an accounting estimate. However, when it is difficult to distinguish a change in an accounting policy from a change in an accounting estimate, the standard requires it to be treated as a change in an accounting estimate, discussed at 4.5 below. *[IAS 8.35]*.

4.5 Changes in accounting estimates

The making of estimates is a fundamental feature of financial reporting reflecting the uncertainties inherent in business activities. IAS 8 notes that the use of reasonable estimates is an essential part of the preparation of financial statements and it does not undermine their reliability. Examples of estimates given by the standard are:

- bad debts;
- inventory obsolescence;
- the fair value of financial assets or financial liabilities;
- the useful lives of, or expected pattern of consumption of the future economic benefits embodied in, depreciable assets; and
- warranty obligations. *[IAS 8.32-33]*.

Of course there are many others, some of the more subjective relating to share-based payments and post-retirement benefits.

Estimates will need revision as changes occur in the circumstances on which they are based or as a result of new information or more experience. The standard observes that, by its nature, the revision of an estimate does not relate to prior periods and is not the correction of an error. *[IAS 8.34]*. Accordingly, IAS 8 requires that changes in estimate be accounted for prospectively; defined as recognising the effect of the change in the accounting estimate in the current and future periods affected by the change. *[IAS 8.5, 36]*. The standard goes on to explain that this will mean (as appropriate):

- adjusting the carrying amount of an asset, liability or item of equity in the statement of financial position in the period of change; and
- recognising the change by including it in profit and loss in:
  - the period of change, if it affects that period only (for example, a change in estimate of bad debts); or
  - the period of change and future periods, if it affects both (for example, a change in estimated useful life of a depreciable asset or the expected pattern of consumption of the economic benefits embodied in it). *[IAS 8.36-38]*.

4.6 Correction of errors

As with all things, financial reporting is not immune to error and sometimes financial statements can be published which, whether by accident or design, contain errors. IAS 8 defines prior period errors as omissions from, and misstatements in, an entity's financial statements for one or more prior periods (including the effects of mathematical mistakes, mistakes in applying accounting policies, oversights or misinterpretations of facts, and fraud) arising from a failure to use, or misuse of, reliable information that:

(a) was available when financial statements for those periods were authorised for issue; and

(b) could reasonably be expected to have been obtained and taken into account in the preparation and presentation of those financial statements. *[IAS 8.5]*.

Errors can arise in respect of the recognition, measurement, presentation or disclosure of elements of financial statements. IAS 8 states that financial statements do not comply with IFRS if they contain errors that are:

(a) material; or

(b) immaterial but are made intentionally to achieve a particular presentation of an entity's financial position, financial performance or cash flows. *[IAS 8.41]*.

The concept in (b) is a little curious. As discussed at 4.1.5.A above, an error is material if it could influence the economic decisions of users taken on the basis of the financial statements. We find it difficult to imagine a scenario where an entity would deliberately seek to misstate its financial statements to achieve a particular presentation of its financial position, performance or cash flows but only in such a way that did not influence the decisions of users. In any event, and perhaps somewhat unnecessarily, IAS 8 notes that potential current period errors detected before the financial statements are authorised for issue should be corrected in those financial statements. This requirement is phrased so as to apply to all potential errors, not just material ones. *[IAS 8.41]*. The standard notes that corrections of errors are distinguished from changes in accounting estimates. Accounting estimates by their nature are approximations that may need revision as additional information becomes known. For example, the gain or loss recognised on the outcome of a contingency is not the correction of an error. *[IAS 8.48]*.

When it is discovered that material prior period errors have occurred, IAS 8 requires that they be corrected in the first set of financial statements prepared after their discovery. *[IAS 8.42]*. The correction should be excluded from profit or loss for the period in which the error is discovered. Rather, any information presented about prior periods (including any historical summaries of financial data) should be restated as far back as practicable. *[IAS 8.46]*. This should be done by:

(a) restating the comparative amounts for the prior period(s) presented in which the error occurred; or

(b) if the error occurred before the earliest prior period presented, restating the opening balances of assets, liabilities and equity for the earliest prior period presented. *[IAS 8.42]*.

This process is described by the standard as retrospective restatement, which it also defines as correcting the recognition, measurement and disclosure of amounts of elements of financial statements as if a prior period error had never occurred. *[IAS 8.5]*.

The implementation guidance accompanying the standard provides an example of the retrospective restatement of errors as follows: *[IAS 8.IG1]*

Example 3.10: Retrospective restatement of errors

During 2018, Beta Co discovered that some products that had been sold during 2017 were incorrectly included in inventory at 31 December 2017 at €6,500.

Beta's accounting records for 2018 show sales of €104,000, cost of goods sold of €86,500 (including €6,500 for the error in opening inventory), and income taxes of €5,250.

In 2017, Beta reported:

	€
Sales	73,500
Cost of goods sold	(53,500)
Profit before income taxes	20,000
Income taxes	(6,000)
Profit	14,000

The 2017 opening retained earnings was €20,000 and closing retained earnings was €34,000.

Beta's income tax rate was 30 per cent for 2018 and 2017. It had no other income or expenses.

Beta had €5,000 of share capital throughout, and no other components of equity except for retained earnings. Its shares are not publicly traded and it does not disclose earnings per share.

Beta Co
Extract from the statement of comprehensive income

	2018	(restated) 2017
	€	€
Sales	104,000	73,500
Cost of goods sold	(80,000)	(60,000)
Profit before income taxes	24,000	13,500
Income taxes	(7,200)	(4,050)
Profit	16,800	9,450

Beta Co
Statement of Changes in Equity

	Share capital	Retained earnings	Total
	€	€	€
Balance at 31 December 2016	5,000	20,000	25,000
Profit for the year ended 31 December 2017 as restated	–	9,450	9,450
Balance at 31 December 2017	5,000	29,450	34,450
Profit for the year ended 31 December 2018	–	16,800	16,800
Balance at 31 December 2018	5,000	46,250	51,250

Extracts from the Notes

1. Some products that had been sold in 2017 were incorrectly included in inventory at 31 December 2017 at €6,500. The financial statements of 2017 have been restated to correct this error. The effect of the restatement on those financial statements is summarised below. There is no effect in 2018.

	Effect on 2017
	€
(Increase) in cost of goods sold	(6,500)
Decrease in income tax expense	1,950
(Decrease) in profit	(4,550)
(Decrease) in inventory	(6,500)
Decrease in income tax payable	1,950
(Decrease) in equity	(4,550)

As is the case for the retrospective application of a change in accounting policy, retrospective restatement for the correction of prior period material errors is not required to the extent that it is impracticable to determine either the period-specific effects or the cumulative effect of the error. *[IAS 8.43]*. This is discussed further at 4.7 below.

4.7 Impracticability of restatement

As noted at 4.4 and 4.6 above, IAS 8 does not require the restatement of prior periods following a change in accounting policy or the correction of material errors if such a restatement is impracticable.

The standard devotes a considerable amount of guidance to discussing what 'impracticable' means for these purposes.

The standard states that applying a requirement is impracticable when an entity cannot apply it after making every reasonable effort to do so. It goes on to note that, for a particular prior period, it is impracticable to apply a change in an accounting policy retrospectively or to make a retrospective restatement to correct an error if:

(a) the effects of the retrospective application or retrospective restatement are not determinable;

(b) the retrospective application or retrospective restatement requires assumptions about what management's intent would have been in that period; or

(c) the retrospective application or retrospective restatement requires significant estimates of amounts and it is impossible to distinguish objectively information about those estimates that:

  (i) provides evidence of circumstances that existed on the date(s) as at which those amounts are to be recognised, measured or disclosed; and

  (ii) would have been available when the financial statements for that prior period were authorised for issue,

  from other information. *[IAS 8.5].*

An example of a scenario covered by (a) above given by the standard is that in some circumstances it may impracticable to adjust comparative information for one or more prior periods to achieve comparability with the current period because data may not have been collected in the prior period(s) in a way that allows either retrospective application of a new accounting policy (or its prospective application to prior periods) or retrospective restatement to correct a prior period error, and it may be impracticable to recreate the information. *[IAS 8.50].*

IAS 8 observes that it is frequently necessary to make estimates in applying an accounting policy and that estimation is inherently subjective, and that estimates may be developed after the reporting period. Developing estimates is potentially more difficult when retrospectively applying an accounting policy or making a retrospective restatement to correct a prior period error, because of the longer period of time that might have passed since the affected transaction, other event or condition occurred.

However, the objective of estimates related to prior periods remains the same as for estimates made in the current period, namely, for the estimate to reflect the circumstances that existed when the transaction, other event or condition occurred. *[IAS 8.51].* Hindsight should not be used when applying a new accounting policy to, or correcting amounts for, a prior period, either in making assumptions about what management's intentions would have been in a prior period or estimating the amounts recognised, measured or disclosed in a prior period. For example, if an entity corrects a prior period error in calculating its liability for employees' accumulated sick leave in accordance with IAS 19, it would disregard information about an unusually severe influenza season during the next period that became available after the financial statements for the prior period were authorised for issue. However, the fact that significant estimates are frequently required when amending comparative information presented for prior periods does not prevent reliable adjustment or correction of the comparative information. *[IAS 8.53]*.

Therefore, retrospectively applying a new accounting policy or correcting a prior period error requires distinguishing information that:

(a) provides evidence of circumstances that existed on the date(s) as at which the transaction, other event or condition occurred; and

(b) would have been available when the financial statements for that prior period were authorised for issue,

from other information. The standard states that for some types of estimates (e.g. a fair value measurement that uses significant unobservable inputs), it is impracticable to distinguish these types of information. When retrospective application or retrospective restatement would require making a significant estimate for which it is impossible to distinguish these two types of information, it is impracticable to apply the new accounting policy or correct the prior period error retrospectively. *[IAS 8.52]*.

IAS 8 addresses the impracticability of restatement separately (although similarly) for changes in accounting policy and the correction of material errors.

4.7.1 *Impracticability of restatement for a change in accounting policy*

When retrospective application of a change in accounting policy is required, the change in policy should be applied retrospectively except to the extent that it is impracticable to determine either the period-specific effects or the cumulative effect of the change. *[IAS 8.23]*. When an entity applies a new accounting policy retrospectively, the standard requires it to be applied to comparative information for prior periods as far back as is practicable. Retrospective application to a prior period is not practicable for these purposes unless it is practicable to determine the cumulative effect on the amounts in both the opening and closing statement of financial position for that period. *[IAS 8.26]*.

When it is impracticable to determine the period-specific effects of changing an accounting policy on comparative information for one or more prior periods presented:

- the new accounting policy should be applied to the carrying amounts of assets and liabilities as at the beginning of the earliest period for which retrospective application is practicable; and
- a corresponding adjustment to the opening balance of each affected component of equity for that period should be made.

The standard notes that this may be the current period. *[IAS 8.24]*.

When it is impracticable to determine the cumulative effect, at the beginning of the current period, of applying a new accounting policy to all prior periods, the standard requires an adjustment to the comparative information to apply the new accounting policy prospectively from the earliest date practicable. *[IAS 8.25]*. Prospective application is defined by the standard as applying the new accounting policy to transactions, other events and conditions occurring after the date as at which the policy is changed. *[IAS 8.5].* This means that the portion of the cumulative adjustment to assets, liabilities and equity arising before that date is disregarded. Changing an accounting policy is permitted by IAS 8 even if it is impracticable to apply the policy prospectively for any prior period. *[IAS 8.27].*

The implementation guidance accompanying the standard illustrates the prospective application of a change in accounting policy as follows: *[IAS 8.IG3]*

Example 3.11: Prospective application of a change in accounting policy when retrospective application is not practicable

During 2018, Delta Co changed its accounting policy for depreciating property, plant and equipment, so as to apply much more fully a components approach, whilst at the same time adopting the revaluation model.

In years before 2018, Delta's asset records were not sufficiently detailed to apply a components approach fully. At the end of 2017, management commissioned an engineering survey, which provided information on the components held and their fair values, useful lives, estimated residual values and depreciable amounts at the beginning of 2018. However, the survey did not provide a sufficient basis for reliably estimating the cost of those components that had not previously been accounted for separately, and the existing records before the survey did not permit this information to be reconstructed.

Delta's management considered how to account for each of the two aspects of the accounting change. They determined that it was not practicable to account for the change to a fuller components approach retrospectively, or to account for that change prospectively from any earlier date than the start of 2018. Also, the change from a cost model to a revaluation model is required to be accounted for prospectively (see 4.4 above). Therefore, management concluded that it should apply Delta's new policy prospectively from the start of 2018.

Additional information:

Delta's tax rate is 30 per cent.	
	€
Property, plant and equipment at the end of 2017:	
Cost	25,000
Depreciation	(14,000)
Net book value	11,000
Prospective depreciation expense for 2018 (old basis)	1,500
Some results of the engineering survey:	
Valuation	17,000
Estimated residual value	3,000
Average remaining asset life (years)	7
Depreciation expense on existing property, plant and equipment for 2018 (new basis)	2,000

Extract from the Notes

1 From the start of 2018, Delta changed its accounting policy for depreciating property, plant and equipment, so as to apply much more fully a components approach, whilst at the same time adopting the revaluation model. Management takes the view that this policy provides reliable and more relevant information because it deals more accurately with the components of property, plant and equipment and is based on up-to-date values. The policy has been applied prospectively from the start of 2018 because it was not practicable to estimate the effects of applying the policy either retrospectively, or prospectively from any earlier date. Accordingly, the adoption of the new policy has no effect on prior years. The effect on the current year is to increase the carrying amount of property, plant and equipment at the start of the year by €6,000; increase the opening deferred tax provision by €1,800; create a revaluation surplus at the start of the year of €4,200; increase depreciation expense by €500; and reduce tax expense by €150.

4.7.2 Impracticability of restatement for a material error

IAS 8 requires that a prior period error should be corrected by retrospective restatement except to the extent that it is impracticable to determine either the period-specific effects or the cumulative effect of the error. *[IAS 8.43]*.

When it is impracticable to determine the period-specific effects of an error on comparative information for one or more prior periods presented, the opening balances of assets, liabilities and equity should be restated for the earliest period for which retrospective restatement is practicable (which the standard notes may be the current period). *[IAS 8.44]*.

When it is impracticable to determine the cumulative effect, at the beginning of the current period, of an error on all prior periods, the comparative information should be restated to correct the error prospectively from the earliest date practicable. *[IAS 8.45]*. The standard explains that this will mean disregarding the portion of the cumulative restatement of assets, liabilities and equity arising before that date. *[IAS 8.47]*.

5 DISCLOSURE REQUIREMENTS

5.1 Disclosures relating to accounting policies

5.1.1 Disclosure of accounting policies

5.1.1.A Summary of significant accounting policies

IAS 1 makes the valid observation that it is important for users to be informed of the measurement basis or bases used in the financial statements (for example, historical cost, current cost, net realisable value, fair value or recoverable amount) because the basis on which the financial statements are prepared significantly affects their analysis. *[IAS 1.118]*.

Accordingly, the standard requires disclosure of significant accounting policies comprising:

(a) the measurement basis (or bases) used in preparing the financial statements; and

(b) the other accounting policies used that are relevant to an understanding of the financial statements. *[IAS 1.117]*.

When more than one measurement basis is used in the financial statements, for example when particular classes of assets are revalued, it is sufficient to provide an indication of the categories of assets and liabilities to which each measurement basis is applied. *[IAS 1.118]*.

It is clearly necessary to apply judgement when deciding on the level of detail required in the disclosure of accounting policies. Of particular note, is that the decision as to whether to disclose a policy should not just be a function of the magnitude of the sums involved. The standard states that an accounting policy may be significant because of the nature of the entity's operations even if amounts for current and prior periods are not material. It is also appropriate to disclose each significant accounting policy that is not specifically required by IFRS, but is selected and applied in accordance with IAS 8 (discussed at 4.3 above). *[IAS 1.121]*. Moreover, the relevance of the disclosure of accounting policies is improved if it specifically addresses how the entity has applied the requirements of IFRS, rather than a giving summary of those requirements.

In deciding whether a particular accounting policy should be disclosed, IAS 1 requires consideration of whether disclosure would assist users in understanding how transactions, other events and conditions are reflected in the reported financial performance and financial position. In doing so, each entity should consider the nature of its operations and the policies that the users of its financial statements would expect to be disclosed for that type of entity. Disclosure of particular accounting policies is especially useful to users when those policies are selected from alternatives allowed in standards and interpretations. An example is disclosure of the choice between the cost and fair value models in IAS 40 – *Investment Property*.

Some standards specifically require disclosure of particular accounting policies, including choices made by management between different policies they allow. For example IAS 16 requires disclosure of the measurement bases used for classes of property, plant and equipment (discussed in Chapter 18 at 8). *[IAS 1.119]*.

5.1.1.B Judgements made in applying accounting policies

The process of applying an entity's accounting policies requires various judgements, apart from those involving estimations, that can significantly affect the amounts recognised in the financial statements. For example, judgements are required in determining:

(a) when substantially all the significant risks and rewards of ownership of financial assets and lease assets are transferred to other entities;

(b) whether, in substance, particular sales of goods are financing arrangements and therefore do not give rise to revenue; and

(c) whether the contractual terms of a financial asset give rise on specified dates to cash flows that are solely payments of principal and interest on the principal amount outstanding. *[IAS 1.123]*.

IAS 1 requires disclosure, along with its significant accounting policies or other notes, of the judgements (apart from those involving estimations, see 5.2.1 below) management has made in the process of applying the entity's accounting policies that have the most significant effect on the amounts recognised in the financial statements. *[IAS 1.122]*.

Some of these disclosures are required by other standards. For example:

- IFRS 12 – *Disclosure of Interests in Other Entities*, requires disclosure of the judgements made in determining if control is present; and
- IAS 40 requires disclosure of the criteria developed by the entity to distinguish investment property from owner-occupied property and from property held for sale in the ordinary course of business, when classification of the property is difficult. *[IAS 1.124]*.

5.1.2 Disclosure of changes in accounting policies

IAS 8 distinguishes between accounting policy changes made pursuant to the initial application of an IFRS and voluntary changes in accounting policy (discussed at 4.4 above). It sets out different disclosure requirements for each, as set out in 5.1.2.A and 5.1.2.B below. Also, if an IFRS is in issue but is not yet effective and has not been applied certain disclosures of its likely impact are required. These are set out in 5.1.2.C below.

5.1.2.A Accounting policy changes pursuant to the initial application of an IFRS

When initial application of an IFRS has an effect on the current period or any prior period, would have such an effect except that it is impracticable to determine the amount of the adjustment, or might have an effect on future periods, an entity should disclose:

(a) the title of the IFRS;
(b) when applicable, that the change in accounting policy is made in accordance with its transitional provisions;
(c) the nature of the change in accounting policy;
(d) when applicable, a description of the transitional provisions;
(e) when applicable, the transitional provisions that might have an effect on future periods;
(f) for the current period and each prior period presented, to the extent practicable, the amount of the adjustment:
   (i) for each financial statement line item affected; and
   (ii) if IAS 33 – *Earnings per Share* – applies to the entity, for basic and diluted earnings per share;
(g) the amount of the adjustment relating to periods before those presented, to the extent practicable; and
(h) if retrospective application required by IAS 8 is impracticable for a particular prior period, or for periods before those presented, the circumstances that led to the existence of that condition and a description of how and from when the change in accounting policy has been applied.

Impracticability of restatement is discussed at 4.7 above. Financial statements of subsequent periods need not repeat these disclosures. *[IAS 8.28].*

5.1.2.B Voluntary changes in accounting policy

When a voluntary change in accounting policy has an effect on the current period or any prior period, would have an effect on that period except that it is impracticable to determine the amount of the adjustment, or might have an effect on future periods, an entity should disclose:

(a) the nature of the change in accounting policy;
(b) the reasons why applying the new accounting policy provides reliable and more relevant information;
(c) for the current period and each prior period presented, to the extent practicable, the amount of the adjustment:
   (i) for each financial statement line item affected; and
   (ii) if IAS 33 applies to the entity, for basic and diluted earnings per share;
(d) the amount of the adjustment relating to periods before those presented, to the extent practicable; and
(e) if retrospective application is impracticable for a particular prior period, or for periods before those presented, the circumstances that led to the existence of that condition and a description of how and from when the change in accounting policy has been applied.

Financial statements of subsequent periods need not repeat these disclosures. *[IAS 8.29].*

Impracticability of restatement is discussed at 4.7 above. Example 3.11 therein illustrates the above disclosure requirements.

5.1.2.C Future impact of a new IFRS

When an entity has not applied a new IFRS that has been issued but is not yet effective, it should disclose:

(a) that fact; and

(b) known or reasonably estimable information relevant to assessing the possible impact that application of the new IFRS will have on the financial statements in the period of initial application. *[IAS 8.30]*.

In producing the above disclosure, the standard requires that an entity should consider disclosing:

(a) the title of the new IFRS;

(b) the nature of the impending change or changes in accounting policy;

(c) the date by which application of the IFRS is required;

(d) the date as at which it plans to apply the IFRS initially; and

(e) either:

  (i) a discussion of the impact that initial application of the IFRS is expected to have on the entity's financial statements; or

  (ii) if that impact is not known or reasonably estimable, a statement to that effect. *[IAS 8.31]*.

5.2 Disclosure of estimation uncertainty and changes in estimates

5.2.1 Sources of estimation uncertainty

Determining the carrying amounts of some assets and liabilities requires estimation of the effects of uncertain future events on those assets and liabilities at the end of the reporting period. Examples given by IAS 1 are that (in the absence of fair values in an active market for identical items used to measure them) the following assets and liabilities require future-oriented estimates to measure them:

- the recoverable amount of classes of property, plant and equipment;
- the effect of technological obsolescence on inventories;
- provisions subject to the future outcome of litigation in progress; and
- long-term employee benefit liabilities such as pension obligations.

These estimates involve assumptions about such items as the risk adjustment to cash flows or discount rates used, future changes in salaries and future changes in prices affecting other costs. *[IAS 1.126]*.

In light of this, IAS 1 requires disclosure of information about the assumptions concerning the future, and other major sources of estimation uncertainty at the end of the reporting period, that have a significant risk of resulting in a material adjustment to the carrying amounts of assets and liabilities *within the next financial year*. In respect of those assets and liabilities, the notes must include details of:

(a) their nature; and

(b) their carrying amount as at the end of the reporting period. *[IAS 1.125]*.

IAS 1 goes on to observe that these assumptions and other sources of estimation uncertainty relate to the estimates that require management's most difficult, subjective or complex judgements. As the number of variables and assumptions affecting the possible future resolution of the uncertainties increases, those judgements become more subjective and complex, and the potential for a consequential material adjustment to the carrying amounts of assets and liabilities normally increases accordingly. *[IAS 1.127]*.

The disclosures are required to be presented in a manner that helps users of financial statements to understand the judgements management makes about the future and about other key sources of estimation uncertainty. The nature and extent of the information provided will vary according to the nature of the assumption and other circumstances. Examples given by the standard of the types of disclosures to be made are:

(a) the nature of the assumption or other estimation uncertainty;

(b) the sensitivity of carrying amounts to the methods, assumptions and estimates underlying their calculation, including the reasons for the sensitivity;

(c) the expected resolution of an uncertainty and the range of reasonably possible outcomes within the next financial year in respect of the carrying amounts of the assets and liabilities affected; and

(d) an explanation of changes made to past assumptions concerning those assets and liabilities, if the uncertainty remains unresolved. *[IAS 1.129]*.

The disclosure of some of these key assumptions is required by other standards. IAS 1 notes the following examples:

- IAS 37 requires disclosure, in specified circumstances, of major assumptions concerning future events affecting classes of provisions; and
- IFRS 13 – *Fair Value Measurement* – requires disclosure of significant assumptions (including the valuation technique(s) and inputs) used when measuring the fair values of assets and liabilities (not just financial ones) that are carried at fair value. *[IAS 1.133]*.

Other examples would include:

- IAS 19 requires disclosure of actuarial assumptions;
- IFRS 2 – *Share-based Payment* – requires disclosure, in certain circumstances, of: the option pricing model used, and the method used and the assumptions made to incorporate the effects of early exercise; and
- IAS 36 – *Impairment of Assets* – requires disclosure, in certain circumstances, of each key assumption on which management has based its cash flow projections.

These assumptions and other sources of estimation uncertainty are not required to be disclosed for assets and liabilities with a significant risk that their carrying amounts might change materially within the next financial year if, at the end of the reporting period, they are measured at fair value based on a quoted price in an active market for an identical asset or liability. *[IAS 1.128]*.

Also, it is not necessary to disclose budget information or forecasts in making the disclosures. *[IAS 1.130]*. Furthermore, the disclosures of particular judgements management made in the process of applying the entity's accounting policies (discussed at 5.1.1.B above) do not relate to the disclosures of sources of estimation uncertainty. *[IAS 1.132]*.

When it is impracticable to disclose the extent of the possible effects of an assumption or another source of estimation uncertainty at the end of the reporting period, the entity should disclose that it is reasonably possible, based on existing knowledge, that outcomes within the next financial year that are different from assumptions could require a material adjustment to the carrying amount of the asset or liability affected. In all cases, the entity should disclose the nature and carrying amount of the specific asset or liability (or class of assets or liabilities) affected by the assumption. *[IAS 1.131]*.

In our view, these requirements of IAS 1 represent potentially highly onerous disclosures. The extensive judgements required in deciding the level of detail to be given has resulted in a wide variety of disclosure in practice. The Basis for Conclusions to the standard reveals that the Board was aware that the requirement could potentially require quite extensive disclosures and explains its attempt to limit this as follows. 'IAS 1 limits the scope of the disclosures to items that have a significant risk of causing a material adjustment to the carrying amounts of assets and liabilities *within the next financial year*. The longer the future period to which the disclosures relate, the greater the range of items that would qualify for disclosure, and the less specific are the disclosures that could be made about particular assets or liabilities. A period longer than the next financial year might obscure the most relevant information with other disclosures.' *[IAS 1.BC84]*. Careful judgement will be required to provide useful and compliant information without reducing the understandability of the financial statement by obscuring material information with immaterial information.

5.2.2 Changes in accounting estimates

IAS 8 requires disclosure of the nature and amount of a change in an accounting estimate that has an effect in the current period or is expected to have an effect in future periods, except for the disclosure of the effect on future periods when it is impracticable to estimate that effect. *[IAS 8.39]*. If the amount of the effect in future periods is not disclosed because estimating it is impracticable, that fact should be disclosed. *[IAS 8.40]*.

5.3 Disclosure of prior period errors

When correction has been made for a material prior period error, IAS 8 requires disclosure of the following:

(a) the nature of the prior period error;

(b) for each prior period presented, to the extent practicable, the amount of the correction:

   (i) for each financial statement line item affected; and

   (ii) if IAS 33 applies to the entity, for basic and diluted earnings per share;

(c) the amount of the correction at the beginning of the earliest prior period presented; and

(d) if retrospective restatement is impracticable for a particular prior period, the circumstances that led to the existence of that condition and a description of how and from when the error has been corrected.

Financial statements of subsequent periods need not repeat these disclosures. *[IAS 8.49].* Example 3.10 at 4.6 above illustrates these disclosure requirements.

5.4 Disclosures about capital

5.4.1 General capital disclosures

The IASB believes that the level of an entity's capital and how it manages it are important factors for users to consider in assessing the risk profile of an entity and its ability to withstand unexpected adverse events. Furthermore, the level of capital might also affect the entity's ability to pay dividends. *[IAS 1.BC86].* For these reasons, IAS 1 requires disclosure of information that enables users of financial statements to evaluate an entity's objectives, policies and processes for managing capital. *[IAS 1.134].*

To achieve this, IAS 1 requires disclosure of the following, which should be based on the information provided internally to the entity's key management personnel: *[IAS 1.135]*

(a) qualitative information about its objectives, policies and processes for managing capital, including:

   (i) a description of what it manages as capital;

   (ii) when an entity is subject to externally imposed capital requirements, the nature of those requirements and how those requirements are incorporated into the management of capital; and

   (iii) how it is meeting its objectives for managing capital;

(b) summary quantitative data about what it manages as capital;

   Some entities regard some financial liabilities (e.g. some forms of subordinated debt) as part of capital. Other entities regard capital as excluding some components of equity (e.g. components arising from cash flow hedges);

(c) any changes in (a) and (b) from the previous period;

(d) whether during the period it complied with any externally imposed capital requirements to which it is subject; and

(e) when the entity has not complied with such externally imposed capital requirements, the consequences of such non-compliance.

IAS 1 observes that capital may be managed in a number of ways and be subject to a number of different capital requirements. For example, a conglomerate may include entities that undertake insurance activities and banking activities, and those entities may also operate in several jurisdictions. When an aggregate disclosure of capital requirements and how capital is managed would not provide useful information or distorts a financial statement user's understanding of an entity's capital resources, the standard requires disclosure of separate information for each capital requirement to which the entity is subject. *[IAS 1.136].*

Examples 3.12 and 3.13 below are based on the illustrative examples of capital disclosures contained in the implementation guidance accompanying IAS 1. *[IAS 1.IG10-11].*

Example 3.12: Illustrative capital disclosures: An entity that is not a regulated financial institution

The following example illustrates the application of the requirements discussed above for an entity that is not a financial institution and is not subject to an externally imposed capital requirement. In this example, the entity monitors capital using a debt-to-adjusted capital ratio. Other entities may use different methods to monitor capital. The example is also relatively simple. An entity should decide, in the light of its circumstances, how much detail to provide.

Facts

Group A manufactures and sells cars. It includes a finance subsidiary that provides finance to customers, primarily in the form of leases. Group A is not subject to any externally imposed capital requirements.

Example disclosure

The Group's objectives when managing capital are:

- to safeguard the entity's ability to continue as a going concern, so that it can continue to provide returns for shareholders and benefits for other stakeholders; and
- to provide an adequate return to shareholders by pricing products and services commensurately with the level of risk.

The Group sets the amount of capital in proportion to risk. The Group manages the capital structure and makes adjustments to it in the light of changes in economic conditions and the risk characteristics of the underlying assets. In order to maintain or adjust the capital structure, the Group may adjust the amount of dividends paid to shareholders, return capital to shareholders, issue new shares, or sell assets to reduce debt.

Consistently with others in the industry, the Group monitors capital on the basis of the debt-to-adjusted capital ratio. This ratio is calculated as net debt ÷ adjusted capital. Net debt is calculated as total debt (as shown in the statement of financial position) less cash and cash equivalents. Adjusted capital comprises all components of equity (i.e. share capital, share premium, non-controlling interests, retained earnings, and revaluation surplus) other than amounts accumulated in equity relating to cash flow hedges, and includes some forms of subordinated debt.

During 2018, the Group's strategy, which was unchanged from 2017, was to maintain the debt-to-adjusted capital ratio at the lower end of the range 6:1 to 7:1, in order to secure access to finance at a reasonable cost by maintaining a BB credit rating. The debt-to-adjusted capital ratios at 31 December 2018 and at 31 December 2017 were as follows:

	2018 €million	2017 €million
Total debt	1,000	1,100
Less: cash and cash equivalents	(90)	(150)
Net debt	910	950
Total equity	110	105
Add: subordinated debt instruments	38	38
Less: amounts accumulated in equity relating to cash flow hedges	(10)	(5)
Adjusted capital	138	138
Debt-to-adjusted capital ratio	6.6	6.9

The decrease in the debt-to-adjusted capital ratio during 2018 resulted primarily from the reduction in net debt that occurred on the sale of subsidiary Z. As a result of this reduction in net debt, improved profitability and lower levels of managed receivables, the dividend payment was increased to €2.8 million for 2018 (from €2.5 million for 2017).

Example 3.13: Illustrative capital disclosures: An entity that has not complied with externally imposed capital requirements

The following example illustrates the application of the requirement to disclose when an entity has not complied with externally imposed capital requirements during the period. Other disclosures would be provided to comply with the other requirements relating to capital.

Facts

Entity A provides financial services to its customers and is subject to capital requirements imposed by Regulator B. During the year ended 31 December 2018, Entity A did not comply with the capital requirements imposed by Regulator B. In its financial statements for the year ended 31 December 2018, Entity A provides the following disclosure relating to its non-compliance.

Example disclosure

Entity A filed its quarterly regulatory capital return for 30 September 2018 on 20 October 2018. At that date, Entity A's regulatory capital was below the capital requirement imposed by Regulator B by $1 million. As a result, Entity A was required to submit a plan to the regulator indicating how it would increase its regulatory capital to the amount required. Entity A submitted a plan that entailed selling part of its unquoted equities portfolio with a carrying amount of $11.5 million in the fourth quarter of 2018. In the fourth quarter of 2018, Entity A sold its fixed interest investment portfolio for $12.6 million and met its regulatory capital requirement.

5.4.2 Puttable financial instruments classified as equity

IAS 32 allows certain liabilities called 'puttable financial instruments' to be classified as equity. Puttable financial instrument is a term defined and discussed at length in IAS 32 (see Chapter 45 at 4.6). The IASB observes that 'Financial instruments classified as equity usually do not include any obligation for the entity to deliver a financial asset to another party. Therefore, the Board concluded that additional disclosures are needed in these circumstances.' *[IAS 1.BC100B].*

The required disclosure for puttable financial instruments classified as equity instruments is as follows:

(a) summary quantitative data about the amount classified as equity;

(b) its objectives, policies and processes for managing its obligation to repurchase or redeem the instruments when required to do so by the instrument holders, including any changes from the previous period;

(c) the expected cash outflow on redemption or repurchase of that class of financial instruments; and

(d) information about how the expected cash outflow on redemption or repurchase was determined. *[IAS 1.136A].*

5.5 Other disclosures

IAS 1 also requires disclosure:

(a) in the notes of:
 (i) the amount of dividends proposed or declared before the financial statements were authorised for issue but not recognised as a distribution to owners during the period, and the related amount per share; and
 (ii) the amount of any cumulative preference dividends not recognised; *[IAS 1.137]*

(b) in accordance with IAS 10 – *Events after the Reporting Period* – the following non-adjusting events in respect of loans classified as current liabilities, if they occur between the end of the reporting period and the date the financial statements are authorised for issue (see Chapter 36 at 2.1.1):
 (i) refinancing on a long-term basis;
 (ii) rectification of a breach of a long-term loan arrangement; and
 (iii) the granting by the lender of a period of grace to rectify a breach of a long-term loan arrangement ending at least twelve months after the reporting period; *[IAS 1.76]*

(c) the following, if not disclosed elsewhere in information published with the financial statements:
 (i) the domicile and legal form of the entity, its country of incorporation and the address of its registered office (or principal place of business, if different from the registered office);
 (ii) a description of the nature of the entity's operations and its principal activities;
 (iii) the name of the parent and the ultimate parent of the group; and
 (iv) if it is a limited life entity, information regarding the length of its life. *[IAS 1.138]*.

6 FUTURE DEVELOPMENTS

The IASB is pursuing a number of matters which relate to the subjects discussed in this chapter.

The board groups its projects into four categories: standard-setting, maintenance, research and other. We discuss below the current projects relevant to this chapter under these headings.[3]

6.1 Standard-setting projects

The board has three relevant standard-setting projects as follows.

6.1.1 Definition of material (amendments to IAS 1 and IAS 8)

The Board will propose clarifying the definition of what information is material in preparing financial statements and at the time of writing intended to publish an exposure draft in 2017.

6.1.2 *Materiality practice statement*

In this project the IASB is considering how materiality is being applied in practice to disclosures in IFRS financial statements. The IASB has decided to provide guidance on the application of materiality, which will take the form of a Practice Statement. In October 2015 the Board published an Exposure Draft: *IFRS Practice Statement Application of Materiality to Financial Statements* to obtain feedback from parties with an interest in financial reporting.

The introduction to the ED explains that its aim is to provide guidance to assist management in applying the concept of materiality to general purpose financial statements prepared in accordance with IFRS. It notes that in this context information is material if omitting or misstating it could influence decisions that users make on the basis of financial information about a specific reporting entity.

In furtherance of this aim, the ED provides guidance in the following three main areas:

- characteristics of materiality;
- how to apply the concept of materiality when making decisions about presenting and disclosing information in the financial statements; and
- how to assess whether omissions and misstatements of information are material to the financial statements.

At the time of writing the IASB website indicates that the Board plans to publish the Practice Statement 'later in 2017'. It will be non-mandatory and will come into effect immediately.

6.1.3 *The IASB's Conceptual Framework*

The IASB is in the process of revising its conceptual framework. Although not actually accounting standard, the framework is relevant to the presentation and disclosure of financial statements; it is discussed in Chapter 2 at 3. The Board expects to publish the revised Conceptual Framework around the end of 2017.

6.2 Maintenance projects

6.2.1 *Distinction between a change in an accounting policy and a change in an accounting estimate*

The IASB is considering amending IAS 8 to clarify the existing distinction between a change in accounting policy and a change in accounting estimate.

In its April 2016 meeting, the Board tentatively decided to amend the definitions of accounting policies and changes in accounting estimates in IAS 8 in order to:

- clarify the definitions of accounting policies and of changes in accounting estimates with the objective of making them more concise and distinctive;
- clarify how accounting policies and estimates relate to each other;
- add guidance about whether changes in valuation techniques and in estimation techniques are changes in accounting estimates; and
- update examples of estimates provided in IAS 8.

At the time of writing the Board was aiming to publish an exposure draft in September 2017.

6.2.2 *Accounting policy changes (amendments to IAS 8)*

The IASB has tentatively decided to amend IAS 8 to lower the 'impracticability' threshold regarding retrospective application of voluntary changes in accounting policies that result from agenda decisions taken by the Interpretations Committee. The proposed threshold would include a consideration of the benefits and costs of applying the change retrospectively. The intention of the board is to publish an exposure draft in the first half of 2018.

6.2.3 *Proposed clarifications to the classification of liabilities*

In February 2015 the IASB published Exposure Draft ED/2015/1 *Classification of Liabilities*. The aim of the proposal is to clarify the criteria for the classification of a liability as current or non-current. To do this, the exposure draft:

- clarifies that the rights which are relevant to the determination are those in existence at the end of the reporting period; and
- proposes limited word changes to make the terminology used in the guidance consistent throughout.

The proposals also contain a clarification of the link between the settlement of a liability and the outflow of resources.

The comment period expired in June 2015. At the time of writing, the website of the IASB indicates that the Board will continue its discussion alongside the final stages of revising the *Conceptual Framework for Financial Reporting*. This is expected to be around the end of 2017 and the Board intends to issue revisions to IAS 1 in the first half of 2018.

6.3 Research projects

The IASB is pursuing two research projects, discussed below.

6.3.1 *Principles of disclosure*

In March 2016 the IASB published Discussion Paper DP/2017/1 *Disclosure Initiative – Principles of Disclosure*.

The main objective of the project is to identify disclosure issues and develop new, or clarify existing, disclosure principles in IFRS Standards to address those issues and to:

- help entities to apply better judgement and communicate information more effectively;
- improve the effectiveness of disclosures for the primary users of financial statements; and
- assist the Board to improve disclosure requirements in Standards.

The Board intends to publish a feedback paper in the first half of 2018.

6.3.2 *Primary financial statements*

The Board is exploring targeted improvements to the structure and content of the primary financial statements, with a focus on the statement(s) of financial performance.

The Board will continue its discussions through the second half of 2017 before deciding whether to publish a Discussion Paper or an Exposure Draft.

References

1 *IFRIC Update*, March 2017.
2 *IFRIC Update*, January 2014.
3 *IASB website*, August 2017.

Chapter 4 Non-current assets held for sale and discontinued operations

List of examples

Chapter 4 Non-current assets held for sale and discontinued operations

1 OBJECTIVE AND SCOPE OF IFRS 5

The objective of IFRS 5 – *Non-current Assets Held for Sale and Discontinued Operations* – is to specify the accounting for assets held for sale, and the presentation and disclosure of discontinued operations. In particular, the standard requires that non-current assets (and, in a 'disposal group', related liabilities and current assets, discussed at 2.1.1 below) meeting its criteria to be classified as held for sale be:

(a) measured at the lower of carrying amount and fair value less costs to sell, with depreciation on them ceasing; and

(b) presented separately on the face of the statement of financial position with the results of discontinued operations presented separately in the statement of comprehensive income. *[IFRS 5.1]*.

The classification and presentation requirements apply to all recognised non-current assets and disposal groups, while there are certain exceptions to the measurement provisions of the standard. *[IFRS 5.2, 5]*. These issues are discussed further at 2.2 below.

The classification, presentation and measurement requirements of IFRS 5 applicable to assets (or disposal groups) classified as held for sale also apply to those classified as held for distribution to owners acting in their capacity as owners. *[IFRS 5.5A]*. This is discussed at 2.1.2 below.

2 NON-CURRENT ASSETS (AND DISPOSAL GROUPS) HELD FOR SALE OR HELD FOR DISTRIBUTION TO OWNERS

2.1 Classification of non-current assets (and disposal groups) held for sale or held for distribution to owners

IFRS 5 frequently refers to current assets and non-current assets. It provides a definition of each term as follows:

'An entity shall classify an asset as current when:

(a) it expects to realise the asset, or intends to sell or consume it in its normal operating cycle;

(b) it holds the asset primarily for the purpose of trading;

(c) it expects to realise the asset within twelve months after the reporting period; or

(d) the asset is cash or a cash equivalent (as defined in IAS 7 – *Statement of Cash Flows*) unless the asset is restricted from being exchanged or used to settle a liability for at least twelve months after the reporting period.'

A non-current asset is 'an asset that does not meet the definition of a current asset'. *[IFRS 5 Appendix A].*

These definitions are the same as those in IAS 1 – *Presentation of Financial Statements* (discussed in Chapter 3 at 3.1.1).

2.1.1 The concept of a disposal group

As its title suggests, IFRS 5 addresses the accounting treatment of non-current assets held for sale, that is assets whose carrying amount will be recovered principally through sale rather than continuing use in the business. *[IFRS 5.6].* However, the standard also applies to certain liabilities and current assets where they form part of a 'disposal group'.

The standard observes that sometimes an entity will dispose of a group of assets, possibly with some directly associated liabilities, together in a single transaction. *[IFRS 5.4].* A common example would be the disposal of a subsidiary. For these circumstances, IFRS 5 introduces the concept of a disposal group, which it defines as a group of assets to be disposed of, by sale or otherwise, together as a group in a single transaction, and liabilities directly associated with those assets that will be transferred in the transaction. The group includes goodwill acquired in a business combination if the group is a cash-generating unit to which goodwill has been allocated in accordance with the requirements of IAS 36 – *Impairment of Assets* (discussed in Chapter 20) or if it is an operation within such a cash-generating unit. *[IFRS 5 Appendix A].*

The use of the phrase 'together in a single transaction' indicates that the only liabilities that can be included in the group are those assumed by the purchaser. Accordingly, any borrowings of the entity which are to be repaid out of the sales proceeds would be excluded from the disposal group.

The standard goes on to explain that a disposal group:

- may be a group of cash-generating units, a single cash-generating unit, or part of a cash-generating unit. Once the cash flows from an asset or group of assets are expected to arise principally from sale rather than continuing use, they become less dependent on cash flows arising from other assets, and a disposal group that was part of a cash-generating unit becomes a separate cash-generating unit; and
- may include any assets and any liabilities of the entity, including current assets, current liabilities and assets outside the scope of the measurement requirements of IFRS 5 (see 2.2 below). *[IFRS 5.4].*

Discontinued operations are discussed at 3 below. As noted there, it seems highly unlikely that the definition of a discontinued operation would ever be met by a single non-current asset. Accordingly, a discontinued operation will also be a disposal group.

2.1.2 Classification as held for sale or as held for distribution to owners

IFRS 5 requires a non-current asset (or disposal group) to be classified as held for sale if its carrying amount will be recovered principally through a sale transaction rather than through continuing use. *[IFRS 5.6].* For these purposes, sale transactions include exchanges of non-current assets for other non-current assets when the exchange has commercial substance in accordance with IAS 16 – *Property, Plant and Equipment* (discussed in Chapter 18 at 4.4). *[IFRS 5.10].* For assets classified according to a liquidity presentation (see Chapter 3 at 3.1.1), non-current assets are taken to be assets that include amounts expected to be recovered more than twelve months after the reporting date. *[IFRS 5.2].*

Determining whether (and when) an asset stops being recovered principally through use and becomes recoverable principally through sale is the critical distinction, and much of the standard is devoted to explaining how to make the determination.

For an asset (or disposal group) to be classified as held for sale:

(a) it must be available for immediate sale in its present condition, subject only to terms that are usual and customary for sales of such assets (or disposal groups);

(b) its sale must be highly probable; *[IFRS 5.7]* and

(c) it must genuinely be sold, not abandoned. *[IFRS 5.13].*

These criteria are discussed further below. If an asset (or disposal group) has been classified as held for sale, but these criteria cease to be met, an entity should cease to classify the asset (or disposal group) as held for sale. *[IFRS 5.26].* Changes in disposal plans are discussed at 2.2.5 below.

Slightly different criteria apply when an entity acquires a non-current asset (or disposal group) exclusively with a view to its subsequent disposal. In that case it should only classify the non-current asset (or disposal group) as held for sale at the acquisition date if:

- the 'one-year requirement' is met subject to its one exception (this is part of being 'highly probable', discussed at 2.1.2.B below); and
- it is highly probable that any other criteria in (a) and (b) above that are not met at that date will be met within a short period following the acquisition (usually within three months). *[IFRS 5.11].*

The standard also makes it clear that the criteria in (a) and (b) above must be met at the reporting date for a non-current asset (or disposal group) to be classified as held for sale in those financial statements. However, if those criteria are met after the reporting date but before the authorisation of the financial statements for issue, the standard requires certain additional disclosures (discussed at 5 below). *[IFRS 5.12]*.

The classification, presentation and measurement requirements of IFRS 5 applicable to assets (or disposal groups) classified as held for sale also apply to those classified as held for distribution to owners acting in their capacity as owners. *[IFRS 5.5A]*. This applies when an entity is committed to distribute the asset (or disposal group) to its owners. For this to be the case, the assets must be available for immediate distribution in their present condition and the distribution must be highly probable.

2.1.2.A Meaning of available for immediate sale

To qualify for classification as held for sale, a non-current asset (or disposal group) must be available for immediate sale in its present condition subject only to terms that are usual and customary for sales of such assets (or disposal groups). This is taken to mean that an entity currently has the intention and ability to transfer the asset (or disposal group) to a buyer in its present condition. The standard illustrates this concept with the following examples. *[IFRS 5.IG1-3]*.

Example 4.1: Meaning of 'available for immediate sale'

1 Disposal of a headquarters building

An entity is committed to a plan to sell its headquarters building and has initiated actions to locate a buyer.

(a) The entity intends to transfer the building to a buyer after it vacates the building. The time necessary to vacate the building is usual and customary for sales of such assets. The criterion of being available for immediate sale would therefore be met at the plan commitment date.

(b) The entity will continue to use the building until construction of a new headquarters building is completed. The entity does not intend to transfer the existing building to a buyer until after construction of the new building is completed (and it vacates the existing building). The delay in the timing of the transfer of the existing building imposed by the entity (seller) demonstrates that the building is not available for immediate sale. The criterion would not be met until construction of the new building is completed, even if a firm purchase commitment for the future transfer of the existing building is obtained earlier.

2 Sale of a manufacturing facility

An entity is committed to a plan to sell a manufacturing facility and has initiated actions to locate a buyer. At the plan commitment date, there is a backlog of uncompleted customer orders.

(a) The entity intends to sell the manufacturing facility with its operations. Any uncompleted customer orders at the sale date will be transferred to the buyer. The transfer of uncompleted customer orders at the sale date will not affect the timing of the transfer of the facility. The criterion of being available for immediate sale would therefore be met at the plan commitment date.

(b) The entity intends to sell the manufacturing facility, but without its operations. The entity does not intend to transfer the facility to a buyer until after it ceases all operations of the facility and eliminates the backlog of uncompleted customer orders. The delay in the timing of the transfer of the facility imposed by the entity (seller) demonstrates that the facility is not available for immediate sale. The criterion would not be met until the operations of the facility cease, even if a firm purchase commitment for the future transfer of the facility were obtained earlier.

3 Land and buildings acquired through foreclosure

An entity acquires through foreclosure a property comprising land and buildings that it intends to sell.

(a) The entity does not intend to transfer the property to a buyer until after it completes renovations to increase the property's sales value. The delay in the timing of the transfer of the property imposed by the entity (seller) demonstrates that the property is not available for immediate sale. The criterion of being available for immediate sale would therefore not be met until the renovations are completed.

(b) After the renovations are completed and the property is classified as held for sale but before a firm purchase commitment is obtained, the entity becomes aware of environmental damage requiring remediation. The entity still intends to sell the property. However, the entity does not have the ability to transfer the property to a buyer until after the remediation is completed. The delay in the timing of the transfer of the property imposed by others *before* a firm purchase commitment is obtained demonstrates that the property is not available for immediate sale (different requirements could apply if this happened *after* a firm commitment is obtained, as illustrated in scenario (b) of Example 4.2 below). The criterion that the asset be available for immediate sale would not continue to be met. The property would be reclassified as held and used in accordance with the requirements discussed at 2.2.5 below.

2.1.2.B Meaning of highly probable

Many observers may consider the meaning of 'highly probable' to be reasonably self-evident, albeit highly judgemental. However, IFRS 5 provides extensive discussion of the topic. As a first step, the term is defined by the standard as meaning 'significantly more likely than probable'. This is supplemented by a second definition – probable is defined as 'more likely than not'. *[IFRS 5 Appendix A]*. Substituting the latter into the former leads to a definition of highly probable as meaning 'significantly more likely than more likely than not'.

The standard goes on to elaborate as follows:

For the sale to be highly probable:

- the appropriate level of management must be committed to a plan to sell the asset (or disposal group);
- an active programme to locate a buyer and complete the plan must have been initiated;
- the asset (or disposal group) must be actively marketed for sale at a price that is reasonable in relation to its current fair value;
- the sale should be expected to qualify for recognition as a completed sale within one year from the date of classification (although in certain circumstances this period may be extended as discussed below); and
- actions required to complete the plan should indicate that it is unlikely that significant changes to the plan will be made or that the plan will be withdrawn. *[IFRS 5.8]*.

As noted above, the classification, presentation and measurement requirements of IFRS 5 applicable to assets (or disposal groups) classified as held for sale also apply to those classified as held for distribution to owners acting in their capacity as owners (see 2.1.2 above). *[IFRS 5.5A]*.

For the distribution to be highly probable, actions to complete the distribution must have been initiated and should be expected to be completed within one year from the date of classification. Actions required to complete the distribution should indicate that it is unlikely that significant changes to the distribution will be made or that the distribution will not be completed. Whilst judgement will be needed in individual circumstances, relevant actions to consider could include: the steps taken by management to prepare for the distribution, board decisions illustrating the commitment to the planned distribution, and steps taken to organise the meeting of shareholders, if their approval is required. The probability of shareholders' approval, if this is required, should be considered as part of the assessment of whether the distribution is highly probable. *[IFRS 5.12A]*.

The basic rule above that for qualification as held for sale the sale should be expected to qualify for recognition as a completed sale within one year from the date of classification (the 'one year rule') is applied quite strictly by the standard. In particular, that criterion would not be met if:

(a) an entity that is a commercial leasing and finance company is holding for sale or lease equipment that has recently ceased to be leased and the ultimate form of a future transaction (sale or lease) has not yet been determined;

(b) an entity is committed to a plan to 'sell' a property that is in use, and the transfer of the property will be accounted for as a sale and finance leaseback. *[IFRS 5.IG4]*.

In (a), the entity does not yet know whether the asset will be sold at all and hence may not presume that it will be sold within a year. In (b), whilst in legal form the asset has been sold it will not be *recognised* as sold in the financial statements.

As indicated above, the standard contains an exception to the one year rule. It states that events or circumstances may extend the period to complete the sale beyond one year. Such an extension would not preclude an asset (or disposal group) from being classified as held for sale if the delay is caused by events or circumstances beyond the entity's control and there is sufficient evidence that the entity remains committed to its plan to sell the asset (or disposal group). This will be the case in the following situations: *[IFRS 5.9]*

(a) at the date an entity commits itself to a plan to sell a non-current asset (or disposal group) it reasonably expects that others (not a buyer) will impose conditions on the transfer of the asset (or disposal group) that will extend the period required to complete the sale; and:
  - (i) actions necessary to respond to those conditions cannot be initiated until after a firm purchase commitment is obtained; and
  - (ii) a firm purchase commitment is highly probable within one year;

(b) an entity obtains a firm purchase commitment and, as a result, a buyer or others unexpectedly impose conditions on the transfer of a non-current asset (or disposal group) previously classified as held for sale that will extend the period required to complete the sale; and
  - (i) timely actions necessary to respond to the conditions have been taken; and
  - (ii) a favourable resolution of the delaying factors is expected;

(c) during the initial one year period, circumstances arise that were previously considered unlikely and, as a result, a non-current asset (or disposal group) previously classified as held for sale is not sold by the end of that period; and
  - (i) during the initial one year period the entity took action necessary to respond to the change in circumstances;
  - (ii) the non-current asset (or disposal group) is being actively marketed at a price that is reasonable, given the change in circumstances; and
  - (iii) the non-current asset (or disposal group) remains available for immediate sale and the sale is highly probable. *[IFRS 5 Appendix B]*.

Firm purchase commitment is a defined term in IFRS 5, meaning an agreement with an unrelated party, binding on both parties and usually legally enforceable, that:

- specifies all significant terms, including the price and timing of the transactions; and
- includes a disincentive for non-performance that is sufficiently large to make performance highly probable. *[IFRS 5 Appendix A].*

The word 'binding' in this definition seems to envisage an agreement still being subject to contingencies. The standard provides an example where a 'firm purchase commitment' exists but is subject to regulatory approval (see scenario (a) in Example 4.2 below). In our view, to be 'binding' in this sense a contingent agreement should be only subject to contingencies outside the control of both parties.

The standard illustrates each of these exceptions to the one year rule with the following examples. *[IFRS 5.IG5-7].*

Example 4.2: Exceptions to the 'one year rule'

Scenario illustrating (a) above

An entity in the power generating industry is committed to a plan to sell a disposal group that represents a significant portion of its regulated operations. The sale requires regulatory approval, which could extend the period required to complete the sale beyond one year. Actions necessary to obtain that approval cannot be initiated until after a buyer is known and a firm purchase commitment is obtained. However, a firm purchase commitment is highly probable within one year. In that situation, the conditions for an exception to the one year requirement would be met.

Scenario illustrating (b) above

An entity is committed to a plan to sell a manufacturing facility in its present condition and classifies the facility as held for sale at that date. After a firm purchase commitment is obtained, the buyer's inspection of the property identifies environmental damage not previously known to exist. The entity is required by the buyer to make good the damage, which will extend the period required to complete the sale beyond one year. However, the entity has initiated actions to make good the damage, and satisfactory rectification of the damage is highly probable. In that situation, the conditions for an exception to the one year requirement would be met.

Scenario illustrating (c) above

An entity is committed to a plan to sell a non-current asset and classifies the asset as held for sale at that date.

(a) During the initial one year period, the market conditions that existed at the date the asset was classified initially as held for sale deteriorate and, as a result, the asset is not sold by the end of that period. During that period, the entity actively solicited but did not receive any reasonable offers to purchase the asset and, in response, reduced the price. The asset continues to be actively marketed at a price that is reasonable given the change in market conditions, and the criteria regarding availability for immediate sale which is highly probable are therefore met. In that situation, the conditions for an exception to the one year requirement would be met. At the end of the initial one year period, the asset would continue to be classified as held for sale.

(b) During the following one year period, market conditions deteriorate further, and the asset is not sold by the end of that period. The entity believes that the market conditions will improve and has not further reduced the price of the asset. The asset continues to be held for sale, but at a price in excess of its current fair value. In that situation, the absence of a price reduction demonstrates that the asset is not available for immediate sale. In addition, to meet the condition that a sale be highly probable also requires an asset to be marketed at a price that is reasonable in relation to its current fair value. Therefore, the conditions for an exception to the one year requirement would not be met. The asset would be reclassified as held and used in accordance with the requirements discussed at 2.2.5 below.

2.1.2.C Abandonment

IFRS 5 stipulates that a non-current asset (or disposal group) that is to be abandoned should not be classified as held for sale. This includes non-current assets (or disposal groups) that are to be used to the end of their economic life and non-current assets (or disposal groups) that are to be closed rather than sold. The standard explains that this is because its carrying amount will be recovered principally through continuing use. *[IFRS 5.13].*

If the disposal group to be abandoned meets the criteria for being a discontinued operation the standard requires it to be treated as such in the period in which the abandonment occurs. *[IFRS 5.13].* This is discussed at 3.1 below. However, a non-current asset that has been temporarily taken out of use should not be accounted for as if it had been abandoned. *[IFRS 5.14].* An example given by the standard is of a manufacturing plant that ceases to be used because demand for its product has declined but which is maintained in workable condition and is expected to be brought back into use if demand picks up. The plant is not regarded as abandoned. *[IFRS 5.IG8].* However, in these circumstances an impairment loss may need to be recognised in accordance with IAS 36 (discussed in Chapter 20).

2.1.3 Partial disposals of operations

2.1.3.A Loss of control of a subsidiary

The standard provides that when an entity is committed to a sale plan involving loss of control of a subsidiary it should classify all the assets and liabilities of that subsidiary as held for sale when the relevant criteria are met (see 2.1 above). This is regardless of whether it will retain a non-controlling interest in the former subsidiary after the sale, such as for instance an interest in an associate or a joint venture. *[IFRS 5.8A].*

If the retained interest represents a joint operation, it could be argued that, since the entity retains a direct interest in the underlying assets and obligations for the liabilities after the disposal, the transaction is in substance a sale of parts of the underlying assets and liabilities. On that basis, only the disposed of parts of the assets and liabilities would be classified as held for sale. The counter argument is that the requirement in IFRS 5 does not scope out situations in which the retained interest represents a joint operation. Furthermore, the loss of control of a subsidiary is a significant economic event in that it changes the relationship between the entity and the investee fundamentally, and therefore it would be appropriate to classify all assets and liabilities of the subsidiary as held for sale. Some further argue that classification as held for sale will depend on whether the operation of the joint operation represents a business. If it does, it could be argued that the principles of IFRS 3 – *Business Combinations* – should be applied, which demonstrates that effectively all assets and liabilities of the subsidiary are being disposed of. On that analysis, classification of all assets and liabilities of the subsidiary as held for sale is appropriate. However, as the standard is not explicit, judgement will be required.

If the subsidiary in question meets the definition of a discontinued operation, the standard's presentation and disclosure requirements for discontinued operations apply (see 3.2 below). *[IFRS 5.36A].*

IFRS 5 does not explicitly extend these requirements to loss of control of a subsidiary in other ways. Given the alignment of the rules on sales with distributions to owners, it seems clear that partial distributions triggering loss of control would result in held for distribution classification.

However, control may be lost in other ways. Examples would include a subsidiary issuing shares to third parties, or control established by contract coming to an end.

The Basis for Conclusions on the standard sheds some light on the views of the Board. In particular, the following:

'At the date control is lost, all the subsidiary's assets and liabilities are derecognised and any investment retained in the former subsidiary is recognised. Loss of control is a significant economic event that changes the nature of an investment. The parent-subsidiary relationship ceases to exist and an investor-investee relationship begins that differs significantly from the former parent-subsidiary relationship. Therefore, the new investor-investee relationship is recognised and measured initially at the date when control is lost.

'The Board concluded that, under the sale plan described above, the controlling interest in the subsidiary is, in substance, exchanged for a non-controlling interest. Therefore, in the Board's view, being committed to a plan involving loss of control of a subsidiary should trigger classification as held for sale.' *[IFRS 5.BC24B-24C]*.

This, and the fact that the standard applies to assets held for distribution to owners, may suggest that the explicit rules for partial *sales* of assets resulting in loss of control should also apply to loss of control from other causes. However, the standard is not explicit, and the IFRIC concluded in January 2016[1] that it could not resolve the issue, and decided it should be considered for a broad-scope project on IFRS 5 (future developments of IFRS 5 are discussed at 6 below). In the meantime, judgement will be required.

2.1.3.B Partial disposal of an associate or joint venture

In accordance with IAS 28 – *Investments in Associates and Joint Ventures*, IFRS 5 will apply to an investment, or a portion of an investment, in an associate or a joint venture that meets the criteria to be classified as held for sale (see 2.1.2 above). Any retained portion of such an investment that has not been so classified should be accounted for using the equity method until disposal of the portion that is classified as held for sale takes place. After the disposal takes place, any retained interest should be accounted for in accordance with IFRS 9 – *Financial Instruments* – unless the retained interest continues to be an associate or a joint venture, in which case the equity method should be used.

If such an investment ceases to be classified as held for sale, it should be accounted for using the equity method retrospectively from the date of its original classification as held for sale. Financial statements for the periods since classification as held for sale should be amended accordingly. *[IAS 28.20, 21]*.

2.2 Measurement of non-current assets (and disposal groups) held for sale

2.2.1 *Scope of the measurement requirements*

IFRS 5's classification and presentation requirements apply to all recognised non-current assets (which is defined in the same way as in IAS 1, discussed at 2.1 above) and disposal groups. However, the measurement provisions of the standard do not apply to the following assets (which remain covered by the standards listed) either as individual assets or as part of a disposal group: *[IFRS 5.2, 5]*

(a) deferred tax assets (dealt with in IAS 12 – *Income Taxes*);

(b) assets arising from employee benefits (dealt with in IAS 19 – *Employee Benefits*);

(c) financial assets within the scope of IFRS 9;

(d) non-current assets that are accounted for in accordance with the fair value model in IAS 40 – *Investment Property*;

(e) non-current assets that are measured at fair value less costs to sell in accordance with IAS 41 – *Agriculture*; and

(f) contractual rights under insurance contracts as defined in IFRS 4 – *Insurance Contracts*.

2.2.2 *Measurement of non-current assets and disposal groups held for sale*

2.2.2.A *Measurement on initial classification as held for sale*

IFRS 5 requires that immediately before the initial classification of an asset (or disposal group) as held for sale, the carrying amount of the asset (or all the assets and liabilities in the group) should be measured in accordance with applicable IFRSs. *[IFRS 5.18]*. In other words, an entity should apply its usual accounting policies up until the criteria for classification as held for sale are met.

Thereafter a non-current asset (or disposal group) classified as held for sale should be measured at the lower of its carrying amount and fair value less costs to sell. *[IFRS 5.15]*. IFRS 13 – *Fair Value Measurement* – defines fair value as 'the price that would be received to sell an asset or paid to transfer a liability in an orderly transaction between market participants at the measurement date' (see Chapter 14). *[IFRS 13.9]*. Costs to sell are defined as 'the incremental costs directly attributable to the disposal of an asset (or disposal group), excluding finance costs and income tax expense.' *[IFRS 5 Appendix A]*. When the sale is expected to occur beyond one year, the costs to sell should be measured at their present value. Any increase in the present value of the costs to sell that arises from the passage of time should be presented in profit or loss as a financing cost. *[IFRS 5.17]*. For disposal groups, the standard adopts a portfolio approach. It requires that if a non-current asset within the scope of its measurement requirements is part of a disposal group, the measurement requirements should apply to the group as a whole, so that the group is measured at the lower of its carrying amount and fair value less costs to sell. *[IFRS 5.4]*. It will still be necessary to apportion any write down to the underlying assets of the disposal group, but no element is apportioned to items outside the scope of the standard's measurement provisions. This is discussed further at 2.2.3 below.

Items held for distribution to owners should be measured at the lower of carrying amount and fair value less costs to distribute. Costs to distribute are incremental costs directly attributable to the distribution, excluding finance costs and income tax expense. *[IFRS 5.15A].*

If a newly acquired asset (or disposal group) meets the criteria to be classified as held for sale (which, as discussed at 2.1.2 above, are subtly different for assets acquired exclusively with a view to subsequent disposal), applying the above requirements will result in the asset (or disposal group) being measured on initial recognition at the lower of its carrying amount had it not been so classified (for example, cost) and fair value less costs to sell. This means that if the asset (or disposal group) is acquired as part of a business combination, it will be measured at fair value less costs to sell. *[IFRS 5.16].*

The implementation guidance accompanying the standard provides the following illustration of a subsidiary acquired with a view to sale. *[IFRS 5.IG13].*

Example 4.3: Measuring and presenting subsidiaries acquired with a view to sale and classified as held for sale

Entity A acquires an entity H, which is a holding company with two subsidiaries, S1 and S2. S2 is acquired exclusively with a view to sale and meets the criteria to be classified as held for sale. Accordingly, S2 is also a discontinued operation (see 3.1 below).

The fair value less costs to sell of S2 is €135. A accounts for S2 as follows:

- initially, A measures the identifiable liabilities of S2 at fair value, say at €40;
- initially, A measures the acquired assets as the fair value less costs to sell of S2 (€135) plus the fair value of the identifiable liabilities (€40), i.e. at €175;
- at the reporting date, A remeasures the disposal group at the lower of its cost and fair value less costs to sell, say at €130. The liabilities are remeasured in accordance with applicable IFRSs, say at €35. The total assets are measured at €130 + €35, i.e. at €165;
- at the reporting date, A presents the assets and liabilities separately from other assets and liabilities in its consolidated financial statements as illustrated in Example 4.5 at 2.2.4 below; and
- in the statement of comprehensive income, A presents the total of the post-tax profit or loss of S2 and the post-tax gain or loss recognised on the subsequent remeasurement of S2, which equals the remeasurement of the disposal group from €135 to €130.

Further analysis of the assets and liabilities or of the change in value of the disposal group is not required.

The final sentence in the above example says no further analysis of the assets and liabilities is required. This must refer to there being no such disclosure requirement for financial statements. A detailed purchase price analysis and tracking of the acquired entity may still be needed, notwithstanding a partial relaxation of what is required to be disclosed by IFRS 5. This may be needed to be able to determine the split between gross assets and liabilities and how movements in the carrying amounts are reflected in profit or loss, or other comprehensive income.

2.2.2.B Subsequent remeasurement

While a non-current asset is classified as held for sale or while it is part of a disposal group classified as held for sale it should not be depreciated or amortised. Interest and other expenses attributable to the liabilities of a disposal group classified as held for sale should continue to be recognised. *[IFRS 5.25]*.

On subsequent remeasurement of a disposal group, the standard requires that the carrying amounts of any assets and liabilities that are not within the scope of its measurement requirements, be remeasured in accordance with applicable IFRSs before the fair value less costs to sell of the disposal group is remeasured. *[IFRS 5.19]*.

2.2.3 Impairments and reversals of impairment

The requirement to measure a non-current asset or disposal group held for sale at the lower of carrying amount and fair value less costs to sell may give rise to a write down in value (impairment loss) and possibly its subsequent reversal. As noted above, the first step is to account for any items outside the scope of the standard's measurement rules in the normal way. After that, any excess of carrying value over fair value less costs to sell should be recognised as an impairment. *[IFRS 5.20]*.

Any subsequent increase in fair value less costs to sell of an asset up to the cumulative impairment loss previously recognised either in accordance with IFRS 5 or in accordance with IAS 36 should be recognised as a gain. *[IFRS 5.21]*. In the case of a disposal group, any subsequent increase in fair value less costs to sell should be recognised:

(a) to the extent that it has not been recognised under another standard in relation to those assets outside the scope of IFRS 5's measurement requirements; but

(b) not in excess of the cumulative amount of losses previously recognised under IFRS 5 or before that under IAS 36 in respect of the non-current assets in the group which are within the scope of the measurement rules of IFRS 5. *[IFRS 5.22]*.

Any impairment loss (or any subsequent gain) recognised for a disposal group should be allocated to the non-current assets in the group that are within the scope of the measurement requirements of IFRS 5. The order of allocation should be:

- first, to reduce the carrying amount of any goodwill in the group; and
- then, to the other non-current assets of the group *pro rata* on the basis of the carrying amount of each asset in the group. *[IFRS 5.23]*.

This is illustrated by the standard with the following example: *[IFRS 5.IG10]*

Example 4.4: Allocation of impairment loss to the components of a disposal group

An entity plans to dispose of a group of its assets (as an asset sale). The assets form a disposal group, and are measured as follows:

	Carrying amount at the reporting date before classification as held for sale	Carrying amount as remeasured immediately before classification as held for sale
	€	€
Goodwill	1,500	1,500
Property, plant and equipment (carried at revalued amounts)	4,600	4,000
Property, plant and equipment (carried at cost)	5,700	5,700
Inventory	2,400	2,200
Investments in equity instruments	1,800	1,500
Total	16,000	14,900

The entity recognises the loss of €1,100 (€16,000 – €14,900) immediately before classifying the disposal group as held for sale. The entity measures the fair value less costs to sell of the disposal group as €13,000. Because an entity measures a disposal group classified as held for sale at the lower of its carrying amount and fair value less costs to sell, the entity recognises an impairment loss of €1,900 (€14,900 – €13,000) when the group is initially classified as held for sale. The impairment loss is allocated to non-current assets to which the measurement requirements of the IFRS are applicable. Therefore, no impairment loss is allocated to inventory and investments in equity instruments. The loss is allocated to the other assets in the order of allocation described above.

The allocation can be illustrated as follows:

First, the impairment loss reduces any amount of goodwill. Then, the residual loss is allocated to other assets *pro rata* based on the carrying amounts of those assets.

	Carrying amount as remeasured immediately before classification as held for sale	Allocated impairment loss	Carrying amount after allocation of impairment loss
	€	€	€
Goodwill	1,500	(1,500)	–
Property, plant and equipment (carried at revalued amounts)	4,000	(165)	3,835
Property, plant and equipment (carried at cost)	5,700	(235)	5,465
Inventory	2,200	–	2,200
Investments in equity instruments	1,500	–	1,500
Total	14,900	(1,900)	13,000

In the first table of this example, it is not particularly clear what the meaning and purpose of the left hand column is. The fact that some of the figures are different in each column, seems to indicate that the column header 'Carrying amount at the reporting date before classification as held for sale' is referring to the opening statement of financial position at the beginning of the period in which the classification is made. As noted at 2.2.2.A above, an entity is required to remeasure

Chapter 4

the assets as normal under the relevant standards immediately before classifying them as held for sale. This would mean the difference of €1,100 reflects routine accounting entries (such as depreciation and revaluation) from the start of the period to the date of classification as held to sale. Also worthy of note is that the example does not say where the entity recognises the loss of €1,100. Given that the disposal group contains investments in equity instruments, some of this amount might be recorded in other comprehensive income rather than in profit or loss. Similarly, movements in property plant and equipment held at revalued amounts may be recorded directly in other comprehensive income.

One thing which the example above fails to illustrate is that the measurement requirements of the standard are incomplete. It is quite possible that the required impairment exceeds the carrying value of the non-current assets within the scope of the standard's measurement rules. IFRS 5 is silent on what to do in such circumstances. Possible approaches would be:

(a) to apply the impairment to current assets;

(b) to apply the impairment to non-current assets outside the scope of the standard's measurement rules;

(c) to recognise a separate provision; or

(d) restrict the impairment to the carrying value of the non-current assets within the scope of the standard's measurement requirements.

For the present, entities will need to apply judgement based on individual circumstances. This issue was brought to the attention of the Interpretations Committee which referred it to the IASB. The IASB intended to address the issue through a future amendment to IFRS 5. The Board decided tentatively to consider amending IFRS 5 as a matter of priority and to work with the FASB to ensure IFRS 5 remains aligned with US GAAP.[2] However, at its December 2009 meeting, the IASB 'decided not to add a project to its agenda to address the impairment measurement and reversal issues at this time.'[3] This matter is one of a number issues which the Board continues to debate. Possible future developments are discussed at 6 below.

The standard contains a reminder that requirements relating to derecognition are set out in IAS 16 for property, plant and equipment (discussed in Chapter 18 at 7), and IAS 38 – *Intangible Assets* – for intangible assets (discussed in Chapter 17 at 9.5) and notes that a gain or loss not previously recognised by the date of the sale of a non-current asset (or disposal group) should be recognised at the date of derecognition. *[IFRS 5.24]*. This may happen, for example, if the fair value less costs to sell of an asset classified as held for sale at the end of the previous period falls during the current period.

2.2.4 Presentation in the statement of financial position of non-current assets and disposal groups held for sale

The general requirement, discussed in Chapter 3 at 3.1.1, to classify items in the statement of financial position as current or non-current (or present them broadly in order of liquidity) is overlaid with further requirements by IFRS 5 regarding non-current assets held for sale and disposal groups. IFRS 5's aim is that entities should present and disclose information that enables users of the financial statements to evaluate the financial effects of disposals of non-current assets (or disposal groups). *[IFRS 5.30].* In pursuit of this aim, IFRS 5 requires:

- non-current assets classified as held for sale and the assets of a disposal group classified as held for sale to be presented separately from other assets in the statement of financial position; and
- the liabilities of a disposal group classified as held for sale to be presented separately from other liabilities in the statement of financial position.

These assets and liabilities should not be offset and presented as a single amount. In addition:

(a) major classes of assets and liabilities classified as held for sale should generally be separately disclosed either on the face of the statement of financial position or in the notes. However, this is not necessary for a disposal group if it is a subsidiary that met the criteria to be classified as held for sale on acquisition; and

(b) any cumulative income or expense recognised directly in other comprehensive income relating to a non-current asset (or disposal group) classified as held for sale should be presented separately. *[IFRS 5.38, 39].*

Chapter 4

The requirement in (b) was included in response to comments made to the IASB during the development of the standard. The Board describes the development as follows: 'Respondents to ED 4 noted that the separate presentation within equity of amounts relating to assets and disposal groups classified as held for sale (such as, for example, unrealised gains and losses on available-for-sale assets and foreign currency translation adjustments) would also provide useful information. The Board agreed and has added such a requirement to the IFRS.' *[IFRS 5.BC58].* On that basis, it might be considered that any non-controlling interest within equity relating to non-current assets (or disposal groups) held for sale should also be presented separately as it would seem to represent equally useful information about amounts within equity. However, such disclosure of non-controlling interests is not specifically required by the standard so would remain voluntary. As noted at 3.2 below, the standard requires an analysis of the income for the period attributable to owners between continuing and discontinued operations.

IFRS 5 is silent as to whether the information specified in (b) above should be on the face of the statement of financial position or in a note. However, the implementation guidance to IFRS 5 shows a caption called 'Amounts recognised in other comprehensive income and accumulated in equity in relation to non-current assets held for sale' and illustrates the requirements as follows: *[IFRS 5.IG12]*

Example 4.5: Presenting non-current assets or disposal groups classified as held for sale

At the end of 2018, an entity decides to dispose of part of its assets (and directly associated liabilities). The disposal, which meets the criteria to be classified as held for sale, takes the form of two disposal groups, as follows:

	Carrying amount after classification as held for sale	
	Disposal group I	Disposal group II
	€	€
Property, plant and equipment	4,900	1,700
Investments in equity instruments	*1,400	–
Liabilities	(2,400)	(900)
Net carrying amount of disposal group	3,900	800

* An amount of €400 relating to these assets has been recognised in other comprehensive income and accumulated in equity.

The presentation in the entity's statement of financial position of the disposal groups classified as held for sale can be shown as follows:

	2018	2017
	€	€
ASSETS		
Non-current assets	×	×
AAA	×	×
BBB	×	×
CCC	×	×
	×	×
Current assets		
DDD	×	×
EEE	×	×
	×	×
Non-current assets classified as held for sale	8,000	–
Total assets	×	×
EQUITY AND LIABILITIES		
Equity attributable to equity holders of the parent		
FFF	×	×
GGG	×	×
Amounts recognised in other comprehensive income and accumulated in equity relating to non-current assets held for sale	400	–
	×	×
Non-controlling (or minority) interests	×	×
Total equity	×	×
Non-current liabilities		
HHH	×	×
III	×	×
JJJ	×	×
	×	×

	2017	2016
	€	€
Current liabilities		
KKK	×	×
LLL	×	×
MMM	×	×
	×	×
Liabilities directly associated with non-current assets classified as held for sale	3,300	–
	×	×
Total liabilities	×	×
Total equity and liabilities	×	×

The presentation requirements for assets (or disposal groups) classified as held for sale at the end of the reporting period do not apply retrospectively. The comparative statements of financial position for any previous periods are therefore not re-presented.

Once assets have been classified as non-current they should not be reclassified as current assets until they meet the criteria to be classified as held for sale in accordance with IFRS 5. So, for example, a mere intention to sell an asset would not trigger held for sale accounting until all the criteria discussed at 2.1.2 above have been met.

Assets of a class that an entity would normally regard as non-current that are acquired exclusively with a view to resale also should not be classified as current unless they meet the slightly relaxed criteria to be classified as held for sale (see 2.1.2 above). *[IFRS 5.3].*

The treatment of comparatives when the classification as held for sale commences or ceases is discussed at 4 below.

2.2.5 Changes to a plan of sale or to a plan of distribution

2.2.5.A Assets (or disposal groups) to be retained by the entity

An asset (or disposal group) should cease to be classified as held for sale (or distribution) if the criteria discussed in 2.1.2 are no longer met. *[IFRS 5.26].*

If an individual asset or liability is removed from a disposal group classified as held for sale or classified as held for distribution, the remaining assets and liabilities of the disposal group should only continue to be measured as a group if the group still meets the criteria to be held for sale (or for distribution) under IFRS 5. Otherwise, the remaining non-current assets of the group that individually meet the criteria should be measured individually at the lower of their carrying amounts and fair values less costs to sell at that date. Any non-current assets that do not meet the criteria should cease to be classified as held for sale or held for distribution. *[IFRS 5.29].*

A non-current asset (or disposal group) that ceases to be classified as held for sale or for distribution (or ceases to be included in a disposal group which is so classified) should be measured at the lower of:

(a) its carrying amount before the asset (or disposal group) was classified as held for sale or for distribution, adjusted for any depreciation, amortisation or revaluations that would have been recognised had the asset (or disposal group) not been so classified; and

(b) its recoverable amount at the date of the subsequent decision not to sell or distribute.

Chapter 4

Regarding (b) above, the standard notes that if the non-current asset is part of a cash-generating unit, its recoverable amount is the carrying amount that would have been recognised after the allocation of any impairment loss arising on that cash-generating unit in accordance with IAS 36. *[IFRS 5.27]*. Recoverable amount is defined as the higher of:

- an asset's fair value less costs to sell; and
- its value in use.

Value in use is defined as 'the present value of estimated future cash flows expected to arise from the continuing use of an asset and from its disposal at the end of its useful life.' *[IFRS 5 Appendix A]*.

Any required adjustment to the carrying amount of a non-current asset that ceases to be classified as held for sale or for distribution should be included:

(a) in profit or loss from continuing operations in the period in which the criteria are no longer met (unless the asset had been revalued in accordance with IAS 16 or IAS 38 before classification as held for sale, in which case the adjustment should be treated as a revaluation increase or decrease); and

(b) in the same caption of the statement of comprehensive income used to present any gain or loss recognised in relation to remeasuring non-current assets (or disposal groups) held for sale or distribution but not meeting the definition of a discontinued operation. *[IFRS 5.28, 37]*.

Financial statements for the periods since classification as held for sale should be amended accordingly if the disposal group or non-current asset that ceases to be classified as held for sale is a subsidiary, joint operation, joint venture, associate, or a portion of an interest in a joint venture or an associate. The adjustment should be presented in the same caption in the statement of comprehensive income described at (b) above.

The treatment of comparative information on the cessation of held-for-sale classification is discussed at 4.2 below.

2.2.5.B Change in method of distribution

An entity may change the manner in which an asset (or disposal group) will be disposed of from being held for sale to being held for distribution to owners (or *vice versa*). Such a change raises the question as to whether the previous accounting treatment under IFRS 5 should be 'unwound' and started afresh based on the new disposal method, or whether a seamless transition from one to the other should be treated as a continuation of one overall disposal plan. In September 2014 the IASB issued *Annual Improvements to IFRS: 2012-2014 Cycle* which clarified the standard to address this issue specifically. The new provision, discussed below, applied prospectively to changes in disposal methods occurring in annual periods beginning on or after 1 January 2016.

When the manner of disposal changes directly from one method to the other, the change in classification is considered to be a continuation of the original plan of disposal. In such cases:

(a) the guidance discussed at 2.2.5.A above does not apply. Rather, the classification, presentation and measurement requirements that are applicable to the new method of disposal should be applied (see 2.1 and 2.2 above); that is, without first treating the asset (or disposal group) as ceasing to be held for sale by reversing the preceding accounting treatment;

(b) any reduction or increase in the fair value less costs to sell/costs to distribute of the non-current asset (or disposal group) should be recognised as discussed at 2.2.3 above; and

(c) the date of classification as held for sale or for distribution does not change; nor does such a change preclude an extension of the 'one year rule' (both as discussed at 2.1.2 above if the relevant conditions are met). *[IFRS 5.26A]*

3 DISCONTINUED OPERATIONS

As discussed at 3.2 below, IFRS 5 requires the presentation of a single amount on the face of the or statement of comprehensive income relating to discontinued operations, with further analysis either on the face of the statement or in the notes.

3.1 Definition of a discontinued operation

IFRS 5 defines a discontinued operation as 'a component of an entity that either has been disposed of, or is classified as held for sale, and

(a) represents a separate major line of business or geographical area of operations,

(b) is part of a single co-ordinated plan to dispose of a separate major line of business or geographical area of operations, or

(c) is a subsidiary acquired exclusively with a view to resale.' *[IFRS 5.32, Appendix A]*.

Classification as held for sale is discussed at 2.1 above. For the purposes of the above definition, a 'component of an entity' is also defined by the standard as comprising 'operations and cash flows that can be clearly distinguished, operationally and for financial reporting purposes, from the rest of the entity. In other words, a component of an entity will have been a cash-generating unit or a group of cash-generating units while being held for use.' *[IFRS 5.31, Appendix A]*. IFRS 5 defines cash generating unit in the same way as IAS 36, that is as 'the smallest identifiable group of assets that generates cash inflows that are largely independent of the cash inflows from other assets or groups of assets.' *[IFRS 5 Appendix A]*. Cash generating units are discussed in Chapter 20 at 3.

It seems unlikely that this definition of a discontinued operation would ever be met by a single non-current asset (for example, a single building or single equity-accounted investment). Accordingly, a discontinued operation will also be a 'disposal group' which is a group of assets to be disposed of, by sale or otherwise, together as a group in a single transaction, and liabilities directly associated with those assets that will be transferred in the transaction (discussed at 2.1.1 above).

The meaning of 'separate major line of business or geographical area' was raised with the Interpretation Committee. It concluded, in January 2016, that it could not provide additional clarity on this matter, and decided it should be considered for a broad-scope project on IFRS 5 (possible future developments of IFRS 5 are discussed at 6 below).[4] In the meantime, judgement will be required.

As discussed at 2.1.2.C above, IFRS 5 stipulates that a non-current asset (or disposal group) that is to be abandoned should not be classified as held for sale. This includes non-current assets (or disposal groups) that are to be used to the end of their economic life and non-current assets (or disposal groups) that are to be closed rather than sold. However, if the disposal group to be abandoned meets the criteria above for being a discontinued operation the standard requires it to be treated as such 'at the date on which it ceases to be used.' *[IFRS 5.13]*. In other words, the treatment as discontinued only starts in the period when abandonment actually occurs (see Example 4.6 below).

A non-current asset that has been temporarily taken out of use should not be accounted for as if it had been abandoned. *[IFRS 5.14]*. Accordingly it would not be disclosed as a discontinued operation. The standard provides an illustration of a discontinued operation arising from abandonment upon which the following example is based. *[IFRS 5.IG9]*

Example 4.6: Discontinued operation arising from abandonment

In October 2017 an entity decides to abandon all of its cotton mills, which constitute a major line of business. All work stops at the cotton mills during the year ended 31 December 2018. In the financial statements for the year ended 31 December 2017, results and cash flows of the cotton mills are treated as continuing operations. In the financial statements for the year ended 31 December 2018, the results and cash flows of the cotton mills are treated as discontinued operations and the entity makes the disclosures required (see 3.2 below).

3.2 Presentation of discontinued operations

IFRS 5 requires the presentation of a single amount on the face of the statement of comprehensive income comprising the total of:

(a) the post-tax profit or loss of discontinued operations; and

(b) the post-tax gain or loss recognised on the measurement to fair value less costs to sell or on the disposal of the assets or disposal group(s) constituting the discontinued operation. *[IFRS 5.33(a)]*.

This single amount should be further analysed (either on the face of the statement or in the notes) into:

(a) the revenue, expenses and pre-tax profit or loss of discontinued operations;

(b) the gain or loss recognised on the measurement to fair value less costs to sell or on the disposal of the assets or disposal group(s) constituting the discontinued operation; and

(c) separately for each of (a) and (b) the related income tax expense as required by IAS 12 (see Chapter 31 at 14.6).

The analysis is not required for disposal groups that are newly acquired subsidiaries that meet the criteria to be classified as held for sale on acquisition (see 2.2.2 above). *[IFRS 5.33(b)]*.

If the required analysis is presented on the face of the statement of comprehensive income it should be presented in a section identified as relating to discontinued operations, i.e. separately from continuing operations. *[IFRS 5.33A]*. The standard also makes clear that any gain or loss on the remeasurement of a non-current asset (or disposal group) classified as held for sale that does not meet the definition of a discontinued operation should not be included within these amounts for discontinued operations, but be included in profit or loss from continuing operations. *[IFRS 5.37]*.

IFRS 5 requires disclosure of the amount of income from continuing operations and discontinued operations attributable to owners of the parent. This may be given either in the notes or on the face of the statement of comprehensive income. *[IFRS 5.33(d)]*.

IFRS 5 requires that all the above disclosures be re-presented for prior periods presented in the financial statements so that the disclosures relate to all operations that have been discontinued by the reporting date for the latest period presented. *[IFRS 5.34]*. Accordingly, adjustments to the comparative information as originally reported will be necessary for those disposal groups categorised as discontinued operations. Comparative information relating to discontinued operations is discussed further at 4 below.

The implementation guidance accompanying IFRS 5 provides the following illustration of the presentation of discontinued operations. *[IFRS 5.IG11]*. (Note that the illustrative example assumes that the entity did not recognise any components of other comprehensive income in the periods presented.)

Example 4.7: Presenting discontinued operations

XYZ GROUP – STATEMENT OF COMPREHENSIVE INCOME FOR THE YEAR ENDED 31 DECEMBER 2018 (illustrating the classification of expenses by function)

(in thousands of Euros)

	2018	2017
Continuing operations		
Revenue	×	×
Cost of sales	(×)	(×)
Gross profit	×	×
Other income	×	×
Distribution costs	(×)	(×)
Administrative expenses	(×)	(×)
Other expenses	(×)	(×)
Finance costs	(×)	(×)
Share of profit of associates	×	×
Profit before tax	×	×
Income tax expense	(×)	(×)
Profit for the period from continuing operations	×	×
Discontinued operations		
Profit for the period from discontinued operations*	×	×
Profit for the period	×	×
Attributable to:		
Owners of the parent		
Profit for the period from continuing operations	×	×
Profit for the period from discontinued operations	×	×
Profit for the period attributable to owners of the parent	×	×
Non-controlling interest		
Profit for the period from continuing operation	×	×
Profit for the period from discontinued operations	×	×
Profit for the period attributable to non-controlling interests	×	×
	×	×

* The required analysis would be given in the notes.

Chapter 4

The above reflects the requirement to disclose the amount of income from continuing operations and discontinued operations attributable to owners of the parent. It is noteworthy that the standard's illustrative example goes beyond what is strictly required by also giving an equivalent analysis for income attributable to non-controlling interests.

Adjustments in the current period to amounts previously presented in discontinued operations that are directly related to the disposal of a discontinued operation in a prior period should be classified separately in discontinued operations. The nature and amount of the adjustments should be disclosed. Examples given by the standard of circumstances in which these adjustments may arise include the following:

(a) the resolution of uncertainties that arise from the terms of the disposal transaction, such as the resolution of purchase price adjustments and indemnification issues with the purchaser;

(b) the resolution of uncertainties that arise from and are directly related to the operations of the component before its disposal, such as environmental and product warranty obligations retained by the seller; and

(c) the settlement of employee benefit plan obligations, provided that the settlement is directly related to the disposal transaction. *[IFRS 5.35]*.

In addition, IFRS 5 requires disclosure of the net cash flows attributable to the operating, investing and financing activities of discontinued operations. The standard allows that these disclosures may be presented either in the notes or on the face of the financial statements. These disclosures are not required for disposal groups that are newly acquired subsidiaries that meet the criteria to be classified as held for sale on acquisition (see 2.2.2 above). *[IFRS 5.33(c)]*.

As a discontinued operation will also be a disposal group, the requirements regarding presentation of disposal groups in the statement of financial position (discussed at 2.2.4 above) also apply to discontinued operations.

3.3 Trading between continuing and discontinued operations

Notwithstanding the one line presentation discussed above, discontinued operations remain consolidated in group financial statements. That means any transactions between discontinued and continuing operations are eliminated as usual in the consolidation. As a consequence, the amounts ascribed to the continuing and discontinued operations will be income and expense only from transactions with counterparties external to the group. Importantly, this means that (unless additional disclosure is presented) the results presented on the face of the statement of comprehensive income will not necessarily represent the activities of the operations as individual entities, particularly when there has been significant trading between the continuing and discontinued operations. Some might consider the results for the continuing and discontinued operations on this basis to be of little use to readers of accounts. An argument could be made that allocating external transactions to or from the discontinued operation would yield more meaningful information.

The Interpretation Committee discussed this matter and published its agenda decision in January 2016.[5] In that decision the committee includes the following. 'The Interpretations Committee noted that neither IFRS 5 nor IAS 1 includes requirements regarding the presentation of discontinued operations that override the consolidation requirements in IFRS 10 – *Consolidated Financial Statements*. The Interpretations Committee also noted that paragraph B86(c) of IFRS 10 requires elimination of, among other things, income and expenses relating to intragroup transactions, and not merely intragroup profit. Consequently, the Interpretations Committee observed that not eliminating intragroup transactions would be inconsistent with the elimination requirements of IFRS 10.'

The Committee went on to observe: 'The Interpretations Committee also noted that paragraph 30 of IFRS 5 requires an entity to present and disclose information that enables users of the financial statements to evaluate the financial effects of discontinued operations and disposal activity. In the light of this objective, the Interpretations Committee observed that, depending on the particular facts and circumstances, an entity may have to provide additional disclosures in order to enable users to evaluate the financial effects of discontinued operations.'

4 COMPARATIVE INFORMATION

As discussed in Chapter 3 at 2.4, IAS 1 requires the presentation of comparative information. IFRS 5 deals with the particular requirements for non-current assets held for sale (and disposal groups) and discontinued operations.

Entities will need to consider whether any (and, if so, what) changes are necessary to comparative information as previously reported whenever:

- non-current assets or disposal groups first become classified as such; and
- that classification ceases.

4.1 Treatment of comparative information on initial classification as held for sale

4.1.1 The statement of comprehensive income

For non-current assets and disposal groups not qualifying as discontinued operations there are no special requirements relating to presentation in the statement of comprehensive income, accordingly no restatement of comparative amounts would be relevant.

When a component of an entity becomes classified as a discontinued operation, separate presentation of the total of its results for the period and any gain or loss on remeasurement is required on the face of the statement (see 3.2 above). IFRS 5 requires that these disclosures be re-presented for prior periods presented in the financial statements so that the disclosures relate to all operations that have been discontinued by the reporting date for the latest period presented. *[IFRS 5.34]*. Accordingly, adjustments to the comparative information as originally reported will be necessary for those disposal groups categorised as discontinued operations.

4.1.2 The statement of financial position

IFRS 5 states that an entity shall not reclassify or re-present amounts presented for non-current assets or for the assets and liabilities of disposal groups classified as held for sale in the statements of financial position for prior periods to reflect the classification in the statement of financial position for the latest period presented. *[IFRS 5.40].* The standard has no separate requirements relating to the statement of financial position for a disposal group also qualifying as a discontinued operation and accordingly comparatives are not adjusted.

4.2 Treatment of comparative information on the cessation of classification as held for sale

As discussed at 2.2.5 above, when a non-current asset ceases to be classified as held for sale the measurement basis for it reverts to what it would have been if it had not been so classified at all (or recoverable amount if lower). Typically this would require a 'catch-up' depreciation charge as depreciation would not have been accounted for while it was held for sale. The standard explicitly requires this to be a current year charge. *[IFRS 5.28].* This seems to indicate that for non-current assets and disposal groups ceasing to be so classified the *measurement* of items in comparative information (statement of comprehensive income and statement of financial position) should not be revisited. This requirement applies equally to discontinued operations.

The above is supplemented with the following. 'Financial statements for the periods since classification as held for sale shall be amended accordingly if the disposal group or non-current asset that ceases to be classified as held for sale is a subsidiary, joint operation, joint venture, associate, or a portion of an interest in a joint venture or an associate. The entity shall present that adjustment in the same caption in the statement of comprehensive income' within continuing operations used to record any gains and losses on non-current assets (or disposal groups) held for sale. *[IFRS 5.28, 37].*

IAS 28 clarifies that, as regards associates and joint ventures, the amendment of financial statements 'for the periods since classification as held for sale' means retrospectively from the date of its original classification as held for sale. *[IAS 28.21].* This clarification is not repeated in IFRS 10 or IFRS 11 – *Joint Arrangements.* However, we believe the clarification should apply to assets or disposal groups within the scope of those standards. As a result, when a disposal group or non-current asset that was classified as held for sale represented an entire subsidiary, joint operation, joint venture or associate or was a portion of an interest in a joint venture or associate, and subsequently no longer qualifies as held for sale, financial statements must be amended retrospectively as though the disposal group or non-current asset never qualified as held for sale.

This area has been considered by the Interpretations Committee. The committee decided not to add it to its agenda, noting that IFRS 5 is a possible subject for a research project by the IASB which would examine a number of areas (possible future developments of IFRS 6 – *Exploration for and Evaluation of Mineral Resources* – are discussed at 6 below). In its agenda decision the Committee observed the following: 'paragraph 28 requires the effects of a remeasurement (upon ceasing to be classified as held for sale) of a non-current asset to be recognised in profit or loss in the current period. Paragraph 28 also requires financial statements for the periods since classification as held for sale or as held for distribution to owners to be "amended accordingly" if the disposal group or non-current asset that ceases to be classified as held for sale or as held for distribution to owners is a subsidiary, joint operation, joint venture, associate, or a portion of an interest in a joint venture or an associate. The issue relates to a situation in which a disposal group that consists of both a subsidiary and other non-current assets ceases to be classified as held for sale. In such a situation, should an entity recognise the remeasurement adjustments relating to the subsidiary and the other non-current assets in different accounting periods, and should any amendment apply to presentation as well as to measurement?'[6] This articulation of the question by the Committee suggests that, until any amendment to the standard is made, judgement may be required.

Regarding the treatment of discontinued operations in the statement of comprehensive income, the standard states that if an entity ceases to classify a component as held for sale, the results of operations of the component previously presented in discontinued operations should be reclassified and included in income from continuing operations for all periods presented. The amounts for prior periods should be described as having been re-presented. *[IFRS 5.36].*

As discussed at 4.1.2 above, the amounts presented for non-current assets or for the assets and liabilities of disposal groups classified as held for sale in the comparative statement of financial position should not be reclassified or re-presented.

5 DISCLOSURE REQUIREMENTS

5.1 Requirements of IFRS 5

As discussed at 2.2.4 and 3.2 above, IFRS 5 sets out detailed requirements for the prominent presentation of amounts relating to non-current assets held for sale, disposal groups and discontinued operations. In particular, and as discussed at 3.2 above, the single amount reflecting the income from discontinued operations must be analysed into its components, either on the face of the statement of comprehensive income or in the notes. In addition, disclosure is required in the notes in the period in which a non-current asset (or disposal group) has been either classified as held for sale or sold:

(a) a description of the non-current asset (or disposal group);

(b) a description of the facts and circumstances of the sale, or leading to the expected disposal, and the expected manner and timing of that disposal;

(c) the gain or loss recognised as a result of measuring the non-current asset (or disposal group) at fair value less costs to sell (discussed at 2.2 above) and, if not separately presented on the face of the statement of comprehensive income, the caption in the statement that includes that gain or loss; and

(d) if applicable, the segment in which the non-current asset (or disposal group) is presented in accordance with IFRS 8 – *Operating Segments* (discussed in Chapter 34 at 3.1). *[IFRS 5.41].*

If a non-current asset (or disposal group) meets the criteria to be classified as held for sale after the reporting date but before the financial statements are authorised for issue, the information specified in (a), (b) and (d) above should also be disclosed in the notes. *[IFRS 5.12]*.

Further, should:

- a non-current asset (or disposal group) cease to be classified as held for sale; or
- an individual asset or liability be removed from a disposal group,

then IFRS 5 requires disclosure, in the period of the decision to change the plan to sell the non-current asset (or disposal group), a description of the facts and circumstances leading to the decision and the effect of the decision on the results of operations for the period and any prior periods presented. *[IFRS 5.42]*.

5.2 Disclosures required by standards other than IFRS 5

IFRS 5 explains that disclosures in other IFRSs do not apply to non-current assets (or disposal groups) classified as held for sale or discontinued operations unless those IFRSs require:

- specific disclosures in respect of non-current assets (or disposal groups) classified as held for sale or discontinued operations; or
- disclosures about the measurement of assets and liabilities within a disposal group that are not within the scope of the measurement requirement of IFRS 5 and such disclosures are not already provided in the other notes to the financial statements.

The requirement in the second bullet above reflects the fact that such assets continue to be measured in accordance with the specific IFRS dealing with them. In practice, much of the requirement will be satisfied by the disclosure of accounting policies. The requirement for other disclosures will depend on the standard concerned. An example would be actuarial assumptions used to measure a pension plan as the surplus or deficit is not within the measurement scope of IFRS 5.

In December 2016 minor amendments were made to IFRS 12 – *Disclosure of Interests in Other Entities* – by the IASB's *Annual Improvements to IFRS Standards 2014-2016 Cycle*. The changes clarify that all the disclosures of that standard apply to interests that are classified as held-for-sale, with the exception only of those disclosures (summarised financial information) identified by IFRS 12 as not being required. The amended provisions apply from 1 January 2017.

The standard goes on to say that additional disclosures about non-current assets (or disposal groups) classified as held for sale or discontinued operations may be necessary to comply with the general requirements of IAS 1, in particular paragraphs 15 and 125 of that Standard. *[IFRS 5.5B]*. Those provisions deal with fair presentation and estimation uncertainty and are discussed in Chapter 3 at 4.1.1 and at 5.2.1.

6 FUTURE DEVELOPMENTS

The IASB has, over recent years, discussed a number of issues related to IFRS 5, as set out below.[7]

(a) The scope of held-for-sale classification;
(b) Accounting for disposal groups consisting mainly of financial instruments;
(c) The 'excess impairment' issue discussed at 2.2.3 above;
(d) The reversal of goodwill impairments in a disposal group;
(e) The allocation of impairments within a disposal group;
(f) The definition of discontinued operation and disclosures;
(g) The presentation of other comprehensive income of disposal groups;
(h) The application of the term 'major line of business';
(i) The treatment of intragroup transactions between continuing and discontinued operations;
(j) The application of the presentation requirements in the standard to a disposal group consisting of a subsidiary and other non-current assets in the case of a change to a plan of sale; and
(k) The applicability of the disclosure requirements in IFRS 12 to a subsidiary classified as held-for-sale.

Item (i) above was referred to the Interpretations Committee for consideration. It published an agenda decision in January 2016, this is discussed at 3.3 above. As regards item (k) above, the Board has amended IFRS 12 (see 5.2 above).

Regarding the rest of the items, the IASB included a reference to them in its request for views regarding its 2015 agenda consultation. In November 2016, the Board published *IASB Work Plan 2017-2021: Feedback Statement on the 2015 Agenda Consultation.* This document notes: 'The Board agreed that the best way to start a review of these issues would be through a post-implementation review of IFRS 5. The Board intends to carry out that review after the forthcoming post-implementation reviews of IFRS 13 and of IFRS Standards 10–12.' Time will tell which, if any, IFRS 5 matters will be pursued by the Board following its agenda consultation.

In January 2016 the Interpretations Committee decided that the IFRS 5 matters referred to it would be better considered as part of a broader scope project, if applicable. For this reason, it has not taken any such matters onto its agenda.

References

1 *IASB Update*, January 2016.
2 *IASB Update*, July 2009.
3 *IASB Update*, December 2009.
4 *IFRIC Update*, January 2016.
5 *IFRIC Update*, January 2016.
6 *IFRIC Update*, January 2016.
7 IASB meeting July 2015, Agenda Paper 12C.

Chapter 5 First-time adoption

List of examples

Chapter 5 First-time adoption

1 INTRODUCTION

1.1 Objectives of first-time adoption

In principle, a first-time adopter should prepare financial statements as if it had always applied IFRSs. Although entities routinely have to apply new accounting standards by way of prior year adjustment, adopting IFRSs, a new basis of accounting, is a challenging undertaking and poses a distinct set of problems. One cannot underestimate the magnitude of the effort involved in adopting a large number of new accounting standards. The requirements of individual standards will often differ significantly from those under an entity's previous GAAP and information may need to be collected that was not required under the previous GAAP.

IFRS 1 – *First-time Adoption of International Financial Reporting Standards* – has a rather limited objective, to ensure that an entity's first IFRS financial statements, and its interim financial reports for part of the period covered by those first IFRS financial statements, contain high quality financial information that

- is transparent for users and comparable over all periods presented;
- provides a suitable starting point for accounting in accordance with IFRSs; and
- can be generated at a cost that does not exceed the benefits. *[IFRS 1.1]*.

It is important for users to be mindful of this objective as it provides the principal rationale underlying many of the decisions reflected in the standard, in particular the various exceptions that require, and exemptions that allow, a first-time adopter to deviate from the general rule.

Although IFRS 1 owes its existence to the 2005 adoption of IFRSs by EU companies whose securities are traded on an EU regulated market,[1] one of the IASB's aims was 'to find solutions that would be appropriate for any entity, in any part of the world, regardless of whether adoption occurs in 2005 or at a different time'. *[IFRS 1.BC3]*. IFRS 1 had to be written in a way that completely ignores a first-time adopter's previous GAAP. This means that first-time adoption exemptions are made available to all first-time adopters, including those whose previous GAAP was very close to IFRSs. A first-time adopter that so desires will be able to make considerable adjustments to its opening IFRS statement of financial position, using the available exemptions in IFRS 1, even if the differences between its previous GAAP and IFRSs were only minor. Yet, it may also be required to make considerable adjustments due to the requirement to use the same IFRS standards for all periods presented in the first IFRS financial statements.

Another issue is the potential for lack of comparability between different first-time adopters, and between first-time adopters and entities already applying IFRSs. *[IFRS 1.BC9].* The IASB ultimately decided that it was more important to achieve 'comparability over time within a first-time adopter's first IFRS financial statements and between different entities adopting IFRSs for the first time at a given date; achieving comparability between first-time adopters and entities that already apply IFRSs is a secondary objective.' *[IFRS 1.BC10].*

A revised IFRS 1 was issued in November 2008, which retains the substance of the previous version of the standard but within a changed structure. *[IFRS 1.IN2].* The standard has been further amended as a result of the IASB's annual improvements process, consequential amendments resulting from issuance of new standards, as well as to provide limited exemptions that address specific matters. This approach always carried the risk that its complexity might eventually overwhelm its practical application. All these amendments are incorporated into the applicable sections of this chapter.

1.2 Authoritative literature

This chapter generally discusses the requirements of IFRS 1 for accounting periods beginning on or after 1 January 2018 unless otherwise stated (for example, for first-time adopters that are insurers, we have retained discussions related to IAS 39 – *Financial Instruments: Recognition and Measurement* – in this chapter.) and reflects the amendments to the original version of IFRS 1 referred to at 1.1 above.

This chapter does not deal with the first-time adoption of the earlier versions of IFRS 1. A detailed discussion of the first-time adoption using the earlier versions of the standard can be found in Chapter 5 of the previous editions of this book, *International GAAP 2017* and prior editions.

1.3 Defined terms

IFRS 1 defines the following terms in connection with the transition to IFRSs: *[IFRS 1 Appendix A]*

Date of transition to IFRSs: The beginning of the earliest period for which an entity presents full comparative information under IFRSs in its first IFRS financial statements.

First IFRS financial statements: The first annual financial statements in which an entity adopts International Financial Reporting Standards, by an explicit and unreserved statement of compliance with IFRSs.

First IFRS reporting period: The latest reporting period covered by an entity's first IFRS financial statements.

First-time adopter: An entity that presents its first IFRS financial statements.

International Financial Reporting Standards: Standards and Interpretations issued by the International Accounting Standards Board (IASB). They comprise:

(a) International Financial Reporting Standards;

(b) International Accounting Standards;

(c) IFRIC Interpretations (Interpretations developed by the IFRS Interpretations Committee); and

(d) SIC Interpretations (Interpretations of the former Standing Interpretations Committee).

Opening IFRS statement of financial position: An entity's statement of financial position (i.e. balance sheet) at the date of transition to IFRSs.

Previous GAAP: The basis of accounting that a first-time adopter used immediately before adopting IFRSs.

1.4 Future developments

As at the time of writing, there was no specific project dealing with IFRS 1. However, the IASB is currently pursuing a number of projects. Consideration will be given at the time of deliberations to how new standards or amendments may impact a first-time adopter of IFRSs and resulting consequential amendments to IFRS 1 will be included in the new standards or amendments. Entities contemplating conversion to IFRSs should monitor the IASB's agenda in order to anticipate how future standards or amendments may affect their conversions.

2 WHO IS A FIRST-TIME ADOPTER?

2.1 The first IFRS financial statements in scope of IFRS 1

An entity's first IFRS financial statements will be subject to IFRS 1 when the entity adopts IFRSs by making in those annual financial statements an explicit and unreserved statement of compliance with IFRSs. *[IFRS 1.3, Appendix A].* The standard provides description of the circumstances in which an entity is a first-time adopter and therefore is within the scope of this standard. These circumstances are discussed below.

An entity's financial statements are considered its first IFRS financial statements, and thus fall within the scope of IFRS 1, when it presented its most recent previous financial statements:

(i) in accordance with national requirements that are not consistent with IFRSs in all respects;

(ii) in conformity with IFRSs in all respects, except that the financial statements did not contain an explicit and unreserved statement that they complied with IFRSs;

(iii) with an explicit statement of compliance with some, but not all, IFRSs;

(iv) in accordance with national requirements, but use some individual IFRSs to account for items for which national requirements did not exist; or

(v) in accordance with national requirements, with a reconciliation of some amounts to the amounts determined in accordance with IFRSs. *[IFRS 1.3(a)].*

An entity whose most recent previous financial statements contained an explicit and unreserved statement of compliance with IFRSs can never be considered a first-time adopter. This is the case even in the following circumstances:

- the entity issued financial statements containing an explicit and unreserved statement of compliance with IFRSs despite the fact that the auditors issued a qualified audit report on those IFRS financial statements. By contrast, an entity that makes a statement of compliance that excludes any IFRSs will still be a first-time adopter (see Example 5.1 below);
- the entity issued financial statements claiming to comply both with national GAAP and IFRSs ; or
- the entity stops presenting a separate set of financial statements under national requirements, which was presented in addition to its IFRS financial statements (see Example 5.2 below). *[IFRS 1.4].*

The IASB could have introduced special rules that would have required an entity that significantly departed from IFRSs to apply IFRS 1. However, the IASB considered that such rules would lead to 'complexity and uncertainty'. *[IFRS 1.BC5].* In addition, this would have given entities applying 'IFRS-lite' (entities not applying IFRSs rigorously in all respects e.g. applying IFRSs except for certain standards and interpretations) an option to side step the requirements of IAS 8 – *Accounting Policies, Changes in Accounting Estimates and Errors* – to disclose departures from IFRSs as errors. *[IFRS 1.BC6].*

The following examples illustrate certain scenarios in connection with determining whether an entity is a first-time adopter.

Example 5.1: Scope of application of IFRS 1

Entity A applied IFRSs in its previous financial statements, but stated that it 'applied IFRSs except for IFRS 2 – *Share-based Payment*.'

Entity A is a first-time adopter because its financial statements did not contain an unreserved statement of compliance with IFRSs. It is irrelevant whether the auditors' report was qualified or not.

Entity B applied IFRSs in its previous financial statements and stated that the 'financial statements are prepared in conformity with IFRSs.' Despite that statement, Entity B had not applied IFRS 2.

Entity B is not a first-time adopter because its financial statements contained an unreserved statement of compliance with IFRSs. Even if the auditors had qualified their report, the entity would still not be a first-time adopter.

It is clear that the scope of IFRS 1 is very much rule-based, which, as the example above illustrates, can lead to different answers in similar situations and sometimes to counter-intuitive answers.

Example 5.2: Entity applying national GAAP and IFRSs

Entity C prepares two sets of financial statements, one set of financial statements based on its national GAAP and the other set based on IFRSs. The IFRS financial statements contained an explicit and unreserved statement of compliance with IFRSs and were made available externally. From 2018 onwards, Entity C stops presenting financial statements based on its national GAAP.

Entity C is not a first-time adopter because it already published financial statements that contained an explicit and unreserved statement of compliance with IFRSs.

Example 5.3: First IFRS financial statements outside the annual report or statutory financial statements

Entity E prepared financial statements under its previous GAAP for the period ending 31 December 2017. In connection with its initial public offering, Entity E published an offering document that includes IFRS financial statements that contain an unreserved statement of compliance with IFRSs. The date of transition to IFRSs for the purposes of those financial statements, which cover the most recent three financial years, was 1 January 2015.

Entity E's annual report (or statutory financial statements) are prepared under IFRSs for the first time for the period ending 31 December 2018.

The IFRS financial statements included in Entity E's offering document were its first IFRS financial statements, containing an unreserved statement of compliance with IFRSs. Therefore, Entity E should not apply IFRS 1 in its first annual report (or statutory financial statements) prepared under IFRSs as it is not a first-time adopter. Although not required by IFRSs, Entity E may want to repeat information about its transition to IFRSs in its statutory financial statements for the year ended 31 December 2018.

If, however, Entity E had included financial statements in its offering document that did not contain an unreserved statement of compliance with IFRSs then the annual report for 2018 (or statutory financial statements) would need to be prepared in accordance with IFRS 1. If those financial statements only included comparative information for the year ended 31 December 2017 then Entity E's date of transition would be 1 January 2017.

An entity may be a first-time adopter if it has previously prepared financial statements in accordance with IFRSs but only for internal purposes. The entity may have:

- prepared financial statements in accordance with IFRSs for internal use only, without making them available to the entity's owners or any other external users;
- prepared a reporting package in accordance with IFRSs for consolidation purposes without preparing a complete set of financial statements as defined in IAS 1 – *Presentation of Financial Statements* (as revised in 2007). *[IFRS 1.3(b)-(c)].*

IFRSs are intended to be applied in the preparation of general-purpose financial statements. Accordingly, financial statements that are restricted for specific use or incomplete reporting packages should not be deemed to comply with IFRSs. An entity that is a subsidiary of an IFRS reporting parent may be able to use the amounts reported for it in the group's financial statements when it adopts IFRSs for its own financial statements (see 5.9.1 below).

Finally, IFRS 1 applies also to a first-time adopter that did not present financial statements for previous periods. *[IFRS 1.3(d)].* For example, when an entity transfers its operations into a new company prior to an issue to the public, the new company would be a first-time adopter if the entity never applied IFRSs in the past.

An entity that is already applying IFRSs in preparing its financial statements cannot apply IFRS 1 to changes in its accounting policies. Instead, such an entity should apply:

- the requirements of IAS 8; and
- specific transitional requirements in other IFRSs. *[IFRS 1.5].*

2.2 When should IFRS 1 be applied?

An entity that presents its first IFRS financial statements is a first-time adopter, *[IFRS 1 Appendix A]*, and should apply IFRS 1 in preparing those financial statements. *[IFRS 1.2(a)].* It should also apply the standard in each interim financial report that it presents in accordance with IAS 34 – *Interim Financial Reporting* – for a part of the period covered by its first IFRS financial statements. *[IFRS 1.2(b)]*. In Extract 5.1 below, AGF Mutual Funds described its adoption of IFRSs in its interim or semi-annual financial statements. Therefore, a first-time adopter does not apply IFRS 1 to a 'trading statement', an 'earnings press release' or other financial report issued at its interim reporting date that is not described as complying with IAS 34 or IFRSs.

Extract 5.1: AGF Mutual Funds (2014)

Notes to Financial Statements (UNAUDITED) [extract]

2. **SUMMARY OF ACCOUNTING POLICIES:** [extract]

Basis of presentation and adoption of International Financial Reporting Standards

These financial statements have been prepared in compliance with International Financial Reporting Standards ("IFRS") applicable to the preparation of interim financial statements, including International Accounting Standard ("IAS") 34, *Interim Financial Reporting* and IFRS 1, *First-time Adoption of International Financial Reporting Standards.* The Funds adopted this basis of accounting effective October 1, 2014 as required by Canadian securities legislation and the Canadian Accounting Standards Board. Previously, the Funds prepared their financial statements in accordance with Canadian generally accepted accounting principles as defined in Part V of the CPA Handbook ("Canadian GAAP"). The Funds have consistently applied the accounting policies used in the preparation of their opening IFRS statements of financial position as at October 1, 2013 and throughout all periods presented, as if these policies had always been in effect. Note 10 includes disclosures of the impact of the transition to IFRS on the Funds' reported financial position and financial performance, including the nature and effect of significant changes in accounting policies from those used in the Funds' financial statements for the year ended September 30, 2014 prepared under Canadian GAAP.

2.2.1 Repeat application of IFRS 1

IFRS 1 does not prohibit an entity from applying IFRS 1 more than once and, in fact, requires it in some cases. *[IFRS 1.3(a)]*. The IASB explained this issue with an example of an entity that had applied IFRS 1 in connection with a foreign listing, subsequently delisted from the foreign exchange and no longer presented IFRS financial statements, but is now adopting IFRSs again together with other entities in its local jurisdiction – see Example 5.4 below. This was clarified by the Board in the *Annual Improvements to IFRSs 2009-2011 Cycle*, issued in May 2012. IFRS 1 was amended to clarify that an entity that stopped applying IFRSs in the past and chooses, or is required, to resume preparing IFRS financial statements has the option to apply IFRS 1 again. *[IFRS 1.4A]*. The Board reasoned that the entity should on cost-benefit grounds be allowed, rather than required, to apply IFRS 1 again. *[IFRS1.BC6C]*. If the entity chooses not to reapply IFRS 1, it must retrospectively restate its financial statements in accordance with IAS 8 as if it had never stopped applying IFRSs while disclosing (in addition to the disclosures required by IAS 8) the reasons why it stopped applying IFRSs and why it resumed applying IFRSs, as well as the reasons for choosing the retrospective restatement method. *[IFRS1.4B, 23A, 23B]*.

Example 5.4: Repeated application of IFRS 1 when an entity does not apply IFRSs for one year

Entity D prepared IFRS financial statements for 2015 and 2016 that contained an explicit and unreserved statement of compliance with IFRSs. However, in 2017 Entity D did not make an unreserved statement of compliance with IFRS.

If Entity D resumes presenting financial statements in accordance with IFRS, it may choose to apply IFRSs as a first-time adopter or it may elect to restate its financial statements retrospectively as if it had never stopped producing IFRS financial statements.

If it elects to apply IFRSs as a first-time adopter for the purposes of its 2018 financial statements, there is no requirement under IFRS 1 for Entity D to base its first IFRS financial statements in 2018 on the IFRS information that it produced before 2018. Therefore, Entity D will apply the IFRS 1 exemptions without regard to the elections it made in its first IFRS financial statements in 2015. In fact, Entity D is unable to apply certain IFRS 1 exemptions by reference to the date of transition that it used in its 2015 financial statements (see 3.5 below).

2.3 Determining the previous GAAP

An entity may prepare two complete sets of financial statements, e.g. one set of financial statements based on its national GAAP and another set for distribution to foreign investors based on US GAAP. Applying the definition of 'previous GAAP' (i.e. 'the basis of accounting that a first-time adopter used immediately before adopting IFRSs' *[IFRS 1 Appendix A]*) to such a dual reporting entity is not straightforward, as the examples below illustrate:

(a) *a dual reporting entity adopts IFRSs and at the same time stops presenting financial statements under its national GAAP and US GAAP:* Both national GAAP and US GAAP meet the definition of 'previous GAAP'. However, the entity can only present one set of IFRS financial statements. Therefore, the entity must choose a 'previous GAAP'. While, at least in theory, this appears to be a free choice there are a number of limiting constraints that should be taken into account:

   (i) national legislation and regulatory requirements may restrict an entity's options and require either national GAAP or US GAAP to be designated as the previous GAAP;

   (ii) comparability with other entities in the same jurisdiction may be increased if all entities in that jurisdiction use the same GAAP as their previous GAAP; and

   (iii) one set of financial statements is considered to be the 'main' set of financial statements, for example:

   - if the national GAAP financial statements received very limited circulation then they are clearly not the entity's 'main' financial statements. Conversely, if the US GAAP financial statements are only prepared for a specific purpose (e.g. to obtain a bank loan) then they may not be the entity's 'main' financial statements; or
   - the relative dominance of shareholder groups might provide an indication as to which set of financial statements is considered to be the 'main' set of financial statements.

   An entity should apply judgement when the constraints above do not all identify the same GAAP as the previous GAAP.

   IFRS 1 only requires disclosure of reconciliations between an entity's previous GAAP and IFRSs. However, it will be advisable for an entity to provide disclosures, on a voluntary basis, that contain sufficient information to enable users to understand the material reconciling items between the IFRS financial statements and the financial statements that were not prepared under its previous GAAP. Some national regulators (e.g. the US Securities and Exchange Commission), in fact, expect such disclosures (see 8.1.2 below).[2]

(b) *a dual reporting entity adopts IFRSs and at the same time continues to present financial statements under its national GAAP but stops presenting financial statements under US GAAP:* While one might expect US GAAP to be treated as the previous GAAP, both national GAAP and US GAAP meet the definition of 'previous GAAP'. An entity should therefore consider the criteria (i) to (iii) under (a) above in determining its previous GAAP.

If an entity treats its national GAAP as its previous GAAP then it may want or need to present an explanation of the differences between US GAAP and IFRSs to aid former users of the US GAAP financial statements.

As illustrated in Extract 5.2 below, when Infosys adopted IFRSs it treated Indian GAAP as its previous GAAP even though it continued to report under Indian GAAP for statutory purposes. However, Infosys provided additional reconciliations between US GAAP and its previous GAAP.

(c) *a dual reporting entity adopts IFRSs and at the same time stops presenting financial statements under US GAAP. Several years later it stops presenting financial statements under its national GAAP:* The entity is not a first-time adopter when it ceases to present financial statements under its national GAAP, even if the entity treated US GAAP as its previous GAAP when it adopted IFRSs. *[IFRS 1.4(a)].* However, the entity may want or need to present an explanation of the differences between its national GAAP and IFRSs to aid former users of its national GAAP financial statements.

Extract 5.2: Infosys Technologies Limited (2009)

2 Notes to the consolidated financial statements [extract]

2.1 Transition to IFRS reporting [extract]

The financial statements of Infosys Technologies Limited and its subsidiaries have been prepared in accordance with IFRS. Infosys Technologies Limited and its subsidiaries adopted all IFRS standards and the adoption was carried out in accordance to IFRS 1, using April 1, 2007 as the transition date. The transition was carried out from Indian GAAP, which was considered as the Previous GAAP. The effect of adopting IFRS has been summarized in the reconciliations provided. The transition to IFRS reporting has resulted in changes in the reported financial statements, notes thereto and accounting principles compared to what had been presented previously. Until the adoption of IFRS, the financial statements included in the Annual Reports on Form 20-F and Quarterly Reports on Form 6-K were prepared in accordance with accounting principles generally accepted in the United States of America (U.S. GAAP) under the historical cost convention on the accrual basis. However, for the purposes of the transition, such transition was carried out from Indian GAAP, which has been considered as the Previous GAAP. The reconciliation statements provided in Note 2.2 describe the differences between IFRS and Indian GAAP. In addition, reconciliations from U.S. GAAP to Indian GAAP have been provided in Note 2.3 for the periods presented.

The Group's financial statements for the year ending March 31, 2009 are the first annual financial statements to comply with IFRS.

2.3 The following voluntary reconciliations provide a quantification of reconciliation items between U.S. GAAP and Previous GAAP: [extract]

- equity as at April 1, 2007 (Note 2.3.1)
- equity as at March 31, 2008 (Note 2.3.2)
- equity as at March 31, 2009 (Note 2.3.3)
- net income for the year ended March 31, 2008 (Note 2.3.4)
- net income for the year ended March 31, 2009 (Note 2.3.5)

2.3.1 Transition to IFRSs from a similar GAAP

One consequence of the ongoing harmonisation of accounting standards around the world is that many national GAAPs are now virtually identical to IFRSs. However, differences between these national GAAPs and IFRSs often exist regarding the scope, transitional provisions, effective dates and actual wording of standards. In addition, some national GAAPs contain accounting alternatives not permitted by IFRSs.

When an entity reporting under such a national GAAP adopts IFRSs there will often not be major changes required in its accounting policies to comply with IFRSs. However, as discussed at 2.1 above, under IFRS 1 it is not relevant whether or not a previous GAAP was very similar to IFRSs. Therefore, regardless of the absence of significant differences in accounting policies, that entity would be a first-time adopter when it includes an explicit and unreserved statement of compliance with IFRSs for the first time. So, even if the entity's accounting policies were already fully aligned with IFRSs:

(a) it would be permitted to apply the IFRS 1 exemptions and required to apply the IFRS 1 exceptions;

(b) it would need to restate items for which the applicable first-time adoption exceptions differ from the transitional rules applicable to ongoing reporters (e.g. classification and measurement of financial assets);

(c) it would not be permitted to apply different versions of IFRSs that were effective at earlier dates; and

(d) it would need to explain the transition to IFRSs.

Notwithstanding the above, we believe an entity that:

- reported under a national GAAP that is identical with IFRSs in all respects;
- applied the national GAAP equivalent of IFRS 1 when the entity adopted that national GAAP;
- made an explicit and unreserved statement of compliance with that national GAAP in its most recent financial statements; and
- could have made an explicit and unreserved statement of compliance with IFRSs in those financial statements, if required,

does not have to re-apply IFRS 1 the first time that it makes an explicit and unreserved statement of compliance with IFRSs.

For example, if an entity that meets the requirements described above decides to make an explicit and unreserved statement of compliance with IFRSs for the first time, either voluntarily or is required to do so by a regulatory requirement related to an IPO, the entity would not be required to re-apply IFRS 1.

3 OPENING IFRS STATEMENT OF FINANCIAL POSITION

At the date of transition to IFRSs, an entity should prepare and present an opening IFRS statement of financial position that is the starting point for its accounting under IFRSs. *[IFRS 1.6]*. The date of transition to IFRSs is the beginning of the earliest comparative period presented in an entity's first IFRS financial statements. *[IFRS 1 Appendix A]*. Therefore the date of transition for an entity reporting under IFRSs for the first time at 31 December 2018 and presenting one year of comparative figures is 1 January 2017. For entities that adopt IFRSs at the beginning of a year, it is recommended that they consider the filing requirements for interim financial reports that a regulator in their jurisdiction may impose. For example, a regulator may require the opening IFRS statement of financial position to be presented in the first IFRS interim period even though this is not an IFRS 1 presentation requirement (see 6.6 below).

3.1 First-time adoption timeline

An entity's first annual IFRS financial statements must include at least three statements of financial position (i.e. balance sheets), two statements of profit or loss and other comprehensive income, two separate statements of profit or loss (if presented), two statements of cash flows and two statements of changes in equity and related notes for all statements presented, including the comparative information. *[IFRS 1.21]*. The beginning of the earliest comparative period for which the entity presents full comparative information under IFRSs will be treated as its date of transition to IFRSs. The diagram below shows how for an entity with a December year-end the above terms are related:

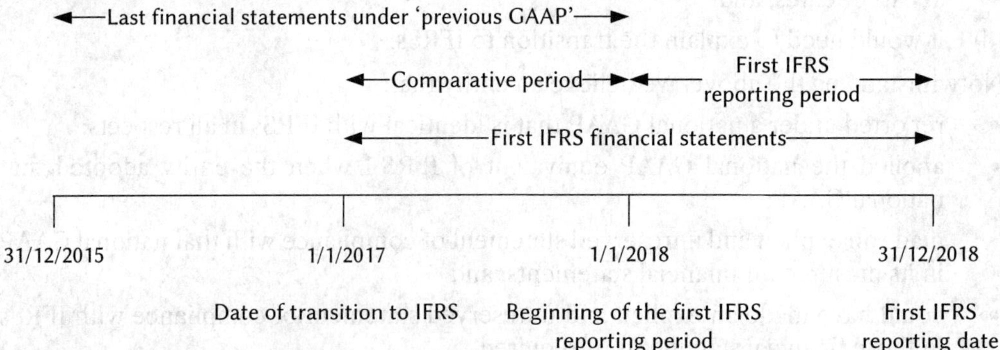

The diagram above also illustrates that there is a period of overlap, for the financial year 2017, which is reported first under the entity's previous GAAP and then as a comparative period under IFRSs. The following example illustrates how an entity should determine its date of transition to IFRSs.

Example 5.5: Determining the date of transition to IFRSs

Entity A's year-end is 31 December and it presents financial statements that include one comparative period. Entity A is required (e.g. by national legislation) to produce IFRS financial statements for the first accounting period starting on or after 1 January 2018.

A's first IFRS financial statements are for the period ending on 31 December 2018. Its date of transition to IFRSs is 1 January 2017, which is the beginning of the single comparative period included in its first IFRS financial statements.

Entity B's year-end is 31 July and it presents financial statements that include two comparative periods. Entity B is required to produce IFRS financial statements for the first annual accounting period starting on or after 1 January 2018.

B's first IFRS financial statements are for the period ending on 31 July 2019. Its date of transition to IFRSs is 1 August 2016, which is the beginning of the earliest period for which full comparative information is included in its first IFRS financial statements.

Entity C's most recent financial statements, under its previous GAAP, are for the period from 1 July 2016 to 31 December 2017. Entity C presents its first IFRS financial statements for the period ending 31 December 2018.

C's date of transition is 1 July 2016. While paragraph 21 of IFRS 1 and paragraph 38 of IAS 1 require presentation of at least one comparative period, IFRSs do not require the comparative period to be a 12-month period. Thus, the entity's date of transition will be the beginning of the earliest comparative period, irrespective of the length of that period. However, paragraph 36 of IAS 1 would require disclosure of the reason why the comparative period is not 12 months and disclosure of the fact that the periods presented are not entirely comparable.

Similarly, it is generally not considered to be a problem if the current or comparative period in an entity's first IFRS financial statements only covers a 52-week period, because IAS 1 does not preclude the practice of presenting financial statements for 52-week financial periods. *[IAS 1.37].*

Chapter 5

3.2 Opening IFRS statement of financial position and accounting policies

The fundamental principle of IFRS 1 is to require full retrospective application of the standards in force at the end of an entity's first IFRS reporting period, but with limited exceptions for the opening IFRS statement of financial position. IFRS 1 requires a first-time adopter to use the same accounting policies in its opening IFRS statement of financial position and for all periods presented in its first IFRS financial statements. However, this may not be straightforward, since to achieve this, the entity should comply with each IFRS effective at the end of its first IFRS reporting period fully retrospectively, after taking into account a number of allowed exemptions from certain IFRSs and mandatory exceptions to retrospective application of other IFRSs in accordance with IFRS 1 (see 3.5 below). *[IFRS 1.7].*

The requirement to apply the same accounting policies to all periods also prohibits a first-time adopter from applying previous versions of standards that were effective at earlier dates. *[IFRS 1.8].* As well as enhancing comparability, the IASB believes that this gives users comparative information that is based on IFRSs that are superior to superseded versions of those standards and avoids unnecessary costs. *[IFRS 1.BC11].*

For similar reasons, IFRS 1 also permits an entity to choose to apply either a current standard or a new standard that is not yet mandatory if that standard allows early application. *[IFRS 1.8].* Whichever standard is selected it would need to be applied consistently throughout the periods presented in its first IFRS financial statements on a retrospective basis, unless IFRS 1 provides an exemption or an exception that permits or requires otherwise. *[IFRS 1.BC11A].*

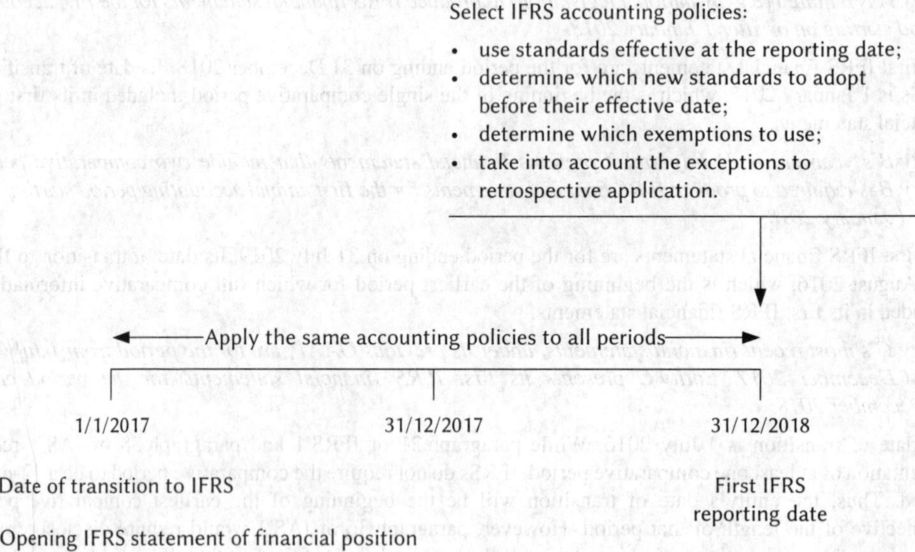

It should be noted that depending on the end of its first IFRS reporting period, an entity may or may not have the option to choose which version of a particular standard it may apply, as can be seen in the example below.

Example 5.6: Prohibition from applying superseded standards

Entity A's date of transition to IFRSs is 1 January 2017 and its first IFRS reporting period ends on 31 December 2018. How should Entity A apply the amendments to IAS 40 – *Transfers of Investment Property – Amendments to IAS 40,* which are effective for annual periods beginning 1 January 2018, in its first IFRS financial statements?

IFRS 1 requires Entity A to apply the amendments to IAS 40 because they are effective in its first IFRS reporting period. Since IFRS 1 prohibits an entity from applying a superseded standard to transactions that occurred before 1 January 2018 while applying the amended standard in the period beginning 1 January 2018, Entity A has to apply the above-mentioned amendments to IAS 40 for all periods presented.

Unless the exceptions and exemptions at 3.5 below apply, in preparing its opening IFRS statement of financial position, an entity should:

(a) recognise all assets and liabilities if recognition is required by IFRSs;
(b) not recognise assets or liabilities if IFRSs do not permit it;
(c) reclassify items recognised under previous GAAP as one type of asset, liability or component of equity, but are a different type of asset, liability or component of equity in accordance with IFRSs; and
(d) measure all recognised assets and liabilities by applying IFRSs. *[IFRS 1.10].*

Any change in accounting policies on adoption of IFRSs may cause changes in the amounts recorded under previous GAAP in respect of events and transactions that occurred before the date of transition. The effects of these changes should be recognised at the date of transition to IFRSs in retained earnings or, if appropriate, in another category of equity. *[IFRS 1.11].* For example, an entity that applies the IAS 16 – *Property, Plant and Equipment* –

revaluation model (see Chapter 18) in its first IFRS financial statements would recognise the difference between cost and the revalued amount of property, plant and equipment in a revaluation reserve. By contrast, an entity that had applied a revaluation model under its previous GAAP, but decided to apply the cost model under IAS 16, would reallocate the revaluation reserve to retained earnings or a separate component of equity not described as a revaluation reserve (see 7.4.3 below).

A first-time adopter is under no obligation to ensure that its IFRS accounting policies are similar to or as close as possible to its previous GAAP accounting policies. Therefore, for example, a first-time adopter could adopt the IAS 16 revaluation model despite the fact that it applied a cost model under its previous GAAP or *vice versa*. However, a first-time adopter would need to take into account the guidance in IAS 8 to ensure that its choice of accounting policy results in information that is relevant and reliable. *[IAS 8.10-12]*.

The requirement to prepare an opening IFRS statement of financial position and 'reset the clock' at that date poses a number of challenges for first-time adopters. Even a first-time adopter that already applies a standard that is directly based on IFRSs may decide to restate items in its opening IFRS statement of financial position (see 2.3.1 above). This happens, for example, in the case of an entity applying a property, plant and equipment standard that is based on IAS 16 before an entity's date of transition to IFRSs because the entity may decide to use a deemed cost exemption for certain of its assets as allowed by IFRS 1.

3.3 Fair value and deemed cost

Some exemptions in IFRS 1 refer to 'fair value' and 'deemed cost', which the standard defines as follows: *[IFRS 1 Appendix A]*

Deemed cost: is an amount used as a surrogate for cost or depreciated cost at a given date. Subsequent depreciation or amortisation assumes that the entity had initially recognised the asset or liability at the given date and that its cost was equal to the deemed cost.

Fair value: is the price that would be received to sell an asset or paid to transfer a liability in an orderly transaction between market participants at the measurement date (see Chapter 14 and IFRS 13 – *Fair Value Measurement*). The fair values determined by a first-time adopter should reflect the conditions that existed at the date for which they were determined, i.e. the first-time adopter should not apply hindsight in measuring the fair value at an earlier date.

3.4 Transitional provisions in other standards

The transitional provisions in other standards only apply to entities that already report under IFRSs. Therefore, a first-time adopter is not able to apply those transitional provisions unless specified by the requirements in IFRS 1. *[IFRS 1.9]*. Exceptions to this general rule are covered in the later parts of this Chapter that deal with the exceptions to the retrospective application of other IFRSs (see 4 below) and the exemptions from other IFRSs (see 5 below).

It is important to note that the transition rules for first-time adopters and entities that already report under IFRSs may differ significantly.

The IASB considers 'case by case when it issues a new IFRS whether a first-time adopter should apply that IFRS retrospectively or prospectively. The Board expects that retrospective application will be appropriate in most cases, given its primary objective of comparability over time within a first-time adopter's first IFRS financial statements. However, if the Board concludes in a particular case that prospective application by a first-time adopter is justified, it will amend the IFRS on first-time adoption of IFRSs.' *[IFRS 1.BC14]*.

IAS 8 allows exceptions from retrospective application for entities that cannot apply a requirement after making every reasonable effort to do so. There is no such relief in IFRS 1. The Interpretations Committee agreed 'that there were potential issues, especially with respect to "old" items, such as property, plant and equipment. However, those issues could usually be resolved by using one of the transition options available in IFRS 1' (see 3.5 below).[3] For example, an entity could elect to use fair value as deemed cost at the transition date if an entity is unable to apply IAS 36 – *Impairment of Assets* – on a fully retrospective basis (see 7.12 below). Therefore no 'impracticability relief' was added to the standard for first-time adopters. The transition options usually involve using certain surrogate values as deemed cost and are discussed at 5.5 below.

3.5 Departures from full retrospective application

IFRS 1 establishes two types of departure from the principle of full retrospective application of standards in force at the end of the first IFRS reporting period: *[IFRS 1.12]*

- it prohibits retrospective application of some aspects of other standards (the 'mandatory exceptions'); and
- it grants a number of exemptions from some of the requirements of other standards ('optional exemptions').

Mandatory exceptions: IFRS 1 prohibits retrospective application of IFRSs in some areas, particularly where this would require judgements by management about past conditions after the outcome of a particular transaction is already known. *[IFRS 1.IN5]*. The mandatory exceptions in the standard cover the following situations: *[IFRS 1.13-17, Appendix B]*

- estimates (see 4.2 below);
- derecognition of financial assets and financial liabilities (see 4.3 below);
- hedge accounting (see 4.4 to 4.7 below);
- non-controlling interests (see 4.8 below);
- classification and measurement of financial assets (see 4.9 below);
- impairment of financial assets (see 4.10 below)
- embedded derivatives (see 4.11 below); and
- government loans (see 4.12 below).

The reasoning behind most of the exceptions is that retrospective application of IFRSs in these situations could easily result in an unacceptable use of hindsight and lead to arbitrary or biased restatements, which would be neither relevant nor reliable.

Optional exemptions: In addition to the mandatory exceptions, IFRS 1 grants limited optional exemptions from the general requirement of full retrospective application of the standards in force at the end of an entity's first IFRS reporting period, considering the fact that the cost of complying with them would be likely to exceed the benefits to users of financial statements. *[IFRS 1.IN5]*. The standard provides exemptions in relation to: *[IFRS 1 Appendix C, D1]*

- business combinations (see 5.2 below);
- share-based payment transactions (see 5.3 below);
- insurance contracts (see 5.4 below);
- deemed cost (see 5.5 below);
- leases (see 5.6 below);
- cumulative translation differences (see 5.7 below);
- investments in subsidiaries, joint ventures and associates (see 5.8 below);
- assets and liabilities of subsidiaries, associates and joint ventures (see 5.9 below);
- compound financial instruments (see 5.10 below);
- designation of previously recognised financial instruments (see 5.11 and 5.12 below);
- designation of contracts to buy or sell a non-financial item (see 5.12.5 below);
- fair value measurement of financial assets or financial liabilities at initial recognition (see 5.13 below);
- decommissioning liabilities included in the cost of property, plant and equipment (see 5.14 below);
- financial assets or intangible assets accounted for in accordance with IFRIC 12 – *Service Concession Arrangements* (see 5.15 below);
- borrowing costs (see 5.16 below);
- extinguishing financial liabilities with equity instruments (see 5.17 below);
- severe hyperinflation (see 5.18 below);
- joint arrangements (see 5.19 below);
- stripping costs in the production phase of a surface mine (see 5.20 below);
- regulatory deferral account (see 5.21 below);
- revenue from contracts with customers (see 5.22 below); and
- foreign currency transactions and advance consideration (see 5.23 below).

In addition to the above, IFRS 1 grants certain short-term exemptions from IFRS 9, which will only be applicable to a first-time adopter that presents its first IFRS financial statements for the periods up to the dates specified in the exemption. These short-term exemptions are contained in Appendix E to IFRS 1 (see 5.24 below).

It is specifically prohibited under IFRS 1 to apply exemptions by analogy to other items. *[IFRS 1.18]*.

Application of these exemptions is entirely optional, i.e. a first-time adopter can pick and choose the exemptions that it wants to apply. Importantly, the IASB did not establish a hierarchy of exemptions. Therefore, when an item is covered by more than one exemption, a first-time adopter has a free choice in determining the order in which it applies the exemptions.

Example 5.7: Order of application of exemptions

Entity A acquired a building in a business combination. If Entity A were to apply the business combinations exemption described at 5.2 below, it would at the date of transition recognise the building at the acquisition date value net of subsequent depreciation and impairment of €120. However, if it were to use the fair value as the deemed cost of the building it would have to recognise it at €150. Which value should Entity A use?

A can choose whether it wants to recognise the building at €120 or €150 in its opening IFRS statement of financial position. The fact that Entity A uses the business combinations exemption does not prohibit it from also applying the 'fair value as deemed cost' exemption in relation to the same assets. Also, Entity A is not required to apply the 'fair value as deemed cost' exemption to all assets or to all similar assets as entities can choose to which assets they want to apply this exemption (see 5.5 below).

4 EXCEPTIONS TO RETROSPECTIVE APPLICATION OF OTHER IFRSs

4.1 Introduction

IFRS 1 provides a number of mandatory *exceptions* that specifically prohibit retrospective application of some aspects of other IFRSs as listed in 3.5 above. Each of the exceptions is explained in detail below.

4.2 Estimates

IFRS 1 requires an entity to use estimates under IFRSs that are consistent with the estimates made for the same date under its previous GAAP – after adjusting for any difference in accounting policy – unless there is objective evidence that those estimates were in error in accordance with IAS 8. *[IFRS 1.14, IAS 8.5].*

Under IFRS 1, an entity cannot apply hindsight and make 'better' estimates when it prepares its first IFRS financial statements. This also means that an entity is not allowed to consider subsequent events that provide evidence of conditions that existed at that date, but that came to light after the date its previous GAAP financial statements were finalised. If an estimate made under previous GAAP requires adjustment because of new information after the relevant date, an entity treats this information in the same way as a non-adjusting event after the reporting period under IAS 10 – *Events after the Reporting Period.* Effectively, the IASB wishes to prevent entities from using hindsight to 'clean up' their balance sheets as part of the preparation of the opening IFRS statement of financial position. In addition, the exception also ensures that a first-time adopter need not conduct a search for, and change the accounting for, events that might have otherwise qualified as adjusting events.

IFRS 1 provides the following guidance on estimates:

- When previous GAAP required estimates of similar items for the date of transition to IFRSs, an entity can be in one of the following two positions: *[IFRS 1.IG3]*
  - its previous GAAP accounting policy was consistent with IFRSs, in which case the estimates under IFRS need to be consistent with those made for that date under previous GAAP, unless there is objective evidence that those estimates were in error under IAS 8; *[IAS 8.5]* or
  - its previous GAAP accounting policy was not consistent with IFRSs, in which case, it adjusts the estimate only for the difference in accounting policies (unless there is objective evidence that those estimates were in error).

In both situations, it accounts for the revisions to those estimates in the period in which it makes the revisions in the same way as a non-adjusting event after the reporting period under IAS 10. *[IFRS 1.15, IG3, IAS 10.10].*

- When an entity needs to make estimates under IFRSs at the transition date that were not required under its previous GAAP, those estimates should reflect conditions that existed at that date. This is consistent with the distinction in IAS 10 between adjusting events and non-adjusting events after the reporting period. In particular, estimates of market prices, interest rates or foreign exchange rates should reflect market conditions at that date. *[IFRS 1.16, IG3].* Entities that are preparing for transition to IFRSs should consider gathering the data necessary for the estimate at the transition date to make the transition easier and to ensure that hindsight is not incorporated into the estimate;

The requirements above apply both to estimates made in respect of the date of transition to IFRSs and to those in respect of any of the comparative periods, in which case the reference to the date of transition to IFRSs above are replaced by references to the end of that comparative period. *[IFRS 1.17].*

The flowchart below shows the decision-making process that an entity needs to apply in dealing with estimates at the transition date and during any of the comparative periods included in its first IFRS financial statements.

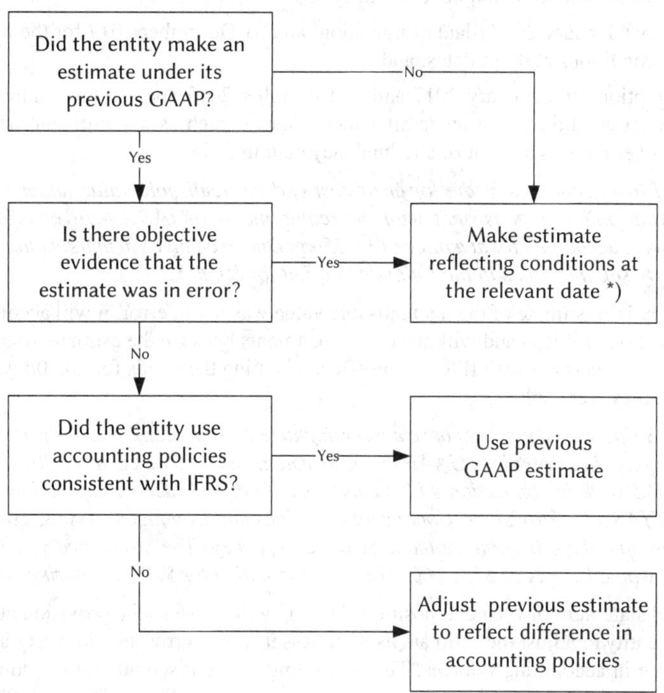

*) the relevant date is the date to which the estimate relates

The general prohibition in IFRS 1 on the use of hindsight in making estimates about past transactions does not override the requirements in other IFRSs that base classifications or measurements on circumstances existing at a particular date, e.g. the distinction between finance leases and operating leases. *[IFRS 1.IG4].*

IFRS 1 requires an entity that is unable to determine whether a particular portion of an adjustment is a transitional adjustment or a change in estimate to treat that portion as a change in accounting estimate under IAS 8, with appropriate disclosures as required by IAS 8. *[IFRS 1.IG58B, IAS 8.32-40].* The distinction between changes in accounting policies and changes in accounting estimates is discussed in detail in Chapter 3.

If a first-time adopter concludes that estimates under previous GAAP were made in error, it should distinguish the correction of those errors from changes in accounting policies in its reconciliations from previous GAAP to IFRSs (see 6.3.1 below). *[IFRS 1.26].* The example below illustrates how an entity should deal with estimates on the transition date and in comparative periods included in its first IFRS financial statements. *[IFRS 1.IG Example 1].*

Example 5.8: Application of IFRS 1 to estimates

Entity A's first IFRS financial statements have a reporting date of 31 December 2018 and include comparative information for one year. In its previous GAAP financial statements for 31 December 2017, Entity A accounted for its pension plan on a cash basis. However, under IAS 19 – Employee Benefits – the plan is classified as a defined benefit plan and actuarial estimates are required.

Entity A will need to make estimates under IFRSs at the relevant date that reflect conditions that existed at the relevant date. This means, for example, that Entity A's:

- discount rates at 1 January 2017 (date of transition) and 31 December 2017 for the pension plan should reflect market conditions at those dates; and
- actuarial assumptions at 1 January 2017 and 31 December 2017 about future employee turnover rates should not reflect conditions that arose after those dates – such as a significant increase in estimated employee turnover rates as a result of a redundancy plan in 2018.

Entity B accounted for inventories at the lower of cost and net realisable value under its previous GAAP. Entity B's accounting policy is consistent with the requirements of IAS 2 – Inventories. Under previous GAAP, the goods were accounted for at a price of £1.25/kg. Due to changes in market circumstances, Entity B ultimately could only sell the goods in the following period for £0.90/kg.

Assuming that Entity B's estimate of the net realisable value was not in error, it will account for the goods at £1.25/kg upon transition to IFRSs and will make no adjustments because the estimate was not in error and its accounting policy was consistent with IFRSs. The effect of selling the goods for £0.90/kg will be reflected in the period in which they were sold.

Entity C's first IFRS financial statements have a reporting date of 31 December 2018 and include comparative information for one year. In its previous GAAP financial statements for 31 December 2016, Entity C accounted for a provision of $150,000 in connection with a court case. Entity C's accounting policy was consistent with the requirements of IAS 37 – Provisions, Contingent Liabilities and Contingent Assets, except for the fact that Entity C did not discount the provision for the time value of money. The discounted value of the provision at 31 December 2016 would have been $135,000. The case was settled for $190,000 during 2017.

In its opening IFRS statement of financial position Entity C will measure the provision at $135,000. IFRS 1 does not permit an entity to adjust the estimate itself, unless it was in error, but does require an adjustment to reflect the difference in accounting policies. The unwinding of the discount and the adjustment due to the under-provision will be included in the comparative statement of profit and loss and other comprehensive income for 2017.

Entity D's first IFRS financial statements have a reporting date of 31 December 2018 and include comparative information for one year. In its previous GAAP financial statements for 31 December 2017, Entity D did not recognise a provision for a court case arising from events that occurred in September 2017. When the court case was concluded on 30 June 2018, Entity D was required to pay €1,000,000 and paid this on 10 July 2018.

In preparing its comparative statement of financial position at 31 December 2017, the treatment of the court case at that date depends on the reason why Entity D did not recognise a provision under its previous GAAP at that date.

Scenario 1 – Previous GAAP was consistent with IAS 37. At the date of preparing its 2017 financial statements, Entity D concluded that the recognition criteria were not met. In this case, Entity D's assumptions under IFRSs are to be consistent with its assumptions under previous GAAP. Therefore, Entity D does not recognise a provision at 31 December 2017 and the effect of settling the court case is reflected in the 2018 statement of profit or loss and other comprehensive income.

Scenario 2 – Previous GAAP was not consistent with IAS 37. Therefore, Entity D develops estimates under IAS 37, which requires that an entity determines whether a present obligation exists at the end of the reporting period by taking account of all available evidence, including any additional evidence provided by events after the end of the reporting period. Similarly, under IAS 10, the resolution of a court case after the end of the reporting period is an adjusting event if it confirms that the entity had a present obligation at that date. In this instance, the resolution of the court case confirms that Entity D had a liability in September 2017 (when the events occurred that gave rise to the court case). Therefore, Entity D recognises a provision at 31 December 2017. Entity D measures that provision by discounting the €1,000,000 paid on 10 July 2018 to its present value, using a discount rate that complies with IAS 37 and reflects market conditions at 31 December 2017.

Some of the potential consequences of applying IAS 37 resulting in changes in the way an entity accounts for provisions are addressed at 7.13 below.

4.3 Derecognition of financial assets and financial liabilities

IFRS 1 requires a first-time adopter to apply the derecognition requirements in IFRS 9 prospectively to transactions occurring on or after the date of transition to IFRSs but need not apply them retrospectively to transactions that had already been derecognised. For example, if a first-time adopter derecognised non-derivative financial assets or non-derivative financial liabilities under its previous GAAP as a result of a transaction that occurred before the date of transition to IFRSs, the entity does not recognise those assets or liabilities under IFRSs unless they qualify for recognition as a result of a later transaction or event. *[IFRS 1.B2]*. However, a first-time adopter may apply the derecognition requirements in IFRS 9 retrospectively from a date of the entity's choosing, provided that the information needed to apply IFRS 9 to financial assets and financial liabilities derecognised as a result of past transactions was obtained at the time of initially accounting for those transactions. *[IFRS 1.B3]*. This will effectively prevent most first-time adopters from restating transactions that occurred before the date of transition to IFRSs.

A first-time adopter that derecognised non-derivative financial assets and financial liabilities before the date of transition to IFRSs and chose not to restate retrospectively will not have to recognise these items under IFRSs even if they meet the IFRS 9 recognition criteria. *[IFRS 1.IG53-54]*. However, IFRS 10 – *Consolidated Financial Statements* – contains no specific transitional or first-time adoption provisions except for those for non-controlling interests (see 4.8 below). Accordingly, its consolidation requirements should be applied fully retrospectively by first-time adopters. For example, an entity may have derecognised, under its previous GAAP, non-derivative financial assets and financial liabilities when they were transferred to a structured entity as part of a securitisation programme. If that entity is considered to be a controlled entity under IFRS 10, those assets and liabilities will be re-recognised on transition to IFRSs by way of the application of IFRS 10 rather than through application of IFRS 9. Of course, if the structured entity itself then subsequently achieved derecognition of the items concerned under the entity's previous GAAP (other than by transfer to another structured entity or member of the entity's group), then the items remain derecognised on transition. Some arrangements for the transfer of assets, particularly securitisations, may last for some time, with the result that transfers might be made both before and after (or on) the date of transition to IFRSs under the same arrangement. IFRS 1 clarifies that transfers made under such arrangements fall within the first-time adoption exception only if they occurred before the date of transition to IFRSs. Transfers on or after the date of transition to IFRSs are subject to the full requirements of IFRS 9. *[IFRS 1.IG53]*.

4.3.1 *First-time adopters applying IAS 39*

The IASB issued four different versions of IFRS 9 between 2009 and 2014, which reflected the progress of its financial instruments project. Each new version added parts of the project that had been completed since the previous version. In July 2014 the IASB issued the final version of IFRS 9 that marks the conclusion of the IASB's financial instruments project, known as the 'complete' version. The IASB decided, upon issuance of the complete version, that earlier versions of IFRS 9 should be withdrawn. This withdrawal was effected by prohibiting entities from adopting earlier versions unless their 'date of initial application' is prior to 1 February 2015. For first time adopters, they have a choice between adopting IAS 39 or the complete version of IFRS 9 if their first IFRS reporting period begins before the mandatory application date of the complete version of IFRS 9, which is 1 January 2018, because paragraph 8 of IFRS 1 allows an entity to apply a new IFRS that is not yet mandatory if that IFRS permits early application. However, for first-time adopters which are insurers, IFRS 4 – *Insurance Contracts* – was amended in September 2016 to permit them, subject to meeting certain criteria, to continue to apply IAS 39 instead of IFRS 9 even after 1 January 2018 (See 5.4 below).

For a first-time adopter that chooses to apply IAS 39 on adoption of IFRSs rather than IFRS 9, all references to IFRS 9 in 4.3 above should be read as references to IAS 39.

4.4 Hedge accounting: general

From 4.4 to 4.7 below, we discuss the hedge accounting treatment for first-time adopters which choose to apply IFRS 9.

First-time adoption issues relating to hedge accounting in the opening IFRS statement of financial position are discussed at 4.5 below and subsequent measurement issues are discussed in 4.6 below. Hedge accounting is dealt with comprehensively in Chapters 52 and 53.

In short:

- If designated as a hedge relationship under previous GAAP and the hedge relationship is of a type that qualifies for hedge accounting under IFRS 9:
  - an entity is required to reflect the hedge relationship in its opening IFRS statement of financial position irrespective of whether the designation and documentation of the hedge relationship under IFRS 9 is completed on or before the transition date; and
  - if the designation or documentation is not completed by the transition date, requirements in IFRS 9 to discontinue hedge accounting apply subsequently.

- If designated as a hedge relationship under previous GAAP, but the hedge relationship is of a type that does not qualify for hedge accounting under IFRS 9:
  - An entity is required to remove that relationship from its opening IFRS statement of financial position (except for a net position as a hedged item under previous GAAP).
- Regardless of the designation under previous GAAP, if hedge designation and documentation that complies with IFRS 9 is completed prior to the transition date:
  - hedge accounting is required from the date the designation and documentation is completed; but
  - retrospective designation under IFRS is not permitted.

4.4.1 Applicability of IAS 39 hedge requirements

A transition requirement of IFRS 9 for hedge accounting permits an existing IFRS user to choose as its accounting policy to continue to apply the hedge accounting requirements of IAS 39 instead of the requirements in Chapter 6 of IFRS 9. *[IFRS 9.7.2.21].* First-time adopters do not have this choice because paragraph 9 of IFRS 1 prohibits first-time adopters from applying the transition provisions in other IFRSs when transitioning to IFRS, except as specified in Appendices B-E. *[IFRS 1.9].* Further, paragraphs B4 to B6 of IFRS 1 contain mandatory exceptions for hedge accounting, but they do not refer to the transition requirements of IFRS 9, and the basis for conclusion attached to IFRS 9 under the heading 'Transition related to the hedge accounting requirements' states 'The IASB decided not to change the requirements of IFRS 1 for hedge accounting. The IASB noted that a first-time adopter would need to look at the entire population of possible hedging relationships and assess which ones would meet the qualifying criteria of the new hedge accounting model'. *[IFRS 9.BC7.52].*

4.4.2 First-time adopters applying IAS 39

For a first-time adopter that chooses to apply IAS 39 on adoption of IFRSs rather than IFRS 9, all references to IFRS 9 in 4.4 above should be read as references to IAS 39.

4.5 Hedge accounting in the opening IFRS statement of financial position

4.5.1 Measurement of derivatives and elimination of deferred gains and losses

Under its previous GAAP an entity's accounting policies might have included a number of accounting treatments for derivatives that formed part of a hedge relationship. For example, accounting policies might have included those where the derivative was:

- not explicitly recognised as an asset or liability (e.g. in the case of a forward contract used to hedge an expected but uncontracted future transaction);
- recognised as an asset or liability but at an amount different from its fair value (e.g. a purchased option recognised at its original cost, perhaps less amortisation; or an interest rate swap accounted for by accruing the periodic interest payments and receipts); or
- subsumed within the accounting for another asset or liability (e.g. a foreign currency denominated monetary item and a matching forward contract or swap accounted for as a 'synthetic' functional currency denominated monetary item).

Chapter 5

Whatever the previous accounting treatment, a first-time adopter should isolate and separately account for all derivatives in its opening IFRS statement of financial position as assets or liabilities measured at fair value. *[IFRS 1.B4(a)].*

All derivatives are measured at fair value through profit or loss, other than those that are financial guarantee contracts, a commitment to provide a loan at a below-market interest rate or a loan commitment that is subject to the impairment requirements of IFRS 9, as well as those that are designated and effective as hedging instruments. Accordingly, the difference between the previous carrying amount of these derivatives (which may have been zero) and their fair value should be recognised as an adjustment of the balance of retained earnings at the date of transition to IFRSs. *[IFRS 1.IG58A].* If an entity cannot determine whether a particular portion of an adjustment is a transition adjustment (i.e. a change in accounting policy) or a change in estimate, it must treat that portion as a change in accounting estimate. *[IFRS 1.IG58B, IAS 8.32-40].* The distinction between changes in accounting policies and changes in accounting estimates is discussed in detail in Chapter 3 at 4.2.

Hedge accounting policies under an entity's previous GAAP might also have included one or both of the following accounting treatments:

- derivatives were measured at fair value but, to the extent they were regarded as hedging future transactions, the gain (or loss) arising was reported as a liability (or asset) such as deferred (or accrued) income;
- realised gains or losses arising on the termination of a previously unrecognised derivative used in a hedge relationship (such as an interest rate swap hedging a borrowing) were included in the statement of financial position as deferred or accrued income and amortised over the remaining term of the hedged exposure.

In all cases, an entity is required to eliminate deferred gains and losses arising on derivatives that were reported in accordance with previous GAAP as if they were assets or liabilities. *[IFRS 1.B4(b)].* In contrast to adjustments made to restate derivatives at fair value, the implementation guidance does not specify in general terms how to deal with adjustments to eliminate deferred gains or losses, i.e. whether they should be taken to retained earnings or a separate component of equity.

The requirement to eliminate deferred gains and losses does not appear to extend to those that have been included in the carrying amount of other assets or liabilities that will continue to be recognised under IFRSs. For example, under an entity's previous GAAP, the carrying amount of non-financial assets such as inventories or property, plant and equipment might have included the equivalent of a basis adjustment (i.e. hedging gains or losses were considered an integral part of the asset's cost). Of course, entities should also consider any other provisions of IFRS 1 that apply to those hedged items, e.g. whether any of the exemptions such as those for business combinations (see 5.2 below) or deemed cost (see 5.5 below) will be taken.

The following diagram illustrates the treatment of hedge accounting in the opening IFRS statement of financial position and after transition to IFRSs. Hedge accounting in the opening IFRS statement of financial position will be discussed in the sub-sections following the diagram and hedge accounting after transition to IFRSs is dealt with at 4.6 below.

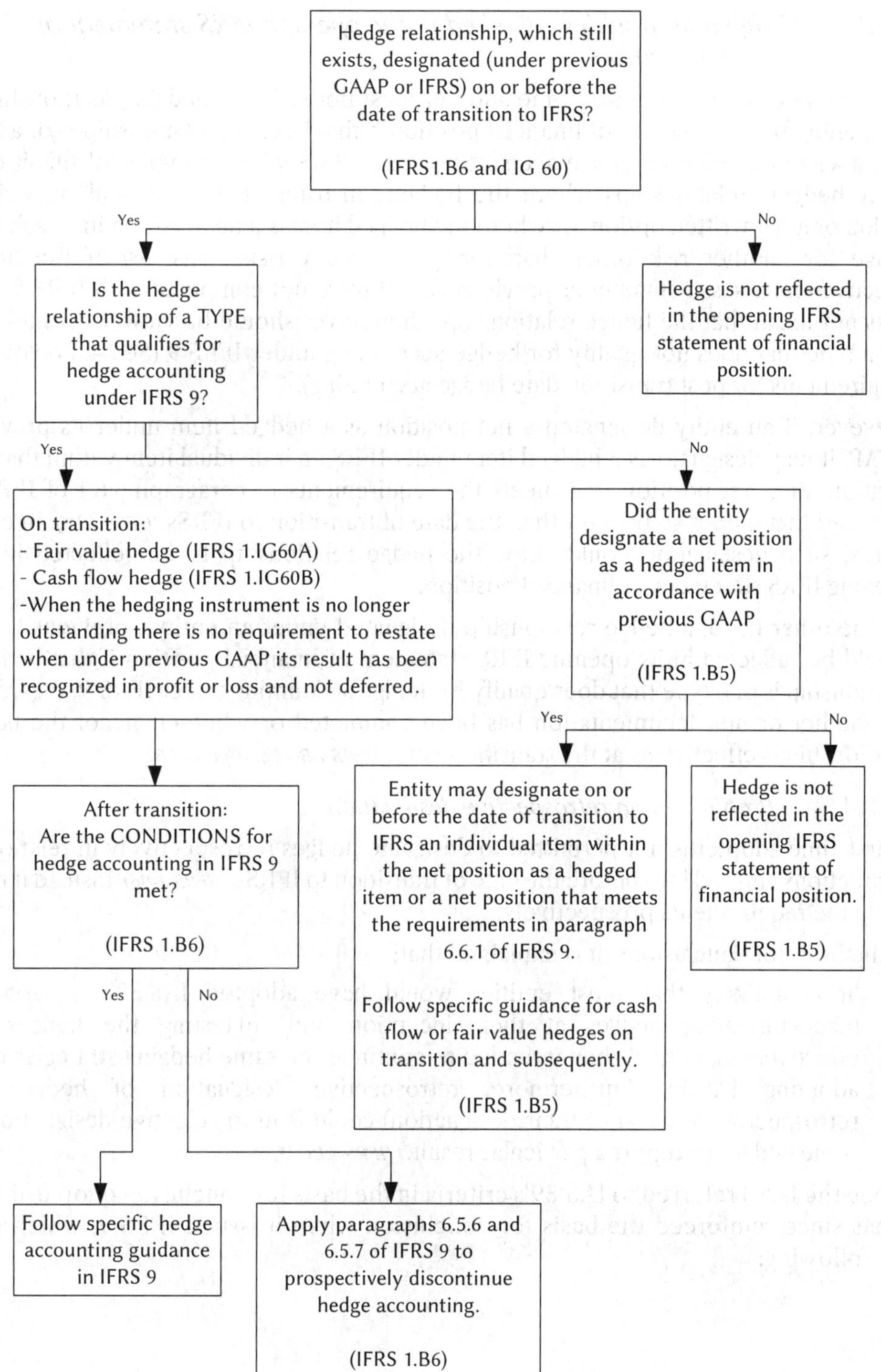
Hedge relationship, which still exists, designated (under previous GAAP or IFRS) on or before the date of transition to IFRS?
(IFRS1.B6 and IG 60)
Yes
No
Is the hedge relationship of a TYPE that qualifies for hedge accounting under IFRS 9?
Hedge is not reflected in the opening IFRS statement of financial position.
Yes
No
On transition:
- Fair value hedge (IFRS 1.IG60A)
- Cash flow hedge (IFRS 1.IG60B)
-When the hedging instrument is no longer outstanding there is no requirement to restate when under previous GAAP its result has been recognized in profit or loss and not deferred.
Did the entity designate a net position as a hedged item in accordance with previous GAAP
(IFRS 1.B5)
Yes
No
After transition:
Are the CONDITIONS for hedge accounting in IFRS 9 met?
(IFRS 1.B6)
Entity may designate on or before the date of transition to IFRS an individual item within the net position as a hedged item or a net position that meets the requirements in paragraph 6.6.1 of IFRS 9.
Follow specific guidance for cash flow or fair value hedges on transition and subsequently.
(IFRS 1.B5)
Hedge is not reflected in the opening IFRS statement of financial position.
(IFRS 1.B5)
Yes
No
Follow specific hedge accounting guidance in IFRS 9
Apply paragraphs 6.5.6 and 6.5.7 of IFRS 9 to prospectively discontinue hedge accounting.
(IFRS 1.B6)

4.5.2 Hedge relationships reflected in the opening IFRS statement of financial position

The standard states that a first-time adopter must not reflect a hedging relationship in its opening IFRS statement of financial position if that hedging relationship is of a type that does not qualify for hedge accounting under IFRS 9. As examples of this it cites many hedging relationships where the hedging instrument is a stand-alone written option or a net written option; or where the hedged item is a net position in a cash flow hedge for another risk other than foreign currency risk. *[IFRS 1.B5]*. If the hedge effectiveness assessments under previous GAAP were not compliant with IFRS 9, that does not mean that the hedge relationships themselves should be viewed as ones that are a type that does not qualify for hedge accounting under IFRS 9 (See 4.6 below for requirements for post transition date hedge accounting).

However, if an entity designated a net position as a hedged item under its previous GAAP, it may designate as a hedged item under IFRS an individual item within that net position, or a net position that meets the requirements in paragraph 6.6.1 of IFRS 9, provided that it does so no later than the date of transition to IFRSs. *[IFRS 1.B5]*. In other words, such designation could allow the hedge relationship to be reflected in the opening IFRS statement of financial position.

On the other hand, a hedge relationship designated under an entity's previous GAAP should be reflected in its opening IFRS statement of financial position if that hedging relationship is of a type that does qualify for hedge accounting under IFRS 9, regardless of whether or not documentation has been completed or whether or not the hedge relationship is effective as at the transition date. *[IFRS 1.B4-B6, IG60A-60B]*.

4.5.2.A Prohibition on retrospective designation

A first-time adopter is not permitted to designate hedges retrospectively in relation to transactions entered into before the date of transition to IFRSs. *[IFRS 1.B6]*. Instead it must apply the requirements prospectively.

In the basis for conclusions, it is explained that:

> 'it is unlikely that most entities would have adopted IAS 39's criteria for (a) documenting hedges at their inception and (b) testing the hedges for effectiveness, even if they intended to continue the same hedging strategies after adopting IAS 39. Furthermore, retrospective designation of hedges (or retrospective reversal of their designation) could lead to selective designation of some hedges to report a particular result.' *[IFRS 1.BC75]*.

While the IASB referred to IAS 39's criteria in the basis for conclusion quoted above, it has since reinforced the basis for conclusion when it issued IFRS 9, which says the following:

'To the extent that an entity wants to apply hedge accounting, those hedging relationships should be documented on or before the transition date. This is consistent with the transition requirements for existing users of IFRSs and the existing transition requirements of IFRS 1...'. *[IFRS 9.BC7.52]*.

4.5.2.B Designation in anticipation of adoption of IFRS

If a first-time adopter, in anticipation of the adoption of IFRS, decides to designate a transaction as a hedge under IFRS 9 and completes the required documentation sometime before the transition date to IFRS, some have questioned whether upon adoption of IFRS hedge accounting should be applied prior to the transition date. In our view, as long as the hedge is properly designated and documented in accordance with IFRS 9 prior to the date of transition, the first-time adopter should apply hedge accounting from the date that it met the designation and documentation requirements of IFRS 9. As explained in 4.5.2.A above, a first-time adopter cannot designate a transaction retrospectively as a hedge under IFRS.

4.5.3 Reflecting cash flow hedges in the opening IFRS statement of financial position

A first-time adopter may have deferred gains and losses on a cash flow hedge of a forecast transaction under its previous GAAP. If, at the date of transition, the hedged forecast transaction is not highly probable, but is expected to occur, the entire deferred gain or loss should be recognised in the cash flow hedge reserve within equity. *[IFRS 1.IG60B]*. This is consistent with the treatment required for a deferred gain or loss expected to be recovered in the future (see Chapter 53). *[IFRS 9.6.5.11]*.

How should an entity deal with such a hedge if, at the date of transition to IFRSs, the forecast transaction *is* highly probable? It would make no sense if the hedge of the transaction that is expected to occur were required to be reflected in the opening IFRS statement of financial position, but the hedge of the highly probable forecast transaction (which is clearly a 'better' hedge) were not.

Therefore, it must follow that a cash flow hedge should be reflected in the opening IFRS statement of financial position in the way set out above if the hedged item is a forecast transaction that is highly probable (see Case 1 of Example 5.9 below). Similarly, it follows that a cash flow hedge of the variability in cash flows attributable to a particular risk associated with a recognised asset or liability (such as all or some future interest payments on variable rate debt) should also be reflected in the opening IFRS statement of financial position. To do otherwise would allow an entity to choose not to designate (in accordance with IFRS 9) certain cash flow hedges, say those that are in a loss position, until one day after its date of transition, thereby allowing associated hedging losses to bypass profit or loss completely. However, this would effectively result in the retrospective de-designation of hedges to achieve a desired result, thereby breaching the general principle of IFRS 1 (i.e. a first-time adopter cannot designate a hedge relationship retrospectively).

If, at the date of transition to IFRSs, the forecast transaction was not expected to occur, consistent with the requirements of paragraphs 6.5.6-6.5.7 and 6.5.12(b) of IFRS 9, a first-time adopter should reclassify any related deferred gains and losses that are not expected to be recovered into retained earnings.

Example 5.9: Unrecognised gains and losses on existing cash flow hedge

Entity A has the euro as its functional currency. In September 2016 it entered into a forward currency contract to sell dollars for euros in twelve months to hedge dollar denominated sales it forecasts are highly probable to occur in September 2017. Entity A will apply IFRS 9 from 1 January 2017, its date of transition to IFRSs. The historical cost of the forward contract is €nil and at the date of transition it had a positive fair value of €100.

Case 1: Gains and losses deferred: Under Entity A's previous GAAP, until the sales occurred the forward contract was recognised in the statement of financial position at its fair value and the resulting gain or loss was deferred in the statement of financial position as a liability or an asset. When the sale occurred, any deferred gain or loss was recognised in profit or loss as an offset to the revenue recognised on the hedged sale.

This relationship must be reflected in Entity A's opening IFRS statement of financial position whether or not it is designated as an effective hedge in accordance with IFRS 9 at the date of transition: there is no restriction on transferring the deferred gain to a separate component of equity and there is no adjustment to the carrying amount of the forward contract.

Case 2: Gains and losses unrecognised: Under Entity A's previous GAAP the contract was not recognised in the statement of financial position. When the sale occurred, any unrecognised gain or loss was recognised in profit or loss as an offset to the revenue recognised on the hedged sales.

Although this Case is more problematic, we consider that it should be accounted for in the same way as Case 1. The difference between the previous carrying amount of a derivative and its fair value would be recognised in other comprehensive income.

4.5.4 Reflecting fair value hedges in the opening IFRS statement of financial position

If a first-time adopter has, under its previous GAAP, deferred or not recognised gains and losses on a fair value hedge of a hedged item that is not measured at fair value, the entity should adjust the carrying amount of the hedged item at the date of transition. The adjustment, which is essentially the effective part of the hedge that was not recognised in the carrying amount of the hedged item under the previous GAAP, should be calculated as the lower of:

(a) that portion of the cumulative change in the fair value of the hedged item that was not recognised under previous GAAP; and

(b) that portion of the cumulative change in the fair value of the hedging instrument and, under previous GAAP, was either (i) not recognised or (ii) deferred in the statement of financial position as an asset or liability. *[IFRS 1.IG60A].*

4.5.5 Reflecting foreign currency net investment hedges in the opening IFRS statement of financial position

IFRS 1 does not provide explicit guidance on reflecting foreign currency net investment hedges in the opening IFRS statement of financial position. However, IFRS 9 requires that ongoing IFRS reporting entities account for those hedges similarly to cash flow hedges. *[IFRS 9.6.5.13].* It follows that the first-time adoption provisions regarding cash flow hedges (see 4.5.3 above) also apply to hedges of foreign currency net investments.

A first-time adopter that applies the exemption to reset cumulative translation differences to zero (see 5.7 below) should not reclassify pre-transition gains and losses on the hedging instruments that were recognised in equity under previous GAAP to profit or loss upon disposal of a foreign operation. Instead, those pre-transition gains and losses should be recognised in the opening balance of retained earnings to avoid a disparity between the treatment of the gains and losses on the hedged item and the hedging instrument. This means that the requirement to reset the cumulative translation differences also applies to related gains and losses on hedging instruments.

4.5.6 First-time adopters applying IAS 39

For a first-time adopter that chooses to apply IAS 39 on adoption of IFRSs rather than IFRS 9, all references to IFRS 9 in 4.5.1 through 4.5.5 above other than the reference to IFRS 9 in 4.5.1 for the exception of measurement at fair value through profit or loss should be read as references to IAS 39.

4.6 Hedge accounting: subsequent treatment

The implementation guidance explains that hedge accounting can be applied prospectively only from the date the hedge relationship is fully designated and documented. In other words, after the transition to IFRS, hedge accounting under IFRS 9 can be applied only if the conditions for hedge accounting in that standard are met. Therefore, if the hedging instrument is still held at the date of transition to IFRSs, the designation and documentation of a hedge relationship must be completed on or before that date if the hedge relationship is to qualify for hedge accounting from that date. *[IFRS 1.IG60].*

Before the date of transition to IFRSs an entity may have designated as a hedge a transaction under previous GAAP that is a type that qualifies for hedge accounting under IFRS 9 but does not meet the conditions for hedge accounting in IFRS 9 at the transition date. In these cases it should follow the general requirements in IFRS 9 for discontinuing hedge accounting subsequent to the date of transition to IFRSs – these are dealt with in Chapter 53. *[IFRS 1.B6].*

For cash flow hedges, any net cumulative gain or loss that was reclassified to the cash flow hedge reserve on the transition date to IFRS (see 4.5.3 above) should remain there until: *[IFRS 1.IG60B]*

(a) the forecast transaction subsequently results in the recognition of a non-financial asset or non-financial liability;

(b) the forecast transaction affects profit or loss; or

(c) subsequently circumstances change and the forecast transaction is no longer expected to occur, in which case any related net cumulative gain or loss that had been reclassified to the cash flow hedge reserve on the transition date to IFRS is reclassified to profit or loss.

The requirements above do little more than reiterate the general requirements of IFRS 9, i.e. that hedge accounting can only be applied prospectively if the qualifying conditions are met, and entities should experience few interpretative problems in dealing with this aspect of the hedge accounting requirements.

4.6.1 First-time adopters applying IAS 39

For a first-time adopter that chooses to apply IAS 39 on adoption of IFRSs rather than IFRS 9, all references to IFRS 9 in 4.6 above should be read as references to IAS 39.

4.7 Hedge accounting: examples

The following examples illustrate the guidance considered at 4.5 to 4.6 above. The examples also are applicable to entities applying IAS 39.

Example 5.10: Pre-transition cash flow hedges

Case 1: All hedge accounting conditions met from date of transition and thereafter

In 2010 Entity A borrowed €10m from a bank. The terms of the loan provide that a coupon of 3 month LIBOR plus 2% is payable quarterly in arrears and the principal is repayable in 2025. In 2013, Entity A decided to 'fix' its coupon payments for the remainder of the term of the loan by entering into a twelve-year pay-fixed, receive-floating interest rate swap. The swap has a notional amount of €10m and the floating leg resets quarterly based on 3 month LIBOR.

In Entity A's final financial statements prepared under its previous GAAP, the swap was clearly identified as a hedging instrument in a hedge of the loan and was accounted for as such. The fair value of the swap was not recognised in Entity A's statement of financial position and the periodic interest settlements were accrued and recognised as an adjustment to the loan interest expense. On 1 January 2017, Entity A's date of transition to IFRSs, the loan and the swap were still in place and the swap had a positive fair value of €1m and a €nil carrying amount. In addition, Entity A met all the conditions in IFRS 9 to permit the use of hedge accounting for this arrangement throughout 2017 and 2018.

In its opening IFRS statement of financial position Entity A should:

- recognise the interest rate swap as an asset at its fair value of €1m; and
- credit €1m to a separate component of equity, to be reclassified to profit or loss as the hedged transactions (future interest payments on the loan) affect profit or loss.

In addition, hedge accounting would be applied throughout 2017 and 2018.

Case 2: Hedge terminated prior to date of transition

The facts are as in Case 1 except that in April 2016 Entity A decided to terminate the hedge and the interest rate swap was settled for its then fair value of €1.5m. Under its previous GAAP, Entity A's stated accounting policy in respect of terminated hedges was to defer any realised gain or loss on terminated hedging instruments where the hedged exposure remained. These gains or losses would be recognised in profit or loss at the same time as gains or losses on the hedged exposure. At the end of December 2016, A's statement of financial position included a liability (unamortised gain) of €1.4m.

IFRS 1 does not explicitly address hedges terminated prior to the date of transition. However, because the terminated hedge relates to a transaction that has an ongoing risk exposure, the provisions of IFRS 9 on hedge discontinuance should be applied to this relationship. Accordingly, in its opening IFRS statement of financial position Entity A should:

- remove the deferred gain of €1.4m from the statement of financial position; and
- credit €1.4m to a separate component of equity, to be reclassified to profit or loss as the hedged transactions (future interest payments on the loan) affect profit or loss.

Example 5.11: Existing fair value hedges

Case 1: All hedge accounting conditions met from date of transition and thereafter (1)

On 15 November 2016, Entity B entered into a forward contract to sell 50,000 barrels of crude oil to hedge all changes in the fair value of certain inventory. Entity B will apply IFRS 9 from 1 January 2017, its date of transition to IFRSs. The historical cost of the forward contract is $nil and at the date of transition the forward had a negative fair value of $50.

In Entity B's final financial statements prepared under its previous GAAP, the forward was clearly identified as a hedging instrument in a hedge of the inventory and was accounted for as such. The contract was recognised in the statement of financial position as a liability at its fair value and the resulting loss was deferred in the statement of financial position as an asset. In the period between 15 November 2016 and 1 January 2017 the fair value of the inventory increased by $47. In addition, Entity B met all the conditions in IFRS 9 to permit the use of hedge accounting for this arrangement throughout 2017 until the forward expired.

In its opening IFRS statement of financial position Entity B should:

- continue to recognise the forward contract as a liability at its fair value of $50;
- derecognise the $50 deferred loss asset on the forward contract;
- recognise the crude oil inventory at its historical cost plus $47 (the lower of the change in fair value of the crude oil inventory, $47, and that of the forward contract, $50); and
- record the net adjustment of $3 in retained earnings.

In addition, hedge accounting would be applied throughout 2017 until the forward expired.

Case 2: All hedge accounting conditions met from date of transition and thereafter (2)

In 2010 Entity C borrowed €10m from a bank. The terms of the loan provide that a coupon of 8% is payable quarterly in arrears and the principal is repayable in 2025. In 2013, Entity C decided to alter its coupon payments for the remainder of the term of the loan by entering into a twelve-year pay-floating, receive-fixed interest rate swap. The swap has a notional amount of €10m and the floating leg resets quarterly based on 3 month LIBOR.

In Entity C's final financial statements prepared under its previous GAAP, the swap was clearly identified as a hedging instrument in a hedge of the loan and accounted for as such. The fair value of the swap was not recognised in Entity C's statement of financial position and the periodic interest settlements on the swap were accrued and recognised as an adjustment to the loan interest expense.

On 1 January 2017, Entity C's date of transition to IFRSs, the loan and the swap were still in place and the swap had a negative fair value of €1m and a €nil carrying amount. The cumulative change in the fair value of the loan attributable to changes in 3 month LIBOR was €1.1m, although this change was not recognised in Entity C's statement of financial position because the loan was accounted for at amortised cost. In addition, Entity C met all the conditions in IFRS 9 to permit the use of hedge accounting for this arrangement throughout 2017 and 2018.

In its opening IFRS statement of financial position Entity C should:

- recognise the interest rate swap as a liability at its fair value of €1m; and
- reduce the carrying amount of the loan by €1m (the lower of the change in its fair value attributable to the hedged risk, €1.1m, and that of the interest rate swap, $1m) to €9m.

In addition, hedge accounting would be applied throughout 2017 and 2018.

Case 3: Hedge terminated prior to date of transition

The facts are as in Case 2 above except that in April 2016 Entity C decided to terminate the fair value hedge and the interest rate swap was settled for its then negative fair value of €1.5m. Under its previous GAAP, Entity C's stated accounting policy in respect of terminated hedges was to defer any gain or loss on the hedging instrument as a liability or an asset where the hedged exposure remained and this gain or loss was recognised in profit or loss at the same time as the hedged exposure. At the end of December 2016 the unamortised loss recognised as an asset in Entity C's statement of financial position was €1.4m. The cumulative change through April 2016 in the fair value of the loan attributable to changes in 3 month LIBOR that had not been recognised was €1.6m.

In its opening IFRS statement of financial position Entity C should:

- remove the deferred loss asset of €1.4m from the statement of financial position; and
- reduce the carrying amount of the loan by €1.4m (the lower of the change in its fair value attributable to the hedged risk, €1.6m, and the change in value of the interest rate swap that was deferred in the statement of financial position, €1.4m).

The €1.4m adjustment to the loan would be amortised to profit or loss over its remaining term.

Case 4: Documentation completed after the date of transition

The facts are as in Case 2 above except that, at the date of transition, Entity C had not prepared documentation that would allow it to apply hedge accounting under IFRS 9. Hedge documentation was subsequently prepared as a result of which the hedge qualified for hedge accounting with effect from the beginning of July 2017 and through 2018.

As in Case 2, in its opening IFRS statement of financial position Entity C should:

- recognise the interest rate swap as a liability at its fair value of €1m; and
- reduce the carrying amount of the loan by €1m (the lower of the change in its fair value attributable to the hedged risk, €1.1m, and that of the interest rate swap, €1m), because the loan was clearly identified as a hedged item.

For the period from January 2017 to June 2017, hedge accounting would not be available. Accordingly, the interest rate swap would be remeasured to its fair value and any gain or loss would be recognised in profit or loss with no offset from remeasuring the loan. With effect from July 2017 hedge accounting would be applied prospectively.

4.8 Non-controlling interests

A first-time adopter must apply IFRS 10 retrospectively, except for the following requirements that apply prospectively from its date of transition to IFRSs: *[IFRS 1.B7]*

(a) the requirement that total comprehensive income is attributed to the owners of the parent and to the non-controlling interests even if this results in the non-controlling interests having a deficit balance; *[IFRS 10.B94]*

(b) the requirements on accounting for changes in the parent's ownership interest in a subsidiary that do not result in a loss of control; *[IFRS 10.23, B96]* and

(c) the requirements on accounting for a loss of control over a subsidiary, and the related requirements in IFRS 5 – *Non-current Assets Held for Sale and Discontinued Operations* – to classify all assets and liabilities of that subsidiary as held for sale. *[IFRS 10.B97-B99, IFRS 5.8A].*

However, if a first-time adopter restates any business combination that occurred prior to its date of transition to comply with IFRS 3 – *Business Combinations* – it must also apply IFRS 10, including these requirements, from that date onwards (see 5.2.2 below). *[IFRS 1.C1].*

4.9 Classification and measurement of financial instruments under IFRS 9

IFRS 9 requires a financial asset to be measured at amortised cost if it meets two tests that deal with the nature of the business that holds the assets and the nature of the cash flows arising on those assets. *[IFRS 9.4.1.2].* Also, the standard requires a financial asset to be measured at fair value through other comprehensive income if certain conditions are met. *[IFRS 9.4.1.2A].* These are described in detail in Chapter 47. Paragraph B8 of IFRS 1 requires a first-time adopter to assess whether a financial asset meets the conditions on the basis of the facts and circumstances that exist at the date of transition to IFRSs.

If it is impracticable to assess a modified time value of money element under paragraphs B4.1.9B-B4.1.9D of IFRS 9 on the basis of the facts and circumstances that exist at the transition date, the first-time adopter should assess the contractual cash flow characteristics of that financial asset on the basis of the facts and circumstances that existed at that date without taking into account the requirements related to the modification of the time value of money element in paragraphs B4.1.9B-B4.1.9D of

IFRS 9. *[IFRS 1.B8A]*. Similarly, if it is impracticable to assess whether the fair value of a prepayment feature is insignificant under B4.1.12(c) of IFRS 9 on the basis of the facts and circumstances that exist at the transition date, paragraphs B8B of IFRS 1 require an entity to assess the contractual cash flow characteristics of that financial asset on the basis of the facts and circumstances that existed at that date without taking into account the exception for prepayment features in B4.1.12 of IFRS 9. These are discussed in more detail in Chapter 47 at 10.2.3.

Paragraph B8C of IFRS 1 states that if it is impracticable (as defined in IAS 8) for an entity to apply retrospectively the effective interest method in IFRS 9, the fair value of the financial asset or the financial liability at the date of transition to IFRSs should be the new gross carrying amount of that financial asset or the new amortised cost of that financial liability at the date of transition to IFRSs.

4.10 Impairment of financial instruments under IFRS 9

Paragraph B8D of IFRS 1 requires a first-time adopter to apply the impairment requirements in section 5.5 of IFRS 9 retrospectively subject to paragraphs 7.2.15 and 7.2.18-7.2.20 of IFRS 9 (see Chapter 50 at 5).

At the date of transition to IFRSs, paragraph B8E of IFRS 1 requires a first-time adopter to use reasonable and supportable information that is available without undue cost or effort to determine the credit risk at the date that the financial instruments were initially recognised (or for loan commitments and financial guarantee contracts the date that the entity became a party to the irrevocable commitment in accordance with paragraph 5.5.6 of IFRS 9) and compare that to the credit risk at the date of transition to IFRSs. *[IFRS 9.B7.2.2-B7.2.3]*.

A first-time adopter may apply the guidance in paragraph B8F of IFRS 1 to determine whether there has been a significant increase in credit risk since initial recognition. However, a first-time adopter would not be required to make that assessment if that would require undue cost or effort. Paragraph B8G of IFRS 1 requires such a first-time adopter to recognise a loss allowance at an amount equal to lifetime expected credit losses at each reporting date until that financial instrument is derecognised (unless that financial asset is low credit risk at a reporting date).

4.11 Embedded derivatives

The treatment of embedded derivatives depends on whether an entity applies IAS 39 or IFRS 9.

4.11.1 Entities applying IAS 39

Under IAS 39, some embedded derivatives are accounted for at fair value separately from their host contracts.

When IAS 39 requires an entity to separate an embedded derivative from a host contract, the initial carrying amounts of the components at the date the instrument first satisfied the recognition criteria in IAS 39 should reflect circumstances that existed at that date. If the initial carrying amounts of the embedded derivative and host contract cannot be determined reliably, the entire combined contract should be designated at fair value through profit or loss (i.e. held for trading). *[IFRS 1.IG55]*.

Further guidance was provided by IFRIC 9 – *Reassessment of Embedded Derivatives* – which stated that, on first-time adoption, an entity should make an assessment of whether an embedded derivative is required to be separated from the host contract and accounted for as a derivative on the basis of conditions that existed at the later of the date it first became a party to the contract and the date a reassessment is required (see Chapter 44). *[IFRIC 9.8]*.

Although the IASB recognised that the equivalent US GAAP requirements provided an option not to account separately for some pre-existing embedded derivatives when that guidance became mandatory, the Board concluded that the failure to measure embedded derivatives at fair value would diminish the relevance and reliability of an entity's first IFRS financial statements. It also observed that IAS 39 addresses an inability to measure an embedded derivative and the host contract separately; in such cases, the entire combined contract is measured at fair value. *[IFRS 1.BC66]*. Accordingly, no exception was granted in this area.

4.11.2 Entities applying IFRS 9

When IFRS 9 requires an entity to separate an embedded derivative from a host contract, the initial carrying amounts of the components at the date the instrument first satisfied the recognition criteria in IFRS 9 should reflect circumstances that existed at that date. If the initial carrying amounts of the embedded derivative and host contract cannot be determined reliably, the entire combined contract should be designated at fair value through profit or loss *(IFRS 1.IG55)*.

Paragraph B9 of IFRS 1 requires a first-time adopter to assess whether an embedded derivative should be separated from the host contract and accounted for as a derivative based on conditions that existed at the later of the date it first became a party to the contract and the date a reassessment is required by IFRS 9. *[IFRS 9.B4.3.11]*. It should be noted that IFRS 9 does not permit embedded derivatives to be separated from host contracts that are financial assets.

4.12 Government loans

It is common practice in certain developing countries for the government to grant loans to entities at below-market interest rates in order to promote economic development. A first-time adopter may not have recognised and measured such loans in its previous GAAP financial statements on a basis that complies with IFRSs. IAS 20 – *Accounting for Government Grants and Disclosure of Government Assistance* – requires such loans to be recognised at fair value with the effect of the below-market interest rate separately accounted for as a government grant. *[IAS 20.10A]*. The IASB has provided transition relief to first-time adopters in the form of an exception that requires government loans received to be classified as a financial liability or an equity instrument in accordance with IAS 32 – *Financial Instruments: Presentation* – and to apply the requirements in IFRS 9 and IAS 20 prospectively to government loans existing at the date of transition to IFRSs. Therefore a first-time adopter will not recognise the corresponding benefit of the government loan at a below-market rate of interest as a government grant. A first-time adopter that did not, under its previous GAAP, recognise and measure a government loan at a below-market rate of interest on a basis consistent with IFRS requirements will use its previous GAAP carrying amount of the loan at the date of transition as the carrying amount of the loan in the opening IFRS statement of financial position and apply IFRS 9 to the measurement of such loans after the date of transition to IFRSs. *[IFRS 1.B10].*

Alternatively, an entity may apply the requirements in IFRS 9 and IAS 20 retrospectively to any government loan originated before the date of transition, provided the information needed to do so had been obtained when it first accounted for the loan under previous GAAP. *[IFRS 1.B11].*

The requirements and guidance above do not preclude an entity from designating previously recognised financial instruments at fair value through profit or loss (see 5.11.2 below). *[IFRS 1.B12].*

The requirements when a government loan with a below-market interest rate is not restated from its previous GAAP amount are illustrated in the following example:

Example 5.12: Government loan with below-market interest rate

A government provides loans at a below-market rate of interest to fund the purchase of manufacturing equipment.

Entity S's date of transition to IFRSs is 1 January 2017.

In 2014 Entity S received a loan of CU 100,000 at a below-market rate of interest from the government. Under its previous GAAP, Entity S accounted for the loan as equity and the carrying amount was CU 100,000 at the date of transition. The amount repayable at 1 January 2020 will be CU 103,030.

No other payment is required under the terms of the loan and there are no future performance conditions attached to it. The information needed to measure the fair value of the loan was not obtained at the time it was initially accounted for.

The loan meets the definition of a financial liability in accordance with IAS 32. Entity S therefore reclassifies it as a liability. It also uses the previous GAAP carrying amount of the loan at the date of transition as the carrying amount of the loan in the opening IFRS statement of financial position, reclassifying it from equity to liability. It calculates the effective interest rate starting 1 January 2017 at 10%. The opening balance of CU 100,000 will accrete to CU 103,030 at 31 December 2019 and interest of CU 1,000, CU 1,010 and CU 1,020 will be charged to interest expense in each of the three years ended 31 December 2017, 2018 and 2019.

5 OPTIONAL EXEMPTIONS FROM THE REQUIREMENTS OF CERTAIN IFRSs

5.1 Introduction

As noted at 3.5 above, IFRS 1 grants limited exemptions from the general requirement of full retrospective application of the standards in force at the end of an entity's first IFRS reporting period. *[IFRS 1.12(b)].* Each of these exemptions is explained in detail below.

5.2 Business combinations and acquisitions of associates and joint arrangements

The business combinations exemption in IFRS 1 is probably the single most important exemption in the standard, as it permits a first-time adopter not to restate business combinations that occurred prior to its date of transition to IFRSs. The detailed guidance on the application of the business combinations exemption is contained in Appendix C to IFRS 1 and is organised as follows in the sections below: *[IFRS 1 Appendix C]*

- option to restate business combinations retrospectively (see 5.2.2 below);
- classification of business combinations (see 5.2.3 below);
- recognition and measurement of assets and liabilities (see 5.2.4 below);
- restatement of goodwill (see 5.2.5 below);
- currency adjustments to goodwill (see 5.2.6 below);
- previously unconsolidated subsidiaries (see 5.2.7 below);
- previously consolidated entities that are not subsidiaries (see 5.2.8 below);
- measurement of deferred taxes and non-controlling interests (see 5.2.9 below); and
- transition accounting for contingent consideration (see 5.2.10 below).

The business combinations exemption applies only to business combinations that occurred before the date of transition to IFRSs and only to the acquisition of businesses as defined under IFRS 3 (see 5.2.1 below). *[IFRS 1 Appendix C]*. Therefore, it does not apply to a transaction that, for example, IFRSs treat as an acquisition of an asset (see 5.2.1.A below).

5.2.1 Definition of a 'business' under IFRSs

As noted above, the business combination exemption applies only to the acquisition of a business as defined under IFRS 3. Therefore, a first-time adopter needs to consider whether past transactions would qualify as business combinations under IFRS 3. That standard defines a business combination as 'a transaction or other event in which an acquirer obtains control of one or more businesses. Transactions sometimes referred to as "true mergers" or "mergers of equals" are also business combinations as that term is used in this IFRS.' *[IFRS 3 Appendix A]*. A business is defined as 'an integrated set of activities and assets that is capable of being conducted and managed for the purpose of providing a return in the form of dividends, lower costs or other economic benefits directly to investors or other owners, members or participants.' *[IFRS 3 Appendix A]*. In addition, IFRS 3 states that 'if the assets acquired are not a business, the reporting entity shall account for the transaction or other event as an asset acquisition' (see 5.2.1.A below). *[IFRS 3.3]*. Distinguishing a business combination from an asset acquisition is described in detail in Chapter 9.

In October 2012, the IASB issued *Investment Entities (Amendments to IFRS 10, IFRS 12 and IAS 27)* effective for annual periods beginning on or after 1 January 2014 (see 5.9.5 below). Amongst other changes, the amendment also makes it clear that Appendix C of IFRS 1, which deals with the business combinations exemption, should be applied only to business combinations within the scope of IFRS 3. This means that the exemption does not apply to mergers of entities that are not business combinations under IFRS 3. So a first-time adopter which had such mergers under previous GAAP should retrospectively apply IFRS to those mergers. If the mergers are those under common control, as there is no specific guidance under IFRS on accounting for them, we discuss this issue in Chapter 10.

5.2.1.A Asset acquisitions

Because IFRS 3 provides such a specific definition of a business combination (as described in Chapter 9), it is possible that under some national GAAPs, transactions that are not business combinations under IFRS 3, e.g. asset acquisitions, may have been accounted for as if they were business combinations. A first-time adopter will need to restate any transactions that it accounted for as business combinations under its previous GAAP, but which are not business combinations under IFRS 3.

Example 5.13: Acquisition of assets

Entity A acquired a company that held a single asset at the time of acquisition. That company had no employees and the asset itself was not in use at the date of acquisition. Entity A accounted for the transaction under its previous GAAP using the purchase method, which resulted in goodwill. Can Entity A apply the business combinations exemption to the acquisition of this asset?

If Entity A concludes that the asset is not a business as defined in IFRS 3, it will not be able to apply the business combinations exemption. Instead, Entity A should account for such transaction as an asset acquisition. The entity may consider applying other applicable optional exemptions under IFRS 1.

If in the example above the entity had accounted for the transaction as an asset acquisition rather than a business combination under previous GAAP, it would need to determine whether the transaction meets the definition of a business combination in IFRS 3 in order to qualify for use of the exemption.

5.2.2 Option to restate business combinations retrospectively

A first-time adopter must account for business combinations occurring after its date of transition under IFRS 3, i.e. any business combinations during the comparative periods need to be restated in accordance with IFRSs. An entity may elect not to apply IFRS 3 to business combinations occurring before the date of transition. However, if a first-time adopter does restate a business combination occurring prior to its date of transition to comply with IFRS 3 it must also restate any subsequent business combinations under IFRS 3 and apply IFRS 10 from that date onwards. *[IFRS 1.C1]*. In other words, as shown on the time line below, a first-time adopter is allowed to choose any date in the past from which it wants to account for all business combinations under IFRS 3 without having to restate business combinations that occurred prior to such date. It must be noted that a first-time adopter availing itself of this option is required to apply the version of IFRS 3 effective at the end of its first IFRS reporting period to any retrospectively restated business combinations.

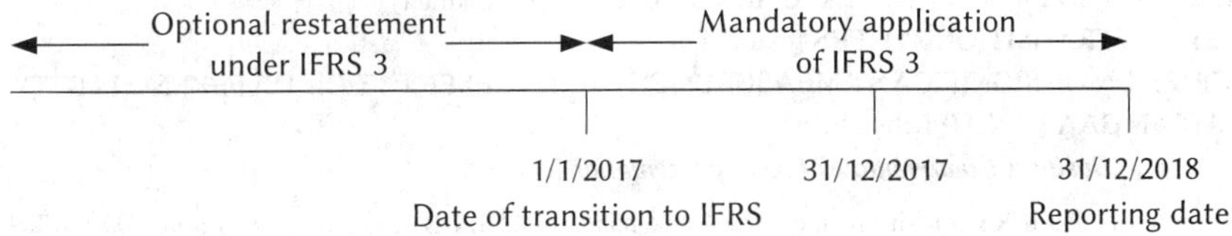

Even if a first-time adopter elects not to restate certain business combinations, it may still need to restate the carrying amounts of the acquired assets and assumed liabilities, as described at 5.2.4 below.

Although there is no restriction that prevents retrospective application by a first-time adopter of IFRS 3 to all past business combinations, in our opinion, a first-time adopter should not restate business combinations under IFRS 3 that occurred before the date of transition when this would require use of hindsight.

Extracts 5.3 below and 5.12 at 6.3 below illustrate the typical disclosure made by entities that opted not to restate business combinations that occurred before their date of transition to IFRSs, while Extract 5.4 below illustrates disclosures by an entity that chose to restate certain business combinations that occurred prior to its date of transition.

Extract 5.3: Husky Energy Inc. (2011)

Notes to the Consolidated Financial Statements[extract]

Note 26 First-Time Adoption of International Financial Reporting Standards [extract]

Key First-Time Adoption Exemptions Applied [extract]

IFRS 1, "First-Time Adoption of International Financial Reporting Standards," allows first-time adopters certain exemptions from retrospective application of certain IFRSs.

The Company applied the following exemptions: [extract]

[...]

- IFRS 3, "Business Combinations," was not applied to acquisitions of subsidiaries or interests in joint ventures that occurred before January 1, 2010.

[...]

i) IFRS 3 Adjustments – *Business Combinations* [extract]

Given that the Company elected to apply the IFRS 1 exemption which permits no adjustments to amounts recorded for acquisitions that occurred prior to January 1, 2010, no retrospective adjustments were required. The Company acquired the remaining interest in the Lloydminster Upgrader from the Government of Alberta in 1995 and is required to make payments to Natural Resources Canada and Alberta Department of Energy from 1995 to 2014 based on average differentials between heavy crude oil feedstock and the price of synthetic crude oil sales. Under IFRS, the Company is required to recognize this contingent consideration at its fair value as part of the acquisition and record a corresponding liability. Under Canadian GAAP, any contingent consideration was not required to be recognized unless amounts were resolved and payable on the date of acquisition. On transition to IFRS, Husky recognized a liability of $85 million, based on the fair value of remaining upside interest payments, with an adjustment to opening retained earnings. For the year ended December 31, 2010, the Company recognized pre-tax accretion of $9 million in finance expenses under IFRS. Changes in forecast differentials used to determine the fair value of the remaining upside interest payments resulted in the recognition of a pre-tax gain of $41 million for the year ended December 31, 2010.

Extract 5.4: The Toronto-Dominion Bank (2011)

CONSOLIDATED FINANCIAL STATEMENTS AND NOTES [extract]

Note 34 TRANSITION TO IFRS [extract]

DESCRIPTION OF SIGNIFICANT MEASUREMENT AND PRESENTATION DIFFERENCES BETWEEN CANADIAN GAAP AND IFRS [extract]

(d) ***Business Combinations: Elective Exemption*** [extract]

As permitted under IFRS transition rules, the Bank has applied IFRS 3, *Business Combinations* (IFRS 3) to all business combinations occurring on or after January 1, 2007. Certain differences exist between IFRS and Canadian GAAP in the determination of the purchase price allocation. The most significant differences are described below.

Under Canadian GAAP, an investment in a subsidiary which is acquired through two or more purchases is commonly referred to as a "step acquisition". Each transaction is accounted for as a step-by-step purchase, and is recognized at the fair value of the net assets acquired at each step. Under IFRS, the accounting for step acquisitions differs depending on whether a change in control occurs. If a change in control occurs, the acquirer remeasures any previously held equity investment at its acquisition-date fair value and recognizes any resulting gain or loss in the Consolidated Statement of Income. Any transactions subsequent to obtaining control are recognized as equity transactions.

Under Canadian GAAP, shares issued as consideration are measured at the market price over a reasonable time period before and after the date the terms of the business combination are agreed upon and announced. Under IFRS, shares issued as consideration are measured at their market price on the closing date of the acquisition.

Under Canadian GAAP, an acquirer's restructuring costs to exit an activity or to involuntarily terminate or relocate employees are recognized as a liability in the purchase price allocation. Under IFRS, these costs are generally expensed as incurred and not included in the purchase price allocation.

Under Canadian GAAP, costs directly related to the acquisition (i.e. finder fees, advisory, legal, etc.) are included in the purchase price allocation, while under IFRS these costs are expensed as incurred and not included in the purchase price allocation.

Under Canadian GAAP, contingent consideration is recorded when the amount can be reasonably estimated at the date of acquisition and the outcome is determinable beyond reasonable doubt, while under IFRS contingent consideration is recognized immediately in the purchase price equation at fair value and marked to market as events and circumstances change in the Consolidated Statement of Income.

The impact of the differences between Canadian GAAP and IFRS to the Bank's IFRS opening Consolidated Balance Sheet is disclosed in the table below.

Business Combinations: Elective Exemption

(millions of Canadian dollars)	As at Nov. 1, 2010
Increase/(decrease) in assets:	
Available-for-sale securities	(1)
Goodwill	(2,147)
Loans – residential mortgages	22
Loans – consumer instalment and other personal	–
Loans – business and government	–
Intangibles	(289)
Land, buildings and equipment and other depreciable assets	2
Deferred tax assets	(12)
Other assets	104
(Increase)/decrease in liabilities:	
Deferred tax liabilities	102
Other liabilities	37
Subordinated notes and debentures	2
Increase/(decrease) in equity	(2,180)

The total impact of business combination elections to the Bank's IFRS opening equity was a decrease of $2,180 million, comprised of a decrease to common shares of $926 million, a decrease to contributed surplus of $85 million and a decrease to retained earnings of $1,169 million.

5.2.2.A Associates and joint arrangements

The exemption for past business combinations applies also to past acquisitions of investments in associates, interests in joint ventures and interests in joint operations (in which the activity of the joint operation constitutes a business, as defined in IFRS 3). The date selected for the first restatement of business combinations will also be applied to the restatement of these other acquisitions. *[IFRS 1.C5]*.

The application of the business combination exemptions in IFRS 1 has the following consequences for that business combination (see 5.2.3 to 5.2.10 below).

Chapter 5

5.2.3 Classification of business combinations

IFRS 3 mandates a business combination to be accounted for as an acquisition or reverse acquisition. An entity's previous GAAP may be based on a different definition of, for example, a business combination, an acquisition, a merger and a reverse acquisition. An important benefit of the business combinations exemption is that a first-time adopter will not have to determine the classification of past business combinations in accordance with IFRS. *[IFRS 1.C4(a)]*. For example, a business combination that was accounted for as a merger or uniting of interests using the pooling-of-interests method under an entity's previous GAAP will not have to be reclassified and accounted for under the acquisition method, nor will a restatement be required if the business combination would have been classified under IFRS 3 as a reverse acquisition by the acquiree. However, an entity may still elect to do so if it so wishes – subject, of course, to the conditions set out under 5.2.2 above.

5.2.4 Assets and liabilities to be recognised in the opening IFRS statement of financial position

In its opening IFRS statement of financial position, a first-time adopter should recognise all assets acquired and liabilities assumed in a past business combination, with the exception of: *[IFRS 1.C4(b)]*

- certain financial assets and liabilities that were derecognised and that fall under the derecognition exception (see 4.3 above); and
- assets (including goodwill) and liabilities that were not recognised in the acquirer's consolidated statement of financial position under its previous GAAP and that would not qualify for recognition under IFRSs in the separate statement of financial position of the acquiree (see 5.2.4.A and Example 5.14 below).

The entity must exclude items it recognised under its previous GAAP that do not qualify for recognition as an asset or liability under IFRSs (see below).

5.2.4.A Assets and liabilities to be excluded

If the first-time adopter recognised under its previous GAAP items that do not qualify for recognition under IFRSs, these must be excluded from the opening IFRS statement of financial position.

An intangible asset, acquired as part of a business combination, that does not qualify for recognition as an asset under IAS 38 – *Intangible Assets* – should be derecognised, with the related deferred tax and non-controlling interests, with an offsetting change to goodwill, unless the entity previously deducted goodwill directly from equity under its previous GAAP (see 5.2.5 below).

All other changes resulting from derecognition of such assets and liabilities should be accounted for as adjustments of retained earnings or another category of equity, if appropriate. *[IFRS 1.C4(c)]*. For example:

- Any restructuring provisions recognised under previous GAAP and which remain at the date of transition to IFRS will need to be assessed against the IFRS recognition criteria. If the criteria are not met, then the provisions must be reversed against retained earnings.

- If an entity has deferred transaction costs (for which the services were received) relating to a business combination that has not been finalised under previous GAAP at the date of transition to IFRS, these deferred transaction costs would need to be recognised in retained earnings as they do not qualify for deferral under IFRSs.
- Assets and liabilities of a structured entity required to be consolidated under previous GAAP but that does not qualify for consolidation under IFRS 10 must be deconsolidated.

5.2.4.B Recognition of assets and liabilities

An asset acquired or a liability assumed in a past business combination may not have been recognised under the entity's previous GAAP. However, this does not mean that such items have a deemed cost of zero in the opening IFRS statement of financial position. Instead, the acquirer recognises and measures those items in its opening IFRS statement of financial position on the basis that IFRSs would require in the statement of financial position of the acquiree. *[IFRS 1.C4(f)].*

If the acquirer had not recognised an acquired contingent liability under its previous GAAP that still exists at the date of transition to IFRSs, the acquirer should recognise that contingent liability at that date unless IAS 37 would prohibit its recognition in the financial statements of the acquiree. *[IFRS 1.C4(f)].*

The change resulting from the recognition of such assets and liabilities should be accounted for as an adjustment of retained earnings or another category of equity, if appropriate. However, if the change results from the recognition of an intangible asset that was previously subsumed within goodwill, it should be accounted for as an adjustment of that goodwill (see 5.2.5 below). *[IFRS 1.C4(b), C4(g)(i)].*

Intangible assets acquired as part of a business combination that were not recognised under a first-time adopter's previous GAAP will rarely be recognised in the opening IFRS statement of financial position because either: (1) they cannot be capitalised in the acquiree's own statement of financial position under IAS 38; or (2) capitalisation would require the use of hindsight which is not permitted under IAS 38 (see 7.14 below).

Example 5.14: Items not recognised under previous GAAP

Entity A acquired Entity B but did not capitalise B's finance leases and internally generated customer lists under its previous GAAP.

Upon first-time adoption of IFRSs, Entity A recognises the finance leases in its opening IFRS statement of financial position using the amounts that Entity B would recognise in its opening IFRS statement of financial position. The resulting adjustment to the net assets at the date of transition is reflected in retained earnings; goodwill is not restated to reflect the net assets that would have been recognised at the date of acquisition (see 5.2.5 below). However, Entity A does not recognise the customer lists in its opening IFRS statement of financial position, because Entity B is not permitted to capitalise internally generated customer lists under IAS 38. Any value that might have been attributable to the customer lists would remain subsumed in goodwill in A's opening IFRS statement of financial position.

Entity C acquired Entity D but did not recognise D's brand name as a separate intangible asset under its previous GAAP.

Upon first-time adoption of IFRSs, Entity C will not recognise D's brand name in its opening IFRS statement of financial position because Entity D would not have been permitted under IAS 38 to recognise it as an asset in its own separate statement of financial position. Again, any value that might have been attributable to the brand name would remain subsumed in goodwill in C's opening IFRS statement of financial position.

Example 5.15: Restructuring provision

Background

Entity C's first IFRS financial statements are for a period that ends on 31 December 2018 and include comparative information for 2017 only. It chooses not to restate previous business combinations under IFRSs. On 1 July 2016, Entity C acquired 100 per cent of Entity D. Under its previous GAAP, Entity C recognised an (undiscounted) restructuring provision of ¥100 million that would not have qualified as an identifiable liability under IFRSs. The recognition of this restructuring provision increased goodwill by ¥100 million. At 1 January 2017 (date of transition to IFRSs), Entity C:

(a) had paid restructuring costs of ¥60 million; and

(b) estimated that it would pay further costs of ¥40 million in 2017 and that the effects of discounting were immaterial. At 1 January 2017, those further costs did not qualify for recognition as a provision under IAS 37.

Application of requirements

In its opening IFRS statement of financial position, Entity C:

(a) Does not recognise a restructuring provision. This is because the recognition criteria to be applied under Appendix C of IFRS 1 are those that generally apply to the specific asset or liability in accordance with the relevant IFRS (in this case IAS 37) rather than the recognition criteria set out under IFRS 3.

(b) Does not adjust the amount assigned to goodwill. However, Entity C tests the goodwill for impairment under IAS 36 and recognises any resulting impairment loss.

5.2.4.C Previous GAAP carrying amount as deemed cost

For assets and liabilities that are accounted for on a cost basis under IFRSs, the carrying amount in accordance with previous GAAP of assets acquired and liabilities assumed in that business combination is their deemed cost immediately after the business combination. This deemed cost is the basis for cost-based depreciation or amortisation from the date of the business combination. *[IFRS 1.C4(e)].*

The standard does not specifically define 'immediately after the business combination', but it is commonly understood that this takes account of the final determination of the purchase price allocation and final completion of purchase accounting. In other words, a first-time adopter would not use the provisionally determined fair values of assets acquired and liabilities assumed in applying the business combinations exemption.

Example 5.16: Provisionally determined fair values

Entity B acquired Entity C in August 2016 and made a provisional assessment of Entity C's identifiable net assets in its 31 December 2016 consolidated financial statements under its previous GAAP. In its 31 December 2017 consolidated financial statements – its last financial statements under previous GAAP – Entity B completed the initial accounting for the business combination and adjusted the provisional values of the identifiable net assets and the corresponding goodwill. Upon first-time adoption of IFRSs, Entity B elects not to restate past business combinations.

In preparing its opening IFRS statement of financial position as of 1 January 2017, Entity B should use the adjusted carrying amounts of the identifiable net assets as determined in its 2017 financial statements rather than the provisional carrying amounts of the identifiable net assets and goodwill at 31 December 2016.

IFRS 1 is silent as to whether the relevant carrying amounts of the identifiable net assets and goodwill are those that appeared in the financial statements drawn up immediately before the transition date or any restated balance appearing in a later set of previous GAAP accounts. Since the adjustments that were made under previous GAAP effectively resulted in a restatement of the balances at the transition date in a manner that is consistent with the approach permitted by IFRSs, it is in our opinion appropriate to reflect those adjustments in the opening IFRS statement of financial position. Since the adjustments are effectively made as at the transition date, it is also appropriate to use the window period permitted by previous GAAP provided that this does not extend into the first IFRS reporting period. This is because any restatements in that period can only be made in accordance with IFRS 3. In effect, the phrase 'immediately after the business combination' in paragraph C4(e) of IFRS 1 should be interpreted as including a window period that ends at the earlier of the end of the window period allowed by the previous GAAP and the beginning of the first IFRS reporting period.

Although the use of cost-based measurements under previous GAAP might be considered inconsistent with the requirements of IFRSs for assets and liabilities that were not acquired in a business combination, the IASB did not identify any situations in a business combination in which it would not be acceptable to bring forward cost-based measurements made under previous GAAP. *[IFRS 1.BC36]*. For example, assume an entity that adopts IFRSs with a transition date of 1 January 2017 and, as required, applies IFRS 3 to business combinations occurring on or after 1 January 2017. Under the entity's previous GAAP, it acquired a business in 2011 and the purchase accounting resulted in negative goodwill. At that time, the negative goodwill was eliminated by reducing the amounts assigned to long-lived assets (PP&E and intangible assets) on a *pro rata* basis. In this situation, the negative goodwill adjustment to PP&E and intangible assets is 'grandfathered' and is not adjusted in the opening IFRS statement of financial position. The negative goodwill adjustment to PP&E and intangible assets was part of the original purchase accounting and is not a subsequent measurement difference between completing the purchase price allocation and 1 January 2017 and therefore the adjustment forms part of the deemed cost of PP&E and intangible assets.

Chapter 5

By contrast, under previous GAAP, the entity may have recognised amortisation of intangible assets from the date of acquisition. If this amortisation is not in compliance with IAS 38, it is not 'grandfathered' under the business combination exemption and therefore should be reversed on transition (note that the adjusted carrying amount should be tested for impairment if there are impairment indicators pursuant to the requirements of IAS 36 at the date of transition: see 7.12 below).

Example 5.17: Items measured on a cost basis

Entity A applies the business combination exemption under IFRS 1. In a business combination Entity A acquired property, plant and equipment, inventory and accounts receivable. Under its previous GAAP, Entity A initially measured these assets at cost (i.e. their fair value at the date originally acquired).

Upon adoption of IFRSs, Entity A determines that its accounting policy for these assets under its previous GAAP complied with the requirements of IFRSs. Therefore, property, plant and equipment, inventory and accounts receivable are not adjusted but recognised in the opening IFRS statement of financial position at the carrying amount under the previous GAAP.

5.2.4.D In-process research and development

IFRS 1 makes it clear that in-process research and development (IPR&D) that was included within goodwill under an entity's previous GAAP should not be recognised separately upon transition to IFRSs unless it qualifies for recognition under IAS 38 in the financial statements of the acquiree. *[IFRS 1.C4(h)(i)].* However, IFRS 1 is silent on the treatment of IPR&D that was identified separately by an entity under the business combinations accounting standard of its previous GAAP, but which was immediately written off to profit or loss.

There are two possible scenarios. If previous GAAP requires IPR&D to be written off as an integral part of the business combination accounting under that GAAP then the carrying amount of IPR&D 'immediately after the business combination' would be zero. While we understand that there may be different views, it is our view that IFRS 1 does not allow reinstatement of the amount of IPR&D that was previously written off under this scenario.

However, if that write-off is not an integral part of the business combination accounting (e.g. the previous GAAP merely requires accelerated amortisation) then the carrying amount 'immediately after the business combination' would be the amount allocated to IPR&D by the business combinations standard under previous GAAP. In our view, reinstatement of the amount of IPR&D that was written off under this scenario is appropriate.

The above distinction may be largely irrelevant if the business combination takes place several years before the transition to IFRSs because, in practice, the IPR&D may have been amortised fully or may be impaired before the date of transition.

5.2.4.E Subsequent measurement under IFRSs not based on cost

IFRSs require subsequent measurement of some assets and liabilities on a basis other than original cost, such as fair value for certain financial instruments or on specific measurement bases for share-based payments (IFRS 2) and employee benefits (IAS 19). Even if a first-time adopter does not apply IFRS 3 retrospectively to a business combination, such assets and liabilities must be measured on that other basis in its opening IFRS statement of financial position. Any change in the carrying amount of those assets and liabilities should be accounted for as an adjustment of retained earnings, or other appropriate category of equity, rather than as an adjustment of goodwill. *[IFRS 1.C4(d)].*

Example 5.18: Items not measured at original cost

Entity A acquired in a business combination a trading portfolio of equity securities and a number of investment properties. Under its previous GAAP, Entity A initially measured these assets at historical cost (i.e. their fair value at the date of original acquisition).

Upon adoption of IFRSs, Entity A measures the trading portfolio of equity securities and the investment properties at fair value in its opening IFRS statement of financial position. The resulting adjustment to these assets at the date of transition is reflected in retained earnings.

5.2.4.F Example of recognition and measurement requirements

The following example, which is based on one within the implementation guidance in IFRS 1, illustrates many of the requirements discussed above. *[IFRS 1.IG Example 2].*

Example 5.19: Business combination example

Background

Entity A's first IFRS financial statements are for a reporting period that ends on 31 December 2018 and include comparative information for 2017 only. On 1 July 2014, Entity A acquired 100 per cent of Entity B. Under its previous GAAP, Entity A:

(a) classified the business combination as an acquisition by Entity A;

(b) measured the assets acquired and liabilities assumed at the following amounts under previous GAAP at 1 January 2017 (date of transition to IFRSs):

  (i) identifiable assets less liabilities for which IFRSs require cost-based measurement at a date after the business combination: €200 (with a tax base of €150 and an applicable tax rate of 30 per cent);

  (ii) pension liability (for which the present value of the defined benefit obligation measured under IAS 19 is €130 and the fair value of plan assets is €100): €nil (because Entity A used a pay-as-you-go cash method of accounting for pensions under its previous GAAP). The tax base of the pension liability is also €nil;

  (iii) goodwill: €180;

(c) did not, at the date of acquisition, recognise deferred tax arising from temporary differences associated with the identifiable assets acquired and liabilities assumed;

In its opening (consolidated) IFRS statement of financial position, Entity A:

(a) classifies the business combination as an acquisition by Entity A even if the business combination would have qualified under IFRS 3 as a reverse acquisition by Entity B; *[IFRS 1.C4(a)]*

(b) does not adjust the accumulated amortisation of goodwill. Entity A tests the goodwill for impairment under IAS 36 and recognises any resulting impairment loss, based on conditions that existed at the date of transition to IFRSs. If no impairment exists, the carrying amount of the goodwill remains at €180; *[IFRS 1.C4(g)]*

(c) for those net identifiable assets acquired for which IFRSs require cost-based measurement at a date after the business combination, treats their carrying amount under previous GAAP immediately after the business combination as their deemed cost at that date; *[IFRS 1.C4(e)]*

(d) does not restate the accumulated depreciation and amortisation of the net identifiable assets in (c) above, unless the depreciation methods and rates under previous GAAP result in amounts that differ materially from those required under IFRSs (for example, if they were adopted solely for tax purposes and do not reflect a reasonable estimate of the asset's useful life under IFRSs). If no such restatement is made, the carrying amount of those assets in the opening IFRS statement of financial position equals their carrying amount under previous GAAP at the date of transition to IFRSs (€200); *[IFRS 1.IG7]*

(e) if there is any indication that identifiable assets are impaired, tests those assets for impairment, under IAS 36, based on conditions that existed at the date of transition to IFRSs (see 7.12 below);

(f) recognises the pension liability, and measures it, at the present value of the defined benefit obligation (€130) less the fair value of the plan assets (€100), giving a carrying amount of €30, with a corresponding debit of €30 to retained earnings. *[IFRS 1.C4(d)]*. However, if Entity B had already adopted IFRSs in an earlier period, Entity A would measure the pension liability at the same amount as in Entity B's individual financial statements; *[IFRS 1.D17, IG Example 9]*

(g) recognises a net deferred tax liability of €6 (€20 at 30 per cent) arising from:

  (i) the taxable temporary difference of €50 (€200 less €150) associated with the identifiable assets acquired and non-pension liabilities assumed; less

  (ii) the deductible temporary difference of €30 (€30 less €nil) associated with the pension liability.

Entity A recognises the resulting increase in the deferred tax liability as a deduction from retained earnings. *[IFRS 1.C4(k)]*. If a taxable temporary difference arises from the initial recognition of the goodwill, Entity A does not recognise the resulting deferred tax liability. *[IAS 12.15(a)]*.

5.2.5 *Restatement of goodwill*

Under the business combinations exemption, a first-time adopter takes the carrying amount of goodwill under its previous GAAP at the date of transition to IFRSs as a starting point and only adjusts it as follows: *[IFRS 1.C4(g)]*

(a) goodwill is increased by the carrying amount of any intangible asset acquired in a business combination under its previous GAAP (less any related deferred tax and non-controlling interests), that does not meet the recognition criteria under IFRSs. The first-time adopter accounts for the change in classification prospectively and does not, for example, reverse the cumulative amortisation on the item that it recognised as an intangible asset under its previous GAAP;

(b) goodwill is decreased if a first-time adopter is required to recognise an intangible asset that was subsumed in goodwill under its previous GAAP. It adjusts deferred tax and non-controlling interests accordingly; and

(c) goodwill must be tested for impairment at the date of transition to IFRSs in accordance with IAS 36 regardless of whether there is any indication that the goodwill may be impaired (see Chapter 20); any resulting impairment loss is recognised in retained earnings unless IAS 36 requires it to be recognised in a revaluation surplus (see Chapter 20). The impairment test must be based on conditions at the date of transition to IFRSs.

Application of the above guidance may sometimes be more complicated than expected as is illustrated in the example below.

Example 5.20: Recognition and derecognition of acquired intangible assets

Before its date of transition to IFRSs, Entity A acquired an online retailer, Entity B. Under its previous GAAP, Entity A recognised an intangible asset of ¥1,200 related to 'deferred marketing costs', which does not meet the recognition criteria under IFRSs. Entity A also acquired customer relationships with a fair value of ¥900 that do meet the recognition criteria under IFRS 3, but which it did not recognise as an intangible asset under its previous GAAP.

Upon adoption of IFRSs, Entity A is required to derecognise the 'deferred marketing costs' intangible asset and increase the carrying amount of goodwill for a corresponding amount. Nevertheless, the customer relationship intangible asset that is subsumed in goodwill cannot be recognised as its carrying amount in the statement of financial position of the acquiree, Entity B, would have been nil under IFRS.

In economic terms it might be contended that the 'deferred marketing costs' intangible asset in the example above comprises the value that would have been attributable under IFRSs to the acquired customer relationships. However, unless Entity A concluded that not recognising a customer relationship intangible asset was an error under its previous GAAP, it would not be able to recognise a customer relationship intangible asset upon adoption of IFRSs.

Under IFRS 1, assets acquired and liabilities assumed in a business combination prior to the date of transition to IFRSs are not necessarily valued on a basis that is consistent with IFRSs. This can lead to 'double counting' in the carrying amount of assets and goodwill as is illustrated in the example below.

Example 5.21: Impairment testing of goodwill on first-time adoption

Entity C acquired a business before its date of transition to IFRSs. The cost of acquisition was €530 and Entity C allocated the purchase price as follows:

	€
Properties, at carry-over cost	450
Liabilities, at amortised cost	(180)
Goodwill	260
Purchase price	530

The goodwill under Entity C's previous GAAP relates entirely to the properties that had a fair value at date of acquisition that was significantly in excess of their value on a carry-over cost basis. In Entity C's opening IFRS statement of financial position the same assets, liabilities and goodwill are valued as follows:

	€
Properties, at fair value	750
Liabilities, at amortised cost	(180)
Provisional IFRS goodwill (before impairment test)	260
Total carrying amount	830

Entity C used the option to measure the properties at fair value at its date of transition in its opening IFRS statement of financial position. However, IFRS 1 does not permit goodwill to be adjusted to reflect the extent to which the increase in fair value relates to other assets recognised at the time of the acquisition. The total carrying amount of the acquired net assets including goodwill of €830 may now exceed the recoverable amount. When Entity C tests the 'provisional IFRS goodwill' for impairment on first-time adoption of IFRSs, the recoverable amount of the business is determined to be €620. Accordingly, it will have to recognise an impairment of goodwill of €210 and disclose this impairment under IFRS 1.

In some cases the write-off will completely eliminate the goodwill and thereby any 'double counting'. However, in this particular case the remaining goodwill of €50 in truth represents goodwill that was internally generated between the date of acquisition and the date of transition to IFRSs.

Chapter 5

The IASB accepted that IFRS 1 does not prevent the implicit recognition of internally generated goodwill that arose after the date of the business combination. It concluded that attempts to exclude such internally generated goodwill would be costly and lead to arbitrary results. *[IFRS 1.BC39]*.

As the business combinations exemption also applies to associates and joint arrangements, a transition impairment review should be carried out on investments in associates and joint arrangements if they include an element of goodwill. However, the goodwill embedded in the amount of an investment in an associate or an investment in a joint venture will not be subject to a separate impairment test. Rather the entire carrying amount of the investment is reviewed for impairment following the requirements of IAS 36. In performing this impairment review of the investment in associate or joint venture, in our view, an investor does not reverse a previous GAAP impairment that was recognised separately on the notional goodwill element embedded in the investment. However, if the previous GAAP impairment had been recognised as a reduction of the entire investment (without attribution to any particular embedded account), the first-time adopter is able to reverse such impairment if it is assessed to no longer be necessary. Consider the two scenarios below:

Example 5.22: Previous GAAP impairment of goodwill embedded in equity method investment

Scenario 1 – Impairment was recognised on the notional goodwill element embedded in the investment under previous GAAP

On 1 January 2011, Entity A acquired an investment in Entity B, which it accounts for using the equity method (the investment would qualify as an associate under IFRSs). The cost of investment was €1,500 compared to B's identifiable net assets of €500; therefore, notional goodwill of €1,000 was included in the carrying value of the investment at that time. The previous GAAP required the entity to:

- Amortise the notional goodwill of the associate on a straight-line basis.
- Test the equity accounted investment for impairment at the investment level.
- Allocate and recognise the impairment loss (if any) against notional goodwill.
- Goodwill impairments (including those on notional goodwill) are not permitted to be reversed and therefore affect future amortisation.

Therefore, under its previous GAAP, Entity A tested its investment in Entity B for impairment, and recognised an impairment loss of €500 in the year ended 31 December 2011. This reduced the notional goodwill to €500, which Entity A amortises over 10 years (€50 annually). By its date of transition to IFRS, 1 January 2017, notional goodwill had been amortised by 5 years × €50 (€250), reducing notional goodwill to €250. Net assets are unchanged since acquisition, leaving the investment with a carrying value of €750.

Entity A applies the exemption from retrospective restatement for past acquisitions of investments in associates. Therefore, at 1 January 2017, its transition date, Entity A also tests the investment for impairment in accordance with IAS 36. At 1 January 2017, the value of the investment in Entity B recovered, and is €1,500 based on its current listed share price. Under this scenario, the previous impairment to notional goodwill is not reversed, since the use of the business combination exemption as it applies to associates means that the goodwill determined under the previous GAAP acquisition accounting together with the subsequent accounting up to the transition date is effectively grandfathered in a similar way in which a subsidiary's goodwill would be, in accordance with paragraph C4(g) of IFRS 1. Therefore, the carrying value of the notional goodwill as determined under previous GAAP becomes the embedded notional goodwill at transition unless specifically required to be adjusted. *[IFRS 1.C4(h)].*

Scenario 2 – Impairment was recognised at the investment level under previous GAAP

The same as Scenario 1, except that Entity A's previous GAAP impairment test was performed at the investment level, using a test similar to that required under IAS 36. Because of applying this approach, when Entity A recognised an impairment loss of €500 in the year ended 31 December 2011, the carrying amount of the investment was €1,000, which remained unchanged until the date of transition, 1 January 2017. Similar to Scenario 1, at 1 January 2017, the value of the investment in Entity B has recovered, and is €1,500 based on its current listed share price.

Under this scenario, the previous impairment of notional goodwill, which is embedded in the full amount of the investment, is reversed. However, the impairment can only be reversed up to the pre-impairment equity accounted value that results from the application of the business combination exemption.

5.2.5.A Prohibition of other adjustments of goodwill

IFRS 1 prohibits restatement of goodwill for most other adjustments reflected in the opening IFRS statement of financial position. Therefore, a first-time adopter electing not to apply IFRS 3 retrospectively is not permitted to make any adjustments to goodwill other than those described above. *[IFRS 1.C4(h)].* For example, a first-time adopter cannot restate the carrying amount of goodwill:

(i) to exclude in-process research and development acquired in that business combination (unless the related intangible asset would qualify for recognition under IAS 38 in the statement of financial position of the acquiree);

(ii) to adjust previous amortisation of goodwill;

(iii) to reverse adjustments to goodwill that IFRS 3 would not permit, but were made under previous GAAP because of adjustments to assets and liabilities between the date of the business combination and the date of transition to IFRSs.

Differences between the goodwill amount in the opening IFRS statement of financial position and that in the financial statements under previous GAAP may arise, for example, because:

(a) goodwill may have to be restated as a result of a retrospective application of IAS 21 – *The Effects of Changes in Foreign Exchange Rates* (see 5.2.6 below);

(b) goodwill in relation to previously unconsolidated subsidiaries will have to be recognised (see 5.2.7 below);

(c) goodwill in relation to transactions that do not qualify as business combinations under IFRSs must be derecognised (see 5.2.1 above); and

(d) 'negative goodwill' that may have been included within goodwill under previous GAAP should be derecognised under IFRSs (see 5.2.5.B below).

Example 5.23: Adjusting goodwill

Entity A acquired Entity B but under its previous GAAP it did not recognise the following items:

- Entity B's customer lists which had a fair value of ¥1,100 at the date of the acquisition and ¥1,500 at the date of transition to IFRSs; and
- Deferred tax liabilities related to the fair value adjustment of Entity B's property, plant and equipment, which amounted to ¥9,500 at the date of the acquisition and ¥7,800 at the date of transition to IFRSs.

What adjustment should Entity A make to goodwill to account for the customer lists and deferred tax liabilities at its date of transition to IFRSs?

As explained at 5.2.4.B above, Entity A cannot recognise the customer lists (internally generated intangible assets of acquiree) when it uses the business combinations exemption. Accordingly, Entity A cannot adjust goodwill for the customer lists.

Entity A must recognise, under IAS 12 – *Income Taxes* – the deferred tax liability at its date of transition because there is no exemption from recognising deferred taxes under IFRS 1. However, Entity A is not permitted to adjust goodwill for the deferred tax liability that would have been recognised at the date of acquisition. Instead, Entity A should recognise the deferred tax liability of ¥7,800 with a corresponding charge to retained earnings or other category of equity, if appropriate.

5.2.5.B Derecognition of negative goodwill

Although IFRS 1 does not specifically address accounting for negative goodwill recognised under a previous GAAP, negative goodwill should be derecognised by a first-time adopter because it is not permitted to recognise items as assets or liabilities if IFRSs do not permit such recognition. *[IFRS 1.10]*. Negative goodwill clearly does not meet the definition of a liability under the IASB's *Conceptual Framework* and its recognition is not permitted under IFRS 3. While not directly applicable to a first-time adopter, the transitional provisions of IFRS 3 specifically require that any negative goodwill is derecognised upon adoption. *[IFRS 3.B69(e)]*.

5.2.5.C Goodwill previously deducted from equity

If a first-time adopter deducted goodwill from equity under its previous GAAP then it should not recognise that goodwill in its opening IFRS statement of financial position. Also, it should not reclassify that goodwill to profit or loss if it disposes of the subsidiary or if the investment in the subsidiary becomes impaired. *[IFRS 1.C4(i)(i)]*. Effectively, under IFRSs such goodwill ceases to exist, as is shown in the following example based on the implementation guidance in IFRS 1. *[IFRS 1.IG Example 5]*.

Example 5.24: Goodwill deducted from equity and treatment of related intangible assets

Entity A acquired a subsidiary before the date of transition to IFRSs. Under its previous GAAP, Entity A:

(a) recognised goodwill as an immediate deduction from equity;

(b) recognised an intangible asset of the subsidiary that does not qualify for recognition as an asset under IAS 38; and

(c) did not recognise an intangible asset of the subsidiary that would qualify under IAS 38 for recognition as an asset in the financial statements of the subsidiary. The subsidiary held the asset at the date of its acquisition by Entity A.

In its opening IFRS statement of financial position, Entity A:

(a) does not recognise the goodwill, as it did not recognise the goodwill as an asset under previous GAAP;

(b) does not recognise the intangible asset that does not qualify for recognition as an asset under IAS 38. Because Entity A deducted goodwill from equity under its previous GAAP, the elimination of this intangible asset reduces retained earnings (see 5.2.4.A above); and

(c) recognises the intangible asset that qualifies under IAS 38 for recognition as an asset in the financial statements of the subsidiary, even though the amount assigned to it under previous GAAP in A's consolidated financial statements was nil (see 5.2.4.B above). The recognition criteria in IAS 38 include the availability of a reliable measurement of cost and Entity A measures the asset at cost less accumulated depreciation and less any impairment losses identified under IAS 36 (see 7.12 below). Because Entity A deducted goodwill from equity under its previous GAAP, the recognition of this intangible asset increases retained earnings. However, if this intangible asset had been subsumed in goodwill recognised as an asset under previous GAAP, Entity A would have decreased the carrying amount of that goodwill accordingly (and, if applicable, adjusted deferred tax and non-controlling interests) (see 5.2.5.A above).

The prohibition on reinstating goodwill that was deducted from equity may have a significant impact on first-time adopters that hedge their foreign net investments.

Example 5.25: Goodwill related to foreign net investments

Entity B, which uses the euro (€) as its functional currency, acquired a subsidiary in the United States whose functional currency is the US dollar ($). The goodwill on the acquisition of $2,100 was deducted from equity. Under its previous GAAP Entity B hedged the currency exposure on the goodwill because it would be required to recognise the goodwill as an expense upon disposal of the subsidiary.

IFRS 1 does not permit reinstatement of goodwill deducted from equity nor does it permit transfer of goodwill to profit or loss upon disposal of the investment in the subsidiary. Under IFRSs, goodwill deducted from equity ceases to exist and Entity B can no longer hedge the currency exposure on that goodwill. Therefore, exchange gains and losses relating to the hedge will no longer be classified in currency translation difference but recognised in profit and loss upon adoption of IFRSs.

If a first-time adopter deducted goodwill from equity under its previous GAAP, adjustments resulting from the subsequent resolution of a contingency affecting the purchase consideration, at or before the date of transition to IFRSs, should be recognised in retained earnings. *[IFRS 1.C4(i)(ii)]*. Effectively, the adjustment is being accounted for in the same way as the original goodwill that arose on the acquisition, rather than having to be accounted for in accordance with IFRS 3. This requirement could affect, for example, the way a first-time adopter accounts for provisional amounts relating to business combinations prior to its date of transition to IFRSs.

Example 5.26: Adjustments made during measurement period to provisional amounts

Entity C acquired Entity D on 30 September 2016. Entity C sought an independent valuation for an item of property, plant and equipment acquired in the combination. However, the valuation was not completed by the date of transition to IFRS (1 January 2017). Under Entity C's previous GAAP, any goodwill was written off against equity as incurred. Five months after the acquisition date (and after the transition date), Entity C received the independent valuation.

In preparing its opening IFRS statement of financial position, Entity C should use the adjusted carrying amounts of the identifiable net assets (see 5.2.4.C above) with the corresponding adjustment being recognised in retained earnings.

5.2.6 Currency adjustments to goodwill

A first-time adopter need not apply IAS 21 retrospectively to fair value adjustments and goodwill arising in business combinations that occurred before the date of transition to IFRSs. *[IFRS 1.C2, IG21A]*. This exemption is different from the 'cumulative translation differences' exemption, which is discussed at 5.7 below.

IAS 21 requires any goodwill arising on the acquisition of a foreign operation and any fair value adjustments to the carrying amounts of assets and liabilities arising on the acquisition of that foreign operation to be treated as assets and liabilities of the foreign operation. Thus they are expressed in the functional currency of the foreign operation and are translated at the closing rate in accordance with the requirements discussed in Chapter 15. *[IAS 21.47]*. For a first-time adopter it may be impracticable, especially after a corporate restructuring, to determine retrospectively the currency in which goodwill and fair value adjustments should be expressed. If IAS 21 is not applied retrospectively, a first-time adopter should treat such fair value adjustments and goodwill as assets and liabilities of the entity rather than as assets and liabilities of the acquiree. As a result, those goodwill and fair value adjustments are either already expressed in the entity's functional currency or are non-monetary foreign currency items that are reported using the exchange rate applied in accordance with previous GAAP. *[IFRS 1.C2]*.

If a first-time adopter chooses not to take the exemption mentioned above, it must apply IAS 21 retrospectively to fair value adjustments and goodwill arising in either: *[IFRS 1.C1, C3]*

(a) all business combinations that occurred before the date of transition to IFRSs; or

(b) all business combinations that the entity elects to restate to comply with IFRS 3.

In practice the exemption may be of limited use for a number of reasons:

First, the exemption permits 'goodwill and fair value adjustments' to be treated as assets and liabilities of the entity rather than as assets and liabilities of the acquiree. Implicit in the exemption is the requirement to treat both the goodwill and the fair value adjustments consistently. However, the IASB apparently did not consider that many first-time adopters,

Chapter 5

under their previous GAAP, will have treated fair value adjustments as assets or liabilities of the acquiree, while at the same time treating goodwill as an asset of the acquirer. As the exemption under IFRS 1 did not foresee this particular situation, those first-time adopters will need to restate either their goodwill or fair value adjustments. In many cases restatement of goodwill is less onerous than restatement of fair value adjustments.

Secondly, the paragraphs in IFRS 1 that introduce the exemption were drafted at a later date than the rest of the Appendix of which they form part. Instead of referring to 'first-time adopter' these paragraphs refer to 'entity'. Nevertheless, it is clear from the context that 'entity' should be read as 'first-time adopter'. This means that the exemption only permits goodwill and fair value adjustments to be treated as assets and liabilities of the first-time adopter (i.e. ultimate parent). In practice, however, many groups have treated goodwill and fair value adjustments as an asset and liabilities of an intermediate parent. Where the intermediate parent has a functional currency that is different from that of the ultimate parent or the acquiree, it will be necessary to restate goodwill and fair value adjustments.

The decision to treat goodwill and fair value adjustments as either items denominated in the parent's or the acquiree's functional currency will also affect the extent to which the net investment in those foreign subsidiaries can be hedged (see also 4.5.5 above).

5.2.7 Previously unconsolidated subsidiaries

Under its previous GAAP a first-time adopter may not have consolidated a subsidiary acquired in a past business combination. In that case, a first-time adopter applying the business combinations exemption should recognise the carrying amounts of the subsidiary's assets and liabilities in its consolidated financial statements at the transition date at either: *[IFRS 1.IG27(a)]*

(a) if the subsidiary has adopted IFRSs, the same carrying amounts as in the IFRS financial statements of the subsidiary, after adjusting for consolidation procedures and for the effects of the business combination in which it acquired the subsidiary; *[IFRS 1.D17]* or

(b) if the subsidiary has not adopted IFRSs, the carrying amounts that IFRSs would require in the subsidiary's statement of financial position. *[IFRS 1.C4(j)].*

The deemed cost of goodwill is the difference at the date of transition between:

(i) the parent's interest in those adjusted carrying amounts; and

(ii) the cost in the parent's separate financial statements of its investment in the subsidiary. *[IFRS 1.C4(j)].*

The cost of a subsidiary in the parent's separate financial statements will depend on which option the parent has taken to measure the cost under IFRS 1 (see 5.8.2 below).

A first-time adopter is precluded from calculating what the goodwill would have been at the date of the original acquisition. The deemed cost of goodwill is capitalised in the opening IFRS statement of financial position. The following example, which is based on one within the guidance on implementation of IFRS 1, illustrates this requirement. *[IFRS 1.IG Example 6].*

Example 5.27: Subsidiary not consolidated under previous GAAP

Background

Entity A's date of transition to IFRSs is 1 January 2017. Under its previous GAAP, Entity A did not consolidate its 75 percent interest in Entity B, which it acquired in a business combination on 15 July 2014. On 1 January 2017:

(a) the cost of Entity A's investment in Entity B is $180; and

(b) under IFRSs, Entity B would measure its assets at $500 and its liabilities (including deferred tax under IAS 12) at $300. On this basis, Entity B's net assets are $200 under IFRSs.

Application of requirements

Entity A consolidates Entity B. The consolidated statement of financial position at 1 January 2017 includes:

(a) Entity B's assets at $500 and liabilities at $300;

(b) non-controlling interests of $50 (25 per cent of [$500 – $300]); and

(c) goodwill of $30 (cost of $180 less 75 per cent of [$500 – $300]). Entity A tests the goodwill for impairment under IAS 36 (see 7.12 below) and recognises any resulting impairment loss, based on conditions that existed at the date of transition to IFRSs.

If the cost of the subsidiary (as measured under IFRS 1, see 5.8.2 below) is lower than the proportionate share of net asset value at the date of transition to IFRSs, the difference is taken to retained earnings, or other category of equity, if appropriate.

Slightly different rules apply to all other subsidiaries (i.e. those not acquired in a business combination but created) that an entity did not consolidate under its previous GAAP, the main difference being that goodwill should not be recognised in relation to those subsidiaries (see 5.8 below). *[IFRS 1.IG27(c)]*.

Note that this exemption requires the use of the carrying value of the investment in the separate financial statements of the parent prepared using IAS 27 – *Separate Financial Statements*. Therefore, if a first-time adopter, in its separate financial statements, does not opt to measure its cost of investment in a subsidiary at its fair value or previous GAAP carrying amount at the date of transition, *[IFRS 1.D15]*, it is required to calculate the deemed cost of the goodwill by comparing the cost of the investment to its share of the carrying amount of the net assets determined on a different date. In the case of a highly profitable subsidiary this could give rise to the following anomaly:

Example 5.28: Calculation of deemed goodwill

Entity C acquired Entity D before the date of transition for $500. The net assets of Entity D would have been $220 under IFRSs at the date of acquisition. Entity D makes on average an annual net profit of $60, which it does not distribute to Entity C.

At the date of transition to IFRSs, the cost of Entity C's investment in Entity D is still $500. However, the net assets of Entity D have increased to $460. Therefore, under IFRS 1 the deemed cost of goodwill is $40.

The deemed goodwill is much lower than the goodwill that was paid at the date of acquisition because Entity D did not distribute its profits. In fact, if Entity D had distributed a dividend to its parent just before its date of transition, the deemed goodwill would have been significantly higher.

5.2.8 Previously consolidated entities that are not subsidiaries

A first-time adopter may have consolidated an investment under its previous GAAP that does not meet the definition of a subsidiary under IFRSs. In this case the entity should first determine the appropriate classification of the investment under IFRSs and then apply the first-time adoption rules in IFRS 1. Generally such previously consolidated investments should be accounted for as either:

- *an associate, a joint venture or a joint operation:* First-time adopters applying the business combinations exemption should also apply that exemption to past acquisitions of investments in associates, joint ventures or joint operations. *[IFRS 1.C5].* If the business combinations exemption is not applicable or the entity did not acquire (i.e. created) the investment in the associate or joint venture, IAS 28 – *Investments in Associates and Joint Ventures* – should be applied retrospectively unless the entity applies the joint arrangements exemption. *[IFRS 1.D31].* (see 5.19 below);
- *an investment under IFRS 9* (see 5.12 below); or
- *an executory contract or service concession arrangement:* There are no first-time adoption exemptions that apply; therefore, IFRSs should be applied retrospectively. However, a practical relief is provided for a service concession arrangement if retrospective application is impracticable (see 5.15 below)

5.2.9 Measurement of deferred taxes and non-controlling interests

Deferred tax is calculated based on the difference between the carrying amount of assets and liabilities and their respective tax base. Therefore, deferred taxes should be recalculated after all assets acquired and liabilities assumed have been adjusted under IFRS 1. *[IFRS 1.C4(k)].*

IFRS 10 defines non-controlling interest as the 'equity in a subsidiary not attributable, directly or indirectly, to a parent.' *[IFRS 10 Appendix A].* This definition is discussed in Chapter 6. Non-controlling interests should be calculated after all assets acquired, liabilities assumed and deferred taxes have been adjusted under IFRS 1. *[IFRS 1.C4(k)].*

Any resulting change in the carrying amount of deferred taxes and non-controlling interests should be recognised by adjusting retained earnings (or, if appropriate, another category of equity), unless they relate to adjustments to intangible assets that are adjusted against goodwill. See Example 5.29 below. *[IFRS 1.IG Example 4].*

In terms of treatment of a deferred tax, there is a difference depending on whether the first-time adopter previously recognised acquired intangible assets in accordance with its previous GAAP or whether it had subsumed the intangible asset into goodwill (in both cases, a deferred tax liability was not recognised under its previous GAAP but is required to be recognised under IFRS). In the first case it must recognise a deferred tax liability and adjust non-controlling interests and opening reserves accordingly. By contrast, in the second case it would have to decrease the carrying amount of goodwill, recognise the intangible assets and a deferred tax liability and adjust non-controlling interests as necessary, as discussed at 5.2.5 above. The IASB discussed this issue in October 2005, but decided not to propose an amendment to address this inconsistency.[4]

Example 5.29: Restatement of intangible assets, deferred tax and non-controlling interests

Entity A's first IFRS financial statements are for a period that ends on 31 December 2018 and include comparative information for 2017 only. On 1 July 2014, Entity A acquired 75% of subsidiary B. Under its previous GAAP, Entity A assigned an initial carrying amount of £200 to intangible assets that would not have qualified for recognition under IAS 38. The tax base of the intangible assets was £nil, giving rise to a deferred tax liability (at 30%) of £60. Entity A measured non-controlling interests as their share of the fair value of the identifiable net assets acquired. Goodwill arising on the acquisition was capitalised as an asset in Entity A's consolidated financial statements.

On 1 January 2017 (the date of transition to IFRSs), the carrying amount of the intangible assets under previous GAAP was £160, and the carrying amount of the related deferred tax liability was £48 (30% of £160).

Under IFRS 1, Entity A derecognises intangible assets that do not qualify for recognition as separate assets under IAS 38, together with the related deferred tax liability of £48 and non-controlling interests, with a corresponding increase in goodwill (see 5.2.5 above). The related non-controlling interests amount to £28 (25% of £112 (£160 minus £48)). Entity A makes the following adjustment in its opening IFRS statement of financial position:

	£	£
Goodwill	84	
Deferred tax liability	48	
Non-controlling interests	28	
Intangible assets		160

Entity A tests the goodwill for impairment under IAS 36 and recognises any resulting impairment loss, based on conditions that existed at the date of transition to IFRSs.

5.2.10 Transition accounting for contingent consideration

The business combination exemption does not extend to contingent consideration that arose from a transaction that occurred before the transition date, even if the acquisition itself is not restated due to the use of the exemption. Therefore, such contingent consideration is recognised at its fair value at the transition date, regardless of the accounting under previous GAAP. If the contingent consideration was not recognised at fair value at the date of transition under previous GAAP, the resulting adjustment is recognised in retained earnings or other category of equity, if appropriate. Subsequent adjustments will be recognised following the provisions of IFRS 3. *[IFRS 3.40, 58].*

5.3 Share-based payment transactions

IFRS 2 applies to accounting for the acquisition of goods or services in equity-settled share-based payment transactions, cash-settled share-based payment transactions and transactions in which the entity or the counterparty has the option to choose between settlement in cash or equity. There is no exemption from recognising share-based payment transactions that have not yet vested at the date of transition to IFRSs. The exemptions in IFRS 1 clarify that a first-time adopter is not required to apply IFRS 2 fully retrospectively to equity-settled share-based payment transactions that have already vested at the date of transition to IFRSs.

IFRS 1 contains the following exemptions and requirements regarding share-based payment transactions:

(a) if a first-time adopter has disclosed publicly the fair value of its equity instruments, determined at the measurement date, as defined in IFRS 2, then it is encouraged to apply IFRS 2 to: *[IFRS 1.D2]*

  (i) equity instruments that were granted on or before 7 November 2002 (i.e. the date the IASB issued ED 2 – *Share-based Payment*);

  (ii) equity instruments that were granted after 7 November 2002 but vested before the date of transition to IFRSs.

  Many first-time adopters that did not use fair value-based share-based payment accounting under previous GAAP will not have published the fair value of equity instruments granted and are, therefore, not allowed to apply IFRS 2 retrospectively to those share-based payment transactions;

(b) for all grants of equity instruments to which IFRS 2 has not been applied a first-time adopter must still make the principal disclosures relating to the nature and extent of share-based payments required by paragraphs 44 and 45 of IFRS 2; *[IFRS 1.D2]*

(c) if a first-time adopter modifies the terms or conditions of a grant of equity instruments to which IFRS 2 has not been applied, the entity is not required to apply the requirements of IFRS 2 (in paragraphs 26-29) if the modification occurred before the date of transition to IFRSs; *[IFRS 1.D2]* and

(d) a first-time adopter is 'encouraged, but not required, to apply IFRS 2 to liabilities arising from share-based payment transactions that were settled before the date of transition to IFRSs'. *[IFRS 1.D3]*.

There are a number of interpretation issues concerning these exemptions and requirements:

- *Meaning of 'disclosed publicly' under (a) above*

  IFRS 1 only permits retrospective application of IFRS 2 if the entity has 'disclosed publicly' the fair value of the equity instruments concerned, but IFRSs do not define what is meant by 'disclosed publicly'. While IFRS 1 does not specifically require public disclosure of the fair value of an entity's share-based payment transactions in its previous financial statements, it is clear that IFRS 1 requires fair value to have been published contemporaneously. In addition, the requirements in IFRS 1 to disclose publicly the fair value of share-based payment transactions can be met even if the fair value is only disclosed in aggregate rather than for individual awards.

- *First-time adopters encouraged to apply IFRS 2 under (a)(ii) and (d) above*

  The 'date of transition to IFRSs' to which those exemptions refer is the first day of the earliest comparative period presented in a first-time adopter's first IFRS financial statements. This effectively means that an entity could accelerate the vesting of an award that was otherwise due to vest after the date of transition to IFRSs, in order to avoid applying IFRS 2 to that award.

- *Consistent selection of the exemptions under (a) and (d) above*

  A first-time adopter can choose which of the exemptions under (a) and (d) it wants to apply, i.e. there is no specific requirement to select the exemptions in a consistent manner.

- *Meaning of 'encouraged' under (a) and (d) above*

  Under IFRS 1, a first-time adopter is 'encouraged', but not required, to apply IFRS 2 to certain categories of share-based payment transactions (see (a) and (d) above). IFRS 1 does not specifically prohibit a literal reading of 'encouraged', which could, for example, allow a first-time adopter to decide to apply IFRS 2 only to some share-based payment transactions granted before 7 November 2002. We believe that it would generally be acceptable for a first-time adopter to apply IFRS 2 only to share-based payment transactions:

  (1) after an earlier date chosen by the entity (e.g. 1 January 2001), while not applying it to earlier transactions;

  (2) for which fair values were disclosed publicly.

- *Treatment of modifications, cancellations and settlements under (c) above*

  There is a slight ambiguity concerning the interpretation of the exemption under (c) above, because paragraph D2 of IFRS 1 refers only to the modification of awards. This could allow a literal argument that IFRS 2 and IFRS 1 do not prescribe any specific treatment when an entity cancels or settles, as opposed to modifying, an award falling within (a) above. However, paragraph D2 also requires an entity to apply paragraphs 26-29 of IFRS 2 to 'modified' awards. These paragraphs deal not only with modification but also with cancellation and settlement; indeed paragraphs 28 and 29 are not relevant to modifications at all. This makes it clear that the IASB intended IFRS 2 to be applied not only to modifications, but also to any cancellation or settlement of an award falling within (a) above, unless the modification, cancellation or settlement occurs before the date of transition to IFRSs. *[IFRS 1.D2, IFRS 2.26-29].*

- *Transactions where the counterparty has a choice of settlement method*

  These are not specifically addressed in the first-time adoption rules. It therefore appears that, where such transactions give rise to recognition of both an equity component and a liability component, the equity component is subject to the transitional rules for equity-settled transactions and the liability component to those for cash-settled transactions. This could well mean that the liability component of such a transaction is recognised in the financial statements, whilst the equity component is not.

- *Application of IFRS 2 to cash-settled transactions settled before the date of transition to IFRSs under (d) above*

  It is not entirely clear what lies behind the exemption under (d) above, since a first-time adopter would never be required to report a share-based payment transaction (or indeed any transaction) settled before the date of transition.

Extract 5.5 from Manulife Financial Corporation (Manulife) provides an illustration of typical disclosures made by entities that applied the share-based payments exemption. In the extract below, Manulife applied the exemption not to apply IFRS 2 to share-based transactions that were fully vested at the transition date. The extract also illustrates the implicit limitation of the share-based payment exemption for awards that were issued after 7 November 2002 and that were still vesting at the date of transition to IFRS.

Extract 5.5: Manulife Financial Corporation (2011)

Notes to Consolidated Financial Statements [extract]

Note 25 First-time Adoption of IFRS [extract]

As outlined in note 1, the Company has adopted IFRS as a replacement of previous Canadian GAAP effective January 1, 2011. References to Canadian GAAP throughout this note relate to Canadian GAAP prior to the adoption of IFRS. The Company's opening Consolidated Statement of Financial Position was prepared at January 1, 2010, the Company's date of transition to IFRS (the "Transition Date") in accordance with the requirements of IFRS 1 "First-Time Adoption of International Financial Reporting Standards". This note explains the principal adjustments made by the Company in preparing the opening IFRS Consolidated Statement of Financial Position as at January 1, 2010 compared to the Consolidated Balance Sheet as at December 31, 2009 under Canadian GAAP and the required adjustments between IFRS and previous Canadian GAAP to total equity and total comprehensive income for the 2010 comparative year.

IFRS has been applied retrospectively, except for certain optional and mandatory exemptions from full retrospective application provided for under IFRS 1, as detailed below.

(a) First-time adoption elections [extract]

Optional exemptions [extract]

Share-based payment transactions – The Company elected to apply IFRS 2 "Share-based Payments" to all equity instruments granted after November 7, 2002 that had not vested by the Transition Date. The Company applied IFRS 2 for all liabilities arising from share-based payment transactions that existed at the Transition Date.

5.3.1 Use of previously published fair values

There is no explicit requirement in IFRS 1 or IFRS 2 that any voluntary retrospective application of IFRS 2 must be based on the fair value previously published. This might appear to allow a first-time adopter the flexibility of using a different valuation for IFRS 2 purposes than that previously used for disclosure purposes. However, the requirements of IFRS 1 in relation to estimates under previous GAAP (see 4.2 above) mean that the assumptions used in IFRS must be consistent with those used in the originally disclosed valuation. The entity will also need to consider the implications of the assertion, in effect, that there is more than one fair value for the same transaction.

5.3.2 Restatement of costs recognised under previous GAAP

A first-time adopter may elect to take advantage of the transitional provisions in IFRS 1 which allow it not to apply IFRS 2 to equity-settled share-based payment transactions that were vested before the date of transition to IFRS, despite having recognised a cost for those transactions in accordance with its previous GAAP. Neither IFRS 1 nor IFRS 2 clearly indicates the appropriate treatment of the costs of share-based payment transactions that were recognised under the previous GAAP. There are mixed views on this issue in different jurisdictions, some of which are being driven by local regulatory expectations. In practice, either of the following approaches is considered acceptable, provided that the treatment chosen is disclosed in the financial statements if the previously recognised costs are material:

- *does not change expense previously recognised under previous GAAP for equity instruments subject to transitional relief under IFRS 1.* This approach is consistent with the approach for cash-settled share-based payment transactions that are settled prior to the date of transition to IFRS, since the entity must reflect the reduction in cash that was actually paid (and therefore the reduction in retained earnings); or

- *derecognise share-based payment expense under previous GAAP for equity instruments subject to transitional relief under IFRS 1.* In other words, reverse cumulative amounts recognised in the retained earnings and equity accounts of the opening IFRS statement of financial position.

5.4 Insurance contracts

A first-time adopter may apply the transitional provisions in IFRS 4. *[IFRS 1.D4].*

The claims development information (see Chapter 55) need not be disclosed for claims development that occurred more than five years before the end of the first IFRS reporting period. For entities taking advantage of this relief, the claims development information will be built up from five to ten years in the five years following adoption of IFRSs. Additionally, if it is 'impracticable' for a first-time adopter to prepare information about claims development that occurred before the beginning of the earliest period for which full comparative information is presented, this fact should be disclosed. *[IFRS 4.44].*

Furthermore, the IASB issued the amendments to IFRS 4 – *Applying IFRS 9 Financial Instruments with IFRS 4 Insurance Contracts* – in September 2016. The amendments permit insurers to either defer the application of IFRS 9 or use an 'overlay approach'. See 10 of Chapter 55 for more details of these approaches and treatments for first-time adopters.

IFRS 17 – *Insurance Contracts* – was issued in May 2017 and will be effective for annual reporting periods beginning on or after 1 January 2021. Early application is permitted for entities that apply IFRS 9 and IFRS 15 – *Revenue from Contracts with Customers* – on or before the date of initial application of IFRS 17. An entity must apply the transition provisions in paragraphs C1 – C24 and C28 in Appendix C of IFRS 17 to contracts within the scope of IFRS 17. The references in those paragraphs in IFRS 17 to the transition date must be read as the date of transition to IFRS. *[IFRS 1.B13].*

5.5 Deemed cost

IFRS 1 requires full retrospective application of standards effective at the end of a first-time adopter's first IFRS reporting period. *[IFRS 1.7].* Therefore, in the absence of the deemed cost exemption, the requirements of, for example, IAS 16, IAS 38, IAS 40 – *Investment Property* – and IFRS 6 – *Exploration for and Evaluation of Mineral Resources* – would have to be applied as if the first-time adopter had always applied these standards. This could be quite onerous because:

- these items are long-lived which means that accounting records for the period of acquisition may not be available anymore. In the case of formerly state-owned businesses, the required accounting records possibly never even existed;
- the entity may have revalued the items in the past as a matter of accounting policy or because this was required under national law; or
- even if the items were carried at depreciated cost, the accounting policy for recognition and depreciation may not have been IFRS compliant.

Given the significance of items like property, plant and equipment in the statement of financial position of most first-time adopters and the sheer number of transactions affecting property, plant and equipment, restatement is not only difficult but would often also involve huge cost and effort. Nevertheless, a first-time adopter needs a cost basis for those assets in its opening IFRS statement of financial position. Therefore, the IASB decided to introduce the notion of a 'deemed cost' that is not the 'true' IFRS compliant cost basis of an asset, but a surrogate that is deemed to be a suitable starting point.

There are five separate deemed cost exemptions in IFRS 1:

- fair value or revaluation as deemed cost (see 5.5.1 below);
- event-driven fair value measurement as deemed cost (see 5.5.2 below);
- deemed cost for oil and gas assets (see 5.5.3 below);
- deemed cost for assets used in operations subject to rate regulation (see 5.5.4 below); and
- deemed cost in determining the cost of an investment in a subsidiary, joint venture or associate (see 5.8.2 below).

5.5.1 Fair value or revaluation as deemed cost

To deal with the problem of restatement of long-lived assets upon first-time adoption of IFRSs, the standard permits a first-time adopter – for the categories of assets listed below – to measure an item in its opening IFRS statement of financial position using an amount that is based on its deemed cost: *[IFRS 1.D5, D6]*

- property, plant and equipment including bearer plants (see 7.4 below); *[IFRS 1.D5]*
- investment property, if an entity elects to use the cost model in IAS 40. *[IFRS 1.D7]*. The fact that the exemption can only be applied to investment property accounted for under the cost model will not pose any problems in practice as the fair value model under IAS 40 requires an entity to measure its investment property at fair value at its date of transition to IFRSs;
- right-of-use assets under IFRS 16 – *Leases; [IFRS 1.D7]* and
- intangible assets (see 7.14 below) that meet:
  - the recognition criteria in IAS 38 (including reliable measurement of original cost); and
  - the criteria in IAS 38 for revaluation (including the existence of an active market). *[IFRS 1.D7]*.

A first-time adopter cannot use this deemed cost approach by analogy for any other assets or for liabilities. *[IFRS 1.D7]*.

The use of fair value or revaluation as deemed cost for intangible assets will be very limited in practice because of the definition of an active market in IFRS 13. An active market is defined as one in which transactions for the item take place with sufficient frequency and volume to provide pricing information on an ongoing basis. *[IFRS 13 Appendix A]*. It is therefore unlikely that a first-time adopter will be able to apply this exemption to any intangible assets (see Chapter 17).

It is important to note that this exemption does not take classes or categories of assets as its unit of measure, but refers to 'an item of property, plant and equipment,' and similarly for investment property, right-of-use assets under IFRS 16 and intangible assets. *[IFRS 1.D5]*. IAS 16 does not 'prescribe the unit of measure for recognition, i.e. what constitutes an item of property, plant and equipment. Thus, judgement is required in applying the recognition criteria to an entity's specific circumstances' (see Chapter 18). *[IAS 16.9]*. A first-time adopter may therefore apply the deemed cost exemption to only some of its assets. For example, it could apply the exemption only to:

- a selection of properties;
- part of a factory; or
- some of the assets leased under a single finance lease under IAS 17 – *Leases*.

The IASB argued that it is not necessary to restrict application of the exemption to classes of assets to prevent selective revaluations, because IAS 36 'requires an impairment test if there is any indication that an asset is impaired. Thus, if an entity uses fair value as deemed cost for assets whose fair value is above cost, it cannot ignore indications that the recoverable amount of other assets may have fallen below their carrying amount. Therefore, the IFRS does not restrict the use of fair value as deemed cost to entire classes of asset.' *[IFRS 1.BC45]*. Nevertheless, it seems doubtful that the quality of financial information would benefit from a revaluation of a haphazard selection of items of property, plant and equipment. Therefore, a first-time adopter should exercise judgement in selecting the items to which it believes it is appropriate to apply the exemption.

Extracts 5.6 and 5.7 below are typical disclosures of the use of the 'fair value or revaluation as deemed cost' exemption.

Chapter 5

Extract 5.6: Suncor Energy Inc (2011)

Notes to the consolidated financial statements [extract]

6. First-Time Adoption of IFRS [extract]

Explanation of Significant Adjustments [extract]

(9) *Fair Value as Deemed Cost* [extract]

The company has applied the IFRS 1 election to record certain assets of property, plant and equipment at fair value on the Transition Date. The exemption has been applied to refinery assets located in Eastern Canada and certain natural gas assets in Western Canada. When estimating fair value, market information for similar assets was used, and where market information was not available, management relied on internally generated cash flow models using discount rates specific to the asset and long-term forecasts of commodity prices and refining margins. The aggregate of these fair values was $1.370 billion, resulting in a reduction of the carrying amount of property, plant and equipment as at January 1, 2010. Under Previous GAAP, impairment losses were recorded in the third quarter of 2010 for certain of these natural gas properties. There were no impairment losses recognized during 2010 under IFRS, as these properties were adjusted to fair value at the Transition Date. The impacts on the financial statements were as follows:

($ millions)	As at and for the year ended Dec 31, 2010
Property, plant and equipment, net	(527)
Retained earnings	(527)
Depreciation, depletion, amortization and impairment	(379)

Extract 5.7: Nexen Inc. (2011)

Notes to Consolidated Financial Statements [extract]

Note 26 Transition to IFRS [extract]

Elected Exemptions from Full Retrospective Application [extract]

In preparing these Consolidated Financial Statements in accordance with IFRS 1 First-time Adoption of International Financial Reporting Standards (IFRS 1), we applied the following optional exemptions from full retrospective application of IFRS.

(II) FAIR VALUE OR REVALUATION AS DEEMED COST

We elected to measure certain producing oil and gas properties at fair value as at the transition date and use that amount as its deemed cost in the opening IFRS balance sheet.

5.5.1.A Determining deemed cost

The deemed cost that a first-time adopter uses is either:

(a) the fair value of the item at the date of transition to IFRSs; *[IFRS 1.D5]* or

(b) a previous GAAP revaluation at or before the date of transition to IFRSs, if the revaluation was, at the date of the revaluation, broadly comparable to: *[IFRS 1.D6]*

  (i) fair value; or

  (ii) cost or depreciated cost in accordance with IFRSs, adjusted to reflect, for example, changes in a general or specific price index.

The revaluations referred to in (b) above need only be 'broadly comparable to fair value or reflect an index applied to a cost that is broadly comparable to cost determined in accordance with IFRSs'. *[IFRS 1.BC47]*. It appears that in the interest of practicality the IASB is allowing a good deal of flexibility in this matter. The IASB explains in the basis for conclusions that 'it may not always be clear whether a previous revaluation was intended as a measure of fair value or differs materially from fair value. The flexibility in this area permits a cost-effective solution for the unique problem of transition to IFRSs. It allows a first-time adopter to establish a deemed cost using a measurement that is already available and is a reasonable starting point for a cost-based measurement.' *[IFRS 1.BC47]*.

IFRS 1 describes the revaluations referred to in (b) above as a 'previous GAAP revaluation'. Therefore, in our view, such revaluations can only be used as the basis for deemed cost if they were recognised in the first-time adopter's previous GAAP financial statements. A previous GAAP impairment (or reversal of an impairment) that resulted in the recognition of the related assets at fair value in the previous GAAP financial statements may be recognised as a previous GAAP revaluation for purposes of applying this exemption if it represents the fair value under IFRS 13 and not another measure such as fair value less costs of disposal. However, when the previous GAAP impairment was determined for a group of impaired assets (e.g. a cash generating unit as defined in IAS 36, see Chapter 20), the recognised value of an individual asset needs to represent its fair value under IFRS 13 and not another measure such as fair value less costs of disposal for purposes of this exemption.

If revaluations under previous GAAP did not satisfy the criteria in IFRS 1, a first-time adopter measures the revalued assets in its opening IFRS statement of financial position on one of the following bases: *[IFRS1.IG11]*

(a) cost (or deemed cost) less any accumulated depreciation and any accumulated impairment losses under the cost model in IAS 16;

(b) deemed cost, being the fair value at the date of transition to IFRSs; or

(c) revalued amount, if the entity adopts the revaluation model in IAS 16 as its accounting policy under IFRSs for all items of property, plant and equipment in the same class.

A first-time adopter that uses the exemption is required to disclose the resulting IFRS 1 adjustment separately (see 6.5.1 below).

5.5.1.B Deemed cost determined before the date of transition to IFRSs

If the deemed cost of an asset was determined before the date of transition then an IFRS accounting policy needs to be applied to that deemed cost in the intervening period to determine what the carrying amount of the asset is in the opening IFRS statement of financial position. This means that a first-time adopter that uses previous GAAP revaluation as the deemed cost of an item of property, plant and equipment will need to start depreciating the item from the date for which the entity established the previous GAAP revaluation and not from its date of transition to IFRSs. *[IFRS 1.IG9]*. The example below illustrates the application of this requirement.

Example 5.30: Deemed cost of property, plant and equipment

Entity A used to revalue items of property, plant and equipment to fair value under its previous GAAP, but changed its accounting policy on 1 January 2011 when it adopted a different accounting policy. Under that accounting policy, Entity A did not depreciate the asset and only recognised the maintenance costs as an expense. Entity A's date of transition to IFRSs is 1 January 2017.

In its balance sheet under previous GAAP the carrying amount of the asset is £80 at the date of transition to IFRSs, which is equal to the last revaluation. Entity A can use the last revalued amount as the deemed cost of the asset on 1 January 2011. However, Entity A will need to apply IAS 16 to the period after 1 January 2011 because the accounting policy under its previous GAAP is not permitted under IFRSs. Assuming that the economic life of the asset is 40 years from 2011 and that the residual value is nil, Entity A would account for the asset at £68 in its opening IFRS statement of financial position, which represents the deemed cost minus 6 years of depreciation.

5.5.1.C Summary

At its date of transition to IFRSs, a first-time adopter is allowed under IFRS 1 to measure each item of property, plant and equipment, investment properties, right-of-use assets under IFRS 16 and intangible assets at an amount based on:

- historical cost determined in accordance with IAS 16, IAS 38, IAS 40 and IFRS 16;
- fair value at the date of transition to IFRSs;
- a previous GAAP revaluation amount that is broadly comparable to:
  - fair value at the date of revaluation; or
  - cost or depreciated cost under IFRS adjusted, for example, for changes in a general or specific index;
- a previous GAAP measure of cost that arose from an event-driven fair value, for example, at the date of an initial public offering or privatisation (see 5.5.2 below);

- in the case of an item acquired in a business combination (see 5.2 above):
  - carrying amount under previous GAAP immediately after the acquisition; or
  - if the item was not recognised under previous GAAP, the carrying amount on the basis that IFRSs would require in the separate statement of financial position of the acquiree;
- in the case of certain oil and gas assets, previous GAAP carrying amount (see 5.5.3 below);
- in the case of certain assets used or previously used in operations subject to rate regulation, previous GAAP carrying amount (see 5.5.4 below); or
- in the case of a lessee under IFRS 16, certain exemptions in IFRS 1 (see 5.6.3 below).

The fact that IFRS 1 offers so many different bases for measurement does not disturb the IASB as it reasons that 'cost is generally equivalent to fair value at the date of acquisition. Therefore, the use of fair value as the deemed cost of an asset means that an entity will report the same cost data as if it had acquired an asset with the same remaining service potential at the date of transition to IFRSs. If there is any lack of comparability, it arises from the aggregation of costs incurred at different dates, rather than from the targeted use of fair value as deemed cost for some assets. The Board regarded this approach as justified to solve the unique problem of introducing IFRSs in a cost-effective way without damaging transparency.' *[IFRS 1.BC43]*. Although this is valid, it still means that an individual first-time adopter can greatly influence its future reported performance by carefully selecting a first-time adoption policy for the valuation of its assets. Users of the financial statements of a first-time adopter should therefore be mindful that historical trends under the previous GAAP might no longer be present in an entity's IFRS financial statements.

5.5.2 Event-driven fair value measurement as deemed cost

A first-time adopter may use fair value measurements that arose from an event such as a privatisation or initial public offering as deemed cost for IFRSs at the date of that measurement. *[IFRS 1.D8]*.

IFRS 1 describes these revaluations as 'deemed cost in accordance with previous GAAP'. Therefore, to the extent that they related to an event that occurred prior to its date of transition or during the period covered by the first IFRS financial statements, they can only be used as the basis for deemed cost if they were recognised in the first-time adopter's previous GAAP financial statements. As discussed in 5.5.2.C below, a first-time adopter is also allowed to use event-driven fair values resulting from such events that occurred subsequent to the first-time adopter's date of transition to IFRSs, but during the period covered by the first IFRS financial statements.

The 'fair value or revaluation as deemed cost' exemption discussed at 5.5.1 above only applies to items of property, plant and equipment, investment property, right-of-use assets under IFRS 16 and certain intangible assets. *[IFRS 1.D5-D7]*. The event-driven deemed cost exemption, however, is broader in scope because it specifies that when a first-time adopter established a deemed cost in accordance with previous GAAP *for some or all of its assets and liabilities* [emphasis added] by measuring them at their fair value at one particular date ... the entity may use such event-driven fair value measurements as deemed cost for IFRSs at the date of that measurement. *[IFRS 1.D8, IFRS 1.BC46]*.

There are two important limitations in the scope of this exemption:

- while it applies, in principle, to all assets and liabilities of an entity, it does not override the recognition criteria in IFRSs. *[IFRS 1.10]*. Consequently, a first-time adopter should derecognise goodwill, assets (e.g. certain intangible assets such as brand names and research) and liabilities that do not qualify for recognition under IFRSs in the statement of financial position of the entity; and
- it cannot be used if the event-driven revaluation did not result in a re-measurement to full fair value (i.e. it cannot be used in the case of a partial step-up towards fair value).

If revaluations under previous GAAP did not satisfy the criteria in IFRS 1, a first-time adopter measures the revalued assets in its opening IFRS statement of financial position on one of the following bases: *[IFRS1.IG11]*

(a) cost (or deemed cost) less any accumulated depreciation and any accumulated impairment losses under the cost model in IAS 16;

(b) deemed cost, being the fair value at the date of transition to IFRSs; or

(c) revalued amount, if the entity adopts the revaluation model in IAS 16 as its accounting policy under IFRSs for all items of property, plant and equipment in the same class.

Finally, although a first-time adopter may use an event-driven fair value measurement as deemed cost for any asset or liability, it does not have to use them for all assets and liabilities that were revalued as a result of the event.

5.5.2.A 'Push down' accounting

Under some previous GAAPs an entity may have prepared its financial statements using 'push down' accounting, that is, the carrying amount of its assets and liabilities is based on their fair value at the date it became a subsidiary of its parent. If such a subsidiary subsequently adopts IFRSs, it will often require a very significant effort to determine the carrying amount of those assets and liabilities on a historical costs basis at the date of transition.

The event-driven deemed cost exemption applies to events 'such as a privatisation or initial public offering.' *[IFRS 1.D8]*. This list of events is clearly not meant to be exhaustive, but rather describes events that result in re-measurement of some or all assets and liabilities at their fair value. An acquisition that results in an entity becoming a subsidiary is a change of control event similar to a privatisation or an initial public offering. In our view, the application of 'push down' accounting results in event-driven fair value measurements that may be used as deemed cost for IFRSs at the date of that measurement.

The exemption can only be used, however, if 'push down' accounting resulted in the recognition of the related assets and liabilities at their fair value. For example, previous GAAP may not have required remeasurement to full fair value in the case of a partial acquisition or a step-acquisition, or if there was a bargain purchase that was allocated, for example, to reduce the fair values of long-lived assets. In these cases, the entity would not qualify for the event-driven deemed cost exemption, since the event did not result in the measurement of its assets and liabilities at their fair value.

5.5.2.B 'Fresh start' accounting

Some previous GAAPs require an entity that emerges from bankruptcy or undertakes a legal reorganisation to apply 'fresh start' accounting, which involves recognition of assets and liabilities at their fair value at that date.

In our view, the application of 'fresh start' accounting results in an event-driven fair value measurement that may be used as deemed cost for IFRSs at the date of that measurement. *[IFRS 1.D8]*. The use of the exemption is limited to instances that resulted in the recognition of the related assets and liabilities at their full fair value (i.e. it cannot be used in the case of a partial step-up towards fair value).

5.5.2.C Exemption for event-driven revaluations after the date of transition

The event-driven revaluation exemption allows a first-time adopter to recognise in its first IFRS financial statements fair values from events whose measurement date is after the date of transition to IFRSs but during the periods covered by the first IFRS financial statements. The event-driven fair value measurements are recognised as deemed cost at the date that the event occurs. An entity should recognise the resulting adjustments directly in retained earnings (or if appropriate, another category of equity) at the measurement date. *[IFRS 1.D8(b)]*.

The Board explicitly considered whether to allow a first-time adopter that uses a revaluation subsequent to the date of transition to 'work back' to the deemed cost on the date of transition to IFRSs by adjusting the revaluation amounts to exclude any depreciation, amortisation or impairment between the date of transition to IFRSs and the date of that measurement. *[IFRS 1.BC46B]*. The Board rejected this approach 'because making such adjustments would require hindsight and the computed carrying amounts on the date of transition to IFRSs would be neither the historical costs of the revalued assets nor their fair values on that date.' *[IFRS 1.BC46B]*. Accordingly, at the date of transition to IFRS, the entity should either establish the deemed cost by applying the criteria in paragraphs D5 – D7 of IFRS 1 or measure assets and liabilities under the other requirements in IFRS 1. *[IFRS 1.D8(b)]*. This restriction seems to limit the usefulness of the exemption for first time adopters; however, it should provide relief from the need to keep two sets of books subsequent to the event.

5.5.3 Deemed cost for oil and gas assets

It is common practice in some countries to account for exploration and development costs for oil and gas properties in development or production phases in cost centres that include all properties in a large geographical area, e.g. under the 'full cost accounting' method. However, this method of accounting generally uses a unit of account that is much larger than that is acceptable under IFRSs. Applying IFRSs fully retrospectively would pose significant problems for first-time adopters because it would also require amortisation 'to be calculated (on a unit of production basis) for each year, using a reserves base that has changed over time because of changes in factors such as geological understanding and prices for oil and gas. In many cases, particularly for older assets, this information may not be available.' *[IFRS 1.BC47A]*. Even when such information is available, the effort and cost to determine the opening balances at the date of transition would usually be very high.

For these entities, use of the fair value as deemed cost exemption (see 5.5.1 above), however, was not considered to be suitable because: *[IFRS 1.BC47B]*

> 'Determining the fair value of oil and gas assets is a complex process that begins with the difficult task of estimating the volume of reserves and resources. When the fair value amounts must be audited, determining significant inputs to the estimates generally requires the use of qualified external experts. For entities with many oil and gas assets, the use of this fair value as deemed cost alternative would not meet the Board's stated intention of avoiding excessive cost.'

The IASB therefore decided to grant an exemption for first-time adopters that accounted under their previous GAAP for 'exploration and development costs for oil and gas properties in the development or production phases ... in cost centres that include all properties in a large geographical area.' *[IFRS 1.D8A]*. Under the exemption, a first-time adopter may elect to measure oil and gas assets at the date of transition to IFRSs on the following basis: *[IFRS 1.D8A]*

(a) exploration and evaluation assets at the amount determined under the entity's previous GAAP; and

(b) assets in the development or production phases at the amount determined for the cost centre under the entity's previous GAAP. This amount should be allocated to the cost centre's underlying assets *pro rata* using reserve volumes or reserve values as of that date.

For this purpose, oil and gas assets comprise only those assets used in the exploration, evaluation, development or production of oil and gas. *[IFRS 1.D8A]*.

A first-time adopter that uses the exemption under (b) should disclose that fact and the basis on which carrying amounts determined under previous GAAP were allocated. *[IFRS 1.31A]*.

To avoid the use of deemed costs resulting in an oil and gas asset being measured at more than its recoverable amount, the Board also decided that oil and gas assets that were valued using this exemption should be tested for impairment at the date of transition to IFRSs as follows: *[IFRS 1.D8A]*

- exploration and evaluation assets should be tested for impairment under IFRS 6; and
- assets in the development and production phases should be tested for impairment under IAS 36.

The deemed cost amounts should be reduced to take account of any impairment charge.

Finally, a first-time adopter that applies the deemed cost exemption for oil and gas assets in the development or production phases in (b) above should also apply the IFRIC 1 – *Changes in Existing Decommissioning, Restoration and Similar Liabilities* – exemption (see 5.14.2 below). *[IFRS 1.D21A]*.

Extract 5.8 below presents disclosure of the use of the 'deemed cost for oil and gas assets' exemption.

Extract 5.8: Zargon Oil & Gas Ltd. (2011)

Notes to the Consolidated Financial Statements [extract]

27 **Reconciliation of Transition from Canadian GAAP to IFRS** [extract]

Explanatory notes [extract]

(b) The Company elected under IFRS 1 to deem the Canadian GAAP carrying value of its oil and gas assets accounted for under the full cost method as at January 1, 2010 as their deemed cost under IFRS as at that date. As such, the Canadian GAAP full cost pool was reallocated upon transition to IFRS and the 2010 comparatives were restated to reflect the new IFRS accounting policies as follows:

i. In accordance with IAS 16, IAS 38 and IFRS 6 on January 1, 2010 the Company reallocated costs of $24.37 million relating to unproved properties from property, plant and equipment to exploration and evaluation assets.

ii. Under Canadian GAAP, all costs incurred prior to having obtained licence rights and lease expiries were included within property, plant and equipment. Under IFRS, such expenditures are expensed as incurred. There was no impact on adoption of IFRS due to the full cost as deemed cost exemption. However, the comparative 2010 balances were restated at December 31, 2010 resulting in a reduction in property, plant and equipment and retained earnings of $2.81 million, and an increase in exploration and evaluation expenses for the year of the same amounts.

iii. The remaining full cost pool was allocated to the developed and producing assets pro rata using reserve values.

iv. Under IFRS, impairment tests must be performed at a more lower reporting level than was required under Canadian GAAP. The Canadian GAAP "ceiling test" incorporated a 2-step approach for testing impairment, while IFRS uses a 1-step approach. Under Canadian GAAP, a discounted cash flow analysis was not required if the undiscounted cash flows from proved reserves exceeded the carrying amount (step 1). If the carrying amount exceeded the undiscounted future cash flows, then a prescribed discounted cash flow test was performed (step 2). Under IFRS, impairment testing is based on discounted cash flows and is calculated at the CGU level. Impairment tests are required to be performed at the transition date, and as at January 1, 2010 no impairment was identified. At December 31, 2010 an impairment test was performed and four of the Company's CGUs were found to have impairment.

5.5.4 Deemed cost for assets used in operations subject to rate regulation

Entities that hold items of property, plant and equipment, right-of-use assets under IFRS 16 or intangible assets that are used, or were previously used, in operations subject to rate regulation might have capitalised, as part of the carrying amounts, amounts that do not qualify for capitalisation in accordance with IFRSs. For example, when setting rates, regulators often permit entities to capitalise an allowance for the cost of financing the asset's acquisition, construction or production. This allowance typically includes an imputed cost of equity. IFRSs do not permit an entity to capitalise an imputed cost of equity. *[IFRS 1.BC47F]*. The IASB decided to permit a first-time adopter with operations subject to rate regulations to elect to use the previous GAAP carrying amount of such an item at the date of transition to IFRSs as deemed cost. *[IFRS 1.D8B]*. In the Board's view, this exemption is consistent with other exemptions in IFRS 1 in that it 'avoids excessive costs while meeting the objectives of the IFRS.' *[IFRS 1.BC47I]*.

Operations are subject to rate regulation if they are governed by a framework for establishing the prices that can be charged to customers for goods or services and that framework is subject to oversight and/or approval by a rate regulator (as defined in IFRS 14 – *Regulatory Deferral Accounts*). *[IFRS 1.D8B, IFRS 14 Appendix A]*.

Without this exemption, a first-time adopter with operations subject to rate regulations would have had either to restate those items retrospectively to remove the non-qualifying amounts, or to use fair value as deemed cost (see 5.5.1 above). Both alternatives, the Board reasoned, pose significant practical challenges, the cost of which can outweigh the benefits. *[IFRS 1.BC47G]*. Typically, once amounts are included in the total cost of an item of property, plant and equipment, they are no longer tracked separately. Therefore, their removal would require historical information that, given the age of some of the assets involved, is probably no longer available and would be difficult to estimate. For many of these assets, it may be impractical to use the fair value exemption as such information may not be readily available. *[IFRS 1.BC47H]*.

A first-time adopter that applies this exemption to an item need not apply it to all items. At the date of transition to IFRSs, the first-time adopter should test for impairment in accordance with IAS 36 each item for which it used the exemption. *[IFRS 1.D8B]*.

Extract 5.9 below illustrates disclosure of the use of the deemed cost exemption for property, plant and equipment and intangible assets subject to rate regulation.

Extract 5.9: Enersource Corporation (2012)

Notes to Consolidated Financial Statements [extract]

Note 5 First-time adoption of IFRS: [extract]

(a) Previous Canadian GAAP carrying amount as deemed costs for PP&E and intangible assets. [extract]

Entities with operations subject to rate regulations may hold items of PP&E or intangible assets where the carrying amount of such items might include amounts that were determined under previous Canadian GAAP but do not qualify for capitalization in accordance with IFRS. If this is the case, a first-time adopter may elect to use the previous Canadian GAAP carrying amount of such an item at the date of transition to IFRS as deemed cost. An entity shall apply this exemption for annual periods beginning on or after 1 January 2011, but earlier application is permitted.

Entities are subject to rate regulation if they provide goods or services to customers at prices (i.e. rates) established by an authorized body empowered to establish rates that bind the customers and that are designed to recover the specific costs the entity incurs in providing the regulated goods or services and to earn a specified return.

Under this exemption the deemed cost at the date of transition becomes the new IFRS cost basis. The accumulated amortization recognized under previous Canadian GAAP prior to the transition date has been included as part of the deemed cost so that the net book values will not be affected.

At the date of transition to IFRS, an entity shall also test for impairment, each item for which this exemption is used.

This exemption does not only apply to individual entities with rate regulated activities but also to the consolidated financial statements of their parent companies.

Based on the definition above, the Corporation qualifies for this IFRS 1 exemption as Enersource Hydro is subject to rate regulations and accordingly the Corporation elected to use the deemed cost election for opening balance sheet values for its PP&E and intangible assets.

At the date of transition, the Corporation's gross book value, accumulated depreciation and net book value for PP&E was $872,359, $422,992 and $449,367 respectively. The gross book value, accumulated amortization and net book value for intangible assets was $18,389, $2,806 and $15,583 respectively.

The Corporation reviewed the additional requirements against the information provided in IAS 36 Impairment of Assets and determined that no impairments would be recorded.

While the current exemption in paragraph D8B of IFRS 1 provides a one-time relief to determine the transition date balances of the eligible property, plant and equipment, right-of-use assets under IFRS 16 and intangible assets, IFRS 14 is wider in scope (see 5.21 below).

5.6 Leases

IFRS 1 does not include any specific exemption from the retrospective application of IAS 17 and SIC-15 – *Operating Leases – Incentives*. Therefore, a first-time adopter is required to classify leases as operating or finance leases under IAS 17 based on the circumstances existing at the inception of the lease and not those existing at the date of transition to IFRSs. *[IFRS 1.IG14]*. However, if 'at any time the lessee and the lessor agree to change the provisions of the lease, other than by renewing the lease, in a manner that would have resulted in a different classification of the lease ... if the changed terms had been in effect at the inception of the lease, the revised agreement is regarded as a new agreement over its term.' *[IAS 17.13]*. In other words, an entity classifies a lease based on the lease terms that are in force at its date of transition to IFRSs; the lease classification is not based on lease terms that are no longer in force.

A first-time adopter should apply SIC-15 retrospectively to all leases, regardless of their starting date. *[IFRS 1.IG16]*.

5.6.1 IFRIC 4 (prior to adoption of IFRS 16)

IFRIC 4 – *Determining whether an Arrangement contains a Lease* – contains specific transitional provisions for existing IFRS-reporting entities that address the practical difficulties of going back potentially many years and making a meaningful assessment of whether the arrangement satisfied the criteria at that time. First-time adopters may apply the same transitional provisions, which allow them to apply IFRIC 4 to arrangements existing at their date of transition on the basis of facts and circumstances existing at that date. *[IFRS 1.D9]*. The example below based on the implementation guidance in IFRS 1 illustrates this exemption. *[IFRS 1.IG Example 202]*.

Example 5.31: Determining whether an arrangement contains a lease

Entity A's first IFRS financial statements are for a period that ends on 31 December 2018 and include comparative information for 2017 only. Its date of transition to IFRSs is 1 January 2017.

On 1 January 2006, Entity A entered into a take-or-pay arrangement to supply gas. On 1 January 2011, there was a change in the contractual terms of the arrangement.

On 1 January 2017, Entity A may determine whether the arrangement contains a lease under IFRIC 4 on the basis of facts and circumstances existing on that date. Alternatively, Entity A may apply the criteria in IFRIC 4 on the basis of facts and circumstances existing on 1 January 2006 and reassess the arrangement on 1 January 2011.

5.6.2 Arrangements assessed for lease accounting under previous GAAP (prior to adoption of IFRS 16)

A first-time adopter may have adopted a standard under its previous GAAP that had the same effect as the requirements of IFRIC 4 and that had the same transitional provisions, even if the wording was not identical and that may have had a different starting date than IFRIC 4. This exemption addresses a first-time adopter that has already assessed whether its existing arrangements contained leases, as required by IFRIC 4. The date at which it made that assessment would be other than that required by IFRIC 4, e.g. it would not have been at inception of the lease and might have been made before IFRIC 4 was issued. The exemption allows the entity not to reassess that determination when it adopts IFRSs. The IASB added that 'for an entity to have made the same determination of whether the arrangement contained a lease in accordance with previous GAAP, that determination would have to have given the same outcome as that resulting from applying IAS 17 and IFRIC 4.' *[IFRS 1.D9A].*

5.6.3 IFRS 16

In January 2016 the IASB issued IFRS 16 – *Leases* – which will be effective for annual reporting periods beginning on or after 1 January 2019 with an earlier application permitted. The consequential amendments to IFRS 1 (paragraph D9-D9E) provide first-time adopters with some exemptions from full retrospective application of IFRS 16.

Firstly, similar to that in 5.6.1 above, a first-time adopter may assess whether a contract existing at the date of transition contains a lease by applying IFRS 16 to these contracts on the basis of facts and circumstances existing at that date.

In addition, a first-time adopter that is a lessee may apply the following approach to all of its leases (subject to the practical expedients described below):

(a) Measure a lease liability at the date of transition to IFRS. A lessee should measure the lease liability at the present value of the remaining lease payments, discounted using the lessee's incremental borrowing rate at the transition date.

(b) Measure a right-of-use asset at the transition date by choosing, on a lease-by-lease basis, to measure that right-of-use asset at either:

  (i) its carrying amount as if IFRS 16 had been applied since that commencement date of the lease, but discounted using the lessee's incremental borrowing rate at the transition date; or

  (ii) an amount equal to the lease liability, adjusted by the amount of any prepaid or accrued lease payments relating to that lease recognised in the statement of financial position immediately before the transition date.

(c) Apply IAS 36 to right-of-use assets at the transition date.

Notwithstanding the exemption above, a first-time adopter that is a lessee should measure the right-of-use asset at fair value at the transition date for leases that meet the definition of investment property in IAS 40 and are measured using the fair value model in IAS 40 from the transition date.

Additionally a first-time adopter that is a lessee may apply one or more of the following practical expedients at the transition date (applied on a lease-by-lease basis):

(a) apply a single discount rate to a portfolio of leases with reasonably similar characteristics (e.g. a similar remaining lease term for a similar class of underlying assets in a similar economic environment);

(b) elect not to apply paragraph D9B to leases for which the lease term ends within 12 months of the transition date. Instead, the entity should account for (including disclosure of information about) these leases as if they were short-term leases accounted for under paragraph 6 of IFRS 16;

(c) elect not to apply paragraph D9B to leases for which the underlying asset is of low value (as described in paragraphs B3-B8 of IFRS 16). Instead, the entity should account for (including disclosure of information about) these leases under paragraph 6 of IFRS 16;

(d) exclude initial direct costs from the measurement of the right-of-use asset at the transition date; and

(e) use hindsight, such as in determining the lease term if the contract contains options to extend or terminate the lease.

Lease payments, lessee, lessee's incremental borrowing rate, commencement date of the lease, initial direct costs and lease term are defined in IFRS 16 and are used in IFRS 1 with the same meaning.

5.7 Cumulative translation differences

IAS 21 requires that, on disposal of a foreign operation, the cumulative amount of the exchange differences deferred in the separate component of equity relating to that foreign operation (which includes, for example, the cumulative translation difference for that foreign operation, the exchange differences arising on certain translations to a different presentation currency and any gains and losses on related hedges) should be reclassified to profit or loss when the gain or loss on disposal is recognised. *[IAS 21.48, IFRS 1.D12]*. This also applies to exchange differences arising on monetary items that form part of a reporting entity's net investment in a foreign operation in its consolidated financial statements. *[IAS 21.32, 39, IFRS 1.D12]*.

Full retrospective application of IAS 21 would require a first-time adopter to restate all financial statements of its foreign operations to IFRSs from their date of inception or later acquisition onwards, and then determine the cumulative translation differences arising in relation to each of these foreign operations. A first-time adopter need not comply with these requirements for cumulative translation differences that existed at the date of transition. If it uses this exemption: *[IFRS 1.D13]*

(a) the cumulative translation differences for all foreign operations are deemed to be zero at the date of transition to IFRSs; and

(b) the gain or loss on a subsequent disposal of any foreign operation must exclude translation differences that arose before the date of transition but must include later translation differences.

If a first-time adopter chooses to use this exemption, it should apply it to all foreign operations at its date of transition, which will include any foreign operations that became first-time adopters before their parent. Any existing separate component of the first-time adopter's equity relating to such translation differences would be transferred to retained earnings at the date of transition.

An entity may present its financial statements in a presentation currency that differs from its functional currency. IFRS 1 is silent on whether the cumulative translation differences exemption should be applied to all translation differences or possibly separately to differences between the parent's functional currency and the presentation currency. However, IAS 21 does not distinguish between the translation differences arising on translation of subsidiaries into the functional currency of the parent and those arising on the translation from the parent's functional currency to the presentation currency. In our opinion, the exemption should therefore be applied consistently to both types of translation differences.

Since there is no requirement to justify the use of the exemption on grounds of impracticality or undue cost or effort, an entity that already has a separate component of equity and the necessary information to determine how much of it relates to each foreign operation in accordance with IAS 21 (or can do so without much effort) is still able to use the exemption. Accordingly, an entity that has cumulative exchange losses in respect of foreign operations may consider it advantageous to use the exemption if it wishes to avoid having to recognise these losses in profit or loss if the foreign operation is sold at some time in the future.

The extract below illustrates how companies typically disclose the fact that they have made use of this exemption.

Extract 5.10: Coca-Cola FEMSA S.A.B. de C.V. (2012)

NOTE 27 First-time adoption of IFRS [extract]

27.3 Explanation of the effects of the adoption of IFRS [extract]

h) Cumulative Translation Effects [extract]

The Company decided to use the exemption provided by IFRS 1, which permits it to adjust at the transition date all the translation effects it had recognized under Mexican FRS to zero and begin to record them in accordance with IAS 21 on a prospective basis. The effect was Ps. 1,000 at the transition date, net of deferred income taxes of Ps. 1,887.

5.7.1 Gains and losses arising on related hedges

Although IFRS 1 is not entirely clear whether this exemption extends to similar gains and losses arising on related hedges, we believe it is entirely appropriate for this exemption to be applied to net investment hedges as well as the underlying gains and losses.

Paragraph D13, which contains the exemption, explains that a first-time adopter need not comply with 'these requirements.' *[IFRS 1.D13].* The requirements referred to are those summarised in paragraph D12 which explain that IAS 21 requires an entity:

(a) to recognise some translation differences in other comprehensive income and accumulate these in a separate component of equity; and

(b) on disposal of a foreign operation, to reclassify the cumulative translation difference for that foreign operation (*including, if applicable, gains and losses on related hedges*) [our emphasis] from equity to profit or loss as part of the gain or loss on disposal. *[IFRS 1.D12].*

The problem arises because paragraph D12 does not refer to the recognition of hedging gains or losses in other comprehensive income and accumulation in a separate component of equity (only the subsequent reclassification thereof). Accordingly, a very literal reading of the standard might suggest that an entity *is* required to identify historical gains and losses on such hedges. However, even if this position is accepted, the basis on which this might be done is not at all clear.

It is clear that the reasons cited by the IASB for including this exemption apply as much to related hedges as they do to the underlying exchange differences. The fact that IFRS 1 can be read otherwise might be seen as little more than poor drafting.

5.8 Investments in subsidiaries, joint ventures and associates

5.8.1 *Consolidated financial statements: subsidiaries and structured entities*

A first-time adopter should consolidate all subsidiaries (as defined in IFRS 10) unless IFRS 10 requires otherwise. *[IFRS 1.IG26]*. First-time adoption of IFRSs may therefore result in the consolidation for the first time of a subsidiary not consolidated under previous GAAP, either because the subsidiary was not regarded as such before, or because the parent did not prepare consolidated financial statements. If a first-time adopter did not consolidate a subsidiary under its previous GAAP, it should recognise the assets and liabilities of that subsidiary in its consolidated financial statements at the date of transition at either: *[IFRS 1.IG27(a)]*

(a) if the subsidiary has adopted IFRSs, the same carrying amounts as in the IFRS financial statements of the subsidiary, after adjusting for consolidation procedures and for the effects of the business combination in which it acquired the subsidiary; *[IFRS 1.D17]* or

(b) if the subsidiary has not adopted IFRSs, the carrying amounts that IFRSs would require in the subsidiary's statement of financial position. *[IFRS 1.C4(j)]*.

If the newly-consolidated subsidiary was acquired in a business combination before the date of the parent's transition to IFRSs, goodwill is the difference between the parent's interest in the carrying amount determined under either (a) or (b) above and the cost in the parent's separate financial statements of its investment in the subsidiary. This is no more than a pragmatic 'plug' that facilitates the consolidation process but does not represent the true goodwill that might have been recorded if IFRSs had been applied to the original business combination (see 5.2.7 above). *[IFRS 1.C4(j), IG27(b)]*. Therefore, if the first-time adopter accounted for the investment as an associate under its previous GAAP, it cannot use the notional goodwill previously calculated under the equity method as the basis for goodwill under IFRSs.

If the parent did not acquire the subsidiary, but established it, it does not recognise goodwill. *[IFRS 1.IG27(c)]*. Any difference between the carrying amount of the subsidiary and the net identifiable assets as determined in (a) or (b) above would be treated as an adjustment to retained earnings, representing the accumulated profits or losses that would have been recognised as if the subsidiary had always been consolidated.

The adjustment of the carrying amounts of assets and liabilities of a first-time adopter's subsidiaries may affect non-controlling interests and deferred tax, as discussed at 5.2.9 above. *[IFRS 1.IG28]*.

5.8.2 *Separate financial statements: Cost of an investment in a subsidiary, joint venture or associate*

When an entity prepares separate financial statements, IAS 27 requires a first-time adopter to account for its investments in subsidiaries, joint ventures and associates either: *[IFRS 1.D14]*

- at cost;
- in accordance with IFRS 9 – *Financial Instruments* – (or IAS 39, as appropriate); or
- using the equity method as described in IAS 28.

However, if a first-time adopter measures such an investment at cost then it can elect to measure that investment at one of the following amounts in its separate opening IFRS statement of financial position: *[IFRS 1.D15]*

(a) cost determined in accordance with IAS 27; or

(b) deemed cost, which is its:

  (i) fair value at the entity's date of transition to IFRSs in its separate financial statements; or

  (ii) previous GAAP carrying amount at that date.

A first-time adopter may choose to use either of these bases to measure its investment in each subsidiary, joint venture or associate where it elects to use a deemed cost. *[IFRS 1.D15]*.

For a first-time adopter that choose to account for such an investment using the equity method procedures in accordance with IAS 28:

(a) the first-time adopter applies the exemption for past business combinations in IFRS 1 (Appendix C) to the acquisition of the investment;

(b) if the entity becomes a first-time adopter for its separate financial statements earlier than for its consolidated financial statements and:

  (i) later than its parent, the entity would apply paragraph D16 of IFRS 1 in its separate financial statements;

  (ii) later than its subsidiary, the entity would apply paragraph D17 of IFRS 1 in its separate financial statements. *[IFRS 1.D15A]*.

A first-time adopter that applies the exemption should disclose certain additional information in its financial statements (see 6.5.2 below).

5.9 Assets and liabilities of subsidiaries, associates and joint ventures

Within groups, some subsidiaries, associates and joint ventures may have a different date of transition to IFRSs than the parent/investor, for example, because national legislation required IFRSs after, or prohibited IFRSs at, the date of transition of the parent/investor. As this could have resulted in permanent differences between the IFRS figures in a subsidiary's own financial statements and those it reports to its parent, the IASB introduced a special exemption regarding the assets and liabilities of subsidiaries, associates and joint ventures.

IFRS 1 contains detailed guidance on the approach to be adopted when a parent adopts IFRSs before its subsidiary (see 5.9.1 below) and when a subsidiary adopts IFRSs before its parent (see 5.9.2 below).

These provisions also apply when IFRSs are adopted at different dates by an investor in an associate and the associate, or a venturer in a joint venture and the joint venture. *[IFRS 1.D16-D17]*. In the discussion that follows 'parent' includes an investor in an associate or a venturer in a joint venture, and 'subsidiary' includes an associate or a joint venture. References to consolidation adjustments include similar adjustments made when applying equity accounting. IFRS 1 also addresses the requirements for a parent that adopts IFRSs at different dates for the purposes of its consolidated and its separate financial statements (see 5.9.4 below).

5.9.1 Subsidiary becomes a first-time adopter later than its parent

If a subsidiary becomes a first-time adopter later than its parent, it should in its financial statements measure its own assets and liabilities at either:

(a) the carrying amounts that would be included in the parent's consolidated financial statements, based on the parent's date of transition, if no adjustments were made for consolidation procedures and for the effects of the business combination in which the parent acquired the subsidiary; or

(b) the carrying amounts required by the rest of IFRS 1, based on the subsidiary's date of transition. These carrying amounts could differ from those described in (a) when:

  (i) exemptions in IFRS 1 result in measurements that depend on the date of transition;

  (ii) the subsidiary's accounting policies are different from those in the consolidated financial statements. For example, under IAS 16 the subsidiary may carry property at cost while the group uses the revaluation model, or *vice versa*. *[IFRS 1.D16]*.

IFRS 1 does not elaborate on exactly what constitute 'consolidation adjustments' but in our view it would encompass adjustments required in order to harmonise a subsidiary's accounting policies with those of the group, as well as purely 'mechanical' consolidation adjustments such as the elimination of intragroup balances, profits and losses.

The following example, which is based on the guidance on implementation of IFRS 1, illustrates how an entity should apply these requirements. *[IFRS 1.IG Example 8]*.

Example 5.32: Parent adopts IFRSs before subsidiary

Entity A presents its (consolidated) first IFRS financial statements in 2011. Its foreign subsidiary B, wholly owned by Entity A since formation, prepares information under IFRSs for internal consolidation purposes from that date, but Subsidiary B will not present its first IFRS financial statements until 2018.

If Subsidiary B applies option (a) above, the carrying amounts of its assets and liabilities are the same in both its opening IFRS statement of financial position at 1 January 2017 and Entity A's consolidated statement of financial position (except for adjustments for consolidation procedures) and are based on Entity A's date of transition.

Alternatively, Subsidiary B may apply option (b) above, and measure all its assets or liabilities based on its own date of transition to IFRSs (1 January 2017). However, the fact that Subsidiary B becomes a first-time adopter in 2018 does not change the carrying amounts of its assets and liabilities in Entity A's consolidated financial statements.

Under option (b) a subsidiary would prepare its own IFRS financial statements, completely ignoring the IFRS elections that its parent used when it adopted IFRSs for its consolidated financial statements.

Under option (a) the numbers in a subsidiary's IFRS financial statements will be as close to those used by its parent as possible. However, differences other than those arising from business combinations will still exist in many cases, for example:

- a subsidiary may have hedged an exposure by entering into a transaction with a fellow subsidiary. Such transaction could qualify for hedge accounting in the subsidiary's own financial statements but not in the group's consolidated financial statements; or
- a pension plan may have to be classified as a defined contribution plan from the subsidiary's point of view, but is accounted for as a defined benefit plan in the group's consolidated financial statements.

The IASB seems content with the fact that the exemption will ease some practical problems, *[IFRS 1.BC62]*, though it will rarely succeed in achieving more than a moderate reduction of the number of reconciling differences between a subsidiary's own reporting and the numbers used by its parent.

More importantly, the choice of option (a) prevents the subsidiary from electing to apply all the other voluntary exemptions offered by IFRS 1, since the parent had already made the choices for the group at its date of transition. Therefore, option (a) may not be appropriate for a subsidiary that prefers to use a different exemption (i.e. fair value as deemed cost) for property, plant and equipment due, for example, to a tax reporting advantage. Also, application of option (a) would be more difficult when a parent and its subsidiary have different financial years. In that case, IFRS 1 would seem to require the IFRS information for the subsidiary to be based on the parent's date of transition to IFRSs, which may not even coincide with an interim reporting date of the subsidiary; the same applies to any joint venture or associate.

A subsidiary may become a first-time adopter later than its parent, because it previously prepared a reporting package under IFRSs for consolidation purposes but did not present a full set of financial statements under IFRSs. The above election may be 'relevant not only when a subsidiary's reporting package complies fully with the recognition and measurement requirements of IFRSs, but also when it is adjusted centrally for matters such as review of events after the reporting period and central allocation of pension costs.' *[IFRS 1.IG31]*. Adjustments made centrally to an unpublished reporting package are not considered to be corrections of errors for the purposes of the disclosure requirements in IFRS 1. However, a subsidiary is not permitted to ignore misstatements that are immaterial to the consolidated financial statements of the group but material to its own financial statements.

If a subsidiary was acquired after the parent's date of transition to IFRSs then it cannot apply option (a) because there are no carrying amounts included in the parent's consolidated financial statements, based on the parent's date of transition. Therefore, the subsidiary is unable to use the values recognised in the group accounts when it was acquired, since push-down of the group's purchase accounting values is not allowed in the subsidiary's financial statements. However, if the subsidiary had recognised those amounts in its previous GAAP financial statements, it may be able to use the same amounts as deemed costs under IFRSs pursuant to the 'event-driven' deemed cost exemption (see 5.5.2 above).

The exemption is also available to associates and joint ventures. This means that in many cases an associate or joint venture that wants to apply option (a) will need to choose which shareholder it considers its 'parent' for IFRS 1 purposes if more than one investor/joint venturer have already applied IFRS and determine the IFRS carrying amount of its assets and liabilities by reference to that parent's date of transition to IFRSs.

5.9.2 *Parent becomes a first-time adopter later than its subsidiary*

If a parent becomes a first-time adopter later than its subsidiary, the parent should, in its consolidated financial statements, measure the subsidiary's assets and liabilities at the carrying amounts that are in the subsidiary's financial statements, after adjusting for consolidation and for the effects of the business combination in which the entity acquired the subsidiary. The same applies for associates or joint ventures, substituting equity accounting adjustments. *[IFRS 1.D17]*.

Unlike other first-time adoption exemptions, this exemption does not offer a choice between different accounting alternatives. In fact, while a subsidiary that adopts IFRSs later than its parent can choose to prepare its first IFRS financial statements by reference to its own date of transition to IFRSs or that of its parent, the parent itself *must* use the IFRS measurements already used in the subsidiary's financial statements, adjusted as appropriate for consolidation procedures and the effects of the business combination in which it acquired the subsidiary. *[IFRS 1.BC63]*. However, this exemption does not preclude the parent from adjusting the subsidiary's assets and liabilities for a different accounting policy, e.g. cost model or revaluation model for accounting for property, plant and equipment.

The following example, which is based on the guidance on implementation of IFRS 1, illustrates how an entity should apply these requirements. *[IFRS 1.IG Example 9]*.

Example 5.33: Subsidiary adopts IFRSs before parent

Entity C presents its (consolidated) first IFRS financial statements in 2018. Its foreign subsidiary D, wholly owned by Entity C since formation, presented its first IFRS financial statements in 2013. Until 2018, Subsidiary D prepared information for internal consolidation purposes under Entity C's previous GAAP.

The carrying amounts of Subsidiary D's assets and liabilities at 1 January 2017 are the same in both Entity C's (consolidated) opening IFRS statement of financial position and Subsidiary D's own financial statements (except for adjustments for consolidation procedures) and are based on Subsidiary D's date of transition to IFRSs. The fact that Entity C becomes a first-time adopter in 2018 does not change the carrying amounts of Subsidiary D's assets and liabilities in the consolidated group financial statements.

When a subsidiary adopts IFRSs before its parent, this will limit the parent's ability to choose first-time adoption exemptions in IFRS 1 freely as related to that subsidiary, as illustrated in the example below. However, this does not mean that the parent's ability to choose first-time adoption exemptions will always be limited. For example, a parent may still be able to deem a subsidiary's cumulative translation differences to be zero because IFRS 1 specifically states that under the option 'the cumulative translation differences for *all* [emphasis added] foreign operations are deemed to be zero at the date of transition to IFRSs' (see 5.7 above). *[IFRS 1.D13]*.

Example 5.34: Limited ability to choose first-time adoption exemptions

Entity E will adopt IFRSs for the first time in 2018 and its date of transition is 1 January 2017. Subsidiary F adopted IFRSs in 2013 and its date of transition was 1 January 2012:

(a) *Subsidiary F and Entity E both account for their property, plant and equipment at historical cost under IAS 16.*

Upon first-time adoption, Entity E may only adjust carrying amounts of Subsidiary F's assets and liabilities to adjust for the effects of consolidation and business combinations. Entity E can therefore not apply the exemption to use fair value as deemed cost for Subsidiary F's property, plant and equipment as at its own date of transition (1 January 2017);

(b) *Subsidiary F accounts for its property, plant and equipment at revalued amounts under IAS 16, while Entity E accounts for its property, plant and equipment at historical cost under IAS 16.*

In this case, Entity E would not be allowed to apply the exemption to use fair value as deemed cost of Subsidiary F's property, plant and equipment because paragraph D17 of IFRS 1 would only permit adjustments for the effects of consolidation and business combinations. Although a consolidation adjustment would be necessary, this would only be to adjust Subsidiary F's revalued amounts to figures based on historical cost.

(c) *Subsidiary F may have deemed the cumulative translation difference for all its foreign subsidiaries to be zero at its date of transition (i.e. 1 January 2012).*

When Entity E adopts IFRSs it can deem Subsidiary F's cumulative translation differences to be zero at its date of transition (1 January 2017).

5.9.3 *Implementation guidance on accounting for assets and liabilities of subsidiaries, associates and joint ventures*

The requirements of IFRS 1 for a parent and subsidiary with different dates of transition do not override the following requirements of IFRS 1: *[IFRS 1.IG30]*

- the parent's election to use the business combinations exemption in Appendix C discussed at 5.2 above, which applies to assets and liabilities of a subsidiary acquired in a business combination that occurred before the parent's date of transition to IFRSs. However, the rules summarised at 5.9.2 above (parent adopting IFRSs after subsidiary) apply only to assets acquired and liabilities assumed by the subsidiary after the business combination and still held and owned by it at the parent's date of transition to IFRSs;
- to apply the requirements in IFRS 1 in measuring all assets and liabilities for which the provisions in paragraphs D16 and D17 of IFRS 1 are not relevant (for example, the use of the exemption in D16(a) to measure assets and liabilities at the carrying amounts in the parent's consolidated financial statements does not affect the use of the exemption in D12-13 to deem the cumulative translation differences for all foreign operations are zero at its date of transition, discussed in 5.7 above); and
- a first-time adopter must give all the disclosures required by IFRS 1 as of its own date of transition to IFRSs – see 6 below.

5.9.4 *Adoption of IFRSs on different dates in separate and consolidated financial statements*

An entity may sometimes become a first-time adopter for its separate financial statements earlier or later than for its consolidated financial statements. Such a situation may arise, for example, when a parent avails itself of the exemption under paragraph 4 of IFRS 10 from preparing consolidated financial statements and prepares its separate financial statements under IFRSs. Subsequently, the parent may cease to be entitled to the exemption or may choose not to use it and would, therefore, be required to apply IFRS 1 in its first consolidated financial statements.

Another example might be that, under local law, an entity is required to prepare its consolidated financial statements under IFRSs, but is required (or permitted) to prepare its separate financial statements under local GAAP. Subsequently the parent chooses, or is required, to prepare its separate financial statements under IFRSs.

If a parent becomes a first-time adopter for its separate financial statements earlier or later than for its consolidated financial statements, it must measure its assets and liabilities at the same amounts in both financial statements, except for consolidation adjustments. *[IFRS 1.D17]*. As drafted, the requirement is merely that the 'same' amounts be used, without being explicit as to which set of financial statements should be used as the benchmark. However, it seems clear from the context that the IASB intends that the measurement basis used in whichever set of financial statements first comply with IFRSs must also be used when IFRSs are subsequently adopted in the other set.

5.9.5 *Application to investment entities under IFRS 10*

IFRS 10 requires a parent that is an 'investment entity' as defined in the standard (see Chapter 6) to account for most of its subsidiaries at fair value through profit or loss in its consolidated financial statements rather than through consolidation. This exception from normal consolidation procedures does not apply to:

- a parent entity that owns a subsidiary which is an investment entity but the parent itself is not an investment entity; *[IFRS 10.33]* or
- a parent that is an investment entity in accounting for subsidiary that is not itself an investment entity and whose main purpose and activities are providing services that relate to the investment entity's investment activities. *[IFRS 10.32]*.

In IFRS 1, there are exemptions relating to a parent adopting IFRSs earlier or later than its subsidiary (see 5.9.1 and 5.9.2 above), in order to deal with situations where:

- a subsidiary that is required to be measured at fair value through profit or loss adopts IFRSs after its parent which is an investment entity (see 5.9.5.A below); or
- a parent that is not an 'investment entity' adopts IFRSs after a subsidiary which is an investment entity (see 5.9.5.B below).

5.9.5.A Subsidiary adopts IFRSs after investment entity parent

In this case, the subsidiary that is required to be measured at fair value through profit or loss is required to measure its assets and liabilities under the general provisions of IFRS 1, based on its own date of transition to IFRSs (i.e. option (b) in 5.9.1 above), *[IFRS 1.D16(a)]*, rather than (as would generally be permitted under option (a) in 5.9.1 above) by reference to the carrying value of its assets and liabilities in the consolidated financial statements of its parent, which is based on the fair value of the subsidiary's equity. This effectively prevents the accounting anomaly of the subsidiary measuring its net assets at the fair value of its own equity on transition to IFRSs.

5.9.5.B Non-investment entity parent adopts IFRSs after investment entity subsidiary

In this case, the parent is required to consolidate its subsidiaries in the normal way. *[IFRS 1.D17]*. If the provisions in 5.9.2 above were to be applied, the effect would be that the parent would bring any investments in subsidiaries accounted for at fair value through profit or loss by the subsidiary into the parent's consolidated statement of financial position at their fair value. This result would be contrary to the intention of the investment entities concept that such an accounting treatment is applied only by a parent that is itself an investment entity.

5.10 Compound financial instruments

IAS 32 requires compound financial instruments (e.g. many convertible bonds) to be split at inception into separate equity and liability components on the basis of facts and circumstances existing when the instrument was issued. *[IAS 32.15, 28]*. If the liability component is no longer outstanding, a full retrospective application of IAS 32 would involve identifying two components, one representing the original equity component and the other (retained earnings) representing the cumulative interest accreted on the liability component, both of which are accounted for in equity (see Chapter 45). A first-time adopter does not need to make this possibly complex allocation if the liability component is no longer outstanding at the date of transition to IFRSs. *[IFRS 1.D18]*. For example, in the case of a convertible bond that has been converted into equity, it is not necessary to make this split.

However, if the liability component of the compound instrument is still outstanding at the date of transition to IFRSs then a split is required to be made (see Chapter 45). *[IFRS 1.IG35-IG36].*

This transitional exemption is of limited value in practice because the number of different compound financial instruments that were outstanding before the date of transition to IFRSs is bound to be limited for any given first-time adopter.

5.11 Designation of previously recognised financial instruments – Entities applying IAS 39

The following discusses the application of the exemption in D19 regarding designation of previously recognised financial instruments to certain financial assets and financial liabilities by an entity using IAS 39.

5.11.1 Available-for-sale financial assets

Subject to the criteria in IAS 39, an entity can only designate such an asset as available-for-sale upon initial recognition (see Chapter 46). However, a first-time adopter that applies IAS 39 is allowed to designate a financial asset, typically one that would otherwise be classified as a loan and receivable, as an available-for-sale financial asset at the date of transition, *[IFRS 1.D19 (a)]*, although it would need to make certain additional disclosures (see 6.4 below). *[IFRS 1.29].*

Retrospective designation as available-for-sale requires a first-time adopter to recognise the cumulative fair value changes in a separate component of equity in the opening IFRS statement of financial position. It must then transfer those fair value changes to profit or loss on subsequent disposal or impairment of the asset.

The IASB recognised that this exemption could allow first-time adopters to designate only those financial instruments with cumulative gains as available-for-sale, but it noted that a first-time adopter could achieve similar results by selectively disposing of some financial assets before the date of transition to IFRSs. Therefore, IFRS 1 does not impose any additional restrictions on a first-time adopter regarding the designation of financial instruments as available-for-sale financial assets at its date of transition to IFRSs.

5.11.2 Financial asset or financial liability at fair value through profit or loss

IAS 39 permits a financial instrument to be designated only on initial recognition as a financial asset or financial liability at fair value through profit or loss. However, a first-time adopter is permitted to designate, at its date of transition, any financial asset or financial liability as at fair value through profit or loss provided it meets the criteria in IAS 39 at that date. *[IFRS 1.D19 (b)].* Broadly, an entity may only designate a financial asset or financial liability at fair value through profit or loss, because either:

- it eliminates or significantly reduces a measurement or recognition inconsistency (sometimes referred to as 'an accounting mismatch') that would otherwise arise;
- a group of financial assets, financial liabilities or both is managed and its performance is evaluated on a fair value basis; or
- if a contract contains one or more embedded derivatives that meets particular conditions (see Chapter 44). *[IAS 39.9, 11A].*

It is clear from the provisions of IFRS 1 that first-time adopters should complete the designation by their date of transition. In other words, designation should be made contemporaneously and cannot be documented retrospectively.

A first-time adopter that applies this exemption needs to make certain additional disclosures (see 6.4 below). *[IFRS 1.29]*.

5.11.3 Implementation guidance on other categories of financial instruments

The implementation guidance to IFRS 1 clarifies how, in preparing its opening IFRS statement of financial position, an entity should apply the criteria in IAS 39 to identify those financial assets and financial liabilities that are measured at fair value and those that are measured at amortised cost. *[IFRS 1.IG56, IG57]*.

5.11.3.A Held-to-maturity investments

Financial assets are classified as held-to-maturity investments based on a designation made at the date of transition that reflects the entity's intention and ability to retain the asset in accordance with IAS 39. *[IFRS 1.IG56(a)]*. This means that sales or transfers of held-to-maturity investments before the date of transition to IFRSs do not trigger the 'tainting' rules in IAS 39. Held-to-maturity investments are described in Chapter 46.

5.11.3.B Financial assets or financial liabilities at fair value through profit or loss

Except for those financial instruments that are designated as at fair value through profit or loss at the date of transition (see 5.11.2 above), non-derivative financial instruments are included within the opening IFRS statement of financial position as at fair value through profit or loss only if the asset or liability was:

- acquired or incurred principally for the purpose of sale or repurchase in the near term; or
- at the date of transition to IFRSs, part of a portfolio of identified financial instruments that were managed together and for which there was evidence of a recent actual pattern of short-term profit taking.

These instruments would be classified as held for trading rather than being designated at fair value through profit and loss. *[IAS 39.9]*. See Chapter 46.

5.11.3.C Loans and receivables

In assessing whether or not a financial asset meets the definition of loans and receivables at the date of transition to IFRSs, a first-time adopter should consider the circumstances that existed when it first met the recognition criteria in IAS 39. *[IFRS 1.IG56(b)]*. See Chapter 46.

5.11.3.D Financial assets and financial liabilities measured at amortised cost

The cost of financial assets and financial liabilities measured at amortised cost in the opening IFRS statement of financial position should be determined on the basis of circumstances existing when the assets and liabilities first satisfied the recognition criteria in IAS 39, unless they were acquired in a past business combination in which case their carrying amount under previous GAAP immediately following the business combination is their deemed cost under IFRSs at that date. *[IFRS 1.IG57]*.

To determine amortised cost using the effective interest method, it is necessary to determine the transaction costs incurred when the instrument was originated. The IASB believes that the unamortised portion of transaction costs at the date of transition to IFRSs is unlikely to be material for most financial instruments. Further, even where the unamortised portion may be material, reasonable estimates are believed possible so no exemption was granted in this area. *[IFRS 1.BC73]*.

5.11.3.E Available-for-sale financial assets

In addition to those financial assets that are designated as available-for-sale, this category includes those non-derivative financial assets that are not in any of the other categories identified by IAS 39. *[IFRS 1.IG56(e)]*.

If an investment is classified as available-for-sale, any revaluation gain under previous GAAP that has been recognised outside profit or loss is recognised in a separate component of equity at the transition date. Subsequently, the entity recognises gains and losses on the available-for-sale financial asset in other comprehensive income and accumulates the gains and losses in that separate component of equity until the investment is impaired, sold, collected or otherwise disposed of, at which point the entity reclassifies to profit or loss the cumulative gain or loss remaining in equity. *[IFRS 1.IG59]*.

The requirement that a first-time adopter should apply IAS 39 retrospectively to available-for-sale financial assets was retained in the standard. The IASB concluded that the costs of retrospective compliance with IAS 39's requirement would be minimal if a first-time adopter carried the available-for-sale financial assets under previous GAAP at cost or the lower of cost and market value. They acknowledged that these costs might be more significant if they were carried at fair value, but in that case those assets might well be classified as held for trading. *[IFRS 1.BC83]*.

Chapter 5

Given the requirements in respect of impairments of available-for-sale equity instruments full retrospective application may not be as straightforward as the IASB thinks.

5.11.3.F Derivatives

All derivatives, except for those that are financial guarantee contracts or designated and effective hedging instruments, are classified as held for trading under IAS 39. Therefore, the difference between their fair value and their previous carrying amount should be recognised as an adjustment to retained earnings at the beginning of the financial year in which IAS 39 is initially applied. *[IFRS 1.IG58A]*.

5.11.4 Loan impairments

An entity's estimates of loan impairments at the date of transition to IFRSs should be consistent with estimates made for the same date under previous GAAP, after adjustments to reflect any difference in accounting policies, unless there is objective evidence that those assumptions were in error. Any later revisions to those estimates should be treated as impairment losses or, if the criteria in IAS 39 are met, reversals of impairment losses, of the period in which the entity makes the revisions. *[IFRS 1.IG58]*.

In the context of the detailed requirements for loan impairments, it is unclear where the dividing line between estimates and accounting policies lies. Therefore, for entities with material impairment provisions, such as banks and similar financial institutions, this requirement is not going to be straightforward. See Chapter 49.

5.12 Designation of previously recognised financial instruments – Entities adopting IFRS 9

The following discusses the application of the exemption in D19 through D19C regarding designation of previously recognised financial instruments to certain financial assets and financial liabilities by an entity using IFRS 9.

5.12.1 Designation of financial asset as measured at fair value through profit or loss

An entity can designate a financial asset as measured at fair value through profit or loss if the entity satisfies the criteria in IFRS 9 at the date the entity becomes a party to the financial instrument. *[IFRS 9.4.1.5].*

Paragraph D19A of IFRS 1 allows a first-time adopter to designate a financial asset as measured at fair value through profit or loss on the basis of facts and circumstances that exist at the date of transition to IFRSs, *[IFRS 1.D19A]*, although paragraph 29 of IFRS 1 would require certain additional disclosures (see 6.4 below).

5.12.2 Designation of financial liability at fair value through profit or loss

IFRS 9 permits a financial liability to be designated as a financial liability at fair value through profit or loss if the entity meets the criteria in IFRS 9 at the date the entity becomes a party to the financial instrument. *[IFRS 9.4.2.2].*

Paragraph D19 of IFRS 1 allows a first-time adopter to designate, at the transition date, a financial liability as measured at fair value through profit or loss provided the liability meets the criteria in paragraph 4.2.2 of IFRS 9 at that date, although paragraph 29A of IFRS 1 would require certain additional disclosures (see 6.4 below).

5.12.3 Designation of investment in equity instruments

At initial recognition, an entity may make an irrevocable election to designate an investment in an equity instrument not held for trading or contingent consideration recognised by an acquirer in a business combination to which IFRS 3 applies as at fair value through other comprehensive income in accordance with IFRS 9. *[IFRS 9.5.7.5].*

Paragraph D19B of IFRS 1 allows a first-time adopter to designate an investment in such an equity instrument as at fair value through other comprehensive income on the basis of facts and circumstances that exist at the date of transition to IFRSs.

5.12.4 Determination of an accounting mismatch for presenting a gain or loss on financial liability

IFRS 9 requires a fair value gain or loss on a financial liability that is designated as at fair value through profit or loss to be presented as follows unless this presentation creates or enlarges an accounting mismatch in profit or loss. *[IFRS 9.5.7.7]*.

- the amount of change in the fair value of the financial liability that is attributable to changes in the credit risk of that liability should be presented in other comprehensive income
- the remaining amount of change in the fair value of the liability should be presented in profit or loss.

Paragraph D19C of IFRS 1 requires a first-time adopter to determine whether the treatment in paragraph 5.7.7 of IFRS 9 would create or enlarge an accounting mismatch in profit or loss on the basis of facts and circumstances that exist at the date of transition to IFRSs (see Chapter 47).

5.12.5 Designation of contracts to buy or sell a non-financial item

IFRS 9 allows some contracts to buy or sell a non-financial item to be designated at inception as measured at fair value through profit or loss. *[IFRS 9.2.5]*. Despite this requirement, paragraph D33 of IFRS 1 allows an entity to designate, at the date of transition to IFRSs, contracts that already exist on that date as measured at fair value through profit or loss but only if they meet the requirements of paragraph 2.5 of IFRS 9 at that date and the entity designates all similar contracts at fair value through profit or loss.

5.13 Fair value measurement of financial assets or financial liabilities at initial recognition

First-time adopters are granted similar transition relief in respect of the day 1 profit requirements of IFRS 9 or IAS 39 as is available to existing IFRS reporters. *[IFRS 1.BC83A]*. Consequently, first-time adopters may apply the requirements of paragraph B5.1.2A(b) of IFRS 9 (or AG76(a) of IAS 39) about a deferral of day 1 gain/loss prospectively to transactions entered into on or after the date of transition to IFRSs. *[IFRS 1.D20]*.

5.14 Decommissioning liabilities included in the cost of property, plant and equipment

5.14.1 IFRIC 1 exemption

Under IAS 16 the cost of an item of property, plant and equipment includes 'the initial estimate of the costs of dismantling and removing the item and restoring the site on which it is located, the obligation for which an entity incurs either when the item is acquired or as a consequence of having used the item during a particular period for purposes other than to produce inventories during that period.' *[IAS 16.16(c)]*. Therefore, a first-time adopter needs to ensure that property, plant and equipment cost includes an item representing the decommissioning provision as determined under IAS 37. *[IFRS 1.IG13]*.

An entity should apply IAS 16 in determining the amount to be included in the cost of the asset, before recognising depreciation and impairment losses which cause differences between the carrying amount of the decommissioning liability and the amount related to decommissioning costs to be included in the carrying amount of the asset.

An entity accounts for changes in decommissioning provisions in accordance with IFRIC 1 but IFRS 1 provides an exemption for changes that occurred before the date of transition to IFRSs and prescribes an alternative treatment if the exemption is used. *[IFRS 1.IG13, IG201-IG203]*. In such cases, a first-time adopter should:

(a) measure the decommissioning liability as at the date of transition in accordance with IAS 37;

(b) to the extent that the liability is within the scope of IFRIC 1, estimate the amount that would have been included in the cost of the related asset when the liability first arose, by discounting it to that date using its best estimate of the historical risk-adjusted discount rate(s) that would have applied for that liability over the intervening period; and

(c) calculate the accumulated depreciation on that amount, as at the date of transition to IFRSs, on the basis of the current estimate of the useful life of the asset, using the entity's IFRS depreciation policy. *[IFRS 1.D21]*.

Example 5.35: Decommissioning component in property, plant and equipment

Entity A's date of transition to IFRSs is 1 January 2017 and the end of its first IFRS reporting period is 31 December 2018. Entity A built a factory that was completed and ready for use on 1 January 2012. Under its previous GAAP, Entity A accrued a decommissioning provision over the expected life of the plant. The facts can be summarised as follows:

Cost of the plant	€1,400
Residual value	€200
Economic life	20 years
Original estimate of decommissioning cost in year 20	€175
Revised estimate on 1 January 2014 of decommissioning cost in year 20	€300
Discount rate applicable to decommissioning liability (the discount rate is assumed to be constant)	5.65%
Discounted value of original decommissioning liability on 1 January 2012	€58
Discounted value on 1 January 2012 of revised decommissioning liability	€100
Discounted value on 1 January 2017 of revised decommissioning liability	€131

If Entity A applies the exemption from full retrospective application, what are the carrying amounts of the factory and the decommissioning liability in A's opening IFRS statement of financial position?

The tables below show how Entity A accounts for the decommissioning liability and the factory under its previous GAAP, under IFRS 1 using the exemption and under IFRS 1 applying IFRIC 1 retrospectively.

	Decommissioning liability		
	Previous GAAP	*Exemption IFRS 1*	*Retrospective application of IFRIC 1*
1 January 2012		100	58
Decommissioning costs €175 ÷ 20 years × 2 =	17.5		
Decommissioning costs €100 × ($1.0565^2 – 1$) =		12	
Decommissioning costs €58 × ($1.0565^2 – 1$) =			7
1 January 2014	17.5	112	65
Revised estimate of decommissioning provision	12.5		47
1 January 2014	30	112	112
Decommissioning costs €300 ÷ 20 years × 3 =	45		
Decommissioning costs €112 × ($1.0565^3 – 1$) =		19	
Decommissioning costs €112 × ($1.0565^3 – 1$) =			19
1 January 2017	75	131	131
Decommissioning costs €300 ÷ 20 years × 2 =	30		
Decommissioning costs €131 × ($1.0565^2 – 1$) =		16	
Decommissioning costs €131 × ($1.0565^2 – 1$) =			16
31 December 2018	105	147	147

In calculating the decommissioning provision, it makes no difference whether Entity A goes back in time and tracks the history of the decommissioning provision or whether it just calculates the decommissioning provision at its date of transition to IFRSs. This is not the case for the calculation of the related asset, as can be seen below.

	Factory		
	Previous GAAP	*Exemption IFRS 1*	*Retrospective application of IFRIC 1*
1 January 2012	1,400	1,500	1,458
Depreciation (€1,400 – €200) ÷ 20 years × 2 =	(120)		
Depreciation (€1,500 – €200) ÷ 20 years × 2 =		(130)	
Depreciation (€1,458 – €200) ÷ 20 years × 2 =			(126)
1 January 2014			1,332
Revised estimate of decommissioning provision			47
1 January 2014			1,379
Depreciation (€1,400 – €200) ÷ 20 years × 3 =	(180)		
Depreciation (€1,500 – €200) ÷ 20 years × 3 =		(195)	
Depreciation (€1,379 – €200) ÷ 18 years × 3 =			(197)
1 January 2017	1,100	1,175	1,182
Depreciation (€1,400 – €200) ÷ 20 years × 2 =	(120)		
Depreciation (€1,500 – €200) ÷ 20 years × 2 =		(130)	
Depreciation (€1,379 – €200) ÷ 18 years × 2 =			(131)
31 December 2018	980	1,045	1,051

As can be seen above, a full retrospective application of IFRIC 1 would require an entity to go back in time and account for each revision of the decommissioning provision in accordance with IFRIC 1. In the case of a long-lived asset there could be a significant number of revisions that a first-time adopter would need to account for. It should also be noted that despite the significant revision of the decommissioning costs, the impact on the carrying amount of the factory is quite modest.

At its date of transition to IFRSs (1 January 2017), Entity A makes the following adjustments:

- the decommissioning liability is increased by €56 (= €131 – €75) to reflect the difference in accounting policy, irrespective of whether Entity A applies the exemption or not; and
- if Entity A applies the exemption it increases the carrying amount of the factory by €75. Whereas if Entity A applies IFRIC 1 retrospectively, the carrying amount of the factory would increase by €82.

It is important to note that in both cases the decommissioning component of the factory will be significantly lower than the decommissioning liability itself.

From the above example it is clear that the exemption reduces the amount of effort required to restate items of property, plant and equipment with a decommissioning component. In many cases the difference between the two methods will be insignificant, except where an entity had to make major adjustments to the estimate of the decommissioning costs near the end of the life of the related assets.

A first-time adopter that elects the deemed cost approaches discussed in 5.5 above and elects to use the IFRIC 1 exemption to recognise its decommissioning obligation should be aware of the interaction between these exemptions that may lead to a potential overstatement of the underlying asset. In determining the deemed cost of the asset, the first-time adopter would need to make sure that the fair value of the asset is exclusive of the decommissioning obligation in order to avoid the potential overstatement of the value of the asset that might result from the application of the IFRIC 1 exemption.

5.14.2 IFRIC 1 exemption for oil and gas assets at deemed cost

A first-time adopter that applies the deemed cost exemption for oil and gas assets in the development or production phases accounted for in cost centres that include all properties in a large geographical area under previous GAAP (see 5.5.3 above) should not apply the IFRIC 1 exemption (see 5.14.1 above) or IFRIC 1 itself, but instead:

(a) measure decommissioning, restoration and similar liabilities as at the date of transition in accordance with IAS 37; and

(b) recognise directly in retained earnings any difference between that amount and the carrying amount of those liabilities at the date of transition determined under previous GAAP. *[IFRS 1.D21A].*

The IASB introduced this requirement because it believed that the existing IFRIC 1 exemption would require detailed calculations that would not be practicable for entities that apply the deemed cost exemption for oil and gas assets. *[IFRS 1.BC63CA].* This is because the carrying amount of the oil and gas assets is deemed already to include the capitalised costs of the decommissioning obligation.

5.15 Financial assets or intangible assets accounted for in accordance with IFRIC 12

Service concession arrangements are contracts between the public and private sector to attract private sector participation in the development, financing, operation and maintenance of public infrastructure (e.g. roads, bridges, hospitals, water distribution facilities, energy supply and telecommunication networks). *[IFRIC 12.1, 2].*

IFRS 1 allows a first-time adopter to apply the transitional provision in IFRIC 12. *[IFRS 1.D22].* IFRIC 12 requires retrospective application unless it is, for any particular service concession arrangement, impracticable for the operator to apply IFRIC 12 retrospectively at the start of the earliest period presented, in which case it should:

(a) recognise financial assets and intangible assets that existed at the start of the earliest period presented, which will be the date of transition for a first-time adopter;

(b) use the previous carrying amounts of those financial and intangible assets (however previously classified) as their carrying amounts as at that date; and

(c) test financial and intangible assets recognised at that date for impairment, unless this is not practicable, in which case the amounts must be tested for impairment at the start of the current period, which will be the beginning of first IFRS reporting period for a first-time adopter. *[IFRIC 12.29, 30].*

This exemption was used by many Brazilian companies with service concession arrangements and a typical disclosure of the use of the exemption is given in Extract 5.11 below from the financial statements of Eletrobras:

Extract 5.11: Centrais Elétricas Brasileiras S.A. – Eletrobras (2010)

Explanatory Notes to the Consolidated Financial Statements [extract]

6 **Transition to IFRS** [extract]

6.1 **Basis of transition to IFRS**

d) **Exemption for initial treatment of IFRIC 12**

Exemption for initial treatment of IFRIC 12. The Company has chosen to apply the exemption provided for in IFRS 1 related to the infrastructure of assets classified as concession assets on the transition date and made the corresponding reclassifications based on the residual book value on January 1, 2009, due to the concession contracts of the Company being substantially old without any possibility to perform a retrospective adjustment.

5.16 Borrowing costs

5.16.1 Borrowing cost exemption

For many first-time adopters, full retrospective application of IAS 23 – *Borrowing Costs* – would be problematic as the adjustment would be required in respect of any asset held that had, at any point in the past, satisfied the criteria for capitalisation of borrowing costs. To avoid this problem, IFRS 1 allows a modified form of the transitional provisions set out in IAS 23, which means that the first-time adopter can elect to apply the requirements of IAS 23 from the date of transition or from an earlier date as permitted by paragraph 28 of IAS 23. From the date on which an entity that applies this exemption begins to apply IAS 23, the entity:

- must not restate the borrowing cost component that was capitalised under previous GAAP and that was included in the carrying amount of assets at that date; and
- must account for borrowing costs incurred on or after that date in accordance with IAS 23, including those borrowing costs incurred on or after that date on qualifying assets already under construction. *[IFRS 1.D23].*

If a first-time adopter established a deemed cost for an asset (see 5.5 above) then it cannot capitalise borrowing costs incurred before the measurement date of the deemed cost (see 5.16.2 below). *[IFRS 1.IG23]*.

5.16.2 Interaction with other exemptions

An entity that uses the 'fair value as deemed cost exemption' described at 5.5 above cannot capitalise borrowing costs incurred before the measurement date of the deemed cost, since there are limitations imposed on capitalised amounts under IAS 23. IAS 23 states that when the carrying amount of a qualifying asset exceeds its recoverable amount or net realisable value, the carrying amount is written down or written off in accordance with the requirement of other standards. *[IAS 23.16]*. Once an entity has recognised an asset at fair value, in our view, the entity should not increase that value to recognise interest capitalised before that date. Interest incurred subsequent to the date of transition may be capitalised on a qualifying asset, subject to the requirements of IAS 23 (see Chapter 21).

5.17 Extinguishing financial liabilities with equity instruments

IFRIC 19 – *Extinguishing Financial Liabilities with Equity Instruments* – deals with accounting for transactions whereby a debtor and creditor might renegotiate the terms of a financial liability with the result that the debtor extinguishes the liability fully or partially by issuing equity instruments to the creditor. The transitional provisions of IFRIC 19 require retrospective application only from the beginning of the earliest comparative period presented. *[IFRIC 19.13]*. The Interpretations Committee concluded that application to earlier periods would result only in a reclassification of amounts within equity. *[IFRIC 19.BC33]*.

The Interpretations Committee provided similar transition relief to first-time adopters, effectively requiring application of IFRIC 19 from the date of transition to IFRSs. *[IFRS 1.D25]*.

5.18 Severe hyperinflation

If an entity has a functional currency that was, or is, the currency of a hyperinflationary economy, it must determine whether it was subject to severe hyperinflation before the date of transition to IFRSs. *[IFRS 1.D26]*. A currency of a hyperinflationary economy has been subject to severe hyperinflation if it has both of the following characteristics:

- a reliable general price index is not available to all entities with transactions and balances in the currency; and
- exchangeability between the currency and a relatively stable foreign currency does not exist. *[IFRS 1.D27]*.

The functional currency of an entity ceases to be subject to severe hyperinflation on the 'functional currency normalisation date', when the functional currency no longer has either, or both, of these characteristics, or when there is a change in the entity's functional currency to a currency that is not subject to severe hyperinflation. *[IFRS 1.D28]*.

If the date of transition to IFRSs is on, or after, the functional currency normalisation date, the first-time adopter may elect to measure all assets and liabilities held before the functional currency normalisation date at fair value on the date of transition and use that fair value as the deemed cost in the opening IFRS statement of financial position. *[IFRS 1.D29]*.

Preparation of information in accordance with IFRSs for periods before the functional currency normalisation date may not be possible. Therefore, entities may prepare financial statements for a comparative period of less than 12 months if the functional currency normalisation date falls within a 12-month comparative period, provided that a complete set of financial statements is prepared, as required by paragraph 10 of IAS 1, for that shorter period. *[IFRS 1.D30]*. It is also suggested that entities disclose non-IFRS comparative information and historical summaries if they would provide useful information to users of financial statements – see 6.7 below. The Board noted that an entity should clearly explain the transition to IFRSs in accordance with IFRS 1's disclosure requirements. *[IFRS 1.BC63J]*. See Chapter 16 regarding accounting during periods of hyperinflation.

5.19 Joint arrangements

A first-time adopter may apply the transition provisions in Appendix C of IFRS 11 – *Joint Arrangements* (see Chapter 12) with the following exception:

- A first-time adopter must apply these transitional provisions at the date of transition to IFRS.
- When changing from proportionate consolidation to the equity method, a first-time adopter must test the investment for impairment in accordance with IAS 36 as at the date of transition to IFRS, regardless of whether there is any indication that it may be impaired. Any resulting impairment must be recognised as an adjustment to retained earnings at the date of transition to IFRS.[5] *[IFRS 1.D31]*.

5.20 Stripping costs in the production phase of a surface mine

In surface mining operations, entities may find it necessary to remove mine waste materials ('overburden') to gain access to mineral ore deposits. This waste removal activity is known as 'stripping'. A mining entity may continue to remove overburden and to incur stripping costs during the production phase of the mine. IFRIC 20 – *Stripping Costs in the Production Phase of a Surface Mine* – considers when and how to account separately for the benefits arising from a surface mine stripping activity, as well as how to measure these benefits both on initial recognition and subsequently. *[IFRIC 20.1, 3, 5]*.

First-time adopters may apply the transitional provisions set out in IFRIC 20, *[IFRIC 20.A1-A4]*, except that the effective date is deemed to be 1 January 2013 or the beginning of the first IFRS reporting period, whichever is later. *[IFRS 1.D32]*.

5.21 Regulatory deferral accounts

IFRS 14 allows a first-time adopter that is a rate-regulated entity the option to continue with the recognition of rate-regulated assets and liabilities under previous GAAP on transition to IFRS. IFRS 14 provides entities with an exemption from compliance with other IFRSs and the conceptual framework on first-time adoption and subsequent reporting periods, until the comprehensive project on rate regulation is completed.

First-time adopters, whose previous GAAP prohibited the recognition of rate-regulated assets and liabilities, will not be allowed to apply IFRS 14 on transition to IFRS. We discuss the requirements of IFRS 14 in detail below.

5.21.1 Defined terms in IFRS 14

IFRS 14 defines the following terms in connection with regulatory deferral accounts. *[IFRS 14 Appendix A].*

Rate regulated activities: An entity's activities that are subject to rate regulation.

Rate regulation: A framework for establishing the prices that can be charged to customers for goods or services and that framework is subject to oversight and/or approval by a rate regulator.

Rate regulator: An authorised body that is empowered by statute or regulation to establish the rate or a range of rates that bind an entity. The rate regulator may be a third-party body or a related party of the entity, including the entity's own governing board, if that body is required by statute or regulation to set rates both in the interest of the customers and to ensure the overall financial viability of the entity.

Regulatory deferral account balance: The balance of any expense (or income) account that would not be recognised as an asset or a liability in accordance with other standards, but that qualifies for deferral because it is included, or is expected to be included, by the rate regulator in establishing the rate(s) that can be charged to customers.

5.21.2 Scope

An entity is permitted to apply IFRS 14 in its first IFRS financial statements, if the entity conducts rate-regulated activities and recognised amounts that qualify as regulatory deferral account balances in its financial statements under its previous GAAP. *[IFRS 14.5].*The entity that is within the scope of, and that elects to apply, IFRS 14 should apply all of its requirements to all regulatory deferral account balances that arise from all of the entity's rate-regulated activities. *[IFRS 14.8].*

The entity that elected to apply IFRS 14 in its first IFRS financial statements should apply IFRS 14 also in its financial statements for subsequent periods. *[IFRS 14.6].*

5.21.3 Continuation of previous GAAP accounting policies (Temporary exemption from paragraph 11 of IAS 8)

In some cases, other standards explicitly prohibit an entity from recognising, in the statement of financial position, regulatory deferral account balances that might be recognised, either separately or included within other line items such as property, plant and equipment, in accordance with previous GAAP accounting policies. However, in accordance with paragraph 9 and 10 of IFRS 14, an entity that elects to apply this standard in its first IFRS financial statements applies the exemption from paragraph 11 of IAS 8. *[IFRS 14.10].* In other words, on initial application of IFRS 14, an entity should continue to apply its previous GAAP accounting policies for the recognition, measurement, impairment, and derecognition of regulatory deferral account balances except for any changes permitted by the standard and subject to any presentation changes required by the standard. *[IFRS 14.11].* Such accounting policies may include, for example, the following practices: *[IFRS 14.B4]*

- recognising a regulatory deferral account debit balance when the entity has the right, as a result of the actual or expected actions of the rate regulator, to increase rates in future periods in order to recover its allowable costs (i.e. the costs for which the regulated rate(s) is intended to provide recovery);
- recognising, as a regulatory deferral account debit or credit balance, an amount that is equivalent to any loss or gain on the disposal or retirement of both items of property, plant and equipment and of intangible assets, which is expected to be recovered or reversed through future rates;
- recognising a regulatory deferral account credit balance when the entity is required, as a result of the actual or expected actions of the rate regulator, to decrease rates in future periods in order to reverse over-recoveries of allowable costs (i.e. amounts in excess of the recoverable amount specified by the rate regulator); and
- measuring regulatory deferral account balances on an undiscounted basis or on a discounted basis that uses an interest or discount rate specified by the rate regulator.

The accounting policy for the regulatory deferral account balances, as explained above, must, of course, be consistent from period to period unless there is an appropriate change in accounting policies. *[IFRS 14.12]*.

5.21.4 Recognition as regulatory deferral account balances

On initial recognition, the regulatory deferral account balances to be recognised are restricted to the incremental amounts from what are permitted or required to be recognised as assets and liabilities under other IFRS and the conceptual framework. *[IFRS 14.7]*. Therefore, the measurement of these balances effectively entails a two-step process:

(a) An entity would first determine the carrying amount of its assets and liabilities under IFRS, excluding IFRS 14.

(b) These amounts would then be compared with the assets and liabilities determined under the entity's previous GAAP (i.e. its rate-regulated balances).

The differences would represent the regulatory deferral account debit or credit balances to be recognised by the entity under IFRS 14.

Some items of expense (income) may be outside the regulated rate(s) because, for example, the amounts are not expected to be accepted by the rate regulator or because they are not within the scope of the rate regulation. Consequently, such an item is recognised as income when earned or expense as incurred, unless another standard permits or requires it to be included in the carrying amount of an asset or liability. *[IFRS 14.B3]*.

The following are examples of the types of costs that rate regulators might allow in rate-setting decisions and that an entity might, therefore, recognise in regulatory deferral account balances: *[IFRS 14.B5]*

- volume or purchase price variances;
- costs of approved 'green energy' initiatives (in excess of amounts that are capitalised as part of the cost of property, plant and equipment in accordance with IAS 16);
- non-directly-attributable overhead costs that are treated as capital costs for rate regulation purposes (but are not permitted, in accordance with IAS 16, to be included in the cost of an item of property, plant and equipment);
- project cancellation costs;
- storm damage costs; and
- deemed interest (including amounts allowed for funds that are used during construction that provide the entity with a return on the owner's equity capital as well as borrowings).

5.21.5 Changes in accounting policies

An entity should not change its accounting policies in order to start to recognise regulatory deferral account balances. *[IFRS 14.13]*. Also, changes in its accounting policies for the recognition, measurement, impairment and derecognition of regulatory deferral account balances are only allowed if it would result in financial statements that are more relevant to the economic decision-making needs of users and no less reliable, or more reliable and no less relevant to those needs. The judgement of relevance and reliability is made using the criteria in IAS 8. *[IFRS 14.13, IAS 8.10]*. It should be noted that IFRS 14 does not exempt entities from applying paragraphs 10 or 14-15 of IAS 8 to changes in accounting policy. *[IFRS 14.14]*.

The application guidance in IFRS 14 clarifies that regulatory deferral account balances usually represent timing differences between the recognition of items of income or expenses for regulatory purposes and the recognition of those items for financial reporting purposes. When an entity changes an accounting policy on the first-time adoption of IFRS or on the initial application of a new or revised standard, new or revised timing differences may arise that create new or revised regulatory deferral account balances. The prohibition in paragraph 13 of this standard that prevents an entity from changing its accounting policy in order to start to recognise regulatory deferral account balances does not prohibit the recognition of the new or revised regulatory deferral account balances that are created because of other changes in accounting policies required by IFRS. This is because the recognition of regulatory deferral account balances for such timing differences would be consistent with the existing recognition policy and would not represent the introduction of a new accounting policy. Similarly, paragraph 13 of this standard does not prohibit the recognition of regulatory deferral account balances arising from timing differences that did not exist immediately prior to the date of transition to IFRS but are consistent with the entity's accounting policies established in accordance with paragraph 11 of IFRS 14, for example, storm damage costs. *[IFRS 14.B6]*.

5.21.6 Presentation and disclosures

5.21.6.A Presentation

This standard requires an entity to present regulatory deferral account debit balances and credit balances and the net movement in those balances as separate line items in the statement of financial position and the statement(s) of profit or loss and other comprehensive income respectively. The totals of regulatory deferral account balances should not be classified as current or non-current. The separate line items should be distinguished from other items that are presented under other IFRSs by the use of sub-totals, which are drawn before the regulatory line items are presented. *[IFRS 14.20, 21, 23, IFRS 14.IE1].*

The net movements in all regulatory deferral account balances for the reporting period that relate to items recognised in other comprehensive income should be presented in the other comprehensive income section of the statement of profit or loss and other comprehensive income. Also, paragraph 22 of IFRS 14 also requires separate line items to be used for the net movement related to items that, in accordance with other standards, either will not or will be reclassified subsequently to profit or loss when specific conditions are met. *[IFRS 14.22, IFRS 14.IE1].*

I Presentation of deferred tax balances

In relation to a deferred tax asset or deferred tax liability that is recognised as a result of recognising regulatory deferral account balances, the entity should not include that deferred tax amount within the total deferred tax asset (liability) balances. Instead, an entity is required to present the deferred tax asset or liability either:

a) with the line items that are presented for the regulatory deferral account debit balances and credit balances; or

b) as a separate line item alongside the related regulatory deferral account debit balances and credit balances. *[IFRS 14.24, IFRS 14.B11].*

Similarly, when an entity recognises the movement in a deferred tax asset (liability) that arises as a result of recognising regulatory deferral account balances, the entity should not include the movement in that deferred tax amount within the tax expense (income) line item that is presented in the statement(s) of profit or loss and other comprehensive income under IAS 12. Instead, the entity should present the movement in the deferred tax asset (liability) that arises as a result of recognising regulatory deferral account balances either:

a) with the line items that are presented in the statement(s) of profit or loss and other comprehensive income for the movements in regulatory deferral account balances; or

b) as a separate line item alongside the related line items that are presented in the statement(s) of profit or loss and other comprehensive income for the movements in regulatory deferral account balances. *[IFRS 14.24, IFRS 14.B12].*

II *Presentation of earnings per share amounts*

IFRS 14 requires additional earnings per share amounts to be presented. When an entity presents earnings per share in accordance with IAS 33 – *Earnings per Share* – the entity has to present additional basic and diluted earnings per share calculated using earnings amount required by IAS 33 but excluding the movements in regulatory deferral account balances. Furthermore, the earnings per share amount under IFRS 14 has to be presented with equal prominence to the earnings per share required by IAS 33 for all periods presented. *[IFRS 14.26, IFRS 14.B14].*

III *Presentation of discontinued operations and disposal groups*

When an entity applying IFRS 14 presents a discontinued operation, paragraph B20 of IFRS 14 requires the movement in regulatory deferral account balances that arose from the rate-regulated activities of the discontinued operation to be excluded from the line items required by paragraph 33 of IFRS 5. Instead, the movement in regulatory deferral account balances that arose from the rate regulated activities of the discontinued operation should be presented either within the line item that is presented for movements in the regulatory deferral account balances related to profit or loss; or as a separate line item alongside the related line item that is presented for movements in the regulatory deferral account balances related to profit or loss. *[IFRS 14.25, IFRS 14.B20].*

Similarly, notwithstanding the requirements of paragraph 38 of IFRS 5, when an entity presents a disposal group, the total of the regulatory deferral account debit balances and credit balances that are part of the disposal group are presented either within the line items that are presented for the regulatory deferral account debit balances and credit balances; or as separate line items alongside the other regulatory deferral account debit balances and credit balances. *[IFRS 14.25, IFRS 14.B21].*

If an entity chooses to include the regulatory deferral account balances and movements in those balances that are related to the disposal group or discontinued operation within the related regulated deferral account line items, it may be necessary to disclose them separately as part of the analysis of the regulatory deferral account line items described by paragraph 33 of IFRS 14. *[IFRS 14.B22].*

5.21.6.B *Disclosures*

The standard requires an entity to disclose information that enables users to assess:

- the nature of, and risks associated with, the rate regulation that establishes the price(s) that the entity can charge customers for the goods or services it provides; and
- the effects of that rate regulation on the entity's financial position, financial performance and cash flows. *[IFRS 14.27].*

I *Explanation of activities subject to rate regulation*

In order to help users of the financial statements assess the nature of, and the risks associated with, an entity's rate-regulated activities, an entity is required to disclose the following for each type of rate-regulated activity: *[IFRS 14.30]*

(a) a brief description of the nature and extent of the rate-regulated activity and the nature of the regulatory rate-setting process;

(b) the identity of the rate regulator(s). If the rate regulator is a related party (as defined in IAS 24 – *Related Party Disclosures*), the entity should disclose that fact, together with an explanation of how it is related;

(c) how the future recovery of each class (i.e. each type of cost or income) of regulatory deferral account debit balance or reversal of each class of regulatory deferral account credit balance is affected by risks and uncertainty, for example:
- demand risk (for example, changes in consumer attitudes, the availability of alternative sources of supply or the level of competition);
- regulatory risk (for example, the submission or approval of a rate-setting application or the entity's assessment of the expected future regulatory actions); and
- other risks (for example, currency or other market risks).

The disclosures required above may be provided in the notes to the financial statements or incorporated by cross-reference from the financial statements to some other statement such as a management commentary or a risk report that is available to users of the financial statements on the same terms as the financial statements and at the same time. *[IFRS 14.31]*.

II Explanation of recognised amounts

IFRS 14 also requires entities to explain the basis on which regulatory deferral account balances are recognised and derecognised, and how they are measured initially and subsequently, including how regulatory deferral account balances are assessed for recoverability and how impairment losses are allocated. *[IFRS 14.32]*.

Furthermore, for each type of rate-regulated activity, an entity is required to disclose the following information for each class of regulatory deferral account balance:

(a) a reconciliation of the carrying amount at the beginning and the end of the period, in a table unless another format is more appropriate. The entity should apply judgement in deciding the level of detail necessary, but the following components would usually be relevant:
- the amounts that have been recognised in the current period in the statement of financial position as regulatory deferral balances;
- the amounts that have been recognised in the statement(s) of profit or loss and other comprehensive income relating to balances that have been recovered (sometimes described as amortised) or reversed in the current period; and
- other amounts, separately identified, that affected the regulatory deferral account balances, such as impairments, items acquired or assumed in a business combination, items disposed of, or the effects of changes in foreign exchange rates or discount rates;

(b) the rate of return or discount rate (including a zero rate or a range of rates, when applicable) used to reflect the time value of money that is applicable to each class of regulatory deferral account balance; and

(c) the remaining periods over which the entity expects to recover (or amortise) the carrying amount of each class of regulatory deferral account debit balance or to reverse each class of regulatory deferral account credit balance. *[IFRS 14.33]*.

It is also important to note that when an entity provides disclosures in accordance with IFRS 12 – *Disclosure of Interests in Other Entities* – for an interest in a subsidiary, associate or joint venture that has rate-regulated activities and for which regulatory deferral account balances are recognised in accordance with IFRS 14, the entity must disclose the amounts that are included for the regulatory deferral account debit and credit balances and the net movement in those balances for the interests disclosed under IFRS 12. *[IFRS 14.35, IFRS 14.B25-B28].*

5.21.7 Interaction with other standards

Any specific exception, exemption or additional requirements related to the interaction of IFRS 14 with other standards are contained within IFRS 14. In the absence of any such exception, exemption or additional requirements, other standards must apply to regulatory deferral account balances in the same way as they apply to assets, liabilities, income and expenses that are recognised in accordance with other standards. The following sections outline how some other IFRSs interact with the requirements of IFRS 14. In particular, the following sections clarify specific exceptions to, and exemptions from, other IFRSs and additional presentation and disclosure requirements that are expected to be applicable. *[IFRS 14.16, IFRS 14.B7-B28].*

5.21.7.A Application of IAS 10 – Events after the Reporting Period

An entity may need to use estimates and assumptions in the recognition and measurement of its regulatory deferral account balances. For events that occur between the end of the reporting period and the date when the financial statements are authorised for issue, an entity has to apply IAS 10 to identify whether those estimates and assumptions should be adjusted to reflect those events. *[IFRS 14.B8].*

5.21.7.B Application of IAS 12 – Income Taxes

Entities are required to apply the requirements of IAS 12 to rate-regulated activities, to identify the amount of income tax to be recognised. *[IFRS 14.B9].* In some rate-regulatory schemes, rate regulators may permit or require an entity to increase its future rates in order to recover some or all of the entity's income tax expense. In such circumstances, this might result in the entity recognising a regulatory deferral account balance in the statement of financial position related to income tax, in accordance with its accounting policies established in accordance with paragraphs 11-12 of IFRS 14. The recognition of this regulatory deferral account balance that relates to income tax might itself create an additional temporary difference for which a further deferred tax amount would be recognised. *[IFRS 14.B10].*

5.21.7.C Application of IAS 36 – Impairment of Assets

As a rate-regulated entity is allowed to continue applying previous GAAP accounting policies, the requirements under IAS 36 do not apply to the separate regulatory deferral account balances recognised. However, IAS 36 may require an entity to perform an impairment test on a CGU that includes regulatory deferral account balances. An impairment test would be required if:

- the CGU contains goodwill; or
- one or more of the impairment indicators described in IAS 36 have been identified relating to the CGU. *[IFRS 14.B15-B16]*.

In such situations, the requirements under paragraphs 74-79 of IAS 36, for identifying the recoverable amount and the carrying amount of a CGU, should be applied to decide whether any of the regulatory deferral account balances recognised are included in the carrying amount of the CGU for the purpose of the impairment test. The remaining requirements of IAS 36 should then be applied to any impairment loss that is recognised as a result of this test (see Chapter 20). *[IFRS 14.B16]*.

5.21.7.D Application of IFRS 3 – Business Combinations

If an entity acquires a business, paragraph B18 of IFRS 14 provides an exception to the core principle of IFRS 3 (that is, to recognise the assets acquired and liabilities assumed at their acquisition-date fair value) for the recognition and measurement of an acquiree's regulatory deferral account balances at the date of acquisition. In other words, the acquiree's regulatory deferral account balances are recognised in the consolidated financial statements of the acquirer in accordance with the acquirer's previous GAAP policies for the recognition and measurement of regulatory deferral account balances, irrespective of whether the acquiree recognises those balances in its own financial statements. *[IFRS 14.B18]*.

5.21.7.E Application of IFRS 10 – Consolidated Financial Statements – and IAS 28 – Investments in Associates and Joint Ventures

If a parent entity recognises regulatory deferral account balances in its consolidated financial statements under IFRS 14, the same accounting policies have to be applied to the regulatory deferral account balances arising in all of its subsidiaries. This should apply irrespective of whether the subsidiaries recognise those balances in their own financial statements. *[IFRS 14.B23, IFRS 10.19]*.

Similarly, accounting policies for the recognition, measurement, impairment and derecognition of regulatory deferral account balances of an associate or joint venture will have to conform to those of the investing entity in applying the equity method. *[IFRS 14.B24, IAS 28.35-36]*.

5.22 IFRS 15 – *Revenue from Contracts with Customers*

IFRS 15 was issued in May 2014 to replace all of the revenue standards and interpretations in IFRS. In April 2016, *Clarification to IFRS 15 – Revenue from Contracts with Customers* – was issued to address implementation questions that were discussed by the Joint Transition Resource Group for Revenue Recognition on: identifying performance obligations; application guidance on principal versus agent and licences of intellectual property (IP); and transition. The amendments are also intended to help ensure a more consistent application when entities adopt IFRS 15 and decrease the cost and complexity of applying it. The requirements of IFRS 15 are discussed in Chapter 30. Paragraph D34 of IFRS 1 requires first-time adopters to apply IFRS 15 on a retrospective basis, with the option of applying the practical expedients in paragraph C5 of IFRS 15. Here are the practical expedients in paragraph C5 of IFRS 15 after the amendments:

- for completed contracts, an entity need not restate contracts that begin and end within the same annual reporting period or contracts that are completed prior to the beginning of the earliest period presented;
- for completed contracts that have variable consideration, an entity may use the transaction price at the date the contract was completed rather than estimating variable consideration amounts in the comparative reporting periods;
- for contracts that were modified before the beginning of the earliest period presented, an entity need not retrospectively restate the contract for those contract modifications in accordance with paragraphs 20-21 of IFRS 15. Instead, an entity should reflect the aggregate effect of all of the modifications that occur before the beginning of the earliest period presented when;
  - identifying the satisfied and unsatisfied performance obligations;
  - determining the transaction price; and
  - allocating the transaction price to the satisfied and unsatisfied performance obligations
- for all reporting periods presented before the beginning of the first IFRS reporting period, an entity need not disclose the amount of the transaction price allocated to the remaining performance obligations and an explanation of when the entity expects to recognise that amount as revenue (see paragraph 120 of IFRS 15). *[IFRS 15.C5]*.

For the purposes of IFRS 15, paragraph D35 of IFRS 1 defines a completed contract as a contract for which the entity has transferred all of the goods or services as identified in accordance with previous GAAP.

A first-time adopter may elect to apply one, some or all of these expedients. However, if an entity elects to use any of them, it must apply that expedient consistently to all contracts within all reporting periods presented. In addition, an entity is required to disclose the following information:

- the expedients that have been used; and
- to the extent reasonably possible, a qualitative assessment of the estimated effect of applying each of those expedients. *[IFRS 15.C6]*.

5.23 Foreign currency transactions and advance consideration

IFRIC 22 – *Foreign Currency Transactions and Advance Consideration* – was issued in December 2016 and is effective for annual reporting periods beginning on or after 1 January 2018. The Interpretation addresses how to determine the date of the transaction for the purpose of determining the exchange rate to use on initial recognition of the related asset, expense or income (or part of it) on the derecognition of a non-monetary asset or non-monetary liability arising from the payment or receipt of advance consideration in a foreign currency. *[IFRIC 22.7]*. The Interpretation applies to a foreign currency transaction (or part of it) when an entity recognises a non-monetary asset or non-monetary liability arising from the payment or receipt of advance consideration before the entity recognises the related asset, expense or income (or part of it). *[IFRIC 22.4]*

A first-time adopter need not apply the interpretation to assets, expenses and income in the scope of the interpretation that were recognised before the date of transition to IFRSs. *[IFRS 1.D36]*.

5.24 Short-term exemptions from restatement of comparative information for IFRS 9

With the issuance of IFRS 9, the IASB introduced a new short-term exemption (paragraph E1 – E2 of IFRS 1) from the requirement to restate comparative information for IFRS 9. If an entity's first IFRS reporting period begins before 1 January 2019 and the entity applies the complete version of IFRS 9 (issued in 2014), the comparative information in the entity's first IFRS financial statements need not comply with IFRS 7 – *Financial Instruments: Disclosures* – or IFRS 9, to the extent that the disclosures required by IFRS 7 relate to items within the scope of IFRS 9. For such entities, references to the 'date of transition to IFRSs' should mean, in the case of IFRS 7 and IFRS 9 only, the beginning of the first IFRS reporting period.

Paragraph E2 of IFRS 1 lists the requirements for entities that choose to present comparative information that does not comply with IFRS 7 and IFRS 9 in their first IFRS financial statements:

- the requirements of previous GAAP must be applied to comparative information about items within the scope of IFRS 9 and disclosure of this fact together with the basis used to prepare this information;
- treat any adjustment between the statement of financial position at the comparative period's reporting date and the statement of financial position at the start of the first IFRS reporting period as arising from a change in accounting policy and give the disclosures required by paragraphs 28(a)–(e) and (f)(i) of IAS 8. Paragraph 28(f)(i) of IAS 8 applies only to amounts presented in the statement of financial position at the comparative period's reporting date;
- additional disclosures must be provided in accordance with paragraph 17(c) of IAS 1 when compliance with the specific requirements in IFRSs is insufficient to enable users to understand the impact of particular transactions, other events and conditions on the entity's financial position and financial performance.

6 PRESENTATION AND DISCLOSURE

An entity's first IFRS financial statements should include at least three statements of financial position, two statements of profit or loss and other comprehensive income, two separate statements of profit or loss (if presented), two statements of cash flows and two statements of changes in equity and related notes, including comparative information for all statements presented. *[IFRS 1.21]*.

A first-time adopter is required to present notes supporting its opening IFRS statement of financial position that is clarified as a part of the *Annual Improvements to IFRSs 2009-2011 Cycle*[6] issued in May 2012. The Board explained that a first-time adopter should not be exempted from presenting three statements of financial position and related notes because it might not have presented this information previously on a basis consistent with IFRSs. *[IFRS 1.BC89B].*

IFRS 1 does not exempt a first-time adopter from any of the presentation and disclosure requirements in other standards, *[IFRS 1.20]*, with the exception of certain presentation and disclosures regarding:

- claims development information under IFRS 4 (see 5.4 above); and
- recognised regulatory deferral account balances under IFRS 14 (see 5.21 above).

6.1 Comparative information

IAS 1 requires, except where a standard or interpretation permits or requires otherwise, comparative information in respect of the previous period for all amounts reported in the current period's financial statements and comparative information for narrative and descriptive information when it is relevant to an understanding of the current period's financial statements. *[IAS 1.38].*

6.2 Non-IFRS comparative information and historical summaries

Normally IFRSs require comparative information that is prepared on the same basis as information relating to the current reporting period. However, if an entity presents historical summaries of selected data for periods before the first period for which they present full comparative information under IFRSs, e.g. information prepared under its previous GAAP, IFRS 1 does not require such summaries to comply with the recognition and measurement requirements of IFRSs. Furthermore, some entities present comparative information under previous GAAP in addition to the comparative information required by IAS 1. *[IFRS 1.22].*

As an entity is only allowed to apply IFRS 1 in its first IFRS financial statements, a literal reading of IFRS 1 would seem to suggest that the above exemption is not available to an entity that prepares its second IFRS financial statements. In practice this need not cause a significant problem because this type of information is generally presented outside the financial statements, where it is not covered by the requirements of IFRSs.

If an entity presents, in the IFRS financial statements, historical summaries or comparative information under its previous GAAP, it should: *[IFRS 1.22]*

(a) label the previous GAAP information prominently as not being prepared in accordance with IFRSs; and

(b) disclose the nature of the main adjustments that would make it comply with IFRSs. Those adjustments need not be quantified.

Although IFRS 1 does not specifically require disclosure of this information when the historical summaries or comparative information are presented outside the financial statements, these explanations would clearly be of benefit to users.

6.3 Explanation of transition to IFRSs

A first-time adopter is required to explain how the transition from its previous GAAP to IFRSs affected its reported financial position, financial performance and cash flows. *[IFRS 1.23]*. The IASB decided 'that such disclosures are essential ... because they help users understand the effect and implications of the transition to IFRSs and how they need to change their analytical models to make the best use of information presented using IFRSs.' *[IFRS 1.BC91]*.

As discussed at 3.5 and 5 above, IFRS 1 offers a wide range of exemptions that a first-time adopter may elect to apply. However, perhaps surprisingly, the standard does not explicitly require an entity to disclose which exemptions it has applied and how it applied them. In the case of, for example, the exemption relating to cumulative translation differences, it will be rather obvious whether or not an entity has chosen to apply the exemption. In other cases, users will have to rely on a first-time adopter disclosing those transitional accounting policies that are relevant to an understanding of the financial statements. In practice most first-time adopters voluntarily disclose which IFRS 1 exemptions they elected to apply and which exceptions apply to them, as is illustrated below by Extract 5.12.

Extract 5.12: Bombardier Inc. (2011)

NOTES TO CONSOLIDATED FINANCIAL STATEMENTS [extract]

For the fiscal years ended December 31, 2011 and January 31, 2011

36. **ADOPTION OF IFRS** [extract]

The Corporation has adopted IFRS effective for its annual consolidated financial statements beginning February 1, 2011. These consolidated financial statements are the Corporation's first annual consolidated financial statements prepared in accordance with IFRS. For all periods up to and including the fiscal year ended January 31, 2011, the Corporation prepared its consolidated financial statements in accordance with previous Canadian GAAP.

This note explains how the transition from previous Canadian GAAP to IFRS affected the Corporation's reported equity as at February 1, 2010 and January 31, 2011, as well as net income, comprehensive income and cash flows for the fiscal year ended January 31, 2011. References to Canadian GAAP in this note refer to Canadian GAAP applicable to the Corporation for reporting periods up to and including the fiscal year ended January 31, 2011.

IFRS 1, *First-time Adoption of International Financial Reporting Standards*, requires a first-time adopter to retrospectively apply all IFRS effective as at the end of its first annual reporting period (December 31, 2011 for the Corporation). IFRS 1 also provides a first-time adopter certain optional exemptions and requires certain mandatory exemptions from full retrospective application. Most of these exemptions, if elected or mandatory, must be applied as at the beginning of the required comparative period (the transition date). The Corporation's transition date to IFRS is February 1, 2010.

The Corporation has not modified the choices made with regard to elections under IFRS 1 or its accounting policies under IFRS during the fiscal year ended December 31, 2011, except for the additional exemption for retirement benefits to recognize all cumulative actuarial gains and losses as at February 1, 2010 in retained earnings as described in the following section.

EXEMPTIONS FROM FULL RETROSPECTIVE APPLICATION OF IFRS

In accordance with the mandatory exemptions from retrospective application of IFRS, the consolidated statement of financial position as at February 1, 2010 does not reflect any hedge relationships which did not satisfy the hedge accounting criteria in IAS 39, *Financial Instruments: Recognition and Measurement*, as of the transition date.

Under IFRS 1, the Corporation elected to apply the following optional exemptions in preparing its opening statement of financial position as at the transition date.

1. ***Business combinations*** – The Corporation elected to apply IFRS prospectively for business combinations from the date of transition to IFRS. Accordingly, the Corporation has not restated the accounting for acquisitions of subsidiaries, interests in joint ventures or associates that occurred before February 1, 2010.

2. ***CCTD*** – At the transition date, the Corporation transferred all cumulative foreign exchange losses, amounting to $117 million, from CCTD to retained earnings. There was no impact on equity as at February 1, 2010 as a result of this election.

3. ***Borrowing costs*** – The Corporation elected to begin capitalization of borrowing costs to qualifying assets under IFRS effective February 19, 2007, the launch date of the *CRJ1000 NextGen* aircraft program. Borrowing costs of $32 million, capitalized under Canadian GAAP prior to that date, were derecognized and applied against retained earnings at the transition date.

4. ***Share-based compensation*** – The Corporation did not apply IFRS 2, *Share-based payment,* to equity instruments granted prior to November 7, 2002 and those that have vested before February 1, 2010. At transition date, there was no adjustment related to these instruments as a result of this election.

5. ***Retirement benefits*** – The Corporation elected to disclose the defined benefit obligations, plan assets, deficit and experience adjustments on retirement benefit liabilities and assets prospectively from the date of transition, progressively building the data to present the four years of comparative information required under IFRS.

6. ***Retirement benefits*** – The Corporation elected to recognize all cumulative actuarial gains and losses as at February 1, 2010 in retained earnings.

If a first-time adopter did not present financial statements for previous periods this fact should be disclosed. *[IFRS 1.28]*. In practice this may apply to entities that did not prepare consolidated accounts under their previous GAAP or a new entity formed for the purpose of performing an IPO. In such cases and others, an explanation of how the transition to IFRSs affected the entity's reported financial position, financial performance and cash flows cannot be presented, because relevant comparative information under the entity's previous GAAP does not exist.

6.3.1 Disclosure of reconciliations

A first-time adopter is required to present:

- reconciliations of its equity reported under previous GAAP to its equity under IFRSs at:
  - the date of transition to IFRSs; and
  - the end of the latest period presented in the entity's most recent annual financial statements under previous GAAP;
- a reconciliation to its total comprehensive income under IFRSs for the latest period in the entity's most recent annual financial statements. The starting point for that reconciliation should be total comprehensive income under previous GAAP for the same period or, if an entity did not report such a total, profit or loss under previous GAAP; *[IFRS 1.24]* and
- an explanation of the material adjustments to the statement of cash flows, if it presented one under its previous GAAP. *[IFRS 1.25]*.

These reconciliations should be sufficiently detailed to enable users to understand the material adjustments to the statement of financial position, statement of profit or loss (if presented) and statement of profit or loss and other comprehensive income. *[IFRS 1.25]*. While the standard does not prescribe a layout for these reconciliations, the implementation guidance contains an example of a line-by-line reconciliation of the statement of financial position, statement of profit or loss and other comprehensive income. *[IFRS 1.IG Example 11]*. This presentation may be particularly appropriate when a first-time adopter needs to make transitional adjustments that affect a significant number of line items in the primary financial statements. If the adjustments are less pervasive a straightforward reconciliation of equity, total comprehensive income and/or profit or loss may provide an equally effective explanation of how the adoption of IFRSs affects the reported financial position, financial performance and cash flows.

If a first-time adopter becomes aware of errors made under previous GAAP, it should distinguish the correction of errors from changes in accounting policies in the above reconciliations. *[IFRS 1.26]*. This means that the adoption of IFRSs should not be used to mask the error.

The example below illustrates how these requirements apply to an entity whose first IFRS financial statements are for the period ending on 31 December 2018 and whose date of transition to IFRSs is 1 January 2017.

Example 5.36: Reconciliations to be presented in first IFRS financial statements

Entity A's date of transition to IFRSs is 1 January 2017 and the end of its first IFRS reporting period is 31 December 2018. Entity A should present the following primary financial statements and reconciliations in its first IFRS financial statements.

	1 January 2017	*31 December 2017*	*31 December 2018*
Statement of financial position	●	●	●
Reconciliation of equity	●	●	‡
For the period ending			
Statement of profit or loss and other comprehensive income *		●	●
Statement of cash flows		●	●
Statement of changes in equity		●	●
Reconciliation of total comprehensive income †		●	‡
Explanation of material adjustments to the statement of cash flows		●	‡

* alternatively the entity should present two statements: a statement of profit or loss and a statement of comprehensive income.

† if an entity did not previously report total comprehensive income then a reconciliation from profit or loss under previous GAAP to total comprehensive income under IFRSs should be presented.

‡ a first-time adopter that ceases to publish financial statements under previous GAAP is not required to present reconciliations of equity and total comprehensive income at the end of the first IFRS reporting period. However, a first-time adopter that continues to publish previous GAAP financial statements may have to reconcile the equity and total comprehensive income and explain material cash flow adjustments as of and for the end of the first IFRS financial reporting period. See 6.3.1.A below for further discussion.

First-time adopters should not apply the requirements of IAS 8 relating to the changes in accounting policies because that standard does not apply to the changes in accounting policies an entity makes when it adopts IFRSs or changes in those policies until after it presents its first IFRS financial statements. *[IFRS 1.27]*.

A first-time adopter should explain changes in accounting policies or in its use of exemptions during the period between its first IFRS interim financial report and its first IFRS annual financial statements (see 6.6 below) and update the reconciliations of equity and total comprehensive income discussed herein. *[IFRS 1.27A]*. This requirement is necessary since the first-time adopter is exempt from the requirements of IAS 8 concerning reporting of such changes. *[IFRS 1.BC97]*.

6.3.1.A Reconciliation by a first-time adopter that continues to publish previous GAAP financial statements

A first-time adopter that continues to publish financial statements under previous GAAP after adopting IFRSs must consider carefully the starting point of the reconciliations required by IFRS 1 in the first IFRS financial statements because the requirements to produce reconciliations do not consider this situation. Paragraph 24 of IFRS 1 results in different applications depending on the timing of issuance of the previous GAAP financial statements in relation to the first-time adopter's first IFRS reporting period. We believe a first-time adopter, that continues to publish previous GAAP financial statements and has already issued those financial statements for the first IFRS reporting period prior to the issuance of the IFRS financial statements, has a choice of presenting reconciliations of equity and total comprehensive income:

(a) respectively as at the end of, and for, the first IFRS reporting period

(b) respectively as at the end of, and for, the first IFRS reporting period, and the comparative period; or

(c) respectively as at the end of, and for, the comparative period

However, if the IFRS financial statements were issued prior to the previous GAAP financial statements for the period, then IFRS 1 can only mean the previous GAAP financial statements for the immediate preceding year.

6.3.2 Line-by-line reconciliations and detailed explanations

The extract below from the 2011 financial statements of Bombardier Inc. complies with the versions of IFRS 1 and IAS 1 that were effective in 2011. However, it still provides a good example of an entity that not only provides summary reconciliations of equity and profit or loss, but also line-by-line reconciliations, as suggested by the Implementation Guidance of IFRS 1, and detailed explanations of the reconciling items.

The exceptions and exemptions used by Bombardier on transition are shown in Extract 5.12 above. The following extract does not include all of Bombardier's detailed explanations of the reconciling items.

Extract 5.13: Bombardier Inc. (2011)

NOTES TO CONSOLIDATED FINANCIAL STATEMENTS [extract]

For the fiscal years ended December 31, 2011 and January 31, 2011

(Tabular figures are in millions of U.S. dollars, unless otherwise indicated)

36. ADOPTION OF IFRS [extract]

RECONCILIATIONS OF EQUITY AND NET INCOME FROM CANADIAN GAAP TO IFRS

The following reconciliations illustrate the measurement and recognition differences in restating equity and net income reported under Canadian GAAP to IFRS for the dates and period indicated.

RECONCILIATION OF EQUITY

	Item	January 31, 2011	February 1, 2010
Equity under Canadian GAAP (as reported)		$ 4,352	$ 3,769
Measurement and recognition differences:			
Retirement benefits	A	(2,110)	(2,198)
Revenues	B	(552)	(554)
Aerospace program tooling	C	(195)	(246)
Sale and leaseback obligations	D	(1)	(6)
Other		(92)	(12)
		(2,950)	(3,016)
Income tax impact of all restatements	E	119	207
Total restatements		(2,831)	(2,809)
Equity under IFRS		$ 1,521	$ 960

RECONCILIATION OF EBIT, NET INCOME AND DILUTED EPS

	Item	BA	BT	EBIT	Net financing expense	Net income	
		Fiscal year ended January 31, 2011					
As reported under Canadian GAAP		$448	$602	$1,050	$ (119)	$769	(1)
Reclassifications		1	–	1	(1)	–	
Restatements to income before income taxes							
Retirement benefits	A	31	66	97	(44)	53	
Revenues	B	24	(15)	9	(7)	2	
Aerospace program tooling	C	55	–	55	(4)	51	
Sale and leaseback obligations	D	10	–	10	(5)	5	
Other		(15)	(2)	(17)	(28)	(45)	
		105	49	154	(88)	66	
Income tax impact of all restatements	E					(60)	
Total restatements		105	49	154	(88)	6	
As restated under IFRS		$554	$651	$1,205	$ (208)	$775	
Diluted EPS under Canadian GAAP (as reported)						$0.42	
Impact of IFRS restatements to net income						–	
Diluted EPS under IFRS						$0.42	

(1) Net of income taxes of $162 million.

The following items explain the most significant restatements to equity and net income resulting from the change in accounting policies upon adoption of IFRS.

A. RETIREMENT BENEFITS

The equity adjustment before income taxes was as follows as at February 1, 2010:

Net unrecognized actuarial loss recorded in deficit	$	(1,826)
Vested past service credits		(32)
Asset ceiling and additional liability test		(97)
Measurement date		(227)
Allocation of retirement benefit costs to inventories and aerospace program tooling		(16)
Equity adjustment, before income taxes	$	(2,198)

The transition date adjustments related to net unrecognized actuarial loss, change of measurement date and asset ceiling and additional liability test, net of income taxes of $177 million, totalled $1,973 million and have been presented as a separate item of the deficit as at February 1, 2010. Cumulative net actuarial gains and losses since February 1, 2010 are also presented in this separate item of the deficit.

The impact on EBT for the fiscal year ended January 31, 2011 was as follows:

Increase in EBIT	$	97
Increase in net financing expense		(44)
Increase in EBT	$	53

Actuarial gains and losses

Under Canadian GAAP, actuarial gains and losses were amortized through net income using a corridor approach over the estimated average remaining service life ("EARSL") of employees. Under IFRS, the Corporation has elected to recognize all actuarial gains and losses in OCI as incurred. As a result of this election, foreign exchange gains and losses on the translation of plan assets and liabilities are also recorded in OCI under IFRS.

Vested past service costs (credits)

Under Canadian GAAP, vested past service costs (credits) of defined benefit plans were amortized over the EARSL of plan participants from their grant date. Under IFRS, vested past service costs (credits) of defined benefit plans must be recognized in net income immediately as granted.

Asset ceiling and additionally liability test

Under IFRS, IFRIC 14, *The limit on a defined benefit asset, minimum funding requirements and their interaction*, requires entities to consider minimum funding requirements when assessing the financial position of defined benefit plans. This interpretation may require either a reduction of the retirement benefit asset or the recognition of an additional liability. Canadian GAAP also set limits on the recognition of the retirement benefit asset, but did not consider minimum funding requirements and as such could not create an additional liability.

Under Canadian GAAP, an adjustment arising from the asset ceiling was recognized in net income. Since the Corporation has elected to recognize all actuarial gains and losses in OCI under IFRS, variations arising from this test are also recognized in OCI in the period in which they occur.

Measurement date

Canadian GAAP allowed entities to use a measurement date for defined benefit obligations and plan assets up to three months prior to the financial year-end date. December 31 was used as the measurement date for all of the Corporation's defined benefit plans under Canadian GAAP.

Measurement of the defined benefit obligations and plan assets is performed at the reporting date under IFRS. Accordingly, defined benefit plans at BA and Corporate Office were measured using a January 31 measurement date under IFRS during the fiscal year ended January 31, 2011. Defined benefit plans at BT continued to use a December 31 measurement date as this is the financial year-end date of BT.

Allocation of retirement benefit costs to inventories and aerospace program tooling

The adjustment to inventories and aerospace program tooling arises from changes in the presentation of retirement benefit costs. The Corporation elected to segregate retirement benefit costs into three components under IFRS:

- retirement benefit expense (including current and past service costs or credits) recorded in EBIT;
- accretion on retirement benefit obligations and expected return on retirement plan assets recorded in financing expense and financing income; and
- actuarial gains and losses, asset ceiling and additional liability test and gains and losses on foreign exchange recorded in OCI.

Under Canadian GAAP these three components were eventually all recorded in EBIT. As a result, only current service costs are considered for capitalization in aerospace program tooling and inventories under IFRS, whereas under Canadian GAAP all three components were considered for capitalization.

[...]

C. AEROSPACE PROGRAM TOOLING

Restatements related to aerospace program tooling are attributed to the following three elements.

Government refundable advances

As an incentive to stimulate R&D, some governments provide advances during the development period, which are usually conditionally repaid upon delivery of the related product.

Under Canadian GAAP, contingently repayable advances received were deducted from aerospace program tooling or R&D expenses, and any repayments were recorded as an expense in cost of sales upon delivery of the aircraft. Under IFRS, a liability is recorded for the expected repayment of advances received if it is probable that the conditions for repayment will be met. Repayments are recorded as a reduction of the liability. Revisions to the estimate of amounts to be repaid result in an increase or decrease in the liability and aerospace program tooling or R&D expense, and a cumulative catch-up adjustment to amortization is recognized immediately in net income.

As a result, aerospace program tooling is recorded gross of government refundable advances under IFRS, resulting in a higher amortization expense in the earlier stages of an aircraft program's life. Recording of government refundable advances as a liability at transition decreased equity by $148 million as a significant portion of the related aerospace program tooling was amortized prior to February 1, 2010 under IFRS.

R&D expenditures incurred by vendors on behalf of the Corporation

As a new aircraft is developed, some vendors invest in the development of new technology (vendor non-recurring costs or "VNR costs"). These costs may be repaid to the vendor as part of the purchase price of the vendor's product, and the technology is transferred to the Corporation once an agreed amount is repaid.

Under Canadian GAAP, the amounts repaid to vendors were recognized as aerospace program tooling ratably as the vendor developed product was purchased. Under IFRS, upon evidence of successful development, which generally occurs at a program's entry-into-service, such VNR costs must be recognized as a liability based on the best estimate of the amount to be repaid to the vendor, with a corresponding increase in aerospace program tooling.

As a result, VNR costs are recorded earlier under IFRS, based on the present value of the best estimate of the amounts repayable, with consequential higher amortization of aerospace program tooling early in the program life. Repayments to vendors are recorded as a reduction of the liability.

The adjustment at transition decreased equity by $70 million as a significant portion of the related aerospace program tooling was amortized prior to February 1, 2010.

[...]

COMBINED IMPACT ON EBT OF ADJUSTMENTS TO AEROSPACE PROGRAM TOOLING

Increase (decrease) in EBT		Fiscal year ended January 31, 2011
Decrease in amortization resulting from overall lower aerospace program tooling balance	$	33
Repayments of government refundable advances no longer recorded in EBIT		47
Change in estimates of the liability for government refundable advances		(14)
Foreign exchange loss upon translation of the liability for government refundable advances		(11)
Accretion expense on the liability for government refundable advances		(19)
Additional capitalization of borrowing costs due to a higher capitalization base for programs under development		15
	$	51

[...]

E. INCOME TAX IMPACT OF ALL RESTATEMENTS

The restatements to equity as at February 1, 2010 totalling $3,016 million affected the accounting values of assets and liabilities but not their tax bases. Applying the Canadian statutory tax rate of 31.3% to these restatements would trigger the recognition of a deferred income tax asset of $944 million at the transition date. However, IFRS allows recognition of a deferred income tax asset only to the extent it is probable that taxable profit will be available against which the deductible temporary differences or unused income tax losses can be utilized. The deferred income tax asset has not been fully recognized under IFRS, as some of the income tax benefits are expected to materialize in periods subsequent to the period meeting the probability of recovery test necessary to recognize such assets. In connection with IFRS restatements to equity at transition, $207 million of additional deferred income tax assets were recognized.

Applying the Canadian statutory tax rate of 30.0% to the IFRS adjustments for the fiscal year ended January 31, 2011 would result in an income tax expense of $20 million. However, the probable future taxable profit that will be available to utilize operating losses and deductible temporary differences is lower under IFRS mainly due to the change in revenue recognition policy for medium and large business aircraft, which delays revenue recognition until completion of the aircraft. As a result, less deferred income tax benefits were recognized under IFRS during the fiscal year ended January 31, 2011. The additional income tax expense as a result of all restatements for the fiscal year ended January 31, 2011 was $60 million.

RECONCILIATIONS OF STATEMENTS OF FINANCIAL POSITION AND INCOME FROM CANADIAN GAAP TO IFRS

The following reconciliations illustrate the reclassifications and restatements from Canadian GAAP to IFRS to the opening statement of financial position and to the statement of income for the fiscal year ended January 31, 2011.

CONSOLIDATED STATEMENT OF FINANCIAL POSITION AS AT FEBRUARY 1, 2010

Canadian GAAP line items	Cdn GAAP	Reclassifications	Restatements	Items	IFRS	IFRS line items
Assets						Assets
Cash and cash equivalents	3,372				3,372	Cash and cash equivalents
Invested collateral	682	(682)				
Receivables	1,897	(137)	(619)	B	1,141	Trade and other receivables
Aircraft financing	473	(473)				
Inventories	5,268	62	2,300	A, B, D	7,630	Inventories
		547	(10)		537	Other financial assets
		500	19	B	519	Other assets
	11,692	(183)	1,690		13,199	Current assets

Canadian GAAP line items	Cdn GAAP	Reclassifications	Restatements	Items	IFRS	IFRS line items
		682	–		682	Invested collateral
PP&E	1,643	46	(15)		1,674	PP&E
		1,439	(54)	(1), C	1,385	Aerospace program tooling
Intangible assets	1,696	(1,696)				
Fractional ownership deferred costs	271	(271)				
Deferred income taxes	1,166		207	E	1,373	Deferred income taxes
Accrued benefit assets	1,070	(44)	(1,026)	A		
Derivative financial instruments	482	(482)				
Goodwill	2,247				2,247	Goodwill
		1,003			1,003	Other financial assets
Other assets	1,006	(455)	6	C, D	557	Other assets
	9,581	222	(882)		8,921	Non-current assets
	21,273	39	808		22,120	

Chapter 5

Canadian GAAP line items	Cdn GAAP	Reclassifications	Restatements	Items	IFRS	IFRS line items
Liabilities						**Liabilities**
Accounts payable and accrued liabilities	7,427	(4,230)	(152)	B, D	3,045	Trade and other payables
		1,180	(40)	B	1,140	Provisions
Advances and progress billings in excess of related long-term contact costs	1,899				1,899	Advances and progress billings in excess of related long-term contact inventories
Advances on aerospace programs	2,092	(1,374)	2,337	B	3,055	Advances on aerospace programs
Fractional ownership deferred revenues	346	(346)				
		359	178	D	537	Other financial liabilities
		1,989	(2)	D	1,987	Other liabilities
	11,764	(2,422)	2,321		11,663	**Current liabilities**
		677	(2)		675	Provisions
		1,373			1,373	Advances on aerospace programs
Deferred income taxes	65	(65)				
Long-term debt	4,162	(11)	(17)		4,134	Non-current portion of long-term debt
Accrued benefit liabilities	1,084	(59)	1,156	A	2,181	Retirement benefits
Derivative financial instruments	429	(429)				
		358	200	C	558	Other financial liabilities
		617	(41)		576	Other liabilities
	5,740	2,461	1,296		9,497	**Non-current liabilities**
	17,504	39	3,617		21,160	
Canadian GAAP line items	**Cdn GAAP**	Reclassifications	Restatements	Items	**IFRS**	**IFRS line items**
Preferred shares	347				347	Preferred shares
Common shares	1,324				1,324	Common shares
Contributed surplus	132				132	Contributed surplus
Retained earnings	2,087		(937)	A-E	1,150	Deficit – Other earnings
			(1,973)	A, E	(1,973)	Deficit – Net actuarial losses
Accumulated OCI – AFS and cash flow hedges	(72)		(6)		(78)	Accumulated OCI – AFS and cash flow hedges
Accumulated OCI – CTA	(117)		117	(1)	–	Accumulated OCI – CCTD
Equity attributable to equity holders of Bombardier Inc.	3,701		(2,799)		902	Equity attributable to equity holders of Bombardier Inc.
Equity attributable to NCI	68		(10)		58	Equity attributable to NCI
	3,769		(2,809)		960	
	21,273	39	808		22,120	

(1) Restatements include effect of IFRS 1 optional exemptions.

CONSOLIDATED STATEMENT OF INCOME FOR THE FISCAL YEAR ENDED JANUARY 31, 2011

Canadian GAAP line items	Cdn GAAP	Reclassi-fications	Restate-ments	Items	IFRS	IFRS line items
Revenues	17,712		180	B, D	17,892	Revenues
Cost of sales	14,668	249	38	A-D	14,955	Cost of sales
	3,044	(249)	142		2,937	Gross margin
SG&A	1,369	7	1	A, B	1,377	SG&A
R&D	193	160	(34)	A, C	319	R&D
Other expense (income)	22	(7)	21	C	36	Other expense (income)
Amortization	410	(410)				
EBIT	1,050	1	154		1,205	EBIT
Financing income	(137)	3	(342)	A	(476)	Financing income
Financing expense	256	(2)	430	A-D	684	Financing expense
EBT	931	–	66		997	EBT
Income taxes	162		60	E	222	Income taxes
Net income	769	–	6		775	Net income
Attributable to shareholders of Bombardier	755		7		762	Attributable to equity holders of Bombardier
Attributable to NCI	14		(1)		13	Attributable to NCI
Basic EPS	0.42		0.01		0.43	Basic EPS
Diluted EPS	0.42		–		0.42	Diluted EPS

RECLASSIFICATIONS FROM CANADIAN GAAP REPORTING TO IFRS

A classified statement of financial position has been presented under IFRS, based on the operating cycle for operating items and based on a 12-month period for non-operating items.

The following are mandatory reclassifications of items in the statement of financial position upon transition to IFRS:

- Financial assets and financial liabilities are presented separately from non-financial assets and non-financial liabilities.
- Provisions are presented separately from other payables.
- Other long-term employment benefits, such as long-term disability and service awards, are segregated from retirement benefits and are presented in other liabilities.

The Corporation has also made the following elective reclassification of items in the statements of financial position to place focus on key accounts under IFRS:

- Aerospace program tooling is presented separately from goodwill and other intangibles.
- *Flexjet* fractional ownership deferred costs and fractional ownership deferred revenues are no longer presented separately and are included in other assets and other liabilities, respectively.
- Aircraft financing is no longer presented separately and is included in other financial assets, except for assets under operating leases which are presented as non-financial assets classified according to their nature.
- Derivative financial instruments are no longer presented separately and are included in other financial assets and other financial liabilities.

The Corporation has made the following mandatory reclassification of items in the statement of income:

- Amortization expense is no longer presented separately and is classified between cost of sales, SG&A and R&D based on the function of the underlying assets.

The Corporation has made the following elective reclassifications of items in the statement of income:

- Expected return on pension plan assets and accretion on retirement benefit obligations are presented in financing expense and financing income and are no longer included in EBIT.
- Other income and expenses related to operations, such as foreign exchange gains and losses, are no longer included in other expense (income) and are instead classified as cost of sales unless the item is unusual and material.
- Under Canadian GAAP, changes in valuation of credit and residual value guarantees, loans and lease receivables, lease subsidies, investments in financing structures and servicing fees are presented in cost of sales or other expense (income). Under IFRS, changes in the value of these items are presented in financing expense or financing income if the changes arise from variation in interest rates. Other changes in valuation of these items are presented in other expense (income) under IFRS.

RECONCILIATION OF COMPREHENSIVE INCOME FROM CANADIAN GAAP TO IFRS

The following reconciliation illustrates the restatements to comprehensive income reported under Canadian GAAP to IFRS for the fiscal year ended January 31, 2011.

RECONCILIATION OF COMPREHENSIVE INCOME

	Item		
Comprehensive income under Canadian GAAP (as reported)		$	799
Differences on net income			6
Differences on OCI			
Retirement benefits	A		35
Other			(35)
Income tax impact of all restatements	E		(28)
			(28)
Comprehensive income under IFRS		$	777

The following items explain the significant restatements to OCI resulting from the change in accounting policies upon adoption of IFRS.

A. RETIREMENT BENEFITS

A net actuarial gain of $35 million was recognized during the fiscal year ended January 31, 2011. This net actuarial gain was comprised of:

Actuarial gains, mainly due to changes in discount rates	$	161
Loss arising from variations in the asset ceiling and additional liability		(70)
Foreign exchange losses on the translation of plan assets and liabilities		(56)
Net actuarial gain	$	35

Actuarial gains and losses are recognized in OCI under IFRS in accordance with the Corporation's choice of accounting policy.

[...]

E. INCOME TAX IMPACT OF ALL RESTATEMENTS

The related deferred income tax assets have not been fully recognized in some countries, as it is not probable that all of the income tax benefits will be realized, and additional income tax expense was recorded in other counties.

6.3.3 Recognition and reversal of impairments

If a first-time adopter recognised or reversed any impairment losses on transition to IFRSs it should disclose the information that IAS 36 would have required if the entity had recognised those impairment losses or reversals in the period beginning with the date of transition to IFRSs (see Chapter 20). *[IFRS 1.24]*. This provides transparency about impairment losses recognised on transition that might otherwise receive less attention than impairment losses recognised in earlier or later periods. *[IFRS 1.BC94]*.

6.3.4 Inclusion of IFRS 1 reconciliations by cross reference

The reconciliation disclosures required by IFRS 1 are generally quite lengthy. While IFRS 1 allows an entity's first interim report under IAS 34 to give certain of these disclosures by way of cross-reference to another published document, *[IFRS 1.32-33]*, there is no corresponding exemption for disclosure in the entity's first annual IFRS financial statements. Therefore, a first-time adopter should include all disclosures required by IFRS 1 within its first annual IFRS financial statements in the same way it would need to include other lengthy disclosures such as those on business combinations, financial instruments and employee benefits. Any additional voluntary information regarding the conversion to IFRSs that was previously published but that is not specifically required by IFRS 1 need not be repeated in the first IFRS financial statements.

6.4 Designation of financial instruments

If, on transition, a first-time adopter designates a previously recognised financial asset or financial liability as a 'financial asset or financial liability at fair value through profit or loss' (see 5.11.2, 5.12.1 and 5.12.2 above), paragraphs 29 – 29A of IFRS 1 require it to disclose:

- the fair value of any financial assets or financial liabilities designated into it at the date of designation; and
- their classification and carrying amount in the previous GAAP financial statements.

If, on transition, a first-time adopter applies IAS 39 and designates a previously recognised financial asset as 'available for sale' (see 5.11.1 above), it should disclose the fair value of financial assets so designated at the date of designation and their classification and carrying amount in the previous GAAP financial statements. *[IFRS 1.29]*.

Although it is related to the designations made under IAS 39, the extract below provides a good illustration of the above disclosure requirement.

Extract 5.14: Industrial Alliance Insurance and Financial Services Inc. (2011)

Notes to consolidated financial statements [extract]

Note 4. Transition to International Financial Reporting Standards (IFRS) [extract]

Exemptions from retrospective application

The Company applied certain optional exemptions to the retrospective application of IFRS when it prepared its opening Statement of Financial Position. The exemptions applied are described below: [...]

5. Designation of previously recognized financial instruments

The Company availed itself of this exemption and reclassified the debentures classified as designated at fair value through profit or loss as a financial liability at amortized cost. Consequently, the financial assets matching these liabilities were reclassified from designated at fair value through profit or loss to available for sale.

Details on adjustments to equity and comprehensive income are presented below: [...]

d) Fair value of financial instruments:

Given that the designation of financial instruments can be changed under IFRS 1, the Company reclassified bonds matching the debentures with a fair value of $305 from designated at fair value through profit or loss to available for sale. This reduced the retained earnings and increased the accumulated other comprehensive income by the same amount.

Furthermore, according to previous GAAP, the Company could classify stocks for which there was no active market as available for sale at cost. These stocks must now be measured at fair value. To do this, the Company uses an internal measurement method. The fair value of these stocks is $54.

Compared to previous accounting standard, IAS 39 added impairment criteria for stocks classified as available for sale. Hence, stocks classified as available for sale should be impaired if the unrealized loss accounted in the Comprehensive Income Statement is significant or prolonged. [...]

f) Reclassification of debentures – reversal of fair value:

The Company used the IFRS 1 exemption on the designation of financial instruments and amended the designation of certain debentures. According to previous GAAP, these debentures were designated at fair value through profit or loss and had a fair value of $327. According to IFRS, these debentures are classified as financial liabilities at amortized cost.

6.5 Disclosures regarding deemed cost

6.5.1 Use of fair value as deemed cost

If a first-time adopter uses fair value as deemed cost for any item of property, plant and equipment, investment property, right-of-use asset under IFRS 16 or an intangible asset in its opening IFRS statement of financial position (see 5.5.1 above), it should disclose for each line item in the opening IFRS statement of financial position: *[IFRS 1.30]*

- the aggregate of those fair values; and
- the aggregate adjustment to the carrying amounts reported under previous GAAP.

This disclosure is illustrated in Extracts 5.6 and 5.7 at 5.5.1 above.

6.5.2 Use of deemed cost for investments in subsidiaries, joint ventures and associates

If a first-time adopter measures its investments in subsidiaries, joint ventures or associates at deemed cost in the parent (or investor) company's opening IFRS statement of financial position (see 5.8.2 above), the entity's first IFRS separate financial statements should disclose:

(a) the aggregate deemed cost of those investments for which deemed cost is their previous GAAP carrying amount;

(b) the aggregate deemed cost of those investments for which deemed cost is fair value; and

(c) the aggregate adjustment to the carrying amounts reported under previous GAAP. *[IFRS 1.31]*.

6.5.3 Use of deemed cost for oil and gas assets

If a first-time adopter uses the deemed cost exemption in paragraph D8A(b) of IFRS 1 for oil and gas assets (see 5.5.3 above), it should disclose that fact and the basis on which carrying amounts determined under previous GAAP were allocated. *[IFRS 1.31A]*.

6.5.4 Use of deemed cost for assets used in operations subject to rate regulation

If a first-time adopter uses the exemption for assets used in operations subject to rate regulation (see 5.5.4 above), it should disclose that fact and the basis on which carrying amounts were determined under previous GAAP. *[IFRS 1.31B]*.

6.5.5 Use of deemed cost after severe hyperinflation

If a first-time adopter uses the exemption to elect fair value as the deemed cost in its opening IFRS statement of financial position for assets and liabilities because of severe hyperinflation (see 5.18 above), it should disclose an explanation of how, and why, the first-time adopter had, and then ceased to have, a functional currency that has both of the following characteristics: *[IFRS 1.31C]*

(a) a reliable general price index is not available to all entities with transactions and balances in the currency; and

(b) exchangeability between the currency and a relatively stable foreign currency does not exist.

Chapter 5

6.6 Interim financial reports

6.6.1 Reconciliations in the interim financial reports

If a first-time adopter presents an interim financial report under IAS 34 for part of the period covered by its first IFRS financial statements: *[IFRS 1.32]*

(a) each such interim financial report should, if the entity presented an interim financial report for the comparable interim period of the immediately preceding financial year, include:
   - a reconciliation of its equity under previous GAAP at the end of that comparable interim period to its equity under IFRSs at that date; and
   - a reconciliation to its total comprehensive income under IFRSs for that comparable interim period (current and year to date). The starting point for that reconciliation is total comprehensive income under previous GAAP for that period or, if an entity did not report such a total, profit or loss under previous GAAP.

(b) in addition, the entity's first interim financial report under IAS 34 for part of the period covered by its first IFRS financial statements should include the reconciliations described at 6.3.1 above or a cross-reference to another published document that includes these reconciliations.

For an entity presenting annual financial statements under IFRSs, it is not compulsory to prepare interim financial reports under IAS 34. Therefore, the above requirements only apply to first-time adopters that prepare interim reports under IAS 34 on a voluntary basis or that are required to do so by a regulator or other party. *[IFRS 1.IG37].*

Examples 5.37 and 5.38 below show which reconciliations should be included in half-year reports and quarterly reports, respectively.

Example 5.37: Reconciliations to be presented in IFRS half-year reports

As in Example 5.36 at 6.3.1 above, Entity A's date of transition to IFRSs is 1 January 2017, the end of its first IFRS reporting period is 31 December 2018 and it publishes a half-year report as at 30 June 2018 under IAS 34. Which primary financial statements and reconciliations should Entity A present in its first IFRS half-year report?

	1 January 2017	*30 June 2017*	*31 December 2017*	*30 June 2018*
Statement of financial position			●	●
Reconciliation of equity	●‡	●	●‡	
For the period ending				
Statement of profit or loss and other comprehensive income *		●		●
Statement of cash flows		●		●
Statement of changes in equity		●		●
Reconciliation of total comprehensive income †		●	●‡	
Explanation of material adjustments to the statement of cash flows			●‡	

* alternatively the entity should present two statements: a statement of profit or loss and a statement of comprehensive income.

† if an entity did not previously report total comprehensive income then a reconciliation from profit or loss under previous GAAP to total comprehensive income under IFRSs should be presented.

‡ these additional reconciliations are required under paragraph 24 and 25 of IFRS 1.

The IAS 34 requirements regarding the disclosure of primary financial statements in interim reports are discussed in Chapter 39.

As can be seen from the tables in Example 5.37, the additional reconciliations and explanations required under (b) above would be presented out of context, i.e. without the statement of financial position, statement of profit or loss (if presented), statement of profit or loss and other comprehensive income and statement of cash flows to which they relate. For this reason, we believe a first-time adopter should either (1) include the primary financial statements to which these reconciliations relate or (2) refer to another document that includes these reconciliations. The following example showing the various reconciliations to be included in the financial statements of a first-time adopter is based on the Illustrative Examples of IFRS 1: *[IFRS 1.IG Example 10]*

Example 5.38: Reconciliations to be presented in IFRS quarterly reports

Entity B's date of transition to IFRSs is 1 January 2017, the end of its first IFRS reporting period is 31 December 2018 and it publishes quarterly reports under IAS 34. Which reconciliations should Entity B present in its 2018 interim IFRS reports and in its first IFRS financial statements?

	Reconciliation of equity	*Reconciliation of total comprehensive income or profit or loss †*	*Explanation of material adjustments to statement of cash flows*
First quarter			
1 January 2017	○		
31 December 2017	○	○	○
31 March 2017 – 3 months ending	●	●	
	Reconciliation of equity	*Reconciliation of total comprehensive income or profit or loss †*	*Explanation of material adjustments to statement of cash flows*
Second quarter			
30 June 2017			
– 3 months ending		●	
– 6 months ending	●	●	
Third quarter			
30 September 2017			
– 3 months ending		●	
– 9 months ending	●	●	
First IFRS financial statements			
1 January 2017	●		
31 December 2017	●	●	●

○ These reconciliations are only required to be presented in an entity's *first* interim financial report under IAS 34 and may be included by way of a cross-reference to another published document in which these reconciliations are presented.

† If an entity did not previously report total comprehensive income, a reconciliation from profit or loss under previous GAAP to total comprehensive income under IFRSs should be presented.

If a first-time adopter issues interim financial report in accordance with IAS 34 for part of the period covered by its first IFRS financial statements and changes accounting policies or its use of exemptions contained in IFRS 1, the first-time adopter is required to explain the changes in each such interim financial report in accordance with paragraph 23 and update the reconciliation required by paragraph 32 (a) and (b) of IFRS 1. *[IFRS 1.32(c)]*.

6.6.2 Disclosures in the interim financial report

Interim financial reports under IAS 34 contain considerably less detail than annual financial statements because they assume that users of the interim financial report also have access to the most recent annual financial statements. *[IFRS 1.33]*. However, they would be expected to provide disclosure relating to material events or transactions to allow users to understand the current interim period. Therefore, a first-time adopter needs to consider what IFRS disclosures are material to an understanding of the current interim period. A full set of IFRS accounting policy disclosures and related significant judgements and estimates should be included as well as information on the IFRS 1 exemptions employed. In addition, consideration should be given to both new disclosures not previously required under previous GAAP, and disclosures made under previous GAAP but for which the amounts contained therein have changed significantly due to changes in accounting policies resulting from the adoption of IFRSs.

It is also important to note that such disclosures apply to balances in both the opening and comparative year-end statement of financial position, each of which could be included in the first interim financial report. First-time adopters should expect to include significantly more information in their first IFRS interim report than would normally be included in an interim report (alternatively, it could cross refer to another published document that includes such information). *[IFRS 1.33]*.

Examples of additional annual disclosures under IFRSs to be included in the entity's first IAS 34 compliant interim financial report could include disclosures relating to retirement benefits, income taxes, goodwill and provisions, amongst other items that significantly differ from previous GAAP and those required IFRS disclosures that are more substantial than previous GAAP.

6.7 Disclosure of IFRS information before adoption of IFRSs

As the adoption of IFRSs may have a significant impact on their financial statements, many entities will want to provide information on its expected impact. There are certain difficulties that arise as a result of the application of IFRS 1 when an entity decides to quantify the impact of the adoption of IFRSs. In particular, IFRS 1 requires an entity to draw up an opening IFRS statement of financial position at its date of transition based on the standards that are effective at the end of its first IFRS reporting period. Therefore, it is not possible to prepare IFRS financial information – and assess the full impact of IFRSs – until an entity knows its date of transition to IFRSs and exactly which standards will be effective at the end of its first IFRS reporting period.

If an entity wanted to quantify the impact of the adoption of IFRSs before its date of transition, it would not be able to do this in accordance with IFRS 1. While an entity would be able to select a date and apply by analogy the requirements of IFRS 1 to its previous GAAP financial information as of that date, it would not be able to claim that such additional information complied with IFRSs. An entity should avoid presenting such additional information if it is believed that the information, despite being clearly marked as not IFRS compliant, would be misleading or misunderstood.

If an entity wants to quantify the impact of the adoption of IFRSs in advance of the release of its first IFRS financial statements but after its date of transition, there may still be some uncertainty regarding the standards that apply. If so, an entity should disclose the nature of the uncertainty, as is illustrated by the extract below from the IFRS announcement of Canadian Imperial Bank of Commerce, and consider describing the information as 'preliminary' IFRS information.

Extract 5.15: Canadian Imperial Bank of Commerce (CIBC). (2011)

Notes to the consolidated financial statements [extract]

Note 32 Transition to International Financial Reporting Standards [extract]

Publicly accountable enterprises are required to adopt IFRS for annual periods beginning on or after January 1, 2011. As a result, our audited consolidated financial statements for the year ending October 31, 2012 will be the first annual financial statements that comply with IFRS, including the application of IFRS 1 "First-time Adoption of International Financial Reporting Standards". IFRS 1 requires an entity to adopt IFRS in its first annual financial statements prepared under IFRS by making an explicit and unreserved statement of compliance with IFRS in those financial statements. We will make this statement of compliance when we issue our 2012 annual consolidated financial statements.

IFRS 1 also requires that comparative financial information be provided. As a result, the first day at which we applied IFRS was as at November 1, 2010 (the Transition Date), and our consolidated opening IFRS balance sheet was prepared as at this date. The opening IFRS balance sheet represents our starting point for financial reporting under IFRS.

In accordance with IFRS 1, we have retrospectively applied our IFRS accounting policies in the preparation of our opening IFRS balance sheet as at November 1, 2010. These IFRS accounting policies are those that we expect to apply in our first annual IFRS financial statements for the year ending October 31, 2012, although IFRS 1 provides certain optional exemptions and mandatory exceptions from retrospective application of IFRS, as described in Section A, Exemptions and exceptions from retrospective application of IFRS.

The following information is provided to allow users of the financial statements to obtain a better understanding of the effect of the adoption of IFRS on our consolidated financial statements. The information below includes our opening IFRS balance sheet as at November 1, 2010, based on the IFRS optional exemptions and accounting policies that we expect to apply in our first annual IFRS financial statements. A description of the differences in accounting policies under IFRS and Canadian GAAP that resulted in transition adjustments as at November 1, 2010 is provided in Section B, Differences in accounting policies. [...]

Notes to the opening IFRS consolidated balance sheet

A. Exemptions and exceptions from retrospective application of IFRS

Set forth below are the applicable IFRS 1 optional exemptions and mandatory exceptions from retrospective application of IFRS accounting policies that have been applied in the preparation of the opening IFRS balance sheet.

IFRS optional exemptions [extract]

1. Actuarial gains and losses for post-employment defined benefit plans – Retrospective application of the 'corridor approach' under IAS 19 "Employee Benefits" would require us to restate the accounting for our post-employment defined benefit plans, including unamortized actuarial gains and losses, from the inception or acquisition of the plans until the Transition Date as if IAS 19 had always been applied. However, IFRS 1 permits entities to instead recognize all unamortized actuarial gains and losses as at the Transition Date in opening retained earnings, except those related to subsidiaries that have applied IFRS in their own financial statements prior to their parent. We elected to apply this 'fresh-start' election, which resulted in the recognition of $1,150 million of after-tax unamortized net actuarial losses on our defined benefit plans that existed under Canadian GAAP as at November 1, 2010 through retained earnings. This amount excludes the unamortized actuarial losses related to CIBC FirstCaribbean which adopted IFRS prior to CIBC. This transition adjustment, together with the other employee benefits IFRS adjustments (see Section B.1), resulted in a decrease in after-tax retained earnings of $1,080 million.

7 ACCOUNTING POLICIES AND PRACTICAL APPLICATION ISSUES

The exceptions and exemptions of IFRS 1 are explained at 4 and 5 above, respectively. This section provides an overview of the detailed application guidance in IFRS 1 (to the extent that it is not covered in 4 and 5 above) and some of the practical application issues that are not directly related to any of the exceptions or exemptions. These issues are discussed on a standard by standard basis as follows:

- IAS 7 – *Statement of Cash Flows* (see 7.1 below);
- IAS 8 – *Accounting Policies, Changes in Accounting Estimates and Errors* (see 7.2 below);
- IAS 12 – *Income Taxes* (see 7.3 below);
- IAS 16 – *Property, Plant and Equipment* – and IAS 40 – *Investment property* (cost model) (see 7.4 below);
- IAS 17 – *Leases* (see 7.5 below);
- IFRS 15 – *Revenue from Contracts with Customers* (see 7.6 below);
- IAS 19 – *Employee Benefits* (see 7.7 below);
- IAS 21 – *The Effects of Changes in Foreign Exchange Rates* (see 7.8 below);
- IAS 28 – *Investments in Associates and Joint Ventures* (see 7.9 below);
- IAS 29 – *Financial Reporting in Hyperinflationary Economies* (see 7.10 below);
- IFRS 11 – *Joint Arrangements* (see 7.11 below);
- IAS 36 – *Impairment of Assets* (see 7.12 below);
- IAS 37 – *Provisions, Contingent Liabilities and Contingent Assets* (see 7.13 below); and
- IAS 38 – *Intangible Assets* (see 7.14 below).

7.1 IAS 7 – *Statement of Cash Flows*

A statement of cash flows prepared under IAS 7 may differ in the following ways from the one prepared under an entity's previous GAAP:

- The definition of cash and cash equivalents under IAS 7 may well differ from the one used under previous GAAP. In particular, IAS 7 includes within cash and cash equivalents those bank overdrafts that are repayable on demand and that form an integral part of an entity's cash management. *[IAS 7.8]*.
- The layout and definition of the categories of cash flows (i.e. operating, investing and financing) is often different from previous GAAP. In addition, IAS 7 contains specific requirements about the classification of interest, dividends and taxes.
- Differences in accounting policies between IFRSs and previous GAAP often have a consequential impact on the statement of cash flows.

IFRS 1 requires disclosure of an explanation of the material adjustments to the statement of cash flows, if a first-time adopter presented one under its previous GAAP (see 6.3.1 above). The extract below illustrates how an IFRS statement of cash flows may differ from the one under previous GAAP.

Extract 5.16: Bombardier Inc. (2011)

NOTES TO CONSOLIDATED FINANCIAL STATEMENTS [extract]

For the fiscal years ended December 31, 2011 and January 31, 2011

(Tabular figures are in millions of U.S. dollars, unless otherwise indicated)

36. ADOPTION OF IFRS [extract]

CHANGES TO THE STATEMENT OF CASH FLOWS FROM CANADIAN GAAP TO IFRS

The net impact on the statement of cash flows as a result of adoption of IFRS was as follows for the fiscal year ended January 31, 2011:

Cash flows from operating activities	$	14
Cash flows from investing activities		(52)
Cash flows from financing activities		38
	$	–

The following items explain the most significant restatements to the statement of cash flows, resulting from the changes in accounting policies upon adoption of IFRS:

- Under Canadian GAAP, payments to and from sale and leaseback facilities for pre-owned aircraft were classified as cash flows from operating activities. Under IFRS, such payments are treated as financing transactions and are classified as cash flows from financing activities. For the fiscal year ended January 31, 2011, cash flows from financing activities increased by $38 million as amounts received from these facilities exceeded repayments to the facilities.
- Under Canadian GAAP, inflows from government refundable advances were netted against additions to PP&E and intangible assets and classified as cash flows from investing activities, with any repayments classified as cash flows from operating activities. Under IFRS, all transactions related to the government refundable advances are classified as cash flows from operating activities. During the fiscal year ended January 31, 2011, $52 million in government refundable advances was received and classified as cash flows from operating activities under IFRS.

Chapter 5

7.2 IAS 8 – *Accounting Policies, Changes in Accounting Estimates and Errors*

Normally when an entity that is already using IFRS changes an accounting policy, it should apply IAS 8 to such a change. IFRS 1 requires that a first-time adopter should apply the same accounting policies in its opening IFRS statement of financial position and throughout all periods presented in its first IFRS financial statements. *[IFRS 1.7]*. Therefore, the change in accounting policies should be treated as a change in the entity's opening IFRS statement of financial position and the policy should be applied consistently in all periods presented under IFRSs.

7.2.1 Changes in IFRS accounting policies during the first IFRS reporting period

A first-time adopter may find that it needs to change IFRS accounting policies after it has issued an IFRS interim report but before issuing its first IFRS financial statements. Such a change in accounting policies could relate either to the ongoing IFRS accounting policies or to the selection of IFRS 1 exemptions.

IAS 8 does not apply to the changes in accounting policies an entity makes when it adopts IFRSs or to changes in those policies until after it presents its first IFRS financial statements. *[IFRS 1.27]*. Therefore, 'if during the period covered by its first IFRS financial statements an entity changes its accounting policies or its use of the exemptions contained in this IFRS', it should explain the changes between its first IFRS interim financial report and its first IFRS financial statements in accordance with paragraph 23 of IFRS 1 (see 6.3.1 above) and update the reconciliations required by paragraphs 24(a) and (b) of IFRS 1 (see 6.3.1 above). *[IFRS 1.27A]*. A similar requirement applies to the disclosures in a first-time adopter's interim financial reports (see 6.6 above). *[IFRS 1.32(c)]*.

The distinction between changes in accounting policies and changes in accounting estimates is discussed in detail in Chapter 3.

7.2.2 Changes in estimates and correction of errors

An entity that adopts IFRSs needs to assess carefully the impact of information that has become available since it prepared its most recent previous GAAP financial statements because the new information:

- may be a new estimate that should be accounted for prospectively (see 4.2 above); or
- may expose an error in the previous GAAP financial statements due to mathematical mistakes, error in applying accounting policies, oversights or misinterpretations of facts and fraud. In the reconciliation from previous GAAP to IFRSs such errors should be disclosed separately from the effect of changes in accounting policies (see 6.3.1 above).

7.3 IAS 12 – *Income Taxes*

There are no particular provisions in IFRS 1 with regard to the first-time adoption of IAS 12, although the implementation guidance notes that IAS 12 requires entities to provide for deferred tax on temporary differences measured by reference to enacted or substantively enacted legislation. *[IFRS 1.IG5-6]*.

The full retrospective application of IAS 12 required by IFRS 1 poses several problems that may not be immediately obvious. First, IAS 12 does not require an entity to account for all temporary differences. For example, an entity is not permitted under IAS 12 to recognise deferred tax on:

- taxable temporary differences arising on the initial recognition of goodwill; *[IAS 12.15, 32A]* and
- taxable and deductible temporary differences arising on the initial recognition of an asset or liability in a transaction that is not a business combination and that, at the time of the transaction, affected neither accounting profit nor taxable profit. *[IAS 12.15, 24]*.

In addition, a change in deferred tax should be accounted for in other comprehensive income or equity, instead of profit or loss, when the tax relates to an item that was originally accounted for in other comprehensive income or equity. *[IAS 12.61A]*.

Therefore, full retrospective application of IAS 12 requires a first-time adopter to establish the history of the items that give rise to temporary differences because, depending on the type of transaction, it may not be necessary to account for deferred tax, or changes in the deferred tax may need to be accounted for in other comprehensive income or equity.

The main issue for many first-time adopters of IFRSs will be that their previous GAAP either required no provision for deferred tax, or required provision under a timing difference approach. They also need to be aware that many of the other adjustments made to the statement of financial position at transition date will also have a deferred tax effect that must be accounted for – see, for example, the potential deferred tax consequences of recognising or derecognising intangible assets where an entity uses the business combinations exemption, described at 5.2.4.A and 5.2.5 above. Entities that reported under US GAAP must also bear in mind that IAS 12, though derived from FASB's Accounting Standard Codification 740 – *Income Taxes*, is different in a number of important respects.

7.3.1 Previous revaluation of plant, property and equipment treated as deemed cost on transition

In some cases IFRS 1 allows an entity, on transition to IFRSs, to treat the carrying amount of plant, property or equipment revalued under its previous GAAP as its deemed cost as of the date of revaluation for the purposes of IFRSs (see 5.5.1 above).

Where an asset is carried at deemed cost on transition but the tax base of the asset remains at original cost, or an amount based on original cost, the previous GAAP revaluation will give rise to a temporary difference which is typically a taxable temporary difference associated with the asset. IAS 12 requires deferred tax to be recognised at transition on any such temporary difference.

If, after transition, the deferred tax is required to be remeasured, e.g. because of a change in tax rate, or a re-basing of the asset for tax purposes, the entity elects the cost model of IAS 16 and the asset concerned was revalued outside profit or loss under previous GAAP, the question arises as to whether the resulting deferred tax income or expense should be recognised in, or outside, profit or loss.

In our view, either approach is acceptable, so long as it is applied consistently.

The essence of the argument for recognising such income or expense in profit or loss is whether the reference in paragraph 61A of IAS 12 to the tax effects of 'items recognised outside profit or loss' means items recognised outside profit or loss under IFRSs, or whether it can extend to the treatment under previous GAAP. *[IAS 12.61A]*.

Those who argue that it must mean solely items recognised outside profit or loss under IFRSs note that an asset carried at deemed cost on transition is not otherwise treated as a revalued asset for the purposes of IFRSs. For example, any impairment of such an asset must be accounted for in profit or loss. By contrast, any impairment of plant, property or equipment treated as a revalued asset under IAS 16 would be accounted for outside profit or loss – in other comprehensive income – up to the amount of the cumulative revaluation gain previously recognised.

Those who hold the contrary view that it need not be read as referring only to items recognised outside profit or loss under IFRSs may do so in the context that the entity's previous GAAP required tax income and expense to be allocated between profit or loss, other comprehensive income and equity in a manner similar to that required by IAS 12.

It is argued that it is inappropriate that the effect of transitioning from previous GAAP to IFRSs should be to require recognition in profit or loss of an item that would have been recognised outside profit or loss under the ongoing application of either previous GAAP or IFRSs. The counter-argument to this is that there are a number of other similar inconsistencies under IFRS 1.

A more persuasive argument for the latter view might be that, whilst IFRSs do not regard such an asset as having been revalued, it does allow the revalued amount to stand. IFRSs are therefore recognising an implied contribution by owners in excess of the original cost of the asset which, although it is not a 'revaluation' under IFRSs, would nevertheless have been recognised in equity on an ongoing application of IFRSs.

7.3.2 Share-based payment transactions subject to transitional provisions of IFRS 1 and IFRS 2

While IFRS 1 provides exemptions from applying IFRS 2 to share-based payment transactions that were fully vested prior to the date of transition to IFRSs, there are no corresponding exemptions from the provisions of IAS 12 relating to the tax effects of share-based payment transactions. Therefore, the provisions of IAS 12 relating to the tax effects of share-based payments apply to all share-based payment transactions, whether they are accounted for in accordance with IFRS 2 or not. A tax-deductible share-based payment is treated as having a carrying amount equivalent to the total cumulative expense recognised in respect of it, irrespective of how, or indeed whether, the share-based payment is itself accounted for.

This means that on transition to IFRSs, and subject to the restrictions on recognition of deferred tax assets (see Chapter 31), a deferred tax asset should be established for all share-based payment awards outstanding at that date, including those not accounted for under the transitional provisions.

Where such an asset is remeasured or recognised after transition to IFRSs, the general rule regarding the 'capping' of the amount of any tax relief recognised in profit or loss to the amount charged to the profit or loss applies (See Chapter 31 at 10.8.1). Therefore, if there was no profit or loss charge for share-based payment transactions under the previous GAAP, all tax effects of share-based payment transactions not accounted for under IFRS 2 should be dealt with within equity.

7.3.3 Retrospective restatements or applications

The adjustments arising from different accounting policies under previous GAAP and IFRS should be recognised directly in retained earnings (or, if appropriate, another category of equity) at the date of transition to IFRSs. *[IFRS 1.11]*.

IAS 12 requires current tax and deferred tax that relates to items that are recognised, in the same or a different period, directly in equity, to be recognised directly in equity. However, as drafted, IAS 12 can also be read as requiring any subsequent remeasurement of such tax effects to be accounted for in retained earnings because the amount to be remeasured was originally recognised in retained earnings. This could give rise to a rather surprising result, as illustrated by Example 5.39 below.

Example 5.39: Remeasurement of deferred tax asset recognised as the result of retrospective application

An entity's date of transition to IFRSs was 1 January 2017. After applying IAS 37, its opening IFRS statement of financial position shows an additional liability for environmental remediation costs of €5 million as an adjustment to retained earnings, together with an associated deferred tax asset at 40% of €2 million.

The environmental liability does not change substantially over the next accounting period, but during the year ended 31 December 2018 the tax rate falls to 30%. This requires the deferred tax asset to be remeasured to €1.5 million giving rise to tax expense of €500,000. Should this expense be recognised in profit or loss for the period or in retained earnings?

We question whether it was really the intention of IAS 12 that these remeasurements be recognised in retained earnings. There is a fundamental difference between an item that by its nature would always be recognised directly outside profit or loss (e.g. certain foreign exchange differences or revaluations of plant, property and equipment) and an item which in the normal course of events would be accounted for in profit or loss, but when recognised for the first time (such as in Example 5.39 above) is dealt with as a 'catch up' adjustment to opening retained earnings. If it had done so, all the charge for environmental costs (and all the related deferred tax) would have been reflected in profit or loss in previous income statements. Therefore, it is our view that subsequent changes to such items recognised as a 'catch-up' adjustment upon transition to IFRSs should be recognised in profit or loss.

7.3.4 Defined benefit pension plans

IAS 19 requires an entity, in accounting for a post-employment defined benefit plan, to recognise actuarial gains and losses relating to the plan in other comprehensive income. At the same time, service cost and net interest on the net defined benefit liability (asset) is recognised in profit or loss.

In many jurisdictions, tax relief for post-employment benefits is given on the basis of cash contributions paid to the plan fund (or benefits paid when a plan is unfunded).

This significant difference between the way in which defined benefit plans are treated for tax and financial reporting purposes can make the allocation of tax between profit or loss and other comprehensive income somewhat arbitrary.

The issue is of particular importance when a first-time adopter has large funding shortfalls on its defined benefit schemes and at the same time can only recognise part of its deferred tax assets. In such a situation the method of allocation may well affect the after-tax profit in a given year. In our view (see Chapter 31), these are instances of the exceptional circumstances envisaged by IAS 12 when a strict allocation of tax between profit or loss and other comprehensive income is not possible. Accordingly, any reasonable method of allocation may be used, provided that it is applied on a consistent basis.

One approach might be to compare the funding payments made to the scheme in the previous few years with the charges made to profit or loss under IAS 19 in those periods. If, for example, it is found that the payments were equal to or greater than the charges to profit or loss, it could reasonably be concluded that any surplus or deficit on the statement of financial position is broadly represented by items that have been accounted for in other comprehensive income.

7.4 IAS 16 – *Property, Plant and Equipment* – and IAS 40 – *Investment Property* (cost model)

The implementation guidance discussed in this section applies to property, plant and equipment as well as investment properties that are accounted for under the cost model in IAS 40. *[IFRS 1.IG62].*

7.4.1 Depreciation method and rate

If a first-time adopter's depreciation methods and rates under its previous GAAP are acceptable under IFRSs then it accounts for any change in estimated useful life or depreciation pattern prospectively from when it makes that change in estimate (see 4.2 above). However, if the depreciation methods and rates are not acceptable and the difference has a material impact on the financial statements, a first-time adopter should adjust the accumulated depreciation in its opening IFRS statement of financial position retrospectively. *[IFRS 1.IG7].* Additional differences may arise from the requirement in IAS 16 to review the residual value and the useful life of an asset at least each financial year end, *[IAS 16.51]*, which may not be required under a first-time adopter's previous GAAP.

If a restatement of the depreciation methods and rates would be too onerous, a first-time adopter could opt instead to use fair value as the deemed cost. However, application of the deemed cost exemption is not always the only approach available. In practice, many first-time adopters have found that, other than buildings, there are generally few items of property, plant and equipment that still have a material carrying amount after more than 30 or 40 years of use. Therefore, the carrying value that results from a fully retrospective application of IAS 16 may not differ much from the carrying amount under an entity's previous GAAP.

7.4.2 Estimates of useful life and residual value

An entity may use fair value as deemed cost for an item of property, plant and equipment still in use that it had depreciated to zero under its previous GAAP (i.e. the asset has already reached the end of its originally assessed economic life). Although IFRS 1 requires an entity to use estimates made under its previous GAAP, paragraph 51 of IAS 16 would require the entity to re-assess the remaining useful life and residual value at least annually. *[IAS 16.51].* Therefore, the asset's deemed cost should be depreciated over its re-assessed economic life and taking into account its re-assessed residual value.

The same applies when an entity does not use fair value or revaluation as deemed cost. If there were indicators in the past that the useful life or residual value changed but those changes were not required to be recognised under previous GAAP, the IFRS carrying amount as of the date of transition should be determined by taking into account the re-assessed useful life and the re-assessed residual value. Often, this is difficult, as most entities would not have re-assessed the useful lives contemporaneously with the issuance of the previous GAAP financial statements. Accordingly, the fair value as deemed cost exemption might be the most logical choice.

7.4.3 Revaluation model

A first-time adopter that chooses to account for some or all classes of property, plant and equipment under the revaluation model needs to present the cumulative revaluation surplus as a separate component of equity. IFRS 1 requires that 'the revaluation surplus at the date of transition to IFRSs is based on a comparison of the carrying amount of the asset at that date with its cost or deemed cost.' *[IFRS 1.IG10]*.

A first-time adopter that uses fair value as the deemed cost for those classes of property, plant and equipment would be required to reset the cumulative revaluation surplus to zero. Therefore any previous GAAP revaluation surplus related to assets valued at deemed cost cannot be used to offset a subsequent impairment or revaluation loss under IFRSs. The following example illustrates the treatment of the revaluation reserve at the date of transition based on different deemed cost exemptions applied under IFRS 1.

Example 5.40: Revaluation reserve under IAS 16

An entity with a date of transition to IFRSs of 1 January 2017 has freehold land classified as property, plant and equipment. The land was measured under previous GAAP using a revaluation model that is comparable to that required by IAS 16. The previous GAAP carrying amount is €185,000, being the revaluation last determined in April 2016. The cost of the land under IFRSs as at 1 January 2017 is €90,000. The fair value of the land on 1 January 2017 is €200,000. The entity elects to apply the revaluation model under IAS 16 to the asset class that includes land.

The revaluation reserve at the date of transition would depend on the exemption applied by the entity:

- if the entity chooses to use the transition date fair value as deemed cost, the IFRS revaluation reserve is zero (€200,000 – €200,000);
- if the entity chooses to use the previous GAAP revaluation as deemed cost, the IFRS revaluation reserve is €15,000 (€200,000 – €185,000);
- if the entity does not use the deemed cost exemption under IFRS 1, the IFRS revaluation reserve is €110,000 (€200,000 – €90,000).

7.4.4 Parts approach

IAS 16 requires a 'parts approach' to the recognition of property, plant and equipment. Thus a large item such as an aircraft is recognised as a series of 'parts' that may have different useful lives. An engine of an aircraft may be a part. IAS 16 does not prescribe the physical unit of measure (the 'part') for recognition i.e. what constitutes an item of property, plant and equipment. *[IFRS 1.IG12]*. Instead the standard relies on judgement in applying the recognition criteria to an entity's specific circumstances. *[IAS 16.9]*. However, the standard does require an entity to:

- apply a very restrictive definition of maintenance costs or costs of day-to-day servicing which it describes as 'primarily the costs of labour and consumables, and may include the cost of small parts. The purpose of these expenditures is often described as for the "repairs and maintenance" of the item of property, plant and equipment'; *[IAS 16.12]*
- derecognise the carrying amount of the parts that are replaced; *[IAS 16.13]* and
- depreciate separately each part of an item of property, plant and equipment with a cost that is significant in relation to the total cost of the item. *[IAS 16.43]*.

Based on this, it is reasonable to surmise that parts can be relatively small units. Therefore, it is possible that even if a first-time adopter's depreciation methods and rates are acceptable under IFRSs, it may have to restate property, plant and equipment because its unit of measure under previous GAAP was based on physical units significantly larger than parts as described in IAS 16. Accounting for parts is described in detail in Chapter 18.

In practice, however, there is seldom a need to account for every single part of an asset separately. Very often there is no significant difference in the reported amounts once all significant parts have been identified. Furthermore, as explained in Chapter 18, an entity may not actually need to identify the parts of an asset until it incurs the replacement expenditure.

7.5 IAS 17 – *Leases*

Other than the IFRIC 4 exemption (see 5.6.1 above) there are no exemptions regarding lease accounting available to a first-time adopter. Therefore, at the date of transition to IFRSs, a lessee or lessor classifies a lease as operating or financing on the basis of circumstances existing at the inception of the lease. *[IAS 17.13]*. If the provisions of the lease have been changed other than by renewing the lease and the change would result in a different classification under IAS 17 than that required pursuant to the original terms of the lease, the revised agreement should be considered a new lease over its term. However, changes in estimate (i.e. change in the estimated economic life or residual value of the property) and changes in circumstances (i.e. a default by the lessee) do not result in a new classification of a lease. *[IFRS 1.IG14]*. See Chapter 24 for further discussion about modifying lease terms under IAS 17.

Sale and leaseback arrangements may be classified differently under IFRSs than under previous GAAP and may need to be restated on transition. Some jurisdictions have special restrictions relating to certain assets that are not present in IAS 17. In other cases applying the qualitative tests in IAS 17 indicates that the asset has been leased back under a finance lease so no revenue can be recognised on the 'sale'. See Chapter 24.

7.5.1 Assets held under finance leases

A first-time adopter should recognise all assets held under finance leases in its statement of financial position. If those assets were not recognised previously, the first-time adopter needs to determine the following:

(a) the fair value of the assets or, if lower, the present value of the minimum lease payments at the date of inception of the lease;

(b) the carrying amount of the assets at the date of transition to IFRSs by applying IFRS accounting policies to their subsequent measurement;

(c) the interest rate implicit in the lease or the lessee's incremental borrowing rate; and

(d) the carrying amount of the lease liability at the date of transition to IFRS in accordance with IAS 17.

When determining the information under (b) above is impracticable, a first-time adopter may want to apply the deemed cost exemption to those assets (see 5.5.1 above). However, no corresponding exemption exists regarding the lease liability.

See Chapter 24 for discussion of the requirements of IAS 17.

7.6 IFRS 15 – *Revenue from Contracts with Customers*

A first-time adopter that has received amounts that do not yet qualify for recognition as revenue under IFRS 15 (e.g. the proceeds of a sale that does not qualify for revenue recognition) should recognise those amounts as a liability in its opening IFRS statement of financial position and adjust the liability for any significant financing component as required by IFRS 15. *[IFRS 1.IG17].* It is therefore possible that revenue that was already recognised under a first-time adopter's previous GAAP will need to be deferred in its opening IFRS statement of financial position and recognised again (this time under IFRSs) as revenue at a later date.

Conversely, it is possible that revenue deferred under a first-time adopter's previous GAAP cannot be recognised as deferred revenue in the opening IFRS statement of financial position. A first-time adopter would not be able to report such revenue deferred under its previous GAAP as revenue under IFRSs at a later date. See Chapter 30 for matters relating to revenue recognition under IFRS 15.

7.7 IAS 19 – *Employee Benefits*

7.7.1 Sensitivity analysis for each significant actuarial assumption

IAS 19 requires the disclosures set out below about sensitivity of defined benefit obligations. Therefore for an entity's first IFRS financial statements careful preparation must be done to compile the information required to present the sensitivity disclosure for the current and comparative periods. IAS 19 requires an entity to disclose: *[IAS 19.145]*

(a) a sensitivity analysis for each significant actuarial assumption as of the end of the reporting period, showing how the defined benefit obligation would have been affected by changes in the relevant actuarial assumption that were reasonably possible at that date;

(b) the methods and assumptions used in preparing the sensitivity analyses required by (a) and the limitations of those methods; and

(c) changes from the previous period in the methods and assumptions used in preparing the sensitivity analyses, and the reasons for such changes.

7.7.2 Full actuarial valuations

An entity's first IFRS financial statements reflect its defined benefit liabilities or assets on at least three different dates, that is, the end of the first IFRS reporting period, the end of the comparative period and the date of transition to IFRSs (four different dates if it presents two comparative periods). If an entity obtains a full actuarial valuation at one or two of these dates, it is allowed to roll forward (or roll back) to another date but only as long as the roll forward (or roll back) reflects material transactions and other material events (including changes in market prices and interest rates) between those dates. *[IFRS 1.IG21].*

7.7.3 Actuarial assumptions

A first-time adopter's actuarial assumptions at its date of transition should be consistent with the ones it used for the same date under its previous GAAP (after adjustments to reflect any difference in accounting policies), unless there is objective evidence that

Chapter 5

those assumptions were in error (see 4.2 above). The impact of any later revisions to those assumptions is an actuarial gain or loss of the period in which the entity makes the revisions. *[IFRS 1.IG19]*.

If a first-time adopter needs to make actuarial assumptions at the date of transition that were not necessary for compliance with its previous GAAP, those actuarial assumptions should not reflect conditions that arose after the date of transition. In particular, discount rates and the fair value of plan assets at the date of transition should reflect the market conditions at that date. Similarly, the entity's actuarial assumptions at the date of transition about future employee turnover rates should not reflect a significant increase in estimated employee turnover rates as a result of a curtailment of the pension plan that occurred after the date of transition. *[IFRS 1.IG20]*.

If there is a material difference arising from a change in assumptions at the transition date, consideration needs to be given to whether there was an error under previous GAAP. Errors cannot be recognised as transition adjustments (see 6.3.1 above).

7.7.4 Unrecognised past service costs

IAS 19 requires immediate recognition of all past service costs. *[IAS 19.103]*. Accordingly, a first-time adopter that has unrecognised past service costs under previous GAAP must recognise such amount in retained earnings at the date of transition, regardless of whether the participants are fully vested in the benefit.

7.8 IAS 21 – *The Effects of Changes in Foreign Exchange Rates*

7.8.1 Functional currency

A first-time adopter needs to confirm whether all entities included within the financial statements have appropriately determined their functional currency. IAS 21 defines an entity's functional currency as 'the currency of the primary economic environment in which the entity operates' and contains detailed guidance on determining the functional currency. *[IAS 21.8-14]*.

If the functional currency of an entity is not readily identifiable, IAS 21 requires consideration of whether the activities of the foreign operation are carried out as an extension of the reporting entity, rather than being carried out with a significant degree of autonomy. *[IAS 21.11]*. This requirement often leads to the conclusion under IFRSs that intermediate holding companies, treasury subsidiaries and foreign sales offices have the same functional currency as their parent.

Many national GAAPs do not specifically define the concept of functional currency, or they may contain guidance on identifying the functional currency that differs from that in IAS 21. Consequently, a first-time adopter that measured transactions in a currency that was not its functional currency under IFRS would need to restate its financial statements because IFRS 1 does not contain an exemption that would allow it to use a currency other than the functional currency in determining the cost of assets and liabilities in its opening IFRS statement of financial position. The exemption that allows a first-time adopter to reset the cumulative exchange differences in equity to zero cannot be applied to assets or liabilities (see 5.7 above). The IFRIC considered whether a specific exemption should be granted to first-time adopter to permit entities to translate all assets and liabilities at the transition date exchange rate rather than applying the functional currency approach in IAS 21 but declined to offer first-time adopters any exemptions on transition on the basis that the position under IFRS 1 and IAS 21 was clear.[7]

The principal difficulty relates to non-monetary items that are measured on the basis of historical cost, particularly property, plant and equipment, since these will need to be re-measured in terms of the IAS 21 functional currency at the rates of exchange applicable at the date of acquisition of the assets concerned, and recalculating cumulative depreciation charges accordingly. It may be that, to overcome this difficulty, an entity should consider using the option in IFRS 1 whereby the fair value of such assets at the date of transition is treated as being their deemed cost (see 5.5.1 above).

7.9 IAS 28 – *Investments in Associates and Joint Ventures*

There are a number of first-time adoption exemptions that have an impact on the accounting for investments in associates and joint ventures:

- the business combinations exemption, which also applies to past acquisitions of investments in associates and interests in joint ventures (see 5.2.2.A above);
- an exemption in respect of determining the cost of an associate and a joint venture within any separate financial statements that an entity may prepare (see 5.8.2 above); and
- separate rules that deal with situations in which an investor adopts IFRSs before or after an associate and a joint venture does so (see 5.9 above).

Otherwise there are no specific first-time adoption provisions for IAS 28, which means that a first-time adopter of IFRSs is effectively required to apply IAS 28 as if it had always done so. For some first-time adopters, this may mean application of the equity method for the first time. For the majority of first-time adopters, however, the issue is likely to be that they are already applying the equity method under their previous GAAPs and will now need to identify the potentially significant differences between the methodologies of the equity method under their previous GAAP and under IAS 28.

In particular there may be differences between:

- the criteria used to determine which investments are associates or joint ventures;
- the elimination of transactions between investors and associates or joint ventures;
- the treatment of loss-making associates or joint ventures;
- the permitted interval between the reporting dates of an investor and an associate or joint ventures with non-coterminous year-ends;
- the treatment of investments in entities formerly classified as associates or joint venture; and
- the requirement for uniform accounting policies between the investor and the associate or joint venture.

7.9.1 Transition impairment review

A first-time adopter of IFRSs is required by IFRS 1 to perform an impairment test in accordance with IAS 36 to any goodwill recognised at the date of transition to IFRSs, regardless of whether there is any indication of impairment. *[IFRS 1.C4(g)(ii)]*. IFRS 1 specifically notes that its provisions with regard to past business combinations apply also to past acquisitions of investments in associates, interests in joint ventures and interests in joint operations (in which the activity of the joint operation constitutes a business, as defined in IFRS 3). *[IFRS 1.C5]*. Therefore, a transition impairment review must be undertaken for investments in associates or joint venture whose carrying value includes an element of goodwill. This impairment review will, however, need to be carried out on the basis required by IAS 28 as described in Chapter 11. See also 5.2.5 above.

7.10 IAS 29 – *Financial Reporting in Hyperinflationary Economies*

The IASB decided not to exempt first-time adopters from retrospective application of IAS 29 because hyperinflation can make unadjusted financial statements meaningless or misleading. *[IFRS 1.BC67]*.

Therefore, in preparing its opening IFRS statement of financial position a first-time adopter should apply IAS 29 to any periods during which the economy of the functional currency or presentation currency was hyperinflationary. *[IFRS 1.IG32]*. However, to make the restatement process less onerous, a first-time adopter may want to consider using fair value as deemed cost for property, plant and equipment (see 5.5.1 above). *[IFRS 1.D5, IG33]*. This exemption is also available to other long-lived assets such as investment properties, right-of-use assets under IFRS 16 and certain intangible assets. *[IFRS 1.D7]*. If a first-time adopter applies the exemption to use fair value or a revaluation as deemed cost, it applies IAS 29 to periods after the date for which the revalued amount or fair value was determined. *[IFRS 1.IG34]*.

7.11 IFRS 11 – *Joint Arrangements*

The 'business combinations' exemption described at 5.2 above is also applicable to joint ventures and joint operations in which the activity of the joint operation constitutes a business, as defined by IFRS 3. Also, the first-time adoption exemptions that are available for investments in associates can also be applied to investments in joint ventures (see 7.9 above) and the requirements to test the investment in associates for impairment at the transition date regardless of whether there were indicators of impairment will need to be applied (see 5.2.5 and 7.9 above). *[IFRS 1.C4(g)(ii)]*.

With respect to joint operations, the requirements of IFRS 11 may well result in the 're-recognition' of assets that were transferred to others and therefore not recognised under previous GAAP. A joint operator is required to recognise its assets and liabilities, including its share of those assets that are jointly held and liabilities that are jointly incurred, based on the requirements of IFRSs applicable to such assets or liabilities. *[IFRS 11.20-23]*.

7.12 IAS 36 – *Impairment of Assets*

As far as goodwill is concerned, first time adopters of IFRSs are required by IFRS 1 to subject all goodwill carried in the statement of financial position at the date of transition to an impairment test, regardless of whether there are any indicators of impairment (see 5.2.5 above). *[IFRS 1.C4(g)(ii)].*

While IFRS 1 does not specifically call for an impairment test of other assets, a first-time adopter should be mindful that there are no exemptions in IFRS 1 from full retrospective application of IAS 36. The implementation guide reminds a first-time adopter to:

(a) determine whether any impairment loss exists at the date of transition to IFRSs; and

(b) measure any impairment loss that exists at that date, and reverse any impairment loss that no longer exists at that date. An entity's first IFRS financial statements include the disclosures that IAS 36 would have required if the entity had recognised those impairment losses or reversals in the period beginning with the date of transition to IFRSs. *[IFRS 1.IG39, IFRS 1.24(c)].*

As impairment losses for non-financial long-lived assets other than goodwill can be reversed under IAS 36, in many instances, there will be no practical difference between applying IAS 36 fully retrospectively and applying it at the transition date. Performing the test at transition date should result in re-measuring any previous GAAP impairment to comply with the approach in IAS 36 and recognition of any additional impairment or reversing any previous GAAP impairment that is no longer necessary.

The estimates used to determine whether a first-time adopter recognises an impairment loss or provision at the date of transition to IFRSs should be consistent with estimates made for the same date under previous GAAP (after adjustments to reflect any difference in accounting policies), unless there is objective evidence that those estimates were in error. *[IFRS 1.IG40].* If a first-time adopter needs to make estimates and assumptions that were not necessary under its previous GAAP, they should not reflect conditions that arose after the date of transition to IFRSs. *[IFRS 1.IG41].*

If a first-time adopter's opening IFRS statement of financial position reflects impairment losses, it recognises any later reversal of those impairment losses in profit or loss unless IAS 36 requires that reversal to be treated as a revaluation. This applies to both impairment losses recognised under previous GAAP and additional impairment losses recognised on transition to IFRSs. *[IFRS 1.IG43].*

An impairment test might be more appropriate if a first-time adopter makes use of any of the deemed cost exemptions. In arguing that it is not necessary to restrict application of the deemed cost exemption to classes of assets to prevent selective revaluations, the IASB effectively relies on IAS 36 to avoid overvaluations:

> 'IAS 36 requires an impairment test if there is any indication that an asset is impaired. Thus, if an entity uses fair value as deemed cost for assets whose fair value is above cost, it cannot ignore indications that the recoverable amount of other assets may have fallen below their carrying amount. Therefore, IFRS 1 does not restrict the use of fair value as deemed cost to entire classes of asset.' *[IFRS 1.BC45].*

7.13 IAS 37 – *Provisions, Contingent Liabilities and Contingent Assets*

The main issue for a first-time adopter in applying IAS 37 is that IFRS 1 prohibits retrospective application of some aspects of IFRSs relating to estimates. This is discussed in detail at 4.2 above. Briefly, the restrictions are intended to prevent an entity from applying hindsight and making 'better' estimates as at the date of transition. Unless there is objective evidence that those estimates were in error, recognition and measurement are to be consistent with estimates made under previous GAAP, after adjustments to reflect any difference in accounting policies. The entity has to report the impact of any later revisions to those estimates as an event of the period in which it makes the revisions. *[IFRS 1.IG40]*. An entity cannot use hindsight in determining the provisions to be included under IAS 37 at the end of the comparative period within its first IFRS financial statements as these requirements also apply at that date. *[IFRS 1.14-17]*.

At the date of transition, an entity may also need to make estimates that were not necessary under its previous GAAP. Such estimates and assumptions must not reflect conditions that arose after the date of transition to IFRSs. *[IFRS 1.IG41]*.

If application of IAS 37 changes the way an entity accounts for provisions it needs to consider whether there are any consequential changes, for example:

- derecognition of a provision for general business risks may mean that assets in the related cash-generating unit are impaired;
- derecognition of a provision for general credit risks may indicate that the carrying amount of related financial assets need to be adjusted to take account of expected credit losses (see Chapter 50); and
- remeasurement of a decommissioning provision may indicate that the decommissioning component of the corresponding asset needs to be reconsidered (see Chapter 28).

The above list is not exhaustive and a first-time adopter should carefully consider whether changes in other provisions have a consequential impact.

7.14 IAS 38 – *Intangible Assets*

An entity's opening IFRS statement of financial position: *[IFRS 1.IG44]*

(a) excludes all intangible assets and other intangible items that do not meet the criteria for recognition under IAS 38 at the date of transition to IFRSs; and

(b) includes all intangible assets that meet the recognition criteria in IAS 38 at that date, except for intangible assets acquired in a business combination that were not recognised in the acquirer's consolidated statement of financial position under previous GAAP and also would not qualify for recognition under IAS 38 in the acquiree's separate statement of financial position (see 5.2.4.B above).

IAS 38 imposes a number of criteria that restrict capitalisation of internally generated intangible assets. An entity is prohibited from using hindsight to conclude retrospectively that the recognition criteria are met, thereby capitalising an amount previously recognised as an expense. *[IAS 38.71]*. A first-time adopter of IFRSs must be particularly careful that, in applying IAS 38 retrospectively as at the date of transition, it does not capitalise costs incurred before the standard's recognition criteria were met. Therefore, a first-time adopter is only permitted to capitalise the costs of internally generated intangible assets when it: *[IFRS 1.IG46]*

(a) concludes, based on an assessment made and documented at the date of that conclusion, that it is probable that future economic benefits from the asset will flow to the entity; and

(b) has a reliable system for accumulating the costs of internally generated intangible assets when, or shortly after, they are incurred.

In other words, it is not permitted under IFRS 1 to reconstruct retrospectively the costs of intangible assets.

If an internally generated intangible asset qualifies for recognition at the date of transition, it is recognised in the entity's opening IFRS statement of financial position even if the related expenditure had been expensed under previous GAAP. If the asset does not qualify for recognition under IAS 38 until a later date, its cost is the sum of the expenditure incurred from that later date. *[IFRS 1.IG47]*. However, a first-time adopter that did not capitalise internally generated intangible assets is unlikely to have the type of documentation and systems required by IAS 38 and will therefore not be able to capitalise these items in its opening IFRS statement of financial position. Going forward, a first-time adopter will need to implement internal systems and procedures that enable it to determine whether or not any future internally generated intangible assets should be capitalised (for example, in the case of development costs).

Capitalisation of separately acquired intangible assets will generally be easier because there is usually contemporaneous documentation prepared to support the investment decisions. *[IFRS 1.IG48]*. However, if an entity that used the business combinations exemption did not recognise an intangible asset acquired in a business combination under its previous GAAP, it would only be able to do so upon first-time adoption if the intangible asset were to qualify for recognition under IAS 38 in the acquiree's statement of financial position (see 5.2.4.B above). *[IFRS 1.IG49]*.

If a first-time adopter's amortisation methods and rates under previous GAAP are acceptable under IFRSs, the entity does not restate the accumulated amortisation in its opening IFRS statement of financial position. Instead, the entity accounts for any change in estimated useful life or amortisation pattern prospectively from the period when it makes that change in estimate. If an entity's amortisation methods and rates under previous GAAP differ from those acceptable in accordance with IFRSs and those differences have a material effect on the financial statements, the entity would adjust the accumulated amortisation in its opening IFRS statement of financial position. *[IFRS 1.IG51].*

The useful life and amortisation method of an intangible asset should be reviewed at least each financial year end (see Chapter 17), which is often something that is not required under a first-time adopter's previous GAAP. *[IAS 38.104].*

8 REGULATORY ISSUES

8.1 First-time adoption by foreign private issuers that are SEC registrants

8.1.1 SEC guidance

A foreign private issuer that is registered with the US Securities and Exchange Commission (SEC) is normally required to present two comparative periods for its statement of profit or loss and other comprehensive income (or statement of profit or loss, if presented), statement of cash flows and statement of changes in equity. Converting two comparative periods to IFRSs was considered to be a significant burden to companies. Therefore, in April 2005, the SEC published amendments to Form 20-F that provided for a limited period a two-year accommodation for foreign private issuers that were first-time adopters of IFRSs.[8] In March 2008, the SEC extended indefinitely the two-year accommodation to all foreign private issuers that are first-time adopters of IFRSs as issued by the IASB.[9]

The amendment states that 'an issuer that changes the body of accounting principles used in preparing its financial statements presented pursuant to Item 8.A.2 of its Form 20-F ("Item 8.A.2") to International Financial Reporting Standards ("IFRS") issued by the International Accounting Standards Board ("IASB") may omit the earliest of three years of audited financial statements required by Item 8.A.2 if the issuer satisfies the conditions set forth in the related Instruction G. For purposes of this instruction, the term "financial year" refers to the first financial year beginning on or after January 1 of the same calendar year.' The accommodation only applies to an issuer that (a) adopts IFRSs for the first time by an explicit and unreserved statement of compliance with IFRSs as issued by the IASB and (b) the issuer's most recent audited financial statements are prepared in accordance with IFRSs.

First-time adopters that rely on the accommodation are allowed, but not required, to include any financial statements, discussions or other financial information based on their previous GAAP. If first-time adopters do include such information, they should prominently disclose cautionary language to avoid inappropriate comparison with information presented under IFRSs. The SEC did not mandate a specific location for any previous GAAP information but did prohibit presentation of previous GAAP information in a side-by-side columnar format with IFRS financial information.

In addition, the accommodation only requires entities to provide selected historical financial data based on IFRSs for the two most recent financial years instead of the normal five years. Selected historical financial data based on US GAAP is not required for the five most recent financial years. Although the SEC does not prohibit entities from including selected financial data based on previous GAAP in their annual reports, side-by-side presentation of data prepared under IFRSs and data prepared under previous GAAP is prohibited. In addition, inclusion of previous GAAP selected financial data will trigger the requirement for the corresponding reconciled US GAAP selected financial data.[10]

Where a narrative discussion of its financial condition is provided, the accommodation requires management to focus on the financial statements prepared under IFRSs as issued by the IASB for the past two financial years.

IFRS 1 requires a first-time adopter to present reconciliations from its previous GAAP to IFRSs in the notes to its financial statements and allows certain exceptions from full retrospective application of IFRSs in deriving the relevant data. Under the SEC's accommodation, any issuer relying on any of the elective or mandatory exceptions from IFRSs that are contained within IFRS 1 will have to disclose additional information which includes:

- to the extent the primary financial statements reflect the use of exceptions permitted or required by IFRS 1:
  - detailed information for each exception used, including:
    - an indication of the items or class of items to which the exception was applied; and
    - a description of what accounting principle was used and how it was applied; and
  - where material, qualitative disclosure of the impact on financial condition, changes in financial condition and results of operations that the treatment specified by IFRSs would have had absent the election to rely on the exception.

8.1.2 IPTF guidance

In November 2008, the Center for Audit Quality SEC Regulations Committee's International Practices Task Force ('IPTF') provided guidance as to the reconciliation requirements of an SEC foreign private issuer the first time it presents IFRS financial statements in its Form 20-F, when that issuer previously used US GAAP for its primary financial statements filed with the SEC.[11] Among others, the IPTF guidance addresses the concern that the reconciliations called for by IFRS 1, which are prepared using the issuer's local GAAP rather than US GAAP, would not have sufficient information to help US investors to bridge from the prior US GAAP financial statements filed with the SEC to IFRSs. Accordingly, the IPTF guidance requires additional detailed reconciliations in these circumstances from US GAAP to IFRSs either in a one step or a two-step format (see below).

Chapter 5

The reconciliation requirements for each of the scenarios are described below:

- *SEC Foreign Private Issuers who currently report under their local GAAP and provide a reconciliation from their local GAAP to US GAAP* – In the year of adoption of IFRSs, these entities will be allowed to file two years rather than three years of profit or loss statements, shareholders' equity and cash flows prepared in accordance with IFRSs. As part of the IFRS transition, these entities will provide the disclosures and reconciliations required under IFRS 1 including:
  - an equity reconciliation as at the date of the transition statement of financial position and as at the comparative year-end balance sheet date;
  - a comprehensive income (or statement of profit or loss, if presented) reconciliation for the comparative year; and
  - an explanation of material adjustments to the statement of cash flows for the comparative year.

  If the IFRS 1 disclosures and reconciliations are prepared using the local GAAP as the issuer's previous GAAP rather than US GAAP, no additional US GAAP to IFRSs or US GAAP to local GAAP reconciliations will be required.
- *SEC foreign private issuers that currently report under US GAAP only* – Some SEC foreign private issuers currently use US GAAP as their primary GAAP in both their home jurisdiction and the United States without reconciliation. These registrants would also be eligible to file two years rather than three years of statements of profit or loss and other comprehensive income, shareholders' equity and cash flows in their first set of IFRS financial statements. In the year of adoption of IFRSs, these entities will be required to provide the IFRS 1 disclosures and reconciliations described above. Such disclosures will be prepared using US GAAP as the issuer's previous GAAP.
- *SEC foreign private issuers that currently report under local GAAP for local reporting and under US GAAP in their SEC Form 20-F filings (assuming these issuers adopt IFRSs in the current period for both local and SEC reporting purposes)* – These registrants would also be eligible to file two years rather than three years of statements of profit or loss and other comprehensive income, shareholders' equity and cash flows in their first set of IFRS financial statements. Under IFRS 1, such entities might conclude their local GAAP is their previous GAAP and their IFRS 1 disclosures and reconciliations would be prepared on that basis. As no reconciliation from their local GAAP to US GAAP was previously provided, the SEC will require additional disclosure in the Form 20-F to enable investors to understand material reconciling items between US GAAP and IFRSs in the year of adoption. Two possible forms of disclosure are acceptable:
  - *One-Step Format* – Registrants can provide an analysis of the differences between US GAAP and IFRSs in a tabular format (consistent with Item 17 of Form 20-F) for the same time period and dates that the IFRS 1 reconciliations are required. The registrant must provide this disclosure for equity as at the beginning and end of the most recent comparative period to the year of adoption and of comprehensive income (or profit or loss) for the most recent

comparative year. A description of the differences between US GAAP and IFRSs for the statement of cash flows is not necessary because registrants are not required to reconcile IAS 7 statement of cash flows to those prepared under US GAAP.

- *Two-Step Format* – Registrants can choose to disclose a two-step reconciliation which would include a quantitative analysis of the differences between US GAAP and their local GAAP and between their local GAAP to IFRSs. The registrant must provide these reconciliations for equity as of the beginning and end of the most recent comparative period to the year of adoption of IFRSs and for comprehensive income (or profit or loss) for the most recent comparative year. Registrants will also be required to provide an explanation of the material differences between the statement of cash flows under US GAAP and the statement of cash flows under their local GAAP for the most recent comparative period to the year of adoption of IFRSs.

- *SEC foreign private issuers that currently report under IFRSs for local reporting and under US GAAP in their SEC Form 20-F filings (assuming these issuers adopted IFRSs for local reporting in a period that preceded the earliest period for which audited financial statements are required in their SEC filing)* – These registrants would not be eligible to file two years of statements of profit or loss and other comprehensive income, shareholders' equity and cash flows the first time they file IFRS financial statements with the SEC, since they are not first-time adopters of IFRSs. Rather, they are required to present a complete set of IFRS financial statements for all periods required by the Form 20-F. In addition, these issuers will be required to present a reconciliation that enables US investors to bridge their previous US GAAP to IFRSs. Such a reconciliation will be similar to the One-Step Format described above, except that the periods presented will be for equity as of the most recent comparative period presented and for comprehensive income (or profit or loss) for the two most recent comparative periods. However, if the issuers are required to present a statement of financial position as of the end of the earliest comparative period, the reconciliation will also be required of the equity as of the end of that period.

8.2 Disclosure of IFRS information in financial statements for periods prior to an entity's first IFRS reporting period

8.2.1 IFRS guidance

Although IFRS 1 provides detailed rules on disclosures to be made in an entity's first IFRS financial statements and in interim reports covering part of its first IFRS reporting period, it does not provide any guidance on presenting a reconciliation to IFRSs in financial reports before the start of the first IFRS reporting period. An entity wishing to disclose information on the impact of IFRSs in its last financial statements under its previous GAAP cannot claim that such information is prepared and presented in accordance with IFRSs because it does not disclose all information required in full IFRS financial statements and it does not disclose comparative information.

As the extract below illustrates, in practice, some entities get around this problem by disclosing pro forma IFRS information and stating that the pro forma information does not comply with IFRSs.

Extract 5.17: ARINSO International SA (2003)

2003 IFRS Consolidated Financial Information [extract]

1. OPENING BALANCE AT JANUARY 1, 2003 [extract]

In 2003, ARINSO decided to anticipate the adoption of the International Financial Reporting Standards (earlier called International Accounting Standards (IAS)). These standards will become mandatory in 2005 for the consolidated financial statements of all companies listed on stock exchanges within the European Union.

As of 2004 ARINSO will publish quarterly reports in full compliance with IFRS. In order to have comparable figures as requested by IFRS, the 2003 financial statements were already prepared on an IFRS basis. In 2003, the impact of the IFRS conversion on the quarterly figures was published in our press releases.

The main differences between Belgian Generally Accepted Accounting Principles (GAAP) and IFRS as well as a reconciliation of the equity to IFRS at the date of conversion are presented hereunder.

3. IFRS VALUATION RULES [extract]

3.2 Adoption of the IFRS

The IFRS standards will be adopted for the first time in the consolidated financial statements for the year ended December 31, 2004. The standard for the first time application of the IFRS, published by the IASB in June 2003, was utilized in the pro forma consolidated IFRS balance sheet, income statement and cash flow statement published for the year ended December 31, 2003.

The information related to accounting year 2003 was converted from Belgian GAAP to IFRS in view of the comparison of information next year. The 2004 annual report will include all necessary comparable information.

Free translation of the Statutory Auditor's Report submitted to the shareholders, originally prepared in Dutch, on the restatement of the consolidated balance sheet, the profit and loss account and cash flow statement from accounting principles generally accepted in Belgium into IFRS [extract]

The financial statements provided, which do not include all notes to the financial statements in accordance with IFRS, have been prepared under the responsibility of the company's management, and do not comply with IFRS.

8.2.2 Disclosure of expected changes in accounting policies

In certain countries, publicly listed companies are required by regulation to disclose the potential impact that recently issued accounting standards will have on their financial statements when such standards are adopted in the future. The Canadian Securities Administrators (the CSA) in their Management's Discussion & Analysis (MD&A form)[12] require this disclosure for changes in accounting policies that registrants expect to make in the future. In connection with the transition to IFRSs, the CSA issued a Staff Notice[13] clarifying that 'changes in an issuer's accounting policies that an issuer expects to make on changeover to IFRSs are changes due to new accounting standards and therefore fall within the scope of the MD&A form.' Among other matters, the CSA Staff Notice requires certain disclosures of companies that have developed an IFRS changeover plan, in interim and annual MD&A forms starting three years before the first IFRS financial statement date, including the following:

- accounting policies, including choices among policies permitted under IFRSs, and implementation decisions such as whether certain changes will be applied on a retrospective or a prospective basis;
- impact on information technology and data systems;
- changes to internal control over financial reporting;
- impact on disclosure controls and procedures, including investor relations and external communications plan;
- enhancements to financial reporting expertise, including training requirements; and
- changes in business activities, such as foreign currency and hedging activities, as well as matters that may be influenced by GAAP measures such as debt covenants, capital requirements and compensation arrangements.

The CSA Staff Notice also specified requirements for update for periods up to the year of changeover, including discussion of the impact of transition for issuers that are well advanced in their plans.

An entity that is planning to adopt IFRS should take note of the regulatory requirements in its jurisdiction or the exchange where it is listed to determine the form of communication that is required in advance of publishing its first IFRS financial statements.

References

1 Regulation (EC) No 1606/2002 of the European Parliament and of the Council of 19 July 2002 on the application of international accounting standards, article 4 defines these companies as follows: 'For each financial year starting on or after 1 January 2005, companies governed by the law of a Member State shall prepare their consolidated accounts in conformity with the international accounting standards adopted in accordance with the procedure laid down in Article 6(2) if, at their balance sheet date, their securities are admitted to trading on a regulated market of any Member State within the meaning of Article 1(13) of Council Directive 93/22/EEC of 10 May 1993 on investment services in the securities field.'

2 *International Practices Task Force – November 25, 2008 – Highlights*, Center for Audit Quality Washington Office, 25 November 2008, pp.2-10.

3 *IFRIC Update*, October 2004, p.3.

4 *IASB Update*, October 2005, p.1.

5 Amendments to IFRS 10, IFRS 11 and IFRS 12, June 2012.

6 *Annual Improvements to IFRSs 2009-2011 Cycle*, IASB, May 2012.

7 *IFRIC Update*, October 2004, p.3.

8 Release No. 33-8567, *First-Time Application of International Financial Reporting Standards*, Securities and Exchange Commission (SEC), 12 April 2005.

9 Release No. 33-8879, *Acceptance from Foreign Private Issuers of Financial Statements Prepared in Accordance with International Financial Reporting Standards without Reconciliation to U.S. GAAP*, Securities and Exchange Commission, 4 March 2008.

10 24 November 2009 IPTF meeting minutes.

11 25 November 2008 IPTF meeting minutes.

12 Canadian Securities Administration Form 51-102F1, *Management's Discussion and Analysis.*

13 Canadian CSA Staff Notice 52-320 – *Disclosure of Expected Changes in Accounting Policies Relating to Changeover to International Financial Reporting Standards, May 9, 2008.*

- accounting policies, including choices among policies permitted under IFRSs, and implementation decisions such as whether certain changes will be applied on a retrospective or prospective basis;
- impact on information technology and data systems;
- changes to internal control over financial reporting;
- impact on disclosure controls and procedures, including investor relations and external communications plan;
- enhancements to financial reporting expertise, including training requirements; and
- changes in business activities, such as foreign currency and hedging activities, as well as matters that may be influenced by GAAP measures such as debt covenants, capital requirements and compensation arrangements.

The CSA Staff Notice also specified requirements for update for periods up to the year of changeover, including discussion of the impact of transition for issuers that are well advanced in their plans.

An entity that is planning to adopt IFRSs should take note of the regulatory requirements of its jurisdiction or the exchange where it is listed to determine the form of communication that is required in advance of publishing its first IFRS financial statements.

References

1 Regulation (EC) No 1606/2002 of the European Parliament and of the Council of 19 July 2002 on the application of international accounting standards. Article 4 defines these companies as follows: "For each financial year starting on or after 1 January 2005, companies governed by the law of a Member State shall prepare their consolidated accounts in conformity with the international accounting standards adopted in accordance with the procedure laid down in Article 6(2) if, at their balance sheet date, their securities are admitted to trading on a regulated market of any Member State within the meaning of Article 1(13) of Council Directive 93/22/EEC of 10 May 1993 on investment services in the securities field."
2 International Practices Task Force, November 25, 2008 – Highlights, Center for Audit Quality, Washington Office, 25 November 2008.
3 IFRIC Update, October 2004.
4 IASB Update, October 2004 [illegible]
5 Amendments to IFRS 10, IFRS 11 and IFRS 12, June 2012.
6 Annual Improvements to IFRSs 2009-2011 Cycle, IASB, May 2012.
7 IFRIC Update, October 2004, p.2.
8 Release No. 33-8567, First-Time Application of International Financial Reporting Standards, Securities and Exchange Commission (SEC), 12 April 2005.
9 Release No. 33-8879, Acceptance from Foreign Private Issuers of Financial Statements Prepared in Accordance with International Financial Reporting Standards without Reconciliation to U.S. GAAP, Securities and Exchange Commission, 4 March 2008.
10 4 November 2008 IPTF meeting minutes.
11 25 November 2008 IPTF meeting minutes.
12 Canadian Securities Administrators Form 52-109F1, Management's Discussion and Analysis.
13 Canadian CSA Staff Notice 52-320, Disclosure of Expected Changes in Accounting Policies Relating to Changeover to International Financial Reporting Standards, May 9, 2008.

Chapter 6 Consolidated financial statements

List of examples

Chapter 6 Consolidated financial statements

1 INTRODUCTION

1.1 Background

An entity may conduct its business not only directly, but also through strategic investments in other entities. IFRS broadly distinguishes between three types of such strategic investments:

- entities controlled by the reporting entity (subsidiaries);
- entities or activities jointly controlled by the reporting entity and one or more third parties (joint arrangements); and
- entities that, while not controlled or jointly controlled by the reporting entity, are subject to significant influence by it (associates).

The first type of investment is accounted for in accordance with IFRS 10 – *Consolidated Financial Statements*.

IFRS 10 establishes a single control model that applies to all entities, including 'structured entities' ('special purpose entities' and 'variable interest entities' under the previous IFRS standards and US GAAP, respectively). In addition, IFRS 10 deals with accounting for subsidiaries by investment entities.

This chapter discusses the requirements of IFRS 10, principally relating to which entities are controlled by a parent and therefore consolidated into the financial statements prepared by that parent (except for certain subsidiaries of investment entities). The requirements of IFRS 10 dealing with consolidation procedures and non-controlling interests are summarised briefly at 1.3 below and dealt with more fully in Chapter 7.

IFRS 10 contains no disclosure requirements. Instead, all disclosures required in respect of an entity's interests in subsidiaries or its interests in structured entities (whether consolidated or unconsolidated) are contained within IFRS 12 – *Disclosure of Interests in Other Entities*. The disclosure requirements in IFRS 12 are discussed in Chapter 13.

When management concludes that an entity does not have control of an investee, the requirements of IFRS 11 – *Joint Arrangements* – and IAS 28 – *Investments in Associates and Joint Ventures* – must be considered to determine whether it has joint control or significant influence, respectively, over the investee. The requirements of IFRS 11 and IAS 28 are dealt with in Chapter 12 and Chapter 11, respectively. The diagram below summarises the identification and accounting for each type of investment, as well as the interaction between IFRS 10, IFRS 11, IFRS 12 and IAS 28.

Figure 6.1: Interaction between IFRS 10, IFRS 11, IFRS 12 and IAS 28

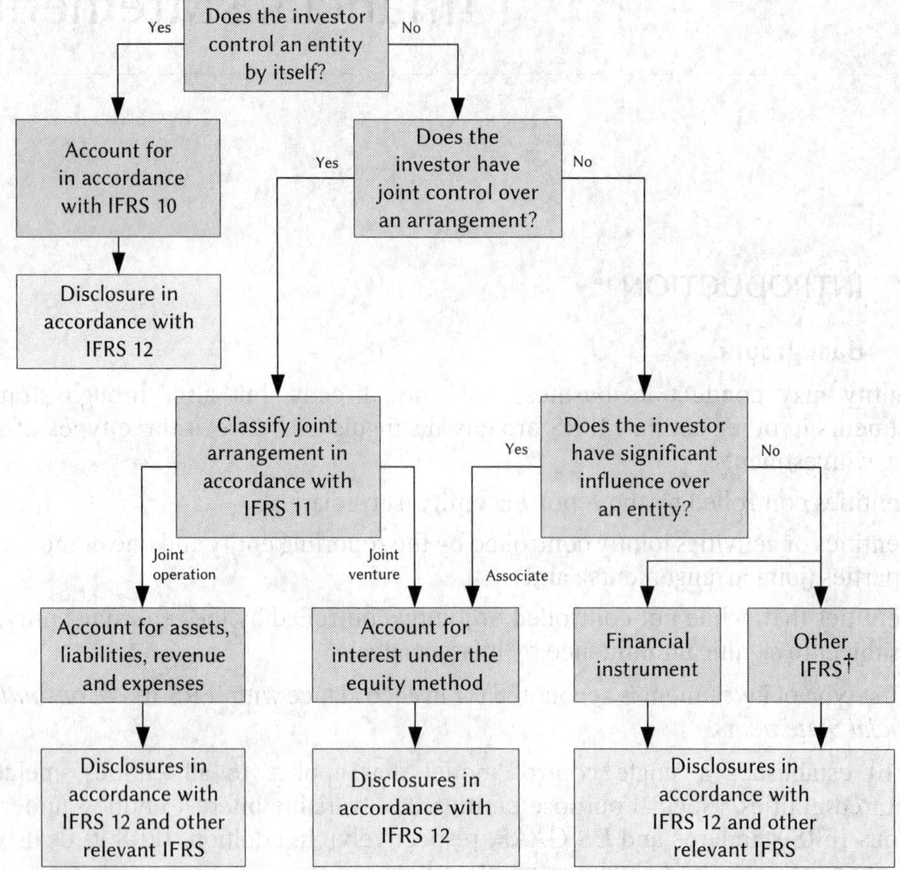

† This would be the case, for example, if an entity has control over (or simply rights to) assets and obligations for liabilities, but *not* control of an entity. In this case, the entity would account for these assets and obligations in accordance with the relevant IFRS.

1.2 Development of IFRS 10

In June 2003, the IASB added a project on consolidation to its agenda to issue a new IFRS to replace the consolidation requirements in IAS 27 – *Consolidated and Separate Financial Statements* ('IAS 27 (2012)') and SIC-12 – *Consolidation – Special Purpose Entities.*

This project was added to the IASB's agenda to deal with divergence in practice in applying the previous standards. In addition, there was a perceived conflict between the definitions of control IAS 27 (2012) and SIC-12 that led to inconsistent application and which was further aggravated by a lack of clear guidance as to which investees were within the scope of IAS 27 (2012) and which were within the scope of SIC-12. *[IFRS 10.BC2-3].*

In December 2008, the IASB published its proposals in an exposure draft, ED 10 – *Consolidated Financial Statements.* ED 10 proposed disclosure requirements for consolidated and unconsolidated investees. However, in its deliberation of the responses to those proposals, the IASB decided to combine the disclosure requirements for interests in subsidiaries, joint arrangements, associates and unconsolidated structured entities within a single comprehensive standard, IFRS 12. Accordingly, IFRS 10 does not include disclosure requirements. *[IFRS 10.BC7].* The requirements of IFRS 12 are dealt with in Chapter 13.

IFRS 10 was issued in May 2011, together with an amended version of IAS 27 with a new title of *Separate Financial Statements* and IFRS 12. In addition, as a result of its project on joint ventures, the IASB issued, at the same time, IFRS 11 and an amended IAS 28. These standards were mandatory for annual periods beginning on or after 1 January 2013.

In October 2012, the IASB issued *Investment Entities (Amendments to IFRS 10, IFRS 12 and IAS 27)* which introduced an exception to the principle that all subsidiaries shall be consolidated. The amendments defined an investment entity and required a parent that is an investment entity to measure its investments in subsidiaries at fair value through profit or loss, with limited exceptions. This amendment applied for annual periods beginning on or after 1 January 2014 but could be adopted early. *[IFRS 10.C1A-B].* The investment entity exception is discussed at 10 below.

In December 2014, the IASB issued *Investment Entities: Applying the Consolidation Exception (Amendments to IFRS 10, IFRS 12 and IAS 28)* which clarifies two aspects of the investment entity exception. This amendment applied for annual periods beginning on or after 1 January 2016 but could be adopted earlier. *[IFRS 10.C1D].* This amendment is discussed at 10 below.

1.3 Consolidation procedures

When an investor determines that it controls an investee, the investor (the parent) consolidates the investee (the subsidiary). The requirements of IFRS 10 relating to consolidation procedures, non-controlling interests and accounting for loss of control are dealt with in Chapter 7.

A parent consolidates a subsidiary from the date on which the parent first obtains control, and continues consolidating that subsidiary until the date on which control is lost. IFRS 3 – *Business Combinations* – defines the date of acquisition, that is, the date on which control is first obtained. *[IFRS 3.8, Appendix A].* The term 'date of acquisition' is used even if a parent gains control without acquiring an interest, or taking any action, as discussed at 9.3 below. IFRS 10 deals with consolidation thereafter (see Chapter 7).

When a parent gains control of a group of assets or an entity that is not a business, such transactions are excluded from the scope of IFRS 3. *[IFRS 3.2].* This is often the case when a parent gains control of a structured entity. Business combinations under common control are also excluded from the scope of IFRS 3, *[IFRS 3.2],* which means that if a parent gains control of a subsidiary (as defined in IFRS 10) that was previously controlled by an entity under common control, IFRS 3 also does not apply.

A parent consolidates all subsidiaries and recognises non-controlling interests for any interests held by investors outside of the group.

1.4 Disclosure requirements

IFRS 10 does not contain any disclosure requirements regarding an entity's interests in subsidiaries included in the consolidated financial statements or its interests in structured entities (whether consolidated or unconsolidated). Such disclosure requirements are contained within IFRS 12.

IFRS 12 contains all disclosure requirements related to an entity's interests in subsidiaries, joint arrangements, associates and structured entities. IFRS 12 requires disclosure of the judgements that were made in determining whether it controls another entity. Even if management concludes that it does not control an entity, the information used to make that judgement will be transparent to users of the financial statements. The required disclosures should also assist users of the financial statements to make their own assessment of the financial impact were management to reach a different conclusion regarding consolidation – by providing information about certain unconsolidated entities. The requirements of IFRS 12 are dealt with in Chapter 13.

2 OBJECTIVE AND SCOPE OF IFRS 10

2.1 Objective

The objective of IFRS 10 is to establish principles for the presentation and preparation of consolidated financial statements when an entity controls one or more other entities. *[IFRS 10.1].*

To meet this objective, the standard:

(a) requires an entity (the parent) that controls one or more other entities (subsidiaries) to present consolidated financial statements;

(b) defines the principle of control, and establishes control as the basis for consolidation;

(c) sets out how to apply the principle of control to identify whether an investor controls an investee and therefore must consolidate the investee;

(d) establishes the accounting requirements for the preparation of consolidated financial statements; and

(e) defines an investment entity and the criteria that must be satisfied for the investment entity exception to be applied. *[IFRS 10.2].*

This chapter deals with (a), (b), (c) and (e). The accounting requirements mentioned in (d) are summarised briefly at 1.3 above, but are dealt with more fully in Chapter 7.

IFRS 10 also states that it does not deal with the accounting requirements for business combinations and their effect on consolidation, including goodwill arising on a business combination; these are covered by IFRS 3 (see Chapter 9). *[IFRS 10.3].*

2.2 Scope

IFRS 10 requires that a parent (unless exempt or an investment entity as discussed below) shall present consolidated financial statements. This means that the financial statements of the group in which the assets, liabilities, equity, income, expenses and cash flows of the parent and its subsidiaries are included, should be presented as those of a single economic entity. A group consists of a parent and its subsidiaries (i.e. entities that the parent controls). *[IFRS 10.4, Appendix A]*.

Under IFRS 10, an entity must assess whether it controls the other entities in which it has an interest (the investees) – see 3 below. This applies to all types of investees including corporations, partnerships, limited liability corporations, trusts, and other types of entities. However, there is a scope exemption for post-employment benefit plans or other long-term employee plans to which IAS 19 – *Employee Benefits* – applies (see 2.2.2 below). In addition, an investment entity generally does not consolidate its subsidiaries (see 2.2.3 below).

IFRS 10 also provides an exemption from preparing consolidated financial statements for entities that are not an ultimate parent, if they meet certain criteria (see 2.2.1 below).

2.2.1 Exemption from preparing consolidated financial statements by an intermediate parent

A parent that prepares financial statements in accordance with IFRS is exempt from presenting (i.e. need not present) consolidated financial statements if it meets all of the following conditions:

(a) it is a wholly-owned subsidiary, or is a partially-owned subsidiary of another entity and all its other owners, including those not otherwise entitled to vote, have been informed about, and do not object to, the parent not presenting consolidated financial statements;

(b) its debt or equity instruments are not traded in a public market (a domestic or foreign stock exchange or an over-the-counter market, including local and regional markets);

(c) it did not file, nor is it in the process of filing, its financial statements with a securities commission or other regulatory organisation for the purpose of issuing any class of instruments in a public market; and

(d) its ultimate or any intermediate parent produces financial statements that are available for public use and comply with IFRSs, in which subsidiaries are consolidated or are measured at fair value through profit or loss in accordance with IFRS 10. *[IFRS 10.4(a)]*.

Where an entity uses this exemption, it may, but is not required, to prepare separate financial statements (see Chapter 8) as its only financial statements. *[IAS 27.8]*. However, if separate financial statements are prepared, they must comply with IAS 27. *[IAS 27.2]*.

The conditions for exemption from preparing consolidated financial statements raise the following interpretation issues.

2.2.1.A Condition (a) – consent of non-controlling shareholders

It is not clear whether a parent is required to obtain explicit consent that the owners of a reporting entity do not object to the use of the exemption.

IFRS 10 requires that, where the parent is itself a partly-owned subsidiary, any non-controlling shareholders must be informed of the parent's intention not to prepare consolidated financial statements. The non-controlling shareholders do not have to give explicit consent – the absence of dissent is sufficient. However, parents that are partly-owned subsidiaries and wish to use the exemption from preparing consolidated financial statements are advised to obtain explicit written consent from non-controlling shareholders in advance.

This is because IFRS 10 sets no time limit on when the non-controlling shareholders can register any objection. Thus, it is possible for the non-controlling shareholders to object to a parent's proposed use of the exemption just before the separate financial statements are printed and even after they have been issued.

IFRS 10 also requires all non-controlling owners 'including those not otherwise entitled to vote' to be informed of the parent's intention not to prepare consolidated financial statements. *[IFRS 10.4(a)]*. Thus, for example, the holders of any voting or non-voting preference shares must be notified of, and consent (or not object) to, the entity's intention to use the exemption.

In our view, the requirement to inform the non-controlling shareholders where the parent 'is a partially-owned subsidiary of another entity' is ambiguous, as illustrated by Examples 6.1 and 6.2 below.

Example 6.1: Consent for not preparing consolidated financial statements (1)

A parent wishing to use the exemption (P) is owned 60% by entity A and 40% by entity B. Entity A and entity B are both wholly-owned by entity C. In this case, P is not obliged to inform its non-controlling shareholder B of its intention not to prepare consolidated financial statements since, although it is a partly-owned subsidiary of A, it is a wholly-owned subsidiary of C (and therefore satisfies condition (a) without regard to its immediate owners).

Example 6.2: Consent for not preparing consolidated financial statements (2)

The facts are the same as in Example 6.1 above, except that A and B are both owned by an individual (Mr X). P is not a wholly-owned subsidiary of any other entity, and therefore the rules applicable to partly-owned subsidiaries apply. Thus, P is required to inform B of any intention not to prepare consolidated financial statements.

2.2.1.B Condition (b) – securities not traded in a public market

It is not clear exactly what constitutes a 'public market'. It is clear that, where quoted prices are available for any of the parent's securities on a generally recognised share exchange, the parent is required to prepare consolidated financial statements, and cannot use the exemption. However, when there are no quoted prices but the parent's shares are occasionally traded, for example, on a matched bargain basis through an exchange (as opposed to by private treaty between individual buyers and sellers), it is not clear whether this would meet the definition of a 'public market' for this condition.

In our view, any security that is traded in circumstances where it is necessary to have filed financial statements with a securities commission or regulator is regarded as 'traded in a public market' for condition (b). It is clear that the IASB regarded conditions (b) and (c) above as linked; in other words, that an entity would fall within (c) before falling within (b). *[IFRS 10.BCZ18]*. Since condition (c) refers to the filing of financial statements with a securities commission or regulator as a precursor to public listing of securities, this forms the basis for our view.

2.2.1.C Condition (c) – not filing financial statements for listing securities

It is not clear whether the 'financial statements' referred to are only those prepared under IFRS, or include those prepared under local GAAP.

In our view, the test is whether the entity currently has, or shortly will have, an ongoing obligation to file financial statements with a regulator in connection with the public trading of any of its securities. This conclusion is based on our view that the phrase 'financial statements' means any financial statements filed in connection with the public trading of securities. The IASB's view is that the information needs of users of financial statements of entities whose debt or equity instruments are traded in a public market are best served when investments in subsidiaries, associates, and jointly controlled entities are accounted for in accordance with IFRS 10, IAS 28, and IFRS 11 respectively. The Board therefore decided that the exemption from preparing such consolidated financial statements is not available to such entities or to entities in the process of issuing instruments in a public market. *[IFRS 10.BCZ18]*.

2.2.1.D Condition (d) – parent's IFRS financial statements are publicly available and includes subsidiaries that are consolidated or measured at fair value through profit or loss in accordance with IFRS 10

The first part of this condition means that the exemption can be used either where a parent of the reporting entity prepares financial statements under IFRS that are publicly available through a regulatory filing requirement, or where those financial statements are available on request. An entity that uses the exemption from preparing consolidated financial statements must disclose the source for obtaining the financial statements of the relevant parent of the reporting entity (see Chapter 8 at 3.1). *[IAS 27.16(a)]*. For example, this information can be provided by providing:

- contact details of a person or an e-mail address from which a hard copy of the document can be obtained; or
- a website address where the financial statements can be found and downloaded.

This condition requires that the parent's financial statements comply with IFRS. There are a number of jurisdictions that have a national GAAP which is virtually identical to IFRS. However, differences between these national GAAPs and IFRS often exist regarding the scope, transitional provisions, effective dates and actual wording of standards. In addition, some national GAAPs contain accounting alternatives not permitted by IFRS. The question arises as to whether a reporting entity, that is a parent entity preparing IFRS financial statements, can claim exemption for the requirement to prepare consolidated accounts on the grounds that it has an ultimate or intermediate parent that produces consolidated financial statements under a national GAAP which is similar to IFRS (e.g. EU-adopted IFRS). In our view, if the ultimate or intermediate parent:

- reports under a national GAAP that is identical with IFRS in all respects;
- applied the national GAAP equivalent of IFRS 1 – *First-time Adoption of International Financial Reporting Standards* – when it adopted that national GAAP;
- makes an explicit and unreserved statement of compliance with that national GAAP in its most recent consolidated financial statements; and
- could have made an explicit and unreserved statement of compliance with IFRS in those consolidated financial statements, if required;

then the exemption from preparing consolidated financial statements is permitted for the reporting entity.

Chapter 6

The second part of condition (d) above confirms that the exemption from preparing consolidated financial statements set out in (a) to (d) above is available to an intermediate parent entity that is a subsidiary of an investment entity. The exemption is available even though the investment entity parent may not prepare consolidated financial statements or consolidate the intermediate parent entity subsidiary. *[IFRS 10.BC28A-B]*. This condition was added by an amendment applicable for accounting periods beginning on or after 1 January 2016. *[IFRS 10.C1D]*.

In making its decision, the IASB observed that, when an investment entity measures its interest in a subsidiary at fair value, the disclosures required by IFRS 12 are supplemented by those required by IFRS 7 – *Financial Instruments: Disclosures* – and IFRS 13 – *Fair Value Measurement*. Accordingly, the IASB decided that this combination of information was sufficient to support the decision to retain an exemption from presenting consolidated financial statements for a subsidiary of an investment entity that is itself a parent entity. The IASB further noted that requiring an intermediate parent that is a subsidiary of an investment entity to prepare consolidated financial statements could result in significant additional costs, without commensurate benefit and this would be contrary to its intention in requiring investment entities to measure investments at fair value, which was to provide more relevant information at a reduced cost. *[IFRS 10.BC28D]*.

However, local law or regulations may conflict with this exemption if it is required that an entity has to be included within the consolidated financial statements of a parent by full consolidation in order to obtain the exemption.

2.2.2 *Employee benefit plans and employee share trusts*

IFRS 10 exempts post-employment benefit plans or other long-term employee benefit plans to which IAS 19 applies. *[IFRS 10.4A]*. However, it is not clear whether this means that an employee benefit plan that controls an investee is not required to consolidate that investee in its financial statements, or whether an investor that controls an employee benefit plan need not consolidate the plan itself.

It seems that the latter was intended: a sponsor of an employee benefit plan need not evaluate whether it controls that employee benefit plan, and, therefore, need not consolidate it. However, the employee benefit plan would need to apply IFRS 10 if it is preparing financial statements under IAS 26 – *Accounting and Reporting by Retirement Benefit Plans*.

In contrast, employee benefit trusts (or similar entities) established for employee share option plans, employee share purchase plans and other share-based payment programmes are not excluded from the scope of IFRS 10. This is because these are outside the scope of IAS 19. The sponsoring entity of these trusts needs to evaluate whether it controls (and therefore consolidates) the trusts. If the trust is treated as an extension of the employer or sponsoring entity (see Chapter 32 at 12.3) its assets and liabilities will already be included in the financial statements of the employer entity that are used for preparing the consolidated financial statements of the group. If the trust is not accounted for as an extension of the employer or sponsoring entity, the parent will need to assess whether the trust, as a separate vehicle, needs to be consolidated according to the control criteria of IFRS 10.

The diagram below illustrates what is in scope and out of scope of IFRS 10.

Figure 6.2: Understanding scope in employee benefit plans and employee share option plans

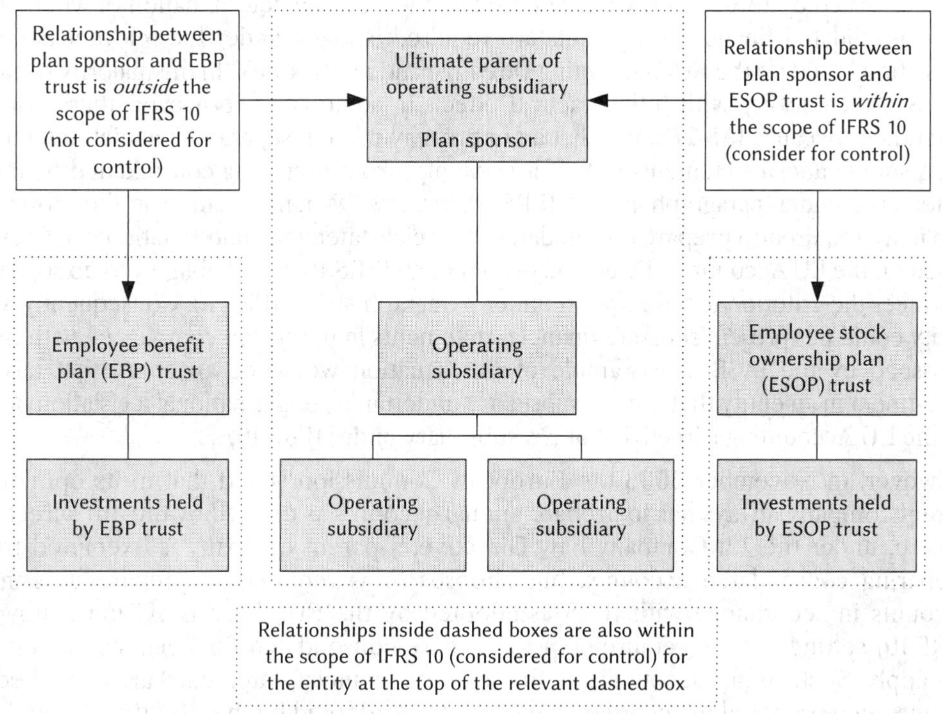

2.2.3 *Investment entity exception*

As an exception to the consolidation rule, a parent that is an investment entity shall not present consolidated financial statements if it is required to measure all of its subsidiaries at fair value through profit or loss. *[IFRS 10.4B].* This is discussed at 10.3 below.

2.2.4 *Entity no longer a parent at the end of the reporting period*

It is not clear whether IFRS 10 requires an entity to prepare consolidated financial statements only if it is a parent at the end of the reporting period or also if it was a parent at any time during the reporting period.

In our view, consolidated financial statements must be prepared by an entity that was a parent during the reporting period, even if that entity is no longer a parent at the end of the reporting period (e.g. because it disposed of all its subsidiaries). IFRS 10 requires a parent to consolidate a subsidiary until the date on which the parent ceases to control the subsidiary. *[IFRS 10.20].* This means that if a parent does not prepare consolidated financial statements pursuant to a concession in local law (see 2.2.5 below), the parent may not present separate financial statements in compliance with IFRS.

Likewise, we believe that an entity that had an associate, or an interest in a joint venture, during the reporting period but no longer does so at end of the reporting period, must apply IAS 28 and/or IFRS 11 to those investments in its financial statements for the reporting period, if not otherwise exempt from doing so.

2.2.5 Interaction of IFRS 10 and EU law

For entities incorporated in the EU there may, in some cases, be a subtle interaction between the requirements to prepare consolidated financial statements in accordance with IFRS as issued by IASB and IFRS as adopted by the EU. The determination of whether or not consolidated financial statements are required is made under the relevant national legislation based on the EU Accounting Directive and not IFRS 10.[1] In the majority of cases this is a technicality with little practical effect. In some cases, however, there will be differences because IAS 27 states that an entity may present separate financial statements as its sole financial statements only if it is exempt from preparing consolidated financial statements under paragraph 4(a) of IFRS 10. *[IAS 27.8].* When an entity is therefore not explicitly required to prepare consolidated financial statements under national legislation based on the EU Accounting Directive, even though IFRS 10 would oblige it to do so, it will not meet the criterion for exemption under paragraph 4(a) of IFRS 10. Consequently, that entity could not present separate financial statements in purported compliance with IFRS as issued by the IASB. An example of this situation would be an entity that has an investment in an entity that is not a subsidiary undertaking under national legislation based on the EU Accounting Directive, but is a subsidiary under IFRS 10.

However, in November 2006 the European Commission stated that in its opinion 'a parent company always has to prepare annual accounts as defined by the 4th Directive. Where, under the 7th Company Law Directive, a parent company is exempted from preparing consolidated accounts, but chooses or is required to prepare its annual accounts in accordance with IFRS as adopted by the EU, those provisions...(now in IFRS 10) setting out the requirement to prepare consolidated financial statements do not apply. Such annual accounts (i.e. the separate financial statements) are described as having been prepared in accordance with IFRS as adopted by the EU'[2] (the 4th and 7th Directives have now been replaced by a single EU Accounting Directive).

2.2.6 Combined and carve-out financial statements

Combined or carve-out financial statements are sometimes prepared under IFRS for a 'reporting entity' that does not comprise a group under IFRS 10. Although some GAAPs draw a distinction between combined and carve-out financial statements, in our view, the determination of whether these financial statements are permitted to be prepared in accordance with IFRS is the same. Accordingly, where the term 'combined' financial statements is used below, the views apply equally to carve-out financial statements. Examples of when combined or carve-out financial statements might be requested include the following:

- two or more legal entities under common control of the same individual or group of individuals (e.g. 'horizontal' groups); or
- a group of business units that are intended to become a group in the future (e.g. following an initial public offering or demerger), which may or may not be separate legal entities.

In 2009, the Interpretations Committee received a request for guidance on whether a reporting entity may, in accordance with IFRS, present financial statements that include a selection of entities that are under common control, rather than being restricted to a parent/subsidiary relationship as defined by IFRS. The Interpretations Committee noted that the ability to include entities within a set of IFRS financial statements depends on the interpretation of 'reporting entity' in the context of common control. The Interpretations Committee decided not to add these issues on to its agenda.[3]

In our view, there are limited circumstances in which such combined financial statements can give a true and fair view in accordance with IFRS and be presented as 'general-purpose' financial statements. As a minimum, there must be both of the following:

- common control for the full or a portion of the reporting period (see 2.2.6.A below); and
- a clear purpose for which the combined financial statements will be used by clearly identified intended users (see 2.2.6.B below).

In addition, the preparer must be able to coherently describe the various legal entities, segments, reportable segments, branches, divisions, geographical jurisdictions, or other 'units' that will be included in the combined financial statements. Careful consideration is required when concluding that it is appropriate to exclude any 'units' from the combined financial statements (such as unprofitable operations) that are similar to the 'units' that are being included in the combined financial statements. Such exclusion must be appropriate when considered in the context of the purpose of the financial statements, the intended users, and the terms and conditions of any relevant agreements (e.g. acquisitions, spin-offs). Other practical considerations related to the preparation of combined financial statements are noted in 2.2.6.C below.

Although IFRS is unclear on this issue, we believe that the fact that *IFRS for Small and Medium-sized Entities* specifically permits the preparation of combined financial statements, and the fact that Exposure Draft ED/2015/3 – *Conceptual Framework for Financial Reporting* – refers to combined financial statements (see 11 below), together provide a basis for preparing combined financial statements in appropriate circumstances.

Chapter 6

2.2.6.A Common control

Determining whether common control exists can be difficult, and requires judgement based on the facts and circumstances (see Chapter 10 at 2.1.1). In our view, general-purpose combined financial statements can only be prepared if the entities are under common control for the full or a portion of the reporting period. Furthermore, the financial results of each combined entity can only be included in the general-purpose combined financial statements for the period in which that entity was under common control. Events that occur after the end of a reporting period that result in common control are non-adjusting events (see Chapter 36 at 2.1.3).

2.2.6.B Purpose and users of combined financial statements

A reporting entity is an entity for which there are users who rely on the financial statements as their major source of financial information about the entity. Therefore, it is a matter of judgement of whether it is appropriate to prepare general-purpose combined financial statements, depending upon the facts and circumstances related to both the purpose and the users of the financial statements, considerations that are interrelated.

For example, the facts and circumstances usually indicate that it is appropriate to prepare general-purpose combined financial statements when required by regulators on behalf of investors. This is because the regulators purport to represent the needs of a wide range of users (investors) for a general purpose, for which the investors cannot otherwise command the financial information. Situations where regulators typically require combined financial statements include:

- carve-out transactions;
- spin-off transactions;
- financing transactions that require approval by a broad group of investors;
- transactions in which the combined entity will become the predecessor financial statements of a new entity; or
- transactions in which the combined entity will be a material acquisition (for the acquirer).

In addition, there may be circumstances when several third parties (banks, acquirers in a private bidding process) all request financial statements that combine the same entities – that is, the same combined financial statements. In such cases, the combined financial statements might be 'general-purpose', because they are used by a wide range of users.

2.2.6.C Preparation of combined financial statements

Combined financial statements must include all normal consolidation entries (such as elimination of group transactions, unrealised profit elimination, etc.). In our view, the combined financial statements should disclose:

- the fact that the financial statements are combined financial statements;
- the reason why combined financial statements are prepared;
- the basis for determining which 'units' are included in the combined financial statements;
- the basis of preparation of the combined financial statements; and
- the related party disclosures required by IAS 24 – *Related Party Disclosures*.

In addition, management should consider who has the appropriate knowledge and authority to authorise the general-purpose combined financial statements for issue (see Chapter 36 at 2.4).

While regulators may require combined or carve-out financial statements, IFRS does not describe how to prepare such information. Accordingly, practical issues frequently arise when preparing financial statements on a combined or carve-out basis, including the items below:

- *Management judgement and hindsight*: Absent clear legal boundaries, determining whether certain items are part of a combined reporting entity often requires significant management judgement and possibly the use of hindsight;
- *Comparative periods:* There is a risk that comparative information is prepared on a basis that reflects the impact of events before they actually occur (e.g. disposals of assets). Once it is determined what 'units' are being included in the combined financial statements, the comparative information presented is the comparative information for such units;
- *Allocation of overhead costs*: Combined reporting entities that are part of a larger group often benefit from certain overheads (e.g. legal or administrative);

- *Transfers of assets*: The group that owns the combined reporting entity may have been reorganised, resulting in the transfer of assets between 'units'. This raises questions about recognising gains or losses on disposals and the appropriate cost basis of assets acquired;
- *Financing costs*: It is often not clear how to allocate a group's liabilities and equity to the individual 'units' that it owns. The individual 'units' may differ considerably in nature, e.g. a group may own both low-risk established 'units' and a high-risk new venture. Therefore, it is not clear how to allocate interest expenses and other aspects of an entity's funding structure (e.g. embedded derivatives and compound financial instruments);
- *Taxation and employee benefits*: Legal and other requirements often create practical issues when determining the amount of the tax or employee benefit liabilities that are recognised in combined or carve-out financial statements; and
- *Designation*: Accounting under IFRS sometimes relies on management's stated intent and other designations (e.g. financial instrument and hedge designations, intent regarding assets held for sale and designation of groups of cash-generating units). It is often not clear how to reflect management's intent and designations in combined or carve-out financial statements.

There is a risk that an inappropriate allocation could result in a set of financial statements that does not offer a 'true and fair view' of the reporting entity. Preparation of financial information on a combined or carve-out basis generally requires a substantial number of adjustments and allocations to be made, and draws heavily on pronouncements of other standard-setting bodies that are referred to by the hierarchy of authoritative guidance in IAS 8 – *Accounting Policies, Changes in Accounting Estimates and Errors*.

Absent clarification by the IASB or the Interpretations Committee, diversity in practice will continue to exist. Therefore, the basis of preparation should disclose:

- which accounting standards have been applied; and
- the significant accounting judgements that were made, including the adjustments and allocations.

2.2.6.D When combined financial statements are not general-purpose

In our view, it is generally not appropriate to present 'general-purpose' combined financial statements when requested by parties that can obtain the desired combined financial information through other means. In such cases, the combined financial statements are often deemed 'special-purpose'. Examples of such parties include:

- lenders (banks) for the purpose of approving a loan or ensuring covenant compliance;
- governments and their agencies other than investor regulators (e.g. tax authorities);
- a single potential acquirer; or
- a board of directors or management.

When a group of family members prepares combined financial statements, judgement is required to assess the facts and circumstances, as to whether such combined financial statements are 'general-purpose' or 'special-purpose,' depending on the purpose for which the family intends to use the combined financial statements.

Where it is not appropriate to present combined financial statements as 'general-purpose,' either because they are requested by a party that has the ability to otherwise command the information, or because there are deviations from IFRS as issued by the IASB due to the specific nature and purpose of the combined or carved-out financial statements, alternative options might include preparing:

- financial statements of each of the entities that would have been included in the combined financial information; or
- special-purpose financial statements.

2.2.6.E The reporting entity in combined financial statements and in consolidated financial statements

In certain circumstances, entities prepare general purpose combined financial statements in compliance with IFRS followed by consolidated financial statements in accordance with IFRS. Sometimes, group entities may be excluded from a parent's combined financial statements despite the fact that they are controlled by the parent, and would otherwise be consolidated by the parent under IFRS 10. For example, a subsidiary that will not form part of a sub-group to be listed may be excluded from the combined financial statements. In our view, the subsequent consolidated financial statements must be prepared according to IFRS 10 and therefore must include all subsidiaries controlled by a parent. This is because IFRS 10 defines consolidated financial statements as those including assets, liabilities, equity, income, expenses and cash flows of the parent and its subsidiaries. *[IFRS 10 Appendix A]*. A subsidiary is derecognised at the date that control is lost. *[IFRS 10.20, 5]*. IFRS 10 does not provide any exceptions to these requirements. Example 6.3 below illustrates the differences in the scope of consolidation that can arise where an entity prepares both combined and consolidated financial statements.

Example 6.3: Preparation of consolidated financial statements after combined financial statements

In 2018, intermediate parent (P), which has three subsidiaries (S1, S2 and S3), is preparing for an IPO. P has historically not prepared consolidated financial statements as it has applied the exemption in IFRS 10.4(a). One of the subsidiaries, S3, is to be transferred to the ultimate parent prior to the listing, and will not form part of the sub-group to be listed. In the prospectus, combined financial statements are presented including P, S1 and S2 for the annual periods ending 31 December 2016 and 2017. The combined financial statements are deemed to be general purpose financial statements in compliance with IFRS, as the combined entities have been under common control for the entire reporting period, and the combined financial statements are required by the regulator on behalf of investors, representing a wide range of users. The transfer of S3 to the ultimate parent occurred in August 2018 and P group was listed in October 2018.

When preparing the 2018 consolidated financial statements, should (now listed) P:

(a) present consolidated financial statements for 2018 (P+S1+S2+S3), showing comparatives for 2017 and consolidating S3 until August 2018; or

(b) present consolidated financial statements for 2019 excluding S3 (P1+S1+S2), showing comparative information for 2017 for only P1+S1+S2, as per the combined financial statements?

The consolidated financial statements must be prepared according to IFRS 10 and therefore the 2018 consolidated financial statements of P must include S3 in the 2017 comparatives and until control ceased in August 2018 (option (a) above).

3 CONTROL

An investor, regardless of the nature of its involvement with an entity (the investee), determines whether it is a parent by assessing whether it controls the investee. *[IFRS 10.5]*.

An investor controls an investee when it is exposed, or has rights, to variable returns from its involvement with the investee and has the ability to affect those returns through its power over the investee. *[IFRS 10.6]*.

Thus, an investor controls an investee if and only if the investor has all of the following:

(a) power over the investee;

(b) exposure, or rights, to variable returns from its involvement with the investee; and

(c) the ability to use its power over the investee to affect the amount of the investor's returns. *[IFRS 10.7]*.

Although not a defined term, IFRS 10 uses the term 'investor' to refer to a reporting entity that potentially controls one or more other entities, and 'investee' to refer to an entity that is, or may potentially be, the subsidiary of a reporting entity. Ownership of a debt or equity interest may be a key factor in determining whether an investor has control. However, it is also possible for a party to be an investor and potentially control an investee, without having an equity or debt interest in that investee.

An investor has to consider all facts and circumstances when assessing whether it controls an investee. *[IFRS 10.8]*.

Only one party, if any, can control an investee. *[IFRS 10.BC69]*. However, IFRS 10 notes that two or more investors collectively can control an investee. To control an investee collectively, investors must act together to direct the relevant activities (see 4.1 below). In such cases, because no investor can direct the activities without the co-operation of the others, no investor individually controls the investee. Each investor would account for its interest in the investee in accordance with the relevant IFRSs, such as IFRS 11, IAS 28 or IFRS 9 – *Financial Instruments* – or (IAS 39 – *Financial Instruments: Recognition and Measurement*). *[IFRS 10.9, C7]*.

3.1 Assessing control

Detailed application guidance is provided by IFRS 10 with respect to the assessment of whether an investor has control over an investee. To determine whether it controls an investee, an investor assesses whether it has all three elements of control described at 3 above. *[IFRS 10.B2]*.

Each of the three control criteria are explored in more detail at 4, 5 and 6 below, respectively.

IFRS 10 notes that consideration of the following factors may assist in making that determination:

(a) the purpose and design of the investee (see 3.2 below);

(b) what the relevant activities are and how decisions about those activities are made (see 4.1 below);

(c) whether the rights of the investor give it the current ability to direct the relevant activities (see 4.2 to 4.6 below);

(d) whether the investor is exposed, or has rights, to variable returns from its involvement with the investee (see 5 below); and

(e) whether the investor has the ability to use its power over the investee to affect the amount of the investor's returns (see 6 below). *[IFRS 10.B3]*.

In addition, when assessing control of an investee, an investor considers the nature of its relationship with other parties (see 7 below). *[IFRS 10.B4]*.

In many cases, when decision-making is controlled by voting rights that also give the holder exposure to variable returns, it is clear that whichever investor holds a majority of those voting rights controls the investee. *[IFRS 10.B6]*. However, in other cases (such as when there are potential voting rights, or an investor holds less than a majority of the voting rights), it may not be so clear. In those instances, further analysis is needed and the criteria need to be evaluated based on all facts and circumstances (considering the factors listed above), to determine which investor, if any, controls an investee. *[IFRS 10.8]*. The diagram below illustrates this assessment.

The control principle outlined above applies to all investees, including structured entities. A structured entity is defined in IFRS 12 as 'an entity that has been designed so that voting or similar rights are not the dominant factor in deciding who controls the entity, such as when any voting rights relate to administrative tasks only and the relevant activities are directed by means of contractual arrangements'. *[IFRS 12 Appendix A]*.

There are no bright lines to determine whether an investor has an exposure, or has rights, to variable returns from its involvement with a structured entity, or whether it has the ability to affect the returns of the structured entity through its power over the structured entity. Rather, as with all investees, all facts and circumstances are considered when assessing whether the investor has control over an investee that is a structured entity. That is, the process outlined in the diagram below is used for structured entities, although the relevant facts and circumstances may differ from when voting rights are a more important factor in determining control.

Figure 6.3: Assessing control

Identify power	Assess returns	Evaluate linkage
Power Determine which party, if any, has power, that is, the current ability to direct the relevant activities. Power arises from the rights which may include: • Voting rights • Potential voting rights (e.g. options or convertible instruments) • Rights to appoint key management personnel • Decision making rights within a management contract • Removal or 'kick-out' rights However, power does not arise from protective rights.	**Returns** Assess whether the investor is exposed, or has rights, to variable returns from its involvement with the investee. Returns can be positive, negative, or both. Examples of returns include: • Dividends • Remuneration • Economies of scale, cost savings, scarce products, proprietary knowledge, synergies, or other returns that are not available to other interest holders	**Linkage** Evaluate whether the investor has the ability to use its power to affect the investor's returns from its involvement with the investee. If applicable, determine whether the investor is a principal or an agent, considering: • Scope of its authority • Rights held by other parties • Remuneration • Exposure to variability from other interests

Understand purpose and design of investee

When management concludes that an entity does *not* have control, the requirements of IFRS 11 and IAS 28 must be considered to determine whether it has joint control or significant influence, respectively, over the investee, as shown in the diagram at 1.1 above.

3.2 Purpose and design of an investee

When assessing control of an investee, an investor considers the purpose and design of the investee in order to identify the relevant activities, how decisions about the relevant activities are made, who has the current ability to direct those activities and who receives returns from those activities. *[IFRS 10.B5]*. Understanding the purpose and design of an investee is therefore critical when identifying who has control.

When an investee's purpose and design are considered, it may be clear that an investee is controlled by means of equity instruments that give the holder proportionate voting rights, such as ordinary shares in the investee. In this case, in the absence of any additional arrangements that alter decision-making, the assessment of control focuses on which party, if any, is able to exercise voting rights (see 4.3 below) sufficient to determine the investee's operating and financing policies. In the most straightforward case, the investor that holds a majority of those voting rights, in the absence of any other factors, controls the investee. *[IFRS 10.B6]*.

To determine whether an investor controls an investee in more complex cases, it may be necessary to consider some or all of the other factors listed at 3.1 above. *[IFRS 10.B7]*.

IFRS 10 notes that an investee may be designed so that voting rights are not the dominant factor in deciding who controls the investee, such as when any voting rights relate to administrative tasks only and the relevant activities are directed by means of contractual arrangements (this is the same wording that IFRS 12 uses in defining a structured entity – see 3.1 above). In such cases, an investor's consideration of the purpose and design of the investee shall also include consideration of the risks to which the investee was designed to be exposed, the risks it was designed to pass on to the parties involved with the investee and whether the investor is exposed to some or all of those risks. Consideration of the risks includes not only the downside risk, but also the potential for upside. *[IFRS 10.B8]*.

Understanding the purpose and design of the investee helps to determine:

- to what risks was the investee designed to be exposed, and what are the risks it was designed to pass on to the parties with which it is involved?
- what are the relevant activities?
- how are decisions about the relevant activities made?
- who has the ability to direct the relevant activities?
- which parties have exposure to variable returns from the investee?
- how do the relevant activities affect returns?
- do the parties that have power, and have exposure to variable returns have the ability to use that power to affect returns?

In short, understanding the purpose and design of the investee helps to understand the goal of each investor; that is, why they are involved with the investee, and what that involvement is.

4 POWER OVER AN INVESTEE

The first criterion to have control relates to power. An investor has power when it has existing rights that give it the current ability to direct the relevant activities. *[IFRS 10.10, B9]*. Therefore, when assessing whether an investor has power, there are two critical concepts:

- relevant activities; and
- existing rights.

These concepts are discussed at 4.1 and 4.2 below, respectively. Power may be achieved through voting rights (see 4.3 below) or through rights arising from contractual arrangements (see 4.4 below). We also discuss other evidence of power (see 4.5 below) and determining whether sponsoring (designing) a structured entity gives power (see 4.6 below).

An investor can have power over an investee even if other entities have existing rights that give them the current ability to participate in the direction of the relevant activities. This may occur when another entity has significant influence, *[IFRS 10.14]*, i.e. the power to participate in the financial and operating policy decisions of the investee but not control or joint control over those policies. *[IAS 28.3]*.

4.1 Relevant activities

In many cases, it is clear that control of an investee is held through voting rights. However, when it is not clear that control of an investee is held through voting rights, a crucial step in assessing control is identifying the relevant activities of the investee, and the way decisions about such activities are made. *[IFRS 10.B10]*. Relevant activities are the activities of the investee that significantly affect the investee's returns. *[IFRS 10.10]*.

For many investees, a range of activities significantly affect their returns. Examples of relevant activities, and decisions about them, include, but are not limited to:

- determining or changing operating and financing policies (which might include the items below);
- selling and purchasing goods and/or services;
- managing financial assets during their life (and/or upon default);
- selecting, acquiring or disposing of assets;
- researching and developing new products or processes;
- determining a funding structure or obtaining funding;
- establishing operating and capital decisions of the investee, including budgets; and
- appointing, remunerating or terminating the employment of an investee's service providers or key management personnel. *[IFRS 10.B11-B12]*.

4.1.1 More than one relevant activity

In many cases, more than one activity will significantly affect an investee's returns.

Under IFRS 10, if two or more unrelated investors each have existing rights that give them the unilateral ability to direct different relevant activities, the investor that has the current ability to direct the activities that most significantly affect the returns of the investee has power over the investee. *[IFRS 10.13].*

In some situations, activities that occur both before or after a particular set of circumstances or events may be relevant activities. When two or more investors have the current ability to direct relevant activities and those activities occur at different times, the investors determine which investor is able to direct the activities that most significantly affect those returns consistently with the treatment of concurrent decision-making rights. The investors reconsider this assessment over time if relevant facts or circumstances change. *[IFRS 10.B13].*

Therefore, when there is more than one activity that significantly affects an investee's returns, and these activities are directed by different investors, it is important to determine which activities most significantly affect the investee's returns. This is illustrated in Example 6.4 below, which is from IFRS 10. *[IFRS 10.B13 Example 1].*

Example 6.4: Identifying relevant activities in life sciences arrangements

Two investors form an investee to develop and market a medical product. One investor is responsible for developing and obtaining regulatory approval of the medical product – that responsibility includes having the unilateral ability to make all decisions relating to the development of the product and to obtaining regulatory approval. Once the regulator has approved the product, the other investor will manufacture and market it – this investor has the unilateral ability to make all decisions about the manufacture and marketing of the project. If all the activities – developing and obtaining regulatory approval as well as manufacturing and marketing of the medical product – are relevant activities, each investor needs to determine whether it is able to direct the activities that most significantly affect the investee's returns. Accordingly, each investor needs to consider whether developing and obtaining regulatory approval or the manufacturing and marketing of the medical product is the activity that most significantly affects the investee's returns and whether it is able to direct that activity. In determining which investor has power, the investors would consider:

(a) the purpose and design of the investee;

(b) the factors that determine the profit margin, revenue and value of the investee as well as the value of the medical product;

(c) the effect on the investee's returns resulting from each investor's decision-making authority with respect to the factors in (b); and

(d) the investors' exposure to variability of returns.

In this particular example, the investors would also consider:

(e) the uncertainty of, and effort required in, obtaining regulatory approval (considering the investor's record of successfully developing and obtaining regulatory approval of medical products); and

(f) which investor controls the medical product once the development phase is successful.

In this example, IFRS 10 does not conclude which of the activities is the most relevant activity (i.e. the activity that most significantly affects the investee's returns). If it were concluded that the most relevant activity is:

- developing and obtaining regulatory approval of the medical product – then the investor that has the power to direct that activity would have power from the date of entering into the arrangement; or
- manufacturing and marketing the medical product – then the investor that has the power to direct that activity would have power from the date of entering into the arrangement.

To determine whether either investor controls the arrangement, the investors would also need to assess whether they have exposure to variable returns from their involvement with the investee (see 5 below) and the ability to use their power over the investee to affect the amount of the investor's returns (see 6 below). *[IFRS 10.7, B2].* The investors are required to reconsider this assessment over time if relevant facts or circumstances change. *[IFRS 10.8].*

Example 6.4 above illustrates a situation when two different activities that significantly affect an investee's returns are directed by different investors. Thus, it is important to identify the activity that *most* significantly affects returns, as part of assessing which investor, if any, has power. This differs from joint control, defined as the contractually agreed sharing of control of an arrangement, which exists only when decisions about the relevant activities require the unanimous consent of the parties sharing control. *[IFRS 11 Appendix A].* Joint control is discussed in more detail in Chapter 12 at 4.

Another example provided by IFRS 10, *[IFRS 10.B13 Example 2]*, is reproduced in Example 6.5 below.

Example 6.5: Identifying relevant activities in an investment vehicle

An investment vehicle (the investee) is created and financed with a debt instrument held by an investor (the debt investor) and equity instruments held by a number of other investors. The equity tranche is designed to absorb the first losses and to receive any residual return from the investee. One of the equity investors who holds 30% of the equity is also the asset manager. The investee uses its proceeds to purchase a portfolio of financial assets, exposing the investee to the credit risk associated with the possible default of principal and interest payments of the assets. The transaction is marketed to the debt investor as an investment with minimal exposure to the credit risk associated with the possible default of the assets in the portfolio because of the nature of these assets and because the equity tranche is designed to absorb the first losses of the investee.

The returns of the investee are significantly affected by the management of the investee's asset portfolio, which includes decisions about the selection, acquisition and disposal of the assets within portfolio guidelines and the management upon default of any portfolio assets. All those activities are managed by the asset manager until defaults reach a specified proportion of the portfolio value (i.e. when the value of the portfolio is such that the equity tranche of the investee has been consumed). From that time, a third-party trustee manages the assets according to the instructions of the debt investor. Managing the investee's asset portfolio is the relevant activity of the investee. The asset manager has the ability to direct the relevant activities until defaulted assets reach the specified proportion of the portfolio value; the debt investor has the ability to direct the relevant activities when the value of defaulted assets surpasses that specified proportion of the portfolio value. The asset manager and the debt investor each need to determine whether they are able to direct the activities that *most* significantly affect the investee's returns, including considering the purpose and design of the investee as well as each party's exposure to variability of returns.

Example 6.6 below illustrates a structured entity in which there is more than one activity that affects the investee's returns.

Example 6.6: Identifying relevant activities in a structured entity

A structured entity buys dollar-denominated assets, issues euro-denominated notes, and hedges the cash flow differences through currency and interest rate swaps. The activities that affect the structured entity's returns include:

- sourcing the assets from the market;
- determining the types of assets that are purchased;
- deciding how the structure is hedged; and
- managing the assets in the event of default.

If each of these activities is managed by different investors (e.g. one investor manages the assets in the event of default, but a different investor determines the types of assets that are purchased), it is necessary to determine which activity most significantly affects the structured entity's returns.

When there are multiple activities that significantly affect an investee's returns, but those activities are all directed by the same investor(s) (which is frequently the case when those activities are directed by voting rights), it is not necessary to determine which activity most significantly affects the investee's returns because the power assessment would be the same in each case.

4.1.2 No relevant activities

We believe that structured entities for which there is no substantive decision making are rare. That is, we believe virtually all structured entities have some level of decision-making and few, if any, are on 'autopilot'. Even if a structured entity operates on 'autopilot' there may be decisions outside the predetermined parameters that may need to be taken if an expected return fails to materialise which could significantly affect the returns of the entity and therefore be relevant activities.

In practice, many entities that may initially have few if any relevant activities can be terminated by at least one of the parties involved in the structure. In this case the choice of whether to terminate may often be viewed as the relevant activity. IFRS 10 would most likely result in such entities being consolidated by an investor that has the power to dissolve the entity, if this power would affect its variable returns. See section 4.6 below for additional guidance on evaluating relevant activities for structured entities and section 6.3.2 below for additional guidance on liquidation and redemption rights.

However, if a structured entity truly has no decision-making then no investor controls that structured entity. This is because no investor has power over the structured entity, that is, no investor has the current ability to direct the activities that significantly affect the structured entity's returns if there are no relevant activities after inception significantly affecting those returns. As discussed above, we believe that such situations where there is no substantive decision-making are rare. An example of a structured entity over which no investor had power was included in the IASB's publication, *Effect analysis: IFRS 10 Consolidated Financial Statements and IFRS 12 Disclosure of Interests in Other Entities.* However, this example caused controversy and the Effect Analysis was re-issued in 2013 with the example deleted.[4]

4.1.3 Single asset, single lessee vehicles

Some structured entities are single asset, single lease vehicles created to lease a single asset to a single lessee. Between November 2014 and May 2015, the Interpretations Committee discussed requests for clarification about the interaction of IFRS 10 and IAS 17 – *Leases* – in two situations which involved the establishment of a structured entity to lease a single asset to a single lessee.

In the first situation, the lease between the structured entity and the lessee was an operating lease and the question was whether the lessee should consolidate the structured entity. In the second situation, the lease between the structured entity and the lessee was a finance lease and the question was whether the junior lender of the structured entity should consolidate the structured entity. In both situations, the consolidation decision would be based on an assessment of whether the entity controls the structured entity. The Interpretations Committee was asked whether the lessee's use of the leased asset was a relevant activity of the structured entity when assessing power over the structured entity.

The Interpretations Committee was of the view that the lessee's right to use the asset for a period of time would not, in isolation, typically give the lessee decision-making rights over the relevant activities of the structured entity and hence would not typically be a relevant activity of the structured entity. This is because on entering into a lease, regardless of whether it is a finance lease or an operating lease, the structured entity (lessor) would have two rights – a right to receive lease payments and a right to the residual value of the leased asset at the end of the lease. Consequently, the activities that would affect the structured entity's returns would relate to managing the returns derived from those rights; for example, managing the credit risk associated with the lease payments or managing the leased asset at the end of the lease term (for example, managing its sale or re-leasing). How the decision-making relating to those activities would significantly affect the structured entity's returns would depend on the particular facts and circumstances.

The Interpretations Committee noted that its conclusion does not mean that a lessee can never control the lessor. For example, a parent that controls another entity for other reasons can lease an asset from that entity. Further, in assessing control, an entity would consider all of the rights that it has in relation to the investee to determine whether it has power over that investee. This would include rights in contractual arrangements other than the lease contract, such as contractual arrangements for loans made to the lessor, as well as rights included within the lease contract, including those that go beyond simply providing the lessee with the right to use the asset.

As a result, the Interpretations Committee concluded that the principles and guidance within IFRS 10 would enable a determination of control to be made based on the relevant facts and circumstances of the scenario and it is not its practice to give case-by-case advice on individual fact patterns. Consequently, the Interpretations Committee concluded that neither an Interpretation nor an amendment to a Standard was required and decided not to add these issues to its agenda.[5]

4.1.4 Management of assets in the event of default

The management of defaults on assets held by a structured entity will frequently be a relevant activity for that entity (see Example 6.5 at 4.1.1 above). However, in practice, if the assets held by the structured entity are bonds, the activities of a decision-maker that is contracted to manage any defaults may be limited to voting at creditors' meetings, as an independent administrator would be appointed to manage the bond default on behalf of all bond holders. Whether the decision-maker has power (i.e. the current ability to direct the management of defaults) or not will probably depend on the size of the structured entity's holding in the individual bonds that have defaulted. The greater the holding, the more likely the decision-maker may be able to control decision-making in a creditors' meeting.

4.2 Existing rights

Once the relevant activities are identified, the next step is to determine which investor, if any, has the current ability to direct those activities (i.e. who has the power). Sometimes, assessing power is straightforward, such as when power over an investee is obtained directly and solely from the voting rights that stem from holding voting interests (e.g. shares), and can be assessed by considering the voting rights from those shareholdings. In other cases, the assessment is more complex and requires many factors to be considered (e.g. instances when power is embedded in one or more contractual arrangements). *[IFRS 10.11]*.

Power arises from rights. To have power over an investee, an investor must have existing rights that give the investor the current ability to direct the relevant activities. The rights that may give an investor power can differ between investees. *[IFRS 10.B14]*.

Examples of rights that, either individually or in combination, can give an investor power include but are not limited to:

(a) rights in the form of voting rights (or potential voting rights) of an investee;

(b) rights to appoint, reassign or remove members of an investee's key management personnel who have the ability to direct the relevant activities;

(c) rights to appoint or remove another entity that directs the relevant activities;

(d) rights to direct the investee to enter into, or veto any changes to, transactions for the benefit of the investor; and

(e) other rights (such as decision-making rights specified in a management contract) that give the holder the ability to direct the relevant activities. *[IFRS 10.B15]*.

Generally, when an investee has a range of operating and financing activities that significantly affect the investee's returns and when substantive decision-making with respect to these activities is required continuously, it will be voting or similar rights that give an investor power, either individually or in combination with other arrangements. *[IFRS 10.B16]*.

4.2.1 Evaluating whether rights are substantive

For a right to convey power, it must provide the current ability to direct the relevant activities. An investor, in assessing whether it has power, considers only substantive rights relating to the investee (held by the investor and others). For a right to be substantive, the holder must have the practical ability to exercise the right. *[IFRS 10.B22]*. An investor that holds only protective rights (see 4.2.2 below) does not have power over an investee, and consequently does not control the investee. *[IFRS 10.14]*. Whether rights are substantive depends on facts and circumstances. The table below (although not exhaustive) describes the factors that should be considered. *[IFRS 10.B23]*.

Figure 6.4: Factors to consider in assessing whether a right is substantive

Factors	Examples
• Are there barriers (economic, operational or otherwise) that would prevent (or deter) the holder(s) from exercising their right(s)?	• Financial penalties • High exercise or conversion price • Narrow exercise periods • Absence of a mechanism to exercise • Lack of information to exercise • Lack of other parties willing or able to take over or provide specialist services • Legal or regulatory barriers (e.g. where a foreign investor is prohibited from exercise)
• Do the holders have the practical ability to exercise their rights, when exercise requires agreement by more than one investor?	• The more parties necessary to come together to exercise this right, the less likely that the right is substantive • A mechanism is in place that provides those parties with the practical ability to exercise their rights collectively if they choose to do so • An independent board of directors may serve as a mechanism for numerous investors to act collectively in exercising their rights
• Would the investor that holds the rights benefit from their exercise or conversion?	• A potential voting right is in-the-money • An investor would obtain benefits from synergies between the investor and the investee

To be substantive, rights also need to be exercisable when decisions about the direction of the relevant activities need to be made. Usually, to be substantive, the rights need to be currently exercisable. However, sometimes rights can be substantive, even though the rights are not currently exercisable. *[IFRS 10.B24]*. This is illustrated by IFRS 10, *[IFRS 10.B24 Example 3-3D]*, as reflected in Example 6.7 below.

Example 6.7: Rights exercisable when decisions need to be made

An investee has annual shareholder meetings at which decisions to direct the relevant activities are made. The next scheduled shareholders' meeting is in eight months. However, shareholders that individually or collectively hold at least 5% of the voting rights can call a special meeting to change the existing policies over the relevant activities, but a requirement to give notice to the other shareholders means that such a meeting cannot be held for at least 30 days. Policies over the relevant activities can be changed only at special or scheduled shareholders' meetings. This includes the approval of material sales of assets as well as the making or disposing of significant investments.

The above fact pattern applies to each scenario described below. Each scenario is considered in isolation.

Scenario A

An investor holds a majority of the voting rights in the investee. The investor's voting rights are substantive because the investor is able to make decisions about the direction of the relevant activities when they need to be made. The fact that it takes 30 days before the investor can exercise its voting rights does not stop the investor from having the current ability to direct the relevant activities from the moment the investor acquires the shareholding.

Scenario B

An investor is party to a forward contract to acquire the majority of shares in the investee. The forward contract's settlement date is in 25 days. The existing shareholders are unable to change the existing policies over the relevant activities because a special meeting cannot be held for at least 30 days, at which point the forward contract will have been settled. Thus, the investor has rights that are essentially equivalent to the majority shareholder in scenario A above (i.e. the investor holding the forward contract can make decisions about the direction of the relevant activities when they need to be made). The investor's forward contract is a substantive right that gives the investor the current ability to direct the relevant activities even before the forward contract is settled.

Scenario C

An investor holds a substantive option to acquire the majority of shares in the investee that is exercisable in 25 days and is deeply in the money. The same conclusion would be reached as in scenario B.

Scenario D

An investor is party to a forward contract to acquire the majority of shares in the investee, with no other related rights over the investee. The forward contract's settlement date is in six months. In contrast to the scenarios A to C above, the investor does not have the current ability to direct the relevant activities. The existing shareholders have the current ability to direct the relevant activities because they can change the existing policies over the relevant activities before the forward contract is settled.

This example illustrates that an investor with the current ability to direct the relevant activities has power even if its rights to direct have yet to be exercised. Evidence that the investor has been directing relevant activities can help determine whether the investor has power, but such evidence is not, in itself, conclusive in determining whether the investor has power over an investee. *[IFRS 10.12]*.

It should be noted that an investor in assessing whether it has power needs to consider substantive rights held by other parties. Substantive rights exercisable by other parties can prevent an investor from controlling the investee to which those rights relate. Such substantive rights do not require the holders to have the ability to initiate decisions. As long as the rights are not merely protective (see 4.2.2 below), substantive rights held by other parties may prevent the investor from controlling the investee even if the rights give the holders only the current ability to approve or block decisions that relate to the relevant activities. *[IFRS 10.B25]*.

It is important to remember that the purpose and design of an investee is critical when assessing whether a right is substantive. For example, the following should be considered when evaluating whether an investor's rights are substantive:

- Why were the rights granted?
- What compensation was given (or received) for the right? Does that compensation reflect fair value?
- Did other investors also receive this right? If not, why?

These questions should be considered both when a right is first granted, but also if an existing right is modified.

To be substantive and convey power, a right must give the investor the 'current ability' to direct the investee's relevant activities. However, 'current ability' does not always mean 'able to be exercised this instant'. The concept of 'current ability' is discussed more in the context of potential voting rights at 4.3.4 below.

4.2.2 Evaluating whether rights are protective

In evaluating whether rights give an investor power over an investee, the investor has to assess whether its rights, and rights held by others, are protective rights. *[IFRS 10.B26].* Under IFRS 10, protective rights are defined as 'rights designed to protect the interest of the party holding those rights without giving that party power over the entity to which those rights relate'. *[IFRS 10 Appendix A].*

Since power is an essential element of control, protective rights do not provide the investor control over the investee. *[IFRS 10.14].* In addition, holding protective rights cannot prevent another investor from having power over an investee. *[IFRS 10.B27].*

Protective rights are typically held to prohibit fundamental changes in the activities of an investee that the holder does not agree with and usually only apply in exceptional circumstances (i.e. upon a contingent event). However, the fact that the right to make decisions is contingent upon an event occurring does not mean that the right is always a protective right. *[IFRS 10.B26].* Examples of protective rights include (but are not limited to) the right to:

- restrict an investee from undertaking activities that could significantly change the credit risk of the investee to the detriment of the investor;
- approve an investee's capital expenditures (greater than the amount spent in the ordinary course of business);
- approve an investee's issuance of equity or debt instruments;
- seize assets if an investee fails to meet specified loan repayment conditions; *[IFRS 10.B28]* and
- veto transactions between the investee and a related party.

In some cases, a right might be deemed protective, such as the ability to sell assets of the investee if an investee defaults on a loan, because default is considered an exceptional circumstance. However, in the event that the investee defaults on a loan (or, say, breaches a covenant), the investor holding that right will need to reassess whether that right has become a substantive right that gives the holder power (rather than merely a protective right), based on the change in facts and circumstances. This issue has been raised with the Interpretations Committee which, in September 2013, concluded that reassessment of control is required when facts and circumstances change in such a way that rights, previously determined to be protective, change (for example upon the breach of a covenant in a borrowing arrangement that causes the borrower to be in default). The Interpretations Committee observed that it did not expect significant diversity in practice to develop on this matter and decided not to add the issue to its agenda. In making its conclusion, the Interpretations Committee observed that:

- paragraph 8 of IFRS 10 requires an investor to reassess whether it controls an investee if facts and circumstances indicate that there are changes to one or more of the three elements of control;
- a breach of a covenant that results in rights becoming exercisable constitutes such a change;
- IFRS 10 does not include an exemption for any rights from this need for reassessment; and
- the IASB's redeliberations of this topic during the development of IFRS 10 concluded that rights initially determined to be protective should be included in a reassessment of control whenever facts and circumstances indicate that there are changes to one or more of the three elements of control.[6]

4.2.2.A Veto rights

Whether veto rights held by an investor are merely a protective right or a right that may convey power to the veto holder will depend on the nature of the veto rights. If the veto rights relate to changes to operating and financing policies that significantly affect the investee's returns, the veto right may not merely be a protective right.

Other veto rights that are common, and are typically protective (because they rarely significantly affect the investee's returns) include veto rights over changes to:

- amendments to articles of incorporation;
- location of investee headquarters;
- name of investee;
- auditors; and
- accounting principles for separate reporting of investee operations.

4.2.2.B Franchises

Many have questioned how to consider franchise rights, and whether they give power (to the franchisor), or whether they are merely protective rights. IFRS 10 notes that a franchise agreement for which the investee is the franchisee often gives the franchisor rights that are designed to protect the franchise brand. Franchise agreements typically give franchisors some decision-making rights with respect to the operations of the franchisee. *[IFRS 10.B29].*

The standard goes on to say that, generally, franchisors' rights do not restrict the ability of parties other than the franchisor to make decisions that have a significant effect on the franchisee's returns. Nor do the rights of the franchisor in franchise agreements necessarily give the franchisor the current ability to direct the activities that significantly affect the franchisee's returns. *[IFRS 10.B30].*

It is necessary to distinguish between having the current ability to make decisions that significantly affect the franchisee's returns and having the ability to make decisions that protect the franchise brand. The franchisor does not have power over the franchisee if other parties have existing rights that give them the current ability to direct the relevant activities of the franchisee. *[IFRS 10.B31].*

Chapter 6

By entering into the franchise agreement the franchisee has made a unilateral decision to operate its business in accordance with the terms of the franchise agreement, but for its own account. *[IFRS 10.B32]*.

Control over such fundamental decisions as the legal form of the franchisee and its funding structure often are not made by the franchisor and may significantly affect the returns of the franchisee. The lower the level of financial support provided by the franchisor and the lower the franchisor's exposure to variability of returns from the franchisee the more likely it is that the franchisor has only protective rights. *[IFRS 10.B33]*.

When analysing whether a franchisor has power over a franchisee, it is necessary to consider the purpose and design of the franchisee. The assessment of whether a franchisor has power hinges on the determination of the relevant activities, and which investor (the franchisor or owner of the franchisee) has the current ability to direct that activity through its rights. The rights held by the franchisor must be evaluated to determine if they are substantive, (i.e. the franchisor has the practical ability to exercise its rights when decisions of the relevant activities need to be made so that it has the current ability to direct the relevant activities), or whether they are merely protective rights. A determination will need to be made in each case, based on the specific facts and circumstances. This is illustrated in Example 6.8 below.

Example 6.8: Rights held by franchisor

A franchisor has certain rights that are designed to protect its brand when it is being licensed by a franchisee. Activities that significantly affect the franchisee's returns include:

- determining or changing its operating policies;
- setting its prices for selling goods;
- selecting suppliers;
- purchasing goods and services;
- selecting, acquiring or disposing of equipment;
- appointing, remunerating or terminating the employment of key management personnel; and
- financing the franchise.

If certain of the activities above are directed by one investor (e.g. the owners of the franchisee), and other activities are directed by another investor (e.g. the franchisor), then the investors will need to determine which activity most significantly affects the franchisee's returns, as discussed at 4.1 above.

4.2.2.C Budget approval rights

Approval rights over budgets are fairly common in shareholders' agreements and form part of the assessment as to the level of power held by investors. If the budget approval rights held by a shareholder (or other investee) are viewed as substantive, that might indicate that the entity having those rights has power over an investee.

However, the purpose and design of arrangements is key to the analysis of who has power. Therefore, the right to approve budgets should not automatically be considered substantive but should be based on a careful consideration of the facts and circumstances. Factors to consider in assessing whether budget approval rights are substantive or protective include (but are not limited to):

- the level of detail of the budget that is required to be approved;
- whether the budget covers the relevant activities of the entity;

- whether previous budgets have been challenged and if so, the practical method of resolution;
- whether there are any consequences of budgets not being approved (e.g. may the operator/directors be removed?);
- whether the entity operates in a specialised business for which only the operator/directors have the specialised knowledge required to draw up the budget;
- who appoints the operator and/or key management personnel of the investee; and
- the nature of the counterparty with budget approval rights and their practical involvement in the business.

4.2.2.D Independent directors

In some jurisdictions, there are requirements that an entity appoints directors who are 'independent'. The phrase 'independent director' has a variety of meanings in different jurisdictions but generally means a director who is independent of a specific shareholder. In some situations, a majority of directors of an entity may be 'independent'.

The fact that a majority of directors of an entity are 'independent' does not mean that no shareholder controls an entity. IFRS 10 requires that all facts and circumstances be considered and in the context of an entity with independent directors it is necessary to determine the role that those directors have in decisions about the relevant activities of the entity. The power to appoint and remove independent directors should be considered as part of this assessment.

Similarly, an entity may have more than one governing body and it should not be assumed that because one body (which may consist of a majority of independent directors) has oversight of another this means that the supervisory body is the one that makes decisions about the relevant activities of the entity.

4.2.3 Incentives to obtain power

There are many incentives to obtain rights that convey power; generally, the more exposure to variable returns (whether positive or negative), the greater that incentive. IFRS 10 notes this in two contexts:

- the greater an investor's exposure, or rights, to variability of returns from its involvement with an investee, the greater the incentive for the investor to obtain rights sufficient to give it power. Therefore, having a large exposure to variability of returns is an indicator that the investor may have power. However, the extent of the investor's exposure is not determinative regarding whether an investor has power over the investee; *[IFRS 10.B20]* and
- an investor may have an explicit or implicit commitment to ensure that an investee continues to operate as designed. Such a commitment may increase the investor's exposure to variability of returns and thus increase the incentive for the investor to obtain rights sufficient to provide it with power. Therefore, a commitment to ensure that an investee operates as designed may be an indicator that the investor has power, but does not, by itself, give an investor power, nor does it prevent another party from having power. *[IFRS 10.B54].*

Thus, even though there may be an incentive to obtain rights that convey power when there is an exposure to variable returns, that incentive, by itself, does not represent power. Rather, the investor must analyse whether it actually does have power through existing rights, which might be in the form of voting rights, or rights through a contractual agreement, as discussed at 4.3 and 4.4 below respectively.

4.3 Voting rights

Power stems from existing rights. Often an investor has the current ability, through voting or similar rights, to direct the relevant activities. *[IFRS 10.B34]*.

In many cases, assessing power can be straightforward. This is often the case when, after understanding the purpose and design of the investee, it is determined that power over an investee is obtained directly and solely from the proportionate voting rights that stem from holding equity instruments, such as ordinary shares in the investee. In this case, in the absence of evidence to the contrary, the assessment of control focuses on which party, if any, is able to exercise voting rights sufficient to determine the investee's operating and financing policies. In the most straightforward case, the investor that holds a majority of those voting rights, in the absence of any other factors, controls the investee. *[IFRS 10.B6]*.

Nevertheless, when taking into account other factors relating to voting rights, an investor can have power even if it holds less than a majority of the voting rights of an investee. An investor can have power with less than a majority of the voting rights of an investee, for example, through:

(a) a contractual arrangement between the investor and other vote holders (see 4.3.5 below);

(b) rights arising from other contractual arrangements (see 4.3.6 below);

(c) the investor's voting rights being sufficient (see 4.3.3 below);

(d) potential voting rights (see 4.3.4 below); or

(e) a combination of (a)-(d). *[IFRS 10.B38]*.

If the relevant activities of an investee are directed through voting rights, an investor needs to consider the requirements of IFRS 10 in relation to such matters as discussed below. *[IFRS 10.B34]*.

In addition, an investor can have control over an investee when it has less than the majority of voting rights but has the practical ability to direct the relevant activities unilaterally (*de facto* control). See 4.3.3 below.

4.4 below discusses cases when voting rights are *not* the right that gives power over an investee.

4.3.1 Power with a majority of the voting rights

In many cases, the legal environment or corporate structure dictate that the relevant activities are directed by the agreement of shareholders who hold more than half of the voting rights of the investee. Alternatively, a governing body, e.g. a Board of Directors, might make decisions regarding the investee and that Board might be appointed by whoever has the majority of the voting rights to direct an investee's relevant activities.

In both cases, when one investor has more than half the voting rights, it has power, assuming that no other facts and circumstances are relevant. *[IFRS 10.B35]*.

However, there may be other facts and circumstances that are relevant, as discussed at 4.3.2 below. In addition, any potential voting rights need to be considered (see 4.3.4 below).

4.3.2 A majority of voting rights without power

In some cases, voting rights do *not* provide the holder the power to direct the relevant activities. This might be the case, when:

- relevant activities are directed by another party with existing rights under a contract, and that party is not an agent of the investor (see 4.4 below); *[IFRS 10.B36]*
- voting rights are not substantive (see 4.2.1 above). For example, if the relevant activities are directed by government, judiciary, administrator, receiver, liquidator, or regulator (see 4.3.2.A below); *[IFRS 10.B37]*
- voting rights have been delegated to a decision-maker, which then holds the voting rights as an agent (see 6 below); or
- voting rights are held as a *de facto* agent of another investor (see 7 below).

4.3.2.A Evaluating voting rights during bankruptcy

Many jurisdictions have laws that offer protection from creditors when an entity is in financial difficulty. For example, an investee in such a position might be placed in the hands of liquidators, receivers or court-appointed managers under a reorganisation plan. Evaluating whether an investor holding the majority of voting rights still has power over an investee in such situations requires the exercise of judgement based on the facts and circumstances. It also requires assessing whether the holder of the voting rights continues to have the current ability to direct the activities that most significantly affect the investee's returns.

In this evaluation, it should be determined whether the shareholders (who hold voting rights) can still direct the operating and financial policies of the investee (assuming that this is the relevant activity), once the investee enters into bankruptcy proceedings. Alternatively, the bankruptcy court (or trustee, or administrator) may direct operating and financial policies. Consideration should be given to the following:

- Who appoints management during the bankruptcy period?
- Who directs management (e.g. the shareholders, or a trustee for the creditors)?
- Does management have to seek approval from parties besides the shareholders (e.g. for significant and/or unusual transactions)?
- Who negotiates the plan of reorganisation?

Even if it appears that the shareholders retain power once the investee enters bankruptcy (i.e. they retain the current ability to direct the relevant activities), this does not mean that a majority shareholder automatically controls the investee. This is because the shareholder may not have any exposure to variable returns (see 5 below), or the ability to affect its returns through its power (see 6 below), which are the other two criteria for having control. Depending on the facts and circumstances, a shareholder might lose power (or control) when the investee files for bankruptcy protection, or when the investee exits from bankruptcy. Determining the appropriate method of accounting for the interest in the investee upon loss of power (or control) requires careful consideration of the nature of the rights and interests, such as whether the shareholder has significant influence over the investee, in which case it would apply the equity method under IAS 28 – see Chapter 11. Alternatively, if the investor does not have significant influence, it would likely account for its investment in the investee as a financial instrument under IFRS 9 (or IAS 39).

When an investee files for bankruptcy, parties holding other rights with respect to that investee might also have to consider whether the control assessment has changed. For example, a right that was previously deemed protective (such as the right to appoint an administrator in the event of a bankruptcy – a right that is frequently held by creditors), may be considered to be a right that now gives power. Alternatively, the trustee itself might have power, through its ability to direct the activities of the investee in bankruptcy.

4.3.3 *Power without a majority of voting rights (de facto control)*

An investor might have control over an investee even when it has less than a majority of the voting rights of that investee if its rights are sufficient to give it power when the investor has the practical ability to direct the relevant activities unilaterally (a concept known as '*de facto* control'). *[IFRS 10.B41]*.

When assessing whether an investor's voting rights are sufficient to give it power, an investor considers all facts and circumstances, including:

(a) the size of the investor's holding of voting rights relative to the size and dispersion of holdings of the other vote holders, noting that:
  - (i) the more voting rights an investor holds, the more likely the investor is to have existing rights that give it the current ability to direct the relevant activities;
  - (ii) the more voting rights an investor holds relative to other vote holders, the more likely the investor is to have existing rights that give it the current ability to direct the relevant activities; and
  - (iii) the more parties that would need to act together to outvote the investor, the more likely the investor is to have existing rights that give it the current ability to direct the relevant activities;

(b) potential voting rights held by the investor, other vote holders or other parties;

(c) rights arising from other contractual arrangements; and

(d) any additional facts and circumstances that indicate the investor has, or does not have, the current ability to direct the relevant activities at the time that decisions need to be made, including voting patterns at previous shareholders' meetings. *[IFRS 10.B42]*.

In addition, IFRS 10 states that if it is not clear that the investor has power, having considered the factors above, then the investor does not control the investee. *[IFRS 10.B46]*.

Whether an investor should include voting rights held by related parties not controlled by the investor (e.g. shareholdings held by its parent, sister companies, associates or shareholdings held by key management personnel or other individuals who are related parties) would depend on the specific facts and circumstances (i.e. whether the related parties are *de facto* agents of the investor). See 7 below.

Potential voting rights and rights arising from other contractual arrangements are discussed at 4.3.4 to 4.3.6 below, respectively. *De facto* control is discussed in more detail below.

IFRS 10 includes several examples illustrating the assessment of power when an investor has less than a majority of voting rights. Some of these are summarised in Examples 6.9 to 6.12 below. Our variation is introduced in Example 6.13 below. In each of the examples, it is assumed that, after understanding the purpose and design of the investee:

- voting rights give an investor the ability to direct activities that most significantly affect the investee's returns (i.e. voting rights give power);
- none of the shareholders has arrangements to consult any of the other shareholders or make collective decisions;
- decisions require the approval of a majority of votes cast at the shareholders' meeting; and
- no other facts or circumstances are relevant.

When the direction of relevant activities is determined by majority vote and an investor holds significantly more voting rights than any other party, and the other shareholdings are widely dispersed, it may be clear, after considering the factors listed in (a)-(c) above alone, that the investor has power over the investee. *[IFRS 10.B43]*. This is illustrated in Example 6.9 below (although factors (b) and (c) are not applicable).

Example 6.9: Less than a majority of voting rights (1)

A holds 48% of the voting rights of B; the remaining 52% of B is widely held by thousands of shareholders (none of whom holds more than 1% of the voting rights).

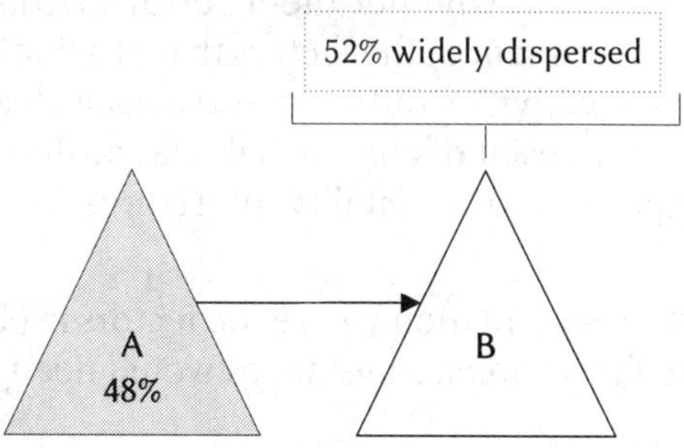

A has power over B, because A has a dominant voting interest (based on the absolute size of its holding, and relative to other shareholders), and a large number of shareholders would have to agree to outvote A. *[IFRS 10.B43 Example 4]*.

In other situations, it may be clear after considering the factors listed in (a)-(c) above alone that an investor does not have power. *[IFRS 10.B44]*. This is illustrated in Example 6.10 below (although factors (b) and (c) are not applicable).

Example 6.10: Less than a majority of voting rights (2)

C holds 45% of the voting rights in D. The other 55% of D is held by two shareholders (each holds 26%), with the remaining 3% held by three other shareholders, each holding 1%.

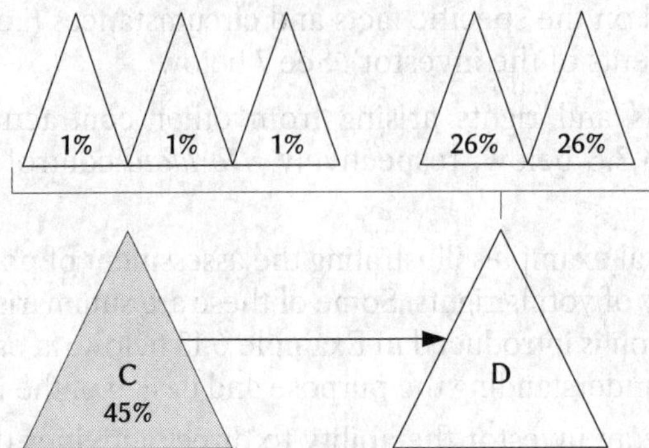

C does *not* have power over D, because the two remaining significant shareholders (i.e. a relatively small number) could easily cooperate to outvote C. The size of C's holding, and size of that holding relative to other shareholders, would *not* give it power. *[IFRS 10.B44 Example 6].*

However, the factors listed in (a)-(c) above alone may not be conclusive. If an investor, having considered those factors, is unclear whether it has power, it considers additional facts and circumstances, such as whether other shareholders are passive in nature as demonstrated by voting patterns at previous shareholders' meetings. When evaluating past voting patterns, significant judgement will be required to determine how far back to review. Judgement will also be required to determine whether past voting patterns may have been influenced by conditions that existed at a point in time, such as how well the entity was operating during the periods reviewed. For example, if an entity was profitable and operating smoothly, other shareholders may have been less motivated to exercise their voting rights.

The fewer voting rights the investor holds, and the fewer parties that would need to act together to outvote the investor, the more reliance would be placed on the additional facts and circumstances to assess whether the investor's rights are sufficient to give it power. This includes the assessment of the factors that provide evidence of the practical ability to direct the relevant activities of the investee, as well as the indicators that the investor may have power as a result of any special relationship with the investee or due to the extent of its exposure to variability of returns as discussed at 4.5 below. *[IFRS 10.B45].*

Example 6.11 below illustrates a situation where the factors in (a)-(c) above alone are not conclusive, and therefore facts and circumstances would need to be considered.

Example 6.11: Less than a majority of voting rights (3)

E holds 45% of the voting rights in F. The rest of F is dispersed among 11 investors, who each hold 5%.

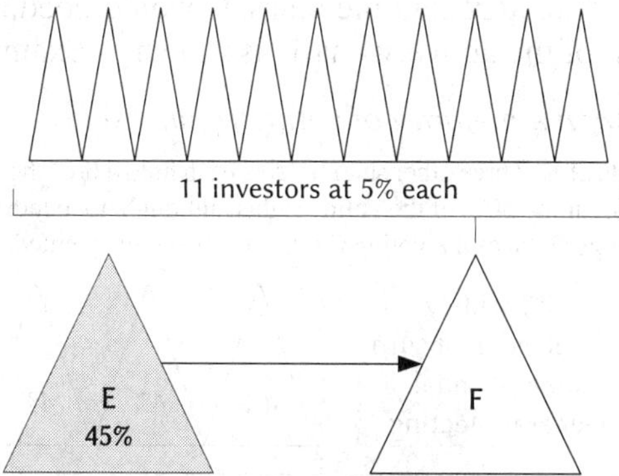

The size of E's holding and the dispersion of the other shareholders are *not* conclusive in determining whether E has power over F. Other relevant facts and circumstances (such as those discussed at 4.5 below) would be considered to determine whether E has power over F. *[IFRS 10.B45 Example 7].*

Comparing Examples 6.10 and 6.11 above illustrates the judgement that will need to be applied in determining whether an investor has power. The IASB considers that it may be easy for two other shareholders to act together to outvote an investor (as in Example 6.10 above), but that it may be more difficult for 11 other shareholders to act together to outvote an investor (as in Example 6.11 above). Where is the line between these two situations?

Example 6.12 below illustrates a situation where additional facts and circumstances need to be considered. For example, this may include whether other shareholders are passive in nature as demonstrated by voting patterns at previous shareholders' meetings.

Example 6.12: Less than a majority of voting rights (4)

G holds 35% of the voting rights in H. Three other shareholders each hold 5% of the voting rights of H. The remaining 50% of the voting rights are held by numerous other shareholders, none individually holding more than 1% of the voting rights. At recent shareholders' meetings, 75% of the voting rights have been represented (including G).

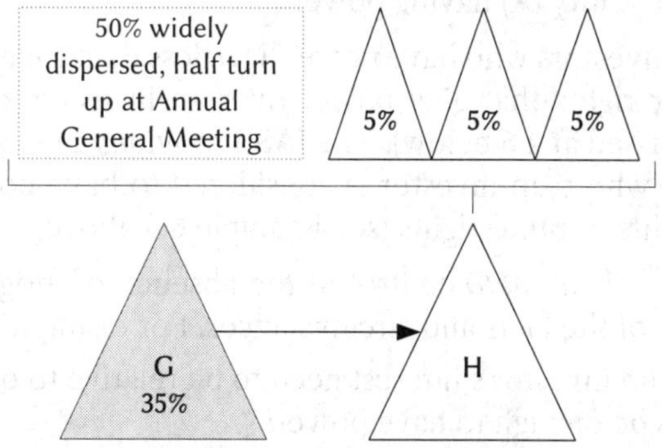

G does not have power over H because the size of G's holding relative to other shareholders, when considering their active participation at recent shareholders' meetings, does not give G the current ability to direct the activities of H. This would be the case regardless of whether there is evidence that G directed H in the past, or whether other shareholders voted in the same way as G. *[IFRS 10.B45 Example 8].*

In Example 6.12 above, G cannot have power because it does not have, at a minimum, more than half the votes of shareholders that have turned up at recent meetings. That is, since 75% have turned up at recent meetings, G would need a minimum of 37.5% to have power. A variation of the above scenario is shown in Example 6.13 below.

Example 6.13: Less than a majority of voting rights (5)

J holds 38% of the voting rights of K. Three other shareholders each hold 4% of the voting rights of K. Numerous other shareholders hold the remaining 50% of the voting rights, although none individually holds more than 1%. At recent shareholders' meetings, 75% of the voting rights have been represented, including J.

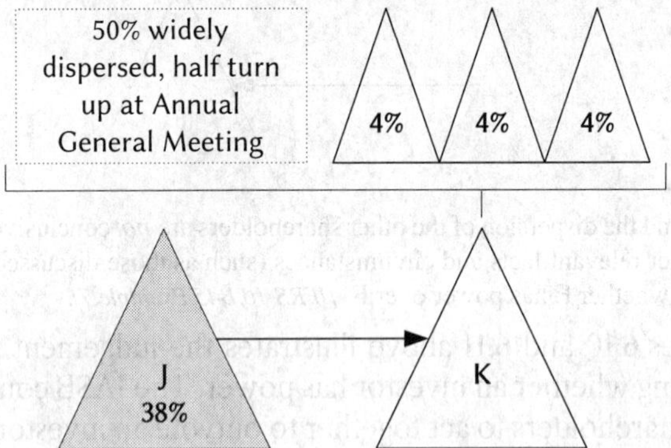

There are diverse views regarding the conclusion on this fact pattern, and judgement will need to be applied in practice. Some believe that J has power, because it has more than half the voting rights of those who have turned up at recent shareholder meetings. (J has more than half the voting rights, because J holds 38%, which is more than 37.5%, or half of 75%). Others believe that it is inconclusive whether J has power, because, while J has more than half the voting rights of those who have turned up at recent shareholder meetings, this is just barely the case. Contrast this fact pattern with Example 6.9 above, where IFRS 10 concludes that, after all relevant facts and circumstances have been considered, holding 48% in combination with remaining ownership that is widely dispersed results in an entity (A) having power.

It is uncommon that investors who have power have less than a majority of voting rights without having other rights that give power over an investee, or other evidence of power (which is discussed at 4.5 below). The IASB provides an example in IFRS 10 that illustrates a situation where an investor is considered to have power with less than a majority of voting rights or other rights (see Example 6.9 above).

Applying the concept of *de facto* control in the absence of 'bright lines' will require significant judgement of the facts and circumstances. For example:

- How large does an investor's interest need to be relative to others? Would 40% of the voting rights be enough to have power?
- How widely dispersed are the other investors? Could three shareholders easily act together?

- Are past voting patterns expected to be indicative of future voting patterns? How much history would be needed to make an assessment?
- Are there other relevant agreements between shareholders?

Generally, the lower the percentage held by one investor (the dominant shareholder, in Examples 6.9 to 6.13 above), the less likely that investor has *de facto* control.

Although perhaps rare, an investor could find itself in control of an investee simply because of circumstances that exist at a point in time, rather than because of deliberate action (see 9.3 below). In addition, while it may be easy to use hindsight to determine whether an investor had (or has) control, it might be difficult to apply this principle on a real-time basis. Information will need to be gathered and analysed (e.g. how widely dispersed are the other shareholders), so that management can reach a timely conclusion. It will also be necessary to monitor the changes in the profile of the other shareholders as this could mean that the investor has gained or lost power over the investee (see 9.3 below).

4.3.4 Potential voting rights

When assessing whether it has power over an investee, an investor also considers the potential voting rights that it holds, as well as potential voting rights held by others. Common examples of potential voting rights include options, forward contracts, and conversion features of a convertible instrument. Those potential voting rights are considered only if the rights are substantive (see 4.2.1 above). *[IFRS 10.B47]*. In the remainder of this section, reference is made to 'options', but the concepts apply to all potential voting rights.

When considering potential voting rights, an investor considers the purpose and design of the entity, including the rights associated with the instrument, as well as those arising from any other involvement the investor has with the investee. This includes an assessment of the various terms and conditions of the instrument as well as the investor's apparent expectations, motives and reasons for agreeing to those terms and conditions. *[IFRS 10.B48]*.

If the investor also has voting or other decision-making rights relating to the investee's activities, the investor assesses whether those rights, in combination with potential voting rights, give the investor power. *[IFRS 10.B49]*.

Substantive potential voting rights alone, or in combination with other rights, may provide an investor the current ability to direct the relevant activities. *[IFRS 10.B50]*. For example, if an investor has less than a majority of voting rights, but holds a substantive option that, if exercised, would give the investor a majority of voting rights, that investor would likely have power. *[IFRS 10.B42, B50]*. Example 6.14 below illustrates when holding an option would likely give an investor power.

Example 6.14: Potential voting rights (1)

A holds 40% of the voting rights of B, and holds a currently exercisable in-the-money option to acquire a further 20% of the voting rights of B.

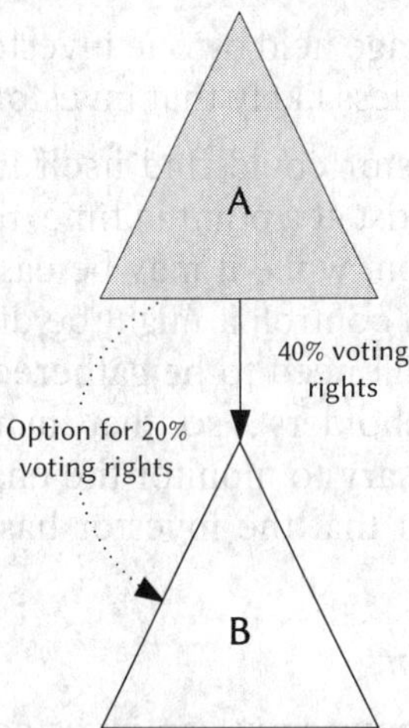

Assuming that voting rights give power over B, the option is substantive and no other facts and circumstances are relevant to this assessment, A would likely have power over B, because A can currently exercise its right to obtain a majority of B's voting shares at any time.

The opposite is also true. If an investor holds a majority of the voting rights, but those voting rights are subject to a substantive option held by another investor, the majority shareholder would likely not have power.

Another example provided by IFRS 10 of a situation where substantive potential voting rights, in combination with other rights, can give an investor the current ability to direct the relevant activities is reflected in Example 6.15 below.

Example 6.15: Potential voting rights (2)

Investor A and two other investors each hold a third of the voting rights of an investee. The investee's business activity is closely related to investor A. In addition to its equity instruments, investor A also holds debt instruments that are convertible into ordinary shares of the investee at any time for a fixed price that is out of the money (but not deeply out of the money). If the debt were converted, investor A would hold 60% of the voting rights of the investee. Investor A would benefit from realising synergies if the debt instruments were converted into ordinary shares. Investor A has power over the investee because it holds voting rights of the investee together with substantive potential voting rights that give it the current ability to direct the relevant activities. *[IFRS 10.B50 Example 10].*

IFRS 10 is silent on whether the intention of the holder (i.e. whether the holder intends to exercise the option or not) is considered in the assessment of potential voting rights. However, IFRS 10 is clear that power arises from rights *per se* and the ability those rights give the investor to direct the relevant activities. *[IFRS 10.B14].* Therefore, an option is only considered in the assessment of power if it is substantive (i.e. the holder has the practical ability to exercise the option when decisions about the direction of relevant activities need to be made). *[IFRS 10.B22, B24, B47].* As discussed at 4.2.1 above, whether an option is substantive depends on facts and circumstances. Common factors to consider when evaluating whether an option is substantive include:

- exercise price or conversion price, relative to market terms;
- ability to obtain financing; and
- timing and length of exercise period.

These factors are each discussed in more detail below, and their implications are indicated in the table below. The evaluation of whether an option is substantive should consider all the factors discussed at 4.2.1 above, rather than limited to only one of the factors.

Figure 6.5: Evaluating whether potential voting rights are substantive

Evaluation	Non-substantive	Depends on facts and circumstances	Substantive
Exercise price	Deeply-out-of-the-money	Out-of-the-money or at market (fair value)	In-the-money
Financial ability to exercise	Holder has no financial ability	Holder would have to raise financing	Holder has cash or financing readily available
Exercise period	Not exercisable	Exercisable before decisions need to be made	Currently exercisable

4.3.4.A Exercise price or conversion price

IFRS 10 is clear that the exercise price (or conversion price) can and should be considered, in evaluating whether an option can give power, because it might represent a barrier to exercise. *[IFRS 10.B23(a)(ii)]*. Factors to consider are:

- deeply-out-of-the-money – Generally, these would be considered non-substantive;
- out-of-the-money (but not deeply) – Judgement will be needed to assess whether the cost of paying more than fair value is worth the potential benefits of exercise, including the exposures to variable returns that are associated with exercising that option (see 5 below for examples of exposures to variable returns);
- at market (fair value) – Consideration should be given as to whether the option conveys rights that differ from those that would be available to third parties in an open market; or
- in-the-money – Generally, in-the-money options would be considered substantive.

IFRS 10 does not define 'deeply-out-of-the-money' or provide a list of indicators for management to consider when exercising judgement in determining whether an option is deeply-out-of-the-money (as opposed to merely out-of-the-money). A call option with a strike price significantly above the value of the underlying interest is normally considered to be deeply-out-of-the-money.

When evaluating the exercise price, consideration is given as to whether the nature of the exercise price (e.g. deeply-out, out, or in-the-money) is expected to remain so for the entire exercise period, or whether the nature of the exercise price may change in the future. That is, the evaluation is not solely based on the nature of the option at inception or as of the end of the reporting period. This is because to convey power, an option must give an investor the current ability to direct the relevant activities when the decisions need to be made. Thus, for example, if an option was deeply-out-of-the-money at the reporting date, but the exercise price was subject to decrease such that the option was expected to become in-the-money before the relevant activities of the investee need to be directed, then the option may be substantive (or *vice versa*). This evaluation will require the exercise of judgement based on all relevant facts and circumstances. As noted above, the evaluation is not solely based on the nature of the option as of the end of the reporting period, i.e. whether a potential voting right is substantive is not based solely on a comparison of the strike or conversion price of the instrument and the then current market price of its underlying share. Although the strike or conversion price is one factor to consider, determining whether potential voting rights are substantive requires a holistic approach, considering a variety of factors. This includes assessing the purpose and design of the instrument, considering whether the investor can benefit for other reasons such as by realising synergies between the investor and the investee, and determining whether there are any barriers (financial or otherwise) that would prevent the holder of potential voting rights from exercising or converting those rights. Accordingly, a change in market conditions (i.e. the market price of the underlying shares) alone would not typically result in a change in the consolidation conclusion. *[IFRS 10.BC124]*.

Example 6.16 below reflects an example from IFRS 10 of an option that is currently exercisable, but is deeply-out-of-the-money and is expected to remain so for the whole of the exercise period. *[IFRS 10.B50 Example 9]*.

Example 6.16: Potential voting rights (3)

Investor A holds 70% of the voting rights of an investee. Investor B has 30% of the voting rights of the investee as well as an option to acquire half of investor A's voting rights. The option is exercisable for the next two years at a fixed price that is deeply out of the money (and is expected to remain so for that two-year period). Investor A has been exercising its votes and is actively directing the relevant activities of the investee. In such a case, investor A is likely to meet the power criterion because it appears to have the current ability to direct the relevant activities. Although investor B has currently exercisable options to purchase additional voting rights (that, if exercised, would give it a majority of the voting rights in the investee), the terms and conditions associated with those options are such that the options are not considered substantive.

4.3.4.B Financial ability

The financial ability of an investor to pay the exercise price should be considered when evaluating whether an option is substantive, because this could be an 'economic barrier' as contemplated by IFRS 10. *[IFRS 10.B23(a)]*. For example, if there is evidence that an investor cannot obtain financing to exercise an in-the-money option, this might indicate that the option is not substantive. However, financial ability is generally considered to be linked to the exercise price, because an investor should be able to obtain financing for an in-the-money option, As such, instances in which an investor would be unable to obtain financing for in-the-money options are expected to be uncommon.

In contrast, it is probably more common that the holder has the financial ability to exercise an option that is out-of-the-money (but not deeply so) and would consider exercising that option to benefit from synergies. This might be the case when the investee has strategic importance to the option holder.

4.3.4.C Exercise period

To have power over an investee, an investor must have existing rights that give the investor the current ability to direct an investee's relevant activities. *[IFRS 10.10]*. This would imply that an option needs to be currently exercisable to give power. However, under IFRS 10, an option can give an investor the current ability to direct an investee's relevant activities even when it is not currently exercisable. Although 'current' often means 'as of today' or 'this instant' in practice, the IASB's use of the term in IFRS 10 broadly refers to the ability to make decisions about an investee's relevant activities when they need to be made. *[IFRS 10.B24]*. This is illustrated in Example 6.17 below.

Example 6.17: Potential voting rights (4)

An investee holds annual shareholder meetings, at which decisions to direct the relevant activities are made. An investor holds an option to acquire the majority of shares in the investee, which is not currently exercisable. However, the option is exercisable before the next scheduled shareholder meeting, and before the next special shareholder meeting could be held (based on the investee's governance policies).

When considering solely the exercise period, the investor's option would be a substantive right that gives the investor power (since it would give the holder a majority of shares). This is because the investor *does have* the current ability to direct the investee's relevant activities when decisions need to be made, i.e. at the next scheduled shareholder meeting or next special shareholder meeting.

However, when concluding whether an investor has power over the investee in real fact patterns, all relevant facts and circumstances would be considered, to evaluate whether the option is substantive, not solely the exercise period.

In contrast, if the next shareholders' meeting occurs (or could be held) before the option is exercisable, that option would not be a right that would give the holder the current ability to direct the investee's activities (and therefore would not give the holder power). This is consistent with the conclusion for Scenario D in Example 6.7 at 4.2.1 above.

IFRS 10 does not contain separate requirements for different types of potential voting rights; that is, employee options are subject to the same requirements as those that are held by a third party. However, it would be unlikely that an option held by an employee would give that employee power (or control) over an investee in practice, usually because the employee options represent a small percentage of the outstanding shares, even if exercised. However, in a very small, privately owned entity it would be possible for an employee (such as a member of management) to have power, if an option gives the employee the current ability to direct the relevant activities, or if the employee has other interests in the investee.

It should be noted that the IASB considered, but did *not* change, similar requirements in IAS 28 related to how options are considered when evaluating whether an investor has significant influence. That is, IAS 28 does not incorporate the IFRS 10 concept of evaluating whether an option is substantive (see Chapter 11 at 4.3). Accordingly, an option might give power under IFRS 10, but the same option might not result in significant influence under IAS 28.

Simply holding a currently exercisable option that, if exercised, would give the investor more than half of the voting rights in an investee is not sufficient to demonstrate control of the investee. All facts and circumstances must be considered to assess whether an investor has power over an investee, including whether an option is substantive (including, but not limited to consideration of the exercise period). This may require considerable judgement to be exercised.

4.3.5 Contractual arrangement with other vote holders

A contractual arrangement between an investor and other vote holders can give the investor the right to exercise voting rights sufficient to give the investor power, even if the investor does not have voting rights sufficient to give it power without the contractual arrangement. However, a contractual arrangement might ensure that the investor can direct enough other vote holders on how to vote to enable the investor to make decisions about the relevant activities. *[IFRS 10.B39]*.

It should be noted that the contractual arrangement has to ensure that investor can direct the other party to vote as required. Where the arrangement is merely that the parties agree to vote the same way, that would only represent joint control; defined as the contractually agreed sharing of control of an arrangement, which exists only when decisions about the relevant activities require the unanimous consent of the parties sharing control. *[IFRS 11 Appendix A]*. Joint control is discussed in more detail in Chapter 12 at 4.

In some jurisdictions, investors holding a certain number of issued shares of a public company may be able to obtain proxy votes from other shareholders by public request or other means for voting at shareholder meetings. The question as to whether the investor has the ability to obtain a majority of votes (and hence power over an investee) through control of proxy votes will depend on the specific facts and circumstances of the process such as, for example, the investor's freedom to use the proxy vote and whether any statements of voting intent must be provided by the investor as a condition of obtaining the proxy vote. A situation where, for example, proxies must be requested each year would make it more difficult to demonstrate that the investor had power as a result of its ability to obtain proxy votes.

4.3.6 Additional rights from other contractual arrangements

Other decision-making rights, in combination with voting rights, can give an investor the current ability to direct the relevant activities. For example, the rights specified in a contractual arrangement in combination with voting rights may be sufficient to give an investor the current ability to direct the manufacturing processes of an investee or to direct other operating or financing activities of an investee that significantly affect the investee's returns. However, in the absence of any other rights, economic dependence of an investee on the investor (such as relations of a supplier with its main customer) does not lead to the investor having power over the investee. *[IFRS 10.B40]*.

Example 6.18 below reflects an example from IFRS 10 of a situation where an investor with less than a majority of the voting rights is considered to have power of the investee, taking into account rights under a contractual arrangement. *[IFRS 10.B43 Example 5]*.

Example 6.18: Less than a majority of voting rights combined with additional rights under a contractual arrangement

Investor A holds 40% of the voting rights of an investee and twelve other investors each hold 5% of the voting rights of the investee. A shareholder agreement grants investor A the right to appoint, remove and set the remuneration of management responsible for directing the relevant activities. To change the agreement, a two-thirds majority vote of the shareholders is required. In this case, investor A concludes that the absolute size of the investor's holding and the relative size of the other shareholdings alone are not conclusive in determining whether the investor has rights sufficient to give it power. However, investor A determines that its contractual right to appoint, remove and set the remuneration of management is sufficient to conclude that it has power over the investee. The fact that investor A might not have exercised this right or the likelihood of investor A exercising its right to select, appoint or remove management shall not be considered when assessing whether investor A has power.

4.4 Contractual arrangements

Power stems from existing rights. Sometimes, the relevant activities are not directed through voting rights, but rather, are directed by other means, such as through one or more contractual arrangements. *[IFRS 10.11].* For example, an investor might have the contractual ability to direct manufacturing processes, operating activities, or determine financing of an investee through a contract or other arrangement.

Similarly, when voting rights cannot have a significant effect on an investee's returns, such as when voting rights relate to administrative tasks only and contractual arrangements determine the direction of the relevant activities, the investor needs to assess those contractual arrangements in order to determine whether it has rights sufficient to give it power over the investee. To determine whether an investor has rights sufficient to give it power, the investor considers the purpose and design of the investee (see paragraphs B5-B8 of IFRS 10 discussed at 3.2 above) and the requirements in paragraphs B51-B54 (discussed below) together with paragraphs B18-B20 (see 4.5 below). *[IFRS 10.B17].*

When these contractual arrangements involve activities that are closely related to the investee, then these activities are, in substance, an integral part of the investee's overall activities, even though they may occur outside the legal boundaries of the investee. Therefore, explicit or implicit decision-making rights embedded in contractual arrangements that are closely related to the investee need to be considered as relevant activities when determining power over the investee. *[IFRS 10.B52].*

When identifying which investor, if any, has power over an investee, it is important to review the contractual arrangements that the investor and the investee entered into. This analysis should include the original formation documents and governance documents of the investee, as well as the marketing materials provided to investors and other contractual arrangements entered into by the investee.

It is common that the relevant activities of a structured entity are directed by contractual arrangement. This is discussed further at 4.4.1 below.

4.4.1 Structured entities

IFRS 12 defines a structured entity as an entity that has been designed so that voting or similar rights are not the dominant factor in deciding who controls the entity, such as when any voting rights relate to administrative tasks only and the relevant activities are directed by means of contractual arrangements. *[IFRS 12 Appendix A]*. Therefore, an entity that is controlled by voting rights is not a structured entity. Accordingly, although it might be thought that an entity that receives funding from third parties following a restructuring is a structured entity, this would not be the case, if that entity continues to be controlled by voting rights after the restructuring. *[IFRS 12.B24]*.

A structured entity often has some or all of the following features:

- restricted activities;
- a narrow and well-defined objective, such as:
  - holding a tax-efficient lease;
  - carrying out research and development activities;
  - funding an entity; or
  - providing investment opportunities for investors by passing on risks and rewards associated with assets to investors;
- insufficient equity to finance its activities without subordinated financial support; and
- financing in the form of multiple contractually-linked instruments to investors that create concentrations of credit or other risks (tranches). *[IFRS 12.B22]*.

Examples of structured entities include:

- securitisation vehicles;
- asset-backed financings; and
- some investment funds. *[IFRS 12.B23]*.

Management needs to evaluate whether it controls a structured entity using the same approach as for 'traditional entities' (those that are controlled through voting rights). That is, management evaluates whether an investor has power over the relevant activities, exposure to variable returns and the ability to affect those returns through its power over the structured entity, as shown in the diagram at 3.1 above. Frequently, as discussed above, the relevant activities of a structured entity are directed by contractual arrangement.

For some investees, relevant activities occur only when particular circumstances arise or events occur. The investee may be designed so that the direction of its activities and its returns are predetermined unless and until those particular circumstances arise or events occur. In this case, only the decisions about the investee's activities when those circumstances or events occur can significantly affect its returns and thus be relevant activities. The circumstances or events need not have occurred for an investor with the ability to make those decisions to have power. The fact that the right to make decisions is contingent on circumstances arising or an event occurring does not, in itself, make those rights protective. *[IFRS 10.B53]*.

This is illustrated in Example 6.19 below, which is summarised from an example included in IFRS 10. *[IFRS 10.B53 Example 11]*.

Example 6.19: Power through contractual arrangements

An investee's only business activity, as specified in its founding documents, is to purchase receivables and service them on a day-to-day basis for its investor. The servicing includes collecting the principal and interest payments as they fall due and passing them on to the investor. For any receivable in default, the investee is required to automatically put the receivable in default to the investor, as contractually agreed in the put agreement between the investor and the investee.

The relevant activity is managing the receivables in default because it is the only activity that can significantly affect the investee's returns. Managing the receivables before default is not a relevant activity because it does not require substantive decisions to be made that could significantly affect the investee's returns – the activities before default are predetermined and amount only to collecting cash flows as they fall due and passing them on to investors.

The purpose and design of the investee gives the investor decision-making authority over the relevant activity. The terms of the put agreement are integral to the overall transaction and the establishment of the investee. Therefore, the put agreement, together with the founding documents of the investee, gives the investor power over the investee. This is the case, even though:

- the investor takes ownership of the receivables only in the event of default; and
- the investor's exposures to variable returns are *not* technically derived from the investee (because the receivables in default are no longer owned by the investee and are managed outside the legal boundaries of the investee).

To conclude whether the investor has control, it would also need to assess whether the other two criteria are met, i.e. it has exposure to variable returns from its involvement with the investee (see 5 below) and the ability to use its power over the investee to affect the amount of its returns (see 6 below). *[IFRS 10.7, B2].*

IFRS 10 also includes a much simpler example where the only assets of an investee are receivables and when the purpose and design of the investee are considered, it is determined that the only relevant activity is managing the receivables upon default. In this situation, the party that has the ability to manage the defaulting receivables has power over the investee, irrespective of whether any of the borrowers have defaulted. *[IFRS 10.B53 Example 12].*

An investor may have an explicit or implicit commitment to ensure that an investee continues to operate as designed. Such a commitment may increase the investor's exposure to variability of returns and thus increase the incentive for the investor to obtain rights sufficient to give it power. Therefore a commitment to ensure that an investee operates as designed may be an indicator that the investor has power, but does not, by itself, give an investor power, nor does it prevent another party from having power. *[IFRS 10.B54].*

Notwithstanding the fact that the same approach is used to evaluate control for structured entities and traditional entities, it is still important to identify which entities are structured entities. This is because certain disclosure requirements of IFRS 12 apply only to structured entities, as discussed in Chapter 13.

4.5 Other evidence of power

In some circumstances, it may be difficult to determine whether an investor's rights give it power over an investee. In such cases, the investor considers other evidence that it has the current ability to direct an investee's relevant activities unilaterally. Consideration is given, but is not limited, to the following factors, which, when considered together with its rights, the indicators of a special relationship with the investee and the extent of the investor's exposure to variability of returns (see below), may provide evidence that the investor's rights are sufficient to give it power over the investee:

- the investor can, without having the contractual right to do so, appoint, approve or nominate the investee's key management personnel (or Board of Directors) who have the ability to direct the relevant activities;
- the investor can, without having the contractual right to do so, direct the investee to enter into, or veto any changes to, significant transactions for the benefit of the investor;
- the investor can dominate either the nominations process for electing members of the investee's governing body, or obtaining proxies from other holders of voting rights;
- the investee's key management personnel are related parties of the investor (for example, the chief executive officer of the investee and the chief executive officer of the investor are the same person); or
- the majority of the members of the investee's governing body are related parties of the investor. *[IFRS 10.B18]*.

When the above factors and the indicators set out below are considered together with an investor's rights, IFRS 10 requires that greater weight is given to the evidence of power described above. *[IFRS 10.B21]*. Sometimes, there will be indications that an investor has a special relationship with the investee, which suggests that the investor has more than a passive interest in the investee. The existence of any individual indicator, or a particular combination of indicators, does not necessarily mean that the power criterion is met. However, having more than a passive interest in an investee may indicate that the investor has other rights that give it power over the investee or provide evidence of existing power over the investee. For example, IFRS 10 states that this might be the case when the investee:

- is directed by key management personnel who are current or previous employees of the investor;
- has significant:
  - obligations that are guaranteed by the investor; or
  - activities that either involve or are conducted on behalf of the investor;
- depends on the investor for:
  - funds for a significant portion of its operations;
  - licenses, trademarks, services, technology, supplies or raw materials that are critical to the investee's operations; or
  - key management personnel, such as when the investor's personnel have specialised knowledge of the investee's operations; or
- the investor's exposure, or rights, to returns from its involvement with the investee is disproportionately greater than its voting or other similar rights. For example, there may be a situation in which an investor is entitled, or exposed, to more than half of the returns of the investee but holds less than half of the voting rights of the investee. *[IFRS 10.B19]*.

As noted at 4.2.3 above, the greater an investor's exposure, or rights, to variability of returns from its involvement with an investee, the greater is the incentive for the investor to obtain rights sufficient to give it power. Therefore, having a large exposure to variability of returns is an indicator that the investor may have power. However, the extent of the investor's exposure does not, in itself, determine whether an investor has power over the investee. *[IFRS 10.B20]*.

4.6 Determining whether sponsoring (designing) a structured entity gives power

IFRS 10 discusses whether sponsoring (that is, designing) a structured entity gives an investor power over the structured entity.

In assessing the purpose and design of an investee, an investor considers the involvement and decisions made at the investee's inception as part of its design and evaluate whether the transaction terms and features of the involvement provide the investor with rights that are sufficient to give it power. Being involved in the design of an investee alone is not sufficient to give an investor control. However, involvement in the design may indicate that the investor had the opportunity to obtain rights that are sufficient to give it power over the investee. *[IFRS 10.B51]*.

An investor's involvement in the design of an investee does not mean that the investor necessarily has control, even if that involvement was significant. Rather, an investor has control of an investee when all three criteria of control are met (see 3.1 above), considering the purpose and design of the investee. Thus, an investor's involvement in the design of an investee is part of the context when concluding if it controls the investee, but is not determinative.

In our view, there are relatively few structured entities that have no substantive decision-making. That is, virtually all structured entities have some level of decision-making and few, if any, are on 'autopilot' (see 4.1.2 above). In such cases, if that decision-making can significantly affect the returns of the structured entity, the investor with the rights to make those decisions would have power. This is because IFRS 10 clarifies that an investor has power when it has existing rights that give it the current ability to direct the relevant activities, even if those relevant activities only occur when particular circumstances arise or specific events occur (see 4.1.1 above).

However, a structured entity with limited decision-making requires additional scrutiny to determine which investor, if any, has power (and possibly control) over the structured entity, particularly for the investors that have a potentially significant explicit or implicit exposure to variable returns. Careful consideration is required regarding the purpose and design of the structured entity.

In addition, the evaluation of power may require an analysis of the decisions made at inception of the structured entity, including a review of the structured entity's governing documents, because the decisions made at formation may affect which investor, if any, has power.

For a structured entity with a limited range of activities, such as certain securitisation entities, power is assessed based on which activities, if any, significantly affect the structured entity's returns, and if so, which investor, if any, has existing rights that give it the current ability to direct those activities. The following considerations may also be relevant when determining which investor, if any, has power (and possibly control):

- an investor's ability to direct the activities of a structured entity only when specific circumstances arise or events occur may constitute power if that ability relates to the activities that most significantly affect the structured entity's returns (see 4.1.1 above);
- an investor does not have to actively exercise its power to have power over a structured entity (see 4.2.1 above); or
- an investor is more incentivised to obtain power over a structured entity the greater its obligation to absorb losses or its right to receive benefits from the structured entity (see 4.2.3 above).

5 EXPOSURE TO VARIABLE RETURNS

The second criterion for assessing whether an investor has control of an investee is determining whether the investor has an exposure, or has rights, to variable returns from its involvement with the investee. *[IFRS 10.B55].* An investor is exposed, or has rights, to variable returns from its involvement with the investee when the investor's returns from its involvement have the potential to vary as a result of the investee's performance. Returns can be positive, negative or both. *[IFRS 10.15].*

Although only one investor can control an investee, more than one party can share in the returns of an investee. For example, holders of non-controlling interests can share in the profits or distributions of an investee. *[IFRS 10.16].*

Variable returns are returns that are not fixed and have the potential to vary as a result of the performance of an investee. As discussed at 5.2 below, returns that appear fixed can be variable. *[IFRS 10.B56].*

Examples of exposures to variable returns include:

- dividends, fixed interest on debt securities that expose the investor to the credit risk of the issuer (see 5.2 below), variable interest on debt securities, other distributions of economic benefits and changes in the value of an investment in an investee;
- remuneration for servicing an investee's assets or liabilities, fees and exposure to loss from providing credit or liquidity support, residual interests in the investee's assets and liabilities on liquidation of that investee, tax benefits and access to future liquidity that an investor has from its involvement with the investee; and
- economies of scale, cost savings, scarce products, proprietary knowledge, synergies, or other exposures to variable returns that are not available to other investors. *[IFRS 10.B57].*

Simply having an exposure to variable returns from its involvement with an investee does not mean that the investor has control. To control the investee, the investor would also need to have power over the investee, and the ability to use its power over the investee to affect the amount of the investor's returns. *[IFRS 10.7].* For example, it is common for a lender to have an exposure to variable returns from a borrower through interest payments that it receives from the borrower, that are subject to credit risk. However, the lender would not control the borrower if it does not have the ability to affect those interest payments (which is frequently the case).

It should be emphasised that with respect to this criterion, the focus is on the existence of an exposure to variable returns, not the amount of the exposure to variable returns.

5.1 Exposure to variable returns can be an indicator of power

Exposure to variable returns can be an indicator of power by the investor. This is because the greater an investor's exposure to the variability of returns from its involvement with an investee, the greater the incentive for the investor to obtain rights that give the investor power. However, the magnitude of the exposure to variable returns is not determinative of whether the investor holds power. *[IFRS 10.B20]*.

When an investor's exposure, or rights, to variable returns from its involvement with the investee are disproportionately greater than its voting or other similar rights, this might be an indicator that the investor has power over the investee when considered with other rights. *[IFRS 10.B19, B20]*.

5.2 Returns that appear fixed can be variable

An investor assesses whether exposures to returns from an investee are variable, based on the substance of the arrangement (regardless of the legal form of the returns). Even a return that appears fixed may actually be variable.

IFRS 10 gives the example of an investor that holds a bond with fixed interest payments. The fixed interest payments are considered an exposure to variable returns, because they are subject to default risk and they expose the investor to the credit risk of the issuer of the bond. How variable those returns are depends on the credit risk of the bond. The same logic would extend to the investor's ability to recover the principal of the bond.

Similarly, IFRS 10 also explains that fixed performance fees earned for managing an investee's assets are considered an exposure to variable returns, because they expose the investor to the performance risk of the investee. That is, the amount of variability depends on the investee's ability to generate sufficient income to pay the fee. *[IFRS 10.B56]*. Performance fees that vary based on the value of an investee's assets are also an exposure to variable returns using the same reasoning.

In contrast, a non-refundable fee received up-front (wherein the investor does not have exposure to credit risk or performance risk) would likely be considered a fixed return.

5.3 Evaluating whether derivatives provide an exposure to variable returns

Investors need to evaluate whether being party to a derivative gives them an exposure to a variable return.

As indicated at 3.2 above, an investee may be designed so that voting rights are not the dominant factor in deciding who controls the investee, such as when any voting rights relate to administrative tasks only and the relevant activities are directed by means of contractual arrangements. In such cases, an investor's consideration of the purpose and design of the investee shall also include consideration of the risks to which the investee was designed to be exposed, the risks that it was designed to pass on to the parties involved with the investee and whether the investor is exposed to some or all of these risks. Consideration of the risks includes not only the downside risk, but also the potential for upside. *[IFRS 10.B8].*

When evaluating whether being party to a derivative is an exposure to a variable return, it is helpful to follow these steps:

- analyse the nature of the risks in the investee – for example, assess whether the purpose and the design of the investee exposes the investor to the following risks:
  - credit risk;
  - interest rate risk (including prepayment risk);
  - foreign currency exchange risk;
  - commodity price risk;
  - equity price risk; and
  - operational risk;
- determine the purpose(s) for which the investee was created – for example, obtain an understanding of the following:
  - activities of the investee;
  - terms of the contracts the investee has entered into;
  - nature of the investee's interests issued;
  - how the investee's interests were negotiated with or marketed to potential investors; and
  - which investors participated significantly in the design or redesign of the entity; and
- determine the variability that the investee is designed to create and pass along to its interest holders – considering the nature of the risks of the investee and the purposes for which the investee was created.

Some might argue that any derivative creates an exposure to variable returns, even if that exposure is only a positive exposure. However, we do not believe that this was the IASB's intention, given the following comments made by the IASB in both the Basis for Conclusions accompanying IFRS 10 and the Application Guidance of IFRS 12.

> 'Some instruments are designed to transfer risk from a reporting entity to another entity. During its deliberations, the Board concluded that such instruments create variability of returns for the other entity but do not typically expose the reporting entity to variability of returns from the performance of the other entity. For example, assume an entity (entity A) is established to provide investment opportunities for investors who wish to have exposure to entity Z's credit risk (entity Z is unrelated to any other party involved in the arrangement). Entity A obtains funding by issuing to those investors notes that are linked to entity Z's credit risk (credit-linked notes) and uses the proceeds to invest in a portfolio of risk-free financial assets. Entity A obtains exposure to entity Z's credit risk by entering into a credit default swap (CDS) with a swap counterparty.

> The CDS passes entity Z's credit risk to entity A, in return for a fee paid by the swap counterparty. The investors in entity A receive a higher return that reflects both entity A's return from its asset portfolio and the CDS fee. The swap counterparty does not have involvement with entity A that exposes it to variability of returns from the performance of entity A because the CDS transfers variability to entity A, rather than absorbing variability of returns of entity A.' *[IFRS 10.BC66, IFRS 12.B9]*.

This principle is applied in the following example.

Example 6.20: Derivatives that create risk for an investee

A structured entity (Entity A) enters into a CDS whereby a bank passes the credit risk of a reference asset to the structured entity and, hence, to the investors of that structured entity. In this example, if the bank has the power to amend the referenced credit risk in the CDS, it would have power over a relevant activity. However, as the bank, through the CDS, creates rather than absorbs risk, the bank is not exposed to a variable return. Consequently, the bank would not be able to use its power to affect its variable returns and so would not control the structured entity.

In our view, a derivative that introduces risk to an investee (e.g. a structured entity) would not normally be considered an exposure to variable returns under IFRS 10. Only a derivative that exposes a counterparty to risks that the investee was designed to create and pass on would be considered an exposure to variable returns under IFRS 10.

This view is consistent with the IASB's intentions. In addition, this view would result in convergence with US GAAP (in most cases). The IASB and FASB have stated that they believe that they have achieved convergence with respect to evaluating control of a structured entity (pending the completion of the FASB's project on principal-agent guidance).[7] It would be difficult to reach converged solutions on many fact patterns involving derivatives and structured entities if the alternative view (that all derivatives create an exposure to variable returns) was taken.

5.3.1 Plain vanilla foreign exchange swaps and interest rate swaps

It is important to consider the purpose and design of the entity when evaluating whether a plain vanilla foreign exchange or interest rate swap should be considered a creator or absorber of variable returns. It is our view that an exposure to variable returns generally absorbs the variability created by the investee's assets, liabilities or other contracts, and the risks the investee was designed to pass along to its investors. Therefore, if a derivative is entered into to reduce the variability of a structured entity's cash flows (such as might arise from movements in foreign currency or interest rates), it is not intended to absorb the cash flows of the entity. Instead, the derivative is entered into to align the cash flows of the assets of the structured entity with those of the investors and so reduce the risks to which the investors in the structured entity are exposed. Accordingly, the counterparty would not have an exposure to a variable return.

Meanwhile, a counterparty to a foreign exchange or interest rate swap typically has a senior claim on any cash flows due under the swap relative to any note holders. Consequently, it is unlikely to be exposed to the credit risk of the assets held by the structured entity, or else that risk will be deemed to be insignificant (i.e. losses on the assets would need to be so large that there would be insufficient funds in the structured entity to settle the derivatives).

However, if payments on a swap were subordinate to the rights of note holders, or contractually referenced to the performance of the underlying assets in the structured entity, the counterparty is exposed to the risk associated with the performance of the underlying assets (i.e. the risk that the structured entity may be unable to fulfil its obligations under the swap). In that case, if the swap counterparty had power over the structured entity because it has the ability to manage its assets, it is likely that it would be deemed to have the ability to affect its variable returns and so would control the structured entity.

The above principles are illustrated in Example 6.21 below.

Example 6.21: Structured entity that enters into foreign currency and interest rate swaps

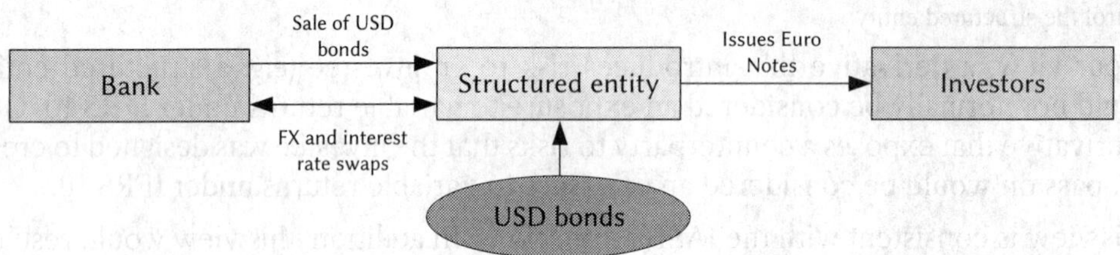

A bank designs a structured entity to meet the requirements of European investors, who wish to be exposed to US corporate bonds without the foreign exchange risk. The structured entity buys dollar-denominated debt securities through the bank, issues Euro-denominated notes and hedges the cash flow differences through a series of swaps entered into with the bank. Subsequently, the structured entity collects and pays the resultant cash flows. The bonds will be held by the structured entity until maturity and cannot be substituted. The bank manages the assets, including in the event of their default and earns a fixed fee for its services. The right to receive the fee ranks more senior than the notes.

Most of the activities of the structured entity are predetermined. It is possible that the relevant activity is the management of the assets in the event of default as discussed at 4.1.4 above. If this is the case, power is held by the bank, since it has the existing rights that give it the current ability to direct this activity. In evaluating the bank's exposure to variable returns from its involvement with the structured entity:

- the foreign currency and interest rate risks were not risks that the structured entity was designed to be exposed to or to pass on to the bank;
- the bank's exposure to movements in foreign exchange and interest rate risks is not affected by its power over the relevant activity;
- the fixed fee that the bank earns is not considered a variable return as its payment is unlikely to be affected by the credit risk of the bonds; and
- the bank's exposure to potential credit risk on its derivatives is considered insignificant, as that risk would only arise if losses on the bonds were so large that there were insufficient funds in the structured entity to settle the derivatives.

In conclusion, even if the bank has power by virtue of managing the defaults (i.e. the relevant activity), the bank has no exposure to variable returns, and thus does not control the structured entity and so would not consolidate it.

5.3.2 Total return swaps

The principles discussed at 5.3.1 above are also relevant where a structured entity enters into a total return swap, since the swap creates an equal, but opposite risk to each party, as illustrated in Example 6.22 below.

Example 6.22: Structured entity that enters into a total return swap

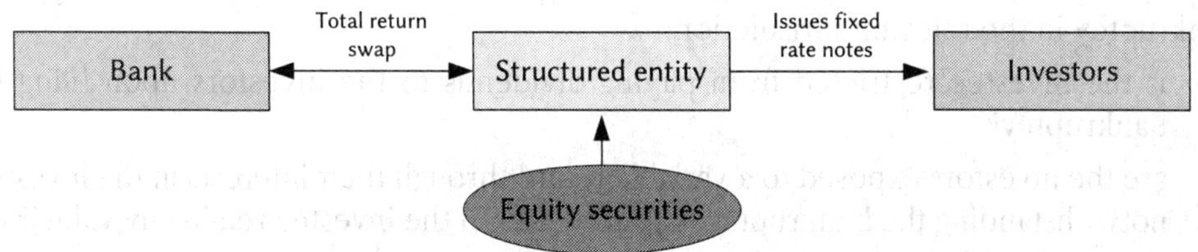

A structured entity acquires a portfolio of equity securities from the market, issues fixed rate notes to investors and hedges the mismatch in cash flows between the equity securities and the notes through entering into a total return swap with a bank. The choice of equity securities that make up the portfolio is pre-agreed by the bank and the note investors. However, the bank also has substitution rights over the equity securities held by the structured entity within certain parameters. The terms of this swap are that the structured entity pays the bank any increase in value of the securities and any dividends received from them, while the bank pays the structured entity any decline in the value of the securities and interest at a fixed rate.

The structured entity was designed to give equity risk to the bank while the note holders earn a fixed rate of interest. The bank's substitution rights over the equity securities is likely the relevant activity, because it may significantly affect the structured entity's returns. Therefore, the bank has power. The bank also has an exposure to variable returns since it absorbs the equity risk. Since it has the ability to use its power to affect its returns from the total return swap, all three criteria for control are met and the bank would consolidate the structured entity.

5.4 Exposures to variable returns not directly received from an investee

When identifying an exposure to variable returns, an investor must include all variable returns resulting from its investment including not only those directly received from the investee but also returns generated as a result of the investment that are not available to other interest holders. *[IFRS 10.B57]*.

Generally, the focus is on the variable returns that are generated by the investee. However, depending on the purpose and design of the arrangements and the investee, when the investor receives variable returns that are not generated by the investee, but stem from involvement with the investee, these variable returns are also considered.

Examples of such variable returns include using assets in combination with the assets of the investee, such as combining operating functions to achieve economies of scale, cost savings, sourcing scare products, gaining access to proprietary knowledge or limiting some operations or assets, to enhance the value of the investor's other assets. *[IFRS 10.B57(c)]*.

5.5 Exposure to variable returns in bankruptcy filings

As discussed at 4.3.2.A above, evaluating whether an investor has control when its investee files for bankruptcy requires the exercise of judgement based on the facts and circumstances. Part of the assessment includes an evaluation of whether the investor has an exposure to variable returns from the investee once the investee files for bankruptcy. For example, based on the requirements for the particular type of bankruptcy in the relevant jurisdiction:

- is the investee restricted from paying dividends to the investors upon filing for bankruptcy?
- are the investors exposed to a variable return through their interests in the investee, notwithstanding the bankruptcy (e.g. do shares in the investee retain any value)?
- do the investors have a loan receivable, or other financial interest in the investee, that is expected to provide a return (or is the loan worthless)?
- do the investors have access to other synergies from the investee?

For an investor to have control, it must also have power (as discussed at 4.3.2.A above) and the ability to use its power over the investee to affect the amount of the investor's returns (see 6 below).

5.6 Interaction of IFRS 10 with the derecognition requirements in IFRS 9 (or IAS 39)

In evaluating whether an entity has an exposure to the variable returns of a structured entity, it is also necessary to consider the interaction with the derecognition requirements set out in IFRS 9 (or IAS 39) (see Chapter 51). Specifically, it is relevant to consider the impact of whether or not the transfer criteria have been satisfied by the transferor on whether a transferor has exposure to variable returns arising from its involvement with a structured entity. The following example will help illustrate this issue.

Example 6.23: Structured entity that enters into a total return swap with the transferor

Assume the same facts as in Example 6.22 at 5.3.2 above, except that the bank originally sold the equity securities to the structured entity (rather than the structured entity acquired the equity securities from the market).

As the bank has, through the total return swap, retained substantially all of the risks and rewards of ownership of the securities, it would not derecognise them. Consequently, the structured entity would not recognise the securities but, instead recognises a loan to the bank, collateralised by the securities. As the bank has not derecognised the securities, it has no variable return from its involvement with the structured entity. Hence, it does not have control of the structured entity and would not consolidate it. The investors have no power over the structured entity, so none of the investors would consolidate it either.

5.7 Reputational risk

The term 'reputational risk' often refers to the risk that failure of an entity could damage the reputation of an investor or sponsor. To protect its reputation, the investor or sponsor might be compelled to provide support to the failing entity, even though it has no legal or contractual obligation to do so. During the financial crisis, some financial institutions stepped in and provided financing for securitisation vehicles that they sponsored, and in some cases took control of these vehicles. The IASB concluded that reputational risk is not an indicator of power in its own right, but may increase an investor's incentive to secure rights that give the investor power over an investee. Accordingly, reputational risk alone would not be regarded as a source of variable returns and so would not require a bank to consolidate a structured entity that it sponsors. *[IFRS 10.BC37-BC39]*.

6 LINK BETWEEN POWER AND RETURNS: PRINCIPAL-AGENCY SITUATIONS

The third criterion for having control is that the investor must have the ability to use its power over the investee to affect the amount of the investor's returns. *[IFRS 10.7]*. An investor controls an investee if the investor not only has power over the investee and exposure or rights to variable returns from its involvement with the investee, but also has the ability to use its power to affect the investor's returns from its involvement with the investee. *[IFRS 10.17]*.

Thus, an investor with decision-making rights shall determine whether it is a principal or an agent. An investor that is an agent in accordance with paragraphs B58-B72 of IFRS 10 does not control an investee when it exercises decision-making rights delegated to it. *[IFRS 10.18]*. This is discussed further at 6.1 below.

In January 2015, the Interpretations Committee noted that a fund manager that concludes that it is an agent in accordance with IFRS 10 should then assess whether it has significant influence in accordance with the guidance in IAS 28.[8] See Chapter 11 at 4.

The link between power over an investee and exposure to variable returns from involvement with the investee is essential to having control. An investor that has power over an investee, but cannot benefit from that power, does not control that investee. An investor that has an exposure to a variable return from an investee, but cannot use its power to direct the activities that most significantly affect the investee's returns, does not control that investee. This is illustrated in Example 6.24 below.

Example 6.24: Link between power and returns is essential for control

A structured entity is created and financed by debt instruments held by a senior lender and a subordinated lender and a minimal equity investment from the sponsor. The subordinated lender transferred receivables to the structured entity. Managing the receivables in default is the only activity of the structured entity that causes its returns to vary, and this power has been given to the subordinated lender by contract. The subordinated loan is designed to absorb the first losses and to receive any residual return from the structured entity. The senior lender has exposure to variable returns due to the credit risk of the structured entity.

When analysing which investor, if any, has control the first step is to identify the relevant activities. In this example, managing the receivables in default is the only activity of the structured entity that causes its returns to vary. Therefore, it would be the relevant activity. The next step is to determine which investor, if any, has the current ability to direct that relevant activity. In this example, the subordinated lender has the power that it was granted by contract. The subordinated lender is exposed to variable returns from its involvement with the structured entity through its subordinated debt. The subordinated lender has the ability to affect those returns through its power to manage the receivables in default. Since all three elements of control are present, the subordinated lender has control over the structured entity. This evaluation is made in the context of understanding the structured entity's purpose and design.

While the senior lender's exposure to variable returns is affected by the structured entity's activities, the senior lender has no power to direct those activities. Thus, the senior lender does *not* control the structured entity, because it is missing two of the elements of control.

6.1 Delegated power: principals and agents

When decision-making rights have been delegated or are being held for the benefit of others, it is necessary to assess whether the decision-maker is a principal or an agent to determine whether it has control. This is because if that decision-maker has been delegated rights that give the decision-maker power, it must be assessed whether those rights give the decision-maker power for its own benefit, or merely power for the benefit of others. An agent is a party primarily engaged to act on behalf of another party or parties (the principal(s)), and therefore does not control the investee when it exercises its decision-making powers. *[IFRS 10.B58]*. As an agent does not control the investee, it does not consolidate the investee. *[IFRS 10.18]*.

While principal-agency situations often occur in the asset management and banking industries, they are not limited to those industries. Entities in the construction, real estate and extractive industries also frequently delegate powers when carrying out their business. This is especially common when an investee is set up and one of the investors (often the lead investor) is delegated powers by the other investors to carry out activities for the investee. Assessing whether the lead investor is making decisions as a principal, or simply carrying out the decisions made by all the investors (i.e. acting as an agent) will be critical to the assessment.

An investor may delegate decision-making authority to an agent on some specific issues or on all relevant activities, but, ultimately, the investor as principal retains the power. This is because the investor treats the decision-making rights delegated to its agent as held by the investor directly. *[IFRS 10.B59]*. Accordingly, a decision-maker that is not an agent is a principal. However, it should be noted that:

- a decision-maker is not an agent simply because others benefit from the decisions that it makes; *[IFRS 10.B58]* and
- an obligation to act in the best interest of those who have delegated the power does not prevent the decision-maker from being a principal.

The terms and conditions of the arrangement are considered to assess whether an entity is an agent or a principal. The determination of whether a decision-maker is an agent or a principal is made based on the following:

- scope of decision-making authority;
- rights held by other parties (e.g. existence of removal rights);
- remuneration of the decision-maker; and
- exposure to variability of returns through other interests. *[IFRS 10.B60]*.

Each of these factors is discussed in more detail below. When reaching a conclusion, each of the factors is weighted according to the facts and circumstances of each case, *[IFRS 10.B60]*, which will require judgement. The only situation that is conclusive by itself is when removal rights are held by a single investor and the decision-maker can be removed without cause. *[IFRS 10.B61]*. This is discussed in more detail at 6.3 below. Accordingly, although each of the factors are discussed in isolation below, a conclusion should be based on all of the factors considered together. Of the four factors that need to be considered when assessing whether the decision-maker is acting as principal or agent, generally it will be the rights held by third parties to remove the decision-maker (see 6.3 below) and the exposure to variability of returns (see 6.5 below) that will require careful consideration.

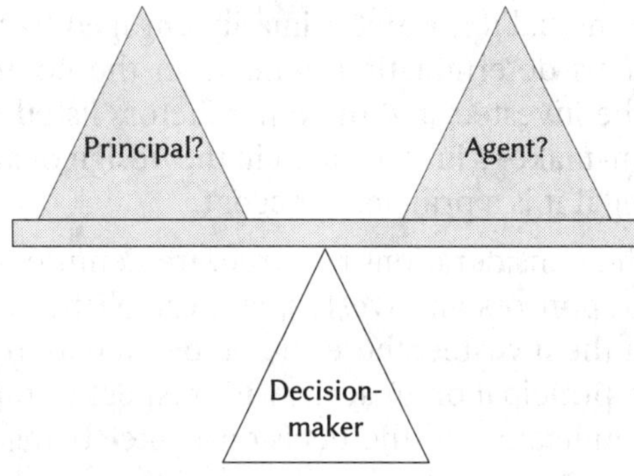

6.2 Scope of decision-making

To assess whether a decision-maker is a principal or an agent, the scope of its authority is evaluated by considering both:

- the activities that the decision-maker is permitted to direct (e.g. by agreement or by law); and
- the discretion that the decision-maker has when making decisions about those activities. *[IFRS 10.B62].*

It is implicit in the definition of control that, for a decision-maker to control the entity over which it has been delegated decision-making authority, the decision-maker must have power. This means that it must have been delegated the rights that give the current ability to direct the relevant activities (the activities that most significantly affect that investee's returns). If a decision-maker has been delegated rights that do not relate to the relevant activities, it would not have control over the investee.

For this reason, it is imperative to understand the purpose and design of the investee, the risks to which it was designed to be exposed and the risk it was designed to pass on to the other parties involved. Understanding the purpose and design of the investee often helps in assessing which rights were delegated, why they were delegated, and which rights have been retained by other parties, and why those rights were retained.

6.2.1 Involvement in design

IFRS 10 requires that a decision-maker considers the purpose and design of the investee, the risks to which the investee was designed to be exposed, the risks it was designed to pass on to the parties involved and the level of involvement the decision-maker had in the design of an investee. For example, if a decision-maker is significantly involved in the design of the investee (including in determining the scope of decision-making authority), that involvement may indicate that the decision-maker had the opportunity and incentive to obtain rights that result in the decision-maker having the ability to direct the relevant activities. *[IFRS 10.B63].*

However, a decision-maker's involvement in the design of an investee does not mean that decision-maker necessarily is a principal, even if that involvement was significant.

A decision-maker is a principal if it is not primarily engaged to act on behalf of and for the benefit of others. This determination is made in the context of considering the purpose and design of the investee, and the other factors listed at 6.1 above. While not determinative, a decision-maker's involvement in the design of an investee is part of the context when concluding if it is a principal or agent.

In our view, similar to the considerations for structured entities discussed at 4.6 above, when a decision-maker sponsors an investee, and establishes certain decisions in the governing documents of the investee, there should be increased scrutiny as to whether that decision-maker is a principal or an agent with respect to the investee, particularly if the other factors are indicative of the decision-maker being a principal. However, when there are many parties involved in the design of an investee, the decisions established in the governing documents might be less relevant.

6.2.2 Assessing whether the scope of powers is narrow or broad

When evaluating whether a decision-maker is a principal or an agent, in considering the scope of its decision-making authority, it appears that a relevant factor is whether the scope of powers that have been delegated (and the discretion allotted) is narrow or broad. In an example in IFRS 10 where a decision-maker (fund manager) establishes, markets and manages a publicly traded, regulated fund according to narrowly defined parameters set out in the investment mandate, it is stated that this is a factor that indicates that the fund manager is an agent. *[IFRS 10.B72 Example 13]*. In another example, where the decision-maker (fund manager) has wide decision-making authority, it is implied that the extensive decision-making authority of the fund manager would be an indicator that it is a principal. *[IFRS 10.B72 Example 14-14A]*. This suggests that where the scope of powers is broad, this would be an indicator that the decision-maker is a principal. However, to conclude whether a decision-maker is an agent or a principal, the scope of power needs to be evaluated with the other three factors in totality.

6.3 Rights held by other parties

The decision-maker may be subject to rights held by other parties that may affect the decision-maker's ability to direct the relevant activities of the investee, such as rights of those parties to remove the decision-maker. Rights to remove are often referred to as 'kick-out' rights. Substantive removal rights may indicate that the decision-maker is an agent. *[IFRS 10.B64]*. Liquidation rights and redemption rights held by other parties, which may in substance be similar to removal rights, are discussed at 6.3.2 below.

Other substantive rights held by other parties that restrict a decision-maker's discretion are considered similarly to removal rights when evaluating whether the decision-maker is an agent. For example, a decision-maker that is required to obtain approval from a small number of other parties for its actions is generally an agent. *[IFRS 10.B66]*.

Figure 6.6: Evaluating rights to remove without cause

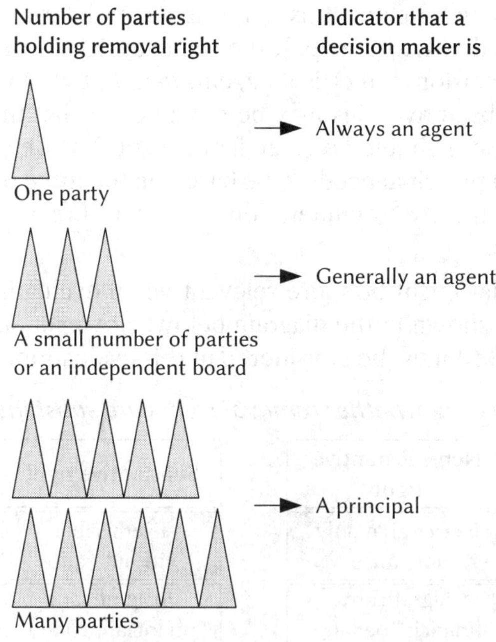

As shown in the diagram above, when a single investor holds substantive rights to remove the decision-maker without cause, that fact in isolation is sufficient to conclude that the decision-maker is an agent. *[IFRS 10.B65]*. That is, the decision-maker does not consolidate the entity.

However, if multiple investors hold such rights (i.e. no individual investor can remove the decision-maker without cause without the others), these rights would not, in isolation, determine whether a decision-maker is an agent or a principal. That is, all other facts and circumstances would need to be considered. The more parties that must act together to remove a decision-maker and the greater the magnitude of, and variability associated with, the decision-maker's other economic interests, the less weighting that is placed on the removal right. *[IFRS 10.B65]*. This is reflected in an example provided by IFRS 10 where there is a large number of widely dispersed unrelated third party investors. Although the decision-maker (the asset manager) can be removed, without cause, by a simple majority decision of the other investors, this is given little weighting in evaluating whether the decision-maker is a principal or agent. *[IFRS 10.B72 Example 15]*.

If an independent Board of Directors (or governing body), which is appointed by the other investors, holds a right to remove without cause, that would be an indicator that the decision-maker is an agent. *[IFRS 10.B23(b), B67]*. This is the position taken in an example in IFRS 10 (see Example 6.31 at 6.6 below) where a fund has a Board of Directors, all of whose members are independent of the decision-maker (the fund manager) and are appointed by the other investors. The Board of Directors appoints the fund manager annually. The example explains that the Board of Directors provides a mechanism to ensure that the investors can remove the fund manager if they decide to do so.

Chapter 6

6.3.1 Evaluating whether a removal right is substantive

When evaluating removal rights, it is important to determine whether they are substantive, as discussed at 4.2.1 above. If the removal right is substantive, this may be an indicator that the decision-maker is an agent. *[IFRS 10.B64]*. On the other hand, if the removal right is not substantive, this may be an indicator that the decision-maker is a principal, but this indicator should be given less weight. The determination of whether the decision-maker is a principal needs to be based on the three other factors, i.e. scope of decision-making authority, remuneration and exposure to variability of returns through other interests.

Some of the criteria that might be more relevant when evaluating whether a removal right is substantive are shown in the diagram below. However, all of the factors noted at 4.2.1 above and IFRS 10 must be considered in this evaluation.

Figure 6.7: Evaluating whether removal rights are substantive

Non-substantive right	Substantive right
Exercisable only for cause	Exercisable without cause
Significant financial penalty to exercise	Insignificant financial penalty to exercise
Skills held by decision- maker are unique	Several other parties could fulfil role of decision-maker
Not currently exercisable	Currently exercisable
Principal	Agent

Decision-maker

Evaluating whether a removal right is substantive will depend on facts and circumstances. *[IFRS 10.B23]*.

6.3.1.A Available replacements

When evaluating whether a removal right is substantive, consideration is given as to whether suitable replacements exist. This is because if there are no (or few) suitable replacements for the decision-maker, this would be an operational barrier that would likely prevent the parties holding the removal right from exercising that removal right. *[IFRS 10.B23(a)(vi)]*.

In the asset management industry, suitable replacements are generally available. However, in other industries (e.g. construction, real estate, extractive), it is more common for the decision-maker to possess unique traits. For example, the decision-maker may have experience with a particular geographic location, local government, or proprietary intellectual property or tools. That might make it more difficult to assess whether there are other parties that could replace the decision-maker if the parties wanted to remove the decision-maker. However, regardless of the industry, an assessment of whether there are available replacements depends upon the specific facts and circumstances, and will require judgement.

6.3.1.B Exercise period

A removal right may not be exercisable until a date in the future. In such cases, judgement must be exercised to determine whether (or when) that right becomes substantive. Similarly, when a removal right can only be exercised during a narrow period (e.g. for one day on the last day of the reporting period), judgement is necessary to determine whether the right is substantive.

When a removal right is exercised, there is typically a period (e.g. six months) until the decision-maker transitions decision-making back to the principal (or to another decision-maker) in an orderly manner. In such cases, judgement will be required to assess whether the principal has the current ability to direct the relevant activities when decisions need to be made, and therefore whether the removal right is substantive.

In our view, even if there is a transition period between when the decision-maker is removed and when the principal (or another decision-maker) becomes responsible for making decisions, the removal right may still be substantive.

6.3.2 Liquidation rights and redemption rights

In some cases, rights held by other parties (such as some liquidation rights and some redemption rights) may have the same effect on the decision-maker's authority as removal rights. When a liquidation right or a redemption right is in substance the same as a removal right, its consideration in the evaluation of whether a decision-maker is a principal or an agent is the same.

For example, if a limited partnership were required to be liquidated upon the withdrawal of one limited partner, that would be considered a removal right if it were substantive (as discussed at 4.2.1 and 6.3.1 above). However, such rights must be analysed carefully, based on the facts and circumstances.

6.4 Remuneration

The third factor to evaluate when assessing whether a decision-maker is a principal or an agent is remuneration.

The greater the magnitude of, and variability associated with, the decision-maker's remuneration relative to the returns expected from the activities of the investee, the more likely the decision-maker is a principal. *[IFRS 10.B68]*. Therefore, when determining if a decision-maker is a principal or an agent, the magnitude and variability of exposure to returns through remuneration are always considered. This applies even if the remuneration is at market rates. However, as discussed at 6.4.1 below, IFRS 10 does not include any examples of remuneration arrangements where it is clear the remuneration is of such significance that it, in isolation, indicates that the decision maker is a principal.

In determining whether it is a principal or an agent the decision-maker also considers whether the following conditions exist:

(a) The remuneration of the decision-maker is commensurate with the services provided.

(b) The remuneration agreement includes only terms, conditions or amounts that are customarily present in arrangements for similar services and level of skills negotiated on an arm's length basis. *[IFRS 10.B69].*

IFRS 10 states that a decision-maker cannot be an agent unless the conditions set out in (a) and (b) above are present. However, meeting those conditions in isolation is not sufficient to conclude that a decision-maker is an agent. *[IFRS 10.B70].*

6.4.1 Evaluating remuneration in the asset management industry

When evaluating whether a decision-maker is a principal or an agent, an entity is required to evaluate the magnitude and the variability of the remuneration relative to the expected returns from the investee. In examples related to the asset management industry, IFRS 10 describes three common remuneration structures:

- 1% of net assets under management; *[IFRS 10.B72 Example 13]*
- 1% of assets under management and performance-related fees of 10% of profits if the investee's profits exceed a specified level; *[IFRS 10.B72 Example 15]* and
- 1% of assets under management and 20% of all the fund's profits if a specified profit level is achieved. *[IFRS 10.B72 Example 14].*

In each case, the examples assume that the remuneration is commensurate with the services provided. In addition, the remuneration aligns the interests of the decision-maker with those of other investors. However, IFRS 10 concludes for each of these cases that the level of remuneration does not create an exposure to variable returns that is of such significance that, in isolation, it indicates that the fund manager is a principal. IFRS 10 does not include any examples of remuneration arrangements where the remuneration is of such significance that, in isolation, it does indicate that the fund manager is a principal. Additionally, IFRS 10 does not provide any examples of remuneration arrangements that are not market-based although this would always need to be assessed.

In our experience, in most asset management scenarios involving retail investors, management will be able to conclude that the remuneration is commensurate with services provided and only includes market terms. This is because otherwise, retail investors would take their business elsewhere. When both of those criteria are met, the decision-maker must evaluate whether the magnitude and exposure to variable returns received through the remuneration, together with other factors, indicates that the decision-maker is an agent or a principal.

6.4.2 Evaluating remuneration in other industries

IFRS 10 does not include any examples of principal-agency evaluations in construction, real estate and extractive industries. In our view, in these industries, it is more common for the decision-maker to possess unique traits (see 6.3.1.A above). That might make it more difficult to assess whether the remuneration is commensurate with the skills provided, and includes only market terms.

6.5 Exposure to variability of returns from other interests

When an investor has exposure to variable returns from its involvement with an investee (e.g. an investment in that investee, or provides a guarantee), and has been delegated decision-making authority by other parties, the investor considers that exposure to variable returns when assessing whether it has control over that investee. *[IFRS 10.B71]*. This is illustrated in Example 6.25 below as well as in the examples provided by IFRS 10 reproduced at 6.6 below.

Example 6.25: Illustration of exposure to variability of returns through other interests

A parent of a fund manager has a 20% direct interest in a fund. The other 80% of the fund is held by third party investors, who have delegated their rights with respect to the fund to the fund manager. When evaluating whether the parent controls the fund, it assesses whether the fund manager (which the parent controls) would use the power that has been delegated to it by the third parties holding the 80% interest, to benefit the parent, since the parent has a 20% direct interest in the fund and could benefit from that power.

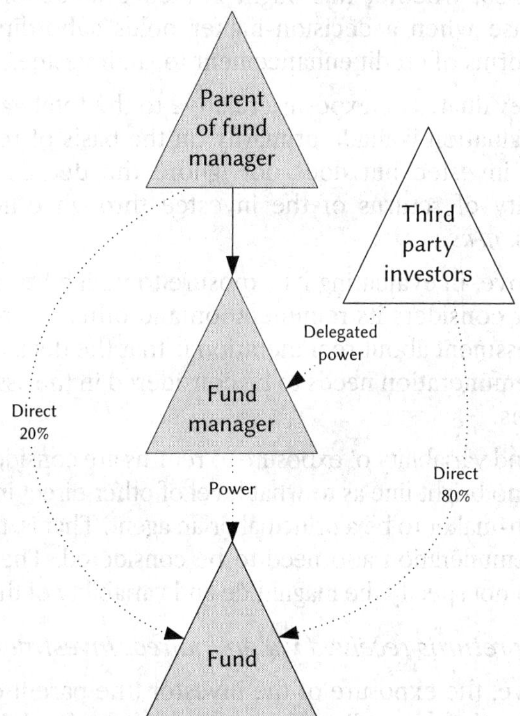

As discussed at 5 above, being an 'investor' and having an 'interest' in an investee is not limited to holding equity or debt instruments. A variety of exposures to variable returns can represent an 'interest' and any potential controlling party is referred to as an 'investor.' IFRS 10 states that if a decision-maker has interests in an investee, just by virtue of holding those other interests, the decision-maker may be a principal. *[IFRS 10.B71]*. In the Basis for Conclusions accompanying IFRS 10, the IASB notes that a decision-maker might use its decision-making authority primarily to affect its exposure to variable returns from that interest. That is, the decision-maker would have power for its own benefit. *[IFRS 10.BC132]*. The IASB also notes in its Basis for Conclusions that it would be inappropriate to conclude that

Chapter 6

every decision-maker that is obliged, by law or contract (i.e. having any fiduciary responsibility) to act in the best interests of other parties is always an agent. This is because it would assume that a decision-maker that is legally or contractually obliged to act in the best interests of other parties will always do so, even if that decision-maker receives the vast majority of the returns that are influenced by its decision-making. *[IFRS 10.BC130]*. Accordingly, IFRS 10 requires an entity to evaluate the magnitude and variability of its other interests when determining if it is a principal or an agent, notwithstanding its fiduciary responsibility.

In evaluating its exposure to variability of returns from other interests in the investee a decision-maker considers the following:

(a) the greater the magnitude of, and variability associated with, its economic interests, considering its remuneration and other interests in aggregate, the more likely the decision-maker is a principal;

(b) whether its exposure to variability of returns is different from that of the other investors and, if so, whether this might influence its actions. For example, this might be the case when a decision-maker holds subordinated interests in, or provides other forms of credit enhancement to, an investee.

The decision-maker evaluates its exposure relative to the total variability of returns of the investee. This evaluation is made primarily on the basis of returns expected from the activities of the investee but does not ignore the decision maker's maximum exposure to variability of returns of the investee through other interests that the decision-maker holds. *[IFRS 10.B72]*.

As indicated at (a) above, in evaluating its exposure to variability of returns from other interests, the investor considers its remuneration and other interests in aggregate. So, even if the initial assessment about remuneration is that the decision-maker is an agent (see 6.4 above), the remuneration needs to be considered in the assessment of exposure to variability of returns.

Since the magnitude and variability of exposure to returns are considered together with the other factors, there is no bright line as to what level of other direct interests, on their own, would cause a decision-maker to be a principal or an agent. That is, the scope of authority, removal rights, and remuneration also need to be considered. The examples in IFRS 10 (see 6.6 below) also do not specify the magnitude and variability of the remuneration.

6.5.1 Evaluating returns received via an indirect investment in another entity

In Example 6.25 above, the exposure of the investor (the parent of the fund manager) to variable returns was through a direct investment in the fund. However, what if the exposure to variable returns arises from an investor's indirect involvement with an investee, e.g. via a joint venture or an associate?

When assessing whether an investor has control of an investee, the investor determines whether it is exposed, or has rights, to variable returns from its involvement with the investee. IFRS 10 discusses 'returns' as a broad term, and the examples in paragraph B57 of the standard (see 5 above) suggest the exposure to variable returns encompasses both direct and indirect involvement with the investee.

The Basis for Conclusions accompanying IFRS 10 further clarifies that the IASB intended the term 'returns' as a broad term, stating that 'The Board confirmed its intention to have a broad definition of "returns" that would include synergistic returns as well as more direct returns, for example, dividends or changes in the value of an investment. In practice, an investor can benefit from controlling an investee in a variety of ways. The Board concluded that to narrow the definition of returns would artificially restrict those ways of benefiting.' *[IFRS 10.BC63]*.

Therefore, in our view, when an investor evaluates the exposure to variable returns from its involvement with another entity, the returns received indirectly via another entity that is not under the control of that investor, are included in that assessment. This is regardless of the structure of the indirect involvement – that is, whether it is held through a joint venture, an associate, or neither influence nor joint control exists such that it is just an investment.

In the case of an indirect interest there are essentially two different ways of assessing the returns – the dividend flow and/or the change in fair value of the intermediate investment. While the dividend flow is not in the control of the investor, it still receives the returns via the change in value of its intermediate investment, and therefore these returns cannot be ignored.

Example 6.26: Illustration of exposure to variability of returns through indirect interests

Company A has a wholly-owned subsidiary, GP, which is the General Partner and fund manager of a Fund. A has a 50% interest in the shares of Company B and, as a result of the contractual arrangement with the other investors in B, has joint control of B. GP has a 1% interest in the Fund, with the remaining 99% of the Fund owned by B.

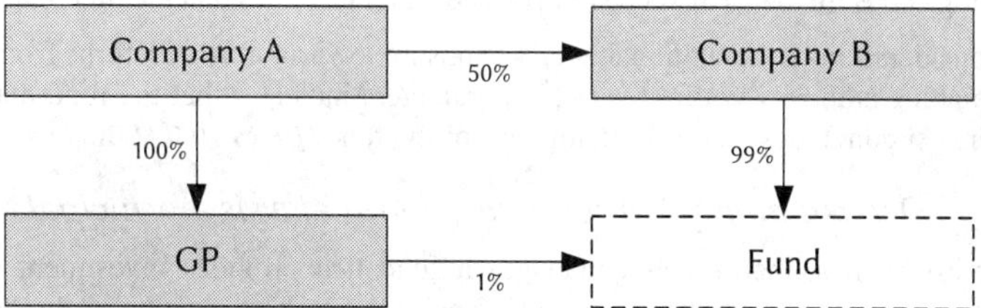

It has been assessed and concluded that GP, in its capacity as the fund manager, has power over the Fund. Therefore, by extension, A has power over the Fund. At the same time, GP also concluded that it is acting on behalf and for the benefit of another party or parties, i.e. as an agent for the investors, and therefore does not control the Fund.

B also evaluated its involvement with the Fund and determined it has no power over the Fund, and therefore does not control it.

A has joint control of B. It does not have control over B and therefore does not control how the returns from the Fund are ultimately distributed to the investors in B.

While A does not control how the returns from the Fund are ultimately distributed, its indirect entitlement to the returns of the Fund is considered with its direct investment through the GP when evaluating whether there is sufficient exposure to variable returns, when combined with power, to conclude that control exists.

6.6 Application examples in IFRS 10

IFRS 10 provides a number of application examples in relation to the determination of whether a decision-maker is a principal or an agent. These are reflected in Examples 6.27 to 6.33 below.

As with all of the examples included in the Application Guidance, the examples portray hypothetical situations. Although some aspects of the examples may be present in actual fact patterns, all relevant facts and circumstances of a particular fact pattern would need to be evaluated when applying IFRS 10. *[IFRS 10.B1]*. When reaching a conclusion on a particular fact pattern, each of the factors discussed above is weighted according to the facts and circumstances of each case, which will require judgement. *[IFRS 10.B60]*.

Example 6.27: Determining whether a decision-maker is a principal or agent (1)

A decision-maker (fund manager) establishes, markets and manages a publicly traded, regulated fund according to narrowly defined parameters set out in the investment mandate as required by its local laws and regulations. The fund was marketed to investors as an investment in a diversified portfolio of equity securities of publicly traded entities. Within the defined parameters, the fund manager has discretion about the assets in which to invest. The fund manager has made a 10% *pro rata* investment in the fund and receives a market-based fee for its services equal to 1% of the net asset value of the fund. The fees are commensurate with the services provided. The fund manager does not have any obligation to fund losses beyond its 10% investment. The fund is not required to establish, and has not established, an independent board of directors. The investors do not hold any substantive rights that would affect the decision-making authority of the fund manager, but can redeem their interests within particular limits set by the fund.

Analysis

Although operating within the parameters set out in the investment mandate and in accordance with the regulatory requirements, the fund manager has decision-making rights that give it the current ability to direct the relevant activities of the fund – the investors do not hold substantive rights that could affect the fund manager's decision-making authority. The fund manager receives a market-based fee for its services that is commensurate with the services provided and has also made a *pro rata* investment in the fund. The remuneration and its investment expose the fund manager to variability of returns from the activities of the fund without creating exposure that is of such significance that it indicates that the fund manager is a principal.

In this example, consideration of the fund manager's exposure to variability of returns from the fund together with its decision-making authority within restricted parameters indicates that the fund manager is an agent. Thus, the fund manager concludes that it does not control the fund. *[IFRS 10.B72 Example 13]*.

Example 6.28: Determining whether a decision-maker is a principal or agent (2)

A decision-maker establishes, markets and manages a fund that provides investment opportunities to a number of investors. The decision-maker (fund manager) must make decisions in the best interests of all investors and in accordance with the fund's governing agreements. Nonetheless, the fund manager has wide decision-making discretion and there are no other rights held by others that affect this discretion. The fund manager receives a market-based fee for its services equal to 1% of assets under management and 20% of all the fund's profits if a specified profit level is achieved. The fees are commensurate with the services provided. The fund manager does not hold a direct interest in the fund.

Analysis

Although it must make decisions in the best interests of all investors, the fund manager has extensive decision-making authority to direct the relevant activities of the fund. The fund manager is paid fixed and performance-related fees that are commensurate with the services provided. In addition, the remuneration aligns the interests of the fund manager with those of the other investors to increase the value of the fund, without creating exposure to variability of returns from the activities of the fund that is of such significance that the remuneration, when considered in isolation, indicates that the fund manager is a principal. Therefore, the fund manager is an agent. *[IFRS 10.B72 Example 14]*.

See Examples 6.29 to 6.31 below for an evaluation of other factors based on the same fact pattern and initial analysis.

Example 6.29: Determining whether a decision-maker is a principal or agent (3)

Assume the fact pattern and initial analysis in Example 6.28 above.

However, in this example the fund manager also has a 2% investment in the fund that aligns its interests with those of the other investors. The fund manager does not have any obligation to fund losses beyond its 2% investment. The investors can remove the fund manager by a simple majority vote, but only for breach of contract.

Analysis

The fund manager's 2% investment increases its exposure to variability of returns from the activities of the fund without creating exposure that is of such significance that it indicates that the fund manager is a principal. The other investors' rights to remove the fund manager are considered to be protective rights because they are exercisable only for breach of contract. In this example, although the fund manager has extensive decision-making authority and is exposed to variability of returns from its interest and remuneration, the fund manager's exposure indicates that the fund manager is an agent. Thus, the fund manager concludes that it does not control the fund. *[IFRS 10.B72 Example 14A].*

Example 6.30: Determining whether a decision-maker is a principal or agent (4)

Assume the fact pattern and initial analysis in Example 6.28 above.

However, in this example, the fund manager has a more substantial *pro rata* investment in the fund (than the 2% in Example 6.29 above), but does not have any obligation to fund losses beyond that investment. The investors can remove the fund manager by a simple majority vote, but only for breach of contract.

Analysis

In this scenario, the other investors' rights to remove the fund manager are considered to be protective rights because they are exercisable only for breach of contract. Although the fund manager is paid fixed and performance-related fees that are commensurate with the services provided, the combination of the fund manager's investment together with its remuneration could create exposure to variability of returns from the activities of the fund that is of such significance that it indicates that the fund manager is a principal. The greater the magnitude of, and variability associated with, the fund manager's economic interests (considering its remuneration and other interests in aggregate), the more emphasis the fund manager would place on those economic interests in the analysis, and the more likely the fund manager is a principal.

For example, having considered its remuneration and the other factors, the fund manager might consider a 20% investment to be sufficient to conclude that it controls the fund. However, in different circumstances (i.e. if the remuneration or other factors are different), control may arise when the level of investment is different. *[IFRS 10.B72 Example 14B].*

Example 6.31: Determining whether a decision-maker is a principal or agent (5)

Assume the fact pattern and initial analysis in Example 6.28 above.

However, in this example, the fund manager has a 20% *pro rata* investment in the fund, but does not have any obligation to fund losses beyond its 20% investment. The fund has a board of directors, all of whose members are independent of the fund manager and are appointed by the other investors. The board appoints the fund manager annually. If the board decided not to renew the fund manager's contract, the services performed by the fund manager could be performed by other managers in the industry.

Analysis

Although the fund manager is paid fixed and performance-related fees that are commensurate with the services provided, the combination of the fund manager's 20% investment together with its remuneration creates exposure to variability of returns from the activities of the fund that is of such significance that it indicates that the fund manager is a principal. However, the investors have substantive rights to remove the fund manager – the board of directors provides a mechanism to ensure that the investors can remove the fund manager if they decide to do so.

In this scenario, the fund manager places greater emphasis on the substantive removal rights in the analysis. Thus, although the fund manager has extensive decision-making authority and is exposed to variability of returns of the fund from its remuneration and investment, the substantive rights held by the other investors indicate that the fund manager is an agent. Thus, the fund manager concludes that it does not control the fund. *[IFRS 10.B72 Example 14C].*

Example 6.32: Determining whether a decision-maker is a principal or agent (6)

An investee is created to purchase a portfolio of fixed rate asset-backed securities, funded by fixed rate debt instruments and equity instruments. The equity instruments are designed to provide first loss protection to the debt investors and receive any residual returns of the investee. The transaction was marketed to potential debt investors as an investment in a portfolio of asset-backed securities with exposure to the credit risk associated with the possible default of the issuers of the asset-backed securities in the portfolio and to the interest rate risk associated with the management of the portfolio. On formation, the equity instruments represent 10% of the value of the assets purchased. A decision-maker (the asset manager) manages the active asset portfolio by making investment decisions within the parameters set out in the investee's prospectus. For those services, the asset manager receives a market-based fixed fee (i.e. 1% of assets under management) and performance-related fees (i.e. 10% of profits) if the investee's profits exceed a specified level. The fees are commensurate with the services provided. The asset manager holds 35% of the equity in the investee.

The remaining 65% of the equity, and all the debt instruments, are held by a large number of widely dispersed unrelated third party investors. The asset manager can be removed, without cause, by a simple majority decision of the other investors.

Analysis

The asset manager is paid fixed and performance-related fees that are commensurate with the services provided. The remuneration aligns the interests of the fund manager with those of the other investors to increase the value of the fund. The asset manager has exposure to variability of returns from the activities of the fund because it holds 35% of the equity and from its remuneration.

Although operating within the parameters set out in the investee's prospectus, the asset manager has the current ability to make investment decisions that significantly affect the investee's returns – the removal rights held by the other investors receive little weighting in the analysis because those rights are held by a large number of widely dispersed investors. In this example, the asset manager places greater emphasis on its exposure to variability of returns of the fund from its equity interest, which is subordinate to the debt instruments. Holding 35% of the equity creates subordinated exposure to losses and rights to returns of the investee, which are of such significance that it indicates that the asset manager is a principal. Thus, the asset manager concludes that it controls the investee. *[IFRS 10.B72 Example 15].*

The conclusions in Examples 6.27 to 6.32 above in respect of whether the fund manager is a principal (and therefore has control) or an agent (and therefore does not have control) can be summarised as follows:

Remuneration	Equity holding	Removal rights	Control?
1% of NAV	10%	None	No
1% of NAV plus 20% profits above a certain level	None	None	No
1% of NAV plus 20% profits above a certain level	2%	Only for breach of contract	No
1% of NAV plus 20% profits above a certain level	20% (illustrative)	Only for breach of contract	Yes
1% of NAV plus 20% profits above a certain level	20%	Yes – annually by board appointed by other investors	No
1% of NAV plus 10% profits above a certain level	35% of equity (0% of debt)	Yes – by simple majority of other widely diverse investors	Yes

Example 6.33 below illustrates a slightly different type of structure where there is an entitlement to a residual return rather than a *pro rata* return.

Example 6.33: Determining whether a decision-maker is a principal or agent (7)

A decision-maker (the sponsor) sponsors a multi-seller conduit, which issues short-term debt instruments to unrelated third party investors. The transaction was marketed to potential investors as an investment in a portfolio of highly rated medium-term assets with minimal exposure to the credit risk associated with the possible default by the issuers of the assets in the portfolio. Various transferors sell high quality medium-term asset portfolios to the conduit. Each transferor services the portfolio of assets that it sells to the conduit and manages receivables on default for a market-based servicing fee. Each transferor also provides first loss protection against credit losses from its asset portfolio through over-collateralisation of the assets transferred to the conduit. The sponsor establishes the terms of the conduit and manages the operations of the conduit for a market-based fee. The fee is commensurate with the services provided. The sponsor approves the sellers permitted to sell to the conduit, approves the assets to be purchased by the conduit and makes decisions about the funding of the conduit. The sponsor must act in the best interests of all investors.

The sponsor is entitled to any residual return of the conduit and also provides credit enhancement and liquidity facilities to the conduit. The credit enhancement provided by the sponsor absorbs losses of up to 5% of all of the conduit's assets, after losses are absorbed by the transferors. The liquidity facilities are not advanced against defaulted assets. The investors do not hold substantive rights that could affect the decision-making authority of the sponsor.

Analysis

Even though the sponsor is paid a market-based fee for its services that is commensurate with the services provided, the sponsor has exposure to variability of returns from the activities of the conduit because of its rights to any residual returns of the conduit and the provision of credit enhancement and liquidity facilities (i.e. the conduit is exposed to liquidity risk by using short-term debt instruments to fund medium-term assets). Even though each of the transferors has decision-making rights that affect the value of the assets of the conduit, the sponsor has extensive decision-making authority that gives it the current ability to direct the activities that most significantly affect the conduit's returns (i.e. the sponsor established the terms of the conduit, has the right to make decisions about the assets (approving the assets purchased and the transferors of those assets) and the funding of the conduit (for which new investment must be found on a regular basis)). The right to residual returns of the conduit and the provision of credit enhancement and liquidity facilities expose the sponsor to variability of returns from the activities of the conduit that is different from that of the other investors. Accordingly, that exposure indicates that the sponsor is a principal and thus the sponsor concludes that it controls the conduit. The sponsor's obligation to act in the best interest of all investors does not prevent the sponsor from being a principal. *[IFRS 10.B72 Example 16].*

Chapter 6

6.7 Other illustrative examples

Example 6.34 below illustrates the application of the guidance relating to the determination of a principal or an agent for a bank that establishes a structured entity to facilitate a securitisation.

Example 6.34: Determining whether a bank is a principal or agent in relation to a securitisation

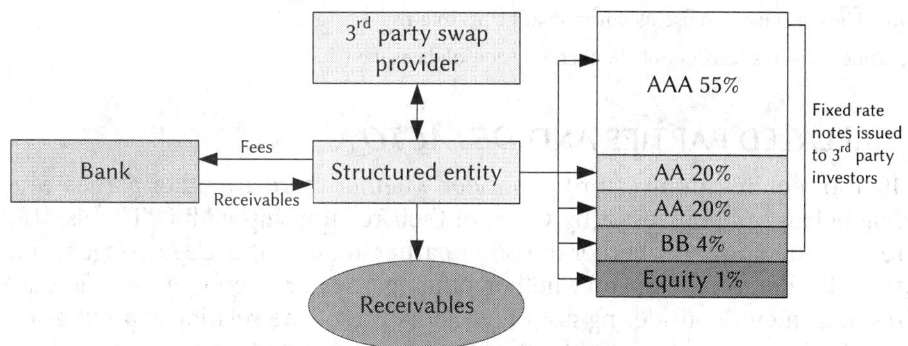

A bank establishes a structured entity to facilitate a securitisation. It transfers floating rate receivables to the structured entity. The structured entity issues tranched fixed rate notes to investors (rated AAA, AA, A and BB) and an equity tranche to the bank. The AAA tranche is the most senior and the equity tranche is the most junior in the event that there is insufficient cash to meet the payments under the terms of the notes.

The bank services the receivables on behalf of the structured entity including the management of defaults (if any), and has substitution rights over the receivables within certain parameters (for example, asset quality).

The bank receives a fee for managing the receivables, that is 1% of the notional amount of the receivables and is commensurate with the level of work performed and only includes market terms. The investors are not able to remove the bank from performing this function, other than in exceptional circumstances, such as negligence by the bank.

A third party provides an interest rate swap to convert the cash flows of the receivables into the cash flows required to be paid to meet the terms of the notes.

As the bank retains only the equity tranche, it concludes that it is no longer exposed to substantially all the risks and rewards of ownership and can derecognise the receivables on transfer to the structured entity and recognises just the equity tranche as its continuing involvement in the receivables.

Analysis

The purpose and design of the structured entity was to:

(a) enable the bank to generate external funding through the securitisation structure; and

(b) provide investors with an attractive investment opportunity.

The activities of the structured entity that significantly affect its returns are:

- selection and transfer of assets at inception;
- determining which assets are held by the structured entity (i.e. asset substitution); and
- management of defaults on the receivables.

The bank has decision-making rights over all of these relevant activities in its capacity as sponsor and service provider, so it has power over the structured entity.

The bank has exposure to variable returns through its holding of the equity tranche of the notes, in addition to the 1% management fee.

However, the question arises as to whether the bank is using its power as principal or as agent. To make that determination, the four factors (scope of decision-making authority, rights held by other investors, remuneration and exposure to variability of returns through other interests) need to be evaluated. Although the bank was involved in the design of the structured entity, the scope of the bank's decision-making authority is considered to be narrow as substitution rights have to be within certain parameters. However, the rights of the investors to remove the bank is not considered to be substantive, as it can only be removed by the investors in exceptional circumstances. In respect of remuneration, the bank earns a modest fee for services rendered that is commensurate with the services provided. Taking account of all the factors, the variability of returns of the equity tranche is likely to be significant relative to the total returns of the entity, such that the bank would be considered to exercise its power as principal rather than as agent. As a result, it is likely that the bank would be considered to use its power to affect its returns.

In conclusion, the bank has control and therefore consolidates the structured entity.

7 RELATED PARTIES AND *DE FACTO* AGENTS

IFRS 10 also requires an investor to consider whether there are other parties who are acting on behalf of the investor by virtue of their relationship with it. That is, IFRS 10 requires consideration of whether the other parties are acting as *de facto* agents for the investor. The determination of whether other parties are acting as *de facto* agents requires judgement, considering not only the nature of the relationship but also how those parties interact with each other and the investor. *[IFRS 10.B73]*.

Such relationships need not be contractual. A party is a *de facto* agent when the investor has, or those that direct the activities of the investor have, the ability to direct that party to act on the investor's behalf. In these circumstances, the investor considers its *de facto* agent's decision-making rights and its indirect exposure, or rights, to variable returns through the *de facto* agent together with its own when assessing control of an investee. *[IFRS 10.B74].*

IFRS 10 lists several examples of parties that might be *de facto* agents for an investor:

(a) the investor's related parties;

(b) a party that received its interest in the investee as a contribution or loan from the investor;

(c) a party that has agreed not to sell, transfer or encumber its interests in the investee without the investor's prior approval (except for situations in which the investor and the other party have the right of prior approval and the rights are based on mutually agreed terms by willing independent parties);

(d) a party that cannot finance its operations without subordinated financial support from the investor;

(e) an investee for which the majority of the members of its governing body or for which its key management personnel are the same as those of the investor; and

(f) a party that has a close business relationship with the investor, such as the relationship between a professional service provider and one of its significant clients. *[IFRS 10.B75].*

However, just because a party falls within the examples above, that does not mean that it *is* necessarily a *de facto* agent for the investor, as shown in the diagram below. It simply means that management must carefully evaluate whether that party is a *de facto* agent for the investor. Parties that are actually *de facto* agents are only a sub-set of the list above. Therefore, management must determine whether the other party is acting on behalf of the investor because of its relationship to the investor. IFRS 10 does not provide much explanation on how this evaluation is to be made; IFRS 10 only states that the evaluation considers the nature of the relationship and how the parties interact with each other. *[IFRS 10.B73].*

Figure 6.8: Identifying parties that might be de facto agents

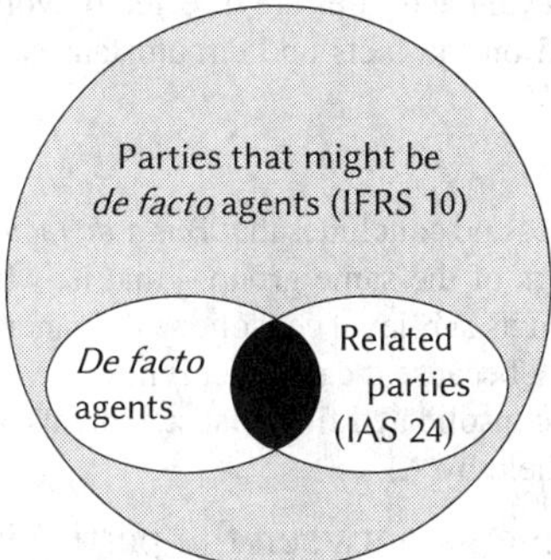

In our view, given the breadth of the parties that might be a *de facto* agent in IFRS 10, there are likely to be numerous parties that need to be evaluated to determine if they are actually *de facto* agents, which requires careful evaluation of the facts and circumstances, including the purpose and design of the investee.

Chapter 6

If a party is determined to be a *de facto* agent, then its rights and exposures to variable returns are considered together with those of the investor when evaluating whether an investor has control of an investee. *[IFRS 10.B74]*. Just because one party is a *de facto* agent of the other party, that does not mean that the *de facto* agent is controlled by the investor. Consolidation procedures in situations when a *de facto* agent exists are discussed at 7.2 below.

7.1 Customer-supplier relationships

Normally, a typical supplier-customer relationship is not expected to result in one party being a *de facto* agent of the other. This is because in a typical supplier-customer relationship, one party cannot direct the other party to act on its behalf. Instead, the activities of each are directed by their respective shareholders (and Board of Directors and management).

However, a party with a 'close business relationship' is an example of a *de facto* agent. *[IFRS 10.B75(f)]*. Accordingly, where a close business relationship exists between a customer and a supplier, consideration needs to be given to whether the supplier is a *de facto* agent of the customer. For example, this might be the case if:

- an entity has only one significant customer;
- the customer and supplier have common management or common shareholders;
- the customer has the ability to direct product design, sales, etc.; or
- the supplier is a service provider (e.g. investment banker, attorney) that assists in structuring a transaction.

7.2 Non-controlling interests when there is a *de facto* agent

When consolidating a subsidiary, a parent only reflects its exposures to variable returns (including those held by its subsidiaries), in its consolidated financial statements. Any rights or exposures to variable returns held by a *de facto* agent that is not in the group would generally be shown as non-controlling interests. This is illustrated in Example 6.35 below.

Example 6.35: Control evaluation and consolidation with a de facto agent

A has a 40% interest in Z, whose relevant activities are directed by voting shares that entitle the holder to a pro rata share of returns of Z. Based on the facts and circumstances, A concludes that, by itself, its 40% interest does not give A control over Z.

B holds a 15% interest in Z.

A evaluates the facts and circumstances and concludes that B is a *de facto* agent of A. This might be concluded if, for example, A and B are members of the same group – that is, when A and B have the same ultimate parent, but B is not part of A's group in its sub-level consolidated financial statements. Based on the combined interest, A concludes that it controls Z, because it can direct B how to vote by virtue of being a *de facto* agent. Accordingly, A consolidates Z in its consolidated financial statements and reflects a non-controlling interest in Z of 60% (that is, all interests not held by A).

Careful evaluation of arrangements between the parties is needed to ensure that there are no other rights and exposures that are required to be accounted for in the consolidated financial statements.

8 CONTROL OF SPECIFIED ASSETS

IFRS 10 requires that an investor has to consider whether it treats a portion of an investee as a deemed separate entity and, if so, whether it controls the deemed separate entity (a 'silo'). *[IFRS 10.B76]*.

It therefore clarifies that an investor can have control over specified assets of an investee (i.e. whether a 'silo' exists within a host entity). IFRS 10 gives a very strict rule as to when a portion of an entity is deemed to be a silo, and therefore, evaluated separately for consolidation from the remainder of the host entity.

Under IFRS 10, an investor treats a portion of an investee as a deemed separate entity if and only if specified assets of the investee (and related credit enhancements, if any) are the only source of payment for specified liabilities of, or specified other interests in, the investee. This means that parties other than those with the specified liability do not have rights or obligations related to the specified assets or to residual cash flows from those assets. In substance, none of the returns from the specified assets can be used by the remaining investee and none of the liabilities of the deemed separate entity are payable from the assets of the remaining investee. Thus, in substance, all the assets, liabilities and equity of that deemed separate entity ('silo') are ring-fenced from the overall investee. *[IFRS 10.B77]*.

It can be seen that the above condition for a silo includes the phrase 'in substance', but it is unclear how this should interpreted. Some proponents take the view that this would allow a portion of an investee to be regarded as ring-fenced if the possibility of using the assets of the silo to meet liabilities of the rest of the investee (or *vice versa*) was remote. In our view, this means that the silo has to be 'legally ring-fenced', and if there is any possibility that the assets could be used to meet liabilities of the rest of the investee, it is not a silo. The phrase 'in substance' is used in the standard to ensure that any terms in the contract that might override a ring fence would need to have substance, not that a silo can be established through 'in substance' ring fencing.

In many cases, where a silo exists, it will be because a trust or similar legal structure exists to ring-fence the assets and liabilities from the host and other silos within the host entity.

Under IFRS 10, it is clear that an investor needs to identify and consolidate any silos that it controls. Accordingly, it is crucial to identify silos (as discussed at 8.1 below).

Identifying whether a silo exists, and whether an investor controls a silo, can be complex. However, the same process outlined in the diagram for assessing control included at 3.1 above can be used for silos, with the initial step of identifying a silo, as shown in the diagram below. Understanding the purpose and design of an investee is critical when identifying whether a silo exists, and if so which investor, if any, has control of that silo.

Chapter 6

Figure 6.9: Identifying and assessing control of a silo

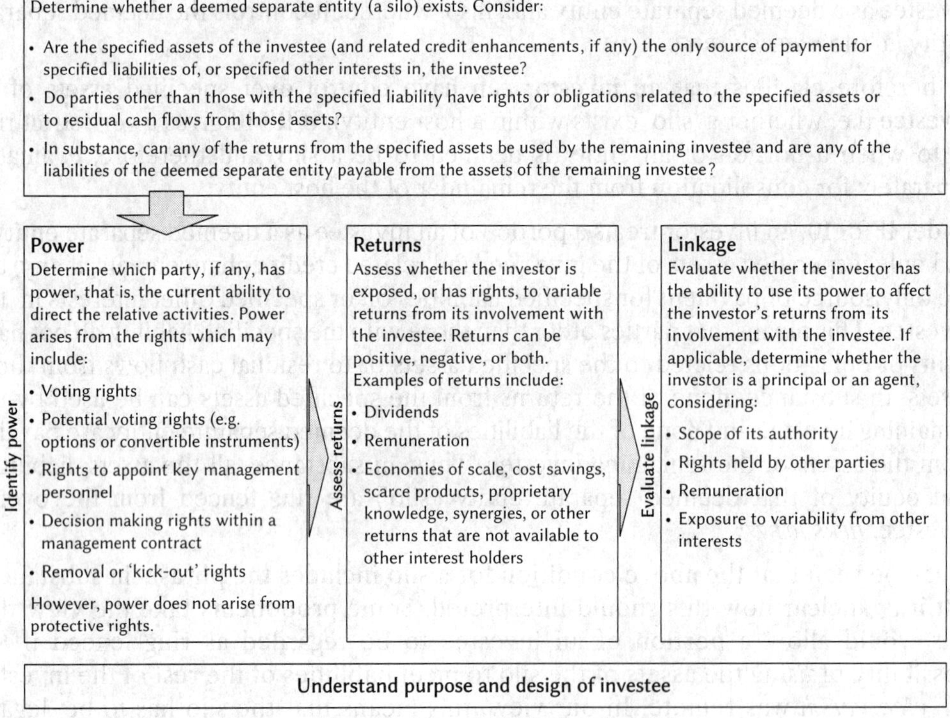

8.1 Identifying a silo

When identifying a silo, it is important to meet the condition that IFRS 10 requires to be satisfied for there to be a silo (see 8 above). Silos occur most often in the following industries:

- insurance (see 8.1.1 below); and
- investment funds (see 8.1.2 below).

8.1.1 Identifying silos in the insurance industry

For insurers, silos may arise in a structure such as a multi-cell reinsurance vehicle, which is an entity comprised of a number of 'cells' where the assets and liabilities are ring-fenced.

Insurers should evaluate whether investments made on behalf of insurance contract holders (policyholders) would be considered silos under IFRS 10. The evaluation will depend on the facts and circumstances of the particular case, and may vary by jurisdiction and by policy, given the differences in regulatory environments and types of policies offered by insurance entities.

When determining whether policies held are ring-fenced (whether a silo exists) relevant facts and circumstances, including local laws and contractual arrangements with the contract holder, must be assessed.

Where a silo exists and the shares in the silo are held by the insurance company on behalf of policyholders and all returns from the sub-funds are passed to the policyholders, the following needs to be considered:

- Does the insurance company have a contractual obligation to hold investments in the sub-funds?
- Are the investments legally ring-fenced such that they may be used to satisfy other liabilities of the insurance company in the event of liquidation?
- Do the policyholders select the investments?
- Will other funds beyond the value of the specified assets in the silo be necessary to fulfil the obligation to the policyholders?
- Is there an exact matching of the policy to the assets held?

All of the relevant facts and circumstances would need to be considered when determining if a silo exists. As discussed at 8.2 below, if a silo exists, control is evaluated for each silo. However, if a silo does *not* exist, this simply means that the control evaluation is made at the entity level.

8.1.2 Identifying silos in the investment funds industry

Silos may exist in the investment fund industry. Certain investment vehicles are set up as 'umbrella funds' with a number of sub-funds, each with its own investment goals and strategies e.g. a sub-fund may specialise in the shares of small companies, or in a particular country, or a particular industry. An assessment will need to be made as to whether a sub-fund should be considered a silo under IFRS 10. The evaluation will depend on the facts and circumstances of the particular case as to whether the sub-funds are legally ring-fenced from each other and the investment vehicle itself, and may vary by jurisdiction, given the differences in regulatory environments and types of such investment vehicles.

8.2 Evaluating control of a silo

If a silo exists, the next step is to identify the relevant activities (the activities that most significantly affect the silo's returns). Only the relevant activities of that silo would be considered, even if other activities affect the returns from other portions of the host.

The next step is then to identify which investor has the ability to direct the relevant activities, (i.e. who has the power over the silo). Only rights that affect the relevant activities of the silo would be considered. Rights that affect the relevant activities for other portions of the host entity would not be considered.

To conclude whether an investor has control over the silo, the investor also evaluates whether the investor has exposure to variable returns from that silo, and whether the investor can use its power over the silo to affect the amount of the investor's returns. Only exposure to variable returns from that silo would be considered; exposures to variable returns from other portions of the host would be excluded. *[IFRS 10.B78]*.

8.3 Consolidation of a silo

If an investor concludes that it controls a silo, it consolidates only the silo. That investor does not consolidate the remaining portions of the host entity.

Similarly, if an investor concludes that it controls a host entity, but not a silo within that entity, it would only consolidate the host entity, but exclude the silo. *[IFRS 10.B79]*.

9 CONTINUOUS ASSESSMENT

IFRS 10 clarifies that an investor is required to reassess whether it controls an investee if the facts and circumstances indicate that there are changes to one of the three elements of control, *[IFRS 10.8, B80]*, which are repeated below. For example, the following would be likely to be triggers:

- power over the investee:
  - an investor increases or decreases its holdings in the investee – see Example 6.36 below;
  - a potential voting right is granted, expires, or changes from being substantive to non-substantive (or *vice versa*) – see Example 6.37 at 9.1 below;
  - a change in how power over an investee can be exercised. For example, changes to decision making rights, which mean that the relevant activities of the investee are no longer governed through voting rights, but instead, are directed by contract (or *vice versa*); *[IFRS 10.B81]*
  - bankruptcy filings – see Example 6.40 at 9.2 below;
  - troubled debt restructurings – see Example 6.41 at 9.2 below;
  - changes in voting patterns;
  - action taken by others without the investor being involved in the event – see Example 6.42 at 9.3 below; *[IFRS 10.B82]*
- exposures, or rights, to variable returns from involvement with the investee – in many cases, these changes occur concurrent with a change in power, such as when acquiring an interest or selling an interest in an investee:
  - an investor can lose control of an investee if it ceases to be entitled to receive returns or to be exposed to obligations because, for example, a contract to receive performance related fees is terminated; *[IFRS 10.B83]* and
- ability of the investor to use its power over the investee to affect the amount of the investor's returns:
  - when the investor is a decision-maker (i.e. a principal or agent), changes in the overall relationship between the investor and other parties can mean that the investor no longer acts as agent, even though it has previously acted as agent or *vice versa*. *[IFRS 10.B84]*.

Therefore, it is possible that a previously unconsolidated investee would need to be consolidated (or *vice versa*) as facts and circumstances change. However, absent a change in facts and circumstances, control assessments are *not* expected to change.

Example 6.36: Providing seed money for a fund

A fund manager provides all of the seed money for a new fund upon inception. Until such times as other investors invest in that fund, the fund manager would likely control that fund. This is because the fund manager has the power to direct the relevant activities of that fund, exposure to variable returns from its involvement with the fund, and the ability to use its power over the fund to affect the amount of its returns.

As third parties invest in the fund and dilute (or acquire) the fund manager's interest, this would likely result in a reassessment of whether the fund manager has control. As the third parties invest, they are likely to obtain rights to direct the relevant activities (that is, the third parties will gain power). In many cases, analysing the facts and circumstances may indicate that the fund manager is acting as an agent of those third parties (as discussed at 6 above). Accordingly, the fund manager would deconsolidate the fund upon its determination that it no longer had control.

9.1 Changes in market conditions

IFRS 10 discusses when a change in market conditions triggers a reassessment of control.

An investor's initial assessment of control or its status as a principal or an agent does not change simply because of a change in market conditions (e.g. a change in the investee's returns driven by market conditions), unless the change in market conditions changes one or more of the three elements of control listed in paragraph 7 of IFRS 10 (see 9 above) or changes the overall relationship between a principal and an agent (see 6 above). *[IFRS 10.B85]*.

In response to concerns, the IASB decided to add this guidance to address the reassessment of control when there are changes in market conditions. The IASB observed that a change in market conditions alone would not generally affect the consolidation conclusion, or the status as a principal or an agent, for two reasons. The first is that power arises from substantive rights, and assessing whether those rights are substantive includes the consideration of many factors, not only those that are affected by a change in market conditions. The second is that an investor is not required to have a particular specified level of exposure to variable returns in order to control an investee. If that were the case, fluctuations in an investor's expected returns might result in changes in the consolidation conclusion. *[IFRS 10.BC152]*.

Accordingly, only a market condition that causes a change in one of the three criteria would trigger a reassessment (see Example 6.42 below). Evaluating whether a change in a market condition triggers a reassessment of control should be considered in the context of the investee's purpose and design.

As discussed at 5 above, with respect to the second criterion, the focus is on the existence of an exposure to variable returns, not the amount of the variable returns. While a change in market conditions often affects the amount of the exposure to variable returns, it typically does not affect whether the exposure exists.

However, when power has been delegated to a decision-maker, a change in market conditions could change whether the magnitude and variability of exposures to variable returns from remuneration and/or other interests are such that they indicate that the decision-maker is a principal (as discussed at 6.4 and 6.5 above, respectively). That is, a change in market conditions could change the evaluation of whether a decision-maker has the ability to use its power over the investee to affect the amount of the decision-maker's returns (the linkage between power and returns). Accordingly, a change in market conditions may trigger a reassessment of control in principal-agency evaluations.

As discussed at 4.3.4.A above, when evaluating the exercise price of an option in the context of whether potential voting rights give control, the evaluation is not solely based on the nature of the option as of the end of the reporting period. During the development of IFRS 10, some constituents raised concerns as to whether frequent changes in the control assessment solely because of market conditions would mean that an investor consolidates and deconsolidates an investee if potential voting rights moved in and out of the money. In response, the IASB noted that determining whether a potential voting right is substantive is not based solely on a comparison of the strike or conversion price of the instrument and the then current market price of its underlying share. Although the strike or conversion price is one factor to consider, determining whether potential voting rights are substantive requires a holistic approach, considering a variety of factors. This includes assessing the purpose and design of the instrument, considering whether the investor can benefit for other reasons such as by realising synergies between the investor and the investee, and determining whether there are any barriers (financial or otherwise) that would prevent the holder of potential voting rights from exercising or converting those rights. Accordingly, a change in market conditions (i.e. the market price of the underlying shares) alone would not typically result in a change in the consolidation conclusion. *[IFRS 10.BC124].*

Example 6.37: Value of option changes from 'in-the-money' to 'out-of-the-money'

A holds 40% of the voting rights of B, and holds a currently exercisable in-the-money option to acquire a further 20% of the voting rights of B. Assuming that voting rights give power over B, the option is substantive and no other facts and circumstances are relevant, A would likely have power over B, because A could currently exercise its right to obtain a majority of B's voting shares.

Consider a situation in which the in-the-money option changed to being slightly (but not deeply) out-of-the-money, due to a change in market conditions (and this change was not previously expected to occur, as discussed at 4.3.4 above). This would probably not trigger reassessment, because the option is likely to remain substantive, and therefore there is no change in how power over B is evaluated.

Consider a second situation in which the option changed to being deeply-out-of-the-money due to a change in market conditions (and this change was not previously expected to occur and it was now expected to remain deeply-out-of-the-money for the remainder of the option period, as discussed at 4.3.4 above). This would likely trigger reassessment, since the option would no longer be substantive, and the fact that the option was previously a substantive right was a critical factor in assessing whether A had power over B.

Example 6.38: Structured entity reassessments

There are two investors in a structured entity; one holds the debt, and the other holds the equity. In the initial assessment, the investors concluded that the equity holder had control because it had the power to direct the relevant activities, exposure to variable returns through its equity interests, and the ability to use its power over the structured entity to affect the equity holder's returns. Due to a change in market conditions, the value of the equity diminishes. This fact, by itself, would probably *not* trigger reassessment, because the equity holder continues to have exposure to variable returns (i.e. it continues to be exposed to further decreases in equity, and has potential upside if market conditions improve). Accordingly, the conclusion that the equity holder had control of the structured entity would probably not change.

However, if, concurrently with the deterioration of the equity, there are other changes in facts and circumstances (e.g. the equity holder loses its ability to direct the relevant activities), this might trigger a reassessment. In this case, the trigger is actually the other change in facts and circumstances, not the decrease in equity itself. In this case, whether the debt holder has control depends on whether it has rights that give it the current ability to direct the relevant activities, and the ability to affect its exposure to variable returns.

Example 6.39: Investee loses money due to change in market conditions

C holds 100% of the voting rights of D, which is a profitable entity. In its initial assessment, C concludes that it controls D.

Due to a change in the market conditions, D begins to lose money and is no longer profitable (e.g. due to a decrease in demand for its products). This would probably *not* trigger reassessment, because the change in market conditions would likely not change the identification of the relevant activities, how those activities are directed, the investors' exposure to variable returns, or the linkage between power and returns.

However, at some point, D might become so unprofitable as to consider restructuring its debt, or filing for bankruptcy. This situation is discussed at 9.2 below.

9.2 Bankruptcy filings and troubled debt restructurings

Filing for bankruptcy or restructuring a debt will usually trigger reassessment as to which investor, if any, controls the investee (see 4.3.2 above). While control should be reassessed at such triggering points, it does not necessarily mean the conclusion as to which entity consolidates will change. Examples 6.40 and 6.41 below illustrate situations when the control conclusion might change, and possibly result in a bank consolidating an entity that it had previously concluded it did not control.

Example 6.40: Bankruptcy filing

A made a loan to B. Because of A's position as a senior creditor, if B defaults on the loan, A has the right to direct B to sell certain assets to repay the loan to A. In its initial assessment of control, A concluded that this right was a protective right, because it concluded that defaulting on the loan would be an exceptional circumstance. Consequently, this right did not give A power over B, and therefore, A did not control B. A concluded that the voting rights, which are held by the equity investors, give the equity investors power over B.

B later defaults on the loan and files for bankruptcy, giving A the right to direct B to sell certain assets to repay the loan to A. Upon B filing for bankruptcy, A would need to evaluate whether having this right, which was previously protective, gives A power.

Before concluding which investors, if any, control B once it files for bankruptcy, consideration would also be given to what rights the equity investors have, if any, to direct the relevant activities of B, and also to whether A and the equity investors have exposure to variable returns from B.

Example 6.41: Troubled debt restructuring

Consider the same facts as Example 6.40 above, except that A and B agree to restructure the loan, rather than B filing for bankruptcy. During the restructuring, A determines which assets will be sold to repay the loan, with management and the equity investors agreeing to this plan. In addition, management agreed to an incentive scheme under which payments are based on asset sale and loan repayment targets.

Upon restructuring the loan, A would need to evaluate whether determining which assets should be sold to repay the loan gives A power. This might be the case if voting rights do not give power over B, because management is required to comply with the asset sale plan mandated by A.

Before concluding which investors, if any, control B, consideration would also be given to what rights the equity investors have, if any, to direct the relevant activities of B, and also to whether A and the equity investors have exposure to variable returns from B.

In some jurisdictions, it is possible that a trustee or court administrator may have power (and possibly control) over an investee that files for bankruptcy. In such situations, consideration needs to be given not only to whether the trustee has power, but also whether it has an exposure to variable returns from the investee, and if so, whether it has the ability to use that power to affect its exposure to variable returns. In many cases, a trustee or court administrator might have power, but this power is held as an agent (see 6 above). However, a determination will need to be made as to whether the trustee or court administrator is an agent for a specific lender, or for the creditors as a group. This will depend on individual facts and circumstances for the jurisdiction.

In the situations in Examples 6.40 and 6.41 above, it might be determined that the lender obtained control over the investee. In this case, judgement will also be needed to determine the date at which the lender obtained control over the investee. Is it the date that the investee filed for bankruptcy or restructured the debt? Or, did the lender obtain control over the investee before the actual filing, or restructuring, when it became evident that the investee would likely have to file for bankruptcy or restructure the debt?

9.3 Control reassessment as a result of action by others

An investor may gain or lose power over an investee as a result of action by others (i.e. without direct involvement in the change in circumstances). For example, an investor can gain power over an investee because decision-making rights held by another party or parties that previously prevented the investor from controlling an investee have elapsed. *[IFRS 10.B82]*. Alternatively, actions of others, such as a government, could cause an investor to lose the ability to make key operational decisions and therefore direct the relevant activities of the investee. Another example would be where other investors acquire rights of other parties. In such cases, it might be more difficult to determine whether an event has happened that would cause an investor to reassess control, because the information might not be publicly available. Consider the situation in Example 6.42 below.

Example 6.42: Control reassessment without being involved

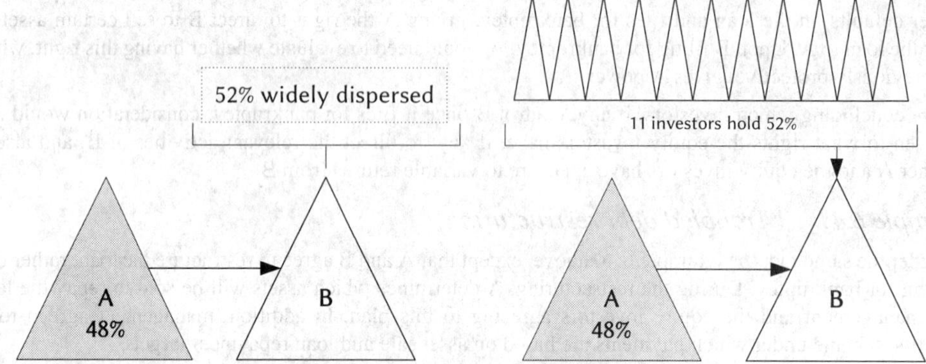

A holds 48% of the voting rights of B, with the remaining 52% being widely dispersed. In its initial assessment, A concludes that the absolute size of its holding, relative to the other shareholdings, gives it power over B.

Over time, some of the shareholders begin to consolidate their interests, such that eventually, the 52% is held by a much smaller group of shareholders. Depending on the regulatory environment, and rights held by A regarding the right to receive information when shareholders acquire other interests in B, it is possible, although perhaps unlikely, that A would not be aware of this occurrence. Nonetheless, it would seem that IFRS 10 would require A to re-evaluate whether it has control over B, because the other shareholders are no longer widely dispersed, and thus A may not have the current ability to direct the relevant activities of B.

While the situation in Example 6.42 above might be uncommon, management should consider what systems and processes are needed to monitor external events for changes that could trigger reassessment. Without knowledge of such events, and a process for gathering this information, it may be difficult to determine the date when the other voters became sufficiently concentrated to conclude that the investor no longer has control. The same might apply where an investor has determined that it does not have control due to there being a relatively small number of other shareholders, but the other voters become sufficiently dispersed or disorganised such that the investor now has control. Depending on the facts and circumstances, there could be a lag in the period between when the facts and circumstances actually change, and when management is able to conclude that the investor has control.

10 INVESTMENT ENTITIES

In October 2012, the IASB issued *Investment Entities (Amendments to IFRS 10, IFRS 12 and IAS 27)*. This introduces an exception to the principle that all subsidiaries shall be consolidated. The amendments define an investment entity and require a parent that is an investment entity to measure its investments in particular subsidiaries at fair value through profit or loss in accordance with IFRS 9 (or IAS 39) with limited exceptions. This amendment applied for annual periods beginning on or after 1 January 2014. *[IFRS 10.C1B]*.

This exception is intended to address what many in the asset management and private equity industries, and users of their financial statements, believe is a significant issue with the consolidation requirements in IFRS 10. As a part of the deliberations ultimately leading to the issuance of IFRS 10, the IASB received many letters noting that for 'investment entities', rather than enhancing decision-useful information, consolidating the controlled investment actually obscures such information. This feedback was persuasive and consequently the IASB decided to issue the investment entity exception.

The Board considers that the entities most likely to be affected by the investment entity exception are:

- private equity or venture capital funds;
- master-feeder or fund of funds structures where an investment entity parent has controlling interests in investment entity subsidiaries;
- some pension funds and sovereign wealth funds which may meet the definition of an investment entity and may hold controlling investments in other entities; and
- other types of entities such as mutual funds and other regulated investment funds, although the Board considers that they tend to hold lower levels of investments in a wider range of entities and therefore the exception from consolidation is less likely to affect them. *[IFRS 10.BC298-BC300]*.

In December 2014, the IASB issued *Investment Entities: Applying the Consolidation Exception (Amendments to IFRS 10, IFRS 12 and IAS 28)* which clarifies two aspects of the investment entity exception. This amendment applied for annual periods beginning on or after 1 January 2016 but could be adopted earlier. *[IFRS 10.C1D]*. This amendment is discussed at 10.2.1.A below.

10.1 Definition of an investment entity

IFRS 10 requires that a parent must determine whether it is an investment entity.

An investment entity is an entity that:

(a) obtains funds from one or more investors for the purpose of providing those investors with investment management services;

(b) commits to its investors that its business purpose is to invest funds solely for returns from capital appreciation, investment income, or both; and

(c) measures and evaluates the performance of substantially all of its investments on a fair value basis. *[IFRS 10.27]*.

An entity shall consider all facts and circumstances when assessing whether it is an investment entity, including its purpose and design. An entity that possesses (all of) the three elements (a) to (c) above is an investment entity. *[IFRS 10.B85A]*.

In addition, when considering the investment entity definition, an entity shall consider whether it has the following typical characteristics:

- it has more than one investment;
- it has more than one investor;
- it has investors that are not related parties of the entity; and
- it has ownership interests in the form of equity or similar interests. *[IFRS 10.28]*.

The absence of any of these typical characteristics does not necessarily disqualify an entity from being classified as an investment entity. However, it indicates that additional judgement is required in determining whether the entity is an investment entity and therefore, where any of these characteristics are absent, disclosure is required by IFRS 12 of the reasons for the entity concluding that it is nonetheless, an investment entity. *[IFRS 10.28, B85N, IFRS 12.9A]*.

In November 2016, the Interpretations Committee discussed a number of questions regarding the investment entity requirements in IFRS 10, including whether an entity qualifies as an investment entity if it does not have one or more of the typical characteristics of an investment entity listed in paragraph 28 of IFRS 10. In its March 2017 agenda decision not to add this question to its standard-setting agenda, the Committee concluded that an entity that possesses all three elements of the definition of an investment entity in paragraph 27 of IFRS 10 is an investment entity, even if that entity does not have one or more of the typical characteristics of an investment entity listed in paragraph 28 of IFRS 10.[9]

If facts and circumstances indicate that there are changes to one or more of the three elements (a) to (c) above, that make up the definition of an investment entity, or changes to the typical characteristics of an investment entity, a parent shall reassess whether it is an investment entity. *[IFRS 10.29]*.

A parent that either ceases to be an investment entity or becomes an investment entity shall account for the change in its status prospectively from the date at which the change in status occurred. *[IFRS 10.30]*.

10.2 Determining whether an entity is an investment entity

The first part of the definition of an investment entity in paragraph 27 of IFRS 10 is the requirement that an investment entity provide investors with investment management services. IFRS 10 does not specify how the investment entity must provide these services. In March 2017 (see 10.1 above), the Interpretations Committee noted that IFRS 10 does not preclude an investment entity from outsourcing the performance of these services to a third party and therefore concluded that an investment entity responsible for providing investment management services to its investors can engage another party to perform some or all of the services on its behalf.

Application guidance is provided in respect of the definition (b) in 10.1 above, as follows:

- Business purpose (see 10.2.1 below);
- Exit strategies (see 10.2.2 below); and
- Earnings from investments (see 10.2.3 below).

Application guidance is provided in respect of definition (c) in 10.1 above, as follows:

- Fair value measurement (see 10.2.4 below).

Application guidance is provided in respect of the four typical characteristics described in 10.1 above, as follows:

- more than one investment (see 10.2.5 below);
- more than one investor (see 10.2.6 below);
- unrelated investors (see 10.2.7 below); and
- ownership interests (see 10.2.8 below).

10.2.1 Business purpose

The definition of an investment entity requires that the purpose of the entity is to invest solely for capital appreciation, investment income (such as dividends, interest or rental income), or both. *[IFRS 10.B85B].*

Documents that include a discussion of an entity's investment objectives, such as offering memoranda, publications distributed by the entity and other corporate or partnership documents, typically provide evidence of an entity's business purpose. Further evidence may include the manner in which an entity presents itself to other parties (such as potential investors or potential investees). *[IFRS 10.B85B].*

However, an entity that presents itself as an investor whose objective is to jointly develop, produce or market products with its investees, has a business purpose that is inconsistent with the business purpose of an investment entity. This is because the entity will earn returns from the development, production and marketing activity as well as from its investments. *[IFRS 10.B85B].*

10.2.1.A Entities that provide investment-related services

An investment entity may provide investment-related services (e.g. investment advisory services, investment management, investment support and administrative services), either directly or through a subsidiary, to third parties as well as its investors and not lose its investment entity status. This applies even if those activities are substantial to the entity, subject to the entity continuing to meet the definition of an investment entity. *[IFRS 10.B85C].* In March 2017, the Interpretations Committee confirmed that an investment entity may provide investment-related services to third parties, either directly or through a subsidiary, as long as those services are ancillary to its core investment activities and thus do not change the business purpose of the investment entity (see 10.1 above).

An investment entity may also participate in the following investment-related activities either directly or through a subsidiary, if these activities are undertaken to maximise the investment return (capital appreciation or investment income) from its investees and do not represent a separate substantial business activity or a separate substantial source of income to the investment entity:

- providing management services and strategic advice to an investee; and
- providing financial support to an investee such as a loan, capital commitment or guarantee. *[IFRS 10.B85D].*

The rationale for these provisions is that investment-related services to third parties are simply an extension of the investment entity's investing activities and should not prohibit an entity from qualifying as an investment entity. *[IFRS 10.BC239]*.

An investment entity must consolidate a subsidiary that is itself not an investment entity and whose main purpose and activities are providing services that relate to the investment entity's investment activities. *[IFRS 10.32]*. If the subsidiary that provides the investment-related services or activities is itself an investment entity, the investment entity parent must measure that subsidiary at fair value through profit or loss. *[IFRS 10.B85E]*.

This means that only those entities that are not investment entities that provide investment related services are consolidated. See 10.3 below for further discussion of the accounting consequences resulting from this requirement.

The requirement to consolidate particular subsidiaries of an investment entity is intended to be a limited exception, capturing only operating subsidiaries that support the investment entity's investing activities as an extension of the operations of the investment entity parent. *[IFRS 10.BC240E]*. When an entity assesses whether it qualifies as an investment entity, it considers whether providing services to third parties is ancillary to its core investing services. However, the definition of an investment entity requires that the purpose of the entity is to invest solely for capital appreciation, investment income or both (see 10.1 above). Consequently, an entity whose main purpose is to provide investment-related services in exchange for consideration from third parties has a business purpose that is different from the business purpose of an investment entity. This is because the entity's main activity is earning fee income in exchange for its services in contrast to an investment entity whose fee income will be derived from its core activities, which are designed for earning capital appreciation, investment income or both. *[IFRS 10.BC240F]*.

If the subsidiary is not an investment entity, the investment entity parent must assess whether the main activities undertaken by the subsidiary support the core investment activities of the parent. If so, the subsidiary's activities are considered to be an extension of the parent's core investing activities and the subsidiary must be consolidated. These support services provided to the parent and other members of the group could include administration, treasury, payroll and accounting services. *[IFRS 10.BC240H]*.

In November 2016, the Interpretations Committee received a question as to whether a subsidiary provides services that relate to its parent investment entity's investment activities by holding an investment portfolio as beneficial owner. In its agenda decision in March 2017, the Committee concluded that an investment entity does not consider the holding of investments by a subsidiary as beneficial owner (and recognised in the subsidiary's financial statements) to be a service that relates to the parent investment entity's investment activities (see 10.1 above), and observed that it had previously discussed a similar question in March 2014 (see 10.2.1.B below).

The requirement that an investment entity measures at fair value through profit or loss all of its subsidiaries that are themselves investment entities is consistent with the decision not to distinguish between investment entity subsidiaries established for different reasons. *[IFRS 10.BC240B]*. See 10.2.1.B below.

10.2.1.B Entities that are intermediate holding companies established for tax optimisation purposes

It is explained in the Basis for Conclusion that some respondents to the original Investment Entities ED suggested that at least some investment entity subsidiaries should be consolidated (for example, wholly-owned investment entity subsidiaries that are created for legal, tax or regulatory purposes). However, the Board considers that fair value measurement of all of an investment entity's subsidiaries (except for subsidiaries providing investment-related services or activities) would provide the most useful information and therefore decided to require fair value management for all investment entity subsidiaries. *[IFRS 10.BC272]*.

Some investment entities establish wholly-owned intermediate subsidiaries in some jurisdictions which own all or part of the portfolio of investments in the group structure. The sole purpose of the intermediate subsidiaries is to minimise the tax paid in the 'parent' investment entity. There is no activity within the subsidiaries and the tax advantage arises from returns being channelled through the jurisdiction of the intermediate subsidiary. In March 2014, the Interpretations Committee discussed a request to clarify whether the 'tax optimisation' described above should be considered investment-related services or activities. The Interpretations Committee noted that the IASB believes that fair value measurement of all of an investment entity's subsidiaries would provide the most useful information, except for subsidiaries providing investment-related services or activities and that the IASB had decided against requiring an investment entity to consolidate investment entity subsidiaries that are formed for tax purposes. The Interpretations Committee further noted that one of the characteristics of the 'tax optimisation' subsidiaries described is 'that there is no activity within the subsidiary'. Accordingly, the Interpretations Committee concluded that the parent should not consolidate such subsidiaries and should account for such intermediate subsidiaries at fair value because they do not provide investment-related services or activities and therefore do not meet the requirements for consolidation. Consequently, the Interpretations Committee considered that sufficient guidance already exists and it decided not to add the issue to its agenda.[10]

10.2.2 Exit strategies

One feature that differentiates an investment entity from other entities is that an investment entity does not plan to hold its investments indefinitely; it holds them for a limited period. *[IFRS 10.B85F]*.

For investments that have the potential to be held indefinitely (typically equity investments and non-financial asset investments), the investment entity must have a documented exit strategy. This documented exit strategy must state how the entity plans to realise capital appreciation from substantially all of these potentially indefinite life investments. An investment entity should also have an exit strategy for any debt instruments that have the potential to be held indefinitely (e.g. perpetual debt instruments). *[IFRS 10.B85F]*.

The investment entity need not document specific exit strategies for each individual investment but should identify different potential strategies for different types or portfolios of investments, including a substantive time frame for exiting the investments. Exit mechanisms that are only put in place for default events, such as breach of contract or non-performance, are not considered exit strategies. *[IFRS 10.B85F]*.

Exit strategies can vary by type of investment. Examples of such strategies for investments in equity securities include an initial public offering, selling the investment in a public market, a private placement, a trade sale of a business, distributions (to investors) of ownership interests in investees and sales of assets (including the sale of an investee's assets followed by a liquidation of an investee). For real estate investments, an example of an exit strategy includes the sale of the real estate through specialised property dealers or the open market. *[IFRS 10.B85G].*

An investment entity may have an investment in another investment entity that is formed in connection with the entity for legal, regulatory, tax or similar business reasons. In this case, the investment entity investor need not have an exit strategy for that investment, provided that the investment entity investee has appropriate exit strategies for its investments. *[IFRS 10.B85H].* This is intended to prevent an entity that conducts most of its investing activities through a subsidiary that is a holding company from failing to qualify as an investment entity. *[IFRS 10.BC248].*

10.2.3 Earnings from investments

An investment entity must commit to its investors that its business purpose is to invest funds solely for returns from capital appreciation, investment income or both.

An entity does not meet this condition when it, or another member of the group containing the entity (i.e. the group that is controlled by the entity's ultimate parent) obtains, or has the objective of obtaining, other benefits from the entity's investments that are not available to other parties that are not related to the investee. 'Other benefits' means benefits in addition to capital appreciation or investment return and such benefits include:

- the acquisition, use, exchange or exploitation of the processes, assets or technology of an investee including the entity or another group member having disproportionate, or exclusive, rights to acquire assets, technology, products or services of any investee; for example by holding an option to purchase an asset from an investee if the asset's development is deemed successful;
- joint arrangements or other agreements between the entity or another group member and an investee to develop, produce, market or provide products or services;
- financial guarantees or assets provided by an investee to serve as collateral for borrowing arrangements of the entity or another group member (however, an investment entity would still be able to use an investment in an investee as collateral for any of its borrowings);
- an option held by a related party of the entity to purchase, from that entity or another group member, an ownership interest in an investee of the entity; and
- except as described below, transactions between the entity or another group member and an investee that:
  - are on terms that are unavailable to entities that are not related parties of either the entity, another group member or the investee;
  - are not at fair value; or
  - represent a substantial portion of the investee's or the entity's business activity, including business activities of other group entities. *[IFRS 10.B85I].*

These requirements in respect of 'other benefits' are anti-avoidance provisions. As explained in the Basis for Conclusions, the Board was concerned that an entity that meets the definition of an investment entity could be inserted into a larger corporate group in order to achieve a particular accounting outcome. This concern is illustrated by an example of a parent entity using an 'internal' investment entity subsidiary to invest in subsidiaries that may be making losses (e.g. research and development activities on behalf of the overall group) and therefore record its investments at fair value, rather than reflecting the underlying activities of the investee. Because of these concerns, the Board has included the requirement that the investment entity, or other members of the group containing the entity, should not obtain benefits from its investees that would be unavailable to other parties that are not related to the investee. *[IFRS 10.BC242]*.

It is also clarified that an entity should demonstrate that fair value is the primary measurement attribute used to evaluate the performance of its investments, both internally and externally. *[IFRS 10.BC252]*.

An entity is not disqualified from being classified as an investment entity because it has investees in the same industry, market or geographical area that trade with each other. This applies where the investment entity has a strategy to invest in more than one investee in that industry, market or geographical area in order to benefit from synergies that increase the capital appreciation and investment income from those investees. *[IFRS 10.B85J]*. The Board decided that trading transactions or synergies that arise between the investments of an investment entity should not be prohibited because their existence does not necessarily mean that the investment entity is receiving any returns beyond solely capital appreciation, investment return, or both. *[IFRS 10.BC243]*.

10.2.4 Fair value measurement

In order to qualify as an investment entity, a reporting entity must measure and evaluate the performance of substantially all of its investments on a fair value basis. This is because using fair value results in more relevant information than, for example, consolidation for subsidiaries or the use of the equity method for interests in associates or joint ventures. In order to demonstrate fair value measurement, an investment entity should:

(a) provide investors with fair value information and measure substantially all of its investments at fair value in its financial statements whenever fair value is permitted in accordance with IFRSs; and

(b) report fair value information to the entity's key management personnel who use fair value as the primary measurement attribute to evaluate the performance of substantially all of its investments and to make investment decisions. *[IFRS 10.B85K]*.

In order to meet the requirements in (a) above, an investment entity would:

- elect to account for any investment property using the fair value model in IAS 40 – *Investment Property;*
- elect the exemption from applying the equity method in IAS 28 for its investments in associates and joint ventures; and
- measure its financial assets at fair value using the requirements in IFRS 9 (or IAS 39). *[IFRS 10.B85L]*.

As described in the Basis for Conclusions, investments measured at fair value in the statement of financial position with fair value changes recognised in other comprehensive income rather than through profit or loss still satisfy the fair value measurement condition of the definition of an investment entity. *[IFRS 10.BC251]*. However, an investment entity should not account for more than an insignificant amount of financial assets at amortised cost under IFRS 9 (or IAS 39), nor fail to elect the fair value measurement options in IAS 28 or IAS 40. *[IFRS 10.BC250]*.

Fair value measurement applies only to an investment entity's investments. There is no requirement to measure non-investment assets such as property, plant and equipment or liabilities such as financial liabilities at fair value. *[IFRS 10.B85M]*.

10.2.5 Holding more than one investment

An investment entity would typically hold several investments to diversify its risk and maximise its returns. These may be held directly or indirectly, for example by holding a single investment in another investment entity that itself holds several investments. *[IFRS 10.B85O]*.

However, holding a single investment does not necessarily prevent an entity from meeting the definition of an investment entity. Examples where an investment entity may hold only a single investment are when the entity:

- is in its start-up period and has not yet identified suitable investments and, therefore, has not yet executed its investment plan to acquire several investments;
- has not yet made other investments to replace those it has disposed of;
- is established to pool investors' funds to invest in a single investment when that investment is unobtainable by individual investors (e.g. when the required minimum investment is too high for an individual investor); or
- is in the process of liquidation. *[IFRS 10.B85P]*.

As holding only one investment is not a typical characteristic of an investment entity, this would require disclosure as a significant judgement (see 10.1 above).

10.2.6 Having more than one investor

An investment entity would typically have several investors who pool their funds to gain access to investment management services and investment opportunities they might not have had access to individually. In the Board's opinion, having more than one investor makes it less likely that the entity, or other members of the group containing the entity, would obtain benefits other than capital appreciation or investment income (see 10.2.3 above). *[IFRS 10.B85Q]*.

Although the Board considers that an investment entity would typically have more than one investor, there is no conceptual reason why an investment fund with a single investor should be disqualified from being an investment entity. Therefore, the presence of more than one investor is a typical characteristic of an investment entity rather than as part of the definition of an investment entity. *[IFRS 10.BC260]*.

An investment entity may be formed by, or for, a single investor that represents or supports the interests of a wider group of investors such as a pension fund, a government investment fund or a family trust. *[IFRS 10.B85R]*.

The Board acknowledges that there may be times when the entity temporarily has a single investor. For example, an investment entity may have a single investor when it:

- is within its initial offering period and the entity is actively identifying suitable investors;
- has not yet identified suitable investors to replace ownership interests that have been redeemed; or
- is in the process of liquidation. *[IFRS 10.B85S]*.

These examples are not stated to be exhaustive and there could be other reasons why an investment entity might have only one investor. Having only one investor is not a typical characteristic of an investment entity. The fact that an entity is considered to be an investment entity despite having only one investor is a significant judgement requiring disclosure (see 10.1 above).

10.2.7 Unrelated investors

An investment entity would typically have several investors that are not related parties of the entity or other members of the group containing the entity. The existence of unrelated investors makes it less likely that the entity, or other members of the group containing the entity, would obtain benefits other than capital appreciation or investment income (see 10.2.3 above). *[IFRS 10.B85T]*.

As the definition of a related party includes an entity which has significant influence over a reporting entity, when read literally this means that, typically, an entity that is significantly influenced by one or more parties by, for example, having investors with a greater than twenty percent ownership interest (see Chapter 11 at 4), cannot be an investment entity.

However, an entity may still qualify as an investment entity even though its investors are related to the entity. To support this, an example is illustrated in which an investment entity sets up a separate 'parallel' fund for a group of its employees (such as key management personnel) or other related party investors, which mirrors the investment of the entity's main investment fund. It is stated that this 'parallel' fund may qualify as an investment entity even though all of its investors are related parties. *[IFRS 10.B85U]*. In this example, the key determinant in concluding that the parallel fund is an investment entity is that it is being managed for capital appreciation or investment income.

Although IFRS 10 provides only one example of a fund which qualifies as an investment entity with investors that are related parties, it is explained in the Basis for Conclusions that respondents to the Investment Entities ED provided 'examples of entities with related investors that they believed should qualify as investment entities'. *[IFRS 10.BC261]*.

10.2.8 Ownership interests

An investment entity is typically, but is not required to be, a separate legal entity. Ownership interests in an investment entity will usually be in the form of equity or similar interests (e.g. partnership interests), to which proportionate shares of the net assets of the investment entity are attributed. However, having different classes of investors, some of which have rights only to a specific investment or groups of investments or which have different proportionate shares of the net assets, does not preclude an entity from being an investment entity. *[IFRS 10.B85V]*.

It is rationalised in the Basis of Conclusions that holding a proportionate share of the net assets of an investment entity explains in part why fair value is more relevant to investors of an investment entity because the value of each ownership interest is linked directly to the fair value of the entity's investments. *[IFRS 10.BC263]*. However, whether there is this form of ownership interest in an entity should not be a deciding factor and would inappropriately exclude certain structures from investment entity status. One example illustrated by the Basis for Conclusions is entities that do not have units of ownership interest in the form of equity or similar interests is a pension fund or sovereign wealth fund with a single direct investor which may have beneficiaries that are entitled to the net assets of the investment fund, but do not have ownership units. Another example is funds with different share classes or funds in which investors have discretion to invest in individual assets. *[IFRS 10.BC264, BC266]*. In both of these examples, the investors are entitled to a proportionate share of at least part of the assets of the fund although not the entire fund.

An entity that has significant ownership interests in the form of debt that does not meet the definition of equity may still qualify as an investment entity, provided that the debt holders are exposed to variable returns from changes in the fair value of the entity's net assets. *[IFRS 10.B85W]*.

10.2.9 Investment entity illustrative examples

The following examples illustrate the application of the investment entity criteria and are based on illustrative examples contained in IFRS 10.

Example 6.43: A limited partnership that is an investment entity

An entity, Limited Partnership (LP) is formed in 2016 with a 10-year life. The offering memorandum states that LP's purpose is to invest in entities with rapid growth potential, with the objective of realising capital appreciation over their life. Entity GP (the general partner of LP) provides 1% of the capital to LP and has responsibility for identifying suitable investments for the partnership. Approximately 75 limited partners, who are unrelated to Entity GP, provide 99% of the capital to the partnership. LP begins its investment activities in 2016 but no investments are identified until 2017 when LP acquires a controlling interest in ABC Corp.

The group structure at 31.12.2017 is illustrated as follows:

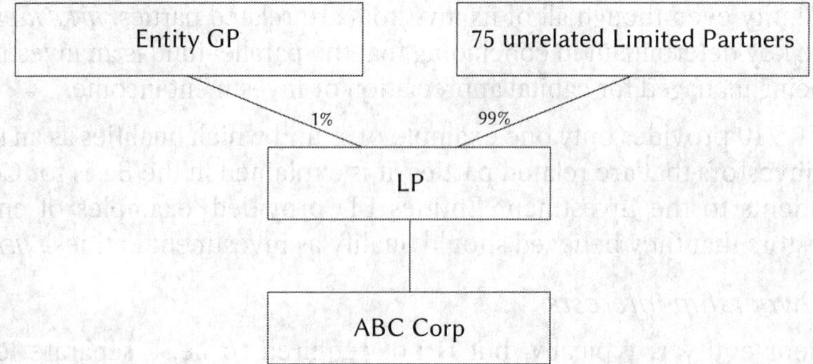

In 2018, LP acquires equity interests in five additional operating companies. Other than acquiring those equity interests, LP conducts no other activities. LP measures and evaluates its investments on a fair value basis and this information is provided to Entity GP and the external investors.

LP plans to dispose of its interests in each of its investees during the 10 year stated life of the partnership. Such disposals include the outright sale for cash, the distribution of marketable equity securities to investors following the successful public offering of the investees' securities and the disposal of investments to the public or other unrelated entities.

In this example, LP meets the definition of an investment entity from formation in 2016 to 31 December 2018 because:

- LP has obtained funds from limited partners and is providing them with investment management services;
- LP's only activity is acquiring equity interests in operating companies with the purpose of realising capital appreciation over the life of the investments. LP has identified and documented exit strategies for its investments, all of which are equity investments; and
- LP measures and evaluates its investments on a fair value basis and reports this financial information to its investors.

In addition, LP displays the following typical characteristics of an investment entity:

- LP is funded by many investors;
- its limited partners are unrelated to LP; and
- ownership in LP is represented by units of partnership interests acquired through a capital contribution.

LP does not hold more than one investment throughout the period. However, this is because it was still in its start-up period and had not identified suitable investment opportunities. *[IFRS 10.IE1-IE6].*

Example 6.44: Start-up high technology fund that is not an investment entity

An entity, High Technology Fund, is formed by Technology Corp. to invest in start-up technology companies for capital appreciation. Technology Corp. holds a 70% interest in High Technology Fund and controls it; the other 30% ownership interest is held by 10 unrelated investors. Technology Corp. holds options to acquire investments held by High Technology Fund, at their fair value, which would be exercised if the technology developed by the investees would benefit the operations of Technology Corp.

The group structure is illustrated below:

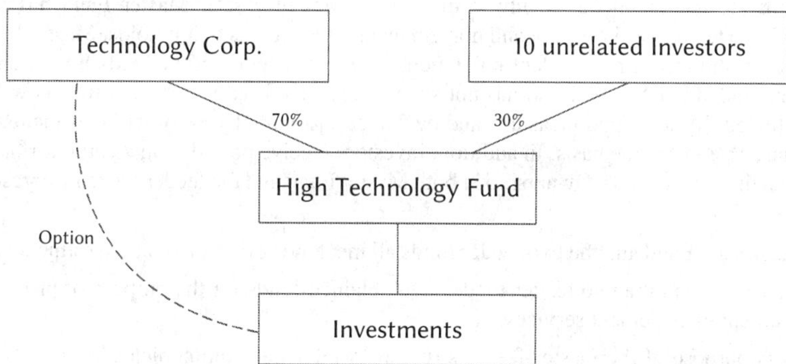

High Technology Fund has no plans for exiting the investments. High Technology Fund is managed by an investment advisor that acts as agent for the investors in High Technology Fund.

In this example, although High Technology Fund's business purpose is investing for capital appreciation and it provides investment management services to its investors, High Technology Fund is not an investment entity because:

- Technology Corp., the parent of High Technology Fund, holds options to acquire investments in investees held by High Technology Fund if assets developed by the investees would benefit the operations of Technology Corp. This provides a benefit in addition to capital appreciation and investment income; and
- the investment plans of High Technology Fund do not include exit strategies for its investments, which are equity instruments. The options held by Technology Corp. are not controlled by High Technology Fund and do not constitute an exit strategy. *[IFRS 10.IE7-IE8].*

Example 6.45: Master and feeder funds that are investment entities

An entity, Master Fund, is formed in 2018 with a 10-year life. The equity of Master Fund is held by two related feeder funds. The feeder funds are established in connection with each other to meet legal, regulatory, tax or similar requirements. The feeder funds are capitalised with a 1% investment from the general partner and 99% from equity investors that are unrelated to the general partner (with no party holding a controlling financial interest).

The group structure is illustrated below:

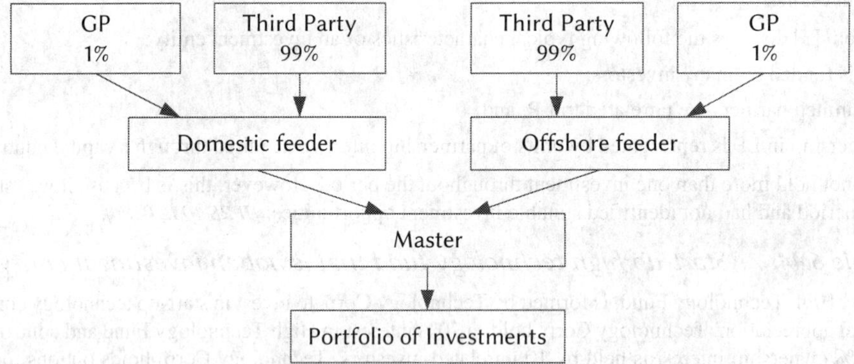

The purpose of Master Fund is to hold a portfolio of investments in order to generate capital appreciation and investment income (such as dividends, interest or rental income). The investment objective communicated to investors is that the sole purpose of the master-feeder structure is to provide investment opportunities for investors in separate market niches to invest in a large pool of assets. Master Fund has identified and documented exit strategies for the equity and non-financial investments that it holds. Master Fund also holds a portfolio of short and medium-term debt instruments, some of which will be held until maturity and some of which will be traded but Master Fund has not specifically identified which investments will be held and which will be traded. Master Fund measures and evaluates substantially all of its investments, including its debt investments, on a fair value basis. In addition, investors receive periodic financial information, on a fair value basis, from the feeder funds. Ownership in both Master Fund and the feeder funds is represented through units of equity.

In this example, Master Fund and the two feeder funds all meet the definition of an investment entity because:

- both Master Fund and the two feeder funds have obtained funds for the purpose of providing investors with investment management services;
- the business purpose of the master-feeder structure, which was communicated directly to investors of the feeder funds, is investing solely for capital appreciation and investment income and Master Fund has identified and documented potential exit strategies for its equity and non-equity financial instruments;
- although the feeder funds do not have an exit strategy for their interests in Master Fund, the feeder funds can nevertheless be considered to have an exit strategy for their investments because Master Fund was formed in connection with the feeder funds and holds investments on behalf of the feeder funds; and
- the investments held by Master Fund are measured and evaluated on a fair value basis and information about the investments made by Master Fund is provided to investors on a fair value basis through the feeder funds.

Master Fund and the feeder funds were formed in connection with each other for legal, regulatory, tax or similar requirements. When considered together, they display the following typical characteristics of an investment entity:

- the feeder fund indirectly holds more than one investment because Master Fund holds a portfolio of investments;
- although Master Fund is wholly capitalised by feeder funds, the feeder funds are funded by many investors who are unrelated to the feeder funds (and to the general partner); and
- ownership in the feeder funds is represented by units of equity interests through a capital contribution. *[IFRS 10.IE12-IE15]*.

10.2.10 Multi-layered fund structures

Example 6.45 above illustrates a multi-layered fund structure. The reason and purpose of these is usually to accomplish one or more of the following:

- regulatory reasons to invest in certain jurisdictions; or
- risk mitigation reasons, that is, to ring fence particular investees; or
- investment-return enhancement, where the after tax returns on an investment can be enhanced by using vehicles in certain jurisdictions.

When an investment entity has a subsidiary that is an intermediate parent that is formed in connection with the parent investment entity for legal, regulatory, tax or similar business reasons, the investment entity investor need not have an exit strategy for that subsidiary. This is on condition that the intermediate investment entity parent has appropriate exit strategies for its investments. *[IFRS 10.B85H]*. In addition, an entity must consider all facts and circumstances in assessing whether it is an investment entity, including its purpose and design. *[IFRS 10.B85A]*. Illustrative Example 4 of IFRS 10, represented by Example 6.45 above, indicates that funds formed in connection with each other for legal, regulatory, tax or similar requirements can be considered together to determine whether they display the characteristics of an investment entity. In Example 6.45 above, both Domestic Feeder and Offshore Feeder are considered to be investment entities.

10.3 Accounting by an investment entity

In its consolidated financial statements, an investment entity shall:

- consolidate any subsidiary that is not an investment entity and whose main purpose and activities are providing services that relate to the investment entity's investment activities and apply the requirements of IFRS 3 to the acquisition of any such subsidiary (see 10.2.1 above); *[IFRS 10.32]* and
- measure all other investments in a subsidiary at fair value through profit or loss in accordance with IFRS 9 (or IAS 39). *[IFRS 10.31]*.

In addition, as discussed at 10.2.4 above, the investment entity must elect to account for its own investments in investment property, associates, joint ventures and financial assets at fair value. However, where applicable, some of these investments could be measured at fair value through other comprehensive income. Other assets (e.g. property, plant and equipment) and financial liabilities need not be measured at fair value unless this is required by the relevant IFRS.

The following diagram illustrates the accounting in the consolidated financial statements of an investment entity in a simple group structure:

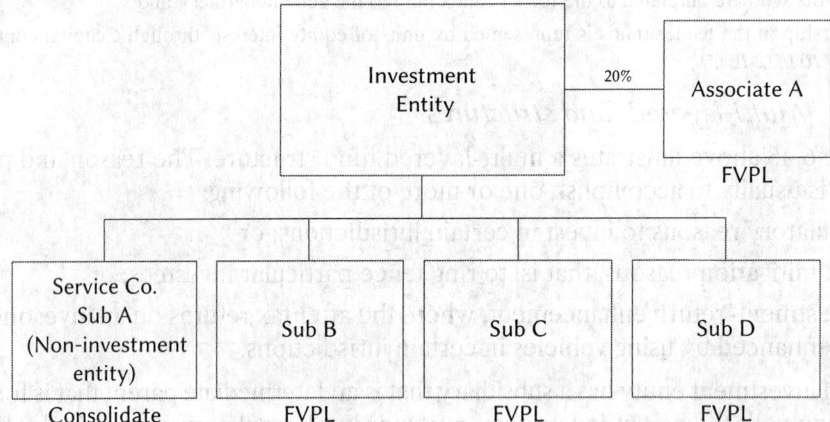

The accounting is less intuitive for investment entities with intermediate holding company subsidiaries. If the intermediate holding company does not meet the conditions for consolidation, then the intermediate holding company, including its investments in subsidiaries, is measured at fair value through profit or loss. The underlying subsidiaries are not measured separately.

The diagram below illustrates the accounting for an investment entity parent using the same group structure as above but with an intermediate parent established for tax optimisation purposes inserted between the investment entity parent and the subsidiaries. As discussed at 10.2.1.B above, the Interpretations Committee has clarified that intermediate holding companies established for tax optimisation purposes should be measured by a parent investment entity at fair value through profit or loss. Therefore, in this situation, the underlying subsidiaries are not separately measured at fair value through profit or loss (or consolidated in the case of the non-investment entity service company). Instead, the intermediate holding entity, including its investments in subsidiaries, is measured at fair value through profit or loss. Parent investment entities with this type of group structure may wish to provide further information in their financial reports to help explain their performance.

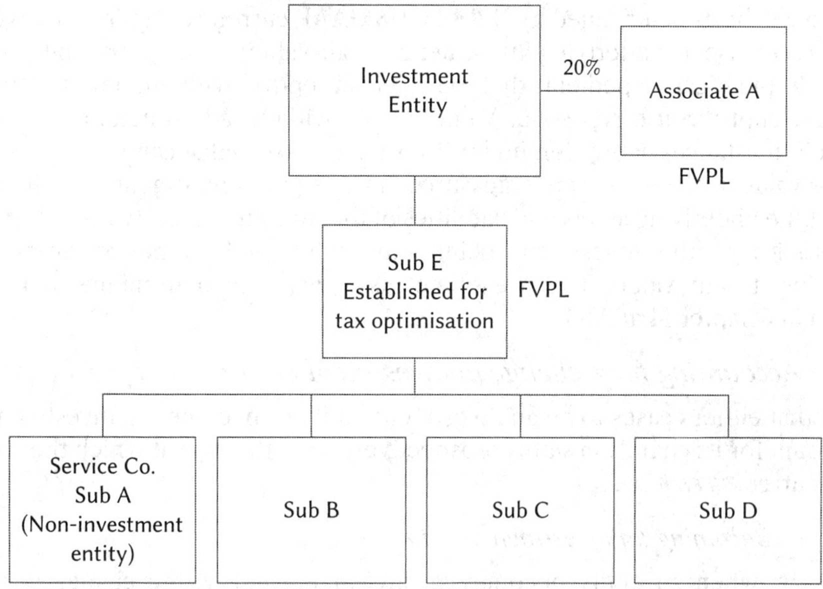

If Subsidiary A (the non-investment entity service company) was owned directly by the investment entity parent, rather than by Subsidiary E, it would be consolidated.

When an investment entity has no subsidiaries that are consolidated (i.e. all subsidiaries are measured at fair value through profit or loss as illustrated above), it presents separate financial statements as its only financial statements. *[IAS 27.8A]*.

When an investment entity parent prepares consolidated financial statements, any subsidiary measured at fair value through profit or loss in those consolidated financial statements must also be accounted for in the same way in its separate financial statements (i.e. at fair value through profit or loss). *[IAS 27.11A]*. When an investment entity parent has subsidiaries that are consolidated in its consolidated financial statements, the parent has an separate accounting policy choice to account for those subsidiaries either at cost, in accordance with IFRS 9 (or IAS 39) or using the equity method in its separate financial statements (see Chapter 8 at 2).

Fair value will be as determined by IFRS 13. US GAAP currently requires an investment entity to recognise its underlying investments at fair value at each reporting period and provides a practical expedient that permits an entity with an investment in an investment entity to use Net Asset Value (NAV), without adjustment, as fair value in specific circumstances. However, under IFRS 13, net asset value cannot be presumed to equal fair value as the asset being measured is the equity investment in an investment entity not the underlying assets and liabilities of the investment entity itself. Instead, the characteristics of the investment being measured need to be considered when determining its fair value. The use of net asset value in determining fair value is discussed in Chapter 14 at 2.5.1.

10.3.1 Accounting for a change in investment entity status

A parent that either ceases to be an investment entity or becomes an investment entity shall account for its change in status prospectively from the date at which the change in status occurred. *[IFRS 10.30]*.

10.3.1.A Becoming an investment entity

In summary, when an entity becomes an investment entity, the change in status is treated as a loss of control of the investment entity subsidiaries. Therefore, when an entity becomes an investment entity, it shall cease to consolidate its subsidiaries from the date of the change in status, except for any non-investment entity subsidiary whose main purpose and activities are providing services that relate to the investment entity's investment activities, and apply the loss of control provisions of IFRS 10. *[IFRS 10.B101]*.

This means that the parent:

- derecognises the assets and liabilities of those subsidiaries from the consolidated statement of financial position;
- recognises any investment retained in those subsidiaries at fair value through profit or loss in accordance with IFRS 9 (or IAS 39); and
- recognises a gain or loss associated with the loss of control attributed to the subsidiaries. *[IFRS 10.25]*.

Similarly, in the separate financial statements of the parent, when an entity becomes an investment entity, it shall account for an investment in a subsidiary at fair value through profit or loss in accordance with IFRS 9 (or IAS 39). The difference between the previous carrying amount of the subsidiary and its fair value at the date of the change in status of the investor shall be recognised as a gain or loss in profit or loss. The cumulative amount of any gain or loss recognised previously in other comprehensive income in respect of those subsidiaries shall be treated as if the investment entity had disposed of those subsidiaries at the date of change in status and recycled through profit or loss. *[IAS 27.11B(b)]*.

IFRS 10 is silent in respect of any accounting changes required when an entity becomes an investment entity in respect of its own investment property, associates, joint ventures and financial assets. However, it is a condition of being an investment entity that a reporting entity must measure and evaluate the performance of substantially all of its investments on a fair value basis. This implies that those assets should have been measured already on a fair value basis in order for the entity to meet the requirements of an investment entity.

10.3.1.B Ceasing to be an investment entity

In summary, when an entity ceases to be an investment entity, the event is treated similar to a business combination. Therefore, when an entity ceases to be an investment entity, it shall apply IFRS 3 to any subsidiary that was previously measured at fair value through profit or loss. This means that all of the individual assets and liabilities of the subsidiary are recognised at fair value (unless IFRS 3 requires otherwise) and the difference between the previous fair value and the value of the individual assets and liabilities is goodwill. The date of change of status is the deemed acquisition date. The fair value of the subsidiary at the deemed acquisition date shall represent the transferred deemed consideration when measuring any goodwill or gain from a bargain purchase that arises from the deemed acquisition. All subsidiaries shall be consolidated in accordance with IFRS 10 from the date of change in status. *[IFRS 10.B100]*.

In the separate financial statements of the parent, when the parent ceases to be an investment entity, it shall account for an investment in a subsidiary either at cost, in accordance with IFRS 9 (or IAS 39), or using the equity method as described in IAS 28. The date of the change in status shall be the deemed acquisition date. The fair value of the subsidiary at the deemed acquisition date when accounting for the investment, under any of the permitted methods, shall represent the transferred deemed consideration. *[IAS 27.11B(a)]*.

10.4 Accounting by a parent of an investment entity

A parent of an investment entity that is not itself an investment entity cannot use the investment entity exception. It must therefore consolidate all entities that it controls including those controlled through an investment entity subsidiary. *[IFRS 10.33]*.

As described in the Basis for Conclusions, the Board considered whether to permit the exception to consolidation to be 'rolled up' to a non-investment entity parent but rejected this approach. This was despite the fact that the majority of respondents to the *Investment Entities* Exposure Draft argued that if fair value information was more relevant than consolidation at an investment entity subsidiary level, it is also more relevant at the non-investment entity parent level. According to the Board, non-investment entities do not have the unique business models of investment entities; they have other substantial activities besides investing or do not manage substantially all of their investments on a fair value basis. Consequently, in the Board's view, the argument for a fair value measurement is weakened at non-investment entity level. *[IFRS 10.BC276-278]*.

The Board also noted the following in arriving at its conclusion:

- concern that a non-investment entity could achieve different accounting outcomes by holding subsidiaries directly or indirectly through an investment entity; *[IFRS 10.BC280]*
- practical difficulties when a non-investment entity parent and an investment entity invest in the same investment or when an investment entity subsidiary holds a subsidiary that invests in the equity of a non-investment entity parent; *[IFRS 10.BC281]*
- although US GAAP permits 'rolled up' accounting in certain circumstances, this is linked to industry-specific guidance that is not generally contained in IFRSs; *[IFRS 10.BC282]* and
- inconsistency with the roll-up of fair value accounting option permitted by IAS 28. However, the Board thought it was important to retain the fair value accounting that is currently allowed for venture capital organisations, mutual funds, unit trusts and similar entities and that the differences between using equity accounting and fair value accounting was considered to be smaller than between consolidation and fair value measurement for investments in subsidiaries. *[IFRS 10.BC283]*.

Ultimately, due to concerns about potential abuses, the Board considered that the investment entity exception is not retained by a non-investment entity parent in its consolidated financial statements.

11 FUTURE DEVELOPMENTS

In May 2015, the IASB issued Exposure Draft ED/2015/3 – *Conceptual framework for Financial Reporting*. The ED contains various concepts (some of which arose from the IASB's earlier 'reporting entity' project) that might, at a future date, result in changes to IFRS 10:

- a reporting entity is an entity that chooses, or is required, to present general purpose financial statements;
- a reporting entity need not be a legal entity, and can comprise a portion of an entity, or two or more entities;
- when one entity (the parent) has control over another entity (the subsidiary), the boundary of the reporting entity can be determined by either direct control only (leading to unconsolidated financial statements) or both direct and indirect control (leading to consolidated financial statements);
- in general, the IASB considers that consolidated financial statements are more likely than unconsolidated financial statements to provide information that is useful to users;
- the IASB is of the view that if an entity chooses, or is required, to prepare unconsolidated financial statements, those unconsolidated financial statements should disclose how users may obtain consolidated financial statements;
- an entity controls an economic resource if it has the present ability to direct the use of the economic resource and obtain the benefits that flow from it;

- financial statements prepared for two or more entities that do not have a parent-subsidiary relationship with each other are referred to as combined financial statements; and
- if a reporting entity is not a legal entity, the boundary of the reporting entity needs to be set in such a way that the financial statements:
  - provide the relevant financial information needed for those existing and potential investors, lenders and other creditors who rely on the financial statements; and
  - faithfully represent the economic activities of the entity.[11]

Comments on the ED were required to be received by 26 October 2015. The IASB is now deliberating the responses to the ED.

References

1 Regulation (EC) No. 1606/2002 of the European Parliament and of the Council of 19 July 2002 on the application of international accounting standards, preamble para. (3).

2 Agenda paper for the meeting of the Accounting Regulatory Committee on 24th November 2006 (document ARC/19/2006), *Subject: Relationship between the IAS Regulation and the 4th and 7th Company Law Directives – Meaning of 'Annual Accounts'*, European Commission: Internal Market and Services DG: Free movement of capital, company law and corporate governance: Accounting/RC MX D(2006), 7 November 2006, para. 5.1.

3 *IFRIC Update*, January 2010, p.2.

4 *Effect analysis IFRS 10 Consolidated Financial Statements and IFRS 12 Disclosure of Interests in Other Entities*, IASB, September 2011, pp.25-26.

5 *IFRIC Update*, May 2015, pp.7-8.

6 *IFRIC Update*, September 2013, p.3.

7 The Project Summary and Feedback Statement on IFRS 10 and IFRS 12 issued in May 2011 on page 22 states 'We think that IFRS 10, in essence, aligns the consolidation guidance for structured entities (or variable interest entities) with US GAAP. Those entities will now have the same basis for consolidation in IFRSs and US GAAP because the same control model is used in both regimes. However, this convergence is dependent on the FASB approving the agent-principal guidance that is included in IFRS 10.'

8 *IFRIC Update*, January 2015, p.10.

9 *IFRIC Update*, March 2017, pp.7-8.

10 *IFRIC Update*, March 2014, p.4.

11 *Exposure Draft ED/2015/3 Conceptual Framework for Financial Reporting*, IASB, May 2015, paras. 3.11-3.25, 4.18.

Chapter 7 Consolidation procedures and non-controlling interests

List of examples

Chapter 7 Consolidation procedures and non-controlling interests

1 INTRODUCTION

Chapter 6 discusses the requirements of IFRS 10 – *Consolidated Financial Statements* – relating to the concepts underlying control of an entity (a subsidiary), the requirement to prepare consolidated financial statements and what subsidiaries are to be consolidated within a set of consolidated financial statements. The development, effective date, objective and scope of IFRS 10 are dealt with in Chapter 6 at 1.2 and 2.

This Chapter deals with the accounting requirements of IFRS 10 relating to the preparation of consolidated financial statements.

One issue that the IASB has been trying to resolve is a conflict between the IFRS 10 requirements relating to loss of control over a subsidiary and those of IAS 28 – *Investments in Associates and Joint Ventures* – for transactions where a parent sells or contributes an interest in a subsidiary to an associate or a joint venture. In order to resolve the conflict, in September 2014, the IASB had issued an amendment – *Sale or Contribution of Assets between an Investor and its Associate or Joint Venture (Amendments to IFRS 10 and IAS 28).* However, in December 2015, the IASB issued a further amendment – *Effective Date of Amendments to IFRS 10 and IAS 28.* This amendment defers the effective date of the September 2014 amendment until the IASB has finalised any revisions that result from the IASB's research project on the equity method, *[IFRS 10.BC190M]*,[1] (although the IASB now plans no further work on this project until the Post-implementation Review of IFRS 11 – *Joint Arrangements* – is undertaken).[2] The September 2014 amendments to IFRS 10 are discussed at 3.2.1.B and 6.1 below.

A similar issue arises in respect of transactions where a parent sells or contributes an interest in a subsidiary to a joint operation (where the entity has joint control or is a party to the joint operation with rights to assets or obligations for liabilities). The Interpretations Committee considered a related issue in July 2016, but decided not to add this issue to its agenda, instead recommending that the IASB considers the issue at the same time that it further considers the accounting for the sale or contribution of assets to an associate or joint venture. See 3.2.1.C and 6.2 below.

2 CONSOLIDATION PROCEDURES

2.1 Basic principles

Consolidated financial statements represent the financial statements of a group (i.e. the parent and its subsidiaries) in which the assets, liabilities, equity, income, expenses and cash flows of the parent and its subsidiaries are presented as those of a single economic entity. *[IFRS 10 Appendix A]*. This approach is referred to as 'the entity concept'. As noted in Chapter 6 at 10, an investment entity measures its investments in particular subsidiaries at fair value through profit or loss in accordance with IFRS 9 – *Financial Instruments* – or IAS 39 – *Financial Instruments: Recognition and Measurement* – with limited exceptions. *[IFRS 10.31-33]*.

When preparing consolidated financial statements, an entity first combines the financial statements of the parent and its consolidated subsidiaries on a 'line-by-line' basis by adding together like items of assets, liabilities, equity, income, expenses and cash flows. IFRS 10 requires a parent to prepare consolidated financial statements using uniform accounting policies for like transactions and other events in similar circumstances (see 2.6 below). *[IFRS 10.19, B87]*. Consolidation of an investee begins from the date the investor obtains control of the investee and ceases when the investor loses control of the investee. *[IFRS 10.20, B88]*.

In order to present financial information about the group as that of a single economic entity, the entity must make adjustments to: *[IFRS 10.B86]*

(a) combine like items of assets, liabilities, equity, income, expenses and cash flows of the parent with those of its subsidiaries;

(b) offset (eliminate) the carrying amount of the parent's investment in each subsidiary and the parent's portion of equity of each subsidiary (IFRS 3 – *Business Combinations* – explains how to account for any related goodwill, *[IFRS 3.B63]* – see Chapter 9 at 13); and

(c) eliminate in full intragroup assets and liabilities, equity, income, expenses and cash flows relating to transactions between entities of the group (profits or losses resulting from intragroup transactions that are recognised in assets, such as inventory and fixed assets, are eliminated in full). Intragroup losses may indicate an impairment that requires recognition in the consolidated financial statements. IAS 12 – *Income Taxes* – applies to temporary differences that arise from the elimination of profits and losses resulting from intragroup transactions. See 2.4 below.

Income and expenses of a subsidiary are based on the amounts of the assets and liabilities recognised in the consolidated financial statements at the acquisition date. IFRS 10's example is depreciation expense, which will be based on the fair values of the related depreciable assets recognised in the consolidated financial statements at the acquisition date, *[IFRS 10.B88]*, but many items will have a fair value on acquisition that will affect subsequent recognition of income and expense.

Point (b) above refers to the elimination of the parent's investment and the parent's portion of equity. The equity in a subsidiary not attributable, directly or indirectly, to the parent represents a non-controlling interest. *[IFRS 10 Appendix A]*. The profit or loss and each component of other comprehensive income of a subsidiary are attributed to the owners of the parent and to the non-controlling interests. *[IFRS 10.B94]*. Non-controlling interests in subsidiaries are presented within equity, separately from the equity of the owners of the parent, *[IFRS 10.22]*, and changes in a parent's ownership interest in a subsidiary that do not result in the parent losing control of the subsidiary are equity transactions. *[IFRS 10.23]*. Accounting for non-controlling interests is discussed in more detail at 2.2 and 4 below.

2.2 Proportion consolidated

The basic procedures described above effectively mean that 100% of the assets, liabilities, income, expenses and cash flows of a subsidiary are consolidated with those of the parent, irrespective of the parent's ownership interest in the subsidiary. However, the profit or loss and each component of other comprehensive income of the subsidiary, and the equity of the subsidiary, are attributed to the parent and the non-controlling interest.

As discussed in Chapter 6 at 4.3.4, when assessing control, an investor considers any potential voting rights that it holds as well as those held by others. Common examples of potential voting rights include options, forward contracts, and conversion features of a convertible instrument.

If there are potential voting rights, or other derivatives containing potential voting rights, the proportion of profit or loss, other comprehensive income and changes in equity allocated to the parent and non-controlling interests (see 4.5 below) in preparing consolidated financial statements is generally determined solely on the basis of existing ownership interests. It does not reflect the possible exercise or conversion of potential voting rights and other derivatives. *[IFRS 10.B89, B94]*.

Usually, there is no difference between the existing ownership interests and the present legal ownership interests in the underlying shares. However, allocating the proportions of profit or loss, other comprehensive income, and changes in equity based on present legal ownership interests is not always appropriate. For example, there may be situations where the terms and conditions of the potential voting rights mean that the existing ownership interest does not correspond to the legal ownership of the shares. IFRS 10 recognises that, in some circumstances, an entity has, in substance, an existing ownership interest as a result of a transaction that currently gives it access to the returns associated with an ownership interest. In such circumstances, the proportion allocated to the parent and non-controlling interests is determined by taking into account the eventual exercise of those potential voting rights and other derivatives that currently give the entity access to the returns. *[IFRS 10.B90]*.

Where this is the case, such instruments are not within scope of IFRS 9 or IAS 39 (since IFRS 9 and IAS 39 do not apply to subsidiaries that are consolidated). *[IFRS 9.2.1(a), IAS 39.2(a)]*. This scope exclusion prevents double counting of the changes in the fair value of such a derivative under IFRS 9 or IAS 39, and of the effective interest created by the derivative in the underlying investment. In all other cases, instruments containing potential voting rights in a subsidiary are accounted for in accordance with IFRS 9 or IAS 39. *[IFRS 10.B91, C7]*.

Example 7.1 below illustrates this principle.

Example 7.1: Potential voting rights

Entities A and B hold 40% and 60%, respectively, of the equity of Entity C. Entity A also holds a currently exercisable option over one third of Entity B's holding (of shares in Entity C) which, if exercised, would give Entity A a 60% interest in Entity C. The terms of the option are such that it leads to the conclusion that Entity C is a subsidiary of Entity A, but does not give Entity A present access to the returns of the underlying shares. Therefore, in preparing its consolidated financial statements, Entity A attributes 60% of profit or loss, other comprehensive income and changes in equity of Entity C to non-controlling interests.

Whether potential voting rights and other derivatives, in substance, already provide existing ownership interests in a subsidiary that currently give an entity access to the returns associated with that ownership interest will be a matter of judgement. Issues raised by put and call options over non-controlling interests, including whether or not such options give an entity present access to returns associated with an ownership interest (generally in connection with a business combination) are discussed further at 5 below. This Chapter uses the term 'present ownership interest' to include existing legal ownership interests together with potential voting rights and other derivatives that, in substance, already provide existing ownership interests in a subsidiary.

The proportion allocated between the parent and a subsidiary might differ when non-controlling interests hold cumulative preference shares (see 4.5 below).

2.2.1 Attribution when non-controlling interests change in an accounting period

Non-controlling interests may change during the accounting period. For example, a parent may purchase shares held by non-controlling interests.

By acquiring some (or all) of the non-controlling interests, the parent will be allocated a greater proportion of the profits or losses of the subsidiary in periods after the additional interests are acquired. *[IFRS 10.BCZ175].*

Therefore, the profit or loss and other comprehensive income of the subsidiary for the part of the reporting period prior to the transaction are attributed to the owners of the parent and non-controlling interests based on their ownership interests prior to the transaction. Following the transaction, the profit or loss and other comprehensive income of the subsidiary are attributed to the owners of the parent and non-controlling interests based on their new ownership interests following the transaction.

2.3 Consolidating foreign operations

IFRS 10 does not specifically address how to consolidate subsidiaries that are foreign operations. As explained in IAS 21 – *The Effects of Changes in Foreign Exchange Rates*, an entity may present its financial statements in any currency (or currencies). If the presentation currency differs from the entity's functional currency, it needs to translate its results and financial position into the presentation currency. Therefore, when a group contains individual entities with different functional currencies, the results and financial position of each entity are translated into the presentation currency of the consolidated financial statements. *[IAS 21.38].* The requirements of IAS 21 in respect of this translation process are explained in Chapter 15 at 6.

A reporting entity comprising a group with intermediate holding companies may adopt either the direct method or the step-by-step method of consolidation. IFRIC 16 – *Hedges of a Net Investment in a Foreign Operation* – refers to these methods as follows: *[IFRIC 16.17]*

- *direct method* – The financial statements of the foreign operation are translated directly into the functional currency of the ultimate parent.
- *step-by-step method* – The financial statements of the foreign operation are first translated into the functional currency of any intermediate parent(s) and then translated into the functional currency of the ultimate parent (or the presentation currency, if different).

An entity has an accounting policy choice of which method to use, which it must apply consistently for all net investments in foreign operations. *[IFRIC 16.17]*. Both methods produce exactly the same outcomes, with the exception of the currency translation differences that arise on consolidation.

IFRIC 16 explains:

> 'The difference becomes apparent in the determination of the amount of the foreign currency translation reserve that is subsequently reclassified to profit or loss. An ultimate parent entity using the direct method of consolidation would reclassify the cumulative foreign currency translation reserve that arose between its functional currency and that of the foreign operation. An ultimate parent entity using the step-by-step method of consolidation might reclassify the cumulative foreign currency translation reserve reflected in the financial statements of the intermediate parent, i.e. the amount that arose between the functional currency of the foreign operation and that of the intermediate parent, translated into the functional currency of the ultimate parent.' *[IFRIC 16.BC36]*.

IFRIC 16 also provides guidance on what does and does not constitute a valid hedge of a net investment in a foreign operation, and on how an entity should determine the amounts to be reclassified from equity to profit or loss for both the hedging instrument and the hedged item, where the foreign operation is disposed of. It notes that in a disposal of a subsidiary by an intermediate parent, the use of the step-by-step method of consolidation may result in the reclassification to profit or loss of a different amount from that used to determine hedge effectiveness. An entity can eliminate this difference by determining the amount relating to that foreign operation that would have arisen if the entity had used the direct method of consolidation. However, IAS 21 does not require an entity to make this adjustment. Instead, it is an accounting policy choice that should be followed consistently for all net investments. *[IFRIC 16.17]*.

IFRIC 16 is discussed in more detail in Chapter 15 at 6.1.5 and 6.6.3 and Chapter 52 at 3.3.

2.4 Intragroup eliminations

IFRS 10 requires intragroup assets and liabilities, equity, income, expenses and cash flows relating to transactions between entities of the group to be eliminated. Profits or losses resulting from intragroup transactions that are recognised in assets, such as inventory and fixed assets, are eliminated in full as shown in Example 7.2 below. *[IFRS 10.B86(c)]*.

Example 7.2: Eliminating intragroup transactions

Entity A holds a 75% interest in its subsidiary, Entity B. Entity A sold inventory costing €100,000 to Entity B for €200,000 giving rise to a profit in Entity A of €100,000. Entity B still held the inventory at the end of the reporting period. Tax effects are ignored in this example.

Under IFRS 10, as well as the intragroup sale between Entity A and Entity B, the unrealised profit is eliminated from the group's point of view in consolidation as follows:

	€'000 DR	€'000 CR
Revenue in Entity A	200	
Cost of sales in Entity A		100
Inventory in Entity B		100

The profit from the sale of inventory of €100,000 is reversed against group profit or loss. As the parent made the sale, no amount of the eliminated profit is attributed to the non-controlling interest.

If the fact pattern was reversed, such that Entity B sold inventory to Entity A, and Entity A still held the inventory at the end of the reporting period, the €100,000 of profit would still be reversed in the consolidated financial statements. However, in this instance, as the subsidiary made the sale, €25,000 of the eliminated profit (i.e. the non-controlling interest's 25% share of the €100,000 profit) would be allocated to the non-controlling interest.

If the inventory held by Entity B had been sold to a third party for €300,000 before the end of the reporting period (resulting in a profit in Entity A of €100,000 for the sale to Entity B at €200,000 and a profit in Entity B of €100,000 for the sale to a third party at €300,000), no intragroup elimination of profit is required. The group has sold an asset with a cost of €100,000 for €300,000 creating a profit to the group of €200,000. In this case, the intragroup elimination is limited to the sale between Entities A and B as follows:

	€'000 DR	€'000 CR
Revenue in Entity A	200	
Cost of sales in Entity B		200

Even though losses on intragroup transactions are eliminated in full, they may still indicate an impairment that requires recognition in the consolidated financial statements. *[IFRS 10.B86(c)]*. For example, if a parent sells a property to a subsidiary at fair value and this is lower than the carrying amount of the asset, the transfer may indicate that the property (or the cash-generating unit to which that property belongs) is impaired in the consolidated financial statements. This will not always be the case as the asset's value-in-use may be sufficient to support the higher carrying value. Transfers between companies under common control involving non-monetary assets are discussed in Chapter 8 at 4.4.1; impairment is discussed in Chapter 20.

Intragroup transactions may give rise to a current and/or deferred tax expense or benefit in the consolidated financial statements. IAS 12 applies to temporary differences that arise from the elimination of profits and losses resulting from intragroup transactions. *[IFRS 10.B86]*. These issues are discussed in Chapter 31 at 7.2.5 and 8.7. The application of IAS 12 to intragroup dividends and unpaid intragroup interest, royalties or management charges is discussed in Chapter 31 at 7.5.4, 7.5.5, 7.5.6 and 8.5.

Where an intragroup balance is denominated in a currency that differs to the functional currency of a transacting group entity, exchange differences will arise. See Chapter 15 at 6.3 for discussion of the accounting for exchange differences on intragroup balances in consolidated financial statements.

2.5 Non-coterminous accounting periods

The financial statements of the parent and its subsidiaries used in the preparation of the consolidated financial statements shall have the same reporting date. If the end of the reporting period of the parent is different from that of a subsidiary, the subsidiary must prepare, for consolidation purposes, additional financial information as of the same date as the financial statements of the parent, unless it is impracticable to do so. *[IFRS 10.B92]*. 'Impracticable' presumably means when the entity cannot apply the requirement after making every reasonable effort to do so (see Chapter 3 at 4.7). *[IAS 1.7]*.

If it is impracticable for the subsidiary to prepare such additional financial information, then the parent consolidates the financial information of the subsidiary using the most recent financial statements of the subsidiary. These must be adjusted for the effects of significant transactions or events that occur between the date of those financial statements and the date of the consolidated financial statements. The difference between the date of the subsidiary's financial statements and that of the consolidated financial statements must not be more than three months. *[IFRS 10.B93]*. It is not necessary, as in some national GAAPs, for the subsidiary's reporting period to end before that of its parent. The length of the reporting periods and any difference between the dates of the financial statements must be the same from period to period. *[IFRS 10.B93]*.

This requirement seems to imply that where a subsidiary previously consolidated using non-coterminous financial statements is now consolidated using coterminous financial statements (i.e. the subsidiary changed the end of its reporting period), comparative information should be restated so that financial information of the subsidiary is included in the consolidated financial statements for an equivalent period in each period presented. However, it may be that other approaches not involving restatement of comparatives would be acceptable, particularly where the comparative information had already reflected the effects of significant transactions or events during the period between the date of the subsidiary's financial statements and the date of the consolidated financial statements. Where comparatives are not restated, additional disclosures might be needed about the treatment adopted and the impact on the current period of including information for the subsidiary for a period different from that of the parent.

IAS 21 addresses what exchange rate should be used in translating the assets and liabilities of a foreign operation that is consolidated on the basis of financial statements made up to a different date to the reporting date used for the reporting entity's financial statements. This issue is discussed further in Chapter 15 at 6.4.

2.6 Consistent accounting policies

If a member of the group uses accounting policies other than those adopted in the consolidated financial statements for like transactions and events in similar circumstances, appropriate adjustments are made to that group member's financial statements in preparing the consolidated financial statements to ensure conformity with the group's accounting policies. *[IFRS 10.B87]*.

IFRS 4 – *Insurance Contracts* – contains an exception to this general rule, as further discussed in Chapter 55 at 8.2.1.C.

3 CHANGES IN OWNERSHIP INTERESTS

3.1 Commencement and cessation of consolidation

A parent consolidates a subsidiary from the date on which the parent first obtains control, and ceases consolidating that subsidiary on the date on which the parent loses control. *[IFRS 10.20]*. IFRS 3 defines the acquisition date, which is the date on which the acquirer obtains control of the acquiree, *[IFRS 3.8, Appendix A]*, (see Chapter 9 at 4.2).

The requirement to continue consolidating (albeit in a modified form) also applies to a subsidiary held for sale accounted for under IFRS 5 – *Non-current Assets Held for Sale and Discontinued Operations* (see Chapter 4).

3.1.1 Acquisition of a subsidiary that is not a business

These basic principles also apply when a parent acquires a controlling interest in an entity that is not a business. Under IFRS 10, an entity must consolidate all investees that it controls, not just those that are businesses, and therefore the parent will recognise any non-controlling interest in the subsidiary (see 4 below). IFRS 3 states that when an entity acquires a group of assets or net assets that is not a business, the acquirer allocates the cost of the group between the individual identifiable assets and liabilities in the group based on their relative fair values at the date of acquisition. Such a transaction or event does not give rise to goodwill. *[IFRS 3.2(b)]*. The cost of the group of assets is the sum of all consideration given and any non-controlling interest recognised. In our view, if the non-controlling interest has a present ownership interest and is entitled to a proportionate share of net assets upon liquidation, the acquirer has a choice to recognise the non-controlling interest at its proportionate share of net assets or its fair value (measured in accordance with IFRS 13 – *Fair Value Measurement*). In all other cases, non-controlling interest is recognised at fair value (measured in accordance with IFRS 13), unless another measurement basis is required in accordance with IFRS (e.g. any share-based payment transaction classified as equity is measured in accordance with IFRS 2 – *Share-based Payment*).

The acquisition of a subsidiary that is not a business is illustrated in Example 7.3 below.

Example 7.3: Acquisition of a subsidiary that is not a business

Entity A pays £160,000 to acquire an 80% controlling interest in the equity shares of Entity B, which holds a single property that is not a business. The fair value of the property is £200,000. An unrelated third party holds the remaining 20% interest in the equity shares. The fair value of the non-controlling interest is £40,000. Tax effects and transaction costs, if any, are ignored in this example.

Entity A therefore records the following accounting entry:

	£'000 DR	£'000 CR
Investment property	200	
Non-controlling interest		40
Cash		160

Variation

The facts are the same as above, except that Entity A pays £170,000 to acquire the 80% interest due to the inclusion of a control premium. In this case, Entity A therefore records the following accounting entry:

	£'000 DR	£'000 CR
Investment property	210	
Non-controlling interest		40
Cash		170

3.2 Accounting for a loss of control

IFRS 10 clarifies that an investor is required to reassess whether it controls an investee if the facts and circumstances indicate that there are changes to one or more of the three elements of control. *[IFRS 10.B80]*. The elements of control are: power over the investee; exposures, or rights, to variable returns from the investor's involvement with the investee; and the investor's ability to use its power over the investee to affect the amount of the investor's returns. *[IFRS 10.7]*. See Chapter 6 at 9 for further discussion, including examples of situation where a change in control may arise.

A parent can lose control of a subsidiary because of a transaction that changes its absolute or relative ownership level. For example, a parent may lose control of a subsidiary if it sells some or all of the ownership interests or if a subsidiary issues new ownership interests to third parties. Alternatively, a parent can lose control without a change in absolute or relative ownership levels. For example, a parent may lose control on expiry of a contractual agreement that previously allowed the parent to control the subsidiary. *[IFRS 10.BCZ180]*. A parent may also lose control if the subsidiary becomes subject to the control of a government, court, administrator, receiver, liquidator or regulator. This evaluation may require the exercise of judgement, based on the facts and circumstances, including the laws in the relevant jurisdiction (see Chapter 6 at 4.3.2 and 9.2).

If a parent loses control of a subsidiary, it is required to: *[IFRS 10.25, B98]*

(a) derecognise the assets (including any goodwill) and liabilities of the former subsidiary at their carrying amounts at the date when control is lost;

(b) derecognise the carrying amount of any non-controlling interests in the former subsidiary at the date when control is lost. This includes any components of other comprehensive income attributable to them;

(c) recognise the fair value of the consideration received, if any, from the transaction, event or circumstances that resulted in the loss of control;

(d) recognise a distribution if the transaction, event or circumstances that resulted in the loss of control involves a distribution of shares of the subsidiary to owners in their capacity as owners;

(e) recognise any investment retained in the former subsidiary at its fair value at the date when control is lost;

(f) reclassify to profit or loss, or transfer directly to retained earnings if required by other IFRSs, the amounts recognised in other comprehensive income in relation to the subsidiary;

    If a parent loses control of a subsidiary, the parent accounts for all amounts previously recognised in other comprehensive income in relation to that subsidiary on the same basis as would be required if the parent had directly disposed of the related assets or liabilities. *[IFRS 10.B99]*. This is discussed at 3.2.3 below; and

(g) recognise any resulting difference as a gain or loss in profit or loss attributable to the parent.

Any amounts owed to or by the former subsidiary (which cease to be eliminated on consolidation) should be accounted for in accordance with the relevant IFRSs. Such balances are often financial assets or financial liabilities, which are initially recognised at fair value in accordance with IFRS 9 or IAS 39, at the date of loss of control. *[IFRS 9.5.1.1, 9.5.1.1A, 5.1.2, 5.1.3, IAS 39.43, 43A, 44]*. See Chapter 48 at 3.

IFRS 5's requirements apply to a non-current asset (or disposal group) that is classified as held for sale. See Chapter 4 at 2. The presentation requirements where the subsidiary for which the parent loses control meets the definition of a discontinued operation are discussed in Chapter 4 at 3.

There is a conflict between the requirements of IFRS 10 and those of IAS 28 for transactions where a parent sells or contributes an interest in a subsidiary to an associate or a joint venture (accounted for using the equity method) and the sale or contribution results in a loss of control of the subsidiary by the parent. This is because IAS 28 restricts any gain arising on the sale of an asset to an associate or joint venture, or on the contribution of a non-monetary asset in exchange for an interest in an associate or a joint venture, to that attributable to the unrelated investors' interests in the associate or joint venture, whereas IFRS 10 does not. This issue is discussed further at 3.2.1.B and 6.1 below.

3.2.1 Interest retained in the former subsidiary

When a parent loses control of a subsidiary, it must recognise any investment retained in the former subsidiary at its fair value at the date when control is lost. Any gain or loss on the transaction will be recorded in profit or loss. The fair value of any investment that it retains at the date control is lost, including any amounts owed by or to the former subsidiary, will be accounted for, as applicable, as:

- the fair value on initial recognition of a financial asset (see Chapter 48 at 3); or
- the cost on initial recognition of an investment in an associate or joint venture (see Chapter 11 at 7.4.1).

The IASB's view is that the loss of control of a subsidiary is a significant economic event that marks the end of the previous parent-subsidiary relationship and the start of a new investor-investee relationship, which is recognised and measured initially at the date when control is lost. *[IFRS 10.BCZ182]*. IFRS 10 is based on the premise that an investor-investee relationship differs significantly from a parent-subsidiary relationship. Therefore, 'any investment the parent has in the former subsidiary after control is lost should be measured at fair value at the date that control is lost and that any resulting gain or loss should be recognised in profit or loss.' *[IFRS 10.BCZ182]*.

If the subsidiary over which control has been lost is a single asset entity, there are some situations in which the transaction should be regarded as a partial sale of the underlying asset rather than a disposal of a subsidiary and a retained interest, as described above. This will affect the gain or loss recognised. This is explored further at 3.2.6 below.

The following discussion addresses the accounting for the loss of control in certain situations – where the interest retained in the former subsidiary is a financial asset (see 3.2.1.A below), where the interest retained in the former subsidiary is an associate or joint venture (see 3.2.1.B below), and where the interest retained in the former subsidiary is a joint operation (see 3.2.1.C below).

3.2.1.A Interest retained in the former subsidiary – financial asset

Example 7.4 below illustrates the above requirement where the interest retained in the former subsidiary is a financial asset.

Example 7.4: Disposal of a subsidiary

A parent sells an 85% interest in a wholly owned subsidiary as follows:

- after the sale the parent elects to account for the interest at fair value through other comprehensive income under IFRS 9 (or accounts for its remaining 15% interest as an available-for-sale investment under IAS 39);
- the subsidiary did not recognise any amounts in other comprehensive income;
- net assets of the subsidiary before the disposal are $500 million;
- cash proceeds from the sale of the 85% interest are $750 million; and
- the fair value of the 15% interest retained by the parent is $130 million.

The parent accounts for the disposal of an 85% interest as follows:

	$m DR	$m CR
Financial asset	130	
Cash	750	
Net assets of the subsidiary derecognised (summarised)		500
Gain on loss of control of subsidiary		380

The gain recognised on the loss of control of the subsidiary is calculated as follows:

	$m	$m
Gain on interest disposed of		
Cash proceeds on disposal of 85% interest	750	
Carrying amount of 85% interest (85% × $500 million)	(425)	
		325
Gain on interest retained		
Carrying amount of 15% investment carried at fair value through other comprehensive income (or available-for-sale investment)	130	
Carrying amount of 15% interest (15% × $500 million)	(75)	
		55
Gain recognised on loss of control of subsidiary		380

Although IFRS 10 requires that any investment retained in the former subsidiary is to be recognised at its fair value at the date when control is lost, no guidance is given in the standard as how such fair value should be determined. However, IFRS 13 provides detailed guidance on how fair value should be determined for financial reporting purposes. IFRS 13 is discussed in detail in Chapter 14.

3.2.1.B Interest retained in the former subsidiary – associate or joint venture

It can be seen that the requirements in IFRS 10 discussed above result in a gain or loss upon loss of control as if the parent had sold all of its interest in the subsidiary, not just that relating to the percentage interest that has been sold.

IFRS 10 envisages that this would be the case where a parent loses control over a subsidiary that has become an associate or a joint venture. However, there is a conflict between these requirements and those of IAS 28 for transactions where a parent sells or contributes an interest in a subsidiary to an associate or a joint venture (accounted for using the equity method) and the sale or contribution results in a loss of control in the subsidiary by the parent. This is because IAS 28 restricts any gain arising on the sale of an asset to an associate or a joint venture, or on the contribution of a non-monetary asset in exchange for an equity interest in an associate or a joint venture, to that attributable to unrelated investors' interests in the associate or joint venture. *[IAS 28.28, 30]*. This conflict is discussed further in Chapter 11 at 7.6.5.C.

In order to resolve the conflict, in September 2014, the IASB had issued an amendment – *Sale or Contribution of Assets between an Investor and its Associate or Joint Venture (Amendments to IFRS 10 and IAS 28).* The amendments are such that the IFRS 10 approach is to be restricted to sales or contributions of businesses, whether or not housed in a subsidiary. The IASB amended IFRS 10 so that the gain or loss resulting from the loss of control of a subsidiary that does not contain a business, as defined in IFRS 3, as a result of a transaction involving an associate or a joint venture that is accounted for using the equity method is recognised only to the extent of the unrelated investors' interests in the associate or joint venture. The same applies if a parent retains an investment in a former subsidiary and the former subsidiary is now an associate or a joint venture that is accounted for using the equity method.[3] However, a full gain or loss would be recognised on the loss of control of a subsidiary that constitutes a business, including cases in which the investor retains joint control of, or significant influence over, the investee.

These amendments were to be applied prospectively to transactions occurring in annual periods beginning on or after 1 January 2016, with earlier application permitted.[4] However, in December 2015, the IASB issued a further amendment – *Effective Date of Amendments to IFRS 10 and IAS 28*. This amendment defers the effective date of the September 2014 amendment until the IASB has finalised any revisions that result from the IASB's research project on the equity method (although the IASB now plans no further work on this project until the Post-implementation Review of IFRS 11 is undertaken).[5] Nevertheless, the IASB has continued to allow early application of the September 2014 amendment as it did not wish to prohibit the application of better financial reporting. *[IFRS 10.BC190O]*.[6] The September 2014 amendments to IFRS 10 are discussed at 6.1 below.

In the meantime, we believe that, where a parent loses control over a subsidiary that has become an associate or a joint venture (accounted for using the equity method) as a result of a transaction involving the sale or contribution of the subsidiary to an associate or joint venture, the former parent has an accounting policy choice as to whether to apply an IFRS 10 or an IAS 28 approach. This means that entities can choose to recognise the gain or loss arising from the transaction in full (IFRS 10 approach) or to restrict the gain or loss to the interest attributable to the other party of the associate or joint venture (IAS 28 approach). Alternatively, entities could adopt the amendments if they choose, as earlier application is permitted.

As indicated at 3.2.1.A above, no guidance is given in IFRS 10 as to how the fair value of the retained interest in the former subsidiary should be determined. However, IFRS 13 provides detailed guidance on how fair value should be determined for financial reporting purposes. IFRS 13 is discussed in detail in Chapter 14. One particular issue that has been discussed by the IASB, that might be relevant in determining the fair value of a retained interest which is an associate or a joint venture, is the unit of account for investments in subsidiaries, joint ventures and associates. In September 2014, the IASB issued an Exposure Draft that proposed, *inter alia*, the following clarifications to the requirements for measuring fair value, in accordance with IFRS 13, for investments in subsidiaries, joint ventures and associates:

- the unit of account for investments in subsidiaries, joint ventures and associates would be the investment as whole; and
- when a quoted price in an active market is available for the individual financial instruments that comprise the entire investment, the fair value measurement would be the product of the quoted price of the financial instrument (P) multiplied by the quantity (Q) of instruments held (i.e. price × quantity, P × Q).[7]

During 2015, the IASB continued its deliberations on these proposals and decided that further research should be undertaken with respect to the fair value measurement of investments in subsidiaries, associates and joint ventures that are quoted in an active market.[8] In January 2016, the IASB decided not to consider this topic further until the Post-implementation Review of IFRS 13 is complete.[9] In May 2017, the IASB published a request for information for the Post-implementation Review of IFRS 13, with comments requested by 22 September 2017.[10] These issues are discussed further in Chapter 14 at 5.1.1.

3.2.1.C Interest retained in the former subsidiary – joint operation

In some transactions, it is possible that an entity would lose control of a subsidiary, but retain an interest in a joint operation to be accounted for under IFRS 11. For example, a parent might contribute an existing business to a newly created joint operation and obtain joint control of the combined operation. Alternatively, it could be achieved by a parent with a 100% subsidiary selling a 50% interest to another party, with the transaction resulting in the formation of a joint operation, with each party having a 50% share of the assets and liabilities of the joint operation.

As set out at 3.2 above, in accounting for a loss of control of a subsidiary, a parent is required, *inter alia*, to:

(a) derecognise the assets and liabilities of the subsidiary;

(b) recognise any investment retained in the former subsidiary at fair value at the date when control is lost; and

(c) recognise any resulting gain or loss in profit or loss.

However, it is unclear how these requirements should be applied when the retained interest is in the assets and liabilities of a joint operation. One view is that the retained interest should be remeasured at fair value. Another view is that the retained interest should not be derecognised or remeasured at fair value, but should continue to be recognised and measured at its carrying amount. This is an issue that the Interpretations Committee has been considering recently as part of a wider discussion of other transactions of changes of interests in a joint operation that is a business, for which there is a lack of guidance, or where there is diversity of views.

In July 2015, the Interpretations Committee agreed an initial scope of the project, which included transactions involving loss of control resulting in the entity having joint control in a joint operation or being a party to a joint operation subsequent to the transaction.[11]

In July 2016, the Interpretations Committee discussed whether an entity should remeasure its retained interest in the assets and liabilities of a joint operation when the entity loses control of a business, or an asset or group of assets that is not a business. In the transaction discussed, the entity either retains joint control of a joint operation or is a party to a joint operation (with rights to assets and obligations for liabilities) after the transaction.

The Interpretations Committee noted that paragraphs B34–B35 of IFRS 11 specify that an entity recognises gains or losses on the sale or contribution of assets to a joint operation only to the extent of the other parties' interests in the joint operation. *[IFRS 11.B34, B35]*. The requirements in these paragraphs could be viewed as conflicting with the requirements in IFRS 10, which specify that an entity remeasures any retained interest when it loses control of a subsidiary.

The Interpretations Committee observed that the IASB had issued amendments to IFRS 10 and IAS 28 in September 2014 to address the accounting for the sale or contribution of assets to an associate or a joint venture. Those amendments address a similar conflict that exists between the requirements in IFRS 10 and IAS 28. The IASB decided to defer the effective date of the amendments to IFRS 10 and IAS 28 and further consider a number of related issues at a later date. The Interpretations Committee observed that the Post-implementation Review of IFRS 10 and IFRS 11 would provide the IASB with an opportunity to consider loss of control transactions and a sale or contribution of assets to an associate or a joint venture.

Because of the similarity between the transaction discussed by the Interpretations Committee and a sale or contribution of assets to an associate or a joint venture (see 3.2.1.B above), the Interpretations Committee concluded that the accounting for the two transactions should be considered concurrently by the IASB. Consequently, the Interpretations Committee decided not to add this issue to its agenda but, instead, to recommend that the IASB consider the issue at the same time that it further considers the accounting for the sale or contribution of assets to an associate or a joint venture.[12]

In the meantime, we believe that, where a parent loses control over a subsidiary but retains an interest in a joint operation that is a business, entities have an accounting policy choice as to whether to remeasure the retained interest at fair value or not.

However, if the subsidiary over which control has been lost is a single asset entity, the transaction should be regarded as a partial sale of the underlying asset rather than a disposal of a subsidiary and a retained interest. This is explored further at 3.2.6 below.

3.2.2 Loss of control in multiple arrangements

If a parent loses control of a subsidiary in two or more arrangements or transactions, sometimes they should be accounted for as a single transaction. *[IFRS 10.B97].* IFRS 10 only allows a parent to recognise a gain or loss on disposal of a subsidiary when the parent loses control over it. This requirement could present opportunities to structure the disposal in a series of disposals, thereby potentially reducing the loss recognised. Example 7.5 below illustrates the issue in IFRS 10 as follows. *[IFRS 10.BCZ185].*

Example 7.5: Step-disposal of a subsidiary (1)

A parent controls 70% of a subsidiary. The parent intends to sell all of its 70% controlling interest in the subsidiary. The parent could structure the disposal in two different ways:

- the parent could initially sell 19% of its ownership interest without loss of control and then, soon afterwards, sell the remaining 51% and lose control; or
- the parent could sell its entire 70% interest in one transaction.

In the first case, any difference between the amount by which the non-controlling interests are adjusted and the fair value of the consideration received upon sale of the 19% interest would be recognised directly in equity, while the gain or loss from the sale of the remaining 51% interest would be recognised in profit or loss. In the second case, however, a gain or loss on the sale of the whole 70% interest would be recognised in profit or loss.

However, even if an entity wanted to conceal losses on a disposal of a subsidiary, the opportunities are limited given the requirements of IAS 36 – *Impairment of Assets* – and IFRS 5, which usually require recognition of an impairment loss even before the completion of any sale (although they do not require reclassification of losses recognised in other comprehensive income).

In determining whether to account for the arrangements as a single transaction, a parent considers all the terms and conditions of the arrangements and their economic effects. One or more of the following circumstances indicate that it is appropriate for a parent to account for multiple arrangements as a single transaction: *[IFRS 10.B97]*

- they are entered into at the same time or in contemplation of each other;
- they form a single transaction designed to achieve an overall commercial effect;
- the occurrence of one arrangement is dependent on the occurrence of at least one other arrangement; or
- one arrangement considered on its own is not economically justified, but it is economically justified when considered together with other arrangements. An example is when one disposal of shares is priced below market and is compensated for by a subsequent disposal priced above market.

These indicators clarify that arrangements that are part of a package are accounted for as a single transaction. However, there is a risk that by casting too wide a net, an entity might end up accounting for a transaction that is truly separate as part of transaction in which the loss of control occurred.

IFRS 10 is silent on how an entity accounts for multiple arrangements that are part of a single transaction. Depending on the facts and circumstances, the parent accounts for these transactions in one of the following ways:

- *Advance payment* – If the parent does not lose control over the subsidiary and access to the benefits associated with ownership until later steps in the transaction, then it accounts for the first step of the transaction as an advance receipt of consideration and continues to consolidate the subsidiary until the later date. In many cases, the assets and liabilities of the consolidated subsidiary would be a disposal group held for sale under IFRS 5 (see Chapter 4 at 2.1.3.A).
- *Immediate disposal* – If the parent loses control and access to benefits associated on the first step of the transaction, then it ceases to consolidate the former subsidiary immediately, recognises a gain or loss on disposal, and accounts for the consideration due in the second step as deferred consideration receivable.

Example 7.6 below illustrates a fact pattern where the entity would need to evaluate how to account for transactions that are linked.

Example 7.6: Step-disposal of a subsidiary (2)

A parent initially controls 70% of a subsidiary that has net assets of $1,000,000 and a foreign currency translation loss that was recognised in other comprehensive income and is accumulated within equity of $100,000. Of this amount, $30,000 was allocated to non-controlling interest, and is included within the non-controlling interest of $300,000. In November 2017, the parent sells 19% of its ownership interest for $200,000. In February 2018, the parent sells the remaining 51% for $550,000 in an arrangement that is considered part of a single overall transaction. It is assumed that there are no gains or losses in the intervening period.

The net assets of the subsidiary are not impaired under IAS 36, which is confirmed by the fact that the total sales price exceeds the parent's share in the net assets by $50,000 ($750,000 less $700,000). The total loss on disposal can be calculated as follows:

	$'000 DR	$'000 CR
Proceeds from the sale ($200,000 + $550,000)	750	
Net assets of the subsidiary derecognised		1,000
Non-controlling interest derecognised	300	
Reclassification of parent's share of the loss in other comprehensive income		70
Loss on disposal of the subsidiary attributable to the parent	20	

If the parent is considered not to have lost control over the investment in the subsidiary until February 2018 then it accounts for the $200,000 received in the first step of the transaction as an advance receipt of consideration. The parent continues to consolidate the subsidiary until the later date, at which point the loss on disposal of $20,000 would be recognised.

If the parent is considered to have lost control over the investment in the subsidiary on the first step of the transaction, then it ceases to consolidate the former subsidiary immediately, recognises a loss on disposal of $20,000, and accounts for the consideration of $550,000 due in the second step as deferred consideration receivable.

3.2.3 Other comprehensive income

If a parent loses control of a subsidiary, all amounts previously recognised in other comprehensive income are accounted for on the same basis as would be required if the parent had directly disposed of the related assets or liabilities. If a gain or loss previously recognised in other comprehensive income would be reclassified to profit or loss on the disposal of the related assets or liabilities, the parent reclassifies the gain or loss from equity to profit or loss (as a reclassification adjustment) when it loses control of the subsidiary. Therefore:

(a) if a revaluation surplus previously recognised in other comprehensive income would be transferred directly to retained earnings on the disposal of the asset, the parent transfers the revaluation surplus directly to retained earnings when it loses control of the subsidiary; *[IFRS 10.B99]*

(b) remeasurement gains or losses on a defined benefit plan recognised in other comprehensive income would not be reclassified to profit or loss when the parent loses control of the subsidiary, but may be transferred within equity; *[IAS 19.122]* and

(c) on disposal of a subsidiary that includes a foreign operation, the cumulative amount of the exchange differences relating to that foreign operation (that is recognised in other comprehensive income and accumulated in the separate component of equity) is reclassified from equity to profit or loss, except for the amounts that have been attributed to the non-controlling interests. Those amounts are derecognised, and not reclassified to profit or loss. *[IAS 21.48-48B]*. This would appear to mean that it is only the parent's share of the cumulative exchange differences that is reclassified; those attributable to the non-controlling interests are not reclassified as they have already been included within the carrying amount of the non-controlling interest that is derecognised as part of calculating the gain or loss attributable to the parent.

There are two different interpretations of how to treat other comprehensive income accumulated in equity that would be reclassified to profit or loss on the disposal of the related assets or liabilities, both of which are acceptable. Approach (1) below is more consistent with the treatment of exchange differences relating to foreign operations, as described under (c) above.

(1) *Reclassification of other comprehensive income related to parent interest only* – IFRS 10 requires derecognition of non-controlling interest (including any components of other comprehensive income attributable to them) at the date when control is lost, which implies derecognition of the non-controlling interests without any need for reclassification. *[IFRS 10.B98(a)].* In addition, IFRS 10 requires recognition of a gain or loss in profit or loss to be attributable to the parent, *[IFRS 10.B98(d)],* which again implies that there should be no reclassification of other comprehensive income in respect of the non-controlling interests.

(2) *Reclassification of other comprehensive income related to parent and the non-controlling interest* – IFRS 10 specifically requires that 'if a gain or loss previously recognised in other comprehensive income would be reclassified to profit or loss on the disposal of the related assets or liabilities, the parent shall reclassify the gain or loss from equity to profit or loss (as a reclassification adjustment) when it loses control of the subsidiary.' *[IFRS 10.B99].* That would clearly require reclassification of the entire balance of other comprehensive income accumulated within equity. However, where this is done, the portion of the reclassification adjustment attributable to the non-controlling interest should be included as part of the profit or loss attributable to non-controlling interests, not as part of the profit or loss attributable to the parent.

Example 7.7 below illustrates the application of the above requirements.

Example 7.7: Reclassification of other comprehensive income

A parent sells a 70% interest in a 90%-owned subsidiary to a third party for cash consideration of €28 million. The fair value of the 20% interest retained by the parent is €8 million.

At the date of disposal, the net assets of the subsidiary were €30 million. Included within those net assets, the subsidiary had recognised, in its own financial statements, the following:

- property, plant and equipment of €5 million that has resulted in a revaluation reserve of €2 million;
- derivative financial assets of €3.2 million (designated in a cash flow hedge) that have resulted in a cash flow hedge reserve of €3 million;
- a net defined benefit liability of €3 million that has resulted in a reserve relating to net remeasurement losses of €1.5 million; and
- net assets of a foreign operation of €10 million that has resulted in a cumulative translation reserve in respect of net translation gains on the foreign operation of €4 million.

In the parent's consolidated financial statements, the parent has recognised 90% of these reserves in equivalent equity reserve balances, with the 10% attributable to the non-controlling interest included as part of the carrying amount of the non-controlling interest.

The impact of the subsidiary on the statement of financial position included in the parent's consolidated financial statements immediately prior to the disposal is as follows:

	€m	€m
Net assets of the subsidiary	30.00	
Equity attributable to parent		
– PP&E revaluation reserve		1.80
– Cash flow hedge reserve		2.70
– IAS 19 net remeasurement loss reserve	1.35	
– Cumulative translation reserve		3.60
– Other equity/retained earnings		20.25
Non-controlling interest		3.00

If the parent follows Approach (1) for the cash flow hedge reserve and makes a reserve transfer for the IAS 19 – *Employee Benefits* – net remeasurement loss reserve, the impact of the disposal on the parent's consolidated financial statements is as follows:

	€m DR	€m CR
Cash proceeds from the disposal	28.00	
Retained 20% investment at fair value	8.00	
Derecognition of net assets of the subsidiary		30.00
Derecognition of non-controlling interest	3.00	
Reserves reclassified to profit or loss		
– Cash flow hedge reserve (a)	2.70	
– Cumulative translation reserve (b)	3.60	
Reserves transferred to retained earnings		
– PP&E revaluation reserve (c)	1.80	
– IAS 19 net remeasurement loss reserve (d)		1.35
Retained earnings resulting from above transfers		0.45
Gain on disposal (attributable to parent)		15.30

The parent:

(a) reclassifies its €2.7 million cash flow hedge reserve to profit or loss for the period. This is reflected in the gain on disposal. The remaining 10% (i.e. €0.3 million) is included as part of the carrying amount of the non-controlling interest that is derecognised as part of the gain or loss recognised on disposal of the subsidiary, but is not reclassified to profit or loss nor is it transferred within equity;

(b) reclassifies its cumulative translation reserve of €3.6 million (90% × €4 million) relating to the parent's interest to profit or loss. Again, this is reflected in the gain on disposal. The €0.4 million (10% × €4 million) relating to the non-controlling interest is included as part of the carrying amount of the non-controlling interest that is derecognised in calculating the gain or loss recognised on disposal of the subsidiary, but is not reclassified to profit or loss nor is it transferred within equity;

(c) transfers its revaluation reserve of €1.8 million relating to its 90% share of the revaluation surplus on property, plant and equipment within equity to retained earnings. It is not reclassified to profit or loss. The remaining 10% attributable to the non-controlling interest is included as part of the carrying amount of the non-controlling interest that is derecognised in calculating the gain or loss recognised on disposal of the subsidiary, but is not reclassified to profit or loss nor is it transferred within equity; and

(d) transfers its reserve of €1.35 million relating to its 90% share of the net remeasurement losses on the defined benefit liability within equity to retained earnings. It is not reclassified to profit or loss. The remaining 10% attributable to the non-controlling interest is included as part of the carrying amount of the non-controlling interest that is derecognised in calculating the gain or loss recognised on disposal of the subsidiary, but is not reclassified to profit or loss nor is it transferred within equity. This results in the same position as if the parent had not recognised a separate reserve for the net remeasurement losses on the defined benefit liability, but had included them within retained earnings.

If, instead, the parent follows Approach (2) for the cash flow hedge reserve, the impact of the disposal on the parent's consolidated financial statements is as follows:

	€m DR	€m CR
Cash proceeds from the disposal	28.00	
Retained 20% investment at fair value	8.00	
Derecognition of net assets of the subsidiary		30.00
Derecognition of non-controlling interest	3.00	
Reserves reclassified to profit or loss		
– Cash flow hedge reserve (a)	2.70	
– Cumulative translation reserve (b)	3.60	
Non-controlling interest (reclassification of cash flow hedge reserve) (a)	0.30	
Reserves transferred to retained earnings		
– PP&E revaluation reserve (c)	1.80	
– IAS 19 net remeasurement loss reserve (d)		1.35
Retained earnings resulting from above transfers		0.45
Gain on reclassification of cash flow hedge reserve (attributable to non-controlling interest) (a)		0.30
Gain on disposal (attributable to parent)		15.30

The parent:

(a) reclassifies the entire €3 million surplus on the cash flow hedge reserve to profit or loss for the period. The 90% of the balance (i.e. €2.7 million) attributable to the parent is included within the gain on disposal that is attributable to the parent, while the remaining 10% (i.e. €0.3 million) attributable to the non-controlling interest is reclassified to profit or loss, and is included within the profit or loss attributable to the non-controlling interest;

(b) reclassifies its cumulative translation reserve of €3.6 million (90% × €4 million) relating to the parent's interest to profit or loss. Again, this is reflected in the gain on disposal. The €0.4 million (10% × €4 million) relating to the non-controlling interest is included as part of the carrying amount of the non-controlling interest that is derecognised in calculating the gain or loss recognised on disposal of the subsidiary, but is not reclassified to profit or loss nor is it transferred within equity;

(c) transfers its revaluation reserve of €1.8 million relating to its 90% share of the revaluation surplus on property, plant and equipment within equity to retained earnings. It is not reclassified to profit or loss. The remaining 10% attributable to the non-controlling interest is included as part of the carrying amount of the non-controlling interest that is derecognised in calculating the gain or loss recognised on disposal of the subsidiary, but is not reclassified to profit or loss nor is it transferred within equity; and

(d) transfers its reserve of €1.35 million relating to its 90% share of the net remeasurement losses on the defined benefit liability within equity to retained earnings. It is not reclassified to profit or loss. The remaining 10% attributable to the non-controlling interest is included as part of the carrying amount of the non-controlling interest that is derecognised in calculating the gain or loss recognised on disposal of the subsidiary, but is not reclassified to profit or loss nor is it transferred within equity. This results in the same position as if the parent had not recognised a separate reserve for the net remeasurement losses on the defined benefit liability, but had included them within retained earnings.

3.2.4 *Deemed disposal*

A subsidiary may cease to be a subsidiary, or a group may reduce its interest in a subsidiary, other than by actual disposal. This is commonly referred to as a 'deemed disposal'. Deemed disposals may arise for many reasons, including:

- a group does not take up its full allocation in a rights issue by a subsidiary in the group;
- a subsidiary declares scrip dividends that are not taken up by its parent, so that the parent's proportional interest is diminished;
- another party exercises its options or warrants issued by a subsidiary;
- a subsidiary issues shares to third parties; or
- a contractual agreement by which a group obtained control over a subsidiary is terminated or changed.

A deemed disposal that results in the loss of control of a subsidiary is accounted for as a regular disposal. This accounting is illustrated in Example 7.8 below.

Example 7.8: Deemed disposal through share issue by subsidiary

A parent entity P owns 600,000 of the 1,000,000 shares issued by its subsidiary S, giving it a 60% interest. The carrying value of S's net identifiable assets in the consolidated financial statements of P is £120 million. P measured the non-controlling interest using the proportionate share of net assets; therefore, the non-controlling interest is £48 million (40% of £120 million). In addition, goodwill of £15 million was recognised upon the original acquisition of S, and has not subsequently been impaired. The goodwill is allocated to S for the purposes of impairment testing.

Subsequently, S issues 500,000 shares to a new investor for £80 million. As a result, P's 600,000 shares now represent 40% of the 1,500,000 shares issued by S in total and S becomes an associate of P.

IFRS 10 requires the remaining interest in the former subsidiary to be recognised at fair value. Therefore, the gain or loss recognised on the loss of control of a subsidiary considers the fair value of the new holding. P considers that, based on the requirements of IFRS 13, the fair value of its 600,000 shares in S is £96 million.

This results in a gain of £9 million on disposal, recognised as follows:

	£m DR	£m CR
Interest in S	96	
Non-controlling interest	48	
Gain on disposal		9
Net assets of S (previously consolidated)		120
Goodwill (previously shown separately)		15

As indicated at 3.2.1.B above, the IASB has been discussing issues relating to the unit of account for investments in subsidiaries, joint ventures and associates, and their fair value measurement under IFRS 13.

3.2.5 Presentation of comparative information for a former subsidiary that becomes an equity-accounted investee

Where a parent loses control of a subsidiary, so that the former subsidiary becomes an associate or a joint venture accounted for under the equity method, the effect is that the former parent/investor's interest in the investee is reported:

- using the equity method from the date on which control is lost in the current reporting period; and
- using full consolidation for any earlier part of the current reporting period, and of any earlier reporting period, during which the investee was controlled.

It is not acceptable for an entity to restate financial information for reporting periods prior to the loss of control using the equity method to provide comparability with the new presentation. Consolidation continues until control is lost, *[IFRS 10.B88]*, and equity accounting starts only from the date on which an entity becomes an associate or joint venture (see Chapter 11 at 7.3).

3.2.6 Subsidiary that is a single-asset entity

It may be that an entity sells a partial interest in a subsidiary that results in the loss of control of that subsidiary, but that subsidiary is a single-asset entity. In that situation, how does the entity determine the gain or loss on the partial sale?

In our view, the accounting depends on an analysis of the type of interest that is retained, which is determined by considering all facts and circumstances.

If the entity retains an interest in a joint operation under IFRS 11, the transaction is regarded as a partial sale of an asset. The entity will recognise a gain or loss for the portion of the asset sold.

In all other cases, the assessment looks through the structure to determine whether the investor retained in substance:

(a) an indirect interest in the underlying asset (for example, because the other (controlling) party cannot sell, pledge the asset or change the overall use of the asset without the investor's permission); or

(b) an investment in an entity.

If (a) is considered appropriate, the entity may be able to regard the transaction as a partial sale of the underlying asset, applying the principles in IAS 16 – *Property, Plant and Equipment* – or IAS 38 – *Intangible Assets* – and a gain or loss is recognised only to the extent of the portion of the asset sold. Neither of these standards addresses part disposals of individual, undivided assets; IAS 16 assumes that the disposal will be of a physical part. However, if the parent retains neither control nor joint control of the underlying asset, it may be appropriate to look through the structure and treat this as a part-disposal of that asset. The parent, in substance, holds an interest in the underlying asset. In that case, how the holding of the interest in the asset is structured does not affect the accounting result or lead to different accounting results when, in substance, an entity sells only a portion of that interest. Therefore, the sale of a portion of the shares in the entity that holds the asset is regarded as a partial sale of the interest in the asset. The conditions in which this may be the appropriate treatment are discussed in Chapter 18 at 7.3.

If (b) is considered appropriate, then the transaction will be accounted for as described at 3.2.1 above. If the retained investment is a financial asset, an IFRS 10 approach is applied; i.e. a gain or loss is recognised as if 100% of the investment in the single-asset entity had been sold (see 3.2.1.A above). If the retained investment is an associate or a joint venture, the gain to be recognised will depend on whether or not the entity is applying the September 2014 amendments to IFRS 10 and IAS 28 (see 3.2.1.B above). If the entity has chosen to early adopt the September 2014 amendments to IFRS 10 and IAS 28, it will apply the IAS 28 approach. If the entity has chosen not to early adopt the September 2014 amendments, based on its accounting policy choice, the entity will apply either an IFRS 10 or an IAS 28 approach:

- a gain or loss is recognised as if 100% of the investment in the single-asset entity had been sold (IFRS 10 approach); or
- the gain is restricted to that attributable to the other investor in the entity (IAS 28 approach).

This is explained further in Example 7.9 below.

Example 7.9: Determination of the gain or loss on the partial sale of an investment in a single-asset entity

A parent M owns 100% of a single-asset entity (SAE). The parent M sells 60% of its stake in its subsidiary to a third party X and as a result loses control of SAE. This is illustrated in the diagrams below.

Before

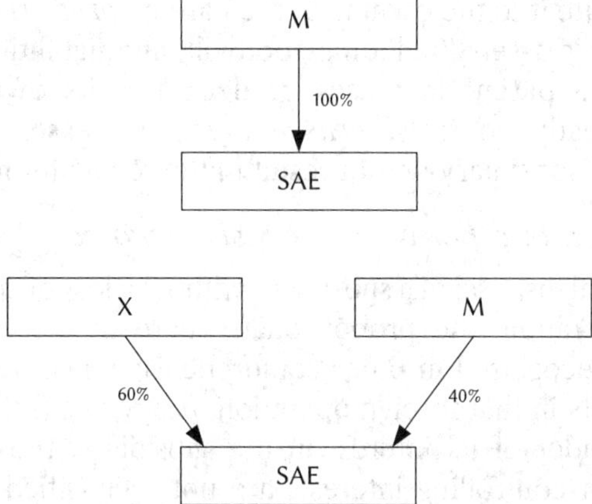

After

X | M
60% | 40%
SAE

Scenario A: Parent M retains a joint operation

At the same time, the parent M that still owns the 40% of the SAE enters into a joint arrangement with X to jointly control the SAE (and therefore the asset). The arrangement is considered to be a joint operation under IFRS 11.

Because the retained investment is a joint operation, it is accounted for as a proportionate share of the asset. Therefore, in scenario A, a gain or loss is recognised only in relation to the 60% sold.

Scenario B: Parent M retains an interest that is not a joint operation

The 40% retained interest does not give joint control over SAE. The entity needs to determine whether the retained interest is in substance an undivided interest in the asset or an investment in an entity, based on an assessment of all facts and circumstances.

- The investor retains an indirect interest in the underlying asset

The transaction is regarded as a partial sale of the underlying asset and a gain or loss is recognised only to the extent of the portion of the asset sold. Therefore, 60% of the asset is considered to be disposed, and the gain or loss calculated on that 60%.

- The investor retains an investment in an entity

The parent does not hold, in substance, an indirect interest in an asset but has an investment in an entity.

If the investment is recognised as an associate (if significant influence is held) or a joint venture (if there is joint control), and the September 2014 amendments to IFRS 10 and IAS 28 have not been early adopted, either 100% of the investment in the SAE is considered to be disposed of and the gain or loss calculated on that 100% or the gain is restricted to the 60% attributable to the other investor in the entity. If the September 2014 amendments have been early adopted, the gain is restricted to the 60% attributable to the other investor in the entity.

If the investment is a financial asset, 100% of the asset is considered to be disposed of and the gain or loss calculated on that 100%.

3.3 Changes in ownership interest without a loss of control

An increase or decrease in a parent's ownership interest that does not result in a loss of control of a subsidiary is accounted for as an equity transaction, i.e. a transaction with owners in their capacity as owners. *[IFRS 10.23]*. A parent's ownership interest may change without a loss of control, e.g. when a parent buys shares from or sells shares to a non-controlling interest, a subsidiary redeems shares held by a non-controlling interest, or when a subsidiary issues new shares to a non-controlling interest.

The carrying amounts of the controlling and non-controlling interests are adjusted to reflect the changes in their relative interests in the subsidiary. IFRS 10 states that 'the entity shall recognise directly in equity any difference between the amount by which the non-controlling interests are adjusted and the fair value of the consideration paid or received, and attribute it to the owners of the parent.' *[IFRS 10.B96]*. In other words, no changes to a subsidiary's assets (including goodwill) and liabilities are recognised in a transaction in which a parent increases or decreases its ownership interest in a subsidiary that it already controls. *[IFRS 10.BCZ173]*. Increases or decreases in the ownership interest in a subsidiary do not result in the recognition of a gain or loss.

3.3.1 Reattribution of other comprehensive income

If there has been a partial disposal of a subsidiary without a loss of control and the disposal includes a foreign operation, the proportionate share of the cumulative amount of exchange differences recognised in other comprehensive income is reattributed to the non-controlling interests in that foreign operation. *[IAS 21.48C]*. If the entity subsequently disposes of the remainder of its interest in the subsidiary, the exchange differences reattributed to the non-controlling interests are not reclassified to profit or loss (see Chapter 15 at 6.6.1.A). *[IAS 21.48B]*. In other words, on loss of control, only the exchange differences attributable to the controlling interest immediately before loss of control are reclassified to profit or loss. The accounting is illustrated in Example 7.12 below.

IFRS also requires the reattribution of other amounts recognised in other comprehensive income and equity. Although not explicitly addressed in IFRS 10 or IAS 21, this requirement was clarified in May 2009, when the IASB considered it in the context of its annual improvements project. The IASB Update noted that in the Board's view 'there is no need to clarify the following points, because the relevant requirements are clear: ...

- When a change in ownership in a subsidiary occurs but does not result in the loss of control, the parent must reattribute other comprehensive income between the owners of the parent and the non-controlling interest.'[13]

Example 7.10 below illustrates accounting for reattribution of other comprehensive income.

Example 7.10: Reattribution of other comprehensive income upon a decrease in ownership interest that does not result in a loss of control

A parent has a wholly owned subsidiary that has net assets of ¥4,000,000, and total other comprehensive income accumulated within equity of ¥1,000,000 related to exchange differences on a foreign operation. The parent sells a 10% interest in the subsidiary for ¥500,000 and does not lose control. The carrying amount of the non-controlling interest is ¥400,000 which includes ¥100,000 (i.e. 10%) of the total other comprehensive income of ¥1,000,000 related to exchange differences on a foreign operation reattributed to the non-controlling interest (as shown below).

The parent accounts for the transaction as follows:

	¥'000 DR	¥'000 CR
Cash	500	
Parent's share of other comprehensive income (¥1,000,000 × 10%)	100	
Parent's other reserves		200
Non-controlling interest's share of other comprehensive income (¥1,000,000 × 10%)		100
Non-controlling interest (excluding share of other comprehensive income) (¥4,000,000 × 10% – (¥1,000,000 × 10%))		300

The IASB's views also clarify that the reattribution approach is also required on an increase in ownership interest without gaining control. Again, neither IFRS 10 nor IAS 21 addresses this explicitly. Example 7.11 below illustrates the reattribution approach upon an increase in ownership interest.

Example 7.11: Reattribution of other comprehensive income upon an increase in ownership interest

A parent holds an 80% interest in a subsidiary that has net assets of ¥4,000,000. The carrying amount of the 20% non-controlling interest is ¥800,000 which includes ¥200,000 that represents the non-controlling interest's share of total other comprehensive income of ¥1,000,000 related to exchange differences on a foreign operation. The parent acquires an additional 10% interest in the subsidiary for ¥500,000, which increases its total interest to 90%. The carrying amount of the non-controlling interest is now ¥400,000 which includes ¥100,000 (i.e. 10%) of the total other comprehensive income of ¥1,000,000 related to exchange differences on a foreign operation, after reattributing ¥100,000 to the parent (as shown below).

The parent accounts for the transaction as follows:

	¥'000 DR	¥'000 CR
Non-controlling interest's share of other comprehensive income (¥1,000,000 × 10%)	100	
Non-controlling interest (excluding share of other comprehensive income) (¥800,000 × 10%/20% – (¥1,000,000 × 10%))	300	
Parent's other reserves	200	
Parent's share of other comprehensive income (¥1,000,000 × 10%)		100
Cash		500

Example 7.12 below illustrates the reclassification of reattributed exchange differences upon subsequent loss of control. This shows that the reattribution of the exchange differences arising on the change in the parent's ownership of the subsidiary (as illustrated in Examples 7.10 and 7.11 above) affects the gain recognised on loss of control of the subsidiary.

Example 7.12: Reclassification of reattributed exchange differences upon subsequent loss of control

Assume the same facts as in Examples 7.10 or 7.11 above. Following those transactions, the parent now holds a 90% interest in a subsidiary that has net assets of ¥4,000,000. The carrying amount of the 10% non-controlling interest is ¥400,000 which includes ¥100,000 of the total other comprehensive income of ¥1,000,000 related to exchange differences on a foreign operation, as reattributed to the non-controlling interest. The parent subsequently sells its 90% interest for ¥4,700,000. For the purposes of illustration, there have been no subsequent changes in net assets nor other comprehensive income up to the date of sale.

The parent accounts for the transaction as follows:

	¥'000 DR	¥'000 CR
Cash proceeds from sale	4,700	
Net assets of subsidiary derecognised		4,000
Non-controlling interest derecognised	400	
Parent's share of other comprehensive income reclassified (¥1,000,000 × 90%)	900	
Gain recognised on disposal of subsidiary attributable to parent		2,000

3.3.2 Goodwill attributable to non-controlling interests

It is not clear under IFRS 10 what happens to the non-controlling interests' share of goodwill, when accounting for transactions with non-controlling interests.

However, we believe that the parent should reallocate a proportion of the goodwill between the controlling and non-controlling interests when their relative ownership interests change. Otherwise, the loss recognised upon loss of control (see 3.2 above) or goodwill impairment would not reflect the ownership interest applicable to that non-controlling interest. Chapter 20 at 9 discusses how an entity tests goodwill for impairment, where there is a non-controlling interest. The issues arising include:

- calculation of the 'gross up' of the carrying amount of goodwill (for the purposes of the impairment test) because non-controlling interest is measured at its proportionate share of net identifiable assets and hence its share of goodwill is not recognised;
- the allocation of impairment losses between the parent and non-controlling interest; and
- reallocation of goodwill between non-controlling interest and controlling interests after a change in a parent's ownership interest in a subsidiary that does not result in loss of control.

Under IFRS 3, the proportion of goodwill that is attributable to the non-controlling interests is not necessarily equal to their ownership percentage. This might happen for one of two reasons. The most common is when the parent recognised the non-controlling interest at its proportionate share of the acquiree's identifiable net assets and therefore does not recognise any goodwill for the non-controlling interest (see Chapter 9 at 5.1 and 8.2). This situation might also occur because goodwill has been recognised for both the parent and the non-controlling interest but the parent's goodwill reflects a control premium that was paid upon acquisition (see Chapter 9 at 8.1).

Example 7.13 below illustrates one approach to reallocating goodwill where there is a change in ownership of the subsidiary with no loss of control (for a situation where the non-controlling interest is recognised initially at its fair value).

Example 7.13: Reallocation of goodwill to non-controlling interests

A parent pays €920 million to acquire an 80% interest in a subsidiary that owns net assets with a fair value of €1,000 million. The fair value of the non-controlling interest at the acquisition date is €220 million.

	Share of net assets €m	Share of goodwill €m	Total €m
Parent	800	120	920
Non-controlling interests	200	20	220
	1,000	140	1,140

Decrease in ownership percentage

A year after the acquisition, the parent sells a 20% interest in the subsidiary to a third party for €265 million. The parent's interest decreases to 60% and its share of net assets decreases to €600 million. Correspondingly, the share of net assets attributable to the non-controlling interest increases from €200 million to €400 million. The parent company sold a 20% interest in its subsidiary. Therefore, one approach for reallocating goodwill is to allocate €30 million (20%/80% × €120 million) of the parent's goodwill to the non-controlling interests. After the transaction, the parent's share of goodwill is €90 million (€120 million – €30 million).

In its consolidated financial statements, the parent accounts for this transaction as follows:

	€m DR	€m CR
Cash	265	
Non-controlling interest ((€400m – €200m) + €30m)		230
Equity of the parent		35

Increase in ownership percentage

Taking the initial fact pattern as a starting point, the parent acquires an additional 10% interest in the subsidiary for €115 million.

The parent's interest increases to 90% and its share of net assets increases to €900 million. Correspondingly, the share of net assets attributable to the non-controlling interest is reduced from €200 million to €100 million. The parent acquired half of the non-controlling interest. Using the proportionate allocation approach discussed above, the parent allocates €10 million (10%/20% × €20 million) of the non-controlling interests' goodwill to the parent.

In its consolidated financial statements, the parent accounts for this transaction as follows:

	€m DR	€m CR
Non-controlling interest ((€200m – €100m) + €10m)	110	
Equity of the parent	5	
Cash		115

In Example 7.13 above, the non-controlling interest was recognised and measured at its fair value at the acquisition date. If the non-controlling interest had been measured based on its proportionate share of net assets, the proportionate allocation approach described in the example would have resulted in the same accounting for the transaction where the parent's ownership interest had decreased. However, where the parent increased its ownership interest, as the carrying amount of the non-controlling interest did not include any amount for goodwill, the adjustment to the non-controlling interest would only have been €100 million resulting in a debit to the parent's equity of €15 million.

The proportionate allocation approach described in Example 7.13 above is just one method that may result in relevant and reliable information. However, other approaches may also be appropriate depending on the circumstances. We consider that an entity is not precluded from attributing goodwill on a basis other than ownership percentages if to do so is reasonable, e.g. because the non-controlling interest is measured on a proportionate share (rather than fair value) and because of the existence of a control premium. In such circumstances, an allocation approach which takes into account the acquirer's control premium will result in a goodwill balance that most closely resembles the balance that would have been recorded had the non-controlling interest been recorded at fair value. An entity may also be able to allocate impairment losses on a basis that recognises the disproportionate sharing of the controlling and the non-controlling interest in the goodwill book value. This is discussed further in Chapter 20 at 9.

3.3.3 *Non-cash acquisition of non-controlling interests*

One issue considered by the Interpretations Committee is the accounting for the purchase of a non-controlling interest by the controlling shareholder when the consideration includes non-cash items, such as an item of property, plant and equipment. More specifically, the submitter asked the Interpretations Committee to clarify whether the difference between the fair value of the consideration given and the carrying amount of such consideration should be recognised in equity or in profit or loss. The submitter asserted that, according to the requirements of the then IAS 27 – *Consolidated and Separate Financial Statements* (now reflected in IFRS 10, as discussed at 3.3 above), the difference described should be recognised in equity, whereas applying IFRIC 17 – *Distributions of Non-cash Assets to Owners* – by analogy the difference should be recognised in profit or loss (see 3.4 below).

The Interpretations Committee noted that the requirements of the then IAS 27 (now reflected in IFRS 10), deal solely with the difference between the carrying amount of the non-controlling interest and the fair value of the consideration given; this difference is required to be recognised in equity. These requirements do not deal with the difference between the fair value of the consideration given and the carrying amount of such consideration. *[IFRS 10.B96].* The difference between the fair value of the assets transferred and their carrying amount arises from the derecognition of those assets. IFRSs generally require an entity to recognise, in profit or loss, any gain or loss arising from the derecognition of an asset.[14]

3.3.4 *Transaction costs*

Although IFRS 10 is clear that changes in a parent's ownership interest in a subsidiary that do not result in the parent losing control of the subsidiary are equity transactions (i.e. transactions with owners in their capacity as owners), *[IFRS 10.23]*, it does not specifically address how to account for related transaction costs. Only incremental costs directly attributable to the equity transaction that otherwise would have been avoided qualify as transaction costs. *[IAS 32.37].*

In our view, any directly attributable incremental transaction costs incurred to acquire outstanding non-controlling interest in a subsidiary or to sell non-controlling interest in a subsidiary without loss of control are deducted from equity. This is regardless of whether the consideration is in cash or shares. This is consistent with both guidance elsewhere in IFRS regarding the treatment of such costs, *[IAS 32.35, 37, IAS 1.106(d), 109]*, and the view expressed by the Interpretations Committee.[15] Although where shares are given as consideration there is no change in total consolidated equity, there are two transactions – an issue of new equity and a repurchase of existing equity. The entity accounts for the transaction costs on the two elements in the same manner as if they had occurred separately. The tax effects of transaction costs of equity instruments are discussed in Chapter 31 at 10.3.5.

IFRS does not specify where to allocate the costs in equity – in particular, whether to the parent (who incurred the costs) or to the non-controlling interest (whose equity was issued/repurchased). Therefore, the parent may choose where to allocate the costs within equity, based on the facts and circumstances surrounding the change in ownership, and any legal requirements of the jurisdiction.

Regardless of the account in equity to which the charge is allocated, the amount is not reclassified to profit or loss in future periods. Consequently, if the costs are allocated to non-controlling interest, this amount must be separately tracked. Therefore, if a subsidiary is later sold in a separate transaction (i.e. loss of control), the transaction costs previously recognised directly in equity to acquire or sell the non-controlling interest are not reclassified from equity to profit and loss, because they do not represent components of other comprehensive income.

3.4 Demergers and distributions of non-cash assets to owners

Groups may dispose of subsidiaries by way of a demerger. This situation typically involves the transfer of the subsidiaries to be disposed of, either:

- directly to shareholders, by way of a dividend in kind; or
- to a newly formed entity in exchange for the issue of shares by that entity to the shareholders of the disposing entity.

IFRS 10 requires recognition of a distribution of shares of the subsidiary to owners in their capacity as owners, but does not describe how to account for such transactions. *[IFRS 10.B98(b)]*. Instead, IFRIC 17 addresses distributions of subsidiary shares to shareholders. The application of IFRIC 17 in the context of demergers is discussed below. The application of IFRIC 17 to assets in general is discussed in Chapter 8 at 2.4.2.

3.4.1 Scope of IFRIC 17

IFRIC 17 applies to the following types of distribution (described by IFRIC 17 as 'non-reciprocal') by an entity to its owners in their capacity as owners: *[IFRIC 17.3]*

(a) distributions of non-cash assets such as items of property, plant and equipment, businesses as defined in IFRS 3 (see Chapter 9 at 3.2), ownership interests in another entity or disposal groups as defined in IFRS 5 (see Chapter 4 at 2.1); and

(b) distributions that give owners a choice of receiving either non-cash assets or a cash alternative.

The scope of IFRIC 17 is limited in several respects:

- it only applies to distributions in which all owners of the same class of equity instruments are treated equally; *[IFRIC 17.4]*
- it does not apply to 'a distribution of a non-cash asset that is ultimately controlled by the same party or parties before and after the distribution', *[IFRIC 17.5]*, which means that IFRIC 17 does not apply when:
  - a group of individual shareholders receiving the distribution, as a result of contractual arrangements, collectively have the power to govern financial and operating policies of the entity making the distribution so as to obtain benefits from its activities; *[IFRIC 17.6]* or
  - 'an entity distributes some of its ownership interests in a subsidiary but retains control of the subsidiary. The entity making a distribution that results in the entity recognising a non-controlling interest in its subsidiary accounts for the distribution in accordance with IFRS 10.' *[IFRIC 17.7]*. In this situation, the requirements of IFRS 10 discussed at 3.3 above would be applied.

  This exclusion applies to 'the separate, individual and consolidated financial statements of an entity that makes the distribution'; *[IFRIC 17.5]* and
- it only addresses the accounting by an entity that makes a non-cash asset distribution. It does not address the accounting by shareholders who receive the distribution. *[IFRIC 17.8]*.

3.4.2 Recognition and measurement in IFRIC 17

An entity making a non-cash distribution to its owners recognises a liability to pay a dividend when the dividend is appropriately authorised and is no longer at the discretion of the entity. This is the date: *[IFRIC 17.10]*

(a) when declaration of the dividend (e.g. by management or the board of directors) is approved by the relevant authority (e.g. shareholders) if the jurisdiction requires such approval; or

(b) when the dividend is declared (e.g. by management or the board of directors) if the jurisdiction does not require further approval.

An entity measures the liability at the fair value of the assets to be distributed. *[IFRIC 17.11]*. If the owners have a choice between receiving a non-cash asset or cash, the entity estimates the dividend payable by considering both the fair value of each alternative and the associated probability of owners selecting each alternative. *[IFRIC 17.12]*. IFRIC 17 does not specify any method of assessing probability nor its effect on measurement. In a demerger involving the distribution of shares in a subsidiary, the fair value will be determined based on the guidance in IFRS 13. As indicated at 3.2.1.B above, the IASB has been discussing issues relating to the unit of account for investments in subsidiaries, joint ventures and associates, and their fair value measurement under IFRS 13.

IFRS 5's requirements apply also to a non-current asset (or disposal group) that is classified as held for distribution to owners acting in their capacity as owners (held for distribution to owners). *[IFRS 5.5A, 12A, 15A]*. This means that a non-current asset (or disposal group) classified as held for sale within scope of IFRS 5 will be carried at the lower of carrying amount and fair value less costs to distribute (i.e. incremental costs directly attributable to the distribution, excluding finance costs and income tax expense). *[IFRS 5.15A]*. Assets not subject to the measurement provisions of IFRS 5 are measured in accordance with the relevant standard. *[IFRS 5.5]*. See further discussion at Chapter 4 at 2.

At the end of each reporting period and at the date of settlement, the carrying amount of the dividend payable is adjusted to reflect any changes in the fair value of the assets being distributed and changes are recognised in equity as adjustments to the amount of the distribution. *[IFRIC 17.13]*.

When the dividend payable is settled, any difference between the carrying amount of the assets distributed and the carrying amount of the dividend payable is recognised as a separate line item in profit or loss. *[IFRIC 17.14-15]*. IFRIC 17 does not express any preference for particular line items or captions in the income statement.

The non-cash assets that are to be distributed are measured in accordance with other applicable IFRSs up to the time of settlement as IFRIC 17 does not override the recognition and measurement requirements of other IFRSs. While the Interpretations Committee recognised concerns about the potential 'accounting mismatch' in equity resulting from measuring the dividend payable and the related assets on a different basis, *[IFRIC 17.BC55]*, it concluded that:

> '... there was no support in IFRSs for requiring a remeasurement of the assets because of a decision to distribute them. The IFRIC noted that the mismatch concerned arises only with respect to assets that are not carried at fair value already. The IFRIC also noted that the accounting mismatch is the inevitable consequence of IFRSs using different measurement attributes at different times with different triggers for the remeasurement of different assets and liabilities.' *[IFRIC 17.BC56]*.

3.4.3 Presentation and disclosure

An entity discloses the following information in respect of distributions of non-cash assets within the scope of IFRIC 17:

- the carrying amount of the dividend payable at the beginning and end of the reporting period; *[IFRIC 17.16]*
- the increase or decrease in the carrying amount recognised in the reporting period as result of a change in the fair value of the assets to be distributed; *[IFRIC 17.16]* and
- if, after the end of a reporting period but before the financial statements are authorised for issue, an entity declares a dividend to distribute a non-cash asset, it discloses: *[IFRIC 17.17]*
  - the nature of the asset to be distributed;
  - the carrying amount of the asset to be distributed as of the end of the reporting period;
  - the fair value of the asset to be distributed as of the end of the reporting period, if it is different from its carrying amount; and
  - information about the method(s) used to determine that fair value required by paragraphs 93(b), (d), (g) and (i) and 99 of IFRS 13 (see Chapter 14 at 20.1 and 20.3).

Chapter 4 at 3 discusses the presentation requirements of IFRS 5 where the demerger meets the definition of a discontinued operation. Chapter 4 at 2.2.4 discusses the presentation of non-current assets and disposal groups held for sale. The same requirements apply to non-current assets and disposal groups held for distribution. *[IFRS 5.5A]*.

4 NON-CONTROLLING INTERESTS

4.1 The definition of non-controlling interest

IFRS 10 defines a non-controlling interest as 'equity in a subsidiary not attributable, directly or indirectly, to a parent.' *[IFRS 10 Appendix A]*. The principle underlying accounting for non-controlling interests is that all residual economic interest holders of any part of the consolidated entity have an equity interest in that consolidated entity. Consequently, non-controlling interest relates to consolidated subsidiaries, and not to those investments in subsidiaries accounted at fair value through profit or loss in accordance with IFRS 9 or IAS 39 by an investment entity (see Chapter 6 at 10.3). *[IFRS 10.31-33, C7]*. This principle applies regardless of the decision-making ability of that interest holder and where in the group that interest is held. Therefore, any equity instruments issued by a subsidiary that are not owned by the parent (apart from those that are required to be classified by IAS 32 – *Financial Instruments: Presentation* – as financial liabilities in the consolidated financial statements, as discussed at 4.4 below) are non-controlling interests, including:

- ordinary shares;
- convertible debt and other compound financial instruments;
- preference shares that are classified as equity (including both those with, and without, an entitlement to a *pro rata* share of net assets on liquidation);
- warrants;
- options over own shares; and
- options under share-based payment transactions.

Options and warrants are non-controlling interests, regardless of whether they are vested and of the exercise price (e.g. whether they are 'in-the-money').

IAS 32 defines an equity instrument as 'any contract that evidences a residual interest in the assets of an entity after deducting all of its liabilities'. *[IAS 32.11]*. This is the same as the definition of 'equity' in the IASB's *Conceptual Framework for Financial Reporting*. *[Framework 4.4(c)]*. Hence, the reference to 'equity' in the definition of a non-controlling interest refers to those 'equity instruments' of a subsidiary that are not held, directly or indirectly, by its parent. This also means that financial instruments that are not classified within equity in accordance with IAS 32 (e.g. total return swaps) are not included within the definition of a non-controlling interest.

4.2 Initial measurement of non-controlling interests

4.2.1 Initial measurement of non-controlling interests in a business combination

IFRS 3 requires any non-controlling interest in an acquiree to be recognised, *[IFRS 3.10]*, but there are differing measurement requirements depending on the type of equity instrument.

There is a choice of two measurement methods for those components of non-controlling interests that are both present ownership interests and entitle their holders to a proportionate share of the entity's net assets in the event of a liquidation ('qualifying non-controlling interests'). They can be measured at either:

a) acquisition-date fair value (consistent with the measurement principle for other components of the business combination); or
b) their proportionate share in the recognised amounts of the acquiree's identifiable net assets.

The choice of method is to be made for each business combination on a transaction-by-transaction basis, rather than being a policy choice. This choice of measurement is discussed in Chapter 9 at 8.

However, this choice is not available for all other components of non-controlling interests, which are required to be measured at their acquisition-date fair values, unless another measurement basis is required by IFRSs. *[IFRS 3.19]*.

Of the items listed in 4.1 above, entities are only given a choice of proportionate share of the acquiree's identifiable net assets or fair value for ordinary shares or preference shares that are entitled to a *pro rata* share of net assets on liquidation.

Another measurement basis (referred to as a 'market-based measure') is required by IFRS 3 for share-based payment transactions classified as equity in accordance with IFRS 2 – these are measured in accordance with the method in IFRS 2. *[IFRS 3.30, B62A, B62B]*. The accounting for replaced and not replaced share-based payment transactions in a business combination is discussed in Chapter 9 at 7.2 and 8.4 and in Chapter 32 at 11.2 and 11.3.

The other items listed in 4.1 above, e.g. the equity component of convertible debt or other compound financial instruments, preference shares classified as equity without an entitlement to a *pro rata* share of net assets upon liquidation, warrants and options over own shares, must be measured at fair value.

These issues are discussed in more detail in Chapter 9 at 8.

The measurement of non-controlling interests in a business combination is illustrated in Example 7.14 below.

Example 7.14: Initial measurement of non-controlling interests in a business combination (1)

Parent acquires 80% of the ordinary shares of Target for €950,000 in cash. The total fair value of the equity instruments issued by Target is €1,165,000 and the fair value of its identifiable net assets is €850,000. The fair value of the 20% of the ordinary shares owned by non-controlling shareholders is €190,000. In addition, the subsidiary has also written gross settled call options over its own shares with a fair value of €25,000, which are considered equity instruments under IAS 32.

Option 1 – Non-controlling interest at fair value

The impact of the business combination and the measurement of non-controlling interests are as follows:

	€'000 DR	€'000 CR
Fair value of identifiable net assets	850	
Goodwill (€950,000 + €215,000 – €850,000)	315	
Cash		950
Non-controlling interest (€190,000 + €25,000)		215

The non-controlling interests are measured at the fair value of all equity instruments issued by Target that are not owned by the parent (i.e. ordinary shares and gross settled call options).

Option 2 – Qualifying non-controlling interests are measured at proportionate share of identifiable net assets

The impact of the business combination and the measurement of non-controlling interests are as follows:

	€'000 DR	€'000 CR
Fair value of identifiable net assets	850	
Goodwill (€950,000 – (80% × €850,000) + €25,000)	295	
Cash		950
Non-controlling interest (20% × €850,000 + €25,000)		195

The non-controlling interests that are present ownership interests and entitle their holders to a proportionate share of the Target's net assets in the event of liquidation (i.e. the ordinary shares) are measured at the non-controlling interest's proportionate share of the identifiable net assets of Target. The non-controlling interests that are not present ownership interests or do not entitle their holders to a proportionate share of the Target's net assets in the event of liquidation (i.e. the gross settled call options) are measured at their fair value.

Reconciliation of goodwill

Goodwill as determined under the two methods can be reconciled as follows:

	€'000
Option 2: Goodwill (€950,000 – 80% × €850,000 + €25,000)	295
Goodwill related to the non-controlling interest in ordinary shares (€190,000 – 20% × €850,000)	20
Option 1: Goodwill (€1,165,000 – €850,000)	315

This makes clear that Option 2 effectively ignores the goodwill related to ordinary shares that are held by non-controlling shareholders.

In Example 7.14 above, under Option 2, the computation of the non-controlling interests represented by the ordinary shares was based solely on the fair value of the identifiable net assets; i.e. no deduction was made in respect of the other component of non-controlling interest. IFRS 3 does not state whether this should be the case. An alternative view would be that such other components of non-controlling interests should be deducted from the value of the net identifiable net assets acquired based on their acquisition-date fair value (or market-based measure) or based on their liquidation rights, as illustrated in Example 7.15 below.

Example 7.15: Initial measurement of non-controlling interests in a business combination (2)

Option 3 – Qualifying non-controlling interests are measured at proportionate share of identifiable net assets net of other components of non-controlling interests

The impact of the business combination and the measurement of non-controlling interests are as follows:

	€'000 DR	€'000 CR
Fair value of identifiable net assets	850	
Goodwill (€950,000 – 80% × (€850,000 – €25,000))	290	
Cash		950
Non-controlling interest ((20% × (€850,000 – €25,000)) + €25,000)		190

The difference between goodwill of €295,000 (Option 2 in Example 7.14 above) and €290,000 is 20% of €25,000, i.e. the amount attributable to the non-controlling interest in the call options.

In Example 7.15 above, Option 2 resulted in no goodwill being attributable to non-controlling interests. However, if the Target had been acquired, not by Parent, but by a 60%-owned subsidiary of Parent, we believe that the goodwill recognised remains the same, but that some of the goodwill is attributable to the non-controlling interests in the acquiring subsidiary as illustrated in Example 7.16 below.

Example 7.16: Initial measurement of non-controlling interests in a business combination by a partly owned subsidiary

Assume the same facts as in Example 7.14 above, except that a 60% Subsidiary of Parent acquires 80% of the ordinary shares of Target for €950,000 in cash.

Under Option 2, the impact of the business combination and the measurement of non-controlling interests in Parent's consolidated financial statements are as follows:

	€'000 DR	€'000 CR
Fair value of identifiable net assets	850	
Goodwill (€950,000 – (80% × €850,000) +€25,000))	295	
Cash		950
Non-controlling interest in Target (20% × €850,000 + €25,000)		195
Non-controlling interest in 60% Subsidiary		–

Although the overall impact on the non-controlling interest in 60% Subsidiary is nil, this is represented by:

	€'000 DR	€'000 CR
Share of fair value of identifiable net assets (40% × 80% × €850,000)		272
Share of goodwill (40% × (€295,000 – €25,000)		108
Share of cash consideration (40% × €950,000)	380	

4.2.2 *Initial measurement of non-controlling interests in a subsidiary (that is not a business combination)*

The initial measurement of non-controlling interests in a subsidiary (that is not a business combination) is discussed at 3.1.1 above.

4.3 Presentation of non-controlling interests

IFRS 10 requires non-controlling interests to be presented in the consolidated statement of financial position within equity, separately from the equity of the owners of the parent. *[IFRS 10.22]*. Profit or loss and each component of other comprehensive income are attributed to the owners of the parent and to the non-controlling interests. Attribution of total comprehensive income to the non-controlling interests continues even if it results in a deficit balance. *[IFRS 10.B94]*. Deficit balances are considered further at 4.5.1 below.

The presentation of non-controlling interests in the primary financial statements is addressed in Chapter 3 at 3.1.5 (statement of financial position), *[IAS 1.54]*, 3.2.2 (statement of profit or loss), *[IAS 1.81B]*, 3.2.4 (statement of comprehensive income), *[IAS 1.81B]*, and 3.3 (statement of changes in equity). *[IAS 1.106]*.

4.4 Non-controlling interests classified as financial liabilities

In spite of the general requirement in IFRS 10 to treat non-controlling interests as equity, a non-controlling interest is classified by IAS 32 as a financial liability and payments to the non-controlling interest as interest expense if the group as a whole has an obligation to deliver cash or another financial asset in respect of the instrument, or to settle it in a manner that results in its classification as a financial liability. *[IAS 32.AG29]*. See Chapter 45 at 4.8.1.

One particular issue considered by the Interpretations Committee is the classification, in the consolidated financial statements of a group, of puttable instruments that are issued by a subsidiary but that are not held, directly or indirectly, by the parent. The question asked was whether these instruments, which are classified as equity instruments in the financial statements of the subsidiary in accordance with IAS 32, *[IAS 32.16A, 16B]*, should be classified as equity or liability in the parent's consolidated financial statements.

The Interpretations Committee noted that paragraphs 16A-16D of IAS 32 state that puttable instruments and instruments that impose on the entity an obligation to deliver to another party a *pro rata* share of the net assets of the entity only on liquidation meet the definition of a financial liability. These instruments are classified as equity in the financial statements of the subsidiary as an exception to the definition of a financial liability if all relevant requirements are met. *[IAS 32.16A, 16B, 16C, 16D]*. This exception applies only to the financial statements of the subsidiary and does not extend to the parent's consolidated financial statements. *[IAS 32.AG29A]*. Consequently, these financial instruments should be classified as financial liabilities in the parent's consolidated financial statements.[16]

In our view, where a non-controlling interest is classified as equity in consolidated financial statements, it is subject to all the requirements of IAS 32 relating to own equity. For example, put or call options over non-controlling interests accounted for as equity should be accounted for in consolidated financial statements as contracts over own equity instruments under IAS 32 (see Chapter 45 at 11).

In some cases, the effect of options over what are in law non-controlling interests may be such that no non-controlling interests are recognised in the financial statements, particularly when such options are issued as part of a business combination (see 5 below).

4.5 Subsequent measurement of non-controlling interests

A proportion of profit or loss, other comprehensive income and changes in equity is only attributed to those instruments included within non-controlling interests if they give rise to an existing ownership interest. Non-controlling interests, that are potential voting rights and other derivatives that require exercise or conversion (such as options, warrants, or share-based payment transactions), generally do not receive an allocation of profit or loss, other comprehensive income and changes in equity. *[IFRS 10.B89, B94]*. However, as discussed at 2.2 above, allocating the proportions of profit or loss, other comprehensive income and changes in equity based on present legal ownership interests is not always appropriate. An entity also considers the eventual exercise of potential rights and other derivatives if, in substance, they provide existing ownership interests that currently give it access to the returns associated with that ownership interest. In that case, the proportion allocated to the parent and non-controlling interest takes into account the eventual exercise of those potential voting rights and other derivatives. *[IFRS 10.B90]*. As noted at 2.2 above, this Chapter uses the term 'present ownership interest' to include existing legal ownership interests, together with potential voting rights and other derivatives that, in substance, already provide existing ownership interests in a subsidiary.

Where a subsidiary has granted options over its own shares under an equity-settled share-based payment transaction, the share-based payment expense recognised in profit or loss will be attributable to the parent and any other non-controlling interest that has a present ownership in the subsidiary. None of the expense is attributed to the non-controlling interest represented by the options under the share-based payment transaction. The corresponding entry taken to equity by the subsidiary in respect of the options under the share-based payment transaction will be recognised as non-controlling interest in the consolidated financial statements.

If a subsidiary has outstanding cumulative preference shares classified as equity that are held by non-controlling interests, the parent is required to compute its share of profits or losses after adjusting for the dividends on these shares, whether or not dividends have been declared. *[IFRS 10.B95]*. This effectively means that the non-controlling interests represented by the cumulative preference shares are being allocated a portion of the profit or loss equivalent to the dividends.

In addition, where an entity has a complicated equity structure with several classes of equity shares that have varying entitlements to net profits, equity or liquidation preferences, the parent needs to assess carefully the rights attaching to each class of equity share in determining the appropriate percentage of ownership interest.

When the proportion of equity held by the non-controlling interest changes, e.g. because a potential voting right is exercised, the carrying amount originally recognised in non-controlling interest is adjusted to reflect the change in the relative interests in the subsidiary. *[IFRS 10.B96]*. In our view, this requirement in IFRS 10 also means that if potential voting rights lapse unexercised, the amount originally recognised in non-controlling interest is reversed, so that the carrying amounts of the controlling and non-controlling interest reflect the relative interests in the subsidiary. Otherwise, amounts previously recognised related to lapsed potential voting rights would remain recognised as part of the non-controlling interest until the next remeasurement of non-controlling interests occurs, which may be an unrelated transaction, or which may never occur.

4.5.1 Loss-making subsidiaries

Total comprehensive income is attributed 'to the owners of the parent and to the non-controlling interests even if this results in the non-controlling interests having a deficit balance.' *[IFRS 10.B94]*. This approach is consistent with the fact that the controlling and the non-controlling interest participate proportionately in the risks and rewards of an investment in the subsidiary. The IASB observed that although it is true that the non-controlling interest has no further obligation to contribute assets to the entity, neither does the parent. *[IFRS 10.BCZ165]*.

Guarantees or other support arrangements by the parent often protect the non-controlling interests from losses of the subsidiary in excess of their equity. The IASB believes that the parent ought to account for such arrangements separately, and that the accounting for these arrangements should not affect how an entity should attribute comprehensive income to the parent and the non-controlling interests. *[IFRS 10.BCZ162-164]*.

These requirements in IFRS 10 in respect of loss-making subsidiaries have been carried forward from those introduced by the IASB when IAS 27 was amended in 2008, and differ from the requirements formerly included in IAS 27. However, a transitional issue that arose when IAS 27 was amended in 2008 that may still have been relevant for certain entities applying IFRS 10 relates to loss-making subsidiaries at the time of transition to IAS 27 (as amended in 2008). *[IFRS 10.C6]*. Since IFRS 1 – *First-time Adoption of International Financial Reporting Standards* – also has a similar transitional exception for measurement of non-controlling interests, *[IFRS 1.B7]*, (see Chapter 5 at 4.8), this issue may also be relevant for entities that applied IFRS 10 (rather than IAS 27, as amended in 2008) on first-time adoption. This issue is discussed in Chapter 7 at 6.1 of EY International GAAP 2016.

5 CALL AND PUT OPTIONS OVER NON-CONTROLLING INTERESTS

Some business combinations involve options over some or all of the outstanding shares. For example, the acquirer might have a call option, i.e. a right to acquire the outstanding shares at a future date for a particular price. Alternatively, the acquirer might have granted a put option to the other shareholders whereby they have the right to sell their shares to the acquirer at a future date for a particular price. In some cases, there may be a combination of such call and put options, the terms of which may be equivalent or may be different.

IFRS 3 gives no guidance as to how to account for such options in a business combination. Therefore, when determining the appropriate accounting in the consolidated financial statements in such situations, IFRS 10, IAS 32, and IFRS 9 or IAS 39 need to be considered. The accounting for call and put options depends on whether or not the acquirer has obtained present access to returns associated with the ownership interest in the shares of the acquiree subject to the call and/or put option. Potential voting rights that represent a present ownership interest are discussed in general at 2.2 and 4.5 above but specific considerations for call and/or put options are discussed at 5.1 and 5.2 below.

While the discussion below deals with options, similar considerations to those discussed at 5.1 and 5.2 below apply where the acquirer entered into a forward purchase contract for the shares held by the other shareholders (see 5.3 below).

Although the discussion at 5.1 and 5.2 below focuses on call and put options entered into at the same time as control of the subsidiary is gained, an entity may enter into the options with non-controlling shareholders after gaining control. As indicated at 5.4 below, the appropriate accounting in the consolidated financial statements will still be based on the discussions in 5.1 and 5.2 below.

5.1 Call options only

Call options are considered when determining whether the entity has obtained control, as discussed at Chapter 6 at 4.3.4. Where it is determined that an entity has control over another entity, the proportions of profit or loss, other comprehensive income and changes in equity allocated to the parent and non-controlling interests are based on present ownership interests, and generally do not reflect the possible exercise or conversion of potential voting rights under call options. *[IFRS 10.B89, B94]*. The eventual exercise of potential voting rights under the call option are reflected in the proportion of profit or loss, other comprehensive income and changes in equity only if in substance the entity already has access to the returns associated with that ownership interest. *[IFRS 10.B90, B94]*. This assessment depends on the terms of the call option, and judgement is required.

5.1.1 Options giving the acquirer present access to returns associated with that ownership interest

A call option is likely to give the acquiring entity present access to returns associated with the ownership interest in the shares subject to the call in limited circumstances, for example:

- when the option price is fixed with a low exercise price and it is agreed between the parties that either no dividends will be paid to the other shareholders or the dividend payments lead to an adjustment of the option exercise price; or
- when the terms are set such that the other shareholders effectively receive only a lender's return.

This is because any accretion in the fair value of the underlying ownership interest under the option (for example, due to improved financial performance of the acquiree subsequent to the granting of the call option) is likely to be realised by the acquirer.

If a call option gives the acquiring entity present access to returns over all of the shares held by non-controlling shareholders, then there will be no non-controlling interest presented in equity. The acquirer accounts for the business combination as though it acquired a 100% interest. The acquirer also recognises a financial liability for the present value of the exercise price to be paid to the non-controlling shareholders under the call option. Changes in the carrying amount of the financial liability are recognised in profit or loss. If the call option expires unexercised, then the acquirer has effectively disposed of a partial interest in its subsidiary in return for the amount recognised as the 'liability' at the date of expiry and accounts for the transaction as a change in ownership interest without a loss of control, as discussed at 3.3 above.

5.1.2 Options not giving the acquirer present access to returns associated with that ownership interest

A call option may not give present access to the returns associated with the ownership interest in the shares subject to the call where the option's terms contain one or more of the following features:

- the option price has not yet been determined or will be the fair value of the shares at the date of exercise (or a surrogate for such a value);
- the option price is based on expected future results or net assets of the subsidiary at the date of exercise; or
- it has been agreed between the parties that, prior to the exercise of the option, all retained profits may be freely distributed to the existing shareholders according to their current shareholdings.

If a call option does not give present access to the returns associated with the ownership interest in the shares subject to the call, IFRS 10 requires that the instruments containing the potential voting rights be accounted for in accordance with IFRS 9 or IAS 39. *[IFRS 10.B91, C7]*. Derivatives on an interest in a subsidiary are accounted for as financial instruments unless the derivative meets the definition of an equity instrument of the entity in IAS 32. *[IFRS 9.2.1(a), IAS 39.2(a)]*. The accounting by the parent in its separate and consolidated financial statements will be as follows.

Separate financial statements: a call option over the shares in the acquired subsidiary is initially recognised as a financial asset at its fair value, with any subsequent changes in its fair value recognised in profit or loss. The call option's fair value may not be significant if it is exercisable at the fair value of the underlying shares at the date of exercise, or at a surrogate for such a value.

Consolidated financial statements: the accounting depends on whether the call option meets the definition of a financial asset or an equity instrument:

- *Financial asset* – A call option is initially recognised as a financial asset at its fair value, with any subsequent changes in its fair value recognised in profit or loss. If the call option is exercised, the fair value of the option at that date is included as part of the consideration paid for the acquisition of the non-controlling interest (see 3.3 above). If it lapses unexercised, any carrying amount is expensed in profit or loss.
- *Equity instrument* – A call option is accounted for in a similar way to a call option over an entity's own equity shares, as discussed in Chapter 45 at 11.2. This is because it is an option over the non-controlling interest in the consolidated financial statements, and IFRS 10 regards the non-controlling interest as 'equity' in those financial statements. Because such a call option over the non-controlling interest's shares will be gross-settled, the initial fair value of the option is recognised as a debit to equity. If the call option is exercised, this initial fair value is included as part of the consideration paid for the acquisition of the non-controlling interest (see 3.3 above). If a call option lapses unexercised, there is no entry required within equity.

5.2 Put options only

Under current IFRS, it is not clear how to account for put options that are granted to holders of non-controlling interests ('NCI puts') at the date of acquiring control of a subsidiary (or, indeed, after gaining control). There is a lack of explicit guidance in IFRS and potential contradictions between the requirements of IFRS 10 and IAS 32.

This issue has been the subject of much debate over the years. Although it is clear that, under current IFRS, the NCI put itself gives rise to a liability representing the exercise price (see 5.2.1 below for a discussion of the measurement of this liability), there are a number of decisions that must be made in order to account for the arrangements, including:

- whether or not the terms of the NCI put mean that it gives the parent a present ownership interest in the underlying securities (see 5.2.2 below); and
- where the parent does not have a present ownership interest, whether or not a non-controlling interest continues to be recognised, i.e. should the parent recognise both the non-controlling interest and the financial liability for the NCI put.

In the latter case, there are a number of additional decisions that must be made, in particular the basis on which the non-controlling interest is recognised.

Although the Interpretations Committee unequivocally confirmed as early as 2006 that an NCI put with an exercise price to be settled in cash is itself a financial liability,[17] the nature of the financial liability remains controversial and has been discussed by the Interpretations Committee and the IASB on a number of occasions. In June 2014, the IASB decided that this issue will be considered as part of the broader project looking at the distinction between liabilities and equity – the Financial Instruments with Characteristics of Equity ('FICE') project.[18]

The previous deliberations have been in the context of an NCI put that is required to be settled for cash. The Interpretations Committee has also considered a request in 2016 regarding how an entity accounts for an NCI put in its consolidated financial statements where the NCI put has a strike price that will be settled by delivery of a variable number of the parent's own equity instruments. Specifically, the Interpretations Committee was asked to consider whether, in its consolidated financial statements, the parent recognises:

(a) a financial liability representing the present value of the option's strike price – in other words, a gross liability; or

(b) a derivative financial liability presented on a net basis measured at fair value.

The Interpretations Committee was also asked whether the parent applies the same accounting in its consolidated financial statements for NCI puts for which the parent has the choice to settle the exercise price either in cash or by way of delivery of a variable number of its own equity instruments to the same value.

However, on the basis of its previous discussions and the IASB's FICE project, the Interpretations Committee decided in November 2016 not to add this issue to its agenda.[19]

These developments are discussed further at 5.5 below.

Like the previous deliberations of the Interpretations Committee and the IASB, the discussion that follows relates to NCI puts that are required to be settled in cash.

5.2.1 The financial liability for the NCI put

As indicated at 4.1 above, IFRS 10 regards the non-controlling interest as 'equity' in the consolidated financial statements. Under current IFRS, any contractual obligation to purchase non-controlling interests – such as a put option granted to non-controlling interests – gives rise to a financial liability measured at the present value of the redemption amount (for example, for the present value of the forward repurchase price, option exercise price or other redemption amount). Subsequently, the financial liability is measured in accordance with IFRS 9 or IAS 39 (see Chapter 45 at 5.3 and 11.3.2). *[IAS 32.23, AG27(b), 97R].*

IAS 32 offers no guidance as to how the financial liability should be measured if the number of shares to be purchased and/or the date of purchase are not known. In our view, it would be consistent with the requirement of IFRS 13 that liabilities with a demand feature such as a demand bank deposit should be measured at not less than the amount payable on demand *[IFRS 13.47]* (see Chapter 14 at 11.5), to adopt a 'worst case' approach. In other words, it should be assumed that the purchase will take place on the earliest possible date for the maximum number of shares.

The accounting for the remaining aspects of the put option is discussed below; this depends in part upon an assessment of the terms of the transaction and, in some areas, involves a choice of accounting policy which, once selected, must be applied consistently.

The following diagram summarises the analysis that we believe should be performed, the questions to be addressed and the approaches that apply.

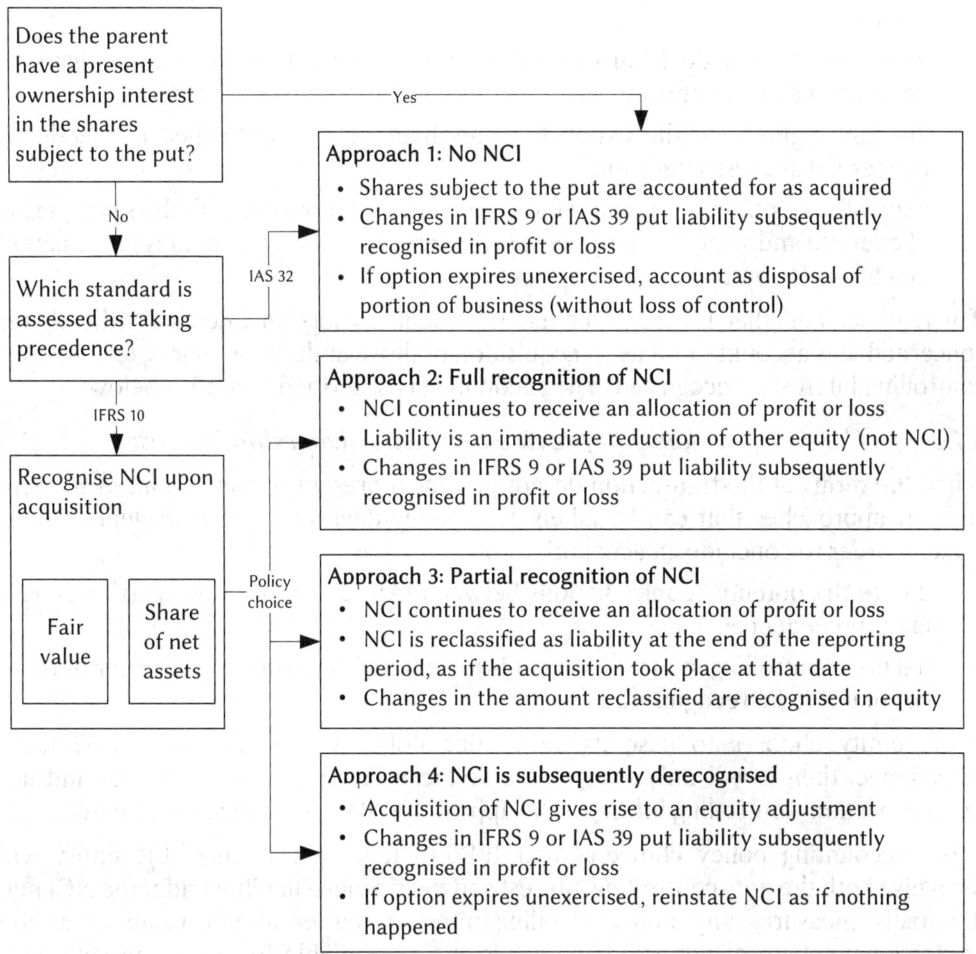

The diagram above indicates that, under approaches 1, 2 and 4, changes in the IFRS 9 or IAS 39 financial liability subsequent to initial recognition are recognised in profit or loss. It is assumed that the financial liability is not designated at fair value in the later discussion of those approaches. However, if the financial liability is designated at fair value under IFRS 9, the fair value changes attributable to changes in credit risk are normally recognised in other comprehensive income (see Chapter 50 at 2.1).

5.2.2 The NCI put provides a present ownership interest

In our view, in the same way as for call options, an entity has to consider whether the terms of the transaction give it present access to the returns associated with the ownership interest in the shares subject to the NCI put. If so, the shares are accounted for as if they had been acquired by the entity.

Factors that indicate that the NCI put might provide a present ownership interest include:

- pricing – to the extent that the price is fixed or determinable, rather than being at fair value;
- voting rights and decision-making – to the extent that the voting rights or decision-making connected to the shares concerned are restricted;
- dividend rights – to the extent that the dividend rights attached to the shares concerned are restricted; and
- issue of call options – a combination of put and call options, with the same period of exercise and same/similar pricing indicates that the arrangement is in the nature of a forward contract.

If it is concluded that the acquirer has a present ownership interest in the shares concerned, it is accounted for as an acquisition of those underlying shares, and no non-controlling interest is recognised. The accounting is described in 5.2.3.A below.

5.2.3 The NCI put does not provide a present ownership interest

When the terms of the transaction do not provide a present ownership interest, there are four approaches that can be taken. Key policy decisions that management must make in order to conclude an accounting approach, are:

- due to the potential contradictions between IAS 32 and IFRS 10, which standard takes precedence; and
- if a non-controlling interest is recognised on initial acquisition – whether or not it continues to be recognised.

If the entity chooses to base its accounting policy on IAS 32, i.e. IAS 32 takes precedence, then it will only recognise a financial liability for the NCI put and not recognise a non-controlling interest. The approach is described in 5.2.3.A below.

If the accounting policy choice is that IFRS 10 takes precedence, the entity will recognise both the non-controlling interest and the financial liability under the NCI put. It initially measures any non-controlling interests, either at fair value or at the proportionate share of net assets, with this choice available for each transaction (as discussed at 4.2.1 above). *[IFRS 3.19]*. There is then a further accounting policy choice as to whether the non-controlling interest that was initially recognised continues to be recognised (as described at 5.2.3.B, 5.2.3.C and 5.2.3.D below).

5.2.3.A Non-controlling interest is not recognised – financial liability recognised (Approach 1)

Approach 1 must be used when the entity has a present ownership interest in the shares concerned (see 5.2.2 above).

Approach 1 may also be used when the entity does not have a present ownership interest, but concludes that IAS 32 takes precedence over IFRS 10. By recognising a liability for the put option over the shares held by the non-controlling interest, no non-controlling interest is recognised. The business combination is accounted for on the basis that the underlying shares subject to the NCI put have been acquired. Thus, if the acquirer has granted a put option over all of the remaining shares, the business combination is accounted for as if the acquirer has obtained a 100% interest in the acquiree. No non-controlling interest is recognised when the acquirer completes the purchase price allocation and determines the amount of goodwill to recognise. The consideration transferred for the business combination includes the present value of the amount payable upon exercise of the NCI put to the 'non-controlling' shareholders.

Approach 1 is based on the requirements and guidance within IAS 32.

IAS 32 requires the NCI put to be recognised as a liability, as discussed in 5.2.1 above. *[IAS 32.23]*. IAS 32 also states that when a subsidiary issues a financial instrument and a parent or another entity in the group agrees additional terms directly with the holders of the instrument (e.g. a guarantee), the group may not have discretion over distributions or redemption. Although the subsidiary may appropriately classify the instrument without regard to these additional terms in its financial statements, the effect of other agreements between members of the group and the holders of the instrument is taken into account in the consolidated financial statements. To the extent that there is such an obligation or settlement provision, the instrument (or the component of it that is subject to the obligation) is classified as a financial liability in the consolidated financial statements. *[IAS 32.AG29]*. The implication is that the underlying financial instruments (i.e. the shares in the subsidiary) are represented by the financial liability. Accordingly, since the shares held by those non-controlling shareholders are not treated as equity interests in the consolidated financial statements, there is no non-controlling interest to be accounted for under IFRS 10. This means that the profit or loss (and changes in other comprehensive income) with respect to the subsidiary are allocated to the parent and not to the non-controlling interest, as there is none.

Under this approach, any dividends paid to the other shareholders are recognised as an expense in the consolidated financial statements, except where they represent a repayment of the liability (e.g. where the exercise price is adjusted by the dividends paid).

The NCI put is accounted for as a financial liability under IFRS 9 or IAS 39. *[IAS 32.23, 97R, IFRS 9.4.2.1, 4.2.2, IAS 39.9]*. Changes in the carrying amount of the financial liability are recognised in profit or loss.

If the NCI put is exercised, the financial liability is extinguished by the payment of the exercise price.

If the NCI put is not exercised, then the entity has effectively disposed of a partial interest in its subsidiary, without loss of control, in return for the amount recognised as the financial liability at the date of expiry. The entity accounts for the transaction as discussed at 3.3 above. The consideration received is the amount of the financial liability extinguished and any difference between this and the carrying amount of the non-controlling interest (as of the date that the NCI put expires) is recognised within equity.

Chapter 7

5.2.3.B Full recognition of non-controlling interest (Approach 2)

Approach 2 is one of the alternatives that may be used when the entity does not have a present ownership interest in the shares concerned, and concludes that IFRS 10 takes precedence. The acquirer initially recognises the non-controlling interest, either at fair value or at the proportionate share of the acquiree's net assets.

Approach 2 takes the view that the non-controlling interest continues to be recognised within equity until the NCI put is exercised. The carrying amount of non-controlling interest changes due to allocations of profit or loss, allocations of changes in other comprehensive income and dividends declared for the reporting period (see 4 above).

The financial liability for the NCI put is recognised at the present value of the amount payable upon exercise of the NCI put, and is subsequently accounted for under IFRS 9 or IAS 39 like any other written put option on equity instruments. On initial recognition, the corresponding debit is made to another component of equity attributable to the parent, not to the non-controlling interest.

All subsequent changes in the carrying amount of the financial liability that result from the remeasurement of the present value of the amount payable upon exercise of the NCI put are recognised in the profit or loss attributable to the parent, and not the non-controlling interest's share of the profit or loss of the subsidiary.

If the NCI put is exercised, the entity accounts for an increase in its ownership interest (see 3.3 above). At the same time, the entity accounts for the settlement of the financial liability by derecognising the financial liability and recognising an offsetting credit in the same component of equity previously reduced (on initial recognition).

If the NCI put expires unexercised, the financial liability is reclassified to the same component of equity that was previously reduced (on initial recognition).

5.2.3.C Partial recognition of non-controlling interest (Approach 3)

Approach 3 is one of the alternatives that may be used when the entity does not have a present ownership interest in the shares concerned but initially applies IFRS 10 and recognises a non-controlling interest, either at fair value or at the proportionate share of the acquiree's net assets.

Under Approach 3, while the NCI put remains unexercised, the accounting at the end of each reporting period is as follows:

(1) the entity determines the amount that would have been recognised for the non-controlling interest, including an update to reflect allocations of profit or loss, allocations of changes in other comprehensive income and dividends declared for the reporting period, as required by IFRS 10 (see 4 above);

(2) the entity derecognises the non-controlling interest as if it was acquired at that date;

(3) the entity recognises a financial liability at the present value of the amount payable on exercise of the NCI put in accordance with IFRS 9 or IAS 39. There is no separate accounting for the unwinding of the discount due to the passage of time; and

(4) the entity accounts for the difference between (2) and (3) as an equity transaction.

If the NCI put is exercised, the same treatment is applied up to the date of exercise. The amount recognised as the financial liability at that date is extinguished by the payment of the exercise price.

If the NCI put expires unexercised, the position is unwound so that the non-controlling interest is recognised at the amount it would have been, as if the put option had never been granted (i.e. measured initially at the date of the business combination, and remeasured for subsequent allocations of profit or loss, other comprehensive income and changes in equity attributable to the non-controlling interest). The financial liability is derecognised, with a corresponding credit to the same component of equity.

5.2.3.D Non-controlling interest is subsequently derecognised (Approach 4)

Approach 4 may be used when the entity does not have a present ownership interest in the shares concerned, and concludes that IFRS 10 takes precedence. When the NCI put is granted in a business combination, the acquirer initially recognises the non-controlling interest, either at fair value or at the proportionate share of the acquiree's net assets.

When the parent recognises the financial liability for the NCI put, it derecognises the non-controlling interest. There are two ways of viewing this but the accounting effect is the same:

- This transaction is an immediate acquisition of the non-controlling interest. The non-controlling interest is treated as having been acquired when the NCI put is granted, as in Approach 1. However, in accordance with IFRS 10, any difference between the liability recognised (at the present value of the amount payable upon exercise of the NCI put) and the amount of non-controlling interest derecognised is recognised directly in equity. (Under Approach 1, the difference is reflected in the measurement of goodwill.)
- This transaction is viewed as a reclassification of an equity instrument to a financial liability. In accordance with IAS 32, when the financial liability is recognised, the present value of the amount payable upon exercise of the NCI put is reclassified from equity with the effect that the non-controlling interest is derecognised. Any difference between the carrying value of non-controlling interest and the liability is adjusted against another component of equity.

The financial liability for the NCI put is subsequently accounted for under IFRS 9 or IAS 39, with all changes in the carrying amount recognised in profit or loss.

Dividends paid to the other shareholders are recognised as an expense of the group, unless they represent a repayment of the liability (e.g. where the exercise price is adjusted by the dividends paid). This means that the profit or loss (and changes in other comprehensive income) with respect to the subsidiary are allocated to the parent and not to the non-controlling interest, as there is none.

If the NCI put is exercised, the carrying amount of the financial liability at that date is extinguished by the payment of the exercise price.

If the NCI put expires unexercised, the liability is derecognised with the non-controlling interest being reinstated as if nothing happened. Any difference between the liability and non-controlling interest is recognised against another component of equity, generally the same component reduced when the liability was initially recognised.

5.2.4 Assessing whether multiple transactions should be accounted for as a single arrangement

As discussed at 3.2.2 above, IFRS 10 provides guidance on when to account for two or more arrangements as a single transaction when a parent loses control of a subsidiary. However, neither IFRS 10 nor IFRS 3 specifically addresses the accounting for a sequence of transactions that begins with an acquirer gaining control over another entity, followed by acquiring additional ownership interests shortly thereafter.

This frequently happens where public offers are made to a group of shareholders and there is a regulatory requirement for an acquirer to make an offer to the non-controlling shareholders of the acquiree.

The Interpretations Committee considered this issue and tentatively agreed that the initial acquisition of the controlling stake and the subsequent mandatory tender offer should be treated as a single transaction. However, there was no consensus among the Interpretations Committee members on whether a liability should be recognised for the mandatory tender offer at the date that the acquirer obtains control of the acquiree. A small majority expressed the view that a liability should be recognised in a manner that is consistent with IAS 32. Other Interpretations Committee members expressed the view that a mandatory tender offer to purchase non-controlling interests is not within the scope of IAS 32 or IAS 37 – *Provisions, Contingent Liabilities and Contingent Assets* – and that a liability should therefore not be recognised. The issue was escalated to the IASB[20] which subsequently decided that the project on put options written on non-controlling interests should be incorporated into the broader project looking at the distinction between liabilities and equity – the Financial Instruments with Characteristics of Equity ('FICE') project (see 6.4 and 6.5 below).

Meanwhile, in the absence of any explicit guidance in IFRS for such transactions, we believe that entities have an accounting policy choice:

- to make an assessment as to whether the transactions should be treated as a single acquisition in which control is gained (a single business combination); or
- to account for the transactions as discrete transactions (a business combination, followed by an acquisition of non-controlling interests).

Where an entity adopts a policy of assessing whether to link the acquisition of the non-controlling interest with the gaining of control, we believe the following guidance should be applied.

5.2.4.A Identifying a linked transaction

The acquisition of the non-controlling interest is accounted for as a linked transaction when it arises from the same transaction as that at which control was gained. This will generally be the case where it arises as part of the same offer, including where legal or regulatory requirements lead to the offer being extended through the creation of a shareholder put, or acquirer compulsory acquisition rights.

In many cases, it will be clear where there is a single offer. Where it is not clear, the existence of all of the following factors indicate a linked transaction:

- the option over the remaining interest and subsequent acquisition is not negotiated separately by the non-controlling shareholders;
- the offer period is short; and
- the price per share offered for subsequent increases is fixed and consistent with the price paid for the controlling interest.

These factors are generally all present in the case of public offers to the entire group of shareholders. They may not all be present for private offers where, for example, some of the options may be for extended terms.

If a put option is granted over the non-controlling interest and the terms of the put option are such that the present ownership interest attached to the underlying shares is gained at the same time as gaining control, this will satisfy the second criterion above. Whilst the put may nominally extend over a long period, the effect is that ownership has already passed to the acquirer. See 5.2.2 above for the factors to be considered in assessing whether or not the acquirer gains present ownership interest over the underlying shares. Where the other criteria above are also met, this is a linked transaction and it is accounted for as one transaction.

5.2.4.B Accounting for the linked transaction

A linked transaction is accounted for as if all ownership interests were acquired at the acquisition date as part of the transaction to gain control.

The consideration transferred is the sum of the amount paid for the controlling and non-controlling interest and the percentage acquired is the sum of the respective shareholdings. If at the date of gaining control the non-controlling interest has not actually been acquired, a financial liability is recognised at the present value of the amount payable upon exercise of the option to acquire the non-controlling interest.

If at the date the non-controlling interest is actually acquired, the percentage acquired differs to that originally accounted for as being acquired, the purchase accounting is adjusted to reflect the actual percentage acquired. A 'true up' exercise is performed to adjust the total consideration paid and therefore the amount of goodwill recognised. It is not accounted for as a partial disposal of non-controlling interest (changes in ownership interest without loss of control are addressed at 3.3 above). The non-controlling interest is measured as of the date of acquisition, not as of the date that the offer expires.

When the transaction is linked because the arrangement provides a present ownership interest in the non-controlling interest, the entity will not recognise a non-controlling interest. Accounting for the transaction is as described in Approach 1 at 5.2.3.A above.

If the granting of the put option and its subsequent exercise are not linked to the transaction in which the acquirer gains control, see 5.4 below for discussion of how the acquirer accounts for the NCI put.

Example 7.17 below illustrates the accounting for a linked transaction.

Example 7.17: Put option and gaining control accounted for as a single transaction

Entity A acquires a 60% controlling interest in listed Entity B. As Entity A has obtained a controlling interest in Entity B, the regulator requires Entity A to offer to purchase the remaining shares of Entity B from all other shareholders of Entity B, paying the same price per share as in the transaction in which Entity A obtained control of Entity B. Entity A makes the offer immediately and the offer period lasts for 30 days.

At the end of 30 days, other shareholders of Entity B owning 30% accept the offer for their shares. The offer to acquire the remaining 10% of shares held in Entity B expires unexercised.

When considering whether the put option (and acquisition of the 30% of Entity B's shares tendered) are linked to the acquisition of 60% of Entity B's shares, in which Entity A gained control, it is relevant that:

- the price per share is fixed and at the same price as paid by Entity A to acquire 60% of Entity B's shares;
- the shareholders of Entity B who own the 30% did not negotiate to receive the offer;
- the offer benefits the shareholders of Entity B (by providing the same opportunity to sell their shares that the shareholder(s) who sold the 60% received);
- although the offer was initiated by Entity A, it stemmed from a regulatory requirement triggered by the acquisition of Entity B (it was not at Entity A's discretion to make the offer); and
- the offer period is relatively short.

Entity A concludes that the acquisition of 30% of Entity B's shares is linked to the transaction when control was gained and is therefore part of the business combination. Therefore, Entity A records the following journal entries:

a) Acquisition of 60% and entering into the put option on the remaining shares (granting the offer):

Dr Net assets (summarised, 100% of fair value of net assets of Entity B, as required by IFRS 3)

Dr Goodwill (as if Entity A acquired 100% of Entity B)

Cr Cash transferred (on acquisition date)

Cr Financial liability (present value of offer price to be paid at the expiry date of the option relating to the 40% of Entity B's shares subject to the offer)

b) Accounting for the liability in accordance with IFRS 9 or IAS 39 (unwinding of the discount during the 30-day period):

Dr Finance expense

Cr Financial liability

c) Acquisition of 30% offered at the end of the 30-day period is accounted for as a reduction of the financial liability:

Dr Financial liability

Cr Cash

d) Reclassification of the financial liability to equity for the 10% outstanding at the end of the offer period – Entity A adjusts the initial purchase price allocation related to Entity B to recognise any non-controlling interest, with an offset to goodwill:

Dr Financial liability (offer price of 10% of shares)

Cr Non-controlling interest (either (1) fair value of the non-controlling interest in Entity B or (2) the 10% shareholders' proportionate share of Entity B's identifiable net assets), measured as of the acquisition date (the date that control was gained, and not the date that the offer expires)

Dr/Cr Goodwill (difference, if applicable).

5.3 Combination of call and put options

In some business combinations, there might be a combination of call and put options, the terms of which may be equivalent or may be different.

The appropriate accounting for such options is determined based on the discussions in 5.1 and 5.2 above. However, where there is a call and put option with equivalent terms, particularly at a fixed price, the combination of the options is more likely to mean that they give the acquirer a present ownership interest.

In such cases, where the options are over all of the shares not held by the parent, the acquirer has effectively acquired a 100% interest in the subsidiary at the date of the business combination. The entity may be in a similar position as if it had acquired a 100% interest in the subsidiary with either deferred consideration (where the exercise price is fixed) or contingent consideration (where the settlement amount is not fixed, but is dependent upon a future event). See Chapter 9 at 7.

As noted at 5 above, similar considerations also apply where the acquirer entered into a forward purchase contract for the shares held by the other shareholders.

5.4 Call and put options entered into in relation to existing non-controlling interests

The discussion in 5.1 and 5.2 above focused on call and put options entered into at the same time as control is gained of the subsidiary. However, an entity may enter into the options with non-controlling shareholders after gaining control. The appropriate accounting policy will still be based on the discussions in 5.1 and 5.2 above.

Where the entity already has a controlling interest and as a result of the options now has a present ownership interest in the remaining shares concerned, or concludes that IAS 32 takes precedence, the non-controlling interest is no longer recognised within equity. The transaction is accounted for as an acquisition of the non-controlling interest, i.e. it is accounted for as an equity transaction (see 3.3 above), because such acquisitions are not business combinations under IFRS 3.

5.5 Put options over non-controlling interests – Interpretations Committee and IASB developments

The Interpretations Committee unequivocally confirmed as early as 2006 that an NCI put to be settled for cash is itself a financial liability.[21] During 2011, the Interpretations Committee developed a proposal that NCI puts be accounted for as if they were derivatives. This means that, initially and subsequently, they would have been measured on a net basis at fair value, rather than being measured on a gross basis at the present value of the option exercise price, as is required by IAS 32. The net treatment would also have resolved issues such as how to account for the receipt of dividends, the component of equity that should be debited when the 'gross' liability is initially recognised (see approaches 2, 3 and 4 in 5.2.3.B, 5.2.3.C and 5.2.3.D above) and how to account for the expiry of the NCI put. These questions only become significant if the liability for the NCI put is measured on a 'gross' basis.

This was never seen as other than a short-term solution but nevertheless it would require a scope exception from IAS 32 for certain NCI puts. However, in September 2011 the IASB rejected the scope amendment proposal.[22]

Consequently, in May 2012, the Interpretations Committee issued a draft Interpretation to clarify that all changes in the measurement of the NCI put must be recognised in profit or loss in accordance with IFRS 9 (paragraphs 5.7.1 and 5.7.2) or IAS 39 (paragraphs 55 and 56).[23] This is on the basis that the changes in the measurement of the financial liability do not change the relative interests in the subsidiary that are held by the parent and the non-controlling-interest and therefore are not equity transactions.[24] Transactions with owners in their capacity as owners that are taken to equity are described at 3.3 above. The proposals would have precluded an entity from applying Approach 3, partial recognition of non-controlling interest, described at 5.2.3.C above. It would not have affected the other three approaches described in 5.2.3 above.

In January 2013, the Interpretations Committee discussed a summary and an analysis of the comments received. The Interpretations Committee reaffirmed the proposals in the draft Interpretation, acknowledging that the draft consensus published in May 2012 is the correct interpretation of existing Standards.

However, the Interpretations Committee expressed the view that better information would be provided if NCI puts were measured on a net basis at fair value, consistently with derivatives that are within the scope of IFRS 9 or IAS 39. It also noted that many respondents to the draft Interpretation think that either the Interpretations Committee or the IASB should address the accounting for NCI puts – or all derivatives written on an entity's own equity – more comprehensively.

Consequently, before finalising the draft Interpretation, the Interpretations Committee decided in January 2013 to ask the IASB to reconsider the requirements in paragraph 23 of IAS 32 for put options and forward contracts written on an entity's own equity. It noted that such work should consider whether NCI puts and NCI forwards should be accounted for differently from other derivatives written on an entity's own equity. The Interpretations Committee directed the staff to report its views as well as the feedback received in the comment letters to the IASB and ask the IASB how it would like to proceed.[25]

At its meeting in March 2013, the IASB discussed the Interpretations Committee's views and the feedback received in the comment letters. The IASB tentatively decided to reconsider the requirements in paragraph 23 of IAS 32, including whether all or particular put options and forward contracts written on an entity's own equity should be measured on a net basis at fair value.[26] However, in June 2014, the IASB decided that the project on put options written on non-controlling interests should be incorporated into the broader project looking at the distinction between liabilities and equity – the Financial Instruments with Characteristics of Equity ('FICE') project.[27] Since resuming this research project in October 2014, the IASB has had discussions on various aspects relating to FICE, but the project is still at an early stage. A discussion paper is planned for publication in the fourth quarter of 2017.[28] The FICE project is discussed further at 6.4 below.

As indicated at 5.2 above, the previous deliberations relating to NCI puts have been in the context of an NCI put that is required to be settled for cash. The Interpretations Committee has also considered in 2016 a request regarding how an entity accounts for an NCI put in its consolidated financial statements where the NCI put has a strike price that will be settled by the exchange of a variable number of the parent's own equity instruments.

Specifically, the IFRS Interpretations Committee was asked to consider whether, in its consolidated financial statements, the parent:

(a) applies paragraph 23 of IAS 32 and, therefore, recognises a financial liability representing the present value of the option's strike price, i.e. a gross liability; or

(b) does not apply paragraph 23 of IAS 32 and, therefore, recognises a derivative financial liability presented on a net basis measured at fair value.

The Interpretations Committee was also asked whether the parent applies the same accounting in its consolidated financial statements for NCI puts for which the parent has the choice to settle the exercise price either in cash or a variable number of its own equity instruments to the same value.

In November 2016, the Interpretations Committee decided not to add this issue to its agenda. In reaching this decision, the Interpretations Committee observed that, in the past, it had discussed issues relating to NCI puts that are settled in cash. Those issues were referred to the IASB and are being considered as part of the FICE project. The Interpretations Committee further noted that, on the basis of its previous discussions, the issue is too broad for the Interpretations Committee to address efficiently within the confines of existing IFRS Standards and that the IASB is currently considering the requirements for all derivatives on an entity's own equity comprehensively as part of the FICE project.[29] The FICE project is discussed further at 6.4 below.

6 FUTURE DEVELOPMENTS

The IASB has been engaged in a number of implementation projects that have led or could lead to 'narrow-scope amendments' to IFRS 10 and other IFRSs and could change the consolidation procedures applied or the accounting for non-controlling interests. However, these have all been put 'on hold' until the finalisation, or are being reconsidered as part, of related research projects.

6.1 Sale or Contribution of Assets between an Investor and its Associate or Joint Venture (Amendments to IFRS 10 and IAS 28)

As discussed at 3.2.1.B above, one issue that the IASB has been trying to resolve was a conflict between the IFRS 10 requirements relating to loss of control over a subsidiary and those of IAS 28 for transactions where a parent sells or contributes an interest in a subsidiary to an associate or a joint venture. In order to resolve the conflict, in September 2014, the IASB had issued an amendment – *Sale or Contribution of Assets between an Investor and its Associate or Joint Venture (Amendments to IFRS 10 and IAS 28).*

These amendments were to be applied prospectively to transactions occurring in annual periods beginning on or after 1 January 2016, with earlier application permitted.[30] However, in December 2015, the IASB issued a further amendment – *Effective Date of Amendments to IFRS 10 and IAS 28.* This amendment defers the effective date of the September 2014 amendment until the IASB has finalised any revisions that result from the IASB's research project on the equity method (although the IASB now plans no further work on this project until the Post-implementation Review of IFRS 11 is undertaken).[31] Nevertheless, the IASB has continued to allow early application of the September 2014 amendment, which must be disclosed, as it did not wish to prohibit the application of better financial reporting. *[IFRS 10.C1C, BC190M-190O, IAS 28.45C, BC37J].*[32]

The main amendment made to IFRS 10 had been to add the following guidance in relation to the accounting for the loss of control of a subsidiary that does not contain a business. Consequently, on the loss of control of a subsidiary that constitutes a business, including cases in which the investor retains joint control of, or significant influence over, the investee, the guidance below is not to apply. In such cases, the full gain or loss determined under the requirements of IFRS 10 (see 3.2 above) is to be recognised. *[IFRS 10.25, 26, B98, B99].*[33]

If a parent loses control of a subsidiary that does not contain a business, as defined in IFRS 3, as a result of a transaction involving an associate or a joint venture that is accounted for using the equity method, the parent is to determine the gain or loss in accordance with paragraphs B98-B99 (see 3.2 above). The gain or loss resulting from the transaction (including the amounts previously recognised in other comprehensive income that would be reclassified to profit or loss in accordance with paragraph B99) is to be recognised in the parent's profit or loss only to the extent of the unrelated investors' interests in that associate or joint venture. The remaining part of the gain is to be eliminated against the carrying amount of the investment in that associate or joint venture. In addition, if the parent retains an investment in the former subsidiary and the former subsidiary is now an associate or a joint venture that is accounted for using the equity method, the parent is to recognise the part of the gain or loss resulting from the remeasurement at fair value of the investment retained in that former subsidiary in its profit or loss only to the extent of the unrelated investors' interests in the new associate or joint venture. The remaining part of that gain is to be eliminated against the carrying amount of the investment retained in the former subsidiary. If the parent retains an investment in the former subsidiary that is now accounted for in accordance with IFRS 9 or IAS 39, the part of the gain or loss resulting from the remeasurement at fair value of the investment retained in the former subsidiary is to be recognised in full in the parent's profit or loss. *[IFRS 10.25, 26, B99A, C7].*[34]

An example provided by IFRS 10 illustrating the application of this guidance is reflected in Example 7.18 below.[35]

Example 7.18: Loss of control of a subsidiary that does not contain a business as a result of a transaction involving an associate

A parent has a 100% interest in a subsidiary that does not contain a business. The parent sells 70% of its interest in the subsidiary to an associate in which it has a 20% interest. As a consequence of this transaction, the parent loses control of the subsidiary. The carrying amount of the net assets of the subsidiary is €100 and the carrying amount of the interest sold is €70 (€100 × 70%). The fair value of the consideration received is €210, which is also the fair value of the interest sold. The investment retained in the former subsidiary is an associate accounted for using the equity method and its fair value is €90. The gain determined in accordance with paragraphs B98-B99 of IFRS 10, before the elimination required by paragraph B99A, is €200 (€210 + €90 – €100). This gain comprises two parts:

(a) the gain (€140) resulting from the sale of the 70% interest in the subsidiary to the associate. This gain is the difference between the fair value of the consideration received (€210) and the carrying amount of the interest sold (€70). According to paragraph B99A, the parent recognises in its profit or loss the amount of the gain attributable to the unrelated investors' interests in the existing associate. This is 80% of this gain, that is €112 (€140 × 80%). The remaining 20% of the gain (€28 = €140 × 20%), is eliminated against the carrying amount of the investment in the existing associate.

(b) the gain (€60) resulting from the remeasurement at fair value of the investment directly retained in the former subsidiary. This gain is the difference between the fair value of the investment retained in the former subsidiary (€90) and 30% of the carrying amount of the net assets of the subsidiary (€30 = €100 × 30%). According to paragraph B99A, the parent recognises in its profit or loss the amount of the gain attributable to the unrelated investors' interests in the new associate. This is 56% (70% × 80%) of the gain, that is €34 (€60 × 56%). The remaining 44% of the gain (€26 = €60 × 44%) is eliminated against the carrying amount of the investment retained in the former subsidiary.

6.2 Sale or contribution of assets to a joint operation (where the entity has joint control or is a party to the joint operation)

In July 2016, the Interpretations Committee discussed whether an entity should remeasure its retained interest in the assets and liabilities of a joint operation when the entity loses control of a business, or an asset or group of assets that is not a business. In the transaction discussed, the entity either retains joint control of a joint operation or is a party to a joint operation (with rights to assets and obligations for liabilities) after the transaction.

Because of the similarity between the transaction being discussed by the Interpretations Committee and a sale or contribution of assets to an associate or joint venture (see 6.1 above), the Interpretations Committee decided not to add the issue to its agenda, but instead to recommend that the IASB consider the issue at the same time that it further considers the accounting for the sale or contribution of assets to an associate or a joint venture. The Interpretations Committee observed that the Post-implementation Review of IFRS 10 and IFRS 11 would provide the IASB with an opportunity to consider loss of control transactions and a sale or contribution of assets to an associate or joint venture.[36]

The decision of the Interpretations Committee, and the accounting for such transactions are discussed further at 3.2.1.C above.

6.3 Fair value measurement: unit of account

As discussed at 3.2.1.B above, although IFRS 10 requires that any investment retained in the former subsidiary is to be recognised at its fair value at the date when control is lost, no guidance is given in the standard as to how such fair value should be determined. In September 2014, the IASB had issued an Exposure Draft that proposed, *inter alia*, some clarifications to the requirements for measuring fair value, in accordance with IFRS 13, for investments in subsidiaries, joint ventures and associates.[37] However, in January 2016, the IASB decided not to consider this topic further until the Post-implementation Review of IFRS 13 is complete.[38] In May 2017, the IASB published a request for information for the Post-implementation Review of IFRS 13, with comments requested by 22 September 2017.[39] These issues are discussed further in Chapter 14 at 5.1.1.

6.4 Financial Instruments with Characteristics of Equity project

As discussed more fully at 5.5 above, the Interpretations Committee and the IASB have been debating the accounting for put options written on non-controlling interests ('NCI puts') over a number of years. At its meeting in March 2013, the IASB tentatively decided to reconsider the requirements in paragraph 23 of IAS 32, including whether all or particular put options and forward contracts written on an entity's own equity should be measured on a net basis at fair value.[40] However, the IASB decided subsequently that this project should be incorporated into the broader project looking at the distinction between liabilities and equity – the Financial Instruments with Characteristics of Equity ('FICE') project.[41] Since resuming this research project in October 2014, the IASB has had discussions on various aspects relating to FICE. A discussion paper is planned for publication in the fourth quarter of 2017.[42]

6.5 Mandatory purchase of non-controlling interests

As discussed more fully at 5.2.4 above, neither IFRS 10 nor IFRS 3 specifically addresses the accounting for a sequence of transactions that begins with an acquirer gaining control over another entity, followed by it acquiring additional ownership interests shortly thereafter. This frequently happens where public offers are made to a group of shareholders and there is a regulatory requirement for an acquirer to make an offer to the non-controlling shareholders of the acquiree. This issue had been considered by the Interpretations Committee and was escalated to the IASB. In June 2014, the IASB decided that the project on put options written on non-controlling interests should be incorporated into the broader project looking at the distinction between liabilities and equity – the Financial Instruments with Characteristics of Equity ('FICE') project[43] (see 6.4 above). In February 2017, the IASB tentatively decided as part of its FICE project to consider whether it should take any action to address the accounting for mandatory tender offers, including potential disclosure requirements.[44]

References

1 *Effective Date of Amendments to IFRS 10 and IAS 28,* IASB, December 2015.
2 Research programme – research pipeline, IASB website, 6 July 2017.
3 *Sale or Contribution of Assets between an Investor and its Associate or Joint Venture, (Amendments to IFRS 10 and IAS 28),* IASB, September 2014, IFRS 10, para. B99A.
4 *Sale or Contribution of Assets between an Investor and its Associate or Joint Venture, (Amendments to IFRS 10 and IAS 28),* IASB, September 2014, IFRS 10, para. C1C and IAS 28, para. 45C.
5 Research programme – research pipeline, IASB website, 6 July 2017.
6 *Effective Date of Amendments to IFRS 10 and IAS 28.*
7 Exposure Draft (ED/2014/4), *Measuring Quoted Investments in Subsidiaries, Joint Ventures and Associates at Fair Value (Proposed amendments to IFRS 10, IFRS 12, IAS 28 and IAS 36 and Illustrative Examples for IFRS 13),* IASB, September 2014.
8 *IASB Update,* July 2015.
9 *IASB Update,* January 2016.
10 Request for Information – Post-implementation Review – IFRS 13 *Fair Value Measurement,* IASB, May 2017.
11 *IFRIC Update,* July 2015.
12 *IFRIC Update,* July 2016.
13 *IASB Update,* May 2009.
14 *IFRIC Update,* January 2013.
15 *IFRIC Update,* May 2009.
16 *IFRIC Update,* November 2013.
17 *IFRIC Update,* November 2006.
18 *Put options written on non-controlling interests (Proposed amendments to IAS 32),* Project news, IASB Website, 23 June 2014.
19 *IFRIC Update,* November 2016.
20 *IASB Update,* May 2013.
21 *IFRIC Update,* November 2006.
22 *IFRIC Update,* January 2012.
23 Draft Interpretation (DI/2012/2) *Put Options Written on Non-controlling Interests,* para. 7.
24 DI/2012/2, para. 8.
25 *IFRIC Update,* January 2013.

26 *IASB Update*, March 2013.
27 *Put options written on non-controlling interests (Proposed amendments to IAS 32)*, Project news, IASB Website (archive), 23 June 2014.
28 IASB Projects – Work plan, IASB website, 8 July 2017.
29 *IFRIC Update*, November 2016.
30 *Sale or Contribution of Assets between an Investor and its Associate or Joint Venture, (Amendments to IFRS 10 and IAS 28)*, IASB, September 2014, IFRS 10, para. C1C and IAS 28, para. 45C.
31 Research programme – research pipeline, IASB website, 8 July 2017.
32 *Effective Date of Amendments to IFRS 10 and IAS 28.*
33 *Sale or Contribution of Assets between an Investor and its Associate or Joint Venture, (Amendments to IFRS 10 and IAS 28)*, IFRS 10, paras. 25, 26, B98 and B99.
34 *Sale or Contribution of Assets between an Investor and its Associate or Joint Venture, (Amendments to IFRS 10 and IAS 28)*, IFRS 10, paras. 25, 26, B99A and C7.
35 *Sale or Contribution of Assets between an Investor and its Associate or Joint Venture, (Amendments to IFRS 10 and IAS 28)*, IFRS 10, para. B99A, Example 17.
36 *IFRIC Update*, July 2016.
37 ED/2014/4.
38 *IASB Update*, January 2016.
39 Request for Information – Post-implementation Review – IFRS 13 *Fair Value Measurement*, IASB, May 2017.
40 *IASB Update*, March 2013.
41 *Put options written on non-controlling interests (Proposed amendments to IAS 32)*, Project news, IASB Website, 23 June 2014.
42 IASB Projects – Work plan, IASB website, 8 July 2017.
43 *Put options written on non-controlling interests (Proposed amendments to IAS 32)*, Project news, IASB Website, 23 June 2014.
44 *IASB Update*, February 2017.

Chapter 8 Separate and individual financial statements

List of examples

Chapter 8 Separate and individual financial statements

1 SEPARATE AND INDIVIDUAL FINANCIAL STATEMENTS

This chapter deals with two aspects of the preparation of financial statements by entities: their separate financial statements, which are defined by IFRS, and some of the consequences of intra-group transactions for their individual financial statements, where guidance in IFRS is limited and incomplete.

Under IFRS, 'separate financial statements' are defined in IAS 27 – *Separate Financial Statements* – as 'those presented by an entity in which the entity could elect, subject to the requirements in this standard, to account for its investments in subsidiaries, joint ventures and associates either at cost, in accordance with IFRS 9 – *Financial Instruments*, or using the equity method as described in IAS 28 – *Investments in Associates and Joint Ventures*'. *[IAS 27.4]*. For periods before IFRS 9 is applicable, IAS 39 – *Financial Instruments: Recognition and Measurement* – will apply. *[IAS 27.19]*. In other words, they are the unconsolidated financial statements or financial statements in which the investments in subsidiaries are not consolidated in accordance with IFRS 10 – *Consolidated Financial Statements*.

The IASB takes the view that the needs of users of financial statements are fully met by requiring entities to consolidate subsidiaries and equity account for associates and joint ventures. It is recognised that entities with subsidiaries, associates or joint ventures may wish, or may be required by local law, to present financial statements in which their investments are accounted for on another basis, e.g. as equity investments or under the equity method. *[IAS 27.2]*.

Accordingly, IFRS does not require the preparation of separate financial statements. However, where an investor with subsidiaries, associates or joint ventures does prepare separate financial statements purporting to comply with IFRS, they must be prepared in accordance with IAS 27. *[IAS 27.3]*.

It follows from this definition that the financial statements of an entity that does not have a subsidiary, associate or joint venture are not 'separate financial statements'. *[IAS 27.7]*.

This chapter also addresses matters that are not exclusive to separate financial statements but relate to any stand-alone financial statements prepared by any entity within a group. We have called these 'individual financial statements', although they may also be referred to (amongst other names) as 'stand-alone', 'solus' or 'single-entity' financial statements. The term 'individual financial statements' for the purpose of this chapter is a broader term than 'separate financial statements' as it covers separate financial statements and financial statements of entities that do not have investments in associates, joint ventures and subsidiaries.

Transactions often take place between a parent entity and its subsidiaries or between subsidiaries within a group that may or may not be carried out at fair value. As a result there may be uncertainty and ambiguity about how these transactions should be accounted for. IAS 24 – *Related Party Disclosures* – requires only that these transactions are disclosed and provides no accounting requirements.

Whilst such transactions do not influence the consolidated financial statements of the ultimate parent (as they are eliminated in the course of consolidation), they can have a significant impact on the individual financial statements of the entities concerned or on the consolidated financial statements prepared for a sub-group.

These issues are discussed at 4 below.

1.1 Consolidated financial statements and separate financial statements

A parent is an entity that controls one or more entities and any parent entity should present consolidated financial statements in which the assets, liabilities, equity, income, expenses and cash flows of the parent and its subsidiaries are presented as those of a single economic entity. *[IFRS 10.4, Appendix A].*

A parent need not present consolidated financial statements if it meets all the following conditions:

'(i) it is a wholly-owned subsidiary or is a partially-owned subsidiary of another entity and all its other owners, including those not otherwise entitled to vote, have been informed about, and do not object to, the parent not presenting consolidated financial statements;

(ii) its debt or equity instruments are not traded in a public market (a domestic or foreign stock exchange or an over-the-counter market, including local and regional markets);

(iii) it did not file, nor is it in the process of filing, its financial statements with a securities commission or other regulatory organisation for the purpose of issuing any class of instruments in a public market; and

(iv) its ultimate or any intermediate parent produces financial statements that are available for public use and comply with IFRSs, in which subsidiaries are consolidated or are measured at fair value through profit or loss in accordance with this IFRS'. *[IFRS 10.4(a)].*

This exemption is discussed further in Chapter 6 at 2.3.1.

An entity that avails itself of the above exemption may, but is not required, to prepare separate financial statements as its only financial statements. *[IAS 27.8].* For example, most intermediate holding companies take advantage of this exemption. If such an entity prepares unconsolidated financial statements that are in accordance with IFRS, they must comply with the provisions of IAS 27 for such statements and they will then be separate financial statements as defined. The requirements for separate financial statements are dealt with in 2 below.

IFRS 10 includes an exception to the consolidation principle for a parent that meets the definition of an investment entity. An investment entity measures its investments in subsidiaries other than those solely providing services that relate to its investment activities at fair value through profit or loss in accordance with IFRS 9 (or IAS 39 if IFRS 9 is not yet applicable) instead of consolidating those subsidiaries. The investment entity exception is discussed in Chapter 6 at 10. Investment entities measure their investments in those subsidiaries in the same way in their separate financial statements as required in the consolidated financial statements. *[IAS 27.11A]*. As a result, IAS 27 clarifies that an investment entity that is required, throughout the current period and all comparative periods presented, to apply the exception to consolidation for all of its subsidiaries in accordance with paragraph 31 of IFRS 10 presents separate financial statements as its only financial statements. *[IAS 27.8A]*. An investment entity that prepares separate financial statements as its only financial statements, discloses that fact and presents the disclosures relating to investment entities required by IFRS 12 – *Disclosure of Interests in Other Entities* – about its interests in subsidiaries. *[IAS 27.16A]*. The exemption from preparing consolidated financial statements, in criterion (iv) above, is available to a parent entity that is a subsidiary of an investment entity, even when the investment entity does not prepare consolidated financial statements but measures its subsidiaries at fair value through profit or loss. *[IFRS 10.BC28A-28B]*.

The requirements to prepare consolidated and separate financial statements in accordance with IFRS are very often subject to local jurisdictional rules. For instance, for entities incorporated in the European Union, local law may exempt the entity from preparing consolidated financial statements under local GAAP if it applies 'IFRS as adopted by the European Union'. However IFRS 10 provides specific IFRS requirements which need to be considered when financial statements are prepared on the basis of IFRS as issued by the IASB. For example, as discussed in Chapter 6 at 2.3.4, in our view, consolidated financial statements must be prepared by an entity that was a parent during the reporting period, even if that entity is no longer a parent at the end of the reporting period (e.g. because it disposed of all its subsidiaries). IFRS 10 requires a parent to consolidate a subsidiary until the date on which the parent ceases to control the subsidiary. *[IFRS 10.20]*. This means that if a parent does not prepare consolidated financial statements pursuant to a concession in local law, the parent may not present separate financial statements in compliance with IFRS. See 1.2 below regarding the interrelationship between IFRS and local European law in respect of consolidated and separate financial statements.

1.1.1 Separate financial statements and interests in associates and joint ventures

IAS 28 must be applied by 'all entities that are investors with joint control of, or significant influence over, an investee'. *[IAS 28.2]*. IAS 28 requires that an investment in an associate or a joint venture be accounted for in the entity's separate financial statements in accordance with paragraph 10 of IAS 27. *[IAS 28.44]*.

An entity that is an investor may present separate financial statements as its only financial statements if it is a parent that is exempt from preparing consolidated financial statements by the scope exemption in paragraph 4(a) of IFRS 10 (see above). If it does not have subsidiaries it may still present separate financial statements as its only financial statements if the same criteria as in (i)-(iv) above apply (they are replicated in paragraph 17 of IAS 28) and all its other owners, including those not otherwise entitled to vote, have been informed about, and do not object to, the entity not applying the equity method to its investees.

A parent cannot prepare financial statements in purported compliance with IFRS in which subsidiaries are consolidated, but associates and joint ventures are not accounted for under IAS 28 but on some other basis (e.g. at cost). Financial statements prepared on such a basis would be neither consolidated financial statements (because of the failure to apply IAS 28) nor separate financial statements (because of the failure to account for subsidiaries on the basis of the direct equity interest).

The conditions for exemption in paragraph 17 of IAS 28 mentioned above are the same as those in IFRS 10. This means that:

- An entity that has subsidiaries and is exempt under IFRS 10 from preparing consolidated accounts is automatically exempt in respect of its associates or joint ventures as well, i.e. it does not have to account for them under IAS 28.
- An entity that has associates or joint ventures but no subsidiaries, and does not meet all the exemption criteria in 1.1 above, is required to apply equity accounting for its associates in its own (non-consolidated) financial statements. Such non-consolidated financial statements include the investment in the associate or joint venture on the basis of the reported results and net assets of the investment. Unless the entity opts to account for associates or joint ventures using the equity method in its separate financial statements (see 2.3. below) such non-consolidated financial statements are *not* 'separate financial statements' as defined in IAS 27 (see definition above) and therefore do not have to meet the additional measurement and disclosure requirements required by IAS 27 for separate financial statements that are described at 3 below in order to comply with IFRS. Most of these disclosures would not be relevant to accounts that include the results of the associate or joint venture as they are based on providing information that is not otherwise given.

  For example a wholly-owned subsidiary that has debt or equity instruments that are traded in a public market must account for its interests in associates and joint ventures in accordance with IAS 28 and the resulting financial statements are not 'separate financial statements' as defined in IAS 27 unless the option to use the equity method in separate financial statements is taken.

  This could be different to some national GAAPs, under which investors that have no subsidiaries (and therefore do not prepare consolidated financial statements) but have associates or joint ventures, are not permitted to account for their share of the profits and net assets of associates or joint ventures in their individual financial statements.

An entity that has held interests in subsidiaries and disposed of any remaining interest in the period is required to prepare consolidated financial statements at the end of that period. This same principle applies to investments in associates and joint ventures when these constitute the only investments of the investor and these investments are sold during the period.

1.1.2 Separate financial statements and interests in joint operations

IFRS 11 – *Joint Arrangements* – differentiates between joint operations and joint ventures. In the separate financial statements, joint ventures are accounted for at cost, in accordance with IFRS 9 (or IAS 39 if IFRS 9 is not yet applicable), or using the equity method as required by paragraph 10 of IAS 27. A joint operator applies paragraphs 20 to 22 of IFRS 11 to account for a joint operation. *[IFRS 11.26].* This means that regardless of the type of financial statements prepared, the joint operator in a joint operation recognises in relation to the joint operation its:

- assets, including its share of any assets held jointly;
- liabilities, including its share of any liabilities incurred jointly;
- revenue from the sale of its share of the output arising from the joint operation;
- share of the revenue from the sale of the output by the joint operation; and
- expenses, including its share of any expenses incurred jointly. *[IFRS 11.20].*

Similarly, in its individual financial statements, a party that participates in, but does not have joint control of, a joint operation, accounts for its interest in the way outlined above provided it has rights to the assets and obligations for the liabilities, relating to the joint operation (see Chapter 12 at 6.4). *[IFRS 11.23].*

In March 2015, the Interpretations Committee published a number of agenda decisions relating to IFRS 11. Two of those are relevant to separate financial statements.[1] The first issue is the accounting by a joint operator in its separate financial statements for its share of the assets and liabilities of a joint operation when it is structured through a separate vehicle. The Interpretations Committee noted that IFRS 11 requires the joint operator to account for its rights and obligations in relation to the joint operation. It also noted that those rights and obligations, in respect of that interest, are the same regardless of whether separate or consolidated financial statements are prepared, by referring to paragraph 26 of IFRS 11. Consequently, the same accounting is required in the consolidated financial statements and in the separate financial statements of the joint operator.

The Interpretations Committee also noted that IFRS 11 requires the joint operator to account for its rights and obligations, which are its share of the assets held by the entity and its share of the liabilities incurred by it. Accordingly, the Interpretations Committee observed that the joint operator would not additionally account in its separate or consolidated financial statements its shareholding in the separate vehicle, whether at cost or fair value.

The second issue relates to the accounting by a joint operation that is a separate vehicle in its financial statements. This issue has arisen because the recognition by joint operators in both consolidated and separate financial statements of their share of assets and liabilities held by the joint operation leads to the question of whether those same assets and liabilities should also be recognised in the financial statements of the joint operation itself. The Interpretations Committee decided not to add the issue to its agenda, because sufficient guidance exists:[2]

(a) IFRS 11 applies only to the accounting by the joint operators and not to the accounting by a separate vehicle that is a joint operation;

(b) the financial statements of the separate vehicle would therefore be prepared in accordance with applicable Standards; and

(c) company law often requires a legal entity/separate vehicle to prepare financial statements. Consequently, the reporting entity for the financial statements would include the assets, liabilities, revenues and expenses of that legal entity/separate vehicle. However, when identifying the assets and liabilities of the separate vehicle, it is necessary to understand the joint operators' rights and obligations relating to those assets and liabilities and how those rights and obligations affect those assets and liabilities.

1.1.3 Publishing separate financial statements without consolidated financial statements or financial statements in which investments in associates or joint ventures are equity accounted

IAS 27 does not directly address the publication requirements for separate financial statements. In some jurisdictions, an entity that prepares consolidated financial statements is prohibited from publishing its separate financial statements without also publishing its consolidated financial statements.

However, in our view, IAS 27 does not prohibit an entity that prepares consolidated financial statements from publishing its separate financial statements compliant with IAS 27 without also publishing its consolidated financial statements, provided that:

(a) the separate financial statements identify the consolidated financial statements prepared under IFRS 10 to which they relate. *[IAS 27.17]*. In other words, they must draw attention to the fact that the entity also prepares consolidated financial statements and disclose the address from where the consolidated financial statements are available, for example, by providing contact details of a person or an e-mail address from which a hard copy of the document can be obtained or a website address where the consolidated financial statements can be found and downloaded; and

(b) the consolidated financial statements have been prepared and approved no later than the date on which the separate financial statements have been approved. Thus, it is not possible to publish the separate financial statements before the consolidated financial statements have been finalised.

The same conditions should be applied by an entity having no subsidiaries that prepares financial statements in which investments in associates or joint ventures are equity accounted, but publishes its separate financial statements (in which the investments in associates and joint ventures are not equity accounted) without also publishing its financial statements in which investments in associates or joint ventures are equity accounted.

Separate financial statements of a parent entity can also be considered compliant with IAS 27 when the exemption to present consolidated financial statements criteria in paragraph 4(a) of IFRS 10 are met.

IAS 27 requires a parent to identify the consolidated financial statements prepared by the parent. *[IAS 27.17]*. Therefore, if the parent has not issued consolidated financial statements prepared in accordance with IFRS at the date the separate financial statements are issued, this requirement cannot be met and therefore the separate financial statements cannot be considered to be in compliance with IAS 27. This will also be the case if the consolidated financial statements are prepared, but are not in accordance with IFRS (e.g. prepared in accordance with local GAAP).

The matter of whether separate financial statements could be issued before the respective consolidated financial statements was explicitly considered by the Interpretations Committee in March 2006. The Interpretations Committee concluded that separate financial statements issued before consolidated financial statements could not comply with IFRS as issued by the IASB, because 'separate financial statements should identify the financial statements prepared in accordance with paragraph 9 of IAS 27 to which they relate (the consolidated financial statements), unless one of the exemptions provided by paragraph 10 is applicable'.[3] Although IAS 27 has changed since the Interpretations Committee has considered that issue, the current version of IAS 27 still requires separate financial statements to identify financial statements prepared in accordance with IFRS 10, IFRS 11 or IAS 28. *[IAS 27.17]*. It therefore implies that consolidated financial statements should be available before or at the same date as separate financial statements. However, the situation may be different if local requirements set specific rules relating to the timing of publication of financial statements. This is for example, the case for an entity that is incorporated in the European Union (EU), as described in 1.2 below.

1.2 Entities incorporated in the EU and consolidated and separate financial statements

The EU Regulation on International Accounting Standards requires IFRS to be applied by certain entities in their consolidated financial statements. As a result of the EU endorsement mechanism, IFRS as adopted in the EU may differ in some respects from the body of Standards and Interpretations issued by the IASB (see Chapter 1 at 4.2.1). In some circumstances a difference between IFRS and IFRS as adopted by the European Union may affect separate financial statements.

The Interpretations Committee had concluded that separate financial statements issued before consolidated financial statements cannot comply with IFRS as issued by the IASB. However, in January 2007 the European Commission stated that 'the Commission Services are of the opinion that, if a company chooses or is required to prepare its annual accounts in accordance with IFRS as adopted by the EU, it can prepare and file them independently from the preparation and filing of its consolidated accounts – and thus in advance, where the national law transposing the Directives requires or permits separate publication'.[4] In other words, under 'IFRS as adopted by the EU' it might be possible to issue separate financial statements before the consolidated financial statements are issued. The details about differences between scope of consolidation under IFRS 10 and European Union national legislation are described in Chapter 6 at 2.3.5.

2 REQUIREMENTS OF SEPARATE FINANCIAL STATEMENTS

In separate financial statements, investments in subsidiaries, associates and joint ventures accounted for at cost or using the equity method that are classified as held for sale (or included in a disposal group that is classified as held for sale) in accordance with IFRS 5 – *Non-current Assets Held for Sale and Discontinued Operations* – are accounted for in accordance with IFRS 5, *[IAS 27.10]*, i.e. at the lower of carrying amount and fair value less cost to sell (see Chapter 4).

All other investments are accounted for either at cost (see 2.1 below), in accordance with IFRS 9 (or IAS 39 if IFRS 9 is not yet applicable) (see 2.2 below) or using the equity method as described in IAS 28 (see 2.3 below). Each 'category' of investment must be accounted for consistently. *[IAS 27.10]*. While 'category' is not defined, we take this to mean, for example, that it would be permissible for a parent that is not an investment entity to account for all subsidiaries at cost and all associates under IFRS 9 (or IAS 39).

Where an investment in an associate or joint venture is accounted for in accordance with IFRS 9 (or IAS 39) in the consolidated financial statements, it must also be accounted for in the same way in the separate financial statements. *[IAS 27.11]*. The circumstances in which IFRS 9 (or IAS 39) is applied in consolidated financial statements are discussed in, respectively, Chapter 11 at 5 and Chapter 12 at 2.

A parent that meets the definition of an investment entity is required to measure its investments in particular subsidiaries at fair value through profit or loss in accordance with IFRS 9 (or IAS 39) in its consolidated financial statements, *[IFRS 10.31]*, and is required to account for them in the same way in the separate financial statements. *[IAS 27.11A]*. When an investment entity parent has shares in subsidiaries that only provide investment related services (and therefore are not subject to obligatory fair value measurement), that parent effectively has shares in two categories of subsidiaries. It therefore has still an accounting policy choice to account for those subsidiaries that only provide investment related services at cost, in accordance with IFRS 9 (or IAS 39), or using the equity method in its separate financial statements.

When an entity becomes an investment entity the difference between the previous carrying value of the investment and its fair value at the date of change in status of the parent is recognised as a gain or loss in profit or loss. When a parent ceases to be an investment entity, it should follow paragraph 10 of IAS 27 and account for the investments in a subsidiary either at cost (the then fair value of the subsidiary at the date of the change in the status becomes the deemed cost), continue to account for the investment in accordance with IFRS 9 (or IAS 39), or apply the equity method. *[IAS 27.11B]*.

IAS 27 contains specific requirements related to the treatment of dividends from investments in subsidiaries, joint ventures or associates that are recognised in profit or loss unless the entity elects to use equity method, in which case the dividend is recognised as a reduction of the carrying amount of the investment. *[IAS 27.12]*. IAS 36 – *Impairment of Assets* – includes specific triggers for impairment reviews on receipt of dividends. These are discussed at 2.4.1 below.

2.1 Cost method

There is no general definition or description of 'cost' in IAS 27. How the term applies in practice is described in 2.1.1 below.

IAS 27 addresses the cost of investment in a new holding company that becomes the parent of an existing parent in a one-for-one share exchange. This is discussed further in 2.1.1.D and 2.1.1.E below.

IAS 27 also indicates that when an entity ceases to be an investment entity and its accounting policy is to account for investments in subsidiaries, associates or joint ventures at cost, the fair value as at the date of the change in status shall be used as the deemed cost. *[IAS 27.11B]*.

IFRS 1 – *First-time Adoption of International Financial Reporting Standards* – allows a 'deemed cost' transitional amendment for those applying IFRS for the first time in separate financial statements (see 2.1.2 below).

2.1.1 Cost of investment

IAS 27 does not define what is meant by 'cost' except in the specific circumstances of certain types of group reorganisation, described below, and when an entity ceases to be an investment entity and accounts for investments in subsidiaries at cost as indicated above.

As discussed further in Chapter 3 at 4.3, IAS 8 – *Accounting Policies, Changes in Accounting Estimates and Errors* – states that, in the absence of specific requirements in IFRS, management should first refer to the requirements and guidance in IFRS that deal with similar and related issues.

The glossary to IFRS defines cost as 'the amount of cash or cash equivalents paid or the fair value of the other consideration given to acquire an asset at the time of its acquisition or construction'.

'Consideration given' is likewise not defined, and therefore we believe that the key sources of guidance in IFRS are:

- 'consideration transferred' in the context of a business combination, as referred to in paragraph 37 of IFRS 3 – *Business Combinations; [IFRS 3.37]* and
- 'cost' as applied in relation to acquisitions of property, plant and equipment in accordance with IAS 16 – *Property, Plant and Equipment*, intangible assets in accordance with IAS 38 – *Intangible Assets* – and investment property in accordance with IAS 40 – *Investment Property*.

Applying the requirements of IFRS 3, the 'consideration transferred' in a business combination comprises the sum of the acquisition date fair values of assets transferred by the acquirer, liabilities incurred by the acquirer to the former owners of the acquiree, and equity interests issued by the acquirer. This includes any liability (or asset) for contingent consideration, which is measured and recognised at fair value at the acquisition date. Subsequent changes in the measurement of the changes in the liability (or asset) are recognised in profit or loss (see Chapter 9 at 7.1).

The Interpretations Committee and IASB have discussed the topic *Variable payments for the separate acquisition of PPE and intangible assets* for a number of years, attempting to clarify how the initial recognition of the variable payments, such as contingent consideration, and subsequent changes in the value of those payments should be recognised. The scope of the past deliberations did not specifically include the cost of an investment in a subsidiary, associate or joint venture. However, as they consider general principles about the recognition of variable payments we believe they can also be considered relevant in determining the cost of such investments.

There was diversity of views about whether the liability for contingent consideration relating to separate acquisition of property, plant and equipment and intangible assets falls within the scope of IAS 37 – *Provisions, Contingent Liabilities and Contingent Assets* – or within the scope of IAS 39 (this will still be relevant after IFRS 9 adoption as well). This affects the initial recognition and also subsequent accounting for changes in the value of the contingent consideration. At their meetings in January and March 2011, the Interpretations Committee took the view that while certain contingent price arrangements would meet the definition of a financial liability, others would not. With respect to subsequent changes, the Interpretations Committee noted that IAS 39 requires changes to a financial liability recognised for the contingent price payable is recognised in profit or loss. Some members of the Interpretations Committee expressed concern about recognising subsequent changes in profit or loss, noting that IFRIC 1 – *Changes in Existing Decommissioning, Restoration and Similar Liabilities* – addressed a similar issue and required an adjustment to the cost of the asset. In November 2012, the Interpretations Committee discussed the initial accounting for variable payments but could not reach a consensus on whether the fair value of variable payments that are dependent on the purchaser's future activity should be excluded from initial measurement of the liability until the activity is performed. The Interpretations Committee put further discussions on hold until the IASB had completed the discussions concerning the treatment of variable payments in the leases project. The Interpretations Committee recommenced discussions in 2015 and in March 2016 stated that they were unable to reach a consensus on whether a purchaser recognises a liability at the date of purchasing an asset for variable payments that depend on future activity or instead recognises a liability only when the related activity occurs. The Interpretations Committee was also unable to reach a consensus on how the purchaser measures the liability, and noted that there are questions about the accounting for variable payments subsequent to the purchase of the asset. The Interpretations Committee decided that the issue is too broad for it to address and concluded that the IASB should address accounting for variable payments more comprehensively.[5]

Until the IASB issues further guidance, differing views remain about the circumstances in which, and to what extent, variable payments such as contingent consideration should be recognised when initially recognising the underlying asset. There are also differing views about the extent to which subsequent changes should be recognised through profit or loss or capitalised as part of the cost of the asset.

The topic is discussed in relation to intangible assets, property, plant and equipment and investment property in Chapter 17 at 4.5, Chapter 18 at 4.1.9 and Chapter 19 at 4.10 respectively.

Where entities have made an accounting policy choice regarding recognition of contingent consideration and accounting for the subsequent changes in separate financial statements, the policy should be disclosed and consistently applied.

Another question relates to the treatment of any transaction costs as, under IFRS 3, these costs are recognised as expenses or in accordance with IAS 32 – *Financial Instruments: Presentation* – and IFRS 9 (i.e. as reduction of the proceeds of the debt or equity securities issued) in the consolidated financial statements rather than being included in goodwill.

At its meeting in July 2009, the Interpretations Committee, in discussing the determination of the initial carrying amount of an equity method investment, noted that IFRSs consistently require assets not measured at fair value through profit or loss to be measured on initial recognition at cost. Generally stated, cost includes the purchase price and other costs directly attributable to the acquisition or issuance of the asset such as professional fees for legal services, transfer taxes and other transaction costs.[6]

Given that IAS 27 does not separately define 'cost', we believe it is appropriate to apply this general meaning of 'cost' in determining the cost of investments in subsidiaries, associates or joint ventures in separate financial statements. Therefore, in our opinion, the cost of investment in a subsidiary in the separate financial statements includes any transaction costs incurred even if such costs are expensed in the consolidated financial statements.

2.1.1.A Investments acquired for own shares or other equity instruments

In some jurisdictions, local law may permit investments acquired for an issue of shares to be recorded at a notional value (for example, the nominal value of the shares issued). In our view, this is not an appropriate measure of cost under IFRS.

A transaction in which an investment in a subsidiary, associate or joint venture is acquired in exchange for an issue of shares or other equity instruments is not specifically addressed under IFRS, since it falls outside the scope of both IFRS 9 (or IAS 39) and also IFRS 2 – *Share-based Payment* (see Chapter 32 at 2.2.3).

However, we believe that it would be appropriate, by analogy with IFRS on related areas (like IFRS 3), to account for such a transaction at the fair value of the consideration given (being fair value of equity instruments issued) or the assets received, if that is more reliably measured, together with directly attributable transaction costs.

2.1.1.B Investments acquired in common control transactions

When an investment in a subsidiary, associate or joint venture is acquired in a common control transaction, in our view, the cost should generally be measured at the fair value of the consideration given (be it cash, other assets or additional shares) plus, where applicable any costs directly attributable to the acquisition. However, when the purchase consideration does not correspond to the fair value of the investment acquired, in our view, the acquirer has an accounting policy choice to account for the investment at fair value of consideration given or may impute an equity contribution or dividend distribution and in effect account for the investment at its fair value.

Example 8.1 below illustrates the determination of the cost of an investment in a subsidiary in separate financial statements as described above.

Example 8.1: Cost of a subsidiary in separate financial statements when the pooling of interest method is applied in consolidated financial statements

Parent has a 100% direct interest in Sub 1 and Sub 2. As part of a group reorganisation, the parent transfers its direct interest in Sub 2 to Sub 1 in exchange for consideration of:

Scenario 1 – €200 (equal to the fair value of Sub 2);

Scenario 2 – €150.

The carrying amount of the investment in Sub 2 in the separate financial statements of Parent is €50. The carrying amount of Sub 2's net assets in the separate financial statements of Sub 2 is €110.

Sub 1 accounts for the acquisition of Sub 2 using the pooling of interest method in its consolidated financial statements.

In Scenario 1, the cost of an investment in a subsidiary that is acquired as part of a group reorganisation is the fair value of the consideration given (be it cash, other assets or additional shares), plus, where applicable, any costs directly attributable to the acquisition. Therefore, the cost to Sub 1 is €200. The cost is not the carrying amount of the investment in Sub 2 in the separate financial statements of Parent (i.e. €50), nor the carrying amount of Sub 2's net assets in the separate financial statements of Sub 2 (i.e. €110).

In Scenario 2, the conclusion in Scenario 1 applies even if the fair value of the consideration given is more or less than the fair value of the acquiree. Therefore, the cost of investment is €150. However, the acquirer may choose to recognise an equity element (equity contribution or dividend distribution). In this case, the cost of investment is €200 with €50 recognised as an equity contribution.

In July and September 2011, the Interpretations Committee discussed group reorganisations in separate financial statements in response to a request asking for clarification on how entities that are established as new intermediate parents within a group determine the cost of their investments when they account for these investments at cost in accordance with paragraph 10(a) of IAS 27. In the agenda decision issued, the Interpretations Committee noted that the normal basis for determining the cost of an investment in a subsidiary under paragraph 10(a) of IAS 27 has to be applied to reorganisations that result in the new intermediate parent having more than one direct subsidiary.[7] This differs from the wording in the original proposed wording for the tentative decision which referred to 'the general principle of determining cost by the fair value of the consideration given'.[8]

Some have read this to mean that 'the normal basis for determining the cost of investment' in a common control transaction is not restricted to using the fair value of the consideration given, but that another basis for determining cost may be appropriate. One situation where we believe that it would be acceptable not to use the fair value of the consideration given is for a common control transaction where an investment in a subsidiary constituting a business is acquired in a share-for-share exchange. In that circumstance, we believe that it is also acceptable to measure the cost based on the carrying amount of the investment in the subsidiary in the transferor entity's separate financial statements immediately prior to the transaction, rather than at the fair value of the shares given as consideration.

Common control transactions are discussed further at 4 below. There are specific measurement requirements applicable to certain arrangements involving the formation of a new parent or intermediate parent, which are described at 2.1.1.D and 2.1.1.E below.

2.1.1.C Cost of investment in subsidiary, associate or joint venture acquired in stages

It may be that an investment in a subsidiary, associate or joint venture was acquired in stages so that, up to the date on which control, significant influence or joint control was first achieved, the initial investment was accounted for at fair value under IFRS 9 (or IAS 39). This raises the question of what the carrying amount should be in the separate financial statements when the cost method is applied.

In our view, in the case of an acquisition in stages, there is only one acceptable method of accounting for the investment in the separate financial statements. The cost of the investment is the sum of the consideration given for each tranche.

The Interpretations Committee discussion in 2009 referred to above at 2.1.1 indicates that cost of investment reflects the consideration given (purchase price) rather than the fair value of any interest held that is 'given up'. In IFRS 3, any investment held prior to a second acquisition that gives control is considered to be 'given up' in exchange for a controlling interest, and is therefore remeasured to its fair value when determining the consideration given for the subsidiary. *[IFRS 3.42]*. However, whilst the change is reflected as a disposal and new acquisition in the consolidated financial statements, there is no change in substance in the investor's *separate* financial statements. That is, the investor has not 'given up' its investment for another interest and continues to have the same ownership entitlement and rights that it always had for that pre-existing investment. Rather, the time of the asset's acquisition is the time at which something is given up or exchanged – which corresponds to the original acquisition dates of each tranche of the investment. Because this date relates to the cash flows or exchanges at the dates of acquisition, any adjustments to this value subsequent to acquisition are not considered an element of 'cost', and are reversed. The reversal will be reflected in the statement of comprehensive income, resulting in an adjustment to the component of equity containing the cumulative valuation gains and losses, e.g. retained earnings, where the investment has been treated as at fair value through profit or loss, or other reserve where the investment has been treated as at fair value through other comprehensive income (if an entity has elected to present gains and losses in other comprehensive income in accordance with paragraph 5.7.5 of IFRS 9).

Example 8.2: Cost of a subsidiary acquired in stages

Entity A has a 10% interest in Entity B, which it acquired in January 2018 for €300. This investment is a financial asset measured at fair value in accordance with IFRS 9, in both the consolidated and separate financial statements of Entity A for the six months ended 30 June 2018. In July 2018, Entity A acquires a further 45% interest in Entity B for €2,160 (its then fair value), giving Entity A control over Entity B. The original 10% interest has a fair value of €480 at that date. In addition, transaction costs were incurred for both tranches, in aggregate amounting to €50.

The cost of investment after both transactions is the sum of the consideration given for each tranche plus transaction costs – €2,510 (€300 + €2,160 + €50). The increase in fair value of €180 (€480 – €300) relating to the first 10% is reversed in the statement of comprehensive income, and reflected in retained earnings (if the change was recognised in profit or loss) or equity reserves (if the change was recognised in other comprehensive income).

If, instead of IFRS 9, an entity were to apply IAS 39 then the accounting would be the same, except where changes to the carrying amount of the investment had resulted from an impairment charge. This charge may not necessarily be reversed. This is because the investment must still be considered for impairment in the separate financial statements of the investor (see 2.4.1 below). Therefore, additional consideration must be given as to whether

IAS 36 and IAS 39 permit reversals of impairment, and whether there are any indicators that the impairment can be reversed, based on the classification of the investment.

The table below summarises the impact on the cost of investment in a subsidiary acquired in stages depending on the accounting policy applied for the measurement of the pre-existing interest and considering any previous impairment recognised:

Classification of tranche prior to subsequent investment	Changes in fair value were previously recognised	Changes in fair value are reversed upon subsequent investment	Impairment permitted to be reversed?
If the entity had chosen to apply the cost basis:			
Cost, as defined in IAS 27	N/A – not remeasured – (see paragraph 10(a) of IAS 27)	N/A – not remeasured – (see paragraph 10(a) of IAS 27)	Yes, through profit or loss in retained earnings. Test performed in accordance with IAS 36
If the entity had chosen to apply IFRS 9:			
Fair value through profit or loss	Recognised in profit or loss (see paragraph 10(b) of IAS 27 and paragraph 5.7.1 of IFRS 9)	Reversed through profit or loss in retained earnings	N/A – remeasured – (see paragraph 5.7.1 of IFRS 9)
Fair value through other comprehensive income (if an entity has elected to present gains and losses in other comprehensive income in accordance with paragraph 5.7.5 of IFRS 9).	Recognised in other comprehensive income (see paragraph 10(b) of IAS 27 and paragraph 5.7.1(b) of IFRS 9)	Reversed through other comprehensive income in equity reserve where other comprehensive income is accumulated	N/A – remeasured – (see paragraph 5.7.1 of IFRS 9)
If the entity had chosen to apply IAS 39 (for periods when IFRS 9 is not yet applicable):			
Cost, as defined in IAS 39 (investment in equity instruments whose fair value cannot be reliably measured)	N/A – not remeasured – (see paragraph 10(b) of IAS 27 and paragraph 46(c) of IAS 39)	N/A – not remeasured – (see paragraph 10(b) of IAS 27 and paragraph 46(c) of IAS 39)	No, not permitted (see paragraph 66 of IAS 39)
Available-for-sale	Recognised in other comprehensive income (see paragraph 10(b) of IAS 27 and paragraph 55(b) of IAS 39)	Reversed through other comprehensive income in equity reserve where other comprehensive income is accumulated (see paragraph 55(b) of IAS 39)	No, not permitted (see paragraph 69 of IAS 39)
Fair value through profit or loss	Recognised in profit or loss (see paragraph 10(b) of IAS 27 and paragraph 55(a) of IAS 39)	Reversed through profit or loss in retained earnings (see paragraph 55(a) of IAS 39)	N/A – remeasured – (see paragraph 55(a) of IAS 39)

2.1.1.D Formation of a new parent

IAS 27 explains how to calculate the cost of the investment when a parent reorganises the structure of its group by establishing a new entity as its parent and meets the following criteria:

(a) the new parent obtains control of the original parent by issuing equity instruments in exchange for existing equity instruments of the original parent;

(b) the assets and liabilities of the new group and the original group are the same immediately before and after the reorganisation; and

(c) the owners of the original parent before the reorganisation have the same absolute and relative interests in the net assets of the original group and the new group immediately before and after the reorganisation.

The new parent measures cost at the carrying amount of its share of the equity items shown in the separate financial statements of the original parent at the date of the reorganisation (see 2.1.1.E below). *[IAS 27.13].*

This approach also applies if the entity that puts a new parent between it and the shareholders is not itself a parent, i.e. it has no subsidiaries. In such cases, references in the three conditions to 'original parent' and 'original group' are to the 'original entity'. *[IAS 27.14].*

The type of reorganisation to which these requirements apply involves an existing entity and its shareholders agreeing to create a new parent between them without changing either the composition of the group or their own absolute and relative interests. This is not a general rule that applies to all common control transactions. Transfers of subsidiaries from the ownership of one entity to another within a group are not within the scope. The IASB has deliberately excluded extending the amendment to other types of reorganisations or to common control transactions more generally because of its plans to address this in its project on common control transactions. *[IAS 27.BC27].*

The IASB has identified business combinations under common control as a priority research project. In June 2014, the Board tentatively decided that the research project should consider business combinations under common control and group restructurings, and to give priority to considering transactions that involve third parties.[9] However, the IASB has not yet considered which entities' financial statements will be covered by the scope of the research project (e.g. acquirer's, the acquiree's, the transferor's, the ultimate parent's) as well as which financial statements the project should address (e.g. consolidated, separate, individual) until the research work on the types of transactions within the scope of the project progresses.[10] During 2016-2017, the IASB has continued discussions on the project, including discussions of a staff paper presented at the Global Preparers Forum Meeting in March 2017 and the next step is likely to be the issuance of a Discussion Paper for public comment in the first half of 2018.[11]

In the meantime, entities will continue to account for such common control transactions in accordance with their accounting policies (see Chapter 10 at 3 and 4.4 below).

As well as the establishment of a new ultimate parent of a group, arrangements that could meet the criteria in paragraph 13 of IAS 27 mentioned above include the following:

(a) Reorganisations in which the new parent does not acquire all classes of the equity instruments issued by the original parent.

For example, the original parent may have preference shares that are classified as equity in addition to ordinary shares; the new parent does not have to acquire the preference shares in order for the transaction to be within scope. *[IAS 27.BC24(a)]*.

(b) A new parent obtains control of the original parent without acquiring all of the ordinary shares of the original parent. *[IAS 27.BC24(a)]*. The absolute and relative holdings must be the same immediately before and after the transaction. *[IAS 27.13(c)]*.

The requirements will apply, for example, if a controlling group of shareholders insert a new entity between themselves and the original parent that holds all of their original shares in the same ratio as before.

Example 8.3: Formation of new parent that does not acquire all of original parent's ordinary shares

Shareholders A and B each hold 35% of the equity instruments of Original Parent. A and B transfer their shares to New Parent in a share-for-share exchange so that both now hold 50% of the shares in New Parent. The absolute and relative interests of A and B and those of the other shareholders in Original Parent are unchanged, so the arrangement is a reorganisation to which the cost method for reorganisations applies.

(c) The establishment of an intermediate parent within a group. *[IAS 27.BC24(b)]*.

The principle is exactly the same as inserting a new parent company over the top of a group. 'Original Parent' will be an intermediate company within a group, owned by another group company. If the transaction is within scope, the intermediate parent will acquire Original Parent from its parent (the Owner) in a share for share swap. The group structure before and after the transaction can be summarised as follows:

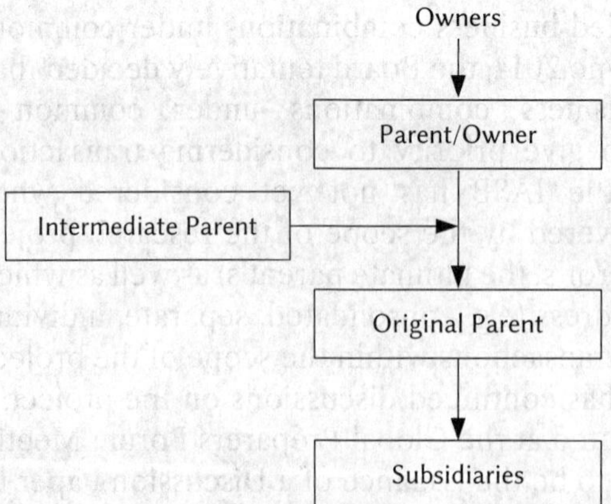

If the composition of the underlying group changes, perhaps because the intermediate parent acquires only part of that group or because it acquires another subsidiary as part of the re-organisation, then the arrangement will not be within scope.

The formation of a new parent was also considered by the Interpretation Committee in 2011. The Interpretations Committee noted 'that the normal basis for determining the cost of an investment in a subsidiary under [...] paragraph 10(a) of IAS 27 [...] has to be applied to reorganisations that result in the new intermediate parent having more than one direct subsidiary. [...] Paragraphs 13 and 14 of IAS 27 [...] apply only when the assets and liabilities of the new group and the original group (or original entity) are the same before and after the reorganisation'. The Interpretations Committee observed that the reorganisations that result in the new intermediate parent having more than one direct subsidiary do not meet the conditions in IAS 27 and therefore the exemptions for group reorganisations in IAS 27 do not apply. They also cannot be applied by analogy because this guidance is an exception to the normal basis for determining the cost of investment in a subsidiary.[12]

For example, if in the group structure as presented above, the Intermediate Parent had been inserted between the Original Parent and its subsidiaries, paragraphs 13 and 14 of IAS 27 would not apply as there are several subsidiaries acquired by the Intermediate Parent. In this case, there has been no 'parent' that has been established by the Intermediate Parent as its new parent.

2.1.1.E Formation of a new parent: calculating the cost and measuring equity

IAS 27 states that the new parent measures cost at the carrying amount of its share of the 'equity items' shown in the separate financial statements of the original parent at the date of the reorganisation. *[IAS 27.13]*. It does not define 'equity items' but the term appears to mean the total equity in the original parent, i.e. its issued capital and reserves attributable to owners. This will be the equity as recorded in IFRS financial statements so it will exclude shares that are classified as liabilities and include, for example, the equity component of a convertible loan instrument.

It is important to stress that the new parent does not record its investment at the consideration given (the shares that it has issued) or at the assets received (the fair value of the investments it has acquired or the book cost of those investments). Instead, it must look down, to the total of the equity in the original parent, which is the acquired entity. Even then, it does not record the investment at the amount of original parent's investments but at the amount of its equity; that is to say, its net assets.

The requirements do not apply to the measurement of any other assets or liabilities in the separate financial statements of either the original parent or the new parent, or in the consolidated financial statements. *[IAS 27.BC25]*.

It is possible for the original parent to have negative equity because its liabilities exceed its assets. IAS 27 does not discuss this but we consider that in these circumstances the investment should be recorded at zero. There is no basis for recording an investment as if it were a liability.

The above applies only when the new parent issues equity instruments but it does not address the measurement of the equity of the new parent. IFRS has no general requirements for accounting for the issue of own equity instruments. Rather, consistent with the position taken by the *Conceptual Framework* that equity is a residual rather than an item 'in its own right', the amount of an equity instrument is normally measured by reference to the item (expense or asset) in consideration for which the equity is issued, as determined in accordance with IFRS applicable to that other item. The new parent will record the increase in equity at the carrying amount of the investments it has acquired (i.e. at cost), regardless of the amount and face value of the equity instruments issued.

The amount at which the new parent's issued share capital is recorded will depend on the relevant law in the jurisdiction applicable to the new parent. The shares may be recorded at fair value, which is the fair value of the investments acquired, or at an amount calculated on some other basis. Local law may allow a company to record its issued share capital at a nominal amount, e.g. the nominal (face) value of the shares. In some jurisdictions, intermediate holding companies that acquire an asset from a parent (the 'transferor') for shares at a premium are required by law to record the share capital issued (its nominal value and share premium) at the carrying value in the transferor's books of the asset transferred; if the nominal value exceeds this book amount, the shares are recorded at their total nominal value.

Once the share capital has been recorded, there will usually need to be an adjustment to equity so that in total the equity is equal to the carrying amount (i.e. cost) of the investments acquired. This adjustment may increase or decrease the acquirer's equity (comparing to share capital value) as it depends on the relative carrying amounts of the investment in the owner, original parent's equity and the number and value of the shares issued as consideration, as shown in the following example.

Example 8.4: Formation of new parent, statutory share capital and adjustments to equity

Intermediate Parent A acquires the investments in Original Parent from Parent; the structure after the arrangement is as illustrated above in 2.1.1.D. Parent carries its investment in Original Parent at £200 but it has a fair value of £750. Original Parent's equity in its separate financial statements is £650. Intermediate Parent A issues shares with a nominal value of £100 to Parent.

In accordance with IAS 27 paragraph 13, Intermediate Company records its investment in Original Parent at £650. Depending on local law, it might record its share capital (including share premium where appropriate) at:

(i) £750, being the fair value of the consideration received for the shares. It records a negative adjustment of £100 elsewhere in equity; or

(ii) £100, being the nominal value of the shares issued. It records a credit adjustment of £550 elsewhere in equity; or

(iii) £200, being the carrying value of the investment in Parent. It records a credit adjustment of £450 elsewhere in equity.

2.1.2 Deemed cost on transition to IFRS

IFRS 1 allows a first-time adopter an exemption with regard to its investments in subsidiaries, joint ventures and associates in its separate financial statements. *[IFRS 1.D15].* If it elects to apply the cost method, it can either measure the investment in its separate opening IFRS statement of financial position at cost determined in accordance with IAS 27 or at deemed cost. Deemed cost is either:

(i) fair value (determined in accordance with IFRS 13 – *Fair Value Measurement*) at the entity's date of transition to IFRSs in its separate financial statements; or

(ii) previous GAAP carrying amount as at the entity's date of transition to IFRSs in its separate financial statements.

As with the other asset measurement exemptions, the first-time adopter may choose either (i) or (ii) above to measure each individual investment in subsidiaries, joint ventures or associates that it elects to measure using a deemed cost. *[IFRS 1.D15].*

2.2 IFRS 9 and IAS 39 methods

2.2.1 IFRS 9 method

Under IFRS 9, the equity investments in subsidiaries, joint ventures or associates would likely be classified as financial assets measured at fair value through profit or loss or, as financial assets measured at fair value through other comprehensive income (OCI), if an entity elects at initial recognition to present subsequent changes in their fair value in OCI. In the former case, changes in the fair value of the investments will be recognised in profit or loss. In the latter case, gains or losses from changes in the fair value will be recognised in OCI and will never be reclassified to profit or loss. The classification requirements of IFRS 9 are discussed in Chapter 47, and the measurement principles of IFRS 9 on initial and subsequent measurement are discussed in detail in Chapters 48 and 50.

2.2.2 IAS 39 method

The measurement rules in IAS 39 on initial and subsequent measurement are complex and discussed in detail in Chapters 48 and 49. In brief, however, they will entail the investments in subsidiaries, joint ventures or associates being recorded initially at cost and then classified as either a 'financial asset at fair value through profit or loss' or an 'available-for-sale financial asset'. In either case, the investment will be measured at fair value. However, the gains and losses arising on periodic remeasurement are generally accounted for:

- in the case of a financial asset at fair value through profit or loss, in profit or loss; and
- in the case of an available-for-sale financial asset, in other comprehensive income.

One issue that has been discussed by the IASB that is relevant in determining the fair value of investments in subsidiaries, joint ventures and associates is the unit of account for such investments.

In September 2014, the IASB issued an Exposure Draft (ED) *Measuring Quoted Investments in Subsidiaries, Joint Ventures and Associates at Fair Value (proposed amendments to IFRS 10, IFRS 12, IAS 27, IAS 28 and IAS 36).* The ED proposed to clarify that the unit of account for investments in subsidiaries, joint ventures and associates be the investment as a whole and not the individual financial instruments that constitute the investment. However, in January 2016, the IASB decided not to consider this topic further until the Post-implementation Review (PIR) of IFRS 13 has been done.[13] In 2017 the Board published a Request for Information for a PIR. Stakeholders can provide feedback on their experiences with IFRS 13 until 22 September 2017.[14]

RSA Insurance Group plc, which publishes its separate financial statements, accounts for its investments as available-for-sale financial assets as can be seen from Extract 8.1 below.

> *Extract 8.1: RSA Insurance Group plc (2015)*
>
> **Notes to the separate financial statements**[extract]
>
> **1) Significant accounting policies** [extract]
>
> **Investment in subsidiaries**
>
> The Company accounts for its investments in directly owned subsidiaries as available for sale financial assets, which are included in the accounts at fair value.
>
> Changes in the fair value of the investments in subsidiaries are recognised directly in equity in the statement of comprehensive income. Where there is a decline in the fair value of a directly owned subsidiary below cost, and there is objective evidence that the investment is impaired, the cumulative loss that has been recognised in equity is removed from equity and recognised in the income statement.

2.3 Equity method

IAS 27 was amended in 2014 to allow entities to use the equity method as described in IAS 28 to account for investments in subsidiaries, joint ventures and associates in their separate financial statements.[15] The amendments introduced applied to annual periods beginning on or after 1 January 2016, and were to be applied retrospectively. *[IAS 27.18J]*. Where the equity method is used, dividends from those investments are recognised as a reduction from the carrying value of the investment.[16] The application of the equity method under IAS 28 is discussed in Chapter 11 at 7. The option to use the equity method was included in response to feedback received from the 2011 Agenda Consultation. Some jurisdictions require the use of the equity method to account for investments in subsidiaries, associates and joint ventures in the separate financial statements. In many cases this was the only GAAP difference to IFRS and hence the IASB reintroduced the option to use the equity method.

In the Basis for Conclusions to IAS 27, the IASB indicates that in general, the application of the equity method to investments in subsidiaries, joint ventures and associates in the separate financial statements of an entity is expected to result in the same net assets and profit or loss attributable to the owners as in the entity's consolidated financial statements. However, there may be situations where this might not be the case, including:[17]

- Impairment testing requirements in IAS 28.

  For an investment in a subsidiary accounted for in separate financial statements using the equity method, goodwill that forms part of the carrying amount of the investment in the subsidiary is not tested for impairment separately. Instead, the entire carrying amount of the investment in the subsidiary is tested for impairment in accordance with IAS 36 as a single asset. However, in the consolidated financial statements of the entity, because goodwill is recognised separately, it is tested for impairment by applying the requirements in IAS 36 for testing goodwill for impairment.

- Subsidiary that has a net liability position.

  IAS 28 requires an investor to discontinue recognising its share of further losses when its cumulative share of losses of the investee equals or exceeds its interest in the investee, unless the investor has incurred legal or constructive obligations or made payments on behalf of the investee, in which case a liability is recognised, whereas there is no such requirement in relation to the consolidated financial statements.
- Capitalisation of borrowing costs incurred by a parent in relation to the assets of a subsidiary.

  IAS 23 – *Borrowing Costs* – notes that, in some circumstances, it may be appropriate to include all borrowings of the parent and its subsidiaries when computing a weighted average of the borrowing costs. When a parent borrows funds and its subsidiary uses them for the purpose of obtaining a qualifying asset, in the consolidated financial statements of the parent the borrowing costs incurred by the parent are considered to be directly attributable to the acquisition of the subsidiary's qualifying asset. However, this would not be appropriate in the separate financial statements of the parent where the parent's investment in the subsidiary is a financial asset which is not a qualifying asset.

In these situations, there will not be alignment of the net assets and profit or loss of an investment in a subsidiary between the consolidated and separate financial statements.

2.3.1 First-time adoption of IFRS

IFRS 1 allows a first-time adopter that accounts for an investment in a subsidiary, joint venture or associate using the equity method in the separate financial statements to apply the exemption for past business combinations to the acquisition of the investment. *[IFRS 1.D15A].* The exemption for past business combinations is discussed in Chapter 5 at 5.2. The first-time adopter can also apply certain exemptions to the assets and liabilities of subsidiaries, associates and joint ventures when it becomes a first-time adopter for the separate financial statements later than its parent or subsidiary. *[IFRS 1.D15A].* These exemptions are discussed in Chapter 5 at 5.9.

2.4 Dividends and other distributions

IAS 27 contains a general principle for dividends received from subsidiaries, joint ventures or associates. This is supplemented by specific indicators of impairment in IAS 36 that apply when a parent entity receives the dividend. The general principle and the specific impairment indicators are discussed in 2.4.1 below.

IFRIC 17 – *Distributions of Non-cash Assets to Owners* – considers in particular the treatment by the entity making the distribution. Details about the requirements of that Interpretation are discussed in 2.4.2 below.

2.4.1 Dividends from subsidiaries, joint ventures or associates

IAS 27 states that an entity recognises dividends from subsidiaries, joint ventures or associates in its separate financial statements when its right to receive the dividend is established. The dividend is recognised in profit or loss unless the entity elects to use the equity method, in which case the dividend is recognised as a reduction from the carrying amount of the investment. *[IAS 27.12].*

Dividends are recognised only when they are declared (i.e. the dividends are appropriately authorised and no longer at the discretion of the entity). IFRIC 17 expands on this point: the relevant authority may be the shareholders, if the jurisdiction requires such approval, or management or the board of directors, if the jurisdiction does not require further approval. *[IFRIC 17.10]*. If the declaration is made after the reporting period but before the financial statements are authorised for issue, the dividends are not recognised as a liability at the end of the reporting period because no obligation exists at that time. Such dividends are disclosed in the notes in accordance with IAS 1 – *Presentation of Financial Statements*. *[IAS 10.13]*. A parent cannot record income or a reduction of the equity accounted investment and recognise an asset until the dividend is a liability of its subsidiary, joint venture or associate, the paying company.

Once dividends are taken to income the investor must determine whether or not the investment has been impaired as a result. IAS 36 requires the entity to assess at each reporting date whether there are any 'indications of impairment'. Only if indications of impairment are present will the impairment test itself have to be carried out. *[IAS 36.8-9]*.

The list of indicators in IAS 36 includes the receipt of a dividend from a subsidiary, joint venture or associate where there is evidence that:

(i) the dividend exceeds the total comprehensive income of the subsidiary, joint venture or associate in the period the dividend is declared; or

(ii) the carrying amount of the investment in the separate financial statements exceeds the carrying amounts in the consolidated financial statements of the investee's net assets, including associated goodwill. *[IAS 36.12(h)]*.

2.4.1.A The dividend exceeds the total comprehensive income

There are circumstances in which receipt of a dividend will trigger the first indicator, even if the dividend is payable entirely from the profit for the period.

First, the indicator states that the test is by reference to the income in the period in which the declaration is made. Dividends are usually declared after the end of the period to which they relate; an entity whose accounting period ends on 31 December 2017 will not normally declare a dividend in respect of its earnings in that period until its financial statements have been drawn up, i.e. some months into the next period ended 31 December 2018. We assume that it is expected that the impairment review itself will take place at the end of the period, in line with the general requirements of IAS 36 referred to above, in which case the dividends received in the period will be compared to the income of the subsidiary for that period. This means that there may be a mismatch in that, say, dividends declared on the basis of 2017 profits will be compared to total comprehensive income in 2018, but at least the indicator of impairment will be by reference to a completed period.

Second, the test is by reference to total comprehensive income, not profit or loss for the period. Total comprehensive income reflects the change in equity during a period resulting from transactions and other events, other than those changes resulting from transactions with owners in their capacity as owners. Total comprehensive income takes into account the components of 'other comprehensive income' that are not reflected in profit or loss that include:

(a) changes in revaluation surpluses of property, plant and equipment or intangible assets (see Chapters 17 and 18);

(b) remeasurements of defined benefit plans (see Chapter 33);

(c) gains and losses arising from translating the financial statements of a foreign operation (see Chapter 15);

(d) gains and losses on remeasuring available-for-sale financial assets (see Chapter 48); and

(e) the effective portion of gains and losses on hedging instruments in a cash flow hedge (see Chapters 52 and 53). *[IAS 1.7].*

This means that all losses on remeasurement that are allowed by IFRS to bypass profit or loss and be taken directly to other components of equity are taken into account in determining whether a dividend is an indicator of impairment. If a subsidiary, joint venture or associate pays a dividend from its profit for the year that exceeds its total comprehensive income because there have been actuarial losses on the pension scheme or a loss on remeasuring its hedging derivatives, then receipt of that dividend is an indicator of impairment to the parent.

The opposite must also be true – a dividend that exceeds profit for the period but does not exceed total comprehensive income (if, for example, the entity has a revaluation surplus on its property) is not an indicator of impairment. However, IAS 36 makes clear that its list of indicators is not exhaustive and if there are other indicators of impairment then the entity must carry out an impairment test in accordance with IAS 36. *[IAS 36.13].*

It must be stressed that this test is solely to see whether a dividend triggers an impairment review. It has no effect on the amount of dividend that the subsidiary, joint venture or associate may pay, which is governed by local law.

2.4.1.B The carrying amount exceeds the consolidated net assets

An indicator of impairment arises if, after paying the dividend, the carrying amount of the investment in the separate financial statements exceeds the carrying amount in the consolidated financial statements of the investee's net assets, including associated goodwill.

It will often be clear when dividends are paid out of profits for the period by subsidiaries, joint ventures or associates, whether the consolidated net assets of the investee in question have declined below the carrying amount of the investment. However this might require the preparation of consolidated financial statements by an intermediate parent which is exempted from the preparation of consolidated financial statements.

Similar issues to those described above may arise, e.g. the subsidiary, joint venture or associate may have made losses or taken some sort of remeasurement to other comprehensive income in the period in which the dividend is paid. However, it is the net assets in the consolidated financial statements that are relevant, not those in the subsidiary's, joint venture's or associate's own financial statements, which may be different if the parent acquired the subsidiary.

Testing assets for impairment is described in Chapter 20. There are particular problems to consider in trying to assess the investments in subsidiaries, joint ventures and associates for impairment. These are discussed in Chapter 20 at 8.1.

2.4.1.C Returns of capital

Returns of share capital are not usually considered to be dividends and hence they are not directly addressed by IAS 27. They are an example of a 'distribution', the broader term applied when an entity gives away its assets to its members.

At first glance, a return of capital appears to be an obvious example of something that ought to reduce the carrying value of the investment in the parent. We do not think that is necessarily the case. Returns of capital cannot easily be distinguished from dividends. For example, depending on local law, entities may be able to:

- make repayments that directly reduce their share capital; or
- create reserves by transferring amounts from share capital into retained earnings and, at the same time or later, pay dividends from that reserve.

Returns of capital can be accounted for in the same way as dividends, i.e. by applying the impairment testing process described above. However, the effect on an entity that makes an investment (whether on initial acquisition of a subsidiary or on a subsequent injection of capital) and immediately receives it back (whether as a dividend or return of capital) generally will be of a return of capital that reduces the carrying value of the parent's investment. In these circumstances there will be an impairment that is equal to the dividend that has been received (provided that the consideration paid as investment was at fair value). If there is a delay between the investment and the dividend or return of capital then the impairment (if any) will be a matter of judgement based on the criteria discussed above.

2.4.2 Distributions of non-cash assets to owners (IFRIC 17)

Entities sometimes make distributions of assets other than cash, e.g. items of property, plant and equipment, businesses as defined in IFRS 3, ownership interests in another entity or disposal groups as defined in IFRS 5. IFRIC 17 has the effect that gains or losses relating to some non-cash distributions to shareholders will be accounted for in profit or loss. The Interpretation addresses only the accounting by the entity that makes a non-cash asset distribution, not the accounting by recipients.

2.4.2.A Scope

IFRIC 17 applies to any distribution of a non-cash asset, including one that gives the shareholder a choice of receiving either non-cash assets or a cash alternative if it is within scope. *[IFRIC 17.3]*.

The Interpretations Committee did not want the Interpretation to apply to exchange transactions with shareholders, *[IFRIC 17.BC5]*, which can include an element of distribution, e.g. a sale to one of the shareholders of an asset having a fair value that is higher than the sales price. Therefore, it applies only to non-reciprocal distributions in which all owners of the same class of equity instruments are treated equally. *[IFRIC 17.4]*.

The Interpretation does not apply to distributions if the assets are ultimately controlled by the same party or parties before and after the distribution, whether in the separate, individual and consolidated financial statements of an entity that makes the distribution. *[IFRIC 17.5]*. This means that it will not apply to distributions made by subsidiaries but only to distributions made by parent entities or individual entities that are not themselves parents. In order to avoid ambiguity regarding 'common control' and to ensure that demergers achieved by way of distribution are dealt with, the Interpretation emphasises that 'common control' is used in the same sense as in IFRS 3. A distribution to a group of individual shareholders will only be out of scope if those shareholders have ultimate collective power over the entity making the distribution as a result of contractual arrangements. *[IFRIC 17.6]*.

If the non-cash asset distributed is an interest in a subsidiary over which the entity retains control, this is accounted for by recognising a non-controlling interest in the subsidiary in equity in the consolidated financial statements of the entity, as required by IFRS 10 paragraph 23 (see Chapter 7 at 4). *[IFRIC 17.7]*.

2.4.2.B Recognition, measurement and presentation

A dividend is not a liability until the entity is obliged to pay it to the shareholders. *[IFRIC 17.10]*. The obligation arises when payment is no longer at the discretion of the entity, which will depend on the requirements of local law. In some jurisdictions, the UK for example, shareholder approval is required before there is a liability to pay. In other jurisdictions, declaration by management or the board of directors may suffice.

The liability is measured at the fair value of the assets to be distributed. *[IFRIC 17.11]*. If an entity gives its owners a choice of receiving either a non-cash asset or a cash alternative, the entity estimates the dividend payable by considering both the fair value of each alternative and the associated probability of owners selecting each alternative. *[IFRIC 17.12]*. IFRIC 17 does not specify any method of assessing probability nor its effect on measurement.

IFRS 5's requirements apply also to a non-current asset (or disposal group) that is classified as held for distribution to owners acting in their capacity as owners (held for distribution to owners). *[IFRS 5.5A, 12A, 15A]*. This means that assets or asset groups within scope of IFRS 5 will be carried at the lower of carrying amount and fair value less costs to distribute. *[IFRS 5.15A]*. Assets not subject to measurement provisions of IFRS 5 are measured in accordance with the relevant standard. In practice, most non-cash distributions of assets out of scope of the measurement provisions of IFRS 5 will be of assets held at fair value in accordance with the relevant standard, e.g. financial instruments and investment property carried at fair value. *[IFRS 5.5]*. Accordingly there should be little difference, if any, between their carrying value and the amount of the distribution.

The liability is adjusted as at the end of any reporting period at which it remains outstanding and at the date of settlement with any adjustment being taken to equity. *[IFRIC 17.13]*. When the liability is settled, the difference, if any, between its carrying amount and the carrying amount of the assets distributed is accounted for as a separate line item in profit or loss. *[IFRIC 17.14-15]*. IFRIC 17 does not express any preference for particular line items or captions in the income statement.

It is rare for entities to distribute physical assets such as property, plant and equipment to shareholders, although these distributions are common within groups and hence out of scope of IFRIC 17. In practice, the Interpretation will have most effect on demergers by way of distribution, as illustrated in the following example.

Example 8.5: Non-cash asset distributed to shareholders

Conglomerate Plc has two divisions, electronics and music, each of which is in a separate subsidiary. On 18 December 2017 the shareholders approve a non-cash dividend in the form of the electronics division, which means that the dividend is a liability when the annual financial statements are prepared as at 31 December 2017. The distribution is to be made on 17 January 2018.

In Conglomerate Plc's separate financial statements at 18 December and 31 December, the investment in Electronics Ltd, which holds the electronics division, is carried at €100 million; the division has consolidated net assets of €210 million. The fair value of the electronics division at 18 December and 31 December is €375 million, so is the amount at which the liability to pay the dividend is recorded in Conglomerate Plc's separate financial statements and in its consolidated financial statements, as follows:

Conglomerate Plc

Separate financial statements			*Consolidated financial statements*		
	€	€		€	€
Dr equity	375		Dr equity	375	
Cr liability		375	Cr liability		375

In Conglomerate's separate financial statements its investment in Electronics Ltd of €100 million is classified as held for distribution to owners. In the consolidated financial statements, the net assets of €210 million are so classified.

If the value of Electronics Ltd had declined between the date of declaration of the dividend and the period end, say to €360 million (more likely if there had been a longer period between declaration and the period end) then the decline would be reflected in equity and the liability recorded at €360 million. Exactly the same entry would be made if the value were €375 million at the period end and €360 million on the date of settlement (Dr liability €15 million, Cr equity €15 million).

The dividend is paid on 17 January 2018 at which point the fair value of the division is €360 million. There was no change in the carrying value of the investment in the separate financial statements and of the net assets in the consolidated financial statements between 31 December and distribution date. The difference between the assets distributed and the liability is recognised as a gain in profit or loss.

Conglomerate Plc

Separate financial statements			*Consolidated financial statements*		
	€	€		€	€
Dr liability	360		Dr liability	360	
Cr profit or loss		260	Cr profit or loss		150
Cr asset held for sale		100	Cr disposal group		210

The entity must disclose, if applicable:

(a) the carrying amount of the dividend payable at the beginning and end of the period: and

(b) the increase or decrease in the carrying amount recognised in the period as a result of a change in the fair value of the assets to be distributed. *[IFRIC 17.16]*.

If an entity declares a dividend that will take the form of a non-cash asset after the end of a reporting period but before the financial statements are authorised the following disclosure should be made:

(a) the nature of the asset to be distributed;

(b) the carrying amount of the asset to be distributed as of the end of the reporting period; and

(c) the estimated fair value of the asset to be distributed as of the end of the reporting period, if it is different from its carrying amount, and the information about the method used to determine that fair value required by IFRS 13 – paragraphs 93(b), (d), (g) and (i) and 99 (see Chapter 14 at 20.3). *[IFRIC 17.17]*.

3 DISCLOSURE

An entity applies all applicable IFRSs when providing disclosures in the separate financial statements. *[IAS 27.15]*. In addition there are a number of specific disclosure requirements in IAS 27 which are discussed below.

3.1 Separate financial statements prepared by parent electing not to prepare consolidated financial statements

When separate financial statements are prepared for a parent that, in accordance with the exemption discussed at 1.1 above, elects not to prepare consolidated financial statements, those separate financial statements are to disclose: *[IAS 27.16]*.

(a) the fact that the financial statements are separate financial statements; that the exemption from consolidation has been used; and the name and the principal place of business (and country of incorporation, if different) of the entity whose consolidated financial statements that comply with IFRS have been produced for public use and the address where those consolidated financial statements are obtainable;

(b) a list of significant investments in subsidiaries, joint ventures and associates, including:

    (i) the name of those investees;

    (ii) the principal place of business (and country of incorporation, if different) of those investees; and

    (iii) its proportion of the ownership interest and, if different, proportion of voting rights held in those investees; and

(c) a description of the method used to account for the investments listed under (b).

These disclosure requirements are illustrated in the extract below.

Extract 8.2: Ageas Insurance Limited (2010)

Significant accounting policies [extract]

(b) Basis of preparation [extract]

The Company has elected not to prepare consolidated financial statements. The accounts as prepared are separate financial statements and the exemption from consolidation, in accordance with IAS 27 Consolidated and Separate Financial Statements, has been used.

(l) Investments in subsidiaries

Investments in group undertakings are stated at the lower of cost or net realisable value. Details of transactions with group companies are included in note 28, Related Party Transactions.

14 Investment in subsidiaries

	2010 £m	2009 £m
Investments in subsidiaries are stated at cost		
At 1 January and 31 December	0.4	0.4

The following companies, which are incorporated in the United Kingdom, were subsidiaries at 31 December 2010 and 31 December 2009.

Company	Activity	% Owned
Ageas Services (UK) Ltd (formerly Fortis Services (UK) Ltd)	Administrative services	100
Bishopsgate Head Office Ltd	Property holding	100

30 Parent company

The Company's results are consolidated into the accounts of Ageas Insurance International N.V. (formerly Fortis Insurance International N.V.), a company incorporated in The Netherlands.

The joint ultimate holding companies of the Company are Ageas N.V. (formerly Fortis N.V.), incorporated in The Netherlands, and Ageas SA/NV (formerly Fortis SA/NV), incorporated in Belgium.

Copies of the above accounts can be obtained from the Company Secretary, Ageas Insurance Limited, Ageas House, Tollgate, Eastleigh, Hants SO53 3YA.

In addition to disclosures required by IAS 27, an entity also has to disclose in its separate financial statements qualitative and quantitative information about its interests in unconsolidated structured entities as required by IFRS 12. IFRS 12 does not generally apply to an entity's separate financial statements to which IAS 27 applies but if it has interests in unconsolidated structured entities and prepares separate financial statements as its only financial statements, it must apply the requirements in paragraphs 24 to 31 of IFRS 12 when preparing those separate financial statements (see Chapter 13 at 6). *[IFRS 12.6(b)].*

The disclosures in IFRS 12 are given only where the parent has taken advantage of the exemption from preparing consolidated financial statements. Where the parent has not taken advantage of the exemption, and also prepares separate financial statements, it gives the disclosures at 3.3 below in respect of those separate financial statements.

3.2 Separate financial statements prepared by an investment entity

When an investment entity that is a parent (other than a parent electing not to prepare consolidated financial statements) prepares separate financial statements as its only financial statements, it discloses that fact. The investment entity also presents disclosures relating to investment entities required by IFRS 12. *[IAS 27.16A]*. See Chapter 13 at 4.6.

3.3 Separate financial statements prepared by an entity other than a parent electing not to prepare consolidated financial statements

As drafted, IAS 27 requires the disclosures at (a), (b) and (c) below to be given by:

- a parent preparing separate financial statements in addition to consolidated financial statements (i.e. whether or not it is required to prepare consolidated financial statements – the disclosures in 3.1 above apply only when the parent has actually taken advantage of the exemption, not merely when it is eligible to do so); and
- an entity (not being a parent) that is an investor in an associate or in a joint venture in respect of any separate financial statements that it prepares, i.e. whether:
  - (i) as its only financial statements (if permitted by IAS 28), or
  - (ii) in addition to financial statements in which the results and net assets of associates or joint ventures are included.

The relevance of certain of these disclosures to financial statements falling within (i) above is not immediately obvious (see 3.3.1 below).

Where an entity is both a parent and either an investor in an associate or in a joint venture, it should follow the disclosure requirements governing parents – in other words, it complies with the disclosures in 3.1 above if electing not to prepare consolidated financial statements and otherwise with the disclosures below.

Separate financial statements prepared by an entity other than a parent electing not to prepare consolidated financial statements must disclose: *[IAS 27.17]*.

(a) the fact that the statements are separate financial statements and the reasons why those statements are prepared if not required by law;

(b) a list of significant investments in subsidiaries, joint ventures and associates, including for each such investment its:
   - (i) name;
   - (ii) principal place of business (and country of incorporation, if different); and
   - (iii) proportion of ownership interest and, if different, proportion of voting power held; and

(c) a description of the method used to account for the investments listed under (b).

The separate financial statements must also identify the financial statements prepared in accordance with the requirements of IFRS 10 (requirement to prepare consolidated financial statements), IFRS 11 and IAS 28 to which they relate. *[IAS 27.17]*. In other words, they must draw attention to the fact that the entity also prepares consolidated financial statements or, as the case may be, financial statements in which the associates or joint ventures are accounted for using the equity method.

The implication of this disclosure requirement is that an entity which publishes both separate and consolidated financial statements under IFRS cannot issue the separate financial statements before the consolidated financial statements have been prepared and approved, since there would not be, at the date of issue of the separate financial statements, any consolidated financial statements 'to which they relate'. This is discussed at 1.1.3 above.

If the parent has issued consolidated financial statements prepared not in accordance with IFRS but with its local GAAP, the parent cannot make reference to the financial statements prepared in accordance with IFRS 10, IFRS 11 or IAS 28, therefore the separate financial statements cannot be considered in compliance with IAS 27.

3.3.1 Entities with no subsidiaries but exempt from applying IAS 28

Entities which have no subsidiaries, but which have investments in associates or joint ventures are permitted by IAS 28 to prepare separate financial statements as their only financial statements if they satisfy the conditions described at 1.1.1 above.

IAS 27 requires such entities to make the disclosures in (a) to (c) above in 3.3. In addition, the entity is supposed to identify the financial statements prepared in accordance with IAS 28, *[IAS 27.17]*, but in this situation, there are no such financial statements.

4 COMMON CONTROL OR GROUP TRANSACTIONS IN INDIVIDUAL FINANCIAL STATEMENTS

4.1 Introduction

Transactions often take place between a parent entity and its subsidiaries or between subsidiaries within a group that may or may not be carried out at fair value.

Whilst such transactions do not affect the consolidated financial statements of the parent as they are eliminated in the course of consolidation, they can have a significant impact on the separate financial statements of the parent and/or subsidiaries and/or a set of consolidated financial statements prepared for a sub-group. IAS 24 requires only that these transactions are disclosed and provides no accounting requirements.

The IASB generally considers that the needs of users of financial statements are fully met by requiring entities to consolidate subsidiaries, equity account for associates and joint ventures. Accounting issues within individual financial statements are not a priority and are usually only addressed when a standard affects consolidated and individual statements in different ways, e.g. accounting for pensions or employee benefits.

We consider that it is helpful to set out some general principles in accounting for these transactions that enhances the consistency of application of IFRS whether for the separate financial statements of a parent, the individual financial statements of an entity that is not a parent or the consolidated financial statements of a sub-group.

Within this section whenever the individual financial statements are discussed it encompasses also separate financial statements except for the legal merger discussion at 4.4.3.B below that differentiates between the parent's separate financial statements and the individual financial statements of the parent that merges with its only subsidiary.

The considerations provided in this section in certain circumstances apply also to sub-parent consolidated financial statements in relation to common control transactions with entities controlled by the ultimate parent or ultimate controlling party or parties, but that are outside the sub-parent group.

We have considered how to apply these principles to certain common types of arrangement between entities under common control, which are described in more detail at 4.4 below:

- sales, exchanges and contributions of non-monetary assets including sales and exchanges of investments not within the scope of IFRS 9 (or IAS 39), i.e. investments in subsidiaries, associates or joint ventures (see 4.4.1 below);
- transfers of businesses, including contributions and distribution of businesses (see 4.4.2 and 4.4.3 below);
- incurring costs and settling liabilities without recharge (see 4.4.4 below).
- loans that bear interest at non-market rates or are interest free (see 4.4.5.A below); and
- financial guarantee contracts given by a parent over a subsidiary's borrowings in the financial statements of a subsidiary (see 4.4.5.B below).

Other arrangements that are subject to specific requirements in particular standards are dealt with in the relevant chapters. These include:

- financial guarantee contracts over a subsidiary's borrowings in the accounts of the parent (see Chapter 43 at 3.4);
- share-based payment plans of a parent (see Chapter 32 at 12); and
- employee benefits (see Chapter 33 at 3.3.2).

In determining how to account for transactions between entities under common control, we believe that the following two aspects need to be considered:

(a) Is the transaction at fair value? Is the price in the transaction the one that would be received to sell an asset or paid to transfer a liability in an orderly transaction between market participants? It is necessary to consider whether the transaction is of a type that market participants could or would enter into. It is also important to remember that an arm's length transaction includes the repayment terms that would be expected of independent parties and this might not be the case in intra-group transactions.

(b) Is it a contractual arrangement and, if so, is the entity whose financial statements are being considered a party to the contract?

If the transaction is at fair value and the entity is a party to the contract, we believe that it should be accounted for in accordance with the terms of the contract and general requirements of IFRS related to this type of transaction.

The principles for accounting for transactions between group entities that are not transacted at fair value are presented in the following flowchart. Detailed comments of the principles are provided further in 4.2 and 4.3 below.

Group entities represent entities under common control of the same parent or the same controlling party or parties. The flowchart therefore does not apply to transactions of group entities with joint ventures or associates of any of the group entities.

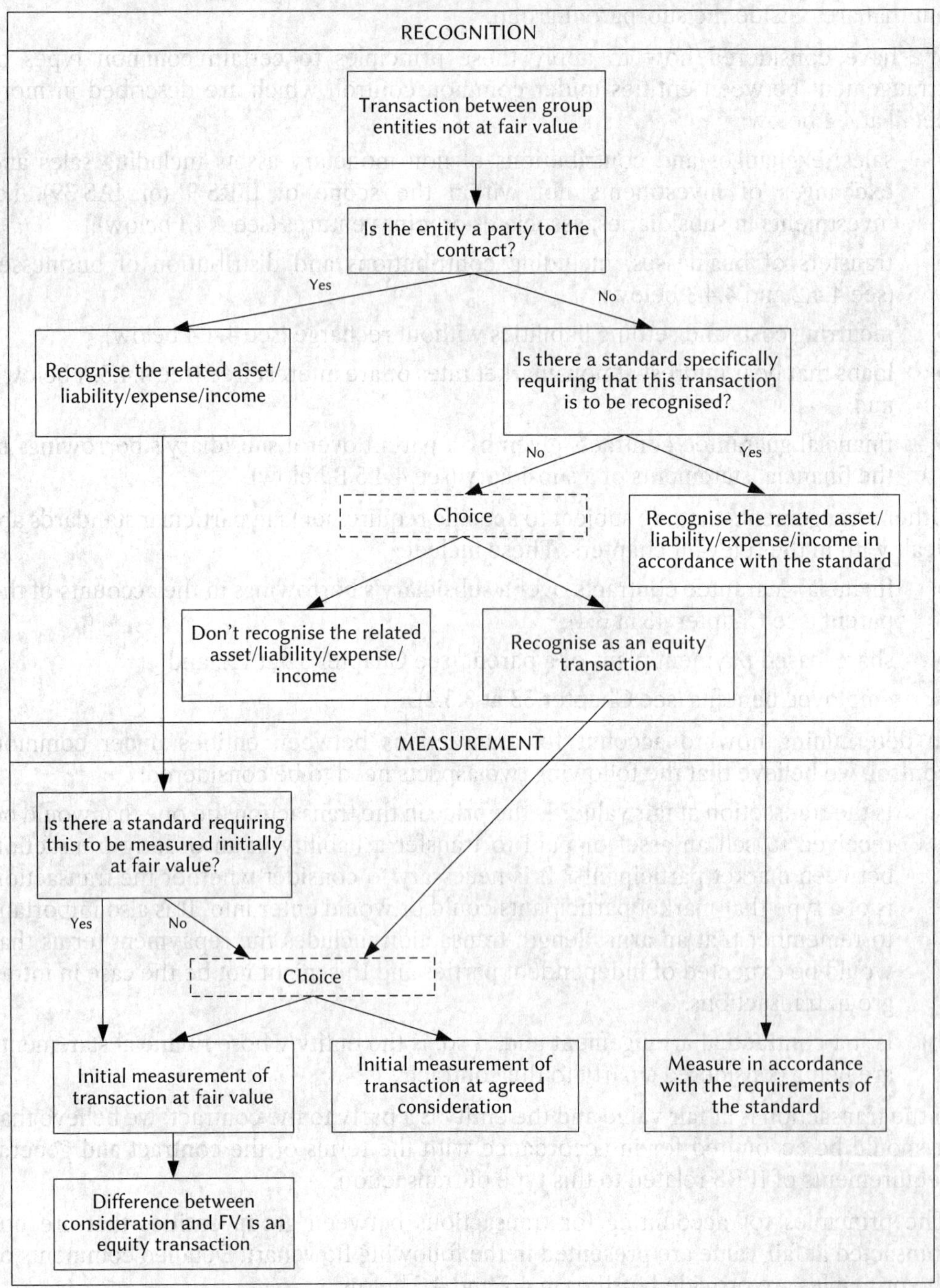

If there is more than one acceptable way of accounting for specific transactions and therefore a choice of accounting policies, the entity should apply its chosen policy consistently to similar arrangements and disclose it if it is material. However, not all group entities need adopt the same accounting policy in their individual financial statements or sub-group consolidated financial statements. Nor is there a requirement for symmetrical accounting by the entities involved in the transaction.

4.2 Recognition

If an entity is a party to a contract under which it receives a right and incurs an obligation, then on the assumption that there is substance to the transaction, it will be recognised in the financial statements of the entity.

An entity may receive a right without incurring an obligation or *vice versa* without being a party to a contract. There are many different types of arrangement that contain this feature, either in whole or in part:

- Some arrangements are not contractual at all, such as capital contributions and distributions, that are in substance gifts made without consideration.
- Some standards require transactions to which the entity is not a party to be reflected in their financial statements. In effect, the accounting treatment is representing that the subsidiary has received a capital contribution from the parent, which the subsidiary has then spent on employee remuneration or *vice versa*. IFRS 2 has such requirements (see Chapter 32 at 12).
- Some are contractual arrangements for the other party, e.g. a parent enters into a contract to engage an auditor for the subsidiary, and pays the audit fees without any recharge.

If an entity is not a party to a contractual relationship and there is no IFRS requiring recognition then the entity may choose not to recognise the transaction at all.

If it chooses to recognise the transaction then recognition will depend on whether the entity is a parent or a subsidiary, as well as the specific nature of the transaction. In some circumstances a parent may treat a debit as either an addition to its investment in its subsidiary or as an expense and a credit as a gain to profit or loss. It is not generally possible for the parent to recognise gains in equity as these are usually transactions with subsidiaries, not shareholders. A subsidiary can only treat the transaction as a credit or debit to income (income or expense) or a debit to asset or credit to liability and an equal and opposite debit or credit to equity (distribution of or contribution to equity).

One example where a subsidiary is required by an IFRS to record an expense when it is not a party to a contractual arrangement is a share-based payment. If the employees of a subsidiary are granted options by the parent company over its shares in exchange for services to the subsidiary, the subsidiary must record a cost for that award within its own financial statements, even though it may not legally be a party to it. The parent must also record the share-based payment as an addition to the investment in the subsidiary (see Chapter 32 at 12.2.4).

Although the entity not party to the contract might have a choice to either record the transaction or not, the other entity within the group that might have entered into the contract on behalf of the entity is required to recognise the transaction. Where a group entity is incurring expenses on behalf of another entity this group entity might be able to capitalise the expenses as part of the cost of the investment (e.g. a parent is incurring expenses of the subsidiary without recharging them), treat them as a distribution (e.g. a sister company is incurring expenses of the entity without recharging them) or to expense them.

The principles apply equally to transactions between a parent and its subsidiaries and those between subsidiaries in a group. If the transaction is between two subsidiaries, and both of the entities are either required or choose to recognise an equity element in the transaction, one subsidiary recognises a capital contribution from the parent, while the other subsidiary recognises a distribution to the parent. The parent may choose whether or not to recognise the equity transfer in its stand-alone financial statements.

4.3 Measurement

If a standard requires the transaction to be recognised initially at fair value, it must be measured at that fair value regardless of the actual consideration. A difference between the fair value and the consideration may mean that other goods or services are being provided, e.g. the transaction includes a management fee. This will be accounted for separately on one of the bases described below. If there is still a difference having taken account of all goods or services, it is accounted for as an equity transaction, i.e. as either a contribution to or distribution of equity.

In all other cases, where there is a difference between the fair value and the consideration after having taken account of all goods or services being provided, there is a choice available to the entity to:

(a) recognise the transaction at fair value, irrespective of the actual consideration; any difference between fair value and agreed consideration will be a contribution to or a distribution of equity for a subsidiary, or an increase in the investment held or a distribution received by the parent; or

(b) recognise the transaction at the actual consideration stated in any agreement related to the transaction.

Except for accounting for the acquisition of businesses where the pooling of interest method can be considered (see 4.4.2 below), the transfer of businesses between a parent and its subsidiary (see 4.4.3 below), and the acquisition of an investment in a subsidiary constituting a business that is acquired in a share-for-share exchange (see 2.1.1.B above), there is no other basis for the measurement of the transactions between entities under common control other than those stated in (a) and (b) above. Therefore, predecessor values accounting (accounting based on the carrying amounts of the transferor) cannot be applied.

4.3.1 Fair value in intra-group transactions

The requirements for fair value measurement included in IFRS 13 should be applied to common control transactions. However, fair value can be difficult to establish in intra-group transactions.

If there is more than one element to the transaction, this means in principle identifying all of the goods and services being provided and accounting for each element at fair value. This is not necessarily straightforward: a bundle of goods and services in an arm's length arrangement will usually be priced at a discount to the price of each of the elements acquired separately and this is reflected in the fair value attributed to the transaction. It can be much harder to allocate fair values in intra-group arrangements where the transaction may not have a commercial equivalent.

As we have already noted, the transaction may be based on the fair value of an asset but the payment terms are not comparable to those in a transaction between independent parties. The purchase price often remains outstanding on intercompany account, whereas commercial arrangements always include agreed payment terms. Interest-free loans are common between group companies; these loans may have no formal settlement terms and, while this makes them technically repayable on demand, they too may remain outstanding for prolonged periods.

As a result, there can be a certain amount of estimation when applying fair values to group arrangements.

Some IFRSs are based on the assumption that one entity may not have the information available to the other party in a transaction, for example:

- a lessee may not know the lessor's internal rate of return, in which case IAS 17 – *Leases* – allows it to substitute its own incremental borrowing rate (see Chapter 24 at 3.4.5); and
- in exchanges of assets, IAS 16 and IAS 38 note that one party may not have information about the fair value of the asset it is receiving, the fair value of the asset it is giving up or it may be able to determine one of these values more easily than the other (see Chapter 18 at 4.4 and 4.4.1.B below).

In an intra-group transaction it will be difficult to assume that one group company knows the fair value of the transaction but the other does not. The approximations allowed by these standards will probably not apply.

However, if a subsidiary is not wholly owned, such transactions are undertaken generally on arm's length terms as non-controlling shareholders are impacted. Therefore, in a situation where such a transaction is not done on arm's length terms the reasons for and implications of the transaction must be assessed and carefully analysed.

4.4 Application of the principles in practice

The following sections deal with common transactions that occur between entities under common control. While the scenarios depict transactions between a parent and its subsidiaries they apply similarly to transactions between subsidiaries. Most of the examples in these sections deal with transactions having a non-arm's length element. As for any other transactions undertaken at fair value (at arm's length), respective IFRSs that are applicable have to be taken into account.

Deferred tax has been ignored for the purposes of the examples.

4.4.1 Transactions involving non-monetary assets

The same principles apply when the asset that is acquired for a consideration different to its fair value is inventory (IAS 2 – *Inventories* – Chapter 22), property, plant and equipment ('PP&E') (IAS 16 – Chapter 18), an intangible asset (IAS 38 Chapter 17) or investment property (IAS 40 – Chapter 19). These standards require assets to be initially recognised at cost.

The same principles generally also apply to the acquisition of an investment in a subsidiary, an associate or joint venture when the purchase consideration does not reflect the fair value of the investment, and such investments are accounted for initially at cost in the separate financial statements as discussed at 2.1 above. Investments acquired in common control transactions are discussed at 2.1.1.B above.

4.4.1.A *Sale of PP&E from the parent to the subsidiary for an amount of cash not representative of the fair value of the asset.*

The parent and subsidiary are both parties to the transaction and both must recognise it. As the asset is recognised by the acquiring entity at cost, and not necessarily at fair value, a choice exists as to how the cost is determined. Does the consideration comprise two elements, cash and equity, or cash alone?

In some jurisdictions, some entities are legally required to conduct such transactions at fair value.

Example 8.6: Sale of PP&E at an undervalue

A parent entity sells PP&E that has a carrying amount of 50 and a fair value of 100 to its subsidiary for cash of 80.

Method (a)			*Method (b)*		
Recognise the transaction at fair value, regardless of the values in any agreement, with any difference between that amount and fair value recognised as an equity transaction. (Note 1)			Recognise the transaction at the consideration agreed between the parties, being the amount of cash paid.		
Subsidiary					
	€	€		€	€
Dr PP&E	100		Dr PP&E	80	
Cr Cash		80	Cr Cash		80
Cr Equity		20			
Parent					
	€	€		€	€
Dr Cash	80		Dr Cash	80	
Dr Investment	20		Cr PP&E		50
Cr PP&E		50	Cr Gain (profit or loss)		30
Cr Gain (profit or loss)		50			

Note 1 This may only be applied where fair value can be measured reliably

However, what if the asset is sold for more than fair value? What are the implications if, in the above example, the PP&E sold for 80 has a carrying value of 80 but its fair value is 75? There are a number of explanations that may affect the way in which the transaction is accounted for:

- The excess reflects additional services or goods included in the transaction, e.g. future maintenance that will be accounted for separately.
- The excess reflects the fact that the asset's value in use ('VIU') is at least 80. It is very common for PP&E to be carried at an amount in excess of fair value because its VIU, or the VIU of the cash-generating unit of which it is a part, is unaffected by falls in fair value. Plant and machinery often has a low resale value; vehicles lose much of their fair value soon after purchase; and falls in property values may not affect the VIU of the head office of a profitable entity (see Chapter 20). In such cases there is no reason why the subsidiary cannot record the asset it has acquired for the cash it has paid, which means that it effectively inherits the transferor's carrying value. An impairment test potentially would not reveal any requirement to write down the asset, assuming of course that other factors do not reduce the asset's VIU (e.g. the fact that the asset will after the sale be part of a different cash generating unit).
- The excess over fair value is a distribution by the subsidiary to the parent that will be accounted for in equity. This treatment is a legal requirement in some jurisdictions, which means that the overpayment must meet the legal requirements for dividends, principally that there be sufficient distributable profits to meet the cost.
- The asset is impaired before transfer, i.e. both its fair value and VIU are lower than its carrying amount, in which case it must be written down by the transferor before the exchange takes place. If it is still sold for more than its fair value, the excess will be accounted for as a distribution received (by the parent) and a distribution made by the subsidiary (as above).

4.4.1.B *The parent exchanges PP&E for a non-monetary asset of the subsidiary.*

The parent and subsidiary are both parties to the transaction and both must recognise it. The exchange of an asset for another non-monetary asset is accounted for by recognising the received asset at fair value, unless the transaction lacks commercial substance (as defined by IAS 16) or the fair value of neither of the exchanged assets can be measured reliably. *[IAS 16.24]*. The requirements of IAS 16 are explained in Chapter 18 at 4.4; the treatment required by IAS 38 and IAS 40 is the same.

The mere fact that an exchange transaction takes place between entities under common control does not of itself indicate that the transaction lacks commercial substance. However, in an exchange transaction between unrelated parties the fair value of the assets is usually the same but this does not necessarily hold true of transactions between entities under common control.

If the fair value of both assets can be measured reliably there may be a difference between the two. IAS 16 suggests that, if an entity is able to determine reliably the fair value of either the asset received or the asset given up, then the fair value of the asset given up is used to measure the cost of the asset received. *[IAS 16.26]*. However, IAS 16 actually requires an entity to base its accounting for the exchange on the asset whose fair value is most clearly evident. *[IAS 16.26]*. If fair values are different it is possible that the group entities have entered into a non-reciprocal transaction. This means that the entity has the policy choice described at 4.3 above, which in this case means that there are three alternative treatments; it can recognise the transaction as follows:

- Method (a) – an exchange of assets at fair value of the asset received with an equity transaction. Any difference between the fair value of the asset received and the fair value of the asset given up is an equity transaction, while the difference between the carrying value of the asset given up and its fair value is recognised in profit or loss;
- Method (b) – an exchange of assets at fair value of the asset received without recognising an equity element. The asset received is recognised at its fair value with any resulting difference to the carrying value of the asset given up is recognised in profit or loss; or
- Method (c) – apply a 'cost' method based on IAS 16 (the fair value of the asset given up is used to measure the cost of the asset received) under which each entity records the asset at the fair value of the asset it has given up. This could result in one of the parties recording the asset it had received at an amount in excess of its fair value, in which case it may be an indicator for impairment of the asset. It would be consistent with the principles outlined at 4.3 above to treat the write down as an equity transaction, i.e. an addition to the carrying value of the subsidiary by the parent and a distribution by the subsidiary.

Example 8.7: Exchange of assets with dissimilar values

A parent entity transfers an item of PP&E to its subsidiary in exchange for an item of PP&E of the subsidiary, with the following values:

Subsidiary			*Parent*		
	€	€		€	€
Carrying Value		20	Carrying Value		50
Fair Value		80	Fair Value		100

The fair value of both assets can be measured reliably.

The accounting for the transaction by the parent and the subsidiary under each of the methods is as follows:

Method (a)

Subsidiary			*Parent*		
	€	€		€	€
Dr PP&E	100		Dr PP&E	80	
Cr PP&E		20	Dr Investment	20	
Cr Gain (profit or loss)		60	Cr PP&E		50
Cr Equity		20	Cr Gain (profit or loss)		50

Method (b)

Subsidiary			*Parent*		
	€	€		€	€
Dr PP&E	100		Dr PP&E	80	
Cr PP&E		20	Cr PP&E		50
Cr Gain (profit or loss)		80	Cr Gain (profit or loss)		30

Method (c)

Subsidiary			*Parent*		
	€	€		€	€
Dr PP&E	80		Dr PP&E (100 – 20)	80	
Cr PP&E		20	Dr Investment	20	
Cr Gain (profit or loss)		60	Cr PP&E		50
			Cr Gain (profit or loss)		50

If the fair value of only one of the exchanged assets can be measured reliably, IAS 16 allows both parties to recognise the asset they have received at the fair value of the asset that can be measured reliably. *[IAS 16.26].* Underlying this requirement is a presumption that the fair value of both assets is the same, but one cannot assume this about common control transactions.

If the fair value of neither of the exchanged assets can be measured reliably, or the transaction does not have commercial substance, both the parent and subsidiary recognise the received asset at the carrying amount of the asset they have given up.

4.4.1.C Acquisition and sale of assets for shares

These transactions include the transfer of inventory, property plant and equipment, intangible assets, investment property and investments in subsidiaries, associates and joint ventures by one entity in return for shares of the other entity. These transactions are usually between a parent and subsidiary where the subsidiary is the transferee that issues shares to the parent in exchange for the assets received.

(a) Accounting treatment by the subsidiary

Transactions that include the transfer of inventory, property plant and equipment, intangible assets, and investment property are within the scope of IFRS 2, as goods have been received in exchange for shares. The assets are recognised at fair value, unless the fair value cannot be estimated reliably, and an increase in equity of the same amount is recognised. If the fair value of the assets cannot be estimated reliably, the fair value of the shares is used instead. *[IFRS 2.10].*

Transactions in which an investment in a subsidiary, associate or joint venture is acquired in exchange for shares is not specifically addressed under IFRS, since it falls outside the scope of both IFRS 9 (or IAS 39) and IFRS 2. However, we believe that it would be appropriate, by analogy with IFRS on related areas (like IFRS 3), to account for such a transaction at the fair value of the consideration given (being fair value of equity instruments issued) or the assets received, if that is more easily measured, together with directly attributable transaction costs. As discussed at 2.1.1.B above, when the purchase consideration does not correspond to the fair value of the investment acquired, in our view, the acquirer has an accounting policy choice to account for the investment at fair value of the consideration given or may impute an equity contribution or dividend distribution and in effect account for the investment at its fair value. Alternatively, if the investment in a subsidiary constitutes a business and is acquired in a share-for-share exchange, it is also acceptable to measure the cost based on the original carrying amount of the investment in the subsidiary in the transferor entity's separate financial statements, rather than at the fair value of the shares given as consideration.

(b) Accounting treatment by the parent

The parent has disposed of an asset in exchange for an increased investment in a subsidiary. Based on what has been said at 2.1.1 above, the cost of investment should be recorded at the fair value of the consideration given i.e. the fair value of the asset sold. Such a transaction has also the nature of an exchange of assets and by analogy to paragraph 24 of IAS 16, the investment should be measured at fair value unless the exchange transaction lacks commercial substance or the fair value of neither the investment received nor the asset given up is reliably measurable. If the investment cannot be measured at fair value, it is measured at the carrying value of the asset given up. *[IAS 16.24]*.

The asset's fair value may be lower than its carrying value but it is not impaired unless its VIU is insufficient to support that carrying value (see 4.4.1.A above). If there is no impairment, the parent is not prevented from treating the carrying value of the asset as an addition to the investment in the subsidiary solely because the fair value is lower. If the asset is impaired then this should be recognised before reclassification, unless the reorganisation affects, and increases, the VIU.

If the fair value is higher than the carrying value and the investment is accounted for at fair value as discussed above, the transferring entity recognises a gain. In certain circumstances it might not be appropriate to account for the transaction at fair value due to lack of commercial substance. For example, exchanging the asset for an investment in the shares of a subsidiary that holds nothing but the asset given as consideration may not give rise to a gain on transfer.

4.4.1.D Contribution and distribution of assets

These transactions include transfers of inventory, property plant and equipment, intangible assets, investment property and investments in subsidiaries, associates and joint ventures from one entity to another for no consideration. These arrangements are not contractual but are equity transactions: either specie capital contributions (an asset is gifted by a parent to a subsidiary) or non-cash distributions (an asset is given by a subsidiary to its parent). IFRIC 17 explicitly excludes intra-group non-cash distributions from its scope (see 2.4.2 above). *[IFRIC 17.5]*.

The relevant standards (IAS 2, IAS 16, IAS 38 and IAS 40) refer to assets being recognised at cost. Similarly, investments in subsidiaries, associates and joint ventures may be recognised at cost under IAS 27 as discussed at 2.1 above. Following the principles described at 4.3 above, the entity receiving the asset has a choice: recognise it at zero or at fair value. It is in practice more common for an entity that has received an asset in what is purely an equity transaction to recognise it at fair value.

The entity that gives away the asset must reflect the transaction. A parent that makes a specie capital contribution to its subsidiary will recognise an increased investment in that subsidiary (in principle at fair value, recognising a gain or loss based on the difference from the carrying amount of the asset) provided the increase does not result in the impairment of the investment, or an expense (based on the carrying amount of the asset given away). A subsidiary that makes a distribution in specie to its parent might account for the transaction by derecognising the distributed asset at its carrying value against retained earnings.

However, the subsidiary could also account for the distribution at fair value, if the fair value could be established reliably. This would potentially result in recognising a gain in profit or loss for the difference between the fair value of the asset and its carrying value. There would also be a charge to equity for the distribution, recognised and measured at the fair value of the asset. This is consistent with IFRIC 17, although the distribution is not in scope.

4.4.1.E Transfers between subsidiaries

As noted at 4.2 above, similar principles apply when the arrangement is between two subsidiaries rather than a subsidiary and parent. To illustrate this, assume that the transaction in Example 8.6 above takes place between two subsidiaries rather than parent and subsidiary.

Example 8.8: Transactions between subsidiaries

The facts are as in Example 8.6 above except that Subsidiary A sells PP&E that has a carrying amount of €50 and a fair value of €100 to its fellow-subsidiary B for cash of €80. As before, it is assumed that fair value can be measured reliably.

Method (a)	*Method (b)*
Recognise the transaction at fair value, regardless of the values in any agreement, with any difference between that amount and fair value recognised as an equity transaction.	Recognise the transaction at the consideration agreed between the parties, being the amount of cash paid.

Subsidiary A

	€	€		€	€
Dr Cash	80		Dr Cash	80	
Dr Equity (Note 1)	20		Cr PP&E		50
Cr PP&E		50	Cr Gain (profit or loss)		30
Cr Gain (profit or loss)		50			

Subsidiary B

	€	€		€	€
Dr PP&E	100		Dr PP&E	80	
Cr Cash		80	Cr Cash		80
Cr Equity (Note 1)		20			

Note 1 From subsidiary A's perspective there is an equity element to the transaction representing the difference between the fair value of the asset and the contractual consideration. This reflects the amount by which the transaction has reduced A's fair value and has been shown as a distribution by A to its parent. From subsidiary B's perspective, the equity element is a capital contribution from the parent.

Parent (Note 2)

	€	€	
Dr Investment in B	20		No entries made
Cr Investment in A		20	

Note 2 Parent can choose to reallocate the equity element of the transaction between its two subsidiaries so as to reflect the changes in value.

In some circumstances the transfer of an asset from one subsidiary to another may affect the value of the transferor's assets to such an extent as to be an indicator of impairment in respect of the parent's investment in its shares. This can happen if the parent acquired the subsidiary for an amount that includes goodwill and the assets generating part or all of that goodwill have been transferred to another subsidiary. As a result, the carrying value of the shares in the parent may exceed the fair value or VIU of the remaining assets. This is discussed further in Chapter 20 at 8.

4.4.2 Acquiring and selling businesses – transfers between subsidiaries

One group entity may sell, and another may purchase, the net assets of a business rather than the shares in the entity. The acquisition may be for cash or shares and both entities must record the transaction in their individual financial statements. There can also be transfers for no consideration. As this chapter only addresses transactions between entities under common control, any arrangement described in this section from the perspective of the transferee will be as common control transactions out of scope of IFRS 3. The common control exemption is discussed in Chapter 10 at 2.

If the arrangement is a business combination for the acquiring entity it will also not be within scope of IFRS 2. *[IFRS 2.5].*

The transferor needs to recognise the transfer of a business under common control. If the consideration received does not represent fair value of the business transferred or there is the transfer without any consideration, the principles described in 4.4.2.C below should be applied to decide whether any equity element is recognised.

4.4.2.A Has a business been acquired?

IFRS 3 defines a business as 'an integrated set of activities and assets that is capable of being conducted and managed for the purpose of providing a return in the form of dividends, lower costs or other economic benefits directly to investors or other owners, members or participants'. *[IFRS 3 Appendix A].* See Chapter 9 at 3.2 for descriptions of the features of a business.

4.4.2.B If a business has been acquired, how should it be accounted for?

As described in Chapter 10 at 3, we believe that until such time as the IASB finalises its conclusions under its project on common control transactions entities should apply either:

(a) the pooling of interest method; or

(b) the acquisition method (as in IFRS 3).

In our view, where the acquisition method of accounting is selected, the transaction must have substance from the perspective of the reporting entity. This is because the method results in a reassessment of the value of the net assets of one or more of the entities involved and/or the recognition of goodwill. Chapter 10 discusses the factors that will give substance to a transaction and although this is written primarily in the context of the acquisition of an entity by another entity, it applies equally to the acquisition of a business by an entity or a legal merger of two subsidiaries.

4.4.2.C Purchase and sale of a business for equity or cash not representative of the fair value of the business

The principles are no different to those described at 4.4.1.A above. The entity may:

- recognise the transaction at fair value, regardless of the values in any agreement, with any difference between that amount and fair value recognised as an equity transaction; or
- recognise the transaction at the consideration agreed between the parties, being the amount of cash paid or fair value of shares issued.

From the perspective of the acquirer of the business, the above choice matters only when the acquisition method is applied in accounting for the business acquired. Depending on which approach is applied, goodwill on the acquisition may be different (or there can even be a gain on bargain purchase recognised). This is discussed further in Chapter 10 at 3.2. When the pooling of interest method is applied, the difference between the consideration paid and carrying value of net assets received is always recognised in equity no matter whether the consideration agreed between the parties represents the fair value of the business. If no consideration is payable for the transfer of the business, this could affect the assessment as to whether the transaction has substance to enable the acquisition method to be applied.

From the perspective of the seller of the business, the choice will impact any gain or loss recognised on the disposal. Recognising the transaction on the basis of the consideration agreed will result in a gain or loss based on the difference between the consideration received and the carrying value of the business disposed. Recognising the transaction at fair value including an equity element imputed will result in the gain or loss being the difference between the fair value of the business and its carrying value. If no consideration is received for the transfer of the business, the transaction may be considered to be more in the nature of a distribution in specie, the accounting for which is discussed at 4.4.1.D above.

4.4.2.D If the net assets are not a business, how should the transactions be accounted for?

Even though one entity acquires the net assets of another, this is not necessarily a business combination. IFRS 3 rules out of scope acquisitions of assets or net assets that are not businesses, noting that:

> 'This IFRS does not apply to [...] the acquisition of an asset or a group of assets that does not constitute a *business*. In such cases the acquirer shall identify and recognise the individual identifiable assets acquired (including those assets that meet the definition of, and recognition criteria for, *intangible assets* in IAS 38 *Intangible Assets*) and liabilities assumed. The cost of the group shall be allocated to the individual identifiable assets and liabilities on the basis of their relative *fair values* at the date of purchase. Such a transaction or event does not give rise to goodwill.' *[IFRS 3.2(b)]*.

If the acquisition is not a business combination, it will be an acquisition of assets for cash or shares or for no consideration (see 4.4.1.A, 4.4.1.C and 4.4.1.D above).

4.4.3 Transfers of businesses between parent and subsidiary

As an acquisition of a business by a subsidiary from its parent in exchange for cash, other assets or equity instruments may meet the definition of a business combination, the guidance provided in 4.4.2 above is applicable. Therefore this section mainly deals with the transfer of a business from a subsidiary to its parent.

A feature that all transfers of businesses to parent entities have in common, whatever the legal form that they take, is that it is difficult to categorise them as business combinations. There is no acquirer whose actions result in it obtaining control of an acquired business; the parent already controlled the business that has been transferred to it.

A transfer without any consideration is comparable to a distribution by a subsidiary to its parent. The transfer can be a dividend but there are other legal arrangements that have similar effect that include reorganisations sanctioned by a court process or transfers after liquidation of the transferor entity. Some jurisdictions allow a legal merger between a parent and subsidiary to form a single entity. The general issues related to distributions of business are addressed in 4.4.3.A below, while the special concerns raised by legal mergers are addressed in 4.4.3.B below.

4.4.3.A Distributions of businesses without consideration – subsidiary transferring business to the parent.

From one perspective the transfer is a distribution and the model on which to base the accounting is that of receiving a dividend. Another view is that the parent has exchanged the investment in shares for the underlying assets and this is essentially a change in perspective from an equity interest to a direct investment in the net assets and results. Neither analogy is perfect, although both have their supporters.

In all circumstances, the following two major features will impact the accounting of the transfer by the parent:

- whether the subsidiary transfers the entirety of its business or only part of it; and
- whether the transfer is accounted for at fair value or at 'book value'.

Book value in turn may depend on whether the subsidiary has been acquired by the parent, in which case the relevant book values would be those reflected in the consolidated financial statements of the parent, rather than those in the subsidiary's financial statements.

The two perspectives (dividend approach and exchange of investment for assets) translate into two approaches to accounting by the parent:

(i) Parent effectively has received a distribution that it accounts for in its income statement at the fair value of the business received. It reflects the assets acquired and liabilities assumed at their fair value, including goodwill, which will be measured as at the date of the transfer. The existing investment is written off to the income statement.

   - This treatment can be applied in all circumstances.
   - This is the only appropriate method when the parent carries its investment in shares at fair value applying IFRS 9 (or IAS 39).
   - When the subsidiary transfers one of its businesses but continues to exist, the investment is not immediately written off to the income statement, but is subject to impairment testing.

(ii) Parent has exchanged its investment or part of its investment for the underlying assets and liabilities of the subsidiary and accounts for them at book values. The values that are reported in the consolidated financial statements become the cost of these assets for the parent.

   - This method is not appropriate if the investment in the parent is carried at fair value, in which case method (i) must be applied.
   - When the subsidiary transfers one of its businesses but continues to exist, the investment is not immediately written off to the income statement, but is subject to impairment testing.

   The two linked questions when using this approach are how to categorise the difference between the carrying value of the investment and the assets transferred and whether or not to reflect goodwill or an 'excess' (negative goodwill) in the parent's financial statements. This will depend primarily on whether the subsidiary had been acquired by the parent (the only circumstances in which this approach allows goodwill in the parent's financial statements after the transfer) and how any remaining 'catch up' adjustment is classified.

These alternative treatments are summarised in the following table:

Subsidiary set up or acquired	Basis of accounting	Goodwill recognised	Effect on income statement
Subsidiary set up by parent	Fair value.	Goodwill or negative goodwill at date of transfer.	Dividend recognised at fair value of the business. Investment written off or tested for impairment.
	Book value from underlying records.	No goodwill or negative goodwill. (note 1)	Catch up adjustment recognised fully in equity or as income, except that the element relating to a transaction recorded directly in equity may be recognised in equity. (note 2) Investment written off or tested for impairment.
Subsidiary acquired by parent	Fair value.	Goodwill or negative goodwill at date of transfer	Dividend recognised at fair value of the business. Investment written off or tested for impairment.
	Book value from consolidated accounts. (note 3)	Goodwill as at date of original acquisition. (note 3)	Catch up adjustment recognised fully in equity or as income, except that the element relating to a transaction recorded directly in equity may be recognised in equity. (note 2) Investment written off or tested for impairment.

Notes

(1) If the parent established the subsidiary itself and its investment reflects only share capital it has injected an excess of the carrying value over the net assets received will not be recognised as goodwill. This generally arises because of losses incurred by the transferred subsidiary.
If the subsidiary's net assets exceed the carrying value of the investment then this will be due to profits or other comprehensive income retained in equity.

(2) The catch up adjustment is not an equity transaction so all of it can be recognised in income. However, to the extent that it has arisen from a transaction that had occurred directly in equity, such as a revaluation, an entity can make a policy choice to recognise this element in equity. In this case the remaining amount is recognised in income. The entity can also take a view that as although the transfer of business is a current period transaction, the differences relate to prior period and hence should be recognised in equity.

(3) Because this was originally an acquisition, the values in the consolidated financial statements (and not the subsidiary's underlying records) become 'cost' for the parent. The assets and liabilities will reflect fair value adjustments made at the time of the business combination. Goodwill or negative goodwill will be the amount as at the date of the original acquisition.

If the business of the acquired subsidiary is transferred to the parent company as a distribution shortly after acquisition of that subsidiary, the accounting shall follow IAS 27 in relation to the dividend payment by the subsidiary. It might be accounted for effectively as a return of capital. The parent eliminates its investment in the subsidiary or part of its investment (based on the relative fair value of the business transferred compared to the value of the subsidiary), recognising instead the assets and liabilities of the business acquired at their fair value including the goodwill that has arisen on the business combination. The effect is to reflect the substance of the arrangement which is that the parent acquired a business. Comparative data is not restated in this case.

4.4.3.B Legal merger of parent and subsidiary

A legal merger can occur for numerous reasons, including facilitating a listing or structuring to transfer the borrowings obtained to acquire an entity to be repaid by the entity itself or to achieve tax benefits. Legal mergers always affect the individual or separate financial statements of the entities involved. As legal mergers are not specifically discussed in IFRS, different views and approaches are encountered in practice.

In many jurisdictions it is possible to effect a 'legal merger' of a parent and its subsidiary whereby the two separate entities become a single entity without any issue of shares or other consideration. This is usually the case when there is a legal merger of a parent with its 100% owned subsidiary. Depending on the jurisdiction, different scenarios might take place.

It is not uncommon for a new entity to be formed as a vehicle used in the acquisition of an entity from a third party in a separate transaction. Subsequently both entities legally merge. Judgement is required to make an assessment as to whether a legal merger occurs 'close to' the date of acquisition, including considering the substance of the transaction and the reasons for structuring. If this is the case i.e. a new entity is formed concurrently with (or near the date of) the acquisition of a subsidiary, and there is a legal merger of the new entity and the subsidiary, these transactions are viewed as a single transaction in which a subsidiary is acquired and is discussed in Chapter 9.

Even though the substance of the legal merger may be the same, whether the survivor is the parent or subsidiary affects the accounting.

a) The parent is the surviving entity

The parent's consolidated financial statements

The legal merger of the parent and its subsidiary does not affect the consolidated financial statements of the group. Only when non-controlling interests (NCI) are acquired in conjunction with the legal merger transaction, is the transaction with the NCI holders accounted for as a separate equity transaction (i.e. transactions with owners in their capacity as owners). *[IFRS 10.23]*.

Even if there is no consolidated group after the legal merger, according to IFRS 10 consolidated financial statements are still required (including comparative financial statements) in the reporting period in which the legal merger occurs. Individual financial statements are the continuation of the consolidated group – in subsequent reporting periods, the amounts are carried forward from the consolidated financial statements (and shown as the comparative financial statements).

In the reporting period in which the legal merger occurs the parent is also permitted, but not required, to present separate financial statements under IFRS.

Separate financial statements

In the parent's separate financial statements two approaches are available, if the investment in the subsidiary was previously measured at cost. An entity chooses its policy and applies it consistently. Under both approaches, any amounts that were previously recognised in the parent's separate financial statements continue to be recognised at the same amount, except for the investment in the subsidiary that is merged into the parent.

We believe that approach (i) below, a distribution at fair value, is the preferable approach, but approach (ii) below, liquidation from the consolidated financial statements, is also acceptable.

(i) The legal merger is in substance the distribution of the business from subsidiary to the parent.

   The investment in the subsidiary is first re-measured to fair value as at the date of the legal merger, with any resulting gain recognised in profit or loss. The investment in the subsidiary is then de-recognised. The acquired assets (including investments in subsidiaries, associates, or joint ventures held by the merged subsidiary) and assumed liabilities are recognised at fair value. Any difference gives rise to goodwill or income (bargain purchase, which is recognised in profit or loss).

(ii) The legal merger is in substance the redemption of shares in the subsidiary, in exchange for the underlying assets of the subsidiary.

   Giving up the shares for the underlying assets is essentially a change in perspective of the parent of its investment, from a 'direct equity interest' to 'the reported results and net assets.' Hence, the values recognised in the consolidated financial statements become the cost of these assets for the parent. The acquired assets (including investments in subsidiaries, associates, or joint ventures held by the merged subsidiary) and assumed liabilities are recognised at the carrying amounts in the consolidated financial statements as of the date of the legal merger. This includes any associated goodwill, intangible assets, or other adjustments arising from measurement at fair value upon acquisition that were recognised when the subsidiary was originally acquired, less the subsequent related amortisation, depreciation, impairment losses, as applicable.

   The difference between:

   (1) the amounts assigned to the assets and liabilities in the parent's separate financial statements after the legal merger; and

   (2) the carrying amount of the investment in the merged subsidiary before the legal merger;

   is recognised in one of the following (accounting policy choice):

   - profit or loss;
   - directly in equity; or
   - allocated to the appropriate component in the separate financial statements in the current period (e.g. current period profit or loss, current period other comprehensive income, or directly to equity) of the parent based on the component in which they were recognised in the financial statements of the merged subsidiary.

If the investment in the subsidiary was measured at fair value in the separate financial statements of the parent then only method (i) is applicable, because there is a direct swap of the investment with the underlying business. The parent would already have reflected the results of transactions that the subsidiary entered into since making its investment. Because the underlying investment in the subsidiary is de-recognised, this also triggers the reclassification of any amounts previously recognised in other comprehensive income and accumulated within a separate component of equity to be recognised in profit or loss.

In the separate financial statements, regardless of which approaches or varieties of approaches are used, comparative information should not be restated to include the merged subsidiary. The financial position and results of operations of the merged subsidiary are reflected in the separate financial statements only from the date on which the merger occurred.

b) The subsidiary is the surviving entity

Some argue that the legal form of a merger is more important in the context of the individual financial statements or separate financial statements of the subsidiary as these have a different purpose, being the financial statements of a legal entity. Others contend that as the legal mergers are not regulated in IFRS the accounting policy selected should reflect the economic substance of transactions, and not merely the legal form. This results in two possible approaches. We believe that approach (i) below, the economic approach, is the preferable approach and generally provides the most faithful representation of the transaction. However, approach (ii) below, the legal approach, may be appropriate when facts and circumstances indicate that the needs of the users of the general-purpose financial statements after the legal merger are best served by using the financial statements of the surviving subsidiary as the predecessor financial statements. This need must outweigh the needs of users who previously relied upon the general-purpose financial statements of the parent (as such information might no longer be available e.g. where following the merger there is no group). Consideration is given as to whether either set of users can otherwise obtain the information needed using special-purpose financial statements.

(i) the economic approach

The legal merger between the parent and subsidiary is considered to have no substance. The amounts recognised after the legal merger are the amounts that were previously in the consolidated financial statements, including goodwill and intangible assets recognised upon acquisition of that subsidiary. The consolidated financial statements after the legal merger also reflect any amounts in the consolidated financial statements (pre-merger) related to subsidiaries, associates, and joint ventures held by the surviving subsidiary. If the surviving subsidiary prepares separate financial statements after the legal merger, the subsidiary recognises the amounts that were previously recognised in the consolidated financial statements of the parent, as a contribution from the parent in equity.

(ii) the legal approach

The financial statements after the legal merger reflect the legal form of the transaction from the perspective of the subsidiary. There are two methods (as described below) with respect to recognising the identifiable assets acquired of the parent or liabilities assumed from the parent; regardless of which is used, amounts recognised previously in the consolidated financial statements with respect to the parent's acquisition of the surviving subsidiary (e.g. goodwill, intangible assets, fair value purchase price adjustments) are not recognised by the subsidiary. The surviving subsidiary does not recognise any change in the basis of subsidiaries, associates and joint ventures that it held before the legal merger.

Fair value method

If a merged parent meets a definition of business, the transaction is accounted for as an acquisition, with the consideration being a 'contribution' from the parent recognised in equity at fair value. Principles in IFRS 3 apply then by analogy.

The subsidiary recognises:

(1) the identifiable assets acquired and liabilities assumed from the parent at fair value;

(2) the fair value of the parent as a business as a contribution to equity; and

(3) the difference between (1) and (2) as goodwill or gain on a bargain purchase.

If the merged parent does not meet the definition of a business, the identifiable assets acquired or liabilities assumed are recognised on a relative fair value basis.

Book value method

Under this method the subsidiary accounts for the transaction as a contribution from the parent at book values. The subsidiary recognises the identifiable assets acquired or liabilities assumed from the parent at the historical carrying amount and the difference in equity. The historical carrying amounts might be the carrying amounts previously recognised in the parent's separate financial statements, the amounts in the ultimate parent's consolidated financial statements, or in a sub-level consolidation (prior to the merger).

Whatever variation of the legal approach is applied, the subsidiary may not recognise amounts that were previously recognised in the consolidated financial statements that related to the operations of the subsidiary, because there is no basis in IFRS for the subsidiary to recognise fair value adjustments to its internally generated assets or goodwill that were recognised by its parent when it was first acquired. Therefore, the carrying amount of the assets (including investments in subsidiaries, associates, and joint ventures) and liabilities held by subsidiary are the same both before and after a legal merger (there is no revaluation to fair value). There is also no push-down accounting of any goodwill or fair value adjustments recognised in the consolidated financial statements related to the assets and liabilities of the subsidiary that were recognised when the parent acquired the subsidiary.

In the separate financial statements, regardless of which approaches or varieties of approaches are used, comparative information should not be restated to include the merged parent. The financial position and results of operations of the merged parent are reflected in the separate financial statements only from the date on which the merger occurred.

4.4.4 Incurring expenses and settling liabilities without recharges

Entities may incur costs that provide a benefit to fellow group entities, e.g. audit, management or advertising fees, and do not recharge the costs. The beneficiary is not party to the transaction and does not directly incur an obligation to settle a liability. It may elect to recognise the cost, in which case it will charge profit or loss and credit equity with equivalent amounts; there will be no change to its net assets. If the expense is incurred by the parent, it could elect to increase the investment in the subsidiary rather than expensing the amount. This could lead to a carrying value that might be impaired. Fellow subsidiaries may expense the cost or recognise a distribution to the parent directly in equity. There is no policy choice if the expense relates to a share-based payment, in which case IFRS 2 mandates that expenses incurred for a subsidiary be added to the carrying amount of the investment in the parent and be recognised by the subsidiary (see Chapter 32 at 12).

Many groups recharge expenses indirectly, by making management charges, or recoup the funds through intra-group dividends, and in these circumstances it would be inappropriate to recognise the transaction in any entity other than the one that makes the payment.

A parent or other group entity may settle a liability on behalf of a subsidiary. If this is not recharged, the liability will have been extinguished in the entity's accounts. This raises the question of whether the gain should be taken to profit or loss or to equity. IAS 18 – *Revenue* – defines revenue as a transaction giving rise to an inflow of benefits other than as contributions from owners. *[IAS 18.7]*. IFRS 15 – *Revenue from Contracts with Customers* – defines revenue in a similar way *[IFRS 15 Appendix A]*. Except in unusual circumstances, the forgiveness of debt will be a contribution from owners and therefore ought to be taken to equity.

It will usually be appropriate for a parent to add the payment to the investment in the subsidiary as a capital contribution, subject always to impairment of the investment but a parent may conclude that it is more appropriate to expense the cost. If one subsidiary settles a liability of its fellow subsidiary, both of the entities may choose to recognise an equity element in the transaction, one subsidiary recognises a capital contribution from the parent, while the other subsidiary recognises a distribution to the parent.

4.4.5 Financial instruments within the scope of IFRS 9 (or IAS 39)

IFRS 9 (except for certain trade receivables) or IAS 39 requires the initial recognition of financial assets and financial liabilities to be at fair value, *[IFRS 9.5.1.1]*, *[IAS 39.43]*, so management has no policy choice. Financial instruments arising from group transactions are initially recognised at their fair value, with any difference between the fair value and the terms of the agreement recognised as an equity transaction.

4.4.5.A Interest-free or non-market interest rate loans

Parents might lend money to subsidiaries on an interest-free or low-interest basis and *vice versa*. A feature of some intra-group payables is that they have no specified repayment terms and are therefore repayable on demand. The fair value of a financial liability with a demand feature is not less than the amount payable on demand, discounted from the first date that the amount could be required to be paid. This means that an intra-group loan payable on demand has a fair value that is the same as the cash consideration given.

Loans are recognised at fair value on initial recognition based on the market rate of interest for similar loans at the date of issue (see Chapter 48 at 3.2.1). *[IFRS 9.B5.1.1, IAS 39.AG64]*. The party making the loan has a receivable recorded at fair value and must on initial recognition account for the difference between the fair value and the loan amount.

If the party making the non-market loan is a parent, it adds this to the carrying value of its investment. The subsidiary will initially record a capital contribution in equity. Subsequently, the parent will recognise interest income and the subsidiary interest expense using the effective interest method so that the loan is stated at the amount receivable/repayable at the redemption date. When the loan is repaid, the overall effect in parent's financial statements is of a capital contribution made to the subsidiary as it has increased its investment and recognised income to the same extent (assuming, of course, no impairment). By contrast, the subsidiary has initially recognised a gain in equity that has been reversed as interest has been charged.

If the subsidiary makes the non-market loan to its parent, the difference between the loan amount and its fair value is treated as a distribution by the subsidiary to the parent, while the parent reflects a gain. Again, interest is recognised so that the loan is stated at the amount receivable and payable at the redemption date. This has the effect of reversing the initial gain or loss taken to equity. Note that the effects in the parent's financial statements are not symmetrical to those when it makes a loan at below market rates. The parent does not need to deduct the benefit it has received from the subsidiary from the carrying value of its investment.

The following example illustrates the accounting for a variety of intra-group loan arrangements.

Example 8.9: Interest-free and below market rate loans within groups

Entity S is a wholly owned subsidiary of Entity P. In each of the following scenarios one of the entities provides an interest free or below market rate loan to the other entity.

1. P provides an interest free loan in the amount of $100,000 to S. The loan is repayable on demand.

On initial recognition the receivable is measured at its fair value, which in this case is equal to the cash consideration given. The loan is classified as a current liability in the financial statements of the subsidiary. The classification in the financial statements of the parent depends upon management intention. If the parent had no intention of demanding repayment in the near term, the parent would classify the receivable as non-current in accordance with paragraph 66 of IAS 1.

If S makes an interest-free loan to parent, the accounting is the mirror image of that for the parent.

2. P provides an interest free loan in the amount of $100,000 to S. The loan is repayable when funds are available.

Generally, a loan that is repayable when funds are available will be classified as a liability. The classification of such a loan as current or non-current and the measurement at origination date will depend on the expectations of the parent and subsidiary of the availability of funds to repay the loan. If the loan is expected to be repaid in three years, measurement of the loan would be the same as in scenario 3.

If S makes an interest-free loan to parent, the accounting is the mirror image of that for the parent.

3. P provides an interest free loan in the amount of $100,000 to S. The loan is repayable in full after 3 years. The fair value of the loan (based on current market rates of 10%) is $75,131.

At origination, the difference between the loan amount and its fair value (present value using current market rates for similar instruments) is treated as an equity contribution to the subsidiary, which represents a further investment by the parent in the subsidiary.

Journal entries at origination:

		Parent	$	$
Dr		Loan receivable from subsidiary	75,131	
Dr		Investment in subsidiary	24,869	
	Cr	Cash		100,000
		Subsidiary	$	$
Dr		Cash	100,000	
	Cr	Loan payable to parent		75,131
	Cr	Equity – capital contribution		24,869

Journal entries during the periods to repayment:

		Parent	$	$
Dr		Loan receivable from subsidiary (Note 1)	7,513	
	Cr	Profit or loss – notional interest		7,513
		Subsidiary	$	$
Dr		Profit or loss – notional interest	7,513	
	Cr	Loan payable to parent		7,513

Note 1 Amounts represent year one assuming no payments before maturity. Year 2 and 3 amounts would be $8,264 and $9,092 respectively i.e. accreted at 10%. At the end of year 3, the recorded balance of the loan will be $100,000.

4. S provides a below market rate loan in the amount of $100,000 to P. The loan bears interest at 4% and is repayable in full after 3 years (i.e. $112,000 at the end of year 3). The fair value of the loan (based on current market rates of 10%) is $84,147.

At origination, the difference between the loan amount and its fair value is treated as a distribution from the subsidiary to the parent.

Journal entries at origination:

		Parent	$	$
Dr		Cash	100,000	
	Cr	Loan payable to subsidiary		84,147
	Cr	Profit or loss – distribution from subsidiary		15,853
		Subsidiary	$	$
Dr		Loan receivable from parent	84,147	
Dr		Retained earnings – distribution	15,853	
	Cr	Cash		100,000

Journal entries during the periods to repayment:

		Parent	$	$
Dr		Profit or loss – notional interest	8,415	
	Cr	Loan payable to subsidiary		8,415
		Subsidiary	$	$
Dr		Loan receivable from parent (Note 1)	8,415	
	Cr	Profit or loss – notional interest		8,415

Note 1 Amounts represent year one assuming no payments before maturity. Year 2 and 3 amounts would be $9,256 and $10,182, respectively i.e. accreted at 10% such that at the end of year 3 the recorded balance of the loan will be $112,000 being the principal of the loan ($100,000) plus the interest payable in cash ($12,000).

4.4.5.B Financial guarantee contracts: parent guarantee issued on behalf of subsidiary

Financial guarantees given by an entity that are within the scope of IFRS 9 (or IAS 39) must be recognised initially at fair value. *[IFRS 9.5.1.1, IAS 39.43]*. If a parent or other group entity gives a guarantee on behalf of an entity, this must be recognised in its separate or individual financial statements. It is normally appropriate for a parent that gives a guarantee to treat the debit that arises on recognising the guarantee at fair value as an additional investment in its subsidiary. This is described in Chapter 43 at 3.4.

The situation is different for the subsidiary or fellow subsidiary that is the beneficiary of the guarantee. There will be no separate recognition of the financial guarantee unless it is provided to the lender separate and apart from the original borrowing, does not form part of the overall terms of the loan and would not transfer with the loan if it were assigned by the lender to a third party. This means that few guarantees will be reflected separately in the financial statements of the entities that benefit from the guarantees.

Example 8.10: Financial guarantee contracts

A group consists of two entities, H plc (the parent) and S Ltd (H's wholly owned subsidiary). Entity H has a stronger credit rating than S Ltd. S Ltd is looking to borrow €100, repayable in five years. A bank has indicated it will charge interest of 7.5% per annum. However, the bank has offered to lend to S Ltd at a rate of 7.0% per annum if H plc provides a guarantee of S Ltd.'s debt to the bank and this is accepted by S Ltd. No charge was made by H plc to S Ltd in respect of the guarantee. The fair value of the guarantee is calculated at €2, which is the difference between the present value of the contractual payments discounted at 7.0% and 7.5%. If the bank were to assign the loan to S Ltd to a third party, the assignee would become party to both the contractual terms of the borrowing with S Ltd as well as the guarantee from H plc.

H plc will record the guarantee at its fair value of €2.

S Ltd will record its loan at fair value including the value of the guarantee provided by the parent. It will simply record the liability at €100 but will not recognise separately the guarantee provided by the parent.

If the guarantee was separate, S Ltd would record the liability at its fair value without the guarantee of €98 with the difference of €2 recorded as a capital contribution.

4.5 Disclosures

Where there have been significant transactions between entities under common control that are not on arm's length terms, it will be necessary for the entity to disclose its accounting policy for recognising and measuring such transactions.

IAS 24 applies whether or not a price has been charged so gifts of assets or services and asset swaps are within scope. Details and terms of the transactions must be disclosed (see Chapter 37 at 2.5).

References

1 *IFRIC Update*, March 2015, p.11.
2 *IFRIC Update*, March 2015, p.11.
3 *IFRIC Update*, March 2006, p.7.
4 Agenda paper for the meeting of the Accounting Regulatory Committee on 2nd February 2007 (document ARC/08/2007), *Subject: Relationship between the IAS Regulation and the 4th and 7th Company Law Directives – Can a company preparing both individual and consolidated accounts in accordance with adopted IFRS issue the individual accounts before the consolidated accounts?*, European Commission: Internal Market and Services DG: Free movement of capital, company law and corporate governance: Accounting/PB D(2006), 15 January 2007, para. 3.1.
5 *IFRIC Update*, March 2016, p.5.
6 *IFRIC Update*, July 2009, p.3.
7 *IFRIC Update*, September 2011, p.3.
8 Staff Paper, IFRS Interpretations Committee Meeting, July 2011, Agenda reference 7, *IAS 27 Consolidated and Separate Financial Statements – Group reorganisations in separate financial statements*, Appendix A.
9 *IASB Update*, June 2014, p.9.
10 Information for Observers (June 2014 IASB meeting), *Business Combinations Under Common Control – Scope of the research project (Agenda Paper 14)*, paras. 5-6.
11 IASB Work plan as at 4 July 2017.
12 *IFRIC Update*, September 2011, p.3.
13 *IASB Update*, January 2016, p.4.
14 IASB Work plan as at 4 July 2017.
15 *Equity Method in Separate Financial Statements* (Amendments to IAS 27), para. 4.
16 *Equity Method in Separate Financial Statements* (Amendments to IAS 27), para. 12.
17 *Equity Method in Separate Financial Statements* (Amendments to IAS 27), para. BC10G.

Chapter 9 Business combinations

Chapter 9

List of examples

Chapter 9 Business combinations

1 INTRODUCTION

A business combination is defined by the IASB ('the Board') as a 'transaction or other event in which an acquirer obtains control of one or more businesses'. *[IFRS 3 Appendix A].*

Over the years, business combinations have been defined in different ways. Whatever definition has been applied, it includes circumstances in which an entity obtains control of an integrated set of activities and assets that constitute a business as well as transactions as a result of which an entity becomes a subsidiary of a parent.

In accounting terms there have traditionally been two distinctly different forms of reporting the effects of a business combination; the purchase method of accounting (or acquisition method of accounting) and the pooling of interests method (or merger accounting).

The two methods of accounting look at business combinations through quite different eyes. An acquisition was seen as the absorption of the target by the acquirer; there is continuity only of the acquiring entity, in the sense that only the post-acquisition results of the target are reported as earnings of the acquiring entity and the comparative figures remain those of the acquiring entity. In contrast, a pooling of interests or merger is seen as the pooling together of two formerly distinct shareholder groups; in order to present continuity of both entities there is retrospective restatement to show the enlarged entity as if the two entities had always been together, by combining the results of both entities pre- and post-combination and also by restatement of the comparatives. However, the pooling of interests method has fallen out of favour with standard setters, including the IASB, as they consider virtually all business combinations as being acquisitions. The purchase method has become the established method of accounting for business combinations. Nevertheless, the pooling of interests method is still sometimes used for business combinations involving entities under common control where the transactions have been scoped out of the relevant standard dealing with business combinations (see Chapter 10).

The other main issues facing accountants have been in relation to accounting for an acquisition. Broadly speaking, the acquiring entity has had to determine the fair values of the identifiable assets and liabilities of the target. Depending on what items are included within this allocation process and what values are placed on them, this will result in a difference to the consideration given that has to be accounted for. Where the amounts allocated to the assets and liabilities are less than the overall consideration given, the difference is accounted for as goodwill. Goodwill is an asset that is not amortised, but subjected to some form of impairment test, although some national standards still require amortisation. Where the consideration given is less than the values allocated to the identifiable assets and liabilities, the issue has then been whether and, if so, when, such a credit should be taken to the income statement.

1.1 IFRS 3 (as revised in 2008) and subsequent amendments

This chapter discusses IFRS 3 – *Business Combinations* – as revised in 2018 and amended subsequently and its associated Basis for Conclusions and Illustrative Examples.

The specific requirements of IAS 38 – *Intangible Assets* – relating to intangible assets acquired as part of a business combination accounted for under IFRS 3 are dealt with as part of the discussion of IFRS 3 in this chapter; the other requirements of IAS 38 are covered in Chapter 17. Impairment of goodwill is addressed in Chapter 20 at 8.

In May 2011, the IASB issued a series of IFRSs that deal broadly with consolidated financial statements. IFRS 10 – *Consolidated Financial Statements* – is a single standard addressing consolidation. The requirements of IFRS 10 are discussed in Chapters 6 and 7 which address, respectively, its consolidation requirements and consolidation procedures. Some consequential amendments were made to IFRS 3, principally to reflect that the guidance on 'control' within IFRS 10 is to be used to identify the acquirer in a business combination.

IFRS 13 – *Fair Value Measurement* – changed the definition of 'fair value' to an explicit exit value, but it did not change when fair value is required or permitted under IFRS. Its impact on IFRS 3 is considered at 5.3 below and reference should be made to Chapter 14 for a full discussion. Unless otherwise indicated, references to fair value in this chapter are to fair value as defined by IFRS 13.

In October 2012, the IASB amended IFRS 10 to provide an exception to the consolidation requirement for entities that meet the definition of an investment entity. As a result of this amendment the scope of IFRS 3 was also amended. The investment entities exception is discussed in Chapter 6 at 10.

In December 2013, the IASB issued two cycles of Annual Improvements – *Cycles* 2010-2012 and 2011-2013 – that had the following impact on IFRS 3.

- Contingent consideration in a business combination that is not classified as equity is subsequently measured at fair value through profit or loss whether or not it falls within the scope of IFRS 9 – *Financial Instruments* (or IAS 39 – *Financial Instruments: Recognition and Measurement*) (see 7.1.2 and 7.1.3 below).
- The formation of joint arrangements, both joint operations and joint ventures, is outside the scope of IFRS 3. The amendment has also clarified that the scope exception applies only to the accounting in the financial statements of the joint arrangement itself (see 2.2.1 below).
- A clarification that the guidance on ancillary services in IAS 40 – *Investment Property*, *[IAS 40.11-14]*, is intended to distinguish an investment property from an owner-occupied property, not whether a transaction is a business combination or an asset acquisition (see 3.2.3 below).

As a result of the issue of IFRS 15 – *Revenue from Contracts with Customers* – in May 2014, a consequential amendment has been made to the requirements for the subsequent measurement of a contingent liability recognised in a business combination (see 5.6.1.B below). IFRS 15 becomes effective for annual periods beginning on or after 1 January 2018, with early adoption permitted. See Chapter 30 for a detailed discussion of IFRS 15.

Some consequential amendments have been made to IFRS 3 as a result of the issue of IFRS 9. These relate principally to the requirements for:

- classifying or designating identifiable assets acquired and liabilities assumed (see 5.4 below);
- business combinations achieved in stages (see 9 below); and
- contingent consideration classified as an asset or liability (see 7.1 below).

The requirements of IFRS 9 are not mandatory until annual periods beginning on or after 1 January 2018, with early adoption permitted. Until that time, entities will apply the requirements of IAS 39.

In January 2016, the IASB issued IFRS 16 – *Leases* – which requires lessees to recognise assets and liabilities for most leases under a single accounting model (i.e. no classification of a lease contract as either operating or finance lease for lessees). For lessors there is little change to the existing accounting in IAS 17 – *Leases*. A number of consequential amendments have been made to IFRS 3 in respect of leases accounted for under IFRS 16. These relate to the requirements for:

- classifying or designating identifiable assets acquired and liabilities assumed (see 5.4 below);
- recognising and measuring particular assets acquired and liabilities assumed (see 5.5.1 below); and
- exceptions to the recognition and/or measurement principles (see 5.6.8 below).

IFRS 16 becomes effective for annual periods beginning on or after 1 January 2019. Early adoption is permitted, provided IFRS 15 has been applied, or is applied at the same date as IFRS 16. See Chapter 25 for a detailed discussion of IFRS 16.

1.1.1 Post-implementation review

In June 2015, the IASB completed the post-implementation review (PIR) of IFRS 3. The PIR was conducted in two phases. The first phase of the PIR began in July 2013. It consisted of an initial assessment of all of the issues that arose on the implementation of IFRS 3 and a consultation with interested parties about those issues. The first phase identified the main questions to be addressed in the PIR of IFRS 3, and these questions were included in the *Request for Information – Post-implementation Review: IFRS 3 Business Combinations* (RFI), issued in January 2014 as a formal request by the IASB to gather information from its constituents. In the second phase the IASB considered the comments received from the RFI along with the information gathered through other consultative activities and a review of relevant academic studies.

The PIR covered the whole Business Combinations project, which resulted in the issue of IFRS 3 (as originally issued in 2004), IFRS 3 (as revised in 2008) and any resulting consequential amendments to other standards.

The accounting for business combinations encompasses a wide range of areas. In the RFI, the IASB focused on the following areas:

- defining a business;
- using fair value measurement in business combinations accounting;
- recognising intangible assets separately from goodwill and accounting for negative goodwill;
- testing for impairment rather than amortising goodwill and indefinite-life intangible assets;
- measuring and presenting non-controlling interests;
- accounting for step acquisitions and for retained investments after loss of control;
- disclosing the nature and effect of a business combination.[1]

In June 2015, the IASB issued its *Report and Feedback Statement – Post-implementation Review of IFRS 3 Business Combinations* (RFS), which summarised the PIR process, the feedback received and conclusions reached by the IASB.

The IASB based its review on information gathered from three main sources:

- a review of academic literature and other reports;
- feedback received from investors and other users of financial statements;
- feedback received from preparers, auditors and regulators.

The review of academic literature provided evidence that generally supported the current requirement on business combinations accounting, particularly in relation to the usefulness of reported goodwill, other intangible assets and goodwill impairment. However, investors expressed mixed views on certain aspects of the current accounting, including subsequent accounting for goodwill, separate recognition of intangible assets, measurement of non-controlling interests and subsequent accounting for contingent consideration. Also, many investors do not support the current requirements on step acquisitions and loss of control, and are asking for additional information about the subsequent performance of an acquired business. Many preparers, auditors and regulators identified implementation challenges in the requirements. In particular, applying the definition of a business, measuring the fair value of contingent consideration, contingent liabilities and intangible assets, testing goodwill for impairment on an annual basis and accounting for contingent payments to selling shareholders who become employees.[2]

Taking into account all of the evidence collected, the IASB decided to add to its research agenda the following areas of focus, assessed as being of high significance:

- effectiveness and complexity of testing goodwill for impairment;
- subsequent accounting for goodwill (i.e. impairment-only approach compared with an amortisation and impairment approach);
- challenges in applying the definition of a business;
- identification and fair value measurement of intangible assets such as customer relationships and brand names.[3]

In June 2016, the IASB proposed amendments to IFRS 3 to address the challenges in applying the definition of a business.[4] These are discussed in detail in 3.2.6 below.

The other three areas of high significance listed above are being considered by the Board within its *Goodwill and Impairment* research project. At the time of writing, the Board is exploring whether the existing impairment test for goodwill can be improved or simplified, whether goodwill should be amortised and which intangible assets should be separated from goodwill. The IASB's work plan indicates that a Discussion Paper is expected in the first half of 2018.[5]

Following the feedback received from the 2015 Agenda Consultation, the IASB decided not to include in its work plan and research pipeline any of the other areas of focus assessed as being of medium or lower significance in the RFI.[6]

1.1.2 Proposed amendments to IFRS 3

In June 2016, the IASB issued an exposure draft *Definition of a Business and Accounting for Previously Held Interests (Proposed amendments to IFRS 3 and IFRS 11)* ('the ED'). The proposed amendments aim to:[7]

- clarify the application of the definition of a business (see 3.2.6 below);
- eliminate diversity in practice in accounting for previously held interests in the assets and liabilities of a joint operation that meets the definition of a business for transactions in which an entity obtains control (see 9.1 below) or joint control of the joint operation (see Chapter 12 at 8.3).

The ED proposes that an entity would be required to apply the proposed amendments to IFRS 3 to any business combination for which the acquisition date is on or after the beginning of the first annual reporting period beginning on or after the effective date of the amendments.[8]

2 SCOPE OF IFRS 3

Entities are required to apply the provisions of IFRS 3 to transactions or other events that meet the definition of a business combination (see 3.2 below). *[IFRS 3.2]*.

2.1 Mutual entities

The acquisition method of accounting applies to combinations involving only mutual entities (e.g. mutual insurance companies, credit unions and cooperatives) and combinations in which separate entities are brought together by contract alone (e.g. dual listed corporations and stapled entity structures). *[IFRS 3.BC58]*. The Board considers that the attributes of mutual entities are not sufficiently different from those of investor-owned entities to justify a different method of accounting for business combinations between two mutual entities. It also considers that such combinations are economically similar to business combinations involving two investor-owned entities, and should be similarly reported. *[IFRS 3.BC71-BC72]*. Similarly, the Board has concluded that the acquisition method should be applied for combinations achieved by contract alone. *[IFRS 3.BC79]*. Additional guidance is given in IFRS 3 for applying the acquisition method to such business combinations (see 7.4 and 7.5 below).

2.2 Arrangements out of scope of IFRS 3

The standard does not apply to:

(a) the accounting for the formation of a joint arrangement in the financial statements of the joint arrangement itself;

(b) the acquisition of an asset or a group of assets that does not constitute a business;

(c) a combination of entities or businesses under common control; or

(d) the acquisition by an investment entity, as defined in IFRS 10 (see Chapter 6 at 10.1), of an investment in subsidiary that is required to be measured at fair value through profit or loss. *[IFRS 3.2, 2A]*.

2.2.1 Formation of a joint arrangement

The scope exception of IFRS 3 for the formation of a joint arrangement relates only to the accounting in the financial statements of the joint arrangement, i.e. the joint venture or joint operation, and not to the accounting for the joint venturer's or joint operator's interest in the joint arrangement. *[IFRS 3.BC61B-BC61D]*.

By contrast, a particular type of arrangement in which the owners of multiple businesses agree to combine their businesses into a new entity (sometimes referred to as a roll-up transaction) does not include a contractual agreement requiring unanimous consent to decisions about the relevant activities. Majority consent on such decisions is not sufficient to create a joint arrangement. Therefore, such arrangements should be accounted for by the acquisition method. *[IFRS 3.BC60]*.

2.2.2 Acquisition of an asset or a group of assets that does not constitute a business

Although the acquisition of an asset or a group of assets is not within the scope of IFRS 3, in such cases the acquirer has to identify and recognise the individual identifiable assets acquired (including intangible assets) and liabilities assumed. The cost of the group is allocated to the individual identifiable assets and liabilities on the basis of their relative fair values at the date of purchase. These transactions or events do not give rise to goodwill. *[IFRS 3.2]*. Thus, existing book values or values in the acquisition agreement may not be appropriate.

The cost of the group of assets is the sum of all consideration given and any non-controlling interest recognised. If the non-controlling interest has a present ownership interest and is entitled to a proportionate share of net assets upon liquidation, the acquirer has a choice to recognise the non-controlling interest at its proportionate share of net assets or its fair value; in all other cases, non-controlling interest is recognised at fair value, unless another measurement basis is required in accordance with IFRS. An example could be the acquisition of an incorporated entity that holds a single property, where this is assessed not to be a business (see Chapter 7 at 3.1.1). In June 2017, the Interpretations Committee considered a request to clarify how an entity accounts for the acquisition of a group of assets that does not constitute a business which may impact the current accounting treatment for asset acquisitions. This is discussed below.

It may be difficult to determine whether or not an acquired asset or a group of assets constitutes a business (see 3.2 below), yet this decision can have a considerable impact on an entity's reported results and the presentation of its financial statements; accounting for a business combination under IFRS 3 differs from accounting for an asset(s) acquisition in a number of important respects:

- goodwill or a gain on bargain purchase only arise on business combinations;
- assets acquired and liabilities assumed are generally accounted for at fair value in a business combination, while they are assigned a carrying amount based on their relative fair values in an asset acquisition;
- directly attributable acquisition-related costs are expensed if they relate to a business combination, but are generally capitalised as part of the cost of the asset in an asset acquisition;
- while deferred tax assets and liabilities must be recognised if the transaction is a business combination, they are not recognised under IAS 12 – *Income Taxes* – if it is an asset acquisition (see Chapter 31);
- where the consideration is in the form of shares, IFRS 2 – *Share-based Payment* – does not apply in a business combination, but will apply in an asset acquisition;
- another difference may arise where the transaction involves contingent consideration. While IFRS 3 provides guidance on the accounting for contingent consideration in the acquisition of a business (see 7.1 below), IAS 16 – *Property, Plant and Equipment* – and IAS 38 provide no clear guidance on accounting for contingent consideration in an asset(s) acquisition (see Chapter 17 at 4.5 and Chapter 18 at 4.1.9); and
- disclosures are much more onerous for business combinations than for asset acquisitions.

The accounting differences above will not only affect the accounting as of the acquisition date, but will also have an impact on future depreciation, possible impairment and other costs.

In June 2017, the Interpretations Committee considered a request to clarify how an entity accounts for the acquisition of a group of assets that does not constitute a business. More specifically, the submitter asked for clarity on how to allocate the transaction price to the identifiable assets acquired and liabilities assumed when:

(a) the sum of the individual fair values of the identifiable assets and liabilities is different from the transaction price; and

(b) the group includes identifiable assets and liabilities initially measured both at cost and at an amount other than cost.

The Interpretations Committee tentatively concluded that a reasonable reading of the requirements in paragraph 2(b) of IFRS 3 on the acquisition of a group of assets that does not constitute a business results in one of the following two approaches:

(a) Under the first approach, an entity accounts for the acquisition of the group as follows:
   (i) it identifies the individual identifiable assets acquired and liabilities assumed that it recognises at the date of the acquisition;
   (ii) it determines the individual transaction price for each identifiable asset and liability by allocating the cost of the group based on the relative fair values of those assets and liabilities at the date of the acquisition; and then
   (iii) it applies the initial measurement requirements in applicable IFRSs to each identifiable asset acquired and liability assumed. The entity accounts for any difference between the amount at which the asset or liability is initially measured and its individual transaction price applying the relevant requirements.

(b) Under the second approach, for any identifiable asset or liability initially measured at an amount other than cost, an entity initially measures that asset or liability at the amount specified in the applicable standard. The entity deducts from the transaction price of the group the amounts allocated to the assets and liabilities initially measured at an amount other than cost, and then allocates the residual transaction price to the remaining identifiable assets and liabilities based on their relative fair values at the date of the acquisition.

The Interpretations Committee also tentatively concluded that an entity should apply its reading of the requirements consistently to all such acquisitions.[9]

2.2.3 Business combinations under common control

The application guidance in Appendix B to IFRS 3 gives some guidance on accounting for business combinations involving entities or businesses under common control and therefore excluded from the requirements of the standard. *[IFRS 3.B1-B4]*. These arrangements are discussed further in Chapter 10.

3 IDENTIFYING A BUSINESS COMBINATION

IFRS 3 requires an entity to determine whether a transaction or event is a *business combination;* the definition requires that the assets acquired and liabilities assumed constitute a *business*. If the assets acquired and liabilities assumed do not constitute a business, the transaction is to be accounted for as an asset acquisition (see 2.2.2 above). *[IFRS 3.3]*.

3.1 Identifying a business combination

IFRS 3 defines a business combination as a 'transaction or other event in which an acquirer obtains control of one or more businesses'. *[IFRS 3 Appendix A].*

IFRS 3 notes that an acquirer might obtain control of an acquiree (i.e. the business or businesses over which the acquirer obtains control) in a variety of ways, for example:

(a) transferring cash, cash equivalents or other assets (including net assets that constitute a business);

(b) incurring liabilities;

(c) issuing equity interests;

(d) providing more than one type of consideration; or

(e) without transferring consideration – including by contract alone (see 7.4 below). *[IFRS 3.B5].*

A business combination may be structured in a variety of ways for legal, taxation or other reasons, which include but are not limited to:

(a) one or more businesses become subsidiaries of an acquirer or the net assets of one or more businesses are legally merged into the acquirer;

(b) one combining entity transfers its net assets, or its owners transfer their equity interests, to another combining entity or its owners;

(c) all of the combining entities transfer their net assets, or the owners of those entities transfer their equity interests, to a newly formed entity (sometimes referred to as a roll-up or put-together transaction); or

(d) a group of former owners of one of the combining entities obtains control of the combined entity. *[IFRS 3.B6].*

3.2 Definition of a business

IFRS 3 defines a business as 'an integrated set of activities and assets that is capable of being conducted and managed for the purpose of providing a return in the form of dividends, lower costs or other economic benefits directly to investors or other owners, members or participants'. *[IFRS 3 Appendix A].* The Basis for Conclusions notes that by focusing on the capability to achieve the purposes of the business, unlike previous versions, it helps avoid the 'unduly restrictive interpretations that existed in accordance with the former guidance' and, in particular, clarifies that start-up activities and activities integrated into those of the acquirer may still be businesses as defined. *[IFRS 3.BC18].*

In June 2016, in response to stakeholder concerns raised during the PIR of IFRS 3, the IASB proposed amendments that aim to clarify how to apply the definition of a business in IFRS 3. These are discussed in detail in 3.2.6 below.

3.2.1 Inputs, processes and outputs

The application guidance to IFRS 3 describes the components of a business as inputs and processes applied to those inputs that have the *ability* to create outputs, which means that outputs do not need to be present for an integrated set of assets and activities to be a business. The elements are described as follows:

- *Input*

  Any economic resource that creates, or has the ability to create, outputs when one or more processes are applied to it. Examples include non-current assets (including intangible assets or rights to use non-current assets), intellectual property, the ability to obtain access to necessary materials or rights and employees.

- *Process*

  Any system, standard, protocol, convention or rule is a process if, when applied to an input or inputs, it either creates or has the ability to create outputs. Examples include strategic management processes, operational processes and resource management processes. These processes typically are documented, but an organised workforce having the necessary skills and experience following rules and conventions may provide the necessary processes that are capable of being applied to inputs to create outputs. Accounting, billing, payroll and other administrative systems typically are not processes used to create outputs so their presence or exclusion generally will not affect whether an acquired set of activities and assets is considered a business.

- *Output*

  The result of inputs and processes applied to those inputs that provide or have the ability to provide a return in the form of dividends, lower costs or other economic benefits directly to investors or other owners, members or participants. Outputs need not be present at the acquisition date for an integrated set of activities and assets to be defined as a business. *[IFRS 3.B7]*.

3.2.2 'Capable of' from the viewpoint of a market participant

IFRS 3 clarifies that an acquired set of activities and assets does not need to include all of the inputs or processes necessary to operate that set of activities and assets as a business, i.e. it does not need to be self-sustaining. If a market participant is capable of utilising the acquired set of activities and assets to produce outputs, e.g. by integrating the acquired set with its own inputs and processes, thereby replacing the missing elements, then the acquired set of activities and assets might constitute a business. It is not necessarily relevant whether the seller historically had operated the transferred set as a business or whether the acquirer intends to operate the acquired set as a business. What is relevant is whether a market participant is capable of operating the acquired set of assets and activities as a business. *[IFRS 3.B8, B11]*. Moreover, if a market participant does not itself have the elements that are missing from the acquired set but they are easily replaced or replicated, i.e. the missing elements are 'minor', we believe a market participant would be capable of operating the acquired set in order to generate a return and the acquired set should be considered a business.

We believe that, in most cases, the acquired set of activities and assets must have at least some inputs and processes in order to be considered a business. If an acquirer obtains control of an input or set of inputs without any processes, we think it is unlikely that the acquired input(s) would be considered a business, even if a market participant had all the processes necessary to operate the input(s) as a business.

The guidance in IFRS 3 also notes that the nature of the elements of a business varies by industry and by the structure of an entity's operations (activities), including the entity's stage of development. Established businesses often have many different types of inputs, processes and outputs, whereas new businesses often have few inputs and processes and sometimes only a single output. Nearly all businesses also have liabilities, but a business need not have liabilities. *[IFRS 3.B9].*

3.2.3 Identifying business combinations

Although the revision of the definition of a business in 2008 was intended to improve consistency in the application of the definition of a business, the term 'capable of' is sufficiently broad that significant judgement continues to be required in determining whether an acquired set of activities and assets constitute a business. The following are examples from extractive industries and real estate that illustrate the issues.

Example 9.1: Extractive industries – definition of a business (1)

E&P Co A (an oil and gas exploration and production company) acquires a mineral interest from E&P Co B, on which it intends to perform exploration activities to determine if reserves exist. The mineral interest is an unproven property and there have been no exploration activities performed on the property.

Inputs – mineral interest

Processes – none

Output – none

Conclusion

In this scenario, we do not believe E&P Co A acquired a business. While E&P Co A acquired an input (mineral interest), it did not acquire any processes. Whether or not a market participant has the necessary processes in place to operate the input as a business is not relevant to the determination of whether the acquired set is a business because no processes were acquired from E&P Co B.

Example 9.2: Extractive industries – definition of a business (2)

E&P Co A acquires a property similar to that in Example 9.1 above, except that oil and gas production activities are in place. The target's employees are not part of the transferred set. E&P Co A will take over the operations by using its own employees.

Inputs – oil and gas reserves

Processes – operational processes associated with oil and gas production

Output – revenues from oil and gas production

Conclusion

In this scenario, we generally consider that E&P Co A acquired a business. The acquired set has all three components of a business (inputs, processes and outputs) and is capable of providing a return to its owners. Although the employees are not being transferred to the acquirer, a market participant would generally be able to produce outputs by:

(1) supplying the employees necessary to continue production; and

(2) integrating the business with its own operations while continuing to produce outputs.

In the real estate industry, IAS 40 notes that where ancillary services (i.e. processes) are provided and they are insignificant to the overall arrangement, this will not prevent the classification of the asset as investment property. *[IAS 40.11]*. The guidance on ancillary services, *[IAS 40.11-14]*, is intended to distinguish an investment property from an owner-occupied property, not whether a transaction is a business combination or an asset acquisition. Entities acquiring investment properties must assess whether the property is a business in terms of IFRS 3. *[IAS 40.14A]*.

Therefore, evaluating whether it is a real estate business where certain processes are transferred involves assessing those processes in the light of the guidance in IFRS 3.

Example 9.3: Real estate – definition of a business (1)

Company A acquires land and a vacant building from Company B. No processes, other assets or employees (for example, leases and other contracts, maintenance or security personnel, or a leasing office) are acquired in the transaction.

Inputs – land and vacant building

Processes – none

Output – none

Conclusion

In this scenario, we do not believe Company A acquired a business. While Company A acquired inputs (land and a vacant building), it did not acquire any processes. Whether or not a market participant has the necessary processes in place to operate the inputs as a business is not relevant to the determination of whether the acquired set is a business, because no processes were acquired from Company B.

Example 9.4: Real estate – definition of a business (2)

Company A acquires an operating hotel, the hotel's employees, the franchise agreement, inventory, reservations system and all 'back office' operations.

Inputs – non-current assets, franchise agreement and employees

Processes – operational and resource management processes associated with operating the hotel

Output – revenues from operating the hotel

Conclusion

In this scenario, we believe Company A acquired a business. The acquired set has all three components of a business (inputs, processes and outputs) and is capable of providing a return to its owners.

Sometimes it may be difficult to determine whether or not an acquired group of assets is a business, and judgement will be required to be exercised based on the particular circumstances. The determination of whether or not an acquired group of assets and activities is a business can have a considerable impact on an entity's reported results and the presentation of its financial statements. Differences between a business combination and an asset(s) acquisition are summarised at 2.2.2 above.

In June 2016, in response to stakeholder concerns raised during the PIR of IFRS 3, the IASB proposed amendments that aim to clarify how to apply the definition of a business in IFRS 3. These are discussed in detail in 3.2.6 below.

3.2.4 Development stage entities

Development stage entities may qualify as businesses, and their acquisition accounted for as business combinations because outputs are not required at the acquisition date. Inputs and processes are not required either if a market participant has access to the necessary inputs or processes or the missing elements are easily replaced. However, we believe that, in most cases, the acquired set of activities and assets must have at least some inputs and processes in order to be considered a business. Various factors need to be considered to determine whether the transferred set of activities and assets is a business, including, but not limited to, the following:

(a) whether the entity has begun its planned principal activities;

(b) whether it has employees, intellectual property and other inputs and processes that could be applied to those inputs;

(c) if it is pursuing a plan to produce outputs; and

(d) if it will be able to obtain access to customers that will purchase the outputs. *[IFRS 3.B10].*

This list of factors should not be considered a checklist; there is no minimum number of criteria that need to be met when determining if a development stage entity is a business. The primary consideration is whether the inputs and processes acquired, combined with the inputs and processes of a market participant are capable of being conducted and managed to produce resulting outputs. We believe that the further an acquired set of assets and activities is in its life cycle, the more difficult it will be to conclude a market participant is not capable of operating the acquired set as a business. For example, if the planned operations of an acquired set of assets and activities have commenced, we generally believe that this would represent a business, as would acquired activities and assets including employees and intellectual property that are capable of producing products.

The application of this guidance may be particularly relevant to transactions in the life sciences industry. This is illustrated in the following examples.

Example 9.5: Life sciences – definition of a business (1)

Biotech A acquires all of the outstanding shares in Biotech B, which is a development stage company with a licence for a product candidate. Due to a loss of funding, Biotech B has no employees and no other assets. Neither clinical trials nor development are currently being performed. When additional funding is obtained, Biotech A plans to commence phase I clinical trials for the product candidate.

Input – licence to product candidate

Processes – none

Outputs – none

Conclusion

In this scenario, we do not consider that Biotech A has acquired a business. While Biotech B has an input (licence), it lacks processes to apply to the licence in order to create outputs. Furthermore, Biotech B has no employees and is not pursuing a plan to produce outputs (no research and development is currently being performed).

Example 9.6: Life sciences – definition of a business (2)

Biotech C acquires all of the outstanding shares in Biotech D, a development stage company that has a licence for a product candidate. Phase III clinical trials are currently being performed by Biotech D employees (one of whom founded Biotech D and discovered the product candidate). Biotech D's administrative and accounting functions are performed by a contract employee.

Inputs – licence for product candidate and employees

Processes – operational and management processes associated with the performance and supervision of the clinical trials

Output – none

Conclusion

In this scenario, we consider that Biotech C has acquired a business because it has acquired inputs and processes. Biotech D has begun operations (development of the product candidate) and is pursuing a plan to produce outputs (i.e. a commercially developed product to be sold or licensed).

3.2.5 Presence of goodwill

There is a rebuttable presumption that if goodwill arises on the acquisition, the acquisition is a business. *[IFRS 3.B12]*. If, for example, the total fair value of an acquired set of activities and assets is $15 million and the fair value of the net identifiable assets is only $10 million, the existence of value in excess of the fair value of identifiable assets (i.e. goodwill) creates a presumption that the acquired set is a business. However, care should be exercised to ensure that all of the identifiable net assets have been identified and measured appropriately. While the absence of goodwill may be an indicator that the acquired activities and assets do not represent a business, it is not presumptive. *[IFRS 3.B12]*.

An acquisition of a business may involve a 'bargain purchase' in which the new bases of the net identifiable assets are actually greater than the fair value of the entity as a whole (see 10 below).

3.2.6 Proposed clarifications to the definition of a business

In June 2016, in response to stakeholder concerns raised during the PIR of IFRS 3, the IASB proposed amendments that aim to clarify how to apply the definition of a business in IFRS 3. The proposed amendments aim to provide additional guidance to help distinguish between the acquisition of a business and the acquisition of a group of assets. The FASB also issued a proposal[10] in response to similar feedback in its PIR regarding difficulties in applying the definition of a business. The FASB and the IASB jointly discussed the clarifications to the definition of a business in IFRS 3 and the FASB's Accounting Standards Codification (ASC) 805. In January 2017, the FASB concluded its project and issued ASU 2017-01, *Business Combinations (Topic 805): Clarifying the Definition of a Business*. At the time of writing, the IASB expects to issue its amendments in the first half of 2018.[11] The IASB's proposed amendments are discussed below.

- *The fair value of the assets acquired is concentrated in a single asset or a group of similar identifiable assets*

  The ED proposes a screening test designed to simplify the evaluation of whether an integrated set of activities and assets constitutes a business. Under the proposed amendments, an integrated set of activities and assets is not a business if substantially all of the fair value of the gross assets acquired is concentrated in a single identifiable asset or group of similar identifiable assets. The proposed screening test is based on the fair value of the gross assets acquired, rather than the fair value of the total consideration paid or the net assets. Thus, the significance of a single asset or a group of similar assets acquired is assessed without considering how they are financed.

If this screening test indicates that an integrated set of activities and assets is not a business, then an entity would not have to evaluate the other guidance included in the definition of a business.[12]

In light of the feedback received, the IASB tentatively decided in April 2017 to:[13]

- make the screening test optional on a transaction-by-transaction basis;
- confirm that, when applied, the screening test is determinative. This means that if an entity has carried out the screening test and concluded that a concentration exists, the entity should treat the transaction as an asset purchase;
- specify that the gross assets considered in the screening test should exclude deferred tax assets and goodwill resulting from the effects of deferred tax liabilities;
- clarify that guidance on 'a single asset' for the screening test also applies when one of the acquired assets is a right-of-use asset, as described in IFRS 16, which is considered together with the asset to which it relates (for example leasehold land and the building on it are a single asset for the screening test);
- clarify that when assessing whether assets are 'similar' for the screening test, an entity should consider the nature of each single asset and the risks associated with managing and creating outputs from the assets; and
- clarify that the new guidance on what assets may be considered a single asset or a group of similar assets is not intended to modify the existing guidance on similar assets in paragraph 36 of IAS 38 and the term 'class' in IAS 16, IAS 38 and IFRS 7 – *Financial Instruments: Disclosures*.

- *Minimum requirements to be a business*

  The IASB decided that in order to be considered a business, an acquisition must include, at a minimum, an input and a substantive process that together have the ability to contribute to the creation of outputs. However, not all of the inputs and processes necessary to create outputs have to be acquired for the integrated set of activities and assets to qualify as a business.[14] In June 2017, the IASB tentatively decided to clarify that to be considered a business an acquired set of activities and assets must include, at a minimum, an input and a substantive process that together are required to contribute *significantly* to the ability to create outputs.[15]

- *Evaluating whether the acquired process is substantive*

  The ED proposes guidance to assist entities in determining whether a substantive process has been acquired. The proposed amendments include different criteria for consideration, depending on whether the acquired integrated set of assets and activities has outputs. When it does not, at the acquisition date, have outputs, then the definition of a business is met only if the inputs acquired include both an organised workforce that performs a process that is critical to the creation of outputs and another input (or inputs) that is intended to be developed into outputs. In contrast, when the acquired set of activities and assets at the acquisition date has outputs, an organised workforce is not required if the acquired set includes a process (or group of processes) that is unique or scarce or is difficult to replace.[16] In June 2017, the IASB tentatively decided to confirm the guidance proposed in the ED to assess whether a substantive process has been acquired. In addition, the IASB tentatively decided to specify that difficulties in replacing an acquired workforce may indicate that the workforce performs a substantive process.[17]

- *Market participant capable of replacing missing elements*

  The IASB decided that the ability of a market participant to replace any missing elements by integrating the acquired set of activities and assets into its own and continuing to produce outputs is no longer a consideration in determining whether the acquisition is a business combination.[18] The Board believes that the assessment should be based on what has been acquired, rather than what a market participant could replace.[19]

- *Revise the definition of outputs*

  The ED proposes to narrow the definition of outputs to focus on goods and services provided to customers and 'other revenues'. Thus, the proposed definition excludes returns in the form of lower costs and other economic benefits provided directly to investors or other owners, members, or participants.[20] The IASB believes that the current definition of outputs does not sufficiently distinguish between an asset and a business. For example, many asset acquisitions (e.g. the purchase of new equipment for a manufacturing facility) may result in lower costs even though they do not involve the acquisition of activities and processes.[21] In June 2017, the IASB tentatively decided to clarify that 'other revenues' includes income arising from contracts that are within the entity's ordinary activities but are outside the scope of IFRS 15. In addition, the IASB tentatively decided that if an acquired set of assets generated revenues before the acquisition, but is integrated by the acquirer and no longer generates revenues after the acquisition, that set of assets is regarded as creating outputs.[22]

The ED also proposes to clarify that an acquired contract is not a substantive process. However, an acquired outsourcing agreement may provide access to an organised workforce that performs a substantive process.[23]

- *Goodwill*

The ED proposed removing from paragraph B12 of IFRS 3 the statement that a set of assets and activities in which goodwill is present is presumed to be a business. The ED also states that the presence of goodwill may be an indicator that a business has been acquired. However, the presence of an insignificant amount of goodwill does not mean that the acquired assets (and activities, if any) should automatically be considered a business.[24] As discussed in 2.2.2 above, the acquisition of an asset or a group of assets (and activities, if any) that do not constitute a business, does not give rise to goodwill. If the consideration paid exceeds the fair value of the individual assets and liabilities acquired in an asset acquisition, the cost of the group is allocated to the individual identifiable assets and liabilities on the basis of their relative fair values at the date of purchase. *[IFRS 3.2].*

The Board also proposes to add illustrative examples to IFRS 3 to assist with the interpretation of what is considered a business.[25]

The ED proposes that an entity would be required to apply the proposed amendments to IFRS 3 to any business combination for which the acquisition date is on or after the beginning of the first annual reporting period beginning on or after the effective date of the amendments.[26]

4 ACQUISITION METHOD OF ACCOUNTING

IFRS 3 requires a business combination to be accounted for by applying the acquisition method. *[IFRS 3.4].* Applying the acquisition method involves the following steps:

(a) identifying an acquirer (4.1 below);

(b) determining the acquisition date (4.2 below);

(c) recognising and measuring the identifiable assets acquired, the liabilities assumed, and any non-controlling interest in the acquiree (5 below); and

(d) recognising and measuring goodwill or a gain in a bargain purchase (6 below). *[IFRS 3.5].*

4.1 Identifying the acquirer

The first step in applying the acquisition method is identifying the acquirer. IFRS 3 requires one of the combining entities to be identified as the acquirer. *[IFRS 3.6].* For this purpose the guidance in IFRS 10 is to be used, i.e. the acquirer is the entity that obtains control of the acquiree. *[IFRS 3.7, B13].* An investor controls an investee when it is exposed, or has rights, to variable returns from its involvement with the investee and has the ability to affect those returns through its power over the investee. *[IFRS 10.6].* This is discussed further in Chapter 6 at 3.

If IFRS 10 does not clearly indicate which of the combining entities is the acquirer, additional guidance in IFRS 3 includes various other factors to take into account. *[IFRS 3.7, B13].*

The various other factors require significant judgement, particularly where the business combination may be a 'reverse acquisition' or where the combination occurred by contract alone.

In a business combination effected primarily by transferring cash or other assets or by incurring liabilities, the acquirer is usually the entity that transfers the cash or other assets or incurs the liabilities. *[IFRS 3.B14].*

In a business combination effected primarily by exchanging equity interests, the acquirer is usually the entity that issues its equity interests, but in some business combinations, so-called 'reverse acquisitions', the issuing entity is the acquiree. Application guidance on the accounting for reverse acquisitions is provided in

Appendix B to IFRS 3 (see 14 below). In identifying the acquirer, IFRS 3 requires that other facts and circumstances should also be considered, including:

- the relative voting rights in the combined entity after the business combination. The acquirer is usually the combining entity whose owners as a group retain or receive the largest portion of the voting rights in the combined entity, after taking due account of any unusual or special voting arrangements and options, warrants or convertible securities;
- the existence of a large minority voting interest in the combined entity if no other owner or organised group of owners has a significant voting interest. The acquirer is usually the combining entity whose single owner or organised group of owners holds the largest minority voting interest in the combined entity;
- the composition of the governing body of the combined entity. The acquirer is usually the combining entity whose owners have the ability to elect or appoint or to remove a majority of the members of the governing body of the combined entity;
- the composition of the senior management of the combined entity. The acquirer is usually the combining entity whose (former) management dominates the management of the combined entity; and
- the terms of the exchange of equity interests. The acquirer is usually the combining entity that pays a premium over the pre-combination fair value of the equity interests of the other combining entity or entities. *[IFRS 3.B15]*.

The acquirer is usually the combining entity whose relative size is significantly greater than that of the other combining entity or entities, whether this be measured by, for example, assets, revenues or profit. *[IFRS 3.B16]*.

If the business combination involves more than two entities, determining the acquirer includes considering, among other things, which of the combining entities initiated the combination, as well as the relative size of the combining entities. *[IFRS 3.B17]*.

4.1.1 New entity formed to effect a business combination

A new entity formed to effect a business combination is not necessarily the acquirer. This will depend on whether it has issued equity interests or paid cash. If it has issued equity interests, one of the combining entities is to be identified as the acquirer by applying the guidance described above. *[IFRS 3.B18]*. The combination between the new entity and the identified acquirer is effectively the same as if a new entity had been inserted above an existing entity. As discussed in Chapter 10 at 4.2, such a transaction should be accounted for as a continuation of the existing entity. The combination of the new entity with the identified acquirer cannot be accounted for as a 'reverse acquisition' because IFRS 3's definition requires the accounting acquiree to meet the definition of a business for a transaction to qualify for this method of accounting. *[IFRS 3.B19]*.

If a new entity transfers cash or other assets or incurs liabilities as consideration, it may be the acquirer. IFRS 3 does not specify in what circumstances this may be the case but it is clear that 'control' is the fundamental concept when identifying an acquirer. An example is where the newly formed entity ('Newco') is used by a group of investors or another entity to acquire a controlling interest in a target entity in an arm's length transaction.

Example 9.7: Business combination effected by a Newco for cash consideration (1)

Entity A intends to acquire the voting shares (and therefore obtain control) of Target Entity. Entity A incorporates Newco and uses this entity to effect the business combination. Entity A provides a loan at commercial interest rates to Newco. The loan funds are used by Newco to acquire 100% of the voting shares of Target Entity in an arm's length transaction.

The group structure post-transaction is as follows:

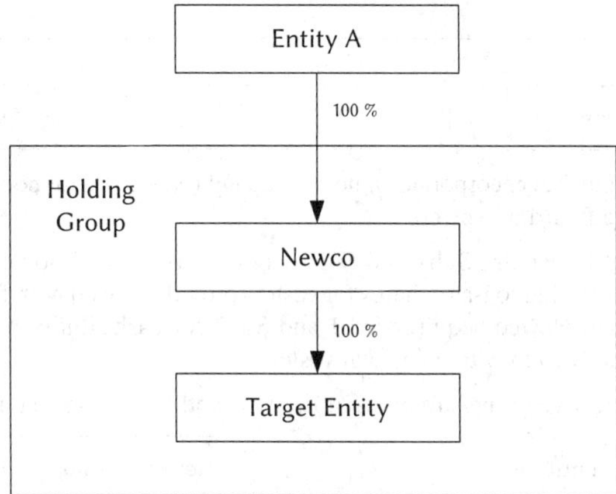

Under its local regulations, Newco is required to prepare IFRS-compliant consolidated financial statements for the Holding Group (the reporting entity). (In most situations like this, Newco would be exempt from preparing consolidated financial statements – see Chapter 6 at 2.3.1.)

The acquirer is the entity that obtains control of the acquiree. Whenever a new entity is formed to effect a business combination other than through the issue of shares, it is appropriate to consider whether Newco is an extension of one of the transacting parties. If it is an extension of the transacting party (or parties) that ultimately gain control of the other combining entities, Newco is the acquirer.

In this situation, Entity A has obtained control of Target Entity in an arm's length transaction, using Newco to effect the acquisition. The transaction has resulted in a change in control of Target Entity and Newco is in effect an extension of Entity A acting at its direction to obtain control for Entity A. Accordingly, Newco would be identified as the acquirer at the Holding Group level.

If, rather than Entity A establishing Newco, a group of investors had established it as the acquiring vehicle through which they obtained control of Target Entity then, we believe, Newco would be regarded as the acquirer since it is an extension of the group of investors.

Another specific situation in which a Newco might be identified as the acquirer is illustrated in Example 9.8 below, where a parent uses a Newco to facilitate a public flotation of shares in a group of subsidiary companies. Although a Newco incorporated by the existing parent of the subsidiaries concerned would not generally be identified as the acquirer, in this particular situation the critical distinguishing factor is that the acquisition of the subsidiaries was conditional on an Initial Public Offering ('IPO') of Newco. This means that there has been a substantial change in the ownership of the subsidiaries by virtue of the IPO. The Interpretations Committee discussed similar fact patterns (see *IFRIC Update*, July 2011) but has subsequently observed that accounting for arrangements involving the creation of a newly formed entity is too broad to be addressed through an interpretation or an annual improvement. The Interpretations Committee concluded that it would be better considered within the context of a broader project on accounting for common control transactions.[27] At the time of writing, the project is on the IASB's active agenda with the next step likely to be a discussion paper in the first half of 2018.[28]

Example 9.8: Business combination effected by a Newco for cash consideration: spin-off transaction (2)

Entity A proposes to spin off two of its existing businesses (currently housed in two separate entities, Sub1 and Sub2) as part of an initial public offering (IPO). The existing group structure is as follows:

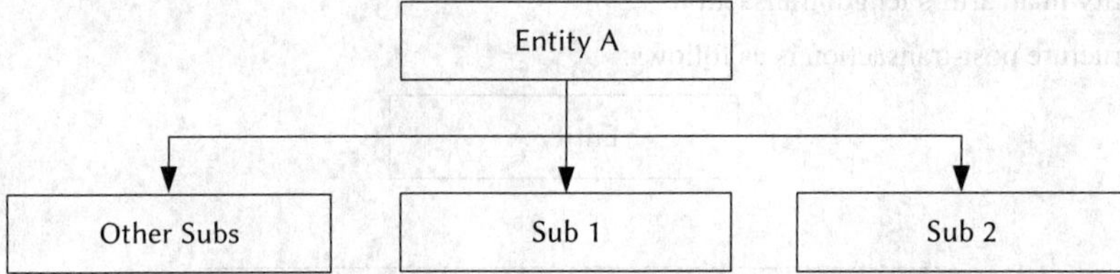

To facilitate the spin off, Entity A incorporates a new company (Newco) with nominal equity and appoints independent directors to the Board of Newco.

Newco signs an agreement to acquire Sub1 and Sub2 from Entity A conditional on the IPO proceeding. Newco issues a prospectus offering to issue shares for cash to provide Newco with funds to acquire Sub1 and Sub2. The IPO proceeds and Newco acquires Sub1 and Sub2 for cash. Entity A's nominal equity leaves virtually 100% ownership in Newco with the new investors.

Following the IPO, the respective group structures of Entity A and Newco appear as follows:

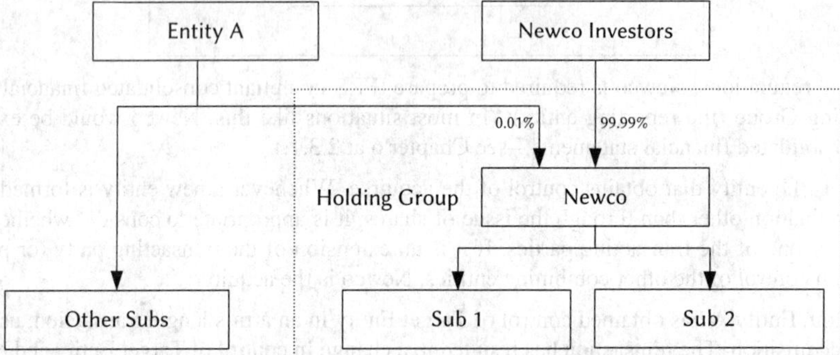

In this case, we believe it might be appropriate to identify Newco as the acquirer. The Newco investors have obtained control and virtually 100% ownership of Sub1 and Sub2 in an arm's length transaction, using Newco to effect the acquisition. The transaction has resulted in a change in control of Sub1 and Sub2 (i.e. Entity A losing control and Newco investors, via Newco, obtaining control). Newco could in effect be considered as an extension of the Newco investors since:

- the acquisition of Sub1 and Sub2 was conditional on the IPO proceeding so that the IPO is an integral part of the transaction as a whole evidencing that Entity A did not have control of the transaction/entities; and
- there is a substantial change in the ownership of Sub1 and Sub2 by virtue of the IPO (i.e. Entity A only retains a negligible ownership interest in Newco).

Accordingly, Newco might be identified as the acquirer at the Holding Group level.

Whether a Newco formed to facilitate an IPO is capable of being identified as an acquirer depends on the facts and circumstances and ultimately requires judgement. If, for example, Entity A incorporates Newco and arranges for it to acquire Sub1 and Sub2 prior to the IPO proceeding, Newco might be viewed as an extension of Entity A or possibly an extension of Sub1 or Sub2. This is because the IPO and the reorganisation may not be seen as being part of one integral transaction, and therefore the transaction would be a combination of entities under common control (see Chapter 10 at 3.1). In that situation, Newco would not be the acquirer.

4.1.2 *Stapling arrangements*

In 2014, the Interpretations Committee considered whether an acquirer identified for the purpose of IFRS 3 is a parent for the purpose of IFRS 10 in circumstances in which a business combination is achieved by contract alone, such as a stapling arrangement, with no combining entity obtaining control of the other combining entities. When considering this issue, the Interpretations Committee thought that the guidance outlined in paragraph B15(a) of IFRS 3, i.e. that the acquirer is usually the combining entity whose owners as a group receive the largest portion of the voting rights in the combined entity, would be relevant to identifying which of the combining entities is the acquirer in the stapling transaction considered.[29]

4.2 Determining the acquisition date

The next step in applying the acquisition method is determining the acquisition date, 'the date on which the acquirer obtains control of the acquiree'. *[IFRS 3.8, Appendix A].* This is generally the 'closing date', i.e. the date on which the acquirer legally transfers the consideration, acquires the assets and assumes the liabilities of the acquiree. *[IFRS 3.9].* However, although the standard refers to the 'closing date', this does not necessarily mean that the transaction has to be closed or finalised at law before the acquirer obtains control over the acquiree.

The acquirer might obtain control on a date that is either earlier or later than the closing date. If a written agreement provides that the acquirer obtains control of the acquiree on a date before the closing date, the acquisition date might precede the closing date. *[IFRS 3.9].* This does not mean that the acquisition date can be artificially backdated or otherwise altered, for example, by the inclusion of terms in the agreement indicating that the acquisition is to be effective as of an earlier date, with the acquirer being entitled to profits arising after that date, even if the purchase price is based on the net asset position of the acquiree at that date.

The Basis for Conclusions accepts that, for convenience, an entity might wish to designate an acquisition date at the beginning or end of a month, the date on which it closes its books, rather than the actual acquisition date during the month. Unless events between the 'convenience' date and the actual acquisition date result in material changes in the amounts recognised, that entity's practice would comply with the requirements of IFRS 3. *[IFRS 3.BC110].*

The date control is obtained will be dependent on a number of factors, including whether the acquisition arises from a public offer or a private deal, is subject to approval by other parties, or is effected by the issue of shares.

For an acquisition by way of a public offer, the date of acquisition could be:

- when the offer has become unconditional because sufficient acceptances have been received; or
- the date that the offer closes.

In a private deal, the date would generally be when an unconditional offer has been accepted by the vendors.

Thus, where an offer is conditional on the approval of the acquiring entity's shareholders, until that approval has been received, it is unlikely that control will have been obtained. Where the offer is conditional upon receiving some form of regulatory approval, then it will depend on the nature of that approval. If it is a substantive hurdle, such as obtaining the approval of a competition authority, it is unlikely that control is obtained prior to that approval. However, where the approval is merely a formality, or 'rubber-stamping' exercise, then this would not preclude control having been obtained at an earlier date.

Where the acquisition is effected by the issue of shares, then the date of control will generally be when the exchange of shares takes place.

However, whether control has been obtained by a certain date is a matter of fact, and all pertinent facts and circumstances surrounding a business combination need to be considered in assessing when the acquirer has obtained control. To evaluate whether control has been obtained the acquirer would need to apply the guidance in IFRS 10 (see Chapter 6 at 3).

5 RECOGNITION AND MEASUREMENT OF ASSETS ACQUIRED, LIABILITIES ASSUMED AND NON-CONTROLLING INTERESTS

The next step in applying the acquisition method involves recognising and measuring the identifiable assets acquired, the liabilities assumed and any non-controlling interest in the acquiree.

5.1 General principles

The identifiable assets acquired and liabilities assumed of the acquiree are recognised as of the acquisition date and measured at fair value as at that date, with certain limited exceptions. *[IFRS 3.10, 14, 18, 20].*

Any non-controlling interest in the acquiree is to be recognised at the acquisition date. Non-controlling interests that are present ownership interests and entitle their holders to a proportionate share of the entity's net assets in the event of liquidation can be measured on one of two bases:

- at fair value at that date; or
- at the non-controlling interest's proportionate share of the acquiree's net identifiable assets.

All other components of non-controlling interests are measured at their acquisition-date fair values, unless another measurement basis is required by IFRSs. *[IFRS 3.10, 19].* See 8 below.

5.2 Recognising identifiable assets acquired and liabilities assumed

To qualify for recognition, an item acquired or assumed must be:

(a) an asset or liability at the acquisition date; and

(b) part of the business acquired (the acquiree) rather than the result of a separate transaction. *[IFRS 3.BC112].*

The identifiable assets acquired and liabilities assumed must meet the definitions of assets and liabilities in the IASB's *Conceptual Framework for Financial Reporting* (*'Framework'*) (see Chapter 2). *[Framework.4.4].* This means that costs that the acquirer expects but is not obliged to incur in the future cannot be provided for. For example, the entity's plans to reorganise the acquiree's activities (e.g. plans to exit from an activity, or terminate the employment of or relocate employees) are not liabilities at the acquisition date. These costs will be recognised by the acquirer in its post-combination financial statements in accordance with other IFRSs. *[IFRS 3.11].* Liabilities for restructuring or exit activities can only be recognised if they meet the definition of a liability at the acquisition date. *[IFRS 3.BC132].* Although the standard no longer contains the explicit requirements relating to restructuring plans, the Basis for Conclusions clearly indicate that the requirements for recognising liabilities associated with restructuring or exit activities remain the same. *[IFRS 3.BC137].* This is discussed further at 11.4 below.

The first condition for recognition makes no reference to reliability of measurement or probability as to the inflow or outflow of economic benefits. This is because the IASB considers them to be unnecessary. Reliability of measurement is a part of the overall recognition criteria in the *Framework* which include the concept of 'probability' to refer to the degree of uncertainty that the future economic benefits associated with an asset or liability will flow to or from the entity. *[IFRS 3.BC125-BC130].* Thus, identifiable assets and liabilities are recognised regardless of the degree of probability that there will be inflows or outflows of economic benefits. However, in recognising a contingent liability, IFRS 3 requires that its fair value can be measured reliably (see 5.6.1.A below).

The second condition requires that the identifiable assets acquired and liabilities assumed must be part of the exchange for the acquiree, rather than the result of separate transactions. *[IFRS 3.12].* Explicit guidance is given in the standard for making such an assessment as discussed at 11 below. An acquirer may recognise some assets and liabilities that had not previously been recognised in the acquiree's financial statements, e.g. intangible assets, such as internally-generated brand names, patents or customer relationships. *[IFRS 3.13].*

Guidance on recognising intangible assets and operating leases, as well as items for which IFRS 3 provides limited exceptions to the recognition principles and conditions are discussed at 5.5 and 5.6 below.

5.3 Acquisition-date fair values of identifiable assets acquired and liabilities assumed

The general principle is that the identifiable assets acquired and liabilities assumed are measured at their acquisition-date fair values. In this chapter, reference to fair value means fair value as measured by IFRS 13.

IFRS 13 provides guidance on how to measure fair value, but it does not change when fair value is required or permitted under IFRS. IFRS 13 is discussed in detail in Chapter 14. IFRS 3 allows some assets and liabilities to be measured at other than fair value on initial recognition, as described at 5.6 below.

IFRS 13 defines 'fair value' as the price that would be received to sell an asset or paid to transfer a liability in an orderly transaction between market participants at the measurement date under current market conditions. It is explicitly an exit price. *[IFRS 13.2].*

Where IFRS 3 requires an identifiable asset acquired or liability assumed to be measured at its fair value at the acquisition date, although an entity applies the IFRS 13 measurement requirements, it does not need to disclose information about those acquisition-date fair value measurements under IFRS 13. However, the IFRS 13 disclosure requirements would apply to any fair value measurement after initial recognition, for example the fair value measurement of contingent consideration obligation classified as a financial liability (see Chapter 14 at 20). *[IFRS 13.91]*.

IFRS 3 specifies those assets and liabilities that are not measured at fair value, including income taxes and employee benefits. *[IFRS 3.20]*. These are discussed at 5.5 and 5.6 below.

5.4 Classifying or designating identifiable assets acquired and liabilities assumed

The acquirer must classify or designate the identifiable assets and liabilities assumed on the basis of its own contractual terms, economic conditions, operating and accounting policies and other relevant conditions as at the acquisition date. *[IFRS 3.15]*.

The standard provides two exceptions:

- classification of leases in accordance with IAS 17 (however, under IFRS 16, this exception will remain relevant only for classification of leases in which the acquiree is the lessor, see discussion below); and
- classification of a contract as an insurance contract in accordance with IFRS 4 – *Insurance Contracts* (however, IFRS 17 – *Insurance Contracts*, will remove this classification exception for entities that apply that standard).[30]

In both of these cases, the contracts are classified on the basis of the contractual terms and other factors at the inception of the contract or at the date of modification. This could be the acquisition date if the terms of the contract have been modified in a manner that would change its classification. *[IFRS 3.17]*.

Thus, if an acquiree is a lessee under a lease contract that has been classified appropriately as an operating lease under IAS 17, the acquirer would continue to account for the lease as an operating lease in the absence of any modification to the terms of the contract. Only if, prior to or as at the acquisition date, the terms of the lease were modified in such a way that it would be reclassified as a finance lease under IAS 17 (see Chapter 24 at 3.2.3), would the acquirer recognise the asset and the related finance lease liability. IFRS 16 introduces a single accounting model for lessees, requiring most leases to be recognised on the balance sheet. Therefore, based on consequential amendments to paragraph 17 of IFRS 3 from IFRS 16, the above exception will remain relevant only for classification of leases in which the acquiree is the lessor. IFRS 16 and its consequential amendments are mandatory for annual periods beginning on or after 1 January 2019, although early adoption is permitted, provided IFRS 15 has been applied, or is applied at the same date as IFRS 16 (for further guidance on IFRS 16, see Chapter 25).

Examples of classifications or designations made by the acquirer on the basis of conditions at the acquisition date include but are not limited to:

(a) classifying financial assets and liabilities as measured at fair value through profit or loss or at amortised cost, or as a financial asset measured at fair value through other comprehensive income, in accordance with IFRS 9 (for entities applying IAS 39, classifying particular financial assets and liabilities as a financial asset or liability at fair value through profit or loss, or as a financial asset available for sale or held to maturity);

(b) designating a derivative instrument as a hedging instrument in accordance with IFRS 9/IAS 39; and

(c) assessing whether an embedded derivative should be separated from the host contract in accordance with IFRS 9/IAS 39 (which is a matter of 'classification' as IFRS 3 uses that term). *[IFRS 3.16].*

In paragraph 16, IFRS 3 refers to IFRS 9, but the classification requirements of that standard are only applicable when IFRS 9 is applied, so they are not mandatory until annual periods beginning on or after 1 January 2018, with early adoption permitted. Until IFRS 9 is applied, entities apply the classifications in IAS 39.

The requirements for the classification of financial assets and liabilities under IFRS 9 are discussed in Chapter 47 and under IAS 39 in Chapter 46. Although, IFRS 9 prohibits reclassifications of financial liabilities and allows reclassifications of financial assets when, and only when, an entity changes its business model for managing financial assets as described in Chapter 47 at 9 and IAS 39 has particular requirements that prohibit the reclassification of items into or out of the fair value through profit or loss category, and permit, and in some situations require, reclassification between held-to-maturity investments and available-for-sale assets, described in Chapter 46 at 6, these do not apply in the circumstances of a business combination. The acquirer has to make its own classification at the acquisition date. If it has not had to consider the classification of such assets or liabilities before, it could choose to adopt the classification applied by the acquiree or adopt a different classification if appropriate. However, if it already has an accounting policy for like transactions, the classification should be consistent with that existing policy.

As discussed in Chapter 53 at 5 and Chapter 52 at 5, there are a number of conditions that need to be met for hedge relationships to qualify for hedge accounting, in particular formal designation and documentation, and an ongoing assessment of the designated hedge. If an acquiree has derivative or other financial instruments that have been used as hedging instruments in a hedge relationship, IFRS 3 requires the acquirer to make its own designation about the hedging relationship that satisfy the conditions for hedge accounting, based on the conditions as they exist at the acquisition date. If the hedging relationship is being accounted for as a cash flow hedge by the acquiree, the acquirer does not inherit the acquiree's existing cash flow hedge reserve, as this clearly represents cumulative pre-acquisition gains and losses. This has implications for the assessment of hedge effectiveness and the measurement of ineffectiveness because, so far as the acquirer is concerned, it has started a new hedge relationship with a hedging instrument that is likely to have a non-zero fair value (see Chapter 52 at 4.2.4). This may mean that although the acquiree can continue to account for the relationship as a cash flow hedge, the acquirer is unable to account for it as a cash flow hedge in its financial statements.

In the situations discussed above, the effect of applying the principle in IFRS 3 only affects the post-business combination accounting for the financial instruments concerned. The financial instruments that are recognised as at the acquisition date, and their measurement at their fair value at that date, do not change.

However, the requirement for the acquirer to assess whether an embedded derivative should be separated from the host contract based on acquisition date conditions could result in additional assets or liabilities being recognised (and measured at their acquisition-date fair value) that differ from those recognised by the acquiree. Embedded derivatives are discussed in Chapter 44.

5.5 Recognising and measuring particular assets acquired and liabilities assumed

IFRS 3 gives some application guidance on recognising and measuring particular assets acquired and liabilities assumed in a business combination, discussed below.

5.5.1 Operating leases

Although existing leases of the acquiree are new leases from the perspective of the acquirer, the classification of the leases between operating and finance in accordance with IAS 17 is not revisited (see 5.4 above). If the acquiree is the lessee to an operating lease and the terms of the lease are favourable (asset) or unfavourable (liability) relative to market terms and prices, the acquirer is required to recognise either an intangible asset or a liability. *[IFRS 3.B28-B29].*

An operating lease at market terms may be associated with an identifiable intangible asset if market participants are willing to pay a price for the lease. A lease of gates at an airport or of retail space in a prime shopping centre may provide entry into a market or other future economic benefits that qualify as identifiable intangible assets, for example, as a customer relationship (see 5.5.2 below). *[IFRS 3.B30].*

For entities applying IFRS 16, as a result of consequential amendments to IFRS 3, the above guidance in paragraphs B28-B29 of IFRS 3 has been removed and a new exception in paragraphs 28A-28B has been introduced to the recognition and measurement principles of IFRS 3 for leases in which the acquiree is the lessee (see 5.6.8 below). IFRS 16 and its consequential amendments are mandatory for annual periods beginning on or after 1 January 2019, although early adoption is permitted, provided IFRS 15 has been applied, or is applied at the same date as IFRS 16 (for further guidance on IFRS 16, see Chapter 25).

If the acquiree is a lessor in an operating lease, i.e. it has an item of property, plant and equipment that is leased to another party, there is no requirement for the acquirer to recognise intangible assets or liabilities if the terms of the lease are favourable or unfavourable relative to market terms and prices. Instead, off-market terms are reflected in the acquisition-date fair value of the asset (such as a building or a patent) subject to the lease. *[IFRS 3.B42].* The IASB sought to avoid any inconsistency with the fair value model in IAS 40, which requires the fair value of investment property to take into account rental income from current leases. *[IFRS 3.BC146].*

The requirement to reflect the off-market terms in the fair value of the asset subject to an operating lease in which the acquiree is the lessor applies to any type of asset, to the extent market participants would take them into consideration when pricing the asset, and is not restricted to investment properties accounted for under the fair value model in IAS 40. Based on the requirements of IAS 16 and IAS 38, an entity would be required to adjust the depreciation or amortisation method for the leased asset so as to reflect the timing of the cash flows attributable to the underlying leases. *[IFRS 3.BC148].*

For entities applying IFRS 16, this guidance in paragraph B42 of IFRS 3 for leases where the acquiree is a lessor effectively remains unchanged, since for lessors the new standard introduces little change to the existing accounting in IAS 17.

5.5.2 Intangible assets

Identifiable intangible assets may have to be recognised by an acquirer although they have not previously been recognised by the acquiree. *[IFRS 3.B31]*. IFRS 3 and IAS 38 give guidance on the recognition of intangible assets acquired in a business combination.

IFRS 3 and IAS 38 both define an 'intangible asset' as 'an identifiable non-monetary asset without physical substance'. *[IFRS 3 Appendix A, IAS 38.8]*. The definition requires an intangible asset to be 'identifiable' to distinguish it from goodwill. *[IAS 38.11]*. Both standards regard an asset as identifiable if it:

(a) is separable, i.e. capable of being separated or divided from the entity and sold, transferred, licensed, rented or exchanged, either individually or together with a related contract, identifiable asset or liability, regardless of whether the entity intends to do so (the 'separability' criterion); or

(b) arises from contractual or other legal rights, regardless of whether those rights are transferable or separable from the entity or from other rights and obligations (the 'contractual-legal' criterion). *[IFRS 3 Appendix A, IAS 38.12]*.

IFRS 3 provides the following application guidance.

- *Separability*

An intangible asset is separable even if the acquirer has no intention of selling, licensing or otherwise exchanging it. An acquired intangible asset is separable if there is evidence of exchange transactions for that type of asset or an asset of a similar type, even if those transactions are infrequent and regardless of whether the acquirer is involved in them. For example, customer and subscriber lists are frequently licensed and thus separable. Even if an acquiree believes its customer lists have characteristics that distinguish them from others, this would not generally prevent the acquired customer list being considered separable. However, if confidentiality terms or other agreements prohibit an entity from selling, leasing or otherwise exchanging information about its customers, then the customer list would not be separable. *[IFRS 3.B33]*.

An intangible asset may be separable from goodwill in combination with a related contract, identifiable asset or liability. Two examples are given by IFRS 3:

(a) market participants exchange deposit liabilities and related depositor relationship intangible assets in observable exchange transactions. Therefore, the acquirer should recognise the depositor relationship intangible asset separately from goodwill;

(b) an acquiree owns a registered trademark and documented but unpatented technical expertise used to manufacture the trademarked product. When it sells the trademark, the owner must also transfer everything else necessary for the new owner to produce a product or service indistinguishable from that produced by the former owner. Because the unpatented technical expertise must be separated from the acquiree or combined entity and sold if the related trademark is sold, it meets the separability criterion. *[IFRS 3.B34]*.

- *Contractual-legal*

An intangible asset that meets the contractual-legal criterion is identifiable, and hence accounted for separately from goodwill, even if the asset is not transferable or separable from the acquiree or from other rights and obligations. For example:

(a) an acquiree leases a manufacturing facility under an operating lease; its terms are favourable relative to market. The lease terms explicitly prohibit transfer, whether by sale or sublease. The amount by which the lease terms are favourable compared to market transactions is an intangible asset that meets the contractual-legal criterion for recognition separately, even though the lease contract cannot be sold or transferred by the acquirer;

(b) an acquiree owns and operates a nuclear power plant. The licence to operate the power plant is a separate intangible asset, even if the acquirer cannot sell or transfer it separately from the power plant itself. IFRS 3 goes on to say that an acquirer may recognise the operating licence and the power plant as a single asset for financial reporting purposes if their useful lives are similar;

(c) an acquiree owns a technology patent that it has licensed to others for their exclusive use outside the domestic market, for which it has received a specified percentage of future foreign revenue. Both the technology patent and the related licence agreement meet the contractual-legal criterion for separate recognition even if it would not be practical to sell or exchange them separately from one another. *[IFRS 3.B32]*.

Accordingly, under IFRS 3, intangible assets are recognised separately from goodwill if they are identifiable, i.e. they either are separable or arise from contractual or other legal rights. *[IFRS 3.B31]*. They must be assigned an acquisition-date fair value.

For entities applying IFRS 16, as a result of consequential amendments, the above example (a) has been removed from paragraph B32 of IFRS 3. This is because IFRS 16 requires the off-market nature of the lease to be captured in the right-of-use asset, rather than recognised separately as an intangible asset or liability (see 5.6.8 below). IFRS 16 and its consequential amendments are mandatory for annual periods beginning on or after 1 January 2019, although early adoption is permitted, provided IFRS 15 has been applied, or is applied at the same date as IFRS 16 (for further guidance on IFRS 16, see Chapter 25).

5.5.2.A Examples of identifiable intangible assets

We have considered above a number of different types of identifiable intangible assets that are recognised separately from goodwill, such as customer and subscriber lists, depositor relationships, registered trademarks, unpatented technical expertise, favourable operating leases under IAS 17, licences and technology patents.

IAS 38 also explicitly requires an acquirer to recognise as a separate intangible asset in-process research and development of the acquiree, in accordance with IFRS 3, if the project meets the definition of an intangible asset. *[IAS 38.34]*. IFRS 3 itself only refers to this in its Basis for Conclusions. *[IFRS 3.BC149-BC156]*. This is discussed at 5.5.2.D below.

IFRS 3's Illustrative Examples list items acquired in a business combination that are identifiable intangible assets, noting that the examples are not intended to be all-inclusive. *[IFRS 3.IE16-IE44]*. The assets listed are designated as being 'contractual', or 'non-contractual', in which case they do not arise from contractual or other legal rights but are separable. It emphasises that assets do not have to be separable to meet the contractual-legal criterion.

The table below summarises the items included in the Illustrative Examples. See the Illustrative Examples for further explanations.

Intangible assets arising from contractual or other legal rights (regardless of being separable)	Other intangible assets that are separable
Marketing-related	
– Trademarks, trade names, service marks, collective marks and certification marks – Trade dress (unique colour, shape or package design) – Newspaper mastheads – Internet domain names – Non-competition agreements	
Customer-related	
– Order or production backlog – Customer contracts and the related customer relationships	– Customer lists – Non-contractual customer relationships
Artistic-related	
– Plays, operas and ballets – Books, magazines, newspapers and other literary works – Musical works such as compositions, song lyrics and advertising jingles – Pictures and photographs – Video and audiovisual material, including motion pictures or films, music videos and television programmes	
Contract-based	
– Licensing, royalty and standstill agreements – Advertising, construction, management, service or supply contracts – Lease agreements – Construction permits – Franchise agreements – Operating and broadcast rights – Servicing contracts such as mortgage servicing contracts – Employment contracts – Use rights such as drilling, water, air, mineral, timber-cutting and route authorities	
Technology-based	
– Patented technology – Computer software and mask works – Trade secrets, such as secret formulas, processes or recipes	– Unpatented technology – Databases, including title plants

Some items have been designated as being 'contractual' due to legal protection, for example, trademarks and trade secrets. The guidance explains that even without that legal protection, they would still normally meet the separability criterion.

Customer relationships established through contracts are deemed identifiable as they meet the contractual-legal criterion. However, there need not be a current contract or any outstanding orders at the date of acquisition for customer relationships to meet the identifiability criteria. Customer relationships can also be recognised as intangible assets if they arise outside a contract but in this case they must be separable to be recognised. This is discussed further in 5.5.2.B below.

5.5.2.B Customer relationship intangible assets

Further guidance on customer relationships acquired in a business combination is provided in IFRS 3's Illustrative Examples, which form the basis of the example below. These demonstrate how an entity should interpret the contractual-legal and separability criteria in the context of acquired customer relationships. *[IFRS 3.IE30].*

Example 9.9: Customer relationship intangible assets

(i) Supply agreement

Acquirer Company (AC) acquires Target Company (TC) in a business combination on 31 December 2018. TC has a five-year agreement to supply goods to Customer. Both TC and AC believe that Customer will renew the agreement at the end of the current contract. The agreement is not separable.

The agreement, whether cancellable or not, meets the contractual-legal criterion. Because TC establishes its relationship with Customer through a contract, both the agreement itself and also TC's customer relationship with Customer meet the contractual-legal criterion.

(ii) Sporting goods and electronics

AC acquires TC in a business combination on 31 December 2018. TC manufactures goods in two distinct lines of business: sporting goods and electronics. Customer purchases both sporting goods and electronics from TC. TC has a contract with Customer to be its exclusive provider of sporting goods but has no contract for the supply of electronics to Customer. Both TC and AC believe that only one overall customer relationship exists between TC and Customer.

The contract to be Customer's exclusive supplier of sporting goods, whether cancellable or not, meets the contractual-legal criterion. In addition, as TC establishes its relationship with Customer through a contract, the customer relationship with Customer meets the contractual-legal criterion. Because TC has only one customer relationship with Customer, the fair value of that relationship incorporates assumptions about TC's relationship with Customer related to both sporting goods and electronics. However, if AC determines that it has two separate customer relationships with Customer, for sporting goods and for electronics, AC would need to assess whether the customer relationship for electronics is separable before it could be recognised as an intangible asset.

(iii) Order backlog and recurring customers

AC acquires TC in a business combination on 31 December 2018. TC does business with its customers solely through purchase and sales orders. At 31 December 2018, TC has a backlog of customer purchase orders from 60 per cent of its customers, all of whom are recurring customers. The other 40 per cent of TC's customers are also recurring customers. However, as at 31 December 2018, TC has no open purchase orders or other contracts with those customers.

Regardless of whether they are cancellable or not, the purchase orders from 60 per cent of TC's customers meet the contractual-legal criterion. Additionally, because TC has established its relationship with 60 per cent of its customers through contracts, not only the purchase orders but also TC's customer relationships meet the contractual-legal criterion. Because TC has a practice of establishing contracts with the remaining 40 per cent of its customers, its relationship with those customers also arises through contractual rights and therefore meets the contractual-legal criterion even though TC does not have contracts with those customers at 31 December 2018.

(iv) Motor insurance contracts

AC acquires TC, an insurer, in a business combination on 31 December 2018. TC has a portfolio of one-year motor insurance contracts that are cancellable by policyholders.

Because TC establishes its relationships with policyholders through insurance contracts, the customer relationship with policyholders meets the contractual-legal criterion.

One of the most difficult areas of interpretation is whether an arrangement is contractual or not. Contractual customer relationships are always recognised separately from goodwill but non-contractual customer relationships are recognised only if they are separable. Consequently, determining whether a relationship is contractual is critical to identifying and measuring customer relationship intangible assets and different conclusions could result in substantially different accounting outcomes.

Paragraph IE28 in the Illustrative Examples explains that a customer relationship is deemed to exist if the entity has information about the customer and regular contact with it and the customer can make direct contact with the entity. A customer relationship 'may also arise through means other than contracts, such as through regular contact by sales or service representatives'. However, the argument is taken a stage further. Regardless of whether any contracts are in place at the acquisition date, 'customer relationships meet the contractual-legal criterion for recognition if an entity has a practice of establishing contracts with its customers'. *[IFRS 3.IE28]*. An example of what is meant by this is given in Example 9.9 above. In the third illustration, 'Order backlog and recurring customers', it states 'Because TC has a practice of establishing contracts with the remaining 40 per cent of its customers, its relationship with those customers also arises through contractual rights and therefore meets the contractual-legal criterion even though TC does not have contracts with those customers at 31 December 2018'.

In 2008 the Interpretations Committee considered the circumstances in which non-contractual customer relationships arise. The staff's survey of Interpretations Committee members indicated that there were diverse practices regarding which customer relationships have a contractual basis and which do not. In addition, valuation experts seemed to be taking different views.[31]

The Interpretations Committee noted that the IFRS Glossary of Terms defined the term 'contract'. Whilst the manner in which a relationship is established is relevant to confirming the existence of a customer relationship, it should not be the primary basis for determining whether an intangible asset is recognised by the acquirer. What might be more relevant is whether the entity has a practice of establishing contracts with its customers or whether relationships arise through other means, such as through regular contact by sales and service representatives (i.e. the matters identified in paragraph IE28). The existence of contractual relationships and information about a customer's prior purchases would be important inputs in valuing a customer relationship intangible asset, but should not determine whether it is recognised.[32] Therefore, a customer base (e.g. customers of a fast food franchise or movie theatres) is an example of a non-contractual customer relationship that would not be recognised in a business combination.

The Interpretations Committee was unable to develop an Interpretation clarifying the distinction between contractual and non-contractual. Given the widespread confusion the matter was referred to the IASB and the FASB with a recommendation to review and amend IFRS 3 by:[33]

- removing the distinction between 'contractual' and 'non-contractual' customer-related intangible assets recognised in a business combination; and
- reviewing the indicators that identify the existence of a customer relationship in paragraph IE28 of IFRS 3 and including them in the standard.

However, the IASB deferred both recommendations of the Interpretations Committee to the PIR of IFRS 3, which was completed in June 2015. As a result of the PIR of IFRS 3 the issue of identification and fair value measurement of intangible assets such as customer relationships and brand names was added to the IASB's active agenda within its *Goodwill and Impairment* research project (see 1.1.1 above). At the time of writing, the IASB is exploring which intangible assets should be separated from goodwill and the IASB's work plan indicates that a Discussion Paper is expected in the first half of 2018.[34] In the meantime, there will be divergent treatments in practice, depending on how entities interpret 'contractual' and 'non-contractual' customer-related intangible assets in a particular business combination.

5.5.2.C *Combining an intangible asset with a related contract, identifiable asset or liability*

IAS 38 was amended as part of the annual improvements issued in April 2009 and is now consistent with IFRS 3. It states that an intangible asset acquired in a business combination might be separable, but only together with a related contract, identifiable asset, or liability. In such cases, the acquirer recognises the intangible assets separately from goodwill, but together with the related item. *[IAS 38.36]*.

Similarly, the acquirer may recognise a group of complementary intangible assets as a single asset provided the individual assets have similar useful lives. For example, 'the terms "brand" and "brand name" are often used as synonyms for trademarks and other marks. However, the former are general marketing terms that are typically used to refer to a group of complementary assets such as a trademark (or service mark) and its related trade name, formulas, recipes and technological expertise.' *[IAS 38.37]*.

It is not clear whether an intangible asset that is only separable in combination with a tangible asset should be recognised together as a single asset for financial reporting purposes in all circumstances. IFRS 3 gives an example of a licence to operate a nuclear power plant, and says that the fair value of the operating licence and the fair value of the power plant may be recognised as a single asset for financial reporting purposes, if the useful lives of those assets are similar (see 5.5.2 above), yet the requirements in IAS 38 only refer to similar useful lives in the context of a group of complementary intangible assets.

In practice entities account for intangible assets separately from the related tangible asset if the useful lives are different. The Rank Group Plc considers that its casino and gaming licences have indefinite useful lives and accounts for them separately from the buildings with which they are acquired, as disclosed in its accounting policy.

Extract 9.1: The Rank Group Plc (2015)

Notes to the financial statements [extract]

1 **General information and accounting policies** [extract]

Summary of significant accounting policies [extract]

1.12 **Intangible assets** [extract]

(b) **Casino and other gaming licences and concessions**

The Group capitalises acquired casino and other gaming licences and concessions. Management believes that licences, with the exception of the two casino concessions in Belgium, have indefinite lives as there is no foreseeable limit to the period over which the licences are expected to generate net cash inflows and each licence holds a value outside the property in which it resides. Each licence is reviewed annually for impairment.

In respect of the two casino concessions in Belgium, their carrying value is amortised over the expected useful life of the concessions.

Any costs in renewing licences or concessions are expensed as incurred.

Guidance on determining asset lives of intangible assets is discussed in Chapter 17 at 9.1.

5.5.2.D In-process research or development project expenditure

IFRS 3 itself only refers to in-process research and development in its Basis for Conclusions, where it is made clear that the acquirer recognises all tangible and intangible research and development assets acquired in a business combination. *[IFRS 3.BC149-BC156].*

IAS 38's general recognition conditions require it to be probable that expected future economic benefits will flow to the entity and that the costs can be measured reliably before an intangible asset can be recognised. *[IAS 38.21].*

IAS 38 states that 'an acquiree's in-process research and development project meets the definition of an intangible asset when it meets the definition of an asset, and is identifiable, i.e. is separable or arises from contractual or other legal rights.' *[IAS 38.34].*

In-process research and development projects, whether or not recognised by the acquiree, are protected by legal rights and are clearly separable as on occasion they are bought and sold by entities without there being a business acquisition. Both of the standard's general recognition criteria, probability of benefits and reliable measurement, are always considered to be satisfied for in-process research and development projects acquired in a business combination. The fair value of an intangible asset reflects expectations about the probability of these benefits, despite uncertainty about the timing or the amount of the inflow. There will be sufficient information to measure the fair value of the asset reliably if it is separable or arises from contractual or other legal rights. If there is a range of possible outcomes with different probabilities, this uncertainty is taken into account in the measurement of the asset's fair value. *[IAS 38.33-35].*

Therefore, recognising in-process research and development as an asset on acquisition applies different criteria to those that are required for internal projects. The research costs of internal projects may under no circumstances be capitalised. *[IAS 38.54].* Before capitalising development expenditure, entities must meet a series of exacting requirements. They must demonstrate the technical feasibility of the intangible assets, their intention and ability to complete the assets and use them or sell them and must be able to measure reliably the attributable expenditure. *[IAS 38.57]*. The probable future economic benefits must be assessed using the principles in IAS 36 – *Impairment of Assets* – which means that they have to be calculated as the net present value of the cash flows generated by the asset or, if it can only generate cash flows in conjunction with other assets, of the cash-generating unit of which it is a part. *[IAS 38.60]*. This process is described further in Chapter 17 at 6.

What this means is that entities will be required to recognise on acquisition some research and development expenditure that they would not have been able to recognise if it had been an internal project. The IASB is aware of this inconsistency, but concluded that this did not provide a basis for subsuming in-process research and development within goodwill. *[IAS 38.BC82]*.

Although the amount attributed to the project is accounted for as an asset, IAS 38 goes on to require that any subsequent expenditure incurred after the acquisition of the project is to be accounted for in accordance with paragraphs 54 to 62 of IAS 38. *[IAS 38.42]*. These requirements are discussed in Chapter 17 at 6.2.

In summary, this means that the subsequent expenditure is:

(a) recognised as an expense when incurred if it is research expenditure;

(b) recognised as an expense when incurred if it is development expenditure that does not satisfy the criteria for recognition as an intangible asset in paragraph 57; and

(c) added to the carrying amount of the acquired in-process research or development project if it is development expenditure that satisfies the recognition criteria in paragraph 57. *[IAS 38.43]*.

The inference is that the in-process research and development expenditure recognised as an asset on acquisition that never progresses to the stage of satisfying the recognition criteria for an internal project will ultimately be impaired, although it may be that this impairment will not arise until the entity is satisfied that the project will not continue. However, since it is an intangible asset not yet available for use, such an evaluation cannot be significantly delayed as it will need to be tested for impairment annually by comparing its carrying amount with its recoverable amount, as discussed in Chapter 20 at 10. *[IAS 36.10]*.

5.5.2.E Emission rights

Emission rights or allowances under a cap and trade emission rights scheme (see Chapter 17 at 11.2) meet the definition of an intangible asset and should therefore be recognised at the acquisition date at their fair value. Likewise, the acquirer is required to recognise a liability at fair value for the actual emissions made at the acquisition date. One approach that is adopted in accounting for such rights is the 'net liability approach' whereby the emission rights are recorded at a nominal amount and the entity will only record a liability once the actual emissions exceed the emission rights granted and still held. As discussed in Chapter 17 at 11.2.5, the net liability approach is not permitted for purchased emission rights and therefore is also not permitted to be applied to emission rights of the acquiree in a business combination. Although the acquiree may not have recognised an asset or liability at the date of acquisition, the acquirer should recognise the emission rights as intangible assets at their fair value and a liability at fair value for the actual emissions made at the acquisition date.

One impact of this is that subsequent to the acquisition, the consolidated income statement will show an expense for the actual emissions made thereafter, as a provision will have to be recognised on an ongoing basis. As discussed in Chapter 17 at 11.2.2, there are different views of the impact that such 'purchased' emission rights have on the measurement of the provision and on accounting for the emissions.

The emission rights held by the acquiree will relate to specific items of property, plant and equipment. Therefore when determining the fair value of these assets, care needs to be taken to ensure that there is no double counting of the rights held.

5.5.2.F Determining the fair values of intangible assets

Little guidance relating to fair value remains in IFRS 3 as it is now included in IFRS 13 (discussed at 5.3 above and in Chapter 14). IAS 38 (as amended by IFRS 13) states that the fair value of an intangible asset will reflect market participants' expectations at the acquisition date about the probability that the expected future economic benefits embodied in the asset will flow to the entity. *[IAS 38.33]*. Like IFRS 3, IAS 38 now incorporates IFRS 13's definition of fair value (see 5.3 above), in place of its previous guidance. *[IAS 38.8]*.

There are three broad approaches to valuing intangible assets that correspond to the valuation approaches referred to in IFRS 13. *[IFRS 13.62]*. These are the market, income and cost approaches. The diagram below shows these valuation approaches, together with some of the primary methods used to measure the fair value of intangible assets that fall under each approach, shown in the boxes on the right.

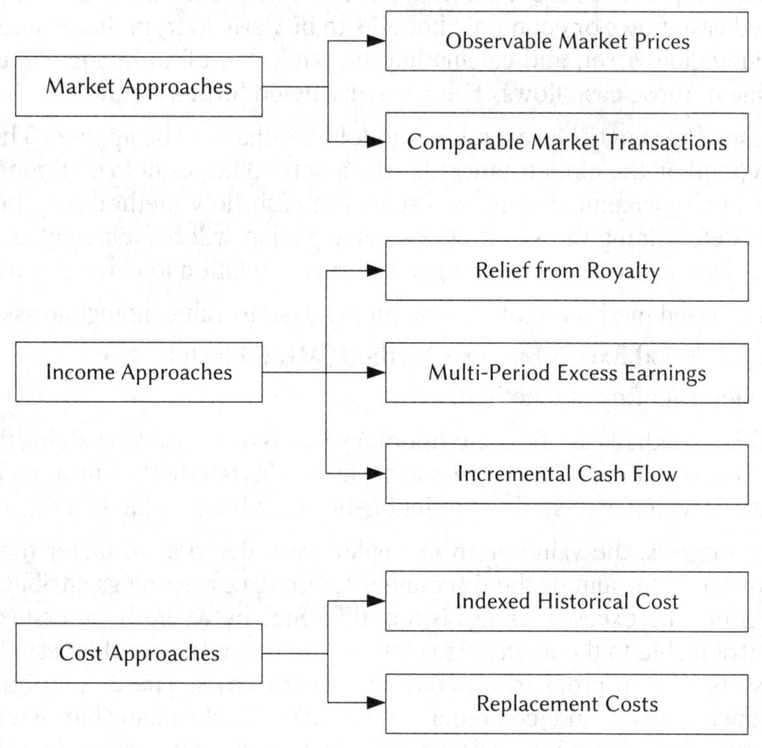

IFRS 13 does not limit the types of valuation techniques an entity might use to measure fair value. Instead the standard indicates that entities should use valuation techniques that are appropriate in the circumstances and for which sufficient data are available, which may result in the use of multiple valuation techniques. Regardless of the technique(s) used, a fair value measurement should 'maximis[e] the use of relevant observable inputs and minimis[e] the use of the unobservable inputs.' *[IFRS 13.61]*. The resulting fair value measurement should also reflect an exit price, i.e. the price to sell an asset. *[IFRS 13.2]*.

In practice, the ability to use a market-based approach is very limited as intangible assets are generally unique and are not typically traded. For example, there are generally no observable transactions for unique rights such as brands, newspaper mastheads, music and film publishing rights, patents or trademarks noted in paragraph 78 of IAS 38, i.e. a number of the intangible assets that IFRS 3 and IAS 38 require an acquirer to recognise in a business combination.

The premise of the cost approach is that an investor would pay no more for an intangible asset than the cost to recreate it. The cost approach reflects the amount that would be required currently to replace the service capacity of an asset (i.e. current replacement cost). It is based on what a market participant buyer would pay to acquire or construct a substitute asset of comparable utility, adjusted for obsolescence. Obsolescence includes physical deterioration, technological (functional) and economic obsolescence so it is not the same as depreciation under IAS 16. *[IFRS 13.B8, B9]*. This approach is most often used for unique intangible assets constructed by the entity, e.g. internally-developed software.

Income-based approaches are much more commonly used. These involve identifying the expected cash flows or economic benefits to be derived from the ownership of the particular intangible asset, and calculating the fair value of an intangible asset at the present value of those cash flows. These are discussed further below.

For each asset, there may be several methodologies that can be applied. The methods used will depend on the circumstances, as the assets could result in additional revenue, cost savings, or replacement time. A discounted cash flow method may be used, for example, in determining the value of cost-savings that will be achieved as a result of having a supply contract with advantageous terms in relation to current market rates.

Two income-based methods that are commonly used to value intangible assets are:

- the Multi Period Excess Earnings Method ('MEEM'); and
- the Relief from Royalty method.

The MEEM is a residual cash flow methodology that is often used in valuing the primary intangible asset acquired. The key issue in using this method is how to isolate the income/cash flow that is related to the intangible asset being valued.

As its name suggests, the value of an intangible asset determined under the MEEM is estimated through the sum of the discounted future excess earnings attributable to the intangible asset. The excess earnings is the difference between the after-tax operating cash flow attributable to the intangible asset and the required cost of invested capital on all other assets used in order to generate those cash flows. These contributory assets include property, plant and equipment, other identifiable intangible assets and net working capital. The allowance made for the cost of such capital is based on the value of such assets and a required rate of return reflecting the risks of the particular assets. As noted at 5.5.4 below, although it cannot be recognised as a separate identifiable asset, an assembled workforce may have to be valued for the purpose of calculating a 'contributory asset charge' in determining the fair value of an intangible asset under the MEEM.

The Relief from Royalty method is often used to calculate the value of a trademark or trade name. This approach is based on the concept that if an entity owns a trademark, it does not have to pay for the use of it and therefore is relieved from paying a royalty. The amount of that theoretical payment is used as a surrogate for income attributable to the trademark. The valuation is arrived at by computing the present value of the after-tax royalty savings, calculated by applying an appropriate royalty rate to the projected revenue, using an appropriate discount rate. The legal protection expenses relating to the trademark and an allowance for tax at the appropriate rate are deducted. The Relief from Royalty method was applied by adidas AG in its 2015 financial statements.

Extract 9.2: adidas AG (2015)

CONSOLIDATED FINANCIAL STATEMENTS [extract]

Notes [extract]

04 ACQUISITION OF SUBSIDIARIES AS WELL AS ASSETS AND LIABILITIES [extract]

The following valuation methods for the acquired assets were applied:

- **Trademarks**: The 'relief-from-royalty method' was applied for the trademarks/brand names. The fair value was determined by discounting notional royalty savings after tax and adding a tax amortisation benefit, resulting from the amortisation of the acquired asset.

It may be that the value of an intangible asset will reflect not only the present value of the future post-tax cash flows as indicated above, but also the value of any tax benefits (sometimes called 'tax amortisation benefits') that might generally be available to the owner if the asset had been bought separately, i.e. not as part of a business combination. Adidas AG discloses in the extract above that fair value of trademarks and similar rights includes a tax amortisation benefit. Whether such tax benefits are included will depend on the nature of the intangible asset and the relevant tax jurisdiction. If tax amortisation benefits are included, an asset that has been purchased as part of a business combination may not actually be tax-deductible by the entity, either wholly or in part. This therefore raises a potential impairment issue that is discussed in Chapter 20 at 8.3.1.

Because fair value is an exit price, the acquirer's intention in relation to intangible assets, e.g. where the acquirer does not intend to use an intangible asset of the acquiree is not taken into account in attributing a fair value. This is explicitly addressed in IFRS 3 and IFRS 13 and discussed at 5.5.6 below and in Chapter 14 at 10.1.

5.5.3 Reacquired rights

A reacquired right, that is a right previously granted to the acquiree to use one or more of the acquirer's recognised or unrecognised assets, must be recognised separately from goodwill. Reacquired rights include a right to use the acquirer's trade name under a franchise agreement or a right to use the acquirer's technology under a technology licensing agreement. *[IFRS 3.B35]*.

A reacquired right is not treated as the settlement of a pre-existing relationship. Reacquisition of, for example, a franchise right does not terminate the right. The difference is that the acquirer, rather than the acquiree by itself, now controls the franchise right. The IASB also rejected subsuming reacquired rights into goodwill, noting that they meet both contractual-legal and separability criteria and therefore qualify as identifiable intangible assets. *[IFRS 3.BC182-BC184].*

Guidance on the valuation of such reacquired rights, and their subsequent accounting, is discussed at 5.6.5 below.

Although the reacquired right itself is not treated as a termination of a pre-existing relationship, contract terms that are favourable or unfavourable relative to current market transactions are accounted for as the settlement of a pre-existing relationship. The acquirer has to recognise a settlement gain or loss. *[IFRS 3.B36].* Guidance on the measurement of any settlement gain or loss is discussed at 11.1 below.

5.5.4 *Assembled workforce and other items that are not identifiable*

The acquirer subsumes into goodwill the value of any acquired intangible asset that is not identifiable as at the acquisition date.

5.5.4.A *Assembled workforce*

A particular example of an intangible asset subsumed into goodwill is an assembled workforce. IFRS 3 regards this as being an existing collection of employees that permits the acquirer to continue to operate an acquired business from the acquisition date without having to hire and train a workforce. *[IFRS 3.B37].*

Although individual employees might have employment contracts with the employer, the collection of employees, as a whole, does not have such a contract. In addition, an assembled workforce is not separable; it cannot be sold, transferred, licensed, rented or otherwise exchanged without causing disruption to the acquirer's business. Therefore, it is not an identifiable intangible asset to be recognised separately from goodwill. *[IFRS 3.BC178].*

Nor does the assembled workforce represent the intellectual capital of the skilled workforce, which is the (often specialised) knowledge and experience that employees of an acquiree bring to their jobs. *[IFRS 3.B37].* Prohibiting an acquirer from recognising an assembled workforce as an intangible asset does not apply to intellectual property and the value of intellectual capital may well be reflected in the fair value of other intangible assets. For example, a process or methodology such as a software program would be documented and generally would be the property of the entity; the employer usually 'owns' the intellectual capital of an employee. The ability of the entity to continue to operate is unlikely to be affected significantly by changing programmers, even replacing the particular programmer who created the program. The intellectual property is part of the fair value of that program and is an identifiable intangible asset if it is separable from the entity. *[IFRS 3.BC180].*

5.5.4.B *Items not qualifying as assets*

The acquirer subsumes into goodwill any value attributed to items that do not qualify as assets at the acquisition date.

- *Potential contracts with new customers*

Potential contracts that the acquiree is negotiating with prospective new customers at the acquisition date might be valuable to the acquirer. The acquirer does not recognise them separately from goodwill because those potential contracts are not themselves assets at the acquisition date. Nor should the acquirer subsequently reclassify the value of those contracts from goodwill for events that occur after the acquisition date. The acquirer should, of course, assess the facts and circumstances surrounding events occurring shortly after the acquisition to determine whether there was a separately recognisable intangible asset at the acquisition date. *[IFRS 3.B38]*.

- *Contingent assets*

If the acquiree has a contingent asset, it should not be recognised unless it meets the definition of an asset in the IASB's *Framework*, even if it is virtually certain that it will become unconditional or non-contingent. Therefore, an asset would only be recognised if the entity has an unconditional right at the acquisition date. This is because it is uncertain whether a contingent asset, as defined by IAS 37 – *Provisions, Contingent Liabilities and Contingent Assets* – actually exists at the acquisition date. Under IAS 37, it is expected that some future event will confirm whether the entity has an asset. *[IFRS 3.BC276]*. Contingent assets under IAS 37 are discussed in Chapter 28 at 3.2.2. *[IAS 37.33]*.

- *Future contract renewals*

In measuring the fair value of an intangible asset, the acquirer would take into account assumptions that market participants would use when pricing the intangible asset, such as expectations of future contract renewals. It is not necessary for the renewals themselves to meet the identifiability criteria. *[IFRS 3.B40]*. Any value attributable to the expected future renewal of the contract is reflected in the value of, for example, the customer relationship, rather than being subsumed within goodwill.

However, any potential contract renewals that market participants would consider in determining the fair value of reacquired rights would be subsumed within goodwill. See the discussion at 5.6.5 below.

5.5.5 Assets with uncertain cash flows (valuation allowances)

Under IFRS 3, the acquirer may not recognise a separate provision or valuation allowance for assets that are initially recognised at fair value. Because receivables, including loans, are to be recognised and measured at fair value at the acquisition date, any uncertainty about collections and future cash flows is included in the fair value measure (see Chapter 48 at 3.2.4). *[IFRS 3.B41]*. Therefore, although an acquiree may have assets, typically financial assets such as receivables and loans, against which it has recognised a provision or valuation allowance for impairment or uncollectible amounts, an acquirer cannot 'carry over' any such valuation allowances nor create its own allowances in respect of those financial assets.

Subsequent measurement of financial instruments under IFRS 9 and IAS 39 is dealt with in Chapters 50 and 49, respectively. Chapter 50 at 5.6.4 deals specifically with the interaction between the initial measurement of debt instruments acquired in a business combination and the impairment model of IFRS 9.

5.5.6 Assets that the acquirer does not intend to use or intends to use in a way that is different from other market participants

An acquirer may intend not to use an acquired asset, for example, a brand name or research and development intangible asset or it may intend to use the asset in a way that is different from the way in which other market participants would use it. IFRS 3 requires the acquirer to recognise all such identifiable assets, and measure them at their fair value determined in accordance with their highest and best use by market participants (see 5.3 above and in Chapter 14 at 10.1). This requirement is applicable both on initial recognition and when measuring fair value less costs of disposal for subsequent impairment testing. *[IFRS 3.B43].* This means that no immediate impairment loss should be reflected if the acquirer does not intend to use the intangible asset to generate its own cash flows, but market participants would.

However, if the entity is not intending to use the intangible asset to generate cash flows, it is unlikely that it could be regarded as having an indefinite life for the purposes of IAS 38, and therefore it should be amortised over its expected useful life. This is likely to be relatively short.

Example 9.10: Acquirer's intention not to use an intangible asset

Entity A acquires a competitor, Entity B. One of the identifiable intangible assets of Entity B is the trade name of one of Entity B's branded products. As Entity A has a similar product, it does not intend to use that trade name post-acquisition. Entity A will discontinue sales of Entity B's product, thereby eliminating competition and enhancing the value of its own branded product. The cash flows relating to the acquired trade name are therefore expected to be nil. Can Entity A attribute a fair value of nil to that trade name?

The fair value of the asset has to be determined in accordance with its use by market participants. Entity A's future intentions about the asset should only be reflected in determining the fair value if that is what other market participants would do.

- There are other market participants that would continue to sell the product;
- Entity A could probably have sold the trade name after acquisition but has chosen not to do so;
- Even if all other market participants would, like Entity A, not sell the product in order to enhance the value of their own products, the trade name is still likely to have some value.

Accordingly, a fair value is attributed to that trade name.

As Entity A is not intending to use the trade name to generate cash flows but to use it defensively by preventing others from using it, the trade name should be amortised over the period it is expected to contribute directly or indirectly to the entity's future cash flows. That period is the period that the trade name provides significant value to Entity A, but would not extend beyond the date Entity A effectively waives its rights to the trade name.

5.5.7 Investments in equity-accounted entities

An acquiree may hold an investment in an associate, accounted for under the equity method (see Chapter 11 at 3). There are no recognition or measurement differences between an investment that is an associate or a trade investment because the acquirer has not acquired the underlying assets and liabilities of the associate. Accordingly, the fair value of the associate should be determined on the basis of the value of the investment, rather than the underlying fair values of the identifiable assets and liabilities of the associate. The impact of having listed prices for investments in associates when measuring fair value is discussed further in Chapter 14 at 5.1.1. Any goodwill relating to the associate is subsumed within the carrying amount for the associate rather than within the goodwill arising on the overall business combination. Nevertheless, although this fair value is effectively the 'cost' to the group to which equity accounting is applied, the underlying fair values of the various identifiable assets and liabilities also need to be determined to apply equity accounting (see Chapter 11 at 7).

This also applies if an acquiree holds an investment in a joint venture that under IFRS 11 – *Joint Arrangements* – is accounted for under the equity method (see Chapter 12 at 7).

5.5.8 Deferred revenue

An acquiree may have recorded deferred revenue at the date of acquisition for a number of reasons. For example, it might represent upfront payments for services or products that have yet to be delivered, or payments for delivered goods or services sold as a part of a multiple-element arrangement that could not be accounted for separately from undelivered items included in the same arrangement. In accounting for a business combination, an acquirer should only recognise a liability for deferred revenue of the acquiree if it relates to an outstanding performance obligation assumed by the acquirer. Such performance obligations would include obligations to provide goods or services or the right to use an asset.

The measurement of the deferred revenue liability should be based on the fair value of the obligation at the date of acquisition, which will not necessarily be the same as the amount of deferred revenue recognised by the acquiree. In general, the fair value would be less than the amount recognised by the acquiree, as the amount of revenue that a market participant would expect to receive for meeting that obligation would not include any profit element relating to the selling or other efforts already completed by the acquiree. IFRS 13 requirements for measuring the fair value of liabilities are discussed in more detail in Chapter 14 at 11.

Example 9.11: Deferred revenue of an acquiree

Target is an electronics company that sells contracts to service all types of electronics equipment for an upfront annual fee of $120,000. Acquirer purchases Target in a business combination. At the acquisition date, Target has one service contract outstanding with 6 months remaining and for which $60,000 of deferred revenue is recorded in Target's pre-acquisition financial statements.

To fulfil the contract over its remaining 6-month term, Acquirer estimates that a market participant would expect to receive $54,000 for fulfilling that obligation. It has estimated that a market participant would incur direct and incremental costs of $45,000, and expect a profit margin for that fulfilment effort of 20%, i.e. $9,000, and would, thus, expect to receive $54,000.

Accordingly, Acquirer will recognise a liability of $54,000 in respect of the deferred revenue obligation.

However, if the acquiree's deferred revenue does not relate to an outstanding performance obligation but to goods or services that have already been delivered, no liability should be recognised by the acquirer.

Where an acquiree has deferred revenue balances as a result of contractual obligations, the acquirer also needs to consider whether it should be recognising customer related intangible assets. In a situation such as that in Example 9.11, this means recognising an acquired customer-related intangible asset at its fair value as well as the liability to fulfil the contract (see 5.5.2 above).

5.6 Exceptions to the recognition and/or measurement principles

There are a number of exceptions to the principles in IFRS 3 that all assets acquired and liabilities assumed should be recognised and measured at fair value. For the particular items discussed below, this will result in some items being:

(a) recognised either by applying additional recognition conditions or by applying the requirements of other IFRSs, with results that differ from applying the recognition principle and conditions; and/or

(b) measured at an amount other than their acquisition-date fair values. *[IFRS 3.21]*.

5.6.1 Contingent liabilities

IAS 37 defines a contingent liability as:

(a) a possible obligation that arises from past events and whose existence will be confirmed only by the occurrence or non-occurrence of one or more uncertain future events not wholly within the control of the entity; or

(b) a present obligation that arises from past events but is not recognised because:

  (i) it is not probable that an outflow of resources embodying economic benefits will be required to settle the obligation; or

  (ii) the amount of the obligation cannot be measured with sufficient reliability. *[IFRS 3.22, IAS 37.10]*.

5.6.1.A Initial recognition and measurement

Under IAS 37, contingent liabilities are not recognised as liabilities; instead they are disclosed in financial statements. However, IFRS 3 does not apply the recognition rules of IAS 37. Instead, IFRS 3 requires the acquirer to recognise a liability at its fair value if there is a present obligation arising from a past event that can be reliably measured, even if it is not probable that an outflow of resources will be required to settle the obligation. *[IFRS 3.23]*. If a contingent liability only represents a possible obligation arising from a past event, whose existence will be confirmed only by the occurrence or non-occurrence of one or more uncertain future events not wholly within the control of the entity, no liability is to be recognised under IFRS 3. *[IFRS 3.BC275]*. No liability is recognised if the acquisition-date fair value of a contingent liability cannot be measured reliably.

5.6.1.B Subsequent measurement and accounting

IFRS 3 requires that after initial recognition and until the liability is settled, cancelled or expires, the acquirer measures a contingent liability that is recognised in a business combination at the higher of:

(a) the amount that would be recognised in accordance with IAS 37; and

(b) the amount initially recognised less, if appropriate, cumulative amortisation recognised in accordance with IAS 18 – *Revenue* (for entities applying IFRS 15, the amount initially recognised less, if appropriate, the cumulative amount of income recognised in accordance with the principles of IFRS 15). *[IFRS 3.56]*.

The implications of part (a) of the requirement are clear. If the acquiree has to recognise a provision in respect of the former contingent liability, and the best estimate of this liability is higher than the original fair value attributed by the acquirer, then the greater liability should now be recognised by the acquirer with the difference taken to the income statement. It would now be a provision to be measured and recognised in accordance with IAS 37. What is less clear is part (b) of the requirement. The reference to 'amortisation recognised in accordance with IAS 18' might relate to the recognition of income in respect of those loan commitments that are contingent liabilities of the acquiree, but have been recognised at fair value at date of acquisition. The requirement would appear to mean that, unless amortisation under IAS 18 is appropriate, the amount of the liability cannot be reduced below its originally attributed fair value until the liability is settled, cancelled or expires.

Despite the fact that the requirement for subsequent measurement discussed above was originally introduced for consistency with IFRS 9/IAS 39, *[IFRS 3.BC245]*, IFRS 3 makes it clear that the requirement does not apply to contracts accounted for in accordance with IFRS 9/IAS 39. *[IFRS 3.56]*. This would appear to mean that contracts that are excluded from the scope of IFRS 9/IAS 39, but are accounted for by applying IAS 37, i.e. loan commitments other than those that are commitments to provide loans at below-market interest rates, will fall within the requirements of IFRS 3 outlined above.

5.6.2 Income taxes

IFRS 3 requires the acquirer to recognise and measure a deferred tax asset or liability, in accordance with IAS 12, arising from the assets acquired and liabilities assumed in a business combination. *[IFRS 3.24]*. The acquirer is also required to account for the potential tax effects of temporary differences and carryforwards of an acquiree that exist at the acquisition date or arise as a result of the acquisition in accordance with IAS 12. *[IFRS 3.25]*.

IAS 12 requires that: *[IAS 12.68]*

(a) acquired deferred tax benefits recognised within the measurement period (see 12 below) reduce the goodwill related to that acquisition if they result from new information obtained about facts and circumstances existing at the acquisition date. If the carrying amount of goodwill is zero, any remaining deferred tax benefits is to be recognised in profit or loss; and

(b) all other acquired tax benefits realised are to be recognised in profit or loss, unless IAS 12 requires recognition outside profit or loss.

It will therefore be necessary to assess carefully the reasons for changes in the assessment of deferred tax made during the measurement period to determine whether it relates to facts and circumstances at the acquisition date or if it is a change in facts and circumstances since acquisition date.

IAS 12 also requires that tax benefits arising from the excess of tax-deductible goodwill over goodwill for financial reporting purposes is accounted for at the acquisition date as a deferred tax asset in the same way as other temporary differences. *[IAS 12.32A]*.

The requirements of IAS 12 relating to the deferred tax consequences of business combinations are discussed further in Chapter 31 at 12.

5.6.3 Employee benefits

IFRS 3 requires the acquirer to recognise and measure a liability (or asset, if any) related to the acquiree's employee benefit arrangements in accordance with IAS 19 – *Employee Benefits* (see Chapter 33), rather than at their acquisition-date fair values. *[IFRS 3.26, BC296-BC300]*.

5.6.4 Indemnification assets

The seller in a business combination may contractually indemnify the acquirer for the outcome of the contingency or uncertainty related to all or part of a specific asset or liability. These usually relate to uncertainties as to the outcome of pre-acquisition contingencies, e.g. uncertain tax positions, environmental liabilities, or legal matters. The amount of the indemnity may be capped or the seller will guarantee that the acquirer's liability will not exceed a specified amount.

IFRS 3 considers that the acquirer has obtained an indemnification asset. *[IFRS 3.27]*.

From the acquirer's perspective, the indemnification is an acquired asset to be recognised at its acquisition-date fair value. However, IFRS 3 makes an exception to the general principles in order to avoid recognition or measurement anomalies for indemnifications related to items for which liabilities are either not recognised or are not required to be measured at fair value (e.g. uncertain tax positions). *[IFRS 3.BC302-BC303]*. Accordingly, under IFRS 3 the acquirer measures an indemnification asset on the same basis as the indemnified item, subject to the need for a valuation allowance for uncollectible amounts.

- If the indemnification relates to an asset or a liability that is measured at fair value, the acquirer will recognise the indemnification asset at its fair value. The effects of uncertainty about future cash flows (i.e. the collectability of the asset) are included in the fair value measure and a separate valuation allowance is not necessary (see 5.5.5 above). *[IFRS 3.27]*.
- The indemnification may relate to an asset or liability that is not measured at fair value. A common example is an indemnification pertaining to a tax liability that is measured in accordance with IAS 12, rather than its fair value (see 5.6.2 above). If the indemnified item is recognised as a liability but is measured on a basis other than fair value, the indemnification asset is recognised and measured using consistent assumptions, subject to management's assessment of collectability and any contractual limitations on the indemnified amount. *[IFRS 3.27-28]*.
- If the indemnified item is not recognised as a liability at the date of acquisition, the indemnification asset is not recognised. An indemnification could relate to a contingent liability that is not recognised at the acquisition date because its fair value is not reliably measurable, *[IFRS 3.28]*, or it is only a possible obligation at that date (see 5.6.1 above).

Thereafter, the indemnification asset continues to be measured using the same assumptions as the indemnified liability or asset. *[IFRS 3.57]*. Thus, where the change in the value of the related indemnified liability or asset has to be recognised in profit or loss, this will be offset by any corresponding change in the value recognised for the indemnification asset. The acquirer derecognises the indemnification asset only when it collects the asset, sells it or otherwise loses the right to it. *[IFRS 3.57]*.

5.6.5 Reacquired rights

If the assets of the acquiree include a right previously granted to it allowing use of the acquirer's assets, IFRS 3 requires it to be recognised as an identifiable intangible asset. Reacquired rights include rights to use the acquirer's trade name under a franchise agreement or the acquirer's technology under a technology licensing agreement. *[IFRS 3.B35]*.

Reacquired rights are valued on the basis of the remaining contractual term of the related contract, regardless of whether market participants would consider potential contractual renewals when measuring their fair value. *[IFRS 3.29]*.

If the terms of the contract giving rise to the reacquired right are favourable or unfavourable relative to current market transactions for the same or similar items, this is accounted for as the settlement of a pre-existing relationship and the acquirer has to recognise a settlement gain or loss. *[IFRS 3.B36]*. Guidance on the measurement of any settlement gain or loss is discussed at 11.1 below. An example of accounting for the settlement gain or loss on the acquisition of a reacquired rights is illustrated in Example 9.5 below.

After acquisition, the intangible asset is to be amortised over the remaining contractual period of the contract, without including any renewal periods. *[IFRS 3.55, BC308]*. As the reacquired right is no longer a contract with a third party it might be thought that the acquirer could assume indefinite renewals of its contractual term, effectively making the reacquired right an intangible asset with an indefinite life. However, the IASB considers that a right reacquired from an acquiree has, in substance, a finite life. *[IFRS 3.BC308]*.

If the acquirer subsequently sells a reacquired right to a third party, the carrying amount of the intangible asset is to be included in determining the gain or loss on the sale. *[IFRS 3.55, BC310]*.

5.6.6 Assets held for sale

Non-current assets or disposal groups classified as held for sale at the acquisition date in accordance with IFRS 5 – *Non-current Assets Held for Sale and Discontinued Operations* – are measured at fair value less costs to sell (see Chapter 4 at 2.2). *[IFRS 3.31]*. This avoids the need to recognise a loss for the selling costs immediately after a business combination (a so-called Day 2 loss).

5.6.7 Share-based payment transactions

Liabilities or equity instruments related to the acquiree's share-based payments are measured in accordance with IFRS 2 (referred to as the 'market-based measure'), rather than at fair value, as are replacement schemes where the acquirer replaces the acquiree's share-based payments with its own. *[IFRS 3.30, IFRS 13.6]*. The measurement rules of IFRS 2 are not based on the fair value of the award at a particular date; measuring share-based payment awards at their acquisition-date fair values would cause difficulties with the subsequent accounting in accordance with IFRS 2. *[IFRS 3.BC311]*.

Additional guidance given in IFRS 3 for accounting for the replacement of share-based payment awards (i.e. vested or unvested share-based payment transactions) in a business combination is discussed at 7.2 and 11.2 below. Any equity-settled share-based payment transactions of the acquiree that the acquirer does not exchange for its own share-based payment transactions will result in a non-controlling interest in the acquiree being recognised, as discussed at 8.4 below.

5.6.8 *Leases in which the acquiree is the lessee (IFRS 16)*

As a result of issue of IFRS 16, consequential amendments have been made to the recognition and measurement principles of IFRS 3. IFRS 16 and its consequential amendments are mandatory for annual periods beginning on or after 1 January 2019, although early adoption is permitted, provided IFRS 15 has been applied, or is applied at the same date as IFRS 16 (for further guidance on IFRS 16, see Chapter 25).

Paragraph 28B of IFRS 3 added as a result of consequential amendments of IFRS 16 requires the acquirer to measure the acquired lease liability as if the lease contract were a new lease at the acquisition date. That is, the acquirer applies IFRS 16's initial measurement provisions, using the present value of the remaining lease payments at the acquisition date. The acquirer follows the requirements for determining the lease term, lease payments and discount rate as discussed in Chapter 25 at 4.

The added paragraph 28B in IFRS 3 also requires the acquirer to measure the right-of-use asset at an amount equal to the recognised liability, adjusted to reflect the favourable or unfavourable terms of the lease, relative to market terms. Because the off-market nature of the lease is captured in the right-of-use asset, the acquirer does not separately recognise an intangible asset or liability for favourable or unfavourable lease terms relative to market terms. Accounting for the favourable or unfavourable terms of the acquiree's operating lease under IAS 17 is discussed at 5.5.1 above.

In accordance with paragraph 28A of IFRS 3 added as a result of consequential amendments of IFRS 16, the acquirer is not required to recognise right-of-use assets and lease liabilities for leases with lease terms which end within 12 months of the acquisition date and leases for low-value assets. As indicated in paragraph BC298 of the Basis for Conclusions of IFRS 16, the IASB considered whether to require an acquirer to recognise assets and liabilities relating to off-market terms for short-term leases and leases of low-value assets. However, the Board observed that the effect of off-market terms would rarely be material for short-term leases and leases of low-value assets and so decided not to require this.

5.6.9 *Insurance contracts within the scope of IFRS 17*

IFRS 17 replaces IFRS 4 and is effective for reporting periods beginning on or after 1 January 2021, with early application permitted. IFRS 17 introduced a new exception to measurement principles in IFRS 3. Under IFRS 3, as amended by IFRS 17, the acquirer in a business combination shall measure a group of contracts within the scope of IFRS 17 as a liability or asset in accordance with paragraphs 39 and B93-B95 of IFRS 17, at the acquisition date.[35]

6 RECOGNISING AND MEASURING GOODWILL OR A GAIN IN A BARGAIN PURCHASE

The final step in applying the acquisition method is recognising and measuring goodwill or a gain in a bargain purchase.

IFRS 3 defines 'goodwill' in terms of its nature, rather than in terms of its measurement. It is defined as 'an asset representing the future economic benefits arising from other assets acquired in a business combination that are not individually identified and separately recognised.' *[IFRS 3 Appendix A].*

However, having concluded that the direct measurement of goodwill is not possible, the standard requires that goodwill is measured as a residual. *[IFRS 3.BC328].*

Goodwill at the acquisition date is computed as the excess of (a) over (b) below:

(a) the aggregate of:
   - (i) the consideration transferred (generally measured at acquisition-date fair value);
   - (ii) the amount of any non-controlling interest in the acquiree; and
   - (iii) the acquisition-date fair value of the acquirer's previously held equity interest in the acquiree.

(b) the net of the acquisition-date fair values (or other amounts recognised in accordance with the requirements of the standard) of the identifiable assets acquired and the liabilities assumed. *[IFRS 3.32].*

Having concluded that goodwill should be measured as a residual, the IASB, in deliberating IFRS 3, considered the following two components to comprise 'core goodwill':

- The fair value of the going concern element of the acquiree's existing business. This represents the ability of the established business to earn a higher rate of return on an assembled collection of net assets than would be expected if those net assets had to be acquired separately. The value stems from the synergies of the net assets of the business, as well as from other benefits, such as factors related to market imperfections, including the ability to earn monopoly profits and barriers to market entry (by potential competitors, whether through legal restrictions or costs of entry);
- The fair value of the expected synergies and other benefits from combining the acquirer's and acquiree's net assets and businesses. These are unique to each combination, and different combinations would produce different synergies and, hence, different values. *[IFRS 3.BC313, BC316].*

However, in practice the amount of goodwill recognised in a business combination will probably not be limited to 'core goodwill'. Items that do not qualify for separate recognition (see 5.5.4 above) and items that are not measured at fair value, e.g. deferred tax assets and liabilities, will also affect the amount of goodwill recognised.

Even though goodwill is measured as a residual, after identifying and measuring all the items in (a) and (b), the acquirer should have an understanding of the factors that make up the goodwill recognised. IFRS 3 requires the disclosure of qualitative description of those factors (see 16.1.1 below).

Where (b) exceeds (a), IFRS 3 regards this as giving rise to a gain on a bargain purchase. *[IFRS 3.34]*. Bargain purchase transactions are discussed further at 10 below.

The measurement of (b) has been discussed at 5 above. The items included within (a) are discussed at 7, 8 and 9 below.

6.1 Subsequent accounting for goodwill

The main issue relating to the goodwill acquired in a business combination is how it should be subsequently accounted for. The requirements of IFRS 3 in this respect are straightforward; the acquirer measures goodwill acquired in a business combination at the amount recognised at the acquisition date less any accumulated impairment losses. *[IFRS 3.B63]*.

Goodwill is not to be amortised. Instead, the acquirer has to test it for impairment annually, or more frequently if events or changes in circumstances indicate that it might be impaired, in accordance with IAS 36. The requirements of IAS 36 relating specifically to the impairment of goodwill are dealt with in Chapter 20 at 8.

7 CONSIDERATION TRANSFERRED

The consideration transferred in a business combination comprises the sum of the acquisition-date fair values of assets transferred by the acquirer, liabilities incurred by the acquirer to the former owners of the acquiree and equity interests issued by the acquirer. The consideration may take many forms, including cash, other assets, a business or subsidiary of the acquirer, and securities of the acquirer (e.g. ordinary shares, preferred shares, options, warrants, and debt instruments). The consideration transferred also includes the fair value of any contingent consideration and may also include some or all of any acquirer's share-based payment awards exchanged for awards held by the acquiree's employees measured in accordance with IFRS 2 rather than at fair value. These are discussed further at 7.1 and 7.2 below. *[IFRS 3.37]*.

The consideration transferred could include assets or liabilities whose carrying amounts differ from their fair values. These are remeasured to fair value at the acquisition date and any resulting gains or losses are recognised in profit or loss. If the transferred assets or liabilities remain within the combined entity after the acquisition date because they were transferred to the acquiree rather than to its former owners, the acquirer retains control of them. They are retained at their existing carrying amounts and no gain or loss is recognised. *[IFRS 3.38]*.

Where the assets given as consideration or the liabilities incurred by the acquirer are financial assets or financial liabilities as defined by IAS 32 – *Financial Instruments: Presentation* (see Chapter 43), the guidance in IFRS 13 on determining the fair values of such financial instruments should be followed. IFRS 13 applies in determining the fair value of financial instruments whether an entity applies IFRS 9 or IAS 39 (see Chapter 14 at 2).

These assets and liabilities might be denominated in a foreign currency, in which case the entity may have hedged the foreign exchange risk. The Interpretations Committee has considered the treatment of gains or losses arising from hedging this risk and in particular whether they would result in an adjustment to the amount that is recognised for goodwill. IAS 39 allows an entity to apply hedge accounting when hedging the movements in foreign currency exchange rates for a firm commitment to acquire a business in a business combination. *[IAS 39.AG98].* When a basis adjustment is made to a hedged item, it is after other applicable IFRSs have been applied. Accordingly, the Interpretations Committee noted that 'such a basis adjustment is made to goodwill (or the gain from a bargain purchase) after the application of the guidance in IFRS 3'.[36]

Where equity interests are issued by the acquirer as consideration, the guidance in IFRS 13 on determining the fair value of an entity's own equity should be followed (see Chapter 14 at 11). *[IFRS 13.34].* IFRS 3 clarifies that they are to be measured at their fair values at the acquisition date, rather than at an earlier agreement date (or on the basis of the market price of the securities for a short period before or after that date). *[IFRS 3.37].*

Although a valid conceptual argument could be made for the use of the agreement date, it was observed that the parties to a business combination are likely to take into account expected changes between the agreement date and the acquisition date in the fair value of the acquirer and the market price of the acquirer's securities issued as consideration. While an acquirer and a target entity both consider the fair value of the target on the agreement date in negotiating the amount of consideration to be paid, the distorting effects are mitigated if acquirers and targets generally consider their best estimates of the fair values on the acquisition dates. In addition, measuring the equity securities on the acquisition date avoids the complexities of dealing with situations in which the number of shares or other consideration transferred can change between the agreement date and the acquisition date. *[IFRS 3.BC342].*

Measuring the fair value of an entity's own equity issued on or close to the agreement date would not result in a consistent measure of the consideration transferred. The fair values of all other forms of consideration transferred are measured at the acquisition date as are the fair values of the assets acquired and liabilities assumed. *[IFRS 3.BC338-BC342].*

The acquisition-date fair value of the acquiree's equity interests may be more reliably measurable than that of the acquirer's equity interests. In that case, IFRS 3 requires goodwill to be calculated using the fair value of the acquiree's equity interests rather than the fair value of the equity interests transferred. *[IFRS 3.33].*

IFRS 3 gives additional guidance if no consideration is transferred by the acquirer. This is discussed at 7.4 below.

7.1 Contingent consideration

Contingent consideration generally arises where the acquirer agrees to transfer additional consideration to the former owners of the acquired business after the acquisition date if certain specified events occur or conditions are met in the future, although it can also result in the return of previously transferred consideration. *[IFRS 3 Appendix A].*

When entering into a business combination, the parties to the arrangement may not always agree on the exact value of the business, particularly if there are uncertainties as to the success or worth of particular assets or the outcome of uncertain events. They therefore often agree to an interim value for the purposes of completing the deal, with additional future payments to be made by the acquirer. That is, they share the economic risks relating to the uncertainties about the future of the business. These future payments may be in cash or shares or other assets and may be contingent upon the achievement of specified events, and/or may be linked to future financial performance over a specified period of time. Examples of such additional payments contingent on future events are:

- earnings above an agreed target over an agreed period;
- components of earnings (e.g. revenue) above an agreed target over an agreed period;
- approval of a patent/licence;
- successful completion of specified contract negotiations;
- cash flows arising from specified assets over an agreed period; and
- remaining an employee of the entity for an agreed period of time.

An arrangement can have a combination of any of the above factors.

While these payments may be negotiated as part of gaining control of another entity, the accounting may not necessarily always reflect this, particularly if these payments are made to those who remain as employees of the business after it is acquired. In the latter case, depending on the exact terms of the arrangement, the payment made may be accounted for as remuneration for services provided subsequent to the acquisition, rather than as part of the consideration paid for the business.

These payments are also often referred to as 'earn-outs'. The guidance in IFRS 3 for determining whether the arrangements involving employees should be accounted for as contingent consideration or remuneration is discussed further at 11.2 below.

The IASB clarified in June 2009 that pre-existing contingent consideration from a prior business combination of an acquiree does not meet the definition of contingent consideration in the acquirer's business combination. It is one of the identifiable liabilities assumed in the subsequent acquisition. Usually it makes no difference whether the pre-existing contingent consideration is treated as contingent consideration or as an identifiable liability as they are both financial liabilities to be accounted for under IFRS 9/IAS 39.[37] As discussed further below, they are initially recognised and measured at fair value at the date of acquisition, with any subsequent remeasurements recognised in profit or loss in accordance with IFRS 9/IAS 39.

7.1.1 Initial recognition and measurement

Contingent consideration is recognised at its fair value as part of the consideration transferred in exchange for the acquiree. *[IFRS 3.39]*.

IFRS 13 has specific requirements with respect to measuring fair value for liabilities. An entity has to determine the price it would need to pay to transfer the liability to a market participant at the measurement date. An entity must assume that the market participant would fulfil the obligation (i.e. it would not be settled or extinguished). *[IFRS 13.34(a)]*. The specific requirements are discussed in detail in Chapter 14 at 11. In light of these requirements, it is likely that the fair value of contingent consideration will need to be measured 'from the perspective of a market participant that holds the identical item as an asset at the measurement date'. *[IFRS 13.37]*. That is, the entity measures the fair value of the liability by reference to the fair value of the corresponding asset held by the counterparty.

The initial measurement of the fair value of contingent consideration is based on an assessment of the facts and circumstances that exist at the acquisition date. Although the fair value of some contingent payments may be difficult to measure, it is argued that 'to delay recognition of, or otherwise ignore, assets or liabilities that are difficult to measure would cause financial reporting to be incomplete and thus diminish its usefulness in making economic decisions'. *[IFRS 3.BC347]*. Information used in negotiations between buyer and seller will often be helpful in estimating the fair value of the contingent consideration. *[IFRS 3.BC348]*.

An estimate of zero for the fair value of contingent consideration would not be reliable. *[IFRS 3.BC349]*. Equally, it would be inappropriate to assume an estimate of 100% for the acquisition-date fair value of the obligation to make the payments under the contingent consideration arrangement.

The fair value of contingent consideration will be measured in accordance with IFRS 13 which does not limit the valuation techniques an entity might use. However, there are two commonly used approaches to estimating the fair value of contingent consideration that an entity might consider:

- the probability-weighted average of payouts associated with each possible outcome ('probability-weighted payout approach'); or
- the payout associated with the probability-weighted average of outcomes ('deterministic approach').

Entities should consider the relationship between the underlying performance metric or outcome and the payout associated with that metric or outcome to determine whether a probability-weighted payout or deterministic approach should be used. A contingent consideration arrangement can be characterised as having either a linear or non-linear relationship between outcomes and payouts. With a linear payout, the relationship between the underlying outcomes and the associated payouts is constant whereas in a non-linear payout the relationship between the underlying outcomes and the associated payouts is not constant. In situations where the payout structure is non-linear, using the deterministic approach is unlikely to give a reliable result.

The method that arguably gives the most reliable result in all circumstances is the probability-weighted payout approach. This method requires taking into account the range of possible outcomes, the payouts associated with each possible outcome and the probability of each outcome arising. The probability-weighted payout is then discounted. This approach is illustrated in the following example.

Example 9.12: Contingent consideration – applying the probability-weighted payout approach to determine fair value

Entity G acquires Entity H and as part of the arrangement, Entity G agrees to pay an additional amount of consideration to the seller in the future, as follows:

- if the 12 month earnings in two years' time (also referred to as the trailing 12 months) are €1 million or less – nothing will be paid;
- if the trailing 12 months' earnings in two years' time are between €1 million and €2 million – 2 × 12 month earnings will be paid;
- if the trailing 12 months' earnings in two years' time are greater than €2 million – 3 × 12 month earnings will be paid.

At the date of acquisition, the possible twelve-month earnings of Entity H in two years' time are determined to be, as follows:

- €0.8 million – 40%
- €1.5 million – 40%
- €2.5 million – 20%

The probability-weighted payout is:

(40% × €0) + (40% × €1.5 million × 2) + (20% × €2.5 million × 3) = €2.7 million

This €2.7 million is then discounted at the date of acquisition to determine its fair value.

Since the liability must be measured at fair value, selecting the discount rate to be applied also requires significant judgement to assess the underlying risks associated with the outcomes and the risks of payment (see 7.1.1.A below for further discussion). The entity's own credit risk will need to be taken into account when measuring fair value, which could include adjusting the discount rate. In addition, IFRS 13 indicates that in those situations where the identical item is held by another party as an asset, the fair value of the liability should be determined from the perspective of a market participant that holds this asset. This guidance applies even if the corresponding asset is not traded or recognised for financial reporting purposes. As such, when determining the fair value of a contingent consideration liability, one should consider market participants' assumptions related to the item when held as an asset. The IASB and the FASB indicated that 'in an efficient market, the price of a liability held by another party as an asset must equal the price for the corresponding asset. If those prices differed, the market participant transferee (i.e. the party taking on the obligation) would be able to earn a profit by financing the purchase of the asset with the proceeds received by taking on the liability. In such cases, the price for the liability and the price for the asset would adjust until the arbitrage opportunity was eliminated.' *[IFRS 13.BC89].*

IFRS 3 also recognises that, in some situations, the agreement may give the acquirer the right to the return of previously transferred consideration if specified future events occur or conditions are met. Such a right falls within the definition of 'contingent consideration', and is to be accounted for as such by recognising an asset at its acquisition-date fair value. *[IFRS 3.39-40, Appendix A].*

7.1.1.A Estimating an appropriate discount rate

As discussed at 7.1.1 above, determining the appropriate discount rate to be applied requires significant judgement and requires that an entity consider the risks and uncertainty related to the asset or liability being measured.

Market participants generally require compensation for taking on the uncertainty inherent in the cash flows of an asset or a liability. This compensation is known as a risk premium. IFRS 13 states that in order to faithfully represent fair value, a present value technique should include a risk premium. The standard acknowledges that determining the appropriate risk premium might be difficult. However, the degree of difficulty alone is not a sufficient reason to exclude a risk premium if market participants would demand one. *[IFRS 13.B16].*

Depending on the present value technique used, risk may be incorporated in the cash flows or in the discount rate. However, identical risks should not be captured in both the cash flows and the discount rate in the same valuation analysis. For example, if the probability of default and loss given default for a liability are already incorporated in the discount rate (i.e. a risk-adjusted discount rate), the projected cash flows should not be further adjusted for the expected losses (see Chapter 14 at 21.2 for further discussion).

When determining the discount rate to use in measuring the fair value of contingent consideration, an entity should consider the risks associated with:

- the underlying outcome;
- the nature of the payout structure (e.g. a constant, fixed payment on achievement of the contingency versus a variable payment based on a multiple of earnings); and
- the ability of the holder to collect the contingent consideration payment (i.e. credit risk).

The first risk, which is associated with the underlying outcome, is generally represented as the required rate of return on the capital necessary to produce the outcome. For example, if the outcome is based on a measure such as revenue or EBIT, the required rates of return on the debt and equity capital used to generate the outcome should provide the starting point for estimating the discount rate. In this case, a weighted-average cost of capital may be an appropriate rate of return. On the other hand, if the outcome is based on net income, the cost of equity may be a more appropriate rate of return because the debt capital has already received its return via the interest payment. Furthermore, since the contingent consideration will be based on the target's performance, the risk should reflect the uncertainty specific to the target, rather than to a hypothetical market participant.

The second risk is inherent in the nature of the payout structure. In some circumstances, the risk of the underlying outcome may be captured in a weighted-average cost of capital or cost of equity. However, they may understate the discount rate. In particular, when the payout structure is non-linear, there may be additional risks that need to be considered. In other words, the contractual features that define the structure of the earn-out could make it a riskier arrangement. For example, assume there is an earn-out with the following characteristics: the payout is three times EBIT if more than €1 million; there is a 50% probability of EBIT being €1 million; and a 50% probability of EBIT being €2 million. The risk of EBIT being €1,000,000 versus €1,000,001 is small. That is, it represents only a fraction of a percentage. However, for the earn-out, there is incremental risk associated with that last € of EBIT. If EBIT is €1,000,000, the earn-out is not triggered, but if it is €1,000,001, the payout is required.

The third risk is the ability of the holder to collect the contingent consideration payment (i.e. credit risk of the buyer). Contingent consideration arrangements generally do not represent a direct claim on the cash flows from the underlying outcome (such as a specified portion of the target's earnings), but rather a subordinate, unsecured claim on the buyer. The credit risk of the buyer should be considered, taking into account the seniority of the contingent consideration claim in the buyer's capital structure and the expected timing of the payout. The buyer's own credit risk is considered in determining fair value because IFRS 13 presumes the liability is transferred to a market participant of equal credit standing. *[IFRS 13.42]*.

As discussed at 7.1.1 above, the fair value of a contingent consideration liability will likely need to be measured from the perspective of a market participant that holds the identical instrument as an asset. If the risk premium of the contingent consideration arrangement were to increase, the fair value would decline (i.e. due to a higher discount rate) for the holder of the contingent consideration asset. This increase in the risk premium would have a symmetrical effect on the liability (i.e. the discount).

7.1.2 Classification of a contingent consideration obligation

Most contingent consideration obligations are financial instruments, and many are derivative instruments. Some arrangements oblige the acquirer to deliver equity securities if specified future events occur, rather than, say, making additional cash payments.

The classification of a contingent consideration obligation that meets the definition of a financial instrument as either a financial liability or equity is to be based on the definitions in IAS 32 (see Chapter 45). *[IFRS 3.40]*.

These requirements, and the impact of subsequent measurement and accounting (which is discussed further at 7.1.3 below), are summarised in the diagram below.

Classification of contingent consideration

Contingent consideration

Initial recognition at fair value

Equity

Other contingent consideration

No remeasurement

Within the scope of IFRS 9/IAS 39

Not within the scope of IFRS 9/IAS 39

Subsequently measured at fair value through profit or loss in accordance with IFRS 9/IAS 39

Subsequently measured at fair value through profit or loss

Contingent consideration will often meet the definition of a financial liability. This includes those arrangements where the acquirer is obliged to deliver equity securities because IAS 32 defines a financial liability to include 'a contract that will or may be settled in the entity's own equity instruments' and is:

- 'a non-derivative for which the entity is or may be obliged to deliver a variable number of the entity's own equity instruments'; or
- 'a derivative that will or may be settled other than by the exchange of a fixed amount of cash or another financial asset for a fixed number of the entity's own equity instruments'. *[IAS 32.11]*.

Most contingent consideration arrangements that are to be settled by delivering equity shares will involve a variable number of shares; e.g. an arrangement obliges the acquirer to issue between zero and 1 million additional equity shares on a sliding scale based on the acquiree's post-combination earnings. This arrangement will be classified as a financial liability. Only in situations where the arrangement involves issuing, say, zero or 1 million shares depending on a specified event or target being achieved would the arrangement be classified as equity. Where the arrangement involves a number of different discrete targets that are independent of one another, which if met will result in additional equity shares being issued as further consideration, we believe that the classification of the obligation to provide such financial instruments in respect of each target is assessed separately in determining whether equity classification is appropriate. However, if the targets are interdependent, the classification of the obligation to provide such additional equity shares should be based on the overall arrangement, and as this is likely to mean that as a variable number of shares may be delivered, the arrangement would be classified as a financial liability.

Example 9.13: Share-settled contingent consideration – financial liability or equity?

Entity P acquires a 100% interest in Entity S on 1 January 2018. As part of the consideration arrangements, additional consideration will be payable based on Entity S meeting certain profit targets over the 3 years ended 31 December 2020, as follows:

Profit target	*Additional consideration*
Year ended 31 December 2018 – €1m+	100,000 shares
Year ended 31 December 2019 – €1.25m+	150,000 shares
Year ended 31 December 2020 – €1.5m+	200,000 shares

Each target is non-cumulative. If the target for a particular year is met, the additional consideration will be payable, irrespective of whether the targets for the other years are met or not. If a target for a particular year is not met, no shares will be issued in respect of that year.

In this scenario, as each of the targets are independent of one another, this arrangement can be regarded as being three distinct contingent consideration arrangements that are assessed separately. As either zero or the requisite number of shares will be issued if each target is met, the obligation in respect of each arrangement is classified as equity.

If the targets were dependent on each other, for example, if they were based on an average for the 3 year period, a specified percentage increase on the previous year's profits, or the later targets were forfeited if the earlier targets were not met, the classification would be assessed on the overall arrangement. As this would mean that a variable number of shares may be delivered, the obligation under such an arrangement would have to be classified as a financial liability.

For those contingent consideration arrangements where the agreement gives the acquirer the right to the return of previously transferred consideration if specified future events occur or conditions are met, IFRS 3 merely requires that such a right is classified as an asset. *[IFRS 3.40]*.

7.1.3 Subsequent measurement and accounting

The IASB has concluded that subsequent changes in the fair value of a contingent consideration obligation generally do not affect the fair value of the consideration transferred to the acquiree. Subsequent changes in value relate to post-combination events and changes in circumstances of the combined entity and should not affect the measurement of the consideration transferred or goodwill. *[IFRS 3.BC357]*.

Accordingly, IFRS 3 requires that changes in the fair value of contingent consideration resulting from events after the acquisition date such as meeting an earnings target, reaching a specified share price, or meeting a milestone on a research and development project are accounted for as follows:

- contingent consideration classified as equity is not subsequently remeasured (consistent with the accounting for equity instruments generally), and its subsequent settlement is accounted for within equity;
- other contingent consideration that:
  - is within the scope of IFRS 9/IAS 39 is remeasured at fair value at each reporting date and changes in fair value are recognised in profit or loss in accordance with IFRS 9/IAS 39; or
  - is not within the scope of IFRS 9/IAS 39 (e.g. the consideration is a non-monetary asset) is remeasured at fair value at each reporting date and changes in fair value are recognised in profit or loss. *[IFRS 3.58]*.

If the changes are the result of additional information about the facts and circumstances that existed at the acquisition date, they are measurement period adjustments and are to be accounted for as discussed at 12 below. *[IFRS 3.58]*.

7.2 Replacement share-based payment awards

Acquirers often exchange share-based payment awards (i.e. replacement awards) for awards held by employees of the acquiree. These exchanges frequently occur because the acquirer wants to avoid the effect of having non-controlling interests in the acquiree, the acquirer's shares are often more liquid than the shares of the acquired business after the acquisition, and/or to motivate former employees of the acquiree toward the overall performance of the combined, post-acquisition business.

If the acquirer replaces any acquiree awards, the consideration transferred will include some or all of any replacement share-based payment awards. However, arrangements that remunerate employees or former owners for future services are excluded from consideration transferred (see 11.2 below).

Replacement awards are modifications of share-based payment awards in accordance with IFRS 2. *[IFRS 3.B56-B62].* Discussion of this guidance, including illustrative examples is dealt with in Chapter 32 at 11.2.

The acquirer is required to include some or all replacement awards (i.e. vested or unvested share-based payment transactions) as part of the consideration transferred, irrespective of whether it is obliged to do so or does so voluntarily. There is only one situation in which none of the market-based measure of the awards is included in the consideration transferred: if acquiree awards would expire as a consequence of the business combination and the acquirer replaces those when it was not obliged to do so. In that case, all of the market-based measure of the awards is recognised as remuneration cost in the post-combination financial statements. *[IFRS 3.B56].*

Any equity-settled share-based payment transactions of the acquiree that the acquirer does not exchange for its own share-based payment transactions will result in non-controlling interest in the acquiree being recognised and measured at their market-based measure as discussed at 8.4 below. *[IFRS 3.B62A, B62B].*

7.3 Acquisition-related costs

IFRS 3 requires acquisition-related costs to be accounted for as expenses in the periods in which the costs are incurred and the related services are received with the exception of the costs of registering and issuing debt and equity securities that are recognised in accordance with IAS 32 and IFRS 9/IAS 39, i.e. as a reduction of the proceeds of the debt or equity securities issued. *[IFRS 3.53].* In addition, IFRS 3 requires that a transaction that reimburses the acquiree or its former owners for paying the acquirer's acquisition-related costs is not to be included in applying the acquisition method (see 11.3 below). This is in order to mitigate concerns about potential abuse, e.g. a buyer might ask a seller to make payments to third parties on its behalf, but the consideration to be paid for the business is sufficient to reimburse the seller for making such payments. *[IFRS 3.51-53, BC370].*

An acquirer's costs incurred in connection with a business combination include:

- direct costs of the transaction, such as costs for the services of lawyers, investment bankers, accountants, and other third parties and issuance costs of debt or equity instruments used to effect the business combination; and
- indirect costs of the transaction, such as recurring internal costs, e.g. the cost of maintaining an acquisition department.

Acquisition-related costs, whether for services performed by external parties or internal staff of the acquirer, are not part of the fair value exchange between the buyer and seller for the acquired business. Accordingly, they are not part of the consideration transferred for the acquiree. Rather, they are separate transactions in which the buyer makes payments in exchange for the services received, to be accounted for separately.

7.4 Business combinations achieved without the transfer of consideration

An acquirer sometimes obtains control of an acquiree without transferring consideration. The standard emphasises that the acquisition method applies to a business combination achieved without the transfer of consideration. *[IFRS 3.43]*. IFRS 3 indicates that such circumstances include:

(a) the acquiree repurchases a sufficient number of its own shares for an existing investor (the acquirer) to obtain control;

(b) minority veto rights lapse that previously kept the acquirer from controlling an acquiree in which the acquirer held the majority voting rights; and

(c) the acquirer and the acquiree agree to combine their businesses by contract alone. In that case, the acquirer transfers no consideration in exchange for control of an acquiree and holds no equity interests in the acquiree, either on the acquisition date or previously. Examples of business combinations achieved by contract alone include bringing two businesses together in a stapling arrangement or forming a dual listed corporation. *[IFRS 3.43]*.

In computing the amount of goodwill in a business combination, IFRS 3 normally requires the acquirer to aggregate:

(i) the consideration transferred;

(ii) the amount of any non-controlling interest in the acquiree; and

(iii) the acquisition-date fair value of the acquirer's previously held equity interest in the acquiree. *[IFRS 3.32]*.

However, where the consideration transferred is nil, IFRS 3 requires the entity to use the acquisition-date fair value of the acquirer's interest in the acquiree instead. *[IFRS 3.33, B46]*.

In the first two circumstances described in (a) and (b) above, the acquirer has a previously-held equity interest in the acquiree. To include the acquisition-date fair value of the previously-held interest would result in double-counting the value of the acquirer's interest in the acquiree. The acquisition-date fair value of the acquirer's interest in the acquiree should only be included once in the computation of goodwill. Nevertheless, it would appear that these two circumstances would also be examples of business combinations achieved in stages (see 9 below).

The fair value of the acquirer's interest in the acquiree is to be measured in accordance with IFRS 13.

7.4.1 Business combinations by contract alone

In a business combination achieved by contract alone ((c) above), IFRS 3 requires that the acquirer attributes to the owners of the acquiree the amount of the acquiree's net assets recognised under the standard (see 2.1 above). In other words, the equity interests in the acquiree held by parties other than the acquirer are a non-controlling interest in the acquirer's consolidated financial statements, even if it results in all of the equity interests in the acquiree being attributed to the non-controlling interest. *[IFRS 3.44]*.

This might suggest that no goodwill is to be recognised in a business combination achieved by contract alone as the second item in part (a) will be equal to part (b) of the goodwill computation set out at 6 above. However, we believe that this requirement to attribute the equity interests in the acquiree to the non-controlling interest is emphasising the presentation within equity in the consolidated financial statements. Thus, where the option of measuring non-controlling interests in an acquiree at its acquisition-date fair value is chosen, goodwill would be recognised. If the option of measuring the non-controlling interest at its proportionate share of the value of net identifiable assets acquired is chosen, no goodwill would be recognised (except to the extent any is recognised as a result of there being other equity instruments that are required to be measured at their acquisition-date fair value or other measurement basis required by IFRSs). These options are discussed at 8 below.

7.5 Combinations involving mutual entities

Combinations involving mutual entities are within the scope of IFRS 3. A mutual entity is defined by IFRS 3 as 'an entity, other than an investor-owned entity, that provides dividends, lower costs or other economic benefits directly to its owners, members or participants. For example, a mutual insurance company, a credit union and a co-operative entity are all mutual entities.' *[IFRS 3 Appendix A]*.

The standard notes that the fair value of the equity or member interests in the acquiree (or the fair value of the acquiree) may be more reliably measurable than the fair value of the member interests transferred by the acquirer. In that situation, the acquirer should determine the amount of goodwill by using the acquisition-date fair value of the acquiree's equity interests as the equivalent to the consideration transferred in the goodwill computation set out at 7.4 above, instead of the acquirer's equity interests transferred as consideration. *[IFRS 3.B47]*.

IFRS 3 clarifies that the acquirer in a combination of mutual entities recognises the acquiree's net assets as a direct addition to capital or equity, not as an addition to retained earnings, which is consistent with the way other types of entity apply the acquisition method. *[IFRS 3.B47]*.

IFRS 3 recognises that mutual entities, although similar in many ways to other businesses, have distinct characteristics that arise primarily because their members are both customers and owners. Members of mutual entities generally expect to receive benefits for their membership, often in the form of reduced fees charged for goods and services or patronage dividends. Patronage dividends are distributions paid to members (or investors) in mutual entities and the portion allocated to each member is often based on the amount of business the member did with the mutual entity during the year. *[IFRS 3.B48]*. The fair value of a mutual entity should include the assumptions that market participants would make about future member benefits. If, for example, a present value technique is used to measure the fair value of the mutual entity, the cash flow inputs should be based on the expected cash flows of the mutual entity, which are likely to reflect reductions for member benefits, such as reduced fees charged for goods and services. *[IFRS 3.B49]*.

8 RECOGNISING AND MEASURING NON-CONTROLLING INTERESTS

IFRS 3 requires any non-controlling interest in an acquiree to be recognised, *[IFRS 3.10]*, but provides a choice of two measurement methods. These apply to those components of non-controlling interests that are present ownership interests and entitle their holders to a proportionate share of the entity's net assets in the event of a liquidation ('qualifying non-controlling interests').

- Option 1, to measure such components of non-controlling interests at acquisition-date fair value (consistent with the measurement principle for other components of the business combination).
- Option 2, to measure such components of non-controlling interests at their proportionate share of the value of net identifiable assets acquired (described at 5 above).

This choice is not available for all other components of non-controlling interests. These are measured at their fair values, unless another measurement basis is required by IFRSs. *[IFRS 3.19]*.

IFRS 3 defines non-controlling interest as 'the equity in a subsidiary not attributable, directly or indirectly, to a parent'. *[IFRS 3 Appendix A]*. This is the same as that in IFRS 10. As discussed in Chapter 7 at 4.1, this definition includes not only equity shares in the subsidiary held by other parties, but also other elements of 'equity' in the subsidiary. These could relate to, say, other equity instruments such as options or warrants, the equity element of convertible debt instruments, and the 'equity' related to share-based payment awards held by parties other than the parent.

The application to particular instruments is set out in the table below.

Instruments issued by the acquiree	Measurement required by IFRS 3
Ordinary shares	Proportionate share of net assets OR fair value
Preference shares entitled to a *pro rata* share of net assets upon liquidation	Proportionate share of net assets OR fair value
Preference shares **not** entitled to a *pro rata* share of net assets upon liquidation	Fair value
Equity component of convertible debt and other compound financial instruments◊	Fair value
Share warrants◊	Fair value
Options over own shares◊	Fair value
Options under share-based payment transactions◊	IFRS 2 'market-based measure'

◊ In practice, because these instruments are generally not entitled to a share of net assets as of the acquisition date, their proportionate share of net assets is nil.

An illustration of the consequences of applying these requirements is given at 8.4 below.

The choice of method is to be made for each business combination on a transaction-by-transaction basis, rather than being a policy choice. This will require management to consider carefully their future intentions about acquiring such non-controlling interests, as each option, combined with the accounting in IFRS 10 for changes in ownership interest of a subsidiary (see Chapter 7 at 3.3) could have a significant effect on the amount recognised for goodwill.

8.1 Measuring qualifying non-controlling interests at acquisition-date fair value

An acquirer will sometimes be able to measure the fair value of a non-controlling interest on the basis of a quoted price in an active market for the equity shares it does not hold. If a quoted price in an active market is unavailable, the acquirer will need to measure the fair value of the non-controlling interest by using other valuation techniques. *[IFRS 3.B44].*

The fair value of the acquirer's interest in the acquiree and the non-controlling interest on a per-share basis might differ. This may happen because the consideration transferred by the acquirer may include a control premium, or conversely, the inclusion of a discount for lack of control (also referred to as a non-controlling interest discount) in the per-share value of the non-controlling interest if market participants would take into account such a premium or discount when pricing the non-controlling interest. *[IFRS 3.B45].* In that case it would not be appropriate to extrapolate the fair value of an acquirer's interest (i.e. the amount that the acquirer paid per share) to determine the fair value of the non-controlling interests.

8.2 Measuring qualifying non-controlling interests at the proportionate share of the value of net identifiable assets acquired

Under this option, the non-controlling interest is measured at the share of the value of the net assets acquired and liabilities assumed of the acquiree (see 5 above). The result is that the amount recognised for goodwill is only the acquirer's share. However, if any part of the outstanding non-controlling interest is subsequently acquired, no additional goodwill is recorded as under IFRS 10 this is an equity transaction (see Chapter 7 at 3.3).

8.3 Implications of method chosen for measuring non-controlling interests

The following example illustrates the impact of the two measurement options on measuring those components of qualifying non-controlling interests.

Example 9.14: Initial measurement of non-controlling interests in a business combination (1)

Entity B has 40% of its shares publicly traded on an exchange. Entity A purchases the 60% non-publicly traded shares in one transaction, paying €630. Based on the trading price of the shares of Entity B at the date of gaining control a value of €400 is assigned to the 40% non-controlling interest, indicating that Entity A has paid a control premium of €30. The fair value of Entity B's identifiable net assets is €700. For the purposes of the illustration, Entity B has no other instruments that would be regarded as non-controlling interests.

Option 1 – Non-controlling interest at fair value

Entity A accounts for the acquisition as follows:

	Dr €	Cr €
Fair value of identifiable net assets acquired	700	
Goodwill	330	
Cash		630
Non-controlling interest in entity B		400

Option 2 – Certain non-controlling interests are measured at proportionate share of identifiable net assets

Entity A accounts for the acquisition as follows:

	€	€
Fair value of identifiable net assets acquired	700	
Goodwill	210	
Cash		630
Non-controlling interest in entity B (€700 × 40%)		280

The IASB has noted that there are likely to be three main differences arising from measuring the non-controlling interest at its proportionate share of the acquiree's net identifiable assets, rather than at fair value. First, the amounts recognised in a business combination for the non-controlling interest and goodwill are likely to be lower (as illustrated in the above example).

Second, if a cash generating unit to which the goodwill has been allocated is subsequently impaired, any resulting impairment of goodwill recognised through income is likely to be lower than it would have been if the non-controlling interest had been measured at fair value. *[IFRS 3.BC217]*. Chapter 20 at 9 discusses testing goodwill for impairment in entities with non-controlling interests. This guidance includes, considerations when an entity applies an allocation methodology that recognises the disproportionate sharing of the controlling and non-controlling interests in the goodwill book value, i.e. taking into account the acquirer's control premium, if any.

The third difference noted by the IASB is that which arises if the acquirer subsequently purchases some or all of the shares held by the non-controlling shareholders. Under IFRS 10, such a transaction is to be accounted for as an equity transaction (see Chapter 7 at 3.3). By acquiring the non-controlling interest, usually at fair value (unless there are some special circumstances surrounding the acquisition), the equity of the group is reduced by the non-controlling interest's share of any unrecognised changes in fair value of the net assets of the business, including goodwill. Measuring the non-controlling interest initially as a proportionate share of the acquiree's net identifiable assets, rather than at fair value, means that the reduction in the reported equity attributable to the acquirer is likely to be larger. *[IFRS 3.BC218]*. If in Example 9.14 above, Entity A were subsequently to acquire all of the non-controlling interest for, say, €500, then assuming that there had been no changes in the carrying amounts for the net identifiable assets and the goodwill, the equity attributable to the parent, Entity A, would be reduced by €220 (€500 – €280) if Option 2 (proportionate share of fair value of identifiable net assets) had been adopted. If Option 1 (full fair value) had been adopted, the reduction would only be €100 (€500 – €400).

In Example 9.14 above, the acquiree had no other instruments that would be regarded as non-controlling interests. This will not always be the case. The impact of the measurement of such non-controlling interests on goodwill is illustrated in Example 9.15 below.

Example 9.15: Initial measurement of non-controlling interests in a business combination (2)

Parent acquires 80% of the ordinary shares of Target, a private entity, for €950 in cash. The total fair value of the equity instruments issued by Target is €1,165 and the fair value of its identifiable net assets is €850. The fair value of the 20% of the ordinary shares owned by non-controlling shareholders is €190. In addition, the subsidiary has also written gross settled call options over its own shares with a fair value of €25, which are considered equity instruments under IAS 32.

Option 1 – Non-controlling interest at fair value

The impact of the business combination, and the measurement of non-controlling interests, are as follows:

	Dr	Cr
	€	€
Fair value of identifiable net assets	850	
Goodwill (€1,165 – €850)	315	
Cash		950
Non-controlling interest (€190 + €25)		215

Under this method, goodwill represents the difference between the fair value of Target and the fair value of its identifiable net assets. The non-controlling interests are measured as the fair value of all equity instruments issued by Target that are not owned by the parent (i.e. ordinary shares and gross settled call options).

Option 2 – Certain non-controlling interests are measured at proportionate share of identifiable net assets

The impact of the business combination, and the measurement of non-controlling interests, are as follows:

	€	€
Fair value of identifiable net assets	850	
Goodwill ((€950 + €195) – €850)	295	
Cash		950
Non-controlling interest (20% × €850 + €25)		195

Under this method, goodwill represents the difference between the total of the consideration transferred and the amount of the non-controlling interests less the fair value of the net assets acquired and liabilities assumed. The non-controlling interests that are present ownership interests and entitle their holders to a proportionate share of the Target's net assets in the event of liquidation (i.e. the ordinary shares) are measured at the non-controlling interest's proportionate share of the identifiable net assets of Target. The non-controlling interests that are not present ownership interests or do not entitle their holders to a proportionate share of the Target's net assets in the event of liquidation (i.e. the gross settled call options) are measured at their fair value.

Reconciliation of goodwill

Goodwill as determined under the two methods can be reconciled as follows:

	€
Option 2: Goodwill (€950 – 80% × €850 + €25)	295
Goodwill related to the non-controlling interest in ordinary shares (€190 – 20% × €850)	20
Option 1: Goodwill (€1,165 – €850)	315

This makes clear that Option 2 effectively ignores the goodwill related to ordinary shares that are held by non-controlling shareholders.

Chapter 9

In Example 9.15 above, under Option 2, the computation of the non-controlling interests represented by the ordinary shares was based solely on the fair value of the identifiable net assets; i.e. no deduction was made in respect of the other component of non-controlling interest. IFRS 3 does not explicitly state whether this should be the case or not. An alternative view would be that other components of non-controlling interests should be deducted from the value of the identifiable net assets based on their acquisition-date fair value (or market-based measure) or based on their liquidation rights (see Chapter 7 at 4.2). This alternative is illustrated in Chapter 7 in Example 7.15.

8.4 Measuring share-based payment and other components of non-controlling interests

These options in measuring the fair values of non-controlling interests only apply to present ownership interests that entitle their holders to a proportionate share of the entity's net assets in the event of a liquidation. All other components of non-controlling interests must be measured at their fair values, unless another measurement basis is required by IFRSs. *[IFRS 3.19]*. For example, a preference share that entitles the holders only to a preferred return of capital and accrued and unpaid dividends (or any other restricted right) in the event of a liquidation does not qualify for the measurement choice in paragraph 19 of IFRS 3 because it does not entitle its holder to a proportionate share of the entity's net assets in the event of liquidation.

The exception to fair values relates to outstanding share-based payment transactions that are not replaced by the acquirer:

- If vested, they are measured at their market-based measure.
- If unvested, they are measured at their market-based measure as if the acquisition date were the grant date. *[IFRS 3.B62A]*.

The market-based measure of unvested share-based payment transactions is allocated to the non-controlling interest on the basis of the ratio of the portion of the vesting period completed to the greater of the total vesting period or the original vesting period of the share-based payment transaction. The balance is allocated to post-combination service. *[IFRS 3.B62B]*.

The above requirements for equity-settled share-based payment transactions of the acquiree are discussed further in Chapter 32 at 11.2.

Example 9.16: Measurement of non-controlling interest represented by preference shares and employee share options

Preference shares

TC has issued 100 preference shares, which are classified as equity. The preference shares have a nominal value of £1 each. The preference shares give their holders a right to a preferential dividend in priority to the payment of any dividend to the holders of ordinary shares. On liquidation of TC, the holders of the preference shares are entitled to receive out of the assets available for distribution the amount of £1 per share in priority to the holders of ordinary shares but there are no further rights on liquidation.

AC acquires all ordinary shares of TC. The acquisition-date fair value of the preference shares is £120.

The non-controlling interests that relate to TC's preference shares do not entitle their holders to a proportionate share of the entity's net assets in the event of liquidation. They are measured at their fair value of £120.

If the preference shares have an equal right and ranking to the ordinary shares in the event of liquidation, they have a present ownership interest and could then be measured at their fair value or at or at their proportionate share in the acquiree's recognised amounts of the identifiable net assets. If the fair value of the preference shares is £160 and the proportionate share of TC's identifiable net assets attributable to the preference shares is £140, the acquirer can elect to measure the preference shares at either of these amounts.

Employee share options

TC has issued share options to its employees. The share options are classified as equity and are vested at the acquisition date. The share options do not expire on the acquisition date and AC does not replace them. They do not represent present ownership interest and do not entitle their holders to a proportionate share of TC's net assets in the event of liquidation. The market-based measure of the share options in accordance with IFRS 2 at the acquisition date is £200. The acquirer measures the non-controlling interests that are related to the share options at their market-based measure of £200.

8.5 Call and put options over non-controlling interests

In some business combinations where less than 100% of the equity shares are acquired, it may be that the transaction also involves options over some or all of the outstanding shares held by the non-controlling shareholders. The acquirer may have a call option, i.e. a right to acquire the outstanding shares at a future date for cash at a particular price. Alternatively, it may have granted a put option to the other shareholders whereby they have the right to sell their shares to the acquirer at a future date for cash at a particular price. In some cases, there may be a combination of call and put options, the terms of which may be equivalent or may be different.

IFRS 3 gives no guidance as to how such options should impact on the accounting for a business combination. This issue is discussed in Chapter 7 at 5.

Similarly, IFRS 3 does not explicitly address the accounting for a sequence of transactions that begin with an acquirer gaining control over another entity, followed by acquiring additional ownership interests shortly thereafter. This frequently happens where public offers are made to a group of shareholders and there is a regulatory requirement for an acquirer to make an offer to the non-controlling shareholders of the acquiree.

The Interpretations Committee considered this issue and tentatively decided that the guidance in IFRS 10 on how to determine whether the disposal of a subsidiary achieved in stages should be accounted for as one transaction, or as multiple transactions, *[IFRS 10.B97]*, should also be applied to circumstances in which the acquisition of a business is followed by successive purchases of additional interests in the acquiree. The Interpretations Committee tentatively agreed that the initial acquisition of the controlling stake and the subsequent mandatory tender offer should be treated as a single transaction. However, there was no consensus among the Interpretations Committee members on whether a liability should be recognised for the mandatory tender offer at the date that the acquirer obtains control of the acquiree. A small majority expressed the view that a liability should be recognised in a manner that is consistent with IAS 32. Other Interpretations Committee members expressed the view that a mandatory tender offer to purchase NCI is not within the scope of IAS 32 or IAS 37 and that a liability should therefore not be recognised. The issue was escalated to the IASB and at its May 2013 meeting the Board tentatively decided to discuss both issues when it discusses the measurement of put options written on NCI.[38] In June 2014, the IASB decided that the project on put options written on NCI should be incorporated into the broader project looking at the distinction between liabilities and equity – the Financial Instruments with Characteristics of Equity ('FICE') project.[39] Since resuming this research project in October 2014, the IASB has had discussions on various aspects relating to FICE, but the project is still at an early stage. A discussion paper is planned for publication in 2017.[40]

Meanwhile, in the absence of any explicit guidance in IFRS for such transactions, we believe that entities have an accounting policy choice as to whether or not they should make an assessment as to whether the transactions should be treated as a single acquisition in which control is gained (a single business combination), or are to be treated as discrete transactions (a business combination, followed by an acquisition of non-controlling interests). This issue is discussed in Chapter 7 at 5.2.4.

9 BUSINESS COMBINATIONS ACHIEVED IN STAGES ('STEP ACQUISITIONS')

The third item in part (a) of the goodwill computation set out at 6 above is the acquisition-date fair value of the acquirer's previously held equity interest in the acquiree.

An acquirer sometimes obtains control of an acquiree in which it held an equity interest immediately before the acquisition date. For example, on 31 December 2018, Entity A holds a 35 per cent non-controlling equity interest in Entity B. On that date, Entity A purchases an additional 40 per cent interest in Entity B, which gives it control of Entity B. IFRS 3 refers to such a transaction as a business combination achieved in stages, sometimes also referred to as a 'step acquisition'. *[IFRS 3.41]*.

If the acquirer holds a non-controlling equity investment in the acquiree immediately before obtaining control, the acquirer remeasures that previously held equity investment at its acquisition-date fair value and recognises any resulting gain or loss in profit or loss. *[IFRS 3.42]*.

In effect, the acquirer exchanges its status as an owner of an investment asset in an entity for a controlling financial interest in all of the underlying assets and liabilities of that entity (acquiree) and the right to direct how the acquiree and its management use those assets in its operations. *[IFRS 3.BC384]*.

In addition, any changes in the value of the acquirer's equity interest in the acquiree recognised in other comprehensive income (e.g. the investment was classified as available-for-sale in accordance with IAS 39), is reclassified into profit or loss. It is recognised on the same basis that would be required if the acquirer had directly disposed of the previously held equity investment.

For entities applying IFRS 9, any resulting gain or loss is to be recognised in profit or loss or other comprehensive income, as appropriate. *[IFRS 3.42]*.

The acquirer's non-controlling equity investment in the acquiree, after remeasurement to its acquisition-date fair value, is then included as the third item of part (a) of the goodwill computation set out at 6 above.

These requirements are illustrated in the following examples.

Example 9.17: Business combination achieved in stages – original investment treated as an available-for-sale investment under IAS 39

Investor acquires a 20 per cent ownership interest in Investee (a service company) on 1 January 2016 for £3,500,000 cash. At that date, the fair value of Investee's identifiable assets is £10,000,000, and the carrying amount of those assets is £8,000,000. Investee has no liabilities or contingent liabilities at that date. The following shows Investee's statement of financial position at 1 January 2016 together with the fair values of the identifiable assets:

Investee's statement of financial position at 1 January 2016	Carrying amounts	Fair values
	£'000	£'000
Cash and receivables	2,000	2,000
Land	6,000	8,000
	8,000	10,000
Issued equity: 1,000,000 ordinary shares	5,000	
Retained earnings	3,000	
	8,000	

During the year ended 31 December 2016, Investee reports a profit of £6,000,000 but does not pay any dividends. In addition, the fair value of Investee's land increases by £3,000,000 to £11,000,000. However, the amount recognised by Investee in respect of the land remains unchanged at £6,000,000. The following shows Investee's statement of financial position at 31 December 2016 together with the fair values of the identifiable assets:

Investee's statement of financial position at 31 December 2016	Carrying amounts	Fair values
	£'000	£'000
Cash and receivables	8,000	8,000
Land	6,000	11,000
	14,000	19,000
Issued equity: 1,000,000 ordinary shares	5,000	
Retained earnings	9,000	
	14,000	

On 1 January 2017, Investor acquires a further 60 per cent ownership interest in Investee for £22,000,000 cash, thereby obtaining control. Before obtaining control, Investor does not have significant influence over Investee, and accounts for its initial 20 per cent investment at fair value with changes in value recognised as a component of other comprehensive income. Investee's ordinary shares have a quoted market price at 31 December 2016 of £30 per share.

Throughout the period 1 January 2016 to 1 January 2017, Investor's issued equity was £30,000,000. Investor's only asset apart from its investment in Investee is cash.

Accounting for the initial investment before obtaining control

Investor's initial 20 per cent investment in Investee is measured at its cost of £3,500,000. However, Investee's 1,000,000 ordinary shares have a quoted market price at 31 December 2016 of £30 per share. Therefore, the carrying amount of Investor's initial 20 per cent investment is remeasured in Investor's financial statements to £6,000,000 at 31 December 2016, with the £2,500,000 increase recognised as a component of other comprehensive income. Therefore, Investor's statement of financial position before the acquisition of the additional 60 per cent ownership interest is as follows:

Investor's statement of financial position at 31 December 2016	£'000
Cash	26,500
Investment in Investee	6,000
	32,500
Issued equity	30,000
Gain on available-for-sale investment	2,500
	32,500

Accounting for the business combination

Assuming Investor adopts option 2 for measuring the non-controlling interest in Investee, i.e. at the proportionate share of the value of the net identifiable assets acquired, it recognises the following amount for goodwill in its consolidated financial statements:

	£'000
Consideration transferred for 60% interest acquired on 1 January 2017	22,000
Non-controlling interest – share of fair values of identifiable net assets at that date (20% × £19,000,000)	3,800
Acquisition-date fair value of initial 20% interest	6,000
	31,800
Acquisition-date fair values of identifiable net assets acquired	19,000
Goodwill	12,800

The existing gain on available-for-sale investment of £2,500,000 is reclassified into profit or loss at the date of obtaining control on 1 January 2017.

The following shows Investor's consolidation worksheet immediately after the acquisition of the additional 60 per cent ownership interest in Investee, together with consolidation adjustments and associated explanations:

	Investor	Investee	Consolidation adjustments		Consolidated	
			Dr	Cr		
	£'000	£'000	£'000	£'000	£'000	
Cash and receivables	4,500	8,000			12,500	
Investment in investee	28,000	–		28,000		
Land		6,000	5,000		11,000	(a)
Goodwill			12,800		12,800	(b)
	32,500	14,000			36,300	
Issued equity	30,000	5,000	5,000		30,000	(c)
Gain on available-for-sale investment	2,500		2,500		–	(d)
Retained earnings		9,000	9,000		–	(e)
Profit for 2017				2,500	2,500	(d)
Non-controlling interest				3,800	3,800	(a)
	32,500	14,000			36,300	

Notes

The above consolidation adjustments result in:

(a) Investee's identifiable net assets being stated at their full fair values at the date Investor obtains control of Investee, i.e. £19,000,000, including land of £11,000,000. The 20 per cent non-controlling interest in Investee is also stated at the non-controlling interest's 20 per cent share of the fair values of Investee's identifiable net assets, i.e. £3,800,000 (20% × £19,000,000).

(b) goodwill being recognised from the acquisition date based on the computation set out at 6 above, i.e. £12,800,000.

(c) issued equity of £30,000,000 comprising the issued equity of Investor of £30,000,000.

(d) profit of £2,500,000 being the amount reclassified from other comprehensive income relating to the previously held investment in Acquiree on the step acquisition. As a result, total retained earnings in the statement of financial position are £2,500,000.

(e) a retained earnings balance of £nil as Investor's share thereof represents pre-acquisition profits.

Investments that were classified as available-for-sale under IAS 39 would likely be classified under IFRS 9 as either:

- financial assets designated as measured at fair value through profit or loss; or
- financial assets measured at fair value through other comprehensive income if an entity made an irrevocable election at initial recognition to present subsequent changes in their fair value in other comprehensive income.

In the latter case, gains or losses from changes in the fair value accumulated in other comprehensive income would never be reclassified to profit or loss (that is, unlike IAS 39, there is no recycling of gains or losses). In the example above, assuming that IFRS 9 was applied retrospectively, this would mean that no reclassification of gains accumulated from the date of initial acquisition of the investment until the date of business combination would be made at the date of business combination as these gains would have already been recognised either in the profit or loss or other comprehensive income.

If the investor in the above example had accounted for its original investment of 20% as an associate using the equity method under IAS 28 – *Investments in Associates and Joint Ventures*, then the accounting would have been as follows:

Example 9.18: Business combination achieved in stages – original investment treated as an associate under IAS 28

This example uses the same facts as in Example 9.17 above, except that Investor does have significant influence over Investee following its initial 20 per cent investment.

Accounting for the initial investment before obtaining control

Investor's initial 20 per cent investment in Investee is included in Investor's consolidated financial statements under the equity method. Accordingly, it is initially recognised at its cost of £3,500,000 and adjusted thereafter for its share of the profits of Investee after the date of acquisition of £1,200,000 (being 20% × £6,000,000). Investor's policy for property, plant and equipment is to use the cost model under IAS 16; therefore in applying the equity method it does not include its share of the increased value of the land held by Investee. IAS 28 requires that on the acquisition of an associate, any difference between the cost of the acquisition and its share of the fair values of the associate's identifiable assets and liabilities is accounted for as goodwill, but is included within the carrying amount of the investment in the associate. Accordingly, Investor has included goodwill of £1,500,000 arising on its original investment of 20%, being £3,500,000 less £2,000,000 (20% × £10,000,000). Therefore, Investor's consolidated statement of financial position at 31 December 2016, before the acquisition of the additional 60 per cent ownership interest, is as follows:

Investor's consolidated statement of financial position at 31 December 2016	£'000
Cash	26,500
Investment in associate	4,700
	31,200
Issued equity	30,000
Retained earnings	1,200
	31,200

In its separate financial statements, Investor includes its investment in the associate at its cost of £3,500,000.

Accounting for the business combination

Although Investor has previously equity accounted for its 20% interest in Investee (and calculated goodwill on that acquisition), the computation of goodwill in its consolidated financial statements as a result of obtaining control over Investee is the same as that in Example 9.17 above:

	£'000
Consideration transferred for 60% interest acquired on 1 January 2017	22,000
Non-controlling interest – share of fair values of identifiable net assets at that date (20% × £19,000,000)	3,800
Acquisition-date fair value of initial 20% interest	6,000
	31,800
Acquisition-date fair values of identifiable net assets acquired	19,000
Goodwill	12,800

Investor recognises a gain of £1,300,000 in profit or loss as a result of remeasuring its existing interest from its equity-accounted amount of £4,700,000 at the date of obtaining control to its acquisition-date fair value of £6,000,000.

The following shows Investor's consolidation worksheet immediately after the acquisition of the additional 60 per cent ownership interest in Investee, together with consolidation adjustments and associated explanations.

	Investor	Investee	Consolidation adjustments Dr	Consolidation adjustments Cr	Consolidated	
	£'000	£'000	£'000	£'000	£'000	
Cash and receivables	4,500	8,000			12,500	
Investment in investee	26,700	–		26,700	–	
Land		6,000	5,000		11,000	(a)
Goodwill			12,800		12,800	(b)
	31,200	14,000			36,300	
Issued equity	30,000	5,000	5,000		30,000	(c)
Retained earnings	1,200	9,000	9,000		1,200	(d)
Profit for 2017				1,300	1,300	(e)
Non-controlling interest				3,800	3,800	(a)
	31,200	14,000			36,300	

Notes

The above consolidation adjustments result in:

(a) Investee's identifiable net assets being stated at their full fair values at the date Investor obtains control of Investee, i.e. £19,000,000, including land of £11,000,000. The 20 per cent non-controlling interest in Investee is also stated at the non-controlling interest's 20 per cent share of the fair values of Investee's identifiable net assets, i.e. £3,800,000 (20% × £19,000,000).

(b) goodwill being recognised from the acquisition date based on the computation set out at 6 above, i.e. £12,800,000.

(c) issued equity of £30,000,000 comprising the issued equity of Investor of £30,000,000.

(d) a retained earnings balance of £1,200,000 being Investor's equity accounted share of Investee while it was an associate.

(e) profit of £1,300,000 being the amount of gain on remeasurement of the previously existing interest in Investee at its acquisition-date fair value (£6,000,000 – £4,700,000). As a result, total retained earnings in the statement of financial position are £2,500,000.

Although the Examples above illustrate the requirements of IFRS 3 when the previously held investment has been accounted for as an available-for-sale investment or as an associate, the requirements in IFRS 3 for step acquisitions apply to all previously held non-controlling equity investments in the acquiree, including those that were accounted for as joint ventures under IFRS 11. IAS 28's requirements also apply to joint ventures. *[IAS 28.2]*.

As a result of obtaining control over a former associate or joint venture, the acquirer accounts for the business combination by applying the other requirements under IFRS 3 as it would in any other business combination. Thus, it needs to recognise the net of the acquisition-date fair values (or other amounts recognised in accordance with the requirements of the standard) of the identifiable assets acquired and the liabilities assumed relating to the former associate or joint venture (see 5 above), i.e. perform a new purchase price allocation. This will include reassessing the classification and designation of assets and liabilities, including the classification of financial instruments, embedded derivatives and hedge accounting, based on the circumstances that exist at the acquisition date (see 5.4 above).

Obtaining control over a former associate or joint venture means that the investor 'loses' significant influence or 'joint control' over it. Therefore, any amounts recognised in other comprehensive income relating to the associate or joint venture should be recognised by the investor on the same basis that would be required if the associate or joint venture had directly disposed of the related assets or liabilities. For associates and joint ventures, this is discussed further in Chapter 11 at 7.12.1.

In Example 9.18 above, a gain was recognised as a result of the step-acquisition of the former associate. However, a loss may have to be recognised as a result of the step-acquisition.

Example 9.19: Business combination achieved in stages – loss arising on step-acquisition

An investor has an equity-accounted interest in a listed associate comprising 1,000 shares with a carrying value of €1,000. The quoted price of the associate's shares is €0.90 per share, i.e. €900 in total. As there is an impairment indicator, the investment is tested for impairment in accordance with IAS 36. However, as the investor determines that the investment's value in use exceeds €1,000, no impairment loss is recognised.

In the following period, the investor acquires all of the other outstanding shares in the associate. Up to the date of obtaining control, the investor has recognised a further share of profits of the associate, such that the equity-accounted interest in the associate is now €1,050. At the date of obtaining control, the fair value of the shares has increased to €0.93. The existing shares are remeasured to fair value at that date and a loss of €120 (€1,050 less €930) is recognised in profit or loss.

9.1 Proposed clarifications to accounting for previously held interests in a joint operation

Currently IFRS provides no specific guidance on accounting for transactions, in which an entity obtains control of a business that is a joint operation and prior to obtaining control the entity held interests in the assets and liabilities of the joint operation.

The IASB observed diversity in practice in the accounting for such transactions. This diversity arises because of differing interpretations of the term 'equity interests' in paragraphs 41-42 of IFRS 3 and, thus, whether the remeasurement requirements for previously held interests in paragraph 42 of IFRS 3 would apply.[41]

In June 2016, the IASB proposed amendments to IFRS 3 in order to reduce that diversity. The proposed amendments aim to clarify that, when an entity obtains control over a business that is a joint operation, in which the entity is already either a joint operator or a party to a joint operation, the previously held interests in the assets and liabilities of the joint operation are remeasured at fair value (see Chapter 12 at 8.3.2).[42] In reaching this conclusion, the IASB observed that obtaining control of a business that is a joint operation is a business combination achieved in stages and remeasurement of previously held interests is consistent with the fair value measurement requirements of IFRS 3.[43]

The ED proposes that an entity would be required to apply the proposed amendments to IFRS 3 to any business combination for which the acquisition date is on or after the beginning of the first annual reporting period beginning on or after the effective date of the amendments.[44]

In April 2017, the IASB tentatively decided to finalise the amendments to IFRS 3 and IFRS 11 with no substantive changes.[45] At the time of writing, the Board plans to issue final amendment at the end of 2017.[46]

10 BARGAIN PURCHASE TRANSACTIONS

IFRS 3 regards a bargain purchase as being a business combination in which:

- the net of the acquisition-date fair values (or other amounts recognised in accordance with the requirements of the standard) of the identifiable assets acquired and the liabilities assumed, exceeds
- the aggregate of:
  - the consideration transferred (generally measured at acquisition-date fair value);
  - the amount of any non-controlling interest in the acquiree; and
  - the acquisition-date fair value of the acquirer's previously held equity interest in the acquiree. *[IFRS 3.34].*

The IASB considers bargain purchases anomalous transactions – business entities and their owners generally do not knowingly and willingly sell assets or businesses at prices below their fair values. *[IFRS 3.BC371].* Nevertheless, occasionally, an acquirer will make a bargain purchase, for example, in a forced sale in which the seller is acting under compulsion. *[IFRS 3.35].* These may occur in a forced liquidation or distress sale (e.g. after the death of a founder or key manager) in which owners need to sell a business quickly. The IASB observed that an economic gain is inherent in a bargain purchase and concluded that, in concept, the acquirer should recognise that gain at the acquisition date. However, there may not be clear evidence that a bargain purchase has taken place, and because of this there remained the potential for inappropriate gain recognition resulting from measurement bias or undetected measurement errors. *[IFRS 3.BC372-BC375].*

Therefore, before recognising a gain on a bargain purchase, the acquirer should reassess all components of the computation to ensure that the measurements are based on all available information as of the acquisition date. This means ensuring that it has correctly identified all of the assets acquired and all of the liabilities assumed and does not have to recognise any additional assets or liabilities. Having done so, the acquirer must review the procedures used to measure all of the following:

(a) the identifiable assets acquired and liabilities assumed;

(b) the non-controlling interest in the acquiree, if any;

(c) for a business combination achieved in stages, the acquirer's previously held equity interest in the acquiree; and

(d) the consideration transferred. *[IFRS 3.36].*

If an excess remains, the acquirer recognises a gain in profit or loss on the acquisition date. All of the gain is attributed to the acquirer. *[IFRS 3.34].*

The computation means that a gain on a bargain purchase and goodwill cannot both be recognised for the same business combination. *[IFRS 3.BC376-BC377].*

IFRS 3 acknowledges that the requirements to measure particular assets acquired or liabilities assumed in accordance with other IFRSs, rather than their fair value, may result in recognising a gain (or change the amount of a recognised gain) on acquisition. *[IFRS 3.35, BC379].*

The computation of a gain on a bargain purchase is illustrated in the following example, which is based on one included within the Illustrative Examples accompanying IFRS 3. *[IFRS 3.IE45-IE49].*

Example 9.20: Gain on a bargain purchase (1)

On 1 January 2018 Entity A acquires 80% of the equity interests of Entity B, a private entity, in exchange for cash of €150m. Because the former owners of Entity B needed to dispose of their investments in Entity B by a specified date, they did not have sufficient time to market Entity B to multiple potential buyers. The management of Entity A initially measures the separately recognisable identifiable assets acquired and the liabilities assumed as of the acquisition date in accordance with the requirements of IFRS 3. The identifiable assets are measured at €250m and the liabilities assumed are measured at €50m. Entity A engages an independent consultant, who determines that the fair value of the 20% non-controlling interest in Entity B is €42m.

Entity B's identifiable net assets of €200m (being €250m – €50m) exceed the fair value of the consideration transferred plus the fair value of the non-controlling interest in Entity B. Therefore, Entity A reviews the procedures it used to identify and measure the assets acquired and liabilities assumed and to measure the fair value of both the non-controlling interest in Entity B and the consideration transferred. After that review, Entity A decides that the procedures and resulting measures were appropriate. Entity A measures the gain on its purchase of the 80% interest as follows:

	€m	€m
Amount of the identifiable net assets acquired (€250m – €50m)		200
Less:		
Fair value of the consideration transferred for Entity A's 80% interest	150	
Fair value of non-controlling interest in Entity B	42	
		192
Gain on bargain purchase of 80% interest in Entity B		8

Entity A would record its acquisition of Entity B in its consolidated financial statements as follows:

	Dr €m	Cr €m
Identifiable net assets acquired	250	
Cash		150
Liabilities assumed		50
Gain on bargain purchase		8
Equity – non-controlling interest in Entity B		42

If Entity A chose to measure the non-controlling interest in Entity B on the basis of its proportionate interest in the identifiable net assets of the acquiree, the gain on the purchase of the 80% interest would have been as follows:

	€m	€m
Amount of the identifiable net assets acquired (€250m – €50m)		200
Less:		
Fair value of the consideration transferred for Entity A's 80% interest	150	
Non-controlling interest in Entity B (20% × €200m)	40	
		190
Gain on bargain purchase of 80% interest in Entity B		10

On that basis, Entity A would record its acquisition of Entity B in its consolidated financial statements as follows:

	Dr €m	Cr €m
Identifiable net assets acquired	250	
Cash		150
Liabilities assumed		50
Gain on bargain purchase		10
Equity – non-controlling interest in Entity B		40

It can be seen from the above example that the amount of the gain recognised is affected by the way in which the non-controlling interest is measured. Indeed, it might be that if the non-controlling interest is measured at its acquisition-date fair value, goodwill is recognised rather than a gain as shown below.

Example 9.21: Gain on a bargain purchase (2)

This example uses the same facts as in Example 9.20 above, except that the independent consultant, determines that the fair value of the 20% non-controlling interest in Entity B is €52m.

In this situation, the fair value of the consideration transferred plus the fair value of the non-controlling interest in Entity B exceeds the amount of the identifiable net assets acquired, giving rise to goodwill on the acquisition as follows:

	€m
Fair value of the consideration transferred for Entity A's 80% interest	150
Fair value of non-controlling interest in Entity B	52
	202
Less: Amount of the identifiable net assets acquired (€250m – €50m)	200
Goodwill on acquisition of 80% interest in Entity B	2

So, although Entity A in the above example might have made a 'bargain purchase', the requirements of IFRS 3 lead to no gain being recognised.

11 ASSESSING WHAT IS PART OF THE EXCHANGE FOR THE ACQUIREE

To be included in the accounting for the business combination, the identifiable assets acquired and liabilities assumed must be part of the exchange for the acquiree, rather than a result of separate transactions. *[IFRS 3.12]*.

IFRS 3 recognises that the acquirer and the acquiree may have a pre-existing relationship or other arrangement before the negotiations for the business combination, or they may enter into an arrangement during the negotiations that is separate from the business combination. In either situation, the acquirer is required to identify any amounts that are separate from the business combination and thus are not part of the exchange for the acquiree. *[IFRS 3.51]*. This requires the acquirer to evaluate the substance of transactions between the parties.

There are three types of transactions that IFRS 3 regards as separate transactions that should not be considered part of the exchange for the acquiree:

- a transaction that effectively settles pre-existing relationships between the acquirer and acquiree, e.g. a lawsuit, supply contract, franchising or licensing arrangement (see 11.1 below);
- a transaction that remunerates employees or former owners of the acquiree for future services (see 11.2 below); or
- a transaction that reimburses the acquiree or its former owners for paying the acquirer's acquisition-related costs (see 11.3 below). *[IFRS 3.52]*.

The acquirer should consider the following factors to determine whether a transaction is part of the exchange for the acquiree or whether it is separate. The standard stresses that these factors are neither mutually exclusive nor individually conclusive. *[IFRS 3.B50].*

- *The reasons for the transaction*

  Understanding the reasons why the parties to the combination, the acquirer and the acquiree and their owners, directors and managers – and their agents – entered into a particular transaction or arrangement may provide insight into whether it is part of the consideration transferred and the assets acquired or liabilities assumed. If a transaction is arranged primarily for the benefit of the acquirer or the combined entity rather than for the benefit of the acquiree or its former owners before the combination, that portion of the transaction price paid (and any related assets or liabilities) is less likely to be part of the exchange for the acquiree. The acquirer would account for that portion separately from the business combination.
- *Who initiated the transaction*

  A transaction or other event that is initiated by the acquirer may be entered into for the purpose of providing future economic benefits to the acquirer or combined entity with little or no benefit received by the acquiree or its former owners before the combination. A transaction or arrangement initiated by the acquiree or its former owners is less likely to be for the benefit of the acquirer or the combined entity and more likely to be part of the business combination transaction.
- *The timing of the transaction*

  A transaction between the acquirer and the acquiree during the negotiations of the terms of a business combination may have been entered into in contemplation of the business combination to provide future economic benefits to the acquirer or the combined entity. If so, the acquiree or its former owners before the business combination are likely to receive little or no benefit from the transaction except for benefits they receive as part of the combined entity.

One particular area that may be negotiated between acquirer and acquiree could be a restructuring plan relating to the activities of the acquiree. This is discussed at 11.4 below.

11.1 Effective settlement of pre-existing relationships

The acquirer and acquiree may have a relationship that existed before they contemplated the business combination, referred to as a 'pre-existing relationship'. This may be contractual, e.g. vendor and customer or licensor and licensee, or non-contractual, e.g. plaintiff and defendant. *[IFRS 3.B51].*

The purpose of this guidance is to ensure that a transaction that in effect settles a pre-existing relationship between the acquirer and the acquiree is excluded from the accounting for the business combination. If a potential acquiree has an asset, a receivable for an unresolved claim against the potential acquirer, the acquiree's owners could agree to settle that claim as part of an agreement to sell the acquiree to the acquirer. If the acquirer makes a lump sum payment to the seller-owner for the business, part of that payment is to settle the claim. In effect, the acquiree relinquished its claim against the acquirer by transferring its receivable as a dividend to the acquiree's owner. Thus, at the acquisition date the acquiree has no receivable to be acquired as part of the combination, and the acquirer should account separately for its settlement payment. *[IFRS 3.BC122]*.

The acquirer is to recognise a gain or a loss on effective settlement of a pre-existing relationship, measured on the following bases:

- for a pre-existing non-contractual relationship, such as a lawsuit, the gain or loss is measured at its fair value;
- for a pre-existing contractual relationship, such as a supply contract, the gain or loss is measured as the lesser of:
  - (a) the amount by which the contract is favourable or unfavourable from the perspective of the acquirer when compared with terms for current market transactions for the same or similar terms. (A contract that is unfavourable in terms of current market terms is not necessarily an onerous contract in which the unavoidable costs of meeting the obligations under the contract exceed the economic benefits expected to be received under it); and
  - (b) the amount of any settlement provisions in the contract available to the counterparty to whom the contract is unfavourable.

  If (b) is less than (a), the difference is included as part of the business combination accounting.

The amount of gain or loss will depend in part on whether the acquirer had previously recognised a related asset or liability, and the reported gain or loss therefore may differ from the amount calculated by applying the above requirements. *[IFRS 3.B52]*.

If there is an 'at market' component to the settlement (i.e. part of the payment reflects the price any market participant would pay to settle the relationship), this is to be accounted for as part of goodwill and may not be treated as a separate intangible asset.[47]

The requirements for non-contractual relationships are illustrated in the following example.

Example 9.22: Settlement of pre-existing non-contractual relationship

On 1 January 2018 Entity A acquires a 100% interest in Entity B for €250m in cash.

At the beginning of 2016 a dispute arose over the interpretation of a contract for the development and implementation by Entity A of an e-business platform for Entity C, which at the end of 2015 was merged with Entity B. The contract, signed in 2011 and for which work was completed in December 2014, provided for payment of part of the contract price by allocating to Entity A 5% of the profit from the platform for five years from the system's installation, i.e. from January 2015 to January 2020. At the end of 2015 the merged Entity ceased to use the platform developed by Entity A as Entity B had its own platform. Entity A, however, believes that 5% of certain profits should be payable by Entity B for the period January 2016 to January 2020 regardless of the system used by Entity B. Several legal hearings took place in 2016 and 2017. However, at the date of acquisition the dispute is still unresolved. Entity B recognised a provision amounting to €12m reflecting the best estimate of the expenditure required to settle the present obligation at 1 January 2018. No assets are recognised by Entity A with respect to the dispute prior to the date of acquisition.

The acquisition by Entity A of Entity B includes the effective settlement of the dispute between Entity A and Entity B which is accounted for as a separate transaction from the business combination. On 1 January 2018 Entity A recognises a gain on effective settlement of the dispute at its fair value, which is not necessarily equal to the amount of the provision reported by Entity B. The amount of consideration transferred for the acquisition of Entity B is increased accordingly. Assuming the fair value of the dispute at 1 January 2018 is assessed to be €15m, Entity A will recognise a gain on effective settlement of €15m, and the consideration transferred for the purposes of determining goodwill will total €265m (€250m + €15m).

The requirements for contractual relationships are illustrated in the following example relating to a supply contract. *[IFRS 3.IE54-IE57]*.

Example 9.23: Settlement of pre-existing contractual relationship – Supply contract

Entity A purchases electronic components from Entity B under a five-year supply contract at fixed rates. Currently, the fixed rates are higher than the rates at which Entity A could purchase similar electronic components from another supplier. The supply contract allows Entity A to terminate the contract before the end of the initial five-year term but only by paying a €6m penalty. With three years remaining under the supply contract, Entity A pays €50m to acquire Entity B, which is the fair value of Entity B based on what other market participants would be willing to pay.

Included in the total fair value of Entity B is €8m related to the fair value of the supply contract with Entity A. The €8m represents a €3m component that is 'at market' because the pricing is comparable to pricing for current market transactions for the same or similar items (selling effort, customer relationships and so on) and a €5 million component for pricing that is unfavourable to Entity A because it exceeds the price of current market transactions for similar items. Entity B has no other identifiable assets or liabilities related to the supply contract, and Entity A has not recognised any assets or liabilities related to the supply contract before the business combination.

In this example, Entity A calculates a loss of €5m (the lesser of the €6m stated settlement amount and the amount by which the contract is unfavourable to the acquirer) separately from the business combination. The €3m 'at-market' component of the contract is part of goodwill.

Whether Entity A had recognised previously an amount in its financial statements related to a pre-existing relationship will affect the amount recognised as a gain or loss for the effective settlement of the relationship. Suppose that Entity A had recognised a €6m liability for the supply contract before the business combination. In that situation, Entity A recognises a €1m settlement gain on the contract in profit or loss at the acquisition date (the €5m measured loss on the contract less the €6m loss previously recognised). In other words, Entity A has in effect settled a recognised liability of €6m for €5m, resulting in a gain of €1m. *[IFRS 3.IE57]*.

Another example of settlement of a pre-existing contractual relationship, which should be recognised separately from the business combination, is where the acquirer has a loan payable to or receivable from the acquiree.

Example 9.24: Settlement of pre-existing contractual relationship – Loan agreement

Entity A acquires a 100% interest in Entity B for €500m in cash.

Before the acquisition, Entity B granted a fixed interest rate loan to Entity A and as at the date of acquisition Entity A has recognised a financial liability in respect of the loan amounting to €50m. Fair value of that financial liability is assessed to be €45m. The fair value of the net identifiable assets and liabilities of Entity B as at the date of acquisition is €460m, including €45m in respect of the fixed rate loan to Entity A.

The amount of consideration transferred for the acquisition of Entity B is decreased by the fair value of the financial liability and the financial liability is derecognised. As such, the consideration transferred for purposes of determining goodwill is €455m (€500m – €45m). The amount by which the loan agreement is favourable to the acquirer is recognised as a gain in the consolidated profit or loss. The net identifiable assets and liabilities of Entity B exclude the receivable due from Entity A.

Entity A accounts for the acquisition of Entity B and settlement of the financial liability as follows:

	€m	€m
Net identifiable assets and liabilities acquired (€460m – €45m)	415	
Loan due to Entity B	50	
Goodwill (€455m – €415m)	40	
Gain on derecognition of loan due to Entity B (€50m – €45m)		5
Cash – consideration for business combination (€500m – €45m)		455
Cash – effective settlement of loan due to Entity B		45

A pre-existing relationship may be a contract that the acquirer recognises as a reacquired right. As indicated at 5.6.5 above, if the contract includes terms that are favourable or unfavourable when compared with pricing for current market transactions for the same or similar items, the acquirer recognises, separately from the business combination, a gain or loss for the effective settlement of the contract, measured in accordance with the requirements described above. *[IFRS 3.B53].*

Example 9.25: Settlement of pre-existing contractual relationship – Reacquired technology licensing agreement

Entity A acquires a 100% interest in Entity B for €350m in cash.

Before the acquisition, Entity A sold to Entity B an exclusive right to use Entity A's technology in a specified territory. Entity B also pays a revenue-based royalty on a monthly basis. The terms of the technology licensing agreement state that if Entity A terminates the arrangement without cause, Entity A would be required to pay a penalty of €30m. Neither Entity A nor Entity B has recognised any assets or liabilities related to the licence agreement.

The fair value of the licence agreement is assessed to be €120m, which includes a value of €20m for the future royalties which are below current market rates. Therefore, the licence agreement is unfavourable to Entity A and favourable to Entity B. The fair value of the net identifiable assets and liabilities of Entity B as at the date of the business combination is €320m, including the fair value of the licence agreement of €120m.

The reacquired licence right is recognised at €100m, being the licence's fair value at current market rates (€120m – €20m). Entity A recognises a loss on settlement of the agreement at the lower of:

- €20m, which is the amount by which the royalty is unfavourable to Entity A compared to market terms;
- €30m, which is the amount that Entity A would have to pay to terminate the right at the date of acquisition.

A loss is therefore recognised of €20m. The amount of consideration transferred for the acquisition of Entity B is decreased accordingly to €330m (€350m – €20m).

Entity A accounts for the acquisition of Entity B and the reacquired technology licensing agreement as follows:

	€m	€m
Net identifiable assets and liabilities acquired (€320m – €20m)	300	
Goodwill (€330m – €300m)	30	
Loss on settlement of technology licensing agreement	20	
Cash – consideration for business combination (€350m – €20m)		330
Cash – effective settlement of technology licensing agreement		20

11.2 Remuneration for future services of employees or former owners of the acquiree

A transaction that remunerates employees or former owners of the acquiree for future services is excluded from the business combination accounting and accounted for separately. *[IFRS 3.52]*.

11.2.1 Arrangements for contingent payments to employees or selling shareholders

Whether arrangements for contingent payments to employees (or selling shareholders) are contingent consideration to be included in the measure of the consideration transferred (see 7.1 above) or are separate transactions to be accounted for as remuneration will depend on the nature of the arrangements.

Such payments are also often referred to as 'earn-outs'. The approach to accounting for earn-out arrangements is summarised in the diagram below:

Approach to accounting for earn-outs

In general, conditions that tie the payment to continuing employment result in the additional payment being considered remuneration for services rather than additional consideration for the business.

Understanding the reasons why the acquisition agreement includes a provision for contingent payments, who initiated the arrangement and when the parties entered into the arrangement may be helpful in assessing the nature of the arrangement. *[IFRS 3.B54]*. If it is not clear whether the arrangement for payments to employees or selling shareholders is part of the exchange for the acquiree or is a transaction separate from the business combination, there are a number of indicators in IFRS 3. *[IFRS 3.B55]*. These are summarised in the table below:

Indicators to consider when classifying payments as remuneration or contingent consideration

Lead to conclusion as remuneration	Indicators to consider when assessing terms of additional payments to selling shareholders that remain employees	Lead to conclusion as contingent consideration
Payments forfeited on termination	Continuing employment	Payments are not affected by termination
Coincides with or exceeds payment period	Duration of required employment	Shorter than the payment period
Not reasonable compared to other key employees of the group	Level of other elements of remuneration	Reasonable compared to the other key employees of the group
Other non-employee selling shareholders receive lower additional payments (on a per share basis)	Incremental payments to other non-employee selling shareholders	Other non-employee selling shareholders receive similar additional payments (on a per share basis)
Selling shareholders remaining as employees owned substantially all shares (in substance profit-sharing)	Number of shares owned when all selling shareholders receive same level of additional consideration (on a per share basis)	Selling shareholders remaining as employees owned only a small portion of shares
Formula for additional payment consistent with other profit-sharing arrangements rather than the valuation approach	Linkage of payments to valuation of business	Initial consideration at lower end of range of business valuation, and formula for additional payment linked to the valuation approach
Formula is based on performance, such as percentage of earnings	Formula for additional payments	Formula is based on a valuation formula, such as multiple of earnings, indicating it is connected to a business valuation

Although these points are supposed to be indicators, continuing employment is an exception. It is categorically stated that 'a contingent consideration arrangement in which the payments are automatically forfeited if employment terminates is remuneration for post-combination services'. *[IFRS 3.B55(a)]*. With this exception, no other single indicator is likely to be enough to be conclusive as to the accounting treatment.

The Interpretations Committee has considered whether payments that are forfeited on termination of employment should automatically be classified as remuneration for post-combination services. The Interpretations Committee observed that an arrangement in which contingent payments are automatically forfeited if employment terminates would lead to a conclusion that the arrangement is compensation for post-combination services rather than additional consideration for an acquisition, unless the service condition is not substantive. The Interpretations Committee reached this conclusion on the basis of the conclusive language used in paragraph B55(a) of IFRS 3. The Interpretations Committee decided not to add this issue to its agenda. The IASB indicated in its *Report and Feedback Statement – Post-implementation Review of IFRS 3 Business Combinations* (June 2015) that many participants asked the Board to revisit the guidance in paragraph B55(a) of IFRS 3 for contingent payments to selling shareholders in circumstances in which those selling shareholders become, or continue as, employees. However, the IASB considered the issue as being of low significance and, having considered the feedback received from the 2015 Agenda Consultation, the Board decided not to include it in its work plan and research pipeline.[48]

The guidance in IFRS 3 expands the points in the table above, but also notes that:

(i) The relevant terms of continuing employment may be included in an employment agreement, acquisition agreement or some other document. *[IFRS 3.B55(a)]*.

(ii) Other pre-acquisition ownership interests may be relevant, e.g. those held by parties related to selling shareholders such as family members, who continue as key employees. *[IFRS 3.B55(e)]*.

Where it is determined that some or all of the arrangement is to be accounted for as contingent consideration, the requirements in IFRS 3 discussed at 7.1 should be applied. If some or all of the arrangement is post-combination remuneration, it will be accounted for under IFRS 2 if it represents a share-based payment transaction (see Chapter 32) or a transaction under IAS 19 (see Chapter 33).

The requirements for contingent payments to employees are illustrated in the following example. *[IFRS 3.IE58-IE60]*.

Example 9.26: Contingent payments to employees

Entity B appointed a candidate as its new CEO under a ten-year contract. The contract required Entity B to pay the candidate $5m if Entity B is acquired before the contract expires. Entity A acquires Entity B eight years later. The CEO was still employed at the acquisition date and will receive the additional payment under the existing contract.

In this example, Entity B entered into the employment agreement before the negotiations of the combination began, and the purpose of the agreement was to obtain the services of CEO. Thus, there is no evidence that the agreement was arranged primarily to provide benefits to Entity A or the combined entity. Therefore, the liability to pay $5m is accounted for as part of the acquisition of Entity B.

In other circumstances, Entity B might enter into a similar agreement with CEO at the suggestion of Entity A during the negotiations for the business combination. If so, the primary purpose of the agreement might be to provide severance pay to CEO, and the agreement may primarily benefit Entity A or the combined entity rather than Entity B or its former owners. In that situation, Entity A accounts for the liability to pay CEO in its post-combination financial statements separately from the acquisition of Entity B.

Not all arrangements relate to judgements about whether an arrangement is remuneration or contingent consideration and other agreements and relationships with selling shareholders may have to be considered. The terms of other arrangements and the income tax treatment of contingent payments may indicate that contingent payments are attributable to something other than consideration for the acquiree. These can include agreements not to compete, executory contracts, consulting contracts and property lease agreements. For example, the acquirer might enter into a property lease arrangement with a significant selling shareholder. If the lease payments specified in the lease contract are significantly below market, some or all of the contingent payments to the lessor (the selling shareholder) required by a separate arrangement for contingent payments might be, in substance, payments for the use of the leased property that the acquirer should recognise separately in its post-combination financial statements. In contrast, if the lease contract specifies lease payments that are consistent with market terms for the leased property, the arrangement for contingent payments to the selling shareholder may be contingent consideration in the business combination.

11.2.2 Share-based payment awards exchanged for awards held by the acquiree's employees

The acquirer may exchange share-based payment awards (i.e. replacement awards) for awards held by employees of the acquiree.

If the acquirer replaces any acquiree awards, the consideration transferred will include some or all of any replacement awards. Any amount not included in the consideration transferred is treated as a post-combination remuneration expense.

IFRS 3 includes application guidance dealing with replacement awards. *[IFRS 3.B56-B62].* Replacement awards are modifications of share-based payment awards in accordance with IFRS 2. Discussion of this guidance, including illustrative examples that reflect the substance of the Illustrative Examples that accompany IFRS 3, *[IFRS 3.IE61-IE71]*, is dealt with in Chapter 32 at 11.2.

11.3 Reimbursement for paying the acquirer's acquisition-related costs

The third example of a separate transaction is included to mitigate concerns about potential abuse. IFRS 3 requires the acquirer to expense its acquisition-related costs – they are not included as part of the consideration transferred for the acquiree. This means that they are not reflected in the computation of goodwill. As a result, acquirers might modify transactions to avoid recognising those costs as expenses. They might disguise reimbursements, e.g. a buyer might ask a seller to make payments to third parties on its behalf; the seller might agree to make those payments if the total amount to be paid to it is sufficient to reimburse it for payments made on the buyer's behalf. *[IFRS 3.BC370].*

The same would apply if the acquirer asks the acquiree to pay some or all of the acquisition-related costs on its behalf and the acquiree has paid those costs before the acquisition date, so that at the acquisition date the acquiree does not record a liability for them. *[IFRS 3.BC120].* This transaction has been entered into on behalf of the acquirer, or primarily for the benefit of the acquirer.

11.4 Restructuring plans

One particular area that could be negotiated between the acquirer and the acquiree or its former owners is a restructuring plan relating to the acquiree's activities.

In our view, a restructuring plan that is implemented by or at the request of the acquirer is not a liability of the acquiree as at the date of acquisition and cannot be part of the accounting for the business combination under the acquisition method, regardless of whether the combination is contingent on the plan being implemented. IFRS 3 does not contain the same explicit requirements relating to restructuring plans that were in the previous version of IFRS 3, but the Basis for Conclusions accompanying IFRS 3 clearly indicate that the requirements for recognising liabilities associated with restructuring or exit activities remain the same. *[IFRS 3.BC137]*. Furthermore, as discussed at 5.2 above, an acquirer recognises liabilities for restructuring or exit activities acquired in a business combination only if they meet the definition of a liability at the acquisition date. *[IFRS 3.BC132]*.

A restructuring plan that is decided upon or put in place between the date the negotiations for the business combination started and the date the business combination is consummated is only likely to be accounted for as a pre-combination transaction of the acquiree if there is no evidence that the acquirer initiated the restructuring and the plan makes commercial sense even if the business combination does not proceed.

If a plan initiated by the acquirer is implemented without an explicit link to the combination this may indicate that control has already passed to the acquirer at this earlier date.

This is discussed further in the following example.

Example 9.27: Recognition or otherwise of a restructuring liability as part of a business combination

The acquirer and the acquiree (or the vendors of the acquiree) enter into an arrangement before the acquisition that requires the acquiree to restructure its workforce or activities. They intend to develop the main features of a plan that involve terminating or reducing its activities and to announce the plan's main features to those affected by it so as to raise a valid expectation that the plan will be implemented. The combination is contingent on the plan being implemented.

Does such a restructuring plan that the acquiree puts in place simultaneously with the business combination, i.e. the plan is effective upon the change in control, but was implemented by or at the request of the acquirer qualify for inclusion as part of the liabilities assumed in accounting for the business combination?

If these facts are analysed:

(a) *the reason:* a restructuring plan implemented at the request of the acquirer is presumably arranged primarily for the benefit of the acquirer or the combined entity because of the possible redundancy expected to arise from the combination of activities of the acquirer with activities of the acquiree, e.g. capacity redundancy leading to closure of the acquiree's facilities;

(b) *who initiated:* if such a plan is the result of a request of the acquirer, it means that the acquirer is expecting future economic benefits from the arrangement and the decision to restructure;

(c) *the timing:* the restructuring plan is usually discussed during the negotiations; therefore, it is contemplated in the perspective of the future combined entity.

Accordingly, a restructuring plan that is implemented as a result of an arrangement between the acquirer and the acquiree is not a liability of the acquiree as at the date of acquisition and cannot be part of the accounting for the business combination under the acquisition method.

Does the answer differ if the combination is not contingent on the plan being implemented?

The answer applies regardless of whether the combination is contingent on the plan being implemented. A plan initiated by the acquirer will most likely not make commercial sense from the acquiree's perspective absent the business combination. For example, there are retrenchments of staff whose position will only truly become redundant once the entities are combined. In that case, this is an arrangement to be accounted for separately rather than as part of the business combination exchange. This arrangement may also indicate that control of acquiree has already passed to the acquirer as otherwise there would be little reason for the acquiree to enter into an arrangement that makes little or no commercial sense to it.

12 MEASUREMENT PERIOD

IFRS 3 contains provisions in respect of a 'measurement period' which provides the acquirer with a reasonable period of time to obtain the information necessary to identify and measure all of the various components of the business combination as of the acquisition date in accordance with the standard, i.e.:

(a) the identifiable assets acquired, liabilities assumed and any non-controlling interest in the acquiree;

(b) the consideration transferred for the acquiree (or the other amount used in measuring goodwill);

(c) in a business combination achieved in stages, the equity interest in the acquiree previously held by the acquirer; and

(d) the resulting goodwill or gain on a bargain purchase. *[IFRS 3.46].*

For most business combinations, the main area where information will need to be obtained is in relation to the acquiree, i.e. the identifiable assets acquired and the liabilities assumed, particularly as these may include items that the acquiree had not previously recognised as assets and liabilities in its financial statements and, in most cases, need to be measured at their acquisition-date fair value (see 5 above). Information may also need to be obtained in determining the fair value of any contingent consideration arrangements (see 7.1 above).

The measurement period ends as soon as the acquirer receives the information it was seeking about facts and circumstances that existed as of the acquisition date or learns that it cannot obtain more information. The measurement period cannot exceed one year from the acquisition date. *[IFRS 3.45].* The Basis for Conclusions notes that in placing this constraint it was 'concluded that allowing a measurement period longer than one year would not be especially helpful; obtaining reliable information about circumstances and conditions that existed more than a year ago is likely to become more difficult as time passes. Of course, the outcome of some contingencies and similar matters may not be known within a year. But the objective of the measurement period is to provide time to obtain the information necessary to measure the fair value of the item as of the acquisition date. Determining the ultimate settlement amount of a contingency or other item is not necessary. Uncertainties about the timing and amount of future cash flows are part of the measure of the fair value of an asset or liability.' *[IFRS 3.BC392].*

Under IFRS 3, if the initial accounting is incomplete at the end of the reporting period in which the combination occurs, the acquirer will include provisional amounts. *[IFRS 3.45].* IFRS 3 specifies particular disclosures about those items (see 16.2 below). *[IFRS 3.BC393].*

Although paragraph 45 refers to the initial accounting being 'incomplete by the end of the reporting period' and the acquirer reporting 'provisional amounts for the items for which the accounting is incomplete', *[IFRS 3.45]*, it is clear from the Illustrative Examples accompanying IFRS 3 that this means being incomplete at the date of authorising for issue the financial statements for that period (see Example 9.28 below). Thus, any items that are finalised up to that date should be reflected in the initial accounting.

12.1 Adjustments made during measurement period to provisional amounts

During the measurement period, the acquirer retrospectively adjusts the provisional amounts recognised at the acquisition date to reflect new information obtained about facts and circumstances at the acquisition date that, if known, would have affected the measurement of the amounts recognised.

Similarly, the acquirer recognises additional assets or liabilities if new information is obtained about facts and circumstances at the acquisition date and, if known, would have resulted in the recognition of those assets and liabilities as of that date. *[IFRS 3.45]*.

IFRS 3 requires the acquirer to consider all pertinent factors to distinguish information that should result in an adjustment to the provisional amounts from that arising from events that occurred after the acquisition date. Factors to be considered include the date when additional information is obtained and whether the acquirer can identify a reason for a change to provisional amounts. Clearly, information obtained shortly after the acquisition date is more likely to reflect circumstances that existed at the acquisition date than information obtained several months later. If the acquirer sells an asset to a third party shortly after the acquisition date for an amount that is significantly different to its provisional fair value, this is likely to indicate an 'error' in the provisional amount unless there is an intervening event that changes its fair value. *[IFRS 3.47]*.

Adjustments to provisional amounts that are made during the measurement period are recognised as if the accounting for the business combination had been completed at the acquisition date. This may be in a prior period, so the acquirer revises its comparative information as needed. This may mean making changes to depreciation, amortisation or other income effects. *[IFRS 3.49]*. These requirements are illustrated in the following example, which is based on one included within the Illustrative Examples accompanying IFRS 3. *[IFRS 3.IE50-IE53]*. The deferred tax implications are ignored.

Example 9.28: Adjustments made during measurement period to provisional amounts

Entity A acquired Entity B on 30 September 2017. Entity A sought an independent valuation for an item of property, plant and equipment acquired in the combination. However, the valuation was not complete by the time Entity A authorised for issue its financial statements for the year ended 31 December 2017. In its 2017 annual financial statements, Entity A recognised a provisional fair value for the asset of €30,000. At the acquisition date, the item of property, plant and equipment had a remaining useful life of five years.

Five months after the acquisition date (and after the date on which the financial statements were issued), Entity A received the independent valuation, which estimated the asset's acquisition-date fair value at €40,000.

In its financial statements for the year ended 31 December 2018, Entity A retrospectively adjusts the 2017 prior year information as follows:

(a) The carrying amount of property, plant and equipment as of 31 December 2017 is increased by €9,500. That adjustment is measured as the fair value adjustment at the acquisition date of €10,000 less the additional depreciation that would have been recognised if the asset's fair value at the acquisition date had been recognised from that date (€500 for three months' depreciation).

(b) The carrying amount of goodwill as of 31 December 2017 is decreased by €10,000.

(c) Depreciation expense for 2017 is increased by €500.

Entity A disclosed in its 2017 financial statements that the initial accounting for the business combination has not been completed because the valuation of property, plant and equipment has not yet been received.

In its 2018 financial statements, Entity A will disclose the amounts and explanations of the adjustments to the provisional values recognised during the current reporting period. Therefore, Entity A will disclose that the 2017 comparative information is adjusted retrospectively to increase the fair value of the item of property, plant and equipment at the acquisition date by €10,000, resulting in an increase to property, plant and equipment of €9,500, offset by a decrease to goodwill of €10,000 and an increase in depreciation expense of €500.

The example below illustrates that adjustments during the measurement period are also made where information is received about the existence of an asset as at the acquisition date:

Example 9.29: Identification of an asset during measurement period

Entity C acquired Entity D on 30 November 2017. Entity C engaged an independent appraiser to assist with the identification and determination of fair values to be assigned to the acquiree's assets and liabilities. However, the appraisal was not finalised by the time Entity C authorised for issue its financial statements for the year ended 31 December 2017, and therefore the amounts recognised in its 2017 annual financial statements were on a provisional basis.

Six months after the acquisition date, Entity C received the independent appraiser's final report, in which it was identified by the independent appraiser that the acquiree had an intangible asset with a fair value at the date of acquisition of €20,000. As this had not been identified at the time when Entity C was preparing its 2017 annual financial statements, no value had been included for it.

In its financial statements for the year ended 31 December 2018, Entity C retrospectively adjusts the prior year information to reflect the recognition of this intangible asset.

Although a change in the provisional amount recognised for an identifiable asset will usually mean a corresponding decrease or increase in goodwill, new information obtained could affect another identifiable asset or liability. If the acquirer assumed a liability to pay damages relating to an accident in one of the acquiree's facilities, part or all of which was covered by the acquiree's liability insurance policy, new information during the measurement period about the fair value of the liability would affect goodwill. This adjustment to goodwill would be offset, in whole or in part, by a corresponding adjustment resulting from a change to the provisional amount recognised for the claim receivable from the insurer. *[IFRS 3.48]*. Similarly, if there is a non-controlling interest in the acquiree, and this is measured based on the proportionate share of the net identifiable assets of the acquiree (see 8 above), any adjustments to those assets that had initially been determined on a provisional basis will be offset by the proportionate share attributable to the non-controlling interest.

12.2 Adjustments made after end of measurement period

After the end of the measurement period, the acquirer can only revise the accounting for a business combination to correct an error in accordance with IAS 8 – *Accounting Policies, Changes in Accounting Estimates and Errors*. *[IFRS 3.50]*. This would probably be the case only if the original accounting was based on a misinterpretation of the facts which were available at the time; it would not apply simply because new information had come to light which changed the acquiring management's view of the value of the item in question.

Adjustments after the end of the measurement period are not made for the effect of changes in estimates. In accordance with IAS 8, the effect of a change in estimate is recognised in the current and future periods (see Chapter 3 at 4.5).

13 SUBSEQUENT MEASUREMENT AND ACCOUNTING

Assets acquired, liabilities assumed or incurred and equity instruments issued in a business combination are usually accounted for in accordance with the applicable IFRSs. However, there is specific guidance on subsequent measurement of and accounting for the following:

(a) reacquired rights (see 5.6.5 above);

(b) contingent liabilities recognised as of the acquisition date (see 5.6.1.B above);

(c) indemnification assets (see 5.6.4 above); and

(d) contingent consideration (see 7.1.3 above). *[IFRS 3.54]*.

Other IFRSs provide guidance on subsequent measurement and accounting: *[IFRS 3.B63]*

(a) IAS 38 prescribes the accounting for identifiable intangible assets acquired in a business combination (see Chapter 17), although accounting for some intangible assets is not prescribed by IAS 38 but by other IFRSs: *[IFRS 3.B39]* see Chapter 17 at 2. Goodwill is measured at the amount recognised at the acquisition date less any accumulated impairment losses, measured in accordance with IAS 36 (see Chapter 20 at 8);

(b) IFRS 4 provides guidance on the subsequent accounting for an insurance contract acquired in a business combination (see Chapter 55); IFRS 17, if adopted, provides guidance on the initial and subsequent measurement of a group of contracts within the scope of IFRS 17 acquired in a business combination (see Chapter 56);

(c) IAS 12 prescribes the subsequent accounting for deferred tax assets (including unrecognised deferred tax assets) and liabilities acquired in a business combination (see Chapter 31);

(d) IFRS 2 provides guidance on subsequent measurement and accounting for the portion of replacement share-based payment awards issued by an acquirer that is attributable to employees' future services (see Chapter 32 at 11); and

(e) IFRS 10 provides guidance on accounting for changes in a parent's ownership interest in a subsidiary after control is obtained (see Chapter 7).

14 REVERSE ACQUISITIONS

The standard takes the view that the acquirer is usually the entity that issues its equity interests, but recognises that in some business combinations, so-called 'reverse acquisitions', the issuing entity is the acquiree.

Under IFRS 3, a reverse acquisition occurs when the entity that issues securities (the legal acquirer) is identified as the acquiree for accounting purposes based on the guidance in the standard as discussed at 4.1 above. Perhaps more accurately, the legal acquiree must be identified as the acquirer for accounting purposes.

Reverse acquisitions sometimes occur when a private operating entity wants to become a public entity but does not want to register its equity shares. The private entity will arrange for a public entity to acquire its equity interests in exchange for the equity interests of the public entity. Although the public entity is the legal acquirer because it issued its equity interests, and the private entity is the legal acquiree because its equity interests were acquired, application of the guidance results in identifying: *[IFRS 3.B19]*

(a) the public entity as the acquiree for accounting purposes (the accounting acquiree); and

(b) the private entity as the acquirer for accounting purposes (the accounting acquirer).

If the transaction is accounted for as a reverse acquisition, all of the recognition and measurement principles in IFRS 3, including the requirement to recognise goodwill, apply. The standard also notes that the legal acquirer must meet the definition of a business (see 3.2 above) for the transaction to be accounted for as a reverse acquisition, *[IFRS 3.B19]*, but does not say how the transaction should be accounted for where the accounting acquiree is not a business. It clearly cannot be accounted for as an acquisition of the legal acquiree by the legal acquirer under the standard either, if the legal acquirer has not been identified as the accounting acquirer based on the guidance in the standard. This is discussed further at 14.8 below.

14.1 Measuring the consideration transferred

The first item to be included in the computation of goodwill in a reverse acquisition is the consideration transferred by the accounting acquirer, i.e. the legal acquiree/subsidiary. In a reverse acquisition, the accounting acquirer usually issues no consideration for the acquiree; equity shares are issued to the owners of the accounting acquirer by the accounting acquiree. The fair value of the consideration transferred by the accounting acquirer is based on the number of equity interests the legal subsidiary would have had to issue to give the owners of the legal parent the same percentage equity interest in the combined entity that results from the reverse acquisition. The fair value of the number of equity interests calculated in that way is used as the fair value of consideration transferred. *[IFRS 3.B20]*.

These requirements are illustrated in the following example, which is based on one included within the Illustrative Examples accompanying IFRS 3. *[IFRS 3.IE1-IE5]*.

Example 9.30: Reverse acquisition – calculating the fair value of the consideration transferred

Entity A, the entity issuing equity instruments and therefore the legal parent, is acquired in a reverse acquisition by Entity B, the legal subsidiary, on 30 September 2018. The accounting for any income tax effects is ignored.

Statements of financial position of Entity A and Entity B immediately before the business combination are:

	Entity A	Entity B
	€	€
Current assets	500	700
Non-current assets	1,300	3,000
Total assets	1,800	3,700
Current liabilities	300	600
Non-current liabilities	400	1,100
Total liabilities	700	1,700
Owner's equity		
Issued equity		
100 ordinary shares	300	
60 Ordinary shares		600
Retained earnings	800	1,400
Total shareholders' equity	1,100	2,000

Other information

(a) On 30 September 2018, Entity A issues 2.5 shares in exchange for each ordinary share of Entity B. All of Entity B's shareholders exchange their shares in Entity B. Therefore, Entity A issues 150 ordinary shares in exchange for all 60 ordinary shares of Entity B.

(b) The fair value of each ordinary share of Entity B at 30 September 2018 is €40. The quoted market price of Entity A's ordinary shares at that date is €16.

(c) The fair values of Entity A's identifiable assets and liabilities at 30 September 2018 are the same as their carrying amounts, except that the fair value of Entity A's non-current assets at 30 September 2018 is €1,500.

Calculating the fair value of the consideration transferred

As a result of Entity A (legal parent/acquiree) issuing 150 ordinary shares, Entity B's shareholders own 60 per cent of the issued shares of the combined entity (i.e. 150 of 250 issued shares). The remaining 40 per cent are owned by Entity A's shareholders. If the business combination had taken the form of Entity B issuing additional ordinary shares to Entity A's shareholders in exchange for their ordinary shares in Entity A, Entity B would have had to issue 40 shares for the ratio of ownership interest in the combined entity to be the same. Entity B's shareholders would then own 60 out of the 100 issued shares of Entity B – 60 per cent of the combined entity.

As a result, the fair value of the consideration effectively transferred by Entity B and the group's interest in Entity A is €1,600 (i.e. 40 shares each with a fair value of €40).

The fair value of the consideration effectively transferred should be based on the most reliable measure. In this example, the quoted market price of Entity A's shares provides a more reliable basis for measuring the consideration effectively transferred than the estimated fair value of the shares in Entity B, and the consideration is measured using the market price of Entity A's shares – 100 shares with a fair value per share of €16, i.e. €1,600.

The final paragraph in the above example would appear to be based on the requirements of paragraph 33 of the standard, i.e. 'in a business combination in which the acquirer and the acquiree (or its former owners) exchange only equity interests, the acquisition-date fair value of the acquiree's equity interests may be more reliably measurable than the acquisition-date fair value of the acquirer's equity interests. If so, the acquirer shall determine the amount of goodwill by using the acquisition-date fair value of the acquiree's equity interests instead of the acquisition-date fair value of the equity interests transferred.' *[IFRS 3.33]*. In the above example, this did not result in a difference as the value of the consideration measured under both approaches was the same. However, the example above indicates that there is a quoted market price for Entity A's shares which is a more reliable basis than the fair value of Entity B's shares. Therefore, if the quoted market price of Entity A's shares had been, say, €14 per share, the fair value of the consideration effectively transferred would have been measured at €1,400.

14.2 Measuring goodwill

As there is no non-controlling interest in the accounting acquiree, and assuming that the accounting acquirer had no previously held equity interest in the accounting acquiree, goodwill is measured as the excess of (a) over (b) below:

(a) the consideration effectively transferred (generally measured at acquisition-date fair value) by the accounting acquirer, i.e. the legal subsidiary;

(b) the net of the acquisition-date fair values (or other amounts recognised in accordance with the requirements of the standard) of the identifiable assets acquired and the liabilities assumed of the accounting acquiree, i.e. the legal parent.

Example 9.31: Reverse acquisition – measuring goodwill (1)

Using the facts in Example 9.30 above, this results in goodwill of €300, measured as follows:

	€	€
Consideration effectively transferred by Entity B		1,600
Net recognised values of Entity A's identifiable assets and liabilities:		
Current assets	500	
Non-current assets	1,500	
Current liabilities	(300)	
Non-current liabilities	(400)	
		1,300
Goodwill		300

Example 9.32: Reverse acquisition – measuring goodwill (2)

If Example 9.31 had been based on the same facts as Example 9.30 except that the quoted market price of Entity A's shares had been €14 per share, and this was considered to be a more reliable measure of the consideration transferred, this would have meant that the fair value of the consideration effectively transferred was €1,400, resulting in goodwill of €100.

14.3 Preparation and presentation of consolidated financial statements

Although the accounting for the reverse acquisition reflects the legal subsidiary as being the accounting acquirer, the consolidated financial statements are issued in the name of the legal parent/acquiree. Consequently they have to be described in the notes as a continuation of the financial statements of the legal subsidiary/acquirer, with one adjustment, which is to adjust retroactively the accounting acquirer's legal capital to reflect the legal capital of the accounting acquiree. Comparative information presented in those consolidated financial statements is therefore that of the legal subsidiary/acquirer, not that originally presented in the previous financial statements of the legal parent/acquiree as adjusted to reflect the legal capital of the legal parent/acquiree. *[IFRS 3.B21]*.

The consolidated financial statements reflect:

(a) the assets and liabilities of the legal subsidiary/acquirer recognised and measured at their pre-combination carrying amounts, i.e. not at their acquisition-date fair values;

(b) the assets and liabilities of the legal parent/acquiree recognised and measured in accordance with IFRS 3, i.e. generally at their acquisition-date fair values;

(c) the retained earnings and other equity balances of the legal subsidiary/acquirer before the business combination, i.e. not those of the legal parent/acquiree;

(d) the amount recognised as issued equity instruments in the consolidated financial statements determined by adding the issued equity of the legal subsidiary/acquirer outstanding immediately before the business combination to the fair value of the legal parent/acquiree. However, the equity structure (i.e. the number and type of equity instruments issued) reflects the equity structure of the legal parent/ acquiree, including the equity instruments issued by the legal parent to effect the combination. Accordingly, the equity structure of the legal subsidiary/acquirer is restated using the exchange ratio established in the acquisition agreement to reflect the number of shares of the legal parent/acquiree issued in the reverse acquisition;

(e) the non-controlling interest's proportionate share of the legal subsidiary's/acquirer's pre-combination carrying amounts of retained earnings and other equity interests (as discussed in 14.4 below); *[IFRS 3.B22]*

(f) the income statement for the current period reflects that of the legal subsidiary/acquirer for the full period together with the post-acquisition results of the legal parent/acquiree based on the attributed fair values.

It is unclear why the application guidance in (d) above refers to using 'the fair value of the legal parent/acquiree', when, as discussed previously at 14.1 above, the guidance for determining 'the fair value of the consideration effectively transferred' uses a different method of arriving at the value of the consideration given. We believe that the amount recognised as issued equity should reflect whichever value has been determined for the consideration effectively transferred.

Continuing with Example 9.30 above, the consolidated statement of financial position immediately after the business combination will be as follows:

Example 9.33: Reverse acquisition – consolidated statement of financial position immediately after the business combination

Using the facts in Example 9.30 above, the consolidated statement of financial position immediately after the date of the business combination is as follows (the intermediate columns for Entity B (legal subsidiary/accounting acquirer) and Entity A (legal parent/accounting acquiree) are included to show the workings):

	Entity B Book values	Entity A Fair values	Consolidated
	€	€	€
Current assets	700	500	1,200
Non-current assets	3,000	1,500	4,500
Goodwill		300	300
Total assets	3,700	2,300	6,000
Current liabilities	600	300	900
Non-current liabilities	1,100	400	1,500
Total liabilities	1,700	700	2,400
Owner's equity			
Issued equity			
250 ordinary shares	600	1,600	2,200
Retained earnings	1,400	–	1,400
Total shareholders' equity	2,000	1,600	3,600

The amount recognised as issued equity interests in the consolidated financial statements (€2,200) is determined by adding the issued equity of the legal subsidiary immediately before the business combination (€600) and the fair value of the consideration effectively transferred (€1,600). However, the equity structure appearing in the consolidated financial statements (i.e. the number and type of equity interests issued) must reflect the equity structure of the legal parent, including the equity interests issued by the legal parent to effect the combination. As noted above, we believe that the amount recognised as issued equity should reflect whichever value has been determined for the consideration effectively transferred.

The application guidance in IFRS 3 only deals with the reverse acquisition accounting in the consolidated financial statements; no mention is made as to what should happen in the separate financial statements, if any, of the legal parent/acquiree. However, the previous version of IFRS 3 indicated that reverse acquisition accounting applies only in the consolidated financial statements, and that in the legal parent's separate financial statements, the investment in the legal subsidiary is accounted for in accordance with the requirements in IAS 27 – *Consolidated and Separate Financial Statements. [IFRS 3.B8 (2007)].*

Example 9.34: Reverse acquisition – legal parent's statement of financial position in separate financial statements

Using the facts in Example 9.30 above, the statement of financial position of Entity A, the legal parent, in its separate financial statements immediately following the business combination will be as follows:

	Entity A
	€
Current assets	500
Non-current assets	1,300
Investment in subsidiary (Entity B)	2,400
Total assets	4,200
Current liabilities	300
Non-current liabilities	400
Total liabilities	700
Owner's equity	
Issued equity	
250 ordinary shares	2,700
Retained earnings	800
	3,500

The investment in the subsidiary is included at its cost of €2,400, being the fair value of the shares issued by Entity A (150 × €16). It can be seen that the issued equity is different from that in the consolidated financial statements and its non-current assets remain at their carrying amounts before the business combination.

14.4 Non-controlling interest

In a reverse acquisition, some of the owners of the legal subsidiary/acquirer might not exchange their equity instruments for equity instruments of the legal parent/acquiree. Those owners are required to be treated as a non-controlling interest in the consolidated financial statements after the reverse acquisition. This is because the owners of the legal subsidiary that do not exchange their equity instruments for equity instruments of the legal parent have an interest only in the results and net assets of the legal subsidiary, and not in the results and net assets of the combined entity. Conversely, even though the legal parent is the acquiree for accounting purposes, the owners of the legal parent have an interest in the results and net assets of the combined entity. *[IFRS 3.B23].*

As indicated at 14.3 above, the assets and liabilities of the legal subsidiary/acquirer are recognised and measured in the consolidated financial statements at their pre-combination carrying amounts. Therefore, in a reverse acquisition the non-controlling interest reflects the non-controlling shareholders' proportionate interest in the pre-combination carrying amounts of the legal subsidiary's net assets even if the non-controlling interests in other acquisitions are measured at fair value at the acquisition date. *[IFRS 3.B24].*

These requirements are illustrated in the following example, which is based on one included within the Illustrative Examples accompanying IFRS 3. *[IFRS 3.IE11-IE15]*.

Example 9.35: Reverse acquisition – non-controlling interest

This example uses the same facts as in Example 9.30 above, except that only 56 of Entity B's 60 ordinary shares are exchanged. Because Entity A issues 2.5 shares in exchange for each ordinary share of Entity B, Entity A issues only 140 (rather than 150) shares. As a result, Entity B's shareholders own 58.3 per cent of the issued shares of the combined entity (i.e. 140 shares out of 240 issued shares).

As in Example 9.30 above, the fair value of the consideration transferred for Entity A, the accounting acquiree) is calculated by assuming that the combination had been effected by Entity B issuing additional ordinary shares to the shareholders of Entity A in exchange for their ordinary shares in Entity A. That is because Entity B is the accounting acquirer, and IFRS 3 requires the acquirer to measure the consideration exchanged for the accounting acquiree (see 14.1 above).

In calculating the number of shares that Entity B would have had to issue, the non-controlling interest is excluded from the calculation. The majority shareholders own 56 shares of Entity B. For that to represent a 58.3 per cent ownership interest, Entity B would have had to issue an additional 40 shares. The majority shareholders would then own 56 out of the 96 issued shares of Entity B and therefore 58.3 per cent of the combined entity.

As a result, the fair value of the consideration transferred for Entity A, the accounting acquiree, is €1,600 (i.e. 40 shares, each with a fair value of €40). That is the same amount as when all 60 of Entity B's shareholders tender all 60 of its ordinary shares for exchange (see Example 9.30 above). The recognised amount of the group's interest in Entity A, the accounting acquiree, does not change if some of Entity B's shareholders do not participate in the exchange.

The non-controlling interest is represented by the 4 shares of the total 60 shares of Entity B that are not exchanged for shares of Entity A. Therefore, the non-controlling interest is 6.7 per cent. The non-controlling interest reflects the proportionate interest of the non-controlling shareholders in the pre-combination carrying amounts of the net assets of Entity B, the legal subsidiary. Therefore, the consolidated statement of financial position is adjusted to show a non-controlling interest of 6.7 per cent of the pre-combination carrying amounts of Entity B's net assets (i.e. €134 or 6.7 per cent of €2,000).

The consolidated statement of financial position at 30 September 2018 (the date of the business combination) reflecting the non-controlling interest is as follows (the intermediate columns for Entity B (legal subsidiary/accounting acquirer), non-controlling interest and Entity A (legal parent/ accounting acquiree) are included to show the workings):

	Entity B Book values	Non-controlling interest	Entity A Fair values	Consolidated
	€	€	€	€
Current assets	700	–	500	1,200
Non-current assets	3,000	–	1,500	4,500
Goodwill	–	–	300	300
Total assets	3,700	–	2,300	6,000
Current liabilities	600	–	300	900
Non-current liabilities	1,100	–	400	1,500
	1,700	–	700	2,400
Owner's equity				
Issued equity				
240 ordinary shares	600	(40)	1,600	2,160
Retained earnings	1,400	(94)	–	1,306
Non-controlling interest	–	134	–	134
	2,000	–	1,600	3,600

The non-controlling interest of €134 has two components. The first component is the reclassification of the non-controlling interest's share of the accounting acquirer's retained earnings immediately before the acquisition (€1,400 × 6.7 per cent or €93.80). The second component represents the reclassification of the non-controlling interest's share of the accounting acquirer's issued equity (€600 × 6.7 per cent or €40.20).

14.5 Earnings per share

The equity structure, i.e. the number and type of equity instruments issued, in the consolidated financial statements following a reverse acquisition reflects the equity structure of the legal parent/acquiree, including the equity instruments issued by the legal parent to effect the business combination. *[IFRS 3.B25].*

Where the legal parent is required by IAS 33 – *Earnings per Share* – to disclose earnings per share information (see Chapter 35), then for the purpose of calculating the weighted average number of ordinary shares outstanding (the denominator of the earnings per share calculation) during the period in which the reverse acquisition occurs:

(a) the number of ordinary shares outstanding from the beginning of that period to the acquisition date is computed on the basis of the weighted average number of ordinary shares of the legal subsidiary/accounting acquirer outstanding during the period multiplied by the exchange ratio established in the acquisition agreement; and

(b) the number of ordinary shares outstanding from the acquisition date to the end of that period is the actual number of ordinary shares of the legal parent/acquiree outstanding during that period. *[IFRS 3.B26].*

The basic earnings per share disclosed for each comparative period before the acquisition date is calculated by dividing:

(a) the profit or loss of the legal subsidiary/acquirer attributable to ordinary shareholders in each of those periods; by

(b) the legal subsidiary's historical weighted average number of ordinary shares outstanding multiplied by the exchange ratio established in the acquisition agreement. *[IFRS 3.B27].*

These requirements are illustrated in the following example, which is based on one included within the Illustrative Examples accompanying IFRS 3. *[IFRS 3.IE9, 10].*

Example 9.36: Reverse acquisition – earnings per share

This example uses the same facts as in Example 9.30 above. Assume that Entity B's earnings for the annual period ended 31 December 2017 were €600, and that the consolidated earnings for the annual period ending 31 December 2018 were €800. Assume also that there was no change in the number of ordinary shares issued by Entity B (legal subsidiary, accounting acquirer) during the annual period ended 31 December 2017 and during the period from 1 January 2018 to the date of the reverse acquisition (30 September 2018), nor by Entity A (legal parent, accounting acquiree) after that date.

Earnings per share for the annual period ended 31 December 2018 is calculated as follows:

Number of shares deemed to be outstanding for the period from 1 January 2018 to the acquisition date (i.e. the number of ordinary shares issued by Entity A (legal parent, accounting acquiree) in the reverse acquisition, or more accurately, the weighted average number of ordinary shares of Entity B (legal subsidiary, accounting acquirer) outstanding during the period multiplied by the exchange ratio established in the acquisition agreement, i.e. 60 × 2.5)	150
Number of shares of Entity A (legal parent, accounting acquiree) outstanding from the acquisition date to 31 December 2018	250
Weighted average number of shares outstanding (150 × 9/12) + (250 × 3/12)	175
Earnings per share (€800 ÷ 175)	€4.57

The restated earnings per share for the annual period ending 31 December 2017 is €4.00 (being €600 ÷ 150, i.e. the earnings of Entity B (legal subsidiary, accounting acquirer) for that period divided by the number of ordinary shares Entity A issued in the reverse acquisition (or more accurately, by the weighted average number of ordinary shares of Entity B (legal subsidiary, accounting acquirer) outstanding during the period multiplied by the exchange ratio established in the acquisition agreement, i.e. 60 × 2.5). Any earnings per share information for that period previously disclosed by either Entity A or Entity B is irrelevant.

14.6 Cash consideration

In some circumstances the combination may be effected whereby some of the consideration given by the legal acquirer (Entity A) to acquire the shares in the legal acquiree (Entity B) is cash.

Normally, the entity transferring cash consideration would be considered to be the acquirer. *[IFRS 3.B14]*. However, despite the form of the consideration, the key determinant in identifying an acquirer is whether it has control over the other (see 4.1 above).

Therefore, if there is evidence demonstrating that the legal acquiree, Entity B, has obtained control over Entity A by being exposed, or having rights, to variable returns from its involvement with Entity A and having the ability to affect those returns through its power over Entity A, Entity B is then the acquirer and the combination should be accounted for as a reverse acquisition.

In that case, how should any cash paid be accounted for?

One approach might be to treat the payment as a pre-acquisition transaction with a resulting reduction in the consideration and in net assets acquired (with no net impact on goodwill). However, we do not believe this is appropriate. Any consideration, whether cash or shares, transferred by Entity A cannot form part of the consideration transferred by the acquirer as Entity A is the accounting acquiree. As discussed at 14.3 above, although the consolidated financial statements following a reverse acquisition are issued under the name of the legal parent (Entity A), they are to be described in the notes as a continuation of the financial statements of the legal subsidiary (Entity B). Therefore, since the consolidated financial statements are a continuation of Entity B's financial statements, in our view the cash consideration paid from Entity A (the accounting acquiree) should be accounted for as a distribution from the consolidated group to the accounting acquirer's (Entity B's) shareholders as at the combination date.

Where a cash payment is made to effect the combination, the requirements of IFRS 3 need to be applied with care as illustrated in the following example.

Example 9.37: Reverse acquisition effected with cash consideration

Entity A has 100,000 ordinary shares in issue, with a market price of £2.00 per share, giving a market capitalisation of £200,000. It acquires all of the shares in Entity B for a consideration of £500,000 satisfied by the issue of 200,000 shares (with a value of £400,000) and a cash payment of £100,000 to Entity B's shareholders. Entity B has 200,000 shares in issue, with an estimated fair value of £2.50 per share. After the combination Entity B's shareholders control the voting of Entity A and, as a result, have been able to appoint Entity B's directors and key executives to replace their Entity A counterparts. Accordingly, Entity B is considered to have obtained control over Entity A. Therefore, Entity B is identified as the accounting acquirer. The combination must be accounted for as a reverse acquisition, i.e. an acquisition of Entity A (legal parent/ accounting acquiree) by Entity B (legal subsidiary/ accounting acquirer).

How should the consideration transferred by the accounting acquirer (Entity B) for its interest in the accounting acquiree (Entity A) be determined?

Applying the requirements of paragraph B20 of IFRS 3 (discussed at 14.1 above) to the transaction might erroneously lead to the following conclusion. Entity A has had to issue 200,000 shares to Entity B's shareholders, resulting in Entity B's shareholders having 66.67% (200,000 ÷ 300,000) of the equity and Entity A's shareholders 33.33% (100,000 ÷ 300,000). If Entity B's share price is used to determine the fair value of the consideration transferred, then under paragraph B20, Entity B would have had to issue 100,000 shares to Entity A's shareholders to result in the same % shareholdings (200,000 ÷ 300,000 = 66.67%). This would apparently give a value of the consideration transferred of 100,000 @ £2.50 = £250,000. This does not seem correct, for the reasons discussed below.

If there had been no cash consideration at all, Entity A would have issued 250,000 shares to Entity B's shareholders, resulting in Entity B's shareholders having 71.43% (250,000 ÷ 350,000) of the equity and Entity A's shareholders 28.57% (100,000 ÷ 350,000). If Entity B's share price is used to determine the value of the consideration transferred, then under paragraph B20, Entity B would have had to issue 80,000 shares to Entity A's shareholders to result in the same % shareholdings (200,000 ÷ 280,000 = 71.43%). This would give a value for the consideration transferred of 80,000 @ £2.50 = £200,000. If it was thought that the fair value of Entity A's shares was more reliably measurable, paragraph 33 of IFRS 3 would require the consideration to be measured using the market price of Entity A's shares. As Entity B has effectively acquired 100% of Entity A, the value of the consideration transferred would be £200,000 (the same as under the revised paragraph B20 calculation above).

In our view, the proper analysis of the paragraph B20 calculation in this case is that of the 100,000 shares that Entity B is deemed to have issued, only 80,000 of them are to acquire Entity A's shares, resulting in consideration transferred of £200,000. The extra 20,000 shares are to compensate Entity A's shareholders for the fact that Entity B's shareholders have received a cash distribution of £100,000, and is effectively a stock distribution to Entity A's shareholders of £50,000 (20,000 @ £2.50), being their share (33.33%) of a total distribution of £150,000. However, since the equity structure (i.e. the number and type of shares) appearing in the consolidated financial statements reflects that of the legal parent, Entity A, this 'stock distribution' will not actually be apparent. The only distribution that will be shown as a movement in equity is the £100,000 cash paid to Entity B's shareholders.

14.7 Share-based payments

In a reverse acquisition, the legal acquirer (Entity A) may have an existing share-based payment plan at the date of acquisition. How does the entity account for awards held by the employees of the accounting acquiree?

Under IFRS 3, accounting for a reverse acquisition takes place from the perspective of the accounting acquirer, not the legal acquirer. Therefore, the accounting for the share-based payment plan of Entity A is based on what would have happened if Entity B rather than Entity A had issued such equity instruments. As indicated at 14.1 above, in a reverse acquisition, the acquisition-date fair value of the consideration transferred by the accounting acquirer for its interest in the accounting acquiree is based on the number of equity interests the legal subsidiary would have had to issue to give the owners of the legal parent the same percentage equity interest in the combined entity that results from the reverse acquisition. The fair value of the number of equity interests calculated in that way can be used as the fair value of consideration transferred in exchange for the acquiree. Therefore, although the legal form of awards made by the accounting acquiree (Entity A) does not change, from an accounting perspective, it is as if these awards have been exchanged for a share-based payment award of the accounting acquirer (Entity B).

As a result, absent any legal modification to the share-based payment awards in Entity A, the acquisition-date fair value of the legal parent/acquiree's (Entity A's) share-based payments awards are included as part of the consideration transferred by the accounting acquirer (Entity B), based on the same principles as those described in paragraphs B56 to B62 of IFRS 3 – see 7.2 above and Chapter 32 at 11.2. *[IFRS 3.B56-B62]*. That is, the portion of the fair value attributed to the vesting period prior to the reverse acquisition is recognised as part of the consideration paid for the business combination and the portion that vests after the reverse acquisition is treated as post-combination expense.

14.8 Reverse acquisitions involving a non-trading shell company

The requirements for reverse acquisitions in IFRS 3, and the guidance provided by the standard, discussed above are based on the premise that the legal parent/acquiree has a business which has been acquired by the legal subsidiary/acquirer. In some situations, this may not be the case, for example where a private entity arranges to have itself 'acquired' by a non-trading public entity as a means of obtaining a stock exchange listing. As indicated at 14 above, the standard notes that the legal parent/acquiree must meet the definition of a business (see 3.2 above) for the transaction to be accounted for as a reverse acquisition, *[IFRS 3.B19]*, but does not say how the transaction should be accounted for where the accounting acquiree is not a business. It clearly cannot be accounted for as an acquisition of the legal acquiree by the legal acquirer under the standard either, if the legal acquirer has not been identified as the accounting acquirer based on the guidance in the standard.

In our view, such a transaction should be accounted for in the consolidated financial statements of the legal parent as a continuation of the financial statements of the private entity (the legal subsidiary), together with a deemed issue of shares, equivalent to the shares held by the former shareholders of the legal parent, and a re-capitalisation of the equity of the private entity. This deemed issue of shares is, in effect, an equity-settled share-based payment transaction whereby the private entity has received the net assets of the legal parent, generally cash, together with the listing status of the legal parent.

Under IFRS 2, for equity-settled share-based payments, an entity measures the goods or services received, and the corresponding increase in equity, directly at the fair value of the goods or services received. If the entity cannot estimate reliably the fair value of the goods and services received, the entity measures the amounts, indirectly, by reference to the fair value of the equity instruments issued. *[IFRS 2.10]*. For transactions with non-employees, IFRS 2 presumes that the fair value of the goods and services received is more readily determinable. *[IFRS 2.13]*. This would suggest that the increase in equity should be based on the fair value of the cash and the fair value of the listing status. As it is unlikely that a fair value of the listing status can be reliably estimated, the increase in equity should be measured by reference to the fair value of the shares that are deemed to have been issued.

Indeed, even if a fair value could be attributed to the listing status, if the total identifiable consideration received is less than the fair value of the equity given as consideration, the transaction should be measured based on the fair value of the shares that are deemed to be issued. *[IFRS 2.13A]*.

This issue was considered by the Interpretations Committee between September 2012 and March 2013. The Interpretations Committee's conclusions, which accord with the analysis given above, are that for a transaction in which the former shareholders of a non-listed operating entity become the majority shareholders of the combined entity by exchanging their shares for new shares of a listed non-trading company, it is appropriate to apply the IFRS 3 guidance for reverse acquisitions by analogy. This results in the non-listed operating entity being identified as the accounting acquirer, and the listed non-trading entity being identified as the accounting acquiree. The accounting acquirer is deemed to have issued shares to obtain control of the acquiree. If the listed non-trading entity is not a business, the transaction is not a business combination, but a share-based payment transaction which should be accounted for in accordance with IFRS 2. Any difference in the fair value of the shares deemed to have been issued by the accounting acquirer and the fair value of the accounting acquiree's identifiable net assets represents a service received by the accounting acquirer. The Interpretations Committee concluded that regardless of the level of monetary or non-monetary assets owned by the non-listed operating entity the entire difference should be considered to be payment for the service of obtaining a stock exchange listing for its shares and no amount should be considered a cost of raising capital.[49]

Example 9.38: Reverse acquisition of a non-trading shell company

Entity A is a non-trading public company with 10,000 ordinary shares in issue. On 31 December 2018, Entity A issues 190,000 ordinary shares in exchange for all of the ordinary share capital of Entity B, a private trading company, with 9,500 ordinary shares in issue.

At the date of the transaction, Entity A has $85,000 of cash and the quoted market price of Entity A's ordinary shares is $12.

The fair value of Entity B has been determined by an independent professional valuer as being $2,185,000, giving a value per share of $230.

Following the transaction, apart from one non-executive director, all of the directors of Entity A resign and four new directors from Entity B are appointed to the Board of Entity A.

As a result of Entity A issuing 190,000 ordinary shares, Entity B's shareholders own 95 per cent of the issued share capital of the combined entity (i.e. 190,000 of the 200,000 issued shares), with the remaining 5 per cent held by Entity A's existing shareholders.

How should this transaction be accounted for in the consolidated financial statements of Entity A?

As the shareholders of Entity A only retain a 5 per cent interest in the combined entity after the transaction, and the Board is dominated by appointees from Entity B, this cannot be accounted for as an acquisition of Entity B by Entity A. Also, as Entity A is a non-trading cash shell company, and therefore not comprising a business (see 3.2 above), it cannot be accounted for as a reverse acquisition of Entity A by Entity B.

The consolidated financial statements should reflect the substance of the transaction which is that Entity B is the continuing entity. Entity B is deemed to have issued shares in exchange for the $85,000 cash held by Entity A together with the listing status of Entity A.

However, the listing status does not qualify for recognition as an intangible asset, and therefore needs to be expensed in profit or loss. As the existing shareholders of Entity A have a 5 per cent interest in the combined entity, Entity B would have had to issue 500 shares for the ratio of ownership interest in the combined entity to be the same. Based on the fair value of an Entity B share of $230, the accounting for the deemed share-based payment transaction is:

	Dr $	Cr $
Cash received	85,000	
Listing expense (income statement)	30,000	
Issued equity (500 × $230)		115,000

As Entity B is a private entity, it may be that a more reliable basis for determining the fair value of the deemed shares issued would have been to use the quoted market price of Entity A's shares at the date of the transaction. On this basis, the issued equity would have been $120,000 (10,000 × $12), giving rise to a listing expense of $35,000.

In summary, the accounting for this transaction is similar in many respects to that which would have been the case if the transaction had been accounted for as a reverse acquisition; the main difference being that no goodwill arises on the transaction, and that any amount that would have been so recognised is accounted for as a listing expense. Indeed, if the transaction had been accounted for as a reverse acquisition, the overall effect may have been the same if an impairment loss on the 'goodwill' had been recognised.

14.9 Reverse acquisitions and acquirers that are not legal entities

In September 2011, the Interpretations Committee considered whether a business that is not a legal entity could be the acquirer in a reverse acquisition. The Interpretations Committee concluded that an acquirer that is a reporting entity, but not a legal entity, can be considered to be the acquirer in a reverse acquisition. The Interpretations Committee observed that IFRSs and the current Conceptual Framework do not require a 'reporting entity' to be a legal entity. Therefore, as long as the business that is not a legal entity obtains control of the acquiree and, in accordance with Appendix A of IFRS 3, the acquiree is 'the business or businesses that the acquirer obtains control of in a business combination' then '...the entity whose equity interests are acquired (the legal acquiree) must be the acquirer for accounting purposes for the transaction to be considered a reverse acquisition.' *[IFRS 3.7, Appendix A, B19].* As this issue is not widespread, the Interpretations Committee did not add this issue to its agenda.[50]

15 PUSH DOWN ACCOUNTING

The term 'push down accounting' relates to the practice adopted in some jurisdictions of incorporating, or 'pushing down', the fair value adjustments which have been made by the acquirer into the financial statements of the acquiree, including the goodwill arising on the acquisition. It is argued that the acquisition, being an independently bargained transaction, provides better evidence of the values of the assets and liabilities of the acquiree than those previously contained within its financial statements, and therefore represents an improved basis of accounting. There are, however, contrary views, which hold that the transaction in question was one to which the reporting entity was not a party, and there is no reason why an adjustment should be made to the entity's own accounting records.

Whatever the theoretical arguments, it is certainly true that push down accounting could be an expedient practice, because it obviates the need to make extensive consolidation adjustments in each subsequent year, based on parallel accounting records. Nevertheless, if the acquiree is preparing its financial statements under IFRS, in our view it cannot apply push down accounting and reflect the fair value adjustments made by the acquirer and the goodwill that arose on its acquisition.

All of the requirements of IFRS must be applied when an entity prepares its financial statements. IFRS requires assets and liabilities to be recognised initially at cost or fair value, depending on the nature of the assets and liabilities. The acquisition of an entity by another party is not a transaction undertaken by that entity itself; hence it cannot be a transaction to determine cost.

Application of push down accounting would result in the recognition and measurement of assets and liabilities that are prohibited by some standards (such as internally generated intangibles and goodwill) and the recognition and measurement of assets and liabilities at amounts that are not permitted under IFRS. While some IFRS standards include an option or requirement to revalue particular assets, this is undertaken as part of a process of determining accounting policies rather than as one-off revaluations. For example:

- IAS 2 – *Inventories* – requires that inventories are measured at the lower of cost and net realisable value (see Chapter 22 at 3);
- IAS 16 requires that items of property, plant and equipment are initially measured at cost. Subsequently, property, plant and equipment can be measured at cost or at revalued amount. However, revaluations must be applied consistently and must be performed on a regular basis. Therefore a one-off revaluation is not permitted (see Chapter 18 at 6);
- IAS 38 requires that intangible assets are initially measured at cost. Subsequently, they can be revalued only in rare circumstances where there is an active market. In addition, IAS 38 specifically prohibits the recognition of internally generated goodwill. Therefore a one-off revaluation is not permitted (see Chapter 17 at 8.2).

16 DISCLOSURES

The disclosure requirements of IFRS 3 are set out below. Note that, although IFRS 13 provides guidance on how to measure fair value, IFRS 13 disclosures are not required for items that are recognised at fair value only at initial recognition. *[IFRS 13.91(a)].* For example, the information about the fair value measurement of non-controlling interest in an acquiree if measured at fair value at the acquisition date is disclosed in accordance with the requirements of IFRS 3. *[IFRS 3.B64(o)(i)].*

16.1 Nature and financial effect of business combinations

The first disclosure objective is that the acquirer discloses information that enables users of its financial statements to evaluate the nature and financial effect of a business combination that occurs either:

(a) during the current reporting period; or

(b) after the end of the reporting period but before the financial statements are authorised for issue. *[IFRS 3.59].*

Information that is required to be disclosed by the acquirer to meet the above objective is specified in the application guidance of the standard. *[IFRS 3.60].*

16.1.1 *Business combinations during the current reporting period*

To meet the above objective, the acquirer is required to disclose the following information for each business combination that occurs during the reporting period: *[IFRS 3.B64]*

(a) the name and a description of the acquiree;
(b) the acquisition date;
(c) the percentage of voting equity interests acquired;
(d) the primary reasons for the business combination and a description of how the acquirer obtained control of the acquiree;
(e) a qualitative description of the factors that make up the goodwill recognised, such as expected synergies from combining operations of the acquiree and the acquirer, intangible assets that do not qualify for separate recognition or other factors;
(f) the acquisition-date fair value of the total consideration transferred and the acquisition-date fair value of each major class of consideration, such as:
    (i) cash;
    (ii) other tangible or intangible assets, including a business or subsidiary of the acquirer;
    (iii) liabilities incurred, for example, a liability for contingent consideration; and
    (iv) equity interests of the acquirer, including the number of instruments or interests issued or issuable and the method of measuring the fair value of those instruments or interests;
(g) for contingent consideration arrangements and indemnification assets:
    (i) the amount recognised as of the acquisition date;
    (ii) a description of the arrangement and the basis for determining the amount of the payment; and
    (iii) an estimate of the range of outcomes (undiscounted) or, if a range cannot be estimated, that fact and the reasons why a range cannot be estimated. If the maximum amount of the payment is unlimited, the acquirer discloses that fact;
(h) for acquired receivables:
    (i) the fair value of the receivables;
    (ii) the gross contractual amounts receivable; and
    (iii) the best estimate at the acquisition date of the contractual cash flows not expected to be collected;

    The disclosures are to be provided by major class of receivable, such as loans, direct finance leases and any other class of receivables;
(i) the amounts recognised as of the acquisition date for each major class of assets acquired and liabilities assumed;
(j) for each contingent liability recognised in accordance with paragraph 23 of the standard (see 5.6.1 above), the information required in paragraph 85 of IAS 37 (see Chapter 28 at 7.1). If a contingent liability is not recognised because its fair value cannot be measured reliably, the acquirer discloses:
    (i) the information required by paragraph 86 of IAS 37 (see Chapter 28 at 7.2); and
    (ii) the reasons why the liability cannot be measured reliably;

(k) the total amount of goodwill that is expected to be deductible for tax purposes;

(l) for transactions that are recognised separately from the acquisition of assets and assumption of liabilities in the business combination in accordance with paragraph 51 of the standard (see 11 above):

  (i) a description of each transaction;

  (ii) how the acquirer accounted for each transaction;

  (iii) the amounts recognised for each transaction and the line item in the financial statements in which each amount is recognised; and

  (iv) if the transaction is the effective settlement of a pre-existing relationship, the method used to determine the settlement amount;

(m) the disclosure of separately recognised transactions required by (l) above includes the amount of acquisition-related costs and, separately, the amount of those costs recognised as an expense and the line item or items in the statement of comprehensive income in which those expenses are recognised. The amount of any issue costs not recognised as an expense and how they were recognised are also to be disclosed;

(n) in a bargain purchase (see 10 above):

  (i) the amount of any gain recognised and the line item in the statement of comprehensive income in which the gain is recognised; and

  (ii) a description of the reasons why the transaction resulted in a gain;

(o) for each business combination in which the acquirer holds less than 100 per cent of the equity interests in the acquiree at the acquisition date (i.e. there is a non-controlling interest – see 8 above):

  (i) the amount of the non-controlling interest in the acquiree recognised at the acquisition date and the measurement basis for that amount; and

  (ii) for each non-controlling interest in an acquiree measured at fair value, the valuation techniques and significant inputs used to measure that value;

(p) in a business combination achieved in stages (see 9 above):

  (i) the acquisition-date fair value of the equity interest in the acquiree held by the acquirer immediately before the acquisition date; and

  (ii) the amount of any gain or loss recognised as a result of remeasuring to fair value the equity interest in the acquiree held by the acquirer before the business combination and the line item in the statement of comprehensive income in which that gain or loss is recognised;

(q) the following information:

  (i) the amounts of revenue and profit or loss of the acquiree since the acquisition date included in the consolidated statement of comprehensive income for the reporting period; and

  (ii) the revenue and profit or loss of the combined entity for the current reporting period as though the acquisition date for all business combinations that occurred during the year had been as of the beginning of the annual reporting period.

If disclosure of any of the information required by this subparagraph is impracticable, the acquirer shall disclose that fact and explain why the disclosure is impracticable. IFRS 3 uses the term 'impracticable' with the same meaning as in IAS 8 (see Chapter 3 at 4.7).

Although it is not explicitly stated in paragraph B64 of the standard, it is evident that the above information is required to be given for each material business combination. This is due to the fact that the standard states that for individually immaterial business combinations occurring during the reporting period that are material collectively, the acquirer has to disclose, in aggregate, the information required by items (e) to (q) above. *[IFRS 3.B65]*.

16.1.2 Business combinations effected after the end of the reporting period

If the acquisition date of a business combination is after the end of the reporting period but before the financial statements are authorised for issue, the acquirer is required to disclose the information set out in 16.1.1 above for that business combination, unless the initial accounting for the business combination is incomplete at the time the financial statements are authorised for issue. In that situation, the acquirer describes which disclosures could not be made and the reasons why they cannot be made. *[IFRS 3.B66]*.

16.2 Financial effects of adjustments recognised in the current reporting period

The second objective is that the acquirer discloses information that enables users of its financial statements to evaluate the financial effects of adjustments recognised in the current reporting period that relate to business combinations that occurred in the period or previous reporting periods. *[IFRS 3.61]*.

Information that is required to be disclosed by the acquirer to meet the above objective is specified in the application guidance of the standard. *[IFRS 3.62]*.

To meet the above objective, the acquirer is required to disclose the following information for each material business combination or in the aggregate for individually immaterial business combinations that are material collectively: *[IFRS 3.B67]*

(a) if the initial accounting for a business combination is incomplete (see 12 above) for particular assets, liabilities, non-controlling interests or items of consideration and the amounts recognised in the financial statements for the business combination thus have been determined only provisionally:

  (i) the reasons why the initial accounting for the business combination is incomplete;

  (ii) the assets, liabilities, equity interests or items of consideration for which the initial accounting is incomplete; and

  (iii) the nature and amount of any measurement period adjustments recognised during the reporting period in accordance with paragraph 49 of the standard (see 12.1 above);

(b) for each reporting period after the acquisition date until the entity collects, sells or otherwise loses the right to a contingent consideration asset, or until the entity settles a contingent consideration liability or the liability is cancelled or expires (see 7.1 above):

   (i) any changes in the recognised amounts, including any differences arising upon settlement;
   (ii) any changes in the range of outcomes (undiscounted) and the reasons for those changes; and
   (iii) the valuation techniques and key model inputs used to measure contingent consideration;

(c) for contingent liabilities recognised in a business combination, the acquirer shall disclose the information required by paragraphs 84 and 85 of IAS 37 for each class of provision (see Chapter 28 at 7.1);

(d) a reconciliation of the carrying amount of goodwill at the beginning and end of the reporting period showing separately:
   (i) the gross amount and accumulated impairment losses at the beginning of the reporting period;
   (ii) additional goodwill recognised during the reporting period, except goodwill included in a disposal group that, on acquisition, meets the criteria to be classified as held for sale in accordance with IFRS 5 (see Chapter 4 at 2.1);
   (iii) adjustments resulting from the subsequent recognition of deferred tax assets during the reporting period in accordance with paragraph 67 of the standard (there should in fact be no such adjustment to disclose as any adjustment is recognised in profit or loss (see 5.6.2 above));
   (iv) goodwill included in a disposal group classified as held for sale in accordance with IFRS 5 and goodwill derecognised during the reporting period without having previously been included in a disposal group classified as held for sale;
   (v) impairment losses recognised during the reporting period in accordance with IAS 36. (IAS 36 requires disclosure of information about the recoverable amount and impairment of goodwill in addition to this requirement (see Chapter 20 at 13.2));
   (vi) net exchange rate differences arising during the reporting period in accordance with IAS 21 – *The Effects of Changes in Foreign Exchange Rates* (see Chapter 15 at 6.5);
   (vii) any other changes in the carrying amount during the reporting period; and
   (viii) the gross amount and accumulated impairment losses at the end of the reporting period;

(e) the amount and an explanation of any gain or loss recognised in the current reporting period that both:
   (i) relates to the identifiable assets acquired or liabilities assumed in a business combination that was effected in the current or previous reporting period; and
   (ii) is of such a size, nature or incidence that disclosure is relevant to understanding the combined entity's financial statements.

16.3 Other necessary information

IFRS 3 includes a catch-all disclosure requirement, that if in any situation the information required to be disclosed set out above, or by other IFRSs, does not satisfy the objectives of IFRS 3, the acquirer discloses whatever additional information is necessary to meet those objectives. *[IFRS 3.63].*

In addition, IAS 7 – *Statement of Cash Flows* – requires disclosures in respect of obtaining control of subsidiaries and other businesses (see Chapter 38 at 6). *[IAS 7.39-42].*

16.4 Illustrative disclosures

An illustration of some of the disclosure requirements of IFRS 3 is given by way of an example in the Illustrative Examples accompanying the standard. The example, which is reproduced below, assumes that the acquirer, AC, is a listed entity and that the acquiree, TC, is an unlisted entity. The illustration presents the disclosures in a tabular format that refers to the specific disclosure requirements illustrated. (The references to paragraph B64 correspond to the equivalent item at 16.1.1 above and those to paragraph B67 correspond to the equivalent item at 16.2 above.) It is also emphasised that an actual footnote might present many of the disclosures illustrated in a simple narrative format. *[IFRS 3.IE72].*

Example 9.39: Footnote X: Acquisitions

Paragraph reference		
B64(a-d)	On 30 June 20X0 AC acquired 15 per cent of the outstanding ordinary shares of TC. On 30 June 20X2 AC acquired 60 per cent of the outstanding ordinary shares of TC and obtained control of TC. TC is a provider of data networking products and services in Canada and Mexico. As a result of the acquisition, AC is expected to be the leading provider of data networking products and services in those markets. It also expects to reduce costs through economies of scale.	
B64(e)	The goodwill of CU2,500 arising from the acquisition consists largely of the synergies and economies of scale expected from combining the operations of AC and TC.	
B64(k)	None of the goodwill recognised is expected to be deductible for income tax purposes. The following table summarises the consideration paid for TC and the amounts of the assets acquired and liabilities assumed recognised at the acquisition date, as well as the fair value at the acquisition date of the non-controlling interest in TC.	
	At 30 June 20X2	
	Consideration	CU
B64(f)(i)	Cash	5,000
B64(f)(iv)	Equity instruments (100,000 ordinary shares of AC)	4,000
B64(f)(iii); B64(g)(i)	Contingent consideration arrangement	1,000
B64(f)	**Total consideration transferred**	10,000
B64(p)(i)	**Fair value of AC's equity interest in TC held before the business combination**	2,000
		12,000

Paragraph reference		
B64(m)	**Acquisition-related costs** (included in selling, general and administrative expenses in AC's statement of comprehensive income for the year ended 31 December 20X2)	1,250
B64(i)	**Recognised amounts of identifiable assets acquired and liabilities assumed**	
	Financial assets	3,500
	Inventory	1,000
	Property, plant and equipment	10,000
	Identifiable intangible assets	3,300
	Financial liabilities	–4,000
	Contingent liability	–1,000
	Total identifiable net assets	12,800
B64(o)(i)	Non-controlling interest in TC	–3,300
	Goodwill	2,500
		12,000

B64(f)(iv) The fair value of the 100,000 ordinary shares issued as part of the consideration paid for TC (CU4,000) was measured using the closing market price of AC's ordinary shares on the acquisition date.

B64(f)(iii)
B64(g)
B67(b) The contingent consideration arrangement requires AC to pay the former owners of TC 5 per cent of the revenues of XC, an unconsolidated equity investment owned by TC, in excess of CU7,500 for 20X3, up to a maximum amount of CU2,500 (undiscounted).

The potential undiscounted amount of all future payments that AC could be required to make under the contingent consideration arrangement is between CU0 and CU2,500.

The fair value of the contingent consideration arrangement of CU1,000 was estimated by applying the income approach. The fair value measurement is based on significant inputs that are not observable in the market, which IFRS 13 – *Fair Value Measurement* – refers to as Level 3 inputs. Key assumptions include a discount rate range of 20-25 per cent and assumed probability-adjusted revenues in XC of CU10,000-20,000.

As of 31 December 20X2, neither the amount recognised for the contingent consideration arrangement, nor the range of outcomes or the assumptions used to develop the estimates had changed.

B64(h) The fair value of the financial assets acquired includes receivables under finance leases of data networking equipment with a fair value of CU2,375. The gross amount due under the contracts is CU3,100, of which CU450 is expected to be uncollectible.

B67(a) The fair value of the acquired identifiable intangible assets of CU3,300 is provisional pending receipt of the final valuations for those assets.

B64(j)
B67(c)
IAS 37.84, 85 A contingent liability of CU1,000 has been recognised for expected warranty claims on products sold by TC during the last three years. We expect that the majority of this expenditure will be incurred in 20X3 and that all will be incurred by the end of 20X4. The potential undiscounted amount of all future payments that AC could be required to make under the warranty arrangements is estimated to be between CU500 and CU1,500. As of 31 December 20X2, there has been no change since 30 June 20X2 in the amount recognised for the liability or any change in the range of outcomes or assumptions used to develop the estimates.

Paragraph reference	
B64(o)	The fair value of the non-controlling interest in TC, an unlisted company, was estimated by applying a market approach and an income approach. The fair value measurements are based on significant inputs that are not observable in the market and thus represent a fair value measurement categorised within Level 3 of the fair value hierarchy as described in IFRS 13. Key assumptions include the following: (a) a discount rate range of 20-25 per cent; (b) a terminal value based on a range of terminal EBITDA multiples between 3 and 5 times (or, if appropriate, based on long term sustainable growth rates ranging from 3 to 6 per cent); (c) financial multiples of companies deemed to be similar to TC; and (d) adjustments because of the lack of control or lack of marketability that market participants would consider when measuring the fair value of the non-controlling interest in TC.
B64(p)(ii)	AC recognised a gain of CU500 as a result of measuring at fair value its 15 per cent equity interest in TC held before the business combination. The gain is included in other income in AC's statement of comprehensive income for the year ending 31 December 20X2.
B64(q)(i)	The revenue included in the consolidated statement of comprehensive income since 30 June 20X2 contributed by TC was CU4,090. TC also contributed profit of CU1,710 over the same period.
B64(q)(ii)	Had TC been consolidated from 1 January 20X2 the consolidated statement of comprehensive income would have included revenue of CU27,670 and profit of CU12,870.

References

1 Request for Information *Post-implementation Review: IFRS 3 Business Combinations,* Request for Information, pp.10-19.
2 Report and Feedback Statement *Post-implementation Review of IFRS 3 Business Combinations,* pp.5-6.
3 Report and Feedback Statement *Post-implementation Review of IFRS 3 Business Combinations,* pp.7-10.
4 Exposure Draft ED/2016/1 – *Definition of a Business and Accounting for Previously Held Interests (Proposed amendments to IFRS 3 and IFRS 11),* IASB, June 2016.
5 *IASB Work Plan as at 4 July 2017.*
6 *IASB Update,* July 2016.
7 ED/2016/1, p.4.
8 ED/2016/1, pp.8-9.
9 *IFRIC Update,* June 2017.
10 The Proposed Accounting Standards Update *Clarifying the Definition of a Business,* FASB, November 2015.
11 *IASB Work Plan as at 4 July 2017.*
12 ED/2016/1, pp.10-11.
13 *IASB Update,* April 2017.
14 ED/2016/1, pp.9-10.
15 *IASB Update,* June 2017.
16 ED/2016/1, pp.11-12.
17 *IASB Update,* June 2017.
18 ED/2016/1, p.9.
19 ED/2016/1, p.16.
20 ED/2016/1, p.9.
21 ED/2016/1, p.17.
22 *IASB Update,* June 2017.
23 ED/2016/1, pp.12-13.
24 ED/2016/1, pp.11-12, 20.
25 ED/2016/1, pp.21-27.

26 ED/2016/1, pp.8-9.
27 *IFRIC Update*, September 2011.
28 *IASB Work Plan as at 4July 2017.*
29 *IFRIC Update*, May 2014.
30 IFRS 17 *Insurance contracts*, Appendix D *Amendments to other IFRS Standards,* IFRS 3 *Business Combinations,* May 2017.
31 *IFRIC Update*, September 2008.
32 *IFRIC Update*, March 2009.
33 *IFRIC Update*, March 2009.
34 *IASB Work Plan as at 4 July 2017.*
35 IFRS 17 *Insurance contracts*, Appendix D *Amendments to other IFRS Standards,* IFRS 3 *Business Combinations,* May 2017.
36 *IFRIC Update,* January 2011.
37 Staff Paper, IASB meeting, June 2009, Agenda reference 13C, *Annual Improvements Process, Contingent consideration of an Acquiree ("pre-existing contingent consideration"),* p.3.
38 *IASB Update,* May 2013.
39 *Put options written on non-controlling interests (Proposed amendments to IAS 32),* Project news, IASB Website, 23 June 2014.
40 *IASB Work plan as at 4 July 2017.*
41 ED/2016/1, p.14.
42 ED/2016/1, p.8.
43 ED/2016/1, p.14.
44 ED/2016/1, pp.8-9.
45 *IASB Update*, April 2017.
46 I*ASB Work plan as at 4 July 2017.*
47 *IFRIC Update*, November 2010.
48 *IASB Update*, July 2016.
49 *IFRIC Update,* March 2013.
50 *IFRIC Update*, September 2011.

Chapter 10 Common control business combinations

List of examples

Chapter 10 Common control business combinations

1 INTRODUCTION

1.1 Background

Transactions between entities under common control occur frequently in business. For example many entities transact their business activities through subsidiaries which often results in transactions between the entities comprising the group.

Transactions between entities under common control can include the sale of goods, property and other assets, the provision of services (including those of employees), leasing and transfers under licence agreements and financing transactions, including provisions of guarantees.

It cannot always be assumed that transactions between entities under common control are undertaken on an arm's length basis or that equal values have been exchanged. Standard setters, including the IASB, have developed standards that require disclosures about related party transactions, rather than requiring the transactions to be measured at fair value on an arm's length basis. Entities that have entered into such transactions need to account for them in their financial statements in accordance with any relevant IFRS applicable to that transaction. Generally there are no exemptions within the standards for transactions between entities under common control. IFRSs do not provide a complete framework for such transactions; there is often more than one acceptable way of accounting for many arrangements and hence a choice of accounting policies. General guidance in accounting for transactions between a parent and its subsidiaries, or between subsidiaries within a group, is included in Chapter 8 at 4.

However, there is an exemption for a business combination that is a combination of entities or businesses under common control. *[IFRS 3.2]*. This chapter discusses the implications of this exemption in IFRS 3 – *Business Combinations* – and the accounting treatments which may be adopted for such transactions.

1.2 Development of the IFRS 3 exemption for business combinations involving entities or businesses under common control

The exemption provided in IFRS 3 for business combinations under common control has been a long-standing exemption under IFRS, having initially been included in IAS 22 – *Business Combinations*. In March 2004, the IASB issued IFRS 3. That version of IFRS 3 retained a scope exclusion, but the Board concluded that it would be better expressed as 'business combinations involving entities or businesses under common control' rather than 'transactions among enterprises under common control' (the exclusion in IAS 22). In addition, authoritative guidance on the application of the exemption was included in the new standard. *[IFRS 3(2007).BC24-26]*.

A revised version of IFRS 3 was issued in January 2008. However, there was no change to the position regarding common control business combinations because the revised version of IFRS 3 essentially retains the scope exclusion and application guidance that was in the previous version of the standard, albeit with some minor changes to the wording. The scope exclusion is now expressed as 'a combination of entities or businesses under common control', *[IFRS 3.2]*, and the application guidance amended accordingly. *[IFRS 3.B1-B4]*.

1.3 Possible future developments: IASB project on business combinations under common control

Historically, the IASB noted that the absence of specific requirements for business combinations under common control has led to diversity in practice. Following views received in response to the Request for Views *Agenda Consultation 2011*, the IASB identified 'business combinations under common control' as one of its priority research projects and commenced the work. The Board's 2015 Agenda Consultation confirmed the importance and urgency of providing guidance on business combinations under common control. Accordingly, as discussed in the November 2016 Feedback Statement on the 2015 Agenda Consultation, the Board decided to retain business combinations under common control as one of the eight projects on the research programme. It was noted that the topic is highly ranked by comment-letter respondents from a wide range of countries, in emerging market outreach and is important to regulators and to members of the Advisory Council.[1]

In March 2017, the Global Preparers Forum discussed the staff's preliminary views on reporting business combinations under common control. The following broad approaches were presented by the staff as having merit if the Board were to decide to proceed with a Discussion Paper:

- Approach 1 – apply the predecessor method to all business combinations under common control and group restructurings; and
- Approach 2 – apply the predecessor method as the default method to business combinations under common control and group restructurings except for transactions that exhibit particular characteristics (for example, those that exhibit characteristics of an arm's-length transaction); apply the acquisition method set out in IFRS 3 to transactions that exhibit those characteristics.

The main advantages of Approach 1 above are its simplicity and that it would provide consistent information about business combinations under common control and group restructurings whereas Approach 2 above could arguably provide information that is most useful for a particular type of transaction and achieve better comparability for transactions with similar economic characteristics (i.e. business combinations that are not under common control would be accounted for in the same way as those transactions).

However, the staff did not think that it was possible to define in a meaningful way a subset of business combinations under common control to which the acquisition method should be applied as such a distinction would be either arbitrary and not achieve better comparability between similar transactions compared to Approach 1, or would be imprecise, requiring the exercise of judgement in practice and potentially resulting in inconsistent application.

The staff did not think that applying the acquisition method set out in IFRS 3 to all business combinations under common control and group restructurings, or applying that method as the default method except for when specified conditions are met, would result in the most useful information. This was because business combinations under common control and group restructurings could exhibit economic characteristics that are very different compared to business combinations that are not under common control. Specifically, they could be undertaken for different reasons and on different terms compared to arm's length transactions between third parties. In those cases, the staff did not think that measuring consideration and transferred net assets at fair value and recognising goodwill or gain would faithfully represent those transactions. Although the fair value information about such transactions could be useful such information could be provided via disclosure.

In relation to the predecessor method the staff thought that an entity's financial statements should reflect the perspective of that entity and accordingly, the combining entities should be treated as combined from the date on which the business combination under common control took place and that comparative information should not be restated. The staff also thought that the carrying amounts used in applying the predecessor method should be those reported by the transferred entity as they did not think that the carrying amounts recognised by the controlling party, including any goodwill that might have arisen on past acquisition of the transferred entity by that controlling party, are relevant from the perspective of the combining entities.

The staff also thought that, within the context of applying the predecessor method, the Board should not prescribe where in equity to recognise any difference between consideration in business combinations under common control and transferred net assets; and how to measure consideration in the form of shares.[2]

Only a few Global Preparers Forum members provided questions or comments on the above preliminary views presented by the staff. Some supported them, in particular to apply the predecessor method to all business combinations under common control and group restructurings. Others suggested that:

(a) it is possible to distinguish business combinations under common control with different economic characteristics; however, no specific suggestions were made;

(b) the Board should clarify the description of business combinations under common control, in particular the description of common control; and

(c) if the predecessor method is used to account for business combinations under common control, a requirement to disclose fair value information would create an extra burden on preparers.[3]

The Discussion Paper is expected in the first half of 2018.[4]

1.4 Scope of this chapter

This chapter deals with two items from the IASB's initial project on common control transactions:

- the exemption in IFRS 3 for business combinations under common control (see 2 below); and
- the accounting for such business combinations in the acquirer's consolidated financial statements (see 3 below).

Although the discussion at 3 below (particularly the Examples contained therein) generally refers to business combinations involving 'entities' and 'consolidated financial statements', the accounting is equally applicable to individual financial statements of an entity that combines with the business of another entity under common control. We believe that the accounting in individual financial statements should be covered by the IASB as it arises from the same IFRS 3 exemption. The IASB has not yet considered which entities' financial statements will be covered by the scope of the research project (e.g. the acquirer's, the acquiree's, the transferor's, the ultimate parent's) as well as which financial statements the project should address (e.g. consolidated, separate, individual) until the research work on the types of transactions within the scope of the project progresses.[5]

This chapter, however, does not deal with the accounting in the acquirer's separate financial statements, which is covered in Chapter 8.

This chapter also does not deal with demergers, such as the spin-off of a subsidiary or business. Demergers are discussed in Chapter 7 at 3.4 and in Chapter 8 at 2.4.2.

Business combinations under common control invariably arise as a result of a group reorganisation. Such reorganisations can take many forms. For some of the entities involved in the reorganisation, there may well be a business combination that needs to be accounted for (see 4 below). Obviously, the transferors in the reorganisation will need to account for their part of the transaction in their own financial statements. In doing so, they will need to consider the requirements of other relevant IFRSs, in particular, the requirements of IFRS 10 – *Consolidated Financial Statements* – relating to disposals of, or loss of control over subsidiaries (see Chapter 7 at 3.2) and the requirements of IFRS 5 – *Non-current Assets Held for Sale and Discontinued Operations* – relating to disposal groups held for sale and discontinued operations (see Chapter 4). The discussion in Chapter 7 at 3.4 and in Chapter 8 at 2.4.2 relating to demergers may also be relevant. Chapter 8 will also be relevant to the accounting in the separate/individual financial statements of the entities involved in the reorganisation.

In addition, any transaction between entities under common control is a related party transaction under IAS 24 – *Related Party Disclosures*, the requirements of which are dealt with in Chapter 37.

2 THE IFRS 3 EXEMPTION

IFRS 3 excludes from its requirements 'a combination of entities or businesses under common control'. *[IFRS 3.2]*.

If the transaction is not a business combination because the entity or assets being acquired do not meet the definition of a business, it is accounted for as an acquisition of assets. The accounting for such common control transactions is discussed in Chapter 8 at 4.4.2.D.

2.1 Common control exemption

For the purpose of the exemption, a business combination involving entities or businesses under common control is 'a business combination in which all of the combining entities or businesses are ultimately controlled by the same party or parties both before and after the business combination, and that control is not transitory'. *[IFRS 3.B1]*. This will include transactions such as the transfer of subsidiaries or businesses between entities within a group.

The extent of non-controlling interests in each of the combining entities before and after the business combination is not relevant to determining whether the combination involves entities under common control. *[IFRS 3.B4]*. This is because a partially-owned subsidiary is nevertheless under the control of the parent entity. Therefore transactions involving partially-owned subsidiaries are also outside the scope of the standard. Similarly, the fact that one of the combining entities is a subsidiary that has been excluded from the consolidated financial statements of the group in accordance with IFRS 10 is not relevant to determining whether a combination involves entities under common control. *[IFRS 3.B4]*.

2.1.1 Common control by an individual or group of individuals

The exclusion is not restricted to transactions between entities within a group. An entity can be controlled by an individual or a group of individuals acting together under a contractual arrangement and they may not be subject to the financial reporting requirements of IFRSs. It is not necessary for combining entities to be included as part of the same consolidated financial statements for a business combination to be regarded as one involving entities under common control. *[IFRS 3.B3]*. Thus if a transaction involves entities controlled by the same individual, including one that results in a new parent entity the acquisition method would not always be applied.

A group of individuals controls an entity if, through contractual arrangements, they collectively have the power to govern its financial and operating policies so as to obtain benefits from its activities. Therefore, a business combination is outside the scope of IFRS 3 if the same group of individuals has ultimate collective power to control each of the combining entities and that ultimate collective power is not transitory. *[IFRS 3.B2]*.

For the exemption to apply to a group of individuals there has to be a 'contractual arrangement' between them such that they have control over the entities involved in the transaction. IFRS 3 also does not indicate what form such an arrangement should take. However, IFRS 11 – *Joint Arrangements* – in its application guidance explains that, in determining what is a 'joint arrangement', 'contractual arrangements can be evidenced in several ways', and a 'contractual arrangement is often, but not always, in writing, usually in the form of a contract or documented discussions between the parties'. *[IFRS 11.B2].* This also implies that it is possible for a contractual arrangement to be in non-written form. If it is not written, great care needs to be taken with all of the facts and circumstances to determine whether it is appropriate to apply the exemption.

One particular situation where this is likely to be the case is where the individuals involved are members of the same family, since there is unlikely to be any written contractual agreement. In such situations, whether common control exists between family members very much depends on the specific facts and circumstances. A starting point can be the definition in IAS 24 of close members of the family of a person as 'those family members who may be expected to influence, or be influenced by, that person in their dealings with the entity and include:

(a) that person's children and spouse or domestic partner;

(b) children of that person's spouse or domestic partner; and

(c) dependants of that person or that person's spouse or domestic partner.' *[IAS 24.9].*

If the individuals concerned are 'close members of the family' as defined in IAS 24, then it is possible that they will act collectively, and the exemption can be applied (see Chapter 37 at 2). This may be the case where one family member may effectively control the voting of a dependent family member, for example, scenario (a) in Example 10.1 below. It is also possible that a highly influential parent may be able to ensure that adult family members act collectively, for example, scenario (b) in Example 10.1 below. In this case there would need to be clear evidence that the family influence has resulted in a pattern of collective family decisions. However, common control is unlikely to exist where the family members concerned are adult siblings, for example, scenario (c) in Example 10.1 below, as such individuals are more likely to act independently. We believe that there should be a presumption that common control does not exist between non-close family members and sufficient evidence that they act collectively, rather than independently, would need to exist to overcome this conclusion.

In all such situations involving family members, whenever there is sufficient evidence that the family members (irrespective of the family relationship) have acted independently then the common control exemption does not apply.

Example 10.1: Common control involving individuals

Entity A has 3 shareholders Mr X, Mr Y, and Mr Z. Mr X and Mr Y are family members who each hold a 30% interest in Entity A. Mr X and Mr Y also each hold a 30% interest in Entity B. There is no written contractual arrangement between Mr X and Mr Y requiring them to act collectively as shareholders in Entity A and Entity B.

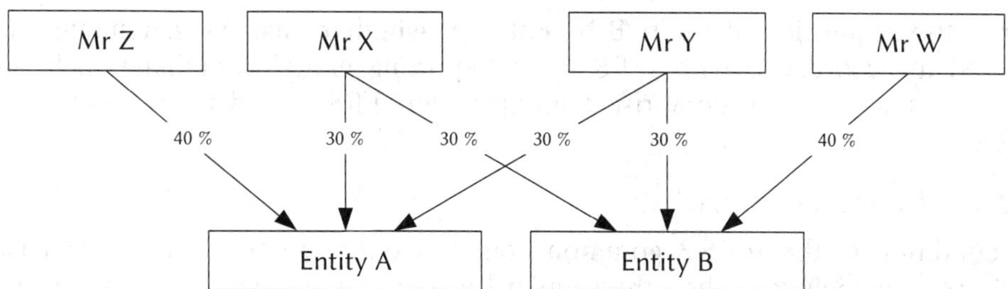

If Entity A acquires 100% of Entity B, is this a business combination involving entities under common control and therefore outside the scope of IFRS 3 when the nature of the family relationship is:

(a) Mr X is the father and Mr Y is his young dependent son; or

(b) Mr X is a patriarchal father and – because of his highly influential standing – his adult son Mr Y has traditionally followed his father's decisions; or

(c) Mr X and Mr Y are adult siblings?

Whether common control exists between family members very much depends on the facts and circumstances, as often there will not be any written agreement between family members. However, the influence that normally arises within relationships between 'close members of the family' as defined in IAS 24 means that it is possible that they will act collectively, such that there is common control. If so, the business combination would be outside the scope of IFRS 3.

Scenario (a)

The business combination may be outside the scope of IFRS 3. The father, Mr X, may effectively control the voting of his dependent son, Mr Y, (particularly a young dependant) by acting on his behalf and thus vote the entire 60% combined holding collectively. However, if there is evidence that they are acting independently, (e.g. by voting differently at shareholder or board meetings), the common control exemption would not apply since the parent and adult family member have not been acting collectively to control the entities.

Scenario (b)

The business combination may be outside the scope of IFRS 3. A highly influential parent may be able to ensure that adult family members act collectively. However, there would need to be clear evidence that the family influence has resulted in a pattern of collective family decisions. If there is any evidence that Mr X and Mr Y are acting independently (e.g. by voting differently at shareholder or board meetings), the common control exemption would not apply since the parent and adult family member have not been acting collectively to control the entities.

Scenario (c)

Common control is unlikely to exist, and therefore the business combination would be in scope of IFRS 3. Where family members are not 'close', there is likely to be less influence between them and adult siblings are more likely to act independently. Therefore, in this scenario where Mr X and Mr Y are adult siblings, it is less likely that an unwritten arrangement will exist, as adult siblings often have less influence over each other. Accordingly there is a presumption that common control does not exist between non-close family members and sufficient evidence that they act collectively, rather than independently, would need to exist to overcome this conclusion.

If in the above example, X and Y had been unrelated, then, in the absence of a written agreement, consideration would need to be given to all of the facts and circumstances to determine whether it is appropriate to apply the exemption. In our view, there would need to be a very high level of evidence of them acting together to control both entities in a collective manner in order to demonstrate that an unwritten contractual agreement really exists, and that such control is not transitory.

Prior to the acquisition of Entity B by Entity A, whether financial statements can be prepared in accordance with IFRS for a 'reporting entity' containing such 'sister' companies that does not comprise a group under IFRS 10 is discussed in Chapter 6 at 2.2.6.

2.1.2 Transitory control

The condition in the IFRS 3 common control exemption that the 'control is not transitory' was included when the standard was first issued and is intended to deal with concerns expressed by some that business combinations between parties acting at arm's length could be structured through the use of 'grooming' transactions so that, for a brief period immediately before and after the combination, the combining entities or businesses are under common control. In this way, it might have been possible for combinations that would otherwise be accounted for in accordance with IFRS 3 using the acquisition method (or the purchase method as it was termed when the standard was first issued) to be accounted for using some other method. *[IFRS 3(2007).BC28].*

IFRS 3 states that when an entity is formed to issue equity instruments to effect a business combination, one of the combining entities that existed before the combination must be identified as the acquirer on the basis of the evidence available. *[IFRS 3.B18].* The Interpretations Committee was asked in 2006 whether a reorganisation involving the formation of a new entity (Newco) to facilitate the sale of part of an organisation is a business combination within the scope of IFRS 3. The Interpretations Committee noted that, to be consistent, the question of whether the entities or businesses are under common control applies to the combining entities that existed before the combination, so excluding the newly formed entity. Accordingly, the Interpretations Committee decided not to add this topic to its agenda.[6] Although the issue was considered in the context of the original IFRS 3, the comments remain valid as the requirements in the standard are unchanged.

Therefore, whether or not a Newco is set up within an existing group to facilitate the disposal of businesses is irrelevant as to whether or not common control is 'transitory'. However, does the fact that the reorganisation results in the parent of the existing group losing control over those businesses, mean that common control is 'transitory'?

In our view, the answer is 'no'. An intention to sell the businesses or go to an initial public offering ('IPO') shortly after the reorganisation does not, by itself, prevent the use of the common control exemption. The reason for the requirement 'that control is not transitory' is intended as an anti-avoidance mechanism to prevent business combinations between parties acting at arm's length from being structured through the use of 'grooming' transactions so that, for a brief period immediately before and after the combination, the combining entities or businesses are under common control. Whether or not control is 'transitory' should be assessed by looking at the duration of control of the businesses in the period both before and after the reorganisation – it is not limited to an assessment of the duration of control only after the reorganisation.

Example 10.2: Formation of Newco to facilitate disposal of businesses

Entity A currently has two businesses operated through Entity X and Entity Y. The group structure (ignoring other entities within the group) is as follows:

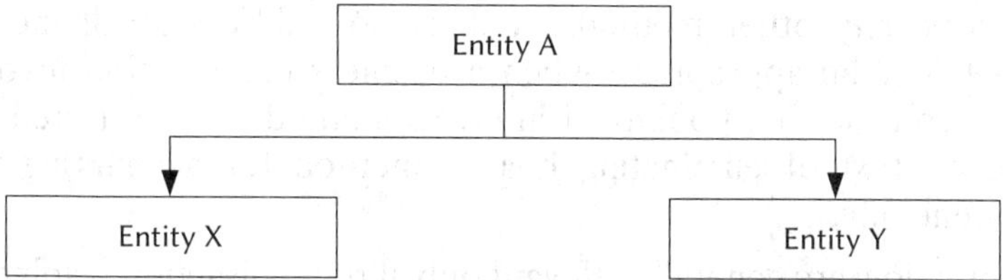

Entity A proposes to combine the two businesses (currently housed in two separate entities, Entity X and Entity Y) into the one entity and then spin-off the combined entity as part of an initial public offering (IPO). Both of the businesses have been owned by Entity A for several years. The internal reconstruction will be structured such that Entity A will establish a new entity (Newco) and transfer its interests in Entity X and Entity Y to Newco, resulting in the following group structure:

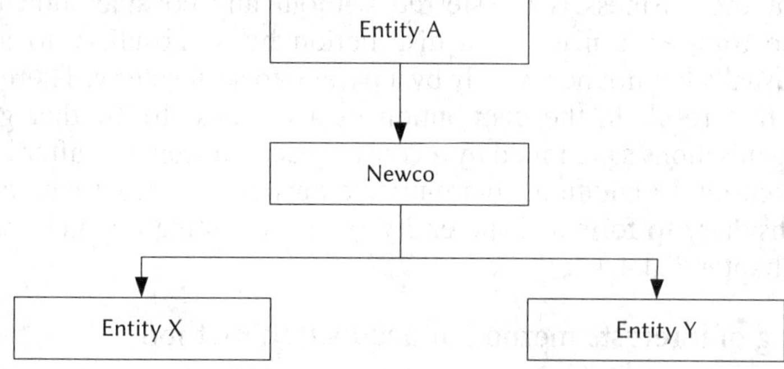

After the IPO, Newco will no longer be under the control of Entity A.

If Newco were to prepare consolidated financial statements, is it entitled to the 'common control' exemption?

The question of whether the entities or businesses are under common control applies to the combining entities that existed before the combination, excluding the newly formed entity, i.e. Entity X and Entity Y. These are clearly entities that have been under the common control of Entity A, and remain so after the transfer.

If Newco was preparing consolidated financial statements without there being an intended IPO, it would be entitled to the exemption. However, as the purpose of the transaction was to facilitate the disposal of the businesses by way of the IPO, such that Entity A no longer has control over Entity X and Entity Y, does this mean that common control is 'transitory'?

In our view, the answer is 'no'. Common control is not considered to be transitory and therefore the reorganisation is excluded from the scope of IFRS 3. This is consistent with the ordinary meaning of 'transitory', something which is fleeting, brief or temporary. The common control of Entity X and Entity Y was not fleeting in the fact pattern as both entities had been controlled by Entity A for several years. By contrast, if Entity Y had only recently come into the group, this may well indicate that control is transitory.

Although the above example involved a new entity, the same considerations apply regardless of the manner in which the internal reconstruction may have been structured. For example, Entity X may have acquired Entity Y or the net assets and trade of Entity Y, with Entity X then being the subject of an IPO. In such a situation, Entity X would be entitled to the common control exemption with respect to the business combination.

3 ACCOUNTING FOR BUSINESS COMBINATIONS INVOLVING ENTITIES OR BUSINESSES UNDER COMMON CONTROL

IFRS 3 prescribes the acquisition method for combinations that are within its scope and does not describe any other methods; it does not address at all the methods of accounting that may be appropriate when a business combination involves entities under common control. The pooling of interests method is not referred to in IFRS 3 except in the context of eliminating it as a method for accounting for business combinations generally.

The discussions below are generally relevant only if the transaction involves a business. If the transaction does not involve a business because the entity or assets being acquired do not meet the definition of a business, it is accounted for as an acquisition of assets. The accounting for such common control transactions is discussed in Chapter 8 at 4.4.2.D.

It may be that the business is transferred without any consideration being given. Commonly the transfer is made as a distribution by a subsidiary to its parent or contribution, usually but not necessarily by a parent, to a subsidiary. There can be legal arrangements that result in the distribution of a business to another group entity, including reorganisations sanctioned by a court process or transfers after liquidation of the transferor entity. In addition, some jurisdictions allow a legal merger between a parent and subsidiary to form a single entity. The accounting for such transactions is discussed in Chapter 8 at 4.4.3.

3.1 Pooling of interests method or acquisition method

IAS 8 – *Accounting Policies, Changes in Accounting Estimates and Errors* – requires that in the absence of specific guidance in IFRS, management shall use its judgement in developing and applying an accounting policy that is relevant and reliable. *[IAS 8.10]*. In making that judgement, in the absence of IFRS dealing with similar or related issues or guidance within the *Conceptual Framework for Financial Reporting ('Framework')*, management may also consider the most recent pronouncements of other standard-setting bodies that use a similar conceptual framework to develop accounting standards, to the extent that these do not conflict with the *Framework* or any other IFRS or Interpretation. *[IAS 8.11-12]*.

Several such bodies have issued guidance and some allow or require the pooling of interests method (or predecessor accounting or merger accounting as it is known in some jurisdictions) in accounting for business combinations involving entities under common control.

IFRS 3 scopes out common control business combinations; it is therefore not prescriptive as to what method must be followed in such transactions. Accordingly, we believe that entities in accounting for business combinations involving entities or businesses under common control should apply either:

(a) the pooling of interests method; or

(b) the acquisition method (as in IFRS 3).

We do not consider that 'fresh start accounting', whereby all combining businesses are restated to fair value, is an appropriate method for accounting for combinations between entities under common control.

Whichever policy is adopted, it should be applied consistently. However, in our view, where the acquisition method of accounting is selected, the transaction must have substance from the perspective of the reporting entity. This is because the acquisition method results in a reassessment of the value of the net assets of one or more of the entities involved and/or the recognition of goodwill. IFRS contains limited circumstances when net assets may be restated to fair value and restricts the recognition of internally generated goodwill, and a common control transaction should not be used to circumvent these limitations. Careful consideration is required of all of the facts and circumstances from the perspective of each entity, before it is concluded that a transaction has substance. If there is no substance to the transaction, the pooling of interests method is the only method that may be applied to that transaction.

When evaluating whether the transaction has substance, the following factors should all be taken into account:

- the purpose of the transaction;
- the involvement of outside parties in the transaction, such as non-controlling interests or other third parties;
- whether or not the transaction is conducted at fair value;
- the existing activities of the entities involved in the transaction;
- whether or not it is bringing entities together into a 'reporting entity' that did not exist before; and
- where a Newco is established, whether it is undertaken in connection with an IPO or spin-off or other change in control and significant change in ownership.

Example 10.3: Accounting for common control business combinations – use of acquisition method? (1)

Entity A currently has two businesses operated through two wholly-owned subsidiaries, Entity B and Entity C. The group structure (ignoring other entities within the group) is as follows:

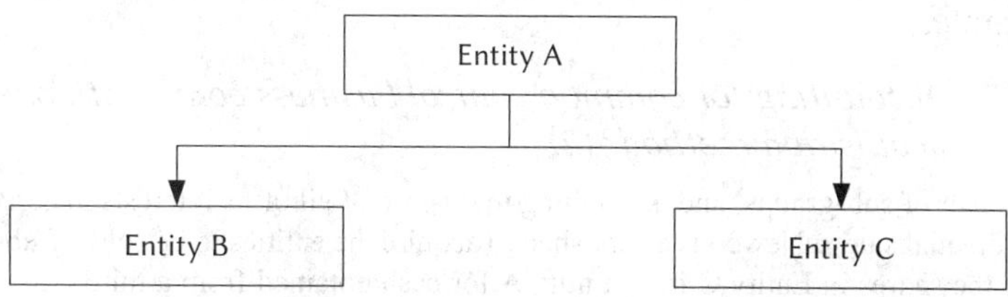

Entity A proposes to combine the two businesses (currently operated by Entity B and Entity C) into one entity in anticipation of spinning off the combined entity as part of an initial public offering (IPO). Both of the businesses have been owned by Entity A for several years. The internal reconstruction will be structured such that Entity C will acquire the shares of the much smaller Entity B from Entity A for cash at its fair value of £1,000. The carrying value of the net assets of Entity B is £200. This also represents the carrying amount of Entity B's net assets in the consolidated financial statements of Entity A. The net of the acquisition-date amounts of the identifiable assets acquired and the liabilities assumed of Entity B measured in accordance with IFRS 3 (generally fair values) are £600.

Assuming that the policy is to apply the acquisition method of accounting to such transactions, how should this business combination be accounted for in the consolidated financial statements of both Entity C and Entity A?

As far as Entity C is concerned, there is substance to this transaction from its perspective. There is a business purpose to the transaction; it has been conducted at fair value; both Entity B and Entity C have existing activities; and they have been brought together to create a reporting entity that did not exist before. Accordingly, Entity C can apply the acquisition method of accounting to this transaction in its consolidated financial statements.

Whether Entity C or Entity B is the acquirer depends on an assessment of the facts and circumstances as to which entity has obtained control of the other. If Entity C now controls Entity B, in summary, this will mean that the net of acquisition-date amounts of the identifiable assets acquired and the liabilities assumed of Entity B will be initially reflected at £600, together with goodwill of £400 (£1,000 less £600), in the consolidated statement of financial position. Only the post-acquisition results of Entity B will be reflected in the consolidated income statement.

As far as Entity A is concerned, from the perspective of the Entity A group, there has been no change in the reporting entity – all that has happened is that Entity B, rather than being directly held and controlled by Entity A, is now indirectly held and controlled through Entity C. Accordingly, there is no business combination that can be accounted for under the acquisition method. The transaction therefore has no impact on the consolidated financial statements of Entity A. Thus, the carrying amounts for Entity B's net assets included in those consolidated financial statements do not change.

In the above example, Entity C had to account for its acquisition of its new subsidiary, Entity B, as it was preparing consolidated financial statements. In some situations, Entity C would not need to account for the business combination at all, as it may be exempt as an intermediate parent company from preparing consolidated financial statements – see Chapter 6 at 2.2.1. If in Example 10.3 above, Entity C had acquired the business of Entity B, rather than the shares, then the same policy choice would have to be made for the business combination in Entity C's financial statements, even if they are not consolidated financial statements.

If the purpose of the transaction in Example 10.3 above had been to combine the complementary businesses of Entity C and Entity B into a reporting entity to facilitate common management, with all other facts in the example remaining the same, there also would have been substance from Entity C's perspective, so it could apply the acquisition method to the transaction. However, in other types of reorganisation there may be no substance from the reporting entity's perspective, as illustrated in the following example.

Example 10.4: Accounting for common control business combinations – use of acquisition method? (2)

Entity A has a number of sub-groups, and is planning to dispose of all of its interests in certain subsidiaries. To facilitate the potential sale, a Newco is established to acquire the entities to be sold – Subgroups C and E. Newco purchases the shares in Entity C from Entity A for cash obtained from a third party bank loan. The group structure before and after this transaction is as follows:

Before

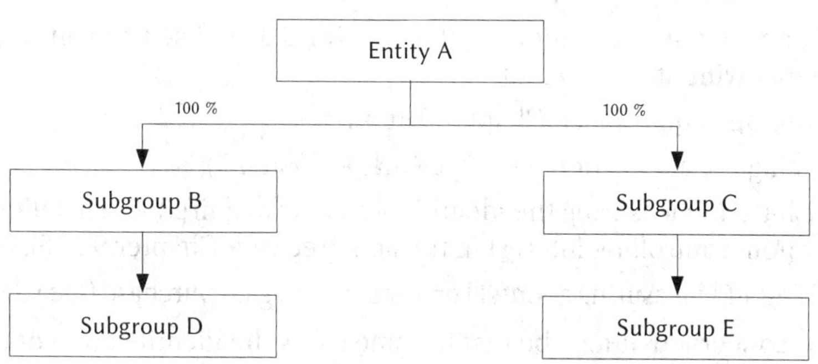

After

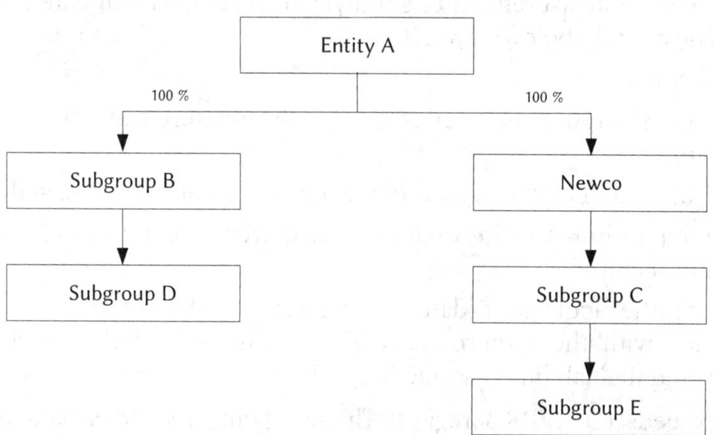

In this situation, there is no substance to the transaction from Newco's perspective as the Newco group is simply a continuation of the existing subgroup comprising Subgroup C's and Subgroup E's activities. Newco is essentially an extension of the parent as it does not have its own operations. In certain circumstances it might also be an extension of Entity C. The change in control is only planned, and it is not an integral part of the transaction. Thus, Newco cannot apply the acquisition method of accounting in preparing its consolidated financial statements. This will be accounted for as a continuation of Subgroup C and Subgroup E as it is not a business combination.

However, if such a restructuring was an integral part of another transaction such as a sale or disposal via an IPO, the circumstances may be such that Newco could be regarded as the acquirer if it is considered to be effectively an extension of the new owners (see Example 9.8 in Chapter 9). Although the Interpretations Committee initially came to a similar conclusion when it discussed the same fact pattern,[7] it has subsequently observed that accounting for arrangements involving the creation of a newly formed entity is too broad to be addressed through an interpretation or an annual improvement. The Interpretations Committee concluded that it would be better considered within the context of a broader project on accounting for common control transactions.[8]

3.2 Application of the acquisition method under IFRS 3

The application of the acquisition method in IFRS 3 is discussed in Chapter 9 and involves the following steps: *[IFRS 3.5]*

(a) identifying an acquirer (see Chapter 9 at 4.1);

(b) determining the acquisition date (see Chapter 9 at 4.2);

(c) recognising and measuring the identifiable assets acquired, the liabilities assumed, and any non-controlling interest in the acquiree (see Chapter 9 at 5); and

(d) recognising and measuring goodwill or a gain on bargain purchase (see Chapter 9 at 6).

As far as (a) is concerned, it may be that in some cases the identification of the acquirer may mean that the business combination needs to be accounted for as a reverse acquisition (see Chapter 9 at 14).

Under (d) above, the measurement of goodwill at the acquisition date is computed as the excess of (a) over (b) below: *[IFRS 3.32]*

(a) the aggregate of:

  (i) the consideration transferred (generally measured at acquisition-date fair value);

  (ii) the amount of any non-controlling interest in the acquiree; and

  (iii) the acquisition-date fair value of the acquirer's previously held equity interest in the acquiree.

(b) the net of the acquisition-date fair values (or other amounts recognised in accordance with the requirements of the standard) of the identifiable assets acquired and the liabilities assumed.

Where (b) exceeds (a), IFRS 3 regards this as giving rise to a gain on a bargain purchase. *[IFRS 3.34]*.

The requirements of IFRS 3 in relation to the acquisition method have clearly been developed for dealing with business combinations between parties on an arm's length basis. The consideration transferred in an arm's length transaction will generally be measured at the acquisition-date fair value of that consideration given (whether it is cash, other assets transferred or equity instruments issued by the acquirer). The value of such consideration given will generally reflect the value of the business that has been received. For business combinations involving entities under common control, this may not be the case. The consideration transferred may not be at arm's length and may not reflect the value of the business received.

Where this is the case, in our view, the entity can either measure the consideration transferred at the acquisition-date fair value of the consideration actually given or elect to impute an additional equity contribution to recognise total consideration equivalent to the fair value of the business received. Whichever method is adopted should be applied consistently, and the entity should disclose its chosen accounting policy.

This is considered in Example 10.5 below. As the example does not include any non-controlling interest in the acquiree nor any previously held interest in the acquiree by the acquirer, the computation of goodwill/gain on bargain purchase only involves the comparison between (a)(i) and (b) above.

Example 10.5: Acquisition method – cash consideration less than the fair value of business acquired

Assume the same facts as in Example 10.3 above, except that Entity C, rather than acquiring Entity B from Entity A for cash at its fair value of £1,000, only pays cash of £700. How should this be reflected by Entity C when applying the acquisition method for its acquisition of Entity B?

In our view, there are two acceptable ways of accounting for this. Either:

(a) the consideration transferred is the fair value of the cash given as consideration, i.e. £700. Accordingly, goodwill of only £100 (£700 less £600) is recognised; or

(b) the consideration transferred is the fair value of the cash given as consideration (£700), together with a deemed capital contribution received from Entity A for the difference up to the fair value of the business of Entity B, i.e. £300 (£1,000 less £700), giving a total consideration of £1,000. Accordingly, goodwill of £400 is recognised. The capital contribution of £300 would be reflected in equity.

Whichever method is adopted, it should be applied on a consistent basis.

If Entity C only paid cash of £500, then the impact under (a) and (b) above would be:

(a) Since the consideration transferred is only £500, then no goodwill is recognised. However, a gain on bargain purchase of £100 (being the excess of the net acquisition-date fair values of the assets acquired less liabilities assumed (£600) over the consideration transferred of £500) is recognised immediately in profit or loss.

(b) As before, goodwill of £400 is recognised, but a capital contribution of £500 would be reflected in equity.

In Example 10.3 and Example 10.5 above, the consideration paid by Entity C was in cash. However, what if Entity C issued shares to Entity A to effect the business combination?

If an acquirer issues equity instruments to effect a business combination, IFRS 3 requires the consideration transferred to be based on the acquisition-date fair value of the equity instruments issued. As discussed in Chapter 9 at 7, in a business combination in which the acquirer and the acquiree (or its former owners) exchange only equity interests, the acquisition-date fair value of the acquiree's equity interests may be more reliably measurable than that of the acquirer's equity interests. In that case, IFRS 3 requires that the calculation of goodwill should use the fair value of the acquiree's equity interests rather than the fair value of the equity interests transferred. *[IFRS 3.33]*. IFRS 3 does not include any guidance on determining the fair value of such consideration. In such circumstances IFRS 13 – *Fair Value Measurement* – is applicable as it provides guidance on how to measure fair value, but does not change when fair value is required or permitted under IFRS. Fair value is defined as 'the price that would be received to sell an asset or paid to transfer a liability in an orderly transaction between market participants at the measurement date'. *[IFRS 13.9]*. IFRS 13 requires that entities maximise the use of relevant observable inputs and minimise the use of unobservable inputs to meet the objective of a fair value measurement. *[IFRS 13.36]*. If either the acquirer's or acquiree's equity shares are quoted, this would indicate which fair value is the more reliably measurable. However, in arrangements between entities under common control, a quoted price for either the acquirer's or the acquiree's shares might not always be available. IFRS 13 is discussed in detail in Chapter 14.

In Example 10.5 above, if Entity C issued shares to Entity A to acquire Entity B, and there is no quoted price for either Entity B's or Entity C's equity shares, then the fair value of the consideration transferred would need to be based on whichever shares are considered to be more reliably measurable. If this were Entity C's shares and their fair value was only £700, then Entity C would apply whichever method in Example 10.5 it has adopted for such transactions, in the same way as for cash consideration less than the fair value of the business acquired. However, if it is considered that the fair value of Entity C's equity shares is not more reliably measurable, the consideration transferred would be based on the fair value of Entity B, i.e. £1,000. Thus, goodwill of £400 would be recognised, with the £1,000 consideration transferred reflected in equity.

3.3 Application of the pooling of interests method

We believe that if entities do not adopt a policy of using the acquisition method under IFRS 3, they should apply the pooling of interests method when accounting for business combinations between entities under common control.

3.3.1 General requirements

IFRS 3 makes no reference to the pooling of interests method, except in the context of eliminating it as a method for accounting for business combinations generally. The pooling of interests method, sometimes known as predecessor accounting or merger accounting, is generally considered to involve the following:[9]

- The assets and liabilities of the combining entities are reflected at their carrying amounts.

  No adjustments are made to reflect fair values, or recognise any new assets or liabilities, at the date of the combination that would otherwise be done under the acquisition method. The only adjustments that are made are to align accounting policies.
- No 'new' goodwill is recognised as a result of the combination.

  The only goodwill that is recognised is any existing goodwill relating to either of the combining entities. Any difference between the consideration paid/transferred and the equity 'acquired' is reflected within equity.
- The income statement reflects the results of the combining entities.

However, apart from the second bullet point, the application of the above general requirements for the pooling of interests method in the context of accounting for business combinations involving entities under common control under IFRS does raise particular issues as discussed below.

3.3.2 Carrying amounts of assets and liabilities

In general, no adjustments would be expected to be required to conform accounting policies of the entities involved in a business combination between entities under common control. This is because in the preparation of the consolidated financial statements of the ultimate parent entity under IFRS, uniform accounting policies should have been adopted by all members of the group. However, it may be necessary to make adjustments where the combining entities have used different accounting policies when preparing their own financial statements.

The main issue relating to the use of carrying amounts when the reporting entity is applying the pooling of interests method for common control combinations is whether the amounts for the entity over which the reporting entity now has control should be based on:

(a) the carrying values reported in the consolidated financial statements of the parent; or

(b) the carrying values reported at the level of the financial statements of the combining entities.

The carrying amounts with respect to the reporting entity are the same as those in its existing financial statements prior to taking over control of the other entity.

In our view, the reporting entity that is accounting under the pooling of interests method for the entity over which it now has control should generally use the amounts in (a) above for the entity which it is now including in its financial statements, i.e. the carrying values for that entity reported in the consolidated financial statements of its parent. Nevertheless, in certain circumstances, it may be acceptable to use the amounts in (b) above, i.e. the carrying values for that entity as reported in that entity's own financial statements. Given it is effectively a new 'sub-set' of an existing group, the use of the carrying values in the existing financial statements of the entity over which the reporting entity now has control in the new consolidated financial statements may not always be appropriate and can be misleading. Hence, when evaluating the circumstances in which to use those carrying values, the following factors should be considered:

- The timing of the transaction in comparison to when the entity over which the reporting entity now has control was established or acquired by the group. The longer the time period the less relevant the values in the entity's own financial statements will be.
- Whether the transaction is a 'grooming transaction' in preparation for a spin-off, sale or similar transaction by the group – the amounts in (a) above will be more relevant in such situation.
- The identity and nature of users of the financial statements (both the financial statements of the reporting entity after the transaction, and the financial statements of the entity over which the reporting entity now has control before the transaction). If the majority of the users of the financial statements of the reporting entity after the transaction are parties that previously relied upon the financial statements of the entity over which the reporting entity now has control, e.g. if there are significant non-controlling interests, using the amounts in (b) might provide more relevant information.
- Whether consistent accounting policies are used with respect to the parent's and subsidiary's financial statements for related transactions (e.g. whether the accounting policy for this transaction is consistent with the accounting policy applied to legal mergers between a parent and a subsidiary – see Chapter 8 at 4.4.3.B).

The rationale for the use of the carrying values reported in the consolidated financial statements of the parent is explained further in Example 10.6 below.

Example 10.6: Pooling of interests method – carrying amounts of assets and liabilities

Entity A currently has two businesses operated through two wholly-owned subsidiaries, Entity B and Entity C. The group structure (ignoring other entities within the group) is as follows:

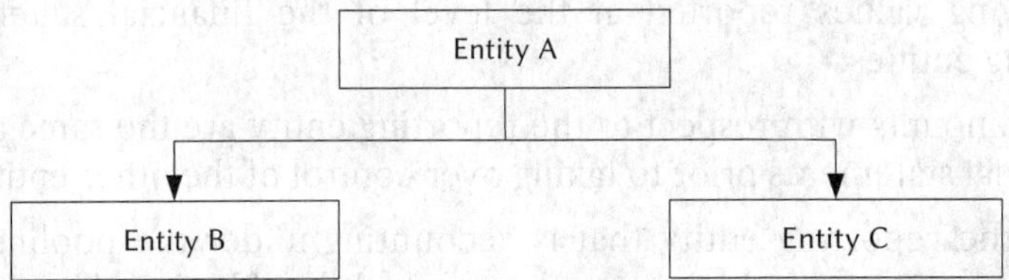

Both entities have been owned by Entity A for a number of years.

On 1 October 2018, Entity A restructures the group by transferring its investment in Entity C which meets the definition of a business under IFRS 3 to Entity B, such that Entity C becomes a subsidiary of Entity B. The policy adopted for business combinations involving entities under common control is to apply the pooling of interests method.

In Entity B's consolidated financial statements for the year ended 31 December 2018, what values should be reflected in respect of Entity C?

Entity B generally should use the carrying values reported in Entity A's consolidated financial statements, rather than the carrying values reported in Entity C's own financial statements.

Accordingly, they will be based on the fair value as at the date Entity C became part of the Entity A group and adjusted for subsequent transactions. Any goodwill relating to Entity C that was recognised in Entity A's consolidated financial statements will also be recognised. Any remaining difference between the equity of Entity C and those carrying values are adjusted against equity. The carrying values of the assets of Entity B will remain as before.

The rationale for applying this approach is that the transaction is essentially a transfer of the assets and liabilities of Entity C from the consolidated financial statements of Entity A to the financial statements of Entity B. From a group perspective of Entity B's shareholder, nothing has changed except the location of those assets and liabilities. Entity B has effectively taken on the group's ownership. Therefore the values used in the consolidated financial statements are the appropriate and most relevant values to apply to the assets and liabilities of Entity C, as they represent the carrying values to the Entity A group.

In our view, an entity should apply the method outlined in the above example when applying the pooling of interests method for common control business combinations – regardless of the legal form of the transaction. Therefore if, in Example 10.6 above, Entity B had acquired the business of Entity C, rather than the shares, or the entities had been merged into one legal entity whereby Entity B was the continuing entity, then the same treatment would apply in Entity B's financial statements even if they are not consolidated financial statements.

3.3.3 Restatement of financial information for periods prior to the date of the combination

Another issue to be considered is the extent to which financial information for periods prior to the date of the business combination, including comparatives, should be restated when applying the pooling of interests method. The pooling of interests method generally is considered to involve the income statement reflecting the results of the combining entities for the full year, irrespective of when the combination took place and comparatives being presented as if the entities had always been combined. The logic of pooling is that there has been no change in control, because the ultimate controlling party has previously had control over the combined resources – it has merely changed the location of its resources. Accordingly, if the ultimate controlling party had control of these resources in the comparative period then the comparatives are restated. Under this view, although IFRS 10 indicates that an entity cannot be included in the consolidated financial statements until the date that it is under the control of the acquirer, i.e. the income and expenses of a subsidiary are included in the consolidated financial statements from the date the entity gains control until the date when it ceases to control the subsidiary, *[IFRS 10.B88]*, this is not considered to be inconsistent with the concept of pooling, which is only a method of presenting the information. That paragraph in the application guidance of IFRS 10 restricts the application of pooling until the entities have actually come under direct control, not how pooling is applied.

Another view is that the requirements of IFRS 10 are viewed as inconsistent with the concept of pooling. Therefore, the financial information in the consolidated financial statements for the combined entity is not restated for periods prior to the combination under common control occurring. This is based on the IFRS 10 requirements that a parent's consolidated financial statements can include the income and expenses of a subsidiary only from the acquisition date as defined in IFRS 3, i.e. the date it obtains control of the subsidiary. Specifically, the scope of IFRS 10 applies to all consolidated financial statements, without any scope exclusions for combinations under common control. The fact that this combination is outside of the scope of IFRS 3 is irrelevant when considering the requirements of IFRS 10. Therefore, the pooling of interests method will affect only the values assigned to the assets and liabilities of the entity now under direct control of the reporting entity (see 3.3.2 above). Such a view would also mean that, when applying the pooling of interests method, the pre-acquisition income and expenses of a subsidiary in the current year should also be excluded.

The Interpretations Committee discussed the presentation of comparatives when applying the 'pooling of interests' method to business combinations between entities under common control at its meeting in November 2009, prior to the issuance of IFRS 10, under the regime of IAS 27 – *Consolidated and Separate Financial Statements* (referred to in this Chapter as IAS 27 (2012)), but it decided (and confirmed in January 2010) not to add the issue to its agenda.

The Interpretations Committee noted that resolving the issue would require interpreting the interaction of multiple IFRSs. It would appear from the Interpretations Committee discussion and agenda decision that the Interpretations Committee did not believe that an approach based on the requirements of IAS 27 (2012) was the only one that could be applied.

It should be noted that there was no change in IFRS 10 from IAS 27 (2012) regarding the measurement of income and expenses of a subsidiary in the consolidated financial statements. IFRS 10 essentially retains the wording of paragraph 26 of IAS 27 (2012), albeit in its application guidance.

Therefore, we believe that, in applying the pooling of interests method, an entity has a choice of two views for its accounting policy:

- View 1 – Restatement of periods prior to the combination under common control

  Restate the financial information in the consolidated financial statements for periods prior to the combination under common control, to reflect the combination as if it had occurred from the beginning of the earliest period presented in the financial statements, regardless of the actual date of the combination.

  However, financial information in the consolidated financial statements for periods prior to the combination is restated only for the period that the entities were under common control.

- View 2 – No restatement of periods prior to the combination under common control

  No restatement of financial information in the consolidated financial statements for the periods prior to the combination under common control.

An entity must consistently apply its chosen accounting policy.

These views are illustrated in Examples 10.7 and 10.8 below.

Example 10.7: Pooling of interests method – restatement of financial information for periods prior to the date of the combination (1)

Assume the same facts as in Example 10.6 above.

In preparing its consolidated financial statements for the year ended 31 December 2018, should Entity B include financial information for Entity C for the period prior to the date of obtaining control on 1 October 2018 (thereby restating the 2017 comparatives) in its consolidated financial statements as if the business combination (and the investment in Entity C) took place as from 1 January 2017?

Entity B has a choice of two views for its accounting policy, which must be applied consistently:

View 1 – Restatement of periods prior to the combination under common control

Since Entity C has been part of the Entity A group for a number of years, then Entity B includes financial information for Entity C as from 1 January 2017, restating the 2017 comparatives in its consolidated financial statements for 2018.

View 2 – No restatement of periods prior to the combination under common control

Entity B does not restate the financial information in its consolidated financial statements for 2018 (including the 2017 comparatives) for any financial information for Entity C prior to 1 October 2018 (the date of the combination).

In the above example, Entity C had been part of the Entity A group for a number of years. What if this had not been the case? Entity B still has a choice of two views, to restate or not to restate. Should it choose restatement, financial information in the consolidated financial statements for periods prior to the combination is restated only for the period that the entities were under common control. If the ultimate controlling party has not always controlled these combined resources, then application of the pooling of interests method reflects that fact. That is, an entity cannot restate the comparative financial information in the consolidated financial statements for a period that common control did not exist.

Example 10.8: Pooling of interests method – restatement of financial information for periods prior to the date of the combination (2)

Assume the same facts as in Example 10.6 above, except that in this situation Entity A acquired Entity C on 1 July 2017 (i.e. the transaction is still considered to be under common control at the date of Entity B's acquisition of Entity C, but Entity B and Entity C were not under common control during the entire comparative period).

In preparing its consolidated financial statements for the year ended 31 December 2018, should Entity B include financial information for Entity C for the period prior to the date of obtaining control on 1 October 2018 (thereby restating the 2017 comparatives) in its consolidated financial statements as if the business combination (and the investment in Entity C) took place as from 1 January 2017?

View 1 – Restatement of periods prior to the combination under common control

If Entity B applies View 1 as its accounting policy, Entity B includes financial information only for Entity C as from 1 July 2017, restating the 2017 comparatives from that date only, in its consolidated financial statements for 2018.

View 2 – No restatement of periods prior to the combination under common control

If Entity B applies View 2 as its accounting policy, this has no impact as Entity B does not restate the financial information in its consolidated financial statements for 2018 (including the 2017 comparatives) for any financial information for Entity C prior to 1 October 2018 (the date of the combination).

Once an entity elects not to restate the financial information in the consolidated financial statements for the periods prior to the combination under common control it is faced with practical challenges as to how to reflect the items of equity (e.g. the equity reserves) that would otherwise be recycled for future events.

One view would be to consider the fact of no restatement as a presentation issue only, and to all intents and purposes, pooling as described in View 1 above is applied in full.

Another view is that the fact that no restatement occurs is considered to be more than a presentation issue – it is viewed as an initial recognition event at that date, and the values assigned to the assets are determined using the concepts of pooling – that is at their carrying values. However this results in the assets and liabilities effectively having a new 'cost base' and the history associated with them is not relevant from the perspective of the new group. That is, for assets/liabilities where changes are recognised directly in equity, the history associated with the past changes in value is lost and the equity reserves will not be rolled forward. This also means that if at the date of the transaction the combination is believed to generate additional value such that previous impairments would reverse at that date, the effect is recognised at that date as part of the adjustment to equity – i.e. as part of the pooling reserve in equity. Similarly, if the combination leads to a change in the tax base of assets, the effect of the change in deferred taxes is recognised as part of the adjustment to equity.

Hence we believe that an entity has an accounting policy choice (View 2a and View 2b):

- View 2a – No restatement of periods prior to the combination under common control but retention of equity balances

  Under View 2a, the view of not restating balances is consistent with the pooling concept and therefore the balance of the reserves are carried over.

  While the financial information for periods prior to the transaction are not restated, the values assigned to the 'acquired' entity, including equity reserves, are determined as if pooling had been applied since the entities were under common control. This means that any equity values associated with 'acquired' entities that would have been recognised in equity are carried over as at the date of transaction. This includes any available-for-sale equity reserves, hedging reserves, foreign currency translation reserves and other asset revaluation reserves.

The history of transactions is retained for such things as recycling available-for-sale reserve movements through the income statement, reversing impairment charges on non-current assets taken in previous periods, foreign currency translation accounts, net investment hedge accounting and cash flow hedge accounting.

If there are changes to the carrying value of assets arising from the combination (e.g. due to revised impairment tests and/or reversals or changes in deferred tax due to changes in the tax base), adjustments are recognised in profit or loss as part of the activity of the business for the year.

- View 2b – No restatement of periods prior to the combination under common control with initial recognition of assets and liabilities at carry-over basis and reset of equity balances.

  Under View 2b, the view is similar to the initial recognition of net assets at book values, in which case the balance of reserves does not carry-over and the history of the equity components is not retained.

  While the financial information for periods prior to the transaction are not restated, the combination gives rise to an initial recognition of assets at the previous carrying values of the assets and liabilities of the acquired entity.

  This means that the assets essentially have a new deemed cost, and there is no history retained of previous transactions or equity reserves. Therefore to the extent there are equity balances arising from past transactions that would have been recognised directly in equity, the equity is not restated. This means that any available-for-sale reserves or hedging reserves will not be retained, and subsequently any future transactions will not give rise to any recycling of amounts from equity that would otherwise have been recycled – even if they still occur in the individual financial statements of one of the entities. Similarly if an asset impairment had been recognised in equity in the past, due to a revaluation reserve relating to the asset, the history is not retained, and there will be no 'impairment reversal' permitted in the consolidated group.

  If there are changes to the carrying value of assets or liabilities arising from the combination (e.g. due to revised impairment tests and/or reversals or changes in deferred tax due to changes in the tax base) these are reflected in the net adjustment to equity at the time of recognising the combination.

  Since any cash flow hedge reserves are not retained, this view may have consequences for hedge effectiveness going forward.

An entity must consistently apply the chosen accounting policy.

Overall, both views result in the same net asset position at the date of the combination. However these views will have a different effect on the components within equity at the date of the transaction and the future treatment of certain transactions relating to equity reserves.

This is illustrated in Example 10.9 below.

Example 10.9: Pooling of interests method – no restatement of financial information for periods prior to the date of the combination – impact on the composition of equity and reflection of the history.

Assume the same facts as in Example 10.7 above, with Entity B adopting View 2 – No restatement of periods prior to the combination under common control.

On 1 October 2018 Entity C had an AFS reserve of €100. At the next reporting date, 31 December 2018, the AFS investment is sold. In Entity B's consolidated financial statements, is the €100 recycled to the income statement?

Entity B has a choice of two views for its accounting policy, which must be applied consistently:

View 2a – No restatement of periods prior to the combination under common control but the pooling concept applies

Entity B recognises an AFS reserve of €100 at the date of the transaction. When the investment is subsequently sold, the €100 is recycled to profit or loss for the year.

View 2b – No restatement of periods prior to the combination under common control with initial recognition at carry-over basis

Entity B does not recognise the AFS reserve at the date of the combination. When the investment is subsequently sold, no additional amount will be recycled to the profit or loss for the year.

3.3.4 Acquisition of a non-controlling interest as part of a common control business combination

The extent of non-controlling interests in each of the combining entities before and after the business combination is not relevant to determining whether the combination involves entities under common control for the purposes of the common control exemption. *[IFRS 3.B4]*. Accordingly, the accounting for business combinations involving entities or businesses under common control is not restricted to combinations involving wholly-owned entities. This is because a partially-owned subsidiary is under the control of the parent entity. Therefore common control transactions involving partially-owned subsidiaries would be outside the scope of IFRS 3.

It may be that in a common control business combination involving a partially-owned subsidiary, any non-controlling interest in that subsidiary is acquired at the same time as the common control transaction.

Where the acquiring entity applies the pooling of interests method, at what date do the consolidated financial statements of the acquiring entity reflect the acquisition of the non-controlling interest? This is particularly pertinent to where the entity restates financial information for periods prior to the date of the combination under View 1 as set out at 3.3.3 above.

In our view, there are two separate transactions to be accounted for:

(a) the acquisition of the non-controlling interest; and

(b) the reorganisation of entities under common control.

Accordingly, the acquisition of the non-controlling interest by the acquiring entity is accounted for from the date the acquisition of these interests. It is not appropriate to reflect the acquisition of the non-controlling interest as if it occurred as of any prior date (as may be done for the controlling interest acquired), even if the acquisition occurs simultaneously with a common control transaction. It is inconsistent with the principles of the pooling of interests method to reflect ownership of a portion or all of businesses that were not owned by the control group prior to the date the control group obtained the ownership interest.

The basic principle of accounting for common control transactions using the pooling of interests method is that the movement of controlled businesses within the control group is discretionary and from the perspective of the controlling party without economic substance. Since the controlling party generally can dictate the structure of ownership within the group at any time, restatement of previous periods presented to reflect the transaction as if it had occurred at an earlier date is permitted. The following are consistent with these principles:

- the acquisition of non-controlling interest is a transaction with economic substance;
- IFRS specifically requires the presentation of income available to the parent's owners (excluding the interest of non-controlling shareholders) and earnings per share based on ordinary shareholders' income; and
- IFRS does not include a principle that a transaction with a third party (e.g. acquisition of non-controlling interest) may be accounted for as of a date earlier than when the transaction is actually consummated.

This is illustrated in Example 10.10 below.

Example 10.10: Pooling of interests method – acquisition of a non-controlling interest as part of a common control business combination

Parent A controls Entity B and Entity C. From the group's perspective, there is a 40% non-controlling interest in Entity C that is held by an unrelated party, Entity Z. Entity B obtains control of Entity C by issuing additional shares on the same date to:

- acquire Parent A's 60% interest in Entity C; and
- acquire Entity Z's 40% interest in Entity C.

The group structure before and after these transactions is as follows:

Before

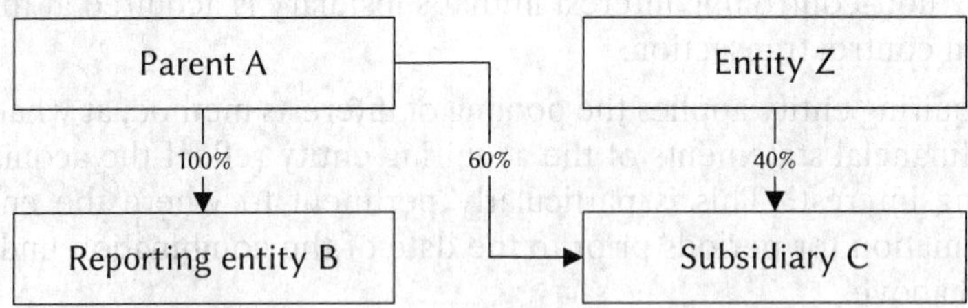

After

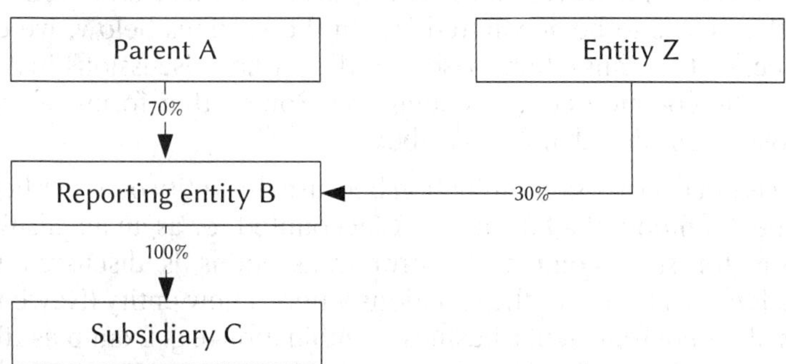

How should Entity B account for the acquisition of Entity Z's 40% interest in Entity C in applying the pooling of interests method?

Entity B should account for the acquisition of Entity Z's 40% interest in Entity C at the date of the transaction. Thus, if Entity B restates its consolidated financial statements to reflect financial information for Entity C for the period before the common control transaction, it will include the non-controlling interest in Entity C within equity until the date of the transaction. The change in ownership interest resulting from the acquisition of Entity Z's 40% interest will be accounted for as an equity transaction at that date. *[IFRS 10.23, B96].*

This applies regardless of whether or not the financial statements for the period before the common control transaction are restated (see 3.3.3 above).

4 GROUP REORGANISATIONS

4.1 Introduction

Group reorganisations involve the restructuring of the relationships between companies in a group (or under common control) and can take many forms, e.g. setting up a new holding company, changing the direct ownership of subsidiaries within the group (possibly involving the creation of a new intermediate holding company), or transferring businesses from one company to another. In principle, most such changes should have no impact on the consolidated financial statements of an existing group, provided there are no non-controlling interests affected, because they are purely internal and cannot affect the group's consolidated financial statements. Some reorganisations may involve transferring businesses outside the group, possibly involving the creation of a new holding company for those businesses.

Group reorganisations may be undertaken for a number of reasons, for example, to improve the co-ordination of diverse businesses, possibly so that the different businesses are conducted through directly owned subsidiaries, or to create a tax grouping in a particular jurisdiction. In some cases, it may be to split up an existing group of companies into two or more separate groups of companies, possibly as a prelude to the disposal of part of the group either by way of sale or by way of an IPO. Similarly, the introduction of a new holding company may be undertaken as part of an IPO of the group.

For some of the entities involved in the reorganisation, there may well be a business combination that needs to be accounted for. In the sections below, we consider this particular aspect of the transaction, based on the earlier discussions in 2 and 3 above with respect to the common control exemption. Some other forms of reorganisation have already been considered in 2 and 3 above.

If a transaction is not a business combination because the entity or assets being acquired do not meet the definition of a business, it is accounted for as an acquisition of assets. The accounting for such common control transactions is discussed in Chapter 8 at 4.4.2.D. In addition, in some of the situations where a new entity (Newco) is involved the transaction does not represent a business combination (e.g. Examples 10.11 and 10.14 at 4.2.1 and 4.4 below respectively).

The transferors in the reorganisation will need to account for their part of the transaction in their own financial statements. In doing so, they will need to consider the requirements of other relevant IFRSs, in particular, the IFRS 10 requirements relating to disposals of, or loss of control over, subsidiaries (see Chapter 7 at 3.2) and the IFRS 5 requirements relating to disposal groups held for sale and discontinued operations (see Chapter 4). The discussion in Chapter 7 at 3.4 and in Chapter 8 at 2.4.2 relating to demergers may also be relevant. Chapter 8 will also be relevant to the accounting in the separate or individual financial statements of the entities involved in the reorganisation.

A business may be transferred without any consideration being given. Commonly the transfer is made as a distribution by a subsidiary to its parent or contribution, usually but not necessarily by a parent, to a subsidiary. There can be legal arrangements that result in the distribution of a business to another group entity, including reorganisations sanctioned by a court process or transfers after liquidation of the transferor entity. In addition, some jurisdictions allow a legal merger between a parent and subsidiary to form a single entity. The accounting for such transactions is discussed in Chapter 8 at 4.4.3.B.

All of the examples that follow at 4.2, 4.3 and 4.4 below involve a new entity (Newco) and assume that all entities are owned 100% by the entity at the top of the particular structure.

4.2 Setting up a new top holding company

In Examples 10.11 and 10.12 below, a holding company has been inserted between shareholders and an existing group or a series of entities with common ownership (but not necessarily common control) in exchange for the issue of equity. In either case the Newco itself is not identified as the acquirer. However, the accounting consequences may differ depending on whether or not there is a group before the setting up of the new holding company. Transactions such as this may be effected for cash or a combination of cash and equity. These arrangements are discussed at 4.2.2 below.

4.2.1 Setting up a new top holding company in exchange for equity

Example 10.11: Newco inserted at the top of an existing group

A Newco is incorporated and inserted at the top of an existing group. Newco issues shares to the existing shareholders of Entity A in exchange for the shares already held in that entity. There are no changes to the shareholder group. The group structure before and after this transaction is as follows:

Before

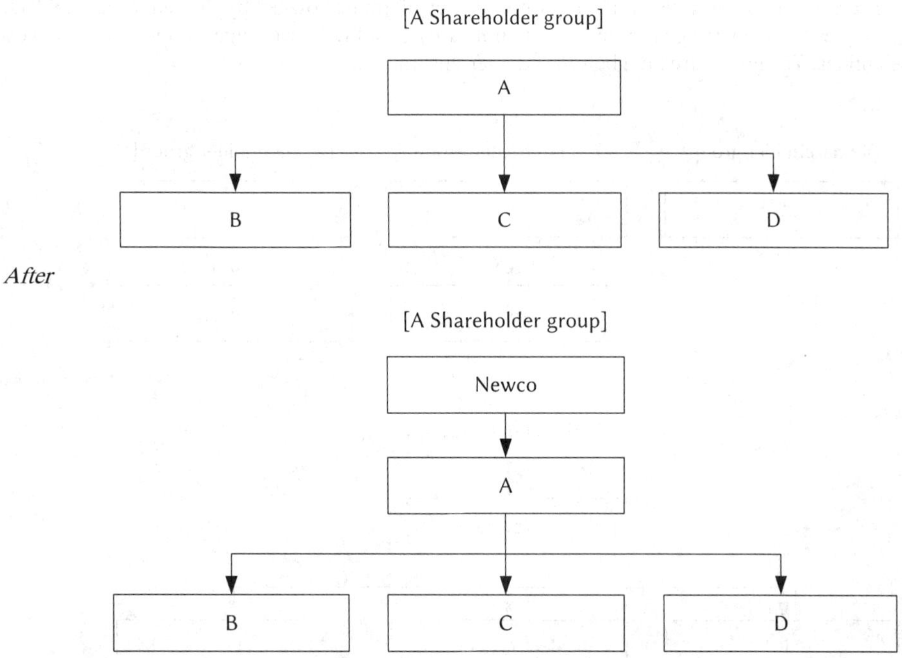

After

[A Shareholder group]

Newco

A

B C D

How should this reorganisation be accounted for in Newco's consolidated financial statements?

The transaction is not a business combination and does not result in any change of economic substance. Accordingly, the consolidated financial statements of Newco are a continuation of the existing group. The consolidated financial statements will reflect any difference in share capital as an adjustment to equity. The group does not recognise this adjustment in any component of equity that may be required to be reclassified to profit or loss at a later date.

In most situations this type of reorganisation will not qualify for the 'common control exemption' since there will be no contractual arrangement between the shareholders (see 2.1.1 above). However, even if the transaction qualified for the exemption because there is one individual, or a sub-group of the shareholders with a contractual arrangement, who controls Entity A and therefore the new Newco group, this is irrelevant.

Entity A did not combine with any other business, since Newco is not a business. On this basis, the transaction is outside the scope of IFRS 3. *[IFRS 3.B19]*. Further, Newco cannot elect to apply the acquisition method in IFRS 3 since there is no economic substance to the transaction in terms of any real alteration to the composition or ownership of the group. Since the substance is that this is a continuation of the existing group, the financial statements reflect that fact.

Even if one argued that the transaction was within the scope of IFRS 3, the transaction does not represent a business combination, since the Newco issued shares. Under IFRS 3, if a new entity is formed to issue equity interests to effect a business combination, one of the combining entities that existed before the business combination shall be identified as the acquirer. *[IFRS 3.B18]*.

In the example above, the reorganisation was effected by Newco issuing shares. If Newco gave cash consideration as part of the transaction, then in most situations this will not affect the analysis above that the arrangement is a continuation of the existing group. The treatment of the cash consideration is described at 4.2.2 below.

Example 10.12: Newco inserted at the top of entities owned by the same shareholders thereby creating a new reporting group

A Newco is incorporated and inserted at the top of a number of entities owned by the same shareholders. Newco issues shares to the existing shareholders of entities B, C and D in exchange for the shares already held in those entities. The group structure before and after this transaction is as follows:

Before

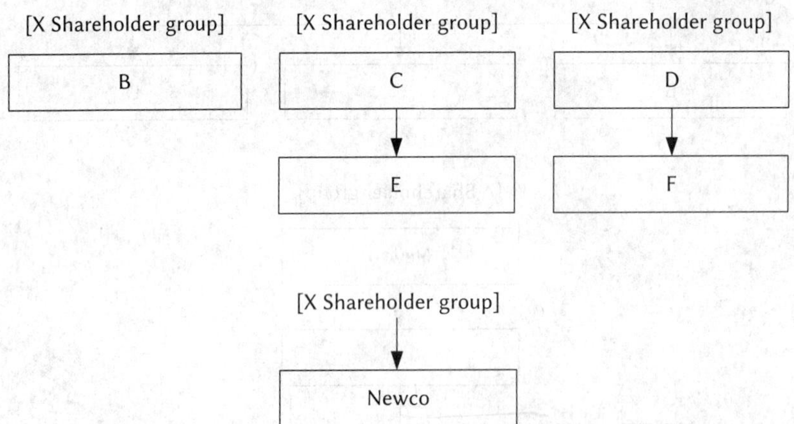

After

Unlike the situation in Example 10.11 above, this is clearly a business combination as defined by IFRS 3 as it is 'a transaction or other event in which an acquirer obtains control of one or more businesses'. *[IFRS 3 Appendix A].* B and sub-groups C and D have been brought together to form a new reporting entity under a new parent entity, Newco. Accordingly, it is within the scope of IFRS 3 unless otherwise exempt.

It may be that this type of reorganisation will qualify for the 'common control exemption' (see 2.1.1 above) since the number of shareholders will generally be relatively few. Accordingly, there may well be one individual, or a sub-group of the shareholders with a contractual arrangement, who controls entities B, C and D. The exemption will apply as long as the common control is not transitory (see 2.1.2 above). In that case, a policy choice should be made as to whether the pooling of interests method or the acquisition method is adopted (see 3.1 above).

If the pooling of interests method is used, as discussed at 3.3.2 above, the consolidated financial statements will reflect the carrying values of each of the entities (although since in this case the entities did not comprise a formal group before, it may be necessary to align accounting policies). Depending on the policy choice made about the restatement of financial information for periods prior to the date of the reorganisation (see 3.3.3 above), the consolidated financial statements may or may not be presented as if the entities had always been combined, including comparative figures for all of the entities 'acquired by Newco' (although this will depend on whether all of those entities were under common control for all of the periods presented).

If the acquisition method in IFRS 3 is to be used, since Newco cannot be the acquirer (Newco issues shares to effect the reorganisation, and there is no change in control arising), one of the existing entities (B, C or D) will need to be identified as the acquirer (see Chapter 9 at 4.1). If, for example, B is identified as the acquirer, the consolidated financial statements will reflect book values for B, and comparative figures comprising those of B; fair values of the assets acquired and liabilities assumed, together with any resulting goodwill, for sub-groups C and D, whose results will be included only from the date of the combination. In addition, IFRS 3 explicitly states that 'the accounting acquiree must meet the definition of a business for the transaction to be accounted for as a reverse acquisition'. *[IFRS 3.B19]*. Accordingly, if the acquisition method is used, Newco cannot be accounted for as a reverse acquisition by the identified acquirer, but will effectively be accounted for under the pooling of interests method.

In the event that the 'common control exemption' is not available, the acquisition method in IFRS 3 would have to be applied as indicated above.

In the example above, the reorganisation was effected by Newco issuing shares. If Newco gave cash consideration as part of the transaction, then in most situations this will not affect the analysis above. The treatment of the cash consideration is described at 4.2.2 below. As discussed at 3.1 above, if the facts and circumstances indicated that there was substance to the transaction such that Newco is the acquirer, the application of IFRS 3's method would result in fair values being attributed to the assets acquired and liabilities assumed of all the existing businesses, and the recognition of goodwill relating to those businesses. This might happen if the transaction was contingent on completion of an IPO that resulted in a change in control of the newly formed Newco group. As we also note in 3.1 above, the Interpretations Committee is expecting arrangements such as this to be considered as part of the IASB's project on common control transactions.

4.2.2 Setting up a new top holding company: transactions including cash consideration

In Examples 10.11 and 10.12 above, a Newco has been inserted between shareholders and either an existing group or a series of entities under common control. In neither case can the Newco itself be identified as the acquirer.

In both of these examples, the reorganisation was effected by Newco issuing shares. If Newco gave cash consideration as part of the transaction, then usually this will not affect the way in which the transaction is accounted for because it will not change the analysis that Newco is not the acquirer.

If the pooling of interests method is applied any cash paid to the shareholders is effectively a distribution to the shareholders and should be accounted for as such. In Example 10.12, if the entity is able to apply acquisition accounting, any cash paid to the shareholders in their capacity as owners of the identified acquirer is accounted for as a distribution. Any cash paid to the shareholders as owners of the acquirees would form part of the consideration transferred for the entities acquired.

4.3 Inserting a new intermediate parent within an existing group

Example 10.13: Newco inserted as a new intermediate parent within an existing group

A Newco is incorporated and inserted above a number of entities within an existing group so as to form a new sub-group. Newco issues shares to its parent A in return for the shares in entities C and D. The group structure before and after this transaction is as follows:

Before

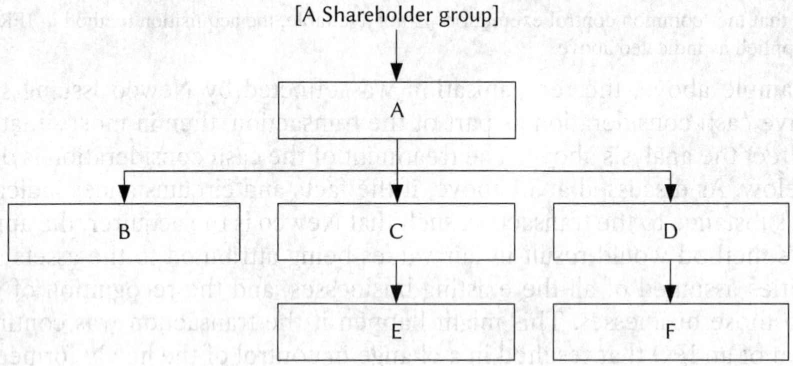

After

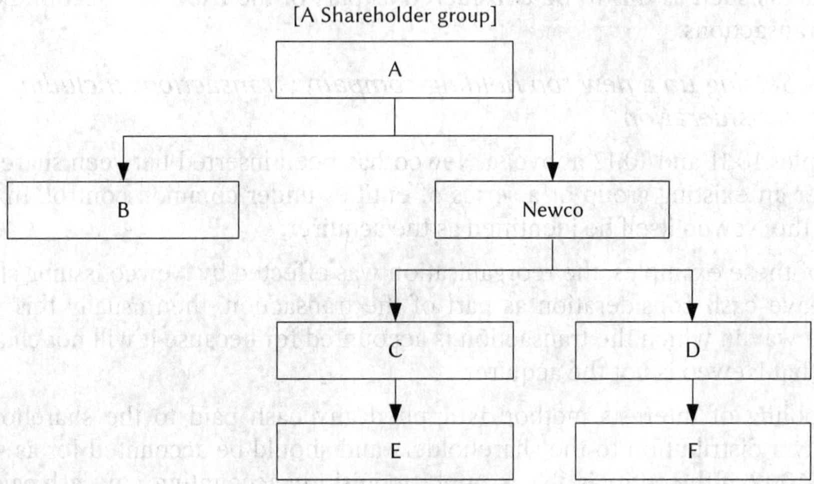

In most situations, Newco will be exempt from preparing consolidated financial statements (see Chapter 6 at 2.2.1). However, if it does prepare consolidated financial statements, consideration will be required as to whether it qualifies as an acquisition or it will be a common control transaction.

This type of reorganisation will generally qualify for the 'common control exemption' in IFRS 3 since sub-group C and sub-group D are controlled by entity A. As discussed at 2.1.2 above, the exemption will apply as long as the common control is not transitory, and in making that assessment the newly formed entity Newco is excluded. If any of the entities within sub-group C and sub-group D had come into the A group recently, this might indicate that control of that entity is transitory. Assuming that the exemption is available, a policy choice should be made as to whether the pooling of interests method or the acquisition method is adopted (see 3.1 above).

If the pooling of interests method is used, as discussed at 3.3.2 above, the consolidated financial statements will reflect carrying values for each of the entities. Depending on the policy choice made about the restatement of financial information for periods prior to the date of the reorganisation (see 3.3.3 above), the consolidated financial statements may or may not be presented as if the entities had always been combined, including comparative figures for all of the entities 'acquired by Newco' (although this will depend on whether all of those entities were under common control for all of the periods presented).

If the acquisition method in IFRS 3 is to be used, since Newco cannot be the acquirer (Newco issues shares to effect the reorganisation, there is no change in control arising, and A already owns/ controls the entities), either C or D will need to be identified as the acquirer (see Chapter 9 at 4.1). If, for example, C is identified as the acquirer, the consolidated financial statements will reflect book values for sub-group C, and comparative figures comprising those of that sub-group; fair values of the assets acquired and liabilities assumed, together with any resulting goodwill, for sub-group D, whose results will be included only from the date of the combination. In addition, if the acquisition method is used, Newco cannot be accounted for as a reverse acquisition by the identified acquirer, but will effectively be accounted for as a recapitalisation in the year of the transaction because IFRS 3 explicitly requires the accounting acquiree to meet the definition of a business for the transaction to be accounted for as a reverse acquisition. *[IFRS 3.B19].*

In the event that the 'common control exemption' is not available, the acquisition method in IFRS 3 would have to be applied as indicated above.

In the example above, the reorganisation was effected by Newco issuing shares. If Newco gave cash consideration as part of the transaction, then in most situations this will not affect the analysis above and the further consequences would be exactly the same as those described in 4.2.2 above. If Newco were identified as the acquirer if the facts and circumstances meant that there was substance to the transaction, the application of the acquisition method in IFRS 3 would result in fair values being attributed to the assets acquired and liabilities assumed of both sub-groups C and D, and the recognition of goodwill, relating to all of those businesses. This might happen if, for example, the transaction was contingent on completion of an IPO that resulted in a change in control of the newly formed Newco group.

4.4 Transferring businesses outside an existing group using a Newco

In some cases, such a transfer involves using a Newco which is owned by the shareholders of the existing group as illustrated below.

Example 10.14: Newco created to take over a business of an existing group ('spin')

Entity C, a subsidiary of Parent A, transfers the shares held in its subsidiary, Entity E, to a newly formed entity, Newco. In return, Newco issues shares to the existing shareholders of Parent A. The group structure before and after this transaction is as follows:

Before

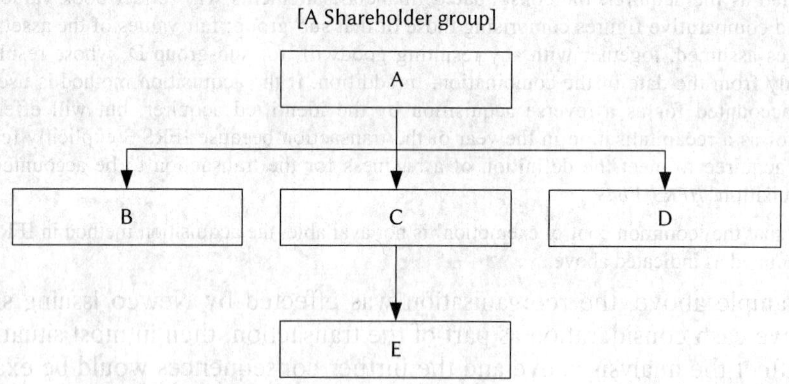

After

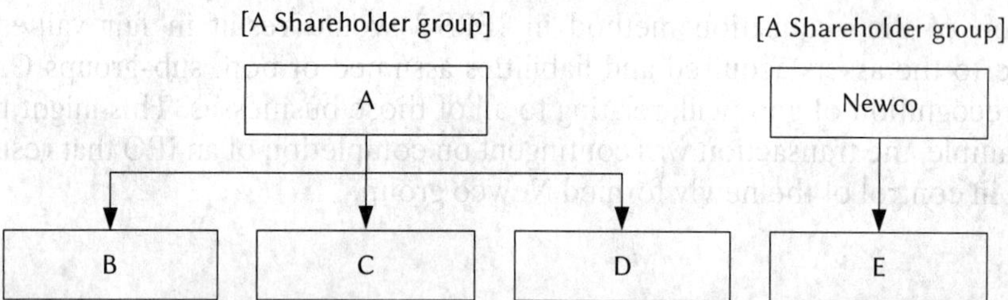

The transaction is not a business combination and does not result in any change of economic substance as far as Newco and E are concerned. Accordingly, the consolidated financial statements of Newco are a continuation of E. The consolidated financial statements will reflect any difference in share capital as an adjustment to equity. Newco does not recognise this adjustment in any component of equity that may be required to be reclassified to profit or loss at a later date.

In most situations this type of reorganisation will not qualify for the 'common control exemption' since there will be no contractual arrangement between the shareholders (see 2.1.1 above). However, even if it did qualify for the exemption because there is one individual, or a sub-group of the shareholders with a contractual arrangement, who controls Entity A and therefore the new Newco group, this is irrelevant.

Entity E did not combine with any other business, since Newco is not a business. On this basis, the transaction is outside the scope of IFRS 3. *[IFRS 3.B19].* Further, Newco cannot elect to apply the acquisition method in IFRS 3 since there is no economic substance to the transaction in terms of any real alteration to the composition or ownership of E. Since the substance is that this is a continuation of E, the financial statements reflect that fact.

Even if one argued that the transaction was within the scope of IFRS 3, the transaction does not represent a business combination, since the Newco issued shares. Under IFRS 3, if a new entity is formed to issue equity interests to effect a business combination, one of the combining entities that existed before the business combination shall be identified as the acquirer. *[IFRS 3.B18].*

In September 2011, the Interpretations Committee discussed a similar situation in which 'the parent company (Entity A), which is wholly owned by Shareholder A, transfers a business (Business A) to a new entity (referred to as "Newco") also wholly owned by Shareholder A'. The only difference to the fact pattern discussed above is that there is a single owner, Shareholder A rather than a shareholder group. The Interpretations Committee concluded that accounting for common control transactions is too broad to be addressed through an interpretation or an annual improvement. The Interpretations Committee concluded that it would be better considered within the context of a broader project on accounting for common control transactions.[10]

In the example above, the reorganisation was effected by Newco issuing shares. If Newco gave cash consideration as part of the transaction, then in most situations this will not affect the analysis above. The only difference is that any cash paid to the shareholders is effectively a distribution to the shareholders and should be accounted for as such (see 4.2.2 above).

Apart from any necessary change in share capital, the accounting set out in the example above is the same as would have been applied if the business was transferred by distributing the shares in E directly to the parent's shareholders, without the use of a Newco. In that case, there would be no question that there had been a business combination at all. Entity E would not reflect any changes in its financial statements. The only impact for E is that rather than only having one shareholder, C, it now has a number of shareholders.

As discussed at 3.1 above, it would only be if Newco paid cash and the facts and circumstances meant that there was substance to the transaction – such that Newco could be regarded as the acquirer – that the application of the acquisition method in IFRS 3 would result in fair values being attributed to the assets acquired and liabilities assumed of E, and the recognition of goodwill. This accounting may be appropriate when the transaction was contingent on completion of an IPO that resulted in a change in control of the newly formed Newco group.

For Entity A, this transaction is a spin-off, or demerger, of Entity E, and therefore the discussion in Chapter 7 at 3.4 and in Chapter 8 at 2.4.2 relating to demergers would be relevant.

4.5 Transferring associates/joint ventures within an existing group

A reorganisation may involve the transfer of associates or joint ventures within an existing group. As indicated at 2.1 above, for the purpose of the common control exemption, a business combination involving entities or businesses under common control 'is a business combination in which all of the combining entities or businesses are ultimately controlled by the same party or parties both before and after the business combination, and that control is not transitory'. *[IFRS 3.B1]*. Although this will include transactions, such as the transfer of subsidiaries or businesses between entities within a group, the issue is whether it can be extended to an entity acquiring an associate or a joint venture from another group entity.

In October 2012, the Interpretations Committee received a request seeking clarification of the accounting for an acquisition of an interest in an associate or joint venture from an entity under common control – whether it is appropriate to apply the IFRS 3 scope exemption for business combinations under common control, by analogy to such acquisitions.[11] The Interpretations Committee observed that IAS 28 – *Investments in Associates and Joint Ventures* – has guidance on the acquisition of an interest in an associate or joint venture and does not distinguish between acquisition of an investment under common control and acquisition of an investment from an entity that is not under common control. *[IAS 28.32]*. The Interpretations Committee also observed that IAS 8 requires management to use its judgement in developing and applying an accounting policy only in the absence of a Standard that specifically applies to a transaction. *[IAS 8.10]*.

The Interpretations Committee also observed that IAS 28 states that many of the procedures that are appropriate for the application of the equity method are similar to the consolidation procedures described in IFRS 10 and that the concepts underlying the procedures used in accounting for the acquisition of a subsidiary are also adopted in accounting for the acquisition of an investment in an associate or a joint venture. *[IAS 28.26]*. The Interpretations Committee also observed that IFRS 3 does not apply to a combination of entities or businesses under common control. *[IFRS 3.2(c)]*. The Interpretations Committee 'observed that some might read these paragraphs as contradicting the guidance in paragraph 32 of IAS 28, and so potentially leading to a lack of clarity. The Interpretations Committee was specifically concerned that this lack of clarity has led to diversity in practice for the accounting of the acquisition of an interest in an associate or joint venture under common control.'[12] Ultimately, the Interpretations Committee noted that accounting for the acquisition of an interest in an associate or joint venture under common control would be better considered within the context of broader projects on accounting for business combinations under common control and the equity method of accounting. Consequently, the Interpretations Committee decided not to take the issue onto its agenda.[13]

Based on the discussions of the Interpretations Committee in October 2012, we believe there are two possible approaches, which are described below, to the accounting by an acquirer/investor applying the equity method when it acquires an investment in an associate or a joint venture from an entity that is under common control. As IFRS 3 and IAS 28 are not clear, there is a question of whether, and how, to apply IFRS 3 principles to investments in associates or joint ventures. An entity should account for such transactions using a consistent accounting policy.

The two approaches are as follows:

- Approach 1 – acquisition accounting

  An acquirer/investor applies the acquisition method in accounting for the acquisition of an associate or a joint venture from a seller that is under common control when the acquirer/investor is applying the equity method. The acquirer/investor compares the fair value of the underlying assets and liabilities of the associate or joint venture against the consideration given up to identify any goodwill or gain on a bargain purchase and adjustments to profit and loss when applying the equity accounting method.

- Approach 2 – pooling of interests

  The scope exemption for business combinations among entities under common control given in IFRS 3 extends to transactions involving associates or joint ventures. The entity uses the pooling of interests method, and carries over equity-accounted values.

These are explained further in Example 10.15 below.

However, at the Interpretations Committee meeting in March 2017, the Interpretations Committee decided to reconsider how an entity should account for the acquisition of an interest in an associate or joint venture from an entity under common control.[14]

In June 2017, the Interpretations Committee tentatively decided that the requirements in IFRS Standards provide an adequate basis for an entity to account for the acquisition of an interest in an associate or joint venture from an entity under common control. The Interpretations Committee observed that IAS 28 does not include a scope exception for the acquisition of an interest in an associate or joint venture from an entity under common control. Accordingly, an entity applies the requirements in IAS 28 when it acquires such an interest and does not apply by analogy the scope exception for business combinations under common control in IFRS 3 as the requirements in paragraph 26 of IAS 28 on the procedures used in accounting for an interest in an associate or joint venture should not be used as a basis to apply paragraph 2(c) of IFRS 3 by analogy. The Interpretations Committee observed that in accounting for the acquisition of the interest, the entity would assess whether the transaction includes a transaction with owners in their capacity as owners – if so, the entity determines the cost of the investment taking into account that transaction with owners.[15]

If the Interpretations Committee finalises its June 2017 tentative agenda decision unchanged then the approach whereby pooling of interests was applied and equity-accounted values were carried over would no longer be available as the accounting policy choice to entities. The only approach to account for an acquirer/investor applying the equity method when it acquires an investment in an associate or a joint venture from an entity under common control would be to apply Approach 1 – acquisition accounting.

Example 10.15: Transfer of an associate within an existing group

Entities B and C are under common control of entity A. Entity C has an investment in an associate D which it sells to entity B for cash. The transaction can be illustrated as follows:

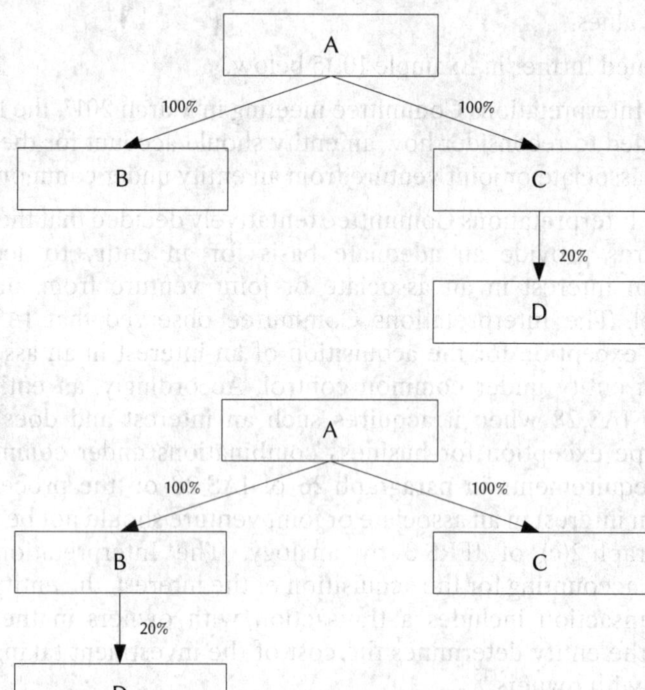

The equity accounted carrying value in Entity C's financial statements of its 20% interest in Associate D is £100, while the fair value of the underlying identifiable assets and liabilities is £800. Entity B gives consideration of £190 to Entity C for the 20% interest in Associate D, which is the fair value of the 20% interest.

The consolidated financial statements prepared by Entity A will not be impacted, because from the group's perspective there has been no change.

How should Entity B account for this transaction when applying the equity accounting method in its own consolidated financial statements (or its stand-alone financial statements where the entity does not have any additional subsidiaries – see Chapter 11 at 5)?

In our view, there are two approaches that Entity B can apply in accounting for this transaction, but whichever approach is adopted it should be applied consistently.

Approach 1 – acquisition accounting

Under this approach, Entity B recognises an investment in an associate with a cost of £190, inclusive of goodwill of £30 and its share of net assets of £160 (20% ×£800).

An acquirer/investor applies the acquisition method in accounting for the acquisition of an associate from a seller that is under common control when the acquirer/investor is applying the equity method. The acquirer/investor compares the fair value of the underlying assets and liabilities of the associate against the consideration given up to identify any goodwill or gain on a bargain purchase and adjustments to profit and loss when applying the equity accounting method.

The basis for this approach is that IAS 28, unlike IFRS 3, does not exempt transactions that are between entities under common control. Furthermore, the IFRS 3 exemption is for business combinations involving entities under common control. The acquisition of an investment in an associate is not a business combination. Therefore, it cannot be a business combination among entities under common control and the acquirer/investor cannot apply the IFRS 3 common control exemption. Accordingly, IAS 28 applies as it does to any other acquisition of an associate (see Chapter 11).

Approach 2 – pooling of interests

Under this approach, Entity B recognises an investment in the associate based on the equity-accounted carrying value in C's financial statements as at the date that B acquires the investment, which is £100. Entity B does not reassess the fair value of Associate D's assets and liabilities. Rather, Entity B continues to recognise any adjustments that Entity C recognised due to differences in fair values at the date Entity C acquired its interest in Associate D.

Entity B recognises the excess of the consideration paid (£190) over the carrying value (£100) of £90 as a distribution.

While IAS 28 does not specifically scope out transactions of this nature between entities under common control, an entity considers the accounting that would most faithfully represent these transactions. Paragraph 26 of IAS 28 indicates that the concepts underlying the procedures used in accounting for the acquisition of a subsidiary are also adopted in accounting for the acquisition of an associate. Therefore, an acquirer/investor cannot apply IFRS 3 literally – otherwise an acquirer/investor could not apply any of the subsidiary-related principles in IFRS 3 to investments in associates. Instead, the underlying principles of IFRS 3 must be established and applied with appropriate modifications to the equity method. Because the principles of IFRS 3 include exempting combinations between entities under common control and the ability to use the pooling of interests method for such exempt transactions – see 3.1 above, this option is also available for the acquisition of an associate.

Although the discussion in Example 10.15 above is expressed in terms of the acquisition of an investment in an associate from another group entity, the two approaches that are available would also apply to transfers of joint ventures within an existing group.

References

1 *IASB Work plan 2017-2021, The Feedback Statement on the 2015 Agenda Consultation*, para. 27.
2 Staff Paper prepared for the Global Preparers Forum Meeting (March 2017, Global Preparers Forum Meeting), *Business Combinations under Common Control - Project update (Agenda ref 5)*, para. 17-25.
3 Minutes from Global Preparers Forum Meeting (March 2017, Global Preparers Forum Meeting), para. 34.
4 *www.ifrs.org*, Projects, Work plan, Business Combinations under Common Control, Project history, Next milestone.
5 Information for Observers (June 2014 IASB meeting), *Business Combinations Under Common Control – Scope of the research project (Agenda Paper 14)*, paras. 5-6.
6 *IFRIC Update*, March 2006, p.6.
7 *IFRIC Update*, July 2011, p.4.
8 *IFRIC Update*, September 2011, p.2.
9 For example, see FASB ASC 805-50; and FRS 6, *Acquisitions and Mergers*, ASB, September 1994, paras. 16-19.
10 *IFRIC Update*, September 2011, p.2.
11 *IFRIC Update*, January 2013, p.8.
12 *IFRIC Update*, May 2013, pp.3-4.
13 *IFRIC Update*, May 2013, pp.3-4.
14 *IFRIC Update*, March 2017, p.11.
15 *IFRIC Update*, June 2017, *Committee's tentative agenda decisions, Agenda Paper* 8.

Chapter 11 Investments in associates and joint ventures

List of examples

Chapter 11 Investments in associates and joint ventures

1 INTRODUCTION

An entity may conduct its business directly or through strategic investments in other entities. IFRS broadly distinguishes three types of such strategic investment:

- entities controlled by the reporting entity (subsidiaries);
- entities jointly controlled by the reporting entity and one or more third parties (joint arrangements classified as either joint operations or joint ventures); and
- entities that, while not controlled or jointly controlled by the reporting entity, are subject to significant influence by it (associates).

The equity method of accounting is generally used to account for investments in associates and joint ventures. It involves a modified form of consolidation of the results and assets of investees in the investor's financial statements. The essence of the equity method of accounting is that, rather than full scale consolidation on a line-by-line basis, it requires incorporation of the investor's share of the investee's net assets in one line in the investor's consolidated statement of financial position, the share of its profit or loss in one line in the investor's consolidated statement of profit or loss and the share of its other comprehensive income in one line in the investor's consolidated statement of other comprehensive income.

2 OBJECTIVE AND SCOPE OF IAS 28

2.1 Objective

The objective of the standard is to prescribe the accounting for investments in associates and to set out the requirements for the application of the equity method when accounting for investments in associates and joint ventures. *[IAS 28.1]*.

IAS 27 – *Separate Financial Statements* – was amended in 2014 to allow an entity, in its separate financial statements, to account for its investments in subsidiaries, joint ventures and associates using the equity method of accounting as described in IAS 28 – *Investments in Associates and Joint Ventures*. This is discussed further in Chapter 8 at 2.3.

2.2 Scope

The standard is applied by all entities that are investors with joint control of a joint venture, or significant influence over an associate. *[IAS 28.2]*. Although there are no exemptions from the standard itself, there are exemptions from applying the equity method by certain types of entities as discussed at 5 below.

3 DEFINITIONS

The following terms are used in IAS 28 with the meanings specified: *[IAS 28.3]*

An *associate* is an entity over which the investor has significant influence.

Consolidated financial statements are the financial statements of a group in which assets, liabilities, equity, income, expenses and cash flows of the parent and its subsidiaries are presented as those of a single economic entity.

The *equity method* is a method of accounting whereby the investment is initially recognised at cost and adjusted thereafter for the post-acquisition change in the investor's share of the investee's net assets. The investor's profit or loss includes its share of the investee's profit or loss and the investor's other comprehensive income includes its share of the investee's other comprehensive income.

A *joint arrangement* is an arrangement of which two or more parties have joint control.

Joint control is the contractually agreed sharing of control of an arrangement, which exists only when decisions about the relevant activities require the unanimous consent of the parties sharing control.

A *joint venture* is a joint arrangement whereby the parties that have joint control of the arrangement have rights to the net assets of the arrangement.

A *joint venturer* is a party to a joint venture that has joint control of that joint venture.

Significant influence is the power to participate in the financial and operating policy decisions of the investee but is not control or joint control of those policies. *[IAS 28.3]*.

IAS 28 also notes that the following terms are defined in paragraph 4 of IAS 27 and in Appendix A of IFRS 10 – *Consolidated Financial Statements* – and are used in IAS 28, with the meanings specified in the IFRS in which they are defined:

- control of an investee;
- group;
- parent;
- separate financial statements; and
- subsidiary. *[IAS 28.4]*.

4 SIGNIFICANT INFLUENCE

Under IAS 28, a holding of 20% or more of the voting power of the investee (held directly or indirectly, through subsidiaries) is presumed to give rise to significant influence, unless it can be clearly demonstrated that this is not the case. Conversely, a holding of less than 20% of the voting power is presumed not to give rise to significant influence, unless it can be clearly demonstrated that there is in fact significant influence. The existence of a substantial or majority interest of another investor does not necessarily preclude the investor from having significant influence. *[IAS 28.5]*. An entity should consider both ordinary shares and other categories of shares in determining its voting rights.

At its November 2016 meeting, the IFRS Interpretations Committee discussed a request to clarify whether, and how, a fund manager assesses if it has significant influence over a fund that it manages and in which it has a direct investment. In the scenario described in the submission, the fund manager applies IFRS 10 and determines that it is an agent, and thus does not control the fund. The fund manager has also concluded that it does not have joint control of the fund. This issue was previously discussed in 2014 and 2015 but at that time the Interpretations Committee decided not to finalise the agenda decision, but instead to place this issue on hold and monitor how any research project on equity accounting progresses. The Interpretations Committee however did not see any benefit in keeping this issue on hold until further progress is made on the research project, which is now part of the IASB's research pipeline. The Interpretations Committee observed that a fund manager assesses whether it has control, joint control or significant influence over a fund that it manages by applying the relevant IFRS standard, which in the case of significant influence is IAS 28. Unlike IFRS 10, IAS 28 does not contemplate whether and how decision-making authority held in the capacity of an agent affects the assessment of significant influence. It believes that developing any such requirements could not be undertaken in isolation of a comprehensive review of the definition of significant influence in IAS 28. Additionally, paragraph 7(b) of IFRS 12 – *Disclosure of Interests in Other Entities* – requires an entity to disclose information about significant judgements and assumptions it has made in determining that it has significant influence over another entity. The Interpretations Committee concluded that it would be unable to resolve the question efficiently within the confines of existing IFRS standards. Consequently, it tentatively decided not to add the issue to its agenda.[1]

IAS 28 states that the exercise of significant influence will usually be evidenced in one or more of the following ways:

(a) representation on the board of directors or equivalent governing body of the investee;

(b) participation in policy-making processes, including participation in decisions about dividends and other distributions;

(c) material transactions between the investor and the investee;

(d) interchange of managerial personnel; or

(e) provision of essential technical information. *[IAS 28.6]*.

Significant influence may also exist over another entity through potential voting rights (see 4.3 below).

An entity loses significant influence over an investee when it loses the power to participate in the financial and operating policy decisions of that investee. The loss of significant influence can occur with or without a change in absolute or relative ownership levels. It could occur as a result of a contractual arrangement. It could also occur, for example, when an associate becomes subject to the control of a government, court, administrator or regulator. *[IAS 28.9]*.

Chapter 11

In some jurisdictions, an entity is able to seek protection from creditors in order to reorganise its business (e.g. under Chapter 11 of the Bankruptcy Code in the United States). In such situations, an investor (which is not under bankruptcy protection itself) with an interest in such an associate will need to evaluate the facts and circumstances to assess whether it is still able to exercise significant influence over the financial and operating policies of the investee. An investor should, when assessing its ability to exercise significant influence over an entity, consider severe long-term restrictions on the transfer of funds from the associate to the investor or other restrictions in exercising significant influence. However, such restrictions do not, in isolation, preclude the exercise of significant influence.

The accounting for loss of significant influence over an associate is discussed at 7.12 below.

4.1 Lack of significant influence

The presumption of significant influence may sometimes be overcome in the following circumstances:

- the investor has failed to obtain representation on the investee's board of directors;
- the investee or other shareholders are opposing the investor's attempts to exercise significant influence;
- the investor is unable to obtain timely or adequate financial information required to apply the equity method; or
- a group of shareholders that holds the majority ownership of the investee operates without regard to the views of the investor.

Determining whether the presumption of significant influence has been overcome requires considerable judgement. IFRS 12 requires that an entity must disclose significant judgements and assumptions made in determining that it does not have significant influence even though it holds 20% or more of the voting rights of another entity.[2] This is discussed further in Chapter 13 at 3. Sufficient evidence that justifies rebutting the presumption is also likely to be required because many regulators are expected to challenge such decisions.

4.2 Holdings of less than 20% of the voting power

Although there is a presumption that an investor that holds less than 20% of the voting power in an investee cannot exercise significant influence, *[IAS 28.5]*, where investments give rise to less than 20% careful judgement is needed to assess whether significant influence may still exist if one of the indicators in IAS 28.6 (a)-(e) at 4 above, are present.

For example, an investor may still be able to exercise significant influence in the following circumstances:

- the investor's voting power is much larger than that of any other shareholder of the investee;
- the corporate governance arrangements may be such that the investor is able to appoint members to the board, supervisory board or significant committees of the investee. The investor will need to apply judgement to the facts and circumstances to determine whether representation on the respective boards or committees is enough to provide significant influence; or
- the investor has the power to veto significant financial and operating decisions.

Determining which policies are significant requires considerable judgement. IFRS 12 requires that an entity must disclose significant judgements and assumptions made in determining that it does have significant influence where it holds less than 20% of the voting rights of another entity.[3] This is discussed further in Chapter 13 at 3. Extract 11.1 below shows how GlaxoSmithKline plc has disclosed how it has significant influence when it has an ownership interest of less than 20%.

Extract 11.1: GlaxoSmithKline plc (2014)

Notes to the financial statements [extract]

20 Investments in associates and joint ventures [extract]

The Group held one significant associate at 31 December 2014, Aspen Pharmacare Holdings Limited. At 31 December 2014, the Group owned 56.5 million shares or 12.4% of Aspen. Aspen, listed on the Johannesburg Stock Exchange, is Africa's largest pharmaceutical manufacturer and a major supplier of branded and generic pharmaceutical, healthcare and nutritional products to the southern African and selected international markets. The investment had a market value of £1,274 million (2013 – £872 million). Although the Group holds less than 20% of the ownership interest and voting control of Aspen, the Group has the ability to exercise significant influence through both its shareholding and its nominated director's active participation on the Aspen Board of Directors.

4.3 Potential voting rights

An entity may own share warrants, share call options, debt or equity instruments that are convertible into ordinary shares, or other similar instruments that have the potential, if exercised or converted, to give the entity voting power or reduce another party's voting power over the financial and operating policies of another entity (potential voting rights). *[IAS 28.7]*.

IAS 28 requires an entity to consider the existence and effect of potential voting rights that are currently exercisable or convertible, including potential voting rights held by another entity, when assessing whether an entity has significant influence over the financial and operating policies of another entity.

Potential voting rights are not currently exercisable or convertible when they cannot be exercised or converted until a future date or until the occurrence of a future event. *[IAS 28.7]*.

IAS 28 adds some further points of clarification. In assessing whether potential voting rights contribute to significant influence, an entity must examine all facts and circumstances (including the terms of exercise of the potential voting rights and any other contractual arrangements whether considered individually or in combination) that affect potential voting rights, except the intention of management and the financial ability to exercise or convert those potential voting rights. *[IAS 28.8]*.

IAS 28 does not include guidance on potential voting rights comparable to that included in IFRS 10. In the amendments introduced to IAS 28 when IFRS 10, 11 and 12 were issued, the IASB did not re-consider the definition of significant influence and concluded that it would not be appropriate to address one element of the definition in isolation. Any such consideration would be done as part of a wider review of accounting for associates. *[IAS 28.BC16]*.

4.4 Voting rights held in a fiduciary capacity

Voting rights on shares held as security remain the rights of the provider of the security, and are generally not taken into account if the rights are only exercisable in accordance with instructions from the provider of the security or in his interest. Similarly, voting rights that are held in a fiduciary capacity may not be those of the entity itself. However, if voting rights are held by a nominee on behalf of the entity, they should be taken into account.

5 EXEMPTIONS FROM APPLYING THE EQUITY METHOD

Under IAS 28, an entity with joint control of, or significant influence over, an investee accounts for its investment in an associate or a joint venture using the equity method, except when that investment qualifies for exemption in accordance with paragraphs 17 to 19 of the standard. *[IAS 28.16]*.

5.1 Parents exempt from preparing consolidated financial statements

An entity need not apply the equity method to its investment in an associate or a joint venture if the entity is a parent that is exempt from preparing consolidated financial statements by the scope exception in paragraph 4(a) of IFRS 10 (see Chapter 6 at 2.3.1). *[IAS 28.17]*.

5.2 Subsidiaries meeting certain criteria

An entity need not apply the equity method to its investment in an associate or a joint venture if *all* the following apply:

(a) the entity is a wholly-owned subsidiary, or is a partially-owned subsidiary of another entity and its other owners, including those not otherwise entitled to vote, have been informed about, and do not object to, the entity not applying the equity method;

(b) the entity's debt or equity instruments are not traded in a public market (a domestic or foreign stock exchange or an over-the-counter market, including local and regional markets);

(c) the entity did not file, nor is it in the process of filing, its financial statements with a securities commission or other regulatory organisation, for the purpose of issuing any class of instruments in a public market;

(d) the ultimate or any intermediate parent of the entity produces financial statements available for public use that comply with IFRSs, in which subsidiaries are consolidated or are measured at fair value through profit or loss in accordance with IFRS 10. *[IAS 28.17]*.

This exemption will apply only where the investor in an associate or a joint venture is not also a parent. If it is a parent, it must look to the similar exemption from preparation of consolidated financial statements in IFRS 10, which also contains the conditions (a) to (d) above for a parent to be exempt from preparing consolidated financial statements under IFRS 10.

This exemption is available only to entities that are themselves either wholly-owned subsidiaries or partially-owned subsidiaries whose non-controlling shareholders do not object to the presentation of financial statements that do not include associates or joint ventures using the equity method. Some of these 'intermediate' entities will not be exempt, for example if none of their parent companies prepares consolidated financial statements in accordance with IFRS. A typical example is that of an entity that is a subsidiary of a US group that prepares consolidated financial statements in accordance with US GAAP only. In addition, any entity that has publicly traded debt or equity, or is in the process of obtaining a listing for such instruments, will not satisfy the criteria for exemption.

Many jurisdictions apply a national GAAP that is based on IFRS but requires some form of endorsement process. The question then arises as to whether the exemption in (d) above can be applied when the ultimate or intermediate parent entity produces financial statements available for public use that comply with a national GAAP that is based on IFRS. In our view, the exemption in (d) can be applied if the parent entity:

- reported under a national GAAP that is identical to IFRS in all respects;
- applied the national GAAP equivalent of IFRS 1 – *First-time Adoption of International Financial Reporting Standards* – when the entity adopted that national GAAP;
- made an explicit and unreserved statement of compliance with that national GAAP in its most recent financial statements; and
- could have made an explicit and unreserved statement of compliance with IFRS in those financial statements.

The effect of the above requirements is that a reporting entity that has associates or joint ventures, but no subsidiaries, and does not meet all the criteria in (a)-(d) above, is required to apply equity accounting for its associates or joint ventures in its own (non-consolidated) financial statements (not to be confused with its 'separate financial statements' – see 9 below). This may be a significant difference from many national GAAPs, where equity accounting is required or permitted only in consolidated financial statements.

5.3 Investments held in associates or joint ventures held by venture capital organisations and similar organisations

When an investment in an associate or a joint venture is held by, or is held indirectly through, an entity that is a venture capital organisation, a mutual fund, unit trust or similar entity including an investment-linked insurance fund, the entity may elect to measure investments in those associates and joint ventures at fair value through profit or loss in accordance with IFRS 9 – *Financial Instruments* (or IAS 39 – *Financial Instruments: Recognition and Measurement* – if IFRS 9 is not yet applied). *[IAS 28.18].*

This exemption is related to the fact that fair value measurement provides more useful information for users of the financial statements than application of the equity method. In the Basis for Conclusions to IAS 28, the IASB clarified that this is an exemption from the requirement to measure interests in joint ventures and associates using the equity method, rather than an exception to the scope of IAS 28 for the accounting for joint ventures and associates held by these entities. *[IAS 28.BC12, BC13].*

This exemption raises the question of exactly which entities comprise 'venture capital organisations, or mutual funds, unit trusts and similar entities including investment-linked insurance funds', since they are not defined in IAS 28. This was a deliberate decision by the IASB given the difficulty of crafting a definition. *[IAS 28.BC12].*

Although IFRS 10 does not have an exemption from consolidation for 'venture capital organisations, or mutual funds, unit trusts and similar entities including investment-linked insurance funds', it does have a scope exclusion for entities that meet the definition of an investment entity as discussed at 5.3.1 below.

5.3.1 Investment entities exception

IFRS 10 requires entities that meet the definition of an investment entity to measure investments in subsidiaries at fair value through profit or loss in accordance with IFRS 9 (or IAS 39). The investment entities exception is discussed further in Chapter 6 at 10.

The application of the investment entity exception is not an accounting policy choice. If an entity meets the definition of an investment entity, it is required to measure its subsidiaries at fair value through profit or loss. In order to meet this definition, an investment entity must elect the exemption from applying the equity method in IAS 28 for its investments in associates and joint ventures. *[IFRS 10.B85L(b)]*.

As discussed further at 7.8 below, if an entity that is not itself an investment entity has an interest in an associate or joint venture that is an investment entity, the investor may retain the fair value measurement applied by that investment entity associate or joint venture to the investment entity associate's or joint venture's interests in subsidiaries. *[IAS 28.36A]*.

5.3.2 Application of IFRS 9 (or IAS 39) to exempt investments in associates or joint ventures

The reason that IAS 28 allows venture capital organisations, mutual funds, unit trusts and similar entities to measure investments in associates and joint ventures at fair value is because such entities often manage their investments on the basis of fair values and so the application of IFRS 9 (or IAS 39) produces more relevant information. Furthermore, the financial statements would be less useful if changes in the level of ownership in an investment resulted in frequent changes in the method of accounting for the investment. Where investments are measured at fair value, the fair value is determined in accordance with IFRS 13 – *Fair Value Measurement* (see Chapter 14 at 5.1).

5.3.2.A Entities with a mix of activities

The exemption clearly applies to venture capital organisations and other similar financial institutions whose main activities consist of managing an investment portfolio comprising investments unrelated to the investor's business. Although the exemption is not intended to apply to other entities that hold investments in a number of associates, there are cases in which entities have significant venture capital activities as well as significant other activities. In those cases, IAS 28 allows an entity to elect to measure the portion of an investment which is held indirectly through a venture capital organisation at fair value through profit or loss in accordance with IFRS 9 (or IAS 39). This is the case regardless of whether the venture capital organisation has significant influence over that portion of the investment. If an entity makes this election, it must apply equity accounting to the remaining portion of the investment not held through the venture capital organisation. *[IAS 28.19]*.

The entity should be able to demonstrate that it runs a venture capital business rather than merely undertaking, on an *ad hoc* basis, transactions that a venture capital business would undertake.

Example 11.1: Entity owning a discrete venture capital organisation

Parent P operates a construction business and owns a venture capital organisation (subsidiary V) that invests in the telecommunications industry. Even though P itself is not a venture capital organisation, subsidiary V would be able to apply the exemption and account for its investments at fair value under IFRS 9 (or IAS 39). In the consolidated financial statements of P, the investments held by V could also be accounted for at fair value under IFRS 9 (or IAS 39), with changes in fair value recognised in profit or loss in the period of change.

Example 11.2: Entity with a venture capital organisation segment

Bank A has a number of separate activities. One segment's business is to acquire all the shares of companies which are then partially sold down to third-party investors. Bank A retains a portion of the shares as a co-investor and has significant influence, but not control, until the investment is exited.

Bank A considers these activities to be in the nature of venture capital. Even though Bank A is itself not a venture capital organisation, it would be able to apply the exemption and account for its investments at fair value under IFRS 9 (or IAS 39), with changes in fair value recognised in profit or loss in the period of change.

5.3.2.B Designation of investments as 'at fair value through profit or loss'

As noted above, venture capital organisations and other similar financial institutions that use the exemption in IAS 28 for their investments in associates or joint ventures are required to apply IFRS 9 (or IAS 39) to those investments. On 8 December 2016, the IASB issued *Annual Improvements to IFRS Standards 2014–2016 Cycle*. An amendment to IAS 28 clarifies that an entity can make the election to use IFRS 9 (or IAS 39) on an investment by investment basis at initial recognition of the associate or joint venture. The amendment will be applicable to accounting periods beginning on or after 1 January 2018, with early application permitted.

5.4 Partial use of fair value measurement of associates

As explained above at 5.3.2.A, an entity may elect to measure a portion of an investment in an associate held indirectly through a venture capital organisation, or a mutual fund, unit trust and similar entities including investment-linked insurance funds at fair value through profit or loss in accordance with IFRS 9 (or IAS 39) regardless of whether the venture capital organisation, or the mutual fund, unit trust and similar entities including investment-linked insurance funds, has significant influence over that portion of the investment.

In the Basis for Conclusions to IAS 28, the IASB noted a discussion of whether the partial use of fair value should be allowed only in the case of venture capital organisations, or mutual funds, unit trusts and similar entities including investment-linked insurance funds, that have designated their portion of the investment in the associate at fair value through profit or loss in their own financial statements. The IASB noted that several situations might arise in which those entities do not measure their portion of the investment in the associate at fair value through profit or loss. In those situations, however, from the group's perspective, the appropriate determination of the business purpose would lead to the measurement of this portion of the investment in the associate at fair value through profit or loss in the consolidated financial statements. Consequently, the IASB decided that an entity should be able to measure a portion of an investment in an associate held by a venture capital organisation, or a mutual fund, unit trust and similar entities including investment-linked insurance funds, at fair value through profit or loss regardless of whether this portion of the investment is measured at fair value through profit or loss in those entities' financial statements. *[IAS 28.BC22]*.

Example 11.3 below (which is based on four scenarios considered by the Interpretations Committee at its meeting in May 2009[4]) illustrates this partial use exemption.

Example 11.3: Venture capital consolidations and partial use of fair value through profit or loss

A parent entity has two wholly-owned subsidiaries (A and B), each of which has an ownership interest in an 'associate', entity C. Subsidiary A is a venture capital business that holds its interest in an investment-linked fund. Subsidiary B is a holding company. Neither of the investments held by subsidiaries A and B is held for trading.

Scenario 1: both investments in the associate result in significant influence on a stand-alone basis

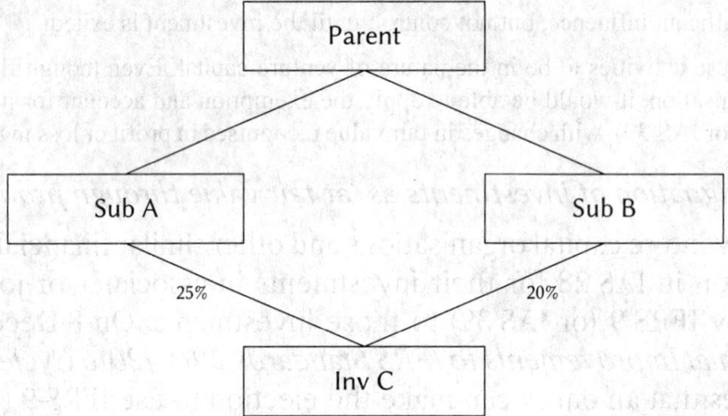

Subsidiary A accounts for its 25% share in the associate at fair value through profit or loss in accordance with IAS 39 (see Chapter 49 at 2.1).

Subsidiary B accounts for its 20% share in the associate using the equity method in accordance with IAS 28 (see 7 below).

The parent entity must equity account for its 20% interest held by B. Under the partial use of fair value exemption, the parent entity may elect to measure the 25% interest held by A at fair value through profit or loss.

Scenario 2: neither of the investments in the associate results in significant influence on a stand-alone basis, but do provide the parent with significant influence on a combined basis.

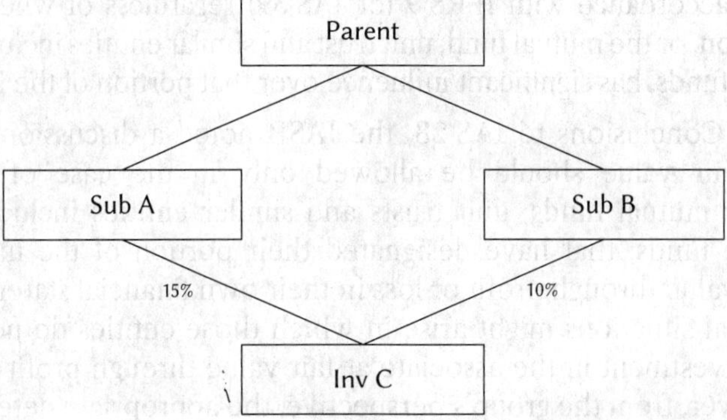

Subsidiary A accounts for its 15% share in the associate at fair value through profit or loss in accordance with IAS 39 (see Chapter 49 at 2.1).

Subsidiary B accounts for its 10% share in the associate as an available-for-sale investment in accordance with IAS 39 (see Chapter 49 at 2.4).

The parent entity must equity account for its 10% interest held by B, even though B would not have significant influence on a stand-alone basis. Under the partial use of fair value exemption, the parent entity may elect to measure the 15% interest held by A at fair value through profit or loss.

Scenario 3: one of the investments in the associate results in significant influence on a stand-alone basis and the other investment in the associate does not result in significant influence on a stand-alone basis

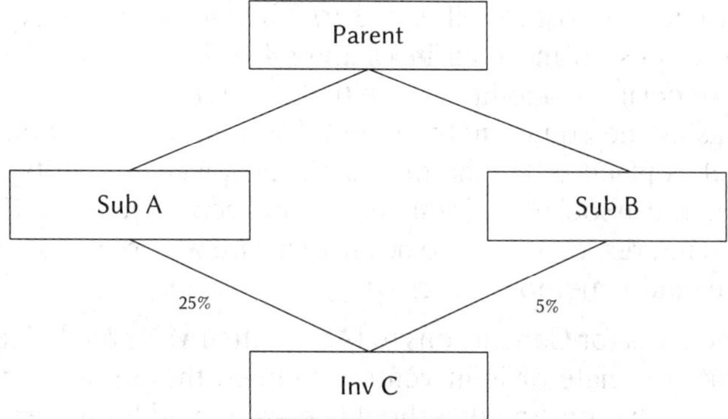

Subsidiary A accounts for its 25% share in the associate at fair value through profit or loss in accordance with IAS 39 (see Chapter 49 at 2.1).

Subsidiary B accounts for its 5% share in the associate as an available-for-sale investment in accordance with IAS 39 (see Chapter 49 at 2.4).

The parent entity must equity account for its 5% interest held by B, even though B would not have significant influence on a stand-alone basis. Under the partial use of fair value exemption, the parent entity may elect to measure the 25% interest held by A at fair value through profit or loss.

Scenario 4: same as scenario 3, but with the ownership interests switched between the subsidiaries

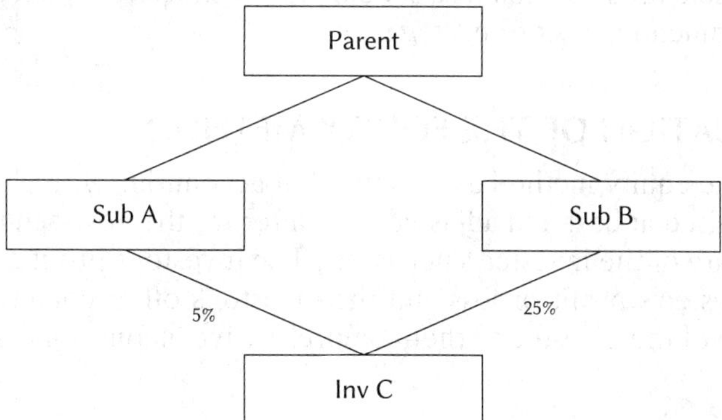

Subsidiary A accounts for its 5% share in the associate at fair value through profit or loss in accordance with IAS 39 (see Chapter 49 at 2.1).

Subsidiary B accounts for its 25% share in the associate using the equity method in accordance with IAS 28 (see 7 below).

The parent entity must equity account for its 25% interest held by B. Under the partial use of fair value exemption, the parent entity may elect to measure the 5% interest held by A at fair value through profit or loss.

6 CLASSIFICATION AS HELD FOR SALE (IFRS 5)

IAS 28 requires that an entity applies IFRS 5 – *Non-current Assets Held for Sale and Discontinued Operations* – to an investment, or a portion of an investment, in an associate or a joint venture that meets the criteria to be classified as held for sale. *[IAS 28.20]*. The detailed IFRS requirements for classification as held for sale are discussed in Chapter 4 at 2.1.2. In this situation, the investor discontinues the use of the equity method from the date that the investment (or the portion of it) is classified as held for sale; instead, the associate or joint venture is then measured at the lower of its carrying amount and fair value less cost to sell. *[IFRS 5.15]*. The measurement requirements as set out in IFRS 5 are discussed in detail in Chapter 4 at 2.2. Any retained portion of an investment in an associate or a joint venture that has not been classified as held for sale is accounted for using the equity method until disposal of the portion that is classified as held for sale takes place. After the disposal takes place, an entity accounts for any retained interest in the associate or joint venture in accordance with IFRS 9 (or IAS 39) unless the retained interest continues to be an associate or a joint venture, in which case the entity uses the equity method. *[IAS 28.20]*.

As explained in the Basis for Conclusions to IAS 28, the IASB concluded that if a portion of an interest in an associate or joint venture fulfilled the criteria for classification as held for sale, it is only that portion that should be accounted for under IFRS 5. An entity should maintain the use of the equity method for the retained interest until the portion classified as held for sale is finally sold. The reason being that even if the entity has the intention of selling a portion of an interest in an associate or joint venture, until it does so it still has significant influence over, or joint control of, that investee. *[IAS 28.BC23-27]*.

When an investment, or a portion of an investment, in an associate or a joint venture previously classified as held for sale no longer meets the criteria to be so classified, it is accounted for using the equity method retrospectively as from the date of its classification as held for sale. Financial statements for the periods since classification as held for sale are amended accordingly. *[IAS 28.21]*.

7 APPLICATION OF THE EQUITY METHOD

IAS 28 defines the equity method as 'a method of accounting whereby the investment is initially recognised at cost and adjusted thereafter for the post-acquisition change in the investor's share of the investee's net assets. The investor's profit or loss includes its share of the investee's profit or loss and the investor's other comprehensive income includes its share of the investee's other comprehensive income.' *[IAS 28.3]*.

7.1 Overview

IAS 28 states that 'Under the equity method, on initial recognition the investment in an associate or a joint venture is recognised at cost, and the carrying amount is increased or decreased to recognise the investor's share of the profit or loss of the investee after the date of acquisition. The investor's share of the investee's profit or loss is recognised in the investor's profit or loss. Distributions received from an investee reduce the carrying amount of the investment. Adjustments to the carrying amount may also be necessary for a change in the investor's proportionate interest in the investee arising from changes in the investee's other comprehensive income. Such changes include those arising from the revaluation of property, plant and equipment and from foreign exchange translation differences. The investor's share of those changes is recognised in the investor's other comprehensive income [...]'. *[IAS 28.10]*. On acquisition of the investment, any difference between the cost of the investment and the entity's share of the net fair value of the investee's identifiable assets and liabilities is accounted for as follows:

- Goodwill relating to an associate or a joint venture is included in the carrying amount of the investment. Amortisation of that goodwill is not permitted.
- Any excess of the entity's share of the net fair value of the investee's identifiable assets and liabilities over the cost of the investment is included as income in the determination of the entity's share of the associate or joint venture's profit or loss in the period in which the investment is acquired.

Appropriate adjustments to the entity's share of the associate's or joint venture's profit or loss after acquisition are made in order to account, for example, for depreciation of the depreciable assets based on their fair values at the acquisition date. Similarly, appropriate adjustments to the entity's share of the associate's or joint venture's profit or loss after acquisition are made for impairment losses, such as for goodwill or property, plant and equipment. *[IAS 28.32]*.

These requirements are illustrated in Example 11.4 below.

Example 11.4: Application of the equity method

On the first day of its financial year, entity A acquires a 35% interest in entity B, over which it is able to exercise significant influence. Entity A paid €475,000 for its interest in B. At the acquisition date the book value of B's net assets was €900,000, and their fair value €1,100,000, the difference of €200,000 relates to an item of property, plant and equipment with a remaining useful life of 10 years. During the year B made a profit of €80,000 and paid a dividend of €120,000. Entity B also owned an investment in securities classified as available-for-sale that increased in value by €20,000 during the year. For the purposes of the example, any deferred tax implications have been ignored.

Entity A accounts for its investment in B under the equity method as follows:

	€	€
Acquisition date of investment in B		
Share in book value of B's net assets: 35% of €900,000	315,000	
Share in fair valuation of B's net assets: 35% of (€1,100,000 – €900,000) *	70,000	
Goodwill on investment in B: €475,000 – €315,000 – €70,000 *	90,000	
Cost of investment		475,000
Profit during the year		
Share in the profit reported by B: 35% of €80,000	28,000	
Adjustment to reflect effect of fair valuation * 35% of ((€1,100,000 – €900,000) ÷ 10 years)	(7,000)	
Share of profit in B recognised in income by A		21,000
Revaluation of available-for-sale asset		
Share in revaluation recognised in other comprehensive income by A: 35% of €20,000		7,000
Dividend received by A during the year		
35% of €120,000		(42,000)
End of the financial year		
Share in book value of B's net assets: €315,000 + 35% (€80,000 – €120,000 + €20,000)	308,000	
Share in fair valuation of B's net assets: €70,000 – €7,000 *	63,000	
Goodwill on investment in B *	90,000	
Closing balance of A's investment in B		461,000

* These line items are normally not presented separately, but are combined with the ones immediately above.

Chapter 11

IAS 28 explains that equity accounting is necessary because recognising income simply on the basis of distributions received may not be an adequate measure of the income earned by an investor on an investment in an associate or a joint venture, since distributions received may bear little relation to the performance of the associate or joint venture. Through its significant influence over the associate, or joint control of the joint venture, the investor has an interest in the associate's or joint venture's performance and, as a result, the return on its investment. The investor accounts for this interest by extending the scope of its financial statements so as to include its share of profits or losses of such an investee. As a result, application of the equity method provides more informative reporting of the net assets and profit or loss of the investor. *[IAS 28.11]*.

7.2 Comparison between equity accounting and consolidation

For some time there has been a debate about whether the equity method of accounting is primarily a method of consolidation or a method of valuing an investment, as IAS 28 does not provide specific guidance either way.

An investor that controls a subsidiary has control over the assets and liabilities of that subsidiary. While an investor that has significant influence over an associate or joint control of a joint venture controls its holding in the shares of the associate or joint venture, it does not control the assets and liabilities of that associate or joint venture. Therefore, the investor does not account for the assets and the liabilities of the associate or joint venture, but only accounts for its investment in the associate or joint venture as a whole.

Although the equity method, in accordance with IAS 28, generally adopts consolidation principles, it also has features of a valuation methodology as discussed below.

IAS 28 notes that many procedures appropriate for the application of the equity method, and described in more detail in 7.3 to 7.12 below, are similar to the consolidation procedures described in IFRS 10 (see Chapter 7). Furthermore, IAS 28 explains that the concepts underlying the procedures used in accounting for the acquisition of a subsidiary are also adopted in accounting for the acquisition of an investment in an associate or a joint venture. *[IAS 28.26]*. However, it is unclear precisely what these concepts are, as no further explanation is given. The position has been confused even further because in the context of an amendment to IAS 39 regarding the application of the exemption in paragraph 2(g) of that standard (see Chapter 43 at 3.7.2), it is stated that 'The Board noted that paragraph 20 of IAS 28 [now paragraph 26 of IAS 28] explains only the methodology used to account for investments in associates. This should not be taken to imply that the principles for business combinations and consolidations can be applied by analogy to accounting for investments in associates and joint ventures.' *[IAS 39.BC24D]*.

The similarities between equity accounting and consolidation include:

- appropriate adjustments to the entity's share of the associate's or joint venture's profits or losses after acquisition are made in order to account, for example, for depreciation of the depreciable assets based on their fair values at the acquisition date;
- recognising goodwill relating to an associate or a joint venture in the carrying amount of the investment;
- non-amortisation of the goodwill;
- any excess of the investor's share of the net fair value of the associate's identifiable assets and liabilities over the cost of the investment is included as income in the determination of the entity's share of the associate or joint venture's profit or loss in the period in which the investment is acquired;
- the elimination of unrealised profits on 'upstream' and 'downstream' transactions (see 7.6.1 below); and
- application of uniform accounting policies for like transactions.

However, there are also a number of differences between equity accounting and consolidation, including:

- the investor ceases to recognise its share of losses of an associate or joint venture once the investment has been reduced to zero;
- the treatment of loans and borrowings (including preference shares classified as debt by the investee) between the reporting entity and its associates or joint ventures (see 7.6.3 below);
- the investor cannot capitalise its own borrowing costs in respect of an associate's or joint venture's assets under construction (an equity accounted investment is not a qualifying asset under IAS 23 – *Borrowing Costs* – regardless of the associate's or joint venture's activities or assets);
- the investor can only apply hedge accounting to the equity accounted investment as a whole, not to individual financial instruments; and
- the investor considers whether there is any additional impairment loss with respect to its net investment.

As there is no clear principle underlying the application of the equity method different views on how to account for certain transactions for which the standard has no clear guidance might be taken, depending on which principle (i.e. consolidation or valuation of an investment) is deemed to take precedence. We address these issues in the following sections.

7.3 Date of commencement of equity accounting

An investor will begin equity accounting for an associate or a joint venture from the date on which it has obtained significant influence over the associate or joint control over the joint venture (and is not otherwise exempt from equity accounting for it). *[IAS 28.32]*. In most situations, this is when the investor acquires the investment in the associate or joint venture. Determining whether an entity has significant influence is discussed at 4 above.

7.4 Initial carrying amount of an associate or joint venture

Under the equity method, an investment is initially recognised at cost. *[IAS 28.3]*. However, 'cost' for this purpose is not defined.

In July 2009, the Interpretations Committee discussed the lack of definition and issued an agenda decision, clarifying that the cost of an investment in an associate at initial recognition comprises its purchase price and any directly attributable expenditures necessary to obtain it.[5] Therefore, any acquisition-related costs are not expensed (as is the case in a business combination under IFRS 3 – *Business Combinations*) but are included as part of the cost of the associate.

The glossary to IFRS defines cost as being the 'amount of cash or cash equivalents paid or the fair value of the other consideration given to acquire an asset at the time of its acquisition or construction ...'.

'Consideration given' is likewise not defined, and therefore we believe that the key sources of guidance in IFRS are:

- 'consideration transferred' in the context of a business combination, as referred to in paragraph 37 of IFRS 3; *[IFRS 3.37]* and
- 'cost' as applied in relation to acquisitions of property, plant and equipment in accordance with IAS 16 – *Property, Plant and Equipment*, intangible assets in accordance with IAS 38 – *Intangible Assets* – and investment property in accordance with IAS 40 – *Investment Property*.

Applying the requirements of IFRS 3, the 'consideration transferred' in a business combination comprises the sum of the acquisition-date fair values of assets transferred by the acquirer, liabilities incurred by the acquirer to the former owners of the acquiree, and equity interests issued by the acquirer. This includes any liability (or asset) for contingent consideration, which is measured and recognised at fair value at the acquisition date. Subsequent changes in the measurement of the changes in the liability (or asset) are recognised in profit or loss (see Chapter 9 at 7.1).

Consequently, in our view, the same treatment may be applied to contingent consideration arrangements in relation to the purchase of an associate or a joint venture, i.e. the initial carrying amount of an associate or joint venture includes the fair value of any contingent consideration arrangement. In this case, subsequent changes in the contingent consideration would be accounted for under IFRS 9 (or IAS 39).

The considerations regarding applying the cost requirements of other standards have previously been discussed by the Interpretations Committee, and the discussions are summarised in Chapter 8 at 2.1.1.

The Interpretations Committee agenda decision did not provide any specific guidance in relation to a piecemeal acquisition of an associate or a joint venture. This is discussed further at 7.4.2 below.

7.4.1 Initial carrying amount of an associate or joint venture following loss of control of an entity

Under IFRS 10, if a parent entity loses control of an entity, the retained interest must be remeasured at its fair value, and this fair value becomes the cost on initial recognition of an investment in an associate or joint venture. *[IFRS 10.25]*.

Example 11.5: Accounting for retained interest in an associate or joint venture following loss of control of an entity

Entity A owns 100% of the shares of Entity B. The interest was originally purchased for £500,000 and £40,000 of directly attributable costs relating to the acquisition were incurred. Upon its reporting date, Entity A sells 60% of the shares to Entity C for £1,300,000. As a result of the sale, Entity C obtains control over Entity B, but by retaining a 40% interest, Entity A determines that it has significant influence over Entity B.

At the date of disposal, the carrying amount of the net assets of Entity B in Entity A's consolidated financial statements is £1,200,000 and there is also goodwill of £200,000 relating to the acquisition of Entity B. The fair value of the identifiable assets and liabilities of Entity B is £1,600,000. The fair value of Entity A's retained interest of 40% of the shares of Entity B is £800,000, which includes goodwill.

Upon Entity A's sale of 60% of the shares of Entity B, it deconsolidates Entity B and accounts for its investment in Entity B as an associate using the equity method of accounting.

Entity A's initial carrying amount of the associate must be based on the fair value of the retained interest, i.e. £800,000. It is not based on 40% of the original cost of £540,000 (purchase price plus directly attributable costs) as might be suggested by the Interpretations Committee statement discussed at 7.4 above, nor is it based on 40% of the carrying amount of the net assets plus goodwill, totalling £1,400,000.

Although it is clear that the initial carrying amount of the associate in the above example is the fair value of the retained interest, i.e. £800,000, does this mean that Entity A in applying the equity method under IAS 28 must:

(a) remeasure the underlying assets and liabilities in Entity B at their fair values at the date Entity B becomes an associate i.e. effectively a new purchase price allocation is performed; and

(b) reassess the classification and designation of assets and liabilities, e.g. the classification of financial instruments, embedded derivatives and hedge accounting, as required by IFRS 3 (see Chapter 9 at 5.4)?

In our view, under IFRS 10, Entity A effectively accounts for the investment in Entity B as if it had acquired the retained investment at fair value as at the date control is lost, and the answer to question (a) is 'yes'. Accordingly, in order to apply the equity method from the date control is lost, Entity A must remeasure *all* of the identifiable assets and liabilities underlying the investment at their fair values (or other measurement basis required by IFRS 3 at that date). As far as question (b) is concerned, we also believe that Entity A should reassess the classification or designation of assets and liabilities in accordance with paragraph 15 of IFRS 3, based on the circumstances that exist at that date. However, in doing so, there is no need to reassess whether an embedded derivative should be separated from a host contract, as 'reassessment of embedded derivatives in contracts held by an associate is not required by IFRIC 9 – *Reassessment of Embedded Derivatives.*

The investment in the associate is the asset the investor controls and recognises, not the underlying assets and liabilities of the associate.' *[IFRIC 9.BC5D]*. We do not believe that the exception provided by IFRIC 9 can be applied by analogy to other reassessments.

IAS 28 indicate that on initial recognition of an investment in an associate, the concepts underlying the procedures used in accounting for the acquisition of a subsidiary are also adopted in accounting for the acquisition of an investment in an associate, and that fair values are applied to measure all of the identifiable assets and liabilities in calculating any goodwill or bargain purchase that exists. *[IAS 28.26, 32]*.

Accordingly, in Example 11.5 above, based on the fair value of the identifiable assets and liabilities of Entity B of £1,600,000, Entity A's initial carrying amount of £800,000 will include goodwill of £160,000, being £800,000 – £640,000 (40% of £1,600,000). IFRS 13 provides detailed guidance about how fair value should be determined, which is discussed in Chapter 14.

In September 2014, the IASB issued an Exposure Draft (ED) *Measuring Quoted Investments in Subsidiaries, Joint Ventures and Associates at Fair Value (proposed amendments to IFRS 10, IFRS 12, IAS 27, IAS 28 and IAS 36)*. The ED proposed to clarify that the unit of account for investments in subsidiaries, joint ventures and associates be the investment as a whole and not the individual financial instruments that constitute the investment. In January 2016, the IASB decided not to consider this topic further until the Post-implementation Review (PIR) of IFRS 13 is complete.

7.4.2 Piecemeal acquisition of an associate or joint venture

7.4.2.A Financial instrument becoming an associate or joint venture

An entity may gain significant influence or joint control over an existing investment upon acquisition of a further interest or due to a change in circumstances. IAS 28 is unclear on how an investor should account for an existing investment, which is accounted for under IFRS 9 (or IAS 39), that subsequently becomes an associate or a joint venture that should be accounted for under the equity method.

IFRS 3 is clear that in a business combination where control over an acquiree is achieved in stages, the previously held (existing) equity investment in that acquiree is required to be revalued to fair value through profit or loss. *[IFRS 3.42]*. If this equity investment was held at fair value through profit and loss this would have happened automatically. If the investment was classified as available-for-sale, any previous fair value remeasurement would be within other comprehensive income and on the date of the business combination, any such amount would be reclassified to profit or loss as if that investment had been directly disposed of. *[IFRS 3.42]*.

It might be argued that a similar approach should be adopted when an associate or joint venture is acquired in stages. Using the IFRS 3 approach, at the date that significant influence or joint control is obtained, the previously held interest would be revalued to fair value and the resulting gain or loss recognised in profit or loss or any fair value measurement recognised previously in other comprehensive income would be reclassified to profit or loss.

Although IAS 28 explains that the concepts underlying the procedures used in accounting for the acquisition of a subsidiary are also adopted in accounting for the acquisition of an investment in an associate or a joint venture, *[IAS 28.26]*, no further explanation is given. This raises the issue as to what impact the concepts inherent within IFRS 3 should have on the accounting for associates and joint ventures.

As discussed at 7.4 above, the Interpretations Committee previously clarified that the initial cost of investment comprises the purchase price and directly attributable expenditures necessary to obtain it. Although the implications for the piecemeal acquisition of an associate are not explicitly addressed, it appeared that, as the Interpretations Committee considered that the initial recognition of the associate is to be based on its cost, the accounting should reflect a cost-based approach.

However, in July 2010, the Interpretations Committee received a request to address the accounting for an investment in an associate when the investment was purchased in stages and classified as available for sale (AFS) until it became an associate.[6] Interestingly, despite the earlier decision in 2009, the Staff Paper produced for the meeting recommended that 'the fair value of an investment classified as AFS prior to the investor obtaining significant influence over that investment should be the deemed cost of that pre-existing interest at the date the investor obtains significant influence over the associate. The accumulated changes in fair value accounted for in OCI should be reclassified to profit or loss at that date.' The Staff Paper further recommended that such a clarification of IAS 28 be included within the Annual Improvements project.[7] Thus, the Staff was recommending that an IFRS 3 approach should be applied, rather than a cost-based approach.

Although the Staff made such recommendations, it is not entirely clear what the Interpretations Committee made of them as the IFRIC Update following the meeting merely states that the Interpretations Committee discussed what amount the investment in an associate should be initially measured at, and the accounting for any accumulated changes in fair value relating to the investment recognised in other comprehensive income (OCI), at the date significant influence is obtained and the investment is no longer categorised as AFS. However, due to the acknowledged diversity in practice in accounting for associates purchased in stages, the Interpretations Committee recommended that the issue be referred to the IASB for consideration.[8] To date this has not yet been considered by the IASB.

In the light of these statements by the Interpretations Committee, we believe that an entity should account for the step acquisition of an associate or a joint venture by applying either:

(a) a cost-based approach; or

(b) a fair value (IFRS 3) approach.

Once selected, the investor must apply the selected policy consistently.

Chapter 11

I Applying a cost-based approach

Where a cost-based approach is applied to accounting for a step acquisition of an associate or a joint venture, this involves the determination of:

(a) the cost of the investment;

(b) whether or not any catch-up adjustment is required when first applying equity accounting (i.e. an adjustment for the share of investee's profits and other equity movements as if the previously held interest was equity accounted; and

(c) the goodwill implicit in the investment (or gain on bargain purchase).

Not all of these aspects of the accounting for a piecemeal acquisition of an associate or a joint venture were addressed by the Interpretations Committee statement in 2009. Accordingly, in our view, the combination of answers to these questions results in four approaches that may be applied to account for a step acquisition of an associate or a joint venture where a cost-based approach is adopted. Once selected, the investor must apply the selected policy consistently.

In all approaches, cost is the sum of the consideration given for each tranche together with any directly attributable costs. However, as a result of the answers to (b) and (c) above, the four approaches are as follows:

	Catch-up equity accounting adjustment for previously held interest	Determination of goodwill/gain on bargain purchase
Approach 1	None	Difference between sum of the cost of each tranche and share of fair value of net assets at date investment becomes an associate or joint venture
Approach 2	None	Difference between the cost of each tranche and the share of fair value of net assets acquired in each tranche
Approach 3	For profits (less dividends), and changes in other comprehensive income (OCI)	Difference between the cost of each tranche and the share of fair value of net assets acquired in each tranche
Approach 4	For profits (less dividends), changes in OCI and changes in fair value of net assets	Difference between the cost of each tranche and the share of fair value of net assets acquired in each tranche

The reasons for using the above cost-based approaches are discussed further below and are illustrated in Example 11.6. Although the example illustrates the step-acquisition of an associate, the accounting would be the same if the transaction had resulted in the step-acquisition of a joint venture.

Example 11.6: Accounting for existing financial instruments on the step-acquisition of an associate (cost-based approach)

In 20X1 an investor acquired a 10% interest in an investee for $100. Three years later in 20X4 the investor acquired a further 15% interest in the investee for $225. The investor now holds a 25% interest and is able to exercise significant influence. For the purposes of the example, directly attributable costs have been ignored. Also, any deferred tax implications have been ignored.

The investor had been accounting for its initial 10% interest at fair value in accordance with IAS 39. The financial information relating to the investee can be summarised as follows:

	20X1		20X4	
	100%	10%	100%	15%
	$	*$*	*$*	*$*
Purchase consideration		100		225
Change in fair value		50		
Fair value of shares in 20X4		150		
Book value of net assets of investee	600		900	
Fair value of net assets of investee *)	800	80	1,200	180
Profit since acquisition in 20X4	500	50		
Dividends declared between 20X1 and 20X4	–200	–20		
Increase in fair value of net assets of investee	400	40		
Cost plus post-acquisition changes in net assets		130		
Other changes in fair value of the investee		10		

*) The fair value uplift from $600 to $800 relates entirely to non-depreciable assets.

The accounting for this step-acquisition under each approach is as follows (all amounts in $):

	Catch-up equity accounting adjustment	**Initial equity accounted amount**	**Goodwill in initial amount of associate**
Approach 1	0	325	Cost less share of fair value of net assets at time investment becomes an associate 325 – (25% × 1200) = 25
Approach 2	0	325	Cost less share of fair value of net assets at each tranche 100 – (10% × 800) = 20 + 225 – (15% × 1200) = 45 Total = 65
Approach 3	10% of profits (less dividends) 10% × (500 – 200) = 30	325 + 30 = 355	Cost less share of fair value of net assets at each tranche 100 – (10% × 800) = 20 + 225 – (15% × 1200) = 45 Total = 65
Approach 4	10% of profits (less dividends) and changes in fair value of assets 10% × (500 – 200 + 400) = 70	325 + 70 = 395	Cost less share of fair value of net assets at each tranche 100 – (10% × 800) = 20 + 225 – (15% × 1200) = 45 Total = 65

Cost of investment

In all four approaches, the cost of the investment is the sum of the consideration given for the two tranches ($325), being the original purchase price of $100 for the existing 10% interest plus the $225 paid for the additional 15% interest.

Therefore, in both the separate and consolidated financial statements, the following occurs:

(a) If the investor measured the original investment at fair value through profit or loss, the changes in fair value previously recognised through profit or loss (excluding dividend income) are reversed through retained earnings to bring the asset back to its original cost.

(b) If the investor measured the original investment at fair value through other comprehensive income (OCI), the changes in fair value previously recognised are reversed through equity reserves to bring the asset back to its original cost.

The investor continues to recognise dividend income in the statement of comprehensive income (in profit or loss) up to the date the entity becomes an associate, irrespective of whether the investor measures the investment at fair value through profit or loss or at fair value through other comprehensive income.

In all four approaches, the difference between the fair value of the original 10% of $150 and the cost of the first tranche of $100 is adjusted against retained earnings within equity or against other equity reserves. The change in the fair value of $50 will be reflected in other comprehensive income in the statement of comprehensive income.

Catch-up adjustment

Approaches 1 and 2 do not recognise a 'catch-up' equity accounting adjustment relating to the first tranche of the investment held by the investor.

On the other hand, Approaches 3 and 4 do recognise a 'catch-up' equity accounting adjustment relating to the first tranche of the investment held by the investor. This adjustment is recognised against the appropriate balance within equity – that is, retained earnings, or other equity reserve. To the extent that they are recognised, these will be reflected in other comprehensive income in the statement of comprehensive income.

Goodwill

Approach 1 determines goodwill in a single calculation based on amounts at the date the investment becomes an associate.

On the other hand, Approaches 2, 3 and 4 determine goodwill based on separate calculations at the date of acquisition of each tranche.

The rationale for each of the four approaches is as follows:

Approach 1

Paragraph 32 of IAS 28 states that 'An investment is accounted for using the equity method from the date on which it becomes an associate or a joint venture.'

Recognising any catch-up adjustments may be interpreted as a form of equity accounting for a period prior to gaining significant influence, which contradicts this principle of IAS 28.

IAS 28 refers to the fact that an investor applies equity accounting to the investment once it is an associate. Therefore, cumulative adjustments for periods prior to this event are not recognised.

Paragraph 32 of IAS 28 also goes on to state that 'on acquisition of the investment, any difference between the cost of the investment and the entity's share of the net fair value of the investee's identifiable assets and liabilities is accounted for as follows:

(a) Goodwill relating to an associate or joint venture is included in the carrying amount of the investment. Amortisation of that goodwill is not permitted.

(b) Any excess of the entity's share of the net fair value of the investee's identifiable assets and liabilities over the cost of the investment is included as income in the determination of the entity's share of the associate or joint venture's profit or loss in the period in which the investment is acquired.'

However, paragraph 32 of IAS 28 does not specify at which dates the fair values of the net assets are to be determined. It may be interpreted to mean only at the date that the investment becomes an associate or a joint venture. This is also consistent with the approach in IFRS 3 whereby the underlying fair values of net assets are only determined at one time rather than determining them several times for individual transactions leading to the change in the economic event.

This approach avoids some of the practical difficulties encountered when applying the other approaches. However, the drawback of this approach is that goodwill may absorb the effects of other events, because a portion of the cost is determined at a different date to the fair value of the assets.

Approach 2

No catch-up adjustment is recognised, similar to the reasons noted in Approach 1. However, paragraph 32 of IAS 28 is interpreted to mean that the fair values of the associate's or joint venture's net assets are determined at a date that corresponds to the date at which consideration was given. Therefore, the fair values are determined for each tranche. This may require the fair values to be determined for previous periods when no such exercise was performed at the date of the original purchase.

The drawback of this approach is that the measurement of the assets and liabilities is based on fair values at different dates.

Approach 3

A catch-up adjustment is recognised to reflect the application of the equity method as described in paragraph 10 of IAS 28 with respect to the first tranche. However, the application of that paragraph restricts the adjustment only to the share of profits and other comprehensive income relating to the first tranche. That is, there is no catch-up adjustment made for changes in the fair value of the net assets not recognised by the investee (except for any adjustments necessary to give effect to uniform accounting policies).

Similar to Approach 2, paragraph 32 of IAS 28 is interpreted to mean that the fair values of the associate's or joint venture's net assets are determined at a date that corresponds to the date at which consideration was given. Therefore, the fair values are determined for each tranche. This may require the fair values to be determined for previous periods when no such exercise was performed at the date of the original purchase.

The drawbacks of this approach are the same as Approach 2.

Approach 4

This approach is based on the underlying philosophy of equity accounting, which is to reflect the investor's share of the underlying net assets plus goodwill inherent in the purchase price. Therefore, where the investment was acquired in tranches, a catch-up adjustment is necessary in order to apply equity accounting from the date the investment becomes an associate or a joint venture as required by paragraph 32 of IAS 28. The catch-up adjustment reflects not only the post-acquisition share of profits and other comprehensive income relating to the first tranche, but also the share of the unrecognised fair value adjustments based on the fair values at the date of becoming an associate or a joint venture.

Similar to Approach 2, paragraph 32 of IAS 28 is interpreted to mean that the fair values of the associate's or joint venture's net assets are determined at a date that corresponds to the date at which consideration was given. Therefore, the fair values are determined for each tranche. This may require the fair values to be determined for previous periods when no such exercise was performed at the date of the original purchase.

By including a catch-up adjustment for the post-acquisition changes in the fair values of the underlying net assets relating to the first tranche, this method overcomes the mixed-measurement drawback of Approach 2.

II Applying a fair value (IFRS 3) approach

Where a fair value (IFRS 3) approach is applied to accounting for a step acquisition of an associate or a joint venture, the fair value of the previously held interest at the date that significant influence or joint control is obtained is deemed to be the cost for the initial application of equity accounting. Because the investment should previously be measured at fair value, this means that there is no further change to its carrying value. If the investment was accounted for as an available-for-sale investment under IAS 39, amounts accumulated in equity are reclassified to profit or loss at the date that significant influence is gained. If the investment was accounted for as a 'fair value through profit or loss' investment, any changes from original cost would already be reflected in profit or loss.

Under this approach, consistent with the guidance in IFRS 3 for acquisitions achieved in stages, the calculation of goodwill at the date the investor obtains significant influence or joint control is made only at that date, using information available at that date. Paragraph 42 of IFRS 3 also requires amounts accumulated within equity that were previously recognised in other comprehensive income to be reclassified to profit or loss on the date control is gained.

This fair value (IFRS 3) approach is illustrated in Example 11.7 below. Although the example illustrates the step-acquisition of an associate, the accounting would be the same if the transaction had resulted in the step-acquisition of a joint venture.

Example 11.7: Accounting for existing financial instruments on the step-acquisition of an associate (fair value (IFRS 3) approach)

Using the same information as in Example 11.6 above, under a fair value (IFRS 3) approach to acquisitions in stages, in the consolidated financial statements of the investor, the fair value of the 10% existing interest would be deemed to be part of the cost for the initial application of equity accounting. The 10% existing interest is effectively revalued through profit or loss to $150. Any amount in other comprehensive income relating to this interest would be reclassified to profit or loss. Goodwill would then be calculated as the difference between $375 (the fair value of the existing 10% interest and the cost of the additional 15% interest) and $300 (25% of the fair value of net assets at the date significant influence is attained of $1,200).

It should be noted that the methodology illustrated in Example 11.7 above is, in fact, consistent with the accounting that is required by IAS 28 in the reverse situation i.e. when there is a loss of significant influence in an associate (or loss of joint control in a joint venture), resulting in the discontinuance of the equity method (see 7.12.2 below).

7.4.2.B Step increase in an existing associate or joint venture without a change in status of the investee

An entity may acquire an additional interest in an existing associate that continues to be an associate accounted for under the equity method. Similarly, an entity may acquire an additional interest in an existing joint venture that continues to be a joint venture accounted for under the equity method. IAS 28 does not explicitly deal with such transactions.

In these situations, we believe that the purchase price paid for the additional interest is added to the existing carrying amount of the associate or the joint venture and the existing interest in the associate or joint venture is not remeasured.

This increase in the investment must still be notionally split between goodwill and the additional interest in the fair value of the net assets of the associate or joint venture. This split is based on the fair value of the net assets at the date of the increase in the associate or joint venture. However, no remeasurement is made for previously unrecognised changes in the fair values of identifiable net assets.

The reasons for using the above treatment are discussed further below and the treatment is illustrated in Example 11.8. This differs from that which is required to be applied under IFRS 3 when as a result of an increased investment in an associate or joint venture an investor obtains control over the investee.

IFRS 3 is clear that where an entity acquires an additional interest in an existing associate or joint venture, revaluation of the previously held interests in equity accounted for investments (with recognition of any gain or loss in profit or loss) is required when the investor acquires control of the investee. *[IFRS 3.41-42]*. However, the reason for this treatment is that there is a significant change in the nature of, and economic circumstances surrounding, that investment and it is this that warrants a change in the classification and measurement of that investment. *[IFRS 3.BC384]*.

When an investor increases its ownership interest in an existing associate that remains an associate after that increase, or increases its ownership interest in an existing joint venture that remains a joint venture, there is no significant change in the nature and economic circumstances of the investment. Hence, there is no justification for remeasurement of the existing ownership interest at the time of the increase. Rather the investor applies a cost-accumulation approach that might be applicable when an entity initially applies equity accounting (as discussed at 7.4.2.A above). Approach 1 discussed at 7.4.2.A above is however not appropriate as there was no change in status of the investee. Therefore, the purchase price paid for the additional interest is added to the existing carrying amount of the associate or joint venture and the existing interest in the associate or joint venture is not remeasured.

Paragraph 32 of IAS 28 establishes the requirement that the cost of an investment in an associate or joint venture is allocated to the purchase of a share of the fair value of net assets and the goodwill. This requirement is not limited to the initial application of equity accounting, but applies to each acquisition of an investment. However, this does not result in any revaluation of the existing share of net assets.

Rather, the existing ownership interests are accounted for under paragraphs 10 and 32 of IAS 28, whereby the carrying value is adjusted only for the investor's share of the associate or joint venture's profits or losses and other recognised equity transactions. No entry is recognised to reflect changes in the fair value of assets and liabilities that are not recognised under the accounting policies applied for the associate or joint venture.

Although Example 11.8 below illustrates an increase in ownership of an associate that continues to be an associate, the accounting would be the same if the transaction had been an increase in ownership of a joint venture.

Example 11.8: Accounting for an increase in the ownership of an associate

Entity A obtains significant influence over Entity B by acquiring an investment of 25% at a cost of £3,000 during 2014. At the date of the acquisition of the investment, the fair value of the associate's net identifiable assets is £10,000. The investment is accounted for under the equity method in the consolidated financial statements of Entity A.

In 2016, Entity A acquires an additional investment of 20% in Entity B at a cost of £4,000, increasing its total investment in Entity B to 45%. The investment is, however, still an associate and still accounted for using the equity method of accounting.

For the purposes of the example, directly attributable costs have been ignored and it is assumed that no profit or loss arose during the period since the acquisition of the first 25%. Therefore, the carrying amount of the investment immediately prior to the additional investment is £3,000. However, an asset held by the associate has increased in value by £5,000 so that the fair value of the associate's net identifiable assets is now £15,000.

To summarise, amounts are as follows:

	£
Fair value of net assets of Entity B in 2014	10,000
Increase in fair value	5,000
Fair value of net assets of Entity B in 2016	15,000

As a result of the additional investment, the equity-accounted amount for the associate increases by £4,000. The notional goodwill applicable to the second tranche of the acquisition is £1,000 [£4,000 – (20% × £15,000)].

The impact of the additional investment on Entity A's equity-accounted amount for Entity B is summarised as follows:

	% held	Carrying amount	Share of net assets	Goodwill included in investment
		£	£	£
Existing investment	25	3,000	2,500	500
Additional investment	20	4,000	3,000	1,000
Total investment	45	7,000	5,500	1,500

The accounting described above applies when the additional interest in an existing associate continues to be accounted for as an associate under the equity method or when the additional interest in an existing joint venture continues to be accounted for as a joint venture under the equity method. The accounting for an increase in an associate or a joint venture that becomes a subsidiary is discussed in Chapter 9 at 9.

7.4.2.C Existing associate that becomes a joint venture, or vice versa

In the situations discussed at 7.4.2.B above, the acquisition of the additional interests did not result in a change in status of the investee i.e. the associate remained an associate or the joint venture remained a joint venture. However, an associate may become a joint venture, either by the acquisition of an additional interest, or through a contractual agreement that gives the investor joint control. Equally, in some situations, a contractual agreement may end or part of an interest may be disposed of and a joint venture becomes an associate. In all of these situations, IAS 28 requires that the entity continues to apply the equity method and does not remeasure the retained interest. *[IAS 28.24]*. Therefore, the accounting described in Example 11.8 above would apply.

7.5 Share of the investee

7.5.1 Accounting for potential voting rights

In applying the equity method to a single investment of a specified number of ordinary shares of the investee, the proportionate share of the associate or joint venture to be accounted for will be based on the investor's ownership interest in the ordinary shares.

This will also generally be the case when potential voting rights or other derivatives containing potential voting rights exist in addition to the single investment in the ordinary shares, as IAS 28 states that an entity's interest in an associate or a joint venture is determined solely on the basis of existing ownership interests and does not reflect the possible exercise or conversion of potential voting rights and other derivative instruments. *[IAS 28.12]*.

However, as an exception to this, IAS 28 recognises that in some circumstances, an entity has, in substance, an existing ownership interest as a result of a transaction that currently gives it access to the returns associated with an ownership interest. In such circumstances, the proportion allocated to the entity is determined by taking into account the eventual exercise of those potential voting rights and other derivative instruments that currently give the entity access to the returns. *[IAS 28.13]*. The standard does not provide any example of such circumstances, but an example might be a presently exercisable option over shares in the investee at a fixed price combined with the right to veto any distribution by the investee before the option is exercised or combined with features that adjust the exercise price with respect to dividends paid.

IFRS 9 (or IAS 39) does not apply to interests in associates and joint ventures that are accounted for using the equity method. When instruments containing potential voting rights in substance currently give access to the returns associated with an ownership interest in an associate or a joint venture, the instruments are not subject to IFRS 9 (or IAS 39). In all other cases, instruments containing potential voting rights in an associate or a joint venture are accounted for in accordance with IFRS 9 (or IAS 39). *[IAS 28.14]*. Once the potential voting rights are exercised and the share in the investee increases, the fair value of such instruments at the exercise date is part of the cost to be recognised in accounting for the step increase.

7.5.2 Cumulative preference shares held by parties other than the investor

If an associate or joint venture has outstanding cumulative preference shares that are held by parties other than the investor and that are classified as equity, the investor computes its share of profits or losses after adjusting for the dividends on such shares, whether or not the dividends have been declared. *[IAS 28.37]*.

Although Example 11.9 below illustrates cumulative preference shares issued by an associate, the accounting would be the same if the shares were issued by a joint venture.

Example 11.9: Cumulative preference shares issued by an associate

An entity holds an investment of 30% in the ordinary shares of an associate that has net assets of £200,000 and net profit for the year of £24,500. The associate has issued 5,000 cumulative preference shares with a nominal value of £10 which entitle its holders to a 9% cumulative preference dividend. The cumulative preference shares are classified by the associate as equity in accordance with the requirements of IAS 32 – *Financial Instruments: Presentation*. The associate has not declared dividends on the cumulative preference shares in the past two years.

The investor calculates its share of the associate's net assets and net profit as follows:

	£
Net assets	200,000
9% Cumulative preference shares	(50,000)
Undeclared dividend on cumulative preference shares	
2 years × 9% × £50,000 =	(9,000)
Net assets value attributable to ordinary shareholders	141,000
Investor's 30% share of the net assets	42,300
Net profit for the year	24,500
Share of profit of holders of cumulative preference shares	
9% of £50,000 =	(4,500)
Net profit attributable to ordinary shareholders	20,000
Investor's 30% share of the net profit	6,000

If the investor also owned all of the cumulative preference shares then its share in the net assets of the associate would be £42,300 + £50,000 + £9,000 = £101,300. Its share in the net profit would be £6,000 + £4,500 = £10,500.

7.5.3 Several classes of equity

When an associate or joint venture has a complicated equity structure with several classes of equity shares that have varying entitlements to net profits, equity or liquidation preferences, the investor needs to assess carefully the rights attaching to each class of equity share in determining the appropriate percentage of ownership interest.

7.5.4 Where the reporting entity is a group

A group's share in an associate or joint venture is the aggregate of the holdings in that associate or joint venture by the parent and its subsidiaries. The holdings of the group's other associates or joint ventures are ignored for this purpose. Example 11.10 below illustrates the group's share in an associate where investments are also held by other entities in the group.

Example 11.10: Share in an associate or a joint venture

Parent A holds a 100% investment in subsidiary B, which in turn holds a 25% investment in associate Z. In addition, parent A also holds a 30% investment in associate C and a 50% investment in joint venture D, each of which holds a 10% investment in associate Z.

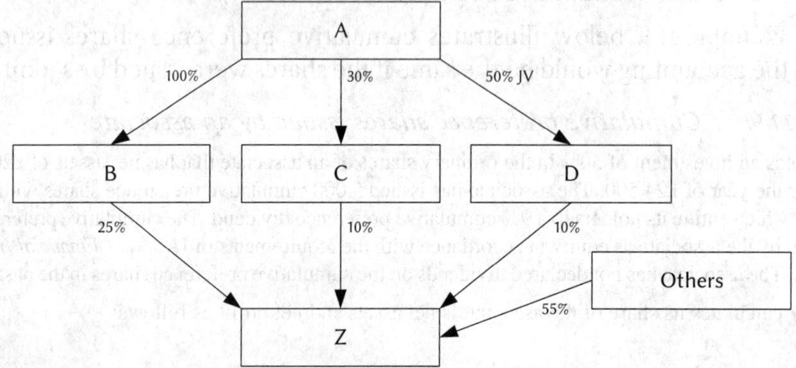

In its consolidated financial statements, parent A accounts for a 25% investment in associate Z under the equity method because:

- the investments in associate Z held by associate C and joint venture D should not be taken into account; and
- parent A fully consolidates the assets of subsidiary B, which include a 25% investment in associate Z.

7.5.5 Where the investee is a group: non-controlling interests in an associate or joint venture's consolidated financial statements

When an associate or joint venture itself has subsidiaries, the profits or losses, other comprehensive income and net assets taken into account in applying the equity method are those recognised in the associate or joint venture's consolidated financial statements, but after any adjustments necessary to give effect to uniform accounting policies (see 7.8 below). *[IAS 28.27]*.

It may be that the associate or joint venture does not own all the shares in some of its subsidiaries, in which case its consolidated financial statements will include non-controlling interests. Under IFRS 10, any non-controlling interests are presented in the consolidated statement of financial position within equity, separately from the equity of the owners of the parent. Profit or loss and each component of other comprehensive income are attributed to the owners of the parent and to the non-controlling interests. *[IFRS 10.22, B94]*. The profit or loss and other comprehensive income reported in the associate or joint venture's consolidated financial statements will include 100% of the amounts relating to the subsidiaries, but the overall profit or loss and total comprehensive income will be split between the amounts attributable to the owners of the parent (i.e. the associate or joint venture) and those attributable to the non-controlling interests. The net assets in the consolidated statement of financial position will also include 100% of the amounts relating to the subsidiaries, with any non-controlling interests in the net assets presented in the consolidated statement of financial position within equity, separately from the equity of the owners of the parent.

IAS 28 does not explicitly say whether the investor should base the accounting for its share of the associate or joint venture's profits, other comprehensive income and net assets under the equity method on the amounts before or after any non-controlling interests in the associate or joint venture's consolidated accounts. However, as the investor's interest in the associate or joint venture is as an owner of the parent, the share is based on the profit or loss, comprehensive income and equity (net assets) that are reported as being attributable to the owners of the parent in the associate or joint venture's consolidated financial statements, i.e. after any amounts attributable to the non-controlling interests. This is consistent with the implementation guidance to IAS 1 – *Presentation of Financial Statements*, where it is indicated that the amounts disclosed for 'share of profits of associates' and 'share of other comprehensive income of associates' represent the amounts 'attributable to owners of the associates, i.e. it is after tax and non-controlling interests in the associates'.[9]

7.6 Transactions between the reporting entity and its associates or joint ventures

7.6.1 Elimination of 'upstream' and 'downstream' transactions

IAS 28 requires gains and losses resulting from what it refers to as 'upstream' and 'downstream' transactions between an entity (including its consolidated subsidiaries) and its associate or joint venture to be recognised in the entity's financial statements only to the extent of unrelated investors' interests in the associate or joint venture. 'Upstream' transactions are, for example, sales of assets from an associate or a joint venture to the investor. 'Downstream' transactions are, for example, sales or contributions of assets from the investor to its associate or its joint venture. The investor's share in the associate's or joint venture's gains or losses resulting from these transactions is eliminated. *[IAS 28.28]*.

IAS 28 is not entirely clear as to how this very generally expressed requirement translates into accounting entries, but we suggest that an appropriate approach might be to proceed as follows:

- in the income statement, the adjustment should be taken against either the investor's profit or the share of the associate's or joint venture's profit, according to whether the investor or the associate or joint venture recorded the profit on the transaction, respectively; and
- in the statement of financial position, the adjustment should be made against the asset which was the subject of the transaction if it is held by the investor or against the carrying amount for the associate or joint venture if the asset is held by the associate or joint venture.

This is consistent with the approach required by IAS 28 in dealing with the elimination of unrealised gains and losses arising on contributions of non-monetary assets to an associate or joint venture in exchange for an equity interest in the associate or joint venture (see 7.6.5 below).

Examples 11.11 and 11.12 below illustrate our suggested approach to this requirement of IAS 28. Both examples deal with the reporting entity H and its 40% associate A. The journal entries are based on the premise that H's financial statements are initially prepared as a simple aggregation of H and the relevant share of its associates. The entries below would then be applied to the numbers at that stage of the process. Although these examples illustrate transactions between the reporting entity and an associate, the accounting would be the same if the transactions occurred between the reporting entity and a joint venture.

Example 11.11: Elimination of profit on sale by investor to associate ('downstream transaction')

One month before its reporting date, H sells inventory costing £750,000 to A for £1 million. Within the first month after the reporting date, A sells the inventory to a third party for £1.2 million. What adjustments are made in the group financial statements of H before and after the reporting date?

Before the reporting date, H has recorded revenue of £1 million and cost of sales of £750,000. However since, at the reporting date, the inventory is still held by A, only 60% of this transaction is regarded by IAS 28 as having taken place (in effect with the other shareholders of A). This is reflected by the equity-accounting entry:

	£	£
Revenue	400,000	
Cost of sales		300,000
Investment in A		100,000

This effectively defers recognition of 40% of the profit on sale (£250,000 × 40%) and offsets the deferred profit against the carrying amount of H's investment in A.

After the reporting date, when the inventory is sold on by A, this deferred profit can be released by H, reflected by the following equity-accounting entry:

	£	£
Opening reserves	100,000	
Cost of sales	300,000	
Revenue		400,000

Opening reserves are adjusted because the financial statement working papers (if prepared as assumed above) will already include this profit in opening reserves, since it forms part of H's opening reserves.

An alternative approach would be to eliminate the profit on 40% of the sale against the cost of sales. Before the reporting date, this is reflected by the equity-accounting entry:

	£	£
Cost of sales	100,000	
Investment in A		100,000

After the reporting date, when the inventory is sold on by A, this deferred profit can be released by H, reflected by the following equity-accounting entry:

	£	£
Opening reserves	100,000	
Cost of sales		100,000

An argument in favour of the alternative approach is that the revenue figures should not be adjusted because the sales to associates or joint ventures need to be disclosed as related party transactions. However, this may be outweighed by the drawback of the approach, namely that it causes volatility in H's reported gross margin as revenue and the related net margin are not necessarily recognised in the same accounting period.

Example 11.12: Elimination of profit on sale by associate to reporting entity ('upstream transaction')

This is the mirror image of the transaction in Example 11.11 above. Before H's reporting date, A sells inventory costing £750,000 to H for £1,000,000. After the reporting date, H sells the inventory to a third party for £1.2 million. What adjustments are made in the group financial statements of H before and after the reporting date?

H's share of the profit of A as included on the financial statement working papers before the reporting date will include a profit of £250,000 (£1,000,000 – £750,000), 40% of which (£100,000) is regarded under IAS 28 as unrealised by H, and is therefore deferred and offset against closing inventory:

	£	£
Share of profit of A	100,000	
Inventory		100,000

In the following period when the inventory is sold H's separate financial statements will record a profit of £200,000, which must be increased by the £100,000 deferred from the previous period. The entry is:

	£	£
Opening reserves	100,000	
Share of profit of A		100,000

Again, opening reserves are adjusted because the financial statement working papers (if prepared as assumed above) will already include this profit in opening reserves, this time, however, as part of H's share of the opening reserves of A.

A slightly counter-intuitive consequence of this treatment is that at the reporting date the investment in A in H's consolidated statement of financial position will have increased by £100,000 more than the share of profit of associates as reported in group profit or loss (and in the following period by £100,000 less). This is because the statement of financial position adjustment at the reporting date is made against inventory rather than the carrying value of the investment in A, which could be seen as reflecting the fact that A has, indeed, made a profit. It might therefore be necessary to indicate in the notes to the financial statements that part of the profit made by A is regarded as unrealised by the group and has therefore been deferred to the following reporting period by offsetting it against inventory.

It may be that a transaction between an investor and its associate or joint venture indicates a reduction in the net realisable value or an impairment loss of the asset that is the subject of the transaction. IAS 28 requires that when downstream transactions

Chapter 11

provide evidence of a reduction in the net realisable value of the assets to be sold or contributed, or of an impairment loss of those assets, those losses shall be recognised in full by the investor. When upstream transactions provide evidence of a reduction in the net realisable value of the assets to be purchased or of an impairment loss of those assets, the investor shall recognise its share in those losses. *[IAS 28.29].*

The effect of these requirements is illustrated in Examples 11.13 and 11.14 below. Although these examples illustrate transactions between the reporting entity and a joint venture, the accounting would be the same if the transactions occurred between the reporting entity and an associate.

Example 11.13: Sale of asset from venturer to joint venture at a loss

Two entities A and B establish a joint arrangement involving the creation of a joint venture C in which A and B each hold 50%. A and B each contribute €5 million in cash to the joint venture in exchange for equity shares. C then uses €8 million of its €10 million cash to acquire from A a property recorded in the financial statements of A at €10 million. €8 million is agreed to be the fair market value of the property. How should A account for these transactions?

The required accounting entry by A is as follows:

	€m	€m
Cash (1)	3	
Investment in C (2)	5	
Loss on sale (3)	2	
Property (4)		10

(1) €8 million received from C less €5 million contributed to C.

(2) Represented by 50% of C's cash €2 million (€10 million from A and B minus €8 million to A), plus 50% of €8 million (carrying value of the property in books of C), not adjusted since the transaction indicated an impairment of A's asset.

(3) Loss on sale of property €2 million (€8 million received from C less €10 million carrying value = €2 million) not adjusted since the transaction indicated an impairment of the property. In effect, it is the result that would have been obtained if A had recognised an impairment charge immediately prior to the sale and then recognised no gain or loss on the sale.

(4) Derecognition of A's original property.

Example 11.14: Sale of asset from joint venture to venturer at a loss

Two entities A and B establish a joint arrangement involving the creation of a joint venture C in which A and B each hold 50%. A and B each contribute €5 million in cash to the joint venture in exchange for equity shares. C then uses €8 million of its €10 million cash to acquire a property from an independent third party D. The property is then sold to A for €7 million settled in cash, which is agreed to be its market value. How should A account for these transactions?

The required accounting entry by A is as follows:

	€m	€m
Property (1)	7.0	
Investment in C (2)	4.5	
Share of loss of C (3)	0.5	
Cash (4)		12.0

(1) €7 million paid to C not adjusted since the transaction indicated an impairment of C's asset.

(2) Represented by 50% of C's cash €9 million (€10 million from A and B minus €8 million to D plus €7 million received from A).

(3) Loss in C's books is €1 million (€8 million cost of property less €7 million proceeds of sale). A recognises its 50% share because the transaction indicates an impairment of the asset. In effect, it is the result that would have been obtained if C had recognised an impairment charge immediately prior to the sale and then recognised no gain or loss on the sale.

(4) €5 million cash contributed to C plus €7 million consideration for property.

7.6.1.A Elimination of 'downstream' unrealised profits in excess of the investment

Occasionally an investor's share of the unrealised profit on the sale of an asset to an associate or a joint venture exceeds the carrying value of the investment held. In that case, to what extent is any profit in excess of the carrying value of the investment eliminated?

IAS 28 is unclear about the elimination of 'downstream' unrealised gains in excess of the investment. Consequently, the Interpretations Committee received a request asking for clarification of the accounting treatment when the amount of gains to eliminate in a 'downstream' transaction in accordance with paragraph 28 of IAS 28 exceeds the amount of the entity's interest in the joint venture. The request specifically asked whether:

- the gain from the transaction should be eliminated only to the extent that it does not exceed the carrying amount of the entity's interest in the joint venture; or
- the remaining gain in excess of the carrying amount of the entity's interest in the joint venture should also be eliminated and if so, what it should be eliminated against.

The Interpretations Committee determined that the entity should eliminate the gain from a 'downstream' transaction to the extent of the related investor's interest in the joint venture, even if the gain to be eliminated exceeds the carrying amount of the entity's interest in the joint venture, as required by paragraph 28 of IAS 28. Any eliminated gain that is in excess of the carrying amount of the entity's interest in the joint venture should be recognised as deferred income.[10] In July 2013, the IASB tentatively agreed with the views of the Interpretations Committee and directed the staff to draft amendments to IAS 28.[11] However, in June 2015, the IASB tentatively decided to defer further work on this topic to the equity accounting research project. This is discussed further at 11 below.

Considering the missing guidance in IAS 28 we believe that, until the IASB issues an amendment to IAS 28, the investor can either recognise the excess as 'deferred income' or restrict the elimination to the amount required to reduce the investment to zero. The treatment chosen is based on the investor's accounting policy choice for dealing with other situations where IAS 28 is unclear, reflecting whether the investor considers the equity method of accounting to be primarily a method of consolidation or a method of valuing an investment. The investor should apply a consistent accounting policy to such situations.

Example 11.15: Elimination of downstream unrealised profits in excess of the investment

An investor has a 40% investment in an associate, which it carries in its statement of financial position at €800,000. The investor sells a property to the associate in exchange for cash, which results in a profit of €3 million. After the sale, 40% of that profit (i.e. €1.2 million) is unrealised from the investor's perspective.

The two approaches for determining to what extent a profit in excess of the carrying value of the investment should be eliminated are as follows:

Method of consolidation approach – excess of the unrealised profit over the carrying value of the investment recognised as 'deferred income'

This approach gives precedence to the requirements in paragraph 26 of IAS 28, which is also consistent with the general requirement to apply IFRS 10 consolidation elimination principles. *[IAS 28.26]*. Although paragraph 38 of IAS 28 requires an investor to discontinue application of the equity method when an investor's share of losses equals or exceeds its interest in the associate (see 7.9 below), *[IAS 28.38]*, the elimination does not represent a real 'loss' to the investor but is simply the non-recognition of a gain as a result of normal consolidation principles. Therefore, paragraph 38 of IAS 28 is subordinate to the requirement to eliminate unrealised profits.

Accordingly, the investor eliminates the investor's total share of the unrealised profit against the carrying amount of the investment in the associate until reaching zero, recognising the excess as a 'deferred income' or similar balance, as follows:

	€	€
Profit on sale of property	1,200,000	
Investment in associate		800,000
'Deferred income'		400,000

This leaves a net profit of €1.8 million recognised in the consolidated financial statements. The investor recognises deferred income as the asset or the investment in the associate is realised (e.g. upon disposal of the investor's investment in the associate, or upon the disposal or depreciation of the asset by the associate.

Method of valuing investment approach – restricts the elimination to the amount required to reduce the investment to zero

This approach views the requirements of paragraph 38 of IAS 28 as taking precedence over the requirements of paragraph 28 of IAS 28 to eliminate unrealised profits from a transaction between the investor and the associate. The elimination of the full amount of the share of unrealised profit effectively results in the recognition of a 'loss' to the investor. Furthermore, by deferring the 'loss', the investor is effectively recognising a negative investment balance, which is not permitted or required under IAS 28 when the investor does not have any further legal or constructive obligations in relation to the asset or the associate.

Accordingly, if the investor does not have any further legal or constructive obligations in relation to the asset or the associate, no liability exists and no further profit is deferred. The investor eliminates the unrealised profit to the extent that it reduces the carrying value of the investment to zero, as follows:

	€	€
Profit on sale of property	800,000	
Investment in associate		800,000

This leaves a net profit of €2.2 million recognised in the consolidated financial statements. The investor does not recognise further profits in the associate until they exceed the unrecognised unrealised profits of €400,000.

7.6.1.B Transactions between associates and/or joint ventures

When transactions take place between associates and/or joint ventures, which are accounted for under the equity method, we believe the investor should apply the requirements of IAS 28 and IFRS 10 by analogy and eliminate its share of any unrealised profits or losses. *[IAS 28.26, 29, IFRS 10.B86]*.

Example 11.16: Elimination of profits and losses resulting from transactions between associates and/or joint ventures

Entity H has a 25% interest in associate A and a 30% interest in joint venture B.

During the reporting period, associate A sold inventory costing £1.0 million to joint venture B for £1.2 million. All of inventory remains on B's statement of financial position at the end of the reporting period.

Entity H eliminates £15,000 (i.e. 30% × 25% × £200,000) as its share of the profits that is unrealised.

Although paragraph 29 of IAS 28 only refers to upstream and downstream transactions between an investor and its associate or its joint venture, we consider this to be an illustration of the of typical transactions to be eliminated as a result of the requirements of paragraph 26 of IAS 28 that 'Many of the procedures that are appropriate for the application of the equity method are similar to the consolidation procedures described in IFRS 10', and are not the only situations to be eliminated by this principle. Therefore, applying the same principles in paragraph 29 of IAS 28 and paragraph B86 of IFRS 10, the unrealised profit in the investor's financial statements arising from any transaction between the associates (and/or joint ventures) is eliminated to the extent of the related investor's interests in the associates (and/or joint ventures) as appropriate.

In practice, however, it may be difficult to determine whether such transactions have taken place.

7.6.2 Reciprocal interests

Reciprocal interests (or 'cross-holdings') arise when an associate itself holds an investment in the reporting entity. It is unlikely that a joint venture would hold an investment in the reporting entity but, in the event that it did, the discussion below would apply equally to such a situation.

7.6.2.A Reciprocal interests in reporting entity accounted for under the equity method by the associate

Where the associate's investment in the reporting entity is such that the associate in turn has significant influence over the reporting entity and accounts for that investment under the equity method, a literal interpretation of paragraph 27 of IAS 28 is that an investor records its share of an associate's profits and net assets, including the associate's equity accounted profits and net assets of its investment in the investor. The reciprocal interests can therefore give rise to a measure of double counting of profits and net assets between the investor and its associate. Paragraph 26 of IAS 28 states that many of the procedures appropriate for the application of the equity method are similar to the consolidation procedures described in IFRS 10. Therefore, the requirement in paragraph B86 of IFRS 10 to eliminate intragroup balances, transactions, income and expenses should be applied by analogy. *[IAS 28.26, IFRS 10.B86]*.

Neither IFRS 10 nor IAS 28 explains how an entity should go about eliminating the double counting that arises from reciprocal holdings. We believe that a direct holding only (or net approach) is applicable, whereby the profit of the investor is calculated by adding its direct investment in the associate to its trading profits, as shown in Example 11.17.

Example 11.17: Elimination of equity-accounted reciprocal interests[12]

Entity A has a 40% equity interest in entity B and conversely, entity B has a 30% interest in entity A. How should entity A and entity B account for their reciprocal investment?

The structure of the reciprocal holdings is shown in the diagram below:

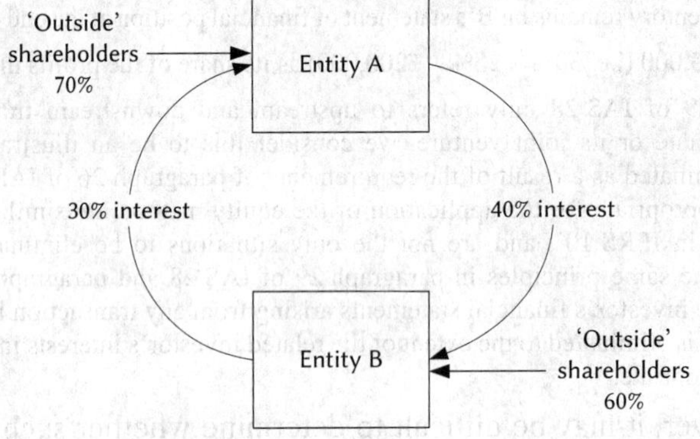

Entity A	
Share in equity of B	40%
Shares in A held by 'outside' shareholders	70%
Trading profit of A (before share in profit of B)	€60,000
Net assets of A (before share in net assets of B)	€600,000
Number of shares in issue	100,000
Entity B	
Share in equity of A	30%
Shares in B held by 'outside' shareholders	60%
Trading profit of B (before share in profit of A)	€110,000
Net assets of B (before share in net assets of A)	€1,100,000
Number of shares in issue	40,000

Income

The profit for the period is calculated by adding the direct interest in the associate's profit:

Profit entity A = €60,000 + 40% × trading profit entity B = €60,000 + 40% × €110,000 = €104,000

Profit entity B = €110,000 + 30% × trading profit entity A = €110,000 + 30% × €60,000 = €128,000

Statement of financial position

A similar approach can be applied to calculate the net assets of A and B:

Net assets of A including share in B without eliminations = €600,000 + 40% × €1,100,000 = €1,040,000

Net assets of B including share in A without eliminations = €1,100,000 + 30% × €600,000 = €1,280,000

Earnings per share

The profits related to the reciprocal interests have been ignored. Therefore, in calculating the earnings per share it is necessary to adjust the number of shares to eliminate the reciprocal holdings: For entity A it can be argued that it indirectly owns 40% of B's 30% interest, i.e. entity A indirectly owns 12% (= 40% × 30%) of its own shares. Those shares should therefore be treated as being equivalent to 'treasury shares' and be ignored for the purposes of the EPS calculation.

Number of A shares after elimination of 'treasury shares' = 100,000 × (100% – 12%) = 88,000 shares

While entity B indirectly owns 30% of A's 40% interest, i.e. entity B indirectly owns 12% (= 30% × 40%) of its own shares.

Number of B shares after elimination of 'treasury shares' = 40,000 × (100% – 12%) = 35,200 shares

The earnings per share for the shareholders of A and B should be calculated as follows:

Earnings per share A = €104,000 ÷ 88,000 = €1.18

Earnings per share B = €128,000 ÷ 35,200 = €3.64

The earnings per share is equivalent to the hypothetical dividend per share in the case of full distribution of all profits.

Conclusion

This method takes up the investor's share of the associate's profits excluding the equity income arising on the reciprocal shareholdings and only eliminates the effects of an entity's indirect investment in its own shares. The financial statements therefore reflect both the interests of the 'outside' shareholders and the interests that B shareholders have in A. It is worthwhile noting that the combined underlying trading profit of A and B is only €170,000 (i.e. €60,000 + €110,000), whereas their combined reported profit is €232,000 (i.e. €104,000 + €128,000). Similarly, the combined underlying net assets of A and B are only €1,700,000, whereas the combined reported net assets are €2,320,000.

The elimination of reciprocal interests was discussed by the Interpretations Committee in August 2002. The Interpretations Committee agreed not to require publication of an Interpretation on this issue, but did state that 'like the consolidation procedures applied when a subsidiary is consolidated, the equity method requires reciprocal interests to be eliminated.'[13]

7.6.2.B Reciprocal interests in reporting entity not accounted for under the equity method by the associate

In some situations the associate's investment in the reporting entity is such that the associate does not have significant influence over the reporting entity and accounts for that investment under IFRS 9 (or IAS 39), either as at fair value through other comprehensive income (or available-for-sale financial asset in terms of IAS 39) or at fair value through profit or loss. Although the associate is not applying the equity method, the reciprocal interest can still give rise to a measure of double counting of profits and net assets between the investor and its associate when the investor accounts for its share of the profits and net assets of the associate. Again, paragraph 26 of IAS 28 states that many of the procedures appropriate for the application of the equity method are similar to the consolidation procedures described in IFRS 10. Therefore, the requirement in paragraph B86 of IFRS 10 to eliminate intragroup balances, transactions, income and expenses should be applied by analogy. Accordingly, in our view, the investor eliminates income from the associate's investment in the investor, in the investor's equity accounting. This elimination includes dividends and changes in fair value recognised either in profit or loss or other comprehensive income.

Example 11.18: Elimination of reciprocal interests not accounted for under the equity method

Investor A has a 20% interest in an Associate B. Associate B has a 10% interest in A, which does not give rise to significant influence.

Scenario 1

Associate B recognises a profit of $1,300 for the year, which includes a dividend of $100 received from Investor A and a gain of $200 from measuring its investment in Investor A at fair value through profit or loss.

In this scenario, Investor A's equity method share of Associate B's profit and loss is $200, being 20% of Associate B's profit of $1,000 after excluding income (dividend of $100 plus fair value gain of $200) on its investment in Investor A.

Scenario 2

Associate B recognises a profit of $1,100 for the year, which includes a dividend of $100 received from Investor A, and recognises $200 in other comprehensive income from measuring its investment in Investor A as an available-for sale financial asset.

In this scenario, Investor A's equity method share of Associate B's profit and loss is $200, being 20% of Associate B's profit of $1,000 after excluding income (dividend of $100) on its investment in Investor A. Investor A's share of Associate B's other comprehensive income also excludes the gain of $200 recognised in other comprehensive income arising from its investment in Investor A.

7.6.3 Loans and borrowings between the reporting entity and its associates or joint ventures

The requirement in IAS 28 to eliminate partially unrealised profits or losses on transactions with associates or joint ventures is expressed in terms of transactions involving the transfer of assets. In our view, the requirement for partial elimination of profits does not apply to items such as interest paid on loans and borrowings between the reporting entity and its associates or joint ventures, since such loans and borrowings do not involve the transfer of assets giving rise to gains or losses. Moreover, they are not normally regarded as part of the investor's share of the net assets of the associate or joint venture, but as separate transactions, except in the case of loss-making associates or joint ventures, where interests in long-term loans and borrowings may be required to be accounted for as if they were part of the reporting entity's equity investment in determining the carrying value of the associate or joint venture against which losses may be offset (see 7.9 below). Likewise, loans and borrowings between the reporting entity and its associates or joint ventures should not be eliminated in the reporting entity's consolidated accounts because the respective assets and liabilities of associates and joint ventures are not recognised by the group.

However, if the associate or joint venture has capitalised the borrowing costs then the investor would need to eliminate a relevant share of its interest income and realise it as the associate depreciates the qualifying asset. The same principle applies to eliminate a share of the capitalised management or advisory fees charged to an associate or joint venture.

7.6.4 Statement of cash flows

In the statement of cash flows (whether in the consolidated or separate financial statements) no adjustment is made in respect of the cash flows relating to transactions with associates or joint ventures. This contrasts with the requirement, in any consolidated statement of cash flows, to eliminate the cash flows between members of the group in the same way that intragroup transactions are eliminated in the profit and loss account and statement of financial position.

7.6.5 Contributions of non-monetary assets to an associate or a joint venture

It is fairly common for an entity to create or change its interest in an associate or a joint venture by contributing some of the entity's existing non-monetary assets to that associate or joint venture. This raises a number of issues as to how such transactions should be accounted for, in particular whether they should be accounted for at book value or fair value.

IAS 28 requires the contribution of a non-monetary asset to an associate or a joint venture in exchange for an equity interest in the associate or joint venture to be accounted for in accordance with paragraph 28, except when the contribution lacks commercial substance, as described in IAS 16 (see 7.6.5.A below and Chapter 18 at 4.4). *[IAS 28.30].* Paragraph 28 requires gains and losses resulting from transactions between an entity and its associate or joint venture to be recognised only to the extent of unrelated interests in the associate or joint venture. The investor's share in the associate's or joint venture's gains or losses resulting from those transactions is eliminated (see 7.6.1 above for a discussion of the requirements relating to such transactions). However, there is a conflict between the requirements of IAS 28 and the requirements in IFRS 10 relating to accounting for the loss of control of a subsidiary, when a subsidiary is contributed by the investor to an associate or joint venture, and control over the subsidiary is consequently lost. This is discussed below at 7.6.5.C below.

If such a contribution lacks commercial substance, the gain or loss is regarded as unrealised and is not recognised unless paragraph 31 also applies. Such unrealised gains and losses are to be eliminated against the investment accounted for using the equity method and are not to be presented as deferred gains or losses in the entity's consolidated statement of financial position or in the entity's statement of financial position in which investments are accounted for using the equity method. *[IAS 28.30].* Where 'unrealised' losses are eliminated in this way, the effect will be to apply what is sometimes referred to as 'asset swap' accounting. In other words, the carrying value of the investment in the associate or joint venture will be the same as the carrying value of the non-monetary assets transferred in exchange for it, subject of course to any necessary provision for impairment uncovered by the transaction.

If, in addition to receiving an equity interest in an associate or a joint venture, an entity receives monetary or non-monetary assets, the entity recognises in full in profit or loss the portion of the gain or loss on the non-monetary contribution relating to the monetary or non-monetary assets received. *[IAS 28.31].*

7.6.5.A 'Commercial substance'

As noted above, IAS 28 requires that a transaction should not be treated as realised when it lacks commercial substance as described in IAS 16. That standard states that an exchange of assets has 'commercial substance' if:

(a) the configuration (risk, timing and amount) of the cash flows of the asset received differs from the configuration of the cash flows of the asset transferred; or

(b) the entity-specific value of the portion of the entity's operations affected by the transaction changes as a result of the exchange; and

(c) the difference in (a) or (b) above is significant relative to the fair value of the assets exchanged. *[IAS 16.25].*

IAS 16's 'commercial substance' test is designed to enable an entity to measure, with reasonable objectivity, whether the asset that it has acquired in a non-monetary exchange is different to the asset it has given up.

The first stage is to determine the cash flows both of the asset given up and of the asset acquired (the latter being the interest in the associate or joint venture). This determination may be sufficient by itself to satisfy (a) above, as it may be obvious that there are significant differences in the configuration of the cash flows. The type of income may have changed. For example, if the entity contributed a non-monetary asset such as a property or intangible asset to the associate or joint venture, the reporting entity may now be receiving a rental or royalty stream from the associate or joint venture, whereas previously the asset contributed to the cash flows of the cash-generating unit of which it was a part.

However, determining the cash flows may not result in a clear-cut conclusion, in which case the entity-specific value will have to be calculated. This is not the same as a value in use calculation under IAS 36 – *Impairment of Assets*, in that the entity is allowed to use a discount rate based on its own assessment of the risks specific to the operations, not those that reflect current market assessments, *[IAS 16.BC22]*, and post-tax cash flows. *[IAS 16.25]*. The transaction will have commercial substance if these entity-specific values are not only different to one another but also significant compared to the fair values of the assets exchanged.

The calculation may not be highly sensitive to the discount rate as the same rate is used to calculate the entity-specific value of both the asset surrendered and the entity's interest in the associate or joint venture. However, if the entity considers that a high discount rate is appropriate, this will have an impact on whether or not the difference is significant relative to the fair value of the assets exchanged. It is also necessary to consider the significance of:

(a) the requirement above that the entity should recognise in its income statement the portion of any gain or loss arising on the transfer attributable to the other investors;
(b) the general requirements of IAS 28 in respect of transactions between investors and their associates or joint ventures; and
(c) the general requirement of IFRS 3 to recognise assets acquired in a business combination at fair value (see Chapter 9 at 5).

As a result, we consider that it is likely that transactions entered into with genuine commercial purposes in mind are likely to pass the 'commercial substance' tests outlined above.

7.6.5.B Contributions of non-monetary assets – practical application

IAS 28 does not give an example of the accounting treatment that it envisages when a gain is treated as 'realised'. We believe that the intended approach is that set out in Example 11.19 below. In essence, this approach reflects the fact that the reporting entity has:

(a) acquired an interest in an associate or joint venture that must be accounted for at fair value under IFRS 3; but

(b) is required by IAS 28 to restrict any gain arising as a result of the exchange relating to its own assets to the extent that the gain is attributable to the other investor in the associate or joint venture. This leads to an adjustment of the carrying amount of the assets of the associate or joint venture.

In Example 11.19 below, we consider the accounting by party A to the transaction where the non-monetary assets it has contributed are intangible assets. On the other hand, party B has contributed an interest in a subsidiary. In some transactions, particularly the formation of joint ventures, both parties may contribute interests in subsidiaries. The requirements in IFRS 10 relating to the accounting for loss of control of a subsidiary are inconsistent with the accounting required by IAS 28, as discussed at 7.6.5.C below. Although Example 11.19 below is based on a transaction resulting in the formation of a joint venture, the accounting treatment by party A would be the same if it had obtained an interest in an associate.

Example 11.19: Contribution of non-monetary assets to form a joint venture

A and B are two major pharmaceutical companies, which agree to form a joint venture (JV Co). A will own 40% of the joint venture, and B 60%. The total fair value of the new business of JV Co is £250 million.

A's contribution to the venture is a number of intangible assets, in respect of which A's consolidated statement of financial position reflects a carrying amount of £60 million. The fair value of the intangible assets contributed by A is considered to be £100 million, i.e. equivalent to 40% of the total fair value of JV Co of £250 million.

B contributes a subsidiary, in respect of which B's consolidated statement of financial position reflects separable net assets of £85 million and goodwill of £15 million. The fair value of the separable net assets is considered to be £120 million. The fair value of the business contributed is £150 million (60% of total fair value of JV Co of £250 million).

The book and fair values of the assets/businesses contributed by A and B can therefore be summarised as follows:

	A		B	
(in £m)	Book value	Fair value	Book value	Fair value
Intangible assets	60	100		
Separable net assets			85	120
Goodwill			15	30
Total	60	100	100	150

How should A apply IAS 28 in accounting for the set-up of the joint venture?

The general principles of IFRS 3 require that A should account at fair value for the acquisition of its 40% interest in the new venture. However, as noted above, any gain or loss recognised by A must reflect only the extent to which it has disposed of the assets to the other partners in the venture (i.e. in this case, 60% – the extent to which A's intangible assets are effectively transferred to B through B's 60% interest in the new venture).

This gives rise to the following accounting entry.

	£m	£m
Share of net assets of JV Co (1)	72	
Goodwill (2)	12	
Intangible assets contributed to JV Co (3)		60
Gain on disposal (4)		24

(1) 40% of fair value of separable net assets (including A's intangible assets) of new entity £88 million (40% of [£100 million + £120 million] as in table above) less elimination of 40% of gain on disposal £16 million (40% of £40 million, being the difference between the book value [£60 million] and fair value [£100 million] of A's intangible assets, as in table above, contributed to JV Co) = £72 million.

This is equivalent to, and perhaps more easily calculated as, 40% of [book value of A's intangible assets + fair value of B's separable net assets], i.e. 40% × [£60 million + £120 million] = £72 million.

Under the equity method, this £72 million together with the £12 million of goodwill (see (2) below) would be included as the equity accounted amount of JV Co.

(2) Fair value of consideration given £100 million (as in table above) less fair value of 40% share of separable net assets of JV Co acquired £88 million (see (1) above) = £12 million.

This is equivalent to, and perhaps more easily calculated as, 40% of the fair value of B's goodwill, i.e. 40% × £30 million = £12 million.

Under the equity method, as noted at (1) above, this £12 million together with the £72 million relating to the separable net assets would be included as the equity accounted amount of JV Co.

(3) Previous carrying amount of intangible assets contributed by A, now deconsolidated.

(4) Fair value of business acquired £100 million (40% of £250 million) less book value of intangible assets disposed of £60 million (as in table above) = £40 million, less 40% of gain eliminated (£16 million) = £24 million. The £16 million eliminated reduces A's share of JV Co's separable net assets by £16 million (see (1) above).

It is common when joint ventures are set up in this way for the fair value of the assets contributed not to be exactly in proportion to the fair values of the venturers' agreed relative shares. Cash 'equalisation' payments are then made between the venturers so that the overall financial position of the venturer does correspond to the agreed relative shares in the venture. Our suggested treatment of such payments in the context of a transaction within the scope of IAS 28 is illustrated in Example 11.20 below. Although the example is based on a transaction resulting in the formation of a joint venture, the accounting treatment by party A would be the same if it had obtained an interest in an associate.

Example 11.20: Contribution of non-monetary assets to form a joint venture with cash equalisation payment between venturers/investors

Suppose that the transaction in Example 11.19 was varied so that A is to have only a 36% interest in JV Co. However, as shown by the introductory table in Example 11.19, A is contributing intangible assets worth 40% of the total fair value of JV Co. Accordingly, B makes good the shortfall by making a cash payment to A equivalent to 4% of the fair value of JV Co, i.e. £10 million (4% of £250 million).

This would require A to make the following accounting entries.

	£m	£m
Share of net assets of JV Co (1)	64.8	
Cash (equalisation payment from B)	10.0	
Goodwill (2)	10.8	
Intangible assets contributed to JV Co (3)		60.0
Gain on disposal (4)		25.6

(1) 36% of fair value of separable net assets of new entity £79.2 million (36% of [£100 million + £120 million] as in table in Example 11.19 above) less elimination of 36% of gain on disposal £14.4 million (36% of £40 million, being the difference between the book value [£60 million] and fair value [£100 million] of A's intangible assets, as in table in Example 11.19 above, contributed to JV Co) = £64.8 million.

This is equivalent to, and perhaps more easily calculated as, 36% of [book value of A's intangible assets + fair value of B's separable net assets], i.e. 36% × [£60 million + £120 million] = £64.8 million.

Under the equity method, this £64.8 million together with the £10.8 million of goodwill (see (2) below) would be included as the equity accounted amount of JV Co.

(2) Fair value of consideration given £100 million (as in table in Example 11.19 above), less cash equalisation payment received £10 million = £90 million less fair value of 36% share of separable net assets of JV Co acquired £79.2 million (see (1) above) = £10.8 million.

This is equivalent to, and perhaps more easily calculated as, 36% of the fair value of B's goodwill], i.e. 36% × £30 million = £10.8 million.

Under the equity method, as noted at (1) above, this £10.8 million together with the £64.8 million relating to the separable net assets would be included as the equity accounted amount of JV Co.

(3) Previous carrying amount of intangible assets contributed by A, now deconsolidated.

(4) Fair value of business acquired £90 million (36% of £250 million) plus cash equalisation payment £10 million = £100 million, less book value of intangible assets disposed of £60 million (as in table in Example 11.19 above) = £40 million, less 36% of gain eliminated (£14.4 million) = £25.6 million. The £14.4 million eliminated reduces A's share of JV Co's separable net assets by £14.4 million (see (1) above).

I 'Artificial' transactions

A concern with transactions such as this is that it is the relative, rather than the absolute, value of the transaction that is of concern to the parties. In other words, in Example 11.19 above, it could be argued that the only clear inference that can be drawn is that A and B have agreed that the ratio of the fair values of the assets/businesses they have each contributed is 40:60, rather than that the business as a whole is worth £250 million. Thus it might be open to A and B, without altering the substance of the transaction, to assert that the value of the combined operations is £500 million (with a view to enlarging their net assets) or £200 million (with a view to increasing future profitability).

Another way in which the valuation of the transaction might be distorted is through disaggregation of the consideration. Suppose that the £60 million net assets contributed by A in Example 11.19 above comprised:

	£m
Cash	12
Intangible assets	48
	60

Further suppose that, for tax reasons, the transaction was structured such that A was issued with 4% of the shares of JV Co in exchange for the cash and 36% in exchange for the intangible assets. This could lead to the suggestion that, as there can be no doubt as to the fair value of the cash, A's entire investment must be worth £120 million (i.e. £12 million × 40 / 4). Testing transactions for their commercial substance will require entities to focus on the fair value of the transaction as a whole and not to follow the strict legal form.

Of course, once cash equalisation payments are introduced, as in Example 11.20 above, the transaction terms may provide evidence as to both the relative and absolute fair values of the assets contributed by each party.

II Accounting for the acquisition of a business on formation of a joint venture

IFRS 3 does not apply to business combinations that arise on the formation of a joint venture. *[IFRS 3.2(a)]*. Therefore, it is not clear under IFRS how the acquisition by JV Co of the former business of B in Example 11.20 above should be accounted for. Indeed, it could also have been the case that A had also contributed a subsidiary, and JV Co would have to account for the former businesses of both A and B. We consider that under the GAAP hierarchy in IAS 8 – *Accounting Policies, Changes in Accounting Estimates and Errors* – the pooling of interests method is still available when accounting for the businesses acquired on the formation of a joint venture and there may be other approaches (including the acquisition method) that will be considered to give a fair presentation in particular circumstances.

Where a new company is formed to create a joint venture and both venturers contribute a business, we believe that it would also be acceptable under the GAAP hierarchy in paragraph 11 of IAS 8 (see Chapter 3 at 4.3) to apply the acquisition method to both businesses, as IFRS does not prevent entities from doing this and it provides useful information to investors. However, in this case, the entity should ensure the disclosures made are sufficient for users of the financial statements to fully understand the transaction.

If JV Co were to apply the acquisition method it could mean that the amounts taken up in the financial statements of B may bear little relation to its share of the net assets of the joint venture as reported in the underlying financial statements of the investee. This would be the case if B accounted for the transaction by applying IAS 28 rather than IFRS 10 (see 7.6.5.C below). For example, B's share of any amortisation charge recorded by JV Co must be based on the carrying amount of B's share of JV Co's intangible assets, not as recorded in JV Co's books (i.e. at fair value) but as recorded in B's books, which will be based on book value for intangible assets contributed by B and at fair value for intangible assets contributed by A. Accordingly it may be necessary for B to keep a 'memorandum' set of books for consolidation purposes reflecting its share of assets originally its own at book value and those originally of A at fair value. The same would apply to A if it had also contributed a subsidiary. In any event, in Example 11.20 above, JV Co will have to account for the intangibles contributed by A at fair value as the transaction represents a share-based payment transaction in terms of IFRS 2 – *Share-based Payment*. Therefore, A will need to keep a 'memorandum' record relating to these intangibles, so that it can make the necessary consolidation adjustments to reflect amortisation charges based on its original book values.

Alternatively, if JV Co were to apply the pooling of interest method, A would need to keep a 'memorandum' set of books for consolidation purposes because its share of assets that were originally those of B should be carried at fair value rather than carry-over cost.

7.6.5.C Conflict between IAS 28 and IFRS 10

In Example 11.19 above, we considered the accounting by party A to the transaction where the non-monetary assets it has contributed are intangible assets. On the other hand, party B has contributed an interest in a subsidiary. The requirements in IFRS 10 relating to the accounting for loss of control of a subsidiary are inconsistent with the accounting required by IAS 28. Under IAS 28, the contributing investor is required to restrict any gain arising as a result of the exchange relating to its own assets to the extent that the gain is attributable to the other party to the associate or joint venture. This leads to an adjustment of the carrying amount of the assets of the associate or joint venture. However, under IFRS 10, where an entity loses control of an entity, but retains an interest that is to be accounted for as an associate or joint venture, the retained interest must be remeasured at its fair value and is included in calculating the gain or loss on disposal of the subsidiary. This fair value becomes the cost on initial recognition of the associate or joint venture. *[IFRS 10.25]*. Consequently, under IFRS 10, the gain is not restricted to the extent that the gain is attributable to the other party to the associate or joint venture, and there is no adjustment to reduce the fair values of the net assets contributed to the associate or joint venture.

In September 2014, the IASB issued *Sale or Contribution of Assets between an Investor and its Associate or Joint Venture* (amendments to IFRS 10 and IAS 28) to address the conflict between IFRS 10 and IAS 28.[14] The amendments require that:

- the partial gain or loss recognition for transactions between an investor and its associate or joint venture only applies to the gain or loss resulting from the sale or contribution of assets that do not constitute a business as defined in IFRS 3; and
- the gain or loss resulting from the sale or contribution of assets that constitute a business as defined in IFRS 3, between an investor and its associate or joint venture be recognised in full.

In December 2015, the IASB deferred the effective date of these amendments indefinitely due to feedback that the recognition of a partial gain or loss when a transaction involves assets that do not constitute a business, even if these assets are housed in a subsidiary, is inconsistent with the initial measurement requirements of IAS 28.32(b) (see 7.4 above). This issue will be reconsidered as part of the equity method research project (see 11 below). However, entities may apply the amendments before the effective date.

We believe that until the amendments become mandatorily effective, and where the non-monetary asset contributed is an interest in a subsidiary that constitutes a business, entities have an accounting policy choice as to whether to apply IFRS 10 or IAS 28, although the requirements of IFRS 10 deal with the specific issue of loss of control, whereas the requirements of IAS 28 are more generic. Once selected, the entity must apply the selected policy consistently. Nevertheless, where the requirements of IFRS 10 are followed for transactions involving a contribution of an interest in a subsidiary, IAS 28 would apply to other forms of non-monetary assets contributed, such as items of property, plant and equipment or intangible assets.

In Example 11.21 below, we illustrate how party B, which has contributed a subsidiary for its interest in the joint venture in the transaction set out in Example 11.19 above, would account for the transaction by applying the requirements of IFRS 10 as amended by the ED above. Although the example is based on a transaction resulting in the formation of a joint venture, the accounting treatment by party B would be the same if it had obtained an interest in an associate.

Example 11.21: Contribution of subsidiary to form a joint venture – applying IFRS 10 as amended in 2014

A and B are two major pharmaceutical companies, which agree to form a joint venture (JV Co). A will own 40% of the joint venture, and B 60%. The parties agree that the total value of the new business of JV Co is £250 million.

A's contribution to the venture is a number of intangible assets, in respect of which A's consolidated statement of financial position reflects a carrying amount of £60 million. The fair value of the intangible assets contributed by A is considered to be £100 million, i.e. equivalent to 40% of the total fair value of JV Co of £250 million.

B contributes a subsidiary, in respect of which B's consolidated statement of financial position reflects separable net assets of £85 million and goodwill of £15 million. The fair value of the separable net assets is considered to be £120 million. The implicit fair value of the business contributed is £150 million (60% of total fair value of JV Co of £250 million).

The book and fair values of the assets/businesses contributed by A and B can therefore be summarised as follows:

	A		B	
(in £m)	Book value	Fair value	Book value	Fair value
Intangible assets	60	100		
Separable net assets			85	120
Goodwill			15	30
Total	60	100	100	150

The application of IFRS 10 to the transaction would result in B reflecting the following accounting entry.

	£m	£m
Share of net assets of JV Co (1)	132	
Goodwill (2)	18	
Separable net assets and goodwill contributed to JV Co (3)		100
Gain on disposal (4)		50

(1) 60% of fair value of separable net assets of new entity £132 million (60% of [£100 million + £120 million] as in table above). There is no elimination of 60% of the gain on disposal.

Under the equity method, this £132 million together with the £18 million of goodwill (see (2) below) would be included as the equity accounted amount of JV Co.

(2) Fair value of consideration given of £60 million (being 40% of £150 million as in table above) plus fair value of retained interest of £90 million (being 60% of £150 million) less fair value of 60% share of separable net assets of JV Co acquired £132 million (see (1) above).

Under the equity method, as noted at (1) above, this £18 million together with the £132 million relating to the separable net assets would be included as the equity accounted amount of JV Co.

(3) Previous carrying amount of net assets contributed by B as in table above, now deconsolidated. In reality there would be a number of entries to deconsolidate these on a line-by-line basis.

(4) Fair value of consideration received of £60 million (being 60% of £100 million as in table above) plus fair value of retained interest of £90 million (being 60% of £150 million) less book value of assets disposed of £100 million (see (3) above) = £50 million.

In Example 11.21 above, B contributed its subsidiary to obtain a 60% interest in the newly formed joint venture. However, rather than contributing its subsidiary, B could have 'transformed' its subsidiary into a joint venture by diluting its interest in the subsidiary by the issue of shares by the subsidiary in return for the intangible assets 'contributed' by A and entering into a contractual arrangement with A, establishing joint control over the former subsidiary. In this case, the legal form of the transaction is that B has not contributed anything for its interest in the joint venture, but the overall substance of the transaction is the same as that in Example 11.21. Indeed, the creation of such a joint venture could be achieved through the sale of shares in an existing subsidiary to another party, and entering into a contractual arrangement with the other party, establishing joint control over the former subsidiary.

7.7 Non-coterminous accounting periods

In applying the equity method, the investor should use the most recent financial statements of the associate or joint venture. Where the reporting dates of the investor and the associate or joint venture are different, IAS 28 requires the associate or joint venture to prepare, for the use of the investor, financial statements as of the same date as those of the investor unless it is impracticable to do so. *[IAS 28.33].*

When the financial statements of an associate or joint venture used in applying the equity method are prepared as of a different reporting date from that of the investor, adjustments must be made for the effects of significant transactions or events, for example a sale of a significant asset or a major loss on a contract, that occurred between that date and the date of the investor's financial statements. In no circumstances can the difference between the reporting date of the associate or the joint venture and that of the investor be more than three months. *[IAS 28.34, BCZ19].* There are no exemptions from this requirement despite the fact that it may be quite onerous in practice, for example, because:

- the associate or joint venture might need to produce interim financial statements so that the investor can comply with this requirement; or
- the associate or joint venture may be a listed company in its own right whose financial information is considered price-sensitive, which means that the associate or joint venture may not be able to provide detailed financial information to one investor without providing equivalent information to all other investors at the same time.

The length of the reporting periods and any difference in the reporting dates must be the same from period to period. *[IAS 28.34].* This implies that where an associate or joint venture was previously equity accounted for on the basis of non-coterminous financial statements and is now equity accounted for using coterminous financial statements, it is necessary to restate comparative information so that financial information in respect of the associate or joint venture is included in the investor's financial statements for an equivalent period in each period presented.

IAS 28 requires merely that a non-coterminous accounting period of an associate or a joint venture used for equity accounting purposes ends within three months of that of the investor. It is not necessary for such a non-coterminous period to end before that of the investor.

7.8 Consistent accounting policies

IAS 28 requires the investor's financial statements to be prepared using uniform accounting policies for like transactions and events in similar circumstances. *[IAS 28.35].* If an associate or joint venture uses accounting policies different from those of the investor for like transactions and events in similar circumstances, adjustments must be made to conform the associate's or joint venture's accounting policies to those of the investor when the associate's or joint ventures financial statements are used by the investor in applying the equity method. *[IAS 28.36].*

In practice, this may be easier said than done, since the investor only has significant influence, and not control, over the associate, and therefore may not have access to the relevant underlying information in sufficient detail to make such adjustments with certainty. Restating the financial statements of an associate to IFRS may require extensive detailed information that may simply not be required under the associate's local GAAP (for example, in respect of business combinations, share-based payments, financial instruments and revenue recognition). Although there may be some practical difficulties where the entity has joint control over a joint venture, we would expect this to arise less often, as joint control is likely to give the investor more access to the information required.

7.9 Loss-making associates or joint ventures

An investor in an associate or joint venture should recognise its share of the losses of the associate or joint venture until its share of losses equals or exceeds its interest in the associate or joint venture, at which point the investor discontinues recognising its share of further losses. For this purpose, the investor's interest in an associate or joint venture is the carrying amount of the investment in the associate or joint venture under the equity method together with any long-term interests that, in substance, form part of the investor's net investment in the associate or joint venture. For example, an item for which settlement is neither planned nor likely to occur in the foreseeable future is, in substance, an extension of the entity's investment in that associate or joint venture. *[IAS 28.38]*. The items that form part of the net investment are discussed further in Chapter 15 at 6.3.1. The IASB argued that this requirement ensures that investors are not able to avoid recognising the loss of an associate or joint venture by restructuring their investment to provide the majority of funding through non-equity investments. *[IAS 28.BCZ39-40]*.

Such items include:

- preference shares; or
- long-term receivables or loans (unless supported by adequate collateral),

but do not include:

- trade receivables;
- trade payables; or
- any long-term receivables for which adequate collateral exists, such as secured loans. *[IAS 28.38]*.

Once the investor's share of losses recognised under the equity method has reduced the investor's investment in ordinary shares to zero, its share of any further losses is applied so as to reduce the other components of the investor's interest in an associate or joint venture in the reverse order of their seniority (i.e. priority in liquidation). *[IAS 28.38]*.

Once the investor's interest is reduced to zero, additional losses are provided for, and a liability is recognised, only to the extent that the investor has incurred legal or constructive obligations or made payments on behalf of the associate or joint venture. If the associate or joint venture subsequently reports profits, the investor resumes recognising its share of those profits only after its share of the profits equals the share of losses not recognised. *[IAS 28.39]*. Whilst IAS 28 does not say so explicitly, it is presumably envisaged that, when profits begin to be recognised again, they are applied to write back the various components of the investor's interest in the associate or joint venture (see previous paragraph) in the reverse order to that in which they were written down (i.e. in order of their priority in a liquidation).

IAS 28 is not explicit about the allocation of losses recognised in the income statement and losses incurred in OCI. Therefore management will need to develop an appropriate policy. The policy chosen should be disclosed and consistently applied.

In addition to the recognition of losses arising from application of the equity method, an investor in an associate or joint venture must consider the additional requirements of IAS 28 in respect of impairment losses (see 8 below).

Example 11.22: Accounting for a loss-making associate

At the beginning of the year entity H invests €5 million to acquire a 30% equity interest in an associate, entity A. In addition, H lends €9 million to the associate, but does not provide any guarantees or commit itself to provide further funding. How should H account for the €20 million loss that the associate made during the year?

H's share in A's loss is €20 million × 30% = €6 million. If H's loan to A is considered part of the net investment in the associate then the carrying amount of the associate is reduced by €6 million, from €14 million (= €5 million + €9 million) to €8 million. That is, the equity interest is reduced to nil and the loan is reduced to €8 million. However, if the loan is not part of the net investment in the associate then H accounts for the loss as follows:

- the equity interest in the associate is reduced from €5 million to zero;
- a loss of €1 million remains unrecognised because H did not provide any guarantees and has no commitments to provide further funding. If in the second year, however, A were to make a profit of €10 million then H would only recognise a profit of €2 million (= €10 million × 30% – €1 million). However, if in the second year H were to provide a €1.5 million guarantee to A and A's net profit were nil, then H would need to recognise an immediate loss of €1 million (i.e. the lower of the unrecognised loss of €1 million and the guarantee of €1.5 million) because it now has a legal obligation pay A's debts; and
- as there are a number of indicators of impairment, the loan from H to A should be tested for impairment in accordance with IFRS 9 (or IAS 39).

7.10 Distributions received in excess of the carrying amount

When an associate or joint venture makes dividend distributions to the investor in excess of the investor's carrying amount it is not immediately clear how the excess should be accounted for. A liability under IAS 37 – *Provisions, Contingent Liabilities and Contingent Assets* – should only be recognised if the investor is obliged to refund the dividend, has incurred a legal or constructive obligation or made payments on behalf of the associate. In the absence of such obligations, it would seem appropriate that the investor recognises the excess in net profit for the period. When the associate or joint venture subsequently makes profits, the investor should only start recognising profits when they exceed the excess cash distributions recognised in net profit plus any previously unrecognised losses (see 7.9 above).

7.11 Equity transactions in an associate's or joint venture's financial statements

The financial statements of an associate or joint venture that are used for the purposes of equity accounting by the investor may include items within its statement of changes in equity that are not reflected in the profit or loss or other components of comprehensive income, for example, dividends or other forms of distributions, issues of equity instruments and equity-settled share-based payment transactions. Where the associate or joint venture has subsidiaries and consolidated financial statements are prepared, those financial statements may include the effects of changes in the parent's (i.e. the associate's or joint venture's) ownership interest and non-controlling interest in a subsidiary that did not arise from a transaction that resulted in loss of control of that subsidiary.

Although the description of the equity method in IAS 28 requires that the investor's share of the profit or loss of the associate or joint venture is recognised in the investor's profit or loss, and the investor's share of changes in items of other comprehensive income of the associate or joint venture is recognised in other comprehensive income of the investor, *[IAS 28.10]*, no explicit reference is made to other items that the associate or joint venture may have in its statement of changes in equity.

Therefore, the guidance in the sections that follow may be considered in determining an appropriate accounting treatment.

7.11.1 Dividends or other forms of distributions

Although paragraph 10 of IAS 28 does not explicitly refer to dividends or other forms of distribution that are reflected in the associate's statement of changes in equity, it does state that distributions received from an investee reduce the carrying amount of the investment. Generally, the distributions received will be the equivalent of the investor's share of the distributions made to the owners of the associate reflected in the associate's statement of changes in equity. Thus, they are effectively eliminated as part of applying the equity method.

However, this may not always be the case. For example, when an associate declares scrip dividends which are not taken up by the investor, the investor's proportionate interest in the associate is reduced. In this situation, the investor should account for this as a deemed disposal (see 7.12.5 below).

7.11.2 Issues of equity instruments

Where an associate or joint venture has issued equity instruments, the effect on its net assets will be reflected in the associate's or joint venture's statement of changes in equity. Where the investor has participated in the issue of these equity instruments, it will account for its cost of doing so by increasing its carrying amount of the associate or joint venture. If, as a consequence of the investor's participation in such a transaction, the investee has become an associate or joint venture of the investor, or the investor has increased its percentage ownership interest in an existing associate or joint venture (but without obtaining control), the investor should account for this as an acquisition of an associate or joint venture or a piecemeal acquisition of an associate or joint venture (see 7.4.2 above). Thus, the amounts reflected in the associate's or joint venture's statement of changes in equity are effectively eliminated as part of applying the equity method.

If, on the other hand, the investor has not participated in the issue of equity instruments reflected in the associate's or joint venture's statement of changes in equity, e.g. shares have been issued to third parties or the investor has not taken up its full allocation of a rights issue by the associate or joint venture, the investor's proportionate interest in the associate or joint venture is diminished. In such situations, it should account for the transaction as a deemed disposal (see 7.12.5 below).

7.11.3 Equity-settled share-based payment transactions

Another item that may feature in an associate's or joint venture's statement of changes in equity is the credit entry relating to any equity-settled share-based payment transactions of the associate or joint venture; the debit entry of such transactions is recognised by the associate or joint venture as an expense within its profit or loss.

How should such a transaction be reflected by the investor in equity accounting for the associate or joint venture, particularly the impact of the credit to equity recognised by the associate or joint venture?

As the share-based payment expense is included within the profit or loss of the associate or joint venture, this will be reflected in the share of the associate's or joint venture's profit or loss recognised in the investor's profit or loss. *[IAS 28.10]*. As far as the credit to equity that is included in the associate's or joint venture's statement of changes in equity is concerned, there are two possible approaches:

(a) ignore the credit entry; or

(b) reflect the investor's share of the credit entry as a 'share of other changes in equity of associates or joint ventures' in the investor's statement of changes in equity.

We believe that approach (a) should be followed, rather than approach (b). The description of the equity method in IAS 28 states that 'the carrying amount [of the investment in an associate or a joint venture] is increased or decreased to recognise the investor's share of the profit or loss of the investee after the date of acquisition. ... Adjustments to the carrying amount may also be necessary for changes in the investor's proportionate interest in the investee arising from changes in the investee's other comprehensive income.' *[IAS 28.10]*.

As far as the credit to shareholders' equity recognised by the associate or joint venture is concerned, this is not part of comprehensive income and given that paragraph 10 of IAS 28 implies that the investor only recognises its share of the elements of profit or loss and of other comprehensive income, the investor should not recognise any portion of the credit to shareholders' equity recognised by the associate or joint venture. If and when the options are exercised, the investor will account for its reduction in its proportionate interest as a deemed disposal (see 7.12.5 below).

This approach results in the carrying amount of the equity investment no longer corresponding to the proportionate share of the net assets of the investee (as reported by the investee). However, this is consistent with the requirement in IAS 28 for dealing with undeclared dividends on cumulative preference shares held by parties other than the investor (see 7.5.2 above). *[IAS 28.37]*. In that situation, the undeclared dividends have not yet been recognised by the investee at all, but the investor still reduces its share of the profit or loss (and therefore its share of net assets). The impact of applying this approach is illustrated in Example 11.23 below. Although the example is based on an equity-settled share based payment transaction of an associate, the accounting treatment would be the same if it been a transaction undertaken by a joint venture.

Example 11.23: Equity-settled share based payment transactions of associate

Entity A holds a 30% interest in Entity B and accounts for its interest in B as an associate using the equity method. This interest arose on incorporation of B. Accordingly, there are no fair value adjustments required related to the assets of B in A's consolidated financial statements and its equity-accounted amount represents an original cost of £1,500 (30% of B's issued equity of £5,000) together with A's 30% share of B's retained profits of £5,000.

Entity B issues share options to its employees which are to be accounted for by B as an equity-settled share-based payment transaction. The options entitle the employees to subscribe for shares of B, representing an additional 20% interest in the shares of B. If the options are exercised, the employees will pay £2,400 for the shares. The grant date fair value of the options issued is £900 and, for the purposes of the example, it is assumed that the options are immediately vested. Accordingly, B has recognised a share-based payment expense of £900 in profit or loss and a credit to equity of the same amount.

Chapter 11

The impact of this equity-settled share-based payment transaction on B's financial statements and on A's consolidated financial statements of accounting for this equity-settled share-based payment transaction is summarised below.

Immediately before the granting of the options

B's financial statements

	£		£
Net assets	10,000	Issued equity	5,000
		Retained earnings	5,000
Total	10,000	Total	10,000

A's consolidated financial statements

	£		£
Investment in B	3,000	Issued equity	10,000
Other net assets	21,000	Retained earnings	14,000
Total	24,000	Total	24,000

*Immediately after the granting of the options**

B's financial statements

	£		£
Net assets	10,000	Issued equity	5,000
		Retained earnings	5,000
		Loss for period	(900)
		Other reserve re options	900
Total	10,000	Total	10,000

A's consolidated financial statements

	£		£
Investment in B	2,730	Issued equity	10,000
Other net assets	21,000	Retained earnings	14,000
		Loss for period	(270)
Total	23,730	Total	23,730

* For the purposes of illustration, B's expense and the corresponding credit to equity have been shown separately within equity as 'loss for period' and 'other reserve re options' respectively. A's 30% share of the expense has similarly been shown separately within equity.

*Immediately after exercise of the options**

B's financial statements

	£		£
Net assets	10,000	Issued equity	5,000
Cash on exercise of options	2,400	Additional equity on exercise of options	2,400
		Retained earnings	5,000
		Loss for period	(900)
		Other reserve re options	900
Total	12,400	Total	12,400

A's consolidated financial statements

	£		£
Investment in B	3,100	Issued equity	10,000
Other net assets	21,000	Retained earnings	14,000
		Loss for period	(270)
		Gain on deemed disposal	370
Total	24,100	Total	24,100

* As a result of the employees exercising the options for £2,400, A's proportionate interest in B has reduced from 30% to 25%. A is considered still to have significant influence over B, which remains an associate of A. This deemed disposal results in A recognising a gain on deemed disposal in its profit or loss for the period. The gain on such a deemed disposal is computed by comparing A's proportionate share of net assets of B before and after the exercise of the options as follows:

	£	
Net assets attributable to A's 30% interest	2,730	(30% of £9,100)
Net assets attributable to A's 25% interest	3,100	(25% of £12,400)
Gain on deemed disposal	370	

As indicated in Example 11.23 above, when the options are exercised, the investor will account for the reduction in its proportionate interest in the associate or joint venture as a deemed disposal (see 7.12.5 below). On the other hand, if the options had lapsed unexercised, having already vested, the associate or joint venture would make no further accounting entries to reverse the expense already recognised, but may make a transfer between different components of equity (see Chapter 32 at 6.1.3). In that situation, as the investor's share of the net assets of the associate or joint venture is now increased as a result (effectively, the impact of the original expense on the share of net assets is reversed), we believe the investor can account for the increase either as a gain in profit or loss or as a credit within equity. Once selected, the investor must apply the selected policy consistently.

7.11.4 Effects of changes in parent/non-controlling interests in subsidiaries

It may be that the associate or joint venture does not own all the shares in some of its subsidiaries, in which case its consolidated financial statements will include non-controlling interests. Under IFRS 10, any non-controlling interests are presented in the consolidated statement of financial position within equity, separately from the equity of the owners of the parent. Profit or loss and each component of other comprehensive income are attributed to the owners of the parent and to the non-controlling interests. *[IFRS 10.22, B94].* The profit or loss and other comprehensive income reported in the associate's or joint venture's consolidated financial statements will include 100% of the amounts relating to the subsidiaries, but the overall profit or loss and total comprehensive income will be split between the amounts attributable to the owners of the parent (i.e. the associate or joint venture) and those attributable to the non-controlling interests. The net assets in the consolidated statement of financial position will also include 100% of the amounts relating to the subsidiaries, with any non-controlling interests in the net assets presented in the consolidated statement of financial position within equity, separately from the equity of the owners of the parent.

The issue of whether the investor's share of the associate's or joint venture's profits, other comprehensive income and net assets under the equity method should be based on the amounts before or after any non-controlling interests in the associate's or joint venture's consolidated accounts is discussed at 7.5.5 above. As the investor's interest in the associate or joint venture is as an owner of the parent, it is appropriate that the share is based on the profit or loss, comprehensive income and equity (net assets) that are reported as being attributable to the owners of the parent in the associate's or joint venture's consolidated financial statements, i.e. after any amounts attributable to the non-controlling interests.

Under IFRS 10, changes in a parent's ownership interest in a subsidiary that do not result in a loss of control are accounted for as equity transactions. *[IFRS 10.23]*. In such circumstances the carrying amounts of the controlling and non-controlling interests are adjusted to reflect the changes in their relative interests in the subsidiary. Any difference between the amount by which the non-controlling interests are adjusted and the fair value of the consideration paid or received is recognised directly in equity and attributed to the owners of the parent. *[IFRS 10.B96]*.

How should such an amount attributed to the owners of the parent that is recognised in the associate's or joint venture's statement of changes in equity be reflected by the investor in equity accounting for the associate or joint venture?

In our view, the investor may account for its share of the change of interest in the net assets/equity of the associate or joint venture as a result of the associate's or joint venture's equity transaction by applying either of the approaches set out below:

(a) reflect it as part of the share of other changes in equity of associates or joint ventures' in the investor's statement of changes in equity; or
(b) reflect it as a gain or loss within the share of associate's or joint venture's profit or loss included in the investor's profit or loss.

Once selected, the investor must apply the selected policy consistently.

Approach (a) reflects the view that although paragraph 10 of IAS 28 only refers to the investor accounting for its share of the investee's profit or loss and other items of comprehensive income, this approach is consistent with the equity method as described in paragraph 10 of IAS 28 since it:

(a) reflects the post-acquisition change in the net assets of the investee; *[IAS 28.3]* and
(b) faithfully reflects the investor's share of the associate's transaction as presented in the associate's consolidated financial statements. *[IAS 28.27]*.

Since, the transaction does not change the investor's ownership interest in the associate it is not a deemed disposal (see 7.12.5 below) and, therefore, there is no question of a gain or loss on disposal arising. Approach (b) reflects the view that:

(a) the investor should reflect the post-acquisition change in the net assets of the investee; *[IAS 28.3]*
(b) from the investor's perspective the transaction is not 'a transaction with owners in their capacity as owners' – the investor does not equity account for the NCI (see 7.5.5 above). So whilst the investee must reflect the transaction as an equity transaction, from the investor's point of view the increase in the investment is a 'gain'. This is consistent with the treatment of unrealised profits between a reporting entity and an associate (see 7.6.1 above). The NCI's ownership is treated as an 'external' ownership interest to the investor's group. Therefore, consistent with this approach, any

transaction which is, from the investor's perspective a transaction with an 'external' ownership interest can give rise to a gain or loss;

(c) the increase in the investee's equity is also not an item of other comprehensive income as referred to in paragraph 10 of IAS 28;

(d) any increase in the amount of an asset should go to profit or loss if not otherwise stated in IFRS. Paragraph 88 of IAS 1 states that an 'entity shall recognise all items of income and expense in a period in profit or loss unless an IFRS requires or permits otherwise.'

These approaches are illustrated in Example 11.24 below. Although the example is based on a transaction by an associate, the accounting would be the same if it had been undertaken by a joint venture.

Example 11.24: Accounting for the effect of transactions with non-controlling interests recognised through equity by an associate

Entity A holds a 20% interest in entity B (an associate) that in turn has a 100% ownership interest in subsidiary C. The net assets of C included in B's consolidated financial statements are €1,000. For the purposes of the example all other assets and liabilities in B's financial statements and in A's consolidated financial statements are ignored.

B sells 20% of its interest in C to a third party for €300. B accounts for this transaction as an equity transaction in accordance with IFRS 10, giving rise to a credit in equity of €100 that is attributable to the owners of B. The credit is the difference between the proceeds of €300 and the share of net assets of C that are now attributable to the non-controlling interest (NCI) of €200 (20% of €1,000).

The financial statements of A and B before the transaction are summarised below:

Before

A's consolidated financial statements

	€		€
Investment in B	200	Equity	200
Total	200	Total	200

B's consolidated financial statements

	€		€
Assets (from C)	1,000	Equity	1,000
Total	1,000	Total	1,000

The financial statements of B after the transaction are summarised below:

After

B's consolidated financial statements

	€		€
Assets (from C)	1,000	Equity	1,000
Cash	300	Equity transaction with non-controlling interest	100
		Equity attributable to owners	1,100
		Non-controlling interest	200
Total	1,300	Total	1,300

As a result of the sale of B's 20% interest in C, B's net assets attributable to the owners of B have increased from €1,000 to €1,100. Although A has not participated in the transaction, the investor's share of net assets in B has increased from €200 to €220.

A should account for this increase in net assets arising from this equity transaction using either of the following approaches:

Approach (a) – 'share of other changes in equity' in investor's statement of changes in equity

The change of interest in the net assets/equity of B as a result of B's equity transaction should be reflected in A's financial statements as 'share of other changes in equity of associates' in its statement of changes in equity.

Therefore, A reflects its €20 share of the change in equity and maintains the same classification as the associate i.e. a direct credit to equity.

Approach (b) – gain or loss within share of associate's profit or loss included in investor's profit or loss

The change of interest in the net assets/equity of B as a result of B's equity transaction should be reflected in A's financial statements as a 'gain' in profit or loss.

Therefore, A reflects its €20 share of the change in equity in profit or loss.

7.12 Discontinuing the use of the equity method

An investor discontinues the use of the equity method on the date that its investment ceases to be either an associate or a joint venture. The subsequent accounting depends upon the nature of the retained investment. If the investment becomes a subsidiary, it will be accounted for in accordance with IFRS 10 and IFRS 3 as discussed at 7.12.1 below. If the retained investment is a financial asset, it will be accounted for in accordance with IFRS 9 (or IAS 39) as discussed at 7.12.2 below. *[IAS 28.22]*. If an investment in an associate becomes an investment in a joint venture, or an investment in a joint venture becomes an investment in an associate, the entity continues to apply the equity method, as discussed at 7.12.3 below. *[IAS 28.24]*.

Where a portion of an investment in an associate or a joint venture meets the criteria to be classified as held for sale, the entity applies IFRS 5 as discussed at 6 above. *[IAS 28.20]*.

7.12.1 Investment in associate or joint venture becoming a subsidiary

If as a result of an increased investment in an associate or joint venture an investor obtains control over the investee, or there is a change in circumstances such that the investor obtains control over the investee, the investment becomes a subsidiary. The entity discontinues the use of the equity method and accounts for its investment in accordance with IFRS 3 and IFRS 10. *[IAS 28.22]*. In this situation, IFRS 3 requires revaluation of the previously held interest in the equity accounted investment at its acquisition-date fair value, with recognition of any gain or loss in profit or loss. *[IFRS 3.41-42]*. The accounting for an increase in an associate or joint venture that becomes a subsidiary is discussed further in Chapter 9 at 9.

In addition, the entity accounts for all amounts previously recognised in other comprehensive income in relation to that investment on the same basis as would have been required if the investee had directly disposed of the related assets or liabilities. *[IAS 28.22]*.

Therefore, if a gain or loss previously recognised in other comprehensive income by the investee would be reclassified to profit or loss on the disposal of the related assets or liabilities, the entity reclassifies the gain or loss from equity to profit or loss (as a reclassification adjustment) when the equity method is discontinued. For example, if an associate or a joint venture has cumulative exchange differences relating to a foreign operation and the entity discontinues the use of the equity method, the entity shall reclassify to profit or loss the gain or loss that had previously been recognised in other comprehensive income in relation to the foreign operation. *[IAS 28.23]*.

7.12.2 Retained investment in the former associate or joint venture is a financial asset

If an investor disposes of a portion of its investment, such that it no longer has significant influence or joint control over the investee, it will discontinue the use of the equity method. If the retained interest is a financial asset, the entity measures the retained interest at fair value. The fair value of the retained interest is to be regarded as its fair value on initial recognition as a financial asset in accordance with IFRS 9 (or IAS 39).

In such situations, the entity recognises in profit or loss any difference between:

(a) the fair value of any retained interest and any proceeds from disposing of a part interest in the associate or joint venture; and

(b) the carrying amount of the investment at the date the equity method was discontinued.

Furthermore, the entity accounts for all amounts previously recognised in other comprehensive income in relation to that investment on the same basis as would have been required if the investee had directly disposed of the related assets or liabilities. *[IAS 28.22]*.

Therefore, if a gain or loss previously recognised in other comprehensive income by the investee would be reclassified to profit or loss on the disposal of the related assets or liabilities, the entity reclassifies the gain or loss from equity to profit or loss (as a reclassification adjustment) when the equity method is discontinued. For example, if an associate or a joint venture has cumulative exchange differences relating to a foreign operation and the entity discontinues the use of the equity method, the entity reclassifies to profit or loss the gain or loss that had previously been recognised in other comprehensive income in relation to the foreign operation. *[IAS 28.23]*.

When the retained interest after the partial disposal of an interest in a joint venture or a partial disposal of an interest in an associate that includes a foreign operation is a financial asset that includes a foreign operation, IAS 21 – *The Effects of Changes in Foreign Exchange Rates* – requires it to be accounted for as a disposal. *[IAS 21.48A]*. As such, it should be noted that the reclassification adjustment from equity to profit or loss is for the full amount that is in other comprehensive income and not just a proportionate amount based upon the interest disposed of. The Basis for Conclusions to IAS 21 explains that the loss of significant influence or joint control is a significant economic event that warrants accounting for the transaction as a disposal under IAS 21, *[IAS 21.BC33-34]*, and hence the transfer of the full exchange difference rather than just the proportionate share that would be required if this was accounted for as a partial disposal under IAS 21.

The accounting described above applies not only when an investor disposes of an interest in an associate or joint venture, but also where it ceases to have significant influence due to a change in circumstances. For example, when an associate issues shares to third parties, changes to the board of directors may result in the investor no longer having significant influence over the associate. Therefore, the investor will discontinue the use of the equity method.

7.12.3 Investment in associate becomes a joint venture (or vice versa)

If an investment in an associate becomes an investment in a joint venture or an investment in a joint venture becomes an investment in an associate, the entity does not discontinue the use of the equity method. In such circumstances, the entity continues to apply the equity method and does not remeasure the retained interest. *[IAS 28.24]*.

When the change in status of the investment results from the acquisition of an additional interest in the investee, the increase in the investment is accounted for as discussed at 7.4.2.C above. When the change in status results from the disposal of an interest in the investee, this is accounted for as explained at 7.12.4 below.

As discussed at 6 and at 7.12 above, if a portion of an interest in an associate or joint venture fulfils the criteria for classification as held for sale, it is only that portion that is accounted for under IFRS 5. An entity maintains the use of the equity method for the retained interest until the portion classified as held for sale is finally sold.

7.12.4 Partial disposals of interests in associate or joint venture where the equity method continues to be applied

IAS 28 does not explicitly state that an entity should recognise a gain or loss when it disposes of a part of its interest in an associate or a joint venture, but the entity continues to apply the equity method. However, as explained below, it is evident that a gain or loss should be recognised on the partial disposal.

The standard requires that when an entity's ownership interest in an associate or a joint venture is reduced, but the entity continues to apply the equity method, the entity reclassifies to profit or loss the proportion of the gain or loss that had previously been recognised in other comprehensive income relating to that reduction in ownership interest if that gain or loss would be required to be reclassified to profit or loss on the disposal of the related assets or liabilities. *[IAS 28.25]*.

In addition, IAS 21 requires for such partial disposals that the investor should 'reclassify to profit or loss only the proportionate share of the cumulative amount of the exchange differences recognised in other comprehensive income'. *[IAS 21.48C]*.

That means that the investor recognises in profit or loss a proportion of:

- foreign exchange differences recognised in other comprehensive income under IAS 21;
- accumulated hedging gains and losses recognised in other comprehensive income under IAS 39 (see Chapter 52); and
- any other amounts previously recognised in other comprehensive income that would have been recognised in profit or loss if the associate had directly disposed of the assets to which they relate, such as gains or losses on available-for-sale financial assets accounted for under IAS 39 (see Chapter 49 at 2.4),

in each case proportionate to the interest disposed of.

IAS 21 requires that the proportion of the foreign exchange differences are reclassified 'when the gain or loss on disposal is recognised'. *[IAS 21.48]*. In addition, the Interpretations Committee in the context of deemed disposals (see 7.12.5 below), noted that reclassification of amounts to profit or loss from other comprehensive income is generally required as part of determining the gain or loss on a disposal.

Although IFRS 10 requires that partial disposals of subsidiaries, where control is retained, are accounted for as equity transactions (see Chapter 7 at 3.3) and no profit or loss is recognised, we do not believe that this has an impact on the accounting for a partial disposal of an associate or a joint venture (which continues to be accounted for under the equity method). Under equity accounting an investor only accounts for its own interest. Given that the other investors' ownership in the associate is not reflected in the accounts of an investor there is no basis for concluding that partial disposals can be treated as equity transactions.

7.12.5 Deemed disposals

An investor's interest in an associate or a joint venture may be reduced other than by an actual disposal. Such a reduction in interest, which is commonly referred to as a deemed disposal, gives rise to a 'dilution' gain or loss. Deemed disposals may arise for a number of reasons, including:

- the investor does not take up its full allocation in a rights issue by the associate or joint venture;
- the associate or joint venture declares scrip dividends which are not taken up by the investor so that its proportional interest is diminished;
- another party exercises its options or warrants issued by the associate or joint venture; or
- the associate or joint venture issues shares to third parties.

In some situations, the circumstances giving rise to the dilution in the investor's interest may be such that the investor no longer has significant influence over the investee. In that case, the investor will account for the transaction as a disposal, with a retained interest in a financial asset measured at fair value. This is described at 7.12.2 above. However, in other situations, the deemed disposal will only give rise to a partial disposal, such that the investor will continue to equity account for the investee.

As discussed in more detail at 7.12.4 above, although IAS 28 does not explicitly state that an entity should recognise a gain or loss on partial disposal of its interest in an associate or a joint venture when the entity continues to apply the equity method, it is evident that a gain or loss should be recognised on partial disposals.

In the absence of further guidance, we believe that gains or losses on deemed disposals should be recognised in profit or loss, and this will include amounts reclassified from other comprehensive income.

However, what is not clear is whether any of the notional goodwill component of the carrying amount of the associate or joint venture should be taken into account in the calculation of the gain or loss on the deemed disposal. We believe that it is appropriate to take into account the entire carrying amount of the associate or joint venture, i.e. including the notional goodwill, as shown in Example 11.25 below. Although the example is based on a deemed disposal of an associate, the accounting would be the same if it had been a deemed disposal of a joint venture.

IAS 28 defines the equity method as 'a method of accounting whereby the investment is initially recognised at cost and adjusted thereafter for the post acquisition change in the investor's share of the investee's net assets. ...' *[IAS 28.3]*. A literal reading of this definition suggests that in calculating the loss on dilution, the investor should only take account of the change in its share of the associate's or joint venture's net assets but not account for a change in the notional goodwill component.

However, paragraph 42 of IAS 28 specifically states that goodwill included in the carrying amount of an investment in an associate or a joint venture is not separately recognised. Hence, we believe that it should not be excluded from the cost of a deemed disposal either.

Although the IASB did not explicitly consider accounting for deemed disposals of associates or joint ventures, paragraph 26 of IAS 28 refers to the concepts underlying the procedures used in accounting for the acquisition of a subsidiary in accounting for acquisitions of an investment in an associate or joint venture. Therefore, it is appropriate to account for deemed disposals of associates or joint ventures in the same way as deemed disposals of subsidiaries.

Example 11.25: Deemed disposal of an associate

At the start of the reporting period, investor A acquired a 30% interest in entity B at a cost of £500,000. Investor A has significant influence over entity B and accounts for its investment in the associate under the equity method. The associate has net assets of £1,000,000 at the date of acquisition, which have a fair value of £1,200,000. During the year entity B recognised a post-tax profit of £200,000, and paid a dividend of £18,000. Entity B also recognised foreign exchange losses of £40,000 in other comprehensive income.

Entity B's net assets at the end of the reporting period can be determined as follows:

	£
Net assets – opening balance	1,000,000
Profit for year	200,000
Dividends paid	(18,000)
Foreign exchange losses	(40,000)
B's net assets – closing balance	1,142,000

Investor A's interest in entity B at the end of the reporting period is calculated as follows:

	£
On acquisition (including goodwill of £500,000 – (30% × £1,200,000) = £140,000):	500,000
Share of profit after tax (30% × £200,000)	60,000
Elimination of dividend (30% of £18,000)	(5,400)
A's share of exchange differences (30% × £40,000)	(12,000)
A's interest in B at the end of the reporting period under the equity method	542,600

which can also be determined as follows:

	£
A's share of B's net assets (30% × £1,142,000)	342,600
Goodwill	140,000
A's share of fair value uplift (30% × £200,000) †	60,000
A's interest in B at the end of the reporting period	542,600

† This assumes that none of the uplift related to depreciable assets, such that the £200,000 did not diminish after the acquisition.

At the start of the next reporting period, entity B has a rights issue that investor A does not participate in. The rights issue brings in an additional £150,000 in cash, and dilutes investor A's interest in entity B to 25%.

Consequently, entity B's net assets at this date are:

	£
Entity B's net assets before the rights issue	1,142,000
Additional cash	150,000
Entity B's net assets after the rights issue	1,292,000

The loss on the deemed disposal, taking into account the entire carrying amount of the associate, including the notional goodwill is calculated as follows:

	£	£
Carrying amount of the investment before the deemed disposal		542,600
Cost of deemed disposal (£542,600 × (30% – 25%) / 30%)	(90,433)	
Share of the contribution (£150,000 × 25%)	37,500	
Reduction in carrying amount of associate	(52,933)	(52,933)
Reclassification of share in currency translation:		
(£40,000 × 30% × (25% – 30%) / 30%)	(2,000)	
Loss on deemed disposal	(54,933)	
Carrying amount of the investment after the deemed disposal		489,667

8 IMPAIRMENT LOSSES

Section 8.1 is applicable while IAS 39 is still effective. Section 8.2 will be relevant once IFRS 9 becomes effective for all reporting periods beginning on or after 1 January 2018.

8.1 IAS 28 and IAS 39

Determining whether an investment in an associate or joint venture is impaired may be more complicated than is apparent at first sight, as it involves carrying out several separate impairment assessments:

- *Assets of the associate or joint venture*

  It is generally not appropriate for the investor simply to multiply the amount of the impairment recognised in the investee's own books by the investor's percentage of ownership, because the investor should measure its interest in an associate's or joint venture's identifiable net assets at fair value at the date of acquisition of an associate or a joint venture. Therefore, if the value that the investor attributes to the associate's or joint venture's net assets differs from the carrying amount of those net assets in the associate's or joint venture's own books, the investor should restate any impairment losses recognised by the associate or joint venture and also needs to consider whether it needs to recognise any impairments that the associate or joint venture itself did not recognise in its own books.

  Any goodwill recognised by an associate or joint venture needs to be separated into two elements. Goodwill that existed at the date the investor acquired its interest in the associate or joint venture is not an identifiable asset of the associate or joint venture from the perspective of the investor. That goodwill should be combined with the investor's goodwill on the acquisition of its interest in the associate or joint venture. However, goodwill that arises on subsequent acquisitions by the associate or joint venture should be accounted for as such in the books of the associate or joint venture and tested for impairment in accordance with IAS 36 by the associate or joint venture. The investor should not make any adjustments to the associate's or joint venture's accounting for that goodwill.

- *Investment in the associate or joint venture*

  As well as applying the equity method as summarised at 7 above, including the recognition of losses (see 7.9 above), IAS 28 requires an investor to apply the requirements of IAS 39 (which are discussed below and in Chapter 49 at 4.1) in order to determine whether it is necessary to recognise any additional impairment loss with respect to the investor's net investment in the associate. *[IAS 28.40]*. Whilst IAS 39 is used to determine whether it is necessary to recognise any further impairment, the amount of any impairment is calculated in accordance with IAS 36 (see Chapter 20 and 8.3 below). *[IAS 28.42]*.

- *Other interests that are not part of the net investment in the associate or joint venture*

  The investor must also apply IAS 39 in order to determine whether it is necessary to recognise any additional impairment loss with respect to that part of the investor's interest in the associate that does not comprise its net investment in the associate. This would include, for example, trade receivables and payables, and collateralised long-term receivables, but might also include preference shares or loans (see 7.9 above). In this case, however, the impairment is calculated in accordance with IAS 39, and not IAS 36. *[IAS 28.41]*.

This has the effect that it is extremely unlikely that any impairment charge recognised in respect of an associate or joint venture will simply be the investor's share of any impairment charge recognised by the associate or joint venture itself, even when the associate or joint venture complies with IFRS.

IAS 28 requires the recoverable amount of an investment in an associate or a joint venture to be assessed individually, unless the associate or joint venture does not generate cash inflows from continuing use that are largely independent of those from other assets of the entity. *[IAS 28.43]*.

The requirements of IFRS 3 with respect to the fair value exercise mean that any goodwill that an associate or joint venture may have recognised in its own financial statements at the date of its acquisition is not considered an identifiable asset from the investor's point of view. Rather, the investor recognises goodwill on its investment in the associate or joint venture in accordance with IAS 28. Goodwill arising on the acquisition of an associate or joint venture is not separately recognised, but is included in the carrying value of that associate. *[IAS 28.32]*. Accordingly such goodwill, unlike that separately recognised, is not separately tested for impairment on an annual basis under IAS 36 – rather the entire carrying value of the investment in the associate or joint venture is tested for impairment as a single asset. *[IAS 28.42]*. Generally, impairment losses of goodwill recognised in the financial statements of an associate or joint venture should be reversed when the investor applies the equity method. However, impairment losses that relate to goodwill on the associate's or joint venture's own business combinations, after the investor acquired its interest in that associate or joint venture, should be taken into account in determining the investor's share of the associate's or joint venture's profits or losses (see 8.1 above).

Whenever application of the requirements in IFRS 9 (or IAS 39) indicates that the investment may be impaired (see below), the entire carrying amount of the investment is tested under IAS 36 for impairment (for a description of impairment reviews under IAS 36 see Chapter 20), by comparing its recoverable amount (the higher of value in use and fair value less costs to sell) with its carrying amount. In determining the value in use of the investment, an entity estimates:

- its share of the present value of the estimated future cash flows expected to be generated by the associate or joint venture, including the cash flows from the operations of the associate or joint venture and the proceeds on the ultimate disposal of the investment; or
- the present value of the estimated future cash flows expected to arise from dividends to be received from the investment and from its ultimate disposal. *[IAS 28.42].*

IAS 28 notes that, under 'appropriate assumptions', both methods give the same result. In effect, IAS 28 requires the investor to regard its investment in an associate or joint venture as a single cash-generating unit, rather than 'drilling down' into the separate cash-generating units determined by the associate or joint venture. The IASB does not explain why it adopted this approach, although we imagine that it may have been for the very practical reason that although an investor has significant influence over an associate, it does not have control and therefore may not have access to the relevant underlying information. Furthermore, IAS 28 requires the investment as a whole to be reviewed for impairment as if it were a financial asset.

Under IAS 39 financial assets are not impaired unless there is 'objective evidence' that one or more events occurring after the initial recognition of the asset ('loss events') have had an impact on the estimated future cash flows of the financial asset or group of financial assets that can be reliably estimated.

Such 'objective evidence' that a financial asset or group of assets is impaired includes observable data that comes to the attention of the holder of the asset about the following loss events:

(a) significant financial difficulty of the issuer or obligor;

(b) a breach of contract, such as a default or delinquency in interest or principal payments;

(c) the lender, for economic or legal reasons relating to the borrower's financial difficulty, granting to the borrower a concession that the lender would not otherwise consider;

(d) it becoming probable that the borrower will enter bankruptcy or other financial reorganisation;

(e) the disappearance of an active market for that financial asset because of financial difficulties; or

Chapter 11

(f) observable data indicating that there is a measurable decrease in the estimated future cash flows from a group of financial assets since the initial recognition of those assets, although the decrease cannot yet be identified with the individual financial assets in the group, including:
   (i) adverse changes in the payment status of borrowers in the group (e.g. an increased number of delayed payments or an increased number of credit card borrowers who have reached their credit limit and are paying the minimum monthly amount); or
   (ii) national or local economic conditions that correlate with defaults on the assets in the group (e.g. an increase in the unemployment rate in the geographical area of the borrowers, a decrease in property prices for mortgages in the relevant area, a decrease in oil prices for loan assets to oil producers, or adverse changes in industry conditions that affect the borrowers in the group). *[IAS 39.59]*.

Many of these considerations can only be applied with difficulty to an investment in an associate or joint venture. We consider that the only practical way in which entities can assess whether interests in associates or joint ventures need to be tested for impairment is by focusing on the cash flow assumptions, in the two bullets earlier in this section, on which the value in use is to be based.

In contrast to the requirement in IAS 36 for annual testing of goodwill relating to subsidiaries, an entity will have to test its associate or joint venture for impairment only if an event has occurred that indicates that it will not recover its carrying value. The most common of these events, trading losses, will automatically have been taken into account in determining the carrying value of the investment, leaving only the remaining net carrying amount (i.e. after deducting the share of trading losses) to be assessed for impairment.

IAS 28 requires that where the entire carrying amount of the investment in an associate or joint venture is tested for impairment in accordance with IAS 36, an impairment loss recognised in these circumstances is not allocated to any asset, including goodwill that forms part of the carrying amount of the associate or joint venture. In addition, any reversal of that impairment loss is recognised in accordance with IAS 36 to the extent that the recoverable amount of the investment subsequently increases. *[IAS 28.42]*.

Consequently, the IAS 36 prohibition on the reversal of impairment losses on goodwill, *[IAS 36.124-125]*, does not apply. The previously recognised impairment of an investment in an associate or joint venture is therefore fully reversible under IFRS.

8.2 IAS 28 and IFRS 9

In July 2014, the IASB issued IFRS 9, which includes consequential amendments to IAS 28 to include the requirement to determine whether there is any objective evidence that the net investment in the associate or joint venture is impaired. IFRS 9 is applicable to annual periods beginning on or after 1 January 2018, although earlier application is permitted.

After application of the equity method, including recognising the associate's or joint venture's losses (see 7.9 above), the entity applies the following requirements to determine whether there is any objective evidence that its net investment in the associate or joint venture is impaired. *[IAS 28.40]*. The entity applies the impairment requirements in IFRS 9 (see Chapter 50 at 5) to its other interests in the associate or joint venture that are in the scope of IFRS 9 and that do not constitute part of the net investment. *[IAS 28.41]*.

- The net investment in an associate or joint venture is impaired and impairment losses are incurred if, and only if, there is objective evidence of impairment as a result of one or more events that occurred after the initial recognition of the net investment (a 'loss event') and that loss event (or events) has an impact on the estimated future cash flows from the net investment that can be reliably estimated. It may not be possible to identify a single, discrete event that caused the impairment. Rather the combined effect of several events may have caused the impairment. Losses expected as a result of future events, no matter how likely, are not recognised. Objective evidence that the net investment is impaired includes observable data that comes to the attention of the entity about the following loss events:
  - significant financial difficulty of the associate or joint venture;
  - a breach of contract, such as a default or delinquency in payments by the associate or joint venture;
  - the entity, for economic or legal reasons relating to its associate's or joint venture's financial difficulty, granting to the associate or joint venture a concession that the entity would not otherwise consider;
  - it becoming probable that the associate or joint venture will enter bankruptcy or other financial reorganisation; or
  - the disappearance of an active market for the net investment because of financial difficulties of the associate or joint venture. *[IAS 28.41A]*.
- The disappearance of an active market because the associate's or joint venture's equity or financial instruments are no longer publicly traded is not evidence of impairment. A downgrade of an associate's or joint venture's credit rating or a decline in the fair value of the associate or joint venture, is not of itself, evidence of impairment, although it may be evidence of impairment when considered with other available information. *[IAS 28.41B]*.
- In addition to the types of events mentioned above, objective evidence of impairment for the net investment in the equity instruments of the associate or joint venture includes information about significant changes with an adverse effect that have taken place in the technological, market, economic or legal environment in which the associate or joint venture operates, and indicates that the cost of the investment in the equity instrument may not be recovered. A significant or prolonged decline in the fair value of an investment in an equity instrument below its cost is also objective evidence of impairment. *[IAS 28.41C]*.

Because goodwill that forms part of the carrying amount of the net investment in an associate or a joint venture is not separately recognised, it is not tested for impairment separately by applying the requirements for impairment testing goodwill in IAS 36. Instead, the entire carrying amount of the investment is tested for impairment in accordance with IAS 36 as a single asset, by comparing its recoverable amount (higher of value in use and fair value less costs to sell) with its carrying amount whenever application of the bullets above indicates that the net investment may be impaired. An impairment loss recognised in those circumstances is not allocated to any asset, including goodwill, that forms part of the carrying amount of the net investment in the associate or joint venture. Accordingly, any reversal of that impairment loss is recognised in accordance with IAS 36 to the extent that the recoverable amount of the net investment subsequently increases. In determining the value in use of the net investment, an entity estimates:

- its share of the present value of the estimated future cash flows expected to be generated by the associate or joint venture, including the cash flows from the operations of the associate or joint venture and the proceeds from the ultimate disposal of the investment; or
- the present value of the estimated future cash flows expected to arise from dividends to be received from the investment and from its ultimate disposal.

Using appropriate assumptions, both methods give the same result. *[IAS 28.42]*

In January 2017, the IASB issued the Exposure Draft *Annual Improvements to IFRS Standards 2015–2017 Cycle* that proposed changes to IAS 28. The IASB proposed to clarify that an entity is required to apply IFRS 9, including its impairment requirements, to long-term interests in an associate or joint venture that, in substance, form part of the net investment in the associate or joint venture but to which the equity method is not applied. After the IASB considered comments on the proposed amendments at the May 2017 meeting, the IASB decided to also clarify that an entity applies the requirements in IFRS 9 to long-term interests before applying the loss allocation and impairment requirements in IAS 28 and in applying IFRS 9, the entity does not take account of any adjustments to the carrying amount of long-term interests that result from the application of IAS 28. It also decided to develop educational material that includes an example illustrating how the requirements in IAS 28 and IFRS 9 interact with respect to long-term interests. This amendment is proposed to be effective for annual periods beginning on or after 1 January 2019 and will require retrospective application and provide transition requirements similar to those in IFRS 9 regarding the classification and measurement of financial assets for entities that apply the amendments after they first apply IFRS 9.[15] The IASB expects to issue the amendments to IAS 28 in September 2017.[16]

9 SEPARATE FINANCIAL STATEMENTS

IAS 27 was amended in August 2014 to allow entities the option to account for investments in subsidiaries, associates and joint ventures using the equity method of accounting.

For the purposes of IAS 28, *separate financial statements* are as defined in IAS 27, *[IAS 28.4]*, as those presented by an entity, in which the entity could elect to account for its investments in subsidiaries, joint ventures and associates either at cost, in accordance with IFRS 9 (or IAS 39) or using the equity method as described in IAS 28.

An investment in an associate or joint venture is accounted for in the entity's separate financial statements in accordance with paragraph 10 of IAS 27. *[IAS 28.44]*. IAS 27 requires that, in separate financial statements, investments in subsidiaries, associates or joint ventures are accounted for either:

- at cost;
- in accordance with IFRS 9 (or IAS 39); or
- using the equity method as described in IAS 28.

The entity applies the same accounting for each category of investments. Investments accounted for at cost or using the equity method are accounted for in accordance with IFRS 5 when they are classified as held for sale (or included in a disposal group that is classified as held for sale). *[IAS 27.10]*.

If an entity elects, in accordance with paragraph 18 of IAS 28, to measure its investments in associates or joint ventures at fair value through profit or loss in accordance with IFRS 9 (or IAS 39) – see 5.3 above, it shall also account for those investments in the same way in its separate financial statements. *[IAS 27.11]*.

IAS 27 requires the investor to recognise all dividends, whether relating to pre-acquisition or post-acquisition profits of the investee, in profit or loss within its separate financial statements once the right to receive payments has been established. *[IAS 27.12]*. The investor then needs to consider whether there are indicators of impairment as set out in paragraph 12(h) of IAS 36 (see Chapter 8 at 2.4.1).

The detailed IFRS requirements for separate financial statements as set out in IAS 27 are discussed more fully in Chapter 8.

9.1 Impairment of investments in associates or joint ventures in separate financial statements

An issue considered by the Interpretations Committee and the IASB is how impairments of investments in associates should be determined in the separate financial statements of the investor. In January 2013 the Interpretations Committee issued an agenda decision[17] stating that according to paragraphs 4 and 5 of IAS 36 and paragraph 2(a) of IAS 39, investments in subsidiaries, joint ventures, and associates that are not accounted for in accordance with IAS 39 are within the scope of IAS 36 for impairment purposes. Consequently, in its separate financial statements, an entity should apply the provisions of IAS 36 to test for impairment its investments in subsidiaries, joint ventures, and associates that are carried at cost or using the equity method.

10 PRESENTATION AND DISCLOSURES

10.1 Presentation

10.1.1 Statement of financial position

Unless an investment, or a portion of an investment, in an associate or a joint venture is classified as held for sale in accordance with IFRS 5 (see 6 above), the investment, or any retained interest in the investment not classified as held for sale, is classified as a non-current asset. *[IAS 28.15]*. The aggregate of investments in associates and joint ventures accounted for using the equity method are presented as a discrete line item in the statement of financial position. *[IAS 1.54(e)]*.

IAS 28 does not explicitly define what is meant by 'investment ... in an associate or a joint venture'. However, paragraph 38 states that 'the interest in an associate or a joint venture is the carrying amount of the investment in the associate or joint venture determined under the equity method together with any long-term interests that, in substance, form part of the investor's net investment in the associate or joint venture. ... Such items may include preference shares and long-term receivables or loans but do not include trade receivables, trade payables or any long-term receivables for which adequate collateral exists, such as secured loans.' *[IAS 28.38].* Some have interpreted this as a requirement to present the investment in ordinary shares and other long-term interests in associates within the same line item.

Yet, when associates are profitable, long-term interests such as loans are normally accounted for under IFRS 9 (or IAS 39) rather than under the equity method. Therefore, it is generally considered acceptable to present the investment in ordinary shares in associates and joint ventures and other long-term interests in associates and joint ventures in separate line items.

Goodwill relating to an associate or joint venture is included in the carrying amount of the investment, *[IAS 28.32]*, as is illustrated in Extract 11.2 below.

Extract 11.2: RWE Aktiengesellschaft (2016)

Notes [extract]

Consolidation principles [extract]

For investments accounted for using the equity method, goodwill is not reported separately, but rather included in the value recognised for the investment. In other respects, the consolidation principles described above apply analogously. If impairment losses on the equity value become necessary, we report such under income from investments accounted for using the equity method. The financial statements of investments accounted for using the equity method are prepared using uniform accounting policies.

10.1.2 Profit or loss

In the statement of comprehensive income or separate income statement, the aggregate of the investor's share of the profit or loss of associates and joint ventures accounted for using the equity method must be shown. *[IAS 1.82(c)].* 'Profit or loss' in this context is interpreted in the implementation guidance to IAS 1 as meaning the 'profit attributable to owners' of the associates and joint ventures, i.e. it is after tax and non-controlling interests in the associates or joint ventures.[18] There is no requirement as to where in the statement of comprehensive income or separate income statement the investor's share of the profit or loss of associates and joint ventures accounted for using the equity method should be shown, and different approaches are therefore seen in practice. As discussed in Chapter 3 at 3.2.2.A, some entities present operating income on the face of the income statement. In this case, equity accounted investments may form part of operating activities with their results included in that measure and with non-operating investments excluded from it. Another acceptable alternative may be to exclude the results of all associates and joint ventures from operating profit.

Nokia for example includes its share of the (post-tax) results of associates after operating profit, but before pre-tax profit:

Extract 11.3: Nokia Corporation (2016)

Consolidated income statement [extract]

For the year ended December 31	Notes	2016 EURm	2015[(1)] EURm	2014[(1)] EURm
Operating (loss)/profit		(1 100)	1 697	1 414
Share of results of associated companies and joint ventures	34	18	29	(12)
Financial income and expenses	11	(287)	(186)	(403)
(Loss)/profit before tax		(1 369)	1 540	999

[(1)] In 2016, following the Acquisition of Alcatel Lucent, the Group adopted a new financial reporting structure which resulted in changes to allocation and presentation principles of certain costs. Comparatives for 2015 and 2014 have been recasted to reflect the new financial reporting structure.

In contrast, Nestlé includes its share of the post-tax results of associates below tax expense:

Extract 11.4: Nestlé S.A. (2016)

Consolidated income statement
for the year ended 31 December 2016 [extract]

In millions of CHF	Notes	2016	2015
Profit before taxes, associates and joint ventures		12 526	11 784
Taxes	13	(4 413)	(3 305)
Income from associates and joint ventures	14	770	988
Profit for the year		8 883	9 467

10.1.2.A Impairment of associates or joint ventures

It is unclear where impairments of associates or joint ventures should be presented in the statement of comprehensive income or separate income statement. IAS 28 requires an impairment test to be performed 'after application of the equity method', *[IAS 28.40]*, which could be read as implying that impairment of an associate or joint venture is not part of the investor's share of the profit or loss of an associate or joint venture accounted for using the equity method. On the other hand, the guidance on accounting for impairment losses on associates is presented under the heading 'Application of the equity method' in IAS 28, which suggests that accounting for impairments of associates is part of the equity method. In practice, both interpretations appear to have gained a degree of acceptance.

RWE, for example, reports impairment losses on associates within income from investments accounted for using the equity method (see Extract 11.2 at 10.1.1 above).

10.1.3 Other items of comprehensive income

The investor's share of items recognised in other comprehensive income by the associate or joint venture is recognised in the investor's other comprehensive income. *[IAS 28.10]*.

In December 2014, the IASB issued *Disclosure Initiative (amendments to IAS 1)*. Paragraph 82A of IAS 1 was amended to clarify that entities must present the share of other comprehensive income of associates and joint ventures accounted for using the equity method, separated into the share of items that, in accordance with other IFRSs:

- will not be subsequently reclassified to profit or loss; and
- will be reclassified subsequently to profit or loss when specific conditions are met. *[IAS 1.82A]*.

The amendment applies to annual periods beginning on or after 1 January 2016.

'Other comprehensive income' in this context is interpreted in the implementation guidance to IAS 1 as meaning the 'other comprehensive income attributable to owners' of the associates and joint ventures, i.e. it is after tax and non-controlling interests in the associates or joint ventures.[19]

10.1.4 Statement of cash flows

IAS 7 – *Statement of Cash Flows* – notes that for an equity accounted investment, reporting in the cash flow statement is limited to cash flows between the investor and the investee, such as dividends received. The question arises as to whether dividends received should be recognised as operating or investing cash flows. As discussed in Chapter 38 at 4.4.1, IAS 7 is not prescriptive; however, entities should select an accounting policy and apply it consistently.

10.2 Disclosures

The disclosure requirements for associates and joint ventures are dealt with in IFRS 12, together with the disclosure requirements for subsidiaries and unconsolidated structured entities. The disclosure requirements in relation to associates and joint ventures are discussed in Chapter 13 at 5.

11 FUTURE DEVELOPMENTS

As discussed in 7.2 above, many procedures appropriate for the application of the equity method are similar to the consolidation procedures described in IFRS 10 (see Chapter 7). Furthermore, IAS 28 explains that the concepts underlying the procedures used in accounting for the acquisition of a subsidiary are also adopted in accounting for the acquisition of an investment in an associate or a joint venture. *[IAS 28.26]*. This does raise a number of practical difficulties, and there has been an ongoing debate about whether the equity method of accounting is a consolidation method or a measurement method. Although IAS 28 generally adopts consolidation principles it nevertheless retains features of a valuation methodology.

In 2015, the IASB tentatively decided to undertake a research project on the equity method.[20] However, in May 2016 the IASB[21] deferred this project until the Post-implementation Reviews (PIR) of IFRS 10, IFRS 11 – *Joint Arrangements* – and IFRS 12 are complete which will include seeking feedback on investors' information needs regarding equity method investments.

References

1 *IFRIC Update*, November 2016.
2 IFRS 12.9(d).
3 IFRS 12.9(e).
4 Staff Paper, Interpretations Committee meeting, May 2009, Agenda reference 3, *Venture capital consolidations and partial use of fair value through profit or loss.*
5 *IFRIC Update*, July 2009.
6 *IFRIC Update*, July 2010.
7 Staff paper, Interpretations Committee meeting, July 2010, Agenda reference 16, *IAS 28 – Investments in Associates – Purchase in stages – fair value as deemed cost*, paras. 24 and 29.
8 *IFRIC Update*, July 2010.
9 IAS 1 IG6 'XYZ Group – Statement of comprehensive income for the year ended 31 December 20X7 (illustrating the presentation of profit and loss and other comprehensive income in one statement and the classification of expenses within profit by function)'.
10 *IFRIC Update*, May 2013.
11 *IASB Update*, July 2013.
12 Detailed worked examples on the elimination cross-holdings in subsidiaries and associates can be found in *Bogie on group accounts*, John C. Shaw (editor), Bristol, 1973.
13 *IFRIC Update*, August 2002, p.3.
14 *Sale or Contribution of Assets between an Investor and its Associate or Joint Venture (amendments to IFRS 10 and IAS 28), September 2014.*
15 *IASB Update*, May 2017.
16 *IASB Update*, June 2017.
17 *IFRIC Update*, January 2013.
18 IAS 1 IG6 'XYZ Group – Statement of comprehensive income for the year ended 31 December 20X7 (illustrating the presentation of profit and loss and other comprehensive income in one statement and the classification of expenses within profit by function)'.
19 IAS 1 IG6 'XYZ Group – Statement of comprehensive income for the year ended 31 December 20X7 (illustrating the presentation of profit and loss and other comprehensive income in one statement and the classification of expenses within profit by function)'.
20 *IASB Update*, May 2016.

Chapter 12 Joint arrangements

Chapter 12

List of examples

Chapter 12 Joint arrangements

1 INTRODUCTION

1.1 The nature of joint arrangements

An entity may pursue an economic activity with one or more third parties and share decision-making relating to those activities. IFRS 11 – *Joint Arrangements* – is applicable when the arrangement establishes joint control over an activity, *[IFRS 11.4]*, between two or more of the parties involved.

A joint arrangement is an arrangement that has the following characteristics:

(a) the parties are bound by a contractual arrangement; and

(b) the contractual arrangement gives two or more of those parties joint control of the arrangement. *[IFRS 11.5]*.

The terms 'joint arrangement,' 'joint control' and 'joint venture' are specifically defined by IFRS 11 and have important accounting consequences. However, these terms also may be used loosely in practice and may appear in legal documents and public statements by management. The terms below also are frequently used in practice because they stem from IAS 31 – *Interests in Joint Ventures* – (the predecessor of IFRS 11), although not defined in IFRS 11:

- Jointly controlled operations in which each party to the arrangement uses its own property, plant and equipment, carries its own inventories, incurs its own expenses and liabilities and raises its own finance to contribute to the economic activities of the arrangement.
- Jointly controlled, and often jointly owned, assets acquired or contributed to be used in the economic activities of the arrangement.
- Jointly controlled entities, which involve the establishment of a corporation, partnership or other entity to conduct the economic activities and in which each party has an interest. *[IFRS 11.BC25]*.

IFRS 11 classifies joint arrangements into one of two types, joint operations and joint ventures. *[IFRS 11.6]*. Parties to a joint operation have rights to the assets, and obligations for the liabilities, whereas parties to a joint venture have rights to the net assets of the arrangement. *[IFRS 11 Appendix A, BC24]*. Whether a separate legal entity is involved is not the definitive issue in classification (see 1.2 below).

A joint operation combines the concepts of a jointly controlled operation and a jointly controlled asset into a single concept for which the accounting is the recognition of assets and liabilities and revenues and expenses. *[IFRS 11.BC25]*. An entity must apply judgement to classify an existing jointly controlled entity either as a joint operation or a joint venture based on an assessment of the parties' rights and obligations that arise from the arrangement. *[IFRS 11.BC28]*.

No matter the terminology used to describe the arrangement, or its purpose, management needs to evaluate the terms of the arrangement, and the relevant facts and circumstances, to determine if it is a joint arrangement as defined in IFRS 11.

1.2 Development of IFRS 11

The IASB developed IFRS 11 to address the following aspects of previous accounting models:

- The existence of a legal entity within the arrangement was the only determinant factor to classify a joint arrangement. *[IFRS 11.IN3, BC8]*. IFRS 11 establishes a principle-based approach to classify a joint arrangement. *[IFRS 11.BC3]*. The principles in IFRS 11 focus more broadly on the rights and obligations arising from the arrangement and are therefore applicable to all joint arrangements irrespective of whether a legal entity exists. *[IFRS 11.IN4]*.
- A party to a jointly controlled entity previously had a choice to account for its interest using the equity method or using proportionate consolidation. *[IFRS 11.IN3]*. The IASB's policy is to exclude options in accounting treatments whenever possible. *[IFRS 11.BC8]*. IFRS 11 removes this choice and prescribes the accounting treatment for a joint operation and joint venture. The removal of proportionate consolidation as an accounting policy choice achieved closer convergence with US GAAP. *[IFRS 11.BC3]*.

The disclosure requirements regarding joint arrangements are in IFRS 12 – *Disclosure of Interests in Other Entities*. Importantly, IFRS 12 requires an entity to disclose the judgements made to determine whether it has joint control over another entity, as well as those made to classify joint arrangements. An entity is also required to disclose summarised financial information for each material joint venture. Chapter 13 at 5 deals with the requirements of IFRS 12 in respect of joint arrangements.

Although the IASB did not fundamentally reconsider the equity method when IFRS 11 was developed, *[IFRS 11.BC5]*, it issued a revised version of IAS 28 – *Investments in Associates and Joint Ventures*. This includes changes in the characterisation of the 'scope exemption' for venture capital organisations and similar entities (see 2.3.1 below) and the accounting where a joint venture becomes an associate, or *vice versa* (see 8.2.4 below).

1.3 Future developments

1.3.1 Research programme on equity method of accounting

In May 2012, the IASB unanimously supported initiating a research programme on several topics, including the equity method of accounting.[1] We supported this move, since the equity method of accounting is currently a significant area of judgement and diversity in practice. In addition, there has been an increase in use of the equity method, as IFRS 11 requires the use of the equity method to account for interests in joint ventures (see 7 below). Following feedback from the 2015 Agenda Consultation and a review of the research findings so far, this project has been deferred until the Post-implementation Reviews (PIR) of IFRS 10, IFRS 11, and IFRS 12[2] have been completed. Chapter 11 discusses the equity method in more detail.

1.3.2 Remeasurement of previously held interests

On 28 June 2016, the IASB issued proposed amendments to IFRS 3 – *Business Combinations* – and IFRS 11 in an ED *Definition of a Business and Accounting for Previously Held Interests (Proposed amendments to IFRS 3 and IFRS 11).* At the time of this publication, this exposure draft has not yet been finalised. This is discussed in 8.3.2. below.

1.3.3 2015 agenda consultation

Recently, we have seen an increase in risk sharing agreements (commonly referred to as 'collaboration arrangements') in, for example, the pharmaceuticals and aerospace and defence industries. Such an arrangement can include a contract to buy an asset, in which the price payable reflects the performance of that asset after the transaction date, thereby sharing the risks and benefits of that asset's performance between the buyer and the seller. It also can include a joint arrangement, and other similar arrangements in which the risks and rewards of a particular activity are shared between the participants. These arrangements may be outside the scope of IFRS 11 when there is not joint control; in which case, other IFRSs should be applied based on the rights and obligations established by the arrangement.

In May 2016, the IASB added variable and contingent consideration for an asset purchase and possible follow-on work on risk-sharing and collaborative arrangements to its research pipeline programme. The IASB expects to begin work on these projects between 2017 and 2021.[3]

2 EFFECTIVE DATE, OBJECTIVE AND SCOPE OF IFRS 11

2.1 Effective date

IFRS 11 was effective for annual periods beginning on or after 1 January 2013 and was effective for a first-time adopter of IFRS on the date of transition to IFRS (see Chapter 5). Early adoption was permitted with disclosure of that fact, if the entity adopted IFRS 10 – *Consolidated Financial Statements*, IFRS 12, IAS 27 (as amended in 2011) and IAS 28 (as amended in 2011) as of the same date. *[IFRS 11.C1].* As noted at 8.3.1. below, paragraphs 21A, B33A-B33D and C1AA and their related headings, which were introduced by the May 2014 amendment to IFRS 11 – *Acquisitions of Interests in Joint Operations*, were effective prospectively for annual periods beginning on or after 1 January 2016.

Chapter 12

2.2 Objective

The objective of IFRS 11 is to establish principles for financial reporting by entities that have an interest in a joint arrangement. *[IFRS 11.1].* As a result, the standard defines and provides guidance on:

- what a joint arrangement is and when joint control is present (see 3 and 4 below);
- the two types of joint arrangements and how to classify an arrangement (see 5 below); and
- how to account for each type of joint arrangement in the financial statements of a party to a joint arrangement (see 6, 7 and 8 below). *[IFRS 11.2].*

2.3 Scope

IFRS 11 applies to all entities that are a party to a joint arrangement. *[IFRS 11.3].* A 'party to a joint arrangement' is defined as 'an entity that participates in a joint arrangement, regardless of whether that entity has joint control of the arrangement'. *[IFRS 11 Appendix A].* Therefore, an entity could be in the scope of IFRS 11 even though it does not have joint control of an arrangement.

2.3.1 Application by venture capital organisations and similar entities

IFRS 11 applies to all entities that are party to a joint arrangement, including venture capital organisations, mutual funds, unit trusts, investment-linked insurance funds and similar entities (referred to hereafter as 'venture capital organisations'). However, venture capital organisations can choose to measure investments in joint ventures at fair value under the measurement exemption in IAS 28 (see Chapter 11 at 5.3), but remain subject to the disclosure requirements of IFRS 12 (see Chapter 13 at 5). *[IFRS 11.BC15-18].*

It should be noted that a venture capital organisation with investments in subsidiaries and associates and/or joint ventures could only qualify as an 'investment entity' under IFRS 10 and measure its investments in subsidiaries at fair value, if it elected to measure its investments in associates and/or joint ventures at fair value through profit or loss. *[IFRS 10.B85L].*

2.3.2 Application to joint arrangements held for sale

As discussed at 8.2.7 below, an investment in a joint venture (or portion thereof) that is classified as held for sale under IFRS 5 – *Non-current Assets Held for Sale and Discontinued Operations* – is accounted for under IFRS 5 and is effectively scoped out of IFRS 11 and IAS 28. *[IAS 28.20].* Similarly, a joint operation that is held for sale under IFRS 5 would be effectively scoped out of IFRS 11 and accounted for under IFRS 5.

2.3.3 Accounting by a joint operation

The scope of IFRS 11 does not address the accounting by the joint operation itself.

In March 2015, the Interpretations Committee published its agenda decision on the issue of the accounting by a joint operation that is a separate vehicle in its financial statements. This issue has arisen because the joint operators recognise their share of assets and liabilities held by the joint operation, which leads to the question of whether those same assets and liabilities should also be recognised in the financial statements of the joint operation itself. The Interpretations Committee decided not to add the issue to its agenda, because the following guidance exists:

- IFRS 11 applies only to the accounting by the joint operators and not to the accounting by a separate vehicle that is a joint operation;
- the financial statements of the separate vehicle would therefore be prepared in accordance with applicable IFRSs. Note that IFRS 3 does not apply to 'the accounting for the formation of a joint arrangement in the financial statements of the joint arrangement itself' (refer Chapter 9 at 2.2.1); *[IFRS 3.2(a)]* and
- company law often requires a legal entity or separate vehicle to prepare financial statements. Consequently, the financial statements would include the assets, liabilities, revenues and expenses of that legal entity/separate vehicle. The determination of which assets and liabilities to recognise and their measurement will depend on rights and obligations of the separate vehicle and specific facts and circumstances.

3 JOINT ARRANGEMENT

IFRS 11 defines a joint arrangement as 'an arrangement of which two or more parties have joint control'. *[IFRS 11 Appendix A]*.

IFRS 11 notes that the contractual arrangement that binds the parties together is often, but not always, in writing. Unwritten agreements are rare in practice. Laws can also create enforceable arrangements, with or without a contract. *[IFRS 11.B2]*. A joint arrangement can be structured through a separate vehicle (see 5.1 below). That entity's articles, charter or by-laws also may include aspects of the contractual arrangement. *[IFRS 11.B3]*.

Contractual arrangements generally specify the following:

- purpose, activity and duration of the joint arrangement;
- appointment of members of the board of directors (or equivalent governing body);
- decision-making processes:
  - matters requiring decisions from the parties;
  - voting rights of the parties; and
  - required level of agreement for those matters;
- capital or other contribution requirements; and
- sharing of assets, liabilities, revenues, expenses or profit or loss relating to the joint arrangement. *[IFRS 11.B4]*.

Understanding the terms of the contractual arrangement is crucial in determining whether joint control exists (see 4 below) and, if so, in deciding whether the joint arrangement is a joint operation or joint venture (see 5 below).

3.1 Unit of account

The unit of account of a joint arrangement is the activity that two or more parties have agreed to control jointly. A party should assess its rights to the assets and obligations for the liabilities, relating to that activity, regardless of whether the activity is conducted in a separate vehicle. *[IFRS 11.BC20, BC35]*. IFRS 11 does not define 'activity'. Therefore, the determination of the unit of account may require judgement in arrangements that are complex.

The purpose and design of an arrangement may provide insight into how to identify the unit of account (see 4.4.2 below). For example, a framework agreement can establish multiple joint arrangements of different types. *[IFRS 11.18]*. The possibility also exists that, within the same separate vehicle, parties to the arrangement may undertake different activities in which they have different rights to the assets, and obligations for the liabilities, resulting in different types of joint arrangements conducted within the same separate vehicle. The IASB believes such situations would be rare in practice. *[IFRS 11.BC36]*. We are aware of scenarios where the activity is larger than a single entity or separate vehicle. We refer to these as 'layered agreements', which are discussed in Example 12.11 at 4.4.2 below.

Example 12.1 below illustrates a case where a master agreement may be accounted for as several distinct joint arrangements, each of which is classified as either a joint operation or a joint venture.

Example 12.1: Master agreement for manufacturing and distribution

A single contract between two parties specifies the terms and conditions related to manufacturing and distribution activities and dictates how these activities are carried out in various jurisdictions through several entities. The activities are carried out concurrently and not sequentially (see 4.1.1 below). In each entity, the parties jointly control the relevant activities.

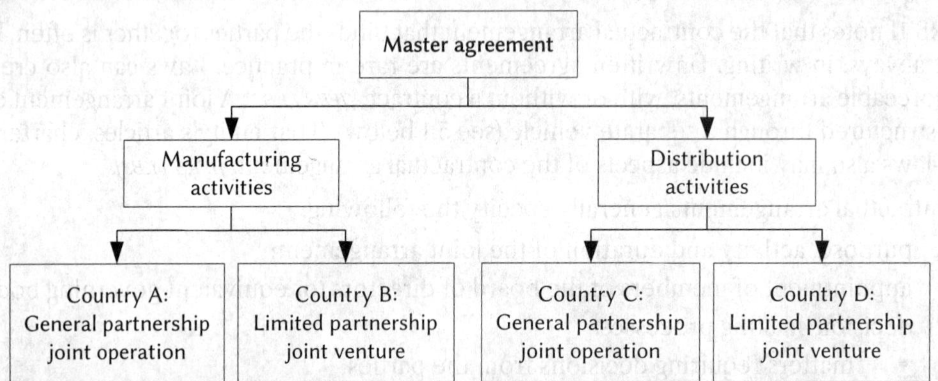

The parties may determine that this agreement contains several discrete joint arrangements (one for each activity in each jurisdiction, which corresponds to an entity). In this case, each entity would likely be classified as a joint venture *or* a joint operation. This would likely be the case if the terms and conditions relating to each activity were distinct for each separate vehicle. Although in this example, it is concluded that the general partnerships are joint operations and the limited partnerships are joint ventures, this may not always be the case depending on the legal form, contractual terms, and facts and circumstances.

In some cases, there will be multiple contractual agreements between parties that relate to the same activities, which may need to be analysed together to determine whether a joint arrangement exists, and if so, the type of joint arrangement.

In other cases, there may be a single master agreement between two parties that covers several different activities. Some of these activities may be controlled solely by one of the two parties, while the parties may jointly control other activities. Careful analysis is required to determine the unit of account and to assess whether any of the arrangements are jointly controlled. Example 12.2 below illustrates a case where a contract contains multiple agreements, only one of which is a joint arrangement.

Example 12.2: Agreements with control and joint control

Assume the same information as per Example 12.1 with the following variation: One party has the ability to direct the marketing activities in the entity in Country A and the other party has the ability to direct the marketing activities in the entity in Country B. As in Example 12.1, in Country C and D the parties jointly control the relevant activities.

In this case, there would *not* be joint control between the two parties in the entities in Country A and B. Rather, each party controls its respective entities, and therefore such entities would not be joint arrangements. The distribution activities conducted in the entities in Country C and D would still be joint arrangements and would each be classified as either a joint operation or a joint venture. See Example 12.17, at 5.5 below, for a case where two parties have two joint arrangements and each joint arrangement relates to a specific activity.

4 JOINT CONTROL

As noted above, the crucial element in having a joint arrangement is joint control, and, therefore, it is important to understand this term.

Joint control is 'the contractually agreed sharing of control of an arrangement, which exists only when decisions about the relevant activities require the unanimous consent of the parties sharing control.' *[IFRS 11.7, Appendix A].*

As discussed under 2.3 above, not all the parties to the joint arrangement need to have joint control of the relevant activities for the arrangement to be classified as a joint arrangement. Therefore, IFRS 11 distinguishes between parties that have joint control of a joint arrangement and those that do not. *[IFRS 11.11].* A joint operator and a joint venturer refer to parties that have joint control of a joint operation and joint venture respectively. *[IFRS 11 Appendix A].* IFRS 11 does not explicitly define a party that participates in, but does not have joint control of, a joint arrangement. We refer to these parties as 'parties that participate in a joint arrangement but do not have joint control'. IFRS 11 specifies the accounting for parties that participate in a joint arrangement but do not have joint control (see 6.4 and 7.1 below).

The following flowchart provided in IFRS 11 illustrates how a party to a joint arrangement should evaluate if joint control exists. *[IFRS 11.B10].*

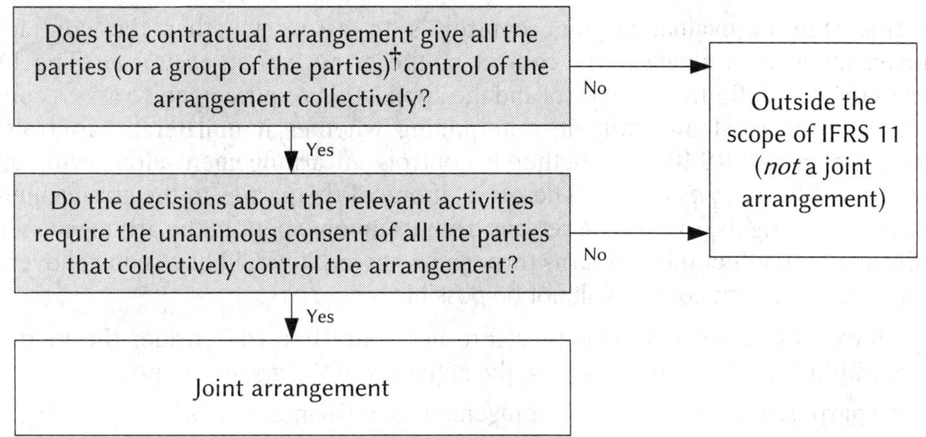

† The reference to 'a group of the parties' refers to a situation in which there is joint control between two or more parties, but other parties to the arrangement are parties that participate in a joint arrangement but do not have joint control.

We discuss key aspects of joint control within this chapter, as follows:

- contractual arrangement – See 3 above;
- assessing control – See 4.1 below;
- rights to control collectively – See 4.2 below;
- unanimous consent – See 4.3 below; and
- other practical issues with assessing joint control – See 4.4 below.

Judgement is required when assessing whether all the parties, or a group of the parties, have joint control of an arrangement by considering all facts and circumstances. *[IFRS 11.12].*

In some cases, it will be clear that there is not collective control (see 4.2 below), or not unanimous consent (see 4.3 below). In cases where it is clear that neither of the two criteria are met, there would not be a joint arrangement, for example, a cooperative advertising cost-sharing agreement (see Chapter 29 at 5.5) between a retailer and a wholesaler that does not establish joint control over the marketing activities. We also believe that it would be rare for a publicly listed entity to be subject to joint control, since it would be unusual to have a contractual agreement among all the shareholders to direct the activities of such an entity.

When it is not clear whether joint control exists, a party to a joint arrangement would need to exercise significant judgement to determine whether there is joint control. In such cases, IFRS 12 requires that an entity disclose information when it has to make significant judgements and assumptions to determine that it has joint control (see Chapter 13 at 3). *[IFRS 12.7].*

When an arrangement is outside the scope of IFRS 11, an entity accounts for its interest in the arrangement in accordance with relevant IFRSs, such as IFRS 10, IAS 28 or IFRS 9 – *Financial Instruments* (or IAS 39 – *Financial Instruments: Recognition and Measurement* – if IFRS 9 is not yet applied). *[IFRS 11.B11, C14].*

4.1 Assessing control

The first step in evaluating joint control is to assess whether the contractual arrangement gives a single party control of the arrangement. *[IFRS 11.10].* The IASB believes that the definition of control and the application requirements to assess control in IFRS 10 will assist an entity in determining whether it unilaterally controls an arrangement per IFRS 10, or whether it controls an arrangement along with other parties, per IFRS 11. *[IFRS 11.BC14].* Therefore, if one of the parties to the arrangement is exposed, or has rights, to variable returns from its involvement in the arrangement and has the ability to affect those returns through its power, it would have control over the arrangement and joint control will not be possible. *[IFRS 11.B5].*

To perform this assessment, it is therefore necessary first to consider the following factors within IFRS 10 as they relate to the activities of the arrangement:

- the purpose and design of the arrangement (see Chapter 6 at 3.2);
- what the relevant activities of the arrangement are and how decisions about those activities are made (see Chapter 6 at 4.1);

- whether the rights of the party give it the current ability to direct the relevant activities (see Chapter 6 at 4.2 to 4.6);
- whether the party is exposed, or has rights, to variable returns from its involvement with the arrangement (see Chapter 6 at 5); and
- whether the party has the ability to use its power over to affect the amount of its returns (see Chapter 6 at 6). *[IFRS 10.B3]*.

4.1.1 Sequential activities

The determination of the relevant activities of an arrangement might be complicated when the arrangement includes different activities that occur at different times. For example, some joint arrangements operate in sequential production phases, such as those in the mining, construction, real estate, and life-sciences industries. These arrangements generally fall into two types of situations:

- parties have rights to direct different activities; or
- parties collectively direct all of the activities.

In the first situation, each party would assess whether it has the rights to direct the activities that most significantly affect returns, and therefore whether they control the arrangement (see Chapter 6 at 4.1.1). The parties to the arrangement should reconsider this assessment over time if relevant facts or circumstances change. *[IFRS 11.13]*.

Example 12.3 and 12.4 illustrate the above principles. They are based on an example taken from IFRS 10. *[IFRS 10.B13 Example 1]*.

Example 12.3: Directing sequential activities separately

Company A and B enter into an arrangement, structured through a separate vehicle, to develop and market a medical product. Company A is responsible for developing and obtaining regulatory approval for the medical product. This includes having the unilateral ability to make all decisions relating to the development of the product and to obtain regulatory approval. Once the regulator has approved the product, Company B will manufacture and market it and has the unilateral ability to make all decisions about the manufacturing and marketing of the project. All of the activities – developing and obtaining regulatory approval as well as manufacturing and marketing of the medical product – are relevant activities. The most relevant activity is the developing and obtaining regulatory approval of the medical product.

In Example 12.3 above, there is no joint control because the parties to the arrangement do not collectively direct the most relevant activity of the arrangement. Rather, one party directs each activity. However, if the fact pattern were different such that they collectively directed the most relevant activity of the arrangement, then there would be joint control. This is described in Example 12.4 below.

Example 12.4: Directing sequential activities jointly

Company A and B enter into an arrangement, structured through a separate vehicle, to develop and market a medical product. Company A and Company B are responsible for developing and obtaining regulatory approval for the medical product. The arrangement establishes joint control over the decisions relating to the development of the product and to obtain regulatory approval. Once the regulator has approved the product, Company B will manufacture and market it and have the unilateral ability to make all decisions about the manufacturing and marketing of the project. All of the activities – developing and obtaining regulatory approval as well as manufacturing and marketing of the medical product – are relevant activities. The most relevant activity is the developing and obtaining regulatory approval of the medical product.

4.2 Rights to control collectively

Joint control can only exist when the parties collectively control the arrangement. *[IFRS 11.B5]*. In other words, all the parties, or a group of the parties, must act together to direct the activities that significantly affect the returns of the arrangement. *[IFRS 11.8]*, which is referred to as 'collective control'. Factors to consider when determining whether a group of parties have collective control are addressed in the following sections.

4.2.1 Protective rights, including some veto rights

IFRS 10 defines protective rights as 'rights designed to protect the interest of the party holding those rights without giving that party power over the entity to which those rights relate'. *[IFRS 10 Appendix A]*.

Protective rights relate to fundamental changes to the activities of the arrangement, or apply in exceptional circumstances. Since power is an essential element of control, protective rights do not give a party control over the arrangement. Holding protective rights cannot prevent another party from having power over an arrangement (see Chapter 6 at 4.2.2). *[IFRS 10.B26-27]*.

Accordingly, when assessing whether a group of the parties collectively control an arrangement, consideration must be given to whether rights held by any of the parties are:

- protective – in which case, the other parties might collectively control the arrangement, and those parties might have joint control; or
- substantive – in which case, such rights could prevent the other parties from having joint control, and possibly give the holder of those rights control.

Example 12.5 below illustrates this point with veto rights, which are often protective rights.

Example 12.5: Protective rights and joint control

A, B and C enter into a joint arrangement to conduct an activity in entity Z. The contractual agreement between A and B states that they must agree to direct all of the activities of Z. The agreement of C is not required, except that C has the right to veto the issuance of debt or equity instruments by Z. The ability to veto the issuance of equity and debt instruments is deemed a protective right because the right is designed to protect C's interest without giving C the ability to direct the activities that most significantly affect Z's returns.

In this fact pattern, A and B have joint control over Z because they collectively have the ability to direct Z and the contractual agreement requires their unanimous consent. Although C is a party to the joint arrangement, C does not have joint control because C only holds a protective right with respect to Z.

An arrangement may be structured such that, rather than giving some parties protective rights, one party has the deciding vote in case of a tie or disagreement (see 4.3.2 below).

4.2.2 Potential voting rights and joint control

Common examples of potential voting rights include options, forward contracts, and conversion features of a convertible instrument that if exercised, would change the decision-making rights of the parties to the arrangement.

IFRS 11 does not explicitly address how to deal with potential voting rights when assessing whether there is joint control. However, since joint control requires the parties collectively to have 'control' as defined in IFRS 10, a party to a joint arrangement must consider the requirements of IFRS 10 regarding potential voting rights. To evaluate whether a potential voting right is substantive, and whether joint control exists, it is necessary to understand the purpose and design of the potential voting right and the context in which it was issued or granted. Guidance on how to assess if a potential voting right is substantive is discussed further in Chapter 6 at 4.3.4.

If the potential voting right is substantive, then the holder could have joint control together with the other parties, if the terms of the contractual arrangement confer joint control.

4.2.3 *Other evidence of joint control*

In some cases, it may be difficult to determine whether the rights of a group of the parties give them collective power over an arrangement. In such cases, the parties consider other evidence to indicate whether they have the current ability to direct the relevant activities collectively. IFRS 10 lists several examples of this evidence (see Chapter 6 at 4.5).

Another fact that may indicate that a group of the parties have collective control, is whether the parties can obtain the financial information needed to account for the arrangement (e.g. to apply the equity method in the case of a joint venture) and to provide the required disclosures. If the group of the parties cannot obtain information regarding an arrangement (e.g. because management of that arrangement refuses to provide it), this might indicate that, the parties do not have collective control (and therefore, no joint control) over that arrangement.

4.2.4 *Delegated decision-making*

In some cases, one of the parties may be appointed as the operational manager of the arrangement. This commonly occurs in the extractive and real estate industries, for example, when one of the parties has extensive experience in the type of activities conducted. The operational manager is frequently referred to as the 'operator', but since IFRS 11 uses the terms 'joint operation' and 'joint operator' with specific meaning, to avoid confusion we refer to such a party as the 'manager'. The other parties to the arrangement may delegate some or all of the decision-making rights to this manager.

To evaluate joint control, a party to the arrangement would need to assess whether the contractual arrangement gives the manager control of the arrangement (see 4.1 above). IFRS 10 also describes how to assess whether the manager is acting as a principal or an agent on behalf of all, or a group of, the parties to the arrangement. Careful consideration of the following will be required (see Chapter 6 at 6):

- The scope of the manager's decision-making authority.
- The rights held by others (e.g. protective rights and removal rights).
- The manager's exposure to the variable returns of the arrangement through management fees earned.
- The manager's exposure to the variable returns of the arrangement through other interests, for example, a direct investment held by the manager in the joint arrangement.

See Chapter 41 at 7.1 for discussion of the application of IFRS 11 to entities in the extractive industries where this situation is more common.

Therefore, depending on the facts and circumstances, it is possible that joint control exists even when a manager is appointed, if the arrangement requires contractually agreed unanimous consent for decisions about the relevant activities. Accordingly, arrangements where the manager appears to have power over the relevant activities should be analysed carefully, to determine whether joint control exists, and if so, which parties share in the joint control.

4.2.5 Related parties and de facto agents

One party to an arrangement may act as a *de facto* agent for another party (see Chapter 6 at 7). *De facto* agents may include related parties (as defined in IAS 24 – *Related Party Disclosures*). A party to a joint arrangement should therefore assess whether any of the parties to the arrangement is acting as a *de facto* agent of another party to determine if joint control is established. Example 12.6 illustrates this point.

Example 12.6: De facto agents in joint control

A contractual arrangement has three parties: A has 50% of the voting rights and B and C each have 25%. The contractual arrangement between A, B and C specifies that at least 75% of the voting rights are required to make decisions about the relevant activities of the arrangement.

Analysis

A, B and C collectively control the relevant activities of the arrangement. However, there is neither control nor joint control, because more than one combination of parties can reach 75% and therefore direct the relevant activities.

Variation – If the facts and circumstances changed, such that C is a *de facto* agent of B, then A and B would have joint control, because effectively B would direct 50% (in combination with C's 25%) and A would need B to agree to direct the relevant activities.

Identifying *de facto* agents can be complex and requires judgement and a careful evaluation of all the facts and circumstances.

4.2.6 Role of a government

In some countries, the government may retain a substantial interest in certain arrangements. When a government entity is party to an arrangement, the arrangement needs to be evaluated carefully to determine whether joint control or control exists. This is illustrated in Example 12.7 below.

Example 12.7: Role of a government

A government owns land, which is believed to contain oil reserves. The government enters into a contractual arrangement with an oil company to drill for oil and sell the product, which the oil company will do through a separate vehicle. The oil company will have to evaluate the contractual terms of the arrangement closely to determine whether it has joint control, control, or some other type of interest. The ownership percentages in the separate vehicle do not necessarily determine whether there is control by one party or joint control.

In some cases, the contractual terms may give all final decision-making authority over the relevant activities to the government, in which case, the government would have control.

However, in other cases, the decision-making authority may require unanimous consent by the government and the oil company to direct the activities, in which case, they would have joint control.

4.3 Unanimous consent

If all the parties, or a group of the parties, control the arrangement collectively, joint control exists only when decisions about the relevant activities require the unanimous consent of the parties that control the arrangement collectively. *[IFRS 11.9, B6]*. Accordingly, it is not necessary for every party to the arrangement to have joint control. Only those parties that collectively control the arrangement must agree.

In a joint arrangement, no single party controls the arrangement. A party with joint control of an arrangement can prevent any of the other parties, or a group of the parties, from controlling the arrangement. *[IFRS 11.10]*. In other words, the requirement for unanimous consent means that any party with joint control of the arrangement can prevent any of the other parties, or a group of the parties, from making unilateral decisions (about the relevant activities) without its consent. *[IFRS 11.B9]*.

IFRS 11 provides additional guidance on when unanimous consent exists. For example, a contractual arrangement can establish unanimous consent implicitly where the proportion of the voting rights needed to make decisions about the relevant activities effectively requires a specified combination of the parties to agree. *[IFRS 11.B7]*. When that minimum proportion voting rights can be achieved by more than one combination of the parties agreeing, the arrangement is not a joint arrangement unless it specifies which parties (or combination of parties) are required to agree unanimously to decisions about the relevant activities of the arrangement. *[IFRS 11.B8]*. IFRS 11 provides some examples to illustrate this point. Examples 1 and 2 are summarised in the following table. *[IFRS 11.B8 Example 1, 2]*.

Chapter 12

Example 1	Example 2
Minimum voting requirement 75% vote to direct relevant activities	**Minimum voting requirement** 75% vote to direct relevant activities
Party A – 50% Party B – 30% Party C – 20%	Party A – 50% Party B – 25% Party C – 25%
Conclusion *Joint control* – A and B collectively control the arrangement (since their votes, and only their votes, together meet the requirement). As there is only one combination of parties that collectively control the arrangement, it is clear that A and B must unanimously agree. C is a 'party that participates in a joint arrangement but does not have joint control' (see 4 above).	**Conclusion** *No joint control* – multiple combinations of parties could collectively control the arrangement (i.e. A and B or A and C could vote together to meet the requirement). Since there are multiple combinations, and the contractual agreement does not specify which parties must agree, there is no unanimous consent.

4.3.1 Arrangements involving parties that participate in a joint arrangement but who do not have joint control

Unanimous consent needs to be explicitly or implicitly established by contract. For example, two parties, A and B, each have 35% of the voting rights in an arrangement with the remaining 30% being widely dispersed and decisions about the relevant activities require approval by a majority of the voting rights. In this situation, A and B have joint control of the arrangement only if the contractual arrangement specifies that decisions about the relevant activities of the arrangement require agreement of both A and B. *[IFRS 11.B8 Example 3]*. The fact that the remaining 30% of the voting rights are widely dispersed does not implicitly create joint control.

4.3.2 Ultimate voting authority

Sometimes an arrangement provides all parties with a voting right, but in the case of a deadlock, or disagreement, one party has the deciding vote (i.e. the final decision, or override powers). If any single party could direct the relevant activities unilaterally, there would not be joint control. Example 12.8 below illustrates this point.

Example 12.8: Ultimate decision-making authority – no joint control (1)

G and H enter into an agreement and set up a joint steering committee. One party has ultimate decision-making authority in cases where the joint steering committee cannot reach an agreement. In this case, there would not be joint control, since the agreement of the other party is not needed.

To evaluate whether the party with the deciding vote has control, one would also need to assess whether it has exposure to variable returns, and the ability to affect those returns through its power, as required by IFRS 10 (see Chapter 6).

Just because one party has a deciding vote does not necessarily mean that it has control, particularly if other parties can act without the agreement of that party. This is illustrated in Example 12.9 below.

Example 12.9: Ultimate decision-making authority – no joint control (2)

I, J and K enter into an agreement and set up a joint steering committee. Each party has one vote and two votes are needed to carry a motion. K has ultimate decision-making authority in cases where the joint steering committee cannot reach an agreement. For example, if no combination of I, J and K can agree with each other, K would have the ultimate decision-making authority.

There is no joint control, since there are multiple combinations of parties that could vote together and the contractual agreement does not specify which parties must agree. For example, I and J could agree together, without the agreement of K.

4.3.3 Arbitration

Contractual arrangements often include terms and conditions relating to the resolution of disputes, and may provide for arbitration. The existence of such terms and conditions does not prevent the arrangement from being jointly controlled and, consequently, from being a joint arrangement. *[IFRS 11.B10]*. Rather, a party to a joint arrangement should evaluate the facts and circumstances related to the arbitration procedures. For example, is the arbitration process neutral to both parties, for example, using a mutually agreed upon arbitrator, in which case, there might be joint control, or do the arbitration procedures favour one party, which might indicate that there is no joint control.

4.3.4 Statutory mechanisms

Statutory mechanisms can create legally enforceable rights and obligations (see 3 above). Accordingly, when evaluating whether an arrangement implicitly results in joint control, an entity should consider the statutory requirements in the relevant jurisdiction under which the contractual arrangement was established.

4.4 Other practical issues with assessing joint control

4.4.1 Undivided share, lease or a joint arrangement

In some cases, it is necessary to consider whether a party owns an undivided share in a commonly-owned asset, has a right to use an asset in return for a payment or series of payments (i.e. a lease), or whether the parties have a joint arrangement. Example 12.10 illustrates this point.

Example 12.10: An undivided share, a lease or a joint arrangement?

Five parties jointly buy an aircraft. By contractual agreement, each party has the right to use the aircraft for a certain number of days each year and shares proportionately in the maintenance costs. They share decision-making regarding the maintenance and disposal of the aircraft, which are the relevant activities for that aircraft. Those decisions require the unanimous agreement of all of the parties. The contractual agreement covers the expected life of the aircraft and can be changed only by unanimous agreement.

Analysis

The agreement is a joint arrangement. Through the contractual agreement, the five parties agreed to share the use and costs of maintaining the aircraft, and decisions require unanimous consent.

Variation – The contractual agreement covers the expected life of the aircraft and can be changed only by agreement of parties holding 75% of the voting rights. There are multiple combinations of how the 75% threshold can be achieved and the contractual agreement does not specify which parties must agree. Therefore, there is no unanimous consent.

Analysis

The agreement is not a joint arrangement, as the contractual agreement does not establish joint control.

4.4.2 Evaluate multiple agreements together

Sometimes, it is necessary to evaluate multiple agreements together, to understand the purpose and design of an arrangement, and to determine if there is joint control. A party may appear to have joint control of a joint arrangement when considering one agreement in isolation, but that party may not have joint control when considered in the full context of its purpose and design. Example 12.11 below illustrates this point.

Example 12.11: Layered agreements

A, B, C and D enter into agreement No.1 to undertake oil and gas exploration. Committee No.1 is formed to direct all activities related to that activity, including review and approval of annual budgets and operating policies. Committee No.1 consists of six members, of whom D nominates three members. The remaining three members are nominated by A, B, and C. The decisions of Committee No.1 require the unanimous vote of the members.

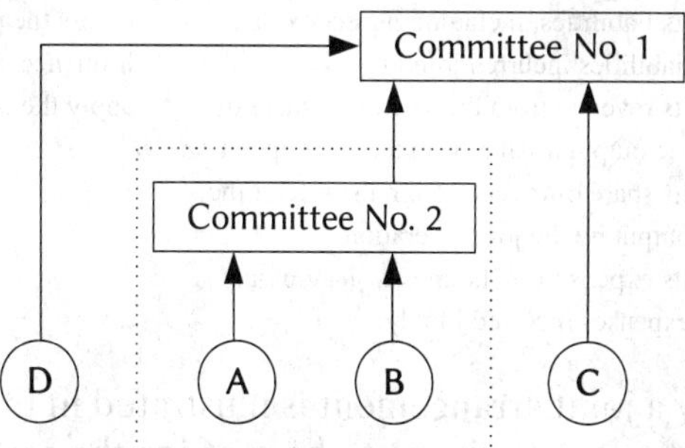

A and B enter into agreement No.2, which establishes Committee No.2 to coordinate cooperation between A and B, with respect to the same oil and gas exploration activity. A and B each appoint one representative to Committee No.2. Committee No.2 has the power to make decisions to be submitted for approval to Committee No.1. Any matter to be decided by Committee No.2 requires the consent of both parties. However, if agreement cannot be reached between A and B, B has the deciding vote. The decisions made in Committee No.2 are binding on A and B and they must vote accordingly in Committee No.1.

In this fact pattern, there are two separate contractual agreements. However, they are evaluated together to determine if there is a joint arrangement, because they relate to the same oil and gas exploration activity. For example, if agreement No.1 were considered in isolation, it would appear that A, B, C and D all have joint control over the arrangement.

However, agreement No. 1 should be evaluated together with agreement No. 2. Accordingly, only B, C and D would have joint control over the joint arrangement. Since B can effectively direct A how to vote (by virtue of agreement No.2) in Committee No.2, A does not have joint control with the other parties, since it is effectively a *de facto* agent of B and will represent a 'party that participates in a joint arrangement but does not have joint control' (see 4.2.5 above).

5 CLASSIFICATION OF A JOINT ARRANGEMENT: JOINT OPERATIONS AND JOINT VENTURES

IFRS 11 requires an entity to determine the type of joint arrangement in which it is involved. *[IFRS 11.14]*. A joint arrangement is classified as either a joint operation or a joint venture. *[IFRS 11.6]*. The classification of a joint arrangement as a joint operation or a joint venture depends upon the rights and obligations of the parties to the arrangement. *[IFRS 11.14]*.

The table below compares the two types of joint arrangements and provides an overview of the accounting for each under IFRS 11. *[IFRS 11.15, 16]*.

Type of arrangement	Joint operation	Joint venture
Definition	The parties with joint control have rights to the assets and obligations for the liabilities of the arrangement.	The parties with *joint control* have rights to the net assets of the arrangement.
Parties with joint control	*Joint operator* is a party with joint control in a joint operation.	*Joint venturer* is a party with joint control in a joint venture.
Accounting overview	A joint operator (and parties that participate in a joint arrangement but who do not have joint control) accounts for the following in accordance with the applicable IFRS: Its assets, including its share of any assets held jointly Its liabilities, including its share of any liabilities incurred jointly Its revenue from the sale of its share of the output arising from the joint operation Its share of revenue from the sale of the output by the joint operation Its expenses, including its share of any expenses incurred jointly.	A joint venturer accounts for its investment in the joint venture using the equity method. Parties that participate in a joint arrangement but who do not have joint control account for the investment in accordance with IFRS 9 (or IAS 39), unless the parties have significant influence, in which case the parties shall apply the equity method.

This process to classify a joint arrangement is illustrated in the following flowchart.[4] The flowchart includes several criteria to be met for the joint arrangement to be a joint venture. The first step is to assess whether there is a separate vehicle. If not, the joint arrangement is automatically a joint operation. However, if there is a separate vehicle, if just one of the additional criteria indicates that the parties have the rights to the assets and obligations for the liabilities, the joint arrangement would be a joint operation. In all other cases it would be classified as a joint venture. IFRS 11 also includes examples illustrating this evaluation, some within the application guidance and others as illustrative examples accompanying the standard (see 5.5 below).

Classifying a joint arrangement

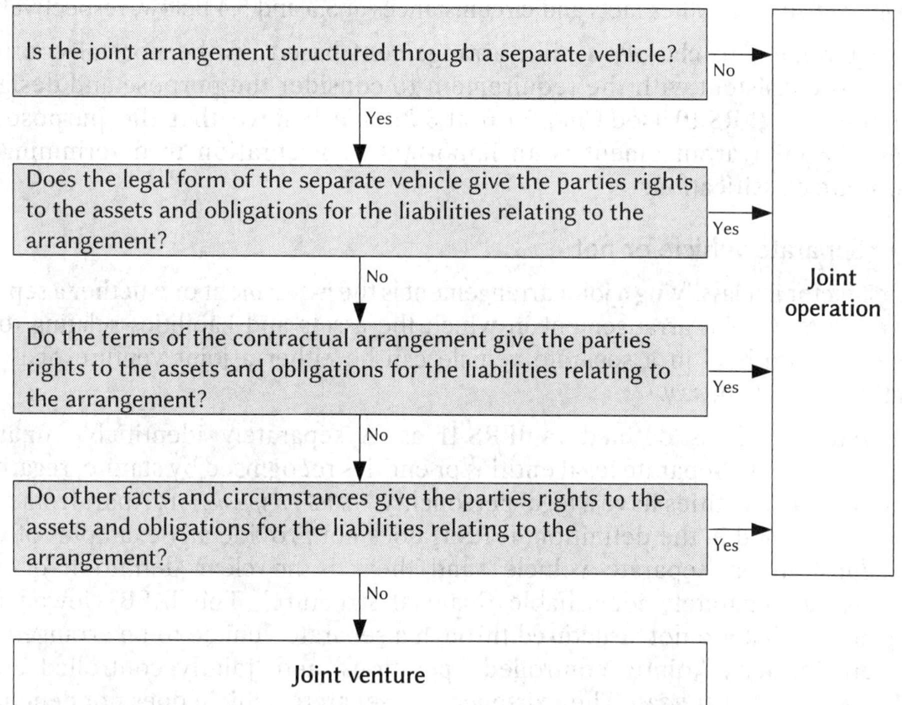

We discuss key aspects of the classification process within this chapter as follows:

- separate vehicle – see 5.1 below;
- legal form of the separate vehicle – see 5.2 below;
- contractual terms – see 5.3 below; and
- other facts and circumstances – see 5.4 below. *[IFRS 11.17, B15].*

Judgement is required in assessing whether a joint arrangement is a joint operation or a joint venture. An entity evaluates its rights and obligations arising from a joint arrangement to classify the arrangement. *[IFRS 11.17].* IFRS 12 requires that an entity shall disclose information when it has to make significant judgements and assumptions to classify the type of joint arrangement, specifically when the arrangement has been structured through a separate vehicle (see Chapter 13 at 3). *[IFRS 12.7].*

When classifying a joint arrangement, parties to the joint arrangement would normally reach the same conclusion regarding classification. To reach different conclusions regarding the classification of a joint arrangement would mean that the parties have different rights to assets and obligations for the liabilities within the same separate vehicle.

When classifying a joint arrangement as either a joint operation or a joint venture, it may be necessary to analyse two (or more) agreements separately, such as when there is a framework or master agreement (see 3.1 above).

The classification of joint arrangements depends upon the parties' rights and obligations arising from the arrangement in the normal course of business. *[IFRS 11.B14].* These concepts are discussed in more detail in the context of analysing the contractual terms of the arrangement, and the other facts and circumstances at 5.3 and 5.4 below, respectively.

The requirement to classify a joint arrangement based on the normal course of business is consistent with the requirement to consider the purpose and design of an investee in IFRS 10 (see Chapter 6 at 3.2). We believe that the purpose and design of a joint arrangement is an important consideration in determining the appropriate classification.

5.1 Separate vehicle or not

The first factor in classifying a joint arrangement is the assessment of whether a separate vehicle exists. A joint arrangement in which the assets and liabilities relating to the arrangement are held in a separate vehicle can be either a joint venture or a joint operation. *[IFRS 11.B19, B20]*.

A separate vehicle is defined in IFRS 11 as 'A separately identifiable financial structure, including separate legal entities or entities recognised by statute, regardless of whether those entities have a legal personality.' *[IFRS 11 Appendix A]*. Apart from those entities mentioned in the definition, IFRS 11 does not provide any examples of what might constitute a 'separate vehicle', and there is no clear definition of what constitutes a 'separately identifiable financial structure'. The IASB viewed joint arrangements that are not structured through a separate vehicle to be arrangements that were formerly 'jointly controlled operations' and 'jointly controlled assets' (see 1.1 above). *[IFRS 11.BC26]*. The existence of a separate vehicle does not depend on whether the assets and liabilities within the vehicle meet the definition of a 'business' in IFRS 3. *[IFRS 11.BC29]*.

The desired economic substance often drives the selection of a particular legal form of a separate vehicle. However, the choice may be driven by tax, regulatory requirements or other reasons that can alter the intended economic substance, necessitating that the parties use contractual arrangements to modify the effects that the legal form would otherwise have on their rights and obligations. *[IFRS 11.BC32]*.

Many common arrangements, such as partnerships, corporations, trusts and syndicates, are likely to be considered separate vehicles, although local laws should be considered. In some jurisdictions, an oral agreement is considered sufficient to create a contractual partnership, and thus, the hurdle for having a separate vehicle could be quite low.

A contract alone may create a separate vehicle, such as when it creates a deemed separate entity (referred to as a 'silo' in IFRS 10), or creates a partnership. A silo exists when specified assets of an arrangement are the only source of payment for specified liabilities of an arrangement, and parties other than those with the specified liability do not have rights or obligations related to the specified assets or to residual cash flows from those assets. That is, a silo exists when, in substance, all the assets, liabilities and equity of that deemed separate entity are ring-fenced from the 'host' arrangement. The identification of silos is discussed further in Chapter 6 at 8.1.

The term 'separate vehicle' is broader than an 'entity' as illustrated in the diagram below. We understand that this was done primarily to address concerns that, in some jurisdictions, separate vehicles created to establish a joint arrangement are not necessarily legal reporting entities or juristic persons.

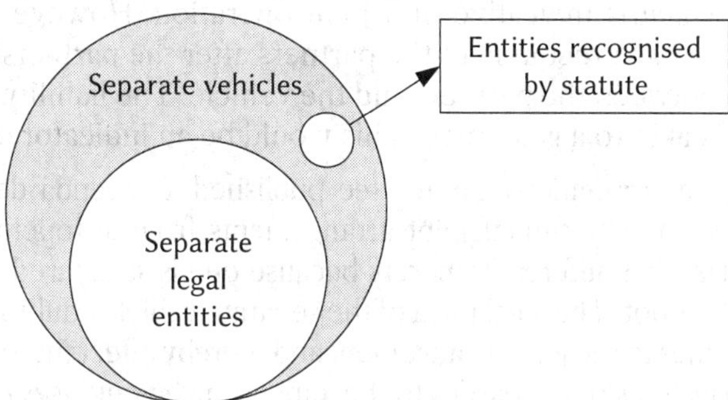

The IASB concluded it would be rare that a joint arrangement would give the parties rights to the net assets without having a separate vehicle. Therefore, they considered that the benefits of introducing an additional assessment in the classification of joint arrangements when these are not structured through separate vehicles would not outweigh the costs of increasing the complexity of the IFRS. *[IFRS 11.BC27].*

5.2 Legal form of the separate vehicle

Once it is determined that a separate vehicle exists, the second step is to analyse the legal form of the separate vehicle to determine whether it gives the parties rights to the net assets, or rights to the assets and obligations for the liabilities of the arrangement. *[IFRS 11.B21].* In other words, does the separate vehicle confer separation between the parties and the separate vehicle?

The legal form of the separate vehicle is relevant as an initial indicator of the parties' rights to the assets, and obligations for the liabilities, relating to the arrangement. The exception is when the legal form of the separate vehicle does not confer separation between the parties and the vehicle, in which case the conclusion is reached that the arrangement is a joint operation. *[IFRS 11.B24, BC31].*

If the legal form of the separate vehicle does confer separation between the parties and the separate vehicle, the classification is not yet conclusive. The terms agreed by the parties in their contractual arrangement (see 5.3 below) and other facts and circumstances (see 5.4 below) can override the assessment of the rights and obligations conferred upon the parties by the legal form of the separate vehicle and the arrangement can still be classified as a joint operation. *[IFRS 11.B23].*

Local laws may affect the form of the separate vehicle. For example, in many countries, a corporation confers separation between the parties and the separate vehicle and provides the parties with rights to net assets. These are indicators of the corporation being a joint venture. That is, the liabilities of the corporation are limited to the corporation. Creditors do not have recourse to the investors in the corporation for those liabilities. However, this may not be true in all countries.

Similarly, partnerships that have unlimited liability, which are common in many countries, often do not confer separation between the parties and the separate vehicle. That is, they provide the partners with rights to the assets and obligations for the liabilities, indicating that the arrangement is a joint operation. When creditors of the partnership have direct recourse to the joint arrangement partners, the partners are the primary obligors, which is indicative of a joint operation. However, in a partnership where creditors only have recourse to the partners after the partnership has defaulted, there is separation between the partners and the vehicle. The liability of the partners as secondary obligor is akin to a guarantee. This would be an indicator of a joint venture.

In March 2015, the Interpretations Committee published an agenda decision in which it observed that two seemingly similar joint arrangements from an operational perspective might need to be classified differently merely because one is structured through a separate vehicle and the other is not. The legal form of the separate vehicle could affect the rights and obligations of the parties to the joint arrangement and thereby affect the economic substance of the rights and obligations of the parties to the joint arrangement. *[IFRS 11.B22, BC43].*

5.3 Contractual terms

The next step in classifying a joint arrangement structured through a separate vehicle is to examine the contractual terms of the arrangement. While the legal form of the separate vehicle gives certain rights and obligations to each of the parties, the contractual terms of the joint arrangement may unwind the effects of the legal form and give the parties different rights and obligations.

IFRS 11 includes examples (which are not exhaustive) of common contractual terms found in joint arrangements, and indicates whether these are examples of joint operations or joint ventures. These are included in the table below. *[IFRS 11.B27].*

Joint operation	Joint venture
Terms of the contractual arrangement	
The parties are provided with rights to the assets, obligations for the liabilities, relating to the arrangement.	The parties are provided with rights to the net assets of the arrangement (i.e. it is the separate vehicle, not the parties, that has rights to the assets and obligations for the liabilities relating to the arrangement).
Rights to assets	
The parties share all interests (e.g. rights, title or ownership) in the assets relating to the arrangement in a specified proportion (e.g. in proportion to the parties' ownership interest in the arrangement or in proportion to the activity carried out through the arrangement that is directly attributed to them).	The assets brought into the arrangement or subsequently acquired by the joint arrangement are the arrangement's assets. The parties have no interests (i.e. no rights, title or ownership) in the assets of the arrangement.
Obligations for liabilities	
The parties share all liabilities, obligations, costs and expenses in a specified proportion (e.g. in proportion to the parties' ownership interest in the arrangement or in proportion to the activity carried out through the arrangement that is directly attributed to them).	The joint arrangement is liable for the debts and obligations of the arrangement. The parties are liable under the arrangement only to the extent of their respective investments in the arrangement, or to their respective obligations to contribute any unpaid or additional capital to the arrangement, or both.
The parties are liable for claims raised by third parties	Creditors of the joint arrangement do not have rights of recourse against any party with respect to debts or obligations of the arrangement.

Joint operation	Joint venture
Revenues and expenses and profits or losses	
Each party receives an allocation of revenues and expenses based on the relative performance of each party to the joint arrangement. For example, the contractual arrangement might establish that revenues and expenses are allocated based on the capacity that each party uses in a plant operated jointly, which could differ from their ownership interest in the joint arrangement. In other instances, the parties might have agreed to share the profit or loss relating to the arrangement based on a specified proportion such as the parties' ownership interest in the arrangement. This would not prevent the arrangement from being a joint operation if the parties have rights to the assets, and obligations for the liabilities, relating to the arrangement.	Each party has a share in the profit or loss relating to the activities of the arrangement.
Guarantees	
The parties to joint arrangements are often required to provide guarantees to third parties that, for example, receive a service from, or provide financing to, the joint arrangement. The provision of such guarantees, or the commitment by the parties to provide them, does not determine, by itself, that the joint arrangement is a joint operation. The feature that determines whether the joint arrangement is a joint operation or a joint venture is whether the parties have obligations for the liabilities relating to the arrangement (for some of which the parties might or might not have provided a guarantee). See 5.3.1 below.	

In many cases, the rights and obligations agreed to by the parties in their contractual arrangements are consistent, or do not conflict, with the rights and obligations conferred on the parties by the legal form of the separate vehicle. *[IFRS 11.B25]*. However, as discussed at 5.2 above, this is not always the case, *[IFRS 11.B26]*, as illustrated in Example 12.12 below. *[IFRS 11 Example 4]*.

Example 12.12: Modification of legal form by contractual terms

A and B jointly start a corporation (C) over which they have joint control. The legal form of the separate vehicle (a corporation) preliminarily indicates that C is a joint venture.

However, the contractual arrangement states that A and B have rights to the assets of C and are obligated for the liabilities of C in a specified proportion. Effectively, this contractual term unwinds the effects of the legal form (corporation). Therefore, C is a joint operation.

When the contractual arrangement specifies that the parties have rights to the assets, and obligations for the liabilities, relating to the joint arrangement, they are parties to a joint operation, and do not further consider other facts and circumstances when classifying the joint arrangement. *[IFRS 11.B28]*.

5.3.1 Guarantees

Parties to joint arrangements may provide guarantees to third parties. For example, a party to a joint arrangement may provide a guarantee or commitment that:

- services provided by the joint arrangement to the third party will be of a certain quality or nature;
- it will support the joint arrangement in the event of distress; or
- it will repay funding received from the third party.

One might think that providing a guarantee (or commitment to provide a guarantee) gives a party an obligation for a liability, which would indicate that the joint arrangement should be classified as a joint operation. However, IFRS 11 states this is not the case. The issuance of guarantees, or a commitment by the parties to provide guarantees, does not determine, by itself, that the joint arrangement is a joint operation. *[IFRS 11.B27]*. Although perhaps counter-intuitive, the fact that a guarantee is not determinative of the classification of a joint operation is consistent with the principles in IFRS 11. This is because the guarantee does not give the guarantor a present obligation for the underlying liabilities. Accordingly, a guarantee is not determinative of having an obligation for a liability.

Similarly, an obligation to contribute unpaid or additional capital to a joint arrangement is not an indicator that the arrangement is a joint operation; it could be a joint venture. *[IFRS 11.B27]*. Cash calls and obligations to contribute unpaid or additional capital are discussed in more detail at 5.4.2.A below.

If the issuer of the guarantee has to pay or perform under that guarantee, this may indicate that facts and circumstances have changed, or this event may be accompanied by a change in the contractual terms of the arrangement. These changes would trigger a reassessment of whether the arrangement is still subject to joint control and, if so, whether the joint arrangement is a joint operation or a joint venture, as discussed at 8 below.

When a guarantee meets the definition of a 'financial guarantee' (see Chapter 42 at 3.4), the party issuing the guarantee must account for the guarantee in accordance with IFRS 9 (or IAS 39), irrespective of the classification of the joint arrangement.

5.3.2 *Contractual terms upon liquidation or dissolution of joint arrangement*

In some joint arrangements, the parties contribute assets to the joint arrangement to use in the activity while it continues to operate. However, if the joint arrangement is liquidated or dissolved, the contributed assets revert to the contributing party. The question is whether this contractual term gives the parties rights to the assets. If so, the joint arrangement is classified as a joint operation.

In our view, a contractual agreement whereby assets contributed to a joint arrangement revert back to the contributing party upon liquidation or dissolution of the joint arrangement, does not necessarily mean that the arrangement is a joint operation. In such a case, the contributing party does not expect to receive the contributed assets in the normal course of business (see 5 above). That is, the purpose and design of the joint arrangement is not intended to give rights to assets, or obligations for liabilities to the contributing party, at least while the joint arrangement continues as a going concern. The joint arrangement should be analysed in the context of its purpose and design.

All relevant facts and circumstances should be considered in reaching a conclusion. If the party contributing the asset has a currently exercisable call option on that asset, it should consider this in evaluating whether it has rights to the assets and obligations for the liabilities of the joint arrangement (i.e. whether it is a joint operation). The call option is accounted for in accordance with the relevant IFRS.

5.4 Other facts and circumstances

When the legal form of the separate vehicle and the terms of the contractual arrangement do not specify that the parties have rights to the assets, and obligations for the liabilities, relating to the arrangement, then the parties must consider all other facts and circumstances to assess whether the arrangement is a joint operation or a joint venture. *[IFRS 11.B29, B30]*. The 'other facts and circumstances' should be substantive and infer rights to the assets and obligations for the liabilities of the separate vehicle to classify the joint arrangement as a joint operation.

In March 2015, the Interpretations Committee published agenda decisions, discussed at 5.4.3 below, that provide a helpful overview of the issues that require judgement and the guidance that should be considered. The assessment of 'other facts and circumstances' can be challenging in practice.

5.4.1 Facts and circumstances indicating rights to assets

When the activities of an arrangement are primarily designed for the provision of output to the parties, this indicates that the parties have rights to substantially all the economic benefits of the assets of the arrangement. The parties to such arrangements often ensure their access to the outputs provided by the arrangement by preventing the arrangement from selling output to third parties. *[IFRS 11.B31]*.

5.4.1.A Output not taken in proportion to ownership

In March 2015, the Interpretations Committee published an agenda decision that addressed the accounting treatment when the joint operator's share of output purchased differs from its share of ownership interest in the joint operation. The Interpretations Committee specifically considered a variation to Example 5 of the application guidance to IFRS 11 where a joint arrangement that is structured through a separate vehicle and for which the parties to the joint arrangement have committed themselves to purchase substantially all of the output produced at a price designed to achieve a break-even result. In that example, the parties to the joint arrangement would be considered to have rights to the assets and obligations for the liabilities and the arrangement would be classified as a joint operation. The variation considered is when the parties' percentage ownership interest in the separate vehicle differs from the percentage share of the output produced, which each party is obliged to purchase.

The Interpretations Committee identified several issues:

- When the joint arrangement agreement does not specify the allocation of assets, liabilities, revenues or expenses, should the share of assets, liabilities, revenue and expenses recognised reflect the percentage of ownership of the legal entity, or should it reflect the percentage of output purchased by each joint operator?
- When the share of output purchased by each party varies over the life of the joint arrangement, over what time horizon should the share of output be considered?
- If the joint operators made a substantial investment in the joint operation that differed from their ownership interest, it would be necessary to determine the other elements of the arrangements that could explain why there is a difference between the percentage of ownership interest and the percentage share of the output produced that each party is obliged to purchase.

The Interpretations Committee noted that it is important to understand why the share of the output purchased differs from the ownership interests in the joint operation and that judgement would be needed to determine the appropriate classification and accounting for the joint arrangement. However, the Interpretations Committee decided not to add the issue to its agenda because it would require the development of additional guidance.[5]

5.4.1.B Consideration of derecognition requirements for financial instruments

When classifying a joint arrangement, one must be mindful of the derecognition requirements with respect to financial instruments. This is particularly important where the activities of the joint arrangement relate to transferred receivables and securitisation arrangements (see Chapter 51 at 3.2).

Therefore, when determining if the facts and circumstances indicate that a party has rights to net assets (a joint venture), or rights to assets, and obligations for liabilities (a joint operation), one should consider whether the assets that have been transferred to the joint arrangement meet the criteria for derecognition by the transferor. The conclusions reached with respect to derecognition would likely also affect the amounts recognised when applying the equity method (if the joint arrangement is a joint venture), or accounting for the rights to the assets (if the joint arrangement is a joint operation).

5.4.2 Facts and circumstances indicating obligations for liabilities

When the parties to a joint arrangement are substantially the only source of cash flows contributing to the continuity of the operations of the arrangement, this indicates that the parties have an obligation for the liabilities relating to the arrangement. *[IFRS 11.B32].*

Many situations may result in the parties to a joint arrangement being substantially the only source of cash flows:

- The parties make payments to third parties under previously issued guarantees on behalf of the joint arrangement.
- The parties are obligated to provide loan financing or working capital funding in the normal course of business.
- The parties commit to provide cash calls in the future (see 5.4.2.A below).
- The parties may be obligated to purchase all the output produced by the joint arrangement, which they may or may not resell to third parties.

5.4.2.A Assessing the obligation related to cash calls or capital contributions

Questions have arisen as to whether parties would be considered 'substantially the only source of cash flows' if they provide cash flows at inception of a joint arrangement, but are not expected to do so thereafter, and no other parties are expected to provide cash flows until the end of an activity. Alternatively, parties might provide cash flows through a series of 'cash calls' throughout the arrangement. IFRS 11 is clear that an obligation to contribute unpaid or additional capital to a joint arrangement, by itself, is not an indicator that the arrangement is a joint operation; it could be a joint venture. *[IFRS 11.B27].*

In our view, the provision of cash flows at the inception of a joint arrangement, and/or the expectation that no other parties will provide cash flows until the end of an activity, are not conclusive in determining whether there is an obligation for a liability. That is, it is not conclusive whether the joint arrangement is a joint operation or a joint venture (see Example 12.13 below).

Example 12.13: Construction and real estate sales

Two parties established a separate vehicle over which they have joint control. Neither the legal form nor the contractual terms of the joint arrangement give the parties rights to the assets or obligations for the liabilities of the arrangement. Other facts and circumstances are as follows:

- the purpose of the joint arrangement is to construct a residential complex for selling residential units to the public;
- contributed equity by the parties is sufficient to purchase land and raise debt finance from third parties to fund construction; and
- sales proceeds will be used as follows (in this priority):
  - repayment of external debt; and
  - remaining profit distributed to parties.

Analysis

Since there is a separate vehicle, and because neither the legal form nor the contractual terms of the joint arrangement give the parties rights to the assets or obligations for the liabilities of the vehicle, the preliminary analysis indicates that this is a joint venture. The fact that the parties are the only source of cash flows at inception is not conclusive as to whether the facts and circumstances indicate that the parties have rights to the assets, or obligations for the liabilities. That is, more information is needed and judgement will be required in determining whether this is a joint venture or a joint operation.

Variation – The contributed equity is not sufficient to purchase the land and raise debt financing. There is an expectation, or requirement, that the parties will have to contribute cash to the joint arrangement through a series of cash calls. The fact that the parties are expected to be a source of cash flows is not sufficiently conclusive to indicate that the parties have rights to the assets, and/or obligations for the liabilities. That is, more information is needed before concluding if this is a joint venture or a joint operation.

The above example refers to the fact that there was third party financing available to fund construction. In March 2015, the Interpretations Committee published an agenda decision confirming that the availability of third party financing does not preclude the classification as a joint operation (see 5.4.3.C below).

5.4.3 Interpretations Committee agenda decisions

In January 2013, the Interpretations Committee received several requests to clarify the application of the 'other facts and circumstances' criterion in IFRS 11, which it discussed during its meetings in 2013 and 2014. In March 2015, the Interpretations Committee issued an agenda decision dealing with the following issues:

- how and why particular facts and circumstances create rights and obligations (see 5.4.3.A below);
- implication of 'economic substance' (see 5.4.3.B below); and
- application of 'other facts and circumstances' to specific fact patterns (see 5.4.3.C below):
  - output sold at a market price;
  - financing from a third party;
  - nature of output (i.e. fungible or bespoke output); and
  - determining the basis for 'substantially all of the output'.

5.4.3.A How and why particular facts and circumstances create rights and obligations

The Interpretations Committee noted the following regarding a joint arrangement that is structured through a separate vehicle, whose legal form causes the separate vehicle to be considered in its own right:[6]

(a) the assessment of other facts and circumstances is performed when there is no contractual arrangement to reverse or modify the rights and obligations conferred by the legal form of the separate vehicle through which the arrangement has been structured;

(b) the assessment focuses on whether the other facts and circumstances establish, for each party to the joint arrangement, rights to the assets and obligations for the liabilities relating to the joint arrangement;

(c) parties to the joint arrangement have rights to the assets of the joint arrangement through other facts and circumstances when they: *[IFRS 11.B31-B32]*

  (i) have rights to substantially all of the economic benefits (for example, 'output') of assets of the arrangement; and

  (ii) have obligations to acquire those economic benefits and thus assume the risks relating to those economic benefits (for example, the risks relating to the output); and

(d) parties to the joint arrangement have obligations for liabilities of the joint arrangement through other facts and circumstances when: *[IFRS 11.B14, B32-B33]*

  (i) as a consequence of their rights to, and obligations for, the assets of the joint arrangement, they provide cash flows that are used to settle liabilities of the joint arrangement; and

  (ii) settlement of the liabilities of the joint arrangement occurs on a continuous basis.

A joint arrangement structured through a separate vehicle is classified as a joint operation only when each party to the joint arrangement meets the above criteria and therefore has both rights to the assets of the joint arrangement and obligations for the liabilities of the joint arrangement through other facts and circumstances.

Although the Interpretations Committee decided not to add this issue to its agenda, it observed that a joint arrangement could only be classified as a joint operation based on other facts and circumstances, if an entity is able to demonstrate that:

(a) each party to the joint arrangement has rights and obligations relating to economic benefits of the assets of the arrangement; and

(b) each party is obliged to provide cash to the arrangement through enforceable obligations, which is used to settle the liabilities of the joint arrangement on a continuous basis.

It is therefore irrelevant whether the activities of the separate vehicle are closely related to the activities of the parties on their own, or whether the parties are closely involved in the operations of the arrangements. *[IFRS 11.BC43].*

In July 2014, the Interpretations Committee discussed the classification of a specific type of joint arrangement structure, established for a bespoke construction project for delivery of a construction service to a single customer. In this specific example, it examined common features of 'project entities' with regard to assessing 'other facts and circumstances.' The staff analysis listed several common features of 'project entities' that would not, by themselves, indicate that the parties have rights to the assets and obligations for the liabilities, i.e. that the joint arrangement is a joint operation.[7]

- The separate vehicle has no workforce of its own.
- The separate vehicle is a limited-life entity that has been set up for a single project.
- The parties are responsible for delivering the goods or services to the customers.
- The parties are jointly or severally liable for all the debts of the separate vehicle.
- The customers of the separate vehicle are obtained through the commercial resources of the parties (for example, their personnel, websites, classified ads, trade name).
- The parties finance any loss or cash needs of the separate vehicle, for example, when there is budget overruns or delivery delays.
- Litigation arising from the operations of the separate vehicle is managed by the parties or is accompanied by legal actions directly against the parties.

5.4.3.B Implication of 'economic substance'

The assessment of other facts and circumstances should focus on whether each party to the joint arrangement has rights to the assets, and obligations for the liabilities, relating to the joint arrangement. This raises questions about the role of the concept of 'economic substance' in the assessment of other facts and circumstances.

The Interpretations Committee determined that the assessment of other facts and circumstances should be undertaken with a view towards whether those facts and circumstances create enforceable rights to assets and obligations for liabilities (see 4.3.4 above). These obligations may be legal or constructive. Therefore, this evaluation should include consideration of the design and purpose of the joint arrangement, its business needs and its past practices to identify all obligations, whether legal or constructive.[8]

5.4.3.C Application of 'other facts and circumstances' to specific fact patterns

The Interpretations Committee also explored the following four fact patterns and considered how 'other facts and circumstances' should be applied in each of these cases:[9]

- Output sold at a market price – The sale of output from the joint arrangement to the parties at market price, on its own, is not a determinative factor for the classification of the joint arrangement. Instead, parties would need to exercise judgement and consider whether the cash flows provided to the joint arrangement through the parties' purchase of the output from the joint arrangement at market price, along with any other funding that the parties are obliged to provide, would be sufficient to enable the joint arrangement to settle its liabilities on a continuous basis.
- Financing from a third party – If the cash flows to the joint arrangement from the sale of output to the parties, along with any other funding that the parties are obliged to provide, satisfy the joint arrangement's liabilities, then third-party financing alone would not affect the classification of the joint arrangement. This conclusion is appropriate irrespective of whether the financing occurs at inception or during the course of the joint arrangement's operations. In this situation, the joint arrangement will, or may, settle some of its liabilities using cash flows from third-party financing,

but the resulting obligation to the third-party finance provider will, in due course, be settled using cash flows that the parties are obliged to provide.

- Nature of output (i.e. fungible or bespoke output) – Whether the output that is produced by the joint arrangement and purchased by the parties is fungible or bespoke, is not a determinative factor for the classification of the joint arrangement. IFRS 11's main focus is on the existence of cash flows flowing from the parties to satisfy the joint arrangement's liabilities.
- Determining the basis for 'substantially all of the output' – The Interpretations Committee noted that the economic benefits of the assets of the joint arrangement would relate to the cash flows arising from the parties' rights to, and obligations for, the assets. *[IFRS 11.B31-B32]*. Therefore, the term 'substantially all of the output' is based on the monetary value of the output, instead of physical quantities.

5.4.4 Comprehensive example illustrating evaluation of facts and circumstances

Example 12.14 below (summarised from Example 5 of IFRS 11) illustrates how the facts and circumstances might indicate that the joint arrangement is a joint operation, even if the legal form and contractual terms point towards the joint arrangement being a joint venture. *[IFRS 11.B32, Example 5]*.

Example 12.14: Modification of legal form and contractual arrangement by facts and circumstances

A and B jointly establish a corporation (C) over which they have joint control. The legal form of C, an incorporated entity, initially indicates that the assets and liabilities held in C are the assets and liabilities of C. The contractual arrangement between the parties does not specify that the parties have rights to the assets or obligations for the liabilities of entity C. Accordingly, the legal form of C and the terms of the contractual arrangement indicate that the arrangement is a joint venture.

However, A and B agree to the following:

- A and B will purchase all the output produced by C in a ratio of 50:50.
- C cannot sell any of the output to third parties, unless A and B approve this. The purpose of the arrangement is to provide A and B with the output they require, so sales to third parties are expected to be uncommon and not material.
- The price of the output sold to A and B is set by the parties at a level that is designed to cover the costs of production and administrative expenses incurred by C. The arrangement is intended to operate at a break-even level.

Analysis

- The obligation of A and B to purchase all of the output produced by C reflects the exclusive dependence of C upon A and B for the generation of cash flows and, thus, implicitly that A and B have an obligation for the liabilities of C.
- The fact that A and B have rights to all of the output produced by C means that they are consuming, and therefore have rights to, all of the economic benefits of the assets of C.

These facts and circumstances indicate that the arrangement is a joint operation.

Variation 1 – If, instead of A and B using their share of the output themselves, they sold their share of the output to third parties, C would still be a joint operation.

Variation 2 – If A and B changed the terms of the contractual arrangement so that the arrangement was able to sell output to third parties, this would result in C assuming demand, inventory and credit risks, such that A and B would not have substantially all of the economic benefits. Accordingly, in this case, the joint arrangement would likely be a joint venture.

5.5 Illustrative examples accompanying IFRS 11

IFRS 11 provides several examples that illustrate aspects of IFRS 11, but are not intended to provide interpretative guidance. The examples portray hypothetical situations illustrating the judgements that might be used when applying IFRS 11 in different situations. Although some aspects of the examples may be present in actual fact patterns, all facts and circumstances of a particular fact pattern are evaluated when applying IFRS 11. *[IFRS 11.IE1].*

Example 12.15: Construction services[10]

A and B (the parties) are two companies whose businesses are the provision of many types of public and private construction services. They set up a contractual arrangement to work together for the purpose of fulfilling a contract with a government for the design and construction of a road between two cities. The contractual arrangement determines the participation shares of A and B and establishes joint control of the arrangement, the subject matter of which is the delivery of the road.

The parties set up a separate vehicle (entity Z) through which to conduct the arrangement. Entity Z, on behalf of A and B, enters into the contract with the government. In addition, the assets and liabilities relating to the arrangement are held in entity Z. The main feature of entity Z's legal form is that the parties, not entity Z, have rights to the assets, and obligations for the liabilities, of the entity.

The contractual arrangement between A and B additionally establishes that:

(a) the rights to all the assets needed to undertake the activities of the arrangement are shared by the parties based on their participation shares in the arrangement;

(b) the parties have several and joint responsibility for all operating and financial obligations relating to the activities of the arrangement on the basis of their participation shares in the arrangement; and

(c) the profit or loss resulting from the activities of the arrangement is shared by A and B based on their participation shares in the arrangement.

For the purposes of co-ordinating and overseeing the activities, A and B appoint an operator, who will be an employee of one of the parties. After a specified time, the role of the operator will rotate to an employee of the other party. A and B agree that the activities will be executed by the operator's employees on a 'no gain or loss' basis.

In accordance with the terms specified in the contract with the government, entity Z invoices the construction services to the government on behalf of the parties.

Analysis

The joint arrangement is carried out through a separate vehicle whose legal form does not confer separation between the parties and the separate vehicle (i.e. the assets and liabilities held in entity Z are the parties' assets and liabilities). This is reinforced by the terms agreed by the parties in their contractual arrangement, which state that A and B have rights to the assets, and obligations for the liabilities, relating to the arrangement that is conducted through entity Z.

The joint arrangement is a joint operation.

A and B each recognise in their financial statements their share of the assets (e.g. property, plant and equipment, accounts receivable) and their share of any liabilities resulting from the arrangement (e.g. accounts payable to third parties) on the basis of their agreed participation share.

Each also recognises its share of the revenue and expenses resulting from the construction services provided to the government through entity Z.

Example 12.16: Shopping centre operated jointly[11]

Two real estate companies (the parties) set up a separate vehicle (entity X) for the purpose of acquiring and operating a shopping centre. The contractual arrangement between the parties establishes joint control of the activities that are conducted in entity X. The main feature of entity X's legal form is that the entity, not the parties, has rights to the assets, and obligations for the liabilities, relating to the arrangement. These activities include the rental of the retail units, managing the car park, maintaining the centre and its equipment, such as lifts, and building the reputation and customer base for the centre as a whole.

The terms of the contractual arrangement are such that:

(a) entity X owns the shopping centre. The contractual arrangement does not specify that the parties have rights to the shopping centre.

(b) the parties are not liable in respect of the debts, liabilities or obligations of entity X. If entity X is unable to pay any of its debts or other liabilities or to discharge its obligations to third parties, the liability of each party to any third party will be limited to the unpaid amount of that party's capital contribution.

(c) the parties have the right to sell or pledge their interests in entity X.

(d) each party receives a share of the income from operating the shopping centre (which is the rental income net of the operating costs) in accordance with its interest in entity X.

Analysis

The joint arrangement is carried out through a separate vehicle whose legal form causes the separate vehicle to be considered in its own right (i.e. the assets and liabilities held in the separate vehicle are the assets and liabilities of the separate vehicle and not the assets and liabilities of the parties). In addition, the terms of the contractual arrangement do not specify that the parties have rights to the assets, or obligations for the liabilities, relating to the arrangement. Instead, the terms of the contractual arrangement establish that the parties have rights to the net assets of entity X.

Based on the description above, there are no other facts and circumstances that indicate that the parties have rights to substantially all the economic benefits of the assets relating to the arrangement, and that the parties have an obligation for the liabilities relating to the arrangement.

The joint arrangement is a joint venture.

The parties recognise their rights to the net assets of entity X as investments and account for them using the equity method.

Example 12.17: Joint manufacturing and distribution of a product[12]

Companies A and B (the parties) have set up a strategic and operating agreement (the framework agreement) in which they have agreed the terms according to which they will conduct the manufacturing and distribution of a product (product P) in different markets.

The parties have agreed to conduct manufacturing and distribution activities by establishing joint arrangements, as described below:

(a) Manufacturing activity: the parties have agreed to undertake the manufacturing activity through a joint arrangement (the manufacturing arrangement). The manufacturing arrangement is structured in a separate vehicle (entity M) whose legal form causes it to be considered in its own right (i.e. the assets and liabilities held in entity M are the assets and liabilities of entity M and not the assets and liabilities of the parties). In accordance with the framework agreement, the parties have committed themselves to purchasing the whole production of product P manufactured by the manufacturing arrangement in accordance with their ownership interests in entity M. The parties subsequently sell product P to another arrangement, jointly controlled by the two parties themselves, that has been established exclusively for the distribution of product P as described below. Neither the framework agreement nor the contractual arrangement between A and B dealing with the manufacturing activity specifies that the parties have rights to the assets, and obligations for the liabilities, relating to the manufacturing activity.

(b) Distribution activity: the parties have agreed to undertake the distribution activity through a joint arrangement (the distribution arrangement). The parties have structured the distribution arrangement in a separate vehicle (entity D) whose legal form causes it to be considered in its own right (i.e. the assets and liabilities held in entity D are the assets and liabilities of entity D and not the assets and liabilities of the parties). In accordance with the framework agreement, the distribution arrangement orders its requirements for product P from the parties according to the needs of the different markets where the distribution arrangement sells the product. Neither the framework agreement nor the contractual arrangement between A and B dealing with the distribution activity specifies that the parties have rights to the assets, and obligations for the liabilities, relating to the distribution activity.

In addition, the framework agreement establishes:

(a) that the manufacturing arrangement will produce product P to meet the requirements for product P that the distribution arrangement places on the parties; and

(b) the commercial terms relating to the sale of product P by the manufacturing arrangement to the parties. The manufacturing arrangement will sell product P to the parties at a price agreed by A and B that covers all production costs incurred. Subsequently, the parties sell the product to the distribution arrangement at a price agreed by A and B.

(c) that any cash shortages that the manufacturing arrangement may incur will be financed by the parties in accordance with their ownership interests in entity M.

Analysis

The framework agreement sets up the terms under which parties A and B conduct the manufacturing and distribution of product P. These activities are undertaken through joint arrangements whose purpose is either the manufacturing or the distribution of product P.

The parties carry out the manufacturing arrangement through entity M whose legal form confers separation between the parties and the entity. In addition, neither the framework agreement nor the contractual arrangement dealing with the manufacturing activity specifies that the parties have rights to the assets, and obligations for the liabilities, relating to the manufacturing activity. However, when considering the following facts and circumstances the parties have concluded that the manufacturing arrangement is a joint operation:

(a) The parties have committed themselves to purchasing the whole production of product P manufactured by the manufacturing arrangement. Consequently, A and B have rights to substantially all the economic benefits of the assets of the manufacturing arrangement.

(b) The manufacturing arrangement manufactures product P to meet the quantity and quality needs of the parties so that they can fulfil the demand for product P of the distribution arrangement. The exclusive dependence of the manufacturing arrangement upon the parties for the generation of cash flows and the parties' commitments to provide funds when the manufacturing arrangement incurs any cash shortages indicate that the parties have an obligation for the liabilities of the manufacturing arrangement, because those liabilities will be settled through the parties' purchases of product P or by the parties' direct provision of funds.

The parties carry out the distribution activities through entity D, whose legal form confers separation between the parties and the entity. In addition, neither the framework agreement nor the contractual arrangement dealing with the distribution activity specifies that the parties have rights to the assets, and obligations for the liabilities, relating to the distribution activity.

There are no other facts and circumstances that indicate that the parties have rights to substantially all the economic benefits of the assets relating to the distribution arrangement or that the parties have an obligation for the liabilities relating to that arrangement.

The distribution arrangement is a joint venture.

A and B each recognise in their financial statements their share of the assets (e.g. property, plant and equipment, cash) and their share of any liabilities resulting from the manufacturing arrangement (e.g. accounts payable to third parties) on the basis of their ownership interest in entity M. Each party also recognises its share of the expenses resulting from the manufacture of product P incurred by the manufacturing arrangement and its share of the revenues relating to the sales of product P to the distribution arrangement.

The parties recognise their rights to the net assets of the distribution arrangement as investments and account for them using the equity method.

Variation

Assume that the parties agree that the manufacturing arrangement described above is responsible not only for manufacturing product P, but also for its distribution to third-party customers.

The parties also agree to set up a distribution arrangement, as the one described above, to distribute product P exclusively to assist in widening the distribution of product P in additional specific markets.

The manufacturing arrangement also sells product P directly to the distribution arrangement. No fixed proportion of the production of the manufacturing arrangement is committed to be purchased by, or to be reserved to, the distribution arrangement.

Analysis

The variation has affected neither the legal form of the separate vehicle in which the manufacturing activity is conducted nor the contractual terms relating to the parties' rights to the assets, and obligations for the liabilities, relating to the manufacturing activity. However, it causes the manufacturing arrangement to be a self-financed arrangement because it is able to undertake trade on its own behalf, distributing product P to third-party customers and, consequently, assuming demand, inventory and credit risks. Even though the manufacturing arrangement might also sell product P to the distribution arrangement, in this scenario the manufacturing arrangement is not dependent on the parties to be able to carry out its activities on a continuous basis.

In this case, the manufacturing arrangement is a joint venture.

The variation has no effect on the classification of the distribution arrangement as a joint venture.

The parties recognise their rights to the net assets of the manufacturing arrangement and their rights to the net assets of the distribution arrangement as investments and account for them using the equity method.

Example 12.18: Bank operated jointly[13]

Banks A and B (the parties) agreed to combine their corporate, investment banking, asset management and services activities by establishing a separate vehicle (bank C). Both parties expect the arrangement to benefit them in different ways. Bank A believes that the arrangement could enable it to achieve its strategic plans to increase its size, offering an opportunity to exploit its full potential for organic growth through an enlarged offering of products and services. Bank B expects the arrangement to reinforce its offering in financial savings and market products.

The main feature of bank C's legal form is that it causes the separate vehicle to be considered in its own right (i.e. the assets and liabilities held in the separate vehicle are the assets and liabilities of the separate vehicle and not the assets and liabilities of the parties). Banks A and B each have a 40 per cent ownership interest in bank C, with the remaining 20 per cent being listed and widely held. The shareholders' agreement between bank A and bank B establishes joint control of the activities of bank C. In addition, bank A and bank B entered into an irrevocable agreement under which, even in the event of a dispute, both banks agree to provide the necessary funds in equal amount and, if required, jointly and severally, to ensure that bank C complies with the applicable legislation and banking regulations, and honours any commitments made to the banking authorities. This commitment represents the assumption by each party of 50 per cent of any funds needed to ensure that bank C complies with legislation and banking regulations.

Analysis

The joint arrangement is carried out through a separate vehicle whose legal form confers separation between the parties and the separate vehicle. The terms of the contractual arrangement do not specify that the parties have rights to the assets, or obligations for the liabilities, of bank C, but it establishes that the parties have rights to the net assets of bank C. The commitment by the parties to provide support if bank C is not able to comply with the applicable legislation and banking regulations is not by itself a determinant that the parties have an obligation for the liabilities of bank C. There are no other facts and circumstances that indicate that the parties have rights to substantially all the economic benefits of the assets of bank C and that the parties have an obligation for the liabilities of bank C.

The joint arrangement is a joint venture.

Both banks A and B recognise their rights to the net assets of bank C as investments and account for them using the equity method.

Example 12.19: Oil and gas exploration, development and production activities[14]

Companies A and B (the parties) set up a separate vehicle (entity H) and a Joint Operating Agreement (JOA) to undertake oil and gas exploration, development and production activities in country O. The main feature of entity H's legal form is that it causes the separate vehicle to be considered in its own right (i.e. the assets and liabilities held in the separate vehicle are the assets and liabilities of the separate vehicle and not the assets and liabilities of the parties).

Country O has granted entity H permits for the oil and gas exploration, development and production activities to be undertaken in a specific assigned block of land (fields).

The shareholders' agreement and JOA agreed by the parties establish their rights and obligations relating to those activities. The main terms of those agreements are summarised below.

Shareholders' agreement

The board of entity H consists of a director from each party. Each party has a 50 per cent shareholding in entity H. The unanimous consent of the directors is required for any resolution to be passed.

Joint Operating Agreement (JOA)

The JOA establishes an Operating Committee. This Committee consists of one representative from each party. Each party has a 50 per cent participating interest in the Operating Committee.

The Operating Committee approves the budgets and work programmes relating to the activities, which also require the unanimous consent of the representatives of each party. One of the parties is appointed as operator and is responsible for managing and conducting the approved work programmes.

The JOA specifies that the rights and obligations arising from the exploration, development and production activities shall be shared among the parties in proportion to each party's shareholding in entity H. In particular, the JOA establishes that the parties share:

(a) the rights and the obligations arising from the exploration and development permits granted to entity H (e.g. the permits, rehabilitation liabilities, any royalties and taxes payable);

(b) the production obtained; and

(c) all costs associated with all work programmes.

The costs incurred in relation to all the work programmes are covered by cash calls on the parties. If either party fails to satisfy its monetary obligations, the other is required to contribute to entity H the amount in default. The amount in default is regarded as a debt owed by the defaulting party to the other party.

Analysis

The parties carry out the joint arrangement through a separate vehicle whose legal form confers separation between the parties and the separate vehicle. The parties reversed the initial assessment of their rights and obligations arising from the legal form of the separate vehicle in which the arrangement is conducted. They have done this by agreeing terms in the JOA that entitle them to rights to the assets (e.g. exploration and development permits, production, and any other assets arising from the activities) and obligations for the liabilities (e.g. all costs and obligations arising from the work programmes) that are held in entity H.

The joint arrangement is a joint operation.

Both company A and company B recognise in their financial statements their own share of the assets and of any liabilities resulting from the arrangement based on their agreed participating interest. On that basis, each party also recognises its share of the revenue (from the sale of their share of the production) and its share of the expenses.

Example 12.20: Liquefied natural gas arrangement[15]

Company A owns an undeveloped gas field that contains substantial gas resources. Company A determines that the gas field will be economically viable only if the gas is sold to customers in overseas markets. To do so, a liquefied natural gas (LNG) facility must be built to liquefy the gas so that it can be transported by ship to the overseas markets.

Company A enters into a joint arrangement with company B to develop and operate the gas field and the LNG facility. Under that arrangement, companies A and B (the parties) agree to contribute the gas field and cash, respectively, to a new separate vehicle, entity C. In exchange for those contributions, the parties each take a 50 per cent ownership interest in entity C. The main feature of entity C's legal form is that it causes the separate vehicle to be considered in its own right (i.e. the assets and liabilities held in the separate vehicle are the assets and liabilities of the separate vehicle and not the assets and liabilities of the parties).

The contractual arrangement between the parties specifies that:

(a) companies A and B must each appoint two members to the board of entity C. The board of directors must unanimously agree the strategy and investments made by entity C.

(b) day-to-day management of the gas field and LNG facility, including development and construction activities, will be undertaken by the staff of company B in accordance with the directions jointly agreed by the parties. Entity C will reimburse B for the costs it incurs in managing the gas field and LNG facility.

(c) entity C is liable for taxes and royalties on the production and sale of LNG as well as for other liabilities incurred in the ordinary course of business, such as accounts payable, site restoration and decommissioning liabilities.

(d) companies A and B have equal shares in the profit from the activities carried out in the arrangement and, are entitled to equal shares of any dividends distributed by entity C.

The contractual arrangement does not specify that either party has rights to the assets, or obligations for the liabilities, of entity C.

The board of entity C decides to enter into a financing arrangement with a syndicate of lenders to help fund the development of the gas field and construction of the LNG facility. The estimated total cost of the development and construction is CU1,000 million.

The lending syndicate provides entity C with a CU700 million loan. The arrangement specifies that the syndicate has recourse to companies A and B only if entity C defaults on the loan arrangement during the development of the field and construction of the LNG facility. The lending syndicate agrees that it will not have recourse to companies A and B once the LNG facility is in production because it has assessed that the cash inflows that entity C should generate from LNG sales will be sufficient to meet the loan repayments. Although at this time the lenders have no recourse to companies A and B, the syndicate maintains protection against default by entity C by taking a lien on the LNG facility.

Analysis

The joint arrangement is carried out through a separate vehicle whose legal form confers separation between the parties and the separate vehicle. The terms of the contractual arrangement do not specify that the parties have rights to the assets, or obligations for the liabilities, of entity C, but they establish that the parties have rights to the net assets of entity C. The recourse nature of the financing arrangement during the development of the gas field and construction of the LNG facility (i.e. companies A and B providing separate guarantees during this phase) does not, by itself, impose on the parties an obligation for the liabilities of entity C (i.e. the loan is a liability of entity C). Companies A and B have separate liabilities, which are their guarantees to repay that loan if entity C defaults during the development and construction phase.

There are no other facts and circumstances that indicate that the parties have rights to substantially all the economic benefits of the assets of entity C and that the parties have an obligation for the liabilities of entity C.

The joint arrangement is a joint venture. The parties recognise their rights to the net assets of entity C as investments and account for them using the equity method.

6 ACCOUNTING FOR JOINT OPERATIONS

For a joint operation, the joint operator recognises its:

- assets, including its share of any assets held jointly;
- liabilities, including its share of any liabilities incurred jointly;
- revenue from the sale of its share of the output arising from the joint operation;
- share of the revenue from the sale of the output by the joint operation; and
- expenses, including its share of any expenses incurred jointly. *[IFRS 11.20]*.

IFRS 11 requires each of these items to be accounted for in accordance with the applicable IFRS. *[IFRS 11.21]*. Careful consideration should be given to the nature of the rights to the assets, and the obligations for the liabilities (or the share of assets, liabilities, revenues, and expenses) if any, of the joint operation (see 6.3 below).

6.1 Joint arrangements not structured through a separate vehicle

For joint arrangements not structured through a separate vehicle, the contractual arrangement establishes the parties' rights to the assets, and obligations for the liabilities, relating to the arrangement, and the parties' rights to the corresponding revenues and obligations for the corresponding expenses. *[IFRS 11.B16]*.

A contractual arrangement often describes the nature of the activities that are the subject of the arrangement and how the parties intend to undertake those activities together. For example, the parties could conduct an activity together, with each party being responsible for a specific task and each using its own assets and incurring its own liabilities and the parties share revenues and expenses. In such a case, each joint operator recognises in its financial statements the assets and liabilities used for the specific task, and recognises its share of the revenues and expenses in accordance with the contractual arrangement. *[IFRS 11.B17]*. When the parties agree, for example, to share and operate an asset together and share the output or revenue from the asset and operating costs, each joint operator accounts for its share of the joint asset, its agreed share of any liabilities, and of the output, revenues and expenses. *[IFRS 11.B18]*.

6.2 Difference from proportionate consolidation

An entity's rights and obligations for the assets, liabilities, revenues and expenses relating to a joint operation as specified in the contractual arrangement, are the basis for accounting for a joint operation under IFRS 11. This may differ from its ownership interest in the joint operation, which would have been the basis for proportionate consolidation. *[IFRS 11.BC38]*.

When the joint operator has differing rights (and percentages) to various assets, and/or different obligations for various liabilities, the financial statements would likely change as a result of accounting for those individual rights and obligations, as compared with the result from proportionately consolidating a blended percentage of all assets and liabilities. Example 12.21 below illustrates joint operation accounting in this case.

Example 12.21: Accounting for rights to assets and obligations for liabilities

D and E establish joint arrangement F, using a separate vehicle, classified as a joint operation. Accordingly, D and E account for their rights to assets and their obligations for liabilities relating to F in accordance with relevant IFRS.

D and E each own 50% of the equity (e.g. shares) in F. However, the contractual terms of the joint arrangement state that D has the rights to all of Building No. 1 and the obligation to pay all the third party debt in F. D and E have rights to all other assets in F, and obligations for all other liabilities in F in proportion to their equity interests (i.e. 50%). F's balance sheet is as follows (in CUs):

Assets		Liabilities and equity	
Cash	20	Debt	120
Building No. 1	120	Employee benefit plan obligation	50
Building No. 2	100	Equity	70
Total assets	240	Total liabilities and equity	240

Under IFRS 11, D would record the following in its financial statements, to account for its rights to the assets in F and its obligations for the liabilities in F. This may differ from the amounts recorded using proportionate consolidation.

Assets		Liabilities and equity	
Cash	10	Debt [(2)]	120
Building No. 1 [(1)]	120	Employee benefit plan obligation	25
Building No. 2	50	Equity	35
Total assets	180	Total liabilities and equity	180

(1) Since D has the rights to all of Building No. 1, it records that amount in its entirety.

(2) D's obligations are for the third-party debt in its entirety.

6.3 Determining the relevant IFRS

As noted at 6 above, joint operators are required to recognise their rights to assets and their obligations for liabilities 'in accordance with the IFRSs applicable'. In some cases, the relevant IFRS is clear, but questions have arisen in other cases.

- Right of use – The illustrative examples of joint operations in IFRS 11 refer to recognising the joint operator's share of assets (e.g. property, plant and equipment, accounts receivable, cash),[16] rather than recognising a 'right of use'. Therefore, a joint operator would recognise its share of an asset in accordance with IAS 16 – *Property, Plant and Equipment,* or IAS 38 – *Intangible Assets,* as applicable. When the contractual terms of the joint operation provide a joint operator with a right to use an asset, not a share of the asset itself, the joint operator would apply IFRIC 4 – *Determining whether an Arrangement contains a Lease* (see Chapter 24 at 2.1), or IFRS 16 – *Leases* – if early adopted (see Chapter 25).
- Liability for entire balance of certain liabilities – One of the joint operators may have a direct legal liability for the entire balance of certain liabilities of the joint operation. It may also have a right to reimbursement by the other parties for their share of that liability of the joint operation. The joint operator would recognise 100 per cent of the joint operation's liabilities and a receivable for the reimbursement due from the other parties for their share of such liability. IFRS prohibits the offsetting of the liability against the receivable. If the other parties were unable to pay, the joint operator would not be able to recognise a receivable for the full amount due. Accordingly, the receivable would be impaired (or less than the third party share of the liability would be recorded), which would result in a reduction in profit in the joint operator's financial statements.
- Jointly and severally liable – In some cases, the joint arrangement (or legal form of the separate vehicle, if applicable) gives joint and several liability for the obligations of the arrangement. This may result in the joint operator recognising the entire obligation due, not just its share. The facts and circumstances need to be assessed in each case, and the liability accounted for in accordance with IAS 37 – *Provisions, Contingent Liabilities and Contingent Assets.*
- Obligation to reimburse other parties – A party to the joint arrangement who has an obligation to reimburse another party would recognise a financial liability for the amount related to the reimbursement.

- Service fee income – In some joint operations, one joint operator receives fees from the other joint operators for providing management services in respect of the joint operation. IFRS 11 does not specifically require that such parties account for any fees received in accordance with IAS 18 – *Revenue*, presumably because it is clear that a party receiving such fees would account for them in accordance with IAS 18, even without this explicit reference. However, paragraph BC55 of IFRS 15 – *Revenue from Contracts with Customers* – explains that a contract with a collaborator or a partner in a joint arrangement could also be within the scope of IFRS 15 if that collaborator or partner meets the definition of a customer for some or all of the terms of the arrangement.
- Inter-company sales – In March 2015, the Interpretations Committee published an agenda decision that addressed the issue of revenue recognition by a joint operator. If a joint arrangement is structured through a separate vehicle, classified as a joint operation, the joint operators' purchase of all the output from the joint operation, is in effect a sale to itself. The Interpretations Committee interpreted paragraph 20(d) of IFRS 11 to mean that a joint operator only would recognise its share of the joint operation's revenue when the joint operation sells its output to third parties (i.e. other parties who have rights to the assets and obligations for the liabilities relating to the joint operation).

6.4 Interest in a joint operation without joint control

A party that participates in a joint arrangement but does not have joint control (see 4 above) is not a joint operator. However, if that party has rights to assets and obligations for liabilities, the accounting is the same as that for a joint operator, as discussed above. *[IFRS 11.23]*.

If the party that participates in a joint arrangement but does not have joint control does not have rights to the assets and obligations for the liabilities relating to the joint operation, it accounts for its interest in the joint operation in accordance with other applicable IFRS. *[IFRS 11.23]*. For example, if it has:

(a) an interest in a separate vehicle over which it has significant influence, it should apply IAS 28;

(b) an interest in a separate vehicle over which it does not have significant influence, it should account for that interest as a financial asset under IAS 39 or IFRS 9; or

(c) an interest in an arrangement without a separate vehicle, it should apply other applicable IFRS (see 4.4.1 above).

Effectively, if the joint arrangement is a joint operation, and the party has rights to the assets and obligations for the liabilities relating to that joint operation, it does not matter whether the parties to that joint arrangement have joint control or not – the accounting is the same. The disclosure requirements of IFRS 12 that may apply are discussed in Chapter 13 at 5.

6.5 Joint operations with a party that participates in a joint arrangement but does not have joint control

A joint operation conducted through a separate vehicle may involve a party that participates in the joint arrangement but does not have joint control (see 4 and 6.4 above). In such cases, a joint operator does not recognise the rights to assets and obligations for the liabilities attributable to such party, or recognise a higher percentage with a 'non-controlling interest'. Rather, a joint operator only recognises its share of any assets held jointly and its obligations for its share of any liabilities incurred jointly. Example 12.22 illustrates this point.

Example 12.22: Joint operation with a party that participates in a joint arrangement but does not have joint control

A and B enter into a joint operation that is structured through a separate vehicle Z. Each of the two entities owns 40% of the shares of the separate vehicle. The remaining 20% of Z is owned by C, which participates in the joint arrangement but does not have joint control. C does has rights to the assets and obligations for the liabilities of Z.

Accordingly, A, B and C (see 6.4 above) recognise their assets, including their share of any assets held jointly, and their liabilities, including their share of any liabilities incurred jointly, in accordance with relevant IFRS.

In A's financial statements, it recognises its assets, liabilities, revenues and expenses in Z, which would be 40% of Z's assets, liabilities, revenues and expenses, in accordance with the relevant IFRS. A does not recognise a 'non-controlling interest' related to C's interest in Z.

6.6 Transactions between a joint operator and a joint operation

IFRS 11 addresses transactions such as the sale, contribution or purchase of assets between a joint operator and a joint operation. *[IFRS 11.22].*

When a joint operator enters into a transaction with its joint operation, such as a sale or contribution of assets to the joint operation, the joint operator is conducting the transaction with the other parties to the joint operation. The joint operator recognises gains and losses resulting from such a transaction only to the extent of the other parties' interests in the joint operation. *[IFRS 11.B34].*

However, when such transactions provide evidence of a reduction in the net realisable value of the assets to be sold or contributed to the joint operation, or of an impairment loss of those assets, those losses are recognised fully by the joint operator. *[IFRS 11.B35].*

When a joint operator enters into a transaction with its joint operation, such as a purchase of assets from the joint operation, it does not recognise its share of the gains and losses until the joint operator resells those assets to a third party. *[IFRS 11.B36].*

However, when such transactions provide evidence of a reduction in the net realisable value of the assets to be purchased or of an impairment loss of those assets, a joint operator recognises its share of those losses. *[IFRS 11.B37].*

When there is a transaction between a joint operator and a joint operation, consideration should be given to whether the transaction changes the nature of the joint operator's rights to assets, or obligations for liabilities. Any such changes should be reflected in the joint operator's financial statements, and the new assets and liabilities should be accounted for in accordance with the relevant IFRS.

6.7 Accounting for a joint operation in separate financial statements

In the separate financial statements, both a joint operator and a party that participates in a joint arrangement but does not have joint control (see 6.4 above) account for their interests in the same manner as accounting for a joint operation in consolidated financial statements. That is, regardless of whether or not the joint operation is structured through a separate vehicle, such a party would recognise in its separate financial statements:

- assets, including its share of any assets held jointly;
- liabilities, including its share of any liabilities incurred jointly;
- revenue from the sale of its share of the output arising from the joint operation;
- share of the revenue from the sale of the output by the joint operation; and
- expenses, including its share of any expenses incurred jointly. *[IFRS 11.20-23, 26(a), 27(a)]*.

Accordingly, the guidance in 6 to 6.6 above also applies to accounting for joint operations in separate financial statements.

7 ACCOUNTING FOR JOINT VENTURES

Joint ventures are accounted for using the equity method. IFRS 11 does not describe how to apply the equity method. Rather, if an entity has joint control over a joint venture, it recognises its interest in the joint venture as an investment and accounts for it by applying the equity method in accordance with IAS 28, unless it is exempted from doing so by IAS 28. *[IFRS 11.24]*. The requirements of IAS 28, including the accounting for transactions between a joint venturer and the joint venture, are discussed in Chapter 11.

As discussed at 2.3.1 above, venture capital organisations, mutual funds, unit trusts and similar entities, including investment-linked insurance funds, can choose to measure investments in joint ventures at fair value or apply the equity method under IAS 28. This is considered a measurement exemption under IFRS 11 and IAS 28 (see Chapter 11 at 5.3).

This means, however, that such entities are subject to the disclosure requirements for joint ventures set out in IFRS 12 (see Chapter 13 at 5).

Although this option included in IAS 28 is available to venture capital organisations and similar entities, IFRS 10 states that an 'investment entity' for the purposes of that standard would elect the exemption from applying the equity method in IAS 28 for its investments in associates and joint ventures. *[IFRS 10.B85L]*.

7.1 Interest in a joint venture without joint control

IAS 28 also applies if a party that participates in a joint arrangement but does not have joint control (see 6.4 above) in a joint venture has significant influence over the entity. *[IFRS 11.25]*. However, the disclosure requirements differ (see Chapter 13 at 5). If the party that participates in a joint arrangement does not have joint control but does have significant influence in a joint venture, but the joint venture is not an entity (i.e. but is in a separate vehicle) (see 5.1 above), IAS 28 would not apply, and the investor would apply the relevant IFRS.

If the party that participates in a joint arrangement but does not have joint control does not have significant influence, its interest in the joint venture would be accounted for as a financial asset under IFRS 9 (or IAS 39 if IFRS 9 is not yet applied). *[IFRS 11.25, C14]*.

7.2 Contributions of non-monetary assets to a joint venture

When an entity contributes a non-monetary asset or liability to a joint venture in exchange for an equity interest in the joint venture, it recognises the portion of the gain or loss attributable to the other parties to the joint venture except when the contribution lacks commercial substance.

The measurement of the non-monetary asset in the financial statements of the joint venture (i.e. not the joint venturer) can differ, depending on the method of settlement. When the consideration given by the joint venture is its own shares, the transaction is an equity-settled share-based payment transaction in the scope of IFRS 2 – *Share-based Payment*. As a result, the joint venture measures the non-monetary asset received at its fair value. When the consideration given by the joint venture is not its own shares, the transaction is outside the scope of IFRS 2; we believe the joint venture should measure the non-monetary asset received at its cost, which is the fair value of the consideration given.

However, when the contributed non-monetary asset is a subsidiary of an entity, a conflict arises between the requirements of IAS 28 and IFRS 10. This is discussed in Chapter 11 at 7.6.5.C and at 8.2.3 below.

7.3 Accounting for a joint venture in separate financial statements

In its separate financial statements, a joint venturer accounts for its interest in the joint venture at cost, as a financial asset per IFRS 9 (or IAS 39, if IFRS 9 is not yet applied), or under the equity method. *[IFRS 11.26(b)]*. These separate financial statements are prepared in addition to those prepared using the equity method. The requirements for separate financial statements are discussed in Chapter 8 at 2.

In its separate financial statements, a party that participates in, but does not have joint control of a joint venture (see 6.4 above) accounts for its interest as a financial asset under IFRS 9 (or IAS 39, if IFRS 9 is not yet applied), unless it has significant influence over the joint venture. *[IFRS 11.27(b)]*. In this case, it may choose whether to account for its interest in the joint venture at cost, as a financial asset per IFRS 9 (or IAS 39, if IFRS 9 is not yet applied), or the equity method. *[IAS 27.10]*.

However, if an entity elects, in accordance with IAS 28, to measure its investments in associates or joint ventures at fair value through profit or loss in accordance with IFRS 9 (or IAS 39), it also accounts for those investments in the same way in its separate financial statements. *[IAS 27.11]*.

8 CONTINUOUS ASSESSMENT

IFRS 11 incorporates the notion of continuous assessment, consistent with the requirements in IFRS 10.

If facts and circumstances change, an entity that is a party in a joint arrangement reassesses whether:

- it still has joint control of the arrangement; and *[IFRS 11.13]*
- the classification of joint arrangement has changed. *[IFRS 11.19]*.

8.1 When to reassess under IFRS 11

A party reassesses upon any change in facts and circumstances whether it has joint control, and whether the classification of joint arrangement has changed. In some cases, such change in facts and circumstances might result in a party having control over the arrangement and therefore losing joint control. A party also may lose joint control upon a change in facts and circumstances. In other cases, an arrangement may remain under joint control, but the classification might change from joint venture to joint operation (or *vice versa*).

Reassessment of a *joint arrangement* occurs upon a change in:

- How activities are directed – For example, A sets up Z to develop a new product or technology. Initially, Z had a Board of Directors elected by shareholders, separate management and the relevant activities were directed by voting rights held exclusively by A. If A enters into an agreement with B so that A and B must agree on all decisions (e.g. they replace the Board and make decisions for management), reassessment would be required to evaluate whether A and B have joint control of Z.
- Legal form – For example, a separate vehicle that initially did not confer separation between the parties and the vehicle (e.g. a general partnership) and was considered a joint operation, is converted into a separate vehicle that now does confer separation between the parties and the vehicle (e.g. a corporation). Reassessment would be required to evaluate whether this indicates a change in classification from a joint operation to a joint venture.
- Contractual terms – For example, the terms of a joint arrangement are renegotiated, such that the parties have rights to the assets or obligations for the liabilities. Reassessment would be required to evaluate whether this indicates a change in classification to a joint operation.
- Other facts and circumstances – For example, the terms and conditions of a joint operation are renegotiated. Initially, a joint arrangement could sell output only to the parties of the joint arrangement. Thereafter, the joint arrangement may also sell output to third-party customers. Reassessment would be required to evaluate whether this indicates a change in classification from a joint operation to a joint venture.

As discussed at 5.3.1 above, another event that might trigger reassessment would be an event that leads a guarantor to have to pay (or perform) under a guarantee.

8.1.1 Changes in ownership

The accounting for changes in ownership of a joint arrangement depends firstly on whether the underlying assets and liabilities constitute a 'business' as defined in IFRS 3. Secondly, it depends on the type of interest held before and after the change in ownership occurred.

The diagram below provides a reference for additional guidance when the assets and liabilities meet the definition of a business. The key questions that arise on these transactions are:

- Should a cost-based approach or a fair value (IFRS 3) approach be used?
- Should any previously held (retained) interest be remeasured?
- Should a profit on sale be recognized and if how should it be measured?

Matrix of transactions involving changes of interest in a business[17]

To: From:	Holder of financial asset	Investee in associate	Joint Venturer	Joint Operator	Parent
Holder of financial asset	IAS 39/IFRS 9 See Chapters 46 and 47	IFRS not clear See Chapter 11 at 7.4.2.A	IFRS not clear 8.2.5 below See Chapter 11 at 7.4.2.A	Proposed amendments to IFRS 3 and IFRS 11 See 8.3.1 below	IFRS 3 See Chapter 9 at 9
Investee in associate or Joint Venturer	IAS 28 and IFRS 9 See Chapter 11 at 7.12.2	IAS 28 See Chapter 11 at 7.4.2.B; 7.4.2.C, 7.12.3, 7.12.4 and 7.12.5		Proposed amendments to IFRS 3 and IFRS 11 See 8.3.1 below	IFRS 3 and IAS 28 See Chapter 11 at 7.12.1
Joint Operator	IFRS not clear See 8.3.4 below	IFRS not clear See 8.3.4 below		Proposed amendments to IFRS 3 and IFRS 11 See 8.3.1 below	Proposed amendments to IFRS 3 and IFRS 11 See 8.3.2 below
Parent	IFRS 10 See Chapter 7 at 3.2	IFRS 10 See Chapter 11 at 7.4.1		IFRS not clear See 8.3.3 below	IFRS 10 See Chapter 7 at 3.3

The rights and obligations of the parties that participate in a joint arrangement but who do not have joint control (see 6.4 above) should determine the appropriate category per the table above.

In 8.2 and 8.3 below, we discuss changes in accounting that result from changes in ownership in joint ventures and joint operations that constitute a business, respectively.

The accounting for a change in an interest in a joint arrangement that does not meet the definition of a business is discussed at 8.4 below.

8.2 Changes in ownership of a joint venture that constitute a business

8.2.1 Acquisition of an interest in a joint venture

The accounting for the acquisition of an interest in a joint venture that meets the definition of a business is accounted for as described in IAS 28 (see Chapter 11 at 7.4) and the procedures are similar to those applied for an acquisition of a business in IFRS 3.

However, it is clear from the scope of IFRS 3 that the formation of a joint venture that constitutes a business, in the financial statements of the joint venture itself, is not covered by IFRS 3. *[IFRS 3.2]*.

8.2.2 Gaining control over a former joint venture

If an entity gains control over a former joint venture, and the acquiree meets the definition of a business, the entity applies IFRS 3 (see Chapter 9 at 9).

8.2.3 Former subsidiary becomes a joint venture

When a subsidiary becomes a joint venture, there is a conflict between the requirements of IAS 28 and IFRS 10 on how to calculate any gain or loss arising in this transaction. This conflict arises when a parent contributes a subsidiary to a joint venture (i.e. the parent loses control over the subsidiary, but retains joint control), and receives an interest in that joint venture in exchange. This may occur, for example, if a parent sells shares in its subsidiary to another party and the arrangement becomes a joint venture, or by dilution (i.e. if the subsidiary issues new shares to another party and the arrangement becomes a joint venture).

If IFRS 10 is applied when an entity loses control of its subsidiary, and obtains joint control of a joint venture, the entity will:

- derecognise the assets and liabilities of the former subsidiary (including any related goodwill and non-controlling interests) from the consolidated statement of financial position;
- recognise the fair value of any consideration received;
- recognise any distribution of shares in the subsidiary to owners;
- recognise the retained investment in the joint venture at its fair value when control is lost and subsequently account for it in accordance with IFRS 11 and IAS 28. The fair value is deemed its cost under the equity method ;
- reclassify to profit or loss, or to retained earnings (based on the applicable IFRS) amounts recognised in other comprehensive income related to that subsidiary; and
- recognise the resulting gain or loss without restriction (that is, the full gain or loss would be recognised and not only the other parties' portion). *[IFRS 10.25, B98]*.

In contrast, as discussed at 7.2 above, if IAS 28 is applied, this will limit the gain recognised, when a subsidiary is contributed to a joint venture, to the portion attributable to the other parties to the joint venture.

To address this conflict, in September 2014, the IASB issued an amendment *Sale or Contribution of Assets between an Investor and its Associate or Joint Venture*. This amended IFRS 10 so that the gain or loss on a transaction that does not involve the transfer of a business is recognised only to the extent of the unrelated investors' interests in the joint venture. If the sale or contribution of assets does involve the transfer of a business, the gain or loss would be recognised in full. The amendment was to apply prospectively to transactions in annual periods beginning on or after 1 January 2016; with early adoption permitted and disclosed.

After the amendments were issued, some constituents noted conflicts arising as a result of the amendments. The IASB then decided to address the issue as part of its research project on equity accounting. Consequently, in December 2015, the IASB amended IFRS 10 and IAS 28 to defer the effective date of the September 2014 amendment indefinitely. However, entities may choose to adopt the September 2014 amendments before an effective date is determined.

In the meantime, we believe that, when a non-monetary asset contributed to a joint venture is an interest in a subsidiary that constitutes a business, entities would have an accounting policy choice as to whether to apply the principles in IFRS 10 or IAS 28. Once selected, the entity must apply the selected policy consistently. Nevertheless, where the requirements of IFRS 10 are applied for transactions involving a contribution of an interest in a subsidiary, IAS 28 would apply to other forms of non-monetary assets contributed, such as items of property, plant and equipment or intangible assets. This issue is discussed further in Chapter 7 at 3.2.1 and 3.2.6, and at Chapter 11 at 7.4.1.

8.2.4 Joint venture becomes an associate (or vice versa)

If a joint venturer loses joint control but retains an interest in an associate, it would continue to apply the equity method. An entity does not remeasure its retained interest in an associate when it loses joint control over a joint venture. The same applies where an entity gains joint control over an associate that becomes an investment in a joint venture. *[IAS 28.24]*. In the Basis for Conclusions to IAS 28, the IASB acknowledged that the nature of the investor-investee relationship changes upon changing from joint venture to associate (or *vice versa*). However, since the investment continues to be accounted for using the equity method (i.e. there is no change in the measurement requirements) and there is no change in the group, it is not an event that warrants remeasurement of the retained interest at fair value. *[IAS 28.BC30]*.

If an entity's ownership interest in an associate or a joint venture is reduced, but the investment continues to be classified either as an associate or a joint venture respectively, the entity shall reclassify to profit or loss the proportion of the gain or loss that had previously been recognised in other comprehensive income relating to that reduction in ownership interest if that gain or loss would be required to be reclassified to profit or loss on the disposal of the related assets or liabilities. *[IAS 28.25]*.

The above requirements of IAS 28 also are discussed in Chapter 11 and at 7.4.2.C and 7.12.3.

8.2.5 Joint venture becomes a financial asset (or vice versa)

If a joint venture becomes a financial asset, the measurement method changes. An entity measures its retained interest in the financial asset at fair value, which becomes its fair value on initial recognition as a financial asset.

The entity recognises in profit or loss any difference between:

(a) the fair value of any retained interest and any proceeds from disposing of a part interest in the joint venture; and

(b) the carrying amount of the interest in the joint venture at the date the equity method was discontinued.

If a gain or loss previously recognised by the entity in other comprehensive income would be reclassified to profit or loss on the disposal of the related assets or liabilities, IAS 28 requires the entity to reclassify the gain or loss from equity to profit or loss when the equity method is discontinued. For example, gains and losses related to foreign currency translation adjustments accumulated in equity would be reclassified to profit or loss. *[IAS 28.22, 23]*.

The above requirements of IAS 28 also are discussed in Chapter 11 at 7.12.2.

An entity may gain joint control over an existing investment (accounted for as a financial asset). IAS 28 is unclear on how piecemeal acquisitions of a joint venture should be treated. This issue is discussed in Chapter 11 at 7.4.2.A.

8.2.6 Disposal of an interest in a joint venture

When an entity disposes of its interest in a joint venture and loses joint control, it ceases to apply the equity method as of that date. It also derecognises its interest and recognises any gain or loss upon sale, as discussed at 8.2.5 above. *[IAS 28.22, 23]*. In such cases, an entity cannot restate its financial statements for the period (or the comparative period) as if it did not have joint control during the reporting period. IAS 28 requires that the entity use the equity method up to the date that the joint venturer disposes of its interest in the joint venture. This assumes that the entity is not exempt from preparing financial statements by IFRS 10, IAS 27 or IAS 28 and that it is not using the fair value measurement exemption (see 2.3.1 above).

8.2.7 Interest in a joint venture held for sale

When a joint venturer plans to dispose of part of its interest in a joint venture, it applies IFRS 5 (see Chapter 4) and only reclassifies the interest to be disposed of as held for sale when that portion meets the criteria for classification as held for sale. The joint venturer continues to account for the retained interest in the joint venture using the equity method until the disposal of that interest occurs. This is because an entity continues to have joint control over its entire interest in the joint venture until it disposes of that interest. Upon disposal, it reassesses the nature of its interest and accounts for that interest accordingly (e.g. as a financial asset). *[IAS 28.20]*.

If an interest (or a portion of an interest) in a joint venture no longer meets the criteria to be classified as held for sale, the interest is accounted for using the equity method retrospectively from the date of its classification as held for sale. *[IAS 28.21]*.

The above requirements of IAS 28 also are discussed in Chapter 11 at 6.

8.3 Changes in ownership of a joint operation that is a business

8.3.1 Acquisition of an interest in a joint operation

An entity that acquires an interest in a joint operation that is a business as defined in IFRS 3 is required to apply, to the extent of its share, all of the principles of IFRS 3 and other IFRSs that do not conflict with IFRS 11, which include:

(a) measuring identifiable assets and liabilities at fair value, other than items for which exceptions are given in IFRS 3 and other IFRSs;

(b) recognising acquisition-related costs as expenses in the periods in which the costs are incurred and the services are received, with the exception that the costs to issue debt or equity securities are recognised in accordance with IAS 32 – *Financial Instruments: Presentation* – and IFRS 9 (or IAS 39 if IFRS 9 has not yet been adopted);

(c) recognising deferred tax assets and deferred tax liabilities that arise from the initial recognition of assets or liabilities, except for deferred tax liabilities that arise from the initial recognition of goodwill;

(d) recognising as goodwill any excess of the consideration transferred over the net amount of identifiable assets acquired and the liabilities assumed; and

(e) testing for impairment a cash-generating unit to which goodwill has been allocated at least annually, and whenever there is an indication that the unit may be impaired, as required by IAS 36 – *Impairment of Assets*. *[IFRS 11.B33A]*.

In addition, the entity should disclose the information that is required in those IFRSs in relation to business combinations.

The IASB recognised that the acquisition of an interest in a joint operation did not meet the definition of a business combination in IFRS 3, but it concluded that it was the most appropriate approach to account for an acquisition of an interest in a joint operation whose activity meets the definition of a business, as defined in IFRS 3. *[IFRS 11.BC45E, BC45F]*.

The above approach also applies to the formation of a joint operation, but only if an existing business (as defined in IFRS 3) is contributed by one of the parties that participates in the joint operation. In other words, the above approach should not be applied if the parties that participate in the joint operation only contribute (groups of) assets that do not constitute businesses to the joint operation on its formation. *[IFRS 11.B33B]*. The amendment applies to the acquisition of both the initial interest and additional interests in a joint operation (while still maintaining joint control) in which the activity of the joint operation constitutes a business. *[IFRS 11.21A]*.

If a joint operator increases its interest in a joint operation that is a business (as defined in IFRS 3) by acquiring an additional interest while still retaining joint control, it should not remeasure its previously held interest in that joint operation. *[IFRS 11.B33C]*.

This requirement does not apply to 'the acquisition of an interest in a joint operation when the parties sharing joint control, including the entity acquiring the interest in the joint operation, are under the common control of the same ultimate controlling party or parties both before and after the acquisition, and that control is not transitory'. *[IFRS 11.B33D]*.

8.3.2 Control or joint control over a former joint operation

In June 2016, the IASB proposed amendments to IFRS 3 and IFRS 11 in an ED *Definition of a Business and Accounting for Previously Held Interests (Proposed amendments to IFRS 3 and IFRS 11).* The proposed amendments aim to eliminate diversity in practice in accounting for previously held interests in the assets and liabilities of a joint operation that constitutes a business when an entity obtains control or joint control of the joint operation. The exposure draft states:

- Obtaining control of a business that is a joint operation for which the acquirer held an interest in its assets and liabilities immediately before the acquisition date (either as a joint operator or as a party to a joint arrangement) is a business combination achieved in stages. Therefore, the acquirer shall remeasure any previously held interests in the joint operation;
- A party that participates in a joint arrangement but that did not have joint control and increases its interest in the joint operation and obtains joint control shall not remeasure previously held interests in the assets and liabilities of the joint operation.

In April 2017, the IASB tentatively decided to finalise amendments to clarify IFRS 3 so that when an entity obtains control of a business that is a joint operation, it remeasures its previously held interest in that joint operation. Readers should monitor developments in this area.

8.3.3 Former subsidiary becomes a joint operation

In some transactions, it is possible that an entity would lose control of a subsidiary, but retain an interest in a joint operation. For example, a parent might contribute an existing business to a newly created joint operation and obtain joint control of the combined operation. Alternatively, it could be achieved by a parent with a 100% subsidiary selling a 50% interest to another party, with the transaction resulting in the formation of a joint operation, with each party having a 50% share of the assets and liabilities of the joint operation.

As set out in Chapter 7 at 3.2, in accounting for a loss of control of a subsidiary, a parent is required to:

(a) derecognise the assets and liabilities of the subsidiary;

(b) recognise any investment retained in the former subsidiary at fair value at the date when control is lost; and

(c) recognise any resulting gain or loss in profit or loss.

However, it is unclear how these requirements should be applied when the retained interest is in the assets and liabilities of a joint operation. One view is that the retained interest should be remeasured at fair value. Another view is that the retained interest should not be derecognised or remeasured at fair value, but should continue to be recognised and measured at its carrying amount.

In July 2016, the Interpretations Committee discussed this issue and noted that paragraphs B34 to B35 of IFRS 11 (see 6.6 above) could be viewed as conflicting with the requirements in IFRS 10, which specify that an entity should remeasure any retained interest when it loses control of a subsidiary. The IASB decided not to add this issue to its agenda but, instead, to recommend that the Board consider the issue at the same time the Board further considers the accounting for the sale or contribution of assets to an associate or a joint venture.

In the meantime, we believe that, when a parent loses control over a subsidiary but retains an interest in a joint operation that is a business, entities have an accounting policy choice as to whether to remeasure the retained interest at fair value.

8.3.4 Other changes in ownership of a joint operation

IFRS 11 does not explicitly address the accounting for a former joint operation, and the situations in which:

- it becomes an associate or a financial instrument – when a former joint operation becomes an associate or financial instrument, it would generally be appropriate to derecognise the assets and liabilities previously recognised in accordance with IFRS 11 and account for the new interest based on the applicable IFRS at that date. This approach may also be appropriate when the rights to assets or obligations for liabilities that the entity held when it was a joint operation differ from its rights or obligations when it ceases to be a party to a joint operation.
- the rights to assets or obligations with respect to that joint operation change – when a joint operator's rights to assets or obligations for liabilities change (e.g. other operators obtain rights to the assets or assume obligations for those liabilities), the joint operator would generally:
  - derecognise the relevant portion of the assets and liabilities;
  - recognise the fair value of any consideration received;
  - recognise the resulting gain or loss; and
  - recognise any rights to assets it acquires from other joint operators, and obligations it assumes from other joint operators, or from the joint arrangement itself.

If an interest in a joint operation (or portion thereof) no longer meets the criteria to be classified as held for sale, an entity restates the financial statements for the periods since classification as held for sale. *[IFRS 5.28]*.

8.3.5 Disposal of interest in a joint operation

When an entity disposes of its interest in a joint operation, it ceases to account for the rights to assets and obligations for liabilities, and recognises any gain or loss as of the disposal date, in accordance with the relevant IFRS. The only exception would be if the same rights to assets or obligations for liabilities replaced that interest directly. In this case, there would be no change in accounting, because, in both cases, the assets and liabilities are recognised in accordance with the relevant IFRS (see 6 and 8.3.4 above).

Consistent with the treatment of joint ventures (see 8.2.6 above) an entity continues to reflect its interest in a joint operation for the reporting period (and comparative period) in which it held that interest. An entity does not restate its financial statements as if it never held the interest in the disposed joint operation.

8.4 Changes in ownership of a joint arrangement that does not constitute a business

8.4.1 Joint operator obtains control or parties that participate in a joint arrangement but do not have joint control obtain joint control

At its January 2016 meeting, the Interpretations Committee discussed whether previously held interests in the assets and liabilities of a joint operation, which does not constitute a business, should be remeasured when:

- a joint operator or a party that participates in a joint arrangement but do not have joint control obtains control of a joint operation; and
- a change of interests resulting in a party that participates in a joint arrangement but does not have joint control obtains joint control over the joint operation.

The Interpretations Committee noted that paragraph 2(b) of IFRS 3 explains the requirements for accounting for an asset acquisition in which the asset or group of assets do not meet the definition of a business. The Interpretations Committee noted that paragraph 2(b) of IFRS 3 specifies that a cost-based approach should be used in accounting for an asset acquisition, and that in a cost-based approach the existing assets generally are not remeasured (see Chapter 9 at 2.2.2). The Interpretations Committee also observed that it was not aware of significant diversity in practice and, therefore, decided not to add this issue to its agenda.[18]

8.4.2 Single-asset subsidiary becomes joint venture or joint operation

When a subsidiary becomes a joint venture, and that former subsidiary was a single-asset entity, in our view, the entity needs to look through the structure to determine whether the investor retained in substance, an indirect interest in the underlying asset or an investment in an entity. The answer would affect the percentage of the profit on transfer to be recognised. This issue is discussed further in Chapter 7 at 3.2.6.

As discussed at 8.3.3 above, the Interpretations Committee discussed in March 2016 whether an entity should remeasure its retained interest in the assets and liabilities of a joint operation when the entity loses control of an asset or group of assets, but decided not to add the issue to its agenda. If the subsidiary over which control has been lost is becomes a joint operation and is a single asset entity, we believe that the transaction should be regarded as a partial sale of the underlying asset rather than a disposal of a subsidiary and a retained interest. This is explored further in Chapter 7 at 3.2.6.

9 DISCLOSURES

The disclosure requirements regarding joint arrangements accounted for under IFRS 11 are included in IFRS 12 and are discussed in Chapter 13 at 5. IFRS 12 combines the disclosure requirements for an entity's interests in subsidiaries, joint arrangements, associates and structured entities into one comprehensive disclosure standard.

References

1 *IASB Update*, May 2012.
2 *IASB Update*, May 2016.
3 *IASB Update*, May 2016.
4 The flowchart is based on those included in paragraphs B21 and B33 of IFRS 11.
5 *IFRIC Update*, March 2015.
6 *IFRIC Update*, March 2015.
7 Staff Paper (March 2014 Interpretations Committee Meeting), IFRS 11 *Joint Arrangements* – Consideration of some common joint arrangement structures (Agenda reference 5B).
8 Staff Paper (March 2015 Interpretations Committee Meeting), IFRS 11 *Joint Arrangements* – Tentative agenda decision comment letter analysis (Agenda reference 4).
9 *IFRIC Update*, March 2015.
10 IFRS 11.IE2-IE8, Example 1.
11 IFRS 11.IE9-IE13, Example 2.
12 IFRS 11.IE14-IE28, Example 3.
13 IFRS 11.IE29-IE33, Example 4.
14 IFRS 11.IE34-IE43, Example 5.
15 IFRS 11.IE44-IE52, Example 6.
16 See, for example, IFRS 11.IE8 and IE21.
17 Staff Paper (July 2015 Interpretations Committee Meeting), IFRS 11 *Joint Arrangements* – Remeasurement of previously held interests (Agenda reference 6).
18 *IFRIC Update*, January 2016.

Chapter 13 Disclosure of interests in other entities

List of examples

Chapter 13 Disclosure of interests in other entities

1 INTRODUCTION

IFRS 12 – *Disclosure of Interests in Other Entities* – is a disclosure standard. It includes all of the disclosure requirements related to interests in subsidiaries, joint arrangements, associates and consolidated and unconsolidated structured entities.

The recognition and measurement of subsidiaries, joint arrangements and associates are dealt with in IFRS 10 – *Consolidated Financial Statements,* IFRS 11 – *Joint Arrangements,* IAS 27 – *Separate Financial Statements* – and IAS 28 – *Investments in Associates and Joint Ventures.*

IFRS 12 was issued in May 2011. It was mandatory for accounting periods beginning on or after 1 January 2013. However, depending on an entity's regulator and jurisdiction, the date at which an entity applies IFRS 12 may have varied from the date prescribed by the IASB. Under EU-adopted IFRS, for example, IFRS 12 was mandatory for accounting periods beginning on or after 1 January 2014 but could be adopted early.

The adoption of IFRS 12 is discussed at 2.3 below.

1.1 The development of IFRS 12

IFRS 12 was never exposed as a draft for comment. It was conceived by the IASB during consideration of the responses to ED 9 – *Joint Arrangements* – and ED 10 – *Consolidated Financial Statements.* The IASB observed that the disclosure requirements of the previous versions of IAS 27 – *Consolidated and Separate Financial Statements* – and IAS 28 – *Investments in Associates* – together with IAS 31 – *Interests in Joint Ventures* – overlapped in many areas. In addition, many respondents to ED 10 commented that its proposed disclosure requirements for interests in unconsolidated structured entities should not be located in a consolidation standard. *[IFRS 12.BC7].*

Consequently, the IASB decided to combine the disclosure requirements for subsidiaries, joint ventures and associates within a comprehensive disclosure standard that would address a reporting entity's involvement with other entities when such involvement was not within the scope of IAS 39 – *Financial Instruments: Recognition and Measurement* – or IFRS 9 – *Financial Instruments.* The disclosure standard would also include the disclosure requirements for joint operations and information that enables users of financial statements to evaluate the nature of, and risks associated with, structured entities that a reporting entity does not control.[1]

The effect of this is that IFRS 12 disclosure requirements replace those contained in the previous versions of IAS 27 and IAS 28 and IAS 31 except for the disclosure requirements that apply only when preparing separate financial statements, which remain in IAS 27. IFRS 12 also contains all disclosures that relate to consolidated financial statements (IFRS 10) and joint operations (IFRS 11). In addition, IFRS 12 includes disclosures related to unconsolidated structured entities (originally proposed to be within IFRS 10).

The IASB has stated that they have heard overwhelming support for the disclosure requirements of IFRS 12 and feel confident that they represent an improvement in the quality of financial reporting.[2]

2 OBJECTIVE, SCOPE AND EFFECTIVE DATE OF IFRS 12

2.1 Objective

The stated objective of IFRS 12 is 'to require an entity to disclose information that enables users of its financial statements to evaluate:

(a) the nature of, and risks associated with, its interest in *other entities*; and

(b) the effects of those interests on its financial position, financial performance and cash flows'. *[IFRS 12.1]*.

To meet the objective of the standard, an entity must disclose:

(a) the significant judgements and assumptions it has made in determining:
   - (i) the nature of its interest in another entity or arrangement;
   - (ii) the type of joint arrangement in which it has an interest;
   - (iii) that it meets the definition of an investment entity if applicable; and

(b) information about its interests in:
   - (i) subsidiaries;
   - (ii) joint arrangements and associates; and
   - (iii) structured entities that are not controlled by the entity (unconsolidated structured entities). *[IFRS 12.2]*.

If the disclosures required by the standard, together with the disclosures required by other IFRSs, do not meet the objective of IFRS 12, an entity must disclose whatever additional information is necessary to meet that objective. *[IFRS 12.3]*.

The standard provides no illustrative examples to support any of its disclosure requirements. In addition, several of the terms used in the standard are undefined. This may well lead to diversity in practice and application where the wording of a disclosure requirement is ambiguous or otherwise unclear.

2.2 Scope

IFRS 12 applies to any entity that has an interest in any of the following:

(a) subsidiaries;

(b) joint arrangements (i.e. joint operations or joint ventures);

(c) associates; and

(d) unconsolidated structured entities. *[IFRS 12.5].*

2.2.1 Definitions

The following definitions from Appendix A to IFRS 12 are relevant to the scope of IFRS 12.

Income from a structured entity 'includes, but is not limited to, recurring and non-recurring fees, interest, dividends, gains or losses on the remeasurement or derecognition of interests in structured entities and gains or losses from the transfer of assets and liabilities to the structured entity'.

Interest in another entity refers to 'contractual and non-contractual involvement that exposes an entity to variability of returns from the performance of the other entity. An interest in another entity can be evidenced by, but is not limited to, the holding of equity or debt instruments as well as other forms of involvement such as the provision of funding, liquidity support, credit enhancement and guarantees. It includes the means by which an entity has control, or joint control of, or significant influence over, another entity. An entity does not necessarily have an interest in another entity solely because of a typical customer supplier relationship'.

A structured entity is an entity 'that has been designed so that voting or similar rights are not the dominant factor in deciding who controls the entity, such as when any voting rights relate to administrative tasks only and the relevant activities are directed by means of contractual arrangements'.

Appendix A to IFRS 12 provides a list of terms defined in IAS 27, IAS 28, IFRS 10 and IFRS 11 which are used in IFRS 12 with the meanings specified in those IFRSs. The terms include the following:

- associate;
- consolidated financial statements;
- control of an entity;
- equity method;
- group;
- investment entity; and
- joint arrangement.

2.2.1.A Interests in other entities

An interest in another entity refers to contractual and non-contractual involvement that exposes the reporting entity to variability of returns from the performance of the other entity. Consideration of the purpose and design of the other entity may help the reporting entity when assessing whether it has an interest in that entity and, therefore, whether it is required to provide the disclosures in IFRS 12. That assessment must include consideration of the risks that the other entity was designed to create and the risks that the other entity was designed to pass on to the reporting entity and other parties. *[IFRS 12.B7]*.

IFRS 10 defines 'variability of returns'. IFRS 10 explains that variable returns are returns that are not fixed and have the potential to vary as a result of the performance of an investee. Variable returns can be only positive, only negative or both positive and negative. An investor assesses whether returns from an interest are variable and how variable these returns are on the basis of the substance of the arrangement and regardless of the legal form of the returns. For example, an investor can hold a bond with fixed interest payments. The fixed interest payments are variable returns for the purpose of IFRS 10 because they are subject to default risk and they expose the investor to the credit risk of the issuer of the bond. The amount of variability (i.e. how variable those returns are) depends on the credit risk of the bond. Similarly, fixed performance fees for managing an investee's assets are variable returns because they expose the investor to the performance risk of the investee. The amount of variability depends on the investee's ability to generate sufficient income to pay the fee. *[IFRS 10.B56]*.

Thus, the definition of an 'interest' in IFRS 12 is much wider than the mere holding of equity instruments in an entity. As IFRS 12 requires disclosures of interests that a reporting entity holds in other entities, preparers will need to ensure that their reporting systems and processes are sufficient to identify those 'interests'.

IFRS 12 clarifies that a reporting entity is typically exposed to variability of returns from the performance of another entity by holding instruments (such as equity or debt instruments issued by the other entity) or having another involvement that absorbs variability. *[IFRS 12.B8]*. This is illustrated in Example 13.1 below.

Example 13.1: Variability of returns arising from issue of credit default swap (1)

A reporting entity issues a credit default swap to a structured entity. The credit default swap protects the structured entity from the default of interest and principal payments on its loan portfolio.

The reporting entity has an involvement in the structured entity that exposes it to variability of returns from the performance of the structured entity because the credit default swap absorbs variability of returns of the structured entity. *[IFRS 12.B8]*.

Some instruments are designed to transfer risk from the reporting entity to another entity. Such instruments create variability of returns for the other entity but do not typically expose the reporting entity to variability of returns from the performance of the other entity. *[IFRS 12.B9]*. This is illustrated in Example 13.2 below.

Example 13.2: Variability of returns arising from issue of credit default swap (2)

A reporting entity enters into a credit default swap with a structured entity. The credit default swap gives the structured entity exposure to Entity Z's credit risk. The purpose of the arrangement is to give the investors in the structured entity exposure to Entity Z's credit risk (Entity Z is unrelated to any party involved in the arrangement).

The reporting entity does not have involvement with the structured entity that exposes it to variable returns from the structured entity because the credit default swap transfers variability to the structured entity rather than absorbing variability of returns of the structured entity.

Purchased call options and written put options (in each case unless the exercise price is at fair value) would also be interests in other entities, because these instruments typically absorb variability created by assets held in the entity. In contrast, some derivative instruments such as interest rate swaps, can both create and absorb variability and judgement will need to be exercised in determining whether these derivatives are interests in other entities.

We believe that plain vanilla swaps and other derivatives that both create and absorb variability, based on market rates or indices and which rank senior to the issued notes, do not absorb the risks the entity was designed to pass on, and are not an exposure to variable returns. They are therefore unlikely to be interests in other entities that would require disclosure under IFRS 12. See Chapter 6 at 5.3.1.

An entity does not necessarily have an interest in another entity because of a typical customer supplier relationship. However, as explained above, IFRS 10 states that fixed performance fees for managing an investee's assets create variable returns for the investor. The fixed performance fees are 'variable' because they expose the investor to the performance risk of the investee. *[IFRS 10.B56]*. Therefore, it would seem closer to the spirit of IFRS 12 that investment management fees are treated as a variable interest rather than a typical customer-supplier relationship in order to present fully the reporting entity's relationships with structured entities. The same principle applies to other fees based on assets under management.

2.2.1.B Structured entities

Whether an entity is a structured entity or not is important because additional disclosures are required by IFRS 12 for interests in structured entities. These disclosures are discussed at 4.4 and 6 below.

As defined at 2.2.1 above, a structured entity is an entity that has been designed so that voting or similar rights are not the dominant factor in deciding who controls the entity, such as when any voting rights relate to administrative tasks only and the relevant activities are directed by means of contractual arrangements.

The guidance to IFRS 12 states that a structured entity often has some or all of the following features or attributes:

(a) restricted activities;

(b) a narrow and well-defined objective, such as:

  (i) to effect a tax-efficient lease;

  (ii) to carry out research and development activities;

  (iii) to provide a source of capital or funding to an entity; or

  (iv) to provide investment opportunities for investors by passing on risks and rewards associated with the assets of the structured entity to investors.

(c) insufficient equity to permit the structured entity to finance its activities without subordinated financial support; and

(d) financing in the form of multiple contractually linked instruments to investors that create concentrations of credit or other risks (tranches). *[IFRS 12.B22]*.

The standard provides the following examples of entities that are regarded as structured entities:

- securitisation vehicles;
- asset-backed financings; and
- some investment funds. *[IFRS 12.B23].*

The IASB's rationale for including specific disclosures of investments in structured entities is that users have requested such disclosures because they believed involvement with these entities posed more risk than involvement with traditional operating entities. The increased risk exposure arises because, for example, the structured entity may have been created to pass risks and returns arising from specified assets to investors, or may have insufficient equity to fund losses on its assets, if they arise.

The Basis for Conclusions explains that the type of entity the Board envisages being characterised as a structured entity is unlikely to differ significantly from an entity that SIC-12 – *Consolidation – Special Purpose Entities* – described as a special purpose entity (SPE). SIC-12 described an SPE as an entity created to accomplish a narrow and well-defined objective, listing as examples entities established to effect a lease, entities established for research and development activities or entities established for the securitisation of financial assets. *[IFRS 12.BC82].*

However, the IFRS 12 definition of a structured entity (i.e. an entity that has been designed so that voting or similar rights are not the dominant factor in deciding who controls the entity) is not the same as the SIC-12 definition of an SPE. The IFRS 12 definition implies that any entity which is not controlled by voting or similar rights is a structured entity. Conversely, any entity controlled by voting or similar rights cannot be a structured entity.

It is not clear what the IASB means by 'similar' (to voting) rights in the definition of a structured entity. No illustrative examples are provided. It seems likely that this will require the exercise of judgement by reporting entities and that there may be diversity in practice about what constitutes a 'similar' right and therefore whether an entity is a structured entity. One example of what the IASB may have had in mind when referring to 'similar' rights is collective investment schemes where investors can vote to remove the manager of the fund without cause as long as a certain proportion of investors demand such a vote. The assessment of whether this right (to remove the fund manager) could be considered substantive rather than administrative, and therefore whether the collective investment scheme is a structured entity, would depend on the number of investors who would need to collaborate in order to force the vote.

IFRS 12 does not state whether the 'features or attributes' of structured entities discussed above are determinative as to whether an entity is a structured entity or whether the features or attributes should always be subordinate to the definition (i.e. if the entity was controlled by voting or similar rights then the features or attributes would be irrelevant). Our view is that the features and attributes are subordinated to the definition. However, the implication from the Basis for Conclusions is that the IASB considers that where some of the features or attributes are present in an entity then it is unlikely that the entity is controlled by voting or similar rights.

The IASB considered, but rejected, defining a structured entity in a way similar to a variable interest entity (VIE) in US GAAP. That approach, in the IASB's opinion, would have introduced complicated guidance solely for disclosure purposes that was not previously in IFRSs. *[IFRS 12.BC83]*. US GAAP defines a VIE, in essence, as an entity whose activities are not directed through voting or similar rights but with an additional condition that the total equity in a VIE is not sufficient to permit the entity to finance its activities without additional subordinated financial support. The IASB had two reasons for not making the definition of a structured entity dependant on total equity at risk (as in US GAAP). First, including insufficient equity at risk in the definition of a structured entity would require extensive application guidance to help determine the sufficiency of the equity, to which the IASB was opposed. Second, the IASB feared that some traditional operating entities might be caught by this definition when it had no intention of catching such entities. *[IFRS 12.BC83-85]*.

The standard clarifies that an entity that is controlled by voting rights is not a structured entity simply, because, for example, it receives funding from third parties following a restructuring. *[IFRS 12.B24]*. However, such funding is likely to give the investee a variable interest in the restructured entity that may still be a subsidiary as defined by IFRS 10.

2.2.1.C Interaction of IFRS 12 and IFRS 5

In July 2015, the IASB was asked to clarify the scope of IFRS 12 with respect to interests in entities within the scope of IFRS 5 – *Non-current Assets Held for Sale and Discontinued Operations*. Paragraph B17 of IFRS 12 states that an entity is not required to disclose summarised financial information in accordance with paragraphs B10–B16 for interests classified as held for sale. However, the requirements in paragraph 5B of IFRS 5 made it unclear whether all the other requirements of IFRS 12 apply to interests in entities classified as held for sale or discontinued operations in accordance with IFRS 5.

The IASB noted that it had not intended to exempt an entity from all of the disclosure requirements in IFRS 12 with respect to interests in entities classified as held for sale or discontinued operations. The objective of IFRS 12 (i.e. to disclose information that enables users of financial statements to evaluate the nature of, and risks associated with, interests in other entities, and the effects of those interests on financial statements) is relevant to interests in other entities, regardless of whether they are within the scope of IFRS 5.

Accordingly, in *Annual Improvements to IFRS Standards 2014–2016 Cycle*, the IASB added paragraph 5A to clarify that, except as described in paragraph B17, the requirements of IFRS 12 apply to an entity's interests listed in paragraph 5 (see 2.2 above) that are classified (or included in a disposal group that is classified) as held for sale or discontinued operations in accordance with IFRS 5.

Paragraph 5A of IFRS 5 clarifies that the requirements in IFRS 5 applicable to a non-current asset (or disposal group) that is classified as held for sale is also applicable to a non-current asset (or disposal group) that is classified as held for distribution to owners acting in their capacity as owners (held for distribution to owners). Paragraph 5B of IFRS 5 specifies the disclosures required in respect of non-current assets (or disposal groups) classified as held for sale or discontinued operations. Paragraph 5B does not refer to non-current assets held for distribution to owners.

The IASB noted that the clarification was required only in respect of interests specified in paragraph 5B of IFRS 5 (i.e. non-current assets (or disposal groups) classified as held for sale or discontinued operations). Clarification was not necessary in respect of paragraph 5A of IFRS 5 (i.e. non-current assets (or disposal groups) classified as held for distribution to owners). Accordingly, paragraph 5A of IFRS 12 refers only to interests that are classified as held for sale or discontinued operations.

Paragraph B17 of IFRS 12 was also amended to clarify that an entity is not required to disclose summarised financial information for a subsidiary, a joint venture or an associate in accordance with paragraphs B10-B16 of IFRS 5 when the entity's interest in that subsidiary, joint venture or associate (or a portion of its interest in a joint venture or an associate) is included in a disposal group that is classified as held for sale in accordance with IFRS 5. Prior to the amendment B17 referred only to interests that are classified as held for sale in accordance with IFRS 5.

The amendments were applicable retrospectively in accordance with IAS 8 – *Accounting Policies, Changes in Accounting Estimates and Errors* – for annual periods beginning on or after 1 January 2017.

2.2.2 *Interests disclosed under IFRS 12*

IFRS 12 requires that an entity must present information separately for interests in:

(a) subsidiaries;

(b) joint ventures;

(c) joint operations;

(d) associates; and

(e) unconsolidated structured entities. *[IFRS 12.B4].*

The standard requires that a reporting entity consider the level of detail necessary to satisfy the disclosure objective and how much emphasis to place on each of the requirements of IFRS 12. Disclosures can be aggregated or disaggregated so that useful information is not obscured by either the inclusion of a large amount of insignificant detail or the aggregation of items that have different characteristics. *[IFRS 12.4].* However, a reporting entity must disclose how it has aggregated its interests in similar entities. *[IFRS 12.B3].*

In determining whether to aggregate information, an entity shall consider qualitative and quantitative information about the different risk and return characteristics of each entity to the reporting entity. The entity must present the disclosures in a manner that clearly explains to users of the financial statements the nature and extent of its interests in those other entities. *[IFRS 12.B5].*

Examples of aggregation levels within classes of entities that the standard considers appropriate are:

- nature of activities (e.g. a research and development entity, a revolving credit card securitisation entity);
- industry classification; and
- geography (e.g. country or region). *[IFRS 12.B6].*

This guidance on aggregation implies latitude for entities to exercise their judgement in determining the appropriate level of disclosure. However, the standard separately requires summarised financial information for each material partly owned subsidiary, each material joint venture and associate and requires minimum disclosures in respect of unconsolidated structured entities.

2.2.2.A Subsidiaries

IFRS 10 defines a subsidiary as 'an entity that is controlled by another entity'. *[IFRS 10 Appendix A]*. IFRS 10 provides guidance as to the circumstances in which an entity is controlled by another entity.

2.2.2.B Joint arrangements

IFRS 11 defines a joint arrangement as 'an arrangement in which two or more parties have joint control'. Joint control is 'the contractually agreed sharing of control of an arrangement, which exists only when decisions about the relevant activities require the unanimous consent of the parties sharing control'. A joint operation is 'a joint arrangement whereby the parties that have joint control of the arrangement have rights to the assets, and obligations for the liabilities, relating to the arrangement'. A joint venture is 'a joint arrangement whereby the parties that have joint control of the arrangement have rights to the net assets of the arrangement'. *[IFRS 11 Appendix A]*. IFRS 11 provides guidance as to the circumstances in which joint control exists and on the characteristics of joint operations and joint ventures.

Interests in joint arrangements which are not structured entities and which do not result in the reporting entity obtaining joint control or significant influence over the joint arrangement are outside the scope of IFRS 12. See 2.2.3.C below.

2.2.2.C Associates

IAS 28 defines an associate as 'an entity over which the investor has significant influence'. *[IAS 28.3]*. IAS 28 provides guidance on the circumstances in which significant influence is exercised.

2.2.2.D Unconsolidated structured entities

'Unconsolidated structured entities' refers to all structured entities which are not consolidated by a reporting entity. Therefore, the definition of 'unconsolidated structured entity' includes structured entities that are joint arrangements and associates (unless specially excluded from the scope of the standard under 2.2.3 below), structured entities that are subsidiaries of parents that prepare separate financial statements (unless consolidated financial statements are also prepared – see 2.2.3.B below) and structured entities over which the reporting entity does not have significant influence.

Where an unconsolidated structured entity is a joint venture or associate then the disclosures required for unconsolidated structured entities at 6 below apply in addition to the separate disclosures at 5 below for interests in joint ventures and associates. The IASB concluded that an entity should capture most, and in some cases all, of the disclosures required for interests in unconsolidated structured entities by providing the disclosures for interests in joint ventures and associates. Accordingly, the IASB considers that the requirement to make both sets of disclosures where applicable should not result in a significant incremental increase in the amount of information that an entity would be required to provide. *[IFRS 12.BC77]*.

As discussed at 2.2.1.A above, the definition of a variable interest is widely drawn so that a derivative issued to a structured entity may result in an interest in an unconsolidated structured entity. This interest would require disclosures under IFRS 12 that would not apply to an identical instrument issued to an entity which is not a structured entity.

Disclosures in respect of unconsolidated structured entities were not previously required by IFRS. These disclosures have been added because the IASB was asked by users of financial statements, regulators and others to improve the disclosure requirements for what are often described as 'off balance sheet' activities. Unconsolidated structured entities, particularly securitisation vehicles and asset-backed financings, were identified as forming part of such activities. *[IFRS 12.BC62]*.

In order to allay suspicions that these disclosures were added simply to cover a lack of 'robust' consolidation requirements, the IASB asserts in the Basis for Conclusions that the disclosure proposals were intended to complement the consolidation criteria. The disclosures focus on an entity's exposure to risk from interests in structured entities that the entity rightly does not consolidate because it does not control them. *[IFRS 12.BC69]*. However, no equivalent disclosures exist in respect of unconsolidated entities that are not structured entities. As IFRS 10 does permit the exercise of judgement, these additional disclosures are intended to help cover the fact that different entities might come to different conclusions on consolidation of structured entities on similar fact patterns.

In determining disclosures in respect of structured entities over which a reporting entity does not have significant influence, the reporting entity should apply the general concept of materiality. Materiality is defined by both IAS 1 – *Presentation of Financial Statements* – and IAS 8 and is discussed in Chapter 3 at 4.1.5.A.

2.2.3 Interests not within the scope of IFRS 12

Having included details of those interests within scope, the standard clarifies that certain interests are not within the scope of IFRS 12.

2.2.3.A Employee benefit plans

Post-employment benefit plans or other long-term employee benefit plans to which IAS 19 – *Employee Benefits* – applies are not within the scope of IFRS 12. *[IFRS 12.6(a)]*. Without this exemption, some employee benefit plans might meet the definition of a structured entity.

2.2.3.B Separate financial statements

An entity's separate financial statements to which IAS 27 applies are not within the scope of IFRS 12. The purpose of this exemption is to prevent a parent duplicating IFRS 12 disclosures in both its consolidated and separate financial statements.

However, an entity that has interests in unconsolidated structured entities and prepares separate financial statements as its only financial statements is required to make the disclosures required by paragraphs 24-31 of IFRS 12 in respect of unconsolidated structured entities (see 6 below). In addition, an investment entity that prepares financial statements in which all of its subsidiaries are measured at fair value through profit or loss (i.e. an investment entity which has subsidiaries but does not prepare consolidated financial statements) shall make the disclosures relating to investment entities discussed at 4.6 below. *[IFRS 12.6(b)].* As discussed at 2.2.2.D above, unconsolidated structured entities include subsidiaries, joint ventures and associates that are structured entities.

The financial statements of an entity that does not have an interest in a subsidiary, associate or a joint venturer's interest in a joint venture are not separate financial statements. *[IAS 27.7].* These financial statements are within the scope of IFRS 12.

2.2.3.C Interests in joint arrangements that result in neither joint control nor significant influence and are not interests in structured entities

An interest held by an entity that participates in, but does not have joint control of, a joint arrangement is outside the scope of IFRS 12 unless that interest results in significant influence in that arrangement or is an interest in a structured entity. *[IFRS 12.6(c)].*

IFRS 11 states that an arrangement can be a joint arrangement even though not all of the parties have joint control of the arrangement. It distinguishes between parties that have joint control of a joint arrangement (joint operators or joint ventures) and parties that participate in, but do not have joint control of, a joint arrangement. *[IFRS 11.11].*

Determining whether an interest in a joint arrangement (which is not a structured entity) results in neither joint control nor significant influence will be a matter of judgement based on the facts and circumstances as explained in IFRS 11.

2.2.3.D Interests in other entities accounted for in accordance with IAS 39 or IFRS 9

An interest in another entity accounted for under either IAS 39 or IFRS 9 is outside the scope of IFRS 12. However, IFRS 12 applies to the following interests:

(i) interests in associates or joint ventures measured at fair value through profit or loss in accordance with IAS 28; or

(ii) interests in unconsolidated structured entities. *[IFRS 12.6(d)].*

In addition, IFRS 12 applies to unconsolidated subsidiaries of an investment entity accounted for at fair value through profit and loss and requires specific disclosures. See 4.6 below.

Interests in unconsolidated structured entities which are not subsidiaries, joint arrangements or associates would normally be measured in accordance with IAS 39 or IFRS 9.

2.3 Effective date

IFRS 12 applies for annual periods beginning on or after 1 January 2013. Earlier application was permitted. *[IFRS 12.C1].*

Depending on an entity's regulator and jurisdiction, the date at which the entity applies the new standards may be later than the date prescribed by the IASB; in such cases, the entity may not state that it prepared financial statements in compliance with IFRS as issued by the IASB. For example, under IFRS as adopted by the EU, the standards were mandatory for accounting periods beginning on or after 1 January 2014 but could be adopted early.

There is no explicit requirement for IFRS 12 disclosures in interim financial statements presented in accordance with IAS 34 – *Interim Financial Reporting*. However, IAS 34 does require an entity to include an explanation of events and transactions that are significant to an understanding of the changes in financial position and performance of the entity since the end of the last annual reporting period. *[IAS 34.15]*.

3 DISCLOSURE OF SIGNIFICANT ESTIMATES AND JUDGEMENTS

IFRS 12 requires that an entity disclose information about significant judgements and assumptions it has made (and changes to those judgements and assumptions) in determining:

(a) that it has control of another entity, i.e. an investee as described in paragraphs 5 and 6 of IFRS 10;

(b) that it has joint control of an arrangement or significant influence over another entity; and

(c) the type of joint arrangement (i.e. joint operation or joint venture) when the arrangement has been structured through a separate vehicle. *[IFRS 12.7]*.

The significant judgements and assumptions disclosed in accordance with the requirements above include those made by an entity when changes in facts and circumstances are such that the conclusion about whether it has control, joint control or significant influence changes during the reporting period. *[IFRS 12.8]*.

In order to comply with the standard, an entity must disclose, for example, significant judgements and assumptions made in determining that:

- it does not control another entity even though it holds more than half of the voting rights of the other entity;
- it controls another entity even though it holds less than half of the voting rights of the other entity;
- it is an agent or principal as defined by IFRS 10;
- it does not have significant influence even though it holds 20 per cent or more of the voting rights of another entity;
- it has significant influence even though it holds less than 20 per cent of the voting rights of another entity. *[IFRS 12.9]*.

The following extract from BP plc's financial statements illustrates disclosure of the significant judgements and assumptions used in determining significant influence with a less than 20 per cent holding of voting rights.

Extract 13.1: BP p.l.c. (2016)

Notes on financial statements [extract]

1. **Significant accounting policies, judgements, estimates and assumptions** [extract]

   Interests in associates [extract]

   Significant judgement: accounting for interests in other entities [extract]

Since 21 March 2013, BP has owned 19.75% of the voting shares of Rosneft Oil Company (Rosneft), a Russian oil and gas company. The Russian federal government, through its investment company JSC Rosneftegaz, owned 50% plus one share of the voting shares of Rosneft at 31 December 2016. BP uses the equity method of accounting for its investment in Rosneft because under IFRS it is considered to have significant influence. Significant influence is defined as the power to participate in the financial and operating policy decisions of the investee but is not control or joint control. IFRS identifies several indicators that may provide evidence of significant influence, including representation on the board of directors of the investee and participation in policy-making processes. BP's group chief executive, Bob Dudley, has been a member of the board of directors of Rosneft since 2013 and he is a member of the Rosneft board's Strategic Planning Committee. A second BP-nominated director, Guillermo Quintero, has been a member of the Rosneft board and its HR ad Remuneration Committee since 2015. BP also holds the voting rights at general meetings of shareholders conferred by its 19.75% stake in Rosneft. In management's judgement, the group has significant influence over Rosneft, as defined by the relevant accounting standard, and the investment is, therefore, classified as an associate and accounted for using the equity method. BP's share of Rosneft's oil and natural gas reserves is included in the estimated net proved reserves of equity-accounted entities.

Chapter 13

The following example illustrates disclosure of significant judgements and assumptions made by an entity in determining whether a joint arrangement is a joint operation or a joint venture.

Example 13.3: Disclosure of significant judgements and assumptions made in determining the type of joint arrangement

The directors have determined that the Group's investment in ABC Inc. should be accounted for as a joint operation rather than a joint venture. Although the legal form of ABC Inc. and the contractual terms of the joint arrangement indicate that the arrangement is a joint venture, sales to third parties by ABC Inc. are expected to be uncommon and not material. In addition, the price of the output sold to the venturers is set by all parties at a level that is designed to cover only the costs of production and administrative expenses incurred by ABC Inc. On this basis, the directors consider that, in substance, the arrangement gives the venturers rights to the assets, and obligations for the liabilities, relating to the arrangement and not rights to the net assets of the arrangements and therefore is a joint operation.

When a parent determines that it is an investment entity in accordance with IFRS 10, the investment entity must disclose information about significant judgements and assumptions it has made in determining that it is an investment entity. If the investment entity does not have one or more of the typical characteristics of an investment entity (as per IFRS 10), it must disclose the reasons for concluding that it is nevertheless an investment entity. *[IFRS 12.9A]*. The definition of an investment entity is discussed in Chapter 6 at 10.1. The following extract from 3i Group plc's financial statements illustrates disclosure of these significant judgements and assumptions.

Extract 13.2: 3i Group plc (2016)

Significant accounting policies [extract]

D **Critical accounting estimates and judgements** [extract]

(a) **Assessment as an investment entity** [extract]

Entities that meet the definition of an investment entity within IFRS 10 are required to account for most investments in controlled entities, as well as investments in associates and joint ventures, at fair value through profit and loss.

The Board has concluded that the Company continues to meet the definition of an investment entity as its strategic objective of investing in portfolio investments and providing investment management services to investors for the purpose of generating returns in the form of investment income and capital appreciation remains unchanged.

The Group is required to determine the degree of control or influence the Group exercises and the form of any control to ensure that the financial treatment is accurate.

IAS 1 requires an entity to disclose the judgements that management has made in the process of applying the entity's accounting policies and that have the most significant effect on the amounts recognised in the financial statements. *[IAS 1.122]*. IFRS 12 adds to those general requirements by specifically requiring an entity to disclose all significant judgements and estimates made in determining the nature of its interest in another entity or arrangement, and in determining the type of joint arrangement in which it has an interest. The IASB's intention is that disclosure should be required for all situations in which an entity exercises significant judgement in assessing the nature of its interest in another entity. *[IFRS 12.BC16]*.

There is no requirement for a reporting entity to disclose significant judgements and assumptions made in determining whether an entity in which it has an interest is a structured entity. Such a judgement or assumption affects disclosure only and not the determination of control, joint control or significant influence. However, where such judgements or assumptions have a significant impact on the volume of disclosures in the financial statements we believe that it would be useful for a reader of the financial statements for such judgements or assumptions to be disclosed.

There is no requirement to disclose quantitative information to help assess the accounting consequences of an entity's decision to consolidate (or not consolidate) another entity. IFRS 3 – *Business Combinations* – already requires disclosures about the nature and effect of a business combination when an entity obtains control of another entity. Where an entity requires significant judgement to conclude that it does not control another entity, that other entity is usually accounted for as a joint venture or as an associate, and IFRS 12 already requires disclosures of quantitative information about an entity's interests in joint ventures and associates and information about risk exposures to unconsolidated structured entities. Therefore, based on this, the IASB concluded that there was no need for a separate disclosure requirement. *[IFRS 12.BC19].*

4 DISCLOSURE OF INTERESTS IN SUBSIDIARIES

An entity must disclose information that enables users of its consolidated financial statements

(a) to understand:

 (i) the composition of the group; and

 (ii) the interest that non-controlling interests have in the group's activities and cash flows; and

(b) to evaluate:

 (i) the nature and extent of significant restrictions on its ability to access or use assets, and settle liabilities, of the group;

 (ii) the nature of, and changes in, the risks associated with its interests in consolidated structured entities;

 (iii) the consequences of changes in its ownership interest in a subsidiary that do not result in loss of control; and

 (iv) the consequences of losing control of a subsidiary during the reporting period. *[IFRS 12.10].*

4.1 Disclosure about the composition of the group

IFRS 12 does not elaborate on what is meant by information that enables users 'to understand' the composition of the group. Judgement will therefore be required as to the extent of the disclosures made.

It may be helpful to users of the financial statements to illustrate the composition of the group via a diagram or group organisation chart.

The Basis for Conclusions implies that the IASB does not intend that entities should be required to disclose financial information about subsidiaries with immaterial non-controlling interests. Separate financial and non-financial disclosures are required for subsidiaries with material non-controlling interests (see 4.2 below). *[IFRS 12.BC28].*

In interpreting the requirement to disclose information that enables users to understand the composition of the group for subsidiaries with immaterial or no non-controlling interests, preparers might wish to refer to the non-financial disclosures required for subsidiaries with non-controlling interests that are material to the entity (see 4.2 below). Applying these disclosures to other material subsidiaries would mean disclosing:

- the names of those entities;
- the principal place of business (and country of incorporation, if different) of those entities; and
- the proportion of ownership interest (and the proportion of the voting rights, if different) held in those entities.

Users of the financial statements are also likely to benefit from a description of the nature of the operations and principal activities of each material subsidiary and an indication of the operating segment(s) to which each material subsidiary has been allocated. A description of the nature of the group's operations and its principal activities is required by IAS 1. *[IAS 1.138(b)]*.

Where the financial statements of a subsidiary used in the preparation of the consolidated financial statements are as of a date or for a period that is different from that of the consolidated financial statements, an entity must disclose:

- the date of the reporting period of the financial statements of that subsidiary; and
- the reason for using a different date or period. *[IFRS 12.11]*.

The following extract shows UBS AG's disclosure of individually significant subsidiaries.

Extract 13.3: UBS Group AG (2016)

Notes to the UBS Group AG consolidated financial statements [extract]

Note 28 Interests in subsidiaries and other entities [extract]

a) Interests in subsidiaries [extract]

UBS defines its significant subsidiaries as those entities that, either individually or in aggregate, contribute significantly to the Group's financial position or results of operations, based on a number of criteria, including the subsidiaries' equity and their contribution to the Group's total assets and profit or loss before tax, in accordance with the requirements set by IFRS 12, Swiss regulations and the rules of the US Securities and Exchange Commission (SEC).

Individually significant subsidiaries

The two tables below list the Group's individually significant subsidiaries as of 31 December 2016. Unless otherwise stated, the subsidiaries listed below have share capital consisting solely of ordinary shares, which are held fully by the Group, and the proportion of ownership interest held is equal to the voting rights held by the Group.

The country where the respective registered office is located is also the principal place of business.

[...]

Individually significant subsidiaries of UBS AG as of 31 December 2016

Company	Registered office	Primary business division	Share capital in million		Equity interest accumulated in %
UBS Americas Holding LLC	Wilmington, Delaware, USA	Corporate Center	USD	2,250.0 [1]	100.0
UBS Asset Management AG	Zurich, Switzerland	Asset Management	CHF	43.2	100.0
UBS Bank USA	Salt Lake City, Utah, USA	Wealth Management Americas	USD	0.0	100.0
UBS Europe SE	Frankfurt, Germany	Wealth Management	EUR	176.0	100.0
UBS Financial Services Inc.	Wilmington, Delaware, USA	Wealth Management Americas	USD	0.0	100.0
UBS Limited	London, United Kingdom	Investment Bank	GBP	226.6	100.0
UBS Securities LLC	Wilmington, Delaware, USA	Investment Bank	USD	1,283.1 [2]	100.0
UBS Switzerland AG	Zurich, Switzerland	Personal & Corporate Banking	CHF	10.0	100.0

1 Comprised of common share capital of USD 1,000 and non-voting preferred share capital of USD 2,250,000,000.
2 Comprised of common share capital of USD 100,000 and non-voting preferred share capital of USD 1,283,000,000.

[...]

UBS Americas Holding LLC, UBS Asset Management AG, UBS Europe SE, UBS Limited and UBS Switzerland AG are fully held by UBS AG. UBS Bank USA, UBS Financial Services Inc. and UBS Securities LLC are fully held, directly or indirectly, by UBS Americas Holding LLC.

4.2 Disclosure of interests of non-controlling interests

A reporting entity must disclose, for each of its subsidiaries that have non-controlling interests that are material:

(a) the name of the subsidiary;
(b) the principal place of business (and country of incorporation if different from the principal place of business) of the subsidiary;
(c) the proportion of ownership interests held by non-controlling interests;
(d) the proportion of voting rights held by non-controlling interests, if different to the proportion of ownership interests held;
(e) the profit or loss allocated to the non-controlling interests of the subsidiary during the reporting period;
(f) accumulated non-controlling interests of the subsidiary at the end of the reporting period; and
(g) summarised financial information about the subsidiary (see below). *[IFRS 12.12]*.

The summarised financial information required to be disclosed is as follows:

(a) dividends paid to non-controlling interests; and
(b) summarised financial information about the assets, liabilities, profit or loss and cash flows of the subsidiary that enables users to understand the interest that non-controlling interests have in the group's activities and cash flows. The information might include but is not limited to, for example, current assets, non-current assets, current liabilities, non-current liabilities, revenue, profit or loss and total comprehensive income. *[IFRS 12.B10]*. The summarised financial information must be presented before inter-company eliminations. *[IFRS 12.B11]*.

The IASB believes that these disclosures will help users when estimating future profit or loss and cash flows by identifying, for example, the assets and liabilities that are held by subsidiaries, the risk exposures of particular group entities (e.g. by identifying which subsidiaries hold debt) and those subsidiaries that generate significant cash flows. *[IFRS 12.BC27]*. From this, one could infer that the summarised financial information should disclose significant amounts of bank loans separately from other liabilities.

The IASB does not believe this requirement is particularly onerous on the grounds that an entity should have the information available in preparing its consolidated financial statements. *[IFRS 12.BC29]*.

Non-controlling interest is equity in a subsidiary not attributable, directly or indirectly, to a parent. *[IFRS 10 Appendix A]*. This means that these disclosures do not apply to instruments that might have the legal characteristics of equity but which are classified as financial liabilities under IFRS. This would also apply to instruments that are classified as equity in the separate financial statements of a subsidiary but classified as financial liabilities in the consolidated financial statements. Similarly, when a parent has concluded that it already has a present ownership interest in shares held by a non-controlling interest by virtue of call or put options in respect of those shares (see Chapter 7 at 5), then IFRS 12 disclosures in respect of those shares are not required by the parent because there is no non-controlling interest in the financial statements.

The standard is clear that this information is required only in respect of non-controlling interests that are material to the reporting entity (i.e. the group). A subsidiary may have a significant non-controlling interest *per se* but disclosure is not required if that interest is not material at group level. Similarly, these disclosures do not apply to non-controlling interests that are material in aggregate but not individually.

In January 2015, the Interpretations Committee discussed a request to clarify the level at which the financial information required by (e) to (g) above should be provided where a subsidiary has non-controlling interests that are material to the group. The issue was whether the information provided should be either:

- at the subsidiary (i.e. entity) level based on the separate financial statements of the subsidiary; or
- at a subgroup level for the subgroup of the subsidiary and based on either (i) the amounts of the subgroup included in the consolidated financial statements of the parent or, (ii) the amounts included in the consolidated financial statements of the subgroup. In both (i) and (ii), transactions and balances between the subgroup and other subsidiaries of the reporting entity outside the subgroup would not be eliminated.

The Interpretations Committee noted that the decision on which approach is used to present the disclosures required by (e) to (g) above should reflect the one that best meets the disclosure objective (see (a) at 4 above) in the circumstances.

In respect of (e) and (f), the Interpretations Committee observed that a reporting entity should apply judgement in determining the level of disaggregation of information about subsidiaries that have material non-controlling interest. That is, whether:

- the entity presents this information about the subgroup of the subsidiary; or
- whether it is necessary in achieving the disclosure objective to disaggregate the information further to present information about the individual subsidiaries that have material non-controlling interest within that subgroup.

In respect of (g) above, the Interpretations Committee observed that, in order to meet the overall disclosure requirement, information would need to be prepared on a basis that was consistent with the information included in the consolidated financial statements from the perspective of the reporting entity. This would mean, for example, that if the subsidiary was acquired in a business combination, the amounts disclosed should reflect the effects of the acquisition accounting (e.g. goodwill and fair value adjustments). The Interpretations Committee further observed that in providing the information, an entity would apply judgement in determining whether this information was presented at a subgroup level or whether further disaggregation was necessary about individual subsidiaries that have material non-controlling interest within that subgroup. However, the Interpretations Committee noted that the information supplied would include transactions between the subgroup/subsidiary and other members of the reporting entity's group without elimination, but that transactions within the subgroup would be eliminated.

On the basis of the above analysis, the Interpretations Committee concluded that neither an Interpretation nor an amendment to IFRS 12 was necessary and decided not to add the issue to its agenda.[3]

Glencore plc's financial statements illustrate disclosure of summarised financial information in respect of subsidiaries that have material non-controlling interests.

Extract 13.4: Glencore plc (2016)

Notes to the financial statements [extract]

31. **PRINCIPAL SUBSIDIARIES WITH MATERIAL NON-CONTROLLING INTERESTS** [extract]

Summarised financial information in respect of Glencore's subsidiaries that have material non-controlling interest as at 31 December 2016, reflecting 100% of the underlying subsidiary's relevant figures, is set out below.

US$ million	Kazzinc	Koniambo	Katanga	Mutanda
31 December 2016				
Non-current assets	4,703	1,226	4,424	4,763
Current assets	1,014	294	652	549
Total assets	**5,717**	**1,520**	**5,076**	**5,312**
Non-current liabilities	719	9,494	3,380	1,885
Current liabilities	391	101	1,848	281
Total liabilities	**1,110**	**9,595**	**5,228**	**2,166**
Net assets	**4,607**	**(8,075)**	**(152)**	**3,146**
Equity attributable to owners of the Company	3,211	(5,422)	359	2,379
Non-controlling interests	1,396	(2,653)	(511) [1]	767
Non-controlling interests in %	30.3%	51.0%	24.7%	31.0%
2016				
Revenue	2,602	152	–	1,322
Expenses	(2,211)	(529)	(625)	(1,147)
Net profit/(loss) for the year	**391**	**(377)**	**(625)**	**175**
Profit attributable to owners of the Company	273	(184)	(310)	121
Profit attributable to non-controlling interests	118	(193)	(315) [1]	54
Other comprehensive income attributable to owners of the Company	–	–	–	–
Other comprehensive income attributable to non-controlling interests	–	–	–	–
Total comprehensive income/(loss) for the year	**391**	**(377)**	**(625)**	**175**

US$ million	Kazzinc	Koniambo	Katanga	Mutanda
Dividends paid to non-controlling interests	(38)	–	–	–
Net cash inflow/(outflow) from operating activities	856	–	(161)	428
Net cash outflow from investing activities	(122)	(263)	(213)	(234)
Net cash (outflow)/inflow from financing activities	(567)	210	338	(195)
Total net cash inflow/(outflow)	**167**	**(53)**	**(36)**	**(1)**

[1] *Glencore has a 75.3% interest in Katanga Mining Limited, which in turn has a 75% interest in Kamoto Copper Company ("KCC") the entity engaged in copper mining activities. The "non-controlling interests" balance includes negative $629 million and the "profit attributable to non-controlling interests" balance includes negative $214 million related to non-controlling interests arising at the KCC level.*

IFRS 12 does not address disclosure of non-controlling interests in the primary statements. IAS 1 requires disclosure of total non-controlling interests within equity in the statement of financial position, profit or loss and total comprehensive income for the period attributable to non-controlling interests and a reconciliation of the opening and closing carrying amount of each component of equity (which would include non-controlling interests) in the statement of changes in equity. *[IAS 1.54, 81B, 106].*

4.3 Disclosure of the nature and extent of significant restrictions

An entity must disclose:

(a) significant restrictions (e.g. statutory, contractual and regulatory restrictions) on its ability to access or use assets and settle the liabilities of the group, such as:
   - (i) those that restrict the ability of a parent or its subsidiaries to transfer cash or other assets to (or from) other entities within the group;
   - (ii) guarantees or other requirements that may restrict dividends and other capital distributions being paid, or loans and advances being made or repaid, to (or from) other entities within the group.

(b) the nature and extent to which protective rights of non-controlling interests can significantly restrict the entity's ability to access or use the assets and settle the liabilities of the group (such as when a parent is obliged to settle liabilities of a subsidiary before settling its own liabilities, or approval of non-controlling interests is required either to settle the assets or settle the liabilities of a subsidiary); and

(c) the carrying amounts in the consolidated financial statements of the assets and liabilities to which the restrictions apply. *[IFRS 12.13].*

These requirements were included in IFRS 12 to clarify that information disclosed in respect of significant restrictions of subsidiaries to transfer funds should include the nature and extent to which protective rights of non-controlling interests can restrict an entity's ability to access and use the assets and settle the liabilities of a subsidiary. *[IFRS 12.BC31].*

The Basis for Conclusions clarifies that these disclosures are intended to be limited to information about the nature and effect of significant restrictions on an entity's ability to access and use assets or settle liabilities of the group. They are not intended, in the IASB's opinion, to require an entity to disclose, for example, a list of all the protective rights held by non-controlling interests that are embedded in law and regulation. *[IFRS 12.BC32].*

The IASB also considers that the restrictions required to be disclosed by IFRS 12 are those that exist because of legal boundaries within the group, such as restrictions on transferring cash between group entities. They are not, in the IASB's opinion, intended to replicate those in other IFRSs relating to restrictions such as those in IAS 16 – *Property, Plant and Equipment* – or IAS 40 – *Investment Property*. *[IFRS 12.BC33]*.

Deutsche Bank AG make the following disclosures about significant restrictions to access or use the group's assets:

Extract 13.5: Deutsche Bank Aktiengesellschaft (2016)

Notes to the Consolidated Financial Statements

Additional Notes [extract]

40 – **Information on Subsidiaries** [extract]

Significant restrictions to access or use the Group's assets [extract]

Statutory, contractual or regulatory requirements as well as protective rights of noncontrolling interests might restrict the ability of the Group to access and transfer assets freely to or from other entities within the Group and to settle liabilities of the Group.

Since the Group did not have any material noncontrolling interests at the balance sheet date, any protective rights associated with these did not give rise to significant restrictions.

The following restrictions impact the Group's ability to use assets:

- The Group has pledged assets to collateralize its obligations under repurchase agreements, securities financing transactions, collateralized loan obligations and for margining purposes for OTC derivative liabilities.
- The assets of consolidated structured entities are held for the benefit of the parties that have bought the notes issued by these entities.
- Regulatory and central bank requirements or local corporate laws may restrict the Group's ability to transfer assets to or from other entities within the Group in certain jurisdictions.

Restricted assets

	Dec. 31, 2016		Dec. 31, 2015	
in € m	**Total assets**	**Restricted assets**	Total assets	Restricted assets
Interest-earning deposits with banks	163,292	1,314	78,263	2,190
Financial assets at fair value through profit or loss	743,781	54,711	820,883	79,222
Financial assets available for sale	56,228	19,870	73,583	11,046
Loans	408,909	74,172	427,749	46,352
Other	218,336	7,693	239,441	9,294
Total	1,590,546	157,760	1,629,130	148,105

4.4 Disclosure of the nature of the risks associated with interests in consolidated structured entities

IFRS 12 requires a number of disclosures in respect of financial or other support provided to consolidated structured entities. Essentially, the standard requires disclosure of certain intra-group transactions that have been eliminated on consolidation and details of certain commitments by a group to itself.

For groups with a number of structured entities, these disclosures are likely to require changes to consolidation reporting packages in order to capture the necessary information. As these transactions will have either been eliminated on consolidation or not (yet) occurred at all, it is unlikely that they will all be reflected in existing consolidation reporting packages. However, some of these transactions are likely to be disclosable as related party transactions in the individual or separate financial statements of the subsidiaries involved.

The IASB concluded that it would help users of financial statements in understanding an entity's exposure to risks if the entity disclosed the terms of contractual arrangements that could require it to provide financial support to a consolidated structured entity, including events or circumstances that could expose the entity to a loss. *[IFRS 12.BC34]*.

It is unclear which 'entity' the IASB considers has suffered a 'loss' in this context since a group does not suffer a loss as a result of one subsidiary providing financial support to another subsidiary as that is an intra-group transaction which is eliminated on consolidation. Any 'loss' suffered by one subsidiary would be offset by the 'profit' in the other subsidiary. However, differing shares held by non-controlling interests in those subsidiaries could affect the overall profit and comprehensive income attributable to non-controlling interests and owners of the parent. Presumably, it is the potential for a 'loss' to the equity holders of the parent from these transactions (rather than a 'loss' to the group) that the IASB is trying to highlight.

For the same reasons, the IASB concluded that an entity should disclose its risk exposure from non-contractual obligations to provide support to both consolidated and unconsolidated structured entities. *[IFRS 12.BC35]*. The question this raises is, assuming the obligation is not contractual, whether an obligation exists at all that requires disclosure.

The IASB also noted that US GAAP requires similar disclosures which, in the opinion of the IASB, 'have been well received by users of financial statements in the US'. *[IFRS 12.BC36]*.

The detailed disclosures that are required in respect of interests in consolidated structured entities are discussed at 4.4.1 to 4.4.4 below.

4.4.1 Terms of contractual arrangements to provide financial support to consolidated structured entities

An entity must disclose the terms of any contractual arrangements that could require the parent or its subsidiaries to provide financial support to a consolidated structured entity, including events or circumstances that expose the reporting entity to a loss (e.g. liquidity arrangements or credit rating triggers associated with obligations to purchase assets of the structured entity or provide financial support). *[IFRS 12.14]*.

As discussed at 4.4 above, the IASB's intent seems to be to address circumstances in which a 'loss' could be suffered by the equity holders of the parent from these transactions rather than a 'loss' suffered by the reporting entity (i.e. the group).

Example 13.4: Illustrative example of disclosure of a contractual arrangement that could require parental support to a consolidated structured entity

The parent company has given a contractual commitment to its subsidiary, SE Limited, whereby if the assets held as collateral by SE Limited for its issued loan notes fall below a credit rating of 'AAA' then the parent will substitute assets of an equivalent fair value with an 'AAA' rating. The maximum fair value of assets to be substituted is €10,000,000. The parent will not suffer a loss on any transaction arising from this commitment but will receive assets with a lower credit rating from those substituted.

4.4.2 Financial or other support to consolidated structured entities with no contractual obligation

If, during the reporting period a parent or any of its subsidiaries has, without having any contractual obligation to do so, provided financial or other support to a consolidated structured entity (e.g. purchasing assets of or instruments issued by the structured entity), the entity must disclose:

(a) the type and amount of support provided, including situations in which the parent or its subsidiaries assisted the structured entity in obtaining financial support; and

(b) the reasons for providing the support. *[IFRS 12.15]*.

The transactions requiring disclosure are intra-group transactions eliminated on consolidation.

'Support' is not defined in IFRS. A literal reading of 'purchasing assets of or instruments issued' is that any transfer of consideration to a structured entity in exchange for an asset is the provision of support requiring disclosure by the standard. The Basis for Conclusions explains that the IASB did not define 'support' because a definition of support would either be so broad that it would be an ineffective definition or invite structuring so as to avoid the disclosure. The IASB believes that support is widely understood as a provision of resources to another entity, either directly or indirectly. In the case of implicit agreements, the support is provided without having the contractual obligation to do so. However, in order to address respondents' concerns about distinguishing the provision of financial support from any other commercial transaction, the IASB clarified that disclosure is required when an entity has provided non-contractual support to a consolidated or unconsolidated structured entity in which it previously had or currently has an interest. *[IFRS 12.BC105-106]*.

Examples of the type of support that the IASB envisages being disclosed for unconsolidated structured entities (see 6.3 below) are liquidity arrangements or credit rating triggers associated with obligations to purchase assets of the structured entity or provide financial support. These examples imply that the IASB does not intend transactions in the ordinary course of business to be caught by the requirement to disclose support provided to consolidated structured entities. By 'asset purchase' they are referring to a 'forced' purchase caused by, for example, liquidity or credit rating triggers.

Interpreting financial or other support is therefore likely to involve judgement. One possible interpretation is that 'support' includes:

- any transaction involving the gifting of funds;
- an equity investment;
- a long-term loan;
- forgiveness of debt;
- a transaction carried out on non-market terms resulting in a net outflow of resources from the reporting entity;
- a transaction not made in the ordinary course of business; or
- implicit or explicit guarantees of a structured entity's performance.

IFRS 12 does not explain what is meant by 'other support' and whether this extends to such non-financial support as the provision of human resources or management services.

Example 13.5: Illustrative example of disclosure of financial or other support provided to a consolidated structured entity

During the reporting period the parent provided financial support in the form of assets with a fair value of €12,000,000 (2016: €0) and a credit rating of 'AAA' to its subsidiary, SE 2 Limited, in exchange for assets with an equivalent fair value. There was no contractual obligation to exchange these assets. The transaction was initiated because the assets held by SE 2 Limited had a credit rating of less than 'AA' and a further ratings downgrade could potentially trigger calls on loan notes issued by SE 2 Limited. The parent did not suffer a loss on the transaction.

These disclosures are also required in respect of unconsolidated structured entities. See 6.2.2 and 6.3 below.

4.4.3 Financial or other support to unconsolidated structured entities which resulted in consolidation of those entities

If, during the reporting period, a parent or any of its subsidiaries has, without having a contractual obligation to do so, provided financial or other support to a previously unconsolidated structured entity and that provision of support resulted in the entity controlling the structured entity, the entity (i.e. the reporting entity) must disclose an explanation of the relevant factors in making that decision. *[IFRS 12.16]*.

The comments at 4.4.2 above regarding the definition of 'support' apply here also.

4.4.4 Current intentions to provide financial or other support

An entity must disclose any current intentions to provide financial or other support to a consolidated structured entity, including intentions to assist the structured entity in obtaining financial support. *[IFRS 12.17]*.

IFRS 12 does not define 'intentions'. The Basis for Conclusions indicates that it means 'the entity has decided' to provide financial support (i.e. it has current intentions to do this). *[IFRS 12.BC104]*. This implies that a decision to provide support has been approved at an appropriately senior level at the entity. Judgement will be required by entities in interpreting this requirement and defining the meaning of 'intention' in this context. The wording in the Basis of Conclusions does not require any such 'intention' to have been communicated to the structured entity that will receive the support or that there has been established a constructive obligation as defined in IAS 37 – *Provisions, Contingent Liabilities and Contingent Assets*.

The comments at 4.4.2 above in respect of the definition of 'support' apply here also.

These disclosures are also required in respect of unconsolidated structured entities. See 6.2.2 below.

4.5 Disclosure of changes in ownership interests in subsidiaries

4.5.1 Changes that do not result in loss of control

An entity must present a schedule that shows the effects on the equity attributable to owners of the parent of any changes in its ownership interests in a subsidiary that do not result in loss of control. *[IFRS 12.18]*. This schedule must be presented in addition to the information required by IAS 1 in the statement of changes in equity.

IAS 1 requires an entity to present, for each component of equity, a reconciliation between the carrying amount at the beginning and the end of the period, separately disclosing changes resulting from transactions with owners in their capacity as owners and changes in ownership interests with subsidiaries that do not result in loss of control. *[IAS 1.106(d)].*

Despite this existing disclosure requirement, the IASB decided to require that if a parent has equity transactions with non-controlling interests, it should disclose in a separate schedule the effects of those transactions on the equity of the owners of the parent.

The IASB's rationale for this duplication is that many respondents to a 2005 exposure draft, which proposed amendments to a previous version of IAS 27, requested more prominent disclosure of the effects of transactions with non-controlling interests on the equity of the owners of the parent. In addition, a schedule showing the effects on the controlling interest's equity of changes in a parent's ownership interests in a subsidiary that do not result in loss of control is required by US GAAP. *[IFRS 12.BC38-39].*

IFRS 12 does not prescribe a format for this additional schedule. An example of the type of disclosure required is illustrated below.

Example 13.6: Illustrative example of disclosure of changes in ownership interest in subsidiary that does not result in loss of control

On 5 October 2017 the Group disposed of 25% of the ownership interests of Subsidiary Limited. Following the disposal, the Group still controls Subsidiary Limited and retains 70% of the ownership interests.

The transaction has been accounted for as an equity transaction with non-controlling interests (NCI), resulting in the following:

	€'000
Proceeds from sale of 25% ownership interest	550
Net assets attributable to NCI	500
Increase in equity attributable to parent	50
Represented by:	
Decrease in currency revaluation reserve	(250)
Decrease in available for sale reserve	(100)
Increase in retained earnings	400
	50

4.5.2 *Changes that do result in loss of control*

An entity must disclose the gain or loss, if any, resulting from the loss of control of a subsidiary calculated in accordance with paragraph 25 of IFRS 10, and:

(a) the portion of that gain or loss attributable to measuring any investment in the retained subsidiary at its fair value at the date that control is lost; and

(b) the line item(s) in profit or loss in which the gain or loss is recognised (if not presented separately). *[IFRS 12.19].*

4.6 Disclosures required by investment entities

An investment entity that is required by IFRS 10 to apply the exception from consolidation and instead account for its investment in a subsidiary at fair value through profit or loss must disclose that fact. *[IFRS 12.19A].*

If an investment entity has a subsidiary that it consolidates because that subsidiary is not an investment entity and whose main purpose and activities are providing services to the investment entity's investment activities, the disclosure requirements in IFRS 12 apply to the financial statements in which the investment entity consolidates that subsidiary. *[IFRS 12.BC61I].*

4.6.1 Disclosures about the composition of the group

For each unconsolidated subsidiary, an investment entity must disclose:

(a) the subsidiary's name;

(b) the principal place of business (and country of incorporation if different from the principal place of business) of the subsidiary; and

(c) the proportion of ownership interest held by the investment entity and, if different, the proportion of voting rights held. *[IFRS 12.19B].*

If an investment entity is the parent of another investment entity, the parent must also provide the disclosures (a) to (c) above for investments that are controlled by its investment entity subsidiary. The disclosures may be provided by including, in the financial statements of the parent, the financial statements of the subsidiary that contain this information. *[IFRS 12.19C].*

We would expect users to apply judgement where the list of subsidiaries is extensive. There is no explicit requirement in IFRS 12 to disclose this information in respect of consolidated subsidiaries (see 4.1 above).

4.6.2 Disclosures required when investment entity status changes

When an entity becomes, or ceases to be, an investment entity it must disclose:

- the change of investment entity status; and
- the reasons for the change.

In addition, an entity that becomes an investment entity must disclose the effect of the change of status on the financial statements for the period presented, including:

- the total fair value, as of the date of change of status, of the subsidiaries that cease to be consolidated;
- the total gain or loss, if any, calculated in accordance with paragraph B101 of IFRS 10; and
- the line item(s) in profit or loss in which the gain or loss is recognised (if not presented separately). *[IFRS 12.9B].*

The accounting effect of becoming or ceasing to become an investment entity is discussed in Chapter 6 at 10.3.1.

4.6.3 Disclosures required in respect of significant restrictions, commitments and financial and other support

An investment entity must disclose:

- the nature and extent of any significant restrictions (e.g. resulting from borrowing arrangements, regulatory requirements or contractual arrangements) on the ability of an unconsolidated subsidiary to transfer funds to the investment entity in the form of cash dividends or to repay loans or advances made to the unconsolidated subsidiary by the investment entity; and
- any current commitments or intentions to provide financial or other support to an unconsolidated subsidiary, including commitments or intentions to assist the subsidiary in obtaining financial support. *[IFRS 12.19D]*.

If, during the reporting period, an investment entity or any of its subsidiaries has, without having a contractual obligation to do so, provided financial or other support to an unconsolidated subsidiary (e.g. purchasing assets of, or instruments issued by, the subsidiary or assisting the subsidiary in obtaining financial support), the entity must disclose:

- the type and amount of support provided to each unconsolidated subsidiary; and
- the reasons for providing the support. *[IFRS 12.19E]*.

In addition, an investment entity must disclose the terms of any contractual arrangements that require the entity or its unconsolidated subsidiaries to provide financial support to an unconsolidated, controlled, structured entity, including events and circumstances that could expose the reporting entity to a loss (e.g. liquidity arrangements or credit rating triggers associated with obligations to purchase assets of the structured entity or to provide financial support). *[IFRS 12.19F]*.

If during the reporting period an investment entity or any of its unconsolidated subsidiaries has, without having a contractual obligation to do so, provided financial or other support to an unconsolidated, structured entity that the investment entity did not control, and if that provision of financial support resulted in the investment entity controlling the structured entity, the investment entity must provide an explanation of the relevant factors in reaching the decision to provide that support. *[IFRS 12.19G]*.

These disclosures are similar to those required for consolidated subsidiaries including consolidated structured entities discussed at 4.3, 4.4.1, 4.4.2 and 4.4.4 – see the comments in these sections.

4.6.4 Valuation methodologies and nature of investing activities

IFRS 12 does not require any disclosure of fair value measurements made by investment entities. The IASB considers that this information is already required by IFRS 7 – *Financial Instruments: Disclosures* – and by IFRS 13 – *Fair Value Measurement* – when reporting investments at fair value through profit or loss or other comprehensive income in accordance with IFRS 9 or IAS 39. *[IFRS 12.BC61C]*.

5 DISCLOSURE OF INTERESTS IN JOINT ARRANGEMENTS AND ASSOCIATES

An entity must disclose information that enables users of its financial statements to evaluate:

(a) the nature, extent and financial effects of its interests in joint arrangements and associates, including the nature and effects of its contractual relationship with other investors with joint control of, or significant influence over, joint arrangements and associates; and

(b) the nature of, and changes in, the risks associated with its interests in joint ventures and associates. *[IFRS 12.20]*.

These requirements, explained in detail at 5.1 and 5.2 below, apply in full to both consolidated financial statements and individual financial statements of entities with joint arrangements and associates.

A reporting entity that prepares separate financial statements, even if it does not prepare consolidated financial statements, is only required to comply with disclosures (a)(i) and (iii) and (b)(i) at 5.1 below. *[IAS 27.16(b), (c)]*.

IFRS 12 does not address disclosures of joint ventures and associates in the primary statements. IAS 1 does not require interests in joint ventures and associates to be disclosed separately in the statement of financial position. This is probably because of the different methods of accounting that can be applied under IAS 28, i.e. equity method or fair value. However, IAS 1 requires separate disclosure of investments accounted for using the equity method on the face of the statement of financial position, although it does not require a split of those investments between joint ventures and associates. *[IAS 1.54]*. IAS 1 also requires a reporting entity's post tax share of the profit or loss of associates and joint ventures accounted for using the equity method to be disclosed on the face of the statement of comprehensive income. *[IAS 1.82]*.

5.1 Disclosure of the nature, extent and financial effects of interests in joint arrangements and associates

An entity must disclose:

(a) for each joint arrangement and associate that is material to the reporting entity:

  (i) the name of the joint arrangement or associate;

  (ii) the nature of the entity's relationship with the joint venture or associate (by, for example, describing the nature of the activities of the joint arrangement or associate and whether they are strategic to the entity's activities);

  (iii) the principal place of business (and country of incorporation, if applicable and different from the principal place of business) of the joint arrangement or associate; and

  (iv) the proportion of ownership interest held by the entity and, if different, the proportion of voting rights held (if applicable).

(b) for each joint venture (but not a joint operation) and associate that is material to the reporting entity:

   (i) whether the investment in the joint venture or associate is measured using the equity method or at fair value;

   (ii) summarised financial information about the joint venture or associate (see 5.1.1 below); and

   (iii) if the joint venture or associate is accounted for using the equity method, the fair value of the investment in the joint venture or associate, if there is a quoted market price for the investment.

(c) financial information (see 5.1.2 below) about the entity's investments in joint ventures and associates that are not individually material:

   (i) in aggregate for all individually immaterial joint ventures and, separately;

   (ii) in aggregate for all individually immaterial associates. *[IFRS 12.21].*

Disclosures (b) and (c) are not required by an investment entity. *[IFRS 12.21A].*

In January 2015, the Interpretations Committee discussed a request to clarify the requirement described above to disclose summary financial information about material joint ventures and associates and its interaction with the aggregation principle of IFRS 12 (see 2.2.2 above). The issue was whether the summary financial information can be disclosed in aggregate for all material joint ventures and associates, or whether such information should be disclosed individually for each material joint venture or associate. The Interpretations Committee also discussed a request to clarify whether an investor should be excused from disclosing information related to a listed joint venture or associate if the local regulatory requirements prevented the investor from disclosing such information until the joint venture or associate has released its own financial statements. The Interpretations Committee noted that it expected the requirement to prepare summarised financial information about a joint venture or associate in IFRS 12 to lead to the disclosure of summarised information on an individual basis for each joint venture or associate that is material to the reporting entity. The Interpretations Committee observed that this reflects the IASB's intentions as described in the Basis for Conclusions to IFRS 12. The Interpretations Committee also noted that there is no provision in IFRS 12 that permits non-disclosure of this information (on the grounds of confidentially or local regulatory requirements) and that outreach performed indicated that there was no significant diversity observed in practice on this issue. Consequently, the Interpretations Committee determined that neither an Interpretation nor an amendment to a standard was necessary and decided not to add this issue to its agenda.[4]

Any entity must also disclose:

(a) the nature and extent of any significant restrictions (e.g. resulting from borrowing arrangements, regulatory requirements or contractual arrangements between investors with joint control of or significant influence over a joint venture or associate) on the ability of the joint ventures or associates to transfer funds to the entity in the form of cash dividends or to repay loans or advances made by the entity;

(b) when the financial statements of a joint venture or associate used in applying the equity method are as of a date or for a period that is different from that of the entity:
   (i) the date of the end of the reporting period of the financial statements of that joint venture or associate; and
   (ii) the reason for using a different date or period.

(c) the unrecognised share of losses of a joint venture or associate, both for the reporting period and cumulatively, if the entity has stopped recognising its share of losses of the joint venture or associate when applying the equity method. *[IFRS 12.22]*.

The implication from this wording is that these disclosures in respect of significant restrictions, reporting dates and unrecognised losses are required separately for each material joint venture or associate.

A summary of the disclosures required for individually material and, collectively for immaterial joint ventures and associates is shown in the table below.

Topic	Material joint ventures and associates	Individually immaterial joint ventures and associates
Accounting policy	✓	×
Summarised financial information	✓	✓ (in aggregate)
Fair value, if quoted market price is available	✓	×
Restrictions on ability to transfer funds	✓	✓ (in aggregate)
Date of financial statements, if different from entity	✓	✓ (in aggregate)
Unrecognised share of losses	✓	✓ (in aggregate)

5.1.1 Summarised financial information of individually material joint ventures and associates

The summarised financial information specified by (b)(ii) of 5.1 above for each material joint venture and associate is as follows:

(a) dividends received;

(b) summarised financial information for the joint venture or associate including, but not necessarily limited to:

  (i) current assets;

  (ii) non-current assets;

  (iii) current liabilities;

  (iv) non-current liabilities;

  (v) revenue;

  (vi) profit or loss from continuing operations;

  (vii) post-tax profit or loss from discontinued operations;

  (viii) other comprehensive income; and

  (ix) total comprehensive income. *[IFRS 12.B12].*

Additionally, for material joint ventures (but not associates) the following information must be disclosed:

(a) cash and cash equivalents included in current assets;

(b) current financial liabilities (excluding trade and other payables and provisions);

(c) non-current financial liabilities (excluding trade and other payables and provisions);

(d) depreciation and amortisation;

(e) interest income;

(f) interest expense; and

(g) income tax expense or income. *[IFRS 12.B13].*

The summarised financial information presented must be the 100 per cent amounts included in the IFRS financial statements of the joint venture or associate (and not the entity's share of those amounts). However, if the entity accounts for the joint venture or associate using the equity method:

(a) the amounts included in the IFRS financial statements of the joint venture or associate must be adjusted to reflect adjustments made by the entity when using the equity method, such as the fair value adjustments made at the time of acquisition and adjustments for differences in accounting policies; and

(b) the entity must provide a reconciliation of the summarised financial information presented to the carrying amount of its interest in the joint venture or associate. *[IFRS 12.B14].*

In January 2015, the Interpretations Committee discussed the basis on which an entity should prepare the required summarised financial information for joint ventures and associates. The Interpretations Committee observed that a reporting entity that has subsidiaries should present the summarised financial information required about a joint venture or associate that is material to the reporting entity based on the consolidated financial statements for the joint venture or associate. If it does not have subsidiaries, the presentation should be based on the financial statements of the joint venture or associate in which its own joint ventures or associates are equity-accounted. The Interpretations Committee noted that these views are consistent with paragraph 14 of IFRS 12, which requires that the amounts included in the financial statements of the joint venture or associate must be adjusted to reflect adjustments made by the reporting entity using the equity method (see (a) above). Consequently, the Interpretations Committee decided that neither an interpretation nor an amendment to a standard was necessary and decided not to add this issue to its agenda.[5]

The standard does not specify what components should be included in the reconciliation required by (b) above. As clarified by the Interpretations Committee, the amounts included in the IFRS financial statements of the joint venture or associate should be adjusted to reflect fair value and accounting policy adjustments per (a) above. The implication is that this should also include the reporting entity's goodwill attributable to the joint venture or associate. However, this is only the goodwill attributable to the reporting entity's share of the joint venture or associate. The goodwill attributable to the rest of the joint venture or associate is presumably not known. Care will therefore be needed in presenting any such goodwill and in adequately explaining how the summarised IFRS financial information reconciles to the carrying amount of the reporting entity's interest in the joint venture or associate. Any pre-existing goodwill in the books of the joint venture or associate at the time it became a joint venture or associate of the reporting entity should be eliminated from the amounts in (a) as a fair value adjustment.

An entity may present the summarised financial information required on the basis of the joint venture's or associate's financial statements if:

(a) the entity measures its interest in the joint venture or associate at fair value in accordance with IAS 28; and

(b) the joint venture or associate does not prepare IFRS financial statements and preparation on that basis would be impracticable or cause undue cost. In that case, the entity must disclose the basis on which the summarised financial information has been prepared. *[IFRS 12.B15].*

This implies that the summarised financial information of the joint venture or associate can be prepared on a non-IFRS basis in those circumstances where both conditions (a) and (b) are satisfied.

Where a joint venture or associate measured at fair value in accordance with IAS 28 does prepare IFRS financial statements, or where the preparation of IFRS financial information would not be impracticable or cause undue cost, it would appear that the summarised financial information disclosed should be the unadjusted IFRS numbers of the joint venture or associate (as compared to the adjusted basis used where the equity method is applied).

In principle, the IASB concluded that the disclosure requirements for joint ventures and associates should be the same for all entities regardless of whether those entities are venture capital organisations, mutual funds, unit trusts or similar entities which are permitted by IAS 28 to hold investments in joint ventures and associates at fair value. *[IFRS 12.BC60].*

Nevertheless, the minimum line item disclosures required for material associates are less than those required for material joint ventures on the grounds that, in the IASB's opinion, an entity is generally more involved with joint ventures than with associates because joint control means that an entity has a veto over decisions relating to the relevant activities of the joint venture. Accordingly, the IASB considers that the different nature of the relationship between a joint venturer and its joint ventures from that between an investor and its associates warrants a different level of detail in the disclosures of summarised financial information. *[IFRS 12.BC50-51].*

IFRS 12 requires that an entity should present the summarised financial information for each material joint venture on a '100 per cent' basis and reconcile that to the carrying amount of its investment in the joint venture or associate. An alternative would be to present summarised financial information for each material joint venture on the basis of the reporting entity's proportionate interest in the joint venture. However, the IASB rejected that alternative approach on the grounds that it would be confusing to present the assets, liabilities and revenue of a joint venture or associate when the entity has neither rights to, nor obligations for, the assets and liabilities of the joint ventures or associates. *[IFRS 12.BC49].*

Summarised financial information is not required for material joint operations since assets and liabilities arising from joint operations are the reporting entity's own assets and liabilities and consequently are recognised separately in the entity's financial statements. They are accounted for in accordance with the requirements of applicable IFRSs, and are therefore subject to the disclosure requirements of those IFRSs. *[IFRS 12.BC52].* Since an investment in a joint operation is not considered to represent an investment in a separate entity, a joint operation also cannot be a structured entity.

BP disclose summarised financial information for material associates as illustrated below.

Extract 13.6: BP p.l.c. (2016)

Notes on financial statements [extract]

16. Investments in associates [extract]

BP owns 19.75% of the voting shares of Rosneft which are listed on the MICEX stock exchange in Moscow and its global depository receipts are listed on the London Stock Exchange. The Russian federal government, through its investment company JSC Rosneftegaz, owned 50.0% plus one share of the voting shares of Rosneft at 31 December 2016.

[...]

The value of BP's 19.75% shareholding in Rosneft based on the quoted market share price of $6.50 per share (2015 $3.48 per share) was $13,604 million at 31 December 2016 (2015 $7,283 million).

The following table provides summarized financial information relating to Rosneft. This information is presented on a 100% basis and reflects adjustments made by BP to Rosneft's own results in applying the equity method of accounting. BP adjusts Rosneft's results for the accounting required under IFRS relating to BP's purchase of its interest in Rosneft and the amortization of the deferred gain relating to the disposal of BP's interest in TNK-BP. These adjustments have increased the reported profit for 2016, as shown in the table below, compared with the equivalent amount in Russian roubles that we expect Rosneft to report in its own financial statements under IFRS.

			$ million
			Gross amount
	2016	2015	2014
Sales and other operating revenues	74,380	84,071	142,856
Profit before interest and taxation	7,094	12,253	19,367
Finance costs	1,747	3,696	5,230
Profit before taxation	5,347	8,557	14,137
Taxation	1,797	1,792	3,428
Non-controlling interests	273	30	71
Profit for the year	3,277	6,735	10,638
Other comprehensive income	4,203	(4,111)	(13,038)
Total comprehensive income	7,480	2,624	(2,400)
Non-current assets	129,403	84,689	
Current assets	37,914	34,891	
Total assets	167,317	119,580	
Current liabilities	46,284	25,691	
Non-current liabilities	71,980	63,554	
Total liabilities	118,264	89,245	
Net assets	49,053	30,335	
Less: non-controlling interests	7,316	982	
	41,737	29,353	

The group received dividends, net of withholding tax, of $332 million from Rosneft in 2016 (2015 $271 million and 2014 $693 million).

5.1.2 Financial information of individually immaterial joint ventures and associates

An entity must disclose, in aggregate, the carrying amount of its interests in all individually immaterial joint ventures or associates that are accounted for using the equity method. An entity must also disclose separately the aggregate amount of its share of those joint ventures' or associates':

(a) profit or loss from continuing operations;

(b) post-tax profit or loss from discontinued operations;

(c) other comprehensive income; and

(d) total comprehensive income.

Separate disclosures are required for joint ventures and associates. *[IFRS 12.B16].*

IFRS 12 does not specifically require a reporting entity's share of (a) to (d) to be disclosed for material joint ventures or associates.

IFRS 12 clarifies that this financial information is not required when a joint venture or associate is held for sale in accordance with IFRS 5. *[IFRS 12.B17].*

Glencore plc disclose the following information about individual immaterial associates:

Extract 13.7: Glencore plc (2016)

Notes to the financial statements [extract]

9. INVESTMENTS IN ASSOCIATES, JOINT VENTURES AND OTHER INVESTMENTS [extract]

Aggregate information of associates that are not individually material:

US$ million	2016	2015
The Group's share of loss	(122)	(48)
The Group's share of other comprehensive income/(loss)	–	(22)
The Group's share of total comprehensive income/(loss)	(122)	(70)
Aggregate carrying value of the Group's interests	1,847	2,554

5.2 Risks associated with interests in joint ventures and associates

An entity must disclose:

(a) commitments that it has relating to its joint ventures separately from the amount of other commitments; and

(b) contingent liabilities (as defined in IAS 37) relating to its interests in joint ventures or associates (including its share of contingent liabilities incurred jointly with other investors with joint control of, or significant influence over, the joint ventures and associates) separately from the amount of other contingent liabilities.

5.2.1 Disclosure of commitments relating to joint ventures

IAS 24 – *Related Party Disclosures* – already requires aggregate commitments relating to joint ventures to be disclosed separately from other commitments. *[IAS 24.18-19].* IFRS 12 clarifies that the commitments required to be disclosed under IAS 24 include an entity's share of commitments made jointly with other investors with joint control of

Chapter 13

a joint venture. Commitments are those that may give rise to a future outflow of cash or other resources. *[IFRS 12.B18]*.

IFRS 12 provides the following illustrative but not exhaustive examples of the type of unrecognised commitments that should be disclosed under IAS 24:

(a) unrecognised commitments to contribute funding or resources as a result of, for example:
   (i) the constitution or acquisition agreements of a joint venture (that, for example, require an entity to contribute funds over a specific period);
   (ii) capital intensive projects undertaken by a joint venture;
   (iii) unconditional purchase obligations, comprising procurement of equipment, inventory or services that an entity is committed to purchasing from, or on behalf of, a joint venture;
   (iv) unrecognised commitments to provide loans or other financial support to a joint venture;
   (v) unrecognised commitments to contribute resources to a joint venture, such as assets or services;
   (vi) other non-cancellable unrecognised commitments relating to a joint venture; and
(b) unrecognised commitments to acquire another party's ownership interest (or a portion of that ownership interest) in a joint venture if a particular event occurs or does not occur in the future. *[IFRS 12.B19]*.

There is no requirement to disclose these commitments at individual joint venture level. However, IAS 24 requires disclosure of information about those transactions and outstanding balances, including commitments, necessary for users to understand the potential effect of the relationship on the financial statements. *[IAS 24.18]*. This implies that there should be separate disclosure of different types of significant commitments. IAS 24 does not require the names of any joint ventures to be disclosed.

5.2.2 Disclosure of contingent liabilities relating to joint ventures and associates

IFRS 12 requires separate disclosure of contingent liabilities relating to an entity's interests in joint ventures and associates from the amount of other contingent liabilities.

IAS 37 defines a contingent liability as an obligation that derives from an entity's actions where:

(a) by an established pattern of past practice, published policies or a sufficiently specific current statement, the entity has indicated to other parties that it will accept certain responsibilities; and
(b) as a result, the entity has created a valid expectation on the part of those other parties that it will discharge those responsibilities. *[IAS 37.10]*.

IAS 37 requires disclosure, for each class of contingent liability at the end of a reporting period, a brief description of the nature of the contingent liability and, where practicable:

(a) an estimate of its financial effect, measured under the requirements of the standard;

(b) an indication of the uncertainties relating to the amount or timing of any outflow; and

(c) the possibility of any reimbursement. *[IAS 37.86].*

IAS 37 further defines what is intended by 'class' and the circumstances in which aggregation of disclosures of contingent liabilities is appropriate.

Further detail on contingent liabilities is contained at Chapter 28.

6 DISCLOSURE OF INTERESTS IN UNCONSOLIDATED STRUCTURED ENTITIES

An entity must disclose information that enables users of its financial statements:

(a) to understand the nature and extent of its interests in unconsolidated structured entities; and

(b) to evaluate the nature of, and changes to, the risks associated with its interests in unconsolidated structured entities. *[IFRS 12.24].*

These disclosures are not required by an investment entity for an unconsolidated structured entity that it controls and for which it presents the disclosures required at 4.6 above. *[IFRS 12.25A].*

Disclosure requirements in respect of risks associated with interests in consolidated structured entities are discussed at 4.4 above.

As discussed at 2.2.2.D above, these disclosures also apply to interests in joint ventures and associates that are also structured entities, in addition to the disclosure required at 5 above for joint ventures and associates.

The information required by (a) and (b) above includes information about an entity's exposure to risk from involvement that it had with unconsolidated structured entities in previous periods (e.g. sponsoring the structured entity) even if the entity no longer has any contractual involvement with the structured entity at the reporting date. *[IFRS 12.25].*

It is likely that some of the disclosure requirements for unconsolidated structured entities will overlap with those of IFRS 7, since many interests in unconsolidated structured entities will be financial assets within the scope of IFRS 7. However, the IASB considers that what is different is that the IFRS 12 disclosures describe an entity's risk exposures, but IFRS 7 requires disclosures about risks associated with financial instruments. IFRS 12 adopts a different perspective and requires an entity to disclose its exposure to risks from its interest in a structured entity. *[IFRS 12.BC72].*

The IASB believes that information from both perspectives assists users of financial statements in their analysis of an entity's exposure to risk – the disclosures in IFRS 7 by identifying those financial instruments that create risk and the disclosures in IFRS 12 by providing, when relevant, information about:

- the extent of an entity's transactions with structured entities;
- concentrations of risk that arise from the nature of the entities with which the entity has transactions; and
- particular transactions that expose the entity to risk. *[IFRS 12.BC73]*.

The IASB was also persuaded by information received from users of financial statements in the US who had been using the disclosures required by US GAAP for variable interest entities in their analysis. According to the IASB, those users confirmed that the new disclosures provided them with information that was not presently available to them, but which they regarded as important for a thorough understanding of an entity's exposure to risk. Many of those users referred also to the global financial crisis and emphasised that a better understanding of an entity's interests in unconsolidated structured entities might have helped to identify earlier the extent of risks to which entities were exposed. Accordingly, those users stated that the new risk disclosures had significantly improved the quality of financial reporting and strongly encouraged the IASB to require similar disclosures for IFRS preparers. *[IFRS 12.BC75-76]*.

No disclosure is required of 'significant' interests in individual unconsolidated structured entities. The IASB decided against adding this requirement because of the overriding concept in IFRSs that an entity would be required to disclose only information that is material as defined and described in the Conceptual Framework and because the word 'significant' is not defined in IFRS. *[IFRS 12.BC79]*. However, as discussed at 6.2.1 below, disclosures of aggregate interests by statement of financial position line item are required.

The IASB decided to retain the wider definition of 'interest in' (i.e. an entity's involvement with another entity, whether contractual or non-contractual, that exposes the entity to variability of returns from the performance of the other entity) which was originally proposed in ED 10, rather than a narrower definition. In making this decision, the IASB was convinced by comments received from US preparers, auditors and users about their experience with the US GAAP requirements to disclose information about involvement with variable interest entities. US preparers and accountants also noted that both the aggregation guidance and the requirement that an entity should determine, in the light of facts and circumstances, how much detail it must give to satisfy the disclosure requirements, provide sufficient flexibility for preparers. Consequently, the IASB decided to include in IFRS 12 the requirement to consider the level of detail necessary to meet the disclosure objectives, and to include aggregation principles and guidance to assist preparers when determining what level of detail is appropriate. *[IFRS 12.BC80-81]*.

The IASB also decided that the objective of its risk disclosures for structured entities is that an entity should provide information about its exposure to risk associated with interests in structured entities, regardless of whether that risk arises from having an existing interest in the entity or from being involved with the entity in previous periods. Therefore the IASB decided to define an interest in a structured entity as contractual or non-contractual involvement that exposes the entity to variability of returns. In addition, the IASB decided to state explicitly that the disclosures about an entity's exposure to risk should include risk that arises from previous involvement with a structured entity, even if an entity no longer has any contractual involvement with the structured entity at the end of the reporting period. *[IFRS 12.BC110].*

6.1 Disclosure of the nature of interests in unconsolidated structured entities

6.1.1 Disclosure of the nature, purpose, size, activities and financing of structured entities

An entity must disclose qualitative and quantitative information about its interests in unconsolidated structured entities, including, but not limited to, the nature, purpose, size and activities of the structured entity and how the structured entity is financed. *[IFRS 12.26].*

The IASB concluded that this requirement should provide users with sufficient information about the assets held by structured entities and the funding of those assets without requiring specific disclosures of the assets of unconsolidated structured entities in which the entity has an interest in all circumstances. If relevant to an assessment of its exposure to risk, an entity would be required to provide additional information about the assets and funding of structured entities. *[IFRS 12.BC96].*

6.1.1.A Nature and purpose

Examples of the nature and purpose of a structured entity might include:

- to manage balance sheet exposure and risk, including securitisation of assets;
- to provide investors with a synthetic exposure to debt and equity instruments such as credit linked notes and equity linked notes;
- to provide investors with a variety of investment opportunities through managed investment strategies; and
- to obtain and facilitate funding.

Old Mutual plc discloses the nature, purpose and type of interest in unconsolidated structured entities in a tabular format as follows:

Extract 13.8: Old Mutual plc (2016)

Notes to the consolidated financial statements [extract]

I: Interests in subsidiaries, associates and joint arrangements [extract]

I3: Structured entities [extract]

(a) Group's involvement in structured entities [extract]

The table below summarises the types of structured entities the Group does not consolidate, but may have an interest in:

Type of structured entity	Nature	Purpose	Interest held by the Group
– Securitisation vehicles for loans and advances	– Finance the Group's own assets through the issue of notes to investors	– Generate: – Funding for the Group's lending activities – Margin through sale of assets to investors – Fees for loan servicing	– Investment in senior notes issued by the vehicles
– Investment funds	– Manage client funds through the investment in assets	– Generate fees from managing assets on behalf of third-party investors	– Investments in units issued by the fund
– Securitisation vehicles for third-party receivables	– Finance third party receivables and are financed through loans from third party note holders and bank borrowing	– Generate fees from arranging the structure. Interest income may be earned on the notes held by the Group	– Interest in these vehicles is through notes that are traded in the market
– Security vehicles	– Hold and realise assets as a result of the default of a client	– These entities seek to protect the collateral of the Group on the default of a loan	– Ownership interest will be in proportion of the lending. At 31 December 2016, the Group held no value in security vehicles
– Clients investment entities	– Hold client investment assets	– Generates various sources of income for the Group	– None
– Black Economic Empowerment (BEE) funding	– Fund the acquisition of shares by a BEE partner	– Generates interest on the funding provided	– None

6.1.1.B Size

The requirement to disclose the size of a structured entity would most likely be met by providing information about the total value of the assets of the entity. However, the Basis for Conclusions states that IFRS 12 does not require specific disclosure of the reported assets of unconsolidated structured entities in which the entity has an interest in all circumstances. *[IFRS 12.BC96]*. This would seem to suggest that measures of size other than asset fair values would be acceptable, including (for example) the notional value of securities issued by structured entities.

6.1.1.C Activities

When disclosing the activities of a structured entity, these activities should include the primary activities for which the entity was designed, which are the activities that significantly affect the entity's returns. Although specific examples are not contained in IFRS 12, we believe that the examples contained previously in SIC-12 would also apply. That is, the entity is involved principally in:

- providing a source of long-term capital to an entity or funding to support a reporting entity's ongoing major or central operations through issuing notes; or
- providing a supply of goods and services that is consistent with a reporting entity's ongoing major or central operations which, without the existence of the structured entity, would have to be provided by the reporting entity itself.

6.1.1.D Financing

This disclosure requirement is not limited to financing provided by the reporting entity to the structured entity and would include financing received by the structured entity from unrelated third parties. It is also not limited to equity financing and would appear to include all forms of financing that allow the structured entity to conduct its business activities.

Barclays PLC's financial statements illustrate disclosures of financing of structured entities.

Extract 13.9: Barclays PLC (2016)

Notes to the financial statements [extract]

37 **Structured entities** [extract]

Lending

The portfolio includes lending provided by the Group to unconsolidated structured entities in the normal course of its lending business to earn income in the form of interest and lending fees and includes loans to structured entities that are generally collateralised by property, equipment or other assets. All loans are subject to the Group's credit sanctioning process. Collateral arrangements are specific to the circumstances of each loan with additional guarantees and collateral sought from the sponsor of the structured entity for certain arrangements. During the period the Group incurred an impairment of £24m (2015: £35m) against such facilities. The main types of lending are £2bn (2015: £3bn) of funding loans to bankruptcy remote structured entities to either invest or develop properties, £3bn (2015: £4bn) of loans to structured entities which have been created by an individual to hold one or more assets, £2bn (2015: £2bn) to entities whose operations are limited to financing or funding the acquisition of specific assets such as schools, hospitals, roads and renewable energy projects under the Private Finance Initiative (PFI), and £1bn (2015: £1bn) of funding loans to bankruptcy remote structured entities to enable them to purchase capital equipment for parent companies and are supported by government export guarantees.

6.1.2 Disclosures of sponsored structured entities for which no interest is held at the reporting date

If an entity has sponsored an unconsolidated structured entity for which it does not disclose the risk information required by 6.2 below (e.g. because it does not have an interest in the entity at the reporting date), the entity must disclose:

(a) how it has determined which structured entities it has sponsored;

(b) income from those structured entities during the reporting period, including a description of the types of income presented; and

(c) the carrying amount (at the time of transfer) of all assets transferred to those structured entities during the reporting period. *[IFRS 12.27]*.

The rationale for this disclosure requirement is that sponsoring a structured entity can create risks for a reporting entity, even though the entity may not retain an interest in the structured entity. The Basis for Conclusions states that 'if the structured entity encounters difficulties, it is possible that the sponsor could be challenged on its advice or actions, or might choose to act to protect its reputation.' *[IFRS 12.BC87]*.

IFRS 12 does not define 'sponsored'. However, SIC-12 defined a sponsor as 'the entity on whose behalf the SPE was created'. *[SIC-12.2]*. An illustrative example in IFRS 10 uses the word 'sponsors' in a similar context when it states that 'a decision maker (the sponsor) sponsors a multi-seller conduit'. In the IFRS 10 example, the sponsor establishes the terms of the conduit and manages the operations of the conduit for a market-based fee. *[IFRS 10.B72 Example 16]*.

Determining whether the reporting entity is the sponsor of a structured entity will be a matter of individual facts and circumstances and may require judgement to be exercised. For example, a structured entity may have been created to achieve two possible objectives that could satisfy both the reporting entity and third party investors in the structured entity. Factors that may indicate that a reporting entity has sponsored a structured entity include:

- the reporting entity established and set up the entity; and
- the reporting entity was involved in the creation and design of the structured entity; or
- the reporting entity is the majority user of the structured entity; or
- the reporting entity's name appears in the name of the structured entity or on the products issued by the structured entity.

The information required by (b) and (c) above must be presented in a tabular format unless some other format is more appropriate and the sponsoring activities must be classified into relevant categories. *[IFRS 12.28]*.

Many financial institutions define 'sponsor' for the purpose of their IFRS 12 disclosures as illustrated by this disclosure from HSBC Holdings plc's financial statements.

Extract 13.10: HSBC Holdings plc (2016)

Notes on the Financial Statements [extract]

1. **Basis of preparation and significant accounting policies** [extract]

1.2 **Summary of significant accounting policies** [extract]

(a) **Consolidation and related policies** [extract]

HSBC sponsored structured entities

HSBC is considered to sponsor another entity if, in addition to ongoing involvement with the entity, it had a key role in establishing that entity or in bringing together relevant counterparties so the transaction that is the purpose of the entity could occur. HSBC is generally not considered a sponsor if the only involvement with the entity is merely administrative.

The information required by (a) and (b) must be disclosed whether or not any assets were transferred to the structured entity during the reporting period. There is no time limit set for these disclosures so, in theory, they could continue indefinitely after the cessation of any interest in the structured entity. IFRS 12 does not specify whether (c) above refers to assets transferred to the structured entity by the reporting entity or to the total assets transferred to the structured entity irrespective of who the transferor may be. However, the Basis for Conclusions states that the IASB concluded that the asset information disclosed should refer not only to assets transferred by the sponsor but to all assets transferred to the structured entity during the reporting period. *[IFRS 12.BC90].*

Income received from structured entities would not be confined to the income derived from the reporting entity's 'interest(s)' as defined by IFRS 12, but would cover all types of income received and reported by the entity. The standard states that 'income from a structured entity' includes, but is not limited to:

- recurring and non-recurring fees (structuring fees, management fees, placing agent fees, etc.);
- interest;
- dividends;
- gains or losses on the remeasurement or derecognition of interests in structured entities; and
- gains or losses from the transfer of assets or liabilities to the structured entity. *[IFRS 12 Appendix A].*

There is no requirement for a quantitative split of the fee income by type although it may be useful for users of the financial statements.

An illustrative example of the disclosures required by (a) to (c) above is shown below.

Example 13.7: Illustrative example of disclosures for sponsored structured entities where no interest exists at the reporting date

The Group considers itself the sponsor of a number of structured entities. The Group designed and established these entities. In some cases, it also transferred assets to them, in others it markets products associated with the entities in its own name and/or provides guarantees regarding the performance of the entities.

For some structured entities, the Group has no interest at the reporting date. However, it has sold assets to those entities during the reporting period in such a way that it has no continuing involvement in those assets and has earned fees for selling those assets and for other transactions carried out for the entities. The table below presents the Group's income recognised during the reporting period and the fair value of any assets transferred to those structured entities during the reporting period as follows:

Income from unconsolidated structured entities in which no interest is held at 31 December 2017	Income 2017 €'000	Income 2016 €'000
Commissions and fees	69	50
Interest income	48	47
Gains and losses on sale of assets	66	–
	183	97
Split by:		
Mortgage-backed securitisations	75	41
CDO's and CLO's	50	20
Asset-backed commercial paper	25	30
Property, credit-related and other investing	33	6
	183	97

Carrying amounts of assets transferred to unconsolidated structured entities in reporting period	Transferred in year 2017 €'000	Transferred in year 2016 €'000
Mortgage-backed securitisations	3,065	–
CDO's and CLO's	2,536	–
Asset-backed commercial paper	1,325	3,000
Property, credit-related and other investing	178	–
	7,104	3,000

Aviva plc made the following disclosures in respect of investment management fees earned in respect of its asset management business.

Extract 13.11: Aviva plc (2016)

Notes to the consolidated financial statements [extract]

25 – Interests in structured entities [extract]

(c) Other interests in unconsolidated structured entities [extract]

The Group receives management fees and other fees in respect of its asset management businesses. The Group does not sponsor any of the funds or investment vehicles from which it receives fees. Management fees received for investments that the Group manages but does not have a holding in also represent an interest in unconsolidated structured entities. As these investments are not held by the Group, the investment risk is borne by the external investors and therefore the Group's maximum exposure to loss relates to future management fees. The table below shows the assets under management of entities that the Group manages but does not have a holding in and the fees earned from those entities. The increase in total assets under management is primarily the result of an increase in total pension fund assets managed by Poland.

	Assets Under Management £m	2016 Investment Management fees £m
Investment funds[1]	9,281	63
Specialised investment vehicles:	3,726	14
Analysed as:		
OEICs	1,536	5
PLPs	2,155	9
SICAVs	35	–
Total	13,007	77

[1] Investment funds relate primarily to the Group's Spanish and Polish pension funds

6.2 Disclosure of the nature of risks of unconsolidated structured entities

The IASB decided that, although it agreed with the concept that an entity should generally be allowed to tailor its disclosures to meet the specific information needs of its users, disclosure requirements should contain a minimum set of requirements that should be applied by all entities. In making this decision, the IASB was convinced by comments from users who pointed out that without any specific disclosure requirements, comparability would be impaired and an entity might not disclose information that users find important. *[IFRS 12.BC94]*.

These minimum disclosures are discussed at 6.2.1 and 6.2.2 below.

6.2.1 Disclosures of interests in structured entities and of the maximum exposure to loss from those interests

An entity must disclose, in a tabular form, unless another format is more appropriate, a summary of:

(a) the carrying amounts of the assets and liabilities recognised in its financial statements relating to its interests in unconsolidated structured entities;

(b) the line items in the statement of financial position in which those assets and liabilities are recognised;

(c) the amount that best represents the entity's maximum exposure to loss from its interests in unconsolidated structured entities, including how the maximum exposure to loss is determined. If an entity cannot quantify its maximum exposure to loss from its interests in consolidated structured entities it must disclose that fact and the reasons; and

(d) a comparison of the carrying amounts of the assets and liabilities of the entity that relate to its interests in unconsolidated structured entities and the entity's maximum exposure to loss from those entities. *[IFRS 12.29]*.

Disclosure of an entity's maximum exposure to loss was considered necessary by the IASB as it was concerned that, if only information about expected losses was required, an entity might often identify a positive expected value of returns from its interests in unconsolidated structured entities and, as a consequence, would not disclose any loss exposure. *[IFRS 12.BC97]*.

The IASB also decided to require an entity to disclose a comparison of the carrying amounts of the assets and liabilities in its statement of financial position and its maximum exposure to loss. This is because the information will provide users with a better understanding of the differences between the expected loss exposure and the expectation of whether it is likely that an entity will bear all or only some of the losses. The IASB reasoned that this information would help an entity explain why the maximum exposure to loss is unrepresentative of its actual exposure if that is the case. *[IFRS 12.BC100].*

IFRS 12 does not define maximum exposure to loss. The IASB decided not to provide such a definition of 'loss' but to leave it to the entity to identify what constitutes a loss in the particular context of that reporting entity. The entity should then disclose how it has determined maximum loss exposure. The IASB acknowledged that an entity might not always be able to calculate the maximum exposure to loss, such as when a financial instrument exposes an entity to theoretically unlimited losses. The IASB decided that when this is the case an entity should disclose the reasons why it is not possible to calculate the maximum exposure to loss. *[IFRS 12.BC98-99].*

We believe that 'maximum exposure to loss' refers to the maximum loss that an entity could be required to record in its statement of comprehensive income as a result of its involvement with a structured entity. Further, this maximum possible loss must be disclosed regardless of the probability of such losses actually being incurred. IFRS 12 is silent on whether the maximum exposure is gross or net of collateral or hedging instruments held that would mitigate any loss. Consistent with the equivalent disclosures required by IFRS 7, we believe that the maximum exposure to loss should be disclosed gross of any collateral or hedging instruments and that separate disclosure should be made in respect of instruments held that would mitigate the loss on a net basis. *[IFRS 7.36].*

UBS AG make the following disclosures in respect of its interests in unconsolidated structured entities.

Extract 13.12: UBS Group AG (2016)

Notes to the UBS Group AG consolidated financial statements [extract]

Note 28 Interests in subsidiaries and other entities [extract]

c) Interests in unconsolidated structured entities [extract]

The table below presents Group's interests in and maximum exposure to loss from unconsolidated SEs as well as the total assets held by the SEs in which UBS had an interest as of year-end, except for investment funds sponsored by third parties, for which the carrying value of UBS's interest as of year-end has been disclosed.

Interests in unconsolidated structured entities

CHF million, except where indicated	31.12.16 Securitization vehicles	Client vehicles	Investment funds	Total	Maximum exposure to loss[1]
Trading portfolio assets	634	394	6,215	7,243	7,243
Positive replacement values	40	76	101	217	217
Loans	0	0	79	79	79
Financial assets designated at fair value	103	83[2]	98	284	1,863
Financial assets available-for-sale	0	3,381	58	3,439	3,439
Other assets	289	37[2]	0	327	1,490
Total assets	1,066[3]	3,971	6,552	11,589	
Negative replacement values	33[4]	346	67	446	90
Total liabilities	33	346	67	446	
Assets held by the unconsolidated structured entities in which UBS had an interest (CHF billion)	72[5]	102[6]	334[7]		

[...]

1 For purposes of this disclosure, maximum exposure to loss amounts do not consider the risk-reducing effects of collateral or other credit enhancements.

2 Represents the carrying value of loan commitments, both designated at fair value and held at amortized cost. The maximum exposure to loss for these instruments is equal to the notional amount.

3 As of 31 December 2016, CHF 1.0 billion of the CHF 1.1 billion (31 December 2015: CHF 0.9 billion of the CHF 1.1 billion) was held in Corporate Center – Non-core and Legacy Portfolio.

4 Comprised of credit default swap (CDS) liabilities and other swap liabilities. The maximum exposure to loss for CDS is equal to the sum of the negative carrying value and the notional amount. For other swap liabilities, no maximum exposure to loss is reported.

5 Represents principal amount outstanding.

6 Represents the market value of total assets.

7 Represents the net asset value of the investment funds sponsored by UBS and the carrying value of UBS's interest in the investment funds not sponsored by UBS.

The Group retains or purchases interests in unconsolidated SEs in the form of direct investments, financing, guarantees, letters of credit, derivatives and through management contracts.

The Group's maximum exposure to loss is generally equal to the carrying value of the Group's interest in the SE, with the exception of guarantees, letters of credit and credit derivatives for which the contract's notional amount, adjusted for losses already incurred, represents the maximum loss that the Group is exposed to. In addition, the current fair value of derivative swap instruments with a positive replacement value only, such as total return swaps, is presented as the maximum exposure to loss. Risk exposure for these swap instruments could change over time with market movements.

The maximum exposure to loss disclosed in the table on the previous page does not reflect the Group's risk management activities, including effects from financial instruments that may be used to economically hedge the risks inherent in the unconsolidated SE or the risk-reducing effects of collateral or other credit enhancements.

6.2.2 Disclosures of actual and intended financial and other support to structured entities

If during the reporting period an entity has, without having a contractual obligation to do so, provided financial or other support to an unconsolidated structured entity in which it previously had or currently has an interest (for example, purchasing assets of or instruments issued by the structured entity), the entity must disclose:

(a) the type and amount of support provided, including situations in which the entity assisted the structured entity in obtaining financial support; and

(b) the reasons for providing the support. *[IFRS 12.30].*

An entity must also disclose any current intentions to provide financial or other support to an unconsolidated structured entity, including intentions to assist the structured entity in obtaining financial support. *[IFRS 12.31].*

See 4.4.2 and 4.4.4 above for discussion of these disclosure requirements.

Example 13.5 above is an illustrative disclosure of the provision of financial support to a structured entity.

6.3 Additional disclosures regarding the nature of risks from interests in unconsolidated structured entities

In addition to the requirements at 6.2 above, IFRS 12 also requires an entity to disclose additional information that is necessary to meet the disclosure objective to disclose information that allows users of a reporting entity's financial statements to evaluate the nature of, and changes to, the risks associated with its interests in unconsolidated structured entities. Examples of additional information that, depending on the circumstances, might be relevant to an assessment of the risks to which a reporting entity is exposed where it has an interest in an unconsolidated structured entity are:

(a) the terms of an arrangement that could require the entity to provide support to a unconsolidated structured entity (e.g. liquidity arrangements or credit rating triggers associated with obligations to purchase assets of the structured entity or provide financial support) including:

  (i) a description of the events or circumstances that could expose the reporting entity to a loss;

  (ii) whether there are any terms that would limit the obligation;

  (iii) whether there are any other parties that provide financial support and, if so, how the reporting entity's obligation ranks with those of other parties;

(b) losses incurred by the entity during the reporting period relating to its interests in unconsolidated structured entities;

(c) the types of income the entity received during the reporting period from its interests in unconsolidated structured entities;

(d) whether an entity is required to absorb losses of an unconsolidated structured entity before other parties, the maximum limit of such losses for the entity and (if relevant) the ranking and amounts of potential losses borne by parties whose interests rank lower than the entity's interest in the unconsolidated structured entity;

(e) information about any liquidity requirements, guarantees or other commitments with third parties that may affect the fair value or risk of the entity's interests in unconsolidated structured entities;

(f) any difficulties an unconsolidated structured entity has experienced in financing its activities during the reporting period; and

(g) in relation to the funding of an unconsolidated structured entity, the forms of funding (e.g. commercial paper or medium term notes) and their weighted-average life. That information might include maturity analyses of the assets and funding of an unconsolidated structured entity if the structured entity has longer-term assets funded by shorter-term funding. *[IFRS 12.B25-26].*

No prescriptive format is suggested for these disclosures. Therefore, a reporting entity will have to decide whether a tabular or narrative format is suitable depending on its individual circumstances. The examples above are not exhaustive.

The IASB does not intend each item in the list of examples above to apply in all circumstances. The IASB's intention regarding the disclosure of risk is that each entity should disclose information that is important when assessing that exposure but not to cloud the information with unnecessary detail that would be considered irrelevant. If an entity has a large exposure to risk because of transactions with a particular unconsolidated structured entity, then the Board would expect extensive disclosure about that exposure. In contrast, if the entity has very little exposure to risk, little disclosure would be required. Therefore, the list of additional information above is a list of examples of information that might be relevant and not a list of requirements that should be applied regardless of the circumstances. *[IFRS 12.BC113-114].*

Given that this information is required in respect of structured entities that the reporting entity does not control, and over which it may not exercise significant influence, some of the disclosures suggested in respect of (d), (f) and (g) above may be difficult to provide. This is because they require current information about the activities of the structured entity, rather than information about the interests held by the reporting entity.

Comments on some of the suggested disclosures are at 6.3.1 to 6.3.7 below.

6.3.1 Disclosure of support

Example 13.5 above illustrates disclosure of a contractual arrangement that could require support to a structured entity.

Example 13.6 above illustrates disclosure of support provided to a structured entity where there is no contractual obligation to provide such support.

The meaning of 'support' is discussed at 4.4.2 above.

6.3.2 Disclosure of losses

The standard does not elaborate on 'losses incurred' but we infer that it refers to both realised and unrealised losses and losses recognised in both profit and loss and other comprehensive income. It may be informative to explain to users of the financial statements the line items in the primary statements in which the losses have been recognised. It would also be informative to disclose the aggregate losses incurred in respect of investments held at the reporting date as well as the losses incurred in the reporting period for those interests disposed of during the period.

Example 13.8: Losses incurred from investments in unconsolidated structured entities

The Group has incurred the following realised and unrealised losses in respect of its investments in unconsolidated structured entities:

	2017	2016
	€'000	€'000
Realised losses	200	200
Unrealised losses (profit and loss)	400	300
Unrealised losses (other comprehensive income)	500	400
	1,100	900
Split by:		
Collateralised debt obligations	800	700
Credit card receivables	300	200
	1,100	900

Aggregate losses incurred	Transferred in year 2017 €'000	Transferred in year 2016 €'000
Collateralised debt obligations	2,300	1,500
Credit card receivables	1,700	1,400
	4,000	2,900

6.3.3 *Disclosure of types of income received*

This disclosure is similar to the disclosure required at 6.1.2 above in respect of unconsolidated structured entities for which the reporting entity does not have an interest at the reporting date. However, (c) above refers only to the types of income received and does not refer to the need for a specific quantification of the income received.

'Income from a structured entity' includes, but is not limited to:

- recurring and non-recurring fees (structuring fees, management fees, placing agent fees, etc.);
- interest;
- dividends;
- gains or losses on the remeasurement or derecognition of interests in structured entities; and
- gains or losses from the transfer of assets or liabilities to the structured entity. *[IFRS 12 Appendix A]*.

6.3.4 *Disclosure of ranking and amounts of potential losses*

Disclosure is required of the maximum limit of losses for a reporting entity where a reporting entity is required to absorb losses of a structured entity before other parties. This requirement is likely to be relevant for reporting entities which hold notes in securitised structured entities or where the interests in the structured entity are held are in the form of multiple contractually linked or 'tranched' notes.

An example of the type of disclosure that could be made is shown below.

Example 13.9: Maximum exposure to and ranking of loss exposure by type of structured entity

The following table shows the maximum exposure to loss for ABC Bank by type of structured entity and by seniority of interest, where ABC Bank's interest ranks lower than those of other investors and so ABC Bank absorbs losses before other parties.

	Seniority of interests				
€'000	Subordinated interests	Mezzanine interests	Senior interests	Most senior interests	Total
Mortgage backed securitisations					
i) ABC Bank's maximum exposure to loss	150	592	850	346	1,938
ii) Potential losses borne by more junior interests	–	897	7,875	10,332	19,104
CDOs and CLOs					
i) ABC Bank's maximum exposure to loss	60	167	243	32	502
ii) Potential losses borne by more junior interests	27	456	4,787	5,311	10,581
Asset backed commercial paper					
i) ABC Bank's maximum exposure to loss	–	–	–	379	379
ii) Potential losses borne by more junior interests	–	–	–	25	25

6.3.5 *Disclosure of liquidity arrangements*

This disclosure might include:

- liquidity arrangements, guarantees or other commitments provided by third parties to the structured entity which affect the fair value or risk of the reporting entity's interests in the structured entity; and
- liquidity arrangements, guarantees or other commitments provided by third parties to the reporting entity which affect the risks of the reporting entity's interests in the structured entity.

We do not believe that this disclosure is intended to include liquidity arrangements, guarantees or other commitments made by the structured entity to third parties as while an arrangement provided to a third party may itself qualify as an interest in a structured entity, it would not normally affect the fair value of an entity's interests in an unconsolidated structured entity.

6.3.6 *Disclosure of funding difficulties*

Disclosure of 'any difficulties' that a structured entity has experienced in financing its activities during a reporting period could potentially be wide-ranging. In practice, we believe that such a disclosure is likely to focus on issues of debt (including short-term commercial paper) and equity securities which have failed either in whole or in part.

6.3.7 Disclosure of the forms of funding of an unconsolidated structured entity

This disclosure appears to refer to the overall funding of the structured entity including forms of funding in which the reporting entity has not participated. A tabular presentation would appear to be the most appropriate way of making this disclosure.

References

1 *IASB Update*, IASB, February 2010, pp.1-2.

2 *Effect analysis: IFRS 10 – Consolidated Financial Statements and IFRS 12 – Disclosure of Interests in Other Entities*, IASB, September 2011, p.11.

3 *IFRIC Update*, January 2015, p.6.

4 *IFRIC Update*, January 2015, p.7.

5 *IFRIC Update*, January 2015, p.7.

Chapter 14 Fair value measurement

List of examples

Chapter 14 Fair value measurement

1 INTRODUCTION AND BACKGROUND

1.1 Introduction

Many IFRSs permit or require entities to measure or disclose the fair value of assets, liabilities or equity instruments. However, until 2011 there was limited guidance in IFRS on how to measure fair value and, in some cases, the guidance was conflicting. To remedy this, the International Accounting Standards Board (IASB or the Board) issued IFRS 13 – *Fair Value Measurement* – in May 2011. The standard was the result of a convergence project between the IASB and the US Financial Accounting Standards Board (FASB) (collectively, the Boards). The standard first applied to annual periods beginning on or after 1 January 2013. *[IFRS 13.C1]*.

IFRS 13 defines fair value, provides principles-based guidance on how to measure fair value under IFRS and requires information about those fair value measurements to be disclosed. *[IFRS 13.1]*. IFRS 13 does not attempt to remove the judgement that is involved in estimating fair value, however, it provides a framework that is intended to reduce inconsistency and increase comparability in the fair value measurements used in financial reporting.

IFRS 13 does not address which assets or liabilities to measure at fair value or when those measurements must be performed. An entity must look to the other standards in that regard. The standard applies to all fair value measurements, when fair value is required or permitted by IFRS, with some limited exceptions, which are discussed later in this chapter (see 2 below). The standard also applies to measurements, such as fair value less costs to sell, that are based on fair value. However, it does not apply to similar measurement bases, such as value in use. *[IFRS 13.IN1, IN2]*.

At the time of writing, the IASB was conducting a Post-implementation Review (PIR) of IFRS 13 to assess the effect of the Standard on financial reporting. In particular, the Board aim was to assess whether:

- the information required by IFRS 13 is useful to users of financial statements;
- areas of IFRS 13 present implementation challenges and might result in inconsistent application of the requirements; and
- unexpected costs have arisen when preparing, auditing or enforcing the requirements of IFRS 13 or when using the information that the Standard requires entities to provide.

The Request for Information was open for comment until 22 September 2017.[1]

This chapter outlines the requirements of IFRS 13, its definitions, measurement framework and disclosure requirements. It addresses some of the key questions that are being asked about how to apply IFRS 13, recognising that some aspects of the standard are still unclear and different views may exist. Further issues and questions may be raised in the future as entities continue to apply the standard and practices evolve.

1.2 Overview of IFRS 13

The framework of IFRS 13 is based on a number of key concepts including unit of account, exit price, valuation premise, highest and best use, principal market, market participant assumptions and the fair value hierarchy. The requirements incorporate financial theory and valuation techniques, but are solely focused on how these concepts are to be applied when determining fair value for financial reporting purposes.

IFRS 13 does not address the issue of *what* to measure at fair value or *when* to measure fair value. The IASB separately considers these issues on a project-by-project basis. Other IFRSs determine which items must be measured at fair value and when. IFRS 13 addresses *how* to measure fair value. The principles in IFRS 13 provide the IASB with a consistent definition that will assist in determining whether fair value is the appropriate measurement basis to be used in any given future project.

The definition of fair value in IFRS 13 is based on an exit price notion, which incorporates the following key concepts:

- Fair value is the price to sell an asset or transfer a liability and, therefore, represents an exit price, not an entry price.
- The exit price for an asset or liability is conceptually different from its transaction price (an entry price). While exit and entry price may be identical in many situations, the transaction price is not presumed to represent the fair value of an asset or liability on its initial recognition.
- Fair value is an exit price in the principal market, i.e. the market with the highest volume and level of activity. In the absence of a principal market, it is assumed that the transaction to sell the asset or transfer the liability would occur in the most advantageous market. This is the market that would maximise the amount that would be received to sell an asset or minimise the amount that would be paid to transfer a liability, taking into account transport and transaction costs. In either case, the entity must have access to the market on the measurement date.

  While transaction costs are considered in determining the most advantageous market, they do not form part of a fair value measurement (i.e. they are not added to or deducted from the price used to measure fair value). However, an exit price would be adjusted for transportation costs if location is a characteristic of the asset or liability being measured. This is discussed further at 9 below.
- Fair value is a market-based measurement, not an entity-specific measurement. When determining fair value, management uses the assumptions that market participants would use when pricing the asset or liability. However, an entity need not identify specific market participants.

These key concepts and the following aspects of the guidance in IFRS 13 require particular focus when applying the standard.

- If another standard provides a fair value measurement exemption that applies when fair value cannot be measured reliably, an entity may need to consider the measurement framework in IFRS 13 in order to determine whether fair value can be reliably measured (see 2 below).
- If there is a principal market for the asset or liability, a fair value measurement represents the price in that market at the measurement date (regardless of whether that price is directly observable or estimated using another valuation technique), even if the price in a different market is potentially more advantageous (see 6 below).
- Fair value measurements should take into consideration the characteristics of the asset or liability being measured, but not characteristics of the transaction to sell the asset or transfer a liability. Transportation costs, for example, must be deducted from the price used to measure fair value when location is a characteristic of the item being measured at fair value (see 5 and 9 below). This principle also clarifies when a restriction on the sale or use of an asset or transfer of a liability affects the measurement of fair value (see 5 below) and when premiums and discounts can be included. In particular, an entity is prohibited from making adjustments for the size of an entity's holding in comparison to current trading volumes (i.e. blockage factors, see 15 below).
- The fair value measurement of non-financial assets must reflect the highest and best use of the asset from a market participant's perspective, which might be its current use or some alternative use. This establishes whether to assume a market participant would derive value from using the non-financial asset on its own or in combination with other assets or with other assets and liabilities (see 10 below).
- The standard clarifies that a fair value measurement of a liability must consider non-performance risk (which includes, but is not limited to, an entity's own credit risk, see 11 below).
- IFRS 13 provides guidance on how to measure the fair value of an entity's own equity instruments, which IFRS did not previously provide (see 11 below), and aligns it with the fair value measurement of liabilities. If there are no quoted prices available for the transfer of an identical or a similar liability or entity's own equity instrument, but the identical item is held by another party as an asset, an entity uses the fair value of the corresponding asset (from the perspective of the market participant that holds that asset) to measure the fair value of the liability or equity instrument. When no corresponding asset exists, the fair value of the liability is measured from the perspective of a market participant that owes the liability (see 11 below).
- A measurement exception in IFRS 13 allows entities to measure financial instruments with offsetting risks on a portfolio basis, provided certain criteria are met both initially and on an ongoing basis (see 12 below).

- The requirements of IFRS 13 in relation to valuation techniques apply to all methods of measuring fair value. Traditionally, references to valuation techniques in IFRS have indicated a lack of market-based information with which to value an asset or liability. Valuation techniques as discussed in IFRS 13 are broader and, importantly, include market-based approaches (see 14 below). When selecting inputs to use, an entity must prioritise observable inputs over unobservable inputs (see 16 below).
- IFRS 13 provides application guidance to assist entities measuring fair value in situations where there has been a decrease in the volume or level of activity (see 8 below).
- Categorisation within the fair value hierarchy is required for all fair value measurements. Disclosures required by IFRS 13 are substantially greater for those fair value measurements that are categorised within Level 3 (see 16 and 20 below).

1.3 Objective of IFRS 13

A primary goal of IFRS 13 is to increase the consistency and comparability of fair value measurements used in financial reporting under IFRS. It provides a common objective whenever IFRS permits or requires a fair value measurement, irrespective of the type of asset or liability being measured or the entity that holds it.

The objective of a fair value measurement is to estimate the price at which an orderly transaction would take place between market participants under the market conditions that exist at the measurement date. *[IFRS 13.2]*.

By highlighting that fair value considers market conditions that exist at the measurement date, the IASB is emphasising that the intent of the measurement is to convey the current value of the asset or liability at the measurement date and not its potential value at some future date. In addition, a fair value measurement does not consider management's intent to sell the asset or transfer the liability at the measurement date. Instead, it represents a market-based measurement that contemplates a hypothetical transaction between market participants at the measurement date (these concepts are discussed further at 6 to 9 below). *[IFRS 13.3]*.

IFRS 13 makes it clear that the objective of a fair value measurement remains the same, regardless of the reason for the fair value measurement (e.g. impairment testing or a recurring measurement) or the extent of observable information available to support the measurement. While the standard requires that the inputs used to measure fair value be prioritised based on their relative observability (see 16 below), the nature of the inputs does not affect the objective of the measurement. That is, the requirement to determine an exit price under current market conditions is not relaxed because the reporting entity cannot observe similar assets or liabilities being transacted at the measurement date. *[IFRS 13.2]*.

Even when fair value is estimated using significant unobservable inputs (because observable inputs do not exist), the goal is to determine an exit price based on the assumptions that market participants would consider when transacting for the asset or liability on the measurement date, including assumptions about risk. This might require the inclusion of a risk premium in the measurement to compensate market participants for the uncertainty inherent in the expected cash flows of the asset or liability being measured. *[IFRS 13.3]*.

IFRS 13 generally does not provide specific rules or detailed 'how-to' guidance. Given the broad use of fair value measurements in accounting for various kinds of assets and liabilities (both financial and non-financial), providing detailed valuation guidance was not deemed practical. As such, the application of IFRS 13 requires significant judgement; but this judgement is applied using the core concepts of the standard's principles-based framework for fair value measurements.

2 SCOPE

IFRS 13 applies whenever another IFRS requires or permits the measurement or disclosure of fair value, or a measure that is based on fair value (such as fair value less costs to sell) *[IFRS 13.5]* with the following exceptions:

(a) The measurement and disclosure requirements do not apply to:

- share-based payment transactions within the scope of IFRS 2 – *Share-based Payment;*
- leasing transactions within the scope of IAS 17 – *Leases* (or accounted for in accordance with IFRS 16 – *Leases,* when effective, see 2.2.2 below); and
- measurements that are similar to fair value, but are not fair value, such as net realisable value in IAS 2 – *Inventories* – or value in use in IAS 36 – *Impairment of Assets* (see 2.2.3 below). *[IFRS 13.6]*.

(b) The measurement requirements in IFRS 13 apply, but the disclosure requirements do not apply to:

- plan assets measured at fair value in accordance with IAS 19 – *Employee Benefits;*
- retirement benefit plan investments measured at fair value in accordance with IAS 26 – *Accounting and Reporting by Retirement Benefit Plans;* and
- assets for which recoverable amount is fair value less costs of disposal in accordance with IAS 36 (see 2.2.4 below). *[IFRS 13.7]*.

Chapter 14

2.1 Items in the scope of IFRS 13

The measurement framework in IFRS 13 applies to both fair value measurements on initial recognition and subsequent fair value measurements, if permitted or required by another IFRS. *[IFRS 13.8]*. Fair value measurement at initial recognition is discussed further at 13 below.

IFRS 13 establishes how to measure fair value. It does not prescribe:

- what should be measured at fair value;
- when to measure fair value (i.e. the measurement date); or
- how (or whether) to account for any subsequent changes in fair value (e.g. in profit or loss or in other comprehensive income). However, the standard does partly address day one gains or losses on initial recognition at fair value, requiring that they be recognised in profit or loss immediately unless the IFRS that permits or requires initial measurement at fair value specifies otherwise.

An entity must consider the relevant IFRSs (e.g. IFRS 3 – *Business Combinations*, IFRS 9 – *Financial Instruments* – or IAS 40 – *Investment Property*) for each of these requirements.

2.1.1 Fair value disclosures

The scope of IFRS 13 includes disclosures of fair value. This refers to situations where an entity is permitted, or may be required, to disclose the fair value of an item whose carrying amount in the financial statements is not fair value. Examples include:

- IAS 40, which requires the fair value to be disclosed for investment properties measured using the cost model; *[IAS 40.79(e)]* and
- IFRS 7 – *Financial Instruments: Disclosures*, which requires the fair value of financial instruments that are subsequently measured at amortised cost in accordance with IFRS 9 (or IAS 39 – *Financial Instruments: Recognition and Measurement*) to be disclosed. *[IFRS 7.25]*.

In such situations, the disclosed fair value must be measured in accordance with IFRS 13 and an entity would also need to make certain disclosures about that fair value measurement in accordance with IFRS 13 (see 20 below).

In certain circumstances, IFRS 7 provides relief from the requirement to disclose the fair value of a financial instrument that is not measured subsequently at fair value. An example is when the carrying amount is considered a reasonable approximation of fair value. *[IFRS 7.29]*. In these situations, an entity would not need to measure the fair value of the financial asset or financial liability for disclosure purposes. However, it would need to consider the requirements of IFRS 13 in order to determine whether the carrying amount is a reasonable approximation of fair value.

2.1.2 Measurements based on fair value

The measurement of amounts (whether recognised or only disclosed) that are based on fair value, such as fair value less costs to sell, are within the scope of IFRS 13. This includes the following:

- a non-current asset (or disposal group) held for sale measured at fair value less costs to sell in accordance with IFRS 5 – *Non-current Assets Held for Sale and Discontinued Operations* – where the fair value less costs to sell is lower than its carrying amount;
- commodity inventories that are held by commodity broker-traders and measured at fair value less costs to sell, as discussed in IAS 2;
- where the recoverable amount for an asset or cash-generating unit(s), determined in accordance with IAS 36, is its fair value less costs of disposal. This includes impairment testing of investments in associates accounted for in accordance with IAS 28 – *Investments in Associates and Joint Ventures* – where that standard requires the test to be performed in accordance with IAS 36; and
- biological assets, agricultural produce and produce growing on a bearer plant measured at fair value less costs to sell in accordance with IAS 41 – *Agriculture*.

In each of these situations, the fair value component is measured in accordance with IFRS 13. Costs to sell or costs of disposal are determined in accordance with the applicable standard, for example, IFRS 5.

2.1.3 Short-term receivables and payables

Prior to the issuance of IFRS 13, Paragraph B5.4.12 of IFRS 9 and paragraph AG79 of IAS 39 allowed entities to measure short-term receivables and payables with no stated interest rate at invoice amounts without discounting, when the effect of not discounting was immaterial. *[IFRS 9 (2012).B5.2.12, IAS 39 (2012).AG79].* Those paragraphs were deleted as a consequence of the IASB issuing IFRS 13.

In the absence of those paragraphs, some questioned whether discounting would be required for such short-term receivables and payables. The IASB amended IFRS 13, as part of its 2010-2012 cycle of *Improvements to IFRSs,* to clarify that, when making those amendments to IFRS 9 and IAS 39, it did not intend to remove the ability to measure such short-term receivables and payables at their invoice amount. The Board also noted that, when the effects of applying them are immaterial, paragraph 8 of IAS 8 – *Accounting Policies, Changes in Accounting Estimates and Errors* – permits entities not to apply accounting policies set out in IFRSs. *[IFRS 13.BC138A, IAS 8.8].*

2.2 Scope exclusions

2.2.1 Share-based payments

IFRS 2 requires certain share-based payments to be measured at grant date fair value (see Chapter 32). However, the objective of an IFRS 2 fair value measurement is not entirely consistent with IFRS 13. Rather than trying to distinguish between these two measures, the IASB decided to exclude share-based payment transactions that are accounted for in accordance with IFRS 2 from the scope of IFRS 13. The grant date fair value of such share-based payments is, therefore, measured and disclosed in accordance with IFRS 2, not IFRS 13. *[IFRS 13.BC21].*

2.2.2 Lease transactions

As noted at 2 above, the standard does not apply to any leasing transactions within the scope of IAS 17 (or any leasing transactions accounted for in accordance with IFRS 16, when effective). The fair value measurement and disclosures requirements in IAS 17 (or IFRS 16) apply instead. This scope exception does not extend to lease assets acquired or liabilities assumed in a business combination in accordance with IFRS 3. IFRS 13 would apply to that measurement of fair value.

At the time of issuing IFRS 13, the IASB noted that applying IFRS 13's requirements might have significantly changed the classification of leases and the timing of recognising gains or losses for sale and leaseback transactions. In addition, at the time that the IASB was undertaking its leases project (which resulted in the issuance of IFRS 16 – that standard replaces IAS 17 (see Chapter 24)), the IASB were concerned that such a requirement may have required entities to make potentially burdensome significant changes to their accounting systems for IFRS 13 and the new leases standard. *[IFRS 13.BC22].*

When effective, IFRS 16 (see Chapter 25) will consequentially amend the scope of IFRS 13 to specify that leasing transactions accounted for in accordance with IFRS 16 are outside the scope of IFRS 13, consistent with the current scope exclusion for IAS 17. However, IFRS 13 may apply to sale and leaseback transactions. IFRS 16 is effective for periods beginning on or after 1 January 2019, with early adoption permitted in certain circumstances.

While it is clear that leasing transactions that are within the scope of IAS 17 are excluded from IFRS 13, finance lease receivables and finance lease liabilities are financial instruments, per paragraph AG9 of IAS 32 – *Financial Instruments: Presentation*, and are, therefore, within the scope of IFRS 7. *[IFRS 7.3, IAS 32.AG9]*. As discussed at 2.1.1 above, paragraph 25 of IFRS 7 requires an entity to disclose, for each class of financial asset and financial liability, a comparison of fair value to carrying amount (except where the carrying amount is a reasonable approximation of fair value). *[IFRS 7.25, 29(a)]*. Since IFRS 7 is not excluded from the scope of IFRS 13, it would appear that the fair value of finance lease receivables and finance lease liabilities would still need to be measured in accordance with IFRS 13, in order to provide these IFRS 7 disclosures.

When effective, IFRS 16 will consequentially amend IFRS 7 such that the fair value of lease liabilities no longer needs to be disclosed.[2]

2.2.3 Measurements similar to fair value

Some IFRSs permit or require measurements that are similar to fair value, but are not fair value. These measures are excluded from the scope of IFRS 13. Such measures may be derived using techniques that are similar to those permitted in IFRS 13. IAS 36, for example, requires value in use to be determined using discounted cash flows (see Chapter 20). An entity may also consider the selling price of an asset, for example, in determining net realisable value for inventories in accordance with IAS 2 (see Chapter 22). Despite these similarities, the objective is not to measure fair value. Therefore, IFRS 13 does not apply to these measurements.

2.2.4 Exemptions from the disclosure requirements of IFRS 13

As noted above, IFRS 13's disclosure requirements do not apply to plan assets measured at fair value in accordance with IAS 19, retirement benefit plan investments measured at fair value in accordance with IAS 26 and assets for which recoverable amount is fair value less costs of disposal in accordance with IAS 36.

In addition, the disclosure requirements in IFRS 13 do not apply to any fair value measurements at initial recognition. That is, the disclosure requirements of IFRS 13 apply to fair value measurements after initial recognition (this is discussed further at 20 below).

The fair value measurement requirements of IFRS 13 still apply to each of these items, even though the disclosure requirements do not. Therefore, an entity would measure the item in accordance with IFRS 13 and then make the required disclosures in accordance with the applicable standard (i.e. IAS 19, IAS 26, IAS 36) or the standard that requires fair value at initial recognition. For example, an entity that acquires a brand as part of a business combination would be required by IFRS 3 to measure the intangible asset at fair value at initial recognition. The acquirer would measure the asset's fair value in accordance with IFRS 13, but would disclose information about that fair value measurement in accordance with IFRS 3 (since those fair values are measured at initial recognition), not IFRS 13.

2.3 Present value techniques

IFRS 13 provides guidance for using present value techniques, such as a discounted cash flow (DCF) analysis, to measure fair value (see 21 below for additional discussion on the application of present value techniques). However, the use of present value techniques does not always result in a fair value measurement. As discussed in 2.2.3 above, some IFRSs use present value techniques to measure assets and liabilities at amounts that are not intended to represent a fair value measurement. Unless the objective is to measure fair value, IFRS 13 does not apply.

2.4 Fair value measurement exceptions and practical expedients in other standards

2.4.1 Fair value measurement exceptions

Some standards provide an exception to a requirement to measure an asset or liability at fair value. IFRS 13 does not eliminate these exceptions. *[IFRS 13.BC8].*

IFRS typically limits fair value measurement exceptions to circumstances where fair value is not reliably measurable and, where applied, requires the application of a cost model. For example, IAS 41 permits the use of a cost model if, on initial recognition of a biological asset, an entity is able to rebut the presumption that fair value can be reliably measured. In addition, it requires an entity to revert to the fair value model if fair value subsequently becomes reliably measurable. *[IAS 41.30].* Additional disclosures are often required to explain why fair value cannot be reliably measured and, if possible, the range of estimates within which fair value is highly likely to lie, as is required in IAS 40 for investment properties, for example. *[IAS 40.79(e)(iii)].*

In these situations, an entity would need to consider the requirements of IFRS 13 in order to determine whether fair value can be reliably measured. If the entity concludes that it could reliably measure fair value based on the requirements of IFRS 13, even in situations where observable information is not available, it would not be able to apply these exceptions.

2.4.2 Practical expedient for impaired financial assets carried at amortised cost (IAS 39 only)

IAS 39 allows, as a practical expedient, creditors to measure the impairment of a financial asset carried at amortised cost based on an instrument's fair value using an observable market price (see Chapter 49). *[IAS 39.AG84].* If the practical expedient is used, IFRS 13 applies to the measurement of fair value.

When the practical expedient is not used, the measurement objective is not intended to be fair value (and IFRS 13 would not apply). Instead, IAS 39's requirements for measuring the impairment of the financial asset carried at amortised cost would apply.

2.5 Measurement exceptions and practical expedients within IFRS 13

2.5.1 Practical expedients in IFRS 13

In addition to maintaining the various practicability exceptions that existed in other IFRSs (as discussed at 2.4 above), IFRS 13 provides its own practical expedients for applying the fair value framework in certain instances. These practical expedients, each of which is discussed separately in this chapter, include the use of mid-market pricing within a bid-ask spread (see 15 below).

Under US GAAP, the equivalent standard, Topic 820 – *Fair Value Measurement* – in the FASB Accounting Standards Codification (ASC 820), provides a practical expedient to measure the fair value of certain investments in investment companies using net asset value (NAV) or its equivalent if certain criteria are met. However, IFRS 13 does not explicitly permit the use of NAV to estimate the fair value of certain alternative investments. Therefore, under IFRS, NAV cannot be presumed to equal fair value, as the asset that is being measured is the equity investment in an investment entity, not the underlying assets (and liabilities) of the investment entity itself. While NAV may represent the fair value of the equity interest in certain situations (for example, in situations where an open-ended fund provides a source of liquidity through on-going subscriptions and redemptions at NAV), one cannot presume this to be the case. Instead, the characteristics of the investment being measured need be considered when determining its fair value (differences from US GAAP are discussed further at 23 below).

If a quoted price in an active market for an identical instrument is available (i.e. a Level 1 input), the fair value of the equity instrument would need to be measured using that price, even if this deviates from NAV. An example where the Level 1 input may differ from NAV is shares in certain closed-end funds that trade on exchanges at prices that differ from the reported NAV of the funds.

In situations where there is no quoted price for an identical instrument, reported NAV may represent a starting point in estimating fair value. However, adjustments may be required to reflect the specific characteristics that market participants would consider in pricing the equity investment in an investment entity. It may be helpful to understand the factors that would reconcile a reported NAV of the investment entity to the fair value used by the reporting entity in order to provide explanations to investors, if necessary, and to support disclosures required by IFRS 13 and other IFRSs. Factors to consider include, but are not limited to, the following:

(a) Is the reported NAV an appropriate input for use in measuring fair value?

Before concluding that the reported NAV is an appropriate input when measuring fair value, a reporting entity should evaluate the effectiveness of the investment entity's valuation practices, by considering the valuation techniques and inputs used by the investment entity when estimating NAV. This assists in determining whether the investment entity's valuation practices and inputs are aligned with those that would need to be used by a market participant in respect of the equity instruments of the investment entity.

(b) Are adjustments to reported NAV needed to reflect characteristics that market participants would consider in pricing an equity investment?

A reporting entity should consider the characteristics of the equity investment that are not reflected in reported NAV. The fair value of the underlying assets within an investment entity would, for example, ignore any restrictions or possible obligations imposed on the holder of an equity investment in an investment entity.

Obligations may take the form of commitments to contribute further capital, as and when called for by the investment entity. If market participants would be expected to place a discount or premium on the reported NAV because of features, risk or other factors relating to the equity investment, then the fair value measurement of the investment would need to be adjusted for that factor.

However, in some cases adjustments to NAV may not be required. For example, if a fund is open to new investors, presumably the fair value of the fund investment would not be expected to exceed the amount that a new investor would be required to invest directly with the fund to obtain a similar interest. Similarly, the hypothetical seller of a fund investment would not be expected to accept lower proceeds than it would receive by redeeming its investment directly with the fund (if possible). As such, the willingness and ability of an investment entity to provide a source of liquidity for the investment through subscriptions and redemptions are important considerations in assessing whether adjustments to NAV would be required in determining the exit price of an investment.

Information related to relevant secondary market transactions should be considered unless they are determined to be disorderly. Limited Partners in such funds may seek to sell their investments for a variety of reasons, including mergers or acquisitions, the need for liquidity or a change in strategy, among others. While premiums have been observed in practice, discounts on sales of investments in investment entities are also common. Likewise, sales of an investment in an investment entity to independent third parties at the reported NAV without a premium or discount, may suggest that no adjustment is needed.

2.5.2 Measurement exception to the fair value principles for financial instruments

IFRS 13 makes it clear that the concepts of 'highest and best use' and 'valuation premise' only apply to the measurement of non-financial assets. Such concepts could have significantly changed the valuation of some over-the-counter (OTC) derivatives, many of which are measured on a portfolio basis. That is, reporting entities typically determine valuation adjustments related to bid-ask spreads and credit risk for OTC derivative contracts considering the net exposure of a portfolio of contracts to a particular market risk or credit risk. To address this concern, IFRS 13 provides an exception to the principles of fair value when measuring financial instruments with offsetting risks, if certain criteria are met.

The exception allows an entity to estimate the fair value of a portfolio of financial instruments based on the sale or transfer of its net position for a particular market risk exposure (rather than to the individual instruments in the portfolio). The exception also enables an entity to consider its credit exposure to a particular counterparty on a net basis, provided there is an arrangement in place that mitigates credit risk upon default (e.g. a master netting agreement).

See 12 below for additional discussion on measuring the fair value of financial assets and financial liabilities with offsetting risks.

3 DEFINITIONS

The following table summarises the terms that are defined in IFRS 13. *[IFRS 13 Appendix A]*.

Figure 14.1: IFRS 13 Definitions

Term	Definition
Active market	A market in which transactions for the asset or liability take place with sufficient frequency and volume to provide pricing information on an ongoing basis.
Cost approach	A valuation technique that reflects the amount that would be required currently to replace the service capacity of an asset (often referred to as current replacement cost).
Entry price	The price paid to acquire an asset or received to assume a liability in an exchange transaction.
Exit price	The price that would be received to sell an asset or paid to transfer a liability.
Expected cash flow	The probability-weighted average (i.e. mean of the distribution) of possible future cash flows.
Fair value	The price that would be received to sell an asset or paid to transfer a liability in an orderly transaction between market participants at the measurement date.
Highest and best use	The use of a non-financial asset by market participants that would maximise the value of the asset or the group of assets and liabilities (e.g. a business) within which the asset would be used.
Income approach	Valuation techniques that convert future amounts (e.g. cash flows or income and expenses) to a single current (i.e. discounted) amount. The fair value measurement is determined on the basis of the value indicated by current market expectations about those future amounts.
Inputs	The assumptions that market participants would use when pricing the asset or liability, including assumptions about risk, such as the following: (a) the risk inherent in a particular valuation technique used to measure fair value (such as a pricing model); and (b) the risk inherent in the inputs to the valuation technique. Inputs may be observable or unobservable.
Level 1 inputs	Quoted prices (unadjusted) in active markets for identical assets or liabilities that the entity can access at the measurement date.
Level 2 inputs	Inputs other than quoted prices included within Level 1 that are observable for the asset or liability, either directly or indirectly.
Level 3 inputs	Unobservable inputs for the asset or liability.
Market approach	A valuation technique that uses prices and other relevant information generated by market transactions involving identical or comparable (i.e. similar) assets, liabilities or a group of assets and liabilities, such as a business.
Market-corroborated inputs	Inputs that are derived principally from or corroborated by observable market data by correlation or other means.

Term	Definition
Market participant	Buyers and sellers in the principal (or most advantageous) market for the asset or liability that have all of the following characteristics: (a) They are independent of each other, i.e. they are not related parties as defined in IAS 24 – *Related Party Disclosures* (see Chapter 37), although the price in a related party transaction may be used as an input to a fair value measurement if the entity has evidence that the transaction was entered into at market terms. (b) They are knowledgeable, having a reasonable understanding about the asset or liability and the transaction using all available information, including information that might be obtained through due diligence efforts that are usual and customary. (c) They are able to enter into a transaction for the asset or liability. (d) They are willing to enter into a transaction for the asset or liability, i.e. they are motivated but not forced or otherwise compelled to do so.
Most advantageous market	The market that maximises the amount that would be received to sell the asset or minimises the amount that would be paid to transfer the liability, after taking into account transaction costs and transport costs.
Non-performance risk	The risk that an entity will not fulfil an obligation. Non-performance risk includes, but may not be limited to, the entity's own credit risk.
Observable inputs	Inputs that are developed using market data, such as publicly available information about actual events or transactions, and that reflect the assumptions that market participants would use when pricing the asset or liability.
Orderly transaction	A transaction that assumes exposure to the market for a period before the measurement date to allow for marketing activities that are usual and customary for transactions involving such assets or liabilities; it is not a forced transaction (e.g. a forced liquidation or distress sale).
Principal market	The market with the greatest volume and level of activity for the asset or liability.
Risk premium	Compensation sought by risk-averse market participants for bearing the uncertainty inherent in the cash flows of an asset or a liability. Also referred to as a 'risk adjustment'.
Transaction costs	The costs to sell an asset or transfer a liability in the principal (or most advantageous) market for the asset or liability that are directly attributable to the disposal of the asset or the transfer of the liability and meet both of the following criteria: (a) They result directly from and are essential to that transaction. (b) They would not have been incurred by the entity had the decision to sell the asset or transfer the liability not been made (similar to costs to sell, as defined in IFRS 5).
Transport costs	The costs that would be incurred to transport an asset from its current location to its principal (or most advantageous) market.
Unit of account	The level at which an asset or a liability is aggregated or disaggregated in an IFRS for recognition purposes.
Unobservable inputs	Inputs for which market data are not available and that are developed using the best information available about the assumptions that market participants would use when pricing the asset or liability.

Credit risk and *market risk* are defined in IFRS 7 (see Chapter 54).

Key management personnel is defined in IAS 24 (see Chapter 37).

4 THE FAIR VALUE FRAMEWORK

4.1 Definition of fair value

Fair value is defined as 'the price that would be received to sell an asset or paid to transfer a liability in an orderly transaction between market participants at the measurement date'. *[IFRS 13.9]*.

The definition of fair value in IFRS 13 is not significantly different from previous definitions in IFRS – that is, 'the amount for which an asset could be exchanged, or a liability settled, between knowledgeable, willing parties in an arm's length transaction'. *[IFRS 13.BC29]*. However, the definition in IFRS 13 and its guidance in the fair value framework clarify the following:

- The definition of fair value in IFRS 13 is a current exit price, not an entry price. *[IFRS 13.BC36]*.

  The exit price for an asset or liability is conceptually different from its transaction price (an entry price). While exit and entry prices may be identical in many situations, the transaction price is not presumed to represent the fair value of an asset or liability on its initial recognition as measured in accordance with IFRS 13.

- The exit price objective of a fair value measurement applies regardless of the reporting entity's intent and/or ability to sell the asset or transfer the liability at the measurement date. *[IFRS 13.BC39, BC40]*. Fair value is the exit price in the principal market (or in the absence of a principal market, the most advantageous market – see 6 below – in which the reporting entity would transact). However, the price in the exit market should not be adjusted for transaction costs – i.e. transaction costs incurred to acquire an item are not added to the price used to measure fair value and transaction costs incurred to sell an item are not deducted from the price used to measure fair value. *[IFRS 13.25]*.

  In addition, fair value is a market-based measurement, not an entity-specific measurement, and, as such, is determined based on the assumptions that market participants would use when pricing the asset or liability. *[IFRS 13.BC31]*.

- A fair value measurement contemplates the sale of an asset or transfer of a liability, not a transaction to offset the risks associated with an asset or liability (see 8 below for further discussion).

- The transaction to sell the asset or transfer the liability is a hypothetical transaction as at the measurement date that is assumed to be orderly and considers an appropriate period of exposure to the market (see 8 below for further discussion). *[IFRS 13.15].*
- The objective of a fair value measurement does not change based on the level of activity in the exit market or the valuation technique(s) used. That is, fair value remains a market-based exit price that considers the current market conditions as at the measurement date, even if there has been a significant decrease in the volume and level of activity for the asset or liability. *[IFRS 13.2, B41].*

4.2 The fair value measurement framework

In addition to providing a single definition of fair value, IFRS 13 includes a framework for applying this definition to financial reporting. Many of the key concepts used in the fair value framework are interrelated and their interaction should be considered in the context of the entire approach.

As discussed at 1.3 above, the objective of a fair value measurement is 'to estimate the price at which an orderly transaction to sell the asset or to transfer the liability would take place between market participants at the measurement date under current market conditions'. *[IFRS 13.B2].*

In light of this objective, when measuring fair value, an entity must determine all of the following:

(a) the particular asset or liability that is the subject of the measurement (consistent with its unit of account – see 5 below);

(b) for a non-financial asset, the valuation premise that is appropriate for the measurement (consistent with its highest and best use – see 10 below);

(c) the principal (or most advantageous) market for the asset or liability (see 6 below); and

(d) the valuation technique(s) appropriate for the measurement (see 14 below), considering the availability of data with which to develop inputs (see 15 below) that represent the assumptions that market participants would use when pricing the asset or liability (see 7 below) and the level of the fair value hierarchy within which the inputs are categorised (see 16 below). *[IFRS 13.B2].*

The following diagram illustrates our view of the interdependence of the various components of the fair value measurement framework in IFRS 13.

Figure 14.2: The fair value measurement framework

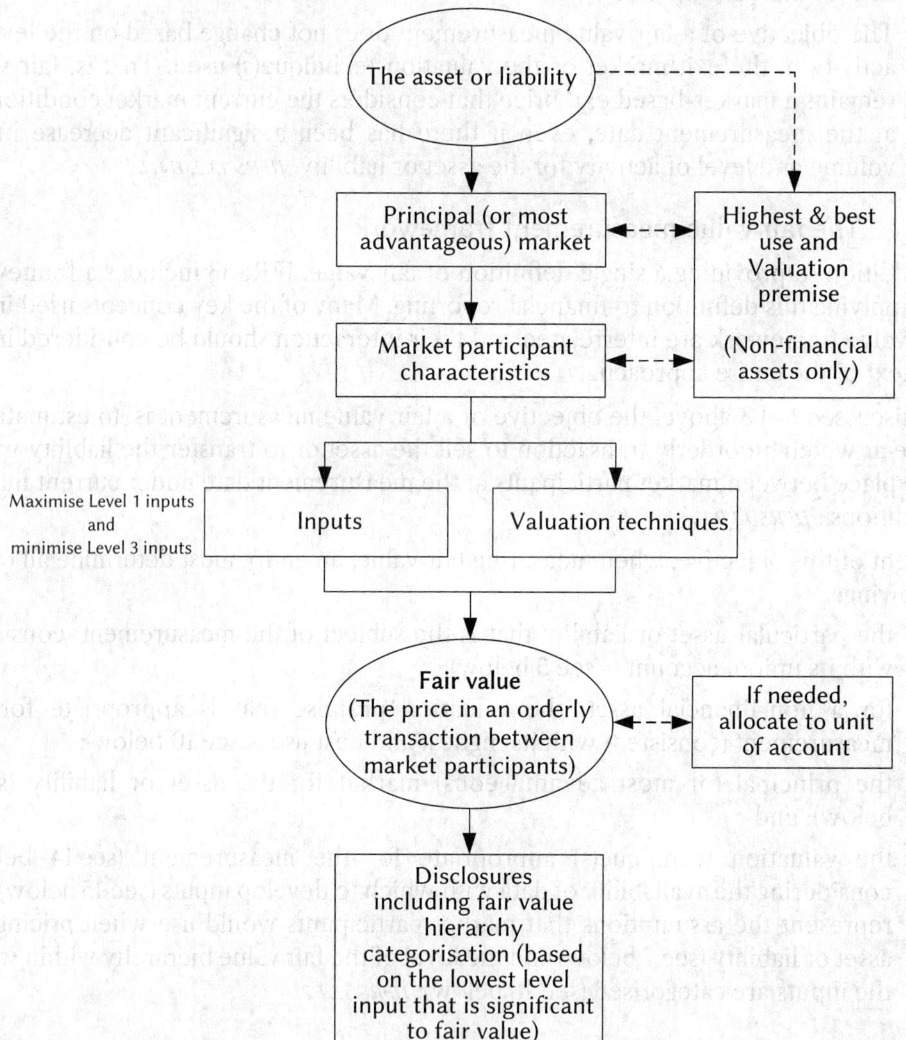

In practice, navigating the fair value framework may be more straight-forward for certain types of assets (e.g. assets that trade in a formalised market) than for others (e.g. intangible assets). For non-financial assets that derive value when used in combination with other assets or for which a developed market does not exist, resolving the circular nature of the relationship between valuation premise, highest and best use and exit market is important in applying the fair value framework (refer to 10 below for additional discussion on the fair value measurement of non-financial assets).

IFRS 13 clarifies that the concepts of 'highest and best use' and 'valuation premise' are only applicable when determining the fair value of non-financial assets. Therefore, the fair value framework is applied differently to non-financial assets versus other items, such as financial instruments, non-financial liabilities and instruments classified in a reporting entity's shareholders' equity (refer to 12 below for additional discussion on the fair value of financial instruments with offsetting positions and to 11 below for the fair value measurement of liabilities and instruments classified in an entity's shareholders' equity). Although there are differences in the application of the fair value framework for non-financial assets, the objective of the fair value measurement remains the same, that is, an exit price in the principal (or most advantageous) market.

As discussed in more detail at 12 below, IFRS 13 provides an exception to the principles of fair value, allowing entities to measure a group of financial instruments based on the price to sell (or transfer) its net position for a particular risk exposure, if certain criteria are met. The use of this exception may require a reporting entity to allocate portfolio-level valuation adjustments to the appropriate unit of account.

5 THE ASSET OR LIABILITY

IFRS 13 states that a fair value measurement is for a particular asset or liability, which is different from the price to offset certain of the risks associated with that particular asset or liability.

This is an important distinction, particularly in the valuation of certain financial instruments that are typically not 'exited' through a sale or transfer, but whose risks are hedged through other transactions (e.g. derivatives). However, IFRS 13 does allow for financial instruments with offsetting risks to be measured based on their net risk exposure to a particular risk, in contrast to the assets or liabilities that give rise to this exposure (see 12 below for additional discussion on the criteria to qualify for this measurement exception and application considerations).

5.1 The unit of account

The identification of exactly what asset or liability is being measured is fundamental to determining its fair value. Fair value may need to be measured for either:

- a stand-alone asset or liability (e.g. a financial instrument or an operating asset); or
- a group of assets, a group of liabilities, or a group of assets and liabilities (e.g. a cash-generating unit or a business).

The unit of account defines what is being measured for financial reporting purposes. It is an accounting concept that determines the level at which an asset or liability is aggregated or disaggregated for the purpose of applying IFRS 13, as well as other standards.

Unless specifically addressed in IFRS 13 (see 5.1.1 and 5.1.2 below), the appropriate unit of account is determined by the applicable IFRS (i.e. the standard that permits or requires the fair value measurement or disclosure). *[IFRS 13.13, 14].* Assume, for example, that an investment property is valued at CU100. Further assume that the investment property is owned by a single asset entity (or corporate wrapper) and the shares in the entity are only valued at CU90. If another entity were to acquire the shares of the single asset entity for CU90, at acquisition, the entity would allocate the purchase price to the property inside it. The property would, therefore, initially be recognised at CU90. Assume that, at year-end, the fair value of the property is CU110 and that the entity measures the property at fair value in accordance with IAS 40. Assume that the fair value of the shares in the single asset entity are CU99. IAS 40 requires that an entity measure an investment property, not the shares of a single entity that owns it. As such, the property would be measured at its fair value of CU110.[3]

5.1.1 Unit of account and P×Q

IFRS 13 does specify the unit of account to be used when measuring fair value in relation to a reporting entity that holds a position in a single asset or liability that is traded in an active market (including a position comprising a large number of identical assets or liabilities, such as a holding of financial instruments). In this situation, IFRS 13 requires an entity to measure the asset or liability based on the product of the quoted price for the individual asset or liability and the quantity held (P×Q).

This requirement is generally accepted when the asset or liability being measured is a financial instrument in the scope of IFRS 9 (or IAS 39). However, when an entity holds an investment in a listed subsidiary, joint venture or associate, some believe the unit of account is the entire holding and the fair value should include an adjustment (e.g. a control premium) to reflect the value of the investor's control, joint control or significant influence over their investment as a whole.

Questions have also arisen as to how this requirement applies to cash-generating units that are equivalent to listed investments. Some argue that, because IAS 36 requires certain assets and liabilities to be excluded from a cash-generating unit (CGU), the unit of account is not identical to a listed subsidiary, joint venture or associate and an entity can include adjustments that are consistent with the CGU as a whole. Some similarly argue that approach is appropriate because, in group financial statements, an entity is accounting for the assets and liabilities of consolidated entities, rather than the investment. However, others argue that if the CGU is effectively the same as an entity's investment in a listed subsidiary, joint venture or associate, the requirement to use P×Q should apply.

IFRS 13 requires entities to select inputs that are consistent with the characteristics of the asset or liability being measured and would be considered by market participants when pricing the asset or liability (see 7.2 below). Apart from block discounts (which are specifically prohibited), determining whether a premium or discount applies to a particular fair value measurement requires judgement and depends on specific facts and circumstances.

As discussed at 15.2 below, the standard indicates that premiums or discounts should not be incorporated into fair value measurements unless all of the following conditions are met:

- the application of the premium or discount reflects the characteristics of the asset or liability being measured;
- market participants, acting in their economic best interest, would consider these premiums or discounts when pricing the asset or liability; and
- the inclusion of the premium or discount is not inconsistent with the unit of account in the IFRS that requires (or permits) the fair value measurement.

Therefore, when an entity holds an investment in a listed subsidiary, joint venture or associate, if the unit of account is deemed to be the entire holding, it would be appropriate to include, for example, a control premium when determining fair value, provided that market participants would take this into consideration when pricing the asset. If, however, the unit of account is deemed to be the individual share of the listed subsidiary, joint venture or associate, the requirement to use P×Q (without adjustment) to measure the fair value would override the requirements in IFRS 13 that permit premiums or discounts to be included in certain circumstances.

In September 2014, in response to these questions regarding the unit of account for an investment in a listed subsidiary, joint venture or associate, the IASB proposed amendments to clarify that:[4]

- The unit of account for investments in subsidiaries, joint ventures and associates should be the investment as a whole and not the individual financial instruments that constitute the investment.
- For investments that are comprised of financial instruments for which a quoted price in an active market is available, the requirement to use P×Q would take precedence, irrespective of the unit of account. Therefore, for all such investments, the fair value measurement would be the product of P×Q, even when the reporting entity has an interest that gives it control, joint control or significant influence over the investee.
- When testing CGUs for impairment, if those CGUs correspond to an entity whose financial instruments are quoted in an active market, the fair value measurement would be the product of P×Q.

  When testing for impairment in accordance with IAS 36, the recoverable amount of a CGU is the higher of its value in use or fair value less costs of disposal. The fair value component of fair value less costs of disposal is required to be measured in accordance with IFRS 13.

  When a CGU effectively corresponds to a listed entity, the same issue arises regarding whether the requirement to use P×Q, without adjustment, to measure fair value applies.

  Consistent with its proposal in relation to listed investments in subsidiaries, joint ventures and associates, the IASB proposed that, if the CGU corresponds to an entity whose financial instruments are quoted in an active market, the requirement to use P×Q would apply.

The exposure draft also included proposed clarifications for the portfolio exception, discussed at 5.1.2 below.

The IASB proposed the following transition requirements:

- For quoted investments in subsidiaries, joint ventures and associates, an entity would recognise a cumulative catch-up adjustment to opening retained earnings for the period in which the proposed amendments are first applied. The entity would then recognise the change in measurement of the quoted investments during that period in profit or loss (i.e. retrospective application).
- For impairment testing in accordance with IAS 36, an entity would apply the requirements on a prospective basis. If an entity incurs an impairment loss or reversal during the period of initial application, it would provide quantitative information about the likely effect on the impairment loss, or reversal amount, had the amendments been applied in the immediately preceding period presented.

The exposure draft did not include a proposed effective date. However, permitting early adoption was proposed. Furthermore, the Board proposed that a first-time adopter of IFRS be able to apply the amendments at the beginning of the earliest period for which it presents full comparative information under IFRS in its first IFRS financial statements (i.e. prospectively from the date of the first-time adopter's transition to IFRS). The comment period for this exposure draft ended on 16 January 2015 and the Board began redeliberations in March 2015. During redeliberations, additional research was undertaken on fair value measurements of investments in subsidiaries, associates and joint ventures that are quoted in an active market and on the measurement of the recoverable amount of cash-generating units on the basis of fair value less costs of disposal when the cash-generating unit is an entity that is quoted in an active market.

Following the redeliberations, in its January 2016 meeting, the IASB concluded that the research would be fed into the Post-implementation Review (PIR) of IFRS 13.[5]

In the Request for Information, the Board specifically asked about prioritising Level 1 inputs in relation to the unit of account. This feedback will be considered to determine if further work on this topic is required.[6]

5.1.2 *Unit of account and the portfolio exception*

There is some debate about whether IFRS 13 prescribes the unit of account in relation to the portfolio exception. Under IFRS 13, a reporting entity that manages a group of financial assets and financial liabilities with offsetting risks on the basis of its net exposure to market or credit risks is allowed to measure the group based on the price that would be received to sell its net long position, or paid to transfer its net short position, for a particular risk (if certain criteria are met).

Some believe the portfolio exception in IFRS 13 specifies the unit of measurement for any financial instruments within the portfolio(s), i.e. that the net exposure of the identified group to a particular risk, and not the individual instruments within the group, represents the new unit of measurement. This may have a number of consequences. For example, the entity may be able to include premiums or discounts in the fair value measurement of the portfolio that are consistent with that unit of account, but not the individual instruments that make up the portfolio. In addition, because the net exposure for the identified group may not be actively traded (even though some financial instruments within the portfolio may be) P×Q may not be applied to the actively traded instruments within the portfolio.

Others believe that the portfolio exception does not override the unit of account as provided in IFRS 9 (or IAS 39). Therefore, any premiums or discounts that are inconsistent with this unit of account, i.e. the individual financial instruments within the portfolio, would be excluded from the fair value measurement under the portfolio exception, including any premiums or discounts related to the size of the portfolio.

Regardless of which view is taken, it is clear in the standard that the portfolio exception does not change the financial statement presentation requirements (see 12 below for further discussion on the portfolio exception and 15 below for further discussion on premiums and discounts).

In the US, ASC 820 has been interpreted by many as prescribing the unit of measurement when the portfolio exception is used. That is, when the portfolio approach is used to measure an entity's net exposure to a particular market risk, the net position becomes the unit of measurement. This view is consistent with how many US financial institutions determined the fair value of their over-the-counter derivative portfolios prior to the amendments to ASC 820 (ASU 2011-04)[7] (see 23 below). We understand that the IASB did not intend application of the portfolio exception to override the requirements in IFRS 13 regarding the use of P×Q to measure instruments traded in active markets and the prohibition on block discounts which raises questions as to how the portfolio exception would be applied to Level 1 instruments.

In 2013, the IFRS Interpretations Committee referred a request to the Board on the interaction between the use of Level 1 inputs and the portfolio exception. The IASB noted that this issue had similarities with the issues of the interaction between the use of Level 1 inputs and the unit of account that arises when measuring the fair value of investments in listed subsidiaries, joint ventures and associates (see 5.1.1 above). The IASB discussed this issue in December 2013, but only in relation to portfolios that comprise only Level 1 financial instruments whose market risks are substantially the same. For that specific circumstance, the Board tentatively decided that the measurement of such portfolios should be the one that results from multiplying the net position by the Level 1 prices (e.g. multiplying the net long or short position by the Level 1 price for either a gross long or short position). Given this tentative decision, in September 2014 the IASB proposed adding a non-authoritative example to illustrate the application of the portfolio exception in this specific circumstance.[8] After reviewing the comments received on the proposal, the Board concluded that it was not necessary to add the proposed non-authoritative illustrative example to IFRS 13 (see 12.2 below for further discussion) because the example would have been non-authoritative and the comments received did not reveal significant diversity in practice for the specific circumstance of portfolios that comprise only Level 1 financial instruments whose market risks are substantially the same.[9]

5.1.3 Unit of account versus the valuation premise

In valuing non-financial assets, the concepts of 'unit of account' and 'valuation premise' are distinct, even though both concepts deal with determining the appropriate level of aggregation (or disaggregation) for assets and liabilities. The unit of account identifies what is being measured for financial reporting and drives the level of aggregation (or disaggregation) for presentation and disclosure purposes (e.g. whether categorisation in the fair value hierarchy is determined at the individual asset level or for a group of assets). Valuation premise is a valuation concept that addresses how a non-financial asset derives its maximum value to market participants, either on a stand-alone basis or through its use in combination with other assets and liabilities.

Since financial instruments do not have alternative uses and their fair values typically do not depend on their use within a group of other assets or liabilities, the concepts of highest and best use and valuation premise are not relevant for financial instruments. As a result, the fair value for financial instruments should be largely based on the unit of account prescribed by the standard that requires (or permits) the fair value measurement.

The distinction between these two concepts becomes clear when the unit of account of a non-financial asset differs from its valuation premise. Consider an asset (e.g. customised machinery) that was acquired other than by way of a business combination, along with other assets as part of an operating line. Although the unit of account for the customised machinery may be as a stand-alone asset (i.e. it is presented for financial reporting purposes at the individual asset level in accordance with IAS 16 – *Property, Plant and Equipment*), the determination of the fair value of the machinery may be derived from its use with other assets in the operating line (see 10 below for additional discussion on the concept of valuation premise).

5.1.4 Does IFRS 13 allow fair value to be measured by reference to an asset's (or liability's) components?

IFRS 13 states that the objective of a fair value measurement is to determine the price that would be received for an asset or paid to transfer a liability at the measurement date. That is, a fair value measurement is to be determined for a particular asset or liability. The unit of account determines what is being measured by reference to the level at which the asset or liability is aggregated (or disaggregated) for accounting purposes.

Unless separation of an asset (or liability) into its component parts is required or allowed under IFRS (e.g. a requirement to separate under IFRS 9 (or IAS 39)), we generally do not believe it is appropriate to consider the unit of account at a level below that of the legal form of the asset or liability being measured. A valuation methodology that uses a 'sum-of-the-parts' approach may still be appropriate under IFRS 13; for example, when measuring complex financial instruments, entities often use valuation methodologies that attempt to determine the value of the entire instrument based on its component parts.

However, in situations where fair value can be determined for an asset or liability as a whole, we would generally not expect that an entity would use a higher amount to measure fair value because the sum of the parts exceeds the whole. Using a higher value inherently suggests that the asset would be broken down and the various components or risk attributes transferred to different market participants who would pay more for the pieces than a market participant would for the asset or liability as a whole. Such an approach is not consistent with IFRS 13's principles, which contemplate the sale of an asset or transfer of a liability (consistent with its unit of account) in a single transaction.

5.2 Characteristics of the asset or liability

When measuring fair value, IFRS 13 requires an entity to consider the characteristics of the asset or liability. For example, age and miles flown are attributes to be considered in determining a fair value measure for an aircraft. Examples of such characteristics could include:

- the condition and location of an asset; and
- restrictions, if any, on the sale or use of an asset or transfer of a liability (see 5.2.2, 10.1 and 11.4 below).

The fair value of the asset or liability must take into account those characteristics that market participants would take into consideration when pricing the asset or liability at the measurement date. *[IFRS 13.11, 12]*. For example, when valuing individual shares in an unlisted company, market participants might consider factors such as the nature of the company's operations; its performance to date and forecast future performance; and how the business is funded, including whether it is highly leveraged.

The requirement to consider the characteristics of the asset or liability being measured is not new to fair value measurement under IFRS. For example, prior to the issuance of IFRS 13, IAS 41 referred to measuring the fair value of a biological asset or agricultural produce in its present location and condition and IAS 40 stated that an entity should identify any differences between the investment property being measured at fair value and similar properties for which observable market prices are available and make the appropriate adjustments for those differences. *[IFRS 13.BC46].*

5.2.1 Condition and location

An asset may not be in the condition or location that market participants would require for its sale at an observable market price. In order to determine the fair value of the asset as it currently exists, the market price needs to be adjusted to the price market participants would be prepared to pay for the asset in its current condition and location. This includes deducting the cost of transporting the asset to the market, if location is a characteristic of the asset being measured, and may include deducting the costs of converting or transforming the asset, as well as a normal profit margin.

For non-financial assets, condition and location considerations may influence, or be dependent on, the highest and best use of an asset (see 10 below). That is, an asset's highest and best use may require an asset to be in a different condition. However, the objective of a fair value measurement is to determine the price for the asset in its current form. Therefore, if no market exists for an asset in its current form, but there is a market for the converted or transformed asset, an entity could adjust this market price for the costs a market participant would incur to re-condition the asset (after acquiring the asset in its current condition) and the compensation they would expect for the effort. Example 14.1 below illustrates how costs to convert or transform an asset might be considered in determining fair value based on the current use of the asset.

Example 14.1: Adjusting fair value for condition and location

An entity owns a forest. The trees take approximately 25 years to mature, after which they can be cut down and sold. The average age of the trees in the forest is 14 years at the end of the reporting period. The current use of the forest is presumed to be its highest and best use.

There is no market for the trees in their current form. However, there is a market for the harvested timber from trees aged 25 years or older. To measure the fair value of the forest, the entity uses an income approach and uses the price for 25 year-old harvested timber in the market today as an input. However, since the trees are not yet ready for harvest, the cash flows must be adjusted for the costs a market participant would incur. Therefore, the estimated cash flows include costs to manage the forest (including silviculture activities, such as fertilising and pruning the trees) until the trees reach maturity; costs to harvest the trees; and costs to transport the harvested logs to the market. The entity estimates these costs using market participant assumptions. The entity also adjusts the value for a normal profit margin because a market participant acquiring the forest today would expect to be compensated for the cost and effort of managing the forest for the period (i.e. 11 years) before the trees will be harvested and the timber is sold (i.e. this would include compensation for costs incurred and a normal profit margin for the effort of managing the forest).

5.2.2 Restrictions on assets or liabilities

IFRS 13 indicates that the effect on fair value of a restriction on the sale or use of an asset will differ depending on whether the restriction is deemed to be a characteristic of the asset or the entity holding the asset. A restriction that would transfer with the asset in an assumed sale would generally be deemed a characteristic of the asset and, therefore, would likely be considered by market participants when pricing the asset. Conversely, a restriction that is specific to the entity holding the asset would not transfer with the asset in an assumed sale and, therefore, would not be considered when measuring fair value. Determining whether a restriction is a characteristic of the asset or of the entity holding the asset may be contractual in some cases. In other cases, this determination may require judgement based on the specific facts and circumstances.

The following illustrative examples highlight the distinction between restrictions that are characteristics of the asset and those of the entity holding the asset, including how this determination affects the fair value measurement. *[IFRS 13.IE28-29]*. Restrictions on non-financial assets are discussed further at 10 below.

Example 14.2: Restrictions on assets

An entity holds an equity instrument for which sale is legally restricted for a specified period. The restriction is a characteristic of the instrument that would transfer to market participants. As such, the fair value of the instrument would be measured based on the quoted price for an otherwise identical unrestricted equity instrument that trades in a public market, adjusted for the effect of the restriction. The adjustment would reflect the discount market participants would demand for the risk relating to the inability to access a public market for the instrument for the specified period. The adjustment would vary depending on:

- the nature and duration of the restriction;
- the extent to which buyers are limited by the restriction; and
- qualitative and quantitative factors specific to both the instrument and the issuer.

Example 14.3: Entity-specific restrictions on assets

A donor of land specifies that the land must be used by a sporting association as a playground in perpetuity. Upon review of relevant documentation, the association determines that the donor's restriction would not transfer to market participants if the association sold the asset (i.e. the restriction on the use of the land is specific to the association). Furthermore, the association is not restricted from selling the land. Without the restriction on the use of the land, the land could be used as a site for residential development. In addition, the land is subject to an easement (a legal right that enables a utility to run power lines across the land).

Under these circumstances, the effect of the restriction and the easement on the fair value measurement of the land is as follows:

(a) Donor restriction on use of land – The donor restriction on the use of the land is specific to the association and thus would not transfer to market participants. Therefore, regardless of the restriction on the use of the land by the association, the fair value of the land would be measured based on the higher of its indicated value:
   (i) As a playground (i.e. the maximum value of the land is through its use in combination with other assets or with other assets and liabilities); or
   (ii) As a residential development (i.e. the fair value of the asset would be maximised through its use by market participants on a stand-alone basis).

(b) Easement for utility lines – Because the easement for utility lines is a characteristic of the land, this easement would be transferred to market participants with the land. The fair value of the land would include the effect of the easement, regardless of whether the land's valuation premise is as a playground or as a site for residential development.

In contrast to Example 14.2 above, Example 14.3 illustrates a restriction on the use of donated land that applies to a specific entity, but not to other market participants.

The calculation of the fair value should take account of any restrictions on the sale or use of an asset, if those restrictions relate to the asset rather than to the holder of the asset and the market participant would take those restrictions into account in his determination of the price that he is prepared to pay.

A liability or an entity's own equity instrument may be subject to restrictions that prevent the transfer of the item. When measuring the fair value of a liability or equity instrument, IFRS 13 does not allow an entity to include a separate input (or an adjustment to other inputs) for such restrictions. This is because the effect of the restriction is either implicitly or explicitly included in other inputs to the fair value measurement. Restrictions on liabilities and an entity's own equity are discussed further at 11 below.

IFRS 13 has different treatments for restrictions on assets and those over liabilities. The IASB believes this is appropriate because restrictions on the transfer of a liability relate to the performance of the obligation (i.e. the entity is legally obliged to satisfy the obligation and needs to do something to be relieved of the obligation), whereas restrictions on the transfer of an asset generally relate to the marketability of the asset. In addition, nearly all liabilities include a restriction preventing the transfer of the liability. In contrast, most assets do not include a similar restriction. As a result, the effect of a restriction preventing the transfer of a liability, theoretically, would be consistent for all liabilities and, therefore, would require no additional adjustment beyond the factors considered in determining the original transaction price. If an entity is aware that a restriction on the transfer of a liability is not already reflected in the price (or in the other inputs used in the measurement), it would adjust the price or inputs to reflect the existence of the restriction. *[IFRS 13.BC99, BC100]*. However, this would be rare because nearly all liabilities include a restriction and, when measuring fair value, market participants are assumed by IFRS 13 to be sufficiently knowledgeable about the liability to be transferred.

5.2.2.A In determining the fair value of a restricted security, is it appropriate to apply a constant discount percentage over the entire life of the restriction?

We generally do not believe a constant discount percentage should be used to measure the fair value of a restricted security because market participants would consider the remaining time on the security's restriction and that time period changes from period to period. Market participants, for example, would generally not assign the same discount for a restriction that terminates in one month, as they would for a two-year restriction.

One approach to value the restriction may be through an option pricing model that explicitly incorporates the duration of the restriction and the characteristics of the underlying security. The principal economic factor underlying a discount for lack of marketability is the increased risk resulting from the inability to quickly and efficiently return the investment to a cash position (i.e. the risk of a price decline during the restriction period). One way in which the price of this risk may be determined is by using an option pricing model that estimates the value of a protective put option. For example, restricted or non-marketable securities are acquired along with a separate option that provides the holder with the right to sell those shares at the current market price for unrestricted securities. The holder of such an option has, in effect, purchased marketability for the shares. The value of the put option may be considered an estimate of the discount for the lack of marketability associated with the restricted security. Other techniques or approaches may also be appropriate in measuring the discount associated with restricted securities.

6 THE PRINCIPAL (OR MOST ADVANTAGEOUS) MARKET

A fair value measurement contemplates an orderly transaction to sell the asset or transfer the liability in either:

(a) the principal market for the asset or liability; or

(b) in the absence of a principal market, the most advantageous market for the asset or liability. *[IFRS 13.16].*

IFRS 13 is clear that, if there is a principal market for the asset or liability, the fair value measurement represents the price in that market at the measurement date (regardless of whether that price is directly observable or estimated using another valuation technique). The price in the principal market must be used even if the price in a different market is potentially more advantageous. *[IFRS 13.18].* This is illustrated in Example 14.4. *[IFRS 13.E19-20].*

Example 14.4: The effect of determining the principal market

An asset is sold in two different active markets at different prices. An entity enters into transactions in both markets and can access the price in those markets for the asset at the measurement date.

	Market A	Market B
	CU	CU
Price that would be received	26	25
Transaction costs in that market	(3)	(1)
Costs to transport the asset to the market	(2)	(2)
Net amount that would be received	21	22

If Market A is the principal market for the asset (i.e. the market with the greatest volume and level of activity for the asset), the fair value of the asset would be measured using the price that would be received in that market, even though the net proceeds in Market B are more advantageous. In this case, the fair value would be CU 24, after taking into account transport costs.

The identification of a principal (or most advantageous) market could be impacted by whether there are observable markets for the item being measured. However, even where there is no observable market, fair value measurement assumes a transaction takes place at the measurement date. The assumed transaction establishes a basis for estimating the price to sell the asset or to transfer the liability. *[IFRS 13.21].*

6.1 The principal market

The principal market is the market for the asset or liability that has the greatest volume or level of activity for the asset or liability. *[IFRS 13 Appendix A].* There is a general presumption that the principal market is the one in which the entity would normally enter into a transaction to sell the asset or transfer the liability, unless there is evidence to the contrary. In practice, an entity would first consider the markets it can access. Then it would determine which of those markets has the greatest volume and liquidity in relation to the particular asset or liability. *[IFRS 13.17].* Management is not required to perform an exhaustive search to identify the principal market; however, it cannot ignore evidence that is reasonably available when considering which market has the greatest volume and level of activity. *[IFRS 13.17]*. For example, it may be appropriate to take into account information available in trade journals, if reliable market information about volumes transacted is available in such journals. Absent evidence to the contrary, the principal market is presumed to be the market in which an entity normally enters into transactions for the asset and liability.

The principal market is considered from the perspective of the reporting entity, which means that the principal market could be different for different entities (this is discussed further at 6.1.1 below). For example, a securities dealer may exit a financial instrument by selling it in the inter-dealer market, while a manufacturing company would sell a financial instrument in the retail market. The entity must be able to access the principal market as at the measurement date. Therefore, continuing with our example, it would not be appropriate for a manufacturing company to assume that it would transact in the inter-dealer market (even when considering a hypothetical transaction) because the company does not have access to this market.

Because IFRS 13 indicates that the principal market is determined from the perspective of the reporting entity, some have questioned whether the principal market should be determined on the basis of: (a) entity-specific volume (i.e. the market where the reporting entity has historically sold, or intends to sell, the asset with the greatest frequency and volume); or (b) market-based volume and activity. However, IFRS 13 is clear that the principal market for an asset or liability should be determined based on the market with the greatest volume and level of activity that the reporting entity can access. It is not determined based on the volume or level of activity of the reporting entity's transactions in a particular market. That is, the determination as to which market(s) a particular entity can access is entity-specific, but once the accessible markets are identified, market-based volume and activity determine the principal market. *[IFRS 13.BC52]*.

The recognition in IFRS 13 that different entities may sell identical instruments in different markets (and therefore at different exit prices) has important implications, particularly with respect to the initial recognition of certain financial instruments, such as derivatives. For example, a derivative contract between a dealer and a retail customer would likely be initially recorded at different fair values by the two entities, as they would exit the derivative in different markets and, therefore, at different exit prices. Day one gains and losses are discussed further at 13.2 below.

Although an entity must be able to access the market at the measurement date, IFRS 13 does not require an entity to be able to sell the particular asset or transfer the particular liability on that date. *[IFRS 13.20]*. For example, if there is a restriction on the sale of the asset, IFRS 13 simply requires that the entity be able to access the market for that asset when that restriction ceases to exist (it is important to note that the existence of the restriction may still affect the price a market participant would pay – see 5.2.2 above for discussion on restrictions on assets and liabilities).

In general, the market with the greatest volume and deepest liquidity will probably be the market in which the entity most frequently transacts. In these instances, the principal market would likely be the same as the most advantageous market (see 6.2 below).

Prior to the adoption of IFRS 13, some entities determined fair value based solely on the market where they transact with the greatest frequency (without considering other markets with greater volume and deeper liquidity). As noted above, IFRS 13 requires an entity to consider the market with the greatest volume and deepest liquidity for the asset. Therefore, an entity cannot presume a commonly used market is the principal market. For example, if an entity previously measured the fair value of agricultural produce based on its local market, but there is a deeper and more liquid market for the same agricultural produce (for which transportation costs are not prohibitive), the latter market would be deemed the principal market and would be used when measuring fair value.

6.1.1 Can an entity have more than one principal market for the same asset or liability?

IFRS 13 states that 'because different entities (and businesses within those entities) with different activities may have access to different markets, the principal (or most advantageous) market for the same asset or liability might be different for different entities (and businesses within those entities). Therefore, the principal (or most advantageous) market (and thus, market participants) shall be considered from the perspective of the entity, thereby allowing for differences between and among entities with different activities.' *[IFRS 13.19]*.

Therefore, in certain instances it may be appropriate for a reporting entity to determine that it has different principal markets for the same asset or liability. However, such a determination would need to be based on the reporting entity's business units engaging in different activities to ensure they were accessing different markets.

Determining the principal market is not based on management's intent. Therefore, we would not expect a reporting entity to have different principal markets for identical assets held within a business unit solely because management has different exit strategies for those assets.

Consider Example 14.5 below, in which multiple exit markets exist for an asset and the reporting entity has access to all of the various exit markets. The fact that a reporting entity (or business unit within a reporting entity) has historically exited virtually identical assets in different markets does not justify the entity utilising different exit markets in determining the fair value of these assets, unless the entity has different business units engaging in different activities. Instead, the concept of a principal market (and most advantageous market) implies that one consistent market should generally be considered in determining the fair value of these identical assets.

Example 14.5: Determining the principal market

The following three markets exist for a particular asset. The company has the ability to transact in all three markets (and has historically done so).

Market	Price
A	CU30,000
B	CU25,000
C	CU22,000

Under the principal market concept, it would not be appropriate to value identical assets at different prices solely because management intends to the sell the assets in different markets. Likewise, a consistent fair value measurement for each asset utilising a blended price that is determined based on the proportion of assets that management intends to sell in each market would not be appropriate. Instead, each of the assets would be measured at the price in the market determined to be the company's principal market.

If Market B were determined to represent the principal market for the asset being measured, each asset would be valued at CU 25,000. Selling the assets in either Market A or Market C would result in a gain or loss for the company. We believe this result is consistent with one of the fundamental concepts in the fair value framework. That is, the consequences of management's decisions (or a company's comparative advantages or disadvantages) should be recognised when those decisions are executed (or those advantages or disadvantages are achieved).

6.1.2 In situations where an entity has access to multiple markets, should the determination of the principal market be based on entity-specific volume and activity or market-based volume and activity?

In most instances, the market in which a reporting entity would sell an asset (or transfer a liability) with the greatest frequency will also represent the market with the greatest volume and deepest liquidity for all market participants. In these instances, the principal market would be the same regardless of whether it is determined based on entity-specific volume and activity or market-based volume and activity. However, when this is not the case, a reporting entity's principal market is determined using market-based volume.

Different entities engage in different activities. Therefore, some entities have access to certain markets that other entities do not. For example, an entity that does not function as a wholesaler would not have access to the wholesale market and, therefore, would need to look to the retail market as its principal market. Once the markets to which a particular entity has access have been identified, the determination of the principal market should not be based on management's intent or entity-specific volume, but rather should be based on the market with the greatest volume and level of activity for the asset or liability.

Example 14.6: Determining the principal market

The following three markets exist for Entity A's fleet of vehicles. Entity A has the ability to transact in all three markets (and has historically done so). As at the measurement date, the entity has 100 vehicles (same make, model and mileage) that it needs to measure at fair value. Volumes and prices in the respective markets are as follows:

Market	Price	The entity's volume for the asset in the market (based on history and/or intent)	Total market-based volume for the asset
A	CU30,000	60%	15%
B	CU25,000	25%	75%
C	CU20,000	15%	10%

Based on this information, Market B would be the principal market as this is the market in which the majority of transactions for the asset occur. As such, the fair value of the 100 cars as at the measurement date would be CU 2.5 million (i.e. CU 25,000 per car). Actual sales of the assets in either Market A or C would result in a gain or loss to the entity, i.e. when compared to the fair value of CU 25,000.

6.2 The most advantageous market

As noted above, if there is a principal market for the asset or liability being measured, fair value should be determined using the price in that market, even if the price in a different market is more advantageous at the measurement date.

Only in situations where there is no principal market for the asset or liability being measured, can an entity consider the most advantageous market. *[IFRS 13.16]*.

The most advantageous market is the one that maximises the amount that would be received to sell the asset or minimises the amount that would be paid to transfer the liability, after considering transaction costs and transport costs. *[IFRS 13 Appendix A]*.

This definition reasonably assumes that most entities transact with an intention to maximise profits or net assets. Assuming economically rational behaviour, the IASB observed that the principal market would generally represent the most advantageous market. However, when this is not the case, the IASB decided to prioritise the price in the most liquid market (i.e. the principal market) as this market provides the most representative input to determine fair value and also serves to increase consistency among reporting entities. *[IFRS 13.BC52]*.

When determining the most advantageous market, an entity must take into consideration the transaction costs and transportation costs it would incur to sell the asset or transfer the liability. The market that would yield the highest price after deducting these costs is the most advantageous market. This is illustrated in Example 14.7. *[IFRS 13.IE19.21-22]*.

Example 14.7: Determining the most advantageous market

Consider the same facts as in Example 14.4. If neither market is the principal market for the asset, the fair value of the asset would be measured using the price in the most advantageous market.

The most advantageous market is the market that maximises the amount that would be received to sell the asset, after taking into account transaction costs and transport costs (i.e. the net amount that would be received in the respective markets).

	Market A CU	Market B CU
Price that would be received	26	25
Transaction costs in that market	(3)	(1)
Costs to transport the asset to the market	(2)	(2)
Net amount that would be received	21	22

Because the entity would maximise the net amount that *would be received* for the asset in Market B (CU 22), that is the most advantageous market. Market B is the most advantageous market even though the fair value that would be recognised in that market (CU 23 = CU 25 – CU 2) is lower than in Market A (CU 24 = CU 26 – CU 2).

It is important to note that, while transaction costs and transportation costs are considered in determining the most advantageous market, the treatment of these costs in relation to measuring fair value differs (transaction costs and transportation costs are discussed further at 9 below).

7 MARKET PARTICIPANTS

When measuring fair value, an entity is required to use the assumptions that market participants would use when pricing the asset or liability. However, IFRS 13 does not require an entity to identify specific market participants. Instead, an entity must identify the characteristics of market participants that would generally transact for the asset or liability being measured. Determining these characteristics takes into consideration factors that are specific to the asset or liability; the principal (or most advantageous) market; and the market participants in that market. *[IFRS 13.22, 23]*. This determination, and how these characteristics affect a fair value measurement, may require significant judgement.

The principal (or most advantageous) market is determined from the perspective of the reporting entity (or business units within a reporting entity). As a result, other entities within the same industry as the reporting entity will most likely be considered market participants. However, market participants may come from outside of the reporting entity's industry, especially when considering the fair value of assets on a stand-alone basis. For example, a residential real estate development entity may be considered a market participant when measuring the fair value of land held by a manufacturing company if the highest and best use of the land is deemed to be residential real estate development.

7.1 Characteristics of market participants

IFRS 13 defines market participants as 'buyers and sellers in the principal (or most advantageous) market for the asset or liability'. *[IFRS 13 Appendix A]*.

IFRS 13 assumes that market participants have *all* of the following characteristics:

- they are independent of each other, that is, they are not related parties, as defined in IAS 24 (see Chapter 37);
- they are knowledgeable, having a reasonable understanding about the asset or liability using all available information, including information obtained through usual and customary due diligence efforts;
- they are able to enter into a transaction for the asset or liability; and
- they are willing to enter into a transaction for the asset or liability, that is, they are motivated but not forced or otherwise compelled to do so. *[IFRS 13.BC55-BC59]*.

Since market participants are independent of each other, the hypothetical transaction is assumed to take place between market participants at the measurement date, not between the reporting entity and another market participant. While market participants are not related parties, the standard does allow the price in a related party transaction to be used as an input in a fair value measurement provided the entity has evidence the transaction was entered into at market terms. *[IFRS 13.BC57]*.

Market participants in the principal (or most advantageous) market should have sufficient knowledge about the asset or liability for which they are transacting. The appropriate level of knowledge does not necessarily need to come from publicly available information, but could be obtained in the course of a normal due diligence process.

When determining potential market participants, certain characteristics should be considered. These include the legal capability and the operating and financial capacity to purchase the asset or assume the liability. Market participants must have both the willingness and the ability to transact for the item being measured. For example, when measuring the fair value less costs of disposal of a cash-generating unit (CGU), as part of testing the CGU for impairment in accordance with IAS 36, the market participants considered in the analysis should be in both a financial and operating position to purchase the CGU.

7.2 Market participant assumptions

IFRS 13 specifies that fair value is not the value specific to one entity, but rather is meant to be a market-based measurement. If market participants would consider adjustments for the inherent risk of the asset or liability, or consider the risk in the valuation technique used to measure fair value, then such risk adjustments should be considered in the fair value assumptions. For example, when measuring the fair value of certain financial instruments, market participants may include adjustments for liquidity, uncertainty and/or non-performance risk.

Fair value is not the value specific to the reporting entity and it is not the specific value to one market participant whose risk assessment or specific synergies may differ from other market participants. The reporting entity should consider those factors that market participants, in general, would consider. Fair value should not be measured based on a single market participant's assumptions or their specific intent or use of the asset or liability. To illustrate, assume a single market participant, Market Participant A, is willing to pay a higher price for an asset than the remaining market participants, due to specific synergies that only Market Participant A could achieve. In such a situation, fair value would not be the price that Market Participant A would be willing to pay for the asset. Instead, fair value would be the price that typical market participants would pay for the asset.

The underlying assumptions used in a fair value measurement are driven by the characteristics of the market participants that would transact for the item being measured and the factors those market participants would consider when pricing the asset or liability. Importantly, IFRS 13 notes that fair value should be based on assumptions that market participants acting in their 'economic best interest' would use when pricing an asset or liability. *[IFRS 13.22].* That is, market participants are assumed to transact in a manner that is consistent with the objective of maximising the value of their business, their net assets or profits. In certain instances, this may result in market participants considering premiums or discounts (e.g. control premiums or discounts for lack of marketability) when determining the price at which they would transact for a particular asset or liability (see 15.2 below for additional discussion on the consideration of premiums and discounts in a fair value measurement).

In situations where market observable data is not available, the reporting entity can use its own data as a basis for its assumptions. However, adjustments should be made to the entity's own data if readily available market data indicates that market participant assumptions would differ from the assumptions specific to that reporting entity (see 19 below for further discussion regarding Level 3 inputs).

The intended use and risk assumptions for an asset or asset group may differ among market participants transacting in the principal market for the asset. For example, the principal market in which the reporting entity would transact may contain both strategic and financial buyers. Both types of buyers would be considered in determining the characteristics of market participants; however, the fair value measurement of an asset may differ among these two types of market participants. The following example from the standard illustrates this point. *[IFRS 13.IE3-6].*

Example 14.8: Asset group

An entity acquires assets and assumes liabilities in a business combination. One of the groups of assets acquired comprises Assets A, B and C. Asset C is billing software integral to the business developed by the acquired entity for its own use in conjunction with Assets A and B (i.e. the related assets). The entity measures the fair value of each of the assets individually, consistently with the specified unit of account for the assets. The entity determines that the highest and best use of the assets is their current use and that each asset would provide maximum value to market participants principally through its use in combination with other assets or with other assets and liabilities (i.e. its complementary assets and the associated liabilities). There is no evidence to suggest that the current use of the assets is not their highest and best use.

In this situation, the entity would sell the assets in the market in which it initially acquired the assets (i.e. the entry and exit markets from the perspective of the entity are the same). Market participant buyers with whom the entity would enter into a transaction in that market have characteristics that are generally representative of both strategic buyers (such as competitors) and financial buyers (such as private equity or venture capital firms that do not have complementary investments) and include those buyers that initially bid for the assets. Although market participant buyers might be broadly classified as strategic or financial buyers, in many cases there will be differences among the market participant buyers within each of those groups, reflecting, for example, different uses for an asset and different operating strategies.

As discussed below, differences between the indicated fair values of the individual assets relate principally to the use of the assets by those market participants within different asset groups:

(a) Strategic buyer asset group – The entity determines that strategic buyers have related assets that would enhance the value of the group within which the assets would be used (i.e. market participant synergies). Those assets include a substitute asset for Asset C (the billing software), which would be used for only a limited transition period and could not be sold on its own at the end of that period. Because strategic buyers have substitute assets, Asset C would not be used for its full remaining economic life. The indicated fair values of Assets A, B and C within the strategic buyer asset group (reflecting the synergies resulting from the use of the assets within that group) are CU 360, CU 260 and CU 30, respectively. The indicated fair value of the assets as a group within the strategic buyer asset group is CU 650.

(b) Financial buyer asset group – The entity determines that financial buyers do not have related or substitute assets that would enhance the value of the group within which the assets would be used. Because financial buyers do not have substitute assets, Asset C (i.e. the billing software) would be used for its full remaining economic life. The indicated fair values of Assets A, B and C within the financial buyer asset group are CU 300, CU 200 and CU 100, respectively. The indicated fair value of the assets as a group within the financial buyer asset group is CU 600.

The fair values of Assets A, B and C would be determined on the basis of the use of the assets as a group within the strategic buyer group (CU 360, CU 260 and CU 30). Although the use of the assets within the strategic buyer group does not maximise the fair value of each of the assets individually, it maximises the fair value of the assets as a group (CU 650).

The example above illustrates that the principal (or most advantageous) market for an asset group may include different types of market participants (e.g. strategic and financial buyers), who would make different assumptions in pricing the assets.

When there are two or more different types of market participants that would transact for the asset, or the asset group, separate fair value estimates of the assets should generally be performed for each type of market participant in order to identify which type of market participant (and the appropriate related assumptions) should be considered in the fair value measurement.

In each of these analyses, the intended use of the asset and any resulting market participant synergies are considered. These include synergies among the assets in the asset grouping and synergies in combination with other assets held by (or available to) market participants generally. The selection of the appropriate market participants is based on the type of market participants that generate the maximum value for the asset group, in aggregate.

This is illustrated in Example 14.8. Fair value would be measured by reference to assumptions made by the Strategic Buyer because the fair value of the group of assets (CU 650) exceeds that of the Financial Buyer (CU 600). Consequently, the fair value of the individual assets within the asset grouping would be estimated based on the indicated values related to the market participants with the highest overall value for the asset grouping. In other words, once the assets are appropriately grouped based on their valuation premise, they should be valued using a consistent set of assumptions (i.e. the assumptions for the same type of market participants and the same related use). As shown in the example, this is true even though the fair value measurement of a specific asset, Asset C in the example, is deemed to be higher for the Financial Buyer.

Example 14.8 also highlights the interdependence between the key concepts within the IFRS 13 fair value framework. Understanding the interrelationships between market participants, exit market and the concepts of valuation premise and highest and best use is important when measuring the fair value of non-financial assets (the concepts of 'valuation premise' and 'highest and best use' are discussed at 10 below).

In the example, the indicated value for the assets as a group is determined based on the valuation premise (i.e. their use in combination with other assets) and market participant assumptions that would maximise the value of the asset group as a whole (i.e. assumptions consistent with strategic buyers). The valuation premise for Assets A, B and C is based on their use in combination with each other (or with other related assets and liabilities held by or available to market participants), consistent with the highest and best use of these assets.

The example also highlights the distinction between the unit of account (i.e. what is being measured and presented for financial reporting purposes) and the valuation premise, which forms the basis of how assets are grouped for valuation purposes (i.e. as a group or on a stand-alone basis). The unit of account may be the individual assets (i.e. Asset A, separate from Asset B and Asset C), but the valuation premise is the asset group comprised of Assets A, B and C. Therefore, the indicated value of the assets in combination (CU 650) must be attributed to the assets based on their unit of account, resulting in the fair value measurement to be used for financial reporting purposes.

8 THE TRANSACTION

As at the measurement date, the transaction to sell an asset or transfer a liability is, by definition, a hypothetical transaction for the particular asset or liability being measured at fair value. If the asset had actually been sold or the liability actually transferred as at the measurement date, there would be no asset or liability for the reporting entity to measure at fair value.

IFRS 13 assumes this hypothetical transaction will take place in the principal (or most advantageous) market (see 6 above) and will:

- be orderly in nature;
- take place between market participants that are independent of each other, but knowledgeable about the asset or liability (see 7 above for additional discussion on market participants);
- take place under current market conditions; and
- occur on the measurement date. *[IFRS 13.15]*.

These assumptions are critical in ensuring that the estimated exit price in the hypothetical transaction is consistent with the objective of a fair value measurement. For example, the concept of an orderly transaction is intended to distinguish a fair value measurement from the exit price in a distressed sale or forced liquidation. Unlike a forced liquidation, an orderly transaction assumes that the asset or liability is exposed to the market prior to the measurement date for a period that is usual and customary to allow for information dissemination and marketing. That is, the hypothetical transaction assumes that market participants have sufficient knowledge and awareness of the asset or liability, including that which would be obtained through customary due diligence even if, in actuality, this process may not have begun yet (or may never occur at all, if the entity does not sell the asset or transfer the liability).

The hypothetical transaction between market participants does not consider whether management actually intends to sell the asset or transfer the liability at the measurement date; nor does it consider the reporting entity's ability to enter into the transaction on the measurement date. *[IFRS 13.20]*. To illustrate, consider a hypothetical transaction to sell a security that, due to a restriction, cannot be sold as at the measurement date. Although the restriction may affect the measurement of fair value, it does not preclude the entity from assuming a hypothetical transaction to sell the security (see 5 above for further discussion on restrictions).

An orderly transaction assumes there will be adequate market exposure, so that market participants would be sufficiently knowledgeable about the asset or liability. This does not mean the hypothetical exchange takes place at some point in the future. A fair value measurement considers market conditions as they exist at the measurement date and is intended to represent the current value of the asset or liability, not the potential value of the asset or liability at some future date. The transaction is therefore assumed to take place on the measurement date and the entity assumes that the marketing activities and due diligence activities have already been performed. For example, assume an entity is required to re-measure an asset to fair value at its reporting date of 31 December 2017. The customary marketing activities and due diligence procedures required for the asset to be sold take six months. The asset's fair value should not be based on the price the entity expects to receive for the asset in June 2018. Instead, it must be determined based on the price that would be received if the asset were sold on 31 December 2017, assuming adequate market exposure had already taken place.

Although a fair value measurement contemplates a price in an assumed transaction, pricing information from actual transactions for identical or similar assets and liabilities is considered in measuring fair value. IFRS 13 establishes a fair value hierarchy (discussed at 16 below) to prioritise the inputs used to measure fair value, based on the relative observability of those inputs. The standard requires that valuation techniques maximise the use of observable inputs and minimise the use of unobservable inputs. As such, even in situations where the market for a particular asset is deemed to be inactive (e.g. due to liquidity issues), relevant prices or inputs from this market should still be considered in the measurement of fair value. It would not be appropriate for an entity to default solely to a model's value based on unobservable inputs (a Level 3 measurement), when Level 2 information is available. Judgement is required in assessing the relevance of observable market data to determine the priority of inputs under the fair value hierarchy, particularly in situations where there has been a significant decrease in market activity for an asset or liability, as discussed at 8.1 below.

Assessing whether a transaction is orderly can require significant judgement. The Boards believe this determination can be more difficult if there has been a significant decrease in the volume or level of activity for the asset or liability in relation to normal market activity. As such, IFRS 13 provides various factors to consider when assessing whether there has been a significant decrease in the volume or level of activity in the market (see 8.1 below) as well as circumstances that may indicate that a transaction is not orderly (see 8.2 below). Making these determinations is based on the weight of all available evidence. *[IFRS 13.B43]*.

8.1 Evaluating whether there has been a significant decrease in the volume and level of activity for an asset or liability

There are many reasons why the trading volume or level of activity for a particular asset or liability may decrease significantly. For example, shifts in supply and demand dynamics, changing levels of investors' risk appetites and liquidity constraints of key market participants could all result in a significant reduction in the level of activity for certain items or class of items. While determining fair value for any asset or liability that does not trade in an active market often requires judgement, the guidance in IFRS 13 is primarily focused on assets and liabilities in markets that have experienced a significant reduction in volume or activity. Prior to a decrease in activity, a market approach is often the primary valuation approach used to estimate fair value for these items, given the availability and relevance of observable data. Under a market approach, fair value is based on prices and other relevant information generated by market transactions involving assets and liabilities that are identical or comparable to the item being measured. As transaction volume or activity for the asset decreases significantly, application of the market approach can prove more challenging and the use of additional valuation techniques may be warranted.

The objective of a fair value measurement remains the same even when there has been a significant decrease in the volume or level of activity for the asset or liability. Paragraph B37 of IFRS 13 provides a number of factors that should be considered when evaluating whether there has been a significant decrease in the volume or level of activity for the asset or liability. The entity must 'evaluate the significance and relevance of factors such as the following:

(a) There are few recent transactions.

(b) Price quotations are not developed using current information.

(c) Price quotations vary substantially either over time or among market-makers (e.g. some brokered markets).

(d) Indices that previously were highly correlated with the fair values of the asset or liability are demonstrably uncorrelated with recent indications of fair value for that asset or liability.

(e) There is a significant increase in implied liquidity risk premiums, yields or performance indicators (such as delinquency rates or loss severities) for observed transactions or quoted prices when compared with the entity's estimate of expected cash flows, taking into account all available market data about credit and other non-performance risk for the asset or liability.

(f) There is a wide bid-ask spread or significant increase in the bid-ask spread.

(g) There is a significant decline in the activity of, or there is an absence of, a market for new issues (i.e. a primary market) for the asset or liability or similar assets or liabilities.

(h) Little information is publicly available (e.g. for transactions that take place in a principal-to-principal market)'. *[IFRS 13.B37]*.

These factors are not intended to be all-inclusive and should be considered along with any additional factors that are relevant based on the individual facts and circumstances. Determining whether the asset or liability has experienced a significant decrease in activity is based on the weight of the available evidence.

IFRS 13 is clear that a decrease in the volume or level of activity, on its own, does not necessarily indicate that a transaction price or quoted price does not represent fair value or that a transaction in that market is not orderly. Additional analysis is required in these instances to assess the relevance of observed transactions or quoted prices in these markets. When market volumes decrease, adjustments to observable prices (which could be significant) may be necessary (see 8.3 below). As discussed at 16 below, an adjustment based on unobservable inputs that is significant to the fair value measurement in its entirety would result in a Level 3 measurement. Observed prices associated with transactions that are not orderly would not be deemed to be representative of fair value.

8.1.1 Can a market exhibit a significant decrease in volume or level of activity and still be considered active?

A significant decrease in the volume of transactions does not automatically imply that a market is no longer active. IFRS 13 defines a market as active if transactions for the asset or liability occur with sufficient frequency and volume to provide pricing information on an ongoing basis. While the same factors may be used to assess whether a market has experienced a significant decrease in activity and to determine whether a market is active or inactive, these are separate and distinct determinations.

The determination that a market has experienced a significant decrease in volume does not change the requirements of IFRS 13 related to the use of relevant observable data from active markets. That is, despite a decrease from recent (or historical) levels of activity, transactions for an asset or liability in a particular market may still occur with sufficient frequency and volume to provide pricing information on an ongoing basis, thereby qualifying as an active market. If there has been a significant decrease in activity, but a market is still deemed to be active, entities would continue to measure the fair value of identical instruments that trade in this market using P×Q (Level 1 measurement).

An example of this is related to 2011 trading activity for Greek sovereign bonds. During that calendar year, the economic situation in Greece had deteriorated and some had questioned whether the Greek sovereign bonds were still being actively traded. In a public statement, ESMA indicated that, '[b]ased on trading data obtained from the Bank of Greece, it [was their] opinion that, as of 30 June 2011, the market was active for some Greek sovereign bonds but could be judged inactive for some others.'[10] While ESMA provided no predictions about the level of trading activity as at 31 December 2011, ESMA clearly stated their expectation that a fair value measurement of Greek sovereign bonds, in interim and annual financial statements during 2011 should be a Level 1 measurement in situations where there was still an active market. Furthermore, ESMA expected entities to use a Level 2 measurement method that maximises the use of observable market data to measure the fair value of those bonds that were traded in inactive markets.

Similar challenges exist for entities assessing whether a market is active for thinly traded investments. While trading volumes may be low, it may be challenging to conclude a market is not active when it regularly provides pricing information. Therefore, significant judgement will be needed to assess whether a market is active, based on the weight of evidence available.

An entity's conclusion that markets were not active for particular investments was recently challenged by ESMA. In its July 2015 enforcement report, ESMA noted that, in order to assess the existence of an active market, the entity had 'calculated a number of ratios and compared them against the following benchmarks:

- daily % of average value of trades / capitalisation lower than 0.05%;
- daily equivalent value of trades lower than CU50,000;
- daily bid-ask spread higher or equal to 3%;
- maximum number of consecutive days with unvaried prices higher than 3;
- % of trading days lower than 100%.'[11]

After performing this analysis and considering the limited trading volume, the issuer concluded that shares held in three of its listed available-for-sale investments were not traded in active markets. As a result, it measured fair value using a valuation technique based on Level 3 inputs. The enforcer disagreed with the issuer's assessment of whether the markets were active and thought that the quoted prices for these investments should have been used to measure fair value. In reaching this decision, the enforcer specifically noted that 'the indicators used by the issuer were insufficient to conclude that the transaction price did not represent fair value or that transactions occurred with insufficient frequency and volume. ... [T]he issuer did not gather sufficient information to determine whether transactions were orderly or took place with sufficient frequency and volume to provide pricing information. Therefore, based on available data, it was not possible to conclude that the markets, where the investments were listed, were not active and further analysis should have been performed to measure fair value.'[12] The enforcer also raised concerns that the valuations based on Level 3 inputs were much higher than the quoted prices. Care will be needed when reaching a conclusion that a market is not active as this is a high hurdle.

8.2 Identifying transactions that are not orderly

IFRS 13 defines an orderly transaction as 'a transaction that assumes exposure to the market for a period before the measurement date to allow for marketing activities that are usual and customary for transactions involving such assets or liabilities; it is not a forced transaction (e.g. a forced liquidation or distress sale)'. *[IFRS 13 Appendix A].* This definition includes two key components:

(i) adequate market exposure is required in order to provide market participants the ability to obtain an awareness and knowledge of the asset or liability necessary for a market-based exchange; and

(ii) the transaction should involve market participants that, while being motivated to transact for the asset or liability, are not compelled to do so.

According to IFRS 13, 'circumstances that may indicate that a transaction is not orderly include the following:

(a) There was not adequate exposure to the market for a period before the measurement date to allow for marketing activities that are usual and customary for transactions involving such assets or liabilities under current market conditions.

(b) There was a usual and customary marketing period, but the seller marketed the asset or liability to a single market participant.

(c) The seller is in or near bankruptcy or receivership (i.e. the seller is distressed).

(d) The seller was required to sell to meet regulatory or legal requirements (i.e. the seller was forced).

(e) The transaction price is an outlier when compared with other recent transactions for the same or a similar asset or liability'. *[IFRS 13.B43].*

These factors are not intended to be all-inclusive and should be considered along with any additional factors that may be pertinent to the individual facts and circumstances.

An entity must consider the following when measuring fair value or estimating market risk premiums:

- if the evidence indicates that a transaction is not orderly, the entity places little, if any, weight (compared with other indications of fair value) on that transaction price;
- if the evidence indicates that a transaction is orderly, the entity must take that transaction price into account. The amount of weight placed on that transaction

price (compared with other indications of fair value) will depend on facts and circumstances, such as:
   (i) the volume of the transaction;
   (ii) the comparability of the transaction to the asset or liability being measured; and
   (iii) the proximity of the transaction to the measurement date; and
- if an entity does not have sufficient information to determine whether a transaction is orderly, it must take that transaction price into account. However, it may not be representative of fair value, particularly where it is not the only or primary measure of fair value or market risk premium. Therefore, the entity must place less weight on those transactions (i.e. transactions the entity cannot conclude are orderly) and more weight on transactions that are known to be orderly. *[IFRS 13.B44]*.

IFRS 13 acknowledges that the determination of whether a transaction is orderly may be more difficult if there has been a significant decrease in the volume or level of activity. However, the standard is clear that, even when there has been a significant decrease in the volume or level of activity for an asset or liability, it is not appropriate to conclude that all transactions in that market are not orderly (i.e. distressed or forced). *[IFRS 13.B43]*. Instead, further assessment as to whether an observed transaction is not orderly generally needs to be made at the individual transaction level.

IFRS 13 does not require an entity to undertake all possible efforts in assessing whether a transaction is orderly. However, information that is available without undue cost and effort cannot be ignored. For instance, when an entity is party to a transaction, the standard presumes it would have sufficient information to conclude whether the transaction is orderly. *[IFRS 13.B44]*. Conversely, the lack of transparency into the details of individual transactions occurring in the market, to which the entity is not a party, can pose practical challenges for many entities in making this assessment. Recognising this difficulty, the IASB provided additional guidance in paragraph B44(c) of IFRS 13, which indicates that while observable data should not be ignored when the reporting entity does not have sufficient information to conclude on whether the transaction is orderly, the entity should place less weight on those transactions in comparison to other transactions that the reporting entity has concluded are orderly (see 8.3 below for further discussion). *[IFRS 13.B44(c)]*.

8.2.1 Are all transactions entered into to meet regulatory requirements or transactions initiated during bankruptcy assumed to be not orderly?

Although an entity may be viewed as being compelled to sell assets to comply with regulatory requirements, such transfers are not necessarily disorderly. If the entity was provided with the usual and customary period of time to market the asset to multiple potential buyers, the transaction price may be representative of the asset's fair value. Similarly, transactions initiated during bankruptcy are not automatically assumed to be disorderly. The determination of whether a transaction is not orderly requires a thorough evaluation of the specific facts and circumstances, including the exposure period and the number of potential buyers.

8.2.2 *Is it possible for orderly transactions to take place in a 'distressed' market?*

Yes. While there may be increased instances of transactions that are not orderly when a market has undergone a significant decrease in volume, it is not appropriate to assume that all transactions that occur in a market during a period of dislocation are distressed or forced. This determination is made at the individual transaction level and requires the use of judgement based on the specific facts and circumstances. While market factors such as an imbalance in supply and demand can affect the prices at which transactions occur in a given market, such an imbalance, in and of itself, does not indicate that the parties to a transaction were not knowledgeable and willing market participants or that a transaction was not orderly. For example, a transaction in a dislocated market is less likely to be considered a 'distressed sale' when multiple buyers have bid on the asset.

In addition, while a fair value measurement incorporates the assumptions that sellers, as well as buyers, would consider in pricing the asset or liability, an entity's conclusion that it would not sell its own asset (or transfer its own liability) at prices currently observed in the market does not mean these transactions should be presumed to be distressed. IFRS 13 makes clear that fair value is a market-based measurement, not an entity-specific measurement, and notes that the entity's intention to hold an asset or liability is not relevant in estimating its fair value. The objective of a fair value measurement is to estimate the exit price in an orderly transaction between willing market participants at the measurement date under current market conditions. This price should include a risk premium that reflects the amount market participants would require as compensation for bearing any uncertainty inherent in the cash flows, and this uncertainty (as well as the compensation demanded to assume it) may be affected by current marketplace conditions. The objective of a fair value measurement does not change when markets are inactive or in a period of dislocation.

8.3 Estimating fair value when there has been a significant decrease in the volume and level of activity

Estimating the price at which market participants would be willing to enter into a transaction if there has been a significant decrease in the volume or level of activity for the asset or liability will depend on the specific facts and circumstances and will require judgement. However, the core concepts of the fair value framework continue to apply. For example, an entity's intentions regarding the asset or liability, e.g. to sell an asset or settle a liability, are not relevant when measuring fair value because that would result in an entity-specific measurement. *[IFRS 13.B42]*.

If there has been a significant decrease in the volume or level of activity for the asset or liability, it may be appropriate to reconsider the valuation technique being used or to use multiple valuation techniques, for example, the use of both a market approach and a present value technique (see 8.3.2 below for further discussion). *[IFRS 13.B40]*.

If quoted prices provided by third parties are used, an entity must evaluate whether those quoted prices have been developed using current information that reflects orderly transactions or a valuation technique that reflects market participant assumptions, including assumptions about risk. This evaluation must take into consideration the nature of a quote (e.g. whether the quote is an indicative price or a binding offer). In weighting a quoted price as an input to a fair value measurement, more weight is given to quotes that reflect the result of actual transactions or those that represent binding offers. Less weight is given to quotes that are not binding, reflect indicative pricing or do not reflect the result of transactions.

In some instances, an entity may determine that a transaction or quoted price requires an adjustment, such as when the price is stale or when the price for a similar asset requires significant adjustment to make it comparable to the asset being measured. *[IFRS 13.B38].* The impact of these adjustments may be significant to the fair value measure and, if so, would affect its categorisation in the fair value hierarchy (see 16.2 below for further discussion on categorisation within the fair value hierarchy).

8.3.1 Assessing the relevance of observable data

While observable prices from inactive markets may not be representative of fair value in all cases, this data should not be ignored. Instead, paragraphs B38 and B44 of IFRS 13 clarify that additional analysis is required to assess the relevance of the observable data. *[IFRS 13.B38, B44].* The relevance of a quoted price from an inactive market is dependent on whether the transaction is determined to be orderly. If the observed price is based on a transaction that is determined to be forced or disorderly, little, if any, weight should be placed on it compared with other indications of value.

If the quoted price is based on a transaction that is determined to be orderly, this data point should be considered in the estimation of fair value. However, the relevance of quoted prices associated with orderly transactions can vary based on factors specific to the asset or liability being measured and the facts and circumstances surrounding the price. Some of the factors to be considered include:

- the condition and(or) location of the asset or liability;
- the similarity of the transactions to the asset or liability being measured (e.g. the extent to which the inputs relate to items that are comparable to the asset or liability);
- the size of the transactions;
- the volume or level of activity in the markets within which the transactions are observed;
- the proximity of the transactions to the measurement date; and
- whether the market participants involved in the transaction had access to information about the asset or liability that is usual and customary.

If the adjustments made to the observable price are significant and based on unobservable data, the resulting measurement would represent a Level 3 measurement.

Figure 14.3: Orderly transactions: measuring fair value and estimating market risk premiums

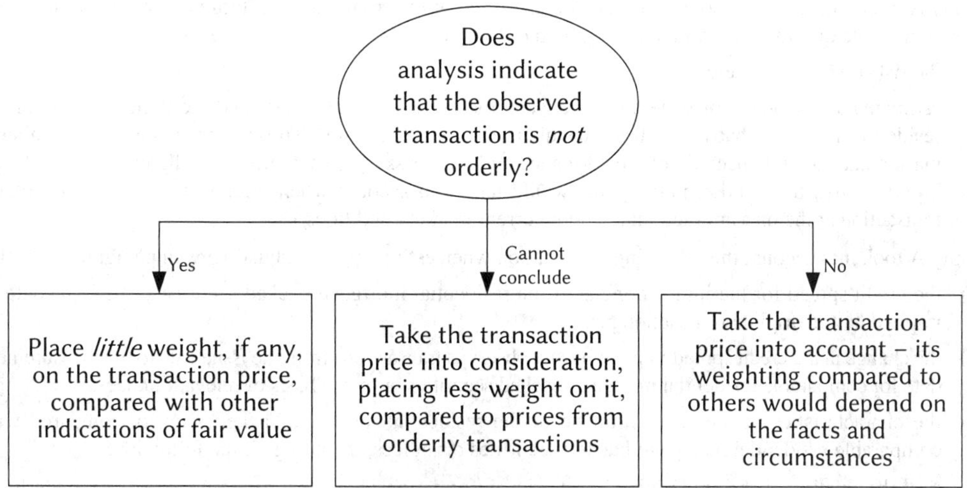

8.3.2 Selection and use of valuation techniques when there has been a significant decrease in volume or level of activity

As discussed above, when activity has significantly decreased for an asset or liability, an assessment of the relevance of observable market data will be required and adjustments to observable market data may be warranted. A significant decrease in volume or activity can also influence which valuation technique(s) are used and how those techniques are applied.

The following example from IFRS 13 highlights some key valuation considerations for assets that trade in markets that have experienced a significant decrease in volume and level of activity. *[IFRS 13.IE49-58]*.

Example 14.9: Estimating a market rate of return when there is a significant decrease in volume or level of activity

Entity A invests in a junior AAA-rated tranche of a residential mortgage-backed security on 1 January 20X8 (the issue date of the security). The junior tranche is the third most senior of a total of seven tranches. The underlying collateral for the residential mortgage-backed security is unguaranteed non-conforming residential mortgage loans that were issued in the second half of 20X6.

At 31 March 20X9 (the measurement date) the junior tranche is now A-rated. This tranche of the residential mortgage-backed security was previously traded through a brokered market. However, trading volume in that market was infrequent, with only a few transactions taking place per month from 1 January 20X8 to 30 June 20X8 and little, if any, trading activity during the nine months before 31 March 20X9.

Entity A takes into account the factors in paragraph B37 of the IFRS to determine whether there has been a significant decrease in the volume or level of activity for the junior tranche of the residential mortgage-backed security in which it has invested. After evaluating the significance and relevance of the factors, Entity A concludes that the volume and level of activity of the junior tranche of the residential mortgage-backed security have significantly decreased. Entity A supported its judgement primarily on the basis that there was little, if any, trading activity for an extended period before the measurement date.

Because there is little, if any, trading activity to support a valuation technique using a market approach, Entity A decides to use an income approach using the discount rate adjustment technique described in paragraphs B18-B22 of the IFRS to measure the fair value of the residential mortgage-backed security at the measurement date. Entity A uses the contractual cash flows from the residential mortgage-backed security (see also paragraphs 67 and 68 of the IFRS).

Entity A then estimates a discount rate (i.e. a market rate of return) to discount those contractual cash flows. The market rate of return is estimated using both of the following:

(a) the risk-free rate of interest.

(b) estimated adjustments for differences between the available market data and the junior tranche of the residential mortgage-backed security in which Entity A has invested. Those adjustments reflect available market data about expected non-performance and other risks (e.g. default risk, collateral value risk and liquidity risk) that market participants would take into account when pricing the asset in an orderly transaction at the measurement date under current market conditions.

Entity A took into account the following information when estimating the adjustments in paragraph IE53(b):

(a) the credit spread for the junior tranche of the residential mortgage-backed security at the issue date as implied by the original transaction price.

(b) the change in the credit spread implied by any observed transactions from the issue date to the measurement date for comparable residential mortgage-backed securities or on the basis of relevant indices.

(c) the characteristics of the junior tranche of the residential mortgage-backed security compared with comparable residential mortgage-backed securities or indices, including all the following:

  (i) the quality of the underlying assets, i.e. information about the performance of the underlying mortgage loans such as delinquency and foreclosure rates, loss experience and prepayment rates;

  (ii) the seniority or subordination of the residential mortgage-backed security tranche held; and

  (iii) other relevant factors.

(d) relevant reports issued by analysts and rating agencies.

(e) quoted prices from third parties such as brokers or pricing services.

Entity A estimates that one indication of the market rate of return that market participants would use when pricing the junior tranche of the residential mortgage-backed security is 12 per cent (1,200 basis points). This market rate of return was estimated as follows:

(a) Begin with 300 basis points for the relevant risk-free rate of interest at 31 March 20X9.

(b) Add 250 basis points for the credit spread over the risk-free rate when the junior tranche was issued in January 20X8.

(c) Add 700 basis points for the estimated change in the credit spread over the risk-free rate of the junior tranche between 1 January 20X8 and 31 March 20X9. This estimate was developed on the basis of the change in the most comparable index available for that time period.

(d) Subtract 50 basis points (net) to adjust for differences between the index used to estimate the change in credit spreads and the junior tranche. The referenced index consists of subprime mortgage loans, whereas Entity A's residential mortgage-backed security consists of similar mortgage loans with a more favourable credit profile (making it more attractive to market participants). However, the index does not reflect an appropriate liquidity risk premium for the junior tranche under current market conditions. Thus, the 50 basis point adjustment is the net of two adjustments:

  (i) the first adjustment is a 350 basis point subtraction, which was estimated by comparing the implied yield from the most recent transactions for the residential mortgage-backed security in June 20X8 with the implied yield in the index price on those same dates. There was no information available that indicated that the relationship between Entity A's security and the index has changed.

  (ii) the second adjustment is a 300 basis point addition, which is Entity A's best estimate of the additional liquidity risk inherent in its security (a cash position) when compared with the index (a synthetic position). This estimate was derived after taking into account liquidity risk premiums implied in recent cash transactions for a range of similar securities.

As an additional indication of the market rate of return, Entity A takes into account two recent indicative quotes (i.e. non-binding quotes) provided by reputable brokers for the junior tranche of the residential mortgage-backed security that imply yields of 15-17 per cent. Entity A is unable to evaluate the valuation technique(s) or inputs used to develop the quotes. However, Entity A is able to confirm that the quotes do not reflect the results of transactions.

Because Entity A has multiple indications of the market rate of return that market participants would take into account when measuring fair value, it evaluates and weights the respective indications of the rate of return, considering the reasonableness of the range indicated by the results.

Entity A concludes that 13 per cent is the point within the range of indications that is most representative of fair value under current market conditions. Entity A places more weight on the 12 per cent indication (i.e. its own estimate of the market rate of return) for the following reasons:

(a) Entity A concluded that its own estimate appropriately incorporated the risks (e.g. default risk, collateral value risk and liquidity risk) that market participants would use when pricing the asset in an orderly transaction under current market conditions.

(b) The broker quotes were non-binding and did not reflect the results of transactions, and Entity A was unable to evaluate the valuation technique(s) or inputs used to develop the quotes.

In Example 14.9 above, Entity A uses an income approach (i.e. discount rate adjustment technique, see 21 below for further discussion regarding present value techniques) to estimate the fair value of its residential mortgage-backed security (RMBS), because limited trading activity precluded a market approach as at the measurement date.

Example 14.9 illustrates that the entity's use of an income approach does not change the objective of the fair value measurement, which is a current exit price. Valuation models should take into account all the factors that market participants would consider when pricing an asset or liability. The discount rate used by Entity A, for example, tries to incorporate all of the risks (e.g. liquidity risk, non-performance risk) market participants would consider in pricing the RMBS under current market conditions. Liquidity, credit or any other risk factors market participants would consider in pricing the asset or liability may require adjustments to model values if such factors are not sufficiently captured in the model.

Entity A prioritises observable inputs (to the extent available) over unobservable inputs in its application of the income approach. Entity A assesses market-based data from various sources to estimate the discount rate. For example, the entity estimates the change in the credit spread of the RMBS since its issuance based on spread changes observed from the most comparable index, for which trades continue to occur. Using the best available market information, the entity adjusts this input to account for differences between the observed index and the RMBS. These adjustments include the entity's assessment of the additional liquidity risk inherent in the RMBS compared to the index.

Paragraph 89 of IFRS 13 indicates that an entity may use its own internal assumptions when relevant observable market data does not exist. *[IFRS 13.89]*. However, if reasonably available data indicates that market participant assumptions would differ, the entity should adjust its assumptions to incorporate that information. Relevant market data is not limited to transactions for the identical asset or liability being measured.

In the above example, Entity A is unable to use a market approach because of limited trading activity for the RMBS. Therefore, Entity A considers implied liquidity risk premiums from recent transactions for a range of similar securities to estimate the incremental premium market participants would demand for its RMBS in the current market (as compared to the benchmark spread). In addition, Entity A considers two indicative broker quotes to estimate an appropriate discount rate for its RMBS. Although these quotes are specific to the RMBS being valued, Entity A puts less weight on these quotes since they are not binding and are not based on actual transactions. Furthermore, Entity A was unable to evaluate the valuation techniques and underlying data used by the brokers.

Importantly, the illustrative example is not intended to imply that an entity's own assumptions carry more weight than non-binding broker quotes. Rather, the example illustrates that each indication of value needs to be assessed based on the extent these indications rely on observable versus unobservable inputs.

Even though the market approach could not be used because of limited trading activity for the RMBS, Entity A was able to corroborate many of the assumptions used in developing the discount rate with relevant observable market data. As a result, the decision by the entity to place additional weight on its own market-corroborated assumptions (and less on the broker quotes) was warranted. When differences between broker quotes or pricing service data and an entity's own determination of value are significant, management should seek to understand the reasons behind these differences, if possible.

9 THE PRICE

'Fair value is the price that would be received to sell an asset or paid to transfer a liability in an orderly transaction in the principal (or most advantageous) market at the measurement date under current market conditions (i.e. an exit price) regardless of whether that price is directly observable or estimated using another valuation technique'. *[IFRS 13.24]*.

IFRS 13 requires the entity to estimate fair value based on the price that would be received to sell the asset or transfer the liability being measured (i.e. an exit price). While the determination of this price may be straightforward in some cases (e.g. when the identical instrument trades in an active market), in others it will require significant judgement. However, IFRS 13 makes it clear that the price used to measure fair value shall not be adjusted for transaction costs, but would consider transportation costs. *[IFRS 13.25, 26]*.

The standard's guidance on the valuation techniques and inputs to these techniques used in determining the exit price (including the prohibition on block discounts) is discussed at 14 and 15 below.

9.1 Transaction costs

Transaction costs are defined as the costs to sell an asset or transfer a liability in the principal (or most advantageous) market for the asset or liability that are directly attributable to the disposal of an asset or the transfer of the liability. In addition, these costs must be incremental, i.e. they would not have been incurred by the entity had the decision to sell the asset or transfer the liability not been made. *[IFRS 13 Appendix A]*. Examples of transaction costs include commissions or certain due diligence costs. As noted above, transaction costs do not include transportation costs.

Fair value is not adjusted for transaction costs. This is because transaction costs are not a characteristic of an asset or a liability; they are a characteristic of the transaction. While not deducted from fair value, an entity considers transaction costs in the context of determining the most advantageous market (in the absence of a principal market – see 6.2 above) because in this instance the entity is seeking to determine the market that would maximise the net amount that would be received for the asset.

9.1.1 Are transaction costs in IFRS 13 the same as 'costs to sell' in other IFRSs?

As discussed at 2.1.2 above, some IFRSs permit or require measurements based on fair value, where costs to sell or costs of disposal are deducted from the fair value measurement. IFRS 13 does not change the measurement objective for assets accounted for at fair value less cost to sell. The 'fair value less cost to sell' measurement objective includes: (1) fair value; and (2) cost to sell. The fair value component is measured in accordance with the IFRS 13.

Consistent with the definition of transaction costs in IFRS 13, IAS 36 describes costs of disposal as 'the direct incremental costs attributable to the disposal of the asset or cash-generating unit, excluding finance costs and income tax expense'. *[IAS 36.6].* IAS 41 and IFRS 5 similarly define costs to sell.

As such, transaction costs excluded from the determination of fair value in accordance with IFRS 13 will generally be consistent with costs to sell or costs of disposal, determined in other IFRSs (listed at 2.1.2 above), provided they exclude transportation costs.

Since the fair value component is measured in accordance with IFRS 13, the standard's disclosure requirements apply in situations where the fair value less cost to sell measurement is required subsequent to the initial recognition (unless specifically exempt from the disclosure requirements, see 20 below). In addition, IFRS 13 clarifies that adjustments used to arrive at measurements based on fair value (e.g. the cost to sell when estimating fair value less cost to sell) should not be considered when determining where to categorise the measurement in the fair value hierarchy (see 16 below).

9.1.2 Transaction costs in IFRS 13 versus acquisition-related transaction costs in other IFRSs

The term 'transaction costs' is used in many IFRSs, but sometimes it refers to transaction costs actually incurred when acquiring an item and sometimes to transaction costs expected to be incurred when selling an item. While the same term might be used, it is important to differentiate between these types of transaction costs.

IAS 36, IAS 41 and IFRS 5 discuss costs to sell or dispose of an item (as discussed at 9.1.1 above).

In contrast, other standards refer to capitalising or expensing transaction costs incurred in the context of acquiring an asset, assuming a liability or issuing an entity's own equity (a buyer's perspective). IFRS 3, for example, requires acquisition-related costs to be expensed in the period incurred. *[IFRS 3.53].*

IFRS 13 indicates that transaction costs are not included in a fair value measurement. As such, actual transaction costs (e.g. commissions paid) that are incurred by an entity when acquiring an asset would not be included at initial recognition when fair value is the measurement objective. Likewise, transaction costs that would be incurred in a hypothetical sales transaction would also not be included in a fair value measurement.

Some standards permit acquisition-related transaction costs to be capitalised at initial recognition, then permit or require the item, to which those costs relate, to be subsequently measured at fair value. In those situations, some or all of the acquisition-related transaction costs that were capitalised will effectively be expensed as part of the resulting fair value gain or loss. This is consistent with current practice. For example, IAS 40 permits transaction costs to be capitalised as part of an investment property's cost on initial recognition. *[IAS 40.20]*. However, if the fair value model is applied to the subsequent measurement of the investment property, transaction costs would be excluded from the fair value measurement.

Similarly, at initial recognition, financial assets or liabilities in the scope of IFRS 9 (or IAS 39) are generally measured at their 'fair value plus or minus, in the case of a financial asset or liability not at fair value through profit or loss, transaction costs that are directly attributable to the acquisition or issue of the financial asset or liability'. *[IFRS 9.5.1.1, IAS 39.43]*. For those items subsequently measured at amortised cost, these transaction costs will be captured as part of the instrument's effective interest rate.

9.2 Transportation costs

Transportation costs represent those that would be incurred to transport an asset or liability to (or from) the principal (or most advantageous) market. If location is a characteristic of the asset or liability being measured (e.g. as might be the case with a commodity), the price in the principal (or most advantageous) market should be adjusted for transportation costs. The following simplified example illustrates this concept.

Example 14.10: Transportation costs

Entity A holds a physical commodity measured at fair value in its warehouse in Europe. For this commodity, the London exchange is determined to be the principal market as it represents the market with the greatest volume and level of activity for the asset that the entity can reasonably access.

The exchange price for the asset is CU 25. However, the contracts traded on the exchange for this commodity require physical delivery to London. Entity A determines that it would cost CU 5 to transport the physical commodity to London and the broker's commission would be CU 3 to transact on the London exchange.

Since location is a characteristic of the asset and transportation to the principal market is required, the fair value of the physical commodity would be CU 20 – the price in the principal market for the asset CU 25, less transportation costs of CU 5. The CU 3 broker commission represents a transaction cost that would not adjust the price in the principal market.

10 APPLICATION TO NON-FINANCIAL ASSETS

Many non-financial assets, either through the initial or subsequent measurement requirements of an IFRS or, the requirements of IAS 36 for impairment testing (if recoverable amount is based on fair value less costs of disposal), are either permitted or required to be measured at fair value (or a measure based on fair value). For example, management may need to measure the fair value of non-financial assets and liabilities when completing the purchase price allocation for a business combination in accordance with IFRS 3. First-time adopters of IFRS might need to measure fair value of assets and liabilities if they use a 'fair value as deemed cost' approach in accordance with IFRS 1 – *First-time Adoption of International Financial Reporting Standards.*

The principles described in the sections above apply to non-financial assets. In addition, the fair value measurement of non-financial assets must reflect the highest and best use of the asset from a market participant's perspective.

The highest and best use of an asset establishes the valuation premise used to measure the fair value of the asset. In other words, whether to assume market participants would derive value from using the non-financial asset (based on its highest and best use) on its own or in combination with other assets or with other assets and liabilities. As discussed below, this might be its current use or some alternative use.

As discussed at 4.2 above, the concepts of highest and best use and valuation premise in IFRS 13 are only relevant for non-financial assets (and not financial assets and liabilities). This is because:

- financial assets have specific contractual terms; they do not have alternative uses. Changing the characteristics of the financial asset (i.e. changing the contractual terms) causes the item to become a different asset and the objective of a fair value measurement is to measure the asset as it exists as at the measurement date;
- the different ways by which an entity may relieve itself of a liability are not alternative uses. In addition, entity-specific advantages (or disadvantages) that enable an entity to fulfil a liability more or less efficiently than other market participants are not considered in a fair value measurement; and
- the concepts of highest and best use and valuation premise were developed within the valuation profession to value non-financial assets, such as land. *[IFRS 13.BC63].*

Chapter 14

10.1 Highest and best use

Fair value measurements of non-financial assets take into account 'a market participant's ability to generate economic benefits by using the asset in its *highest and best use* or by selling it to another market participant that would use the asset in its highest and best use'. *[IFRS 13.27].*

Highest and best use refers to 'the use of a non-financial asset by market participants that would maximise the value of the asset or the group of assets and liabilities (e.g. a business) within which the asset would be used'. *[IFRS 13 Appendix A].*

The highest and best use of an asset considers uses of the asset that are:

(a) physically possible: the physical characteristics of the asset that market participants would take into account when pricing the asset (e.g. the location or size of a property);

(b) legally permissible: any legal restrictions on the use of the asset that market participants would take into account when pricing the asset (e.g. the zoning regulations applicable to a property); and

(c) financially feasible: whether a use of the asset that is physically possible and legally permissible generates adequate income or cash flows (taking into account the costs of converting the asset to that use) to produce an investment return that market participants would require from an investment in that asset put to that use. *[IFRS 13.28].*

Highest and best use is a valuation concept that considers how market participants would use a non-financial asset to maximise its benefit or value. The maximum value of a non-financial asset to market participants may come from its use: (a) in combination with other assets or with other assets and liabilities; or (b) on a stand-alone basis.

In determining the highest and best use of a non-financial asset, paragraph 28 of IFRS 13 indicates uses that are physically possible, legally permissible (see 10.1.1 below for further discussion) and financially feasible should be considered. As such, when assessing alternative uses, entities should consider the physical characteristics of the asset, any legal restrictions on its use and whether the value generated provides an adequate investment return for market participants.

Provided there is sufficient evidence to support these assertions, alternative uses that would enable market participants to maximise value should be considered, but a search for potential alternative uses need not be exhaustive. In addition, any costs to transform the non-financial asset (e.g. obtaining a new zoning permit or converting the asset to the alternative use) and profit expectations from a market participant's perspective are also considered in the fair value measurement.

If there are multiple types of market participants who would use the asset differently, these alternative scenarios must be considered before concluding on the asset's highest and best use. While applying the fair value framework may be straightforward in many situations, in other instances, an iterative process may be needed to consistently apply the various components. This may be required due to the interdependence among several key concepts in IFRS 13's fair value framework (see Figure 14.2 at 4.2 above). For example, the highest and best use of a non-financial asset determines its valuation premise and affects the identification of the appropriate market participants. Likewise, the determination of the principal (or most advantageous) market can be important in determining the highest and best use of a non-financial asset.

Determining whether the maximum value to market participants would be achieved either by using an asset in combination with other assets and liabilities as a group, or by using the asset on a stand-alone basis, requires judgement and an assessment of the specific facts and circumstances.

A careful assessment is particularly important when the highest and best use of a non-financial asset is in combination with one or more non-financial assets.

As discussed at 10.2 below, assets in an asset group should all be valued using the same valuation premise. For example, if the fair value of a piece of machinery on a manufacturing line is measured assuming its highest and best use is in conjunction with other equipment in the manufacturing line, those other non-financial assets in the asset group (i.e. the other equipment on the manufacturing line) would also be valued using the same premise. As highlighted by Example 14.13 at 10.2.2 below, once it is determined that the value for a set of assets is maximised when considered as a group, all of the assets in that group would be valued using the same premise, regardless of whether any individual asset within the group would have a higher value on a stand-alone basis.

10.1.1 Highest and best use: determining what is legally permissible

To be legally permissible, the standard indicates a use of a non-financial asset need not be legal (or have legal approval) at the measurement date, but it must not be legally prohibited in the jurisdiction. *[IFRS 13.BC69]*.

What is legally permissible is a matter of law. However, the IASB seems to be distinguishing between a use that is explicitly prohibited and a use that would be permitted if the jurisdiction's specific legal requirements were met. However, in some situations it may be difficult to determine whether a use is capable of being legally permitted when, at the measurement date, it is subject to legal restrictions that are not easily overcome.

The standard gives the example of a land development. Assume the government has prohibited building on or developing certain land (i.e. the land is a protected area). For the entity to develop the land, a change of law would be required. Since development of this land would be illegal, it cannot be the highest and best use of the land. Alternatively, assume the land has been zoned for commercial use, but nearby areas have recently been developed for residential use and, as such, market participants would consider residential development as a potential use of the land. Since re-zoning the land for residential development would only require approval from an authority and that approval is usually given, this alternative use could be deemed to be legally permissible.

It is assumed that market participants would consider all relevant factors, as they exist at the measurement date, in determining whether the legally permissible use of the non-financial asset may be something other than its current use. That is, market participants would consider the probability, extent and timing of different types of approvals that may be required in assessing whether a change in the legal use of the non-financial asset could be obtained.

The scenarios, of protected land and re-zoning of land, considered above illustrate either end of the spectrum; uses that are unlikely and likely to be legally permissible, respectively. However, consider the protected land example above. Assume the government were expected to change the law in the near future to permit residential development, but there had not been any similar changes in law to date. An entity would need to consider the weight of evidence available and whether market participants would have similar expectations. This may be more difficult without past history of similar changes in law. However, an entity might consider factors such as whether expectations are based on verbal assurances or written evidence; whether the process to change the law has begun; and the risk that the change in law will not be approved. It may also help to determine whether market participants would pay for this potential. However, this fact, on its own, is unlikely to be sufficient to support a use being legally permissible.

In our view, an entity would need to have sufficient evidence to support its assumption about the potential for an alternative use, particularly in light of IFRS 13's presumption that the highest and best use is an asset's current use. In the example above of re-zoning land for residential development, the entity's belief that re-zoning was possible (or even likely) is unlikely to be sufficient evidence that the re-zoning is legally permissible.

However, the fact that nearby areas had recently been re-zoned for residential use may provide additional evidence as to the likelihood that the land being measured could similarly be re-zoned. If obtaining re-zoning permission is not merely perfunctory, there may be a significant burden on the entity to prove that market participants would consider commercial use of the land 'legally permissible'.

10.1.2 Highest and best use versus current use

Although IFRS 13 presumes that an entity's current use of an asset is its highest and best use, market or other factors may suggest that a different use by market participants would maximise the value of that asset. *[IFRS 13.29]*. Because the highest and best use of an asset is determined based on market participants' expectations, reporting entities may need to consider alternative uses of an asset (e.g. land) in their analysis of fair value. An entity's current or intended use of a non-financial asset might not be the highest and best use of the asset, and thus would not determine its premise of value. Instead, the highest and best use of the asset (or asset group) should be determined based on how market participants would maximise the asset's value. For example, market participants may maximise the value of land, currently used as a site for a manufacturing facility, for residential housing instead.

The consideration of alternative uses is not intended to be exhaustive. It is not necessary that all possible alternatives be considered. Instead, judgement is required in assessing those alternative uses that market participants would consider in pricing the asset. As noted above, consideration of what is physically possible, legally permissible and financially feasible would be part of this assessment. Example 14.11, based on an example in IFRS 13, illustrates this further. If an entity determines that the highest and best use of an asset is different from its current use, IFRS 13 requires that fact to be disclosed as well as the reason why the non-financial asset is being used in a manner that differs from its highest and best use (disclosures are discussed further at 20 below). *[IFRS 13.93(i)]*.

It is important to note that even if the current use of a non-financial asset is the same as its highest and best use, the underlying assumptions used to value the asset should not be entity-specific, but instead should be based on the assumptions that market participants would use when transacting for the asset in its current condition. Entity-specific synergies, if they would differ from market participant synergies, would not be considered in the determination of the highest and best use of the asset. This is illustrated in Example 14.11. *[IFRS 13.IE7-8]*.

Example 14.11: Highest and best use versus current use

An entity acquires land in a business combination. The land is currently developed for industrial use as a site for a factory. The current use of the land is presumed to be its highest and best use unless market or other factors suggest a different use. Nearby sites have recently been developed for residential use as sites for high-rise apartment buildings. On the basis of that development and recent zoning and other changes to facilitate that development, the entity determines that the land currently used as a site for a factory could be developed as a site for residential use (i.e. for high-rise apartment buildings) because market participants would take into account the potential to develop the site for residential use when pricing the land.

The highest and best use of the land would be determined by comparing both of the following:

(a) the value of the land as currently developed for industrial use (i.e. the land would be used in combination with other assets, such as the factory, or with other assets and liabilities).

(b) the value of the land as a vacant site for residential use, taking into account the costs of demolishing the factory and other costs (including the uncertainty about whether the entity would be able to convert the asset to the alternative use) necessary to convert the land to a vacant site (i.e. the land is to be used by market participants on a stand-alone basis).

The highest and best use of the land would be determined on the basis of the higher of those values. In situations involving real estate appraisal, the determination of highest and best use might take into account factors relating to the factory operations, including its assets and liabilities.

Assume that the fair value of the land in-use as a manufacturing operation is determined to be CU 4,000,000 and that the fair value for the land as a vacant site that can be used for residential purposes is CU 5,000,000. In order to convert the land from a manufacturing operation to a vacant site for residential use, the manufacturing facility must be removed. Assuming demolition and other costs of CU 500,000, the fair value of the land as a vacant lot for residential use would be CU 4,500,000.* In order to determine the fair value of the land, the price of the land as a residential development site (CU 5,000,000) would need to be adjusted for the transformation costs (CU 500,000) necessary to prepare the land for residential use. Therefore, the amount of CU 4,500,00 must be used as the fair value of the land.

* For simplicity purposes, this example does not specifically discuss other types of costs that may need to be considered in determining the fair value of the land for residential use (such as the effect of intangible or other assets related to the manufacturing facility).

10.1.3 Highest and best use versus intended use (including defensive value)

An entity's intended use of an asset, at the time it is acquired, may not be the same as how market participants would use the asset. If the highest and best use and the entity's intended use of an asset are not the same, it could result in differences between the price to acquire the asset and fair value measured in accordance with IFRS 13 (see 13 below). IFRS 13 requires that the highest and best use of an asset be determined from the perspective of market participants, even if management intends a different use, *[IFRS 13.29, 30]*, as is illustrated in Example 14.12.

In certain instances, the highest and best use of an asset may be to not actively use it, but instead to lock it up or 'shelve it' (commonly referred to as a defensive asset). That is, the maximum value provided by an asset may be its defensive value. IFRS 13 clarifies that the fair value of an asset used defensively is not assumed to be zero or a nominal amount. Instead, an entity should consider the incremental value such a use provides to the assets being protected, such as the incremental value provided to an entity's existing brand name by acquiring and shelving a competing brand. Generally speaking, a nominal fair value is appropriate only when an asset is abandoned (i.e. when an entity would be willing to give the asset away for no consideration).

Importantly, an entity's decision to use an asset defensively does not mean that market participants would necessarily maximise the asset's value in a similar manner. Likewise, an entity's decision to actively use an asset does not preclude its highest and best use to market participants as being defensive in nature. The following example in IFRS 13 illustrates these points. *[IFRS 13.IE9]*.

Example 14.12: Highest and best use versus intended use

An entity acquires a research and development (R&D) project in a business combination. The entity does not intend to complete the project. If completed, the project would compete with one of its own projects (to provide the next generation of the entity's commercialised technology). Instead, the entity intends to hold (i.e. lock up) the project to prevent its competitors from obtaining access to the technology. In doing this the project is expected to provide defensive value, principally by improving the prospects for the entity's own competing technology. To measure the fair value of the project at initial recognition, the highest and best use of the project would be determined on the basis of its use by market participants. For example:

(a) The highest and best use of the R&D project would be to continue development if market participants would continue to develop the project and that use would maximise the value of the group of assets or of assets and liabilities in which the project would be used (i.e. the asset would be used in combination with other assets or with other assets and liabilities). That might be the case if market participants do not have similar technology, either in development or commercialised. The fair value of the project would be measured on the basis of the price that would be received in a current transaction to sell the project, assuming that the R&D would be used with its complementary assets and the associated liabilities and that those assets and liabilities would be available to market participants.

(b) The highest and best use of the R&D project would be to cease development if, for competitive reasons, market participants would lock up the project and that use would maximise the value of the group of assets or of assets and liabilities in which the project would be used. That might be the case if market participants have technology in a more advanced stage of development that would compete with the project if completed and the project would be expected to improve the prospects for their own competing technology if locked up. The fair value of the project would be measured on the basis of the price that would be received in a current transaction to sell the project, assuming that the R&D would be used (i.e. locked up) with its complementary assets and the associated liabilities and that those assets and liabilities would be available to market participants.

(c) The highest and best use of the R&D project would be to cease development if market participants would discontinue its development. That might be the case if the project is not expected to provide a market rate of return if completed and would not otherwise provide defensive value if locked up. The fair value of the project would be measured on the basis of the price that would be received in a current transaction to sell the project on its own (which might be zero).

If the highest and best use in this example was (a), then that is the value that the entity must ascribe to the R&D project, even though its intended use is to lock-up the project.

The fair value of the in-process research and development project in Example 14.12 above depends on whether market participants would use the asset offensively, defensively or abandon it (as illustrated by points (a), (b) and (c) in the example, respectively). As discussed at 10.1 above, if there are multiple types of market participants who would use the asset differently, these alternative scenarios must be considered before concluding on the asset's highest and best use.

10.2 Valuation premise for non-financial assets

Dependent on its highest and best use, the fair value of the non-financial asset will either be measured based on the value it would derive on a stand-alone basis or in combination with other assets or other assets and liabilities – i.e. the asset's valuation premise.

10.2.1 Valuation premise – stand-alone basis

If the highest and best use of the asset is to use it on a stand-alone basis, an entity measures the fair value of the asset individually. In other words, the asset is assumed to be sold to market participants for use on its own. Fair value is the price that would be received in a current transaction under those circumstances. *[IFRS 13.31(b)]*. For instance, alternative (c) of Example 14.12 above suggests the highest and best use of the research and development project could be to cease development. Since its highest and best use is on a stand-alone basis, the fair value of the project would be the price that would be received in a current transaction to sell the project on its own and assuming a market participant would cease development of the project. In addition, the asset should be measured based only on its current characteristics, potentially requiring an adjustment for transformation costs. For example, if land that is used as a factory site is to be valued on a stand-alone basis, transformation costs (e.g. the cost of removing the factory) should be considered in the fair value measurement.

When the valuation premise of one non-financial asset in an asset group is valued on a stand-alone basis, all of the other assets in the group should also be valued using a consistent valuation premise. For example, based on Example 14.11 at 10.1.2 above, if the highest and best use of the land is determined to be on a stand-alone basis (i.e. as vacant land), the fair value of the equipment in the factory could be determined under two alternative valuation premises: (a) stand-alone (i.e. the value of the equipment sold on a stand-alone basis); or (b) in conjunction with other equipment on the operating line, but in a different factory (i.e. not in combination with the land, since the land would be valued on a stand-alone basis). Regardless of the valuation premise used to measure the equipment, market participant assumptions regarding the cost of redeployment, such as costs for disassembling, transporting and reinstalling the equipment should be considered in the fair value measurement.

10.2.2 Valuation premise – in combination with other assets and/or liabilities

If the highest and best use of a non-financial asset is in combination with other assets as a group or in combination with other assets and liabilities, the fair value of the asset is the price that would be received in a current transaction to sell the asset and would assume that:

(i) market participants would use the asset together with other assets or with other assets and liabilities; and

(ii) those assets and liabilities (i.e. its complementary assets and the associated liabilities) would be available to market participants. *[IFRS 13.31(a)(i)]*. That is, the fair value of the asset would be measured from the perspective of market participants who are presumed to hold the complementary assets and liabilities (see 10.2.3 below for further discussion regarding associated liabilities).

Once an entity determines that the valuation premise for a non-financial asset is its use in combination with a set of assets (or assets and liabilities), all of the complementary non-financial assets in that group should be valued using the same valuation premise (i.e. assuming the same highest and best use), regardless of whether any individual asset within the group would have a higher value under another premise. *[IFRS 13.31(a)(iii)].* Example 14.13 illustrates this further.

Example 14.13: Consistent assumptions about highest and best use in an asset group

A wine producer owns and manages a vineyard and produces its own wine onsite. The vines are measured at fair value less costs to sell in accordance with IAS 41 at the end of each reporting period. The grapes are measured at the point of harvest at fair value less costs to sell in accordance with IAS 41 (being its 'cost' when transferred to IAS 2). Before harvest, the grapes are considered part of the vines. The wine producer elects to measure its land using IAS 16's revaluation model (fair value less any subsequent accumulated depreciation and accumulated impairment). All other non-financial assets are measured at cost.

At the end of the reporting period, the entity assesses the highest and best use of the vines and the land from the perspective of market participants. The vines and land could continue to be used, in combination with the entity's other assets and liabilities, to produce and sell its wine (i.e. its current use). Alternatively, the land could be converted into residential property. Conversion would include removing the vines and plant and equipment from the land.

Scenario A

The entity determines that the highest and best use of these assets in combination as a vineyard (i.e. its current use). The entity must make consistent assumptions for assets in the group (for which highest and best use is relevant, i.e. non-financial assets). Therefore, the highest and best use of all non-financial assets in the group is to produce and sell wine, even if conversion into residential property might yield a higher value for the land on its own.

Scenario B

The entity determines that the highest and best use of these assets is to convert the land into residential property, even if the current use might yield a higher value for the vines on their own. The entity would need to consider what a market participant would do to convert the land, which could include the cost of rezoning, selling cuttings from the vines or simply removing the vines, and the sale of the buildings and equipment either individually or as an asset group.

Since the highest and best use of these assets is not their current use in this scenario, the entity would disclose that fact, as well as the reason why those assets are being used in a manner that differs from their highest and best use.

When the asset's highest and best use is in combination with other items, the effect of the valuation premise on the measurement of fair value will depend on the specific circumstances. IFRS 13 gives the following examples.

(a) The fair value of the asset might be the same whether it's on a stand-alone basis or in an asset group.

This may occur if the asset is a business that market participants would continue to operate, for example, when a business is measured at fair value at initial recognition in accordance with IFRS 3. The transaction would involve valuing the business in its entirety. The use of the assets as a group in an ongoing business would generate synergies that would be available to market participants (i.e. market participant synergies that, therefore, should affect the fair value of the asset on either a stand-alone basis or in combination with other assets or with other assets and liabilities).

(b) An asset's use in an asset group might be incorporated into the fair value measurement through adjustments to the value of the asset used on a stand-alone basis.

For example, assume the asset to be measured at fair value is a machine that is installed and configured for use. If the fair value measurement is determined using an observed price for a similar machine that is not installed or otherwise configured for use, it would need to be adjusted for transport and installation costs so that the fair value measurement reflects the current condition and location of the machine.

(c) An asset's use in an asset group might be incorporated into the fair value measurement through the market participant assumptions used to measure the fair value of the asset.

For example, the asset might be work in progress inventory that is unique and market participants would convert the inventory into finished goods. In that situation, the fair value of the inventory would assume that market participants have acquired or would acquire any specialised machinery necessary to convert the inventory into finished goods.

(d) An asset's use in combination with other assets or with other assets and liabilities might be incorporated into the valuation technique used to measure the fair value of the asset.

That might be the case when using the multi-period excess earnings method to measure the fair value of an intangible asset because that valuation technique specifically takes into account the contribution of any complementary assets and the associated liabilities in the group in which such an intangible asset would be used.

(e) In more limited situations, when an entity uses an asset within a group of assets, the entity might measure the asset at an amount that approximates its fair value when allocating the fair value of the asset group to the individual assets of the group.

For example, this might be the case if the valuation involves real property and the fair value of improved property (i.e. an asset group) is allocated to its component assets (such as land and improvements). *[IFRS 13.B3]*.

Although the approach used to incorporate the valuation premise into a fair value measurement may differ based on the facts and circumstances, the determination of a non-financial asset's valuation premise (based on its highest and best use) and the inputs applied in the valuation technique used to estimate fair value should always be considered from the perspective of market participants, not the reporting entity.

10.2.3 How should associated liabilities be considered when measuring the fair value of a non-financial asset?

As discussed at 10.2.2 above, an asset's highest and best use might be in combination with associated liabilities and complementary assets in an asset group. IFRS 13.B3(d), for example, notes that an asset's use in combination with other assets and liabilities might be incorporated when using the multi-period excess earnings method to measure the fair value of an intangible asset that has been acquired in a business acquisition. *[IFRS 13.B3]*. The multi-period excess earnings method specifically takes into account the contribution of any complementary assets and the associated liabilities in the group in which such an intangible asset would be used.

'Associated liabilities' is not defined and IFRS 13 provides limited guidance on the types of liabilities that could be considered associated to a non-financial asset. IFRS 13 provides some guidance, stating that associated liabilities can include those that fund working capital, but must exclude liabilities used to fund assets other than those within the group of assets. *[IFRS 13.31(a)(ii)]*.

Management will need to exercise judgement in determining which liabilities to include or exclude from the group, based on the specific facts and circumstances. This assessment must reflect what market participants would consider when determining the non-financial asset's highest and best use. Entities will need to be careful to exclude entity-specific assumptions when valuing liabilities, particularly if valuation techniques are used that are based on their own data (valuation techniques are discussed further at 14 below).

The clarification on considering associated liabilities when measuring the fair value of non-financial assets was generally intended to align the guidance in IFRS 13 with current practice for measuring the fair value of certain non-financial assets (e.g. intangible assets). We generally would not expect this clarification to result in significant changes to the valuation of most non-financial assets. For example, real estate should generally be valued independently from any debt used to finance the property.

10.2.4 Unit of account versus the valuation premise

Fair value measurement of a non-financial asset assumes the asset is sold consistently with its unit of account (as specified in other IFRSs), irrespective of its valuation premise. This assumption applies even if the highest and best use of the asset is in combination with other assets and/or liabilities. This is because the fair value measurement contemplates the sale of the individual asset to market participants that already hold, or are able to obtain, the complementary assets and liabilities. *[IFRS 13.32]*. Only when the unit of account of the item being measured at fair value is an asset group (which may be the case when measuring non-financial assets for impairment as part of a cash-generating unit), can one consider the sale of an asset group. That is, the valuation premise for a non-financial asset does not override the unit of account as defined by the applicable IFRS. However, this can be confusing in practice as both concepts deal with determining the appropriate level of aggregation or disaggregation for assets and liabilities.

Unit of account is an accounting concept. It identifies what is being measured for financial reporting purposes. When applying IFRS 13, this drives the level of aggregation (or disaggregation) for presentation and disclosure purposes, for example, whether the information presented and disclosed in the financial statements is for an individual asset or for a group of assets.

The valuation premise is a valuation concept (sometimes referred to as the 'unit of valuation'). It determines how the asset or liability is measured, i.e. based on the value it derives on a stand-alone basis or the value it derives in conjunction with other assets and liabilities. As discussed above, the unit of account established by an IFRS may be an individual item. However, that item may need to be grouped with others for the purpose of measuring fair value, i.e. the valuation premise may differ from the unit of account.

For example, an entity may own an investment property that is attached to land and contains other assets, such as fixtures and fittings. The unit of account for the investment property would likely be the stand-alone asset in accordance with IAS 40. However, the value of this asset on a stand-alone basis may have little meaning since it is physically attached to the land and derives its benefit in combination with the fixtures and fittings in the building. Therefore, when determining fair value, the valuation premise would likely reflect its use in combination with other assets.

It is important to note that when the valuation premise for measuring the fair value of a non-financial asset (or group of assets and corresponding liabilities) differs from its unit of account, categorisation within IFRS 13's fair value hierarchy (for disclosure purposes) must be determined at a level consistent with the unit of account for the asset or liability (see 16.2 below).

11 APPLICATION TO LIABILITIES AND AN ENTITY'S OWN EQUITY

IFRS 13 applies to liabilities, both financial and non-financial, and an entity's own equity whenever an IFRS requires those instruments to be measured at fair value. For example, in accordance with IFRS 3, in a business combination management might need to determine the fair value of liabilities assumed, when completing the purchase price allocation, and the fair value of its own equity instruments to measure the consideration given.

For financial liabilities and an entity's own equity that are within the scope of IAS 32 or IFRS 9 (or IAS 39), it is important to note that IFRS 13 would apply to any initial and subsequent fair value measurements that are recognised in the Statement of Financial Position. In addition, if those instruments are not subsequently measured at fair value in the Statement of Financial Position, for example financial liabilities may be subsequently measured at amortised cost, an entity may still need to disclose their fair value in the notes to the financial statements. At a minimum, this would be a requirement for financial liabilities. In these situations, IFRS 13 would also need to be applied to measure the instruments' fair value for disclosure.

The classification of an instrument as either a liability or equity instrument by other IFRSs may depend on the specific facts and circumstances, such as the characteristics of the transaction and the characteristics of the instrument. Examples of these instruments include contingent consideration issued in a business combination in accordance with IFRS 3 or equity warrants issued by an entity in accordance with IFRS 9 (or IAS 39). In developing the requirements in IFRS 13 for measuring the fair value of liabilities and an entity's own equity, the Boards concluded the requirements should generally be consistent between these instruments. That is, the accounting classification of an instrument, as either a liability or own equity, should not affect that instrument's fair value measurement. *[IFRS 13.BC106]*.

Prior to the issuance of IFRS 13, IFRS did not provide guidance on how to measure the fair value of an entity's own equity instruments. While IFRS 13 may be consistent with how many entities valued their own equity prior to adoption of IFRS 13, it changed practice for entities that concluded the principal market for their own equity (and therefore the assumption of market participants in that market) would be different when valuing the instrument as an asset. For example, this might have been the case if an entity measuring the fair value of a warrant previously assumed a volatility that differs from the volatility assumptions market participants would use in pricing the warrant as an asset.

11.1 General principles

Under IFRS 13, a fair value measurement assumes that a liability or an entity's own equity instrument is transferred to a market participant at the measurement date and that:

- for liabilities – the liability continues and the market participant transferee would be required to fulfil the obligation. That is, the liability is not settled with the counterparty or otherwise extinguished; and
- for an entity's own equity – the equity instrument would remain outstanding and the market participant transferee would take on the rights and responsibilities associated with the instrument. The instrument would not be cancelled or otherwise extinguished on the measurement date. *[IFRS 13.34]*.

11.1.1 Fair value of a liability

IFRS 13 states that the fair value measurement of a liability contemplates the transfer of the liability to a market participant at the measurement date. The liability is assumed to continue (i.e. it is not settled or extinguished), and the market participant to whom the liability is transferred would be required to fulfil the obligation.

The fair value of a liability also reflects the effect of non-performance risk. Non-performance risk is the risk that an obligation will not be fulfilled. This risk includes, but may not be limited to, the entity's own credit risk (see 11.2 below). The requirement that non-performance risk remains unchanged before and after the transfer implies that the liability is hypothetically transferred to a market participant of equal credit standing.

The clarification in IFRS 13 that fair value is not based on the price to settle a liability with the existing counterparty, but rather to transfer it to a market participant of equal credit standing, affects the assumptions about the principal (or most advantageous) market and the market participants in the exit market for the liability (see 11.1.3 below for further detail on the distinction between the settlement notion for liabilities and the transfer notion in IFRS 13).

11.1.2 Fair value of an entity's own equity

For an entity's own equity, IFRS 13 states that the fair value measurement would contemplate a transfer of the equity instrument. The equity instrument would remain outstanding and the market participant transferee would take on the rights and responsibilities associated with the instrument. The instrument would not be cancelled or otherwise extinguished on the measurement date.

The requirements for measuring the fair value of an entity's own equity are generally consistent with the requirements for measuring liabilities, except for the requirement to incorporate non-performance risk, which does not apply directly to an entity's own equity.

11.1.3 Settlement value versus transfer value

While IFRS 13 requires the use of an exit price to measure fair value, an entity might not intend (or be able) to transfer its liability to a third party. For example, it might be more beneficial for the entity to fulfil or settle a liability or the counterparty might not permit the liability to be transferred to another party. The issuer of an equity instrument may only be able to exit from that instrument if it ceases to exist or if the entity repurchases the instrument from the holder. Even if an entity is unable to transfer a liability, the IASB believes the transfer notion is necessary for measuring fair value, because 'it captures market participants' expectations about the liquidity, uncertainty and other associated factors whereas, a settlement notion may not because it may consider entity-specific factors'. *[IFRS 13.BC82].*

Under a transfer notion, the fair value of a liability is based on the price that would be paid to market participants to assume the obligation. The guidance is clear that an entity's intention to settle or otherwise fulfil the liability or exit the equity instrument is not relevant when measuring its fair value. Because the fair value of the liability is considered from the perspective of market participants, and not the entity itself, any relative efficiencies (or inefficiencies) of the reporting entity in settling the liability would not be considered in the fair value measurement.

Unlike a transfer notion, a settlement notion may allow for the consideration of a reporting entity's specific advantages (or disadvantages) in settling (or performing) the obligation. However, the Boards concluded that 'when a liability is measured at fair value, the relative efficiency of an entity in settling the liability using its own internal resources appears in profit or loss over the course of its settlement, and not before'. *[IFRS 13.BC81].*

While similar thought processes are needed to estimate both the amount to settle a liability and the amount to transfer that liability, *[IFRS 13.BC82],* IFRS 13 requires the fair value of a liability to be measured on the assumption that the liability is transferred to a market participant. Therefore, an entity cannot presume that the fair value of a liability is the same as its settlement value. In particular, the requirement to reflect the effect of non-performance risk in the fair value measurement of a liability could result in a difference between the fair value of a liability and the settlement value because it is unlikely that the counterparty would accept a different amount as settlement of the obligation if the entity's credit standing changed (i.e. the settlement value would not necessarily consider changes in credit risk). The IASB is expected to address this issue in its project on non-financial liabilities (see Chapter 28). At the time of writing, further development on this research project was on hold pending developments in the *Conceptual Framework* project, which is expected to be issued towards the end of 2017.[13]

11.2 Measuring the fair value of a liability or an entity's own equity when quoted prices for the liability or equity instruments are not available

In many cases, there may be no quoted prices available for the transfer of an instrument that is identical or similar to an entity's own equity or a liability, particularly as liabilities are generally not transferred. For example, this might be the case for debt obligations that are legally restricted from being transferred, or for decommissioning liabilities that the entity does not intend to transfer. In such situations, an entity must determine whether the identical item is held by another party as an asset:

- if the identical item is held by another party as an asset – an entity is required to measure the fair value of a liability or its own equity from the perspective of a market participant that holds the asset (see 11.2.1 below); *[IFRS 13.37]* and
- if the identical item is *not* held by another party as an asset – an entity measures the fair value of the liability or equity instrument using a valuation technique from the perspective of a market participant that owes the liability or has issued the claim on equity (see 11.2.2 below). *[IFRS 13.40]*.

Regardless of how an entity measures the fair value of a liability or its own equity, the entity is required to maximise the use of relevant observable inputs and minimise the use of unobservable inputs to meet the objective of a fair value measurement. That is, it must estimate the price at which an orderly transaction to transfer the liability or its own equity would take place between market participants at the measurement date under current market conditions. *[IFRS 13.36]*.

11.2.1 Liabilities or an entity's own equity that are held by other parties as assets

If there are no quoted prices available for the transfer of an identical or a similar liability or the entity's own equity instrument and the identical item is held by another party as an asset, an entity uses the fair value of the corresponding asset to measure the fair value of the liability or equity instrument. *[IFRS 13.37]*. The fair value of the asset should be measured from the perspective of the market participant that holds that asset at the measurement date. This approach applies even when the identical item held as an asset is not traded (i.e. when the fair value of the corresponding asset is a Level 3 measurement). For example, under the guidance in IFRS 13, the fair value of a contingent consideration liability should equal its fair value when held as an asset despite the fact that the asset would likely be a Level 3 measurement.

In these situations, the entity measures the fair value of the liability or its own equity by:

(a) using the quoted price in an active market for the identical item held by another party as an asset, if that price is available. This is illustrated in Example 14.14 below;

(b) if that price is not available, using other observable inputs, such as the quoted price in a market that is not active for the identical item held by another party as an asset; or

(c) if the observable prices in (a) and (b) are not available, using another valuation technique (see 14 below for further discussion), such as:

   (i) an income approach, as is illustrated in Example 14.15 below; or

   (ii) a market approach. *[IFRS 13.38]*.

As with all fair value measurements, inputs used to determine the fair value of a liability or an entity's own equity from the perspective of a market participant that holds the identical instrument as an asset must be prioritised in accordance with the fair value hierarchy. Accordingly, IFRS 13 indicates that the fair value of a liability or equity instrument held by another party as an asset should be determined based on the quoted price of the corresponding asset in an active market, if available. This is illustrated in

Example 14.14 below. If such a price is not available, other observable inputs for the identical asset would be used, such as a quoted price in an inactive market. In the absence of quoted prices for the identical instrument held as an asset, other valuation techniques, including an income approach (as is illustrated in Example 14.15 below) or a market approach, would be used to determine the liability's or equity's fair value. In these instances, the objective is still to determine the fair value of the liability or equity from the perspective of a market participant that holds the identical instrument as an asset.

In some cases, the corresponding asset price may need to be adjusted for factors specific to the identical item held as an asset but not applicable to the liability, such as the following:

- the quoted price for the asset relates to a similar (but not identical) liability or equity instrument held by another party as an asset. IFRS 13 gives the example of a liability or equity instrument where the credit quality of the issuer is different from that reflected in the fair value of the similar liability or equity instrument held as an asset; and
- the unit of account for the asset is not the same as for the liability or equity instrument. For instance, assume the price for an asset reflected a combined price for a package that comprised both the amounts due from the issuer and a third-party credit enhancement. If the unit of account for the liability is only its own liability, not the combined package, the entity would adjust the observed price for the asset to exclude the effect of the third-party credit enhancement. *[IFRS 13.39]*.

In addition, IFRS 13 states that when using the price of a corresponding asset to determine the fair value of a liability or entity's own equity, the fair value of the liability or equity should not incorporate the effect of any restriction preventing the sale of that asset. *[IFRS 13.39]*. If the quoted price did reflect the effect of a restriction, it would need to be adjusted. That is, all else being equal, the liability's or equity's fair value would be the same as the fair value of an otherwise unrestricted corresponding asset.

The fair value of a liability may also differ from the price of its corresponding asset when the instrument is priced within a bid-ask spread. In these instances, the liability should be valued based on the price within the bid-ask spread that is most representative of where the liability would be exited, not the corresponding asset (see 15.3 below for discussion on pricing within the bid-ask spread).

The Boards believe the fair value of a liability or equity instrument will equal the fair value of a properly defined corresponding asset (i.e. an asset whose features mirror those of the liability), assuming an exit from both positions in the same market. This assumes markets are efficient and arbitrage free. For example, if the prices differed for a liability and the corresponding asset, the market participant taking on the liability would be able to earn a profit by financing the purchase of the asset with the proceeds received by taking on the liability. In an efficient market, the price for the liability and the price for the asset would adjust until the arbitrage opportunity was eliminated. In the Boards' view, the price for the liability or equity instrument and the corresponding asset would generally only differ if the entity was measuring an asset relating to a similar (not identical) instrument or the unit of account was different. The Boards did consider whether the effects of illiquidity could create a difference but noted that they are difficult to differentiate from credit-related effects. *[IFRS 13.BC88, BC89]*.

The following two examples extracted from IFRS 13 include factors to consider when measuring the fair value of a liability or entity's own equity by estimating the fair value of the corresponding asset held by another party. *[IFRS 13.IE40-42]*. The first example highlights how entities need to assess whether the quoted price for a corresponding asset includes the effects of factors not applicable to the liability. However, for the sake of simplicity, the example does not consider bid-ask spread considerations.

Example 14.14: Debt obligation: quoted price

On 1 January 20X1 Entity B issues at par a CU 2 million BBB-rated exchange-traded five-year fixed rate debt instrument with an annual 10% coupon. Entity B designated this financial liability as at fair value through profit or loss.

On 31 December 20X1 the instrument is trading as an asset in an active market at CU 929 per CU 1,000 of par value after payment of accrued interest. Entity B uses the quoted price of the asset in an active market as its initial input into the fair value measurement of its liability (CU 929 × [CU 2,000,000/CU 1,000] = CU 1,858,000).

In determining whether the quoted price of the asset in an active market represents the fair value of the liability, Entity B evaluates whether the quoted price of the asset includes the effect of factors not applicable to the fair value measurement of a liability, for example, whether the quoted price of the asset includes the effect of a third-party credit enhancement if that credit enhancement would be separately accounted for from the perspective of the issuer. Entity B determines that no adjustments are required to the quoted price of the asset. Accordingly, Entity B concludes that the fair value of its debt instrument at 31 December 20X1 is CU 1,858,000. Entity B categorises and discloses the fair value measurement of its debt instrument within Level 1 of the fair value hierarchy.

The second example provides factors that would be incorporated when using a present value technique to estimate the fair value of a financial liability (e.g. changes in credit spreads for the liability), as well as factors that would be excluded (e.g. adjustments related to transferability restrictions or profit margin). *[IFRS 13.IE43-47]*.

Example 14.15: Debt obligation: present value technique

On 1 January 20X1 Entity C issues at par in a private placement a CU 2,000,000 BBB-rated five-year fixed rate debt instrument with an annual 10% coupon. Entity C designated this financial liability as at fair value through profit or loss.

At 31 December 20X1 Entity C still carries a BBB credit rating. Market conditions, including available interest rates, credit spreads for a BBB-quality credit rating and liquidity, remain unchanged from the date the debt instrument was issued. However, Entity C's credit spread has deteriorated by 50 basis points because of a change in its risk of non-performance. After taking into account all market conditions, Entity C concludes that if it was to issue the instrument at the measurement date, the instrument would bear a rate of interest of 10.5% or Entity C would receive less than par in proceeds from the issue of the instrument.

For the purpose of this example, the fair value of Entity C's liability is calculated using a present value technique. Entity C concludes that a market participant would use all the following inputs when estimating the price the market participant would expect to receive to assume Entity C's obligation:

(a) the terms of the debt instrument, including all the following:
  (i) coupon of 10%;
  (ii) principal amount of CU 2,000,000; and
  (iii) term of four years.
(b) the market rate of interest of 10.5% (which includes a change of 50 basis points in the risk of non-performance from the date of issue).

On the basis of its present value technique, Entity C concludes that the fair value of its liability at 31 December 20X1 is CU 1,968,641.

Entity C does not include any additional input into its present value technique for risk or profit that a market participant might require for compensation for assuming the liability. Because Entity C's obligation is a financial liability, Entity C concludes that the interest rate already captures the risk or profit that a market participant would require as compensation for assuming the liability. Furthermore, Entity C does not adjust its present value technique for the existence of a restriction preventing it from transferring the liability.

While the example above assumes that relevant market data on the non-performance risk of the debt obligation is readily available, estimating the appropriate credit spreads is often the most challenging aspect of using a present value technique to value a debt instrument. Credit spreads on identical or similar liabilities issued by the same obligor represent high quality market data. But even when issued by the same obligor, credit spreads on liabilities with significantly different features or characteristics may not appropriately capture the credit risk of the liability being measured. When spreads on identical instruments do not exist and data from comparable debt instruments (e.g. option adjusted spreads (OAS)) is used, the specific characteristics of these comparable liabilities (e.g. tenor, seniority, collateral, coupon, principal amortisation, covenant strength, etc.) should be analysed carefully. In addition, credit default swap (CDS) spreads, which represent the compensation required by the CDS issuer to accept the default risk of a debt issuer (i.e. the reference obligor), may also provide useful market data.

In some instances, observable market data is not available for a specific debt issuer, but the issuer has a reported credit rating. In these circumstances, credit spreads or CDS spreads of similarly rated entities or debt instruments may be used as a proxy to evaluate the credit risk of the liability being measured. Once again, the specific characteristics of these similar debt instruments and the subject liability should be compared.

Other situations may involve a liability with no observable credit quality measures (e.g. credit spreads) issued by an entity that is not rated. In these circumstances, techniques such as a regression or other quantitative analysis may be performed to determine the credit quality of the issuer. Comparing financial metrics such as profit margins, leverage ratios, and asset sizes between the non-rated issuer of the liability being measured to rated entities may allow a credit rating to be estimated. Once a credit rating has been determined, an appropriate credit spread could be quantified from other comparable (i.e. similarly rated) debt instruments.

11.2.2 Liabilities or an entity's own equity not held by other parties as assets

While many liabilities are held by market participants as corresponding assets, some are not. For example, there is typically no corresponding asset holder for a decommissioning liability. When no observable price is available for a liability and no corresponding asset exists, the fair value of the liability is measured from the perspective of a market participant that owes the liability, using an appropriate valuation technique (e.g. a present value technique). *[IFRS 13.40]*.

Generally, an instrument classified as an entity's own equity would have a corresponding asset. However, if no corresponding asset exists and no observable price is available for an entity's own equity, fair value is measured from the perspective of a market participant that has issued the claim on equity, using an appropriate valuation technique.

IFRS 13 gives two examples of what an entity might take into account in measuring fair value in this situation:

(a) the future cash outflows that a market participant would expect to incur in fulfilling the obligation (i.e. a present value technique). This includes any compensation a market participant would require for taking on the obligation. This approach is discussed further at 11.2.2.A below; and

(b) the amount that a market participant would receive to enter into an identical liability, or issue an identical equity instrument. This approach is discussed further at 11.2.2.B below. *[IFRS 13.41]*.

11.2.2.A Use of present value techniques to measure fair value for liabilities and an entity's own equity instruments not held by other parties as assets

If an entity uses a present value technique to measure the fair value of a liability or its own equity not held by other parties as assets, IFRS 13 requires the entity to estimate the future cash outflows that a market participant would expect to incur in fulfilling the obligation, among other things. The estimated cash flows include:

- market participants' expectations about the costs of fulfilling the obligation; and
- compensation that a market participant would require for taking on the obligation. This compensation includes the return that a market participant would require for the following:
  - (i) undertaking the activity (i.e. the value of fulfilling the obligation) – for example, by using resources that could be used for other activities; and
  - (ii) assuming the risk associated with the obligation (i.e. a *risk premium* that reflects the risk that the actual cash outflows might differ from the expected cash outflows). *[IFRS 13.B31]*.

In some cases, the components of the return a market participant would require will be indistinguishable from one another. In other cases, an entity will need to estimate those components separately. For example, assume an entity uses the price a third-party contractor would charge as part of the discounted cash flows. If the contract is priced on a fixed fee basis, both the return for undertaking the activity and the risk premium would be indistinguishable. However, as is shown in Example 14.16 below, if the contractor would charge on a cost plus basis, an entity would need to estimate the components separately, because the contractor in that case would not bear the risk of future changes in costs. *[IFRS 13.B32]*.

A risk premium can be included in such fair value measurements, either by:

(a) adjusting the cash flows (i.e. as an increase in the amount of cash outflows); or

(b) adjusting the rate used to discount the future cash flows to their present values (i.e. as a reduction in the discount rate).

However, an entity must ensure adjustments for risk are not double-counted or omitted. *[IFRS 13.B33]*.

IFRS 13 provides the following example, which illustrates how these considerations would be captured when using a valuation technique to measure the fair value of a liability not held by another party as an asset. *[IFRS 13.IE35-39]*.

Example 14.16: Decommissioning liability

On 1 January 20X1 Entity A assumes a decommissioning liability in a business combination. The entity is legally required to dismantle and remove an offshore oil platform at the end of its useful life, which is estimated to be 10 years. Entity A uses the expected present value technique to measure the fair value of the decommissioning liability.

If Entity A were contractually allowed to transfer its decommissioning liability to a market participant, Entity A would conclude that a market participant would use all the following inputs, probability-weighted as appropriate, when estimating the price it would expect to receive:

(a) labour costs;

(b) allocation of overhead costs;

(c) the compensation that a market participant would require for undertaking the activity and for assuming the risk associated with the obligation to dismantle and remove the asset. Such compensation includes both of the following:

  (i) profit on labour and overhead costs; and

  (ii) the risk that the actual cash outflows might differ from those expected, excluding inflation;

(d) effect of inflation on estimated costs and profits;

(e) time value of money, represented by the risk-free rate; and

(f) non-performance risk relating to the risk that Entity A will not fulfil the obligation, including Entity A's own credit risk.

The significant assumptions used by Entity A to measure fair value are as follows:

(a) Labour costs are developed on the basis of current marketplace wages, adjusted for expectations of future wage increases and a requirement to hire contractors to dismantle and remove offshore oil platforms. Entity A assigns probability assessments to a range of cash flow estimates as follows:

Cash flow estimate CU	Probability assessment	Expected cash flows CU
100,000	25%	25,000
125,000	50%	62,500
175,000	25%	43,750
		131,250

The probability assessments are developed on the basis of Entity A's experience with fulfilling obligations of this type and its knowledge of the market.

(b) Entity A estimates allocated overhead and equipment operating costs using the rate it applies to labour costs (80% of expected labour costs). This is consistent with the cost structure of market participants.

(c) Entity A estimates the compensation that a market participant would require for undertaking the activity and for assuming the risk associated with the obligation to dismantle and remove the asset as follows:

  (i) A third-party contractor typically adds a mark-up on labour and allocated internal costs to provide a profit margin on the job. The profit margin used (20%) represents Entity A's understanding of the operating profit that contractors in the industry generally earn to dismantle and remove offshore oil platforms. Entity A concludes that this rate is consistent with the rate that a market participant would require as compensation for undertaking the activity.

  (ii) A contractor would typically require compensation for the risk that the actual cash outflows might differ from those expected because of the uncertainty inherent in locking in today's price for a project that will not occur for 10 years. Entity A estimates the amount of that premium to be 5% of the expected cash flows, including the effect of inflation.

(d) Entity A assumes a rate of inflation of 4% over the 10-year period on the basis of available market data.

(e) The risk-free rate of interest for a 10-year maturity on 1 January 20X1 is 5%. Entity A adjusts that rate by 3.5% to reflect its risk of non-performance (i.e. the risk that it will not fulfil the obligation), including its credit risk. Therefore, the discount rate used to compute the present value of the cash flows is 8.5%.

Entity A concludes that its assumptions would be used by market participants. In addition, Entity A does not adjust its fair value measurement for the existence of a restriction preventing it from transferring the liability even if such a restriction exists. As illustrated in the following table, Entity A measures the fair value of its decommissioning liability as CU 194,879.

	Expected cash flows CU
Expected labour costs	131,250
Allocated overhead and equipment costs (0.80 × CU 131,250)	105,000
Contractor's profit mark-up [0.20 × (CU 131,250 + CU 105,000)]	47,250
Expected cash flows before inflation adjustment	283,500
Inflation factor (4% for 10 years)	1.4802
Expected cash flows adjusted for inflation	419,637
Market risk premium (0.05 × CU 419,637)	20,982
Expected cash flows adjusted for market risk	440,619
Expected present value using discount rate of 8.5% for 10 years	194,879

In practice, estimating the risk premium for a decommissioning liability, such as in the example above, requires significant judgement, particularly in circumstances where the decommissioning activities will be performed many years in the future. Information about the compensation market participants would demand to assume decommissioning liability may be limited, because very few decommissioning liabilities are transferred in the manner contemplated by IFRS 13.

Because of these data limitations, entities might look to risk premiums observed from business combinations where decommissioning liabilities are assumed, including their own business combination transactions. IFRS 13 indicates that when market information is not reasonably available, an entity may consider its own data in developing assumptions related to the market risk premium (see 19 below for additional discussion on the use of an entity's own data to determine unobservable inputs).

Alternatively, as noted above, the market risk premium might be estimated by considering the difference between a fixed-price arrangement and a cost-plus arrangement with a third party to complete the remediation and monitor the site. The difference between the fixed-price arrangement and the cost-plus arrangement may provide insight into the risk premium market participants would demand to fulfil the obligation.

While all available evidence about market participant assumptions regarding the market risk premium should be considered, circumstances may exist when an explicit assumption cannot be determined. In such cases, based on the specific guidance in IFRS 13 – which acknowledges that explicit assumptions in some cases may not be able to be incorporated into the measurement of decommissioning liability – we believe the market risk premium may be incorporated into the fair value measurement on an implicit basis.

11.2.2.B Consideration of an entry price in measuring a liability or entity's own equity not held as an asset

Although fair value represents an exit price, IFRS 13 indicates that in certain situations an entry price may be considered in estimating the fair value of a liability or an entity's own equity instrument. This approach uses assumptions that market participants would use when pricing the identical item (e.g. having the same credit characteristics) in the principal (or most advantageous) market – that is, the principal (or most advantageous) market for issuing a liability or equity instrument with the same contractual terms.

The standard allows for entry prices to be considered in estimating the fair value of a liability because the IASB believes that a liability's entry and exit prices will be identical in many instances. As a result, the price at which a market participant could enter into the identical liability on the measurement date (e.g. an obligation having the same credit characteristics) may be indicative of its fair value.

However, an entry price may differ from the exit price for a liability for a number of reasons. For example, an entity may transfer the liability in a different market from that in which the obligation was incurred. When entry and exit prices differ, IFRS 13 is clear that the objective of the measurement remains an exit price.

11.3 Non-performance risk

IFRS 13 requires a fair value measurement of a liability to incorporate non-performance risk (i.e. the risk that an obligation will not be fulfilled). Conceptually, non-performance risk encompasses more than just an entity's credit risk. It may also include other risks, such as settlement risk. In the case of non-financial instruments, such as commodity contracts, non-performance risk could represent the risk associated with physically extracting and transferring an asset to the point of delivery. When measuring the fair value of a liability, an entity must:

- Take into account the effect of its credit risk (credit standing) and any other factors that could influence the likelihood whether or not the obligation will be fulfilled.
- Assume that non-performance risk will be the same before and after the transfer of a liability.
- Ensure the effect of non-performance risk on the fair value of the liability is consistent with its unit of account for financial reporting purposes.

  If a liability is issued with a third-party credit enhancement that the issuer accounts for separately from the liability, the fair value of the liability does not include the effect of the credit enhancement (e.g. a third-party guarantee of debt). That is, the issuer would take into account its own credit standing and not that of the third-party guarantor when measuring the fair value of the liability (see 11.3.1 below). *[IFRS 13.42-44]*.

An entity takes into account the effect of its credit risk (credit standing) on the fair value of the liability in all periods in which the liability is measured at fair value because market participants valuing the entity's obligations as assets would take into account the effect of the entity's credit standing when estimating the prices at which they would transact. *[IFRS 13.IE31]*. Valuation techniques continue to evolve and new concepts are developing in relation to considering non-performance risk. Whether an entity should incorporate them into an IFRS 13 fair value measurement depends on whether market participants would take them into account.

Incorporating non-performance risk into subsequent fair value measurements of a liability is also consistent with the notion that credit risk affects the initial measurement of a liability. Since the terms of a liability are determined based on an entity's credit standing at the time of issuance (and since IFRS 13 assumes the liability is transferred to another party with the same credit standing at the measurement date), subsequent changes in an entity's credit standing will result in the obligation's terms being favourable or unfavourable relative to current market requirements. The standard gives the following example illustrating how the fair value of the same instrument could be different depending on the credit risk of the issuer. *[IFRS 13.IE32]*.

Example 14.17: Non-performance risk

Assume that Entity X and Entity Y each enter into a contractual obligation to pay cash (CU 500) to Entity Z in five years. Entity X has a AA credit rating and can borrow at 6%, and Entity Y has a BBB credit rating and can borrow at 12%. Entity X will receive about CU 374 in exchange for its promise (the present value of CU 500 in five years at 6%). Entity Y will receive about CU 284 in exchange for its promise (the present value of CU 500 in five years at 12%). The fair value of the liability to each entity (i.e. the proceeds) incorporates that entity's credit standing.

The effect of non-performance risk on the fair value measurement of the liability will depend on factors, such as the terms of any related credit enhancement or the nature of the liability – that is, whether the liability is an obligation to deliver cash (a financial liability) or an obligation to deliver goods or services (a non-financial liability). The following example, from the standard, illustrates changes in fair value measurement due to changes in non-performance risk. As indicated in this example, changes to an entity's non-performance risk does not require there to be a change in credit rating. Instead, such changes are often based on changes in credit spreads. *[IFRS 13.IE34]*.

Example 14.18: Structured note

On 1 January 20X7 Entity A, an investment bank with a AA credit rating, issues a five-year fixed rate note to Entity B. The contractual principal amount to be paid by Entity A at maturity is linked to an equity index. No credit enhancements are issued in conjunction with or otherwise related to the contract (i.e. no collateral is posted and there is no third-party guarantee). Entity A designated this note as at fair value through profit or loss. The fair value of the note (i.e. the obligation of Entity A) during 20X7 is measured using an expected present value technique. Changes in fair value are as follows:

(a) *Fair value at 1 January 20X7* – The expected cash flows used in the expected present value technique are discounted at the risk-free rate using the government bond curve at 1 January 20X7, plus the current market observable AA corporate bond spread to government bonds, if non-performance risk is not already reflected in the cash flows, adjusted (either up or down) for Entity A's specific credit risk (i.e. resulting in a credit-adjusted risk-free rate). Therefore, the fair value of Entity A's obligation at initial recognition takes into account non-performance risk, including that entity's credit risk, which presumably is reflected in the proceeds.

(b) *Fair value at 31 March 20X7* – During March 20X7 the credit spread for AA corporate bonds widens, with no changes to the specific credit risk of Entity A. The expected cash flows used in the expected present value technique are discounted at the risk-free rate using the government bond curve at 31 March 20X7, plus the current market observable AA corporate bond spread to government bonds, if non-performance risk is not already reflected in the cash flows, adjusted for Entity A's specific credit risk (i.e. resulting in a credit-adjusted risk-free rate). Entity A's specific credit risk is unchanged from initial recognition. Therefore, the fair value of Entity A's obligation changes as a result of changes in credit spreads generally. Changes in credit spreads reflect current market participant assumptions about changes in non-performance risk generally, changes in liquidity risk and the compensation required for assuming those risks.

(c) *Fair value at 30 June 20X7* – As at 30 June 20X7 there have been no changes to the AA corporate bond spreads. However, on the basis of structured note issues corroborated with other qualitative information, Entity A determines that its own specific creditworthiness has strengthened within the AA credit spread. The expected cash flows used in the expected present value technique are discounted at the risk-free rate using the government bond yield curve at 30 June 20X7, plus the current market observable AA corporate bond spread to government bonds (unchanged from 31 March 20X7), if non-performance risk is not already reflected in the cash flows, adjusted for Entity A's specific credit risk (i.e. resulting in a credit-adjusted risk-free rate). Therefore, the fair value of the obligation of Entity A changes as a result of the change in its own specific credit risk within the AA corporate bond spread.

The standard's assumption that the non-performance risk related to a liability is the same before and after its transfer is not intended to reflect reality. In most cases, the reporting entity and the market participant transferee will have different credit standings. However, this assumption is important when measuring fair value under IFRS 13 for the following reasons:

- if the transaction results in changes to the non-performance risk associated with the liability, the market participant taking on the obligation would not enter into the transaction without reflecting that change in the price.

  IFRS 13 gives the following examples; a creditor would not generally permit a debtor to transfer its obligation to another party of lower credit standing, nor would a transferee of higher credit standing be willing to assume the obligation using the same terms negotiated by the transferor if those terms reflect the transferor's lower credit standing;
- if IFRS 13 did not specify the credit standing of the entity taking on the obligation, there could be fundamentally different fair values for a liability depending on an entity's assumptions about the characteristics of the market participant transferee; and
- those who might hold the entity's liability as an asset would consider the effect of the entity's credit risk and other risk factors when pricing those assets (see 11.2.1 above). *[IFRS 13.BC94]*.

The requirements of IFRS 13 regarding non-performance risk, when measuring fair value for liabilities, are consistent with the fair value measurement guidance in IFRSs prior to the issuance of IFRS 13. Specifically, IFRS 9 (or IAS 39) both referred to making adjustments for credit risk if market participants would reflect that risk when pricing a financial instrument. However, the IASB acknowledged that there was inconsistent application of that principle for two reasons. Firstly, IFRS 9 (or IAS 39) referred to credit risk generally and did not specifically refer to the reporting entity's own credit risk. Secondly, there were different interpretations about how an entity's own credit risk should be reflected in the fair value of a liability using the settlement notion, under the previous definition of fair value, because it was unlikely that the counterparty would accept a different amount as settlement of the obligation if the entity's credit standing changed. *[IFRS 13.BC92, BC93]*. As such, adoption of IFRS 13 may have resulted in a change for some entities in this regard.

In developing IFRS 13, there was some debate among constituents about the usefulness of including non-performance risk after initial recognition because this might lead to counter-intuitive and potentially confusing reporting (i.e. gains for credit deterioration and losses for credit improvements). However, in the IASB's view, this does not affect how to measure fair value, but rather whether an IFRS should require fair value measurement subsequent to initial recognition, which is outside the scope of IFRS 13. The standard is clear that a measurement that does not consider the effect of an entity's non-performance risk is not a fair value measurement. *[IFRS 13.BC95]*. The adoption of IFRS 9 may resolve some of these concerns. For financial liabilities designated at fair value through profit or loss (using the fair value option), IFRS 9 requires fair value changes that are the result of changes in an entity's own credit risk to be presented in other comprehensive income, unless doing so would introduce an accounting mismatch. If it would introduce an accounting mismatch, the whole fair value change is presented in profit or loss (see Chapter 50 at 2 for further discussion). *[IFRS 9.5.7.7]*.

11.3.1 Liabilities issued with third-party credit enhancements

As discussed at 11.3 above, IFRS 13 requires entities to measure the fair value of a liability issued with an inseparable third-party credit enhancement from the issuer's perspective, i.e. considering the issuer's credit risk rather than that of the third-party providing the credit enhancement. This would apply in situations where a credit enhancement (or guarantee) is purchased by an issuer, then combined with a liability and issued as a combined security to an investor. IFRS 13's requirements are based on the fact that the third-party credit enhancement does not relieve the issuer of its ultimate obligation under the liability. Generally, if the issuer fails to meet its payment obligations to the investor, the guarantor has an obligation to make the payments on the issuer's behalf and the issuer has an obligation to the guarantor. By issuing debt combined with a credit enhancement, the issuer is able to market its debt more easily and can either reduce the interest rate paid to the investor or receive higher proceeds when the debt is issued.

IFRS 13 requires the fair value measurement of a liability to follow the unit of account of the liability for financial reporting purposes. The standard anticipates that there may be instances where, even though it may be inseparable, the credit enhancement may need to be separated (i.e. separately recognised) for financial reporting purposes. However, this assumes that: (i) the unit of account is clear in other standards, which may not be the case; and (ii) that standards, such as IFRS 9 (or IAS 39), may permit or require separation when a credit enhancement is inseparable.

As discussed in Figure 14.4 below, if the unit of account excludes the credit enhancement, the fair value of the liability measured from the issuer's perspective in accordance with IFRS 13, will not equal its fair value as a guaranteed liability held by another party as an asset. The fair value of the asset held by the investor considers the credit standing of the guarantor. However, under the guarantee, any payments made by the guarantor result in a transfer of the issuer's debt obligation from the investor to the guarantor. That is, the amount owed by the issuer does not change; the issuer must now pay the guarantor instead of the investor. Therefore, as discussed at 11.2.1 above, if the fair value of a third-party guaranteed liability is measured based on the fair value of the corresponding asset, it would need to be adjusted. *[IFRS 13.BC96-BC98]*.

Figure 14.4: Liabilities with credit enhancements

	Issuer's perspective (i.e. the obligor)	Perspective of the entity that holds the corresponding asset
Credit enhancement provided by the issuer (e.g. collateral or master netting agreement)		
Separate unit of account?	Dependent on the relevant IFRS (e.g. IFRS 9 (or IAS 39)). Depending on the nature of the credit enhancement, it may be recognised (e.g. collateral recognised as an asset in the financial statements of the issuer) or unrecognised (e.g. a master netting agreement).	Dependent on the relevant IFRS (e.g. IFRS 9 (or IAS 39)) and the nature of the credit enhancement.
Considered in the fair value measurement?	Generally, yes. The fair value measurement of a liability takes into consideration the credit standing of the issuer. The effect may differ depending on the terms of the related credit enhancement.	Possibly. If the credit enhancement is not accounted for separately, the fair value of the corresponding asset would take into consideration the effect of the related the credit enhancement.
Credit enhancement provided by a third-party (e.g. financial guarantee)		
Separate unit of account?	Dependent on the relevant IFRS (e.g. IFRS 9 (or IAS 39)). Likely to be a separate unit of account and remain unrecognised, unless the issuer fails to meet its obligations under the liability.	Dependent on the relevant IFRS (e.g. IFRS 9 (or IAS 39)) and the nature of the credit enhancement.
Considered in the fair value measurement?	Generally, no. If the credit enhancement is accounted for separately from the liability, the issuer would take into account its own credit standing and not that of the third party guarantor when measuring the fair value of the liability.	Possibly. If the credit enhancement is not accounted for separately, the fair value of the corresponding asset would take into consideration the effect of the related third-party credit enhancement.

11.3.1.A Do the requirements of IFRS 13 regarding third-party credit enhancements in a fair value measurement apply to liabilities other than debt?

The requirements of IFRS 13 for liabilities issued with third-party credit enhancements apply to all liabilities that are measured or disclosed at fair value on a recurring basis. Although the requirements would not affect financial liabilities after their initial recognition if they are subsequently measured at amortised cost in accordance with IFRS 9 (or IAS 39), it would apply to the disclosure of the fair value of those liabilities, as required by IFRS 7.

While an issuer's accounting for guaranteed debt may be the most common application of this guidance, the clarification with respect to the unit of account for certain types of credit enhancements could affect other liabilities, including derivative instruments measured at fair value in accordance with IFRS 9 (or IAS 39). Many OTC derivative contracts are subject to credit support requirements under an International Swaps and Derivatives Association[14] (ISDA) Master Agreement between the derivative counterparties. The application of this guidance to OTC derivatives will depend on the nature of the credit support provided. For example, while credit support is typically provided through the posting of collateral, in certain industries posting a letter of credit (LOC) for the benefit of a derivative counterparty is not uncommon.

In those instances where a LOC is posted for the benefit of a derivative counterparty, we believe the requirement in paragraph 44 of IFRS 13, to consider the issuer's credit risk rather than that of the third party providing the LOC, would generally apply. *[IFRS 13.44]*. If an entity defaults on its derivative contracts, the bank issuing the LOC will pay the counterparty and the entity's obligation merely transfers from the original counterparty to the issuing bank. In other words, the entity will have a continuing obligation, even in the event it defaults on the derivative. As such, the entity's non-performance risk (not that of the bank providing the LOC) would be considered in determining the fair value of the derivative liability. We believe this generally would apply even if the LOC were deemed separable from the derivative contract. In our view, including the effect of separable credit enhancements while excluding the effect of inseparable credit enhancements would contradict the principles of IFRS 13.

11.3.2 Does IFRS 13 require an entity to consider the effects of both counterparty credit risk and its own credit risk when valuing its derivative transactions?

IFRS 13 addresses the issue of credit risk both explicitly and implicitly. As discussed at 11.3 above, in relation to an entity's own credit risk in the valuation of liabilities, the guidance is explicit; the fair value of a liability should reflect the effect of non-performance risk, which includes own credit risk.

The standard's requirements are less explicit regarding counterparty credit risk. IFRS 13 requires the fair value of an asset or liability to be measured based on market participant assumptions. Because market participants consider counterparty credit risk in pricing a derivative contract, an entity's valuation methodology should incorporate counterparty credit risk in its measurement of fair value.

11.3.3 How should an entity incorporate credit risk into the valuation of its derivative contracts?

As discussed at 11.3.2 above, IFRS 13 requires entities to consider the effects of credit risk when determining a fair value measurement, e.g. by calculating a debit valuation adjustment (DVA) or a credit valuation adjustment (CVA) on their derivatives.

As no specific method is prescribed in IFRS 13, various approaches are used in practice by derivatives dealers and end-users to estimate the effect of credit risk on the fair value of OTC derivatives.

The degree of sophistication in the credit adjustment valuation method used by a reporting entity is influenced by the qualitative factors noted below. Estimation can be complex and requires the use of significant judgement which is often influenced by various qualitative factors, including:

- the materiality of the entity's derivative's carrying value to its financial statements;
- the number and type of contracts for derivatives in the entity's portfolio;
- the extent to which derivative instruments are either deeply in or out of the money;
- the existence and terms of credit mitigation arrangements (e.g. collateral arrangements in place);
- the cost and availability of technology to model complex credit exposures;
- the cost and consistent availability of suitable input data to calculate an accurate credit adjustment; and
- the credit worthiness of the entity and its counterparties.

While the degree of sophistication and complexity may differ by entity and by the size and nature of the derivative portfolio, any inputs used under any methodology should be consistent with assumptions market participants would use. The complexity and judgement involved in selecting and consistently applying a method may require entities to provide additional disclosures to assist users of financial statements (see 20 below). 11.3.3.A to 11.3.4.B below provide further insights into some of the considerations for determining valuation adjustments for credit risk on derivatives measured at fair value, except for which a quoted price in an active market is available (i.e. over-the-counter derivatives).

In situations where an entity has a master netting agreement or credit support annex[15] (CSA) with a counterparty, the entity may consider the credit risk of its derivative instruments with that counterparty on a net basis if it qualifies to use the measurement exception noted at 2.5.2 above (see 12 below for more detail on applying the measurement exception for financial instruments with offsetting credit risks).

11.3.3.A How do credit adjustments work?

In simple terms, the requirement for a credit adjustment as a component of fair value measurement can be analogised to the need for a provision on a trade receivable or an impairment charge on an item of property, plant and equipment. Whilst this analogy helps conceptualise the requirement, the characteristics of derivatives mean that the calculation itself can be significantly more complex than for assets measured at amortised cost.

Consistent with the fact that credit risk affects the initial measurement of a derivative asset or liability, IFRS 13 requires that changes in counterparty credit risk or an entity's own credit standing be considered in subsequent fair value measurements. It cannot be assumed that the parties to the derivative contract will perform.

The terms of the asset or liability were determined based on the counterparty's or entity's credit standing at the time of entering into the contract. In addition, IFRS 13 assumes a liability is transferred to another party with the same credit standing at the measurement date. As a result, subsequent changes in a counterparty's or entity's credit standing will result in the derivative's terms being favourable or unfavourable relative to current market conditions.

Unlike the credit exposure of a 'vanilla' receivable, which generally remains constant over time (typically at the principal amount of the receivable), the bilateral nature of the credit exposure in many derivatives varies, whereby both parties to the contract may face potential exposure in the future. As such, many instruments may possibly have a value that is either positive (a derivative asset) or negative (a derivative liability) at different points in time based on changes in the underlying variables of the contract.

Figure 14.5 below illustrates the effect on the income statement and on the statement of financial position of CVA and DVA adjustments as a component of fair value measurement on a single derivative asset or liability.

Figure 14.5: Accounting for CVA and DVA

	Derivative asset example – CVA	CU		Derivative liability example – DVA	CU
Derivative position valued using the risk-free curve (1)	Risk-free derivative asset	100,000		Risk-free derivative liability	(100,000)
Credit adjustment required (2)	Counterparty credit adjustment	(10,000)		Debit adjustment based on own credit	5,000
Credit-adjusted derivative position	Derivative asset	90,000		Derivative liability	(95,000)

Subsequent credit movements

Counterparty credit improves	A gain arises in the income statement and is reflected by a larger derivative asset in the statement of financial position	Own credit improves	A loss arises in the income statement and is reflected by a larger derivative liability in the statement of financial position
Counterparty credit deteriorates	A further CVA charge is required in the income statement and is reflected by a reduced derivative asset in the statement of financial position	Own credit deteriorates	A further DVA credit is required to the income statement and is reflected by a reduced derivative liability in the statement of financial position

Notes:

(1) The table represents a point-in-time during the life of a derivative asset or liability

(2) For illustrative purposes, we have assumed the counterparty credit valuation adjustment is CU 10,000 and the debit valuation adjustment is CU 5,000. These credit adjustments are not intended to reflect reality

11.3.3.B Valuation methods

The determination of a credit adjustment can be complex. Part of the complexity stems from the particular nature of credit risk in many OTC derivative contracts. Credit risk associated with a derivative contract is similar to other forms of credit risk in that the cause of economic loss is an obligor's default on its contractual obligation. However, for many derivative products, two features set credit risk apart from traditional forms of credit risk in instruments such as debt:

- the uncertainty of the future exposure associated with the instrument – this is due to the uncertainty of future changes in value of the derivative, as the cash flows required under the instrument stem from: (a) movements in underlying variables that drive the value of the contract; and (b) the progression of time towards the contract's expiry; and

- the bilateral nature of credit exposure in many derivatives, whereby both parties to the contract may face potential exposure in the future – this can occur in instruments, such as swaps and forwards, given the potential for these derivatives to 'flip' from an asset to a liability (or *vice versa*), based on changes in the underlying variables to the contract (e.g. interest rates or foreign exchange rates).

As previously noted at 11.3.3 above, IFRS does not prescribe any specific valuation methods to quantify the impact of non-performance risk on derivatives' fair value. IFRS 13 is a principles-based standard intended to provide a general framework for measuring fair value. It was not intended to provide detailed application guidance for calculating the fair value of various types of assets and liabilities. Likewise, IFRS 9 (and IAS 39) does not provide specific valuation guidance related to derivatives. As a result, extensive judgement needs to be applied, potentially resulting in diversity in the methods and approaches used to quantify credit risk, particularly as it pertains to derivatives. As discussed at 11.3.3 above, a variety of factors may influence the method an entity chooses for estimating credit adjustments. In addition, the cost and availability of technology and input data to model complex credit exposures will also be a contributing factor.

In recent years, some derivative dealers have started to include a funding valuation adjustment (FVA) in the valuation of their uncollateralised derivative positions, as is illustrated in Extract 14.1 at 20.2 below. FVA is included in order to capture the funding cost (or benefit) that results from posting (or receiving) collateral on inter-bank transactions that are used to economically hedge the market risk associated with these uncollateralised trades. The methods for determining FVA can vary. As such, determining whether these methods comply with IFRS 13 requires judgement based on the specific facts and circumstances. A number of valuation adjustments have also emerged in addition to CVA, DVA and FVA. Examples include self-default potential hedging (LVA), collateral (CollVA) and market hedging positions (HVA), as well as tail risk (KVA), collectively these are now referred to as X-Value Adjustments (XVA). It is important to note that some of these valuation adjustments may be useful for internal reporting, but may not be appropriate to use when measuring fair value in accordance with IFRS 13. As noted above, the inputs used in measuring fair value must reflect the assumptions of market participants transacting for the asset or liability in the principal (or most advantageous) market at the measurement date.

11.3.3.C Data challenges

In addition to the method employed to determine a credit adjustment, the inputs used in the various approaches can often require significant judgement. Regardless of the method used, probability of default, loss given default (i.e. the amount that one party expects not to recover if the other party defaults) or credit spread assumptions are important inputs. While the sources of information may vary, the objective remains unchanged – that is, to incorporate inputs that reflect the assumptions of market participants in the current market.

Where available, IFRS 13 requires entities to make maximum use of market-observable credit information. For example, credit default swap (CDS) spreads may provide a good indication of the market's current perception of a particular reporting entity's or counterparty's creditworthiness. However, CDS spreads will likely not be available for smaller public companies or private entities. In these instances, reporting entities may need to consider other available indicators of creditworthiness, such as publicly traded debt or loans.

In the absence of any observable indicator of creditworthiness, a reporting entity may be required to combine a number of factors to arrive at an appropriate credit valuation adjustment. For example, it may be necessary to determine an appropriate credit spread using a combination of own issuance credit spread data, publicly available information on competitors' debt pricing, sector specific CDS spreads or relevant indices, or historical company or sector-specific probabilities of default.

In all cases, identifying the basis for selecting the proxy, benchmark or input, including any analysis performed and assumptions made, should be documented. Such an analysis may include calculating financial ratios to evaluate the reporting entity's financial position relative to its peer group and their credit spreads. These metrics may consider liquidity, leverage and general financial strength, as well as comparable attributes such as credit ratings, similarities in business mix and level of regulation or geographic footprint.

The use of historical default rates would seem to be inconsistent with the exit price notion in IFRS 13, particularly when credit spread levels in the current environment differ significantly from historical averages. Therefore, when current observable information is unavailable, management should adjust historical data to arrive at its best estimate of the assumptions that market participants would use to price the instrument in an orderly transaction in the current market.

Figure 14.6 below highlights some of the common sources of credit information and the advantages and disadvantages of using each input for the credit adjustment calculation.

Figure 14.6: Credit data requirements

Data requirements	Advantages	Disadvantages
CDS curve (own or counterparty)	• Market observable • Information is current (for counterparties with adequate CDS trading volume) • Easy to source from third party data providers • Exposure specific data available for most banking counterparties	• Not available for many entities • May not be representative of all the assets of the entity • May have liquidity issues due to low trading volumes, resulting in higher-than-expected spreads and additional volatility in calculations • CDS quotes may be indicative quotes, not necessarily reflective of actual trades
Current debt credit spread	• Market observable • Available for some publicly traded debt instruments • Easy to source from third party data providers	• May require an adjustment for illiquidity • May require a judgemental adjustment due to maturity mismatch and amount of security of debt issuance and derivative to be valued

Sector-specific CDS Index or competitor CDS Curve	• Market-observable • Information is current • Easy to source from third party data providers • Proxy CDS curve mapping is possible for almost all entities	• Not exposure-specific; may require judgemental adjustments to reflect differences between proxy and entity (e.g. size, credit rating, etc.) • Index CDS curves can be influenced by macro-economic factors, which do not affect entity or affect entity to a lesser or greater extent
Debt issuance credit spread	• Market observable • Information can be current, in case a recent issuance can be referenced (or where pricing terms are available ahead of debt issuance) • Easy to source from third party data providers and/or from treasurer, through communications with the banks	• Information can be outdated and may require an adjustment for illiquidity • As it is not always possible to reference a recent issuance, a judgemental adjustment may be required to bridge gap between debt issue date and derivative valuation date (i.e. financial reporting date) • May require a judgemental adjustment due to maturity mismatch of debt issuance and derivative to be valued
Credit rating/ historical default information (e.g. Moody's publication of Historic Probability of Default)	• Rating agency data available for most entities • Easy to source from third party data providers	• Information can be outdated • Conversion to probability of default may be based on historical information • May require an adjustment from long-term average measure to a 'point-in-time' measure • Not associated with a specific maturity; ratings are generally long term average estimates of creditworthiness, which may not be appropriate for short term derivatives
Internal credit risk analysis	• May be applied by most entities • Ability to customise internal models	• Based on unobservable information • Information can be outdated • May not be consistent with what other market participants would use

11.3.4 Does the existence of master netting agreements and/or CSAs eliminate the need to consider an entity's own credit risk when measuring the fair value of derivative liabilities?

IFRS 13 is clear that non-performance risk should be considered from the perspective of the liability being measured, not the entity obligated under the liability. As such, non-performance risk may differ for various liabilities of the same entity. This difference may result from the specific terms of the liability (e.g. seniority or priority in the event of liquidation) or from specific credit enhancements related to the liability (e.g. collateral).

Bilateral collateral arrangements, master netting agreements and other credit enhancement or risk mitigation tools will reduce the credit exposure associated with a liability (or asset) and should be considered in determining the fair value of the liability. Although these agreements reduce credit exposure, they typically do not eliminate the exposure completely. For example, most CSAs do not require collateral to be posted until a certain threshold has been reached, and once reached require collateral only for the exposure in excess of the threshold. Therefore, while the existence of master netting agreements or CSAs mitigates the effect of own credit risk on the fair value of a liability, their presence alone would not enable an entity to ignore its own credit risk. Entities should assess their credit exposure to a specific liability when determining how their own credit risk would affect its fair value.

11.3.4.A Portfolio approaches and credit mitigation arrangements

When calculating derivative credit adjustments, reporting entities may factor in their ability to reduce their counterparty exposures through any existing netting or collateral arrangements. The measurement exception in IFRS 13 (see 12 below) allows a reporting entity to measure the net credit risk of a portfolio of derivatives to a single counterparty, assuming there is an enforceable arrangement in place that mitigates credit risk upon default (e.g. a master netting agreement). *[IFRS 13.48].*

- *Netting arrangements*

  A master netting agreement is a legally binding contract between two counterparties to net exposures under other agreements or contracts (e.g. relevant ISDA agreements, CSAs and any other credit enhancements or risk mitigation arrangements in place) between the same two parties. Such netting may be effected with periodic payments (payment netting), settlement payments following the occurrence of an event of default (close-out netting) or both. In cases of default, such an agreement serves to protect the parties from paying out on the gross amount of their payable positions, while receiving less than the full amount on their gross receivable positions with the same counterparty.

  IFRS 7 requires disclosure of the effects of set-off and related netting on an entity's financial position (see Chapter 54 for further discussion).

  In situations where an entity meets the criteria to apply the measurement exception in IFRS 13 (discussed at 12 below), it will still need to assess whether it has the practical ability to implement a credit valuation method which reflects the net counterparty exposure. This can be challenging, particularly for those entities that do not have systems in place to capture the relevant net positions by debtor/counterparty. Also, an allocation of the portfolio level adjustments is required, as discussed at 11.3.4.B below.

  A further complication arises if the net exposure represents the position across different classes of derivatives (e.g. interest rate swaps and foreign exchange forwards). Basic valuation methods can attempt to approximate a net position through the creation of an appropriate 'modelled net position' representing the net risk.

- *Collateral arrangements*

  In many instances, counterparty credit exposure in derivative transactions can be further reduced through collateral requirements. Such arrangements serve to limit the potential exposure of one counterparty to the other by requiring the out-of-the-money counterparty to post collateral (e.g. cash or liquid securities) to the in-the-money counterparty. While these and other credit mitigation arrangements often serve to reduce credit exposure, they typically do not eliminate the exposure completely.

> Many collateral agreements, for example, do not require collateral to be posted until a certain threshold has been reached, and then, collateral is required only for the exposure in excess of the threshold. In addition, even when transactions with a counterparty are subject to collateral requirements, entities remain exposed to what is commonly referred to as 'gap risk' (i.e. the exposure arising from fluctuations in the value of the derivatives before the collateral is called and between the time it is called and the time it is actually posted).
>
> Finally, collateral arrangements may be either unilateral or bilateral. Unilateral arrangements require only one party to the contract to post collateral. Under bilateral agreements, both counterparties are subject to collateral requirements, although potentially at different threshold levels.

Given their ability to reduce credit exposure, netting and collateral arrangements are typically considered in determining the CVA for a portfolio of derivatives. This can add to the complexity of the calculation as total expected credit exposure should be determined not just for a single derivative contract (whose value changes over time), but for a portfolio of derivative contracts (which can include both derivative assets and derivative liabilities). Simply taking the sum of the CVA of individual trades could dramatically overstate the potential credit exposure, as it would not take into account positions in the portfolio with offsetting exposures. Consequently, when netting agreements and collateral arrangements are in place, and a company has elected to measure its derivative positions with offsetting credit risk using the measurement exception in IFRS 13, the expected exposure is generally analysed at the portfolio level (i.e. on a net basis).

11.3.4.B Portfolio-level credit adjustments

The measurement exception (the portfolio approach) permits measuring non-performance risk of derivatives with the same counterparty on a portfolio basis (see 12 below), allowing the mitigating effect of CSAs and master netting agreements to have their full effect in the financial statements taken as a whole. The use of the measurement exception does not change the fact that the unit of account is the individual derivative contract, a concept particularly important when an individual derivative is designated as a hedging instrument in a hedging relationship.

There is no specific guidance under IFRS on how portfolio level credit adjustments should be allocated to individual derivatives. A number of quantitative allocation methods have been observed in practice and have been accepted as long as a reporting entity is able to support that the method is: (a) appropriate for its facts and circumstances; and (b) applied consistently. Given the renewed focus on credit adjustments, it is likely that valuation methods will become more sophisticated and new techniques and refinements to the above portfolio allocation techniques will arise.

11.4 Restrictions preventing the transfer of a liability or an entity's own equity

A liability or an entity's own equity may be subject to restrictions that prevent the transfer of the item. When measuring the fair value of a liability or equity instrument, IFRS 13 does not allow an entity to include a separate input (or an adjustment to other inputs) for such restrictions. This is because the effect of the restriction is either implicitly or explicitly included in other inputs to the fair value measurement. The standard gives the example of both a creditor and an obligor accepting a transaction price for a liability with full knowledge that the obligation includes a restriction that prevents its transfer. In this case, the restriction is implicitly included in the price. Therefore, further adjustment would be inappropriate. *[IFRS 13.45, 46]*. In Example 14.16 above, the fair value of the decommissioning liability was not adjusted for the existence of a restriction because that restriction was contemplated in developing the inputs to the valuation techniques used to measure fair value.

Paragraph 46 of IFRS 13 states that a separate adjustment for lack of transferability is not necessary for either the initial or subsequent fair value measurement of a liability. This differs from the treatment of asset restrictions. *[IFRS 13.46]*. IFRS 13 considers liability restrictions and asset restrictions differently because:

- restrictions on the transfer of a liability relate to the performance of the obligation (i.e. the entity is legally obliged to satisfy the obligation and needs to do something to be relieved of the obligation), whereas restrictions on the transfer of an asset relate to the marketability of the asset; and
- unlike assets, virtually all liabilities include a restriction preventing their transfer. As a result, the effect of a restriction preventing the transfer of a liability would, in theory, be consistent for all liabilities.

The standard also appears to assume that the effect of a restriction on the fair value of a liability remains constant over the life of the liability. Therefore, no additional adjustments are required in subsequent measurements if the effect of the restriction was already captured in the initial pricing of the liability. Unlike restrictions on assets, which typically expire and whose effect on fair value changes over time, restrictions on liabilities usually remain throughout the life of the obligation.

The Basis for Conclusions to IFRS 13 states that if an entity is aware that a restriction on transfer is not already reflected in the price (or in the other inputs used in the measurement), it would adjust the price or inputs to reflect the existence of the restriction. *[IFRS 13.BC99, BC100]*. However, in our view this would be rare because nearly all liabilities include a restriction and, when measuring fair value, market participants are assumed by IFRS 13 to be sufficiently knowledgeable about the liability to be transferred.

11.5 Financial liability with a demand feature

IFRS 13 states that the 'fair value of a financial liability with a demand feature (e.g. a demand deposit) is not less than the amount payable on demand, discounted from the first date that the amount could be required to be paid'. *[IFRS 13.47]*. This is consistent with the requirements in IFRS 9 (and IAS 39). In many cases, the observed market price for these financial liabilities would be the demand amount, i.e. the price at which they are originated between the customer and the deposit-taker. Recognising such a financial liability at less than the demand amount may give rise to an immediate gain on the origination of the deposit, which the IASB believes is inappropriate. *[IFRS 13.BCZ102-BCZ103]*.

12 FINANCIAL ASSETS AND LIABILITIES WITH OFFSETTING POSITIONS

IFRS 13 specifies that the concepts of 'highest and best use' and 'valuation premise' are not relevant when measuring the fair value of financial instruments. Therefore, the fair value of financial assets and financial liabilities is based on the unit of account prescribed by the IFRS that requires (or permits) the fair value measurement, which is generally the individual financial instrument. However, IFRS 13 provides a measurement exception that allows an entity to determine the fair value of a group of financial assets and liabilities with offsetting risks based on the sale or transfer of its *net* exposure to a particular risk (or risks), if certain criteria are met. *[IFRS 13.48]*. This measurement approach is an exception to the principles of fair value because it represents an entity-specific measure (i.e. an entity's net risk exposure is a function of the other financial instruments specifically held by that entity and its unique risk preferences).

It may be possible for entities to offset multiple risks (e.g. both market and credit risks) within the same portfolio. In addition, since the focus is on offsetting risks, entities may offset credit and market risks stemming from a group of financial instruments at different levels of aggregation. For example, under IFRS 13, management could continue its existing practice of offsetting credit risk at the counterparty level (e.g. based on its portfolio of interest rate swaps with a particular counterparty) while offsetting market risks on a more aggregated portfolio basis (e.g. based on its portfolio of interest rate swaps with all counterparties), provided all of the criteria in 12.1 below are met.

This guidance is largely consistent with practice under IFRS prior to adoption of IFRS 13 when determining valuation adjustments for derivative instruments related to bid-ask spreads and credit risk.

12.1 Criteria for using the portfolio approach for offsetting positions

Entities that hold a group of financial assets and liabilities are generally exposed to market risks (e.g. interest rate risk, currency risk or other price risk) and to the credit risk of each of its counterparties. IFRS 13 allows entities to make an accounting policy choice (see 12.1.1 below) to measure the fair value of a group of financial assets and liabilities based on the price that would be received to sell a net long position or transfer a net short position for a particular risk exposure (that is, a portfolio approach). In order to use the portfolio approach, entities are required to meet all of the following criteria, both initially and on an ongoing basis:

- the entity manages the group of financial assets and financial liabilities on the basis of the entity's net exposure to a particular market risk(s) or credit risk, in accordance with the entity's documented risk management or investment strategy;
- the entity provides information based on the group of financial assets and financial liabilities to the entity's key management personnel; and
- the entity measures (either by requirement or by choice) the financial assets and financial liabilities at fair value in the statement of financial position at each reporting date. *[IFRS 13.49]*.

The measurement exception for offsetting positions only applies to financial assets and financial liabilities within the scope of IFRS 9 or IAS 39. *[IFRS 13.52]*. Also, as indicated by these criteria, the portfolio approach only applies to financial instruments with offsetting risks. As such, a group of financial instruments comprised of only financial assets (e.g. a portfolio of loans) would not qualify for the exception and would need to be valued in a manner consistent with the appropriate unit of account. However, an entity need not maintain a static portfolio to use the measurement exception, i.e. the entity could have assets and liabilities within the portfolio that are traded.

When IFRS 13 was issued, paragraph 52 stated that the measurement exception only applied to financial assets and financial liabilities within the scope of IFRS 9 or IAS 39. However, it was not the Boards' intention to exclude contracts to buy or sell a non-financial item (e.g. physically settled commodity derivative contracts) that are within the scope of IFRS 9 and IAS 39 (and that are measured at fair value) from the scope of the measurement exception. *[IFRS 13.BC119A, BC119B]*. If a contract to buy or sell a non-financial item is within the scope of IFRS 9 or IAS 39, those standards treat that contract as if it were a financial instrument. Therefore, as part of the 2011-2013 cycle of *Improvements to IFRSs*, the IASB amended paragraph 52 to clarify that all contracts within the scope of IFRS 9 or IAS 39 are eligible for the measurement exception, regardless of whether they meet the definitions of financial assets or financial liabilities in IAS 32. *[IFRS 13.52]*.

12.1.1 Accounting policy considerations

As noted above, the use of the portfolio approach is an accounting policy decision, to be made in accordance with IAS 8 (see Chapter 3), which must include an entity's policy regarding measurement assumptions – i.e. for both allocating bid-ask adjustments and credit adjustments (see 12.2 below).

An entity can choose to use the portfolio approach on a portfolio-by-portfolio basis. In addition, if entities choose this policy for a particular portfolio, they are not required to apply the portfolio approach to all of the risks of the financial assets and liabilities that make up the particular group. For example, an entity could choose to measure only the credit risk associated with a group of financial instruments on a net basis, but not the group's exposure to market risk.

An entity may also decide to apply the portfolio approach to only certain market risks related to the group. For example, an entity that is exposed to both interest rate and foreign currency risk in a portfolio of financial assets and liabilities could choose to measure only its interest rate risk exposure on a net basis.

The accounting policy decision can be changed if an entity's risk exposure preferences change, for example, a change in strategy to have fewer offsetting positions. In that case, the entity can decide not to use the exception but instead to measure the fair value of its financial instruments on an individual instrument basis. We generally expect that an entity's use of the portfolio approach would be consistent from period to period as changes in risk management policies are typically not common. *[IFRS 13.51, BC121]*.

12.1.2 Presentation considerations

IFRS 13 is clear that applying the portfolio approach for measurement purposes does not affect financial statement presentation. For example, an entity might manage a group of financial assets and liabilities based on the net exposure(s) for internal risk management or investment strategy purposes, but be unable to present those instruments on a net basis in the statement of financial position because the entity does not have a positive intention and ability to settle those instruments on a net basis, as is required by IAS 32. *[IAS 32.42].*

If the requirements for presentation of financial instruments in the statement of financial position differ from the basis for the measurement, an entity may need to allocate the portfolio-level adjustments (see 12.2 below) to the individual assets or liabilities that make up the portfolio. Entities may also need to allocate portfolio-level adjustments for disclosure purposes when items in the group would be categorised within different levels of the fair value hierarchy (see 16 below for additional discussion on the allocation of portfolio-level adjustments related to the fair value hierarchy disclosures).

IFRS 13 does not prescribe any methodologies for allocating portfolio-level adjustments; instead, it states that the allocation should be performed in a reasonable and consistent manner that is appropriate in the circumstances. *[IFRS 13.50].*

12.1.3 Is there a minimum level of offset required to use the portfolio approach?

While there are explicit criteria that an entity must meet in order to use the portfolio approach, IFRS 13 does not specify any minimum level of offset within the group of financial instruments. For example, if an entity has positions with offsetting credit risk to a particular counterparty, we believe use of the portfolio approach is appropriate even if the extent of offset is minimal (provided that the entity has in place a legally enforceable agreement, as discussed at 12.2.2 below, that provides for offsetting upon default and all the other required criteria are met). To illustrate, even if the gross credit exposure was CU 100,000 (long) and CU 5,000 (short), upon counterparty default the entity would be exposed to a credit loss of only CU 95,000 under the terms of its master netting agreement.

With respect to market risk, considering the degree of offset may require additional judgement. Entities should assess the appropriateness of using the portfolio approach based on the nature of the portfolio being managed (e.g. derivative versus cash instruments) and its documented risk management policies (or investment strategies). An entity should use the portfolio approach in a manner consistent with the IASB's basis for providing the measurement exception and not in a manner to circumvent other principles within the standard.

12.1.4 Can Level 1 instruments be included in a portfolio of financial instruments with offsetting risks when calculating the net exposure to a particular market risk?

It is our understanding that Level 1 instruments can be included when using the exception to value financial instruments with offsetting risks. An entity is allowed to consider the effect of holding futures contracts when evaluating its net exposure to a particular market risk, such as interest rate risk. Paragraph 54 of IFRS 13 gives an example stating that 'an entity would not combine the interest rate risk associated with a financial asset with the commodity price risk associated with a financial liability because doing so would not mitigate the entity's exposure to interest rate risk or commodity price risk'. *[IFRS 13.54]*.

We understand that some constituents believe that the requirement in IFRS 13 to measure instruments that trade in active markets based on P×Q does not apply to the measurement of the net exposure when the portfolio exception is used, since the net exposure does not trade in an active market. As such, these constituents argue that the measurement of the net exposure and the allocation of this value back to the instruments that comprise the group are not constrained by the price at which the individual instruments trade in active markets. Others believe that although Level 1 instruments, such as futures contracts, may be considered when calculating an entity's net exposure to a particular market risk, the quoted price (unadjusted) for these Level 1 instruments should be used when allocating the fair value to the individual units of account for presentation and disclosure purposes, to comply with the requirement in IFRS 13 to measure Level 1 instruments at P×Q. However, depending on the extent of Level 1 instruments in the group, it may not always be possible to allocate the fair value determined for the net exposure back to the individual instruments in a manner that results in each of these instruments being recorded at P×Q. For this reason, there are constituents who believe that the use of the portfolio exception should never result in the measurement of Level 1 instruments at an amount other than P×Q. That is, the determination of the fair value of the net exposure is constrained by the requirement that all Level 1 instruments within the group are recorded at a value based on P×Q.

As discussed at 5.1.2 above, we understand that the IASB did not intend the portfolio exception to change existing practice under IFRS or override the requirement in IFRS 13 to measure Level 1 instruments at P×Q or the prohibition on block discounts. However, given the lack of clarity, some have asked questions about how these requirements would apply in practice. In 2013, the IFRS Interpretations Committee referred a request to the Board on the interaction between the use of Level 1 inputs and the portfolio exception. The IASB discussed this issue in December 2013, but only in relation to portfolios that comprise only Level 1 financial instruments whose market risks are substantially the same. The Board tentatively decided that the measurement of such portfolios should be the one that results from multiplying the net position by the Level 1 prices. Therefore, in September 2014, the IASB proposed adding a non-authoritative example to illustrate the application of the portfolio exception in these circumstances.

As discussed at 5.1.2 above and 12.2 below, in April 2015, after considering responses to this proposal from constituents, the IASB concluded it was not necessary to add the proposed illustrative example to IFRS 13.

12.2 Measuring fair value for offsetting positions

If the portfolio approach is used to measure an entity's net exposure to a particular market risk, the net risk exposure becomes the unit of measurement. That is, the entity's net exposure to a particular market risk (e.g. the net long or short Euro interest rate exposure within a specified maturity bucket) represents the asset or liability being measured.

In applying the portfolio approach, an entity must assume an orderly transaction between market participants to sell or transfer the net risk exposure at the measurement date under current market conditions. The fair value of the portfolio is measured on the basis of the price that would be received to sell a net long position (i.e. an asset) for a particular risk exposure or transfer a net short position (i.e. a liability) for a particular risk exposure. *[IFRS 13.48]*. That is, the objective of the valuation is to determine the price that market participants would pay (or receive) in a single transaction for the entire net risk exposure, as defined. Some argue that, as a result, an adjustment based on the size of the net exposure could be considered in the valuation if market participants would incorporate such an adjustment when transacting for the net exposure. Since the unit of measurement is the net exposure, size is considered a characteristic of the asset (net long position) or liability (net short position) being measured, not a characteristic of the entity's specific holdings. Many have interpreted the equivalent requirements in US GAAP in this way. Others believe that the portfolio exception does not override the unit of account guidance provided in IFRS 9 (or IAS 39) and, therefore, any premiums or discounts that are inconsistent with that unit of account, i.e. the individual financial instruments within the portfolio, must be excluded. This would include any premiums or discounts related to the size of the portfolio. As discussed at 5.1.2 above, we understand the IASB did not intend the portfolio exception to override the requirement in IFRS 13 to measure Level 1 instruments at P×Q or the prohibition on block discounts which raises questions as to how the portfolio exception would be applied to Level 1 instruments.

In 2013, the IFRS Interpretations Committee referred a request to the Board on the interaction between the use of Level 1 inputs and the portfolio exception. The IASB discussed this issue in December 2013, but only in relation to portfolios that comprise only Level 1 financial instruments whose market risks are substantially the same. The Board tentatively decided that the measurement of such portfolios should be the one that results from multiplying the net position by the Level 1 prices. In September 2014, the IASB proposed adding the following non-authoritative example to illustrate the application of the portfolio exception in these circumstances.

Example 14.19: Applying the portfolio approach to a group of financial assets and financial liabilities whose market risks are substantially the same and whose fair value measurement is categorised within Level 1 of the fair value hierarchy[16]

Entity A holds a group of financial assets and financial liabilities consisting of a long position of 10,000 financial assets and a short position of 9,500 financial liabilities whose market risks are substantially the same. Entity A manages that group of financial assets and financial liabilities on the basis of its net exposure to market risks. The fair value measurement of all the financial instruments in the group is categorised within Level 1 of the fair value hierarchy.

The mid-price and the most representative bid and ask prices are as follows:

	Bid	Mid	Ask
Most representative exit price	CU 99	CU 100	CU 101

Entity A applies the exception in paragraph 48 of the IFRS that permits Entity A to measure the fair value of the group of financial assets and financial liabilities on the basis of the price that would be received to sell, in

Chapter 14

this particular case, a net long position (i.e. an asset) in an orderly transaction between market participants at the measurement date under current market conditions.

Accordingly, Entity A measures the net long position (500 financial assets) in accordance with the corresponding Level 1 prices. Because the market risks arising from the financial instruments are substantially the same, the measurement of the net position coincides with the measurement of the exposure arising from the group of financial assets and financial liabilities. Consequently, Entity A measures the group of financial assets and financial liabilities on the basis of the price that it would receive if it would exit or close out its outstanding exposure as follows:

	Quantity held (Q)	Level 1 price (P)	P×Q
Net long position	500	CU 99	CU 49,500

Entity A would have also achieved the same measurement of CU 49,500 by measuring the net long position at the mid-price (i.e. CU 100 × 500 = CU 50,000) adjusted by a bid-offer reserve (CU 1 × 500 = CU 500).

Entity A allocates the resulting measurement (i.e. CU 49,500) to the individual (10,000) financial assets and (9,500) financial liabilities. In accordance with paragraph 51 of the IFRS, Entity A performs this allocation on a reasonable basis that is consistent with previous allocations of that nature using a methodology appropriate to the circumstances.

In response to this proposal, some respondents raised concerns because they believed there was a risk that constituents may infer principles from this simple example that could lead to unintended consequences. Respondents noted that the illustrative example did not address:

- other scenarios and circumstances to which the portfolio approach would apply. For example, situations where the instruments in the portfolio are categorised within Level 2 or Level 3 of the fair value hierarchy or for which different Level 1 prices are available; and
- allocation of the resulting measurement to each instrument in the portfolio for disclosure purposes.

The proposed illustrative example also raised questions about the interaction between the portfolio exception and the use of mid-market pricing as a practical expedient in accordance with paragraph 71 of IFRS 13 and may have required clarification of the term 'bid-offer reserve adjustment' used in the example. Despite these concerns, the majority of the respondents agreed that the proposed additional illustrative example appropriately illustrated application of the portfolio approach.[17]

As discussed at 5.1.2 above, in April 2015, after considering responses to this proposal from constituents, the IASB concluded that it was not necessary to add the proposed illustrative example to IFRS 13. However, in reaching this decision, the Board noted that the proposed illustrative example appropriately illustrated the application of the portfolio approach. 'That is, if an entity elects to use the exception in paragraph 48 of IFRS 13, the appropriate fair value measurement of the net risk exposure arising from a group of financial assets and financial liabilities whose market risks are substantially the same, and whose fair value measurement is categorised within Level 1 of the fair value hierarchy, would be determined by multiplying the financial instruments included in the resulting net position by the corresponding unadjusted Level 1 price'.[18] *[IFRS 13.48].*

While the proposed non-authoritative example provides one approach to consider, in light of the above discussion, entities will need to use judgement to determine the most appropriate approach to employ when applying the portfolio exception.

When measuring fair value using the portfolio approach, IFRS 13 also requires that the market risks be substantially the same (see 12.2.1 below) and that the fair value measurement must take into consideration any exposure to the credit risk of a particular counterparty (see 12.2.2 below).

It is also important to note that when applying the portfolio approach, entities may offset credit and market risks at different levels of aggregation. This approach is consistent with risk management practices employed by many entities. Such an approach may be required because it is unlikely that all of the financial assets and liabilities giving rise to the net exposure for a particular market risk will be with the same counterparty. The example below illustrates this concept.

Example 14.20: Calculating net exposure

Entity XYZ holds a portfolio of long and short derivative positions (USD interest rate swaps and USD/JPY foreign currency forwards) with various counterparties as follows:

- Counterparties A, B and C: only interest rate swaps
- Counterparty D: interest rate swaps and foreign currency forwards
- Counterparties E, F and G: only foreign currency forwards

Entity XYZ has executed master netting agreements in respect of credit risk with each of its counterparties except counterparty G. In addition, the agreement in place with counterparty D can be applied across products.

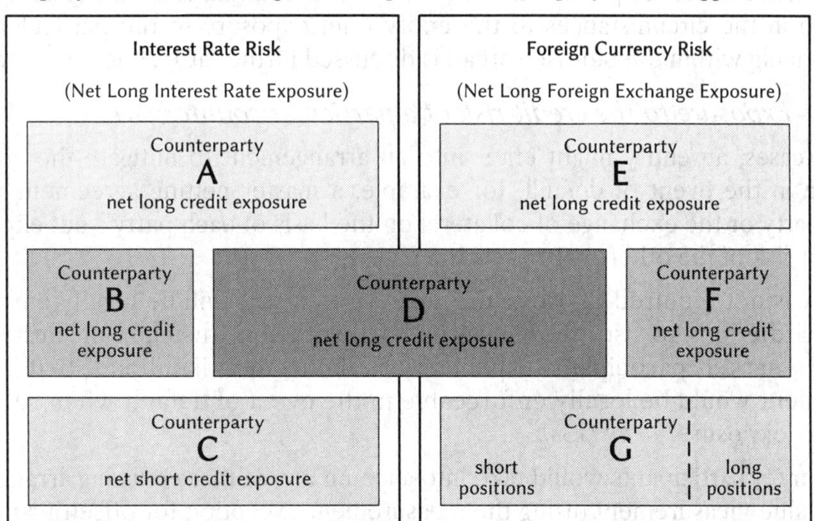

Using the measurement exception, Entity XYZ may consider its credit risk exposure to each individual counterparty except counterparty G on a net basis (i.e. net long credit exposure to Counterparty A, net short credit exposure to Counterparty C, etc.).

At the same time, the entity may consider its net long exposure to USD interest rate risk from its portfolio of derivatives with counterparties A, B, C and D. The entity may also consider its net long exposure to foreign currency risk (Japanese yen risk) from its portfolio of derivatives with counterparties D, E, F and G.

12.2.1 Exposure to market risks

When measuring fair value using the measurement exception for offsetting positions, the entity is required to ensure the following in relation to market risks:

- Market risk (or risks), to which the entity is exposed within that portfolio, is substantially the same. For example, combining the interest rate risk associated with a financial asset with the commodity price risk associated with a financial liability would not be appropriate because it would not mitigate the entity's exposure to interest rate risk or commodity price risk.

  The standard requires any basis risk resulting from the market risk parameters not being identical to be taken into account in the fair value measurement of the financial assets and financial liabilities within the group. *[IFRS 13.54]*.

- The duration of the entity's exposure to a particular market risk (or risks) must be substantially the same. *[IFRS 13.55]*.

  The standard gives the example of an entity that uses a 12-month futures contract against the cash flows associated with 12 months' worth of interest rate risk exposure on a five-year financial instrument. The futures and five-year financial instruments are within a group that is made up of only those financial assets and financial liabilities. The entity measures the fair value of the exposure to 12-month interest rate risk on a net basis and the remaining interest rate risk exposure (i.e. years 2-5) on a gross basis.

Management selects the price within the bid-ask spread that is most representative of fair value in the circumstances to the entity's net exposure to the particular market risk(s) (pricing within the bid-ask spread is discussed further at 15.3 below). *[IFRS 13.53]*.

12.2.2 Exposure to the credit risk of a particular counterparty

In some cases, an entity might enter into an arrangement to mitigate the credit risk exposure in the event of default, for example, a master netting agreement with the counterparty or the exchange of collateral on the basis of each party's net exposure to the credit risk of the other party.

An entity is not required to prove that such agreements will be legally enforceable in all jurisdictions to use the measurement exception. Instead, an entity should consider market participant expectations about the likelihood that such an arrangement would be legally enforceable in the event of default when valuing the net credit exposure. *[IFRS 13.56]*.

When market participants would take into account any of these existing arrangements, the fair value measurement (using the measurement exception for offsetting positions) must include the effect of the entity's net exposure to the credit risk of that counterparty and/or the counterparty's net exposure to the credit risk of the entity.

13 FAIR VALUE AT INITIAL RECOGNITION

13.1 Exit price versus entry price

IFRS 13 defines fair value as the price that would be received to sell the asset or paid to transfer the liability; this is an exit price notion. When an entity acquires an asset, or assumes a liability, the price paid (or the transaction price) is an entry price. Conceptually, entry prices and exit prices are different. Entities do not necessarily sell assets at the prices paid to acquire them. Similarly, entities do not necessarily transfer liabilities at the prices received to assume them. This distinction is significant and can have important implications on the initial recognition of assets and liabilities at fair value. However, IFRS 13 acknowledges that, in many cases, an entry price may equal an exit price (e.g. when the transaction takes place in the entity's principal market); since one party is selling an asset, that transaction is also an exit transaction. *[IFRS 13.57, 58]*.

13.1.1 Assessing whether the transaction price equals fair value at initial recognition

Prior to the issuance of IFRS 13, it was common for entities to use the transaction price as fair value of an asset or liability on its initial recognition. While IFRS 13 acknowledges that in many situations, an entry price may equal an exit price, it does not presume that these prices are equal. Therefore, an entity must determine whether the transaction price represents the fair value of an asset or liability at initial recognition. *[IFRS 13.59]*.

Paragraph B4 of IFRS 13 provides certain factors that an entity should consider in making this determination. For example, a transaction price may not represent fair value if the unit of account represented by the transaction price is different from the unit of account for the asset or liability measured at fair value. *[IFRS 13.B4(c)]*. This may be the case with a complex financial instrument where the transaction price includes a fee for structuring the transaction or when an entity acquires a block and the transaction price includes a block discount.

Another factor to consider is whether the market in which an entity acquired the asset (or assumed the liability) is different from the principal (or most advantageous) market in which the entity will sell the asset (or transfer the liability). *[IFRS 13.B4(d)]*. For example, a securities dealer may acquire an asset in the retail market but sell it in the inter-dealer market. However, the fair value measurement should consider the fact that, while the inter-dealer price (i.e. the exit price in a hypothetical transaction) may differ from the retail price (i.e. transaction price), another dealer would also expect to earn a profit on the transaction. Accordingly, a pricing model's value should incorporate assumptions regarding the appropriate profit margin that market participants (i.e. other dealers) would demand when estimating the instrument's fair value at inception.

Other examples identified by paragraph B4 of IFRS 13 include:

- the transaction is between related parties – although IFRS 13 does allow the price in a related party transaction to be used as an input into a fair value measurement if the entity has evidence that the transaction was entered into at market terms; and
- the transaction takes place under duress or the seller is forced to accept the price in the transaction – for example, if the seller is experiencing financial difficulty. *[IFRS 13.B4(a)-(b)]*.

In addition, the measurement of fair value in accordance with IFRS 13 should take into consideration market participant assumptions about risk. Adjustments for uncertainty associated with a valuation technique or certain inputs used to measure fair value are required if market participants would incorporate such risk adjustments when pricing the asset or liability. A measurement (e.g. a 'mark-to-model' measurement) that ignores these market participant adjustments for risk is not representative of fair value.

While helpful in identifying the factors entities should consider in assessing whether a transaction price would equal fair value, the examples provided in the standard are not intended to be exhaustive.

13.2 Day one gains and losses

IFRS 13's measurement framework applies to initial fair value measurements, if permitted or required by another IFRS. At initial recognition, if the measurement of fair value in accordance with IFRS 13 and the transaction price differ, the entity recognises the resulting gain or loss in profit or loss unless the related IFRS (i.e. the IFRS that permits or requires the initial measurement at fair value) specifies otherwise. *[IFRS 13.60].*

As noted in Example 14.21 below, IFRS 9 and IAS 39 have specific requirements with regard to the recognition of inception (or 'day one') gains and losses for financial instruments within the scope of those standards (see Chapter 48 at 3). In developing IFRS 13, the IASB did not change the recognition threshold in those standards in relation to day one gains or losses. However, IFRS 9 and IAS 39 were both amended to clarify that an entity: (i) measures the fair value of financial instruments at initial recognition in accordance with IFRS 13, then; (ii) considers the requirements of IFRS 9 or IAS 39 in determining whether (and when) the resulting difference (if any) between fair value at initial recognition and the transaction price is recognised. *[IFRS 13.BC138].*

13.2.1 Day one losses for over-the-counter derivative transactions

The definition of fair value as an exit price affects the accounting by retail customers as much as financial institutions (i.e. dealers). For example, retail customers whose entry and exit market for a financial asset (or financial liability) measured at fair value is with a wholesaler (e.g. a dealer) could experience a day one loss, because the price at which a wholesaler would sell a financial asset to a retail customer would generally exceed the price a wholesaler would pay to acquire that financial asset from a retail customer (this difference in price is commonly referred to as the bid-ask spread in many financial markets).

The following example from IFRS 13 discusses how an interest rate swap at initial recognition may be measured differently by a retail counterparty (i.e. an end-user) and a dealer. *[IFRS 13.IE24-26].*

Example 14.21: Interest rate swap at initial recognition

Entity A (a retail counterparty) enters into an interest rate swap in a retail market with Entity B (a dealer) for no initial consideration (i.e. the transaction price is zero). Entity A can access only the retail market. Entity B can access both the retail market (i.e. with retail counterparties) and the dealer market (i.e. with dealer counterparties).

From the perspective of Entity A, the retail market in which it initially entered into the swap is the principal market for the swap. If Entity A were to transfer its rights and obligations under the swap, it would do so with a dealer counterparty in that retail market. In that case the transaction price (zero) would represent the fair value of the swap to Entity A at initial recognition, i.e. the price that Entity A would receive to sell or pay to transfer the swap in a transaction with a dealer counterparty in the retail market (i.e. an exit price). That price would not be adjusted for any incremental (transaction) costs that would be charged by that dealer counterparty.

From the perspective of Entity B, the dealer market (not the retail market) is the principal market for the swap. If Entity B were to transfer its rights and obligations under the swap, it would do so with a dealer in that market. Because the market in which Entity B initially entered into the swap is different from the principal market for the swap, the transaction price (zero) would not necessarily represent the fair value of the swap to Entity B at initial recognition. If the fair value differs from the transaction price (zero), Entity B applies IFRS 9 (or IAS 39) to determine whether it recognises that difference as a gain or loss at initial recognition.

This example seems to indicate that a retail counterparty may not have any gain or loss at initial recognition because the retail counterparty would likely be presumed to transact both at inception and on disposal (i.e. a hypothetical exit) in the same principal market (i.e. the retail market with securities dealers). However, this example does not address the bid-ask spread.

The bid-ask spread is the difference between the price a prospective dealer is willing to pay for an instrument (the 'bid' price) and the price at which the dealer would sell that same instrument (the 'ask' price), allowing the dealer to earn a profit for its role as a 'market maker' in the over-the-counter marketplace. The bid-ask spread may differ by dealer, as well as by the market and type of instrument that is being transacted.

IFRS 13 requires that instruments that trade in markets with bid-ask spreads (e.g. a dealer market) be measured at the price within the bid-ask spread that is most representative of fair value in the circumstances (pricing within the bid-ask spread is discussed further at 15.3 below). Therefore, an inception loss could be experienced by the retail counterparty due to a difference in the price within the bid-ask spread that the retail counterparty could hypothetically exit the instrument and the price within the bid-ask spread that the retail counterparty actually transacted.

The IASB has acknowledged that the fair value of an interest rate swap may differ from its transaction price because of the bid-ask spread, even when the entry and exit markets for the swap are identical. *[IFRS 13.BC165]*. In addition to the bid-ask spread, retail counterparties may recognise additional losses or expenses at the inception of derivative contracts. For example, if the transaction price for a complex derivative includes a structuring fee, the retail counterparty would likely recognise a loss when measuring the fair value of the derivative. Because the transaction price includes the price for the derivative instrument, as well as the fee paid by the retail counterparty to the dealer for structuring the transaction, the unit of account represented by the transaction price differs from the unit of account for the instrument being measured, as discussed in paragraph B4(c) of IFRS 13. *[IFRS 13.B4(c)]*.

13.2.2 Day one gains and losses when entry and exit markets for the transaction are deemed to be the same

IFRS 13 contains no explicit prohibitions on the recognition of day one gains or losses, even in situations where the entry and exit markets are the same. For example, it may be acceptable in certain situations for a dealer to recognise a day one gain or loss on a transaction where the entry and exit markets are deemed to be the same (e.g. inter-dealer market). A difference in the price within the bid-ask spread at which a dealer could exit a transaction versus where it entered the transaction could be one reason to record an inception gain or loss. IFRS 13 clarifies that the exit price within the bid-ask spread that is most representative of fair value in the circumstances should be used to measure fair value, regardless of where in the fair value hierarchy the input falls (pricing within the bid-ask spread is discussed further at 15.3 below).

Notwithstanding the guidance in IFRS 13, IFRS 9 (or IAS 39) provide specific requirements in relation to the recognition of any day one gains or losses. For example, where fair value is not measured using a quoted price in an active market (without adjustment), recognition of day one gains or losses is generally prohibited (see Chapter 48 at 3).

13.3 Related party transactions

As discussed at 7 above, the definition of market participants makes it clear that buyers and sellers for the item being measured are not related parties (as defined in IAS 24). That is, the hypothetical transaction used to determine fair value in IFRS 13 is assumed to take place between market participants that are independent from one another. However, IFRS 13 indicates that the price in a related party transaction may be used as an input into a fair value measurement if there is evidence the transaction was entered into at market terms. The Boards believe such an approach is consistent with the requirements of IAS 24. As with disclosures made in accordance with IAS 24, evidence to support that a related party transaction was executed at market terms may be difficult to substantiate absent corroborating market data from transactions between independent parties.

14 VALUATION TECHNIQUES

There are two key distinctions between the way previous IFRSs considered valuation techniques and the approach in IFRS 13. On adoption of the standard, these distinctions, in and of themselves, may not have changed practice. However, they may have required management to reconsider their methods of measuring fair value.

Firstly, IFRS 13's requirements in relation to valuation techniques apply to all methods of measuring fair value. Traditionally, references to valuation techniques in IFRS have indicated a lack of market-based information with which to value an asset or liability. Valuation techniques as discussed in IFRS 13 are broader and, importantly, include market-based approaches.

Secondly, IFRS 13 does not prioritise the use of one valuation technique over another, unlike existing IFRSs, or require the use of only one technique (with the exception of the requirement to measure identical financial instruments that trade in active markets at price multiplied by quantity (P×Q)). Instead, the standard establishes a hierarchy for the inputs used in those valuation techniques, requiring an entity to maximise observable inputs and minimise the use of unobservable inputs (the fair value hierarchy is discussed further at 16 below). *[IFRS 13.74]*. In some instances, the approach in IFRS 13 may be consistent with previous requirements in IFRS. For example, the best indication of fair value continues to be a quoted price in an active market. However, since IFRS 13 indicates that multiple techniques should be used when appropriate and sufficient data is available, judgement will be needed to select the techniques that are appropriate in the circumstances. *[IFRS 13.61]*.

14.1 Selecting appropriate valuation techniques

IFRS 13 recognises the following three valuation approaches to measure fair value.

- *Market approach:* based on market transactions involving identical or similar assets or liabilities.
- *Income approach:* based on future amounts (e.g. cash flows or income and expenses) that are converted (discounted) to a single present amount.
- *Cost approach:* based on the amount required to replace the service capacity of an asset (frequently referred to as current replacement cost).

IFRS 13 requires that an entity use valuation techniques that are consistent with one or more of the above valuation approaches (these valuation approaches are discussed in more detail at 14.2 to 14.4 below). *[IFRS 13.62].* These approaches are consistent with generally accepted valuation methodologies used outside financial reporting. Not all of the approaches will be applicable to all types of assets or liabilities. However, when measuring the fair value of an asset or liability, IFRS 13 requires an entity to use valuation techniques that are appropriate in the circumstances *and* for which sufficient data is available. As a result, the use of multiple valuation techniques may be required. *[IFRS 13.61, 62].*

The determination of the appropriate technique(s) to be applied requires: significant judgement; sufficient knowledge of the asset or liability; and an adequate level of expertise regarding the valuation techniques. Within the application of a given approach, there may be a number of possible valuation techniques. For instance, there are a number of different techniques used to value intangible assets under the income approach (such as the multi-period excess earnings method and the relief-from-royalty method) depending on the nature of the asset.

As noted above, the fair value hierarchy does not prioritise the valuation techniques to be used; instead, it prioritises the inputs used in the application of these techniques. As such, the selection of the valuation technique(s) to apply should consider the exit market (i.e. the principal (or most advantageous) market) for the asset or liability and use valuation inputs that are consistent with the nature of the item being measured. Regardless of the technique(s) used, the objective of a fair value measurement remains the same – i.e. an exit price under current market conditions from the perspective of market participants.

Selection, application, and evaluation of the valuation techniques can be complex. As such, reporting entities may need assistance from valuation professionals.

14.1.1 Single versus multiple valuation techniques

The standard does not contain a hierarchy of valuation techniques because particular valuation techniques might be more appropriate in some circumstances than in others.

Selecting a single valuation technique may be appropriate in some circumstances, for example, when measuring a financial asset or liability using a quoted price in an active market. However, in other situations, more than one valuation technique may be deemed appropriate and multiple approaches should be applied. For example, it may be appropriate to use multiple valuation techniques when measuring fair value less costs of disposal for a cash-generating unit to test for impairment.

The nature of the characteristics of the asset or liability being measured and the availability of observable market prices may contribute to the number of valuation techniques used in a fair value analysis. For example, the fair value of a business is often estimated by giving consideration to multiple valuation approaches; such as an income approach that derives value from the present value of the expected future cash flows specific to the business and a market approach that derives value from market data (such as EBITDA or revenue multiples) based on observed transactions for comparable assets. On the other hand, financial assets that frequently trade in active markets are often valued using only a market approach given the availability and relevance of observable data.

Even when the use of a single approach is deemed appropriate, entities should be aware of changing circumstances that could indicate using multiple approaches may be more appropriate. For example, this might be the case if there is a significant decrease in the volume and level of activity for an asset or liability in relation to normal market activity. Observable transactions that once formed the basis for the fair value estimate may cease to exist altogether or may not be determinative of fair value and, therefore, require an adjustment to the fair value measurement (this is discussed further at 8.3 above). As such, the use of multiple valuation techniques may be more appropriate.

14.1.2 Using multiple valuation techniques to measure fair value

When the use of multiple valuation techniques is considered appropriate, their application is likely to result in a range of possible values. IFRS 13 requires that management evaluate the reasonableness of the range and select the point within the range that is *most representative* of fair value in the circumstances. *[IFRS 13.63].*

As with the selection of the valuation techniques, the evaluation of the results of multiple techniques requires significant judgement. The merits of each valuation technique applied, and the underlying assumptions embedded in each of the techniques, will need to be considered. Evaluation of the range does not necessarily require the approaches to be calibrated to one another (i.e. the results from different approaches do not have to be equal). The objective is to find the point in the range that most reflects the price to sell an asset or transfer a liability between market participants.

If the results from different valuation techniques are similar, the issue of weighting multiple value indications becomes less important since the assigned weights will not significantly alter the fair value estimate. However, when indications of value are disparate, entities should seek to understand why significant differences exist and what assumptions might contribute to the variance. Paragraph B40 of IFRS 13 indicates that when evaluating results from multiple valuation approaches, a wide range of fair value measurements may be an indication that further analysis is needed. *[IFRS 13.B40].* For example, divergent results between a market approach and income approach may indicate a misapplication of one or both of the techniques and would likely necessitate additional analysis.

The standard gives two examples that illustrate situations where the use of multiple valuation techniques is appropriate and, when used, how different indications of value are assessed.

Firstly, an entity might determine that a technique uses assumptions that are not consistent with market participant assumptions (and, therefore, is not representative of fair value). This is illustrated in Example 14.22 below, where the entity eliminates use of the cost approach because it determines a market participant would not be able to construct the asset itself. *[IFRS 13.IE15-17]*.

Example 14.22: Multiple valuation techniques – software asset

An entity acquires a group of assets. The asset group includes an income-producing software asset internally developed for licensing to customers and its complementary assets (including a related database with which the software asset is used) and the associated liabilities. To allocate the cost of the group to the individual assets acquired, the entity measures the fair value of the software asset. The entity determines that the software asset would provide maximum value to market participants through its use in combination with other assets or with other assets and liabilities (i.e. its complementary assets and the associated liabilities). There is no evidence to suggest that the current use of the software asset is not its highest and best use. Therefore, the highest and best use of the software asset is its current use. (In this case the licensing of the software asset, in and of itself, does not indicate that the fair value of the asset would be maximised through its use by market participants on a stand-alone basis.)

The entity determines that, in addition to the income approach, sufficient data might be available to apply the cost approach but not the market approach. Information about market transactions for comparable software assets is not available. The income and cost approaches are applied as follows:

(a) The income approach is applied using a present value technique. The cash flows used in that technique reflect the income stream expected to result from the software asset (licence fees from customers) over its economic life. The fair value indicated by that approach is CU 15 million.

(b) The cost approach is applied by estimating the amount that currently would be required to construct a substitute software asset of comparable utility (i.e. taking into account functional and economic obsolescence). The fair value indicated by that approach is CU 10 million.

Through its application of the cost approach, the entity determines that market participants would not be able to construct a substitute software asset of comparable utility. Some characteristics of the software asset are unique, having been developed using proprietary information, and cannot be readily replicated. The entity determines that the fair value of the software asset is CU 15 million, as indicated by the income approach.

Secondly, as is illustrated in Example 14.23 below, *[IFRS 13.IE11-14]*, an entity considers the possible range of fair value measures and considers what is most representative of fair value by taking into consideration that:

- one valuation technique may be more representative of fair value than others;
- inputs used in one valuation technique may be more readily observable in the marketplace or require fewer adjustments (inputs are discussed further at 15 below);
- the resulting range in estimates using one valuation technique may be narrower than the resulting range from other valuation techniques; and
- divergent results from the application of the market and income approaches would indicate that additional analysis is required, as one technique may have been misapplied, or the quality of inputs used in one technique may be less reliable.

Example 14.23: Multiple valuation techniques – machine held and used

An entity acquires a machine in a business combination. The machine will be held and used in its operations. The machine was originally purchased by the acquired entity from an outside vendor and, before the business combination, was customised by the acquired entity for use in its operations. However, the customisation of the machine was not extensive. The acquiring entity determines that the asset would provide maximum value to market participants through its use in combination with other assets or with other assets and liabilities (as installed or otherwise configured for use). There is no evidence to suggest that the current use of the machine is not its highest and best use. Therefore, the highest and best use of the machine is its current use in combination with other assets or with other assets and liabilities.

The entity determines that sufficient data are available to apply the cost approach and, because the customisation of the machine was not extensive, the market approach. The income approach is not used because the machine does not have a separately identifiable income stream from which to develop reliable estimates of future cash flows. Furthermore, information about short-term and intermediate-term lease rates for similar used machinery that otherwise could be used to project an income stream (i.e. lease payments over remaining service lives) is not available. The market and cost approaches are applied as follows:

(a) The market approach is applied using quoted prices for similar machines adjusted for differences between the machine (as customised) and the similar machines. The measurement reflects the price that would be received for the machine in its current condition (used) and location (installed and configured for use). The fair value indicated by that approach ranges from CU 40,000 to CU 48,000.

(b) The cost approach is applied by estimating the amount that would be required currently to construct a substitute (customised) machine of comparable utility. The estimate takes into account the condition of the machine and the environment in which it operates, including physical wear and tear (i.e. physical deterioration), improvements in technology (i.e. functional obsolescence), conditions external to the condition of the machine such as a decline in the market demand for similar machines (i.e. economic obsolescence) and installation costs. The fair value indicated by that approach ranges from CU 40,000 to CU 52,000.

The entity determines that the higher end of the range indicated by the market approach is most representative of fair value and, therefore, ascribes more weight to the results of the market approach. That determination is made on the basis of the relative subjectivity of the inputs, taking into account the degree of comparability between the machine and the similar machines. In particular:

(a) the inputs used in the market approach (quoted prices for similar machines) require fewer and less subjective adjustments than the inputs used in the cost approach.

(b) the range indicated by the market approach overlaps with, but is narrower than, the range indicated by the cost approach.

(c) there are no known unexplained differences (between the machine and the similar machines) within that range.

Accordingly, the entity determines that the fair value of the machine is CU 48,000.

If customisation of the machine was extensive or if there were not sufficient data available to apply the market approach (e.g. because market data reflect transactions for machines used on a stand-alone basis, such as a scrap value for specialised assets, rather than machines used in combination with other assets or with other assets and liabilities), the entity would apply the cost approach. When an asset is used in combination with other assets or with other assets and liabilities, the cost approach assumes the sale of the machine to a market participant buyer with the complementary assets and the associated liabilities. The price received for the sale of the machine (i.e. an exit price) would not be more than either of the following:

(a) the cost that a market participant buyer would incur to acquire or construct a substitute machine of comparable utility; or

(b) the economic benefit that a market participant buyer would derive from the use of the machine.

Both Examples 14.22 and 14.23 highlight situations where it was appropriate to use more than one valuation approach to estimate fair value. Although the indication of value from the cost approach was ultimately not given much weight in either example, performing this valuation technique was an important part of the estimation process. Even when a particular valuation technique is given little weight, its application can highlight specific characteristics of the item being measured and may help in assessing the value indications from other techniques.

Determining the point in a range of values that is 'most representative of fair value' can be subjective and requires the use of judgement by management. In addition, although Example 14.23 refers to 'weighting' the results of the valuation techniques used, in our view, this is not meant to imply that an entity must explicitly apply a percentage weighting to the results of each technique to determine fair value. However, this may be appropriate in certain circumstances.

The standard does not prescribe a specific weighting methodology (e.g. explicit assignment of percentages versus qualitative assessment of value indications). As such, evaluating the techniques applied in an analysis will require judgement based on the merits of each methodology and their respective assumptions.

Identifying a single point within a range is not the same as finding the point within the range that is most representative of fair value. As such, simply assigning arbitrary weights to different indications of value is not appropriate. The weighting of multiple value indications is a process that requires significant judgement and a working knowledge of the different valuation techniques and inputs. Such knowledge is necessary to properly assess the relevance of these methodologies and inputs to the asset or liability being measured. For example, in certain instances it may be more appropriate to rely primarily on the fair value indicated by the technique that maximises the use of observable inputs and minimises the use of unobservable inputs. In all cases, entities should document how they considered the various indications of value, including how they evaluated qualitative and quantitative factors, in determining fair value.

14.1.3 Valuation adjustments

In certain instances, adjustments to the output from a valuation technique may be required to appropriately determine a fair value measurement in accordance with IFRS 13. An entity makes valuation adjustments if market participants would make those adjustments when pricing an asset or liability (under the market conditions at the measurement date). This includes any adjustments for measurement uncertainty (e.g. a risk premium).

Valuation adjustments may include the following:

(a) an adjustment to a valuation technique to take into account a characteristic of an asset or a liability that is not captured by the valuation technique (the need for such an adjustment is typically identified during calibration of the value calculated using the valuation technique with observable market information – see 14.1.3.A below);

(b) applying the point within the bid-ask spread that is most representative of fair value in the circumstances (see 15.3 below);

(c) an adjustment to take into account credit risk (e.g. an entity's non-performance risk or the credit risk of the counterparty to a transaction); and

(d) an adjustment to take into account measurement uncertainty (e.g. when there has been a significant decrease in the volume or level of activity when compared with normal market activity for the asset or liability, or similar assets or liabilities, and the entity has determined that the transaction price or quoted price does not represent fair value). *[IFRS 13.BC145]*.

14.1.3.A Adjustments to valuation techniques that use unobservable inputs

Regardless of the valuation technique(s) used, the objective of a fair value measurement remains the same – i.e. an exit price under current market conditions from the perspective of market participants. As such, if the transaction price is determined to represent fair value *at* initial recognition (see 13 above) *and* a valuation technique that uses unobservable inputs will be used to measure the fair value of an item in subsequent periods, the valuation technique must be calibrated to ensure the valuation technique reflects current market conditions. *[IFRS 13.64]*.

Calibration ensures that a valuation technique incorporates current market conditions. The calibration also helps an entity to determine whether an adjustment to the valuation technique is necessary by identifying potential deficiencies in the valuation model. For example, there might be a characteristic of the asset or liability that is not captured by the valuation technique.

If an entity measures fair value *after* initial recognition using a valuation technique (or techniques) that uses unobservable inputs, an entity must ensure the valuation technique(s) reflect observable market data (e.g. the price for a similar asset or liability) at the measurement date. *[IFRS 13.64]*. That is, it should be calibrated to observable market data, when available.

14.1.4 Making changes to valuation techniques

The standard requires that valuation techniques used to measure fair value be applied on a consistent basis among similar assets or liabilities and across reporting periods. *[IFRS 13.65]*. This is not meant to preclude subsequent changes, such as a change in its weighting when multiple valuation techniques are used or a change in an adjustment applied to a valuation technique.

An entity can make a change to a valuation technique or its application (or a change in the relative importance of one technique over another), provided that change results in a measurement that is equally representative (or more representative) of fair value in the circumstances.

IFRS 13 provides the following examples of circumstances that may trigger a change in valuation technique or relative weights assigned to valuation techniques:

(a) new markets develop;

(b) new information becomes available;

(c) information previously used is no longer available;

(d) valuation techniques improve; or

(e) market conditions change. *[IFRS 13.65]*.

In addition, a change in the exit market, characteristics of market participants that would transact for the asset or liability, or the highest and best use of an asset by market participants could also warrant a change in valuation techniques in certain circumstances.

Changes to fair value resulting from a change in the valuation technique or its application are accounted for as a change in accounting estimate in accordance with IAS 8. However, IFRS 13 states that the disclosures in IAS 8 for a change in accounting estimate are not required for such changes. *[IFRS 13.65, 66]*. Instead, information would be disclosed in accordance with IFRS 13 (see 20.3.5 below for further discussion). If a valuation technique is applied in error, the correction of the technique would be accounted as a correction of an error in accordance with IAS 8.

14.2 Market approach

IFRS 13 describes the market approach as a widely used valuation technique. As defined in the standard, the market approach 'uses prices and other relevant information generated by market transactions involving identical or comparable (i.e. similar) assets, liabilities or a group of assets and liabilities, such as a business'. *[IFRS 13.B5]*. Hence, the market approach uses prices that market participants would pay or receive for the transaction, for example, a quoted market price. The market price may be adjusted to reflect the characteristics of the item being measured, such as its current condition and location, and could result in a range of possible fair values.

Valuation techniques consistent with the market approach use prices and other market data derived from observed transactions for the same or similar assets, for example, revenue, or EBITDA multiples. Multiples might be in ranges with a different multiple for each comparable asset or liability. The selection of the appropriate multiple within the range requires judgement, considering qualitative and quantitative factors specific to the measurement. *[IFRS 13.B6]*.

Another example of a market approach is matrix pricing. Matrix pricing is a mathematical technique used principally to value certain types of financial instruments, such as debt securities, where specific instruments (e.g. cusips) may not trade frequently. The method derives an estimated price of an instrument using transaction prices and other relevant market information for benchmark instruments with similar features (e.g. coupon, maturity or credit rating). *[IFRS 13.B7]*.

14.3 Cost approach

'The cost approach reflects the amount that would be required currently to replace the service capacity of an asset'. This approach is often referred to as current replacement cost. *[IFRS 13.B8]*. The cost approach (or current replacement cost) is typically used to measure the fair value of tangible assets, such as plant or equipment.

From the perspective of a market participant seller, the price that would be received for the asset is based on the cost to a market participant buyer to acquire or construct a substitute asset of comparable utility, adjusted for obsolescence.

Obsolescence is broader than depreciation, whether for financial reporting or tax purposes. According to the standard, obsolescence encompasses:

- physical deterioration;
- functional (technological) obsolescence; and
- economic (external) obsolescence. *[IFRS 13.B9]*.

Physical deterioration and functional obsolescence are factors specific to the asset. Physical deterioration refers to wear, tear or abuse. For example, machines in a factory might deteriorate physically due to high production volumes or a lack of maintenance. Something is functionally obsolete when it does not function in the manner originally intended (excluding any physical deterioration). For example, layout of the machines in the factory may make their use, in combination, more labour intensive, increasing the cost of those machines to the entity. Functional obsolescence also includes the impact of technological change, for example, if newer, more efficient and less labour-intensive models were available, demand for the existing machines might decline, along with the price for the existing machines in the market.

Economic obsolescence arises from factors external to the asset. An asset may be less desirable or its economic life may reduce due to factors such as regulatory changes or excess supply. Consider the machines in the factory; assume that, after the entity had purchased its machines, the supplier had flooded the market with identical machines. If demand was not as high as the supplier had anticipated, it could result in an oversupply and the supplier would be likely to reduce the price in order to clear the excess stock.

14.3.1 Use of depreciated replacement cost to measure fair value

As discussed at 14.3 above, IFRS 13 permits the use of a cost approach for measuring fair value. However, care is needed in using depreciated replacement cost to ensure the resulting measurement is consistent with the requirements of IFRS 13 for measuring fair value.

Before using depreciated replacement cost as a method to measure fair value, an entity should ensure that both:

- the highest and best use of the asset is its current use (see 10 above); and
- the exit market for the asset (i.e. the principal market or in its absence, the most advantageous market, see 6 above) is the same as the entry market (i.e. the market in which the asset was/will be purchased).

In addition, an entity should ensure that both:

- the inputs used to determine replacement cost are consistent with what market participant buyers would pay to acquire or construct a substitute asset of comparable utility; and
- the replacement cost has been adjusted for obsolescence that market participant buyers would consider – i.e. that the depreciation adjustment reflects all forms of obsolescence (i.e. physical deterioration, technological (functional) and economic obsolescence), which is broader than depreciation calculated in accordance with IAS 16.

Even after considering these factors, the resulting depreciated replacement cost must be assessed to ensure market participants would actually transact for the asset, in its current condition and location, at this price. The Illustrative Examples to IFRS 13 reflect this stating that 'the price received for the sale of the machine (i.e. an exit price) would not be more than either of the following:

(a) the cost that a market participant buyer would incur to acquire or construct a substitute machine of comparable utility; or

(b) the economic benefit that a market participant buyer would derive from the use of the machine.' *[IFRS 13.IE11-IE14].*

14.4 Income approach

The income approach converts future cash flows or income and expenses to a single current (i.e. discounted) amount. A fair value measurement using the income approach will reflect current market expectations about those future cash flows or income and expenses. *[IFRS 13.B10].*

The income approach includes valuation techniques such as:

(a) present value techniques (see 21 below);

(b) option pricing models – examples include the Black-Scholes-Merton formula or a binomial model (i.e. a lattice model) – that incorporate present value techniques and reflect both the time value and the intrinsic value of an option; and

(c) the multi-period excess earnings method. This method is used to measure the fair value of some intangible assets. *[IFRS 13.B11]*.

The standard does not limit the valuation techniques that are consistent with the income approach to these examples; an entity may consider other valuation techniques.

The standard provides some application guidance, but only in relation to present value techniques (see 21 below for further discussion regarding this application guidance).

15 INPUTS TO VALUATION TECHNIQUES

15.1 General principles

When selecting the inputs to use in a valuation technique, IFRS 13 requires that they:

- be consistent with the characteristics of the asset or liability that market participants would take into account (see 5.2 above);
- exclude premiums or discounts that reflect size as a characteristic of the entity's holding, rather than a characteristic of the item being measured (for example, blockage factors); and
- exclude other premiums or discounts if they are inconsistent with the unit of account (see 5.1 above for discussions regarding unit of account). *[IFRS 13.69]*.

Premiums, discounts and blockage factors are discussed further at 15.2 below.

In all cases, if there is a quoted price in an active market (i.e. a Level 1 input) for the identical asset or a liability, an entity shall use that price without adjustment when measuring fair value. Adjustments to this price are only permitted in certain circumstances, which are discussed at 17.1 below.

Regardless of the valuation techniques used to estimate fair value, IFRS 13 requires that these techniques maximise the use of relevant observable inputs and minimise the use of unobservable inputs. *[IFRS 13.67]*. This requirement is consistent with the idea that fair value is a market-based measurement and, therefore, is determined using market-based observable data, to the extent available and relevant.

The standard provides some examples of markets in which inputs might be observable.

(a) *Exchange markets* – where closing prices are both readily available and generally representative of fair value, e.g. the Hong Kong Stock Exchange.

(b) *Dealer markets* – where dealers stand ready to trade for their own account. Typically, in these markets, bid and ask prices (see 15.3 below) are more readily available than closing prices. Dealer markets include over-the-counter markets, for which prices are publicly reported.

(c) *Brokered markets* – where brokers attempt to match buyers with sellers but do not stand ready to trade for their own account. The broker knows the prices bid and asked by the respective parties, but each party is typically unaware of another party's price requirements. In such markets, prices for completed transactions may be available. Examples of brokered markets include electronic communication networks in which buy and sell orders are matched, and commercial and residential real estate markets.

(d) *Principal-to-principal markets* – where transactions, both new and re-sales, are negotiated independently with no intermediary. Little, if any, information about these transactions in these markets may be publicly available. *[IFRS 13.68, B34]*.

The standard clarifies that the relevance of market data must be considered when assessing the priority of inputs in the fair value hierarchy. When evaluating the relevance of market data, the number and range of data points should be considered, as well as whether this data is directionally consistent with pricing trends and indications from other more general market information.

Relevant market data reflects the assumptions that market participants would use in pricing the asset or liability being measured. Recent transaction prices for the reference asset or liability (or similar assets and liabilities) are typically considered to represent relevant market data, unless the transaction is determined not to be orderly (see 8 above for a discussion of factors to consider when determining if a transaction is orderly). However, even in situations where a transaction is considered to be orderly, observable transaction prices from inactive markets may require adjustment to address factors, such as timing differences between the transaction date and the measurement date or differences between the asset being measured and a similar asset that was the subject of the transaction. In those instances where the adjustments to observable data are significant and are determined using unobservable data, the resulting measurement would be considered a Level 3 measurement.

Whether observable or unobservable, all inputs used in determining fair value should be consistent with a market-based measurement. As such, the use of unobservable inputs is not intended to allow for the inclusion of entity-specific assumptions in a fair value measurement. While IFRS 13 acknowledges that unobservable inputs may sometimes be developed using an entity's own data, the guidance is clear that these inputs should reflect market participant assumptions. When valuing an intangible asset using unobservable inputs, for example, an entity should take into account the intended use of the asset by market participants, even though this may differ from the entity's intended use. The entity may use its own data, without adjustment, if it determines that market participant assumptions are consistent with its own assumptions (see 19.1 below for additional discussion on how an entity's own assumptions may be applied in a fair value measurement).

The term 'input' is used in IFRS 13 to refer broadly to the assumptions that market participants would use when pricing an asset or liability, rather than to the data entered into a pricing model. This important distinction implies that an adjustment to a pricing model's value (e.g. an adjustment for the risk that a pricing model might not replicate a market price due to the complexity of the instrument being measured) represents an input, which should be evaluated when determining the measurement's category in the fair value hierarchy. For example, when measuring a financial instrument, an adjustment for model risk would be considered an input (most likely a Level 3 input) that, if deemed significant (see 16.2.1 below for further discussion on assessing the significance of inputs) may render the entire fair value estimate a Level 3 measurement.

It is also important to note that an input is distinct from a characteristic. IFRS 13 requires an entity to consider the characteristics of the asset or liability (if market participants would take those characteristics into account when pricing the asset or liability at the measurement date). *[IFRS 13.11].* As discussed at 5.1 above, examples of such characteristics could include:

- the condition and location of an asset; and
- restrictions, if any, on the sale or use of an asset or transfer of a liability.

To draw out the distinction between an input and a characteristic, consider the example of a restricted security that has the following characteristics, which would be considered by a market participant:

- the issuer is a listed entity; and
- the fact that the security is restricted.

An entity is required to select inputs in pricing the asset or liability that are consistent with its characteristics. In some cases those characteristics result in the application of an adjustment, such as a premium or discount. In our example, the inputs could be:

- a quoted price for an unrestricted security; and
- a discount adjustment (to reflect the restriction).

The quoted price for the unrestricted security may be an observable and a Level 1 input. However, given the restriction and the standard's requirement that inputs be consistent with the characteristics of the asset or liability being measured, the second input in measuring fair value is an adjustment to the quoted price to reflect the restriction. If this input is unobservable, it would be a Level 3 input and, if it is considered to be significant to the entire measurement, the fair value measurement of the asset would also be categorised within Level 3 of the fair value hierarchy.

15.2 Premiums and discounts

IFRS 13 indicates that when measuring fair value, entities should select inputs that: (i) are consistent with the characteristics of the asset or liability being measured; and (ii) would be considered by market participants when pricing the asset or liability. In certain instances, these characteristics could result in a premium or discount being incorporated into the fair value measurement.

Determining whether a premium or discount applies to a particular fair value measurement requires judgement and depends on specific facts and circumstances.

IFRS 13 distinguishes between premiums or discounts that reflect size as a characteristic of the entity's holding (specifically, a blockage factor) and control premiums, discounts for non-controlling interests and discounts for lack of marketability that are related to characteristics of the asset or liability being measured.

Control premiums, discounts for non-controlling interests and discounts for lack of marketability reflect characteristics of the asset or liability being measured at fair value. Provided these adjustments are consistent with the unit of account (see 5.1 above) of the asset or liability being measured they can be taken into consideration when measuring fair value. *[IFRS 13.69]*.

Apart from block discounts (discussed at 15.2.1 below), IFRS 13 does not provide explicit guidance on the types of premiums or discounts that may be considered, or when they should be applied to a fair value measurement. Instead, the guidance indicates that premiums and discounts (e.g. control premiums or discounts for lack of marketability) should be incorporated into non-Level 1 fair value measurements if all of the following conditions are met:

- the application of the premium or discount reflects the characteristics of the asset or liability being measured;
- market participants, acting in their 'economic best interest' (see 7.2 above), would consider these premiums or discounts when pricing the asset or liability; and
- the inclusion of the premium or discount is not inconsistent with the unit of account in the IFRS that requires (or permits) the fair value measurement (see 5.1 above).

IFRS 13 emphasises that prices of instruments that trade in active markets (i.e. Level 1 measurements) should generally not be adjusted and should be measured based on the quoted price of the individual instrument multiplied by the quantity held (P×Q).

Figure 14.7: Differentiating between blockage factors and other premiums and discounts

Examples of premiums and discounts	Blockage factor (or block discount)	Control premium	Discount for lack of marketability
Can fair value be adjusted for the premium or discount?	No	Yes, in certain circumstances.	Yes, in certain circumstances.
In what situations would these arise?	When an entity sells a large holding of instruments such that the market's normal daily trading volume is not sufficient to absorb the entire quantity (i.e. flooding the market). IFRS 13 does not permit an entity to take block discounts into consideration in the measurement of fair value.	When an entity transacts for a controlling interest in another entity (and the unit of account is deemed to be the controlling interest and not the individual shares).	When an asset or liability is not readily marketable, for example, where there is no established market of readily-available buyers and sellers or as a result of restrictions.

Example	An entity holds a 20% investment in a listed company. The normal daily trading for those shares on the exchange is 1-2%. If the entity were to sell its entire holding, the price per share would be expected to decrease by 30%.	An entity transacts for a controlling interest in a private business and determines that the fair value of the business is greater than the aggregate value of the individual shares due to its ability to control the acquired entity.	The shares of a private company for which no liquid market exists.
What does the premium or discount represent?	The difference between the price to sell: • the individual asset or liability; and • an entity's entire holding. IFRS 13 does not permit an entity to include such a difference in the measurement of fair value.	The difference between the price to sell: • the individual shares in the controlled entity; and • the entire controlling interest.	The difference between the price to sell: • an asset or liability does not trade in a liquid market; and • an identical asset or liability for which a liquid market exists.

15.2.1 Blockage factors (or block discounts)

IFRS 13 explicitly prohibits the consideration of blockage factors (or block discounts) in a fair value measurement. *[IFRS 13.69, 80]*. While the term blockage factor may be subject to different interpretations, during their deliberations the Boards indicated that they view a blockage factor as an adjustment to the quoted price of an asset or liability because the market's normal trading volume is not sufficient to absorb the quantity held by a reporting entity.

Regardless of the hierarchy level in which a measurement is categorised, blockage factors are excluded from a fair value measurement because such an adjustment is specific to the size of an entity's holding and its decision to transact in a block. That is, the Boards believe such an adjustment is entity-specific in nature. *[IFRS 13.BC157]*. However, the standard clarifies that there is a difference between size being a characteristic of the asset or liability being measured (based on its unit of account) and size being a characteristic of the reporting entity's holding. While any adjustment for the latter is not permitted, the former should be considered if it is consistent with how market participants would price the asset or liability. *[IFRS 13.69]*.

The following example illustrates how IFRS 13 distinguishes between size as a characteristic of the item being measured and size as a characteristic of an entity's holding.

Example 14.24: Blockage factors

Bank X has one outstanding OTC derivative contract with Dealer A.

The notional amount of this contract is CU 1 billion, which is significantly larger than the market norm for these types of contracts.

Bank Y has 100 identical OTC derivative contracts outstanding with various dealers (whose risks are not offsetting because all the contracts are assets and therefore are not measured using the measurement exception).

Each of the 100 contracts has a notional amount of CU 10 million, which is consistent with the market norm for these types of contracts.

Although Bank X and Bank Y have virtually identical market exposures (ignoring credit risk for simplicity), IFRS 13 would allow Bank X to consider a discount for lack of marketability but would preclude Bank Y from applying a similar discount.

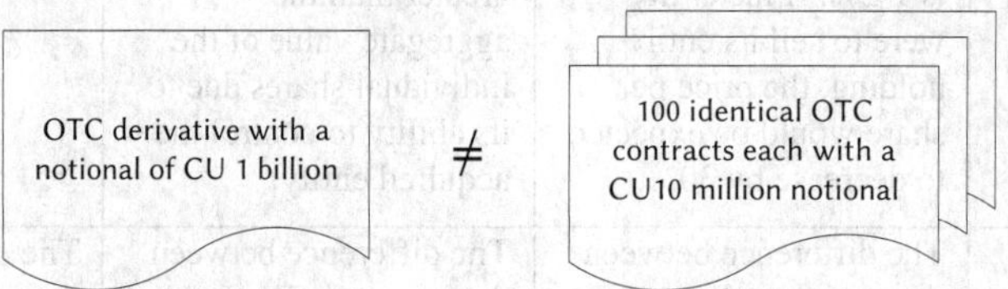

For Bank X, the large notional amount (CU 1 billion) is a characteristic of the instrument being measured and would likely be considered by market participants when transacting for the derivative based on its unit of account (the derivative contract). As such, the fair value of the individual derivative should incorporate an adjustment for size if market participants would consider one in pricing the instrument.

In contrast, the unit of account for Bank Y's 100 derivative contracts is the individual OTC contracts, not the aggregate gross exposure stemming from the 100 contracts (i.e. the block). In pricing the individual contracts, market participants would likely not consider a discount associated with the size of the contracts, since the notional amount for each contract is consistent with the market norm. In accordance with IFRS 13, Bank Y would be prohibited from applying a discount based on the size of its entire holding (i.e. the 100 contracts) as this would represent a block discount that cannot be considered in a fair value measurement.

As discussed at 5.1 above, the unit of account is determined by the relevant IFRS that permits or requires an asset or liability to be measured at fair value, unless IFRS 13 states otherwise. In some cases, the unit of account may be clear, for example, the unit of account for financial instruments in the scope of IFRS 9 (or IAS 39) is typically the individual instrument. However, it may be less clear in other standards, for example, the unit of account for a cash-generating unit when testing non-financial assets for impairment in accordance with IAS 36. At the time of writing, the IASB had issued a Request for Information as part of its PIR of IFRS 13, which asks constituents about prioritising Level 1 inputs or the unit of account. This is discussed further at 5.1.1 above.

15.3 Pricing within the bid-ask spread

The 'bid price' represents the price at which a dealer or market maker is willing to buy an asset (or dispose of a liability). The 'ask price' (or offer price) represents the price at which a dealer or market maker is willing to sell an asset (or assume a liability). The spread between these two prices represents the profit a dealer requires for making a market in a particular security (i.e. providing two-way liquidity).

The use of bid prices to measure assets and ask prices to measure liabilities is permitted, but not required. Instead, for assets and liabilities that are bought and sold in markets where prices are quoted using a bid-ask spread (e.g. over-the-counter markets), the entity must use the price within the bid-ask spread that is most representative of fair value in the circumstances to measure fair value. In making this assessment, entities should evaluate their recent transaction history to support where in the bid-ask spread they are able to exit their positions. For some entities this could result in valuing assets at the bid price and liabilities at the ask price, but in other instances judgement is required to determine the point in the bid-ask spread that is most indicative of fair value. The use of the price within the bid-ask spread that is most representative of fair value applies regardless of whether the input (i.e. the bid or ask price) is observable or not (i.e. regardless of its categorisation in the fair value hierarchy – see 16 below for further discussion). *[IFRS 13.70]*.

Entities need to be consistent in their application of this concept. It would not be appropriate for an entity to measure similar assets at different prices within the bid-ask spread, without evidence indicating that the exit prices for those assets would be at different points within the bid-ask spread.

15.3.1 Mid-market pricing

As a practical expedient, IFRS 13 allows the use of mid-market pricing, or other pricing conventions that are used by market participants, when measuring fair value within the bid-ask spread. *[IFRS 13.71]*. Use of a mid-market pricing convention results in a valuation of an asset or liability at the mid-point of the bid-ask spread. Extract 14.1 at 20.2 below illustrates use of mid-market pricing.

The guidance does not limit or restrict the use of mid-market pricing to specific types of instruments or entities. However, as discussed at 14 above, valuation techniques used to measure fair value should be consistently applied. *[IFRS 13.65]*.

15.3.2 What does the bid-ask spread include?

The commentary in the Basis for Conclusions acknowledges that the previous guidance in paragraph AG70 of IAS 39 only includes transaction costs in the bid-ask spread. The Boards chose not to specify what is included in the bid-ask spread, except for transaction costs. However, they did make it clear that, in their view, the bid-ask spread does not include adjustments for counterparty credit risk. *[IFRS 13.BC164]*.

The IASB has not provided any clarity regarding the interaction between the guidance in IFRS 13 on transaction costs (i.e. transaction costs are not considered an attribute of the asset or liability and, accordingly, are excluded from fair value measurements) and the guidance on the use of prices within the bid-ask spread. If transaction costs are included in the bid-ask spread, measuring an asset at the bid price would include certain future transaction costs in the fair value measurement for the asset.

Given the lack of any specific guidance on this issue, there may be some diversity in practice between entities with respect to how transaction costs are considered. However, we would expect an entity to apply a consistent approach to all of its own fair value measurements.

15.4 Risk premiums

IFRS 13 defines a risk premium as 'compensation sought by risk-averse market participants for bearing the uncertainty inherent in the cash flows of an asset or a liability'. *[IFRS 13 Appendix A]*. Regardless of the valuation technique(s) used, a fair value measurement is intended to represent an exit price and, as such, should include a risk premium that reflects the compensation market participants would demand for bearing the uncertainty inherent in the cash flows of an asset or liability. *[IFRS 13.B16, B39]*. While this risk premium should reflect compensation required in an orderly transaction (not a forced or distressed sale), it should also capture market participant assumptions regarding risk under current market conditions. Example 14.9 discussed at 8.3.2 above illustrates that this risk adjustment may include assumptions about liquidity and uncertainty based on relevant market data.

IFRS 13 explicitly states that '[a] fair value measurement should include a risk premium reflecting the amount market participants would demand as compensation for the uncertainty inherent in the cash flows. Otherwise, the measurement would not faithfully represent fair value. In some cases, determining the appropriate risk premium might be difficult. However, the degree of difficulty alone is not a sufficient reason to exclude a risk premium'. *[IFRS 13.B16]*.

The objective of a risk premium is often misunderstood. Many incorrectly assume that a risk premium is unnecessary when fair value is determined using probability-weighted cash flows. That is, they believe it is appropriate to discount probability-weighted cash flows using a risk-free rate under the assumption that all uncertainty is captured by probability-weighting the cash flows. While expected cash flows (i.e. the probability-weighted average of possible future cash flows) incorporate the uncertainty in the instrument's cash flows, they do not incorporate the compensation that market participants demand for bearing that uncertainty. *[IFRS 13.B25-B29]*. In order to capture this required compensation in the measurement, a market risk premium must be added (either as an adjustment to the discount rate or to the expected cash flows). IFRS 13's application guidance addresses this point when discussing systematic and unsystematic risk and certainty-equivalent cash flows (see 21 below for additional discussion on how risk premiums are applied in a present value technique).

It is important to note that increased risk associated with an asset generally decreases the fair value of that asset, whereas increased risk associated with a liability generally increases the fair value of that liability (with the exception of non-performance risk). Uncertainty associated with an asset reduces the amount a market participant would pay for the asset. In contrast, all else being equal, compensation for an uncertainty related to a liability results in an increase to the amount that the market participant would expect to receive for assuming the obligation. If that compensation is accounted for in the discount rate, rather than in the cash flows, it would result in an increase in the discount rate used to measure the fair value of an asset. However, it would result in a reduction of the discount rate used in the fair value measurement of the liability (i.e. the discount rate must be lower so that the resulting fair value of the liability is higher). *[IFRS 13.BC91]*. This concept only applies when measuring the fair value of a liability that does not have a corresponding asset using an income approach. As discussed at 11.2.1 above, when a quoted price for the transfer of an identical or similar liability or entity's own equity instrument is held by another party as an asset, the fair value of this liability or own equity instrument should be determined from the perspective of the market participant that holds the identical item as an asset.

15.5 Broker quotes and pricing services

When quoted prices from brokers or pricing services are used to measure fair value, it is the entity's responsibility to understand the source and nature of this information to accurately assess its relevance. When there has been a significant decrease in the volume or level of activity for the asset or liability, management should evaluate whether the prices received from brokers or pricing services are based on current information from orderly transactions or valuation techniques that appropriately reflect market participant assumptions regarding risk. IFRS 13 states that entities should place less reliance on third-party quotes that are not based on transactions, compared to other value indications that are based on market transactions. *[IFRS 13.B46]*.

When information from brokers and pricing services is based on transaction data, entities should assess whether, and to what extent, the observed prices are a result of orderly transactions when determining the weight to place on these data points, compared to other value indications (see 8.2 above for additional information on the factors an entity may consider when assessing whether transactions are orderly). Facts and circumstances will determine the weight that an entity should place on a transaction price, including:

- the comparability of the transaction to the asset or liability being measured at fair value;
- the proximity of the transaction to the measurement date;
- the size of the transaction; and
- the nature of the quote (e.g. binding versus indicative quote) and the number of quotes received.

See 16.2.3 below for additional discussion on fair value hierarchy considerations when using quoted prices from brokers and pricing services.

15.5.1 How should values provided by central clearing organisations for margin purposes be evaluated when determining the fair value of centrally cleared derivatives for financial reporting?

For OTC derivatives that are centrally cleared, counterparties are typically required on an ongoing basis to post collateral based on the change in value of the derivative (sometimes referred to as 'variation margin'). As a result, entities with centrally cleared OTC derivatives will periodically receive a 'value mark' from a clearing organisation that states the amount of variation margin to be posted or received.

However, this value should not be presumed to represent fair value (an exit price) in accordance with IFRS 13. Different clearing organisations may have different approaches for calculating variation margin requirements and while practice may continue to evolve, it is our understanding that the 'value marks' provided generally do not represent an actual transaction price (i.e. a price at which the reporting entity could execute a trade to buy or sell the contract). Instead, this value may be based on a clearing organisation's analysis of information provided by clearing members and certain of its own assumptions. While this value may potentially be an appropriate estimate of fair value in certain instances, the reporting entity should understand how this value is determined and evaluate whether it includes only those factors that would be considered by market participants in an orderly transaction to sell or transfer the derivative. For example, to provide themselves with additional protection, some clearing organisations may include an incremental amount in their variation margin requirement in excess of the 'true' change in the value of the derivative.

As with pricing information provided by brokers or third-party pricing services, reporting entities are responsible for understanding the source and nature of information provided by central clearing organisations. An entity should assess whether the value indication represents fair value in accordance with IFRS 13 or whether an adjustment may be needed. See 16.2.4 below for a discussion of the classification of centrally cleared OTC derivatives in the fair value hierarchy.

16 THE FAIR VALUE HIERARCHY

The fair value hierarchy is intended to increase consistency and comparability in fair value measurements and the related disclosures. *[IFRS 13.72]*. Application of the hierarchy requires an entity to prioritise observable inputs over those that are unobservable when measuring fair value. In addition, for disclosures, it provides a framework for users to consider the relative subjectivity of the fair value measurements made by the reporting entity.

16.1 The fair value hierarchy

The fair value hierarchy classifies the inputs used to measure fair value into three levels, which are described in Figure 14.8.

Figure 14.8: Fair value hierarchy

	Level 1	Level 2	Level 3
Definition *[IFRS 13 Appendix A]*	Quoted prices (unadjusted) in active markets for identical assets or liabilities that the entity can access at the measurement date.	Inputs other than quoted prices included within level 1 that are observable for the asset or liability, either directly or indirectly.	Unobservable inputs for the asset or liability.
Example	The price for a financial asset or financial liability for the identical asset is traded on an active market (e.g. Tokyo Stock Exchange).	Interest rates and yield curves observable at commonly quoted intervals, implied volatilities, and credit spreads.	Projected cash flows used in a discounted cash flow calculation.

Valuation techniques used to measure fair value must maximise the use of relevant observable inputs and minimise the use of unobservable inputs. The best indication of fair value is a quoted price in an active market (i.e. 'a market in which transactions for the asset or liability take place with sufficient frequency and volume to provide pricing information on an ongoing basis' *[IFRS 13 Appendix A]*).

The fair value hierarchy focuses on prioritising the inputs used in valuation techniques, not the techniques themselves. *[IFRS 13.74]*. While the availability of inputs might affect the valuation technique(s) selected to measure fair value, as discussed at 14 above, IFRS 13 does not prioritise the use of one technique over another (with the exception of the requirement to measure identical financial instruments that trade in active markets at P×Q). The determination of the valuation technique(s) to be used requires significant judgement and will be dependent on the specific characteristics of the asset or liability being measured and the principal (or most advantageous) market in which market participants would transact for the asset or liability.

Although the valuation techniques themselves are not subject to the fair value hierarchy, a risk adjustment that market participants would demand to compensate for a risk inherent in a particular valuation technique (e.g. a model adjustment) is considered an input that must be assessed within the fair value hierarchy. As discussed at 16.2 below, if this type of risk adjustment is included, it should be considered when categorising the fair value measurement within the fair value hierarchy.

16.2 Categorisation within the fair value hierarchy

IFRS 13 distinguishes between where in the fair value hierarchy an individual input to a valuation technique may fall and where the entire measurement is categorised for disclosure purposes.

Inputs used in a valuation technique may fall into different levels of the fair value hierarchy. However, for disclosure purposes, the fair value measurement must be categorised in its entirety (i.e. the fair value measure for the asset or liability or the group of assets and/or liability, depending on the unit of account) within the hierarchy. Categorising the entire measurement (and the required disclosure of this information, see 20.3.3 below) provides users of financial statements with an indication of the overall observability or subjectivity of a fair value measurement.

The appropriate categorisation may be obvious when only a single input is used, for example, when measuring fair value using a quoted price in an active market, without adjustment. However, an asset or liability that is not traded in an active market with a quoted price will often require more than one input to determine its fair value. For example, an over-the-counter option on a traded equity security measured at fair value using an option pricing model requires the following market-based inputs: (i) expected volatility; (ii) expected dividend yield; and (iii) the risk-free rate of interest.

IFRS 13 clarifies that the hierarchy categorisation of a fair value measurement, in its entirety, is determined based on the lowest level input that is significant to the entire measurement. The standard also makes it clear that adjustments to arrive at measurements based on fair value (e.g. 'costs to sell' when measuring fair value less costs to sell) are not be taken into account in this determination. *[IFRS 13.73]*. In the over-the-counter equity option example, assume that the risk-free interest rate and the dividend yield were determined to be Level 2 inputs, but the expected volatility was determined to be a Level 3 input. If expected volatility was determined to be significant to the overall value of the option, the entire measurement would be categorised within Level 3 of the fair value hierarchy.

If an observable input requires an adjustment using an unobservable input and that adjustment actually results in a significantly higher or lower fair value measurement, the standard is clear that the resulting fair value measurement would be categorised within Level 3 of the fair value hierarchy. *[IFRS 13.75]*. Consider our example of a restricted security discussed at 15.1 above. While the quoted price for the unrestricted security may be observable, if Level 3 inputs are needed to determine the effect of the restriction on the instrument's fair value, and this effect is significant to the measurement, the asset would be categorised within Level 3 of the fair value hierarchy. In addition, as discussed at 8 above, in certain situations adjustments to a transaction price in an inactive market may be required. If these adjustments are based on unobservable inputs and significant to the measurement, the item would be categorised within Level 3 of the fair value hierarchy.

It is important to understand that the determination of the hierarchy level in which the fair value measure falls (and, therefore, the category in which it will be disclosed – see 20.3.3 below) is based on the fair value measurement for the specific item being measured, which will be dependent on the unit of account for the asset or liability. This may create practical challenges in relation to fair value measurements for non-financial assets and financial assets and liabilities with offsetting risk measured using the measurement exception discussed at 12 above. For example, in situations where the unit of account for a non-financial asset is the individual item, but the valuation premise is in combination with other assets (or other assets and liabilities), the value of the asset group would need to be attributed to the individual assets or liabilities or to the various instruments within each level of the fair value hierarchy. For example, consider Example 14.13 at 10.2.2 above. The unit of account for the vines and the land was that specified by IAS 41 and IAS 16 respectively. However, their highest and best use was in combination, together and with other assets. The value of that group would need to be attributed to each of the assets, including both the vines and land, as the fair value of these individual assets should be categorised within the fair value hierarchy.

16.2.1 Assessing the significance of inputs

Assessing the significance of a particular input to the entire measurement requires judgement and consideration of factors specific to the asset or liability (or group of assets and/or liabilities) being measured. *[IFRS 13.73]*.

IFRS 13 does not provide specific guidance on how entities should evaluate the significance of individual inputs. This determination will require judgement and consideration of factors specific to the asset or liability (or group of assets and liabilities) being measured.

The standard is clear that it considers significance in relation to 'the entire measurement'. In our view, this requires the assessment to consider the fair value measure itself, rather than any resulting change in fair value, regardless of whether that change is recognised (i.e. in profit or loss or other comprehensive income) or unrecognised. For example, assume an investment property is measured at fair value at the end of each reporting period. In the current reporting period the fair value of the investment property reduces by CU 200,000 to CU 500,000. The significance of any inputs to the fair value measurement would be assessed by reference to the CU 500,000, even though CU 200,000 is the amount that will be recognised in profit or loss. However a reporting entity may deem it appropriate to also consider significance in relation to the change in fair value from prior periods, in addition to considering the significance of an input in relation to the entire fair value measurement. Such an approach may be helpful in relation to cash-based instruments (e.g. loans or structured notes with embedded derivatives) whose carrying amounts, based on fair value, are heavily affected by their principal or face amount.

As noted in 16.2 above, if an observable input requires an adjustment using an unobservable input and that adjustment actually results in a significantly higher or lower fair value measurement, the standard is clear that the resulting fair value measurement would be categorised within Level 3 of the hierarchy. *[IFRS 13.75]*. What is not clear, however, is the appropriate categorisation when an observable input requires an adjustment using an unobservable input and: (a) that adjustment does not actually result in a significantly higher or lower fair value in the current period; but (b) the potential adjustment from using a different unobservable input would result in a significantly higher or lower fair value measurement. As noted in 16.2 above, the categorisation of a fair value measurement indicates the overall observability or subjectivity of a measurement, in its entirety. To this end, in some cases, the use of sensitivity analysis or stress testing (i.e. using a range of reasonably possible alternative input values as of the measurement date) might be appropriate to assess the effects of unobservable inputs on a fair value measure. In situations where more than one unobservable input is used in a fair value measure, the assessment of significance should be considered based on the aggregate effect of all the unobservable inputs.

Entities should have a documented policy with respect to their approach to determining the significance of unobservable inputs on its fair value measurements and apply that policy consistently. This is important in light of the disclosure requirements in IFRS 13, particularly for fair value measurements categorised within Level 3 of the fair value hierarchy (see 20.3 below).

16.2.2 Transfers between levels within the fair value hierarchy

For assets or liabilities that are measured at fair value (or measurements based on fair value) at the end of each reporting period, their categorisation within the fair value hierarchy may change over time. This might be the case if the market for a particular asset or liability that was previously considered active (Level 1) becomes inactive (Level 2 or Level 3) or if significant inputs used in a valuation technique that were previously unobservable (Level 3) become observable (Level 2) given transactions that were observed around the measurement date. Such changes in categorisation within the hierarchy are referred to in IFRS 13 as transfers between levels within the fair value hierarchy.

An entity is required to select, and consistently apply, a policy for determining when transfers between levels of the fair value hierarchy are deemed to have occurred, that is, the timing of recognising transfers. This policy must be the same for transfers into and out of the levels. Examples of policies for determining the timing of transfers include:

- the date of the event or change in circumstances that caused the transfer;
- the beginning of the reporting period; or
- the end of the reporting period. *[IFRS 13.95]*.

The standard requires an entity to disclose this policy (see 20.2 below). In addition, the selected timing (i.e. when transfers are deemed to have occurred) has a direct impact on the information an entity needs to collate in order to meet the disclosure requirements in IFRS 13 – specifically those required by IFRS 13.93(c) and (e)(iv) – for both transfers between Levels 1 and 2 and transfers into and out of Level 3 (these disclosure requirements are discussed at 20.3.2 below). *[IFRS 13.93(c), 93(e)(iv)].*

16.2.3 Information provided by third-party pricing services or brokers

IFRS 13 does not preclude the use of quoted prices provided by third parties, such as pricing services or brokers, provided those quoted prices are developed in accordance with the standard. Quoted prices provided by third parties represent an important source of information in estimating fair value for many entities. While not precluded, the standard makes it clear that the use of broker quotes, third-party pricing services, or a third-party valuation specialist does not alleviate management's responsibility for the fair value measurements (and the related disclosures) that will be included in its financial statements. *[IFRS 13.B45].*

It is important for entities to understand the source of information received from brokers and pricing services, particularly when there has been a significant decrease in the volume or level of activity for the asset or liability, as management needs to assess the relevance of these quotes. This is discussed further at 8.3 above.

As discussed at 15.5 above, an entity should evaluate whether quotes from brokers and pricing services are based on current information that reflects orderly transactions or were determined using valuation techniques that appropriately reflect market participant assumptions regarding risk. Entities should place less weight on third-party quotes that are not based on transactions compared to fair value indications that are based on market transactions.

Determining the level in which assets and liabilities are categorised within the fair value hierarchy for disclosure purposes often requires judgement. Information provided by third-party pricing services or brokers could represent Level 1, Level 2, or Level 3 inputs depending on the source of the information and the type of instrument being measured. For example, pricing services may provide quoted market prices (e.g. closing price) for financial instruments traded in active markets. These prices are Level 1 measurements.

Alternatively, a pricing service may provide an entity with consensus pricing information (e.g. information obtained by polling dealers for indications of mid-market prices for a particular asset class). The non-binding nature of consensus pricing would generally result in its categorisation as Level 3 information, assuming no additional corroborating evidence.

Pricing services may also use valuation models to estimate values for certain instruments. For example, pricing services may use matrix pricing to determine the value of many fixed-income securities. The hierarchy level in which these instruments would be categorised depends on the observability of the valuation model's inputs. Therefore, entities that use pricing services should understand the data sources and valuation methods used to derive those third-party quotes. This information will determine where the entity's instruments would be categorised within the fair value hierarchy.

Similarly, the level within the hierarchy in which a broker quote is categorised depends on the nature of the quote. *[IFRS 13.B47]*. In certain brokered markets, firm quotes are disclosed and an entity has the ability to 'hit' or execute a transaction at the quoted price. Depending on the level of activity in these markets, those quotes may be categorised as Level 1 or Level 2. However, when an entity has to solicit a quote from a broker, the quotes are often non-binding and may include a disclaimer that releases the broker from being held to that price in an actual transaction. On their own, non-binding quotes would generally represent a Level 3 input. In addition, when the quote includes explanatory language or a disclaimer, the entity should assess whether the quote represents fair value (exit price) or whether an adjustment is needed.

If an entity uses multiple quotes within a narrow range when measuring fair value, it will likely provide stronger evidence of fair value than a single quote or quotes that are widely dispersed. However, the number of quotes should not, in and of itself, affect the categorisation within the fair value hierarchy. An entity would still need to consider the nature of those quotes. For example, multiple Level 3 inputs, within a reasonable range, would not result in a Level 2 measurement without additional observable corroborating evidence.

In August 2014, the IFRS Interpretations Committee received a request to clarify the circumstances in which a fair value measurement, in its entirety, that uses prices that are provided by third parties (e.g. consensus prices) could be categorised within Level 1 of the fair value hierarchy, particularly in relation to debt securities that are actively traded. The submitter highlighted that categorisation within the fair value hierarchy for debt securities is not straightforward and that there were divergent views on the appropriate level within the hierarchy such fair value measurements should be categorised.

After considering the analyses and outreach performed by its staff, the Interpretations Committee decided not to add this issue to its agenda, noting the following:[19]

- The guidance in IFRS 13 relating to the categorisation within the fair value hierarchy was sufficient to draw an appropriate conclusion on this issue.
- The fair value hierarchy prioritises the inputs to valuation techniques, not the valuation techniques used to measure fair value. When the fair value of assets or liabilities is measured based on prices provided by third parties, the categorisation of those measurements within the fair value hierarchy depends on the evaluation of the inputs used by the third party to derive those prices; not on the pricing methodology the third party has used.
- Only unadjusted quoted prices in active markets for identical assets or liabilities that the entity can access at the measurement date qualify as Level 1 measurement. Therefore, a fair value measurement that is based on prices provided by third parties can only be categorised within Level 1 of the fair value hierarchy if that measurement relies solely on unadjusted quoted prices in an active market for an identical instrument that the entity can access at the measurement date (i.e. P×Q, without adjustment).

16.2.4 Categorisation of over-the-counter derivative instruments

Depending on the observability of the inputs used, fair value measurements of over-the-counter derivatives that are not centrally cleared would likely be within either Level 2 or Level 3 of the fair value hierarchy.

Although these instruments may initially be executed in active markets, quoted prices for the identical asset or liability will often not be available when measuring fair value subsequently. For example, consider a 10-year plain vanilla interest-rate swap entered into on 1 January 20X9 that is not centrally cleared. While there may be quoted prices for 10-year swaps, when measuring the fair value of the swap on 31 March 20X9, the subject instrument would represent a 9.75 year swap for which quoted prices are generally not available. As a result, most over-the-counter derivative contracts that are not centrally cleared are valued based on inputs used in pricing models.

In addition, centrally cleared derivatives would not be categorised within Level 1 unless their fair value was determined based on an unadjusted quoted price in active markets for an identical instrument. Some constituents have questioned whether a 'value mark', periodically provided by a central clearing organisation for variation margin purposes, represents a Level 1 measurement. As discussed at 15.5.1 above, a reporting entity should not presume that the value provided by a central clearing organisation for margin purposes represents fair value in accordance with IFRS 13. Instead, entities need to understand the source and nature of the information provided by the central clearing organisation and assess whether the value indication represents fair value in accordance with IFRS 13 or whether an adjustment may be needed.

Even in those circumstances where an entity determines that the information received from the central clearing organisation is representative of fair value and does not require adjustment, it is our understanding that the 'value marks' provided typically do not represent actual trades of the identical instrument and therefore would not be a Level 1 measurement. See 15.5.1 above for additional discussion on the consideration of values provided by central clearing organisations when determining the fair value.

17 LEVEL 1 INPUTS

'Level 1 inputs are quoted prices (unadjusted) in active markets for identical assets or liabilities that the entity can access at the measurement date'. *[IFRS 13.76]*. According to IFRS 13, this price represents the most reliable evidence of fair value. If a quoted price in an active market is available, an entity *must use* this price to measure fair value without adjustment; although adjustments are permitted in limited circumstances (see 17.3 below). *[IFRS 13.77]*.

17.1 Use of Level 1 inputs

As a general principle, IFRS 13 mandates the use of quoted prices in active markets for identical assets and liabilities whenever available. With limited exceptions, quoted prices in active markets should not be adjusted when determining the fair value of identical assets and liabilities, as the IASB believes these prices provide the most reliable evidence of fair value.

Adjustments can only be made to a quoted price in an active market (a Level 1 input) in the following circumstances:

(a) when an entity holds a large number of similar (but not identical) assets or liabilities (e.g. debt securities) that are measured at fair value and a quoted price in an active market is available but is not readily accessible for each of those assets or liabilities individually. That is, since the assets or liabilities are not identical and given the large number of similar assets or liabilities held by the entity, it would be difficult to obtain pricing information for each individual asset or liability at the measurement date.

    In this situation, IFRS 13 provides a practical expedient; an entity may measure fair value using an alternative pricing method that does not rely exclusively on quoted prices (e.g. matrix pricing);

(b) when a quoted price in an active market does not represent fair value at the measurement date.

    This may be the case, for example, if significant events, such as transactions in a principal-to-principal market, trades in a brokered market or announcements, take place after the close of a market but before the measurement date. An entity must establish and consistently apply a policy for identifying those events that might affect fair value measurements; or

(c) when measuring the fair value of a liability or an entity's own equity instrument using the quoted price for the identical item traded as an asset in an active market and that price needs to be adjusted for factors specific to the item or the asset. *[IFRS 13.79]*.

These exceptions are discussed further at 17.1.1, 17.2 and 17.3 below. Level 1 inputs are most commonly associated with financial instruments, for example, shares that are actively traded on a stock exchange. It may be that an asset or liability is traded in multiple active markets, for example, shares that are listed on more than one stock exchange. In light of this, the standard emphasises the need within Level 1 to determine both, the principal (or most advantageous) market (see 6 above) and whether the entity can enter into a transaction for the asset or liability at the price in that market at the measurement date (see 8 above). *[IFRS 13.78]*.

As discussed at 16.2 above, if no adjustment is made to a Level 1 input, the result is the entire fair value measurement being categorised within Level 1 of the fair value hierarchy. However, any adjustment made to a Level 1 input or use of the practical expedient in (a) above would result in categorisation within a lower level of the fair value hierarchy. If the adjustment uses significant unobservable inputs, it would need to be categorised within Level 3. *[IFRS 13.75]*.

17.1.1 Level 1 liabilities and instruments classified in an entity's own equity

Quoted prices in active markets for identical liabilities and instruments classified as an entity's own equity are Level 1 measurements. These instruments would likewise be categorised within Level 1 when a quoted price exists for the identical instrument traded as an asset in an active market, provided no adjustment to the quoted price is required.

The fair value of corporate debt issued by a reporting entity, for example, would be a Level 1 measurement if the asset corresponding to the issuer's liability (i.e. the corporate bond) trades in an active market and no adjustment is made to the quoted price. While the liability itself is not transferred in an active market, the IASB concluded that Level 1 categorisation is appropriate when the identical instrument trades as an asset in an active market.

If an adjustment to the corresponding asset's price is required to address differences between the asset and the liability or equity instrument (as discussed at 11 above), *[IFRS 13.79(c)]*, the adjusted price would not be a Level 1 measurement. For example, an adjustment to the quoted price of an asset that includes the effect of a third-party credit enhancement would be warranted when measuring the fair value of the liability. In this case, the corresponding asset and the liability would have different units of account (as discussed at 11.3.1 above).

17.2 Alternative pricing methods

When an entity holds a large number of similar assets and liabilities for which quoted prices exist, but are not easily accessible, IFRS 13 allows for the use of alternative pricing methods (e.g. matrix pricing) as a practical expedient. *[IFRS 13.79(a)]*. The IASB provided this practical expedient to ease the administrative burden associated with obtaining quoted prices for each individual instrument. However, if the practical expedient is used, the resulting fair value measurement would not be considered a Level 1 measurement.

17.3 Quoted prices in active markets that are not representative of fair value

IFRS 13 recognises that in certain situations a quoted price in an active market might not represent the fair value of an asset or liability, such as when significant events occur on the measurement date, but after the close of trading. In these situations, entities would adjust the quoted price to incorporate this new information into the fair value measurement. *[IFRS 13.79(b)]*. However, if the quoted price is adjusted, the resulting fair value measurement would no longer be considered a Level 1 measurement.

An entity's valuation policies and procedures should address how these 'after-hour' events will be identified and assessed. Controls should be put in place to ensure that any adjustments made to quoted prices are appropriate under IFRS 13 and are applied in a consistent manner.

17.4 Unit of account

Although the unit of account is generally determined in accordance with other IFRSs, IFRS 13 addresses the unit of account for Level 1 assets and liabilities. Paragraph 80 of IFRS 13 states that 'if an entity holds a position in a single asset or liability (including a position comprising a large number of identical assets or liabilities, such as a holding of financial instruments) and the asset or liability is traded in an active market, the fair value of the asset or liability shall be measured within Level 1 as the product of the quoted price for the individual asset or liability and the quantity held by the entity'. *[IFRS 13.80]*. By dictating that fair value be determined based on P×Q, IFRS 13 effectively prescribes the unit of account as the individual asset or liability in these situations.

This requirement is generally accepted when the asset or liability being measured is a financial instrument in the scope of IFRS 9 (or IAS 39). However, when an entity holds an investment in a listed subsidiary, joint venture or associate, some believe the fair value should include an adjustment (e.g. a control premium) to reflect the value of the investor's control, joint control or significant influence over their investment as a whole. In September 2014, the IASB issued an exposure draft that proposed clarifying that the requirement in IFRS 13 to use P×Q, without adjustment, to measure fair value would apply even in situations where the unit of account is the entire investment. After considering the responses from constituents, the IASB had directed its staff to perform additional research before they deliberated further. Following that work the IASB has decided that further research would be fed into the PIR of IFRS 13. At the time of writing, the IASB had issued a Request for Information as part of its PIR of IFRS 13, which asks for feedback on prioritising level 1 inputs. The Board will consider this feedback to determine if further work on this topic is needed. This is discussed further at 5.1.1 above.

Chapter 14

18 LEVEL 2 INPUTS

18.1 Level 2 inputs

Level 2 inputs include quoted prices (in non-active markets or in active markets for similar assets or liabilities), observable inputs other than quoted prices and inputs that are not directly observable, but are corroborated by observable market data. *[IFRS 13.82]*.

The inclusion of market-corroborated inputs is significant because it expands the scope of Level 2 inputs beyond those directly observable for the asset or liability. Inputs determined through mathematical or statistical techniques, such as correlation or regression, may be categorised as Level 2 if the inputs into, and/(or) the results from, these techniques can be corroborated with observable market data.

IFRS 13 requires that a Level 2 input be observable (either directly or indirectly through corroboration with market data) for substantially the full contractual term of the asset or liability being measured. *[IFRS 13.81]*. Therefore, a long-term input extrapolated from short-term observable market data (e.g. a 30-year yield extrapolated from the observable 5-, 10- and 15-year points on the yield curve) would generally not be considered a Level 2 input.

18.2 Examples of Level 2 inputs

IFRS 13's application guidance provides a number of examples of Level 2 inputs for specific assets or liabilities. These examples are included in Figure 14.9 below.

Figure 14.9: Examples of Level 2 inputs [IFRS 13.B35]

Asset or Liability	Example of a Level 2 Input
Receive-fixed, pay-variable interest rate swap based on the London Interbank Offered Rate (LIBOR) swap rate	The LIBOR swap rate if that rate is observable at commonly quoted intervals for substantially the full term of the swap.
Receive-fixed, pay-variable interest rate swap based on a yield curve denominated in a foreign currency	The swap rate based on a yield curve denominated in a foreign currency that is observable at commonly quoted intervals for substantially the full term of the swap. This would be a Level 2 input if the term of the swap is 10 years and that rate is observable at commonly quoted intervals for 9 years, provided that any reasonable extrapolation of the yield curve for year 10 would not be significant to the fair value measurement of the swap in its entirety.
Receive-fixed, pay-variable interest rate swap based on a specific bank's prime rate	The bank's prime rate derived through extrapolation if the extrapolated values are corroborated by observable market data, for example, by correlation with an interest rate that is observable over substantially the full term of the swap.
Three-year option on exchange-traded shares	The implied volatility for the shares derived through extrapolation to year 3 if both of the following conditions exist: (i) Prices for one-year and two-year options on the shares are observable. (ii) The extrapolated implied volatility of a three-year option is corroborated by observable market data for substantially the full term of the option. In this situation, the implied volatility could be derived by extrapolating from the implied volatility of the one-year and two-year options on the shares and corroborated by the implied volatility for three-year options on comparable entities' shares, provided that correlation with the one-year and two-year implied volatilities is established.
Licensing arrangement	For a licensing arrangement that is acquired in a business combination and was recently negotiated with an unrelated party by the acquired entity (the party to the licensing arrangement), a Level 2 input would be the royalty rate in the contract with the unrelated party at inception of the arrangement.
Cash-generating unit	A valuation multiple (e.g. a multiple of earnings or revenue or a similar performance measure) derived from observable market data, e.g. multiples derived from prices in observed transactions involving comparable (i.e. similar) businesses, taking into account operational, market, financial and non-financial factors.

Finished goods inventory at a retail outlet	For finished goods inventory that is acquired in a business combination, a Level 2 input would be either a price to customers in a retail market or a price to retailers in a wholesale market, adjusted for differences between the condition and location of the inventory item and the comparable (i.e. similar) inventory items so that the fair value measurement reflects the price that would be received in a transaction to sell the inventory to another retailer that would complete the requisite selling efforts. Conceptually, the fair value measurement will be the same, whether adjustments are made to a retail price (downward) or to a wholesale price (upward). Generally, the price that requires the least amount of subjective adjustments should be used for the fair value measurement.
Building held and used	The price per square metre for the building (a valuation multiple) derived from observable market data, e.g. multiples derived from prices in observed transactions involving comparable (i.e. similar) buildings in similar locations.

18.3 Market corroborated inputs

Level 2 inputs, as discussed at 18.1 above, include market-corroborated inputs. That is, inputs that are not directly observable for the asset or liability, but, instead, are corroborated by observable market data through correlation or other statistical techniques.

IFRS 13 does not provide any detailed guidance regarding to the application of statistical techniques, such as regression or correlation, when attempting to corroborate inputs to observable market data (Level 2) inputs. However, the lack of any specific guidance or 'bright lines' for evaluating the validity of a statistical inference by the IASB should not be construed to imply that the mere use of a statistical analysis (such as linear regression) would be deemed valid and appropriate to support Level 2 categorisation (or a fair value measurement for that matter). Any statistical analysis that is relied on for financial reporting purposes should be evaluated for its predictive validity. That is, the statistical technique should support the hypothesis that the observable input has predictive value with respect to the unobservable input.

In Example 14.12 at 10.1.3 above, for the three-year option on exchange-traded shares, the implied volatility derived through extrapolation has been categorised as a Level 2 input because the input was corroborated (through correlation) to an implied volatility based on an observable option price of a comparable entity. In this example, the determination of an appropriate proxy (i.e. a comparable entity) is a critical component in supporting that the implied volatility of the actual option being measured is a market-corroborated input.

In practice, identifying an appropriate benchmark or proxy requires judgement that should appropriately incorporate both qualitative and quantitative factors. For example, when valuing equity-based instruments (e.g. equity options), an entity should consider the industry, nature of the business, size, leverage and other factors that would qualitatively support the expectation that the benchmarks are sufficiently comparable to the subject entity. Qualitative considerations may differ depending on the type of input being analysed or the type of instrument being measured (e.g. a foreign exchange option versus an equity option).

In addition to the qualitative considerations discussed above, quantitative measures are used to validate a statistical analysis. For example, if a regression analysis is used as a means of corroborating non-observable market data, the results of the analysis can be assessed based on statistical measures.

18.4 Making adjustments to a Level 2 input

The standard acknowledges that, unlike a Level 1 input, adjustments to Level 2 inputs may be more common, but will vary depending on the factors specific to the asset or liability. *[IFRS 13.83]*.

There are a number of reasons why an entity may need to make adjustments to Level 2 inputs. Adjustments to observable data from inactive markets (see 8 above), for example, might be required for timing differences between the transaction date and the measurement date, or differences between the asset being measured and a similar asset that was the subject of the transaction. In addition, factors such as the condition or location of an asset should also be considered when determining if adjustments to Level 2 inputs are warranted.

If the Level 2 input relates to an asset or liability that is similar, but not identical to the asset or liability being measured, the entity would need to consider what adjustments may be required to capture differences between the item being measured and the reference asset or liability. For example, do they have different characteristics, such as credit quality of the issuer in the case of a bond? Adjustments may be needed for differences between the two. *[IFRS 13.83]*.

If an adjustment to a Level 2 input is significant to the entire fair value measurement, it may affect the fair value measurement's categorisation within the fair value hierarchy for disclosure purposes. If the adjustment uses significant unobservable inputs, it would need to be categorised within Level 3 of the hierarchy. *[IFRS 13.84]*.

18.5 Recently observed prices in an inactive market

Valuation technique(s) used to measure fair value must maximise the use of *relevant* observable inputs and minimise the use of unobservable inputs. While recently observed transactions for the same (or similar) items often provide useful information for measuring fair value, transactions or quoted prices in inactive markets are not necessarily indicative of fair value. A significant decrease in the volume or level of activity for the asset or liability may increase the chances of this. However, transaction data should not be ignored, unless the transaction is determined to be disorderly (see 8 above).

The relevance of observable data, including last transaction prices, must be considered when assessing the weight this information should be given when estimating fair value and whether adjustments are needed (as discussed at 18.4 above). Adjustments to observed transaction prices may be warranted in some situations, particularly when the observed transaction is for a similar, but not identical, instrument. Therefore, it is important to understand the characteristics of the item being measured compared with an item being used as a benchmark.

When few, if any, transactions can be observed for an asset or liability, an index may provide relevant pricing information if the underlying risks of the index are similar to the item being measured. While the index price may provide general information about market participant assumptions regarding certain risk features of the asset or liability, adjustments are often required to account for specific characteristics of the instrument being measured or the market in which the instrument would trade (e.g. liquidity considerations). While this information may not be determinative for the particular instrument being measured, it can serve to either support or contest an entity's determination regarding the relevance of observable data in markets that are not active.

IFRS 13 does not prescribe a methodology for applying adjustments to observable transactions or quoted prices when estimating fair value. Judgement is needed when evaluating the relevance of observable market data and determining what (if any) adjustments should be made to this information. However, the application of this judgement must be within the confines of the stated objective of a fair value measurement within the IFRS 13 framework. Since fair value is intended to represent the exit price in a transaction between market participants in the current market, an entity's intent to hold the asset due to current market conditions, or any entity-specific needs, is not relevant to a fair value measurement and is not a valid reason to adjust observable market data.

19 LEVEL 3 INPUTS

All unobservable inputs for an asset or liability are Level 3 inputs. The standard requires an entity to minimise the use of Level 3 inputs when measuring fair value. As such, they should only be used to the extent that relevant observable inputs are not available, for example, in situations where there is limited market activity for an asset or liability. *[IFRS 13.86, 87]*.

19.1 Use of Level 3 inputs

A number of IFRSs permit or require the use of fair value measurements regardless of the level of market activity for the asset or liability as at the measurement date (e.g. the initial measurement of intangible assets acquired in a business combination). As such, IFRS 13 allows for the use of unobservable inputs to measure fair value in situations where observable inputs are not available. In these cases, the IASB recognises that the best information available with which to develop unobservable inputs may be an entity's own data. However, IFRS 13 is clear that while an entity may begin with its own data, this data should be adjusted if:

- reasonably available information indicates that other market participants would use different data; or
- there is something particular to the entity that is not available to other market participants (e.g. an entity-specific synergy). *[IFRS 13.89]*.

For example, when measuring the fair value of an investment property, we would expect that a reporting entity with a unique tax position would consider the typical market participant tax rate in its analysis. While this example is simplistic and is meant only to illustrate a concept, in practice significant judgement will be required when evaluating what information about unobservable inputs or market data may be reasonably available.

It is important to note that an entity is not required to undertake exhaustive efforts to obtain information about market participant assumptions when pricing an asset or liability. Nor is an entity required to establish the absence of contrary data. As a result, in those situations where information about market participant assumptions does not exist or is not reasonably available, a fair value measurement may be based primarily on the reporting entity's own data. *[IFRS 13.89]*.

Even in situations where an entity's own data is used, the objective of the fair value measurement remains the same – i.e. an exit price from the perspective of a market participant that holds the asset or owes the liability. As such, unobservable inputs should reflect the assumptions that market participants would use, which includes the risk inherent in a particular valuation technique (such as a pricing model) and the risk inherent in the inputs. As discussed at 7.2 above, if a market participant would consider those risks in pricing an asset or liability, an entity must include that risk adjustment; otherwise the result would not be a fair value measurement. When categorising the entire fair value measurement within the fair value hierarchy, an entity would need to consider the significance of the model adjustment as well as the observability of the data supporting the adjustment. *[IFRS 13.87, 88]*.

19.2 Examples of Level 3 inputs

IFRS 13's application guidance provides a number of examples of Level 3 inputs for specific assets or liabilities, as outlined in Figure 14.10 below. *[IFRS 13.B36]*.

Figure 14.10: Examples of Level 3 inputs

Asset or Liability	Example of a Level 3 Input
Long-dated currency swap	An interest rate in a specified currency that is not observable and cannot be corroborated by observable market data at commonly quoted intervals or otherwise for substantially the full term of the currency swap. The interest rates in a currency swap are the swap rates calculated from the respective countries' yield curves.
Three-year option on exchange-traded shares	Historical volatility, i.e. the volatility for the shares derived from the shares' historical prices. Historical volatility typically does not represent current market participants' expectations about future volatility, even if it is the only information available to price an option.
Interest rate swap	An adjustment to a mid-market consensus (non-binding) price for the swap developed using data that are not directly observable and cannot otherwise be corroborated by observable market data.
Decommissioning liability assumed in a business combination	A current estimate using the entity's own data about the future cash outflows to be paid to fulfil the obligation (including market participants' expectations about the costs of fulfilling the obligation and the compensation that a market participant would require for taking on the obligation to dismantle the asset) if there is no reasonably available information that indicates that market participants would use different assumptions. That Level 3 input would be used in a present value technique together with other inputs, e.g. a current risk-free interest rate or a credit-adjusted risk-free rate if the effect of the entity's credit standing on the fair value of the liability is reflected in the discount rate rather than in the estimate of future cash outflows.
Cash-generating unit	A financial forecast (e.g. of cash flows or profit or loss) developed using the entity's own data if there is no reasonably available information that indicates that market participants would use different assumptions.

20 DISCLOSURES

The disclosure requirements in IFRS 13 apply to fair value measurements recognised in the statement of financial position, after initial recognition, and disclosures of fair value (i.e. those items that are not measured at fair value in the statement of financial position, but whose fair value is required to be disclosed). However, as discussed at 2.2.4 above, IFRS 13 provides a scope exception in relation to disclosures for:

- plan assets measured at fair value in accordance with IAS 19;
- retirement benefit plan investments measured at fair value in accordance with IAS 26; and
- assets for which recoverable amount is fair value less costs of disposal in accordance with IAS 36.

In addition to these scope exceptions, the IASB decided not to require the IFRS 13 disclosures for items that are recognised at fair value only at initial recognition. Disclosure requirements in relation to fair value measurements at initial recognition are covered by the standard that is applicable to that asset or liability. For example, IFRS 3 requires disclosure of the fair value measurement of assets acquired and liabilities assumed in a business combination. *[IFRS 13.BC184].*

However, it should be noted that, unlike IAS 19, IAS 26 and IAS 36, there is no scope exemption for IFRS 3 or other standards that require fair value measurements (or measures based on fair value) at initial recognition. Therefore, if those standards require fair value measurements (or measures based on fair value) after initial recognition, IFRS 13's disclosure requirements would apply.

20.1 Disclosure objectives

IFRS 13 requires a number of disclosures designed to provide users of financial statements with additional transparency regarding:

- the extent to which fair value is used to measure assets and liabilities;
- the valuation techniques, inputs and assumptions used in measuring fair value; and
- the effect of Level 3 fair value measurements on profit or loss (or other comprehensive income).

The standard establishes a set of broad disclosure objectives and provides the minimum disclosures an entity must make (see 20.2 to 20.5 below for discussion regarding the minimum disclosure requirements in IFRS 13).

The objectives of IFRS 13's disclosure requirements are to:

(a) enable users of financial statements to understand the valuation techniques and inputs used to develop fair value measurements; and

(b) help users to understand the effect of fair value measurements on profit or loss and other comprehensive income for the period when fair value is based on unobservable inputs (Level 3 inputs). *[IFRS 13.91].*

After providing the minimum disclosures required by IFRS 13 and other standards, such as IAS 1 – *Presentation of Financial Statements* – or IAS 34 – *Interim Financial Reporting*, an entity must assess whether its disclosures are sufficient to meet the disclosure objectives in IFRS 13. If not, additional information must be disclosed in order to meet those objectives. *[IFRS 13.92]*. This assessment requires judgement and will depend on the specific facts and circumstances of the entity and the needs of the users of its financial statements.

An entity must consider all the following:

- the level of detail needed to satisfy the disclosure requirements;
- how much emphasis to place on each of the various requirements;
- the level of aggregation or disaggregation (see 20.1.2 below); and
- whether users of financial statements need additional information to evaluate the quantitative information disclosed. *[IFRS 13.92]*.

An entity might, for example, disclose the nature of the item being measured at fair value, including the characteristics of the item being measured that are taken into account in the determination of relevant inputs. In addition, when describing the valuation techniques and inputs used for fair value measurements categorised within Levels 2 and 3, the entity might disclose how third-party information (such as broker quotes, pricing services, net asset values and relevant market data) was taken into account when measuring fair value. For example, for residential mortgage-backed securities, an entity might disclose the following:

(i) the types of underlying loans (e.g. prime loans or sub-prime loans);
(ii) collateral;
(iii) guarantees or other credit enhancements;
(iv) seniority level of the tranches of securities;
(v) the year of issue;
(vi) the weighted-average coupon rate of the underlying loans and the securities;
(vii) the weighted-average maturity of the underlying loans and the securities;
(viii) the geographical concentration of the underlying loans; and
(ix) information about the credit ratings of the securities. *[IFRS 13.IE64(a)]*.

IFRS 13 includes the above example to illustrate the type of additional information an entity might disclose based on the considerations outlined in paragraph 92 of IFRS 13. These additional disclosures are intended to help financial statement users better understand and evaluate the quantitative information provided by the entity (e.g. the quantitative information the entity disclosed regarding the valuation of its residential mortgage-backed securities holdings).

20.1.1 Format of disclosures

IFRS 13's requirements, with regard to the format of disclosures, are limited to the presentation of quantitative information. An entity is required to use a tabular format to present the quantitative disclosures required by IFRS 13, unless another format is more appropriate. *[IFRS 13.99]*.

20.1.2 Level of disaggregation

IFRS 13 requires disclosures to be presented by class of asset or liability (the definition of a class of asset or liability is discussed at 20.1.2.A below). Unlike certain other IFRSs, IFRS 13 does not specify the level of aggregation or disaggregation an entity must use when complying with its disclosure requirements. Instead, as discussed below, it simply provides the basis for making this determination. As such, the appropriate class of assets and liabilities may depend on the entity's specific facts and circumstances and the needs of users of its financial statements.

According to the standard, a class of assets and liabilities will often require greater disaggregation than the line items presented in the statement of financial position. Therefore, an entity must present information in sufficient detail to permit reconciliation back to the statement of financial position. *[IFRS 13.99].* Such a reconciliation could be presented through the use of subtotals that correspond to line items disclosed in the statement of financial position; however, other approaches may be acceptable.

20.1.2.A Determining appropriate classes of assets and liabilities for disclosure

Determining appropriate classes of assets and liabilities requires judgement. An entity bases this determination on the nature, characteristics and risks of the asset or liability and the level of the fair value hierarchy within which the fair value measurement is categorised (see 16.2 above for further discussion). *[IFRS 13.94].* In addition, the standard specifies that the number of classes may need to be greater for fair value measurements categorised within Level 3 of the fair value hierarchy because they have a greater degree of uncertainty and subjectivity.

Other IFRSs may specify classes for asset or liability. For example, IAS 16 and IAS 38 – *Intangible Assets* – require disclosures by class of property, plant and equipment or intangible respectively. If another IFRS specifies the class for an asset or a liability and that class meets the requirements for determining a class in accordance with IFRS 13, an entity may use that class in providing IFRS 13's required disclosures. *[IFRS 13.99].*

The determination of a class includes considering the fair value measurement's categorisation within the fair value hierarchy as noted above with respect to Level 3 measurements. IFRS 13 requires disclosure of this categorisation for each class of asset or liability (see 20.3 to 20.4 below). While an entity takes the fair value categorisation into consideration when determining a class, this does not mean assets or liabilities within a single class cannot be categorised within different levels of the hierarchy. For example, assume an entity has grouped all its buildings within one class in accordance with IAS 16 and measures all those buildings using the revaluation approach in that standard. Further assume that the fair value measurements of some buildings are categorised within Level 2, while others are categorised within Level 3, based on the availability of observable inputs used in the fair value measurement. In and of itself, the assets' categorisation within two levels of the hierarchy does not necessarily mean the entity would need to further disaggregate the IAS 16 class of buildings into two classes for disclosure in accordance with IFRS 13. However, it may be appropriate to do that if the differing categorisation indicated the buildings categorised within Level 2 were different in their nature, characteristics or risks compared to those categorised within Level 3.

20.1.3 Differentiating between 'recurring' and 'non-recurring'

IFRS 13 has different disclosure requirements for those fair value measurements that are recognised (rather than just disclosed), depending on whether those measurements are recurring or non-recurring in nature (see 20.3 below). Therefore, it is important to understand the distinction.

- *Recurring* fair value measurements are those that another IFRS requires or permits to be recognised in the statement of financial position at the end of each reporting period. For example, the fair value of a financial asset classified as fair value through profit or loss in accordance with IFRS 9 (or IAS 39) would need to be measured at the end each reporting period. Other examples include a liability to distribute non-cash assets to shareholders, measured at fair value in accordance with IFRIC 17 – *Distributions of Non-cash Assets to Owners*.

  In our view, revaluations of property, plant and equipment in accordance with IAS 16 represent a recurring fair value measurement. The revaluation model in IAS 16 requires that revaluations be made 'with sufficient regularity to ensure that the carrying amount does not differ materially from that which would be determined using fair value at the end of the reporting period'. *[IAS 16.31]*. Furthermore, 'the frequency of revaluations depends upon the changes in fair values of the items of property, plant and equipment being revalued. When the fair value of a revalued asset differs materially from its carrying amount, a further revaluation is required'. *[IAS 16.34]*. Therefore, while an entity might not revalue an asset each year, the objective is to ensure the carrying amount approximates fair value, subject to materiality.

- *Non-recurring* fair value measurements are those that another IFRS requires or permits to be recognised in the statement of financial position in particular circumstances. For example, IFRS 5 requires an entity to measure an asset held for sale at the lower of its carrying amount and fair value less costs to sell. Since the asset's fair value less costs to sell is only recognised in the statement of financial position when it is lower than its carrying amount, that fair value measurement is non-recurring. However, it should be noted that in a disposal group, not all assets and liabilities are subject to the measurement requirements of IFRS 5. If financial assets categorised as fair value through other comprehensive income in accordance of IFRS 9 (or as available for sale in accordance with IAS 39) were included in a disposal group, an entity would continue to measure these assets in accordance with IFRS 9 (or IAS 39) at fair value. These fair value measurements would continue to be recurring. *[IFRS 13.93]*.

20.2 Accounting policy disclosures

In general, the requirements to disclose an entity's accounting policies will be addressed by the standard that requires or permits an item to be measured at fair value. In addition, the disclosure requirements of IAS 8 would address any changes to an entity's accounting policies (see Chapter 3). In addition to these, IFRS 13 requires the disclosure of two policies. *[IFRS 13.95, 96]*.

Firstly, if an entity makes an accounting policy decision to use the exception in relation to the measurement of fair value for financial assets and financial liabilities with offsetting positions, it must disclose that fact (see 12 above for further discussion regarding the measurement exception and criteria for selecting this accounting policy choice). *[IFRS 13.96].*

Secondly, an entity must disclose its policy for determining when transfers between levels of the fair value hierarchy are deemed to have occurred (see 16.2.2 above for further discussion regarding this policy choice). *[IFRS 13.95].*

As discussed at 14.1.4 above, changes to fair value resulting from a change in the valuation technique or its application are accounted for as a change in accounting estimate in accordance with IAS 8 (unless the valuation technique is applied in error, which would be accounted for as a correction of an error in accordance with IAS 8). However, information would be disclosed in accordance with IFRS 13, not IAS 8; specifically, that there has been a change in valuation technique and the reasons for the change (see 20.3.5 below for further discussion).

Extract 14.1: ING Groep N.V. (2014)

Notes to the consolidated annual accounts [Extract]

1 Accounting policies [Extract]

Critical accounting policies [Extract]

Fair values of real estate

Real estate investments are reported at fair value. The fair value of real estate investments is based on regular appraisals by independent qualified valuers. The fair values are established using valuation methods such as: comparable market transactions, capitalisation of income methods or discounted cash flow calculations. The underlying assumption used in the valuation is that the properties are let or sold to third parties based on the actual letting status. The discounted cash flow analyses and capitalisation of income method are based on calculations of the future rental income in accordance with the terms in existing leases and estimations of the rental values for new leases when leases expire and incentives like rental free periods. The cash flows are discounted using market based interest rates that reflect appropriately the risk characteristics of real estate.

Market conditions in recent years have led to a reduced level of real estate transactions. Transaction values were significantly impacted by low volumes of actual transactions. As a result comparable market transactions have been used less in valuing ING's real estate investments by independent qualified valuers. More emphasis has been placed on discounted cash flow analysis and capitalisation of income method.

Reference is made to Note 43 'Fair value of assets and liabilities' for more disclosure on fair values of real estate investments.

The valuation of real estate involves various assumptions and techniques. The use of different assumptions and techniques could produce significantly different valuations. Consequently, the fair values presented may not be indicative of the net realisable value. In addition, the calculation of the estimated fair value is based on market conditions at a specific point in time and may not be indicative of future fair values. To illustrate the uncertainty of our real estate investments valuation, a sensitivity analysis on the changes in fair value of real estate is provided in the 'Risk management' section.

Fair values of financial assets and liabilities

Fair values of financial assets and liabilities are based on unadjusted quoted market prices where available. Such quoted market prices are primarily obtained from exchange prices for listed instruments. Where an exchange price is not available, market prices may be obtained from independent market vendors, brokers or market makers. In general, positions are valued taking the bid price for a long position and the offer price for a short position or are valued at the price within the bid-offer spread that is most representative of fair value in the circumstances. In some cases where positions are marked at mid-market prices, a fair value adjustment is calculated.

When markets are less liquid there may be a range of prices for the same security from different price sources, selecting the most appropriate price requires judgement and could result in different estimates of fair value.

For certain financial assets and liabilities quoted market prices are not available. For these financial assets and liabilities, fair value is determined using valuation techniques. These valuation techniques range from discounting of cash flows to valuation models, where relevant pricing factors including the market price of underlying reference instruments, market parameters (volatilities, correlations and credit ratings) and customer behaviour are taken into account. All valuation techniques used are subject to internal review and approval. Most data used in these valuation techniques are validated on a daily basis.

To include credit risk in the fair valuation, ING applies both credit and debit valuation adjustments (CVA, DVA). Own issued debt and structured notes that are valued at fair value are adjusted for credit risk by means of a DVA. Additionally, derivatives valued at fair value are adjusted for credit risk by a CVA. The CVA is of a bilateral nature as both the credit risk on the counterparty as well as the credit risk on ING are included in the adjustment. All market data that is used in the determination of the CVA is based on market implied data. Additionally, wrong-way risk (when exposure to a counterparty is increasing and the credit quality of that counterparty decreases) and right-way risk (when exposure to a counterparty is decreasing and the credit quality of that counterparty increases) are included in the adjustment. ING also applies CVA for pricing credit risk into new external trades with counterparties. To address the risk associated with the illiquid nature of the derivative portfolio, ING applies an additional 'liquidity valuation adjustment'. The adjustment is based on the market price of funding liquidity and is applied to the uncollateralised derivatives. This additional discounting is taken into account in both the credit and debit valuation adjustments.

Valuation techniques are subjective in nature and significant judgement is involved in establishing fair values for certain financial assets and liabilities. Valuation techniques involve various assumptions regarding pricing factors. The use of different valuation techniques and assumptions could produce significantly different estimates of fair value.

Price testing is performed to assess whether the process of valuation has led to an appropriate fair value of the position and to an appropriate reflection of these valuations in the profit and loss account. Price testing is performed to minimise the potential risks for economic losses due to incorrect or misused models.

Reference is made to Note 43 'Fair value of assets and liabilities' and the 'Risk management' section for the basis of the determination of the fair value of financial instruments and related sensitivities.

20.3 Disclosures for recognised fair value measurements

Paragraph 93 of IFRS 13 establishes the minimum disclosure requirements for fair value measurements (and those based on fair value) that are recognised in the statement of financial position after initial recognition. The requirements vary depending on whether the fair value measurements are recurring or non-recurring and their categorisation within the fair value hierarchy (i.e. Level 1, 2, or 3 – see 16 above for further discussion regarding the fair value hierarchy).

Irrespective of the frequency with which the fair value is measured, the disclosures under IFRS 13 are intended to provide financial statement users with additional insight into the relative subjectivity of various fair value measurements and enhance their ability to broadly assess an entity's quality of earnings.

In order to meet the disclosure objectives, the following information, at a minimum, must be disclosed for all fair value measurements. Disclosures are required for each class of asset and liability, whether recurring or non-recurring, that are recognised in the statement of financial position after initial recognition: *[IFRS 13.93]*

(a) The fair value measurement at the end of the reporting period (see Example 14.25 at 20.3.3 below).

(b) For non-financial assets, if the highest and best use differs from its current use, an entity must disclose that fact and why the non-financial asset is being used in a manner that differs from its highest and best use.

(c) The fair value measurement's categorisation within the fair value hierarchy (Level 1, 2 or 3 – see Example 14.25 at 20.3.3 below).

(d) If categorised within Level 2 or Level 3 of the fair value hierarchy:
   (i) a description of the valuation technique(s) used in the fair value measurement;
   (ii) the inputs used in the fair value measurement;
   (iii) if there has been a change in valuation technique (e.g. changing from a market approach to an income approach or the use of an additional valuation technique):
      - the change; and
      - the reason(s) for making it.

(e) Quantitative information about the significant unobservable inputs used in the fair value measurement for those categorised within Level 3 of the fair value hierarchy. Example 14.27 at 20.3.5.A below illustrates how this information might be disclosed.

(f) If categorised within Level 3 of the fair value hierarchy, a description of the valuation processes used by the entity (including, for example, how an entity decides its valuation policies and procedures and analyses changes in fair value measurements from period to period).

   This requirement focuses on valuation processes rather than the specific valuation techniques, which are covered by the requirements in (d) above.

In addition to these requirements, an entity must provide the disclosures discussed at 20.3.1 and 20.3.2 below depending on whether the measurement is recurring or non-recurring.

20.3.1 Disclosures for recognised recurring fair value measurements

The disclosure requirements in paragraph 93 of IFRS 13 (see 20.3 above and 20.3.1.A and 20.3.1.B below) apply to all fair value measurements that are recognised in the financial statements on a recurring basis. Given the increased subjectivity, IFRS 13 requires additional disclosures for fair value measurements categorised within Level 3 of the fair value hierarchy than for those categorised within Levels 1 or 2 (see 20.3.1.B below).

20.3.1.A Recurring fair value measurements categorised as Level 1 or Level 2

For recurring fair value measurements that are categorised within either Level 1 or Level 2 of the fair value hierarchy, an entity must disclose both:

- information required to comply with the disclosure requirements discussed at 20.3 above; and

- for any transfers between Level 1 and Level 2 of the fair value hierarchy:
  - (i) the amounts of any transfers between Level 1 and Level 2 of the fair value hierarchy;
  - (ii) the reasons for those transfers; and
  - (iii) the entity's policy for determining when transfers between levels are deemed to have occurred (see 16.2.2 and 20.2 above for further discussion).

  The standard requires transfers into each level to be disclosed and discussed separately from transfers out of each level. *[IFRS 13.93]*.

20.3.1.B Recurring fair value measurements categorised as Level 3

In addition to the disclosure requirements listed at 20.3 above, recurring fair value measurements that are categorised within Level 3 of the fair value hierarchy are subject to additional disclosure requirements:

(a) a reconciliation from the opening balances to the closing balances, disclosing separately changes during the period (also referred to as the Level 3 roll-forward);

(b) a narrative description of the sensitivity of Level 3 fair value measurements to changes in unobservable inputs; and

(c) for financial assets and financial liabilities only, quantitative sensitivity analysis for Level 3 fair value measurements. *[IFRS 13.93]*.

These additional disclosure requirements for Level 3 fair value measurements are discussed further at 20.3.5 to 20.3.8 below.

20.3.2 Disclosures for recognised non-recurring fair value measurements

Certain disclosure requirements in IFRS 13 do not apply to fair value measurements that are non-recurring in nature (e.g. a non-current asset (or disposal group) held for sale measured at fair value less costs to sell in accordance with IFRS 5 where the fair value less costs to sell is lower than its carrying amount). Specifically, the following disclosures are *not* required for non-recurring recognised fair value measurements:

- information about any transfers between Level 1 and Level 2 of the fair value hierarchy;
- a reconciliation of the opening balances to the closing balances for Level 3 measurements (also referred to as the Level 3 roll-forward);
- a narrative description of the sensitivity of Level 3 fair value measurements to changes in unobservable inputs; and
- for financial assets and financial liabilities, quantitative sensitivity analysis for Level 3 fair value measurements. *[IFRS 13.93]*.

Information regarding transfers between hierarchy levels and the Level 3 reconciliation do not lend themselves to non-recurring measurements and, therefore, are not required. While discussing the sensitivity of Level 3 measurements to changes in unobservable inputs might provide financial statement users with some information about how the selection of these inputs affects non-recurring valuations, the Boards ultimately decided that this information is most relevant for recurring measurements.

However, entities are required to disclose the reason for any non-recurring fair value measurements made subsequent to the initial recognition of an asset or liability. *[IFRS 13.93]*.

For example, the entity may intend to sell or otherwise dispose of it, thereby resulting in the need for its measurement at fair value less costs to sell based on the requirements of IFRS 5, if lower than the asset's carrying amount.

While obvious for recurring measurements, determining the periods in which the fair value disclosures should be made for non-recurring measurements is less clear. For example, assume a listed entity classifies a building as held for sale in accordance with IFRS 5 at the end of its second quarter and appropriately decreases the carrying value of the asset to its then fair value less costs to sell. In its interim financial statements, the entity would make all of the disclosures required by IFRS 13 for non-recurring fair value measurements. During the second half of the financial year, the sale falls through and the asset is no longer held for sale. In accordance with IFRS 5, the asset is measured at its carrying amount before the asset (or disposal group) was classified as held for sale, adjusted for any depreciation, as this is lower than it's recoverable amount. The entity continues to account for the asset in accordance with IAS 16. While the carrying value of the asset at the end of the financial year is no longer *at* fair value less costs to sell, the asset was adjusted to fair value less costs to sell during the year. Therefore, in its annual financial statements, the entity would again disclose the information required by IFRS 13 for non-recurring fair value measurements. While not explicit in IFRS 13, we believe this approach is consistent with the interim and annual disclosure requirements for assets subsequently measured under the revaluation model in IAS 34 and IFRS 5.

In these situations, we recommend that the disclosures clearly indicate that the fair value information presented is not current, but rather as at the date fair value was measured. Entities should also indicate if the carrying amount of the asset no longer equals its fair value.

20.3.3 Fair value hierarchy categorisation

IFRS 13 requires entities to disclose the fair value hierarchy level in which each fair value measurement is categorised. As noted at 16.2 above, the categorisation of a fair value measurement of an asset or liability in the fair value hierarchy is based on the lowest level input that is significant to the fair value measurement in its entirety. Although the hierarchy disclosure is presented by class of asset or liability, it is important to understand that the determination of the hierarchy level in which a fair value measurement falls (and therefore the category in which it will be disclosed) is based on the fair value measurement for the specific item being measured and is, therefore, driven by the unit of account for the asset or liability.

For example, in situations where the unit of account for a financial instrument is the individual item, but the measurement exception for financial instruments is used (as discussed at 12 above), entities may need to allocate portfolio-level adjustments to the various instruments that make up the net exposure for purposes of hierarchy categorisation.

This may seem inconsistent to certain constituents given the discussion at 12 above about the consideration of size as a characteristic of the net risk exposure when the measurement exception for financial instruments is used. However, the IASB and FASB staffs have indicated that the determination of the net risk exposure as the unit of measurement applies only for measurement considerations and was not intended to change current practice with respect to disclosures. As such, the entire net exposure would not be categorised within a single level of the fair value hierarchy (e.g. Level 2), unless all of the individual items that make up the net exposure would fall within that level.

To illustrate, consider an individual derivative that is valued using the measurement exception as part of a group of derivative instruments with offsetting credit risk (due to the existence of a legally enforceable netting agreement). Assuming the portfolio included instruments that on their own must be categorised within different levels of the fair value hierarchy (i.e. Level 2 and Level 3), for disclosure purposes, the portfolio-level adjustment for credit risk (considering the effect of master netting agreements) may need to be attributed to the individual derivative transactions within the portfolio or to the group of transactions that fall within each of the levels of the hierarchy. This example assumes that the portfolio-level adjustment for credit risk is based on observable market data. If the portfolio-level adjustment was determined using unobservable inputs, the significance of the adjustment to the measurement of the individual derivative instruments would need to be considered in order to determine if categorisation in Level 2 or Level 3 was appropriate.

The following example from IFRS 13 illustrates how an entity might disclose, in tabular format, the fair value hierarchy category for each class of assets and liabilities measured at fair value at the end of each reporting period. *[IFRS 13.IE60].*

Example 14.25: Disclosure of assets measured at fair value and their categorisation in the fair value hierarchy

(CU in millions)	Fair value measurements at the end of the reporting period using:				
Description	31/12/X9	Quoted prices in active markets for identical assets (Level 1)	Significant other observable inputs (Level 2)	Significant unobservable inputs (Level 3)	Total gains (losses)
Recurring fair value measurements					
Trading equity securities(a):					
Real estate industry	93	70	23		
Oil and gas industry	45	45			
Other	15	15			
Total trading equity securities	153	130	23		
Other equity securities(a):					
Financial services industry	150	150			
Healthcare industry	163	110		53	
Energy industry	32			32	
Private equity fund investments(b)	25			25	
Other	15	15			
Total other equity securities	385	275		110	

Debt securities:					
Residential mortgage-backed securities	149		24	125	
Commercial mortgage-backed securities	50			50	
Collateralised debt obligations	35			35	
Risk-free government securities	85	85			
Corporate bonds	93	9	84		
Total debt securities	412	94	108	210	
Hedge fund investments:					
Equity long/short	55		55		
Global opportunities	35		35		
High-yield debt securities	90			90	
Total hedge fund investments	180		90	90	
Derivatives:					
Interest rate contracts	57		57		
Foreign exchange contracts	43		43		
Credit contracts	38			38	
Commodity futures contracts	78	78			
Commodity forward contracts	20		20		
Total derivatives	236	78	120	38	
Investment properties:					
Commercial – Asia	31			31	
Commercial – Europe	27			27	
Total investment properties	58			58	
Total recurring fair value measurements	1,424	577	341	506	
Non-recurring fair value measurements					
Assets held for sale[c]	26		26		(15)
Total non-recurring fair value measurements	26		26		(15)

(a) On the basis of its analysis of the nature, characteristics and risks of the securities, the entity has determined that presenting them by industry is appropriate.

(b) On the basis of its analysis of the nature, characteristics and risks of the investments, the entity has determined that presenting them as a single class is appropriate.

(c) In accordance with IFRS 5, assets held for sale with a carrying amount of CU 35 million were written down to their fair value of CU 26 million, less costs to sell of CU 6 million (or CU 20 million), resulting in a loss of CU 15 million, which was included in profit or loss for the period.

(Note: A similar table would be presented for liabilities unless another format is deemed more appropriate by the entity.)

In the above example, the gain or loss recognised during the period for assets and liabilities measured at fair value on a non-recurring basis is separately disclosed and discussed in the notes to the financial statements.

20.3.4 Transfers between hierarchy levels for recurring fair value measurements

IFRS 13 requires entities to disclose information regarding all transfers between fair value hierarchy levels (i.e. situations where an asset or liability was categorised within a different level in the fair value hierarchy in the previous reporting period). *[IFRS 13.93(c), 93(e)(iv)]*. However, this disclosure requirement only applies to assets and liabilities held at the end of the reporting period which are measured at fair value on a recurring basis. Information regarding transfers into or out of Level 3 is captured in the Level 3 reconciliation (discussed at 20.3.6 below) as these amounts are needed to roll forward Level 3 balances from the beginning to the end of the period being disclosed. The amounts of any transfers between Level 1 and Level 2 of the fair value hierarchy are also required to be disclosed. Regardless of the hierarchy levels involved, transfers into each level of the hierarchy are disclosed separately from transfers out of each level. That is, all transfers are required to be presented on a gross basis by hierarchy level, whether included in the Level 3 reconciliation or disclosed separately.

For all transfer amounts disclosed, an entity is required to discuss the reasons why the categorisation within the fair value hierarchy has changed (i.e. transferred between hierarchy levels). *[IFRS 13.93(c), 93(e)(iv)]*. Reasons might include the market for a particular asset or liability previously considered active (Level 1) becoming inactive (Level 2 or Level 3), or significant inputs used in a valuation technique that were previously unobservable (Level 3) becoming observable (Level 2) given transactions that were observed around the measurement date.

As discussed at 16.2.2 and 20.2 above, IFRS 13 also requires that entities disclose and consistently follow their policy for determining when transfers between fair value hierarchy levels are deemed to have occurred. That is, an entity's policy about the timing of recognising transfers into the hierarchy levels should be the same as the policy for recognising transfers out, and this policy should be used consistently from period to period. Paragraph 95 of IFRS 13 includes the following examples of potential policies: the actual date of the event or change in circumstances that caused the transfer, the beginning of the reporting period or the end of the reporting period. In practice, some variation of these approaches may also be used by entities. For example, some entities may use an intra-period approach using a transfer amount based on the fair value as at the month-end in which the transfer occurred, as opposed to the actual date within the month. *[IFRS 13.95]*. The following illustrative example demonstrates the differences between the three methods noted above.

Example 14.26: Comparison of policies for recognising transfers

Assume an entity acquires an asset at 31 December 20X7 for CU 1,000 that was categorised within Level 2 of the fair value hierarchy at year end 20X7 and throughout Q1 20X8. At the end of Q1 20X8, the fair value of the asset based on market observable information was CU 950, and, as such, the asset was excluded from the Level 3 reconciliation. During Q2 20X8, observable market information was no longer available, so the entity categorised the asset in Level 3 at the end of Q2 20X8. During Q2 20X8, the fair value of the asset decreased from CU 950 to CU 750, with CU 50 of the change in fair value arising subsequent to the time when market observable information was no longer available.

Under the three approaches described above, the Level 3 reconciliation for Q2 20X8 would be as follows.

	Transferred to Level 3 at:		
	Beginning of the period	Actual date	End of the period
Beginning fair value	–	–	–
Purchases, issuances and settlements	–	–	–
Transfers in	CU 950	CU 800	CU 750
Total losses	CU (200)	CU (50)	–
Ending fair value	CU 750	CU 750	CU 750

As previously noted, the disclosures under IFRS 13 are intended to provide information that enables users to identify the effects of fair value measurements that are more subjective in nature on reported earnings, and, thereby, enhance financial statement users' ability to make their own assessment regarding earnings quality. We believe that this objective is best met by considering the level of observability associated with the fair value measurement made at the end of the reporting period (i.e. the observability of the inputs used to determine fair value on the last day in the period). As such, while no specific approach is required under IFRS, we believe a beginning-of-period approach for recognising transfers provides greater transparency on the effect that unobservable inputs have on fair value measurements and reported earnings. Under this view, all changes in fair value that arise during the reporting period of the transfer are disclosed as a component of the Level 3 reconciliation.

While the 'actual date' approach more precisely captures the date on which a change in the observability of inputs occurred, its application can be more operationally complex. In addition, in our view, it does not necessarily provide more decision-useful information than the beginning-of-period approach. This is because, for a given period, the intra-period approach results in an allocation of the fair value changes between hierarchy levels that is inconsistent with the actual categorisation of the item as at the end of the reporting period. As such, the intra-period approach implies that a portion of the earnings recognised during the period is of a higher (or lower) quality solely because there was observable information regarding the value of the instrument at some point during the period.

To further illustrate this point, assume an entity acquires an investment in a private company in Q1 for CU 1,000. In the middle of Q2, the company completes an initial public offering that values the investment at CU 1,500. At the end of Q2, the fair value of the investment is CU 2,200 based on a quoted market price. Under the intra-period approach for the six-month period ended Q2, CU 500 would be included as an unrealised gain in the Level 3 reconciliation, despite the fact that the entire CU 1,200 unrealised gain recognised during the six-month period is supported by observable market information (i.e. a quoted price less cash paid).

Of the three alternatives, we believe the end-of-period approach is the least effective in achieving IFRS 13's disclosure objectives. Under this approach, the Level 3 reconciliation would not reflect any unrealised gains or losses for items that move from Level 2 to Level 3 during the reporting period.

20.3.5 *Disclosure of valuation techniques and inputs*

Entities are required to describe the valuation techniques and inputs used to measure the fair value of items categorised within Level 2 or Level 3 of the fair value hierarchy. In addition, entities are required to disclose instances where there has been a change in the valuation technique(s) used during the period, and the reason for making the change. As discussed at 20.3.5.A below, the standard also requires quantitative information about the significant unobservable inputs to be disclosed for Level 3 fair value measurements. *[IFRS 13.93(d)]*.

Importantly, the disclosures related to valuation techniques and inputs (including the requirement to disclose quantitative information about unobservable inputs) apply to both recurring and non-recurring fair value measurements. *[IFRS 13.93(d)]*.

20.3.5.A *Significant unobservable inputs for Level 3 fair value measurements*

For Level 3 measurements, IFRS 13 specifically requires that entities provide quantitative information about the significant unobservable inputs used in the fair value measurement. *[IFRS 13.93(d)]*. For example, an entity with asset-backed securities categorised within Level 3 would be required to quantitatively disclose the inputs used in its valuation models related to prepayment speed, probability of default, loss given default and discount rate (assuming these inputs were all unobservable and deemed to be significant to the valuation).

Consistent with all of the disclosures in IFRS 13, entities are required to present this information separately for each class of assets or liabilities based on the nature, characteristics and risks of their Level 3 measurements. *[IFRS 13.93]*. As such, we expect that entities will likely disclose both the range and weighted average of the unobservable inputs used across a particular class of Level 3 assets or liabilities. In addition, entities should assess whether the level of disaggregation at which this information is provided results in meaningful information to users, consistent with the objectives of IFRS 13.

In some situations significant unobservable inputs may not be developed by the reporting entity itself, such as when an entity uses third-party pricing information without adjustment. In these instances, IFRS 13 states that an entity is not required to create quantitative information to comply with its disclosure requirements. However, when making these disclosures, entities cannot ignore information about significant unobservable inputs that is 'reasonably available'.

Determining whether information is 'reasonably available' will require judgement, and there may be some diversity in practice stemming from differences in entities' access to information and information vendors may be willing or able to provide. If the valuation has been developed, either by the entity or an external valuation expert at the direction of the entity, quantitative information about the significant unobservable inputs would be expected to be reasonably available and therefore should be disclosed. As a result, entities need to ensure any valuers they use provide them with sufficient information to make the required disclosures.

In contrast, when an entity receives price quotes or other valuation information from a third-party pricing service or broker, the specific unobservable inputs underlying this information may not always be reasonably available to the entity. While determining whether information is reasonably available in these instances will require judgement, we would expect entities to make good-faith efforts to obtain the information needed to meet the disclosure requirements in IFRS 13. In addition, some diversity in practice may stem from differences in entities' access to information and the nature of information that various vendors may be willing or able to provide. However, in all cases, any adjustments made by an entity to the pricing data received from a third party should be disclosed if these adjustments are not based on observable market data and are deemed to be significant to the overall measurement.

The following example from IFRS 13 illustrates the type of information an entity might provide to comply with the requirement to disclose quantitative information about Level 3 fair value measurements. *[IFRS 13.IE63]*. Extract 14.3 from BP p.l.c. and Extract 14.4 from Rio Tinto plc at 20.3.8.A below also illustrates this disclosure in relation to derivatives categorised within Level 3.

Example 14.27: Significant unobservable inputs (Level 3)

Quantitative information about fair value measurements using significant unobservable inputs (Level 3)				
(CU in millions) Description	Fair value at 31/12/X9	Valuation technique(s)	Unobservable input	Range (weighted average)
Other equity securities:				
Healthcare industry	53	Discounted cash flow	weighted average cost of capital	7%-16% (12.1%)
			long-term revenue growth rate	2%-5% (4.2%)
			long-term pre-tax operating margin	3%-20% (10.3%)
			discount for lack of marketability[(a)]	5%-20% (17%)
			control premium[(a)]	10%-30% (20%)
		Market comparable companies	EBITDA multiple[(b)]	10-13 (11.3)
			revenue multiple[(b)]	1.5-2.0 (1.7)
			discount for lack of marketability[(a)]	5%-20% (17%)
			control premium[(a)]	10%-30% (20%)
Energy industry	32	Discounted cash flow	weighted average cost of capital	8%-12% (11.1%)
			long-term revenue growth rate	3%-5.5% (4.2%)
			long-term pre-tax operating margin	7.5%-13% (9.2%)
			discount for lack of marketability[(a)]	5%-20% (10%)
			control premium[(a)]	10%-20% (12%)
		Market comparable companies	EBITDA multiple[(b)]	6.5-12 (9.5)
			revenue multiple[(b)]	1.0-3.0 (2.0)
			discount for lack of marketability[(a)]	5%-20% (10%)
			control premium[(a)]	10%-20% (12%)
Private equity fund investments(b)	25	Net asset value[(c)]	n/a	n/a
(CU in millions) Description	Fair value at 31/12/X9	Valuation technique(s)	Unobservable input	Range (weighted average)
Debt securities:				
Residential mortgage-backed securities	125	Discounted cash flow	constant prepayment rate	3.5%-5.5% (4.5%)
			probability of default	5%-50% (10%)
			loss severity	40%-100% (60%)
Commercial mortgage-backed securities	50	Discounted cash flow	constant prepayment rate	3%-5% (4.1%)
			probability of default	2%-25% (5%)
			loss severity	10%-50% (20%)
Collateralised debt obligations	35	Consensus pricing	offered quotes	20-45
			comparability adjustments (%)	–10%-+15% (+5%)
Hedge fund investments:				
High-yield debt securities	90	Net asset value[(c)]	n/a	n/a

(CU in millions) Description	Fair value at 31/12/X9	Valuation technique(s)	Unobservable input	Range (weighted average)
Derivatives:				
Credit contracts	38	Option model	annualised volatility of credit[(d)]	10%-20%
			counterparty credit risk[(e)]	0.5%-3.5%
			own credit risk[(e)]	0.3%-2.0%
Investment properties:				
Commercial – Asia	31	Discounted cash flow	long-term net operating income margin	18%-32% (20%)
			cap rate	0.08-0.12 (0.10)
		Market comparable companies	price per square metre (USD)	\$3,000-\$7,000 (\$4,500)
Commercial – Europe	27	Discounted cash flow	long-term net operating income margin	15%-25% (18%)
			cap rate	0.06-0.10 (0.08)
		Market comparable companies	price per square metre (EUR)	€4,000-€12,000 (€8,500)

(a) Represents amounts used when the entity has determined that market participants would take into account these premiums and discounts when pricing the investments.

(b) Represents amounts used when the entity has determined that market participants would use such multiples when pricing the investments.

(c) The entity has determined that the reported net asset value represents fair value at the end of the reporting period.

(d) Represents the range of volatility curves used in the valuation analysis that the entity has determined market participants would use when pricing the contracts.

(e) Represents the range of the credit default swap curves used in the valuation analysis that the entity has determined market participants would use when pricing the contracts.

(Note: A similar table would be presented for liabilities unless another format is deemed more appropriate by the entity.)

20.3.6 Level 3 reconciliation

IFRS 13 requires a reconciliation (also referred to as the Level 3 roll-forward) of the beginning and ending balances for any recurring fair value measurements that utilise significant unobservable inputs (i.e. Level 3 inputs). Therefore, any asset or liability (measured at fair value on a recurring basis) that was determined to be a Level 3 measurement at either the beginning or the end of a reporting period would need to be considered in the Level 3 reconciliation.

To reconcile Level 3 balances for the period presented, entities must present the following information for each class of assets and liabilities:

- balance of Level 3 assets or liabilities (as at the beginning of the period);
- total gains or losses;
- purchases, sales, issues and settlements (presented separately);
- transfers in and/or out of Level 3 (presented separately); and
- balance of Level 3 assets or liabilities (as at the end of the period).

In addition, entities are required to separately present gains or losses included in earnings from those gains or losses recognised in other comprehensive income, and to describe in which line items these gains or losses are reported in profit or loss, or in other comprehensive income. To enhance the ability of financial statement users to assess an entity's quality of earnings, IFRS 13 also requires entities to separately disclose the amount of total gains and losses reported in profit or loss (for the period) that are attributable to changes in unrealised gains and losses for assets and liabilities categorised within Level 3 and are still held at the end of the reporting period. Effectively, this requires an entity to distinguish its unrealised gains and losses from its realised gains and losses for Level 3 measurements.

The following example from IFRS 13 illustrates how an entity could comply with the Level 3 reconciliation requirements. *[IFRS 13.IE61]*. Extract 14.3 from BP p.l.c. and Extract 14.4 from Rio Tinto plc at 20.3.8.A below also illustrates these disclosure requirements in relation to derivatives categorised within Level 3.

Example 14.28: Reconciliation of fair value measurements categorised within Level 3 of the fair value hierarchy

	Fair value measurements using significant unobservable inputs (Level 3)										
(CU in millions)	Other equity securities			Debt securities			Hedge fund invest-ments	Deriv-atives	Investment properties		
	Healthcare industry	Energy industry	Private equity fund	Residential mortgage-backed securities	Commercial mortgage-backed securities	Collateralised debt obligations	High-yield debt securities	Credit contracts	Asia	Europe	Total
Opening balance	49	28	20	105	39	25	145	30	28	26	495
Transfers into Level 3				(a)(b) 60							60
Transfers out of Level 3				(b)(c) (5)							(5)
Total gains or losses for the period											
Included in profit or loss			5	(23)	(5)	(7)	7	5	3	1	(14)
Included in other comprehensive income	3	1									4
Purchases, issues, sales and settlements											
Purchases	1	3			16	17		18			55
Issues											
Sales				(12)			(62)				(74)
Settlements								(15)			(15)
Closing balance	53	32	25	125	50	35	90	38	31	27	506

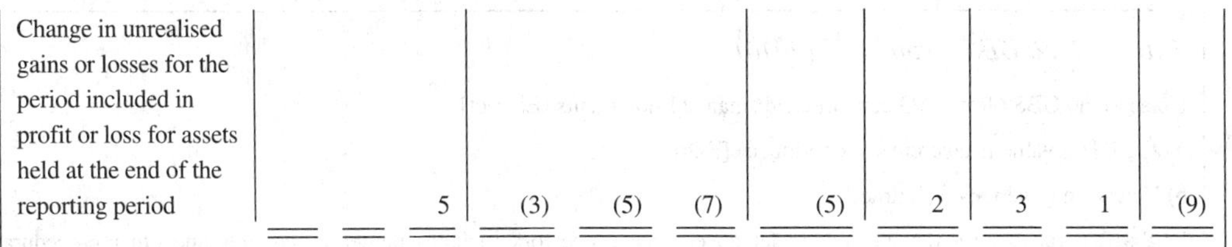

Change in unrealised gains or losses for the period included in profit or loss for assets held at the end of the reporting period			5	(3)	(5)	(7)	(5)	2	3	1	(9)

(a) Transferred from Level 2 to Level 3 because of a lack of observable market data, resulting from a decrease in market activity for the securities.

(b) The entity's policy is to recognise transfers into and transfers out of Level 3 as at the date of the event or change in circumstances that caused the transfer.

(c) Transferred from Level 3 to Level 2 because observable market data became available for the securities.

(Note: A similar table would be presented for liabilities unless another format is deemed more appropriate by the entity.)

IFRS 13 also provides the following example to illustrate how an entity could comply with the requirements to separately disclose the amount of total gains and losses reported in profit or loss that are attributable to changes in unrealised gains and losses for assets and liabilities categorised within Level 3 and are still held at the end of the reporting period. *[IFRS 13.IE62]*.

Example 14.29: Gains and losses

(CU in millions)	Financial income	Non-financial income
Total gains or losses for the period included in profit or loss	(18)	4
Change in unrealised gains or losses for the period included in profit or loss for assets held at the end of the reporting period	(13)	4

(Note: A similar table would be presented for liabilities unless another format is deemed more appropriate by the entity.)

20.3.7 Disclosure of valuation processes for Level 3 measurements

Entities are required to describe the valuation processes used for fair value measurements categorised within Level 3 of the fair value hierarchy, whether on a recurring or non-recurring basis. This is illustrated in the extract below from the financial statements of UBS Group AG. The Boards decided to require these disclosures for Level 3 measurements because they believe this information, in conjunction with the other Level 3 disclosures, will help users assess the relative subjectivity of these measurements.

Extract 14.2: UBS Group AG (2016)

Notes to the UBS Group AG consolidated financial statements [Extract]

Note 22 Fair value measurement (continued) [Extract]

b) Valuation governance [Extract]

UBS's fair value measurement and model governance framework includes numerous controls and other procedural safeguards that are intended to maximize the quality of fair value measurements reported in the financial statements. New products and valuation techniques must be reviewed and approved by key stakeholders from risk and finance control functions. Responsibility for the ongoing measurement of financial and non-financial instruments at fair value resides with the business divisions. In carrying out their valuation responsibilities, the businesses are required to consider the availability and quality of external market data and to provide justification and rationale for their fair value estimates.

Fair value estimates are validated by risk and finance control functions, which are independent of the business divisions. Independent price verification is performed by finance through benchmarking the business divisions' fair value estimates with observable market prices and other independent sources. Controls and governance are in pace to ensure the quality of third-party pricing sources where used. For instruments where valuation modes are used to determine fair value, independent valuation and model control groups within finance and risk evaluate UBS's models on a regular basis, including valuation and model input parameters as well as pricing. As a result of the valuation controls employed, valuation adjustments may be made to the business divisions' estimates of fair value to align with independent market data and the relevant accounting standard.

IFRS 13 provides an example of how an entity could comply with the requirements to disclose the valuation processes for its Level 3 fair value measurements, suggesting this disclosure might include the following:

(i) for the group within the entity that decides the entity's valuation policies and procedures:
   - its description;
   - to whom that group reports; and
   - the internal reporting procedures in place (e.g. whether and, if so, how pricing, risk management or audit committees discuss and assess the fair value measurements);

(ii) the frequency and methods for calibration, back testing and other testing procedures of pricing models;

(iii) the process for analysing changes in fair value measurements from period to period;

(iv) how the entity determined that third-party information, such as broker quotes or pricing services, used in the fair value measurement was developed in accordance with the IFRS; and

(v) the methods used to develop and substantiate the unobservable inputs used in a fair value measurement. *[IFRS 13.IE65]*.

20.3.8 Sensitivity of Level 3 measurements to changes in significant unobservable inputs

IFRS 13 requires entities to provide a narrative description of the sensitivity of recurring Level 3 fair value measurements to changes in the unobservable inputs used, if changing those inputs would significantly affect the fair value measurement. However, except in relation to financial instruments (see 20.3.8.A below) there is no requirement to quantify the extent of the change to the unobservable input, or the quantitative effect of this change on the measurement (i.e. only discuss directional change).

At a minimum, the unobservable inputs quantitatively disclosed based on the requirements described at 20.3.5 above must be addressed in the narrative description. In addition, entities are required to describe any interrelationships between the unobservable inputs and discuss how they might magnify or mitigate the effect of changes on the fair value measurement.

This disclosure, combined with the quantitative disclosure of significant unobservable inputs, is designed to enable financial statement users to understand the directional effect of certain inputs on an item's fair value and to evaluate whether the entity's views about individual unobservable inputs differ from their own. The Boards believe these disclosures can provide meaningful information to users who are not familiar with the pricing models and valuation techniques used to measure a particular class of assets or liabilities (e.g. complex structured instruments).

The following example from IFRS 13 illustrates how an entity could comply with the disclosure requirements related to the sensitivity of Level 3 measurements to changes in significant unobservable inputs. *[IFRS 13.IE66]*.

Example 14.30: Narrative description of sensitivity to significant unobservable inputs

The significant unobservable inputs used in the fair value measurement of the entity's residential mortgage-backed securities are prepayment rates, probability of default and loss severity in the event of default. Significant increases (decreases) in any of those inputs in isolation would result in a significantly lower (higher) fair value measurement. Generally, a change in the assumption used for the probability of default is accompanied by a directionally similar change in the assumption used for the loss severity and a directionally opposite change in the assumption used for prepayment rates.

We note that the above example is fairly general in nature, because no numbers relating to how the unobservable inputs might be changed, or how such a change would affect fair value, are required to be disclosed. However, in making this disclosure we would encourage entities to avoid over-generalisations that may not hold true in all cases.

20.3.8.A Quantitative sensitivity of Level 3 measurements of financial instruments to changes in significant unobservable inputs

In addition to the qualitative sensitivity analysis, IFRS 13 requires quantitative sensitivity analysis for Level 3 fair value measurements of financial assets and financial liabilities (as noted at 20.3.2 above, this is only for recurring fair value measurements), which is generally consistent with the existing disclosure requirement in IFRS 7 (see Chapter 54). If changing one or more of the unobservable inputs to reflect reasonably possible alternative assumptions would change fair value significantly, an entity must disclose the fact and the effect of those changes.

The entity must also disclose how the effect of a change to reflect a reasonably possible alternative assumption was calculated. For the purpose of this disclosure requirement, significance is judged with respect to profit or loss, and total assets or total liabilities, or, when changes in fair value are recognised in other comprehensive income and total equity.

The following extracts from BP p.l.c. and Rio Tinto plc illustrates the disclosures required for Level 3 measurements.

Extract 14.3: BP p.l.c. (2014)

28. Derivative financial instruments [Extract]

Level 3 derivatives

The following table shows the changes during the year in the net fair value of derivatives held for trading purposes within level 3 of the fair value hierarchy.

					$ million
	Oil price	Natural gas price	Power price	Other	Total
Net fair value of contracts at 1 January 2014	(18)	313	86	475	856
Gains recognized in the income statement	350	152	141	94	737
Settlements	(86)	(56)	(13)	(180)	(335)
Transfers out of level 3	–	(228)	–	–	(228)
Net fair value of contracts at 31 December 2014	246	181	214	389	1,030

					$ million
	Oil price	Natural gas price	Power price	Other	Total
Net fair value of contracts at 1 January 2013	105	304	(43)	71	437
Gains (losses) recognized in the income statement	(47)	62	81	–	96
Purchases	110	1	–	–	111
New contracts	–	–	–	475	475
Settlements	(143)	(52)	10	(71)	(256)
Transfers out of level 3	(43)	(1)	36	–	(8)
Exchange adjustments	–	(1)	2	–	1
Net fair value of contracts at 31 December 2013	(18)	313	86	475	856

The amount recognized in the income statement for the year relating to level 3 held for trading derivatives still held at 31 December 2014 was a $456 million gain (2013 $110 million gain related to derivatives still held at 31 December 2013).

The most significant gross assets and liabilities categorized in level 3 of the fair value hierarchy are US natural gas contracts. At 31 December 2014, the gross US natural gas price instruments dependent on inputs at level 3 of the fair value hierarchy were an asset of $586 million and liability of $526 million (net fair value of $60 million), with $126 million, net, valued using level 2 inputs. US natural gas price derivatives are valued using observable market data for maturities up to 60 months in basis locations that trade at a premium or discount to the NYMEX Henry Hub price, and using internally developed price curves based on economic forecasts for periods beyond that time. The significant unobservable inputs for fair value measurements categorized within level 3 of the fair value hierarchy for the year ended 31 December 2014 are presented below.

	Unobservable inputs	Range $/mmBtu	Weighted average $/mmBtu
Natural gas price contracts	Long-dated market price	3.44-6.39	4.64

If the natural gas prices after 2019 were 10% higher (lower), this would result in a decrease (increase) in derivative assets of $85 million, and decrease (increase) in derivative liabilities of $64 million, and a net decrease (increase) in profit before tax of $21 million.

Extract 14.4: Rio Tinto plc (2016)

Notes to the 2016 financial statements [Extract]

30 Financial instruments and risk management [Extract]

C (c) Level 3 financial assets and financial liabilities

The table below shows the summary of changes in the fair value of the Group's Level 3 financial assets and financial liabilities.

	31 December 2016 Level 3 financial assets and financial liabilities US$m	31 December 2015 Level 3 financial assets and financial liabilities US$m
Opening balance	456	282
Currency translation adjustments	(2)	(43)
Total realised gains/(losses) included in:		
– Consolidated sales revenue	1	–
– Net operating costs	(28)	6
Total unrealised gains included in:		
– Net operating costs	11	196
Total unrealised gains transferred into other comprehensive income	–	15
Additions	43	–
Impairment	(2)	–
Closing balance	479	456
Total gains/(losses) for the year included in the income statement for assets and liabilities held at year end	11	(15)

Sensitivity analysis in respect of Level 3 derivatives

Forward contracts and options whose carrying value are valued using unobservable inputs are calculated using appropriate discounted cashflow and option model valuation techniques. The most significant of these assumptions relate to long-term pricing wherein internal pricing assumptions are used after the ten year LME curve. A ten per cent increase in long-term metal pricing assumptions would result in a US$38 million (31 December 2015: US$38 million) decrease in carrying value. A ten per cent decrease in long-term metal pricing assumptions would result in a US$64 million (31 December 2015: US$39 million) increase in carrying value.

20.3.9 Highest and best use

As discussed at 10 above, if the highest and best use of a non-financial asset differs from its current use, entities are required to disclose this fact and why the non-financial asset is being used in a manner that differs from its highest and best use. *[IFRS 13.93(i)]*. The Boards believe this information is useful to financial statement users who project expected cash flows based on how an asset is actually being used.

20.4 Disclosures for unrecognised fair value measurements

For each class of assets and liabilities not measured at fair value in the statement of financial position, but for which the fair value is disclosed (e.g. financial assets carried at amortised cost whose fair values are required to be disclosed in accordance with IFRS 7), entities are required to disclose the following:

(a) the level of the fair value hierarchy within which the fair value measurements are categorised in their entirety (Level 1, 2 or 3);

(b) if categorised within Level 2 or Level 3 of the fair value hierarchy:
   (i) a description of the valuation technique(s) used in the fair value measurement;
   (ii) a description of the inputs used in the fair value measurement;
   (iii) if there has been a change in valuation technique (e.g. changing from a market approach to an income approach or the use of an additional valuation technique):
   - the change; and
   - the reason(s) for making it; and

(c) for non-financial assets, if the highest and best use differs from its current use, an entity must disclose that fact and why the non-financial asset is being used in a manner that differs from its highest and best use. *[IFRS 13.97]*.

None of the other IFRS 13 disclosures are required for assets and liabilities whose fair value is only disclosed. For example, even though certain fair value disclosures are categorised within Level 3, entities are not required to provide quantitative information about the unobservable inputs used in their valuation because these items are not measured at fair value in the statement of financial position.

20.5 Disclosures regarding liabilities issued with an inseparable third-party credit enhancement

IFRS 13 includes an additional disclosure requirement for liabilities measured at fair value that have been issued with an inseparable third-party credit enhancement (refer to 11.3.1 above for further discussion regarding these instruments). The standard requires that an issuer disclose the existence of the third-party credit enhancement and whether it is reflected in the fair value measurement of the liability. *[IFRS 13.98]*.

21 APPLICATION GUIDANCE – PRESENT VALUE TECHNIQUES

This section focuses on the application guidance in IFRS 13 regarding the use of present value techniques to estimate fair value.

21.1 General principles for use of present value techniques

A present value technique is an application of the income approach, which is one of the three valuation approaches prescribed by IFRS 13. Valuation techniques under the income approach, such as present value techniques or option pricing models, convert expected future amounts to a single present amount. That is, a present value technique uses the projected future cash flows of an asset or liability and discounts those cash flows at a rate of return commensurate with the risk(s) associated with those cash flows. Present value techniques, such as discounted cash flow analyses, are frequently used to estimate the fair value of business entities, non-financial assets and non-financial liabilities, but are also useful for valuing financial instruments that do not trade in active markets.

The standard does not prescribe the use of a single specific present value technique, nor does it limit the use of present value techniques to those discussed. The selection of a present value technique will depend on facts and circumstances specific to the asset or liability being measured at fair value and the availability of sufficient data. *[IFRS 13.B12]*.

The application guidance in IFRS 13 regarding the use of present value techniques specifically focuses on three techniques: a discount rate adjustment technique and two methods of the expected cash flow (expected present value) technique. These approaches are summarised in the following table.

Figure 14.11: Comparison of present value techniques described in IFRS 13

	Discount rate adjustment technique	**Expected present value technique**	
		Method 1	**Method 2**
	(see 21.3 below)	(see 21.4 below)	(see 21.4 below)
Nature of cash flows	Conditional cash flows – may be contractual or promised or the most likely cash flows	Expected cash flows	Expected cash flows
Cash flows based on probability weighting?	No	Yes	Yes
Cash flows adjusted for certainty?	No	Yes – cash risk premium is deducted. Cash flows represent a certainty-equivalent cash flow	No
Cash flows adjusted for other market risk?	No	Yes	Yes – to the extent not already captured in the discount rate
Discount rate adjusted for the uncertainty inherent in the cash flows?	Yes – uses an observed or estimated market rate of return, which includes adjustment for the possible variation in cash flows.	No – already captured in the cash flows	No – already captured in the cash flows
Discount rate adjusted for the premium a market participant would require to accept the uncertainty?	Yes	No – represents time value of money only (i.e. the risk-free rate is used)	Yes – represents the expected rate of return (i.e. the risk-free rate is adjusted to include the risk premium)

Additional considerations when applying present value techniques to measuring the fair value of a liability and an entity's own equity instrument not held by other parties as assets are discussed at 11 above.

21.2 The components of a present value measurement

Present value measurements use future cash flows or values to estimate amounts in the present, using a discount rate. Present value techniques can vary in complexity depending on the facts and circumstances of the item being measured. Nevertheless, for the purpose of measuring fair value in accordance with IFRS 13, the standard requires a present value technique to capture all the following elements from the perspective of market participants at the measurement date:

- an estimate of future cash flows for the asset or liability being measured;
- expectations about the uncertainty inherent in the future cash flows (i.e. the possible variations in the amount and timing of the cash flows);
- the time value of money – represented by a risk-free interest rate. That is, the rate on risk-free monetary assets that have maturity dates (or durations) that coincide with the period covered by the cash flows and pose neither uncertainty in timing nor risk of default to the holder;
- a risk premium (i.e. the price for bearing the uncertainty inherent in the cash flows);
- other factors that market participants would take into account in the circumstances; and
- for a liability, the non-performance risk relating to that liability, including the entity's (i.e. the obligor's) own credit risk. *[IFRS 13.B13]*.

Since present value techniques may differ in how they capture these elements, IFRS 13 sets out the following general principles that govern the application of any present value technique used to measure fair value:

(a) both cash flows and discount rates should:
   - reflect assumptions that market participants would use when pricing the asset or liability;
   - take into account only the factors attributable to the asset or liability being measured; and
   - have internally consistent assumptions.

   For example, if the cash flows include the effect of inflation (i.e. nominal cash flows), they would be discounted at a rate that includes the effect of inflation, for example, a rate built off the nominal risk-free interest rate. If cash flows exclude the effect of inflation (i.e. real cash flows), they should be discounted at a rate that excludes the effect of inflation. Similarly, post-tax and pre-tax cash flows should be discounted at a rate consistent with those cash flows; and

(b) discount rates should also:
   - be consistent with the underlying economic factors of the currency in which the cash flows are denominated; and
   - reflect assumptions that are consistent with those assumptions inherent in the cash flows.

   This principle is intended to avoid double-counting or omitting the effects of risk factors. For example, a discount rate that reflects non-performance (credit) risk is appropriate if using contractual cash flows of a loan (i.e. a discount rate adjustment technique – see 21.3 below). The same rate would not be appropriate when using probability-weighted cash flows (i.e. an expected present value technique – see 21.4 below) because the expected cash flows already reflect assumptions about the uncertainty in future defaults. *[IFRS 13.B14]*.

21.2.1 Time value of money

The objective of a present value technique is to convert future cash flows into a present amount (i.e. a value as at the measurement date). Therefore, time value of money is a fundamental element of any present value technique. *[IFRS 13.B13(c)]*. A basic principle in finance theory, time value of money holds that 'a dollar today is worth more than a dollar tomorrow', because the dollar today can be invested and earn interest immediately. Therefore, the discount rate in a present value technique must capture, at a minimum, the time value of money. For example, a discount rate equal to the risk-free rate of interest encompasses only the time value element of a present value technique. If the risk-free rate is used as a discount rate, the expected cash flows must be adjusted into certainty-equivalent cash flows to capture any uncertainty associated with the item being measured and the compensation market participants would require for this uncertainty.

21.2.2 Risk and uncertainty in a present value technique

At its core, the concept of value measures expected rewards against the risks of realising those rewards. Present value techniques implicitly contain uncertainty as they generally deal with estimates rather than known amounts. In many cases, both the amount and timing of the cash flows are uncertain. The standard notes that even contractually fixed amounts are uncertain if there is risk of default. *[IFRS 13.B15]*.

Market participants generally require compensation for taking on the uncertainty inherent in the cash flows of an asset or a liability. This compensation is known as a risk premium. IFRS 13 states that in order to faithfully represent fair value, a present value technique should include a risk premium. The standard acknowledges that determining the appropriate risk premium might be difficult. However, the degree of difficulty alone is not a sufficient reason to exclude a risk premium if market participants would demand one. *[IFRS 13.B16]*.

Depending on the present value technique used, risk may be incorporated in the cash flows or in the discount rate. However, identical risks should not be captured in both the cash flows and the discount rate in the same valuation analysis. For example, if the probability of default and loss given default for a liability are already incorporated in the discount rate (i.e. a risk-adjusted discount rate), the projected cash flows should not be further adjusted for the expected losses.

The present value techniques discussed in the application guidance to IFRS 13 differ in how they adjust for risk and in the type of cash flows they use.

- The discount rate adjustment technique uses a risk-adjusted discount rate and contractual, promised or most likely cash flows (see 21.3 below).
- Method 1 of the expected present value technique uses cash certain equivalent cash flows and a risk-free rate (see 21.4 below).
- Method 2 of the expected present value technique uses expected cash flows that are not risk-adjusted and a discount rate adjusted to include the risk premium that market participants require. That rate is different from the rate used in the discount rate adjustment technique (see 21.4 below). *[IFRS 13.B17]*.

If the risks are accounted for fully and appropriately, the three present value techniques noted above should all produce an identical fair value measurement, regardless of whether risk is captured in the cash flows or the discount rate (see 21.4.1 below for a numerical example illustrating this point).

21.3 Discount rate adjustment technique

The discount rate adjustment technique attempts to capture all of the risk associated with the item being measured in the discount rate and is most commonly used to value assets and liabilities with contractual payments, such as debt instruments. This technique uses a single set of cash flows from the range of possible estimated amounts and discounts those cash flows using a rate that reflects all of the risk related to the cash flows.

According to the standard, the cash flows may be contractual or promised or the most likely cash flows. In all cases, those cash flows are conditional upon the occurrence of specified events. For example, contractual or promised cash flows for a bond are conditional on the event of no default by the debtor. *[IFRS 13.B18].*

The discount rate is derived from observable rates of return for comparable assets and liabilities that are traded in the market and incorporates the following:

- the risk-free interest rate;
- market participants' expectations about possible variations in the amount or timing of the cash flows;
- the price for bearing the uncertainty inherent in these cash flows (or risk premium); and
- other risk factors specific to the asset or liability.

As such, under this technique the cash flows are discounted at an observed or estimated market rate appropriate for such conditional cash flows (that is, a market rate of return).

The discount rate adjustment technique requires an analysis of market data for comparable assets or liabilities. Comparability is established by considering:

- the nature of the cash flows – for example, whether the cash flows are contractual or non-contractual and whether the cash flows are likely to respond similarly to changes in economic conditions; and
- other factors, such as credit standing, collateral, duration, restrictive covenants and liquidity. *[IFRS 13.B19].*

Alternatively, if a single comparable asset or liability does not fairly reflect the risk inherent in the cash flows of the asset or liability being measured, it may be possible to derive a discount rate using a 'build-up' approach. That is, the entity should use data for several comparable assets or liabilities in conjunction with the risk-free yield curve. Example 14.31 at 21.3.1 below illustrates this further.

If the discount rate adjustment technique is applied to fixed receipts or payments, the adjustment for any risk inherent in the cash flows is included in the discount rate. In some applications of the discount rate adjustment technique to cash flows that are not fixed receipts or payments, an entity may need to make an adjustment to the cash flows to achieve comparability with the observed asset or liability from which the discount rate is derived. *[IFRS 13.B22].*

Although IFRS 13 does not prescribe when a particular present value technique should be used, the extent of market data available for a particular type of asset or liability will influence when use of the discount rate adjustment technique is appropriate. Paragraph B19 of IFRS 13 states that the 'discount rate adjustment technique requires an analysis of market data for comparable assets or liabilities'. *[IFRS 13.B19]*. Therefore, certain assets and liabilities may not lend themselves to the use of the discount rate adjustment technique, even though it may be possible to derive discount rates using market data from several comparable items when no single observable rate of return reflects the risk inherent in the item being measured.

The most challenging aspect of applying this technique is the identification of market observable rates of return that appropriately capture the risk inherent in the asset or liability being measured. Understanding the various risk factors associated with certain types of assets and liabilities is not always easy, and quantifying the effect of these factors is even more difficult. However, it may be helpful to deconstruct a discount rate into its component parts to understand what risks are being considered; beginning with the risk-free rate, which represents the time value of money. In addition to the risk-free rate, entities should consider credit or non-performance risk, if the subject asset or liability requires performance in the future (including, but not limited to, a cash payment). For example, in the case of a financial asset, the discount rate would include compensation required by market participants to assume the risk that the counterparty will be unable to fulfil its obligation. Not all discount rates require an explicit adjustment for credit (or non-performance) risk. Equity interests, for example, may assume perpetual residual cash flows from the operations of a business, rather than a contractual future payment. In this case, an additional component of risk is captured through an equity risk premium, instead of a credit risk adjustment. The long-term incremental rate of return of equity interests over long-term risk-free interest rates may generally represent an identifiable component of risk.

When applying the discount rate adjustment technique, the credit spread (above the risk-free rate) will implicitly include assumptions about probabilities of default and losses given default without requiring an adjustment to the projected cash flows used in the analysis. However, a credit adjusted risk-free rate may not sufficiently capture all the risk related to the subject asset or liability. Depending on facts and circumstances of the item being measured, the observable rate of return should also capture other potential variability with respect to the timing and amount of the cash flows (e.g. potential variability due to prepayment risk for financial instruments such as mortgage backed securities) and the price for bearing such uncertainty (risk premium).

In addition, when assessing discount rates, it is important to keep in mind the exit price objective of a fair value measurement in IFRS 13. Because the discount rate represents the rate of return required by market participants in the current market, it should also incorporate factors such as illiquidity and the current risk appetite of market participants.

21.3.1 Illustrative example of the discount rate adjustment technique

The following example from IFRS 13 illustrates how a build-up approach is applied when using the discount rate adjustment technique. *[IFRS 13.B20-21]*

Example 14.31: Discount rate adjustment technique

Assume that Asset A is a contractual right to receive CU 800 in one year (i.e. there is no timing uncertainty). There is an established market for comparable assets, and information about those assets, including price information, is available. Of those comparable assets:

Asset B is a contractual right to receive CU 1,200 in one year and has a market price of CU 1,083. Therefore, the implied annual rate of return (i.e. a one-year market rate of return) is 10.8% [(CU 1,200/CU1,083) – 1].

Asset C is a contractual right to receive CU 700 in two years and has a market price of CU 566. Therefore, the implied annual rate of return (i.e. a two-year market rate of return) is 11.2% [(CU 700/CU 566)^0.5 – 1].

All three assets are comparable with respect to risk (i.e. dispersion of possible pay-offs and credit).

(i) *Comparability based nature of the cash flows and other factors*

On the basis of the timing of the contractual payments to be received for Asset A relative to the timing for Asset B and Asset C (i.e. one year for Asset B versus two years for Asset C), Asset B is deemed more comparable to Asset A. Using the contractual payment to be received for Asset A (CU 800) and the one-year market rate derived from Asset B (10.8%), the fair value of Asset A is CU 722 (CU 800/1.108).

(ii) *Using the build-up approach*

In the absence of available market information for Asset B, the one-year market rate could be derived from Asset C using the build-up approach. In that case the two-year market rate indicated by Asset C (11.2%) would be adjusted to a one-year market rate using the term structure of the risk-free yield curve. Additional information and analysis might be required to determine whether the risk premiums for one-year and two-year assets are the same. If it is determined that the risk premiums for one-year and two-year assets are not the same, the two-year market rate of return would be further adjusted for that effect.

As evidenced in the example above, using a build-up approach requires that market data for comparable assets be available. In addition, when applying the build-up approach, significant judgement may be required in determining comparability between the item being measured and the available benchmarks, as well as quantifying the appropriate adjustments necessary to account for any differences that may exist between the item being measured and the applicable benchmark (e.g. differences in credit risks, nature and timing of the cash flows, etc.).

21.4 Expected present value technique

The expected present value technique is typically used in the valuation of business entities, assets and liabilities with contingent or conditional payouts and items for which discount rates cannot be readily implied from observable transactions.

This technique uses, as a starting point, a set of cash flows that represent the probability-weighted average of all possible future cash flows (i.e. the expected cash flows). Unlike the cash flows used in the discount rate adjustment technique (i.e. contractual, promised or most likely amounts), expectations about possible variations in the amount and/or timing of the cash flows are explicitly incorporated in the projection of the expected cash flows themselves, rather than solely in the discount rate. *[IFRS 13.B23]*.

The application guidance in IFRS 13 identifies two types of risk, based on portfolio theory:

(a) *unsystematic (diversifiable) risk* – the risk specific to a particular asset or liability; and

(b) *systematic (non-diversifiable) risk* – the common risk shared by an asset or a liability with the other items in a diversified portfolio (i.e. market risk). *[IFRS 13.B24].*

According to portfolio theory, in a market in equilibrium, market participants will be compensated only for bearing the systematic risk inherent in the cash flows. If the market is inefficient or is out of equilibrium, other forms of return or compensation might be available.

While, in theory, all possible future cash flows are meant to be considered, in practice, a discrete number of scenarios are often used to capture the probability distribution of potential cash flows.

- The number of possible outcomes to be considered will generally depend on the characteristics of the specific asset or liability being measured. For example, the outcome of a contingency may be binary, therefore, only two possible outcomes need be considered. In contrast, certain complex financial instruments are valued using option pricing models, such as Monte Carlo simulations, that generate thousands of possible outcomes.
- Estimating the probability distribution of potential outcomes requires judgement and will depend on the nature of the item being measured.

Assuming the entity's use of the asset is consistent with that of market participants, an entity might look to its own historical performance, current and expected market environments (including expectations of volatility) and budgetary considerations to develop expectations about future cash flows and appropriate weightings. However, as discussed at 19.1 above, the use of an entity's own data can only be a starting point when measuring fair value. Adjustments may be needed to ensure that the measurement is consistent with market participant assumptions. For example, synergies that can be realised by the entity should not be considered unless they would similarly be realised by market participants.

The concept of a risk premium is just as important under an expected present value technique as it is under the discount rate adjustment technique. The use of probability-weighted cash flows under an expected present value technique does not remove the need to consider a market risk premium when estimating fair value. While 'expected cash flows' capture the uncertainty in the amount and timing of the future cash flows, the probability weighting does not include the compensation market participants would demand for bearing this uncertainty. For example, assume Asset A is a contractual right to receive CU 10,000. Asset B has a payout that is conditional upon the toss of a coin: if 'heads', Asset B pays CU 20,000; and if 'tails' it pays nothing. Assuming no risk of default, both assets have an expected value of CU 10,000 (i.e. CU 10,000 × 100% for Asset A, and CU 20,000 × 50% + CU 0 × 50% for Asset B). However, risk-averse market participants would find Asset A more valuable than Asset B, as the cash-certain payout of CU 10,000 for Asset A is less risky than the expected cash flow of CU 10,000 for Asset B.

Although the variability in the cash flows of Asset B has been appropriately captured by probability-weighting all the possible cash flows (i.e. there is no subjectivity involved in the determination of the probability weighting in the simplified example since the payout is based on a coin toss), Asset B's expected value does not capture the compensation market participants would require for bearing the uncertainty in the cash flows. As such, all else being equal, the price for Asset B would be lower than the price for Asset A. That is, the required rate of return for Asset B would be higher than that for Asset A, in order to compensate the holder for the incremental risk in Asset B's cash flows (relative to Asset A).

21.4.1 Expected present value technique – method 1 and method 2

The standard describes two methods of the expected present value technique. The key difference between Method 1 and Method 2 is where the market risk premium is captured. However, either method should provide the same fair value measurement, i.e. where the risk premium is treated should have no effect on relative fair values.

- *Method 1* – the expected cash flows are adjusted for the systematic (market) risk by subtracting a cash risk premium. This results in risk-adjusted expected cash flows that represent a certainty-equivalent cash flow. The cash flows are then discounted at a risk-free interest rate. *[IFRS 13.B25].*

  Because all of the risk factors have been incorporated into the cash flows under Method 1, the discount rate used would only capture the time value of money. That is, use of a risk-free discount rate is appropriate when using this technique, provided that credit risk considerations are not applicable or have already been considered in the cash flows.

  A certainty-equivalent cash flow is an expected cash flow adjusted for risk so that a market participant is indifferent to trading a certain cash flow for an expected cash flow. For example, if a market participant was willing to trade an expected cash flow of CU 1,200 for a cash flow that the market participant is certain to receive of CU 1,000, the CU 1,000 is the certainty-equivalent of the CU 1,200 (i.e. the CU 200 would represent the cash risk premium). *[IFRS 13.B25].*

- *Method 2* – adjusts for systematic (market) risk by applying a risk premium to the risk-free interest rate (i.e. the risk premium is captured in the discount rate). As such, the discount rate represents an expected rate of return (i.e. the expected rate associated with probability-weighted cash flows). In Method 2, the expected cash flows are discounted using this rate. *[IFRS 13.B26].*

  The use of a risk-free discount rate is not appropriate under Method 2, because the expected cash flows, while probability weighted, do not represent a certainty-equivalent cash flow. The standard suggests that models used for pricing risky assets, such as the capital asset pricing model, could be used to estimate the expected rate of return. As discussed at 21.3 above, the discount rate used in the discount rate adjustment technique also uses a rate of return, but it is related to conditional cash flows. A discount rate determined in accordance with the discount rate adjustment technique is likely to be higher than the discount rate used in Method 2, which is an *expected* rate of return relating to expected or probability-weighted cash flows. *[IFRS 13.B26].*

Capturing the risk premium in the cash flows versus the discount rate has no effect on relative fair values under each method. That is, Method 1 and Method 2 should result in the same fair value measurement, all else being equal.

Example 14.32 below illustrates the application of Method 1 and Method 2 when measuring fair value. *[IFRS 13.B27-B29]*. The selection of Method 1 or Method 2 will depend on facts and circumstances specific to the asset or liability being measured, the extent to which sufficient data are available and the judgements applied. *[IFRS 13.B30]*. However, in practice, Method 1 is rarely used because in most cases, to mathematically estimate the cash certainty adjustment, one must already know the market risk premium that would be applied to the discount rate under Method 2.

Example 14.32: Expected present value techniques

An asset has expected cash flows of CU 780 in one year determined on the basis of the possible cash flows and probabilities shown below. The applicable risk-free interest rate for cash flows with a one-year horizon is 5% and the systematic risk premium for an asset with the same risk profile is 3%.

Possible cash flows CU	Probability	Probability-weighted cash flows CU
500	15%	75
800	60%	480
900	25%	225
	Expected cash flows	780

In this simple example, the expected cash flows of CU 780 represent the probability-weighted average of the three possible outcomes. In more realistic situations, there could be many possible outcomes. However, to apply the expected present value technique, it is not always necessary to take into account distributions of all possible cash flows using complex models and techniques. Rather, it might be possible to develop a limited number of discrete scenarios and probabilities that capture the array of possible cash flows. For example, an entity might use realised cash flows for some relevant past period, adjusted for changes in circumstances occurring subsequently (e.g. changes in external factors, including economic or market conditions, industry trends and competition as well as changes in internal factors affecting the entity more specifically), taking into account the assumptions of market participants.

In theory, the present value (i.e. the fair value) of the asset's cash flows is the same whether determined using Method 1 or Method 2, as follows:

(a) Using Method 1, the expected cash flows are adjusted for systematic (i.e. market) risk. In the absence of market data directly indicating the amount of the risk adjustment, such adjustment could be derived from an asset pricing model using the concept of certainty equivalents. For example, the risk adjustment (i.e. the cash risk premium of CU 22) could be determined using the systematic risk premium of 3% (CU 780 – [CU 780 × (1.05/1.08)]), which results in risk-adjusted expected cash flows of CU 758 (CU 780 – CU 22). The CU 758 is the certainty equivalent of CU 780 and is discounted at the risk-free interest rate (5%). The present value (i.e. the fair value) of the asset is CU 722 (CU 758/1.05).

(b) Using Method 2, the expected cash flows are not adjusted for systematic (i.e. market) risk. Rather, the adjustment for that risk is included in the discount rate. Thus, the expected cash flows are discounted at an expected rate of return of 8% (i.e. the 5% risk-free interest rate plus the 3% systematic risk premium). The present value (i.e. the fair value) of the asset is CU 722 (CU 780/1.08).

In Example 14.33 below, we have expanded the example from IFRS 13 to include the discount rate adjustment technique (described at 21.3 above). Example 14.33 shows how all three techniques converge to the same fair value measurement, while highlighting the difference in the discount rates applied under each approach.

Example 14.33: Comparison of present value techniques

An entity is estimating the fair value of an asset that will expire in one year and has determined that the probability distribution of the future cash flows is as follows.

Possible cash flows CU	Probability	Probability-weighted cash flows CU
500	15%	75
800	60%	480
900	25%	225
	Expected cash flows	780

Assume that the risk-free interest rate is 5% and the risk premium is 3%. The table below shows that all three present value techniques yield identical results:

Method	Contractual cash flows	Most likely cash flows	Expected cash flows	Certainty-equivalent adjustment	Certainty-equivalent cash flows	Discount rate	Present value
Discount rate adjustment technique	N/A	CU 800	N/A	N/A	N/A	10.8%	CU 722
EPV Method 1 – Adjust expected cash flows for risk premium	N/A	N/A	CU 780	CU (22)	CU 758	5.0%	CU 722
EPV Method 2 – Adjust discount rate for risk premium	N/A	N/A	CU 780	N/A	N/A	8.0%	CU 722

Method	Fair value	Calculation
Discount rate adjustment technique	CU 722	= Most likely cash flow / (1 + risk-free rate + adjustment for cash flow uncertainty + risk premium)
EPV Method 1	CU 722	= (Expected cash flow – certainty-equivalent adjustment[(a)]) / (1 + risk-free rate)
EPV Method 2	CU 722	= Expected cash flow / (1 + risk-free rate + risk premium)

(a) Certainty-equivalent adjustment = Expected cash flow – [Expected cash flow x (1 + risk-free rate) / (1 + risk-free rate + risk premium)]

The three techniques differ in the manner in which the risks in the cash flows are captured, but not the level of the risk inherent in those cash flows. In the discount rate adjustment technique, the most likely cash flow (CU 800) is discounted at a rate that reflects all the risk inherent in the investment (i.e. time value of money, possible variations in the amount of cash flows, risk premium).

Method 1 of the expected present value technique incorporates asset-specific and systematic uncertainty directly into the cash flows (certainty-equivalent cash flow of CU 758) and therefore uses the risk-free rate for discounting, as all the risks associated with the investment are incorporated in the cash flows. The adjustment to the cash flows for systematic risk is based on the 3% risk premium.

Instead of using the risk premium to estimate a certainty-equivalent cash flow, Method 2 of the expected present value technique incorporates the risk premium in the discount rate. The difference between the discount rate in Method 1 and Method 2 is the market risk premium.

22 EFFECTIVE DATE AND TRANSITION

IFRS 13 mandatorily applied to annual periods beginning on or after 1 January 2013. Entities were permitted to early adopt the standard, provided that fact was disclosed. *[IFRS 13.C1-C2].*

The standard applied prospectively from the beginning of the annual period in which it was initially applied. Assuming an entity had a reporting date of 30 June and did not early adopt the standard, the date of initial application would have been 1 July 2013. Any fair value measurements and disclosures (and those based on fair value) that occurred on or after 1 July 2013 would be measured in accordance with IFRS 13. Any changes to fair value resulting from the initial application of IFRS 13 would be recognised during the year to 30 June 2014 in the same way as a change in accounting estimate. *[IFRS 13.BC229].*

In the first year of application, disclosures for comparative periods were not required. Disclosures required by IFRS 13 must be provided for the periods after the date of initial application. *[IFRS 13.C3].* In our example, the entity would have provided the required disclosures for the year ending 30 June 2014, but need not have disclosed the same information for the comparative period to 30 June 2013.

23 CONVERGENCE WITH US GAAP

23.1 The development of IFRS 13

IFRS 13 was the result of a convergence project between the IASB and the US Financial Accounting Standards Board (FASB). However, the Boards began developing their fair value measurement standards separately. The FASB issued Statement of Financial Accounting Standards No. 157 – *Fair Value Measurements* (SFAS 157, now ASC 820) in 2006. The IASB's initial discussion paper, issued in 2006, and subsequent exposure draft, issued in 2009, were developed using the requirements of SFAS 157. However, the proposed requirements were not wholly consistent with that guidance and responses from constituents emphasised the need for a common set of requirements regarding the determination of fair value measurements under both IFRS and US GAAP. As a result, the Boards began joint discussions in 2010. From the IASB's perspective, the project had four main objectives:

- 'to establish a single set of requirements for all fair value measurements required or permitted by IFRSs to reduce complexity and improve consistency in their application, thereby enhancing the comparability of information reported in financial statements;
- to clarify the definition of fair value and related guidance to communicate the measurement objective more clearly;
- to enhance disclosures about fair value measurements that will help users of financial statements assess the valuation techniques and inputs used to develop fair value measurements; and
- to increase the convergence' of IFRSs and US GAAP. *[IFRS 13.BC6].*

The Boards' joint discussions resulted in the issuance of IFRS 13 and ASU 2011-04 (formerly SFAS 157) and created a generally uniform framework for applying fair value measurement in both IFRS and US GAAP (refer to 23.2 below for further discussion).

IFRS 13 was also part of the IASB's response to G20 requests in relation to the financial crisis. Therefore, the disclosures required by the standard are intended to help users assess the valuation techniques and inputs used to measure fair value. The IASB had originally proposed to require entities to disclose a quantitative sensitivity analysis for non-financial assets and liabilities measured at fair value. While the proposed disclosures were favoured by users and were consistent with the recommendations from the IASB's Expert Advisory Panel, the proposals were heavily criticised by preparers. Their concerns included the additional cost involved. Therefore, the Boards decided not to include this requirement until additional outreach could be completed. Until such time that this project is completed, sensitivity disclosures are only required for financial assets and liabilities (this continues the current disclosure requirements in IFRS 7). *[IFRS 13.BC208].*

23.2 US GAAP differences

As noted above, the Boards' joint fair value measurement project resulted in both the issuance of IFRS 13 and amendments to particular aspects of ASC 820. These standards now have a consistent definition of fair value and represent converged guidance in relation to how to measure fair value. However, some differences still remain. The main differences are discussed at 23.2.1 to 23.2.4 below.

It is also worth noting that there continue to be differences between IFRS and US GAAP as to *what* is measured at fair value, but those differences were outside the scope of the joint project, which focused on *how* to measure fair value.

In 2014, the Financial Accounting Foundation issued its post-implementation review of SFAS 157, concluding that the standard met its intended objectives.[20] While agreeing that a comprehensive review of the fair value guidance was not needed, the FASB noted that it plans to potentially address more challenging aspects of the standard in the years ahead.[21] In addition, at the time of writing, the FASB was in the process of evaluating existing fair value disclosure requirements as part of its broader Disclosure Framework project. The FASB issued an exposure draft for changes to disclosure requirements, but is currently redeliberating the comments received on exposure draft.[22]

23.2.1 Practical expedient for alternative investments

ASC 820 provides a practical expedient to measure the fair value of certain investments in investment companies (e.g. investments in hedge funds or private equity funds that do not have readily determinable fair values) using net asset value (NAV), without adjustment.[23] Furthermore, in May 2015, the FASB issued ASU 2015-07 – *Fair Value Measurement (Topic 820): Disclosures for Investments in Certain Entities That Calculate Net Asset Value per Share (or Its Equivalent)*, which eliminates the requirement to categorise in the fair value hierarchy investments measured using the NAV practical expedient.[24] This amendment was effective for public business entities for fiscal years beginning after 15 December 2015 and interim periods within those fiscal years, with early adoption permitted. While this exemption provides some relief for entities, they now have additional disclosure requirements specific to investments that are measured using the NAV practical expedient. These requirements are intended to help financial statement users reconcile amounts reported to the face of the financial statements and better understand the nature and risk of these investments, including whether the investments, if sold, are probable of being sold at amounts different from their NAV.

IFRS 13 does not have a similar practical expedient. Nor does it provide a similar disclosure exemption or requirements specific to such investments. Therefore, IFRS preparers cannot presume that NAV, or an equivalent measure, will be the same as fair value as measured in accordance with IFRS 13 (this is discussed further at 2.5.1 above). In addition, entities will need to categorise such investments within the fair value hierarchy and comply with the general disclosure requirements in IFRS 13.

At the time IFRS 13 was issued, the IASB believed it would be difficult to identify when such a practical expedient would be applied, given the different practices entities across the world use to calculate NAV. This difference was expected to be addressed as part of the IASB's project on Investment Entities. However, when the IASB issued *Investment Entities (Amendments to IFRS 10, IFRS 12 and IAS 27)* in October 2012, a footnote was added to paragraph 238(a) of the Basis for Conclusions to IFRS 13 which confirmed it had reconsidered providing a net asset value practical expedient, but decided against providing one for the reason outlined above and because it was outside the scope of the Investment Entities project to provide fair value measurement guidance for investments in investment entities. *[IFRS 13.BC238(a)]*.

23.2.2 Fair value of liabilities with a demand feature

The guidance in IFRS on measuring the fair value of a financial liability with a demand feature differs slightly from US GAAP. IFRS 13 states that the fair value of a liability with a demand feature cannot be less than the present value of the amount payable on demand, which is consistent with the existing requirements in IFRS. US GAAP has specific industry guidance for banks and depository institutions.[25] The industry specific guidance states that the fair value of deposit liabilities with no defined maturities is the amount payable on demand at the reporting date. Since deposit liabilities, withdrawable on demand, of banks and depository institutions are excluded from the scope of the fair value option guidance in ASC 825, the industry guidance in US GAAP around how to fair value these liabilities is applicable to disclosure, only. *[IFRS 13.BC238(b)]*.

23.2.3 Recognition of day-one gains and losses

While fair value is defined in IFRS 13 as an exit price (which can differ from an entry price), the standard defers to other IFRSs on whether to recognise any difference between fair value and transaction price at initial recognition, that is, day-one gains or losses. IFRS 9 (or IAS 39) restricts the recognition of day-one gains and losses when fair value is determined using unobservable inputs.

US GAAP contains no specific threshold regarding the observability of fair value inputs. As such, US GAAP does not specifically prohibit the recognition of day-one gains or losses even when the fair value measurement is based on significant unobservable inputs (i.e. a Level 3 measurement – see 16.2 above for further discussion regarding categorisation within the fair value hierarchy).

23.2.4 Disclosures

IFRS 13 and ASC 820 have some differences in the disclosure requirements for fair value measurements. For example, IFRS 13 does not provide exceptions to its disclosure requirements for non-public entities, whereas ASC 820 does. The IASB believes that *IFRS for Small and Medium-Sized Entities* addresses the accounting for entities that do not have public accountability, and the disclosures about their fair value measurements. *[IFRS 13.BC238(c)].*

Other examples of disclosure differences include:

(a) quantitative sensitivity analysis disclosures for Level 3 financial instruments – IFRS 13 currently requires a quantitative sensitivity analysis disclosure for Level 3 financial instruments. That is, if different inputs could have reasonably been used in place of one or more of the unobservable inputs used to measure fair value (and those inputs would have significantly changed the fair value measurement), entities are required to state that fact, disclose the effect on their fair value measurements and describe how they calculated those effects (note, this disclosure was previously required by IFRS 7). No similar disclosure is currently required under US GAAP;

(b) other Level 3 disclosures – IFRS generally does not allow for derivative assets and liabilities to be presented on a net basis. As such, amounts disclosed for fair value measurements categorised within Level 3 might differ between US GAAP and IFRS because US GAAP allows a net presentation in some cases; and

(c) retirement benefit plan investments measured at fair value in accordance with IAS 26 – As discussed at 2 above, retirement benefit plans that measure their investments at fair value in accordance with IAS 26 are required to measure fair value in accordance with IFRS 13 but are exempt from IFRS 13's disclosure requirements. Instead, the disclosure requirements in IAS 26 apply. Under US GAAP, retirement benefit plans have no similar exemption from ASC 820's disclosure requirements.

(d) a disclosure exemption and additional disclosure requirements for investments measured using the NAV practical expedient, as discussed at 23.2.1 above.

References

1 Request for Information: *Post Implementation review – IFRS 13 Fair Value Measurement*, May 2017.

2 IFRS 7.25, 29(d) as amended by IFRS 16, effective 1 January 2019.

3 *IFRIC Update*, July 2014.

4 Exposure Draft ED/2014/4 *Measuring Quoted Investments in Subsidiaries, Joint Ventures and Associates at Fair Value (Proposed amendments to IFRS 10, IFRS 12, IAS 27, IAS 28, IAS 36 and Illustrative Examples for IFRS 13)*, IASB, September 2014.

5 *IASB Update*, January 2016.

6 Request for Information: *Post Implementation review – IFRS 13 Fair Value Measurement*, May 2017.

7 FASB Accounting Standards Update 2011-04, *Amendments to Achieve Common Fair Value Measurement and Disclosure Requirements in U.S. GAAP and IFRSs*.

8 Exposure Draft ED/2014/4 *Measuring Quoted Investments in Subsidiaries, Joint Ventures and Associates at Fair Value (Proposed amendments to IFRS 10, IFRS 12, IAS 27, IAS 28, IAS 36 and Illustrative Examples for IFRS 13)*, IASB, September 2014.
9 *IASB Update*, April 2015.
10 European Securities and Markets Authority public statement *Sovereign Debt in IFRS Financial Statements* issued in November 2011.
11 Decision ref EECS/0115-03, European Securities and Markets Authority report *17th Extract from the EECS's Database of Enforcement*, July 2015, pp.7-8.
12 Decision ref EECS/0115-03, European Securities and Markets Authority report *17th Extract from the EECS's Database of Enforcement*, July 2015, pp.7-8.
13 Website of the IFRS Foundation and IASB, http://www.ifrs.org/projects/work-plan/ (accessed21 August 2017).
14 The International Swaps and Derivatives Association (ISDA) agreement is part of a framework of documents designed to enable OTC derivatives to be documented fully and flexibly. The ISDA master agreement sets out the standard terms that apply to all transactions and is published by the International Swaps and Derivatives Association.
15 A credit support annex (CSA) is a legal document that regulates the credit support (collateral) for derivative transactions and forms part of an ISDA Master Agreement.
16 Proposed illustrative example 13A, paragraphs IE47A-IE47G, Exposure Draft ED/2014/4 *Measuring Quoted Investments in Subsidiaries, Joint Ventures and Associates at Fair Value (Proposed amendments to IFRS 10, IFRS 12, IAS 27, IAS 28, IAS 36 and Illustrative Examples for IFRS 13)*, IASB, September 2014.
17 IASB Staff Paper, Agenda Paper reference 6 for the February 2014 IASB meeting – *Measuring Quoted Investments in Subsidiaries, Joint Ventures and Associates at Fair Value (Proposed amendments to IFRS 10, IFRS 12, IAS 27, IAS 28 and IAS 36 and Illustrative Examples for IFRS 13) – Illustrative Example for IFRS 13 – Portfolios.*
18 *IASB Update*, April 2015.
19 *IFRIC Update*, January 2015.
20 Financial Accounting Foundation, *Post-Implementation Review Report – FASB Statement No. 157, Fair Value Measurements (Codified in Accounting Standards Codification Topic 820, Fair Value Measurements and Disclosures)*, February 2014.
21 FASB, Response to FAF Post-implementation Review Report of FAS 157 on *Fair Value Measurement*, dated 10 March 2014.
22 Website of the FASB, www.fasb.org/jsp/FASB/FASBContent_C/ProjectUpdatePage&cid=1176164227350 (accessed 21 August 2017).
23 FASB Accounting Standards Codification Topic 820 – Fair Value Measurements and Disclosures – sections 10-35-59 – 10-35-62.
24 FASB Accounting Standards Codification Topic 820 – Fair Value Measurements and Disclosures – section 10-35-54B, which is added by ASU 2015-07 – *Fair Value Measurement (Topic 820): Disclosures for Investments in Certain Entities That Calculate Net Asset Value per Share (or Its Equivalent).*
25 FASB Accounting Standards Codification Topic 825 – *Financial Instruments* and Topic 942 – *Financial Services – Depository and Lending.*

Chapter 15 Foreign exchange

Chapter 15

List of examples

Chapter 15 Foreign exchange

1 INTRODUCTION

1.1 Background

An entity can engage in foreign currency activities in two ways. It may enter directly into transactions which are denominated in foreign currencies, the results of which need to be translated into the currency in which the company measures its results and financial position. Alternatively, it may conduct foreign operations through a foreign entity, such as a subsidiary, associate, joint arrangement or branch which keeps its accounting records in terms of its own currency. In this case it will need to translate the financial statements of the foreign entity for the purposes of inclusion in the consolidated financial statements.

Before an international standard was developed, there were four distinct methods which could be used in the translation process:

(a) *current rate method* – all assets and liabilities are translated at the current rate of exchange, i.e. the exchange rate at the end of the reporting period;

(b) *temporal method* – assets and liabilities carried at current prices (e.g. cash, receivables, payables, and investments at market value) are translated at the current rate of exchange. Assets and liabilities carried at past prices (e.g. property, investments at cost, prepayments) are translated at the rate of exchange in effect at the dates to which the prices pertain;

(c) *current/non-current method* – all current assets and current liabilities are translated at the current rate of exchange. Non-current assets and liabilities are translated at historical rates, i.e. the exchange rate in effect at the time the asset was acquired or the liability incurred; and

(d) *monetary/non-monetary method* – monetary assets and liabilities, i.e. items which represent the right to receive or the obligation to pay a fixed amount of money, are translated at the current rate of exchange. Non-monetary assets and liabilities are translated at the historical rate.

There was no consensus internationally on the best theoretical approach to adopt. In essence, the arguments surround the choice of exchange rates to be used in the translation process and the subsequent treatment of the exchange differences which arise.

1.2 Relevant pronouncements

The principal international standard dealing with this topic is IAS 21 – *The Effects of Changes in Foreign Exchange Rates,* the original version of which dates back to 1983. In December 2003, the IASB issued a revised version of IAS 21 as part of a wide ranging project to improve its standards and this forms the core of the current standard, although it has been subject to a number of subsequent amendments.

One interpretation of the earlier version of IAS 21 issued by the SIC remains applicable. SIC-7 – *Introduction of the Euro* – deals with the application of IAS 21 to the changeover from the national currencies of participating Member States of the European Union to the euro and is covered at 8 below. IFRIC 16 – *Hedges of a Net Investment in a Foreign Operation* – is not actually an interpretation of IAS 21, but provides guidance on applying certain aspects of the standard and is discussed at 6.1.5 and 6.6.3 below.

IFRIC 22 – *Foreign Currency Transactions and Advance Consideration* – provides guidance on determining the date of a transaction for the purposes of applying IAS 21 when consideration is paid or received in advance. This interpretation, which was published in December 2016, is effective for periods commencing on or after 1 January 2018 and is discussed at 5.1.2 below.

2 IAS 21: OBJECTIVE, SCOPE AND DEFINITIONS

2.1 Objective of the standard

An entity may carry on foreign activities in two ways. It may have transactions in foreign currencies or it may have foreign operations. In addition, an entity may present its financial statements in a foreign currency. IAS 21 does not set out what the objective of foreign currency translation should be, but just states that the objective of the standard is 'to prescribe how to include foreign currency transactions and foreign operations in the financial statements of an entity and how to translate financial statements into a presentation currency'. *[IAS 21.1]*.

It also indicates that the principal issues to be addressed are 'which exchange rate(s) to use and how to report the effects of changes in exchange rates in the financial statements'. *[IAS 21.2]*.

2.2 Scope

IAS 21 should be applied: *[IAS 21.3]*

(a) in accounting for transactions and balances in foreign currencies, except for those derivative transactions and balances that are within the scope of IAS 39 – *Financial Instruments: Recognition and Measurement* – or, when applied, IFRS 9 – *Financial Instruments;*

(b) in translating the results and financial position of foreign operations that are included in the financial statements of the entity by consolidation or the equity method; and

(c) in translating an entity's results and financial position into a presentation currency.

IAS 39, and IFRS 9, apply to many foreign currency derivatives and, accordingly, these are excluded from the scope of IAS 21. However, those foreign currency derivatives that are not within the scope of IAS 39 and IFRS 9 (e.g. some foreign currency derivatives that are embedded in other contracts) are within the scope of IAS 21. In addition, IAS 21 applies when an entity translates amounts relating to derivatives from its functional currency to its presentation currency. *[IAS 21.4]*.

IAS 21 also does not apply to hedge accounting for foreign currency items, including the hedging of a net investment in a foreign operation. *[IAS 21.5]*. This is dealt with in IAS 39 or IFRS 9, which have detailed rules on hedge accounting that are different from the requirements of IAS 21 (see Chapters 52 and 53). *[IAS 21.27]*.

The requirements of IAS 21 are applicable to financial statements that are described as complying with International Financial Reporting Standards. They do not apply to translations of financial information into a foreign currency that do not meet these requirements, although the standard does specify information to be disclosed in respect of such 'convenience translations' (see 10.3 below). *[IAS 21.6]*.

IAS 21 does not apply to the presentation in a statement of cash flows of the cash flows arising from transactions in a foreign currency, or to the translation of cash flows of a foreign operation. *[IAS 21.7]*. These are dealt with in IAS 7 – *Statement of Cash Flows* (see Chapter 38 at 5.3).

2.3 Definitions of terms

The definitions of terms which are contained in IAS 21 are as follows: *[IAS 21.8]*

Closing rate is the spot exchange rate at the end of the reporting period.

Exchange difference is the difference resulting from translating a given number of units of one currency into another currency at different exchange rates.

Exchange rate is the ratio of exchange for two currencies.

Fair value is the price that would be received to sell an asset or paid to transfer a liability in an orderly transaction between market participants at the measurement date.

Foreign currency is a currency other than the functional currency of the entity.

Foreign operation is an entity that is a subsidiary, associate, joint arrangement or branch of a reporting entity, the activities of which are based or conducted in a country or currency other than those of the reporting entity.

Functional currency is the currency of the primary economic environment in which the entity operates.

A *group* is a parent and all its subsidiaries.

Monetary items are units of currency held and assets and liabilities to be received or paid in a fixed or determinable number of units of currency.

Net investment in a foreign operation is the amount of the reporting entity's interest in the net assets of that operation.

Presentation currency is the currency in which the financial statements are presented.

Spot exchange rate is the exchange rate for immediate delivery.

The terms 'functional currency', 'monetary items' and 'net investment in a foreign operation' are elaborated on further within the standard. These are discussed at 4, 5.4 and 6.3.1 below.

3 SUMMARY OF THE APPROACH REQUIRED BY IAS 21

Many reporting entities comprise a number of individual entities (e.g. a group is made up of a parent and one or more subsidiaries). Various types of entities, whether members of a group or otherwise, may have investments in associates or joint arrangements. They may also have branches or divisions (see 4.4 below). It is necessary for the results and financial position of each individual entity included in the reporting entity to be translated into the currency in which the reporting entity presents its financial statements (if this presentation currency is different from the individual entity's functional currency). *[IAS 21.18]*.

In preparing financial statements, the following approach should be followed:

- Each entity – whether a stand-alone entity, an entity with foreign operations (such as a parent) or a foreign operation (such as a subsidiary or branch) – determines its functional currency. *[IAS 21.17]*. This is discussed at 4 below.

  In the case of group financial statements, it should be emphasised that there is not a 'group' functional currency; each entity included within the group financial statements, be it the parent, or a subsidiary, associate, joint arrangement or branch, has its own functional currency.

- Where an entity enters into a transaction denominated in a currency other than its functional currency, it translates those foreign currency items into its functional currency and reports the effects of such translation in accordance with the provisions of IAS 21 discussed at 5 below. *[IAS 21.17]*.

- The results and financial position of any individual entity within the reporting entity whose functional currency differs from the presentation currency are translated in accordance with the provisions of IAS 21 discussed at 6 below. *[IAS 21.18]*.

  Since IAS 21 permits the presentation currency of a reporting entity to be any currency (or currencies), this translation process will also apply to the parent's figures if its functional currency is different from the presentation currency.

  The standard also permits a stand-alone entity preparing financial statements or an entity preparing separate financial statements in accordance with IAS 27 – *Separate Financial Statements* – to present its financial statements in any currency (or currencies). If the entity's presentation currency differs from its functional currency, its results and financial position are also translated into the presentation currency in accordance with this process. *[IAS 21.19]*.

4 DETERMINATION OF AN ENTITY'S FUNCTIONAL CURRENCY

4.1 General

Functional currency is defined as the currency of 'the primary economic environment in which the entity operates' (see 2.3 above). This will normally be the one in which it primarily generates and expends cash. *[IAS 21.9]*.

IAS 21 sets out a number of factors or indicators that any entity should or may need to consider in determining its functional currency. When the factors or indicators are mixed and the functional currency is not obvious, management should use its judgement to determine the functional currency that most faithfully represents the economic effects of the underlying transactions, events and conditions. As part of this approach, management should give priority to the primary indicators before considering the other indicators, which are designed to provide additional supporting evidence to determine an entity's functional currency. *[IAS 21.12]*.

The primary factors that IAS 21 requires an entity to consider in determining its functional currency are as follows: *[IAS 21.9]*

(a) the currency:

 (i) that mainly influences sales prices for goods and services (this will often be the currency in which sales prices for its goods and services are denominated and settled); and

 (ii) of the country whose competitive forces and regulations mainly determine the sales prices of its goods and services.

(b) the currency that mainly influences labour, material and other costs of providing goods or services (this will often be the currency in which such costs are denominated and settled).

Where the functional currency of the entity is not obvious from the above, the following factors may also provide evidence of an entity's functional currency: *[IAS 21.10]*

(a) the currency in which funds from financing activities (i.e. issuing debt and equity instruments) are generated; and

(b) the currency in which receipts from operating activities are usually retained.

An operation that is 'integral' to its parent, i.e. it carries on business as if it were an extension of the parent's operations, will always have the same functional currency as the parent. (In this context, the term parent is drawn broadly and is the entity that has the foreign operation as its subsidiary, branch, associate or joint arrangement). *[IAS 21.BC6]*. Therefore the following additional factors are also considered in determining the functional currency of a foreign operation, particularly whether its functional currency is the same as that of the reporting entity: *[IAS 21.11]*

(a) whether the activities of the foreign operation are carried out as an extension of the reporting entity, rather than being carried out with a significant degree of autonomy. An example of the former is when the foreign operation only sells goods imported from the reporting entity and remits the proceeds to it. An example of the latter is when the operation accumulates cash and other monetary items, incurs expenses, generates income and arranges borrowings, all substantially in its local currency;

(b) whether transactions with the reporting entity are a high or a low proportion of the foreign operation's activities;

(c) whether cash flows from the activities of the foreign operation directly affect the cash flows of the reporting entity and are readily available for remittance to it; and

(d) whether cash flows from the activities of the foreign operation are sufficient to service existing and normally expected debt obligations without funds being made available by the reporting entity.

Although the standard says that these factors 'are' considered in determining the functional currency of a foreign operation, this contradicts the requirement in the standard that management gives priority to the primary indicators before considering the other indicators. If it is obvious from the primary indicators what the entity's functional currency is, then there is no need to consider any of the other factors.

Example 15.1: Factors to be considered when determining the functional currency

A French entity (Parent A) has a US subsidiary (Subsidiary B) that produces and sells knitwear in the United States.

It is clear from the primary factors in IAS 21 that Subsidiary B's functional currency is the US dollar, because the US dollar mainly influences sales prices for goods, labour, material and other costs of providing goods, and the competitive forces and regulations that mainly determine the sales prices of the goods are located in the United States.

However, suppose Subsidiary B is financed by an inter-company loan denominated in euros granted from Parent A and the cash flows generated by Subsidiary B are transferred to Parent A on a regular basis. Should these additional factors be taken into account in determining the functional currency of Subsidiary B?

In our view, they should not. These additional factors only have to be considered when it is not obvious from the primary factors what Subsidiary B's functional currency is.

However, in practice, there are occasions when the functional currency is not completely clear from the primary factors and it will often be necessary to consider the other indicators. For example, if Subsidiary B was not producing the knitwear itself, but purchasing it from sources outside of the US (such that its operating costs were not predominantly in US dollars) this would mean that it was no longer obvious based on the primary factors that its functional currency was the US dollar and the additional factors would be taken into account in determining Subsidiary B's functional currency.

Since an entity's functional currency reflects the underlying transactions, events and conditions that are relevant to it, once it is determined, IAS 21 requires that the functional currency is not changed unless there is a change in those underlying transactions, events and conditions. *[IAS 21.13]*. The implication of this is that management of an entity cannot decree what the functional currency is – it is a matter of fact, albeit subjectively determined fact based on management's judgement of all the circumstances.

4.2 Intermediate holding companies or finance subsidiaries

For many entities the determination of functional currency may be relatively straightforward. However, for some entities, particularly entities within a group, this may not be the case. One particular difficulty is the determination of the functional currency of an intermediate holding company or finance subsidiary within an international group.

Example 15.2: Functional currency of intermediate holding companies or finance subsidiaries

An international group is headquartered in the UK. The UK parent entity has a functional currency of pound sterling, which is also the group's presentation currency. The group has three international sub-operations, structured as follows:

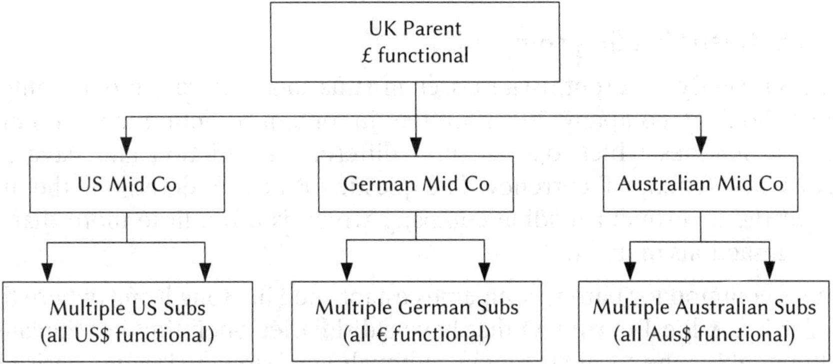

What is the functional currency of the three Mid Cos?

There are a variety of factors to be considered for intermediate holding companies or finance subsidiaries when deciding on the appropriate functional currency. Therefore, there will not be a single analysis applicable to all such entities.

IAS 21 defines a 'foreign operation' as 'an entity that is a subsidiary...the activities of which are based or conducted in a country or currency other than those of the reporting entity' (see 2.3 above). This definition would seem to suggest that a foreign operation must have its own 'activities'.

Also, paragraph 9 of the standard states that the functional currency is 'the currency of the primary economic environment in which the entity operates'. However, under paragraph 9 this is determined by reference to the currency that mainly influences sales prices and the operation's costs, and is therefore not directly relevant to intermediate holding companies or finance subsidiaries (see 4.1 above). Paragraphs 10 and 11 set out a number of factors to consider in determining the functional currency of a foreign operation. The theme running through these factors is the extent to which the activities and cash flows of the foreign operation are independent of those of the reporting entity.

In the case of an intermediate holding company or finance subsidiary, the acid-test question to consider is whether it is an extension of the parent and performing the functions of the parent – i.e. whether its role is simply to hold the investment in, or provide finance to, the foreign operation on behalf of the parent company or whether its functions are essentially an extension of a local operation (e.g. performing selling, payroll or similar activities for that operation) or indeed it is undertaking activities on its own account.

This means that subsidiaries that do nothing but hold investments or borrow money on behalf of the parent will normally have the functional currency of the parent. The borrowings of such companies are frequently guaranteed by the parent, which is itself likely to be a relevant factor. In other words, on whose credit is the lender relying? If the lender is looking to the ultimate parent, then the functional currency is likely to be that of the ultimate parent. However, if the lender is looking to the sub-group, then the functional currency of the companies in the sub-group will be relevant. Accordingly, any analysis that such a company has a functional currency other than that of the parent will require careful consideration of the features of the entity which give rise to that conclusion. Complex situations are likely to require the application of careful management judgement as indicated by the standard.

As for other entities within a group, each entity should be reviewed for its particular circumstances against the indicators and factors set out in the standard. This review requires management to use its judgement in determining the functional currency that most faithfully represents the economic effects of the underlying transactions, events and conditions applicable to that entity.

4.3 Investment holding companies

A similar, but subtly different, issue arises in situations where a group comprises an investment holding company incorporated in one jurisdiction and a number of operating subsidiaries which operate in a different jurisdiction and have the local currency as their functional currency. The question is how to determine the functional currency of the investment holding company which is often little more than a 'shell' with few transactions of its own.

This issue is common for parent companies established in Hong Kong (where the Hong Kong dollar is the local currency) that have subsidiaries operating in Mainland China (where Renminbi is the local currency), although very similar situations arise in other jurisdictions. Often the investment holding company will be listed in Hong Kong, incur some expenses, e.g. directors' remuneration, limited staff costs and office rental payments, in Hong Kong dollars and raise capital (shares and borrowings) in Hong Kong dollars. Furthermore, dividends from subsidiaries will either be received in Hong Kong dollars or be converted into Hong Kong dollars on receipt.

In 2010, the IFRS Interpretations Committee was asked to consider this issue and the staff identified two broad approaches being used in practice, namely:

- the parent uses the currency of its local environment, i.e. the one in which its operating expenses are denominated, it receives dividends from its subsidiaries and it raises funding; and
- the parent uses the currency of the local environment of its subsidiaries as its functional currency as this is the environment which drives the dividend income it receives, which is its primary source of revenue, i.e. the parent is seen as an extension of its subsidiaries.

The Interpretations Committee chose not to take the issue onto its agenda because any guidance it could provide would be in the nature of application guidance and simply emphasised that judgement needed to be applied.[1] In practice the judgement will often be based on whether the holding company's operations are considered sufficiently substantive to enable it to have a different functional currency from its subsidiaries.

4.4 Branches and divisions

IAS 21 uses the term 'branch' to describe an operation within a legal entity that may have a different functional currency from the entity itself. However, it contains no definition of that term, nor any further guidance on what arrangements should be regarded as a branch.

Many countries' governments have established legal and regulatory regimes that apply when a foreign entity establishes a place of business (often called a branch) in that country. Where an entity has operations that are subject to such a regime, it will normally be appropriate to regard them as a branch and evaluate whether those operations have their own functional currency. In this context, the indicators in paragraph 11 of the standard used to assess whether an entity has a functional currency that is different from its parent (see 4.1 above) will be particularly relevant.

An entity may also have an operation, e.g. a division, that operates in a different currency environment to the rest of the entity but which is not subject to an overseas branch regime. If that operation represents a sufficiently autonomous business unit it may be appropriate to view it as a branch and evaluate whether it has a functional currency that is different to the rest of the legal entity. However, in our experience, this situation will not be a common occurrence.

4.5 Documentation of judgements made

Since the determination of an entity's functional currency is critical to the translation process under IAS 21, we believe that an entity should clearly document its decision about its functional currency, setting out the factors taken into account in making that determination, particularly where it is not obvious from the primary factors set out in paragraph 9 of the standard. We recommend that the ultimate parent entity of a group should do this for each entity within the group and agree that determination with the local management of those entities, particularly where those entities are presenting financial statements in accordance with IFRS. Although the determination of functional currency is a judgemental issue, it would be expected that within the group the same determination would be made as to the functional currency of a particular entity. If local management has come up with a different analysis of the facts from that of the parent, it should be discussed to ensure that both parties have considered all the relevant facts and circumstances and a final determination made.

By documenting the decision about the functional currency of each entity, and the factors taken into account in making that determination, the reporting entity will be better placed in the future to determine whether a change in the underlying transactions, events and conditions relating to that entity warrant a change in its functional currency.

5 REPORTING FOREIGN CURRENCY TRANSACTIONS IN THE FUNCTIONAL CURRENCY OF AN ENTITY

Where an entity enters into a transaction denominated in a currency other than its functional currency then it will have to translate those foreign currency items into its functional currency and report the effects of such translation. The general requirements of IAS 21 are as follows.

5.1 Initial recognition

A foreign currency transaction is a transaction that is denominated or requires settlement in a foreign currency, including transactions arising when an entity: *[IAS 21.20]*

(a) buys or sells goods or services whose price is denominated in a foreign currency;

(b) borrows or lends funds when the amounts payable or receivable are denominated in a foreign currency; or

(c) otherwise acquires or disposes of assets, or incurs or settles liabilities, denominated in a foreign currency.

On initial recognition, foreign currency transactions should be translated into the functional currency using the spot exchange rate between the foreign currency and the functional currency on the date of the transaction. *[IAS 21.21]*. The date of a transaction is the date on which it first qualifies for recognition in accordance with IFRS. For convenience, an average rate for a week or month may be used for all foreign currency transactions occurring during that period, if the exchange rate does not fluctuate significantly. *[IAS 21.22]*.

5.1.1 *Identifying the date of transaction*

The date of a transaction is the date on which it first qualifies for recognition in accordance with IFRS. Although this sounds relatively straightforward, the following example illustrates the difficulty that can sometimes arise in determining the transaction date:

Example 15.3: Establishing the transaction date (1)

A Belgian entity buys an item of inventory from a Canadian supplier. The dates relating to the transaction, and the relevant exchange rates, are as follows:

Date	Event	€1=C$
14 April 2018	Goods are ordered	1.50
5 May 2018	Goods are shipped from Canada and invoice dated that day	1.53
7 May 2018	Invoice is received	1.51
10 May 2018	Goods are received	1.54
14 May 2018	Invoice is recorded	1.56
7 June 2018	Invoice is paid	1.60

IAS 2 – *Inventories* – does not make any reference to the date of initial recognition of inventory. However, IAS 39 or, when applied, IFRS 9 deal with the initial recognition of financial liabilities. They require the financial liability to be recognised when, and only when, the entity becomes a party to the contractual provisions of the instrument. *[IAS 39.14, IFRS 9.3.1.1]*. In discussing firm commitments to purchase goods, they indicate that an entity placing the order does not recognise the liability at the time of the commitment, but delays recognition until the ordered goods have been shipped or delivered, *[IAS 39.AG35, IFRS 9.B3.1.2(b)]*, normally on the date that the risks and rewards of ownership are considered to have passed.

Accordingly, it is unlikely that the date the goods are ordered should be used as the date of the transaction.

If the goods are shipped free on board (f.o.b.) then the risks and rewards of ownership are normally considered to pass on shipment (5 May) and this date should be used. If, however, the goods are not shipped f.o.b. then the risks and rewards of ownership will often be considered to pass on delivery (10 May) and therefore the date the goods are received should be treated as the date of the transaction. In practice, the transaction date will depend on the precise terms of the agreement (which are often based on standardised agreements such as the Incoterms rules).

The dates on which the invoice is received and is recorded are irrelevant to when the risks and rewards of ownership pass and therefore should not in principle be considered to be the date of the transaction. In practice, it may be acceptable that as a matter of administrative convenience that the exchange rate at the date the invoice is recorded is used, particularly if there is no undue delay in processing the invoice. If this is done then care should be taken to ensure that the exchange rate used is not significantly different from that ruling on the 'true' date of the transaction.

It is clear from IAS 21 that the date the invoice is paid is not the date of the transaction because if it were then no exchange differences would arise on unsettled transactions.

In the example above, one of the difficulties in identifying the date of transaction is the fact that IAS 2 contains little guidance on determining when purchased inventory should be recognised as an asset. Some standards, particularly those published more recently such as IFRS 15 – *Revenue from Contracts with Customers* – contain more detailed guidance in this respect. Nevertheless, determining the date of transaction may still require the application of judgement and the date that a transaction is recorded in an entity's books and records will not necessarily be the same as the date at which it qualifies for recognition under IFRS. Other situations where this issue is likely to arise is where an entity is recording a transaction that relates to a period, rather than one being recognised at a single point in time, as illustrated below:

Example 15.4: Establishing the transaction date (2)

On 30 September 2018 Company A, whose functional currency is the euro, acquires a US dollar bond for US$8,000. The bond carries fixed interest of 5% per annum paid quarterly, i.e. US$100 per quarter. The exchange rate on acquisition is US$1 to €1.50.

On 31 December 2018, the US dollar has appreciated and the exchange rate is US$1 to €2.00. Interest received on the bond on 31 December 2018 is US$100 (= €200).

Although the interest might only be recorded on 31 December 2018, the rate on that date is not the spot rate ruling at the date of the transaction. Since the interest has accrued over the 3 month period, it should be translated at the spot rates applicable to the accrual of interest during the 3 month period. Accordingly, a weighted average rate for the 3 month period should be used. Assuming that the appropriate average rate is US$1 to €1.75 the interest income is €175 (= US$100 × 1.75).

Accordingly, there is also an exchange gain on the interest receivable of €25 (= US$100 × [2.00 – 1.75]) to be reflected in profit or loss. The journal entry for recording the receipt of the interest on 31 December 2018 is therefore as follows:

	€	€
Cash	200	
Interest income (profit or loss)		175
Exchange gain (profit or loss)		25

5.1.2 Deposits and other consideration received or paid in advance

An entity might receive (or pay) a deposit in a foreign currency in advance of delivering (or receiving) goods or services in circumstances where the resulting liability (or asset) is considered a non-monetary item – see 5.4.1 below. To many it seems clear that in these circumstances the date of transaction is the date on which the deposit is recognised. However, historically, some have argued it should be a subsequent date (or dates) when the goods or services are actually delivered. *[IFRIC 22.1-3]*.

The Interpretations Committee, noting diversity in practice particularly in the construction industry, published IFRIC 22 in December 2016 addressing this issue. It explains that, in general, the appropriate application of IAS 21 is to use the exchange rate at the date the advance payment is recognised, normally the payment date. *[IFRIC 22.8]*. If there are multiple payments or receipts in advance, an entity should determine a date of transaction for each payment or receipt of advance consideration. *[IFRIC 22.9]*.

IFRIC 22 applies to a foreign currency transaction (or part of it) when an entity recognises a non-monetary asset or non-monetary liability arising from the payment or receipt of advance consideration before the related asset, expense or income (or part of it) is recognised. *[IFRIC 22.4]*. It does not apply when an entity measures the asset, income or expense arising from the advance payment at fair value or at the fair value of the consideration paid or received at a date other than the date of initial recognition of the non-monetary asset or non-monetary liability, for example the measurement of goodwill when applying IFRS 3 – *Business Combinations*. *[IFRIC 22.5]*.

The interpretation need not be applied to income taxes or insurance contracts (including reinsurance contracts) issued or reinsurance contracts held. *[IFRIC 22.6]*. In fact, once IFRS 17 – *Insurance Contracts* – is applied, a group of insurance contracts is treated as a monetary item (see Chapter 56 at 7.1) and therefore the interpretation is unlikely to be relevant. *[IFRIC 22.BC8, IFRS 17.30]*.

The interpretation is effective for periods commencing on or after 1 January 2018. Earlier application is permitted, but disclosure of this fact is required. *[IFRIC 22.A1]*. On initial application, an entity should apply the requirements either: *[IFRIC 22.A2]*

(a) retrospectively in accordance with IAS 8 – *Accounting Policies, Changes in Accounting Estimates and Errors*; or

(b) prospectively to all assets, expenses and income in the scope of the interpretation initially recognised on or after:

   (i) the beginning of the reporting period in which the entity first applies the interpretation; or

   (ii) the beginning of a prior reporting period presented as comparative information in the financial statements of the reporting period in which the entity first applies the interpretation.

An entity applying the interpretation prospectively should apply it to assets, expenses and income initially recognised on or after the beginning of the first reporting period to which it is applied (see (b) above) for which the entity has recognised non-monetary assets or non-monetary liabilities arising from advance consideration before that date. *[IFRIC 22.A3]*.

5.1.3 Using average rates

Rather than using the actual rate ruling at the date of the transaction 'an average rate for a week or month may be used for all foreign currency transactions occurring during that period', if the exchange rate does not fluctuate significantly (see 5.1 above). *[IAS 21.22]*. For entities which engage in a large number of foreign currency transactions it will be more convenient for them to use an average rate rather than using the exact rate for each transaction. If an average rate is to be used, what guidance can be given in choosing and using such a rate?

(a) Length of period

   As an average rate should only be used as an approximation of actual rates then care has to be taken that significant fluctuations in the day-to-day exchange rates do not arise in the period selected. For this reason the period chosen should not be too long. We believe that the period should be no longer than one month and where there is volatility of exchange rates it will be better to set rates on a more frequent basis, say, a weekly basis, especially where the value of transactions is significant;

(b) Estimate of average rate relevant to date of transaction

   The estimation of the appropriate average rate will depend on whether the rate is to be applied to transactions which have already occurred or to transactions which will occur after setting the rate. Obviously, if the transactions have already occurred then the average rate used should relate to the period during which those transactions occurred; e.g. purchase transactions for the previous week should be translated using the average rate for that week, not an average rate for the week the invoices are being recorded;

If the rate is being set for the following period the rate selected should be a reasonable estimate of the expected exchange rate during that period. This could be done by using the closing rate at the end of the previous period or by using the actual average rate for the previous period. We would suggest that the former be used. Whatever means is used to estimate the average rate, the actual rates during the period should be monitored and if there is a significant move in the exchange rate away from the average rate then the rate being applied should be revised;

(c) Application of average rate to type of item

We believe that average rates should be used only as a matter of convenience where there are a large number of transactions. Even where an average rate is used, we recommend that the actual rate should be used for large one-off transactions such as the purchase of a fixed asset or an overseas investment or taking out a foreign loan. Where the number of foreign currency transactions is small it will probably not be worthwhile setting and monitoring average rates and therefore actual rates should be used.

5.1.4 Dual rates or suspension of rates

One practical difficulty in translating foreign currency amounts is where there is more than one exchange rate for that particular currency depending on the nature of the transaction. In some cases the difference between the exchange rates can be small and therefore it probably does not matter which rate is actually used. However, in other situations the difference can be quite significant. In these circumstances, what rate should be used? IAS 21 states that 'when several exchange rates are available, the rate used is that at which the future cash flows represented by the transaction or balance could have been settled if those cash flows had occurred at the measurement date'. *[IAS 21.26]*. Companies should therefore look at the nature of the transaction and apply the appropriate exchange rate.

Another practical difficulty which could arise is where for some reason exchangeability between two currencies is temporarily lacking at the transaction date or subsequently at the end of the reporting period. In this case, IAS 21 requires that the rate to be used is 'the first subsequent rate at which exchanges could be made'. *[IAS 21.26]*.

5.1.5 Longer term lack of exchangeability

The standard does not address the situation where there is a longer-term lack of exchangeability and the Interpretations Committee has considered this in the context of a number of issues associated with the Venezuelan currency, the Bolivar. The background to these discussions involves strict government controls over exchanging Bolivars and concerns about the consequences of applying IAS 21 and IAS 29 – *Financial Reporting in Hyperinflationary Economies* – given the hyperinflationary status of the Venezuelan economy. A number of official exchange mechanisms have been operating in the country, each with different exchange rates and each theoretically available for specified types of transaction. In practice, however, there have been significant restrictions on entities' ability to make more than very limited remittances out of the country using these mechanisms.

The committee noted it is not entirely clear how IAS 21 applies in such situations. Further, the committee thought that addressing this issue was a broader-scope project than it could address and decided not to take it onto its agenda.[2] Consequently, determining the appropriate exchange rate(s) for financial reporting purposes for any particular entity will require the application of judgement. The rate(s) selected will depend on the entity's individual facts and circumstances, particularly its legal ability to convert currency or to settle transactions using a specific rate and its intent to use a particular mechanism, including whether the rate available through that mechanism is published or readily determinable.

The committee did, however, draw attention to disclosure requirements in IFRS that might be relevant in these circumstances and these are covered at 10.4 below.

5.2 Reporting at the ends of subsequent reporting periods

At the end of each reporting period: *[IAS 21.23]*

(a) foreign currency monetary items should be translated using the closing rate;

(b) non-monetary items that are measured in terms of historical cost in a foreign currency should be translated using the exchange rate at the date of the transaction; and

(c) non-monetary items that are measured at fair value in a foreign currency should be translated using the exchange rate at the date when the fair value was determined.

The carrying amount of an item should be determined in conjunction with the relevant requirements of other standards. For example, property, plant and equipment may be measured in terms of fair value or historical cost in accordance with IAS 16 – *Property, Plant and Equipment.* Irrespective of whether the carrying amount is determined on the basis of historical cost or fair value, if the amount is determined in a foreign currency, IAS 21 requires that amount to be translated into the entity's functional currency. *[IAS 21.24].*

The carrying amount of some items is determined by comparing two or more amounts. For example, IAS 2 requires the carrying amount of inventories to be determined as the lower of cost and net realisable value. Similarly, in accordance with IAS 36 – *Impairment of Assets* – the carrying amount of an asset for which there is an indication of impairment should be the lower of its carrying amount before considering possible impairment losses and its recoverable amount. When such an asset is non-monetary and is measured in a foreign currency, the carrying amount is determined by comparing:

- the cost or carrying amount, as appropriate, translated at the exchange rate at the date when that amount was determined (i.e. the rate at the date of the transaction for an item measured in terms of historical cost); and
- the net realisable value or recoverable amount, as appropriate, translated at the exchange rate at the date when that value was determined (e.g. the closing rate at the end of the reporting period).

The effect of this comparison may be that an impairment loss is recognised in the functional currency but would not be recognised in the foreign currency, or *vice versa. [IAS 21.25].*

5.3 Treatment of exchange differences

5.3.1 Monetary items

The general rule in IAS 21 is that exchange differences on the settlement or retranslation of monetary items should be recognised in profit or loss in the period in which they arise. *[IAS 21.28]*.

When monetary items arise from a foreign currency transaction and there is a change in the exchange rate between the transaction date and the date of settlement, an exchange difference results. When the transaction is settled within the same accounting period as that in which it occurred, all the exchange difference is recognised in that period. However, when the transaction is settled in a subsequent accounting period, the exchange difference recognised in each period up to the date of settlement is determined by the change in exchange rates during each period. *[IAS 21.29]*.

These requirements can be illustrated in the following examples:

Example 15.5: Reporting an unsettled foreign currency transaction in the functional currency

A French entity purchases plant and equipment on credit from a Canadian supplier for C$328,000 in January 2018 when the exchange rate is €1=C$1.64. The entity records the asset at a cost of €200,000. At the French entity's year end at 31 March 2018 the account has not yet been settled. The closing rate is €1=C$1.61. The amount payable would be retranslated at €203,727 in the statement of financial position and an exchange loss of €3,727 would be reported as part of the profit or loss for the period. The cost of the asset would remain as €200,000.

Example 15.6: Reporting a settled foreign currency transaction in the functional currency

A UK entity sells goods to a German entity for €87,000 on 28 February 2018 when the exchange rate is £1=€1.45. It receives payment on 31 March 2018 when the exchange rate is £1=€1.50. On 28 February the UK entity will record a sale and corresponding receivable of £60,000. When payment is received on 31 March the actual amount received is only £58,000. The loss on exchange of £2,000 would be reported as part of the profit or loss for the period.

There are situations where the general rule above will not be applied. The first exception relates to exchange differences arising on a monetary item that, in substance, forms part of an entity's net investment in a foreign operation (see 6.3.1 below). In this situation the exchange differences should be recognised initially in other comprehensive income until the disposal of the investment (see 6.6 below). However, this treatment only applies in the financial statements that include the foreign operation and the reporting entity (e.g. consolidated financial statements when the foreign operation is a consolidated subsidiary or equity method investment). It does not apply to the reporting entity's separate financial statements or the financial statements of the foreign operation. Rather, the exchange differences will be recognised in profit or loss in the period in which they arise in the financial statements of the entity that has the foreign currency exposure. *[IAS 21.32]*. This is discussed further at 6.3.1 below.

The next exception relates to hedge accounting for foreign currency items, to which IAS 39 or IFRS 9 apply. The application of hedge accounting requires an entity to account for some exchange differences differently from the treatment required by IAS 21. For example, IAS 39 and IFRS 9 require that exchange differences on monetary items that qualify as hedging instruments in a cash flow hedge or a hedge of a net investment in a foreign operation are recognised initially in other comprehensive income to the extent the hedge is effective. Hedge accounting is discussed in more detail in Chapters 52 and 53.

Another situation where exchange differences on monetary items are not recognised in profit or loss in the period they arise would be where an entity capitalises borrowing costs under IAS 23 – *Borrowing Costs* – since that standard requires exchange differences arising from foreign currency borrowings to be capitalised to the extent that they are regarded as an adjustment to interest costs (see Chapter 21 at 5.4). *[IAS 23.6]*.

One example of a monetary item given by IAS 21 is 'provisions that are to be settled in cash'. In most cases it will be appropriate for the exchange differences arising on provisions to be recognised in profit or loss in the period they arise. However, it may be that an entity has recognised a decommissioning provision under IAS 37 – *Provisions, Contingent Liabilities and Contingent Assets*. One practical difficulty with such a provision is that due to the long timescale of when the actual cash outflows will arise, an entity may not be able to say with any certainty the currency in which the transaction will actually be settled. Nevertheless if it is determined that it is expected to be settled in a foreign currency it will be a monetary item. The main issue then is what should happen to any exchange differences. IFRIC 1 – *Changes in Existing Decommissioning, Restoration and Similar Liabilities* – applies to any decommissioning or similar liability that has been both included as part of the cost of an asset and measured as a liability in accordance with IAS 37 (see Chapter 28 at 6.3.1). IFRIC 1 requires, *inter alia*, that any adjustment to such a provision resulting from changes in the estimated outflow of resources embodying economic benefits (e.g. cash flows) required to settle the obligation should not be recognised in profit or loss as it occurs, but should be added to or deducted from the cost of the asset to which it relates. The requirement of IAS 21 to recognise the exchange differences arising on the provision in profit or loss in the period in which they arise conflicts with this requirement in IFRIC 1. Accordingly, we believe that either approach could be applied as an accounting policy choice. However, in our experience, such exchange differences are most commonly dealt with in accordance with IFRIC 1, particularly by entities with material long-term provisions.

5.3.2 Non-monetary items

When non-monetary items are measured at fair value in a foreign currency they should be translated using the exchange rate as at the date when the fair value was determined. Therefore, any re-measurement gain or loss will include an element relating to the change in exchange rates. In this situation, the exchange differences are recognised as part of the gain or loss arising on the fair value re-measurement.

When a gain or loss on a non-monetary item is recognised in other comprehensive income, any exchange component of that gain or loss should also be recognised in other comprehensive income. *[IAS 21.30]*. For example, IAS 16 requires some gains and losses arising on a revaluation of property, plant and equipment to be recognised in other comprehensive income (see Chapter 18 at 6.2). When such an asset is measured in a foreign currency, the revalued amount should be translated using the rate at the date the value is determined, resulting in an exchange difference that is also recognised in other comprehensive income. *[IAS 21.31]*.

Conversely, when a gain or loss on a non-monetary item is recognised in profit or loss, e.g. financial instruments that are measured at fair value through profit or loss in accordance with IAS 39 or IFRS 9 (see Chapter 49 at 2.1 or Chapter 50 at 2.1) or an investment property accounted for using the fair value model (see Chapter 19 at 6), any exchange component of that gain or loss should be recognised in profit or loss. *[IAS 21.30]*.

An example of an accounting policy dealing with the reporting of foreign currency transactions in the functional currency of an entity is illustrated below.

Extract 15.1: ING Groep N.V. (2015)

Notes to the consolidated annual accounts of ING Group [extract]

1 ACCOUNTING POLICIES [extract]

FOREIGN CURRENCY TRANSLATION [extract]

Functional and presentation currency

Items included in the financial statements of each of the Group's entities are measured using the currency of the primary economic environment in which the entity operates ('the functional currency'). The consolidated financial statements are presented in euros, which is ING Group's functional and presentation currency.

Transactions and balances [extract]

Foreign currency transactions are translated into the functional currency using the exchange rate prevailing at the date of the transactions. Exchange rate differences resulting from the settlement of such transactions and from the translation at year-end exchange rates of monetary assets and liabilities denominated in foreign currencies are recognised in the profit and loss account, except when deferred in equity as part of qualifying cash flow hedges or qualifying net investment hedges.

Exchange rate differences on non-monetary items, measured at fair value through profit and loss, are reported as part of the fair value gain or loss. Non-monetary items are retranslated at the date fair value is determined. Exchange rate differences on non-monetary items measured at fair value through the revaluation reserve are included in the revaluation reserve in equity.

5.4 Determining whether an item is monetary or non-monetary

IAS 21 generally requires that monetary items denominated in foreign currencies be retranslated using closing rates at the end of the reporting period and non-monetary items should not be retranslated (see 5.2 above). Monetary items are defined as 'units of currency held and assets and liabilities to be received or paid in a fixed or determinable number of units of currency'. *[IAS 21.8]*. The standard elaborates further on this by stating that 'the essential feature of a monetary item is a right to receive (or an obligation to deliver) a fixed or determinable number of units of currency'. Examples given by IAS 21 are pensions and other employee benefits to be paid in cash; provisions that are to be settled in cash; cash dividends that are recognised as a liability; and, once IFRS 16 – *Leases* – is applied (see Chapter 25), lease liabilities. *[IAS 21.16]*. More obvious examples are cash and bank balances; trade receivables and payables; and loan receivables and payables.

IAS 39 also indicates that where a foreign currency bond is held as an available-for-sale financial asset, then it should first be accounted for at amortised cost in the underlying currency, thus effectively treating that amount as if it was a monetary item. IFRS 9 contains similar guidance for debt instruments measured at fair value through other comprehensive income. This guidance is discussed further in Chapter 49 at 5.1 and Chapter 50 at 4.1 respectively.

IAS 21 also states that 'a contract to receive (or deliver) a variable number of the entity's own equity instruments or a variable amount of assets in which the fair value to be received (or delivered) equals a fixed or determinable number of units of currency is a monetary item'. *[IAS 21.16]*. No examples of such contracts are given in IAS 21. However, it would seem to embrace those contracts settled in the entity's own equity shares that under IAS 32 – *Financial Instruments: Presentation* – would be presented as financial assets or liabilities (see Chapter 45 at 5.2).

Conversely, the essential feature of a non-monetary item is the absence of a right to receive (or an obligation to deliver) a fixed or determinable number of units of currency. Examples given by the standard are amounts prepaid for goods and services (e.g. prepaid rent, at least until IFRS 16 is applied); goodwill; intangible assets; inventories; property, plant and equipment; provisions that are to be settled by the delivery of a non-monetary asset; and, once IFRS 16 is applied, right-of-use assets. *[IAS 21.16]*. IAS 39 indicates (and IFRS 9 states) that investments in equity instruments are non-monetary items. *[IAS 39.AG83, IFRS 9.B5.7.3]*. It follows that equity investments in subsidiaries, associates or joint ventures are non-monetary items.

Even with this guidance there will clearly be a number of situations where the distinction may not be altogether clear.

5.4.1 Deposits or progress payments

Entities may be required to pay deposits or progress payments when acquiring certain assets, such as property, plant and equipment or inventories, from foreign suppliers. The question then arises as to whether such payments should be retranslated as monetary items or not.

Example 15.7: Deposits or progress payments

A Dutch entity contracts to purchase an item of plant and machinery for US$10,000 on the following terms:

Payable on signing contract (1 August 2018)	– 10%
Payable on delivery (19 December 2018)	– 40%
Payable on installation (7 January 2019)	– 50%

At 31 December 2018 the entity has paid the first two amounts on the due dates when the respective exchange rates were €1=US$1.25 and €1=US$1.20. The closing rate at the end of its reporting period, 31 December 2018, is €1=US$1.15.

		(i)	(ii)
		€	€
First payment	– US$1,000	800	870
Second payment	– US$4,000	3,333	3,478
		4,133	4,348

(i) If the payments made are regarded as prepayments or as progress payments then the amounts should be treated as non-monetary items and included in the statement of financial position at €4,133. This would appear to be consistent with US GAAP which in defining 'transaction date' states: 'A long-term commitment may have more than one transaction date (for example, the due date of each progress payment under a construction contract is an anticipated transaction date).'

(ii) If the payments made are regarded as deposits, and are refundable, then the amounts could possibly be treated as monetary items and included in the statement of financial position at €4,348 and an exchange gain of €215 recognised in profit or loss. A variant of this would be to only treat the first payment as a deposit until the second payment is made, since once delivery is made it is less likely that the asset will be returned and a refund sought from the supplier.

In practice, it will often be necessary to consider the terms of the contract to ascertain the nature of the payments made in order to determine the appropriate accounting treatment and this may well require the application of judgement, something acknowledged in IFRIC 22 (see 5.1.2 above). *[IFRIC 22.BC17]*.

5.4.2 Investments in preference shares

Entities may invest in preference shares of other entities. Whether such shares are monetary items or not will depend on the rights attaching to the shares. IAS 39 indicates (and IFRS 9 states) that investments in equity instruments are non-monetary items (see 5.4 above). *[IAS 39.AG83, IFRS 9.B5.7.3]*. Thus, if the terms of the preference shares are such that they are classified by the issuer as equity, rather than as a financial liability, then they are non-monetary items. However, if the terms of the preference shares are such that they are classified by the issuer as a financial liability (e.g. a preference share that provides for mandatory redemption by the issuer for a fixed or determinable amount at a fixed or determinable future date), then it would appear that they should be treated as monetary items. Indeed, IAS 39 would allow such an instrument to be classified within loans and receivables by the holder provided the definition in IAS 39 is otherwise met (see Chapter 46 at 4). However, even where an investment in such redeemable preference shares is not classified within loans and receivables, but as a held-to-maturity investment or as an available-for-sale financial asset, then it would seem that it should be treated as a monetary item (in the latter case, to the extent that it would be measured at amortised cost, similar to an investment in a bond as discussed at 5.4 above).

5.4.3 Foreign currency share capital

An entity may issue share capital denominated in a currency that is not its functional currency or, due to changes in circumstances that result in a re-determination of its functional currency, may find that its share capital is no longer denominated in its functional currency. Neither IAS 21, IAS 39 nor IFRS 9 address the treatment of translation of share capital denominated in a currency other than the functional currency. In theory two treatments are possible: the foreign currency share capital (and any related share premium or additional paid-in capital) could be maintained at a fixed amount by being translated at a historical rate of exchange, or it could be retranslated annually at the closing rate as if it were a monetary amount. In the latter case a second question would arise: whether to recognise the difference arising on translation in profit or loss or in other comprehensive income or to deal with it within equity.

Where the shares denominated in a foreign currency are ordinary shares, or are otherwise irredeemable and classified as equity instruments, in our experience the most commonly applied view is that the shares should be translated at historical rates and not remeasured. This view reflects the fact that the effect of rate changes is not expected to have an impact on the entity's cash flows associated with those shares. Such capital items are included within the examples of non-monetary items listed in US GAAP (FASB ASC 830 – *Foreign Currency Matters*) as accounts to be remeasured using historical exchange rates when the temporal method is being applied. IAS 21 requires non-monetary items that are measured at historical cost in a foreign currency to be translated using the historical rate (see 5.2 above).

Where such share capital is retranslated at the closing rate, we do not believe that it is appropriate for the exchange differences to be recognised in profit or loss, since they do not affect the cash flows of the entity. Further, because the retranslation of such items has no effect on assets or liabilities it is not an item of income or expense to be recognised in other comprehensive income. Instead, the exchange differences should be taken to equity. Consequently, whether such share capital is maintained at a historical rate, or is dealt with in this way, the treatment has no impact on the overall equity of the entity.

Where the shares are not classified as equity instruments, but as financial liabilities, under IAS 32, e.g. preference shares that provide for mandatory redemption by the issuer for a fixed or determinable amount at a fixed or determinable future date, then, as with investments in such shares (see 5.4.2 above), they should be treated as monetary items and translated at the closing rate. Any exchange differences will be recognised in profit or loss, unless the shares form part of a hedging relationship and IAS 39 or IFRS 9 would account for the exchange differences differently (see Chapter 52 or 53).

5.4.4 Deferred tax

One of the examples of a monetary item included within the exposure draft that preceded IAS 21 was deferred tax.[3] However, this was dropped from the list of examples in the final standard. No explanation is given in IAS 21 as to why this is the case. Until 2007, IAS 12 – *Income Taxes* – suggested that any deferred foreign tax assets or liabilities are monetary items since it stated that 'where exchange differences on deferred foreign tax liabilities or assets are recognised in the income statement, such differences may be classified as deferred tax expense (income) if that presentation is considered to be the most useful to financial statement users'.[4] The reference to 'income statement' has now been changed to 'statement of comprehensive income', although the suggestion remains the same.

5.4.5 Post-employment benefit plans – foreign currency assets

For most entities, benefits payable under a defined benefit post-employment plan will be payable in the functional currency of the entity. However, such a plan may have monetary assets that are denominated in a foreign currency and/or non-monetary assets, the fair value of which are determined in a foreign currency. (Where benefits are payable in a currency that is different to the entity's functional currency, the considerations at 5.4.6 below will be relevant.)

Consider, for example, a UK company with the pound sterling as its functional currency which has a funded pension scheme in which benefit payments are based on the employees' sterling denominated salaries and are paid in sterling. The majority of plan assets comprise a mix of sterling denominated bonds, UK equities and UK properties. However, those assets also include a number of US dollar denominated bonds and equities issued by US companies that are listed on a US stock exchange. IAS 19 – *Employee Benefits* – requires all these assets to be measured at their fair value at the end of the reporting period, but how should the entity deal with any exchange differences or changes in fair value attributable to changes in exchange rates arising on the US assets?

IAS 21 gives as an example of a monetary item 'pensions and other employee benefits to be paid in cash'. Further, the accounting for defined benefit schemes under IAS 19 requires an entity to reflect net interest on the net defined benefit asset or liability in profit or loss and any difference between this amount and the actual return on plan assets in other comprehensive income (see Chapter 33 at 10.2 and 10.3.2). *[IAS 19.120, 127(b)]*. Consequently, it would seem appropriate to view the net pension asset or liability as a single unit of account measured in sterling. Therefore the gains and losses on all the US plan assets attributable to changes in foreign exchange rates would be dealt with as remeasurements in accordance with IAS 19 and recognised in other comprehensive income.

5.4.6 Post-employment benefit plans – foreign currency plans

For some entities the pension benefits payable under a post-employment benefit plan will not be payable in the functional currency of the entity. For example, a UK entity in the oil and gas industry may determine that its functional currency is the US dollar, but its employee costs including the pension benefits are payable in sterling. How should such an entity account for its post-employment benefit plan?

One of the examples of a monetary item given by IAS 21 is 'pensions and other employee benefits to be paid in cash'. However, the standard does not expand on this, and does not appear to make any distinction between pensions provided by defined contribution plans or defined benefit plans. Nor does it distinguish between funded or unfunded defined benefit plans.

Clearly for pensions that are payable under a defined contribution plan (or one that is accounted for as such) this is straightforward. Any liability for outstanding contributions at the end of the reporting period is a monetary item that should be translated at the closing rate, with any resulting exchange differences recognised in profit or loss. For an unfunded defined benefit plan in which the benefit payments are denominated in a foreign currency, applying IAS 21 would also seem to be straightforward. The defined benefit obligation is regarded as a monetary liability and exchange differences on the entire balance are recognised in profit or loss.

A funded defined benefit plan is a more a complex arrangement to assess under IAS 21, particularly if the plan assets include items that considered in their own right would be non-monetary and/or foreign currency monetary items. However, in the light of the guidance in IAS 21 noted above, our preferred view is to consider such arrangements as a single monetary item denominated in the currency in which the benefit payments are made. Therefore the requirements of IAS 19 will be applied in the currency in which the benefit payments are denominated and foreign currency gains or losses on the net asset or liability would be recognised in profit or loss.

Another approach would be to argue that a funded scheme is more akin to a non-monetary item and the exchange differences relating to the defined benefit obligation are similar to actuarial gains and losses. The calculation of the obligation under IAS 19 will be based on actuarial assumptions that reflect the currency of the obligation to the employee (for example, the discount rate used 'shall be consistent with the currency and estimated term' of the obligation *[IAS 19.83]*). Any variations from those assumptions on both the obligation and the assets are dealt with in the same way under IAS 19. Actuarial assumptions are 'an entity's best estimates of the variables that will determine the ultimate cost of providing post-employment benefits' and include financial assumptions. *[IAS 19.76]*. Although IAS 19 does not refer to exchange rates, it is clearly a variable that will determine the ultimate cost to the entity of providing the post-employment benefits. On that basis, the exchange differences relating to the defined benefit obligation would be accounted for in a similar manner to actuarial gains and losses. Although not our preferred accounting treatment, we consider this to be an acceptable approach.

Some might argue that the plan should be regarded as a 'foreign operation' under IAS 21 (see 2.3 above). However, in this situation it is very difficult to say that its 'functional currency' can be regarded as being different from that of the reporting entity given the relationship between the plan and the reporting entity (see 4 above). Thus, it would appear that the entity cannot treat the plan as a foreign operation with a different functional currency from its own.

5.5 Change in functional currency

IAS 21 requires management to use its judgement to determine the entity's functional currency such that it most faithfully represents the economic effects of the underlying transactions, events and conditions that are relevant to the entity (see 4 above). Accordingly, once the functional currency is determined, it may be changed only if there is a change to those underlying transactions, events and conditions. For example, a change in the currency that mainly influences the sales prices of goods and services may lead to a change in an entity's functional currency. *[IAS 21.36]*.

When there is a change in an entity's functional currency, the entity should apply the translation procedures applicable to the new functional currency prospectively from the date of the change. *[IAS 21.35]*.

In other words, an entity translates all items into the new functional currency using the exchange rate at the date of the change. The resulting translated amounts for non-monetary items are treated as their historical cost. Exchange differences arising from the translation of a foreign operation recognised in other comprehensive income are not reclassified from equity to profit or loss until the disposal of the operation (see 6.6 below). *[IAS 21.37]*.

Example 15.8: Change in functional currency

The management of Entity A has considered the functional currency of the entity to be the euro. However, as a result of a change in circumstances affecting the operations of the entity, management determines that on 1 January 2018 the functional currency of the entity is now the US dollar. The exchange rate at that date is €1=US$1.20. Entity A's statement of financial position at 1 January 2018 in its old functional currency is as follows:

	€
Property, plant and equipment	200,000
Current assets	
Inventories	10,000
Receivables	20,000
Cash	5,000
	35,000
Current liabilities	
Payables	15,000
Taxation	3,000
	18,000
Net current assets	17,000
	217,000
Long-term loans	120,000
	97,000

Included within the statement of financial position at 1 January 2018 are the following items:

- Equipment with a cost of €33,000 and a net book value of €16,500. This equipment was originally purchased for £20,000 in 2012 and has been translated at the rate ruling at the date of purchase of £1=€1.65.
- Inventories with a cost of €6,000. These were purchased for US$6,000 and have been translated at the rate ruling at the date of purchase of €1=US$1.00.
- Payables of €5,000 representing the US$6,000 due in respect of the above inventories, translated at the rate ruling at 1 January 2018.
- Long-term loans of €15,000 representing the outstanding balance of £10,000 on a loan originally taken out to finance the acquisition of the above equipment, translated at £1=€1.50, the rate ruling at 1 January 2018.

Entity A applies the translational procedures applicable to its new functional currency prospectively from the date of change. Accordingly, all items in its statement of financial position at 1 January 2018 are translated at the rate of €1=US$1.20 giving rise to the following amounts:

	$
Property, plant and equipment	240,000
Current assets	
Inventories	12,000
Receivables	24,000
Cash	6,000
	42,000
Current liabilities	
Payables	18,000
Taxation	3,600
	21,600
Net current assets	20,400
	260,400
Long-term loans	144,000
	116,400

As far as the equipment that was originally purchased for £20,000 is concerned, the cost and net book value in terms of Entity A's new functional currency are US$39,600 and US$19,800 respectively, being €33,000 and €16,500 translated at €1=US$1.20. Entity A does not go back and translate the £20,000 cost at whatever the £ sterling/US dollar exchange rate was at the date of purchase and calculate a revised net book value on that basis.

Similarly, the inventories purchased in US dollars are included at $7,200, being €6,000 translated at €1=US$1.20. This is despite the fact that Entity A knows that the original cost was $6,000.

As far as the payables in respect of the inventories are concerned, these are included at $6,000, being €5,000 translated at €1=US$1.20. This represents the original amount payable in US dollars. However, this is as it should be since the original payable had been translated into euros at the rate ruling at 1 January 2018 and has just been translated back into US dollars at the same rate. The impact of the change in functional currency is that whereas Entity A had recognised an exchange gain of €1,000 while the functional currency was the euro, no further exchange difference will be recognised in respect of this amount payable. Exchange differences will now arise from 1 January 2018 on those payables denominated in euros, whereas no such differences would have arisen on such items prior to that date.

Similarly, the £10,000 amount outstanding on the loan will be included at $18,000, being €15,000 translated at €1=US$1.20. This is equivalent to the translation of the £10,000 at a rate of £1=US$1.80, being the direct exchange rate between the two currencies at 1 January 2018. In this case, whereas previously exchange gains and losses would have been recognised on this loan balance based on movements of the £/€ exchange rate, as from 1 January 2018 the exchange gains and losses will be recognised based on the £/$ exchange rate.

Often an entity's circumstances change gradually over time and it may not be possible to determine a precise date on which the functional currency changes. In these circumstances an entity will need to apply judgement to determine an appropriate date from which to apply the change, which might coincide with the beginning or end of an interim or annual accounting period.

5.6 Books and records not kept in functional currency

Occasionally, an entity may keep its underlying books and records in a currency that is not its functional currency under IAS 21. For example, it could record its transactions in terms of the local currency of the country in which it is located, possibly as a result of local requirements. In these circumstances, at the time the entity prepares its financial statements all amounts should be converted into the functional currency in accordance with the requirements of the standard discussed at 5.1 to 5.3 above.[5] This process is intended to produce the same amounts in the functional currency as would have occurred had the items been recorded initially in the functional currency. For example, monetary items should be translated into the functional currency using the closing rate, and non-monetary items that are measured on a historical cost basis should be translated using the exchange rate at the date of the transaction that resulted in their recognition which will result in local currency denominated transactions giving rise to exchange differences. *[IAS 21.34]*.

6 USE OF A PRESENTATION CURRENCY OTHER THAN THE FUNCTIONAL CURRENCY

An entity may present its financial statements in any currency (or currencies) (see 3 above). If the presentation currency differs from the entity's functional currency, it needs to translate its results and financial position into the presentation currency. For example, when a group contains individual entities with different functional currencies, the results and financial position of each entity are expressed in a common currency so that consolidated financial statements may be presented. *[IAS 21.38]*. There is no concept of a 'group' functional currency. Each entity within the group has its own functional currency, and the results and financial position of each entity have to be translated into the presentation currency that is used for the consolidated financial statements. *[IAS 21.18]*.

The requirements of IAS 21 in respect of this translation process are discussed below. The procedures to be adopted apply not only to the inclusion of foreign subsidiaries in consolidated financial statements but also to the incorporation of the results of associates and joint arrangements. *[IAS 21.44]*. They also apply when the results of a foreign branch are to be incorporated into the financial statements of an individual entity or a stand-alone entity preparing financial statements or when an entity preparing separate financial statements in accordance with IAS 27 presents its financial statements in a currency other than its functional currency.

In addition to these procedures, IAS 21 has additional provisions that apply when the results and financial position of a foreign operation are translated into a presentation currency so that the foreign operation can be included in the financial statements of the reporting entity by consolidation or the equity method. *[IAS 21.44]*. These additional provisions are covered at 6.3 to 6.5 below.

6.1 Translation to the presentation currency

Under IAS 21, the method of translation depends on whether the entity's functional currency is that of a hyperinflationary economy or not, and if it is, whether it is being translated into a presentation currency which is that of a hyperinflationary economy or not. A hyperinflationary economy is defined in IAS 29 (see Chapter 16 at 2.3). The requirements of IAS 21 discussed below can be summarised as follows:

	Presentation currency	
	Non-hyperinflationary	**Hyperinflationary**
Non-hyperinflationary functional currency		
Assets/liabilities		
– current period	Closing rate (current B/S date)	Closing rate (current B/S date)
– comparative period	Closing rate (comparative B/S date)	Closing rate (comparative B/S date)
Equity items		
– current period	Not specified	Not specified
– comparative period	Not specified	Not specified
Income/expenses (including those recognised in other comprehensive income)		
– current period	Actual rates (or appropriate average for current period)	Actual rates (or appropriate average for current period)
– comparative period	Actual rates (or appropriate average for comparative period)	Actual rates (or appropriate average for comparative period)
Exchange differences	Separate component of equity	Separate component of equity
Hyperinflationary functional currency		
Assets/liabilities		
– current period	Closing rate (current B/S date)	Closing rate (current B/S date)
– comparative period	Closing rate (comparative B/S date)	Closing rate (current B/S date)
Equity items		
– current period	Closing rate (current B/S date)	Closing rate (current B/S date)
– comparative period	Closing rate (comparative B/S date)	Closing rate (current B/S date)
Income/expenses (including those recognised in other comprehensive income)		
– current period	Closing rate (current B/S date)	Closing rate (current B/S date)
– comparative period	Closing rate (comparative B/S date)	Closing rate (current B/S date)
Exchange differences	Not specified	Not applicable

6.1.1 Functional currency is not that of a hyperinflationary economy

The results and financial position of an entity whose functional currency is not the currency of a hyperinflationary economy should be translated into a different presentation currency using the following procedures: *[IAS 21.39]*

(a) assets and liabilities for each statement of financial position presented (i.e. including comparatives) are translated at the closing rate at the reporting date;

(b) income and expenses for each statement of comprehensive income or separate income statement presented (i.e. including comparatives) are translated at exchange rates at the dates of the transactions; and

(c) all resulting exchange differences are recognised in other comprehensive income.

For practical reasons, the reporting entity may use a rate that approximates the actual exchange rate, e.g. an average rate for the period, to translate income and expense items. However, if exchange rates fluctuate significantly, the use of the average rate for a period is inappropriate. *[IAS 21.40]*.

As discussed at 5.1.2 above, IFRIC 22 explains how to determine the 'date of transaction' for the purposes of an entity recording a foreign currency transaction in its functional currency, particularly when payments are made or received in advance of the associated transaction occurring. However, in our view, this guidance does not apply to the translation of an entity's results into a presentation currency; instead the date of transaction for this purpose is the date on which income or expense is recorded in profit or loss or other comprehensive income of the foreign operation.

A foreign operation may have reclassification adjustments to profit or loss of gains or losses previously recognised in other comprehensive income, for example as a result of the application of cash flow hedge accounting. However, IAS 21 does not explicitly address how these adjustments should be translated into the presentation currency. In our experience the most commonly applied approach is to regard them as income or expenses of the foreign operation to be translated at the exchange rate at the date of reclassification in accordance with paragraph 39(b). For cash flow hedges, this better reflects the hedge accounting reported in the foreign operation's own financial statements. Nevertheless, some would argue that reclassification adjustments do not represent income or expenses. Consequently, paragraph 39(b) would not apply and the reclassification is translated using the historical exchange rates at the dates the original gains or losses arose. In our view, each of these approaches represents an acceptable accounting policy choice.

The translational process above makes only limited reference to the translation of equity items, although the selection of accounting policy for translating reclassification adjustments is likely to influence whether an entity translates the associated equity balance in order to prevent a residual amount being left within the reserve. The treatment of such items is discussed at 6.2 below.

IAS 21 indicates that the exchange differences referred to in item (c) above result from: *[IAS 21.41]*

- translating income and expenses at the exchange rates at the dates of the transactions and assets and liabilities at the closing rate. Such exchange differences arise both on income and expense items recognised in profit or loss and on those recognised in other comprehensive income; and
- translating the opening net assets at a closing rate that differs from the previous closing rate.

This is not in fact completely accurate since if the entity has had any transactions with equity holders that have resulted in a change in the net assets during the period there are likely to be further exchange differences that need to be recognised to the extent that the closing rate differs from the rate used to translate the transaction. This will particularly be the case where a parent has subscribed for further equity shares in a subsidiary.

The reason why these exchange differences are not recognised in profit or loss is because the changes in exchange rates have little or no direct effect on the present and future cash flows from operations. *[IAS 21.41]*.

The application of these procedures is illustrated in the following example.

Example 15.9: Translation of a non-hyperinflationary functional currency to a non-hyperinflationary presentation currency

An Australian entity owns 100% of the share capital of a foreign entity which was set up a number of years ago when the exchange rate was A$1=FC2. It is consolidating the financial statements of the subsidiary in its consolidated financial statements for the year ended 31 December 2018. The exchange rate at the year-end is A$1=FC4 (2017: A$1=FC3). For the purposes of illustration, it is assumed that exchange rates have not fluctuated significantly and the appropriate weighted average rate for the year was A$1=FC3.5, and that the currency of the foreign entity is not that of a hyperinflationary economy. The income statement of the subsidiary for that year and its statement of financial position at the beginning and end of the year in its functional currency and translated into Australian dollars are as follows:

Income statement

	FC	A$
Sales	35,000	10,000
Cost of sales	(33,190)	(9,483)
Depreciation	(500)	(143)
Interest	(350)	(100)
Profit before taxation	960	274
Taxation	(460)	(131)
Profit after taxation	500	143

Statements of financial position	2017 FC	2018 FC	2017 A$	2018 A$
Property, plant and equipment	6,000	5,500	2,000	1,375
Current assets				
Inventories	2,700	3,000	900	750
Receivables	4,800	4,000	1,600	1,000
Cash	200	600	67	150
	7,700	7,600	2,567	1,900
Current liabilities				
Payables	4,530	3,840	1,510	960
Taxation	870	460	290	115
	5,400	4,300	1,800	1,075
Net current assets	2,300	3,300	767	825
	8,300	8,800	2,767	2,200
Long-term loans	3,600	3,600	1,200	900
	4,700	5,200	1,567	1,300
Share capital	1,000	1,000	500	500
Retained profits*	3,700	4,200	1,500	1,643
Exchange reserve*			(433)	(843)
	4,700	5,200	1,567	1,300

* The opening balances for 2017 in A$ have been assumed and represent cumulative amounts since the foreign entity was set up.

The movement of A$(410) in the exchange reserve included as a separate component of equity is made up as follows:

(i) the exchange loss of A$392 on the opening net investment in the subsidiary, calculated as follows:

Opening net assets at opening rate	– FC4,700 at FC3 = A$1 =	A$1,567
Opening net assets at closing rate	– FC4,700 at FC4 = A$1 =	A$1,175
Exchange loss on net assets		A$392

(ii) the exchange loss of A$18, being the difference between the income account translated at an average rate, i.e. A$143, and at the closing rate, i.e. A$125.

When the exchange differences relate to a foreign operation that is consolidated but not wholly-owned, accumulated exchange differences arising from translation and attributable to non-controlling interests are allocated to, and recognised as part of, non-controlling interests in the consolidated statement of financial position. *[IAS 21.41]*.

An example of an accounting policy dealing with the translation of entities whose functional currency is not that of a hyperinflationary economy is illustrated in the following extract.

Extract 15.2: Lloyds Banking Group plc (2015)

Notes to the consolidated financial statements [extract]

Note 2 Accounting policies [extract]

(O) Foreign currency translation

Items included in the financial statements of each of the Group's entities are measured using the currency of the primary economic environment in which the entity operates (the functional currency). The consolidated financial statements are presented in sterling, which is the Company's functional and presentation currency.

Foreign currency transactions are translated into the appropriate functional currency using the exchange rates prevailing at the dates of the transactions. Foreign exchange gains and losses resulting from the settlement of such transactions and from the translation at year end exchange rates of monetary assets and liabilities denominated in foreign currencies are recognised in the income statement, except when recognised in other comprehensive income as qualifying cash flow or net investment hedges. Non-monetary assets that are measured at fair value are translated using the exchange rate at the date that the fair value was determined. Translation differences on equities and similar non-monetary items held at fair value through profit and loss are recognised in profit or loss as part of the fair value gain or loss. Translation differences on available-for-sale non-monetary financial assets, such as equity shares, are included in the fair value reserve in equity unless the asset is a hedged item in a fair value hedge.

The results and financial position of all group entities that have a functional currency different from the presentation currency are translated into the presentation currency as follows:

- The assets and liabilities of foreign operations, including goodwill and fair value adjustments arising on the acquisition of a foreign entity, are translated into sterling at foreign exchange rates ruling at the balance sheet date.
- The income and expenses of foreign operations are translated into sterling at average exchange rates unless these do not approximate to the foreign exchange rates ruling at the dates of the transactions in which case income and expenses are translated at the dates of the transactions.

Foreign exchange differences arising on the translation of a foreign operation are recognised in other comprehensive income and accumulated in a separate component of equity together with exchange differences arising from the translation of borrowings and other currency instruments designated as hedges of such investments (see (F)(3) above). On disposal or liquidation of a foreign operation, the cumulative amount of exchange differences relating to that foreign operation are reclassified from equity and included in determining the profit or loss arising on disposal or liquidation.

The IASB had considered an alternative translation method, which would have been to translate all amounts (including comparatives) at the most recent closing rate. This was considered to have several advantages: it is simple to apply; it does not generate any new gains and losses; and it does not change ratios such as return on assets. Supporters of this method believed that the process of merely expressing amounts in a different currency should preserve the same relationships among amounts as measured in the functional currency. *[IAS 21.BC17]*. These views were probably based more on the IASB's proposals for allowing an entity to present its financial statements in a currency other than its functional currency, rather than the translation of foreign operations for inclusion in consolidated financial statements. Such an approach does have theoretical appeal. However, the major drawback is that it would require the comparatives to be restated from those previously reported.

The IASB rejected this alternative and decided to require the method that the previous version of IAS 21 required for translating the financial statements of a foreign operation. *[IAS 21.BC20]*. It is asserted that this method results in the same amounts in the presentation currency regardless of whether the financial statements of a foreign operation are first translated into the functional currency of another group entity and then into the presentation currency or translated directly into the presentation currency. *[IAS 21.BC18]*. We agree that it will result in the same amounts for the statement of financial position, regardless of whether the translation process is a single or two-stage process. However, it does not necessarily hold true for income and expense items particularly if an indirectly held foreign operation is disposed of – this is discussed further at 6.1.5 and 6.6.3 below. Differences will also arise between the two methods if an average rate is used, although these are likely to be insignificant.

The IASB states that the method chosen avoids the need to decide the currency in which to express the financial statements of a multinational group before they are translated into the presentation currency. In addition, it produces the same amounts in the presentation currency for a stand-alone entity as for an identical subsidiary of a parent whose functional currency is the presentation currency. *[IAS 21.BC19]*. For example, if a Swiss entity with the Swiss franc as its functional currency wishes to present its financial statements in euros, the translated amounts in euros should be the same as those for an identical entity with the Swiss franc as its functional currency that are included within the consolidated financial statements of its parent that presents its financial statements in euros.

6.1.2 *Functional currency is that of a hyperinflationary economy*

The results and financial position of an entity whose functional currency is the currency of a hyperinflationary economy should be translated into a different presentation currency using the following procedures: *[IAS 21.42]*

(a) all amounts (i.e. assets, liabilities, equity items, income and expenses, including comparatives) are translated at the closing rate at the date of the most recent statement of financial position, except that

(b) when amounts are translated into the currency of a non-hyperinflationary economy, comparative amounts are those that were presented as current year amounts in the relevant prior year financial statements (i.e. not adjusted for subsequent changes in the price level or subsequent changes in exchange rates). Similarly, in the period during which the functional currency of a foreign operation such as a subsidiary becomes hyperinflationary and applies IAS 29 for the first time, the parent's consolidated financial statement for the comparative period should not in our view be restated for the effects of hyperinflation.

When an entity's functional currency is the currency of a hyperinflationary economy, the entity should restate its financial statements in accordance with IAS 29 before applying the translation method set out above, except for comparative amounts that are translated into a currency of a non-hyperinflationary economy (see (b) above). *[IAS 21.43]*.

When the economy ceases to be hyperinflationary and the entity no longer restates its financial statements in accordance with IAS 29, it should use as the historical costs for translation into the presentation currency the amounts restated to the price level at the date the entity ceased restating its financial statements. *[IAS 21.43]*.

Example 15.10: Translation of a hyperinflationary functional currency to a non-hyperinflationary presentation currency

Using the same basic facts as Example 15.9 above, but assuming that the functional currency of the subsidiary is that of a hyperinflationary economy, the income statement of the subsidiary for that year and its statement of financial position at the beginning and end of the year in its functional currency and translated into Australian dollars are as shown below. For the purposes of illustration, any adjustments resulting from the restatement in accordance with IAS 29 have been ignored. See Chapter 16 for a discussion of such adjustments.

Income statement	FC	A$
Sales	35,000	8,750
Cost of sales	(33,190)	(8,298)
Depreciation	(500)	(125)
Interest	(350)	(87)
Profit before taxation	960	240
Taxation	(460)	(115)
Profit after taxation	500	125

Statements of financial position	2017 FC	2018 FC	2017 A$	2018 A$
Property, plant and equipment	6,000	5,500	2,000	1,375
Current assets				
Inventories	2,700	3,000	900	750
Receivables	4,800	4,000	1,600	1,000
Cash	200	600	67	150
	7,700	7,600	2,567	1,900
Current liabilities				
Payables	4,530	3,840	1,510	960
Taxation	870	460	290	115
	5,400	4,300	1,800	1,075
Net current assets	2,300	3,300	767	825
	8,300	8,800	2,767	2,200
Long-term loans	3,600	3,600	1,200	900
	4,700	5,200	1,567	1,300

Statements of financial position (cont.)	2017 FC	2018 FC	2017 A$	2018 A$
Share capital	1,000	1,000	333	250
Retained profits*	3,700	4,200	1,234	1,050
	4,700	5,200	1,567	1,300

*The movement in retained profits is as follows:

	A$
Balance brought forward	1,234
Profit for year	125
Exchange difference	(309)
	1,050

The exchange loss of A$309 represents the reduction in retained profits due the movements in exchange, calculated as follows:

Opening balance at opening rate	– FC3,700 at FC3 = A$1 =	A$1,234
Opening balance at closing rate	– FC3,700 at FC4 = A$1 =	A$925
Exchange loss		A$(309)

Chapter 15

It is unclear what should happen to such an exchange difference (and also the movement in share capital caused by the change in exchange rates) since paragraph 42 of IAS 21 makes no reference to any possible exchange differences arising from this process. However, in the absence of any requirement to recognise them in other comprehensive income (as in Example 15.9 above) or to profit or loss, it would seem that they are to be included as movements in the equity balances to which they relate.

An example of an accounting policy dealing with the translation of entities whose functional currency is that of a hyperinflationary economy is illustrated in the following extract.

Extract 15.3: Sberbank of Russia (2015)

Notes to the Consolidated Financial Statements – 31 December 2015 [extract]

3 **Basis of Preparation and Significant Accounting Policies** [extract]

Foreign currency translation. The functional currency of each of the Group's consolidated entities is the currency of the primary economic environment in which the entity operates. The Bank's functional currency and the Group's presentation currency is the national currency of the Russian Federation, Russian Rouble ("RR").

Monetary assets and liabilities are translated into each entity's functional currency at the applicable exchange rate at the respective reporting dates. Foreign exchange gains and losses resulting from the settlement of the transactions performed by the companies of the Group and from the translation of monetary assets and liabilities into each entity's functional currency are recognized in profit or loss. Effects of exchange rate changes on the fair value of equity instruments are recorded as part of the fair value gain or loss.

The results and financial position of each group entity (except for the subsidiary bank in Belarus the economy of which was considered hyperinflationary before 2015) are translated into the presentation currency as follows:

(I) assets and liabilities for each statement of financial position presented are translated at the applicable closing rate at the respective reporting date;

(II) income and expenses for each statement of profit or loss and statement of other comprehensive income are translated either at the rates prevailing at the dates of the transactions or at average exchange rates (in case this average is a reasonable approximation of the cumulative effect of the rates prevailing on the transaction dates).

The results and financial position of an entity whose functional currency is the currency of a hyperinflationary economy shall be translated into a different presentation currency using the following procedure: all amounts (i.e. assets, liabilities, equity items, income and expenses, including comparatives) shall be translated at the closing rate at the date of the most recent statement of financial position.

When amounts are translated into the currency of a non-hyperinflationary economy, comparative amounts shall be those that were presented as current year amounts in the relevant prior year financial statements (i.e. not adjusted for subsequent changes in the price level or subsequent changes in exchange rates).

Exchange differences arising on the translation of results and financial position of each of the Group's consolidated entities are included in Net foreign currency translation effect in other comprehensive income and taken to a separate component of equity – Foreign currency translation reserve.

6.1.3 Dual rates, suspension of rates and longer-term restrictions on exchangeability

The problems of dual rates and suspension of rates in relation to the translation of foreign currency transactions and balances into an entity's functional currency and the related requirements of IAS 21 dealing with such issues have already been discussed in 5.1.4 and 5.1.5 above. However, the standard makes no reference to them in the context of translating the results and financial position of an entity into a different presentation currency, particularly where the results and financial position of a foreign operation are being translated for inclusion in the financial statements of the reporting entity by consolidation or the equity method.

Where the problem is one of a temporary suspension of rates, the predominant practice noted by the Interpretations Committee is for the requirement in IAS 21 relating to transactions and balances to be followed; i.e. by using 'the first subsequent rate at which exchanges could be made'. In this context the rate will be the one at which future cash flows could be settled when viewing the net investment as a whole.[6] This approach is broadly consistent with US GAAP which states that the rate to be used to translate foreign financial statements should be, in the absence of unusual circumstances, the rate applicable to dividend remittance.

The standard does not address the situation where there is a longer-term lack of exchangeability. In these circumstances the discussion at 5.1.5 above, including the Interpretations Committee's consideration of this issue in the context of the Venezuelan currency, will be relevant. Determining the appropriate exchange rate(s) to use will require the application of judgement. The rate(s) selected will depend on the entity's individual facts and circumstances, particularly its legal ability to convert currency or to settle transactions using a specific rate and its intent to use a particular mechanism, including whether the rate available through that mechanism is published or readily determinable. The disclosure requirements highlighted by the committee and covered at 10.4 below will also be relevant in these circumstances.

6.1.4 Calculation of average rate

When translating the results of an entity whose functional currency is not that of a hyperinflationary economy, for practical reasons, the reporting entity may use a rate that approximates the actual exchange rate, e.g. an average rate for the period, to translate income and expense items. *[IAS 21.40].*

The standard does not give any guidance on the factors that should be taken into account in determining what may be an appropriate average rate for the period – it merely says that 'if exchange rates fluctuate significantly, the use of the average rate for the period is inappropriate'. *[IAS 21.40].* What methods are, therefore, available to entities to use in calculating an appropriate average rate? Possible methods might be:

(a) mid-year rate;

(b) average of opening and closing rates;

(c) average of month end/quarter end rates;

(d) average of monthly average rates;

(e) monthly/quarterly results at month end/quarter end rates; or

(f) monthly/quarterly results at monthly/quarterly averages.

Example 15.11: Calculation of average rate

A Spanish entity has a foreign subsidiary and is preparing its consolidated financial statements for the year ended 30 April 2018. It intends to use an average rate for translating the results of the subsidiary. The relevant exchange rates for €1=FC are as follows:

Month	Month end	Average for month	Average for quarter	Average for year
April 2017	1.67			
May 2017	1.63	1.67		
June 2017	1.67	1.64		
July 2017	1.64	1.65	1.65	
August 2017	1.67	1.64		
September 2017	1.70	1.63		
October 2017	1.67	1.68	1.65	
November 2017	1.65	1.70		
December 2017	1.66	1.66		
January 2018	1.64	1.67	1.68	
February 2018	1.60	1.65		
March 2018	1.61	1.63		
April 2018	1.61	1.62	1.63	1.65

Average of month end rates – 1.65

Average of quarter end rates – 1.64

The results of the subsidiary for each of the 12 months to 30 April 2018 and the translation thereof under each of the above methods (using monthly figures where appropriate) are shown below:

Method (a)	FC31,050 @ 1.67 = €18,593
Method (b)	FC31,050 @ 1.64 = €18,933
Method (c) – monthly	FC31,050 @ 1.65 = €18,818
Method (c) – quarterly	FC31,050 @ 1.64 = €18,933
Method (d)	FC31,050 @ 1.65 = €18,818

Month	FC	(e) quarterly €	(e) monthly €	(f) quarterly €	(f) monthly €
May 2017	1,000		613		599
June 2017	1,100		659		671
July 2017	1,200	2,012	732	2,000	727
August 2017	1,300		778		793
September 2017	1,300		765		798
October 2017	1,350	2,365	808	2,394	804
November 2017	1,400		848		824
December 2017	1,400		843		843
January 2018	2,000	2,927	1,220	2,857	1,198
February 2018	5,000		3,125		3,030
March 2018	10,000		6,211		6,135
April 2018	4,000	11,801	2,484	11,656	2,469
Total	31,050	19,105	19,086	18,907	18,891

It can be seen that by far the simplest methods to use are the methods (a) to (d).

In our view methods (a) and (b) should not normally be used as it is unlikely in times of volatile exchange rates that they will give appropriate weighting to the exchange rates which have been in existence throughout the period in question. They are only likely to give an acceptable answer if the exchange rate has been static or steadily increasing or decreasing throughout the period.

Method (c) based on quarter end rates has similar drawbacks and therefore should not normally be used.

Method (c) based on month end rates and method (d) are better than the previous methods as they do take into account more exchange rates which have applied throughout the year, with method (d) being more precise, as this will have taken account of daily exchange rates. Average monthly rates for most major currencies are likely to be given in publications issued by the government, banks and other sources and therefore it is unnecessary for entities to calculate their own. The work involved in calculating an average for the year, therefore, is not very onerous. Method (d) will normally give reasonable and acceptable results when there are no seasonal variations in items of income and expenditure.

Where there are seasonal variations in items of income and expenditure, using a single average rate for the entire reporting period is unlikely to result in a reasonable approximation of applying actual rates. In these situations appropriate exchange rates should be applied to the appropriate items. This can be done by using either of methods (e) or (f) preferably using figures and rates for each month. Where such a method is being used care should be taken to ensure that the periodic accounts are accurate and that cut-off procedures have been adequate, otherwise significant items may be translated at the wrong average rate.

Where there are significant one-off items of income and expenses then it is likely that actual rates at the date of the transaction will need to be used to translate such items.

6.1.5 Accounting for foreign operations where sub-groups exist

A reporting entity comprising a group with intermediate holding companies may adopt either the direct or the step-by-step method of consolidation. The direct method involves the financial statements of foreign operations being translated directly into the presentation currency of the ultimate parent. The step-by-step method involves the financial statements of the foreign operation first being translated into the functional currency of any intermediate parent(s) and then into the presentation currency of the ultimate parent. *[IFRIC 16.17]*.

It is asserted that both methods will result in the same amounts being reported in the presentation currency. *[IAS 21.BC18]*. However, as set out at 6.6.3 below, particularly in Example 15.19, and as acknowledged by the Interpretations Committee,[7] this assertion is demonstrably untrue in certain situations.

Whilst the various requirements of the standard appear to indicate that the direct method should be used and the Interpretations Committee has indicated it is the conceptually correct method,[8] IAS 21 does not require an entity to use the direct method or to make adjustments to produce the same result. Rather, an entity has an accounting policy choice as to which of the two methods it should use and the method selected should be used consistently for all net investments. *[IFRIC 16.17]*.

6.2 Translation of equity items

The method of translation of the results and financial position of an entity whose functional currency is not the currency of a hyperinflationary economy is discussed at 6.1.1 above. The translation process makes only limited reference to the translation of equity items. The exposure draft that preceded the standard had proposed that '... equity items other than those resulting from income and expense recognised in the period ... shall be translated at the closing rate'. However, the IASB decided not to specify in the standard the translation rate for equity items,[9] but no explanation has been given in the Basis for Conclusions about this matter.

So how should entities deal with the translation of equity items?

6.2.1 Share capital

Where an entity presents its financial statements in a currency other than its functional currency, it would seem more appropriate that its share capital (whether they are ordinary shares, or are otherwise irredeemable and classified as equity instruments) should be translated at historical rates of exchange. Such capital items are included within the examples of non-monetary items listed in US GAAP as accounts to be remeasured using historical exchange rates when the temporal method is being applied (see 5.4.3 above). IAS 21 requires non-monetary items that are measured at historical cost in a foreign currency to be translated using the historical rate (see 5.2 above). Translation at an historical rate would imply using the rate ruling at the date of the issue of the shares. However, where a subsidiary is presenting its financial statements in the currency of its parent, it may be that the more appropriate historical rate for share capital that was in issue at the date it became a subsidiary would be that ruling at the date it became a subsidiary of the parent, rather than at earlier dates of issue.

Where such share capital is retranslated at the closing rate, we do not believe that it is appropriate for the exchange differences to be recognised in other comprehensive income nor for them to be taken to the separate component of equity required by IAS 21 (since to do so could result in them being reclassified from equity to profit or loss upon disposal of part of the entity's operations in the future), but should either be taken to retained earnings or some other reserve. Consequently, whether such share capital is maintained at a historical rate, or is dealt with in this way, the treatment has no impact on the overall equity of the entity.

6.2.2 Other equity balances resulting from transactions with equity holders

In addition to share capital, an entity may have other equity balances resulting from the issue of shares, such as a share premium account (additional paid-in capital). Like share capital, the translation of such balances could be done at either historical rates or at the closing rate. However, we believe that whichever method is adopted it should be consistent with the treatment used for share capital. Again, where exchange differences arise through using the closing rate, we believe that it is not appropriate for them to be recognised in other comprehensive income or taken to the separate component of equity required by IAS 21.

A similar approach should be adopted where an entity has acquired its own equity shares and has deducted those 'treasury shares' from equity as required by IAS 32 (see Chapter 45 at 9).

6.2.3 *Other equity balances resulting from income and expenses being recognised in other comprehensive income*

Under IAS 21, income and expenses recognised in other comprehensive income are translated at the exchange rates ruling at the dates of the transaction. *[IAS 21.39(b), 41]*. Examples of such items include certain gains and losses on:

- revalued property, plant and equipment under IAS 16 (see Chapter 18 at 6.2) and revalued intangible assets under IAS 38 – *Intangible Assets* (see Chapter 17 at 8.2);
- available-for-sale financial assets under IAS 39 (see Chapter 49 at 2.4);
- debt instruments measured at fair value through other comprehensive income, investments in equity instruments designated at fair value through other comprehensive income and financial liabilities designated at fair value through profit or loss under IFRS 9 (see Chapter 50 at 2.3, 2.2 and 2.1 respectively);
- gains and losses on cash flow hedges under IAS 39 or IFRS 9 (see Chapter 52 at 4.2.1 or Chapter 53); and
- any amounts of current and deferred tax recognised in other comprehensive income under IAS 12 (see Chapter 31 at 10).

This would suggest that where these gains and losses are accumulated within a separate reserve or component of equity, then any period-end balance should represent the cumulative translated amounts of such gains and losses. However, as IAS 21 is silent on the matter it would seem that it would be acceptable to translate these equity balances at the closing rate.

The treatment of equity balances that are subsequently reclassified to profit or loss, for example cash flow hedge reserves of a foreign operation, typically depends on the exchange rate used to translate the reclassification adjustments (a topic which is discussed at 6.1.1 above). Where reclassification adjustments are translated using the exchange rate at the date of reclassification, translating the equity balance at closing rate should mean no residual balance is left in the reserve once the hedge accounting is completely accounted for. Conversely, where reclassification adjustments are translated using exchange rates at the dates the original gains or losses arose, an entity would avoid a residual balance remaining in the reserve by not retranslating the equity balance.

Any exchange differences arising on retranslating an equity reserve are not taken to the separate component of equity required by IAS 21. The differences would be taken to retained earnings or some other reserve, effectively as a transfer between the reserves. Consequently, whether such balances are maintained at the original translated rates, or are translated at closing rates, the treatment has no impact on the overall equity of the entity.

6.3 Exchange differences on intragroup balances

The incorporation of the results and financial position of a foreign operation with those of the reporting entity should follow normal consolidation procedures, such as the elimination of intragroup balances and intragroup transactions of a subsidiary. *[IAS 21.45]*. On this basis, there is a tendency sometimes to assume that exchange differences on intragroup balances should not impact on the reported profit or loss for the group in the consolidated financial statements. However, an intragroup monetary asset (or liability), whether short-term or long-term, cannot be eliminated against the corresponding intragroup liability (or asset) without the entity with the currency exposure recognising an exchange difference on the intragroup balance.

This exchange difference will be reflected in that entity's profit or loss for the period (see 5.3.1 above) and, except as indicated below, IAS 21 requires this exchange difference to continue to be included in profit or loss in the consolidated financial statements. This is because the monetary item represents a commitment to convert one currency into another and exposes the reporting entity to a gain or loss through currency fluctuations.

6.3.1 Monetary items included as part of the net investment in a foreign operation – general

As an exception to the general rule at 6.3 above, where an exchange difference arises on an intragroup balance that, in substance, forms part of an entity's net investment in a foreign operation, then the exchange difference is not to be recognised in profit or loss in the consolidated financial statements, but is recognised in other comprehensive income and accumulated in a separate component of equity until the disposal of the foreign operation (see 6.6 below). *[IAS 21.32, 45].*

The 'net investment in a foreign operation' is defined as being 'the amount of the reporting entity's interest in the net assets of that operation'. *[IAS 21.8].* This will include a monetary item that is receivable from or payable to a foreign operation for which settlement is neither planned nor likely to occur in the foreseeable future (often referred to as a 'permanent as equity' loan) because it is, in substance, a part of the entity's net investment in that foreign operation. Such monetary items may include long-term receivables or loans. They do not include trade receivables or trade payables. *[IAS 21.15].*

In our view, trade receivables and payables can be included as part of the net investment in the foreign operation, but only if cash settlement is not made or planned to be made in the foreseeable future. However, if a subsidiary makes payment for purchases from its parent, but is continually indebted to the parent as a result of new purchases, then in these circumstances, since individual transactions are settled, no part of the inter-company balance should be regarded as part of the net investment in the subsidiary. Accordingly, exchange differences on such balances should be recognised in profit or loss.

These requirements are illustrated in the following example.

Example 15.12: Receivables/payables included as part of net investment in a foreign operation

A UK entity, A, has a Belgian subsidiary, B. A has a receivable due from B amounting to £1,000,000.

In each of the following scenarios, could the receivable be included as part of A's net investment in B?

Scenario 1

The receivable arises from the sale of goods, together with interest payments and dividend payments which have not been paid in cash but have been accumulated in the inter-company account. A and B agree that A can claim at any time the repayment of this receivable. It is likely that there will be a settlement of the receivable in the foreseeable future.

Although the standard states that trade receivables and payables are not included, we do not believe that it necessarily precludes deferred trading balances from being included. In our view, such balances can be included as part of the net investment in the foreign operation, but only if cash settlement is not made or planned to be made in the foreseeable future.

In this scenario, the settlement of A's receivable due from B is not planned; however, it is likely that a settlement will occur in the foreseeable future. Accordingly, the receivable does not qualify to be treated as part of A's net investment in B. The term 'foreseeable future' is not defined and no specific time period is implied. It could be argued that the receivable should only be considered as part of the net investment if it will be repaid only when the reporting entity disinvests from the foreign operation. However, it is recognised that in most circumstances this would be unrealistic and therefore a shorter time span should be considered in determining the foreseeable future.

Scenario 2

The receivable represents a loan made by A to B and it is agreed that the receivable will be repaid in 20 years.

In this scenario, A's receivable due from B has a specified term for repayment. This suggests that settlement is planned. Accordingly, the receivable does not qualify to be treated as part of A's investment in B.

Scenario 3

A and B have previously agreed that the receivable under scenario 2 will be repaid in 20 years but A now decides that it will replace the loan on maturity either with a further inter-company loan or with an injection of equity. This approach is consistent with A's intention to maintain the strategic long-term investment in B.

In this scenario, the words from paragraph 15 of IAS 21 '... settlement is neither planned nor likely to occur in the foreseeable future ...' are potentially problematic, since a loan with a fixed maturity must, *prima facie*, have a planned settlement. However, from the date A decides that it will re-finance the inter-company debt upon maturity with a further long-term instrument, or replace it with equity, the substance of the inter-company loan is that it is part of the entity's net investment in the foreign operation, and there is no actual 'intent' to settle the investment without replacement. On this basis, loans with a stated maturity may qualify to be treated in accordance with paragraph 32 of IAS 21, with foreign currency gains and losses recognised in other comprehensive income and accumulated in a separate component of equity in the consolidated financial statements. However, in our view, management's intention to refinance the loan must be documented appropriately, for example in the form of a minute of a meeting of the management board or board of directors. In addition, there should not be any established historical pattern of the entity demanding repayment of such inter-company debt without replacement.

Consequently, when the purpose of the loan is to fund a long-term strategic investment then it is the entity's overall intention with regard to the investment and ultimate funding thereof, rather than the specific terms of the inter-company loan funding the investment, that should be considered.

Scenario 4

The receivable arises from the sale of goods, together with interest payments and dividend payments which have not been paid in cash but have been accumulated in the inter-company account. However, in this scenario, A and B agree that A can claim the repayment of this receivable only in the event that the subsidiary is disposed of. A has no plans to dispose of entity B.

In this scenario, the settlement of A's receivable due from B is not planned nor is it likely to occur in the foreseeable future. Although the term 'foreseeable future' is not defined, it will not go beyond a point of time after the disposal of a foreign operation. Accordingly, the receivable does qualify for being treated as part of a net investment in a foreign operation.

The question of whether or not a monetary item is as permanent as equity can, in certain circumstances, require the application of significant judgement.

6.3.2 Monetary items included as part of the net investment in a foreign operation – currency of the monetary item

When a monetary item is considered to form part of a reporting entity's net investment in a foreign operation and is denominated in the functional currency of the reporting entity, an exchange difference will be recognised in profit or loss for the period when it arises in the foreign operation's individual financial statements. If the item is denominated in the functional currency of the foreign operation, an exchange difference will be recognised in profit or loss for the period when it arises in the reporting entity's separate financial statements. Such exchange differences are only recognised in other comprehensive income and accumulated in a separate component of equity in the financial statements that include the foreign operation and the reporting entity (i.e. financial statements in which the foreign operation is consolidated or accounted for using the equity method). *[IAS 21.32, 33]*.

Example 15.13: Monetary item in functional currency of either the reporting entity or the foreign operation

A UK entity has a Belgian subsidiary. On the last day of its financial year, 31 March 2017, the UK entity lends the subsidiary £1,000,000. Settlement of the loan is neither planned nor likely to occur in the foreseeable future, so the UK entity regards the loan as part of its net investment in the Belgian subsidiary. The exchange rate at 31 March 2017 was £1=€1.40. Since the loan was made on the last day of the year there are no exchange differences to recognise for that year. At 31 March 2018, the loan has not been repaid and is still regarded as part of the net investment in the Belgian subsidiary. The relevant exchange rate at that date was £1=€1.50. The average exchange rate for the year ended 31 March 2018 was £1=€1.45.

In the UK entity's separate financial statements no exchange difference is recognised since the loan is denominated in its functional currency of pound sterling. In the Belgian subsidiary's financial statements, the liability to the parent is translated into the subsidiary's functional currency of euros at the closing rate at €1,500,000, giving rise to an exchange loss of €100,000, i.e. €1,500,000 less €1,400,000 (£1,000,000 @ £1=€1.40). This exchange loss is reflected in the Belgian subsidiary's profit or loss for that year. In the UK entity's consolidated financial statements, this exchange loss included in the subsidiary's profit or loss for the year will be translated at the average rate for the year, giving rise to a loss of £68,966 (€100,000@ £1=€1.45). This will be recognised in other comprehensive income and accumulated in the separate component of equity together with an exchange gain of £2,299, being the difference between the amount included in the Belgian subsidiary's income statement translated at average rate, i.e. £68,966, and at the closing rate, i.e. £66,667 (€100,000@ £1=€1.50). The overall exchange loss recognised in other comprehensive income is £66,667. This represents the exchange loss on the increased net investment of €1,400,000 in the subsidiary made at 31 March 2017, i.e. £1,000,000 (€1,400,000 @ £1=€1.40) less £933,333 (€1,400,000 @ £1=€1.50).

If, on the other hand, the loan made to the Belgian subsidiary had been denominated in the equivalent amount of euros at 31 March 2017, i.e. €1,400,000, the treatment would have been as follows:

In the UK entity's separate financial statements, the amount receivable from the Belgian subsidiary would be translated at the closing rate at £933,333 (€1,400,000 @ £1=€1.50), giving rise to an exchange loss of £66,667, i.e. £1,000,000 (€1,400,000 @ £1=€1.40) less £933,333, which is included in its profit or loss for the year. In the Belgian subsidiary's financial statements, no exchange difference is recognised since the loan is denominated in its functional currency of euros. In the UK entity's consolidated financial statements, the exchange loss included in its profit or loss for the year in its separate financial statements will be recognised in other comprehensive income and accumulated in the separate component of equity. As before, this represents the exchange loss on the increased net investment of €1,400,000 in the subsidiary made at 31 March 2017, i.e. £1,000,000 (€1,400,000 @ £1=€1.40) less £933,333 (€1,400,000 @ £1=€1.40).

In most situations, intragroup balances for which settlement is neither planned nor likely to occur in the foreseeable future will be denominated in the functional currency of either the reporting entity or the foreign operation. However, this will not always be the case. If a monetary item is denominated in a currency other than the functional currency of either the reporting entity or the foreign operation, the exchange difference arising in the reporting entity's separate financial statements and in the foreign operation's individual financial statements are also recognised in other comprehensive income and accumulated in the separate component of equity in the financial statements that include the foreign operation and the reporting entity (i.e. financial statements in which the foreign operation is consolidated or accounted for using the equity method). *[IAS 21.33]*.

6.3.3 *Monetary items included as part of the net investment in a foreign operation – treatment in the individual financial statements*

The exception for exchange differences on monetary items forming part of the net investment in a foreign operation applies only in the financial statements that include the foreign operation (for example consolidated financial statements when the foreign operation is a subsidiary). In the individual financial statements of the entity (or entities) with the currency exposure the exchange differences have to be reflected in that entity's profit or loss for the period.

6.3.4 *Monetary items transacted by other members of the group*

As illustrated in the examples above, the requirements of IAS 21 whereby exchange differences on a monetary item that forms part of the net investment in a foreign operation are recognised in other comprehensive income clearly apply where the monetary item is transacted between the parent preparing the consolidated financial statements and the subsidiary that is the foreign operation. However, loans from any entity (and in any currency) qualify for net investment treatment, so long as the conditions of paragraph 15 are met. *[IAS 21.15A]*.

6.3.5 *Monetary items becoming part of the net investment in a foreign operation*

An entity's plans and expectations in respect of an intragroup monetary item may change over time and the status of such items should be assessed each period. For example, a parent may decide that its subsidiary requires refinancing and instead of investing more equity capital in the subsidiary decides that an existing inter-company account, which has previously been regarded as a normal monetary item, should become a long-term deferred trading balance and no repayment of such amount will be requested within the foreseeable future. In our view, such a 'capital injection' should be regarded as having occurred at the time it is decided to redesignate the inter-company account. Consequently, the exchange differences arising on the account up to that date should be recognised in profit or loss and the exchange differences arising thereafter would be recognised in other comprehensive income on consolidation. This is discussed further in the following example.

Example 15.14: Monetary item becoming part of the net investment in a foreign operation

A UK entity has a wholly owned Canadian subsidiary whose net assets at 31 December 2017 were C$2,000,000. These net assets were arrived at after taking account of a liability to the UK parent of £250,000. Using the closing exchange rate of £1=C$2.35 this liability was included in the Canadian company's statement of financial position at that date at C$587,500. On 30 June 2018, when the exchange rate was £1=C$2.45, the parent decided that in order to refinance the Canadian subsidiary it would regard the liability of £250,000 as a long-term liability which would not be called for repayment in the foreseeable future. Consequently, the parent thereafter regarded the loan as being part of its net investment in the subsidiary. In the year ended 31 December 2018 the Canadian company made no profit or loss other than any exchange difference to be recognised on its liability to its parent. The relevant exchange rate at that date was £1=C$2.56. The average exchange rate for the year ended 31 December 2018 was £1=C$2.50.

The financial statements of the subsidiary in C$ and translated using the closing rate are as follows:

Statement of financial position	31 December 2018		31 December 2017	
	C$	£	C$	£
Assets	2,587,500	1,010,742	2,587,500	1,101,064
Amount due to parent	640,000	250,000	587,500	250,000
Net assets	1,947,500	760,742	2,000,000	851,064
Income statement				
Exchange difference	(52,500)			

If the amount due to the parent is not part of the parent's net investment in the foreign operation, this exchange loss would be translated at the average rate and included in the consolidated profit and loss account as £21,000. As the net investment was C$2,000,000 then there would have been an exchange loss recognised in other comprehensive income of £69,814, i.e. £851,064 less £781,250 (C$2,000,000 @ £1=C$2.56), together with an exchange gain of £492, being the difference between profit or loss translated at average rate, i.e. £21,000, and at the closing rate, i.e. £20,508.

However, the parent now regards the amount due as being part of the net investment in the subsidiary. The question then arises as to when this should be regarded as having happened and how the exchange difference on it should be calculated. No guidance is given in IAS 21.

In our view, the 'capital injection' should be regarded as having occurred at the time it is decided to redesignate the inter-company account. The exchange differences arising on the account up to that date should be recognised in profit or loss. Only the exchange difference arising thereafter would be recognised in other comprehensive income on consolidation. The inter-company account that was converted into a long-term loan becomes part of the entity's (UK parent's) net investment in the foreign operation (Canadian subsidiary) at the moment in time when the entity decides that settlement is neither planned nor likely to occur in the foreseeable future, i.e. 30 June 2018. Accordingly, exchange differences arising on the long-term loan are recognised in other comprehensive income and accumulated in a separate component of equity from that date. The same accounting treatment would have been applied if a capital injection had taken place at the date of redesignation.

At 30 June 2018 the subsidiary would have translated the inter-company account as C$612,500 (£250,000 @ £1=C$2.45) and therefore the exchange loss up to that date was C$25,000. Translated at the average rate this amount would be included in consolidated profit or loss as £10,000, with only an exchange gain of £234 recognised in other comprehensive income, being the difference between profit or loss translated at average rate, i.e. £10,000, and at the closing rate, i.e. £9,766. Accordingly, £11,000 (£21,000 less £10,000) offset by a reduction in the exchange gain on the translation of profit or loss of £258 (£492 less £234) would be recognised in other comprehensive income. This amount represents the exchange loss on the 'capital injection' of C$612,500. Translated at the closing rate this amounts to £239,258 which is £10,742 less than the original £250,000.

Some might argue that an approach of regarding the 'capital injection' as having occurred at the beginning of the accounting period would have the merit of treating all of the exchange differences for this year in the same way. However, for the reasons provided above we do not regard such an approach as being acceptable.

Suppose, instead of the inter-company account being £250,000, it was denominated in dollars at C$587,500. In this case the parent would be exposed to the exchange risk; what would be the position?

The subsidiary's net assets at both 31 December 2017 and 2018 would be:

Assets	C$2,587,500
Amount due to parent	C$587,500
Net assets	C$2,000,000

As the inter-company account is expressed in Canadian dollars, there will be no exchange difference thereon in the subsidiary's profit or loss.

There will, however, be an exchange loss in the parent as follows:

C$587,500	@ 2.35 =	£250,000
	@ 2.56 =	£229,492
		£20,508

Again, in the consolidated financial statements as the inter-company account is now regarded as part of the equity investment some of this amount should be recognised in other comprehensive income. For the reasons stated above, in our view it is only the exchange differences that have arisen after the date of redesignation, i.e. 30 June 2018,that should be recognised in other comprehensive income.

On this basis, the exchange loss would be split as follows:

C$587,500	@ 2.35 =	£250,000	
	@ 2.45 =	£239,796	
			£10,204
	@ 2.45 =	£239,796	
	@ 2.56 =	£229,492	
			£10,304

The exchange loss up to 30 June 2018 of £10,204 would be recognised in consolidated profit or loss and the exchange loss thereafter of £10,304 would be recognised in other comprehensive income. This is different from when the account was expressed in sterling because the 'capital injection' in this case is C$587,500 whereas before it was effectively C$612,500.

6.3.6 Monetary items ceasing to be part of the net investment in a foreign operation

The previous section dealt with the situation where a pre-existing monetary item was subsequently considered to form part of the net investment in a foreign operation. However, what happens where a monetary item ceases to be considered part of the net investment in a foreign operation, either because the circumstances have changed such that it is now planned or is likely to be settled in the foreseeable future or indeed that the monetary item is in fact settled?

Where the circumstances have changed such that the monetary item is now planned or is likely to be settled in the foreseeable future, then similar issues to those discussed at 6.3.1 above apply; i.e. are the exchange differences on the intragroup balance to be recognised in profit or loss only from the date of change or from the beginning of the financial year? For the same reasons set out in Example 15.14 above, in our view, the monetary item ceases to form part of the net investment in the foreign operation at the moment in time when the entity decides that settlement is planned or is likely to occur in the foreseeable future. Accordingly, exchange differences arising on the monetary item up to that date are recognised in other comprehensive income and accumulated in a separate component of equity. The exchange differences that arise after that date are recognised in profit or loss.

Consideration also needs to be given as to the treatment of the cumulative exchange differences on the monetary item that have been recognised in other comprehensive income, including those that had been recognised in other comprehensive income in prior years. The treatment of these exchange differences is to recognise them in other comprehensive income and accumulate them in a separate component of equity until the disposal of the foreign operation. *[IAS 21.45]*. The principle question is whether the change in circumstances or actual settlement in cash of the intragroup balance represents a disposal or partial disposal of the foreign operation and this is considered in more detail at 6.6 below.

6.3.7 Dividends

If a subsidiary pays a dividend to the parent during the year the parent should record the dividend at the rate ruling when the dividend was declared. An exchange difference will arise in the parent's own financial statements if the exchange rate moves between the declaration date and the date the dividend is actually received. This exchange difference is required to be recognised in profit or loss and will remain there on consolidation.

The same will apply if the subsidiary declares a dividend to its parent on the last day of its financial year and this is recorded at the year-end in both entities' financial statements. There is no problem in that year as both the intragroup balances and the dividends will eliminate on consolidation with no exchange differences arising. However, as the dividend will not be received until the following year an exchange difference will arise in the parent's financial statements in that year if exchange rates have moved in the meantime. Again, this exchange difference should remain in consolidated profit or loss as it is no different from any other exchange difference arising on intragroup balances resulting from other types of intragroup transactions. It should not be recognised in other comprehensive income.

It may seem odd that the consolidated results can be affected by exchange differences on inter-company dividends. However, once the dividend has been declared, the parent now effectively has a functional currency exposure to assets that were previously regarded as part of the net investment. In order to minimise the effect of exchange rate movements entities should, therefore, arrange for inter-company dividends to be paid on the same day the dividend is declared, or as soon after the dividend is declared as possible.

6.3.8 Unrealised profits on intragroup transactions

The other problem area is the elimination of unrealised profits resulting from intragroup transactions when one of the parties to the transaction is a foreign subsidiary.

Example 15.15: Unrealised profits on an intragroup transaction

An Italian parent has a wholly owned Swiss subsidiary. On 30 November 2018 the subsidiary sold goods to the parent for CHF1,000. The cost of the goods to the subsidiary was CHF700. The goods were recorded by the parent at €685 based on the exchange rate ruling on 30 November 2018 of €1=CHF1.46. All of the goods are unsold by the year-end, 31 December 2018. The exchange rate at that date was €1=CHF1.52. How should the intragroup profit be eliminated?

IAS 21 contains no specific guidance on this matter. However, US GAAP requires the rate ruling at the date of the transaction to be used.

The profit shown by the subsidiary is CHF300 which translated at the rate ruling on the transaction of €1=CHF1.46 equals €205. Consequently, the goods will be included in the statement of financial position at:

Per parent company statement of financial position	€685
Less unrealised profit eliminated	€205
	€480

It can be seen that the resulting figure for inventory is equivalent to the original euro cost translated at the rate ruling on the date of the transaction. Whereas if the subsidiary still held the inventory it would be included at €461 (CHF700 @ €1=CHF1.52).

If in the above example the goods had been sold by the Italian parent to the Swiss subsidiary then the approach in US GAAP would say the amount to be eliminated is the amount of profit shown in the Italian entity's financial statements. Again, this will not necessarily result in the goods being carried in the consolidated financial statements at their original cost to the group.

6.4 Non-coterminous period ends

IAS 21 recognises that in preparing consolidated financial statements it may be that a foreign operation is consolidated on the basis of financial statements made up to a different date from that of the reporting entity (see Chapter 7 at 2.5). In such a case, the standard initially states that the assets and liabilities of the foreign operation are to be translated at the exchange rate at the end of the reporting period of the foreign operation rather than at the date of the consolidated financial statements. However, it then goes on to say that adjustments are made for significant changes in exchange rates up to the end of the reporting period of the reporting entity in accordance with IFRS 10 – *Consolidated Financial Statements.* The same approach is used in applying the equity method to associates and joint ventures in accordance with IAS 28 – *Investments in Associates and Joint Ventures* (see Chapters 11 and 12). *[IAS 21.46].*

The rationale for this approach is not explained in IAS 21. The initial treatment is that required by US GAAP and the reason given in that standard is that this presents the functional currency performance of the subsidiary during the subsidiary's financial year and its position at the end of that period in terms of the parent company's reporting (presentation) currency. The subsidiary may have entered into transactions in other currencies, including the functional currency of the parent, and monetary items in these currencies will have been translated using rates ruling at the end of the subsidiary's reporting period. The income statement of the subsidiary will reflect the economic consequences of carrying out these transactions during the period ended on that date. In order that the effects of these transactions in the subsidiary's financial statements are not distorted, the financial statements should be translated using the closing rate at the end of the subsidiary's reporting period.

However, an alternative argument could have been advanced for using the closing rate ruling at the end of the parent's reporting period. All subsidiaries within a group should normally prepare financial statements up to the same date as the parent entity so that the parent can prepare consolidated financial statements that present fairly the financial performance and financial position about the group as that of a single entity. The use of financial statements of a subsidiary made up to a date earlier than that of the parent is only an administrative convenience and a surrogate for financial statements made up to the proper date. Arguably, therefore the closing rate that should have been used is that which would have been used if the financial statements were made up to the proper date, i.e. that ruling at the end of the reporting period of the parent. Another reason for using this rate is that there may be subsidiaries that have the same functional currency as the subsidiary with the non-coterminous year end that do make up their financial statements to the same date as the parent company and therefore in order to be consistent with them the same rate should be used.

6.5 Goodwill and fair value adjustments

The treatment of goodwill and fair value adjustments arising on the acquisition of a foreign operation should depend on whether they are part of: *[IAS 21.BC27]*

(a) the assets and liabilities of the acquired entity (which would imply translating them at the closing rate); or

(b) the assets and liabilities of the parent (which would imply translating them at the historical rate).

In the case of fair value adjustments these clearly relate to the acquired entity. However, in the case of goodwill, historically different views have been held as set out in the following example.

Example 15.16: Translation of goodwill

A UK company acquires all of the share capital of an Australian company on 30 June 2018 at a cost of A$3m. The fair value of the net assets of the Australian company at that date was A$2.1m. In the consolidated financial statements at 31 December 2018 the goodwill is recognised as an asset in accordance with IFRS 3. The relevant exchange rates at 30 June 2018 and 31 December 2018 are £1=A$2.61 and £1=A$2.43 respectively. At what amount should the goodwill on consolidation be included in the statement of financial position?

		(i)	(ii)
	A$	£	£
Goodwill	900,000	344,828	370,370

(i) This method regards goodwill as being an asset of the parent and therefore translated at the historical rate. Supporters of this view believe that, in economic terms, the goodwill is an asset of the parent because it is part of the acquisition price paid by the parent, particularly in situations where the parent acquires a multinational operation comprising businesses with many different functional currencies. *[IAS 21.BC30]*.

(ii) This method regards goodwill as being part of the parent's net investment in the acquired entity and therefore translated at the closing rate. Supporters of this view believe that goodwill should be treated no differently from other assets of the acquired entity, in particular intangible assets, because a significant part of the goodwill is likely to comprise intangible assets that do not qualify for separate recognition; the goodwill arises only because of the investment in the foreign entity and has no existence apart from that entity; and the cash flows that support the continued recognition of the goodwill are generated in the entity's functional currency. *[IAS 21.BC31]*.

The IASB was persuaded by the arguments set out in (ii) above. *[IAS 21.BC32]*. Accordingly, IAS 21 requires that any goodwill arising on the acquisition of a foreign operation and any fair value adjustments to the carrying amounts of assets and liabilities arising on the acquisition of that foreign operation should be treated as assets and liabilities of the foreign operation. Thus they are expressed in the functional currency of the foreign operation and are translated at the closing rate in accordance with the requirements discussed at 6.1 above. *[IAS 21.47]*.

Clearly, if an entity acquires a single foreign entity this will be a straightforward exercise. Where, however, the acquisition is of a multinational operation comprising a number of businesses with different functional currencies this will not be the case. The goodwill needs to be allocated to the level of each functional currency of the acquired operation. However, the standard gives no guidance on how this should be done.

In our experience, the most commonly applied way of allocating goodwill to different functional currencies is an economic value approach. This approach effectively calculates the goodwill relating to each different functional currency operation by allocating the cost of the acquisition to the different functional currency operations on the basis of the relative economic values of those businesses and then deducting the fair values that have been attributed to the net assets of those businesses as part of the fair value exercise in accounting for the business combination (see Chapter 9 at 5). We consider that any other basis for allocating goodwill to different functional currencies would need to be substantiated.

The level to which goodwill is allocated for the purpose of foreign currency translation may be different from the level at which the goodwill is tested for impairment under IAS 36 (see Chapter 20 at 8.1). *[IAS 21.BC32]*. In many cases the allocation under IAS 21 will be at a lower level. This will apply not only on the acquisition of a multinational operation but could also apply on the acquisition of a single operation where the goodwill is allocated to a larger cash generating unit under IAS 36 that is made up of businesses with different functional currencies.

As a consequence of this different level of allocation one particular difficulty that entities are likely to face is how to deal with an impairment loss that is recognised in respect of goodwill under IAS 36. If the impairment loss relates to a larger cash generating unit made up of businesses with different functional currencies, again some allocation of this impairment loss will be required to determine the amount of the remaining carrying amount of goodwill in each of the functional currencies for the purposes of translation under IAS 21.

6.6 Disposal or partial disposal of a foreign operation

The requirements relating to disposals and partial disposals of foreign operations have been amended a number of times in recent years and the current requirements are considered at 6.6.1 and 6.6.2 below. However, these amendments have given rise to a number of application issues, some of which were considered by the Interpretations Committee in 2010, although their deliberations were ultimately inconclusive.

6.6.1 Disposals and transactions treated as disposals

6.6.1.A Disposals of a foreign operation

Exchange differences resulting from the translation of a foreign operation to a different presentation currency are to be recognised in other comprehensive income and accumulated within a separate component of equity (see 6.1 above).

On the disposal of a foreign operation, the exchange differences relating to that foreign operation that have been recognised in other comprehensive income and accumulated in the separate component of equity should be recognised in profit or loss when the gain or loss on disposal is recognised. *[IAS 21.48]*. This will include exchange differences arising on an intragroup balance that, in substance, forms part of an entity's net investment in a foreign operation (see 6.3 above).

Example 15.17: Disposal of a foreign operation

A German entity has a Swiss subsidiary which was set up on 1 January 2015 with a share capital of CHF200,000 when the exchange rate was €1=CHF1.55. The subsidiary is included in the parent's separate financial statements at its original cost of €129,032. The profits of the subsidiary, all of which have been retained by the subsidiary, for each of the three years ended 31 December 2017 were CHF40,000, CHF50,000 and CHF60,000 respectively, so

Chapter 15

that the net assets at 31 December 2017 are CHF350,000. In the consolidated financial statements the results of the subsidiary have been translated at the respective average rates of €1=CHF1.60, €1=CHF1.68 and €1=CHF1.70 and the net assets at the respective closing rates of €1=CHF1.71, €1=CHF1.65 and €1=CHF1.66. All exchange differences have been recognised in other comprehensive income and accumulated in a separate exchange reserve. The consolidated reserves have therefore included the following amounts in respect of the subsidiary:

	Retained profit	Exchange reserve
	€	€
1 January 2015	–	–
Movement during 2015	25,000	(13,681)
31 December 2015	25,000	(13,681)
Movement during 2016	29,762	5,645
31 December 2016	54,762	(8,036)
Movement during 2017	35,294	(209)
31 December 2017	90,056	(8,245)

The net assets at 31 December 2017 of CHF350,000 are included in the consolidated financial statements at €210,843.

On 1 January 2018 the subsidiary is sold for CHF400,000 (€240,964), thus resulting in a gain on disposal in the parent entity's books of €111,932, i.e. €240,964 less €129,032.

In the consolidated financial statements for 2018, IAS 21 requires the cumulative exchange losses of €8,245 to be recognised in profit or loss for that year. Assuming they were included as part of the gain on disposal (which was explicitly required by earlier versions of IAS 27)[10] this gain would be reduced to €21,876, being €30,121 (the difference between the proceeds of €240,964 and net asset value of €210,843 at the date of disposal) together with the cumulative exchange losses of €8,245.

In this example, this gain on disposal of €21,876 represents the parent's profit of €111,932 less the cumulative profits already recognised in group profit or loss of €90,056.

The following accounting policies of Pearson reflect these requirements as shown below.

Extract 15.4: Pearson plc (2015)

Notes to the consolidated financial statements [extract]

1 **Accounting policies** [extract]

c. **Foreign currency translation** [extract]

3. Group companies – The results and financial position of all Group companies that have a functional currency different from the presentation currency are translated into the presentation currency as follows:

i) Assets and liabilities are translated at the closing rate at the date of the balance sheet

ii) Income and expenses are translated at average exchange rates

iii) All resulting exchange differences are recognised as a separate component of equity.

On consolidation, exchange differences arising from the translation of the net investment in foreign entities, and of borrowings and other currency instruments designated as hedges of such investments, are taken to shareholders' equity. The Group treats specific inter-company loan balances, which are not intended to be repaid in the foreseeable future, as part of its net investment. When a foreign operation is sold, such exchange differences are recognised in the income statement as part of the gain or loss on sale.

The principal overseas currency for the Group is the US Dollar. The average rate for the year against sterling was $1.53 (2012: $1.65) and the year end rate was $1.47 (2012: $1.56).

This treatment is to be adopted not only when an entity sells an interest in a foreign entity, but also when it disposes of its interest through liquidation, repayment of share capital, or abandonment of that entity. *[IAS 21.49]*.

The requirement to reclassify the cumulative exchange differences to profit or loss cannot be avoided, for example, by an entity merely disposing of the net assets and business of the foreign operation, rather than disposing of its interest in the legal entity that is the foreign operation. This is because paragraph 49 refers to the disposal of a foreign operation, and a foreign operation as defined by IAS 21 must have 'activities' (see 2.3 above). Following the disposal of the net assets and business, there no longer are 'activities'. Furthermore, a foreign operation need not be an incorporated entity but may be a branch, the disposal of which would necessarily take the form of an asset sale. The legal form of the entity should make no difference to the accounting treatment of exchange differences, including the reclassification of cumulative exchange differences from equity to profit or loss. It also follows that reclassification of exchange differences could potentially be required on the disposal of a branch or similar operation within a legal entity if it represents a separate foreign operation (see 4.4 above).

Where it is a subsidiary that is disposed of, the related exchange differences that have been attributed to the non-controlling interests should be derecognised and therefore included in the calculation of the gain or loss on disposal, but should not be reclassified to profit or loss. *[IAS 21.48B]*. This is illustrated in the following example.

Example 15.18: Disposal of a partially owned foreign subsidiary

Entity P, which is incorporated in France and has the euro as its functional currency, owns 80% of Entity S which has US dollars as its functional currency. In P's consolidated financial statements, the following amounts have been recognised in relation to its investment in S:

- net assets of €1,000 and associated non-controlling interests of €200;
- foreign exchange gains of €100 were recognised in other comprehensive income, of which €20 was attributable to non-controlling interests and is therefore included in the €200 non-controlling interests;
- €80 of foreign exchange gains have therefore been accumulated in a separate component of equity relating to P's 80% share in S.

P sells its 80% interest in S for €1,300 and records the following amounts:

Dr Cash	1,300	
Dr NCI	200	
Dr OCI	80	
Cr Net assets		1,000
Cr Profit on disposal		580

It can be seen that €80 of the foreign currency gains previously recognised in OCI, i.e. the amount attributed to P, is reclassified to profit or loss (profit on disposal) and reported as a loss in OCI. However, the €20 of such gains attributed to the non-controlling interests is not reclassified in this way and is simply derecognised along with the rest of the NCI balance.

6.6.1.B Transactions treated as disposals

In addition to the disposal of an entity's entire interest in a foreign operation, the following partial disposals are accounted for as disposals: *[IAS 21.48A]*

(a) when the partial disposal involves the loss of control of a subsidiary that includes a foreign operation, regardless of whether the entity retains a non-controlling interest in its former subsidiary after the partial disposal; and

(b) when the retained interest after the partial disposal of an interest in a joint arrangement or a partial disposal of an interest in an associate that includes a foreign operation is a financial asset that includes a foreign operation.

Therefore all exchange differences accumulated in the separate component of equity relating to that foreign operation are reclassified on its disposal even if the disposal results from a sale of only part of the entity's interest in the operation, for example if a parent sold 60% of its shares in a wholly owned subsidiary which as a result became an associate.

The treatment of exchange differences relating to an investment in an associate or joint venture that becomes a subsidiary in a business combination is not clearly specified in IAS 21. However, in these circumstances, IAS 28 clearly requires the reclassification of equity accounted exchange differences of the associate or joint venture that were recognised in other comprehensive income (see Chapter 9 at 9 and Chapter 11 at 7.12.1) and, in our view, the same treatment should apply to the exchange differences arising on the associate or joint venture itself.

6.6.2 Partial disposals

6.6.2.A What constitutes a partial disposal?

A partial disposal of an entity's interest in a foreign operation is any reduction in its ownership interest, except for those that are accounted for as disposals (see 6.6.1 above). *[IAS 21.48D]*.

A write-down of the carrying amount of a foreign operation, either because of its own losses or because of an impairment recognised by the investor, does not constitute a partial disposal, therefore no deferred exchange difference should be reclassified from equity to profit or loss at the time of the write-down. *[IAS 21.49]*. Similarly, it is implicit in the requirement of IFRS 5 – *Non-current Assets Held for Sale and Discontinued Operations* – for separate disclosure of cumulative gains and losses recognised in equity relating to a disposal group (see Chapter 4 at 2.2.4) that the classification of a foreign operation as held for sale under IFRS 5 does not give rise to a reclassification of foreign exchange differences to profit or loss at that time.

Also, a dividend made by a foreign operation that is accounted for as revenue by its parent, investor or venturer in its separate financial statements (see Chapter 8 at 2.4.1) should not be treated as a disposal or partial disposal of a net investment. *[IAS 21.BC35]*.

The term 'ownership interest' is not defined within IFRS, although it is used in a number of standards,[11] normally to indicate an investor's proportionate interest in an entity. This might seem to indicate that a partial disposal arises only when an investor reduces its proportionate interest in the foreign operation. However, the Interpretations Committee has indicated that a partial disposal may also be interpreted to mean an absolute reduction in ownership interest[12] (other than those indicated above), for example the repayment by a foreign operation of a permanent as equity loan made to it by the reporting entity.

Accordingly, in our view, entities will need to apply judgement and select an appropriate accounting policy for determining what constitutes a partial disposal.

6.6.2.B Partial disposal of a proportionate interest in a subsidiary

On the partial disposal of a proportionate interest in a subsidiary that includes a foreign operation, the proportionate share of the cumulative amount of exchange differences recognised in other comprehensive income should be reattributed to the non-controlling interests in that foreign operation. *[IAS 21.48C]*. In other words, these exchange differences will not be reclassified to profit or loss. Further, if the entity subsequently disposes of the remainder of its interest in the subsidiary, the exchange differences reattributed will not be reclassified to profit or loss at that point either (see 6.6.1 above).

6.6.2.C Repayment of a permanent as equity loan by a subsidiary

Where an entity considers the repayment by a subsidiary of a permanent as equity loan a partial disposal (see 6.6.2.A above), IAS 21 is unclear whether related foreign currency differences should be reclassified from equity to profit and loss. Consequently, in our opinion, entities should select an appropriate accounting policy and apply that policy consistently.

In our experience the most commonly applied policy is for entities not to reclassify exchange differences in these circumstances. This is consistent with the explicit requirements of IAS 21 which require only that an entity reattribute to the non-controlling interests any exchange differences in that foreign operation. *[IAS 21.48C]*.

However, in analysing the issue for the Interpretations Committee in 2010, the IFRIC staff indicated, albeit without any technical analysis, that in their opinion exchange differences should be reclassified to profit or loss on settlement of such a monetary item.[13] The Interpretations Committee, which did not take the issue onto its agenda, noted that diversity may exist in practice[14] and, consequently, we also consider this treatment to be an acceptable policy choice. A logical extension of this accounting policy choice would involve reclassifying exchange differences as a result of similar transactions, for example the repayment of share capital by a foreign subsidiary.

6.6.2.D Partial disposal of interest in an associate or joint arrangement

In a partial disposal of an associate or joint arrangement where the retained interest remains or becomes an associate or joint arrangement, the proportionate share of the cumulative amount of exchange differences recognised in other comprehensive income should be reclassified from equity to profit or loss. *[IAS 21.48C]*. There is an equivalent requirement in IAS 28 applying to all gains and losses recognised in other comprehensive income that would be reclassified to profit or loss on disposal of the related assets or liabilities. *[IAS 28.25]*. In this context, the Interpretations Committee has concluded that this treatment applies however an investor's ownership interest is reduced, for example if an associate that is a foreign operation issues shares to third parties.[15]

Whether the repayment by an associate or joint arrangement of a permanent as equity loan made to it by the reporting entity results in reclassification of exchange differences to profit or loss depends on whether the reporting entity considers such a transaction to represent a partial disposal (see 6.6.2.A above). In other words it will be an entity's accounting policy choice.

6.6.3 Comparison of the effect of step-by-step and direct methods of consolidation on accounting for disposals

We illustrated the basic requirement to reclassify cumulative exchange differences from equity to profit or loss on the disposal of a foreign operation in Example 15.17 at 6.6.1 above where a parent sold a direct interest in a subsidiary. This requirement also applies on the sale of an indirect subsidiary. However, where the intermediate holding company and the subsidiary each have different functional currencies, the method of consolidation can have an impact on the amount of exchange differences reclassified from equity to profit or loss on the disposal of the subsidiary.

If the step-by-step method is used, this amount will have been measured based on the functional currencies of the intermediate holding company and the subsidiary. The translation of that amount into the presentation currency of the ultimate parent will not be the same as if the ultimate parent had consolidated the subsidiary individually. In this second case (the direct method), the exchange differences on translation of the subsidiary would have been measured based on the functional currency of the subsidiary and the presentation currency used by the ultimate parent. This is illustrated in the following example.

Example 15.19: Disposal of an indirectly held foreign operation

On 1 January 2017, Entity A is incorporated in the UK with share capital of £300m. It sets up a wholly-owned Swiss subsidiary, Entity B, on the same day with share capital of CHF200m. Entity B in turn sets up a wholly-owned German subsidiary, Entity C, with share capital of €45m. All of the capital subscribed in each of the entities, to the extent that it has not been invested in a subsidiary, is used to acquire operating assets in their country of incorporation. The functional currency of each of the entities is therefore pound sterling, the Swiss franc and the euro respectively. The relevant exchange rates at 1 January 2017 are £1=CHF2.50=€1.50.

For the purposes of the example, it is assumed that in the year ended 31 December 2017 each of the entities made no profit or loss. The relevant exchange rates at that date were £1=CHF3.00=€1.25.

On 1 January 2018, the German subsidiary, Entity C, is sold by Entity B for €45m.

The exchange differences relating to Entity C that will be reclassified from equity to profit or loss in the consolidated financial statements of the Entity A group for the year ended 31 December 2018 on the basis that each of the subsidiaries are consolidated individually (the direct method) will be as follows:

Consolidating each subsidiary individually (the direct method)

The opening consolidated statement of financial position of the Entity A group at 1 January 2017 is as follows:

	Entity A	Entity B		Entity C		Adjustments	Consolidated
Millions	£	CHF	£	€	£	£	£
Investment in B	80.0					(80.0)	
Investment in C		75.0	30.0			(30.0)	
Other net assets	220.0	125.0	50.0	45.0	30.0		300.0
	300.0	200.0	80.0	45.0	30.0		300.0
Share capital	300.0						300.0
Share capital		200.0	80.0			(80.0)	
Share capital				45.0	30.0	(30.0)	

The consolidated statement of financial position of the Entity A group at 31 December 2017 is as follows:

	Entity A	Entity B			Entity C	Adjustments	Consolidated
Millions	£	CHF	£	€	£	£	£
Investment in B	80.0					(80.0)	
Investment in C		75.0	25.0			(25.0)	
Other net assets	220.0	125.0	41.7	45.0	36.0		297.7
	300.0	200.0	66.7	45.0	36.0		297.7
Share capital	300.0						300.0
Share capital		200.0	80.0			(80.0)	
Share capital				45.0	30.0	(30.0)	
Exchange – B			(13.3)			5.0	(8.3)
Exchange – C					6.0		6.0
	300.0	200.0	66.7	45.0	36.0		297.7

The exchange differences in respect of Entity B and Entity C are only shown for illustration purposes; the consolidated statement of financial position would only show the net amount of £(2.3)m as a separate component of equity. The exchange difference of £6.0m in respect of Entity C is that arising on the translation of its opening net assets of €45m into the presentation currency of pound sterling based on the opening and closing exchange rates of £1=€1.50 and £1=€1.25 respectively, as required by paragraph 39 of IAS 21. Accordingly, it is this amount of £6.0m that will be reclassified from equity to profit or loss for the year ended 31 December 2018 upon the disposal of Entity C as required by paragraph 48 of IAS 21.

If the consolidated statement of financial position for the Entity A group at 31 December 2017 had been prepared on the basis of a sub-consolidation of the Entity B sub-group incorporating Entity C, the position would have been as follows.

Consolidating using a sub-group consolidation (the step-by-step method)

The exchange rates at 1 January 2017 and 31 December 2017 are the equivalent of €1=CHF1.667 and €1=CHF2.400.

The sub-consolidation of Entity B and Entity C at 31 December 2017 is as follows:

	Entity B	Entity C		Adjustments	Consolidated
Millions	CHF	€	CHF	CHF	CHF
Investment in C	75.0			(75.0)	
Other net assets	125.0	45.0	108.0		233.0
	200.0	45.0	108.0		233.0
Share capital	200.0				200.0
Share capital		45.0	75.0	(75.0)	
Exchange – C			33.0		33.0
	200.0	45.0	108.0		233.0

The exchange difference of CHF33.0m in respect of Entity C is that arising on the translation of its opening net assets of €45m into the functional currency of that of Entity B, the Swiss franc, based on the opening and closing exchange rates of €1=CHF1.667 and €1=CHF2.400 respectively.

In the consolidated financial statements of the Entity B sub-group for the year ended 31 December 2018, it is this amount of CHF33.0m that would be reclassified from equity to profit or loss upon the disposal of Entity C.

The consolidated statement of financial position of the Entity A group at 31 December 2017 prepared using this sub-consolidation would be as follows:

	Entity A		Entity B sub-group	Adjustments	Consolidated
Millions	£	CHF	£	£	£
Investment in B	80.0			(80.0)	
Other net assets	220.0	233.0	77.7		297.7
	300.0	233.0	77.7		297.7
Share capital	300.0				200.0
Share capital		200.0	80.0	(80.0)	
Exchange – C		33.0	11.0		11.0
Exchange – B group			(13.3)		(13.3)
	300.0	233.0	77.7		297.7

The exchange differences in respect of Entity C and those for the Entity B sub-group are only shown for illustration purposes; the consolidated statement of financial position would only show the net amount of £(2.3)m as a separate component of equity. As can be seen, the consolidated position for the Entity A group is the same as that using the direct method. However, using the step-by-step method, the exchange difference of £11.0m in respect of Entity C is the exchange difference of CHF33.0 included in the Entity B sub-consolidation translated into the presentation currency used in the Entity A consolidated financial statements.

As indicated above, it is this amount of CHF33.0m that would be reclassified from equity to profit or loss upon the disposal of Entity C in the consolidated financial statements of the Entity B sub-group for the year ended 31 December 2018. In the consolidated financial statements of the Entity A group for the year ended 31 December 2018, it would be the translated amount of exchange differences of £11.0m that would be reclassified from equity to profit or loss on the disposal of Entity C.

Although the Interpretations Committee has indicated that the direct method is conceptually correct, IFRIC 16 permits the use of either approach as an accounting policy choice (see 6.1.5 above).

In certain situations, the methods of consolidation seem to result in more extreme differences. For example, consider the disposal of a US subsidiary by a US intermediate holding company (both of which have the US dollar as their functional currency) within a group headed by a UK parent (which has sterling as its functional and presentation currency). The US subsidiary that is disposed of is a foreign operation so exchange differences accumulated in the separate component of equity relating to it should be reclassified from equity to profit or loss on its disposal. Under the direct method of consolidation, this amount will represent exchange differences arising from translating the results and net assets of the US subsidiary directly into sterling. However, under the step-by-step method, these exchange differences will be entirely attributable to the intermediate parent undertaking and so there would be no reclassification from equity to profit or loss.

7 CHANGE OF PRESENTATION CURRENCY

IAS 21 does not address how an entity should approach presenting its financial statements if it changes its presentation currency. This is a situation that is commonly faced when the reporting entity determines that its functional currency has changed (the accounting implications of which are set out in IAS 21 and discussed at 5.5 above). However, because entities have a free choice of their presentation currency, it can occur in other situations too.

Changing presentation currency is, in our view, similar to a change in accounting policy, the requirements for which are set out in IAS 8. Therefore, when an entity chooses to change its presentation currency, we consider it appropriate to follow the approach in IAS 8 which requires retrospective application except to the extent that this is impracticable (see Chapter 3 at 4.4). It will also require the presentation of a statement of financial position at the beginning of the comparative period (see Chapter 3 at 2.3 and 2.4).

It almost goes without saying that the comparatives should be restated and presented in the new presentation currency. Further, they should be prepared as if this had always been the entity's presentation currency (at least to the extent practicable). The main issue arising in practice is determining the amount of the different components of equity, particularly the exchange differences that IAS 21 requires to be accumulated in a separate component of equity, and how much of those differences relate to each operation within the group. The following example illustrates the impact of a change in presentation currency of a relatively simple group.

Example 15.20: Change of presentation currency

A Canadian parent, P, was established on 1 January 2016 and issued new shares for C$20 million. On the same date it established two wholly owned subsidiaries, S1 and S2 incorporated in Canada and the UK respectively and subscribed C$10 million and £4.5 million for their entire share capital. The functional currency of each group company was determined to be its local currency, i.e. Canadian dollars for P and S1 and the pound sterling for S2.

During 2016, S1 made a profit of C$800,000, S2 made a profit of £350,000 and P made a loss of C$25,000. On 30 September 2016, P issued new shares for C$10 million of which £4 million was used immediately to subscribe for additional shares in S2.

During 2017, S1 made a profit of C$700,000, S2 made a profit of £750,000 and P made a loss of C$30,000 before dividends received from S2. On 30 June 2017, S2 paid dividends (out of profits then made) of £700,000 to P and on 30 September 2017 P paid dividends of C$1,000,000 to its shareholders.

The relevant exchange rates for C$1=£ were as follows:

1 January 2016	2.10
30 September 2016	2.28
31 December 2016	2.35
Average for 2016	2.24
30 June 2017	2.55
30 September 2017	2.63
31 December 2017	2.40
Average for 2017	2.52

Consequently, the statement of changes in equity in P's consolidated financial statements for 2016 and 2017 can be summarised as follows:

	Paid-in capital C$	Retained earnings C$	Foreign exchange C$	Total C$
1 January 2016	–	–	–	–
Issue of shares	30,000,000	–	–	30,000,000
Comprehensive income	–	1,559,000	1,443,500	3,002,500
31 December 2016	30,000,000	1,559,000	1,443,500	33,002,500
Comprehensive income	–	2,560,000	457,500	3,017,500
Dividends	–	(1,000,000)	–	(1,000,000)
31 December 2017	30,000,000	3,119,000	1,901,000	35,020,000

The comprehensive income reflected within retained earnings represents the profit for each year, calculated as follows:

2016: C$800,000 + (£350,000 × 2.24) – C$25,000 = C$1,559,000

2017: C$700,000 + (£750,000 × 2.52) – C$30,000 = C$2,560,000

The foreign exchange differences recognised in other comprehensive income, which are entirely attributable to S2, can be calculated as follows:

	2016 £	*2016* Rate	*2016* C$	*2017* £	*2017* Rate	*2017* C$
Opening net assets*	4,500,000	2.10	9,450,000	8,850,000	2.35	20,797,500
		2.35	10,575,000		2.40	21,240,000
Exchange gain			1,125,000			442,500
Additional capital	4,000,000	2.28	9,120,000	–	–	–
		2.35	9,400,000			–
Exchange gain			280,000			–
Dividend	–	–	–	(700,000)	2.55	(1,785,000)
		–	–		2.40	(1,680,000)
Exchange gain			–			105,000
Profit	350,000	2.24	784,000	750,000	2.52	1,890,000
		2.35	822,500		2.40	1,800,000
Exchange gain/(loss)			38,500			(90,000)
	8,850,000		1,443,500	8,900,000		457,500

*for 2016, includes the proceeds received for issuing shares on 1 January.

For the year ended 31 December 2018, P decided to change its presentation currency to sterling. (This may or may not have coincided with a change of P's functional currency.) In P's consolidated financial statements for the year ended 31 December 2018, what amounts should be included in respect of the comparative period?

Direct method

If P's accounting policy was to use the direct method of consolidation (see 6.1.5 above), its financial statements for 2016 and 2017 would have been prepared by translating the financial statements of each entity within the group directly into sterling (where necessary). The revised statement of changes in equity in P's consolidated financial statements can be summarised as follows and these are the amounts that will be reflected as comparative amounts in P's consolidated financial statements for the year ended 31 December 2018:

	Paid-in capital £	Retained earnings £	Foreign exchange £	Total £
1 January 2016	–	–	–	–
Issue of shares	13,909,775	–	–	13,909,775
Comprehensive income	–	695,982	(562,140)	133,842
31 December 2016	13,909,775	695,982	(562,140)	14,043,617
Comprehensive income	–	1,015,873	(87,595)	928,278
Dividends	–	(380,228)	–	(380,228)
31 December 2017	13,909,775	1,331,627	(649,735)	14,591,667

The table above assumes that P will record its paid-in capital at historical exchange rates (£13,909,775 = C$20,000,000 ÷ 2.10 + C$10,000,000 ÷ 2.28). Alternatively, P could retranslate those amounts at year end rates although any difference arising would simply be recorded in another component of equity (but not the foreign exchange reserve) and this difference would not affect profit or loss or other comprehensive income in any period (see 6.2.1 and 6.2.2 above).

The calculations showing how these amounts have been determined are shown below.

The comprehensive income reflected within retained earnings represents the profit for each year, calculated as follows:

2016: (C$800,000 ÷ 2.24) + £350,000 – (C$25,000 ÷ 2.24) = £695,982

2017: (C$700,000 ÷ 2.52) + £750,000 – (C$30,000 ÷ 2.52) = £1,015,873

In this case, the profit calculated in this way results in the same amount as translating the consolidated profit of C$1,559,000 and C$2,560,000 presented in Canadian dollars at the average rate for the period of C$2.24=£1 and C$2.52=£1 respectively. In practice minor differences can arise as a result of imperfections in the average rates used.

Similarly, the net assets presented above are the same as the amounts obtained by translating consolidated net assets of C$33,002,500 and C$35,020,000 at the closing rates at the end of the relevant period, C$2.35=£1 and C$2.40=£1 respectively. This should always be the case.

However, the foreign exchange reserve is fundamentally different to that in the financial statements presented in Canadian dollars. In this case it represents exchange differences arising from the translation of both P's and S1's financial statements into sterling whereas previously it represented exchange differences arising from the translation of S2's financial statements into Canadian dollars.

The foreign exchange differences recognised in other comprehensive income that are attributable to P can be calculated as follows:

	2016 C$	Rate	£	*2017* C$	Rate	£
Opening net assets*	550,000	2.10	261,905	1,405,000	2.35	597,872
		2.35	234,042		2.40	585,417
Exchange loss			(27,863)			(12,455)
Additional capital**	880,000	2.28	385,965	–	–	–
		2.35	374,468		–	–
Exchange loss			(11,497)			–
Dividend received	–	–	–	1,785,000	2.55	700,000
		–	–		2.40	743,750
Exchange gain			–			43,750
Dividend paid	–	–	–	(1,000,000)	2.63	(380,228)
		–	–		2.40	(416,667)
Exchange loss			–			(36,439)
Loss	(25,000)	2.24	(11,161)	(30,000)	2.52	(11,905)
		2.35	(10,638)		2.40	(12,500)
Exchange gain/(loss)			523			(595)
	1,405,000		(38,837)	2,160,000		(5,739)

*for 2016, includes the proceeds received for issuing shares on 1 January (C$20,000,000) less amounts invested in S1 (C$10,000,000) and S2 (C$9,450,000 = £4,500,000 × 2.10) on the same date.

**reduced by the amounts invested in S2 on the same date.

The foreign exchange differences recognised in other comprehensive income that are attributable to S1 can be calculated as follows:

	2016 C$	Rate	£	*2017* C$	Rate	£
Opening net assets*	10,000,000	2.10	4,761,905	10,800,000	2.35	4,595,745
		2.35	4,255,319		2.40	4,500,000
Exchange loss			(506,586)			(95,745)
Profit	800,000	2.24	357,143	700,000	2.52	277,778
		2.35	340,426		2.40	291,667
Exchange (loss)/gain			(16,717)			13,889
	10,800,000		(523,303)	11,500,000		(81,856)

* for 2016, includes the proceeds received for issuing shares on 1 January.

Therefore the total foreign exchange loss arising in 2016 is £562,140 (£38,837 + £523,303) and in 2017 is £87,595 (£5,739 + £81,856).

Under this method amounts in the foreign exchange reserve would be reclassified to profit or loss on the subsequent disposal of S1, but not on the subsequent disposal of S2.

Step-by-step method

If P's accounting policy was to use the step-by-step method of consolidation (see 6.1.5 above), the first step in producing its consolidated financial statements for 2016 and 2017 would have been to translate the financial statements of S2 into Canadian dollars, the functional currency of P, to produce consolidated financial statements in Canadian dollars (effectively those that P had prepared historically). The second step involves translating these consolidated financial statements into sterling.

These financial statements (and hence the comparative amounts included in the financial statements for the year ended 31 December 2018) will appear to be the same as those produced under the direct method (assuming equity items are dealt with similarly, i.e. paid-in capital is translated at the relevant rate at the date of issue and that retained earnings represent each element translated at the relevant rates, being 2016 and 2017 profit at the average rate for the year, and dividends at the date of payment). However, the balance on the foreign exchange reserve will be attributable to different entities within the group (see 6.6.3 above). The calculations showing how these amounts have been determined are shown below.

The foreign exchange differences recognised in other comprehensive income in the financial statements presented in Canadian dollars that are attributable to S2 will remain attributable to S2, albeit that they are translated into sterling at the average rate:

2016: C$1,443,500 ÷ 2.24 = £644,420

2017: C$457,500 ÷ 2.52 = £181,548

The remaining exchange differences recognised in other comprehensive income, which arise from retranslating P's consolidated financial statements presented in Canadian dollars into sterling, are attributable to P. They can be calculated as follows:

		2016			*2017*	
	C$	Rate	£	C$	Rate	£
Opening net assets*	20,000,000	2.10	9,523,809	33,002,500	2.35	14,043,617
		2.35	8,510,638		2.40	13,751,042
Exchange loss			(1,013,171)			(292,575)
Additional capital	10,000,000	2.28	4,385,965	–		
		2.35	4,255,319			
Exchange loss			(130,646)			–
Dividend paid	–	2.24	–	(1,000,000)	2.63	(380,228)
		2.35	–		2.40	(416,667)
Exchange loss			–			(36,439)
Comprehensive income	3,002,500	2.24	1,340,402	3,017,500	2.52	1,197,421
		2.35	1,277,660		2.40	1,257,292
Exchange (loss)/gain			(62,742)			59,871
	33,002,500		(1,206,559)	35,020,000		(269,143)

* for 2016, includes the proceeds received for issuing shares on 1 January.

In contrast to the direct method, under this method amounts in the foreign exchange reserve would be reclassified to profit or loss on the subsequent disposal of S2, but not on the subsequent disposal of S1.

In the example above, it was reasonably straightforward to recreate the consolidated equity balances and identify the amounts of accumulated exchange differences related to each entity within the group using the new presentation currency. This is because the group had a very simple structure with operations having only two functional currencies, a short history and few (external and internal) equity transactions. Whilst entities should strive for a theoretically perfect restatement, in practice it is unlikely to be such an easy exercise.

As noted above, where an accounting policy is changed, IAS 8 requires retrospective application except to the extent that this is impracticable, in which case an entity should adjust the comparative information to apply the new accounting policy prospectively from the earliest practicable date. A similar approach is, in our view, appropriate when an entity changes its presentation currency. In this context the most important component of equity to determine correctly (or as near correctly as possible) is normally the foreign exchange reserve because that balance, or parts of it, has to be reclassified from equity to profit or loss in the event of any future disposal of the relevant foreign operation, and could therefore affect future earnings.

Where an entity applies the direct method of consolidation, it could be impracticable to determine precisely the amount of exchange differences accumulated within the separate component of equity relating to each individual entity within the group. In these circumstances, approximations will be necessary to determine the amounts at the beginning of the earliest comparative period presented, although all subsequent exchange differences should be accumulated in accordance with the requirements of IAS 21. For an entity that set its foreign exchange reserve to zero on transition to IFRS (see Chapter 5 at 5.7) it may be able to go back to that date and recompute the necessary components of equity. This should be less of an issue for entities applying the step-by-step method.

BBA Aviation changed its presentation currency in 2011 and included the following explanation in its accounting policies.

Extract 15.5: BBA Aviation plc (2011)

Accounting policies [extract]

Presentation currency

The Group's revenues, profits and cash flows are primarily generated in US dollars, and are expected to remain principally denominated in US dollars in the future. During the year, the Group changed the currency in which it presents its consolidated financial statements from pounds sterling to US dollars, in order to better reflect the underlying performance of the Group.

A change in presentation currency is a change in accounting policy which is accounted for retrospectively. Statutory financial information included in the Group's Annual Report and Accounts for the year ended 31 December 2010 previously reported in sterling has been restated into US dollars using the procedures outlined below:

– assets and liabilities denominated in non-US dollar currencies were translated into US dollars at the closing rates of exchange on the relevant balance sheet date;
– non-US dollar income and expenditure were translated at the average rates of exchange prevailing for the relevant period;
– the cumulative hedging and translation reserves were set to nil at 1 January 2004, the date of transition to IFRS, and these reserves have been restated on the basis that the Group has reported in US dollars since that date. Share capital, share premium and the other reserves were translated at the historic rates prevailing at 1 January 2004, and subsequent rates prevailing on the date of each transaction;
– all exchange rates were extracted from the Group's underlying financial records.

8 INTRODUCTION OF THE EURO

From 1 January 1999, the effective start of Economic and Monetary Union (EMU), the euro became a currency in its own right and the conversion rates between the euro and the national currencies of those countries who were going to participate in the first phase were irrevocably fixed, such that the risk of subsequent exchange differences related to these currencies was eliminated from that date on.

In October 1997, the SIC issued SIC-7 which deals with the application of IAS 21 to the changeover from the national currencies of participating Member States of the European Union to the euro. Consequential amendments have been made to this interpretation as a result of the IASB's revised version of IAS 21.

Although the Interpretation is no longer relevant with respect to the national currencies of those countries that participated in the first phase, SIC-7 makes it clear that the same rationale applies to the fixing of exchange rates when countries join EMU at later stages. *[SIC-7.3]*.

Under SIC-7, the requirements of IAS 21 regarding the translation of foreign currency transactions and financial statements of foreign operations should be strictly applied to the changeover. *[SIC-7.3]*.

This means that, in particular:

(a) Foreign currency monetary assets and liabilities resulting from transactions should continue to be translated into the functional currency at the closing rate. Any resultant exchange differences should be recognised as income or expense immediately, except that an entity should continue to apply its existing accounting policy for exchange gains and losses related to hedges of the currency risk of a forecast transaction. *[SIC-7.4]*.

    The effective start of the EMU after the reporting period does not change the application of these requirements at the end of the reporting period; in accordance with IAS 10 – *Events after the Reporting Period* – it is not relevant whether or not the closing rate can fluctuate after the reporting period. *[SIC-7.5]*.

    Like IAS 21, the Interpretation does not address how foreign currency hedges should be accounted for. The effective start of EMU, of itself, does not justify a change to an entity's established accounting policy related to hedges of forecast transactions because the changeover does not affect the economic rationale of such hedges. Therefore, the changeover should not alter the accounting policy where gains and losses on financial instruments used as hedges of forecast transactions are initially recognised in other comprehensive income and reclassified from equity to profit or loss to match with the related income or expense in a future period; *[SIC-7.6]*

(b) Cumulative exchange differences relating to the translation of financial statements of foreign operations recognised in other comprehensive income should remain accumulated in a separate component of equity and be reclassified from equity to profit or loss only on the disposal (or partial disposal) of the net investment in the foreign operation. *[SIC-7.4]*.

    The fact that the cumulative amount of exchange differences will be fixed under EMU does not justify immediate recognition as income or expenses since the wording and the rationale of IAS 21 clearly preclude such a treatment. *[SIC-7.7]*.

9 TAX EFFECTS OF ALL EXCHANGE DIFFERENCES

Gains and losses on foreign currency transactions and exchange differences arising on translating the results and financial position of an entity (including a foreign operation) into a different currency may have tax effects to which IAS 12 applies. *[IAS 21.50]*. The requirements of IAS 12 are discussed in Chapter 31. In broad terms the tax effects of exchange differences will follow the reporting of the exchange differences, i.e. they will be recognised in profit or loss except to the extent they relate to exchange differences recognised in other comprehensive income, in which case they will also be recognised in other comprehensive income. *[IAS 12.58]*.

The tax base of a non-monetary asset such as property, plant or equipment, will sometimes be determined in a currency other than the entity's functional currency. Consequently, changes in the exchange rate will give rise to temporary differences that result in a recognised deferred tax liability or asset (subject to recoverability). The resulting deferred tax should be recognised in profit or loss *[IAS 12.41]* and presented with other deferred taxes rather than with foreign exchange gains or losses (see Chapter 31 at 10.1.1).[16]

10 DISCLOSURE REQUIREMENTS

10.1 Exchange differences

IAS 21 requires the amount of exchange differences recognised in profit or loss (except for those arising on financial instruments measured at fair value through profit or loss in accordance with IAS 39 or IFRS 9) to be disclosed. *[IAS 21.52]*. Since IAS 21 does not specify where such exchange differences should be presented in the income statement entities should apply judgement in the light of the requirements of IAS 1 – *Presentation of Financial Statements* – to determine the appropriate line item(s) in which exchange differences are included. For example, an entity which has an operating and a financing section within its income statement might include exchange differences arising on operating items (such as trade payables and receivables) in other operating income or expense and exchange differences on financing items (such as loans and borrowings) in the financing section. In the light of this, we recommend that entities in disclosing the amount of such exchange differences indicate the line item(s) in which they are included. Further, the classification of exchange differences (both gains and losses) arising from transactions of a similar nature should be classified consistently throughout the periods presented.

The standard also requires disclosure of the net exchange differences recognised in other comprehensive income and accumulated in a separate component of equity, and a reconciliation of such amounts at the beginning and end of the period. *[IAS 21.52]*.

10.2 Presentation and functional currency

When the presentation currency is different from the functional currency, that fact should be stated, together with disclosure of the functional currency and the reason for using a different presentation currency. *[IAS 21.53]*. For this purpose, in the case of a group, the references to 'functional currency' are to that of the parent. *[IAS 21.51]*.

When there is a change in the functional currency of either the reporting entity or a significant foreign operation, that fact and the reason for the change in functional currency should be disclosed. *[IAS 21.54]*.

10.3 Convenience translations of financial statements or other financial information

Paragraph 55 of IAS 21 indicates that when an entity presents its financial statements in a currency that is different from its functional currency, it should describe the financial statements as complying with IFRS only if they comply with all the requirements of each applicable standard and interpretation of those standards, including the translation method set out in IAS 21 (see 6.1 above). *[IAS 21.55]*.

However, the standard recognises that an entity sometimes presents its financial statements or other financial information in a currency that is not its functional currency without meeting the above requirements. Examples noted by IAS 21 are where an entity converts into another currency only selected items from its financial statements or where an entity whose functional currency is not the currency of a hyperinflationary economy converts the financial statements into another currency by translating all items at the most recent closing rate. Such conversions are not in accordance with IFRS; nevertheless IAS 21 requires disclosures to be made. *[IAS 21.56]*.

The standard requires that when an entity displays its financial statements or other financial information in a currency that is different from either its functional currency or its presentation currency and the requirements of paragraph 55 are not met, it should: *[IAS 21.57]*

(a) clearly identify the information as supplementary information to distinguish it from the information that complies with IFRS;

(b) disclose the currency in which the supplementary information is displayed; and

(c) disclose the entity's functional currency and the method of translation used to determine the supplementary information.

For the purpose of these requirements, in the case of a group, the references to 'functional currency' are to that of the parent. *[IAS 21.51]*.

10.4 Judgements made in applying IAS 21 and related disclosures

IAS 1 requires disclosure of the significant judgements that management has made in the process of applying the entity's accounting policies and that have the most significant effect on the amounts recognised in the financial statements (see Chapter 3 at 5.1.1.B). *[IAS 1.122]*. The application of IAS 21 can, in certain circumstances, require the exercise of significant judgement, particularly the determination of functional currency (see 4 above) and assessing whether intragroup monetary items are permanent as equity (see 6.3.1 above). Where relevant, information about these particular judgements should be disclosed.

Whilst considering a number of issues associated with the Venezuelan currency (see 5.1.5 and 6.1.3 above), the Interpretations Committee drew attention to a number of disclosure requirements in IFRS that might be relevant when an entity has material foreign operations subject to extensive currency controls, multiple exchange rates and/or a long-term lack of exchangeability. In addition to the significant judgements in applying those policies, the more important of these disclosures were:[17]

- significant accounting policies applied; *[IAS 1.117-121]*
- sources of estimation uncertainty that have a significant risk of resulting in a material adjustment to the carrying amounts of assets and liabilities within the next financial year, which may include a sensitivity analysis; *[IAS 1.125-133]* and
- the nature and extent of significant restrictions on an entity's ability to access or use assets and settle the liabilities of the group, or its joint ventures or associates. *[IFRS 12.10, 13, 20, 22].*

In addition, the following may also be relevant:[18]

- the nature and extent of risks (including foreign exchange risk) arising from financial instruments (from a qualitative and quantitative perspective and including sensitivity analyses); *[IFRS 7.31-42, B6-B24]*
- significant cash held by the entity that is not available for use by the group, including due to exchange controls; *[IAS 7.48, 49]* and
- the amount of foreign exchange differences recognised in profit or loss and other comprehensive income. *[IAS 21.52].*

11 FUTURE DEVELOPMENTS

IAS 21 has caused a degree of concern in recent years, especially in certain emerging economies. In particular, some have criticised IAS 21 as designed for companies that operate in a reserve currency, e.g. the US dollar or euro; and volatility in exchange rates, including during the financial crisis, led some to ask the IASB to reconsider IAS 21.

However, after performing research and outreach as part of its periodic agenda consultations, the IASB decided in May 2016 not to include in its work plan any further work on the topic.[19] Therefore it seems unlikely there will be any significant changes to the standard in the foreseeable future, although it is possible that narrow-scope amendments or interpretative guidance will be considered.

References

1 *IFRIC Update*, March 2010, Staff Paper (Agenda reference 13), *Determining the functional currency of an investment holding company*, IASB, January 2010 and Staff Paper (Agenda reference 4A), *Determining the functional currency of an investment holding company*, IASB, March 2010.

2 *IFRIC Update*, November 2014.

3 *Exposure Draft of Revised IAS 21*, IASB, May 2002, para. 14.

4 IAS 12 (2007), *Income Taxes*, 2007 Bound Volume, IASB, para. 78.

5 In this context, IAS 21 does not actually refer to those requirements relating to the treatment of exchange differences arising from the translation process. However, we believe that any resulting exchange differences should be recognised as discussed at 5.3 above.

6 *IFRIC Update*, November 2014 and Staff Paper (Agenda reference 16), *Foreign exchange restrictions and hyperinflation*, IASB, July 2014.
7 *IFRIC Update*, March 2008, p.2.
8 *IFRIC Update*, March 2008, p.2.
9 *IASB Update*, February 2003, p.5.
10 IAS 27 (2007), *Consolidated and Separate Financial Statements*, IASB, 2007 Bound Volume, para. 30.
11 For example, IAS 27, *Separate Financial Statements*, IASB, paras. 16(b)(iii) and 17(b)(iii), IFRS 3, *Business Combinations*, IASB, para. B63(e) and IFRS 10, *Consolidated Financial Statements*, IASB, para. 23.
12 *IFRIC Update*, September 2010, p.2.
13 Staff Paper (Agenda reference 7D), *CTA Recycling in IAS 27R Transactions*, IASB, March 2010 and Staff Paper (Agenda reference 11), *Repayment of investment/CTA*, IASB, July 2010, paras. 10(a) and 11.
14 *IFRIC Update*, September 2010, p.2.
15 *IFRIC Update*, July 2009.
16 *IFRIC Update*, January 2016.
17 *IFRIC Update*, November 2014.
18 Staff Paper (Agenda reference 16), *Foreign exchange restrictions and hyperinflation*, IASB, July 2014.
19 *IASB Update*, May 2016.

Chapter 16 Hyperinflation

List of examples

Chapter 16 Hyperinflation

1 INTRODUCTION

1.1 Background

Accounting standards are applied on the assumption that the value of money (the unit of measurement) is constant over time, which normally is an acceptable practical assumption. However, when the effect of inflation on the value of money is no longer negligible, the usefulness of historical cost based financial reporting is often significantly reduced. High rates of inflation give rise to a number of problems for entities that prepare their financial statements on a historical cost basis, for example:

- historical cost figures expressed in terms of monetary units do not show the 'value to the business' of assets;
- holding gains on non-monetary assets that are reported as operating profits do not represent real economic gains;
- financial information presented for the current period is not comparable with that presented for the prior periods; and
- 'real' capital can be reduced because profits reported do not take account of the higher replacement costs of resources used in the period. Therefore, if calculating a nominal 'return on capital' based on profit, and not distinguishing this properly from a real 'return of capital', the erosion of capital may go unnoticed in the financial statements. This is the underlying point in the concept of capital maintenance.

The IASB's *The Conceptual Framework for Financial Reporting* discusses the concept of capital maintenance, which raises the issue of how an entity defines capital. In general terms, an entity maintains its capital if it has as much capital at the end of the period as it had at the beginning, the issue being how this evaluation is measured. Whilst there are different concepts of capital maintenance, IFRS is ultimately based on the financial capital maintenance concept (see Chapter 2 at 2.6.5).

Under the financial capital maintenance concept, the capital of the entity will be maintained if the financial amount of net assets at the end of a period is at least equal to the financial amount of net assets at the beginning of that period, excluding contributions from and distributions to owners during the period. *[CF 4.59(a)]*. To facilitate the evaluation of capital maintenance in a hyperinflationary environment, IAS 29 – *Financial Reporting in Hyperinflationary Economies* – was adopted in April 2001.

The IASB and IFRS Interpretations Committee (Interpretations Committee) have only since addressed the subject of hyperinflation to clarify the provisions of the standard. In 2005, IFRIC 7 – *Applying the Restatement Approach under IAS 29 Financial Reporting in Hyperinflationary Economies* – was issued to provide guidance on applying IAS 29 in the reporting period in which an entity's functional currency first becomes hyperinflationary (see 10.1 below). In 2010 the IASB issued an amendment to IFRS 1 – *First-time Adoption of International Financial Reporting Standards* – for countries that exit severe hyperinflation (see 10.3 below).

1.2 Hyperinflationary economies

For entities used to working in economies with low inflation it is easy to overlook that there are countries where inflation is a major economic concern. In some of these countries, inflation has reached such levels that (1) the local currency is no longer a useful measure of value in the economy and (2) the general population may prefer not to hold its wealth in the local currency. Instead, they hold their wealth in a stable foreign currency or non-monetary assets. Such a condition is often referred to as hyperinflation.

There are several characteristics that need to be considered under IFRS to determine whether hyperinflation exists. The IASB does not monitor inflation rates in specific jurisdictions, nor conclude on the applicability of the characteristics to these jurisdictions. Conversely, under US GAAP hyperinflation is clearly defined and deemed to exist when the cumulative rate of inflation over a three-year period exceeds 100%. For the purposes of reporting under US accounting standards, the International Practices Task Force (IPTF), a task force of the SEC Regulations Committee, monitors the inflation status of different countries.

As the IPTF's criteria are similar to those used under IFRS, this provides a useful guide for entities reporting under IFRS. However, it should be noted that hyperinflation accounting may need to be applied earlier under IFRS than US accounting standards as IAS 29 applies from the beginning of the reporting period in which hyperinflation is identified and the IPTF usually only meet in May and November each year. Minutes of these meetings are publicly available.[1]

In practice, few countries are considered hyperinflationary by the IPTF. For the purposes of IAS 29, the same countries are usually considered hyperinflationary, but where the assessment of the characteristics is unclear, consensus is at times facilitated by local regulators and professional bodies.

1.3 Restatement approach

The problems of historical cost based financial reporting may reach such a magnitude under hyperinflationary circumstances that financial reporting in the hyperinflationary currency is no longer useful. Therefore, a solution is needed to allow meaningful financial reporting by entities that operate in these hyperinflationary economies.

IAS 29 requires a restatement approach, whereby financial information recorded in the hyperinflationary currency is adjusted by applying a general price index and expressed in the measuring unit current at the end of the reporting period (i.e. the accounting value is adjusted for a factor of current purchasing power. This process aims to improve comparability between periods by restating financial information for changes in the purchasing power of money.

2 THE REQUIREMENTS OF IAS 29

2.1 The context of IAS 29

The underlying premise of IAS 29 is that 'reporting of operating results and financial position in the local [hyperinflationary] currency without restatement is not useful'. *[IAS 29.2].* The standard's approach is therefore to require that:

(a) the financial statements of an entity whose functional currency is the currency of a hyperinflationary economy shall be stated in terms of the measuring unit current at the end of the reporting period;

(b) the corresponding figures for the previous period required by IAS 1 – *Presentation of Financial Statements* – and any information in respect of earlier periods shall also be stated in terms of the measuring unit current at the end of the reporting period; and

(c) the gain or loss on the net monetary position shall be included in profit or loss and separately disclosed. *[IAS 29.8-9].*

IAS 29 requires amounts recorded in the statement of financial position, not already expressed in terms of the measuring unit current at the end of the reporting period, to be restated in terms of the current measuring unit at the end of the reporting period, by applying a general price index. *[IAS 29.11].* The example below illustrates how this would apply to the statement of financial position of an entity:

Example 16.1: Accounting for hyperinflation under IAS 29

An entity that operates in a hyperinflationary economy is required under IAS 29 to restate all non-monetary items in its statement of financial position to the measuring unit current at the end of the reporting period by applying a general price index as follows:

	Before restatement (HC)	Historical general price index*	Year-end general price index	After restatement (HC)
Plant and equipment	225	150	600	900
Inventory	250	500	600	300
Cash	100			100
Total assets	575			1,300
Accounts payable	180			180
Long-term debt	250			250
Equity **	145			870
	575			1,300

* General price index at the date of purchase

** The restatement of equity is not illustrated here, but discussed at 5 below.

Chapter 16

The simplified example above already raises a number of questions, such as:

- Which items are monetary and which are non-monetary?
- How does the entity select the appropriate general price index?
- What was the general price index when the assets were acquired?

The standard provides guidance on the restatement to the measuring unit current at the end of the reporting period, but concedes that the consistent application of these inflation accounting procedures and judgements from period to period is more important than the precise accuracy of the resulting amounts included in the restated financial statements. *[IAS 29.10]*. The requirements of the standard look deceptively straightforward but their application may represent a considerable challenge. These difficulties and other aspects of the practical application of the IAS 29 method of accounting for hyperinflation are discussed below.

2.2 Scope

IAS 29 shall be applied by all entities whose functional currency is the currency of a hyperinflationary economy. *[IAS 29.1]*.

The standard should be applied in an entity's separate financial statements (if prepared) and its consolidated financial statements, as well as by parents that include such an entity in their consolidated financial statements.

If an entity whose functional currency is that of a hyperinflationary economy wishes to present the financial statements in a different presentation currency, or if their parent has a different presentation currency, the financial statements of the entity first have to be restated under IAS 29. Only then, can the financial statements be translated under IAS 21 – *The Effects of Changes in Foreign Exchange Rates* (see 11 below).

Almost all entities operating in hyperinflationary economies will be subject to the accounting regime of IAS 29, unless they can legitimately argue that the local hyperinflationary currency is not their functional currency as defined by IAS 21 (see Chapter 15 at 4). *[IAS 21.14]*.

2.3 Definition of hyperinflation

Determining whether an economy is hyperinflationary in accordance with IAS 29 requires judgement. The standard does not establish an absolute inflation rate at which hyperinflation is deemed to arise. Instead, it considers the following characteristics of the economic environment of a country to be strong indicators of the existence of hyperinflation:

(a) the general population prefers to keep its wealth in non-monetary assets or in a relatively stable foreign currency. Amounts of local currency held are immediately invested to maintain purchasing power;

(b) the general population regards monetary amounts not in terms of the local currency but in terms of a relatively stable foreign currency. Prices may be quoted in that currency;

(c) sales and purchases on credit take place at prices that compensate for the expected loss of purchasing power during the credit period, even if the period is short;

(d) interest rates, wages and prices are linked to a price index; and

(e) the cumulative inflation rate over three years is approaching, or exceeds, 100%. *[IAS 29.3]*.

The above list is not exhaustive and there may be other indicators that an economy is hyperinflationary, such as the existence of price controls and restrictive exchange controls. In determining whether an economy is hyperinflationary, condition (e) is quantitatively measurable while the other indicators require reliance on more qualitative evidence.

IAS 29 expresses a preference that all entities that report in the currency of the same hyperinflationary economy apply this Standard from the same date. Nevertheless, once an entity has identified the existence of hyperinflation, it should apply IAS 29 from the beginning of the reporting period in which it identified the existence of hyperinflation. *[IAS 29.4]*.

Identifying when a currency becomes hyperinflationary, and, just as importantly, when it ceases to be so, is not easy in practice and is frequently hampered by a lack of reliable statistics. The consideration of trends and the application of common sense is important in this judgement, as are consistency of measurement and of presentation. As discussed at 1.2 above, the IPTF monitors hyperinflationary countries for US GAAP and this may be useful for IFRS reporters. Transition into and out of hyperinflationary economies are discussed further at 10 below.

2.4 The IAS 29 restatement process

Restatement of financial statements in accordance with IAS 29 can be seen as a process comprising the following steps:

(a) selection of a general price index (see 3 below);
(b) analysis and restatement of the statement of financial position (see 4 below);
(c) restatement of the statement of changes in equity (see 5 below);
(d) restatement of the income statement and statement of comprehensive income (see 6 below);
(e) calculation of the gain or loss on the net monetary position (see 6.2 below);
(f) restatement of the statement of cash flows (see 7 below); and
(g) restatement of comparative figures (see 8 below).

3 SELECTION OF A GENERAL PRICE INDEX

The standard requires entities to use a general price index that reflects changes in general purchasing power. Ideally all entities that report in the same hyperinflationary currency should use the same price index. *[IAS 29.37].*

3.1 Selecting a general price index

It is generally accepted practice to use a Consumer Price Index (CPI) for this purpose, unless that index is clearly flawed. National statistical offices in most countries issue several price indices that potentially could be used for the purposes of IAS 29. Important characteristics of a good general price index include the following:

- a wide range of goods and services has been included in the price index;
- continuity and consistency of measurement techniques and underlying assumptions;
- free from bias;
- frequently updated; and
- available for a long period.

The entity should use the above criteria to choose the most reliable and most readily available general price index and use that index consistently. It is important that the index selected is representative of the real position of the hyperinflationary currency concerned.

3.2 General price index not available for all periods

IAS 29 requires an entity to make an estimate of the price index if the general price index is not available for all periods for which the restatement of long-lived assets is required. The entity could base the estimate, for example, on the movements in the exchange rate between the functional currency and a relatively stable foreign currency. *[IAS 29.17].* It should be noted that this method is only appropriate if the currency of the hyperinflationary economy is freely exchangeable, i.e. not subject to currency controls and 'official' exchange rates. Entities should also be mindful that, especially in the short term, the exchange rate may fluctuate significantly in response to factors other than changes in the domestic price level.

Entities could use a similar approach when they cannot find a general price index that meets the minimum criteria for reliability (e.g. because the national statistical office in the hyperinflationary economy may be subject to significant political bias).

However, this would only be acceptable if there was a widespread consensus that all available general price indices are fatally flawed.

4 ANALYSIS AND RESTATEMENT OF THE STATEMENT OF FINANCIAL POSITION

A broad outline of the process to restate assets and liabilities in the statement of financial position in accordance with the requirements of IAS 29 is shown in the diagram below:

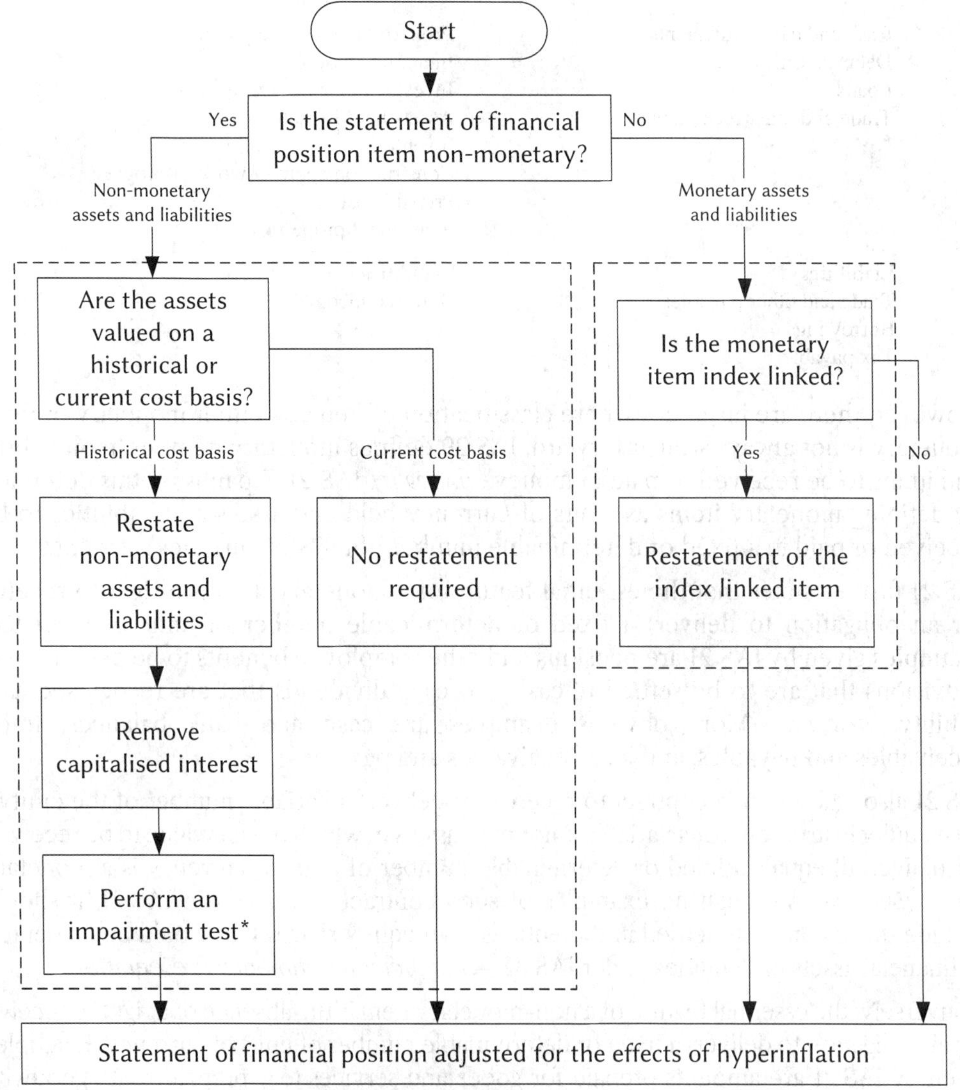

* IAS 29 requires the restated amount of a non-monetary item to be reduced in accordance with the appropriate IFRS when the restated amount exceeds its recoverable amount. *[IAS 29.19]*.

The above flowchart does not illustrate the restatement of investees and subsidiaries (see 4.3 below), deferred taxation (see 4.4 below) and equity (see 5 below).

4.1 Monetary and non-monetary items

4.1.1 Monetary or non-monetary distinction

Monetary items are not restated as they are already expressed in the measurement unit current at the end of the reporting period. Therefore an entity needs to determine whether or not an item is monetary in nature. Most statement of financial position items are readily classified as either monetary or non-monetary as is shown in the table below:

Monetary items	Non-monetary items
Assets	**Assets**
Cash and cash equivalents	Property, plant and equipment
Debt securities	Intangible assets
Loans	Investments in equity securities
Trade and other receivables	Assets held for sale
	Inventories
	Construction contract work-in-progress
	Prepaid costs
	Investment properties
Liabilities	**Liabilities**
Trade and other payables	Deferred income
Borrowings	
Tax payable	

However, there are instances where classification of items as either monetary or non-monetary is not always straightforward. IAS 29 defines monetary items as 'money held and items to be received or paid in money'. *[IAS 29.12]*. IAS 21 expands on this definition by defining monetary items as 'units of currency held and assets and liabilities to be received or paid in a fixed or determinable number of units of currency'. *[IAS 21.8]*.

IAS 21 further states that the essential feature of a monetary item is a right to receive (or an obligation to deliver) a fixed or determinable number of units of currency. Examples given by IAS 21 are pensions and other employee benefits to be paid in cash, provisions that are to be settled in cash and cash dividends that are recognised as a liability. *[IAS 21.16]*. More obvious examples are cash and bank balances, trade receivables and payables, and loan receivables and payables.

IAS 21 also states that 'a contract to receive (or deliver) a variable number of the entity's own equity instruments or a variable amount of assets in which the fair value to be received (or delivered) equals a fixed or determinable number of units of currency is a monetary item.' *[IAS 21.16]*. Although no examples of such contracts are given in IAS 21, it should include those contracts settled in the entity's own equity shares that would be presented as financial assets or liabilities under IAS 32 – *Financial Instruments: Presentation.*

Conversely, the essential feature of a non-monetary item is the absence of a right to receive (or an obligation to deliver) a fixed or determinable number of units of currency. Examples given by IAS 21 are amounts prepaid for goods and services (e.g. prepaid rent); goodwill; intangible assets; inventories; property, plant and equipment; and provisions that are to be settled by the delivery of a non-monetary asset. *[IAS 21.16]*. IAS 39 – *Financial Instruments: Recognition and Measurement* – indicates that equity instruments that are held as available-for-sale financial assets are non-monetary items. *[IAS 39.AG83]*. Likewise, guidance in

IFRS 9 – *Financial Instruments* – states that all equity instruments are non-monetary. *[IFRS 9.B5.7.3]*. Therefore, equity investments in subsidiaries, associates or joint ventures would also be considered non-monetary items. IAS 29 provides separate rules on restatement of such investees (see 4.3 below).

Even with this guidance there may be situations where the distinction is not clear. Certain assets and liabilities may require careful analysis before they can be classified. Examples of items that are not easily classified as either monetary or non-monetary include:

(a) *provisions:* these can be monetary, non-monetary or partly monetary. For example, a warranty provision would be:

    (i) entirely monetary when customers only have a right to return the product and obtain a cash refund equal to the amount they originally paid;

    (ii) non-monetary when customers have the right to have any defective product replaced; and

    (iii) partly monetary if customers can choose between a refund and a replacement of the defective product.

    Classification as either a monetary or a non-monetary item is not acceptable in (iii) above. To meet the requirements of IAS 29, part of the provision should be treated as a non-monetary item and the remainder as a monetary item;

(b) *deferred tax assets and liabilities:* characterising these as monetary or non-monetary can be difficult as explained in 4.4 below;

(c) *associates and joint ventures:* IAS 29 provides separate rules on restatement of investees that do not rely on the distinction between monetary and non-monetary items (see 4.3 below);

(d) *deposits or progress payments paid or received:* if the payments made are regarded as prepayments or as progress payments then the amounts should be treated as non-monetary items. However, if the payments made are in effect refundable deposits then the amounts should probably be treated as monetary items; and

(e) *index-linked assets and liabilities:* classification is particularly difficult when interest rates, lease payments or prices are linked to a price index.

In summary, the practical application of the monetary/non-monetary distinction can be complex and will require judgement on the part of preparers of financial statements. Further examples of problem areas in the application of the monetary/non-monetary distinction are discussed in Chapter 15 at 5.4.

4.1.2 Monetary items

Generally, monetary items are not restated to reflect the effect of inflation, because they already reflect their purchasing power at the end of the reporting period. However, monetary assets and liabilities linked by agreement to changes in prices, such as index-linked bonds and loans, should be adjusted in accordance with the terms of the underlying agreement to show the repayment obligation at the end of the reporting period. *[IAS 29.13]*. This adjustment should be offset against the gain or loss on the net monetary position (see 6.2 below). *[IAS 29.28]*.

This type of restatement is not a hyperinflation accounting adjustment, but rather a gain or loss on a financial instrument. Accounting for inflation linked bonds and loans under IAS 39 (or IFRS 9) may well lead to complexity in financial reporting. Depending on the specific wording of the inflation adjustment clause, such contracts may give rise to embedded derivatives and gains or losses will have to be recorded either in profit or loss or other comprehensive income depending on how the instrument is classified under IFRS 9 (or IAS 39) (see Chapter 44 at 5.1.5 and Chapter 47 at 6.3.5).

4.1.3 Non-monetary items carried at current cost

Non-monetary items carried at current cost are not restated because they are already expressed in terms of the measuring unit current at the end of the reporting period. *[IAS 29.29]*. Current cost is not defined by the standard, but the IASB's *Conceptual Framework* provides the following definition: 'Assets are carried at the amount of cash or cash equivalents that would have to be paid if the same or an equivalent asset was acquired currently. Liabilities are carried at the undiscounted amount of cash or cash equivalents that would be required to settle the obligation currently'. *[Framework 4.55(b)]*. IAS 29 expands this definition by including net realisable value and fair value into the concept of 'amounts current at the end of the reporting period'. *[IAS 29.14]*. In summary, this would include items carried at a value that reflects purchasing power at the balance sheet date.

It is important to note that non-monetary items that were revalued at some earlier date are not necessarily carried at current cost, and need to be restated from the date of their latest revaluation. *[IAS 29.18]*.

In many hyperinflationary economies, national legislation may require entities to adjust historical cost based financial information in a way that is not in accordance with IAS 29 (for example, national legislation may require entities to adjust the carrying amount of tangible fixed assets by applying a multiplier). Though financial information adjusted in accordance with national legislation is sometimes described as 'current cost' information, it will seldom meet the definition of current cost in accordance with the *Conceptual Framework*. *[Framework 4.55(b)]*. Where this is the case, entities must first determine the carrying value on the historical cost basis for these assets and liabilities before applying the requirements of IAS 29.

4.1.4 Non-monetary items carried at historical cost

Non-monetary items carried at historical cost, or cost less depreciation, are stated at amounts that were current at the date of their acquisition. The restated cost, or cost less depreciation, of those items is calculated as follows:

$$\text{net book value restated for hyperinflation} = \text{historical cost} \times \frac{\text{general price index at the end of the reporting period}}{\text{general price index at the date of acquisition}}$$

Application of this formula to property, plant and equipment, inventories of raw materials and merchandise, goodwill, patents, trademarks and similar assets appears to be straightforward, but does require detailed records of their acquisition dates and accurate price indices at those dates. *[IAS 29.15]*. It should be noted though that IAS 29 permits certain approximations as long as the procedures and judgements are consistent from period to period. *[IAS 29.10]*. Where sufficiently detailed records are not available or capable of estimation, IAS 29 suggests that it may be necessary to obtain an 'independent professional assessment' of the value of the items as the basis for their restatement in the first period of application of the standard, but also notes that this will only be in rare circumstances. *[IAS 29.16]*.

Example 16.2: Restatement of property, plant and equipment

The table below illustrates how the restatement of a non-monetary item (for example, property, plant and equipment) would be calculated in accordance with the requirements of IAS 29. When IAS 29 is first applied, the item is restated from the date of acquisition. In subsequent periods it is restated from the previous reporting period as shown below.

Net book value of property, plant and equipment	Historical restatements	Conversion factor	Restated for hyperinflation	
Opening balance, 1 January	510	2.40	1,224	(a)
– Additions (May)	360	1.80	648	(b)
– Disposals (March)	(105)	2.40	(252)	(c)
– Depreciation	(200)		(448)	(d)
Closing balance, 31 December	565		1,172	(e)

(a) The opening balance is restated by adjusting the historical balance for the increase in the price index between the beginning and the end of the reporting period;

(b) The additions are restated for the increase in the price index from May to December;

(c) The disposals are restated for the increase in the price index between the beginning and the end of the reporting period, assuming all disposals were acquired in a previous reporting period;

(d) Depreciation has been recalculated using the cost balance restated for hyperinflation on an asset by asset basis as a starting point. The alternative approach, to restate the depreciation charge by applying the appropriate conversion factor, could be easier to apply but may not be accurate enough when there is a significant level of additions and disposals during the reporting period;

(e) The closing balance is in practice determined by adding up items (a)-(d). Alternatively, the entity could calculate the closing balance by restating the acquisition cost of the individual assets for the change in the price index during the period of ownership.

The calculations described under (a)-(e) all require estimates regarding the general price index at given dates and are sometimes based on averages or best estimates of the actual date of the transaction.

When an entity purchases an asset and payment is deferred beyond normal credit terms, it would normally recognise the present value of the cash payment as its cost. *[IAS 16.23]*. When it is impracticable to determine the amount of interest, IAS 29 provides relief by allowing such assets to be restated from the payment date rather than the date of purchase. *[IAS 29.22]*.

Once the calculation discussed above has been completed, additional adjustments may need to be made. In order to arrive at the final restated cost of the non-monetary items, the provisional restated cost needs to be adjusted for borrowing costs and impairment, if applicable, as follows: *[IAS 29.19, 21]*

restated costs	=	net book value restated for hyperinflation	–	borrowing costs that compensate for inflation capitalised under IAS 23	–	adjustment to recoverable amount

IAS 29 only permits partial capitalisation of borrowing costs, unlike the full capitalisation that is ordinarily required by IAS 23 – *Borrowing Costs* (see Chapter 21), because of the risk of double counting as the entity would both restate the capital expenditure financed by borrowing and capitalise that part of the borrowing costs that compensates for the inflation during the same period. *[IAS 29.21]*. The difficulty when borrowing costs are capitalised is that IAS 29 only permits capitalisation of borrowing costs to the extent that those costs do not compensate for inflation. The standard does not provide any guidance on how an entity should go about determining the component of borrowing costs that compensates for the effects of inflation. Therefore, entities will need to develop an appropriate methodology.

It is possible that an IAS 29 inflation adjustment based on the general price index leads to non-monetary assets being stated above their recoverable amount. Therefore, IAS 29 requires that the restated amount of a non-monetary item is reduced, in accordance with the appropriate standard, when it exceeds its recoverable amount from the item's future use (including sale or other disposal). *[IAS 29.19]*. This requirement should be taken to mean that any overstatement of non-monetary assets not within the scope of IAS 39 should be calculated and accounted for in accordance with IAS 36 – *Impairment of Assets* – or the measurement provisions of IAS 2 – *Inventories* (see 4.2 below). That is, the asset is written down to its recoverable amount or net realisable value and the loss is recognised in profit or loss.

The example below illustrates how, after it has restated the historical cost based carrying amount of property, plant and equipment by applying the general price index, an entity adjusts the net book value restated for hyperinflation:

Example 16.3: Borrowing costs and net realisable value adjustments

After the entity has restated the historical cost based carrying amount of property, plant and equipment by applying the general price index, it needs to adjust the net book value restated for hyperinflation to take account of borrowing costs capitalised since the acquisition of the asset as follows:

Net book value restated for hyperinflation (inclusive of borrowing costs)		1,725	
Borrowing costs capitalised at historical cost under IAS 23	42		
Borrowing costs that compensated for inflation	(30)		
Borrowing costs permitted to be capitalised under IAS 29	12		
Borrowing costs that compensated for inflation	(30)		
Relevant conversion factor for the borrowing costs	2.10 ×		
		(63)	(a)
Net book value restated for hyperinflation and after adjustment of capitalised borrowing costs		1,662	
Net book value restated for hyperinflation and after adjustment of capitalised borrowing costs	1,662		
Amount recoverable from the item's future use	1,550		
	112		
Adjustment to lower recoverable amount		(112)	(b)
Carrying amount restated under IAS 29		1,550	

(a) The borrowing costs capitalised in the original historical cost financial statements are reversed, as they are not permitted under IAS 29;

(b) To the extent that the 'net book value restated for hyperinflation and after adjustment of capitalised borrowing costs' exceeds the 'amount recoverable from the item's future use', the restated amount should be reduced to the lower 'amount recoverable from the item's future use'.

4.2 Inventories

Inventories of finished and partly finished goods should be restated from the dates on which the costs of purchase and of conversion were incurred. *[IAS 29.15]*. This means that the individual components of finished goods should be restated from their respective purchase dates. Similarly, if production takes place in several distinct phases, the costs associated with each of those phases should be restated from the date that the cost was incurred.

Given the large number of transactions affecting an entity's inventory position, it may be difficult to determine the date of acquisition of individual items of inventory. Therefore, entities commonly approximate the ageing of inventories based on inventory turnover. Similarly, the level of the general price index at the date of acquisition is often determined at the average level for the month because an up-to-date price index is not available for each day of the month. Determining the appropriate level of the general price index can be difficult when the price index is updated relatively infrequently and the entity's business is highly seasonal.

IAS 29 requires restatement of inventory by applying a general price index, which could result in an overvaluation when the price of inventory items increases at a different rate from the general price index. At the end of each period it is therefore essential to ensure that items of inventory are not valued in excess of their net realisable value. Any overstated inventories should be written down to net realisable value under IAS 2. *[IAS 29.19]*.

4.3 Restatement of associates, joint ventures and subsidiaries

IAS 29 provides separate rules for the restatement of associates and joint ventures that are accounted for under the equity method. If the investee itself operates in the same hyperinflationary currency, the entity should restate the statement of financial position, income statement and the statement of comprehensive income of the investee in accordance with the requirements of IAS 29 in order to calculate its share of the investee's net assets and results of operations. *[IAS 29.20]*. The standard does not permit the investment in the investee to be treated as a single indivisible item for the purposes of the IAS 29 restatement. Restating the financial statements of an associate before application of the equity method will often be difficult because the investor may not have access to the detailed information required. The fact that the investor can exercise significant influence or has joint control over an investee often does not mean that the investor has unrestricted access to the investee's books and records at all times.

When the investor does not operate in the hyperinflationary currency, but the investee does, the same processes described above are still required to be completed prior to the equity accounting process. Once restated, the results of the investee are translated into the investor's presentation currency at the closing rate. *[IAS 29.20]*. IAS 21 contains a similar provision that requires that all current year amounts related to an entity (i.e. investee), whose functional currency is the currency of a hyperinflationary economy, to be translated at the closing rate at the date of the most recent statement of financial position (see Chapter 15 at 6.1). *[IAS 21.42]*.

If a parent that reports in the currency of a hyperinflationary economy has a subsidiary that also reports in the currency of a hyperinflationary economy, then the financial statements of that subsidiary must first be restated by applying a general price index of the country in whose currency it reports before they are included in the consolidated financial statements issued by its parent. *[IAS 29.35]*. When an investor has a subsidiary whose functional currency is the currency of a hyperinflationary economy, IAS 21 further clarifies that all current year amounts related to the subsidiary should be translated at the closing rate at the date of the most recent statement of financial position (see Chapter 15 at 6.1). *[IAS 21.42]*.

If a parent that reports in the currency of a hyperinflationary economy has a subsidiary that reports in a currency that is not hyperinflationary, the financial statements of that subsidiary should be translated in accordance with paragraph 39 of IAS 21 (see Chapter 15 at 6.1). *[IAS 21.39]*.

In addition, IAS 29 requires that when financial statements with different reporting dates are consolidated, all items, whether non-monetary or monetary are restated into the measuring unit current at the date of the consolidated financial statements. *[IAS 29.36]*.

4.4 Calculation of deferred taxation

Determining whether deferred tax assets and liabilities are monetary or non-monetary is difficult because:

- deferred taxation could be seen as a valuation adjustment that is either monetary or non-monetary depending on the asset or liability it relates to, or
- it could also be argued that any deferred taxation payable or receivable in the very near future is almost identical to current tax payable and receivable. Therefore, at least the short-term portion of deferred taxation, if payable or receivable, should be treated as if it were monetary.

IFRIC 7 provides guidance to facilitate the first time application of IAS 29. Although the interpretation notes that there continues to be a difference of opinion as to whether deferred taxation is monetary or non-monetary, *[IFRIC 7.BC21-BC22]*, the debate has been settled for practical purposes because:

- IAS 12 – *Income Taxes* – requires deferred taxation in the closing statement of financial position for the year to be calculated based on the difference between the carrying amount and the tax base of assets and liabilities, irrespective of the monetary/non-monetary distinction; and
- IFRIC 7 requires an entity to remeasure the deferred tax items in any comparative period in accordance with IAS 12 after it has restated the nominal carrying amounts of its non-monetary items at the date of the opening statement of financial position of the reporting period by applying the measuring unit at that date. These remeasured deferred tax items are then restated for the change in the measuring unit between the beginning and the end of reporting period. *[IFRIC 7.4]*.

The following example, which is based on the illustrative example in IFRIC 7, shows how an entity should restate its deferred taxation in the comparative period. *[IFRIC 7.IE1-IE6]*.

Example 16.4: Restatement of deferred taxation

Entity A owns a building that it acquired in December 2015. The carrying amount and tax base of the building, and the deferred tax liability are as follows:

Before IAS 29 restatement	2017	2016
Building (not restated)	300	400
Tax base	200	333
Tax rate	30%	30%
Deferred tax liability:		
(300 – 200) × 30% =	30	
(400 – 333) × 30% =		20

Entity A has identified the existence of hyperinflation in 2017 and therefore applies IAS 29 from the beginning of 2017. Entity A will use the following general price index and conversion factors to restate its financial statements:

	General price index
December 2015	95
December 2016	135
December 2017	223

The table below shows the method required by IFRIC 7:

	2017	2016	
Building (not restated)	300	400	
Building (restated in 2017 financial statements):			
300 × (223 ÷ 95) =	704		
400 × (223 ÷ 95) =		939	
Building (restated in 2016 financial statements):			
400 × (135 ÷ 95) =		568	(a)
Tax base	200	333	(b)
Deferred tax liability (restated in 2017 financial statements):			
(704 – 200) × 30% =	151		
(568 – 333) × 30% = 71; 71 × (223 ÷ 135) =		117	

Entity A measures the temporary difference at the end of 2015 by comparing (a) the restated carrying amount of the building in 2016 accounts to (b) its tax base at that date. The temporary difference calculated in that manner is then multiplied by the applicable tax rate and the resulting amount is then adjusted for the hyperinflation during 2017, resulting in a deferred tax liability of 116.

After entity A has restated its financial statements for a given year, all corresponding figures in the financial statements for a subsequent reporting period, including deferred tax items, are restated by applying the change in the measuring unit for that subsequent reporting period only to the restated financial statements for the previous reporting period. *[IFRIC 7.5].*

IAS 29 refers to IAS 12 for guidance on the calculation of deferred taxation by entities operating in hyperinflationary economies. *[IAS 29.32].* IAS 12 recognises that IAS 29 restatements of assets and liabilities may give rise to temporary differences when equivalent adjustments are not allowed for tax purposes. *[IAS 12.IE.A18].* Where IAS 29 adjustments give rise to temporary differences, IAS 12 requires the following accounting treatment:

(1) the deferred tax income or expense is recognised in profit or loss; and

(2) if, in addition to the restatement, non-monetary assets are also revalued, the deferred tax movement relating to the revaluation is recognised in other comprehensive income and the deferred tax relating to the restatement is recognised in profit or loss. *[IAS 12.IE.A18].*

For example, deferred taxation arising on revaluation of property, plant and equipment is recognised in other comprehensive income, just as it would be if the entity were not operating in a hyperinflationary economy. On the other hand, restatement in accordance with IAS 29 of property, plant and equipment that is measured at historical cost is recognised in profit or loss. Thus the treatment of deferred taxation related to non-monetary assets valued at historical cost and those that are revalued, is consistent with the general requirements of IAS 12.

5 RESTATEMENT OF THE STATEMENT OF CHANGES IN EQUITY

At the beginning of the first period when an entity applies IAS 29, it restates the components of owners' equity as follows:

- the components of owners' equity, except retained earnings and any revaluation surplus, are restated by applying a general price index from the dates the components were contributed or otherwise arose;
  - any revaluation surplus that arose in previous periods is eliminated; and
  - restated retained earnings are derived from all the other amounts in the restated statement of financial position. *[IAS 29.24].*

At the end of the first period and in subsequent periods, all components of owners' equity are restated by applying a general price index from the beginning of the period or the date of contribution, if later. *[IAS 29.25].* Subsequent revaluations may give rise to a revaluation surplus within equity.

IFRS does not define retained earnings and many jurisdictions require entities to appropriate part of the balance into specific (often non-distributable) reserves. In such cases, entities will need to apply judgement to determine whether these reserves are essentially part of retained earnings (and so are not restated by applying the general price index as described in paragraph 24 of IAS 29). If they are considered a separate component of equity, then they are restated by applying the general price index as explained above, both at the beginning of the first period when an entity applies IAS 29 and at the end of the first period and subsequent periods. Where entities have made such judgements concerning the types of reserves held, we believe this should be disclosed to users of the financial statements.

Though IAS 29 provides guidance on the restatement of assets, liabilities and individual components of shareholders' equity, national laws and regulations with which the entity needs to comply might not permit such revaluations. This can mean that IAS 29 may require restatement of distributable reserves, but that from the legal point of view in the jurisdiction concerned, those same reserves remain unchanged. That is, it is possible that 'restated retained earnings' under IAS 29 will not all be legally distributable.

It may therefore be unclear to users of financial statements restated under IAS 29 to what extent components of equity are distributable. Because of its global constituents, the IASB's standards cannot deal with specific national legal requirements relating to a legal entity's equity. Entities reporting under IAS 29 should therefore disclose the extent to which components of equity are distributable where this is not obvious from the financial statements. In our view it is important for entities to give supplementary information in the circumstances where the IAS 29 adjustments have produced large apparently distributable reserves that are in fact not distributable.

Example 16.5: Restatement of equity

The table below shows the effect of a hypothetical IAS 29 restatement on individual components of equity. Issued share capital and share premium increase by applying the general price index, the revaluation reserve is eliminated as required, and retained earnings is the balancing figure derived from all other amounts in the restated statement of financial position.

	Amounts before restatement	Amounts after IAS 29 restatement	Components of equity under national law
Issued capital and share premium	1,500	3,150	1,500
Revaluation reserve	800	–	800
Retained earnings	350	1,600	350
Total equity	2,650	4,750	2,650

A user of the financial statements of the entity might get the impression, based on the information restated in accordance with IAS 29, that distributable reserves have increased from 350 to 1,600. However, if national law does not permit revaluation of assets, liabilities and components of equity then distributable reserves remain unchanged.

6 RESTATEMENT OF THE STATEMENT OF COMPREHENSIVE INCOME AND INCOME STATEMENT

IAS 29 requires that all items in historical cost based statements of comprehensive income (and income statements if presented) be expressed in terms of the measuring unit current at the end of the reporting period. *[IAS 29.26]*. The standard contains a similar requirement for current cost based statements of comprehensive income (and income statements if presented), because the underlying transactions or events are recorded at current cost at the time they occurred rather than in the measuring unit current at the end of the reporting period. *[IAS 29.30]*. Therefore, all amounts in the statements of comprehensive income (and income statements if presented) need to be restated as follows:

$$\text{restated amount} = \text{amount before restatement} \times \frac{\text{general price index at the end of the reporting period}}{\text{general price index when the underlying income or expenses were initially recorded}}$$

Actually performing the above calculation on a real set of financial statements is often difficult because an entity would need to keep a very detailed record of when it entered into transactions and when it incurred expenses. Instead of using the exact price index for a transaction it may be more practical to use an average price index that approximates the actual rate at the date of the transaction. For example, an average rate for a week or a month might be used for all transactions occurring during that period. However, it must be stressed that if price indices fluctuate significantly, the use of an average for the period may be inappropriate.

There may be items in statements of comprehensive income (and income statements if presented), e.g. interest income and expense, that comprise an element that is intended to compensate for the effect of hyperinflation. However, even those items need to be restated as IAS 29 specifically requires that 'all amounts need to be restated' (see 6.1 below). *[IAS 29.26, 30]*.

Example 16.6 illustrates how an entity might, for example, restate its revenue to the measuring unit current at the end of the reporting period. A similar calculation would work well for other items in statements of comprehensive income (and income statements if presented), with the exception of:

(a) depreciation and amortisation charges which are often easier to restate by using the cost balance restated for hyperinflation as a starting point;

(b) deferred taxation which should be based on the temporary differences between the carrying amount and tax base of assets and liabilities, the restated opening balance carrying amount of statement of financial position items, and the underlying tax base of those items; and

(c) the net monetary gain or loss which results from the IAS 29 restatements (see 6.2 below).

Example 16.6: Restatement of historical cost income statement

An entity would restate its revenue for the period ending 31 December 2016, when the general price index was 2,880, as shown in the table below.

	General price index	Conversion factor	Revenue before restatement	Restated revenue
31 January 2016	1,315	(2,880 ÷ 1,315) = 2.19	40	87.6
28 February 2016	1,345	(2,880 ÷ 1,345) = 2.14	35	74.9
31 March 2016	1,371	etc. = 2.10	45	94.5
30 April 2016	1,490	1.93	45	87.0
31 May 2016	1,600	1.80	65	117.0
30 June 2016	1,846	1.56	70	109.2
31 July 2016	1,923	1.50	70	104.8
31 August 2016	2,071	1.39	65	90.4
30 September 2016	2,163	1.33	75	99.9
31 October 2016	2,511	1.15	75	86.0
30 November 2016	2,599	1.11	80	88.6
31 December 2016	2,880	1.00	80	80.0
			745	1,119.9

Inevitably, in practice there is some approximation in this process because of the assumptions that the entity is required to make, for example the use of weighted averages rather than more detailed calculations and assumptions as to the timing of the underlying transactions (e.g. the calculation above assumes the revenues for the month are earned on the final day of the month, which is not realistic).

6.1 Restatement of interest and exchange differences

A common question is whether an entity should restate exchange differences under IAS 29, because the standard considers that 'foreign exchange differences related to invested or borrowed funds, are also associated with the net monetary position'. *[IAS 29.28]*. Nevertheless, the standard requires that all items in the income statement and statement of comprehensive income are expressed in terms of the measuring unit current at the end of the reporting period. 'Therefore all amounts need to be restated by applying the change in the general price index from the dates when the items of income and expenses were initially recorded in the financial statements'. *[IAS 29.26]*.

Interest and exchange differences should therefore be restated for the effect of inflation, as are all other items in the statement of comprehensive income (and income statements if presented), and be presented on a gross basis. However, it may be helpful if they are presented together with the gain or loss on net monetary position in the statement of comprehensive position. *[IAS 29.28]*.

6.2 Calculation of the gain or loss on the net monetary position

In theory, hyperinflation only affects the value of money and monetary items and does not affect the value, as distinct from the price, of non-monetary items. Therefore, any gain or loss because of hyperinflation will be the gain or loss on the net monetary position of the entity. By arranging the items in an ordinary statement of financial position, it can be shown that the monetary position minus the non-monetary position is always equal to zero:

	Total	Monetary items	Non-monetary items
Monetary assets	280	280	
Non-monetary assets	170		170
Monetary liabilities	(200)	(200)	
Non-monetary liabilities	(110)		(110)
Assets minus liabilities	140		
Shareholders' equity	(140)		(140)
Net position	0	80	(80)

Theoretically, the gain or loss on the net monetary position can be calculated by applying the general price index to the entity's monetary assets and liabilities. This would require the entity to determine its net monetary position on a daily basis, which would be entirely impracticable given the resources required to prepare daily IFRS compliant accounts as well as the difficulties in making the monetary/non-monetary distinction (see 4.1 above). The standard therefore allows the gain or loss on the net monetary position to be estimated by applying the change in a general price index to the weighted average for the period of the difference between monetary assets and monetary liabilities. *[IAS 29.27, 31]*. Due care should be exercised in estimating the gain or loss on the net monetary position, as a calculation based on averages for the period (or monthly averages) can be unreliable if addressed without accurate consideration of the pattern of hyperinflation and the volatility of the net monetary position.

However, as shown in the above table, any restatement of the non-monetary items must be met by an equal restatement of the monetary items. Therefore, in preparing financial statements it is more practical to assume that the gain or loss on the net monetary position is exactly the reverse of the restatement of the non-monetary items. A stand-alone calculation of the net gain or loss can be used to verify the reasonableness of the restatement of the non-monetary items.

The gain or loss on the net monetary position as calculated above, as well as any adjustments on inflation linked instruments (see 4.1.2 above), should be included in profit or loss and disclosed separately. It may be helpful to present it together with items that are also associated with the net monetary position such as interest income and expense, and foreign exchange differences related to invested or borrowed funds. *[IAS 29.28].*

6.3 Measurement of reclassification adjustments within equity

IAS 29 does not provide guidance on the measurement basis of reclassifications from other comprehensive income. For example, it is not clear when an available-for-sale instrument is sold, whether the amount reclassified into profit and loss is based on the amounts historically recorded in other comprehensive income, or alternatively based on an inflation adjusted amount. Another example is the case of cash flow hedges where gains or losses in an earlier reporting period are recycled to profit and loss to offset against the gains or losses of the hedged item at a later date.

The conflict arises due to the manner in which the statement of comprehensive income is constructed, including the need to classify items in other comprehensive income as amounts to be recycled, or not. The need to classify items in other comprehensive income into items that are recycled to profit or loss, or not, would indicate that amounts initially recorded in other comprehensive income should be recycled at amounts as originally recorded. While this may satisfy the requirements for other comprehensive income, this leads to a loss of relevant information in the income statement, or the profit or loss section of the statement of comprehensive income (if this is presented as one statement). Using the examples cited above, the gain or loss on disposal of an available for sale instrument would no longer be presented in terms of the index being used for purposes of restating amounts in profit or loss. In the case of a cash flow hedge, the offset that would also be expected in the income statement is also lost. The alternative view would be to recycle amounts that have been restated in terms of the current index that is being applied. This is illustrated in the example below.

Example 16.7: Measurement of reclassification adjustments

An entity acquired an item of PPE for FCU 3,000 on 31 December 2017. The exchange rate on the date of acquisition was CU10 to FCU1, therefore the cost to the entity was CU 30,000. The entity entered, before the acquisition was made, into a fully effective cash flow hedge that resulted in a gain of CU 6,000. The entity's accounting policy for cash flow hedges is to reclassify from equity to profit or loss as a reclassification adjustment in the same period or periods during which the asset acquired affects profit or loss. The useful life of the asset is three years, therefore in a non-hyperinflationary environment, for each of these three years, depreciation would amount to CU 10,000, and CU 2,000 would be reclassified from other comprehensive income to profit or loss.

IAS 29 is not explicit on whether the reclassification from other comprehensive income should be adjusted for the effects of hyperinflation. The following example illustrates the difference between adjusting and not adjusting the reclassification of the cash flow hedge gains for the effect of hyperinflation. For the purpose of this example, assume the general price index was 100 at 31 December 2017 and 150 at 31 December 2018.

	2018 – Hyperinflationary Adjusted	2018 – Hyperinflationary Non-Adjusted	2018 – Non-hyperinflationary
Depreciation	(a) –15,000	(a) –15,000	–10,000
Reclassification of cash flow hedge gains	(b) 3,000	2,000	2,000
Net profit			
Other comprehensive income			
Reclassification of cash flow hedge gains	–3,000	–2,000	–2,000

(a) 30,000 × (150/100) / 3

(b) 6,000 × (150/100) / 3

If the entity had made the policy choice to include gains or losses in the initial cost or carrying amount of the asset as a basis adjustment, the result would be consistent with the outcome of the adjusted reclassification approach.

While this would ensure relevant information in the income statement, this would lead to different amounts being originally recorded and subsequently recycled in other comprehensive income.

As no direct guidance is given in IAS 29, the development of an accounting policy in terms of the IAS 8 – *Accounting Policies, Changes in Accounting Estimates and Errors* – hierarchy would be required. In developing such an accounting policy an entity would need to apply judgement and consider the objective of the standard that gives to amounts that are recycled to profit or loss. The basic accounting requirements before the application of IAS 29 for the hedge accounting example cited above is currently contained in IAS 39 (or IFRS 9 if already adopted). Understanding the objective of hedge accounting and what risks have been hedged in the designated relationship would be relevant inputs in developing an appropriate accounting policy. Once developed, the general recommendation of IFRS to apply procedures and judgements consistently should be followed for a particular class of equity reclassification. As there are numerous different types of reclassifications within equity, an entity may need to determine a relevant policy for each class of adjustment that could occur.

7 RESTATEMENT OF THE STATEMENT OF CASH FLOWS

The standard requires that all items in the statement of cash flows be expressed in terms of the measuring unit current at the end of the reporting period. *[IAS 29.33]*. This is a difficult requirement to fulfil in practice.

IAS 7 – *Statement of Cash Flows* – requires the following information to be presented:

(a) cash flows from operating activities, which are the principal revenue-producing activities of the entity and other activities that are not investing or financing activities;

(b) cash flows from investing activities, which are the acquisition and disposal of long-term assets and other investments not included in cash equivalents; and

(c) cash flows from financing activities, which are activities that result in changes in the size and composition of the equity capital and borrowings of the entity. *[IAS 7.6, 10]*.

In effect IAS 29 requires restatement of most items in a statement of cash flows, therefore implying that the actual cash flows at the time of the transactions will be different from the numbers presented in the statement of cash flows itself. However, not all items are restated using the same method and many of the restatements are based on estimates. For example, items in the income statement or statement of comprehensive income are restated using an estimate of the general price index at the time that the revenues were earned and the costs incurred. Unavoidably this will give rise to some inconsistencies. Similarly, the restatement of statement of financial position items will give rise to discrepancies because some items are not easily classified as either monetary or non-monetary. This raises the question of how an entity should classify the monetary gain or loss relating to a statement of financial position item in its statement of cash flows.

It is not clear from IAS 29 how a monetary gain or loss should be presented in the statement of cash flows. In practice different approaches have been adopted such as:

(a) presenting the effect of inflation on operating, investing and financing cash flows separately for each of these activities and presenting the net monetary gain or loss as a reconciling item in the cash and cash equivalents reconciliation;

(b) presenting the monetary gain or loss on cash and cash equivalents and the effect of inflation on operating, investing and financing cash flows as one number; and

(c) attributing the effect of inflation on operating, investing and financing cash flows to the underlying item and presenting the monetary gain or loss on cash and cash equivalents separately.

Irrespective of the method chosen, users of statements of cash flows prepared in the currency of a hyperinflationary economy should be mindful of the fact that figures presented in the statement of cash flows may have been restated in accordance with IAS 29 and may differ from the actual underlying cash flows. In our view it is important for entities that have a significant proportion of their activities in hyperinflationary economies to consider whether the entity should provide sufficient additional disclosures to ensure that the financial statements are fully understood. Whether this is limited to a general explanation of the mismatch between reported and actual amounts, or specific information on major transactions is provided, would depend on the nature and materiality of transactions affected.

8 RESTATEMENT OF COMPARATIVE FIGURES

The standard requires that all financial information be presented in terms of the measurement unit current at the end of the current reporting period, therefore:

- corresponding figures for the previous reporting period, whether they were based on a historical cost approach or a current cost approach, are restated by applying a general price index; and
- information that is disclosed in respect of earlier periods is also expressed in terms of the measuring unit current at the end of the reporting period. *[IAS 29.34]*.

Where IAS 29 was applied in the previous reporting period, this will be a straightforward mathematical computation to apply the measuring unit current at the end of the reporting period to the prior year comparative figures. An example of this can be seen in the restatement of the opening balance of property, plant and equipment in Example 16.2 above.

9 INTERIM REPORTING

The illustrative examples to IAS 34 – *Interim Financial Reporting* – state that interim financial reports in hyperinflationary economies are prepared using the same principles as at financial year end. *[IAS 34.B32].* This means that the financial statements must be stated in terms of the measuring unit current at the end of the interim period and that the gain or loss on the net monetary position is included in net income (profit or loss). The comparative financial information reported for prior periods must also be restated to the current measuring unit. *[IAS 34.B33].* Hence, an entity that reports quarterly information must restate the comparative statements of financial position, income statements and other primary financial statements each quarter.

In restating its financial information an entity may not 'annualise' the recognition of the gain or loss on the net monetary position or use an estimated annual inflation rate in preparing an interim financial report in a hyperinflationary economy. *[IAS 34.B34].*

Interim reporting of a group containing a subsidiary that reports in a hyperinflationary currency results in particular issues in the year that the subsidiary's functional currency becomes hyperinflationary. These are discussed further at 10.1 below.

10 TRANSITION

10.1 Economies becoming hyperinflationary

When the functional currency of an entity becomes hyperinflationary it must start applying IAS 29. The standard requires that the financial statements and any information in respect of earlier periods should be stated in terms of the measuring unit current at the end of the reporting period. *[IAS 29.8].* IFRIC 7 clarifies that items should be restated fully retrospectively. In the first year in which the entity identifies the existence of hyperinflation, the requirements of IAS 29 should be applied as if the economy had always been hyperinflationary. The opening statement of financial position at the beginning of the earliest period presented in the financial statements should be restated as follows:

- non-monetary items measured at historical cost should be restated to reflect the effect of inflation from the date the assets were acquired and the liabilities were incurred or assumed; and
- non-monetary items carried at amounts current at dates other than those of acquisition or incurrence should be restated to reflect the effect of inflation from the dates those carrying amounts were determined. *[IFRIC 7.3].*

What is less obvious is how an entity (a parent), which does not operate in a hyperinflationary economy, should account for the restatement of an entity (a subsidiary) that operates in an economy that became hyperinflationary in the current reporting period when incorporating it within its consolidated financial statements. This issue has been clarified by IAS 21 which specifically prohibits restatement of comparative figures when the presentation currency is not hyperinflationary. *[IAS 21.42(b)]*. This means that when the financial statements of a hyperinflationary subsidiary are translated into the non-hyperinflationary presentation currency for consolidation into the financial statements of the parent, the comparative amounts are not adjusted.

However, the impact on interim financial statements of such a parent may be more difficult to resolve. For example, a parent (with a December year-end) may own a subsidiary, whose functional currency is considered hyperinflationary from 31 August 2017 onwards. Questions arising in respect of the preparation of quarterly interim financial statements would include:

- Would the parent entity need to re-issue interim reports that had been issued earlier in the current year?
- In the period that the subsidiary's economy become hyperinflationary, would the parent entity adjust the comparative interim information for hyperinflation (and year to date interim information) for the same interim period in the prior year?
- In the first quarter of the following financial period (2018), would the parent entity adjust the comparative information for hyperinflation (and year to date interim information) for the same interim period in the prior year (2017)?

Although the subsidiary will apply the requirements of IAS 29 on a retrospective basis, the parent will incorporate the results of the subsidiary into the group financial statements as required by IAS 21. Hence in response to the first question, the parent would not restate prior interim financial statements in the year that the subsidiary's functional currency becomes hyperinflationary. Hyperinflationary adjustments would only occur in the interim financial statements of the parent from the date that the subsidiary became hyperinflationary onwards. Further, IAS 21 would preclude the restatement of comparative interim financial statements as contemplated in the second question above. *[IAS 21.42(b)]*. The issue addressed in the third question is not specifically addressed by IAS 21 or IAS 34. We consider that the parent entity is allowed but not required to adjust its comparative interim statements. These specific requirements of IAS 34 are considered in Chapter 39 at 9.6.2.

10.2 Economies ceasing to be hyperinflationary

Determining when a currency stops being hyperinflationary is not easy in practice. It is important to review trends, not just at the end of the reporting period but also subsequently. In addition, consistency demands that the financial statements do not unnecessarily fall in and out of a hyperinflationary presentation, where a more careful judgement would have avoided it.

When an economy ceases to be hyperinflationary, entities should discontinue preparation and presentation of financial statements in accordance with IAS 29. The amounts expressed in the measuring unit current at the end of the previous reporting period will be treated as the deemed cost of the items in the subsequent statement of financial position. *[IAS 29.38]*.

The previous reporting period used as the basis for the carrying amounts going forward may be the last annual reporting period or it may be an interim period depending on whether the entity prepares interim reports. Therefore, for interim reporters, it should be noted that, an amalgamation of interim periods during which IAS 29 was applied with those where it was not, may result in financial statements that are difficult to interpret. This is shown in Example 16.8 below.

Example 16.8: Economies ceasing to be hyperinflationary in an interim period

An entity has a financial year end of 31 December and prepares interim financial statements on a quarterly basis. The last annual financial statements were prepared for the period ending 31 December 2016 when the economy was hyperinflationary. In August 2017 the economy ceased to be hyperinflationary. The table below shows the impact on the financial statements.

Period	Impact on financial statements
Annual 31 December 2016	Hyperinflationary accounting.
Interim 31 March 2017	Hyperinflationary accounting.
Interim 30 June 2017	Hyperinflationary accounting.
Interim 30 September 2017	No longer in the scope of IAS 29. Balances at 30 June 2017 used as the basis for carrying amounts going forward. Comparatives will include adjustments for hyperinflation up to 30 June 2017.
Annual 31 December 2017	No longer in the scope of IAS 29. Balances at 31 December 2017 will use 30 June 2017 as the basis for carrying amounts going forward. Comparatives will include adjustments for hyperinflation up to 30 June 2017.

The following extract illustrates the effect of ceasing to be hyperinflationary on financial results.

Extract 16.1: Belarusian National Reinsurance Organisation (2015)

Statement of profit or loss and other comprehensive income for the year ended 31 December 2015 [extract]

All amounts in millions of BYR

	Notes	2015	2014
Loss on net monetary position due to hyperinflation effect		–	(210 592)
Profit before tax		230 687	(68 498)
Income tax expense	19	(73 600)	(30 413)
Profit /(loss) for the year		157 087	(98 911)

Notes to the financial statements [extract]

(2) BASIS OF PREPARATION [extract]

The accompanying financial statements have been prepared in accordance with International Financial Reporting Standards ("IFRS").

Hyperinflation

In 2014 and earlier the economy of the Republic of Belarus was classified as a hyperinflationary economy under the criteria included in IAS 29, and IAS 29. Starting from 1 January 2015 the economy of the Republic of Belarus ceased to be classified as a hyperinflationary economy. Therefore, all non-monetary items (assets, liabilities and equity) are presented in units of measure as of 31 December 2014 as the opening balances as at 1 January 2015. In the statement of profit or loss and other comprehensive income for the period ended 31 December 2015, non-monetary items have been presented as the opening balances as at 1 January 2015 units of measure as at 31 December 2014.

10.3 Economies exiting severe hyperinflation

IFRS 1 includes an exemption for entities that have been subject to severe hyperinflation before the date of transition to IFRS, or on reapplication into IFRS after being unable to prepare IFRS compliant financial statements. Severe hyper-inflation has both of the following characteristics:

(a) a reliable general price index is not available to all entities with transactions and balances in the currency; and

(b) exchangeability between the currency and a relatively stable foreign currency does not exist. *[IFRS 1.D27].*

This exemption was included in response to a specific issue that occurred in Zimbabwe in 2008. In Zimbabwe the ability to produce financial statements had been completely undermined by severe hyperinflation. In response to this situation, an exemption was created in IFRS 1 which would be available to any entity that is either adopting IFRS for the first time, or is reapplying IFRS due to severe hyperinflation. In practice, the existence of severe hyperinflation (as described by the standard) is a rare economic occurrence (see Chapter 5 at 5.18).

11 TRANSLATION TO A DIFFERENT PRESENTATION CURRENCY

IAS 21 requires an entity to determine its functional currency as the currency of the primary economic environment in which it operates. If the functional currency is that of a hyperinflationary economy, the entity's financial statements are restated in accordance with IAS 29. An entity cannot avoid restatement by adopting as its functional currency, a currency other than the functional currency as determined in accordance with IAS 21. *[IAS 21.14].*

However, an entity is permitted to present its financial statements in any presentation currency it chooses. A different presentation currency will not alter the entity's functional currency or the requirement to apply IAS 29. However, it is noted that determining an appropriate exchange rate may be difficult in jurisdictions where there are severe exchange controls, and where judgement has been used to determine an appropriate rate, this should be disclosed. The Interpretations Committee noted that predominant practice is to apply by extension the principle in paragraph 26 of IAS 21 (see Chapter 15 at 6.1.3), which gives guidance on which exchange rate to use when reporting foreign currency transactions in the functional currency when several exchange rates are available.[2]

If an entity, whose functional currency is hyperinflationary, wants to translate its financial statements into a different presentation currency it must first restate its financial statements in accordance with IAS 29 and then apply the following procedures under IAS 21:

'(a) all amounts (i.e. assets, liabilities, equity items, income and expenses, including comparatives) shall be translated at the closing rate at the date of the most recent statement of financial position, except that

(b) when amounts are translated into the currency of a non-hyperinflationary economy, comparative amounts shall be those that were presented as current year amounts in the relevant prior year financial statements (i.e. not adjusted for subsequent changes in the price level or subsequent changes in exchange rates).' *[IAS 21.42].*

In other words, when an entity that applies IAS 29 translates its financial statements into a non-hyperinflationary presentation currency, the comparative information should not be restated under IAS 29. Instead IAS 21 should be applied and the comparative amounts should be those that were presented as current year amounts in the prior period. For a more detailed discussion of these requirements see Chapter 15 at 6.1.

When the economy ceases to be hyperinflationary, and restatement in accordance with IAS 29 is no longer required, an entity uses the amounts restated to the price level at the date it ceased restating its financial statements as the historical costs for translation into the presentation currency. *[IAS 21.43].*

12 DISCLOSURES

IAS 29 requires that entities should disclose the following information when they apply the provisions of the standard:

(a) the fact that the financial statements and the corresponding figures for previous periods have been restated for the changes in the general purchasing power of the functional currency and, as a result, are stated in terms of the measuring unit current at the end of the reporting period;

(b) whether the financial statements are based on a historical cost approach or a current cost approach; and

(c) the identity and level of the price index at the end of the reporting period and the movement in the index during the current and the previous reporting period. *[IAS 29.39].*

It should be noted that disclosure of financial information that is restated under IAS 29 as a supplement to unrestated financial information is not permitted. This is to prevent entities from giving the historical cost based financial information greater prominence than the information that is restated under IAS 29. The standard also discourages separate presentation of unrestated financial information, but does not explicitly prohibit it. *[IAS 29.7].* However, such unrestated financial statements would not be in accordance with IFRS and should be clearly identified as such. An entity that is required (for example by local tax authorities or stock exchange regulators) to present unrestated financial statements needs to ensure that the IFRS financial statements are perceived to be the main financial statements rather than mere supplemental information.

The following excerpt illustrates the disclosure of the loss on net monetary position, the basis of preparation and the required disclosures in respect of the relevant price index.

Extract 16.2: Priorbank JSC (2014)

Consolidated income statement for the year ended 31 December 2014 [extract]
(in millions of Belarusian rubles in terms of purchasing power of the Belarusian ruble as at 31 December 2014)

	Notes	2014	2013
Loss on net monetary position		(414,573)	(336,754)
Income before income tax expense		**1,141,881**	**1,251,055**
Income tax expense	14	(373,037)	(310,069)
Profit for the year		**768,844**	**940,986**
Attributable to:			
– shareholders of the Bank		746,437	923,141
– non-controlling interests		22,407	17,845
		768,844	**940,986**

Notes to 2014 IFRS Consolidated financial statements [extract]

2. Basis of preparation [extract]

General [extract]

These consolidated financial statements have been prepared in accordance with International Financial Reporting Standards ("IFRS").

Inflation accounting

With the effect from 1 January 2011, the Belarusian economy is considered to be hyperinflationary in accordance with the criteria in IAS 29 "*Financial Reporting in Hyperinflationary Economies*" ("IAS 29"). Accordingly, adjustments and reclassifications for the purposes of presentation of IFRS financial statements include restatement, in accordance with IAS 29, for changes in the general purchasing power of the Belorussian ruble. The standard requires that the financial statements prepared in the currency of a hyperinflationary economy be stated in terms of the measuring unit current at the reporting date.

On the application of IAS 29 the Bank used the conversion coefficient derived from the consumer price index in the Republic of Belarus ("CPI") published by the National Statistics Committee. The CPIs for the nine-year period and corresponding conversion coefficient since the time when the Republic of Belarus previously ceased to be considered hyperinflationary, i.e. since 1 January 2006, were as follows:

Year	**Index, %**	**Conversion coefficient**
2006	106.6	528.9
2007	112.1	471.8
2008	113.3	416.4
2009	110.1	378.2
2010	109.9	344.2
2011	208.7	164.9
2012	121.7	135.4
2013	116.6	116.2
2014	116.2	100

Monetary assets and liabilities are not restated because they are already expressed in terms of the monetary unit current as at 31 December 2014. Non-monetary assets and liabilities (items which are not already expressed in terms of the monetary unit as at 31 December 2014) are restated by applying the relevant index. The effect of inflation on the Bank's net monetary position is included in the consolidated income statement as loss on net monetary position.

The application of IAS 29 results in an adjustment for the loss of purchasing power of the Belarusian ruble recorded in the income statement. In a period of inflation, an entity holding an excess of monetary assets over monetary liabilities loses purchasing power, which results in a loss on the net monetary position. This loss/gain is derived as the difference resulting from the restatement of non-monetary assets and liabilities, equity and items in the statement of comprehensive income. Corresponding figures for the year ended 31 December 2013 have also been restated so that they are presented in terms of the purchasing power of the Belarusian Ruble as at 31 December 2014.

Telefónica, S.A. is an example of a parent entity that has subsidiaries that operate in an economy subject to hyperinflation. As a parent entity, Telefónica, S.A. would not restate the comparative amounts and, therefore, has reported a reconciling item for the effect of hyperinflation adjustments.

Extract 16.3: Telefónica, S.A. and subsidiaries (2016)

Notes to the consolidated financial statements (consolidated annual accounts) for the year ended December 31, 2016 [extract]

Note 7. Goodwill [extract]

The movement in this heading assigned to each Group segment was the following:

2016

Millions of euros	Balance at 12/31/15	Acquisitions	Write-offs	Translation differences and hyperinflation adjustments	Balance at 12/31/16
Telefónica Spain	4,306	–	–	–	4,306
Telefónica Brazil	9,345	–	–	2,220	11,565
Telefónica Germany	4,787	–	–	–	4,787
Telefónica United Kingdom	5,621	–	–	(797)	4,824
Telefonica Hispanoamérica	3,187	–	(215)	68	3,040
Others	149	26	(13)	2	164
Total	27,395	26	(228)	1,493	28,686

Chapter 16

References

1 Minutes of the meetings of the International Practices Task Force are available at www.thecaq.org

2 *IFRIC Update*, July 2014, p.11.

Chapter 17 Intangible assets

List of examples

Chapter 17 Intangible assets

1 INTRODUCTION

1.1 Background

IAS 38 – *Intangible Assets* – is structured along similar lines as IAS 16 – *Property, Plant and Equipment*.

Why was the standard needed? Accounting practice had largely developed on an issue-by-issue basis, with the result being a variety of treatments for particular types of intangible assets. There have been many topical issues over the years: research and development (as long ago as the 1970s), brands and similar assets, particularly those arising in business combinations, and today's assets and costs that are directly and indirectly related to the internet and personal communications. In time, it came to be seen that two different types of intangible rights shared characteristics that made a single standard meaningful. First, there were internal costs incurred by entities from which they expect to benefit. The critical issue is identifying whether, when and how much of these costs should be recognised as assets, which means distinguishing between assets and expenses. There are many types of expenditure from which an entity may expect to benefit where it is not possible to identify an asset or where the relationship between the cost and future benefits is too tenuous to allow capitalisation. The second arose from business combinations and the premiums paid by acquirers for intangible rights. This brought an additional issue: were these rights distinguishable from goodwill? This has become more important as a consequence of goodwill not being amortised, which means that entities must identify as separate intangible assets certain rights, e.g. customer relationships that had historically been subsumed within goodwill.

Unlike IAS 16 whose scope is defined by its title (it applies to property, plant and equipment), IAS 38 includes a definition of the assets to which it applies. However, this is so general (an intangible asset is an identifiable non-monetary asset without physical substance) that the standard must exclude certain assets and items of expenditure that would otherwise fall within it. The definition could include assets generated by other standards, which are therefore excluded from scope. Incidentally, this shows just how broad the definition could be as the list of scope exemptions includes deferred tax assets, leases and assets arising from employee benefits which are within scope of, respectively, IAS 12 – *Income Taxes*, IAS 17 – *Leases* – and IAS 19 – *Employee Benefits*. *[IAS 38.3]*.

Additional clarification comes from the prohibition on recognising internally-generated goodwill. This means that expenditure on brands and similar assets cannot be recognised as an intangible asset as it is not possible to distinguish these costs from the costs of developing the business as a whole. *[IAS 38.63, 64]*. However, arguably the opposite approach is taken with the intangible assets identified in a business combination where the standard encourages separate recognition through a broad approach given to concepts such as separability. This remains a difficult and controversial area, discussed at 5 below. The requirements of IFRS 3 – *Business Combinations* – are discussed in Chapter 9.

This chapter addresses the specific provisions of IAS 38, with the requirements relating to intangible assets acquired as part of a business combination being covered both at 5 below and in Chapter 9. IFRS 13 – *Fair Value Measurement* – includes the guidance relating to the determination of fair values (see Chapter 14). Impairment of intangible assets is addressed in IAS 36 – *Impairment of Assets*, covered in Chapter 20.

Other intangible assets are dealt with by specific accounting pronouncements. The amount spent on the operation and development of websites led to the issue of SIC-32 – *Intangible Assets – Web Site Costs* – that is discussed at 6.2.5 below. Although IAS 38 addresses acquisition by way of government grant, this has not proved sufficient to address accounting for various schemes designed to influence business behaviour, especially in environmental areas. Emissions trading schemes give rise to intangible rights and the attempts to devise a satisfactory accounting model for these and similar schemes are considered at 11.2 below.

1.2 Terms used in IAS 38

The following terms are used in IAS 38 with the meanings specified:

Term	Definition
Intangible asset	An identifiable non-monetary asset without physical substance. *[IAS 38.8]*.
Asset	An asset is a resource: *[IAS 38.8]* (a) controlled by an entity as a result of past events; and (b) from which future economic benefits are expected to flow to the entity.
Monetary assets	Money held and assets to be received in fixed or determinable amounts of money. *[IAS 38.8]*.
Identifiable	An asset is identifiable if it either: *[IAS 38.12]* (a) is separable, i.e. capable of being separated or divided from the entity and sold, transferred, licensed, rented or exchanged, either individually or together with a related contract, identifiable asset or liability, regardless of whether the entity intends to do so; or (b) arises from contractual or other legal rights, regardless of whether those rights are transferable or separable from the entity or from other rights and obligations.
Control	The power to obtain the future economic benefits flowing from the underlying resource and to restrict the access of others to those benefits. *[IAS 38.13]*.

Cost	The amount of cash or cash equivalents paid or the fair value of other consideration given to acquire an asset at the time of its acquisition or construction, or, when applicable, the amount attributed to that asset when initially recognised in accordance with the specific requirements of other IFRSs, e.g. IFRS 2 – *Share-based Payment. [IAS 38.8].*
Carrying amount	The amount at which the asset is recognised in the statement of financial position after deducting any accumulated amortisation and accumulated impairment losses thereon. *[IAS 38.8].*
Amortisation	The systematic allocation of the depreciable amount of an intangible asset over its useful life. *[IAS 38.8].*
Depreciable amount	The cost of an asset, or other amount substituted for cost, less its residual value. *[IAS 38.8].*
Residual value	The estimated amount that the entity would currently obtain from disposal of the intangible asset, after deducting the estimated costs of disposal, if the intangible asset were already of the age and in the condition expected at the end of its useful life. *[IAS 38.8].*
Useful life	(a) the period over which an asset is expected to be available for use by an entity; or (b) the number of production or similar units expected to be obtained from the asset by an entity. *[IAS 38.8].*
Impairment loss	The amount by which the carrying amount of the asset exceeds its recoverable amount. *[IAS 38.8].*
Research	Original and planned investigation undertaken with the prospect of gaining new scientific or technical knowledge and understanding. *[IAS 38.8].*
Development	The application of research findings or other knowledge to a plan or design for the production of new or substantially improved materials, devices, products, processes, systems or services before the start of commercial production or use. *[IAS 38.8].*
Entity-specific value	The present value of the cash flows an entity expects to arise from the continuing use of an asset and from its disposal at the end of its useful life or expects to incur when settling a liability. *[IAS 38.8].*
Fair value	The price that would be received to sell an asset or paid to transfer a liability in an orderly transaction between market participants at the measurement date. (See Chapter 14). *[IAS 38.8].*
Active market	A market in which transactions for the asset or liability take place with sufficient frequency and volume to provide pricing information on an ongoing basis. *[IFRS 13 Appendix A].*

2 OBJECTIVE AND SCOPE OF IAS 38

The objective of IAS 38 is to prescribe the accounting treatment for intangible assets that are not specifically dealt with in another standard. *[IAS 38.1].*

IAS 38 does not apply to accounting for:

(a) intangible assets that are within the scope of another standard;
(b) financial assets, as defined in IAS 32 – *Financial Instruments: Presentation*;
(c) the recognition and measurement of exploration and evaluation assets within the scope of IFRS 6 – *Exploration for and Evaluation of Mineral Resources*; and
(d) expenditure on the development and extraction of, minerals, oil, natural gas and similar non-regenerative resources. *[IAS 38.2]*.

Examples of specific types of intangible asset that fall within the scope of another standard include: *[IAS 38.3]*

(a) intangible assets held by an entity for sale in the ordinary course of business, to which IAS 2 – *Inventories* – or IAS 11 – *Construction Contracts* – applies (see Chapters 22 and 23);
(b) deferred tax assets, which are governed by IAS 12 (see Chapter 31);
(c) leases that are within the scope of IAS 17 (see Chapter 24), or leases of intangible assets accounted for in accordance with IFRS 16 – *Leases*, if this standard has been adopted (see Chapter 25). However, an entity that applies IAS 17 and leases an intangible asset under a finance lease should apply IAS 38 to account for the underlying asset after its initial recognition. *[IAS 38.6]*. Rights under licensing agreements for such items as motion picture films, video recordings, plays, manuscripts, patents and copyrights that are outside the scope of IAS 17 *[IAS 17.2]* and IFRS 16 *[IFRS 16.3]* are within the scope of IAS 38; *[IAS 38.6]*
(d) assets arising from employee benefits, for which IAS 19 is relevant (see Chapter 33);
(e) financial assets as defined in IAS 32. The recognition and measurement of some financial assets are covered by IFRS 10 – *Consolidated Financial Statements,* IAS 27 – *Separate Financial Statements* – and IAS 28 – *Investments in Associates and Joint Ventures* (see Chapters 6, 8, 11 and 42 to 54);
(f) goodwill acquired in a business combination, which is determined under IFRS 3 (see Chapter 9);
(g) deferred acquisition costs, and intangible assets, arising from an insurer's contractual rights under insurance contracts within the scope of IFRS 4 – *Insurance Contracts*, or IFRS 17 – *Insurance Contracts* – if applied. IFRS 4 sets out specific disclosure requirements for those deferred acquisition costs but not for those intangible assets. Therefore, the disclosure requirements in this standard apply to those intangible assets (see Chapter 55);
(h) non-current intangible assets classified as held for sale, or included in a disposal group that is classified as held for sale, in accordance with IFRS 5 – *Non-current Assets Held for Sale and Discontinued Operations* (see Chapter 4); and
(i) assets arising from contracts with customers that are recognised in accordance with IFRS 15 – *Revenue from Contracts with Customers*, if that standard has been adopted.

IAS 38 excludes insurance contracts and expenditure on the exploration for, or development and extraction of oil, gas and mineral deposits in extractive industries from its scope because activities or transactions in these areas are so specialised that they give rise to accounting issues that need to be dealt with in a different way. However, the standard does apply to other intangible assets used in extractive industries or by insurers (such as computer software), and other expenditure incurred by them (such as start-up costs). *[IAS 38.7]*.

Finally, the standard makes it clear that it applies to expenditures on advertising, training, start-up and research and development activities. *[IAS 38.5]*.

2.1 What is an intangible asset?

IAS 38 defines an asset as 'a resource controlled by an entity as a result of past events; and from which future economic benefits are expected to flow to the entity'. *[IAS 38.8]*. Intangible assets form a sub-section of this group and are further defined as 'an identifiable non-monetary asset without physical substance'. *[IAS 38.8]*. The IASB considers that the essential characteristics of intangible assets are that they are:

- controlled by the entity;
- will give rise to future economic benefits for the entity;
- lack physical substance; and
- are identifiable.

An item with these characteristics is classified as an intangible asset regardless of the reason why an entity might hold that asset. *[IAS 38.BC5]*. There is one exception: intangible assets held for sale (either in the ordinary course of business or as part of a disposal group) and accounted for under IAS 2, IAS 11 or IFRS 5 are specifically excluded from the scope of IAS 38. *[IAS 38.3]*.

Businesses frequently incur expenditure on all sorts of intangible resources such as scientific or technical knowledge, design and implementation of new processes or systems, licences, intellectual property, market knowledge, trademarks, brand names and publishing titles. Examples that fall under these headings include computer software, patents, copyrights, motion picture films, customer lists, mortgage servicing rights, fishing licences, import quotas, franchises, customer or supplier relationships, customer loyalty, market share and marketing rights. *[IAS 38.9]*.

Although these items are mentioned by the standard, not all of them will meet the standard's eligibility criteria for recognition as an intangible asset, which requires identifiability, control over a resource and the existence of future economic benefits. Expenditure on items that do not meet all three criteria will be expensed when incurred, unless they have arisen in the context of a business combination as discussed at 5 below. *[IAS 38.10]*.

2.1.1 Identifiability

IAS 38's requirement that an intangible asset must be 'identifiable' was introduced to try to distinguish it from internally generated goodwill (which, outside a business combination, should not be recognised as an asset *[IAS 38.48]*), but also to emphasise that, especially in the context of a business combination, there will be previously unrecorded items that should be recognised in the financial statements as intangible assets separately from goodwill. *[IAS 38.BC7, BC8]*.

IFRS 3 defines goodwill as 'representing the future economic benefits arising from other assets acquired in a business combination that are not individually identified and separately recognised.' *[IFRS 3 Appendix A].* For example, future economic benefits may result from synergy between the identifiable assets acquired or from assets that, individually, do not qualify for recognition in the financial statements. *[IAS 38.11].*

IAS 38 states that an intangible asset is identifiable when it either: *[IAS 38.12]*

(a) is separable, meaning that it is capable of being separated or divided from the entity and sold, transferred, licensed, rented or exchanged, either individually or together with a related contract, identifiable asset or liability, regardless of whether the entity intends to do so; or

(b) arises from contractual or other legal rights, regardless of whether those rights are transferable or separable from the entity or from other rights and obligations.

The explicit requirement to recognise assets arising from contractual rights alone confirms the IASB's position that the existence of contractual or legal rights is a characteristic that distinguishes an intangible asset from goodwill, even if those rights are not readily separable from the entity as a whole. The Board cites as an example of such an intangible asset a licence that, under local law, is not transferable except by sale of the entity as a whole. *[IAS 38.BC10].* Therefore, the search for intangible assets is not restricted to rights that are separable.

However, preparers should not restrict their search for intangible assets to those embodied in contractual or other legal rights, since the definition of identifiability merely requires such rights to be *capable* of separation. Non-contractual rights are required to be recognised as an intangible asset if the right *could be* sold, transferred, licensed, rented or exchanged. In considering the responses to ED 3 – *Business Combinations* – the Board observed that the existence of an exchange transaction for a non-contractual relationship provides evidence both that the item is separable, and that the entity is able to control the expected future economic benefits flowing from it, meaning that the relationship should be recognised as an intangible asset. Only in the absence of exchange transactions for the same or similar non-contractual customer relationships would an entity be unable to demonstrate that such relationships are separable or that it can control the expected future economic benefits flowing from those relationships. *[IAS 38.BC13].*

2.1.2 Control

IAS 38 defines control as the power to obtain the future economic benefits generated by the resource and the ability to restrict the access of others to those benefits. Control normally results from legal rights, in the way that copyright, a restraint of trade agreement or a legal duty on employees to maintain confidentiality protects the economic benefits arising from market and technical knowledge. *[IAS 38.13-14].* While it will be more difficult to demonstrate control in the absence of legal rights, the standard is clear that legal enforceability of a right is not a necessary condition for control, because an entity may be able to control the future economic benefits in some other way. *[IAS 38.13].* The existence of exchange transactions for similar non-contractual rights can provide sufficient evidence of control to require separate recognition as an asset. *[IAS 38.16].* Obviously, determining that this is the case in the absence of observable contractual or other legal rights requires the exercise of judgement based on an understanding of the specific facts and circumstances involved.

For example, the standard acknowledges that an entity usually has insufficient control over the future economic benefits arising from an assembled workforce (i.e. a team of skilled workers, or specific management or technical talent) or from training for these items to meet the definition of an intangible asset. *[IAS 38.15]*. There would have to be other legal rights before control could be demonstrated.

Example 17.1: Demonstrating control over the future services of employees

Entity A acquires a pharmaceutical company. A critical factor in the entity's decision to acquire the company was the reputation of its team of research chemists, who are renowned in their field of expertise. However, in the absence of any other legal rights it would not be possible to show that the entity can control the economic benefits embodied in that team and its skills because any or all of those chemists could leave. Therefore, it is most unlikely that Entity A could recognise an intangible asset in relation to the acquiree's team of research chemists.

Entity B acquires a football club. A critical factor in the entity's decision to acquire the club was the reputation of its players, many of whom are regularly selected to play for their country. A footballer cannot play for a club unless he is registered with the relevant football authority. It is customary to see exchange transactions involving players' registrations. The payment to a player's previous club in connection with the transfer of the player's registration enables the acquiring club to negotiate a playing contract with the footballer that covers a number of seasons and prevents other clubs from using that player's services. In these circumstances Entity B would be able to demonstrate sufficient control to recognise the cost of obtaining the players' registrations as an intangible asset.

In neither of the above examples is an asset being recognised for the assembled workforce. In the case of the football team, the asset being recognised comprises the economic benefits embodied in the players' registrations, arising from contractual rights. In particular, it is the ability to prevent other entities from using that player's services (i.e. restricting the access of others to those benefits), *[IAS 38.13]*, combined with the existence of exchange transactions involving similar players' registrations, *[IAS 38.16]*, that distinguishes this type of arrangement from a normal contract of employment. In cases when the transfer fee is a stand-alone payment and not part of a business combination, i.e. when an entity separately acquires the intangible resource, it is much more likely that it can demonstrate that its purchase meets the definition of an asset (see 4 below).

Similarly, an entity would not usually be able to recognise an asset for an assembled portfolio of customers or a market share. In the absence of legal rights to protect or other ways to control the relationships with customers or the loyalty of its customers, the entity usually has insufficient control over the expected economic benefits from these items to meet the definition of an intangible asset. However, exchange transactions, other than as part of a business combination, involving the same or similar non-contractual customer relationships may provide evidence of control over the expected future economic benefits in the absence of legal rights. In that case, those customer relationships could meet the definition of an intangible asset. *[IAS 38.16]*. IFRS 3 includes a number of examples of customer-related intangible assets acquired in business combinations that meet the definition of an intangible asset, which are discussed in more detail at 5 below. *[IFRS 3.IE23-31]*.

It is worth emphasising that intangible assets should only be recognised when they meet both the definition of an intangible asset and the applicable recognition criteria in IAS 38, *[IAS 38.18]*, which are discussed at 3.1 below. All that is established in the discussion above is whether the intangible right meets the definition of an asset.

The extract below illustrates the range of intangible assets that require recognition under IAS 38.

> *Extract 17.1: RELX PLC and RELX NV (2016)*
>
> **Notes to the consolidated financial statements**
> for the year ended 31 December 2016 [extract]
> **16 Intangible assets** [extract]
> **Accounting policy** [extract]
>
> Intangible assets acquired as part of business combinations comprise: market-related assets (e.g. trademarks, imprints, brands); customer-related assets (e.g. subscription bases, customer lists, customer relationships); editorial content; software and systems (e.g. application infrastructure, product delivery platforms, in-process research and development); contract-based assets (e.g. publishing rights, exhibition rights, supply contracts); and other intangible assets. Internally generated intangible assets typically comprise software and systems development where an identifiable asset is created that is probable to generate future economic benefits.

2.1.3 *Future economic benefits*

Future economic benefits include not only future revenues from the sale of products or services but also cost savings or other benefits resulting from the use of the asset by the entity. For example, the use of intellectual property in a production process may reduce future production costs rather than increase future revenues. *[IAS 38.17]*.

2.2 Is IAS 38 the appropriate IFRS?

An asset is defined generally and in IAS 38 as 'a resource controlled by an entity as a result of past events; and from which future economic benefits are expected to flow to the entity'. *[IAS 38.8]*. Intangible assets form a sub-section of this group and are further defined as 'an identifiable non-monetary asset without physical substance'. *[IAS 38.8]*. As we have discussed earlier, this definition could include assets covered by another standard which are therefore excluded from its scope (see 2 above). However, in some circumstances it is not clear whether IAS 38 or another standard applies.

2.2.1 *Whether to record a tangible or intangible asset*

Before the advent of IAS 38 many entities used to account for assets without physical substance in the same way as property, plant and equipment. Indeed, the standard notes that intangible assets can be contained in or on a physical medium such as a compact disc (in the case of computer software), legal documentation (in the case of a licence or patent) or film, requiring an entity to exercise judgement in determining whether to apply IAS 16 or IAS 38. *[IAS 38.4]*. For example:

- software that is embedded in computer-controlled equipment that cannot operate without it is an integral part of the related hardware and is treated as property, plant and equipment; *[IAS 38.4]*
- application software that is being used on a computer is treated as an intangible asset because it is generally easily replaced and is not an integral part of the related hardware, whereas the operating system normally is integral to the computer and is included in property, plant and equipment; *[IAS 38.4]*

- a database that is stored digitally is considered to be an intangible asset where the value of the physical medium is wholly insignificant compared to that of the data collection; and
- research and development expenditure may result in an asset with physical substance (e.g. a prototype), but as the physical element is secondary to its intangible component, the related knowledge, it is treated as an intangible asset. *[IAS 38.5]*.

It is worthwhile noting that the 'parts approach' in IAS 16 requires an entity to account for significant parts of an asset separately because they have a different economic life or are often replaced, *[IAS 16.44]*, (see Chapter 18). This raises 'boundary' problems between IAS 16 and IAS 38 when software and similar expenditure is involved. We believe that where IAS 16 requires an entity to identify parts of an asset and account for them separately, the entity needs to evaluate whether any intangible-type part is actually integral to the larger asset or whether it is really a separate asset in its own right. The intangible part is more likely to be an asset in its own right if it was developed separately or if it can be used independently of the item of property, plant and equipment of which it apparently forms part.

This view is consistent with that taken in IFRS 3, when it asserts that related tangible and intangible components of an asset with similar useful lives (meaning that IAS 16 would not require separate accounting of parts of an asset) can be combined into a single asset for financial reporting purposes. *[IFRS 3.B32(b)]*.

2.2.2 Classification of programme and other broadcast rights as inventory or intangible assets

Ultimately, the appropriate classification of broadcast rights will depend on the particular facts and circumstances as they apply to an entity. However, it is possible for an entity to conclude that some of its broadcast rights are intangible assets while others should be treated as inventory.

Programme and other broadcast rights meet the definition of intangible assets because they are identifiable non-monetary assets without physical substance. IAS 38 specifically includes within its scope rights under licensing agreements for items such as motion picture films and video recordings. *[IAS 38.6]*. In addition, a broadcast right meets the other criteria for recognition as an intangible asset, being identifiable, as it arises from contractual rights *[IAS 38.12(b)]* and controlled by the entity. *[IAS 38.13]*.

Rights to programmes held exclusively for sale to other parties also meet the definition of inventory and are therefore within the scope of IAS 2. *[IAS 38.3]*. It is possible to argue that programmes held with a view to broadcasting them to an audience are comparable to 'materials or supplies to be consumed in the production process or in the rendering of services', *[IAS 2.6]*, which would mean that they could also be treated as inventory. Equally, it can be argued that such programme rights are intangible assets as they are used in the production or supply of services but not necessarily consumed because they can be used again.

Therefore, it is possible for entities to choose whether programme or other broadcast rights are classified as intangible assets or as inventory. However, the classification of income, expenses and cash flows in respect of those rights should be consistent with the manner of their classification in the statement of financial position.

Accordingly, where a broadcast right is classified as an intangible asset:

- it is classified in the statement of financial position as current or non-current according to the entity's operating cycle (see 10.2 below);
- the intangible asset is amortised, with amortisation included in the statement of profit or loss within the depreciation and amortisation expense, or within a functional expense category (such as cost of sales);
- in the cash flow statement, payments for the acquisition of intangible broadcast rights are classified as an investing activity (if the asset is classified as non-current on acquisition) or as an operating activity if the asset is classified as current; and
- rights are measured at a revalued amount only if the criteria in IAS 38 are met (see 8.2 below). Otherwise the asset is carried at cost less accumulated amortisation and impairments. Any impairment of the asset is determined in accordance with IAS 36.

Where a broadcast right is classified as inventory:

- it is classified in the statement of financial position as a current asset either as part of inventory or as a separate category;
- the entity recognises an expense in cost of sales as the right is consumed;
- payments for the acquisition of inventory are classified as operating activities in the statement of cash flows; and
- rights are carried at the lower of cost and net realisable value.

Both of these classifications are found in practice. Vivendi accounts for its film and television rights catalogues as intangible assets (see Extract 17.3 at 3.1.1 below). ITV on the other hand, presents its programme rights as current assets under the caption 'Programme rights and other inventory'.

Extract 17.2: ITV plc (2016)

Notes to the financial statements [extract]

Section 3: Operating Assets and Liabilities [extract]

Broadcast programme rights [extract]

Acquired programme rights (which include films), and sports rights, are purchased for the primary purpose of broadcasting on the ITV Family channels, including VOD and SVOD platforms. These are recognised within current assets as payments are made or when the rights are ready for broadcast. The Group generally expenses these rights through operating costs over a number of transmissions reflecting the pattern and value in which the right is consumed.

Commissions, which primarily comprise programmes purchased based on editorial specification and over which the Group has some control, are recognised in current assets as payments are made and are generally expensed to operating costs in full on first transmission. Where a commission is repeated on any platform, incremental costs associated with the broadcast are included in operating costs. […]

The Broadcast programme rights and other inventory at the year end are shown in the table below:

	2016 £m	2015 £m
Acquired programme rights	157	111
Commissions	69	61
Sports rights	27	30
	253	202

3 RECOGNITION AND MEASUREMENT

3.1 Recognition

An item that meets the definition of an intangible asset (see 2.1 above) should only be recognised if, at the time of initial recognition of the expenditure:

(a) it is probable that the expected future economic benefits that are attributable to the asset will flow to the entity; and

(b) the cost of the asset can be measured reliably. *[IAS 38.21]*.

Although IAS 38 does not define 'probable', it is defined in other standards as 'more likely than not'. *[IAS 37.23, IFRS 5 Appendix A]*. In assessing whether expected future economic benefits are probable, the entity should use reasonable and supportable assumptions that represent management's best estimate of the set of economic conditions that will exist over the useful life of the asset. *[IAS 38.22]*. In making this judgement the entity considers the evidence available at the time of initial recognition, giving greater weight to external evidence. *[IAS 38.23]*.

This test (that the item meets both the definition of an intangible asset and the criteria for recognition) is performed each time an entity incurs potentially eligible expenditures, whether to acquire or internally generate an intangible asset or to add to, replace part of, or service it subsequent to initial recognition. *[IAS 38.18]*. If these criteria are not met at the time the expenditure is incurred, an expense is recognised and it is never reinstated as an asset. *[IAS 38.68, 71]*.

The guidance in IAS 38 on the recognition and initial measurement of intangible assets takes account of the way in which an entity obtained the asset. Separate rules for recognition and initial measurement apply for intangible assets depending on whether they were:

- acquired separately (see 4 below);
- acquired by way of government grant (see 4.6 below);
- obtained in an exchange of assets (see 4.7 below);
- acquired as part of a business combination (see 5 below); and
- generated internally (see 6 below). *[IAS 38.19]*.

The difficulties that may arise in applying these criteria when an entity enters into a contract to buy an intangible asset for delivery in some future period are discussed in detail (in the context of programme broadcast rights) at 3.1.1 below.

For recognition purposes IAS 38 does not distinguish between an internally and an externally developed intangible asset other than when considering the treatment of goodwill. When the definition of an intangible asset and the relevant recognition criteria are met, all such assets should be recognised. *[IAS 38.BCZ40]*. Preparers do not have the option to decide, as a matter of policy, that costs relating to internally generated intangible assets are expensed if the recognition criteria in the standard are met. *[IAS 38.BCZ41]*.

3.1.1 When to recognise programme and other broadcast rights

Television stations frequently enter into contracts to buy programme rights related to long-running televisions series or future sports events that are not yet available for broadcast, sometimes over a specified period or for a certain number of showings or viewings. Payments might be made at the beginning of or during the broadcast period, which raises the question of when those programme rights and the related obligations for payment should be recognised in the statement of financial position.

The IASB's *Conceptual Framework* recognises that in practice 'obligations under contracts that are equally proportionately unperformed (for example, liabilities for inventory ordered but not yet received) are generally not recognised as liabilities in the financial statements'. *[Framework 4.46].* For example, liabilities in connection with non-cancellable orders of inventory or items of property, plant and equipment are generally not recognised in an entity's statement of financial position until the goods have been delivered. The same approach can also be applied to broadcast rights.

Accordingly, an entity recognises a broadcast right at the first date that it controls an asset. The meaning of control is discussed at 2.1.2 above.

Determining the date at which control is obtained is a complex matter that depends on the specific facts and circumstances of each case. Factors that may be relevant include whether:

(a) the underlying resource is sufficiently developed to be identifiable. For example, a right to broadcast a film or play might not be sufficiently developed until a manuscript or screenplay is written or a director and actors are hired. For a right to broadcast a sporting event to be identifiable it might be appropriate to establish the existence of a venue, participants or the number or timing of events subject to the right;

(b) the entity has legal, exclusive rights to broadcast (with exclusivity potentially defined in terms of a defined period or geographical area);

(c) there is a penalty payable for non-delivery of the content (e.g. the film or sporting event subject to the broadcast right);

(d) it is probable that the event will occur or the content will be delivered (e.g. completion of a film or a lack of history of cancellations, strikes or rain-outs); and

(e) it is probable that economic benefits will flow to the entity.

Example 17.2: Determining when to recognise a broadcast right

A sporting competition – rights secured over a number of seasons

Entity A (the licensee) signs a contract with a licensor for the exclusive rights to broadcast matches in a long-established sporting competition covering the whole season for a number of years. The entity is required to pay agreed amounts at the start of each season, with the rights to that season and future seasons reverting to the licensor if payment is not made on time. Entity A concludes that an obligation does not exist until the beginning of each season for the amount payable to secure rights for that season.

Based on an evaluation of the factors above, the entity concludes that it has an asset for the rights to broadcast matches in each season and recognises that asset at the start of each season. The entity discloses a commitment for amounts payable in future years without recognising any asset or liability at that time.

Rights to broadcast the future output of a film production company

Entity B (the licensee) signs a contract with a film production company (the licensor) whereby the entity agrees to pay amounts in the future for a specified number of films that the licensor will release in that year, but neither the licensee not the licensor knows which films will be released when they sign the contract.

Based on an evaluation of the facts and circumstances, Entity B concludes that the underlying resource (the films) is not sufficiently developed to be identifiable at the time of signing the contract. Instead, the entity concludes that the criteria for recognising an intangible asset are not met until delivery of the films by the licensor.

This approach is illustrated in the extract from Vivendi below, which distinguishes between contracts requiring recognition and commitments to pay amounts in future periods when content is delivered.

Extract 17.3: Vivendi S.A. (2016)

Notes to the Consolidated Financial Statements [extract]

10.2. Contractual content commitments [extract]

Commitments given recorded in the Statement of Financial Position: content liabilities [extract]

	Minimum future payments as of December 31, 2016				Total minimum future payments as of
		Due in			
(in millions of euros)	Total	2017	2018-2021	After 2021	December 31, 2015
Music royalties to artists and repertoire owners	1,938	1,920	18	–	1,848
Film and television rights (a)	175	175	–	–	196
Sports rights	461	461	–	–	455
Creative talent, employment agreements and others	69	48	19	2	90
Content liabilities	**2,643**	**2,604**	**37**	**2**	**2,589**

Off-balance sheet commitments given/(received) [extract]

	Minimum future payments as of December 31, 2016				Total minimum future payments as of
		Due in			
(in millions of euros)	Total	2017	2018-2021	After 2021	December 31, 2015
Film and television rights (a)	2,785	1,259	1,523	3	3,080
Sport rights (b)	2,661	879	1,682	100	2,965
Creative talent, employment agreements and others (c)	1,003	464	506	33	790
Given commitments	6,449	2,602	3,711	136	6,835
Film and television rights (a)	(189)	(100)	(89)	–	(174)
Sport rights	(25)	(10)	(15)	–	(39)
Creative talent, employment agreements and others (c)			not available		
Received commitments	(214)	(110)	(104)	–	(213)
Total net	6,235	2,492	3,607	136	6,622

As illustrated in Extract 17.2 at 2.2.2 below, ITV follows a similar type of approach for acquired programme rights under which an asset is recognised as payments are made and is recognised in full when the acquired programming is available for transmission.

3.2 Measurement

On initial recognition an intangible asset should be measured at cost. *[IAS 38.24]*. The standard defines this as the amount of cash or cash equivalents paid or the fair value of other consideration given to acquire an asset at the time of its acquisition or construction.

When the nature of the consideration given is governed by other IFRSs, the cost of the asset is the amount initially recognised in accordance with the specific requirements of that standard, e.g. IFRS 2. *[IAS 38.8]*.

IAS 38's initial measurement depends, in part, on the manner in which the asset is acquired and these are discussed in more detail at 4 to 7 below. The components of the cost of an internally generated intangible asset are discussed in more detail at 6.3 below.

3.3 Subsequent expenditure

Although IAS 38 is based on a general recognition principle that applies to both initial acquisition and subsequent expenditures, the hurdle for the recognition of subsequent expenditure as an addition to an intangible asset is set higher, because it must first be confirmed that the expenditure is not associated with the replacement of an existing asset (see 9.5.1 below) or the creation of an internally generated intangible that would not be eligible for recognition under the standard (see 6 below). The standard presumes that only rarely will subsequent expenditure, i.e. expenditure incurred after the initial recognition of an acquired intangible asset or after completion of an internally generated intangible asset, be recognised in the carrying amount of an asset. In most cases, subsequent expenditures are likely to maintain the expected future economic benefits embodied in an existing intangible asset rather than meet the definition of an intangible asset and the recognition criteria in IAS 38. The standard also notes that it is often difficult to attribute subsequent expenditure directly to a particular intangible asset rather than to the business as a whole. *[IAS 38.20]*.

Capitalisation of subsequent expenditure on brands, mastheads, publishing titles, customer lists and similar items is expressly forbidden even if they were initially acquired externally, which is consistent with the general prohibition on recognising them if internally generated. This is because the standard argues that such expenditure cannot be distinguished from the cost of developing the business of which they are a part. *[IAS 38.20, 63]*. Thus, at best such expenditure creates unrecognised internally generated goodwill that might be crystallised only in a business combination.

4 SEPARATE ACQUISITION

4.1 Recognition

Separately acquired intangible rights will normally be recognised as assets. IAS 38 assumes that the price paid to acquire an intangible asset usually reflects expectations about the probability that the future economic benefits embodied in it will flow to the entity. In other words, the entity always expects there to be a flow of economic benefits, even if it is uncertain about the timing or amount. *[IAS 38.25]*. Therefore, the standard assumes that the cost of a separately acquired intangible asset can usually be measured reliably, especially in the case of cash or other monetary purchase considerations. *[IAS 38.26]*.

Not all external costs incurred to secure intangible rights automatically qualify for capitalisation as separately acquired assets, because they do not meet the definition of an intangible asset in the first place. An entity that subcontracts the development of intangible assets (e.g. development-and-supply contracts or R&D contracts) to other parties (its suppliers) must exercise judgement in determining whether it is acquiring an intangible asset or whether it is obtaining goods and services that are being used in the development of an intangible asset by the entity itself. In the latter case, the entity will only be able to recognise an intangible asset if the expenditure meets IAS 38's requirements for internally-generated assets (see 6 below).

In determining whether a supplier is providing services to develop an internally generated intangible asset, the terms of the supply agreement should be examined to see whether the supplier is bearing a significant proportion of the risks associated with a failure of the project. For example, if the supplier is always compensated under a development-and-supply contract for development services and tool costs irrespective of the project's outcome, the entity on whose behalf the development is undertaken should account for those activities as its own.

If the entity pays the supplier upfront or by milestone payments during the course of a project, it will not necessarily recognise an intangible asset on the basis of those payments. Only costs incurred after it becomes probable that economic benefits are expected to flow to the entity will be part of the cost of an intangible asset (see 6.2 below).

4.2 Components of cost

The cost of a separately acquired intangible asset comprises:

- its purchase price, including import duties and non-refundable purchase taxes, after deducting trade discounts and rebates; and
- any directly attributable cost of preparing the asset for its intended use, *[IAS 38.27]*, for example:
  - costs of employee benefits arising directly from bringing the asset to its working condition;
  - professional fees arising directly from bringing the asset to its working condition; and
  - costs of testing whether the asset is functioning properly. *[IAS 38.28]*.

Capitalisation of expenditure ceases when the asset is in the condition necessary for it to be capable of operating in the manner intended by management. *[IAS 38.30]*. This may well be before the date on which it is brought into use.

If payment for an intangible asset is deferred beyond normal credit terms, its cost is the cash price equivalent. The difference between this amount and the total payments is recognised as interest expense over the period of credit unless it is capitalised in accordance with IAS 23 – *Borrowing Costs* (see Chapter 21). *[IAS 38.32]*.

4.3 Costs to be expensed

The following types of expenditure are not considered to be part of the cost of a separately acquired intangible asset:

- costs of introducing a new product or service, including costs of advertising and promotional activities;
- costs of conducting business in a new location or with a new class of customer, including costs of staff training;
- administration and other general overhead costs;
- costs incurred in using or redeploying an intangible asset;
- costs incurred while an asset capable of operating in the manner intended by management has yet to be brought into use; and
- initial operating losses, such as those incurred while demand for the asset's output builds up. *[IAS 38.29-30]*.

Accordingly, start-up costs, training costs, advertising and promotional activities, and relocation or reorganisation costs should be expensed (see 7 below).

4.4 Income from incidental operations while an asset is being developed

When an entity generates income while it is developing or constructing an asset, the question arises as to whether this income should reduce the initial carrying value of the asset being developed or be recognised in profit or loss. IAS 38 requires an entity to consider whether the activity giving rise to income is necessary to bring the asset to the condition necessary for it to be capable of operating in the manner intended by management, or not. The income and related expenses of incidental operations (being those not necessary to develop the asset for its intended use) should be recognised immediately in profit or loss and included in their respective classifications of income and expense. *[IAS 38.31]*. Such incidental operations can occur before or during the development activities. The example below illustrates these requirements.

Example 17.3: Incidental operations

Entity A is pioneering a new process for the production of a certain type of chemical. Entity A will be able to patent the new production process. During the development phase, A is selling quantities of the chemical that are produced as a by-product of the development activities that are taking place. The expenditure incurred comprises labour, raw materials, assembly costs, costs of equipment and professional fees.

The revenues and costs associated with the production and sale of the chemical are accounted for in profit or loss for the period, while the development costs that meet the strict recognition criteria of IAS 38 are recognised as an intangible asset. Development costs that fail the IAS 38 recognition test are also expensed.

As the above example suggests, identifying the revenue from incidental operations will often be much easier than allocating costs to incidental operations. Furthermore, it will often be challenging to determine when exactly a project moves from the development phase into its start-up phase.

Whilst IAS 38 is not explicit on the matter, it follows that when the activity is determined to be necessary to bring the intangible asset into its intended use, any income should be deducted from the cost of the asset. (Note that IAS 16 mandates this treatment; see Chapter 18 at 4.2.1). An example would be where income is generated from the sale of samples produced during the testing of a new process or from the sale of a production prototype. However, care must be taken to confirm whether the incidence of income indicates that the intangible asset is ready for its intended use, in which case capitalisation of costs would cease, revenue would be recognised in profit or loss and the related costs of the activity would include a measure of amortisation of the asset.

4.5 Measurement of intangible assets acquired for contingent consideration

Transactions involving contingent consideration are often very complex and payment is dependent on a number of factors. In the absence of specific guidance in IAS 38, entities trying to determine an appropriate accounting treatment are required not only to understand the commercial complexities of the transaction itself, but also to negotiate a variety of accounting principles and requirements.

Consider a relatively simple example where an entity acquires an intangible asset for consideration comprising a combination of up-front payment, guaranteed instalments for a number of years and additional amounts that vary according to future activity (revenue, profit or number of units output).

Where the goods and services in question have been delivered, there is no doubt that there is a financial liability under IAS 39 – *Financial Instruments: Recognition and Measurement*. A contingent obligation to deliver cash meets the definition of a financial liability (see Chapter 45). However, where the purchaser can influence or control the crystallisation of the contingent payments or they are wholly dependent on its future activities, the circumstances are more difficult to interpret. Many consider that these arrangements contain executory contracts that are only accounted for when one of the contracting parties performs.

Further complications arise when the terms of the agreement indicate that a future payment relates to the completion of a separate performance obligation, or the delivery of intangible rights in addition to those conferred by the exchange of the original asset.

In practice there are two general approaches. One includes the fair value of all contingent payments in the initial measurement of the asset. The other excludes executory payments from initial measurement. Under both approaches, contingent payments are either capitalised when incurred if they meet the definition of an asset, or expensed as incurred.

The issue of contingent consideration has been considered by the Interpretations Committee, which separated costs into two types according to whether or not they depend on the purchaser's future activity. The Committee proposed that the fair value of contingent payments that do not depend on the purchaser's future activity should be included in the initial measurement of the asset. The Committee could not reach a consensus on variable payments that depend on the purchaser's future activity.[1]

For the subsequent accounting the Committee recommended that, for a financial liability that is not a floating rate instrument, in specified circumstances the cost of the corresponding asset should be adjusted when the carrying amount of that financial liability is remeasured. The proposed amendment would not address initial recognition of the contingent (variable) costs that depend on the purchaser's future activity, so it did not address subsequent measurement of these costs should they be excluded from initial recognition.[2]

These proposals were rejected by the IASB. The Board wanted initial and subsequent recognition of both types of contingent payments to be addressed; moreover, the leases exposure draft proposed yet another treatment of variable payments so the Board recommended that the Committee wait for the comment letter responses to the lease ED before proceeding with their analysis.[3] In March 2016, the Interpretations Committee re-discussed accounting for contingent payments for acquiring tangible and intangible assets. However, it decided that this issue was too broad for the Committee to address and it was referred back to the Board.[4] In May 2016, the IASB tentatively agreed that this issue would be included in the research pipeline between 2017 and 2021.[5] This is not currently an active project for the IASB.

Until this matter is resolved, an entity should adopt and apply a consistent accounting policy to initial recognition and subsequent costs. For intangible assets, these approaches are illustrated in the following example. Note that this example does not include a number of common contingent payments, e.g. those related to usage or revenue, or non-floating rate changes in finance costs.

Example 17.4: Contingent consideration relating to a football player's registration

Entity A is a football club which signs a new player on a 4 year contract. In securing the registration of the new player, Entity A agrees to make the following payments to the player's former club:

- €5.5 million on completion of the transfer;
- €2.8 million on the first anniversary of the transfer;
- €1 million as soon as the player has made 25 appearances for the club;
- €0.2 million when the player is first selected to play for his country; and
- 25% of the gross proceeds from any onward sale of the player before the expiry of the initial contract term.

It is determined that the expenditure meets the definition of an intangible asset because it allows Entity A to negotiate a playing contract with the footballer that covers 4 seasons and prevents other clubs from using that player's services over that time. How does Entity A determine the cost of the player registration?

View 1 – All of the above payments are contractual and a financial liability arises under IAS 39 as soon as that the player signs for the club. Accordingly, the cost of the intangible asset comprises the initial payment of €5.5 million, plus an amount representing the present value of the €2.8 million payable in one year and an amount to reflect the fair value of the other contingent payments (most likely determined using some kind of probability-weighted estimation technique).

View 2 – The contractual terms requiring a payment of €1 million on the player achieving 25 appearances for the club and another payment of 25% of the gross proceeds from any onward sale of the player are not liabilities of Entity A at the inception of the contract, as there is no obligation on the part of Entity A to use the player in more than 24 fixtures or to sell the player before the end of the 4 year contract term. Accordingly, these elements of the contract are excluded from the initial cost of the intangible asset and are not recognised until the obligating event occurs. However, the element that is contingent on the player being selected to play for his country is not within the entity's control and is included in the initial measurement of cost.

An entity taking view 2 would not include the appearance payment or the share of sale proceeds within the cost of the intangible asset, even when the related obligation is eventually recognised. The entity would most likely regard the €1 million appearance payment as an expense on the grounds that this is subsequent expenditure that does not qualify for recognition as an intangible asset (see 3.3 above).

4.6 Acquisition by way of government grant

An intangible asset may sometimes be acquired free of charge, or for nominal consideration, by way of a government grant. Governments frequently allocate airport-landing rights, licences to operate radio or television stations, emission rights (see 11.2 below), import licences or quotas, or rights to access other restricted resources. *[IAS 38.44]*.

Government grants should be accounted for under IAS 20 – *Accounting for Government Grants and Disclosure of Government Assistance* – which permits initial recognition of intangible assets received either at fair value or a nominal amount. *[IAS 20.23]*.

This represents an accounting policy choice for an entity that should be applied consistently to all intangible assets acquired by way of a government grant.

It may not be possible to measure reliably the fair value of all of the permits allocated by governments because they may have been allocated for no consideration, may not be transferable and may only be bought and sold as part of a business. Some of the issues surrounding the determination of fair value in the absence of an active market are considered in Chapter 14. Other allocated permits such as milk quotas are freely traded and therefore do have a readily ascertainable fair value.

4.7 Exchanges of assets

Asset exchanges are transactions that have challenged standard-setters for many years. An entity might swap certain intangible assets that it does not require or is no longer allowed to use for those of a counterparty that has other surplus assets. For example, it is not uncommon for airlines and media groups to exchange landing slots and newspaper titles, respectively, to meet demands of competition authorities. The question arises whether such transactions should be recorded at cost or fair value, which would give rise to a gain in the circumstances where the fair value of the incoming asset exceeds the carrying amount of the outgoing one. Equally, it is possible that a transaction could be arranged with no real commercial substance, solely to boost apparent profits.

Three separate International Accounting Standards contain virtually identical guidance on accounting for exchanges of assets: IAS 16 (see Chapter 18), IAS 40 – *Investment Property* (see Chapter 19) and IAS 38.

4.7.1 Measurement of assets exchanged

In the context of asset exchanges, the standard contains guidance on the reliable determination of fair values in the circumstances where market values do not exist. Note that while fair value is defined by reference to IFRS 13 (see Chapter 14), the requirements in this section are specific to asset exchanges in IAS 38.

IAS 38 requires all acquisitions of intangible assets in exchange for non-monetary assets, or a combination of monetary and non-monetary assets, to be measured at fair value. The acquired intangible asset is measured at fair value unless: *[IAS 38.45]*

(a) the exchange transaction lacks commercial substance; or

(b) the fair value of neither the asset received nor the asset given up is reliably measurable.

The acquired asset is measured in this way even if an entity cannot immediately derecognise the asset given up. If an entity is able to reliably determine the fair value of either the asset received or the asset given up, then it uses the fair value of the asset given up to measure cost unless the fair value of the asset received is more clearly evident. *[IAS 38.47]*. If the fair value of neither the asset given up, nor the asset received can be measured reliably the acquired intangible asset is measured at the carrying amount of the asset given up. *[IAS 38.45]*.

In this context the fair value of an intangible asset is reliably measurable if the variability in the range of reasonable fair value measurements is not significant for that asset or the probabilities of the various estimates within the range can be reasonably assessed and used when measuring fair value. *[IAS 38.47]*.

4.7.2 Commercial substance

A gain or loss is only recognised on an exchange of non-monetary assets if the transaction is determined to have commercial substance. Otherwise, the acquired asset is measured at the cost of the asset given up. *[IAS 38.45]*.

The commercial substance test for asset exchanges was put in place to prevent gains being recognised in income when the transaction had no discernible effect on the entity's economics. *[IAS 16.BC21]*. The commercial substance of an exchange is determined by forecasting and comparing the future cash flows expected to be generated by the incoming and outgoing assets. Commercial substance means that there must be a significant difference between the two forecasts. An exchange transaction has commercial substance if: *[IAS 38.46]*

(a) the configuration (i.e. risk, timing and amount) of the cash flows of the asset received differs from the configuration of the cash flows of the asset transferred; or
(b) the entity-specific value of the portion of the entity's operations affected by the transaction changes as a result of the exchange; and
(c) the difference in (a) or (b) is significant relative to the fair value of the assets exchanged.

IAS 38 defines the entity-specific value of an intangible asset as the present value of the cash flows an entity expects to arise from its continuing use and from its disposal at the end of its useful life. *[IAS 38.8]*. In determining whether an exchange transaction has commercial substance, the entity-specific value of the portion of the entity's operations affected by the transaction should reflect post-tax cash flows. *[IAS 38.46]*. This is different to the calculation of an asset's value in use under IAS 36 (see Chapter 20), as it uses a post-tax discount rate based on the entity's own risks rather than IAS 36, which requires use of the pre-tax rate that the market would apply to a similar asset.

The standard acknowledges that the result of this analysis might be clear without having to perform detailed calculations. *[IAS 38.46]*.

5 ACQUISITION AS PART OF A BUSINESS COMBINATION

The requirements of IFRS 3 apply to intangible assets acquired in a business combination. The recognition and initial measurement requirements are discussed in detail in Chapter 9 and a summary is given below. The emphasis in IFRS 3 is that, in effect, it does not matter whether assets meeting the definition of an intangible asset have to be combined with other intangible assets, incorporated into the carrying value of a complementary item of property, plant and equipment with a similar useful life or included in the assessment of the fair value of a related liability. The important requirement is that the intangible asset is recognised separately from goodwill.

The process of identifying intangible assets in a business combination might involve, for example:

- reviewing the list of items that meet the definition of an intangible asset in IFRS 3 (see 5.2 below);
- a review of documents such as those related to the acquisition, other internal documents produced by the entity, public filings, press releases, analysts' reports, and other externally available documents; and
- comparing the acquired business to similar businesses and their intangible assets.

Intangible assets that are used differ considerably between industries and between individual entities. Therefore, considerable expertise and careful judgement is required in determining whether there are intangible assets that need to be recognised and valued separately.

IFRS 3 provides a long list of items that should be recognised separately from goodwill (see 5.2 below). The list is not intended to be exhaustive.

5.1 Recognition of intangible assets acquired in a business combination

As noted at 3.1 above, an intangible asset should only be recognised if: *[IAS 38.21]*

(a) it is probable that the expected future economic benefits that are attributable to the asset will flow to the entity; and

(b) the cost of the asset can be measured reliably.

5.1.1 Probable inflow of benefits

In the case of a business combination, the probability recognition criterion is always considered to be satisfied. The cost of the intangible asset is its fair value at the acquisition date. The standard indicates that the fair value reflects expectations about the probability that the future economic benefits embodied in the asset will flow to the entity. *[IAS 38.33]*. In other words, the existence of a fair value means that an inflow of economic benefits is considered to be probable, in spite of any uncertainties about timing or amount.

5.1.2 Reliability of measurement

Under IFRS 3, the cost of the intangible asset acquired in a business combination can always be measured reliably. *[IAS 38.BC19A]*.

In developing IFRS 3, the Board concluded that the needs of users were better served by recognising intangible assets, on the basis of an estimate of fair value, rather than subsuming them in goodwill, even if a significant degree of judgement is required to estimate fair value. *[IAS 38.BC19B]*. Accordingly, if an asset acquired in a business combination is separable or arises from contractual or other legal rights, there is sufficient information to measure reliably the fair value of the asset. Thus, the requirement at 3.1 above for reliable measurement of cost is always considered to be satisfied for intangible assets acquired in business combinations. *[IAS 38.33]*.

5.1.3 Identifiability in relation to an intangible asset acquired in a business combination

Intangible assets need to be identifiable to distinguish them from goodwill and the two elements of identifiability are the existence of contractual or other legal rights and separability. Separability means that the asset is capable of being sold, transferred, licensed, rented or exchanged without having to dispose of the whole business. An intangible asset is considered to be separable regardless of whether the entity intends to sell or otherwise transfer it. *[IAS 38.12]*.

The IASB recognised that an intangible asset acquired in a business combination might be separable, but only together with a related contract, identifiable asset or liability. In such cases, IAS 38 requires the acquirer to recognise the intangible asset separately from goodwill, but together with the related contract, asset or liability. *[IAS 38.36]*.

Acquirers are permitted to recognise a group of complementary intangible assets as a single asset provided the individual assets in the group have similar useful lives. For example, the terms 'brand' and 'brand name' are often used as synonyms for trademarks and other marks. However, 'brands' are regarded as general marketing terms that are typically used to refer to a group of complementary assets such as a trademark or service mark and its related trade name, formulas, recipes and technological expertise. *[IAS 38.37]*.

Heineken, for example, acknowledges the relationship between brands and customer-related intangible assets acquired in business combinations.

Extract 17.4: Heineken N.V. (2016)

Notes to the Consolidated Financial Statements [extract]

3. Significant accounting policies [extract]

(g) Intangible assets [extract]

(ii) Brands [extract]

Brands acquired, separately or as part of a business combination, are capitalised if they meet the definition of an intangible asset and the recognition criteria are satisfied.

[...]

(iii) Customer-related, contract-based intangibles and reacquired rights [extract]

Customer-related and contract-based intangibles are capitalised if they meet the definition of an intangible asset and the recognition criteria are satisfied. If the amounts are not material, these are included in the brand valuation. The relationship between brands and customer-related intangibles is carefully considered so that brands and customer-related intangibles are not both recognised on the basis of the same cash flows.

IFRS 3 contains additional guidance on the application of the contractual-legal and separability criteria that indicate how far the IASB expects entities to go to ensure that intangible assets acquired in a business combination are recognised separately from goodwill.

5.1.3.A Contractual-legal rights

An intangible asset that arises from contractual or other legal rights is recognised separately from goodwill even if it is not transferable or separable from the acquiree or from other rights and obligations. For example:

(a) an acquiree leases a manufacturing facility from a lessor under an operating lease that has terms that are favourable relative to market terms. The lease terms explicitly prohibit transfer of the lease (through either sale or sublease). The amount by which the lease terms are favourable compared with the terms of current market transactions for the same or similar items is an intangible asset that meets the contractual-legal criterion for recognition separately from goodwill, even though the acquirer cannot sell or otherwise transfer the lease contract. See Chapter 9.

(b) an acquiree owns and operates a nuclear power plant. The licence to operate that power plant is an intangible asset that meets the contractual-legal criterion for recognition separately from goodwill, even if the acquirer cannot sell or transfer it separately from the acquired power plant. However, IFRS 3 goes on to say that an acquirer may recognise the fair value of the operating licence and the fair value of the power plant as a single asset for financial reporting purposes if the useful lives of those assets are similar.

(c) an acquiree owns a technology patent. It has licensed that patent to others for their exclusive use outside the domestic market, receiving a specified percentage of future foreign revenue in exchange. Both the technology patent and the related licence agreement meet the contractual-legal criterion for recognition separately from goodwill even if selling or exchanging the patent and the related licence agreement separately from one another would not be practical. *[IFRS 3.B32]*.

5.1.3.B Separability

IFRS 3 emphasises that the separability criterion means that an acquired intangible asset is *capable* of being separated or divided from the acquiree, regardless of the intentions of the acquirer. It adds that an acquired intangible asset is recognised separately from goodwill if there is evidence of exchange transactions for that type of asset or an asset of a similar type, even if those transactions are infrequent and regardless of whether the acquirer is involved in them. For example, customer and subscriber lists are frequently licensed and thus merit recognition as intangible assets. The standard acknowledges that an acquiree might try to distinguish its customer lists from those that are frequently licensed generally, in order to justify no recognition. However, in the absence of a truly distinguishing feature, such as confidentiality or other agreements that prohibit an entity from selling, leasing or otherwise exchanging information about its customers, these non-contractual rights should be recognised separately from goodwill. *[IFRS 3.B33]*.

An intangible asset that is not individually separable from the acquiree or combined entity should still be recognised separately from goodwill if it could be separable in combination with a related contract, identifiable asset or liability. For example, an acquiree owns a registered trademark and documented but unpatented technical expertise used to manufacture the trademarked product. The entity could not transfer ownership of the trademark without everything else necessary for the new owner to produce an identical product or service. Because the unpatented technical expertise must be transferred if the related trademark is sold, it is separable and not included in the carrying value of goodwill. *[IFRS 3.B34]*.

The requirements described above demonstrate how IFRS 3 and IAS 38 define intangible assets in a way that eliminates as much as possible any barrier to recognising them separately from goodwill.

5.2 Examples of intangible assets acquired in a business combination

IFRS 3 provides a long list of examples of items acquired in a business combination that meet the definition of an intangible asset and should therefore be recognised separately from goodwill. *[IFRS 3.IE16-44]*. The list is not intended to be exhaustive and other items acquired in a business combination might still meet the definition of an intangible asset. *[IFRS 3.IE16]*.

The table below summarises the items included in the IASB's Illustrative Example. Reference should be made to the Illustrative Example itself for any further explanation about some of these items.

Intangible assets arising from contractual or other legal rights (regardless of being separable)	Other intangible assets that are separable
Marketing-related	
– Trademarks, trade names, service marks, collective marks and certification marks	
– Internet domain names	
– Trade dress (unique colour, shape or package design)	
– Newspaper mastheads	
– Non-competition agreements	
Customer-related	
– Order or production backlog	– Customer lists
– Customer contracts and the related customer relationships	– Non-contractual customer relationships
Artistic-related	
– Plays, operas and ballets	
– Books, magazines, newspapers and other literary works	
– Musical works such as compositions, song lyrics and advertising jingles	
– Pictures and photographs	
– Video and audiovisual material, including films, music videos and television programmes	
Contract-based	
– Licensing, royalty and standstill agreements	
– Advertising, construction, management, service or supply contracts	
– Lease agreements	
– Construction permits	
– Franchise agreements	
– Operating and broadcast rights	
– Servicing contracts such as mortgage servicing contracts	
– Employment contracts that are beneficial contracts from the perspective of the employer because the pricing of those contracts is below their current market value	
– Use rights such as drilling, water, air, mineral, timber-cutting and route authorities	
Technology-based	
– Patented technology	– Unpatented technology
– Computer software and mask works	– Databases, including title plants
– Trade secrets such as secret formulas, processes and recipes	

Further details on the requirements relating to intangible assets acquired as part of a business combination are covered in Chapter 9.

5.3 Measuring the fair value of intangible assets acquired in a business combination

IFRS 3 assumes that there will always be sufficient information to measure reliably the fair value of an intangible asset acquired in a business combination if it is separable or arises from contractual or other legal rights.

The issues underlying the initial measurement of these intangible assets are discussed further in Chapter 9. The requirements of IFRS 13 are discussed in Chapter 14, which also addresses the challenges of applying IFRS 13 at initial recognition since fair value is defined as an exit price. In particular, the selection of appropriate valuation techniques, inputs to those valuation techniques and the application of the fair value hierarchy are discussed in Chapter 14.

5.4 Customer relationship intangible assets acquired in a business combination

Further guidance on customer relationships acquired in a business combination is provided by IFRS 3 in the Illustrative Examples, which form the basis of the example below. These demonstrate how the contractual-legal and separability criteria, discussed at 2.1.1 above, interact in the recognition of acquired customer relationships. *[IFRS 3.IE30]*.

Example 17.5: Customer relationship intangible assets acquired in a business combination

Supply agreement

Acquirer Company (A) acquires Target Company (T) in a business combination. T has a five-year agreement to supply goods to Customer (C). Both T and A believe that C will renew the supply agreement at the end of the current contract. The supply agreement is not separable.

Because T establishes its relationship with C through a contract, not only the supply agreement (whether cancellable or not) but also T's customer relationship with C meet the contractual-legal criterion for identification as an intangible asset. Therefore, both the supply agreement and the customer relationship intangible asset are recognised separately from goodwill.

Sporting goods and electronics

A acquires T in a business combination. T manufactures goods in two distinct lines of business: sporting goods and electronics. Customer (C) purchases both sporting goods and electronics from T. T has a contract with C to be its exclusive provider of sporting goods, but has no contract for the supply of electronics to C. Both T and A believe that there is only one overall customer relationship between T and C.

As in the previous example, both the contract for the exclusive supply of sporting goods (whether cancellable or not) and the related customer relationship qualify for identification as an intangible asset because the contractual-legal criterion is met. Because T and A believe that there is only one customer relationship, the fair value of the intangible asset incorporates assumptions regarding T's relationship with C for both sporting goods and electronics.

However, if A determined that there were two customer relationships with C – one for sporting goods and another for electronics – the customer relationship for electronics would only be recognised if it meets the separability criterion for identification as an intangible asset (because there is not a current or past contract it can be linked to).

Order backlog and recurring customers

A acquires T in a business combination on 31 December 2017. T does business with its customers solely through purchase and sales orders. At 31 December 2017, T has a backlog of customer purchase orders from 60 per cent of its customers, all of whom are recurring customers. The other 40 per cent of T's customers are also recurring customers. However, as of 31 December 2017, T has no open purchase orders or other contracts with those customers.

The purchase orders from 60 per cent of T's customers (whether cancellable or not) meet the contractual-legal criterion, so the order backlog is recognised as an intangible asset separate from goodwill. Additionally, because T has a practice of establishing contracts (purchase and sales orders) with all of its customers, its relationship with all of its customers (not just the 60 per cent in respect of which there is a backlog of purchase orders) also arises through contractual rights, and therefore meets the contractual-legal criterion for identification as an intangible asset, even though T does not have contracts with 40% of those customers at 31 December 2017.

Motor insurance contracts

A acquires T, an Insurer, in a business combination. T has a portfolio of one-year motor insurance contracts that are cancellable by policyholders.

Because T establishes its relationships with policyholders through insurance contracts, the customer relationship with policyholders meets the contractual-legal criterion for identification as an intangible asset.

One of the most difficult areas of interpretation is whether an arrangement is contractual or not. Contractual customer relationships are always recognised separately from goodwill but non-contractual customer relationships are recognised only if they are separable. Consequently, determining whether a relationship is contractual is critical to identifying and measuring customer relationship intangible assets and different conclusions could result in substantially different accounting outcomes. This is discussed in more detail in Chapter 9 at 5.5.2.B.

Given the widespread confusion the matter was referred to the IASB and the FASB with a recommendation to review and amend IFRS 3 by:

- removing the distinction between 'contractual' and 'non-contractual' customer-related intangible assets recognised in a business combination; and
- reviewing the indicators that identify the existence of a customer relationship in paragraph IE28 of IFRS 3 and including them in the standard.

When it considered the issue in March 2009, the Interpretations Committee was unable to develop an Interpretation clarifying the distinction between contractual and non-contractual.

The IASB deferred both recommendations of the Interpretations Committee to the post-implementation review (PIR) of IFRS 3, which was completed in June 2015. As a result of the PIR of IFRS 3 the issue of the identification and fair value measurement of intangible assets such as customer relationships and brand names was added to the IASB's active agenda within its *Goodwill and Impairment* research project. At the time of writing, the Board is exploring which intangible assets should be separated from goodwill and the IASB's work plan indicates that Discussion Paper is expected in the first half of 2018.[6] This project is covered in further detail in Chapter 9 at 1.1.1 and 5.5.2.B.

In the meantime, there will be divergent treatments in practice, depending on how entities interpret 'contractual' and 'non-contractual' customer-related intangible assets in a particular business combination.

5.5 In-process research and development

The term 'in-process research and development' (IPR&D) refers to those identifiable intangible assets resulting from research and development activities that are acquired in a business combination. An acquirer should recognise IPR&D separately from goodwill if the project meets the definition of an intangible asset. This is the case when the IPR&D project meets the definition of an asset and is identifiable, i.e. it is separable or arises from contractual or other legal rights. *[IAS 38.34]*.

IPR&D projects, whether or not recognised by the acquiree, are protected by legal rights and are clearly separable, as they can be bought and sold by entities in the normal course of business.

Any subsequent expenditure incurred on the project after its acquisition should be accounted for in accordance with the general rules in IAS 38 on internally generated intangible assets which are discussed at 6.2 below. *[IAS 38.42]*. In summary, this means that the subsequent expenditure is accounted for as follows: *[IAS 38.43]*

- research expenditure is recognised as an expense when incurred;
- development expenditure that does not satisfy the criteria for recognition as an intangible asset is recognised as an expense when incurred; and
- development expenditure that satisfies the recognition criteria is added to the carrying value of the acquired in-process research or development project.

This approach results in some IPR&D projects acquired in business combinations being treated differently from similar projects started internally because there are different criteria for recognition. The IASB acknowledged this point but decided that it could not support a treatment that allowed acquired IPR&D to be subsumed within goodwill. *[IAS 38.BC82]*. Until the Board finds time to address this issue, users of financial statements will have to live with the problem that an asset can be recognised for acquired research and development projects despite the fact that the entity might recognise as an expense the costs of internal projects at a similar stage of development.

The implication is that if an acquired project is ultimately successful, the asset recognised will have a higher carrying amount and related amortisation charged to profit and loss over its useful life than an equivalent internal project.

If the carrying value cannot be justified, the acquired asset will be impaired. An impairment test will be performed before the end of the period of acquisition and annually thereafter in accordance with the requirements of IAS 36 for intangible assets not yet available for use (see Chapter 20). *[IAS 36.10]*. Any impairment loss will be reflected in the entity's statement of profit or loss as a post-acquisition event.

6 INTERNALLY GENERATED INTANGIBLE ASSETS

6.1 Internally generated goodwill

IAS 38 explicitly prohibits the recognition of internally generated goodwill as an asset because internally generated goodwill is neither separable nor does it arise from contractual or legal rights. *[IAS 38.48]*. As such, it is not an identifiable resource controlled by the entity that can be measured reliably at cost. *[IAS 38.49]*. It therefore does not meet the definition of an intangible asset under the standard or that of an asset under the IASB's *Conceptual Framework*. The standard maintains that the difference between the fair value of an entity and the carrying amount of its identifiable net assets at any time may capture a range of factors that affect the fair value of the entity, but that such differences do not represent the cost of intangible assets controlled by the entity. *[IAS 38.50].*

6.2 Internally generated intangible assets

The IASB recognises that it may be difficult to decide whether an internally generated intangible asset qualifies for recognition because of problems in:

(a) confirming whether and when there is an identifiable asset that will generate expected future economic benefits; and

(b) determining the cost of the asset reliably, especially in cases where the cost of generating an intangible asset internally cannot be distinguished from the cost of maintaining or enhancing the entity's internally generated goodwill or of running day-to-day operations. *[IAS 38.51].*

To avoid the inappropriate recognition of an asset, IAS 38 requires that internally generated intangible assets are not only tested against the general requirements for recognition and initial measurement (discussed at 3 above), but also meet criteria which confirm that the related activity is at a sufficiently advanced stage of development, is both technically and commercially viable and includes only directly attributable costs. *[IAS 38.51].* Those criteria comprise detailed guidance on accounting for intangible assets in the research phase (see 6.2.1 below), the development phase (see 6.2.2 below) and on components of cost of an internally generated intangible asset (see 6.3 below).

If the general recognition and initial measurement requirements are met, the entity classifies the generation of the internally developed asset into a research phase and a development phase. *[IAS 38.52].* Only expenditure arising from the development phase can be considered for capitalisation, with all expenditure on research being recognised as an expense when it is incurred. *[IAS 38.54].* If it is too difficult to distinguish an activity between a research phase and a development phase, all expenditure is treated as research. *[IAS 38.53].*

The standard distinguishes between research and development activities as follows:

Research is original and planned investigation undertaken with the prospect of gaining new scientific or technical knowledge and understanding. *[IAS 38.8].*

The standard gives the following examples of research activities: *[IAS 38.56]*

(a) activities aimed at obtaining new knowledge;

(b) the search for, evaluation and final selection of, applications of research findings or other knowledge;

(c) the search for alternatives for materials, devices, products, processes, systems or services; and

(d) the formulation, design, evaluation and final selection of possible alternatives for new or improved materials, devices, products, processes, systems or services.

Development is the application of research findings or other knowledge to a plan or design for the production of new or substantially improved materials, devices, products, processes, systems or services before the start of commercial production or use. *[IAS 38.8].*

The standard gives the following examples of development activities:

(a) the design, construction and testing of pre-production or pre-use prototypes and models;

(b) the design of tools, jigs, moulds and dies involving new technology;

(c) the design, construction and operation of a pilot plant that is not of a scale economically feasible for commercial production; and

(d) the design, construction and testing of a chosen alternative for new or improved materials, devices, products, processes, systems or services. *[IAS 38.59]*.

6.2.1 Research phase

An entity cannot recognise an intangible asset arising from research or from the research phase of an internal project. Instead, any expenditure on research or the research phase of an internal project should be expensed as incurred because the entity cannot demonstrate that there is an intangible asset that will generate probable future economic benefits. *[IAS 38.54-55]*.

If an entity cannot distinguish the research phase from the development phase, it should treat the expenditure on that project as if it were incurred in the research phase only and recognise an expense accordingly. *[IAS 38.53]*.

6.2.2 Development phase

The standard requires recognition of an intangible asset arising from development (or the development phase of an internal project) while it imposes stringent conditions that restrict recognition. These tests create a balance, ensuring that the entity does not recognise unrecoverable costs as an asset.

An intangible asset arising from development or from the development phase of an internal project should be recognised if, and only if, an entity can demonstrate all of the following:

(a) the technical feasibility of completing the intangible asset so that it will be available for use or sale;

(b) its intention to complete the intangible asset and use or sell it;

(c) its ability to use or sell the intangible asset;

(d) how the intangible asset will generate probable future economic benefits. Among other things, the entity can demonstrate the existence of a market for the output of the intangible asset or the intangible asset itself or, if it is to be used internally, the usefulness of the intangible asset;

(e) the availability of adequate technical, financial and other resources to complete the development and to use or sell the intangible asset; and

(f) its ability to measure reliably the expenditure attributable to the intangible asset during its development. *[IAS 38.57]*.

The fact that an entity can demonstrate that the asset will generate probable future economic benefits distinguishes development activity from the research phase, where it is unlikely that such a demonstration would be possible. *[IAS 38.58]*.

It may be challenging to obtain objective evidence on each of the above conditions because:

- condition (b) relies on management intent;
- conditions (c), (e) and (f) are entity-specific (i.e. whether development expenditure meets any of these conditions depends both on the nature of the development activity itself and the financial position of the entity); and
- condition (d) above is more restrictive than is immediately apparent because the entity needs to assess the probable future economic benefits using the principles in IAS 36, i.e. using discounted cash flows. If the asset will generate economic benefits only in conjunction with other assets, the entity should apply the concept of cash-generating units. *[IAS 38.60]*. The application of IAS 36 is discussed in Chapter 20.

IAS 38 indicates that evidence may be available in the form of:

- a business plan showing the technical, financial and other resources needed and the entity's ability to secure those resources;
- a lender's indication of its willingness to fund the plan confirming the availability of external finance; *[IAS 38.61]* and
- detailed project information demonstrating that an entity's costing systems can measure reliably the cost of generating an intangible asset internally, such as salary and other expenditure incurred in securing copyrights or licences or developing computer software. *[IAS 38.62]*.

In any case, an entity should maintain books and records in sufficient detail that allow it to prove whether it meets the conditions set out by IAS 38.

Certain types of product (e.g. pharmaceuticals, aircraft and electrical equipment) require regulatory approval before they can be sold. Regulatory approval is not one of the criteria for recognition under IAS 38 and the standard does not prohibit an entity from capitalising its development costs in advance of approval. However, in some industries regulatory approval is vital to commercial success and its absence indicates significant uncertainty around the possible future economic benefits. This is the case in the pharmaceuticals industry, where it is rarely possible to determine whether a new drug will secure regulatory approval until it is actually granted. Accordingly, it is common practice in this industry for costs to be expensed until such approval is obtained. See Extract 17.6 and the discussion at 6.2.3 below.

The standard does not define the terms 'research phase' and 'development phase' but explains that they should be interpreted more broadly than 'research' and 'development' which it does define. *[IAS 38.52]*. The features characterising the research phase have less to do with what activities are performed, but relate more to an inability to demonstrate at that time that there is an intangible asset that will generate probable future benefits. *[IAS 38.55]*. This means that the research phase may include activities that do not necessarily meet the definition of 'research'. For example, the research phase for IAS 38 purposes may extend to the whole period preceding a product launch, regardless of the fact that activities that would otherwise characterise development are taking place at the same time, because certain features that would mean the project has entered its development phase are still absent (such as confirming an ability to use or sell the asset; demonstrating sufficient market demand for a product; or uncertainty regarding the source of funds to complete the project). As a result, an entity might not be able to distinguish the research phase from the development phase of an internal project to create an intangible asset, in which case it should treat the expenditure on that project as if it were incurred in the research phase only and recognise an expense accordingly. *[IAS 38.53].* It also means that the development phase may include activities that do not necessarily meet the definition of 'development'. The example below illustrates how an entity would apply these rules in practice.

Example 17.6: Research phase and development phase under IAS 38

Entity K is working on a project to create a database containing images and articles from newspapers around the world, which it intends to sell to customers over the internet. K has identified the following stages in its project:

(a) Research stage – gaining the technical knowledge necessary to transfer images to customers and assessing whether the project is feasible from a technological point of view;

(b) Development stage – performing market analysis to identify potential demand and customer requirements; developing the ability to exploit the image capture technology including configuration of the required database software and acquiring the required data to populate the database, designing the customer interface and testing a prototype of the system; and

(c) Production stage – before and after the commercial launch of the service, debugging the system and improving functionality to service higher user volumes; updating and managing the database to ensure its currency.

The above can be summarised as follows:

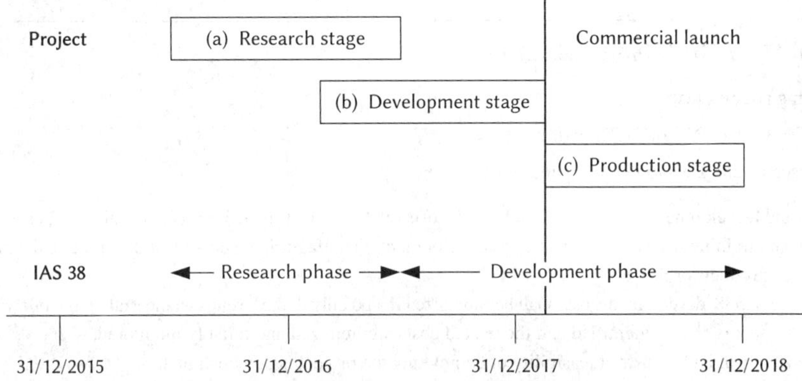

The activities in the research stage included under (a) meet the definition of research under IAS 38 and would be accounted for as part of the research phase of the project, as an expense.

The activities in the development stage included under (b) meet the definition of development under IAS 38. However, whilst K has started to plan the commercial exploitation of its image and data capture technology, it will not be immediately apparent that the project is economically viable. Until this point is reached, for example when the entity has established there is demand for the database and it is likely that a working prototype of the system will be available, the development activities cannot be distinguished from the research activities taking place at the same time. Accordingly, the initial development activities are accounted for as if they were incurred in the research phase. Only once it becomes possible to demonstrate the existence of an intangible asset that will generate future income streams, can project expenditure be accounted for under IAS 38 as part of the development phase.

There may be a period after the commercial launch of the service that would still be accounted for as part of the development phase. For example, activities to improve functionality to deal with higher actual customer volumes could constitute development. This does not necessarily mean that K can capitalise all this expenditure because it needs to pass the double hurdle of:

- the presumption in IAS 38.20 that 'there are no additions to such an asset or replacements of part of it'; and
- the six criteria in IAS 38.57 for recognition of development costs as an asset (see above).

Activity to ensure that the database is up-to-date is a routine process that does not involve major innovations or new technologies. Therefore, these activities in the production stage do not meet the definition of 'research' or 'development' and the related costs are recognised as an expense.

As the above example illustrates, the guidance in IAS 38 seems to take a somewhat restricted view as to how internally generated intangible assets are created and managed in practice, as well as the types of internally generated intangible assets. It requires activity to be classified into research and development phases, but this analysis does not easily fit with intangible assets that are created for use by the entity itself. The standard therefore does not address the everyday reality for software companies, television production companies, newspapers and data vendors that produce intangible assets in industrial-scale routine processes.

Many of the intangible assets produced in routine processes (e.g. software, television programmes, newspaper content and databases) meet the recognition criteria in the standard, but no specific guidance is available that could help an entity in dealing with the practical problems that arise when accounting for them.

Generally, entities disclose little detail of the nature of their research and development activities and the costs that they incur, instead focusing on the requirements of IAS 38 that must be met before development expenditure can be capitalised.

Extract 17.5: L'Air Liquide S.A. (2016)

Accounting policies [extract]

5. **NON-CURRENT ASSETS** [extract]

b. **Research and Development expenditures**

Research and Development expenditures include all costs related to the scientific and technical activities, patent work, education and training necessary to ensure the development, manufacturing, start-up, and commercialization of new or improved products or processes.

According to IAS38, development costs shall be capitalized if, and only if, the Group can meet all of the following criteria:

- the project is clearly identified and the related costs are itemized and reliably monitored;
- the technical and industrial feasibility of completing the project is demonstrated;
- there is a clear intention to complete the project and to use or sell the intangible asset arising from it;
- the Group has the ability to use or sell the intangible asset arising from the project;
- the Group can demonstrate how the intangible asset will generate probable future economic benefits;
- the Group has adequate technical, financial and other resources to complete the project and to use or sell the intangible asset.

When these conditions are not satisfied, development costs generated by the Group are recognized as an expense when incurred.

Research expenditure is recognized as an expense when incurred.

c. **Internally generated intangible assets**

Internally generated intangible assets primarily include the development costs of information management systems. These costs are capitalized only if they satisfy the criteria as defined by IAS38 and described above.

Internal and external development costs on management information systems arising from the development phase are capitalized. Significant maintenance and improvement costs are added to the initial cost of assets if they specifically meet the capitalization criteria.

Internally generated intangible assets are amortized over their useful lives.

The difficulty in applying the IAS 38 recognition criteria for development costs in the pharmaceutical industry are discussed further at 6.2.3 below. Technical and economic feasibility are typically established very late in the process of developing a new product, which means that usually only a small proportion of the development costs is capitalised.

When the development phase ends will also influence how the entity recognises revenue from the project. As noted at 4.4 above, during the development phase an entity can only recognise income from incidental operations, being those not necessary to develop the asset for its intended use, as revenue in profit or loss. *[IAS 38.31]*. During the phase in which the activity is necessary to bring the intangible asset into its intended use, any income should be deducted from the cost of the development asset. Examples include income from the sale of samples produced during the testing of a new process or from the sale of a production prototype. Only once it is determined that the intangible asset is ready for its intended use would revenue be recognised from such activities. At the same time capitalisation of costs would cease and the related costs of the revenue generating activity would include a measure of amortisation of the asset.

6.2.3 *Research and development in the pharmaceutical industry*

Entities in the pharmaceutical industry consider research and development to be of primary importance to their business. Consequently, these entities spend a considerable amount on research and development every year and one might expect them to carry significant internally generated development intangible assets on their statement of financial position. However, their financial statements reveal that they often consider the uncertainties in the development of pharmaceuticals to be too great to permit capitalisation of development costs.

One of the problems is that, in the case of true 'development' activities in the pharmaceutical industry, the final outcome can be uncertain and the technical and economic feasibility of new products or processes is typically established very late in the development phase, which means that only a small proportion of the total development costs can ever be capitalised. In particular, many products and processes require approval by a regulator such as the US Food and Drug Administration (FDA) before they can be applied commercially and until that time the entity may be uncertain of their success. After approval, of course, there is often relatively little in the way of further development expenditure.

In the pharmaceutical sector, the capitalisation of development costs for new products or processes usually begins at the date on which the product or process receives regulatory approval. In most cases that is the point when the IAS 38 criteria for recognition of intangible assets are met. It is unlikely that these criteria will have been met before approval is granted by the regulator.

Extracts 17.6 and 17.7 below illustrate some of the difficulty in applying the IAS 38 recognition criteria for development costs in the pharmaceutical industry.

Extract 17.6: Merck Kommanditgesellschaft auf Aktien (2016)

Notes to the Consolidated Financial Statements [extract]

(53) Research and development costs

Research and development costs comprise the costs of research departments and process development, the expenses incurred as a result of research and development collaborations as well as the costs of clinical trials (both before and after approval is granted).

The costs of research cannot be capitalized and are expensed in full in the period in which they are incurred. As internally generated intangible assets, it is necessary to capitalize development expenses if the cost of the internally generated intangible asset can be reliably determined and the asset can be expected to lead to future economic benefits. The condition for this is that the necessary resources are available for the development of the asset, technical feasibility of the asset is given, its completion and use are intended, and marketability is given. Owing to the high risks up to the time that pharmaceutical products are approved, these criteria are not met in the Healthcare business sector. Costs incurred after regulatory approval are usually insignificant and are therefore not recognized as intangible assets. Owing to the risks existing up until market launch, development expenses in the Life Science and Performance Materials business sectors can likewise not be capitalized.

Reimbursements for R&D are offset against research and development costs.

Extract 17.7: Bayer AG (2016)

Consolidated Financial Statements [extract]

Notes to the Consolidated Financial Statements of the Bayer Group [extract]

4 Basic principles, methods and critical accounting estimates [extract]

Research and development expenses

For accounting purposes, research expenses are defined as costs incurred for current or planned investigations undertaken with the prospect of gaining new scientific or technical knowledge and understanding. Development expenses are defined as costs incurred for the application of research findings or specialist knowledge to plans or designs for the production, provision or development of new or substantially improved products, services or processes, respectively, prior to the commencement of commercial production or use.

Research and development expenses are incurred in the Bayer Group for in-house research and development activities as well as numerous research and development collaborations and alliances with third parties.

Research and development expenses mainly comprise the costs for active ingredient discovery, clinical studies, research and development activities in the areas of application technology and engineering, field trials, regulatory approvals and approval extensions.

Research costs cannot be capitalized. The conditions for capitalization of development costs are closely defined: an intangible asset must be recognized if, and only if, there is reasonable certainty of receiving future cash flows that will cover an asset's carrying amount. Since our own development projects are often subject to regulatory approval procedures and other uncertainties, the conditions for the capitalization of costs incurred before receipt of approvals are not normally satisfied.

In the case of research and development collaborations, a distinction is generally made between payments on contract signature, upfront payments, milestone payments and cost reimbursements for work performed. If an intangible asset (such as the right to the use of an active ingredient) is acquired in connection with any of these payment obligations, the respective payment is capitalized even if it is uncertain whether further development work will ultimately lead to the production of a saleable product. Reimbursements of the cost of research or development work are recognized in profit or loss, except where they are required to be capitalized.

6.2.4 *Internally generated brands, mastheads, publishing titles and customer lists*

IAS 38 considers internally generated brands, mastheads, publishing titles, customer lists and items similar in substance to be indistinguishable from the cost of developing a business as a whole so it prohibits their recognition. *[IAS 38.63-64].* As discussed at 3.3 above, the same applies to subsequent expenditures incurred in connection with such intangible assets even when originally acquired externally. *[IAS 38.20].* For example, expenditure incurred in redesigning the layout of newspapers or magazines, which represent subsequent expenditure on publishing titles and mastheads, should not be capitalised.

6.2.5 *Website costs (SIC-32)*

SIC-32 clarifies how IAS 38 applies to costs in relation to websites designed for use by the entity in its business. An entity's own website that arises from development and is for internal or external access is an internally generated intangible asset under the standard. *[SIC-32.7].* A website designed for external access may be used for various purposes such as to promote and advertise an entity's own products and services, provide electronic services to customers, and sell products and services. A website may be used within the entity to give staff access to company policies and customer details, and allow them to search relevant information. *[SIC-32.1].*

SIC-32 does not apply to items that are accounted for under another standard, such as the development or operation of a website (or website software) for sale to another entity (IAS 2, IAS 11 and IFRS 15); acquiring or developing hardware supporting a website (IAS 16); or in determining the initial recognition of an asset for a website subject to a leasing arrangement (IAS 17). However, the Interpretation should be applied by lessors providing a web site under an operating lease and by lessees considering the treatment of subsequent expenditure relating to a web site asset leased under a finance lease, *[SIC-32.5-6],* because the related website asset will be carried on the entity's statement of financial position.

Under SIC-32, an intangible asset should be recognised for website development costs if and only if, it meets the general recognition requirements in IAS 38 (see 3.1 above) and the six conditions for recognition as development costs (see 6.2.2 above). Most important of these is the requirement to demonstrate how the website will generate probable future economic benefits. *[SIC-32.8].* The Interpretation deems an entity unable to demonstrate this for a website developed solely or primarily for promoting and advertising its own products and services. All expenditure on developing such a website should be recognised as an expense when incurred. Accordingly, it is unlikely that costs will be eligible for capitalisation unless an entity can demonstrate that the website is used directly in the income-generating process, for example where customers can place orders on the entity's website. *[SIC-32.8].*

The following stages of a website's development are identified by the interpretation: *[SIC-32.2, 9]*

(a) *planning* includes undertaking feasibility studies, defining objectives and specifications, evaluating alternatives and selecting preferences. Expenditures incurred in this stage are similar in nature to the research phase and should be recognised as an expense when they are incurred;

(b) *application and infrastructure development* includes obtaining a domain name, purchasing and developing hardware and operating software, installing developed applications and stress testing. The requirements of IAS 16 are applied to expenditure on physical assets. Other costs are recognised as an expense, unless they can be directly attributed, or allocated on a reasonable and consistent basis, to preparing the website for its intended use and the project to develop the website meets the SIC-32 criteria for recognition as an intangible asset;

(c) *graphical design development* includes designing the appearance of web pages. Costs incurred at this stage should be accounted for in the same way as expenditure incurred in the 'application and infrastructure development' stage described under (b) above;

(d) *content development* includes creating, purchasing, preparing and uploading information, either textual or graphical in nature, on the website before the completion of the website's development. The costs of content developed to advertise and promote an entity's own products and services are always expensed as incurred. Other costs incurred in this stage should be recognised as an expense unless the criteria for recognition as an asset described in (b) above are satisfied; and

(e) the *operating stage*, which starts after completion of the development of a website, when an entity maintains and enhances the applications, infrastructure, graphical design and content of the website. *[SIC-32.3]*. Expenditure incurred in this stage should be expensed as incurred unless it meets the asset recognition criteria in IAS 38.

In making these assessments, the entity should evaluate the nature of each activity for which expenditure is incurred, independently of its consideration of the website's stage of development. *[SIC-32.9]*. This means that even where a project has been determined to qualify for recognition as an intangible asset, not all costs incurred in relation to a qualifying stage of development are eligible for capitalisation. For example, whilst the direct costs of developing an online ordering system might qualify for recognition as an asset, the costs of training staff to operate that system should be expensed because training costs are deemed not necessary to creating, producing or preparing the website for it to be capable of operating (see 6.3 above). *[IAS 38.67]*. Examples of other costs that would be recognised as an expense regardless of the stage of the project are given in the Illustrative Example to SIC-32, including:

(a) selling, administrative and other general overhead expenditure unless it can be directly attributed to preparing the web site for use to operate in the manner intended by management;

(b) clearly identified inefficiencies in the project, such as those relating to alternative solutions explored and rejected; and

(c) initial operating losses incurred before the web site achieves planned performance.

A website qualifying for recognition as an intangible asset should be measured after initial recognition by applying the cost model or the revaluation model in IAS 38 as discussed at 8.1 and 8.2 below. In respect of the useful life of website assets, the expectation is that it should be short. *[SIC-32.10].*

The criteria for recognition as an asset are restrictive. On-line fashion retailer, ASOS, does not capitalise website development costs, as demonstrated in the extract below.

Extract 17.8: ASOS plc (2016)

NOTES TO THE FINANCIAL STATEMENTS

For the year to 31 August 2016 [extract]

25 ACCOUNTING POLICIES [extract]

i) Other intangible assets [extract]

The costs of acquiring and developing software that is not integral to the related hardware is capitalised separately as an intangible asset. This does not include internal website development and maintenance costs which are expensed as incurred unless representing a technological advance leading to future economic benefit. Capitalised software costs include external direct costs of material and services and the payroll and payroll-related costs for employees who are directly associated with the project.

6.3 Cost of an internally generated intangible asset

On initial recognition, an intangible asset should be measured at cost, *[IAS 38.24]*, which the standard defines as the amount of cash or cash equivalents paid or the fair value of other consideration given to acquire an asset at the time of its acquisition or construction. When applicable, cost is the amount attributed to that asset when initially recognised in accordance with the specific requirements of other IFRSs, e.g. IFRS 2. *[IAS 38.8].* It is important to ensure that cost includes only the expenditure incurred after the recognition criteria are met and to confirm that only costs directly related to the creation of the asset are capitalised.

6.3.1 Establishing the time from which costs can be capitalised

The cost of an internally generated intangible asset is the sum of the expenditure incurred from the date when the intangible asset first meets the recognition criteria of the standard, *[IAS 38.65]*, and meets the detailed conditions for recognition of development phase costs as an asset (see 6.2.2 above).

Costs incurred before these criteria are met are expensed, *[IAS 38.68]*, and cannot be reinstated retrospectively, *[IAS 38.65]*, because IAS 38 does not permit recognition of past expenses as an intangible asset at a later date. *[IAS 38.71].*

The following example, which is taken from IAS 38, illustrates how these above rules should be applied in practice.

Example 17.7: Recognition of internally generated intangible assets

An entity is developing a new production process. During 2017, expenditure incurred was €1,000, of which €900 was incurred before 1 December 2017 and €100 was incurred between 1 December 2017 and 31 December 2017. The entity is able to demonstrate that, at 1 December 2017, the production process met the criteria for recognition as an intangible asset. The recoverable amount of the know-how embodied in the process (including future cash outflows to complete the process before it is available for use) is estimated to be €500.

At the end of 2017, the production process is recognised as an intangible asset at a cost of €100 (expenditure incurred since the date when the recognition criteria were met, that is, 1 December 2017). The €900 expenditure incurred before 1 December 2017 is recognised as an expense because the recognition criteria were not met until 1 December 2017. This expenditure does not form part of the cost of the production process recognised in the statement of financial position.

During 2018, expenditure incurred is €2,000. At the end of 2018, the recoverable amount of the know-how embodied in the process (including future cash outflows to complete the process before it is available for use) is estimated to be €1,900.

At the end of 2018, the cost of the production process is €2,100 (€100 expenditure recognised at the end of 2017 plus €2,000 expenditure recognised in 2018). The entity recognises an impairment loss of €200 to adjust the carrying amount of the process before impairment loss (€2,100) to its recoverable amount (€1,900). This impairment loss will be reversed in a subsequent period if the requirements for the reversal of an impairment loss in IAS 36 are met.

6.3.2 Determining the costs eligible for capitalisation

The cost of an internally generated intangible asset comprises all directly attributable costs necessary to create, produce, and prepare the asset to be capable of operating in the manner intended by management. Examples of directly attributable costs are:

(a) costs of materials and services used or consumed in generating the intangible asset;

(b) costs of employee benefits arising from the generation of the intangible asset;

(c) fees to register a legal right;

(d) amortisation of patents and licences that are used to generate the intangible asset; and

(e) borrowing costs that meet the criteria under IAS 23 for recognition as an element of cost. *[IAS 38.66].*

Indirect costs and general overheads, even if they can be allocated on a reasonable and consistent basis to the development project, cannot be recognised as part of the cost of any intangible asset. The standard also specifically prohibits recognition of the following items as a component of cost:

(a) selling, administrative and other general overhead expenditure unless this expenditure can be directly attributed to preparing the asset for use;

(b) identified inefficiencies and initial operating losses incurred before the asset achieves planned performance; and

(c) expenditure on training staff to operate the asset. *[IAS 38.67].*

For these purposes it does not make any difference whether the costs are incurred directly by the entity or relate to services provided by third parties.

7 RECOGNITION OF AN EXPENSE

Unless expenditure is incurred in connection with an item that meets the criteria for recognition as an intangible asset, and is an eligible component of cost, it should be expensed. The only exception is in connection with a business combination, where the cost of an item that cannot be recognised as an intangible asset will form part of the carrying amount of goodwill at the acquisition date. *[IAS 38.68].*

Some of the ineligible components of cost are identified at 4.3 and 6.3 above and include costs that are not directly related to the creation of the asset, such as costs of introducing a new product or costs incurred to redeploy an asset. IAS 38 provides other examples of expenditure that is recognised as an expense when incurred:

(a) start-up costs, unless they qualify for recognition as part of the cost of property, plant and equipment under IAS 16 (see Chapter 18). Start-up costs recognised as an expense may consist of establishment costs such as legal and secretarial costs incurred in setting up a legal entity, expenditure to open a new facility or business or expenditures for starting new operations or launching new products or processes;

(b) training costs;

(c) advertising and promotional activities (including mail order catalogues); and

(d) relocation or reorganisation costs. *[IAS 38.69].*

For these purposes no distinction is made between costs that are incurred directly by the entity and those that relate to services provided by third parties. However, the standard does not prevent an entity from recording a prepayment if it pays for the delivery of goods before obtaining a right to access those goods. Similarly, a prepayment can be recognised when payment is made before the services are received. *[IAS 38.70].*

7.1 Catalogues and other advertising costs

The Board considers that advertising and promotional activities do not qualify for recognition as an intangible asset because their purpose is to enhance or create internally generated brands or customer relationships, which themselves cannot be recognised as intangible assets. *[IAS 38.BC46B].* An entity has a different asset, a prepayment, if it has paid for goods or services before they are provided, as described above. However, the Board did not believe this justified an asset being recognised beyond the point at which the entity gained the right to access the related goods or received the related services. *[IAS 38.BC46D].* Entities cannot, therefore maintain a prepayment asset and defer recognising an expense in the period between receiving the material from a supplier and delivery to its customers or potential customers. *[IAS 38.BC46E].*

Accordingly, the IASB is deliberate in using the phrase 'obtaining the right to access those goods' when it defines the point that an expense is recognised. This is because the date of physical delivery could be altered without affecting the substance of the commercial arrangement with the supplier. *[IAS 38.BC46E].* Recognition is determined by the point when the goods have been constructed by the supplier in accordance with the terms of the customer contract and the entity could demand delivery in return for payment. *[IAS 38.69A].* Therefore an entity must recognise an expense for customer catalogues once they are ready for delivery from the printer, even if the entity has arranged for the printer to send catalogues directly to customers when advised by the entity's sales department. Similarly in the case of services, an expense is recognised when those services are received by the entity, and not deferred until the entity uses them in the delivery of another service, for example, to deliver an advertisement to its customers. *[IAS 38.69A].*

The Board rejected calls to make a special case for mail order catalogues, where it was argued that they created a distribution network, on the grounds that their primary objective was to advertise goods to customers. *[IAS 38.BC46G].* For this reason the wording in the standard cites mail order catalogues as an example of expenditure on advertising and promotional activities that is recognised as an expense. *[IAS 38.69].*

8 MEASUREMENT AFTER INITIAL RECOGNITION

IAS 38, in common with a number of other standards, provides an entity the option to choose between two alternative treatments: *[IAS 38.72]*

- the *cost model*, which requires measurement at cost less any accumulated amortisation and any accumulated impairment losses; *[IAS 38.74]* or
- the *revaluation model*, which requires measurement at a revalued amount, being its fair value at the date of the revaluation, less any subsequent accumulated amortisation and any subsequent accumulated impairment losses. *[IAS 38.75]*.

The revaluation option is only available if there is an active market for the intangible asset. *[IAS 38.75, 81-82]*. Active market is defined by IFRS 13; see Chapter 14 at 3. There are no provisions in IAS 38 that allow fair value to be determined indirectly, for example by using the techniques and financial models applied to estimate the fair value of intangible assets acquired in a business combination. Therefore, in accordance with IFRS 13, an entity must measure the fair value of an intangible under the revaluation model using the price in an active market for an identical asset, i.e. a Level 1 price. For further guidance on the price in an active market, see Chapter 14 at 17. If an entity chooses an accounting policy to measure an intangible asset at revalued amount, it must apply the revaluation model to all the assets in that class, unless there is no active market for those other assets. *[IAS 38.72]*. A class of intangible assets is a grouping of assets of a similar nature and use in an entity's operations. *[IAS 38.73]*. Examples of separate classes of intangible asset include:

(a) brand names;

(b) mastheads and publishing titles;

(c) computer software;

(d) licences and franchises;

(e) copyrights, patents and other industrial property rights, service and operating rights;

(f) recipes, formulae, models, designs and prototypes; and

(g) intangible assets under development. *[IAS 38.119]*.

The standard requires assets in the same class to be revalued at the same time, as to do otherwise would allow selective revaluation of assets and the reporting of a mixture of costs and values as at different dates within the same asset class. *[IAS 38.73]*.

8.1 Cost model for measurement of intangible assets

Under the cost model, after initial recognition, the carrying amount of an intangible asset is its cost less any accumulated amortisation and accumulated impairment losses. *[IAS 38.74]*. The rules on amortisation of intangible assets are discussed at 9.2 and 9.3 below; and impairment is discussed at 9.4 below.

8.2 Revaluation model for measurement of intangible assets

An entity can only apply the revaluation model if the fair value can be determined by reference to an active market. *[IAS 38.75, 81-82]*. An active market will rarely exist for intangible assets (see 8.2.1 below). *[IAS 38.78]*.

After initial recognition an intangible asset should be carried at a revalued amount, which is its fair value at the date of the revaluation less any subsequent accumulated amortisation and any subsequent accumulated impairment losses. *[IAS 38.75]*. To prevent an entity from circumventing the recognition rules of the standard, the revaluation model does not allow:

- the revaluation of intangible assets that have not previously been recognised as assets; or
- the initial recognition of intangible assets at amounts other than cost. *[IAS 38.76]*.

These rules are designed to prevent an entity from recognising at a 'revalued' amount an intangible asset that was never recorded because its costs were expensed as they did not at the time meet the recognition rules. As noted at 6.3.1 above, IAS 38 does not permit recognition of past expenses as an intangible asset at a later date. *[IAS 38.71]*.

However, it is permitted to apply the revaluation model to the whole of an intangible asset even if only part of its cost was originally recognised as an asset because it did not meet the criteria for recognition until part of the way through the process. *[IAS 38.77]*. Since the prohibition on initial recognition of intangible assets at amounts other than cost would also prevent the revaluation of quotas and permits allocated by governments and similar bodies – which are amongst the few intangible assets that do have an active market – the standard specifically makes an exception and allows the revaluation model to be applied to 'an intangible asset that was received by way of a government grant and recognised at a nominal amount'. *[IAS 38.77]*.

The example below illustrates how this would work in practice.

Example 17.8: Application of revaluation model to intangible assets that are partially recognised or received by way of government grant

Entity C spent €12,000,000 in preparing its application for a number of taxi licences, which it expensed because of the uncertain outcome of the process. The application was successful and C was granted a number of freely transferable taxi licences and paid a nominal registration fee of €50,000, which it recognised as an asset. There is an active and liquid market in these taxi licences.

C can apply the revaluation model under IAS 38 to these taxi licences, because it previously recognised the licence (even if it only recognised part of the costs as an asset) and there is an active market in these licences.

Entity D obtained a number of freely transferable fishing quotas free of charge, which it recognised at a nominal amount as permitted under IAS 20. There is an active and liquid market in these quotas.

D can apply the revaluation model under IAS 38 to these fishing quotas, because it previously recognised the quota (even if it only recognised it at a nominal amount) and there is an active market in these quotas.

8.2.1 Revaluation is only allowed if there is an active market

An entity can only elect to apply the revaluation model if the fair value can be determined by reference to an active market for the intangible asset. *[IAS 38.81-82]*. An active market is defined in IFRS 13 as one in which transactions for the item take place with sufficient frequency and volume to provide pricing information on an ongoing basis. *[IFRS 13 Appendix A]*.

Few intangible assets will be eligible for revaluation and indeed the standard concedes that such an active market would be uncommon. Nevertheless, in some jurisdictions, an active market may exist for freely transferable taxi licences, fishing licences or production quotas. *[IAS 38.78]*. However, by their very nature most intangible assets are unique or entity-specific. The standard lists brands, newspaper mastheads, music and film publishing rights, patents or trademarks as items that are ineligible for revaluation because each such asset is unique. *[IAS 38.78]*. The existence of a previous sale and purchase transaction is not sufficient evidence for the market to be regarded as active because of the requirement in the definition for a sufficient frequency and volume of transactions to allow the provision of ongoing pricing information. The standard notes that where contracts are negotiated between individual buyers and sellers or when transactions are relatively infrequent, the price of a previous transaction for one intangible asset may not provide sufficient evidence of the fair value of another. In addition, if prices are not available to the public, this is taken as evidence that an active market does not exist. *[IAS 38.78]*.

An entity should stop revaluing an asset if the market used to determine its fair value ceases to meet the criteria for an active market. The valuation is 'frozen' from that date, and reduced thereafter by subsequent amortisation and any subsequent impairment losses. *[IAS 38.82]*. The IASB believes that the disappearance of a previously active market may indicate that the asset needs to be tested for impairment in accordance with IAS 36. *[IAS 38.83]*.

If an active market for the previously revalued asset emerges at a later date, the entity is required to apply the revaluation model from that date. *[IAS 38.84]*.

8.2.2 Frequency of revaluations

IAS 38 requires revaluations to be performed 'with such regularity that at the end of the reporting period the carrying amount of the asset does not differ materially from its fair value'. *[IAS 38.75]*. The standard lets entities judge for themselves the frequency of revaluations depending on the volatility of the fair values of the underlying intangible assets. Significant and volatile movements in fair value would necessitate annual revaluation, whereas a less frequent update would be required for intangibles whose price is subject only to insignificant movements. *[IAS 38.79]*. Nevertheless, since an entity can only revalue assets for which a price is quoted in an active market, there should be no impediment to updating that valuation at each reporting date. As noted above, when an entity has a number of items in the same class of intangible assets, the standard requires that they are all valued at the same time. *[IAS 38.73]*.

8.2.3 Accounting for revaluations

Increases in an intangible asset's carrying amount as a result of a revaluation should be credited to other comprehensive income under the heading of revaluation surplus, except to the extent that the revaluation reverses a revaluation decrease of the same asset that was previously recognised in profit or loss. *[IAS 38.85]*. Conversely, decreases in an intangible asset's carrying amount as a result of a revaluation should be recognised in profit or loss, unless the decrease reverses an earlier upward revaluation, in which case the decrease should first be recognised in other comprehensive income to extinguish the revaluation surplus in respect of the asset. *[IAS 38.86]*. The example below illustrates how this works.

Example 17.9: Accounting for upward and downward revaluations

Entity E acquired an intangible asset that it accounts for under the revaluation model. The fair value of the asset changes as follows:

	£	£ Change
Acquisition	530	–
Date A	550	+20
Date B	520	–30
Date C	510	–10
Date D	555	+45

The table below shows how entity E should account for the upward and downward revaluations.

	Value of asset	*Cumulative revaluation reserve*	*Revaluation recognised in other comprehensive income*	*Revaluation recognised in profit or loss*
	£	£	£	£
Acquisition	530	–	–	–
Date A	550	20	20	–
Date B	520	–	(20)	(10)
Date C	510	–	–	(10)
Date D	555	25	25	20

The diagram below summarises this information (the impact of amortisation on the carrying amount and revaluation surplus has been ignored in this example for the sake of simplicity).

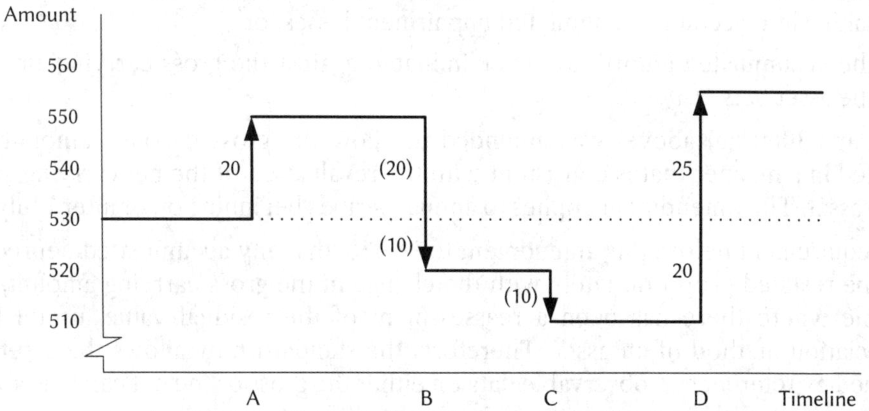

The upward revaluation at Date A is accounted for in other comprehensive income. The downward revaluation at Date B first reduces the revaluation reserve for that asset to nil and the excess of £10 is recognised as a loss in profit or loss. The second downward revaluation at Date C is recognised as a loss in profit or loss. The upward revaluation at Date D first reverses the cumulative loss recognised in profit or loss and the excess is accounted for in other comprehensive income.

In the example above, the impact of amortisation on the carrying amount of the assets and the revaluation surplus was ignored for the sake of simplicity. However, the cumulative revaluation surplus included in other comprehensive income may be transferred directly to retained earnings when the surplus is realised, which happens either on the retirement or disposal of the asset, or as the asset is used by the entity. *[IAS 38.87]*. In the latter case, the amount of the surplus regarded as realised is the amount of amortisation in excess of what would have been charged based on the asset's historical cost. *[IAS 38.87]*. See Chapter 18 at 6.2 for an example. In practice this means two things:

- an entity applying the revaluation model would need to track both the historical cost and revalued amount of an asset to determine how much of the revaluation surplus has been realised; and
- any revaluation surplus is amortised over the life of the related asset. Therefore, in the case of a significant downward revaluation there is a smaller revaluation surplus available against which the downward revaluation can be offset before recognition in the statement of profit or loss.

The transfer from revaluation surplus to retained earnings is not made through profit or loss. *[IAS 38.87]*. It is not the same as recycling a gain or loss previously recognised in other comprehensive income. Accordingly, the transfer will appear as a line item in the Statement of Changes in Equity rather than in other comprehensive income.

When an intangible asset is revalued, the carrying amount of that asset is adjusted to the revalued amount. At the date of the revaluation, the asset is treated in one of the following ways:

(a) the gross carrying amount is adjusted in a manner that is consistent with the revaluation of the carrying amount of the asset. For example, the gross carrying amount may be restated by reference to observable market data or it may be restated proportionately to the change in the carrying amount. The accumulated amortisation at the date of the revaluation is adjusted to equal the difference between the gross carrying amount and the carrying amount of the asset after taking into account accumulated impairment losses; or

(b) the accumulated amortisation is eliminated against the gross carrying amount of the asset. *[IAS 38.80]*.

Paragraph 80(a) ((a) above) was amended to allow the gross carrying amount to be adjusted in a manner that is consistent with the revaluation of the net carrying amount of the asset. This amendment applies to annual periods beginning on or after 1 July 2014.

The requirement before this amendment to IAS 38, that any accumulated depreciation must be restated proportionately with the change in the gross carrying amount, is not possible where there has been a reassessment of the residual value, useful life or depreciation method of an asset. Therefore, the standard now allows the asset to be revalued by reference to observable data on either the gross or the net carrying amount; and the accumulated amortisation is simply the difference between the gross and net carrying amounts of the asset.

The example below illustrates how the adjustments are calculated.

Example 17.10: Restatement of accumulated amortisation after a revaluation

Entity F revalued an intangible asset from its carrying amount of £120 to its fair value of £150. The gross carrying amount is adjusted to £345 by reference to the observable market data. The adjustment is in a manner consistent with the revaluation of the intangible asset. Under the observable market data approach (in the column, approach (a)), the accumulated depreciation is adjusted to £195, which is the difference between the gross revalued amount of £345 and the net revalued amount of £150. The proportionate restatement approach (in the column, approach (b)) leads to grossing up of both gross carrying amount and the accumulated amortisation. The elimination approach (in the column, approach (c)) results in elimination of the accumulated amortisation.

	Before revaluation	*After revaluation*		
		Observable market data (a)	*Proportionate restatement (b)*	*Eliminating amortisation (c)*
	£	£	£	£
Gross carrying amount	300	345	375	150
Accumulated amortisation	(180)	(195)	(225)	–
Net carrying amount	120	150	150	150

9 AMORTISATION OF INTANGIBLE ASSETS

9.1 Assessing the useful life of an intangible asset as finite or indefinite

IAS 38 defines the useful life of an intangible asset as:

(a) the period over which an asset is expected to be available for use by an entity; or

(b) the number of production or similar units expected to be obtained from the asset by an entity. *[IAS 38.8].*

The standard requires an entity to assess whether the useful life of an intangible asset is finite or indefinite. *[IAS 38.88].* An intangible asset with a finite useful life is amortised over its useful life or the number of production units (or similar units) constituting that useful life, whereas an intangible asset with an indefinite useful life is not amortised. *[IAS 38.89].*

The standard requires an intangible asset to be classified as having an indefinite useful life 'when, based on an analysis of all of the relevant factors, there is no foreseeable limit to the period over which the asset is expected to generate net cash inflows for the entity'. *[IAS 38.88].* Therefore, for this purpose the term 'indefinite' does not mean 'infinite'. *[IAS 38.91].*

Entities should not confuse the absence of a foreseeable limit to an asset's life with an ability to renew, refresh or upgrade an asset to ensure it continues to generate future cash flows. Some intangible assets are based on legal rights that are conveyed in perpetuity rather than for finite terms, whether or not those terms are renewable. If the cash flows are expected to continue indefinitely, the useful life is indefinite. *[IAS 38.BC62].*

An important underlying assumption in making the assessment of the useful life of an intangible asset is that it 'reflects only that level of future maintenance expenditure required to maintain the asset at its standard of performance assessed at the time of estimating the asset's useful life, and the entity's ability and intention to reach such a level. A conclusion that the useful life of an intangible asset is indefinite should not depend on planned future expenditure in excess of that required to maintain the asset at that standard of performance.' *[IAS 38.91].* Determining exactly what constitutes the level of expenditure 'required to maintain the asset at that standard of performance' is a matter of judgement. However, a clear distinction exists between this type of expenditure and costs that might be incurred to renew, refresh or upgrade an asset to ensure it continues to generate future cash flows. Expenditure to ensure that an intangible asset does not become obsolete is not the type of maintenance expenditure that, though very necessary to ensure continuing future cash flows, would be indicative of an indefinite life. Indeed, the standard asserts that assets subject to technological change would be expected to have a short useful life. *[IAS 38.92]*.

9.1.1 Factors affecting the useful life

The standard identifies a number of factors that may affect the useful life of an intangible asset:

(a) the expected usage of the asset by the entity and whether the asset could be managed efficiently by another management team;

(b) typical product life cycles for the asset and public information on estimates of useful lives of similar assets that are used in a similar way;

(c) technical, technological, commercial or other types of obsolescence;

(d) the stability of the industry in which the asset operates and changes in the market demand for the products or services output from the asset;

(e) expected actions by competitors or potential competitors;

(f) the level of maintenance expenditure required to obtain the expected future economic benefits from the asset and the entity's ability and intention to reach such a level;

(g) the period of control over the asset and legal or similar limits on the use of the asset, such as the expiry dates of related leases, discussed further at 9.1.2 below; and

(h) whether the useful life of the asset is dependent on the useful life of other assets of the entity. *[IAS 38.90]*.

The standard explicitly warns against both:

- overestimating the useful life of an intangible asset. For example, a history of rapid changes in technology means that the useful lives of computer software and many other intangible assets that are susceptible to technological obsolescence will be short; *[IAS 38.92]* and
- underestimating the useful life. Whilst uncertainty justifies estimating the useful life of an intangible asset on a prudent basis, it does not justify choosing a life that is unrealistically short. *[IAS 38.93]*.

Where an intangible asset is acquired in a business combination, but the acquiring entity does not intend to use it to generate future cash flows, it is unlikely that it could have anything other than a finite useful life. Indeed, whilst in our view an entity would not recognise an immediate impairment loss on acquisition, the estimated useful life of the asset is likely to be relatively short (see Chapter 9 at 5.5.6).

The following examples, based on those in IAS 38's Illustrative Examples, show how some of the features that affect the useful life are taken into account in assessing that life.

Example 17.11: Assessing the useful life of an intangible asset

Acquired customer list

A direct-mail marketing company acquires a customer list and expects that it will be able to derive benefit from the information on the list for at least one year, but no more than three years.

The customer list would be amortised over management's best estimate of its useful life, say 18 months. Although the direct-mail marketing company may intend to add customer names and other information to the list in the future, the expected benefits of the acquired customer list relate only to the customers on that list at the date it was acquired. The customer list also would be reviewed for indicators of impairment in accordance with IAS 36 at the end of each reporting period. *[IAS 36.9].*

An acquired trademark used to identify and distinguish a leading consumer product that has been a market-share leader for the past eight years

The trademark has a remaining legal life of five years but is renewable every 10 years at little cost. The acquiring entity intends to renew the trademark continuously and evidence supports its ability to do so. An analysis of product life cycle studies, market, competitive and environmental trends, and brand extension opportunities provides evidence that the trademarked product will generate net cash inflows for the acquiring entity for an indefinite period.

The trademark would be treated as having an indefinite useful life because it is expected to contribute to net cash inflows indefinitely. Therefore, the trademark would not be amortised until its useful life is determined to be finite. It would be tested for impairment in accordance with IAS 36 annually and whenever there is an indication that it may be impaired. *[IAS 36.10].*

It is clear from the above discussion that despite the fairly detailed guidance in the standard an entity will need to exercise judgement in estimating the useful life of intangible assets.

9.1.2 Useful life of contractual or other legal rights

Where an intangible asset arises from contractual or other legal rights, the standard requires an entity to take account of both economic and legal factors influencing its useful life and determine the useful life as the shorter of:

- the period of the contractual or other legal rights; and
- the period (determined by economic factors) over which the entity expects to obtain economic benefits from the asset. *[IAS 38.94-95].*

If the contractual or other legal rights can be renewed, the useful life of the intangible asset should include the renewal period only if there is evidence to support renewal by the entity without significant cost.

However, renewal periods must be ignored if the intangible asset is a reacquired right that was recognised in a business combination. *[IAS 38.94].* The existence of the following factors may indicate that an entity is able to renew the contractual or other legal rights without significant cost:

(a) there is evidence, possibly based on experience, that the contractual or other legal rights will be renewed. If renewal is contingent upon the consent of a third party, this includes evidence that the third party will give its consent;

(b) there is evidence that any conditions necessary to obtain renewal will be satisfied; and

(c) the cost to the entity of renewal is not significant when compared with the future economic benefits expected to flow to the entity from renewal. *[IAS 38.96].*

A renewal period is only added to the estimate of useful life if its cost is insignificant when compared with the future economic benefits expected to flow to the entity from renewal. *[IAS 38.94].* If this is not the case, then the original asset's useful life ends at the contracted renewal date and the renewal cost is treated as the cost to acquire a new intangible asset. *[IAS 38.96].* An entity needs to exercise judgement in assessing what it regards as a significant cost.

In the case of a reacquired contractual right, recognised as an intangible asset in a business combination accounted for under IFRS 3, its useful life is the remaining contractual period of the contract in which the right was granted. Renewal periods may not be taken into account. *[IAS 38.94]*.

The following examples are derived from those in IAS 38's Illustrative Examples and show the effect of contractual or other legal rights on the useful life of an intangible asset, when assessed together with other factors. The useful life may be shorter than the legal rights or, if supported by facts and circumstances, renewal rights could mean that the intangible asset's life is indefinite.

Example 17.12: Legal rights and useful life

An acquired copyright that has a useful life that is shorter than its remaining legal life of 50 years

An analysis of consumer habits and market trends provides evidence that the copyrighted material will generate net cash inflows for only 30 more years.

The copyright would be amortised over its 30-year estimated useful life and not over the term of the legal rights of 50 years. The copyright also would be reviewed for impairment in accordance with IAS 36 by assessing at the end of each reporting period whether there is any indication that it may be impaired.

An acquired broadcasting licence that expires in five years but is assessed as having an indefinite useful life

The broadcasting licence is renewable every 10 years if the entity provides at least an average level of service to its customers and complies with the relevant legislative requirements. The licence may be renewed indefinitely at little cost and has been renewed twice before the most recent acquisition. The acquiring entity intends to renew the licence indefinitely and evidence supports its ability to do so. Historically, there has been no compelling challenge to the licence renewal. The technology used in broadcasting is not expected to be replaced by another technology at any time in the foreseeable future. Therefore, the licence is expected to contribute to the entity's net cash inflows indefinitely.

The broadcasting licence would be treated as having an indefinite useful life because it is expected to contribute to the entity's net cash inflows indefinitely. Therefore, the licence would not be amortised until its useful life is determined to be finite. The licence would be tested for impairment in accordance with IAS 36 annually (as part of a cash-generating unit) and whenever there is an indication that it may be impaired.

An acquired airline route authority between two European cities that expires in three years but is assessed as having an indefinite useful life

The route authority may be renewed every five years, and the acquiring entity intends to comply with the applicable rules and regulations surrounding renewal. Route authority renewals are routinely granted at a minimal cost and historically have been renewed when the airline has complied with the applicable rules and regulations. The acquiring entity expects to provide service indefinitely between the two cities from its hub airports and expects that the related supporting infrastructure (airport gates, slots, and terminal facility leases) will remain in place at those airports for as long as it has the route authority. An analysis of demand and cash flows supports those assumptions.

Because the facts and circumstances support the acquiring entity's ability to continue providing air service indefinitely between the two cities, the intangible asset related to the route authority is treated as having an indefinite useful life. Therefore, the route authority would not be amortised until its useful life is determined to be finite. It would be tested for impairment in accordance with IAS 36 annually (as part of a cash-generating unit) and whenever there is an indication that it may be impaired.

9.2 Intangible assets with a finite useful life

9.2.1 Amortisation period and method

Amortisation is the systematic allocation of the depreciable amount of an intangible asset over its useful life. The depreciable amount is the cost of an asset, or other amount substituted for cost (e.g. revaluation), less its residual value. *[IAS 38.8]*. The depreciable amount of an intangible asset with a finite useful life should be allocated on a systematic basis over its useful life in the following manner: *[IAS 38.97]*

- amortisation should begin when the asset is available for use, i.e. when it is in the location and condition necessary for it to be capable of operating in the manner intended by management. Therefore, even if an entity is not using the asset, it should still be amortised because it is available for use, although there may be exceptions from this general rule (see 9.2.3 below);
- amortisation should cease at the earlier of:
  - the date that the asset is classified as held for sale, or included in a disposal group that is classified as held for sale, in accordance with IFRS 5; and
  - the date that the asset is derecognised.
- the amortisation method should reflect the pattern of consumption of the economic benefits that the intangible asset provides. If that pattern cannot be reliably determined, a straight-line basis should be used.

Amortisation of an intangible asset with a finite useful life continues until the asset has been fully depreciated or is classified as held for sale, as noted above, or derecognised. Amortisation does not cease simply because an asset is not being used, *[IAS 38.117]*, although this fact might give rise to an indicator of impairment.

The standard allows a variety of amortisation methods to be used to depreciate the asset on a systematic basis over its useful life, such as the straight-line method, the diminishing balance method and the unit of production method. *[IAS 38.98]*. The factors to consider in determining the most appropriate amortisation method are similar to those that are relevant for the depreciation of property, plant and equipment in accordance with IAS 16 (see Chapter 18). For example, entities can adopt a 'sum of the digits' methodology, where amortisation reflects higher consumption of benefits in the earlier part of the asset's useful life, as this is a variant of the diminishing balance method (see Chapter 18).

The amortisation charge for each period should be recognised in profit or loss unless IFRS specifically permits or requires it to be capitalised as part of the carrying amount of another asset (e.g. inventory or work in progress). *[IAS 38.97, 99]*.

IAS 38 was amended in May 2014 to confirm that there is a rebuttable presumption that an amortisation method based on the pattern of expected revenues is not appropriate. This is because a revenue-based method reflects a pattern of generation of economic benefits from operating the business (of which the asset is a part), rather than the consumption of the economic benefits embodied in the asset itself (see 9.2.2 below). By contrast, an amortisation method based on estimated total output (a unit of production method) is appropriate.

The future economic benefits of some intangible assets are clearly consumed on a declining balance basis. This often applies to customer relationships and similar assets acquired as part of a business combination. Both the fair value and the future economic benefits from the customer relationship or similar asset decline over time as the consumption of the economic benefits embodied in the asset declines. Therefore amortising the customer relationship on a declining balance method would be appropriate.

It is important to distinguish this from an asset whose fair value shows a declining balance profile over its life but where the future economic benefits are consumed on a time basis, e.g. a motor vehicle where the entity will obtain as much benefit in year 4 as in year 1. A straight-line method of amortisation properly reflects the consumption of benefits from the motor vehicle.

9.2.1.A Amortising customer relationships and similar intangible assets

In practice entities rarely use declining balance methods for amortisation. One reason for customer relationships and similar intangible assets is the uncertainty about the future economic benefits that might arise several years in the future and the difficulty in distinguishing them from cash flows that have been generated by internally-generated assets of the business. As a pragmatic solution, supported by valuations experts, entities often use a straight-line method over a shorter period so that at all points the amortised carrying amount of the asset is below the curve for the expected benefits. This is illustrated in the following example and chart. As long as the benefits expected to arise in the period after the intangible asset is fully amortised are not expected to be significant and the entity applies the requirements of IAS 38 to review the useful life and amortisation method (see 9.2.3 below), this method will give a reasonable approximation of the consumption of economic benefits.

Example 17.13: Amortisation method and useful life for customer relationships

An entity identifies a customer relationship on acquiring another business. The entity completes its initial accounting at the end of 20X0 and the customer relationship is valued at €4 million. The valuations expert consulted by the entity assesses the total period from which benefits will be derived from the customer relationship is 9 years but that the benefits will show a declining balance over this period. After discussions with the valuer, the entity concludes that the best estimate of the useful life of the customer relationship for accounting purposes is 5 years and a straight-line method over this period will adequately reflect the consumption of future economic benefits from the customer relationship, given that the amount and timing of benefits after 5 years is inherently uncertain as to timing or amount. The entity notes that a straight-line method over 9 years would not adequately reflect the consumption of future economic benefits.

The relationship between the total economic life, useful life and amortisation method is illustrated in the following chart.

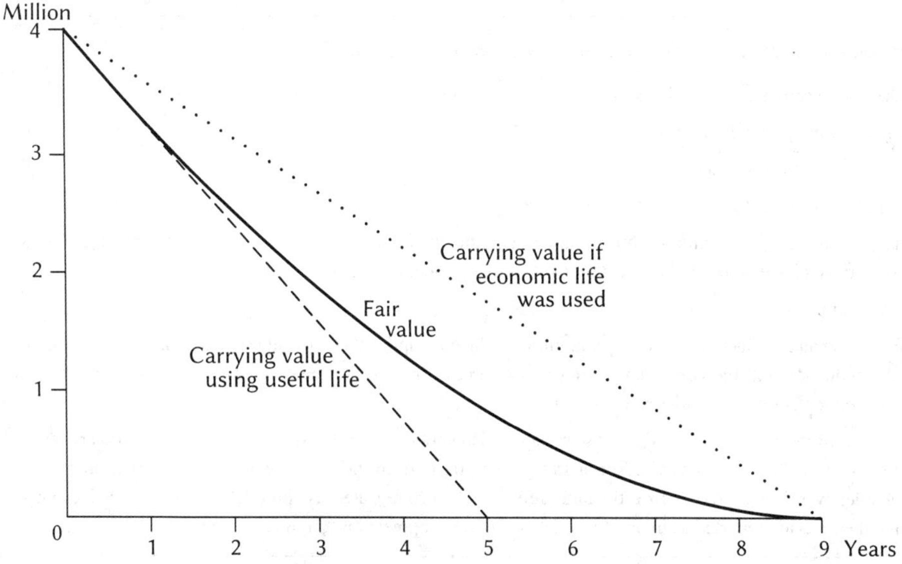

9.2.1.B Amortisation of programme and other broadcast rights

The value of programme and other broadcast rights diminishes because the programmes or events have been broadcast to the same audience before and as result of the passage of time, e.g. audiences lose interest in old programmes or repeats of events for which the result is known or the right is for a limited period. In accounting for this diminution in value, in practice, entities usually take into account how often a programme has been broadcast and, less frequently, the passage of time as such.

When an entity accounts for broadcast rights as inventory, the problem arises that IAS 2 requires valuation 'at the lower of cost and net realisable value' and does not appear to recognise the concept of amortisation of inventories. *[IAS 2.9]*. However, it has been argued that a programme right embodies a series of identifiable components, i.e. first transmission, second transmission, etc., which an entity should account for separately. This appears to be the approach that ITV applies in writing off its programme rights (see Extract 17.2 at 2.2.2 above).

An entity that accounts for programme and other broadcast rights as intangible assets would need to comply with the requirements of IAS 38, which requires that the amortisation method reflects the pattern in which the asset's future economic benefits are expected to be consumed by the entity. *[IAS 38.97]*. As discussed at 9.2.1 above, the standard permits a range of amortisation methods (e.g. the straight-line method, the diminishing balance method and the unit of production method), provided that the chosen method reflects the pattern in which the asset's future economic benefits are expected to be consumed. *[IAS 38.97-98]*.

RAI is an example of a company that amortises some of its programme rights on a straight-line basis.

Extract 17.9: RAI – Radiotelevisione italiana S.p.A. (2015)

Notes to the separate financial statements as at 31 December 2015 [extract]

4) Accounting principles [extract]

Non-current assets [extract]

Intangible assets [extract]

Intangible assets with a finite useful life are systematically amortised over their useful life, which is the estimated period in which the assets will be used by the Company and are structured as follows:

a) Programmes:

Acquisition and production costs for programmes, which comprise the external costs that can be allocated directly to each production and the costs of the internal resources used for the creation of the individual programmes, are accounted for as follows:

1) costs for repeated-use TV productions are capitalised under intangible assets. If such productions are ready for use at year-end the costs are amortised on a straight-line basis from the month when they are realised or the right is available, over the period of their estimated useful life. If such repeated-use productions are not yet useable at period –end, the costs are reported as intangible assets under development and payments on account.

9.2.2 Revenue-based amortisation

Consumption of the future economic benefits of an asset is the principle on which amortisation is based. Whether this completely precluded revenue-based methods of amortisation had become a matter of debate, particularly in the context of service concession arrangements that are accounted for using the intangible asset model (see Chapter 27 at 4.3.1).

In May 2014, the IASB amended IAS 16 and IAS 38 to clarify acceptable methods of depreciation and amortisation, based on this principle. The amendments apply to annual periods beginning on or after 1 January 2016. Earlier application is permitted, subject to an entity disclosing that fact. *[IAS 38.130J]*.

Following the amendment, there is a rebuttable presumption that under IAS 38, a revenue-based approach is not appropriate. Revenue reflects the output of the intangible asset but it also measures the impact of other factors, such as changes in sales volumes and selling prices, the effects of selling activities and changes to inputs and processes. The price component of revenue may be affected by inflation. *[IAS 38.98A]*.

The following example illustrates how a revenue-based method of amortisation diverges from the units-of-production method when the price per unit is not fixed.

Example 17.14: Output-based versus revenue-based amortisation

Entity Z acquires a five-year licence to manufacture a product for a cost of £1,220,000. It is expected that the production line used for making the product has a capacity of 100,000 units per year. The entity plans to produce at full capacity each year and to sell all of its output. However, it expects the price per unit to be £10 in year 1 and increase by 10% each year thereafter. On this basis, the profile of amortisation on a unit of production basis (UoP) and on a revenue basis would be as follows:

	Units	UoP charge	Revenue	Charge
Year 1	100,000	244,000	1,000,000	200,000
Year 2	100,000	244,000	1,100,000	220,000
Year 3	100,000	244,000	1,210,000	242,000
Year 4	100,000	244,000	1,330,000	266,000
Year 5	100,000	244,000	1,460,000	292,000
Total	500,000	1,220,000	6,100,000	1,220,000

The IASB acknowledged certain 'limited circumstances' that would allow revenue-based amortisation. Therefore, the presumption that they are not acceptable is rebuttable only:

(a) when the rights embodied in that intangible asset are expressed as a measure of revenue; or

(b) when it can be demonstrated that revenue and the consumption of the economic benefits embodied in the intangible asset are highly correlated. *[IAS 38.98A]*.

A 'highly correlated' outcome would only be achieved where a revenue-based method of amortisation is expected to give a similar answer as one of the other methods permitted by IAS 38. For example, if revenue is earned evenly over the expected life of the asset, the pattern of amortisation would be similar to a straight-line basis. In situations where unit prices are fixed and all production is sold, the pattern of amortisation would replicate the use of the units-of-production method. However, when unit prices are not fixed, revenue would not provide the same answer and its use would therefore be inappropriate (as in the example above). *[IAS 38.98B]*. The revised standard notes that revenue is the predominant limiting factor that is inherent in the intangible asset in circumstances in which it is appropriate to use it as the basis of amortisation. In other words, in these circumstances, revenue determines the useful life of the asset, rather than, for example, a number of years or the number of units produced.

The amended standard includes two examples in which revenue earned can be regarded as a measure of consumption of an intangible asset.

- A contract may allow the extraction of gold from a mine until total cumulative revenue from the sale of gold reaches $2 billion; or
- The right to operate a toll road could be based on a fixed total amount of revenue to be generated from cumulative tolls, i.e. the operator can collect up to €100 million from the tolls collected. *[IAS 38.98C]*.

Some respondents had argued that a units of production method did not seem practicable when the units of production were not homogeneous. For example, a producer of a motion picture generates revenue through showing the picture in theatres, selling DVDs, licensing the rights to characters to toy manufacturers and licensing the broadcast rights to television. The IASB acknowledges that such situations require the exercise of judgement. The Board did consider whether an intangible asset should be divided into components for amortisation purposes 'but refrained from developing guidance in this respect for intangible assets'. *[IAS 38.BC72H-72I]*.

9.2.3 Review of amortisation period and amortisation method

An entity should review the amortisation period and the amortisation method for an intangible asset with a finite useful life at least at each financial year-end. If the expected useful life of the asset has changed, the amortisation period should be changed accordingly. *[IAS 38.104].* An entity may, for example, consider its previous estimate of the useful life of an intangible asset inappropriate upon recognition of an impairment loss on the asset. *[IAS 38.105].*

If the expected pattern of consumption of the future economic benefits embodied in the asset has changed, the amortisation method should be changed to reflect the new pattern. *[IAS 38.104].* The standard provides two examples of when this might happen:

- if it becomes apparent that a diminishing balance method of amortisation is appropriate rather than a straight-line method; *[IAS 38.106]* and
- if use of the rights represented by a licence is deferred pending action on other components of the business plan. In this case, economic benefits that flow from the asset may not be received until later periods. *[IAS 38.106].* This implies that circumstances may exist in which it is appropriate not to recognise an amortisation charge in relation to an intangible asset, because the entity may not yet be ready to use it. For example, telecommunication companies acquired UMTS (3G) licences, before constructing the physical network necessary to use the licence. Note that an entity must perform an impairment test at least annually for any intangible asset that has not yet been brought into use. *[IAS 36.10].*

Both changes in the amortisation period and the amortisation method should be accounted for as changes in accounting estimates in accordance with IAS 8 – *Accounting Policies, Changes in Accounting Estimates and Errors* – which requires such changes to be recognised prospectively by revising the amortisation charge in the current period and for each future period during the asset's remaining useful life. *[IAS 8.36, 38, IAS 38.104].*

9.2.4 Residual value

The residual value of an intangible asset is the estimated amount that an entity would currently obtain from disposal of the asset, after deducting the estimated costs of disposal, if the asset were already of the age and in the condition expected at the end of its useful life. *[IAS 38.8].*

IAS 38 requires entities to assume a residual value of zero for an intangible asset with a finite useful life, unless there is a commitment by a third party to purchase the asset at the end of its useful life *or* there is an active market (as defined by IFRS 13) for the asset from which to determine its residual value and it is probable that such a market will exist at the end of the asset's useful life. *[IAS 38.100].* This presumption has been retained from the previous version of IAS 38 as an anti-abuse measure to prevent entities from circumventing the requirement to amortise all intangible assets. *[IAS 38.BC59].*

Given the definition of 'active market' (see 8.2.1 above) it seems highly unlikely that, in the absence of a commitment by a third party to buy the asset, an entity will ever be able to prove that the residual value is other than zero. A residual value other than zero implies that the entity intends to dispose of the asset before the end of its economic life. *[IAS 38.101].* Third party commitments can be found in contracts in the scope of IFRIC 12 – *Service Concession Arrangements* (see Chapter 27) and one of IAS 38's Illustrative examples includes a residual value; see Example 17.15 below.

If an entity can demonstrate a case for estimating a residual value other than zero, its estimate should be based on current prices for the sale of a similar asset that has reached the end of its useful life and has operated under conditions similar to those in which the asset will be used. *[IAS 38.102]*. The standard requires a review of the residual value at each financial year end. This review can result in an upward or downward revision of the estimated residual value and thereby affect the depreciable amount of the asset; that change to depreciation should be accounted for prospectively as a change in an accounting estimate in accordance with IAS 8. *[IAS 38.102]*.

The following example is based on one of IAS 38's Illustrative Examples. The intangible asset being considered has a residual value at the end of its useful life.

Example 17.15: Amortisation of an intangible asset with a residual value

An acquired patent that expires in 15 years

A product protected by patented technology is expected to be a source of net cash inflows for at least 15 years. The entity has a commitment from a third party to purchase that patent in five years for 60 per cent of the fair value of the patent at the date it was acquired, and the entity intends to sell the patent in five years.

The patent will be amortised over its five-year useful life to the entity, with a residual value equal to 60 per cent of the patent's fair value at the date it was acquired. The patent will also be reviewed for impairment in accordance with IAS 36 by assessing at the end of each reporting period whether there is any indication that it may be impaired.

The standard does not permit negative amortisation in the event that the residual value of an intangible asset increases to an amount greater than the asset's carrying amount. Instead, the asset's amortisation charge will be zero until its residual value decreases to an amount below the asset's carrying amount. *[IAS 38.103]*.

9.3 Intangible assets with an indefinite useful life

IAS 38 prohibits amortisation of an intangible asset with an indefinite useful life. *[IAS 38.107]*. Instead, IAS 36 requires such an asset to be tested for impairment annually and whenever there is an indication that the intangible asset may be impaired. *[IAS 38.108]*.

An entity should review and validate at the end of each reporting period its decision to classify the useful life of an intangible asset as indefinite. *[IAS 38.109]*. If events and circumstances no longer support an indefinite useful life, the change from indefinite to finite life should be accounted for as a change in accounting estimate under IAS 8, *[IAS 38.109]*, which requires such changes to be recognised prospectively (i.e. in the current and future periods). *[IAS 8.36]*. Furthermore, reassessing the useful life of an intangible asset as finite rather than indefinite is an indicator that the asset may be impaired. *[IAS 38.110]*. See Chapter 20 for a discussion on impairment.

The following examples from IAS 38's Illustrative Examples illustrate circumstances in which an entity considers whether the useful life of an intangible asset is still indefinite.

Example 17.16: Review of indefinite useful lives

A broadcasting licence is no longer to be renewed

The facts are as in Example 17.12 above. A licensing authority has allowed broadcast licences to be renewed indefinitely at little cost and an entity, having renewed the licence twice, had concluded that it had an indefinite useful life. However, the licensing authority subsequently decides that it will no longer renew broadcasting licences, but rather will auction the licences. At the time the licensing authority's decision is made, the entity's broadcasting licence has three years until it expires. The entity expects that the licence will continue to contribute to net cash inflows until the licence expires.

Because the broadcasting licence can no longer be renewed, its useful life is no longer indefinite. Thus, the acquired licence would be amortised over its remaining three-year useful life and immediately tested for impairment in accordance with IAS 36.

A trademark for a line of products acquired several years ago in a business combination

At the time of the business combination the acquiree had been producing the line of products for 35 years with many new models developed under the trademark. At the acquisition date the acquirer expected to continue producing the line, and an analysis of various economic factors indicated there was no limit to the period the trademark would contribute to net cash inflows, so the trademark was not amortised by the acquirer. However, management has recently decided that production of the product line will be discontinued over the next four years.

Because the useful life of the acquired trademark is no longer regarded as indefinite, the carrying amount of the trademark would be tested for impairment in accordance with IAS 36, written down to recoverable amount as appropriate and the carrying amount amortised over its remaining four-year useful life.

9.4 Impairment losses

An impairment loss is the amount by which the carrying amount of an asset exceeds its recoverable amount. *[IAS 38.8].* An entity applies IAS 36 in determining whether an intangible asset is impaired (see Chapter 20). *[IAS 38.111].*

IAS 36 requires an entity to perform an annual impairment test on every intangible asset that has an indefinite useful life and every intangible asset that is not yet available for use. Many intangible assets with indefinite lives do not generate independent cash inflows as individual assets and so are tested for impairment with other assets of the cash-generating unit of which they are part (see Chapter 20). *[IAS 36.10, 22].* This means that impairment losses, if any, will be allocated in accordance with IAS 36 and, if any goodwill allocated to the cash-generating unit has been written off, the other assets of the cash-generating unit, including the intangible asset, will be reduced *pro rata* to their carrying amount (see Chapter 20 at 11.2). *[IAS 36.104].*

Example 17.17: Impairment of an intangible asset with an indefinite useful life

A trademark acquired 10 years ago that distinguishes a leading consumer product

The trademark was regarded as having an indefinite useful life when it was acquired because the trademarked product was expected to generate cash inflows indefinitely. However, unexpected competition has recently entered the market and will reduce future sales of the product. Management estimates that cash inflows generated by the product will be 20 per cent less for the foreseeable future. However, management expects that the product will continue to generate cash inflows indefinitely at those reduced amounts.

As a result of the projected decrease in future cash inflows, the entity determines that the estimated recoverable amount of the trademark and the assets that comprise the cash-generating unit is less than its carrying amount. An impairment loss is recognised for the cash-generating unit of which it is a part. Because it is still regarded as having an indefinite useful life, the trademark would continue not to be amortised but would be tested for impairment in accordance with IAS 36 annually, i.e. as part of the cash-generating unit, and whenever there is an indication that it may be impaired.

Note that a trademark may generate independent cash inflows if, for example, it is licenced to another party; otherwise, as in Example 17.17 above, it will be part of a cash-generating unit.

9.5 Retirements and disposals

An intangible asset should be derecognised on disposal (e.g. by sale, by entering into a finance lease, or by donation) or when no future economic benefits are expected from its use or disposal. *[IAS 38.112, 114]*.

For an entity that applies IFRS 15, the date of disposal of an intangible asset is the date the recipient obtains control of that asset in accordance with the requirements for determining when a performance obligation is satisfied in IFRS 15. *[IAS 38.114]*. In the case of a disposal by a sale and leaseback, an entity should apply IAS 17 (see Chapter 24) *[IAS 38.114]* or, when applied, IFRS 16 (see Chapter 25).

An entity that is not yet applying IFRS 15 should apply the criteria for recognising revenue from the sale of goods in IAS 18 – *Revenue* – in determining the date of disposal of an intangible asset (see Chapter 29).

The gain or loss on derecognition, which is determined as the difference between the net disposal proceeds and the carrying amount of the asset, should be accounted for in profit or loss unless IAS 17 or, when applied, IFRS 16 requires otherwise on a sale and leaseback. Gains on disposal should not be presented as revenue because they are incidental to the entity's main revenue-generating activities. *[IAS 38.113]*.

The consideration to be included in the calculation of the gain or loss is determined in accordance with the requirements for determining the transaction price in paragraphs 47 to 72 of IFRS 15 (see Chapter 30 at 5). *[IAS 38.116]*. If the transaction price includes variable consideration, subsequent changes to the estimated amount of the consideration included in the gain or loss on disposal are accounted for in accordance with the requirements for changes in the transaction price in IFRS 15 (see Chapter 30 at 6.5). *[IAS 38.116]*.

If the receipt of the consideration does not match the timing of the transfer of the asset (e.g. the consideration is prepaid or paid after the date of disposal), then the arrangement may also contain a financing component for which the transaction price will need to be adjusted, if significant (see Chapter 30 at 5.5).

For an entity that applies IAS 18, the consideration receivable on disposal of an intangible asset is recognised initially at its fair value. This means that, if payment for the intangible asset is deferred, the consideration received is recognised initially at the cash price equivalent. The difference between the nominal amount of the consideration and the cash price equivalent is recognised as interest using the effective interest method under IAS 18.

In the case of a reacquired contractual right, recognised as an intangible asset in a business combination accounted for under IFRS 3, if the right is subsequently reissued or sold to a third party, any gain or loss is determined using the remaining carrying amount of the reacquired right. *[IAS 38.115A]*.

9.5.1 Derecognition of parts of intangible assets

The standard requires an entity to recognise the cost of replacing a part of an intangible asset as a component of the asset's carrying amount and to derecognise that component when the part is replaced. 'If it is not practicable for an entity to determine the carrying amount of the replaced part, it may use the cost of the replacement as an indication of what the cost of the replaced part was at the time it was acquired or internally generated.' *[IAS 38.115]*. As noted by the standard, the nature of intangible assets is such that, in many cases, there are no additions or replacements that would meet its recognition criteria, so this should be an unlikely event (see 3.3 above). *[IAS 38.20]*.

However, this requirement raises the question of how to account for the disposal of a part of a larger intangible item, acquired in a single transaction but capable of being subdivided for separate disposal. An example would be the division of the global rights to sell a particular product into a number of agreements providing exclusive rights over a particular continent or other geographic territory. In this case, the part disposed of is an identifiable and separable part of the original intangible asset. Because the rights are exclusive, the part still meets the definition of an intangible asset because it is embodied in legal rights that allow the acquirer to control the benefits arising from the asset, either by providing access to earn revenues in that geographic market or by restricting the access of others to that market. *[IAS 38.13]*. In that case, an entity would apply the requirements above for the derecognition of a replacement part of an asset, by determining the carrying amount of the separate part or, if to do so is impracticable, deducting the proceeds of disposal from the depreciated replacement cost of the original asset (in effect treating the value of the newly separated part as an indicator of original cost).

Where the subdivision of rights is not established on an exclusive basis, it would be more difficult to regard a separable component of the original intangible as having been disposed of. For example, rights might be assigned to a third party over a geographic area, but the entity retains the ability to sell goods in that market as well. In such circumstances it may not be appropriate to derecognise a portion of the original intangible asset. Instead the entity may have transferred a right of use (or lease) over the asset to the third party, or entered into a form of joint arrangement. The issues raised by the partial disposal of previously undivided interests in property, plant and equipment are discussed in Chapter 18.

Accounting for the partial derecognition of goodwill on the disposal of an operation that forms part of a cash-generating unit is discussed in Chapter 20 at 8.5.

10 DISCLOSURE

The main requirements in IAS 38 are set out below, but it may be necessary to refer to the disclosure requirements of IFRS 5 in Chapter 4, the disclosure requirements of IAS 36 in Chapter 20 in the event of a disposal or impairment, and the fair value disclosures in IFRS 13 in Chapter 14 when fair value is used or disclosed.

10.1 General disclosures

IAS 38 requires certain disclosures to be presented by class of intangible assets. A class of intangible assets is defined as a grouping of assets of a similar nature and use in an entity's operations. The standard provides examples of classes of assets, which may be disaggregated (or aggregated) into smaller (or larger) groups if this results in more relevant information for the users of the financial statements (see 8 above for examples of classes of intangible assets). *[IAS 38.119].* Although separate information is required for internally generated intangible assets and other intangible assets, these categories are not considered to be separate classes when they relate to intangible assets of a similar nature and use in an entity's operations. Hence the standard requires the following disclosures to be given for each class of intangible assets, distinguishing between internally generated intangible assets and other intangible assets:

(a) whether the useful lives are indefinite or finite and, if finite, the useful lives or the amortisation rates used;

(b) the amortisation methods used for intangible assets with finite useful lives;

(c) the gross carrying amount and any accumulated amortisation (aggregated with accumulated impairment losses) at the beginning and end of the period;

(d) the line item(s) of the statement of comprehensive income in which any amortisation of intangible assets is included; and

(e) a reconciliation of the carrying amount at the beginning and end of the period showing:

    (i) additions, indicating separately those from internal development, those acquired separately, and those acquired through business combinations;

    (ii) assets classified as held for sale or included in a disposal group classified as held for sale in accordance with IFRS 5 and other disposals;

    (iii) increases or decreases during the period resulting from revaluations and from impairment losses recognised or reversed in other comprehensive income in accordance with IAS 36 (if any);

    (iv) impairment losses recognised in profit or loss during the period in accordance with IAS 36 (if any);

    (v) impairment losses reversed in profit or loss during the period in accordance with IAS 36 (if any);

    (vi) any amortisation recognised during the period;

    (vii) net exchange differences arising on the translation of the financial statements into the presentation currency, and on the translation of a foreign operation into the presentation currency of the entity; and

    (viii) other changes in the carrying amount during the period. *[IAS 38.118].*

The standard permits an entity to present the reconciliation required under (e) above either for the net carrying amount or separately for the gross carrying amount and the accumulated amortisation and impairments.

IAS 1.38 requires comparative information for the reconciliation in (e) above.

An entity may want to consider separate disclosure of intangible assets acquired by way of government grant or obtained in an exchange of assets, even though disclosure is not specifically required under (e)(i) above.

An example of these general disclosures is given by International Consolidated Airlines Group, S.A.

Extract 17.10: International Consolidated Airlines Group, S.A. (2016)

Notes to the consolidated financial statements [extract]

2. **Significant accounting policies** [extract]

Intangible assets [extract]

a Goodwill

Goodwill arises on the acquisition of subsidiaries, associates and joint ventures and represents the excess of the consideration paid over the net fair value of the identifiable assets and liabilities of the acquiree. Where the net fair value of the identifiable assets and liabilities of the acquiree is in excess of the consideration paid, a gain on bargain purchase is recognised immediately in the Income statement.

For the purposes of assessing impairment, goodwill is grouped at the lowest levels for which there are separately identifiable cash flows (cash generating units). Goodwill is tested for impairment annually and whenever indicators exist that the carrying value may not be recoverable.

b Brands

Brands arising on the acquisition of subsidiaries are initially recognised at fair value at the acquisition date. Long established brands that are expected to be used indefinitely are not amortised but assessed annually for impairment.

c Customer loyalty programmes

Customer loyalty programmes arising on the acquisition of subsidiaries are initially recognised at fair value at the acquisition date. A customer loyalty programme with an expected useful life is amortised over the expected remaining useful life. Established customer loyalty programmes that are expected to be used indefinitely are not amortised but assessed annually for impairment.

d Landing rights

Landing rights acquired in a business combination are recognised at fair value at the acquisition date. Landing rights acquired from other airlines are capitalised at cost.

Capitalised landing rights based outside the EU are amortised on a straight-line basis over a period not exceeding 20 years.

Capitalised landing rights based within the EU are not amortised, as regulations provide that these landing rights are perpetual.

e Contract based intangibles

Contract based intangibles acquired in a business combination are recognised initially at fair value at the acquisition date and amortised over the remaining life of the contract.

f Software

The cost to purchase or develop computer software that is separable from an item of related hardware is capitalised separately and amortised on a straight-line basis generally over a period not exceeding five years, with certain specific software developments amortised over a period of up to 10 years.

g Emissions allowances

Purchased emissions allowances are recognised at cost. Emissions allowances are not revalued or amortised but are tested for impairment whenever indicators exist that the carrying value may not be recoverable.

16. **Intangible assets and impairment review** [extract]

a **Intangible assets**

€ million	Goodwill	Brand	Customer loyalty programmes	Landing rights[1]	Other[2]	Total
Cost						
Balance at January 1, 2015	328	341	253	1,442	749	3,113
Additions	–	–	–	–	168	168
Acquired through Business combination	272	110	–	172	40	594
Disposals	–	–	–	–	(114)	(114)
Reclassifications	–	–	–	–	20	20
Exchange movements	5	–	–	70	42	117
Balance at December 31, 2015	605	451	253	1,684	905	3,898
Additions	–	–	–	–	154	154
Disposals	–	–	–	–	(19)	(19)
Reclassifications	–	–	–	–	20	20
Exchange movements	(7)	–	–	(128)	(100)	(235)
December 31, 2016	**598**	**451**	**253**	**1,556**	**960**	**3,818**
Amortisation and impairment						
Balance at January 1, 2015	249	–	–	77	349	675
Charge for the year	–	–	–	3	72	75
Disposals	–	–	–	–	(78)	(78)
Reclassifications	–	–	–	–	8	8
Exchange movements	–	–	–	6	17	23
Balance at December 31, 2015	249	–	–	86	368	703
Charge for the year	–	–	–	6	98	104
Impairment charge recognised during the year[3]	–	–	–	14	–	14
Reclassifications	–	–	–	–	9	9
Exchange movements	–	–	–	(8)	(41)	(49)
December 31, 2016	**249**	**–**	**–**	**98**	**434**	**781**
Net book values						
December 31, 2016	349	451	253	1,458	526	3,037
December 31, 2015	356	451	253	1,598	537	3,195

1 The net book value includes non-EU based landing rights of €113 million (2015: €123 million) that have a finite life. The remaining life of these landing rights is 19 years.

2 Other intangible assets consists primarily of software with a net book value of €474 million (2015: €487 million), and also include purchased emissions allowances.

3 The impairment charge of €14 million relates to landing rights associated with British Airways' Openskies operation, €11 million of which relates to landing rights in the EU that have an indefinite life.

In addition to the disclosures required above, any impairment of intangible assets is to be disclosed in accordance with IAS 36, which is discussed in Chapter 20 at 13, *[IAS 38.120]*, while the nature and amount of any change in useful life, amortisation method or residual value estimates should be disclosed in accordance with the provisions of IAS 8. *[IAS 38.121]*.

There are a number of additional disclosure requirements, some of which only apply in certain circumstances:

(a) for an intangible asset assessed as having an indefinite useful life, the carrying amount of that asset and the reasons supporting the assessment of an indefinite useful life. In giving these reasons, the entity should describe the factor(s) that played a significant role in determining that the asset has an indefinite useful life;

(b) a description, the carrying amount and remaining amortisation period of any individual intangible asset that is material to the entity's financial statements;

(c) for intangible assets acquired by way of a government grant and initially recognised at fair value (see 4.6 above):

    (i) the fair value initially recognised for these assets;

    (ii) their carrying amount; and

    (iii) whether they are measured after recognition under the cost model or the revaluation model.

(d) the existence and carrying amounts of intangible assets whose title is restricted and the carrying amounts of intangible assets pledged as security for liabilities;

(e) the amount of contractual commitments for the acquisition of intangible assets. *[IAS 38.122]*.

In describing the factors (as required under (a) above) that played a significant role in determining that the useful life of an intangible asset is indefinite, an entity considers the list of factors in IAS 38.90 (see 9.1.1 above). *[IAS 38.123]*.

Finally, an entity is encouraged, but not required, to disclose the following information:

(a) a description of any fully amortised intangible asset that is still in use; and

(b) a brief description of significant intangible assets controlled by the entity but not recognised as assets because they did not meet the recognition criteria in this Standard or because they were acquired or generated before the version of IAS 38 issued in 1998 was effective. *[IAS 38.128]*.

10.2 Statement of financial position presentation

IAS 1 – *Presentation of Financial Statements* – uses the term 'non-current' to include tangible, intangible and financial assets of a long-term nature, although it does not prohibit the use of alternative descriptions as long as the meaning is clear. *[IAS 1.67]*. Although most intangible assets are non-current, an intangible asset may meet the definition of a current asset (i.e. it has an economic life of less than 12 months) when it is acquired and should be classified accordingly.

IAS 1 requires intangible assets to be shown as a separate category of asset on the face of the statement of financial position. *[IAS 1.54]*. Intangible assets will, therefore, normally appear as a separate category of asset in the statement of financial position at a suitable point within non-current assets, or at a point in an undifferentiated statement of financial position that reflects their relative liquidity, *[IAS 1.60]*, that is the time over which they are to be amortised or sold. An entity that holds a wide variety of different intangible assets may need to present these in separate line items on the face of the statement of financial position if such presentation is relevant to an understanding of the entity's financial position. *[IAS 1.55]*.

While the figure for intangible assets may include goodwill, the relevant standards require more detailed disclosures of the constituent elements to be included in the notes to the financial statements. In many cases though, entities will be able to aggregate the intangible assets into slightly broader categories in order to reduce the number of lines items on the face of their statement of financial position.

Nestlé is an example of an entity that chooses to present goodwill separately from other intangible assets on the face of the statement of financial position.

Extract 17.11: Nestlé S.A. (2016)

Consolidated balance sheet as at 31 December 2016 [extract]

In million CHF	Notes	2016	2015
Assets			
Non-current assets			
Property, plant and equipment	8	27 554	26 576
Goodwill	9	33 007	32 772
Intangible assets	9	20 397	19 236
Investments in associates and joint ventures	14	10 709	8 675
Financial assets	12	5 719	5 419
Employee benefits assets	10	310	109
Current income tax assets		114	128
Deferred tax assets	13	2 049	1 643
Total non-current assets		99 859	94 558

10.3 Profit or loss presentation

No specific guidance is provided within IAS 1, and only limited guidance is available within IAS 38, on the presentation of amortisation, impairment, and gains or losses related to intangible assets in the statement of profit or loss.

- Gains on the sale of intangible assets should not be presented within revenue. *[IAS 38.113]*.
- An entity should disclose the line item(s) of the statement of comprehensive income in which any amortisation of intangible assets is included. *[IAS 38.118(d)]*.

In the absence of detailed guidance on how to present such items in the statement of profit or loss, it will, in practice, usually be appropriate to present them in a similar way as those related to property, plant and equipment.

10.4 Additional disclosures when the revaluation model is applied

IAS 38 requires an entity, which accounts for intangible assets at revalued amounts, to disclose the following additional information:

(a) by class of intangible assets:
   (i) the effective date of the revaluation;
   (ii) the carrying amount of revalued intangible assets; and
   (iii) the carrying amount that would have been recognised had the revalued class of intangible assets been measured after recognition using the cost model; and

(b) the amount of the revaluation surplus that relates to intangible assets at the beginning and end of the period, indicating the changes during the period and any restrictions on the distribution of the balance to shareholders. *[IAS 38.124]*.

Classes of revalued assets can be aggregated for disclosure purposes. However, an entity cannot combine classes of intangible asset measured under the revaluation model with other classes measured at cost. *[IAS 38.125]*. Where assets are carried at fair value, an entity will also have to comply with the disclosure requirements of IFRS 13, as appropriate. These requirements are discussed in Chapter 14.

10.5 Disclosure of research and development expenditure

An entity should disclose the aggregate total amount of research or development expenditure (see 6.2 above) that is recognised in profit or loss as an expense during the period. *[IAS 38.126-127]*.

11 SPECIFIC ISSUES REGARDING INTANGIBLE ASSETS

11.1 Rate-regulated activities

In many countries the provision of utilities (e.g. water, natural gas or electricity) to consumers is regulated by the national government. Regulations differ between countries but often regulators operate a cost-plus system under which a utility is allowed to make a fixed return on investment. A regulator may allow a utility to recoup its investment by increasing the prices over a defined period. Consequently, the future price that a utility is allowed to charge its customers may be influenced by past cost levels and investment levels.

Under a number of national GAAPs accounting practices have developed whereby an entity accounts for the effects of regulation by recognising a 'regulatory' asset or liability that reflects the increase or decrease in future prices approved by the regulator. Such 'regulatory assets' may have been classified as intangible assets under those national GAAPs.

This issue has been a matter of significant interest for entities in those countries adopting IFRS, because the recognition of these regulatory assets and liabilities is prohibited under IFRS. Just as the requirement to charge a lower price for the delivery of goods and services in the future does not meet the definition of a past obligating event, or a liability, in IAS 37 – *Provisions, Contingent Liabilities and Contingent Assets* (see Chapter 28), the ability to charge higher prices for goods services to be rendered in the future does not meet the definition of an intangible asset in IAS 38. In particular, the right obtained from the regulator to set higher prices is not accompanied by a legal requirement for a customer to buy those goods and services in future, meaning that the entity cannot demonstrate sufficient control over the related benefits to meet the definition of an intangible asset.

In order to permit certain assets and liabilities to achieve recognition under very limited circumstances and to ease the adoption of IFRS for rate-regulated entities, the IASB issued on 30 January 2014, IFRS 14 – *Regulatory Deferral Accounts*. IFRS 14 allows rate-regulated entities to continue recognising regulatory deferral accounts in connection with their first-time adoption of IFRS, e.g. Canadian utility entities. This allows those entities to avoid making major changes in accounting policy for regulatory deferral accounts on transition to IFRS until a comprehensive IASB project is completed. Existing IFRS preparers are prohibited from adopting this standard. Entities that adopt IFRS 14 must present the regulatory deferral accounts as separate line items on the statement of financial position and present movements in these account balances as separate line items in the statement of profit or loss and other comprehensive income. The standard requires disclosures on the nature of, and risks associated with, the entity's rate regulation and the effects of that rate regulation on its financial statements. The standard is effective for annual periods beginning on or after 1 January 2016. Earlier application is permitted. The further application of IFRS 14 is discussed in Chapter 5.

The IASB is continuing its comprehensive rate-regulated activities project, which could result in a standard on rate regulation or a decision not to develop specific requirements. In September 2014 the IASB issued a Discussion Paper – *Reporting the Financial Effects of Rate Regulation*. Based on a defined type of rate regulation, the Discussion Paper considers four possible approaches to reporting the financial effects of rate regulation:

- recognising the package of rights and obligations as an intangible asset (i.e. a licence);
- adopting the regulatory accounting requirements as an exemption to the general requirements of IFRS;
- developing specific IFRS requirements for rate regulation; or
- prohibiting the recognition of regulatory deferral account balances.[7]

At the time of writing, the IASB had not indicated which approach, if any, it prefers. In May 2017 the IASB resumed its discussions and held meetings in June and July 2017 to consider examples that demonstrated the operation of a possible accounting model for rate-regulated activities.[8]

11.2 Emissions trading schemes

Governments around the world have introduced or are in the process of developing schemes to encourage corporations and individuals to reduce emissions of pollutants. These schemes comprise tradable emissions allowances or permits, an example of which is a 'cap and trade' model whereby participants are allocated emission rights or allowances equal to a cap (i.e. a maximum level of allowable emissions, usually less than the entity's current quantity) and are permitted to trade those allowances.

While there are variants to these arrangements, a cap and trade emission rights scheme typically has the following features:

- an entity participating in the scheme (participant) sets a target to reduce its emissions to a specified level (the cap). The participant is issued allowances equal in number to its cap by a government or government agency. Allowances may be issued free of charge, or participants may have to pay the government for them (see below);
- the scheme operates for defined compliance periods;
- participants are free to buy and sell allowances at any time;
- if at the end of the compliance period a participant's actual emissions exceed its emission rights, the participant will have to buy additional rights in the market or it will incur a penalty;
- in some schemes emission rights surpluses and deficits may be carried forward to future periods; and
- the scheme may provide for brokers – who are not themselves participants – to buy and sell emission rights.

The EU Emissions Trading Scheme, still by far the biggest international scheme for trading greenhouse gas emission allowances, now allocates many allowances by auction, not free allocation.[9]

A number of attempts have been made by the Interpretations Committee and the IASB to formulate guidance on how these schemes might be accounted for, but without reaching a definitive conclusion. IFRIC 3 – *Emission Rights* – was issued in 2004 (see 11.2.1 below). However, the interpretation met with significant resistance and was withdrawn in 2005, despite the IASB considering it to be an appropriate interpretation of existing IFRSs.[10]

Until the IASB completes a new project on emissions trading schemes, an entity has the option either:

(a) to apply IFRIC 3, which despite having been withdrawn, is considered to be an appropriate interpretation of existing IFRS; or

(b) to develop its own accounting policy for cap and trade schemes based on the hierarchy of authoritative guidance in IAS 8.

In April 2016, the IASB provided an update on its Pollutant Pricing Mechanisms (formerly referred to as Emissions Trading Schemes) Project in which it noted the diversity in how Pollutant Pricing Mechanisms (which include emissions trading schemes) are accounted for and that some of the issues identified related to possible gaps and inconsistencies in IFRSs.[11] No further work is planned by the IASB until the revised Conceptual Framework is closer to finalisation.[12]

11.2.1 Emissions trading schemes – IFRIC 3

IFRIC 3 dealt with accounting for cap and trade schemes by entities that participated in them.[13] The provisions of the interpretation were also considered to be relevant to other schemes designed to encourage reduced levels of emissions and share some of the features outlined above.[14]

IFRIC 3 took the view that a cap and trade scheme did not give rise to a net asset or liability, but that it gave rise to various items that were to be accounted for separately:[15]

(a) *an asset for allowances held* – Allowances, whether allocated by government or purchased, were to be regarded as intangible assets and accounted for under IAS 38. Allowances issued for less than fair value were to be measured initially at their fair value;[16]

(b) *a government grant* – When allowances are issued for less than fair value, the difference between the amount paid and fair value was a government grant that should be accounted for under IAS 20. Initially the grant was to be recognised as deferred income in the statement of financial position and subsequently recognised as income on a systematic basis over the compliance period for which the allowances were issued, regardless of whether the allowances were held or sold;[17]

(c) *a liability for the obligation to deliver allowances equal to emissions that have been made* – As emissions are made, a liability was to be recognised as a provision that falls within the scope of IAS 37. The liability was to be measured at the best estimate of the expenditure required to settle the present obligation at the reporting date. This would usually be the present market price of the number of allowances required to cover emissions made up to the reporting date.[18]

The interpretation also noted that the existence of an emission rights scheme could represent an indicator of impairment of the related assets, requiring an IAS 36 impairment test to be performed, because the additional costs of compliance could reduce the cash flows expected to be generated by those assets.[19]

Those who called for the withdrawal of IFRIC 3 identified a number of accounting mismatches arising from its application:[20]

- a measurement mismatch between the assets and liabilities recognised in accordance with IFRIC 3;
- a mismatch in the location in which the gains and losses on those assets are reported; and
- a possible timing mismatch because allowances would be recognised when they are obtained – typically at the start of the year – whereas the emission liability would be recognised during the year as it is incurred.

In light of these accounting mismatches, it is perhaps no surprise that in practice very few companies have applied IFRIC 3 on a voluntary basis. Instead companies have developed a range of different approaches in accounting for cap and trade emission rights schemes, which are discussed below:

- 'net liability' approaches;
- 'government grants' approach.

Whatever approach is used, companies should disclose their accounting policies regarding grants of emission rights, the emission rights themselves, the liability for the obligation to deliver allowances equal to emissions that have been made and the presentation in the statement of profit or loss. *[IAS 1.117, 121].*

11.2.2 Emissions trading schemes – Net liability approaches

Under the 'net liability' approach emission allowances received by way of grant are recorded at a nominal amount and the entity will only recognise a liability once the actual emissions exceed the emission rights granted and still held, thereby requiring the entity to purchase additional allowances in the market or incur a regulatory penalty. Purchased grants are initially recognised at cost.

We believe that an entity can apply such a 'net liability' approach, because in the absence of specific guidance on the accounting for emission rights, IAS 20 allows non-monetary government grants and the related asset (in this case the emission rights) received to be measured at a nominal amount (i.e. nil). *[IAS 20.23]*.

Under IAS 37, a provision can only be recorded if the recognition criteria in the standard are met, including that the entity has a present obligation as a result of a past event, it is probable that an outflow of economic resources will be required to settle the obligation and a reliable estimate can be made, *[IAS 37.14]*, (see Chapter 28). As far as emissions are concerned, the 'obligating event' is the emission itself, therefore a provision is considered for recognition as emissions are made, but an outflow of resources is not probable until the reporting entity has made emissions in excess of any rights held. This means that an entity should not recognise a provision for any anticipated future shortfall of emission rights, nor should it accrete a provision over the period of the expected shortfall.

Under IAS 37 the entire obligation to deliver allowances should be measured on the basis of the best estimate of the expenditure required to settle the present obligation at the end of the reporting period (see Chapter 28). *[IAS 37.36]*. Accordingly any provision is based on the lower of the expected cost to purchase additional allowances in the market or the amount of any regulatory penalty.

Although it has been criticised for using a nominal value for the rights and a net approach for measuring the liability, the 'net liability' approach appears to have gained acceptance in practice.

Example 17.18: Application of 'net liability' approach

Company A received allowances representing the right to produce 10,000 tonnes of CO_2 for the year to 31 December 2017. The expected emissions for the full year are 12,000 tonnes of CO_2. At the end of the third quarter, it has emitted 9,000 tonnes of CO_2. The market price of the allowances at the end of the each quarter is €10/tonne, €12/tonne, €14/tonne and €16/tonne respectively.

Under the 'net liability' approach, the provision at the end of the first, second and third quarters would be nil, because the company has not yet exceeded its emissions target. Only in the fourth quarter is a provision recognised, for the excess tonnage emitted, at 2,000 tonnes × €16/tonne = €32,000.

In the above example, the company cannot anticipate the future shortfall of 2,000 tonnes before the fourth quarter by accreting the provision over the year, nor can it recognise on day one the full provision for the 2,000 tonnes expected shortfall. This is because there is no past obligating event to be recognised until the emissions target has actually been exceeded.

Some schemes operate over a period of more than one year, such that the entity is unconditionally entitled to receive allowances for, say, a 3-year period, and it is possible to carry over unused emission rights from one year to the next. In our view, these circumstances would justify application of the net liability approach for the entire period concerned, not just the reporting period for which emission rights have been transferred to the entity. When applying the net liability approach, an entity may choose an accounting policy that measures deficits on the basis of:

- an annual allocation of emission rights; or
- an allocation that covers the entire first period of the scheme (e.g. 3 years) provided that the entity is unconditionally entitled to all the allowances for the first period concerned.

For such schemes, the entity must apply the chosen method consistently at every reporting date. If the entity chooses the annual allocation basis, a deficit is measured on that basis and there can be no carrying over of rights from one year to the next or back to the previous year.

In Example 17.18 above, the entity had an expected shortfall of 2,000 tonnes. Suppose that during the year it had purchased emission rights to cover some or all of the expected shortfall. How should these be accounted for?

Example 17.19: Impact of purchased emission rights on the application of 'net liability' approach

In Example 17.18 above, Company A had an expected shortfall of 2,000 tonnes. The same facts apply, except that at the end of the second quarter, it purchases emission rights for 1,000 tonnes at €12/tonne, i.e. a cost of €12,000. It records these rights as an intangible asset at cost. No impairment has been necessary.

In recognising the provision for its excess emissions of 2,000 tonnes at the end of the year, can the entity apply a method whereby the provision is based on the carrying amount of the emission rights it already owns (the 'carrying value method'), with the balance based on the market price at the year end? That is, can the entity recognise a provision of €28,000, being €12,000 (1,000 tonnes at €12/tonne) plus €16,000 (1,000 tonnes at €16/tonne)?

Because the cost of emissions can only be settled by delivering allowances and the liability to the government cannot be transferred, it is argued that the cost to the entity of settling the obligation is represented by the current carrying value of the emission rights held.

Another view is that measurement of the obligation should be determined independently of considerations as to how settlement may be funded by the entity. Accordingly, the provision would be measured, as in Example 17.18, at €32,000 (based on the market value of emission rights at the year-end). However, the entity may consider the emission rights it holds as a reimbursement right under IAS 37, which is recognised at an amount not exceeding the related provision (see Chapter 28). *[IAS 37.53]*.

Under this alternative 'net liability / reimbursement rights' approach, the entity would re-measure (to fair value) the emission rights that it holds. So although Company A has recognised a provision (and an expense) of €32,000, at the same time it would revalue its purchased emission rights, as a reimbursement right, from €12/tonne to €16/tonne. It would thus recognise a gain of €4,000 (1,000 tonnes × €4/tonne), resulting in a net expense of €28,000 in the statement of profit or loss. This is the same as the profit or loss effect of applying the 'net liability / carrying value' approach.

In practice both the 'net liability' approach and the 'net liability / reimbursement rights' approach have gained acceptance.

In the extract below, MOL Hungarian Oil and Gas Plc applies a 'net liability' approach, i.e. emission rights granted free of charge are accounted for at their nominal value of zero and no government grant is recognised. A liability for the obligation to deliver allowances is only recognised when the level of emissions exceed the level of allowances granted. MOL Hungarian Oil and Gas Plc measures the liability at the cost of purchased allowances up to the level of purchased allowances held, and then at the market price of allowances ruling at the reporting date, with movements in the liability recognised in operating profit.

Extract 17.12: MOL Hungarian Oil and Gas Plc (2016)

Notes to the financial statements [extract]

9. Property, plants and equipment and intangible assets [extract]

b) Intangible assets [extract]

Accounting policies [extract]

Emission rights

Free granted quotas are not recorded in the financial statements, while purchased quotas are initially recognised as intangible assets at cost at the emitting segments subsequently remeasured to fair value through profit or loss.

[...]

16. Provisions [extract]

Accounting policies [extract]

Emission rights

The Group recognizes provisions for the estimated CO_2 emissions costs when actual emission exceeds the emission rights granted and still held. When actual emission exceeds the amount of emission rights granted, provision is recognised for the exceeding emission rights based on the purchase price of allowance concluded in forward contracts or market quotations at the reporting date.

11.2.3 Emissions trading schemes – Government grant approach

Another approach which has gained acceptance in practice is to recognise the emission rights granted by the government initially at their fair value and record a corresponding government grant in the statement of financial position. The government grant element is subsequently recognised as income in accordance with the requirements of IAS 20. To that extent, the approach follows that required by IFRIC 3. However, rather than measuring the liability for the obligation to deliver allowances at the present market price of those allowances, the liability is measured instead by reference to the amounts recorded when those rights were first granted.

As with the 'net liability' approach, critics have argued that the government grant approach would not be in line with the 'best estimate' determined under IAS 37 as the amount that an entity would rationally pay to settle the obligation at the reporting date or to transfer it to a third party at that time. *[IAS 37.37]*.

Repsol initially recognises the emission rights at fair value as a government grant under IAS 20 and illustrates clearly that the measurement of the liability follows that of the related emission rights. To the extent that emissions are not covered by emission rights, the liability is recognised at the fair value of such allowances at the reporting date.

Extract 17.13: Repsol, S.A. (2016)

NOTES TO THE 2016 CONSOLIDATED FINANCIAL STATEMENTS [extract]

(2) **BASIS OF PRESENTATION** [extract]

2.2) **Applicable standards to financial reporting** [extract]

7. ***Other intangible assets*** [extract]

c) **Carbon emission allowances** [extract]

Emission allowances are recognized as an intangible asset and are initially recognized at acquisition cost.

Allowances received free of charge under the emissions trading system for the period 2013-2020, are initially recognized at the market price prevailing at the beginning of the year in which they are issued, and a balancing item is recognized as a grant for the same amount as deferred income. As the corresponding tons of CO_2 are issued, the deferred income is reclassified to profit or loss.

The allowance rights are not amortized as their carrying amount equals their residual value and, therefore, the depreciable basis is zero. Emission allowances are subject to an impairment test based on their recoverable amount, as measured with reference to the price of the benchmark contract in the futures market provided by the ECX – European Climate Exchange.

The Group records an expense under "*Other operating expenses*" in the income statement for the CO_2 *emissions released during the year, recognizing a provision calculated based on the tons of* CO_2 emitted, measured at: (i) their carrying amount in the case of the allowances of which the Group is in possession at year end; and (ii) the closing list price in the case of allowances of which it is not in possession at year end.

When the emissions allowances for the CO_2 tons emitted are delivered to the authorities, the intangible assets as well as their corresponding provision are derecognized from the balance sheet without any effect on the income statement.

The fair value on initial recognition of emission rights that are accounted as intangible assets will be based on the requirements of IFRS 13 which are discussed in Chapter 14. If there is no active market for emission rights, the selection of appropriate valuation techniques, inputs to those valuation techniques and the application of the fair value hierarchy are discussed in Chapter 14.

11.2.4 Amortisation and impairment testing of emission rights

In the case of cap and trade schemes, emission rights that are accounted for as intangible assets are unlikely to be amortised as their depreciable amount is usually nil. Their expected residual value at inception will be equal to their fair value. Thereafter, although their residual value is equal to their market value, there is no consumption of economic benefit while the emission right is held. The economic benefits are realised instead by surrendering the rights to settle obligations under the scheme for emissions made, or by selling rights to another party. It is necessary to perform an IAS 36 impairment test whenever there is an indication of impairment (see Chapter 20). If the market value of an emission right drops below its carrying amount, this does not automatically result in an impairment charge because emission rights are likely to be tested for impairment as part of a larger cash generating unit.

11.2.5 Emission rights acquired in a business combination

At the date of acquisition of a business, an acquirer is required to recognise the acquiree's identifiable intangible assets, in this case emission rights, at their fair values. *[IFRS 3.18].*

However, an acquirer should only recognise a provision for actual emissions that have occurred up to that date. This means that an acquirer cannot apply the 'net liability' approach to emission rights acquired in a business combination. Instead, an acquirer should treat acquired emission rights in the same way as purchased emission rights (see 11.2.2 above). An acquirer that applies IFRIC 3 or the 'government grant' approach would recognise acquired emission rights at their fair value, but cannot recognise a deferred credit for a 'government grant' as it acquired the emission rights by way of a business combination.

Consequently, an acquirer may report a higher emission expense in its statement of profit or loss in the compliance period in which it acquires a business.

11.2.6 Sale of emission rights

The sale of emission rights that are accounted for as intangible assets should be recognised in accordance with IAS 38. This means that they should be derecognised on disposal or when no future economic benefits are expected from their use or disposal. *[IAS 38.112]*. The gain or loss arising from derecognition of the emission rights should be determined as the difference between the net disposal proceeds and the carrying amount of emission rights. *[IAS 38.113]*.

Prior to the sale the entity may not have recognised the obligation, to deliver allowances equal to the emissions caused, at its fair value at the date of derecognition. If that were the case then the entity would need to ensure that the liability in excess of the emission rights held by the company after the sale is recognised at the present fair value of the emission rights.

Both the gain or loss on the derecognition of the emission rights and the adjustment of the liability should be recognised when the emission rights are derecognised. Any gain should not be classified as revenue. *[IAS 38.113]*.

If an entity that applies the 'net liability' approach were to sell all its emission rights at the start of the compliance period, it would not be permitted to defer the gain on that sale even if it was certain that the entity would need to repurchase emission rights later in the year to cover actual emissions. A gain is recognised immediately on the sale and a provision is recognised as gases are emitted.

If an entity enters into a forward contract to sell an emission right, it may be acting effectively as a broker-trader. The entity should determine whether the contract is a derivative within the scope of IAS 39 (or, when applied, IFRS 9 – *Financial Instruments*) by applying the requirements in that Standard (see Chapter 44).

11.2.7 Accounting for emission rights by brokers and traders

IFRIC 3 did not address accounting by brokers and traders that are not themselves participants in a cap and trade scheme. However, they hold emission rights as assets held for sale in the ordinary course of business, which means that they meet the definition of inventories in IAS 2. *[IAS 2.6]*. Under that standard a broker-trader may choose between measuring emission rights at the lower of cost and net realisable value or at fair value less costs to sell. Commodity broker-traders who measure their inventories at fair value less costs to sell may recognise changes in fair value less costs in profit or loss in the period of the change. *[IAS 2.3]*.

When a company trades derivatives based on the emission rights, they fall within the scope of IAS 39 (or, when applied, IFRS 9) and are accounted for at fair value through profit or loss unless they hedge the fair value of the emission rights granted to the company or qualify for the 'own use exemption'. *[IAS 39.5, IFRS 9.2.4].*

When an entity holds emission rights for own use and also has a trading department trading in emission rights, the company should split the books between emission rights held for own use and those held for trading. The emission rights should be treated as intangible assets and inventory respectively.

11.3 Accounting for green certificates or renewable energy certificates

Some governments have launched schemes to promote power production from renewable sources, based on green certificates, renewable energy certificates, green tags or tradable renewable certificates. There are similarities between green certificates and emission rights, except that whilst emission rights are granted to reflect a future limit on emissions, green certificates are awarded on the basis of the amount of green energy already produced.

In a typical scheme, producers of electricity are granted certificates by the government based on the power output (kWh) derived from renewable sources. Entities distributing electricity (produced from both renewable and traditional sources) are required to hand over to the government a number of certificates based on the total kWh of electricity sold to consumers during the year, or pay a penalty to the extent that an insufficient number of certificates is rendered. It is this requirement that creates a valuable market for the certificates, allowing producers to sell their certificates to distributors, using the income to subsidise in effect the higher cost of generation from renewable sources.

11.3.1 Accounting by producers using renewable energy sources

As in the case of emission rights, the award of green certificates is treated as a government grant by a producer. An intangible asset representing an entitlement to that grant is recognised at the point in time when the green electricity is produced. As with any government grant, the entitlement is initially measured at either fair value or a nominal amount, depending on the entity's chosen policy. *[IAS 20.23].*

Where the entitlement asset is initially recognised at fair value, a credit entry is recorded in the statement of profit or loss as either a reduction in production costs for the period (on the basis that the purpose of the grant is to compensate the producer for the higher cost of using renewable energy sources) or as other income, but not as revenue. *[IAS 20.29].* Subsequent revaluation of the intangible asset is only allowed if an active market exists for the green certificates, and the other requirements of IAS 38 are applied (see 8.2 above). The intangible is derecognised when the certificate is sold by the producer.

11.3.2 Accounting by distributors of renewable energy

When the distributor is also a producer of renewable energy, it has the option to use certificates granted to it or to sell them in the market. Accordingly, the permissible accounting treatments of green certificates are in principle the same as those for emission rights discussed at 11.2 above. The distributor is obliged to remit certificates and therefore recognises a provision as sales are recorded (in the same way that a provision for emission rights is recognised as emissions are made). The distributor might apply a 'net liability' approach, discussed at 11.2.2 above, and only start to recognise a provision once it has achieved a level of sales exceeding that covered by certificates granted to the entity in its capacity as a producer.

If a distributor is not also a producer of renewable energy, it recognises a provision as sales are made, measured at the fair value of green certificates to be remitted. A corresponding cost is included in cost of sales. The provision is remeasured to fair value at each reporting date. If the entity purchases certificates in the market, they are recognised as an intangible asset and initially measured at cost. Subsequent revaluation is only allowed if an active market exists for the green certificates, and the other requirements of IAS 38 are applied (see 8.2 above).

Alternatively, as discussed in Example 17.19 at 11.2.2 above, the asset held may be designated by management as a reimbursement right in respect of the associated liability, allowing remeasurement to fair value. Similarly, the entity could apply a carrying value method, measuring the provision based on the value and extent of certificates already held and applying fair value only to the extent that it has an obligation to make further purchases in the market or to incur a penalty if it fails to do so.

11.3.3 Accounting by brokers and traders

As discussed at 11.2.7 above, brokers and traders should apply IAS 2 where green certificates are held for sale in the ordinary course of business; account for derivatives based on green certificates in accordance with IAS 39 (or, when applied, IFRS 9); and properly distinguish those held for own use (carried within intangible assets) from certificates held for trading (included in inventory).

11.4 Accounting for REACH costs

The European Regulation[21] concerning the Registration, Evaluation, Authorisation and Restriction of Chemicals (REACH) came into force on 1 June 2007. The regulation requires manufacturers or importers of substances to register them with a central European Chemicals Agency (ECHA). An entity will not be able to manufacture or supply unregistered substances. As a consequence, entities will incur different types of costs, such as:

- costs of identifying the substances that need to be registered;
- testing and other data collection costs, including outsourcing services from external laboratories, costs of tests in own laboratories – testing materials, labour costs and related overheads;
- registration fees payable to ECHA; and
- legal fees.

These costs may be part of the development of a new manufacturing process or product, or in the use of a new chemical in an existing manufacturing process or product. They might be incurred solely by an entity or shared with other entities (clients, partners or even competitors). Under the REACH legislation, cost sharing might be achieved by the submission of a joint registration (whereby testing and other data collection costs are shared before the registration is filed) or by reimbursement (whereby an entity pays an existing registrant for access to the registration and testing data used in its earlier application for registration). Accordingly, questions arise as to whether such costs should be capitalised or recognised as an expense and, if capitalised, on what basis the related intangible asset should be amortised.

In our view, a registration under the REACH regulation is an intangible asset as defined by IAS 38. *[IAS 38.8]*. As it gives rise to a legal right, the registration is identifiable. *[IAS 38.12(b)]*. Because a registration cannot be arbitrarily withdrawn and also establishes intellectual property rights over the data used in the application for registration, a resource is controlled. *[IAS 38.13]*. The future economic benefits relating to the registration arise from either the right to reimbursement for the use by others of data supporting the entity's earlier application; or from the revenues to be earned and cost savings to be achieved by the entity from the use of registered substances in its business activities. *[IAS 38.17]*.

The appropriate accounting treatment under IAS 38 depends upon whether the required data is collected by the entity or acquired from an existing registrant and on whether the registration being completed is for a substance already used in an existing process or product (an existing substance) or intended to be used for the first time or in a new process or product (a new substance). The flow chart below demonstrates how these different features interact with the requirements of IAS 38.

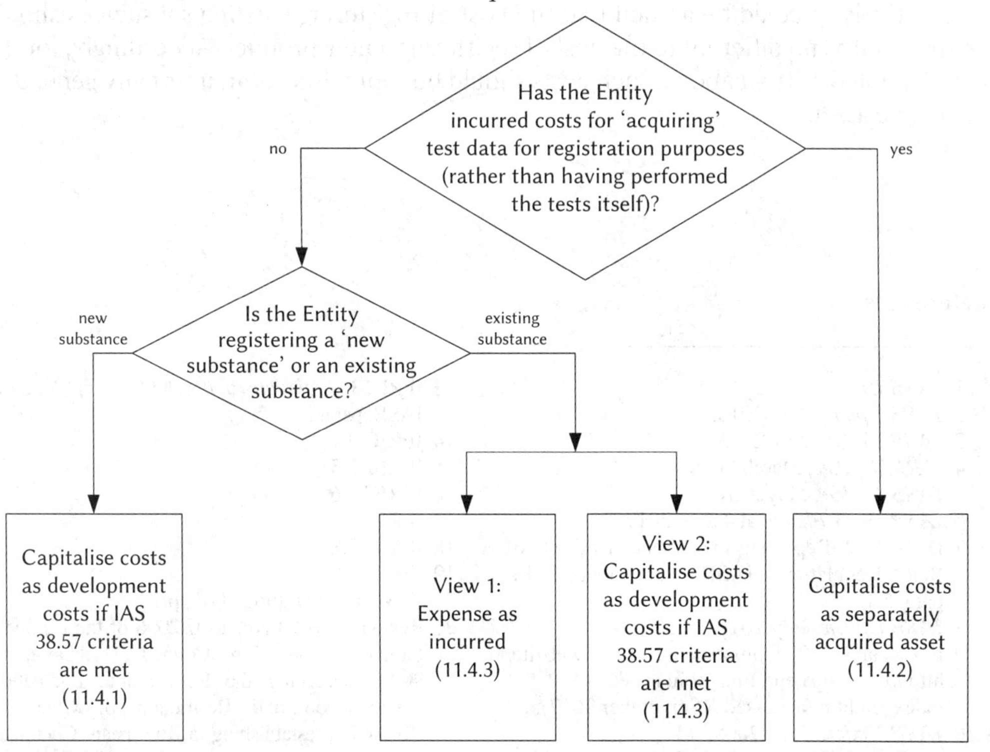

11.4.1 Costs of registering a new substance performed by the entity itself

If the entity itself incurs REACH costs, these activities meet the definition of development in IAS 38. *[IAS 38.8]*. Accordingly, the entity must also meet the rigorous rules in the standard described at 6.2.2 above which confirm that the related development project is at a sufficiently advanced stage, is economically viable and includes only directly attributable costs. *[IAS 38.57].*

Costs of identifying the substances that need to be registered would have to be recognised as an expense when incurred, as this activity is regarded as research. *[IAS 38.56].*

11.4.2 Costs of acquiring test data from an existing registrant

An entity may acquire test data from an existing registrant that has already been used by it in its earlier application for registration. These costs should be capitalised as a separately acquired intangible asset (see 4 above).

11.4.3 Costs of registering an existing substance performed by the entity itself

In this case two alternative treatments are acceptable. If the costs of obtaining a REACH registration for existing substances used in existing processes are regarded as subsequent expenditure on an existing intangible asset, the related costs should be recognised as an expense as incurred, *[IAS 38.20]*, (see 3.3 above). As unregistered substances will no longer be available for use, this might indicate that the registration maintains the economic benefits associated with the related production process or product and does not improve it.

Alternatively, it could be argued that the cost of registering existing substances should be regarded as no different to the cost of registering a new product. Accordingly, for the reasons noted at 11.4.1 above, such costs should be capitalised as an internally generated intangible asset.

References

1 *IASB Update*, July 2013.
2 *IASB Update*, July 2013.
3 *IASB Update*, July 2013.
4 *IFRIC Update,* March 2016.
5 *IASB Update*, May 2016.
6 *IASB Work Plan* as at 4 July 2017.
7 DP/2014/2, Reporting the Financial Effects of Rate Regulation, IASB September 2014, para. 5.1.
8 *IASB Update*, July 2017.
9 European Commission website, http://ec.europa.eu/clima/policies/ets/index_en.htm (accessed 5 September 2017).
10 *IASB Update*, June 2005, p.1.
11 IASB Staff Paper, *Pollutant Pricing Mechanisms, Project update and response to the Agenda Consultation*, April 2016.
12 IFRS Foundation website, http://www.ifrs.org/projects/research-programme/#the-research-pipeline (accessed 5 September 2017).
13 IFRIC 3, *Emission Rights*, 2005 Bound Volume, IASB, para. 2.
14 IFRIC 3.3.
15 IFRIC 3.5.
16 IFRIC 3.6.
17 IFRIC 3.7.
18 IFRIC 3.8.
19 IFRIC 3.9.
20 *IASB Update*, June 2005, p.1.
21 Regulation (EC) No. 1907/2006 of the European Parliament and of the Council of 18 December 2006 concerning the Registration, Evaluation, Authorisation and Restriction of Chemicals (REACH), establishing a European Chemicals Agency, amending Directive 1999/45/EC and repealing Council Regulation (EEC) No. 793/93 and Commission Regulation (EC) No. 1488/94 as well as Council Directive 76/769/EEC and Commission Directives 91/155/EEC, 93/67/EEC, 93/105/EC and 2000/21/EC.

Chapter 18 Property, plant and equipment

List of examples

Chapter 18 Property, plant and equipment

1 INTRODUCTION

One fundamental problem in financial reporting is how to account periodically for performance when many of the expenditures an entity incurs in the current period also contribute to future accounting periods. Expenditure on property, plant and equipment ('PP&E') is the best example of this difficulty.

The accounting conventions permitted by the IASB are the subject of this chapter, although the underlying broad principles involved are among the first that accountants and business people learn in their business life. The cost of an item of PP&E is capitalised when acquired (i.e. recorded in the statement of financial position as an asset); then subsequently a proportion of the cost is charged each year to profit or loss (i.e. the cost is spread over the future accounting periods expected to benefit). Ideally, at the end of the item's working life the cost remaining on the statement of financial position should be equal to the disposal proceeds of the item, or be zero if there are none.

The principal standard is IAS 16 – *Property, Plant and Equipment.* The objective of this standard is to prescribe the accounting treatment for PP&E so that users of the financial statements can discern information about an entity's investment in its PP&E and the changes in such investment. The principal issues in accounting for PP&E are the recognition of the assets, the determination of their carrying amounts and the depreciation charges and impairment losses to be recognised in relation to them. *[IAS 16.1].* Impairment is a major consideration in accounting for PP&E, as this procedure is intended to ensure PP&E costs that are not fully recoverable are immediately written down to a level that is fully recoverable. Impairment is covered by IAS 36 – *Impairment of Assets* – and dealt with as a separate topic in Chapter 20. In addition, there is a separate standard, IAS 40 – *Investment Property* – that deals with that particular category of PP&E which is discussed in Chapter 19.

IFRS 5 – *Non-current Assets Held for Sale and Discontinued Operations* – deals with the accounting required when items of PP&E are held for sale and is discussed in Chapter 4.

This chapter discusses the most recent version of IAS 16, which was published in March 2004 and became effective for periods beginning on or after 1 January 2005, as subsequently updated by various narrow-scope amendments, including minor consequential amendments arising from other standards.

In May 2014, the IASB issued a new revenue standard, IFRS 15 – *Revenue from Contracts with Customers* – which supersedes all revenue recognition standards and interpretations in IFRS. This means that the recognition of revenue in certain transactions involving PP&E including the disposal of fixed assets are now within scope of or affected by the new standard (see 7 below). Entities are required to apply IFRS 15 and its consequential amendments to other standards for annual reporting periods beginning on or after 1 January 2018. Early application is permitted. *[IAS 16.81J]*.

In January 2016, the IASB issued a new leasing standard, IFRS 16 – *Leases*, which will supersede the current leases standard and interpretations in IFRS. Under IFRS 16, lessees apply a single model for most leases recognising these leases (i.e. rental contracts) in their statement of financial position as lease liabilities with corresponding right-of-use assets. Therefore, lessees no longer need to classify leases as finance or operating leases. Accordingly, lessee accounting for PP&E held under leases classified as finance leases under IAS 17 – *Leases* – will be affected by the new standard. IFRS 16 and its consequential amendments to other standards are effective for annual periods beginning on or after 1 January 2019. Early application is permitted provided that IFRS 15 has been applied, or is applied, at the same date as IFRS 16.

In May 2017, the IASB issued IFRS 17 – *Insurance Contracts*, a comprehensive new accounting standard for insurance contracts covering recognition and measurement, presentation and disclosure. Once effective, IFRS 17 will replace IFRS 4 – *Insurance Contracts* – that was issued in 2005. As part of the consequential amendments arising from IFRS 17, the subsequent measurement requirements in IAS 16 will be amended (see 5 below). IFRS 17 and its consequential amendments to other standards are effective for annual periods beginning on or after 1 January 2021, with adjusted comparative figures required. Early application is permitted provided that both IFRS 9 – *Financial Instruments* – and IFRS 15 have already been applied, or are applied for the first time, at the date on which IFRS 17 is first applied.

IFRS 15, IFRS 16 and IFRS 17 make consequential amendments to IAS 16, these are indicated in the sections of this chapter, where appropriate. For those entities early adopting IFRS 16 and IFRS 17, and for the detailed discussions and requirements of IFRS 15, IFRS 16 and IFRS 17, see Chapter 30, Chapter 25 and Chapter 56, respectively.

2 THE REQUIREMENTS OF IAS 16

2.1 Scope

All PP&E is within the scope of IAS 16 except as follows:

- when another standard requires or permits a different accounting treatment, for example, IAS 40 for investment properties held at fair value (but investment properties held using the cost model under IAS 40 should use the cost model in IAS 16 which is discussed at 5 below);
- PP&E classified as held for sale in accordance with IFRS 5;
- biological assets related to agricultural activity (covered by IAS 41 – *Agriculture*) other than bearer plants (see 3.1.7 below);
- the recognition and measurement of exploration and evaluation assets (covered by IFRS 6 – *Exploration for and Evaluation of Mineral Resources*); and
- mineral rights and mineral reserves such as oil, gas, and similar 'non-regenerative' resources. *[IAS 16.2-3, 5]*.

Although the standard scopes out non bearer plant biological assets and mineral rights and reserves, it includes any PP&E used in developing or maintaining such resources. *[IAS 16.3]*. Therefore, exploration PP&E is included in the scope of the standard (see Chapter 41), as is agricultural PP&E (see Chapter 40).

Other standards may require an item of PP&E to be recognised on a basis different from that required by IAS 16. For example, IAS 17 requires an entity to evaluate its recognition of an item of leased PP&E on the basis of the transfer of risks and rewards. IAS 17 has its own rules regarding recognition and measurement – see Chapter 24 for a description of how an item of PP&E held under a finance lease is recognised and initially measured. However, once an item of PP&E has been recognised as a finance lease under IAS 17, its treatment thereafter is in accordance with IAS 16. *[IAS 16.4]*.

When IFRS 16 is adopted, it will supersede IAS 17 in its entirety. Accordingly, IFRS 16 amends the scope of IAS 16 so that paragraph 4 of IAS 16 as described above, will be deleted. Under IFRS 16, lessees apply a single model for most leases so that they no longer need to classify leases as finance leases or as operating leases. Lessees recognise most leases in their statement of financial position as lease liabilities with corresponding right-of-use assets. Consequently, accounting for right-of-use assets should be in accordance with IFRS 16. IFRS 16 is discussed in detail in Chapter 25.

Also, IFRS 16 amends paragraph 5 of IAS 16 (described above) to clarify that an entity should use the cost model in IAS 16 for its owned investment property if the entity chooses the cost model to account for its investment property under IAS 40.

2.2 Definitions used in IAS 16

IAS 16 defines the main terms it uses throughout the standard as follows: *[IAS 16.6]*

Bearer plant is a living plant that:

- is used in the production or supply of agricultural produce;
- is expected to bear produce for more than one period; and
- has a remote likelihood of being sold as agricultural produce, except for incidental scrap sales (see 3.1.7 below).

Carrying amount is the amount at which an asset is recognised after deducting any accumulated depreciation and accumulated impairment losses.

Cost is the amount of cash or cash equivalents paid or the fair value of other consideration given to acquire an asset at the time of its acquisition or construction or, where applicable, the amount attributed to that asset when initially recognised in accordance with the specific requirements of other IFRSs, e.g. IFRS 2 – *Share-based Payment.*

Depreciable amount is the cost of an asset, or other amount substituted for cost, less its residual value.

Depreciation is the systematic allocation of the depreciable amount of an asset over its useful life.

Entity-specific value is the present value of the cash flows an entity expects to arise from the continuing use of an asset and from its disposal at the end of its useful life or expects to incur when settling a liability.

Fair value is the price that would be received to sell an asset or paid to transfer a liability in an orderly transaction between market participants at the measurement date. (See IFRS 13 – *Fair Value Measurement* – discussed in Chapter 14).

An *impairment loss* is the amount by which the carrying amount of an asset exceeds its recoverable amount.

Property, plant and equipment are tangible items that:

(a) are held for use in the production or supply of goods or services, for rental to others, or for administrative purposes; and

(b) are expected to be used during more than one period.

Recoverable amount is the higher of an asset's fair value less costs to sell and its value in use.

The *residual value* of an asset is the estimated amount that an entity would currently obtain from disposal of the asset, after deducting the estimated costs of disposal, if the asset were already of the age and in the condition expected at the end of its useful life.

Useful life is:

(a) the period over which an asset is expected to be available for use by an entity; or

(b) the number of production or similar units expected to be obtained from the asset by an entity.

These definitions are discussed in the relevant sections below.

3 RECOGNITION

An item of PP&E should be recognised (i.e. its cost included as an asset in the statement of financial position) only if it is probable that future economic benefits associated with the item will flow to the entity and its cost can be measured reliably. *[IAS 16.7].* This requirement for recognition is directly taken from the IASB's *The Conceptual Framework for Financial Reporting* ('the *Framework*'), which is discussed in Chapter 2. *[Framework 4.4, 4.38].*

Extract 18.1 below describes Skanska's criteria for the recognition of PP&E.

Extract 18.1: Skanska AB (2016)

Notes including accounting and valuation principles [extract]

Note 1. Consolidated accounting and valuation principles [extract]

IAS 16 Property, Plant and Equipment [extract]

Property, plant and equipment are recognized as assets if it is probable that the Group will derive future economic benefits from them and the cost of the assets can be reliably calculated. Property, plant and equipment are recognized at cost minus accumulated depreciation and any impairment losses. Cost includes purchase price plus expenses directly attributable to the asset in order to bring it to the location and condition to be used in the intended manner. Examples of directly attributable expenses are delivery and handling costs, installation, ownership documents, consultant fees and legal services. Borrowing costs are included in the cost of property, plant and equipment produced by the Group. Impairment losses are applied in compliance with IAS 36.

The cost of self-constructed property, plant and equipment includes expenditures for materials and remuneration to employees, plus other applicable manufacturing costs that are considered attributable to the asset.

Further expenditures are added to cost only if it is probable that the Group will derive future economic benefits from the asset and the cost can be reliably calculated. All other further expenditures are recognized as expenses in the period when they arise.

The decisive factor in determining when a further expenditure is added to cost is whether the expenditure is related to replacement of identified components, or parts thereof, at which time such expenditures are capitalized. In cases where a new component is created, this expenditure is also added to cost. Any undepreciated carrying amounts for replaced components, or parts thereof, are disposed of and recognized as an expense at the time of replacement. If the cost of the removed component cannot be determined directly, its cost may be estimated as the cost of the new component adjusted by a suitable price index to take into account inflation. Repairs are recognized as expenses on a continuous basis.

3.1 Aspects of recognition

3.1.1 Spare parts and minor items

Items such as spare parts, stand-by equipment and servicing equipment are inventory unless they meet the definition of PP&E (see 2.2 above). *[IAS 16.8].* This treatment is illustrated in Extract 18.2 below.

> *Extract 18.2: Heineken Holding N.V. (2016)*
>
> **NOTES TO THE CONSOLIDATED FINANCIAL STATEMENTS** [extract]
>
> 3. **SIGNIFICANT ACCOUNTING POLICIES** [extract]
>
> (f) **Property, plant and equipment** [extract]
>
> (i) Owned assets [extract]
>
> Spare parts that are acquired as part of an equipment purchase and only to be used in connection with this specific equipment or purchased software that is integral to the functionality of the related equipment are capitalised and amortised as part of that equipment. In all other cases, spare parts are carried as inventory and recognised in the income statement as consumed.

Materiality judgements are considered when deciding how an item of PP&E should be accounted for. Major spare parts, for example, qualify as PP&E, while smaller spares would be carried as inventory and as a practical matter many companies have a minimum value for capitalising assets.

Some types of business may have a very large number of minor items of PP&E such as spare parts, tools, pallets and returnable containers, which nevertheless are used in more than one accounting period. There are practical problems in recording them on an asset-by-asset basis in an asset register; they are difficult to control and frequently lost. The main consequence is that it becomes very difficult to depreciate them. Generally, entities write off such immaterial assets as expenses in the period of addition. Skanska in Extract 18.7 below immediately depreciates such minor equipment, achieving the same result. The standard notes that there are issues concerning what actually constitutes a single item of PP&E. The 'unit of measurement' for recognition is not prescribed and entities have to apply judgement in defining PP&E in their specific circumstances. The standard suggests that it may be appropriate to aggregate individually insignificant items (such as tools, moulds and dies) and to apply the standard to the aggregate amount (presumably without having to identify the individual assets). *[IAS 16.9].*

3.1.2 Environmental and safety equipment

The standard acknowledges that there may be expenditures forced upon an entity by legislation that requires it to buy 'assets' that do not meet the recognition criteria because the expenditure does not directly increase the future economic benefits expected to flow from the asset. Examples would be safety or environmental protection equipment. IAS 16 explains that these expenditures qualify for recognition as they allow an entity to derive future economic benefits from related assets in excess of those that would flow if such expenditure had not been made. For example, a chemical manufacturer may install new chemical handling processes to comply with environmental requirements for the production and storage of dangerous chemicals; related plant enhancements are recognised as an asset because without them the entity is unable to manufacture and sell the chemicals or a plant might have to be closed down if these safety or environmental expenditures were not made. *[IAS 16.11]*.

An entity may voluntarily invest in environmental equipment even though it is not required by law to do so. The entity can capitalise those investments in environmental and safety equipment in the absence of a legal requirement as long as:

- the expenditure meets the definition of an asset; or
- there is a constructive obligation to invest in the equipment.

If the entity can demonstrate that the equipment is likely to increase the economic life of the related asset, the expenditure meets the definition of an asset. Otherwise, the expenditure can be capitalised when the entity can demonstrate all of the following:

- the entity can prove that a constructive obligation exists to invest in environmental and safety equipment (e.g. it is standard practice in the industry, environmental groups are likely to raise issues or employees demand certain equipment to be present);
- the expenditure is directly related to improvement of the asset's environmental and safety standards; and
- the expenditure is not related to repairs and maintenance or forms part of period costs or operational costs.

Whenever safety and environmental assets are capitalised, the standard requires the resulting carrying amount of the asset, and any related asset, to be reviewed for impairment in accordance with IAS 36 (see 5.7 below). *[IAS 16.11]*.

3.1.3 Property economic benefits and property developments

The standard requires that PP&E only be recognised when it is probable that future economic benefits associated with the item will flow to the entity.

For example, in relation to property development, many jurisdictions require permissions prior to development whilst developers, including entities developing property for their own use, typically incur significant costs prior to such permissions being granted.

In assessing whether such pre-permission expenditures can be capitalised – assuming they otherwise meet the criteria – a judgement must be made at the date the expenditure is incurred of whether it is sufficiently probable that the relevant permission will be granted. Such expenditure does not become part of the cost of the land; to the extent that it can be recognised it is part of the costs of a separate building. Furthermore, if during the application and approval process of such permits it is no longer expected that necessary permits will be granted, capitalisation of pre-permission expenditure should cease, any related amounts that were previously capitalised should be written off in accordance with IAS 36 and accordingly, the carrying amount of any related item of PP&E subject to development or redevelopment (or, if appropriate, the cash generating unit where such an asset belongs) should be tested for impairment, where applicable (see 5.7 below).

3.1.4 Classification as PP&E or intangible asset

The restrictions in IAS 38 – *Intangible Assets* – in respect of capitalising certain internally-generated intangible assets focus attention on the treatment of many internal costs. In practice, items such as computer software purchased by entities are frequently capitalised as part of a tangible asset, for example as part of an accounting or communications infrastructure. Equally, internally written software may be capitalised as part of a tangible production facility, and so on. Judgement must be exercised in deciding whether such items are to be accounted for under IAS 16 or IAS 38 and this distinction becomes increasingly important if the two standards prescribe differing treatments in any particular case. IAS 16, unlike IAS 38, does not refer to this type of asset. IAS 38 states that an entity needs to exercise judgement in determining whether an asset that incorporates both intangible and tangible elements should be treated under IAS 16 or as an intangible asset under IAS 38, for example:

- computer software that is embedded in computer-controlled equipment that cannot operate without that specific software is an integral part of the related hardware and is treated as PP&E;
- application software that is being used on a computer is generally easily replaced and is not an integral part of the related hardware, whereas the operating system normally is integral to the computer and is included in PP&E; and
- a database that is stored on a compact disc is considered to be an intangible asset because the value of the physical medium is wholly insignificant compared to that of the data collection. *[IAS 38.4].*

It is worthwhile noting that as the 'parts approach' in IAS 16 requires an entity to account for significant parts of an asset separately, this raises 'boundary' problems between IAS 16 and IAS 38 when software and similar expenditure are involved. We believe that where IAS 16 requires an entity to identify significant parts of an asset and account for them separately, the entity needs to evaluate whether any software-type intangible part is actually integral to the larger asset or whether it is really a separate asset in its own right. The intangible part is more likely to be an asset in its own right if it was developed separately or if it can be used independently of the item of PP&E.

3.1.5 Classification of items as inventory or PP&E when minimum levels are maintained

Entities may acquire items of inventory on a continuing basis, either for sale in the ordinary course of business or to be consumed in a production process or when rendering services.

This means there will always be a core stock of that item (i.e. a minimum level of inventory is maintained). This does not in itself turn that inventory into an item of PP&E, since each individual item will be consumed within a single operating cycle. However, there may be cases where it is difficult to judge whether an item is part of inventory or is an item of PP&E. This may have implications on measurement because, for example, PP&E has a revaluation option (see 6 below) that is not available for inventory.

In our view, an item of inventory is accounted for as an item of PP&E if it:

- is not held for sale or consumed in a production process or during the process of rendering services;
- is necessary to operate or benefit from an asset during more than one operating cycle; and
- cannot be recouped through sale (or is significantly impaired after it has been used to operate the asset or benefit from that asset).

This applies even if the part of inventory that is an item of PP&E cannot be physically separated from the rest of inventories.

Consider the following examples:

- An entity acquires the right to use an underground cave for gas storage purposes for a period of 50 years. The cave is filled with gas, but a substantial part of that gas will only be used to keep the cave under pressure in order to be able to get gas out of the cave. It is not possible to distinguish the gas that will be used to keep the cave under pressure and the rest of the gas.
- An entity operates an oil refining plant. In order for the refining process to take place, the plant must contain a certain minimum quantity of oil. This can only be taken out once the plant is abandoned and would then be polluted to such an extent that the oil's value is significantly reduced.
- An entity sells gas and has at any one time a certain quantity of gas in its gas distribution network.

In the first example, therefore, the total volume of gas must be virtually split into (i) gas held for sale and (ii) gas held to keep the cave under pressure. The former must be accounted for under IAS 2 – *Inventories*. The latter must be accounted for as PP&E and depreciated over the period the cave is expected to be used.

In the second example the part of the crude that is necessary to operate (in technical terms) the plant and cannot be recouped (or can be recouped but would then be significantly impaired), even when the plant is abandoned, should be considered as an item of PP&E and amortised over the life of the plant.

In the third example the gas in the pipeline is not necessary to operate the pipeline. It is held for sale or to be consumed in the production process or process of rendering services. Therefore this gas is accounted for as inventory.

3.1.6 Production stripping costs of surface mines

IFRIC 20 – *Stripping Costs in the Production Phase of a Surface Mine* – states that costs associated with a 'stripping activity asset' (i.e. the costs associated with gaining access to a specific section of the ore body) are accounted for as an additional component of an existing asset. Other routine stripping costs are accounted for as current costs of production (i.e. inventory).

The Interpretations Committee's intention was to maintain the principle of IAS 16 by requiring identification of the component of the ore body for which access had been improved, as part of the criteria for recognising stripping costs as an asset. An entity will have to allocate the stripping costs between the amount capitalised (as it reflects the future access benefit) and the amount that relates to the current-period production of inventory. This allocation should be based on a relevant production measure.

This component approach follows the principle of separating out parts of an asset that have costs that are significant in relation to the entire asset and when the useful lives of those parts are different. *[IAS 16.45].*

This interpretation is discussed in more detail in Chapter 41 at 15.5.

3.1.7 Bearer plants

Bearer plants, defined as living plants that are used in the production or supply of agricultural produce, are expected to bear produce for more than one period and have a remote likelihood of being sold as a plant or harvested as agricultural produce, (except for incidental scrap sales such as for use as firewood). *[IAS 16.6, IAS 41.5B].*

Bearer plants are within the scope of IAS 16 and subject to all of the requirements therein. This includes the ability to choose between the cost model and revaluation model for subsequent measurement. Agricultural produce growing on bearer plants, e.g. the fruit growing on a tree, remains within the scope of IAS 41 (see Chapter 40). *[IAS 16.3(b), IAS 41.5C].*

The following are not included within the definition of bearer plants:

- plants cultivated to be harvested as agricultural produce, e.g. trees grown for use as lumber;
- plants cultivated to produce agricultural produce when there is more than a remote likelihood that the entity will also harvest and sell the plant as agricultural produce, other than as incidental scrap sales, e.g. trees that are cultivated both for their fruit and their lumber; and
- annual crops such as maize and wheat. *[IAS 41.5A].*

Bearer plants are accounted for in the same way as self-constructed items of PP&E before they are brought to the location and condition necessary to be capable of operating in the manner intended by management. Consequently, references to 'construction' in IAS 16, with respect to bearer plants, cover the activities that are necessary to cultivate such plants before they are brought in to the location and condition necessary to be capable of operating in the manner intended by management. *[IAS 16.22A].*

Bearer plants are subject to the requirements of IAS 16, and so entities will need to consider the correct unit of account, analyse which costs can be capitalised prior to maturity, set useful lives for depreciation purposes and consider the possibility of impairment.

For a more detailed discussion of the requirements, including some of the measurement challenges for bearer plants under IAS 16, see Chapter 40 at 1, 2.2.1.A, 2.3.3, and 3.2.3.A.

3.2 Accounting for parts ('components') of assets

IAS 16 has a single set of recognition criteria, which means that subsequent expenditure must also meet these criteria before it is recognised.

Parts of an asset are to be identified so that the cost of replacing a part may be recognised (i.e. capitalised as part of the asset) and the previous part derecognised. These parts are often referred to as 'components'. 'Parts' are distinguished from day-to-day servicing but they are not otherwise identified and defined; moreover, the unit of measurement to which the standard applies (i.e. what comprises an item of PP&E) is not itself defined.

IAS 16 requires 'significant parts' of an asset to be depreciated separately. These are parts that have a cost that is significant in relation to the total cost of the asset. An entity will have to identify the significant parts of the asset on initial recognition in order for it to depreciate each such part of the asset properly. *[IAS 16.43, 44]*. There is no requirement to identify all parts. IAS 16 requires entities to derecognise an existing part when it is replaced, regardless of whether it has been depreciated separately, and allows the carrying value of the part that has been replaced to be estimated, if necessary:

'If it is not practicable for an entity to determine the carrying amount of the replaced part, it may use the cost of the replacement as an indication of what the cost of the replaced part was at the time it was acquired or constructed.' *[IAS 16.70]*.

As a consequence, an entity may not actually identify the parts of an asset until it incurs the replacement expenditure, as in the following example.

Example 18.1: Recognition and derecognition of parts

An entity buys a piece of machinery with an estimated useful life of ten years for €10 million. The asset contains two identical pumps, which are assumed to have the same useful life as the machine of which they are a part. After seven years one of the pumps fails and is replaced at a cost of €200,000. The entity had not identified the pumps as separate parts and does not know the original cost. It uses the cost of the replacement part to estimate the carrying value of the original pump. With the help of the supplier, it estimates that the cost would have been approximately €170,000 and that this would have a remaining carrying value after seven year's depreciation of €51,000. Accordingly it derecognises €51,000 and capitalises the cost of the replacement.

If the entity has no better information than the cost of the replacement part, it appears that it is permitted to use a depreciated replacement cost basis to calculate the amount derecognised in respect of the original asset.

3.3 Initial and subsequent expenditure

IAS 16 makes no distinction in principle between the initial costs of acquiring an asset and any subsequent expenditure upon it. In both cases any and all expenditure has to meet the recognition rules, and be expensed in profit or loss if it does not. IAS 16 states:

'An entity evaluates under this recognition principle all its property, plant and equipment costs at the time they are incurred. These costs include costs incurred initially to acquire or construct an item of property, plant and equipment and costs incurred subsequently to add to, replace part of, or service it.' *[IAS 16.10].*

The standard draws a distinction between servicing and more major expenditures. Day-to-day servicing, by which is meant the repair and maintenance of PP&E that largely comprises labour costs, consumables and other minor parts, should be recognised in profit or loss as incurred. *[IAS 16.12].* However, if the expenditure involves replacing a significant part of the asset, this part should be capitalised as part of the PP&E, if the recognition criteria are met. The carrying amount of the part that has been replaced should be derecognised (see 7 below). *[IAS 16.13].* Examples of this treatment of major maintenance expenditure are shown in Extract 18.1 above and in Extract 18.3 and Extract 18.4 below.

Extract 18.3: Akzo Nobel N.V. (2016)

Notes to the Consolidated financial statements [extract]

1 **Note 1: Summary of significant accounting policies** [extract]

Property, plant and equipment (Note 9) [extract]

Costs of major maintenance activities are capitalized and depreciated over the estimated useful life. Maintenance costs which cannot be separately defined as a component of property, plant and equipment are expensed in the period in which they occur.

When IFRS 16 is adopted, lessees are required to recognise most leases in their statement of financial position as lease liabilities with corresponding right-of-use assets. Consequently, IFRS 16 amends paragraph 10 of IAS 16 (described above) to clarify that the cost of an item of PP&E may include costs incurred relating to leases of assets that are used to construct, add to, replace part of or service an item of PP&E, such as depreciation of right-of-use assets.

3.3.1 Types of parts

IAS 16 identifies two particular types of parts of assets. The first is an item that requires replacement at regular intervals during the life of the asset such as relining a furnace after a specified number of hours of use, or replacing the interiors of an aircraft (e.g. seats and galleys) several times during the life of the airframe. The second type involves less frequently recurring replacements, such as replacing the interior walls of a building, or to make a nonrecurring replacement. The standard requires that under the recognition principle described at 3 above, an entity recognises in the carrying amount of an item of PP&E the cost of replacing part of such an item when that cost is incurred and the recognition criteria are met while derecognising the carrying amount of the parts that have been replaced (see 7 below). *[IAS 16.13].*

IAS 16 does not state that these replacement expenditures necessarily qualify for recognition. Some of its examples, such as aircraft interiors, are clearly best treated as separate assets as they have a useful life different from that of the asset of which they are part. With the other examples, such as interior walls, it is less clear why they meet the recognition criteria. However, replacing internal walls or similar expenditures may extend the useful life of a building while upgrading machinery may increase its capacity, improve the quality of its output or reduce operating costs. Hence, this type of expenditure may give rise to future economic benefits.

This parts approach is illustrated by British Airways Plc in Extract 18.4 below and by Skanska in Extract 18.7 below.

Extract 18.4: British Airways Plc (2016)

Notes to the financial statements [extract]

2 **Significant accounting policies** [extract]

Property, plant and equipment [extract]

b **Fleet**

All aircraft are stated at the fair value of the consideration given after taking account of manufacturers' credits. Fleet assets owned, or held on finance leases, are depreciated at rates calculated to write down the cost to the estimated residual value at the end of their planned operational lives on a straight-line basis. Depreciation rates are specific to aircraft type, based on the Group's fleet plans, within overall parameters of seven and 29 years. For engines maintained under 'pay-as-you-go' contracts, the depreciation lives and residual values are the same as the aircraft to which the engines relate. For all other engines, the engine core is depreciated to its residual value over the average remaining life of the related fleet.

Cabin interior modifications, including those required for brand changes and relaunches, are depreciated over the lower of five years and the remaining life of the aircraft.

Aircraft and engine spares acquired on the introduction or expansion of a fleet, as well as rotable spares purchased separately, are carried as property, plant and equipment and generally depreciated in line with the fleet to which they relate.

Major overhaul expenditure, including replacement spares and labour costs, is capitalised and amortised over the average expected life between major overhauls. All other replacement spares and other costs relating to maintenance of fleet assets (including maintenance provided under 'pay-as-you-go' contracts) are charged to the income statement on consumption or as incurred respectively.

Note that 'Pay-as-you-go' contracts are not described in the financial statements above. These are comprehensive turbine engine maintenance and overhaul contracts, usually based on a fixed hourly fee for each hour flown and including loan engines when required.

3.3.2 Major inspections

The standard also allows a separate part to be recognised if an entity is required to perform regular major inspections for faults, regardless of whether any physical parts of the asset are replaced. *[IAS 16.14]*.

The reason for this approach is to maintain a degree of consistency with IAS 37 – *Provisions, Contingent Liabilities and Contingent Assets* – which forbids an entity to make provisions if there is no obligations. Therefore an entity is prohibited by IAS 37 from making, for example, a provision to overhaul an owned aircraft engine by annually providing for a quarter of the cost for four years and then utilising the provision when the engine is overhauled in the fourth year. *[IAS 37 IE Example 11A, 11B]*. This had been a common practice in the airline and oil refining industries, although it had never been universally applied in either sector; some companies accounted for the expenditure when incurred, others capitalised the cost and depreciated it over the period until the next major overhaul – as illustrated in Extract 18.4 above.

IAS 16 applies the same recognition criteria to the cost of major inspections. Inspection costs are not provided for in advance, rather they are added to the asset's cost if the recognition criteria are satisfied and any amount remaining from the previous inspection (as distinct from physical parts) is derecognised. This process of recognition and derecognition should take place regardless of whether the cost of the previous inspection was identified (and considered a separate part) when the asset was originally acquired or constructed. Therefore, if the element relating to the inspection had previously been identified, it would have been depreciated between that time and the current overhaul. However, if it had not previously been identified, the recognition and derecognition rules still apply, but the standard allows the estimated cost of a future similar inspection to be used as an indication of what the cost of the existing inspection component was when the item was acquired or constructed that must be derecognised. *[IAS 16.14]*. This appears to allow the entity to reconstruct the carrying amount of the previous inspection (i.e. to estimate the net depreciated carrying value of the previous inspection that will be derecognised) rather than simply using a depreciated replacement cost approach.

4 MEASUREMENT AT RECOGNITION

IAS 16 draws a distinction between measurement at recognition (i.e. the initial recognition of an item of PP&E on acquisition) and measurement after recognition (i.e. the subsequent treatment of the item). Measurement after recognition is discussed at 5 and 6 below.

The standard states that 'an item of property, plant and equipment that qualifies for recognition as an asset shall be measured at its cost'. *[IAS 16.15]*. What may be included in the cost of an item is discussed below.

4.1 Elements of cost and cost measurement

IAS 16 sets out what constitutes the cost of an item of PP&E on its initial recognition, as follows:

'The cost of an item of property, plant and equipment comprises:

(a) its purchase price, including import duties and non-refundable purchase taxes, after deducting trade discounts and rebates.

(b) any costs directly attributable to bringing the asset to the location and condition necessary for it to be capable of operating in the manner intended by management.

(c) the initial estimate of the costs of dismantling and removing the item and restoring the site on which it is located, the obligation for which an entity incurs either when the item is acquired or as a consequence of having used the item during a particular period for purposes other than to produce inventories during that period.' *[IAS 16.16]*.

The purchase price of an individual item of PP&E may be an allocation of the price paid for a group of assets. If an entity acquires a group of assets that do not comprise a business ('the group'), the principles in IFRS 3 – *Business Combinations* – are applied to allocate the entire cost to individual items (see Chapter 9 at 2.2.2). In such cases the acquirer should identify and recognise the individual identifiable assets acquired (including those assets that meet the definition of, and recognition criteria for, intangible assets in IAS 38) and liabilities assumed. The cost of the group should be allocated to the individual identifiable assets and liabilities on the basis of their relative fair values at the date of purchase. Such a transaction or event does not give rise to goodwill. *[IFRS 3.2(b)]*. In its June 2017 meeting, the Interpretations Committee considered two possible ways of applying the requirements in paragraph 2(b) of IFRS 3 (as described above) on the acquisition of the group particularly when the sum of individual fair values of the identifiable assets and liabilities is different from the transaction price and the group includes identifiable assets and liabilities initially measured both at cost and at an amount other than cost.[1] These two approaches are discussed in detail in Chapter 9 at 2.2.2. See also similar discussion relating to investment property in Chapter 19 at 4.1.1.

If an asset is used to produce inventories during a particular period, the costs of obligations that are incurred during that period to dismantle, remove or restore the site on which such asset has been located are dealt with in accordance with IAS 2, as a consequence of having used the asset to produce inventories during that period (see Chapter 22). *[IAS 16.18]*.

Note that all site restoration costs and other environmental restoration and similar costs must be estimated and capitalised at initial recognition, in order that such costs can be recovered over the life of the item of PP&E, even if the expenditure will only be incurred at the end of the item's life. The obligations are calculated in accordance with IAS 37 and IFRIC 1 – *Changes in Existing Decommissioning, Restoration and Similar Liabilities* (see 4.3 below and Chapter 28 at 4 and 6.3). *[IAS 16.18]*. This is illustrated in Extract 18.5 below.

Extract 18.5: Bayer Aktiengesellschaft (2015)

Notes to the Consolidated Financial Statements of the Bayer Group [extract]

4 Basic principles, methods and critical accounting estimates [extract]

Property, plant and equipment [extract]

Where an obligation exists to dismantle or remove an asset or restore a site to its former condition at the end of its useful life, the present value of the related future payments is capitalized along with the cost of acquisition or construction upon completion and a corresponding liability is recognized.

A common instance of (c) above is dilapidation obligations in lease agreements, under which a lessee is obliged to return premises to the landlord in an agreed condition. Arguably, a provision is required whenever the 'damage' is incurred. Therefore, if a retailer rents two adjoining premises and knocks down the dividing wall to convert the premises into one and has an obligation to make good at the end of the lease term, the tenant should immediately provide for the costs of so doing. The 'other side' of the provision entry is an asset that will be amortised over the lease term, notwithstanding the fact that some of the costs of modifying the premises may also have been capitalised as leasehold improvement assets. This is discussed in more detail in Chapter 28 at 6.9.

4.1.1 'Directly attributable' costs

This is the key issue in the measurement of cost. The standard gives examples of types of expenditure that are, and are not, considered to be directly attributable. The following are examples of those types of expenditure that are considered to be directly attributable and hence may be included in cost at initial recognition: *[IAS 16.17]*

(a) costs of employee benefits (as defined in IAS 19 – *Employee Benefits*) arising directly from the construction or acquisition of the item of PP&E. This means that the labour costs of an entity's own employees (e.g. site workers, in-house architects and surveyors) arising directly from the construction, or acquisition, of the specific item of PP&E may be recognised;

(b) costs of site preparation;

(c) initial delivery and handling costs;

(d) installation and assembly costs;

(e) costs of testing whether the asset is functioning properly, after deducting the net proceeds from selling any items produced while bringing the asset to that location and condition such as samples produced when testing equipment (see 4.2.1 below); and

(f) professional fees.

Income received during the period of construction of PP&E is considered further in 4.2.2 below.

In our view, amounts charged under operating leases during the construction period of an asset may also be a directly attributable cost that may be included as part of the cost of the PP&E if those lease costs are 'directly attributable to bringing the asset to the location and condition necessary for it to be capable of operating in the manner intended by management'. *[IAS 16.16]*. This may be the case, for example, where a building is constructed on land that is leased under an operating lease. This approach must be applied consistently.

The view above is consistent with IFRS 16, which, when adopted, will amend paragraph 10 of IAS 16 to clarify that the cost of an item of PP&E may include costs incurred relating to leases of assets that are used to construct, add to, replace part of or service an item of PP&E, such as depreciation of right-of-use assets (see 3.3 above).

Also, under IFRS 16, lessees are required to recognise all leases in their statement of financial position as lease liabilities with corresponding right-of-use assets, except for short-term leases and low-value assets if they choose to apply such exemptions. Lessees can make an accounting policy election to apply accounting similar to accounting for operating leases under IAS 17 to short-term leases (i.e. leases that, at the commencement date, have a lease term of 12 months or less and do not include an option to purchase the underlying asset) and to leases of low-value assets, subject to certain criteria. IFRS 16 is discussed in detail in Chapter 25.

4.1.2 Borrowing costs

Borrowing costs must be capitalised in respect of certain qualifying assets, if those assets are measured at cost. Therefore, an entity will capitalise borrowing costs on a self-constructed item of PP&E if it meets the criteria in IAS 23 – *Borrowing Costs*, as discussed at 4.1.5 below. *[IAS 16.22].*

Entities are not required to capitalise borrowing costs in respect of assets that are measured at fair value. This includes revalued PP&E which is measured at fair value through Other Comprehensive Income ('OCI'). Generally, an item of PP&E within scope of IAS 16 will only be carried at revalued amount once construction is completed, so capitalisation of borrowing costs will have ceased (see 4.1.4 below). This is not necessarily the case with investment property in the course of construction (see Chapter 19 at 2.5). The cost of the asset, before adopting a policy of revaluation, will include capitalised borrowing costs. However, to the extent that entities choose to capitalise borrowing costs in respect of assets still in the course of construction that are carried at fair value, the methods allowed by IAS 23 should be followed. The treatment of borrowing costs is discussed separately in Chapter 21.

For disclosure purposes, an entity will still need to monitor the carrying amount of PP&E measured under revaluation model, including those borrowing costs that would have been recognised had such an asset been carried under the cost model (see 8.2 below).

4.1.3 Administration and other general overheads

Administration and other general overhead costs are not costs of an item of PP&E. This means that employee costs not related to a specific asset, such as site selection activities and general management time do not qualify for capitalisation. Entities are also not allowed to recognise so-called 'start up costs' as part of the item of PP&E. These include costs related to opening a new facility, introducing a new product or service (including costs of advertising and promotional activities), conducting business in a new territory or with a new class of customer (including costs of staff training) and similar items. *[IAS 16.19].* These costs should be accounted for (in general, expensed as incurred) in the same way as similar costs incurred as part of the entity's on-going activities.

4.1.4 Cessation of capitalisation

Cost recognition ceases once an item of PP&E is in the location and condition necessary for it to be capable of operating in the manner intended by management. This will usually be the date of practical completion of the physical asset. IAS 16 therefore prohibits the recognition of relocation and reorganisation costs, costs incurred in using the asset or during the run up to full use once the asset is ready to be used, and any initial operating losses. *[IAS 16.20].* An entity is not precluded from continuing to capitalise costs during an initial commissioning period that is necessary for running in machinery or testing equipment. By contrast no new costs should be capitalised if the asset is fully operational but is not yet achieving its targeted profitability because demand is still building up, for example in a new hotel that initially has high room vacancies or a partially let investment property. In these cases, the asset is clearly in the location and condition necessary for it to be capable of operating in the manner intended by management.

4.1.5 Self-built assets

If an asset is self-built by the entity, the same general principles apply as for an acquired asset. If the same type of asset is made for resale by the business, the cost of such asset is usually the same as the cost of constructing of an asset for sale, i.e. without including any internal profit element but including attributable overheads in accordance with IAS 2 (see Chapter 22). The costs of abnormal amounts of wasted resources, whether labour, materials or other resources, are not included in the cost of such self-built assets. IAS 23, discussed in Chapter 21, contains criteria relating to the recognition of any interest as a component of the carrying amount of a self-built item of PP&E. *[IAS 16.22]*.

KAZ Minerals PLC provides an example of an accounting policy for self-built assets.

Extract 18.6: KAZ Minerals PLC (2016)

NOTES TO THE CONSOLIDATED FINANCIAL STATEMENTS [extract]

35. **Summary of significant accounting policies** [extract]

(d) **Property, plant and equipment** [extract]

(i) **Initial Measurement** [extract]

The cost of self-constructed assets includes the cost of materials, direct labour and an appropriate proportion of production overheads.

4.1.6 *Deferred payment*

IAS 16 specifically precludes the capitalisation of hidden credit charges as part of the cost of an item of PP&E, so the cost of an item of PP&E is its cash price equivalent at the recognition date. This means that if payment is made in some other manner, the cost to be capitalised is the normal cash price. Thus, if the payment terms are extended beyond 'normal' credit terms, the cost to be recognised must be the cash price equivalent and any difference between the cash price equivalent and the total payment must be treated and recognised as an interest expense over the period of credit unless such interest is capitalised in accordance with IAS 23 (see 4.1.2 above). *[IAS 16.23]*. Assets held under finance leases in accordance with IAS 17 and right-of-use assets under IFRS 16, if adopted, are discussed in Chapters 24 and 25, respectively. Assets partly paid for by government grants are discussed in Chapter 26.

4.1.7 *Land and buildings to be redeveloped*

It is common for property developers to acquire land with an existing building where the planned redevelopment necessitates the demolition of that building and its replacement with a new building that is to be held to earn rentals or will be owner occupied. Whilst IAS 16 requires that the building and land be classified as two separate items (see 5.4.2 below), in our view it is appropriate, if the existing building is unusable or likely to be demolished by any party acquiring it, that the entire or a large part of the purchase price be allocated to the land. Similarly, subsequent demolition costs should be treated as being attributable to the cost of the land.

Owner-occupiers may also replace existing buildings with new facilities for their own use or to rent to others. Here the consequences are different and the carrying amount of the existing building cannot be rolled into the costs of the new development. The existing building must be depreciated over its remaining useful life to reduce the carrying amount of the asset to its residual value (presumably nil) at the point at which it is demolished. Consideration will have to be given as to whether the asset is impaired in accordance with IAS 36 (see 5.7 below). Many properties do not directly generate independent cash inflows (i.e. they are part of a cash-generating unit) and reducing the useful life will not necessarily lead to an impairment of the cash-generating unit, although by the time the asset has been designated for demolition it may no longer be part of a cash-generating unit (see Chapter 20 at 2.1.3 and 3).

Developers or owner-occupiers replacing an existing building with a building to be sold in the ordinary course of their business will deal with the land and buildings under IAS 2 (see Chapter 22 at 4.2.2).

4.1.8 Transfers of assets from customers (IFRIC 18)

Customer consideration may be in the form of goods, services or other non-cash consideration (e.g. PP&E). When an entity (i.e. the seller or vendor) receives, or expects to receive, non-cash consideration, the fair value of the non-cash consideration is included in the transaction price. *[IFRS 15.66].* The IFRS 15 requirements regarding non-cash consideration are discussed in detail in Chapter 30 at 5.6.

Before adoption of IFRS 15, IFRIC 18 – *Transfers of Assets from Customers* – provided guidance when entities receive contributions of PP&E from customers.

Examples include:

- a supplier who receives a contribution to the development costs of specific tooling equipment from another manufacturer to whom the supplier will sell parts, using that specific tooling equipment under a supply agreement;
- suppliers of utilities who receive items of PP&E from customers that are used to connect them to a network through which they will receive ongoing services (e.g. electricity, gas, water or telephone services). A typical arrangement is one in which a builder or individual householder must pay for power cables, pipes, or other connections; and
- in outsourcing arrangements, the existing assets are often contributed to the service provider, or the customer must pay for assets, or both.

This raises questions about recognising assets for which the entity has not paid. In what circumstances should the entity recognise these assets, at what carrying amount and how is the 'other side' of the accounting entry dealt with? Is it revenue and if so, how and over what period is it recognised? There are a number of potential answers to this and, unsurprisingly, practice had differed.

IFRIC 18 applied to all agreements under which an entity receives from a customer, or another party, an item of PP&E (or cash for the acquisition or construction of such items) that the entity must then use either to connect the customer to a network or to provide the customer with ongoing access to a supply of goods or services or both. Transfers that are government grants within the scope of IAS 20 – *Accounting for Government Grants and Disclosure of Government Assistance* – or assets used in a service concession within the scope of IFRIC 12 – *Service Concession Arrangements* – were out of scope of IFRIC 18.

If the item of PP&E meets the definition of an asset as set out in the *Framework*, as described at 3 above, then the transferred asset is measured at its fair value and this becomes its cost on initial recognition. *[IFRIC 18.11].* This means that the entity has to demonstrate that it controls the asset. It does not have to own it but 'control' generally means that it can deal with the asset as it pleases, for example use it to produce goods and services, lease it to others, sell it or scrap it and replace it without the consent of others.

Control of assets is discussed in the following examples, extracted from IFRIC 18's illustrative examples 1 and 2. In both cases it is noteworthy that the utility receives the asset from another party (a builder) and not the ultimate customer.

Example 18.2: IFRIC 18 and control of assets

Situation 1

A real estate company is building a residential development in an area that is not connected to the electricity network. In order to have access to the electricity network, the real estate company is required to construct an electricity substation that is then transferred to the network company responsible for the transmission of electricity. It is assumed in this example that the network company concludes that the transferred substation meets the definition of an asset. The network company then uses the substation to connect each house of the residential development to its electricity network. In this case, it is the homeowners that will eventually use the network to access the supply of electricity, although they did not initially transfer the substation.

Alternatively, the network company could have constructed the substation and received a transfer of an amount of cash from the real estate company that had to be used only for the construction of the substation. The amount of cash transferred would not necessarily equal the entire cost of the substation. It is assumed that the substation remains an asset of the network company

In this example, the IFRIC 18 applied to the network company that receives the electricity substation from the real estate company. The network company recognises the substation as an item of PP&E and measures its cost on initial recognition at its fair value or at its construction cost in the circumstances described in the preceding paragraph.

Situation 2

A house builder constructs a house on a redeveloped site in a major city. As part of constructing the house, the house builder installs a pipe from the house to the water main in front of the house. Because the pipe is on the house's land, the owner of the house can restrict access to the pipe. The owner is also responsible for the maintenance of the pipe. In this example, the facts indicate that the definition of an asset is not met for the water company.

Alternatively, a house builder constructs multiple houses and installs a pipe on the commonly owned or public land to connect the houses to the water main. The house builder transfers ownership of the pipe to the water company that will be responsible for its maintenance. In this example, the facts indicate that the water company controls the pipe and should recognise it.

If the entity does control the asset then it is recognised as PP&E and accounted for thereafter in the same manner as any other item of PP&E.

The transaction is treated as an exchange transaction involving dissimilar goods and services under IAS 18 – *Revenue* – not as an exchange of assets under IAS 16 as described at 4.4 below and revenue is recognised. It will be necessary to identify the separate services that are to be provided in exchange for the item of PP&E. *[IFRIC 18.14].* This is in order to allocate revenue to these elements and to determine the manner in which that revenue should be recognised. If the only service is connection to the network, usually evidenced by the contributing customer paying the same as others who have not made contributions, then revenue will be recognised on connection. Allocation and recognition of revenue is described in more detail in Chapter 29.

IFRIC 18 did not provide guidance on how the fair value of the PP&E should be allocated to any separately identifiable services, but the Basis for Conclusions referred to both IFRIC 12 and IFRIC 13 – *Customer Loyalty Programmes* – where it noted that such guidance (which is based upon fair values of the separate components) was provided. IFRIC 12 is discussed in Chapter 27 and IFRIC 13 in Chapter 29 at 5.15. Revenue recognition under IFRIC 18 is discussed further in Chapter 29 at 5.14.

IAS 18, IFRIC 13 and IFRIC 18 were superseded by IFRS 15, which must be applied to financial statements for periods beginning on or after 1 January 2018 (see 1 above). For further discussion of IFRS 15, see Chapter 30.

4.1.9 Variable pricing

The final purchase price of an item of PP&E is not always known when the terms include a variable or contingent amount that is linked to future events that cannot be determined at the date of acquisition. The total consideration could vary based on the performance of an asset – for example, the revenue or EBITDA generated, for a specified future period, by the asset or a business in which the asset is used. Generally, we would believe that a financial liability relating to variable consideration arises on the purchase of an item of PP&E and any measurement changes to that liability would be recorded in the statement of profit or loss as required by IFRS 9 (or IAS 39 – *Financial Instruments: Recognition and Measurement*). However, in some instances contracts are more complex and it can be argued that the subsequent changes to the initial estimate of the purchase price should be capitalised as part of the asset value, similar to any changes in a decommissioning liability recorded under IFRIC 1 (see 4.3 below). The Interpretations Committee and the IASB discussed this issue for a number of years, in order to clarify how the initial recognition and subsequent changes should be recognised, but no conclusion has been reached to date of writing this chapter.

In March 2016, the Interpretations Committee determined that this issue was too broad for it to address within the confines of existing IFRSs. The Interpretations Committee decided not to add this issue to its agenda and concluded that the IASB should address the accounting for variable payments comprehensively.[2] In May 2016 the IASB tentatively decided to include '*Variable and Contingent Consideration*' in its pipeline of future research projects. The IASB expects to begin work on projects in its research pipeline between 2017 and 2021.[3]

In the meantime, an entity should develop an accounting policy for variable consideration relating to the purchase of PP&E in accordance with the hierarchy in IAS 8 – *Accounting Policies, Changes in Accounting Estimates and Errors.* In practice, there are different approaches for treating the estimated future variable payments. Some entities do not capitalise these amounts upon initial recognition of the asset and then either expense or capitalise any payments as they are incurred. Other entities include an estimate of future amounts payable on initial recognition with a corresponding liability being recorded. Under this approach subsequent changes in the liability are either capitalised or expensed. An entity should exercise judgement in developing and consistently applying an accounting policy that results in information that is relevant and reliable in its particular circumstances. *[IAS 8.10]*. For more discussion see Chapter 17 at 4.5.

4.2 Incidental and non-incidental income

Under IAS 16, the cost of an item of PP&E includes any costs directly attributable to bringing the asset to the location and condition necessary for it to be capable of operating in the manner intended by management. *[IAS 16.16(b)].* However, before or during the construction of an asset, an entity may enter into incidental operations that are not, in themselves, necessary to meet this objective. *[IAS 16.21].*

The standard gives the example of income earned by using a building site as a car park prior to starting construction. Because incidental operations are not required in order to bring an asset to the location or condition necessary for it to be capable of operating in the manner intended by management, the income and related expenses of incidental operations are recognised in profit or loss and included in their respective classifications of income and expense. *[IAS 16.21].* Such incidental income and related expenses are not included in determining the cost of the asset.

If, however, some income is generated wholly and necessarily as a result of the process of bringing the asset into the location and condition for its intended use, for example from the sale of samples produced when testing the equipment concerned, then the income should be credited to the cost of the asset (see 4.2.1 below). *[IAS 16.17].*

On the other hand, if the asset is already in the location and condition necessary for it to be capable of being used in the manner intended by management then IAS 16 requires capitalisation to cease and depreciation to start. *[IAS 16.20].* In these circumstances all income earned from using the asset must be recognised as revenue in profit or loss and the related costs should include an element of depreciation of the asset.

4.2.1 Income earned while bringing the asset to the intended location and condition

As noted above, the directly attributable costs of an item of PP&E include the costs of testing whether the asset is functioning properly, after deducting the net proceeds from selling any items produced while bringing the asset to that location and condition. *[IAS 16.17].* The standard gives the example of samples produced when testing equipment.

There are other situations in which income may be earned whilst bringing the asset to the intended location and condition. This issue is common in the mining and oil and gas sectors, where test production may be sold during the commission stage of a mine or oil well (see Chapter 41 at 12). In these and other examples, it is possible that the net proceeds from selling items produced while testing the plant under construction may exceed the cost of related testing. IAS 16 is not clear as to whether such excess proceeds should be recognised in profit or loss or as a deduction from the cost of the asset.

The Interpretations Committee received a request to clarify two specific aspects of IAS 16, including:

(a) whether the proceeds referred to in IAS 16 relate only to items produced from testing; and

(b) whether an entity deducts from the cost of an item of PP&E any proceeds that exceed the cost of testing.

After exploring different approaches to the issue, the Interpretations Committee recommended, and the IASB agreed, to propose an amendment to IAS 16.

In June 2017, the IASB issued the exposure draft ('ED') *Property, Plant and Equipment – Proceeds before Intended Use (Proposed amendments to IAS 16).* It proposes to amend paragraph 17(e) of IAS 16 to prohibit deducting from the cost of an item of PP&E, any proceeds from selling items produced while bringing that asset to the location and condition necessary for it to be capable of operating in the manner intended by management (i.e. the point up until it is available for intended use). Instead, the ED proposes to add paragraph 20A to clarify that such proceeds and the costs of producing those items would be recognised in profit or loss in accordance with applicable standards.

The ED indicates that there would be no basis on which to conclude that such items would not be output from the entity's ordinary activities. Consequently, proceeds from selling inventories produced would represent revenue from contracts with customers in the scope of IFRS 15, i.e. the sales proceeds of items produced by PP&E before it is ready for its intended use would be required to be accounted for and disclosed in accordance with IFRS 15 in profit or loss.

The IASB also decided that additional disclosure requirements were not required because the existing requirements of relevant standards were sufficient. If revenue and the cost of inventories produced before an item of PP&E is available for its intended use have a material effect on an entity's financial statements, the entity would disclose the information required by IFRS 15 (in particular, revenue from sale of these pre-production inventories might be considered as a category of revenue when disclosing disaggregated revenue information) and the information required by IAS 2 (the disclosures regarding the costs of producing inventories, e.g. the accounting policy adopted, the carrying amount of inventories (if any) and the amount of inventories recognised as an expense).

The ED proposes that an entity apply the amendments retrospectively only to items of PP&E brought to the location and condition necessary for them to be capable of operating in the manner intended by management on or after the beginning of the earliest period presented in the financial statements in which the entity first applies the amendments. The cumulative effect of initially applying the amendments would be presented as an adjustment to the opening balance of retained earnings (or other component of equity, as appropriate) at the beginning of that earliest period presented. The IASB will decide on the effective date when it finalises the proposed amendments.[4]

For more details of the development of the interpretation and considerations for extractive industries, see Chapter 41 at 12.1.2 and 12.1.2.A.

4.2.2 *Income received during the construction of property*

One issue that commonly arises is whether rental and similar income generated by existing tenants in a property development may be capitalised and offset against the cost of developing that property.

The relevant question is whether the leasing arrangements with the existing tenants are a necessary activity to bring the development property to the location and condition necessary for it to be capable of operating in the manner intended by management. Whilst the existence of the tenant may be a fact, it is not a necessary condition for the building to be developed to the condition intended by management; the building could have been developed in the absence of any existing tenants.

Therefore, rental and similar income from existing tenants are incidental to the development and should not be capitalised. Rather rental and similar income should be recognised in profit or loss in accordance with the requirements of IAS 17 (or IFRS 16, once adopted) together with related expenses.

4.2.3 Liquidated damages during construction

Income may arise in other ways, for example, liquidated damages received as a result of delays by a contractor constructing an asset. Normally such damages received should be set off against the asset cost – the purchase price of the asset is reduced to compensate for delays in delivery.

4.3 Accounting for changes in decommissioning and restoration costs

IAS 16 requires the initial estimate of the costs of dismantling and removing an item of PP&E and restoring the site on which it is located to be included as part of the item's cost. This applies whether the obligation is incurred either when the item is acquired or as a consequence of having used the item during a particular period for purposes other than to produce inventories during that period. *[IAS 16.16]*. See 4.1 above. However, IAS 16 does not address the extent to which an item's carrying amount should be affected by changes in the estimated amount of dismantling and site restoration costs that occur after the estimate made upon initial measurement. This issue is the subject of IFRIC 1, which applies to any decommissioning, restoration or similar liability that has been both included as part of the cost of an asset measured in accordance with IAS 16 and recognised as a liability in accordance with IAS 37. *[IFRIC 1.2]*. It deals with the impact of events that change the measurement of an existing decommissioning, restoration or similar liability. Events include a change in the estimated cash flows, a change in the discount rate and the unwinding of the discount. *[IFRIC 1.3]*. This is discussed in detail in Chapter 28 at 6.3.

4.4 Exchanges of assets

An entity might swap an asset it does not require in a particular area, for one it does in another – the opposite being the case for the counterparty. Such exchanges are not uncommon in the telecommunications, media and leisure businesses, particularly after an acquisition. Governmental competition rules sometimes require such exchanges. The question arises whether such transactions give rise to a gain in circumstances where the carrying value of the outgoing facility is less than the fair value of the incoming one. This can occur when carrying values are less than market values, although it is possible that a transaction with no real commercial substance could be arranged solely to boost apparent profits.

IAS 16 requires all acquisitions of PP&E in exchange for non-monetary assets, or a combination of monetary and non-monetary assets, to be measured at fair value, subject to conditions:

'The cost of such an item of property, plant and equipment is measured at fair value unless (a) the exchange transaction lacks commercial substance or (b) the fair value of neither the asset received nor the asset given up is reliably measurable. The acquired item is measured in this way even if an entity cannot immediately derecognise the asset given up.' *[IAS 16.24]*.

The IASB concluded that the recognition of income from an exchange of assets does not depend on whether the assets exchanged are dissimilar. *[IAS 16.BC19]*.

If at least one of the two fair values can be measured reliably, that value is used for measuring the exchange transaction; if not, then the exchange is measured at the carrying value of the asset the entity no longer owns. *[IAS 16.24]*. For example, if the new asset's fair value is higher than the carrying amount of the old asset, a gain may be recognised.

This requirement is qualified by a 'commercial substance' test. If it is not possible to demonstrate that the transaction has commercial substance as defined by the standard (see 4.4.1 below), assets received in exchange transactions will be recorded at the carrying value of the asset given up. *[IAS 16.24]*.

If the transaction passes the 'commercial substance' test then IAS 16 requires the exchanged asset to be recorded at its fair value. As discussed in 7 below, the standard requires gains or losses on items that have been derecognised to be included in profit or loss in the period of derecognition but does not allow gains on derecognition to be classified as revenue, except for certain assets previously held for rental. *[IAS 16.68]*. It gives no further indication regarding their classification in profit or loss. It should be noted that prior to adoption of IFRS 15, the exchange of goods and services arising in the course of an entity's ordinary activities was dealt with in IAS 18 which in general took a different approach from IAS 16. Under IAS 18, when such goods or services are exchanged or swapped for goods or services that are of a similar nature and value, the exchange was not regarded as a transaction that generated revenue (see Chapter 29 at 3.9). *[IAS 18.12]*. Such exchanges of goods and services are also excluded from the scope of IFRS 15 if the non-monetary exchange is between entities in the same line of business to facilitate sales to customers or potential customers (see Chapter 30 at 2). *[IFRS 15.5(d)]*.

4.4.1 Commercial substance

The commercial substance test was put in place as an anti-abuse provision to prevent gains from being recognised in income when the transaction had no discernible effect on the entity's economics. *[IAS 16.BC21]*. The commercial substance of an exchange is to be determined by forecasting and comparing the future cash flows budgeted to be generated by the incoming and outgoing assets. For there to be commercial substance, there must be a significant difference between the two forecasts. The standard sets out this requirement as follows:

'An entity determines whether an exchange transaction has commercial substance by considering the extent to which its future cash flows are expected to change as a result of the transaction. An exchange transaction has commercial substance if:

(a) the configuration (risk, timing and amount) of the cash flows of the asset received differs from the configuration of the cash flows of the asset transferred; or

(b) the entity-specific value of the portion of the entity's operations affected by the transaction changes as a result of the exchange; and

(c) the difference in (a) or (b) is significant relative to the fair value of the assets exchanged.' *[IAS 16.25]*.

As set out in the definitions of the standard, entity-specific value in item (b) above is the net present value of the future predicted cash flows from continuing use and disposal of the asset (see 2.2 above). Post-tax cash flows should be used for this calculation. The standard contains no guidance on the discount rate to be used for this exercise, nor on any of the other parameters involved, but it does suggest that the result of these analyses might be clear without having to perform detailed calculations. *[IAS 16.25]*. Care will have to be taken to ensure that the transaction has commercial substance as defined in the standard if an entity receives a similar item of PP&E in exchange for a similar asset of its own. Commercial substance may be difficult to demonstrate if the entity is exchanging an asset for a similar one in a similar location. However, in the latter case, the risk, timing and amount of cash flows could differ if one asset were available for sale and the entity intended to sell it whereas the previous asset could not be realised by sale or only sold over a much longer timescale. It is feasible that such a transaction could meet conditions (a) and (c) above. Similarly, it would be unusual if the entity-specific values of similar assets differed enough in any arm's length exchange transaction to meet condition (c).

Other types of exchange are more likely to pass the 'commercial substance' test, for example exchanging an interest in an investment property for one that the entity uses for its own purposes. The entity has exchanged a rental stream and instead has an asset that contributes to the cash flows of the cash-generating unit of which it is a part. In this case it is probable that the risk, timing and amount of the cash flows of the asset received would differ from the configuration of the cash flows of the asset transferred.

4.4.2 Reliably measurable

In the context of asset exchanges, the standard contains guidance on the reliable determination of fair values in the circumstances where market values do not exist. The 'reliable measurement' test for using fair value was included to measure these exchanges to minimise the risk that entities could 'manufacture' gains by attributing inflated values to the assets exchanged. *[IAS 16.BC23]*. Note that fair value is defined by reference to IFRS 13 and that the requirements below are specific to asset exchanges in IAS 16.

'The fair value of an asset is reliably measurable if (a) the variability in the range of reasonable fair value measurements is not significant for that asset or (b) the probabilities of the various estimates within the range can be reasonably assessed and used when measuring fair value. If an entity is able to measure reliably the fair value of either the asset received or the asset given up, then the fair value of the asset given up is used to measure the cost of the asset received unless the fair value of the asset received is more clearly evident.' *[IAS 16.26]*. If the fair value of neither the asset given up nor the asset received can be measured reliably (i.e. neither (a) nor (b) above are met), the cost of the asset is measured at the carrying amount of the asset given up; this means there is no gain on the transaction. *[IAS 16.24]*.

No further guidance is given in IAS 16 on how to assemble a 'range of reasonable fair value measurements' and the guidance in IFRS 13 should be followed (see Chapter 14).

4.5 Assets held under finance leases

The cost at initial recognition of assets held by a lessee under finance leases is determined in accordance with IAS 17, as described in Chapter 24. *[IAS 16.27]*.

When IFRS 16 is adopted, it will delete paragraph 27 of IAS 16 (described above) and will instead require lessees to initially measure the right-of-use asset at the amount of lease liability, adjusted for lease prepayments, lease incentives received, initial direct costs and an estimate of restoration, removal and dismantling costs. IFRS 16 is discussed in detail in Chapter 25.

4.6 Assets acquired with the assistance of government grants

The carrying amount of an item of PP&E may be reduced by government grants in accordance with IAS 20. *[IAS 16.28]*. This is one of the accounting treatments available which are discussed further in Chapter 26.

5 MEASUREMENT AFTER RECOGNITION: COST MODEL

IAS 16 allows one of two alternatives to be chosen as the accounting policy for measurement of PP&E after initial recognition. The choice made must be applied to an entire class of PP&E, which means that not all classes are required to have the same policy. *[IAS 16.29]*.

The first alternative is the cost model whereby the item, after recognition as an asset, is carried at cost less any accumulated depreciation and less any accumulated impairment losses. *[IAS 16.30]*. The alternative, the revaluation model, is discussed at 6 below. *[IAS 16.29]*.

Some entities operate, either internally or externally, an investment fund that provides investors with benefits determined by units in the fund. Similarly, some entities issue groups of insurance contracts with direct participation features and hold the underlying items. Some such funds or underlying items include owner-occupied property. For many contracts that specify a link to returns on underlying items, those underlying items include a mix of assets that are almost all measured at fair value through profit or loss. Accordingly, the Board decided that measurement of owner-occupied property at fair value through profit or loss would be consistent with the measurement of the majority of the underlying assets and would prevent accounting mismatches. *[IFRS 17.BC65(c)]*.

Consequently, when IFRS 17 is adopted (see 1 above), the subsequent measurement requirements in IAS 16 will be amended by adding paragraphs 29A and 29B to permit entities to elect to measure owner-occupied properties in such specified circumstances as if they were investment properties measured at fair value through profit or loss in accordance with IAS 40, despite paragraph 29 (as described above). For the purposes of this election, insurance contracts include investment contracts with discretionary participation features. An entity shall treat owner-occupied property measured using the investment property fair value model as a separate class of PP&E.

5.1 Significant parts of assets

IAS 16 links its recognition concept of a 'part' of an asset, discussed at 3.2 above, with the analysis of assets for the purpose of depreciation. Each part of an asset with a cost that is significant in relation to the total cost of the item must be depreciated separately, which means that the initial cost must be allocated between the significant parts by the entity. *[IAS 16.43, 44]*. The standard once again refers to the airframe and engines of an aircraft (whether owned or subject to a finance lease) but also sets out that if an entity acquires PP&E subject to an operating lease in which it is the lessor, it may be appropriate to depreciate separately amounts reflected in the cost of that item that are attributable to favourable or unfavourable lease terms relative to market terms. *[IAS 16.44]*. IFRS 16, when adopted, will amend paragraph 44 of IAS 16 (described above) by deleting the phrase 'whether owned or subject to a finance lease' when referring to the example given above (i.e. airframe and engines of an aircraft).

A determination of the significant parts of office buildings can be seen in Extract 18.7 below from Skanska. This policy may have been based on the construction methods used for the particular buildings as it is unusual to see a separation between foundation and frame for office buildings. In addition, Extract 19.1 in Chapter 19 shows an example of the allocation for investment property, although favourable or unfavourable lease terms are not identified as a separate part.

Extract 18.7: Skanska AB (2016)

Notes including accounting and valuation principles [extract]

Note 1. Consolidated accounting and valuation principles [extract]

IAS 16 Property, Plant and Equipment [extract]

Property, plant and equipment that consist of parts with different periods of service are treated as separate components of property, plant and equipment. Depreciation occurs on a straight-line basis during the estimated useful life or based on degree of use, taking into account any residual value at the end of the period. Office buildings are divided into foundation and frame, with a depreciation period of 50 years, installations of 35 years, and non-weight-bearing parts of 15 years. In general, industrial buildings are depreciated over a 20-year period without allocation into different parts. Stone crushing and asphalt plants as well as concrete mixing plants are depreciated over 10 to 25 years depending on their condition when acquired and without being divided into different parts. For other buildings and equipment, division into different components occurs only if major components with different useful lives can be identified. For other machinery and equipment, the depreciation period is normally between five and 10 years. Minor equipment is depreciated immediately. Gravel pits and stone quarries are depreciated as materials are removed. Land is not depreciated. Assessments of an asset's residual value and period of service are performed annually.

Because parts of an item of PP&E are identified by their significant cost rather than their effect on depreciation, they may have the same useful lives and depreciation method and the standard allows them to be grouped for depreciation purposes. *[IAS 16.45]*. It also identifies other circumstances in which the significant parts do not correspond to the depreciable components within the asset. To the extent that an entity depreciates separately some parts of an item of PP&E, it also depreciates separately the remainder of the item. The remainder of such asset that has not separately been identified into parts may consist of other parts that are individually not significant and if the entity has varying expectations for these parts, it may need to use approximation techniques to calculate an appropriate depreciation method for all of these parts in a manner that faithfully represents the consumption pattern and/or useful life of such parts. *[IAS 16.46]*. The standard also allows an entity to depreciate separately such parts that are not significant in relation to the total cost of the whole asset. *[IAS 16.47]*.

The depreciation charge for each period is recognised in profit or loss unless it forms part of the cost of another asset and included in its carrying amount. *[IAS 16.48]*. Sometimes, the future economic benefits embodied in an asset are absorbed in producing other assets, for example, the depreciation of manufacturing plant and equipment is included as part of the cost of conversion of finished manufactured goods held in inventory in accordance with IAS 2, and similarly, depreciation of PP&E used for development activities may be included as part of the cost of an intangible asset recognised in accordance with IAS 38. *[IAS 16.49]*.

5.2 Depreciable amount and residual values

The depreciable amount of an item of PP&E is its cost, or other amount substituted for cost (e.g. valuation), less its estimated residual value. *[IAS 16.6]*. The standard states that an entity should review the residual value of an item of PP&E, and therefore all parts of it, at least at each financial year-end. If the estimated residual value differs from the previous estimate, the change should be accounted for prospectively as a change in accounting estimate in accordance with IAS 8 (see Chapter 3 at 4.5). *[IAS 16.51]*.

The residual value of an item of PP&E is the estimated amount that an entity would currently obtain from disposal of the asset, after deducting the estimated costs of disposal, if the asset were already of the age and assuming that it was already in the condition it will be in at the end of its useful life. *[IAS 16.6]*. Therefore, IAS 16 contains an element of continuous updating of one component of an asset's carrying value because it is the current disposal amount (e.g. value at financial reporting date) of an asset's future state (i.e. asset's condition in the future when the entity expects to dispose of it). This means that only the changes up to the financial reporting date are taken into account and that expected future changes in residual value other than the effects of expected wear and tear are not taken into account. *[IAS 16.BC29]*.

As any change in the residual value directly affects the depreciable amount, it may also affect the depreciation charge. This is because the depreciable amount (i.e. the amount actually charged to profit or loss over the life of the asset) is calculated by deducting the residual value from the cost (or other amount substituted for cost, such as valuation) of the asset. Sometimes, the residual value of an asset may increase to an amount equal to or greater than the asset's carrying amount. If it does, the residual value is capped at the asset's carrying amount. This means that in such a case, the asset's depreciation charge is zero unless and until its residual value subsequently decreases to an amount below the asset's carrying amount. *[IAS 16.53, 54]*.

In practice, many items of PP&E have a negligible residual value. *[IAS 16.54]*. This is usually because they are kept for significantly all of their useful lives. Residual values are of no relevance if the entity intends to keep the asset for significantly all of its useful life. If an entity uses residual values based on prices fetched in the market for a type of asset that it holds, it must also demonstrate an intention to dispose of that asset before the end of its economic life.

The requirement concerning the residual values of assets highlights how important it is that residual values are considered and reviewed in conjunction with the review of useful lives. The useful life is the period over which the entity expects to use the asset, not the asset's economic life.

5.3 Depreciation charge

The standard requires the depreciable amount of an asset to be allocated on a systematic basis over its useful life. *[IAS 16.50]*.

The standard makes it clear that depreciation must be charged on all items of PP&E, including those carried under the revaluation model, even if the fair value of an asset is higher than its carrying amount, as long as the residual value of the asset is lower than its carrying amount. *[IAS 16.52]*. If the residual value exceeds the carrying amount, no depreciation is charged until the residual value once again decreases to less than the carrying amount (see 5.2 above). *[IAS 16.54]*. IAS 16 makes it clear that the repair and maintenance of an asset do not, of themselves, negate the need to depreciate it. *[IAS 16.52]*.

There is no requirement in IAS 16 for an automatic impairment review if no depreciation is charged.

5.4 Useful lives

One of the critical assumptions on which the depreciation charge depends is the useful life of the asset. The standard requires the useful life of an asset to be estimated on a realistic basis and reviewed at least at the end of each financial year. The effects of changes in useful life are to be recognised prospectively as changes in accounting estimates in accordance with IAS 8 (see Chapter 3 at 4.5), over the remaining useful life of the asset. *[IAS 16.51]*.

As described in 2.2 above, the useful life of an asset is defined in terms of the asset's expected utility to the entity. *[IAS 16.57]*. It is the period over which the present owner will benefit from using the asset and not the total potential life of the asset; the two will often not be the same.

It is quite possible for an asset's useful life to be shorter than its economic life. The estimation of the useful life of the asset is a matter of judgement based on the experience of the entity with similar assets. Many entities have an asset management policy that may involve disposal of assets after a specified time or after consumption of a specified proportion of the future economic benefits embodied in the assets. *[IAS 16.57]*. This often occurs when disposing of assets when they still have a residual value, which means that another user can benefit from the asset. This is particularly common with property and motor vehicles, where there are effective second-hand markets, but less usual for plant and machinery. For example, an entity may have a policy of replacing all of its motor vehicles after three years, so this will be their estimated useful life for depreciation purposes. The entity will depreciate them over this period down to the estimated residual value. The residual values of motor vehicles are often easy to obtain and the entity will be able to reassess these residuals in line with the requirements of the standard. Thus, the estimation of the useful life of the asset is a matter of judgement based on the experience of the entity with similar assets. *[IAS 16.57]*.

The future economic benefits embodied in an asset are consumed principally through usage. Other factors, however, should be taken into account such as technical or commercial obsolescence and wear and tear while an asset remains idle because they often result in the diminution of the economic benefits expected to be obtained from the asset. Consequently, IAS 16 provides guidance that all the following factors are to be considered when estimating the useful life of an asset:

(a) expected usage of the asset. Usage is assessed by reference to the asset's expected capacity or physical output.

(b) expected physical wear and tear, which depends on operational factors such as the number of shifts for which the asset is to be used and the repair and maintenance programme, and the care and maintenance of the asset while idle (see 5.4.1 below).

(c) technical or commercial obsolescence arising from changes or improvements in production, or from a change in the market demand for the product or service output of the asset. Expected future reductions in the selling price of an item that was produced using an asset could indicate the expectation of technical or commercial obsolescence of the asset, which, in turn, might reflect a reduction of the future economic benefits embodied in the asset (see 5.4.3 below).

(d) legal or similar limits on the use of the asset, such as the expiry dates of related leases. *[IAS 16.56]*.

Factor (d), above, states that the 'expiry dates of related leases' is considered when determining the asset's useful life. Generally, the useful life of the leasehold improvement is the same or less than the lease term, as defined by IAS 17 or IFRS 16, once adopted. However, a lessee may be able to depreciate an asset whose useful life exceeds the lease term over a longer period if the lease includes an option to extend that the lessee expects to exercise, even if the option is not considered 'reasonably certain' at inception (a higher threshold than the estimate of useful life in IAS 16). In such a case, the asset may be depreciated either over the lease term or over the shorter of the asset's useful life and the period for which the entity expects to extend the lease. 'Lease term' under IAS 17 and IFRS 16, if adopted, is discussed in Chapters 24 and 25, respectively.

ArcelorMittal is an example of an entity depreciating an asset over its expected usage by reference to the production period.

> *Extract 18.8: ArcelorMittal (2016)*
>
> Notes to the consolidated financial statements [extract]
>
> Note 5: Goodwill, intangible and tangible assets [extract]
>
> 5.2 Property, plant and equipment and biological assets [extract]
>
> Property, plant and equipment used in mining activities is depreciated over its useful life or over the remaining life of the mine, if shorter, and if there is no alternative use. For the majority of assets used in mining activities, the economic benefits from the asset are consumed in a pattern which is linked to the production level and accordingly, assets used in mining activities are primarily depreciated on a units-of-production basis. A unit-of-production is based on the available estimate of proven and probable reserves.

5.4.1 Repairs and maintenance

The initial assessment of the useful life of the asset will take into account the expected routine spending on repairs and expenditure necessary for it to achieve that life. Although IAS 16 implies that this refers to an item of plant and machinery, care and maintenance programmes are relevant to assessing the useful lives of many other types of asset. For example, an entity may assess the useful life of a railway engine at thirty-five years on the assumption that it has a major overhaul every seven years. Without this expenditure, the life of the engine would be much less certain and could be much shorter. Maintenance necessary to support the fabric of a building and its service potential will also be taken into account in assessing its useful life. Eventually, it will always become uneconomic for the entity to continue to maintain the asset so, while the expenditure may lengthen the useful life, it is unlikely to make it indefinite.

Note that this applies whether the expenditure is capitalised because it meets the definition of a 'major inspection' (see 3.3.2 above) or if it is repairs and maintenance that is expensed as incurred.

5.4.2 Land

The standard requires the land and the building elements of property to be accounted for as separate components, even when they are acquired together. Land, which usually has an unlimited life, is not usually depreciated, while buildings are depreciable assets because they have limited useful life. IAS 16 states that the determination of the depreciable amount and useful life of a building is not affected by an increase in the value of the land on which it stands. *[IAS 16.58]*.

There are circumstances in which depreciation may be applied to land. In those instances in which land has a finite life (e.g. land that is used either for extractive purposes such as a quarry or mine, or for some purpose such as landfill), it will be depreciated in an appropriate manner that reflects the benefits to be derived from it, but it is highly unlikely that there will be any issue regarding separating the interest in land from any building element. *[IAS 16.58, 59]*. Further, the cost of such land may include an element for site dismantlement, removal or restoration, e.g. the initial estimate of the costs of dismantling and removing the item and restoring the site on which it is located, and any subsequent changes thereto (described in 4.3 above). *[IAS 16.16]*. This element will have to be separated from the land element and depreciated over an appropriate period. The standard describes this as 'the period of benefits obtained by incurring these costs' which will often be the estimated useful life of the site for its purpose and function. *[IAS 16.59]*. An entity engaged in landfill on a new site may make a provision for restoring it as soon as it starts preparation by removing the overburden. It will separate the land from the 'restoration asset' and depreciate the restoration asset over the landfill site's estimated useful life. If the land has an infinite useful life, an appropriate depreciation basis will have to be chosen that reflects the period of benefits obtained from the restoration asset.

If the estimated costs are revised in accordance with IFRIC 1, the adjusted depreciable amount of the asset is depreciated over its useful life. Therefore, once the related asset has reached the end of its useful life, all subsequent changes in the liability will be recognised in profit or loss as they occur, irrespective of whether the entity applies the cost or revaluation model. *[IFRIC 1.7]*.

5.4.3 Technological change

A current or expected future reduction in the market demand for the product or service output of an asset may be evidence of technical or commercial obsolescence, which, in turn, might reflect a reduction of the future economic benefits embodied in the asset. If an entity anticipates such technical or commercial obsolescence, it should reassess both the useful life of an asset and the pattern of consumption of future economic benefits. *[IAS 16.56(c), 61]*. In such cases, it might be more appropriate to use a diminishing balance method of depreciation to reflect the pattern of consumption (see 5.6.1 below).

The effects of technological change are often underestimated. It affects many assets, not only high technology plant and equipment such as computer systems. For example, many offices that have been purpose-built can become obsolete long before their fabric has physically deteriorated, for reasons such as the difficulty of introducing computer network infrastructures or air conditioning, poor environmental performance or an inability to meet new legislative requirements such as access for people with disabilities. Therefore, the estimation of an asset's useful life is a matter of judgement and the possibility of technological change must be taken into account. *[IAS 16.56, 57]*.

5.5 When depreciation starts

The standard is clear on when depreciation should start and finish, and sets out the requirements succinctly as follows:

- Depreciation of an asset begins when it is available for use, which is defined by the standard as occurring when the asset is in the location and condition necessary for it to be capable of operating in the manner intended by management. This is usually the point at which capitalisation of costs relating to the asset ceases as the physical asset is operational or ready for intended use (see 4.1.4 above).
- Depreciation of an asset ceases at the earlier of the date that the asset is classified as held for sale (or included in a disposal group that is classified as held for sale) in accordance with IFRS 5 and the date that the asset is derecognised (see 7 below). *[IAS 16.55]*.

Therefore, an entity does not stop depreciating an asset merely because it has become idle or has been retired from active use unless the asset is fully depreciated. However, if the entity is using a usage method of depreciation (e.g. the units-of-production method), the charge can be zero while there is no production. *[IAS 16.55]*. Of course, a prolonged period in which there is no production may raise questions as to whether the asset is impaired because an asset becoming idle is a specific example of an indication of impairment in IAS 36 (see Chapter 20 at 2.1). *[IAS 36.12(f)]*.

Assets held for sale under IFRS 5 are discussed below at 7.1 below.

5.6 Depreciation methods

There is a variety of depreciation methods that can be used to allocate the depreciable amount of an asset on a systematic basis over its useful life. The standard is not prescriptive about what methods of depreciation should be used. It simply says that 'the depreciation method used shall reflect the pattern in which the asset's future economic benefits are expected to be consumed by the entity', mentioning the possible methods that can be used such as the straight-line method (which is the most common method where the depreciation results in a constant charge over the useful life if the asset's residual value does not change), the diminishing balance method (see 5.6.1 below) and the units of production method (see 5.6.2 below). The overriding requirement is to select the depreciation method that most closely reflects the expected pattern of consumption of the future economic benefits the asset brings over its useful life; and that the selected method is applied consistently from period to period unless there is a change in the expected pattern of consumption of those future economic benefits. *[IAS 16.60-62]*.

IAS 16 contains an explicit requirement that the depreciation method be reviewed at least at each financial year-end to determine if there has been a significant change in the pattern of consumption of an asset's future economic benefits. If there has been such a change, the depreciation method should be changed to reflect it. *[IAS 16.60]*. However, under IAS 8, this change is a change in accounting estimate and not a change in accounting policy. *[IAS 8.32(d), IAS 16.60]*. This means that the consequent depreciation adjustment should be made prospectively, i.e. the asset's depreciable amount should be written off over current and future periods using the new and more appropriate method of depreciation. *[IAS 8.36]*.

A revenue-based approach, e.g. using the ratio of revenue generated to total revenue expected to be generated, is not a suitable basis for depreciation. Depreciation is an estimate of the economic benefits of the asset consumed in the period. The revenue generated by an activity that requires the use of an asset generally reflects factors other than the consumption of the economic benefits of the asset. Revenue reflects the output of the asset, but it also reflects other factors that do not affect depreciation, such as changes in sales volumes and selling prices, the effects of selling activities and other inputs and processes. The price component of revenue may be affected by inflation or foreign currency exchange rates. This means that revenue does not, as a matter of principle, reflect how an asset is used or consumed. *[IAS 16.62A]*. While revenue-based methods of depreciation are considered inappropriate under IAS 16, the standard does permit other methods of depreciation that reflect the level of activity, such as the units of production method (see 5.6.2 below).

5.6.1 *Diminishing balance methods*

The diminishing balance method involves determining a percentage depreciation that will write off the asset's depreciable amount over its useful life. This involves solving for a rate that will reduce the asset's net book value to its residual value at the end of the useful life. The diminishing balance method results in a decreasing depreciation charge over the useful life of the asset. *[IAS 16.62]*.

Example 18.3: Diminishing balance depreciation

An asset costs €6,000 and has a life of four years and a residual value of €1,500. It calculates that the appropriate depreciation rate on the declining balance is 29% and that the depreciation charge in years 1-4 will be as follows:

		€
Year 1	Cost	6,000
	Depreciation at 29% of €6,000	1,757
	Net book value	4,243
Year 2	Depreciation at 29% of €4,243	1,243
	Net book value	3,000
Year 3	Depreciation at 29% of €3,000	879
	Net book value	2,121
Year 4	Depreciation at 29% of €2,121	621
	Net book value	1,500

The sum of digits method is another form of the reducing balance method, but one that is based on the estimated life of the asset and which can easily be applied if the asset has a residual value. If an asset has an estimated useful life of four years then the digits 1, 2, 3, and 4 are added together, giving a total of 10. Depreciation of four-tenths, three-tenths and so on, of the cost of the asset, less any residual value, will be charged in the respective years. The method is sometimes called the 'rule of 78', 78 being the sum of the digits 1 to 12.

Example 18.4: Sum of the digits depreciation

An asset costs €10,000 and is expected to be sold for €2,000 after four years. The depreciable amount is €8,000 (€10,000 – €2,000). Depreciation is to be provided over four years using the sum of the digits method.

		€
Year 1	Cost	10,000
	Depreciation at 4/10 of €8,000	3,200
	Net book value	6,800
Year 2	Depreciation at 3/10 of €8,000	2,400
	Net book value	4,400
Year 3	Depreciation at 2/10 of €8,000	1,600
	Net book value	2,800
Year 4	Depreciation at 1/10 of €8,000	800
	Net book value	2,000

5.6.2 *Unit-of-production method*

Under this method, the asset is written off in line with its expected use or estimated total output. *[IAS 16.62]*. By relating depreciation to the proportion of productive capacity utilised to date, it reflects the fact that the useful economic life of certain assets, principally machinery, is more closely linked to its usage and output than to time. This method is normally used in extractive industries, for example, to amortise the costs of development of productive oil and gas facilities.

The essence of choosing a fair depreciation method is to reflect the consumption of economic benefits provided by the asset concerned. In most cases the straight-line basis will give perfectly acceptable results, and the vast majority of entities use this method. Where there are instances, such as the extraction of a known proportion of a mineral resource, or the use of a certain amount of the total available number of working hours of a machine, it may be that a unit of production method will give fairer results.

5.7 Impairment

All items of PP&E accounted for under IAS 16 are subject to the impairment requirements of IAS 36. Impairment is discussed in Chapter 20. *[IAS 16.63]*.

The question has arisen about the treatment of any compensation an entity may be due to receive as a result of an asset being impaired. For example an asset that is insured might be destroyed in a fire, so repayment from an insurance company might be expected. IAS 16 states that these events – the impairments or losses of items of PP&E, the related claims for or payments of compensation from third parties and any subsequent purchase or construction of replacement assets – are 'separate economic events' and should be accounted for separately as follows:

- impairments of PP&E are recognised in accordance with IAS 36 (see Chapter 20);
- derecognition of items of PP&E retired or disposed of should be determined in accordance with IAS 16 (see 7 below);
- compensation from third parties for items of PP&E that were impaired, lost or given up is included in determining profit and loss when it becomes receivable; and
- the cost of items of PP&E restored, purchased or constructed as replacements is determined in accordance with IAS 16 (see 3 and 4 above). *[IAS 16.65, 66]*.

6 MEASUREMENT AFTER RECOGNITION: REVALUATION MODEL

If the revaluation model is adopted, PP&E is initially recognised at cost and subsequently carried at a revalued amount, being its fair value (if it can be measured reliably) at the date of the revaluation, less subsequent accumulated depreciation and impairment losses. *[IAS 16.29, 31]*. In practice, 'fair value' will usually be the market value of the asset. There is no requirement for a professional external valuation or even for a professionally qualified valuer to perform the appraisal, although in practice professional advice is often sought.

Valuation frequency is not prescribed by IAS 16. Instead it states that revaluations are to be made with sufficient regularity to ensure that the carrying amount does not differ materially from that which would be determined using fair value at the end of the reporting period. *[IAS 16.31]*. Therefore, the frequency of revaluations depends upon the changes in fair values of the items of PP&E being revalued. When the fair value of a revalued asset differs materially from its carrying amount, a further revaluation is necessary. The standard suggests that some items of PP&E have frequent and volatile changes in fair value and these should be revalued annually. This is true for property assets in many jurisdictions, but even in such cases there may be quieter periods in which there is little movement in values. If there are only insignificant changes in fair value, frequent revaluations are unnecessary and it may only be necessary to perform revaluations at three or five-year intervals. *[IAS 16.34]*.

If the revaluation model is adopted, IAS 16 specifies that all items within a class of PP&E are to be revalued simultaneously to prevent selective revaluation of assets and the reporting of amounts in the financial statements that are a mixture of costs and values as at different dates. *[IAS 16.29, 36, 38]*. A class of PP&E is a grouping of assets of a similar nature and use in an entity's operations. This is not a precise definition. IAS 16 suggests that the following are examples of separate classes of PP&E:

(i) land;

(ii) land and buildings;

(iii) machinery;

(iv) ships;

(v) aircraft;

(vi) motor vehicles;

(vii) furniture and fixtures;

(viii) office equipment; and

(ix) bearer plants. *[IAS 16.37]*.

These are very broad categories of PP&E and it is possible for them to be classified further into groupings of assets of a similar nature and use. Office buildings and factories or hotels and fitness centres, could be separate classes of asset. If the entity used the same type of asset in two different geographical locations, e.g. clothing manufacturing facilities for similar products or products with similar markets, say in Sri Lanka and Guatemala, it is likely that these would be seen as part of the same class of asset. However, if the entity manufactured pharmaceuticals and clothing, both in European facilities, then few would argue that these could be assets with a sufficiently different nature and use to be a separate class. Ultimately it must be a matter of judgement in the context of the specific operations of individual entities.

IAS 16 permits a rolling valuation of a class of assets provided the revaluation of such class of assets is completed within a short period of time and 'provided the revaluations are kept up to date'. *[IAS 16.38]*. This final condition makes it difficult to see how rolling valuations can be performed unless the value of the assets changes very little (in which case the standard states that valuations need only be performed every three to five years) because if a large change is revealed, then presumably a wholesale revaluation is required.

An entity that uses the cost model for its investment property, as allowed by IAS 40, should apply the cost model in IAS 16 (see 5 above). *[IAS 16.5]*. IFRS 16, if adopted, will amend paragraph 5 of IAS 16 (described above) to clarify that an entity should use the cost model in IAS 16 for its 'owned investment property' if it chooses the cost model to account for its investment property under IAS 40. Investment property held by a lessee as a right-of-use asset will be measured in accordance with IFRS 16 (see Chapter 25 at 5.3.1).

6.1 The meaning of fair value

Fair value is defined in IFRS 13. IFRS 13 does not prescribe when to measure fair value but provides guidance on how to measure it under IFRS when fair value is required or permitted by IFRS.

IFRS 13 clarifies that fair value is an exit price from the perspective of market participants. 'Fair value' is defined as 'the price that would be received to sell an asset or paid to transfer a liability in an orderly transaction between market participants at the measurement date'. *[IAS 16.6, IFRS 13 Appendix A].*

6.1.1 Revaluing assets under IFRS 13

IFRS 13 specifies that 'fair value is a market-based measurement, not an entity-specific measurement'. *[IFRS 13.2].* Some of the new principles that affect the revaluation of PP&E are the concept of highest and best use and the change in focus of the fair value hierarchy from valuation techniques to inputs. IFRS 13 also requires a significant number of disclosures, including the categorisation of a fair value measurement with the fair value measurement hierarchy.

The requirements of IFRS 13 are discussed in Chapter 14.

The following sections consider some of the key considerations when measuring the fair value of an item of PP&E.

6.1.1.A Highest and best use

IFRS 13 states that 'a fair value measurement of a non-financial asset takes into account a market participant's ability to generate economic benefits by using the asset in its highest and best use or by selling it to another market participant that would use the asset in its highest and best use'. *[IFRS 13.27].* This evaluation will include uses that are 'physically possible, legally permissible and financial feasible'. *[IFRS 13.28].*

The highest and best use is determined from the perspective of market participants that would be acquiring the asset, but the starting point is the asset's current use. It is presumed that an entity's current use of the asset is the asset's highest and best use, unless market or other factors suggest that a different use of the asset by market participants would maximise its value. *[IFRS 13.29].*

Prior to the adoption of IFRS 13, IAS 16 did not imply that fair value and market value were synonymous, which allowed a broader meaning of the term 'fair value'. The term could certainly have been interpreted as encompassing the following two commonly used, market derived, valuation bases:

- market value in existing use, an entry value for property in continuing use in the business which is based on the concept of net current replacement cost; and
- open market value, which is an exit value and based on the amount that a property that is surplus to requirements could reach when sold.

Both of these bases are market-derived, yet they can differ for a variety of reasons. A property may have a higher value on the open market if it could be redeployed to a more valuable use. On the other hand, the present owner may enjoy some benefits that could not be passed on in a sale, such as planning consents that are personal to the present occupier. Market value in existing use will be presumed to be fair value under IFRS 13 for many types of business property unless market or other factors suggest that open market value is higher (i.e. open market value represents highest and best use). For most retail sites market value in existing use will be fair value; if there is market evidence that certain types of property have an alternative use with a higher value, e.g. pubs or warehouses that can be converted to residential use, this will have to be taken into account.

The fair value of an item of PP&E will either be measured based on the value it would derive on a standalone basis or in combination with other assets or other assets and liabilities, i.e. the asset's 'valuation premise'. 'Valuation premise' is a valuation concept that addresses how a non-financial asset derives its maximum value to market participants. The highest and best use of an item of PP&E 'might provide maximum value to market participants through its use in combination with other assets as a group or in combination with other assets and liabilities (e.g. a business)' or it 'might have maximum value to market participants on a stand-alone basis'. *[IFRS 13.31(a)-(b)]*.

The following example is derived from IFRS 13 and illustrates highest and best use in establishing fair value. *[IFRS 13.IE7-IE8]*.

Example 18.5: Highest and best use

An entity acquires land in a business combination. The land is currently developed for industrial use as a site for a factory. The current use of land is presumed to be its highest and best use unless market or other factors suggest evidence for a different use.

Scenario (1): In the particular jurisdiction, it can be difficult to obtain consents to change use from industrial to residential use for the land and there is no evidence that the area is becoming desirable for residential development. The fair value is based on the current industrial use of the land

Scenario (2): Nearby sites have recently been developed for residential use as sites for high-rise apartment buildings. On the basis of that development and recent zoning and other changes that facilitated the residential development, the entity determines that the land currently used as a site for a factory could also be developed as a site for residential use because market participants would take into account the potential to develop the site for residential use when pricing the land.

This determination can be highly judgemental. For further discussion on highest and best use and valuation premise see Chapter 14 at 10.

6.1.1.B Valuation approaches

Prior to the adoption of IFRS 13, IAS 16 had a hierarchy of valuation techniques for measuring fair value. Only if there was no market-based evidence could an entity estimate fair value using an income or a depreciated replacement cost approach under IAS 16. However, the implementation of IFRS 13 removed these from IAS 16, which now refers to the valuation techniques in IFRS 13.

IFRS 13 does not limit the types of valuation techniques an entity might use to measure fair value but instead focuses on the types of inputs that will be used. The standard requires the entity to use the valuation technique that maximises the use of relevant observable inputs and minimises the use of unobservable inputs. *[IFRS 13.61]*. The objective is that the best available inputs should be used in valuing the assets. These inputs could be used in any valuation technique provided they are consistent with the three valuation approaches in the standard: the market approach, the cost approach and the income approach. *[IFRS 13.62].*

The *market approach* uses prices and other relevant information generated by market transactions involving identical or comparable (i.e. similar) assets, liabilities or a group of assets and liabilities, such as a business. *[IFRS 13.B5].* For PP&E, market techniques will usually involve market transactions in comparable assets or, for certain assets valued as businesses, market multiples derived from comparable transactions. *[IFRS 13.B5, B6].*

The *cost approach* reflects the amount that would be required currently to replace the service capacity of an asset (i.e. current replacement cost). It is based on what a market participant buyer would pay to acquire or construct a substitute asset of comparable utility, adjusted for obsolescence. Obsolescence includes physical deterioration, functional (technological) and economic (external) obsolescence so it is broader than and not the same as depreciation under IAS 16. *[IFRS 13.B8, B9].*

The *income approach* converts future amounts (e.g. cash flows or income and expenses) to a single discounted amount. The fair value reflects current market expectations about those future amounts. In the case of PP&E, this will usually mean using a present value (i.e. discounted cash flow) technique. *[IFRS 13.B10, B11].*

See Chapter 14 at 14 for a further discussion of these valuation techniques.

IFRS 13 does not place any preference on the techniques. An entity can use any valuation technique, or use multiple techniques, as long as it applies the valuation technique consistently. A change in a valuation technique is considered a change in an accounting estimate in accordance with IAS 8. *[IFRS 13.66].*

Instead, the inputs used to measure the fair value of an asset have a hierarchy. Level 1 inputs are those that are quoted prices in active markets (i.e. markets in which transactions take place with sufficient frequency and volume to provide pricing information on an ongoing basis) for identical assets that the entity can access at the measurement date. *[IFRS 13.76].* Level 1 inputs have the highest priority, followed by inputs, other than quoted prices, that are observable for the asset either directly or indirectly (Level 2). The lowest priority inputs are those based on unobservable inputs (Level 3). *[IFRS 13.72].* The valuation techniques, referred to above, will use a combination of inputs to determine the fair value of the asset.

As stated above, land and buildings are the most commonly revalued items of PP&E. These types of assets use a variety of inputs such as other sales, multiples or discounted cash flows. While some of these maybe Level 1 inputs, we generally expect the fair value measurement as a whole to be categorised within Level 2 or Level 3 of the fair value hierarchy for disclosure purposes (see 8.2 below).

IFRS 13 also requires additional disclosure in the financial statements that are discussed at 8.2 below of this chapter and in Chapter 14 at 20.

6.1.1.C The cost approach: current replacement cost and depreciated replacement cost (DRC)

IFRS 13 permits the use of a cost approach for measuring fair value, for example current replacement costs. Before using current replacement cost as a method to measure fair value, an entity should ensure that both:

- the highest and best use of the assets is consistent with their current use; and
- the principal market (or in its absence, the most advantageous market) is the same as the entry market.

The resulting current replacement cost should also be assessed to ensure market participants would actually transact for the asset in its current condition and location at this price. In particular, an entity should ensure that both:

- the inputs used to determine replacement cost are consistent with what market participant buyers would pay to acquire or construct a substitute asset of comparable utility; and
- the replacement cost has been adjusted for obsolescence that market participant buyers would consider so that the depreciation adjustment reflects all forms of obsolescence (i.e. physical deterioration, technological (functional) and economic obsolescence and environmental factors), which is broader than depreciation calculated in accordance with IAS 16.

Before IAS 16 was amended by IFRS 13, DRC was permitted to measure the fair value of specialised properties. In some ways DRC is similar to current replacement cost. The crucial difference is that under IAS 16 entities were not obliged to ensure that the resulting price is one that would be paid by a market participant (i.e. it is an exit price). The objective of DRC is to make a realistic estimate of the current cost of constructing an asset that has the same service potential as the existing asset. DRC therefore has a similar meaning to current replacement cost under IFRS 13 except that current replacement cost is an exit price and its use is not restricted to specialised assets as IFRS 13 requires entities to use the best available inputs in valuing any assets.

DRC can still be used, but care is needed to ensure that the resulting measurement is consistent with the requirements of IFRS 13 for measuring fair value. Since DRC measures the current entry price, it can only be used when the entry price equals the exit price. For further discussion see Chapter 14 at 14.3.1.

6.2 Accounting for valuation surpluses and deficits

Increases in the carrying amount of PP&E as a result of revaluations should be credited to OCI and accumulated in a revaluation surplus account in equity. To the extent that a revaluation increase of an asset reverses a revaluation decrease of the same asset that was previously recognised as an expense in profit or loss, such increase should be credited to income in profit or loss. Decreases in valuation should be charged to profit or loss, except to the extent that they reverse the existing accumulated revaluation surplus on the same asset and therefore such decrease is recognised in OCI. The decrease recognised in OCI reduces the amount accumulated in equity under revaluation surplus account. *[IAS 16.39, 40].* This means that it is not permissible under the standard to carry a negative revaluation reserve in respect of any item of PP&E.

The same rules apply to impairment losses. An impairment loss on a revalued asset is first used to reduce the revaluation surplus for that asset. Only when the impairment loss exceeds the amount in the revaluation surplus for that same asset is any further impairment loss recognised in profit or loss (see Chapter 20 at 11.1). *[IAS 36.61].*

IAS 16 generally retains a model in which the revalued amount substitutes for cost in both statement of financial position and statement of profit or loss and on derecognition there is no recycling to profit and loss of amounts taken directly to OCI. The revaluation surplus included equity in respect of an item of PP&E may be transferred directly to retained earnings when the asset is derecognised (i.e. transferring the whole of the surplus when the asset is retired or disposed of). *[IAS 16.41]*.

IAS 16 also allows some of the revaluation surplus to be transferred to retained earnings as the asset is used by an entity. In such a case, the difference between depreciation based on the revalued carrying amount of the asset and depreciation based on its original cost may be transferred from revaluation surplus to retained earnings in equity. This is illustrated in the Example 18.6 below. This recognises that any depreciation on the revalued part of an asset's carrying value has been realised by being charged to profit or loss. Thus, a transfer should be made of an equivalent amount from the revaluation surplus to retained earnings. Any remaining balance may also be transferred when the asset is disposed of. These transfers should be made directly from revaluation surplus to retained earnings and not through the statement of profit or loss. *[IAS 16.41]*.

Example 18.6: Effect of depreciation on the revaluation reserve

On 1 January 2015 an entity acquired an asset for €1,000. The asset has an economic life of ten years and is depreciated on a straight-line basis. The residual value is assumed to be €nil. At 31 December 2018 (when the cost net of accumulated depreciation is €600) the asset is valued at €900. The entity accounts for the revaluation by debiting the carrying value of the asset (using either of the methods discussed below) €300 and crediting €300 to the revaluation reserve. At 31 December 2018 the useful life of the asset is considered to be the remainder of its original life (i.e. six years) and its residual value is still considered to be €nil. In the year ended 31 December 2019 and in later years, the depreciation charged to profit or loss is €150 (€900/6 years remaining).

The usual treatment thereafter for each of the remaining 6 years of the asset's life, is to transfer €50 (€300/6 years) each year from the revaluation reserve to retained earnings (not through profit or loss). This avoids the revaluation reserve being maintained indefinitely even after the asset ceases to exist, which does not seem sensible.

Any effect on taxation, both current and deferred, resulting from the revaluation of PP&E is recognised and disclosed in accordance with IAS 12 – *Income Taxes*. *[IAS 16.42]*. This is dealt with in Chapter 31.

When an item of PP&E is revalued, the carrying amount of that asset is adjusted to the revalued amount. As alluded to in Example 18.5 above, there are two methods of accounting for accumulated depreciation when an item of PP&E is revalued. At the date of revaluation, the asset is treated in one of the following ways:

- the accumulated depreciation is eliminated against gross carrying amount of the asset; or
- the gross carrying amount is adjusted in a manner that is consistent with the revaluation of the carrying amount of the asset. For example, the gross carrying amount may be restated by reference to observable market data or it may be restated proportionately to the change in the carrying amount. The accumulated depreciation at the date of the revaluation is adjusted to equal the difference between the gross carrying amount and the carrying amount of the asset after taking into account accumulated impairment losses. *[IAS 16.35]*.

The first method available eliminates the accumulated depreciation against the gross carrying amount of the asset. After the revaluation, the gross carrying amount and the net carrying amount are same (i.e. reflecting the revalued amount). This is illustrated in Example 18.7 below.

Example 18.7: Revaluation by eliminating accumulated depreciation

On 31 December, a building has a carrying amount of €40,000, being the original cost of €70,000 less accumulated depreciation of €30,000. A revaluation is performed and the fair value of the asset is €50,000. The entity would record the following journal entries:

	Dr	Cr
	€	€
Accumulated depreciation	30,000	
Building		20,000
Asset revaluation reserve		10,000

	Before	After
	€	€
Building at cost	70,000	
Building at valuation		50,000
Accumulated depreciation	30,000	–
Net book value	40,000	50,000

Under the observable market data approach, the gross carrying amount will be restated and the difference compared to the revalued amount of the asset will be absorbed by the accumulated depreciation. Using the example above, assuming the gross carrying amount is restated to €75,000 by reference to the observable market data, the accumulated depreciation will be adjusted to €25,000 (i.e. the gross carrying amount of €75,000 less the carrying amount adjusted to its revalued amount of €50,000). The revaluation gain recognised is the same as the first method above at €10,000.

Alternatively, the gross carrying amount is restated proportionately to the change in carrying amount (i.e. a 25% uplift) resulting in the same revaluation gain as the methods above but the cost and accumulated depreciation carried forward reflect the gross cost of the asset of €87,500 and accumulated depreciation of €37,500. This method may be used if an asset is revalued using an index to determine its depreciated replacement cost (see 6.1.1.C above).

Notice that the revaluation gain recognised remained at €10,000 whichever method described above is used.

6.3 Reversals of downward valuations

IAS 16 requires that, if an asset's carrying amount is increased as a result of a revaluation, the increase should be credited directly to OCI and accumulated in equity under the heading of revaluation surplus. However, the increase should be recognised in profit or loss to the extent that it reverses a revaluation decrease of the same asset previously recognised in profit or loss (see 6.2 above). *[IAS 16.39]*.

The same rules apply to a reversal of an impairment loss – see discussion in Chapter 20 at 11.4.2.

If the revalued asset is being depreciated, we consider that the full amount of any reversal should not be taken to profit or loss. Rather, the reversal should take account of the depreciation that would have been charged on the previously higher book value. The text of IAS 16 does not specify this treatment but other interpretations would be inconsistent with IAS 36, which states:

> 'The increased carrying amount of an asset other than goodwill attributable to a reversal of an impairment loss shall not exceed the carrying amount that would have been determined (net of amortisation or depreciation) had no impairment loss been recognised for the asset in prior years.' *[IAS 36.117]*.

The following example demonstrates a way in which this could be applied.

Example 18.8: Reversal of a downward valuation

An asset has a cost of £1,000,000, a life of 10 years and a residual value of £nil. At the end of year 3, when the asset's NBV is £700,000, it is revalued to £350,000. This write down below cost of £350,000 is taken through profit or loss.

The entity then depreciated its asset by £50,000 per annum, so as to write off the carrying value of £350,000 over the remaining 7 years.

At the end of year 6, the asset's depreciated cost is £200,000 but it is now revalued to £500,000. The effect on the entity's asset is as follows:

	£000
Valuation	
At the beginning of year 6	350
Surplus on revaluation	150
At the end of the year	500
Accumulated depreciation	
At beginning of year 6 *	100
Charge for the year	50
Accumulated depreciation written back on revaluation	(150)
At the end of the year	–
Net book value at the end of year 6	500
Net book value at the beginning of year 6	250

* Two years' depreciation (years 4 and 5) at £50,000 per annum.

The total credit for the uplift in value is £300,000 on the revaluation in year 6 (i.e. £500,000 less £200,000). However, only £200,000 is taken through profit or loss. £100,000 represents depreciation that would otherwise have been charged to profit or loss in years 4 and 5. This will be taken directly to the revaluation surplus in OCI.

From the beginning of year 7, the asset at revalued amount of £500,000 will be written off over the remaining four years at £125,000 per annum.

In the example the amount of the revaluation that is credited to the revaluation surplus in OCI represents the difference between the net book value that would have resulted had the asset been held on a cost basis (£400,000) and the net book value on a revalued basis (£500,000).

Of course this is an extreme example. Most assets that are subject to a policy of revaluation would not show such marked changes in value and it would be expected that there would be valuation movements in the intervening years rather than dramatic losses and gains in years 3 and 6. However, we consider that in principle this is the way in which downward valuations should be recognised.

There may be major practical difficulties for any entity that finds itself in the position of reversing revaluation deficits on depreciating assets, although whether in practice this eventuality often occurs is open to doubt. If there is any chance that it is likely to occur, the business would need to continue to maintain asset registers on the original, pre-write down basis.

6.4 Adopting a policy of revaluation

Although the initial adoption of a policy of revaluation by an entity that has previously used the cost model is a change in accounting policy, it is not dealt with as a prior period adjustment in accordance with IAS 8. Instead, the change is treated as a revaluation during the current period as set out in 6.2 above. *[IAS 8.17]*. This means that the entity is not required to obtain valuation information about comparative periods.

6.5 Assets held under finance leases

Once assets held under finance leases have been capitalised as items of PP&E, their subsequent accounting is the same as for any other asset so they do not constitute a separate class of assets. Therefore such assets may also be revalued using the revaluation model but, if the revaluation model is used, then the entire class of assets (both owned and those held under finance lease) must be revalued. *[IAS 16.36]*.

Whilst it is not explicit in IAS 16, in our view, to obtain the fair value of an asset held under a finance lease for financial reporting purposes, the assessed value must be adjusted to take account of any recognised finance lease liability. This follows the treatment required by IAS 40. *[IAS 40.50(d)]*. The mechanism for achieving this is set out in detail in Chapter 19 at 6.7.

For disclosure purposes PP&E acquired under a finance lease should be considered to be the same class of asset as those with a similar nature that are owned. Consequently, there is no need to provide separate reconciliations of movements in owned assets from assets held under finance leases (see 8.1 below).

When IFRS 16 is adopted, lessees no longer classify leases as finance leases or as operating leases, instead lessees are required to recognise most leases in their statement of financial position as lease liabilities with corresponding right-of-use assets. A lessee subsequently measures the right-of-use asset using a cost model under IFRS 16, unless it applies one of the following measurement models allowed by IFRS 16 (see Chapter 25):

- the fair value model in IAS 40, but only if the lessee applies this to its investment property and the right-of-use asset meets the definition of investment property in IAS 40; or
- if the lessee applies the revaluation model in IAS 16 to a class of PP&E, the lessee would also have the option to revalue all of the right-of-use assets that relate to that class of PP&E.

7 DERECOGNITION AND DISPOSAL

Derecognition, i.e. removal of the carrying amount of an item of PP&E from the financial statements of the entity, occurs when an item of PP&E is either disposed of, or when no further economic benefits are expected to flow from its use or disposal. *[IAS 16.67].* The disposal of an item of PP&E may occur in a variety of ways (e.g. by sale, by entering into a finance lease or by donation). IFRS 15 requires that revenue (and a gain or loss on disposal of a non-current asset not in the ordinary course of business) be recognised upon satisfaction of performance obligation by transferring control. Accordingly, the actual date of disposal of an item of PP&E is the date the recipient obtains control of that item in accordance with the requirements for determining when a performance obligation is satisfied in IFRS 15 (see Chapter 30 at 7). IAS 17 applies to disposal by way of a sale and leaseback. *[IAS 16.69].* Prior to adoption of IFRS 15, the actual date of disposal was determined in accordance with the criteria in IAS 18 for the recognition of revenue from the sale of goods. Revenue recognition under IAS 18 is discussed in Chapter 29.

All gains and losses on derecognition must be included in profit and loss for the period when the item is derecognised, unless another standard applies; e.g. under IAS 17 a sale and leaseback transaction might not give rise to a gain (see Chapter 24 at 7). *[IAS 16.68].* IFRS 16, when adopted, will amend paragraphs 68 and 69 of IAS 16 (described above) to refer to IFRS 16 replacing the references to IAS 17. Sale and leaseback accounting under IFRS 16 is discussed in Chapter 25 at 8.

Gains are not to be classified as revenue, although in some limited circumstances presenting gross revenue on the sale of certain assets may be appropriate (see 7.2 below). *[IAS 16.68].* Gains and losses are to be calculated as the difference between any net disposal proceeds and the carrying value of the item of PP&E. *[IAS 16.71].* This means that any revaluation surplus in equity relating to the asset disposed of is transferred directly to retained earnings when the asset is derecognised and not reflected in profit or loss (see 6.2 above). *[IAS 16.41].*

Replacement of 'parts' of an asset requires derecognition of the carrying value of the replaced part, even if that part had not been depreciated separately. In these circumstances, the standard allows the cost of the replacement part to be a guide in estimating the original cost of the replaced part at the time it was acquired or constructed, if that cannot be determined. *[IAS 16.70].*

The amount of consideration to be included in the gain or loss arising from the derecognition of an item of PP&E is determined in accordance with the requirements for determining the transaction price in paragraphs 47–72 of IFRS 15 (see Chapter 30 at 5). Any subsequent changes to the estimated amount of the consideration included in the gain or loss should be accounted for in accordance with the requirements for changes in the transaction price in IFRS 15 (see Chapter 30 at 6.5). *[IAS 16.72].*

Prior to adoption of IFRS 15, the amount of consideration receivable on the disposal of an item of PP&E should be recognised initially at its fair value. If deferred credit terms are given, the consideration received for the sale is initially recognised at the cash price equivalent. The difference between the nominal amount of the consideration and the cash price equivalent is treated as interest revenue using the effective yield method as required by IAS 18 (see Chapter 29 at 3.5).

7.1 IFRS 5 – *Non-current Assets Held for Sale and Discontinued Operations*

IFRS 5 introduced a category of asset, 'held for sale', and PP&E within this category is outside the scope of IAS 16, although IAS 16 requires certain disclosures about assets held for sale to be made, as set out at 8.1 below.

IFRS 5 requires that an item of PP&E should be classified as held for sale if its carrying amount will be recovered principally through a sale transaction rather than continuing use, though continuing use is not in itself precluded for assets classified as held for sale. *[IFRS 5.6]*. An asset can also be part of a 'disposal group' (that is a group of assets that are to be disposed of together), in which case such group can be treated as a whole. Once this classification has been made, depreciation ceases, even if the asset is still being used, but the assets must be carried at the lower of their previous carrying amount and fair value less costs to sell. For assets (or disposal group) to be classified as held for sale, they must be available for immediate sale in their present condition, and the sale must be highly probable. *[IFRS 5.7]*.

Additionally, the sale should be completed within one year from the date of classification as held for sale, management at an 'appropriate level' must be committed to the plan, and an active programme of marketing the assets at current fair value must have been started. *[IFRS 5.8]*.

The requirements of IFRS 5 are dealt with in Chapter 4. IFRS 5 does not apply when assets that are held for sale in the ordinary course of business are transferred to inventories (see 7.2 below). *[IAS 16.68A]*.

7.2 Sale of assets held for rental

If an entity, in the course of its ordinary activities, routinely sells PP&E that it has held for rental to others, it should transfer such assets to inventories at their carrying amount when they cease to be rented and are then held for sale. The proceeds from the sale of such assets should be recognised as revenue in accordance with IFRS 15 (or IAS 18). *[IAS 16.68A]*. In contrast, the sale of investment property is generally not recognised as revenue. The rationale and possible treatment of investment property in such cases is discussed in detail in Chapter 19 at 9 and 10.

A number of entities sell assets that have previously been held for rental, for example, car rental companies that may acquire vehicles with the intention of holding them as rental cars for a limited period and then selling them. An issue was whether the sale of such assets, which arguably have a dual purpose of being rented out and then sold, should be presented gross (revenue and cost of sales) or net (gain or loss) in profit or loss.

The IASB concluded that the presentation of gross revenue, rather than a net gain or loss, would better reflect the ordinary activities of some such entities and amended IAS 16 accordingly.

The IASB also made a consequential adjustment to IAS 7 – *Statement of Cash Flows* – to require that both (i) the cash payments to manufacture or acquire assets held for rental and subsequently held for sale; and (ii) the cash receipts from rentals and sales of such assets are presented as from operating activities. *[IAS 7.14]*. This amendment to IAS 7 is intended to avoid initial expenditure on purchases of assets being classified as investing activities while inflows from sales are recorded within operating activities.

7.3 Partial disposals and undivided interests

IAS 16 requires an entity to derecognise 'an item' of PP&E on disposal or when it expects no future economic benefits from its use or disposal. *[IAS 16.67]*.

Items of PP&E are recognised when their costs can be measured reliably and it is probable that future benefits associated with the asset will flow to the entity. *[IAS 16.7]*. The standard 'does not prescribe the unit of measure for recognition, i.e. what constitutes an item of property, plant and equipment'. *[IAS 16.9]*.

However, items that are derecognised were not necessarily items on initial recognition. The item that is being disposed of may be part of a larger 'item' bought in a single transaction that can be subdivided into parts (i.e. separate items) for separate disposal; an obvious example is land or many types of property. The principle is the same as for the replacement of parts, which may only be identified and derecognised so that the cost of the replacement part may be recognised (see 3.2 above). The entity needs to identify the cost of the part disposed of by allocating the carrying value on a systematic and appropriate basis.

In these cases, the part disposed of is a physical part of the original asset. The standard assumes that disposal will be of a physical part (except in the specific case of major inspections and overhauls – see 3.3.2 above). However, some entities enter into arrangements in which they dispose of part of the benefits that will be derived from the assets.

Although IAS 16 defines an asset by reference to the future economic benefits that will be controlled by the entity as a result of the acquisition, it does not address disposals of a proportion of these benefits. An entity may dispose of an undivided interest in the whole asset (sometimes called an ownership 'in common' of the asset). This means that all owners have a proportionate share of the entire asset (e.g. the purchaser of a 25% undivided interest in 100 acres of land owns 25% of the whole 100 acres). These arrangements are common in, but are not restricted to, the extractive and property sectors. Vendors have to determine how to account for the consideration they have received from the purchaser. This will depend on the details of the arrangement and, in particular, whether the entity continues to control the asset or there is joint control.

(a) Joint control

In some cases there may be joint control over the asset, in which case the arrangement will be within scope of IFRS 11 – *Joint Arrangements* – which will determine how to account for the disposal and the subsequent accounting. Joint control is discussed in detail in Chapter 12.

The accounting treatment may depend on whether the disposing entity holds an asset directly or holds it within a single-asset subsidiary. If the entity is disposing of an interest in an asset that is not held within a single-asset subsidiary and if the retained interest represents an investment in an entity a gain or loss is recognised as if 100% of asset had been sold because control has been lost. If the transaction is with other parties to a joint operation, the vendor will only recognise gains and losses to the extent of the other parties' interests. *[IFRS 11.B34]*. In other words, it will recognise a part disposal. The retained interest will be analysed as a joint operation or a joint venture.

In the former case, the entity will account for its own assets, liabilities, revenue etc. while in the latter case it will apply the equity method to account for its interests in the joint venture (see Chapter 12 at 6 and 7, respectively). Undivided interests cannot be accounted for as joint arrangements in the absence of joint control.

In many jurisdictions it is common for certain assets, particularly properties, to be bought and sold by transferring ownership of a separate legal entity formed to hold the asset (a 'single-asset' entity) rather than the asset itself. If the asset is held in a single-asset subsidiary entity that becomes a joint venture, there is a conflict between the requirements of IFRS 10 – *Consolidated Financial Statements* – and IAS 28 – *Investments in Associates and Joint Ventures*. In September 2014, the IASB issued amendments to IFRS 10 and IAS 28, in dealing with the sale or contribution of assets between an investor and its associate or joint venture. The main consequence of the amendments is that a full gain or loss is recognised when a transaction involves a business (whether it is housed in a subsidiary or not). A partial gain or loss is recognised when a transaction involves assets that do not constitute a business, even if these assets are housed in a subsidiary. The amendments are currently effective for annual periods commencing on or after 1 January 2016; however, the IASB is considering deferring the mandatory application date until such time as it has finalised any amendments that result from its research project on the equity method. This issue is discussed further in Chapter 7 at 3.2.1.B and 3.2.6, Chapter 11 at 7.6.5.C and in Chapter 12 at 8.2.3.

(b) Vendor retains control

If the asset is not jointly controlled in the subsequent arrangement, the vendor might retain control over the asset. The vendor will recognise revenue or it will be a financing arrangement. If it is the former, then the issue is the period and pattern over which revenue is recognised.

If the vendor retains control, then it will not meet the requirements in IFRS 15 for treating the transaction as a sale, i.e. recognising revenue on entering into the arrangement. IFRS 15 requires that revenue (and a gain or loss on disposal of a non-current asset not in the ordinary course of business) be recognised upon satisfaction of performance obligation by transferring control (see Chapter 30 at 7). Prior to adoption of IFRS 15, such scenario would not have met the criteria in IAS 18 for treating the transaction as a sale because the entity must have retained neither continuing managerial involvement to the degree usually associated with ownership nor effective control over the goods sold in order to recognise revenue from the sale of goods (see Chapter 29 at 3.7). *[IAS 18.14]*.

The arrangement could be akin to a lease, especially if the disposal is for a period of time. However, arrangements are only within the scope of IAS 17, or IFRS 16, once adopted, if they relate to a specified asset. Generally, a portion of a larger asset that is not physically distinct is not considered to be a specified asset. The related detailed requirements of IAS 17 and IFRS 16 are discussed in Chapter 24 at 2.1.2 and Chapter 25 at 3.1.2, respectively.

If it is not a lease and the vendor continues to control the asset, the arrangement might be best characterised as a performance obligation for services to be spread over the term of the arrangement. That is, the initial receipt would be a liability and recognised in profit and loss over time.

Alternatively, it could be a financing-type arrangement, in which case the proceeds would be classified as a financial liability. In effect, the vendor is trading a share of any revenue to which it is entitled in exchange for funding by the purchaser of one or more activities relating to the asset. The purchaser receives a return that is comparable to a lender's rate of return out of the proceeds of production. This could be by receiving a disproportionate share of output until it has recovered its costs (the financing it has provided) as well as the agreed rate of return for the funding. These arrangements are found in the extractive sector, e.g. carried interests and farm-outs (Chapter 41 at 6). In the development stage of a project, the asset in question will be classified as PP&E or as an intangible asset under IAS 38. Under a carried interest arrangement the carried party transfers a *portion* of the risks and rewards of a property, in exchange for a funding commitment from the carrying party.

(c) Partial disposal

In some circumstances it is argued that the rights transferred by the vendor are such that it neither controls nor jointly controls the whole of the original asset and the question arises as to whether there is a part disposal of the asset. The arrangement cannot be accounted for as a joint operation as there is no joint control. Classification as a joint operation would allow a part disposal of an item of PP&E. It is noted that a party that participates in a joint operation but does not have joint control records its interests in the same way as a participant in a joint operation, accounting for its own assets and liabilities. *[IFRS 11.23].* This is unaffected by the fact that the asset in question may be an interest in an undivided asset; it will still classify its interest in the asset as an item of PP&E. In those sectors where these arrangements are common and where an entity will be simultaneously vendor and acquirer in different arrangements, it is argued that the transactions should be treated symmetrically, i.e. as a part disposal of the undivided asset and an acquisition of an interest in PP&E. However, this interpretation depends entirely on the vendor ceding control of part of its rights and applying IAS 16 principles to obtain symmetry of accounting between acquisitions and disposals.

8 IAS 16 DISCLOSURE REQUIREMENTS

The main disclosure requirements of IAS 16 are set out below, but it should be noted that the related disclosure requirements in other standards such as IFRS 13, IAS 1 – *Presentation of Financial Statements* – and IAS 36 may also be relevant. See Chapters 14, 3 and 20, respectively.

8.1 General disclosures

For each class of PP&E the following should be disclosed in the financial statements:

(a) the measurement bases used for determining the gross carrying amount (e.g. cost or revaluation). *[IAS 16.73(a)].* When more than one basis has been used, the gross carrying amount for that basis in each category may have to be disclosed (however the standard requires that if revaluation is adopted the entire class of PP&E must be revalued);

(b) the depreciation methods used. Selection of the depreciation method adopted is a matter of judgement and its disclosure provides information that allows users of financial statements to review the policies selected by management and enables them to compare with other entities. For similar reasons, it is necessary to disclose depreciation (in item (e)(vii) below), whether recognised in profit or loss or as a part of the cost of other assets, during a period; and accumulated depreciation at the end of the period (in item (d) below); *[IAS 16.73(b), 75]*

(c) the useful lives or the depreciation rates used. Selection of the useful lives or depreciation rates used is a matter of judgement and its disclosure provides information that allows users of financial statements to review the policies selected by management and enables them to compare with other entities; *[IAS 16.73(c), 75]*

(d) the gross carrying amount and the accumulated depreciation (aggregated with accumulated impairment losses) at the beginning and end of the period; *[IAS 16.73(d)]* and

(e) a reconciliation of the carrying amount at the beginning and end of the period showing:
   (i) additions;
   (ii) disposals, and assets classified as held for sale or included in a disposal group held for sale in accordance with IFRS 5;
   (iii) acquisitions through business combinations;
   (iv) increases or decreases resulting from revaluations and from impairment losses recognised or reversed directly in other comprehensive income under IAS 36;
   (v) impairment losses recognised in profit or loss during the period under IAS 36;
   (vi) impairment losses reversed in profit or loss during the period under IAS 36;
   (vii) depreciation;
   (viii) the net exchange differences arising on the translation of the financial statements from the functional currency into a different presentation currency, including the translation of a foreign operation into the presentation currency of the reporting entity; and
   (ix) other changes. *[IAS 16.73(e)]*.

Extract 18.9 below illustrates an accounting policy on PP&E together with the movement and reconciliation note (a comparative is provided in the financial statements but is not reproduced here).

Extract 18.9: Volkswagen Aktiengesellschaft (2016)

Notes to the Consolidated Financial Statements [extract]

Accounting policies [extract]

PROPERTY, PLANT AND EQUIPMENT [extract]

Property, plant and equipment is carried at cost less depreciation and – where necessary – write-downs for impairment. Investment grants are generally deducted from cost. Cost is determined on the basis of the direct and indirect costs that are directly attributable. Special tools are reported under other equipment, operating and office equipment. Property, plant and equipment is depreciated using the straight-line method over its estimated useful life. The useful lives of items of property, plant and equipment are reviewed on a regular basis and adjusted if required.

Depreciation is based mainly on the following useful lives:

	Useful life
Buildings	20 to 50 years
Site improvements	10 to 20 years
Technical equipment and machinery	6 to 12 years
Other equipment, operating and office equipment, including special tools	3 to 15 years

Balance sheet disclosures [extract]

13. **Property, plant and equipment** [extract]

CHANGES IN PROPERTY, PLANT AND EQUIPMENT IN THE PERIOD JANUARY 1 TO DECEMBER 31, 2016 [extract]

€ million	Land, land rights and buildings, including buildings on third-party land	Technical equipment and machinery	Other equipment, operating and office equipment	Payments on account and assets under construction	Total
Cost					
Balance at Jan. 1, 2016	31,036	39,836	58,243	7,717	136,832
Foreign exchange differences	228	429	498	51	1,206
Changes in consolidated Group	42	26	30	1	98
Additions	742	1,843	5,150	5,025	12,760
Transfers	1,639	2,296	1,879	–5,758	55
Disposals	154	1,076	1,203	28	2,461
Balance at Dec. 31, 2016	33,534	43,353	64,595	7,008	148,490
Depreciation and impairment					
Balance at Jan. 1, 2016	12,789	28,148	45,645	79	86,661
Foreign exchange differences	90	305	397	5	796
Changes in consolidated Group	6	14	16	–	36
Additions to cumulative depreciation	1,000	2,918	4,707	–	8,625
Additions to cumulative impairment losses	67	143	291	8	508
Transfers	17	21	15	–46	7
Disposals	81	1,011	1,071	0	2,164
Reversal of impairment losses	–	7	0	7	13
Balance at Dec. 31, 2016	13,887	30,531	49,999	39	94,456
Carrying amount at Dec. 31, 2016	19,647	12,822	14,596	6,969	54,033
of which assets leased under finance leases					
Carrying amount at Dec. 31, 2016	318	9	45	–	372

Options to purchase buildings and plant leased under the terms of finance leases exist in most cases, and are also expected to be exercised.

IAS 16 also requires the disclosure of the following information, which is useful to gain a fuller understanding of the entire position of the entity's holdings of and its commitments to purchase property plant and equipment:

(a) the existence and amounts of restrictions on title, and PP&E pledged as security for liabilities;

(b) the amount of expenditures recognised in the carrying amount of an item of PP&E in the course of construction;

(c) the amount of contractual commitments for the acquisition of PP&E; and

(d) if it is not disclosed separately in the statement of comprehensive income, the amount of compensation from third parties for items of PP&E that were impaired, lost or given up that is included in profit or loss. *[IAS 16.74].*

In addition there is a reminder in the standard that, in accordance with IAS 8, the nature and effect of any change in an accounting estimate (e.g. depreciation methods, useful lives, residual values, and the estimated cost of dismantling, removing or restoring items of PP&E) that has an effect on the current period or is expected to have an effect in future periods must be disclosed. *[IAS 16.76].*

8.2 Additional disclosures for revalued assets

In addition to the disclosures required by IFRS 13, the disclosure requirements in IAS 16 if the revaluation method is adopted are:

(a) the effective date of the revaluation;

(b) whether an independent valuer was involved;

(c) for each revalued class of PP&E, the carrying amount that would have been recognised had the assets been carried under the cost model; and

(d) the revaluation surplus, indicating the change for the period and any restrictions on the distribution of the balance to shareholders. *[IAS 16.77].*

In particular the requirement under (c) is quite onerous for entities, as it entails their keeping asset register information in some detail in order to meet it.

In May 2014, the Interpretations Committee received a request to clarify whether an entity is required to reflect the capitalisation of borrowing costs to meet the disclosure requirement of IAS 16 for assets stated at revalued amounts and for which borrowing costs are not capitalised. Since the capitalisation of borrowing costs for such assets is not required (see Chapter 21 at 3.2), the determination of the amount of borrowing costs that would have been capitalised under a cost model – solely to meet a disclosure requirement – might be considered burdensome.

The Interpretations Committee noted that the requirements in paragraph 77(e) of IAS 16 (i.e. item (c) above) are clear. This paragraph requires an entity to disclose the amount at which assets stated at revalued amounts would have been stated had those assets been carried under the cost model. The amount to be disclosed includes borrowing costs capitalised in accordance with IAS 23 (see Chapter 21).[5]

IFRS 13 has a number of disclosure requirements for assets measured at fair value. Some of the significant disclosures under IFRS 13 which would apply to revalued PP&E are: *[IFRS 13.93]*

- if the highest and best use differs from its current use, an entity must disclose that fact and why the asset is being used in a manner different from its highest and best use;
- the fair value measurement's categorisation within the fair value measurement hierarchy (i.e. Level 1, 2 or 3);
- if categorised within Level 2 or 3 of the fair value hierarchy (which most revalued PP&E is likely to be):
  - (i) a description of the valuation technique(s) used in the fair value measurement;
  - (ii) the inputs used in the fair value measurement;
  - (iii) if there has been a change in the valuation technique (e.g. changing from a market approach to an income approach or use of an additional technique):
    - the change; and
    - the reason(s) for making it;
- quantitative information about the significant unobservable inputs used in the fair value measurement for those categorised within Level 3 of the fair value measurement hierarchy;
- if categorised within Level 3 of the fair value measurement hierarchy, a description of the valuation processes used by the entity (including, for example, how an entity decides its valuation policies and procedures and analyses changes in fair value measurements from period to period).

In addition to these requirements, an entity must also provide the disclosures depending on whether the fair value measurement is recurring or non-recurring. Revalued PP&E are considered recurring fair value measurements and are subject to additional disclosure requirements, which include a qualitative sensitivity analysis. The disclosures for revalued PP&E categorised under Level 3 include a reconciliation from the opening balance to the closing balance, disclosing separately changes during the period to the following:

(i) total gains and losses for the period recognised in profit or loss, and the line item(s) in profit or loss in which these gains or losses are recognised;

(ii) total gains and losses for the period recognised in other comprehensive income, and the line item(s) in other comprehensive income in which those gains or losses are recognised;

(iii) purchases, sales, issues and settlements (separately disclosing each of those types of changes);

(iv) transfers into or out of Level 3 of the fair value hierarchy (separately disclosing and discussing transfers into Level 3 from those out of Level 3) including:

- the amounts of any transfers into or out of Level 3;
- the reasons for those transfers; and
- the entity's policy for determining when transfers between levels are deemed to have occurred. *[IFRS 13.93]*.

These requirements and examples of the requirements are discussed in more detail in Chapter 14 at 20.

8.3 Other disclosures

In addition to the disclosures required by IAS 1, IAS 16 (i.e. those discussed in 8.1 and 8.2 above) and IFRS 13, the standard emphasises that entities are also required to disclose information on impaired PP&E in accordance with IAS 36 (see Chapter 20 at 13.2.1 and 13.2.2). *[IAS 16.78]*.

As users of financial statements may find other information relevant to their needs, the standard encourages, but does not require, entities to disclose other additional information such as the carrying amount of any temporarily idle PP&E, the gross carrying amount of any fully depreciated PP&E that is still in use and the carrying amount of any PP&E retired from active use but not classified as held for disposal in accordance with IFRS 5. For any PP&E measured using the cost model, the disclosure of its fair value is also encouraged when this is materially different from the carrying amount. *[IAS 16.79]*.

References

1 *IFRIC Update*, June 2017.
2 *IFRIC Update*, March 2016.
3 *IASB Update*, May 2016.
4 *Exposure Draft (ED/2017/4) – Property, Plant and Equipment – Proceeds before Intended Use (Proposed amendments to IAS 16)*, IASB, June 2017.
5 *IFRIC Update*, May 2014.

Chapter 19 Investment property

List of examples

List of examples

Chapter 19 Investment property

1 INTRODUCTION

IAS 40 – *Investment Property* – is an example of the particular commercial characteristics of an industry resulting in the special accounting treatment of a certain category of asset, i.e. investment property. However, it is not only investment property companies that hold investment property; any property that meets the investment property definition in IAS 40 is so classified, irrespective of the nature of the business of the reporting entity. This standard should be applied in the recognition, measurement and disclosure of investment property. *[IAS 40.1, 2]*.

The original standard, which was approved in 2000, was the first international standard to introduce the possibility of applying a fair value model for non-financial assets where all valuation changes from one period to the next are reported in profit or loss. This contrasts with the revaluation approach allowed under IAS 16 – *Property, Plant and Equipment* (see Chapter 18 at 6) where increases above cost, and their reversals, are recognised directly in Other Comprehensive Income ('OCI').

The exposure draft that preceded IAS 40 proposed that fair value should be the sole measurement model for investment property. However, some respondents were concerned that, in certain parts of the world, property markets were not sufficiently liquid to support fair value measurement for financial reporting purposes. Consequently, the cost option was introduced into the standard, as the Board believed, at that stage, that it was impracticable to require a fair value model for all investment property.

Despite the free choice of model available, IAS 40 has a rebuttable presumption that, other than in exceptional cases, an entity can measure the fair value of a completed investment property reliably on a continuing basis.

The question of the reliability of valuations was given greater focus following the change in scope of the standard in 2009 to include investment property under construction (see 2.5 below) because, following that change, the standard allows investment property under construction to be measured at cost if the fair value cannot be measured reliably. However, in this case, the standard is not explicit on whether this should be confined to 'exceptional cases' or not.

This chapter discusses the revised version of IAS 40, which was published in December 2003, as updated by various narrow-scope amendments, including *Transfers of Investment*

Property (Amendments to IAS 40) and minor consequential amendments arising from other standards including IFRS 15 – *Revenue from Contracts with Customers*.

In May 2014, the IASB issued a new revenue standard, IFRS 15 which supersedes all revenue recognition standards and interpretations in IFRS including IAS 11 – *Construction Contracts*, IAS 18 – *Revenue* – and IFRIC 15 – *Agreements for the Construction of Real Estate*. The consequential amendments arising from IFRS 15 include updated example of items that are not investment property (see 2.6 below). The new standard also provides a model for the measurement and recognition of gains and losses on the sale of certain non-financial assets, such as investment properties, when that disposal is not in the ordinary course of business. As a consequence, the existing requirements for the recognition of a gain or loss on the disposal of a non-financial asset in IAS 40 have been amended (see 10 and 10.1 below). Entities are required to apply IFRS 15 and its consequential amendments to other standards for annual reporting periods beginning on or after 1 January 2018. Early application is permitted. For the detailed discussions and requirements of IFRS 15, see Chapter 30.

In December 2016, the IASB issued narrow-scope amendments – *Transfers of Investment Property (Amendments to IAS 40)* – which clarify when an entity should transfer property, including property under construction or development into, or out of investment property. Entities are required to apply these amendments for annual reporting periods beginning on or after 1 January 2018. Early application is permitted. See 9.1 below for further discussion.

IFRS 16 – *Leases* – and IFRS 17 – *Insurance Contracts* – will result in further changes to IAS 40 in later accounting periods (see 13 below).

2 DEFINITIONS AND SCOPE

An investment property is defined in IAS 40 as 'property (land or a building – or part of a building – or both) held (by the owner or by the lessee under a finance lease) to earn rentals or for capital appreciation or both, rather than for:

(a) use in the production or supply of goods or services or for administrative purposes; or
(b) sale in the ordinary course of business.' *[IAS 40.5]*.

This means that any entity, whatever the underlying nature of its business, can hold investment property assets if its intention on initial recognition (either by acquisition or change in use – see 9 below) is to hold them for rent or for capital appreciation or both. Subsequent to initial recognition, assets might be reclassified into and from investment property (see 9 below). It is also of note that an investment property can be held under an operating lease (see 2.1 below).

In contrast, 'owner-occupied' property is defined as 'property held (by the owner or by the lessee under a finance lease) for use in the production or supply of goods or services or for administrative purposes.' *[IAS 40.5]*. Such property falls outside the scope of IAS 40 and is accounted for under IAS 16 (see Chapter 18), together with IAS 17 – *Leases* (see Chapter 24), if relevant.

IAS 40 applies to the measurement in a lessee's financial statements of investment property interests held under a finance lease and to the measurement in a lessor's financial statements of investment property provided to a lessee under an operating lease (see 2.3 below). However, it does not deal with other accounting matters that are dealt with in IAS 17 (see Chapter 24), including:

- Classification of leases as finance or operating leases.
- Recognition of lease income arising from the leasing of investment property.
- Measurement in a lessee's financial statements of property interests held under a lease accounted for as an operating lease. However, such property interests held under operating leases can be within the scope of IAS 40 if certain criteria are met (see 2.1 below).
- Measurement in a lessor's financial statements of its net investment in a finance lease.
- Accounting for sale and leaseback transactions.
- Disclosure about finance leases and operating leases. *[IAS 40.3].*

Note that in January 2016, the new leases standard, IFRS 16, was issued and will supersede IAS 17 when it becomes effective in 2019. IFRS 16 will amend the scope of IAS 40 so that paragraph 3 of IAS 40 described above will be deleted. Also paragraph 5 of IAS 40 will be amended so that the definitions of 'investment property' and 'owner-occupied property', as set out above, will include both owned investment property and investment property held by a lessee as a right-of-use asset. See 13.1 below for further discussion.

IAS 40 does not apply to:

- biological assets related to agricultural activity (see IAS 41 – *Agriculture* – and IAS 16); and
- mineral rights and mineral reserves such as oil, natural gas and similar non-regenerative resources. *[IAS 40.4].*

Biological assets that are physically attached to land (for example, trees in a plantation forest) are measured at their fair value less estimated point-of-sale costs separately from the land. *[IAS 41.12].* However, the land related to the agricultural activity is accounted for either as property under IAS 16 or investment property under IAS 40. *[IAS 41.2].*

What primarily distinguishes investment property from other types of property interest is that its cash flows (from rental or sale) are largely independent of those from other assets held by the entity. By contrast, owner-occupied property used by an entity for administrative purposes or for the production or supply of goods or services does not generate cash flows itself but does so only in conjunction with other assets used in the production or supply process. IAS 16 applies to owner-occupied property. *[IAS 40.7].*

However, even with this distinction, it may not be easy to distinguish investment property from owner-occupied property. The standard therefore gives guidance to help determine whether or not an asset is an investment property (see 2.1 to 2.10 below). Note that when IFRS 16 is adopted (see 13.1 below), IAS 40 will be amended so that it will refer to IAS 16 for owned owner-occupied property and to IFRS 16 for owner-occupied property held by a lessee as a right-of-use asset.

It is also worthy of note that the Interpretations Committee has discussed the accounting for a structure that 'lacks the physical characteristics of a building', i.e. whether it should be accounted for as investment property in accordance with IAS 40. This primarily related to an emerging business model in which an entity owns telecommunication towers and leases spaces in the towers to telecommunication operators to which the operators attach their own devices. The entity may also provide some basic services to the telecommunication operators such as maintenance services.[1]

The request specifically sought clarification on whether a telecommunication tower should be viewed as a 'building' and thus 'property', as described in paragraph 5 of IAS 40 and how any service element in the leasing agreement and business model of the entity should be taken into consideration when analysing the issue.

The Interpretations Committee observed that the tower has some of the characteristics of investment property, in that spaces in the tower were let to tenants to earn rentals (e.g. leasing of spaces for telecommunication operators to which operators attach their own devices) but questioned whether the tower qualifies as a 'building' because it lacks features usually associated with a building such as walls, floors and a roof. They also observed that the same question could arise about other structures, such as gas storage tanks and advertising billboards.[2]

The Interpretations Committee observed that there would be merit in exploring approaches to amending IAS 40 to include structures that lack the physical characteristics associated with a building.[3] However, following research on this issue, the IASB decided not to pursue this issue because there appeared to be limited demand for fair value accounting for these types of structures and limited diversity in practice.[4]

2.1 Property interests held under operating leases

Entities are permitted to treat property interests held under operating leases as investment property – providing that they would otherwise meet the definition of investment property and that the fair value model is applied (see 6 below). This classification alternative is available on a property-by-property basis so that the entity need not classify all property interests held under operating leases as investment property. *[IAS 40.6]*.

However, IAS 40 requires that once one operating leasehold interest is classified as an investment property, all property classified as investment property must be accounted for using the fair value model. These leasehold interests are subject also to the same disclosure requirements as other investment properties accounted for under the fair value method (see 12 below). *[IAS 40.6, 34]*.

Note that the guidance on the classification alternative of leased property described above will be superseded by IFRS 16 which is effective in 2019. Consequently, paragraphs 6 and 34 of IAS 40 (as described above and in 5.1 below) will be deleted so that the classification alternative for a property interest held under an operating lease will no longer be available. This means that if a leased property meets the definition of investment property and the lessee elects the fair value model in IAS 40 as an accounting policy, the right-of-use asset arising from the leased property will be measured in accordance with the fair value model of IAS 40. For further discussion, see 13.1 below and Chapter 25.

IAS 17 or, if adopted, IFRS 16, generally requires leases to be separated into land and building components unless either such allocation cannot be made reliably or the land element is immaterial (see Chapter 24 at 3.3.3 and Chapter 25 at 6.1.2). However, if the interest is to be an investment property carried at fair value in accordance with IAS 40, there is no requirement under IAS 17 to separate the land and buildings elements of the lease. *[IAS 17.18]*. IFRS 16 does not contain similar specific provisions for investment property.

2.2 Land

Land is investment property if it is held to earn rentals or for capital appreciation or for both; or for a currently undetermined future use. This is in contrast to land that is held for sale in the ordinary course of business (typically in the shorter term) or held for the production or supply of goods and services or for administrative purposes. *[IAS 40.7, 8]*.

If, on initial recognition, land is held for a currently undetermined future use, i.e. if an entity has not determined whether it will use the land as owner-occupied property or for sale in the ordinary course of business, it is deemed to be held for capital appreciation and must be classified as investment property. *[IAS 40.8]*.

2.3 Property leased to others

Properties leased to third parties under one or more operating lease are generally investment properties, whether they are owned freehold by the reporting entity or held under a leasehold interest (or if IFRS 16 is adopted (see 13.1 below), whether they are right-of-use assets relating to properties held by the reporting entity). This will also apply if the property is currently vacant while tenants are being sought. *[IAS 40.8]*.

However, in our opinion, an exception should be made in those cases where, despite being leased out, properties have been held for sale in the ordinary course of business since their initial recognition (either by acquisition or change in use – see 9 below). Leasing of property prior to sale is a common practice in the real estate industry in order to minimise cash outflows whilst the entity seeks a buyer and because prospective buyers may view the existence of such lease contracts positively, especially those that wish to acquire property for investment purposes.

In those circumstances – and notwithstanding that they are leased to tenants under operating leases – they should be accounted for as inventory under IAS 2 – *Inventories* – as long as it remains the intention to hold such properties for short-term sale in the ordinary course of business. The rent received would be recorded in profit or loss and would not be treated as a reduction in the cost of inventory.

Property that is leased to a third party under a finance lease is not an investment property but is accounted for under IAS 17 (see Chapter 24) or, if adopted, IFRS 16 (see Chapter 25). *[IAS 40.9]*.

2.4 Property held for own use ('owner-occupied')

As noted above, owner-occupied property, that is property held for use in the production or supply of goods or services or for administrative purposes, is specifically excluded from being treated as investment property and is subject to the provisions of IAS 16 and, if adopted, IFRS 16 (see 13.1 below). Owner-occupied property includes:

- property that is going to be owner-occupied in the future (whether or not it has first to be redeveloped);
- property occupied by employees (whether or not they pay rent at market rates); and
- owner-occupied property awaiting disposal. *[IAS 40.9]*.

Note that the treatment in the consolidated accounts can be different from the treatment by individual group entities. For example, it may be the case that a property owned by one group company is held for occupation by another group company. This will be owner-occupied from the perspective of the group as a whole but can be classified as an investment property in the accounts of the individual entity that owns it, provided it meets the definition of an investment property. *[IAS 40.15]*. This classification in the individual entity's financial statements will apply even if the rental is not at arm's length and the individual entity is not in a position to benefit from capital appreciation. The IASB concluded that the more significant factor is that the property itself will generate cash flows that are largely independent from other assets held by the entity. *[IAS 40.7]*.

Associates and joint ventures are not part of the group. Therefore, a property owned by the group but occupied by an associate or a joint venture would be accounted for as investment property in the consolidated financial statements (provided, of course, it meets the investment property definition).

2.5 Investment property under construction

Prior to 1 January 2009, IAS 16 applied to property that was being constructed or developed for future use as investment property until construction or development was complete, at which time the property became investment property. Amendments to IAS 40 with effect from 1 January 2009 brought investment property under construction within the scope of IAS 40. *[IAS 40.8]*.

The fair value of investment property under construction is further discussed in 6.3 below.

2.6 Property held or under construction for sale in the ordinary course of business

Property held, or being constructed, with the intention of sale in the ordinary course of business is not an investment property. This includes:

- property acquired exclusively for sale in the near future or for development and resale (such property is accounted for as inventory under IAS 2 (see Chapter 22)); *[IAS 40.9(a)]* and
- prior to adoption of IFRS 15, property being built or developed under a construction contract for third parties which was covered by IAS 11 and discussed in Chapter 23. *[IAS 40.9(b)]*. As part of the consequential amendments arising from IFRS 15, paragraph 9(b) of IAS 40 is deleted to exclude such property from the examples of items that are not investment property (see also 1 above).

In practice, the classification between investment property and property intended for sale in the ordinary course of business is often a difficult judgement. There is only a fine line between:

- a property held for capital appreciation, and therefore classified as investment property; and
- a property intended for sale in the ordinary course of business, which would be classified as inventory. This might be the case where, for example, the owner will undertake activities to increase the property's value prior to sale or where there is uncertainty in obtaining permits required from relevant authorities prior to commencing construction activities. In the latter case, the property, e.g. land, may continue to appreciate in value during the period where there are no development activities – see 3.1 below.

As set out in 2.3 above, the receipt of rental income from a property would not necessarily be the deciding factor. Certainly, other than for land (see 2.2 above), IAS 40 provides no explicit 'default' classification when the future use of a property has not yet been determined.

However, this judgement is important because whilst IAS 40 allows property held as inventory to be reclassified as investment property when there is a change in use and an operating lease with a third party is entered into, it is more difficult to reclassify investment property as inventory (see 9.1 and 9.2 below). Accordingly, an entity should develop criteria so that it can exercise that judgement consistently in accordance with the definition of investment property and with the related guidance in IAS 40. Such criteria are required to be disclosed when classification is difficult (see 12.1 below). *[IAS 40.14]*.

2.7 Property with dual uses

A property may be used partly to derive rental income and partly as owner-occupied property. For example, an office could be sub-divided by the owner with some floors being rented to tenants whilst retaining others for own use.

IAS 40 states that if a property has both investment property and non-investment property uses, providing the parts of the property could be sold or leased out under a finance lease separately, they should be accounted for separately. *[IAS 40.10]*.

However, to meet these requirements we consider that a property must actually be in a state and condition to enable it to be disposed of or leased out separately at the end of the reporting period. The fact that a property could be divided in future periods if the owner so chose is insufficient to conclude that the portions can be accounted for separately. Consequently, if a property requires sub-division before the portions could be disposed of separately, then those parts should not, in our view, be accounted for as separate portions until such sub-divisions occur unless sub-division is a non-substantive legal requirement (see below).

In our view, an intention to lease out, or the action of leasing out a portion of a property under an operating lease is *prima facie* evidence that, if it so wished, the entity could also lease out the property under a finance lease – the difference between the two commonly being just the length of the lease. If however, there is evidence that the property could not be leased out under a finance lease then IAS 40 could not be applied to that portion.

It also seems clear that 'separately' needs to be assessed both in terms of the physical separation (for example, mezzanine floors and partitioning walls) of the property and legal separation such as legally defined boundaries.

In many jurisdictions, properties that are physically sub-divided into different portions (for example, different floors) are registered in a land or property registry as one single property and need to be legally sub-divided before a portion can be leased out to a third party or disposed of. Often, these legal proceedings are undertaken only at or near the point of sale or the assignment of a lease on that portion of the property concerned. At the end of the reporting period the legal sub-division may not have occurred.

Accordingly, judgement is required to determine whether legal separation is a substantive requirement that will restrict the property being considered currently separable or whether it is a non-substantive requirement where the property is currently separable. For example:

- If the entity owning the property could not be prevented from legally sub-dividing the property then it is already in a condition to be sold separately and this would not prevent the portion of the property concerned being accounted for as investment property. This would be the case where, for example: the process of sub-dividing the property was entirely within the control of the entity and did not require permission from a third party (which would include the relevant authorities); or if permission from a third party was required, but this was no more than a formality.
- Conversely, if the entity was required to obtain the permission of third parties before legally sub-dividing the property, and such permission could realistically be withheld, the portions of the property concerned are not accounted for separately until such legal sub-division occurs.

Therefore, if the portion of the property concerned otherwise meets the definition of investment property at the end of the reporting period, judgement is required to assess the legal position of the property in determining whether it is appropriate to account for a portion separately under IAS 40. Criteria used in the assessment should be disclosed and applied consistently (see 12.1 below). *[IAS 40.14]*.

In the event that no separation is possible, the property is an investment property only if an insignificant proportion is used for non-investment property purposes. *[IAS 40.10]*.

The setting of a threshold to evaluate whether or not something is significant or insignificant depends on judgement and circumstances. In the extract below, PSP Swiss Property discloses its judgement about dealing with property that it partially uses, but other entities will need to make their own assessment.

> *Extract 19.1: PSP Swiss Property Ltd (2016)*
>
> **Notes to the consolidated 2016 financial statements** [extract]
>
> 2 **Summary of significant accounting policies**[extract]
>
> 2.6 **Accounting and valuation principles** [extract]
>
> **Own-used properties**
>
> In accordance with IAS 16, properties used by the Company itself are stated at historical cost and depreciated over their economically useful life according to their significant components. Depreciable life (linear) is 40 years for buildings and 20 years for facilities (such as air-conditioning, elevators, ventilation etc.). Land belonging to the property is not depreciated. Where the Company uses only part of a property it owns, utilisation of less than 25% is regarded as immaterial, which means that the whole property is stated at market value as an investment property.

2.8 Property with the provision of ancillary services

If the owner supplies ancillary services to the user of the investment property, the property will not qualify as an investment property unless these services are an insignificant component of the arrangement as a whole. For example, security and maintenance services are described by the standard as being insignificant. *[IAS 40.11]*.

The crucial issue is the extent to which the owner retains significant exposure to the risks of running a business. The standard uses the example of a hotel. An owner-managed hotel, for example, would be precluded from being an investment property as the services provided to guests are a significant component of the commercial arrangements. *[IAS 40.12-13]*. However, the nature of the asset in question is not the key factor; rather it is the nature of the owner's interest in the asset. If the owner's position is, in substance, that of a passive investor, any property may be treated as investment property. If, in contrast, the owner has outsourced day-to-day functions while retaining significant exposure to variation in the cash flows generated by the operations that are being executed in the building, a property should rather be treated as owner-occupied property. *[IAS 40.13]*.

The standard refers to owner-managed hotels as being precluded from being investment property. Hotel properties that are leased on arm's length terms to hotel operators may, however, fall to be accounted for as investment property. This is more likely to be the case when:

- the payments under the lease are not significantly determined by the results of the hotel operator (see 2.9 below), rather they reflect the general market for such properties; and
- the nature of the owner's rights in the arrangements with the operator is not divergent from those usually expected under a property lease.

The standard acknowledges that this question of significance can require judgements to be made. It specifies that an entity should develop consistent criteria for use in such instances that reflect the provisions described above. These criteria must be disclosed in those cases where classification is difficult. *[IAS 40.14]*.

See also 3.3 below where the question of classification of a property as a business or as an asset is considered.

2.9 Property where rentals are determined by reference to the operations in the property

It may also be inappropriate to consider a property as investment property if the owner is significantly exposed to the operation of the business in the property through a linkage between the rentals charged and the performance of the business.

A common example is the incidence of turnover- or profit-related rents in retail leases. If the turnover- or profit-related element is a very significant proportion of total rental then consideration should be given to whether the landlord is so exposed to the performance of the underlying retail business as to make classification of the property as investment property inappropriate. This will be a matter of judgement, including the consideration of any other facts and circumstances (for example, the length of the lease to the tenant).

2.10 Group of assets leased out under a single operating lease

It is sometimes the case in practice that a group of assets comprising land, buildings and 'other assets' is leased out by a lessor under a single lease contract in order to earn rentals. In such a case, the 'other assets' would generally comprise assets that relate to the manner in which the land and buildings are used under the lease. The issue that arises is under what circumstances the 'other assets' should be regarded by the lessor as part of an investment property rather than as a separate item of property, plant and equipment. This is illustrated in the following example:

Example 19.1: Definition of an investment property: a group of assets leased out under a single operating lease

A lessor enters into the following two single contract leases in order to earn rentals. All the individual assets subject to the leases meet the test of being classified as an operating lease. The lessor applies the fair value measurement model for subsequent measurement of investment property.

Lease 1: Vineyard and winery

A vineyard including a winery is leased out under an operating lease. The vineyard comprises the following assets:

- land;
- vineyard infrastructure (e.g. trellises);
- winery building structures;
- winery plant and machinery (crushing equipment, distilling equipment); and
- vines (grapes are excluded, as they belong to the lessee).

Lease 2: Port

A port is leased out under an operating lease. The port comprises the following assets:

- land;
- warehouses;
- transport infrastructure to and from the port (roads, rail tracks, bridges);
- wharves;
- light towers (that enable the 24-hour operation of the port); and
- specialised container cranes (to be able to move containers around).

To what extent can the 'other assets' included in the leases (but which are not considered to constitute a piece of land or a building) be included in the investment property definition under IAS 40?

The consequence of including plant and equipment in the definition of investment property is that if the investment property is accounted for at fair value, changes in the fair value of that plant and equipment will, like changes in the fair value of the land and buildings, be recognised in profit or loss.

From a literal reading of the definition of an investment property in paragraph 5 of IAS 40, it could be argued that an investment property can consist only of a building (or part of a building), a piece of land, or both and cannot include 'other assets'. However, such an interpretation is inconsistent with paragraph 50 of IAS 40, which implies that a broader interpretation is more appropriate. Paragraphs 50(a) and (b) of IAS 40 read as follows:

'In determining the carrying amount of investment property under the fair value model, an entity does not double-count assets or liabilities that are recognised as separate assets or liabilities. For example:

(a) equipment such as lifts or air-conditioning is often an integral part of a building and is generally included in the fair value of the investment property, rather than recognised separately as property, plant and equipment.

(b) if an office is leased on a furnished basis, the fair value of the office generally includes the fair value of the furniture, because the rental income relates to the furnished office. When furniture is included in the fair value of investment property, an entity does not recognise that furniture as a separate asset.' *[IAS 40.50(a), 50(b)]*.

Although paragraph 50 addresses the fair valuation of investment property, it nevertheless implies that other assets that are integral to the land and buildings or are otherwise required to be included in the lease in order to generate rental income under the lease concerned should also be regarded as being part of the investment property.

Consequently, in our view, an item other than a piece of land or a building should be regarded by a lessor as being part of an investment property if this item is an integral part of it, that is, it is necessary for the land and buildings to be used by a lessee in the manner intended and is leased to the lessee on the same basis (e.g. as a package with the same lease term) as the land and buildings. The determination as to whether or not an item constitutes an integral part of an investment property requires judgement and will depend on the particular facts and circumstances. However, it is our view that in order for all the assets to be classified as investment property, the following conditions should be present:

- the land and buildings should be the 'dominant assets' that form the investment property;
- the 'other assets' are leased to the lessee together with the land and building as a whole; and
- the entire group of assets is generating the income stream from the lease contract.

This means that, in the case of Lease 1, the investment property comprises the land, the vineyard infrastructure, the winery building structures and the winery plant and machinery. Vines, which meet the definition of biological assets, are subject to the requirements of IAS 41. They are excluded because 'biological assets related to agricultural activity' are outside the scope of IAS 40. *[IAS 40.4(a)]*.

In the case of Lease 2, the investment property comprises all of the assets, i.e. the land, the warehouses, the transport infrastructure, the wharves, the light towers, and the specialised container cranes.

3 RECOGNITION

An investment property should be recognised as an asset when, and only when, it is probable that the future economic benefits that are associated with the investment property will flow to the entity and its cost can be measured reliably. *[IAS 40.16]*.

These recognition criteria apply for any costs incurred, whether initially or subsequently. This means that all costs related to investment property, whether on initial recognition or thereafter (for example, to add to, or replace part of, or service a property) must meet the recognition criteria at the point at which the expenditure is incurred if they are to be capitalised. *[IAS 40.17]*.

Note that when IFRS 16 is adopted (see 13.1 below), paragraph 16 of IAS 40 is amended so that an owned investment property will continue to be recognised as described above. IFRS 16 adds a new paragraph 19A to IAS 40 so that an investment property held by a lessee as a right-of-use asset will be recognised in accordance with IFRS 16.

3.1 Expenditure prior to planning permissions/zoning consents

In many jurisdictions, permissions from relevant authorities are required prior to development of new or existing property, and the ability to start physical construction of the development depends on these permissions.

Application for such permissions supports the entity's intention as to the use of the property and may be considered as a factor in classifying the asset. However, unless an entity is considering a number of possible uses of the asset at its initial recognition, the uncertainty in obtaining relevant permission would usually not affect the classification of the property which, as set out in 2 above, is mainly based on the entity's intention when the property is first acquired. Subsequent to initial recognition, assets might be reclassified into and from investment property (see 9 below).

The likelihood of obtaining such permissions, however, is relevant in recognition and measurement of any additional costs to the property. Developers typically incur significant costs prior to such permissions being granted and such permissions are rarely guaranteed. Therefore, in assessing whether such pre-permission expenditure can be capitalised – assuming it otherwise meets the criteria – a judgement must be made, at the date the expenditure is incurred, of whether there is sufficient probability that the relevant permissions will be granted. Conversely, if during the application and approval process of such permits it is no longer expected that necessary permits will be granted, capitalisation of pre-permission expenditure should cease and any related amounts that were previously capitalised should be written off (either under the fair value model in IAS 40 (see 6 below) or in accordance with IAS 36 – *Impairment of Assets*, if the cost model is applied (see 7.3 below)). Further, if the cost model is used, the carrying amount of any related property subject to development or redevelopment (or, if appropriate, the cash generating unit where such an asset belongs) should be tested for impairment, where applicable, in accordance with IAS 36 (see 7.3 below).

3.2 Other aspects of cost recognition

3.2.1 Repairs and maintenance

Day-to-day servicing, by which is meant the repairs and maintenance of the property which largely comprises labour costs, consumables and minor parts, should be recognised in profit or loss as incurred. *[IAS 40.18]*. However, the treatment is different if large parts of the properties have been replaced – the standard cites the example of interior walls that are replacements of the original walls. In this case, the cost of replacing the part will be recognised at the time that cost is incurred if the recognition criteria are met, while the carrying amount of the original part is derecognised (see 10.3 below). *[IAS 40.19]*.

The inference is that by restoring the asset to its originally assessed standard of performance, the new part will meet the recognition criteria and future economic benefits will flow to the entity once the old part is replaced. The inference is also that replacement is needed for the total asset to be operative. This being the case, the new walls will therefore meet the recognition criteria and the cost will therefore be capitalised.

Other than interior walls, large parts that might have to be replaced include elements such as lifts, escalators and air conditioning equipment.

3.2.2 Allocation into parts

IAS 40 does not explicitly require an analysis of investment properties into components or parts. However, this analysis is needed for the purposes of recognition and derecognition of all expenditure after the asset has initially been recognised and (if the parts are significant) for depreciation of those parts (see Chapter 18 at 5.1). Some of this is not relevant to assets held under the fair value model that are not depreciated because the standard expects the necessary adjustments to the carrying value of the asset as a whole to be made via the fair value mechanism (see 6 below). However, entities that adopt the cost model are obliged to account for assets after initial recognition in accordance with the requirements of IAS 16. The cost model is discussed further at 7 below.

3.3 Acquisition of investment property or a business combination?

IFRS 3 – *Business Combinations* – defines a business as '[a]n integrated set of activities and assets that is capable of being conducted and managed for the purpose of providing a return in the form of dividends, lower costs or other economic benefits...'. *[IFRS 3 Appendix A]*. However, the standard goes on to say that a business need not include all of the inputs or processes that the seller used in operating that business if market participants are 'capable of' acquiring the business and continuing to produce outputs, for example, by integrating the business with their own. *[IFRS 3.B8, B11]*.

The phrase 'capable of' is sufficiently broad that judgement will be required in assessing if an acquired set of activities and assets, such as investment property, constitutes a business. In isolation this requirement could be interpreted to mean that the acquisition of most investment properties should be dealt with as a business combination under IFRS 3 (and therefore be recognised in accordance with IFRS 3 rather than IAS 40). If dealt with under IFRS 3, then the initial accounting for investment property is considerably more complex. For example, amongst other requirements:

- initial direct costs are expensed (IAS 40 allows these to be capitalised – see 4.1 below);
- the initial recognition exception for deferred taxation does not apply (IAS 12 – *Income Taxes* – does not allow deferred taxation to be provided on existing temporary differences for acquisitions that are not business combinations); and
- goodwill is recognised (often itself 'created' by the provision of deferred taxation).

Judging whether an acquisition is a business combination or not is therefore of considerable importance. *[IAS 40.14A]*.

IAS 40 notes, in relation to the need to distinguish investment property from owner-occupied property, that where certain ancillary processes exist in connection with an investment property they are often insignificant to the overall arrangement (see 2.8 above). Consequently, it may be appropriate to conclude that, where such acquired processes are considered by IAS 40 to be insignificant, an investment property acquisition is within the scope of IAS 40 rather than IFRS 3. However, it should be noted that IAS 40 and IFRS 3 are not mutually exclusive and this determination is not the specific purpose of the standard's observation about ancillary services.

In July 2011, the Interpretations Committee received a request seeking clarification on precisely this point – whether the acquisition of a single investment property, with lease agreements with multiple tenants over varying periods and associated processes, such as cleaning, maintenance and administrative services such as rent collection, constitutes a business as defined in IFRS 3.[5]

Consequently, the IASB issued the *Annual Improvements to IFRSs 2011-2013 Cycle* on 12 December 2013 which amended IAS 40 to state explicitly that the judgement required to determine whether the acquisition of investment property is the acquisition of an asset or a group of assets – or a business combination within the scope of IFRS 3 – should only be made with reference to IFRS 3.

This clarified that the discussion about 'ancillary services' in paragraphs 7-14 of IAS 40 (see 2.8 above) relates to whether or not property is owner-occupied property or investment property and not to determining whether or not a property is a business as defined in IFRS 3. Determining whether a specific transaction meets the definition of a business combination as defined in IFRS 3 and includes an investment property as defined in IAS 40 requires the separate application of both standards. *[IAS 40.14A]*.

It will be a matter of judgement for preparers, but it may still be appropriate to conclude that, when applying the guidance in IFRS 3, if acquired processes are considered to be insignificant (whether by reference to guidance in IAS 40 or otherwise) an investment property acquisition is within the scope of IAS 40 rather than IFRS 3. This judgement will rest upon the facts and circumstances of each acquisition. If significant, disclosure of this judgement would be required by IAS 1 – *Presentation of Financial Statements*. *[IAS 1.122]*.

The definition of a business is applied regardless of whether the entity purchases a property directly or, in the case of consolidated financial statements, via the shares in another entity.

We discuss at 3.3.1 below a recent Exposure Draft relating to the definition of a business. See also Chapter 9 at 3 for additional discussion in identifying a business combination.

3.3.1 Possible future developments – exposure draft on definition of a business

The IASB recognises the difficulties in determining whether an acquisition meets the definition of a business – which are not just limited to investment property – and explored this issue in its post-implementation review of IFRS 3 which was completed in June 2015. As a result, in June 2016 the IASB issued an Exposure Draft ED/2016/1 – *Definition of a Business and Accounting for Previously Held Interests (Proposed amendments to IFRS 3 and IFRS 11)* ('the Exposure Draft'). The proposed amendments include clarification of the application of the definition of a business. The IASB aims to provide additional guidance to help distinguish between the acquisition of a business and the acquisition of a group of assets.

The Exposure Draft proposes a screening test designed to simplify the evaluation of whether an integrated set of activities and assets constitutes a business. Under the proposed amendments, an integrated set of activities and assets is not a business if a concentration of fair value exists. A concentration would exist if substantially all of the fair value of the gross assets acquired is concentrated in a single identifiable asset or group of similar identifiable assets. This proposed 'screening test' is based on the fair value of the gross assets acquired (i.e. any acquired input, contract, process, workforce and any other intangible asset that is not identifiable), rather than the fair value of the total consideration paid or the net assets. Thus, the significance of a single asset or a group of similar assets acquired is assessed without considering how they are financed.

For this screening test, a single identifiable asset is any asset or group of assets that would be recognised and measured as a single identifiable asset in a business combination. In addition, for this screening test, tangible assets that are attached to, and cannot be physically removed and used separately from, other tangible assets without incurring significant cost, or significant diminution in utility or fair value to either asset, should be considered a single identifiable asset.

If this screening test indicates that an integrated set of activities and assets is not a business, then an entity would not have to evaluate the other guidance included in the definition of a business. This is discussed further in Chapter 9 at 3.

The Exposure Draft also proposed a number of examples to IFRS 3 to assist with the interpretation of what is considered a business. These include examples relating to the acquisition of investment properties.

One of the proposed examples describes an entity that purchases a multi-tenant corporate office park with six 10-storey office buildings that are fully leased. The acquired set of activities and assets includes the land, buildings, leases and contracts for outsourced cleaning and security. No employees, other assets, or other activities are transferred. The contracts for outsourced cleaning and security are ancillary and have a fair value of nil.

After considering the guidance proposed in the Exposure Draft as described above, the entity concludes that:

(a) the buildings and the land are considered as a single asset for the purpose of assessing the concentration of fair value because, although they are different classes of tangible assets, the buildings are attached to the land and cannot be removed without incurring significant cost;

(b) the building and the leases are considered as a single asset, because they would be recognised and measured as a single identifiable asset in a business combination in line with paragraph B42 of IFRS 3;

(c) the group of six 10-storey office buildings is a group of similar assets (all office buildings); and

(d) the fair value associated with the acquired contracts for cleaning and security is nil.

Consequently, the fair value of the gross assets acquired is concentrated in a group of similar assets and so the set of activities and assets purchased is not a business.[6]

A second example assumes the same facts as in the example above except that the purchased set of activities and assets includes the employees responsible for leasing, tenant management, and managing and supervising all operational processes and the purchase price is significantly higher because of the employees and processes acquired.

In these circumstances, the entity concludes that there is significant fair value associated with the acquired workforce, i.e. the fair value of the gross assets purchased is not concentrated in a group of similar identifiable assets. The set of activities and assets has outputs as it generates revenues through the in-place leases. Consequently, the entity will need to apply the criteria in the other proposed guidance included in the definition of a business to determine whether the set includes both an input and a substantive process. See Chapter 9 at 3 for detailed discussion.

In this specific example in the Exposure Draft, the entity concludes that the set of activities and assets acquired is a business because the set includes an organised workforce that performs processes (i.e. leasing, tenant management and supervision of the operational processes) critical to the ability to continue producing outputs when applied to the acquired inputs (i.e. the land, buildings, and in-place leases).[7]

In its April 2017 meeting the IASB discussed the comments received on the Exposure Draft particularly relating to the screening test (as described above) and tentatively decided to:

- make the screening test optional on a transaction-by-transaction basis. Thus an entity could on a transaction-by-transaction basis elect to bypass the screening test and assess directly whether a substantive process has been acquired;
- confirm that the screening test is determinative. This means that if an entity has carried out the screening test and concluded that a concentration exists, the entity should treat the transaction as an asset purchase. There is no further assessment that might change that conclusion. If no concentration exists, the entity then should assess whether it has acquired a substantive process;
- specify that the gross assets considered in the screening test exclude: i) goodwill resulting from the effects of deferred tax liabilities, and ii) deferred tax assets;
- clarify that guidance on 'a single asset' for the screening test also applies when one of the acquired assets is a right-of-use asset, as described in IFRS 16 (for example leasehold land and the building on it are a single asset for the screening test);
- clarify that when assessing whether assets are 'similar' for the screening test, an entity should consider the nature of each single asset and the risks associated with managing and creating outputs from the assets; and
- clarify that the new guidance on what assets may be considered a single asset or a group of similar assets is not intended to modify the existing guidance on similar assets in paragraph 36 of IAS 38 – *Intangible Assets* – and the term 'class' in IAS 16, IAS 38 and IFRS 7 – *Financial Instruments: Disclosures.*[8]

The IASB subsequently continued discussing the comments received on various aspects of the Exposure Draft and, in its June 2017 meeting, tentatively decided to reaffirm a number of items already included in the Exposure Draft and clarify certain principles used – see Chapter 9 at 3.2.6 for detailed discussion of these updates.[9]

4 INITIAL MEASUREMENT

4.1 Attributable costs

IAS 40 requires an investment property to be measured initially at cost, which includes transaction costs. *[IAS 40.20]*. If a property is purchased, cost means purchase price and any directly attributable expenditure such as professional fees, property transfer taxes and other transaction costs. *[IAS 40.21]*.

As noted in 2.5 above, prior to 2009, investment property under construction was subject to IAS 16 until completed at which time it became investment property to which IAS 40 applied. This meant that only those elements of cost that were allowed by IAS 16 could be capitalised and that capitalisation ceased when the asset has reached the condition necessary for it to be capable of operating in the manner intended by management. *[IAS 16.16(b)]*.

Although there is no longer a specific reference to IAS 16, we consider that the principles in IAS 16 must still be applied to the recognition of costs in IAS 40. These principles are set out in detail in Chapter 18 at 4.

Note that when IFRS 16 is adopted (see 13.1 below), paragraph 20 of IAS 40 will be amended so that an owned investment property will be measured initially at cost as described above and an investment property held by a lessee as a right-of-use asset will be measured initially at cost in accordance with IFRS 16 – see Chapter 25 at 5.2.1.

4.1.1 Acquisition of a group of assets that does not constitute a business ('the group')

The purchase price of an investment property may result from an allocation of the price paid for a group of assets. If an entity acquires a group of assets that do not comprise a business, the principles in IFRS 3 are applied to allocate the entire cost to individual items (see Chapter 9 at 2.2.2). In such cases the acquirer should identify and recognise the individual identifiable assets acquired and liabilities assumed and allocate the cost of the group to the individual identifiable assets and liabilities on the basis of their relative fair values at the date of purchase. Such a transaction or event does not give rise to goodwill. *[IFRS 3.2(b)]*.

In its June 2017 meeting, the Interpretations Committee considered a request for clarification on how to allocate the transaction price to the identifiable assets acquired and liabilities assumed when:

(a) the sum of individual fair values of the identifiable assets and liabilities is different from the transaction price; and

(b) the group includes identifiable assets and liabilities initially measured both at cost and at an amount other than cost.

The Interpretations Committee noted the requirement of paragraph 2(b) of IFRS 3 as described above and also noted that other IFRSs include initial measurement requirements for particular assets and liabilities, including IAS 40 for investment property. It observed that if an entity initially considers that there might be a difference as described in (a) above, the entity should first review the procedures it has used to determine those individual fair values to assess whether such a difference truly exists before allocating the transaction price.

The Interpretations Committee considered two possible ways of accounting for the acquisition of the group. These two approaches are discussed in detail in Chapter 9 at 2.2.2.

Under the first approach an entity:

- identifies the individual identifiable assets acquired and liabilities assumed that it recognises at the date of the acquisition;
- determines the individual transaction price for each identifiable asset and liability by allocating the cost of the group based on the relative fair values of those assets and liabilities at the date of the acquisition; and then
- applies the initial measurement requirements in applicable standards to each identifiable asset acquired and liability assumed. The entity accounts for any difference between the amount at which the asset or liability is initially measured and its individual transaction price applying the relevant requirements.

Applying the second approach, for any identifiable asset or liability initially measured at an amount other than cost, an entity initially measures that asset or liability at the amount specified by the applicable standard. The entity deducts from the transaction price of the group the amounts allocated to the assets and liabilities initially measured at an amount other than cost, and then allocates the residual transaction price to the remaining identifiable assets and liabilities based on their relative fair values at the date of acquisition.

The Interpretations Committee tentatively concluded that a reasonable reading of the requirements in paragraph 2(b) of IFRS 3 on the acquisition of the group results in one of the two approaches outlined above and an entity should apply its reading of the requirements consistently to all such acquisitions.

The Interpretations Committee tentatively decided not to add this matter to its standard-setting agenda.[10]

For investment properties acquired as part of the group, the first approach could mean that a revaluation gain or loss may need to be recognised in profit or loss at the date of acquisition of the group to account for the difference between the allocated individual transaction price and the fair value of the investment property acquired. Using the second approach, investment properties are recorded at fair value as at acquisition date with no immediate impact on profit or loss at the date of the acquisition.

4.1.2 Deferred taxes when acquiring a 'single asset' entity that is not a business

In many jurisdictions, it is usual for investment property to be bought and sold by transferring ownership of a separate legal entity formed to hold the asset (a 'single asset' entity) rather than the asset itself.

When an entity acquires all of the shares of another entity that has an investment property as its only asset (i.e. the acquisition of a 'single asset' entity that is not a business) and the acquiree had recognised in its statement of financial position a deferred tax liability arising from measuring the investment property at fair value as allowed by IAS 40, a specific issue arises as to whether or not the acquiring entity should recognise a deferred tax liability on initial recognition of the transaction.

This specific situation was considered by the Interpretations Committee and, in its March 2017 meeting, it was concluded that the initial recognition exception in paragraph 15(b) of IAS 12 applies because the transaction is not a business combination. Accordingly, on acquisition, the acquiring entity recognises only the investment property and not a deferred tax liability in its consolidated financial statements. The acquiring entity therefore allocates the entire purchase price to the investment property.[11]

For an example and further discussions on the application of the initial recognition exception to assets acquired in the circumstances described above, see Chapter 31 at 7.2.9.

4.2 Start-up costs and self-built property

IAS 40 specifies that start-up costs (unless necessary to bring the property into working condition) and operating losses incurred before the investment property achieves the planned occupancy level, are not to be capitalised. *[IAS 40.23(a), 23(b)].*

IAS 40 therefore prohibits a practice of capitalising costs until a particular level of occupation or rental income is achieved because at the date of physical completion the asset would be capable of operating in the manner intended by management. This forestalls an argument, sometimes advanced in the past, that the asset being constructed was not simply the physical structure of the building but a fully tenanted investment property, and its cost correspondingly included not simply the construction period but also the letting period.

If a property is self-built by an entity, the same general principles apply as for an acquired property (see 4.1 above). However, IAS 40 prohibits capitalisation of abnormal amounts of wasted material, labour or other resources incurred in constructing or developing the property. *[IAS 40.23(c)].*

4.3 Deferred payments

If payment for a property is deferred, the cost to be recognised is the cash price equivalent (which in practice means the present value of the deferred payments due) at the recognition date. Any difference between the cash price and the total payments to be made is recognised as interest expense over the credit period. *[IAS 40.24].*

4.4 Reclassifications from property, plant and equipment ('PP&E') or from inventory

When an entity uses the cost model, transfers between investment property, owner-occupied property and inventories do not change the carrying amount of the property transferred and they do not change the cost of that property for measurement or disclosure purposes. *[IAS 40.59].*

The treatment of transfers of properties measured using the revaluation option in IAS 16 to investment property is set out in 9.3 below.

4.5 Initial measurement of property held under a lease

The same accounting is applied both to property acquired under finance leases and to operating leases where the property interests otherwise meet the definition of investment properties and have been classified as such. For an entity that does not yet apply IFRS 16 (see 13.1 below), this means that a property interest that is held by a lessee under an operating lease and classified as an investment property must be accounted for as if it were a finance lease and be measured using the fair value model (see 6 below). *[IAS 17.19]*.

At the commencement of the lease term, the entity recognises the property asset and related liability in its statement of financial position in accordance with IAS 17, at amounts equal to the fair value of the leased property or, if lower, at the present value of the minimum lease payments, each determined at the inception of the lease (see Chapter 24 at 4). *[IAS 40.25]*. The entity's initial direct costs are added to the asset – these might include similar costs to those described in 4.1 above, such as professional fees. *[IAS 17.20]*. The treatment of initial direct costs by a lessee applying IFRS 16 is discussed at 4.9 below.

If the entity pays a premium for the lease, this is part of the minimum lease payments and is included in the cost of the asset; however, it is, of course, excluded from the liability as it has already been paid. *[IAS 40.26]*.

The standard emphasises that the property interest, the fair value of which is to be determined, is the leasehold interest and not the underlying property. When the fair value is used as cost for initial recognition purposes, guidance on measuring the fair value of a property interest as set out for the fair value model in IAS 40 (see 6 below) and in IFRS 13 – *Fair Value Measurement* (see Chapter 14) should be followed. *[IAS 40.26]*.

Note that the guidance above in determining the initial cost of a property interest held under a lease and classified as investment property, and IAS 17 in its entirety, will be superseded by IFRS 16 (see 13.1 below and Chapter 25). Paragraphs 25 and 26 of IAS 40 (as described above) will be deleted and a new paragraph 29A will be added so that an investment property held by a lessee as a right-of-use asset will be measured initially at its cost in accordance with IFRS 16 – see Chapter 25 at 5.2.1. Also, IFRS 16 will add a new paragraph 40A to IAS 40 so that when a lessee uses the fair value model to measure an investment property that is held as a right-of-use asset, it will measure the right-of-use asset, and not the underlying property, at fair value.

4.6 Initial measurement of assets acquired in exchange transactions

The requirements of IAS 40 for investment properties acquired in exchange for non-monetary assets, or a combination of monetary and non-monetary assets, are the same as those of IAS 16. *[IAS 40.27-29]*. These provisions are discussed in detail in Chapter 18 at 4.4.

4.7 Initial recognition of tenanted investment property subsequently measured using the cost model

During the development of the current IFRS 3 the IASB considered whether it would be appropriate for any favourable or unfavourable lease aspect of an investment property to be recognised separately.

The IASB concluded that this was not necessary for investment property that will be measured at fair value because the fair value of investment property takes into account rental income from leases and therefore the contractual terms of leases and other contracts in place.

However, a different position has been taken for investment property measured using the cost model. In this case the IASB observed that the cost model requires:

- the use of a depreciation or amortisation method that reflects the pattern in which the entity expects to consume the asset's future economic benefits; and
- each part of an item of property, plant and equipment that has a cost that is significant in relation to the total cost of the item to be depreciated separately.

Therefore, an acquirer of investment property in a business combination that is subsequently measured using the cost model will need to adjust the depreciation method for the investment property to reflect the timing of cash flows attributable to the underlying leases. *[IFRS 3.BC148].*

In effect, therefore, this requires that the favourable or unfavourable lease aspect of the investment property – measured with reference to market conditions at the date of the business combination – be separately identified in order that it may be subsequently depreciated or amortised, usually over the remaining lease term. Any such amount is not presented separately in the financial statements.

This approach has also been extended to acquisition of all property, i.e. including those acquired outside a business combination (see 7.1.2 below).

4.8 Borrowing costs

IAS 23 – *Borrowing Costs* – generally mandates capitalisation of borrowing costs in respect of qualifying assets. However, application of IAS 23 to borrowing costs directly attributable to the acquisition, construction or production of qualifying assets that are measured at fair value, such as investment property, is not required because it would not affect the measurement of the investment property in the statement of financial position; it would only affect presentation of interest expense and fair value gains and losses in the income statement. Nevertheless, IAS 23 does not prohibit capitalisation of eligible borrowing costs to such assets as a matter of accounting policy.

To the extent that entities choose to capitalise eligible borrowing costs in respect of such assets, in our view, the methods allowed by IAS 23 should be followed.

The treatment of borrowing costs is discussed further in Chapter 21.

4.9 Lease incentives and initial costs of leasing a property

SIC-15 – *Operating Leases – Incentives* – requires that such incentives granted to a lessee are recognised as a reduction in lease income over the term of the lease. Consequently, they do not form part of the cost of the investment property (see also 6.6.1 below for the requirement to adjust the fair value of an investment property to avoid 'double counting' in circumstances where a lease incentive exists and is recognised separately). It is therefore relevant to distinguish between lease incentives and other capital expenditure.

Lease incentives are described in SIC-15 as follows:

'In negotiating a new or renewed operating lease, the lessor may provide incentives for the lessee to enter into the agreement. Examples of such incentives are an up-front cash payment to the lessee or the reimbursement or assumption by the lessor of costs of the lessee (such as relocation costs, leasehold improvements and costs associated with a pre-existing lease commitment of the lessee). Alternatively, initial periods of the lease term may be agreed to be rent-free or at a reduced rent.' *[SIC-15.1].*

There is no additional guidance in SIC-15 to assist in the identification of incentives, but a similar requirement existed in previous United Kingdom GAAP (in UITF abstract 28 – *Operating lease incentives*) and provides helpful additional detail:

'A payment (or other transfer of value) from a lessor to (or for the benefit of) a lessee should be regarded as a lease incentive when that fairly reflects its substance. A payment to reimburse a lessee for fitting-out costs should be regarded as a lease incentive where the fittings are suitable only for the lessee and accordingly do not add to the value of the property to the lessor. On the other hand, insofar as a reimbursement of expenditure enhances a property generally and causes commensurate benefit to flow to the lessor, it should be treated as reimbursement of expenditure on the property. For example, where the lifts in a building are to be renewed and a lease has only five years to run, a payment made by the lessor may not be an inducement to enter into a lease but payment for an improvement to the lessor's property.'[12]

The distinction between costs that enhance the value of the property, and those that are of value to the tenant, can be seen in Extract 19.2 below.

While IAS 40 does not contain specific guidance on the accounting treatment of initial direct costs of arranging leases over a property, such as legal and agency fees, such costs should be recognised as an expense over the term of the resultant lease. This practice can also be seen in Extract 19.2 below. In practice, this means, if the cost model is used, such costs are presented as part of the cost of the investment property, even if they do not strictly form part of it and are then amortised separately over the lease term.

An entity using the fair value model should also initially include these costs as part of the carrying value of the investment property. However, in our view, at the next reporting date such initial costs would be recognised in profit and loss in the reported fair value gain or loss, as they would otherwise exceed the fair value of the related investment property. This is consistent with the treatment of transaction costs incurred on acquisition of a property discussed in 6.4 below.

Adding initial direct costs to the carrying amount of the leased property as described above is consistent with the guidance provided by IAS 17 applicable to an entity that holds the leased property in a lease arrangement, i.e. a lessee in a finance lease and a lessor in an operating lease (see Chapter 24 at 4 and 5.2). *[IAS 17.20, 24, 52].*

Extract 19.2: The British Land Company PLC (2015)

NOTES TO THE ACCOUNTS [extract]

1 **Basis of preparation, significant accounting policies and accounting judgements** [extract]

Net rental income [extract]

Initial direct costs incurred in negotiating and arranging a new lease are amortised on a straight-line basis over the period from the date of lease commencement to the earliest termination date.

Where a lease incentive payment, including surrender premia paid, does not enhance the value of a property, it is amortised on a straight-line basis over the period from the date of lease commencement to the earliest termination date.

Note that when IFRS 16 is adopted (see 13.1 below), it will supersede SIC-15. However, lessors' treatment of lease incentives paid or payable to lessees will not change. On the other hand, for lessees, lease incentives received or receivable will be deducted from lease payments and will reduce the initial measurement of a lessee's right-of-use asset. *[IFRS 16.23].* Lease incentives that are payable to the lessee at lease commencement will reduce a lessee's lease liability. *[IFRS 16.27].*

Further, when IFRS 16 is adopted, the requirement on initial direct costs will be consistent with the concept of incremental costs of obtaining a contract in IFRS 15 (see Chapter 30 at 9.3.1). IFRS 16 defines initial direct costs as 'incremental costs of obtaining a lease that would not have been incurred if the lease had not been obtained ...'. *[IFRS 16 Appendix A].* Examples of such costs are commissions and payments made to an existing tenant as an incentive to terminate its lease. In addition to excluding allocated costs (e.g. salaries), which also are excluded under IAS 17, initial direct costs exclude costs incurred regardless of whether the lease is successfully finalised (e.g. fees for certain legal advice, estate agent fees not contingent upon success). Lessees and lessors apply the same definition of initial direct costs.

IFRS 16 requires lessors to include initial direct costs in the carrying amount of the underlying asset in an operating lease. These initial direct costs are recognised as an expense over the lease term on the same basis as lease income. *[IFRS 16.83].* IFRS 16 requires lessees to include their initial direct costs in their initial measurement of the right-of-use asset. *[IFRS 16.24].*

For further discussion, see Chapter 25 at 4.5.2, 4.7, 5.2.1, 5.2.2 and 6.3.

4.10 Contingent costs

The terms of purchase of investment property may sometimes include a variable or contingent amount that cannot be determined at the date of acquisition. For example, the vendor may have the right to additional consideration from the purchaser in the event that a certain level of income is generated from the property; or its value reaches a certain level; or if certain legislative hurdles, such as the receipt of zoning or planning permission, are achieved.

A common issue is whether these liabilities should be accounted for as a financial liability or as a provision. This is important because remeasurement of a financial liability is taken to profit or loss, whilst changes in a provision could, by analogy to IFRIC 1 – *Changes in Existing Decommissioning, Restoration and Similar Liabilities* – be recorded as an adjustment to the cost of the asset.

The Interpretations Committee took this question onto its agenda in January 2011,[13] but in May 2011 chose to defer further work on it until the IASB concluded on its discussions on the accounting for the liability for variable payments as part of the leases project.[14]

At its July 2013 meeting, the IASB considered this issue again and noted that the initial accounting for variable payments affects their subsequent accounting. Some IASB members expressed the view that the initial and subsequent accounting for variable payments for the purchase of assets are linked and should be addressed comprehensively. The IASB noted that accounting for variable payments is a topic that was discussed as part of the Leases and Conceptual Framework projects and decided that it would reconsider this issue after the proposals in the Exposure Draft – *Leases* (published in May 2013) had been redeliberated.[15]

The Interpretations Committee revisited this issue at its meetings in September 2015, November 2015 and March 2016. It determined that this issue is too broad for it to address within the confines of existing IFRSs. Consequently, the Interpretations Committee decided not to add this issue to its agenda and concluded that the IASB should address the accounting for variable payments comprehensively.[16]

As a result, in May 2016 the IASB tentatively decided to include '*Variable and Contingent Consideration*' in its pipeline of future research projects and noted that it expected to begin work on projects in its research pipeline between 2017 and 2021.[17]

Until such time as the IASB implements any changes, in our view, the treatment as either a provision or as a financial liability is a matter of accounting policy choice. Of course, for investment property held at fair value, this policy choice primarily affects classification within the income statement.

It is important to note that this policy choice is not available for the contingent costs of acquiring investment property as part of a business combination. The treatment of contingent costs in these circumstances is described in Chapter 9 at 7.1.

For more related discussions see Chapter 17 at 4.5 and Chapter 18 at 4.1.9.

4.11 Income from tenanted property during development

An issue that can arise is whether rental and similar income generated by existing tenants in a property development may be capitalised and offset against the cost of developing that property.

IAS 16 requires that the income and related expenses of incidental operations are recognised in profit or loss and included in their respective classifications of income and expense (see Chapter 18 at 4.2). *[IAS 16.21]*. We consider that rental and similar income from existing tenants are incidental operations to the development.

In our view there should not be a measurement difference between the cost of a property development dealt with under IAS 40 and the cost of development dealt with under IAS 16. Therefore, rental and similar income generated by existing tenants in a property dealt with under IAS 40 and now intended for redevelopment should not be capitalised against the costs of the development. Rather rental and similar income should be recognised in profit or loss in accordance with the requirements of IAS 17 (or

IFRS 16, if adopted – see 13.1 below) together with related expenses. For these purposes it is irrelevant whether the investment property is held at cost or fair value.

4.12 Payments by the vendor to the purchaser

On occasion, a transaction for the purchase of an investment property may include an additional element where the vendor repays an amount to the purchaser – perhaps described as representing a rental equivalent for a period of time.

The question then arises whether, in the accounts of the purchaser, this payment should be recorded as income (albeit perhaps recognised over a period of time) or as a deduction from the acquisition cost of the investment property on initial recognition.

In our view such amounts are an integral part of the acquisition transaction and should invariably be treated as a deduction from the acquisition cost of the investment property because the payment is an element of a transaction between a vendor and purchaser of the property, rather than a landlord and tenant. In the event that the repayments by the vendor are spread over time, the present value of those payments should be deducted from the cost of the investment property and an equivalent receivable recognised against which those payments are amortised.

5 MEASUREMENT AFTER INITIAL RECOGNITION

Once recognised, IAS 40 allows an entity to choose one of the two methods of accounting for investment property as its accounting policy (except as noted in 5.1 below):

- fair value model (see 6 below); or
- cost model (see 7 below).

An entity has to choose one model or the other, and apply it to all its investment property (unless the entity is an insurer or similar entity, in which case there are exemptions that are described briefly at 5.2 below). *[IAS 40.30]*.

The standard does not identify a preferred alternative; although the fair value model currently seems to be the more widely adopted model among entities in the real estate sector (see 7.2 below).

The standard discourages changes from the fair value model to the cost model, stating that it is highly unlikely that this will result in a more relevant presentation, which is a requirement of IAS 8 – *Accounting Policies, Changes in Accounting Estimates and Errors* – for any voluntary change in accounting policy. *[IAS 40.31]*.

All entities, regardless of which measurement option is chosen, are required to determine the fair value of their investment property, because even those entities that use the cost model are required to disclose the fair value of their investment property (see 12.3 below). *[IAS 40.32, 79(e)]*.

5.1 Property held under an operating lease

There is an exception to the choice of measurement: a property interest that is held by a lessee under an operating lease may be classified as an investment property – provided that the fair value model is applied for the asset recognised. This classification choice is available on a property-by-property basis (see 2.1 above) but, once an entity has classified one such property as investment property, it then has to apply the fair value model to all of its recognised investment properties. *[IAS 40.6, 34].*

When IFRS 16 is adopted, the classification alternative for property interests under operating lease will no longer be available (see 2.1 above). Under IFRS 16, if a lessee applies the fair value model in IAS 40 to its investment property, the lessee will also apply that fair value model to the right-of-use assets that meet the definition of investment property in IAS 40. *[IFRS 16.34].*

5.2 Measurement by insurers and similar entities

There is an exception to the requirement that an entity must apply its chosen measurement policy to all of its investment properties. This is applicable to insurance companies and other entities that hold specified assets, including investment properties, whose fair value or return is directly linked to the return paid on specific liabilities (i.e. liabilities that are secured by such investment properties).

These entities are permitted to choose either the fair value or the cost model for all such properties without it affecting the choice available for all other investment properties that they may hold. *[IAS 40.32A].* However, for an insurer or other entity that operates an internal property fund that issues notional units, with some units held by investors in linked contracts and others held by the entity, all properties within such a fund must be held on the same basis because the standard does not permit the entity to measure the property held by such a fund partly at cost and partly at fair value. *[IAS 40.32B].*

If an entity elected a model for those properties described above that is different from the model used for the rest of its investment properties, sales of investment properties between these pools of assets are to be recognised at fair value with any applicable cumulative change in fair value recognised in profit or loss. Consequently, if an investment property is sold from a pool in which the fair value model is used into a pool in which the cost model is used, the fair value of the property sold at the date of the sale becomes its deemed cost. *[IAS 40.32C].*

When IFRS 17 is adopted (see 13.2 below), paragraph 32B of IAS 40 (as discussed above) will be amended. The previous reference to 'insurers and other entities [operating] an internal property fund that issues notional units' will be replaced by '[s]ome entities operate, either internally or externally, an investment fund that provides investors with benefits determined by units in the fund.' The revised paragraph will also refer to entities that issue insurance contracts with direct participation features, for which the underlying items include investment property, and will specify that for the purposes of applying paragraph 32A (as discussed above) and the amended paragraph 32B of IAS 40 only, insurance contracts include investment contracts with discretionary participation features.

The amended paragraph 32B of IAS 40 will clarify that an entity is not permitted to measure the property held by the fund (as described above) or property that is an underlying item partly at cost and partly at fair value.

6 THE FAIR VALUE MODEL

Under this model all investment property is measured at its fair value at the end of the reporting period (except in the cases described in 6.2 and 6.3 below) and a gain or loss arising from changes in the fair value in the reporting period is recognised in profit or loss for that period. *[IAS 40.33, 35]*.

IFRS 13 provides a fair value measurement framework that applies whenever fair value measurement is permitted or required (see Chapter 14). IFRS 13 does not specify when an entity is required to use fair value, but rather, provides guidance on how to measure fair value under IFRS when fair value is required or permitted by IFRS.

IFRS 13 defines fair value as 'the price that would be received to sell an asset or paid to transfer a liability in an orderly transaction between market participants at the measurement date.' *[IFRS 13.9, IAS 40.5]*.

While entities cannot presume this to be the case, in practice, the fair value estimate arrived at under IFRS 13 may be similar to that estimated for 'market value' as defined by the Royal Institution of Chartered Surveyors ('RICS') and the International Valuation Standards Council ('IVSC'). Their definition of 'market value' being 'the estimated amount for which an asset or liability should exchange on the valuation date between a willing buyer and a willing seller in an arm's length transaction, after proper marketing and where the parties had each acted knowledgeably, prudently and without compulsion.'[18]

Many entities use an external valuer to estimate fair value based on the RICS and/or IVSC Valuation Standards. Indeed, the use of an independent valuer with a recognised and relevant professional qualification and with recent experience in the location and category of the investment property being valued is encouraged by IAS 40, albeit not required. *[IAS 40.32]*.

The price in the principal (or most advantageous) market used to measure fair value shall not be adjusted for transaction costs. This is because transaction costs are not a characteristic of an asset or a liability; rather, they are specific to a transaction and will differ depending on how an entity enters into a transaction for the asset or liability. *[IFRS 13.25]*.

Transaction costs incurred by a purchaser on acquisition are dealt with at 6.4 below and in Chapter 14 at 9.1.2.

6.1 Estimating fair value

When estimating the fair value of the property in accordance with IFRS 13, the objective is to estimate the price that would be received to sell an investment property in an orderly transaction between market participants at the measurement date under current market conditions. *[IFRS 13.2]*. This objective applies regardless of the techniques and inputs used to measure fair value.

IAS 40 has certain requirements in addition to those in IFRS 13. In particular, IAS 40 requires that the fair value reflects, among other things, rental income from current leases and other assumptions that market participants would use when pricing investment property under current market conditions. *[IAS 40.40]*. For example, in a transaction to sell an investment property, it is likely that market participants would consider the existing lease agreements in place.

This is consistent with the general requirement in IFRS 13 that an entity should measure the fair value using the assumptions that market participants would use when pricing the asset or liability, assuming that market participants act in their economic best interest. *[IFRS 13.22].*

Extract 19.3 below describes Unibail-Rodamco's approach to valuations:

Extract 19.3: Unibail-Rodamco SE (2016)

4.2. **Notes to the Consolidated Financial Statements** [extract]

Note 5 – **Investment properties, tangible and intangible assets, goodwill** [extract]

5.1. **Investment properties** [extract]

5.1.1. **Accounting principles** [extract]

Investment properties (IAS 40 & IFRS 13)

Under the accounting treatment recommended by IAS 40, investment properties are shown at their market value. According to IFRS 13, the fair value is defined as the price that would be received to sell an asset or paid to transfer a liability in an orderly transaction between market participants at the measurement date (*i.e.* an exit price). Expectations about future improvements or modifications to be made to the property interest to reflect its highest and best use have to be considered in the appraisal, such as the renovation of or an extension to the property interest.

Unibail-Rodamco complies with the IFRS 13 fair value measurement rule and the position paper[(1)] on IFRS 13 established by EPRA, the representative body of the publicly listed real estate industry in Europe.

Transaction costs incurred for an asset deal are capitalised in the value of the investment property. Capitalised expenses include capital expenditures, evictions costs, capitalised financial interests, letting fees and other internal costs related to development projects.

Investment Properties Under Construction (IPUC) are covered by IAS 40 and are eligible to be measured at fair value. In accordance with the Group's investment properties valuation method, they are valued at fair value by an external appraiser twice a year. Projects for which the fair value is not reliably determinable are valued at cost until such time that a fair value valuation becomes reliable, or until one year before the construction completion.

According to the Group, a development project is eligible for a fair value measurement once all three of the following criteria are fulfilled:

- all administrative authorisations needed to complete the project are obtained;
- the construction has started and costs are committed toward the contractor; and
- substantial uncertainty in future rental income has been eliminated.

If the time to delivery is less than one year, the project has to be taken at fair value.

(1) EPRA Position Paper on IFRS 13 – Fair value measurement and illustrative disclosures, February 2013.

For properties measured at fair value, the market value adopted by Unibail-Rodamco is determined on the basis of appraisals by independent external experts, who value the Group's portfolio as at June 30 and December 31 of each year. The gross value is reduced by disposal costs and transfer taxes[(1)], depending on the country and on the tax situation of the property, in order to arrive at a net market value.

For the Shopping Centres and Offices portfolios, the independent appraisers determine the fair market value based on the results of two methods: the discounted cash flow methodology as well as the yield methodology. Furthermore, the resulting valuations are cross-checked against the initial yield, value per m^2 and the fair market values established through actual market transactions.

Appraisers have been given access to all information relevant for valuations, such as the Group's rent rolls, including information on vacancy, break options, expiry dates and lease incentives, performance indicators (*e.g.* footfall and sales where available), letting evidence and the Group's cash flow forecasts from annually updated detailed asset business plans. Appraisers make their independent assessments of current and forward looking cash flow profiles and usually reflect risk either in the cash flow forecasts (*e.g.* future rental levels, growth, investment requirements, void periods, incentives) or in the applied required returns or discount rates.

The sites of the Convention & Exhibition portfolio are qualified as Investment property.

For the Convention & Exhibition portfolio, the valuation methodology adopted is mainly based on a discounted cash flow model applied to total net income projected over the life of the concession, or over the life of the long-term lease (notably the Porte de Versailles long-term lease) or leasehold, if it exists or otherwise over a 10-year period, with an estimation of the asset's value at the end of the given time period, based either on the residual contractual value for concessions or on capitalised cash flows over the last year. The valuations carried out by the appraisers took into account total net income, which comprised net rents and ancillary services, as well as net income from car parks. The cost of maintenance works, major repairs, refurbishments, redevelopments and extensions, as well as concession or leasehold fees, are included in projected cash flow figures.

The income statement for a given year (Y) records the change in value for each property, which is determined as follows: market value Y – [market value Y–1 + amount of works and other costs capitalised in year Y].

Capital gains on disposals of investment properties are calculated by comparison with their latest market value recorded in the closing statement of financial position for the previous financial year.

Properties under construction carried at cost are subject to impairment tests, determined on the basis of the estimated fair value of the project. The fair value of a project is assessed by the Development & Investment teams through a market exit capitalisation rate and the targeted net rents at completion. When the fair value is lower than net book value, an impairment provision is booked.

Properties held for sale are identified separately in the statement of financial position.

(1) Transfer taxes are valued on the assumption that the property is sold directly, even though the cost of these taxes can, in certain cases, be reduced by selling the property's holding company.

6.1.1 Methods of estimation

IFRS 13 does not specify or rank the techniques an entity must use to measure fair value. However, it requires them to be consistent with one or more of the three broad approaches: the market approach; the income approach; and the cost approach. *[IFRS 13.62].* As discussed at 6.1.2 below, IFRS 13 does require an entity to prioritise observable inputs over unobservable inputs. See Chapter 14 at 14 for further discussion on selecting appropriate techniques and inputs.

IAS 40 notes that in a lease negotiated at market rates, the fair value of an interest in a leased property at acquisition, net of all expected lease payments (including those relating to recognised liabilities), should be zero ('acquisition' means the inception of the lease as defined by IAS 17, which is before any lease payments are due or any other accounting entries are required to be made, see Chapter 24 at 3.4.1). This applies regardless of whether the asset and liability are initially recognised at fair value (as is usually the case with a finance lease) or at the present value of the minimum lease payments (for an interest under an operating lease). Consequently, re-measuring an interest in a lease to fair value will only give rise to a gain or loss if the fair value model is applied after initial recognition and upon subsequent re-measurement. *[IAS 40.41].*

When an entity first acquires an investment property (or when an existing property first becomes investment property after a change in use – see 9 below) there could be an indication that its fair value will not be reliably measurable on a continuing basis. For example, there might be clear evidence that the variability in the range of reasonable fair value measurements will be so great, and the probabilities of the various outcomes so difficult to assess, that the usefulness of a single measure of fair value will be negated. However, it cannot be over-emphasised that IAS 40 describes such circumstances as 'exceptional cases'. *[IAS 40.48]*. This is discussed further at 6.2 below.

When IFRS 16 is adopted (see 13.1 below), paragraph 41 of IAS 40 (as described above) will be amended to refer to investment property held by a lessee as a right-of-use asset. IFRS 16 specifies the basis for initial recognition of the cost of an investment property held by a lessee as a right-of-use asset (see 4.5 above). In line with the discussion in 5.1 above, paragraph 33 of IAS 40 will require the investment property held by a lessee as a right-of-use asset to be remeasured, if necessary, to fair value if the entity chooses the fair value model. When lease payments are at market rates, the fair value of an investment property held by a lessee as a right-of-use asset at acquisition, net of all expected lease payments (including those relating to recognised lease liabilities), should be zero. Thus, remeasuring a right-of-use asset from cost in accordance with IFRS 16 to fair value (taking into account the requirements in paragraph 50 of IAS 40 – see 6.1.4 below) should not give rise to any initial gain or loss, unless fair value is measured at different times. This could occur when an election to apply the fair value model is made after initial recognition.

IFRS 16 also adds a new paragraph 40A to IAS 40 requiring that when a lessee uses the fair value model to measure an investment property that is held as a right-of-use asset, it will measure the right-of-use asset, and not the underlying property, at fair value.

6.1.2 Observable data

When selecting the most appropriate inputs to a fair value measurement from multiple available inputs, those that maximise the use of observable data, rather than unobservable data, should be selected. *[IFRS 13.67]*. Just because the volume or level of activity in a market has significantly decreased, it does not mean that transactions in that market are not orderly or do not represent fair value. *[IFRS 13.B43]*.

Entities will need to consider the individual facts and circumstances in making this assessment. Notwithstanding the need for judgement, an entity must have a reasonable basis for concluding that a current observable market price can be ignored based on a view that it represents a liquidation or distressed sale value. *[IFRS 13.B43]*. This is discussed further in Chapter 14 at 8.

6.1.3 Comparison with value in use

Fair value is not the same as 'value in use' as defined in IAS 36. In particular, it does not take account of the entity specific factors of the holder that would not generally be available to knowledgeable willing buyers such as additional value derived from holding a portfolio of investment property assets, synergies between the properties and other assets or legal rights or tax benefits or burdens pertaining to the current owner. Fair value is also not the same as net realisable value as, for example, net realisable value does not have to take account of market required returns but would have to take into account cost to sell. *[IFRS 13.6(c), BC24]*. See also Chapter 14 at 2.2.3.

However, in most cases, it is unlikely that the 'value in use' of an individual property will exceed the fair value of that property – see 7.3 below.

6.1.4 'Double counting'

An entity must take care, when determining the carrying amount of investment property under the fair value model, not to double count assets or liabilities that are recognised separately. IAS 40 describes a number of situations where this might otherwise happen as follows:

- Equipment such as lifts or air-conditioning is often an integral part of a building and is generally included in the fair value of the investment property, rather than recognised separately as property, plant and equipment (see 6.5 below).
- If an office is leased on a furnished basis, the fair value of the office generally includes the fair value of the furniture, because the rental income relates to the furnished office. When furniture is included in the fair value of investment property, an entity does not recognise that furniture as a separate asset (see 6.5 below).
- The fair value of investment property excludes prepaid or accrued operating lease income, because the entity recognises it as a separate liability or asset (see 6.6 below).
- The fair value of investment property held under a lease reflects expected cash flows (including contingent rent that is expected to become payable). Accordingly, if a valuation obtained for a property is net of all payments expected to be made, it will be necessary to add back any recognised lease liability, to arrive at the carrying amount of the investment property using the fair value model (see 6.7 below). *[IAS 40.50]*.

Where an entity applies IFRS 16 (see 13.1 below), paragraph 50 of IAS 40 described in the final bullet above is amended so that the fair value of investment property held by a lessee as a right-of-use asset reflects expected cash flows (including variable lease payments that are expected to become payable).

6.2 Inability to determine fair value of completed investment property

It is a rebuttable presumption that an entity can determine the fair value of a property reliably on a continuing basis, that is, on each subsequent occasion in which it records the investment property in its financial statements. *[IAS 40.53]*.

The standard emphasises that it is only in exceptional cases and only on initial recognition (either by acquisition or change in use – see 9 below) that the entity will be able to conclude that it will not be able to reliably measure the investment property's fair value on a continuing basis. *[IAS 40.53]*.

Additionally, entities are strongly discouraged from arguing that fair value cannot be reliably measured. It may be a possible argument when, and only when, the market for comparable properties is inactive (e.g. there are few recent transactions, price quotations are not current or observed transaction prices indicate that the seller was forced to sell) and alternative reliable measurements of fair value (for example, based on discounted cash flow projections) are not available. In such exceptional cases, the property should be measured using the cost model in IAS 16 until its disposal and assumed to have a nil residual value. *[IAS 40.53].* This means that it has to be carried at cost and the building and its component parts depreciated over their useful lives (see 7 below). In these circumstances, IAS 16's revaluation model, under which assets may be revalued to fair value, is specifically ruled out. If this exceptional situation occurs, the cost model of IAS 16 should continue to be applied until disposal of such property. Although an entity measures an individual property at cost for this reason, all other investment property must continue to be carried at fair value. *[IAS 40.54].*

The above exception is not permitted for investment property that has been previously measured using the fair value model. Once a property is initially recognised at its fair value, it must always be so recognised until disposed of or reclassified for owner-occupation or development for subsequent sale in the ordinary course of the business, even if comparable market transactions become less frequent or market prices become less easily available. *[IAS 40.55].*

If an entity has adopted IFRS 16 (see 13.1 below), paragraphs 53 and 54 of IAS 40 are amended to include reference to the cost model under IFRS 16 so that owned investment property will be measured using the cost model in IAS 16 and investment property held by a lessee as a right-of-use asset will be measured in accordance with IFRS 16 (see Chapter 25 at 5.3.1).

6.3 The fair value of investment property under construction

Entities who wish to measure their completed investment property at fair value will also need to measure their investment property under construction at fair value (subject to fair value being reliably determinable). *[IAS 40.33, 53].*

Determining the fair value of investment property under construction will often be more judgemental than for completed property because:

- There are generally no observable transactions for investment property under construction. Where such assets are transacted, this is typically when they are in the very early stages of development or when they are nearly complete and substantially let.
- Additional assumptions must be made about the risks and costs of any incomplete construction.

In January 2009, the International Valuation Standards Board ('IVSB') released an Interim Position Statement – *The Valuation of Investment Property under Construction under IAS 40.* This Position Statement acknowledged that few investment properties under construction are transferred between market participants except as part of a sale of the owning entity or where the seller is either insolvent or facing insolvency and therefore unable to complete the project.

Despite this, the Position Statement set out that since the property is being developed for either income or capital appreciation, the cash flows associated with its construction and completion should normally be readily identifiable and capable of reliable estimation. Consequently, the IVSB considered that it would be rare for the fair value of an investment property under construction not to be capable of reliable determination.

However, this latter comment was excluded from the subsequent draft – *Proposed Guidance Note – The Valuation of Investment Property under Construction* – issued in August 2009 and the IVSB invited views as to whether such a comment is outside of the scope of the Guidance Note. The IVSB seems to have concluded that it was not its role to comment on this area because when the final Guidance Note was issued in February 2010, no comment about the reliability of estimation was included.

It is worth noting that, in light of the requirements of IFRS 13, an entity will have to determine whether fair value can be reliably measured or not under the requirements in that standard. This is discussed in Chapter 14 at 2.4.1.

In any event, some entities do consider that not all of their investment property under construction can be reliably measured and have developed criteria to make that assessment, see Extract 19.3 above for an example.

There were persistent concerns that, in some situations, the fair value of investment property under construction could not be measured reliably. Where an entity that chooses the fair value model for its investment property determines that the fair value of an investment property under construction is not reliably measurable but it expects the fair value to be reliably measurable when construction is complete, the IASB decided to allow such investment property under construction to be measured at cost until such time as the fair value becomes reliably measurable or construction is completed (whichever comes earlier). *[IAS 40.53]*.

IAS 40 also sets out the following:

- Once an entity becomes able to measure reliably the fair value of an investment property under construction that it has previously measured at cost (see 7 below), it should measure that property at its fair value. *[IAS 40.53A]*.
- Once construction of such property is complete, it is presumed that fair value can be measured reliably. If this is not the case, and this will be only in exceptional situations, the property should be accounted for using the cost model in accordance with IAS 16 (see 7 below) and the general requirements discussed in 6.2 above, i.e. use the cost model until disposal of the property (even if subsequently its fair value becomes reliably determinable) and assume that it has a nil residual value. *[IAS 40.53A]*.
- The presumption that the fair value of investment property under construction can be measured reliably can be rebutted only on initial recognition. Therefore, an entity that has measured an item of investment property under construction at fair value may not subsequently conclude that the fair value of the completed investment property cannot be measured reliably. *[IAS 40.53B]*.

If an entity has adopted IFRS 16 (see 13.1 below), paragraph 53A of IAS 40 is amended so that owned investment property will be accounted for using the cost model in IAS 16 and investment property held by a lessee as a right-of-use asset will be accounted for in accordance with IFRS 16 (see Chapter 25 at 5.3.1).

6.4 Transaction costs incurred by the reporting entity on acquisition

An issue that arises in practice is whether transaction costs that have been incurred by the reporting entity on purchase of an investment property should be taken into account in determining the subsequent fair value of the property when applying the fair value model. This is illustrated in the following example:

Example 19.2: The fair value model and transaction costs incurred at acquisition

On 1 January 2018 Entity A acquired an investment property for a purchase price of €10,000. In addition, Entity A incurred legal costs of €200 in connection with the purchase and paid property transfer tax of €400. Accordingly, the investment property was initially recorded at €10,600. Entity A applies the fair value model for subsequent measurement of investment property:

	Development of prices in property market	Appraised market value of property	Cost of property initially recognised	Difference
		€	€	€
Scenario 1	Unchanged	10,000	10,600	(600)
Scenario 2	Slightly increased	10,250	10,600	(350)
Scenario 3	Significantly increased	11,000	10,600	400
Scenario 4	Decreased	9,500	10,600	(1,100)

The issue that arises in practice is whether or not the acquisition-related transaction costs that were incurred by Entity A on 1 January 2018 can be considered in determining the fair value of the investment property at the next reporting date.

In our view, the acquisition-related transaction costs incurred by Entity A may not be considered separately in determining the fair value of an investment property. In the example above, on the next reporting date the carrying value to be recorded in the statement of financial position is its fair value. Changes from the initial carrying amount to the appraised market value at the subsequent reporting date (reflected in the 'Difference' column in the table) are recognised in profit or loss.

Although IAS 40 states that transaction costs incurred by a purchaser on the acquisition of an investment property are included in the cost of the investment property at initial recognition, *[IAS 40.21]*, if an entity applies the fair value model, the same investment property that was recorded at cost on initial recognition is subsequently measured at fair value in accordance with IFRS 13. The fact that the cost of the investment property recorded on initial recognition included legal and other transaction costs is irrelevant to the subsequent fair valuation of the asset.

IFRS 13 clarifies that '[t]he price in the principal (or most advantageous) market used to measure the fair value of the asset or liability shall not be adjusted for transaction costs. Transaction costs shall be accounted for in accordance with other IFRSs. Transaction costs are not a characteristic of an asset or a liability; rather, they are specific to a transaction and will differ depending on how an entity enters into a transaction for the asset or liability.' *[IFRS 13.25]*. See Chapter 14 at 9.1.2 for further discussion.

Likewise, when measuring the fair value of an investment property, it is not appropriate to add the acquisition-related transaction costs incurred by the purchaser to fair value, as these have no relevance to the fair value of the property. Therefore, some or all of the transaction costs incurred when acquiring the investment property that were capitalised in accordance with IAS 40 will effectively be expensed as part of the subsequent fair value gain or loss.

6.5 Fixtures and fittings subsumed within fair value

Fixtures and fittings such as lifts or air conditioning units are usually reflected within the fair value of the investment property rather than being accounted for separately. *[IAS 40.50(a)]*. In other cases, additional assets may be necessary in order that the property can be used for its specific purposes. The standard refers to furniture within a property that is being let as furnished offices, and argues that this should not be recognised as a separate asset if it has been included in the fair value of the investment property. *[IAS 40.50(b)]*.

The entity may have other assets that have not been included within the valuation, in which case these will be recognised separately and accounted for in accordance with IAS 16.

6.6 Prepaid and accrued operating lease income

6.6.1 Accrued rental income and lease incentives

The requirement in IAS 40 not to double-count assets or liabilities recognised separately is most commonly encountered when the carrying value of an investment property is reduced below its fair value to the extent that a separate asset arises under SIC-15 (or IFRS 16, when adopted – see 13.1 below). For example, when an entity offers an initial rent-free period to a lessee, it will recognise an asset in the rent-free period and then amortise it over the remaining lease term, thereby spreading the reduction in rental income over the term of the lease. The amount of the separate asset should therefore be deducted from the carrying value of the investment property in order to avoid double counting and therefore ensure the carrying value does not exceed fair value. *[IAS 40.50(c)]*.

The British Land Company PLC explains the treatment in its accounting policies:

Extract 19.4: The British Land Company PLC (2015)

NOTES TO THE ACCOUNTS [extract]

1 **Basis of preparation, significant accounting policies and accounting judgements** [extract]

Net rental income [extract]

Where a rent-free period is included in a lease, the rental income foregone is allocated evenly over the period from the date of lease commencement to the earliest termination date.

Rental income from fixed and minimum guaranteed rent reviews is recognised on a straight-line basis to the earliest termination date. Where such rental income is recognised ahead of the related cash flow, an adjustment is made to ensure that the carrying value of the related property including the accrued rent does not exceed the external valuation.

This treatment can also be seen in Extracts 19.5 and 19.6 below.

6.6.2 Prepaid rental income

The same principles are applied when rental income arising from an operating lease is received in advance. This is demonstrated in the example below:

Example 19.3: Investment property and rent received in advance

A company owns land with an estimated value of £10m as at 1 January 2017 that is accounted for as investment property. The company applies the fair value option in IAS 40 and has a reporting period ending on 31 December each year.

The land was not let until, on 30 December 2017, a lease of 50 years was granted for consideration of £9.5m. The lease is considered to be an operating lease. No rental income was recognised in 2017 as it was considered immaterial.

An external valuer estimated that, after the grant of the 50 year lease, the fair value of the company's interest in the land as at 31 December 2017 was £1m. As at 31 December 2018 the external valuer estimated the fair value of the interest in the property was £1.2m.

The resultant accounting entries are summarised below.

Extracts from the ledgers for the year ended 31 December 2017

	As at 1 January 2017	Journal (1)	Journal (2)	Journal (3)	As at 31 December 2017
Investment property	10.0	–	(9.0)	9.5	10.5
Cash	–	9.5	–	–	9.5
Deferred Income	–	(9.5)	–	–	(9.5)
Net Assets	10.0	–	(9.0)	9.5	10.5
Share capital	10.0	–	–	–	10.0
Retained profit	–	–	(9.0)	9.5	0.5
Total Equity	10.0	–	(9.0)	9.5	10.5

Journals:

(1) Issue of lease (£9.5m received on issue of lease).

(2) Write down investment property to £1m external valuation.

(3) Write up book value of property by the amount of unamortised deferred revenue in the statement of financial position.

Extracts from the ledgers for the year ended 31 December 2018

	As at 1 January 2018	Journal (1)	Journal (2)	Journal (3)	As at 31 December 2018
Investment property	10.5	–	(9.3)	9.31	10.51
Cash	9.5	–	–	–	9.5
Deferred Income	(9.5)	0.19	–	–	(9.31)
Net Assets	10.5	0.19	(9.3)	9.31	10.7
Share capital	10.0	–	–	–	10.0
Retained profit	0.5	0.19	(9.3)	9.31	0.7
Total Equity	10.5	0.19	(9.3)	9.31	10.7

Journals:

(1) Amortise rent (one year of the £9.5m received for 50 years).

(2) Write down investment property to £1.2m external valuation.

(3) Write up the book value of property by the amount of unamortised deferred revenue in the statement of financial position (£9.31m).

An example of an entity dealing with this in practice can be seen in Extract 19.5 below:

Extract 19.5: The Crown Estate (2017)

Notes forming part of the group and parent consolidated financial statements [extract]

18. Investment properties [extract]

Group Continuing Operations						As at 31 March 2017
Portfolio	Central London £m	Regional Retail £m	Rural & Coastal £m	Windsor £m	Energy Minerals and Infrastructure £m	Total £m
Opening fair value	7,755.0	1,685.9	1,450.7	188.1	950.9	12,030.6
Less: deferred income from lease premiums received	(1,325.3)	(55.2)	–	–	–	(1,380.5)
Less: Head lease liabilities	–	(2.4)	–	–	–	(2.4)
At opening valuation	6,429.7	1,628.3	1,450.7	188.1	950.9	10,647.7
Acquisitions	34.1	68.6	13.2	–	–	115.9
Capital expenditure	315.2	96.4	16.8	4.1	1.5	434.0
Capital receipts	(0.2)	(2.4)	(1.0)	–	(14.5)	(18.1)
Disposals	(144.3)	(4.3)	(180.3)	0.1	–	(328.8)
Revaluation	84.9	(30.9)	24.4	(0.4)	186.6	264.6
Impairment of discontinued operation	–	–	–	–	–	–
At closing valuation (before lease incentives)	6,719.4	1,755.7	1,323.8	191.9	1,124.5	11,115.3
Deferred income from lease premiums received	1,508.6	62.9	–	–	–	1,571.5
Head lease liabilities	–	2.4	–	–	–	2.4
Closing fair value	8,228.0	1,821.0	1,323.8	191.9	1,124.5	12,689.2
Reconciliation to valuation						
At closing valuation (before lease incentives)	6,719.4	1,755.7	1,323.8	191.9	1,124.5	11,115.3
Add lease incentives	–	16.8	–	–	–	16.8
At valuation	6,719.4	1,772.5	1,323.8	191.9	1,124.5	11,132.1

6.7 Valuation adjustment to the fair value of properties held under a lease

IAS 40 states that the fair value of investment property held under a lease reflects expected cash flows (including contingent rent that is expected to become payable). If an entity has adopted IFRS 16 (see 13.1 below), the fair value of investment property held by a lessee as a right-of-use asset will reflect expected cash flows, including variable lease payments that are expected to become payable. Accordingly, if a valuation obtained for a property is net of all payments expected to be made, it will be necessary to add back any recognised lease liability, to arrive at the carrying amount of the investment property using the fair value model. *[IAS 40.50(d)].*

Therefore, if the entity obtains a property valuation net of the valuer's estimate of the present value of future lease obligations (which is usual practice), to the extent that the lease obligations have already been accounted for in the statement of financial position as a lease obligation, an amount is to be added back to arrive at the fair value of the investment property for the purposes of the financial statements.

Where an entity subsequently measures its investment properties using the fair value model, there is no difference in accounting for investment property held under a finance lease or investment property held under an operating lease (or, if IFRS 16 is adopted (see 13.1 below), a right-of-use asset that meets the definition of investment property) (see also 4.5 above).

The valuation adjustment referred to above is achieved by adjusting for the finance lease obligation recognised in the financial statements.

This is illustrated using the information in the following example:

Example 19.4: Valuation of a property held under a finance lease

Entity A pays €991,000 for a 50-year leasehold interest in a property which is classified as an investment property using the fair value model. In addition, a ground rent of €10,000 is payable annually during the lease term, the present value of which is calculated at €99,000 using a discount rate of 10% which reflects the rate implicit in the lease at that time. The company has initially recognised the investment property at the following amount:

	€'000
Amount paid	991
Present value of the ground rent obligation on acquisition	99
Cost recorded for financial reporting purposes	1,090

Assume at the next reporting date the leasehold interest in the property has a fair value of €1,006,000 measured (based on market participant assumptions) as follows:

	€'000
Present value of estimated future lease income	1,089
Less: Present value of the ground rent obligation at the reporting date *	(83)
Fair value	1,006

* The market required yield has changed to 12%. Therefore, the present value of the ground rent obligations of €10,000 per annum for the remaining 49 years is now €83,000.

At the same time the ground rent finance lease liability has reduced to €98,000 as payments are made.

This would give the following results:

	€'000
Fair value	1,006
Add recognised finance lease liability	98
Carrying value for financial reporting purposes	1,104

The statement of financial position of Entity A would therefore contain the following items:

	Investment property €'000	Finance lease liability €'000
On acquisition	1,090	99
End of year 1	1,104	98

An example of this in practice can be seen in Extract 19.6 below:

Extract 19.6: Land Securities Group PLC (2017)

Notes to the financial statements [extract]

Section 3 – Properties [extract]

14. **Investment properties** [extract]

The market value of the Group's investment properties, as determined by the Group's external valuer, differs from the net book value presented in the balance sheet due to the Group presenting lease incentives, tenant finance leases and head leases separately. The following table reconciles the net book value of the investment properties to the market value.

	Group 2017 Group (excl. joint ventures) £m
Net book value	**12,144**
Plus: tenant lease incentives	**311**
Less: head leases capitalised	**(31)**
Plus: properties treated as finance leases	**238**
Market value	**12,662**
Net (deficit)/surplus on revaluation of investment properties	**(186)**

6.8 Future capital expenditure and development value ('highest and best use')

It is common for the value of land to reflect its potential future use and the value of land may increase in the event that the owner obtains any required permissions for a change in the use of that land.

It may be, for example, that a permission to change from an industrial to residential use will increase the value of the property as a whole, notwithstanding that the existing industrial buildings are still in place. This increase in value is typically attributable to the land, rather than the buildings.

It is therefore important to note that IFRS 13 requires consideration of all relevant factors in determining whether the highest and best use of a property can be something other than its current use at the measurement date. IFRS 13 presumes that an entity's current use of an asset is generally its highest and best use unless market or other factors suggest that a different use of that asset by market participants would maximise its value. *[IFRS 13.29]*. IFRS 13 states:

'A fair value measurement of a non-financial asset takes into account a market participant's ability to generate economic benefits by using the asset in its highest and best use or by selling it to another market participant that would use the asset in its highest and best use. The highest and best use of a non-financial asset takes into account the use of the asset that is physically possible, legally permissible and financially feasible, as follows:

(a) A use that is physically possible takes into account the physical characteristics of the asset that market participants would take into account when pricing the asset (e.g. the location or size of a property).

(b) A use that is legally permissible takes into account any legal restrictions on the use of the asset that market participants would take into account when pricing the asset (e.g. the zoning regulations applicable to a property).

(c) A use that is financially feasible takes into account whether a use of the asset that is physically possible and legally permissible generates adequate income or cash flows (taking into account the costs of converting the asset to that use) to produce an investment return that market participants would require from an investment in that asset put to that use.' *[IFRS 13.27-28]*.

Considerable judgement may then have to be applied in determining when an anticipated change is legally permissible. For example, if approval is required for rezoning land or for an alternative use of existing property interests, it may be necessary to assess whether such approval is a substantive legal requirement or not. See Chapter 14 at 10.1 for further discussion on determining highest and best use and the assessment of 'legally permissible'.

If management determines that the highest and best use of an asset is something other than its current use, certain valuation matters must be considered. Appraisals that reflect the effect of a reasonably anticipated change in what is legally permissible should be carefully evaluated. If the appraised value assumes that a change in use can be obtained, the valuation must also reflect the cost associated with obtaining approval for the change in use and transforming the asset, as well as capture the risk that the approval might not be granted (that is, uncertainty regarding the probability and timing of the approval).

Expectations about future improvements or modifications to be made to the property to reflect its highest and best use may be considered in the appraisal, such as the renovation of the property or the conversion of an office into condominiums, but only if and when other market participants would also consider making these investments and reflect only the cash flows that market participants would take into account when assessing fair value.

See Chapter 14 at 10 for further discussion on application of IFRS 13 requirements to non-financial assets which includes determining highest and best use.

6.9 Negative present value

In some cases, an entity expects that the present value of its payments relating to an investment property (other than payments relating to recognised liabilities) will exceed the present value of the related cash receipts. An entity should apply IAS 37 –

Provisions, Contingent Liabilities and Contingent Assets – to determine whether a liability should be recognised and, if so, how that liability should be measured. *[IAS 40.52]*.

6.10 Deferred taxation for property held by a 'single asset' entity

It is common in many jurisdictions for investment property to be bought and sold by transferring ownership of a separate legal entity formed to hold the asset (a 'single asset' entity) rather than the asset itself. In addition to the issue on initial recognition discussed in 4.1.2 above, this matter created diversity in practice when determining the expected manner of recovery of the asset for the purposes of IAS 12, i.e. whether or not the parent entity should reflect the fact that an asset held by a single asset entity is likely to be disposed of by selling the shares of the entity rather than the asset itself, and if so, whether the deferred taxation would be recognised with reference to the shares rather than the underlying property.

However, the Interpretations Committee clarified in its July 2014 meeting that IAS 12 requires the parent to recognise in its consolidated financial statements both the deferred tax related to the property inside the single asset entity and the deferred tax related to the shares of that single asset entity (the outside), if:

- tax law attributes separate tax bases to the asset inside and to the shares;
- in the case of deferred tax assets, the related deductible temporary differences can be utilised; and
- no specific exceptions in IAS 12 apply.[19]

Accordingly, in determining the expected manner of recovery of a property held by a single asset entity for the purposes of IAS 12, the parent entity should have regard to the asset itself. In line with this, it would not be appropriate to measure deferred taxation with reference to selling the shares of the single asset entity or include the related effects of tax in the valuation of the underlying property.

For further discussions on recognition of deferred taxes for investment property and for single asset entities, see Chapter 31 at 8.4.7 and 8.4.10, respectively.

7 THE COST MODEL

Except in the cases described in 8 below, the cost model requires that all investment property be measured after initial recognition under the cost model set out in IAS 16 (or in accordance with IFRS 16, when adopted, if the property is held by a lessee as a right-of-use asset – see 13.1 below). *[IAS 40.56]*.

Under IAS 16, this means that the asset must be recognised at cost, depreciated systematically over its useful life and impaired when appropriate. *[IAS 16.30]*. The residual value and useful life of each investment property must be reviewed at least at each financial year-end and, if expectations differ from previous estimates, the changes must be accounted for as a change in accounting estimate in accordance with IAS 8. *[IAS 16.51]*.

For further discussion of IFRS 16, see 13.1 below and Chapter 25.

If an entity adopts the cost model, the fair value of its investment property must be disclosed (see 12.3 below).

7.1 Initial recognition

7.1.1 Identification of tangible parts

The cost of the property must be analysed into appropriate significant components, each of which will have to be depreciated separately (see also Chapter 18 at 5.1).

The analysis into significant components is rarely a straightforward exercise since properties typically contain a large number of components with varying useful lives. Klépierre, which adopted the cost model for investment property prior to 2016 (see 7.2 below), disclosed its approach to this exercise – see Extract 19.7 below.

Extract 19.7: Klépierre (2015)

6. Consolidated financial statements as of December 31, 2015

6.5. Appendices [extract]

Note 2. Accounting principles and methods [extract]

2.10. Investment property [extract]

2.10.2 The component method

The component method is applied based on the recommendations of the Fédération des Sociétés Immobilières et Foncières (French Federation of Property Companies) for components and useful life:

– for properties developed by the companies themselves, assets are classified by component type and recognized at cost;

– for other properties, components are broken down into four categories: business premises, shopping centers, offices and residential properties.

Four components have been identified for each of these asset types (in addition to land):

– structures;

– facades, cladding and roofing;

– general and technical installations (GTI);

– fittings.

Components are broken down based on the history and technical characteristics of each building.

Klépierre uses the following matrix to determine components:

	Shopping centers		Retail stores	
	Period	QP	Period	QP
Structures	30 to 50 years	50%	30 to 40 years	50%
Facades	25 years	15%	15 to 25 years	15%
GTI	20 years	25%	10 to 20 years	25%
Fitting	10 to 15 years	10%	5 to 15 years	10%

A wear and tear ratio is applied when the acquired property is not new. Purchase costs are split between land and buildings. The proportion allocated to buildings is amortized over the useful life of the structures. The residual value is equivalent to the current estimate of the amount the Company would achieve if the asset concerned were already of an age and condition commensurate with the end of its useful life, less disposal expenses.

Given the useful life periods applied, the residual value of components is zero.

The entity is also required to recognise replacement parts and derecognise the replaced part as described in Chapter 18 at 7.

7.1.2 Identification of intangible parts

IAS 16 sets out that if an entity acquires PP&E subject to an operating lease in which it is the lessor, it may be appropriate to depreciate separately amounts reflected in the cost of that item that are attributable to favourable or unfavourable lease terms relative to market terms. *[IAS 16.44].* This will therefore apply to investment property accounted for under the cost model (see 4.7 above).

7.2 Incidence of use of the cost model

It appears less common for entities to measure investment property using the cost model than the fair value model.

In previous years, EY real estate financial statement surveys have consistently found that over 90% of the companies in those surveys used the fair value model. There also seems to be a general, although not universal, market consensus among existing IFRS reporters that the fair value model is the more appropriate. For example, in its latest *Best Practices Recommendations* issued in November 2016, the European Public Real Estate Association ('EPRA') recommends to its members that 'Real estate companies should account for their property investments based upon the fair value model.'[20]

Some IFRS reporters have moved from the cost model. For example, Klépierre adopted the cost model until the middle of 2016 when the fair value model was adopted. It made the following statement in its 2016 financial statements:

Extract 19.8: Klépierre (2016)

3 FINANCIAL STATEMENTS

3.1 **Consolidated financial statements as of December 31, 2016**

3.1.5 **Appendices** [extract]

NOTE 2 Significant accounting policies [extract]

2.4 **Change in accounting policies (IAS 8) – Fair value option according to IAS 40**

In the second half of 2016, Klépierre decided to choose the fair value method of IAS 40 for the accounting of its investment properties. Therefore the group presents comparative financial statements for 2015 (Consolidated statements of comprehensive income and Consolidated statements of financial position) showing the items affected by this change in accounting method. The fair value method is the preferential method under the provisions of IAS 40 and also the one recommended by the EPRA (European Public Real Estate Association). The fair value option facilitates comparisons with the financial statements of other property companies of which the majority applies this model. The change of accounting method was motivated by these elements.

The use of the cost model (rather than the fair value model) removes the need to recognise gains from increases in the fair value of property within profit or loss. However, it is unlikely to insulate an entity from reporting falls in the fair value of investment property below the depreciated cost of the property – see 7.3 below.

7.3 Impairment

Investment property measured at cost is subject to the requirements of IAS 36 in respect of impairment. As set out in Chapter 20, IAS 36 requires a recoverable amount to be determined as the higher of (i) value in use and (ii) fair value less costs of disposal. *[IAS 36.18]*.

Both value in use calculation and fair value calculation (where there is no price quoted for identical assets on an active market) are typically based on discounted cash flow models. The former will typically use entity specific cash flows, whilst the latter would generally use market expected cash flows. Both would use a market determined discount rate.

For a rental generating asset such as an investment property, the future cash flows to be taken into account in any projection would, in simple terms, be (i) the rental stream under the existing lease arrangements and (ii) an estimate of any rental stream thereafter. The cash flows expected to be generated from the existing lease would be the same whether the basis was entity specific or market expected cash flows.

The estimate of any rental stream thereafter would also be the same unless the entity forecast it would outperform the market and achieve superior cash flows. This is unlikely to be an acceptable basis for a forecast as no entity can realistically expect to outperform the market for its whole portfolio or do so for more than the short term. Therefore, a forecast that cash flows from individual properties will outperform the market would have to be considered with scepticism.

Consequently, we would regard it as being a rare circumstance where the value in use of an individual investment property could be said to be higher than the fair value of that property. Indeed, in some circumstances – for example, where a fair value is partly dependent on a gain from planned future development (see 6.8 above) but where that expenditure is not to be allowed to be considered in a value in use calculation – value in use may be lower than fair value.

8 IFRS 5 AND INVESTMENT PROPERTY

Investment property measured using the cost model (under IAS 16 or, when adopted, IFRS 16 – see 13.1 below) which meets the criteria to be classified as held for sale, or is included within a disposal group classified as held for sale, is measured in accordance with IFRS 5 – *Non-current Assets Held for Sale and Discontinued Operations*. *[IAS 40.56]*. This means that such property will be held at the lower of carrying amount and fair value less costs to sell, and depreciation of the asset will cease. *[IFRS 5.15, 25]*.

As set out in Chapter 4 at 2.2.1, investment property measured at fair value is not subject to the measurement requirements of IFRS 5. However, such property is subject to the presentation requirements of that standard. Consequently, investment property that meets the definition of held for sale is required to be presented separately from other assets in the statement of financial position. This does not necessarily mean that such property must be presented within current assets (see Chapter 4 at 2.2.4).

An example of an entity applying the presentation requirements of IFRS 5 to investment property measured at fair value is Land Securities Group PLC in its 2015 financial statements – see Extract 19.9 below.

Extract 19.9: Land Securities Group PLC (2015)

FINANCIAL STATEMENTS [extract]

BALANCE SHEETS [extract]

at 31 March 2015

		Group
	Notes	2015 £m
Non-current assets		
Investment properties	15	12,158.0
Intangible assets	41	34.7
Other property, plant and equipment	20	9.6
Net investment in finance leases	19	185.1
Loan investment	31	49.5
Investments in joint ventures	16	1,433.5
Investments in subsidiary undertakings	32	–
Other investments		12.8
Trade and other receivables	28	54.0
Derivative financial instruments	25	–
Pension surplus	34	7.0
Total non-current assets		13,944.2
Current assets		
Trading properties and long-term development contracts	17	222.3
Trade and other receivables	28	402.7
Monies held in restricted accounts and deposits	23	10.4
Cash and cash equivalents	24	14.3
Total current assets		649.7
Non-current assets held for sale	42	283.4
Total assets		14,877.3

[...]

NOTES TO THE FINANCIAL STATEMENTS [extract]

42. **Non-current assets held for sale**

On 23 March 2015, the Group exchanged contracts for the sale of Times Square, EC4 for consideration of £284.6m. The risks and returns of ownership had not fully transferred to the buyer as at 31 March 2015. As a result the property was classified as a Non-current asset held for sale with carrying value of **£283.4m.**

Investment property measured using the cost model is subject to both the measurement and presentation requirements of IFRS 5. Klépierre, which previously used the cost model for its investment property (see 7.2 above), provides an accounting policy for such property held for sale in its 2015 financial statements – see Extract 19.10 below.

Extract 19.10: Klépierre (2015)

6.5. **Appendices** [extract]

Note 2. Accounting principles and methods [extract]

2.11. **Investment property held for sale**

Investment properties under promise or mandate of sale are presented according to IFRS 5.

The accounting impacts are as follows:

- reclassification as held for sale at the lower of its carrying amount and fair value less costs to sell;
- investment properties concerned are presented separately in current assets;
- depreciation ceases.

9 TRANSFER OF ASSETS TO OR FROM INVESTMENT PROPERTY

9.1 Transfers to or from investment property (requirements before and after December 2016 amendments to IAS 40)

IAS 40 specifies the circumstances in which a property becomes, or ceases to be, an investment property. As discussed in 1 above, narrow-scope amendments issued in December 2016 – *Transfers of Investment Property (Amendments to IAS 40)* – have amended paragraphs 57 and 58 of IAS 40 to clarify when an entity should transfer property, including property under construction or development into, or out of, investment property. These amendments apply to accounting periods beginning on or after 1 January 2018 and are discussed further below.

Prior to the amendments referred to above, paragraph 57 stated that a transfer is made to, or from, investment property when, and only when, there is a change in use, evidenced by:

(a) commencement or end of owner-occupation for a transfer from investment property to owner-occupied property (or *vice versa*);

(b) commencement of development with a view to sale, at which point an investment property would be transferred to inventory; or

(c) commencement of an operating lease to another party, for a transfer from inventory to investment property (but see 2.3 above).

Extract 19.11 below describes how Land Securities Group PLC dealt with the requirements of (b) above.

Extract 19.11: Land Securities Group PLC (2017)

Notes to the financial statements [extract]
Section 3 – Properties [extract]
Accounting policy [extract]

Transfers between investment properties and trading properties

When the Group begins to redevelop an existing investment property for continued future use as an investment property, the property continues to be held as an investment property. When the Group begins to redevelop an existing investment property with a view to sell, the property is transferred to trading properties and held as a current asset. The property is re-measured to fair value as at the date of the transfer with any gain or loss being taken to the income statement. The re-measured amount becomes the deemed cost at which the property is then carried in trading properties.

Some interpreted the instances of change set out in the unamended paragraph 57 as exhaustive, given the reference to 'evidenced by' in that paragraph, and, therefore, applied this guidance in a very narrow sense. There was also a notion that the paragraph only applied to completed investment properties and not to those still under construction.

The Interpretations Committee received a request to clarify whether paragraph 57 prohibits transfers of a property under construction or development, previously classified as inventory, to investment property when there is an evident change in use.

The Interpretations Committee observed that the principle in IAS 40 for classification as investment property is based on how an asset is used, and consequently, an entity should reclassify investment property under construction or development into, or out of, investment property if, and only if, there is evidence that a change in the use of such property has occurred.

The Interpretations Committee also noted that the words 'when, and only when' in paragraph 57 are important to ensure that a reclassification is limited appropriately to changes in use that have taken place, but observed that the list of circumstances set out in paragraphs 57(a)-(d), prior to amendment, should be re-presented as examples of evidence that a change in use has occurred and not as an exhaustive list.

Accordingly, the Interpretations Committee recommended, and the IASB agreed, that paragraph 57 of IAS 40 should be amended to reinforce the principle for transfers into, or out of, investment property in IAS 40 to specify that:

- a transfer into, or out of investment property should be made only when there has been a change in use of the property; and
- such a change in use would involve an assessment of whether the property qualifies as an investment property. That change in use should be supported by evidence.

As recommended by the Interpretations Committee, the IASB also decided that the list of circumstances set out in paragraph 57(a)-(d), prior to amendment, should be re-presented as examples of evidence that a change in use has occurred rather than as an exhaustive list.[21]

Accordingly, the narrow-scope amendments issued in December 2016 clarify paragraph 57 as follows: 'An entity shall transfer a property to, or from, investment property when, and only when, there is a change in use. A change in use occurs when the property meets, or ceases to meet, the definition of investment property and there is evidence of the change in use. In isolation, a change in management's intentions for the use of a property does not provide evidence of a change in use. Examples of evidence of a change in use include:

(a) commencement of owner-occupation, or of development with a view to owner-occupation, for a transfer from investment property to owner-occupied property;

(b) commencement of development with a view to sale, for a transfer from investment property to inventories;

(c) end of owner-occupation, for a transfer from owner-occupied property to investment property; and

(d) inception of an operating lease to another party, for a transfer from inventories to investment property' (but see 2.3 above). *[IAS 40.57]*.

We illustrate the application of this principle with an example below:

Example 19.5: Transfers from inventory

In 2017, an entity purchased land with the intention of constructing an apartment building on the land and selling the apartments to private customers. Accordingly, the land was classified as inventory. During 2017, the prices for residential properties decreased and the entity decided to change its original business plans at the beginning of 2018. Instead of constructing an apartment building and selling the apartments, the entity decided to construct an office building that it would lease out to tenants. The entity holds and manages other investment property as well.

During the first half of 2018, the entity obtained permission from the relevant authorities to commence the construction and hired an architect to design the office building. The physical construction of the office building began in August 2018. No operating leases had been agreed with other parties for the lease of office space. However, negotiations had been held with potential tenants.

The inception of an operating lease is generally evidence of a change in use for a transfer from inventories to investment property. *[IAS 40.57(d)]*. However, even in the absence of the inception of an operating lease, there may be other circumstances that provide evidence of a change in use. We would generally conclude that there is sufficient evidence for a change in use from inventory to investment property if all of the following criteria are met:

- the entity has prepared a business plan that reflects the future rental income generated by the property and this is supported with evidence that there is demand for rental space;
- the entity can demonstrate that it has the resources, including the necessary financing or capital, to hold and manage an investment property (which requires different skills than developing a property). If the entity also owns other investment property, this could be more easily demonstrated. However, if this property would be the entity's only investment property, it may be harder to demonstrate this;
- the change in use is legally permissible. That is, the entity has obtained permission from relevant authorities for the change in use. In cases where the approval of the change in use is merely a routine or a non-substantive legal requirement (i.e. not at the discretion of the authorities), the entity's request for permission may be sufficient evidence; and
- if the property must be further developed for the change in use, development has commenced.

For the scenario described in the fact pattern above, the entity met the above criteria at the point in time when it obtained permission from the relevant authorities to change the use of the property and commenced development of the property by hiring an architect. At that time, the land would be transferred from inventory to investment property.

The amendments are expected to eliminate diversity in practice. The amended paragraph 57 of IAS 40 establishes a guiding principle regarding transfers to or from investment property based on whether there is evidence of a change in use and provides a non-exhaustive list of examples of such evidence. *[IAS 40.BC26]*.

Actions toward effecting a change in use must have been taken by the entity during the reporting period to provide evidence that such a change has occurred. The assessment of whether a change in use has occurred is based on an assessment of all the facts and circumstances.

9.1.1 Transfers of investment property: effective date and transitional provisions of the December 2016 amendments

The amendments are effective for annual periods on or after 1 January 2018. Early application of the amendments is permitted and must be disclosed. *[IAS 40.85G]*.

Entities should apply the amendments prospectively to changes in use that occur on or after the beginning of the annual reporting period in which the entity first applies the amendments. An entity should reassess the classification of property held at that date and, if applicable, reclassify property (applying paragraphs 7-14 of IAS 40, discussed in 2.2 to 2.8 above) to reflect the conditions that exist at that date. *[IAS 40.84C]*.

If an entity reclassifies property at the date of initial application, the entity should:

- account for the reclassification applying the requirements in paragraphs 59-64 of IAS 40 (discussed in 9.3 below). Accordingly, an entity should:
  - read any reference to the date of change in use as the date of initial application; and
  - recognise any amount that, in accordance with paragraphs 59-64 of IAS 40 (discussed in 9.3 below), would have been recognised in profit or loss as an adjustment to the opening balance of retained earnings at the date of initial application.
- disclose the amounts reclassified to, or from, investment property in accordance with paragraph 84C of IAS 40 (as described above) as part of the reconciliation of the carrying amount of investment property at the beginning and end of the period as required by paragraphs 76 and 79 of IAS 40 (discussed respectively in 12.2 and 12.3 below). *[IAS 40.84E]*.

Notwithstanding the prospective application referred to above, retrospective application in accordance with IAS 8 is permitted but only if that is possible without the use of hindsight. *[IAS 40.84D]*.

9.2 Transfers from investment property to inventory

Transfers to inventory are more difficult to deal with by way of the application of a general principle since IFRS 5 explicitly deals with investment property held for sale. IAS 40 allows a transfer to inventory only when there is a change in use as evidenced, for example, by the start of development with a view to subsequent sale. *[IAS 40.57]*.

If an entity decides to dispose of an investment property without development with a view to sale, it is unlikely to be transferred to inventory as IFRS 5 is applied to property held for sale to the extent that the requirements therein are met (see 8 above).

The IASB is aware of this inconsistency in the application of IFRS 5 and IAS 2 to investment property and in 2010 it asked the Interpretations Committee to consider any necessary interpretation to resolve it. However, the Interpretations Committee decided to recommend proposals that indicated no change to existing practice.

Consequently, this means that, unless there is development with a view to sale, it may not be possible to reclassify investment property as inventory even if the entity holding that property changes its intentions and is no longer holding that property for rental or capital appreciation. Accordingly, when an entity decides to dispose of an investment property without development, it should continue to classify the property as an investment property until it is derecognised (see 10 below) and should not reclassify it as inventory. Similarly, if an entity begins to redevelop an existing investment property for continued future use as investment property, the property remains an investment property and is not reclassified as owner-occupied property during the redevelopment. *[IAS 40.58].*

9.3 Accounting treatment of transfers

When an entity uses the cost model for investment property, transfers between investment property, owner-occupied property and inventories do not change the carrying amount of the property transferred and they do not change the cost of that property for measurement or disclosure purposes. *[IAS 40.59].*

Transfers to and from investment property under the fair value model are accounted for as follows:

- *Transfers from inventory*: any difference between the fair value of the property at date of change in use and its previous carrying amount should be recognised in profit or loss. *[IAS 40.63].* This treatment is consistent with the treatment of sales of inventories. *[IAS 40.64].*
- *Transfers to inventory or owner-occupation*: the cost for subsequent accounting under IAS 2 or IAS 16 (or IFRS 16, when adopted – see 13.1 below) respectively should be the property's fair value at the date of change in use. *[IAS 40.60].*
- *Transfers from owner-occupation*: IAS 16 will be applied up to the date of change in use (or if IFRS 16 is adopted (see 13.1 below), IAS 16 will be applied for owned property and IFRS 16 for property held by a lessee as a right-of-use asset up to the date of change in use). At that date, any difference between the carrying amount under IAS 16 (or IFRS 16, when adopted) and the fair value should be treated in the same way as a revaluation under IAS 16. *[IAS 40.61].*

If the owner-occupied property had not previously been revalued, the transfer does not imply that the entity has now chosen a policy of revaluation for other property accounted for under IAS 16 in the same class. The treatment depends on whether it is a decrease or increase in value and whether the asset had previously been revalued or impaired in value.

The treatment required by IAS 40 is as follows. Up to the date when an owner-occupied property becomes an investment property carried at fair value, an entity depreciates the property (or the right-of use asset, if IFRS 16 is adopted – see 13.1 below) and recognises any impairment losses that have occurred. The entity treats any difference at that date between the carrying amount of the property in accordance with IAS 16 (or IFRS 16, if adopted) and its fair value in the same way as a revaluation in accordance with IAS 16.

'In other words:

(a) any resulting decrease in the carrying amount of the property is recognised in profit or loss. However, to the extent that an amount is included in revaluation surplus for that property, the decrease is recognised in other comprehensive income and reduces the revaluation surplus within equity.

(b) any resulting increase in the carrying amount is treated as follows:

  (i) to the extent that the increase reverses a previous impairment loss for that property, the increase is recognised in profit or loss. The amount recognised in profit or loss does not exceed the amount needed to restore the carrying amount to the carrying amount that would have been determined (net of depreciation) had no impairment loss been recognised.

  (ii) any remaining part of the increase is recognised in other comprehensive income and increases the revaluation surplus within equity. On subsequent disposal of the investment property, the revaluation surplus included in equity may be transferred to retained earnings. The transfer from revaluation surplus to retained earnings is not made through profit or loss.' *[IAS 40.62]*.

IAS 40 also reconfirms that when an entity completes the construction or development of a self-constructed investment property that will be carried at fair value (i.e. no actual reclassification to investment property), any difference between the fair value of the property at that date and its previous carrying amount shall be recognised in profit or loss. *[IAS 40.65]*.

Under IAS 17, if a premium is paid for an interest in a property held under operating lease, e.g. in a lease of land, and the property is occupied by the lessee, the amount paid as a premium is recognised as prepayment and is amortised over the lease term in accordance with the expected pattern of consumption of the economic benefits embodied in the land-use right (see Chapter 24 at 3.3). However, if subsequently the occupation of the land ends and the land is leased to third parties, the leasehold will meet the definition of an investment property and could be transferred to and classified as investment property provided the fair value model is applied (see 2.1 and 5.1 above).

Neither IAS 40 nor IAS 17 specifies the accounting treatment of a resulting gain or loss on such a transfer. Some consider that any result from such a transfer should be recognised in profit or loss in line with the requirement in IAS 1 that all items of income and expense should be recognised in profit or loss unless an IFRS requires or permits otherwise. *[IAS 1.88]*. However, others may argue that it may be appropriate to adopt the approach in IAS 40 applicable to the transfer of an owner-occupied property to an investment property (see discussion above) since strictly, the property was previously owner-occupied before it becomes an investment property. Management will therefore need to exercise judgement in determining its policy and apply it consistently. If significant, clear disclosure of such policy and judgement would be required by IAS 1. *[IAS 1.117, 122]*.

Note that when IFRS 16 is adopted (see 13.1 below), lessees are required to include any lease payments made at or before lease commencement date in their initial measurement of the right-of-use asset (which may include premium paid for a right-of-use asset) (see Chapter 25 at 5.2.1). *[IFRS 16.23]*. Also, IFRS 16 amends paragraph 61 of IAS 40, as set out above, to include guidance on transfers to investment property of owner-occupied property held by a lessee as a right-of-use asset. Accordingly, IFRS 16 will be applied for property held by a lessee as a right-of-use asset up to the date of change in use. At that date, any difference between the carrying amount under IFRS 16 and the fair value should be treated in the same way as a revaluation under IAS 16.

9.4 Transfers of investment property held under operating leases

An entity applying the fair value model is allowed to classify interests held under operating leases as investment properties in the same manner as if they were held under finance leases (see 4.5 above). IAS 17 requires this treatment to continue even if the property interest ceases to be classified as an investment property by the lessee and gives two examples:

- the lessee occupies the property, in which case it is transferred to owner-occupied property at a deemed cost equal to its fair value at the date of change in use; or
- the lessee grants a sublease that transfers substantially all of the risks and rewards incidental to ownership of the interest to an unrelated third party. It will treat the sublease as a finance lease to the third party even though the interest may well be accounted for as an operating lease by that party. *[IAS 17.19]*.

Therefore, on transfer, the treatment of interests held under operating leases mirrors that of other ownership interests.

See also the discussion in Chapter 24 at 3.3.3.

Note that when IFRS 16 is adopted, the guidance above and IAS 17 in its entirety, will be superseded (see 13.1 below). Under IFRS 16, lessees will apply a single model for most leases and will recognise most rental contracts in their statement of financial position as lease liabilities with corresponding right-of-use assets. Subsequent to initial recognition, the IASB indicated that a lease liability should be accounted for in a manner similar to other financial liabilities (i.e. on amortised cost basis). *[IFRS 16.BC182]*. For further discussion on subsequent measurements of lease liabilities and right-of-use assets, see Chapter 25 at 5.3.

10 DISPOSAL OF INVESTMENT PROPERTY

IAS 40 requires that an investment property should be removed from the statement of financial position ('derecognised') on disposal or when it is permanently withdrawn from use and no future economic benefits are expected from its disposal. *[IAS 40.66]*.

A disposal of an investment property may be achieved by:

- its sale; or
- when it becomes the subject of a finance lease (the owner becoming the lessor); or
- when it becomes the subject of a sale and leaseback deal resulting in an operating lease (the original owner becoming the lessee). *[IAS 40.67]*.

These derecognition rules also apply to a part of the investment property that has been replaced (see 10.3 below).

IAS 17 (or IFRS 16, if adopted – see 13.1 below) applies if a property is disposed of by the owner becoming a lessor in a finance lease, or if a property is the subject of a sale and leaseback transaction (see Chapter 24 or if applicable, Chapter 25). *[IAS 40.67]*.

If disposal of investment property is achieved by sale, the determination of the timing of recognition of any gain or loss should be in accordance with IFRS 15. Consequently, the date of disposal for investment property that is sold is the date the recipient obtains control of the investment property in accordance with the requirements for determining when a performance obligation is satisfied in IFRS 15. *[IAS 40.67]*. IFRS 15 requires revenue (and a gain or loss on disposal of a non-current asset not in the ordinary course of business) to be recognised when a performance obligation is satisfied, which will be when control of the asset is transferred to the customer. Control may be transferred at a point in time or over time. *[IFRS 15.31, 32]*. Accordingly, entities that dispose of an investment property through sale should recognise a gain or loss on disposal when control of the property transfers, which may be at a point in time. In many cases, control will transfer when the buyer obtains legal title and physical possession of the asset. However, this may occur prior to legal settlement if it can be demonstrated that control has passed to the buyer before that date. For the detailed discussion and requirements of IFRS 15 on satisfaction of performance obligations, see Chapter 30 at 7.

Prior to adoption of IFRS 15, IAS 18 was applied in determining the timing of recognition of any gain or loss on disposal of investment property achieved upon a sale. Accordingly, such a gain or loss was recognised when the conditions in that standard were met. This had the effect that while the sale might be recognised when legal title passed, in some jurisdictions the risks and rewards of ownership passed to the buyer before legal title had passed. In such cases, provided that the seller had no further substantial acts to complete under the contract, it might be appropriate to recognise the sale. Capital & Counties Properties PLC has taken this approach.

Extract 19.12: Capital & Counties Properties PLC (2016)

Notes to the accounts [extract]

1 **PRINCIPAL ACCOUNTING POLICIES** [extract]

Revenue recognition [extract]

Where revenue is obtained by the sale of property, it is recognised when the significant risks and rewards have been transferred to the buyer. This will normally take place on exchange of contracts unless there are conditions that suggest insufficient probability of future economic benefits flowing to the Group. For conditional exchanges, sales are recognised when these conditions are satisfied.

10.1 Calculation of gain or loss on disposal

Gains and losses on retirement or disposal of investment property are calculated based on the difference between the net disposal proceeds (after deducting direct costs of disposal) and the carrying amount of the asset. *[IAS 40.69]*. IAS 40 does not give guidance on how to determine the carrying amount of the asset. Possible alternatives would include the use of (i) the carrying amount in the financial statements of the last full period of account, or (ii) the carrying amount in the latest interim financial statements, or (iii) the updated carrying amount at the date of disposal. In our view, this is a policy choice for an entity to make and is primarily a matter of income statement presentation to the extent that an entity presents gains and losses on disposal separately from gains and losses on revaluation. This choice is illustrated in Extract 19.3 above where Unibail-Rodamco uses the 'full period of account' approach.

Gains and losses on retirement or disposal of investment property are recognised in profit or loss, unless it is a sale and leaseback and IAS 17 requires a different treatment, in the period of retirement or disposal (see also 12.4 below). *[IAS 40.69]*. IAS 17 allows only the immediate recognition of profits and losses on a sale and operating leaseback if the transaction is established at fair value; no gains would be recognised if the transaction resulted in a finance leaseback. Refer to Chapter 24 at 7 for a discussion of sale and leaseback under IAS 17. Note that the new leases standard, IFRS 16, will supersede IAS 17 when it becomes effective in 2019 (see 13.1 below). Refer to Chapter 25 at 8 for a discussion of sale and leaseback under IFRS 16.

The amount of consideration to be included in the gain or loss arising from the derecognition of an investment property is determined in accordance with the requirements for determining the transaction price in paragraphs 47-72 of IFRS 15. *[IAS 40.70]*. Under IFRS 15, an entity is required to consider the terms of the contract and its customary business practices in determining the transaction price. Transaction price is defined as the amount of consideration to which an entity expects to be entitled in exchange for transferring the property to a buyer, excluding amounts collected on behalf of third parties (e.g. sales taxes). The consideration in a contract may include fixed amounts, variable amounts, or both. *[IFRS 15.47]*.

In many cases, the transaction price may be readily determined if the entity receives payment when it transfers the property and the price is fixed. In other situations, it could be more challenging as it may be affected by the nature, timing and amounts of consideration.

Determining the transaction price is discussed in detail in Chapter 30 at 5.

Subsequent changes to the estimated amount of the consideration included in the gain or loss should be accounted for in accordance with the requirements for changes in the transaction price in IFRS 15. *[IAS 40.70]*. This is further discussed in Chapter 30 at 6.5.

An entity that has not adopted IFRS 15 initially recognises the consideration receivable on the disposal at fair value. If the payment is deferred (deferral is not defined but must mean beyond normal credit terms) the consideration received is recognised initially at the cash price equivalent (which in practice means the present value of the consideration). Any difference between the total payments receivable and this 'cash price equivalent' is treated as interest revenue under IAS 18 using the effective interest method.

If an entity retains any liabilities after disposing of an investment property these are measured and accounted for in accordance with IAS 37 or other relevant standards. *[IAS 40.71]*. Accounting for such liabilities depends on specific facts and circumstances as such a liability may represent a provision or a contingent liability under IAS 37, or a financial liability under IFRS 9 – *Financial Instruments* (or IAS 39 – *Financial Instruments: Recognition and Measurement*), or a separate performance obligation or variable consideration under IFRS 15.

Under IAS 18, retention of liabilities on sale of goods may indicate that the significant risks and rewards of ownership have not passed to the buyer or that the seller has continuing involvement to the extent usually associated with ownership (see Chapter 29 at 3.7). In both instances, this would preclude revenue recognition. In contrast, under IFRS 15, retention of liabilities or the existence of continuing managerial involvement might indicate that control of goods has not passed to a buyer, but on their own do not affect whether an entity can recognise a sale and the associated profit from the transfer of the property. Instead, an entity might need to consider whether it represents an assurance-type or service-type warranty or consideration payable to a customer and whether variable consideration requirements would apply. See also related discussions in Chapter 30 at 5.2.1.B.

10.2 Sale prior to completion of construction

Prior to adoption of IFRS 15, IFRIC 15 dealt with real estate sales in which an agreement for sale is reached before the construction of property is complete. IFRIC 15 addressed:

- whether such an agreement is within the scope of IAS 11 or IAS 18; and
- when revenue from the construction of real estate should be recognised. *[IFRIC 15.6].*

It should be noted that property that is subject to sale prior to completion of construction, if not previously classified as investment property, is likely to be property intended for sale in the ordinary course of business (see 2.6 above) and is therefore not likely to be investment property. IFRIC 15 is discussed in more detail in Chapter 29 at 5.12.

As discussed at 1 above, IFRS 15 supersedes IFRIC 15, IAS 11 and IAS 18. For further discussion of IFRS 15, see Chapter 30.

10.3 Replacement of parts of investment property

When an entity that applies the fair value model wishes to capitalise a replacement part (provided it meets the criteria at 3 above), the question arises of how to deal with the cost of the new part and the carrying value of the original. The basic principle in IAS 40 is that the entity derecognises the carrying value of the replaced part. However, the problem frequently encountered is that even if the cost of the old part is known, its carrying value – at fair value – is usually by no means clear. It is possible also that the fair value may already reflect the loss in value of the part to be replaced, because the valuation reflected the fact that an acquirer would reduce the price accordingly. *[IAS 40.68].*

As all fair value changes are taken to profit or loss, the standard concludes that it is not necessary to identify separately the elements that relate to replacements from other fair value movements. Therefore, if it is not practical to identify the amount by which fair value should be reduced for the part replaced, the cost of the replacement is added to the carrying amount of the asset and the fair value of the investment property as a whole is reassessed. The standard notes that this is the treatment that would be applied to additions that did not involve replacing any existing part of the property. *[IAS 40.68].*

If the investment property is carried under the cost model, then the entity should derecognise the carrying amount of the original part. A replaced part may not have been depreciated separately, in which case, if it is not practicable to determine the carrying amount of the replaced part, the standard allows the entity to use the cost of the replacement as an indication of an appropriate carrying value. This does not mean that the entity has to apply depreciated replacement cost, rather that it can use the cost of the replacement as an indication of the original cost of the replaced part in order to reconstruct a suitable carrying amount for the replaced part. *[IAS 40.68]*.

10.4 Compensation from third parties

IAS 40 applies the same rules as IAS 16 to the treatment of compensation from third parties if property has been impaired, lost or given up (see Chapter 18 at 5.7). It stresses that impairments or losses of investment property, related claims for or payments of compensation from third parties and any subsequent purchase or construction of replacement assets are separate economic events that have to be accounted for separately. *[IAS 40.73]*.

Impairment of investment property will be recorded automatically if the fair value model is used; but if the property is accounted for using the cost model, it is to be calculated in accordance with IAS 36 (see Chapter 20). If the entity no longer owns the asset, for example because it has been destroyed or subject to a compulsory purchase order, it will be derecognised (see 10 above). Compensation from third parties (for example, from an insurance company) for property that was impaired, lost or given up is recognised in profit or loss when it becomes receivable. The cost of any replacement asset is accounted for wholly on its own merits according to the recognition rules covered in 3 above. *[IAS 40.72, 73]*.

11 INTERIM REPORTING AND IAS 40

IAS 34 – *Interim Financial Reporting* – requires the use of the same principles for the recognition and the definitions of assets, liabilities, income and expenses for interim periods as will be used in annual financial statements.

IAS 40 requires, for those entities using the fair value model, investment property to be presented at fair value at the end of the reporting period. Accordingly, investment property measured using the fair value model should also be measured at fair value in any interim financial reports. IAS 34 expects this as it includes the following guidance in Part C of the illustrative examples accompanying the standard:

'IAS 16 *Property, Plant and Equipment* allows an entity to choose as its accounting policy the revaluation model whereby items of property, plant and equipment are revalued to fair value. Similarly, IAS 40 requires an entity to measure the fair value of investment property. For those measurements, an entity may rely on professionally qualified valuers at annual reporting dates though not at interim reporting date.' *[IAS 34 IE Example C7]*.

The United Kingdom regulator made a similar point in its 2009 report on its activities. It stated that:

'A key principle of IAS 34, "Interim Financial Reporting", is that interim accounts should be prepared applying the same accounting policies as those applied to the annual accounts. IAS 40, "Investment Property" requires companies applying the fair value model to carry their properties at fair value with changes reported in the income statement. Properties are therefore required to be carried at fair value at the half-year stage.'[22]

For those entities using the cost model in annual financial statements, IAS 40 requires the disclosure of the fair value of investment property (see 12.3 below). For interim financial statements prepared under IAS 34, there is no such explicit disclosure requirement. Preparers of the financial statements should therefore consider the principle of IAS 34 which is that:

'Timely and reliable interim financial reporting improves the ability of investors, creditors, and others to understand an entity's capacity to generate earnings and cash flows and its financial condition and liquidity.' *[IAS 34 Objectives].*

It is likely that an understanding of the fair value of investment property at the end of an interim reporting period would help this purpose.

In addition, Part C of the illustrative examples to IAS 34 sets out that IAS 40 requires an entity to estimate the fair value of investment property. It does not distinguish between those entities that measure investment property at fair value and those entities that use the cost model and disclose fair value.

Consequently, it is our view that the fair value of investment property at the end of the interim period should usually be disclosed in interim financial reports for those entities using the cost model in IAS 40.

IAS 34 is discussed in more detail in Chapter 39.

12 THE DISCLOSURE REQUIREMENTS OF IAS 40

For entities that adopt the fair value option in IAS 40, attention will focus on the judgemental and subjective aspects of property valuations, because they will be reported in profit or loss. IAS 40 requires significant amounts of information to be disclosed about these judgements and the cash-related performance of the investment property, as set out below.

Note also that the disclosures below apply in addition to those in IAS 17 which require the owner of an investment property to provide lessors' disclosures about leases into which it has entered (see Chapter 24 at 9). IAS 40 also requires an entity that holds an investment property under a lease to provide lessees' disclosures for finance leases and lessors' disclosures for any operating leases into which it has entered. *[IAS 40.74].*

When IFRS 16 is adopted (see 13.1 below), IAS 17 will be superseded. Accordingly, the disclosures below apply in addition to those in IFRS 16. In accordance with IFRS 16, the owner of an investment property will provide lessors' disclosures about leases into which it has entered. A lessee that holds an investment property as a right-of-use asset will provide lessees' disclosures as required by IFRS 16 and lessors' disclosures as required by IFRS 16 for any operating leases into which it has entered.

12.1 Disclosures under both fair value and cost models

Whichever model is chosen, fair value or cost, IAS 40 requires all entities to disclose the fair value of their investment property. Therefore, the following disclosures are required in both instances:

- whether the entity applies the cost model or the fair value model;
- if it applies the fair value model, whether, and in what circumstances, property interests held under operating leases are classified and accounted for as investment property (if IFRS 16 is adopted (see 13.1 below), this disclosure will no longer be required because IFRS 16 will remove the classification alternative for property interests held under operating leases – as discussed in 2.1 and 5.1 above);
- when classification is difficult, the criteria it uses to distinguish investment property from owner-occupied property and from property held for sale in the ordinary course of business;
- the extent to which the fair value of investment property (as measured or disclosed in the financial statements) is based on a valuation by an independent valuer who holds a recognised and relevant professional qualification and has recent experience in the location and category of the investment property being valued. If there has been no such valuation, that fact shall be disclosed (e.g. a statement that the fair value of investment property is based on internal appraisals rather than on a valuation by an independent valuer as described above);
- the amounts recognised in profit or loss for:
  - rental income from investment property;
  - direct operating expenses (including repairs and maintenance) arising from investment property that generated rental income during the period (see 12.1.3 below);
  - direct operating expenses (including repairs and maintenance) arising from investment property that did not generate rental income during the period (see 12.1.3 below); and
  - the cumulative change in fair value recognised in profit or loss on sale of an investment property from a pool of assets in which the cost model is used into a pool in which the fair value model is used (see 5.2 above);
- the existence and amounts of restrictions on the realisability of investment property or the remittance of income and proceeds of disposal; and
- contractual obligations to purchase, construct or develop investment property or for repairs, maintenance or enhancements. *[IAS 40.75]*.

12.1.1 Methods and assumptions in fair value estimates

IFRS 13 includes a fair value hierarchy which prioritises the inputs used in a fair value measurement. The hierarchy is defined as follows:

- Level 1 inputs – Quoted prices (unadjusted) in active markets for identical assets or liabilities that the entity can access at the measurement date;
- Level 2 inputs – Inputs other than quoted prices included with Level 1 that are observable for the asset or liability, either directly or indirectly; and
- Level 3 inputs – Unobservable inputs for the asset or liability. *[IFRS 13 Appendix A]*.

IFRS 13 also uses its fair value hierarchy to categorise each fair value measurement in its entirety for disclosure purposes. Categorisation within the hierarchy is based on the lowest level input that is significant to the fair value measurement as a whole. This is discussed further in Chapter 14 at 16.2.

Significant differences in disclosure requirements apply to fair value measurements categorised within each level of the hierarchy to provide users with insight into the observability of the fair value measurement (the full disclosure requirements of IFRS 13 are discussed further in Chapter 14 at 20).

In our view, due to the lack of an active market for identical assets, it would be rare for real estate to be categorised within Level 1 of the fair value hierarchy.

In market conditions where similar real estate is actively purchased and sold, and the transactions are observable, the fair value measurement might be categorised within Level 2. This categorisation will be unusual for real estate, but that determination will depend on the facts and circumstances, including the significance of adjustments to observable data.

In this regard, IFRS 13 provides a real-estate specific example stating that a Level 2 input would be the price per square metre for the property interest derived from observable market data, e.g. multiples derived from prices in observed transactions involving comparable (i.e. similar) property interests in similar locations. *[IFRS 13.B35(g)]*. Accordingly, in active and transparent markets for similar assets (perhaps those that exist in some of the capital cities of developed economies), real estate valuations might be able to be categorised within Level 2, provided that no significant adjustments have been made to the observable data.

However, and likely to be much more common for real estate, if an adjustment to an observed transaction is based on unobservable data and that adjustment is significant to the fair value measurement as a whole, the fair value measurement would be categorised within Level 3 of the fair value hierarchy for disclosure purposes.

A Level 3 categorisation is likely to be the most common. For example, in February 2013, EPRA published its position paper on IFRS 13 – *EPRA Position Paper on IFRS 13, Fair Value Measurement & Illustrative Disclosures.* In this publication it is stated that:

'Estimating the fair value of an investment property inevitably requires a significant range of methodologies, inputs, and adjustments to reflect the wide range of factors which contribute towards the value of a property e.g. state and condition, location, in-place leases, development potential, infrastructure, etc. Consequently, even in the most transparent and liquid markets – and depending on the valuation technique – it is very likely that valuers will use one or more significant unobservable inputs or make at least one significant adjustment to an observable input. Accordingly, it is likely that the vast majority of property valuations will fall within the level 3 category.'[23]

IFRS 13 expands the disclosures related to fair value to enable users of financial statements to understand the valuation techniques and inputs used to develop fair value measurements.

In summary, it requires the following additional disclosures for all entities regardless of the model of measurement or the valuation technique used in measuring investment property:

- the level of the fair value hierarchy within which the fair value measurement in its entirety is categorised; *[IFRS 13.93(b)]*
- for Level 2 and Level 3 measurements, valuation technique and the inputs used, and changes in the valuation technique, if applicable, and the reasons for those changes; *[IFRS 13.93(d)]* and
- if the highest and best use of a non-financial asset differs from its current use, disclose that fact and the reason for it. *[IFRS 13.93(i)]*.

For entities applying the fair value model in measuring investment property, the following additional disclosure should be made:

- for Level 3 measurements, quantitative information regarding the significant unobservable inputs; *[IFRS 13.93(d)]*
- amount of transfers between Level 1 and Level 2, the reasons and related accounting policies; *[IFRS 13.93(c)]*
- for Level 3 measurements, a reconciliation from the opening balances to the closing balances (including gains and losses, purchases, sales, issues, settlements, transfers in and out of Level 3 and reasons and policies for transfer and where all such amounts are recognised); *[IFRS 13.93(e)]*
- for Level 3 measurements, the total gains or losses included in profit or loss that are attributable to the change in unrealised gains or losses relating to those assets and liabilities held at the reporting date, and a description of where such amounts are recognised; *[IFRS 13.93(f)]*
- for Level 3 measurements, a description of the valuation process used by the entity; *[IFRS 13.93(g)]* and
- for Level 3 measurements, a narrative description of the sensitivity of the fair value measurement to changes in unobservable inputs if a change in those inputs might result in a significantly different amount and, if applicable, a description of interrelationships between those inputs and other unobservable inputs and of how they might magnify or mitigate the effect of changes in the unobservable inputs. *[IFRS 13.93(h)]*.

Unibail-Rodamco included the following disclosures in its 2016 financial statements, in addition to those disclosed in Extract 19.3 above.

Extract 19.13: Unibail-Rodamco SE (2016)

4.2.	**Notes to the Consolidated Financial Statements** [extract]
Note 5 –	**Investment properties, tangible and intangible assets, goodwill** [extract]
5.1.	**Investment properties** [extract]
5.1.2.	**Investment properties at fair value** [extract]

(€Mn)	31/12/2016
Shopping centres	**29,580.8**
France	13,724.1
Central Europe	3,576.5
Spain	3,359.3
Nordic	3,337.3
Austria	2,278.5
Germany	2,032.0
The Netherlands	1,273.1
Offices	**3,182.8**
France	2,902.4
Other countries	280.4
Convention & Exhibition	**2,663.4**
TOTAL	35,426.9

(€Mn)	Shopping Centres	Offices	Convention & Exhibition	Total investment properties	Properties held for sale	Total
31/12/2015	27,062.8	3,487.4	2,451.7	33,001.8	268.8	33,270.6
Acquisitions[(1)]	135.2	2.3	–	137.5	–	137.5
Entry into scope of consolidation	9.2	–	–	9.2	–	9.2
Capitalised expenses[(2)]	611.1	50.7	153.7	815.4	0.1	815.6
Disposals/exits from the scope of consolidation[(3)]	(64.3)	(526.7)	0.0	(591.0)	(268.9)	(860.0)
Reclassification and transfer of category[(4)]	266.0	(53.7)	(0.0)	212.2	–	212.2
Discounting impact	(6.4)	–	–	(6.4)	–	(6.4)
Valuation movements	1,734.4	234.8	58.0	2,027.2	–	2,027.2
Currency translation	(167.0)	(12.0)	–	(179.0)	–	(179.0)
31/12/2016	29,580.8	3,182.8	2,663.4	35,426.9[(4)]	–	35,426.9

(1) The acquisitions refer mainly to Forum des Halles, Rosny 2 and La Part Dieu.

(2) Capitalised expenses mainly include:
– shopping centres in France, Sweden, Spain and Austria;
– offices in France;
– convention & exhibition site such as Parc des Expositions de la Porte de Versailles.

(3) Disposals are mainly office buildings in France: 2-8 Ancelle, So Ouest Office, Nouvel Air and 70-80 Wilson (see Note 1).

(4) Refers mainly to the transfer from IPUC at cost of Parly 2, Carré Sénart, Centrum Chodov extension and renovation projects as well as Wroclavia project which are assessed at fair value as at December 31, 2016. It is partly offset by the transfer to IPUC at cost of Leidsenhage due to extension/renovation project for The Mall of The Netherlands.

Acquisitions of investment properties and entry into scope of consolidation

The main acquisitions include:

- Retail units in Rosny 2 (Paris region), La Part Dieu (Lyon) and Les Quatre Temps (La Défense);
- Additional plots acquired in France such as Forum des Halles (Paris) and Vélizy 2 (Paris region).

Valuation assumptions and sensitivity

Considering the limited public data available, the complexity of real estate asset valuations, as well as the fact that appraisers use in their valuations the non-public rent rolls of the Group's assets, Unibail-Rodamco believes it appropriate to classify its assets under Level 3. In addition, unobservable inputs, including appraisers' assumption on growth rates and exit yields, are used by appraisers to determine the fair values of Unibail-Rodamco's assets.

As at December 31, 2016, independent experts have appraised 97% of Unibail-Rodamco's portfolio.

The outstanding balances of deferred lease incentives and key monies amortised over the firm term of the lease, which corrected the appraisal value, represented –€51.3 Mn.

The following tables provide a number of quantitative elements used by the appraisers to assess the fair valuation of the Group's assets.

Shopping Centres

All Shopping Centres are valued using the discounted cash flow and/or yield methodologies.

Shopping Centres – December 31, 2016		Net initial yield	Rent in € per sqm[(1)]	Discount Rate[(2)]	Exit yield[(3)]	CAGR of NRI[(4)]
	Max	7.5%	853	13.0%	9.5%	10.4%
France	Min	3.5%	110	5.3%	3.7%	1.3%
	Weighted average	4.1%	491	5.8%	4.2%	4.1%
	Max	6.6%	554	7.9%	7.5%	2.8%
Central Europe	Min	4.7%	188	6.5%	4.7%	2.2%
	Weighted average	4.9%	389	6.8%	5.1%	2.6%
	Max	12.1%	513	9.5%	8.3%	4.3%
Nordic	Min	3.9%	100	6.5%	4.1%	1.1%
	Weighted average	4.4%	356	7.0%	4.4%	3.5%
	Max	7.8%	785	11.0%	7.8%	4.1%
Spain	Min	4.0%	95	7.2%	4.2%	1.6%
	Weighted average	4.8%	288	7.8%	4.8%	3.3%
	Max	7.2%	453	8.0%	6.6%	4.7%
Germany	Min	4.0%	244	6.2%	4.0%	2.3%
	Weighted average	4.5%	303	6.5%	4.6%	3.4%
	Max	4.4%	382	6.2%	4.1%	3.0%
Austria	Min	4.1%	359	6.2%	4.1%	2.6%
	Weighted average	4.3%	370	6.2%	4.1%	2.8%
	Max	9.3%	404	8.8%	8.9%	5.5%
The Netherlands	Min	4.5%	113	5.8%	4.2%	n.m
	Weighted average	5.0%	247	6.2%	4.9%	3.4%

Net initial yield, discount rate and exit yield weighted by GMV.

(1) Average annual rent (minimum guaranteed rent + sales based rent) per asset per m².

(2) Rate used to calculate the net present value of future cash flows.

(3) Rate used to capitalise the exit rent to determine the exit value of an asset.

(4) Compounded Annual Growth Rate of Net Rental Income determined by the appraiser (between 6 and 10 years depending on duration of DCF model used).

Based on an asset value excluding estimated transfer taxes and transaction costs, the shopping centre division's net initial yield as at December 31, 2016, decreased to 4.4% from 4.6% as at December 31, 2015.

A change of +25 basis points of the net initial yield would result in a downward adjustment of –€1.630 Mn (–5.4%) of the total shopping centres portfolio value (excluding assets under development or accounted for using the equity method), including transfer taxes and transaction costs.

Offices

Appraisers value the Group's Offices using the discounted cash flow and yield methodologies.

Offices – December 31, 2016		**Net initial yield on occupied space**	**Rent in € per sqm(1)**	**Discount Rate(2)**	**Exit yield(3)**	**CAGR of NRI(4)**
	Max	11.2%	536	9.5%	8.2%	15.3%
France	Min	3.9%	105	5.0%	3.8%	–4.1%
	Weighted average	5.7%	439	5.8%	4.8%	3.6%
	Max	10.7%	218	9.4%	7.8%	3.0%
Nordic	Min	6.2%	104	7.1%	5.2%	2.3%
	Weighted average	7.5%	183	7.8%	6.4%	2.6%
	Max	18.3%	48	13.8%	9.8%	11.2%
The Netherlands	Min	n.m	n.m	6.3%	4.6%	n.m
	Weighted average	17.3%	40	9.7%	7.0%	11.0%
	Max	7.9%	152	8.4%	7.5%	12.2%
Germany	Min	4.8%	48	6.5%	4.5%	1.7%
	Weighted average	5.5%	114	6.8%	4.9%	2.8%
	Max	6.8%	130	7.6%	7.0%	5.0%
Austria	Min	6.6%	118	7.5%	6.5%	2.0%
	Weighted average	6.7%	124	7.6%	6.8%	3.7%

Net initial yield, discount rate and exit yield weighted by GMV. Central Europe region only encompasses one asset (excluding shares in Zlote Tarasy offices, Lumen and Skylight) and is therefore not displayed. Vacant assets, assets considered at bid value and assets under restructuring are not included in this table.

(1) Average annual rent (minimum guaranteed rent) per asset per m². The computation takes into account the areas allocated to company restaurants.

(2) Rate used to calculate the net present value of future cash flows.

(3) Rate used to capitalise the exit rent to determine the exit value of an asset.

(4) Compounded Annual Growth Rate of NRI determined by the appraiser (between 3 and 10 years, depending on duration of DCF model used).

For occupied offices and based on an asset value excluding estimated transfer taxes and transaction costs, the office division's net initial yield as at December 31, 2016 fell by –15 bps to 5.8%.

A change of +25 basis points of the net initial yield would result in a downward adjustment of –€168 Mn (–4.9%) of the total Office portfolio value (occupied and vacant spaces, excluding assets under development or accounted for using the equity method), including transfer taxes and transaction costs.

Convention & Exhibition

Based on these valuations, the average EBITDA yield (recurring earnings before interest, tax, depreciation and amortisation divided by the value of assets, excluding estimated transfer taxes and transaction costs) as at December 31, 2016 decreased by –96 basis points from December 31, 2015 to 5.4%.

A change of +25 basis points of the yield and WACC as determined at the end of the year would result in an adjustment of –€120.4 Mn (–5.1%).

5.1.3. Investment properties under construction at cost [extract]

(€Mn)	31/12/2016
Shopping centres	685.2
France	236.3
Central Europe	31.3
Spain	124.9
Nordic	–
Austria	–
Germany	67.1
The Netherlands	225.6
Offices	260.5
France	260.5
Other countries	–
Convention & Exhibition	8.3
TOTAL	954.0

As at December 31, 2016, assets under construction valued at cost are notably:

- offices developments such as Trinity and Phare-Sisters in La Défense;
- shopping centres extension and renovation projects such as Mall of The Netherlands (Leidsenhage)

Assets still stated at cost were subject to impairment tests as at December 31, 2016. Allowances were booked for a total amount of €4.7 Mn.

(€Mn)	Gross value	Impairment	Total investment properties at cost
31/12/2015	775.0	(66.8)	708.2
Acquisitions(1)	41.3	–	41.3
Entry into scope of consolidation(2)	32.0	–	32.0
Capitalised expenses(3)	349.2	–	349.2
Disposals/exits from the scope of consolidation	(0.1)	–	(0.1)
Reclassification and transfer of category(4)	(170.9)	–	(170.9)
Discounting impact	0.6	–	0.6
Impairment/reversal	–	(4.7)	(4.7)
Currency translation	(1.6)	–	(1.6)
31/12/2016	1,025.4	(71.5)	954.0

(1) *Mostly relates to acquisitions in Spain, The Netherlands and one office building in Paris region.*

(2) *Relates to an asset previously accounted for using the equity method and fully consolidated as at December 31, 2016.*

(3) *Capitalised expenses mainly refer to investments in Carré Sénart and Centrum Chodov extension and renovation projects before their transfers to IPUC at fair value, and to Trinity, Uberseequartier and Wroclavia new development projects.*

(4) *Refers mainly to the transfer to investment properties at fair value of Parly 2, Carré Sénart, Centrum Chodov extension and renovation projects as well as Wroclavia project which are assessed at fair value as at December 31, 2016. It is partly offset by the transfer to IPUC at cost of Leidsenhage due to extension/renovation project for The Mall of The Netherlands.*

12.1.2 Level of aggregation for IFRS 13 disclosures

IFRS 13 disclosures are required for each class of assets (and liabilities). These classes are determined based on:

- the nature, characteristics and risks of the asset or liability; and
- the level of the fair value hierarchy within which the fair value measurement is categorised. *[IFRS 13.94].*

The determination of the appropriate class of assets will require significant judgement. See Chapter 14 at 20.1.2 for further discussion on this determination.

At one end of the spectrum, the properties in an operating segment (as defined by IFRS 8 – *Operating Segments*) may be a class of assets for the purpose of the disclosures required by IFRS 13. This may be the case if the properties have the same risk profile (for example, the segment comprises residential properties in countries with property markets of similar characteristics) even if there are a large number of properties in the segment.

At the other end of the spectrum, IFRS 13 disclosures may be required for individual properties or small groups of properties if the individual properties or groups of properties have different risk profiles (for example, a real estate entity with two properties – an office building in a developed country and a shopping centre in a developing country).

The number of classes may need to be greater for fair value measurements categorised within Level 3 of the fair value hierarchy because those measurements have a greater degree of uncertainty and subjectivity.

A class of assets and liabilities will often require greater disaggregation than the line items presented in the statement of financial position. However, sufficient information must be provided to permit reconciliation to the line items presented in the statement of financial position.

When determining the appropriate classes, entities should also consider all of the following:

- the level of detail necessary to satisfy the disclosure requirements;
- how much emphasis to place on each of the various requirements;
- how much aggregation or disaggregation to undertake; and
- whether users of financial statements need additional information to evaluate the quantitative information disclosed. *[IFRS 13.92].*

Determining appropriate classes of assets and liabilities for which disclosures about fair value measurements should be provided requires considerable judgement. *[IFRS 13.94].*

12.1.3 Disclosure of direct operating expenses

As set out in 12.1 above, entities are required to disclose both the direct operating expenses arising from investment property that generated rental income during the period and the amounts arising from investment property that did not generate rental income during the period.

In practice, this requirement can be interpreted in different ways and the outcome will depend upon a number of judgements, for example, the unit of account for the investment property. In the instance of a multi-tenanted property, the relevant unit may be considered either the entire building or a separately let floor.

It will therefore be necessary for an entity to interpret this requirement and apply that interpretation, as an accounting policy and judgement, consistently.

12.2 Additional disclosures for the fair value model

A reconciliation between the carrying amounts of investment property at the start and end of the period must be given showing the following:

- additions, disclosing separately those additions resulting from acquisitions and those resulting from subsequent expenditure recognised in the carrying amount of an asset;
- additions resulting from acquisitions through business combinations;
- assets classified as held for sale or included in a disposal group classified as held for sale in accordance with IFRS 5 and other disposals;
- net gains or losses from fair value adjustments;
- the net exchange differences arising on the translation of the financial statements into a different presentation currency, and on translation of a foreign operation into the presentation currency of the reporting entity;
- transfers to and from inventories and owner-occupied property; and
- other changes. *[IAS 40.76]*.

When a valuation obtained for investment property is adjusted significantly for the purpose of the financial statements, for example to avoid double-counting of assets or liabilities that are recognised separately (see 6.1.4 above), the entity must disclose a reconciliation between the valuation obtained and the adjusted valuation included in the financial statements, showing separately the aggregate amount of any recognised lease obligations (or lease liabilities, if IFRS 16 is adopted – see 13.1 below) that have been added back, and any other significant adjustments. *[IAS 40.77]*. Extracts 19.5 and 19.6 above provide examples of such disclosure.

12.2.1 Presentation of changes in fair value

Neither IAS 1 nor IAS 40 specifies how changes in the fair value of investment property should be presented. The Extracts below show two different approaches. In Extract 19.14 below the change in fair value (here referred to as a 'Gain on revaluation') is presented together with the profit or loss on disposal of properties with an analysis of the components included in the notes to the accounts. By contrast, in Extract 19.15 below, the change in fair value is analysed and presented separately from the profit or loss on disposal of properties.

Extract 19.14: Capital & Counties Properties PLC (2016)

Consolidated income statement [extract]
For the year ended 31 December 2016

	Notes	2016 £m	2015 £m
Revenue	2	127.4	114.9
Rental income		104.0	99.7
Rental expenses		(22.0)	(24.4)
Net rental income	2	82.0	75.3
Profit on sale of trading property	3	5.6	3.5
Other income		4.6	4.0
(Loss)/gain on revaluation and sale of investment and development property	4	(235.0)	453.9
Profit/(loss) on sale of available-for-sale investments		0.4	(0.2)
Impairment of other receivables	5	(14.8)	(12.2)
Other costs	6	(5.0)	(0.2)
		(162.2)	524.1
Administration expenses		(50.6)	(52.1)
Operating (loss)/profit		(212.8)	472.0

Extract 19.15: Unibail-Rodamco SE (2016)

4.1. **Consolidated Financial Statements** [extract]

4.1.1. **Consolidated statement of comprehensive income** [extract]

Presented under IFRS format *(€Mn)*	Notes	2016	2015
NET RENTAL INCOME		1,528.5	1,452.8
Corporate expenses		(116.8)	(104.0)
Development expenses		(5.9)	(4.5)
Depreciation of other tangible assets		(2.2)	(2.2)
ADMINISTRATIVE EXPENSES	4.3.4	(124.9)	(110.7)
ACQUISITION AND RELATED COSTS	3.3	(1.3)	(1.6)
Revenues from other activities		261.3	293.4
Other expenses		(175.1)	(219.7)
NET OTHER INCOME	4.3.3	86.2	73.7
Proceeds from disposal of investment properties		973.9	342.4
Carrying value of investment properties sold		(882.7)	(341.0)
RESULT ON DISPOSAL OF INVESTMENT PROPERTIES	5.1	91.2	1.4
Proceeds from disposal of shares		25.9	114.4
Carrying value of disposed shares		(20.9)	(100.7)
RESULT ON DISPOSAL OF SHARES	3.3.1	5.0	13.7
Valuation gains on assets		2,244.0	2,137.4
Valuation losses on assets		(238.2)	(318.6)
VALUATION MOVEMENTS ON ASSETS	5.5	2,005.8	1,818.8
NET OPERATING RESULT BEFORE FINANCING COST		3,590.5	3,248.2

Some companies include the change in fair value within their definition of operating profit. This approach appears to be just one of the available accounting policy choices but it is worth noting that at least one European regulator has concluded that fair value changes arising from investment property must be taken into account when determining operating results. This decision was reported in the European Securities and Markets Authority's ('ESMA') *Report – 11th Extract from the EECS's Database of Enforcement (ESMA/2011/265).*

The regulator's rationale for this decision was that fair value changes in investment property are a normal part of the activities of a real estate company and feature in the description of the business model of that real estate business.[24]

12.2.2 Extra disclosures where fair value cannot be determined reliably

If an entity chooses the fair value model, but in an exceptional case cannot measure the fair value of the property reliably and accounts for the property under the cost model in IAS 16 (or, when adopted, in accordance with IFRS 16), the reconciliation described in 12.2 above should disclose the amounts for such investment property separately from amounts relating to other investment property. In addition to this, the following should be disclosed:

- a description of the investment property;
- an explanation of why fair value cannot be measured reliably;
- if possible, the range of estimates within which fair value is highly likely to lie; and
- on disposal of investment property not carried at fair value:
    - the fact that the entity has disposed of investment property not carried at fair value;
    - the carrying amount of that investment property at the time of sale; and
    - the amount of gain or loss recognised. *[IAS 40.78].*

The standard makes it clear that this situation, at least for completed investment property, would be exceptional (see 6.2 above). The situation for investment property under construction is discussed at 6.3 above.

12.3 Additional disclosures for the cost model

If investment property is measured using the cost model, the following disclosures are required by IAS 40 in addition to those at 12.1 above:

- the depreciation methods used;
- the useful lives or the depreciation rates used;
- the gross carrying amount and the accumulated depreciation (aggregated with accumulated impairment losses) at the beginning and end of the period;
- a reconciliation of the carrying amount of investment property at the beginning and end of the period, showing the following:
    - additions, disclosing separately those additions resulting from acquisitions and those resulting from subsequent expenditure recognised as an asset;
    - additions resulting from acquisitions through business combinations;

- assets classified as held for sale or included in a disposal group classified as held for sale in accordance with IFRS 5 and other disposals;
- depreciation;
- the amount of impairment losses recognised, and the amount of impairment losses reversed, during the period in accordance with IAS 36 (see Chapter 20);
- the net exchange differences arising on the translation of the financial statements into a different presentation currency, and on translation of a foreign operation into the presentation currency of the reporting entity;
- transfers to and from inventories and owner-occupied property; and
- other changes;

- the fair value of investment property. In the exceptional cases when an entity cannot measure the fair value of the investment property reliably (see 6.2 above), it shall disclose:
  - a description of the investment property;
  - an explanation of why fair value cannot be measured reliably; and
  - if possible, the range of estimates within which fair value is highly likely to lie. *[IAS 40.79].*

12.4 Presentation of sales proceeds

IAS 16 allows an entity that, in the course of its ordinary activities, routinely sells items of property, plant and equipment that it has held for rental to transfer such assets to inventories at their carrying amount when they cease to be rented and become held for sale. The proceeds from the sale of such assets are then recognised as revenue (see Chapter 29 at 5.11.1).

However, investment property, by definition, is held to earn rentals or for capital appreciation rather than for sale in the ordinary course of business. Consequently, we consider that this IAS 16 accounting treatment may not be applied by analogy to IAS 40 and proceeds from the sale of investment property may not be presented as revenue.

Despite this, however, it may be appropriate to present separately the material gains or losses on retirement or disposal of investment property elsewhere in the financial statements, either as part of the income statement or in the notes. *[IAS 1.97].* For example, Unibail-Rodamco has chosen to present proceeds from disposal of investment properties, together with the carrying amount derecognised and the net gain/loss on disposal on the face of its statement of comprehensive income (see Extract 19.15 above).

13 FUTURE DEVELOPMENTS

13.1 New leases standard: IFRS 16

In January 2016, the IASB issued the new leases standard, IFRS 16, which will supersede IAS 17, IFRIC 4 – *Determining whether an Arrangement contains a Lease*, SIC-15 and SIC-27 – *Evaluating the Substance of Transactions Involving the Legal Form of a Lease*. As a consequence, IFRS 16 amended the scope of IAS 40 by defining investment property to include both owned investment property and property held by a lessee as a right-of-use asset. Further, IFRS 16 extensively amended, added and deleted a number of paragraphs in IAS 40 – these are indicated in the earlier sections of this chapter, where appropriate.

Leases of property that meet the definition of investment property in IAS 40 are included in the scope of IFRS 16.

The new leases standard significantly changes the accounting for lessees, requiring them to recognise most leases (i.e. rental contracts) in their statement of financial position as lease liabilities with corresponding right-of-use assets. In addition, IFRS 16 requires a lessee to measure right-of-use assets arising from leased property in accordance with the fair value model of IAS 40 if the leased property meets the definition of investment property and the lessee elects the fair value model in IAS 40 as an accounting policy. This represents a change from the existing requirements of IAS 40. Under existing requirements, the classification of property held under an operating lease as an investment property is an accounting policy election that is available on a property-by-property basis (see 2.1 and 5.1 above).

Under IFRS 16 tenants apply a single model for most leases i.e. they no longer need to classify leases as finance leases or as operating leases. Generally, the profit or loss recognition pattern will change as interest and depreciation expense are recognised separately in profit or loss (similar to the accounting for a finance lease under IAS 17). However, tenants can make an accounting policy election, by class of underlying asset to which the right-of-use relates, to apply accounting similar to IAS 17's operating lease accounting to 'short-term' leases – i.e. leases that, at the commencement date, have a lease term of 12 months or less. A lease that contains a purchase option is not a short-term lease (see Chapter 25 at 5.1.1).

Lessor accounting is substantially unchanged from current accounting. As with IAS 17, IFRS 16 requires landlord lessors to classify their rental contracts into two types, finance and operating leases. Lease classification determines how and when a landlord recognises lease revenue and what assets a landlord records. The profit or loss recognition pattern for landlords is not expected to change.

IFRS 16 and its consequential amendments are effective for annual periods beginning on or after 1 January 2019. Early application is permitted provided IFRS 15 has been applied, or is applied, at the same date as IFRS 16. Further, IFRS 16 adds a new paragraph 84B to IAS 40 so that an entity applying IFRS 16, and its related amendments to IAS 40, for the first time will apply the transition requirements in Appendix C of IFRS 16 to its investment property held as a right-of-use asset (see Chapter 25 at 10).

For those entities adopting IFRS 16 early and for the detailed discussion and requirements of this new standard, see Chapter 25.

13.2 New standard for insurance contracts: IFRS 17

In May 2017, the IASB issued IFRS 17. Once effective, IFRS 17 will replace IFRS 4 – *Insurance Contracts*.

As part of the consequential amendments arising from IFRS 17, the subsequent measurement requirements in IAS 40 will be amended and this is indicated in 5.2 above. IFRS 17 and its consequential amendments to other standards are effective for annual periods beginning on or after 1 January 2021, with adjusted comparative figures required. Early application is permitted provided that both IFRS 9 and IFRS 15 have already been applied, or are applied for the first time, at the date on which IFRS 17 is first applied.

For those entities early adopting IFRS 17 and for the detailed discussions and requirements of this new standard, see Chapter 56.

References

1 *IFRIC Update*, September 2012.
2 *IFRIC Update*, September 2012.
3 *IFRIC Update*, January 2013.
4 *IASB Update*, December 2014.
5 *IFRIC Update*, July 2011.
6 *Example H – acquisition of investment properties, Exposure Draft – Definition of a Business and Accounting for Previously Held Interests, Proposed amendments to IFRS 3 and IFRS 11 – (ED/2016/1)*, IASB, June 2016, p.25.
7 *Example I – acquisition of investment properties, Exposure Draft – Definition of a Business and Accounting for Previously Held Interests, Proposed amendments to IFRS 3 and IFRS 11 – (ED/2016/1)*, IASB, June 2016, pp.25-26.
8 *IASB Update*, April 2017.
9 *IASB Update*, June 2017.
10 *IFRIC Update*, June 2017.
11 *IFRIC Update*, March 2017.
12 *UITF abstract 28 – Operating lease incentives*, UK Accounting Standards Board, February 2001, para 3.
13 *IFRIC Update*, January 2011.
14 *IFRIC Update*, May 2011.
15 *IASB Update*, July 2013.
16 *IFRIC Update*, March 2016.
17 *IASB Update*, May 2016.
18 *The IVS Framework*, International Valuation Standards 2013, IVSC, June 2013, para. 29.
19 *IFRIC Update*, July 2014.
20 *Best Practices Recommendations*, EPRA, November 2016, p.19, section 4.1.
21 *IASB Update*, April 2015.
22 *Review Findings and Recommendations – 2009*, Financial Reporting Review Panel, July 2009, p.11.
23 *EPRA Position Paper on IFRS 13, Fair Value Measurement & Illustrative Disclosures*, EPRA, February 2013, p.4.
24 *Report – 11th Extract from the EECS's Database of Enforcement (ESMA/2011/265)*, European Securities and Markets Authority (ESMA), August 2011, paras. 76-81.

Chapter 20 Impairment of fixed assets and goodwill

List of examples

Chapter 20

Chapter 20 Impairment of fixed assets and goodwill

1 INTRODUCTION

In principle an asset is impaired when an entity will not be able to recover that asset's carrying value, either through using it or selling it. If circumstances arise which indicate assets might be impaired, a review should be undertaken of their cash generating abilities either through use or sale. This review will produce an amount which should be compared with the assets' carrying value, and if the carrying value is higher, the difference must be written off as an impairment in the statement of comprehensive income. The provisions within IAS 36 – *Impairment of Assets* – that set out exactly how this is to be done, and how the figures involved are to be calculated, are detailed and quite complex.

1.1 The theory behind the impairment review

The purpose of the impairment review is to ensure that intangible assets, including goodwill, and tangible assets are not carried at a figure greater than their recoverable amount (RA). This recoverable amount is compared with the carrying value (or carrying amount (CA)) of the asset to determine if the asset is impaired.

Recoverable amount is defined as the higher of fair value less costs of disposal (FVLCD) and value in use (VIU); the underlying concept being that an asset should not be carried at more than the amount it could raise, either from selling it now or from using it.

Fair value less costs of disposal essentially means what the asset could be sold for, having deducted costs of disposal (incrementally incurred direct selling costs). Value in use is defined in terms of discounted future cash flows, as the present value of the cash flows expected from the future use and eventual sale of the asset at the end of its useful life. As the recoverable amount is to be expressed as a present value, not in nominal terms, discounting is a central feature of the impairment test.

Diagrammatically, this comparison between carrying value and recoverable amount, and the definition of recoverable amount, can be portrayed as follows:

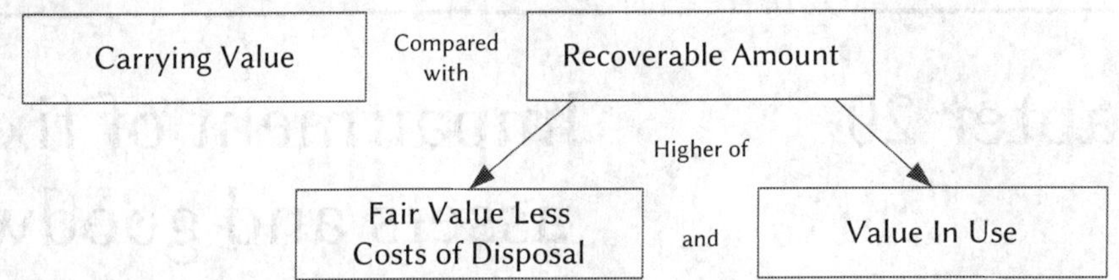

It may not always be necessary to identify both VIU and FVLCD, as if either of VIU or FVLCD is higher than the carrying amount then there is no impairment and no write-down is necessary. Thus, if FVLCD is greater than the carrying amount then no further consideration need be given to VIU, or to the need for an impairment write down. The more complex issues arise when the FVLCD is not greater than the carrying value, and so a VIU calculation is necessary.

1.2 Key features of the impairment review

Although an impairment review might theoretically be conducted by looking at individual assets, this will not always be possible. Goodwill does not have a separate FVLCD at all. Even if FVLCDs can be obtained for individual items of property, plant and equipment, estimates of VIUs usually cannot be. This is because the cash flows necessary for the VIU calculation are not usually generated by single assets, but by groups of assets being used together.

Often, therefore, the impairment review cannot be done at the level of the individual asset and it must be applied to a group of assets. IAS 36 uses the term cash generating unit (CGU) for the smallest identifiable group of assets that together have cash inflows that are largely independent of the cash inflows from other assets and that therefore can be the subject of a VIU calculation. This focus on the CGU is fundamental, as it has the effect of making the review essentially a business-value test. Goodwill cannot always be allocated to a CGU and may therefore be allocated to a group of CGUs. IAS 36 has detailed guidance in respect of the level of goodwill impairment testing which is discussed at 8 below.

Most assets and CGUs need only be tested for impairment if there are indicators of impairment. The 'indications' of impairment may relate to either the assets themselves or to the economic environment in which they are operated. IAS 36 gives examples of indications of impairment, but makes it clear this is not an exhaustive list, and states explicitly that the entity may identify other indications that an asset is impaired, that would equally trigger an impairment review. *[IAS 36.13]*. There are more onerous requirements for goodwill, intangible assets with an indefinite useful life and intangible assets that are not available for use on the reporting date. These must be tested for impairment at least on an annual basis, irrespective of whether there are any impairment indicators. This is because the first two, goodwill and indefinite-lived intangible assets, are not subject to annual amortisation while it is argued that intangible assets are intrinsically subject to greater uncertainty before they are brought into use. Impairment losses are recognised as expenses in profit or loss except in the case of an asset carried at revalued amount where the impairment loss is recorded first against any previously recognised revaluation gains in respect of that asset in other comprehensive income.

Figure 20.1 below illustrates the key stages in the process of measuring and recognising impairment losses under IAS 36. The key components of the diagram are discussed in detail in the remainder of this chapter.

Figure 20.1: Determining and accounting for impairment

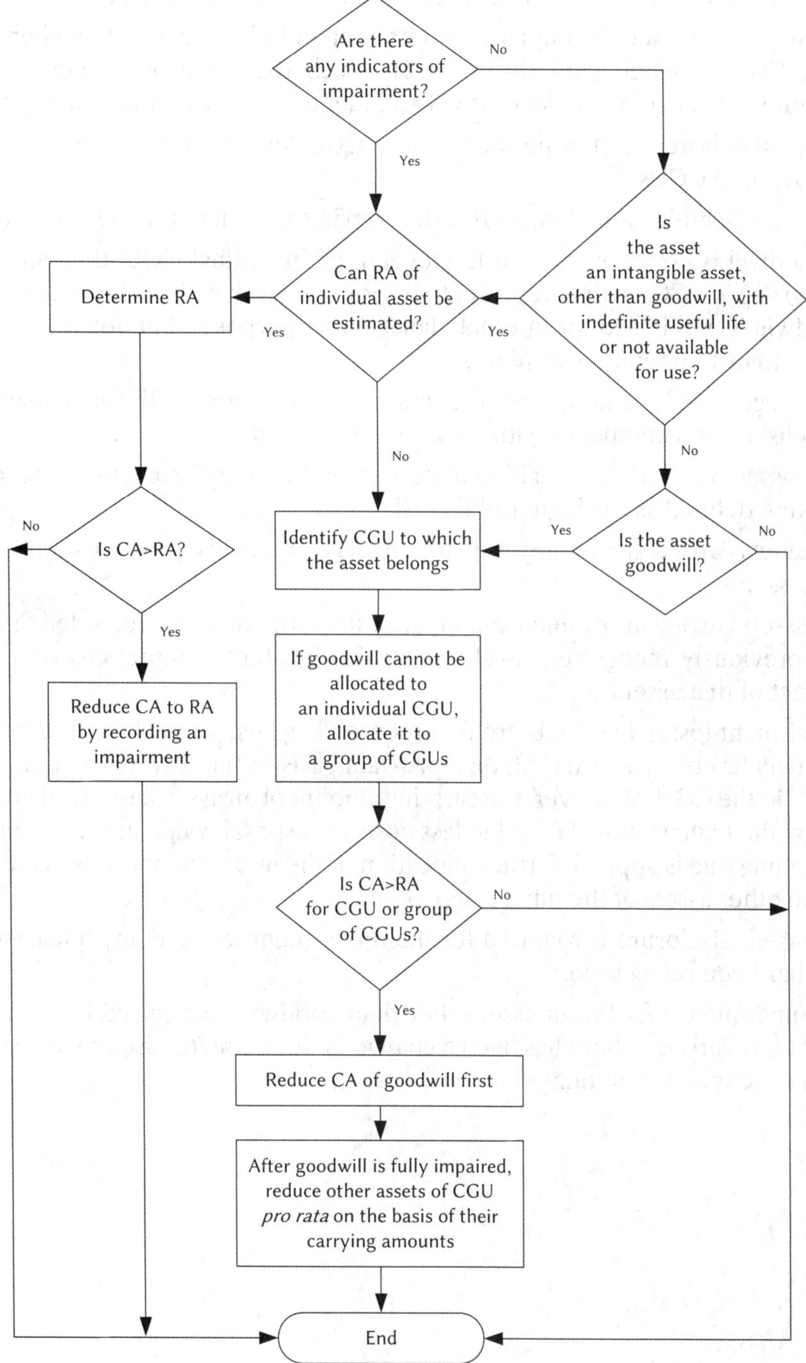

The entity assesses, at each reporting date, whether an impairment assessment is required and acts accordingly:

- If there is an indication that an asset may be impaired, an impairment test is required.
- For goodwill, intangible assets with an indefinite useful life and intangible assets that are not available for use on the reporting date an annual impairment test is required.
- An asset is assessed for impairment either at an individual asset level or the level of a CGU depending on the level of which the recoverable amount can be determined, meaning the level at which independent cash inflows are generated.
- If the impairment test is performed at a CGU level then the entity needs to be divided into CGUs.
- After the identification of the CGUs, the carrying amount of the CGUs is determined.
- If goodwill is not monitored at the level of an individual CGU, then allocate it to the group of CGUs that represent the lowest level within the entity at which goodwill is monitored for internal management purposes, but not at a level that is larger than an operating segment.
- The recoverable amount of the asset or CGU assessed for impairment is established and compared with the carrying amount.
- The asset or CGU is impaired if its carrying amount exceeds its recoverable amount, defined as the higher of FVLCD and VIU.
- For assets carried at cost, any impairment loss is recognised as an expense in profit or loss.
- For assets carried at revalued amount, any impairment loss is recorded first against any previously recognised revaluation gains in other comprehensive income in respect of that asset.
- Impairment losses in a CGU are first recorded against goodwill and second, if the goodwill has been written off, on a pro-rata basis to the carrying amount of other assets in the CGU. However, the carrying amount of an asset should not be reduced below the highest of its fair value less costs of disposal, value in use or zero. If the preceding rule is applied, further allocation of the impairment loss is made pro rata to the other assets of the unit (group of units).
- Extensive disclosure is required for the impairment test and any impairment loss that has been recognised.
- An impairment loss for an asset other than goodwill recognised in prior periods must be reversed if there has been a change in the estimates used to determine the asset's recoverable amount.

1.3 Scope

The standard is a general impairment standard and its provisions are referred to in other standards, for example IAS 16 – *Property, Plant and Equipment*, IAS 38 – *Intangible Assets* – and IFRS 3 – *Business Combinations* – where impairment is to be considered.

The standard has a general application to all assets, but the following are outside its scope:

- inventories (IAS 2 – *Inventories*);
- assets arising from construction contracts (for periods before IFRS 15 – *Revenue from Contracts with Customers* – applies), contract assets and assets arising from costs to obtain or fulfil a contract that are recognised in accordance with IFRS 15 (for periods after IFRS 15 applies);
- deferred tax assets (IAS 12 – *Income Taxes*);
- assets arising from employee benefits under IAS 19 – *Employee Benefits*;
- financial assets that are included in the scope of IFRS 9 – *Financial Instruments*;
- investment property that is measured at fair value under IAS 40 – *Investment Property*;
- biological assets under IAS 41 – *Agriculture*, except bearer plants, e.g. apple trees, which are in the scope of IAS 16 and therefore fall under the IAS 36 impairment guidance;
- deferred acquisition costs and intangible assets arising from an insurer's contractual rights under insurance contracts within the scope of IFRS 4 – *Insurance Contracts*; and
- non-current assets (or disposal groups) classified as held for sale in accordance with IFRS 5 – *Non-current Assets Held for Sale and Discontinued Operations*. *[IAS 36.2]*.

This, the standard states, is because these assets are subject to specific recognition and measurement requirements. *[IAS 36.3]*. The effect of these exclusions is to reduce the scope of IAS 36. While investment properties measured at fair value are exempt, investment properties not carried at fair value are in the scope of IAS 36. If a company has recorded oil and mineral exploration and evaluation assets and has chosen to carry them at cost, then these assets are to be tested under IAS 36 for impairment, once they have been assessed for impairment indicators in accordance with IFRS 6 – *Exploration for and Evaluation of Mineral Resources*. *[IFRS 6.2(b)]*. Financial assets classified as subsidiaries as defined by IFRS 10 – *Consolidated Financial Statements*, joint ventures as defined in IFRS 11 – *Joint Arrangements* – and associates as defined in IAS 28 – *Investments in Associates and Joint Ventures* – are within its scope. *[IAS 36.4]*. This will generally mean only those investments in the separate financial statements of the parent. Interests in joint ventures and associates included in the consolidated accounts by way of the equity method are brought into scope by IAS 28. *[IAS 28.42]*.

The standard applies to assets carried at revalued amounts, e.g. under IAS 16 (or rarely IAS 38). *[IAS 36.4]*.

2 WHEN AN IMPAIRMENT TEST IS REQUIRED

There is an important distinction in IAS 36 between assessing whether there are indications of impairment and actually carrying out an impairment test. The standard has two different general requirements governing when an impairment test should be carried out:

- For goodwill and all intangible assets with an indefinite useful life the standard requires an annual impairment test. The impairment test may be performed at any time in the annual reporting period, but it must be performed at the same time every year. Different intangible assets may be tested for impairment at different times. *[IAS 36.10].* In addition, the carrying amount of an intangible asset that has not yet been brought into use must be tested at least annually. This, the standard argues, is because intangible assets are intrinsically subject to greater uncertainty before they are brought into use. *[IAS 36.11].*
- For all other classes of assets within the scope of IAS 36, the entity is required to assess at each reporting date (year-end or any interim period end) whether there are any indications of impairment. The impairment test itself only has to be carried out if there are such indications. *[IAS 36.8-9].*

The particular requirements of IAS 36 concerning the impairment testing of goodwill and of intangible assets with an indefinite life are discussed separately at 8 (goodwill) and 10 (intangible assets with indefinite useful life) below, however the methodology used is identical for all types of assets.

For all other assets, an impairment test, i.e. a formal estimate of the asset's recoverable amount as set out in the standard, must be performed if indications of impairment exist. *[IAS 36.9].* The only exception is where there was sufficient headroom in a previous impairment calculation that would not have been eroded by subsequent events or the asset or CGU is not sensitive to a particular indicator; the indicators and these exceptions are discussed further in the following section. *[IAS 36.15].*

2.1 Indicators of impairment

Identifying indicators of impairment is a crucial stage in the impairment assessment process. IAS 36 lists examples of indicators but stresses that they represent the minimum indicators that should be considered by the entity and that the list is not exhaustive. *[IAS 36.12-13].* They are divided into external and internal indicators.

External sources of information:

(a) A decline in an asset's value during the period that is significantly more than would be expected from the passage of time or normal use.

(b) Significant adverse changes that have taken place during the period, or will take place in the near future, in the technological, market, economic or legal environment in which the entity operates or in the market to which an asset is dedicated.

(c) An increase in the period in market interest rates or other market rates of return on investments if these increases are likely to affect the discount rate used in calculating an asset's value in use and decrease the asset's recoverable amount materially.

(d) The carrying amount of the net assets of the entity exceeds its market capitalisation.

Internal sources of information:

(e) Evidence of obsolescence or physical damage of an asset.

(f) Significant changes in the extent to which, or manner in which, an asset is used or is expected to be used, that have taken place in the period or soon thereafter and that will have an adverse effect on it. These changes include the asset becoming idle, plans to dispose of an asset sooner than expected, reassessing its useful life as finite rather than indefinite or plans to restructure the operation to which the asset belongs.

(g) Internal reports that indicate that the economic performance of an asset is, or will be, worse than expected. *[IAS 36.12]*.

The standard amplifies and explains relevant evidence from internal reporting that indicates that an asset may be impaired:

(a) cash flows for acquiring the asset, or subsequent cash needs for operating or maintaining it, are significantly higher than originally budgeted;

(b) operating profit or loss or actual net cash flows are significantly worse than those budgeted;

(c) a significant decline in budgeted net cash flows or operating profit, or a significant increase in budgeted loss; or

(d) operating losses or net cash outflows for the asset, if current period amounts are aggregated with budgeted amounts for the future. *[IAS 36.14]*.

The presence of indicators of impairment will not necessarily mean that the entity has to calculate the recoverable amount of the asset in accordance with IAS 36. A previous calculation may have shown that an asset's recoverable amount was significantly greater than its carrying amount and it may be clear that subsequent events have been insufficient to eliminate this headroom. Similarly, previous analysis may show that an asset's recoverable amount is not sensitive to one or more of these indicators. *[IAS 36.15]*.

If there are indications that the asset is impaired, it may also be necessary to examine the remaining useful life of the asset, its residual value and the depreciation method used, as these may also need to be adjusted even if no impairment loss is recognised. *[IAS 36.17]*.

2.1.1 Market capitalisation

If market capitalisation is lower than carrying value of equity, this is a powerful indicator of impairment as it suggests that the market considers that the business value is less than the carrying value. However, the market may have taken account of factors other than the return that the entity is generating on its assets. For example, an individual entity may have a high level of debt that it is unable to service fully. A market capitalisation below equity will not necessarily be reflected in an equivalent impairment loss. An entity's response to this indicator depends very much on facts and circumstances. Most entities cannot avoid examining their CGUs in these circumstances unless there was sufficient headroom in a previous impairment calculation that would not have been eroded by subsequent events or none of the assets or CGUs is sensitive to market capitalisation as an indicator. If a formal impairment review is required when the market capitalisation is below equity, great care must be taken to ensure that the discount rate used to calculate VIU is consistent with current market assessments. IAS 36 does not require a formal reconciliation between market capitalisation of the entity, FVLCD and VIU. However, entities need to be able to understand the reason for the shortfall and consider whether they have made sufficient disclosures describing those factors that could result in impairment in the next periods. *[IAS 36.134(f)].*

2.1.2 (Future) performance

Another significant element is an explicit reference in (b), (c) and (d) above to internal evidence that future performance will be worse than expected. Thus IAS 36 requires an impairment review to be undertaken if performance is or will be significantly below that previously budgeted. In particular, there may be indicators of impairment even if the asset is profitable in the current period if budgeted results for the future indicate that there will be losses or net cash outflows when these are aggregated with the current period results.

2.1.3 Individual assets or part of CGU?

Some of the indicators are aimed at individual fixed assets rather than the CGU of which they are a part, for example a decline in the value of an asset or evidence that it is obsolete or damaged. Such indicators may also imply that a wider review of the business or CGU is required. However, this is not always the case. For example, if there is a slump in property prices and the market value of the entity's new head office falls below its carrying value this would constitute an indicator of impairment and trigger a review. At the level of the individual asset, as FVLCD is below carrying amount, this might indicate that a write-down is necessary. However, the building's recoverable amount may have to be considered in the context of a CGU of which it is a part. This is an example of a situation where it may not be necessary to re-estimate an asset's recoverable amount because it may be obvious that the CGU has suffered no impairment. In short, it may be irrelevant to the recoverable amount of the CGU that it contains a head office whose market value has fallen.

2.1.4 Interest rates

Including interest rates as indicators of impairment could imply that assets are judged to be impaired if they are no longer expected to earn a market rate of return, even though they may generate the same cash flows as before. However, it may well be that an upward movement in general interest rates will not give rise to a write-down in assets because they may not affect the rate of return expected from the asset or CGU itself. The standard indicates that this may be an example where the asset's recoverable amount is not sensitive to a particular indicator.

The discount rate used in a VIU calculation should be based on the rate specific for the asset. An entity is not required to make a formal estimate of an asset's recoverable amount if the discount rate used in calculating the asset's VIU is unlikely to be affected by the increase in market rates. For example recoverable amount for an asset that has a long remaining useful life may not be materially affected by increases in short-term rates. Further an entity is not required to make a formal estimate of an asset's recoverable amount if previous sensitivity analyses of the recoverable amount show that it is unlikely that there will be a material decrease in recoverable amount because future cash flows are also likely to increase to compensate for the increase in market rates. Consequently, the potential decrease in recoverable amount may simply be unlikely to result in a material impairment loss. *[IAS 36.16]*.

Events in the financial crisis of 2008/2009 demonstrated that this may also be true for a decline in market interest rates. A substantial decline in short-term market interest rates did not lead to an equivalent decline in the (long term) market rates specific to assets.

3 DIVIDING THE ENTITY INTO CASH-GENERATING UNITS (CGUS)

If an impairment assessment is required, one of the first tasks will be to identify the individual assets affected and if those assets do not have individually identifiable and independent cash inflows, to divide the entity into CGUs. The group of assets that is considered together should be as small as is reasonably practicable, i.e. the entity should be divided into as many CGUs as possible and an entity must identify the lowest aggregation of assets that generate largely independent cash inflows. *[IAS 36.6, 68]*.

It must be stressed that CGUs are identified from cash inflows, not from net cash flows or indeed from any basis on which costs might be allocated (this is discussed further below).

The existence of a degree of flexibility over what constitutes a CGU is obvious. Indeed, the standard acknowledges that the identification of CGUs involves judgement. *[IAS 36.68]*. The key guidance offered by the standard is that CGU selection will be influenced by 'how management monitors the entity's operations (such as by product lines, businesses, individual locations, districts or regional areas) or how management makes decisions about continuing or disposing of the entity's assets and operations'. *[IAS 36.69]*. While monitoring by management may help identify CGUs, it does not override the requirement that the identification of CGUs is based on the lowest level at which largely independent cash inflows can be identified.

Example 20.1: Identification of cash-generating units and largely independent cash inflows

An entity obtains a contract to deliver mail to all users within a country, for a price that depends solely on the weight of the item, regardless of the distance between sender and recipient. It makes a significant loss in deliveries to outlying regions. Because of the entity's contractual service obligations, the CGU is the whole region covered by its mail services.

The division should not go beyond the level at which each income stream is capable of being separately monitored. For example, it may be difficult to identify a level below an individual factory as a CGU but of course an individual factory may or may not be a CGU.

An entity may be able to identify independent cash inflows for individual factories or other assets or groups of assets such as offices, retail outlets or assets that directly generate revenue such as those held for rental or hire.

Intangible assets such as brands, customer relationships and trademarks used by an entity for its own activities are unlikely to generate largely independent cash inflows and will therefore be tested together with other assets at a CGU level. This is also the case with intangible assets with indefinite useful lives and those that have not yet been brought into use, even though the carrying amount must be tested at least annually for impairment (see 2 above and 3.1 below).

Focusing on cash inflows avoids a common misconception in identifying CGUs. Management may argue that the costs for each of their retail outlets are not largely independent because of purchasing synergies and therefore these outlets cannot be separate CGUs. In fact, this will not be the deciding feature. IAS 36 explicitly refers to the allocation of cash outflows that are necessarily incurred to generate the cash inflows. If they are not directly attributed, cash outflows can be 'allocated on a reasonable and consistent basis'. *[IAS 36.39(b)]*. Goodwill and corporate assets may also have to be allocated to CGUs as described in 8.1 and 4.2 below.

Management may consider that the primary way in which they monitor their business is for the entity as a whole or on a regional or segmental basis, which could also result in CGUs being set at too high a level. It is undoubtedly true, in one sense, that management monitors the business as a whole but in most cases they also monitor at a lower level that can be identified from the lowest level of independent cash inflows. For example, while management of a chain of cinemas will make decisions that affect all the cinemas such as the selection of films and catering arrangements, it will also monitor individual cinemas. Management of a chain of branded restaurants will monitor both the brand and the individual restaurants. In both cases, management may also monitor at an intermediate level, e.g. a level based on regions. In most cases, each restaurant or cinema will be a CGU, as illustrated in Example 20.2 Example B below, because each will generate largely independent cash inflows, but brands and goodwill may be tested at a higher level.

In Example 20.2 below Example A illustrates a practical approach which involves working down to the smallest group of assets for which a stream of cash inflows can be identified. These groups of assets will be CGUs unless the performance of their cash inflow-generating assets is dependent on those generated by other assets, or their cash inflows are affected by those of other assets. If the cash inflows generated by the group of assets are not largely independent of those generated by other assets, other assets should be added to the group to form the smallest collection of assets that generates largely independent cash inflows.

Example 20.2: Identification of cash-generating units

Example A – newspapers

An entity publishes 10 suburban newspapers, each with a different mast-head, across 4 distinct regions within a major city. The price paid for a purchased mast-head is recognised as an intangible asset. The newspapers are distributed to residents free of charge. No newspaper is distributed outside its region. All of the revenue generated by each newspaper comes from advertising sales. An analysis of advertising sales shows that for each mast-head:

- Approximately 90% of sales come from advertisers purchasing 'bundled' advertisements that appear in all those newspapers published in one particular region of the city;
- Approximately 6% of sales come from advertisers purchasing 'bundled' advertisements that appear in all 10 newspapers in the major city; and
- Approximately 4% of sales come from advertisers purchasing advertisements that appear in one newspaper only.

What is the cash-generating unit for an individual mast-head?

Identify the smallest aggregation of assets for which a stream of cash inflows can be identified.

The fact that it is possible to use a pro-rata allocation basis to determine the cash inflows attributable to each newspaper means that each mast-head is likely to represent the smallest aggregation of assets for which a stream of cash inflows can be identified.

Are the cash inflows generated by an individual mast-head largely independent of those of other mast-heads and, conversely, is that individual mast-head affecting the cash inflows generated by other mast-heads?

As approximately 96% of cash inflows for each mast-head arise from 'bundled' advertising sales across multiple mast-heads, the cash inflows generated by an individual mast-head are not largely independent.

Therefore, the individual mast-heads would most likely need to be aggregated to form the smallest collection of assets that generates largely independent cash inflows. On the basis that approximately 90% of cash inflows for each mast-head arise from 'bundled' advertising sales across all of the newspapers published in a particular region, it is likely that those mast-heads published in one region will together form a cash-generating unit.

Example B – retail outlets

An entity has a chain of retail outlets located in the same country. The business model of the entity is highly integrated and the majority of the entity's revenue generating decisions, such as decisions about investments and monitoring of performance, are carried out at an entity level by the executive committee, with some decisions (such as product range and marketing) delegated to the regional or store levels. The majority of the operations, such as purchasing, are centralised. Management operates its business on a regional basis; but sales are monitored at the individual store level.

The outlets are usually bought and sold in packages of outlets that are subject to common economic characteristics, e.g. outlets of similar size or location such as a shopping centre or city or region. Only in rare situations has the entity sold or closed down an individual outlet.

The determining factor for CGUs is the level at which largely independent cash inflows are generated, and not the manner in which the entity's operations are organised and monitored. The fact that operations and costs are managed centrally does not in itself affect the source and independence of the cash inflows. The interdependence of cash outflows is unlikely to be relevant to the identification of CGUs.

The key issue in deciding whether CGUs should be identified at the level of the individual store as opposed to a group of stores is whether, if a store is closed down, all the customers of that store would seek out another of the entity's stores such that there is no significant 'leakage' of customers from the store closure. Unless the customers transfer their business to another of the entity's stores, the individual stores are separate CGUs.

Management in Example B may consider that the primary way in which they monitor their business is on a regional or segmental basis, but cash inflows are monitored at the level of an individual store. Individual stores generate independent cash inflows in most circumstances and the overriding requirement under IAS 36 is that the identification of CGUs is based on largely independent cash inflows.

However, the business models of some retailers have significantly changed over the last years and with the increased importance of internet sales will probably further change in the years ahead. The following example illustrates a new evolving omni-channel business model and its potential impact on the identification of CGUs in the retail sector.

Example 20.3: Omni-channel business model

Retailer A sells a wide range of general household merchandise online and through its retail stores which are located in most large and medium-sized cities in the same country. In order to cater to the changing habits of consumers and significant growth of online shoppers, A established an online platform. Retailer A offers the same products in each of its stores and on the online platform.

A uses the 'click and collect' business model. With 'click and collect' a customer is able to place an order online for items and then choose from which store to collect. If the preferred store runs out of an item, the customer might choose another store in the same city instead of waiting until the item arrives in its preferred store. This is the case for both customers buying online for store collection and for customers wanting to purchase the product directly in the store. The customer could either choose to pay online for the goods or make payment in store at the point of pick up. The customer could also purchase an item online and wait for it to be delivered in 3 working days. Sales generated online account for a significant portion of total sales, ranging from 20% to 25% depending on the city, and are projected to grow steadily in the coming years. The stores also serve as a point of return for products that customers ordered online. A product purchased online or in a store can be returned in any store and experience shows that customers make use of this option by returning products to stores in the same city where the product was originally purchased, picked up or delivered. The customers may exchange the products returned with products from the store shelves or they may purchase other products within the store when picking up or returning products. Hence, the activity of picking up and returning products also triggers sales in the stores. Retailer A considers the stores as well as showrooms for the online business whereby customers get professional buying advice and are able to experience the look and feel of the products, but then acquire the products only later through the online platform. For supply chain optimisation purposes Retailer A through its store personnel also encourages its customers to order online.

The performance of the stores together with the relevant online sales is assessed by city and not on an individual store-level. The employees of the stores are paid on an hourly basis and have performance-based compensation which is based on sales in all stores in one city together with online sales generated by customers located in the same city.

In assessing the CGU level for impairment purposes the key question is at which level of the retailer's organisation are independent cash inflows generated? In the specific fact pattern above, customers treat stores in the same city as an alternative means of making purchases and transacting returns which seems to indicate that all stores in one city might be one CGU. In addition, in the above described integrated omni-channel business model, the cash-inflows generated by stores and the cash-inflows generated by the online channel may not be largely independent from each other as the online revenues influence the store revenues and *vice versa.* Online customers treat stores as a collection and return point for online sales and as showrooms to experience the products. All of this together, as well as the fact that the performance of the stores and of the employees is assessed by city including online sales for the city, suggests that independent cash inflows are generated at the city level. Therefore, in the specific fact pattern above, it would be reasonable to treat the stores in a city together with the allocated assets of the online sales channel as one CGU for impairment testing purposes. The recoverable amount would consider the sales in the stores in a city plus the online sales to customers in the city.

Alternatively, if the sales generated online are an insignificant component of total sales and stores are not treated to a large extent as substitutes for each other by customers, then each single store may be considered a CGU for impairment testing purposes, even if the performance of the stores are monitored together at a higher level.

As explained above, IAS 36 states that the identification of CGUs involves judgment and that in identifying CGUs an entity should consider various factors including how management monitors the entity's operations (such as by product line, business, individual location, district or regional area) or how management makes decisions about continuing or disposing of the entity's assets and operations. *[IAS 36.68-69].*

Applying this guidance, the following quantitative and qualitative criteria might be considered in determining the appropriate CGUs in an omni-channel business model for impairment testing purposes:

- Whether the interdependency of the revenues from different sales channels (online, stores) is evidenced in the business model.
- Whether the retailer is able to measure the interdependencies of the revenues (i.e. online and stores).

- Whether the business model provides evidence that the sales channels are monitored together (e.g. on the level of customers allocated based on ZIP-Codes to stores in an area).
- Whether the profitability as well as the remuneration system are monitored/assessed on the combined basis of online and store revenues on a regional level (e.g. cities in Example 20.3 above).
- Whether in deciding about store openings and closures, the revenues of the online-business in the region (city in the example above) are considered.
- Whether online revenues are reaching a significant quantitative proportion of the overall revenues of the retailer's CGUs. It is important to note that IAS 36 does not give any specific guidance on when cash inflows are largely independent and therefore judgement is required. The level of interdependent online sales in Example 20.3 above is not meant to be a bright line but rather part of the specific fact pattern in the example and in practice the determination of CGUs will have to be made in the context of the overall facts and circumstances.

As illustrated in Example 20.4 below, it may be that the entity is capable of identifying individual cash inflows from assets but this is not conclusive. It may not be the most relevant feature in determining the composition of its CGUs which also depends on whether cash inflows are independent from cash inflows of other assets and on how cash inflows are monitored. If, however, the entity were able to allocate VIU on a reasonable basis, this might indicate that the assets are separate CGUs.

Example 20.4: Identification of cash-generating units – grouping of assets

Example A – A tour operator's hotels

A tour operator owns three hotels of a similar class near the beach at a large holiday resort. These hotels are advertised as alternatives in the operator's brochure, at the same price. Holidaymakers are frequently transferred from one to another and there is a central booking system for independent travellers. In this case, it may be that the hotels can be regarded as offering genuinely substitutable products by a sufficiently high proportion of potential guests and can be grouped together as a single cash-generating unit. Effectively, the hotels are being run as a single hotel on three sites. The entity will have to bear in mind that disposal decisions may still be made on a hotel-by-hotel basis and have to weight this appropriately in its determination of its CGUs.

Example B – Flagship stores

Store Z is a flagship store located in a prime site location in a capital city. Although store Z is loss making, its commercial performance is in line with expectations and with budgets. How should the impairment issues of the flagship store Z be considered?

It is difficult to conclude that a flagship store is a corporate asset as it does generate separate cash inflows (corporate assets are discussed at 4.2 below). It may be possible to argue for the aggregation of a flagship store with other stores in the vicinity into a single CGU as flagship stores are usually designed to enhance the image of the brand and hence other stores as well. They may be budgeted to run with negative cash flows; perhaps in substance the losses are not an impairment. However, this argument for not recognising an impairment would generally only be acceptable during a start-up phase and it must be borne in mind that the added function of the flagship store is largely marketing. As marketing expenditures are expensed, it would not necessarily be inconsistent to take an impairment loss and the entity may have to consider whether it should capitalise these costs in the first place.

Example C – Container ships

A shipping company operates a series of container vessels of similar size in a specific region that it considers to be a single CGU. As well as this shipping business, it has other types and regions of shipping operations where CGUs are established on an appropriate basis.

Management can identify the actual cash inflows from the individual vessels but it determines that the following are the principal features that indicate that these container ships comprise a single CGU:

- the vessels are interchangeable within the contracts and none is on a long-term hire to any individual client, meaning that the allocation of the estimated cash inflows to individual vessels becomes arbitrary;
- the pricing of the contract is not vessel specific;
- a reasonable portion of the contracts require the operator to have a certain level of capacity available, comprising multiple vessels;
- the investment, continuance and disposal decisions are made by class of vessel and not linked to the actual revenue generated by that vessel;
- the class of vessels has a clear and distinctive market and management views and makes decisions by reference to the CGU, not individual assets.

The fact that one or more of the assets could be used individually, i.e. taken out of the 'pool', would not in itself prevent the assets being considered part of a single CGU.

Example C is illustrated in Extract 20.1 below.

Extract 20.1: A.P. Møller – Mærsk A/S (2016)

NOTES

NOTE 23 SIGNIFICANT ACCOUNTING ESTIMATES AND JUDGEMENTS [extract]

INTANGIBLE ASSETS AND PROPERTY, PLANT AND EQUIPMENT [extract]

The determination of cash generating units differs for the various businesses. Maersk Line operates its fleet of container vessels in an integrated network for which reason the global container shipping activities are tested for impairment as a single cash generating unit. Maersk Oil tests fields individually or combined, when connected through shared infrastructure. APM terminals considers each terminal individually in impairment tests, unless when the capacity is managed as a portfolio, which is the case for certain terminals in Northern Europe and Global Ports Investments (Russia). Maersk Drilling considers rigs with the similar functionality and operating environment as cash generating units due to largely interdependent cash flows. Maersk Tankers, Svitzer and Maersk Supply Service group vessels according to type, size, etc. in accordance with the structure governing management's ongoing follow-up.

In Example C above, an analogy can be made to the conclusion in illustrative example IE11-IE16 of IAS 36 that plants B and C of entity M are part of one CGU which is illustrated in the following example 20.5:

Example 20.5: Identification of cash-generating units – single product entity

Entity M produces a single product and owns plants A, B, C. Each plant is located in a different continent. A produces a component that is assembled in either B or C. The combined capacity of B and C is not fully utilised. M's products are sold worldwide from either plant B or C. For example, B's product can be sold in C's continent if the products can be delivered faster from B than from C. Utilisation levels from B and C depend on the allocation of sales between the two sites. There is no active market for A's products.

Most likely A, B and C together, therefore M as a whole, are the smallest identifiable group of assets that generates cash inflows that are largely independent. This is due to

(a) A's cash inflows depend on sales of the final product by B and C, and

(b) cash inflows for B and C depend on the allocation of the production across the two sites.

As explained at 3.2 below, the conclusion would be different if an active market for A's product existed, resulting in A being one CGU and B and C together another CGU.

As a result of applying the methodology illustrated in Example 20.2, an entity could identify a large number of CGUs. However, the standard allows reasonable approximations and one way in which entities may apply this in practice is to group together assets that are separate CGUs, but which if considered individually for impairment would not be material. Retail outlets, usually separate CGUs, may be grouped if they are in close proximity to one another, e.g. all of the retail outlets in a city centre owned by a branded clothes retailer, if they are all subject to the same economic circumstances and grouping rather than examining individually will have an immaterial effect. However, the entity will still have to scrutinise the individual CGUs to ensure that those that it intends to sell or that have significantly underperformed are not supported by the others with which they are grouped. They would need to be identified and dealt with individually.

In practice, different entities will inevitably have varying approaches when determining their CGUs. There is judgement to be exercised in determining an income stream and in determining whether it is largely independent of other streams. Given this, entities may tend towards larger rather than smaller CGUs, to keep the complexity of the process within reasonable bounds.

IAS 36 also requires that identification of cash generating units be consistent from period to period unless the change is justified; if changes are made and the entity records or reverses an impairment, disclosures are required. *[IAS 36.72, 73]*.

Assets held for sale cannot remain part of a CGU. They generate independent cash inflows being the proceeds expected to be generated by sale. Once they are classified as held for sale they will be accounted for in accordance with IFRS 5 and carried at an amount that may not exceed their FVLCD (see 5.1 below and Chapter 4 for a further discussion of IFRS 5's requirements).

3.1 CGUs and intangible assets

IAS 36 requires certain intangible assets to be tested at least annually for impairment (see 2 above). These are intangible assets with an indefinite life and intangible assets that have not yet been brought into use. *[IAS 36.10-11]*.

Although these assets must be tested for impairment at least once a year, this does not mean that they have to be tested by themselves. The same requirements apply as for all other assets. The recoverable amount is the higher of the FVLCD or VIU of the individual asset or of the CGU to which the asset belongs (see 3 above). If the individual intangible asset's FVLCD is lower than the carrying amount and it does not generate largely independent cash flows then the CGU to which it belongs must be reviewed for impairment.

Many intangible assets do not generate independent cash inflows as individual assets and so they are tested for impairment with other assets of the CGU of which they are part. A trade mark, for example, will generate largely independent cash flows if it is licensed to a third party but more commonly it will be part of a CGU.

If impairment is tested by reference to the FVLCD or VIU of the CGU, impairment losses, if any, will be allocated in accordance with IAS 36. Any goodwill allocated to the CGU has to be written off first. After that, the other assets of the CGU, including the intangible asset, will be, reduced pro rata based on their carrying amount (see 11.2 below). *[IAS 36.104]*.

However, the carrying amount of an asset should not be reduced below the highest of its fair value less costs of disposal, value in use or zero. If the preceding rule is applied, further allocation of the impairment loss is made pro rata to the other assets of the unit (group of units).

If the intangible asset is no longer useable then it must be written off, e.g. an in-process research and development project that has been abandoned, so it is no longer part of the larger CGU and its own recoverable amount is nil. Intangible assets held for sale are treated in the same way as all other assets held for sale – see 5.1 below.

3.2 Active markets and identifying CGUs

The standard stresses the significance of an active market for the output of an asset or group of assets in identifying a CGU. An active market is a market in which transactions take place with sufficient frequency and volume to provide pricing information on an ongoing basis. *[IFRS 13 Appendix A]*. If there is an active market for the output produced by an asset or group of assets, the assets concerned are identified as a cash-generating unit, even if some or all of the output is used internally. *[IAS 36.70]*. The reason given for this rule is that the existence of an active market means that the assets or CGU could generate cash inflows independently from the rest of the business by selling on the active market. *[IAS 36.71]*. There are active markets for many metals, energy products (various grades of oil product, natural gas) and other commodities that are freely traded. When estimating cash inflows for the selling CGU or cash outflows for the buying CGU, the entity will replace internal transfer prices with management's best estimate of the price in a future arm's length transaction. Note that this is a general requirement for all assets and CGUs subject to internal transfer pricing (see 7.1.6 below).

Example A below, based on Example 1B in IAS 36's accompanying section of illustrative examples, illustrates the point. Example B describes circumstances in which the existence of an active market does not necessarily lead to the identification of a separate CGU.

Example 20.6: Identification of cash-generating units – internally-used products

Example A – Plant for an Intermediate Step in a Production Process

A significant raw material used for plant Y's final production is an intermediate product bought from plant X of the same entity. X's products are sold to Y at an internal price that passes all margins to X. 60 per cent of X's final production is sold to Y and the remaining 40 per cent is sold to customers outside of the entity. Y sells 80 per cent of its products to customers outside of the entity. Transfer pricing is discussed at 7.1.6 below.

If X can sell its products in an active market and generate cash inflows that are largely independent of the cash inflows from Y, it is likely that X is a CGU even though part of its production is used by Y. Therefore, its cash inflows can be regarded as being largely independent. It is likely that Y is also a separate CGU. However, internal transfer prices do not reflect market prices for X's output. Therefore, in determining value in use of both X and Y, the entity adjusts financial budgets/forecasts to reflect management's best estimate of future prices that could be achieved in arm's length transactions for those of X's products that are used internally.

If, on the other hand, there is no active market, it is likely that the recoverable amount of each plant cannot be assessed independently of the recoverable amount of the other plant. The majority of X's production is used internally and could not be sold in an active market. Cash inflows of X depend on demand for Y's products. Therefore, X cannot be considered to generate cash inflows that are largely independent of those of Y. In addition, the two plants are managed together. As a consequence, it is likely that X and Y together are the smallest group of assets that generates cash inflows that are largely independent. *[IAS 36.IE5-10]*.

Example B – 'Market' for intermediate product not relevant to identification of a separate CGU

A vertically integrated operation located in Australia produces an intermediate product that is fully used internally to manufacture the end product. The Australian market is the principal market for the intermediate product and there is no active market as defined by IFRS 13 (see Chapter 14) for it in Australia. The entity has only one other competitor in Australia, which is also vertically integrated and, likewise, uses the intermediate product internally. Both entities are, and have always been, very profitable when looking at their vertically integrated manufacturing processes to the end-stage product.

There is an active market for the intermediate product in China, but the prices at which the product can be sold are so low that a company based in Australia whose sole activity is to sell the intermediate product into China would never be profitable and a company would never set up manufacturing operations in Australia in order to sell into China.

Each of the Australian companies will occasionally sell small surpluses of their intermediate products into the active market in China, rather than make that product available to their competitor in Australia.

The existence of an active market for the intermediate product in China might suggest that the operations involved should be treated as a separate CGU. However, the mere existence of an active market somewhere in the world does not mean that the asset or CGU could realistically generate cash inflows independently from the rest of the business by selling on that active market. If such sales are a genuine incidental activity (i.e. if it is genuinely a case of obtaining some proceeds from excess product that would otherwise be scrapped), it may be appropriate not to regard that market as an active market for the intermediate product for IAS 36 purposes.

If the market is not regarded as an active market for IAS 36 purposes, the assets/operations involved in producing the intermediate product will not be treated as a separate CGU.

4 IDENTIFYING THE CARRYING AMOUNT OF CGU ASSETS

After an entity has established its CGU(s) for the impairment assessment, it needs to determine the carrying amount of the CGU(s). The carrying amount must be determined on a basis that is consistent with the way in which the recoverable amount is determined. *[IAS 36.75]*.

The carrying amount of a CGU includes only those assets that can be attributed directly, or allocated on a reasonable and consistent basis. These must be the assets that will generate the future cash inflows used in determining the CGU's recoverable amount. It does not include the carrying amount of any recognised liability, unless the recoverable amount of the cash-generating unit cannot be determined without taking it into account. Both FVLCD and VIU of a CGU are determined excluding cash flows that relate to assets that are not part of the cash-generating unit and liabilities that have been recognised. *[IAS 36.76]*.

The standard emphasises the importance of completeness in the allocation of assets to CGUs. Every asset used in generating the cash flows of the CGU being tested must be included in the CGU; otherwise an impaired CGU might appear to be unimpaired, as its carrying value would be understated by having missed out assets. *[IAS 36.77]*.

There are exceptions to the rule that recognised liabilities are not included in arriving at the CGU's carrying value or VIU. If the buyer would have to assume a liability if it acquired an asset or group of assets, then the fair value less costs of disposal would be the price to sell the assets or group of assets and the liability together. The liability would then need to be deducted from the CGU's carrying amount and VIU. This will enable a meaningful comparison between carrying amount and recoverable amount, whether the latter is based on FVLCD or VIU. *[IAS 36.78]*. See 4.1.1 below.

For practical reasons the entity may determine the recoverable amount of a CGU after taking into account assets and liabilities such as receivables or other financial assets, trade payables, pensions and other provisions that are outside the scope of IAS 36 and therefore not part of the CGU. *[IAS 36.79]*. If the value in use calculation for a CGU or its FVLCD are determined taking into account these sorts of items, then it is essential that the carrying amount of the CGU is determined on a consistent basis. However, this frequently causes confusion in practice, as described in 4.1 below.

Other assets such as goodwill and corporate assets may not be able to be attributed on a reasonable and consistent basis and the standard has separate rules regarding their treatment. The allocation of goodwill is dealt with separately at 8.1 below and corporate assets at 4.2 below.

4.1 Consistency and the impairment test

Consistency is a very important principle underlying IAS 36. In testing for impairment entities must ensure that the carrying amount of the CGU is consistent for VIU and FVLCD. In calculating VIU, or using a discounted cash flow methodology for FVLCD, entities must ensure that there is consistency between the assets and liabilities of the CGU and the cash flows taken into account, as there must also be between the cash flows and discount rate.

4.1.1 below describes the exceptions to the rule that recognised liabilities are not included in arriving at the CGU's carrying value. If the buyer would have to assume a liability if it acquired an asset or group of assets (CGU), then the fair value less costs of disposal of the CGU would be the price to sell the assets of the CGU and the liability together, less the costs of disposal. *[IAS 36.78]*. To provide a meaningful comparison this liability should then be deducted as well from the VIU and the carrying amount of the asset or group of assets (CGU).

The standards requirement to deduct the liability from both the CGU's carrying amount and from its VIU avoids the danger of distortion that can arise when cash flows that will be paid to settle the contractual obligation are included in the VIU discounted cash flow calculation. If the liability cash flows are included in the VIU discounted cash flow calculation, they would potentially be discounted using a different discount rate to the rate used to calculate the carrying value of the liability causing distortion. See 4.1.1 below for further discussion.

From a practical point of view an entity could simply calculate the VIU of a CGU excluding the liability cash outflows and compare that to the CGU carrying amount excluding the liability. While this would mean that the VIU is not comparable to the FVLCD, this would not cause an issue as long as the calculated VIU is above the CGU's carrying amount, therefore providing evidence that the CGU is not impaired.

It is also accepted in IAS 36 that an entity might for practical reasons determine the recoverable amount of a CGU after taking into account assets and liabilities such as receivables or other financial assets, trade payables, pensions and other provisions that are outside the scope of IAS 36.

In all cases:

- the carrying amount of the CGU must be calculated on the same basis for VIU and FVLCD, i.e. including the same assets and liabilities; and
- it is essential that cash flows are prepared on a consistent basis to the assets and liabilities within CGUs.

In addition, some of these assets and liabilities have themselves been calculated using discounting techniques. Therefore a danger of distortion arises resulting from differing discount rates, as discussed above.

4.1.1 Environmental provisions and similar provisions and liabilities

IAS 36.78 illustrates liabilities that should be deducted from the carrying amount of the assets of a CGU because a buyer would assume the liability using an example of a mine in a country in which there is a legal obligation to restore the site by replacing the overburden. The restoration provision, which is the present value of the restoration costs, has been provided for and deducted from the carrying value of the assets of the CGU. It will be taken into account in the estimation of FVLCD but must also be deducted in arriving at VIU so that both methods of estimating recoverable amount are calculated on a comparable basis that aligns with the carrying amount of the CGU.

There are other provisions for liabilities that would be taken over by the purchaser of a CGU, e.g. property dilapidations or similar contractual restoration provisions. These may relate to an off-balance sheet leasehold interest in property or equipment rather than a fixed asset. The provision will be accrued as the 'damage' is incurred and hence expensed over time rather than capitalised. If the provision is deducted from the assets of the CGU then it must also be deducted in arriving at VIU and it has to be taken into account in the estimation of FVLCD.

Indeed, many provisions made in accordance with IAS 37 – *Provisions, Contingent Liabilities and Contingent Assets* – may be reflected in the CGU's carrying amount as long as they will be considered appropriately in arriving at the recoverable amount of the CGU.

Including the cash outflows that will be paid to settle the contractual obligation in the VIU discounted cash flow calculation bears the danger of distortion as the cash flows for impairment purposes will be discounted using a different rate to the rate used to calculate the provision itself. The carrying amount of this class of liability will reflect a discount rate suitable for provisions, based on the time value of money and the risks relating to the provision. This is likely to be considerably lower than a suitable discount rate for an asset and the distortion caused by this would have to be considered and adjusted if the effect is significant. A simple illustration is that the present value of a cash outflow of €100 in 10 years' time is €39 discounted at 10% but €68 if a discount rate of 4% is used. Deducting the respective cash flows discounted at the asset discount rate could result in an overstatement of the CGU's recoverable amount.

Therefore, to avoid the danger of distortion and to allow for a meaningful comparison between the carrying amount of the CGU and the recoverable amount, IAS 36 requires the carrying amount of the provision to be deducted in determining both the CGU's carrying amount and its VIU. *[IAS 36.78]*.

In 2015 the Interpretations Committee received a request to clarify the application of paragraph 78 of IAS 36. The submitter observed that the approach of deducting the liability from both the VIU and the CGU's carrying amount would produce a null result and therefore asked whether this was really the intention or whether an alternative approach should be required.

In its November 2015 meeting the Interpretations Committee observed that when the CGU's fair value less costs of disposal (FVLCD) considers a recognised liability then IAS 36.78 requires adjusting both the CGU's carrying amount and its VIU by the carrying amount of the liability. In the Interpretations Committee's view this approach provides a straightforward and cost-effective method to perform a meaningful comparison of the recoverable amount and the carrying amount of the CGU. Moreover, it observed that this approach is consistent with the requirement in IAS 36 to reflect the risks specific to the asset in the present value measurement of the assets in the CGU and the requirements in IAS 37 to reflect the risk specific to the liability in the present value calculation of the liability.

The Interpretations Committee therefore decided that neither an interpretation nor an amendment to a Standard was necessary and not to add this issue to its agenda.

As mentioned under 4.1 from a practical point of view an entity could calculate the VIU of a CGU without deducting the liability cash outflow and compare that to the CGU excluding the liability. As long as the calculated VIU is above the CGU's carrying amount no impairment would be required and the lack of comparability to the FVLCD would not cause an issue.

4.1.2 Finance leases

A CGU may include assets held under finance leases. IAS 17 – *Leases* – requires an entity to apply IAS 36 in determining whether leased assets have become impaired in value. When testing VIU, an entity excludes the finance lease liability from the carrying amount as well as excluding the rental payments under the lease from the recoverable amount.

If for practical reasons an entity deducts the related liabilities from the assets of the CGU then it has to deduct the liabilities as well from the VIU as described at 4.1-4.1.1 above. The entity will have to ensure consistent treatment of the carrying value. In addition if an entity deducts the finance lease liability from the carrying value of the CGU and includes the rental payments in the cash flows for the VIU, instead of deducting the finance lease liability from the VIU, the entity would need to consider any discount rate distortion if significant to the outcome of the test.

4.1.3 Trade debtors and creditors

Whether an entity includes or excludes trade debtors and creditors in the assets of the CGU, it must avoid double counting the cash flows that will repay the receivable or pay those liabilities. This may be tricky because cash flows do not normally distinguish between cash flows that relate to working capital items and others. A practical solution often applied is to include working capital items in the carrying amount of the CGU and include the effect of changes in the working capital balances in the cash flow forecast.

The following simplified example illustrates the effects of including and excluding initial working capital items.

Example 20.7: The effects of working capital on impairment tests

At the end of the year, Entity A's net assets comprise:

	€
Carrying value of assets in CGU	100,000
Working capital: net liability	(800)

Its budgeted cash flows before interest and tax for the following five years, including and excluding changes in working capital, and their net present value using a 10% discount rate are as follows:

Year	1	2	3	4	5	6
	€	€	€	€	€	€
Pre-tax cash flow [(1)]	10,000	20,000	30,000	40,000	50,000	
Opening working capital	(800)	(1,500)	(3,000)	(4,500)	(6,000)	(7,500)
Closing working capital	(1,500)	(3,000)	(4,500)	(6,000)	(7,500)	
Change in working capital	700	1,500	1,500	1,500	1,500	(7,500)

Notes

(1) cash flow before interest, excluding working capital changes

Year 5's closing working capital is treated as a cash outflow in year 6.

Cash flow including opening working capital	10,700	21,500	31,500	41,500	51,500	(7,500)
NPV at 10% discount rate	107,251					
Cash flow excluding opening working capital	11,500	21,500	31,500	41,500	51,500	(7,500)
NPV at 10% discount rate	107,979					

Including opening working capital:

	€
Carrying value of CGU net of working capital	99,200
NPV of cash flow including opening working capital	107,251
Headroom	8,051

Excluding working capital:

	€
Carrying value of CGU	100,000
NPV of cash flow excluding opening changes in working capital	107,979
Headroom	7,979

Note that the headroom is not exactly the same in both cases, due to the discounting effect of differences in the periods in which cash flows are incurred. Typically, the distortion caused by discounting will not be significant in relation to short term working capital items. However, in our view, if significant, such distortion should be adjusted.

Any other combination will not treat assets and cash flows consistently and will either overstate or understate headroom, e.g. it would be incorrect to compare the carrying value of the CGU net of the working capital (99,200) and the cash flows excluding the opening changes in working capital (107,979).

4.1.4 Pensions

As mentioned under 4 above, recognised liabilities are in general not included in arriving in the recoverable amount or carrying amount of a CGU.

IAS 36.79 mentions pension obligations as items that might for practical reasons be included in calculating the recoverable amount of a CGU. In such a case, the carrying amount of the CGU is decreased by the carrying amount of those liabilities.

In practice, including cash flows for a pension obligation in the recoverable amount could be fraught with difficulty, especially if it is a defined benefit scheme, as there can be so much difference between the measurement basis of the pension liability and the cash flows that relate to pensions. Deducting the carrying amount of the pension obligation from both the value in use and the carrying amount of the CGU avoids this issue. If the pension liability is excluded from the carrying amount of the CGU, then any cash flows in relation to it should not be considered in the value in use calculation and the pension liability should not be deducted from the VIU.

Cash flows in relation to future services on the other hand, whether for defined contributions or defined benefit arrangements, should always be included in calculating the recoverable amount as these are part of the CGU's ongoing employee costs. In practice, it can be difficult to distinguish between cash flows reflecting repayment of the pension liability and cash flows that are future employee costs of the CGU.

4.1.5 Cash flow hedges

In the case of a cash flow hedge in relation to highly probable forecasted transactions, it often makes no significant difference for short term hedging arrangements if the hedging asset or liability and the hedging cash flows are included in the calculation of recoverable amount. The result is to gross up or net down the assets of the CGU and the relevant cash flows by an equivalent amount, after taking account of the distorting effects of differing discount rates. However, some entities argue that they ought to be able to take into account cash flows from instruments hedging their sales or purchases that are designated as cash flow hedges under IFRS 9 or IAS 39 – *Financial Instruments: Recognition and Measurement* – because not to do so misrepresents their economic position. In order to do this, they wish to include the cash flows and either exclude the derivative asset or liability from the CGU or, alternatively, include the derivative asset or liability and reflect the related cash flow hedge reserve in the CGU as well (this latter treatment would not be a perfect offset to the extent of ineffectiveness). They argue that the cash flow hedges protect the fair value of assets through their effect on price risk. They also note that not taking cash flows from instruments hedging their sales or purchases introduces a profit or loss mismatch by comparison with instruments that meet the 'normal purchase/normal sale' exemption under which the derivative remains off balance sheet until exercised.

Although logical from an income perspective, IAS 36 does not support these arguments. The derivative asset or liability can only be included in the CGU as a practical expediency and the hedge reserve is neither an asset nor liability to be reflected in the CGU. As the carrying amount of the hedge instrument is a net present value, any impairment loss might be similar to that calculated by excluding the derivative financial instrument and its cash flows. However, there may be a difference between the two due to different discount rates being applied in the determination of the derivative's fair value and the determination of the VIU. Neither IFRS 9 nor IAS 39 would not permit an entity to mitigate the effects of impairment by recycling the appropriate amount from the hedging reserve. Finally, entities must be aware that cash flow hedges may have negative values as well as positive ones.

Example 20.8: Cash flow hedges and testing for impairment

Entity A, which only has one CGU, enters into derivative contracts to hedge its commodity sales. These derivatives are accounted for as cash flow hedges and there is no ineffectiveness.

The entity is required to perform an impairment test.

Entity A's statement of financial position as at the impairment testing date is as follows:

	€
Asset/CGU	3,000
Derivatives fair value	1,125
Equity – other reserves	(3,000)
Equity – cash flow hedge reserve	(1,125)

As at the impairment testing date, the entity's cash flow forecasts are as follows:

Year	*20X0*	*20X1*	*20X2*	*20X3*
Forecast sales cash inflows		750	750	750
Forecast hedge cash inflows		450	450	450
Total cash inflows		1,200	1,200	1,200
NPV sales cash inflows	1,875	1,307	684	0
NPV total cash inflows	3,000	2,091	1,094	0
Fair value of hedge	1,125	784	410	0

IAS 36 requires the entity to exclude the cash flows from hedge transactions when calculating VIU. The carrying amount of the derivative is therefore excluded from the carrying amount of the cash-generating unit. The entity recognises an impairment loss of €1,125 as follows:

	€
Asset carrying amount	3,000
Recoverable amount (VIU)	1,875
Impairment loss	(1,125)

The entity is not prohibited from including within the VIU calculation the cash flows from a hedge instrument, provided the instrument's carrying amount is included within the carrying amount of the cash-generating unit and the effects of discounting are taken into account, thereby ensuring that the cash flows and carrying amount are consistently discounted. This approach would result in the same impairment of €1,125.

4.2 Corporate assets

An entity may have assets that are inherently incapable of generating cash inflows independently, such as headquarters buildings or central IT facilities that contribute to more than one CGU. IAS 36 calls such assets corporate assets. Corporate assets are defined as '...assets other than goodwill that contribute to the future cash flows of both the cash-generating unit under review and other cash-generating units'.

The characteristics that distinguish corporate assets are that they do not generate cash inflows independently of other assets or groups of assets and their carrying amount cannot be fully attributed to the CGU under review. *[IAS 36.100]*. Nevertheless, in order to test properly for impairment, the corporate asset's carrying value has to be tested for impairment along with CGUs. Corporate assets therefore have to be allocated to the CGUs to which they belong and then tested for impairment along with those CGUs. *[IAS 36.101]*.

This presents a problem in the event of those assets themselves showing indications of impairment. It also raises a question of what those indications might actually be, in the absence of cash inflows directly relating to this type of asset. Some, but not all, of these assets may have relatively easily determinable fair values but while this is usually true of a headquarters building, it could not be said for a central IT facility. We have already noted at 2.1.3 above that a decline in value of the asset itself may not trigger a need for an impairment review and it may be obvious that the CGUs of which corporate assets are a part are not showing any indications of impairment – unless, of course, management has decided to dispose of the asset. It is most likely that a corporate asset will show indications of impairment if the CGU or group of CGUs to which it relates are showing indications and this is reflected in the methodology by which corporate assets are tested.

If possible, the corporate assets are to be allocated to individual CGUs on a 'reasonable and consistent basis'. *[IAS 36.102]*. This is not expanded upon and affords some flexibility, although plainly consistency is vital; the same criteria must be applied at all times. If the carrying value of a corporate asset can be allocated on a reasonable and consistent basis between individual CGUs, each CGU has its impairment test done separately and its carrying value includes its share of the corporate asset. If the corporate asset's carrying value cannot be allocated to an individual CGU, there are three steps. As noted above, indicators of impairment for corporate assets that cannot be allocated to individual CGUs are likely to relate to the CGUs that use the corporate asset as well. First the CGU is tested for impairment and any impairment is recognised. Then a group of CGUs is identified to which, as a group, all or part of the carrying value of the corporate asset can be allocated. This group must include the CGU that was the subject of the first test. Finally, all CGUs in this group have to be tested to determine if the group's carrying value (including the allocation of the corporate asset's carrying value) is in excess of the group's recoverable amount. *[IAS 36.102]*. If it is not sufficient, the impairment loss will be allocated pro-rata, subject to the limitations of IAS 36.105, to all assets in the group of CGUs and the allocated portion of the corporate asset, as described at 11.2 below.

Some entities include a charge for the use of corporate assets rather than allocating the assets to CGUs and CGU groups. This is an acceptable approximation as long as entities ensure that the allocation is reasonable and that the total charge has the same NPV as the carrying amount of those assets and there is no impairment. Otherwise, there could be double counting or the omission of assets or cash outflows from CGUs or the misallocation of impairment to the assets of the CGU. Overheads are discussed further at 7.1.7 below.

In IAS 36's accompanying section of illustrative examples, Example 8 has a fully worked example of the allocation of corporate assets and calculation of a VIU. *[IAS 36.IE69-IE79]*. The table below is included in it, and serves to illustrate the allocation of the corporate asset to CGUs:

Example 20.9: Allocation of corporate assets

An entity comprises three CGUs and a headquarters building. The carrying amount of the headquarters building of 150 is allocated to the carrying amount of each individual cash-generating unit. A weighted allocation basis is used because the estimated remaining useful life of A's cash-generating unit is 10 years, whereas the estimated remaining useful lives of B and C's cash-generating units are 20 years.

Schedule 1. Calculation of a weighted allocation of the carrying amount of the headquarters building

End of 20X0	A	B	C	Total
Carrying amount	100	150	200	450
Remaining useful life	10 years	20 years	20 years	
Weighting based on useful life	1	2	2	
Carrying amount after weighting	100	300	400	800
Pro-rata allocation of the building	(100/800)= 12%	(300/800)= 38%	(400/800)= 50%	100%
Allocation of the carrying amount of the building (based on pro-rata above)	19	56	75	150
Carrying amount (after allocation of the building)	119	206	275	600

The allocation need not be made on carrying value or financial measures such as revenue – employee numbers or a time basis might be a valid basis in certain circumstances.

One effect of this pro-rata process is that the amount of the head office allocated to each CGU will change as the useful lives and carrying values change. In the above example, the allocation of the head office to CGU A will be redistributed to CGUs B and C as A's remaining life shortens. Similar effects will be observed if the sizes of any other factor on which the allocation to the CGUs is made change relative to one another.

5 RECOVERABLE AMOUNT

The standard requires the carrying amount of the asset or CGU to be compared with the recoverable amount, which is the higher of VIU and FVLCD. *[IAS 36.18]*. If either the FVLCD or the VIU is higher than the carrying amount, no further action is necessary as the asset is not impaired. *[IAS 36.19]*. Recoverable amount is calculated for an individual asset, unless that asset does not generate cash inflows that are largely independent of those from other assets or groups of assets, in which case the recoverable amount is determined for the CGU to which the asset belongs. *[IAS 36.22]*.

Recoverable amount is the higher of FVLCD and VIU. IAS 36 defines VIU as the present value of the future cash flows expected to be derived from an asset or CGU. FVLCD is the fair value as defined in IFRS 13 – *Fair Value Measurement*, the price that would be received to sell an asset or paid to transfer a liability in an orderly transaction between market participants at the measurement date, less the costs of disposal. *[IAS 36.6]*.

Estimating the VIU of an asset involves estimating the future cash inflows and outflows that will be derived from the use of the asset and from its ultimate disposal, and discounting them at an appropriate rate. *[IAS 36.31]*. There are complex issues involved in determining the cash flows and choosing a discount rate and often there is no agreed methodology to follow (refer to 7.1 and 7.2 below for a discussion of some of these difficulties).

It may be possible to estimate FVLCD even in the absence of quoted prices in an active market for an identical asset but if there is no basis for making a reliable estimate then the value of an asset must be based on its VIU. *[IAS 36.20]*.

There are two practical points to emphasise. First, IAS 36 allows the use of estimates, averages and computational shortcuts to provide a reasonable approximation of FVLCD or VIU. *[IAS 36.23]*. Second, if the FVLCD is greater than the asset's carrying value, no VIU calculation is necessary. It is not uncommon for the FVLCD of an asset to be readily obtainable while the asset itself does not generate largely independent cash inflows, as is the case with many property assets held by entities. If the FVLCD of the asset is lower than its carrying value then the recoverable amount will have to be calculated by reference to the CGU of which the asset is a part. However, as explained in 2.1.3 above, it may be obvious that the CGU to which the property belongs has not suffered an impairment. In such a case it would not be necessary to assess the recoverable amount of the CGU.

5.1 Impairment of assets held for sale

The standard describes circumstances in which it may be appropriate to use an asset or CGU's FVLCD without calculating its VIU, as the measure of its recoverable amount. There may be no significant difference between FVLCD and VIU, in which case the asset's FVLCD may be used as its recoverable amount. This is the case, for example, if management is intending to dispose of the asset or CGU, as apart from its disposal proceeds there will be few if any cash flows from further use. *[IAS 36.21]*.

The asset may also be held for sale as defined by IFRS 5, by which stage it will be outside the scope of IAS 36, although IFRS 5 requires such assets to be measured immediately before their initial classification as held for sale 'in accordance with applicable IFRSs'. *[IFRS 5.18]*. A decision to sell is a triggering event for an impairment review, which means that any existing impairment will be recognised at the point of classification and not be rolled into the gain or loss on disposal of the asset. See Chapter 4 for a description of the subsequent measurement of the carrying amounts of the assets.

Clearly IFRS 5's requirement to test for impairment prior to reclassification is intended to avoid impairment losses being recognised as losses on disposal. However, one effect is that this rule may require the recognition of impairment losses on individual assets that form part of a single disposal group subsequently sold at a profit, as in the following example.

Example 20.10: Impairment of assets held for sale

Entity A decided to sell three assets in one transaction to the same acquirer. Each asset had been part of a different CGU. The decision to sell was made on 20 December 20X0, just prior to Entity A's year end of 31 December. The assets met IFRS 5's requirements for classification as a disposal group on 10 January 20X1.

The information about the carrying amounts and fair values less cost of disposal of individual assets at 20 December 20X0 and the disposal group on 10 January 20X1 is summarised below. There was no change in the fair values of these assets between the two dates.

Asset	*Carrying amount*	*FVLCD of separate assets*	*Aggregate of the lower of the carrying amount and FVLCD*	*Fair value of the group*
	€	€	€	€
X	4,600	4,300	4,300	n/a
Y	5,700	5,800	5,700	n/a
Z	2,400	2,500	2,400	n/a
Total	12,700	12,600	12,400	12,600

Although these assets were classified as held for sale subsequent to the year end, the decision to sell them was an indicator of impairment. Accordingly, it is necessary to determine whether the three assets together comprise a new CGU. If so, impairment would be assessed on the three assets together, prior to reclassification and remeasurement under IFRS 5.

If the three assets together do not comprise a CGU, they would have to be tested for impairment individually at the year end, which would result in an impairment loss on Asset X of €300. As there is no change in the recoverable amount between the year end and immediately before the classification under IFRS 5, the aggregate value of these assets prior to classification under IFRS 5 would be €12,400 (4,300 + 5,700 + 2,400). The FVLCD of the disposal group at the date of the first application of IFRS 5 (10 January 20X1) is €12,600. Therefore, according to the measurement criteria under IFRS 5 the carrying amount of the disposal group remains at €12,400 and the impairment loss previously recognised on Asset X would only be reversed, should the FVLCD of the disposal group exceed €12,600.

IAS 36 does not allow an asset to be written down below the higher of its VIU or FVLCD. *[IAS 36.105]*. An entity might, however, expect to sell a CGU for less than the apparent aggregate FVLCD of individual assets, e.g. because the potential buyer expects further losses. If this happens, the carrying amount of the disposal group under IFRS 5 is capped at its FVLCD so the impairment loss is allocated to all non-current assets, even if their carrying amounts are reduced below their FVLCD. See Chapter 4.

6 FAIR VALUE LESS COSTS OF DISPOSAL

IFRS 13 specifies how to measure fair value, but does not change when fair value is required or permitted under IFRS. IFRS 13 is discussed in detail in Chapter 14.

The standard defines fair value as the price that would be received to sell an asset or paid to transfer a liability in an orderly transaction between market participants at the measurement date. It is explicitly an exit price. *[IFRS 13.2]*. When measuring FVLCD, fair value is measured in accordance with IFRS 13. Costs of disposal are calculated in accordance with IAS 36. IFRS 13 specifically excludes VIU from its scope. *[IFRS 13.6]*.

Fair value, like FVLCD, is not an entity-specific measurement but is focused on market participants' assumptions for a particular asset or liability. *[IFRS 13.11]*. For non-financial assets, fair value has to take account of the highest and best use by a market participant to which the asset could be put. *[IFRS 13.27]*. An entity's current use of a non-financial asset is presumed to be its highest and best use unless market or other factors suggest that a different use by market participants would maximise the value of the asset. *[IFRS 13.29]*.

Entities are exempt from the disclosures required by IFRS 13 when the recoverable amount is FVLCD. *[IFRS 13.7(c)]*. IAS 36's disclosure requirements are broadly aligned with those of IFRS 13. See IAS 36's disclosure requirements at 13 below.

While IFRS 13 makes it clear that transaction costs are not part of a fair value measurement, in all cases, FVLCD should take account of estimated disposal costs. These include legal costs, stamp duty and other transaction taxes, costs of removing the asset and other direct incremental costs. Business reorganisation costs and employee termination costs (as defined in IAS 19, see Chapter 33) may not be treated as costs of disposal. *[IAS 36.28]*.

If the disposal of an asset would entail the buyer assuming a liability and there is only a single FVLCD for both taken together, then, to enable a meaningful comparison, the obligation must also be taken into account in calculating VIU and the carrying value of the asset. This is discussed at 4.1 above. *[IAS 36.29, 78]*.

6.1 Estimating FVLCD

IFRS 13 does not limit the types of valuation techniques an entity might use to measure fair value but instead focuses on the types of inputs that will be used. The standard requires the entity to use the valuation technique that 'maximis[es] the use of relevant observable inputs and minimis[es] the use of unobservable inputs'. *[IFRS 13.61]*. The objective is that the best available inputs should be used in valuing the assets. These inputs could be used in any valuation technique provided they are consistent with (one of) the three valuation approaches in the standard: the market approach, the cost approach and the income approach. *[IFRS 13.62]*. IFRS 13 does not place any preference on the techniques that are used as long as the entity achieves the objective of a fair value measurement, which means it must use the best available inputs. In some cases, a single valuation technique will be appropriate, while in other cases, multiple valuation techniques will need to be used to meet this objective. An entity must apply the valuation technique(s) consistently. A change in a valuation technique is considered a change in an accounting estimate in accordance with IAS 8 – *Accounting Policies, Changes in Accounting Estimates and Errors*. *[IFRS 13.66]*.

The market approach uses prices and other relevant information generated by market transactions involving identical or comparable (i.e. similar) assets, liabilities or a group of assets and liabilities, such as a business. *[IFRS 13.B5]*. For items within scope of IAS 36, market techniques will usually involve market transactions in comparable assets or, for certain assets valued as businesses, market multiples derived from comparable transactions. *[IFRS 13.B5, B6]*.

The cost approach reflects the amount that would be required currently to replace the service capacity of an asset (i.e. current replacement cost). It is based on what a market participant buyer would pay to acquire or construct a substitute asset of comparable utility, adjusted for obsolescence. Obsolescence includes physical deterioration, technological (functional) and economic obsolescence so it is not the same as depreciation under IAS 16. *[IFRS 13.B8, B9]*. See also 6.1.2 below.

The income approach converts future amounts (e.g. cash flows or income and expenses) to a single discounted amount. The fair value reflects current market expectations about those future amounts. This will usually mean using a discounted cash flow technique or one of the other techniques that fall into this classification (e.g. option pricing and multi-period excess earnings methods). *[IFRS 13.B10, B11]*.

See Chapter 14 for a further discussion of these valuation approaches.

The inputs used in these valuation techniques to measure the fair value of an asset have a hierarchy. Those that are quoted prices in an active market for identical assets (Level 1) have the highest priority, followed by inputs, other than quoted prices, that are observable (Level 2). The lowest priority inputs are those based on unobservable inputs (Level 3). *[IFRS 13.72]*. The valuation techniques, referred to above, will use a combination of inputs to determine the fair value of the asset.

An active market is a market in which transactions take place with sufficient frequency and volume to provide pricing information on an ongoing basis. *[IFRS 13 Appendix A]*.

Using the IFRS's approach, most estimates of fair value for IAS 36 purposes will use Level 2 inputs that are directly or indirectly observable and Level 3 inputs that are not based on observable market data but reflect assumptions used by market participants, including risk.

If Level 2 information is available then entities must take it into account in calculating FVLCD because this is a relevant observable input, and cannot base their valuation only on Level 3 information. Deutsche Telekom calculated the FVLCD of one of its CGUs and took a third party transaction in the same sector and geographical area into account in its valuation model. Although this transaction, shown in the following extract, long pre-dates IFRS 13, the principles are the same as those that would be applied under the new IFRS.

Extract 20.2: Deutsche Telekom AG (2007)

Notes to the consolidated income statement [extract]

16. Depreciation, amortization and impairment losses [extract]

In the 2005 financial year, Deutsche Telekom recognized an impairment loss of EUR 1.9 billion at the T-Mobile UK cash-generating unit. Telefónica announced its offer to acquire the UK group O2 at a price of 200 pence per share (approximately GBP 17.7 billion) on October 31, 2005. When determining the fair value less costs to sell, the purchase prices paid in comparable transactions must generally be given preference over internal DCF calculations. The fair value of the cash-generating unit T-Mobile UK was derived from the Telefónica offer in accordance with a valuation model based on multipliers.

IFRS 13 allows entities to use unobservable inputs, which can include the entity's own data, to calculate fair value, as long as the objectives (an exit price from the perspective of a market participant) and assumptions about risk are met. *[IFRS 13.87-89]*. This means that a discounted cash flow technique may be used if this is commonly used in that industry to estimate fair value. Cash flows used when applying the model may only reflect cash flows that market participants would take into account when assessing fair value. This includes the type, e.g. future capital expenditure, as well as the estimated amount of such cash flows. For example, an entity may wish to take into account cash flows relating to future capital expenditure, which would not be permitted for a VIU calculation (see 7.1.2 below). These cash flows can be included if, and only if, other market participants would consider them when evaluating the asset. It is not permissible to include assumptions about cash flows or benefits from the asset that would not be available to or considered by a typical market participant.

The entity cannot ignore external evidence. It must use the best information that is available to it and adjust its own data if 'reasonably available information indicates that other market participants would use different data or there is something particular to the entity that is not available to other market participants such as an entity-specific synergy'. An entity need not undertake exhaustive efforts to obtain information about market participant assumptions. 'However, an entity shall take into account all information about market participant assumptions that is reasonably available.' *[IFRS 13.89]*. This means using a relevant model, which requires consideration of industry practice, for example, multiples based on occupancy, revenue and EBITDA might be inputs in estimating the fair value of a hotel but the value of an oilfield would depend on its reserves. The fair value of an oil field would include the costs that would be incurred in accessing those reserves based on the costs a market participant expects to incur instead of the entity's own specific cost structure.

IAS 36 notes that sometimes it is not possible to obtain reliable evidence regarding the assumptions and techniques that market participants would use (IAS 36 uses the phrase 'no basis for making a reliable estimate'); if so, the recoverable amount of the asset must be based on its VIU. *[IAS 36.20]*. Therefore, the IASB accepts that there are some circumstances in which market conditions are such that it will not be possible to calculate a reliable estimate of the price at which an orderly transaction to sell the asset would take place under current market conditions. *[IAS 36.20]*. IFRS 13 includes guidance for identifying transactions that are not orderly. *[IFRS 13.B43]*. These are discussed in Chapter 14 at 8.2.

6.1.1 FVLCD and the unit of account

In determining FVLCD it is critical to determine the relevant unit of account appropriately.

IFRS 13 does specify the unit of account to be used when measuring fair value in relation to a reporting entity that holds a position in a single asset or liability that is traded in an active market (including a position comprising a large number of identical assets or liabilities, such as a holding of financial instruments). In this situation, IFRS 13 requires an entity to measure the asset or liability based on the product of the quoted price for the individual asset or liability and the quantity held (P×Q).

This requirement is generally accepted when the asset or liability being measured is a financial instrument in the scope of IFRS 9 or IAS 39. However, when an entity holds an investment in a listed subsidiary, joint venture or associate, some believe the unit of account is the entire holding and the fair value should include an adjustment (e.g. a control premium) to reflect the value of the investor's control, joint control or significant influence over their investment as a whole.

Questions have also arisen as to how this requirement applies to cash-generating units that are equivalent to listed investments. Some argue that, because IAS 36 requires certain assets and liabilities to be excluded from a CGU, the unit of account is not identical to a listed subsidiary, joint venture or associate and an entity can include adjustments that are consistent with the CGU as a whole. Some similarly argue that approach is appropriate because, in group financial statements, an entity is accounting for the assets and liabilities of consolidated entities, rather than the investment. However, others argue that if the CGU is effectively the same as an entity's investment in a listed subsidiary, joint venture or associate, the requirement to use P×Q should apply.

IFRS 13 requires entities to select inputs that are consistent with the characteristics of the asset or liability being measured and would be considered by market participants when pricing the asset or liability. Apart from block discounts (which are specifically prohibited), determining whether a premium or discount applies to a particular fair value measurement requires judgement and depends on specific facts and circumstances.

The standard indicates that premiums or discounts should not be incorporated into fair value measurements unless all of the following conditions are met:

- the application of the premium or discount reflects the characteristics of the asset or liability being measured;
- market participants, acting in their economic best interest, would consider these premiums or discounts when pricing the asset or liability; and
- the inclusion of the premium or discount is not inconsistent with the unit of account in the IFRS that requires (or permits) the fair value measurement.

Therefore, when an entity holds an investment in a listed subsidiary, joint venture or associate and if the unit of account is deemed to be the entire holding, it seems to be appropriate to include, for example, a control premium when determining fair value, provided that market participants would take this into consideration when pricing the asset. If, however, the unit of account is deemed to be the individual share of the listed subsidiary, joint venture or associate, the requirement to use P×Q (without adjustment) to measure the fair value would override the requirements in IFRS 13 that permit premiums or discounts to be included in certain circumstances. In September 2014, in response to these questions regarding the unit of account for an investment in a listed subsidiary, joint venture or associate, the IASB proposed amendments to clarify that:

- The unit of account for investments in subsidiaries, joint ventures and associates be the investment as a whole and not the individual financial instruments that constitute the investment.
- For investments that are comprised of financial instruments for which a quoted price in an active market is available, the requirement to use P×Q would take precedence, irrespective of the unit of account. Therefore, for all such investments, the fair value measurement would be the product of P×Q, even when the reporting entity has an interest that gives it control, joint control or significant influence over the investee.
- When testing CGUs for impairment, if those CGUs correspond to an entity whose financial instruments are quoted in an active market, the fair value measurement would be the product of P×Q.

Based on the feedback received on the proposed amendments, the Board decided that, before further deliberating, additional research was required on this topic. In January 2016 the Board decided to consider the findings from the 2014 Exposure draft and subsequent research during the Post-implementation Review (PIR) of IFRS 13. In May 2017 the Board issued the request for information in relation to the PIR of IFRS 13 with one section covering questions around prioritising Level 1 inputs or the unit account. Until the IASB issues additional guidance, we expect that diversity in practice will continue.

This issue is discussed in more detail in Chapter 14 at 5.1.1.

6.1.2 Depreciated replacement cost or current replacement cost as FVLCD

Cost approaches, e.g. depreciated replacement cost (DRC) or current replacement cost, are one of the three valuation approaches that IFRS 13 considers to be appropriate for establishing FVLCD. Yet, the Basis for Conclusions of IAS 36 indicates that DRC is not suitable:

> 'Some argue that the replacement cost of an asset should be adopted as a ceiling for its recoverable amount. They argue that the value of an asset to the business would not exceed the amount that the enterprise would be willing to pay for the asset at the balance sheet date.
>
> 'IASC believed that replacement cost techniques are not appropriate to measuring the recoverable amount of an asset. This is because replacement cost measures the cost of an asset and not the future economic benefits recoverable from its use and/or disposal.' *[IAS 36.BCZ28-BCZ29].*

We do not consider that this means that FVLCD cannot be based on DRC. Rather, this means that DRC can only be used if it meets the objective of IFRS 13 by being a current exit price and not the cost of an asset. If the entity can demonstrate that the price that would be received for the asset is based on the cost to a market participant buyer to acquire or construct a substitute asset of comparable utility, adjusted for obsolescence, then (and only then) is DRC an appropriate basis for FVLCD. See Chapter 14 at 14.3.

7 DETERMINING VALUE IN USE (VIU)

IAS 36 defines VIU as the present value of the future cash flows expected to be derived from an asset or CGU. IAS 36 requires the following elements to be reflected in the VIU calculation:

(a) an estimate of the future cash flows the entity expects to derive from the asset;

(b) expectations about possible variations in the amount or timing of those future cash flows;

(c) the time value of money, represented by the current market risk-free rate of interest;

(d) the price for bearing the uncertainty inherent in the asset; and

(e) other factors, such as illiquidity that market participants would reflect in pricing the future cash flows the entity expects to derive from the asset. *[IAS 36.30].*

The calculation requires the entity to estimate the future cash flows and discount them at an appropriate rate. *[IAS 36.31]*. It also requires uncertainty as to the timing of cash flows or the market's assessment of risk in those assets ((b), (d) and (e) above) to be taken into account either by adjusting the cash flows or the discount rate. *[IAS 36.32]*. The intention is that the VIU should be the expected present value of those future cash flows.

If possible, recoverable amount is calculated for the individual asset. However, it will frequently be necessary to calculate the VIU of the CGU of which the asset is a part. *[IAS 36.66]*. This is because the single asset may not generate sufficiently independent cash inflows, *[IAS 36.67]*, as is often the case.

Goodwill cannot be tested by itself so it always has to be tested as part of a CGU or group of CGUs (see 8 below).

Where a CGU is being reviewed for impairment, this will involve calculation of the VIU of the CGU as a whole unless a reliable estimate of the CGU's FVLCD can be made and the resulting FVLCD is above the total carrying amount of the CGU's net assets.

VIU calculations at the level of the CGU will thus be required when no satisfactory FVLCD is available or FVLCD is below the CGU's carrying amount and:

- the CGU includes goodwill, indefinite lived intangibles or intangibles not yet brought into use which must be tested annually for impairment;
- a CGU itself is suspected of being impaired; or
- intangible assets or other fixed assets are suspected of being impaired and individual future cash flows cannot be identified for them.

The standard contains detailed requirements concerning the data to be assembled to calculate VIU that can best be explained and set out as a series of steps. The steps also contain a discussion of the practicalities and difficulties in determining the VIU of an asset. The steps in the process are:

1: Dividing the entity into CGUs (see 3 above).

2: Allocating goodwill to CGUs or CGU groups (see 8.1 below).

3: Identifying the carrying amount of CGU assets (see 4 above).

4: Estimating the future pre-tax cash flows of the CGU under review (see 7.1 below).

5: Identifying an appropriate discount rate and discounting the future cash flows (see 7.2 below).

6: Comparing carrying value with VIU (assuming FVLCD is lower than carrying value) and recognising impairment losses (if any) (see 11.1 and 11.2 below).

Although this process describes the determination of the VIU of a CGU, steps 3 to 6 are the same as those that would be applied to an individual asset if it generated cash inflows independently of other assets. Impairment of goodwill is discussed at 8 below.

7.1 Estimating the future pre-tax cash flows of the CGU under review

In order to calculate the VIU the entity needs to estimate the future cash flows that it will derive from its use and consider possible variations in their amount or timing. *[IAS 36.30]*. In estimating future cash flows the entity must:

(a) Base its cash flow projections on reasonable and supportable assumptions that represent management's best estimate of the range of economic conditions that will exist over the remaining useful life of the asset. Greater weight must be given to external evidence.

(b) Base cash flow projections on the most recent financial budgets/forecasts approved by management, excluding any estimated future cash inflows or outflows expected to arise from future restructurings or from improving or enhancing the asset's performance. These projections can only cover a maximum period of five years, unless a longer period can be justified.

(c) Estimate cash flow projections beyond the period covered by the most recent budgets/forecasts by extrapolating them using a steady or declining growth rate for subsequent years, unless an increasing rate can be justified. This growth rate must not exceed the long-term average growth rate for the products, industries, or country or countries in which the entity operates, or for the market in which the asset is used, unless a higher rate can be justified. *[IAS 36.33]*.

7.1.1 Budgets and cash flows

The standard describes in some detail the responsibilities of management towards the estimation of cash flows. Management is required to ensure that the assumptions on which its current cash flow projections are based are consistent with past actual outcomes by examining the causes of differences between past cash flow projections and actual cash flows. If actual cash flows have been consistently below projected cash flows then management has to investigate the reason for it and assess whether the current cash flow projections are realistic or require adjustment. *[IAS 36.34]*.

IAS 36 states that the cash flows should be based on the most recent budgets and forecasts for a maximum of five years because reliable forecasts are rarely available for a longer period. If management is confident that its projections are reliable and can demonstrate this from past experience, it may use a longer period. *[IAS 36.35]*. In using budgets and forecasts, management is required to consider whether these really are the best estimate of economic conditions that will exist over the remaining useful life of the asset. *[IAS 36.38]*. It may be appropriate to revise forecasts where the economic environment or conditions have changed since the most recent financial budgets and forecasts were approved by management.

Cash flows for the period beyond that covered by the forecasts or budgets assume a steady, declining or even negative rate of growth. An increase in the rate may be used if it is supported by objective information. *[IAS 36.36]*.

Therefore, only in exceptional circumstances should an increasing growth rate be used, or should the period before a steady or declining growth rate be assumed to extend to more than five years. This five year rule is based on general economic theory that postulates above-average growth rates will only be achievable in the short-term, because such above-average growth will lead to competitors entering the market. This increased competition will, over a period of time, lead to a reduction of the growth rate, towards the average for the economy as a whole. IAS 36 suggests that entities will find it difficult to exceed the average historical growth rate for the products, countries or markets over the long term, say twenty years. *[IAS 36.37]*.

This stage of the impairment review illustrates the point that it is not only fixed assets that are being assessed. The future cash flows to be forecast are all cash flows – receipts from sales, purchases, administrative expenses, etc. It is akin to a free cash flow valuation of a business with the resulting valuation then being compared to the carrying value of the assets in the CGU.

The cash flow forecast should include three elements:

- cash inflows from the continuing use of the asset;
- the cash outflows necessary to generate these cash inflows, including cash outflows to prepare the asset for use, that can either be directly attributed, or allocated on a reasonable and consistent basis; and
- the net cash flows, if any, that the entity may receive or pay for the disposal of the asset at the end of its useful life. *[IAS 36.39]*.

Cash flows can be estimated by taking into account general price changes caused by inflation, or on the basis of stable prices. If inflation is excluded from the cash flow then the discount rate selected must also be adjusted to remove the inflationary effect. *[IAS 36.40]*. Generally, entities will use whichever method is most convenient to them that is consistent with the method they use in their budgets and forecasts. It is, of course, fundamental that cash flows and discount rate are both estimated on a consistent basis.

To avoid the danger of double counting, the future cash flows exclude those relating to financial assets, including receivables and liabilities such as payables, pensions and provisions. *[IAS 36.43]*. However, 4 above notes that paragraph 79 allows the inclusion of such assets and liabilities for practical reasons, in which case the cash flows must be reflected as well, and includes a discussion of some of the assets and liabilities that may or may not be reflected together with the implications of so doing. *[IAS 36.79]*.

The expected future cash flows of the CGU being assessed for impairment should not include cash inflows or outflows from financing activities or tax receipts or payments. This is because the discount rate used represents the financing costs and the future cash flows are themselves determined on a pre-tax basis. *[IAS 36.50, 51]*.

7.1.2 Cash inflows and outflows from improvements and enhancements

Whilst a part-completed asset must have the costs to complete it included in the cash flows, *[IAS 36.42]*, the general rule is that future cash flows should be forecast for CGUs or assets in their current condition. Forecasts should not include estimated future cash inflows or outflows that are expected to arise from improving or enhancing the asset's performance. *[IAS 36.44]*. Projections in the cash flow should include costs of day-to-day servicing that can be reasonably attributed to the use of the asset (for overheads see 7.1.7 below). *[IAS 36.41]*.

While the restriction on enhanced performance may be understandable, it adds an element of unreality that is hard to reconcile with other assumptions made in the VIU process. For example, the underlying forecast cash flows that the standard requires management to use will obviously be based on the business as it is actually expected to develop in the future, growth, improvements and all. Producing a special forecast based on unrealistic assumptions, even for this limited purpose, may be difficult.

Nevertheless, paragraph 48 explicitly states that improvements to the current performance of an asset may not be included in the estimates of future cash flows until the entity incurs the expenditure that provides those improvements. The treatment of such expenditure is illustrated in Example 6 in the standard's accompanying section of illustrative examples. *[IAS 36.48]*. The implication of this requirement is that if an asset is impaired, and even if the entity is going to make the future expenditure to reverse that impairment, the asset will still have to be written down. Subsequently, the asset's impairment can be reversed, to the degree appropriate, after the expenditure has taken place. Reversal of asset impairment is discussed at 11.4 below.

IAS 36 makes it clear that for a part-completed asset, all expected cash outflows required to make the asset ready for use or sale should be considered in the estimate of future cash flows, and mentions a building under construction or a development project as examples. *[IAS 36.42]*. The standard is also clear that the estimate of future cash flows should not include the estimated future cash inflows that are expected to arise from the increase in economic benefits associated with cash outflows to improve or enhance an asset's performance until an entity incurs these cash outflows. *[IAS 36.48]*. This raises the question of what to do once a project to enhance or improve the performance of an asset or a CGU has commenced and it has started to incur cash outflows. In our view, once a project has been committed to and has substantively commenced, an entity should consider future cash inflows that are expected to arise from the increase in economic benefits associated with the cash outflows to improve or enhance the asset. Important to note is that it must take into consideration all future cash outflows required to complete the project and any risks in relation with the project, reflected either in the cash flows or the discount rate.

An assumption of new capital investment is in practice intrinsic to the VIU test. What has to be assessed are the future cash flows of a productive unit such as a factory or hotel. The cash flows, out into the far future, will include the sales of product, cost of sales, administrative expenses, etc. They must necessarily include capital expenditure as well, at least to the extent required to keep the CGU functioning as forecast. This is explicitly acknowledged as follows:

> 'Estimates of future cash flows include future cash outflows necessary to maintain the level of economic benefits expected to arise from the asset in its current condition. When a cash-generating unit consists of assets with different estimated useful lives, all of which are essential to the ongoing operation of the unit, the replacement of assets with shorter lives is considered to be part of the day-to-day servicing of the unit when estimating the future cash flows associated with the unit. Similarly, when a single asset consists of components with different estimated useful lives, the replacement of components with shorter lives is considered to be part of the day-to-day servicing of the asset when estimating the future cash flows generated by the asset.' *[IAS 36.49]*.

Accordingly, some capital expenditure cash flows must be built into the forecast cash flows. Whilst improving capital expenditure may not be recognised, routine or replacement capital expenditure necessary to maintain the function of the asset or assets in the CGU has to be included. Entities must therefore distinguish between maintenance, replacement and enhancement expenditure. This distinction may not be easy to draw in practice, as shown in the following example.

Example 20.11: Distinguishing enhancement and maintenance expenditure

A telecommunications company provides fixed line, telephone, television and internet services. It must develop its basic transmission infrastructure (by overhead wires or cables along streets or railway lines, etc.) and in order to service a new customer it will have to connect the customer's home via cable and other equipment. It will extend its network to adjoining areas and perhaps acquire an entity with its own network. It will also reflect changes in technology, e.g. fibre optic cables replacing copper ones.

Obviously, when preparing the budgets which form the basis for testing the network for impairment, it will make assumptions regarding future revenue growth and will include the costs of connecting those customers. However, its infrastructure maintenance spend will inevitably include replacing equipment with the current technology. There is no option of continuing to replace equipment with something that has been technologically superseded. Once this technology exists, it will be reflected in the entity's budgets and taken into account in its cash flows when carrying out impairment tests, even though this new equipment will enhance the performance of the transmission infrastructure.

Further examples indicate another problem area – the effects of future expenditure that the entity has identified but which the entity has not yet incurred. An entity may have acquired an asset with the intention of enhancing it in future and may, therefore, have paid for future synergies which will be reflected in the calculation of goodwill. Another entity may have plans for an asset that involve expenditure that will enhance its future performance and without which the asset may be impaired.

Examples could include:

- a TV transmission company that, in acquiring another, would expect to pay for the future right to migrate customers from analogue to digital services; or
- an aircraft manufacturer that expects to be able to use one of the acquired plants for a new model at a future point, a process that will involve replacing much of the current equipment.

In both cases the long-term plans reflect both the capital spent and the cash flows that will flow from it. There is no obvious alternative to recognising an impairment when calculating the CGU or CGU group's VIU as IAS 36 insists that the impairment test has to be performed for the asset in its current condition. This means that it is not permitted to include the benefit of improving or enhancing the asset's performance in calculating its VIU.

In the TV example above, it does not appear to matter whether the entity recognises goodwill or has a separable intangible right that it has not yet brought into use.

An entity in this situation may attempt to avoid or reduce an impairment write down by calculating the appropriate FVLCD, as this is not constrained by rules regarding future capital expenditure. As discussed above, these cash flows can be included only to the extent that other market participants would consider them when evaluating the asset. It is not permissible to include assumptions about cash flows or benefits from the asset that would not be available to or considered by a typical market participant.

7.1.3 Restructuring

The standard contains similar rules with regard to any future restructuring that may affect the VIU of the asset or CGU. The prohibition on including the results of restructuring applies only to those plans to which the entity is not committed. Again, this is because of the general rule that the cash flows must be based on the asset in its current condition so future events that may change that condition are not to be taken into account. *[IAS 36.44, 45]*. When an entity becomes committed to a restructuring (as set out in IAS 37 – see Chapter 28), IAS 36 then allows an entity's estimates of future cash inflows and outflows to reflect the cost savings and other benefits from the restructuring, based on the most recent financial budgets/forecasts approved by management. *[IAS 36.46, 47]*. Treatment of such a future restructuring is illustrated by Example 5 in the standard's accompanying section of illustrative examples. The standard specifically points out that the increase in cash inflows as a result of such a restructuring may not be taken into account until after the entity is committed to the restructuring. *[IAS 36.47]*.

Entities will sometimes be required to recognise impairment losses that will be reversed once the expenditure has been incurred and the restructuring completed.

7.1.4 Terminal values

In the case of non-current assets, a large component of value attributable to an asset or CGU arises from its terminal value, which is the net present value of all of the forecast free cash flows that are expected to be generated by the asset or CGU after the explicit forecast period. IAS 36 includes specific requirements if the asset is to be sold at the end of its useful life. The disposal proceeds and costs should be based on current prices and costs for similar assets, adjusted if necessary for price level changes if the entity has chosen to include this factor in its forecasts and selection of a discount rate. The entity must take care that its estimate is based on a proper assessment of the amount that would be received in an arm's length transaction. *[IAS 36.52, 53]*.

Whether the life of an asset or CGU is considered to be finite or indefinite will have a material impact on the terminal value. It is therefore of the utmost importance for management to assess carefully the cash generating ability of the asset or CGU and whether the period over which this asset or CGU is capable of generating cash flows is defined or not. While many CGUs containing goodwill will have an indefinite life, the same is not necessarily true for CGUs without allocated goodwill. For example, if a CGU has one main operating asset with a finite life, as in the case of a mine, the cash flow period may need to be limited to the life of the mine. Whether it would be reasonable to assume that an entity would replace the principal assets of a CGU and therefore whether it would be appropriate to calculate the terminal value under consideration of cash flows into perpetuity will depend on the specific facts and circumstances.

In the case of assets or CGUs with indefinite useful lives, the terminal value is calculated by having regard to the forecast maintainable cash flows that are expected to be generated by the assets or CGUs in the final year of the explicit forecast period ('the terminal year'). It is essential that the terminal year cash flows reflect maintainable cash flows as otherwise any material one-off or abnormal cash flows that are forecast for the terminal year will inappropriately increase or decrease the valuation.

The maintainable cash flow expected to be generated by the asset or CGU is then capitalised by a perpetuity factor based on either:

- the discount rate if cash flows are forecast to remain relatively constant; or
- the discount rate less the long term growth rate if cash flows are forecast to grow.

Care is required in assessing the growth rate to ensure consistency between the long term growth rate used and the assumptions used by the entity generally in its business planning. IAS 36 requires an entity to use in the VIU calculation a steady or declining growth rate for subsequent years, unless an increasing rate can be justified. This growth rate must not exceed the long-term average growth rate for the products, industries, or country or countries in which the entity operates, or for the market in which the asset is used, unless a higher rate can be justified. *[IAS 36.33]*.

7.1.5 Foreign currency cash flows

Foreign currency cash flows should first be estimated in the currency in which they will be generated and then discounted using a discount rate appropriate for that currency. An entity should translate the present value calculated in the foreign currency using the spot exchange rate at the date of the value in use calculation. *[IAS 36.54]*. This is to avoid the problems inherent in using forward exchange rates, which are based on differential interest rates. Using such a rate would result in double-counting the time value of money, first in the discount rate and then in the forward rate. *[IAS 36.BCZ49]*. However, the method requires an entity to perform, in effect, separate impairment tests for cash flows generated in different currencies but make them consistent with one another so that the combined effect is meaningful. This is an extremely difficult exercise. Many different factors need to be taken into account including relative inflation rates and relative interest rates as well as appropriate discount rates for the currencies in question. Because of this, the possibility for error is great and the greatest danger is understating the present value of cash outflows by using too high a discount rate. In practice, valuers may assist entities to obtain a sufficiently accurate result by assuming that cash flows are generated in a single currency even though they may be received or paid in another. Significantly, the rate used to translate the cash flows could well be different from that used to translate the foreign currency assets, goodwill and liabilities of a subsidiary at the period end. For example, a non-monetary asset such as an item of property, plant and equipment may be carried at an amount based on exchange rates on the date on which it was acquired but generates foreign currency cash flows. In order to determine its recoverable amount if there are indicators of impairment, IAS 21 – *The Effects of Changes in Foreign Exchange Rates* – states that the recoverable amount will be calculated in accordance with IAS 36 and the present value of the cash flows translated at the exchange rate at the date when that value was determined. *[IAS 21.25]*. IAS 21 notes that this may be the rate at the reporting date. The VIU is then compared to the carrying value and the item is then carried forward at the lower of these two values.

7.1.6 Internal transfer pricing

If the cash inflows generated by the asset or CGU are based on internal transfer pricing, the best estimate of an external arm's length transaction price should be used in estimating the future cash flows to determine the asset's or CGU's VIU. *[IAS 36.70]*. Note that this applies to any cash inflow once a CGU has been identified; it is not restricted to CGUs that have been identified because there is an active market for their outputs, which are described at 3.2 above.

In practice, transfer pricing may be based on estimated market values, perhaps with a discount or other adjustment, be a cost-based price or be based on specific negotiation between the group companies. Transfer prices will reflect the taxation consequences to the transferring and acquiring companies and the prices may be agreed with the relevant taxation authorities. This is especially important to multinational companies but may affect transfer prices within a single jurisdiction.

Transfer pricing is extremely widespread. The following example describes a small number of bases for the pricing and the ways in which it might be possible to verify whether they approximate to an arm's length transaction price (and, of course, even where the methodology is appropriate, it is still necessary to ensure that the inputs into the calculation are reasonable). An arm's length price may not be a particular price point but rather a range of prices.

Example 20.12: Transfer prices

A vehicle manufacturer, Entity A has a CGU that manufactures parts, transferring them to the vehicle assembly division. The parts are specific to the manufacturer's vehicles and the manufacturer cannot immediately source them on the open market. However, Entity A and other manufacturers in the sector do enter into parts supply arrangements with third parties, which set up the specific tooling necessary to manufacture the parts and could provide an external comparable transaction to help validate that the parts' internal transfer price is equivalent to an arm's length transaction. If not, the forecasts should be adjusted.

Entity B is an oil company that transfers crude oil from the drilling division to the refinery, to be used in the production of gasoline. There are market prices for crude oil that can be used to estimate cash inflows in the drilling division CGU and cash outflows for the refinery CGU.

7.1.7 Overheads and share-based payments

Projections in the cash flows should include overheads that are necessarily incurred to generate the cash inflow from continuing use and can be reasonably attributed to the use of the asset (or the CGU of which it is part). *[IAS 36.41].* This means that entities must take care to ensure that all relevant cash outflows are reflected in its impairment tests of CGUs. This is similar to the requirement that all assets, including goodwill and corporate assets that do not directly generate cash inflows, be tested for impairment by being allocated to CGUs and CGU groups.

Overheads often include salary and other employee costs which may include directors' costs, all of which should in principle be allocated to CGUs and CGU groups.

Many entities make internal charges, often called 'management charges', that purport to transfer overhead charges to other group entities. Care must be taken before using these charges as a surrogate for actual overheads as they are often based on what is permitted, e.g. by the taxation authorities, rather than actual overhead costs.

There is also a danger of double counting if a management charge includes an element for the use of corporate assets, e.g. an internal rent charge. In such cases, the management charge for the use of the corporate asset should be reversed and the impairment test carried out using an appropriate allocation of the corporate asset.

In many jurisdictions employees' remuneration packages include share-based payments. Share-based payments may be cash-settled, equity-settled or give the entity or the counterparty the choice of settlement in equity or in cash. In practice, many share-based payment transactions undertaken by entities are awards of equity settled shares and options. This gives the entity the possibility of rewarding employees without incurring any cash outflows and instead the cash costs are ultimately borne by the shareholders through dilution of their holdings.

When it comes to impairment assessment a question that often faces entities is whether and how to consider share-based payments in the recoverable amount, in particular the VIU calculation? IAS 36 itself does not provide any specific guidance in respect whether or how share-based payments should be considered in determining the recoverable amount.

As IAS 36 focuses on cash flows in determining VIU, it seems that expected cash outflows in relation to cash-settled share-based payments would need to be reflected in the VIU calculation. The future expected cash outflow could for example be reflected by the fair value of the award at the balance sheet date, through including the amount of that fair value expected to vest and be paid out in excess of the liability already recognised at that date in the VIU calculation. In such a case the liability already recognised at the date of the VIU determination would not form part of the carrying value of the CGU.

While theoretically this seems to be straight forward, in practice it can be quite a challenging and judgemental task in particular when the entity consists of a large number of CGUs. Share-based payments are in general awarded by the parent to employees within the group and any change in the value of share-based payments after the grant date might be disconnected from the performance of the employing CGU which may be relevant in assessing whether and how such changes in value and the ultimate expected cash flows are allocated to a specific CGU.

What is even less clear is whether an entity should reflect in the VIU calculation equity-settled share-based payments. Such share-based payment transactions will never result in any cash outflows for the entity, and therefore a literal reading of IAS 36 may indicate that they can be ignored in determining the recoverable amount. However, some might argue an entity should appropriately reflect all share-based payments in the VIU calculation, whether or not these result in a real cash outflow to the entity. Such share-based payments are part of an employee's remuneration package and therefore costs (in line with the treatment under IFRS 2 – *Share-based Payment*) by the entity for services from the employee, which are necessary as part of the overall cash flow generating capacity of the entity. Others may argue that they need to be considered through adjusting the discount rate in order to reflect a higher return to equity holders to counter the dilutive effects of equity settled share based payment awards.

The time span over which the recoverable amount is calculated is often much longer than the time period for which share-based payments have been awarded. Companies and their employees would often expect that further share-based payment awards will be made in the future during the time period used for the recoverable amount calculation. Depending on the respective facts and circumstances an entity would need to consider whether to include the effect of share-based payments over a longer period, considering the discussion above.

7.1.8 Events after the reporting period

Events after the reporting period and information received after the reporting period end should be considered in the impairment assessment only if changes in assumptions provide additional evidence of conditions that existed at the end of the reporting period. Judgement of all facts and circumstances is required to make this assessment.

Information available after the year end might provide evidence that conditions were much worse than assumed. Whether an adjustment to the impairment assessment would be required or not would depend on whether the information casts doubts on the assumptions made in the estimated cash flows for the impairment assessment.

Competitive pressures resulting in price reductions after the year end do not generally arise overnight but normally occur over a period of time and may be more a reaction to conditions that already existed at the year-end in which case management would reflect this in the year end impairment assessment.

IAS 10 – *Events after the Reporting Period* – distinguishes events after the reporting period into adjusting and non-adjusting events (see Chapter 36). IAS 10 mentions abnormally large changes after the reporting period in asset prices or foreign exchange rates as examples of non-adjusting events and therefore would in general not be a reason to update year end impairment calculations. The Standard implies that abnormally large changes must be due to an event that occurred after the period end and therefore more or less assumes that the cause of such abnormally large changes are not conditions that already existed at the year-end. However, management would need to carefully assess the reason for the abnormally large change and consider whether it is due to conditions which already existed at the period end.

7.1.9 'Traditional' and 'expected cash flow' approach to present value

7 above described the elements that must be taken into account in calculating VIU. IAS 36 requires an estimate of the future cash flows the entity expects to derive from the asset and the time value of money, represented by the current market risk-free rate of interest, to be reflected in the VIU calculation. However, the other elements that must be taken into account, all of which measure various aspects of risk, may be dealt with either as adjustments to the discount rate or to the cash flows. These elements are:

- expectations about possible variations in the amount or timing of those future cash flows;
- the price for bearing the uncertainty inherent in the asset; and
- other factors, such as illiquidity that market participants would reflect in pricing the future cash flows the entity expects to derive from the asset. *[IAS 36.30].*

Adjusting for these factors in the discount rate is termed the 'traditional approach' in Appendix A to IAS 36. Alternatively, under the 'expected cash flow' approach these adjustments are made in arriving at the risk-adjusted cash flows. Either method may be used to compute the VIU of an asset or CGU. *[IAS 36.A2].*

The traditional approach uses a single set of estimated cash flows and a single discount rate, often described as 'the rate commensurate with the risk'. This approach assumes that a single discount rate convention can incorporate all expectations about the future cash flows and the appropriate risk premium and therefore places most emphasis on the selection of the discount rate. *[IAS 36.A4].*

Due to the problems and difficulties around capturing and reflecting all of the variables into a single discount rate, IAS 36 notes that the expected cash flow approach may be the more effective measurement tool. *[IAS 36.A6, A7].*

The expected cash flow approach is a probability weighted net present value approach. This approach uses all expectations about possible cash flows instead of a single most likely cash flow and assigns probabilities to each cash flow scenario to arrive at a probability weighted net present value. The use of probabilities is an essential element of the expected cash flow approach. *[IAS 36.A10].* The discount rate then considers the risks and variability for which the cash flows have not been adjusted. Appendix A notes some downsides of this approach, e.g. that the probabilities are highly subjective and that it might be inappropriate for measuring a single item or one with a limited number of outcomes. Nonetheless, it considers the most valid objection to the method to be the costs of obtaining additional information when weighed against its 'greater reliability'. *[IAS 36.A10-13].*

Whichever method is used, an entity needs to ensure that consistent assumptions are used for the estimation of cash flows and the selection of an appropriate discount rate in order to avoid any double-counting or omissions.

7.2 Identifying an appropriate discount rate and discounting the future cash flows

Finally, although probably inherent in their identification, the forecast cash flows of the CGU have to be allocated to different periods for the purpose of the discounting step. The present value of these cash flows should then be calculated by discounting them. The discount rate is to be a pre-tax rate that reflects current market assessments of the time value of money and the risks specific to the asset for which the future cash flow estimates have not been adjusted. *[IAS 36.55].*

This means the discount rate to be applied should be an estimate of the rate that the market would expect on an equally risky investment. The standard states:

> 'A rate that reflects current market assessments of the time value of money and the risks specific to the asset is the return that investors would require if they were to choose an investment that would generate cash flows of amounts, timing and risk profile equivalent to those that the entity expects to derive from the asset.' *[IAS 36.56].*

Therefore, if at all possible, the rate is to be obtained from market transactions or market rates, which means the rate implicit in current market transactions for similar assets or the weighted average cost of capital (WACC) of a listed entity that has a single asset (or a portfolio of assets) with similar service potential and risks to the asset under review. *[IAS 36.56].* If such a listed entity could be found, care would have to be taken in using its WACC as the standard specifies for the VIU the use of a pre-tax discount rate that is independent of the entity's capital structure and the way it financed the purchase of the asset (see below). The effect of gearing and its effect on calculating an appropriate WACC is illustrated in Example 20.13.

Only in rare cases (e.g. property assets) can such market rates be obtained. If an asset-specific rate is not available from the market, surrogates should be used. *[IAS 36.A16]*. The discount rate that investors would require if they were to choose an investment that would generate cash flows of amounts, timing and risk profile equivalent to those that the entity expects to derive from the asset will not be easy to determine. IAS 36 suggests that, as a starting point, the entity may take into account the following rates:

(a) the entity's weighted average cost of capital determined using techniques such as the Capital Asset Pricing Model;

(b) the entity's incremental borrowing rate; and

(c) other market borrowing rates. *[IAS 36.A17]*.

Appendix A also gives the following guidelines for selecting the appropriate discount rate:

- it should be adjusted to reflect the specific risks associated with the projected cash flows (such as country, currency, price and cash flow risks) and to exclude risks that are not relevant; *[IAS 36.A18]*
- to avoid double counting, the discount rate does not reflect risks for which future cash flow estimates have been adjusted; *[IAS 36.A18]*
- the discount rate is independent of the entity's capital structure and the way it financed the purchase of the asset; *[IAS 36.A19]*
- if the basis for the rate is post-tax (such as a weighted average cost of capital), it is adjusted for the VIU calculation to reflect a pre-tax rate; *[IAS 36.A20]* and
- normally the entity uses a single discount rate but it should use separate discount rates for different future periods if the VIU is sensitive to different risks for different periods or to the term structure of interest rates. *[IAS 36.A21]*.

The discount rate specific for the asset or CGU will take account of the period over which the asset or CGU is expected to generate cash inflows and it may not be sensitive to changes in short-term rates – this is discussed in 2.1.4 above. *[IAS 36.16]*.

It is suggested that the incremental borrowing rate of the business is relevant to the selection of a discount rate. This could only be a starting point as the appropriate discount rate should be independent of the entity's capital structure or the way in which it financed the purchase of the asset. In addition, the incremental borrowing rate may include an element of default risk for the entity as a whole, which is not relevant in assessing the return expected from the assets.

In practice, many entities use the WACC to estimate the appropriate discount rate. The appropriate way to calculate the WACC is an extremely technical subject, and one about which there is much academic literature and no general agreement. The selection of the rate is obviously a crucial part of the impairment testing process and in practice it will probably not be possible to obtain a theoretically perfect rate. The objective, therefore, must be to obtain a rate which is sensible and justifiable. There are probably a number of acceptable methods of arriving at the appropriate rate and one method is set out below. While this illustration may appear to be quite complex, it has been written at a fairly general level as the calculation of the appropriate discount rate may be difficult and specialist advice may be needed.

Example 20.13: Calculating a discount rate

This example illustrates how to estimate a discount rate (WACC) for a CGU. As it is highly unlikely that a listed company with a similar risk profile to the CGU in questions exists, the WACC has to be simulated by looking at a hypothetical company with a similar risk profile.

When estimating the WACC for the CGU, the following three elements needs to be estimated:

- gearing, i.e. the ratio of market value of debt to market value of equity;
- cost of debt; and
- cost of equity.

Gearing can best be obtained by reviewing quoted companies operating predominantly in the same industry as the CGU and identifying an average level of gearing for such companies. The companies need to be quoted so that the market value of equity can be readily determined.

Where companies in the sector typically have quoted debt, the cost of such debt can be determined directly. In order to calculate the cost of debt for bank loans and borrowings more generally, one method is to take the rate implicit in fixed interest government bonds – with a period to maturity similar to the expected life of the assets being reviewed for impairment – and to add to this rate a bank's margin, i.e. the commercial premium that would be added to the bond rate by a bank lending to the hypothetical company in this sector. In some cases, the margin being charged on existing borrowings to the company in question will provide evidence to help with establishing the bank's margin. Obviously, the appropriateness of this will depend upon the extent to which the risks facing the CGU being tested are similar to the risks facing the company or group as a whole.

If goodwill or intangible assets with an indefinite life were being included in a CGU reviewed for impairment (see 8 and 10 below) the appropriate Government bond rate to use might have to be adjusted towards that for irredeemable bonds. The additional bank's margin to add would be a matter for judgement but would vary according to the ease with which the sector under review was generally able to obtain bank finance and, as noted above, there might be evidence from the borrowings actually in place of the likely margin that would be chargeable. Sectors that invest significantly in tangible assets such as properties that are readily available as security for borrowings, would require a lower margin than other sectors where such security could not be found so easily.

Cost of equity is the hardest component of the cost of capital to determine. One technique referred to in the standard, frequently used in practice and written up in numerous textbooks is the 'Capital Asset Pricing Model' (CAPM). The theory underlying this model is that the cost of equity is equal to the risk-free rate plus a multiple, known as the beta, of the market risk premium. The risk-free rate is the same as that used to determine the nominal cost of debt and described above as being obtainable from government bond yields with an appropriate period to redemption. The market risk premium is the premium that investors require for investing in equities rather than government bonds. There are also reasons why this rate may be loaded in certain cases, for instance to take account of specific risks in the CGU in question that are not reflected in its market sector generally. Loadings are typically made when determining the cost of equity for a small company. The beta for a quoted company is a number that is greater or less than one according to whether market movements generally are reflected in a proportionately greater (beta more than one) or smaller (beta less than one) movement in the particular stock in question. Most betas fall into the range 0.4 to 1.5.

Various bodies, such as The London Business School, publish betas on a regular basis both for individual stocks and for industry sectors in general. Published betas are in general levered, i.e. they reflect the level of gearing in the company or sector concerned (although unlevered betas (based on risk as if financed with 100% equity) are also available and care must be taken not to confuse the two).

In addition to the volatility expressed in the beta, investors also reflect the exposure of the stock to a limited niche sector or exposure to a limited customer base. As a result, size premium could be required when the CGU is smaller size compared to its direct competitors.

The cost of equity for the hypothetical company having a similar risk profile to the CGU is:

Cost of equity = risk-free rate + (levered beta × market risk premium) + size premium (if deemed required)

Having determined the component costs of debt and equity and the appropriate level of gearing, the WACC for the hypothetical company having a similar risk profile to the CGU in question is:

$$\text{WACC} = (1 - t) \times D \times \frac{g}{1+g} + E \times \left[1 - \frac{g}{1+g}\right]$$

where:

D is the cost of debt;
E is the cost of equity;
g is the gearing level (i.e. the ratio of debt to equity) for the sector; and
t is the rate of tax relief available on the debt servicing payments.

IAS 36 requires that the forecast cash flows are before tax and finance costs, though it is more common in discounted cash flow valuations to use cash flows after tax. However, as pre-tax cash flows are being used, the standard requires a pre-tax discount rate to be used. *[IAS 36.55].* This will theoretically involve discounting higher future cash flows (before deduction of tax) with a higher discount rate. This higher discount rate is the post-tax rate adjusted to reflect the specific amount and timing of the future tax flows. In other words, the pre-tax discount rate is the rate that gives the same present value when discounting the pre-tax cash flows as the post-tax cash flows discounted at the post-tax rate of return. *[IAS 36.BCZ85].*

Once the WACC has been calculated, the pre-tax WACC can be calculated. If a simple gross up is appropriate, it can be calculated by applying the fraction 1/(1–t). Thus, if the WACC comes out at, say, 10% the pre-tax WACC will be 10% divided by 0.7, if the relevant tax rate for the reporting entity is 30%, which will give a pre-tax rate of 14.3%. However, the standard warns that in many circumstances a gross up will not give a good enough answer as the pre-tax discount rate also depends on the timing of future tax cash flows and the useful life of the asset; these tax flows can be scheduled and an iterative process used to calculate the pre-tax discount rate. *[IAS 36.BCZ85].* The relationship between pre- and post-tax rates is discussed further at 7.2.2 below.

The selection of discount rates leaves considerable room for judgement in the absence of more specific guidance, and it is likely that many very different approaches will be applied in practice, even though this may not always be evident from the financial statements. However, once the discount rate has been chosen, the future cash flows are discounted in order to produce a present value figure representing the VIU of the CGU or individual asset that is the subject of the impairment test.

7.2.1 Discount rates and the weighted average cost of capital

The WACC is often used in practice. It is usually acceptable to auditors as it is supported by valuation experts and is an accepted methodology based on a well-known formula and widely available information. In addition, many entities already know their own WACC. However, it can only be used as a starting point for determining an appropriate discount rate and some of the issues that must be taken into account are as follows:

a) the WACC is a post-tax rate and IAS 36 requires VIU to be calculated using pre-tax cash flows and a pre-tax rate. In the majority of cases, converting the former into the latter is not simply a question of grossing up the post-tax rate by the effective tax rate;

b) an entity's own WACC may not be suitable as a discount rate if there is anything atypical about the entity's capital structure compared with 'typical' market participants;

c) the WACC must reflect the risks specific to the asset and not the risks relating to the entity as a whole, such as default risk; and

d) the entity's WACC is an average rate derived from its existing business, yet entities frequently operate in more than one sector. Within a sector, different types of projects may have different levels of risk (e.g. a start-up as against an established product).

These issues are discussed further below.

One of the most difficult areas in practice is the effect of taxation on the WACC. In order to determine an appropriate pre-tax discount rate it is likely to be necessary to adjust the entity's actual tax cash flows.

Ultimately, the appropriate discount rate to select is one that reflects current market assessments of the time value of money and the risks specific to the asset in question, including taxation. Such a rate is one that reflects 'the return that investors would require if they were to choose an investment that would generate cash flows of amounts, timing and risk profile equivalent to those that the entity expects to derive from the asset'. *[IAS 36.56]*.

7.2.2 Calculating a pre-tax discount rate

VIU is primarily an accounting concept rather than a business valuation of the asset or CGU. One fundamental difference is that IAS 36 requires pre-tax cash flows to be discounted using a pre-tax discount rate. Why not calculate VIU on a post-tax basis? The reason is the complexities created by tax losses carried forward, temporary tax differences and deferred taxes.

The standard explains in the Basis for Conclusions that, future income tax cash flows may affect recoverable amount. It is convenient to analyse future tax cash flows into two components:

(a) the future tax cash flows that would result from any difference between the tax base of an asset (the amount attributed to it for tax purposes) and its carrying amount, after recognition of any impairment loss. Such differences are described in IAS 12 as 'temporary differences'; and

(b) the future tax cash flows that would result if the tax base of the asset were equal to its recoverable amount. *[IAS 36.BCZ81]*.

The concepts are complex but it refers to the following issues.

An impairment test, say at the end of 2016, takes account of estimated future cash flows. The tax that an entity will pay in future years that will be reflected in the actual tax cash flows that it expects may depend on tax depreciation that the entity has already taken (or is yet to take) in respect of the asset or CGU being tested for impairment. The value of the asset to the business on a post-tax basis must take account of all tax effects including those relating to the past and not only those that will only arise in future.

Although these 'temporary differences' are accounted for as deferred taxation, IAS 12:

(i) does not allow entities to recognise all deferred tax liabilities or deferred tax assets;

(ii) does not recognise deferred tax assets using the same criteria as deferred tax liabilities; and

(iii) deferred tax is not recognised on a discounted basis.

Therefore, deferred taxation as provided in the income statement and statement of financial position is not sufficient to take account of the actual temporary differences relating to the asset or CGU.

At the same time, an asset valuation implicitly assumes that the carrying amount of the asset is deductible for tax. For example, if the tax rate is 25%, an entity must receive pre-tax cash flows with a present value of 400 in order to recover a carrying amount of 300. *[IAS 36.BCZ88]*. In principle, therefore, VIU on a post-tax basis would include the present value of the future tax cash flows that would result if the tax base of the asset were equal to its value in use. Hence, IAS 36 indicates that the appropriate tax base to calculate VIU in a post-tax setting, is the VIU itself. *[IAS 36.BCZ84]*. Therefore, the calculated VIU should also be used to derive the pre-tax discount rate. It follows from this that the 'tax cash flows' to be taken into account will be those reflected in the post-tax VIU, so they will be neither the tax cash flows available in relation to the asset (based on its cost) nor the actual tax cash flows payable by the entity.

For these reasons, the (then) IASC decided to require an enterprise to determine value in use by using pre-tax future cash flows and a pre-tax discount rate.

This means that there is a different problem, calculating an appropriate pre-tax discount rate because there are no observable pre-tax discount rates. Two important points must be taken into account:

- The pre-tax discount rate is not always the post-tax discount rate grossed up by a standard rate of tax. There are some circumstances in which a gross-up will give a reasonable approximation, discussed further at 7.2.4 below.
- The pre-tax discount rate is not the post-tax rate grossed up by the effects of the entity's actual tax cash flows. As discussed above, a post-tax discount rate such as the WACC is based on certain assumptions about the tax-deductibility of the asset and not the actual tax cash flows experienced by the entity.

Recognising this, paragraph BCZ85 of IAS 36 states that 'in theory, discounting post-tax cash flows at a post-tax discount rate and discounting pre-tax cash flows at a pre-tax discount rate should give the same result, as long as the pre-tax discount rate is the post-tax discount rate adjusted to reflect the specific amount and timing of the future tax cash flows'. *[IAS 36.BCZ85]*.

Therefore, the only accurate way to calculate a pre-tax WACC is to calculate the VIU by applying a post-tax rate to post-tax cash flows, tax cash flows being based on the allowances and charges available to the asset and to which the revenue is subject (see discussion at 7.2.3 below). The effective pre-tax rate is calculated by removing the tax cash flows and, by iteration, one can identify the pre-tax rate that makes the present value of the adjusted cash flows equal the VIU calculated using post tax cash flows.

Paragraph BCZ85 includes an example of how to calculate a pre-tax discount rate where the tax cash flows are irregular because of the availability of tax deductions for the asset's capital cost. See also the calculations in Example 20.14 below – (a) illustrates a calculation of a pre-tax discount rate. This is a relatively straightforward calculation for a single asset at the inception of the relevant project.

It may be far more complex at a later date. This is because entities may be attempting to calculate a discount rate starting with post-tax cash flows and a post-tax discount rate at a point in time when there are already temporary differences relating to the asset. A discount rate based on an entity's prospective tax cash flows may under- or overstate IAS 36's impairment charge unless it reflects these previous allowances or disallowances. This is the same problem that will be encountered if an entity attempts to test VIU using post-tax cash flows as described at 7.2.3 below.

A notional adjustment will have to be made if the entity is not paying tax because it is making, or has made, tax losses. It is unwarranted to assume that the post- and pre-tax discount rates will be the same if the entity pays no tax because of its own tax losses as this will be double counting. It is taking advantage of the losses in the cash flows but excluding that value from the assets of the CGU.

Entities may attempt to deal with the complexity of determining a pre-tax rate by trying to calculate VIU on a post-tax basis but this approach means addressing all of the many difficulties that have been identified by the IASB and the reasons why it mandated a pre-tax approach in testing for impairment in the first place.

Some approximations and short cuts that may give an acceptable answer in practice are dealt with at 7.2.4 below.

7.2.3 Calculating VIU using post-tax cash flows

Because of the challenges in calculating an appropriate pre-tax discount rate and because it aligns more closely with their normal business valuation approach, some entities attempt to perform a VIU calculation based on a post-tax discount rate and post-tax cash flows.

In support of the post-tax approach, the example in paragraph BCZ85 of IAS 36, which explains how to calculate a pre-tax discount rate, is mistakenly understood as a methodology for a post-tax VIU calculation using an entity's actual tax cash flows.

Entities that try a post-tax approach generally use the year-end WACC and estimated post-tax cash flows for future years that reflect the actual tax that they expect to pay in those years. A calculation on this basis will only by chance correspond to an impairment test in accordance with IAS 36 because it is based on inappropriate assumptions, i.e. it does not take account of the temporary differences that affect the entity's future tax charges and will not be based on the assumption that the VIU is tax deductible. Some include in the post-tax calculation the benefit of tax deductions or tax losses by bringing them into the cash flows in the years in which the tax benefit is expected to be received. In these cases the calculation will not correctly take account of the timing differences reflected in the tax cash flows and may not accurately reflect the differences created by the assumption that the VIU is tax deductible.

In order to calculate a post-tax VIU that is the equivalent to the VIU required by IAS 36, an entity will usually have to make adjustments to the actual tax cash flows or otherwise adjust its actual post-tax cash flows.

There are two approaches that can give a post-tax VIU that is equivalent to IAS 36's pre-tax calculation:

(1) Post-tax cash flows based on notional tax cash flows. The assumptions that need to be made are the same as those used in calculating a pre-tax discount rate as described in paragraph BCZ85. Therefore, there must be no temporary differences associated with the asset which means including only the future cash flows that would result if the tax base of the asset were equal to its VIU. In addition, no account is taken of the existing tax losses of the entity. Both of these assumptions will probably mean making appropriate notional adjustments.

(2) Post-tax cash flows reflecting actual tax cash flows. The relevant deferred tax asset or liability, discounted as appropriate, should be treated as part of the net assets of the relevant CGU.

It is very important to note that these are methodologies to determine IAS 36's required VIU and they will only be acceptable if the result can be shown to be materially the same as a pre-tax impairment calculation as required by IAS 36.

Note that for illustrative purposes all of the following examples assume that there is no headroom, i.e. the NPV of the relevant cash flows is exactly equal to the carrying value of the asset. This is to make it easier to observe the relationship between pre- and post-tax calculations. See 7.2.5 below for worked examples including headroom.

Example 20.14: Impairment calculations using pre- and post-tax cash flows and discount rates

The following examples illustrate impairment calculations using pre- and post-tax cash flows and discount rates.

(a) Comparing pre- and post-tax rates

An entity has invested €2,139 in a facility with a 10 year life. Revenue and operating costs are expected to grow by 5% annually. The net present value of the post-tax future cash flows, discounted at the WACC of 8.1%, is equal to the cost of the plant.

The budgeted pre-tax cash flows are as follows:

Year	1	2	3	4	5	6	7	8	9	10
	€	€	€	€	€	€	€	€	€	€
Revenues	500	525	551	579	608	638	670	703	739	776
Operating expenses	200	210	220	232	243	255	268	281	296	310
Pre-tax cash flow	300	315	331	347	365	383	402	422	443	466

The following tax amortisation and tax rate apply to the business:

Tax and accounting depreciation	straight line
Tax rate	30%

These apply to the budgeted cash flows as follows:

Year	1	2	3	4	5	6	7	8	9	10
	€	€	€	€	€	€	€	€	€	€
Tax amortisation	214	214	214	214	214	214	214	214	214	214
Taxation	26	30	35	40	45	51	56	62	69	75
Post-tax cash flow	274	285	296	307	320	332	346	360	374	390

The pre-tax rate can be calculated using an iterative calculation and this can be compared to a gross up using the standard rate of tax. The NPV using these two rates is as follows:

Pre-tax rate (day 1) – iterative calculation	10.92%
Cost of investment at NPV future cash flows	€2,139
Standard gross up (day 1) (8.1% ÷ 70%).	11.57%
NPV at standard gross up	€2,077

The NPV of the pre-tax cash flows at 11.57% is €2,077. This is only 2.9% lower than the number calculated using the true pre-tax rate. In many circumstances, this difference would not have a material effect.

If the tax and accounting depreciation are straight line then the distortion introduced by a standard gross-up can be relatively small and could be of less significance to an impairment test than, for example, the potential variability in cash flows. See also 7.2.4 below.

(b) *Comparing pre- and post-tax rates when the asset is impaired*

Assume that the facility is much less successful than had previously been assumed and that the revenues are 20% lower than the original estimates. The pre- and post-tax cash flows are as follows.

Year	1	2	3	4	5	6	7	8	9	10
	€	€	€	€	€	€	€	€	€	€
Revenues	400	420	441	463	486	511	536	563	591	621
Operating expenses	200	210	220	232	243	255	268	281	296	310
Pre-tax cash flow	200	210	221	232	243	255	268	281	295	310
Tax amortisation	214	214	214	214	214	214	214	214	214	214
Taxation	(4)	(1)	2	5	9	12	16	20	24	29
Post-tax cash flow	204	211	219	226	234	243	252	261	271	281

The asset is clearly impaired as the previous cash flows were just sufficient to recover the carrying amount of the investment. If these revised cash flows are discounted using the pre- and post-tax discount rates discussed above, the resulting impairment is as follows:

		NPV	Impairment	Deferred tax	Net loss
Original investment		2,139			
Pre-tax cash flows, discounted at pre-tax discount rate	10.92%	1,426	713	214	499
Post-tax cash flows discounted at post-tax discount rate	8.1%	1,569	570	171	399

Unless adjustments are made to the post-tax calculation, it will understate the impairment loss by 143 (pre-tax) and 100 (post-tax, assuming full provision for the deferred tax asset). This difference is the present value of the deferred tax on the actual impairment loss, a point explored in more detail in (d) below.

(c) *Impairment and variable tax cash flows*

The assumption of straight-line amortisation for taxation and accounting purposes does not reflect the circumstances of certain sectors, particularly where there are significant deductions for tax for the cost of the asset being tested for impairment, e.g. in the extractive sector. Impairment tests have to be calculated on finite life assets and variable tax cash flows. In many jurisdictions there are, or have been, substantial tax allowances for the construction of the asset but high rates of tax in the production phase.

The following example assumes that the entity gets a tax deduction for the cost of the asset in year 1. Once again, this assumes that in year 1 the cost of the investment is equal to the NPV of the cash flows.

Year	1	2	3	4	5	6	7	8	9	10
	€	€	€	€	€	€	€	€	€	€
Revenues	500	525	551	579	608	638	670	704	739	776
Operating expenses	200	210	220	232	243	255	268	281	296	310
Pre-tax cash flow	300	315	331	347	365	383	402	422	443	465
Tax amortisation	2,367									
Taxation	(620)	95	99	104	109	115	121	127	133	140
Post-tax cash flow	920	220	232	243	256	268	281	295	310	325

Assuming the same post-tax WACC of 8.1%, the pre-tax WACC is now considerably lower owing to the effect of the tax deduction in the first year. It can be calculated using an iterative process at 8.76%, rather than 10.92%, which is the pre-tax rate in (a) and (b) above. Therefore, the NPV of the pre- and post-tax cash inflows is €2,367 rather than €2,139 – the first year tax allowances enhance the VIU of the project. If the entity discounted the pre-tax cash flows at 11.57%, the post-tax rate grossed up at the standard rate of taxation, these cash flows would have a NPV of €2,077, which is approximately 12% lower than the actual NPV. It is clear that a standardised gross up will not give a reasonable approximation in these circumstances.

(d) Correctly measuring impairment using post-tax information

If an entity applies a post-tax rate to post-tax cash flows, what can it do to ensure that impairment is correctly measured in accordance with IAS 36?

Assume, in example (c) above, that cash inflows decline by 20% commencing at the beginning of year 2. The net present value of the pre-tax cash flows at 8.76% is €1,516.

Year	2	3	4	5	6	7	8	9	10
	€	€	€	€	€	€	€	€	€
Pre-tax cash flow	210	221	232	243	255	268	281	295	310
Taxation	63	66	69	73	77	80	84	89	93
Post-tax cash flows	147	155	163	170	178	188	197	206	217

The asset's book value, assuming straight line depreciation over 10 years, is €2,130. Impairment calculated using pre-tax cash flows and discount rates is as follows:

		€
Original investment		2,367
Net book value (end of year 1)		2,130
Pre-tax cash flows, discounted at pre-tax discount rate	8.76%	1,516
Impairment		614
Deferred tax asset (reduction in deferred tax liability)		(184)
Net impairment loss		430

A post-tax calculation overstates the impairment, as follows:

		€
Original investment		2,367
Net book value (end of year 1)		2,130
Post-tax cash flows, discounted at post-tax discount rate	8.1%	1,092
Impairment – overstated by 424		1,038
Deferred tax asset (reduction in deferred tax liability)		(311)
Net impairment loss – overstated by 297		727

It can be seen that unless adjustments are made to the post-tax calculation, it will overstate the impairment loss. There are two ways in which the post-tax calculation can be adjusted so as to give the right impairment charge.

Method (1): Post-tax cash flows based on notional tax cash flows. The assumptions that need to be made are the same as those used in calculating a pre-tax discount rate. Therefore, there must be no temporary differences associated with the asset which means including only the future cash flows that would result if the tax base of the asset were equal to its VIU.

This means assuming that the VIU of the asset (1,516) is deductible for tax purposes in year 2. This would usually be calculated iteratively

Year	2	3	4	5	6	7	8	9	10
	€	€	€	€	€	€	€	€	€
Pre-tax cash flow	210	221	232	243	255	268	281	295	310
Deemed tax amortisation	1,516								
Taxation	(392)	66	69	73	77	80	84	89	93
Post-tax cash flows	602	155	163	170	178	188	197	206	217

The present value of the notional post-tax cash flows at the post-tax discount rate of 8.1% is now €1,516, i.e. the VIU of the asset is fully deductible for tax purposes, so the impairment charge, before taxation, is €614, which is the same impairment as calculated above under the pre-tax cash flow model.

Method (2): Post-tax cash flows reflecting actual tax cash flows as adjusted for deferred tax. Again, this is an iterative calculation.

Year	2	3	4	5	6	7	8	9	10
	€	€	€	€	€	€	€	€	€
Pre-tax cash flow	210	221	232	243	255	268	281	295	310
Deferred tax	(455)								
Taxation	63	66	69	73	77	80	84	89	93
Post-tax cash flows	147	155	163	170	178	188	197	207	217
Post-tax cash flows as adjusted for deferred tax	602	155	163	170	178	188	197	206	217

The net present value of the post-tax cash flows at the post-tax discount rate is €1,092. The NPV of the post-tax cash flows as adjusted for deferred tax (see bottom line in the table), which is the VIU of the asset being tested for impairment, is €1,516 and the gross deferred tax liability relating to the asset is 1,516 at 30%, i.e. €455. The NPV of €455, discounted for one year at the post-tax discount rate of 8.1%, is €424. The deferred tax liability is discounted for one year due to the assumption used that all tax cash flows take place at the end of the year. Revised, the post-tax calculation is a follows:

		€
Original investment		2,367
Net book value (end of year 1)		2,130
Post-tax cash flows, discounted at post-tax discount rate	8.1%	1,092
Discounted deferred tax		424
Impairment (2,130 – (1,092 + 424))		614

The impairment loss will impact the deferred tax calculation in the usual way, i.e.614 at 30% = €184.

It will rarely be practicable to apply this methodology to calculate a discount rate for a CGU, as so many factors need to be taken into account. Even if all assets within the CGU are individually acquired or self-constructed, they may have a range of lives for depreciation and tax amortisation purposes, up to and including indefinite lives.

If goodwill is being tested it has an indefinite life whilst the underlying assets in the CGU or CGU group to which it has been allocated will usually have finite lives. It is likely that a reasonable approximation to the 'true' discount rate is the best that can be achieved and this is discussed further below.

7.2.4 Approximations and short cuts

The illustrations in Example 20.14 at 7.2.3 above are of course simplified, and in reality it is unlikely that entities will need to schedule all of the tax cash flows and tax consequences in order to calculate a pre-tax discount rate every time they perform an impairment review. In practice, it will probably not be possible to obtain a rate that is theoretically perfect – the task is just too intractable for that. The objective, therefore, must be to obtain a rate which is sensible and justifiable. Some of the following may make the exercise a bit easier.

An entity may calculate a pre-tax rate using adjusted tax cash flows based on the methods and assumptions described above and then apply that rate to discount pre-tax cash flows for the VIU calculation. This pre-tax rate will only need to be reassessed in following years when there is an external factor that affects risks, relevant market rates or the taxation basis of the asset or CGU.

The market may conclude that the risks relating to a particular asset are higher or lower than had previously been assumed. The market might consider risks to have reduced if, for example, a new project, process or product proves to be successful; the converse would also be true if there were previously unforeseen problems with an activity. Relevant changes in market rates are those for instruments with a period to maturity similar to the expected life of the assets being reviewed for impairment, so these will not necessarily need to be recalculated every time an impairment review is carried out. Short-term market rates may increase or decrease without affecting the rate of return that the market would require on long-term assets. Significant changes in the basis of taxation could also affect the discount rate, e.g. if tax deductions are applied or removed for all of a class of asset or activity. The discount rate will not necessarily be affected if the entity ceases to make taxable profits.

Valuation practitioners often use approximations when computing tax cash flows that may also make the task more straightforward. It may often be a valid approximation to assume that the tax amortisation of assets equals their accounting depreciation. Tax cash flows will be based on the relevant corporate tax rate and the forecast earnings before interest and taxation to give post-tax 'cash flows' that can then be discounted using a post-tax discount rate. The circumstances in which this could lead to a material distortion (perhaps in the case of an impairment test for an individual asset) will probably be obvious. This approach is consistent with the overall requirement of IAS 36, which is that the appropriate discount rate to select is one that reflects current market assessments of the risks specific to the asset in question.

The circumstances in which a standardised gross up at the corporation tax rate will give the relevant discount rate are:

- no growth in cash flows;
- a perpetuity calculation; and
- tax cash flows that are a constant percentage of total cash flows.

As long as these conditions remain unchanged, it will be straightforward to determine the discount rate for an impairment review at either the pre- or post-tax level.

There may be a close approximation to these criteria for some CGUs, particularly if accounting and tax amortisation of assets is similar. This is illustrated in Example 20.15 below – see the comparison of discount rates at the end of the example. A simple gross up may be materially correct. The criteria are unlikely to apply to the VIU of individual assets because these are rarely perpetuity calculations and the deductibility for tax purposes may not resemble accounting depreciation. If it is inappropriate to make such a gross up, an iterative calculation may be necessary to compute the appropriate pre-tax discount rate.

7.2.5 Disclosing pre-tax discount rates when using a post-tax methodology

If an entity calculates impairment using a post-tax methodology, it must still disclose the appropriate pre-tax discount rate. *[IAS 36.134(d)(v)].* There is a widely-held view that the relevant pre-tax discount rate is the rate that will discount the pre-tax cash flows to the same VIU as the post-tax cash flows discounted using the post-tax discount rate. This will not necessarily give an answer that is consistent with IAS 36, which makes it clear that pre- and post-tax discount rates will only give the same answer if 'the pre-tax discount rate is the post-tax discount rate adjusted to reflect the specific amount and timing of the future tax cash flows'. *[IAS 36.BCZ85].* It is no different in principle whether grossing up for a pre-tax rate or grossing up for disclosure purposes.

IAS 36 indicates that the appropriate tax base to calculate VIU in a post-tax setting, is the VIU itself. Therefore, the calculated (post-tax) VIU should also be used to derive the pre-tax discount rate. Depreciation for tax purposes must also be based on the calculated VIU.

Assuming that there is no impairment, the post-tax VIU will be higher than the carrying value of the asset. To calculate the pre-tax rate, the tax amortisation must be based on this figure. If tax amortisation is based on the cost of the asset, the apparent pre-tax discount rate will show a rising trend over the life of the asset as the ratio of pre- to post-tax cash flows changes and the effect of discounting becomes smaller. These effects can be very marked.

Example 20.15: Calculating pre-tax discount rates from post-tax VIUs

The assumptions underlying these calculations are as follows:

	€
Tax rate	25%
Post-tax discount rate	10%
Carrying amount beginning of year 1	1,500
Remaining useful life (years)	5
Straight line tax amortisation	

If the tax amortisation is based on the cost of the asset, the apparent pre-tax discount rate in each of the five years is as follows:

Year	1	2	3	4	5
	€	€	€	€	€
Revenue	1,000	1,020	1,040	1,061	1,082
Pre-tax cash flow	500	510	520	531	541
Tax amortisation	(300)	(300)	(300)	(300)	(300)
Taxation	50	53	55	58	60
Post-tax cash flows	450	458	465	473	481
NPV of post-tax cash flows using a 10% discount rate	1,756	1,484	1,175	827	437

The apparent pre-tax discount rate in any year will be the rate that discounts the pre-tax cash flows to the same NPV as the post-tax cash flows using the post-tax discount rate.

Apparent pre-tax discount rate	14.4%	15.4%	16.7%	19.1%	23.8%

It is quite clear that these apparent pre-tax discount rates are incorrect. Although pre-tax rates are not observable in the market, they are derived from market rates and would not increase in a mechanical fashion over the life of the asset.

The correct way to calculate the tax amortisation is based on the VIU. Years 1 and 2 are illustrated in the following table:

Year	1	2	3	4	5
	€	€	€	€	€
Revenue	1,000	1,020	1,040	1,061	1,082
Pre-tax cash flow	500	510	520	531	541
Year 1					
Notional tax amortisation (VIU 1,819/5)	(364)	(364)	(364)	(364)	(364)
Taxation	34	37	39	42	44
Post-tax cash flows	466	473	481	489	497
Year 2					
Notional tax amortisation (VIU 1,554/5)		(389)	(389)	(389)	(389)
Taxation		30	33	36	38
		480	487	495	503

The NPV of the post-tax cash flows, which is the VIU of the asset being tested for impairment, is €1,819 in year 1 and €1,554 in year 2, and the tax base allowing for a tax amortisation is based on these VIUs as well, both solved iteratively. Years 3, 4 and 5 are calculated in the same way, with tax amortisation based on the VIUs in the following table:

Year	1	2	3	4	5
	€	€	€	€	€
VIU (NPV of post-tax cash flows)	1,819	1,554	1,247	890	478
Annual depreciation for remaining term	364	389	416	445	478
	(1,819/5)	(1,554/4)	(1,247/3)	(890/2)	478
Pre-tax discount rate	13.1%	13.1%	13.2%	13.3%	13.3%

We can now compare the correct and incorrectly computed pre-tax discount rates. A rate based on grossing up the post-tax rate at the standard rate of tax is included for comparison.

Year	1	2	3	4	5
Post-tax discount rate	10%	10%	10%	10%	10%
Pre-tax discount rate – correct	13.1%	13.1%	13.2%	13.3%	13.3%
Pre-tax discount rate – incorrect, based on cost	14.4%	15.4%	16.7%	19.1%	23.8%
Pre-tax rate – approximation based on gross-up	13.3%	13.3%	13.3%	13.3%	13.3%

Note that in circumstances where tax amortisation is equal to accounting depreciation, a straightforward gross-up at the tax rate may give a satisfactory discount rate.

A rate based on actual post-tax cash flows will also vary from year to year depending on the tax situation.

Neither of these distortions is consistent with the principle that the pre-tax discount rate is the rate that reflects current market assessments of the time value of money and the risks specific to the asset. *[IAS 36.55]*.

7.2.6 Determining pre-tax rates taking account of tax losses

A common problem relates to the effect of tax losses on the impairment calculation, as they may reduce the total tax paid in the period under review or even eliminate it altogether. As noted above, however, a post-tax discount rate is based on certain assumptions about the tax-deductibility of the asset and not the actual tax cash flows. It is therefore unwarranted to assume that the post- and pre-tax discount rates will be the same if the entity pays no tax because of its own tax losses. The pre-tax rate should not include the benefit of available tax benefits and any deferred tax asset arising from tax losses carried forward at the reporting date must be excluded from the assets of the CGU if the impairment review is based on VIU. Similarly, if the entity calculates a post-tax VIU (see 7.2.3 above), it will also make assumptions about taxation and not base the calculation on the actual tax cash flows.

In many circumstances, the past history of tax losses affects the level of risk in the cash flows in the period under review, but one must take care not to increase the discount rate to reflect risks for which the estimated cash flows have been adjusted. *[IAS 36.A15]*. To do so would be to double count.

7.2.7 Entity-specific WACCs and different project risks within the entity

The entity's WACC is an average rate derived from its existing business, yet entities frequently operate in more than one sector. Within a sector, different types of projects may have different levels of risk, e.g. a start-up against an established product. Therefore, entities must ensure that the different business risks of different CGUs are properly taken into account when determining the appropriate discount rates.

It must be noted that these areas of different risk will not always coincide with the assets or CGUs that are being tested for impairment as this is a test for impairment and not necessarily a determination of business value.

Example 20.16: Different project risks and CGUs

An aircraft manufacturer makes both civilian and military aircraft. The risks for both sectors are markedly different as they are much lower for defence contractors than for the civilian market. The assembly plants for civilian and military aircraft are separate CGUs. In this sector there are entities that are based solely in one or other of these markets, i.e. they are purely defence or civilian contractors, so there will be a basis for identifying the different discount rates for the different activities. If the entity makes its own components then the defence CGU or CGUs could include the manufacturing activity if defence is vertically integrated and components are made solely for military aircraft. Manufacturing could be a separate CGU if components are used for both activities and there is an external market for the products.

A manufacturer of soft drinks uses the same plant to produce various flavours of carbonated and uncarbonated drinks. Because the market for traditional carbonated drinks is declining, it develops and markets a new uncarbonated 'health' drink, which is still produced using the same plant. The risks of the product are higher than those of the existing products but it is not a separate CGU.

Many sectors generate many new products but have a high attrition rate as most of their new products fail (pharmaceuticals and biotechnology, for example) and this is likely built into industry WACCs. If the risk of failure is not reflected in the industry WACC because the entity is not typical of the industry then either the WACC or the cash flows ought to be adjusted to reflect the risk (but not so as to double count).

7.2.8 Entity-specific WACCs and capital structure

The discount rate is a pre-tax rate that reflects current market assessments of the time value of money and the risks specific to the asset for which the future cash flow estimates have not been adjusted. *[IAS 36.55]*. An entity's own WACC may not be suitable as a discount rate if there is anything atypical about the entity's capital structure compared with 'typical' market participants. In other words, would the market assess the cash flows from the asset or unit as being riskier or less risky than the entity-wide risks reflected in the entity-wide WACC? Some of the risks that need to be thought about are country risk, currency risks and price risk.

Country risk will reflect the area in which the assets are located. In some areas assets are frequently nationalised by governments or the area may be politically unstable and prone to violence. In addition, the potential impact of physical instability such as weather or earthquakes, and the effects of currency volatility on the expected return from the asset, must be considered.

Two elements of price risk are the gearing ratio of the entity in question (if, for example, it is much more or less geared than average) and any default risk built into its cost of debt. However, IAS 36 explicitly notes that the discount rate is independent of the entity's capital structure and the way the entity financed the purchase of the asset, because the future cash flows expected to arise from an asset do not depend on these features. *[IAS 36.A19]*.

Example 20.17: Effect of entity default risk on its WACC

The formula for calculating the (post tax) WACC, as given in Example 20.13 at 7.2 above, is

$$\text{WACC} = (1-\text{t}) \times \text{D} \times \frac{\text{g}}{1+\text{g}} + \text{E} \times \left[1 - \frac{\text{g}}{1+\text{g}}\right]$$

where:

t is the rate of tax relief available on the debt servicing payments;
D is the pre-tax cost of debt;
E is the cost of equity;
g is the gearing level (i.e. the ratio of debt to equity) for the sector.

The cost of equity is calculated as follows:

Cost of equity = risk-free rate + (levered beta (β*) × market risk premium) + size premium (if deemed required)

Assume that the WACC of a typical sector participant is as follows:

Cost of equity	
Risk free rate	4%
Levered beta (β)	1.1
Market risk premium	6%
Cost of equity after tax (market risk premium × β + risk-free rate)	10.6%
Cost of debt	
Risk free rate	4%
Credit spread	3%
Tax rate	25%
Cost of debt (pre-tax)	7%
Cost of debt (post-tax)	5.25%
Capital structure	
Debt / (debt + equity)	25%
Equity / (debt + equity)	75%
Post-tax cost of equity (10.6 × 75%)	8%
Post-tax cost of debt (5.25 × 25%)	1.3%
WACC (Post tax, nominal)	9.3%

* The beta is explained in Example 20.13 at 7.2 above.

However, the company has borrowed heavily and is in some financial difficulties. Its gearing ratio is 75% and its actual cost of debt, based on the market price of its listed bonds, is 18% (13.5% after taking account of tax at 25%). This makes its individual post-tax WACC 12.8% (10.6 × 25% + 13.5 × 75%). As a matter of fact the entity's individual post-tax WACC might actually be even higher than 12.8% as this rate is based on a levered beta for a typical sector participant, while the entity's own beta will probably be higher. Having said this, the entity's WACC is not an appropriate WACC for impairment purposes because it does not represent a market rate of return *on the assets.* Its entity WACC has been increased by default risk.

Ultimately, it might be acceptable to use the entity's own WACC, but an entity cannot conclude on this without going through the exercise of assessing for risk each of the assets or units and concluding on whether or not they contain additional risks that are not reflected in the WACC.

7.2.9 Use of discount rates other than the WACC

IAS 36 allows an entity to use rates other than the WACC as a starting point in calculating the discount rate. These include:

(a) the entity's incremental borrowing rate; and

(b) other market borrowing rates. *[IAS 36.A17]*.

If borrowing rates (which are, of course, pre-tax) were used as a starting point, could this avoid some of the problems associated with adjusting the WACC for the effects of taxation? Unfortunately, this is unlikely. Debt rates reflect the entity's capital structure and do not reflect the risk inherent in the asset. A pure asset/business risk would be obtained from an entity funded solely by equity and equity risk premiums are always observed on a post-tax basis. Therefore, the risk premium that must be added to reflect the required (increased) return over and above a risk free rate by an investor will always have to be adjusted for the effects of taxation.

It must be stressed that the appropriate discount rate, which is the one that reflects current market assessments of the time value of money and the risks specific to the asset in question, ought to be the same whatever the starting point for the calculation of the rate.

Vodafone in its description of its pre-tax discount rate starts from the relevant bond (i.e. debt) rate (Extract 20.3 at 13.3 below). However, this note also describes many of the elements of the WACC calculation and how Vodafone has obtained these; it does not suggest that Vodafone has used anything other than an adjusted WACC as a discount rate for the purposes of the impairment test.

7.3 Differences between fair value and value in use

IFRS 13 is explicit that it does not apply to value in use, noting that its measurement and disclosure requirements do not apply to 'measurements that have some similarities to fair value, such as [..] value in use ...'. *[IFRS 13.7(c)]*. IAS 36 includes an explanation of the ways in which fair value is different to value in use. Fair value, it notes, 'reflects the assumptions market participants would use when pricing the asset. In contrast, value in use reflects the effects of factors that may be specific to the entity and not applicable to entities in general.' *[IAS 36.53A]*. It gives a number of specific examples of factors that are excluded from fair value to the extent that they would not be generally available to market participants: *[IAS 36.53A]*

- the additional value derived from the grouping of assets. IAS 36's example is of the creation of a portfolio of investment properties in different locations;
- synergies between the asset being measured and other assets;
- legal rights or legal restrictions that are specific only to the current owner of the asset; and
- tax benefits or tax burdens that are specific to the current owner of the asset.

By contrast, an entity calculating FVLCD may include cash flows that are not permitted in a VIU calculation but only to the extent that other market participants would consider them when evaluating the asset. For example, cash inflows and outflows relating to future capital expenditure could be included if they would be taken into account by market participants (see 7.1.2 above).

8 IMPAIRMENT OF GOODWILL

8.1 Goodwill and its allocation to cash-generating units

By definition, goodwill can only generate cash inflows in combination with other assets which means that an impairment test cannot be carried out on goodwill alone. Testing goodwill for impairment requires it to be allocated to a CGU or to a group of CGUs of the acquirer. This is quite different to the process by which CGUs themselves are identified as that depends on identifying the smallest group of assets generating largely independent cash inflows. The cash flows of the CGU, or those of a CGU group if appropriate, must be sufficient to support the carrying value both of the assets and any allocated goodwill.

IFRS 3 states that the acquirer measures goodwill acquired in a business combination at the amount recognised at the acquisition date less any accumulated impairment losses and refers to IAS 36. *[IFRS 3.B63]*. Initial recognition and measurement of goodwill acquired in a business combination is discussed in Chapter 9 at 6.

From the acquisition date, acquired goodwill is to be allocated to each of the acquirer's CGUs, or to a group of CGUs, that are expected to benefit from the synergies of the combination. This is irrespective of whether other assets or liabilities of the acquiree are assigned to those CGUs or group of CGUs. *[IAS 36.80]*.

The standard recognises that goodwill sometimes cannot be allocated on a non-arbitrary basis to an individual CGU, so permits it to be allocated to a group of CGUs. However, each CGU or group of CGUs to which the goodwill is so allocated must:

(a) represent the lowest level within the entity at which the goodwill is monitored for internal management purposes; and

(b) not be larger than an operating segment determined in accordance with IFRS 8 – *Operating Segments* – before aggregation. *[IAS 36.80, 81]*.

All CGUs or groups of CGUs to which goodwill has been allocated have to be tested for impairment on an annual basis.

The standard takes the view that applying these requirements results in goodwill being tested for impairment at a level that reflects the way an entity manages its operations and with which the goodwill would naturally be associated. Therefore, the development of additional reporting systems is typically not necessary. *[IAS 36.82]*.

This is, of course, consistent with the fact that entities do not monitor goodwill directly. Rather, they monitor the business activities, which means that goodwill allocated to the CGUs or CGU groups that comprise those activities will be 'monitored' indirectly. This also means, because goodwill is measured as a residual, that the goodwill balance in the statement of financial position may include elements other than goodwill relating to synergies. Some of these issues and their implications are discussed at 8.1.1 below. It also means that internally-generated goodwill will be taken into account when calculating the recoverable amount because the impairment test itself does not distinguish between purchased and internally-generated goodwill.

However, the difficulties with the concept of monitoring goodwill do not mean that entities can default to testing at an arbitrarily high level, e.g. at the operating segment level or for the entire entity by arguing that goodwill is not monitored.

IAS 36 emphasises that a CGU to which goodwill is allocated for the purpose of impairment testing may not coincide with the level at which goodwill is allocated in accordance with IAS 21 for the purpose of measuring foreign currency gains and losses (see Chapter 15). *[IAS 36.83]*. In many cases, the allocation under IAS 21 will be at a lower level. This will apply not only on the acquisition of a multinational operation but could also apply on the acquisition of a single operation where the goodwill is allocated to a larger cash generating unit under IAS 36 that is made up of businesses with different functional currencies. However, IAS 36 clarifies that the entity is not required to test the goodwill for impairment at that same level unless it also monitors the goodwill at that level for internal management purposes. *[IAS 36.83]*.

Groups that do not have publicly traded equity or debt instruments are not required to apply IFRS 8. In our view, these entities are still obliged to allocate goodwill to CGUs and CGU groups in the same way as entities that have to apply IFRS 8 as the restriction in IAS 36 refers to the definition of operating segment in IFRS 8, not to entities within scope of that standard.

IAS 36 does not provide any methods for allocating goodwill. This means that once the acquirer's CGUs or CGU groups that benefit from the synergies have been identified, discussed at 8.1.2 below, the entity must use an appropriate methodology to allocate that goodwill between them. Some approaches are described at 8.1.3 below.

8.1.1 The composition of goodwill

IAS 36 requires an entity to allocate goodwill to the CGUs that are expected to benefit from the synergies of the business combination, a challenging task because, in accounting terms, goodwill is measured as a residual (see Chapter 9 at 6). This means that in most cases goodwill includes elements other than the synergies on which the allocation to CGUs is based.

The IASB and FASB argue that what it refers to as 'core goodwill' is an asset. *[IFRS 3.BC323]*.

Core goodwill, conceptually, comprises two components: *[IFRS 3.BC313]*

(a) the fair value of the going concern element of the acquiree's existing business. 'The going concern element represents the ability of the established business to earn a higher rate of return on an assembled collection of net assets than would be expected if those net assets had to be acquired separately. That value stems from the synergies of the net assets of the business, as well as from other benefits (such as factors related to market imperfections, including the ability to earn monopoly profits and barriers to market entry – either legal or because of transaction costs – by potential competitors).'

(b) the fair value of the expected synergies and other benefits from combining the acquirer's and acquiree's net assets and businesses. Those synergies and other benefits are unique to each combination, and different combinations would produce different synergies and, hence, different values.

The problem for the allocation process is, firstly, that (a) relates to the acquired business taken as a whole and any attempt to allocate it to individual CGUs or CGU groups in the combined entity may well be futile. IFRS 3 refers to part of element (a) above, the value of an assembled workforce, which may not be recognised as a separate intangible asset. This is the existing collection of employees that permits the acquirer to continue to operate an acquired business from the acquisition date without having to hire and train a workforce. *[IFRS 3.B37]*. This has to be allocated to all the CGUs and CGU groups that benefit from the synergies.

Secondly, synergies themselves fall into two broad categories, operating synergies, which allow businesses to increase their operating income, e.g. through economies of scale or higher growth, or financial synergies that may result in a higher cash flow or lower cost of capital and includes tax benefits. Some financial synergies are quite likely to relate to the combined business rather than individual CGUs or CGU groups. Even though the expected future cash flows of the CGU being assessed for impairment should not include cash inflows or outflows from financing activities or tax receipts, *[IAS 36.50, 51]*, there is no suggestion in IAS 36 that these synergies cannot be taken into account in allocating goodwill.

In addition, goodwill measured as a residual may include amounts that do not represent core goodwill. IFRS 3 attempts to minimise these amounts by requiring an acquirer:

- to measure the consideration accurately, thus reducing any overvaluation of the consideration paid;
- to recognise the identifiable net assets acquired at their fair values rather than their carrying amounts; and
- to recognise all acquired intangible assets meeting the relevant criteria so that they are not subsumed into the amount initially recognised as goodwill. *[IFRS 3.BC317]*.

However, this process is not perfect. The acquirer might for example attribute value to potential contracts the acquiree is negotiating with prospective customers at the acquisition date but these are not recognised under IFRS 3 and neither are contingent assets, so their fair value is subsumed into goodwill. *[IFRS 3.B38, IFRS 3.BC276]*. Employee benefits and share-based payments are not recognised at their fair value. *[IFRS 3.26, 30]*. In practice, the most significant mismatch arises from deferred taxation, which is not recognised at fair value and can lead to the immediate recognition of goodwill. This is discussed at 8.3.1 below.

In summary, this means that the goodwill that is allocated to a CGU or CGU group may well include an element that relates to the whole of the acquired business or to an inconsistency in the measurement process as well as the synergies that follow from the acquisition itself. This point has been acknowledged by the IASB during the development of the standard:

> 'However, the Board was concerned that in the absence of any guidance on the precise meaning of "allocated on a reasonable and consistent basis", some might conclude that when a business combination enhances the value of all of the acquirer's pre-existing cash-generating units, any goodwill acquired in that business combination should be tested for impairment only at the level of the entity itself. The Board concluded that this should not be the case.' *[IAS 36.BC139]*.

In spite of the guidance in the standard, the meaning of the monitoring of goodwill as well as the allocation process remains somewhat elusive. Nevertheless, all goodwill arising in a business combination must be allocated to CGUs or CGU groups that benefit from the synergies, none may be allocated to CGUs or CGU groups that do not benefit and entities are not permitted to test at the level of the entity as a whole as a default. This means that identifying CGUs and CGU groups that benefit from the synergies is a crucial step in the process of testing goodwill for impairment.

8.1.2 Identifying synergies and identifying CGUs or CGU groups for allocating goodwill

IAS 36 requires goodwill to be allocated to CGUs or CGU groups that are expected to benefit from the synergies of the combination and only to those CGUs and CGU groups. This is irrespective of whether other assets or liabilities of the acquiree are assigned to those CGUs or group of CGUs. *[IAS 36.80].*

Operating synergies fall into two broad groups, those that improve margin (e.g. through cost savings and economies of scale) and those that give an opportunity for future growth (e.g. through the benefits of the combined talent and technology).

Example 20.18: Identifying synergies

In all of the following cases, the acquiring entity can identify the synergies and the CGU or CGU group that benefits from them. Goodwill will be allocated to the relevant CGU or CGU group.

- A mining entity (group) extracts a metal ore that does not have an active market until it has been through a smelting and refining process. The entity considers the CGU to comprise the smelter together with the individual mines. When the entity acquires a mine, the synergies relate to cost savings as the mine's fixed costs are already covered by the existing refining operations. Goodwill is therefore allocated to the CGU comprising the smelter, the existing mines and the newly acquired mine.
- An airline is subject to cost pressures common in the sector. It acquires another operation with similar international operations on the basis that it can reduce its workforce and asset base. It will combine its operational management, including its sales, reporting and human resources functions, into one head office and consolidate all aircraft maintenance in a single site that currently has capacity. These cost savings are the synergies of the business combination and goodwill would therefore be allocated to the CGU or group of CGUs that benefit from these cost savings.
- A global consumer products company, which allocates goodwill at the operating segment level, purchases a company best-known for razors and razor blades. It has not previously manufactured razors although its 'grooming products' operating segment does manufacture other shaving products. The acquirer expects that it will be able to increase sales of its shaving products through association with the target company's razors and through branding. No assets of the acquired business are allocated to the grooming products operating segment but this segment will benefit from the synergies of the business combination and therefore goodwill from the acquisition will be allocated to it.

The process is further illustrated in the following example which shows the differences for the purposes of testing impairment between the CGU/CGU groups to which goodwill is allocated and the identification of CGUs.

Example 20.19: Allocating goodwill and identifying CGUs

Entity A operates three different types of fish restaurant: fifteen restaurants, twenty five pubs that contain restaurants serving fish and forty fish bars. Each is separately branded, although the brand is clearly identified with the Entity A identity, e.g. the restaurant range is branded 'Fish by A'. Each brand is identified as a separate operating segment: restaurants, pubs and fish bars.

Entity A acquired Entity B, which had a similar range of restaurants and bars (thirty in total) although that entity had not applied any branding to the types of restaurant.

Entity A recognised goodwill on acquisition and determined that ten of Entity B's outlets were to be allocated to each of its brands where they would be rebranded and included in the relevant operating segment.

Each restaurant, pub or fish bar is a separate CGU because it has separately identifiable largely independent cash inflows.

Management notes that it manages the 'A' brand at group (entity) level. This is not appropriate for testing goodwill as IAS 36 states that CGUs or CGU groups to which goodwill is allocated cannot be larger than an operating segment determined in accordance with IFRS 8. Also, management monitors operating segments that correspond to the three individual brands to which it has allocated the acquired outlets.

There are costs that cannot be clearly identified as relating to an individual restaurant, including marketing costs, sourcing of fish for the different brands and bulk purchasing. However, these costs are related to the brands which underlie Entity A's operating segments and the branding is evidence that there are synergies at this level. It is appropriate to allocate goodwill to the operating segments in order to test it for impairment. This does not prevent the separate outlets being identified as CGUs as IAS 36 allows an apportionment of costs. The independence of cash inflows is decisive.

8.1.3 Measuring the goodwill allocated to CGUs or CGU groups

Although goodwill has to be allocated IAS 36 does not provide any allocation methodologies. One allocation method is a 'direct' method, which is based on the difference between the fair value of the net assets and the fair value of the acquired business (or portion thereof) to be assigned to the CGUs, thereby calculating goodwill directly by reference to the allocated net assets. However, this method will not allocate any goodwill to a CGU if no assets or liabilities are assigned to the CGU and, arguably, it will allocate too little goodwill to CGUs that may benefit disproportionately because of synergies with the acquired business. A method that does not have these shortcomings is a 'with and without' method that requires the entity to calculate the fair value of the CGU or CGU groups that are expected to benefit before and after the acquisition; the difference represents the amount of goodwill to be allocated to that reporting unit. This will take account of buyer-specific synergies that relate to a CGU or CGU group. These methods are illustrated in the following example.

Example 20.20: Allocating goodwill to more than one CGU

Entity A acquires Entity B for $50 million, of which $35 million is the fair value of the identifiable assets acquired and liabilities assumed. The acquisition is to be integrated into two of Entity A's CGUs with the net assets being allocated as follows.

	CGU 1	CGU 2	Total
	$m	$m	$m
Acquired identifiable tangible and intangible assets	25	10	35

In addition to the net assets acquired that are assigned to CGU 2, the acquiring entity expects CGU 2 to benefit from certain synergies related to the acquisition (e.g. CGU 2 is expected to realise higher sales of its products because of access to the acquired entity's distribution channels). There is no synergistic goodwill attributable to other CGUs.

Entity A calculates that the fair value of the acquired businesses allocated to CGU 1 and CGU 2 is $33 million and $17 million respectively. If goodwill is allocated to the CGUs based on the difference between the fair value of the net assets and the fair value of the acquired business, i.e. the direct method, the allocation would be as follows:

	CGU 1	CGU 2	Total
	$m	$m	$m
Acquired identifiable tangible and intangible assets	25	10	35
Fair value of acquired business allocated based on direct method	33	17	50
Goodwill assigned to CGUs	8	7	15

Alternatively, Entity A assigns goodwill to the CGUs based on the difference between the fair value of the net assets to be assigned and the fair value of the acquired business (or portion thereof), including the beneficial synergies that CGU 2 is expected to achieve. In this case, the fair value of the acquired business (or portion thereof) is determined using a 'with and without' method.

	CGU 1	CGU 2	Total
	$m	$m	$m
Fair value of CGU after acquisition	90	85	175
Fair value of CGU prior to acquisition	(62)	(63)	(125)
Fair value of acquired business allocated based on the 'with and without' method	28	22	50
Acquired identifiable tangible and intangible assets	(25)	(10)	(35)
Goodwill assigned to CGUs	3	12	15

In this case, the 'with and without' method may be more appropriate but this would depend on the availability and reliability of inputs. The 'direct' method may in other circumstances give a reasonable allocation of goodwill.

8.1.4 The effect of IFRS 8 – Operating Segments – on impairment tests

Goodwill to be tested for impairment cannot be allocated to a CGU or CGU group larger than an operating segment as defined by IFRS 8. *[IAS 36.80, 81, IFRS 8.11-12].* IFRS 8 is discussed in Chapter 34.

Organisations managed on a matrix basis cannot test goodwill for impairment at the level of internal reporting, if this level crosses more than one operating segment as defined in IFRS 8. *[IFRS 8.5].* In addition, the operating segments selected by the entities may not correspond with their CGUs.

These are entities that manage their businesses simultaneously on two different bases; for example, some managers may be responsible for different product and service lines while others are responsible for specific geographical areas. IFRS 8 notes that the characteristics that define an operating segment may apply to two or more overlapping sets of components for which managers are held responsible. Financial information is available for both and the chief operating decision maker may regularly review both sets of operating results of components. In spite of this, IFRS 8 requires the entity to characterise one of these bases as determining its operating segments. *[IFRS 8.10]*. Similarly, the entity will have to allocate its goodwill to CGUs or groups of CGUs no larger than operating segments even if this means an allocation of goodwill between segments on a basis that does not correspond with the way it is monitored for internal management purposes.

8.1.4.A Changes to operating segments

Changes to the way in which an entity manages its activities may result in changes to its operating segments. An entity may have to reallocate goodwill if it changes its operating segments, particularly if the entity has previously allocated goodwill at or close to segment level. Such a reallocation of goodwill is due to a change in circumstances and therefore will not be a change in accounting policy under IAS 8. *[IAS 8.34]*. This means that the previous impairment test will not need to be re-performed retrospectively.

In two situations, the disposal of an operation within a CGU and a change in the composition of CGUs due to a reorganisation, which are described at 8.5 below, IAS 36 proposes a reallocation based on relative values, unless another basis is more appropriate. A reallocation of goodwill driven by the identification of new operating segments is another form of reorganisation of the reporting structure, so the same methodology is appropriate. The entity should use a relative value approach, unless it can demonstrate that some other method better reflects the goodwill associated with the reorganised units (see 8.5.1 below). *[IAS 36.87]*.

This means a method based on the activities in their current state; e.g. an entity should not attempt to revert to the historical goodwill as it arose on the various acquisitions.

Generally an impairment review would be performed prior to the reallocation of goodwill.

An important issue in practice is the date from which the revised goodwill allocation applies. The goodwill allocation must be based on the way in which management is actually monitoring activities and cannot be based on management intentions. Under IFRS 8, operating segments are identified on the basis of internal reports that are regularly reviewed by the entity's chief operating decision maker in order to allocate resources to the segment and assess its performance. *[IFRS 8.5]*. Therefore, goodwill cannot be allocated to the revised operating segments until it can be demonstrated that the chief operating decision maker is receiving the relevant internal reports for the revised segments.

8.1.4.B Aggregation of operating segments for disclosure purposes

IFRS 8 allows an entity to aggregate two or more operating segments into a single reporting segment if this is 'consistent with the core principles' and, in particular, the segments have similar economic characteristics. *[IFRS 8.12]*. Whilst this is specifically in the context of segmental reporting, it might also, in isolation, have suggested that individual operating segments could also be aggregated to form one operating segment that would also apply for impairment purposes. The 'unit of accounting' for goodwill impairment is before any aggregation. *[IAS 36.80(b)]*.

8.1.5 Goodwill initially unallocated to cash-generating units

IFRS 3 allows a 'measurement period' after a business combination to provide the acquirer with a reasonable time to obtain the information necessary to identify and measure all of the various components of the business combination as of the acquisition date in accordance with the standard. *[IFRS 3.46]*. The measurement period ends as soon as the acquirer receives the information it is seeking and cannot exceed one year from the acquisition date. *[IFRS 3.45]*.

IAS 36 recognises that in such circumstances, it might also not be possible to complete the initial allocation of the goodwill to a CGU or group of CGUs for impairment purposes before the end of the annual period in which the combination is effected. *[IAS 36.85]*. Where this is the case the goodwill (or part of it) is left unallocated for that period. Goodwill must then be allocated before the end of the first annual period beginning after the acquisition date. *[IAS 36.84]*. The standard requires disclosure of the amount of the unallocated goodwill together with an explanation as to why that is the case (see 13.3 below).

The question arises as to whether the entity ought to test in such circumstances the goodwill acquired during the current annual period before the end of the current annual period or in the following year if the annual impairment testing date is before the allocation of goodwill is completed.

In our view, it will depend on whether an entity is able during the 'measurement period' and until the initial allocation of goodwill is completed to quantify goodwill with sufficient accuracy and allocate goodwill on a provisional basis to CGUs or group of CGUs.

If the entity is able to quantify goodwill with sufficient accuracy, a provisional allocation of goodwill could be made in the following circumstances:

(a) the entity might know that all goodwill relates to a single CGU or to a group of CGUs no larger than a single operating segment; or

(b) the entity may know that the initial accounting for the combination is complete in all material respects, although some details remain to be finalised.

In circumstances where a provisional allocation of goodwill could be made, an entity should, in our view, tests this provisional goodwill for impairment in accordance with IAS 36 during the annual period in which the acquisition occurred and in the following years annual impairment test, even if this is before the allocation of goodwill is completed.

In addition, we believe an entity should carry out an impairment test where there are indicators of impairment. This is the case even if the fair values have not been finalised and the goodwill amount is only provisional or goodwill has not necessarily been allocated to the relevant CGUs or CGU groups and the test therefore has to be carried out at a higher, potentially even at the reporting entity, level.

In our view, an entity would not need to test the goodwill for impairment until the allocation of goodwill has been finalised, if a provisional allocation of goodwill could not be made and there are no indications of impairment.

When the allocation of goodwill is finalised, in the first annual period after the acquisition date, the entity must consider appropriate actions.

In our view, the acquirer should test in some circumstances the final allocated goodwill for impairment retrospectively, on the basis that the test on provisional goodwill was in fact the first impairment test applying IAS 36. In the following cases an entity should update the prior year's impairment test retrospectively:

- the entity allocated provisional goodwill to CGUs, although it had not completed its fair value exercise, and tested provisional goodwill for impairment in accordance with IAS 36 (see above); or
- the entity did not allocate provisional goodwill to the related CGUs but there were indicators for impairment and the entity tested the provisional goodwill potentially at a different level to the ultimate allocation and the impairment test resulted in an impairment (see above).

If the entity did not allocate provisional goodwill to CGUs, there were indicators that the provisional goodwill may have been impaired and the impairment test at a higher, potentially entity, level, did not result in an impairment, the entity can choose whether to update the prior year's impairment test retrospectively, but is not required to do so.

In all other scenarios, the acquirer performs only a current year impairment test (i.e. after the allocation has been completed) on a prospective basis.

If the acquirer updates the prior year's impairment test as outlined above, this update could decrease the original goodwill impairment recognised. Such a decrease is an adjustment to the original goodwill impairment. This will not qualify as a reversal and does not violate the prohibition on reversing any goodwill impairments in IAS 36.124. See 11.3 below.

If an entity were to change its annual reporting date, it could mean that it has a shorter period in which to allocate goodwill as IAS 36 requires that allocation of goodwill for impairment purposes is completed by the end of the first annual period after the acquisition and not within 12 months as required by IFRS 3. *[IAS 36.84]*.

Example 20.21: Impact of shortened accounting period

Entity A prepares its financial statements for annual periods ending on 31 December. It acquired Entity B on 30 September 20X0. In accounting for this business combination in its financial statements for the year ended 31 December 20X0, Entity A has only been able to determine the fair values to be assigned to Entity B's assets, liabilities and contingent liabilities on a provisional basis and has not allocated the resulting provisional amount of goodwill arising on the acquisition to any CGU (or group of CGUs). During 20X1, Entity A changes its annual reporting date to June and is preparing its financial statements as at its new period end of 30 June 20X1. IFRS 3 does not require the fair values assigned to Entity B's net assets (and therefore the initial amount of goodwill) to be finalised by that period end, since Entity A has until 30 September 20X1 to finalise the values. However, IAS 36 would appear to require the allocation of the goodwill to CGUs for impairment purposes be completed by the date of the 30 June 20X1 financial statements since these are for the first annual period beginning after the acquisition date, despite the fact that the initial accounting under IFRS 3 is not yet complete. The entity would therefore need to test goodwill for impairment for the financial reporting period ending 30 June 20X1.

8.2 When to test cash-generating units with goodwill for impairment

IAS 36 requires a CGU or group of CGUs to which goodwill has been allocated to be tested for impairment annually by comparing the carrying amount of the CGU or group of CGUs, including the goodwill, with its recoverable amount. *[IAS 36.90]*. The requirements of the standard in relation to the timing of such an annual impairment test (which need not be at the period end) are discussed below. This annual impairment test is not a substitute for management being aware of events occurring or circumstances changing between annual tests that might suggest that goodwill is impaired. *[IAS 36.BC162]*. IAS 36 requires an entity to assess at each reporting date whether there is an indication that a CGU may be impaired. *[IAS 36.9]*. So, whenever there is an indication that a CGU or group of CGUs may be impaired it is to be tested for impairment by comparing the carrying amount, including the goodwill, with its recoverable amount. *[IAS 36.90]*.

If the carrying amount of the CGU (or group of CGUs), including the goodwill, exceeds the recoverable amount of the CGU (or group of CGUs), then an impairment loss has to be recognised in accordance with paragraph 104 of the standard (see 11.2 below). *[IAS 36.90]*.

8.2.1 Timing of impairment tests

IAS 36 requires an annual impairment test of CGUs or groups of CGUs to which goodwill has been allocated. The impairment test does not have to be carried out at the end of the reporting period. The standard permits the annual impairment test to be performed at any time during an annual period, provided the test is performed at the same time every year. Different CGUs may be tested for impairment at different times.

However, if some or all of the goodwill allocated to a CGU or group of CGUs was acquired in a business combination during the current annual period, that unit must be tested for impairment before the end of the current annual period. *[IAS 36.96]*.

The IASB observed that acquirers can sometimes 'overpay' for an acquiree, so that the amount initially recognised for the business combination and the resulting goodwill exceeds the recoverable amount of the investment. The Board was concerned that without this requirement it might be possible for entities to delay recognising such an impairment loss until the annual period after the business combination. *[IAS 36.BC173]*.

It has to be said that the wording of the requirement may not achieve that result, as the goodwill may not have been allocated to a CGU in the period in which the business combination occurs. The time allowed for entities to allocate goodwill may mean that this is not completed until the period following the business combination. *[IAS 36.84]*. The potential consequences of this are discussed at 8.1.5 above.

Consider also the following example.

Example 20.22: Testing for impairment of goodwill allocated in the period after acquisition after the annual impairment testing date

Entity A prepares its financial statements for annual reporting periods ending on 31 December. It performs its annual impairment test for all cash-generating units (CGUs) to which it has allocated goodwill at 30 September.

On 31 October 20X0, Entity A acquires Entity B. Entity A completes the initial allocation of goodwill to CGUs at 31 October 20X1, before the end of the annual reporting period on 31 December 20X1. Therefore, Entity A does not allocate the goodwill until after its annual date for testing goodwill, 30 September 20X1.

There are no indicators of impairment of goodwill at 31 December 20X0. If there is any such indicator, Entity A is required to test goodwill for impairment at that date, regardless of the date of its annual impairment test. At 31 December 20X0, the entity had not yet allocated its goodwill and did not test it for impairment, because there were no impairment indications at that time. During 20X1, Entity A receives the information it was seeking about facts and circumstances that existed as of the acquisition date, but it does not finalise the fair values assigned to Entity B's net assets (and therefore the initial amount of goodwill) until 31 October 20X1. IAS 36 requires Entity A to allocate the goodwill to CGUs by the end of the financial year. It does this by December 20X1.

In this case, at the time of carrying out its annual impairment tests at 30 September 20X1, Entity A has not yet allocated the goodwill relating to Entity B; therefore no impairment test of that goodwill needs to be carried out at that time, provided there are no indicators of impairment. When it does allocate the goodwill by December 20X1, the requirement to perform an impairment test for the CGUs to which this goodwill is allocated does not seem to be applicable since the goodwill does not relate to a business combination during the current annual period. It actually relates to a business combination in the previous period; it is just that it has only been allocated for impairment purposes in the current period. Nevertheless Entity A should perform an updated impairment test for the CGUs to which this goodwill is allocated for the purposes of its financial statements for the year ended 31 December 20X1 since this would seem to be the intention of the IASB. Not to do so, would mean that the goodwill would not be tested for impairment until September 20X2, nearly 2 years after the business combination.

IAS 36 requires the annual impairment test for a CGU to which goodwill has been allocated to be performed at the same time every year but is silent on whether an entity can change the timing of the impairment test. We believe a change in timing of the annual impairment test is acceptable if there are valid reasons for the change, the period between impairment tests does not exceed 12 months and the change is not made to avoid an impairment charge. The requirement that the period between impairment tests should not exceed 12 months could mean that an entity would need to test a CGU twice in a year if for example it would want to change the test from October to December. In our view it would in general not be appropriate to change the date of the impairment test again in consecutive years.

8.2.2 Sequence of impairment tests for goodwill and other assets

When a CGU to which goodwill has been allocated is tested for impairment, there may also be an indication of impairment of an asset within the unit. IAS 36 requires the entity to test the asset for impairment first and recognise any impairment loss on it before carrying out the impairment test for the goodwill, although this is unlikely to have any practical impact as the assets within the CGU by definition will not generate separate cash flows. An entity will have to go through the same process if there is an indication of an impairment of a CGU within a group of CGUs containing the goodwill. The entity must test the CGU for impairment first, and recognise any impairment loss for that CGU, before testing the group of CGUs to which the goodwill is allocated. *[IAS 36.97-98].*

8.2.3 Carry forward of a previous impairment test calculation

IAS 36 permits the most recent detailed calculation of the recoverable amount of a CGU or group of CGUs to which goodwill has been allocated to be carried forward from a preceding period provided all of the following criteria are met:

(a) the assets and liabilities making up the CGU or group of CGUs have not changed significantly since the most recent recoverable amount calculation;

(b) the most recent recoverable amount calculation resulted in an amount that exceeded the carrying amount of the CGU or group of CGUs by a substantial margin; and

(c) based on an analysis of events that have occurred and circumstances that have changed since the most recent recoverable amount calculation, the likelihood that a current recoverable amount determination would be less than the current carrying amount of the CGU or group of CGUs is remote. *[IAS 36.99].*

The Basis for Conclusions indicates that the reason for this dispensation is to reduce the costs of applying the impairment test, without compromising its integrity. *[IAS 36.BC177].* However, clearly it is a matter of judgement as to whether each of the criteria is actually met.

8.2.4 Reversal of impairment loss for goodwill prohibited

Once an impairment loss has been recognised for goodwill, IAS 36 prohibits its reversal in a subsequent period. *[IAS 36.124].* The standard justifies this on the grounds that any reversal 'is likely to be an increase in internally generated goodwill, rather than a reversal of the impairment loss recognised for the acquired goodwill', and IAS 38 prohibits the recognition of internally generated goodwill. *[IAS 36.125].* The impairment test itself though does not distinguish between purchased and internally generated goodwill.

8.3 Impairment of assets and goodwill recognised on acquisition

There are a number of circumstances in which the fair value of assets or goodwill acquired as part of a business combination may be measured at a higher amount through recognition of deferred tax or notional tax benefits. This raises the question of how to test for impairment and even whether there is, in fact, a 'day one' impairment in value. In other circumstances, deferred tax assets may or may not be recognised as part of the fair value exercise and this, too, may affect subsequent impairment tests of the assets and goodwill acquired as part of the business combination.

8.3.1 Testing goodwill 'created' by deferred tax for impairment

As described in Chapter 31 at 12, the requirement of IAS 12 to recognise deferred tax on all temporary differences arising on net assets acquired in a business combination may have an impact on the amount of goodwill recognised. In a business combination, there is no initial recognition exemption for deferred tax and the corresponding accounting entry for a deferred tax asset or liability forms part of the goodwill arising or the bargain purchase gain recognised. *[IAS 12.22(a)].* Where an intangible asset, which was not recognised in the acquiree's financial statements, is acquired in a business combination and the intangible's tax base is zero, a deferred tax liability based on the fair value of the intangible and the prevailing tax rate will be recognised. The corresponding debit entry will increase goodwill. This then begs the question of how to consider this in the VIU when performing an impairment test on that goodwill and whether there is indeed an immediate impairment that would need to be recognised. We explore the issues in the following examples.

Example 20.23: Apparent 'day one' impairment arising from recognition of deferred tax in a business combination

Entity A, which is taxed at 40%, acquires Entity B for €100m in a transaction that is a business combination. For simplicity assume the only asset of the entity is an intangible asset with a fair value of €60m.

It is assumed that the entity cannot get a deduction for tax purposes for the goodwill and the intangible asset, as is often the case for assets that arise only on consolidation. It also assumes that the fair value of the intangible asset does not reflect the benefits of any tax deductions had the asset been tax deductible, which may not be an appropriate assumption and is discussed further below.

The fair value and tax base of the intangible are as follows:

	Fair value	*Tax base*
	€m	€m
Intangible asset	60	nil

This will give rise to the following initial entries on consolidation:

	€m	€m
Goodwill (balance)	64	
Intangible asset	60	
Deferred tax liability[1]		24
Cost of investment		100

[1] 40% of €60m

Of the goodwill of €64m, €24m is created through deferred tax on the intangible asset.

The carrying value of the consolidated assets of the subsidiary (excluding deferred tax) is now €124m consisting of goodwill of €64m and the intangible asset of €60m. However the fair value of the subsidiary is only €100m. Clearly €24m of the goodwill arises solely from the recognition of deferred tax. However, IAS 36.50, explicitly requires tax to be excluded from the estimate of future cash flows used to calculate any impairment. This raises the question of whether there should be an immediate impairment write-down of the assets to €100m.

We think that an immediate write down of goodwill created by deferred tax is unlikely to have been the intention of IAS 36 because certain assumptions about taxation have been incorporated into the carrying amount of goodwill that are represented by the deferred tax liability recorded in relation of the intangible asset recognised on consolidation. In order to remove all tax effects from the CGU, the carrying amount of goodwill that relates to taxation and the deferred tax liability should be removed for impairment testing purposes; otherwise it might not be possible to determine the appropriate pre-tax discount rate. This means, in effect, that as at the point of acquisition, the goodwill can be reduced by the deferred tax liability recorded on consolidation in order to test that goodwill for impairment. As a result, the entity does not have to recognise an immediate loss.

Not recognising an immediate loss is consistent with the fact that the goodwill due to deferred tax that is being recognised as part of this acquisition is not part of 'core goodwill' (see 8.1.1 above), but is a consequence of the exceptions in IFRS 3 to the basic principle that assets and liabilities be measured at fair value, deferred tax being one of these exceptions (see 8.1.1 above and Chapter 9 at 5.6.2).

Another way of describing this is the lack of tax basis inherent in the asset has already been reflected in the fair value assigned to the asset. As a result, the incremental fair value of the deferred tax liability is nil. Goodwill is reduced by the nominal versus fair value difference of the deferred tax liability which in this case is the full amount of the deferred tax liability related to the intangible.

Continuing with this simplified example, if it is assumed that the intangible asset is amortised over a finite useful life then the deferred tax relating to that asset (€24m in this example) will be released over that life with the effect that the net amount charged to the income statement of €36m (total amortisation less deferred tax, €60m – €24m) will be the same as if the amortisation charge were tax deductible.

At future impairment testing dates, one would adjust for any remaining deferred tax liability at the impairment testing date that resulted in an increase in goodwill at the acquisition date.

In many jurisdictions the amortisation of intangible assets is deductible for tax purposes. This generates additional benefits, called tax amortisation benefit (TAB), impacting the fair value of the intangible. Therefore, the fair value as part of a business acquisition for many intangible assets includes assumptions about the tax amortisation benefit that would be available if the asset were acquired separately. For example, the value of a trademark using the 'relief from royalty' method would be assumed to be the net present value of post-tax future royalty savings, under consideration of TAB, in the consolidated financial statements, based on the hypothetical case of not owning the trademark. In order to reach the fair value of the asset, its value before amortisation would be adjusted by a tax amortisation factor reflecting the corporate tax rate, a discount rate and a tax amortisation period (this is the period allowed for tax purposes, which is not necessarily the useful life for amortisation purposes of the asset). In a market approach, fair value is estimated from market prices paid for comparable assets and the prices will contain all benefits of owning the assets, including any tax amortisation benefit.

This means that the difference between the tax amortisation benefit and the gross amount of the deferred tax liability remains part of goodwill.

This is demonstrated in the following example:

Example 20.24: Impairment testing assets whose fair value reflects tax amortisation benefits

Assume that the entity in Example 20.23 above has acquired an intangible asset that would be tax deductible if separately acquired but that has a tax base of zero.

The entity concludes that the fair value of the intangible will reflect the tax benefit, whose gross amount is €40m (€60m × 40% / 60%) but in calculating the fair value this will be discounted to its present value – say €30m. The initial entry is now as follows:

	€m	€m
Goodwill (balance)	46	
Intangible asset (€(60m + 30m))	90	
Deferred tax liability[1]		36
Cost of investment		100

[1] 40% of €90m

Overall, the assets that cost €100m will now be recorded at €136m, as against the total of €124m in Example 20.23. This increase has come about because of recognition of deferred tax of €12m, which is 40% of €30m, the assumed tax amortisation benefit.

In this example, only €6m goodwill results from the recognition of deferred tax [€46m – (€100m – €60m)] and its treatment is discussed above. The €6m represents the difference between the nominal amount of deferred tax of €36m and the fair value of the tax amortization benefit included in the intangible asset of €30m.

Unlike goodwill, the intangible asset will only have to be tested for impairment if there are indicators of impairment, if it has an indefinite useful life or if it has not yet been brought into use. *[IAS 36.10]*. If the intangible asset is being tested by itself for impairment, i.e. not as part of a CGU, its FVLCD would need to be determined on the same basis as for the purposes of the business combination, making the same assumptions about taxation. If FVLCD exceeds the carrying amount, there is no impairment.

However, as mentioned under 3.1 above, many intangible assets do not generate independent cash inflows as individual assets and so they are being tested as part of a CGU. Assuming there is no goodwill in the CGU being tested, then the VIU of the CGU might be calculated on an after-tax basis using notional tax cash flows assuming the asset's tax basis is equal to its VIU as discussed in 7.2.3 above.

When goodwill is a part of the CGU, the carrying amount of goodwill that results from the recognition of deferred tax (e.g. the €6m in Example 20.24 above) should be removed for impairment testing purposes. At future impairment testing dates, one should adjust for any remaining difference between the nominal deferred tax liability at the impairment testing date and the original fair value of the assumed tax basis embedded in the intangible asset carrying value that remains at the impairment testing date. This is consistent with the assumption that it could not have been the IASB's intention to have an immediate impairment at the time of acquisition and the same logic and approach is being carried forward from day 1 to future impairment tests.

Another way of describing this is the fair value of the deferred tax liability in the above example is equal to 30 being the tax amortization benefit embedded in the fair value of the intangible asset which tax amortization benefit does not actually exist given the intangible asset's tax basis is in fact nil. Goodwill is reduced by the nominal versus fair value difference of the deferred tax liability which in this case is 6. If one tests the CGU including both the intangible asset and goodwill for impairment, and when calculating VIU following the approach in 7.2.3 above on an after tax basis using notional tax cash flows assuming tax basis equal to VIU, this should not lead to day 1 impairment given the VIU calculation assumes full tax basis similar to what was assumed in the intangible carrying value and goodwill has been reduced by the nominal versus fair value difference of the deferred tax liability of 6.

An entity might not continue to make this adjustment if it becomes impracticable to identify reliably the amount of the adjustment, in which case the entity would use VIU without this adjustment or use FVLCD of the CGU as the recoverable amount.

This is illustrated in the following example:

Example 20.25: Impairment testing assets whose fair value reflects tax amortisation benefits (continued)

Assume that the entity in Example 20.24 above amortises the intangible asset on a straight line basis over 10 years. When the entity performs its impairment test at the end of year one the carrying amount of the deferred tax liability and remaining fair value of the tax benefits embedded in the carrying amount of the intangible are as follow:

	acquisition date	amortisation year 1	end of year 1
	€m	€m	€m
Intangible asset	60	6	54
Tax amortisation benefit (TAB)	30	3	27
Carrying value of intangible asset incl. TAB	90	9	81
Deferred tax[1]	36	3.6	32.4

1 year 1: 40% of €90m and end of year 1 40% of €81m

In the impairment test at the end of year 1, goodwill would be adjusted for the difference between the remaining nominal deferred tax liability of €32.4m and the remaining tax benefit reflected in the carrying value of the intangible asset of €27m resulting in an adjustment of €5.4m to goodwill. The impairment test would therefore incorporate goodwill of €40.6m (€46m – €5.4m).

The standard's disclosure requirements including the pre-tax discount rate, principally described at 13.3 below, will apply.

8.3.2 Deferred tax assets and losses of acquired businesses

Deferred tax assets arising from tax losses carried forward at the reporting date must be excluded from the assets of the CGU for the purpose of calculating its VIU. However, tax losses may not meet the criteria for recognition as deferred tax assets in a business combination, which means that their value is initially subsumed within goodwill. Under IFRS 3 and IAS 12, only acquired deferred tax assets that are recognised within the measurement period (through new information about circumstances at the acquisition date) are to reduce goodwill, with any excess once goodwill has been reduced to zero being taken to profit or loss. After the end of the measurement period, all other acquired deferred tax assets are taken to profit or loss. *[IFRS 3.67, IAS 12.68]*.

Unless and until the deferred tax asset is recognised, this raises the same problems as in 8.3.1 above. Certain assumptions regarding future taxation are built into the carrying value of goodwill and one should consider excluding these amounts from the carrying amount of the CGU when testing for impairment. However, if at a later date it transpires that any tax losses carry forwards subsumed in goodwill cannot be utilised then excluding these amounts from the carrying amount of the CGU for impairment testing is not appropriate and therefore might lead to an impairment.

8.4 Impairment testing when a CGU crosses more than one operating segment

While IAS 36 is clear that goodwill cannot be tested at a level that is larger than an operating segment determined in accordance with IFRS 8, it does not contain similar guidance for other assets. Therefore, in our view, the basic principle of IAS 36 applies, meaning assets or a group of assets are tested at the lowest level at which largely independent cash inflows can be identified. In practice a CGU determined based on the lowest level of independent cash inflows could be larger than an operating segment and therefore could cross more than one operating segment. For example, in the telecom industry, the entire telecom fixed line network may be one CGU, while at the same time an entity may identify its operating segments based on types of clients (e.g. individual clients, business clients, other operators, etc.). The general guidance in IAS 36 would require an entity to assess at each reporting date whether there are impairment indicators for the CGU and if such impairment indicators exist, perform a formal impairment assessment at CGU level. Regardless of whether a CGU crosses more than one operating segment, goodwill would need to be tested at a lower operating segment level. For this operating segment level impairment test, the assets of the larger CGU, in particular the cross operating segment assets e.g. the fixed line network in the example above, would need to be allocated to the operating segments. The application of these principles in practice can be complex and may require judgement.

8.5 Disposal of operation within a cash-generating unit to which goodwill has been allocated

If goodwill has been allocated to a CGU (or a group of CGUs) and the entity disposes of an operation within that CGU, IAS 36 requires that the goodwill associated with the operation disposed of is included in the carrying amount of the operation when determining the gain or loss on disposal. For that purpose, the standard requires that the amount to be included is measured on the basis of the relative values of the operation disposed of and the portion of the CGU retained, unless the entity can demonstrate that some other method better reflects the goodwill associated with the operation disposed of. *[IAS 36.86]*.

The standard refers to the 'relative values' of the parts without specifying how these are to be calculated. The recoverable amount of the part that it has retained will be based on the principles of IAS 36, i.e. at the higher of FVLCD and VIU. This means that the VIU or FVLCD of the part retained may have to be calculated as part of the allocation exercise on disposal.

In addition, the VIU and FVLCD of the part disposed of will be materially the same. This is because the VIU will consist mainly of the net disposal proceeds; it cannot be based on the assumption that the sale would not take place.

Example 20.26: Goodwill attributable to the disposal of an operation based on relative values

An entity sells for €100 an operation that was part of a CGU to which goodwill of €60 has been allocated. The goodwill allocated to the CGU cannot be identified or associated with an asset group at a level lower than that CGU, except arbitrarily. The recoverable amount of the portion of the CGU retained is €300. Because the goodwill allocated to the CGU cannot be non-arbitrarily identified or associated with an asset group at a level lower than that CGU, the goodwill associated with the operation disposed of is measured on the basis of the relative values of the operation disposed of and the portion of the CGU retained. Therefore, 25 per cent of the goodwill allocated to the CGU, i.e. €15 is included in the carrying amount of the operation that is sold.

It will not necessarily follow, for example, that the business disposed of generated 25% of the net cash flows of the combined CGU. Therefore, the relative value method suggested by the standard to be applied in most circumstances may be based on a mismatch in the valuation bases used on the different parts of the business, reflecting the purchaser's assessment of the value of the part disposed of at the point of sale rather than that of the vendor at purchase.

The standard allows the use of some other method if it better reflects the goodwill associated with the part disposed of. The IASB had in mind a scenario in which an entity buys a business, integrates it with an existing CGU that does not include any goodwill in its carrying amount and immediately sells a loss-making part of the combined CGU. It is accepted that in these circumstances it may be reasonable to conclude that no part of the carrying amount of the goodwill has been disposed of. *[IAS 36.BC156]*. The loss-making business being disposed of could, of course, have been owned by the entity before the acquisition or it could be part of the acquired business. However, the standard is not clear in what other circumstances a base other than relative values would better reflect the goodwill associated with the part disposed of. Any other method must take account of the basic principle, which is that this is an allocation of the carrying amount of goodwill and not an impairment test. It is not relevant, for example, that the part retained may have sufficient headroom for all of the goodwill without any impairment. One has to bear in mind that any basis of allocation of goodwill on disposal other than that recommended by the standard could be an indication that goodwill should have been allocated on a different basis on acquisition. It could suggest that there may have been some reasonable basis of allocating goodwill to the CGUs within a CGU group.

However, as demonstrated in Example 20.28 below, in some circumstances the allocation based on relative values might lead to an immediate impairment which is not intuitive and therefore an alternative method may, depending on facts and circumstances, therefore better reflect the goodwill associated with the operation disposed of. In our view, an approach that is based on current relative values of notional goodwill in the part disposed of and the part retained could, depending on facts and circumstances, be seen as an acceptable alternative for the goodwill allocation as illustrated in 8.5.1 below.

8.5.1 Changes in composition of cash-generating units

If an entity reorganises the structure of its operations in a way that changes the composition of one or more CGUs to which goodwill has been allocated, IAS 36 requires that the goodwill be reallocated to the units affected. For this purpose, the standard requires the reallocation to be performed using a relative value approach similar to that discussed above when an entity disposes of an operation within a CGU, unless the entity can demonstrate that some other method better reflects the goodwill associated with the reorganised units. *[IAS 36.87]*. Generally an impairment review would need to be performed prior to the reallocation of goodwill. As a result, if the reorganisation is triggered by underperformance in any of the affected operations, it cannot mask any impairment.

Example 20.27: Reallocation of goodwill to CGUs based on relative values

Goodwill of €160 had previously been allocated to CGU A. A is to be divided and integrated into three other CGUs, B, C and D. Because the goodwill allocated to A cannot be non-arbitrarily identified or associated with an asset group at a level lower than A, it is reallocated to CGUs B, C and D on the basis of the relative values of the three portions of A before those portions are integrated with B, C and D. The recoverable amounts of these portions of A before integration with the other CGUs are €200, €300 and €500 respectively. Accordingly, the amounts of goodwill reallocated to CGUs B, C and D are €32, €48 and €80 respectively.

When goodwill is reallocated based on relative values, it may be necessary to assess impairment immediately following the reallocation, as the recoverable amount of the CGUs will be based on the principles of IAS 36 and the reallocation could lead to an immediate impairment.

Again, the standard gives no indication as to what other methods might better reflect the goodwill associated with the reorganised units.

As illustrated in Example 20.28 below, the reallocation based on relative values could lead to an immediate impairment after the reallocation. This is not intuitive given that an impairment review would have been performed immediately before the goodwill reallocation and the restructuring of a business would not be expected to result in an impairment of goodwill.

In our view an allocation based on the relative current value of notional goodwill could, depending on facts and circumstances, be seen as an acceptable alternative to the IAS 36 suggested approach of relative values. This method calculates the current value of notional goodwill in each of the components to be allocated to new CGUs by performing a notional purchase price allocation for each affected CGU. To do this the components' fair value is compared with the fair value of the net identifiable assets to obtain the current value of notional goodwill. The carrying amount of the goodwill to be reallocated is then allocated to the new CGUs based on the relative current values of notional goodwill. This approach together with an example of circumstances under which the approach may be acceptable is illustrated in Example 20.28:

Example 20.28: Reallocation of goodwill to CGUs based on relative current values of notional goodwill

A US company acquired a European sub-group in 20X0 and recorded goodwill of €30 million. At the time Europe was a new market for the company and goodwill was fully allocated to one CGU A based on the geographic location Europe. Two years later the group fundamentally restructured its business in Europe. The restructuring resulted in the split of the existing CGU into three new CGUs B, C and D based on products. The goodwill of €30 million was assessed for impairment immediately prior to the restructuring and no impairment was identified. When the recoverable amount of each component of A allocated to B, C and D was assessed,

FVLCD was higher than VIU for each component allocated and is therefore used as basis for the recoverable amount based in the relative value approach. For simplicity purposes the examples assume that there are no material disposal costs and therefore the fair value of the components equals the fair value less costs of disposal. The fair value of the net identifiable assets and the fair value of each new CGU are given in the following table:

CGU	B €m	C €m	D €m	Total
Fair value of net identifiable assets	20	40	40	100
Book value of net identifiable assets	10	35	35	80
Fair value/FVLCD	40	80	40	160

The allocation based on the relative values of the three components of A allocated to B, C and D, as the required default method by the standard, would result in the following allocation of goodwill:

CGU	B €m	C €m	D €m	Total
Goodwill allocation	7.5	15	7.5	30
Book value of net identifiable assets	10	35	35	80
Total	17.5	50	42.5	110
Recoverable amount of CGU (FVLCD)	40	80	40	160
Immediate impairment	–	–	2.5	2.5

Goodwill of €7.5m (goodwill of €30m × recoverable amount €40m/overall recoverable amount €160m) is allocated to CGU B and D and €15m (goodwill of €30m × recoverable amount €80m/overall recoverable amount €160m) to CGU C. As can be seen, the relative value approach would result in an immediate impairment of €2.5m in CGU D. This is not intuitive, given that no impairment existed immediately prior to the restructuring and the restructuring of the business would not be expected to result in an immediate impairment. Another method of allocation might therefore better reflect the goodwill associated with the reorganised units. In our view, an allocation based on relative current values of notional goodwill could be an acceptable alternative method in this case. This would lead to the following allocation:

CGU	B €m	C €m	D €m	Total
CGU's fair value	40	80	40	160
Fair value net identifiable assets	20	40	40	100
Current value of notional goodwill	20	40	0	60
Historic goodwill allocated	10	20	–	30

This would allocate goodwill of €10m (goodwill of €30m × relative current value of notional goodwill €20 / overall current value of notional goodwill €60m) to CGU B, €20m (goodwill of €30m × relative current value of notional goodwill €40 / overall current value of notional goodwill €60m) to CGU C and €0m (goodwill of €30m × relative current value of notional goodwill €0 / overall current value of notional goodwill €60m) to CGU D. This allocation would not cause an immediate impairment directly after the reallocation as the following table shows.

CGU	B €m	C €m	D €m	Total
Goodwill allocation	10	20	0	30
Book value of net identifiable assets	10	35	35	80
Total	20	55	35	110
Recoverable amount (based on FVLCD)	40	80	40	160
Immediate impairment	–	–	–	–

The above example is based on a fact pattern where an existing CGU is split into three new CGUs. However, the method could be applied as well in circumstances where components of an existing CGU are allocated to other existing CGUs. The current values of notional goodwill used for reallocation purposes in such a case would need to be based only on the goodwill in the components being reallocated ignoring any goodwill in the existing CGUs to which the components are being allocated.

While the method illustrated above might be seen as an alternative method for goodwill reallocation it requires an entity to perform notional purchase price allocations for the components of each affected CGU and therefore potentially involves a significant time, effort and cost commitment. It is important to note that IAS 36 is not entirely clear whether an entity would need to use an alternative method that might better reflect the goodwill associated with the reorganised units, if the entity is aware of it, or whether an entity could always just default to the IAS 36.87 stated relative value method.

In practice, situations may be considerably more complex than Examples 20.26, 20.27 and 20.28 above. For example, after an acquisition, a combination of disposal of acquired businesses together with a reorganisation and integration may arise. The entity may sell some parts of its acquired business immediately but may also use the acquisition in order to replace part of its existing capacity, disposing of existing elements. In addition, groups frequently undertake reorganisations of their statutory entities. It is often the case that CGUs do not correspond to these individual entities and the reorganisations may be undertaken for taxation reasons so the ownership structure within a group may not correspond to its CGUs. This makes it clear how important it is that entities identify their CGUs and the allocation of goodwill to them, so that they already have a basis for making any necessary allocations when an impairment issue arises or there is a disposal.

9 NON-CONTROLLING INTERESTS – THE IMPACT ON GOODWILL IMPAIRMENT TESTING

The amount of goodwill recorded by an entity when it acquires a controlling stake in a subsidiary that is less than 100% of its equity depends on which of the two following methods have been used to calculate it. Under IFRS 3 an entity has a choice between two methods:

(i) Goodwill attributable to the non-controlling interests is not recognised in the parent's consolidated financial statements as the non-controlling interest is stated at its proportion of the net fair value of the net identifiable assets of the acquiree.

(ii) The non-controlling interest is measured at its acquisition-date fair value, which means that its share of goodwill will also be recognised.

Under method (i) above the carrying amount of that CGU comprises:

(a) both the parent's interest and the non-controlling interest in the identifiable net assets of the CGU; and

(b) the parent's interest in goodwill.

But part of the recoverable amount of the CGU determined in accordance with IAS 36 is attributable to the non-controlling interest in goodwill.

IFRS 3 allows both measurement methods. The choice of method is to be made for each business combination, rather than being a policy choice, and could have a significant effect on the amount recognised for goodwill. *[IFRS 3.19, IAS 36.C1]*.

Previous acquisitions under IFRS 3 (2007) were required to be accounted for using method (i) and were not restated on transition to the revised standard. *[IFRS 3.64]*.

These methods are described in more detail in Chapter 9 at 8.

The IASB itself has noted that there are likely to be differences arising from measuring the non-controlling interest at its proportionate share of the acquiree's net identifiable assets, rather than at fair value. First, the amounts recognised in a business combination for the non-controlling interest and goodwill are likely to be lower (as illustrated in the example given in Chapter 9 at 8.3). Second, if a CGU to which the goodwill has been allocated is subsequently impaired, any impairment of goodwill recognised through income is likely to be lower than it would have been if the non-controlling interest had been measured at fair value.

The Standard is clear that not all of the goodwill arising will necessarily be allocated to a CGU or group of CGUs which includes the subsidiary with the non-controlling interest. *[IAS 36.C2]*.

Guidance is given on the allocation of impairment losses:

(a) If a subsidiary, or part of a subsidiary, with a non-controlling interest is itself a CGU, the impairment loss is allocated between the parent and the non-controlling interest on the same basis as that on which profit or loss is allocated. *[IAS 36.C6]*.

(b) If it is part of a larger CGU, goodwill impairment losses are allocated to the parts of the CGU that have a non-controlling interest and the parts that do not on the following basis: *[IAS 36.C7]*

  (i) to the extent that the impairment relates to goodwill in the CGU, the relative carrying values of the goodwill of the parts before the impairment; and

  (ii) to the extent that the impairment relates to identifiable assets in the CGU, the relative carrying values of these assets before the impairment. Any such impairment is allocated to the assets of the parts of each unit pro-rata on the basis of the carrying amount of each asset in the part.

  In those parts that have a non-controlling interest the impairment loss is allocated between the parent and the non-controlling interest on the same basis as that on which profit or loss is allocated.

However, it is not always clear how an entity should test for impairment when there is a NCI. The issues include:

- calculating the 'gross up' of the carrying amount of goodwill because NCI is measured at its proportionate share of net identifiable assets and hence its share of goodwill is not recognised (see 9.1 below);
- allocation of impairment losses between the parent and NCI; and
- reallocation of goodwill between NCI and controlling interests after a change in a parent's ownership interest in a subsidiary that does not result in a loss of control.

Each of these issues arises in one or more of the following situations:

(a) NCI is measured on a proportionate share, rather than fair value;

(b) because of the existence of a control premium there are indications that it would be appropriate to allocate goodwill between the parent and NCI on a basis that is disproportionate to the percentage of equity owned by the parent and the NCI shareholders; and

(c) there are subsequent changes in ownership between the parent and NCI shareholders, but the parent maintains control.

Increases in the parent's share are discussed at 9.1.1 below and disposals at 8.5 above.

The Interpretations Committee considered these issues in 2010 but declined to propose an amendment to IAS 36 as part of the Annual Improvements. They were concerned that there could be possible unintended consequences of making any changes, and recommended that the Board should consider the implication of these issues as part of the IFRS 3 post-implementation review.[1] While these issues were not specifically addressed in the IFRS 3 post-implementation review, participants informed the Board that in their view the required impairment test is complex, time-consuming and expensive and involves significant judgements. The Board therefore decided to undertake research to consider improvements, in particular on whether there is scope for simplification when it comes to impairment testing. At the time of writing this research is still ongoing.

In the absence of any guidance, we consider that an entity is not precluded from grossing up goodwill on a basis other than ownership percentages if to do so is reasonable. A rational gross up will result in a goodwill balance that most closely resembles the balance that would have been recorded had non-controlling interest been recorded at fair value. This is explored further at 9.3 below.

9.1 Testing for impairment in entities with non-controlling interests measured at the proportionate share of net identifiable assets

If an entity measures NCI at its proportionate interest in the net identifiable assets of a subsidiary at the acquisition date, rather than at the fair value, goodwill attributable to the NCI is included in the recoverable amount of the CGU but is not recognised in the consolidated financial statements. To enable a like-for-like comparison, IAS 36 requires the carrying amount of a non-wholly-owned CGU to be notionally adjusted by grossing up the carrying amount of goodwill allocated to the CGU to include the amount attributable to the non-controlling interest. This notionally adjusted carrying amount is then compared with the recoverable amount. *[IAS 36.C3, C4].* If there is an impairment, the entity allocates the impairment loss as usual, first reducing the carrying amount of goodwill allocated to the CGU (see 11.2 below). However, because only the parent's goodwill is recognised, the impairment loss is apportioned between that attributable to the parent and that attributable to the non-controlling interest, with only the former being recognised. *[IAS 36.C8].*

If any impairment loss remains, it is allocated in the usual way to the other assets of the CGU *pro rata* on the basis of the carrying amount of each asset in the CGU (the allocation of impairment losses to CGUs is discussed at 11.2 below). *[IAS 36.104].*

These requirements are illustrated in the following example. *[IAS 36.IE62-68]*. Note that in these examples goodwill allocation and impairment is based on the ownership interests. At 9.3 below we discuss alternative allocation methodologies when there is a control premium.

Example 20.29: A CGU with goodwill and non-controlling interest

Entity X acquires an 80 per cent ownership interest in Entity Y for €1,600 on 1 January 20X0. At that date, Entity Y's identifiable net assets have a fair value of €1,500. Entity X recognises in its consolidated financial statements:

(a) goodwill of €400, being the difference between the cost of the business combination of €1,600 and the non-controlling interest of €300 (20% of €1,500) and the identifiable net assets of Entity Y of €1,500;

(b) Entity Y's identifiable net assets at their fair value of €1,500; and

(c) a non-controlling interest of €300.

At the end of 20X0 the carrying amount of Entity Y's identifiable assets has reduced to €1,350 (excluding goodwill) and Entity X determines that the recoverable amount of CGU Y is €1,000.

The carrying amount of CGU Y must be notionally adjusted to include goodwill attributable to the non-controlling interest, before being compared with the recoverable amount of €1,000. Goodwill attributable to Entity X's 80% interest in Entity Y at the acquisition date is €400. Therefore, goodwill notionally attributable to the 20% non-controlling interest in Entity Y at the acquisition date is €100, being (€400 ÷ 80% × 20%).

Testing CGU Y for impairment at the end of 20X0 gives rise to an impairment loss of €850 calculated as follows:

	Goodwill	Identifiable net assets	Total
	€	€	€
Carrying amount	400	1,350	1,750
Unrecognised non-controlling interest	100	–	100
Notionally adjusted carrying amount	500	1,350	1,850
Recoverable amount			1,000
Impairment loss			850

The impairment loss of €850 is allocated to the assets in the CGU by first reducing the carrying amount of goodwill to zero. Therefore, €500 of the €850 impairment loss for the CGU is allocated to the goodwill. However, because Entity X only holds a 80% ownership interest in Entity Y, it recognises only 80 per cent of that goodwill impairment loss (i.e. €400). The remaining impairment loss of €350 is recognised by reducing the carrying amounts of Entity Y's identifiable assets, as follows:

	Goodwill	Identifiable net assets	Total
	€	€	€
Carrying amount	400	1,350	1,750
Impairment loss	(400)	(350)	(750)
Carrying amount after impairment loss	–	1,000	1,000

Of the impairment loss of €350 relating to Entity Y's identifiable assets, €70 (i.e. 20% thereof) would be attributed to the non-controlling interest.

In this example the same result would have been achieved by just comparing the recoverable amount of €1,000 with the carrying amount of €1,750. However, what if the recoverable amount of the CGU had been greater than the carrying amount of the identifiable net assets prior to recognising the impairment loss?

Assume the same facts as above, except that at the end of 20X0, Entity X determines that the recoverable amount of CGU Y is €1,400. In this case, testing CGU Y for impairment at the end of 20X0 gives rise to an impairment loss of €450 calculated as follows:

	Goodwill €	Identifiable net assets €	Total €
Carrying amount	400	1,350	1,750
Unrecognised non-controlling interest	100	–	100
Notionally adjusted carrying amount	500	1,350	1,850
Recoverable amount			1,400
Impairment loss			450

All of the impairment loss of €450 is allocated to the goodwill. However, Entity X recognises only 80 per cent of that goodwill impairment loss, i.e. €360. This allocation of the impairment loss results in the following carrying amounts for CGU Y in the financial statements of Entity X at the end of 20X0:

	Goodwill €	Identifiable net assets €	Total €
Carrying amount	400	1,350	1,750
Impairment loss	(360)	–	(360)
Carrying amount after impairment loss	40	1,350	1,390

Of the impairment loss of €360, none of it is attributable to the non-controlling interest since it all relates to the majority shareholder's goodwill.

In this case the total carrying amount of the identifiable net assets and the goodwill has not been reduced to the recoverable amount of €1,400, but is actually less than the recoverable amount. This is because the recoverable amount of goodwill relating to the non-controlling interest (20% of [€500 – €450]) is not recognised in the consolidated financial statements.

9.1.1 Acquisitions of non-controlling interests measured at the proportionate share of net identifiable assets

As described above, in order to enable a like-for-like comparison, IAS 36 requires the carrying amount of a non-wholly-owned CGU to be notionally adjusted by grossing up the carrying amount of goodwill allocated to the CGU to include the amount attributable to the non-controlling interest.

What happens if the non-controlling interest is acquired by the entity so that it is now wholly owned? IFRS 10 now requires these purchases to be reflected as equity transactions, which means that there is no change to goodwill (see Chapter 7 at 3.3). *[IFRS 10.23].* Other methods have been used in the past that may still be reflected in the carrying amounts of goodwill. These could have partially or wholly reflected the fair value of the additional interest acquired.

No notional adjustment is required when the remaining non-controlling interest is acquired and the carrying amount of the unit, including the recognised goodwill, i.e. the goodwill paid in the acquisition where control was obtained, should be tested against 100% of the recoverable amount of the unit.

9.2 Testing for impairment in entities with non-controlling interests initially measured at fair value

The following examples in which the non-controlling interest is initially measured at fair value, are based on the Examples 7B and 7C in IAS 36's Illustrative Examples and illustrate the requirements for testing for impairment when non-controlling interest is initially measured at fair value. Note that in these examples goodwill impairment is allocated on the basis of the ownership interests. At 9.3 below we discuss alternative allocation methodologies when there is a control premium.

Example 20.30: Non-controlling interests measured initially at fair value

Entity X acquires an 80 per cent ownership interest in Entity Y for €2,100 on 1 January 20X0. At that date, Entity Y's identifiable net assets have a fair value of €1,500. Entity X chooses to measure the non-controlling interests at its fair value of €350. Goodwill is €950, which is the aggregate of the consideration transferred and the amount of the non-controlling interests (€2,100 + €350) less the net identifiable assets (€1,500).

(a) **The acquired subsidiary is a stand-alone CGU**

Entity Y is a CGU but part of the goodwill is allocated to other of Entity X's CGUs that are expected to benefit from the synergies of the combination. Goodwill of €450 is allocated to the Entity Y CGU and €500 to the other CGUs.

At the end of 20X0, the carrying amount of Entity Y's identifiable assets excluding goodwill has reduced to €1,350 and Entity X determines that the recoverable amount of CGU Y is €1,650.

	Goodwill	Identifiable net assets	Total
	€	€	€
Carrying amount	450	1,350	1,800
Recoverable amount			1,650
Impairment loss			150

Of the goodwill impairment loss of €150, €30 (20%) will be allocated to the non-controlling interest because the goodwill is allocated to the controlling interest and non-controlling interest on the same basis as profit or loss.

(b) **The acquired subsidiary is part of a larger CGU**

Entity Y becomes part of a larger CGU, Z. As before, €500 of the goodwill is allocated to other of Entity X's CGUs that are expected to benefit from the synergies of the combination. Goodwill of €450 is allocated to Z. Z's goodwill related to previous business combinations is €800.
At the end of 20X0, Parent determines that the recoverable amount of the Z CGU is €3,300. The carrying amount of its net assets excluding goodwill is €2,250.

	Goodwill	Identifiable net assets	Total
	€	€	€
Carrying amount	1,250	2,250	3,500
Recoverable amount			3,300
Impairment loss			200

All of the impairment loss of €200 is allocated to the goodwill. As the partially-owned subsidiary forms part of a larger CGU, the goodwill impairment loss must be allocated first to the parts of the cash-generating unit Z, and then to the controlling and non-controlling interests of Entity Y.

The impairment loss is allocated on the basis of the relative carrying values of the goodwill of the parts before the impairment. Entity Y is allocated 36% of the impairment (450 ÷ 1,250), in this case €72, of which €14.40 (20%) will be allocated to the non-controlling interest.

9.3 Testing for impairment in entities with non-controlling interests: alternative allocation methodologies

At 9 above we noted that in the absence of any guidance, we consider that an entity is not precluded from grossing up goodwill on a basis other than ownership percentages if to do so is reasonable. A rational gross up will result in a goodwill balance that most closely resembles the balance that would have been recorded had non-controlling interest been recorded at fair value.

There are therefore two broad methods of grossing up goodwill for impairment testing purposes when non-controlling interest is measured at its proportionate interest in the net identifiable assets of the subsidiary at the acquisition date:

(a) a 'mechanical' gross up of the controlling interest's goodwill on the basis of ownership interests; and

(b) a 'rational' gross up of the controlling interest's goodwill that takes into account the acquirer's control premium, if any.

Similarly, there are two broad methods of allocating goodwill impairment:

(a) a 'mechanical' allocation in which the impairment loss is allocated on the basis of ownership interests; and

(b) a 'rational' allocation, in which the entity applies an allocation methodology that recognises the disproportionate sharing of the controlling and non-controlling interests in the goodwill book value. The rational allocation takes into account the acquirer's control premium, if any.

When non-controlling interest is measured at its proportionate interest in the net identifiable assets of the subsidiary, there are alternatives for both the gross up and allocation methods. The following are all acceptable:

- rational gross up and rational allocation;
- rational gross up and mechanical allocation; and
- mechanical gross up and mechanical allocation.

A mechanical gross up and a rational allocation is not appropriate because a mechanical gross up results in the controlling and non-controlling interests having goodwill carrying values which are proportionate to their ownership interests.

Although the above methods of allocating goodwill and grossing up the NCI are acceptable, entities would be expected to be consistent year on year in the approach that they apply in testing any particular CGU or CGU group. This does not prevent an entity from applying different approaches to different CGUs or CGU groups, should that be appropriate in the circumstances. Both Examples 20.29 and 20.30 in 9.1 and 9.2 above are examples of mechanical allocation of impairment losses. In Example 20.30 the NCI is recorded initially at fair value, so there is no gross up methodology for goodwill but in Example 20.29, goodwill is grossed up mechanically.

The examples below illustrate the various methods. Depending on the circumstances, the gross up and allocation process could be much more complex than in the examples below. For example, where goodwill is being tested for impairment for a group of CGUs with multiple non-controlling interests measured at both fair value and proportionate interest in net identifiable assets, other (practical) approaches, not illustrated below may result in a reasonable measurement and allocation of goodwill impairment. Also, detailed records may need to be maintained to facilitate the gross up and allocation process.

Example 20.31: Measurement and allocation of goodwill impairment losses when there are non-controlling interests

An entity purchases 80% of a business for €160. The controlling and non-controlling interests share in profits on the basis of their ownership interests. The fair value of the net identifiable assets is €140 and the fair value of the non-controlling interest is €36. Goodwill is allocated to the business acquired.

Subsequent to the acquisition, the entity performs an impairment test and determines that the recoverable amount of the CGU is €160.

Scenario 1 – Non-controlling interest recorded at fair value

The entity elects to record the non-controlling interest at fair value, rather than the non-controlling interest's proportionate share of the recognised amounts of the acquiree's identifiable net assets. Accordingly, goodwill of €56 is recorded (= €160 + €36 – €140).

The initial carrying amount of the CGU is €196 (= €140 + €56). Assuming for simplicity that at the time of the impairment test the carrying amounts are unchanged, there is impairment of €36 (= €196 – €160). The entire impairment loss is applied against the goodwill balance of €56, reducing recorded goodwill to €20. The entity is required to allocate the impairment loss between the controlling and non-controlling interests.

Rational allocation: the goodwill impairment loss is allocated on a rational basis using a methodology that recognises the disproportionate sharing of the controlling and non-controlling interests in the goodwill book value. The rational allocation takes into account the acquirer's control premium, if any. Goodwill of €48 (= €160 – (€140 × 80%)) relates to the controlling interest and goodwill of €8 (= €36 – (€140 × 20%)) relates to the non-controlling interest. Therefore, a rational allocation method would result in impairment of €48 / €56 × €36 = €31 being allocated to the controlling interest and impairment of €8 / €56 × €36 = €5 being allocated to the non-controlling interest.

Mechanical allocation: the goodwill impairment loss is allocated on the basis of ownership interests. Therefore, impairment of €29 (= €36 × 80%) is allocated to the controlling interest while impairment of €7 (= €36 × 20%) is allocated to the non-controlling interest [Note 1].

Scenario 2 – Non-controlling interest recorded at fair value of identifiable assets

The entity elects to record non-controlling interest at its proportionate share of the fair value of the acquiree's identifiable net assets, i.e. €28 (= €140 × 20%). Therefore, goodwill of €48 is recorded (= €160 + €28 – €140). In this case, the carrying amount of the CGU is €188 (= €140 + €48). The entity is required to gross up the carrying amount of the CGU for the purposes of determining whether the CGU is impaired.

Rational gross up and rational allocation: goodwill attributable to the non-controlling interest is calculated by grossing up the recognised goodwill using a factor which takes into account the premium, if any, relating to the fact that the entity has a controlling 80% interest. Assume the relevant gross up factor results in goodwill attributable to the non-controlling interest of €8 [Note 2]. Therefore, the adjusted carrying value of the reporting unit is €196 (= €188 + €8). There is impairment of €36 (= €196 – €160). The total impairment of €36 is then allocated between the controlling and non-controlling interest on a rational basis. Using the same rational allocation methodology as in Scenario 1 results in impairment of €31 being allocated to the controlling interest and impairment of €5 being allocated to the non-controlling interest. The impairment of €5 associated with the non-controlling interest is not recognised because no goodwill is recorded in the financial statements relating to the non-controlling interest.

Rational gross up and mechanical allocation: as above, assume the relevant gross up factor results in goodwill attributable to the non-controlling interest of €8 and the adjusted carrying value of the reporting unit is €196 (= €188 + €8). The total impairment of €36 is then allocated between the controlling and non-controlling interest based on their ownership interests, resulting in impairment of €29 (= €36 × 80%) being allocated to the controlling interest and impairment of €7 (= €36 × 20%) being allocated to the non-controlling interest. The impairment of €7 associated with the non-controlling interest is not recognised because no goodwill is recorded in the financial statements relating to the non-controlling interest.

Mechanical gross up and mechanical allocation: goodwill attributable to the non-controlling interest is €12 (= €48 ÷ (80/20)). Therefore, the adjusted carrying value of the reporting unit is €200 (= €188 + €12). There is impairment of €40 (= €200 (adjusted carrying value) less €160 (= recoverable amount). Impairment of €32 (= 80% × €40) is allocated to the controlling interest and impairment of €8 (= 20% × €40) is allocated to the non-controlling interest. The impairment of €8 associated with the non-controlling interest is not recognised because no goodwill is recorded in the financial statements relating to the non-controlling interest.

Note [1]: As a further illustration of the difference between the two methods, suppose that the entity determined that the recoverable amount was nil. In this case, under the rational allocation in Scenario 1, the non-controlling interest of €36 would be reduced to zero, as an impairment of €8 to goodwill and an impairment of €28 (= 20% of €140) to other identifiable assets would be each allocated to non-controlling interest. However, under mechanical allocation in Scenario 1, the non-controlling interest would be reduced by €39 (= 20% of the carrying value of €196) with the result being a non-controlling interest debit balance of €3.

Note [2]: Note that this results in total adjusted goodwill of €56, which is the same goodwill figure that is recorded in Scenario 1 when non-controlling interest is recorded at fair value.

Chapter 20

10 IMPAIRMENT OF INTANGIBLE ASSETS WITH AN INDEFINITE USEFUL LIFE

IAS 38 makes the point that 'indefinite' does not mean 'infinite', and unforeseeable factors may affect the entity's ability and intention to maintain the asset at its standard of performance assessed at the time of estimating the asset's useful life. *[IAS 38.91]*. The requirements of IAS 36 for this type of asset can be summarised as follows:

1. all intangible assets with indefinite useful lives must be tested for impairment at least once per year and at the same time each year; *[IAS 36.10]*
2. any intangible asset with an indefinite useful life recognised during the reporting period must be tested for impairment before the end of the period; *[IAS 36.10]*
3. any intangible asset (regardless of whether it has an indefinite useful life or not) that is not yet available for use recognised during the reporting period must be tested for impairment before the end of the period; *[IAS 36.10-11]*
4. if an intangible asset that has an indefinite useful life or is not yet available for use can only be tested for impairment as part of a CGU, then that CGU must be tested for impairment at least annually; *[IAS 36.89]*
5. if there are indicators of impairment a period end test must also be performed; *[IAS 36.9]* and
6. for an intangible asset that has an indefinite useful life that is part of a CGU, there are specific concessions, discussed below, allowing an impairment test in a previous period to be used if that test showed sufficient headroom. *[IAS 36.24]*.

Any intangible asset not yet ready for use must be tested annually because its ability to generate sufficient future economic benefits to recover its carrying amount is usually subject to greater uncertainty before the asset is available for use than after it is available for use. *[IAS 36.11]*.

This will obviously affect any entity that capitalises development expenditure in accordance with IAS 38 where the period of development may straddle more than one accounting period. The requirement will also apply to in-process research and development costs recognised in a business combination (see Chapter 9 at 5.5.2.D).

An intangible asset with an indefinite useful life may generate independent cash inflows as an individual asset, in which case the impairment testing procedure for a single asset as set out in 7 above applies. Most intangible assets form part of the assets within a CGU, in which case the procedures relevant to testing a CGU as set out above apply. In particular IAS 36 makes it clear that if an intangible asset with an indefinite useful life, or any intangible asset not yet ready for use, is included in the assets of a CGU, then that CGU has to be tested for impairment annually. *[IAS 36.89]*. As with other assets, it may be that the FVLCD of the intangible asset with an indefinite useful life can be ascertained but the asset itself does not generate largely independent cash flows. If its individual FVLCD is lower than the carrying amount, this does not necessarily mean that the asset is impaired. The impairment test is still based on the CGU of which the asset is a part, and if the recoverable amount of the CGU is higher than the carrying amount of the CGU, there is no impairment loss.

IAS 36 allows a concession that applies to those intangible assets with an indefinite useful life that form part of a CGU, which is similar to the concession for goodwill. It allows the most recent detailed calculation of such an asset's recoverable amount made in a preceding period to be used in the impairment test in the current period if all of the following criteria are met:

(a) if the intangible asset is part of a CGU, the assets and liabilities making up that unit have not changed significantly since the most recent recoverable amount calculation;

(b) that calculation of the asset's recoverable amount exceeded its carrying amount by a substantial margin; and

(c) the likelihood that an updated calculation of the recoverable amount would be less than the asset's carrying amount is remote, based on an analysis of events and circumstances since the most recent calculation of the recoverable amount. *[IAS 36.24]*.

Thus if there was sufficient headroom on the last calculation and little has changed in the CGU to which the asset belongs, it can be revisited and re-used rather than having to be entirely started from scratch, which considerably reduces the work involved in the annual test. The impairment test cannot be rolled forward forever, of course, and an entity will have to take a cautious approach to estimating when circumstances have changed sufficiently to require a new test.

Impairment losses experienced on intangible assets with an indefinite useful life are recognised exactly as set out in 11 below, either as an individual asset or as part of a CGU, depending upon whether the intangible concerned is part of a CGU or not. Note that there is an important distinction concerning the allocation of losses in a CGU between the treatment of goodwill and that of intangible assets with an indefinite useful life. If goodwill forms part of the assets of a CGU, any impairment loss first reduces the goodwill and thereafter the remaining assets are reduced pro-rata. However, if an intangible asset is part of a CGU that is impaired, there is no requirement to write down the intangible before the other assets in the CGU, rather all assets are written down *pro-rata*. For the *pro-rata* allocation it is important to keep in mind that the carrying amount of an asset should not be reduced below the highest of its fair value less costs of disposal, value in use or zero. If the preceding rule is applied, further allocation of the impairment loss is made *pro rata* to the other assets of the unit (group of units).

11 RECOGNISING AND REVERSING IMPAIRMENT LOSSES

If the carrying value of an individual asset or of a CGU is equal to or less than its calculated VIU, there is no impairment. On the other hand, if the carrying value of the CGU is greater than its recoverable amount, an impairment write-down should be recognised.

There are three scenarios: an impairment loss on an individual asset, an impairment loss on an individual CGU and an impairment loss on a group of CGUs. The last of these may occur where there are corporate assets (see 4.2 above) or goodwill (see 11.2 below) that have been allocated to a group of CGUs rather than to individual ones.

11.1 Impairment losses on individual assets

For individual assets IAS 36 states:

> 'If, and only if, the recoverable amount of an asset is less than its carrying amount, the carrying amount of the asset shall be reduced to its recoverable amount. That reduction is an impairment loss. *[IAS 36.59]*.
>
> 'An impairment loss shall be recognised immediately in profit or loss, unless the asset is carried at revalued amount in accordance with another Standard (for example, in accordance with the revaluation model in IAS 16). Any impairment loss of a revalued asset shall be treated as a revaluation decrease in accordance with that other Standard'. *[IAS 36.60]*.

If there is an impairment loss on an asset that has not been revalued, it is recognised in profit or loss. An impairment loss on a revalued asset is first used to reduce the revaluation surplus in other comprehensive income for that asset. Only when the impairment loss exceeds the amount in the revaluation surplus for that same asset is any further impairment loss recognised in profit or loss.

IAS 36 does not require impairment losses to be shown in any particular position in the income statement, although the requirements of IAS 1 – *Presentation of Financial Statements* – should always be considered. It may be necessary to add an appropriate line item in profit or loss if it is relevant for an understanding of the entity's financial performance. *[IAS 1.85]*.

Any amounts written off a fixed asset should be shown as part of the accumulated depreciation when an entity discloses the gross carrying amount and the accumulated depreciation at the beginning and the end of the period. *[IAS 16.73(d)]*. In the reconciliation required by IAS 16.73(e) any impairment recognised or reversed through profit and loss should be shown in a separate line item. If the asset is held at revalued amount then any impairment losses recognised or reversed should be shown in the reconciliation in one line item together with the revaluations. *[IAS 16.73(e)(iv)]*.

An impairment loss greater than the carrying value of the asset does not give rise to a liability unless another standard requires it, presumably as this would be equivalent to providing for future losses. *[IAS 36.62]*. An impairment loss will reduce the depreciable amount of an asset and the revised amount will be depreciated or amortised prospectively over the remaining life. *[IAS 36.63]*. However, an entity ought also to review the useful life and residual value of its impaired asset, as both of these may need to be revised. The circumstances that give rise to impairments frequently affect these as well.

Finally, an impairment loss will have implications for any deferred tax calculation involving the asset. The standard makes clear that if an impairment loss is recognised then any related deferred tax assets or liabilities are determined in accordance with IAS 12, by comparing the revised carrying amount of the asset with its tax base. *[IAS 36.64]*. Example 3 in the standard's accompanying section of illustrative examples, on which the following is based, illustrates the possible effects.

Example 20.32: Recognition of an impairment loss creates a deferred tax asset

An entity has an asset with a carrying amount of €2,000 whose recoverable amount is €1,300. The tax rate is 30% and the tax base of the asset is €1,500. Impairment losses are not deductible for tax purposes. The effect of the impairment loss is as follows:

	Before impairment €	Effect of impairment €	After impairment €
Carrying amount	2,000	(700)	1,300
Tax base	1,500	–	1,500
Taxable (deductible) temporary difference	500	(700)	(200)
Deferred tax liability (asset) at 30%	150	(210)	(60)

The entity will recognise the deferred tax asset to the extent that the respective recognition criteria of IAS 12 are met.

11.2 Impairment losses and CGUs

Impairment losses in a CGU can occur in two ways:

(i) an impairment loss is incurred in a CGU on its own, and that CGU may or may not have corporate assets or goodwill included in its carrying value; and

(ii) an impairment loss is identified that must be allocated across a group of CGUs because a corporate asset or goodwill is involved whose carrying value could only be allocated to a group of CGUs as a whole, rather than to individual CGUs (the allocation of corporate assets to CGUs is discussed in 4.2 above, and goodwill is discussed at 8 above). Note that if there are indicators of impairment in connection with a CGU with which goodwill is associated, i.e. the CGU is part of a CGU group to which the goodwill is allocated, this CGU should be tested and any necessary impairment loss taken, before goodwill is tested for impairment (see 8.2.2 above). *[IAS 36.88]*.

The relevant paragraphs from the standard deal with both instances but are readily understandable only if the above distinction is appreciated. The standard lays down that impairment losses in CGUs should be recognised to reduce the carrying amount of the assets of the unit (group of units) in the following order:

(a) first, to reduce the carrying amount of any goodwill allocated to the CGU or group of units; and

(b) second, if the goodwill has been written off, to reduce the other assets of the CGU (or group of CGUs) *pro rata* to their carrying amount, subject to the limitation that the carrying amount of an asset should not be reduced to the highest of fair value less costs of disposal, value in use or zero. *[IAS 36.104, 105].*

The important point is to be clear about the order set out above. Goodwill must be written down first, and if an impairment loss remains, the other assets in the CGU or group of CGUs are written down pro-rata to their carrying values subject to the limitation stated at (b) above.

This pro-rating is in two stages if a group of CGUs is involved:

(i) the loss reduces goodwill (which by definition in this instance is unallocated to individual CGUs in the group); and

(ii) any remaining loss is pro-rated between the carrying values of the individual CGUs in the group and within each individual CGU the loss is again pro-rated between the individual assets' carrying values.

Unless it is possible to estimate the recoverable amount of each individual asset within a CGU, it is necessary to allocate impairment losses to individual assets in such a way that the revised carrying amounts of these assets correspond with the requirements of the standard. Therefore, the entity does not reduce the carrying amount of an individual asset below the highest of its FVLCD or VIU (if these can be established), or zero. The amount of the impairment loss that would otherwise have been allocated to the asset is then allocated pro-rata to the other assets of the CGU or CGU group. *[IAS 36.105].* The standard argues that this arbitrary allocation to individual assets when their recoverable amount cannot be individually assessed is appropriate because all assets of a CGU 'work together'. *[IAS 36.106].*

If corporate assets are allocated to a CGU or group of CGUs, then any remaining loss at (ii) above (i.e. after allocation to goodwill) is pro-rated against the allocated share of the corporate asset and the other assets in the CGU.

This process, then, writes down the carrying value attributed or allocated to a CGU until the carrying value of the net assets is equal to the computed recoverable amount. Due to the restriction of not reducing the carrying amount of an asset below its FVLCD or VIU, it is logically possible, after all assets and goodwill are either written off or down to their FVLCD or VIU, for the carrying value of the CGU to be higher than the computed recoverable amount. There is no suggestion that the net assets should be reduced any further because at this point the FVLCD would be the relevant impairment figure. The remaining amount will only be recognised as a liability if that is a requirement of another standard. *[IAS 36.108].*

IAS 36 includes in the standard's accompanying section of illustrative examples Example 2 which illustrates the calculation, recognition and allocation of an impairment loss across CGUs.

However, the standard stresses that no impairment loss should be reflected against an individual asset if the CGU to which it belongs has not been impaired, even if its carrying value exceeds its FVLCD. This is expanded in the following example, based on that in paragraph 107 of the standard:

Example 20.33: Individually impaired assets within CGUs

A machine has suffered physical damage but is still working, although not as well as before it was damaged. The machine's FVLCD is less than its carrying amount. The machine does not generate independent cash inflows. The smallest identifiable group of assets that includes the machine and generates cash inflows that are largely independent of the cash inflows from other assets is the production line to which the machine belongs. The recoverable amount of the production line shows that the production line taken as a whole is not impaired.

Assumption 1: budgets/forecasts approved by management reflect no commitment of management to replace the machine.

The recoverable amount of the machine alone cannot be estimated because its VIU may be different from its FVLCD (because the entity is going to continue to use it) and can be determined only for the CGU to which it belongs (the production line).

As the production line is not impaired, no impairment loss is recognised for the machine. Nevertheless, the entity may need to reassess the depreciation period or the depreciation method for the machine. Perhaps a shorter depreciation period or a faster depreciation method is required to reflect the expected remaining useful life of the machine or the pattern in which economic benefits are expected to be consumed by the entity.

Assumption 2: budgets/forecasts approved by management reflect a commitment of management to replace the machine and sell it in the near future.

Cash flows from continuing use of the machine until its disposal are estimated to be negligible. The machine's VIU can be estimated to be close to its FVLCD. Therefore, the recoverable amount of the machine can be determined and no consideration is given to the CGU (the production line) to which it belongs. As the machine's carrying amount exceeds its FVLCD, an impairment loss is recognised to write it down to FVLCD. *[IAS 36.107].*

Note that it is assumed that the asset is still useable (otherwise it would not be contributing to the cash flows of the CGU and would have to be written off) and that it is not held for sale as defined by IFRS 5. If the asset is no longer part of the CGU, it will have to be tested for impairment on a stand-alone basis. For IFRS 5's requirements when an asset is held for sale, see 5.1 above.

11.3 Reversal of impairment loss relating to goodwill prohibited

As mentioned in 8.2.4, IAS 36 does not permit an impairment loss on goodwill to be reversed under any circumstances. *[IAS 36.124].* The standard justifies this on the grounds that such a reversal would probably be an increase in internally generated goodwill, rather than a reversal of the impairment loss recognised for the acquired goodwill, and that recognition of internally generated goodwill is prohibited by IAS 38. *[IAS 36.125].*

Example 20.34: Impairment of goodwill

Company A has a CGU that has a carrying value of $2,000,000 at 31 December 20X0. This carrying value comprises $500,000 relating to goodwill and $1,500,000 relating to net tangible assets.

In 20X1, as a result of losses, net tangible assets have decreased to $1,400,000 reducing the total carrying value of the unit to $1,900,000. Changes in the regulatory framework surrounding its business mean that the cash-generating unit has a recoverable amount of $1,600,000 and has thus suffered an impairment loss of $300,000. This is charged to profit or loss. The carrying value of goodwill is reduced to $200,000.

In 20X2 the company develops a new product with the result that the recoverable amount of the cash-generating unit rises to $1,700,000. Net tangible assets have remained at $1,400,000. Despite the recoverable amount of the business unit now being $1,700,000 compared to its carrying value of $1,600,000, it is not possible to reverse $100,000 of the prior year's impairment loss of $300,000.

11.4 Reversal of impairment losses relating to assets other than goodwill

For all other assets, including intangible assets with an indefinite life, IAS 36 requires entities to assess at each reporting date whether there is any indication that an impairment loss may no longer exist or may have decreased. If there is any such indication, the entity has to recalculate the recoverable amount of the asset. *[IAS 36.110]*.

Therefore if there are indications that a previously recognised impairment loss has disappeared or reduced, it is necessary to determine again the recoverable amount (i.e. the higher of FVLCD or VIU) so that the reversal can be quantified. The standard sets out examples of what it notes are in effect 'reverse indications' of impairment. *[IAS 36.111]*. These are the reverse of those set out in paragraph 12 of the standard as indications of impairment (see 2.1 above). *[IAS 36.112]*. They are arranged, as in paragraph 12, into two categories: *[IAS 36.111]*

External sources of information:

(a) A significant increase in the asset's value.

(b) Significant changes during the period or expected in the near future in the entity's technological, market, economic or legal environment that will have a favourable effect.

(c) Decreases in market interest rates or other market rates of return on investments and those decreases are likely to affect the discount rate used in calculating the asset's value in use and increase the asset's recoverable amount materially.

Internal sources of information:

(d) Significant changes during the period or expected in the near future that will affect the extent to which, or manner in which, the asset is used. These changes include costs incurred during the period to improve or enhance the asset's performance or restructure the operation to which the asset belongs.

(e) Evidence from internal reporting that the economic performance of the asset is, or will be, better than expected.

Compared with paragraph 12, there are two notable omissions from this list of 'reverse indicators', one external and one internal.

The external indicator not included is the mirror of the impairment indicator 'the carrying amount of the net assets of the reporting entity is more than its market capitalisation'. No explanation is provided as to why, if a market capitalisation below shareholders' funds is an indication of impairment, its reversal should not automatically be an indication of a reversal. However, the most likely reason is that all of the facts and circumstances need to be considered before assuming that an impairment has reversed. In any event, deficits below market capitalisation may affect goodwill so the impairment charge cannot be reversed.

The internal indicator omitted from the list of 'reverse indicators' is that evidence of obsolescence or physical deterioration has been reversed. Once again no reason is given. It may be that the standard-setters have assumed that no such reversal could take place without the entity incurring costs to improve or enhance the performance of the asset or the CGU so that this is, in effect, covered by indicator (d) above.

The standard also reminds preparers that a reversal, like an impairment, is evidence that the depreciation method or residual value of the asset should be reviewed and may need to be adjusted, whether or not the impairment loss is reversed. *[IAS 36.113]*.

A further restriction is that impairment losses should be reversed only if there has been a change in the estimates used to determine the impairment loss, e.g. a change in cash flows or discount rate (for VIU) or a change in FVLCD. The 'unwinding' of the discount will increase the present value of future cash flows as they become closer but IAS 36 does not allow the mere passage of time to trigger the reversal of an impairment. In other words the 'service potential' of the asset must genuinely improve if a reversal is to be recognised. *[IAS 36.114-116]*. However, this inability to recognise the rise in value can give rise to what is in effect a double recognition of losses, which may seem illogical, as demonstrated by the following example:

Example 20.35: Double counted losses

At the end of 20X0, an entity with a single CGU is carrying out an impairment review. The discounted forecast cash flows for years 20X2 and onwards would be just enough to support the carrying value of the entity's assets. However, 20X1 is forecasted to produce a loss and net cash outflow. The discounted value of this amount is accordingly written off the carrying value of the fixed assets in 20X0 as an impairment loss. It is then suffered again in 20X1 (at a slightly higher amount being now undiscounted) as the actual loss. Once that loss is past, the future cash flows are sufficient to support the original unimpaired value of the fixed assets. Nevertheless, the assets cannot be written back up through profit or loss to counter the double counting effect as the increase in value does not derive from a change in economic conditions or in the expected use of an asset.

In this type of scenario, which is common in practice, the entity will only 'benefit' as the assets are depreciated or amortised at a lower amount.

If, on the other hand, the revival in cash flows is the result of expenditure by the entity to improve or enhance the performance of the asset or the CGU or on a restructuring of the CGU, there may be an obvious improvement in the service potential and the entity may be able to reverse some or all of the impairment write down.

In the event of an individual asset's impairment being reversed, the reversal may not raise the carrying value above the figure it would have stood at taking into account depreciation, if no impairment had originally been recognised. *[IAS 36.117]*. Any increase above this figure would really be a revaluation, which would have to be accounted for in accordance with the standard relevant to the asset concerned. *[IAS 36.118]*.

Example 20.36: Reversal of impairment losses

At the beginning of year 1 an entity acquires an asset with a useful life of 10 years for $1,000. The asset generates net cash inflows that are largely independent of the cash inflows of other assets or groups of assets. At the end of year 3, when the carrying amount after depreciation is $700, the entity recognises that there has been an impairment loss of $210. The entity writes the asset down to $490. As the useful life is not affected, the entity commences amortisation at $70 per annum which, if applied in each of the years 4-10, would amortise the carrying value over the remaining useful life, as follows:

Table 1

	Year									
	1	2	3	4	5	6	7	8	9	10
	$	$	$	$	$	$	$	$	$	$
NBV – beginning of the year	1,000	900	800	490	420	350	280	210	140	70
Depreciation	100	100	100	70	70	70	70	70	70	70
Impairment			210							
NBV – end of the year	900	800	490	420	350	280	210	140	70	–
NBV without impairment	900	800	700	600	500	400	300	200	100	–

At the beginning of year 5, before depreciation for the year, the asset's carrying value is $420. Thanks to improvements in technology, the entity is able to increase the asset's VIU to $550 by spending $120 on parts that improve and enhance its performance.

At the end of year 5, the asset can therefore be written up to the *lower* of:

- $600, which is the net book value of the asset after the additional expenditure, assuming that there had never been any impairment. This is the balance brought forward at the beginning of year 5 of $600 (Table 1 bottom row) plus expenditure of $120 less depreciation for the year of (720/6) = $120; and
- $550, which is the VIU at the end of year 5.

Therefore it can write the asset's net book value back up to $550. The entity can reverse $100 of the impairment write down and amortise the remaining net book value of the asset of $550 to zero over the remaining five years, year 6 to year 10, at $110 per annum (see table 2 below).

Table 2

	Year					
	5	6	7	8	9	10
	$	$	$	$	$	$
Cost	1,000	1,120	1,120	1,120	1,120	1,120
Expenditure in the year	120					
Cost carried forward	1,120	1,120	1,120	1,120	1,120	1,120
Accumulated depreciation brought forward	580	570	680	790	900	1,010
Charge for the year (70 plus 20 (120/6))	90	110	110	110	110	110
Reversal of impairment	(100)					
Accumulated depreciation carried forward	570	680	790	900	1,010	1,120
NBV	550	440	330	220	110	–

The Standard includes an illustration of the reversal of an impairment loss in the standard's accompanying section of illustrative examples, in Example 4.

All reversals are to be recognised in the income statement immediately, except for revalued assets which are dealt with below. *[IAS 36.119]*.

If an impairment loss is reversed against an asset, its depreciation or amortisation is adjusted to allocate its revised carrying amount less residual value over its remaining useful life. *[IAS 36.121]*.

11.4.1 Reversals of impairments – cash-generating units

Where an entity recognises a reversal of an impairment loss on a CGU, the increase in the carrying amount of the assets of the unit should be allocated by increasing the carrying amount of the assets, other than goodwill, in the unit on a pro-rata basis. However, the carrying amount of an individual asset should not be increased above the lower of its recoverable amount (if determinable) and the carrying amount that would have resulted had no impairment loss been recognised in prior years. Any 'surplus' reversal is to be allocated to the remaining assets pro-rata, always remembering that goodwill, if allocated to an individual CGU, may not be increased under any circumstances. *[IAS 36.122, 123]*.

11.4.2 Reversals of impairments – revalued assets

If an asset is recognised at a revalued amount under another standard any reversal of an impairment loss should be treated as a revaluation increase under that other standard. Thus a reversal of an impairment loss on a revalued asset is credited to other comprehensive income. However, to the extent that an impairment loss on the same revalued asset was previously recognised as an expense in the income statement, a reversal of that impairment loss is recognised as income in the income statement. *[IAS 36.119, 120]*.

As with assets carried at cost, after a reversal of an impairment loss is recognised on a revalued asset, the depreciation charge should be adjusted in future periods to allocate the asset's revised carrying amount, less any residual value, on a systematic basis over its remaining useful life. *[IAS 36.121]*.

12 GROUP AND SEPARATE FINANCIAL STATEMENT ISSUES

The application of IAS 36 in group situations is not always straight forward and can give rise to a number of challenging questions. We explore some of these questions in the following sections, including:

- How to identify CGUs and relevant cash flows in the financial statements of an individual entity within a group; the consolidated financial statements of a subgroup; or when impairment testing equity accounted investments or those carried at cost; and
- Whether the cash flows mentioned above need to be on an arm's length basis i.e. at fair value, and the extent the restrictions imposed by IAS 36 need to be applied.

Note that we have used the term 'individual financial statements' for any stand-alone financial statements that apply IFRS, prepared by any entity within a group, whether or not those financial statements are within scope of IAS 27 – *Separate Financial Statements*. The term 'individual financial statements' includes separate financial statements, individual financial statements for subsidiary companies with no investments and, where the context requires, consolidated financial statements for a subgroup or, for a subgroup that does not have any subsidiaries, unconsolidated financial statements whose associates and joint ventures are accounted for using the equity method.

The distinction between individual financial statements and 'separate financial statements', a term that applies only to financial statements prepared in accordance with the provisions of IAS 27, is explained in Chapter 8 at 1.

12.1 VIU: relevant cash flows and non-arm's length prices (transfer pricing)

When it comes to impairment testing of:

- equity accounted investments;
- investments in subsidiaries, associates or joint ventures carried at cost in the separate financial statements of the parent; or
- assets/CGUs in individual group companies or subgroups financial statements;

the key questions are how to determine the cash flows for intra-group transactions and whether those cash flows need to be on an arm's length basis.

Many individual group companies or subgroups do not have truly independent cash flows because of the way in which groups allocate activities between group entities. Transactions between a parent entity and its subsidiaries, between subsidiaries within a group or between subsidiaries/parents and investments in associates and joint ventures may not be carried out on an arm's length basis. Entities may benefit from transactions entered into by others that are not reflected in their financial statements, e.g. management and other facilities provided by another group company, or may incur those expenses on their behalf without recharge.

In the context of impairment testing, this means that an entity needs to consider whether the relevant cash flows should be those actually generated by the asset (investment in subsidiary, joint venture, associate or individual asset or CGU) or those that it could generate on an arm's length basis. IAS 36 gives no clear answer to this question. There are two broad approaches, and preference for one view or the other will often depend on local jurisdictions. Either:

- the VIU must be based on the cash flows directly generated under current arrangements, e.g. those received and receivable; or
- the cash flows must take into consideration the manner in which the group has organised its activities and make notional adjustments to reflect arm's length amounts.

Those arguing that notional adjustments are required, refer to the IAS 36 requirement to replace transfer prices with arm's length prices for CGUs within the some reporting entity/group once a CGU has been identified (see 7.1.6 above). *[IAS 36.70]*. The argument is that the same principle should apply in intra-group arrangements and therefore the internal transfer prices of the group entities in question should be substituted with arm's length prices. This may not be straightforward in practice, as it can be difficult to allocate arm's length prices in intra-group arrangements where there is often a 'bundle' of goods and services and where transactions may not have commercial equivalents.

A method that may work in practice, (and that should give broadly the same answer) as it reflects the arm's length prices of inputs and outputs, and therefore the substitution of transfer prices, is to start from the VIU of the CGU in the consolidated financial statements of which the subsidiary being tested for impairment is a part. This VIU could be apportioned between the various subsidiaries.

This approach rests, at least notionally, on the assumption that the group has allocated its activities between its various subsidiaries for its own benefit. Group companies may make transactions at off-market values at the request of the parent but at least in principle there would be a basis for charging arm's length prices.

It is necessary to avoid two potential pitfalls:

- taking account of a notional increase in income or VIU to one subsidiary but neglecting to reflect the notional increase in costs or loss of VIU to another; and
- including benefits or costs that cannot be converted into cash flows to the entity. This can be particularly problematic when testing goodwill, including the carrying value of investments when the purchase price reflects goodwill on acquisition. Most would consider this a constraint on the cash flows reflected in this impairment test. This may be revealed if there is a major difference between the subsidiary-based and CGU-based recoverable amount as there could be cash flows or synergies elsewhere in the group that cannot be reasonably attributed to the subsidiary or subgroup in question.

Those arguing notional adjustments are not required refer to the lack of guidance in IAS 36. The argument is that it is not clear that the same principle should apply, particularly in circumstances when using the contractual agreed cash flows would lead to an impairment which would be avoided by substitution of contractual agreed cash flows with arm's length prices.

12.2 Goodwill in individual (or subgroup) financial statements and the interaction with the group financial statements

In many jurisdictions, subsidiary entities are not exempt from preparing financial statements and these may be required to comply with IFRSs. These may be consolidated accounts for the subgroup that it heads. Such individual or subgroup financial statements might include goodwill for which an annual impairment test is required. Along with the question of whether intra-group cash flows need to be on an arm's length basis for impairment testing purposes, as discussed at 12.1 above, other principal questions are:

- how to treat synergies arising outside of the reporting entity/subgroup (see 12.2.1 below);
- whether the guidance in IFRS 8 applies in determining the level at which goodwill has to be tested for impairment in the consolidated financial statements of the subgroup or in individual financial statements (see 12.2.2 below); and
- how to deal with goodwill, arising at a subgroup level, in the group financial statements (see 12.2.3)?

12.2.1 Goodwill synergies arising outside of the reporting entity/subgroup

If goodwill is being tested in consolidated subgroup or individual financial statements, it may be that the synergies that gave rise to the goodwill are in another part of the larger group because the subgroup is part of a CGU containing other subsidiary companies. It may not be possible to translate some synergies such as economies of scale into cash flows to the entity or subgroup in question. Although there is no impairment at the level of the CGU in the group consolidated financial statements, the entity may not be able to avoid writing down the goodwill in the individual or subgroup statements at the time the first impairment test is performed in the year of the acquisition. In our view, it would not be appropriate to consider synergies arising outside the individual or subgroup financial statements when testing impairment in the individual or subgroup financial statements unless these synergies would be available to market participants and therefore could be built into the FVLCD. Whether this write down needs to be recorded in the statement of profit or loss or whether it is appropriate to treat it as an equity transaction in form of distribution to the parent is a matter of judgement.

12.2.2 The effect of IFRS 8 – Operating segments – when allocating goodwill to CGU's in individual (or subgroup) financial statements

As discussed in 8.1 above, goodwill is not necessarily tested at the lowest level of CGUs (however defined in the context of these group entities or subgroups), but at the level of a CGU group at which goodwill is monitored. However, that CGU group cannot be larger than an operating segment, before aggregation (see 8.1.4 above). *[IAS 36.80]*.

We believe that for purposes of testing goodwill in the individual or subgroup's financial statements, companies must apply the guidance in IFRS 8 to determine its operating segments even if IFRS 8 is not applicable because the subsidiary (subgroup) is not public. Therefore, if the application of IFRS 8 would result in the identification of separate operating segments in the individual or subgroup's financial statements, goodwill cannot be tested for impairment at a level above the operating segments in those financial statements (i.e. the operating segments would serve as a ceiling). It would not be appropriate to apply IAS 36.80 in these circumstances based on the operating segments as determined by the ultimate parent entity for its consolidated financial statements.

However, the CGU/CGU group for purposes of goodwill impairment testing could be at a level lower than the subgroup's operating segments.

Example 20.37: A subgroup with goodwill that is not an operating segment for the group

A mining entity (group) extracts a metal ore that does not have an active market until it has been through a smelting and refining process. Each mine is held in a separate subsidiary, as is the refinery, and in two joint ventures. The refinery, subsidiaries and joint ventures are located in several different countries. The entity considers the CGU to comprise the subsidiary that holds the smelter together with the subsidiaries that hold the individual mines and the interests in the joint ventures.

The entity acquires a group of mine-holding subsidiaries in a country where there is a requirement to prepare consolidated financial statements at the highest level within that country. These consolidated financial statements, which are prepared using the acquisition method by the relevant intermediate parent, include goodwill. The entity does not consider the subgroup to be an operating segment. However, in the subgroup's financial statements, first of all the relevant operating segments would need to be determined from the subgroup's perspective. If it was concluded that from the subgroup's perspective there was only one operating segment, this would be the maximum level at which goodwill is tested for impairment in the subgroup's consolidated financial statements.

12.2.3 Acquisitions by subsidiaries and determining the level at which the group tests goodwill for impairment

IAS 36 requires goodwill to be allocated to the lowest level within the entity at which the goodwill is monitored for internal management purposes. If a subsidiary undertakes acquisitions and recognises goodwill in its own financial statements, the level at which the subsidiary's management monitors the goodwill may differ from the level at which the parent's or group's management monitors goodwill from the group's perspective.

If a subsidiary's management monitors its goodwill at a lower level than the level at which the parent's or group's management monitors its goodwill, a key issue is whether that lower level should, from the group's perspective, be regarded as the 'lowest level within the entity at which the goodwill is monitored for internal management purposes'? The answer is not necessarily, as is demonstrated in the following example.

Example 20.38: Monitoring goodwill arising from acquisitions by subsidiaries

A parent acquired 100% of the issued shares of a company that operates autonomously and is required to prepare IFRS-compliant financial statements. The subsidiary has acquired various businesses both before and after becoming part of the group. Those business combinations have included significant amounts of goodwill.

The subsidiary's management monitors its acquired goodwill at the level of the subsidiary's operating segments identified in accordance with IFRS 8. However, management of the parent/group monitors its acquired goodwill at the level of the group's operating segments, which is a higher level than the subsidiary's operating segments. The subsidiary's operations form part of two of the group's six operating segments.

The subsidiary's goodwill comprises goodwill arising on its acquisitions, some of which took place *before*, and some *after*, the subsidiary became part of the group.

In contrast, the goodwill recognised by the group comprises:

- Goodwill acquired by the parent in the acquisition of the subsidiary;
- Goodwill acquired by the subsidiary since becoming part of the group;
- Goodwill acquired by the parent in other operating combinations (i.e. goodwill that relates to other subsidiaries and businesses that make up the group).

The goodwill acquired in the acquisition of the subsidiary that is recognised by the parent in its consolidated financial statements is therefore different from the goodwill recognised by the subsidiary (which relates only to the acquisitions made by the subsidiary itself and was measured at the date of the acquisition concerned, as any other goodwill would be internally generated goodwill from the subsidiary's perspective and therefore not recognised by the subsidiary).

In such circumstances the actions of the subsidiary's management in deciding the level at which it tests its goodwill for impairment will *not* cause the group to be 'locked in' to testing goodwill at the same level in the consolidated financial statements.

Rather, the group should test its goodwill for impairment at the level at which management of the group (i.e. of the parent) monitors its various investments in goodwill, namely, in this example, at the group's operating segment level.

12.3 Group reorganisations and the carrying value of investments in subsidiaries

A common form of group reorganisation involves the transfer of the entire business of a subsidiary to another subsidiary of the same parent. These transactions often take place at the book value of the transferor's assets rather than at fair value. If the original carrying value was a purchase price that included an element of goodwill, the remaining 'shell', i.e. an entity that no longer has any trade or activities, may have a carrying value in the parent company's statement of financial position in excess of its net worth/recoverable amount. It could be argued that as the subsidiary is now a shell with no possibility in its current state of generating sufficient profits to support its value, a loss should be recognised by the parent in its separate financial statements to reduce its investment in the shell company to its net worth/recoverable amount. However, the transfer of part of the group's business from one controlled entity to another has no substance from the perspective of the group and will have no effect in the consolidated accounts. There has also been no loss overall to the parent as a result of this reorganisation as the loss in net worth/recoverable amount in one subsidiary results in an increase in the net worth/recoverable amount in the other subsidiary.

This is, of course, a transaction between companies under common control as all of the combining entities or businesses are ultimately controlled by the same party or parties both before and after the business combination, and that control is not transitory. *[IFRS 3.B1]*. This means that the treatment by the acquirer is out of the scope of IFRS 3.

From the transferor entity's perspective, the transaction combines a sale of its assets at an undervalue to the acquirer, by reference to the fair value of the transferred assets, and a distribution of the shortfall in value to its parent. The fair value of those assets to the parent may well not be reflected in the transferor's own statement of financial position because there is no push-down accounting under IFRS. The transferor is not obliged to record the 'distribution' to its parent at fair value. IFRIC 17 – *Distributions of Non-cash Assets to Owners* – issued in November 2008, requires gains or losses measured by reference to fair value of the assets distributed to be taken to profit or loss but, amongst other restrictions, excludes from its scope non-cash distributions made by wholly-owned group companies (see Chapter 8 at 2.4.2).

This interpretation of the transferor's transaction (as a sale at an undervalue and a deemed distribution to the parent) is wholly consistent with a legal analysis in some jurisdictions, for example the United Kingdom, where a company that does not have zero or positive distributable reserves is unable to sell its assets at an undervalue because it cannot make any sort of distribution.

The parent, in turn, could be seen as having made a capital contribution of the shortfall in value to the acquirer. The parent may choose to record the distribution from the transferor (and consequent impairment in its carrying value) and the contribution to the acquirer (and consequent increase in its carrying value). This is consistent with our analysis in Chapter 8 at 4.2 regarding intra-group transactions.

The acquirer will not necessarily record the capital contribution even if this is an option available to it.

However, the underlying principles are not affected by whether or not the acquirer makes this choice – there has been a transfer of value from one subsidiary to another. This demonstrates why the business transfer alone does not necessarily result in an impairment charge in the parent entity.

If the above analysis is not supportable in a particular jurisdiction then an impairment write down may have to be taken.

Actual circumstances may be less straightforward. In particular, the transferor and the acquirer may not be held directly by the same parent. This may make it necessary to record an impairment against the carrying value of the transferor ('shell') company in its intermediate parent to reflect its loss in value, which will be treated as an expense or as a distribution, depending on the policy adopted by the entity and the relevant facts and circumstances. See Chapter 8 at 4.4.1 for a discussion of the policy choices available to the entity. There may be another, higher level within the group at which the above arguments against impairment will apply.

Example 20.39: Group reorganisations and impairment

Topco has two directly held subsidiaries, Tradeco and Shellco. It acquired Shellco for £30 million and immediately thereafter transferred all of its trade and assets to its fellow subsidiary Tradeco for book value of £10 million with the proceeds being left outstanding on intercompany account. Shellco now has net assets of £10 million (its intercompany receivable) but a carrying value in Topco of £30 million. On the other hand, the value of Tradeco has been enhanced by its purchase of the business at an undervalue.

In our view, there are two acceptable ways in which Tradeco may account for this. The cost of the investment in Tradeco's individual financial statements may be the fair value of the cash given as consideration, i.e. £10 million. Alternatively, it is the fair value of the cash given as consideration (£10 million), together with a deemed capital contribution received from Topco for the difference up to the fair value of the business of Shellco of £20 million, which will be recognised in equity, giving a total consideration of £30 million.

The capital contribution measured under the second method represents the value distributed by Shellco to its parent Topco and thence to Tradeco. Meanwhile Topco could record a transfer of £20 million from the carrying value of Shellco to the carrying value of Topco.

If there is an intermediate holding company between Topco and Shellco but all other facts remain the same, then it would appear that an impairment ought to be made against the carrying value of Shellco in its immediate parent, which will be treated as an expense or as a distribution, depending on the policy adopted by the entity and the relevant facts and circumstances. The argument against impairment would still apply in Topco.

12.4 Investments in subsidiaries, associates and joint ventures

Investment in subsidiaries, associates and joint ventures carried at cost in separate financial statements of the parent and equity accounted investments are within the scope of IAS 36.

While a parent entity could elect to account for investments in subsidiaries, associates and joint ventures under IFRS 9 or IAS 39, most parent entities choose to carry these investments at cost as permitted by IAS 27. *[IAS 36.4, IAS 27.10].* IAS 27 was amended in 2014 to give parent entities the option to use the equity method to account for these investments in an entity's separate financial statements.

The recoverable amount for investments carried at cost or under the use of the equity method is the higher of FVLCD and VIU. Specific questions around FVLCD are dealt with at 12.4.1. Challenges in respect of VIU for investments carried at cost or under the equity method are dealt with at 12.4.2.

Important to note is that testing an investment in an associate or joint venture carried under the equity method using IAS 28 in group financial statements cannot always provide assurance about the recoverability of the cost of shares in the investor's separate financial statements, if they are carried at cost. *[IAS 27.10(a)].* Accounting for the group's share of losses may take the equity interest below cost and an impairment test could reveal no need for an impairment loss in the consolidated financial statements. This might not necessarily provide any assurance about the (higher) carrying value of shares in the separate financial statements.

12.4.1 Fair value less costs of disposal (FVLCD) for investments in subsidiaries, associates and joint ventures

In order to establish FVLCD an entity must apply IFRS 13's requirements as outlined at 6 above and described in detail in Chapter 14.

If an entity holds a position in a single asset or liability that is traded in an active market, IFRS 13 requires an entity to measure fair value using that price, without adjustment. This requirement is accepted when the asset or liability being measured is a financial instrument in the scope of IAS 39 or IFRS 9. However, when an entity holds an investment in a subsidiary, joint venture or associate the question is what the unit of account is, the individual shares or the investment as a whole, and whether it would be appropriate to include a control premium when determining fair value provided that market participants take this into consideration when pricing the asset. See 6.1.1 above and Chapter 14 at 5.1.1 for consideration and recent developments in respect of this.

Unlike investments with quoted prices, discussed above, there are less issues if FVLCD is used to determine the recoverable amount of an asset that does not have a quoted price in an active market and is either:

- an investment in a subsidiary, joint venture or associate; or
- a CGU comprising the investment's underlying assets.

Using FVLCD may avoid some of the complexities of determining appropriate cash flows because of transfer pricing and other intra-group transactions issues, described in 12.1 above and 12.4.2 below.

12.4.2 VIU for investments in subsidiaries, associates and joint ventures

Unlike most other assets, an investment in a subsidiary, joint venture or associate can be viewed as either:

- an individual asset that can generate income, e.g. in the form of dividends; or
- as an asset that represents the underlying assets and liabilities that are under the control of the subsidiary, joint venture or the associate.

IAS 28 acknowledges this by stating:

> 'In determining the value in use of the investment, an entity estimates:
>
> (a) its share of the present value of the estimated future cash flows expected to be generated by the associate or joint venture, including the cash flows from the operations of the associate or joint venture and the proceeds on the ultimate disposal of the investment; or
>
> (b) the present value of the estimated future cash flows expected to arise from dividends to be received from the investment and from its ultimate disposal.
>
> Under appropriate assumptions, both methods give the same result.' *[IAS 28.42]*.

This means that there are broadly two approaches in testing for impairment: one focuses on the investment and the cash flows the parent receives (dividends and ultimate disposal proceeds) and the other considers the recoverable amount of the underlying assets of the investment and the cash flows generated by these assets. These two approaches are considered at 12.4.2.A and 12.4.2.B respectively. Whichever view is taken, the entity needs to ensure that the cash flows are appropriate (see 12.1 above in respect of considerations around intra-group transfer pricing).

It is important to note that, whether an entity calculates VIU using its share of present value of estimated cash flows of the underlying assets or the dividends expected to be received, it is necessary to adjust them to reflect IAS 36 restrictions, e.g. those in respect of improvements and enhancements (see 7.1.2 above) and restructuring (see 7.1.3 above) and as well as growth (see 7.1 and 7.1.1 above) and discount rates (see 7.2 above). A practical challenge in practice may be to obtain sufficiently detailed information to make such adjustments for investments in entities that are not controlled by the parent, in which case the entity may have to use FVLCD to establish the recoverable amount.

12.4.2.A VIU of investments in subsidiaries, associates and joint ventures using dividend discount models

IAS 28 allows the VIU of the equity accounted interest to be based on the present value of the estimated future cash flows expected to arise from dividends to be received from the investment. This describes in broad terms what is also known as a dividend discount model (DDM). DDMs are financial models frequently used by financial institutions that value shares at the discounted value of future dividend payments. These models value a company on the basis of future cash flows that may be distributed to the shareholders in compliance with the capital requirements provided by law, discounted at a rate expressing the cost of risk capital. By analogy this approach can be used to calculate the VIU for investments in subsidiaries, associates and joint ventures carried at cost in the separate financial statements of a parent and for equity accounted investments.

The Interpretations Committee considered the use of DDMs in testing for impairment under IAS 36. The Interpretations Committee rejected 'in general' the use of DDMs as an appropriate basis for calculating the VIU of a CGU in consolidated financial statements.[2] It was of the view that calculations using DDMs may be appropriate when calculating the VIU of a single asset, for example when determining whether an investment is impaired in the separate financial statements of an entity. It did not consider whether the cash flows used in the DDMs should be adjusted to reflect IAS 36 assumptions and restrictions, as discussed more fully under 12.4.2 above. However, in order to use a DDM for calculating VIU, IAS 36's requirements should be reflected in the future dividends calculated for use in the model.

12.4.2.B VIU of investments in subsidiaries, associates and joint ventures based on cash flows generated by underlying assets

When testing investments in subsidiaries, associates and joint ventures based on cash flows generated by underlying assets entities need to ensure that the cash flows are appropriate (see 12.1 above in respect of intra-group transfer pricing) and that the restrictions of IAS 36 are appropriately applied (see 12.4.2 above).

If an entity is testing its investments in subsidiaries, associates and joint ventures for impairment and it can demonstrate that the investment contains one or more CGUs in their entirety then it may in some circumstances be able to use the results of the group impairment tests of the underlying CGUs to test the investment for impairment. If the aggregate VIU (or FVLCD) of the CGU or CGUs is not less than the carrying value of the investment, then the investment may not be impaired. Note that the entity's investment reflects the net assets of the subsidiary, associates or joint venture while the CGU reflects the assets and liabilities on a gross basis, so appropriate adjustments will have to be made.

It may not be so straightforward in practice. There are particular problems if the asset (the investment) and the underlying CGU are not the same. CGUs may overlap individual subsidiaries so, for example, a single CGU may contain more than one such subsidiary. Even if the CGU and investment coincide, the shares may have been acquired in a business combination. It is quite possible that the synergies that gave rise to goodwill on acquisition are in another part of the group not controlled by the intermediate parent in question. In such a case an entity might not be able to use the result of the group impairment test and so would have to calculate the recoverable amount of the investment.

12.4.3 Equity accounted investment and indicators of impairment

In connection with issuing IFRS 9, the IASB amended IAS 28 to include the impairment indicators an entity needs to use to determine whether it is necessary to recognise any additional impairment loss once it has accounted for losses, if any, under IAS 28. *[IAS 28.40-41A].* These impairment indicators are the same indicators as previously stated in IAS 39 for financial assets.

Before this amendment, IAS 28 required an entity to use IAS 39 to determine whether it is necessary to recognise an additional impairment loss.

The indicators of impairment require 'objective evidence of impairment as a result of one or more events that have occurred after the initial recognition'. *[IAS 28.41A, IAS 39.59].* However, one would not expect any significant difference in the impairment indicators under IAS 36 and IAS 28 because both look for objective evidence, sometimes in virtually identical terms[3] and neither claims that its list of indicators is exclusive. *[IAS 36.13, IAS 28.41A].* This means that an impairment test should not be avoided because an impairment indicator is not mentioned specifically in IAS 28.

If an entity has reason to believe that the carrying amount of an investment in an associate or joint venture is higher than the recoverable amount, this is most likely a sufficient indicator on its own to require an impairment test.

12.4.4 Equity accounted investments and long term loans

Investors frequently make long-term loans to associates or joint ventures that, from their perspective, form part of the net investment in the associate or joint venture. Under current IFRS guidance, it is not clear whether these should be accounted for, in particular tested for impairment, as part of the net investment under IAS 28 and IAS 36, or as stand-alone investments by applying the requirements of IFRS 9 (or IAS 39 where applicable).

After receiving a request related to the interaction between IFRS 9 (or IAS 39 where applicable) and IAS 28 and whether the measurement of long-term interests that form part of the net investment in associates and joint ventures should be governed by IFRS 9 (or IAS 39 where applicable), IAS 28 or a combination of both, the IASB, in its October 2016 meeting, tentatively decided to propose amendments to IAS 28 to clarify that an entity applies IFRS 9, in addition to IAS 28, to long-term interests that form part of the net investment and to include the proposed amendments in the next cycle of annual improvements (2015–2017). Exposure Draft ED/2017/1 which was subsequently published in January 2017, proposes to amend IAS 28 to clarify that:

- the scope exemption of IFRS 9 applies only to interests in an associate or a joint venture that an entity accounts for using the equity method; and
- long-term interests that, in substance, form part of the entity's investment are not accounted for using the equity method, therefore these instruments are in the scope of IFRS 9.

In response to comments letter received the Board tentatively decided in its May 2017 meeting to finalise the proposed amendments to IAS 28 and to clarify that:

- an entity applies the requirements in IFRS 9 to long-term interests before applying the loss allocation and impairment requirements in IAS 28; and
- in applying IFRS 9, the entity does not take account of any adjustments to the carrying amount of long-term interest that result from the application of IAS 28.

In respect of application, the Board tentatively decided to set an effective date of 1 January 2019, with earlier application permitted. At the time of writing, the IASB had not yet finalised the proposed amendments.

12.4.5 Equity accounted investments and CGUs

IAS 28 states that the recoverable amount of an investment in an associate or a joint venture should be assessed for each associate or joint venture, unless it does not generate cash inflows from continuing use that are largely independent of those from other assets of the entity. *[IAS 28.43]*. This means that each associate or joint venture is a separate CGU unless it is part of a larger CGU including other assets, which could include other associates or joint ventures.

Example 20.40: Joint ventures are part of larger CGU

A mining entity (group) extracts a metal ore that does not have an active market until it has been through a smelting and refining process. Each mine is held in a separate subsidiary, as is the refinery, and in two joint ventures. The refinery, subsidiaries and joint ventures are located in several different countries. The entity considers the CGU to comprise the subsidiary that holds the smelter together with the subsidiaries that hold the individual mines and the interests in the joint ventures.

If there is goodwill in the carrying amount of an associate or joint venture, this is not tested separately. *[IAS 28.42]*. However, there may be additional goodwill in the group that will be allocated to a CGU that includes an associate or joint venture, that will be tested for impairment by reference to the combined cash flows of assets and associates and joint ventures.

12.4.6 Equity accounted investments and testing goodwill for impairment

When calculating its share of an equity accounted investee's results, an investor makes adjustments to the investee's profit or loss to reflect depreciation and impairments of the investee's identifiable assets based on their fair values at the date the investor acquired its investment. This is covered in IAS 28 which states that:

> 'Appropriate adjustments to the investor's share of the associate's or joint venture's profits or losses after acquisition are also made to account, for example, for depreciation of the depreciable assets, based on their fair values at the acquisition date. Similarly, appropriate adjustments to the investor's share of the associate's or joint venture's profits or losses after acquisition are made for impairment losses recognised by the associate, such as for goodwill or property, plant and equipment.' *[IAS 28.32]*.

Although this refers to 'appropriate adjustments' for goodwill impairment losses, this should not be interpreted as requiring the investor to recalculate the goodwill impairment on a similar basis to depreciation and impairment of tangible and intangible assets. The 'appropriate adjustment' is to reverse that goodwill impairment that relates to pre-acquisition goodwill in the investee before calculating the investor's share of the investee's profit. After application of the equity method the entire equity-accounted carrying amount of the investor's investment, including the goodwill included in that carrying amount, is tested for impairment in accordance with IAS 28. *[IAS 28.40-43]*. Note that there is no requirement to test investments in associates or joint ventures for impairment annually but only when there are indicators that the amount may not be recoverable. These requirements are described in detail in Chapter 11 at 9.

Impairment write-offs made against investments accounted for under the equity method may be reversed if an impairment loss no longer exists or has decreased (see 11.4 above). Although IAS 36 does not allow impairments of goodwill to be reversed, *[IAS 36.124]*, this impairment is not a write-off against goodwill, but a write-off against the equity investment, so this prohibition does not apply. IAS 28 states that 'an impairment loss recognised in those circumstances is not allocated to any asset, including goodwill, that forms part of the carrying amount of the investment in the associate or joint venture. Accordingly, any reversal of that impairment loss is recognised in accordance with IAS 36 to the extent that the recoverable amount of the investment subsequently increases'. *[IAS 28.42]*.

13 DISCLOSURES REQUIRED BY IAS 36

13.1 Introduction

This section sets out the principal disclosures for impairment required in financial statements as set out in IAS 36. Any disclosures required relating to impairment by other standards are dealt with in the chapter concerned. Disclosures that may be required by other authorities such as national statutes or listing authorities are not included.

13.2 IAS 36 disclosures

The disclosures required fall into two broad categories:

(i) disclosures concerning any actual impairment losses or reversals made in the period, that are obviously only required if such a loss or reversal has occurred, regardless of the type of asset involved; and

(ii) yearly disclosures concerning the annual impairment tests required for goodwill and intangible assets with an indefinite useful life, that are required regardless of whether an impairment adjustment to these types of assets has occurred or not.

13.2.1 Disclosures required for impairment losses or reversals

For each class of assets the entity must disclose:

'(a) the amount of impairment losses recognised in profit or loss during the period and the line item(s) of the statement of comprehensive income in which those impairment losses are included.

(b) the amount of reversals of impairment losses recognised in profit or loss during the period and the line item(s) of the statement of comprehensive income in which those impairment losses are reversed.

(c) the amount of impairment losses on revalued assets recognised directly in other comprehensive income during the period.

(d) the amount of reversals of impairment losses on revalued assets recognised directly in other comprehensive income during the period.' *[IAS 36.126]*.

A class of assets is a grouping of assets of similar nature and use in an entity's operations. *[IAS 36.127]*.

These disclosures can be made as an integral part of the other disclosures, for example the property, plant and equipment note reconciling the opening and closing values (as set out in Chapter 18 at 8) may contain the required information. *[IAS 36.128]*.

Additionally, IAS 36 links disclosure of impairments with segment disclosures. Thus, if an entity reports segment information in accordance with IFRS 8 then any impairments or reversals must be disclosed by reportable segment as follows:

(a) the amount of impairment losses recognised in profit or loss and directly in other comprehensive income during the period; and

(b) the amount of reversals of impairment losses recognised in profit or loss and directly in other comprehensive income during the period. *[IAS 36.129]*.

13.2.2 Material impairments

If an impairment loss for an individual asset or a cash-generating unit is recognised or reversed during the period and is material to the financial statements of the reporting entity as a whole, the following disclosures are required:

(a) the events and circumstances that led to the recognition or reversal of the impairment loss;

(b) the amount of the impairment loss recognised or reversed;

(c) for an individual asset:

    (i) the nature of the asset; and

    (ii) if the entity reports segmental information in accordance with IFRS 8, the reportable segment to which the asset belongs.

(d) for a cash-generating unit:

    (i) a description of the cash-generating unit (such as whether it is a product line, a plant, a business operation, a geographical area, or a reportable segment as defined in IFRS 8);

(ii) the amount of the impairment loss recognised or reversed by class of assets and if the entity reports segment information in accordance with IFRS 8, by reportable segment; and

(iii) if the aggregation of assets for identifying the cash-generating unit has changed since the previous estimate of the cash-generating unit's recoverable amount (if any), a description of the current and former way of aggregating assets and the reasons for changing the way the cash-generating unit is identified.

(e) the recoverable amount of the asset or CGU and whether the recoverable amount of the asset or cash-generating unit is its fair value less costs of disposal (FVLCD) or its value in use (VIU);

(f) if the recoverable amount is FVLCD:

(i) the level of the fair value hierarchy (as defined by IFRS 13, see 6.1 above) within which the fair value measurement of the asset or CGU is classified, without taking into account whether the costs of disposal are observable;

(ii) if the fair value measurement is classified as Level 2 or Level 3 of the fair value hierarchy, a description of the valuation technique(s) used to measure FVLCD. The entity must disclose any change in valuation technique and the reason(s) for making it; and

(iii) if the fair value measurement is classified as Level 2 or Level 3 of the fair value hierarchy, each key assumption on which management has based its determination of fair value less costs of disposal. Key assumptions are those to which the asset's or CGU's recoverable amount is most sensitive.

The entity must also disclose the discount rate(s) used in the current measurement and previous measurement if FVLCD is measured using a present value technique; and

(g) if the recoverable amount is VIU, the discount rate used in the current estimate and previous estimate (if any) of VIU. *[IAS 36.130]*.

It is logically possible for impairment adjustments in aggregate to be material, yet no single one material in itself, in which case the previous requirement that relates to individual assets or CGUs could theoretically be circumvented. Therefore the following 'catch all' requirement is added:

'An entity shall disclose the following information for the aggregate impairment losses and the aggregate reversals of impairment losses recognised during the period for which no information is disclosed in accordance with paragraph 130:

(a) the main classes of assets affected by impairment losses and the main classes of assets affected by reversals of impairment losses.

(b) the main events and circumstances that led to the recognition of these impairment losses and reversals of impairment losses.' *[IAS 36.131]*.

In addition, in these circumstances, if there are any cases of impairment adjustments where intangible assets with indefinite useful life and goodwill are not involved, IAS 36 encourages the disclosure of key assumptions made in the recoverable amount calculations used to determine any impairments recognised in the period. *[IAS 36.132]*.

However, as set out below, an entity is required to give this type of disclosure when goodwill or intangible assets with an indefinite useful life are tested for impairment.

13.3 Annual impairment disclosures required for goodwill and intangible assets with an indefinite useful life

Paragraph 84 of IAS 36 accepts that following a business combination it may not have been possible to allocate all the goodwill to individual CGUs or groups of CGUs by the end of the period in which the acquisition has been made (see 8.1.5 above). In these circumstances the standard requires that the amount of any such unallocated goodwill be disclosed, together with the reasons why it has not been allocated. *[IAS 36.133]*.

The annual disclosures are intended to provide the user with information about the types of estimates that have been used in arriving at the recoverable amounts of goodwill and intangible assets with an indefinite useful life, that are included in the assets of the entity at the period end. They are divided into two broad categories:

(i) those concerning individual CGUs or group of CGUs in which the carrying amount of goodwill or of intangible assets with an indefinite useful life is 'significant' in comparison with the entity's total carrying amount of these items. In this category disclosures are to be made separately for each significant CGU or group of CGUs; and

(ii) those concerning CGUs or groups of CGUs in which the carrying amount of goodwill or of intangible assets with an indefinite useful life is not 'significant' individually in comparison with the entity's total carrying amount of these items. In this case the disclosures can be made in aggregate.

For each cash-generating unit or group of units for which the carrying amount of goodwill or intangible assets with indefinite useful lives allocated to that unit or group of units is significant, the following disclosures are required every year:

(a) the carrying amount of goodwill allocated to the CGU (group of CGUs);

(b) the carrying amount of intangible assets with indefinite useful lives allocated to the CGU (group of CGUs);

(c) the basis on which the CGU's or group of CGUs' recoverable amount has been determined (i.e. VIU or FVLCD):

(d) if the CGU's or group of CGUs' recoverable amount is based on VIU:

   (i) a description of each key assumption on which management has based its cash flow projections for the period covered by the most recent budgets/forecasts. Key assumptions are those to which the unit's (group of units') recoverable amount is most sensitive;

   (ii) a description of management's approach to determining the value(s) assigned to each key assumption, whether those value(s) reflect past experience or, if appropriate, are consistent with external sources of information, and, if not, how and why they differ from past experience or external sources of information;

   (iii) the period over which management has projected cash flows based on financial budgets/forecasts approved by management and, when a period greater than five years is used for a cash-generating unit (group of units), an explanation of why that longer period is justified;

  (iv) the growth rate used to extrapolate cash flow projections beyond the period covered by the most recent budgets/forecasts, and the justification for using any growth rate that exceeds the long-term average growth rate for the products, industries, or country or countries in which the entity operates, or for the market to which the unit (group of units) is dedicated;

  (v) the discount rate(s) applied to the cash flow projections.

(e) if the CGU's or group of CGUs' recoverable amount is based on FVLCD, the valuation technique(s) used to measure FVLCD. An entity is not required to provide the disclosures required by IFRS 13. If fair value less costs of disposal is not measured using a quoted price for an identical CGU or CGU group, an entity must disclose the following information:

  (i) a description of each key assumption on which management has based its determination of FVLCD. Key assumptions are those to which the unit's (group of units') recoverable amount is most sensitive;

  (ii) a description of management's approach to determining the value(s) assigned to each key assumption, whether those value(s) reflect past experience or, if appropriate, are consistent with external sources of information, and, if not, how and why they differ from past experience or external sources of information;

  (iiA) the level of the fair value hierarchy (see IFRS 13) within which the fair value measurement is categorised in its entirety (without giving regard to the observability of 'costs of disposal');

  (iiB) if there has been a change in valuation technique, the change and the reason(s) for making it;

  If FVLCD is determined using discounted cash flow projections, the following information shall also be disclosed:

  (iii) the period over which management has projected cash flows;

  (iv) the growth rate used to extrapolate cash flow projections;

  (v) the discount rate(s) applied to the cash flow projections.

(f) if a reasonably possible change in a key assumption on which management has based its determination of the CGU's or group of CGUs' recoverable amount would cause the CGU's or group of CGUs' carrying amount to exceed its recoverable amount:

  (i) the amount by which the CGU's or group of CGUs' recoverable amount exceeds its carrying amount;

  (ii) the value assigned to the key assumption;

  (iii) the amount by which the value assigned to the key assumption must change, after incorporating any consequential effects of that change on the other variables used to measure recoverable amount, in order for the CGU's or group of CGUs' recoverable amount to be equal to its carrying amount. *[IAS 36.134]*.

As set out above, there are separate disclosure requirements for those CGUs or groups of CGUs that taken individually do not have significant amounts of goodwill in comparison with the total carrying value of goodwill or of intangible assets with an indefinite useful life. *[IAS 36.135]*.

First, an aggregate disclosure has to be made of the 'not significant' amounts of goodwill or of intangible assets with an indefinite useful life. If some or all of the carrying amount of goodwill or intangible assets with indefinite useful lives is allocated across multiple CGUs or group of CGUs, and the amount so allocated to each CGU or group of CGUs is not significant in comparison with the entity's total carrying amount of goodwill or intangible assets with indefinite useful lives, that fact shall be disclosed, together with the aggregate carrying amount of goodwill or intangible assets with indefinite useful lives allocated to those CGUs or group of CGUs.

In addition, if the recoverable amounts of any of those CGUs or group of CGUs are based on the same key assumption(s) and the aggregate carrying amount of goodwill or intangible assets with indefinite useful lives allocated to them is significant in comparison with the entity's total carrying amount of goodwill or intangible assets with indefinite useful lives, an entity shall disclose that fact, together with:

(a) the aggregate carrying amount of goodwill allocated to those CGUs or group of CGUs);

(b) the aggregate carrying amount of intangible assets with indefinite useful lives allocated to those CGUs or group of CGUs;

(c) a description of the key assumption(s);

(d) a description of management's approach to determining the value(s) assigned to the key assumption(s), whether those value(s) reflect past experience or, if appropriate, are consistent with external sources of information, and, if not, how and why they differ from past experience or external sources of information;

(e) if a reasonably possible change in the key assumption(s) would cause the aggregate of the CGU's or group of CGUs' carrying amounts to exceed the aggregate of their recoverable amounts:

   (i) the amount by which the aggregate of the CGU's or group of CGUs' recoverable amounts exceeds the aggregate of their carrying amounts;

   (ii) the value(s) assigned to the key assumption(s);

   (iii) the amount by which the value(s) assigned to the key assumption(s) must change, after incorporating any consequential effects of the change on the other variables used to measure recoverable amount, in order for the aggregate of the CGU's or group of CGUs' recoverable amounts to be equal to the aggregate of their carrying amounts. *[IAS 36.135].*

Example 9 in IAS 36's Illustrative Examples gives an indication of the types of assumptions and other relevant information the IASB envisages being disclosed under this requirement. The IASB expects disclosure of: budgeted gross margins, average gross margins, expected efficiency improvements, whether values assigned to key assumptions reflect past experience, what improvements management believes are reasonably achievable each year, forecast exchange rates during the budget period, forecast consumer price indices during the budget period for raw materials, market share and anticipated growth in market share. If a reasonable possible change in a key assumption would cause the CGU's carrying amount to exceed its recoverable amount then the standard would require an entity to give disclose the value assigned to this key assumption and the amount by which the value assigned to the key assumption must change in order to cause an impairment. *[IAS 36.134(f)(ii)].*

An example of disclosures including key assumptions and sensitivities is given by Vodafone Group Plc. The following extract from the annual report of Vodafone plc focuses on the current period disclosures. While disclosures for comparative years are required, and given by Vodafone in the annual report, these were for simplicity purposes not included in the following extract.

Extract 20.3: Vodafone Group Plc (2017)

Notes to the consolidated financial statements [extract]

4. **Impairment losses** [extract]

Following our annual impairment review, the impairment charges in the consolidated income statement within operating profit in respect of goodwill are stated below. The impairment losses were based on value in use calculations.

Cash generating unit:	Reportable segment:	2017 £m	Restated 2016 £m	Restated 2015 £m
Romania	Other Europe	–	569	–

In addition to the impairment losses above, in the first half of 2017 financial year, the Group recorded a non-cash impairment of €6.4 billion, relating to Indian business. This was driven by lower projected cash flows within our business plan as a result of increased competition in the market. Impairment testing at 31 March 2017, following the announcement of the merger of Vodafone Indian with Idea Cellular, gave rise to a partial reversal of that impairment. As a result, the Group recorded an overall impairment loss of €4,515 million (2016: €nil, 2015: €nil) in respect of the fair value of Group's investment in India which, together with the recognition of an associated €840 million deferred tax assets, led to an overall €3,675 million reduction in the carrying value of Vodafone India, the results of which are included discontinued operations. See note 7 "Discontinued operations and assets held for resale" for further details.

Goodwill

The remaining carrying value of goodwill at 31 March was as follows:

	2017 £m	Restated 2016 £m
Germany	12,479	12,479
Italy	3,654	3,654
Spain	3,814	3,814
	19,947	19,947
Other	6,861	8,291
	26,808	28,238

Key assumptions used in the value in use calculations

The key assumptions used in determining the value in use are:

Assumption	How determined
Projected adjusted EBITDA	Budgeted EBITDA has been based on past experience adjusted for the following: > voice and messaging revenue is expected to benefit from increased usage from new customers, especially in emerging markets, the introduction of new services and traffic moving from fixed networks to mobile networks, though these factors will be offset by increased competitor activity, which may result in price declines, and the trend of falling termination and other regulated rates; > non-messaging data revenue is expected to continue to grow as the penetration of 3G (plus 4G where available) enabled devices and smartphones rise along with higher data bundle attachment rates, and new products and services are introduced; and > margins are expected to be impacted by negative factors such as the cost of acquiring and retaining customers in increasingly competitive markets and the expectation of further termination rate cuts by regulators and by positive factors such as the efficiencies expected from the implementation of Group initiatives.
Projected capital expenditure	The cash flow forecasts for capital expenditure are based on past experience and include the ongoing capital expenditure required to roll out networks in emerging markets, to provide voice and data products and services and to meet the population coverage requirements of certain of the Group's licences. Capital expenditure includes cash outflows for the purchase of property, plant and equipment and computer software.
Projected licence and spectrum payments	The cash flow forecasts for licence and spectrum payments for each operating company for the initial five years include amounts for expected renewals and newly available spectrum. Beyond that period, a long-run cost of spectrum is assumed.
Long-term growth rate	For businesses where the five year management plans are used for the Group's value in use calculations, a long-term growth rate into perpetuity has been determined as the lower of: > the nominal GDP rates for the country of operation; and > the long-term compound annual growth rate in adjusted EBITDA in years six to ten estimated by management.
Pre-tax risk adjusted discount rate	The discount rate applied to the cash flows of each of the Group's operations is generally based on the risk free rate for ten year bonds issued by the government in the respective market. Where government bond rates contain a material component of credit risk, high quality local corporate bond rates may be used. These rates are adjusted for a risk premium to reflect both the increased risk of investing in equities and the systematic risk of the specific Group operating company. In making this adjustment, inputs required are the equity market risk premium (that is the required increased return required over and above a risk free rate by an investor who is investing in the market as a whole) and the risk adjustment, beta, applied to reflect the risk of the specific Group operating company relative to the market as a whole. In determining the risk adjusted discount rate, management has applied an adjustment for the systematic risk to each of the Group's operations determined using an average of the betas of comparable listed mobile telecommunications companies and, where available and appropriate, across a specific territory. Management has used a forward-looking equity market risk premium that takes into consideration both studies by independent economists, the average equity market risk premium over the past ten years and the market risk premiums typically used by investment banks in evaluating acquisition proposals.

Year ended 31 March 2017

As discontinued operation, Vodafone India has been valued at fair value less costs to sell. Vodafone India's fair value less costs to sell is not observable in a quoted market and accordingly it has been determined with reference to the outcomes from the application of a number of potential valuation techniques, which are considered to result in a "level 2" valuation. As such significant judgement is required and involves the use of estimates. The two basis of valuation which were given the strongest weighing in the overall assessment of fair value are set out below. Fair value has been assessed to be €14.0 billion. See note 7 "Discontinued operations and assets held for resale" for further details.

> The contracted cash price for the sale of a portion of the entity to the Aditya Birla Group as part of the planned disposal of Vodafone India, adjusted for the agreed level of debt which is an observable price relating to Vodafone India; and

> The share price of Idea Cellular prior to the announcement of the plan to dispose of Vodafone India and participate with Idea Cellular in the planned jointly controlled entity, adjusted for transaction specific factors. Idea Cellular equity shares are the primary component of the consideration for Vodafone India to be received by the Group, and the value of the Idea Cellular shares has been adjusted to reflect 50% of the estimated cost synergies that management expects to be realised by the jointly controlled entity. A 10% increase or reduction in the expected cost synergies included in this determination of fair value would result in a €220 million increase or reduction, respectively, in the fair value less costs to sell of Vodafone India calculated using this approach.

The table below shows the key assumptions used in the value in use calculations.

	Assumptions used in value in use calculation			
	Germany	Spain	Italy	Romania
	%		%	%
Pre-tax risk adjusted discount rate	8.4	9.7	10.3	9.0
Long-term growth rate	0.5	1.5	1.0	1.0
Projected adjusted EBITDA[1]	3.0	7.9	(0.8)	0.1
Projected capital expenditure[2]	14.9-16.5	14.3-15.8	12.7-14.2	12.6-15.9

Notes:

1 Projected adjusted EBITDA is expressed as the compound annual growth rates in the initial five years for all cash-generating units of the plans used for impairment testing.

2 Projected capital expenditure, which excludes licenses and spectrum, is expressed as the range of capital expenditure as a percentage of revenue in the initial five years for all cash-generating units of the plans used for impairment testing.

Sensitivity analysis

Other than as disclosed below, management believes that no reasonably possible change in any of the above key assumptions would cause the carrying value of any cash generating unit to exceed its recoverable amount.

The estimated recoverable amounts of the Group's operations in Germany, Spain and Romania exceed their carrying values by €3.5 billion, €1.0 billion and €0.2 billion respectively. The changes in the following table to assumptions used in the impairment review would, in isolation, lead to an impairment loss being recognised for the year ended 31 March 2017:

	Change required for carrying value to equal the recoverable amount		
	Germany	**Spain**	**Romania**
	pps	pps	pps
Pre-tax risk adjusted discount rate	0.9	0.6	1.5
Long-term growth rate	(1.0)	(0.7)	(1.7)
Projected adjusted EDITDA[1]	(1.6)	(1.1)	(1.9)
Projected capital expenditure[2]	7.6	4.4	7.1

Chapter 20

Notes:

1 Projected adjusted EBITDA is expressed as the compound annual growth rates in the initial five years for all cash-generating units of the plans used for impairment testing.

2 Projected capital expenditure, which excludes licenses and spectrum, is expressed as the range of capital expenditure as a percentage of revenue in the initial five years for all cash-generating units of the plans used for impairment testing.

The carrying values for Vodafone UK, Portugal, Ireland and Czech Republic include goodwill arising from their acquisition by the Group and/or the purchase of operating licences or spectrum rights. While the recoverable amounts for these operating companies are not materially greater than their carrying value, each has a lower risk of giving rise to impairment that would be material to the Group given their relative size or the composition of their carrying value. The changes in the following table to assumptions used in the impairment review would have, in isolation, led to an impairment loss being recognised in the year ended 31 March 2017.

	Changes required for carrying value to equal recoverable amount			
	UK pps	Ireland pps	Portugal pps	Czech Republic pps
Pre-tax risk adjusted discount rate	0.5	0.8	0.6	2.1
Long-term growth rate	(0.6)	(0.9)	(0.6)	(2.4)
Projected adjusted EBITDA[1]	(0.8)	(1.2)	(0.9)	(2.8)
Projected capital expenditure[2]	3.2	4.3	3.9	12.0

1 Projected adjusted EBITDA is expressed as the compound annual growth rates in the initial five years for all cash-generating units of the plans used for impairment testing.

2 Projected capital expenditure, which excludes licenses and spectrum, is expressed as the range of capital expenditure as a percentage of revenue in the initial five years for all cash-generating units of the plans used for impairment testing.

References

1 *IFRIC Update,* September 2010.

2 *IFRIC Update,* September 2010.

3 IAS 39 para. 61 refers to '... information about significant changes with an adverse effect that have taken place in the technological, market, economic or legal environment in which the entity/issuers operates...', which is almost identical to the wording in IAS 36 para. 12(b).

Chapter 21 Capitalisation of borrowing costs

List of examples

Chapter 21 Capitalisation of borrowing costs

1 INTRODUCTION

A common question when determining the initial measurement of an asset is whether or not finance costs incurred on its acquisition or during the period of its construction should be capitalised. There have always been a number of strong arguments in favour of the capitalisation of directly attributable finance costs. For example, it is argued that they are just as much a cost as any other directly attributable cost; that expensing finance costs distorts the choice between purchasing and constructing an asset; that capitalising the costs leads to a carrying value that is far more akin to the market value of the asset; and that the financial statements are more likely to represent the true results of the project.

In accounting periods commencing prior to 1 January 2009, entities were permitted to capitalise borrowing costs as an alternative to expensing them in the period they were incurred. However, in March 2007, the IASB issued a revised version of IAS 23 – *Borrowing Costs* – mandating capitalisation of borrowing costs directly attributable to the acquisition, construction or production of a qualifying asset. This was done to achieve convergence in principle with US GAAP. *[IAS 23.BC2]*. It thereby eliminated some (but not all) of the differences with SFAS 34 – *Capitalization of Interest Cost*.[1]

The revised standard applied for the first time to accounting periods commencing on or after 1 January 2009, although early implementation was permitted. *[IAS 23.29]*. In this chapter we consider the requirements of this revised standard, as subsequently updated by minor consequential amendments arising from other standards including IFRS 15 – *Revenue from Contracts with Customers* (see 3.3 below) and IFRS 9 – *Financial Instruments* (see 4 below). These new standards apply to annual reporting periods beginning on or after 1 January 2018, with early application permitted subject to certain conditions.

In January 2016, the IASB issued a new leasing standard, IFRS 16 – *Leases*, which will supersede the current leases standard and interpretations in IFRS. The consequential amendments arising from IFRS 16 include an updated definition of borrowing costs to reflect the requirements of IFRS 16 (see 4 below) when it becomes effective on 1 January 2019. Early application is permitted provided that IFRS 15 has been, or is, applied at the same date as IFRS 16. For the detailed discussion and requirements of this new standard, see Chapter 25.

2 THE REQUIREMENTS OF IAS 23

2.1 Core principle

IAS 23 requires borrowing costs to be capitalised if they are directly attributable to the acquisition, construction or production of a qualifying asset (whether or not the funds have been borrowed specifically). These borrowing costs are included in the cost of the asset; all other borrowing costs are recognised as an expense in the period in which they are incurred. *[IAS 23.1, 8].*

2.2 Scope

An entity should apply IAS 23 in accounting for borrowing costs. *[IAS 23.2].* IAS 23 deals with the treatment of borrowing costs in general, rather than solely focusing on capitalising borrowing costs as part of the carrying value of assets.

The standard does not deal with the actual or imputed costs of equity used to fund the acquisition or construction of an asset. *[IAS 23.3].* This means that any distributions or other payments made in respect of equity instruments, as defined by IAS 32 – *Financial Instruments: Presentation*, are not within the scope of IAS 23. Conversely, interest and dividends payable on instruments classified as financial liabilities appear to be within the scope of the standard (see 4.2 below).

An entity is not required to apply the standard (i.e. application is optional) to borrowing costs directly attributable to the acquisition, construction or production of:

- a qualifying asset measured at fair value (see 3.2 below); or
- inventories that are manufactured, or otherwise produced, in large quantities on a repetitive basis (see 3.1 below). *[IAS 23.4].*

3 QUALIFYING ASSETS

IAS 23 defines a qualifying asset as 'an asset that necessarily takes a substantial period of time to get ready for its intended use or sale'. *[IAS 23.5].*

Assets that are ready for their intended use or sale when acquired are not qualifying assets. *[IAS 23.7].*

IAS 23 does not define 'substantial period of time' and this will therefore require the exercise of judgement after considering the specific facts and circumstances. In practice, an asset that normally takes twelve months or more to be ready for its intended use will usually be a qualifying asset.

The standard indicates that, depending on the circumstances, the following may be qualifying assets: manufacturing plants, power generation facilities, investment properties, inventories, intangible assets and bearer plants. *[IAS 23.7].*

3.1 Inventories

Inventories are within the scope of IAS 23 as long as they meet the definition of a qualifying asset and require a substantial period of time to bring them to a saleable condition. This means inventories that are manufactured, or otherwise produced, over a short period of time are not qualifying assets and are out of scope of IAS 23.

However, even if inventories meet the definition of a qualifying asset and take a substantial period of time to get ready for sale, an entity is not required to apply the standard to borrowing costs directly attributable to the acquisition, construction or production of inventories if these are routinely manufactured or otherwise produced in large quantities on a repetitive basis. *[IAS 23.4(b), BC6]*.

Therefore an entity may choose whether to apply the requirements of IAS 23 to such inventories as a matter of accounting policy. This optional scope exemption has been allowed because of the difficulty of calculating and monitoring the amount to be capitalised, i.e. the costs of capitalisation are likely to exceed the potential benefits. *[IAS 23.BC6]*. There are many examples of such inventories, including large manufactured or constructed items that take some time to complete but are basically sold as standard items, such as aircraft and large items of equipment, or food and drink that take a long time to mature, such as cheese or alcohol that matures in bottle or cask.

Conversely, IAS 23 is required to be applied to bespoke inventories (i.e. those made according to the unique specifications of a particular customer) that are occasionally manufactured or produced on a single item by item basis and take a substantial period of time to get ready for sale.

3.2 Assets measured at fair value

IAS 23 does not require entities to capitalise borrowing costs directly attributable to the acquisition, construction or production of assets measured at fair value that would otherwise be qualifying assets, for example, biological assets within the scope of IAS 41 – *Agriculture*. *[IAS 23.4(a)]*. If the assets are held under a fair value model (or a fair value less costs to sell model) with all changes going to profit or loss, then capitalisation would not affect measurement in the statement of financial position and would involve no more than a reallocation between finance costs and the fair value movement in profit or loss. However, this scope exemption is optional and would still allow an entity to choose whether to apply the requirements of IAS 23 to such assets as a matter of accounting policy.

IAS 23 does not restrict the exemption to assets where the fair value movement is taken to profit or loss. Assets measured at fair value that fall under the revaluation model of IAS 16 – *Property, Plant and Equipment* – are also eligible for this scope exemption even though the revaluation gain or loss goes to other comprehensive income, not profit or loss (see Chapter 18 at 4.1.2). While such assets may be subject to the scope exemption, the revaluation model in IAS 16 is only applied subsequent to initial recognition. *[IAS 16.31]*. Therefore, such assets might be qualifying assets at initial recognition, but subject to the scope exemption subsequently.

For example, assume that an entity borrows specific funds to construct a building, that the building is a qualifying asset and that the entity has a policy of revaluing all its land and buildings. When the constructed building is initially recognised, it will be measured at cost, which would include the directly attributable borrowing costs. *[IAS 16.15, 16(b)]*. Assume that the entity subsequently renovates the building, that the renovation takes a substantial amount of time to complete and that those costs qualify for capitalisation under IAS 16. Since the asset is being revalued it would fall under the scope exemption in IAS 23. Therefore, the entity would not be required to capitalise any directly attributable borrowing costs relating to this subsequent renovation even if it takes a substantial amount of time to complete.

However, for disclosure purposes, an entity will still need to monitor the carrying amount of such an asset, including those borrowing costs that would have been recognised had such an asset been carried under the cost model.

In May 2014 the Interpretations Committee received a request for clarification as to whether an entity is required to reflect the capitalisation of borrowing costs to meet the disclosure requirement of IAS 16 for assets stated at revalued amounts (see Chapter 18 at 8.2) and for which borrowing costs are not capitalised. Since, as discussed above, the capitalisation of borrowing costs for such assets is not required, the determination of the amount of borrowing costs that would have been capitalised under a cost model – solely to meet a disclosure requirement – might be considered burdensome.

The Interpretations Committee noted that the requirements in paragraph 77(e) of IAS 16 are clear. This paragraph requires an entity to disclose the amount at which assets stated at revalued amounts would have been stated had those assets been carried under the cost model. The amount to be disclosed includes borrowing costs capitalised in accordance with IAS 23.

The Interpretations Committee determined that, in the light of the existing IFRS requirements, neither an interpretation nor an amendment to a standard was necessary and consequently decided not to add this issue to its agenda.[2]

3.3 Construction contracts

IFRS 15, which supersedes all revenue recognition standards and interpretations in IFRS including IAS 11 – *Construction Contracts*, applies to accounting periods beginning on or after 1 January 2018 (see 1 above). For the detailed discussion and requirements of this new standard, see Chapter 30.

Prior to adoption of IFRS 15, IAS 11 allows borrowing costs to be treated as contract costs when they can be attributed to contract activity in general and can be allocated to specific contracts (see Chapter 23). *[IAS 11.18]*. If an entity includes borrowing costs in its IAS 11 contract costs, it will affect the presentation of those costs when they are recognised in profit or loss. However, this does not preclude the borrowing costs from being capitalised in accordance with IAS 23, if the criteria for capitalisation in the standard are met.

3.4 Financial assets

IAS 23 excludes all financial assets (which we consider include equity accounted investments) from the definition of qualifying assets. *[IAS 23.7]*.

4 DEFINITION OF BORROWING COSTS

4.1 The definition of borrowing costs in IAS 23

Borrowing costs are interest and other costs that an entity incurs in connection with the borrowing of funds. *[IAS 23.5]*. Borrowing costs are defined in the standard to include:

- interest expense calculated using the effective interest method as described in IFRS 9 (or, for entities that have not yet adopted IFRS 9, IAS 39 – *Financial Instruments: Recognition and Measurement*);
- finance charges in respect of finance leases recognised in accordance with IAS 17 – *Leases* (or, for entities that have adopted IFRS 16, interest in respect of liabilities recognised in accordance with IFRS 16); and
- exchange differences arising from foreign currency borrowings to the extent that they are regarded as an adjustment to interest costs (see 5.4 below). *[IAS 23.6]*.

The standard addresses whether or not to capitalise borrowing costs as part of the cost of the asset. *[IAS 23.8, 9]*. The identification and measurement of finance costs are not dealt with in IAS 23 (see 4.2 below).

4.2 Other finance costs

IAS 23 does not address many of the ways in which an entity may finance its operations or other finance costs that it may incur. For example, the standard does not address any of the following:

- the many derivative financial instruments such as interest rate swaps, floors, caps and collars that are commonly used to manage interest rate risk on borrowings;
- gains and losses on derecognition of borrowings, for example early settlement of directly attributable borrowings that have been renegotiated prior to completion of an asset in the course of construction; and
- dividends payable on shares classified as financial liabilities (such as certain redeemable preference shares) that have been recognised as an expense in profit or loss.

The eligibility of these other finance costs for capitalisation under IAS 23 is discussed at 5.5 below.

IAS 23 does not preclude the classification of costs, other than those it identifies, as borrowing costs. However, they must meet the basic criterion in the standard, i.e. that they are costs that are directly attributable to the acquisition, construction or production of a qualifying asset, which would, therefore, preclude treating the unwinding of discounts as borrowing costs. Many unwinding discounts are treated as finance costs in profit or loss. These include discounts relating to various provisions such as those for onerous leases and decommissioning costs. These finance costs will not be borrowing costs under IAS 23 because they do not arise in respect of funds borrowed by the entity that can be attributed to a qualifying asset. Therefore, they cannot be capitalised. In addition, as in the case of exchange differences, capitalisation of such costs should be permitted only 'to the extent that they are regarded as an adjustment to interest costs' (see 5.4 below). *[IAS 23.6(e)]*.

5 BORROWING COSTS ELIGIBLE FOR CAPITALISATION

5.1 Directly attributable borrowing costs

Borrowing costs are eligible for capitalisation as part of the cost of an asset if they are directly attributable to the acquisition, construction or production of a qualifying asset, it is probable that such costs will result in future economic benefits to the entity and the costs can be measured reliably. *[IAS 23.8, 9]*.

The standard starts from the premise that borrowing costs that are directly attributable to the acquisition, construction or production of a qualifying asset are those that would have been avoided if the expenditure on the qualifying asset had not been made. *[IAS 23.10]*. Recognising that it may not always be easy to identify a direct relationship between particular borrowings and a qualifying asset and to determine the borrowings that could otherwise have been avoided, the standard includes separate requirements for specific borrowings and general borrowings.

5.2 Specific borrowings

When an entity borrows funds specifically to obtain a particular qualifying asset, the borrowing costs that are directly related to that qualifying asset can be readily identified. *[IAS 23.10]*. The borrowing costs eligible for capitalisation would be the actual borrowing costs incurred on that specific borrowing during the period. *[IAS 23.12]*.

Entities frequently borrow funds in advance of expenditure on qualifying assets and may temporarily invest the borrowings. The standard makes it clear that any investment income earned on the temporary investment of those borrowings needs to be deducted from the borrowing costs incurred and only the net amount capitalised (see Example 21.2 below). *[IAS 23.12, 13]*.

There is no restriction in IAS 23 on the type of investment in which the funds can be invested but, in our view, to maintain the conclusion that the funds are specific borrowings, the investment must be of a nature that does not expose the principal amount to the risk of not being recovered. The more risky the investment, the greater is the likelihood that the borrowing is not specific to the qualifying asset. If the investment returns a loss rather than income, such losses are not added to the borrowing costs to be capitalised.

5.3 General borrowings

IAS 23 concedes that there may be practical difficulties in identifying a direct relationship between particular borrowings and a qualifying asset and in determining the borrowings that could otherwise have been avoided. *[IAS 23.11]*. This could be the case if the financing activity of an entity is co-ordinated centrally, for example, if an entity borrows to meet its funding requirements as a whole and the construction of the qualifying asset is financed out of general borrowings. Other circumstances that may cause difficulties are identified by the standard as follows:

- a group has a treasury function that uses a range of debt instruments to borrow funds at varying rates of interest and lends those funds on various bases to other entities in the group; or
- loans are denominated in or linked to foreign currencies and the group operates in highly inflationary economies or there are fluctuations in exchange rates. *[IAS 23.11]*.

In these circumstances, determining the amount of borrowing costs that are directly attributable to the acquisition of a qualifying asset may be difficult and require the exercise of judgement. *[IAS 23.11]*.

When general borrowings are used in part to obtain a qualifying asset, IAS 23 requires the application of a capitalisation rate to the expenditure on that asset in determining the amount of borrowing costs eligible for capitalisation. However, the amount of borrowing costs capitalised during a period cannot exceed the amount of borrowing costs incurred during that period. *[IAS 23.14]*.

The capitalisation rate applied should be the weighted average of the borrowing costs applicable to the borrowings of the entity that are outstanding during the period, other than borrowings made specifically for the purpose of obtaining a qualifying asset. *[IAS 23.14]*. The capitalisation rate is then applied to the expenditure on the qualifying asset.

Expenditure on a qualifying asset includes only that expenditure resulting in the payment of cash, the transfer of other assets or the assumption of interest-bearing liabilities. Such expenditure must be reduced by any progress payments and grants received in connection with the asset (see IAS 20 – *Accounting for Government Grants and Disclosure of Government Assistance* – and Chapter 26). The standard accepts that, when funds are borrowed generally, the average carrying amount of the asset during a period, including borrowing costs previously capitalised, is normally a reasonable approximation of the expenditure to which the capitalisation rate is applied in that period. *[IAS 23.18]*.

The standard does not provide specific guidance regarding interest income earned from temporarily investing excess general funds. However, any interest income earned is unlikely to be directly attributable to the acquisition or construction of a qualifying asset. In addition, the capitalisation rate required by IAS 23 focuses on the borrowings of the entity outstanding during the period of construction or acquisition and does not include temporary investments. As such, borrowing costs capitalised should not be reduced by interest income earned from the investment of general borrowings nor should such income be included in determining the appropriate capitalisation rate.

In some circumstances, it is appropriate for all borrowings made by the group (i.e. borrowings of the parent and its subsidiaries) to be taken into account in determining the weighted average of the borrowing costs. In other circumstances, it is appropriate for each subsidiary to use a weighted average of the borrowing costs applicable to its own borrowings. *[IAS 23.15]*. It is likely that this will largely be determined by the extent to which borrowings are made centrally (and, perhaps, interest expenses met in the same way) and passed through to individual group companies via intercompany accounts and intra-group loans. The capitalisation rate is discussed further at 5.3.2 below.

5.3.1 Definition of general borrowings

5.3.1.A General borrowings related to specific non-qualifying assets

As noted at 5.3 above, determining general borrowings will not always be straightforward and, as a result, the determination of the amount of borrowing costs that are directly attributable to the acquisition of a qualifying asset is difficult and the exercise of judgement is required.

In July 2009, the Interpretations Committee received a request for guidance on what borrowings comprise 'general borrowings' for the purpose of capitalising borrowing costs in accordance with IAS 23. The request asked for guidance on the treatment of general borrowings used to purchase a specific asset other than a qualifying asset.

The Interpretations Committee noted that paragraph 14 of IAS 23 states that '[t]o the extent that an entity borrows funds generally and uses them for the purpose of obtaining a qualifying asset, the entity shall determine the amount of borrowing costs eligible for capitalisation by applying a capitalisation rate to the expenditures on that asset. The capitalisation rate shall be the weighted average of the borrowing costs applicable to the borrowings of the entity that are outstanding during the period, other than borrowings made specifically for the purpose of obtaining a qualifying asset.'

The Interpretations Committee also noted that because paragraph 14 refers only to qualifying assets:

- some conclude that borrowings related to specific assets other than qualifying assets cannot be excluded from determining the capitalisation rate for general borrowings; and
- others note the general principle in paragraph 10 that the borrowing costs that are directly attributable to the acquisition, construction or production of a qualifying asset are borrowing costs that would have been avoided if the expenditure on the qualifying asset had not been made.

Consequently, the Interpretations Committee concluded that any guidance it could provide would be in the nature of application guidance rather than an interpretation. In light of this and because the IASB was due to consider whether to add this issue to the annual improvements project, the Committee decided not to add the issue to its agenda.[3]

The IASB subsequently considered the issue of whether debt incurred specifically to acquire a non-qualifying asset could be excluded from general borrowings but, as IAS 23 excludes only debt used to acquire qualifying assets from the determination of the capitalisation rate, decided not to include this issue in the annual improvements project.[4] However, in June 2017, the Interpretations Committee recommended that the IASB clarify this issue when finalising the proposed amendments to paragraph 14 of IAS 23 – see discussion in 5.3.1.B below.

5.3.1.B Borrowing costs on borrowings related to completed qualifying assets

Another question that arises is whether a specific borrowing undertaken to obtain a qualifying asset ever changes its nature into a general borrowing. Differing views exist as to whether or not borrowings change their nature throughout the period they are outstanding. Some consider that once the asset for which the borrowing was incurred has been completed, and the entity chooses to use its funds on constructing other assets rather than repaying the loan, this changes the nature of the loan into a general borrowing. However, to the extent that the contract links the repayment of the loan to specific proceeds generated by the entity, its nature as a specific borrowing would be preserved. Others take the view that once the borrowing has been classified as specific, its nature does not change while it remains outstanding.

The Interpretations Committee received a request for clarification on this matter. The request sought clarification on whether funds borrowed specifically to finance the construction of a qualifying asset, the construction of which has now been completed, must be included as part of the general borrowings for the purposes of determining the capitalisation rate for other qualifying assets that have been funded from the entity's general borrowings as described in paragraph 14 of IAS 23 (see 5.3.1.A above).

On the basis of the wording in paragraph 14 of IAS 23, the Interpretations Committee concluded that any outstanding specific borrowings would be included within the general borrowings when the related qualifying asset is ready for its intended use or sale. However, the Interpretations Committee noted that there is diversity in practice, which arises from a perceived lack of clarity in the wording in paragraph 14 of IAS 23.

Accordingly, the Interpretations Committee recommended, and the IASB agreed, that the wording in IAS 23 should be clarified through an annual improvement. Consequently, the IASB decided that:

- the amendment should be included in the next cycle of annual improvements (2015-2017); and
- the proposed amendment should be applied prospectively with early application permitted.[5]

As a result, an Exposure Draft of *Annual Improvements to IFRSs 2015-2017 Cycle* was issued in January 2017 with proposals to amend paragraph 14 of IAS 23 to read as follows:

'The capitalisation rate shall be the weighted average of the borrowing costs applicable to the borrowings of the entity that are outstanding during the period. *An entity shall exclude from this calculation* borrowings made specifically for the purpose of obtaining a qualifying asset *until substantially all the activities necessary to prepare that asset for its intended use or sale are complete.*'[6]

The Interpretations Committee discussed feedback on the proposed amendments in its June 2017 meeting and recommended that the IASB finalise the proposed amendments subject to drafting changes. In finalising the amendments, it was also recommended that the IASB clarify that an entity includes funds borrowed specifically to obtain an asset other than a qualifying asset as part of its general borrowings.[7]

In its July 2017 meeting, the IASB tentatively decided to finalise the proposed amendments with no substantive changes and to clarify that an entity also includes funds borrowed specifically to obtain an asset other than a qualifying asset as part of its general borrowings. The IASB will consider the effective date and due process steps at a future meeting.[8]

5.3.2 Calculation of capitalisation rate

As the standard acknowledges that determining general borrowings will not always be straightforward, it will be necessary to exercise judgement to meet the main objective – a reasonable measure of the directly attributable finance costs.

The following example illustrates the practical application of the method of calculating the amount of finance costs to be capitalised:

Example 21.1: Calculation of capitalisation rate (no investment income)

On 1 April 2018 a company engages in the development of a property, which is expected to take five years to complete, at a cost of £6,000,000. The statements of financial position at 31 December 2017 and 31 December 2018, prior to capitalisation of interest, are as follows:

	31 December 2017	31 December 2018
	£	£
Development property	–	1,200,000
Other assets	6,000,000	6,000,000
	6,000,000	7,200,000
Loans		
5.5% debenture stock	2,500,000	2,500,000
Bank loan at 6% p.a.	–	1,200,000
Bank loan at 7% p.a.	1,000,000	1,000,000
	3,500,000	4,700,000
Shareholders' equity	2,500,000	2,500,000

The bank loan with an effective interest rate of 6% was drawn down to match the development expenditure on 1 April 2018, 1 July 2018 and 1 October 2018.

Expenditure was incurred on the development as follows:

	£
1 April 2018	600,000
1 July 2018	400,000
1 October 2018	200,000
	1,200,000

If the bank loan at 6% p.a. is a new borrowing specifically to finance the development then the amount of interest to be capitalised for the year ended 31 December 2018 would be the amount of interest charged by the bank of £42,000 ((£600,000 × 6% × 9/12) + (£400,000 × 6% × 6/12) + (£200,000 × 6% × 3/12)).

However, if all the borrowings were general (i.e. the bank loan at 6% was not specific to the development) and would have been avoided but for the development, then the amount of interest to be capitalised would be:

$$\frac{\text{Total interest expense for period}}{\text{Weighted average total borrowings}} \times \text{Development expenditure}$$

Total interest expense for the period

	£
£2,500,000 × 5.5%	137,500
£1,200,000 (as above)	42,000
£1,000,000 × 7%	70,000
	249,500

Therefore the capitalisation rate would be calculated as:

$$\frac{249{,}500}{3{,}500{,}000 + 700{,}000} = 5.94\%$$

The capitalisation rate would then be applied to the expenditure on the qualifying asset, resulting in an amount to be capitalised of £41,580 as follows:

	£
£600,000 × 5.94% × 9/12	26,730
£400,000 × 5.94% × 6/12	11,880
£200,000 × 5.94% × 3/12	2,970
	41,580

In this example, all borrowings are at fixed rates of interest and the period of construction extends at least until the end of the period, simplifying the calculation. The same principle is applied if borrowings are at floating rates i.e. only the interest costs incurred during that period, and the weighted average borrowings for that period, will be taken into account.

Note that the company's shareholders' equity (i.e. equity instruments – see further discussion in 5.5.4 below) cannot be taken into account. Also, at least part of the outstanding general borrowings is presumed to finance the acquisition or construction of qualifying assets. Regardless of whether they are financing qualifying or non-qualifying assets, all of the outstanding borrowings are presumed to be general borrowings – unless they are specific borrowings used to obtain the same or another qualifying asset (see discussion in 5.3.1.A above).

The above example also assumes that loans are drawn down to match expenditure on the qualifying asset. If, however, a loan is drawn down immediately and investment income is received on the unapplied funds, then the calculation differs from that in Example 21.1 above. This is illustrated in Example 21.2 below.

Example 21.2: Calculation of amount to be capitalised – specific borrowings with investment income

On 1 April 2018 a company engages in the development of a property, which is expected to take five years to complete, at a cost of £6,000,000. In this example, a bank loan of £6,000,000 with an effective interest rate of 6% was taken out on 31 March 2018 and fully drawn. The total interest charge for the year ended 31 December 2018 was consequently £270,000.

However, investment income was also earned at 3% on the unapplied funds during the period as follows:

	£
£5,400,000 × 3% × 3/12	40,500
£5,000,000 × 3% × 3/12	37,500
£4,800,000 × 3% × 3/12	36,000
	114,000

Consequently, the amount of interest to be capitalised for the year ended 31 December 2018 is:

	£
Total interest charge	270,000
Less: investment income	(114,000)
	156,000

5.3.3 Accrued costs and trade payables

As noted in 5.3 above, IAS 23 states that expenditure on qualifying assets includes only that expenditure resulting in the payment of cash, the transfer of other assets or the assumption of interest-bearing liabilities. *[IAS 23.18]*. Therefore, in principle, costs of a qualifying asset that have only been accrued but have not yet been paid in cash should be excluded from the amount on which interest is capitalised, as by definition no interest can have been incurred on an accrued payment. The same principle can be applied to non-interest bearing liabilities e.g. non-interest-bearing trade payables or retention money that is not payable until the asset is completed.

The effect of applying this principle is often merely to delay the commencement of the capitalisation of interest since the capital expenditure will be included in the calculation once it has been paid in cash. If the time between incurring the cost and cash payment is not that great, the impact of this may not be material.

5.3.4 Assets carried below cost in the statement of financial position

An asset may be recognised in the financial statements during the period of production on a basis other than cost, i.e. it may have been written down below cost as a result of being impaired. An asset may be impaired when its carrying amount or expected ultimate cost, including costs to complete and the estimated capitalised interest thereon, exceeds its estimated recoverable amount or net realisable value (see 6.2.1 below).

The question then arises as to whether the calculation of interest to be capitalised should be based on the cost or carrying amount of the impaired asset. In this case, cost should be used, as this is the amount that the entity or group has had to finance. In the case of an impaired asset, the continued capitalisation based on the cost of the asset may well necessitate a further impairment. Accordingly, although the amount capitalised will be different, this should not affect net profit or loss as this is simply an allocation of costs between finance costs and impairment expense.

5.4 Exchange differences as a borrowing cost

An entity may borrow funds in a currency that is not its functional currency e.g. a US dollar loan financing a development in a company which has the Russian rouble as its functional currency. This may have been done on the basis that, over the period of the development, the borrowing costs, even after allowing for exchange differences, were expected to be less than the interest cost of an equivalent rouble loan.

IAS 23 defines borrowing costs as including exchange differences arising from foreign currency borrowings to the extent that they are regarded as an adjustment to interest costs. *[IAS 23.6(e)]*. The standard does not expand on this point. In January 2008, the Interpretations Committee considered a request for guidance on the treatment of foreign exchange gains and losses and on the treatment of any derivatives used to hedge such foreign exchange exposures. The Interpretations Committee decided not to add the issue to its agenda because:

- the standard acknowledges that judgement will be required in its application and appropriate disclosure of accounting policies and judgements would provide users with the information they need to understand the financial statements; and
- the IASB had considered this issue when developing the new IAS 23 and had decided not to provide any guidance.[9]

In our view, as exchange rate movements are partly a function of differential interest rates, in many circumstances the foreign exchange differences on directly attributable borrowings will be an adjustment to interest costs that can meet the definition of borrowing costs. However, care is needed if there are fluctuations in exchange rates that cannot be attributed to interest rate differentials. In such cases, we believe that a practical approach is to limit exchange losses taken as borrowing costs such that the total borrowing costs capitalised do not exceed the amount of borrowing costs that would be incurred on functional currency equivalent borrowings, taking into consideration the corresponding market interest rates and other conditions that existed at inception of the borrowings.

If this approach is used and the construction of the qualifying asset takes more than one accounting period, there could be situations where in one period only a portion of foreign exchange differences could be capitalised. However, in subsequent years, if the borrowings are assessed on a cumulative basis, foreign exchange losses previously expensed may now meet the recognition criteria. The two methods of dealing with this are illustrated in Example 21.3 below.

In our view, whether foreign exchange gains and losses are assessed on a discrete period basis or cumulatively over the construction period is a matter of accounting policy, which must be consistently applied. As alluded to above, IAS 1 – *Presentation of Financial Statements* – requires clear disclosure of significant accounting policies and judgements that are relevant to an understanding of the financial statements (see 7.2 below).

Example 21.3: Foreign exchange differences in more than one period

Method A – The discrete period approach

The amount of foreign exchange differences eligible for capitalisation is determined for each period separately. Foreign exchange losses that did not meet the criteria for capitalisation in previous years are not capitalised in subsequent years.

Method B – The cumulative approach

The borrowing costs to be capitalised are assessed on a cumulative basis based on the cumulative amount of interest expense that would have been incurred had the entity borrowed in its functional currency. The amount of foreign exchange differences capitalised cannot exceed the amount of foreign exchange losses incurred on a cumulative basis at the end of the reporting period. The cumulative approach looks at the construction project as a whole as the unit of account ignoring the occurrence of reporting dates. Consequently, the amount of the foreign exchange differences eligible for capitalisation as an adjustment to the borrowing cost in the period is an estimate, which can change as the exchange rates vary over the construction period.

An illustrative calculation of the amount of foreign exchange differences that may be capitalised under Method A and Method B is set out below.

	Year 1	Year 2	Total
	$	$	$
Interest expense in foreign currency (A)	25,000	25,000	50,000
Hypothetical interest expense in functional currency (B)	30,000	30,000	60,000
Foreign exchange loss (C)	6,000	3,000	9,000
Method A – Discrete Approach			
Foreign exchange loss capitalised – lower of C and (B minus A)	5,000	3,000	8,000
Foreign exchange loss expensed	1,000	–	1,000
Method B – Cumulative Approach			
Foreign exchange loss capitalised	5,000 *	4,000 **	9,000
Foreign exchange loss expensed	1,000	(1,000)	–

* Lower of C and (B minus A) in Year 1.

** Lower of C and (B minus A) in total across the two years. In this example this represents the sum of the foreign exchange loss of $3,000 capitalised using the discrete approach plus the $1,000 not capitalised in year 1.

5.5 Other finance costs as a borrowing cost

5.5.1 *Derivative financial instruments*

The most straightforward and commonly encountered derivative financial instrument used to manage interest rate risk is a floating to fixed interest rate swap, as in the following example.

Example 21.4: Floating to fixed interest rate swaps

Entity A has borrowed €4 million for five years at a floating interest rate to fund the construction of a building. In order to hedge the cash flow interest rate risk arising from these borrowings, A has entered into a matching pay-fixed receive-floating interest rate swap, based on the same underlying nominal sum and duration as the original borrowing, that effectively converts the interest on the borrowings to fixed rate. The net effect of the periodic cash settlements resulting from the hedged and hedging instruments is as if A had borrowed €4 million at a fixed rate of interest.

These instruments are not addressed in IAS 23. IFRS 9 (or IAS 39) sets out the basis on which such instruments are recognised and measured. See Chapter 53 (or Chapter 52) regarding how to account for effective hedges and the conditions that these instruments must meet.

An entity may consider that a specific derivative financial instrument, such as an interest rate swap, is directly attributable to the acquisition, construction or production of a qualifying asset. If the instrument does not meet the conditions for hedge accounting then the effects on income will be different from those if it does, and they will also be dissimilar from year to year. What is the impact of the derivative on borrowing costs eligible for capitalisation? In particular, does the accounting treatment of the derivative financial instrument affect the amount available for capitalisation? If hedge accounting is not adopted, does this affect the amount available for capitalisation?

The following examples illustrate the potential differences.

Example 21.5: Cash flow hedge of variable-rate debt using an interest rate swap

Entity A is constructing a building and expects it to take 18 months to complete. To finance the construction, on 1 January 2017 the entity issues an eighteen month, €20,000,000 variable-rate note payable, due on 30 June 2018 at a floating rate of interest plus a margin of 1%. At that date the market rate of interest is 8%. Interest payment dates and interest rate reset dates occur on 1 January and 1 July until maturity. The principal is due at maturity. On 1 January 2017, the entity also enters into an eighteen month interest rate swap with a notional amount of €10,000,000 from which it will receive periodic payments at the floating rate and make periodic payments at a fixed rate of 9%, with settlement and rate reset dates every 30 June and 31 December. The fair value of the swap is zero at inception.

On 1 January 2017, the debt is recorded at €20,000,000. No entry is required for the swap on that date because its fair value was zero at inception.

During the eighteen month period, floating interest rates change as follows:

	Cash payments	
	Floating rate on principal	Rate paid by Entity A
Period to 30 June 2017	8%	9%
Period to 31 Dec 2017	8.5%	9.5%
Period to 30 June 2018	9.75%	10.75%

Under the interest rate swap, Entity A receives interest at the market floating rate as above and pays at 9% on the nominal amount of €10,000,000 throughout the period.

At 31 December 2017, the swap has a fair value of €37,500, reflecting the fact that it is now in the money as Entity A is expected to receive a net cash inflow of this amount in the period until the instrument is terminated. There are no further changes in interest rates prior to the maturity of the swap and the fair value of the swap declines to zero at 30 June 2018. Note that this example excludes the effect of issue costs and discounting. In addition, it is assumed that, if Entity A is entitled to, and applies, hedge accounting, there will be no ineffectiveness.

The cash flows incurred by the entity on its borrowing and interest rate swap are as follows:

	Cash payments		
	Interest on principal	Interest rate swap (net)	Total
	€	€	€
30 June 2017	900,000	50,000	950,000
31 Dec 2017	950,000	25,000	975,000
30 June 2018	1,075,000	(37,500)	1,037,500
Total	2,925,000	37,500	2,962,500

There are a number of different ways in which Entity A could calculate the borrowing costs eligible for capitalisation, including the following:

(i) The interest rate swap meets the conditions for, and entity A applies, hedge accounting. The finance costs eligible for capitalisation as borrowing costs will be €1,925,000 in the year to 31 December 2017 and €1,037,500 in the period ended 30 June 2018.

(ii) Entity A does not apply hedge accounting. Therefore, it will reflect the fair value of the swap in income in the year ended 31 December 2017, reducing the net finance costs by €37,500 to €1,887,500 and increasing the finance costs by an equivalent amount in 2018 to €1,075,000. However, it considers that it is inappropriate to reflect the fair value of the swap in borrowing costs eligible for capitalisation so it capitalises costs based on the net cash cost on an accruals accounting basis. In this case this will give the same result as in (i) above.

(iii) Entity A does not apply hedge accounting and considers only the costs incurred on the borrowing, not the interest rate swap, as eligible for capitalisation. The borrowing costs eligible for capitalisation would be €1,850,000 in 2017 and €1,075,000 in 2018.

In our view, all these methods are valid interpretations of IAS 23; however, the preparer will need to consider the most appropriate method in the particular circumstances after taking into consideration the discussion below.

In particular, if using method (ii), it is necessary to demonstrate that the gains or losses on the derivative financial instrument are directly attributable to the construction of a qualifying asset. In making this assessment it is necessary to consider the term of the derivative and this method may not be appropriate if the derivative has a different term to the underlying directly attributable borrowing.

Based on the facts in this example, and assuming that entering into the derivative financial instrument is considered to be related to the borrowing activities of the entity, method (iii) may not be an appropriate method to use because it appears to be inconsistent with the underlying principle of IAS 23 – that the costs eligible for capitalisation are those costs that would have been avoided if the expenditure on the qualifying asset had not been made. *[IAS 23.10]*. However, method (iii) may be an appropriate method to use in certain circumstances where it is not possible to demonstrate that the gains or losses on a specific derivative financial instrument are directly attributable to a particular qualifying asset, rather than being used by the entity to manage its interest rate exposure on a more general basis.

Note that method (i) appears to be permitted under US GAAP for fair value hedges. IAS 23 makes reference in its basis of conclusion that under US GAAP, derivative gains and losses (arising from the effective portion of a derivative instrument that qualifies as a fair value hedge) are considered to be part of the capitalised interest cost. IAS 23 does not address such derivative gains and losses. *[IAS 23.BC21]*.

Whichever policy is chosen by an entity, it needs to be consistently applied in similar situations.

5.5.2 Gains and losses on derecognition of borrowings

If an entity repays borrowings early, in whole or in part, then it may recognise a gain or loss on the early settlement. Such gains or losses include amounts attributable to expected future interest rates; in other words, the settlement includes an estimated prepayment of the future cash flows under the instrument. The gain or loss is a function of relative interest rates and how the interest rate of the instrument differs from current and anticipated future interest rates. There may be circumstances in which a loan is repaid while the qualifying asset is still under construction. IAS 23 does not address this issue.

IFRS 9 (or IAS 39) requires that gains and losses on extinguishment of debt should be recognised in profit or loss (see Chapter 51 at 6.3). Accordingly, in our view, gains and losses on derecognition of borrowings are not eligible for capitalisation. It would be extremely difficult to determine an appropriate amount to capitalise and it would be inappropriate thereafter to capitalise any interest amounts (on specific or general borrowings) if doing so would amount to double counting. Decisions to repay borrowings early are not usually directly attributable to the qualifying asset but to other circumstances of the entity.

The same approach would be applied to gains and losses arising from a refinancing when there is a substantial modification of the terms of borrowings as this is accounted for as an extinguishment of the original financial liability and the recognition of a new financial liability (see Chapter 51 at 6.2 to 6.3).

5.5.3 Gains or losses on termination of derivative financial instruments

If an entity terminates a derivative financial instrument, for example, an interest rate swap, before the end of the term of the instrument, it will usually have to either make or receive a payment, depending on the fair value of the instrument at that time. This fair value is typically based on expected future interest rates; in other words it is an estimated prepayment of the future cash flows under the instrument.

The treatment of the gain or loss for the purposes of capitalisation will depend on the following:

- the basis on which the entity capitalises the gains and losses associated with derivative financial instruments attributable to qualifying assets (see 5.5.1 above); and
- whether the derivative is associated with a borrowing that has also been terminated.

Entities must adopt a treatment that is consistent with their policy for capitalising the gains and losses from derivative financial instruments that are attributable to qualifying investments (see 5.5.1 above).

The accounting under IFRS 9 (or IAS 39) will differ depending on whether the instrument has been designated as a hedge or not; in the former case, and assuming that the borrowing has not also been repaid, the entity will usually continue to account for the cumulative gain or loss on the instrument as if the hedge were still in place. In such a case, the amounts that are reclassified from other comprehensive income will be eligible for capitalisation for the remainder of the period of construction.

If the entity is not hedge accounting for the derivative financial instrument, but considers it to be directly attributable to the construction of the qualifying asset then it will have to consider whether part of the gain or loss relates to a period after construction is complete.

If the underlying borrowing is also terminated then the gain or loss will not be capitalised and the treatment will mirror that applied on derecognition of the borrowing, as described in 5.5.2 above.

5.5.4 Dividends payable on shares classified as financial liabilities

An entity might finance its operations in whole or in part by the issue of preference shares and in some circumstances these will be classified as financial liabilities (see Chapter 45 at 4.5). In some circumstances the dividends payable on these instruments would meet the definition of borrowing costs. For example, an entity might have funded the development of a qualifying asset by issuing redeemable preference shares that are redeemable at the option of the holder and so are classified as financial liabilities under IAS 32. In this case, the 'dividends' would be treated as interest and meet the definition of borrowing costs and so should be capitalised following the principles on specific borrowings discussed in 5.2 above.

Companies with outstanding preference shares which are treated as liabilities under IAS 32 might subsequently obtain a qualifying asset. In such cases, these preference share liabilities would be considered to be part of the company's general borrowings.

The related 'dividends' would meet the definition of borrowing costs and could be capitalised following the principles on general borrowings discussed in 5.3 above – i.e. that they are directly attributable to a qualifying asset.

If these shares were both irredeemable, but still treated as liabilities under IAS 32 (see Chapter 45 at 4.5.2), and the only general borrowings, it would generally be difficult to demonstrate that such borrowings would have been avoided if the expenditure on the qualifying asset had not been made. In such a case capitalisation of related 'dividends' would not be appropriate, unless the qualifying asset is demonstrably funded (at least partly) by such borrowings. In cases where such instruments were just a part of a general borrowing 'pool', it would be appropriate to include applicable 'dividends' in determining the borrowing costs eligible for capitalisation (see 5.3.2 above), notwithstanding the fact that these instruments are irredeemable, provided that:

- at least part of any of the general borrowings in the pool was applied to obtain the qualifying asset; or
- it can be demonstrated that at least part of the fund specifically allocated for repaying any of the redeemable part of the pool was used to obtain the qualifying asset.

Capitalisation of dividends or other payments made in respect of any instruments that are classified as equity in accordance with IAS 32 is not appropriate as these instruments would not meet the definition of financial liabilities. In addition, as discussed in 2.2 above, IAS 23 does not deal with the actual or imputed cost of equity, including preferred capital not classified as a liability. *[IAS 23.3]*.

5.6 Capitalisation of borrowing costs in hyperinflationary economies

In situations where IAS 29 – *Financial Reporting in Hyperinflationary Economies* – applies, an entity needs to distinguish between borrowing costs that compensate for inflation and those incurred in order to acquire or construct a qualifying asset.

IAS 29 states that '[t]he impact of inflation is usually recognised in borrowing costs. It is not appropriate both to restate the capital expenditure financed by borrowing and to capitalise that part of the borrowing costs that compensates for the inflation during the same period. This part of the borrowing costs is recognised as an expense in the period in which the costs are incurred.' *[IAS 29.21]*.

Accordingly, IAS 23 specifies that when an entity applies IAS 29, the borrowing costs that can be capitalised should be restricted and the entity must expense the part of borrowing costs that compensates for inflation during the same period in accordance with paragraph 21 of IAS 29 (as described above). *[IAS 23.9]*.

For detailed discussion and requirements of IAS 29, see Chapter 16.

5.7 Group considerations

5.7.1 Borrowings in one company and development in another

A question that can arise in practice is whether it is appropriate to capitalise interest in the group financial statements on borrowings that appear in the financial statements of a different group entity from that carrying out the development. Based on the underlying principle of IAS 23, capitalisation in such circumstances would only be appropriate if the amount capitalised fairly reflected the interest cost of the group on borrowings from third parties that could have been avoided if the expenditure on the qualifying asset were not made.

Although it may be appropriate to capitalise interest in the group financial statements, the entity carrying out the development should not capitalise any interest in its own financial statements as it has no borrowings. If, however, the entity has intra-group borrowings then interest on such borrowings may be capitalised in its own financial statements.

5.7.2 Qualifying assets held by joint arrangements

A number of sectors carry out developments through the medium of joint arrangements (see Chapter 12) – this is particularly common with property developments. In such cases, the joint arrangement may be financed principally by equity and the joint operators or joint venturers may have financed their participation in this equity through borrowings.

In situations where the joint arrangement is classified as a joint venture in accordance with IFRS 11 – *Joint Arrangements*, it is not appropriate to capitalise interest in the joint venture on the borrowings of the venturers as the interest charge is not a cost of the joint venture. Neither would it be appropriate to capitalise interest in the financial statements of the venturers, whether separate or consolidated financial statements, because the qualifying asset does not belong to them. The investing entities have an investment in a financial asset (i.e. an equity accounted investment), which is excluded by IAS 23 from being a qualifying asset (see 3.4 above).

In situations where the joint arrangement is classified as a joint operation in accordance with IFRS 11 and the operators are accounting for their own share of the assets, liabilities, revenue and expenses of the joint operation, then the operators should capitalise borrowing costs incurred that relate to their share of any qualifying asset. Borrowing costs eligible for capitalisation would be based on the operator's obligation for the loans of the joint operation together with any direct borrowings of the operator itself if the operator funds part of the acquisition of the joint operation's qualifying asset.

6 COMMENCEMENT, SUSPENSION AND CESSATION OF CAPITALISATION

6.1 Commencement of capitalisation

IAS 23 requires that capitalisation of borrowing costs as part of the cost of a qualifying asset commences when the entity first meets all of the following conditions:

(a) it incurs expenditures for the asset;

(b) it incurs borrowing costs; and

(c) it undertakes activities that are necessary to prepare the asset for its intended use or sale. *[IAS 23.17]*.

The standard is explicit that only that expenditure on a qualifying asset that has resulted in payments of cash, transfers of other assets or the assumption of interest-bearing liabilities, may be included in determining borrowing costs (see 5.3.3 above). Such expenditure must be reduced by any progress payments and grants received in connection with the asset (see 5.3 above). *[IAS 23.18]*.

The activities necessary to prepare an asset for its intended use or sale can include more than the physical construction of the asset. Necessary activities can start before the commencement of physical construction and include, for example, technical and administrative work such as the activities associated with obtaining permits prior to the commencement of the physical construction. *[IAS 23.19]*. However, this does not mean that borrowing costs can be capitalised if the permits that are necessary for the construction are not expected to be obtained. Borrowing costs are capitalised as part of the cost of an asset when it is probable that they will result in future economic benefits to the entity and the costs can be measured reliably. *[IAS 23.9]*. Therefore, in assessing whether borrowing costs can be capitalised in advance of obtaining permits – assuming the borrowing costs otherwise meet the criteria – a judgement must be made, at the date the expenditure is incurred, as to whether it is sufficiently probable that the relevant permits will be granted. Conversely, if during the application and approval process of such permits it is no longer expected that the necessary permits will be granted, capitalisation of borrowing costs should cease, any related borrowing costs that were previously capitalised should be written off in accordance with IAS 36 – *Impairment of Assets* – and accordingly, the carrying amount of any related qualifying asset subject to development or redevelopment (or, if appropriate, the cash generating unit where such an asset belongs) should be tested for impairment, where applicable (see 6.2.1 below).

Borrowing costs may not be capitalised during a period in which there are no activities that change the condition of the asset. For example a house-builder or property developer may not capitalise borrowing costs on its 'land bank' i.e. that land which is held for future development. Borrowing costs incurred while land is under development are capitalised during the period in which activities related to the development are being undertaken. However, borrowing costs incurred while land acquired for building purposes is held without any associated development activity represent a holding cost of the land. Such costs do not qualify for capitalisation and hence would be considered a period cost (i.e. expensed as incurred). *[IAS 23.19]*.

An entity may make a payment to a third party contractor before that contractor commences construction activities. It is unlikely to be appropriate to capitalise borrowing costs in such a situation until the contractor commences activities that are necessary to prepare the asset for its intended use or sale.

In its accounting policy, KAZ Minerals describes the period during which borrowing costs are capitalised, as well as noting that it uses either an actual rate or a weighted average cost of borrowings.

Extract 21.1: KAZ Minerals PLC (2016)

NOTES TO THE CONSOLIDATED FINANCIAL STATEMENTS [extract]

35. Summary of significant accounting policies [extract]

(r) Borrowing costs

Borrowing costs directly relating to the acquisition, construction or production of a qualifying capital project under construction are capitalised and added to the project cost during construction until such time as the assets are considered substantially ready for their intended use, i.e. when they are capable of commercial production. Where funds are borrowed specifically to finance a project, the amount capitalised represents the actual borrowing costs incurred. Where surplus funds are available for a short period of time from money borrowed specifically to finance a project, the income generated from the temporary investment of such amounts is also capitalised and deducted from the total capitalised borrowing cost. Where the funds used to finance a project form part of general borrowings, the amount capitalised is calculated using a weighted average of rates applicable to relevant general borrowings of the Group during the year. All other borrowing costs are recognised in the income statement in the period in which they are incurred using the effective interest rate method.

Borrowing costs that represent avoidable costs not related to the financing arrangements of the development projects and are therefore not directly attributable to the construction of these respective assets are expensed in the period as incurred. These borrowing costs generally arise where the funds are drawn down under the Group's financing facilities, whether specific or general, which are in excess of the near term cash flow requirements of the development projects for which the financing is intended, and the funds are drawn down ahead of any contractual obligation to do so.

6.2 Suspension of capitalisation

An entity may incur borrowing costs during an extended period in which it suspends the activities necessary to prepare an asset for its intended use or sale. In such a case, IAS 23 states that capitalisation of borrowing costs should be suspended during extended periods in which active development is interrupted. *[IAS 23.20, 21].* Such costs are costs of holding partially completed assets and do not qualify for capitalisation. However, the standard distinguishes between extended periods of interruption (when capitalisation would be suspended) and periods of temporary delay that are a necessary part of preparing the asset for its intended purpose (when capitalisation is not normally suspended). *[IAS 23.21].*

An entity does not normally suspend capitalising borrowing costs during a period when it carries out substantial technical and administrative work. Also, capitalising borrowing costs would not be suspended when a temporary delay is a necessary part of the process of getting an asset ready for its intended use or sale. For example, capitalisation would continue during the extended period in a situation where construction of a bridge is delayed by temporary adverse weather conditions or high water levels, if such conditions are common during the construction period in the geographical region involved. *[IAS 23.21].* Similarly, capitalisation continues during periods when inventory is undergoing slow transformation – the example is given of inventories taking an extended time to mature (presumably such products as Scotch whisky or Cognac, although the relevance of this may be limited as these products are likely to meet the optional exemption for 'routinely manufactured' products – see 3.1 above).

Borrowing costs incurred during extended periods of interruption caused, for example, by a lack of funding or a strategic decision to hold back project developments during a period of economic downturn are not considered a necessary part of preparing the asset for its intended purpose and should not be capitalised.

6.2.1 Impairment considerations

When it is determined that capitalisation is appropriate, an entity continues to capitalise borrowing costs that are directly attributable to the acquisition, construction or production of a qualifying asset as part of the cost of the asset even if the capitalisation causes the expected ultimate cost of the asset to exceed its recoverable amount or net realisable value.

When the carrying amount of the qualifying asset exceeds its recoverable amount or net realisable value (depending on the type of asset), the carrying amount of the asset must be written down or written off in accordance with the relevant IFRSs. In certain circumstances, the amount of the write-down or write-off is written back in accordance with those relevant IFRSs. If the asset is incomplete, this assessment is performed by considering the expected ultimate cost of the asset. *[IAS 23.16]*. The expected ultimate cost, which will be compared to recoverable amount or net realisable value, must include costs to complete and the estimated capitalised interest thereon.

IAS 36 will apply if the qualifying asset is property, plant and equipment accounted for in accordance with IAS 16 or if the asset is otherwise within the scope of IAS 36 (see Chapter 20). For inventories that are qualifying assets, the requirements of IAS 2 – *Inventories* – on net realisable value will apply (see Chapter 22).

6.3 Cessation of capitalisation

The standard requires capitalisation of borrowing costs to cease when substantially all the activities necessary to prepare the qualifying asset for its intended use or sale are complete. *[IAS 23.22]*.

An asset is normally ready for its intended use or sale when the physical construction of the asset is complete, even though routine administrative work might still continue. If minor modifications, such as the decoration of a property to the purchaser's or user's specification, are all that are outstanding, this indicates that substantially all the activities are complete. *[IAS 23.23]*. In some cases there may be a requirement for inspection (e.g. to ensure that the asset meets safety requirements) before the asset can be used. Usually 'substantially all the activities' would have been completed before this point in order to be ready for inspection. In such a situation, capitalisation would cease prior to the inspection.

When the construction of a qualifying asset is completed in parts and each part is capable of being used while construction continues on other parts, capitalisation should cease for the borrowing costs on the portion of borrowings attributable to that part when substantially all the activities necessary to prepare that part for its intended use or sale are completed. *[IAS 23.24]*. An example of this might be a business park comprising several buildings, each of which is capable of being fully utilised individually while construction continues on other parts. *[IAS 23.25]*. This principle also applies to single buildings where one part is capable of being fully utilised even if the building as a whole is incomplete.

For a qualifying asset that needs to be complete in its entirety before any part can be used as intended, it would be appropriate to capitalise related borrowing costs until all the activities necessary to prepare the entire asset for its intended use or sale are substantially complete. An example of this is an industrial plant, such as a steel mill, involving several processes which are carried out in sequence at different parts of the plant within the same site. *[IAS 23.25]*.

However, other circumstances may not be as straightforward. It will therefore depend on particular facts and circumstances and may require the exercise of judgement as to what constitutes a 'part'. Disclosure of this judgement is required if it is significant to the understanding of the financial statements (see 7.2 below).

7 DISCLOSURE REQUIREMENTS

7.1 The requirements of IAS 23

An entity shall disclose:

- the amount of borrowing costs capitalised during the period; and
- the capitalisation rate used to determine the amount of borrowing costs eligible for capitalisation. *[IAS 23.26]*.

KAZ Minerals discloses in its 'finance income and finance costs' note its capitalisation rates used to determine its borrowing costs. The amount of borrowing costs capitalised during the period is also disclosed within the table that precedes this narrative disclosure and within the table of movements in the property, plant and equipment note.

Extract 21.2: KAZ Minerals PLC (2016)

NOTES TO THE CONSOLIDATED FINANCIAL STATEMENTS [extract]

11. Finance income and finance costs [extract]

1 Total interest expense includes $197 million of interest incurred on borrowings and $8 million relating to the unwinding of the discount on the NFC deferral agreement (see note 27).

2 In 2016, the Group capitalised to the cost of qualifying assets $155 million (2015: $132 million) of borrowing costs incurred on the outstanding debt during the period on the CDB-Bozshakol and Bozymchak facilities at an average rate of interest (net of interest income) of 5.40% (2015: 4.97%) and on the CDB-Aktogay US$ and CNY facilities at an average rate of interest of 5.12% and 4.33% respectively (2015: 4.64% and 3.93%). Interest capitalised includes $8 million of unwinding of interest on the deferred NFC payable (see note 27).

27. Other liabilities [extract]

(a) Payables to NFC

On 17 November 2015, the Group reached an agreement with its principal construction contractor at Aktogay, NFC, to defer payment of $300 million. Under these terms, $300 million scheduled for payment in 2016 and 2017, was deferred for settlement in the first half of 2018, with $250 million becoming payable shortly after 31 December 2017 and $50 million shortly after 30 June 2018. The extended credit terms arising from the agreement were discounted using a rate of US$ LIBOR plus 4.20% on the estimated cost of services. The discount rate applied is in line with CBD Aktogay facility. The unwinding of the interest will be charged to property, plant and equipment as a borrowing cost (see note 11) until the date the sulphide plant has reached commercial production, after which it will be charged to the income statement within finance costs. At 31 December 2016, the full liability, discounted to its present value, was recognised.

7.2 Disclosure requirements in other IFRSs

In addition to the disclosure requirements in IAS 23, an entity may need to disclose additional information in relation to its borrowing costs in order to comply with requirements in other IFRSs. For example, disclosures required by IAS 1 include:

- the nature and amount of material items included in profit or loss; *[IAS 1.97]*
- the measurement bases used in preparing the financial statements and other accounting policies used that are relevant to an understanding of the financial statements (see an example at Extract 21.1 above); *[IAS 1.117]* and
- the significant judgements made in the process of applying an entity's accounting policies that have the most significant effect on the recognised amounts (e.g. criteria in determining a qualifying asset or a 'part' of a qualifying asset, including definition of 'substantial period of time'). *[IAS 1.122]*.

As noted in 5.4 above, the Interpretations Committee considered a request for guidance on the treatment of foreign exchange gains and losses and on the treatment of any derivatives used to hedge such foreign exchange exposures.

The Interpretations Committee decided not to add the issue to its agenda but concluded both that (i) how an entity applies IAS 23 to foreign currency borrowings is a matter of accounting policy requiring an entity to exercise judgement and (ii) IAS 1 requires disclosure of significant accounting policies and judgements that are relevant to an understanding of the financial statements.[10] The requirements of IAS 1 are discussed in Chapter 3.

References

1 Effective from 15 September 2009, FASB Statement No. 34 (SFAS 34) – *Capitalization of Interest Cost* – was superseded by FASB Accounting Standards Codification (ASC) Topic 835-20 – *Capitalization of Interest*, a subtopic to FASB ASC Topic 835 – *Interest*.

2 *IFRIC Update*, May 2014.

3 *IFRIC Update*, July 2009.

4 *IASB Update*, July 2009.

5 *IASB Update*, October 2015.

6 *Exposure Draft (ED/2017/1) – Annual Improvements to IFRS Standards 2015–2017 Cycle*, IASB, January 2017, p.16.

7 *IFRIC Update*, June 2017.

8 *IASB Update*, July 2017.

9 *IFRIC Update*, January 2008.

10 *IFRIC Update*, January 2008.

Chapter 22 Inventories

Chapter 22 Inventories

1 INTRODUCTION

Under IFRS the relevant standard for inventories is IAS 2 – *Inventories*. The term 'inventories' includes raw materials, work-in-progress, finished goods and goods for resale, although the standard does not include all instances of these categories; some are covered by other standards, for example growing crops are covered by IAS 41 – *Agriculture* (see Chapter 40). This chapter deals only with the inventories within the scope of IAS 2.

Prior to adoption of IFRS 15 – *Revenue from Contracts with Customers* – which applies to accounting periods beginning on or after 1 January 2018, entities accounted for long-term contracts and the associated work in progress under a separate standard, IAS 11 – *Construction Contracts* (see Chapter 23). IFRS 15 only applies when there is a contract with a customer. This means that IFRS 15 has an impact on the accounting for construction contracts, previously accounted for under IAS 11, but does not apply to inventory in the absence of a contract. The requirements of IFRS 15 are addressed in Chapter 30.

Under the historical cost accounting system, costs of inventories comprise expenditure which has been incurred in the normal course of business in bringing the product or service to its present location and condition. All costs incurred in respect of inventories are charged as period costs, except for those which relate to those unconsumed inventories which are expected to be of future benefit to the entity. These are carried forward as an asset, to be matched with the revenues that they will generate in the future. Inventories in the statement of financial position have characteristics similar to those of prepaid expenses or property, plant and equipment – they are effectively deferred costs.

When IAS 2 was revised in 2003 all references to matching and to the historical cost system were deleted, even though historical cost was retained as the primary measurement approach for IAS 2 inventories. However, there have been no recent developments suggesting a move away from this widely accepted and traditional cost-based inventory measurement model to one based on fair value.

2 IAS 2: OBJECTIVE, SCOPE AND DEFINITIONS

The objective of IAS 2 is to prescribe the accounting treatment for inventories. The standard notes that a primary issue in accounting for inventories is the cost to be recognised as an asset until the related revenues are recognised. The standard provides guidance on the determination of cost and its subsequent recognition as an expense, including any write-down to net realisable value. Further to this, it provides guidance on the cost formulas that are used to assign costs to inventories. *[IAS 2.1]*.

IAS 2 applies to all inventories in financial statements except:

- financial instruments (see Chapters 42 to 54); and
- biological assets related to agricultural activity and agricultural produce at the point of harvest (see Chapter 40). *[IAS 2.2]*.

Prior to amendment as a consequence of IFRS 15, in addition to financial instruments and biological assets, IAS 2 excluded from its scope work-in-progress arising under construction contracts including directly related service contracts (both of which were dealt with by IAS 11, see Chapter 23).

Agricultural produce that has been harvested by the entity from its biological assets is in scope; it is initially recognised at its fair value less costs to sell at the point of harvest, as set out in IAS 41 (see Chapter 40). This figure becomes the cost of inventories at that date for the purposes of IAS 2. *[IAS 2.20]*.

The measurement provisions of IAS 2 do not apply to the measurement of inventories held by:

(a) producers of agricultural and forest products, agricultural produce after harvest, and minerals and mineral products, to the extent that they are measured at net realisable value in accordance with well-established practices in those industries. When such inventories are measured at net realisable value, changes in that value are recognised in profit or loss in the period of the change. *[IAS 2.3]*. This occurs, for example, when agricultural crops have been harvested or minerals have been extracted and sale is assured under a forward contract or a government guarantee, or when an active market exists and there is a negligible risk of failure to sell. *[IAS 2.4]*. However, in practice this approach is not common; and

(b) commodity broker-traders who measure their inventories at fair value less costs to sell. If these inventories are measured at fair value less costs to sell, the changes in fair value less costs to sell are recognised in profit or loss in the period of the change. *[IAS 2.3]*. Broker-traders are those who buy or sell commodities for others or on their own account and these inventories are principally acquired with the purpose of selling in the near future and generating a profit from fluctuations in price or broker-traders' margin. *[IAS 2.5]*.

In both cases, the standard stresses that these inventories are only scoped out from the measurement requirements of IAS 2; the standard's other requirements, such as disclosure, continue to apply. Fair value and net realisable value (NRV) are discussed at 3.1 below.

Inventories are defined by IAS 2 as:

(a) assets held for sale in the ordinary course of business;

(b) assets in the process of production for such sale; or

(c) assets in the form of materials or supplies to be consumed in the production process or in the rendering of services. *[IAS 2.6]*.

Inventories can include all types of goods purchased and held for resale including, for example, merchandise purchased by a retailer and other tangible assets such as land and other property, although investment property accounted for under IAS 40 – *Investment Property* – is not treated as an inventory item. The term also encompasses finished goods produced, or work in progress being produced, by the entity and includes materials and supplies awaiting use in the production process. If the entity is a service provider, its inventories may be intangible, e.g. the costs of the service for which the entity has not yet recognised the related revenue). The inventory of service providers will probably consist mainly of the labour costs of the people providing the service. As noted at 1 above, costs incurred to fulfil a contract with a customer that do not give rise to inventories (or assets within the scope of another Standard) are accounted for in accordance with IFRS 15. *[IAS 2.8]*.

Collectibles, for example paintings or sculptures, acquired for short-term investment purposes and traded in the ordinary course of business could be within scope of IAS 2. Depending on the facts and circumstances, these could be either:

- inventories measured at the lower of cost and net realisable value; or
- commodities, measured at fair value less costs to sell.

There is a separate standard, IFRS 5 – *Non-current Assets Held for Sale and Discontinued Operations* – that governs the accounting treatment of non-current assets held for sale, for example a group of assets held for sale such as a business being disposed of. An entity would apply IFRS 5 to any inventories that form part of a disposal group. IFRS 5 is discussed in Chapter 4.

2.1 Scope issues: IAS 2 or another IFRS

2.1.1 Core inventories and spare parts – IAS 2 or IAS 16

It is our view that an item of inventory that is not held for sale or consumed in a production process should be accounted for as an item of property, plant and equipment (PP&E) under IAS 16 – *Property, Plant and Equipment* – if it is necessary to the operation of a facility during more than one operating cycle and its cost cannot be recouped through sale (or it is significantly impaired). This applies even if the part of inventory that is deemed to be an item of PP&E cannot physically be separated from other inventory.

By contrast, spare parts are classified as inventory unless they meet the definition of PP&E. The recognition of spare parts as PP&E and the accounting treatment of core inventories are discussed further in Chapter 18 at 3.1.5.

2.1.2 Transfers of rental assets to inventory

An entity may, in the course of its ordinary activities, routinely sell items that had previously been held for rental and classified as property, plant and equipment. For example, car rental companies may acquire vehicles with the intention of holding them as rental cars for a limited period and then selling them. IAS 16 requires that when such items become held for sale rather than rental they be transferred to inventory at their carrying value. *[IAS 16.68A]*. Revenue from the subsequent sale is then recognised gross rather than net, as discussed in Chapter 18 at 7.2.

2.1.3 Broadcast rights – IAS 2 or IAS 38

Broadcasters purchase programmes under a variety of different arrangements. Often they commit to purchasing programmes that are at a very early stage of development, perhaps merely being concepts. The broadcaster may have exclusive rights over the programme or perhaps only have the rights to broadcast for a set period of time or on a set number of occasions. IFRS is not clear on how these rights should be classified and when they should be recognised.

We believe that an entity may either treat these rights as intangible assets and classify them under IAS 38 – *Intangible Assets,* see Chapter 17 at 2.2, or classify them as inventory under IAS 2. Such rights would certainly seem to meet the definition of inventory under IAS 2. Given that the acquisition of these rights forms part of the cost of the broadcaster's programming schedule, they meet the general IAS 2 definition in that they are:

(a) held for sale in the ordinary course of business;

(b) in the process of production for such sale; or

(c) in the form of materials or supplies to be consumed in the production process or in the rendering of services. *[IAS 2.6].*

When classified as inventory, the rights will need to be disclosed within current assets, even if the intention is not to consume them within 12 months. *[IAS 1.68].* As with costs of other inventory the cash outflow from acquisition will be classified as an operating cash flow and the expense will be presented within cost of sales when the right is consumed.

There is also the issue of the timing of recognition of these rights. In accordance with paragraph 4.4 of *The Conceptual Framework for Financial Reporting* an asset is a resource controlled by an entity as a result of past events and from which future economic benefits are expected to flow to the entity. Hence it is necessary to determine when control is obtained. Under IFRS, executory contracts where both parties are still to perform (such as purchase orders where neither payment nor delivery has taken place) do not generally result in the recognition of assets and liabilities. When a broadcaster initially contracts to purchase a programme it will not usually result in immediate recognition of an asset relating to that programme. At this point there will not normally be an asset under the control of the broadcaster. Factors that may be relevant in determining when the entity controls an asset include whether:

- the underlying resource is sufficiently developed to be identifiable (e.g. whether the manuscript or screenplay has been written, and whether directors and actors have been hired);
- the entity has legal, exclusive rights to broadcast, which may be in respect of a defined period or geographic area;
- there is a penalty to the licensor for non-delivery of the content;
- it is probable that content will be delivered; and
- it is probable that economic benefits will flow to the entity.

Where there is difficulty in determining when control of the asset is obtained it may be helpful to assess at what point any liability arises, since a liability will generally indicate that an asset has been acquired. In practice an entity might recognise an asset and liability for a specific broadcast right on the following trigger dates:

- when a screening certificate is obtained;
- when programming is available for exhibition;
- the beginning of the season;
- the beginning of the license period; or
- the date the event occurs (e.g. game-by-game basis).

The issue of when a licensor recognises revenue under IFRS 15 on the sale of such broadcast rights is covered in Chapter 30 (entities applying IAS 18 – *Revenue* – prior to the adoption of IFRS 15 see Chapter 29 at 5.10).

2.1.4 *Emission rights – IAS 2 or IAS 38*

In order to encourage entities to reduce emissions of pollutants, governments around the world have introduced schemes that comprise tradable emissions allowances or permits. Entities using emission rights for their own purposes may elect to record the rights as intangible assets, whether at cost, revalued amount or, under the so-called 'net liability' approach, as rights that are re-measured to fair value. See Chapter 17 at 11.2.

It may also be appropriate to recognise emission rights, whether granted by the government or purchased by an entity, as inventory in accordance with IAS 2 if they are held for sale in the ordinary course of business or to settle an emissions liability in the ordinary course of business. If the purchased emission rights are recognised as inventories, they are subsequently measured at the lower of cost or net realisable value in accordance with IAS 2, unless they are held by commodity broker-traders.

Broker-traders account for emission rights as inventory. A broker-trader may recognise emission rights either at the lower of cost and net realisable value, or at fair value less costs to sell as permitted by IAS 2. An integrated entity may hold emission rights both for own-use and for trading. An entity accounts for these emission rights separately.

3 MEASUREMENT

The standard's basic rule is that inventories are measured at the lower of cost and net realisable value, apart from those inventories scoped out of its measurement requirements as explained at 2 above. *[IAS 2.9]*. Net realisable value is 'the estimated selling price in the ordinary course of business less the estimated costs of completion and the estimated costs necessary to make the sale'. *[IAS 2.6]*. This is different to fair value, which IAS 2 defines in accordance with IFRS 13 – *Fair Value Measurement*, as 'the price that would be received to sell an asset or paid to transfer a liability in an orderly transaction between market participants at the measurement date'. *[IAS 2.6]*.

The standard points out that net realisable value is an entity-specific value, the amount that the entity actually expects to make from selling that particular inventory, while fair value is not. Fair value reflects the price at which an orderly transaction to sell the same inventory in the principal (or most advantageous) market for that inventory would take place between market participants at the measurement date. Therefore, net realisable value may not be the same as fair value less costs to sell. *[IAS 2.7]*. This is illustrated in the following extract in which AngloGold Ashanti discloses that net realisable value is based on estimated future sales prices of the product.

Extract 22.1: AngloGold Ashanti Limited (2016)

GROUP – NOTES TO THE FINANCIAL STATEMENTS

For the year ended 31 December [extract]

1 ACCOUNTING POLICIES [extract]

1.2 SIGNIFICANT ACCOUNTING JUDGEMENTS AND ESTIMATES [extract]

Use of estimates [extract]

Stockpiles and metals in process [extract]

Costs that are incurred in or benefit the production process are accumulated as stockpiles and metals in process. Net realisable value tests are performed at least annually and represent the estimated future sales price of the product, based on prevailing and long-term metals prices, less estimated costs to complete production and bring the product to sale.

If there has been a downturn in a cyclical business such as real estate, an entity may argue that net realisable value is higher than fair value because the entity intends to hold the asset until prices recover. This is rarely supportable as the decline in fair value usually indicates that the price that will be achieved in the ordinary course of business has declined and time taken to dispose of assets has increased. Net realisable value is discussed at 3.4 below.

This basic measurement rule inevitably raises the question of what may be included in the cost of inventory.

3.1 What may be included in cost?

The costs attributed to inventories under IAS 2 comprise all costs of purchase, costs of conversion and other costs incurred in bringing the inventories to their present location and condition. *[IAS 2.10]*. Costs include import duties and unrecoverable taxes, transport, handling and other costs directly attributable to the inventories. *[IAS 2.11]*. This definition allows for significant interpretation of the costs to be included in inventory.

Trade discounts and similar rebates should be deducted from the costs attributed to inventories. *[IAS 2.11]*. For example a supplier may pay to its customer an upfront cash incentive when entering into a contract. This is a form of rebate and the incentive should be accounted for as a liability by the customer until it receives the related inventory, which is then shown at cost net of this incentive.

Costs of conversion include direct costs such as direct labour and materials, as well as an allocation of fixed and variable production overheads. It must be remembered that the inclusion of overheads is not optional. Overheads may comprise indirect labour and materials or other indirect costs of production. For the most part there are few problems over the inclusion of direct costs in inventories although difficulties may arise over the inclusion of certain types of overheads and over the allocation of overheads into the inventory valuation. Overhead costs must be apportioned using a 'systematic allocation of fixed and variable production overheads that are incurred in converting materials into finished goods'. *[IAS 2.12]*. Overheads should be allocated to the cost of inventory on a consistent basis from year to year, and should not be omitted in anticipation of a net realisable value problem.

Variable production overheads are indirect costs that vary directly, or nearly directly, with the volume of production such as indirect material and indirect labour. *[IAS 2.12]*.

Variable production overheads are allocated to each unit of production on the basis of the actual use of the production facilities. *[IAS 2.13]*.

Fixed production overheads are indirect costs that remain relatively constant regardless of the volume of production, such as building and equipment maintenance and depreciation, and factory management expenses. IFRS 16 – *Leases* – which is mandatory for accounting periods beginning on or after 1 January 2019 amends paragraph 12 of IAS 2 to add 'right-of-use assets used in the production process' as an example of fixed production overheads. *[IAS 2.40G]*.

The allocation of fixed production overheads is based on the normal capacity of the facilities. Normal capacity is defined as 'the production expected to be achieved on average over a number of periods or seasons under normal circumstances, taking into account the loss of capacity resulting from planned maintenance'. *[IAS 2.13]*. While actual capacity may be used if it approximates to normal capacity, increased overheads may not be allocated to production as a result of low output or idle capacity. In these cases the unallocated overheads must be expensed. Similarly, in periods of abnormally high production, the fixed overhead absorption must be reduced, as otherwise inventories would be recorded at an amount in excess of cost. *[IAS 2.13]*.

In computing the costs to be allocated via the overhead recovery rate, costs such as distribution and selling must be excluded, together with the cost of storing raw materials and work in progress, unless it is necessary that storage costs be incurred prior to further processing, which may occasionally be the case (see 3.1.1 below).

The assumptions about normal levels of activity relate to all costs including direct costs. Although determining the normal level of activity when allocating overheads is a judgemental area, it is relatively straightforward when dealing with the manufacturing and processing of physical inventory. It is far harder to establish what this can mean in the context of service industries where the 'inventory' is intangible and based on work performed for customers that has not yet been recognised as income. There really is no equivalent to the normal capacity of production facilities in these cases. However, the standard still requires the inclusion of attributable overheads, and entities must take care to establish an appropriate benchmark to avoid the distortions that could occur if overheads were attributed on the basis of actual 'output'.

Extract 22.2 below shows how Syngenta AG describes its inventory valuation policies.

Extract 22.2: Syngenta AG (2016)

Notes to the Syngenta Group Consolidated Financial Statements [extract]

29. New IFRSs and accounting policies [extract]

Inventories

Purchased products are recorded at acquisition cost while own-manufactured products are recorded at manufacturing cost including a share of production overheads based on normal capacity. Cost of inventories is determined on a first-in-first-out basis. Allowances are made for inventories with a net realizable value less than cost, or which are slow moving. Net realizable value is the estimated selling price in the ordinary course of business, less the estimated costs of completion and costs to sell. Costs to sell include direct marketing, selling and distribution costs. Unsaleable inventories are fully written off.

Although not specifically referred to in IAS 2, when the revaluation model in IAS 16 is applied, depreciation of property, plant and equipment is based on the revalued amount, less the residual value of the asset and it is the revalued depreciation that, in our view, should be utilised in inventory valuation.

IAS 2 mentions the treatment to be adopted when a production process results in the simultaneous production of more than one product, for example a main product and a by-product. If the costs of converting each product are not separately identifiable, they should be allocated between the products on a rational and consistent basis. For example, this might be the relative sales value of each of the products either at the stage in the production process when the products become separately identifiable, or at the completion of production. If the value of the by-product is immaterial, it may be measured at net realisable value and this value deducted from the cost of the main product. *[IAS 2.14]*.

Other costs are to be included in inventories only to the extent that they bring them into their present location and condition. Often judgement will be necessary to make this assessment. An example is given in IAS 2 of design costs for a special order for a particular customer and the standard notes that it may be appropriate to include such costs or other non-production overheads. *[IAS 2.15]*. However a number of examples are given of costs that are specifically disallowed. These include:

(a) abnormal amounts of wasted materials, labour, or other production costs;

(b) storage costs, unless those costs are necessary in the production process prior to a further production stage;

(c) administrative overheads that do not contribute to bringing inventories to their present location and condition; and

(d) selling costs. *[IAS 2.16]*.

3.1.1 Storage and distribution costs

Storage costs are not permitted as part of the cost of inventory unless they are necessary in the production process. *[IAS 2.16(b)]*. This appears to prohibit including the costs of the warehouse and the overheads of a retail outlet as part of inventory, as neither of these is a prelude to a further production stage.

Where it is necessary to store raw materials or work in progress prior to a further processing or manufacturing stage, the costs of such storage should be included in production overheads. For example, it would appear reasonable to allow the costs of storing maturing stocks, such as cheese, wine or whisky, in the cost of production.

Although distribution costs are obviously a cost of bringing an item to its present location, the question arises as to whether costs of transporting inventory from one location to another are eligible.

Costs of distribution to the customer are not allowed as they are selling costs, which are prohibited by the standard from being included in the carrying value of inventory. It therefore seems probable that distribution costs of inventory whose production process is complete should not normally be included in its carrying value. If the inventory is transferred from one of the entity's storage facilities to another and the condition of the inventory is not changed at either location, none of the warehousing costs may be included in inventory costs. It follows that transportation costs between the two storage facilities should not be included in the carrying value of inventory.

A question arises about the meaning of 'production' in the context of large retailers with distribution centres, for example supermarkets. As the transport and logistics involved are essential to their ability to put goods on sale at a particular location in an appropriate condition, it seems reasonable to conclude that such costs are an essential part of the production process and can be included in the cost of inventory. The circumstances of the entity may warrant the inclusion of distribution or other costs into cost of sales even though they have been excluded from the cost of inventory. *[IAS 2.38]*. Disclosure is discussed at 6 below.

3.1.2 General and administrative overheads

IAS 2 specifically disallows administrative overheads that do not contribute to bringing inventories to their present location and condition. *[IAS 2.16(c)]*. Other costs and overheads that do contribute are allowable as costs of production. There is a judgement to be made about such matters, as under a very broad interpretation any department could be considered to make a contribution. For example, the accounts department will normally support the following functions:

(a) production – by paying direct and indirect production wages and salaries, by controlling purchases and related payments, and by preparing periodic financial statements for the production units;

(b) marketing and distribution – by analysing sales and by controlling the sales ledger; and

(c) general administration – by preparing management accounts and annual financial statements and budgets, by controlling cash resources and by planning investments.

Only those costs of the accounts department that can be allocated to the production function can be included in the cost of conversion. Part of the management and overhead costs of a large retailer's logistical department may be included in cost if it can be related to bringing the inventory to its present location and condition. These types of cost are unlikely to be material in the context of the inventory total held by organisations. An entity wishing to include a material amount of overhead of a borderline nature must ensure it can sensibly justify its inclusion under the provisions of IAS 2 by presenting an analysis of the function and its contribution to the production process similar to the above.

3.1.3 Borrowing costs and purchases on deferred terms

IAS 2 states that, in limited circumstances, borrowing costs are to be included in the costs of inventories. *[IAS 2.17]*. IAS 23 – *Borrowing Costs* – requires that borrowing costs be capitalised on qualifying assets but the scope of that standard exempts inventories that are manufactured in large quantities on a repetitive basis. *[IAS 23.4, 8]*. In addition, IAS 23 clarifies that inventories manufactured over a short period of time are not qualifying assets. *[IAS 23.7]*. However, any manufacturer that is producing small quantities over a long time period has to capitalise borrowing costs. This is further discussed in Chapter 21.

IAS 2 also states that on some occasions, an entity might purchase inventories on deferred settlement terms, accompanied by a price increase that effectively makes the arrangement a combined purchase and financing arrangement. Under these circumstances the price difference is recognised as an interest expense over the period of the financing. *[IAS 2.18]*.

Entities might also make prepayments for inventory, particularly raw materials in long-term supply contracts, raising the question of whether there is a financing component that should be accounted for separately.

If a purchaser accretes interest on long-term prepayments by recognising interest income, this will result in an increase in the cost of inventories and, ultimately, the cost of sales. The Interpretations Committee considered this in July 2015, noting that IAS 16 and IAS 38 include similar requirements when payment for an asset is deferred (see Chapter 18 at 4.1.6 and Chapter 17 at 4.2).

Historically there has been no explicit requirement in IFRS to accrete interest income but the Interpretations Committee noted that IFRS 15 includes the requirement that the financing component of a transaction should be recognised separately in circumstances of both prepayment and deferral of payment (see Chapter 30 at 5.5). They concluded, therefore, that when a financing component is identified in a long-term supply contract of raw materials, that financing component should be accounted for separately. They acknowledged that judgement is required to identify when individual arrangements contain a financing component.[1]

3.1.4 Service providers

Costs to fulfil a contract, as defined in IFRS 15, are divided into two categories: (a) costs that give rise to an asset; and (b) costs that are expensed as incurred (see Chapter 30 at 9.3.2) *[IFRS 15.95-96]*. When determining the appropriate accounting treatment for such costs IAS 2 (or any other more specific IFRS) is considered first and if costs incurred in fulfilling the contract are within the scope of this standard, those costs should be accounted for in accordance with IAS 2 (or other IFRS). If costs incurred to fulfil a contract are not within the scope of this standard, an entity would need to consider the criteria in IFRS 15 for capitalisation of such costs (see Chapter 30 at 9.3.2).

Prior to adoption of IFRS 15, cost of inventories of a service provider – effectively their work-in-progress – was specifically addressed in paragraph 19 of IAS 2 (deleted by the consequential amendments arising from IFRS 15). For this type of business, IAS 2 required the labour and other costs of personnel directly engaged in providing the service, including supervisory personnel and attributable overheads, to be included in the cost of inventories. However, labour and other costs relating to sales and general administrative personnel had to be expensed as incurred. Inventories would not have included profit margins or non-attributable overheads. As discussed in 3.1 above, service providers may have found it a challenge to establish 'normal capacity' for the purposes of allocating attributable overheads.

3.1.5 Forward contracts to purchase inventory

The standard scopes out commodity broker-traders that measure inventory at fair value less costs to sell from its measurement requirements (see 2 above). If a broker-trader had a forward contract for purchase of inventory this contract would be accounted for as a derivative under IFRS 9 – *Financial Instruments* – or IAS 39 – *Financial Instruments: Recognition and Measurement* – since it would not meet the normal purchase or sale exemption (see Chapter 43 at 4.2) and when the contract was physically settled the inventory would likewise be shown at fair value less costs to sell. *[IAS 2.3(b)]*. However, if such an entity were not measuring inventory at fair value less costs to sell it would be subject to the measurement requirements of IAS 2 and would therefore have to record the inventory at the lower of cost and net realisable value. This raises the question: what is cost when such an entity takes delivery of inventory that has been purchased with a forward contract?

On delivery, the cash paid (i.e. the fixed price agreed in the forward contract) is in substance made up of two elements:

(i) an amount that settles the forward contract; and

(ii) an amount that represents the 'cost of purchase', being the market price at the date of purchase.

This 'cost of purchase' represents the forward contract price adjusted for the derivative asset or liability. For example, assume that the broker-trader was purchasing oil and the forward contracted price was $40 per barrel of oil, but at the time of delivery the spot price of oil was $50 and the forward contract had a fair value of $10 at that date. The oil would be recorded at the fair value on what is deemed to be the purchase date of $50. The $40 cash payment would in substance consist of $50 payment for the inventory offset by a $10 receipt on settlement of the derivative contract, which would be separately accounted for. This is exactly the same result as if the entity had been required to settle the derivative immediately prior to, and separate from, the physical delivery of the oil.

If the entity purchasing the oil in the example above is not a broker-trader, and the acquisition meets the normal purchase or sale exemption given in IAS 32 – *Financial Instruments: Presentation*, the purchase of oil would be recognised at the entity's cost thereof, in terms of IAS 2, that is $40 per barrel of oil.

3.1.6 Drug production costs within the pharmaceutical industry

After the development stage, pharmaceutical companies often commence production of drugs prior to obtaining the necessary regulatory approval to sell them. As long as the regulatory approval has been applied for and it is believed highly likely that this will be successfully obtained then it is appropriate to be recognising an asset and classifying this as inventory. Prior to this application for regulatory approval being made any costs would need to be classified as research and development costs rather than inventory and the criteria within IAS 38 assessed to determine if capitalisation was appropriate (see Chapter 17 at 6.2.3).

3.2 Measurement of cost

IAS 2 specifically allows the use of the standard cost method, or of the retail method, provided that the chosen method gives a result which approximates to cost. Standard costs should take into account normal levels of materials and supplies, labour, efficiency and capacity utilisation. They must be regularly reviewed and revised where necessary. *[IAS 2.21]*. Normal levels of activity are discussed in 3.1 above.

The retail method is often used in the retail industry for measuring inventories with high volumes of rapidly changing items with similar margins. *[IAS 2.22]*. It may be unnecessarily time-consuming to determine the cost of the period-end inventory on a conventional basis. Consequently, the most practical method of determining period-end inventory may be to record inventory on hand at selling prices, and then convert it to cost by adjusting for a normal margin.

Judgement is applied in the retail method in determining the margin to be removed from the selling price of inventory in order to convert it back to cost. The percentage has to take account of circumstances in which inventories have been marked down to below original selling price. Adjustments have to be made to eliminate the effect of these markdowns so as to prevent any item of inventory being valued at less than both its cost and its net realisable value. In practice, however, entities that use the retail method apply a gross profit margin computed on an average basis appropriate for departments and/or ranges, rather than applying specific mark-up percentages. This practice is, in fact, acknowledged by IAS 2, which states that, 'an average percentage for each retail department is often used'. *[IAS 2.22]*.

Items that are not interchangeable and goods or services produced for specific projects should have their costs specifically identified and these costs will be matched with the goods physically sold. *[IAS 2.23]*. In practice this is a relatively unusual method of valuation, as the clerical effort required does not make it feasible unless there are relatively few high value items being bought or produced. Consequently, it would normally be used where the inventory comprised items such as antiques, jewellery and automobiles in the hands of dealers. This method is inappropriate where there are large numbers of items that are interchangeable, as specific identification of costs could distort the profit or loss arising from these inventories through the method applied to selecting items that remain in inventories. *[IAS 2.24]*.

Where it is necessary to use a cost-flow assumption (i.e. when there are large numbers of ordinarily interchangeable items), IAS 2 allows either a FIFO (first-in, first-out) or a weighted average cost formula to be used. *[IAS 2.25]*.

FIFO – In the vast majority of businesses it will not be practicable to keep track of the cost of identical items of inventory on an individual unit basis; nevertheless, it is desirable to approximate to the actual physical flows as far as possible. The FIFO method probably gives the closest approximation to actual cost flows, since it is assumed that when inventories are sold or used in a production process, the oldest are sold or used first. Consequently the balance of inventory on hand at any point represents the most recent purchases or production. *[IAS 2.27]*. This can best be illustrated in the context of a business which deals in perishable goods (e.g. food retailers) since clearly such a business will use the first goods received earliest. The FIFO method, by allocating the earliest costs incurred against revenue, matches actual cost flows with the physical flow of goods reasonably accurately. In any event, even in the case of businesses which do not deal in perishable goods, this would reflect what would probably be a sound management policy. In practice, the FIFO method is generally used where it is not possible to value inventory on an actual cost basis;

Weighted average – This method, which like FIFO is suitable where inventory units are identical or nearly identical, involves the computation of an average unit cost by dividing the total cost of units by the number of units. The average unit cost then has to be revised with every receipt of inventory, or alternatively at the end of predetermined periods. *[IAS 2.27]*. In practice, weighted average systems are widely used in packaged inventory systems that are computer controlled, although its results are not very different from FIFO in times of relatively low inflation, or where inventory turnover is relatively quick.

LIFO (last-in, first-out), as its name suggests, is the opposite of FIFO and assumes that the most recent purchases or production are used first. In certain cases this could represent the physical flow of inventory (e.g. if a store is filled and emptied from the top). However it is not an acceptable method under IAS 2. LIFO is an attempt to match current costs with current revenues so that profit or loss excludes the effects of holding gains or losses. Essentially, therefore, LIFO is an attempt to achieve something closer to replacement cost accounting for the statement of profit or loss, whilst disregarding the statement of financial position. Consequently, the period-end balance of inventory on hand represents the earliest purchases of the item, resulting in inventories being stated in the statement of financial position at amounts which may bear little relationship to recent cost levels. Unlike under IFRS, LIFO is allowable under US GAAP, and is popular in the US as the Internal Revenue Service officially recognises LIFO as an acceptable method for the computation of tax provided that it is used consistently for tax and financial reporting purposes.

The standard makes it clear that the same cost formula should be used for all inventories having a similar nature and use to the entity, although items with a different nature and use may justify the use of a different cost formula. *[IAS 2.25]*. For example the standard acknowledges that inventories used in one operating segment may have a use to the entity different from the same type of inventories used in another operating segment. However, a difference in geographical location of inventories (or in their respective tax rules) is not sufficient, by itself, to justify the use of different cost formulas. *[IAS 2.26]*.

An entity may choose, as a result of particular facts and circumstances, to change its cost formula, for instance, from a FIFO-based cost formula to a weighted average cost formula. The change in a cost formula represents a change in the basis on which the value of the inventory has been determined, rather than a change in valuation of the inputs used to determine the cost of the inventory. An accounting policy is defined in IAS 8 – *Accounting Policies, Changes in Accounting Estimates and Errors* – as including specific bases applied by an entity in preparing and presenting financial statements. Therefore a change in the cost formula represents a change in accounting policy which should only be made if it results in the financial statements providing reliable and more relevant information. If material, the change in accounting policy will have to be dealt with as a prior period adjustment in accordance with IAS 8 (see Chapter 3 at 4.4).

3.3 Net realisable value

IAS 2 carries substantial guidance on the identification of net realisable value. When this is below cost, inventory must be written down.

The cost of inventory may have to be reduced to its net realisable value if the inventory has become damaged, is wholly or partly obsolete, or if its selling price has declined. The costs of inventory may not be recovered from sale because of increases in the costs to complete, or the estimated selling costs. *[IAS 2.28]*. However the costs to consider in making this assessment should only comprise direct costs to complete and sell the inventory.

Selling costs are excluded from the cost of inventory and are expensed as incurred; of course, the selling price takes account of the expected costs of sale. Selling costs include direct costs that are only incurred when the item is sold, e.g. sales commissions, and indirect costs, which are those overheads that enable sales to take place, including sales administration and the costs of retail activities. If inventory is not impaired then the distinction between direct and indirect selling costs is not relevant as both are expensed as incurred. *[IAS 2.16]*. It is clear that costs to be reflected in the write down to NRV must be incremental but Paragraph 28 does not distinguish between direct and indirect costs. This allows for different interpretations. In practice there may be few incremental increases in indirect costs that will cause inventory to be sold at a loss. An example of this is reflected in Extract 22.2 above in which Syngenta AG describes its inventory valuation policies, including using only direct costs in costs to sell.

Writing inventory down to net realisable value should normally be done on an item-by-item basis. IAS 2 specifically states that it may be appropriate to group similar or related items but it is not appropriate to write down an entire class of inventory, such as finished goods, or all the inventory of a particular segment. However, it may be necessary to write down an entire product line or group of inventories in a given geographical area if the items cannot be practicably evaluated separately. *[IAS 2.29]*.

For a service provider that has not yet adopted IFRS 15, paragraph 29 of IAS 2 prior to amendment by IFRS 15 stated that costs associated with a service contract would generally be accumulated in respect of each service for which a separate selling price is charged. It is on this basis that the net realisable value would be considered and each such service would therefore be treated as a separate item.

Estimates of net realisable value must be based on the most reliable evidence available and take into account fluctuations of price or cost after the end of the period if this is evidence of conditions existing at the end of the period. *[IAS 2.30]*. A loss realised on a sale of a product after the end of the period may well provide evidence of the net realisable value of that product at the end of the period. However if this product is, for example, an exchange traded commodity, and the loss realised can be attributed to a fall in prices on the exchange after the period end date, then this loss would not, in itself, provide evidence of the net realisable value at the period end date.

Estimates of net realisable value must also take into account the purpose for which the inventory is held. Therefore inventory held for a particular contract has its net realisable value based on the contract price, and only any excess inventory held would be based on current market prices. If there is a firm contract to sell quantities in excess of inventory quantities that the entity holds or is able to obtain under a firm purchase contract, this may give rise to an onerous contract liability that should be provided for in accordance with IAS 37 – *Provisions, Contingent Liabilities and Contingent Assets* (see Chapter 28). *[IAS 2.31]*.

IAS 2 explains that materials and other supplies held for use in the production of inventories are not written down below cost if the final product in which they are to be used is expected to be sold at or above cost. *[IAS 2.32]*. This is the case even if these materials in their present condition have a net realisable value that is below cost and would therefore otherwise require write down. Thus, a whisky distiller would not write down an inventory of grain because of a fall in the grain price, so long as it expected to sell the whisky at a price which is sufficient to recover cost. If a decline in the price of materials indicates that the cost of the final product will exceed net realisable value then a write down is necessary and the replacement cost of those materials may be the best measure of their net realisable value. *[IAS 2.32]*. If an entity writes down any of its finished goods, the carrying value of any related raw materials should also be reviewed to see if they too need to be written down.

Often raw materials are used to make a number of different products. In these cases it is normally not possible to arrive at a particular net realisable value for each item of raw material based on the selling price of any one type of finished item. If the current replacement cost of those raw materials is less than their historical cost, a provision is only required to be made if the finished goods into which they will be made are expected to be sold at a loss. No provision should be made just because the anticipated profit will be less than normal.

When the circumstances that previously caused inventories to be written down below cost no longer exist, or when there is clear evidence of an increase in net realisable value because of changed economic circumstances, the amount of the write-down is reversed. The reversal cannot be greater than the amount of the original write-down, so that the new carrying amount will always be the lower of the cost and the revised net realisable value. *[IAS 2.33]*.

3.4 Consignment stock and sale and repurchase agreements

A seller may enter into an arrangement with a distributor where the distributor sells inventory on behalf of the seller. Such consignment arrangements are common in certain industries, such as the automotive industry. For entities applying IFRS 15 revenue would generally not be recognised for stock delivered to the consignee because control has not yet transferred (see Chapter 30 at 4.5). Despite the approach to analysing revenue contracts with customers changing on the adoption of IFRS 15, in practice the accounting for these transactions may remain the same as under the previous standard on revenue, IAS 18. IAS 18 required entities to recognise revenue (and therefore derecognise inventory) only if the substantial risks and rewards of ownership had been transferred to the customer (see Chapter 29 at 5.1).

Similarly, entities may enter into sale and repurchase agreements with a customer where the seller agrees to repurchase inventory under particular circumstances. For example, the seller may agree to repurchase any inventory that the customer has not sold to a third party after six months. In the new revenue standard, IFRS 15, repurchase agreements are generally categorised into forward, put and call options; this is considered further in Chapter 30 at 7.4. In practice the accounting may remain unchanged from the previous standard on revenue, IAS 18, despite the different approaches to analysing revenue contracts. IAS 18 gave some guidance on when revenue could be recognised in these types of transaction in the illustrative examples to the standard. Recognition of revenue under IAS 18 for sale and repurchase transactions is considered in Chapter 29 at 5.1.

Prior to adopting IFRS 15 there is no other specific guidance on these types of inventories in IFRS and so entities need to ensure they adopt an appropriate and consistent accounting policy for derecognising inventory and recognising revenue that reflects the commercial substance of these transactions.

> *Extract 22.3: Volkswagen Aktiengesellschaft (2016)*
>
> **Notes to the Consolidated Financial Statements** [extract]
>
> **Accounting policies** [extract]
>
> **REVENUE AND EXPENSE RECOGNITION** [extract]
>
> Income from assets for which a Group company has a buy-back obligation is recognized only when the assets have definitively left the Group. If a fixed repurchase price was agreed when the contract was entered into, the difference between the selling price and the present value of the repurchase price is recognized as income ratably over the term of the contract. Prior to that time, the assets are carried as inventories in the case of short contract terms and as lease assets in the case of long contract terms.

The entity will also have to consider appropriate disclosure for material amounts of inventory that is held on consignment or sale and return at a third party's premises.

4 REAL ESTATE INVENTORY

4.1 Classification of real estate as inventory

Many real estate businesses develop and construct residential properties for sale, and these developments often consist of several units. The strategy is to make a profit from the development and construction of the property rather than to make a profit in the long term from general price increases in the property market. The intention is to sell the property units as soon as possible following their construction and the sale is therefore in the ordinary course of the entity's business. When construction is complete it is not uncommon for individual property units to be leased at market rates to earn revenues to partly cover expenses such as interest, management fees, and real estate taxes. Large-scale buyers of commercial property, such as insurance companies, are often reluctant to buy unless a property has been let, as this assures immediate cash flows from the investment.

It is our view that if it is in the entity's ordinary course of business (supported by its strategy) to hold property for short-term sale rather than for long-term capital appreciation or rental income, the entire property (including the leased units) should be accounted for and presented as inventory. This will continue to be the case as long as it remains the intention to sell the property in the short term. Rent received should be included in other income as it does not represent a reduction in the cost of inventory.

Investment property is defined in IAS 40 as 'property ... held ... to earn rentals or for capital appreciation or both, rather than for ... use in the production or supply of goods or services or for administrative purposes; or ... sale in the ordinary course of business'. *[IAS 40.5]*. Therefore in the case outlined above, the property does not meet the definition of investment property. Properties intended for sale in the ordinary course of business, no matter whether leased out or not, are outside the scope of IAS 40. However, if a property is not intended for sale, IAS 40 requires it to be transferred from inventory to investment property when there is a change in use. The change can be evidenced by the commencement of an operating lease to another party (see Chapter 19 at 9).

4.2 Costs of real estate inventory

4.2.1 Allocation of costs to individual units in multi-unit developments

A real estate developer of a multi-unit complex will be able to track and record various costs that are specific to individual units, such as individual fit out costs. However there will also be various costs that are incurred which are not specific to any individual unit, such as the costs of land and any shared facilities, and a methodology will be required to allocate these costs to the individual units. This will of course impact the profit that is recognised on the sale of each individual unit.

There are two general approaches to this allocation, both of which we believe are acceptable under IAS 2. The first approach is to allocate these non-unit specific costs based on some relative cost basis. A reasonable proxy of relative cost is likely to be the size of each unit and hence an appropriate methodology would be to allocate the non-unit specific cost per square metre to the individual units based upon the floor area of each unit. Another proxy of (total) relative cost may be the use of the specific cost of each unit. Marking up the specific cost that is attributable to each unit by a fixed percentage so as to cover and account for the non-unit specific costs would also seem reasonable. This relative cost approach is consistent with the guidance under IAS 2 in respect of allocation of overheads which requires a 'systematic allocation of fixed and variable production overheads'. *[IAS 2.12]*.

The second approach would be to allocate these non-unit specific costs based on the relative sales value of each unit. This methodology is specifically referred to by the standard in the context of a production process that results in more than one product being produced simultaneously. *[IAS 2.14]*. Whichever approach is adopted it must be used consistently. In addition the developer should initially, as far as is practicable, segregate the non-unit specific costs between any commercial, retail and residential components before applying these methodologies.

4.2.2 Property demolition and operating lease costs

During the course of a property redevelopment project, an existing building may need to be demolished in order for the new development to take place. Should the cost of the building to be demolished be capitalised as part of the construction cost for the new building or should the cost be charged to profit or loss?

In all such cases an entity will need to exercise judgement in assessing the facts and circumstances. There are three distinct scenarios to consider:

(a) the entity is the owner-occupier, in which case the matter falls under IAS 16;

(b) the entity holds the property to earn rentals, in which case the matter falls under IAS 40;

(c) the entity sells such properties in its normal course of business.

IAS 2 defines inventories as assets (a) held for sale in the ordinary course of business; or (b) in the process of production for such sale; or (c) in the form of materials or supplies to be consumed in the production process or in the rendering of services. *[IAS 2.6]*. The cost of inventories must comprise all costs of purchase, costs of conversion and other costs incurred in bringing the inventories to their present location and condition. *[IAS 2.10]*.

If it is the strategy of the developer to sell the developed property after construction, the new development falls within the scope of IAS 2, as it would be considered held for sale in the normal course of business by the developer. The cost of the old building as well as demolition costs and costs of developing the new one would be treated as inventory, but must still be subject to the normal 'lower of cost and net realisable value' requirements.

In our view a similar approach can be applied to lease costs for the land upon which a building is being constructed. The amount that can be included in inventory will depend on whether the entity considers the land lease to be a finance lease or an operating lease.

- If it is a finance lease, depreciation is an example of a fixed cost that can be considered a cost of conversion. *[IAS 2.12].* IAS 2 states that, in limited circumstances, borrowing costs are to be included in the costs of inventories. *[IAS 2.17].* It is quite possible that buildings constructed for disposal under a finance lease could meet these criteria. See the discussion at 3.1.3 above.
- If the entity considers it to be an operating lease, the operating lease costs could be considered costs of conversion.

Alternatively, the entity could consider that the operating lease costs are for the right to control the land during the lease period rather than costs in bringing this inventory to any particular condition, in which case it may be appropriate to expense the costs.

For accounting periods beginning on or after 1 January 2019, IFRS 16 is mandatory. Paragraph 12 of IAS 2 will be amended by IFRS 16 to include a reference to the depreciation charge on right-of use assets used in the production process. The detailed requirements of IFRS 16 are discussed in Chapter 25.

5 RECOGNITION IN PROFIT OR LOSS

IAS 2 specifies that when inventory is sold, the carrying amount of the inventory must be recognised as an expense in the period in which the revenue is recognised. *[IAS 2.34].*

Judging when to recognise revenue, and therefore to charge the inventory expense, is one of the more complex accounting issues that can arise, particularly in the context of extended payment arrangements and manufacturer financing of sales to customers. In some industries, for example automobile manufacturing and retailing, aircraft manufacturing, railway carriage manufacturing and maintenance, and mobile phone handset retailing, it is customary for the goods concerned to be subject to extended and complex delivery, sales and settlement arrangements. For these types of transactions, the accounting problem that arises principally concerns when to recognise revenue, the consequent derecognition of inventory being driven by the revenue recognition judgement, not vice-versa.

Revenue recognition in accordance with IFRS 15 is dealt with in Chapter 30 (entities applying IAS 18 see Chapter 29), to which reference should be made in considering such issues.

Inventory that goes into the creation of another asset, for instance into a self-constructed item of property, plant or equipment, would form part of the cost of that asset. Subsequently these costs are expensed through the depreciation of that item of property, plant and equipment during its useful life. *[IAS 2.35].*

Any write-downs or losses of inventory must be recognised as an expense when the write-down or loss occurs. Reversals of previous write-downs are recognised as a reduction in the inventory expense recognised in the period in which the reversal occurs. *[IAS 2.34]*.

6 DISCLOSURE REQUIREMENTS OF IAS 2

The financial statements should disclose:

(a) the accounting policies adopted in measuring inventories, including the cost formula used;

(b) the total carrying amount of inventories and the carrying amount in classifications appropriate to the entity;

(c) the carrying amount of inventories carried at fair value less costs to sell;

(d) the amount of inventories recognised as an expense during the period;

(e) the amount of any write-down of inventories recognised as an expense in the period;

(f) the amount of any reversal of any write-down that is recognised as a reduction in the amount of inventories recognised as expense in the period;

(g) the circumstances or events that led to the reversal of a write-down of inventories; and

(h) the carrying amount of inventories pledged as security for liabilities. *[IAS 2.36]*.

IAS 2 does not specify the precise classifications that must be used to comply with (b) above. However it states that 'information about the carrying amounts held in different classifications of inventories and the extent of the changes in these assets is useful to financial statement users', and suggests suitable examples of common classifications such as merchandise, production supplies, materials, work-in-progress, and finished goods. *[IAS 2.37]*.

Extract 22.4 below shows how the Unilever Group disclosed the relevant information.

Extract 22.4: Unilever PLC and Unilever N.V. (2016)

NOTES TO THE CONSOLIDATED FINANCIAL STATEMENTS [extract]

12. INVENTORIES [extract]

Inventories	€ million 2016	€ million 2015
Raw materials and consumables	1,385	1,381
Finished goods and goods for resale	2,893	2,954
	4,278	4,335

Inventories with a value of €110 million (2015: €100 million) are carried at net realisable value, this being lower than cost. During 2016, €113 million (2015: €119 million) was charged to the income statement for damaged, obsolete and lost inventories. In 2016, €113 million (2015: €123 million) was utilised or released to the income statement from inventory provisions taken in earlier years.

The amount of inventory recognised as an expense in the period is normally included in cost of sales; this category includes unallocated production overheads and abnormal costs as well as the costs of inventory that has been sold. However, the circumstances of the entity may warrant the inclusion of distribution or other costs in cost of sales. *[IAS 2.38]*.

Hence when a company presents its profit or loss based upon this IAS 1 – *Presentation of Financial Statements* – 'function of expense' or 'cost of sales' method it will normally be disclosing costs that are greater than those that have previously been classified as inventory, but this appears to be explicitly allowable by the standard.

Extract 22.5 below shows how Stora Enso classified its inventories in its 2016 financial statements.

Extract 22.5: Stora Enso Oyj (2016)

Notes to the Consolidated financial statements [extract]

Note 16 Inventories [extract]

EUR million	As at 31 December 2016	2015
Materials and supplies	332	343
Work in progress	77	81
Finished goods	651	664
Spare parts and consumables	282	283
Other inventories	15	13
Advance payments and cutting rights	102	108
Obsolescence allowance – spare parts and consumables	–98	–106
Obsolescence allowance – finished goods	–9	–9
Net realisable value allowance	–6	–4
Total	1 346	1 373

EUR 14 (EUR 10) million of inventory write-downs have been recognised as an expense. EUR 7 (EUR 6) million have been recognised as a reversal of previous write-downs.

Some entities adopt a format for profit or loss that results in amounts other than the cost of inventories being disclosed as an expense during the period. This will happen if an entity presents an analysis of expenses using a classification based on the nature of expenses. The entity then discloses the costs recognised as an expense for raw materials and consumables, labour costs and other costs together with the amount of the net change in inventories for the period. *[IAS 2.39]*.

Formats for the presentation of profit or loss are discussed in Chapter 3.

The requirement to disclose the amount of any write-down of inventories recognised as an expense in the period in (e) above only relates to write-downs of inventory held at the end of the reporting period. The notion of 'write-down' is used in the context of the lower of cost and net realisable value test. An entity only performs this test at a reporting date.

References

1 *IFRIC Update*, July 2015.

Chapter 23 Construction contracts (IAS 11)

List of examples

Chapter 23 Construction contracts (IAS 11)

1 INTRODUCTION

IAS 11 – *Construction Contracts* – deals with the accounting treatment of revenues and costs arising from construction contracts for accounting periods beginning before 1 January 2018. Like a number of other older standards that have not yet been revised significantly by the IASB (IAS 11 was last revised in 1993), the focus of the standard is on the statement of comprehensive income and the basis on which revenue and expenditure should be recognised.

The IASB issued a new revenue recognition standard, IFRS 15 – *Revenue from Contracts with Customers* – in 2014, which was developed in conjunction with the FASB. The new standard replaces both IAS 11 and IAS 18 – *Revenue* – and related Interpretations (e.g. IFRIC 15 – *Agreements for the Construction of Real Estate*) and is effective for annual periods beginning on or after 1 January 2018. The IFRS 15 requirements could significantly affect the manner in which revenue is recognised for construction contracts. See Chapter 30 for a discussion on IFRS 15 and the amendments to IFRS 15 that the IASB issued in April 2016.

1.1 Scope and definitions of IAS 11

IAS 11 applies to accounting for construction contracts in the financial statements of the contractor. *[IAS 11.1]*.

A construction contract is defined as follows:

> 'a contract specifically negotiated for the construction of an asset or a combination of assets that are closely interrelated or interdependent in terms of their design, technology and function or their ultimate purpose or use.' *[IAS 11.3]*.

The meaning of 'specifically negotiated for the construction of an asset' has been considered by the Interpretations Committee. Although IFRIC 15 has been written in the specific context of the construction of real estate, it includes an analysis of the distinguishing features of construction contracts and it is, therefore, relevant in determining whether any contract that involves the construction of an asset is within the scope of IAS 11 or is a sale of goods within the scope of IAS 18 and IAS 2 – *Inventories* (see 1.2 below).

Something that may be accounted for as a single construction contract can comprise a number of different elements. Single constructions could include a bridge, a building, a dam, a pipeline, a road, a ship or a tunnel. Other single contracts include groups of interrelated assets, such as an oil refinery or complex pieces of plant and equipment. *[IAS 11.4]*. Whether a contract is, in fact, a single construction contract or one that should be separated into components (each of which would be dealt with individually) is one of the more difficult and subjective areas of contract accounting and one that has also been considered by the Interpretations Committee (see 2 below).

Contracts for services directly related to construction contracts are covered by IAS 11 and not by IAS 18. These include contracts for the services of project managers and architects. Contracts for the demolition and restoration of assets and restoration of the environment after an asset is demolished are also construction contracts. *[IAS 11.5]*.

IAS 11 does not specify any minimum period of duration for a construction contract and if the contract meets the definition of a construction contract, it will need to be accounted for under this standard. The standard identifies two specific types of construction contract:

'A *fixed price contract* is a construction contract in which the contractor agrees to a fixed contract price, or a fixed rate per unit of output, which in some cases is subject to cost escalation clauses;

'A *cost plus contract* is a construction contract in which the contractor is reimbursed for allowable or otherwise defined costs, plus a percentage of these costs or a fixed fee.' *[IAS 11.3]*.

These types of construction contract determine the basis on which revenue is recognised, as discussed at 3.3.1 below.

Contracts that contain elements of both types, e.g. a cost plus contract that has an agreed maximum price, will have to be analysed in order to determine when to recognise contract revenue and expenses. *[IAS 11.6]*.

1.2 Whether an arrangement is a construction contract

Determining whether an arrangement is a construction contract is critical as this determines whether revenue is recognised using the percentage of completion method under IAS 11. Otherwise arrangements are governed by IAS 18 and revenue is not recognised until the risks and rewards of ownership and control have passed. In developing IFRIC 15, the meaning of the term 'construction contract' as defined in IAS 11 was addressed, which helps to clarify the scope of this standard.

For a contract to meet the definition of a construction contract in IAS 11 it must be 'specifically negotiated for the construction of an asset or a combination of assets ...'. *[IAS 11.3]*.

Although IFRIC 15 provides guidance in the particular context of real estate, as described below, paragraph BC6 of the Basis for Conclusions on IFRIC 15 states that the interpretation can be applied by analogy to other arrangements that do not include real estate. *[IFRIC 15.BC6]*. IFRIC 15 is discussed further in Chapter 29 at 5.12.

Under the Interpretation:

- an agreement for the construction of real estate meets the definition of a construction contract when the buyer is able to specify the major structural elements of the design of the real estate before construction begins and/or specify major structural changes once construction is in progress, whether or not it exercises that ability. When IAS 11 applies, the construction contract also includes any contracts or components for the rendering of services that are directly related to the construction of the real estate. *[IFRIC 15.11]*.
- an agreement for the construction of real estate in which buyers have only limited ability to influence the design of the real estate, for example to select a design from a range of options specified by the entity, or to specify only minor variations to the basic design, is an agreement for the sale of goods and, therefore, within the scope of IAS 18. *[IFRIC 15.12]*.

Within a single agreement, an entity may contract to deliver goods or services in addition to the construction of real estate (for example a sale of land or provision of property management services – see 3.3.8 below). Such an agreement may need to be split into separately identifiable components, which may include one for the construction of real estate. The fair value of the total consideration received or receivable for the agreement must be allocated to each component. *[IFRIC 15.8]*. The Basis for Conclusions to the Interpretation points to IFRIC 12 – *Service Concession Arrangements* – and IFRIC 13 – *Customer Loyalty Programmes* – for guidance on allocating the fair value. *[IFRIC 15.BC11]*. These Interpretations discuss two approaches, the relative fair value approach and residual approach. *[IFRIC 12.13, IFRIC 13.BC14]*. The segmentation of contracts is discussed at 2 below.

IFRIC 15 assumes that there is revenue to be recognised, i.e. it assumes that the entity retains neither continuing managerial involvement to the degree usually associated with ownership nor effective control over the constructed real estate to an extent that would preclude recognition of some or all of the consideration as revenue. *[IFRIC 15.7]*.

With these types of contracts, in general, there are a range of contractual arrangements for similar products from, at one end, sales of 'off the shelf' items through to large projects where a similar type of asset is constructed to a purchaser's specification. Determining whether an arrangement is a construction contract, which should be accounted for under IAS 11, or a sale of goods, which should be accounted for under IAS 18, is relatively simple in arrangements at either end of this spectrum but can be less clear in other cases.

An example of an entity whose activities cover this range is Vestas Wind Systems A/S whose revenue recognition policy is as follows:

Extract 23.1: Vestas Wind Systems A/S (2016)

Consolidated financial statements

1. Result for the year [extract]

1.2. Revenue [extract]

Group accounting policies

Revenue comprises sale of wind turbines and wind power plants, after-sales service, and sale of spare parts.

Sale of individual wind turbines and small wind power plants based on standard solutions (supply-only and supply-and-installation projects) as well as spare parts sales are recognised in the income statement provided that risk has been transferred to the buyer in the reporting period, and provided that the income can be measured reliably and is expected to be received. Revenue from contracts to deliver wind power plants with a high degree of customisation are recognised as the wind power plants are constructed based on the stage of completion of the individual contracts (turnkey projects). Where the profit from a contract cannot be estimated reliably, revenue is only recognised equalling the cost incurred to the extent that it is probable that the costs will be recovered.

Service sales, comprising service and maintenance agreements as well as extended warranties regarding wind turbines and wind power plants sold, are recognised as revenue over the term of the agreement as the services are provided.

1.3 Service concession agreements

Service concession agreements commonly include the construction of an asset followed by a period in which the constructor maintains and services that asset. This secondary period may include asset replacement and refurbishment, as well as service elements. Alternatively, the contract might provide for the refurbishment of an existing infrastructure asset together with related services. These agreements provide particular accounting difficulties because they combine contract accounting issues and issues arising from a number of other accounting standards including IAS 11, IAS 17 – *Leases* – and IAS 18. The accounting issues raised by IFRIC 12 are discussed further in Chapter 27.

1.4 Sale of real estate based on a third party's specifications

The revenue standard that applies, either IAS 11 or IAS 18, will depend on the nature of the arrangement between all of the parties. In some situations, it could depend on the nature of the relationship with a third party. For example, a real estate developer has access to a piece of land and intends to develop it into an office and sell it. It finds a user/lessee with whom it negotiates the major structural elements of the design. It enters into a lease contract with the user. Before construction starts, or shortly after, the real estate developer (together with the lessee) finds a property investment company prepared to buy the office when finished and take over the lease agreement from the real estate developer. Legal title only transfers to the buyer on completion of the office. In our view, the standard that applies to the developer will depend on the type of lease. We believe that if the lease arrangement is an operating lease IAS 18 will most likely apply, but if the lease arrangement is a finance lease IAS 11 will likely apply. This is because IFRIC 15 indicates an agreement for the construction of real estate meets the definition of a construction contract when the buyer is able to specify the major structural elements of the design of the real estate before construction begins and/or specify major structural changes once construction is in progress. An operating lessee does not have substantially all the risks and rewards of the leased asset and, therefore, there has not been a negotiation with respect to the major structural design with the buyer in the real estate sales contract. On the other hand, a finance lessee can be considered, in substance, the buyer. As noted in paragraph 10 of IFRIC 15 'determining whether an agreement for the construction of real estate is within the scope of IAS 11 or IAS 18 depends on the terms of the agreement and all the surrounding facts and circumstances. Such a determination requires judgement with respect to each agreement.' *[IFRIC 15.10]*. See Chapter 25 for more discussion on the new leasing standard that was issued by the IASB in January 2016, IFRS 16 – *Leases*.

2 COMBINATION AND SEGMENTATION OF CONTRACTS

IAS 11 should be applied separately to each construction contract. However, in order to reflect the substance of the transaction it may be necessary for a contract to be sub-divided and the standard to be applied individually to each component, or for a group of contracts to be treated as one. *[IAS 11.7]*.

IAS 11 provides guidance in three separate cases.

The first case is where a single contract covers the construction of a number of separate assets, each of which is in substance a separate contract, i.e. when:

(a) separate proposals have been submitted for each asset;

(b) the contractor and customer have negotiated separately for each asset and can accept or reject that part of the contract relating to each asset; and

(c) the costs and revenues relating to each asset can be identified. *[IAS 11.8]*.

The second case is effectively the reverse of the first. It deals with situations in which, in substance, there is only a single contract with a customer, or a group of customers. This group of contracts should be treated as a single contract where:

(a) the group of contracts is negotiated as a single package;

(b) the contracts are so closely interrelated that they are, in effect, part of a single project with an overall profit margin; and

(c) the contracts are performed concurrently or in a continuous sequence. *[IAS 11.9]*.

The third case is where a contract anticipates the construction of a further asset at the customer's discretion. Whether these options should be accounted for in combination with, or separately from, the original contract is discussed at 2.1 below.

IAS 11 contains little guidance on combining and segmenting contracts. It only considers the issues in very clear circumstances. Specifically, where a number of separate contracts have been negotiated as a single package or where a series of separate contracts have been subsumed within a single contract document, but where the individual contracts should be dealt with separately. There is no further guidance in the standard on whether or how individual contracts or groups of contracts should be separated or combined and contract revenue and costs recognised on the basis of the individually separated or combined contracts. These treatments can have a major effect on the recognition of revenue. Separating a contract can affect the profile of revenue recognition, perhaps allowing earlier recognition of revenue. If a series of contracts is negotiated as a package with the objective of achieving an overall profit margin, this will not be reflected if the individual contracts are accounted for separately. Inappropriate combining of contracts could result in the timing of profits or losses not being recognised on the basis required by the standard.

The Interpretations Committee has discussed whether some of the detailed guidance under US GAAP for combining and segmenting contracts (ASC 605-35 – *Revenue Recognition – Construction-Type and Production-Type Contracts*) should be incorporated into IAS 11, but concluded that it was not appropriate to do so. The Interpretations Committee members were not aware of any significant divergence in practice. They also concluded that, because of differences between the two standards, full convergence of the conditions for combining and separating construction contracts could not be achieved simply through interpretation.[1] With the issuance of the new revenue standard the future requirements for combining and segmenting contracts are converged between IFRS and US GAAP. See Chapter 30 for discussion of IFRS 15.

2.1 Options for the construction of an additional asset

Another area where it is necessary to consider whether contracts should be combined is contract options and additions. Once again, combining contracts is important because of its potential impact on the recognition of revenue and profits on transactions. If an optional asset is treated as part of the original contract, contract revenue will be recognised using the percentage of completion method over the combined contract.

IAS 11 considers the circumstances in which a contract gives a customer an option for an additional asset (or is amended in this manner) and concludes that this should be treated as a separate construction contract if:

(a) the asset differs significantly in design, technology or function from the asset or assets covered by the original contract; or

(b) the price of the asset is negotiated without regard to the original contract price. *[IAS 11.10].*

This means, for example, that the contract for an additional, identical asset would be treated as a separate contract if its price was negotiated separately from the original contract price. Costs often decline with additional production, not only because of the effects of initial costs, but also because of the 'learning curve' (the time taken by the workforce to perform activities decreases with practice and repetition). This could result in a much higher profit margin on the additional contract since the expected costs could be less. Assume, for example, a government department takes up its option with a defence contractor for five more aircraft, in addition to the original twenty-five for which it had already contracted. Further assume that the option was not priced and the new contract is priced afresh. In our view, this additional contract cannot be combined with the original contract, regardless of the difference in profit margins.

The combining of contracts may also have unexpected results. If, for example, an entity has a contract with a government to build two satellites and a priced option to build a third, it may be obliged to combine the contracts at the point at which the option is exercised. This could be in a different accounting period to the commencement of the contract. Using the requirements outlined in 3.3.3 below, there will be a cumulative catch-up, or reversal, of revenue and probably also of profits, depending on the pricing of the option. In subsequent periods, results will be based on the combined contracts.

3 CONTRACT REVENUE, COSTS AND EXPENSES

3.1 Contract revenue

Contract revenue comprises the amount of revenue initially agreed by the parties together with any variations, claims and incentive payments, as long as it is probable that they will result in revenue and can be measured reliably. *[IAS 11.11].* The standard states that such revenue is to be measured at the fair value of the consideration received and receivable. Fair value is as defined in IFRS 13 – *Fair Value Measurement*, which is discussed in Chapter 14. In this context, 'fair value' includes the re-measurement of the consideration as events occur and uncertainties are resolved. These may include contractual matters, such as increases in revenue in a fixed price contract as a result of cost escalation clauses or, when a contract involves a fixed price per unit of output, contract revenue may increase as the number of units is increased. Penalties for delays may reduce revenue. In addition, variations and claims must be taken into account. *[IAS 11.12].* If deferred payments are due after completion of the contract, for example retention payments, such payments will be brought into account at their present value. Similarly, if advance payments are received, and these constitute financing transactions, it may be appropriate to accrue interest on them (see Chapter 29 at 5.1.4).

Variations are instructions by the customer to change the scope of the work to be performed under the contract, including changes to the specification or design of the asset or to the duration of the contract. Variations may only be included in contract revenue when it is probable that the customer will approve the variation and the amount to be charged for it, and the amount can be measured reliably. *[IAS 11.13].*

Given the extended periods over which contracts are carried out and changes in circumstances prevailing whilst the work is in progress, it is quite normal for a contractor to submit claims for additional amounts to a customer. Claims may be made for costs not included in the original contract or arising as an indirect consequence of approved variations, such as customer-caused-delays, errors in specifications or design and disputed variations. Because their settlement is by negotiation, which can in practice be long and drawn-out, they are subject to a high level of uncertainty. Consequently, no revenue should be taken for them unless negotiations have reached an advanced stage such that:

- it is probable that the customer will accept the claim; and
- the amount that is probable will be accepted by the customer can be measured reliably. *[IAS 11.14].*

This means that, at a minimum, the claims must have been agreed in principle and, in the absence of an agreed sum, the amount to be accrued must have been carefully assessed.

Contracts may provide for incentive payments, for example, for early completion or superior performance. They may only be included in contract revenue when the contract is at such a stage that it is probable the required performance will be achieved and the amount can be measured reliably. *[IAS 11.15]*.

3.1.1 Foreign currency revenues

Where contract revenue is denominated in a foreign currency it will be necessary to apply an appropriate exchange rate to record that revenue in the functional currency of the entity concerned. IAS 21 – *The Effects of Changes in Foreign Exchange Rates* – requires that foreign currency transactions be recorded at the spot exchange rate at the date of a transaction. *[IAS 21.21]*. Where work is performed on a steady basis over a period of time it may be appropriate to use an average exchange rate for that period.

IAS 11 does not provide explicit guidance on how to incorporate the effect of foreign currency denominated contracts when costs and revenues are denominated in different currencies. For example, an entity with a functional currency of GBP sterling may construct an asset where the revenues received are denominated in US dollars and some of the costs are denominated in Euros. IAS 11 requires an entity to apply percentage of completion when it can establish a reliable estimate of costs and revenues. At the reporting date, costs and revenues (still to be recognised) are generally translated using the spot exchange rate on that date in line with the requirements of IAS 21. Where revenue and costs are denominated in different currencies and are translated at their respective spot rates, this may affect the calculated percentage of completion where the entity determines the stage of completion using the proportion of total costs incurred to date compared to the total estimated contract costs (see 3.3.2 below). Where there is evidence that a different foreign exchange rate provides for a better estimate, an entity applies that other rate provided it can be supported by market information. In such cases, disclosures about management judgements would be necessary in the financial statements.

Progress billings and cost accruals incurred during construction will be recognised at the spot rate on the date the transaction occurs, which may differ from the spot rate at the end of the reporting period. Any re-measurement at the reporting date is presented in profit or loss with other foreign exchange gains or losses (see Chapter 15). *[IAS 21.28]*.

Changes in foreign exchange rates will only affect the calculated percentage of completion where it is measured using the proportion of total costs incurred to date compared to the total estimated contract costs. Entities using an alternative basis for determining the percentage of completion, such as a survey of the work performed, will not be impacted.

An entity might receive consideration in a foreign currency in advance of delivering goods or services in circumstances where the resulting liability is considered a non-monetary item. This raises the question of whether the date of transaction, when applying IAS 21, is the date on which the consideration received in advance is recognised or a subsequent date (or dates) when the goods or services are actually delivered. In December 2016, the Interpretations Committee published IFRIC 22 – *Foreign Currency Transactions and*

Advance Consideration – which addresses this issue. IFRIC 22 concludes that the appropriate application of IAS 21 is to use the exchange rate at the date the advanced receipt is recognised, normally the payment date. IFRIC 22 has an effective date of 1 January 2018 and is discussed further in Chapter 15 at 5.1.2).

3.2 Contract costs

Contract costs are those that relate directly to the specific contract and to those that are attributable to contract activity in general that can be allocated to the contract. In addition, they include costs that are specifically chargeable to the customer under the terms of the contract. *[IAS 11.16]*.

Directly related costs include:

(a) direct labour costs, including site supervision;

(b) costs of materials used in construction;

(c) depreciation of plant and equipment used on the contract;

(d) costs of moving plant, equipment and materials to and from the contract site;

(e) costs of hiring plant and equipment;

(f) costs of design and technical assistance that is directly related to the contract;

(g) the estimated costs of rectification and guarantee work, including expected warranty costs; and

(h) claims from third parties. *[IAS 11.17]*.

If the contractor generates incidental income from any directly related cost (e.g. by selling surplus materials and disposing of equipment at the end of the contract) this is treated as a reduction in contract costs. *[IAS 11.17]*.

The second category of costs comprises those attributable to contract activity in general that can be allocated to a particular contract. These include design and technical assistance not directly related to an individual contract, insurance and construction overheads, such as the costs of preparing and processing the payroll for the personnel actually working on the contract. These must be allocated using a systematic and rational method, consistently applied to all costs having similar characteristics. Allocation must be based on the normal level of construction activity. *[IAS 11.18]*.

There are various costs that, in most circumstances, are specifically precluded by IAS 11 from being attributed to contract activity or allocated to a contract. These include general administration costs, selling costs, research and development costs and the depreciation of idle plant and equipment that is not used on a particular contract. *[IAS 11.20]*. However, the entity is allowed to classify general administration costs and research and development as contract costs if they are specifically reimbursable under the terms of the contract. *[IAS 11.19-20]*.

An example is given by Airbus Group SE, which discloses the following:

Extract 23.2: Airbus Group SE (2016)

2. Notes to the IFRS Consolidated Financial Statements [extract]

2.1 **Basis of Presentation** [extract]

2. **Significant Accounting Policies** [extract]

Research and development expenses [extract] – Research and development activities can be either contracted or self-initiated.

The costs for contracted research and development activities, carried out in the scope of externally financed research and development contracts, are expensed when the related revenues are recorded.

3.2.1 Costs incurred in securing a contract

Costs may be attributed to a contract from the date on which it is secured until its final completion. In addition, costs relating directly to the contract that have been incurred in gaining the business may be included in contract costs if they have been incurred once it is probable the contract will be obtained. The word 'probable' is defined in the Glossary as 'more likely than not', which is similar to how it is used in IAS 37 – *Provisions, Contingent Liabilities and Contingent Assets* – see Chapter 28. These costs must also be separately identified and measured reliably. *[IAS 11.21].* This is not dissimilar to the general rules for recognition of an asset. An asset is defined in the Framework as 'a resource controlled by the entity as a result of past events and from which future economic benefits are expected to flow to the entity'. *[Framework 4.4(a)].* Therefore, we believe that this should be read restrictively and that these costs should not be recognised until they can, themselves, be seen as an asset of the entity through its control of the future economic benefits from the contract.

Costs that have been written off cannot be reinstated if the contract is obtained in a subsequent period. *[IAS 11.21].*

Costs incurred in securing a contract include such things as the building of models (including computer modelling exercises) for tender purposes, travelling costs of technicians to survey sites, technical tendering costs and similar expenses relating specifically to a given contract. However, costs incurred in securing a contract do not form part of the contract costs incurred for the purpose of determining stage of completion and are, therefore, excluded from the calculation (see 3.3.2 below).

3.2.2 Borrowing costs

Borrowing costs may be specific to individual contracts or attributable to contract activity in general. IAS 11 paragraph 18 states that 'costs that may be attributable to contract activity in general and can be allocated to specific contracts also include borrowing costs.' *[IAS 11.18].* Attributing borrowing costs to contracts is not a matter of capitalisation. Rather, it is a matter of identifying the contract costs. The inclusion of borrowing costs in contract costs affects the presentation of borrowing costs in profit or loss. It does not affect the recognition of borrowing costs as specified in IAS 23 – *Borrowing Costs. [IAS 23.BC27].* See Chapter 21 for a discussion on borrowing costs.

3.3 The recognition of contract revenue and expenses

If the basic requirements of accounting for inventories were applied to contracts, it would result in an annual income statement that reflected only the outcome of contracts completed during the year. For a contracting company this might bear no relation to the company's actual level of activity for that year. IAS 11, therefore, requires revenue and expenses to be recognised on uncompleted contracts in order to present a consistent view of the results of the company's activities during the period and from one period to the next. The underlying principle in IAS 11 is that, once the outcome of a construction contract can be estimated reliably, revenue and expense associated with the construction contract should be recognised by reference to the stage of completion of the contract activity at the end of the reporting period. *[IAS 11.22]*. The standard does not define the attributable profit in a contract, which will be the balancing figure once revenue and expenses are known.

If it is anticipated that the contract will be loss-making, the expected loss must be recognised immediately. *[IAS 11.22]*. This is discussed further in 3.3.6 below.

3.3.1 Types of construction contract

IAS 11 identifies two types of construction contract, fixed price and cost plus contracts.

3.3.1.A Fixed price contracts

In the case of a fixed price contract, the standard states that the outcome of a construction contract can be estimated reliably when the conditions discussed below are satisfied:

- it must be probable that the economic benefits associated with the contract will flow to the entity, which must be able to measure total contract revenue reliably. As discussed further below, these conditions will usually be satisfied when there are adequate contractual arrangements between the parties;
- both the contract costs to complete the contract and the stage of contract completion at the end of the reporting period must be able to be measured reliably; and
- the entity must be able to identify and reliably measure the contract costs attributable to the contract so that actual contract costs incurred can be compared with prior estimates. *[IAS 11.23]*. This means that it must have adequate reporting and budgeting systems.

3.3.1.B Cost plus contracts

Cost plus contracts are not subject to all of the same uncertainties as fixed price contracts. As with any transaction, it must be probable that the economic benefits associated with the contract will flow to the entity in order to recognise income at all. In most contracts this will be evidenced by the contract documentation. The fundamental criterion for a cost plus contract is the proper measurement of contract costs. Therefore, the contract costs attributable to the contract, whether or not specifically reimbursable, must be clearly identified and reliably measured. *[IAS 11.24]*.

3.3.2 The stage of completion method

There are certain general principles that apply whether the contract is classified as fixed cost or as cost plus. Recognition of revenue is by reference to the 'stage of completion', also known as the 'percentage of completion method'. Contract revenue and costs are recognised as revenue and expenses in profit or loss in the period in which the work is performed. Any anticipated excess of contract costs over contract revenue (i.e. a loss on the contract) is recognised as soon as it is anticipated. *[IAS 11.25-26]*.

This does not mean that contract activity is necessarily based on the total costs that have been incurred by the entity. Contract costs that relate to future contract activity (i.e. that activity for which revenue has not yet been recognised) may be deferred and recognised as an asset as long as it is probable that they will be recovered. These costs are usually classified as contract work in progress. *[IAS 11.27]*. An example of this may be materials purchased and stored for future use on a contract. Otherwise, contract costs are recognised in profit or loss as they are incurred.

Importantly, this does not mean that an entity can determine what it considers to be an appropriate profit margin for the whole contract and spread costs over the contract so as to achieve this margin (thereby classifying deferred costs as work in progress). As noted at 3.3 above, IAS 11 describes contract revenue and contract costs, not attributable profit. The standard does not seek to achieve a uniform profit margin throughout the contract, unless, of course, it is a cost plus contract.

An entity does not adjust the cumulative revenue it has recognised if it transpires in a subsequent period that there are doubts about the collectability of an amount it has recognised as revenue and it, consequently, has to make provision against its debtor. Instead the amount that is no longer considered collectable is written off as an expense (e.g. bad debt expense). *[IAS 11.28]*.

In order to be able to recognise revenue, the construction entity must be able to make reliable estimates of its revenue and costs. It is usually possible to do so once the parties have agreed to a contract that establishes both parties' enforceable rights, the contract consideration and the manner and terms of settlement. However, the entity must also be able to review and, where necessary, revise the estimates of contract revenue and contract costs as the contract progresses. This means that the entity must have effective systems for internal financial budgets and reporting. *[IAS 11.29]*.

The standard allows the stage of completion of a contract to be determined in a number of ways, but requires the entity to use the method that reliably measures the work performed. Depending on the nature of the contract, the methods may include:

- the proportion that contract costs incurred for work performed to date bear to the estimated total contract costs;
- surveys of work performed; or
- completion of a physical proportion of the contract work. *[IAS 11.30]*.

These could, of course, give different answers regarding the stage of completion of a contract as demonstrated in the following example.

Example 23.1: Determination of revenue

A company is engaged in a construction contract with an expected sales value of £10,000. It is the end of the accounting period during which the company commenced work on this contract and it needs to compute the amount of revenue to be reflected in profit and loss for this contract.

Scenario (i) **Stage of completion is measured by the proportion that contract costs incurred for work performed to date bear to the estimated total contract costs**

The company has incurred and applied costs of £4,000. £3,000 is the best estimate of costs to complete, resulting in total estimated costs of £7,000. The company should, therefore, recognise revenue of £5,714, being the appropriate proportion of total contract value, and computed, as follows:

$$\frac{4{,}000}{7{,}000} \times 10{,}000 = 5{,}714$$

Scenario (ii) **Stage of completion is measured by surveys of work performed**

An independent surveyor has certified that at the period-end the contract is 55% complete and that the company is entitled to apply for cumulative progress payments of £5,225 (after a 5% retention). In this case the company would record revenue of £5,500 being the sales value of the work done (if it is anticipated that rectification work will have to be carried out to secure the release of the retention money then this should be taken into account in computing the stage of completion. However, the fact that there is retention of an amount does not, in itself, directly impact the amount of revenue to be recognised).

Scenario (iii) **Stage of completion is measured by completion of a physical proportion of the contract work**

The company's best estimate of the physical proportion of the work it has completed is that it is 60% complete. The value of the work done and, therefore, the revenue to be recognised is £6,000.

Note that in each of the above scenarios the computation of the amount of revenue is independent of the question of how much (if any) profit should be taken. This is because, even if a contract is loss-making, the sales price will be earned and this should be reflected by recording revenue as the contract progresses. In the final analysis, any loss arises because costs are greater than revenue and costs should be reflected through cost of sales. Different methods of determining revenue will, as discussed above, produce different results, which highlights the importance of disclosing the method adopted by the entity.

Where an entity uses a method for determining stage of completion, other than by measuring the proportion of costs incurred to date compared to the total estimated contract cost, an entity may find that the profit margin recognised is not in line with expectations due to the timing of the recognition of costs. For example, a survey of work performed may indicate that the work is 70% complete, but significantly more costs may have been incurred, resulting in a lower than expected profit margin. It is not clear within IAS 11 how such costs could be treated as work in progress. Likewise, if costs incurred are lower than expected, it would normally be inappropriate for entities to accrue for costs not yet incurred. In this circumstance, entities may need to reassess whether the method selected for determining the stage of completion is the most appropriate. The method chosen should accurately reflect progress in the contract and should be applied consistently.

An entity that discloses that it uses different methods to determine revenue depending on the nature of its contracts (e.g. as technical milestones are reached or units are delivered) is Airbus Group SE, as shown in the following extract.

Extract 23.3: Airbus Group SE (2016)

2. **Notes to the IFRS Consolidated Financial Statements** [extract]

2.1 **Basis of Presentation** [extract]

2. **Significant Accounting Policies** [extract]

Revenue from construction contracts [extract]

When the outcome can be estimated reliably, revenues and contract costs are recognised as revenue and expensed respectively by reference to the percentage of completion of the contract activity at the end of the reporting period ("PoC method"). Contract revenues include the purchase price agreed with the customer considering escalation formulas, contract amendments and claims and penalties when assessed as probable. The PoC method used depends on the contract. The method is based either on inputs (*i.e.* costs incurred for development contracts) or outputs (*i.e.* contractually agreed technical milestones, delivered units).

Whenever the outcome of a construction contract cannot be estimated reliably – for example during the early stages of a contract or during the course of a contract's completion – all related contract costs that are incurred are immediately expensed and revenues are recognised only to the extent of those costs being recoverable (the "early stage", also called "zero profit margin" method of accounting).

By contrast, many entities use just one principal method to calculate the percentage of completion.

The Royal BAM Group nv considers contract costs incurred as a proportion of total costs.

Extract 23.4: Royal BAM Group nv (2016)

Notes to the consolidated financial statements [extract]

2. **Summary of significant accounting policies** [extract]

2.24 **Revenue recognition** [extract]

(a) *Construction contracts* [extract]

When the outcome of a construction contract can be estimated reliably and it is probable that the contract will be profitable, contract revenue is recognised over the period of the contract by reference to the stage of completion. The net contract position as per period end is included on the balance sheet. […]

The Group uses the 'percentage-of-completion method' to determine the appropriate amount to recognise in a given period. The stage of completion is measured by reference to the contract costs incurred up to the end of the reporting period as a percentage of total forecasted costs for each contract. Costs incurred in the year in connection with future activity on a contract are excluded from contract costs in determining the stage of completion.

When it is probable that total contract costs will exceed total contract revenue, the expected loss is recognised as an expense immediately.

When the outcome of a construction contract cannot be estimated reliably, contract revenue is recognised only to the extent of contract costs incurred that are likely to be recoverable.

Variations in contract work, claims and incentive payments are included in contract revenue to the extent that may have been agreed with the customer and are capable of being reliably measured.

The Taylor Wimpey Group relies on surveys of work completed:

> *Extract 23.5: Taylor Wimpey plc (2016)*
>
> NOTES TO THE CONSOLIDATED FINANCIAL STATEMENTS [extract]
>
> 1. **Significant accounting policies** [extract]
>
> **Revenue** [extract]
>
> (d) ***Contracting work and partnership housing contracts***
>
> Where the outcome of a long term contract can be estimated reliably, revenue and costs are recognised by reference to the stage of completion of the contract activity at the balance sheet date. This is normally measured by surveys of work performed to date. Variations in contract work, claims and incentive payments are included to the extent that it is probable that they will result in revenue and they are capable of being reliably measured.
>
> Where the outcome of a long term contract cannot be estimated reliably, contract revenue that is probable will be recovered is recognised to the extent of contract costs incurred. Contract costs are recognised as expenses in the period in which they are incurred. When it is probable that total contract costs will exceed total contract revenue, the expected loss is recognised as an expense immediately.

There are other ways of measuring work done (e.g. labour hours), which, depending upon the exact circumstances, might lead to a more appropriate basis for computing revenue.

The above examples apply only to fixed-price contracts. Where a contract is on a cost-plus basis, it is necessary to examine the costs incurred to ensure they are of the type and size envisaged in the terms of the contract. Only once this is done and the recoverable costs identified can the amount be grossed up to arrive at the appropriate revenue figure.

If the stage of completion is determined by reference to the contract costs incurred to date, it is fundamental that this amount includes only those contract costs that reflect work actually performed so far. Any contract costs that relate to future activity on the contract must be excluded. This includes the costs of materials that have been delivered to a contract site or set aside for use in a contract but not yet installed, used or applied during contract performance, unless the materials have been made especially for the contract. Payments made to sub-contractors in advance of work performed under the sub-contract would similarly not relate to work performed to date and would need to be excluded. *[IAS 11.31]*.

Example 23.2: Determination of revenue – exclusion of unapplied costs

The circumstances are as in Scenario (i) of Example 23.1 above. The entity has incurred and applied costs of £4,000. £3,000 is the best estimate of costs to complete. If the costs incurred to date included £500 in respect of unapplied raw materials, then the revenue to be recognised falls to £5,000 being:

$$\frac{\text{costs incurred and applied}}{\text{total costs}} = \frac{(4{,}000 - 500)}{7{,}000} \times 10{,}000 = 5{,}000$$

3.3.3 *Changes in estimates*

The percentage of completion method is applied on a cumulative basis in each accounting period to the current estimates of contract revenues and costs. The effect of any changes in estimates of revenue and costs, or the effect of any change in the estimate of the outcome of a contract, must be treated as a change in accounting estimate, in accordance with IAS 8 – *Accounting Policies, Changes in Accounting Estimates and Errors.* The revised estimates must be used in determining the amount of revenue and expenses recognised in profit or loss in the period in which the change is made and in subsequent periods. *[IAS 11.38].*

Where an entity makes assumptions about the future and is subject to major sources of estimation uncertainty at the end of the reporting period (i.e. that have a significant risk of resulting in a material adjustment to the carrying amounts of assets and liabilities within the next financial year) this must be disclosed. *[IAS 1.125].* An example of an entity that makes disclosures about the uncertainties is Royal BAM Group nv.

Extract 23.6: Royal BAM Group nv (2016)

Notes to the consolidated financial statements [extract]

4. **Critical accounting judgements and key sources of estimation uncertainties** [extract]

Estimates and judgements are continually evaluated and are based on historical experience and other factors, including expectations of future events that are believed to be reasonable under the circumstances.

The critical judgements including those involving estimations assumptions concerning the future, that the Group has made in the process of applying the accounting policies and that have the most significant effect on the amounts recognised in the consolidated financial statements are addressed below.

(a) Contract revenue and costs

When the outcome of a construction contract can be estimated reliably and it is probable that the contract will be profitable, contract revenue and costs are recognised over the period of the contract by reference to the stage of completion using the 'percentage-of-completion method' to determine the appropriate amount to recognise in a given period. When it is probable that total contract costs will exceed total contract revenue, the expected loss is recognised as an expense immediately.

In determining the stage of completion the Group has efficient, coordinated systems for cost estimating, forecasting and revenue and costs reporting. The system also requires a consistent judgment (forecast) of the final outcome of the project, including variance analyses of divergences compared with earlier assessment dates. Estimates are an inherent part of this assessment and actual future outcome may deviate from the estimated outcome, specifically for major and complex construction contracts. However, historical experience has also shown that estimates are, on the whole, sufficiently reliable.

(b) Claims receivable

In the normal course of business the Group recognises amounts receivable in connection with claims for completed work due from the principal and/or insurance claims as reimbursement for certain loss events on projects. Project related claims on principals are recognised when it is probable that the claim amount will be received. Insurance claims can be recognised only if it is virtually certain that the amount recognised will be reimbursed.

3.3.4 The determination of contract revenue and expenses

These estimates are used to calculate the timing and measurement of contract revenue and expenses throughout the term of a construction contract. The following example, based on the Illustrative Examples in IAS 11, illustrates how contract revenue and expenses are determined:

Example 23.3: Determination of contract revenue and expenses

The following example illustrates the determination of the stage of completion of a contract and the timing of the recognition of contract revenue and expenses, measured by the proportion that contract costs incurred for work performed to date bear to the estimated total contract costs.

A construction contractor has a fixed price contract to build a bridge. The initial amount of revenue agreed in the contract is €9,000. The contractor's initial estimate of contract costs is €8,000. It will take 3 years to build the bridge.

By the end of year 1, the contractor's estimate of contract costs has increased to €8,050.

In year 2, the customer approves a variation resulting in an increase in contract revenue of €200 and estimated additional contract costs of €150. At the end of year 2, costs incurred include €100 for standard materials stored at the site to be used in year 3 to complete the project.

The contractor determines the stage of completion of the contract by calculating the proportion that contract costs incurred for work performed to date bear to the latest estimated total contract costs. A summary of the financial data during the construction period is as follows:

	Year 1	Year 2	Year 3
	€	€	€
Initial amount of revenue agreed in contract	9,000	9,000	9,000
Variation	–	200	200
Total contract revenue	9,000	9,200	9,200
Contract costs incurred to date	2,093	6,168	8,200
Contract costs to complete	5,957	2,023	–
Total estimated contract costs	8,050	8,200	8,200
Estimated profit	950	1,000	1,000
Stage of completion	26%	74%	100%

The constructor uses the percentages calculated as above to calculate the revenue, contract costs and profits over the term of the contract. The stage of completion for year 2 (74%) is determined by excluding from contract costs incurred for work performed to date the €100 of standard materials stored at the site for use in year 3.

The amounts of revenue, expenses and profit recognised in profit or loss in the three years are as follows:

	To date	Recognised in prior years	Recognised in current years
	€	€	€
Year 1			
Revenue (€9,000 × 26%)	2,340	–	2,340
Expenses	2,093	–	2,093
Profit	247	–	247
Year 2			
Revenue (€9,200 × 74%)	6,808	2,340	4,468
Expenses (€6,168 incurred less €100 of materials in storage)	6,068	2,093	3,975
Profit	740	247	493
Year 3			
Revenue (€9,200 × 100%)	9,200	6,808	2,392
Expenses	8,200	6,068	2,132
Profit	1,000	740	260

3.3.5 *Inability to estimate the outcome of a contract reliably*

When the outcome of a construction contract cannot be estimated reliably, an entity will need to determine whether it is probable that the costs incurred will be recovered under the contract. It can then recognise revenue to the extent of these costs. Contract costs should be recognised as an expense in the period in which they are incurred, *[IAS 11.32]*, unless they relate to future contract activity, such as materials purchased for future use on the contract, as explained at 3.3.2 above.

It is often difficult to estimate the outcome of a contract reliably during its early stages. This means that it is not possible to recognise contract profit. However, the entity may be satisfied that, at least, some of the contract costs it has incurred will be recovered and it will be able to recognise revenue to this extent.

If it is probable that total costs will exceed total revenues, even if the outcome of the contract cannot be estimated reliably, any expected excess of contract costs must be expensed immediately. *[IAS 11.33]*. The standard also identifies a number of situations that may give rise to unrecoverable contract costs that must be recognised as expenses immediately. There may be deficiencies in the contract, which means that it is not fully enforceable. Other problems may be caused by the legal environment, such as the outcome of pending litigation or legislation or the expropriation of property. The customer or the contractor may no longer be able to meet their obligations or the contractor may be unable for some reason to complete the contract. *[IAS 11.34]*.

If these uncertainties, which prevent the outcome of the contract being estimated reliably, are resolved, revenue and expenses are recognised using the stage of completion method. *[IAS 11.35]*. As discussed at 3.3.3 above, this may require a cumulative catch up adjustment for previous years in the period in which the uncertainties are resolved.

3.3.6 *Loss-making contracts*

When an entity determines that it is probable that the contract costs will exceed contract revenue it must immediately recognise the expected loss as an expense. It is irrelevant whether work has commenced on the contract or the stage of completion of contract activity. In addition, the entity may not take into account any anticipated profits on other contracts with the same customer, unless all of these contracts are treated as a single construction contract. *[IAS 11.36-37]*.

Provisions for losses are set off against amounts due from customers (if an asset) or added to amounts due to customers (if a liability). *[IAS 11.43-44]*.

3.3.7 *Contract inefficiencies*

IAS 2 explicitly excludes from the costs of inventories 'abnormal amounts of wasted materials, labour or other production costs'. *[IAS 2.16(a)]*. There is no such requirement in IAS 11 and this is reflected in a degree of uncertainty about how to account for inefficiencies and 'abnormal costs' incurred during the course of a construction contract. If such costs are simply added to the total contract costs, this may affect the stage of completion if contract activity is estimated based on the total costs that have been incurred (see 3.3.2 above).

The issue is often a practical one of how to distinguish such abnormal costs and inefficiencies so as not to overstate the stage of completion on a contract. Usually, abnormal costs and inefficiencies that result from an observable event can be identified. If a major supplier collapses, the costs of securing the materials from another source (e.g. acquisition costs, construction delays) may be an abnormal cost or inefficiency that ought not to be included in contract costs used to measure the stage of completion. By contrast, an unexpected increase in costs of materials might be included in contract costs used to measure the stage of completion and also lead to a revision to the estimate of total contract costs. There are more marginal situations. A load of bricks may develop an off colour and not be suitable for their designated purpose. This is a natural, but intermittent defect that builders may face. In such circumstances, it is less clear whether it is an inefficiency excluded from contract costs used to measure the stage of completion or not. In any particular situation, an assessment may have to be based on the significance to the project. It is relatively easy to distinguish situations at either extreme, but much less so when the issues are marginal, where judgement will have to be exercised.

Note that these inefficiencies must be distinguished from cost increases that will result in the contract becoming loss-making, as an expected loss on a contract must be expensed immediately (see 3.3.6 above).

3.3.8 Contracts that contain sales of assets and construction contracts

In some real estate markets an entity may enter into a contract to construct a building on land that the entity owns and then – after construction is complete – to deliver the entire property to a customer.

If the contract can be separated into a construction contract and the sale of the land, the delivery of land follows the revenue recognition guidance of IAS 18 for sale of land. The construction of the building follows the revenue recognition requirements of either IAS 11 or IAS 18 as appropriate, as it may be necessary to apply IFRIC 15's requirements to the construction of the building (see 1.2 above). The effect of this can be seen below:

Example 23.4: Construction contract that is separated

On 1 January 2017, Entity A entered into a contract to construct a building on a piece of land it has acquired and, when construction is complete, to deliver the entire property to a customer. A applies the percentage of completion method to account for contract revenues and expenses. The relative percentage of cost incurred is considered a reliable method for measuring the progress of the contract.

- Total cost of land: $2m
- Estimated total cost of construction: $8m
- Estimated total cost of contract: $10m
- Agreed sales price of the completed building: $11m

Construction has commenced and at the end of the reporting period (31 December 2017) total construction costs incurred amount to $2m.

Entity A considers that the amount of revenue in the contract attributable to the construction is $8.5m and the amount to the sale of land is $2.5m.

The percentage of completion of the construction contract is 25% – calculated as $2m costs incurred as a proportion of the $8m estimated total cost of construction.

Accordingly, as at 31 December 2017 the following amounts are recorded:

Revenue	($8.5m × 25%)	$2.13m
Contract expense		$2.00m
Gross amount due from customer	(Revenue of $2.13m)	$2.13m
Inventory	(Cost of the land)	$2.00m

The revenue and cost relating to the land will be recognised when the revenue recognition criteria of IAS 18 are met – this is often when legal title passes.

4 DISCLOSURE REQUIREMENTS OF IAS 11

IAS 11 has detailed disclosure requirements. The following disclosures must be given by entities in respect of construction contracts:

(a) the amount of contract revenue recognised as revenue in the period;

(b) the methods used to determine the contract revenue recognised in the period; and

(c) the methods used to determine the stage of completion of contracts in progress. *[IAS 11.39].*

The standard includes, in its Appendix, an illustrative example of accounting policy disclosures, shown below. *[IAS 11.IE].*

Example 23.5: Disclosure of accounting policies

Revenue from fixed price construction contracts is recognised on the percentage of completion method, measured by reference to the percentage of labour hours incurred to date compared to estimated total labour hours for each contract.

Revenue from cost plus contracts is recognised by reference to the recoverable costs incurred during the period plus the fee earned, measured by the proportion that costs incurred to date bear to the estimated total costs of the contract.

The following is the accounting policy of Thales, which also refers to the treatment of the related balances in the balance sheet.

Extract 23.7: Thales (2016)

1.2.6 Notes to the consolidated financial statements [extract]

NOTE 14. ACCOUNTING POLICIES [extract]

c) **Revenue recognition** [extract]

Construction contracts

A construction contract is a contract specifically negotiated for the construction of an asset or group of assets that are closely linked or interrelated in terms of their design, technology, function, purpose or use.

According to its characteristics, a notified construction contract can either be accounted for separately, be segmented into several components which are each accounted for separately, or be combined with another construction contract in progress in order to form the scope of the contract for accounting purposes in respect of which sales and expenses will be recognised.

Sales and expenses on construction contracts are recognised in accordance with the technical percentage-of-completion method. However, when there is no significant time difference between technical percentage of completion and contractual dates of transfer of ownership, the percentage of completion is determined according to the contractual transfer of ownership.

> Penalties for late payment or the improper execution of a contract are recognised as a deduction from sales. In the balance sheet, provisions for penalties are deducted from assets related to the contract.
>
> Expected losses on contracts are fully recognised as soon as they are identified.
>
> Selling, administrative and interest expenses are directly charged to the profit and loss account in the period in which they are incurred.
>
> Estimates of work remaining on loss-making contracts do not include sales from claims made by the Group, except when it is highly probable that such claims will be accepted by the customer.
>
> Progress payments received on construction contracts are deducted from contract assets as the contract is completed. Progress payments received before the corresponding work has been performed are classified in "advances received from customers on contracts" in balance sheet liabilities.
>
> The cumulative amount of costs incurred and profit recognised, less any recognised losses and progress billings, is determined on a contract-by-contract basis. If this amount is positive, it is recognised under "Construction contracts: assets" in the balance sheet. If it is negative, it is recognised under "Construction contracts: liabilities".

Airbus Group SE identifies different features by which its contract revenue is recognised, as disclosed in Extract 23.3 at 3.3.2 above.

In the case of contracts in progress at the end of the reporting period, an entity shall disclose each of the following:

(a) the aggregate amount of costs incurred and recognised profits (less recognised losses) to date;

(b) the amount of advances received; and

(c) the amount of retentions. *[IAS 11.40]*.

Retentions, progress billings and advances are defined as follows:

> 'Retentions are amounts of progress billings that are not paid until the satisfaction of conditions specified in the contract for the payment of such amounts or until defects have been rectified. Progress billings are amounts billed for work performed on a contract whether or not they have been paid by the customer. Advances are amounts received by the contractor before the related work is performed.' *[IAS 11.41]*.

In addition, an entity shall present:

(a) an asset, being the gross amount due from customers for contract work, for all contracts in progress for which costs incurred plus recognised profits (less recognised losses) exceed progress billings; and

(b) a liability, being the gross amount due to customers for contract work, for all contracts in progress for which progress billings exceed costs incurred plus recognised profits (less recognised losses). *[IAS 11.42-44]*.

The following example is based on the Illustrative Examples in IAS 11 and serves to illustrate the financial statement disclosure requirements of the standard as they apply to the various circumstances that might arise concerning construction contracts. It is followed by an example of the disclosures in practice from the financial statements of Thales.

Example 23.6: Disclosure of numerical information regarding construction contracts

A contractor has reached the end of its first year of operations. All its contract costs incurred have been paid for in cash and all its progress billings and advances have been received in cash. Contract costs incurred for contracts B, C and E include the cost of materials that have been purchased for the contract but which have not been used in contract performance to date.

For contracts B, C and E, the customers have made advances to the contractor for work not yet performed.

The status of the entity's five contracts in progress at the end of year 1 is as follows:

Contract	A	B	C	D	E	Total
	£	£	£	£	£	£
Contract revenue recognised in accordance with IAS 11.22 (see 3.3 above)	145	520	380	200	55	1,300
Contract expenses recognised in accordance with IAS 11.22 (see 3.3 above)	110	450	350	250	55	1,215
Expected losses recognised in accordance with IAS 11.36 (see 3.3.6 above)	–	–	–	40	30	70
Recognised profits less recognised losses	35	70	30	(90)	(30)	15
Contract costs incurred in the period	110	510	450	250	100	1,420
Contract costs incurred recognised as contract expenses in the period in accordance with IAS 11.22	110	450	350	250	55	1,215
Contract costs that relate to future activity recognised as an asset in accordance with IAS 11.27	–	60	100	–	45	205
Contract revenue	145	520	380	200	55	1,300
Progress billings (IAS 11.41: see above)	100	520	380	180	55	1,235
Unbilled contract revenue	45	–	–	20	–	65
Advances (IAS 11.41: see above)	–	80	20	–	25	125

The amounts to be disclosed in accordance with IAS 11 are as follows:	£
Contract revenue recognised as revenue in the period	1,300
Contract costs incurred and recognised profits (less recognised losses) to date	1,435
Advances received	125
Gross amount due from customers for contract work (presented as an asset)	220
Gross amount due to customers for contract work (presented as a liability)	(20)

These amounts are calculated as follows:

Contract	A	B	C	D	E	Total
	£	£	£	£	£	£
Contract costs incurred	110	510	450	250	100	1,420
Recognised profits less recognised losses	35	70	30	(90)	(30)	15
	145	580	480	160	70	1,435
Progress billings	100	520	380	180	55	1,235
Due from customers	45	60	100	–	15	220
Due to customers	–	–	–	(20)	–	(20)

The amount disclosed in accordance with IAS 11.40(a) (the aggregate amount of costs incurred and recognised profits (less recognised losses) to date) is the same as the amount for the current period because the disclosures relate to the first year of operation.

Thales discloses its contracts in progress as follows:

Extract 23.8: Thales (2014)

Notes to the Consolidated Financial Statements [extract]

Note 10 **CURRENT OPERATING ASSETS AND LIABILITIES** [extract]

10.2 **Construction contracts**

Balances presented in the balance sheet are analysed as follows:

	31/12/2014	31/12/2013
Construction contracts: assets	1,996.4	1,995.2
Construction contracts: liabilities	(1,072.3)	(1,073.9)
NET	**924.1**	**921.3**
This balance is analysed as follows:		
Work-in-progress on construction contracts	898.1	889.6
Unbilled receivables on construction contracts	1,346.0	1,326.2
Reserves for losses at completion on construction contracts[(a)]	(518.2)	(590.1)
Other reserves on construction contracts	(801.8)	(704.4)
NET	**924.1**	**921.3**
Advances received from customers on construction contracts	2,679.2	2,790.8

(a) *The variations of reserves for losses at completion between 2013 and 2014 are mainly explained by the utilisation of reserves booked during the previous years.*

In addition, the entity is required to disclose any contingent liabilities and contingent assets in accordance with IAS 37 (see Chapter 28). Contingent liabilities and contingent assets may arise from such items as warranty costs, claims, penalties or possible losses. *[IAS 11.45]*.

Chapter 23

References

1 *IFRIC Update*, April 2005, p.4.

Index of extracts from financial statements

Index of standards

Framework

IFRS 1

IFRS 2

IFRS 3 (2007)

IFRS 3

IFRS 4

IFRS 5

IFRS 6

IFRS 7 (2010)

IFRS 7

IFRS 8

IFRS 9 (2012)

IFRS 9

IFRS 10

IFRS 11

IFRS 12

IFRS 13

IFRS 14

IFRS 15

IFRS 16

IFRS 17

IAS 1

IAS 2

IAS 7

IAS 8

IAS 10

IAS 11

IAS 12

IAS 16

IAS 17

IAS 18 (2008)

IAS 18

IAS 19

IAS 20

IAS 21

IAS 23

IAS 24

IAS 27

IAS 28

IAS 29

IAS 32

IAS 33

IAS 34

IAS 36

IAS 37

IAS 38

IAS 39 (2012)

IAS 39 (2017)

IAS 39

IAS 40

IAS 41 (2008)

IAS 41 (2012)

IAS 41

IFRIC 1

IFRIC 2

IFRIC 4

IFRIC 5

IFRIC 6

IFRIC 7

IFRIC 9

IFRIC 10

IFRIC 12 (2007)

IFRIC 12

IFRIC 13

IFRIC 14

IFRIC 15

IFRIC 16

IFRIC 17

IFRIC 18

IFRIC 19

IFRIC 20

IFRIC 21

IFRIC 22

IFRIC 23

SIC-7

SIC-10

SIC-12

SIC-15

SIC-25

SIC-27

SIC-29

SIC-31

SIC-32

Management Commentary

Index

Note: This index uses chapter number followed by section number for locators. A section number includes all its sub-sections. For example the locator Ch. 37, 2.7 will include subsections 2.7.1 and 2.7.2 in chapter 37. The locator Ch. 21, 5.3.1 will include subsections 5.3.1.A and 5.3.1.B. Where a range is indicated, for example, Ch. 3, 2–3, this means the topic starts from the beginning of section 2 to the end of section 3.